The Bedford Anthology of

World Literature

The Ancient World,
Beginnings–100 C.E.

Book 1

The Bedford Anthology of
*W*orld Literature

The Ancient World, Beginnings–100 C.E.

EDITED BY

Paul Davis
Gary Harrison
David M. Johnson
Patricia Clark Smith
John F. Crawford

THE UNIVERSITY OF NEW MEXICO

BEDFORD / ST. MARTIN'S   Boston ♦ New York

For Bedford/St. Martin's

Executive Editor: Alanya Harter
Associate Developmental Editor: Joshua Levy
Senior Production Editor: Ara Salibian
Senior Production Supervisor: Nancy Myers
Marketing Manager: Jenna Bookin Barry
Art Editor: Genevieve Hamilton
Editorial Assistant: Jeffrey Voccola
Production Assistants: Kerri Cardone, Kendra LeFleur
Copyeditor: Melissa Cook
Map Coordinator: Tina Samaha
Text and Cover Design: Anna George
Cover Art: Wallpainting from tomb of Nebamun, 18th Dynasty (1550–1295 B.C.E.). Thebes, Egypt. Werner Forman / Art Resource, NY
Composition: Stratford Publishing Services, Inc.
Printing and Binding: R. R. Donnelley & Sons Company

President: Joan E. Feinberg
Editorial Director: Denise B. Wydra
Editor in Chief: Karen S. Henry
Director of Marketing: Karen Melton
Director of Editing, Design, and Production: Marcia Cohen
Managing Editor: Elizabeth M. Schaaf

Library of Congress Control Number: 2002112262

Manufactured in the United States of America.

4 3 2
m l k

For information, write: Bedford / St. Martin's, 75 Arlington Street, Boston, MA 02116 (617-399-4000)

ISBN-10: 0–312–24873–3
ISBN-13: 978-0–312–24873–4

Acknowledgments

Aeschylus, "Agamemnon" and "The Eumenides" from *The Oresteian Trilogy, Revised Edition,* translated by Philip Vellacott. Copyright © 1956, 1959 by Philip Vellacott. Reprinted with the permission of Penguin Books, Ltd.

PREFACE

The Bedford Anthology of World Literature has a story behind it. In 1985, a group of us received a grant from the National Endowment for the Humanities. Our task: to develop and team teach a new kind of literature course—one that drew from the rich literary traditions of Asia, India, the Middle East, and the Americas as well as from the masterpieces of the Western world. We learned so much from that experience—from our students and from each other—that we applied those lessons to an anthology published in 1995, *Western Literature in a World Context.*

In that first edition of our anthology, our goal was to add works that truly represented *world* literature to the list of Western classics and to place great literary works in their historical and cultural contexts. We've kept that focus in the newly titled *Bedford Anthology*—but we've also drastically reshaped, redesigned, and reimagined it to make it the book you hold today. We talked to hundreds of instructors and students in an effort to identify and confirm what they considered challenging about the world literature course. The design and content of these pages represent our attempt to meet these challenges.

The study and teaching of world literature have changed significantly in the past twenty to thirty years. Formerly, most world literature courses consisted of masterpieces of Western literature, while the literary traditions of Asia, Africa, and Latin America were virtually ignored. The movement to broaden the canon to more accurately represent our world—and to better represent oral and marginalized traditions in the West—has greatly increased the number of texts taught in world literature courses today. Although the specifics remain controversial, nearly all teachers of literature are committed to the ongoing revaluation and expansion of the canon.

The last few decades have also seen instructors reconsidering the traditional methods of teaching world literature. In the past, most world literature courses were designed along formalistic or generic principles. But the expanded canon has complicated both of these approaches. There are no developed criteria for defining masterworks in such formerly ignored genres as letters and diaries or for unfamiliar forms from non-Western cultures, and we are frequently reminded that traditional approaches sometimes impose inappropriate Eurocentric perspectives on such works. As content and methodology for the course have been evolving, recent critical theory has reawakened interest in literature's historical and cultural contexts. All of these factors have both complicated and enriched the study of world literature. With this multivolume literature anthology, we don't claim to be presenting the definitive new canon of world literature or the last word on how to teach it. We have, however, tried to open new perspectives and possibilities for both students and teachers.

One anthology — six individual books. *The Bedford Anthology of World Literature* is now split into six separate books that correspond to the six time periods most commonly taught. These books are available in two packages: Books 1–3 and Books 4–6. Our motivation for changing the packaging is twofold and grows out of the extensive market research we did before shaping the development plan for the book. In our research, instructors from around the country confirmed that students just don't want to cart around a 2,500-page book — who would? Many also said that they focus on ancient literatures in the first semester of the course and on the twentieth

The Bedford Anthology of World Literature *has been dynamically reimagined, redesigned, and restructured. We've added a second color, four hundred images, three hundred pronunciation guides, forty maps, six comparative time lines — and much more.*

Portuguese Caravels Leaving to Explore the World, 1775 *The eighteenth century was a time of unprecedented global communication — political, social, economic, and literary. These painted blue tiles are found on the walls of the town of Paco de Arcos, near Lisbon, Portugal. (The Art Archive / Dagli Orti.)*
The Eighteenth Century
1650 - 1800

century in the second semester. In addition, many instructors teach an introduction to world literature that is tailored specifically to the needs of their students and their institution and thus want a text that can be adapted to *many* courses.

We believe that the extensive changes we've made to *The Bedford Anthology of World Literature*—breaking the anthology into six books rather than only two, creating a new two-color design, increasing the trim size, and adding maps, illustrations, numerous pedagogical features, an expanded instructor's manual, and a new companion Web site—will make the formidable task of teaching and taking a world literature course both manageable and pleasurable.

An expanded canon for the twenty-first century. In each of the six books of *The Bedford Anthology*, you'll find a superb collection of complete longer works, plays, prose, and poems—the best literature available in English or English translation. Five of the books are organized geographically and then by author in order of birth date. The exception to this rule is Book 6, which, reflecting our increasingly global identities, is organized by author without larger geographical groupings.

Aphra Behn's Oroonoko *is one of the texts we include in its entirety—highlighting important issues of race, gender, and slavery in the eighteenth century.*

APHRA BEHN
1640–1689

Aphra Behn, Engraving from *Histories and Novels*, 1696
This is the earliest surviving image of Behn. (The Huntington Library, San Marino, CA)

Poet, playwright, and novelist Aphra Behn was one of the most prolific writers of her time. During a period in England when women were strongly discouraged from seeking literary recognition, she not only managed to earn a living as a professional writer but also directly engaged such traditionally "masculine" themes as political corruption, sexual politics, and social reform. In *Oroonoko* (1688), she openly addresses the complexities of rulership, sexual desire, and social injustice. Though her talent as a writer earned her much popularity and praise, the supposed presumptuousness and boldness of her work resulted in vicious attacks on her moral integrity. Associating her entrance into the public sphere of print and stage with prostitution, the satirist Robert Gould labeled her a vile "Punk[1] and Poetesse." Largely because of this stigma of indecency, publishers and scholars ignored Behn's work for years after her death. Only recently has she returned to center stage as a great literary talent, a major contributor to the development of the early English NOVEL, and a revolutionary figure in the tradition of women's writing in English.

Mystery, Travel, and Espionage. It is difficult to pin down the facts of Behn's early life. According to many sources, she was born near Canterbury to Bartholomew Johnson, a barber, and Elizabeth Denham. Her surprisingly advanced education and language skills (she was learned in Latin and French), which would have been unusual for a barber's daughter, might be attributed to a close association with the well-to-do family of Colonel Colepeper and to frequent exposure to Huguenot[2] and Dutch immigrants in Canterbury. Some recent scholarship, however, claims she was born in Kent and the daughter of John and Amy Amis or Amies. This would make her a possible relation, through her father, of Francis, Lord Willoughby of Parham, who at one time held a position for the British government in the West Indies. We know that in 1663 Behn traveled to the West Indies with her family after her father was named lieutenant-general of the colony of Surinam.[3] Though the stay in Surinam only lasted two months (her father died on the voyage), this experience influenced the writing of her most famous narrative work, *Oroonoko*.

The circumstances surrounding the adoption of Aphra Behn's last name are even more cloudy than those of her birth. Though there is no extant marriage record, scholars speculate that after the trip to Surinam, Behn wed a London merchant or seaman of Dutch or German descent. If

[1] **punk:** Prostitute.

[2] **Huguenots:** French Protestants who were members of the Reformed Church established in France by John Calvin circa 1555. Because of religious persecution, they fled to other countries in the sixteenth and seventeenth centuries.

[3] **Surinam:** A British sugar colony on the South American coast below Venezuela.

88

Aphra Behn, 1640–1689 89

she married, she and her husband were together for only a short time before either he died or the two parted ways to live separate lives. More interesting is the suggestion that Behn imagined a spouse for herself so that she could gain the respectable title of widow. Several critics comment that, assuming Behn's maiden name was Johnson, taking the last name Behn creates an intriguing allusion to the famous seventeenth-century playwright Ben (Behn) Jonson.

The creation of a fictional husband may well seem like a bold act for a woman of the seventeenth century, but Behn was not one to shy away from taking chances or embarking on daring adventures. In 1666, for example, she served as a spy for Charles II (r. 1660–85) in the Anglo-Dutch War.[4] Recruited by her associate Thomas Killigrew, she was charged with convincing one William Scot to be a double agent, reporting on expatriots, and providing information on Dutch military plans. Her foray into espionage was unsuccessful—what information she provided to the English crown was largely ignored, and she was never repaid for her expenses. Deep in debt and forced to borrow money for the cost of her return to England, it is likely that she spent some time in debtor's prison in 1688.

WWW For links to more information about Behn and a quiz on *Oroonoko*, see *World Literature Online* at bedfordstmartins.com/worldlit.

Writing Politics and the Politics of Writing. Aphra Behn lived through a period of monumental political unrest and social change. In 1642, two years after her birth, England became embroiled in a bloody civil war over religious authority, class privileges, and economic practices, among other issues. Charles I (r. 1625–49) was brought to trial and executed in 1649. Despite the promise of a new kind of governance, the ensuing rule of Oliver Cromwell[5]—under whom Britain was called the "Commonwealth," then the "Protectorate"—proved only that a citizen given the power to govern may be more ineffective and tyrannical than a monarch. The period known as the Restoration, beginning in 1660 with the restoration of Charles II as king of England, saw a newfound celebration of, and freedom in, the arts but did not provide long-term political stability. Charles's successor, James II (r. 1685–88), was quickly ousted and sent into exile, primarily because he was a professed Roman Catholic. In what is called the "Glorious Revolution" of 1688,[6] the Dutch Protestant William of Orange and his wife Mary came to power.

As shown by her service as a spy for Charles II, Behn was dedicated to the preservation of the monarchy and to the system of aristocratic rule. Much of her work is informed by this sociopolitical agenda. In texts

[4] **Anglo-Dutch War:** Battles between the British and the Dutch for control of the seas and trade routes (1652–84).

[5] **Oliver Cromwell** (1599–1658): A soldier, politician, and staunch Puritan who attacked the bishops of the Church of England and advocated widespread political and religious reform. He came to power as "Lord Protector" of England (1653–58) shortly after the execution of Charles I.

[6] **Glorious Revolution:** The birth of a son to the Catholic James II led prominent statesmen in England to invite Dutchman William of Orange and his wife, Mary, to assume the throne. William arrived in 1688, promised to protect the Protestant faith and the liberties of the English, and took the throne without opposition. James II, denounced by Parliament, fled to France.

We've tried to assemble a broad selection of the world's literatures. We've updated our selection of European texts; we have also included American writers who have had significant contact with world culture and who have influenced or defined who we are as Americans. And of course we have added many works from non-Western traditions, both frequently anthologized pieces and works unique to this anthology, including texts from Mesopotamia, Egypt, Israel, India, Persia, China, Japan, Arab countries of the Middle East, Africa, native America, Latin America, and the Caribbean.

Over thirty-five complete, longer works. These include Homer's *Odyssey* and *The Epic of Gilgamesh* in Book 1, Dante's *Inferno* and Kalidasa's *Shakuntala* in Book 2, Marlowe's *Doctor Faustus* and Shakespeare's *The Tempest* in Book 3, Bashō's *Narrow Road through the Backcountry* in Book 4, Dostoevsky's *Notes from Underground* in Book 5, and Achebe's *Things Fall Apart* in Book 6.

When a work is too long to be produced in its entirety, we've presented carefully edited selections from it; examples include the Rig Veda, *Ramayana, Mahabharata,* Qur'an, *The Song of Roland,* Ibn Hazm's *The Dove's Necklace, The Book of Margery Kempe,* Attar's *Conference of the Birds,* Cervantes's *Don Quixote,* Swift's *Gulliver's Travels,* Equiano's *Interesting Narrative,* Benjamin Franklin's *Autobiography,* Chikamatsu's *The Love Suicides at Amijima,* and Cao Xueqin's *The Story of the Stone.* In most cases the excerpts are not fragments but substantial selections wherein the structure and themes of the whole work are evident. The anthology also contains a generous selection of prose writing—short stories, letters, and essays.

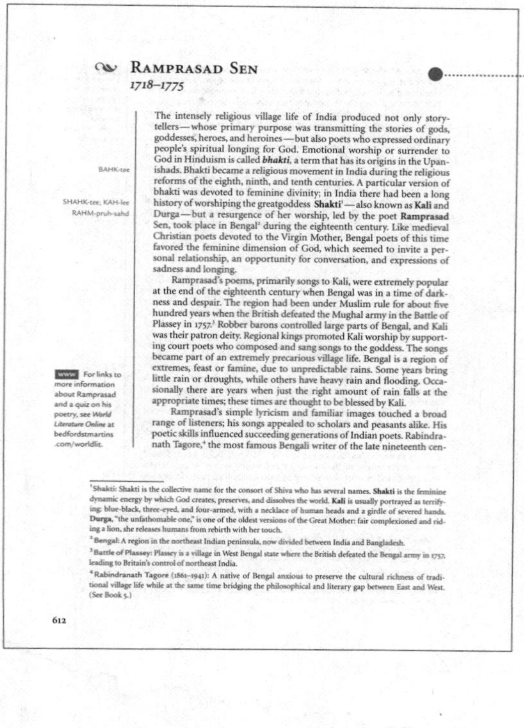

RAMPRASAD SEN
1718–1775

The intensely religious village life of India produced not only storytellers—whose primary purpose was transmitting the stories of gods, goddesses, heroes, and heroines—but also poets who expressed ordinary people's spiritual longing for God. Emotional worship or surrender to God in Hinduism is called ***bhakti***, a term that has its origins in the Upanishads. Bhakti became a religious movement in India during the religious reforms of the eighth, ninth, and tenth centuries. A particular version of bhakti was devoted to feminine divinity; in India there had been a long history of worshiping the greatgoddess **Shakti**[1]—also known as **Kali** and Durga—but a resurgence of her worship, led by the poet **Ramprasad** Sen, took place in Bengal[2] during the eighteenth century. Like medieval Christian poets devoted to the Virgin Mother, Bengal poets of this time favored the feminine dimension of God, which seemed to invite a personal relationship, an opportunity for conversation, and expressions of sadness and longing.

BAHK-tee

SHAHK-tee; KAH-lee

RAHM-pruh-sahd

Ramprasad's poems, primarily songs to Kali, were extremely popular at the end of the eighteenth century when Bengal was in a time of darkness and despair. The region had been under Muslim rule for about five hundred years when the British defeated the Mughal army in the Battle of Plassey in 1757.[3] Robber barons controlled large parts of Bengal, and Kali was their patron deity. Regional kings promoted Kali worship by supporting court poets who composed and sang songs to the goddess. The songs became part of an extremely precarious village life. Bengal is a region of extremes, feast or famine, due to unpredictable rains. Some years bring little rain or droughts, while others have heavy rain and flooding. Occasionally there are years when just the right amount of rain falls at the appropriate times; these times are thought to be blessed by Kali.

Ramprasad's simple lyricism and familiar images touched a broad range of listeners; his songs appealed to scholars and peasants alike. His poetic skills influenced succeeding generations of Indian poets. Rabindranath Tagore,[4] the most famous Bengali writer of the late nineteenth cen-

WWW For links to more information about Ramprasad and a quiz on his poetry, see *World Literature Online* at bedfordstmartins.com/worldlit.

[1] Shakti: Shakti is the collective name for the consort of Shiva who has several names. **Shakti** is the feminine dynamic energy by which God creates, preserves, and dissolves the world. **Kali** is usually portrayed as terrifying: blue-black, three-eyed, and four-armed, with a necklace of human heads and a girdle of severed hands. **Durga**, "the unfathomable one," is one of the oldest versions of the Great Mother: fair complexioned and riding a lion, she releases humans from rebirth with her touch.

[2] Bengal: A region in the northeast Indian peninsula, now divided between India and Bangladesh.

[3] Battle of Plassey: Plassey is a village in West Bengal state where the British defeated the Bengal army in 1757, leading to Britain's control of northeast India.

[4] Rabindranath Tagore (1861–1941): A native of Bengal anxious to preserve the cultural richness of traditional village life while at the same time bridging the philosophical and literary gap between East and West. (See Book 5.)

612

Several hundred lyric poems. *The Bedford Anthology* includes the work of such fine poets as Sappho, Bhartrhari, Nezahualcoyotl, Petrarch, Kakinomoto Hitomaro, Rumi, Li Bai, Heine, Mirabai, Ramprasad, Baudelaire, Dickinson, Ghalib, Akhmatova, Neruda, Rich, and Walcott. Unique *In the Tradition* clusters collect poems that share a tradition or theme: poetry about love in Books 1, 2, and 3, Tang dynasty poetry in Book 2, Indian devotional poetry in Book 3, and poetry on war in Book 6.

Literature in context. In addition to individual authors presented in chronological order, *The Bedford Anthology* features two types of cross-cultural literary groupings. In the more than thirty ***In the World*** clusters, five to six in each book, writings around a single theme—such as the history of religions, science, love, human rights, women's rights, colonialism, the meeting of East and West, imperialism, and existentialism—and from different countries and cultural traditions are presented side by side, helping students understand that people of every culture have had their public gods, heroes, and revolutions, their private loves, lives, and losses. Titles include "Changing Gods: From Religion to Philosophy," in Book 1; "Muslim and Christian at War," in Book 2; "Humanism, Learning, and Education" in Book 3; "Love, Marriage, and the Education of Women," in Book 4; "Emancipation," in Book 5; and "Imagining Africa," in Book 6. The second type of grouping, ***In the Tradition,*** presents poetry on love in Books 1, 2, and 3 and literature on war and American multiculturalism in Book 6. These clusters gather together such widely disparate writers as Hammurabi, Heraclitus, Marcus Aurelius, Ibn Battuta, Marco Polo, Sei Shonagon, Galileo, Bartolomé de las Casas, Mary Wollstonecraft, Mary Astell, Shen Fu, Karl Marx, Elizabeth Cady Stanton, Swami Vivekananda, Aimé Césaire, and Bharati Mukherjee.

In the World *clusters bring together texts from different literary traditions and help students make thematic connections and comparisons.*

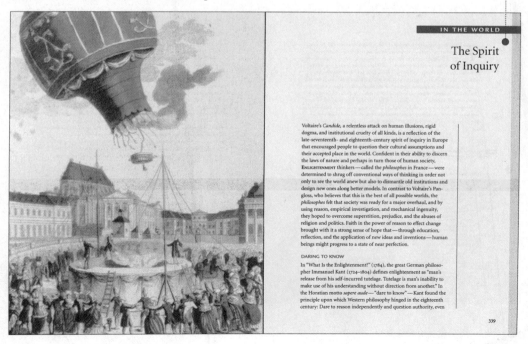

IN THE WORLD

The Spirit of Inquiry

Voltaire's *Candide,* a relentless attack on human illusions, rigid dogma, and institutional cruelty of all kinds, is a reflection of the late-seventeenth- and eighteenth-century spirit of inquiry in Europe that encouraged people to question their cultural assumptions and their accepted place in the world. Confident in their ability to discern the laws of nature and perhaps in turn those of human society, ENLIGHTENMENT thinkers—called the *philosophes* in France—were determined to shrug off conventional ways of thinking in order not only to see the world anew but also to dismantle old institutions and design new ones along better models. In contrast to Voltaire's Pangloss, who believes that this is the best of all possible worlds, the *philosophes* felt that society was ready for a major overhaul, and by using reason, empirical investigation, and mechanical ingenuity, they hoped to overcome superstition, prejudice, and the abuses of religion and politics. Faith in the power of reason to effect change brought with it a strong sense of hope that—through education, reflection, and the application of new ideas and inventions—human beings might progress to a state of near perfection.

DARING TO KNOW

In "What Is the Enlightenment?" (1784), the great German philosopher Immanuel Kant (1724–1804) defines enlightenment as "man's release from his self-incurred tutelage. Tutelage is man's inability to make use of his understanding without direction from another." In the Horatian motto *sapere aude*—"dare to know"—Kant found the principle upon which Western philosophy hinged in the eighteenth century: Dare to reason independently and question authority, even

339

Helping students and teachers navigate the wide world of literature. The hundreds of instructors we talked to before embarking on *The Bedford Anthology* shared with us their concerns about teaching an introduction to world literature course, no matter what their individual agendas were. One concern was the sheer difficulty for students of reading literature that not only spans the period from the beginning of recorded literatures to the present but also hails from vastly different cultures and historical moments. Another was the fact that no one instructor is an expert in *all* of world literature. We've put together *The Bedford Anthology of World Literature* with these factors in mind and hope that the help we offer both around and with the selected texts goes a long way toward bringing clarity to the abundance and variety of world writings.

Helping students understand the where and when of the literature in the anthology. Each book of *The Bedford Anthology* opens with an extended overview of its time period as well as with a **comparative time line** that lists what happened, where, and when in three overarching categories: history and politics; literature; and science, culture, and technology. An interactive version of each time line serves as the portal to the online support offered on our Book Companion Site. In addition,

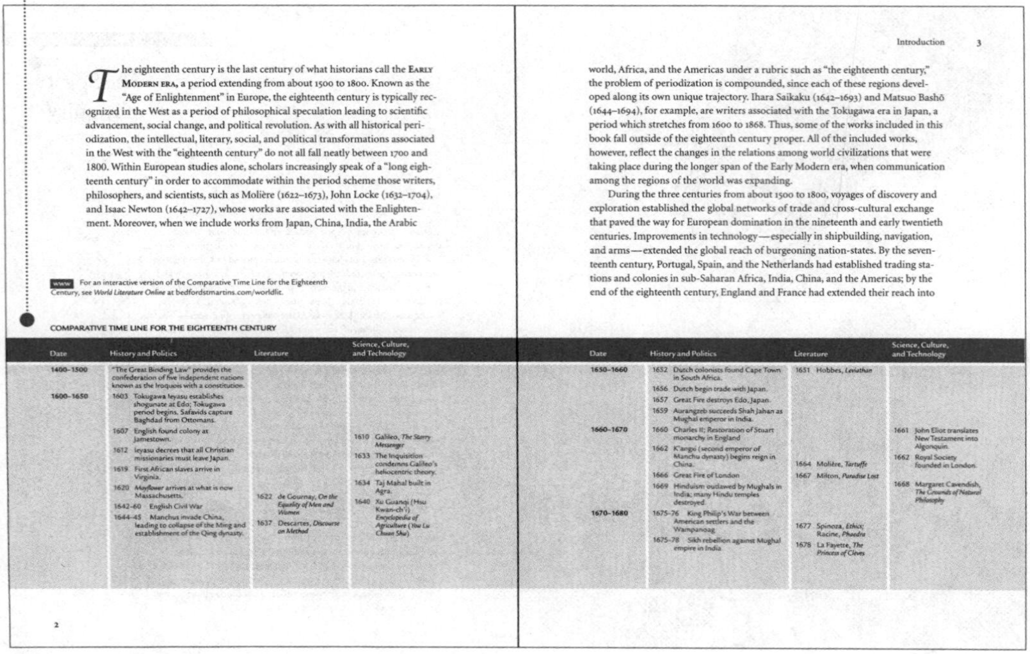

The eighteenth century is the last century of what historians call the EARLY MODERN ERA, a period extending from about 1500 to 1800. Known as the "Age of Enlightenment" in Europe, the eighteenth century is typically recognized in the West as a period of philosophical speculation leading to scientific advancement, social change, and political revolution. As with all historical periodization, the intellectual, literary, social, and political transformations associated in the West with the "eighteenth century" do not all fall neatly between 1700 and 1800. Within European studies alone, scholars increasingly speak of a "long eighteenth century" in order to accommodate within the period scheme those writers, philosophers, and scientists, such as Molière (1622–1673), John Locke (1632–1704), and Isaac Newton (1642–1727), whose works are associated with the Enlightenment. Moreover, when we include works from Japan, China, India, the Arabic

WWW For an interactive version of the Comparative Time Line for the Eighteenth Century, see *World Literature Online* at bedfordstmartins.com/worldlit.

COMPARATIVE TIME LINE FOR THE EIGHTEENTH CENTURY

Date	History and Politics	Literature	Science, Culture, and Technology
1400–1500	"The Great Binding Law" provides the confederation of five independent nations known as the Iroquois with a constitution.		
1600–1650	1603 Tokugawa Ieyasu establishes shogunate at Edo; Tokugawa period begins. Safavids capture Baghdad from Ottomans. 1607 English found colony at Jamestown. 1612 Ieyasu decrees that all Christian missionaries must leave Japan. 1619 First African slaves arrive in Virginia. 1620 *Mayflower* arrives at what is now Massachusetts. 1642–60 English Civil War 1644–45 Manchus invade China, leading to collapse of the Ming and establishment of the Qing dynasty.	1622 de Gournay, *On the Equality of Men and Women* 1637 Descartes, *Discourse on Method*	1610 Galileo, *The Starry Messenger* 1633 The Inquisition condemns Galileo's heliocentric theory. 1634 Taj Mahal built in Agra. 1640 Xu Guangqi (Hsu Kwan-ch'i) *Encyclopedia of Agriculture* (*You Lu Chuan Shu*)

2

Introduction 3

world, Africa, and the Americas under a rubric such as "the eighteenth century," the problem of periodization is compounded, since each of these regions developed along its own unique trajectory. Ihara Saikaku (1642–1693) and Matsuo Bashō (1644–1694), for example, are writers associated with the Tokugawa era in Japan, a period which stretches from 1600 to 1868. Thus, some of the works included in this book fall outside of the eighteenth century proper. All of the included works, however, reflect the changes in the relations among world civilizations that were taking place during the longer span of the Early Modern era, when communication among the regions of the world was expanding.

During the three centuries from about 1500 to 1800, voyages of discovery and exploration established the global networks of trade and cross-cultural exchange that paved the way for European domination in the nineteenth and early twentieth centuries. Improvements in technology—especially in shipbuilding, navigation, and arms—extended the global reach of burgeoning nation-states. By the seventeenth century, Portugal, Spain, and the Netherlands had established trading stations and colonies in sub-Saharan Africa, India, China, and the Americas; by the end of the eighteenth century, England and France had extended their reach into

Date	History and Politics	Literature	Science, Culture, and Technology
1650–1660	1652 Dutch colonists found Cape Town in South Africa. 1656 Dutch begin trade with Japan. 1657 Great Fire destroys Edo, Japan. 1659 Aurangzeb succeeds Shah Jahan as Mughal emperor in India.	1651 Hobbes, *Leviathan*	
1660–1670	1660 Charles II; Restoration of Stuart monarchy in England 1662 K'angxi (second emperor of Manchu dynasty) begins reign in China. 1666 Great Fire of London 1669 Hinduism outlawed by Mughals in India; many Hindu temples destroyed.	1664 Molière, *Tartuffe* 1667 Milton, *Paradise Lost*	1661 John Eliot translates New Testament into Algonquin. 1662 Royal Society founded in London. 1668 Margaret Cavendish, *The Grounds of Natural Philosophy*
1670–1680	1675–76 King Philip's War between American settlers and the Wampanoag 1675–78 Sikh rebellion against Mughal empire in India	1677 Spinoza, *Ethics*; Racine, *Phaedra* 1678 La Fayette, *The Princess of Cleves*	

"Time and Place" boxes in the introductions to the different geographical groupings of writers further orient students in the era and culture connected with the literature they're reading by spotlighting something interesting and specific about a certain place and time.

Maps included throughout the anthology show students where in the world various literatures came from. Besides the maps that open each geographical section and show countries in relation to the larger world at a given time in history, we've supplied maps that illustrate the shifting of national boundaries; industrial growth; the effects of conquest, conquerors, and colonialism; and the travels of Odysseus, Ibn Battuta, and Bashō.

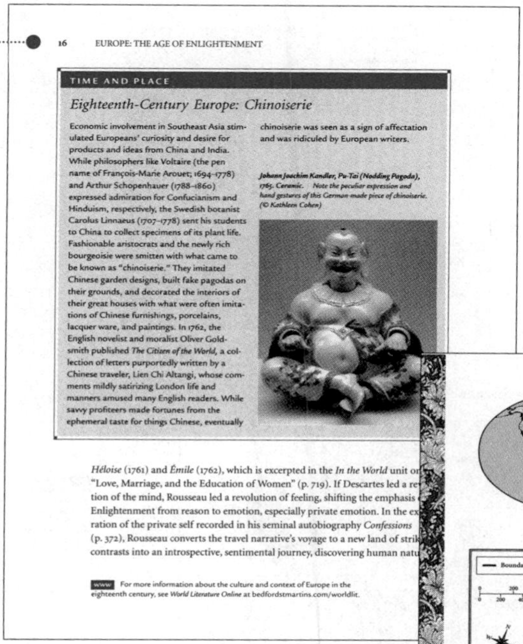

16 EUROPE: THE AGE OF ENLIGHTENMENT

TIME AND PLACE

Eighteenth-Century Europe: Chinoiserie

Economic involvement in Southeast Asia stimulated Europeans' curiosity and desire for products and ideas from China and India. While philosophers like Voltaire (the pen name of François-Marie Arouet; 1694–1778) and Arthur Schopenhauer (1788–1860) expressed admiration for Confucianism and Hinduism, respectively, the Swedish botanist Carolus Linnaeus (1707–1778) sent his students to China to collect specimens of its plant life. Fashionable aristocrats and the newly rich bourgeoisie were smitten with what came to be known as "chinoiserie." They imitated Chinese garden designs, built fake pagodas on their grounds, and decorated the interiors of their great houses with what were often imitations of Chinese furnishings, porcelains, lacquer ware, and paintings. In 1762, the English novelist and moralist Oliver Goldsmith published *The Citizen of the World*, a collection of letters purportedly written by a Chinese traveler, Lien Chi Altangi, whose comments mildly satirizing London life and manners amused many English readers. While savvy profiteers made fortunes from the ephemeral taste for things Chinese, eventually chinoiserie was seen as a sign of affectation and was ridiculed by European writers.

Johann Joachim Kandler, Pu-Tai (Nodding Pagoda), 1765. Ceramic. *Note the peculiar expression and hand gestures of this German-made piece of chinoiserie. (© Kathleen Cohen)*

Héloise (1761) and *Émile* (1762), which is excerpted in the *In the World* unit o[n] "Love, Marriage, and the Education of Women" (p. 719). If Descartes led a re[volu]tion of the mind, Rousseau led a revolution of feeling, shifting the emphasis [of the] Enlightenment from reason to emotion, especially private emotion. In the ex[plo]ration of the private self recorded in his seminal autobiography *Confessions* (p. 372), Rousseau converts the travel narrative's voyage to a new land of strik[ing] contrasts into an introspective, sentimental journey, discovering human natu[re]

WWW For more information about the culture and context of Europe in the eighteenth century, see *World Literature Online* at bedfordstmartins.com/worldlit.

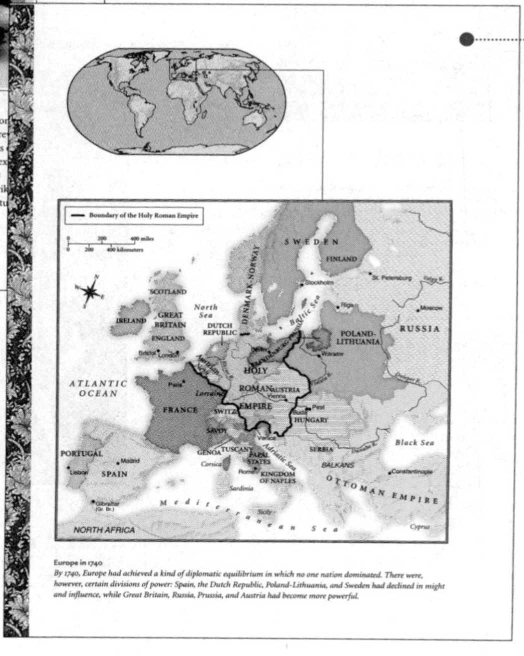

Europe in 1740

By 1740, Europe had achieved a kind of diplomatic equilibrium in which no one nation dominated. There were, however, certain divisions of power: Spain, the Dutch Republic, Poland-Lithuania, and Sweden had declined in might and influence, while Great Britain, Russia, Prussia, and Austria had become more powerful.

The anthology's many illustrations—art, photographs, frontispieces, cartoons, and cultural artifacts—are meant to bring immediacy to literature that might otherwise feel spatially and temporally remote. A few examples are a photo of the Acropolis today juxtaposed with an artist's rendering of what it looked like newly built, a sketch of the first seven circles of Dante's hell, a scene from Hogarth's *Marriage à la Mode,* the ad Harriet Jacobs's owner ran for her capture and return, an editorial cartoon mocking Darwin's evolutionary theories, and a woodcut depicting Japanese boats setting out to greet Commodore Perry's warship in their harbor.

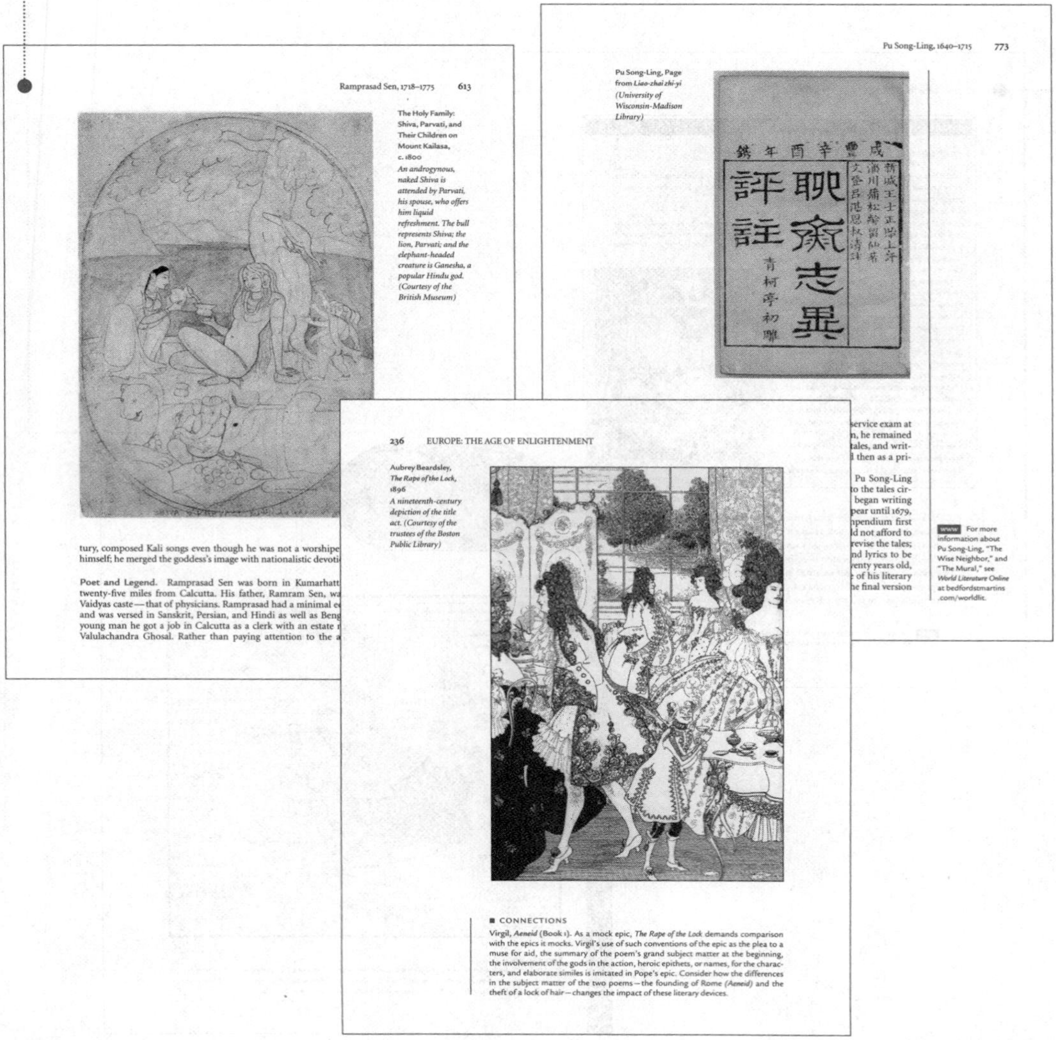

Practical and accessible editorial apparatus helps students understand what they read. Each author in the anthology is introduced by an informative and accessible literary and biographical discussion. The selections themselves are complemented with generous footnotes, marginal notes, cross-references, and critical quotations. Phonetic pronunciation guides are supplied in the margins of introductory material and before the selections for unfamiliar character and place names. Providing help with literary and historical vocabulary, bold-faced key terms throughout the text refer students to the comprehensive glossary at the end of each book.

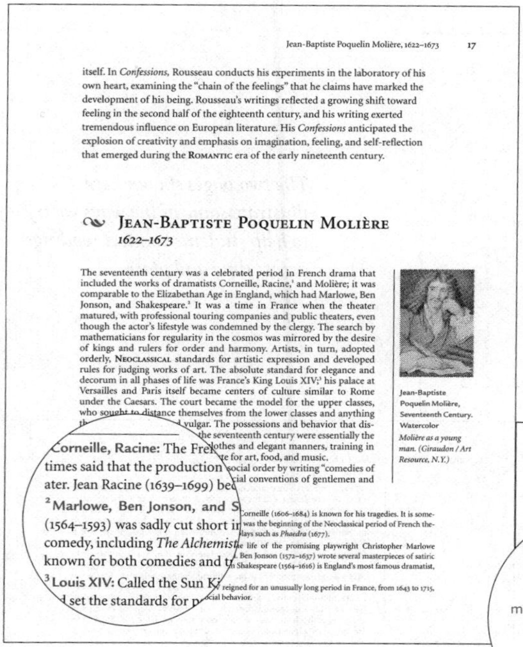

Jean-Baptiste Poquelin Molière, 1622–1673 17

itself. In *Confessions,* Rousseau conducts his experiments in the laboratory of his own heart, examining the "chain of the feelings" that he claims have marked the development of his being. Rousseau's writings reflected a growing shift toward feeling in the second half of the eighteenth century, and his writing exerted tremendous influence on European literature. His *Confessions* anticipated the explosion of creativity and emphasis on imagination, feeling, and self-reflection that emerged during the **Romantic** era of the early nineteenth century.

JEAN-BAPTISTE POQUELIN MOLIÈRE
1622–1673

The seventeenth century was a celebrated period in French drama that included the works of dramatists Corneille, Racine,[1] and Molière; it was comparable to the Elizabethan Age in England, which had Marlowe, Ben Jonson, and Shakespeare.[2] It was a time in France when the theater matured, with professional touring companies and public theaters, even though the actor's lifestyle was condemned by the clergy. The search by mathematicians for regularity in the cosmos was mirrored by the desire of kings and rulers for order and harmony. Artists, in turn, adopted orderly, **Neoclassical** standards for artistic expression and developed rules for judging works of art. The absolute standard for elegance and decorum in all phases of life was France's King Louis XIV;[3] his palace at Versailles and Paris itself became centers of culture similar to Rome under the Caesars. The court became the model for the upper classes, who sought to distance themselves from the lower classes and anything ... vulgar. The possessions and behavior that dis... the seventeenth century were essentially the ...lothes and elegant manners, training in ...te for art, food, and music. ...social order by writing "comedies of ...cial conventions of gentlemen and

Jean-Baptiste Poquelin Molière, Seventeenth Century. Watercolor
Molière as a young man. (Giraudon / Art Resource, N.Y.)

Corneille, Racine: The Fre... times said that the production ... ater. Jean Racine (1639–1699) be...
[2] Marlowe, Ben Jonson, and S... (1564–1593) was sadly cut short i... comedy, including *The Alchemist* ... known for both comedies and t...
[3] Louis XIV: Called the Sun K... set the standards for p...

...orneille (1606–1684) is known for his tragedies. It is some... was the beginning of the Neoclassical period of French the... ...lays such as *Phaedra* (1677).
...e life of the promising playwright Christopher Marlowe ... Ben Jonson (1572–1637) wrote several masterpieces of satiric ...n Shakespeare (1564–1616) is England's most famous dramatist.
... reigned for an unusually long period in France, from 1643 to 1715, ...ocial behavior.

These two pages show a sampling of the apparatus we include for each author in the book, including helpful footnotes, pronunciation guides, critical quotations, and much more.

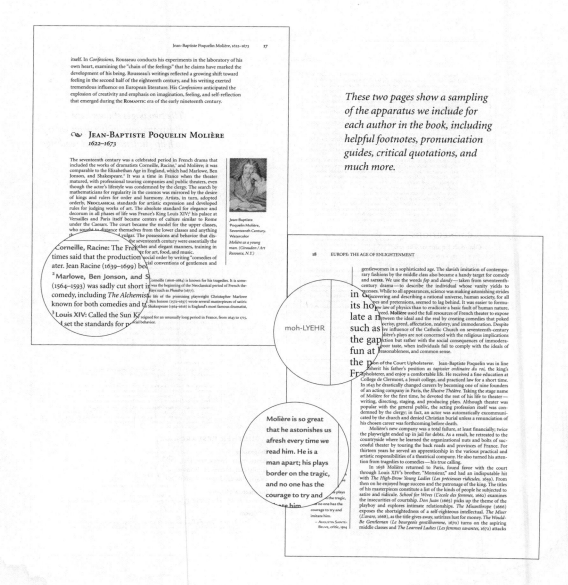

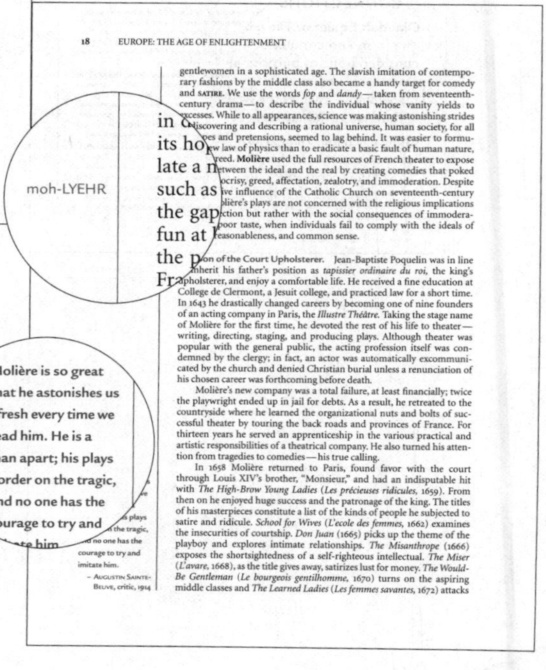

18 EUROPE: THE AGE OF ENLIGHTENMENT

gentlewomen in a sophisticated age. The slavish imitation of contemporary fashions by the middle class also became a handy target for comedy and **satire.** We use the words *fop* and *dandy*—taken from seventeenth-century drama—to describe the individual whose vanity yields to ...xcesses. While to all appearances, science was making astonishing strides ...discovering and describing a rational universe, human society, for all ...es and pretensions, seemed to lag behind. It was easier to formu... ...w law of physics than to eradicate a basic fault of human nature, ...reed. **Molière** used the full resources of French theater to expose ...etween the ideal and the real by creating comedies that poked ...ocrisy, greed, affectation, zealotry, and immoderation. Despite ...ive influence of the Catholic Church on seventeenth-century ...lière's plays are not concerned with the religious implications ...ction but rather with the social consequences of immoderate... poor taste, when individuals fail to comply with the ideals of ...easonableness, and common sense.

...on of the Court Upholsterer. Jean-Baptiste Poquelin was in line ...herit his father's position as *tapissier ordinaire du roi,* the king's ...pholsterer, and enjoy a comfortable life. He received a fine education at College de Clermont, a Jesuit college, and practiced law for a short time. In 1643 he drastically changed careers by becoming one of nine founders of an acting company in Paris, the *Illustre Théâtre.* Taking the stage name of Molière for the first time, he devoted the rest of his life to theater—writing, directing, staging, and producing plays. Although theater was popular with the general public, the acting profession itself was condemned by the clergy; in fact, an actor was automatically excommunicated by the church and denied Christian burial unless a renunciation of his chosen career was forthcoming before death.

Molière's new company was a total failure, at least financially; twice the playwright ended up in jail for debts. As a result, he retreated to the countryside where he learned the organizational nuts and bolts of successful theater by touring the back roads and provinces of France. For thirteen years he served an apprenticeship in the various practical and artistic responsibilities of a theatrical company. He also turned his attention from tragedies to comedies—his true calling.

In 1658 Molière returned to Paris, found favor with the court through Louis XIV's brother, "Monsieur," and had an indisputable hit with *The High-Brow Young Ladies* (*Les précieuses ridicules,* 1659). From then on he enjoyed huge success and the patronage of the king. The titles of his masterpieces constitute a list of the kinds of people he subjected to satire and ridicule. *School for Wives* (*L'ecole des femmes,* 1662) examines the insecurities of courtship. *Don Juan* (1665) picks up the theme of the playboy and explores intimate relationships. *The Misanthrope* (1666) exposes the shortsightedness of a self-righteous intellectual. *The Miser* (*L'avare,* 1668), as the title gives away, satirizes lust for money. *The Would-Be Gentleman* (*Le bourgeois gentilhomme,* 1670) turns on the aspiring middle classes and *The Learned Ladies* (*Les femmes savantes,* 1672) attacks

moh-LYEHR

in ... its ho... late a n... such as the gap... fun at the p... Fr...

Molière is so great that he astonishes us afresh every time we read him. He is a man apart; his plays border on the tragic, and no one has the courage to try and imitate him.
– Augustin Sainte-Beuve, critic, 1914

These terms cover the generic conventions of fiction, poetry, and drama; historical forms such as epic, epigram, and myth; and relevant historical periods such as the European Enlightenment or the Edo period in Japan.

Making connections among works from different times and places. At the end of each author introduction are two catalysts for further thought and discussion. **Questions** in the Connections apparatus tie together Western and world texts, both those within a single book and selections from other centuries, making the six books more of a unit and aiding in their interplay. **Further Research bibliographies**

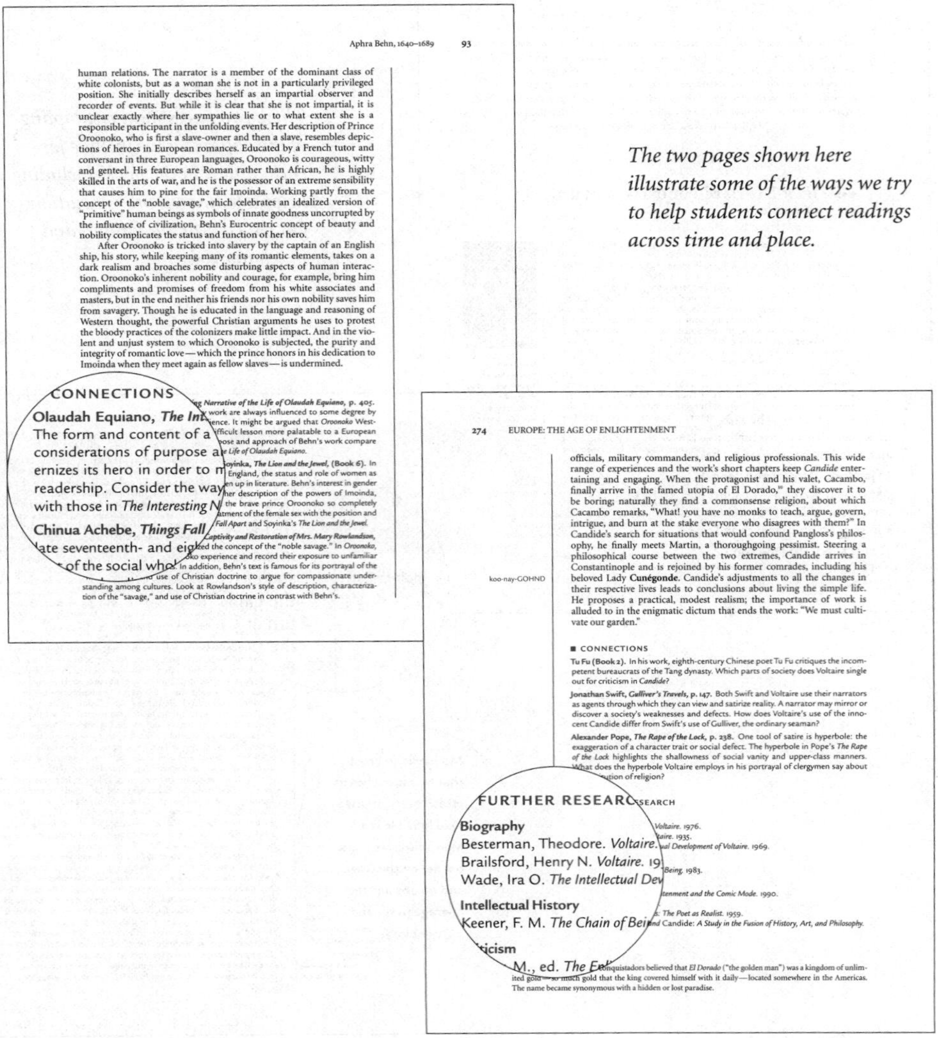

Aphra Behn, 1640–1689 93

human relations. The narrator is a member of the dominant class of white colonists, but as a woman she is not in a particularly privileged position. She initially describes herself as an impartial observer and recorder of events. But while it is clear that she is not impartial, it is unclear exactly where her sympathies lie or to what extent she is a responsible participant in the unfolding events. Her description of Prince Oroonoko, who is first a slave-owner and then a slave, resembles depictions of heroes in European romances. Educated by a French tutor and conversant in three European languages, Oroonoko is courageous, witty and genteel. His features are Roman rather than African, he is highly skilled in the arts of war, and he is the possessor of an extreme sensibility that causes him to pine for the fair Imoinda. Working partly from the concept of the "noble savage," which celebrates an idealized version of "primitive" human beings as symbols of innate goodness uncorrupted by the influence of civilization, Behn's Eurocentric concept of beauty and nobility complicates the status and function of her hero.

After Oroonoko is tricked into slavery by the captain of an English ship, his story, while keeping many of its romantic elements, takes on a dark realism and broaches some disturbing aspects of human interaction. Oroonoko's inherent nobility and courage, for example, bring him compliments and promises of freedom from his white associates and masters, but in the end neither his friends nor his own nobility saves him from savagery. Though he is educated in the language and reasoning of Western thought, the powerful Christian arguments he uses to protest the bloody practices of the colonizers make little impact. And in the violent and unjust system to which Oroonoko is subjected, the purity and integrity of romantic love—which the prince honors in his dedication to Imoinda when they meet again as fellow slaves—is undermined.

CONNECTIONS

Olaudah Equiano, *The Int* ***g Narrative of the Life of Olaudah Equiano,* p. 405.**
The form and content of a work are always influenced to some degree by considerations of purpose a ence. It might be argued that *Oroonoko* Westernizes its hero in order to m fficult lesson more palatable to a European readership. Consider the way ose and approach of Behn's work compare with those in *The Interesting N e Life of Olaudah Equiano.*

oyinka, *The Lion and the Jewel,* (Book 6). In England, the status and role of women as en up in literature. Behn's interest in gender her description of the powers of Imoinda, the brave prince Oroonoko so completely atment of the female sex with the position and

Chinua Achebe, *Things Fall* *Fall Apart* and Soyinka's *The Lion and the Jewel.*

aptivity and Restoration of Mrs. Mary Rowlandson, late seventeenth- and eig ed the concept of the "noble savage." In *Oroonoko,* oko experience and record their exposure to unfamiliar of the social who . In addition, Behn's text is famous for its portrayal of the use of Christian doctrine to argue for compassionate understanding among cultures. Look at Rowlandson's style of description, characterization of the "savage," and use of Christian doctrine in contrast with Behn's.

274 EUROPE: THE AGE OF ENLIGHTENMENT

officials, military commanders, and religious professionals. This wide range of experiences and the work's short chapters keep *Candide* entertaining and engaging. When the protagonist and his valet, Cacambo, finally arrive in the famed utopia of El Dorado,[10] they discover it to be boring; naturally they find a commonsense religion, about which Cacambo remarks, "What! you have no monks to teach, argue, govern, intrigue, and burn at the stake everyone who disagrees with them?" In Candide's search for situations that would confound Pangloss's philosophy, he finally meets Martin, a thoroughgoing pessimist. Steering a philosophical course between the two extremes, Candide arrives in Constantinople and is rejoined by his former comrades, including his beloved Lady **Cunégonde**. Candide's adjustments to all the changes in their respective lives leads to conclusions about living the simple life. He proposes a practical, modest realism; the importance of work is alluded to in the enigmatic dictum that ends the work: "We must cultivate our garden."

koo-nay-GOHND

■ CONNECTIONS

Tu Fu (Book 2). In his work, eighth-century Chinese poet Tu Fu critiques the incompetent bureaucrats of the Tang dynasty. Which parts of society does Voltaire single out for criticism in *Candide*?

Jonathan Swift, *Gulliver's Travels,* p. 147. Both Swift and Voltaire use their narrators as agents through which they can view and satirize reality. A narrator may mirror or discover a society's weaknesses and defects. How does Voltaire's use of the innocent Candide differ from Swift's use of Gulliver, the ordinary seaman?

Alexander Pope, *The Rape of the Lock,* p. 238. One tool of satire is hyperbole: the exaggeration of a character trait or social defect. The hyperbole in Pope's *The Rape of the Lock* highlights the shallowness of social vanity and upper-class manners. What does the hyperbole Voltaire employs in his portrayal of clergymen say about ution of religion?

FURTHER RESEARC SEARCH

Biography
Besterman, Theodore. *Voltaire.* 1976.
Brailsford, Henry N. *Voltaire.* 19 aire. 1935.
Wade, Ira O. *The Intellectual Dev ual Development of Voltaire.* 1969.

Intellectual History
Keener, F. M. *The Chain of Bei Being.* 1983.
tenment and the Comic Mode. 1990.

ticism
M., ed. *The En* : *The Poet as Realist.* 1959.
nd Candide: *A Study in the Fusion of History, Art, and Philosophy.*

Conquistadors believed that *El Dorado* ("the golden man") was a kingdom of unlimited gold—so much gold that the king covered himself with it daily—located somewhere in the Americas. The name became synonymous with a hidden or lost paradise.

The two pages shown here illustrate some of the ways we try to help students connect readings across time and place.

provide sources for students who want to read more critical, biographical, or historical information about an author or a work.

Print and online ancillaries further support the anthology's material. Two instructor's manuals, *Resources for Teaching* THE BEDFORD ANTHOLOGY OF WORLD LITERATURE, accompany Books 1–3 and Books 4–6 (one for each package), providing additional information about the anthology's texts and the authors, suggestions for discussion and writing prompts in the classroom and beyond, and additional connections among texts in the six books.

We are especially enthusiastic about our integrated Book Companion Site, *World Literature Online*, which provides a wealth of content and information that only the interactive medium of the Web can offer. **Web links** throughout the anthology direct

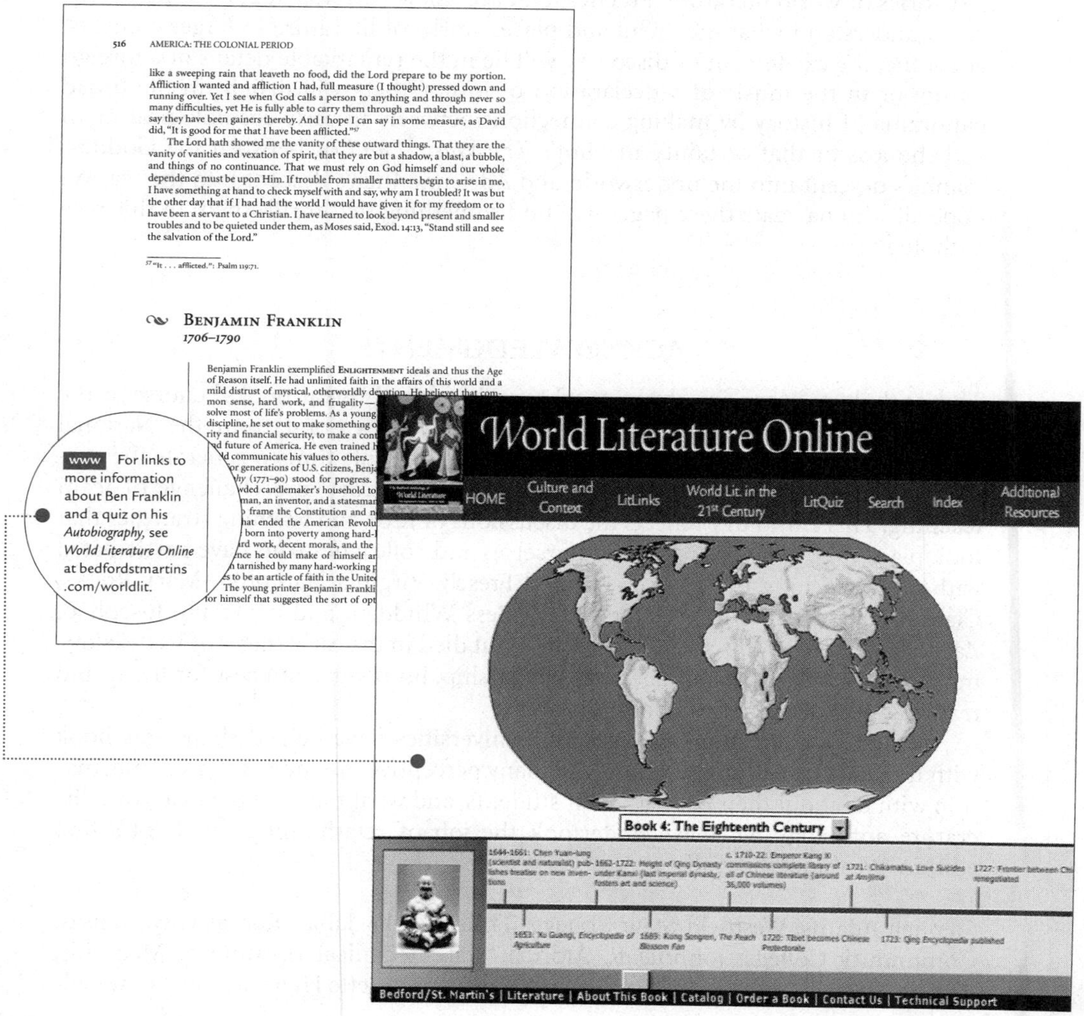

students to additional content on the Web site, where interactive illustrated time lines and maps serve as portals to more information about countries, texts, and authors. Culture and Context overviews offer additional historical background and annotated research links that students can follow to learn more on their own. Illustrated World Literature in the Twenty-First Century discussions trace the enduring presence in contemporary culture of the most frequently taught texts in world literature courses. Maps from the book are available online. Quizzes in LitQuiz offer an easy way for instructors to assess students' reading and comprehension. And LitLinks—annotated research links—provide a way for students to learn more about individual authors.

This wide variety of supplementary materials, as well as the broad spectrum of literary texts, offers teachers choices for navigating the familiar and the unfamiliar territories of world literature. Practical and accessible editorial apparatus helps students understand what they read and places works of literature in larger contexts. For some, the excitement of discovery will lie in the remarkable details of a foreign setting or in the music of a declaration of love. Others will delight in the broad panorama of history by making connections between an early cosmological myth and the loss of that certainty in Eliot's *The Waste Land* or between the Goddess Inanna's descent into the underworld and Adrienne Rich's descent into the sea. We hope all who navigate these pages will find something that thrills them in this new anthology.

ACKNOWLEDGMENTS

This anthology began in a team-taught, multicultural "great books" course at the University of New Mexico, initially developed with a grant from the National Endowment for the Humanities. The grant gave us ample time to generate the curriculum for the course, and it also supported the luxury and challenge of team teaching. This anthology reflects the discussions of texts and teaching strategies that took place over many years among ourselves and colleagues who have participated with us in teaching the course—Cheryl Fresch, Virginia Hampton, Mary Rooks, Claire Waters, Richard K. Waters, Mary Bess Whidden, and especially Joseph B. Zavadil, who began this anthology with us but died in the early stages of its development. Joe's spirit—his courage, wit, scholarship, humanity, and zest for living and teaching—endures in this book.

Reviewers from many colleges and universities have helped shape this book with their advice and suggestions. And many perceptive instructors shared information with us about their courses, their students, and what they wanted in a world literature anthology when we undertook the job of refashioning this book's first edition. We thank them all:

Stephen Adams, Westfield State College; Tamara Agha-Jaffar, Kansas City, Kansas, Community College; Johnnie R. Aldrich, State Technical Institute at Memphis; Allison Alison, Southeastern Community College; Jannette H. Anderson, Snow College; Kit Andrews, Western Oregon University; Joan Angelis, Woodbury University; Shirley Ariker, Empire State College; Sister Elena F. Arminio, College of Saint Elizabeth; Rose Lee Bancroft, Alice Lloyd College; John Bartle, Hamilton College; Amy M. Bawcom, University of Mary Hardin-Baylor; M. Susan Beck, University of Wisconsin-River Falls; Frank Beesley, Dalton State College; Peter Benson, Farleigh Dickinson University; Michael Bielmeier, Silver Lake College; Dale B. Billingsley, University of Louisville; Mark Bingham, Union University; Stephen Black, Dyersburg State Community College; Neil Blackadder, Knox College; Tyler Blake, MidAmerica Nazarene University; Gene Blanton, Jacksonville State University; James Boswell Jr., Harrisburg Area Community College; Lisa S. Bovelli, Itasca Community College; Lois Bragg, Gallaudet University; Kristin Ruth Brate, Arizona Western College; Marie Brenner, Bethel College; Linda Brown, Coastal Georgia Community College; Keith Callis, Crichton College; Charles P. Campbell, New Mexico Tech.; Zuoya Cao, Lincoln University; William Carpenter, College of ME Atlantic; May Charles, Wheeling Jesuit College; R. J. Clougherty, Tennessee Technical College; Helen Connell, Barry University; Lynn Conroy, Seton Hill College; Sue Coody, Weatherford College; Thomas A. Copeland, Youngstown State University; Peter Cortland, Quinnipiac College; R. Costomiris, Georgia Southern University; H. J. Coughlin, Eastern Connecticut State University; Marc D. Cyr, Georgia Southern University; Sarah Dangelantonio, Franklin Pierce College; James Davis, Troy State University; Barbara Dicey, Wallace College; Wilfred O. Dietrich, Blinn College; Michael Dinielli, Chaffey College; Matt Djos, Mesa State College; Marjorie Dobbin, Brewton-Parker College; Brian L. Dose, Martin Luther College; Dawn Duncan, Concordia College; Bernie Earley, Tompkins-Cortland Community College; Sarah M. Eichelman, Walters State Community College; Robert H. Ellison, East Texas Baptist University; Joshua D. Esty, Harvard University; Robert J. Ewald, University of Findlay; Shirley Felt, Southern California College; Lois Ferrer, CSU Dominguez Hills; Patricia Fite, University of the Incarnate Word; Sr. Agnes Fleck, St. Scholastica College; Robert Fliessner, Central State University; M. L. Flynn, South Dakota State University; Keith Foster, Arkansas State University; John C. Freeman, El Paso Community College; Doris Gardenshire, Trinity Valley Community College; Susan Gardner, University of North Carolina-Charlotte; Jerry D. Gibbens, Williams Baptist College; Susan Gilbert, Meredith College; Diana Glyer, Azusa Pacific University; Irene Gnarra, Kean University; R. C. Goetter, Glouster Community College; Nancy Goldfarb, Western Kentucky University; Martha Goodman, Central Virginia Community College; Lyman Grant, Austin Community College; Hazel Greenberg, San Jacinto College South; Janet Grose, Union University; Sharon Growney-Seals, Ouachita Technical College; Rachel Hadas, Rutgers University; Laura Hammons, East Central Community College; Carmen Hardin, University of Louisville; Darren Harris-Fain, Shawnee State University; Patricia B. Heaman, Wilkes University; Charles Heglan, University of South Florida; Dennis E. Hensley, Taylor University; Kathleen M. Herndon, Weber State University; Betty Higdon, Reedley College; David Hoegberg, Indiana University; Diane Long Hoeveler, Marquette University; Tyler Hoffman, Rutgers University; Lynn Hoggard, Midwestern State University; Greg Horn, Southwest VA Community College; Roger Horn, Charles County Community

College; Malinda Jay-Bartels, Gulf Coast Community College; Mell Johnson, Wallace State Community College; Kathryn Joyce, Santa Barbara City College; Steven Joyce, Ohio State University-Mansfield; Ronald A. T. Judy, University of Pittsburgh; Alan Kaufman, Bergen Community College; Tim Kelley, Northwest-Shoals Community College; Shoshanna Knapp, Virginia Technical College; Jim Knox, Roane State Community College; Mary Kraus, Bob Jones University; F. Kuzman, Bethel College; Kate Kysa, Anoka-Ramsey Community College; Linda L. Labin, Husson College; Barbara Laman, Dickinson State University; R. Scott Lamascus, GA-Southwestern State University; Sandi S. Landis, St. Johns River Community College; Ben Larson, York College; Craig Larson, Trinidad State Junior College; Linda M. Lawrence, Georgia Military College; Simon Lewis, C. of Charleston; Gary L. Litt, Moorhead State University; H. W. Lutrin, Borough of Manhattan Community College; Dennis Lynch, Elgin Community College; Donald H. Mager, Johnson C. Smith University; Barbara Manrique, California State University; W. E. Mason, Mid-Continent College; Judith Matsunobu, Atlantic Community College; Noel Mawer, Edward Waters College; Patrick McDarby, St. John's University; Judy B. McInnis, University of Delaware; Becky McLaughlin, University of Southern Alabama; Edward E. Mehok, Notre Dame College of Ohio; Patricia Menhart, Broward Community College; Arthur McA. Miller, New College of Florida; Mark James Morreale, Marist College; Toni Morris, University of Indianapolis; Philip Mosley, Penn State–Worthington; George Mower, Community College of Alleghany County; L. Carl Nadeau, University of St. Francis; Walter Nelson, Red Rocks Community College; Steven Neuwirth, Western Connecticut State University; Carol H. Oliver, St. Louis College of Pharmacy; Richard Orr, York Technical College; Geoffrey Orth, Longwood College; Ramenga M. Osotsi, James Madison University; Bonnie Pavlis, Riverside Community College; Craig Payne, Indian Hills College; Leialoha Perkins, University of Hawaii; Ralph Perrico, Mercyhurst College; Charles W. Pollard, Calvin College; Michael Popkin, Touro College; Victoria Poulakis, Northern Virginia Community College; Alan Powers, Bristol Community College; Andrew B. Preslar, Lamar University; Evan Radcliffe, Villanova University; Belle Randall, Cornish College of the Arts; Elaine Razzano, Lyndon State College; Lucia N. Robinson, Okaloosa-Walton Community College; John Rooks, Morris College; William T. Ross, University of South Florida; Andrew Rubenfeld, Stevens Institute of Technology; Elizabeth S. Ruleman, Tennessee Wesleyan College; Olena H. Saciuk, Inter-American University; Mary Lynn Saul, Worcester State College; MaryJane Schenck, University of Tampa; Kevin Schilbrack, Wesleyan College; Deborah Schlacks, University of Wisconsin; Michael Schroeder, Savannah State University; Helen Scott, Wilkes University; Asha Sen, University of Wisconsin; Mary Sheldon, Washburn University; Lisa Shoemaker, State Technical Community College; Jack Shreve, Allegany College of Maryland; Meg Simonton, Albertson College; Susan Sink, Joliet Junior College; Henry Sloss, Anne Arundel Community College; T. Sluberski, Concordia University; Betty Smith, The Criswell College; Jane Bouman Smith, Winthrop University; John Somerville, Hillsdale College; Claudia Stanger, Fullerton College; Patrick Sullivan, Manchester Community-Technical College; Joan S. Swartz, Baptist

Bible College of PA; Leah Swartz, Maryville University; Sister Renita Tadych, Silver Lake College; Janet Tarbuck, Kennebee Valley Technical College; Gina Teel, Southeast Arkansas College; Daniel Thurber, Concordia University; John Paul Vincent, Asbury College; Paul Vita, Morningside College; Tim Walsh, Otera Junior College; Julia Watson, Ohio State University; Patricia J. Webb, Maysville Community College; Lynne Weller, John Wood Community College; Roger West, Trident Technical College; Katherine Wikoff, Milwaukee School of Engineering; Evelyn M. Wilson, Tarrant County College; Carmen Wong, John Lyle Community College; Paul D. Wood, Paducah Community College; Fay Wright, North Idaho College; and finally, Pamela G. Xanthopoulos, Jackson State Community College.

We also want to thank a special group of reviewers who looked in depth at the manuscript for each book, offering us targeted advice about its strengths and weaknesses:

Cora Agatucci, Central Oregon Community College; Michael Austin, Shepherd College; Maryam Barrie, Washtenaw Community College; John Bartle, Hamilton College; Jeffry Berry, Adrian College; Lois Bragg, Gallaudet University; Ron Carter, Rappahannock Community College; Robin Clouser, Ursinus College; Eugene R. Cunnar, New Mexico State University; Karen Dahr, Ellsworth Community College; Kristine Daines, Arizona State University; Sarah Dangelantonio, Franklin Pierce College; Jim Doan, Nova SE University; Melora Giardetti, Simpson College; Audley Hall, North West Arkansas Community College; Dean Hall, Kansas State University; Wail Hassan, Illinois State University; Joris Heise, Sinclair Community College; Diane Long Hoeveler, Marquette University; Glenn Hopp, Howard Payne University; Mickey Jackson, Golden West College; Feroza Jussawalla, University of New Mexico; Linda Karch, Norwich University; David Karnos, Montana State University; William Laskowski, Jamestown College; Pat Lonchar, University of the Incarnate Word; Donald Mager, The Mott University; Judy B. McInnis, University of Delaware; Becky McLaughlin, University of South Alabama; Tony J. Morris, University of Indianapolis; Deborah Schlacks, University of Wisconsin; James Snowden, Cedarville University; David T. Stout, Luzerne County Community College; Arline Thorn, West Virginia State College; Ann Volin, University of Kansas; Mary Wack, Washington State University; Jayne A. Widmayer, Boise State University; and William Woods, Wichita State University.

No anthology of this size comes into being without critical and supportive friends and advisors. Our thanks go to the Department of English at the University of New Mexico (UNM); its chair, Scott Sanders, who encouraged and supported our work; and Margaret Shinn and the office staff, who provided administrative and technical assistance. Among our colleagues at UNM, we particularly want to thank Gail Baker, Helen Damico, Reed Dasenbrock, Patrick Gallacher, Feroza Jussawalla, Michelle LeBeau, Richard Melzer, Mary Power, Diana Robin, and Hugh Witemeyer. Several graduate students also helped with this project: Jana Giles contributed the final section on American multicultural literature; Mary Rooks wrote the sections on Aphra Behn and Wole Soyinka and served heroically as our assistant, record keeper, all-purpose editor, and consultant.

We have benefited from the knowledge and suggestions of those who have corrected our misunderstandings, illuminated topics and cultures with which we were unfamiliar, critiqued our work, and suggested ways to enrich the anthology: Paula Gunn Allen, Reynold Bean, Richard Bodner, Machiko Bomberger, Robert Dankoff, Kate Davis, Robert Hanning, Arthur Johnson, Dennis Jones, James Mischke, Harlan Nelson, Barrett Price, Clayton Rich, Julia Stein, Manjeet Tangri, William Witherup, Diane Wolkstein, and William Woods.

Resources for Teaching THE BEDFORD ANTHOLOGY OF WORLD LITERATURE was expertly developed, edited, and assembled by Mary Rooks, assisted by Julia Berrisford. Along with Mary, Shari Evans, Gabriel Gryffyn, Rick Mott, Susan Reese, Kenneth Kitchell, Randall Colaizi, Bainard Cowan, William Flesch, Fidel Fajardo-Acosta, Yigal Levin, John Phillips, and Donald R. Reese each wrote a section of the manual. The manual itself was a large and challenging endeavor; we are grateful to its authors for their enthusiasm and hard work.

A six-volume anthology is an undertaking that calls for a courageous, imaginative, and supportive publisher. Chuck Christensen, Joan Feinberg, Karen Henry, and Steve Scipione at Bedford/St. Martin's possess these qualities; we especially appreciate their confidence in our ability to carry out this task. Our editor, Alanya Harter, and her associate, Joshua Levy, have guided the project throughout, keeping us on track with a vision of the whole when we were discouraged and keeping the day-to-day work moving forward. In particular, they helped us to reconceptualize the anthology's format and content. Without their suggestions, unacknowledged contributions, and guidance, this anthology would not be what it is today. They were assisted by many others who undertook particular tasks: The brilliant design was conceived by Anna George; Genevieve Hamilton helped to manage the art program, and together with Julia Berrisford she managed the final stages of development. Martha Friedman served as photo researcher, and Tina Samaha was design consultant and map coordinator. Jeff Voccola acted as editorial assistant, taking on many tasks, including the onerous ones of pasting up and numbering the manuscript. Ben Fortson expertly and efficiently supplied the pronunciation guides. Harriet Wald tirelessly and imaginatively oversaw the content and production of the Web site, an enormous task; she was helped along the way by Coleen O'Hanley, Chad Crume, and Dave Batty. Jenna Bookin Barry enthusiastically developed and coordinated the marketing plan, especially challenging when six books publish over a span of six months.

We were blessed with a superb production team who took the book from manuscript to final pages. For Books 4 and 6, we owe special thanks to Senior Production Editor Karen Baart, whose dedication and eye for detail made the project better in every way. Stasia Zomkowski efficiently served as production editor for Books 3 and 5, Ara Salibian for Book 1, and Paula Carroll for Book 2; they were ably assisted by Courtney Jossart, Kerri Cardone, and Tina Lai. Melissa Cook's careful and thoughtful copyediting helped to give consistency and clarity to the different voices that contributed to the manuscript. Managing Editor Elizabeth Schaaf oversaw the whole process and Senior Production Supervisor Nancy Myers realized our final vision of design and content in beautifully bound and printed books.

Most of all, we thank our families, especially Mary Davis, Marlys Harrison, and Mona Johnson, for their advice, stamina, and patience during the past three years while this book has occupied so much of our time and theirs.

Paul Davis
Gary Harrison
David M. Johnson
Patricia Clark Smith
John F. Crawford

A NOTE ON TRANSLATION

Some translators of literary works into English tended to sacrifice form for literal meaning, while others subordinated literal meaning to the artistry of the original work. With the increasing number of translations of world literature available by a range of translators, it has become possible to select versions that are clear and accessible as well as literally and aesthetically faithful to the original. Thus our choice of Robert Fitzgerald's *Iliad* and *Odyssey*, Horace Gregory's poems by Catullus, Mary Barnard's poems by Sappho, Theodore Morrison's *Canterbury Tales*, Edward Seidensticker's *Tale of Genji*, and Willa and Edwin Muir's *The Metamorphosis*, among others.

There are those who question whether poetry can ever be adequately translated from one language and culture into another; our concern, however, is not with what might be lost in a translation but with what is gained. The best translations do not merely duplicate a work but re-create it in a new idiom. Coleman Barks's poems of Rumi, Stephen Mitchell's poems of Rilke, Miguel León-Portilla's translations of Nahuatl poetry, and David Hinton's poems of the Tang dynasty are in a way outstanding English poems in their own right. And William Kelly Simpson's love poems of ancient Egypt, Robert and Jean Hollander's *Inferno*, Richard Wilbur's *Tartuffe*, W. S. Merwin's poems of Ghalib, Judith Hemschemeyer's poems of Anna Akhmatova, and Robert Bly's poems of Pablo Neruda are examples of translations done by major poets whose renderings are now an important part of their own body of work.

Barbara Stoler Miller's translation of the Bhagavad Gita and Donald Keene's translation of Chikamatsu's *Love Suicides at Amijima* communicate the complexity of a literary work. Richard Bodner's contemporary translation of Bashō's *Narrow Road through the Backcountry*, especially commissioned, does justice to both the prose and the resonant haiku in that work. David Luke's excellent translation of *Death in Venice* pays tribute to Thomas Mann's original German and is at the same time very readable.

More is said about the translations in this book in the notes for individual works.

About the Editors

Paul Davis (Ph.D., University of Wisconsin), professor emeritus of English at the University of New Mexico, has been the recipient of several teaching awards and academic honors, including that of Master Teacher. He has taught courses since 1962 in composition, rhetoric, and nineteenth-century literature and has written and edited many scholarly books, including *The Penguin Dickens Companion* (1999), *Dickens A to Z* (1998), and *The Life and Times of Ebeneezer Scrooge* (1990). He has also written numerous scholarly and popular articles on solar energy and Victorian book illustration.

Gary Harrison (Ph.D., Stanford University), professor and director of undergraduate studies at the University of New Mexico, has won numerous fellowships and awards for scholarship and teaching. He has taught courses in world literature, British Romanticism, and literary theory at the University of New Mexico since 1987. Harrison's publications include a critical study on William Wordsworth, *Wordsworth's Vagrant Muse: Poetry, Poverty and Power* (1994); and many articles on the literature and culture of the early nineteenth century.

David M. Johnson (Ph.D., University of Connecticut), professor emeritus of English at the University of New Mexico, has taught courses in world literature, mythology, the Bible as literature, philosophy and literature, and creative writing since 1965. He has written, edited, and contributed to numerous scholarly books and collections of poetry, including *Fire in the Fields* (1996) and *Lord of the Dawn: The Legend of Quetzalcoatl* (1987). He has also published scholarly articles, poetry, and translations of Nahuatl myths.

Patricia Clark Smith (Ph.D., Yale University), professor emerita of English at the University of New Mexico, has taught courses in world literature, creative writing, American literature, and Native American literature since 1971. Her many publications include a collection of poetry, *Changing Your Story* (1991); the biography *As Long as the Rivers Flow* (1996); and *On the Trail of Elder Brother* (2000).

John F. Crawford (Ph.D., Columbia University), associate professor of English at the University of New Mexico–Valencia, has taught medieval, world, and other literature courses since 1965 at a number of institutions, including California Institute of Technology, Herbert Lehmann College of CUNY, and, most recently, the University of New Mexico. The publisher of West End Press, Crawford has also edited *This Is About Vision: Interviews with Southwestern Writers* (1990) and written articles on multicultural women poets of the Southwest.

Pronunciation Key

This key applies to the pronunciation guides that appear in the margins and before most selections in *The Bedford Anthology of World Literature*. The syllable receiving the main stress is CAPITALIZED.

a	mat, alabaster, laugh	MAT, AL-uh-bas-tur, LAF
ah	mama, Americana, Congo	MAH-mah, uh-meh-rih-KAH-nuh, KAHNG-goh
ar	cartoon, Harvard	kar-TOON, HAR-vurd
aw	saw, raucous	SAW, RAW-kus
ay (or a)	may, Abraham, shake	MAY, AY-bruh-ham, SHAKE
b	bet	BET
ch	church, matchstick	CHURCH, MACH-stik
d	desk	DESK
e	Edward, melted	ED-wurd, MEL-tid
ee	meet, ream, petite	MEET, REEM, puh-TEET
eh	cherub, derriere	CHEH-rub, DEH-ree-ehr
f	final	FIGH-nul
g	got, giddy	GAHT, GIH-dee
h	happenstance	HAP-un-stans
i	mit, Ipswich, impression	MIT, IP-swich, im-PRESH-un
igh (or i)	eyesore, right, Anglophile	IGH-sore, RITE, ANG-gloh-file
ih	Philippines	FIH-luh-peenz
j	judgment	JUJ-mint
k	kitten	KIT-tun
l	light, allocate	LITE, AL-oh-kate
m	ramrod	RAM-rahd
n	ran	RAN
ng	rang, thinker	RANG, THING-ker
oh (or o)	open, owned, lonesome	OH-pun, OHND, LONE-sum
ong	wrong, bonkers	RONG, BONG-kurz
oo	moot, mute, super	MOOT, MYOOT, SOO-pur
ow	loud, dowager, how	LOWD, DOW-uh-jur, HOW
oy	boy, boil, oiler	BOY, BOYL, OY-lur
p	pet	PET
r	right, wretched	RITE, RECH-id
s	see, citizen	SEE, SIH-tuh-zun
sh	shingle	SHING-gul
t	test	TEST
th	thin	THIN
th	this, whether	*TH*IS, WEH-*th*ur
u	until, sumptuous, lovely	un-TIL, SUMP-choo-us, LUV-lee
uh	about, vacation, suddenly	uh-BOWT, vuh-KAY-shun, SUH-dun-lee
ur	fur, bird, term, beggar	FUR, BURD, TURM, BEG-ur
v	vacuum	VAK-yoo-um
w	western	WES-turn
y	yesterday	YES-tur-day
z	zero, loser	ZEE-roh, LOO-zur
zh	treasure	TREH-zhur

Where a name is given two pronunciations, usually the first is the most familiar pronunciation in English and the second is a more exact rendering of the native pronunciation.

In the pronunciations of French names, nasalized vowels are indicated by adding "ng" after the vowel.

Japanese words have no strong stress accent, so the syllables marked as stressed are so given only for the convenience of English speakers.

CONTENTS

THE ANCIENT HEBREWS: The Path of Righteousness and the Ten Commandments 127

CHINA: The Ancient Way: Ancestors, Emperors, and Society *1563*

Osmand Hamdy Bay, Excavation at Nippur, 1903
Mesopotamian cities were among the earliest urban centers in antiquity. With the invention of writing in Egypt and Mesopotamia sometime around 3000 B.C.E., rulers were able to oversee larger and larger administrative areas. One of the earliest uses of writing was in keeping track of the practical and myriad details of government, from taxes and birth and death records to business transactions. This extremely realistic painting shows the early twentieth-century excavation at Nippur, a major Mesopotamian city. (University of Pennsylvania Museum [Negative #S8-6807])

The Ancient World

Beginnings
- 100 C.E.

Prior to the development of urban civilizations about five thousand years ago, much of the world's population lived on farms or in small villages. Many anthropologists believe that women were central figures in this life, and that the people of this time widely worshipped goddesses. Village life was often organized around the health and fertility of crops, herds, and people, and women were the childbearers, the nurturers, and the principal tenders of crops. Men tended to herd domestic animals and hunt wild game. Eventually, as farming populations increased in the rich alluvial plains along major rivers, like the Nile in Egypt, the Indus in Pakistan, and the Tigris and Euphrates in Mesopotamia, people began to produce a surplus of food. Small trading centers gradually grew into cities. As labor became more specialized and efficient, more workers were drawn away from cyclical, seasonal, agricultural communities, where women were impor-

www For an interactive version of the Comparative Time Line for the Ancient World, see *World Literature Online* at bedfordstmartins.com/worldlit.

COMPARATIVE TIME LINE FOR THE ANCIENT WORLD

Date	History and Politics	Literature	Science, Culture, and Technology
B.C.E. **7000–2000**	7000–1500 Neolithic, agricultural communities; mother goddesses; weaving, metallurgy.		
	3500–3000 Beginning of cities along rivers in Mesopotamia and Egypt; development of irrigation, mathematics, calendars, bureaucracies, patriarchal institutions.		c. 3400 First walled towns along the Nile in Egypt
			c. 3200 Development of cuneiform writing in Mesopotamia, hieroglyphic writing in Egypt
	c. 3100 Egypt: Upper and lower Egypt unified by Narmer.		
	c. 3000 Beginning of the Minoan civilization on Crete		c. 3000 Earliest surviving Egyptian papyri
	c. 2700 Gilgamesh, legendary king of Uruk in Mesopotamia		c. 2700–2500 Egypt: the building of the Pyramids
	c. 2620–c. 2170 Old Kingdom in Egypt		
	2600–1500 India: The Harappan civilization along the Indus River; the development of writing (as yet undeciphered).		
	c. 2340–c. 2305 Mesopotamia: the Akkadian Sargon I establishes the first empire in history.	c. 2350–2150 Egypt: Pyramid Texts	
	c. 2080–1760 Middle Kingdom in Egypt		c. 2060 Mesopotamia: Ziggurat at Ur

tant, to these newer, more urban centers; power became more centralized and the organization of larger public projects gained in importance. The creation of a military marked the increasing importance of men in urban society.

The new urban dwellers developed systems of mathematics and bookkeeping. Political organizations and bureaucracies evolved that coordinated the building of palaces, temples, pyramids, and statues. Priests created yearly calendars to mark the passage of seasons and to regulate annual ceremonies. The invention of writing was the glue that held these urban complexities together. Writing was first used to keep business accounts and tax records. It was later used to record and thus preserve an extensive religious literature that had previously been transmitted orally: myths about the origins of the world, hymns to the presiding deities, and stories about the creation of human culture. With the written word, epics were composed to honor famous warriors and their exploits; histories of kings who had created empires or dynasties and then lost them were chronicled; and an extensive history of warfare was set down. New, increased attention was paid to this world and to individuals' needs, which led to a new consciousness of the self. Poems dealt with

Date	History and Politics	Literature	Science, Culture, and Technology
B.C.E. **2000–1000**	c. 2000 Greek-speaking Achaeans enter Greece.	c. 2000 Mesopotamia: *The Descent of Inanna*	
	2000–1400 Age of the Patriarchs in Hebrew history: Abraham, Isaac, Jacob, Joseph; sojourn in Egypt.	Egypt: "Creating the World and Defeating Apophis: A Ritual Hymn"	18th century Mesopotamia: Code of Hammurabi
	c. 1800 First Dynasty of Babylon	c. 1800 Mesopotamia: *The Epic of Creation*	
	c. 1700 Minoan sea-empire at its height	Mesopotamia: *The Epic of Gilgamesh*	c. 1700 Crete: Development of writing called Linear A (as yet undeciphered)
	c. 1600–c. 1028 Shang dynasty in China	c. 1570 Egypt: "Hymn to Osiris"	c. 1600 Chariots used in China.
	1539–1078 New Kingdom in Egypt		c. 1546–1200 Worship of Osiris in Egypt
	c. 1500–1100 Mycenaean Age (Heroic Age) on the Greek mainland		1500–1000 India: Spread of the Vedic religion; creation of the caste system.
	c. 1500–c. 700 India: Invasion of Aryan tribes; the Vedic Age.		
	c. 1450 Downfall of Minoans on Crete		r. 1353–1336 Egypt: Amenhotep IV (Akhenaten) promotes monotheism.
	13th century Hebrews' Exodus from Egypt	c. 1320 Egypt: "Hymn to Aten"	13th century Moses and the Ten Commandments
	c. 1250 Hebrew conquest of Canaan	1290–1078 Egypt: Ancient love poems	

love, sadness, and loss. Midway through the first millennium B.C.E., new religions emerged that spoke of virtue and suffering, and philosophical treatises expounded the secular ingredients of a good life.

THE IDEA OF COSMOGONY

COSMOGONY is a picture or model of the cosmos that demonstrates how life on earth with its rulers and systems of government is coordinated with the powers and patterns of the heavens. The discovery by Mesopotamian mathematicians and astronomers of the movement of planets through constellations of fixed stars led to what was probably the earliest systematic cosmogony, one that mapped out basic celestial relationships and cyclical patterns of movement. A hierarchy of deities reflecting heavenly patterns became the model and justification for an earthly hierarchical system of kings, priests, and underlings. The organization of gods into various roles was the glorified example of the specialization of earthly culture into religion, politics, education, and agriculture and the division of society into social classes. The temple, or **ZIGGURAT**, the earthly residence of the god or gods, took its place in the center of the city-state, where rulers (often deified) and nobility

Date	History and Politics	Literature	Science, Culture, and Technology
B.C.E. **2000–1000 (cont.)**	c. 1200 Trojan War and the fall of Troy 1200–1030 Israel: Period of Judges 1200–1000 Iron Age invasions; further conquest of India by Aryans, who spread the Vedic religion. 1100 Dorian invasion of Greece; destruction of Mycenaean fortresses; migration of Greeks to Asia Minor. c. 1027–221 Zhou (Chou) dynasty in China		c. 1200 China: Development of a writing system Phoenician alphabet of twenty-two letters Olmecs create urban centers in Mesoamerica.
1000–500	1000–922 Israel: Reigns of Kings David and Solomon c. 1000–600 India: the Brahmanic period 922 Israel divided into two kingdoms 826 Founding of Carthage	c. 1000 India: Rig Veda c. 1000–600 China: Shi jing (*Book of Songs*) 900–500 Israel: Book of Genesis, Book of Exodus (Hebrew Scriptures) 9th century India: Upanishads 8th century Greece: Hesiod, *Theogony* and *Works and Days*	c. 800 Lycurgus, the legendary lawgiver of Sparta (Greece) Greece adopts an alphabet.

mirrored the divine pantheon of deities by ordering the course of civic and social life and participating in the fertility cycles of nature. About the third millennium B.C.E. the ancient Egyptians developed a similar cosmogony, an orderly and eternal system that they believed had been created by the gods even though chaos and the forces of disorder periodically threatened it.

Behind both the Mesopotamian and Egyptian models of heaven and earth was the idea of immutability, or permanence, an abstract force thought to hold the cosmic hierarchy in place, ensuring its functioning, its rightness in the midst of change or flux. This idea was at the core of all civilizations that were sustained for any length of time. Sumerians, who created the first Mesopotamian civilization in the fourth millennium B.C.E., called the collective rules and regulations governing the universe the ***ME***'s, and first entrusted them to the goddess Inanna. The Egyptians referred to cosmic order as ***MAAT***, which was the responsibility of the sun-god Re and eventually became the goddess Maat, who accompanied Re in his sun-boat. The priests of India called the principle of justice ***DHARMA***, while the ancient Chinese invoked the principle of the **DAO**. The principle of justice in ancient Greece was named **MOIRA**; it eventually evolved into **LOGOS**. In Israel, a just universe was

Date	History and Politics	Literature	Science, Culture, and Technology
B.C.E. **1000–500 (cont.)**	753 Legendary founding of Rome by Romulus 721 Northern Kingdom of Israel is conquered by Assyria (Shalmaneser V) and disappears. 721–705 Assyrian dynasty founded by Sargon II 605–562 Babylonia: Nebuchadnezzar's reign 594 Greece: Solon's reforms in Athens	8th century (cont.) Greece: Homer, *The Iliad* and *The Odyssey* Mesopotamia: Sargon II, *Annalistic Reports* c. 800 China: Shu jing (Book of History) 7th century Mesopotamia: *The Epic of Gilgamesh*, standard version 6th century India: *Ramayana* 6th–3rd centuries China: Laozi (Lao Tzu) 6th century B.C.E.–1st century C.E. India: Uttardhyayana Sutra (Jain Text) c. 600 Greece: Sappho, poems 5th century China: Confucius (Kongfuzi), *The Analects* Israel: Book of Job (Hebrew Scriptures)	776 First Olympic Games 7th–6th centuries Zoroastrianism in Persia; Hebrew prophets in Israel r. 669–633 Mesopotamia: Assurbanipal, king of Assyria, creates an extensive library. 621 The Book of Deuteronomy, "discovered" by Josiah, leads to religious reforms in Judah. 6th century Rise of Doric and Ionic architecture in Greece. Rome: Latin alphabet is developed. 6th–3rd centuries China: period of the "Hundred Philosophers" c. 539–468 India: Mahavira (founder of Jainism)

guaranteed by the Jewish god **YAHWEH**, who, the Jews believed, personally intervened in history to uphold righteousness.

WRITING AND LITERATURE

Urban civilization would not have been possible without the invention of writing. About 3200 B.C.E., both the Mesopotamians and the Egyptians began to develop a writing system—commonly defined as a system of human communication by means of conventional visible marks linked to spoken language. It is not known which culture was actually first. After a **PICTOGRAPHIC** stage, which tends to be an early stage in all writing systems, the Mesopotamians developed **CUNEIFORM**, a series of wedge-shaped marks that designated syllables and were capable of expressing a full range of meaning. The ancient Egyptian priesthood produced a picture-based system that the Greeks called "sacred carvings," or **HIEROGLYPHICS**. Other major writing systems followed in the Indus Valley in India (2600–1900 B.C.E.), in China (1200 B.C.E. to the present), and in Phoenicia and Greece in the Levant (1050 B.C.E. to the present). In the Americas, a writing system was invented by the Maya (250 C.E. to 900).

Date	History and Politics	Literature	Science, Culture, and Technology
B.C.E. 1000–500 (cont.)	587–586 Israel: Jerusalem is destroyed by Nebuchadnezzar; Babylonian captivity of the Jews. c. 550 Cyrus the Great establishes Persian empire. 546 Fall of Ionia (western Turkey) to Persia 539 Fall of Babylon to Cyrus (Persia) 509 Rome: Brutus establishes Roman Republic 507 Greece: Cleisthenes' democratic reforms in Athens		563–483 India: Siddhartha Gautama (founder of Buddhism) 551–479 China: Confucius (Kongfuzi) c. 550 Zoroastrianism becomes official religion of Persia. c. 544 Beginnings of Attic tragedy in Greece c. 520–515 Palestine: Second Temple is built.
500–300	490 Greece: Athenians defeat Persians at the Battle of Marathon. 461–429 Greece: Age of Pericles (Golden Age) in Athens 431–404 Greece: Peloponnesian War	c. 475 Greece: Heraclitus, *Fragments* 458 Greece: Aeschylus, *The Oresteia* (*Agamemnon, The Libation Bearers, The Eumenides*) c. 441 Greece: Sophocles, *Antigone* 431 Greece: Euripides, *Medea*	5th century Athens: Phidias sculpts Athena Parthenos and Zeus. 486 Athens: Contests for best comedy c. 450 Invention of the crossbow in China 432 The Parthenon in Athens is completed.

Creation myths, often the earliest literature of ancient civilizations, were written to express a cosmogony: how the world came into being, who runs it, and how humans participate in it. A religious interpretation of the sky and the cosmos in early stories is usually balanced by a concern with the earth, the cycle of seasons that becomes the basis of religious ritual. The transformation of a seed into a plant is compared to the phases in the life of a spiritual being, a god or a goddess. Out of this natural process came the complex rituals or ceremonies in which the birth, growth, and death of the god of nature were dramatized and acted out. Often these dramas contain the secrets of immortality and life after death. In ancient Sumer, the story of the descent of the goddess Inanna into the underworld reflects the vegetation cycle; in Egypt the same cycle is dramatized in the story of Isis and the death and resurrection of Osiris. In Greece, the yearly agricultural cycles are invoked by the story of Demeter and Persephone; and in Syria, in the story of Attis. The Christian Easter services and rituals seem a successor to these ceremonies. The celebrated correlation between gods and humankind, between the heavens and the earth was institutionalized in an astronomically based religious calendar that marked the major annual festivals. Since then, priests and rulers throughout the

Date	History and Politics	Literature	Science, Culture, and Technology
B.C.E. 500–300 (cont.)	c. 403–221 China: Warring States period	c. 430 Greece: Herodotus, *History of the Persian Wars* Greece: Sophocles, *Oedipus Rex* c. 420 Greece: Thucydides, *History of the Peloponnesian War* 411 Greece: Aristophanes, *Lysistrata* 4th century–1st century B.C.E. India: *Majjhima Nikaya, Samyutta Nikaya, Mahaparinibbana Sutta* (Buddhist texts) 4th century B.C.E.–4th century C.E. India: *Mahabharata* 4th century Dao De Jing (Tao Te Ching) China: Zhuangzi's (Chuang Tzu's) writings	c. 400 Rise of Daoism (Taoism) in China Brahmi syllabic script in India 399 Execution of Socrates in Athens c. 386 Plato founds the Academy in Athens c. 371–c. 288 Mencius (Mengzi), Chinese philosopher c. 370 Hippocrates, the Greek Father of Medicine, dies. c. 336 Aristotle founds the Lyceum. c. 330 Egypt: Founding of the library at Alexandria

ancient Near East and the Mediterranean have validated their agendas and creeds with celestial authority, as if to say, "This is the way that the gods intended it!"

EMPIRES AND HEROES

The negative side of civilization has always been its organized warfare, slavery, rape, theft, and destruction. The spread of a patriarchal warrior culture characterized the third millennium B.C.E. in both Mesopotamia and Egypt. Both peoples in those regions devoted their resources to waging war with neighboring city-states and empire-building. Ruling bureaucracies became more and more complex, while religion and law became increasingly codified. In the third millennium B.C.E., migrant tribes from the north called Aryans invaded India and imposed patriarchal institutions, such as the caste system, on settlements along the Indus River—an indigenous culture now called Harappan. These Aryan tribes, which gradually moved across India, were part of a larger nomadic group from Central Asia called Indo-Europeans that swept in a series of waves into Greece and Italy, overwhelming the agricultural communities in their path. A similar pattern of conquest occurred in China during the Shang dynasty (c. 1600–c. 1028 B.C.E.), when a

Date	History and Politics	Literature	Science, Culture, and Technology
B.C.E. 500–300 (cont.)	331 Egypt: Founding of Alexandria. 323 Death of Alexander the Great c. 322–c. 185 India: the Maurya empire 305 Ptolemy becomes the ruler of Egypt.	4th century (cont.) China: Mencius (Mengzi), philosophical writings Greece: Plato, *Apology, Phaedo, The Republic,* and *Timaeus* Greece: Aristotle, Poetics and Metaphysics	
300–1		c. 300 Israel: Song of Songs (Hebrew Scriptures) Greece: Euhemerus, *Sacred History* 3rd century B.C.E.–1st century C.E. India: Uttaradhyayana Sutra (Jain text) 3rd century India: Ashoka Maurya, *Asokavadana* India: Kautilya, *Arthashastra* (*The Treatise on Material Gain*)	3rd century First Great Wall of China is completed during Qin dynasty. 250–100 Egypt: Hebrew Scriptures translated into Greek (Septuagint).

nomadic Eurasian people brought a militaristic culture to the mainland, introducing horses, the chariot, metallurgy, and a class-based society to the region.

Later literature romanticizes these early periods of empire-building and immortalizes warrior-kings and other heroes in magnificent epic poems about what historians refer to as the Heroic Ages. The most famous such eras are the Greek Heroic Age, which occurred near the end of the second millennium B.C.E.; the Heroic Age of India, which followed a few centires later; and the Heroic Age of northern Europe, which is dated from the fourth to the sixth centuries C.E. There was, however, the much earlier Heroic Age that flourished some fifteen-hundred years before Greece—the Sumerian Heroic Age of Mesopotamia. It inspired several cycles of epic poems, only one of which has survived, *The Epic of Gilgamesh.* The most famous epics of ancient times—*The Iliad* and *The Odyssey* from Greece, the *Ramayana* and *Mahabharata* from India, and the Old English *Beowulf*—share characteristics. They celebrate the unusual and sometimes miraculous exploits of individual heroes, men assisted or thwarted by divine beings. They abound in epithets, formulas, catalogs, and speeches, features that testify to their stories' origins in an earlier oral tradition. The Greek Heroic tradition is the one that is most

Date	History and Politics	Literature	Science, Culture, and Technology
B.C.E. **300–1 (cont.)**	r. c. 273–c. 232 India: Ashoka, the first Buddhist emperor in history. 270 Rome rules all of Italy. 264–146 Punic Wars: Rome versus Carthage 221–206 The first Chinese empire: Qin (Ch'in) dynasty 206 B.C.E.–220 C.E. China: Han dynasty 200 Roman conquest of Greece begins. 63 Rome seizes control of Palestine. 60 Rome: First Triumvirate (Julius Caesar, Pompey, Crassus) 44 Rome: Assassination of Caesar 43 Rome: Second Triumvirate (Antony, Octavian, Lepidus) 27 Rome: Establishment of empire by Augustus Caesar	3rd century (cont.) Greece: Epicurus, *Letter to Menoeceus* Greece: Cleanthes, "Invocation," and "Hymn to Zeus" 2nd century B.C.E. Greece: Apollodorus, *Bibliotheca* 2nd century B.C.E.–1st century C.E. Israel: Dead Sea Scrolls 1st century B.C.E.–1st century C.E. India: Bhagavad Gita c. 145–85 China: Sima Qian (Ssu-ma Ch'ien), *Historical Records* (first history of China) 1st century Rome: Lucretius, *The Nature of the Universe* Rome: Catullus, poems c. 19 Rome: Virgil, *The Aeneid*	c. 170 First paved roads in Rome 165 Invention of parchment (vellum) in Asia Minor 136 Confucianism becomes official doctrine in China.

known in the West; in addition to the warrior's code of honor and courage, the Greek epic values the intelligence and beauty of individuals, including women. The heroes of the *Ramayana*—Rama, the incarnation of the god Vishnu, and Sita, his wife—became models of love, heroism, and friendship for millions of Hindus. The central action of *Mahabharata*, a war among cousins and bands of brothers, is complemented with moral digressions, elaborate rituals, and romantic episodes that have been a source of education, art, and literature in India to the present day.

RELIGION AND PHILOSOPHY

A profound change of a religious and moral nature took place in Europe and Asia in the period 700–400 B.C.E. evidenced by a decrease of interest in the mythic stories about the cosmic realm and the emergence of a literature concerned with the philosophical challenges of this world. **Zoroastrianism**, which had been founded by Zoroaster perhaps as early as 1200 B.C.E. and saw the world in terms of a struggle between good and evil, became the religion of the Persian state during this time. In India, some teachers rejected the ritual life prescribed by the **Vedas** and the dominance of the **Brahmins**, or the caste of priests, and turned to the

Date	History and Politics	Literature	Science, Culture, and Technology
B.C.E. **300–1 (cont.)**	27 B.C.E.–180 C.E. Rome: *Pax Romana* (Two hundred plus years of peace)		c. 5 B.C.E.–c. 30 C.E. Palestine: Jesus of Nazareth (founder of Christianity)
C.E. **1–300**		1st century C.E. Israel: Flavius Josephus, *The Jewish War*	
		Egypt: Philo Judaeus, *On the Creation of the World*	
		Rome: Petronius, *The Satyricon*	
		c. 8 Rome: Ovid, *Metamorphoses*	
	25–220 Later Han dynasty in China	c. 50 Paul's letters to Christian churches	c. 46 C.E. Palestine: Paul's missionary journeys begin.
	70 Titus destroys the First Temple in Jerusalem and exiles Jews.	65–70 Gospel of Mark (Christian Scriptures)	61–113 Pliny, the great Roman naturalist
			70 Colosseum begun at Rome.
		late 80s Gospel of Matthew (Christian Scriptures)	90 Council of Jamnia; rabbis settle canon of Hebrew Bible.
		c. 95 The Revelation of St. John the Divine (Christian Scriptures)	

program of personal development described in the **Upanishads. Buddhism**, one of the earliest world religions, was founded at this time. In China this was the age of Confucius, Laozi (Lao Tzu), and the great Chinese schools of philosophy. The transformation in Greece began with such sixth-century-B.C.E. philosophers as Heraclitus and Pythagoras and continued in Periclean Athens with Socrates, Plato, and Aristotle. In the seventh and sixth centuries B.C.E., the great Hebrew prophets of Israel—Isaiah, Jeremiah, and Ezekiel—transformed Judaism. These revolutionary thinkers as well as others focused attention on "historical reality"; that is, a shift of focus from a preoccupation with the transcendent reality of the heavens and issues of faith to a concern with the phenomenal, physical world of the present that can be discovered by rational thought.

During this period, moral and religious philosophers struggled to discover a basic principle that governed life. Some proposed that humans were primarily motivated by desire or pleasure. Others saw humans as essentially rational creatures capable of creating a just society. The concept of sin was developed to explain the existence of evil in the world. The doctrine of karma articulated the relationship between action and consequences, extending even into previous lifetimes. In

Date	History and Politics	Literature	Science, Culture, and Technology
C.E. 1–300 (cont.)	c. 100–240 Kushan empire in India	c. 100 India: Ashvaghosha, *The Life of Buddha* 2nd century Greece: Plutarch, *Moralia* Rome: Suetonius, *The Lives of the Twelve Caesars* Rome: Marcus Aurelius, *Meditations* 3rd century Greece: Diogenes Laertius, *Lives of Eminent Philosophers*	c. 100 Buddhism enters China. c. 105 China: Invention of paper 118–126 Construction of the Pantheon at Rome c. 250 Mesoamerica: The Maya invent a writing system.
300–500	313 Emperor Constantine proclaims religious toleration, including Christianity. 320–c. 550 Gupta empire in India 410 The Visigoth Alaric sacks Rome. 476 The barbarian Odoacer replaces the last emperor and ends the Roman Empire.	413–426 St. Augustine, *The City of God*	

poetry, parables, sermons, maxims, and proverbs, the great prophets and teachers of this period created ethical systems that described the nature of the good life and its possible fruits. Some individual belief systems pointed to a variety of rewards available in this lifetime: prosperity, enlightenment, peace of mind, nirvana. Others emphasized punishment, depicting the physical and mental pain one would suffer—usually after death—if one failed to follow a particular path.

THE LEGACY OF LITERATURE

It is difficult to overestimate the role of writing and literacy in the history of the world. However ancient texts are interpreted or even misunderstood, their very longevity offers a potential link between the peoples of ancient civilizations and the present day. A Sanskrit text from the first century C.E. may be the inspiration for a Chinese novel of a thousand years later. The power of writing and the almost magical possibility of immortality that it holds were understood by the Egyptian scribe who wrote:

> Man dies, his body is dust,
> his family all brought low to the earth;
> But writing shall make him remembered,
> alive in the mouths of any who read.
> Better a book than a builded mansion,
> better than body's home in the West,
> Splendid above a fine house in the country
> or stone-carved deeds in the precinct of God.
>
> –(from *Papyrus Chester Beatty IV*, C. 1300–1100 B.C.E.)

A comparison of writing with nonwriting cultures shows the profound impact of the written word. The first use of writing appears to have been record keeping. It is thought that Mesopotamian scribes were associated with temples and palaces and considered so important that special schools were established to train them. They kept business records and transcribed sacred knowledge that in part validated the importance of priests. As written documentation accumulated, it provided a means of attending to the evolution of a society's political, social, and religious institutions.

Ownership of written texts was sometimes exploited for power. Rulers and priests often guarded written records thought to be magical and powerful. Writing made it possible to manipulate the letters of god's name for purposes of divination, for example the use of runes by the Scandinavians and the practices of the Jewish cabalists. Ceremonial texts of Egypt, Mesopotamia, and India were not shared with ordinary mortals since they were seen as privileged communications from the gods. The **Brahmins**, the priest caste of India, took another tack. They preserved an oral tradition for passing down their teachings as a means of restricting access to sacred lore. The guru tradition in Hinduism and Buddhism, by contrast to all of the above, combines literate and oral modes of communication in order to better *share* wisdom; a guru's talks or information addresses are an essential addition to what has been recorded in books.

Literacy altered oral literatures by "fixing" their stories. Once they were written down, these literatures could be analyzed, canonized, and re-created in art and philosophy. Written texts became the basis for schools of religion and philosophy. Theologians, philosophers, and critics have argued about the meaning of the particular words and literal and allegorical interpretations of religious writings ever since they were published. Lengthy commentaries have been written on minute particulars of religious doctrine, sometimes causing schisms or even wars.

Literacy constitutes the very core of modern society. The teachings of Confucius, passed down for more than two thousand years, continue to shape Chinese society today. The poetry of Laozi is probably more popular today than ever, with new translations appearing regularly. Following the dictates of the Vedas and the Upanishads for almost three thousand years, Hinduism is practiced by almost a billion people today. The Hebrew Scriptures, with their ideals of law and righteousness, spawned Judaism and two additional world religions: Christianity, with more than a billion and a half followers, and Islam, whose followers approach one billion. And the various literatures of Greece, which greatly expanded the boundaries of human potential and creativity, are ever present in almost every aspect of Western politics, art, literature, and philosophy.

A note on dating ancient literatures: The designations B.C. and A.D., proposed by a Scythian monk, Dionysius Exiguus, in 525 C.E. in response to a request by Pope John I to prepare a chronology, stand for "before Christ" and "anno Domini," or "in the year of the Lord." Revising Diocletian's calendar from the third century, Dionysius Exiguus fixed December 25 as the date of Jesus' birth and made the following January 1 the start of 1 A.D. He called the previous year 1 B.C. and numbered preceding years accordingly, back to the date of creation. Dionysius' calendar was adopted in Europe by the eighth century, with other parts of the world following in later years. Today, however, as a way of recognizing the diversity of religions and cultures around the globe, publishing houses, scholars, and writers are increasingly substituting B.C.E. ("before the common era") and C.E. ("common era") for B.C. and A.D., which refer to the same periods of time, respectively.

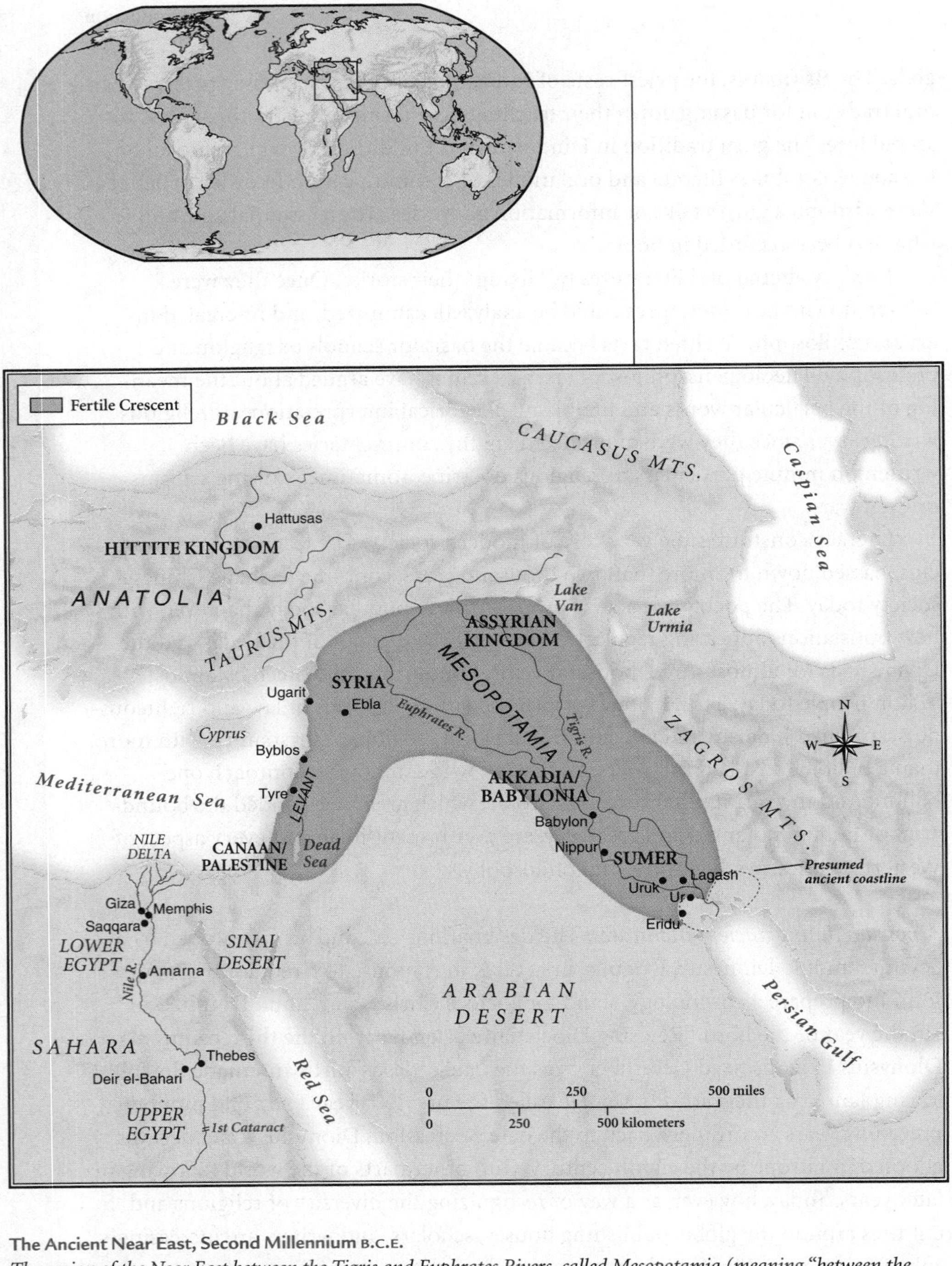

The Ancient Near East, Second Millennium B.C.E.

The region of the Near East between the Tigris and Euphrates Rivers, called Mesopotamia (meaning "between the rivers"), is thought to be the birthplace of civilization—non-nomadic societies characterized by agriculture and cities. The inhabitants of Mesopotamia raised crops on this rich but dry land by developing and using complex irrigation systems so successful they resulted in a surplus of food. This in turn led to population growth and the emergence of cities.

MESOPOTAMIA
The Formation of Cities and the Earliest Literatures

The various peoples who created the city-states and empires along the Tigris and Euphrates Rivers in what is today Iraq are referred to collectively as Mesopotamians—from the Greek meaning "between the rivers." Some time before 3500 B.C.E., a remarkable, dark-haired people called Sumerians settled in this area and with sophisticated irrigation systems developed the agricultural surplus necessary for the building of cities like Uruk, Nippur, and Eridu. Still, life was precarious. There were storms, floods, and drought, and early communities were vulnerable to invasions from nomadic raiders from the desert. Walled cities were constructed to protect domestic life from robbers and foreign armies.

Written and archeological records indicate that Sumerians created a complex, interwoven theocracy, a system of government in which the fortunes of individual city-states were controlled by individual gods who actually owned religious real estate in each city. The assembly of citizens who determined earthly, urban affairs was mirrored in the PANTHEON of gods: four gods controlled the heavens, the earth, the sea, and the air, while numerous other deities dealt with the fates, influenced human events, and determined patterns of weather, agricultural crops, and military engagements. The prestige of a deity depended on whether his or her city prospered. The earthly residence of the deity was a temple, or ZIGGURAT, from the Akkadian *ziqqurratu,* meaning "mountaintop," located in the center of the city-state. The root meaning of *ziggurat* seems to indicate that the Sumerians originally came from a mountainous region. Like the pyramids of Egypt and ancient Mexico, these tall temples rose high above the plains toward communion with the powers of heaven. Social and political roles eventually became specialized. A labor force was developed to build public structures. A strong military was needed to protect domestic food supplies and to raid granaries in rival cities. Village chieftains evolved into generals and kings, and Sumerian women were involved in the business activities of the temple, owned real estate in their own names, and were

Cylinder Seal Showing the Goddess Inanna/Ishtar, 2254–2193 B.C.E.
Cylinder seals served a practical purpose in ancient cultures. They were used to guarantee authenticity, mark ownership, formalize legal transactions, and protect property against theft. The images carved into the seals were most often those of gods, goddesses, and rulers—and no two were alike. The winged goddess Inanna/Ishtar is shown here with her right foot atop a roaring lion. (Courtesy of the Oriental Institute of the University of Chicago)

moneylenders. The status of Sumerian women is reflected in the respect paid to goddess figures in Sumerian mythology, especially to the goddess Inanna. There are indications that women had more privileges in Sumerian society around 3000 B.C.E. than they did later, in 1800 B.C.E. or so.

CUNEIFORM WRITING

The Sumerians and the Egyptians were the earliest peoples to develop writing systems, starting in about 3200 B.C.E. The Sumerians first used pictographic symbols for keeping business records, but pictograms were limited to lists and catalogs. By 2800 B.C.E. **CUNEIFORM** was developed—from the Latin *cuneus*, meaning "wedge"—so named for the wedge-shaped reed stylus used by scribes to inscribe characters on wet clay, which dried into a semipermanent record (clay tablets are subject to breakage). Cuneiform signs stood for syllables or sounds, not individual letters, as is true of alphabetic writing. Because someone reading cuneiform had to memorize a great number of signs, literacy tended to be limited to a special class, professional specialists trained for government service. Sumerian script was used to create written literature on clay tablets at least by 2750 B.C.E., perhaps earlier. Cuneiform spread to other Near Eastern cultures and was employed by successors to the Sumerians in the region—the Akkadians, Babylonians, Hittites, and Assyrians. It slowly fell into disuse after Alexander the Great's death in 323 B.C.E., when that ruler's empire broke up and Mesopotamia became part of the Seleucid kingdom late in the fourth century B.C.E.

Sumerian Cuneiform Tablet, 2350 B.C.E.
The Sumerians were one of the earliest literate peoples. Here, an accounting tablet records the number of goats and sheep someone owned. (The Art Archive/Musée du Louvre, Paris/Dagli Orti)

AKKADIANS AND BABYLONIANS

About 2300 B.C.E., a Semitic people from the interior of the Arabian peninsula called Akkadians conquered the non-Semitic Sumerians and under Sargon I (c. 2340–c. 2305 B.C.E.) established the first known empire in history—stretching from the Persian Gulf to the Mediterranean Sea. In a remarkable text written in his own words, Sargon the Great describes his secret birth from an *enitum,* a priestess who participated in the sacred marriage ritual with the king. The following passage is reminiscent of the story of Moses in the Book of Exodus and Karna's birth in the Mahabharata.

My mother, an *enitum,* conceived me; in secret she bore me,
She set me in a basket of rushes, with bitumen she sealed my lid,
She cast me into the river, which rose not over me,

> The river bore me up and carried me to Akki, the drawer of water.
> Akki, the drawer of water, lifted me out as he dipped his bucket.
> Akki, the drawer of water, took me as his son and reared me,
> Akki, the drawer of water, appointed me as his gardener.
> While I was a gardener, Ishtar [goddess of fertility] granted me her love,
> And for four and . . . years I exercised kingship,
> The black-headed people I ruled, I governed.

The Akkadians transformed Sumerian sociopolitical institutions by gradually replacing Sumerian goddesses' powers with those of Akkadian gods. While integrating Sumerian myths, literature, and technical expertise into their culture, the Akkadians ensured the dominance of males in their society through private property rights, class distinctions, the superiority of sky-gods, and the centralization of authority. Women, who had previously held positions as priestesses and diviners, managers of property, and owners of businesses, slowly lost power.

Around 2000 B.C.E., other Semitic peoples entered the region and created three separate kingdoms: Assyria, Babylonia, and Elam (Persia) to the east. The whole region from the Persian Gulf to the Mediterranean Sea was again united under King Hammurabi (r. c. 1792–1750 B.C.E.), who is known for an extensive set of laws called the Code of Hammurabi (p. 230) and for establishing Babylon as the seat of his authority and the home temple for the storm-god Marduk.

ASTRONOMY, COSMOGONY, AND ASTROLOGY

The earliest written records in the Western hemisphere describing the workings of the cosmos come from Mesopotamia. Babylonians devised mathematics and geometry, which were important not only for city planning, large-scale irrigation projects, and business records but also for mapping the heavens. The earliest accurate observation noted on the clay tablets of Babylonian astronomers was the rising and setting of the planet Venus. Eventually the astronomer-priests of the three major schools of astronomy in the cities of Uruk, Sippar, and Babylon were sophisticated enough to predict the eclipses of the sun and moon.

From their correct observations of astronomical events, astronomers created a vast map of the universe that traced the passages of planets through the constellations of the fixed stars. They conceived of these patterns as the dramatic movement, the ebb and flow, of vast cycles of time and space regulated by various deities. As they developed the idea that life on earth should reflect patterns in the heavens, they had the basis for astrology. Vast compilations of astrological data were preserved on clay tablets in extensive ziggurat libraries and consulted for purposes of divination. To Mesopotamians, the planetary patterns not only suggested

Babylonian Globe, 500 B.C.E. *Babylonian astronomers mapped the heavens and could even predict eclipses of the sun and moon. (British Museum, London, UK/The Bridgeman Art Library)*

order but also an influence and significance that was related to the classes of society as well as to an individual's body and psyche.

A detailed religious calendar marking the major festivals of the year and a large body of religious literature—myths, poems, hymns, prayers, and moral teachings—institutionalized the array of beliefs concerning the relationship between life on earth and the heavens. Backed by this literature and religious institutions themselves, priests and rulers assumed a kind of celestial authority that permeated the ancient Near East. Mesopotamian astronomy and astrology had their golden age under the Chaldean ruler Nebuchadnezzar, king of Babylon from 605 to 562 B.C.E. Nebuchadnezzar is infamous in Jewish history for conquering Jerusalem, destroying the Temple, and deporting many Jews to Babylonia in 586 B.C.E.

MESOPOTAMIAN LITERATURE

Scholars have pieced together Sumerian literature from thousands of clay cuneiform tablets—and fragments of tablets—that date from about the second millennium B.C.E. Unearthed at various sites in Iraq, many toward the close of the nineteenth century, these texts display a rich variety similar to that found in early Egyptian writings and in the Hebrew Scriptures. They include myths, hymns of praise to deities, epic histories, lamentations, and wisdom literature. Scholars have assembled *The Descent of Inanna,* a cycle of stories about the goddess Inanna, from thirty different tablets and fragments. In addition to the grand *Epic of Creation, The Epic of Gilgamesh* contains the earliest known epic hero. In 1983 Samuel Noah Kramer, the renowned scholar of Sumerian literature, was able to write that "many a text is still lying buried in the tells of southern Iraq, awaiting the spade of the lucky future excavator."

The oldest extant goddess stories in the West come from Sumer and center around Inanna, the Queen of Heaven and Earth, the morning and evening star, and the goddess of love, agriculture, and warfare. Stories involving this goddess date from 3500 to 1900 B.C.E. and perhaps even earlier. The myth of Inanna's descent into the underworld, probably the earliest surviving literary text in the world, symbolizes the death of nature in winter and its rebirth in spring. *The Epic of Creation,* also known as *Enuma Elish,* is the most famous creation story to come out of the Babylonian empire, which succeeded the rule of the Sumerians in the third millennium. This extended account describes how order was first created out of primordial chaos when the god Marduk defeated Tiamat, a serpentine female. The epic story of the hero Gilgamesh is essentially the maturation journey of a young king whose name has been found in Sumerian king-lists and is associated with the kingship of Uruk on the Euphrates River around 2500 B.C.E. In the epic, after battling a giant and grieving the death of his dear friend Enkidu, Gilgamesh embarks on a grievous journey, searching for a balm for human mortality and answers about the ultimate meaning of life. On his journey, he is told a story of a flood very similar to the one found in the Book of Genesis.

ASSURBANIPAL'S LIBRARY

By about 800 B.C.E., Assyrians established complete dominion over Mesopotamia under the city-state Assur. The last great king of Assyria, Assurbanipal (r. 669–633 B.C.E.), known for his cruelty to enemies, was also an intellectual. From his royal palace at Nineveh he sent scribes to the ancient centers of learning to collect information, creating an extensive library of some twenty thousand clay tablets with their findings. Assyria was conquered in 626 B.C.E., and Nineveh was leveled

TIME AND PLACE

Ancient Mesopotamia: The Flood Myth

Stories of a great flood or deluge often seen as a warning or punishment have appeared in all parts of the world except Africa. The gods send a flood in the Mesopotamian *Epic of Gilgamesh* (c. 1800 B.C.E.), in which a human couple along with relatives and cattle survive on an ark sealed with pitch and asphalt. When the ark comes aground on a mountain top, birds are sent out to test whether the waters have subsided. God also sends the flood survived by Noah in his ark, a punishment for evil, in Genesis (c. 900 B.C.E.). The couple in the Mesoamerican story of the great flood float in a hollow log. Zeus sends the flood in the Greek myth "Deucalion's Flood," in which Deucalion and Pyrrha replace humankind by throwing stones behind them in a field.

The Woolley Excavation at Ur. Photo taken 1933–34. *Evidence of the flood mythologized by many ancient cultures in the Near East may have been unearthed during the excavation of Ur by Sir Leonard Woolley. Archeologists have dated the flood at about 4000 B.C.E. (University of Pennsylvania Museum [Negative #S4-141589])*

Interpretations of flood myths depend on the richness of water as a symbol. Water is often seen as the source of all life, similar to the amniotic fluid of the womb; water is used for ritual baths and rebirth ceremonies such as baptism. But water is also connected to the end of life; flood stories are told about the end of an era and the destruction of the earth. These flood stories may be accounts of an actual deluge. Sir Leonard Woolley of the British Museum began excavating in 1926 at Ur, near the Persian Gulf, in the delta of the Tigris and Euphrates Rivers, the legendary home of the great Hebrew patriarch Abraham. In the summer of 1929, after excavating the remains of a rich civilization, Woolley sent a shaft down below what the archeologists thought was the last strata of ruins. At forty feet it hit mud, a layer more than eight feet thick beneath which was an even older strata of ancient habitation. A simple river flood could not account for the depth of the mud; whatever was responsible for it was an event of such magnitude that it ended a way of life. There is possible evidence that after the flood life began anew at the location of the dig and spread out in different directions. The flood layer was dated about 4000 B.C.E. To this day there are expeditions to Mount Ararat on the eastern border of Turkey, the reasonable terminus of the Mesopotamian flood, in search of evidence of Noah's ark in the frozen wastes of the mountain.

in 612 B.C.E. by Babylonians, Medes, and Scythians. The library was buried under sand for two millennia. In the mid nineteenth century, archeologists discovered clay tablets at Nineveh and other sites along the Tigris and Euphrates, rewriting ancient history. Assurbanipal's library is the primary source of most information about Akkad and Babylon before 1000 B.C.E. In addition to administrative records, the unearthed library contained a vast literature of Sumer and Babylon.

After translating Mesopotamian tablets, scholars concluded that myths and epics written in Akkadian (dialects of Babylonia and Assyria), which predate Greek and Hebrew literature by about a thousand years, were widely known throughout the ancient Near East. In 1872 George Smith announced to the newly founded Society of Biblical Archeology that in *The Epic of Gilgamesh* he had found a flood story very similar to the one told in Genesis. Because of the questions about meaning and chronology raised by Middle Eastern archeology and the comparison of literary texts from the Bible with other literatures from the region, biblical scholarship was permanently transformed. Similarities between Gilgamesh and the Greek heroes Achilles and Odysseus suggest a line of transmission from *The Epic of Gilgamesh* to the Homeric epics: both Gilgamesh and Achilles are partly of divine origin and both are fated to die; and the relationship between Achilles and Patroclus resembles that of Gilgamesh and Enkidu. Gilgamesh and Odysseus each go on arduous quests and are aided by mysterious women—Siduri and Circe, respectively—and both must cross the water to the edge of the world.

WWW For more information about the culture and context of Mesopotamia in the ancient world, see *World Literature Online* at bedfordstmartins.com/worldlit.

The Descent of Inanna

c. 2000 B.C.E.

The Descent of Inanna is the oldest text in this anthology. It was set down by scribes in cuneiform on clay tablets early in the second millennium B.C.E. The repetition and the formulaic phrasing in the text suggest that previous oral versions of it must have existed and that the stories of the goddess Inanna may easily go back to 3500 B.C.E. if not earlier. Inanna played an essential role in ancient Sumer, a kingdom of cities that flourished in the third millennium B.C.E. on the irrigated plains along the Tigris and Euphrates Rivers in what is now southern Iraq, between Baghdad and the Persian Gulf. So highly regarded was Sumer's culture that even after the Babylonian conquest of the region c. 1800 B.C.E., when Semitic Akkadian became the area's common tongue, Sumerian remained the learned language of writers and scholars, just as classical Greek and Latin

The Goddess Inanna, 2000 B.C.E.
Before patriarchal societies became dominant during the second millennium B.C.E., the ancient Sumerians worshipped a host of goddesses, the most important among them the great goddess Inanna. Here she is seen in relief with her traditional wings and with horned animals at her feet. (Z. Radovan, Jerusalem)

WWW For a quiz on *The Descent of Inanna,* see *World Literature Online* at bedfordstmartins.com/worldlit.

and Sanskrit were employed long after they ceased to be everyday spoken languages. Sumerian myths were also integrated into the new culture, though adjusted, for example by substituting Babylonian names.

In contrast with the Jewish, Christian, and Islamic sacred texts that eventually replaced Sumerian stories, the chief actors in *The Descent of Inanna* are not a male god and an assemblage of desert patriarchs, but rather the shining Inanna—Queen of Heaven and Earth, Goddess of Love and Beauty, she of the Morning and Evening Star—and her grim shadow-sister **Ereshkigal**, Queen of the Great Below. These sisters are incarnations of the Triple Goddess[1] who, in her three aspects of fresh maiden, ripe lover-mother, and frightening death-crone, was once worshipped under different names in the Mediterranean area. With the development of cities and the emergence of patriarchal societies, she was mostly eradicated or demoted to secondary status as the consort of a male deity. Yet the literature of these new societies bears traces of her—in sensuous nature worship; in the virginal nature powers of Artemis and Diana; in the fearful representations of bloodthirsty revenge-spirits like the Greek Erinyes or the Hebrew Lilith; in the reverent adoration of the Christian Madonna and the Muslim Fatima; in the celebrations or condemnations of the goddess's human sisters—Eve, Helen of Troy, Clytemnestra, Cleopatra, Deidre, the Wife of Bath, Dante's Beatrice, and Petrarch's Laura, among others. It is fitting both thematically and chronologically that Book 1 of this anthology begins with a story that deals openly and primarily with Inanna.

eh-RESH-kee-gawl

A Goddess with Many Roles. Stories of Inanna have been pieced together from thousands of clay fragments inscribed with cuneiform writing excavated from various sites in Iraq and later translated by Samuel Noah Kramer and other scholars.

In the earliest parts of these stories, Inanna is an adolescent goddess laying claim to her powers, first by witnessing the growth of a special tree and then by encouraging the human hero Gilgamesh to make a bed for her out of it; these episodes are echoed in Homer's ***Odyssey*** and in **Genesis**, in the tree of the knowledge of good and evil. Inanna then challenges an elder generation of parental god-figures such as Enki, Sumerian sea-god and god of wisdom. After Enki has been enticed into a beer-drinking bout, he lets his guard down, and with drunken generosity, grants Inanna guardianship of the *me*. The *me* are not easily described; there are more than one hundred of them listed, and ancient Egyptian texts suggest there are many more. The best way to describe them might be to say they are the qualities, characteristics, and skills of human civilization, for good

p. 421; p. 140

[1] **Triple Goddess:** Name given to the earliest manifestations of the Great Goddess, who dates from the neolithic villages of the eighth millennium B.C.E. Her trinity of aspects became the model for subsequent trinities—whether female, male, or mixed (as in father, mother, and child). In India, the Virgin-Mother-Crone was called Parvati-Durga-Uma; in Greece, Hebe-Hera-Hecate and Persephone-Demeter-Hecate; and in Rome, Juventas-Juno-Minerva. Her personas were related to the phases of the moon as well as to the agricultural cycle.

or for ill. They include such diverse gifts as the attributes and duties of kingship and the priesthood; the techniques of sexual pleasure, arts and crafts, agriculture, cookery, and oratory; and abstractions such as truth, fear, comfort, and the ability to make choices.

Inanna's story goes on to show her as a young fertility goddess discovering her allure and sexuality. She falls in love with the shepherd **Dumuzi**, woos and is wooed by him in sensual words that clearly parallel parts of the biblical **Song of Songs**, joyously sleeps with him, and then begins to learn that the intensity of romance does not necessarily last.

doo-moo-ZEE

p. 208

Not only was Inanna of primary importance in Sumerian religion, but women enjoyed an elevated status in Sumerian culture. Women were involved in temple business, owned real estate, and negotiated money transactions. The patriarchal institutions of the second millennium B.C.E. gradually curbed or eliminated women's role in society, and Inanna was reduced to a deity of fertility alone.

The Descent of Inanna, one section of the entire goddess's story, contains a good many LACUNAE (gaps in the text) and references to beings, objects, or customs that scholars have not yet identified. The story recounts a journey to the underworld or kingdom of death, a type of journey undertaken by mythological heroes in cultures throughout the world and throughout literary history; Persephone, Attis, Orpheus, Osiris, and Jesus[2] are among the many figures from Mediterranean and Middle Eastern literature who make such a descent and return. In part, such descents into darkness and reemergence into light reflect the agricultural cycle: spring flowering, summer fruition, harvest, the apparent death of winter dormancy, and the renewal of spring. *The Descent of Inanna* may in part describe an actual ritual wherein priestesses staged Inanna's descent, death, and return, thereby ensuring another season of fertility in the fields as well as in the homes of Sumer.

Inanna's descent is a shamanic journey, a venturing into the void, the unknown, into the dark womb of the inner Earth for the wisdom it holds. In this symbolic death, she hangs on a peg, a rotting corpse, but gains essential insight and experience into the full cycle of existence.

– Elinor Gadon, scholar, 1989

Inanna's passage is divided into three parts: She first descends into the underworld and dies; she is then revived and ascends to the upper world; finally, a substitute, Dumuzi, is found and takes Inanna's place in the region of death. The lines of repeated text at the beginning of this story suggest that it was originally recited, perhaps chanted during annual reenactments. The consequences of Inanna's death are told in a later Akkadian version of the story (c. 1200 B.C.E.), "The Descent of Ishtar," in which winter is described as an absence of fertility: "No bull mounted a cow, [no donkey impregnated a jenny], / No young man impregnated a girl in [the street (?)] / The young man slept in his private room, / The girl slept in the company of her friends" (Stephanie Dalley,

[2] **Persephone . . . Jesus:** The story of Persephone's abduction, residence in the underworld, and reunion with her mother, Demeter, is recounted in the Greek "Hymn to Demeter." The cult of Attis, in which the goddess is named Cybele, originated in Asia Minor and spread to Rome in the third century B.C.E. Orpheus is the Greek musician who descended into Hades to retrieve his dead wife, Eurydice. Osiris is the Egyptian god who dies and comes back to life; the cult of Isis—Osiris' wife and lover—spread throughout Greece and Rome. Jesus' descent, recorded in the Gospel of Nicodemus and the Apostles' Creed, is called the Harrowing of Hell. Easter has its roots in ancient springtime celebrations of death and rebirth.

trans.). The conclusion of *The Descent of Inanna* suggests an actual shift in the ritual and an accommodation to the agricultural cycle. In the beginning of the story the goddess herself dies and is reborn, but at the end of the story we learn that her husband Dumuzi will become the substitute for Inanna. As in other fertility stories, the goddess will now symbolize the eternal, immutable Mother Nature, while Dumuzi, symbolizing plant life and the annual agricultural cycle that takes place within the context of Nature herself, will make the annual journey to the underworld, where he will remain for half the year—the winter period. When Dumuzi ascends, the new shoots and buds and leaves come with him, and spring returns to the land, a mythic pattern seen again in the Christian Easter celebration. This pattern provides roles for a profound ritual drama, since a priestess or queen can play the role of Inanna and a king or priest the role of Dumuzi, whereby human fertility is thus linked to the fertility of the earth. Diane Wolkstein explains: "Inanna's journey to the underworld has brought a new world order to Sumer . . . By giving Dumuzi eternal life half the year, Inanna changes the cosmic pattern. Love, which parallels the normal course of the human life cycle—budding, blooming, and dying—is henceforth guaranteed, by being linked to the seasons, an annual renewal. The king who enters the underworld once a year will emerge every six months renewed in feminine wisdom and inner strength to take over leadership and vitality of the nation."

Descent stories may be about how people experience alternating periods of flagging energy and renewed strength. They have to do with the human quest for the kind of knowledge that adds to spiritual power, and they hint at where that knowledge lies. Inanna, already Queen of Heaven and Earth, knows somehow that her honor and glory are not enough, just as apparently happy and successful people in every age and culture often ask, "Is this all?" In the face of grief, disappointment, fear, or simply a sense of something lacking, we may retreat deeply into our own psyches, descend into the psychological depths to do battle with our own demons, which are almost always aspects of ourselves. Indeed, death or despair are very possible outcomes of daring to explore the depths. But Inanna says to us that with luck, courage, and good helpers, we may eventually emerge from those experiences with new power and hope and heightened understanding. That is a story worth knowing, a great gift from Sumer.

. . . [Inanna] Queen of Heaven and Earth, a young and radiant goddess adorned with all "powers" of her office, wishes to experience that unknown dimension of the underworld. "Opening her ear" to the Great Below, she makes the shamanic journey to the hidden face of life in order to achieve a deeper understanding of its mysteries. Inanna's journey seems to mirror the need of a culture for a ritual that would reconnect it with its psychic roots—the underworld. Her descent is not only a dramatization of the ancient rituals associated with the moon cycle that had influenced human consciousness for so many thousands of years; it also dramatizes an initiation into a feared dimension that was conceived as *geographically* remote from the "upper" light world of everyday life and practical concerns.

—Anne Baring and Jules Cashford, historians, 1991

■ CONNECTIONS

Homer, *The Odyssey*, p. 421; Virgil, *The Aeneid*, p. 1181. In the ancient world the underworld was associated not only with death, rebirth, and fertility but also with unusual or special knowledge. Does Inanna emerge from the underworld a changed person? What does Odysseus learn from his time in Hades? What does Aeneas gain from his descent into the world below?

Plato, "Allegory of the Cave," p. 1111. Dominantly patriarchal societies commonly deemphasize the role of the feminine by replacing the mythologized descent into the feminine underworld with ascent. Plato's "Allegory of the Cave" is an example of such a reversal. How might Plato's emergence from the cave symbolize masculine qualities?

Exodus, p. 162. In the patriarchal religion of Judaism, the path of righteousness is also an ascent—as seen in Moses' ascent of Mt. Sinai in the Book of Exodus—as opposed to the descent into the underworld of Inanna. How do Moses' experiences on Mt. Sinai associate him with a masculine god?

Dante, *Inferno* (Book 2). By the time of Dante, c. 1300 C.E., the underworld had become known as Hell, but its identity as a realm of special knowledge was still intact. How is Dante's journey both similar and different from Odysseus's and Aeneas's?

Joseph Conrad, *Heart of Darkness* (Book 6). Modern psychology has interpreted the descent into the underworld as an inner journey, an exploration of the hidden reaches of the psyche. How might *Heart of Darkness* be seen as a journey into both the interior of Africa and the unknown realms of the soul?

Inanna's journey to the underworld has brought a new world order to Sumer. The ramifications of her proclamation are manifold. By giving Dumuzi eternal life half the year, Inanna changes the cosmic pattern. Love, which parallels the normal course of the human life cycle—budding, blooming, and dying—is henceforth guaranteed, by being linked to the seasons, an annual renewal. The king who enters the underworld once a year will emerge every six months renewed in feminine wisdom and inner strength to take over leadership and vitality of the nation.

– Diane Wolkstein, critic, 1983

■ FURTHER RESEARCH

Literary Texts

Dalley, Stephanie. *Myths from Mesopotamia.* 1991.

De Strong Meador, Betty, and Judy Grahn. *Inanna, Lady of Largest Heart: Poems of the Sumerian High Priestess Enheduanna.* 2000.

Kramer, Samuel Noah, and Diane Wolkstein. *Inanna, Queen of Heaven and Earth: Her Stories and Hymns from Sumer.* 1983.

Mendelsohn, Isaac, ed. *Religions of the Ancient Near East: Sumer-Akkadian Religious Texts and Ugaritic Epics.* 1955.

History and Background

Baring, Anne, and Jules Cashford. *The Myth of the Goddess: Evolution of an Image.* 1991.

Gadon, Elinor W. *The Once & Future Goddess.* 1989.

Lerner, Gerda. *The Creation of Patriarchy.* 1986.

■ PRONUNCIATION

Badtibira: bahd-tih-BEE-rah
Dumuzi: doo-moo-ZEE
Ereshkigal: eh-RESH-kee-gawl
Galatur: gah-lah-TOOR
Gugalanna: goo-gahl-AH-nah
kurgarra: koor-GAH-rah
Ninshubur: nin-SHOO-boor
shugurra: shoo-GOO-rah

FROM

The Descent of Inanna

Translated by Diane Wolkstein and Samuel Noah Kramer

From the Great Above she opened her ear to the Great Below.
From the Great Above the goddess opened her ear to the Great Below.
From the Great Above Inanna opened her ear to the Great Below.

My Lady abandoned heaven and earth to descend to the underworld.
Inanna abandoned heaven and earth to descend to the underworld.
She abandoned her office of holy priestess to descend to the underworld.

In Uruk[1] she abandoned her temple to descend to the underworld.
In Badtibira she abandoned her temple to descend to the underworld.
In Zabalam she abandoned her temple to descend to the underworld.
In Adab she abandoned her temple to descend to the underworld.
In Nippur she abandoned her temple to descend to the underworld.
In Kish she abandoned her temple to descend to the underworld.
In Akkad she abandoned her temple to descend to the underworld.
She gathered together the seven *me.*

The Descent of Inanna. The story of how this poem was pieced together is a remarkable bit of history and scholarship that reveals a great deal about why the West has been slow to acknowledge the religious and literary importance of ancient Sumer. The text was translated from thirty clay tablets that had been initially inscribed c. 1750 B.C.E. by mythographers, then buried in the ruins of Nippur, Sumer's spiritual center, for some four thousand years. Egyptian hieroglyphs were visible on temple and tomb walls long before they were translated, but *The Descent of Inanna* was a text found through difficult excavations at the ancient site of Nippur in today's Iraq between 1889 and 1900. Iraq was then part of the Turkish empire, and the thousands of clay fragments found at the site were divided between the Istanbul Museum of the Ancient Orient and the University Museum of the University of Pennsylvania. Three pieces stored in Philadelphia and two fragments kept in Istanbul contained the first five sections of Inanna's descent—incomplete and obscure—and were published in 1914. In 1937 Samuel Noah Kramer reconstructed the first half of the story and revealed its coherence, and in 1942 he added fragments that brought the story to the point at which Inanna emerges from the underworld. After two more fragments of the story were found in 1951, Kramer published the next section, which describes how Inanna hands over her husband Dumuzi to the demons of the underworld. Finally, in 1963, after fifty years of scholarly detective work, the

---

[1] **Uruk:** Inanna's seven sacred cities and temples are listed here; Uruk is her major city, her primary residence. Seven appears several times in the text as a sacred number. Some speculate that the number came to be considered sacred because it was the number of visible bodies—the sun, the moon, and the five planets; others suggest it could be related to the menstrual cycle, since a twenty-eight-day month is divisible by seven. The number seven reappears in the Hebrew creation story.

She took them into her hands.
With the *me* in her possession, she prepared herself:

She placed the *shugurra,* the crown of the steppe, on her head.
She arranged the dark locks of hair across her forehead.
She tied the small lapis beads around her neck,
Let the double strand of beads fall to her breast,
And wrapped the royal robe around her body.
She daubed her eyes with ointment called "Let him come, Let him come,"
Bound the breastplate called "Come, man, come!" around her chest,
Slipped the gold ring over her wrist,
And took the lapis measuring rod and line in her hand.

Inanna set out for the underworld.
Ninshubur, her faithful servant, went with her.
Inanna spoke to her, saying:
    "Ninshubur, my constant support,
    My *sukkal* who gives me wise advice,
    My warrior who fights by my side,
    I am descending to the *kur,* to the underworld.
    If I do not return,
    Set up a lament for me by the ruins.
    Beat the drum for me in the assembly places.
    Circle the houses of the gods.
    Tear at your eyes, at your mouth, at your thighs.
    Dress yourself in a single garment like a beggar.

---

poem's last section was added, which begins with a fly giving information about Dumuzi's location to Inanna and concludes with Inanna's decree that Dumuzi's residence in the underworld would last half the year—roughly corresponding to winter—and Geshtinanna, his sister, would take his place the other half of the year. This incredibly important section ties the myth of Inanna's descent to the underworld to agricultural myths found in the Middle East and the Mediterranean that involve either the death and resurrection of the goddess herself, such as in the case of the Babylonian Ishtar, or the death and resurrection of the goddess's lover or child, such as in the stories of Attis and Adonis in Syria and Asia Minor, and those of Demeter and Persephone in Greece.

The importance of *The Descent of Inanna* lies not only in its antiquity and its influence on subsequent literature in the region but also in its revelation of a unique time in history when the rulers and subjects of Sumer paid reverence to a goddess whose rituals determined nothing less than the process of growing food and the sexual potency of the king, whose annual consummation of marriage with a goddess-priestess ensured the fertility of the land and legitimized his rule. In the Akkadian version of this myth, which dates from 1250 B.C.E., the goddess's name is Ishtar, her lover is Tammuz, and the dark sister of the underworld is still Ereshkigal.

A note on the translation: This translation is a reworking of Samuel Noah Kramer's rendering by noted folklorist and storyteller Diane Wolkstein. In the interests of readability, the translators have chosen not to indicate gaps or uncertainties in the text. All notes are the editors'.

Go to Nippur, to the temple of Enlil.[2]
When you enter his holy shrine, cry out:
'O Father Enlil, do not let your daughter
Be put to death in the underworld.
Do not let your bright silver
Be covered with the dust of the underworld.
Do not let your precious lapis
Be broken into stone for the stoneworker.
Do not let your fragrant boxwood
Be cut into wood for the woodworker.
Do not let the holy priestess of heaven
Be put to death in the underworld.'

If Enlil will not help you,
Go to Ur, to the temple of Nanna.
Weep before Father Nanna.
If Nanna will not help you,
Go to Eridu, to the temple of Enki.[3]
Weep before Father Enki.
Father Enki, the God of Wisdom, knows the food of life,
He knows the water of life;
He knows the secrets.
Surely he will not let me die."

Inanna continued on her way to the underworld.
Then she stopped and said:
"Go now, Ninshubur—
Do not forget the words I have commanded you."

When Inanna arrived at the outer gates of the underworld,
She knocked loudly.
She cried out in a fierce voice:
"Open the door, gatekeeper!
Open the door, Neti!
I alone would enter!"

Neti, the chief gatekeeper of the *kur,* asked:
"Who are you?"

She answered:
"I am Inanna, Queen of Heaven,
On my way to the East."

[2] **Enlil:** A god of unknown attributes; perhaps the god of wind and air. His symbol is a horned crown on a shrine. [3] **Eridu . . . Enki:** Eridu was an ancient city on the shore of the Persian Gulf; Enki is the god of water and wisdom.

Neti said:
"If you are truly Inanna, Queen of Heaven,
On your way to the East,
Why has your heart led you on the road
From which no traveler returns?"

Inanna answered:
"Because . . . of my older sister, Ereshkigal,
Her husband, Gugalanna, the Bull of Heaven, has died.
I have come to witness the funeral rites.
Let the beer of his funeral rites be poured into the cup.
Let it be done."

Neti spoke:
"Stay here, Inanna, I will speak to my queen.
I will give her your message."

Neti, the chief gatekeeper of the *kur,*
Entered the palace of Ereshkigal,[4] the Queen of the Underworld, and said:
"My queen, a maid
As tall as heaven,
As wide as the earth,
As strong as the foundations of the city wall,
Waits outside the palace gates.

She has gathered together the seven *me.*
She has taken them into her hands.
With the *me* in her possession, she has prepared herself:

On her head she wears the *shugurra,* the crown of the steppe.
Across her forehead her dark locks of hair are carefully arranged.
Around her neck she wears the small lapis beads.
At her breast she wears the double strand of beads.
Her body is wrapped with the royal robe.
Her eyes are daubed with the ointment called 'Let him come, let him come.'
Around her chest she wears the breastplate called 'Come, man, come!'
On her wrist she wears the gold ring.
In her hand she carries the lapis measuring rod and line."

When Ereshkigal heard this,
She slapped her thigh and bit her lip.

[4] **Ereshkigal:** Although here Ereshkigal is Inanna's sister, it is probable that in different contexts they were treated as two sides of the same deity, the goddess of life and death, light and dark. In the Sumerian myth, Ereshkigal is portrayed as spiteful and unfulfilled.

She took the matter into her heart and dwelt on it.
Then she spoke:
"Come, Neti, my chief gatekeeper of the *kur,*
Heed my words:
Bolt the seven gates of the underworld.
Then, one by one, open each gate a crack.
Let Inanna enter.
As she enters, remove her royal garments.[5]
Let the holy priestess of heaven enter bowed low."

Neti heeded the words of his queen.
He bolted the seven gates of the underworld.
Then he opened the outer gate.
He said to the maid:
"Come, Inanna, enter."

When she entered the first gate,
From her head, the *shugurra,* the crown of the steppe, was removed.

Inanna asked:
"What is this?"

She was told:
"Quiet, Inanna, the ways of the underworld are perfect.
They may not be questioned."

When she entered the second gate,
From her neck the small lapis beads were removed.

Inanna asked:
"What is this?"

She was told:
"Quiet, Inanna, the ways of the underworld are perfect.
They may not be questioned." [. . .]

[Inanna's strand of beads, breastplate, gold ring, and lapis measuring rod were taken from her at gates three to six, respectively.]

When she entered the seventh gate,
From her body the royal robe was removed.

---

[5] **remove . . . garments:** The symbols of power and prestige in the world above have no value in the underworld; Inanna will be naked when she confronts death.

Inanna asked:
"What is this?"

She was told:
"Quiet, Inanna, the ways of the underworld are perfect.
They may not be questioned."

Naked and bowed low, Inanna entered the throne room.
Ereshkigal rose from her throne.
Inanna started toward the throne.
The Anunna,[6] the judges of the underworld, surrounded her.
They passed judgment against her.

Then Ereshkigal fastened on Inanna the eye of death.
She spoke against her the word of wrath.
She uttered against her the cry of guilt.

She struck her.

Inanna was turned into a corpse,
A piece of rotting meat,
And was hung from a hook on the wall.

When, after three days and three nights,[7] Inanna had not returned,
Ninshubur set up a lament for her by the ruins.
She beat the drum for her in the assembly places.
She circled the houses of the gods.
She tore at her eyes; she tore at her mouth; she tore at her thighs.
She dressed herself in a single garment like a beggar.

[Ninshubur seeks help from Enlil and Nanna (the moon god), both of whom refuse.]

Ninshubur went to Eridu and the temple of Enki.
When she entered the holy shrine,
She cried out:
"O Father Enki, do not let your daughter
Be put to death in the underworld.
Do not let your bright silver

[6] **Anunna:** Also called the Anunnaki, these are the deities of the underworld, seven in number.

[7] **three days and three nights:** A period of time found throughout the literature of the ancient Near East: In Hebrew scriptures, Jonah is in a whale's belly for three days and nights, and in the New Testament Jesus is in the tomb for the same amount of time. The origin of this three-day period may have been the three days in the lunar cycle when the moon disappears from view, since the moon was a favored symbol of death and rebirth in the ancient world.

Be covered with the dust of the underworld.
Do not let your precious lapis
Be broken into stone for the stoneworker.
Do not let your fragrant boxwood
Be cut into wood for the woodworker.
Do not let the holy priestess of heaven
Be put to death in the underworld."

Father Enki said:
"What has happened?
What has my daughter done?
Inanna! Queen of All the Lands! Holy Priestess of Heaven!
What has happened?
I am troubled. I am grieved."

From under his fingernail Father Enki brought forth dirt.
He fashioned the dirt into a *kurgarra,* a creature neither male nor female.
From under the fingernail of his other hand he brought forth dirt.
He fashioned the dirt into a *galatur,*[8] a creature neither male nor female.
He gave the food of life to the *kurgarra.*
He gave the water of life to the *galatur.*
Enki spoke to the *kurgarra* and *galatur,* saying:
"Go to the underworld,
Enter the door like flies.
Ereshkigal, the Queen of the Underworld, is moaning
With the cries of a woman about to give birth.
No linen is spread over her body.
Her breasts are uncovered.
Her hair swirls about her head like leeks.
When she cries, 'Oh! Oh! My inside!'
Cry also, 'Oh! Oh! Your inside!'
When she cries, 'Oh! Oh! My outside!'
Cry also, 'Oh! Oh! Your outside!'
The queen will be pleased.
She will offer you a gift.
Ask her only for the corpse that hangs from the hook on the wall.
One of you will sprinkle the food of life on it.
The other will sprinkle the water of life.
Inanna will arise."

[8] ***kurgarra . . . galatur:*** These beings are able to cross from the living realm to the realm of the dead and back without dying, either because they are sexless or androgynous. The Greek messenger-god Hermes shares some of this sexual ambiguity.

The *kurgarra* and the *galatur* heeded Enki's words.
They set out for the underworld.
Like flies, they slipped through the cracks of the gates.
They entered the throne room of the Queen of the Underworld.
No linen was spread over her body.
Her breasts were uncovered.
Her hair swirled around her head like leeks.

Ereshkigal was moaning:
"Oh! Oh! My inside!"

They moaned:
"Oh! Oh! Your inside!"

She moaned:
"Ohhhh! Oh! My outside!"

They moaned:
"Ohhhh! Oh! Your outside!"

She groaned:
"Oh! Oh! My belly!"

They groaned:
"Oh! Oh! Your belly!"

She groaned:
"Oh! Ohhhh! My back!!"

They groaned:
"Oh! Ohhhh! Your back!!"

She sighed:
"Ah! Ah! My heart!"

They sighed:
"Ah! Ah! Your heart!"

She sighed:
"Ah! Ahhhh! My liver!"

They sighed:
"Ah! Ahhhh! Your liver!"

Ereshkigal stopped.
She looked at them.
She asked:
"Who are you,
Moaning—groaning—sighing with me?
If you are gods, I will bless you.
If you are mortals, I will give you a gift.
I will give you the water-gift, the river in its fullness."

The *kurgarra* and *galatur* answered:
"We do not wish it."

Ereshkigal said:
"I will give you the grain-gift, the fields in harvest."

The *kurgarra* and *galatur* said:
"We do not wish it."

Ereshkigal said:
"Speak then! What do you wish?"

They answered:
"We wish only the corpse that hangs from the hook on the wall."

Ereshkigal said:
"The corpse belongs to Inanna."

They said:
"Whether it belongs to our queen,
Whether it belongs to our king,
That is what we wish."

The corpse was given to them.

The *kurgarra* sprinkled the food of life on the corpse.
The *galatur* sprinkled the water of life on the corpse.
Inanna arose. . . .

Inanna was about to ascend from the underworld
When the Anunna, the judges of the underworld, seized her.
They said:
"No one ascends from the underworld unmarked.
If Inanna wishes to return from the underworld,
She must provide someone in her place."

As Inanna ascended from the underworld,
The *galla,* the demons of the underworld, clung to her side.
The *galla* were demons who know no food, who know no drink,
Who eat no offerings, who drink no libations,
Who accept no gifts.
They enjoy no lovemaking.
They have no sweet children to kiss.
They tear the wife from the husband's arms,
They tear the child from the father's knees,
They steal the bride from her marriage home.

The demons clung to Inanna.
The small *galla* who accompanied Inanna
Were like reeds the size of low picket fences.
The large *galla* who accompanied Inanna
Were like reeds the size of high picket fences.

The one who walked in front of Inanna was not a minister,
Yet he carried a sceptre.
The one who walked behind her was not a warrior,
Yet he carried a mace.
Ninshubur, dressed in a soiled sackcloth,
Waited outside the palace gates.
When she saw Inanna
Surrounded by the *galla,*
She threw herself in the dust at Inanna's feet.

The *galla* said:
    "Walk on, Inanna,
    We will take Ninshubur in your place."

Inanna cried:
    "No! Ninshubur is my constant support. [. . .]

[The demons suggest taking first Shara and then Lulal in Inanna's stead, but Inanna will not let them go, as they are her sons.]

The *galla* said:
    "Walk on to your city, Inanna.
    We will go with you to the big apple tree in Uruk."

In Uruk, by the big apple tree,
Dumuzi, the husband of Inanna, was dressed in his shining *me*-garments.
He sat on his magnificent throne; (he did not move).

The *galla* seized him by his thighs.
They poured milk out of his seven churns.
They broke the reed pipe which the shepherd was playing.

Inanna fastened on Dumuzi the eye of death.
She spoke against him the word of wrath.
She uttered against him the cry of guilt:
"*Take him! Take Dumuzi away!*"

The *galla,* who know no food, who know no drink,
Who eat no offerings, who drink no libations,
Who accept no gifts, seized Dumuzi.
They made him stand up; they made him sit down.
They beat the husband of Inanna.
They gashed him with axes.

Dumuzi let out a wail.
He raised his hands to heaven to Utu, the God of Justice, and beseeched him:
"O Utu, you are my brother-in-law,
I am the husband of your sister.
I brought cream to your mother's house,
I brought milk to Ningal's house.
I am the one who carried food to the holy shrine.
I am the one who brought wedding gifts to Uruk.
I am the one who danced on the holy knees, the knees of Inanna.

Utu, you who are a just god, a merciful god,
Change my hands into the hands of a snake.
Change my feet into the feet of a snake.
Let me escape from my demons;
Do not let them hold me."

The merciful Utu accepted Dumuzi's tears.
He changed the hands of Dumuzi into snake hands.
He changed the feet of Dumuzi into snake feet.
Dumuzi escaped from his demons.
They could not hold him. . . .

[After Dumuzi runs away and hides, a fly tells Inanna where to find him.]

Then a fly appeared.[9]
The holy fly circled the air above Inanna's head and spoke:

---

[9] **a fly appeared:** The messengers sent to the underworld to rescue Inanna took the form of flies; it is not known if this fly is related to them.

"If I tell you where Dumuzi is,
What will you give me?"

Inanna said:
"If you tell me,
I will let you frequent the beer-houses and taverns.
I will let you dwell among the talk of the wise ones.
I will let you dwell among the songs of the minstrels."

The fly spoke:
"Lift your eyes to the edges of the steppe,
Lift your eyes to Arali.
There you will find Geshtinanna's brother,
There you will find the shepherd Dumuzi."

Inanna and Geshtinanna went to the edges of the steppe.
They found Dumuzi weeping.
Inanna took Dumuzi by the hand and said:
"You will go to the underworld
Half the year.
Your sister, since she has asked,
Will go the other half.
On the day you are called,
That day you will be taken.
On the day Geshtinanna is called,
That day you will be set free."

Inanna placed Dumuzi in the hands of the eternal.

Holy Ereshkigal! Great is your renown!
Holy Ereshkigal! I sing your praises!

THE EPIC OF CREATION

C. 1800 B.C.E.

The Epic of Creation is the most famous creation story to come out of the Babylonian empire. The poem is not an EPIC in the traditional sense—the story of a mortal hero of national importance who undergoes trials and challenges, such as ***The Epic of Gilgamesh***. *The Epic of Creation* might better be called the Babylonian Genesis, since it is a religious text that tells of the origins of the universe. Most world cultures and religions have a CREATION MYTH, a kind of blueprint of the cosmos and its origins: How did it all begin? What gods and/or goddesses were involved? What or who keeps the present world from collapsing into chaos? and Where is the whole thing headed? After presenting a picture of the world, creation myths usually define the role that human beings play in the universe and how they might participate in the upkeep and purpose of the world. Such participation is typically embodied in a series of religious rituals performed throughout the year, in which the needs of human beings are intertwined with the seasons of the year. *The Epic of Creation*, for example, was recited annually at the Babylonian New Year's celebration, where the reciprocal relationship between human fertility and the agricultural cycle was dramatized. The cosmic picture or image in *The Epic of Creation* is a COSMOGONY. The book of Genesis in Hebrew Scripture served the same purpose for Judaism, and later, Christianity; Hesiod's ***Theogony***[1] conjured a fathomable and meaningful world for the ancient Greeks.

p. 62

p. 263

Creation stories contain much more than prehistoric or primitive theories about the world's beginnings; in them can be seen the fundamental attitudes and beliefs that shape the present. The process of creation provides a repository of images and actions that people use to shape their attitudes and guide their behavior. Creation stories usually employ analogies involving the human mind or body: For example, creation is spoken of as dreaming or speaking or being born. It can also be represented as emergence from a cosmic egg, the trunk of a tree, or Mother Earth. Sumerian creation myths before 2000 B.C.E. pit a primordial dragon of chaos against a warrior-champion, like the storm-god Ninurta.[2] A pattern of warrior-kings defeating the forces of chaos in the guise of serpentine monsters of the sea—often female—is later found throughout the literature of the ancient Near East and the Mediterranean: In Greek myth, Zeus or Apollo defeats Python, Typhon, or Typhoeus; in India, Indra defeats the water serpent Vritra; in Egypt, the

WWW For a quiz on *The Epic of Creation*, see *World Literature Online* at bedfordstmartins.com/worldlit.

[1] ***Theogony:*** Hesiod (eighth century B.C.E.), a Greek poet from an area north of Athens known for two primary works: *Theogony*, an orderly presentation of the generations of the gods and goddesses, and *Works and Days*, a body of advice about the proper treatment of deities. The latter delineates the "five ages of man," the Greek version of the decline of humanity—similar to the Fall in Hebrew myth. A theogony is a story of the origin of the gods; a cosmogony narrates the origins of the cosmos.

[2] **Ninurta:** A Sumerian warrior-god and predecessor to Marduk in *The Epic of Creation*.

dragonlike serpent is Apep or Apophis; in Hebrew Scripture, a battle ensues between Yahweh and Rahab or Leviathan.[3]

This recurring story of battle suggests that combat or conflict was an early view of how the world functioned. The myths, saying the world was originally created by way of a struggle between two forces, may also be comments on the world's essential nature, its functional paradigm. Darwin's theory of "survival of the fittest"[4] is a modern expression of such a cosmogony. The fact that the forces of chaos are often female in these ancient stories indicates a cultural shift away from female earth-deities to male sky-deities. The primordial battles of the gods and goddesses against the forces of chaos became the model for Babylonian kings, whose battles were thought to imitate divine warfare.

[*The Epic of Creation*] is religiously of great profundity, leading in its picture of Marduk toward the aspects of awe and majesty. Moreover, it is intellectually admirable in providing a unifying concept of existence: political order pervades both nature and society. Finally it is humanly satisfying: ultimate power is not estranged from mankind, but resides in gods in human form who act understandably.

– THORKILD JACOBSEN, historian, 1971

The Epic of Creation. The seven tablets on which this epic is inscribed date from the first millennium B.C.E., but it seems likely that the poem was composed much earlier, probably during the Old Babylonian period (c. 1800–1500 B.C.E.), when Marduk, the epic's hero, was worshiped as the titular deity of Babylon. The epic is organized in three sections: the creation of the primordial deities, the combat between Marduk and Tiamat,[5] and the creation of the world and human beings.

The epic begins with Apsu and Tiamat, who symbolize the origins of life itself, the mingling of masculine fresh water and feminine salt water in the southern marshes of Mesopotamia. All life was thought to have emerged from the luxuriant growth produced from the meeting of the Euphrates and Tigris Rivers with the sea in the delta region. This couple spawns the first generation of gods, individual deities who assume the roles of nature-gods—the gods of water, wind, sky, earth, and other elements—representing the basic powers of the universe.

The next generation of gods, however, are unruly, and the parents cannot tolerate the noisy children; Father Apsu complains to Mother Tiamat, threatening to exterminate them. In a preemptive strike, the children, sensing repression, murder Apsu. At first rather passive, Tiamat eventually angers and threatens revenge against her children. For assistance, she creates a formidable army of monsters, beings with a mixture of animal and human features. The children consult intensely in the face

---

[3] **Leviathan:** The process of editing Hebrew Scripture in the first millennium B.C.E. apparently eliminated this story from canonized books until only vestiges of the old combat myth remained; a dragon or sea monster, called by various names, such as Leviathan and Tannin, is mentioned in several places: Isaiah 51:9–10 and 27:1; Psalms 74:12–14 and 89:10; and Job 26:12–13.

[4] **"survival of the fittest":** An explanation of the way that life on earth is ordered, proposed by Charles Darwin (1809–1882), the English biologist who popularized the theory of evolution in *Origin of Species* (1859). "Survival of the fittest" means that nature intends for individual organisms to compete with one another; the strongest, the smartest, or the most adaptable survive; the rest perish prematurely.

[5] **Tiamat:** The Hebrew word for "deep" in Genesis 1:2 is *tehom,* a word linguistically connected to the Sumerian sea monster Tiamat. The New English Bible translates *tehom* as "abyss," a word suggestive of the ancient chaos often personified as a dragon, and notes that the "mighty wind that swept over the surface of the waters" is related to the mythical storm-gods said to have created the cosmos. In *The Epic of Creation,* Tiamat becomes Chaos.

> **For the Mesopotamian, the entire world which surrounded him was filled with life. Every contact between man and nature was an encounter between two living entities facing each other and pitting their will power against each other.**
>
> – SILVESTRO FIORE, medievalist, 1965

of Tiamat's threat. The process by which they choose a leader reflects the political structures of the time: After Anshar directs his son to meet the challenge and his son is intimidated by Tiamat's might, an assembly is called and new nominations for a leader are presented. The magnificent storm-god Marduk, after setting down terms for supreme rule, is elected the champion of the new order of gods. Marduk and Tiamat then meet in a primordial battle, a cosmic conflagration.

The final section of the poem begins with Tiamat's defeat and the imprisoning of her forces—imprisoned rather than destroyed since chaos has the potential to return. Marduk takes the Tablets of Destiny from Qingu, who is killed. The world is created out of Tiamat's carcass; she is split in two and transformed into heaven and earth—which suggests a feminine basis for nature. Marduk then puts order to the cosmos by assigning gods to various tasks; Marduk sanctifies the sun, moon, stars, and their pathways in the heavens—the discoveries of Mesopotamia's own astronomers. Humankind is created from Qingu's blood—perhaps a reference to the essential rebelliousness of man's nature. Humans, as in much world mythology, are also given work: Ea "imposed the toil of the gods (on man) and released the gods from it." Humans are created to serve the gods; that is their purpose. Marduk then assigns various tasks to the gods. Finally, the destinies are fixed for the next year, and all the gods gather at a banquet to celebrate creation.

Though Tiamat is defeated, she continues to exist as the embodiment of chaos, as the potential threat of the sea and the power of tidal waves, a continuing threat to the lowland cities of Mesopotamia. One version of the end of time says that Marduk will defeat Tiamat again when she arises from chaos. Another view claims that the Chaos Mother swallows the world and returns it to formlessness in order to begin anew.

The Akitu. The Babylonian New Year Festival, or Akitu, was typically a twelve-day event held in spring whose purpose was the renewal of life, both human and cosmic. Throughout the twelve-day period, Babylonians reenacted the major events of the creation story and their implications for the king and his kingdom through story and pantomime. World order was reestablished, the king was reenthroned, and Marduk determined all human destinies for the coming twelve months. On the ninth day a group of actors dramatized Marduk's defeat of Tiamat, and a statute of his likeness was paraded through the streets, then placed in a special shrine. On the tenth day a ritual marriage—*hieros gamos*[6]—took place atop a ziggurat, or sacred temple—in which the king—as Marduk—consummated the rites of fertility with a priestess, ensuring the fertility of crops for the next year. On the last day of the festival, the statues of the gods were returned to their home temples in surrounding cities, and the work of the new year began.

[6] ***hieros gamos:*** Greek for "sacred marriage"; a fertility ritual in which a god-king or priest-king is united with a goddess or priestess-queen as a model for the kingdom and to establish the king's right to rule for another year.

Scholar Theodor Gaster points out that such ceremonies are not so far removed from present-day rituals: "Ceremonies of this kind, involving mimetic combats with dragons . . . triumphal parades, and the formal deposition and reinstatement of the king, are common in many parts of the world. The curious reader need be referred only to the mass of examples collected by the late Sir James Frazer in his classic work, *The Golden Bough.* He may be reminded also that the kings and queens of May, so familiar from folk custom—and even our own "beauty queens" and "Miss Rheingolds"—are but a dim survival of the annual reenthronement of the sovereign."

■ CONNECTIONS

Genesis, p. 140. Creation myths reflect the values and times of their cultures. Most creator gods are portrayed as powerful, and the deities of both the Mesopotamians and the Hebrews promote warfare. The God in the first chapter of Genesis, however, uses a more sophisticated method than combat for bringing the cosmos into being. How does the use of speech reflect a set of values?

Hesiod, *Theogony,* p. 263. Early myths often separate creation into a series of stages or ages in which different generations come into conflict. Hesiod's depiction of the first generations of gods, with its battles between fathers and sons, parallels the story of the first family of deities in *The Epic of Creation.* Why might family conflict be a useful theme in a culture's earliest stories?

"Creating the World and Defeating Apophis," p. 109. Creation stories involving combat often show a sky-deity defeating a water monster (who is sometimes feminine). The defeat of Apophis in the Egyptian creation myth is similar to the fate of Tiamat in *The Epic of Creation.* How are serpents and dragons associated with primordial chaos, and the powers of the sky, like the sun and the stars, linked to order?

■ FURTHER RESEARCH

Background

Black, Jeremy, and Anthony Green. *Gods, Demons and Symbols of Ancient Mesopotamia, an Illustrated Dictionary.* 1992.

Gray, John. *Near Eastern Mythology: Mesopotamia, Syria, Palestine.* 1969.

Jacobsen, Thorkild. *The Treasures of Darkness: A History of Mesopotamian Religion.* 1976.

McCall, Henrietta. *Mesopotamian Myths.* 1990.

The Epic of Creation

Budge, E. A., and Sidney Smith. *The Babylonian Legends of the Creation.* 1931.

Dalley, Stephanie. *Myths from Mesopotamia.* 1991.

Fiore, Silvestro. *Voices from the Clay: The Development of Assyro-babylonian Literature.* 1965.

Heidel, Alexander. *The Babylonian Genesis: The Story of Creation.* 1951.

Kramer, Samuel Noah. *From the Poetry of Sumer: Creation, Glorification, Adoration.* 1979.

FROM

The Epic of Creation

Translated by Stephanie Dalley

Tablet I

When skies above[1] were not yet named
Nor earth below pronounced by name,
Apsu,[2] the first one, their begetter
And maker Tiamat,[3] who bore them all,
Had mixed their waters together,
But had not formed pastures, nor discovered reed-beds;
When yet no gods were manifest,
Nor names pronounced, nor destinies decreed,
Then gods were born within them.
Lahmu (and) Lahamu emerged,[4] their names pronounced.
As soon as they matured, were fully formed,

The Epic of Creation. The exact date of composition of this poem has not been determined. The most complete version of the epic was found on tablets from King Assurbanipal's library (seventh century B.C.E.) at Nineveh, the ancient capital of Assyria. The hero of this epic is Marduk, the principal deity of Babylon, the old Babylonian metropolis. And the great temple Esagila that is erected in Marduk's honor at the end of the epic has been located in Babylon. It seems probable, therefore, that this creation story was handed down over a period of years during which the names of the gods changed according to current rulers, capital cities, and patron deities. In an earlier Sumerian version of the poem, the storm-god was called Ninurta; another version centered around the storm-god Enlil of Nippur. Yet another, discovered at Ashur, the capital of Assyria, features the hero Ashur. *The Epic of Creation* was known in Akkadian as *Enuma Elish,* from the poem's opening words, meaning "when skies above." The story was recited each year by a high priest on the fourth day of the Babylonian New Year Festival, or Akitu, which reenacted the primordial events of creation in preparation for the coming year.

A note on the translation: This recent translation by Stephanie Dalley contains a number of acknowledged lacunae, or gaps. Repetitious sections, appropriate for ritual purposes but unnecessary to advance the story, have been cut. All notes are the editors' unless otherwise indicated. The translator provides the following explanation for gaps in the text: "[ ] Square brackets indicate short gaps in text due to damage of tablet clay. Text inside brackets is restored, often from parallel versions. ( ) Round brackets indicate words inserted to give a better rendering in English, or explanatory insertions. [( )] Square brackets enclosing round brackets indicate uncertainty as to whether or not there is a gap in the text. . . . Omission dots indicate an unknown word or phrase."

---

[1] **When skies above:** The first words in Akkadian are *Enuma elish,* sometimes used as the epic's name.

[2] **Apsu:** The sweet, fresh waters.

[3] **Tiamat:** At this point, salt water or the sea; she becomes the mother of the first generation of the gods and later a monstrous sea creature.

[4] **Lahmu (and) Lahamu emerged:** Perhaps the silt forming in the waters, the first land emerging as mud.

Anshar (and) Kishar[5] were born, surpassing them.
They passed the days at length, they added to the years.
Anu[6] their first-born son rivalled his forefathers:
Anshar made his son Anu like himself,
And Anu begot Nudimmud[7] in his likeness.
He, Nudimmud, was superior to his forefathers:
Profound of understanding, he was wise, was very strong at arms.
Mightier by far than Anshar his father's begetter,
He had no rival among the gods his peers.
The gods of that generation would meet together
And disturb Tiamat, and their clamour reverberated.
They stirred up Tiamat's belly,
They were annoying her by playing inside Anduruna.[8]
Apsu could not quell their noise
And Tiamat became mute before them;
However grievous their behaviour to her,
However bad their ways, she would indulge them.
Finally Apsu, begetter of the great gods,
Called out and addressed his vizier Mummu,[9]
'O Mummu, vizier who pleases me!
Come, let us go to Tiamat!'
They went and sat in front of Tiamat,
And discussed affairs concerning the gods their sons.
Apsu made his voice heard
And spoke to Tiamat in a loud voice,
'Their ways have become very grievous to me,
By day I cannot rest, by night I cannot sleep.
I shall abolish their ways and disperse them!
Let peace prevail, so that we can sleep.'
When Tiamat heard this,
She was furious and shouted at her lover;
She shouted dreadfully and was beside herself with rage,
But then suppressed the evil in her belly.
'How could we allow what we ourselves created to perish?
Even though their ways are so grievous, we should bear it patiently.'
(Vizier) Mummu replied and counselled Apsu;
The vizier did not agree with the counsel of his earth mother.
'O father, put an end to (their) troublesome ways,
So that she may be allowed to rest by day and sleep at night.'
Apsu was pleased with him, his face lit up
At the evil he was planning for the gods his sons.

[5] **Anshar (and) Kishar:** Akin to "Grandfather Sky or Horizon" and Mother Earth. [6] **Anu:** The sky. [7] **Nudimmud:** Same as the Sumerian Ea, god of fresh water, wisdom, and incantations. [8] **Anduruna:** The gods' dwelling. [9] **vizier Mummu:** A porter or servant.

(Vizier) Mummu hugged him,
Sat on his lap and kissed him rapturously.
But everything they plotted between them
Was relayed to the gods their sons.
The gods listened and wandered about restlessly;
They fell silent, they sat mute.
Superior in understanding, wise and capable,
Ea[10] who knows everything found out their plot,
Made for himself a design of everything, and laid it out correctly,
Made it cleverly, his pure spell was superb.
He recited it and it stilled the waters.
He poured sleep upon him so that he was sleeping soundly,
Put Apsu to sleep, drenched with sleep.
Vizier Mummu the counsellor (was in) a sleepless daze.
He (Ea) unfastened his belt, took off his crown,
Took away his mantle of radiance and put it on himself.
He held Apsu down and slew him;
Tied up Mummu and laid him across him.
He set up his dwelling on top of Apsu,
And grasped Mummu, held him by a nose-rope.
When he had overcome and slain his enemies,
Ea set up his triumphal cry over his foes.
Then he rested very quietly inside his private quarters
And named them Apsu[11] and assigned chapels,
Founded his own residence there,
And Ea and Damkina[12] his lover dwelt in splendour.
In the chamber of destinies, the hall of designs,
Bel,[13] cleverest of the clever, sage of the gods, was begotten.
And inside Apsu, Marduk[14] was created;
Inside pure Apsu, Marduk was born.
Ea his father created him,
Damkina his mother bore him.
He suckled the teats of goddesses;
The nurse who reared him filled him with awesomeness.
Proud was his form, piercing his stare,
Mature his emergence, he was powerful from the start.
Anu his father's begetter beheld him,
And rejoiced, beamed; his heart was filled with joy.
He made him so perfect that his godhead was doubled.
Elevated far above them, he was superior in every way.

[10] **Ea:** God of fresh water, wisdom, and incantations. [11] **Apsu:** Name given by Ea to his temple in Eridu. He names it such after slaying Apsu. [12] **Damkina:** Means "faithful wife." [13] **Bel:** The title "lord," which was used by patron deities such as Marduk and Assur in their temples. [14] **Marduk:** The patron god of Babylon; his name might mean "bull-calf of the sun." At the end of *The Epic of Creation,* he assimilates a number of deities into himself.

His limbs were ingeniously made beyond comprehension,
Impossible to understand, too difficult to perceive.
Four were his eyes, four were his ears;[15]
When his lips moved, fire blazed forth.
The four ears were enormous
And likewise the eyes; they perceived everything.
Highest among the gods, his form was outstanding.
His limbs were very long, his height (?) outstanding.

(Anu cried out)

'Mariutu, Mariutu,[16]
Son, majesty, majesty of the gods!'
Clothed in the radiant mantle of ten gods, worn high above his head
Five fearsome rays were clustered above him.
Anu created the four winds and gave them birth,
Put them in his (Marduk's) hand, 'My son, let them play!'
He fashioned dust and made the whirlwind carry it;
He made the flood-wave and stirred up Tiamat.
Tiamat was stirred up, and heaved restlessly day and night.
The gods, unable to rest, had to suffer . . .
They plotted evil in their hearts, and
They addressed Tiamat their mother, saying,
'Because they slew Apsu your lover and
You did not go to his side but sat mute,
He has created the four, fearful winds
To stir up your belly on purpose, and we simply cannot sleep!
Was your lover Apsu not in your heart?
And (vizier) Mummu who was captured? No wonder you sit alone!
Are you not a mother? You heave restlessly
But what about us, who cannot rest? Don't you love us?
Our grip(?) [is slack], (and) our eyes are sunken.
Remove the yoke of us restless ones, and let us sleep!
Set up a [battle cry] and avenge them!
Con[quer the enemy] and reduce them to nought!'
Tiamat listened, and the speech pleased her.
'Let us act now, (?) as you were advising!
The gods inside him (Apsu) will be disturbed,
Because they adopted evil for the gods who begot them.'
They crowded round and rallied beside Tiamat.
They were fierce, scheming restlessly night and day.

---

[15] **Four . . . ears:** Marduk is a cosmic being, lord of the four directions of space. [16] **Mariutu:** This appears to be a play on the logogram for Marduk's name AMAR.UTU; it has also been interpreted as a possible diminutive of the word *son*. (Translator's note.)

They were working up to war, growling and raging.
They convened a council and created conflict.
Mother Hubur,[17] who fashions all things,
Contributed an unfaceable weapon: she bore giant snakes,
Sharp of tooth and unsparing of fang (?).
She filled their bodies with venom instead of blood.
She cloaked ferocious dragons with fearsome rays
And made them bear mantles of radiance, made them godlike,

(chanting this imprecation)

'Whoever looks upon them shall collapse in utter terror!
Their bodies shall rear up continually and never turn away!'
She stationed a horned serpent, a *mušhuššu*-dragon, and a *lahmu*-hero,[18]
An *ugallu*-demon,[19] a rabid dog, and a scorpion-man,
Aggressive *ūmu*-demons,[20] a fish-man, and a bull-man
Bearing merciless weapons, fearless in battle.
Her orders were so powerful, they could not be disobeyed.
In addition she created eleven more likewise.
Over the gods her offspring who had convened a council for her
She promoted Qingu and made him greatest among them,
Conferred upon him leadership of the army, command of the assembly,
Raising the weapon to signal engagement, mustering combat-troops,
Overall command of the whole battle force.
And she set him upon a throne.
'I have cast the spell for you and made you greatest in the gods' assembly!
I have put into your power rule over all the gods!
You shall be the greatest, for you are my only lover!
Your commands shall always prevail over all the Anukki!'[21]
Then she gave him the Tablet of Destinies[22] and made him clasp it to his breast.
'Your utterance shall never be altered! Your word shall be law!'
When Qingu was promoted and had received the Anu-power
And had decreed destinies for the gods his sons, (he said),
'What issues forth from your mouths shall quench Fire!
Your accumulated venom (?) shall paralyse the powerful!' [. . .]

[The gods must decide how to deal with Tiamat's threat; the old father god Anshar sends his son Anu to fight Tiamat, but Anu turns back, as does Nudimmud (Ea). Anshar then announces that Marduk has been chosen to face Tiamat and lays down certain conditions.]

---

[17] **Mother Hubur:** A chthonic, or underworld, being who personifies the river of the underworld; the Greek goddess Styx is comparable. [18] ***mušhuššu*-dragon . . . *lahmu*-hero:** These are composite, theriomorphic (having an animal's form) beings or demons: *mušhuššu* means "red furious"; see note 4. [19] ***ugallu*-demon:** A demon with a lion's body. [20] ***ūmu*-demons:** Storm-demons. [21] **Anukki:** Or Anunnaki; the chthonic deities who became the seven judges in the underworld. [22] **Tablet of Destinies:** Like a book of fate, the Tablet or Tablets of Destinies control events for the coming year; whoever controls the Tablet controls the destiny of the world.

'I sent Anu, but he was unable to face her.
Nudimmud panicked and turned back.
Then Marduk, sage of the gods, your son, came forward.
He wanted of his own free will to confront Tiamat.
He addressed his words to me,
"If indeed I am to be your champion,
To defeat Tiamat and save your lives,
Convene the council, name a special fate,
Sit joyfully together in Ubshu-ukkinakku:"'[23] [. . .]

Tablet IV

They founded a princely shrine for him,
And he took up residence as ruler before his fathers, (*who proclaimed*)
'You are honoured among the great gods.
Your destiny is unequalled, your word (has the power of) Anu!
O Marduk, you are honoured among the great gods.
Your destiny is unequalled, your word (has the power of) Anu!
From this day onwards your command shall not be altered.
Yours is the power to exalt and abase.
May your utterance be law, your word never be falsified.
None of the gods shall transgress your limits.
May endowment, required for the gods' shrines
Wherever they have temples, be established for your place.
O Marduk, you are our champion!
We hereby give you sovereignty over all of the whole universe.
Sit in the assembly and your word shall be pre-eminent!
May your weapons never miss (the mark), may they smash your enemies!
O lord, spare the life of him who trusts in you,
But drain the life of the god who has espoused evil!'
They set up in their midst one constellation,
And then they addressed Marduk their son,
'May your decree, O lord, impress the gods!
Command to destroy and to recreate, and let it be so!
Speak and let the constellation vanish![24]
Speak to it again and let the constellation reappear.'
He spoke, and at his word the constellation vanished.
He spoke to it again and the constellation was recreated.
When the gods his fathers saw how effective his utterance was,
They rejoiced, they proclaimed: 'Marduk is King!'
They invested him with sceptre, throne, and staff-of-office.

[23] **Ubshu-ukkinakku:** Assembly hall for deities, usually included in a temple complex. [24] **Speak . . . vanish:** A test to establish Marduk's authority and the power of his word.

They gave him an unfaceable weapon to crush the foe.
'Go, and cut off the life of Tiamat!
Let the winds bear her blood to us as good news!'
The gods his fathers thus decreed the destiny of the lord
And set him on the path of peace and obedience.
He fashioned a bow, designated it as his weapon,
Feathered the arrow, set it in the string.
He lifted up a mace and carried it in his right hand,
Slung the bow and quiver at his side,
Put lightning in front of him,
His body was filled with an ever-blazing flame.
He made a net to encircle Tiamat within it,
Marshalled the four winds so that no part of her could escape:
South Wind, North Wind, East Wind, West Wind,
The gift of his father Anu, he kept them close to the net at his side.
He created the *imhullu*-wind (evil wind), the tempest, the whirlwind,
The Four Winds, the Seven Winds, the tornado, the unfaceable facing wind.
He released the winds which he had created, seven of them.
They advanced behind him to make turmoil inside Tiamat.
The lord raised the flood-weapon,[25] his great weapon,
And mounted the frightful, unfaceable storm-chariot.
He had yoked to it a team of four and had harnessed to its side
'Slayer', 'Pitiless', 'Racer', and 'Flyer';
Their lips were drawn back, their teeth carried poison.
They know not exhaustion, they can only devastate.
He stationed on his right Fiercesome Fight and Conflict,
On the left Battle to knock down every contender (?).
Clothed in a cloak of awesome armour,
His head was crowned with a terrible radiance.
The Lord set out and took the road,
And set his face towards Tiamat who raged out of control.
In his lips he gripped a spell,
In his hand he grasped a herb to counter poison.
Then they thronged about him, the gods thronged about him;
The gods his fathers thronged about him, the gods thronged about him.
The Lord drew near and looked into the middle of Tiamat:
He was trying to find out the strategy of Qingu her lover.
As he looked, his mind[26] became confused,

---

[25] **flood-weapon:** Marduk was originally a weather god, as were many gods in the ancient Near East. The Greek Zeus, for example, is often pictured with a thunderbolt; Yahweh led the Israelites with cloud and fire—possibly storm clouds and lightning or volcanic eruption. Marduk's *imhullu*-wind is possibly a tornado.

[26] **As he . . . mind:** Probably refers to Qingu rather than Marduk.

His will crumbled and his actions were muddled.
As for the gods his helpers, who march(ed) at his side,
When they saw the warrior, the leader, their looks were strained.
Tiamat cast her spell. She did not even turn her neck.
In her lips she was holding falsehood, lies, (wheedling),
'[How powerful is] your attacking force, O lord of the gods!
The whole assembly of them has gathered to your place!'

(But he ignored her blandishments)

The Lord lifted up the flood-weapon, his great weapon
And sent a message to Tiamat who feigned goodwill, saying:
'Why are you so friendly on the surface
When your depths conspire to muster a battle force?
Just because the sons were noisy (and) disrespectful to their fathers,
Should you, who gave them birth, reject compassion?
You named Qingu as your lover,
You appointed him to rites of Anu-power, wrongfully his.
You sought out evil for Anshar, king of the gods,
So you have compounded your wickedness against the gods my fathers!
Let your host prepare! Let them gird themselves with your weapons!
Stand forth, and you and I shall do single combat!'
When Tiamat heard this,
She went wild, she lost her temper.
Tiamat screamed aloud in a passion,
Her lower parts shook together from the depths.
She recited the incantation and kept casting her spell.
Meanwhile the gods of battle were sharpening their weapons.
Face to face they came, Tiamat and Marduk, sage of the gods.
They engaged in combat, they closed for battle.
The Lord spread his net and made it encircle her,
To her face he dispatched the *imhullu*-wind, which had been behind:
Tiamat opened her mouth to swallow it,
And he forced in the *imhullu*-wind so that she could not close her lips.
Fierce winds distended her belly;
Her insides were constipated and she stretched her mouth wide.
He shot an arrow which pierced her belly,
Split her down the middle and slit her heart,
Vanquished her and extinguished her life.
He threw down her corpse and stood on top of her.
When he had slain Tiamat, the leader,
He broke up her regiments; her assembly was scattered.
Then the gods her helpers, who had marched at her side,
Began to tremble, panicked, and turned tail.

Although he allowed them to come out and spared their lives,
They were surrounded, they could not flee.
Then he tied them up and smashed their weapons.
They were thrown into the net and sat there ensnared.
They cowered back, filled with woe.
They had to bear his punishment, confined to prison.
And as for the dozens of creatures, covered in fearsome rays,
The gang of demons who all marched on her right,
He fixed them with nose-ropes and tied their arms.
He trampled their battle-filth (?) beneath him.
As for Qingu, who had once been the greatest among them,
He defeated him and counted him among the dead gods,[27]
Wrested from him the Tablet of Destinies, wrongfully his,
Sealed it with (his own) seal and pressed it to his breast.
When he had defeated and killed his enemies
And had proclaimed the submissive (?) foe his slave,
And had set up the triumphal cry of Anshar over all the enemy,
And had achieved the desire of Nudimmud, Marduk the warrior
Strengthened his hold over the captive gods,
And to Tiamat, whom he had ensnared, he turned back.
The Lord trampled the lower part of Tiamat,
With his unsparing mace smashed her skull,
Severed the arteries of her blood,
And made the North Wind carry it off as good news.
His fathers saw it and were jubilant: they rejoiced,
Arranged to greet him with presents, greetings, gifts.
The Lord rested, and inspected her corpse.
He divided the monstrous shape and created marvels (from it).
He sliced her in half like a fish for drying:
Half of her he put up to roof the sky,[28]
Drew a bolt across and made a guard hold it.
Her waters he arranged so that they could not escape.
He crossed the heavens and sought out a shrine;
He levelled Apsu, dwelling of Nudimmud.
The Lord measured the dimensions of Apsu
And the large temple (Eshgalla), which he built in its image, was Esharra:
In the great shrine Esharra, which he had created as the sky,
He founded cult centres for Anu, Ellil,[29] and Ea. [. . .]

---

[27] **the dead gods:** The meaning here is unclear; usually gods cannot be killed, only imprisoned or contained. Although Tiamat is split in half to create earth and sky, she is a "living" universe. [28] **to roof the sky:** Ancient peoples thought that the sky was a dome, called a firmament in Genesis. [29] **Anu, Ellil:** Perhaps gods of wind or air.

Tablet V

He fashioned stands for the great gods.
As for the stars, he set up constellations corresponding to them.
He designated the year and marked out its divisions,
Apportioned three stars each to the twelve months.
When he had made plans of the days of the year,
He founded the stand of Neberu to mark out their courses,
So that none of them could go wrong or stray.
He fixed the stand of Ellil and Ea together with it,
Opened up gates in both ribs,
Made strong bolts to left and right.
With her liver he located the Zenith;
He made the crescent moon appear, entrusted night (to it)
And designated it the jewel of night to mark out the days.
'Go forth every month without fail in a corona,
At the beginning of the month, to glow over the land.
You shine with horns to mark out six days;
On the seventh day the crown is half.
The fifteenth day[30] shall always be the mid-point, the half of each month.
When Shamash[31] looks at you from the horizon,
Gradually shed your visibility and begin to wane.
Always bring the day of disappearance close to the path of Shamash,
And on the thirtieth day, the [year] is always equalized, for Shamash is
(responsible for) the year.
A sign [shall appear (?)]: sweep along its path.
Then always approach the [ ] and judge the case.
[ ] the Bowstar to kill and rob.
[. . .]

(15 lines broken)

[After the gods proclaim their allegiance to Marduk, he makes Babylon the center of his cult and creates the first humans from the blood of the rebel Qingu. The primary duty of humans is to serve the gods.]

Tablet VI

When Marduk heard the speech of the gods,
He made up his mind to perform miracles.
He spoke his utterance to Ea,

---

[30] **The fifteenth day:** The word for the fifteenth day of the month, *šabattu*, is cognate with the Sabbath. (Translator's note.) [31] **Shamash:** Sun-god.

And communicated to him the plan that he was considering.
'Let me put blood together, and make bones too.
Let me set up primeval man: Man shall be his name.
Let me create a primeval man.
The work of the gods shall be imposed (on him), and so they shall be at leisure.
Let me change the ways of the gods miraculously,
So they are gathered as one yet divided in two.'
Ea answered him and spoke a word to him,
Told him his plan for the leisure of the gods.
'Let one who is hostile to them be surrendered (up),
Let him be destroyed, and let people be created (from him).
Let the great gods assemble,
Let the culprit be given up, and let them convict him.'
Marduk assembled the great gods,
Gave (them) instructions pleasantly, gave orders.
The gods paid attention to what he said.
The king addressed his words to the Anunnaki,
'Your election of me shall be firm and foremost.
I shall declare the laws, the edicts within my power.
Whosoever started the war,
And incited Tiamat, and gathered an army,
Let the one who started the war be given up to me,
And he shall bear the penalty for his crime, that you may dwell in peace.'
The Igigi, the great gods, answered him,
Their lord Lugal-dimmer-ankia, counsellor of gods,
'It was Qingu who started the war,
He who incited Tiamat and gathered an army!'
They bound him and held him in front of Ea,
Imposed the penalty on him and cut off his blood.
He created mankind from his blood,
Imposed the toil of the gods (on man) and released the gods from it.
When Ea the wise had created mankind,
Had imposed the toil of the gods on them—
That deed is impossible to describe,
For Nudimmud performed it with the miracles of Marduk—
Then Marduk the king divided the gods,
The Anunnaki, all of them, above and below.
He assigned his decrees to Anu to guard,
Established three hundred as a guard in the sky;
Did the same again when he designed the conventions of earth,
And made the six hundred dwell in both heaven and earth. [. . .]

[After they divide the heavens and the earth by lots among themselves, the gods build a ziggurat for Apsu. Then Ishtar, designated as the bow, is given her place in the heavens and in the assembly of gods.]

Anu raised (the bow) and spoke in the assembly of gods,
He kissed the bow. 'May she go far!'[32]
He gave to the bow her names, saying,
'May Long and Far be the first, and Victorious the second;
Her third name shall be Bowstar, for she shall shine in the sky.'
He fixed her position among the gods her companions.
When Anu had decreed the destiny of the bow,
He set down her royal throne. 'You are highest of the gods!'
And Anu made her sit in the assembly of gods.
The great gods assembled
And made Marduk's destiny highest; they themselves did obeisance.
They swore an oath for themselves,
And swore on water and oil, touched their throats.
Thus they granted that he should exercise the kingship of the gods
And confirmed for him mastery of the gods of heaven and earth. [. . .]

[The conclusion is a recitation of the fifty gods now assimilated into the figure of Marduk.]

[32] **'May she go far!':** Probably Ishtar; the bow belongs to the goddess of the hunt.

The Epic of Gilgamesh
c. 1800 B.C.E.

The Epic of Gilgamesh is the most influential literary epic to come out of ancient Mesopotamia. It narrates the journey of Gilgamesh, a young king of Uruk, whose search for solace from despair and human mortality leads to the threshold of life itself. Although the story is more than four millennia old and from a culture long past, Gilgamesh is familiar; he is an individual, a person with deep feelings who treats life as an adventure, makes mistakes, battles giants, grieves for the death of a friend, and embarks on a long quest into the unknown in search of a way out of the pain of loss and the meaning of life. Gilgamesh is someone with whom a modern reader can sympathize, even identify. Historian William Irwin Thompson sees Gilgamesh as man himself: "Just as Faust's story was the medieval legend which became the myth of modern scientific man and was given

WWW For a quiz on *The Epic of Gilgamesh,* see *World Literature Online* at bedfordstmartins .com/worldlit.

Just as Faust's story was the medieval legend which became the myth of modern scientific man and was given such different artistic renderings by Marlowe, Goethe, and Mann, so Gilgamesh is the central legend of ancient civilized humanity that becomes *the* myth of humanity and civilization.
– WILLIAM IRWIN THOMPSON, historian, 1981

such different artistic renderings by Marlowe, Goethe, and Mann,[1] so Gilgamesh is the central legend of ancient civilized humanity that becomes *the* myth of humanity and civilization."

This narration is called an **EPIC** because it contains the basic features of the form later established as standard by Homer:[2] a hero of national stature performing extraordinary deeds in a world setting, whose mortal challenges and triumphs are associated with the immortal arena of gods and goddesses. Unlike Homer's epics, however, which were performed or recited at religious and literary festivals, it is not clear that the Gilgamesh narration was ever used for the purpose of ritual or entertainment. A line from a poetic translation of the prologue by Stephanie Dalley suggests a didactic role for the story: "He journeyed far and wide, weary and at last resigned. / He engraved all toils on a memorial monument of stone." It seems that *Gilgamesh* is not simply a series of adventures written to glorify a king, but a story that points to the wisdom of acceptance.

The Epic of Gilgamesh is apparently based on a historical figure. The name Gilgamesh has been found in lists of Sumerian kings, and it is believed that Gilgamesh reigned in the city of Uruk—the modern Warka—on the Euphrates River sometime between 2800 and 2500 B.C.E. Uruk had been a major religious center in the fourth millennium B.C.E. Since Mesopotamian gods and goddesses were thought to actually reside in their temples, religious cities were treated as reflections or models of the cosmos. Uruk, for example, was balanced between two deities: One half of the city was devoted to the sky-god An or Anu; the other half was devoted to the earth-goddess Inanna. Her temple was named Eanna, meaning the house of An. In the narration, Gilgamesh's father is a mortal; in the Sandars translation used here, Gilgamesh's spirit guardian is called **Lugulbanda**, and the name Lugulbanda (or **Lugalbanda**) is also found on the king-lists of Uruk, two kings before Gilgamesh. It is probable that Lugulbanda was Gilgamesh's father, though another king reigned between them. In the narration, Gilgamesh's mother is Ninsun, a goddess who provides his partial divinity. Tablets from this period indicate that after his reign Gilgamesh was considered a god—a deification not unlike that of the Greek Heracles or Orpheus that occurred when an extraordinary mortal warranted eternal elevation.

loo-gool-BAHN-dah; loo-gahl-BAHN-dah

Though evidence of its actual transmission is missing, it is believed that *The Epic of Gilgamesh* influenced the literature of the region for many years, from Persia to Palestine to Greece and Rome. The tablets on which

[1] **Marlowe . . . Mann:** Faust, with his deep yearning for knowledge about the self and human life, was the hero of medieval legends. His story later was dramatized by the English playwright Christopher Marlowe (1564–1593) in *Doctor Faustus* (c. 1589). Johann Wolfgang von Goethe (1749–1832), one of the great German writers, authored *Faust* (1832), a poetic drama, and several novels, including *The Sorrows of Young Werther* (1774). Thomas Mann (1875–1955) wrote the novels *The Magic Mountain* (1924) and *Death in Venice* (1911); he published *Doctor Faustus* in 1947.

[2] **Homer** (c. 700 B.C.E.): Author of two epics about the Trojan War (c. 1200 B.C.E.), *The Iliad,* a war among the Greeks, and *The Odyssey,* the story of Odysseus' arduous return home to the Greek island of Ithaca after the Trojan War.

Gilgamesh, 721–705 B.C.E.
In this relief from the palace of Sargon II, the Sumerian hero Gilgamesh holds a tamed lion cub. (Giraudon / Art Resource, NY)

the epic was inscribed also tell of a flood that bears an unmistakable resemblance to the flood spoken of in the Book of Genesis in the Hebrew Scriptures. Either the writer of the biblical story was acquainted with the Babylonian account, or the two accounts drew on a common source. N. K. Sandars explains the possible link to Greece: "It is less a case of prototypes and parentage than of similar atmosphere. The world inhabited by Greek bards and Assyrian scribes, in the eighth and seventh centuries [B.C.E.], was small enough for there to have been some contact between them, and the trading voyages of Greek merchants and adventurers provide a likely setting for the exchange of stories . . . Therefore it is not surprising that Gilgamesh, Enkidu, and Humbaba should seem to inhabit the same universe as the gods and mortals of the *Homeric Hymns*, Hesiod's ***Theogony***,[3] and ***The Odyssey***."

p. 263, p. 421

The Story of Gilgamesh. Gilgamesh's tale begins with a celebration of the feats that made him famous and secured for him a place in history. He was a wise king known for his building projects, especially for the great wall circling the city. The stories that follow cluster around two major events: Gilgamesh's friendship with Enkidu and his grand journey to the edge of the world in search of immortality.

Characteristic of most great heroes down through the ages, Gilgamesh is of mixed parentage, divine and human, which sets him apart from ordinary men and raises his destiny to a cosmic level. As a young untested king, Gilgamesh's youthful energy creates problems: He indulges in an antiquated custom of claiming first sexual rights to brides and other women in Uruk. He also alienates sons from their fathers. The people are fed up and cry out to the father of the gods, Anu, for assistance. Anu provides for the creation of **Enkidu**, a young man capable of challenging Gilgamesh and diverting him from his present lifestyle.

ENG-kee-doo

Because Enkidu initially lives with animals and frees them from traps, he comes to the attention of trappers, who complain about him. The translated text says that a temple prostitute is used to domesticate Enkidu, but *prostitute* has perhaps an inappropriate connotation for a woman who was probably a temple priestess familiar with the arts of sexuality and well suited to initiate Enkidu into carnal mysteries. After six days and seven nights of lovemaking, Enkidu finds himself estranged from the animals and ready to enter civilized society in order to confront Gilgamesh, who knows of Enkidu from his dreams, an important source of visionary knowledge for the Sumerians.

---

[3] ***Homeric Hymns . . . Theogony:*** The *Homeric Hymns* (seventh–sixth centuries B.C.E.) at one time were attributed to Homer but are now believed to have been written by poets from a Homeric school or to be simply hymns written in the style of Homer. Five of the longer hymns are important sources of stories about the gods Demeter, Dionysus, Apollo, Aphrodite, and Hermes. Hesiod was a Greek poet (eighth century B.C.E.) from an area north of Athens. He is known for two primary works: *Theogony,* an orderly presentation of creation stories and the generations of the gods and goddesses, and *Works and Days,* a body of advice about the proper treatment of deities. The latter contains the "five ages of man," the Greek version of the decline of humanity—similar to the Fall in Hebrew myth.

Gilgamesh and Enkidu. After they test each other's strength in a wrestling match, Enkidu and Gilgamesh become close friends and soul mates, reminiscent of other friendships from antiquity, such as Achilles and Patroclus in ***The Iliad*** and David and Jonathan in the Bible, male friendships said by Plato to be deeper than those between men and women. In some ways, however, the two men appear to be opposites: Gilgamesh is a civilized ruler, while Enkidu is a hairy man of nature; Gilgamesh is at home in the court, Enkidu lives in the wild with animals. If Gilgamesh represents the urban male, then Enkidu complements him by being the natural man, the man of instinct and intuition. The pair might in fact represent wholeness or health, as if Enkidu were a psychological extension or alter ego of Gilgamesh.

p. 288

Together they are well prepared to face their first challenge—a rite of passage for young warriors coming of age. They confront the giant Humbaba, who dwells in cedar forests on the other side of the mountains. The defeat of this giant symbolizes the extension of civilization, and it gives the two men the confidence to return to Uruk as independent, self-reliant warriors. The first part of the epic reaches a climax when Gilgamesh encounters the goddess Ishtar, who asks him to be her lover. This is not a simple request for sexual pleasure; she represents the earth's fertility and is proposing that Gilgamesh become the year-king. As such, he would symbolize the annual vegetative cycle and would be sacrificed to the Great Mother in order to guarantee the harvest at the end of the season. Gilgamesh's negative response includes a litany of Ishtar's former lovers,[4] all of whom were sacrificed in some manner. Gilgamesh's rejection of this role amounts to a major turning point in masculine consciousness. Free from the annual agricultural cycle of the Mother Goddess, Gilgamesh is charting a new destiny for the patriarchal hero as a solitary individual meeting challenges on his own and searching for personal answers.

If a superman and demigod like Gilgamesh failed to attain everlasting life, or at least ever recurrent youth, how utterly futile it is for a mere mortal to aspire to such a blessed estate and to hope to escape death! It is true, Utnapishtim and his wife obtained eternal life, but that was an exceptional case; and, furthermore, it was by divine favor, not through their own efforts. The rule still holds good that all men must die.

–Alexander Heidel, historian and linguist, 1949

Rejected and angry, Ishtar tries to punish the young warriors with the Bull of Heaven, which they kill in what amounts to the first bullfight in literature. As a final insult, Enkidu tears out the bull's right thigh (symbolic of genitals?) and flings it in Ishtar's face.

A price must be paid, however, for the destruction of Humbaba and the Bull of Heaven, and for the humiliation of Ishtar and the old religion. The two heroes, after all, have defied the gods and created a new independence for humans. In some sense they have gone too far, which is always the initial appearance of extending psychological boundaries and developing a new consciousness. The Greek story of Prometheus explores a similar transition from an old to a new order with tragic consequences,

[4] **Ishtar's . . . lovers:** Refers to the king-lovers who become replacements for the goddess in the underworld. The lovers then are part of the annual agricultural cycles, the growth of grains, in the ancient Near East. It is not known whether the king-lovers were actually sacrificed in an imitation of harvesting or whether they were part of a religious ceremony. Gilgamesh's rejection of Ishtar seems to point to a change in Sumerian culture whereby the role of the goddess was deemphasized and the status of warriors, kings, and sky-gods was elevated.

as does the Renaissance tale of Faustus.[5] Enkidu must die, not a glorious death in battle, but a withering away in illness. Enkidu dreams of the Sumerian land of the dead, where the deceased resemble bats residing in dust and darkness. The real price therefore of individual consciousness is not death, but dread of death, which drives Gilgamesh to question his mortality and to seek answers in a faraway land.

The Journey to the Edge of the World. Following the path of the sun, Gilgamesh embarks on his great journey to find **Utnapishtim**, the one mortal who has been granted immortality by the gods. Although it is impossible to determine the exact influence that *Gilgamesh* had on later works of literature in Greece and Israel, a number of patterns or motifs in *Gilgamesh* later appear as standard fare in epic works. On the other side of the mountains, Gilgamesh confronts guardians who are part human and part animal,[6] signifying their allegiance to two worlds. He meets a mysterious woman, Siduri, in a paradisal garden. She assists him in dealing with **Urshanabi** the ferryman.[7] To reach Utnapishtim they must cross the waters of death or chaos. Finally, Gilgamesh accomplishes his goal by questioning Utnapishtim about mortality.

oot-nah-PISH-tim

oor-shah-NAH-bee

If Gilgamesh is not the first human hero, he is the first tragic hero of whom anything is known. The narrative is incomplete and may remain so; nevertheless it is today the finest surviving epic poem from any period until the appearance of Homer's *Iliad:* and it is immeasurably older.

– N. K. Sandars, archeologist, 1964

There are two parts to Utnapishtim's answer. First, he explains that the essence of life is change. Then he tells Gilgamesh his life story, which largely is the story of a great flood, complete with ark, rain, and birds as emissaries. Gilgamesh does not, however, learn how to obtain immortality from the gods. Gilgamesh then begs Utnapishtim and is granted a chance to obtain eternal life magically through passing a test—but Gilgamesh fails. He is then told where to find the plant of eternal youth, which he says he will call "The Old Men Are Young Again," but once he has retrieved it, it is stolen and eaten by a snake[8]—another failure. An all-too-human picture of mortality emerges at the close of Gilgamesh's journey.

It is impossible to conclude with certainty about the lessons learned by Gilgamesh from Siduri and Utnapishtim, but it appears that the advice he receives recommends a gentle kind of hedonism, of the sort found in Ecclesiastes: Although one cannot completely understand the mysteries of life, the essence of life is change, and death is the end result; one should accept this and live life to its fullest. Gilgamesh returns to

[5] **Prometheus . . . Faustus:** The Greek Prometheus was imprisoned for his rebellion against Zeus; the medieval and Renaissance figure of Faustus was willing to trade his soul for knowledge and understanding. Marlowe's play about Faustus ends with the hero's descent into hell.

[6] **a mixture . . . animal:** Deities who are a combination of animal and human forms are called theriomorphic figures; power or wisdom results from their connection to two different realms. An angel is powerful, for example, because it is linked to both the earth and the sky.

[7] **Urshanabi the ferryman:** The traditional ferryman in myth and religious tales transports souls into the realm of the dead. The Greek ferryman is called Charon. The ferryman in Buddhist tradition carries individuals across a river to the shore of enlightenment.

[8] **eaten by a snake:** Possibly a tale that explains a snake's capacity for "rebirth" through its shedding of skin.

Uruk and becomes a great king about whom stories are told for generations. It is remarkable that his story should seem so contemporary, so relevant to the experience of life today.

■ CONNECTIONS

Homer, *The Odyssey*, p. 421; Virgil, *The Aeneid*, p. 1181. The motif of the hero journey in the literature of the ancient Mediterranean region involved either a descent into the underworld or a trip to the world's edge in order to gain knowledge or an elixir or boon. How is Gilgamesh's quest both similar to and different from Odysseus' and Aeneas' journeys to Hades?

***Ramayana*, p. 1357.** Epic heroes prove themselves through tests of physical strength. Gilgamesh is quite obviously related to Greek heroes like Achilles and Heracles in his physical prowess, but the Indian hero Rama appears to use physical conflict as a way of obtaining spiritual knowledge. Is Gilgamesh also after self-knowledge?

***Beowulf* (Book 2).** Water and its association with the unconscious often play important roles in the maturation journeys of epic heroes. Gilgamesh must engage a ferryman to cross the waters of the dead. Beowulf must descend in waters in order to defeat Grendel's dam. What role does water play in both stories, and what are the possible psychological meanings of a hero's encounter with water?

■ FURTHER RESEARCH

Translations

Dalley, Stephanie. *Myths from Mesopotamia.* 1991.
Ferry, David. *Gilgamesh: A New Rendering in English Verse.* 1992.
Mason, Herbert. *Gilgamesh: A Verse Narrative.* 1970.
Sandars, N. K. *The Epic of Gilgamesh.* 1960. A detailed, informative introduction.

Background and Criticism

Heidel, Alexander. *The Gilgamesh Epic and Old Testament Parallels.* 1963.
Jacobsen, Thorkild. *The Treasure of Darkness: A History of Mesopotamian Religion.* 1976.
Kramer, Samuel Noah. *Sumerian Mythology.* 1944.
Thompson, William Irwin. *The Time Falling Bodies Take to Light: Mythology, Sexuality & The Origins of Culture.* 1981. An insightful discussion of *Gilgamesh* and the transition from neolithic to Sumerian civilization.

■ PRONUNCIATION

Enkidu: ENG-kee-doo
Lugulbanda: loo-gool-BAHN-dah (more commonly written Lugalbanda: loo-gahl-BAHN-dah)
Urshanabi: oor-shah-NAH-bee
Utnapishtim: oot-nah-PISH-tim

The Epic of Gilgamesh

Translated by N. K. Sandars

PROLOGUE

Gilgamesh King in Uruk

I will proclaim to the world the deeds of Gilgamesh. This was the man to whom all things were known; this was the king who knew the countries of the world. He was wise, he saw mysteries and knew secret things, he brought us a tale of the days before the flood. He went on a long journey, was weary, worn-out with labour, returning he rested, he engraved on a stone the whole story.

When the gods created Gilgamesh they gave him a perfect body. Shamash[1] the glorious sun endowed him with beauty, Adad the god of the storm endowed him with courage, the great gods made his beauty perfect, surpassing all others, terrifying like a great wild bull. Two thirds they made him god and one third man.

In Uruk[2] he built walls, a great rampart, and the temple of blessed Eanna[3] for the god of the firmament Anu,[4] and for Ishtar the goddess of love. Look at it still today:

The Epic of Gilgamesh. Individual Sumerian stories about Gilgamesh, such as "Gilgamesh and the Giant Humbaba" and "Gilgamesh and the Bull of Heaven," were passed down orally until poets around 2100 B.C.E. began to record some of his adventures. These stories, written in cuneiform on clay tablets, were shaped into the longest and finest Akkadian composition of the Old Babylonian period (1900–1600 B.C.E.). Unfortunately, a complete text from this period does not exist. Other fragments of versions have been found in the Hittite and Hurrian languages from the late second millennium B.C.E. The most complete version of the epic, called the Standard Version, was found in Assurbanipal's library at Nineveh and dates from the first half of the seventh century B.C.E. Its author is traditionally given as Sin-leqe-unnini, but it is not known whether he actually contributed to the composition of the text or merely transcribed the epic in clay.

The story of Gilgamesh is about kingship and the necessary preparations for becoming a great king. The narration also tells of civilization and its progress as well as the shift in Babylonian culture from goddess to god worship. But most of all, this epic is a wonderful story of an individual's maturation and search for enlightenment regarding friendship and death. N. K. Sandars states its importance: "If Gilgamesh is not the first human hero, he is the first tragic hero of whom anything is known . . . The narrative is incomplete and may remain so; nevertheless it is today the finest surviving epic poem from any period until the appearance of Homer's *Iliad:* and it is immeasurably older."

A note on the translation: In order to provide what the translator terms a "straightforward narrative," she does not indicate gaps or omissions in the poetry of the original Akkadian version; she has also chosen to render the text in prose. All notes are the editors'.

---

[1] **Shamash:** Also the god of law and the husband of Ishtar, Queen of Heaven and goddess of love and fertility.

[2] **Uruk:** An important city in southern Babylonia; after the flood it was the seat of a dynasty of kings. Gilgamesh was the fifth and most famous king of this dynasty.

[3] **walls . . . Eanna:** A temple precinct sacred to Anu and Ishtar.

[4] **Anu:** Father of the gods and god of the firmament or "Great Above."

the outer wall where the cornice runs, it shines with the brilliance of copper; and the inner wall, it has no equal. Touch the threshold, it is ancient. Approach Eanna the dwelling of Ishtar, our lady of love and war, the like of which no latter-day king, no man alive can equal. Climb upon the wall of Uruk; walk along it, I say; regard the foundation terrace and examine the masonry: is it not burnt brick and good? The seven sages[5] laid the foundations.

1

The Coming of Enkidu

Gilgamesh went abroad in the world, but he met with none who could withstand his arms till he came to Uruk. But the men of Uruk muttered in their houses "Gilgamesh sounds the tocsin for his amusement, his arrogance has no bounds by day or night. No son is left with his father, for Gilgamesh takes them all, even the children; yet the king should be a shepherd to his people. His lust leaves no virgin to her lover, neither the warrior's daughter nor the wife of the noble; yet this is the shepherd of the city, wise, comely, and resolute."

The gods heard their lament, the gods of heaven cried to the Lord of Uruk, to Anu the god of Uruk: "A goddess made him strong as a savage bull, none can withstand his arms. No son is left with his father for Gilgamesh takes them all; and is this the king, the shepherd of his people? His lust leaves no virgin to her lover, neither the warrior's daughter nor the wife of the noble." When Anu had heard their lamentation the gods cried to Aruru, the goddess of creation, "You made him, O Aruru, now create his equal; let it be as like him as his own reflection, his second self, stormy heart for stormy heart. Let them contend together and leave Uruk in quiet."

So the goddess conceived an image in her mind, and it was of the stuff of Anu of the firmament. She dipped her hands in water and pinched off clay, she let it fall in the wilderness, and noble Enkidu was created. There was virtue in him of the god of war, of Ninurta himself. His body was rough, he had long hair like a woman's; it waved like the hair of Nisaba, the goddess of corn. His body was covered with matted hair like Samuqan's, the god of cattle. He was innocent of mankind; he knew nothing of the cultivated land.

Enkidu ate grass in the hills with the gazelle and lurked with wild beasts at the water-holes; he had joy of the water with the herds of wild game. But there was a trapper who met him one day face to face at the drinking-hole, for the wild game had entered his territory. On three days he met him face to face, and the trapper was frozen with fear. He went back to his house with the game that he had caught, and he was dumb, benumbed with terror. His face was altered like that of one who has made a long journey. With awe in his heart he spoke to his father: "Father, there is a man, unlike any other, who comes down from the hills. He is the strongest in the world, he is like an immortal from heaven. He ranges over the hills with wild beasts and eats grass; he ranges through your land and comes down to the wells. I am afraid and

[5] **seven sages:** Wise men who brought civilization to the seven oldest cities of Mesopotamia.

dare not go near him. He fills in the pits which I dig and tears up my traps set for the game; he helps the beasts to escape and now they slip through my fingers."

His father opened his mouth and said to the trapper, "My son, in Uruk lives Gilgamesh; no one has ever prevailed against him, he is strong as a star from heaven. Go to Uruk, find Gilgamesh, extol the strength of this wild man. Ask him to give you a harlot, a wanton[6] from the temple of love; return with her, and let her woman's power overpower this man. When next he comes down to drink at the wells she will be there, stripped naked; and when he sees her beckoning he will embrace her, and then the wild beasts will reject him."

So the trapper set out on his journey to Uruk and addressed himself to Gilgamesh saying, "A man unlike any other is roaming now in the pastures; he is as strong as a star from heaven and I am afraid to approach him. He helps the wild game to escape; he fills in my pits and pulls up my traps." Gilgamesh said, "Trapper, go back, take with you a harlot, a child of pleasure. At the drinking-hole she will strip, and when he sees her beckoning he will embrace her and the game of the wilderness will surely reject him."

Now the trapper returned, taking the harlot with him. After a three days' journey they came to the drinking-hole, and there they sat down; the harlot and the trapper sat facing one another and waited for the game to come. For the first day and for the second day the two sat waiting, but on the third day the herds came; they came down to drink and Enkidu was with them. The small wild creatures of the plains were glad of the water, and Enkidu with them, who ate grass with the gazelle and was born in the hills; and she saw him, the savage man, come from far-off in the hills. The trapper spoke to her: "There he is. Now, woman, make your breasts bare, have no shame, do not delay but welcome his love. Let him see you naked, let him possess your body. When he comes near uncover yourself and lie with him; teach him, the savage man, your woman's art, for when he murmurs love to you the wild beasts that shared his life in the hills will reject him."

She was not ashamed to take him, she made herself naked and welcomed his eagerness; as he lay on her murmuring love she taught him the woman's art. For six days and seven nights they lay together, for Enkidu had forgotten his home in the hills; but when he was satisfied he went back to the wild beasts. Then, when the gazelle saw him, they bolted away; when the wild creatures saw him they fled. Enkidu would have followed, but his body was bound as though with a cord, his knees gave way when he started to run, his swiftness was gone. And now the wild creatures had all fled away; Enkidu was grown weak, for wisdom was in him, and the thoughts of a man were in his heart. So he returned and sat down at the woman's feet, and listened intently to what she said. "You are wise, Enkidu, and now you have become like a god. Why do you want to run wild with the beasts in the hills? Come with me. I will take you to strong-walled Uruk, to the blessed temple of Ishtar and of Anu, of love and of heaven: There Gilgamesh lives, who is very strong, and like a wild bull he lords it over men."

[6] **harlot . . . wanton:** "Harlot" or "wanton" has perhaps an inappropriate connotation for someone who is probably a temple priestess of Ishtar.

When she had spoken Enkidu was pleased; he longed for a comrade, for one who would understand his heart. "Come, woman, and take me to that holy temple, to the house of Anu and of Ishtar, and to the place where Gilgamesh lords it over the people. I will challenge him boldly, I will cry out aloud in Uruk, 'I am the strongest here, I have come to change the old order, I am he who was born in the hills, I am he who is strongest of all.'"

She said, "Let us go, and let him see your face. I know very well where Gilgamesh is in great Uruk. Ò Enkidu, there all the people are dressed in their gorgeous robes, every day is holiday, the young men and the girls are wonderful to see. How sweet they smell! All the great ones are roused from their beds. O Enkidu, you who love life, I will show you Gilgamesh, a man of many moods; you shall look at him well in his radiant manhood. His body is perfect in strength and maturity; he never rests by night or day. He is stronger than you, so leave your boasting. Shamash the glorious sun has given favours to Gilgamesh, and Anu of the heavens, and Enlil, and Ea the wise has given him deep understanding. I tell you, even before you have left the wilderness, Gilgamesh will know in his dreams that you are coming."

Now Gilgamesh got up to tell his dream to his mother, Ninsun, one of the wise gods. "Mother, last night I had a dream. I was full of joy, the young heroes were round me and I walked through the night under the stars of the firmament, and one, a meteor of the stuff of Anu, fell down from heaven. I tried to lift it but it proved too heavy. All the people of Uruk came round to see it, the common people jostled and the nobles thronged to kiss its feet; and to me its attraction was like the love of woman. They helped me, I braced my forehead and I raised it with thongs and brought it to you, and you yourself pronounced it my brother."

Then Ninsun, who is well-beloved and wise, said to Gilgamesh, "This star of heaven which descended like a meteor from the sky; which you tried to lift, but found too heavy, when you tried to move it it would not budge, and so you brought it to my feet; I made it for you, a goad and spur, and you were drawn as though to a woman. This is the strong comrade, the one who brings help to his friend in his need. He is the strongest of wild creatures, the stuff of Anu; born in the grass-lands and the wild hills reared him; when you see him you will be glad; you will love him as a woman and he will never forsake you. This is the meaning of the dream."

Gilgamesh said, "Mother, I dreamed a second dream. In the streets of strong-walled Uruk there lay an axe; the shape of it was strange and the people thronged round. I saw it and was glad. I bent down, deeply drawn towards it; I loved it like a woman and wore it at my side." Ninsun answered, "That axe, which you saw, which drew you so powerfully like love of a woman, that is the comrade whom I give you, and he will come in his strength like one of the host of heaven. He is the brave companion who rescues his friend in necessity." Gilgamesh said to his mother, "A friend, a counsellor has come to me from Enlil, and now I shall befriend and counsel him." So Gilgamesh told his dreams; and the harlot retold them to Enkidu.

And now she said to Enkidu, "When I look at you you have become like a god. Why do you yearn to run wild again with the beasts in the hills? Get up from the ground, the bed of a shepherd." He listened to her words with care. It was good advice that she gave. She divided her clothing in two and with the one half she clothed him and with the other herself; and holding his hand she led him like a child to the sheepfolds, into the shepherds' tents. There all the shepherds crowded round to see him, they put down bread in front of him, but Enkidu could only suck the milk of wild animals. He fumbled and gaped, at a loss what to do or how he should eat the bread and drink the strong wine. Then the woman said, "Enkidu, eat bread, it is the staff of life; drink the wine, it is the custom of the land." So he ate till he was full and drank strong wine, seven goblets. He became merry, his heart exulted and his face shone. He rubbed down the matted hair of his body and anointed himself with oil. Enkidu had become a man; but when he had put on man's clothing he appeared like a bridegroom. He took arms to hunt the lion so that the shepherds could rest at night. He caught wolves and lions and the herdsmen lay down in peace; for Enkidu was their watchman, that strong man who had no rival.

He was merry living with the shepherds, till one day lifting his eyes he saw a man approaching. He said to the harlot, "Woman, fetch that man here. Why has he come? I wish to know his name." She went and called the man saying, "Sir, where are you going on this weary journey?" The man answered, saying to Enkidu, "Gilgamesh has gone into the marriage-house and shut out the people. He does strange things in Uruk, the city of great streets. At the roll of the drum work begins for the men, and work for the women. Gilgamesh the king is about to celebrate marriage with the Queen of Love, and he still demands to be first with the bride, the king to be first and the husband to follow, for that was ordained by the gods from his birth, from the time the umbilical cord was cut. But now the drums roll for the choice of the bride and the city groans." At these words Enkidu turned white in the face. "I will go to the place where Gilgamesh lords it over the people, I will challenge him boldly, and I will cry aloud in Uruk, 'I have come to change the old order, for I am the strongest here.'"

Now Enkidu strode in front and the woman followed behind. He entered Uruk, that great market, and all the folk thronged round him where he stood in the street in strong-walled Uruk. The people jostled; speaking of him they said, "He is the spit of Gilgamesh." "He is shorter." "He is bigger of bone." "This is the one who was reared on the milk of wild beasts. His is the greatest strength." The men rejoiced: "Now Gilgamesh has met his match. This great one, this hero whose beauty is like a god, he is a match even for Gilgamesh."

In Uruk the bridal bed was made, fit for the goddess of love. The bride waited for the bridegroom, but in the night Gilgamesh got up and came to the house. Then Enkidu stepped out, he stood in the street and blocked the way. Mighty Gilgamesh came on and Enkidu met him at the gate. He put out his foot and prevented Gilgamesh from entering the house, so they grappled, holding each other like bulls. They broke the doorposts and the walls shook, they snorted like bulls locked together. They shattered the doorposts and the walls shook. Gilgamesh bent his knee with his foot planted on the ground and with a turn Enkidu was thrown. Then immediately his fury died. When Enkidu was thrown he said to Gilgamesh, "There is not another like you in the world. Ninsun, who is as strong as a wild ox in the byre, she was the mother who bore you, and now you are raised above all men, and Enlil has given you the kingship, for your strength surpasses the strength of men." So Enkidu and Gilgamesh embraced and their friendship was sealed.

2

The Forest Journey

Enlil[7] of the mountain, the father of the gods, had decreed the destiny of Gilgamesh. So Gilgamesh dreamed and Enkidu said, "The meaning of the dream is this. The father of the gods has given you kingship, such is your destiny, everlasting life is not your destiny. Because of this do not be sad at heart, do not be grieved or oppressed. He has given you power to bind and to loose, to be the darkness and the light of mankind. He has given you unexampled supremacy over the people, victory in battle from which no fugitive returns, in forays and assaults from which there is no going back. But do not abuse this power, deal justly with your servants in the palace, deal justly before Shamash."

The eyes of Enkidu were full of tears and his heart was sick. He sighed bitterly and Gilgamesh met his eye and said, "My friend, why do you sigh so bitterly?" But Enkidu opened his mouth and said, "I am weak, my arms have lost their strength, the cry of sorrow sticks in my throat, I am oppressed by idleness." It was then that the lord Gilgamesh turned his thoughts to the Country of the Living; on the Land of Cedars the lord Gilgamesh reflected. He said to his servant Enkidu, "I have not established my name stamped on bricks as my destiny decreed; therefore I will go to the country where the cedar is felled. I will set up my name in the place where the names of famous men are written, and where no man's name is written yet I will raise a monument to the gods. Because of the evil that is in the land, we will go to the forest and destroy the evil; for in the forest lives Humbaba[8] whose name is 'Hugeness,' a ferocious giant." But Enkidu sighed bitterly and said, "When I went with the wild beasts ranging through the wilderness I discovered the forest; its length is ten thousand leagues in every direction. Enlil has appointed Humbaba to guard it and armed him in sevenfold terrors, terrible to all flesh is Humbaba. When he roars it is like the torrent of the storm, his breath is like fire, and his jaws are death itself. He guards the cedars so well that when the wild heifer stirs in the forest, though she is sixty leagues distant, he hears her. What man would willingly walk into that country and explore its depths? I tell you, weakness overpowers whoever goes near it: it is not an equal struggle when one fights with Humbaba; he is a great warrior, a battering-ram. Gilgamesh, the watchman of the forest never sleeps."

Gilgamesh replied: "Where is the man who can clamber to heaven? Only the gods live for ever with glorious Shamash, but as for us men, our days are numbered, our occupations are a breath of wind. How is this, already you are afraid! I will go first although I am your lord, and you may safely call out, 'Forward, there is nothing to fear!' Then if I fall I leave behind me a name that endures; men will say of me, 'Gilgamesh has fallen in fight with ferocious Humbaba.' Long after the child has been born in my house, they will say it, and remember." Enkidu spoke again to Gilgamesh, "O my lord, if you will enter that country, go first to the hero Shamash, tell the Sun God, for the land is his. The country where the cedar is cut belongs to Shamash."

---

[7] **Enlil:** As god of earth, wind, and spirit, Enlil is the active manifestation of Anu.

[8] **Humbaba:** A nature divinity, guardian spirit of the forest.

Gilgamesh took up a kid, white without spot, and a brown one with it; he held them against his breast, and he carried them into the presence of the sun. He took in his hand his silver sceptre and he said to glorious Shamash, "I am going to that country, O Shamash, I am going; my hands supplicate, so let it be well with my soul and bring me back to the quay of Uruk. Grant, I beseech, your protection, and let the omen be good." Glorious Shamash answered, "Gilgamesh, you are strong, but what is the Country of the Living to you?"

"O Shamash, hear me, hear me, Shamash, let my voice be heard. Here in the city man dies oppressed at heart, man perishes with despair in his heart. I have looked over the wall and I see the bodies floating on the river, and that will be my lot also. Indeed I know it is so, for whoever is tallest among men cannot reach the heavens, and the greatest cannot encompass the earth. Therefore I would enter that country: because I have not established my name stamped on brick as my destiny decreed, I will go to the country where the cedar is cut. I will set up my name where the names of famous men are written; and where no man's name is written I will raise a monument to the gods." The tears ran down his face and he said, "Alas, it is a long journey that I must take to the Land of Humbaba. If this enterprise is not to be accomplished, why did you move me, Shamash, with the restless desire to perform it? How can I succeed if you will not succour me? If I die in that country I will die without rancour, but if I return I will make a glorious offering of gifts and of praise to Shamash."

So Shamash accepted the sacrifice of his tears; like the compassionate man he showed him mercy. He appointed strong allies for Gilgamesh, sons of one mother, and stationed them in the mountain caves. The great winds he appointed: the north wind, the whirlwind, the storm and the icy wind, the tempest and the scorching wind. Like vipers, like dragons, like a scorching fire, like a serpent that freezes the heart, a destroying flood and the lightning's fork, such were they and Gilgamesh rejoiced.

He went to the forge and said, "I will give orders to the armourers; they shall cast us our weapons while we watch them." So they gave orders to the armourers and the craftsmen sat down in conference. They went into the groves of the plain and cut willow and boxwood; they cast for them axes of nine score pounds, and great swords they cast with blades of six score pounds each one, with pommels and hilts of thirty pounds. They cast for Gilgamesh the axe "Might of Heroes" and the bow of Anshan;[9] and Gilgamesh was armed and Enkidu; and the weight of the arms they carried was thirty score pounds.

The people collected and the counsellors in the streets and in the market-place of Uruk; they came through the gate of seven bolts and Gilgamesh spoke to them in the market-place: "I, Gilgamesh, go to see that creature of whom such things are spoken, the rumour of whose name fills the world. I will conquer him in his cedar wood and show the strength of the sons of Uruk, all the world shall know of it. I am committed to this enterprise: to climb the mountain, to cut down the cedar, and leave behind me an enduring name." The counsellors of Uruk, the great market,

[9] **Anshan:** A district in southwest Persia, probably the source of wood for making bows.

answered him, "Gilgamesh, you are young, your courage carries you too far, you cannot know what this enterprise means which you plan. We have heard that Humbaba is not like men who die, his weapons are such that none can stand against them; the forest stretches for ten thousand leagues in every direction; who would willingly go down to explore its depths? As for Humbaba, when he roars it is like the torrent of the storm, his breath is like fire and his jaws are death itself. Why do you crave to do this thing, Gilgamesh? It is no equal struggle when one fights with Humbaba, that battering-ram."

When he heard these words of the counsellors Gilgamesh looked at his friend and laughed, "How shall I answer them; shall I say I am afraid of Humbaba, I will sit at home all the rest of my days?" Then Gilgamesh opened his mouth again and said to Enkidu, "My friend, let us go to the Great Palace, to Egalmah,[10] and stand before Ninsun the queen. Ninsun is wise with deep knowledge, she will give us counsel for the road we must go." They took each other by the hand as they went to Egalmah, and they went to Ninsun the great queen. Gilgamesh approached, he entered the palace and spoke to Ninsun. "Ninsun, will you listen to me; I have a long journey to go, to the Land of Humbaba, I must travel an unknown road and fight a strange battle. From the day I go until I return, till I reach the cedar forest and destroy the evil which Shamash abhors, pray for me to Shamash."

Ninsun went into her room, she put on a dress becoming to her body, she put on jewels to make her breast beautiful, she placed a tiara on her head and her skirts swept the ground. Then she went up to the altar of the Sun, standing upon the roof of the palace; she burnt incense and lifted her arms to Shamash as the smoke ascended: "O Shamash, why did you give this restless heart to Gilgamesh, my son; why did you give it? You have moved him and now he sets out on a long journey to the Land of Humbaba, to travel an unknown road and fight a strange battle. Therefore from the day that he goes till the day he returns, until he reaches the cedar forest, until he kills Humbaba and destroys the evil thing which you, Shamash, abhor, do not forget him; but let the dawn, Aya, your dear bride, remind you always, and when day is done give him to the watchman of the night to keep him from harm." Then Ninsun the mother of Gilgamesh extinguished the incense, and she called to Enkidu with this exhortation: "Strong Enkidu, you are not the child of my body, but I will receive you as my adopted son; you are my other child like the foundlings they bring to the temple. Serve Gilgamesh as a foundling serves the temple and the priestess who reared him. In the presence of my women, my votaries and hierophants, I declare it." Then she placed the amulet for a pledge round his neck, and she said to him, "I entrust my son to you; bring him back to me safely."

And now they brought to them the weapons, they put in their hands the great swords in their golden scabbards, and the bow and the quiver. Gilgamesh took the axe, he slung the quiver from his shoulder, and the bow of Anshan, and buckled the sword to his belt; and so they were armed and ready for the journey. Now all the people came and pressed on them and said, "When will you return to the city?" The counsellors blessed Gilgamesh and warned him, "Do not trust too much in your

---

[10] **Egalmah:** The palace home of the goddess Ninsun.

own strength, be watchful, restrain your blows at first. The one who goes in front protects his companion; the good guide who knows the way guards his friend. Let Enkidu lead the way, he knows the road to the forest, he has seen Humbaba and is experienced in battles; let him press first into the passes, let him be watchful and look to himself. Let Enkidu protect his friend, and guard his companion, and bring him safe through the pitfalls of the road. We, the counsellors of Uruk entrust our king to you, O Enkidu; bring him back safely to us." Again to Gilgamesh they said, "May Shamash give you your heart's desire, may he let you see with your eyes the thing accomplished which your lips have spoken; may he open a path for you where it is blocked, and a road for your feet to tread. May he open the mountains for your crossing, and may the nighttime bring you the blessings of night, and Lugulbanda,[11] your guardian god, stand beside you for victory. May you have victory in the battle as though you fought with a child. Wash your feet in the river of Humbaba to which you are journeying; in the evening dig a well, and let there always be pure water in your water-skin. Offer cold water to Shamash and do not forget Lugulbanda."

Then Enkidu opened his mouth and said, "Forward, there is nothing to fear. Follow me, for I know the place where Humbaba lives and the paths where he walks. Let the counsellors go back. Here is no cause for fear." When the counsellors heard this they sped the hero on his way. "Go, Gilgamesh, may your guardian god protect you on the road and bring you safely back to the quay of Uruk."

After twenty leagues they broke their fast; after another thirty leagues they stopped for the night. Fifty leagues they walked in one day; in three days they had walked as much as a journey of a month and two weeks. They crossed seven mountains before they came to the gate of the forest. Then Enkidu called out to Gilgamesh, "Do not go down into the forest; when I opened the gate my hand lost its strength." Gilgamesh answered him, "Dear friend, do not speak like a coward. Have we got the better of so many dangers and travelled so far, to turn back at last? You, who are tried in wars and battles, hold close to me now and you will feel no fear of death; keep beside me and your weakness will pass, the trembling will leave your hand. Would my friend rather stay behind? No, we will go down together into the heart of the forest. Let your courage be roused by the battle to come; forget death and follow me, a man resolute in action, but one who is not foolhardy. When two go together each will protect himself and shield his companion, and if they fall they leave an enduring name."

Together they went down into the forest and they came to the green mountain. There they stood still, they were struck dumb; they stood still and gazed at the forest. They saw the height of the cedar, they saw the way into the forest and the track where Humbaba was used to walk. The way was broad and the going was good. They gazed at the mountain of cedars, the dwelling-place of the gods and the throne of Ishtar. The hugeness of the cedar rose in front of the mountain, its shade was beautiful, full of comfort; mountain and glade were green with brushwood.

There Gilgamesh dug a well before the setting sun. He went up the mountain and poured out fine meal on the ground and said, "O mountain, dwelling of the

[11] **Lugulbanda:** The third king in the king-list, the hero of several poems, and the spirit guardian of Gilgamesh.

gods, bring me a favourable dream." Then they took each other by the hand and lay down to sleep; and sleep that flows from the night lapped over them. Gilgamesh dreamed, and at midnight sleep left him, and he told his dream to his friend. "Enkidu, what was it that woke me if you did not? My friend, I have dreamed a dream. Get up, look at the mountain precipice. The sleep that the gods sent me is broken. Ah, my friend, what a dream I have had! Terror and confusion; I seized hold of a wild bull in the wilderness. It bellowed and beat up the dust till the whole sky was dark, my arm was seized and my tongue bitten. I fell back on my knee; then someone refreshed me with water from his water-skin."

Enkidu said, "Dear friend, the god to whom we are travelling is no wild bull, though his form is mysterious. That wild bull which you saw is Shamash the Protector; in our moment of peril he will take our hands. The one who gave water from his water-skin, that is your own god who cares for your good name, your Lugulbanda. United with him, together we will accomplish a work the fame of which will never die."

Gilgamesh said, "I dreamed again. We stood in a deep gorge of the mountain, and beside it we two were like the smallest of swamp flies; and suddenly the mountain fell, it struck me and caught my feet from under me. Then came an intolerable light blazing out, and in it was one whose grace and whose beauty were greater than the beauty of this world. He pulled me out from under the mountain, he gave me water to drink and my heart was comforted, and he set my feet on the ground."

Then Enkidu the child of the plains said, "Let us go down from the mountain and talk this thing over together." He said to Gilgamesh the young god, "Your dream is good, your dream is excellent, the mountain which you saw is Humbaba. Now, surely, we will seize and kill him, and throw his body down as the mountain fell on the plain."

The next day after twenty leagues they broke their fast, and after another thirty they stopped for the night. They dug a well before the sun had set and Gilgamesh ascended the mountain. He poured out fine meal on the ground and said, "O mountain, dwelling of the gods, send a dream for Enkidu, make him a favourable dream." The mountain fashioned a dream for Enkidu; it came, an ominous dream; a cold shower passed over him, it caused him to cower like the mountain barley under a storm of rain. But Gilgamesh sat with his chin on his knees till the sleep which flows over all mankind lapped over him. Then, at midnight, sleep left him; he got up and said to his friend, "Did you call me, or why did I wake? Did you touch me, or why am I terrified? Did not some god pass by, for my limbs are numb with fear? My friend, I saw a third dream and this dream was altogether frightful. The heavens roared and the earth roared again, daylight failed and darkness fell, lightning flashed, fire blazed out, the clouds lowered, they rained down death. Then the brightness departed, the fire went out, and all was turned to ashes fallen about us. Let us go down from the mountain and talk this over, and consider what we should do."

When they had come down from the mountain Gilgamesh seized the axe in his hand: he felled the cedar. When Humbaba heard the noise far off he was enraged; he cried out, "Who is this that has violated my woods and cut down my cedar?" But glorious Shamash called to them out of heaven, "Go forward, do not be afraid." But now

Gilgamesh was overcome by weakness, for sleep had seized him suddenly, a profound sleep held him; he lay on the ground, stretched out speechless, as though in a dream. When Enkidu touched him he did not rise, when he spoke to him he did not reply. "O Gilgamesh, Lord of the plain of Kullab,[12] the world grows dark, the shadows have spread over it, now is the glimmer of dusk. Shamash has departed, his bright head is quenched in the bosom of his mother Ningal. O Gilgamesh, how long will you lie like this, asleep? Never let the mother who gave you birth be forced in mourning into the city square."

At length Gilgamesh heard him; he put on his breastplate, "The Voice of Heroes," of thirty shekels' weight; he put it on as though it had been a light garment that he carried, and it covered him altogether. He straddled the earth like a bull that snuffs the ground and his teeth were clenched. "By the life of my mother Ninsun who gave me birth, and by the life of my father, divine Lugulbanda, let me live to be the wonder of my mother, as when she nursed me on her lap." A second time he said to him, "By the life of Ninsun my mother who gave me birth, and by the life of my father, divine Lugulbanda, until we have fought this man, if man he is, this god, if god he is, the way that I took to the Country of the Living will not turn back to the city."

Then Enkidu, the faithful companion, pleaded, answering him, "O my lord, you do not know this monster and that is the reason you are not afraid. I who know him, I am terrified. His teeth are dragon's fangs, his countenance is like a lion, his charge is the rushing of the flood, with his look he crushes alike the trees of the forest and reeds in the swamp. O my Lord, you may go on if you choose into this land, but I will go back to the city. I will tell the lady your mother all your glorious deeds till she shouts for joy: and then I will tell the death that followed till she weeps for bitterness." But Gilgamesh said, "Immolation and sacrifice are not yet for me, the boat of the dead shall not go down, nor the three-ply cloth be cut for my shrouding. Not yet will my people be desolate, nor the pyre be lit in my house and my dwelling burnt on the fire. Today, give me your aid and you shall have mine: what then can go amiss with us two? All living creatures born of the flesh shall sit at last in the boat of the West, and when it sinks, when the boat of Magilum[13] sinks, they are gone; but we shall go forward and fix our eyes on this monster. If your heart is fearful throw away fear; if there is terror in it throw away terror. Take your axe in your hand and attack. He who leaves the fight unfinished is not at peace."

Humbaba came out from his strong house of cedar. Then Enkidu called out, "O Gilgamesh, remember now your boasts in Uruk. Forward, attack, son of Uruk, there is nothing to fear." When he heard these words his courage rallied; he answered, "Make haste, close in, if the watchman is there do not let him escape to the woods where he will vanish. He has put on the first of his seven splendours[14] but not yet the other six, let us trap him before he is armed." Like a raging wild bull he snuffed the ground; the watchman of the woods turned full of threatenings, he cried out. Humbaba came from his strong house of cedar. He nodded his head and shook it,

[12] **Kullab:** Part of Uruk. [13] **boat of Magilum:** Possibly the "boat of the dead." [14] **seven splendours:** Unclear, but probably natural armaments like winds.

menacing Gilgamesh; and on him he fastened his eye, the eye of death. Then Gilgamesh called to Shamash and his tears were flowing, "O glorious Shamash, I have followed the road you commanded but now if you send no succour how shall I escape?" Glorious Shamash heard his prayer and he summoned the great wind, the north wind, the whirlwind, the storm and the icy wind, the tempest and the scorching wind; they came like dragons, like a scorching fire, like a serpent that freezes the heart, a destroying flood and the lightning's fork. The eight winds rose up against Humbaba, they beat against his eyes; he was gripped, unable to go forward or back. Gilgamesh shouted, "By the life of Ninsun my mother and divine Lugulbanda my father, in the Country of the Living, in this Land I have discovered your dwelling; my weak arms and my small weapons I have brought to this Land against you, and now I will enter your house."

So he felled the first cedar and they cut the branches and laid them at the foot of the mountain. At the first stroke Humbaba blazed out, but still they advanced. They felled seven cedars and cut and bound the branches and laid them at the foot of the mountain, and seven times Humbaba loosed his glory on them. As the seventh blaze died out they reached his lair. He slapped his thigh in scorn. He approached like a noble wild bull roped on the mountain, a warrior whose elbows are bound together. The tears started to his eyes and he was pale, "Gilgamesh, let me speak. I have never known a mother, no, nor a father who reared me. I was born of the mountain, he reared me, and Enlil made me the keeper of this forest. Let me go free, Gilgamesh, and I will be your servant, you shall be my lord; all the trees of the forest that I tended on the mountain shall be yours. I will cut them down and build you a palace." He took him by the hand and led him to his house, so that the heart of Gilgamesh was moved with compassion. He swore by the heavenly life, by the earthly life, by the underworld itself: "O Enkidu, should not the snared bird return to its nest and the captive man return to his mother's arms?" Enkidu answered, "The strongest of men will fall to fate if he has no judgement. Namtar, the evil fate that knows no distinction between men, will devour him. If the snared bird returns to its nest, if the captive man returns to his mother's arms, then you my friend will never return to the city where the mother is waiting who gave you birth. He will bar the mountain road against you, and make the pathways impassable."

Humbaba said, "Enkidu, what you have spoken is evil: you, a hireling, dependent for your bread! In envy and for fear of a rival you have spoken evil words." Enkidu said, "Do not listen, Gilgamesh: this Humbaba must die. Kill Humbaba first and his servants after." But Gilgamesh said, "If we touch him the blaze and the glory of light will be put out in confusion, the glory and glamour will vanish, its rays will be quenched." Enkidu said to Gilgamesh, "Not so, my friend. First entrap the bird, and where shall the chicks run then? Afterwards we can search out the glory and the glamour, when the chicks run distracted through the grass."

Gilgamesh listened to the word of his companion, he took the axe in his hand, he drew the sword from his belt, and he struck Humbaba with a thrust of the sword to the neck, and Enkidu his comrade struck the second blow. At the third blow Humbaba fell. Then there followed confusion for this was the guardian of the forest whom they had felled to the ground. For as far as two leagues the cedars shivered when Enkidu felled the watcher of the forest, he at whose voice Hermon and Lebanon used to tremble. Now the mountains were moved and all the hills, for the guardian of the forest was killed. They attacked the cedars, the seven splendours of Humbaba were extinguished. So they pressed on into the forest bearing the sword of eight talents. They uncovered the sacred dwellings of the Anunnaki[15] and while Gilgamesh felled the first of the trees of the forest Enkidu cleared their roots as far as the banks of Euphrates. They set Humbaba before the gods, before Enlil; they kissed the ground and dropped the shroud and set the head before him. When he saw the head of Humbaba, Enlil raged at them. "Why did you do this thing? From henceforth may the fire be on your faces, may it eat the bread that you eat, may it drink where you drink." Then Enlil took again the blaze and the seven splendours that had been Humbaba's: he gave the first to the river, and he gave to the lion, to the stone of execration, to the mountain and to the dreaded daughter of the Queen of Hell.

O Gilgamesh, king and conqueror of the dreadful blaze; wild bull who plunders the mountain, who crosses the sea, glory to him, and from the brave the greater glory is Enki's![16]

3
Ishtar and Gilgamesh, and the Death of Enkidu

Gilgamesh washed out his long locks and cleaned his weapons; he flung back his hair from his shoulders; he threw off his stained clothes and changed them for new. He put on his royal robes and made them fast. When Gilgamesh had put on the crown, glorious Ishtar lifted her eyes, seeing the beauty of Gilgamesh. She said, "Come to me Gilgamesh, and be my bridegroom; grant me seed of your body, let me be your bride and you shall be my husband. I will harness for you a chariot of lapis lazuli and of gold, with wheels of gold and horns of copper; and you shall have mighty demons of the storm for draftmules. When you enter our house in the fragrance of cedar-wood, threshold and throne will kiss your feet. Kings, rulers, and princes will bow down before you; they shall bring you tribute from the mountains and the plain. Your ewes shall drop twins and your goats triplets; your pack-ass shall outrun mules; your oxen shall have no rivals, and your chariot horses shall be famous far-off for their swiftness."

Gilgamesh opened his mouth and answered glorious Ishtar, "If I take you in marriage, what gifts can I give in return? What ointments and clothing for your body? I would gladly give you bread and all sorts of food fit for a god. I would give you wine to drink fit for a queen. I would pour out barley to stuff your granary; but as for making you my wife—that I will not. How would it go with me? Your lovers have found you like a brazier which smoulders in the cold, a backdoor which keeps out neither squall of wind nor storm, a castle which crushes the garrison, pitch that blackens the bearer, a water-skin that chafes the carrier, a stone which falls from the

[15] **Anunnaki:** Gods of the underworld and judges of the dead. [16] **Enki:** God of sweet water and wisdom.

parapet, a battering-ram turned back from the enemy, a sandal that trips the wearer. Which of your lovers did you ever love for ever? What shepherd of yours has pleased you for all time? Listen to me while I tell the tale of your lovers. There was Tammuz,[17] the lover of your youth, for him you decreed wailing, year after year. You loved the many-coloured roller, but still you struck and broke his wing; now in the grove he sits and cries, "kappi, kappi, my wing, my wing." You have loved the lion tremendous in strength: seven pits you dug for him, and seven. You have loved the stallion magnificent in battle, and for him you decreed whip and spur and a thong, to gallop seven leagues by force and to muddy the water before he drinks; and for his mother Silili[18] lamentations. You have loved the shepherd of the flock; he made meal-cake for you day after day, he killed kids for your sake. You struck and turned him into a wolf, now his own herd-boys chase him away, his own hounds worry his flanks. And did you not love Ishullanu,[19] the gardener of your father's palm-grove? He brought you baskets filled with dates without end; every day he loaded your table. Then you turned your eyes on him and said, 'Dearest Ishullanu, come here to me, let us enjoy your manhood, come forward and take me, I am yours.' Ishullanu answered, 'What are you asking from me? My mother has baked and I have eaten; why should I come to such as you for food that is tainted and rotten? For when was a screen of rushes sufficient protection from frosts?' But when you had heard his answer you struck him. He was changed to a blind mole deep in the earth, one whose desire is always beyond his reach. And if you and I should be lovers, should not I be served in the same fashion as all these others whom you loved once?"

When Ishtar heard this she fell into a bitter rage, she went up to high heaven. Her tears poured down in front of her father Anu, and Antum her mother. She said, "My father, Gilgamesh has heaped insults on me, he has told over all my abominable behaviour, my foul and hideous acts." Anu opened his mouth and said, "Are you a father of gods? Did not you quarrel with Gilgamesh the king, so now he has related your abominable behaviour, your foul and hideous acts."

Ishtar opened her mouth and said again, "My father, give me the Bull of Heaven to destroy Gilgamesh. Fill Gilgamesh, I say, with arrogance to his destruction; but if you refuse to give me the Bull of Heaven I will break in the doors of hell and smash the bolts; there will be confusion of people, those above with those from the lower depths. I shall bring up the dead to eat food like the living; and the hosts of dead will outnumber the living." Anu said to great Ishtar, "If I do what you desire there will be seven years of drought throughout Uruk when corn will be seedless husks. Have you saved grain enough for the people and grass for the cattle?" Ishtar replied. "I have saved grain for the people, grass for the cattle; for seven years of seedless husks there is grain and there is grass enough."

When Anu heard what Ishtar had said he gave her the Bull of Heaven to lead by the halter down to Uruk. When they reached the gates of Uruk the Bull went to the river; with his first snort cracks opened in the earth and a hundred young men fell down to death. With his second snort cracks opened and two hundred fell down to

[17] **Tammuz:** God of vegetation who is born in the spring and dies in the fall. [18] **Silili:** Perhaps a divine mare.
[19] **Ishullanu:** The gardener of Anu.

death. With his third snort cracks opened, Enkidu doubled over but instantly recovered, he dodged aside and leapt on the Bull and seized it by the horns. The Bull of Heaven foamed in his face, it brushed him with the thick of its tail. Enkidu cried to Gilgamesh, "My friend, we boasted that we would leave enduring names behind us. Now thrust in your sword between the nape and the horns." So Gilgamesh followed the Bull, he seized the thick of its tail, he thrust the sword between the nape and the horns and slew the Bull. When they had killed the Bull of Heaven they cut out its heart and gave it to Shamash, and the brothers rested.

But Ishtar rose up and mounted the great wall of Uruk; she sprang on to the tower and uttered a curse: "Woe to Gilgamesh, for he has scorned me in killing the Bull of Heaven." When Enkidu heard these words he tore out the Bull's right thigh and tossed it in her face saying, "If I could lay my hands on you, it is this I should do to you, and lash the entrails to your side." Then Ishtar called together her people, the dancing and singing girls, the prostitutes of the temple, the courtesans. Over the thigh of the Bull of Heaven she set up lamentation.

But Gilgamesh called the smiths and the armourers, all of them together. They admired the immensity of the horns. They were plated with lapis lazuli two fingers thick. They were thirty pounds each in weight, and their capacity in oil was six measures, which he gave to his guardian god, Lugulbanda. But he carried the horns into the palace and hung them on the wall. Then they washed their hands in Euphrates, they embraced each other and went away. They drove through the streets of Uruk where the heroes were gathered to see them, and Gilgamesh called to the singing girls, "Who is most glorious of the heroes, who is most eminent among men?" "Gilgamesh is the most glorious of heroes, Gilgamesh is most eminent among men." And now there was feasting, and celebrations and joy in the palace, till the heroes lay down saying, "Now we will rest for the night."

When the daylight came Enkidu got up and cried to Gilgamesh, "O my brother, such a dream I had last night. Anu, Enlil, Ea, and heavenly Shamash took counsel together, and Anu said to Enlil, 'Because they have killed the Bull of Heaven, and because they have killed Humbaba who guarded the Cedar Mountain one of the two must die.' Then glorious Shamash answered the hero Enlil, 'It was by your command they killed the Bull of Heaven, and killed Humbaba, and must Enkidu die although innocent?' Enlil flung round in rage at glorious Shamash, 'You dare to say this, you who went about with them every day like one of themselves!' "

So Enkidu lay stretched out before Gilgamesh; his tears ran down in streams and he said to Gilgamesh, "O my brother, so dear as you are to me, brother, yet they will take me from you." Again he said, "I must sit down on the threshold of the dead and never again will I see my dear brother with my eyes."

While Enkidu lay alone in his sickness he cursed the gate as though it was living flesh, "You there, wood of the gate, dull and insensible, witless, I searched for you over twenty leagues until I saw the towering cedar. There is no wood like you in our land. Seventy-two cubits high and twenty-four wide, the pivot and the ferrule and the jambs are perfect. A master craftsman from Nippur has made you; but O, if I had known the conclusion! If I had known that this was all the good that would come of it, I would have raised the axe and split you into little pieces and set up here a gate of wattle instead. Ah, if only some future king had brought you here, or some god had fashioned you. Let him obliterate my name and write his own, and the curse fall on him instead of on Enkidu."

With the first brightening of dawn Enkidu raised his head and wept before the Sun God, in the brilliance of the sunlight his tears streamed down. "Sun God, I beseech you, about that vile Trapper, that Trapper of nothing because of whom I was to catch less than my comrade; let him catch least, make his game scarce, make him feeble, taking the smaller of every share, let his quarry escape from his nets."

When he had cursed the Trapper to his heart's content he turned on the harlot. He was roused to curse her also. "As for you, woman, with a great curse I curse you! I will promise you a destiny to all eternity. My curse shall come on you soon and sudden. You shall be without a roof for your commerce, for you shall not keep house with other girls in the tavern, but do your business in places fouled by the vomit of the drunkard. Your hire will be potter's earth, your thievings will be flung into the hovel, you will sit at the cross-roads in the dust of the potter's quarter, you will make your bed on the dunghill at night, and by day take your stand in the wall's shadow. Brambles and thorns will tear your feet, the drunk and the dry will strike your cheek and your mouth will ache. Let you be stripped of your purple dyes, for I too once in the wilderness with my wife had all the treasure I wished."

When Shamash heard the words of Enkidu he called to him from heaven: "Enkidu, why are you cursing the woman, the mistress who taught you to eat bread fit for gods and drink wine of kings? She who put upon you a magnificent garment, did she not give you glorious Gilgamesh for your companion, and has not Gilgamesh, your own brother, made you rest on a royal bed and recline on a couch at his left hand? He has made the princes of the earth kiss your feet, and now all the people of Uruk lament and wail over you. When you are dead he will let his hair grow long for your sake, he will wear a lion's pelt and wander through the desert."

When Enkidu heard glorious Shamash his angry heart grew quiet, he called back the curse and said, "Woman, I promise you another destiny. The mouth which cursed you shall bless you! Kings, princes and nobles shall adore you. On your account a man though twelve miles off will clap his hand to his thigh and his hair will twitch. For you he will undo his belt and open his treasure and you shall have your desire; lapis lazuli, gold and carnelian from the heap in the treasury. A ring for your hand and a robe shall be yours. The priest will lead you into the presence of the gods. On your account a wife, a mother of seven, was forsaken."

As Enkidu slept alone in his sickness, in bitterness of spirit he poured out his heart to his friend. "It was I who cut down the cedar, I who levelled the forest, I who slew Humbaba and now see what has become of me. Listen, my friend, this is the dream I dreamed last night. The heavens roared, and earth rumbled back an answer; between them stood I before an awful being, the sombre-faced man-bird; he had directed on me his purpose. His was a vampire face, his foot was a lion's foot, his hand was an eagle's talon. He fell on me and his claws were in my hair, he held me fast and I smothered; then he transformed me so that my arms became wings covered with feathers. He turned his stare towards me, and he led me away to the palace of Irkalla, the Queen of Darkness,[20] to the house from which none who enters ever returns, down the road from which there is no coming back.

"There is the house whose people sit in darkness; dust is their food and clay their meat. They are clothed like birds with wings for covering, they see no light, they sit in darkness. I entered the house of dust and I saw the kings of the earth, their crowns put away for ever; rulers and princes, all those who once wore kingly crowns and ruled the world in the days of old. They who had stood in the place of the gods like Anu and Enlil, stood now like servants to fetch baked meats in the house of dust, to carry cooked meat and cold water from the water-skin. In the house of dust which I entered were high priests and acolytes, priests of the incantation and of ecstasy; there were servers of the temple, and there was Etana, that king of Kish whom the eagle carried to heaven in the days of old. I saw also Samuqan, god of cattle, and there was Ereshkigal the Queen of the Underworld; and Belit-Sheri squatted in front of her, she who is recorder of the gods and keeps the book of death. She held a tablet from which she read. She raised her head, she saw me and spoke: 'Who has brought this one here?' Then I awoke like a man drained of blood who wanders alone in a waste of rushes; like one whom the bailiff has seized and his heart pounds with terror."

Gilgamesh had peeled off his clothes, he listened to his words and wept quick tears, Gilgamesh listened and his tears flowed. He opened his mouth and spoke to Enkidu: "Who is there in strong-walled Uruk who has wisdom like this? Strange things have been spoken, why does your heart speak strangely? The dream was marvellous but the terror was great; we must treasure the dream whatever the terror; for the dream has shown that misery comes at last to the healthy man, the end of life is sorrow." And Gilgamesh lamented, "Now I will pray to the great gods, for my friend had an ominous dream."

This day on which Enkidu dreamed came to an end and he lay stricken with sickness. One whole day he lay on his bed and his suffering increased. He said to Gilgamesh, the friend on whose account he had left the wilderness, "Once I ran for you, for the water of life, and I now have nothing." A second day he lay on his bed and Gilgamesh watched over him but the sickness increased. A third day he lay on his bed, he called out to Gilgamesh, rousing him up. Now he was weak and his eyes were blind with weeping. Ten days he lay and his suffering increased, eleven and twelve days he lay on his bed of pain. Then he called to Gilgamesh, "My friend, the great goddess cursed me and I must die in shame. I shall not die like a man fallen in battle; I feared to fall, but happy is the man who falls in the battle, for I must die in shame." And Gilgamesh wept over Enkidu. With the first light of dawn he raised his voice and said to the counsellors of Uruk:

"Hear me, great ones of Uruk,
I weep for Enkidu, my friend,
Bitterly moaning like a woman mourning

[20] **Irkalla . . . Darkness:** She is also called Ereshkigal.

I weep for my brother.
O Enkidu, my brother,
You were the axe at my side,
My hand's strength, the sword in my belt,
The shield before me,
A glorious robe, my fairest ornament;
An evil Fate has robbed me.
The wild ass and the gazelle
That were father and mother,
All long-tailed creatures that nourished you
Weep for you,
All the wild things of the plain and pastures;
The paths that you loved in the forest of cedars
Night and day murmur.
Let the great ones of strong-walled Uruk
Weep for you;
Let the finger of blessing
Be stretched out in mourning;
Enkidu, young brother. Hark,
There is an echo through all the country
Like a mother mourning.
Weep all the paths where we walked together;
And the beasts we hunted, the bear and hyena,
Tiger and panther, leopard and lion,
The stag and the ibex, the bull and the doe.
The river along whose banks we used to walk,
Weeps for you,
Ula of Elam and dear Euphrates
Where once we drew water for the water-skins.
The mountain we climbed where we slew the Watchman,
Weeps for you.
The warriors of strong-walled Uruk
Where the Bull of Heaven was killed,
Weep for you.
All the people of Eridu
Weep for you Enkidu.
Those who brought grain for your eating
Mourn for you now;
Who rubbed oil on your back
Mourn for you now;
Who poured beer for your drinking
Mourn for you now.
The harlot who anointed you with fragrant ointment
Laments for you now;
The women of the palace, who brought you a wife,
A chosen ring of good advice,
Lament for you now.
And the young men your brothers
As though they were women

Go long-haired in mourning.
What is this sleep which holds you now?
You are lost in the dark and cannot hear me."

He touched his heart but it did not beat, nor did he lift his eyes again. When Gilgamesh touched his heart it did not beat. So Gilgamesh laid a veil, as one veils the bride, over his friend. He began to rage like a lion, like a lioness robbed of her whelps. This way and that he paced round the bed, he tore out his hair and strewed it around. He dragged off his splendid robes and flung them down as though they were abominations.

In the first light of dawn Gilgamesh cried out, "I made you rest on a royal bed, you reclined on a couch at my left hand, the princes of the earth kissed your feet. I will cause all the people of Uruk to weep over you and raise the dirge of the dead. The joyful people will stoop with sorrow; and when you have gone to the earth I will let my hair grow long for your sake, I will wander through the wilderness in the skin of a lion." The next day also, in the first light, Gilgamesh lamented; seven days and seven nights he wept for Enkidu, until the worm fastened on him. Only then he gave him up to the earth, for the Anunnaki, the judges, had seized him.

Then Gilgamesh issued a proclamation through the land, he summoned them all, the coppersmiths, the goldsmiths, the stone-workers, and commanded them, "Make a statue of my friend." The statue was fashioned with a great weight of lapis lazuli for the breast and of gold for the body. A table of hardwood was set out, and on it a bowl of carnelian filled with honey, and a bowl of lapis lazuli filled with butter. These he exposed and offered to the Sun; and weeping he went away.

4
The Search for Everlasting Life

Bitterly Gilgamesh wept for his friend Enkidu; he wandered over the wilderness as a hunter, he roamed over the plains; in his bitterness he cried, "How can I rest, how can I be at peace? Despair is in my heart. What my brother is now, that shall I be when I am dead. Because I am afraid of death I will go as best I can to find Utnapishtim[21] whom they call the Faraway, for he has entered the assembly of the gods." So Gilgamesh travelled over the wilderness, he wandered over the grasslands, a long journey, in search of Utnapishtim, whom the gods took after the deluge; and they set him to live in the land of Dilmun, in the garden of the sun; and to him alone of men they gave everlasting life.

At night when he came to the mountain passes Gilgamesh prayed: "In these mountain passes long ago I saw lions, I was afraid and I lifted my eyes to the moon; I prayed and my prayers went up to the gods, so now, O moon god Sin, protect me." When he had prayed he lay down to sleep, until he was woken from out of a dream. He saw the lions round him glorying in life; then he took his axe in his hand, he drew

[21] **Utnapishtim:** A wise king and priest of Shurrupak who survived the primordial flood and was taken by the gods to live in Dilmun, the Sumerian garden paradise. He is similar to the biblical Noah.

his sword from his belt, and he fell upon them like an arrow from the string, and struck and destroyed and scattered them.

So at length Gilgamesh came to Mashu, the great mountains about which he had heard many things, which guard the rising and the setting sun. Its twin peaks are as high as the wall of heaven and its paps reach down to the underworld. At its gate the Scorpions stand guard, half man and half dragon; their glory is terrifying, their stare strikes death into men, their shimmering halo sweeps the mountains that guard the rising sun. When Gilgamesh saw them he shielded his eyes for the length of a moment only; then he took courage and approached. When they saw him so undismayed the Man-Scorpion called to his mate, "This one who comes to us now is flesh of the gods." The mate of the Man-Scorpion answered, "Two thirds is god but one third is man."

Then he called to the man Gilgamesh, he called to the child of the gods: "Why have you come so great a journey; for what have you travelled so far, crossing the dangerous waters; tell me the reason for your coming?" Gilgamesh answered, "For Enkidu; I loved him dearly, together we endured all kinds of hardships; on his account I have come, for the common lot of man has taken him. I have wept for him day and night, I would not give up his body for burial, I thought my friend would come back because of my weeping. Since he went, my life is nothing; that is why I have travelled here in search of Utnapishtim my father; for men say he has entered the assembly of the gods, and has found everlasting life. I have a desire to question him concerning the living and the dead." The Man-Scorpion opened his mouth and said, speaking to Gilgamesh, "No man born of woman has done what you have asked, no mortal man has gone into the mountain; the length of it is twelve leagues of darkness; in it there is no light, but the heart is oppressed with darkness. From the rising of the sun to the setting of the sun there is no light." Gilgamesh said, "Although I should go in sorrow and in pain, with sighing and with weeping, still I must go. Open the gate of the mountain." And the Man-Scorpion said, "Go, Gilgamesh, I permit you to pass through the mountain of Mashu and through the high ranges; may your feet carry you safely home. The gate of the mountain is open."

When Gilgamesh heard this he did as the Man-Scorpion had said, he followed the sun's road to his rising, through the mountain. When he had gone one league the darkness became thick around him, for there was no light, he could see nothing ahead and nothing behind him. After two leagues the darkness was thick and there was no light, he could see nothing ahead and nothing behind him. After three leagues the darkness was thick, and there was no light, he could see nothing ahead and nothing behind him. After four leagues the darkness was thick and there was no light, he could see nothing ahead and nothing behind him. At the end of five leagues the darkness was thick and there was no light, he could see nothing ahead and nothing behind him. At the end of six leagues the darkness was thick and there was no light, he could see nothing ahead and nothing behind him. When he had gone seven leagues the darkness was thick and there was no light, he could see nothing ahead and nothing behind him. When he had gone eight leagues Gilgamesh gave a great cry, for the darkness was thick and he could see nothing ahead and nothing behind him. After nine leagues he felt the north wind on his face, but the darkness was thick and there was no light, he could see nothing ahead and nothing behind him. After ten leagues the end was near. After eleven leagues the dawn light appeared. At the end of twelve leagues the sun streamed out.

There was the garden of the gods; all round him stood bushes bearing gems. Seeing it he went down at once, for there was fruit of carnelian with the vine hanging from it, beautiful to look at; lapis lazuli leaves hung thick with fruit, sweet to see. For thorns and thistles there were haematite and rare stones, agate, and pearls from out of the sea. While Gilgamesh walked in the garden by the edge of the sea Shamash saw him, and he saw that he was dressed in the skins of animals and ate their flesh. He was distressed, and he spoke and said, "No mortal man has gone this way before, nor will, as long as the winds drive over the sea." And to Gilgamesh he said, "You will never find the life for which you are searching." Gilgamesh said to glorious Shamash, "Now that I have toiled and strayed so far over the wilderness, am I to sleep, and let the earth cover my head for ever? Let my eyes see the sun until they are dazzled with looking. Although I am no better than a dead man, still let me see the light of the sun."

Beside the sea she lives, the woman of the vine, the maker of wine; Siduri[22] sits in the garden at the edge of the sea, with the golden bowl and the golden vats that the gods gave her. She is covered with a veil; and where she sits she sees Gilgamesh coming towards her, wearing skins, the flesh of the gods in his body, but despair in his heart, and his face like the face of one who has made a long journey. She looked, and as she scanned the distance she said in her own heart, "Surely this is some felon; where is he going now?" And she barred her gate against him with the cross-bar and shot home the bolt. But Gilgamesh, hearing the sound of the bolt, threw up his head and lodged his foot in the gate; he called to her, "Young woman, maker of wine, why do you bolt your door; what did you see that made you bar your gate? I will break in your door and burst in your gate, for I am Gilgamesh who seized and killed the Bull of Heaven, I killed the watchman of the cedar forest, I overthrew Humbaba who lived in the forest, and I killed the lions in the passes of the mountain."

Then Siduri said to him, "If you are that Gilgamesh who seized and killed the Bull of Heaven, who killed the watchman of the cedar forest, who overthrew Humbaba that lived in the forest, and killed the lions in the passes of the mountain, why are your cheeks so starved and why is your face so drawn? Why is despair in your heart and your face like the face of one who has made a long journey? Yes, why is your face burned from heat and cold, and why do you come here wandering over the pastures in search of the wind?"

Gilgamesh answered her, "And why should not my cheeks be starved and my face drawn? Despair is in my heart and my face is the face of one who has made a long journey, it was burned with heat and with cold. Why should I not wander over the pastures in search of the wind? My friend, my younger brother, he who hunted the wild ass of the wilderness and the panther of the plains, my friend, my younger

[22] **Siduri:** A divine wine-maker who has advice for Gilgamesh.

brother who seized and killed the Bull of Heaven and overthrew Humbaba in the cedar forest, my friend who was very dear to me and who endured dangers beside me, Enkidu my brother, whom I loved, the end of mortality has overtaken him. I wept for him seven days and nights till the worm fastened on him. Because of my brother I am afraid of death, because of my brother I stray through the wilderness and cannot rest. But now, young woman, maker of wine, since I have seen your face do not let me see the face of death which I dread so much."

She answered, "Gilgamesh, where are you hurrying to? You will never find that life for which you are looking. When the gods created man they allotted to him death, but life they retained in their own keeping. As for you, Gilgamesh, fill your belly with good things; day and night, night and day, dance and be merry, feast and rejoice. Let your clothes be fresh, bathe yourself in water, cherish the little child that holds your hand, and make your wife happy in your embrace; for this too is the lot of man."

But Gilgamesh said to Siduri, the young woman, "How can I be silent, how can I rest, when Enkidu whom I love is dust, and I too shall die and be laid in the earth. You live by the seashore and look into the heart of it; young woman, tell me now, which is the way to Utnapishtim, the son of Ubara-Tutu? What directions are there for the passage; give me, oh, give me directions. I will cross the Ocean if it is possible; if it is not I will wander still farther in the wilderness." The wine-maker said to him, "Gilgamesh, there is no crossing the Ocean; whoever has come, since the days of old, has not been able to pass that sea. The Sun in his glory crosses the Ocean, but who beside Shamash has ever crossed it? The place and the passage are difficult, and the waters of death are deep which flow between. Gilgamesh, how will you cross the Ocean? When you come to the waters of death what will you do? But Gilgamesh, down in the woods you will find Urshanabi,[23] the ferryman of Utnapishtim; with him are the holy things, the things of stone. He is fashioning the serpent prow of the boat. Look at him well, and if it is possible, perhaps you will cross the waters with him; but if it is not possible, then you must go back."

When Gilgamesh heard this he was seized with anger. He took his axe in his hand, and his dagger from his belt. He crept forward and he fell on them like a javelin. Then he went into the forest and sat down. Urshanabi saw the dagger flash and heard the axe, and he beat his head, for Gilgamesh had shattered the tackle of the boat in his rage. Urshanabi said to him, "Tell me, what is your name? I am Urshanabi, the ferryman of Utnapishtim the Faraway." He replied to him, "Gilgamesh is my name, I am from Uruk, from the house of Anu." Then Urshanabi said to him, "Why are your cheeks so starved and your face drawn? Why is despair in your heart and your face like the face of one who has made a long journey; yes, why is your face burned with heat and with cold, and why do you come here wandering over the pastures in search of the wind?"

Gilgamesh said to him, "Why should not my cheeks be starved and my face

[23] **Urshanabi:** A boatman comparable to the Greek Charon.

drawn? Despair is in my heart, and my face is the face of one who has made a long journey. I was burned with heat and with cold. Why should I not wander over the pastures? My friend, my younger brother who seized and killed the Bull of Heaven, and overthrew Humbaba in the cedar forest, my friend who was very dear to me, and who endured dangers beside me, Enkidu my brother whom I loved, the end of mortality has overtaken him. I wept for him seven days and nights till the worm fastened on him. Because of my brother I am afraid of death, because of my brother I stray through the wilderness. His fate lies heavy upon me. How can I be silent, how can I rest? He is dust and I too shall die and be laid in the earth for ever. I am afraid of death, therefore, Urshanabi, tell me which is the road to Utnapishtim? If it is possible I will cross the waters of death; if not I will wander still farther through the wilderness."

Urshanabi said to him, "Gilgamesh, your own hands have prevented you from crossing the Ocean; when you destroyed the tackle of the boat you destroyed its safety." Then the two of them talked it over and Gilgamesh said, "Why are you so angry with me, Urshanabi, for you yourself cross the sea by day and night, at all seasons you cross it." "Gilgamesh, those things you destroyed, their property is to carry me over the water, to prevent the waters of death from touching me. It was for this reason that I preserved them, but you have destroyed them, and the *urnu* snakes with them. But now, go into the forest, Gilgamesh; with your axe cut poles, one hundred and twenty, cut them sixty cubits long, paint them with bitumen, set on them ferrules and bring them back."

When Gilgamesh heard this he went into the forest, he cut poles one hundred and twenty; he cut them sixty cubits long, he painted them with bitumen, he set on them ferrules, and he brought them to Urshanabi. Then they boarded the boat, Gilgamesh and Urshanabi together, launching it out on the waves of Ocean. For three days they ran on as it were a journey of a month and fifteen days, and at last Urshanabi brought the boat to the waters of death. Then Urshanabi said to Gilgamesh, "Press on, take a pole and thrust it in, but do not let your hands touch the waters. Gilgamesh, take a second pole, take a third, take a fourth pole. Now, Gilgamesh, take a fifth, take a sixth and seventh pole. Gilgamesh, take an eighth, and ninth, a tenth pole. Gilgamesh, take an eleventh, take a twelfth pole." After one hundred and twenty thrusts Gilgamesh had used the last pole. Then he stripped himself, he held up his arms for a mast and his covering for a sail. So Urshanabi the ferryman brought Gilgamesh to Utnapishtim, whom they call the Faraway, who lives in Dilmun at the place of the sun's transit, eastward of the mountain. To him alone of men the gods had given everlasting life.

Now Utnapishtim, where he lay at ease, looked into the distance and he said in his heart, musing to himself, "Why does the boat sail here without tackle and mast; why are the sacred stones destroyed, and why does the master not sail the boat? That man who comes is none of mine; where I look I see a man whose body is covered with skins of beasts. Who is this who walks up the shore behind Urshanabi, for surely he is no man of mine?" So Utnapishtim looked at him and said, "What is your name, you who come here wearing the skins of beasts, with your cheeks starved and your face drawn? Where are you hurrying to now? For what reason have you made this great journey, crossing the seas whose passage is difficult? Tell me the reason for your coming."

He replied, "Gilgamesh is my name. I am from Uruk, from the house of Anu." Then Utnapishtim said to him, "If you are Gilgamesh, why are your cheeks so starved and your face drawn? Why is despair in your heart and your face like the face of one who has made a long journey? Yes, why is your face burned with heat and cold, and why do you come here, wandering over the wilderness in search of the wind?"

Gilgamesh said to him, "Why should not my cheeks be starved and my face drawn? Despair is in my heart and my face is the face of one who has made a long journey. It was burned with heat and with cold. Why should I not wander over the pastures? My friend, my younger brother who seized and killed the Bull of Heaven and overthrew Humbaba in the cedar forest, my friend who was very dear to me and endured dangers beside me, Enkidu, my brother whom I loved, the end of mortality has overtaken him. I wept for him seven days and nights till the worm fastened on him. Because of my brother I am afraid of death; because of my brother I stray through the wilderness. His fate lies heavy upon me. How can I be silent, how can I rest? He is dust and I shall die also and be laid in the earth for ever." Again Gilgamesh said, speaking to Utnapishtim, "It is to see Utnapishtim whom we call the Faraway that I have come this journey. For this I have wandered over the world, I have crossed many difficult ranges, I have crossed the seas, I have wearied myself with travelling; my joints are aching, and I have lost acquaintance with sleep which is sweet. My clothes were worn out before I came to the house of Siduri. I have killed the bear and hyena, the lion and panther, the tiger, the stag and the ibex, all sorts of wild game and the small creatures of the pastures. I ate their flesh and I wore their skins; and that was how I came to the gate of the young woman, the maker of wine, who barred her gate of pitch and bitumen against me. But from her I had news of the journey; so then I came to Urshanabi the ferryman, and with him I crossed over the waters of death. Oh, father Utnapishtim, you who have entered the assembly of the gods, I wish to question you concerning the living and the dead, how shall I find the life for which I am searching?"

Utnapishtim said, "There is no permanence. Do we build a house to stand for ever, do we seal a contract to hold for all time? Do brothers divide an inheritance to keep for ever, does the flood-time of rivers endure? It is only the nymph of the dragon-fly who sheds her larva and sees the sun in his glory. From the days of old there is no permanence. The sleeping and the dead, how alike they are, they are like a painted death. What is there between the master and the servant when both have fulfilled their doom? When the Anunnaki, the judges, come together, and Mammetun the mother of destinies, together they decree the fates of men. Life and death they allot but the day of death they do not disclose."

Nothing lives Forever

Then Gilgamesh said to Utnapishtim the Faraway, "I look at you now, Utnapishtim, and your appearance is no different from mine; there is nothing strange in your features. I thought I should find you like a hero prepared for battle, but you lie here taking your ease on your back. Tell me truly, how was it that you came to enter the company of the gods and to possess everlasting life?" Utnapishtim said to Gilgamesh; "I will reveal to you a mystery, I will tell you a secret of the gods."

5

The Story of the Flood

"You know the city Shurrupak, it stands on the banks of Euphrates? That city grew old and the gods that were in it were old. There was Anu, lord of the firmament, their father, and warrior Enlil their counsellor, Ninurta the helper, and Ennugi watcher over canals; and with them also was Ea. In those days the world teemed, the people multiplied, the world bellowed like a wild bull, and the great god was aroused by the clamour. Enlil heard the clamour and he said to the gods in council, 'The uproar of mankind is intolerable and sleep is no longer possible by reason of the babel.' So the gods agreed to exterminate mankind. Enlil did this, but Ea because of his oath warned me in a dream. He whispered their words to my house of reeds, 'Reed-house, reed-house! Wall, O wall, hearken reed-house, wall reflect; O man of Shurrupak, son of Ubara-Tutu; tear down your house and build a boat, abandon possessions and look for life, despise worldly goods and save your soul alive. Tear down your house, I say, and build a boat. These are the measurements of the barque as you shall build her: let her beam equal her length, let her deck be roofed like the vault that covers the abyss; then take up into the boat the seed of all living creatures.'

"When I had understood I said to my lord, 'Behold, what you have commanded I will honour and perform, but how shall I answer the people, the city, the elders?' Then Ea opened his mouth and said to me, his servant, 'Tell them this: I have learnt that Enlil is wrathful against me, I dare no longer walk in his land nor live in his city; I will go down to the Gulf to dwell with Ea my lord. But on you he will rain down abundance, rare fish and shy wild-fowl, a rich harvest-tide. In the evening the rider of the storm will bring you wheat in torrents.'

"In the first light of dawn all my household gathered round me, the children brought pitch and the men whatever was necessary. On the fifth day I laid the keel and the ribs, then I made fast the planking. The ground-space was one acre, each side of the deck measured one hundred and twenty cubits, making a square. I built six decks below, seven in all, I divided them into nine sections with bulk-heads between. I drove in wedges where needed, I saw to the punt-poles, and laid in supplies. The carriers brought oil in baskets, I poured pitch into the furnace and asphalt and oil; more oil was consumed in caulking, and more again the master of the boat took into his stores. I slaughtered bullocks for the people and every day I killed sheep. I gave the shipwrights wine to drink as though it were river water, raw wine and red wine and oil and white wine. There was feasting then as there is at the time of the New Year's festival; I myself anointed my head. On the seventh day the boat was complete.

"Then was the launching full of difficulty; there was shifting of ballast above and below till two thirds was submerged. I loaded into her all that I had of gold and of living things, my family, my kin, the beast of the field both wild and tame, and all the craftsmen. I sent them on board, for the time that Shamash had ordained was already fulfilled when he said, 'In the evening, when the rider of the storm sends down the destroying rain, enter the boat and batten her down.' The time was fulfilled, the evening came, the rider of the storm sent down the rain. I looked out at the weather and it was terrible, so I too boarded the boat and battened her down. All was now complete, the battening and the caulking; so I handed the tiller to Puzur-Amurri the steersman, with the navigation and the care of the whole boat.

"With the first light of dawn a black cloud came from the horizon; it thundered within where Adad, lord of the storm, was riding. In front over hill and plain Shullat and Hanish, heralds of the storm, led on. Then the gods of the abyss rose up; Nergal pulled out the dams of the nether waters, Ninurta the war-lord threw down the dykes, and the seven judges of hell, the Anunnaki, raised their torches, lighting the land with their livid flame. A stupor of despair went up to heaven when the god of the storm turned daylight to darkness, when he smashed the land like a cup. One whole day the tempest raged, gathering fury as it went, it poured over the people like the tides of battle; a man could not see his brother nor the people be seen from heaven. Even the gods were terrified at the flood, they fled to the highest heaven, the firmament of Anu; they crouched against the walls, cowering like curs. Then Ishtar the sweet-voiced Queen of Heaven cried out like a woman in travail: 'Alas the days of old are turned to dust because I commanded evil; why did I command this evil in the council of all the gods? I commanded wars to destroy the people, but are they not my people, for I brought them forth? Now like the spawn of fish they float in the ocean.' The great gods of heaven and of hell wept, they covered their mouths.

Flood came and turned everyone to clay

"For six days and six nights the winds blew, torrent and tempest and flood overwhelmed the world, tempest and flood raged together like warring hosts. When the seventh day dawned the storm from the south subsided, the sea grew calm, the flood was stilled; I looked at the face of the world and there was silence, all mankind was turned to clay. The surface of the sea stretched as flat as a roof-top; I opened a hatch and the light fell on my face. Then I bowed low, I sat down and I wept, the tears streamed down my face, for on every side was the waste of water. I looked for land in vain, but fourteen leagues distant there appeared a mountain, and there the boat grounded; on the mountain of Nisir the boat held fast, she held fast and did not budge. One day she held, and a second day on the mountain of Nisir she held fast and did not budge. A third day, and a fourth day she held fast on the mountain and did not budge; a fifth day and a sixth day she held fast on the mountain. When the seventh day dawned I loosed a dove and let her go. She flew away, but finding no resting-place she returned. Then I loosed a swallow, and she flew away but finding no resting-place she returned. I loosed a raven, she saw that the waters had retreated, she ate, she flew around, she cawed, and she did not come back. Then I threw everything open to the four winds, I made a sacrifice and poured out a libation on the mountain top. Seven and again seven cauldrons I set up on their stands, I heaped up wood and cane and cedar and myrtle. When the gods smelled the sweet savour, they gathered like flies over the sacrifice. Then, at last, Ishtar also came, she lifted her necklace with the jewels of heaven that once Anu had made to please her. 'O you gods here present, by the lapis lazuli round my neck I shall remember these days as I remember the jewels of my throat; these last days I shall not forget. Let all the gods gather round the sacrifice, except Enlil. He shall not approach this offering, for without reflection he brought the flood; he consigned my people to destruction.'

"When Enlil had come, when he saw the boat, he was wrath and swelled with anger at the gods, the host of heaven, 'Has any of these mortals escaped? Not one was to have survived the destruction.' Then the god of the wells and canals Ninurta opened his mouth and said to the warrior Enlil, 'Who is there of the gods that can devise without Ea? It is Ea alone who knows all things.' Then Ea opened his mouth and spoke to warrior Enlil, 'Wisest of gods, hero Enlil, how could you so senselessly bring down the flood?

> Lay upon the sinner his sin,
> Lay upon the transgressor his transgression,
> Punish him a little when he breaks loose,
> Do not drive him too hard or he perishes;
> Would that a lion had ravaged mankind
> Rather than the flood,
> Would that a wolf had ravaged mankind
> Rather than the flood,
> Would that famine had wasted the world
> Rather than the flood,
> Would that pestilence had wasted mankind
> Rather than the flood.

It was not I that revealed the secret of the gods; the wise man learned it in a dream. Now take your counsel what shall be done with him.'

"Then Enlil went up into the boat, he took me by the hand and my wife and made us enter the boat and kneel down on either side, he standing between us. He touched our foreheads to bless us saying, 'In time past Utnapishtim was a mortal man; henceforth he and his wife shall live in the distance at the mouth of the rivers.' Thus it was that the gods took me and placed me here to live in the distance, at the mouth of the rivers."

6
The Return

Utnapishtim said, "As for you, Gilgamesh, who will assemble the gods for your sake, so that you may find that life for which you are searching? But if you wish, come and put it to the test: only prevail against sleep for six days and seven nights." But while Gilgamesh sat there resting on his haunches, a mist of sleep like soft wool teased from the fleece drifted over him, and Utnapishtim said to his wife, "Look at him now, the strong man who would have everlasting life, even now the mists of sleep are drifting over him." His wife replied, "Touch the man to wake him, so that he may return to his own land in peace, going back through the gate by which he came." Utnapishtim said to his wife, "All men are deceivers, even you he will attempt to deceive; therefore bake loaves of bread, each day one loaf, and put it beside his head; and make a mark on the wall to number the days he has slept."

So she baked loaves of bread, each day one loaf, and put it beside his head, and she marked on the wall the days that he slept; and there came a day when the first loaf was hard, the second loaf was like leather, the third was soggy, the crust of the fourth had mould, the fifth was mildewed, the sixth was fresh, and the seventh was still on the embers. Then Utnapishtim touched him and he woke. Gilgamesh said to Utnapishtim the Faraway, "I hardly slept when you touched and roused me." But Utnapishtim said, "Count these loaves and learn how many days you slept, for your first is hard, your second like leather, your third is soggy, the crust of your fourth has mould, your fifth is mildewed, your sixth is fresh and your seventh was still over the glowing embers when I touched and woke you." Gilgamesh said, "What shall I do, O Utnapishtim, where shall I go? Already the thief in the night has hold of my limbs, death inhabits my room; wherever my foot rests, there I find death."

Then Utnapishtim spoke to Urshanabi the ferryman: "Woe to you Urshanabi, now and for ever more you have become hateful to this harbourage; it is not for you, nor for you are the crossings of this sea. Go now, banished from the shore. But this man before whom you walked, bringing him here, whose body is covered with foulness and the grace of whose limbs has been spoiled by wild skins, take him to the washing-place. There he shall wash his long hair clean as snow in the water, he shall throw off his skins and let the sea carry them away, and the beauty of his body shall be shown, the fillet on his forehead shall be renewed, and he shall be given clothes to cover his nakedness. Till he reaches his own city and his journey is accomplished, these clothes will show no sign of age, they will wear like a new garment." So Urshanabi took Gilgamesh and led him to the washing-place, he washed his long hair as clean as snow in the water, he threw off his skins, which the sea carried away, and showed the beauty of his body. He renewed the fillet on his forehead, and to cover his nakedness gave him clothes which would show no sign of age, but would wear like a new garment till he reached his own city, and his journey was accomplished.

Then Gilgamesh and Urshanabi launched the boat on to the water and boarded it, and they made ready to sail away; but the wife of Utnapishtim the Faraway said to him, "Gilgamesh came here wearied out, he is worn out; what will you give him to carry him back to his own country?" So Utnapishtim spoke, and Gilgamesh took a pole and brought the boat in to the bank. "Gilgamesh, you came here a man wearied out, you have worn yourself out; what shall I give you to carry you back to your own country? Gilgamesh, I shall reveal a secret thing, it is a mystery of the gods that I am telling you. There is a plant that grows under the water, it has a prickle like a thorn, like a rose; it will wound your hands, but if you succeed in taking it, then your hands will hold that which restores his lost youth to a man."

When Gilgamesh heard this he opened the sluices so that a sweet-water current might carry him out to the deepest channel; he tied heavy stones to his feet and they dragged him down to the water-bed. There he saw the plant growing; although it pricked him he took it in his hands; then he cut the heavy stones from his feet, and the sea carried him and threw him on to the shore. Gilgamesh said to Urshanabi the ferryman, "Come here, and see this marvellous plant. By its virtue a man may win back all his former strength. I will take it to Uruk of the strong walls; there I will give it to the old men to eat. Its name shall be 'The Old Men Are Young Again'; and at last

I shall eat it myself and have back all my lost youth." So Gilgamesh returned by the gate through which he had come, Gilgamesh and Urshanabi went together. They travelled their twenty leagues and then they broke their fast; after thirty leagues they stopped for the night.

Gilgamesh saw a well of cool water and he went down and bathed; but deep in the pool there was lying a serpent, and the serpent sensed the sweetness of the flower. It rose out of the water and snatched it away, and immediately it sloughed its skin and returned to the well. Then Gilgamesh sat down and wept, the tears ran down his face, and he took the hand of Urshanabi; "O Urshanabi, was it for this that I toiled with my hands, is it for this I have wrung out my heart's blood? For myself I have gained nothing; not I, but the beast of the earth has joy of it now. Already the stream has carried it twenty leagues back to the channels where I found it. I found a sign and now I have lost it. Let us leave the boat on the bank and go."

After twenty leagues they broke their fast, after thirty leagues they stopped for the night; in three days they had walked as much as a journey of a month and fifteen days. When the journey was accomplished they arrived at Uruk, the strong-walled city. Gilgamesh spoke to him, to Urshanabi the ferryman, "Urshanabi, climb up on to the wall of Uruk, inspect its foundation terrace, and examine well the brickwork; see if it is not of burnt bricks; and did not the seven wise men lay these foundations? One third of the whole is city, one third is garden, and one third is field, with the precinct of the goddess Ishtar. These parts and the precinct are all Uruk."

This too was the work of Gilgamesh, the king, who knew the countries of the world. He was wise, he saw mysteries and knew secret things, he brought us a tale of the days before the flood. He went a long journey, was weary, worn out with labour, and returning engraved on a stone the whole story.

7
The Death of Gilgamesh

The destiny was fulfilled which the father of the gods, Enlil of the mountain, had decreed for Gilgamesh: "In nether-earth the darkness will show him a light: Of mankind, all that are known, none will leave a monument for generations to come to compare with his. The heroes, the wise men, like the new moon have their waxing and waning. Men will say, 'Who has ever ruled with might and with power like him?' As in the dark month, the month of shadows, so without him there is no light. O Gilgamesh, this was the meaning of your dream. You were given the kingship, such was your destiny, everlasting life was not your destiny. Because of this do not be sad at heart, do not be grieved or oppressed; he has given you power to bind and to loose, to be the darkness and the light of mankind. He has given unexampled supremacy over the people, victory in battle from which no fugitive returns, in forays and assaults from which there is no going back. But do not abuse this power, deal justly with your servants in the palace, deal justly before the face of the Sun."

The king has laid himself down and will not rise again,
The Lord of Kullab will not rise again;

He overcame evil, he will not come again;
Though he was strong of arm he will not rise again;

He had wisdom and a comely face, he will not come again;
He is gone into the mountain, he will not come again;
On the bed of fate he lies, he will not rise again,
From the couch of many colours he will not come again.

The people of the city, great and small, are not silent; they lift up the lament, all men of flesh and blood lift up the lament. Fate has spoken; like a hooked fish he lies stretched on the bed, like a gazelle that is caught in a noose. Inhuman Namtar is heavy upon him, Namtar that has neither hand nor foot, that drinks no water and eats no meat.

For Gilgamesh, son of Ninsun, they weighed out their offerings; his dear wife, his son, his concubine, his musicians, his jester, and all his household; his servants, his stewards, all who lived in the palace weighed out their offerings for Gilgamesh the son of Ninsun, the heart of Uruk. They weighed out their offerings to Ereshkigal, the Queen of Death, and to all the gods of the dead. To Namtar, who is fate, they weighed out the offering. Bread for Neti the Keeper of the Gate, bread for Ningizzida the god of the serpent, the lord of the Tree of Life; for Dumuzi[24] also, the young shepherd, for Enki and Ninki, for Endukugga and Nindukugga,[25] for Enmul and Ninmul, all the ancestral gods, forbears of Enlil. A feast for Shulpae the god of feasting. For Samuqan, god of the herds, for the mother Ninhursag, and the gods of creation in the place of creation, for the host of heaven, priest and priestess weighed out the offering of the dead.

Gilgamesh, the son of Ninsun, lies in the tomb. At the place of offerings he weighed the bread-offering, at the place of libation he poured out the wine. In those days the lord Gilgamesh departed, the son of Ninsun, the king, peerless, without an equal among men, who did not neglect Enlil his master. O Gilgamesh, lord of Kullab, great is thy praise.

[24] **Dumuzi:** The Sumerian version of Tammuz. [25] **Enki . . . Nindukugga:** Gods of the underworld.

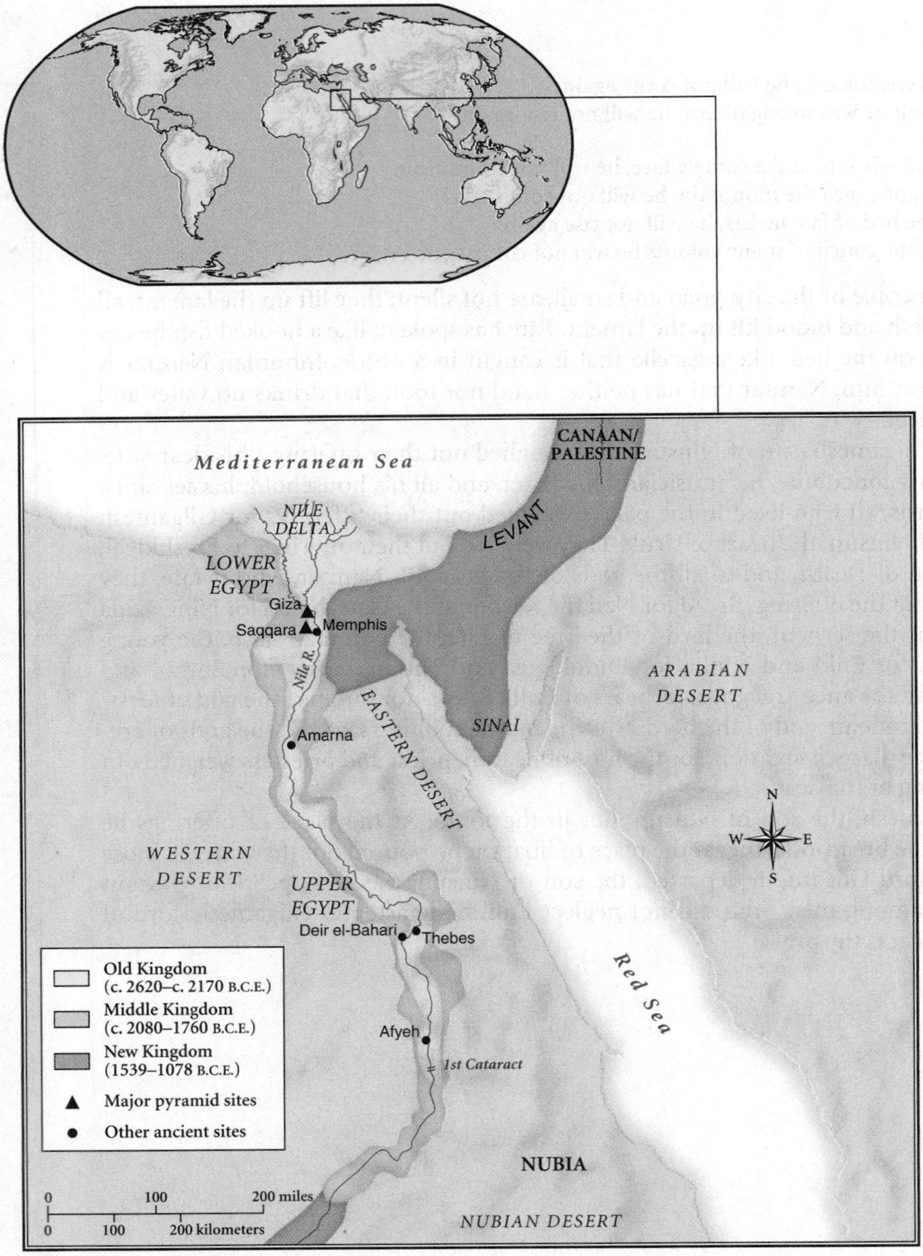

Ancient Egypt

Like the people of Mesopotamia, the Egyptians took advantage of a water source, the Nile River, to irrigate arid land and produce a surplus of food. The river also acted as a highway for traveling north to the Mediterranean and south to Nubia (present-day Sudan). Egypt enjoyed a degree of safety because of its location: The only easy land route into and out of Egypt lay through the northern Sinai Peninsula to the coast of the Levant. Egyptian rulers always fought for control of these areas.

EGYPT

The Seasons of the Nile: Pyramids, Tombs, and Hieroglyphics

Unlike Mesopotamia, which had to be reconstructed out of sand dunes, broken columns, and clay fragments, much of ancient Egypt survives to this day and has long intrigued the historian, archeologist, and tourist with its artistic brilliance and mystery: the immensity of its pyramids, the fantastic colors and painted figures inside its tombs, the giant pillars supporting numerous surviving temples. A wealth of information about ancient Egypt has been garnered from paintings, inscriptions, and artistic artifacts wondrously preserved by an exceptionally dry climate that hasn't changed for millennia. Because of the culture's very antiquity, however, it is a challenge to fully appreciate its influence on the Mediterranean region. Despite the diligent work of Egyptologists for more than a hundred years, it is still not known how ancient Egypt's vast writings, for example, influenced Israel, the Minoan Greeks on Crete, and the city-states on the Greek mainland, as they almost certainly did.

THE NILE

The oldest continuous civilization in the Western world developed along the longest river in the world. The White Nile, which originates in the lakes of central Africa, and the Blue Nile, which begins in the mountains of Ethiopia, join and become a single river at Khartoum, flowing about four thousand miles from there to the delta and the Mediterranean Sea. The annual flooding of the river brought silt from the highlands of Ethiopia to fertilize the Nile Valley, providing the basis for an abundance of food in a country with mostly no rainfall. (The Aswan Dam prevents flooding today.) While Mesopotamians had to develop complicated irrigation systems to lead water from the Tigris and Euphrates Rivers to the land, water came to the Egyptians each summer as snows melted in the highlands, flooding the Nile. Farmers could often harvest two crops of grain before winter set in.

The extensive farmlands in the delta region became the breadbasket for other regions on the Mediterranean Sea, such as Greece and Rome.

The Nile Valley, predictably, sustained the core of Egyptian settlements, which were conveniently ruled by a central government, and the surrounding desert protected from invasion. The valley was divided into two kingdoms—Upper Egypt, to the south, and Lower Egypt, to the north—in the fourth millennium, and then unified around 3100 B.C.E. by a ruler named Narmer (also known as Menes), who established his capital at Memphis. At this time Egyptians developed the basic forms of government, architecture, religion, and **HIEROGLYPHIC** writing that would serve them for another two thousand years. Historians also date Egyptian history from 3100 B.C.E. following the example of Manetho, an Egyptian priest who wrote in Greek c. 280 B.C.E. Menetho devised the plan for dividing the period of Egyptian history from 3100 to 332 B.C.E. into thirty-one dynasties, which were linked to particular rulers. Later scholars grouped the dynasties into the major periods of Old Kingdom (c. 2620–c. 2170 B.C.E.), Middle Kingdom (c. 2080–1760 B.C.E.), and New Kingdom (1539–1078 B.C.E.), with intermediate periods that mark political unrest. Because of the lack of documentary evidence, the period 3100–2620 B.C.E. is usually called the Archaic Period, although some historians include it in the Old Kingdom. The years between 1078 and 332 B.C.E. were a period of foreign occupation in Egypt.

THE OLD KINGDOM AND COSMOGONY

Religion was a part of every aspect of life in ancient Egypt; as in other ancient civilizations, religion in Egypt was a set of stories and rituals that connected the realm of the invisible with the domain of the visible. Such a linking together is a **COSMOGONY**, a model by which earthly powers are matched up with celestial powers and each is assigned a role. Also as in most ancient civilizations, this cosmogony was elaborated on in a creation story that explained how the gods and the world first came into being. In the Egyptian story creation begins with a small island emerging in a boundless chaos—perhaps analogous to a silt island in the Nile—and with a creating, organizing force that the Egyptians called Atum, the "Undifferentiated One." Out of his body Atum creates the major deities, or the **ENNEAD** (the nine great gods), and the material world. Underlying this world is the fundamental principle of ***MAAT***, the idea of "right order" or "justice" that manifests in a moral society based on laws, rules, and customs. *Maat* was the responsibility of both king and commoner. The sun-god Re is called "lord of *maat*," and later the goddess Ma'at' rides with Re in his sun-boat. Forces of order in this universe are cosmically balanced by forces of chaos and disorder, represented by a dragonlike serpent, Apophis or Apep. The hymn "Creating the World and Defeating Apophis"

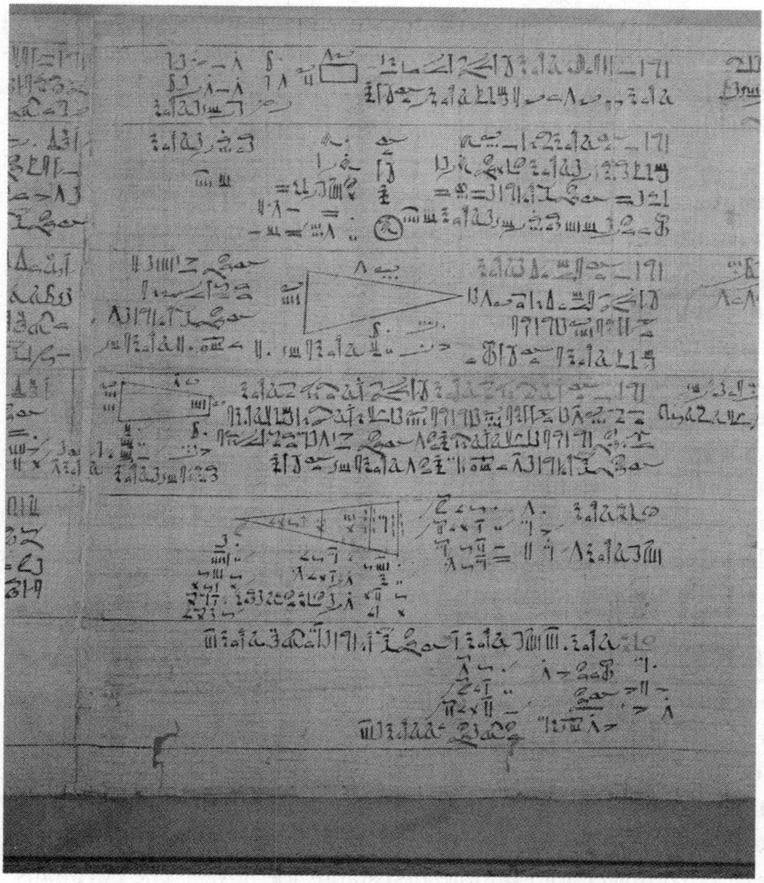

Rhind Papyrus, 1550 B.C.E.
The ancient Egyptians were sophisticated mathematicians—they needed to be in order to conceptualize and plan their monumental building programs. Complex geometric formulas are illustrated on this papyrus. (British Museum, London, UK/The Bridgeman Art Library)

(c. 2000 B.C.E.) describes how Apophis attempts to block Re's sun-boat in its passage through the underworld en route to rebirth each morning; each night Apophis is defeated.

During the time of the Old Kingdom (c. 2620–c. 2170 B.C.E.), the king was literally considered a god. (The term *pharaoh* was not used until the time of the New Kingdom.) The king enjoyed supreme power; indeed, as god-king he owned all of Egypt. Kings came to be called sons of Re, the sun-god, sometimes adding *re* as a suffix to their own names: Khafre, Mendure, Neuserre. The king represented the fertility of the land and summoned the flooding of the Nile each year. The king and his court were inextricably tied to the various priesthoods of the time, their temples and rituals. The priest who daily stood in front of a god's image acted as a substitute for the king, who represented his people to the gods as surely as he personified the gods to his people. Food was plentiful because of the gods' concern; in turn, people set aside a portion of their produce or profits for the deities. Priest-philosophers established the principal shrine of Re at Heliopolis, some twenty-five miles north of Memphis, in about 2500 B.C.E. The ancient Egyptians had called the city On, a name also used in the Book of Genesis; it was the Greeks who renamed it Heliopolis, meaning "city of the sun-god," sometime after their presence was felt in Egypt in the fourth century B.C.E. At On, Egyptians developed astronomy, mathematics, and a precise architecture for designing buildings as expressions and validations of their cosmogony.

The most celebrated priest-architect was Imhotep, who designed the Step Pyramid at Saqqara for King Djoser, which was begun c. 2630 B.C.E.; it was the first truly monumental building in the world, six tiers rising more than two hundred feet above the desert. The three gigantic pyramids—Khufu, Khafre, and Mendure—built at Giza between c. 2600 and c. 2500 B.C.E. are testaments to Egyptian economic power, social organization, and engineering skill. The pyramid built for Khufu (called Cheops by the Greeks) is 482 feet high; it was the tallest structure in the world until the ninth century C.E.

EGYPTIAN WRITING

Egyptians developed a writing system called hieroglyphics, from the Greek meaning "sacred carvings." The earliest hieroglyphs, like other picture-writing, attempted, with some 600 pictures, to imitate objects; a small oval, for example, signified "mouth." These pictographs, in which an image of an object stands for the object, take a great deal of space and are limited or ambiguous with reference to abstract ideas: What object, for example, best stands for "love"? The Egyptians used the "dung beetle" to signify the "universe." At some time in the Old Kingdom about 130 pictographs evolved into phonetic signs, which gave the written language the necessary flexibility for expressing the spoken language and recording literature. Like other ancient culture, the Egyptians considered writing so important and magical they attributed its invention to a god; in addition to the invention of writing, the god Thoth was credited with geometry and astronomy. The many hieroglyphs inscribed on the walls of pyramids and temples were a complete mystery until the Rosetta stone was discovered in Egypt in 1799 by Napoleon's army. On the stone were inscribed three parallel texts—one in Greek characters, one in Egyptian hieroglyphics, and one in *demotic.* The hieroglyphics were deciphered by the French scholar Champollion (1790–1832), but not until 1824. The earliest hieroglyphics were found as recently as 1998 in southern Egypt, when excavations unearthed clay tablets with "sacred carvings" from the tomb of a king named Scorpian that have been carbon-dated between 3300 and

***Three Scribes,* 2446–2426 B.C.E.**
One of the earliest and most advanced cultures of the ancient world, the Egyptians were an extremely literate people, producing written works of all kinds, from bureaucratic records to religious hymns to love poems. This bas-relief showing three scribes at work comes from the tomb of Ti, a Fifth Dynasty official. (The Art Archive / Dagli Orti)

3200 B.C.E. The tablets contained lists of kings and records of shipments of linen and oil.

PYRAMID TEXTS

Early writing (c. 3200 B.C.E.) was devoted primarily to the business of creating and maintaining an urban bureaucracy: tax records, epithets, and dynastic records. But in about 2400 B.C.E., Egyptians began to create the largest body of literature in the ancient Near East and Mediterranean region. Together with texts from ancient Sumer, the Pyramid Texts from the Fifth and Sixth Dynasties (c. 2465–c. 2170 B.C.E.) are the oldest religious texts in the world. (With one exception: Extant Sumerian texts are actually first millennium B.C.E. copies from an earlier period.)

Pyramid Texts is a collection of translations of the hieroglyphs that were inscribed on the chambers and corridors of the pyramids of Saqqara (Sakkara), the necropolis for the royalty of Memphis: the pyramids of Unas, Teti, Pepi, Merenre, Pepi II, and Ibi, as well as Pepi II's three queens (c. 2350–c. 2150 B.C.E.).

The inscriptions are not narratives but rather a collection of spells, incantations, and hymns or prayers that reflect Egyptian religion. Most are devoted to aiding the king in his ascent into the heavens to join the other gods and secure a happy afterlife. The Egyptians were uniquely concerned with death and afterlife. The writings from this early period tend to be somewhat repetitious.

COFFIN TEXTS AND PAPYRI

When the Old Kingdom collapsed from a weakened pharaoh and a possible drought, a faction from Thebes reunited Egypt and the balance of power shifted to the south, where the god Amen was supreme. As was true for many ancient religions, when the centers of power within a country shifted, local deities merged with deities from other regions, resulting in gods with compound names. Re, the highly visible sun-god, was combined with Amen, whose name means "Hidden One." Together they symbolized an Egypt unified under a powerful and wealthy priesthood, whose influence expanded into Palestine as well as southward, beyond the First Cataract of the Nile. Their temple at Karnak is the largest temple ever erected to an ancient god. Pharaohs, considered the sons of Amen-Re, sometimes incorporated Amen into their names during the Twelfth, Thirteenth, and Eighteenth Dynasties; four were named Amenemhet.

A great variety of form characterizes the literature of the second millennium B.C.E. During the Middle Kingdom (c. 2080–1760 B.C.E.) various spells and maps were written on the coffins of governmental officials, again with the intent of providing guidance in the afterlife. Other types of literature include autobiographies, prayers, parables, proverbs, stories, and works of philosophy. The Egyptians had a strong wisdom tradition that instructed individuals on how to comport themselves at work and on the importance of loyalty and dedication. In addition to inscribing stones, Egyptians wrote on sheets of **PAPYRUS**, a reed that grew in abundance along the Nile. Thousands of papyri (from which the English *paper* is derived) have survived from ancient times due to the region's dry climate.

OSIRIS

No complete creation myth involving the gods of ancient Egypt has been found. Stories about individual gods have been pieced together from fragments of texts from numerous pyramids, coffins, and papyri. In some cases, the most complete English version of a story of a particular god is a translation of a Greek story. The

Greek biographer Plutarch (46?–120? C.E.) collected the most detailed account of Osiris, one of the most important deities of ancient Egypt. His story, which frames the "Hymn to Osiris," touched all aspects of Egyptian life. Osiris was the god of vegetation who was annually harvested and then reborn after the flooding of the Nile. The Nile flooded from July until October, when the waters receded. Seeding took place in November. Seth's murder of Osiris, whose body is dumped in the Nile, symbolizes the harvest. The goddess Isis's search for Osiris and his resurrection under her care correspond to the rebirth of plant life in the spring. Seth is the antagonist, the dryness of the desert that threatens the growth of cereals and, therefore, the very existence of the city-state.

Osiris, in addition to being the fertility god, similar to Mesopotamian Dumuzi, was Lord of the Underworld and the rationale for the Egyptian mortuary cults. Egypt developed the most complex and elaborate ideas concerning death and the afterlife found in the ancient Mediterranean and Near East. The Egyptian afterlife, unlike in many other traditions, is a happy one—a time when the dead continue their earthly tasks but with more pleasure and success. The Egyptian Book of the Dead is a collection of texts and magical incantations that focus on the transition from this life to the next.

From early times, Egyptian kings were identified with Horus during their reigns and with Osiris when they died. From the time of the Middle Kingdom

Scene from The Book of the Dead, 1240 B.C.E. *Egyptians spent much of their lives preparing for their death and for life in the afterworld—a happy and positive place. Here, in a scene from The Book of the Dead, the deceased appear before the god Osiris, the supreme judge. (The Art Archive/Egyptian Museum Cairo/Dagli Orti)*

onward, the cult of Osiris was extended to all Egyptians. Thus all bodies were mummified, the heart removed and replaced by a gold scarab, representing the power of the sun to bring forth new life, just as the scarab or dung beetle miraculously brought forth life from the spherical pellets it rolled along the ground. Every dead Egyptian bore his name, "Osiris So-and-So," as if he were the god himself. Sir James Frazer explains: "The thousands of inscribed and pictured tombs that have been opened in the valley of the Nile prove that the mystery of the resurrection was performed for the benefit of every dead Egyptian. . . . The dead man, conceived to be lying, like Osiris, with mangled body, was comforted by being told that the heavenly goddess Nut, the mother of Osiris, was coming to gather up his poor scattered limbs and mould them with her own hands into a form immortal and divine. 'She gives thee thy head, she brings thee thy bones, she sets thy limbs together and puts thy heart in thy body.' Thus the resurrection of the dead was conceived like that of Osiris, not merely as spiritual but also as bodily."

The "Hymn to Aten" by Akhenaten represents a strange twist in Egypt's religious history, one which nevertheless had a permanent effect on the arts. It started when Amenhotep IV, or Akhenaten (r. 1353–1336 B.C.E.), attempted to reform Egyptian religion and institute the worship of a single god, Aten. Prior to Akhenaten's reign, Egyptian schools had preserved the literary language of the Twelfth Dynasty for five hundred years, while the colloquial language of Egypt evolved and changed. After Akhenaten wrote the magnificent "Hymn to Aten," in the language of the day, however, a new literature called New Egyptian flourished. Akhenaten also encouraged artists to break away from the stylized conventions of the past and to paint nature in ordinary settings, such as the harvesting of grain. With Akhenaten's death, Egypt returned to the worship of Amen-Re.

SECULAR LITERATURE

In addition to business inventories and religious texts, a few pieces of nonreligious literature and a selection of lyric poetry from ancient Egypt have survived. The earliest tales, probably written in the Twelfth Dynasty of the Middle Kingdom (c. 1850 B.C.E.), are filled with the wondrous and the miraculous. A single, complete papyrus exists on which is written the stories "The Shipwrecked Sailor," "The Tale of Two Brothers," and "The Contendings of Horus and Seth." Other stories exist in part, such as "King Cheops and the Magicians," "The Teaching for the Vizier Kagemni," and "The Man Who Was Tired of Life." A collection of love poems, originally written on papyri and dating from 1300–1100 B.C.E., are presented here in translation. They cover a broad range of emotions and exhibit a lively use of image and metaphor; their passionate honesty is similar to that in the biblical Song of

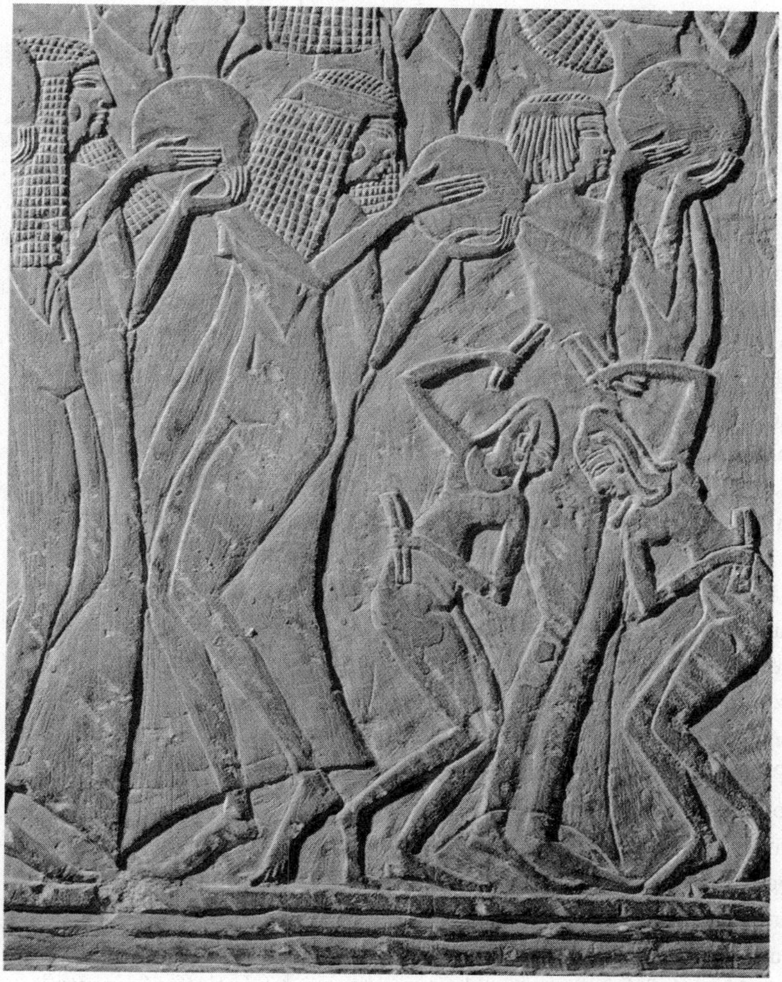

Female Musicians, 1300–1200 B.C.E.
In this scene from a Nineteenth-Dynasty tomb, dancing women play the tambourine and shake clappers in a musical funerary procession. (The Art Archive / Egyptian Museum Cairo / Dagli Orti)

Songs. Several works by women, a rarity in ancient literature, are part of this collection. Their poets join the Greek Sappho (c. 600 B.C.E.) as part of a minority of ancient literary women known today.

ALEXANDER THE GREAT AND ALEXANDRIA

A succession of pharaohs, all named Ramses, closed out the New Kingdom. The height of power and riches was reached by Ramses II, who reigned for nearly seventy years (c. 1292–1225 B.C.E.) and controlled a vast empire from Syria in the north to the Fourth Cataract of the Nile in the Nubian Desert in the south.

Monuments to him were built throughout Egypt. He was probably the pharaoh who initially forbade the Exodus of the Israelites from Egypt in the story of Moses in the Hebrew Scriptures. The splendor of Egyptian temples and tombs along with a wealthy class of nobles attracted invaders gathering on various borders. Because of internal dissension, rulers from Libya to the west dominated Egypt from 1075 to 715 B.C.E. Nubians from the south and Persians from the northeast controlled Egypt from 715 to 332 B.C.E., at which time Alexander the Great seized power and founded the city of Alexandria on the Mediterranean. Alexandria, one of the greatest cities of the period, became the capital of the Ptolemy rulers (305–30 B.C.E.) and a cultural crossroads and prominent center for **Hellenistic** and Jewish learning, attracting philosophers, historians, scientists, and poets from Greece, Rome, and the eastern Mediterranean.

The literature of the ancient world was collected in two magnificent libraries in Alexandria, in the form of approximately six hundred thousand volumes, the backbone of a university and a medical school. Any books found on ships landing in Alexandria were confiscated and copied. The Ptolemies were kept current on world affairs; Ptolemy IV even dedicated a temple to Homer. Manetho, an Egyptian priest, wrote a history of Egypt in Greek, *Aegyptiaca* (c. 280 B.C.E.), in which he covered the period from Menes in 2950 B.C.E. to the conquest of Alexander the Great in 332 B.C.E.

Another Alexandrian was the outstanding thinker of his day, the Jewish philosopher Philo Judaeus (c. 20 B.C.E.–50 C.E.). He is responsible for creating a blend of Platonism and Judaism that influenced early Christianity. Because the Jews of Alexandria had dropped Hebrew as well as Aramaic, their vernacular language, and spoke only Greek, a translation of the Hebrew Scriptures (Old Testament) into Greek was made, the extremely important **Septuagint**. According to legend, the translation was done by seventy-two scholars from Jerusalem who labored over their work for seventy-two days—*septuagint* is Latin for "seventy." The Septuagint is still used by the Greek and Russian Orthodox Church.

Unfortunately, most of the literature of Alexandria has been lost. After Octavian's army defeated Queen Cleopatra of Egypt and her ally Marc Antony in 31 B.C.E., Alexandria became part of the Roman Empire. Its two libraries later came under attack: The main library was destroyed during a civil war late in the third century C.E.; the smaller library was destroyed by Christians in 391 C.E.

WWW For more information about the culture and context of Egypt in the ancient world, see *World Literature Online* at bedfordstmartins.com/worldlit.

TIME AND PLACE

Ancient Egypt: The Rosetta Stone

Archeologists could not read Egyptian hieroglyphs until the Rosetta stone, discovered in Egypt by an unknown soldier in Napoleon's army in 1799, was deciphered by a scholar from Figeac, in southern France, in 1824. Named after the town in Egypt near which it was uncovered, the Rosetta stone is a piece of basalt about 3½ ft. × 2½ ft. × 1 ft. Inscribed on one side of the slab are three distinct groups of writings: fourteen lines of hieroglyphs, thirty-two lines of *demotic* script (a popular, cursive script used for business), and fifty-four lines of Greek. (Greek had become the official language of Egypt after Alexander's invasion in 332 B.C.E.)

Immediately after its discovery, excellent copies of the Rosetta stone writings were circulated to scholars. Among those who entered the race to decipher the Rosetta stone was Jean-François Champollion (1790–1832). Champollion, who had exhibited brilliance in Latin, Greek, and Hebrew at the early age of eleven, was invited as a child to the home of Jean-Baptiste Fourier, a famous mathematician and physicist, to see his collection of Egyptian artifacts. Champollion was entranced by hieroglyphic inscriptions on fragments of papyrus and asked if anyone could read them. When Fourier replied in the negative, Champollion predicted, "I am going to do it." He went on to learn Arabic, Syrian, Chaldean, and Coptic, and in 1807, at the age of seventeen, he wrote an extended outline of a book, *Egypt under the Pharaohs.* At nineteen, after studying Sanskrit and Persian, he became a university lecturer of history in Grenoble.

The Rosetta Stone, 205–180 B.C.E. *One of the most famous slabs of basalt in history, the Rosetta stone discovered in 1799 was the key to deciphering ancient Egyptian hieroglyphics — opening a window onto a five-thousand-year-old culture. (© Archivo Iconografico, S.A. / CORBIS)*

Champollion believed, as did other scholars before him, that the writing on the Rosetta stone represented three parallel texts, and he had learned to recognize certain dates and titles of rulers found on a number of obelisks. In 1822, using a clue from Abbé Rémusat's study of Chinese, which examined the phonetic features of Chinese characters, Champollion determined the key for deciphering the Egyptian writing: The hieroglyphs, he said, could be both logograms (a symbol for a word) *and* phonetic symbols. He then took about two years to translate Egyptian hieroglyphics, publishing *Summary of the Hieroglyphic System of the Ancient Egyptians* in 1824. Champollion identified a total of 864 hieroglyphics; of these, he said, 130 were used phonetically and most frequently. Champollion's scholarship had its detractors, but in 1866 another inscription was found in Greek, hieroglyphic, and *demotic* describing the honors given to Ptolemy III and his queen, Berenice, that finally vindicated Champollion; he had indeed correctly deciphered Egyptian hieroglyphics four decades earlier.

HYMNS

C. 2000–1300 B.C.E.

WWW For a quiz on Egyptian hymns, see *World Literature Online* at bedfordstmartins.com/worldlit.

Songs written in honor of deities—HYMNS—were one of the predominant forms of literature in ancient cultures. Written to celebrate and praise a particular god or goddess as well as to request guidance and protection, hymns could also be supplications for inspiration and forgiveness. Egyptian hymns were addressed to the major Egyptian gods, but in particular they voiced peoples' concerns with the sun, the Nile, and cycles of fertility. "Creating the World and Defeating Apophis," which contains a brief account of how the sun-god Atum-Re[1] created the world, celebrates that god's nightly defeat of the serpent of chaos in the underworld. This hymn is a picture of the Egyptian cosmos and the primary gods who administer it—the Egyptian cosmogony. "Hymn to Osiris" is directed to the deity who was both the fertility god associated with the annual cycle of crops, from planting to harvest, and the Lord of the Underworld, the judge of individual souls who doled out rewards and punishments in the afterlife and held the key to immortality. And "Hymn to Aten" was written in honor of a new sun-god and is attributed to the pharaoh Akhenaten, who attempted to create a religious revolution soon after he inherited the throne from his father in 1353 B.C.E. by forcing Egyptians to worship Aten rather than the longstanding deity Amun-Re (Amon-Re).

p. 109

"Creating the World and Defeating Apophis." Egyptian priests recited or chanted this hymn in nightly ceremonies to assist the sun-god Re on his journey through what the Egyptians called the "two heavens": the heaven in the sky and the heaven in the underworld. While Re travels through the underworld, the serpent Apophis, symbolizing darkness and chaos, attempts to block his passage and thereby prohibit the "rebirth" of the sun each morning.

In the Beginning, There Was Water. Much like the creation story in Genesis, which begins with darkness over a watery deep, the Egyptian cosmogony begins with a boundless body of water, an abyss called Nun or Nu. Out of the waters, which undoubtedly represent the annual flooding of the Nile, emerges a small island and a creator-deity, Atum, "Lord of Heliopolis," who identifies himself as Khepri, the sun-god with the head of a scarab beetle. Khepri rolls the sun across the sky just as beetles roll balls of dung along the ground. The scarab beetle was associated with the energy of the sun as well as with the power of creation, since new beetles were born out of the balls of dung.[2] Scarabs carved from precious stones

[1] **Atum-Re:** Names of gods were combined as the Egyptian religion evolved, as a dominant deity like the sun-god Re, for example, "absorbed" the gods of another region or time period. Atum was probably the original sun-god at Heliopolis; when he was merged with Re, Atum was linked to the nighttime journey of the sun.

[2] **Khepri . . . dung:** Because Khepri was associated with creation and birth, scarabs carved from precious stones were used in funerals: They took the place of the deceased's heart in a rite of rebirth and immortality.

were substituted for human hearts in mummies, further associating the creature with birth and immortality. Atum as Khepri creates the other deities and the rest of the world.

Egyptian priests attempted to answer the question faced by all ancient religions with male creators: How does a solitary male god create anything, since the natural or organic model for creation usually involves the female body? The ancient Babylonian creation story depicts a male god defeating a female goddess in combat; the dismembered body of the female deity then becomes the various parts of creation. An earlier Mesopotamian version from Sumer pictures Enki, the god of fresh water, essentially ejaculating the sparkling waters of the Tigris River, the fertilizing water that eventually brings vegetation and grain to the desert, the basis for all life and the primary condition for civilization. And in the Egyptian story, the male creator-god gives birth to the rest of the deities out of his own body through masturbation. He first creates Shu, the god of air, and Tefnut, the goddess of moisture. They in turn create Geb, the male earth-god, and Nut, the female sky-goddess. In other mythologies the genders of these deities are often reversed: The earth is usually female and the sky is male. But the Egyptians, who equated the earth with the land of Egypt and therefore with the figure of the king, saw the earth deity as a male. Geb and Nut create Osiris (who symbolizes vegetation as well as being Lord of the Underworld), Seth (chaos and desert heat), Isis (goddess of love and maternity), and Nephthys (goddess of the household). Scholars call this core group of deities the **Ennead**, a Greek term

Akhenaten Offering Lotus Flowers to Aten, 1353–1336 B.C.E. *King Akhenaten imposed monotheism, worship of the sun-god Aten, on the Egyptians. (© Archivo Iconografico, S.A. / CORBIS)*

Religion was the dominant factor in virtually every aspect of the life of ancient Egyptians. Food production and the economy prospered because of the gods' concern; in turn, men set aside a certain part of their produce, profits, or labor for the gods. The kings were worshiped as supreme because they were considered the gods' representatives on earth; meanwhile the king and his court were inextricably involved with the various priesthoods, their temples, and the many rituals. Scientific knowledge, the arts, architecture—including the construction of the magnificent pyramids and tombs—were all intertwined with religious beliefs.

– T. G. H. James, critic, 1971

meaning a set of nine. (In the translation chosen here, Horus is also listed, but usually he appears as the son of Osiris and Isis, a relationship explored in the text.) The Ennead attack Apophis, the serpent of darkness and destruction.

Defeating Apophis. In the ancient Egyptian religion centered at Heliopolis, the sun-god Re traverses the sky in a boat (the Boat of Millions[3]) and at sunset rides his boat through the underworld towed by the spirits of the dead. In the underworld, the serpent or dragon of chaos, Apophis, attempts to block Re's passage; nightly Re and some lesser gods battle the serpent. If Apophis ever halted the sun's passage, the world would come to an end, so Egyptian priests throughout the land assisted Re by praying the sun-boat through the dark hours of the underworld. Apophis also stands for all the problems that might impede the orderly affairs of the kingdom. In effect, the nightly defeat of chaos repeats the event of creation when Atum first emerged from the waters of the abyss.

p. 111

"Hymn to Osiris." This hymn celebrates Osiris's importance to Egypt. Osiris reached out to all Egyptians at the time of their deaths and was central to the idea of kingship. No complete version of the Osiris story has yet been found, but it seems Osiris may have been a historical king who was martyred or who sacrificed himself for the good of the people, was deified, and became a cultural hero. Tradition says that a great voice proclaimed at Osiris's birth: "Here comes the Universal Lord of All." As king, Osiris provided the basis for civilization: He gave Egypt laws and temple rituals, and he discovered the cultivation of wheat, barley, and grapes, traveling throughout Egypt with his teachings. He also invented two kinds of flutes. He married his sister Isis (the Throne),[4] who taught women to grind corn, spin, and weave and instructed Egyptians in medicine and healing.

Osiris's jealous brother Set (or Seth) tricked Osiris into getting into a coffin that he and his accomplices then nailed shut and threw into the Nile. Osiris drifted to Byblos (Phoenicia), followed by Isis, who retrieved the coffin from a pillar of tamarisk and returned with it to Egypt. But Set came across the coffin, opened it, and cut the body of Osiris into fourteen pieces, which he either scattered over the land of Egypt or flung into the Nile. Isis again went in search of Osiris. In one version of the story, all the pieces are recovered; in another, Isis buries each piece of Osiris wherever she finds it. In still another, Isis buries an image of Osiris in every city, pretending it is his body so that Osiris will be worshiped in many places and Set will never find Osiris's real grave. Isis makes an image of

[3] **Millions:** Millions of years.

[4] **Throne:** Isis is often pictured in hieroglyphs wearing a throne that symbolizes her roles: Not only was she the wife of the king, but as a mother goddess and the mother of Horus she provided the divine authority by which the earthly king ruled. Her throne is also reminiscent of the primal mound that emerges out of the primordial waters in the Egyptian creation story.

Osiris's phallus, which was eaten by fish; that image became part of Egyptian festivals.

In the versions of the myth in which Isis recovers all the pieces of Osiris, the goddess fans the cold body of Osiris with her wings and revives him, at which point Horus is conceived. Rather than return to rule Egypt, Osiris chooses to become the ruler of the Kingdom of the Dead, the land of the West, the region of darkness. Isis cares for her son Horus, who undergoes a series of trials; when he becomes old enough, he challenges Set for the throne. After a tribunal before the gods and a fight between Horus and Set in which Horus loses his left eye, Horus finally wins the throne and becomes ruler of Egypt. Horus journeys to the underworld, presents Osiris with his eye,[5] which restores Osiris to eternal life, and the pageant of the new year recommences.

> **Seth is the opposing principle to Osiris; he is the perpetual antagonist. Where Osiris is moisture, Seth is aridity and dryness; where Osiris is the Nile, Seth is the desert that threatens to cover it over, or the winds that scatter the burning sand, or the scorching heat of the sun that evaporates the waters . . . he is the darkness that engulfs the sun each night.**
>
> **– Anne Baring and Jules Cashford, historians, 1991**

The Importance of Osiris. The story of Osiris provided a model for the transition of power in ancient Egypt: When a king died he joined Osiris, and the prince, as Horus, inherited the throne. Osiris also granted immortality, not only to kings and pharaohs, but to the common people as well. By assimilating Osiris in death, every devotee believed he would be raised to a new life in the next world where, as in life, a good and just king ruled. To qualify for a blessed afterlife, a person must have worshiped Osiris and lived a virtuous life according to *maat*—cosmic truth and justice. He or she then had to appear before forty-two judges in the Hall of Two Truths, a trial over which Osiris presided. The deceased's heart was literally weighed on the scales of justice against a feather, and, depending on the result, the individual received either punishment in a sea of fire or life eternal filled with such pleasures as hunting and banqueting. This scenario helped to make sense of death while skirting the issue of the origin of death itself.

"Hymn to Aten." When Akhenaten ascended the throne during the Eighteenth Dynasty (c. 1570–1290 B.C.E.) in Egypt, he was called Amenhotep IV, after his father, Amenhotep III. Although most of the kings and conquerors of ancient Egypt are shrouded in mystery, Akhenaten emerges as a distinct personage, one of the earliest in the ancient Near East and Mediterranean region, though his exact beliefs and motivations remain unknown. What is known is that he created a religious revolution. In the fifth year of his reign he changed his name to Akhenaten, for "in the service of Aten," abolished polytheistic temples, rituals, and festivals devoted to Amen-Re, the supreme deity in the Egyptian pantheon, and maintained that the sun-god Aten was the sole god—considered by scholars to be the first instance of MONOTHEISM. He then moved his wife, the beautiful Nefertiti, his children, and his court to a new city in Middle Egypt named Akhetaten for "the glory of Aten." Akhenaten is also known

p. 114

[5] **his eye:** The eye of Horus is called *Wedjat*-eye, the Eye of Eternity, which protects against all harm. It is pictured on its own in artworks.

to have fostered a new direction in Egyptian art, with an emphasis on themes from nature; some artistic works from this period show Akhenaten's rather deformed body as well as his delight in his wife and children.

The Counterrevolution. Depriving his subjects of their traditional religious activity probably proved to be Akhenaten's undoing. It is very likely that the religious establishment of his day created ferment, and as it turned out, the worship of Amen was restored immediately following the succession of Tutankhamen (King Tut). Just as Akhenaten had removed symbols of Amen in the temples, so efforts were made to obliterate traces of Akhenaten's reign, including the destruction of the city of Aten and the removal of Akhenaten's name from monuments.

Because "Hymn to Aten" bears a strong resemblance to Psalm 104 in Hebrew Scriptures, there has been speculation that Akhenaten's monotheism influenced the Hebrew faith. According to legend, the Hebrews resided in Egypt for several centuries prior to their Exodus in the thirteenth century B.C.E. In any case, the "Hymn to Aten" stands on its own as a triumphant poem celebrating Aten as the "sole God, like whom there is no other."

■ CONNECTIONS

***Epic of Creation*, p. 44.** The geography of Sumer and Egypt, especially the deserts and rivers, shaped the culture and the beliefs of the lands' inhabitants. The Sumerian goddess of the salt sea and of chaos, Tiamat, must be defeated. The Egyptian Seth as the desert seems to represent more of a threat than the Nile. What about the Nile was different from the delta of the Tigris and Euphrates Rivers?

***The Descent of Inanna*, p. 28.** In several mythologies of the ancient world, a goddess went on a journey in search of a young god who represented the annual agricultural cycle: His death and resurrection was linked to the death and birth of plants during the winter and spring seasons. The Sumerian version involved Inanna and Dumuzi; the Egyptian cycle involved Isis and Osiris. What might be the reasons for drawing parallels between human fertility and the plant cycle? How did this relationship contribute to the ritual drama in the religious life of a people?

Genesis, p. 140. A number of ancient creation stories begin with a large body of water, an ocean, a watery abyss. Water is the primordial condition of the world in both Genesis and the Egyptian cosmogony. What qualities of water and its relationship to the human psyche make it prime material from which to create the cosmos?

Rig Veda, p. 1338. Chaos in ancient literature is often represented by monsters like serpents and dragons. An important Indian myth, comparable to the Egyptian story of Re's defeat of Apophis, involves the defeat of the dragon Vritra by the god Indra. Which of their characteristics make serpents and dragons good adversaries?

■ FURTHER RESEARCH

Literary Texts

Erman, Adolf, ed. *The Ancient Egyptians: A Sourcebook of Their Writings.* 1927, 1966.
Foster, John L. *Echoes of Egyptian Voices.* 1992.
Lichtheim, Miriam, ed. *Ancient Egyptian Literature: A Book of Readings* (3 vols.). 1973.
Parkinson, R. B., ed. *Voices from Ancient Egypt.* 1991.
Pritchard, J. B., ed. *Ancient Near Eastern Texts Relating to the Old Testament.* 1969.

Simpson, William Kelly. *The Literature of Ancient Egypt: An Anthology of Stories, Instructions, and Poetry.* 1972.

Historical Background

Baring, Anne, and Jules Cashford. *The Myth of the Goddess: The Evolution of an Image.* 1991.

Donoughue, Carol. *The Mystery of the Hieroglyphs: The Story of the Rosetta Stone and the Race to Decipher Egyptian Hieroglyphs.* 1999.

Forman, Werner. *Hieroglyphs and the Afterlife in Ancient Egypt.* 1996.

Hart, George. *Dictionary of Egyptian Gods and Goddesses.* 1986.

Kramer, Samuel Noah, ed. *Mythologies of the Ancient World.* 1961.

Shafer, B. E., ed. *Religion in Ancient Egypt: Gods, Myths and Personal Practice.* 1991.

Thompson, William Irwin. *The Time Falling Bodies Take to Light: Mythology, Sexuality & the Origins of Culture.* 1981.

FROM

Creating the World and Defeating Apophis: A Ritual Hymn

Translated by John A. Wilson

(xxvi 21) . . . THE BOOK OF KNOWING THE CREATIONS OF RE AND OF OVERTHROWING APOPHIS. THE WORDS TO BE SPOKEN.

The All-Lord[1] said, after he had come into being:

I am he who came into being as Khepri.[2] When I had come into being, being

---

"Creating the World and Defeating Apophis." This text comes from the *Papyrus Bremner-Rhind* (British Museum #10188), on which are written a group of texts under the heading, "THE BEGINNING OF THE BOOK OF OVERTHROWING APOPHIS, THE ENEMY OF RE AND THE ENEMY of King Wen-nofer—life, prosperity, health!—the justified, performed in the course of every day in the Temple of Amon-Re, Lord of the Thrones of the Two Lands, Presiding over Karnak." Although the papyrus itself is dated c. 310 B.C.E., scholars believe that the texts are from an earlier period, since they imitate a language used some two thousand years earlier. King Wen-nofer is another name for Osiris. The reference to Karnak, the monumental temple at Thebes, points to sometime during the Middle Kingdom (c. 2080–1760 B.C.E.) when Thebes was the political and religious center of Egypt. Amon-Re (or Amen-Re or Amun-Re, depending on the translator) is a combination name; Amen was the primary god at Thebes who was absorbed into the figure of Re toward the end of the Middle Kingdom.

A note on the translation: In our translation italics are used to indicate a doubtful translation of a known text; words in parentheses indicate additions for a better understanding of the translation. Ellipses indicate missing materials. Capital letters show words that are highlighted in the manuscript, usually in red. All notes are the editors' unless otherwise indicated.

[1] **All-Lord:** Probably the creator-god Atum, whose name means "the one who contains all beings." He is the primordial being from whom all other beings issue. Atum is also another name for Re, the sun-god. As the lord of creation, Atum precedes the later worship of Amen (Amon, Amun) at Thebes.

[2] **Khepri:** Khepri is the scarab beetle that represents the sun-god in the morning.

(itself) came into being, and all beings came into being after I came into being. Many were the beings where came forth from my mouth,[3] before heaven came into being, before earth came into being, before the ground and creeping things had been created in this place. I put together (some) of them in Nun as weary ones, before I could find a place in which I might stand.[4] It (seemed) advantageous to me in my heart; I planned with my face; and I made (in concept) every form when I was alone, before I had spat out what was Shu, before I had sputtered out what was Tefnut,[5] and before (any) other had come into being who could act with me.

I planned in my own heart, and there came into being a multitude of forms of beings, the forms of children and the forms of their children. I was the one who copulated with my fist, I masturbated with my hand. Then I spewed with my own mouth. I spat out what was Shu, and I sputtered out what was Tefnut. It was my father Nun who brought them up, and my Eye[6] followed after them since the ages when they were distant from me.

After I had come into being as the sole god, there were three gods beside me.[7] I came into being in this land, whereas Shu and Tefnut rejoiced in Nun, in which they were. They brought to me my Eye with them. After I had joined together my members, I wept over them.[8] That is how men came into being from the tears which came forth from my Eye. It was angry with me, after it returned and found that I had made another in its place, having replaced it with the Glorious Eye, which I had made. Then I advanced its place on my head,[9] and after it had ruled this entire land, *its rage fell away to its roots,* for I had replaced what had been taken away from it. I came forth from the roots,[10] and I created all creeping things and whatever lives among them. Then Shu and Tefnut brought forth (5) Geb and Nut. Then Geb and Nut brought forth Osiris, Horus, Seth, Isis, and Nephthys[11] from the body, one of them after another; and they brought forth their multitudes in this land.

---

[3] **Many . . . mouth:** As one form of creation, the All-Lord actually creates a multitude of beings through verbal commands.

[4] **a place . . . stand:** Nun is the god of the primordial ocean or watery abyss; he also symbolizes the annual flooding of the Nile. As such, Nun is male, since the Nile fertilizes the land. In the cosmogonies of other civilizations, the primordial ocean is female. "A place in which I might stand" refers to the island that emerges out of the primordial ocean, a place from which the rest of creation might occur.

[5] **Shu . . . Tefnut:** Shu is the god of air; Tefnut is the goddess of moisture; their emergence contains a play on words: *ishesh,* "spit" and Shu; *tef,* "sputter" and Tefnut. (Translator's note.)

[6] **my Eye:** The eye of the sun-god is separable and has its own adventures.

[7] **three . . . me:** Nun, Shu, and Tefnut.

[8] **I wept . . . them:** Apparently Re wept when he found that his Eye was missing from his body. He made a substitute eye, which displeased his missing Eye when it returned to him. The labored point of the context is a play on the words *remit* "tears" and *romet* "mankind," in explanation of human creation. (Translator's note.)

[9] **I advanced . . . head:** Re appeased his wrathful Eye by making it the uraeus, the Eye of Horus, which is the figure of the sacred asp or cobra on the headdress of Egyptian rulers.

[10] **I came . . . roots:** Reference to the creation of vegetation.

[11] **Shu . . . Nephthys:** The children of Shu and Tefnut: Geb, the earth; Nut, the sky; Osiris, vegetation and Lord of the Underworld; Seth, the desert and murderer of Osiris; Isis, the goddess of love, maternity, and the "throne"; and Nephthys, goddess of the household. Atum-Re and his eight children are the nine ruling gods, or the Ennead (Greek for "a set of nine"). Horus is ordinarily considered the child of Osiris and Isis.

When (these gods) rich in magic spoke, it was the (very) spirit[12] of magic, for they were ordered to annihilate my enemies by the effective charms of their speech, and I sent out these who came into being from my body TO OVERTHROW THAT EVIL ENEMY.

HE IS ONE FALLEN TO THE FLAME, APOPHIS with a knife on his head. He *cannot* see, and his name is no (more) in this land. I have commanded that *a curse* be cast upon him; I have consumed his bones; I have annihilated his soul in the course of every day; I have cut his vertebrae at his neck, severed with a knife which hacked up his flesh and pierced into his hide.[13] [. . .]

(Thus) thou shalt be in thy shrine, thou shalt journey in the evening-barque, thou shalt rest in the morning-barque, thou shalt cross thy two heavens in peace,[14] thou shalt be powerful, thou shalt live, thou shalt be healthy, thou shalt make thy states of glory to endure, thou shalt drive away thy every enemy by thy command [. . . .]

[12] **spirit:** The Egyptian word is *ka,* which means a person's vital force or life force as well as his or her personality.

[13] The narration continues at this point with repetitious details of the destruction of Apophis and the roles of various gods.

[14] **journey . . . in peace:** This section seems to suggest that the sun travels in two different boats in his journey across the two heavens, one for the heaven above and another for the heaven of the underworld.

Hymn to Osiris

Translated by Aylward M. Blackman

Praise to thee, Osiris! Thou lord of eternity, king of gods! Thou with many names and lordly of being! With mysterious ceremonies in the temples.[1]

He it is that hath the noble ka[2] in Busiris and the abundant sustenance (?) in Letopolis; to whom men shout for joy in the nome of Busiris, and that hath many victuals in Heliopolis.[3]

Hymn to Osiris. This hymn was inscribed on a tombstone of the Eighteenth Dynasty, c. 1539 B.C.E. The translator has used the following typographical marks in his translation: An interpolation or a free rendering of a passage is set in italics; brackets indicate restorations. Gaps in the text are marked in two ways: An ellipsis (. . .) indicates a single word is missing; a dashed line (– – – –) appears where a sentence or more was indecipherable or missing. A question mark in parentheses (?) signals ambiguity in the original language. All notes are the editors' unless otherwise indicated.

[1] **ceremonies . . . temples:** Refers to the dramatic performances of Osiris's life—the Osirian mysteries—performed in his sanctuaries; the most important took place at Busiris in the delta and at Abydos.

[2] **ka:** Vital force in an individual or the personality.

[3] **Busiris . . . Heliopolis:** Places where Osiris was worshiped; a nome was a province in Egypt.

He whom men call to mind in . . . , the mysterious soul of the lord of Kerert; that is lordly in Memphis, the soul of Rē and his own body.[4]

He that went to rest in Herakleopolis,[5] and to whom men raised goodly shouts of joy in the Naret-tree, which came into being in order to raise up his soul.[6]

Lord of the Great Hall in Hermopolis, and very terrible in Shashotep; lord of eternity in Abydos, that hath his seat in To-zoser.[7]

He whose name endureth in the mouth of men, that was in Primæval Time for the Two Lands together;[8] sustenance and food at the head of the Ennead; the most excellent glorified one among the glorified.[9]

Nun[10] hath offered to him his water, and the north wind journeys southward to him; the sky createth air for his nose, for the contentment of his heart. The plants grow according to his desire, and the field createth for him its food.

The firmament and its stars hearken unto him, and the great portals open to him; to whom men shout for joy in the southern sky, whom men adore in the northern sky.[11] The imperishable stars are under his authority, and the never-wearying ones are his place of abode.

Offering is made to him by the command of Kēb,[12] and the Nine Gods adore him; they that are in the underworld kiss the ground, and they that are in the necropolis make an obeisance. The . . . shout for joy when they behold him, they that are there[13] are in fear of him. The Two Lands together give him praise at the approach of his majesty.

The lordly noble at the head of the nobles, with enduring office and established rule. The goodly Mighty One for the Nine Gods, he with the kindly face, on whom men love to look.

He that put the fear of him in all lands, to the intent that they might make mention of his name *in respect of all that they offered (?) unto him;* he that is remembered in heaven and on earth. *To whom many shouts of joy are raised* at the Wag-festival,[14] over whom the Two Lands rejoice together. The most chiefest of his brethren, the eldest of the Nine Gods.[15]

He that established right throughout the Two River-banks, and placed the son upon his father's seat; praised of his father Kēb, beloved of his mother Nut.

Great of strength when he overthrew the adversary, powerful of arm when he slew his foe. He that put the fear of him in the enemies, and reached (?) the boundaries of them that plotted mischief. Firm of heart when he trod down (?) the foemen.

The heir of Kēb in the kingship of the Two Lands. He[16] saw how excellent he was, and he entrusted it to him to lead the Two Lands to good fortune.

---

[4] **His . . . body:** Religious connections to other deities. [5] **Herakleopolis:** A city in Middle Egypt. [6] **men raised . . . soul:** Events in the Osiris story about which scholars are ignorant. [7] **To-zoser:** The name for the necropolis of Abydos. [8] **Two Lands together:** Reference to the unification of Upper and Lower Egypt (c. 3100 B.C.E.). [9] **Ennead . . . glorified:** The Ennead is the group of nine primary gods; Osiris is glorified as ruler of the dead. [10] **Nun:** God of the primeval ocean that preceded creation, Nun is called upon by Osiris annually for the flooding of the Nile. [11] **The firmament . . . sky:** A reference to the resurrection and ascension of Osiris. [12] **Kēb:** The earth-god. [13] **they . . . there:** The dead. [14] **Wag-festival:** Probably a harvest festival. [15] **eldest . . . Gods:** Meaning Osiris; a poetic exaggeration, since Osiris is not the eldest. [16] **He:** Kēb.

He placed this land in his hand, its water and its air, its herbs and all its cattle. All that flieth and all that fluttereth, its worms and its wild beasts, were made over to the son of Nut, and the Two Lands were contented therewith.

He that appeared upon the throne of his father, like Rē when he ariseth in the horizon, that he might give light to him that was in darkness. He illumined – – – – and flooded the Two Lands, like the sun at dawn of day.

His crown cleft the sky and consorted with the stars; he, the leader of every god, admirable in command, whom the Great Ennead of gods praised, and the Lesser Ennead[17] loved.

His sister protected him, she that held the foes aloof and warded off the deeds of the *miscreant* by the beneficent things of her mouth,[18] she with the excellent tongue, whose words come not to nought, and admirable in command.

Beneficent Isis, that protected her brother, that sought for him without wearying, that traversed this land mourning, and took no rest until she found him.

She that afforded him shade with her feathers, and with her wings created air. She that cried aloud for joy and brought her brother to land.

She that revived the faintness of the Weary One, that took in his seed and provided an heir, that suckled the child in solitude, the place where he was being unknown, that brought him, when his arm was strong, into the hall of Kēb.

The Ennead cried out full of joy:

"Welcome, Horus, son of Osiris!
Stalwart hearted, justified![19]
Son of Isis, heir of Osiris!"

The Tribunal of Truth assembled for him, the Ennead and the Lord of All himself, the lords of truth that were united therein, that turned their backs on iniquity.

They sat them down in the hall of Kēb with the intent to assign the office to its lord, the kingdom to whom it should be given.

It was found that the word of Horus was true, and the office of his father was given unto him. He came forth crowned by the command of Kēb, he received the lordship of the Two River-banks, and the crown rested securely on his head.

The earth was accounted unto him for his possession (?), and heaven and earth were under his authority. Men, folk, people, mankind, were made over to him, Egypt and the Northerners,[20] and what the sun encircleth, were under his governance, the north wind, the river, the flood, the fruit-tree, and all plants.

The corn-god gave all his herbage and (?) sustenance to the glorified one; he brought (?) satiety and placed it in all lands.

All people were happy, cheerful of mind, and with glad hearts; all men cried out

[17] **Lesser Ennead:** After the first nine gods, which constitute the Great Ennead, the rest of the gods constitute the Lesser Ennead. [18] **beneficent . . . mouth:** Isis uses magical spells to protect Osiris; the murder is too terrible to mention. [19] **Horus . . . justified:** Horis is actually not yet justified; his case still has to be presented to a tribunal of the gods, who will decide between him and Seth. [20] **Northerners:** Probably peoples of the Mediterranean.

for joy, and all people adored his goodness: "How deeply we love him! His goodness traverseth the hearts, and great in all is the love of him.

"They have given his enemies to the son of Isis – – – –. Evil hath been inflicted on the miscreant (?) – – – –.

"The son of Isis hath protected his father, and his name hath been made noble and excellent. Might hath taken its seat, and Prosperity endureth by its ordinances. The roads lie outspread, and the ways are open.[21]

"How contented are the Two Lands! Wickedness hath vanished, and evil hath fled. The land is happy under its lord. Right is established for its lord, and the back is turned on iniquity.

"Be glad of heart, Wennōfre![22] The son of Isis hath assumed the diadem. The office of his father hath been assigned unto him in the hall of Kēb. Rē, he speaketh, Thōth, he writeth,[23] and the tribunal assenteth thereto. Thy father Kēb hath given command for thee (?) and it is done according to that which he spake."

[21] **Might . . . open:** These are expressions used with the ordinances of an earthly king. [22] **Wennōfre:** Osiris.
[23] **Thōth . . . writeth:** Thōth, the moon-god with the head of an ibis, inventor of writing.

FROM

Hymn to Aten

Translated by William Kelly Simpson

You rise in perfection on the horizon of the sky,
living Aten, who started life.
Whenever you are risen upon the eastern horizon
you fill every land with your perfection.
You are appealing, great, sparkling, high over every land;
your rays hold together the lands as far as everything you have made.
Since you are Re, you reach as far as they do,

"Hymn to Aten." This text is inscribed on the tomb of one of Akhenaten's successors, Eye or Aye (r. 1325–1321 B.C.E.), in the area called el-Amarna, the site of Akhenaten's old capital. As an artist and poet himself, it is probable that Akhenaten is the hymn's author or at least its sponsor, since he is mentioned as the earthly son of Aten. Several hymns to Aten were found in the tombs of nobility at Amarna, but the most beautiful tribute to the sun-god is this one, in which Aten is pictured as a benevolent, universal creator.

A note on the translation: The translator has used the following conventions to indicate problems with the text: "Brackets are employed for text which has been restored when there is a gap in the manuscript, and half brackets when the word or phrase is uncertain or imperfectly understood; three dots are used when the gap cannot be filled with any degree of certainty and represent an omission of indeterminate length. . . . Parentheses are used for phrases not in the original added as an aid to the reader; angle brackets are used for words which the copyist erroneously omitted. . . ." Unless otherwise indicated, the footnotes are the editors'.

and you curb them for your beloved son.
Although you are far away, your rays are upon the land;
you are in their faces, yet your departure is not observed.

Whenever you set on the western horizon,
the land is in darkness in the manner of death.
They sleep in a bedroom with heads under the covers,
and one eye does not see another.
If all their possessions which are under their heads were stolen,
they would not know it.
Every lion who comes out of his cave and all the serpents bite,
for darkness is a blanket.
The land is silent now, because he who made them
is at rest on his horizon.

But when day breaks you are risen upon the horizon,
and you shine as the Aten in the daytime.
When you dispel darkness and you give forth your rays
the two lands are in festival,
alert and standing on their feet,
now that you have raised them up.
Their bodies are clean, / and their clothes have been put on;
their arms are <lifted> in praise at your rising.

The entire land performs its work:
all the cattle are content with their fodder,
trees and plants grow,
birds fly up to their nests,
their wings <extended> in praise for your Ka.[1]
All the kine prance on their feet;
everything which flies up and alights,
they live when you have risen for them.
The barges sail upstream and downstream too,
for every way is open at your rising.
The fishes in the river leap before your face
when your rays are in the sea.

You who have placed seed in woman
and have made sperm into man,
who feeds the son in the womb of his mother,
who quiets him with something to stop his crying;
you are the nurse in the womb,
giving breath to nourish all that has been begotten.

[1] **Ka:** Life force, personality; sometimes translated as soul.

When he comes down from the womb to breathe
on the day he is born,
you open up his mouth ⌈completely⌉, and supply his needs.
When the fledgling in the egg speaks in the shell,
you give him air inside it to sustain him.
When you grant him his allotted time to break out from the egg,
he comes out from the egg to cry out at his fulfillment,
and he goes upon his legs when he has come forth from it.

How plentiful it is, what you have made,
although they are hidden from view,
sole god, without another beside you;
you created the earth as you wished,
when you were by yourself, <before>
mankind, all cattle and kine,
all beings on land, who fare upon their feet,
and all beings in the air, who fly with their wings.

The lands of Khor and Kush[2]
and the land of Egypt:
you have set every man in his place,
you have allotted their needs,
every one of them according to his diet,
and his lifetime is counted out.
Tongues are separate in speech,
and their characters / as well;
their skins are different,
for you have differentiated the foreigners.
In the underworld you have made a Nile
that you may bring it forth as you wish
to feed the populace,
since you made them for yourself, their utter master,
growing weary on their account, lord of every land.
For them the Aten of the daytime arises,
great in awesomeness.

All distant lands,
you have made them live,
for you have set a Nile in the sky[3]
that it may descend for them
and make waves upon the mountains like the sea

[2] **Khor and Kush:** Khor is Syro-Palestine in the northeast, and Kush is the Nubian region in the Sudan to the south. (Translator's note.)

[3] **a Nile . . . sky:** Egypt is watered by the Nile River, not by rain; "Nile in the sky" means rain.

to irrigate the fields in their towns.
How efficient are your designs,
Lord of eternity:
a Nile in the sky for the foreigners
and all creatures that go upon their feet,
a Nile coming back from the underworld for Egypt.

Your rays give suck to every field:
when you rise they live,
and they grow for you.
You have made the seasons
to bring into being all you have made:
the Winter to cool them,
the Heat that you may be felt.
You have made a far-off heaven
in which to rise
in order to observe everything you have made.
Yet you are alone,
rising in your manifestations as the Living Aten:
appearing, glistening, being afar, coming close;
you make millions of transformations of yourself.
Towns, harbors, fields, roadways, waterways:
every eye beholds you upon them,
for you are the Aten of the daytime on the face of the earth.
When you go forth
every eye [is upon you].
You have created their sight
but not to see (only) the body . . .
which you have made. [. . .]

Love Poems
c. 1290–1078 B.C.E.

. . . I would argue that the splendor of pharaonic visual art has its worthy parallel in Egyptian literature: It is indeed a full-blooded verbal equivalent to the richness, elegance, vitality, and variety of Egypt's visual remains. Egyptians honored words as they became flesh in hymns and prayers, instructions, stories, and even love songs; and Egyptian writers — the poets particularly — delighted in working (or playing) with the nuances of words and meaning, and in the sounds and images of the language.

–John L. Foster, critic and translator, 1992

The love poems in this section reflect the aesthetic revolution of the Nineteenth and Twentieth Dynasties of the New Kingdom (c. 1290–1078 B.C.E.), a movement initiated by Amenhotep IV (or Akhenaten) and exemplified in his famous "Hymn to Aten" (see page 114), which like other literature of the time uses the vernacular of the day, called New Egyptian, to create a new kind of poetry. While in Egyptian prose tales the personality of the storyteller tends to remain hidden, the voice of the poet emerges in Egyptian lyrics, and with it, across these many years and into diverse cultures, his or her personal feelings are revealed. Similarly, while some aspects of Egyptian religion seem quite foreign today, Egyptian love poetry is readily accessible. Ancient Egyptian poets explore the full range of romantic love's emotions, from feelings of rejection to great eroticism.

Selected Poems. The poems by one or more women in the following selections exhibit a remarkable freshness and honesty. "If I am [not] with you, where will you set your heart?" makes sensuous use of the human body. Intimacy is approached indirectly in "I wish I were her washerman." The bird and animal metaphors in "My love for you is mixed" add interest to the love situation in the poem. "Please come quick to the lady love" compares a lover to a hunted gazelle, but as if the man were both the seeker and the sought. "I sail downstream in the ferry" includes analogies to Egyptian gods. And "Seven days have passed" talks about love as a sickness, a motif later found in European medieval and Renaissance poetry.

Several of the selected poems combine the sacred and the secular and so seem part of the literary tradition that influenced the biblical Song of Songs (Song of Solomon). In fact, writings from the later New Kingdom are filled with borrowed foreign words, primarily from Palestine, which attests to a close relationship between Egypt and Palestine during this period and helps to account for the similarities between Egyptian writings and the poetry in Hebrew Scripture. The Egyptian convention of repeating the theme of the first line of a couplet in the second line is also found in Hebrew poetry.

The Challenges of Translation. Translation of ancient Egyptian literature is more complex than the translation of more modern works for several reasons. To begin with, papyrus becomes brittle over time and can break; it is also vulnerable to insects. Most texts written on papyrus have sections missing. Scribes used black ink for the text and red ink for headings (some translations set these rubrics in small capitals). Hieroglyphics lack conjunctions and indications of tense, and the exact meaning of many hieroglyphs is unknown. In poetry, stanzas are not clearly indicated. Add to these challenges the fact that copying was done rather carelessly. At times, translators must make an informed guess about a particular word

www For a quiz on ancient love poems, see *World Literature Online* at bedfordstmartins.com/worldlit.

***Pair Statue of Memi and Sabu Standing,* 2575–2465 B.C.E.** *Relaxed portraits of men and women expressing affection for each other were not uncommon in any period of Egyptian art. (The Metropolitan Museum of Art, Rogers Fund, 1948 [48.111]. All rights reserved, The Metropolitan Museum of Art)*

or phrase. William Kelly Simpson's translations were chosen for this anthology for their readability and liveliness as well as for their acknowledgment of gaps and difficulties in the text. Two other editions of ancient Egyptian love lyrics are notable for their modernity, but they also embellish on the originals. The following translations of the conclusion to Poem 20 from *The Songs of Papyrus Harris 500* are a good example of how different the rendering can be. The first is Simpson's, the second is by Ezra Pound and Noel Stock, and the last by John L. Foster.

> Then I'll go into the water at your bidding,
> and I'll come out to you with a red fish

Under the Nineteenth and Twentieth Dynasties there burst forth into flower a vigorous literature, written in the new language, which we call New Egyptian . . . their productions have now a more lively tone than they had in the old epoch. And this liveliness is, moreover, characteristic of the literature of this period; men saw the world as it is and took a pleasure in it.

– William Kelly Simpson, historian, 1972

who will be happy in my fingers . . .
So come and look me over.

Let us admit, I find you attractive
I swim away, but soon I'm back,
Splashing, chattering,
Any excuse at all to join your party.

Look! a redfish flashed through my fingers!
You'll see it better
If you come over here,
Hear me.

Couldn't I coax you to wade in with me?
    Let the cool creep slowly around us?
Then I'd dive deep down
    And come up for you dripping,
Let you fill your eyes
    With the little red fish that I'd catch.

And I'd say, standing there tall in the shadows:
Look at my fish, love,
    how it lies in my hand,
How my fingers caress it,
    slip down its sides . . .

But then I'd say softer,
    eyes bright with your seeing:
        A gift, love. No words.
    Come closer and
        look, it's all me.

■ CONNECTIONS

Song of Songs, p. 208. Love lyrics often make use of sensuous imagery to create a passionate atmosphere. How is the sensuous imagery in Egyptian lyrics similar to the erotic imagery in the biblical Song of Songs? How do the uses of plant and animal imagery contribute to the passion of the love lyrics?

Courtly Love Lyrics (Book 2). In order to evoke depth of feeling, romantic love is sometimes compared to a sickness or a wound. What instances of the theme of love as a sickness or an obsession can you find in Egyptian love lyrics and the courtly love lyrics of France and Spain?

***Book of Songs*, p. 1573.** Are there similarities between the love poems written from the point of view of a woman in ancient Egypt and China?

Li Po, poems (Book 2). Poems written about human passion often employ a language of excess, extravagant metaphors, hyperbole. How do the poems of Li Po and Egyptian love lyrics approach excess?

■ FURTHER RESEARCH

Literary Texts

Erman, Adolf. *The Ancient Egyptians: A Sourcebook of Their Writings.* 1927, 1966.
Foster, John L. *Love Songs of Ancient Egypt.* 1992.

———. *Hymns, Prayers, and Songs: An Anthology of Ancient Egyptian Lyric Poetry.* 1995.
Lichtheim, Miriam. *Ancient Egyptian Literature: A Book of Readings.* 3 vols. 1973.
Parkinson, R. B., ed. and trans. The Tale of Sinuhe *and Other Ancient Egyptian Poems: 1940–1640 BC.* 1997.
Pound, Ezra, and Noel Stock. *Love Poems of Ancient Egypt.* 1962.
Simpson, William Kelly, ed. *The Literature of Ancient Egypt: An Anthology of Stories, Instructions, and Poetry.* 1972.

Historical and Cultural Background
Fox, Michael V. *The Song of Songs and the Ancient Egyptian Love Songs.* 1985.
Shafer, B. E., ed. *Religion in Ancient Egypt: Gods, Myths and Personal Practice.* 1991.

■ PRONUNCIATION

Ankh-Tawy: ahngk-TAH-wee
Khor: KORE
Kush: KOOSH
Nefertum: neh-fehr-TOOM, NEF-ehr-toom
Ptah: PTAH
Sekmet: SEK-met

Egyptian Love Poems

Translated by William Kelly Simpson

1: If I am [not] with you, where will you set your heart?

. . . .
If I am [not] with you, where will you set your heart?
If you do [not] embrace [me], [where will you go?]
If good fortune comes your way, [you still cannot find] happiness.
But if you try to touch my thighs and breasts,
[Then you'll be satisfied.]

Egyptian Love Poems. The poems "If I am [not] with you, where will you set your heart?"; "My love for you is mixed"; "My heart is not yet happy with your love"; "I sail downstream in the ferry"; "My god, my [lover . . .]"; "I embrace her"; and "I wish I were her washerman" are from *Papyrus Harris 500* (London) and were written in the Nineteenth or Twentieth Dynasty (c. 1290–1078 B.C.E.). "Seven days have passed" and "Please come quick to the lady love," from *Papyrus Chester Beatty I* (British Museum), are from the same time period.

A note on the translation: About the following poems, translator William Kelly Simpson comments: "Some of the manuscripts are particularly difficult . . . and in cases I have intentionally adopted rather personal, idiosyncratic renderings. . . ." The translator has used the following conventions to indicate problems with the text: "Brackets are employed for text which has been restored when there is a gap in the manuscript, and half brackets when the word or phrase is uncertain or imperfectly understood; three dots are used when the gap cannot be filled with any degree of certainty and represent an omission of indeterminate length . . . angle brackets are used for words which the copiest erroneously omitted. . . ." Unless otherwise indicated, the footnotes are the editors'.

Because you remember you are hungry
  would you then leave?
Are you a man
  thinking only of his stomach?
Would you [walk off from me
  concerned with] your stylish clothes
and leave me the sheet?

Because of hunger
  would you then leave me?
  [or because you are thirsty?]
Take then my breast:
  for you its gift overflows.
Better indeed is one day in your arms . . .
  than a hundred thousand [anywhere] on earth.

2: My love for you is mixed throughout my body

My love for you is mixed throughout my body
like [salt] dipped in water,
like a medicine to which gum is added,
like milk shot through [water] . . .

So hurry to see your lady,
like a stallion on the track,
or like a falcon [swooping down] to its papyrus marsh.

Heaven sends down the love of her
as a flame falls in the ⌜hay⌝ . . .
. . . .

4: My heart is not yet happy with your love

My heart is not yet happy with your love,
my wolf cub, so be lascivious unto drunkenness.

Yet I will not leave it unless sticks beat me off
to dally in the Delta marshes
or <driven> to the land of Khor with cudgels and maces
to the land of Kush[1] with palm switches

---

[1] **Khor . . . Kush:** Khor is the region of Syria and Palestine; Kush is Nubia, the southern area south of the First Cataract at Aswan. (Translator's note.)

to the highground with staves
to the lowland with rushes.

So I'll not heed their arguments
to leave off needing you.

5: I SAIL DOWNSTREAM IN THE FERRY BY ⌜THE PULL OF THE CURRENT⌝

I sail downstream in the ferry by ⌜the pull of the current⌝,
my bundle of reeds in my arms.
I'll be at Ankh-towy,[2]
and say to Ptah,[3] the lord of truth,
give me my girl tonight.

The sea is wine,
Ptah its reeds,
Sekhmet its ⌜kelp⌝,
the Dew Goddess its buds,
Nefertum[4] its lotus flower.

[The Golden Goddess] rejoices
and the land grows bright at her beauty.
For Memphis is a flask of mandrake wine
placed before the good-looking god.[5]

20: MY GOD, MY [LOVER . . .]

My god, my [lover . . .]
it is pleasant to go to the [canal]
. . . .
and to bathe in your presence.
I shall let [you see . . .] my perfection
in a garment of royal linen, wet [and clinging].

Then I'll go into the water at your bidding,
and I'll come out to you with a red fish

[2] **Ankh-towy:** "Life of the Two Lands," a designation for Memphis or a part of it. (Translator's note.)

[3] **Ptah:** The creator-god of Memphis; essentially, he plays the same role as Atum and Re at Heliopolis.

[4] **Sekhmet . . . Nerfertum:** Sekhmet, a lion-headed goddess, and Nefertum, the god on the lotus, are also Memphite deities. (Translator's note.)

[5] **[The Golden . . . god:** The Golden Goddess is Hathor; in many ways she is the patron goddess of women. The phrase "good-looking god," lit. "beautiful of countenance," applies to Ptah. (Translator's note.)

who will be happy in my fingers . . .
So come and look me over.

23: I embrace her

I embrace her,
and her arms open wide,
I am like a man in Punt,[6]
like someone overwhelmed with drugs.
I kiss her,
her lips open,
and I am drunk
without a beer.

26: I wish I were her washerman

I wish I were her washerman,
if only for a single month,
then I would be [entranced],
washing out the Moringa oils
in her diaphanous garments . . .

37: Seven days have passed, and I've not seen my lady love

Seven days have passed, and I've not seen my lady love;
a sickness has shot through me.
I have become sluggish,
I have forgotten my own body.

If the best surgeons come to me,
my heart will not be comforted with their remedies.
And the prescription sellers, there's no help through them;
my sickness will not be cut out.

Telling me "she's come" is what will bring me back to life.
It's only her name which will raise me up.
It's the coming and going of her letters
which will bring my heart to life.

To me the lady love is more remedial than any potion;
she's better than the whole Compendium.

---

[6] **Punt:** A romantic, mysterious place on the east coast of Africa invoked in love poems.

My only salvation is her coming inside.
Seeing her, then I'm well.

When she opens her eyes my body is young,
when she speaks I'll grow strong,
when I embrace her she drives off evil from me.
But by now the days of her absence amount to Seven.

40: Please come quick to the lady love

Please come quick to the lady love
like a gazelle
running in the desert
its feet are wounded
its limbs are exhausted
fear penetrates its body

the hunters are after it
the hounds are with them
they cannot see
because of the dust

its sees its rest place like a ⌜mirage⌝
it takes a canal as its road.

Before you have kissed your hand four times,
you shall have reached her hideaway
as you chase the lady love.
For it is the Golden Goddess
who has set her aside for you, friend.

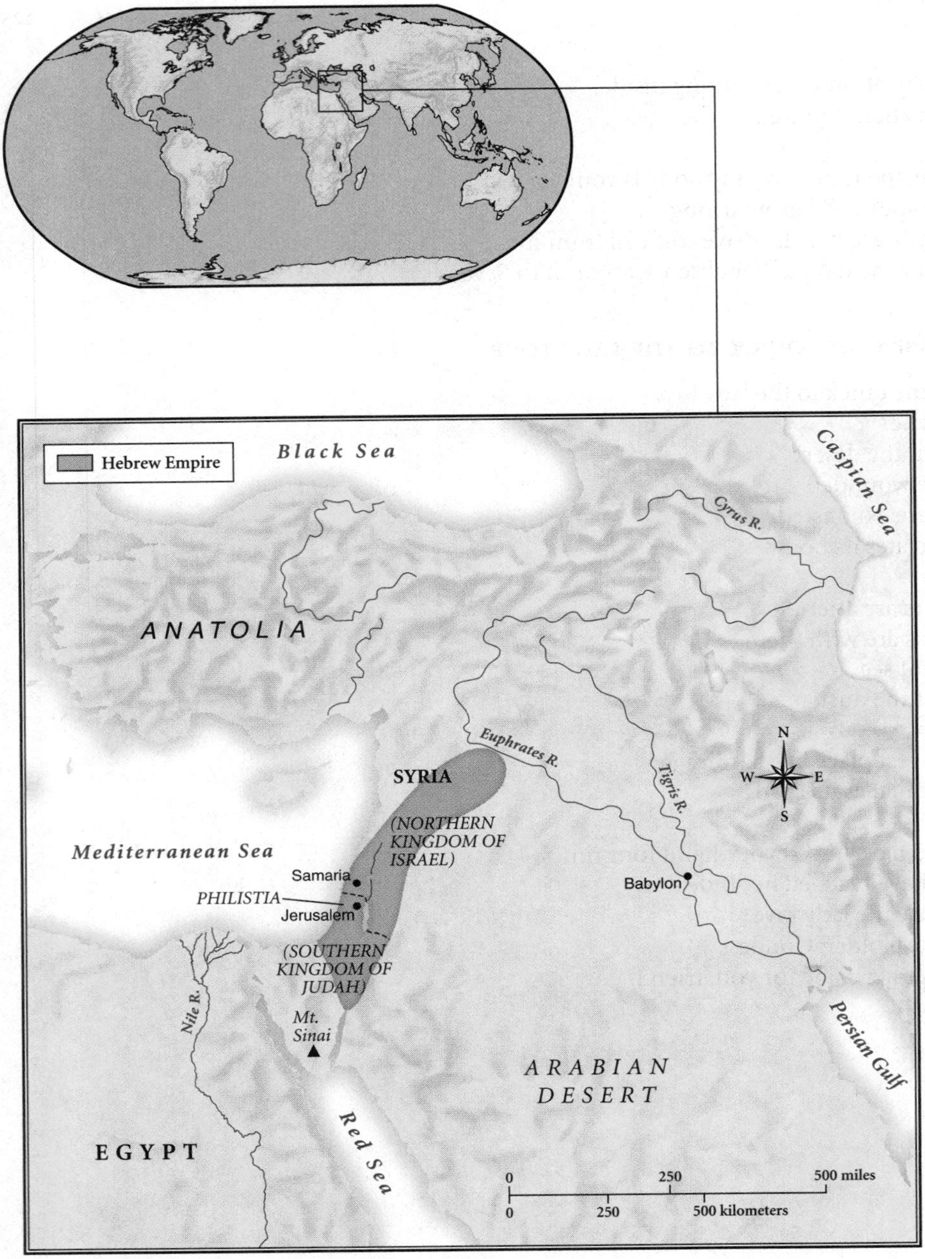

Israel and Judah

King Solomon ruled Israel from 960 to 922 B.C.E. *This "Golden Age of Israel" was prosperous and peaceful. After Solomon's death, however, the kingdom was divided into two states, Israel in the north and Judah in the south. Israel vanished as a political entity in 722* B.C.E.*, and its peoples were dispersed throughout the Near East. In 597* B.C.E. *Judah was conquered by King Nebuchadnezzar of Babylon, and in 586* B.C.E. *most of the Jewish survivors were deported to Babylon, becoming the first diaspora community.*

THE ANCIENT HEBREWS

The Path of Righteousness and the Ten Commandments

The history of the ancient Hebrews is the story of the Hebrews' search for God's blessings and their transformation from a nomadic, tribal people into a settled kingdom in Palestine. For hundreds of years, Israel was caught between Egypt's and Mesopotamia's struggles for control of Palestine (a narrow strip of land, 150 miles long and 70 miles wide, between the eastern end of the Mediterranean Sea and the inland deserts), enduring a mixture of victories and defeats. Eventually, they were exiled. Throughout this time, Israel's poets, priests, and prophets assembled the Hebrew Scriptures—what Christians refer to as the Old Testament—a remarkable collection of history, religion, and literature. If the heroic outlook of the Greeks and Romans celebrated the human potential of individuals in their grandiose and often tragic confrontation with destiny, the great poets and prophets of Israel continually recast the material world in terms of its spiritual destiny, its relationship to a transcendent authority, and the human capacity for righteousness and blessings. From the nation of Israel came a consciousness of personal morality, a code of ethics based on allegiance to a single deity and an awareness of divine purpose in history.

THE EXODUS AND THE TEN COMMANDMENTS

Early in the second millennium B.C.E., nomadic tribes of Hebrews followed the Fertile Crescent southward through Palestine to Egypt, where they were enslaved by the Egyptians sometime between c. 1500–1300 B.C.E. According to Hebrew Scripture, God (referred to by the letters YHWH and known as Yahweh) reveals himself to Moses telling Moses to free his people from slavery. Under Moses' guidance, the Hebrews escape from Egypt about 1250 B.C.E. and cross the Sinai Desert to Mt. Sinai, where they receive the spiritual and legal foundation of their religion in the form of the Ten Commandments. Prepared for conquest, they journey to the land of Canaan (also known as Palestine), invade towns and villages, and

Sacrifice of Isaac, **Mosaic Pavement from the Beth-Alpha Synagogue, Hefzibah, early sixth century**
One of the most important stories in Hebrew Scriptures tells of the near sacrifice of Isaac by his father, the Hebrew patriarch Abraham. Ordered by God to murder his son, Abraham prepares to do so before he is stopped by the hand of God and rewarded for his willingness to perform the ultimate sacrifice. (Z. Radovan, Jerusalem)

eventually settle down. Yahweh proved to be a fierce partisan; he was wrathful whether dealing with Hebrew backsliders at Mt. Sinai, Sodom and Gomorrah, or the Canaanite enemy. For the next five hundred years or so—until the time of military defeat and exile in 586 B.C.E.—the religion of Mt. Sinai and the polytheistic practices of the indigenous religion, the Canaanite religion of Baal and Ashtorath, struggled for supremacy within the Israelite community. Hebrew scriptures record a number of times when Canaanite elements had to be purged from the religion of Yahweh.

DAVID, SOLOMON, AND A KINGDOM DIVIDED

The twelfth and eleventh centuries B.C.E. were a time of warfare when Hebrew military leaders, called judges, arose. These leaders defended various groups against invasion and then played a unifying, political role in the region. Substantial progress toward national unity was made by Saul, the first king of Israel (c. 1020 B.C.E.),

***Samuel Anoints David,* Wall Painting from Dura Europos, early fourth century**
King David united the tribes of Israel, founding a dynasty and creating the first successful Jewish kingdom. (Z. Radovan, Jerusalem)

when the people banded together in the face of their common enemy, the Philistines. Credit for finally creating a united kingdom, however, is given to David, who reigned from c. 1000 to 960 B.C.E. King David consolidated his rule through military victories and by establishing Jerusalem as Israel's national capital, but like Saul's, David's life was tragically marred by rebellion and personal conflicts—a pattern that harkens back to the Book of Genesis. Solomon's reign, from 960 to 922 B.C.E., the Golden Age of Israel, was a time of peace and prosperity. At this time the Israelites fortified their cities and built a magnificent temple in Jerusalem, where the worship of Yahweh was centered.

When Solomon died, the kingdom was divided into a large northern state of Israel, with a capital at Shechem, and a small southern state of Judah. Caught in the middle of the rivalry between Egypt and Assyria, the northern kingdom—Israel—disappeared in 722 B.C.E., its former inhabitants becoming the "Ten Lost Tribes" of Israel. In 621 B.C.E. Josiah became king of Judah and, discovering the Book of Deuteronomy during a temple renovation, instituted broad religious reforms, such as the destruction of pagan shrines and the reinstitution of Passover, in accordance with its instructions. Nebuchadnezzar of Babylon established control over the region by defeating Egypt in 605 B.C.E. Unwise successors to Josiah rebelled against

Babylonian rule, and Nebuchadnezzar defeated Jerusalem in 587 B.C.E., burning buildings and leveling the Temple. Jewish survivors were deported to Babylon, the start of a long succession of Jewish settlements outside of Palestine known by the Greek term ***DIASPORA***, meaning dispersion.

FOREIGN OCCUPATION

After the Persian king Cyrus captured Babylon in 539 B.C.E., he allowed the Hebrews in captivity, now referred to as Jews, to return to Jerusalem in 538 B.C.E.; meanwhile a number of outsiders, like the Persians, the Greeks, and the Ptolemies, ruled the region. When the Syrian king Antiochus IV (175–163 B.C.E.) attempted to force the Jews to accept **HELLENISTIC** culture—Greek language, art, and religion—the Jews answered with the Maccabeean Revolt (167–160 B.C.E.) and, victorious, enjoyed some independence during the next hundred years, until 64 B.C.E. when Pompey annexed Syria, and Palestine came under the control of the Romans. Herod the Great, a builder who renovated the Temple in Jerusalem, was made king of Judea (the Greco-Roman name for Judah) in 37 B.C.E. by Octavius Caesar. When Herod died in 4 B.C.E., Judea was split up into three portions, provinces governed by procurators who answered directly to the emperor. Pontius Pilate, the procurator of Judea from 26–36 C.E., condemned the Jewish teacher, Jesus of Nazareth, to death.

The Jews and their council of elders, the Sanhedrin, were granted a great degree of self-governance until the ascension of the Roman emperor Caligula in 37 C.E. Sanctioning persecution of the Jews, Caligula had his own image hung in the Temple in Jerusalem. Unrest eventually led to a Jewish revolt in 66 C.E., to which Rome responded under Emperor Vespasian and his son General Titus by destroying Jerusalem in 70 C.E., ending that city's role as a religious center for 1900 years. After the Council at Jamnia in 90 C.E., when Jewish rabbis decided on the contents of the Hebrew Scriptures, one further revolt against Rome took place under the leadership of Simon bar Kochba in 135 C.E. The Jews, who were defeated, were forbidden to set foot in Jerusalem, and the province of Judea was renamed Palestine.

BIBLICAL LITERATURE

Outside of Judaism, the Hebrew Scriptures are usually included in the Bible, from the Greek *biblia,* meaning "little books," under the title of "Old Testament." The Bible is indeed a collection of little books: thirty-nine in the Old Testament and twenty-seven in the New Testament. The classification "Old Testament" is a Christian one that divides the Bible into the "old" covenant between God and his people and the "new" covenant (New Testament) established by Jesus with his followers.

For religious Jews, there is still only one covenant. What Christians call the Old Testament, Jews call Tanach (***Tanak***) a word whose consonants stand for the three major groups of books in the Hebrew Bible: the Torah (the Law), the Nebi'im (the Prophets), and the Ketubim (the Writings).

As the all-time best-seller and the most translated book in the world—translated into most of the written languages on earth—the Bible is probably the single most influential book in Western history. As a history of ancient Judaism and early Christianity the Bible covers a period of about two thousand years, and for approximately two millennia the Bible, with its belief in a Father-God, its code of ethics, its attitude toward women, its view of history, and its prophecies for the future, has had an impact on all aspects of Western society. Although science has challenged the truth of certain portions of the Bible, it remains the basic religious document for about fifteen million Jews and for some two billion Christians throughout the world today. The Hebrew Scriptures are also a foundation document for Islam, which has approximately 1.2 billion followers. In addition to its influence on religion, the Bible as a literary document has had a pervasive influence on Western writing: from Dante's *Divine Comedy* and Chaucer's *Canterbury Tales* in the Middle Ages to the twentieth-century poetry of T. S. Eliot and W. H. Auden and the novels of William Faulkner and Toni Morrison.

AUTHORSHIP

The authorship of the Hebrew Scriptures was once thought a simple matter. Some scholars, even into the twentieth century, thought that Moses wrote the Torah and the Book of Job, Joshua wrote the Book of Joshua, and Samuel wrote Samuel, Judges, and Ruth—in other words, that the names of the biblical books roughly indicated their authorship. But over the years textual scholars have noted stylistic differences, inconsistencies, and chronological oddities in the writings. A basic inconsistency, for example, is found in the first two creation stories in Genesis, in which the Hebrew names for God differ: His name in the first creation story (Genesis 1:1–2:3) is *Elohim;* His names, plural, in the second creation story, beginning with Genesis 2:4, are *Yahweh* and *Yahweh Elohim.* In the nineteenth century a document theory arose that stated that four major historical narrations were combined by editors to constitute the Torah, or Pentateuch (meaning "first five books"), as well as the Books of Joshua, Samuel, and Kings: the "J" document originating around 900 B.C.E.; the "E" document, from around 700 B.C.E.; the "D" document, from around 650 B.C.E.; and the "P" document, from around 500 B.C.E. These various strands were joined together and officially recognized around 400 B.C.E. by Ezra, a postexilic Jewish priest, or the school of Ezra. The entire Hebrew Bible was finally canonized at the Council of Jamnia, 90 C.E., when an official list of books was selected by religious leaders to be the official Jewish Scripture or Bible.

The Hebrew Scriptures comprise a wide variety of literature originally written primarily in Hebrew. The written Hebrew language was derived from the Phoenicians who, between 1500 and 1000 B.C.E., had created a new syllabary out of the syllabic Egyptian signs, about thirty in number, dropping all Egyptian logograms. The Hebrews adopted a version of the Phoenician system c. 1000 B.C.E., when they began to record their literature, a collection of myths, folk tales, history, poetry, drama, short stories, biographies, philosophy, and prophecies. This system was later replaced by a newer script called "square writing," after the square shape of its letters. The Book of Genesis, which acts as a foundation for the rest of the Bible, describes the creation of the world, the adventures of the first humans, and the nomadic wanderings of the Hebrew patriarchs in myth, folklore, and legend. Through poetry and histories, the Book of Exodus portrays the struggles of the Hebrews as they escape slavery, survive their crossing of the desert, and reach the Promised Land. The Book of Joshua documents the Hebrews' invasion and conquering of Canaanite settlements.

A number of biblical stories have become part of the cultural heritage of the West: Adam and Eve in the Garden of Eden, Noah and his ark, Joseph and his brothers. Stories about King David deal with his courage against Goliath, his friendship for Jonathan, and his indiscretions with Bathsheba. Whereas works of Western literature are almost always attributed to an individual author, the literature of the Hebrew Bible often seems the work of a collective voice, a community's songs and stories that tell about its sufferings, dreams, and joys. It is not a single hero who escapes the clutches of Egyptian slave masters but a whole people who assume heroic stature on their journey to the Promised Land. And even when an individual such as Job is speaking, the forceful debate of an entire intellectual community that has wrestled with the issues of God's justice and the meaning of suffering can be heard. Lyric poetry, which appears throughout the Bible, celebrates victories and laments sorrows. The Psalms remain the primary collection of biblical lyric poetry, but the Song of Songs is a masterpiece of image and metaphor that evokes the passion of love. The Book of Job is the one biblical work that resembles Greek drama. Both the Greeks and the Hebrews saw a world made up of conflict, adventure, and war, but focusing on obedience to God, the Hebrews participated in a spiritual odyssey with religious earnestness and conscience.

WWW For more information about the culture and context of Hebrews in the ancient world, see *World Literature Online* at bedfordstmartins.com/worldlit.

TIME AND PLACE

The Ancient Hebrews: The Great Temple

The great Temple in Jerusalem was King Solomon's (r. 960 to 922 B.C.E.) crowning achievement and the Hebrews' premier religious monument. Its construction marked a period of unprecedented growth and prosperity. Decorated with gold leaf—a striking symbol of Israel's wealth and political power—the Temple was the house of the Hebrew god, Yahweh, and the home of the Ark of the Covenant, the revered chest that reputedly contained the stones on which were inscribed the Ten Commandments.

***Bronze Calf, twelfth century** B.C.E.* *When Moses descended from Mt. Sinai, where he had received the Ten Commandments, he found the Hebrews venerating a golden calf. He destroyed the calf and banned the worship of foreign idols forever. (Z. Radovan, Jerusalem)*

The Hebrews, as chronicled in their scriptures, had endured a long history of hardship and slavery and had never had the opportunity to rule themselves. That history came to an end in 1020 B.C.E. with the rise of King Saul and King David. David united the disparate Hebrew tribes, creating the first Hebrew nation in 1000 B.C.E. David's unification of the Hebrew peoples—accomplished by unifying Israel and Judah—created the first nation the Hebrews could call their own. It was in this nation that the Temple was built. The building of the Temple by David's son, Solomon, solidified and symbolized the new, united nation of Israel.

The Temple was destroyed by Babylonians four hundred years later, in 587 B.C.E. For a time, Judaism (the religion of the Jews) became centered more around the Hebrew Scriptures than temple rituals and the calendar for prescribed sacrifices. A second temple was built on the site of the first seventy years later. It was to survive for more than five hundred years. Jerusalem was eventually taken over by Rome, and Herod the Great, king of Judea (40–4 B.C.E.) even reconstructed and built an elaborate third temple. Under Roman rule, however, the Jews were more and more distrusted. One complaint had to do with the Temple itself, which was criticized for its bald display of wealth. Even Jesus disapproved of the proliferation of gold and the materialism that had enveloped the Temple.

The Third Temple was destroyed in 70 C.E., coinciding with the expulsion of the Hebrews from Jerusalem. The ruins of the Temple came to symbolize the dispersion of the Hebrew people all over the world, the Jewish Diaspora. The Temple is still invoked today as a symbol of lost nationhood. On the site where it once was now stands one of the most sacred sites in the Muslim world, the Dome of the Rock.

Hebrew Scriptures

c. 900–100 B.C.E.

The National Epic. The first five books of the Hebrew Bible, the most important portion of the Scriptures to Orthodox Jews, are called the Pentateuch or the Torah (the Law). The Torah was originally divided into books because in its entirety it was too long for a single roll of papyrus or parchment. The most important writer of this section is identified as "J," so named because he uses Jahweh (Yahweh) for God's name. This author constructed a national epic that begins with the creation of the world and the lives of the first humans in Genesis 2:5. Using the folk materials of his day, "J" tells the story of how humans were tempted by a talking snake and rebelled against Yahweh, causing him to curse the natural world, inflict pain on women in childbirth, and drive these first ancestors out of Eden. He describes the founding of the Hebrews' tribal identity under a series of patriarchs and chronicles this people's escape from Egyptian bondage under a heroic leader called Moses. After receiving an ethical code from their god on Mt. Sinai, the Hebrews triumphantly enter the land of Canaan, which had been promised to their first patriarch, Abraham. With its central themes of obedience, rebellion, and reconciliation, this story became the founding story of the nation of Israel and of the Jews, in the same way that the Trojan War story for the Greeks and the story of Aeneas for the Romans were founding tales. Herman Wouk in *This is My God* summarizes this theme for Judaism:

> The Hebrew Bible read as living literature is a tragic epic with a single long plot: the tale of the fall of a hero through his weaknesses. The hero is Israel, a people given a destiny almost too high for human beings, the charge of God's law. . . . Unlike all other epic tragedies, it does not end in death. The hero has eternal life, and the prospect of ages of pain in which to rise at long last to the destiny which he cannot escape.

Through a variety of literatures—myth, history, poetry, drama, biography, philosophy, and prophecy—the Hebrew Scriptures record a people's struggle to understand the all-powerful, complex, and seemingly contradictory deity Yahweh and to live up to the terms of a series of agreements or covenants with Him. On one hand Yahweh is a god of violence and destruction, wiping out cities, flooding the world, demanding death without mercy for his enemies. On the other, He is a giving deity, as revealed in the terms of the covenant: In return for His peoples' obedience, faithfulness, and loyalty, He will bestow blessings on the chosen ones of Israel. Yahweh is very much like a stern but loving father who both reprimands and rewards his children.

WWW For quizzes on the Hebrew Scriptures, see *World Literature Online* at bedfordstmartins .com/worldlit.

The Jewish focus on Yahweh, on monotheism, and on a comprehensive code of ethics was shaped by Hebrew poets and prophets and formulated into basic concepts that influenced Western civilization.

Moses Guiding the Hebrews
Detail from a late Roman sarcophagus. (The Art Archive / Archaeological Museum Naples / Dagli Orti)

Genesis. The first book of the Hebrew Scriptures divides into two parts: primeval history (chapters 1–11) and patriarchal tales (chapters 12–50). It begins with the origins of heaven and earth, the first humans, the beginnings of sin and death, the first murder, the Flood, and the Tower of Babel. The materials of this portion of the Book of Genesis are called myth or folklore by some scholars, not because they are considered false but because they deal with God and human relationships in a timeless, prehistorical manner and share similarities with the creation stories of other cultures in the ancient Near East. The Babylonian flood story from the second millennium B.C.E., in particular, helped shape the biblical version.

Early biblical stories contain truths about human nature and have been studied seriously for their lessons about families and nations.

Patriarchs. The second part of Genesis begins in Chapter 12, with stories of tribal fathers, rivalry between brothers, and conflict between fathers and sons. Scholars tend to interpret these legendary stories of the patriarchs Abraham, Isaac, Jacob, and Joseph as histories of whole clans or tribes over a period of some six hundred years, c. 2000–1400 B.C.E. They believe the patriarchal patterns of conflict within these biblical tribal families parallel the rivalries among the Semitic tribes of nomads

Many readers feel that the Book of Job is the literary masterpiece of the Bible. A poem, a drama, a philosophical debate, it fits into no clearly defined category. Yet it is the work of a great artist.

–JOSEPH FRANK, critic, 1963

who were migrating from the Arabian peninsula into the Fertile Crescent and formulating their religion and culture during this time period. The writer of those biblical stories stresses the unique identity of the Hebrews, their having been chosen by a personal deity who entered into a series of covenants with the founding fathers and promised them a prosperous future.

According to Hebrew Scriptures, Abraham, the first patriarch, came from Ur of the Chaldees, an ancient Sumerian city in Mesopotamia, sometime around 2000 B.C.E. His journey apparently represents the movement of Amorites into the southern portion of Canaan (the land of Palestine). The stories about Abraham and his descendants are full of twists and unexpected ironies: Concubines assist their own sons in the competition for the patriarchal inheritance, Jacob wins a wrestling match with an angel, and Joseph shows his brilliance interpreting dreams and managing an empire.

In 1700 B.C.E. a number of Canaanite and Amorite tribes moved farther on, to Egypt, where they were known as Hyksos (foreign chiefs). The migration of Joseph and his brothers southward into Egypt mirrors this historical event. Egyptians eventually enslaved the Hyksos interlopers, a fact to which the story of the Hebrew slaves at the beginning of the Book of Exodus may allude.

Exodus. The Book of Exodus describes the emergence of the extraordinary leader Moses, the historical founder of Judaism and the person primarily responsible for the transition of the Hebrew people from a tribal to a national culture. Moses is believed to have led his people out of slavery in Egypt sometime in the thirteenth century B.C.E., during the Nineteenth Dynasty ruled by the famous pharaohs Seti (1308–1290 B.C.E.) and Ramses II (1292–1225 B.C.E.). The song of Miriam, dating from the thirteenth century B.C.E., celebrates a victory over the Egyptian chariots and is probably the oldest piece of literature in the Bible.

I will sing unto the Lord, for he hath triumphed gloriously:
The horse and his rider hath he thrown into the sea.

During the forty years of crossing the Sinai Desert (the exact route is uncertain), Moses prepared his people for settling down in Canaan—the Promised Land—by transforming tribal groups with various deities into a more or less unified group under the worship of a single God, Yahweh. Moses provided the Israelites with a fundamental religious code, as symbolized by the receiving of the Ten Commandments at Mt. Sinai and detailed in the books of Leviticus and Deuteronomy. This code, influenced by the Code of Hammurabi[1] and the Hittite legal system, circumscribed the Hebrews' sacred calling as the chosen people of Yahweh and provided them with a legal foundation for communal life and, eventually, nationhood.

The Book of Joshua, named after the successor to Moses, concludes

[1] **Code of Hammurabi:** An elaborate body of laws that King Hammurabi (r. 1792–1750 B.C.E.) used to sustain his Babylonian empire. (See p. 229.)

the "J" epic with the migration of the Hebrews into Canaan and an idealized description of absolute victories over Canaanite towns. Yahweh's origin as a tribal deity is revealed in Deuteronomy (chapters 6, 7, and 20), in which Yahweh prescribes ruthless treatment for defeated populations. Overall, the Hebrews' Exodus story—from slavery to migration to arrival in the Promised Land—served as an inspirational model and narrative pattern for later Christians and Jews as well as a symbol of hope for numerous groups throughout history who were living in bondage.

The Bible, once thought of as a source of secular literature yet somehow apart from it, now bids fair to become part of the literary canon . . . Indeed, it seems we have reached a turning point in the history of criticism, for the Bible, under a new aspect, has reoccupied the literary culture.

– Robert Alter and Frank Kermode, critics, 1987

Job. The Book of Job is considered one of the great masterpieces of Western literature, although its literary form is difficult to classify. Victor Hugo, the nineteenth-century French poet and novelist, proclaimed that "the Book of Job is perhaps the greatest masterpiece of the human mind."

Dating probably from the sixth century B.C.E., Job is a series of dialogues on the nature of God and divine justice. Even though, in general, the book belongs to the wisdom tradition of the ancient Near East, it is unusual in that it calls into question the validity of the conventional wisdom that a good, pious person will ultimately be rewarded in this lifetime (with a large family and material prosperity) while an evil person will be punished. The problem with the conventional wisdom is simply that experience provides contradictory evidence: Some good or innocent people suffer; some evil people prosper.

It is around this basic issue of cosmic justice that the author of Job creates his debate, which is framed by prose folk material from an earlier age. The book begins with a description of Job, a righteous man, and a discussion in a fictional land between God and Satan—the "accuser"—who wonders whether Job's piety depends on his wealth. Job is then put to a test. When he is finally deprived of all the good things of his life, including his health, Job complains to God about his treatment, and three friends respond in the first cycle of speeches. His friends, in effect, reaffirm conventional wisdom, which argues that God is just and that Job must have sinned in order to have deserved his suffering.

As Job reaffirms his innocence and becomes increasingly isolated in his position, he demands that he be allowed to make his case in person and hear God's response. The climax arrives when God breaks his silence and responds in a whirlwind to Job's request with a discourse on power. The meaning and appropriateness of God's response have been subjects of discussion ever since. Because God does not answer Job's questions directly, it appears as if the author of the Book of Job understands faith to involve a transcendent deity whose connection to this world cannot be readily understood or experienced by human beings, even exemplary ones.

Psalms. The word *psalm* means a song sung to a harp, indicating that the Book of Psalms, made up of 150 poems, was originally a hymnbook for temple services and for private prayers and meditations. Martin Luther[2]

[2] **Martin Luther:** Luther (1483–1546 C.E.) was the father of the Lutheran Reformation in the fifteenth century; he also translated the Bible into German and composed hymns in German that brought religious literature to ordinary people.

[The purpose of the Old Testament] is to record the Hebrews' continuous quest for God — his nature, his will, and his plans — as a basis for the teaching of divine law and morality. Every mood and every condition of human life — sorrow, joy, loneliness, companionship, love, hate, conspiracy, falsehood, truth, loyalty, heroism, cowardice, war, peace, kindness, brutality, hunger, luxury — all are depicted in simple, direct terms as part of the divine stream of history, teaching the lessons of the past as admonitions, sermons, and guides for all who will listen.

– Buckner B. Trawick, critic, 1970

used psalms to create his hymnbook and Johann Sebastian Bach[3] set a number of psalms to music. The verses in the Book of Psalms are known for their concrete imagery and emotional sincerity.

Although as many as seventy-three psalms have been ascribed to David, the authorship of most, probably written after the Babylonian captivity, between 400 and 100 B.C.E., is unknown. There are various types of psalms: royal psalms, associated with enthronement and the kingship of God; psalms of praise and thanksgiving; psalms of lament and confession.

Psalm 23, "The Lord is my shepherd," with its lyric beauty and comforting message, may be the most well known psalm of all. Psalm 104, "Bless the Lord, my soul," a creation hymn, has often been compared with the Egyptian "Hymn to Aten" and the Mesopotamian "Epic of Creation." Psalm 137, "By the rivers of Babylon we sat down and wept," is a lament the people of Israel sang in exile in Babylon after the destruction of Jerusalem by the Babylonians in 587 B.C.E.

Song of Songs. Because of its rather explicit sexual imagery, the Song of Songs is an unusual book to include in a collection of religious writings. It appears to have been integrated in Jewish Scripture at the end of the first century C.E. as an allegory of the love of God for the Israelites: King Solomon represented God, the Shulamite represented the Hebrews, and the love was spiritual rather than carnal. Early Christians interpreted the courtship songs as poetic expressions of the love of Christ for his Church, called the bride of Christ in the New Testament. Anthropologists have suggested that the songs are adaptations of pagan fertility ceremonies, like the annual wedding of the Babylonian Tammuz to the goddess Ishtar in the spring, the Egyptian ceremonies involving Osiris and Isis, and the Syrian rites between Adonis and Astarte. In a related interpretation, sociologists see the Song of Songs as a description of an ancient Far Eastern wedding celebration involving a week-long pageant of song and dance. Whatever its influences or origins, there is no doubt as to the richness of the imagery and symbolism in the Song of Songs or its passionate and energetic expression of attraction.

The New English Bible. The New English Bible, from which the following selections are taken, does not enjoy the literary reputation of the earlier King James Version, of 1611, which influenced numerous English writers and was brought to the United States by Pilgrims and carried westward by American pioneers. But it is an unusually clear and readable Bible. Back in 1947 the Church of Scotland, the Church of England, and the Methodist, Baptist, and Congregational Churches organized a committee to oversee a new translation of the Bible, one that would incorporate modern scholarship and use a contemporary idiom rather than the traditional "biblical" English. The translation of the New Testament was published in 1961; the Old Testament and the Apocrypha were published in 1970.

[3] **Johann Sebastian Bach** (1685–1750): German organist and composer.

■ CONNECTIONS

***Epic of Creation*, p. 44; "Creating the World and Defeating Apophis," p. 109; "Indra Slays the Dragon Vritra," p. 1338.** Stories in which male gods create the cosmos differ in their use of metaphors: a Mesopotamian creation story tells of a male deity bringing the world into being through combat; an Egyptian god does so by masturbating; and male Indian gods resort to a variety of methods ranging from combat to thought. In chapter one of the Book of Genesis, God creates the world through speech, and in chapter two the deity is comparable to a potter in his formation of the first man. How are these modes of creation either appropriate or inappropriate for a patriarchal god?

"Hymn to Aten," p. 114. Because of the close proximity of the countries in the Fertile Crescent, a region that stretches from present-day Iraq to Egypt, the literatures of the area influenced one another. How is Psalm 104 in the Hebrew Scriptures similar to the Egyptian "Hymn to Aten"? How are their images of the sun and rich imagery from the natural world similar or different?

***Book of Songs*, p. 1573.** The legendary histories of ancient cultures often feature strong and wise patriarchs who provide models or paradigms for succeeding generations. The Chinese *Book of Songs* contains poems that describe the storied patriarchs of China; what are the characteristics of the Hebrew patriarchs found in the Book of Genesis and how are these men similar to Chinese patriarchs?

John Milton, *Paradise Lost* (Book 3). Creation stories almost universally depict the appearance of the first man and the first woman. The story of Adam and Eve in the Book of Genesis is probably the most famous of these in the Western world. How is Milton's rendering of humans' first sin different from the account in Genesis?

■ FURTHER RESEARCH

History and Background

Anderson, Bernhard. *Understanding the Old Testament.* 1986.

Armstrong, Karen. *A History of God: The 4000-Year Quest of Judaism, Christianity and Islam.* 1993.

Buttrick, George A. et al., eds., *The Interpreter's Dictionary of the Bible.* 1962, 1976. (5 vols.)

———. *The Interpreter's Bible.* 1952. (12 vols.)

Kaufmann, Yehezkel. *The Religion of Israel: From Its Beginnings to the Babylonian Exile.* 1961.

Smith, Mark S. *The Early History of God: Yahweh and the Other Deities in Ancient Israel.* 1990.

The Bible as Literature

Alter, Robert, and Frank Kermode. *The Literary Guide to the Bible.* 1987.

Chase, Mary Ellen. *The Bible and the Common Reader.* 1952.

Frye, Northrop. *The Great Code: The Bible and Literature.* 1982.

Harris, Stephen L. *Understanding the Bible.* 1992.

Moulton, Richard G. *A Short Introduction to the Literature of the Bible.* 1903.

Trawick, Buckner B. *The Bible as Literature: The Old Testament and the Apocrapha.* 1970. Part of the Barnes & Noble Outline Series.

Approaches and Commentary

Fromm, Erich. *You Shall Be As Gods: A Radical Interpretation of the Old Testament and Its Tradition.* 1966.

Kushner, Harold S. *When Bad Things Happen to Good People.* 1981.

Terrien, Samuel. *The Psalms and Their Meaning Today.* 1952.

Genesis

The Creation of the World[1]

1

1, 2 In the beginning of creation, when God made heaven and earth, the earth was
without form and void, with darkness over the face of the abyss,[2] and a mighty wind[3]
3 that swept over the surface of the waters. God said, 'Let there be light,' and there was
4, 5 light; and God saw that the light was good, and he separated light from darkness. He
called the light day, and the darkness night. So evening[4] came, and morning came,
the first day.

6 God said, 'Let there be a vault[5] between the waters, to separate water from water.'
7 So God made the vault, and separated the water under the vault from the water
8 above it, and so it was; and God called the vault heaven. Evening came, and morning
came, a second day.

9 God said, 'Let the waters under heaven be gathered into one place, so that dry
10 land may appear'; and so it was. God called the dry land earth, and the gathering of
11 the waters he called seas; and God saw that it was good. Then God said, 'Let the earth
produce fresh growth, let there be on the earth plants bearing seed, fruit-trees bear-
12 ing fruit each with seed according to its kind.' So it was; the earth yielded fresh
growth, plants bearing seed according to their kind and trees bearing fruit each with
13 seed according to its kind; and God saw that it was good. Evening came, and morning
came, a third day.

14 God said, 'Let there be lights[6] in the vault of heaven to separate day from night,
15 and let them serve as signs both for festivals and for seasons and years. Let them also

---

The Book of Genesis. According to modern scholarship the stories in the Book of Genesis were written and edited between 900 and 500 B.C.E. Chapters 1 through 11, which have been called the Mythological Cycle, include two accounts of creation as well as stories of the Fall of man, the first murder, a great deluge, and the Tower of Babel. These stories have influenced modern ideas about gender roles, the origins of sin or evil, the relationship of God to humans and to nature, the idea of estrangement from Eden, and the human yearning for paradise. The legends of the four patriarchs in the second half of Genesis explore family relationships and Yahweh's role in setting a direction for the nation of Israel.

Unless otherwise indicated all the footnotes have been adapted from the Oxford Study Edition of the New English Bible.

---

[1] **World:** Genesis 1–2.4 is a creation account composed by priests. Order evolves from chaos by divine command, followed by God's resting.

[2] **abyss:** In ancient Near Eastern thought, the sea, personified as a dragon, fathered [or gave birth to] the great sea serpents.

[3] **wind:** In non-Hebrew epics, the wind god was the creator. Here, however, the sea and wind are portrayed as creations, subject to God.

[4] **evening:** Day began at sundown and hence the order given here.

[5] **vault:** A solid dome retaining the upper waters whence the rains come.

[6] **lights:** Israel's neighbors regarded celestial bodies as deities. Here, they are mere results of God's creation.

16 shine in the vault of heaven to give light on earth.' So it was; God made the two great
lights, the greater to govern the day and the lesser to govern the night; and with them
17 he made the stars. God put these lights in the vault of heaven to give light on earth,
18 to govern day and night, and to separate light from darkness; and God saw that it
19 was good. Evening came, and morning came, a fourth day.
20 God said, 'Let the waters teem with countless living creatures, and let birds fly
21 above the earth across the vault of heaven.' God then created the great sea-monsters
and all living creatures that move and swarm in the waters, according to their kind,
22 and every kind of bird; and God saw that it was good. So he blessed them and said,
'Be fruitful and increase, fill the waters of the seas; and let the birds increase on land.'
23 Evening came, and morning came, a fifth day.
24 God said, 'Let the earth bring forth living creatures, according to their kind:
25 cattle, reptiles, and wild animals, all according to their kind.' So it was; God made
wild animals, cattle, and all reptiles, each according to its kind; and he saw that it was
26 good. Then God said, 'Let us[7] make man in our image and likeness to rule the fish in
the sea, the birds of heaven, the cattle, all wild animals on earth, and all reptiles that
27 crawl upon the earth.' So God created man in his own image; in the image of God he
28 created him; male and female he created them. God blessed them and said to them,
'Be fruitful and increase, fill the earth and subdue it,[8] rule over the fish in the sea, the
29 birds of heaven, and every living thing that moves upon the earth.' God also said, 'I
give you all plants that bear seed everywhere on earth, and every tree bearing fruit
30 which yields seed: They shall be yours for food. All green plants I give for food to the
wild animals, to all the birds of heaven, and to all reptiles on earth, every living crea-
31 ture.' So it was; and God saw all that he had made, and it was very good. Evening
came, and morning came, a sixth day.

2

1, 2 Thus heaven and earth were completed with all their mighty throng. On the
sixth day God completed all the work he had been doing, and on the seventh day he
3 ceased from all his work. God blessed the seventh day and made it holy, because on
that day he ceased from all the work he had set himself to do.
4 This is the story of the making of heaven and earth when they were created.

The Beginnings of History[9]

5 When the Lord God[10] made earth and heaven, there was neither shrub nor
plant growing wild upon the earth, because the Lord God had sent no rain on the

---

[7] **us:** The plural *us* may be a majestic plural, or else refer to the minor divine beings thought to surround God, like the courtiers of a human king.

[8] **subdue it:** To *subdue* the earth is to be free from nature's tyranny and from idolizing mere objects. [The meaning of *subdue* has troubled ecologists, especially if *subdue* means "willful dominance and exploitation." Editor's note.]

[9] **History:** Genesis 2.5–3.24 is a second account of primeval time. This account is generally regarded as more ancient than 1.1–2.4.

[10] **Lord God:** A compound designation [Yahweh God or Yahweh Elohim] largely confined to this section.

6 earth; nor was there any man to till the ground. A flood[11] used to rise out of the earth
7 and water all the surface of the ground. Then the LORD God formed a man from the
dust of the ground[12] and breathed into his nostrils the breath of life. Thus the man
8 became a living creature. Then the LORD God planted a garden in Eden[13] away to the
9 east, and there he put the man whom he had formed. The LORD God made trees
spring from the ground, all trees pleasant to look at and good for food; and in the
middle of the garden he set the tree of life[14] and the tree of the knowledge of good
and evil.

10 There was a river flowing from Eden to water the garden, and when it left the
11 garden it branched into four streams. The name of the first is Pishon, that is the river
12 which encircles all the land of Havilah, where the gold is. The gold of that land is
13 good; bdellium and cornelians are also to be found there. The name of the second
14 river is Gihon; this is the one which encircles all the land of Cush.[15] The name of the
third is Tigris; this is the river which runs east of Asshur. The fourth river is the
Euphrates.[16]

15 The LORD God took the man and put him in the garden of Eden to till it and
16, 17 care for it. He told the man, 'You may eat from every tree in the garden, but not from
the tree of the knowledge of good and evil; for on the day that you eat from it, you
18 will certainly die.' Then the LORD God said, 'It is not good for the man to be alone. I
19 will provide a partner for him.' So God formed out of the ground all the wild animals and all the birds of heaven. He brought them to the man to see what he would
20 call them, and whatever the man called each living creature, that was its name. Thus
the man gave names to all cattle, to the birds of heaven, and to every wild animal; but
21 for the man himself no partner had yet been found. And so the LORD God put the
man into a trance, and while he slept, he took one of his ribs[17] and closed the flesh
22 over the place. The LORD God then built up the rib, which he had taken out of the
23 man, into a woman. He brought her to the man, and the man said:

'Now this, at last—
bone from my bones,
flesh from my flesh!—

---

[11] **flood:** The earth was thought to be suspended upon the abyss which could break through with great force.

[12] **ground:** A pun here links man and earth; the Hebrew for "man" is *adam,* the Hebrew for "ground" is *adamah.*

[13] **Eden:** Originally not a place name, it means "plain," "steppe," and is equivalent to "delight." In some other Near Eastern cultures, the gods inhabit a fertile garden; most often it lies in the east where the life-giving sun rises.

[14] **tree of life:** The notion that immortality could be attained by eating a magic plant is found elsewhere in the ancient world.

[15] **Cush:** The land of the Kassites, to the east, in Mesopotamia.

[16] **Euphrates:** The headwaters of the Tigris and Euphrates were sacred to the Assyrians. The other two of the four "original" rivers are unknown.

[17] **ribs:** The selection of the rib may be the result of borrowing a pun from the ancient Sumerians; the same word means both "rib" and "to make alive" in Sumerian.

this shall be called woman,
for from man was this taken.'[18]

24 That is why a man leaves his father and mother and is united to his wife, and the
25 two become one flesh.[19] Now they were both naked, the man and his wife, but they
had no feeling of shame towards one another.

3

1 The serpent[20] was more crafty than any wild creature that LORD God had made.
He said to the woman, 'Is it true that God has forbidden you to eat from any tree in
2 the garden?' The woman answered the serpent, 'We may eat the fruit of any tree in
3 the garden, except for the tree in the middle of the garden; God has forbidden us
4 either to eat or to touch the fruit of that; if we do, we shall die.' The serpent said, 'Of
5 course you will not die. God knows that as soon as you eat it, your eyes will be
6 opened and you will be like gods knowing both good and evil.' When the woman saw
that the fruit of the tree was good to eat, and that it was pleasing to the eye and tempting to contemplate, she took some and ate it. She also gave her husband some and he
7 ate it. Then the eyes of both of them were opened and they discovered that they were
naked; so they stitched fig-leaves together and made themselves loincloths.
8 The man and his wife heard the sound of the LORD God walking in the garden at
the time of the evening breeze and hid from the LORD God among the trees of the
9 garden. But the LORD God called to the man and said to him, 'Where are you?' He
10 replied, 'I heard the sound as you were walking in the garden, and I was afraid
11 because I was naked, and I hid myself.' God answered, 'Who told you that you were
12 naked? Have you eaten from the tree which I forbade you?' The man said, 'The
woman you gave me for a companion, she gave me fruit from the tree and I ate it.'
13 Then the LORD God said to the woman, 'What is this that you have done?' The woman
14 said, 'The serpent tricked me, and I ate.' Then the LORD God said to the serpent:

'Because you have done this you are accursed
more than all cattle and all wild creatures.
On your belly you shall crawl, and dust you shall eat
all the days of your life.
15 I will put enmity between you and the woman,
between your brood and hers.
They shall strike at your head,
and you shall strike at their heel.'

---

[18] **man:** Another Hebrew word for "man," *ish* (compare note 12), is used to distinguish him from "woman," *ishshah.* [Editors' note.]

[19] **one flesh:** Sex is not regarded as evil here, but as a God-given impulse. [Editors' note.]

[20] **serpent:** An ancient extrabiblical story, the Mesopotamian *Epic of Gilgamesh,* tells how a serpent stole the plant which would have given immortality to humans. It was believed that when the snake shed his skin, he was rejuvenated. The idea of the serpent as a primeval adversary of God, or as the Devil, arose much later; so too the fixing of blame on the woman arose at a much later time.

16 To the woman he said:

'I will increase your labour and your groaning,
and in labour you shall bear children.
You shall be eager for your husband,
and he shall be your master.'

17 And to the man he said:

'Because you have listened to your wife
and have eaten from the tree which I forbade you,
accursed shall be the ground on your account.
With labour you shall win your food from it
all the days of your life.
18 It will grow thorns and thistles for you,
none but wild plants for you to eat.
19 You shall gain your bread by the sweat of your brow
until you return to the ground;
for from it you were taken.
Dust you are, to dust you shall return.'[21]

20, 21 The man called his wife Eve[22] because she was the mother of all who live. The
22 LORD God made tunics of skins for Adam[23] and his wife and clothed them. He said,
'The man has become like one of us, knowing good and evil; what if he now reaches
23 out his hand and takes fruit from the tree of life also, eats it and lives for ever?' So the
LORD God drove him out of the garden of Eden to till the ground from which he had
24 been taken. He cast him out, and to the east of the garden of Eden he stationed the
cherubim[24] and a sword whirling and flashing to guard the way to the tree of life.

CAIN AND ABEL: THE FIRST MURDER

4

1 The man lay with his wife Eve, and she conceived and gave birth to Cain. She
2 said, 'With the help of the LORD I have brought a man into being.' Afterwards she
had another child, his brother Abel.[25] Abel was a shepherd and Cain a tiller of the
3 soil. The day came when Cain brought some of the produce of the soil as a gift to the
4 LORD; and Abel brought some of the first-born of his flock, the fat portions of them.
5 The LORD received Abel and his gift with favour; but Cain and his gift he did not
6 receive. Cain was very angry and his face fell. Then the LORD said to Cain, 'Why are
you so angry and cast down?

[21] **return:** Verses 14–19 contain a series of originally independent folk explanations: Why is mankind hostile to serpents? Why is childbirth painful? Why is woman's social position subordinate? Why must man work?

[22] **Eve:** That is, *life;* see note 17.

[23] **Adam:** The word "man" occurs here for the first time without the definite article, becoming a name.

[24] **cherubim:** Winged semidivine creatures, half human and half lion, often the guardians of sacred areas.

[25] **Abel:** *Cain,* "smith" or "metallurgist," and *Abel,* "herdsman," may personify a culture conflict between the settled farmer and the seminomadic shepherd.

7 If you do well, you are accepted;
if not, sin is a demon crouching at the door.
It shall be eager for you, and you will be mastered by it.'

8 Cain said to his brother Abel, 'Let us go into the open country.' While they were
9 there, Cain attacked his brother Abel and murdered him. Then the LORD said to
Cain, 'Where is your brother Abel?' Cain answered, 'I do not know. Am I my
10 brother's keeper?' The LORD said, 'What have you done? Hark! your brother's blood[26]
11 that has been shed is crying out to me from the ground. Now you are accursed, and
banished from the ground which has opened its mouth wide to receive your
12 brother's blood, which you have shed. When you till the ground, it will no longer
13 yield you its wealth. You shall be a vagrant and a wanderer on earth.' Cain said to the
14 LORD, 'My punishment is heavier than I can bear; thou hast driven me today from
the ground, and I must hide myself from thy presence. I shall be a vagrant and a
15 wanderer on earth, and anyone who meets me can kill me.' The LORD answered him,
'No: if anyone kills Cain, Cain shall be avenged sevenfold.' So the LORD put a mark[27]
16 on Cain, in order that anyone meeting him should not kill him. Then Cain went out
from the LORD's presence and settled in the land of Nod to the east of Eden. [. . .]

THE FLOOD

6

1 When mankind began to increase and to spread all over the earth and daughters
2 were born to them, the sons of the gods[28] saw that the daughters of men were beauti-
3 ful; so they took for themselves such women as they chose. But the LORD said, 'My
life-giving spirit shall not remain in man for ever; he for his part is mortal flesh: he
shall live for a hundred and twenty years.'

4 In those days, when the sons of the gods had intercourse with the daughters of
men and got children by them, the Nephilim[29] were on earth. They were the heroes
of old, men of renown.

5 When the LORD saw that man had done much evil on earth and that his
6 thoughts and inclinations were always evil, he was sorry that he had made man on
7 earth, and he was grieved at heart. He said, 'This race of men whom I have created, I
will wipe them off the face of the earth—man and beast, reptiles and birds. I am
8 sorry that I ever made them.' But Noah had won the LORD's favour.[30]

[26] **blood:** Regarded as the seat of the life-force.

[27] **mark:** Devotees of deities wore distinctive emblems. Cain is designated here as a ward of the Lord.

[28] **sons of the gods:** Verses 1–4 are an ancient fragment, a folk explanation for a race of giants. It is used here to illustrate man's growing wickedness, to explain the decreasing lifespan, and to set the stage for the deluge. "Sons of the gods" is a term of Canaanite origin for members of the pantheon ("assembly of the gods").

[29] **Nephilim:** Giants.

[30] **favour:** God's judgment takes the form of a punishing flood, while preserving a remnant through which a new beginning can take place. The story was adapted from the Babylonian *Epic of Gilgamesh,* itself possibly the "explanation" of a local but catastrophic flood in the Tigris-Euphrates Valley.

9 This is the story of Noah. Noah was a righteous man, the one blameless man of
10, 11 his time; he walked with God. He had three sons, Shem, Ham and Japheth. Now God
12 saw that the whole world was corrupt and full of violence. In his sight the world had
13 become corrupted, for all men had lived corrupt lives on earth. God said to Noah,
'The loathsomeness of all mankind has become plain to me, for through them the
14 earth is full of violence. I intend to destroy them, and the earth with them. Make
yourself an ark with ribs of cypress; cover it with reeds and coat it inside and out
15 with pitch. This is to be its plan: the length of the ark shall be three hundred cubits,[31]
16 its breadth fifty cubits, and its height thirty cubits. You shall make a roof for the ark,
giving it a fall of one cubit when complete; and put a door in the side of the ark, and
17 build three decks, upper, middle, and lower. I intend to bring the waters of the flood
over the earth to destroy every human being under heaven that has the spirit of life;
18 everything on earth shall perish. But with you I will make a covenant, and you shall
19 go into the ark, you and your sons, your wife and your sons' wives with you. And you
shall bring living creatures of every kind into the ark to keep them alive with you,
20 two of each kind, a male and a female; two of every kind of bird, beast, and reptile,
21 shall come to you to be kept alive. See that you take and store every kind of food that
22 can be eaten; this shall be food for you and for them.' Exactly as God had commanded him, so Noah did.

7

1 The LORD said to Noah, 'Go into the ark, you and all your household; for I have
2 seen that you alone are righteous before me in this generation. Take with you seven
pairs, male and female, of all beasts that are ritually clean, and one pair, male and
3 female, of all beasts that are not clean; also seven pairs, male and female, of every
4 bird—to ensure that life continues on earth. In seven days' time I will send rain over
the earth for forty days and forty nights, and I will wipe off the face of the earth
5 every living thing that I have made.' Noah did all that the LORD had commanded
6 him. He was six hundred years old when the waters of the flood came upon the
earth.

7 And so, to escape the waters of the flood, Noah went into the ark with his sons,
8 his wife, and his sons' wives. And into the ark with Noah went one pair, male and
female, of all beasts, clean and unclean, of birds and of everything that crawls on the
9, 10 ground, two by two, as God had commanded. Towards the end of the seven days the
11 waters of the flood came upon the earth. In the year when Noah was six hundred
years old, on the seventeenth day of the second month, on that very day, all the
12 springs of the great abyss broke through, the windows[32] of the sky were opened, and
13 rain fell on the earth for forty days and forty nights. On that very day Noah entered
the ark with his sons, Shem, Ham and Japheth, his own wife, and his three sons'
14 wives. Wild animals of every kind, cattle of every kind, reptiles of every kind that
15 move upon the ground, and birds of every kind—all came to Noah in the ark, two

[31] **cubits:** Modern estimates of the Hebrew cubit range from 12 to 25.2 inches.

[32] **windows:** The earth was threatened with a return to the pre-creation chaos.

16 by two of all creatures that had life in them. Those which came were one male and
one female of all living things; they came in as God had commanded Noah, and the
17 LORD closed the door on him. The flood continued upon the earth for forty days,
and the waters swelled and lifted up the ark so that it rose high above the ground.
18 They swelled and increased over the earth, and the ark floated on the surface of the
19 waters. More and more the waters increased over the earth until they covered all the
20 high mountains everywhere under heaven. The waters increased and the mountains
21 were covered to a depth of fifteen cubits. Every living creature that moves on earth
22 perished, birds, cattle, wild animals, all reptiles, and all mankind. Everything died
23 that had the breath of life in its nostrils, everything on dry land. God wiped out
every living thing that existed on earth, man and beast, reptile and bird; they were all
wiped out over the whole earth, and only Noah and his company in the ark survived.
24 When the waters had increased over the earth for a hundred and fifty days,[33]

8

1 God thought of Noah and all the wild animals and the cattle with him in the
2 ark, and he made a wind pass over the earth, and the waters began to subside. The
springs of the abyss were stopped up, and so were the windows of the sky; the down-
3 pour from the skies was checked. The water gradually receded from the earth, and by
4 the end of a hundred and fifty days it had disappeared. On the seventeenth day of the
5 seventh month the ark grounded on a mountain in Ararat.[34] The water continued to
recede until the tenth month, and on the first day of the tenth month the tops of the
mountains could be seen.
6, 7 After forty days Noah opened the trap-door that he had made in the ark, and
released a raven to see whether the water had subsided, but the bird continued flying
8 to and fro until the water on the earth had dried up. Noah waited for seven days, and
then released a dove from the ark to see whether the water on the earth had subsided
9 further. But the dove found no place where she could settle, and so she came back to
him in the ark, because there was water over the whole surface of the earth. Noah
10 stretched out his hand, caught her and took her into the ark. He waited another
11 seven days and again released the dove from the ark. She came back to him towards
evening with a newly plucked olive leaf in her beak. Then Noah knew for certain that
12 the water on the earth had subsided still further. He waited yet another seven days
13 and released the dove, but she never came back. And so it came about that, on the
first day of the first month of his six hundred and first year, the water had dried up
on the earth, and Noah removed the hatch and looked out of the ark. The surface of
the ground was dry.
14, 15 By the twenty-seventh day of the second month the whole earth was dry. And
16 God said to Noah, Come out of the ark, you and your wife, your sons and their
17 wives. Bring out every living creature that is with you, live things of every kind, bird

[33] **a hundred and fifty days:** This precise number may reflect an effort to bind the events to a liturgical calendar.

[34] **Ararat:** A region of upper Mesopotamia.

and beast and every reptile that moves on the ground, and let them swarm over the
18 earth and be fruitful and increase there.' So Noah came out with his sons, his wife,
19 and his sons' wives. Every wild animal, all cattle, every bird, and every reptile that
20 moves on the ground, came out of the ark by families. Then Noah built an altar to
the LORD. He took ritually clean beasts and birds of every kind, and offered whole-
21 offerings on the altar. When the LORD smelt the soothing odour, he said within
himself, 'Never again will I curse the ground because of man, however evil his inclinations may be from his youth upwards. I will never again kill every living creature,
as I have just done.

22 While the earth lasts
seedtime and harvest, cold and heat,
summer and winter, day and night,
shall never cease.'

9

1 God blessed Noah and his sons and said to them, 'Be fruitful and increase, and
2 fill the earth. The fear and dread of you shall fall upon all wild animals on earth, on
all birds of heaven, on everything that moves upon the ground and all fish in the sea;
3 they are given into your hands. Every creature that lives and moves shall be food for
4 you;[35] I give you them all, as once I gave you all green plants. But you must not eat
5 the flesh with the life, which is the blood, still in it. And further, for your life-blood I
will demand satisfaction; from every animal I will require it, and from a man also I
will require satisfaction for the death of his fellow-man.

6 He that sheds the blood of a man,
for that man his blood shall be shed;
for in the image of God
has God made man.

7 But you must be fruitful and increase, swarm throughout the earth and rule over it.'
8, 9 God spoke to Noah and to his sons with him: 'I now make my covenant[36] with
10 you and with your descendants after you, and with every living creature that is with
you, all birds and cattle, all the wild animals with you on earth, all that have come
11 out of the ark. I will make my covenant with you: Never again shall all living creatures be destroyed by the waters of the flood, never again shall there be a flood to lay
waste the earth.'
12 God said, 'This is the sign of the covenant which I establish between myself and
you and every living creature with you, to endless generations:

13 My bow[37] I set in the cloud,
sign of the covenant

[35] **for you:** Eating meat is sanctioned but possibly not desirable.

[36] **covenant:** A binding agreement. This covenant involves the whole of humankind; other covenants involve individuals or the Hebrew people.

[37] **bow:** In ancient mythology, the [rain] *bow* was a weapon of the deity and regarded as a sign of victory.

between myself and earth.
14 When I cloud the sky over the earth,
the bow shall be seen in the cloud. [. . .]

The Tower of Babel

11

1 Once upon a time all the world spoke a single language and used the same
2 words. As men journeyed in the east, they came upon a plain in the land of Shinar[38]
3 and settled there. They said to one another, 'Come, let us make bricks and bake them
4 hard'; they used bricks for stone and bitumen for mortar. 'Come,' they said, 'let us
build ourselves a city and a tower[39] with its top in the heavens, and make a name for
5 ourselves; or we shall be dispersed all over the earth.' Then the LORD came down to
6 see the city and tower which mortal men had built, and he said, 'Here they are, one
people with a single language, and now they have started to do this; henceforward
7 nothing they have a mind to do will be beyond their reach. Come, let us go down
there and confuse their speech, so that they will not understand what they say to one
8 another.' So the LORD dispersed them from there all over the earth, and they left off
9 building the city. That is why it is called Babel,[40] because the LORD there made a
babble of the language of all the world; from the place the LORD scattered men all
over the face of the earth. [. . .]

Abraham and Isaac

21

1 The LORD showed favour to Sarah as he had promised, and made good what he
2 had said about her. She conceived and bore a son to Abraham for his old age, at the
3 time which God had appointed. The son whom Sarah bore to him, Abraham named
4 Isaac.[41] When Isaac was eight days old Abraham circumcised him, as God had com-
5, 6 manded. Abraham was a hundred years old when his son Isaac was born. Sarah said,
'God has given me good reason to laugh, and everybody who hears will laugh with
7 me.' She said, 'Whoever would have told Abraham that Sarah would suckle children?
8 Yet I have borne him a son for his old age.' The boy grew and was weaned, and on the
9 day of his weaning Abraham gave a feast. Sarah saw the son whom Hagar the Egyp-
10 tian had borne to Abraham laughing at him, and she said to Abraham, 'Drive out
this slave-girl and her son; I will not have this slave-girl's son sharing the inheritance

---

[38] **Shinar:** Sumeria.

[39] **tower:** The center of the Mesopotamian city was a complex of buildings including a pyramidal temple called a ziggurat, the top of which was a threshold or gate for the heavenly deities.

[40] **Babel:** This term, which for the Babylonians meant "the gate of the gods," is punned on through the verb *balal,* "to confuse," "make babble."

[41] **Isaac:** That is, *He laughed.*

11, 12 with my son Isaac.'[42] Abraham was vexed at this on his son Ishmael's account, but
God said to him, 'Do not be vexed on account of the boy and the slave-girl. Do what
13 Sarah says, because you shall have descendants through Isaac. I will make a great
nation of the slave-girl's son too, because he is your own child.'[43]

14 Abraham rose early in the morning, took some food and a waterskin full of
water and gave it to Hagar; he set the child on her shoulder and sent her away, and
15 she went and wandered in the wilderness of Beersheba. When the water in the skin
16 was finished, she thrust the child under a bush, and went and sat down some way off,
about two bowshots away, for she said, 'How can I watch the child die?' So she sat
17 some way off, weeping bitterly. God heard the child crying, and the angel of God
called from heaven to Hagar, 'What is the matter, Hagar? Do not be afraid: God had
18 heard the child crying where you laid him. Get to your feet, lift the child up and hold
19 him in your arms, because I will make of him a great nation.' Then God opened her
eyes and she saw a well full of water; she went to it, filled her waterskin and gave the
20 child a drink. God was with the child, and he grew up and lived in the wilderness of
21 Paran. He became an archer, and his mother found him a wife from Egypt. [. . .]

22

1 The time came when God put Abraham to the test. 'Abraham', he called and
2 Abraham replied, 'Here I am.' God said, 'Take your son Isaac, your only son, whom
you love, and go to the land of Moriah. There you shall offer him as a sacrifice on one
3 of the hills which I will show you.' So Abraham rose early in the morning and
saddled his ass, and he took with him two of his men and his son Isaac; and he split
4 the firewood for the sacrifice, and set out for the place of which God had spoken. On
5 the third day Abraham looked up and saw the place in the distance. He said to his
men, 'Stay here with the ass while I and the boy go over there; and when we have
6 worshipped we will come back to you.' So Abraham took the wood for the sacrifice
and laid it on his son Isaac's shoulder; he himself carried the fire and the knife, and
7 the two of them went on together. Isaac said to Abraham, 'Father', and he answered,
'What is it, my son?' Isaac said, 'Here are the fire and the wood, but where is the
8 young beast for the sacrifice?' Abraham answered, 'God will provide himself with a
9 young beast for a sacrifice, my son.' And the two of them went on together and came
to the place of which God had spoken. There Abraham built an altar and arranged
the wood. He bound his son Isaac and laid him on the altar on top of the wood.
10, 11 Then he stretched out his hand and took the knife to kill his son; but the angel of the
12 LORD called to him from heaven, 'Abraham, Abraham.' He answered, 'Here I am.' The
angel of the LORD said, 'Do not raise your hand against the boy; do not touch him.
Now I know that you are a God-fearing man. You have not withheld from me your

[42] **my son Isaac:** In chapter 16, when Sarah finds that she cannot bear children, she tells Abraham to father a child by the slave girl Hagar and thus Ishmael was born. Ancient Near Eastern law stipulated that the offspring of a slave wife could either inherit with the children of the free woman or be set free. Sarah demands the latter option.

[43] **child:** The Arab nations.

13 son, your only son.' Abraham looked up, and there he saw a ram caught by its horns
in a thicket.[44] So he went and took the ram and offered it as a sacrifice instead of his
14 son. Abraham named that place Jehovah-jireh; and to this day the saying is: 'In the
15 mountain of the Lord it was provided.' Then the angel of the Lord called from
16 heaven a second time to Abraham, 'This is the word of the Lord: By my own self I
swear: inasmuch as you have done this and have not withheld your son, your only
17 son, I will bless you abundantly and greatly multiply your descendants until they are
as numerous as the stars in the sky and the grains of sand on the sea-shore. Your
18 descendants shall possess the cities of their enemies. All nations on earth shall
pray to be blessed as your descendants are blessed, and this because you have obeyed
me.' [. . .]

Joseph and His Brothers

37

1, 2 So Jacob lived in Canaan, the country in which his father had settled. And this is
the story of the descendants of Jacob.
When Joseph was a boy of seventeen, he used to accompany his brothers, the
sons of Bilhah and Zilpah, his father's wives, when they were in charge of the flock;
3 and he brought their father a bad report of them. Now Israel loved Joseph more than
any other of his sons, because he was a child of his old age, and he made him a long,
4 sleeved robe. When his brothers saw that their father loved him more than any of
them, they hated him and could not say a kind word to him.
5 Joseph had a dream; and when he told it to his brothers, they hated him still
6, 7 more. He said to them, 'Listen to this dream I have had. We were in the field binding
sheaves, and my sheaf rose on end and stood upright, and your sheaves gathered
8 round and bowed low before my sheaf.' His brothers answered him, 'Do you think
you will one day be a king and lord it over us?' and they hated him still more because
9 of his dreams and what he said. He had another dream, which he told to his father
and his brothers. He said, 'Listen: I have had another dream. The sun and moon and
10 eleven stars[45] were bowing down to me.' When he told it to his father and his brothers, his father took him to task: 'What is this dream of yours?' he said. 'Must we come
11 and bow low to the ground before you, I and your mother and your brothers?' His
brothers were jealous of him, but his father did not forget.
12, 13 Joseph's brothers went to mind their father's flocks in Shechem. Israel said to
him, 'Your brothers are minding the flocks in Shechem; come, I will send you to
14 them,' and he said, 'I am ready.' He said to him, 'Go and see if all is well with your
brothers and the sheep, and bring me back word.' So he sent off Joseph from the vale
15 of Hebron and he came to Shechem. A man met him wandering in the open country

[44] **thicket:** The earliest form of this story may have been directed against child sacrifice, proposing that the deity desires the substitution of animals.

[45] **eleven stars:** The zodiac is possibly meant, since the number of constellations in it agrees with that of the members of the tribal league.

16 and asked him what he was looking for. He replied, 'I am looking for my brothers.
17 Tell me, please, where they are minding the flocks.' The man said, 'They have gone
away from here; I heard them speak of going to Dothan.' So Joseph followed his
18 brothers and he found them in Dothan. They saw him in the distance, and before he
19 reached them, they plotted to kill him. They said to each other, 'Here comes that
20 dreamer. Now is our chance; let us kill him and throw him into one of these pits and
say that a wild beast has devoured him. Then we shall see what will come of his
21 dreams.' When Reuben heard, he came to his rescue, urging them not to take his life.
22 'Let us have no bloodshed', he said. 'Throw him into this pit in the wilderness, but do
him no bodily harm.' He meant to save him from them so as to restore him to his
23 father. When Joseph came up to his brothers, they stripped him of the long, sleeved
24 robe which he was wearing, took him and threw him into the pit. The pit was empty
and had no water in it.
25 Then they sat down to eat some food and, looking up, they saw an Ishmaelite
caravan coming in from Gilead on the way down to Egypt, with camels carrying
26 gum tragacanth and balm and myrrh. Judah said to his brothers, 'What shall we gain
27 by killing our brother and concealing his death? Why not sell him to the Ishmaelites?
Let us do him no harm, for he is our brother, our own flesh and blood'; and his
28 brothers agreed with him. Meanwhile some Midianite merchants passed by and
drew Joseph up out of the pit. They sold him for twenty pieces of silver to the Ish-
29 maelites, and they brought Joseph to Egypt.[46] When Reuben went back to the pit,
30 Joseph was not there. He rent his clothes and went back to his brothers and said, 'The
boy is not there. Where can I go?'
31 Joseph's brothers took his robe, killed a goat and dipped it in the goat's blood.
32 Then they tore the robe, the long, sleeved robe, brought it to their father and said,
33 'Look what we have found. Do you recognize it? Is this your son's robe or not?' Jacob
did recognize it, and he replied, 'It is my son's robe. A wild beast has devoured him.
34 Joseph has been torn to pieces.' Jacob rent his clothes, put on sackcloth and mourned
his son for a long time. His sons and daughters all tried to comfort him, but he
35 refused to be comforted. He said, 'I will go to my grave mourning for my son.' Thus
36 Joseph's father wept for him. Meanwhile the Midianites had sold Joseph in Egypt to
Potiphar, one of Pharaoh's eunuchs, the captain of the guard.

39

1 When Joseph was taken down to Egypt, he was bought by Potiphar, one of
Pharaoh's eunuchs, the captain of the guard, an Egyptian. Potiphar bought him
2 from the Ishmaelites who had brought him there. The LORD was with Joseph and he
3 prospered. 'He lived in the house of his Egyptian master, who saw that the LORD was
4 with him and was giving him success in all that he undertook. Thus Joseph found
favour with his master, and he became his personal servant. Indeed, his master put
5 him in charge of his household and entrusted him with all that he had. From the

---

[46] **Egypt:** This material sets the stage for the Egyptian bondage and the exodus led by Moses. Parts of Joseph's story have a very close Egyptian parallel, in "The Story of Two Brothers."

time that he put him in charge of his household and all his property, the LORD
blessed the Egyptian's household for Joseph's sake. The blessing of the LORD was on
6 all that was his in house and field. He left everything he possessed in Joseph's care,
and concerned himself with nothing but the food he ate.
7 Now Joseph was handsome and good-looking, and a time came when his mas-
8 ter's wife took notice of him and said, 'Come and lie with me.' But he refused and
said to her, 'Think of my master. He does not know as much as I do about his own
9 house, and he has entrusted me with all he has. He has given me authority in this
house second only to his own, and has withheld nothing from me except you,
10 because you are his wife. How can I do anything so wicked, and sin against God?' She
kept asking Joseph day after day, but he refused to lie with her and be in her com-
11 pany. One day he came into the house as usual to do his work, when none of the men
12 of the household were there indoors. She caught him by his cloak, saying, 'Come and
13 lie with me', but he left the cloak in her hands and ran out of the house. When she
14 saw that he had left his cloak in her hands and had run out of the house, she called
out to the men of the household, 'Look at this! My husband has brought in a Hebrew
15 to make a mockery of us. He came in here to lie with me, but I gave a loud scream.
16 When he heard me scream and call out, he left his cloak in my hand and ran off.' She
17 kept his cloak with her until his master came home, and then she repeated her tale.
She said, 'That Hebrew slave whom you brought in to make a mockery of me, has
18 been here with me. But when I screamed for help and called out, he left his cloak in
19 my hands and ran off.' When Joseph's master heard his wife's story of what his slave
20 had done to her, he was furious. He took Joseph and put him in the Round Tower,
21 where the king's prisoners were kept; and there he stayed in the Round Tower. But
the LORD was with Joseph and kept faith with him, so that he won the favour of the
22 governor of the Round Tower. He put Joseph in charge of all the prisoners in the
23 tower and of all their work. He ceased to concern himself with anything entrusted to
Joseph, because the LORD was with Joseph and gave him success in everything.

40

1 It happened later that the king's butler and his baker offended their master the
2 king of Egypt. Pharaoh was angry with these two eunuchs, the chief butler and the
3 chief baker, and he put them in custody in the house of the captain of the guard, in
4 the Round Tower where Joseph was imprisoned. The captain of the guard appointed
5 Joseph as their attendant, and he waited on them. One night, when they had been in
prison for some time, they both had dreams, each needing its own interpretation—
the king of Egypt's butler and his baker who were imprisoned in the Round Tower.
6, 7 When Joseph came to them in the morning, he saw that they looked dejected. So he
asked these eunuchs, who were in custody with him in his master's house, why they
8 were so downcast that day. They replied, 'We have each had a dream and there is no
one to interpret it for us.' Joseph said to them, 'Does not interpretation belong to
9 God? Tell me your dreams.' So the chief butler told Joseph his dream: 'In my dream',
10 he said, 'there was a vine in front of me. On the vine there were three branches, and
11 as soon as it budded, it blossomed and its clusters ripened into grapes. Now I had

Pharaoh's cup in my hand, and I plucked the grapes, crushed them into Pharaoh's
12 cup and put the cup into Pharaoh's hand.' Joseph said to him, 'This is the interpreta-
13 tion. The three branches are three days: within three days Pharaoh will raise you and
restore you to your post, and then you will put the cup into Pharaoh's hand as you
14 used to do when you were his butler. But when things go well with you, if you think
of me, keep faith with me and bring my case to Pharaoh's notice and help me to get
15 out of this house. By force I was carried off from the land of the Hebrews, and I have
done nothing here to deserve being put in this dungeon.'

16 When the chief baker saw that Joseph had given a favourable interpretation, he
said to him, 'I too had a dream, and in my dream there were three baskets of white
17 bread on my head. In the top basket there was every kind of food which the baker
prepares for Pharaoh, and the birds were eating out of the top basket on my head.'
18, 19 Joseph answered, 'This is the interpretation. The three baskets are three days: within
three days Pharaoh will raise you and hang you up on a tree, and the birds of the air
will eat your flesh.'

20 The third day was Pharaoh's birthday and he gave a feast for all his servants. He
21 raised the chief butler and the chief baker in the presence of his court. He restored
22 the chief butler to his post, and the butler put the cup into Pharaoh's hand; but he
hanged the chief baker. All went as Joseph had said in interpreting the dreams for
23 them. Even so the chief butler did not remember Joseph, but forgot him.

41

1, 2 Nearly two years later Pharaoh had a dream: he was standing by the Nile, and
there came up from the river seven cows, sleek and fat, and they grazed on the reeds.
3 After them seven other cows came up from the river, gaunt and lean, and stood on
4 the river-bank beside the first cows. The cows that were gaunt and lean devoured the
5 cows that were sleek and fat. Then Pharaoh woke up. He fell asleep again and had a
6 second dream: he saw seven ears of corn, full and ripe, growing on one stalk. Grow-
7 ing up after them were seven other ears, thin and shrivelled by the east wind.[47] The
thin ears swallowed up the ears that were full and ripe. Then Pharaoh woke up and
8 knew that it was a dream. When morning came, Pharaoh was troubled in mind; so
he summoned all the magicians and sages of Egypt. He told them his dreams, but
9 there was no one who could interpret them for him. Then Pharaoh's chief butler
10 spoke up and said, 'It is time for me to recall my faults. Once Pharaoh was angry with
his servants, and he imprisoned me and the chief baker in the house of the captain of
11, 12 the guard. One night we both had dreams, each needing its own interpretation. We
had with us a young Hebrew, a slave of the captain of the guard, and we told him our
dreams and he interpreted them for us, giving each man's dream its own interpreta-
13 tion. Each dream came true as it had been interpreted to us: I was restored to my
position, and he was hanged.'

14 Pharaoh thereupon sent for Joseph, and they hurriedly brought him out of the
15 dungeon. He shaved and changed his clothes, and came in to Pharaoh. Pharaoh said

[47] **east wind:** A seasonal wind *(hamsin)* from the desert which destroys the vegetation.

to him, 'I have had a dream, and no one can interpret it to me. I have heard it said
16 that you can understand and interpret dreams.' Joseph answered, 'Not I, but God,
17 will answer for Pharaoh's welfare.' Then Pharaoh said to Joseph, 'In my dream I was
18 standing on the bank of the Nile, and there came up from the river seven cows, fat
19 and sleek, and they grazed on the reeds. After them seven other cows came up that
were poor, very gaunt and lean; I have never seen such gaunt creatures in all Egypt.
20, 21 These lean, gaunt cows devoured the first cows, the fat ones. They were swallowed
up, but no one could have guessed that they were in the bellies of the others, which
22 looked as gaunt as before. Then I woke up. After I had fallen asleep again, I saw in a
23 dream seven ears of corn, full and ripe, growing on one stalk. Growing up after them
24 were seven other ears, shrivelled, thin, and blighted by the east wind. The thin ears
swallowed up the seven ripe ears. When I told all this to the magicians, no one could
explain it to me.'

25 Joseph said to Pharaoh, 'Pharaoh's dreams are one dream. God has told Pharaoh
26 what he is going to do. The seven good cows are seven years, and the seven good ears
27 of corn are seven years. It is all one dream. The seven lean and gaunt cows that came
up after them are seven years, and the empty ears of corn blighted by the east wind
28 will be seven years of famine. It is as I have said to Pharaoh: God has let Pharaoh see
29 what he is going to do. There are to be seven years of great plenty throughout the
30 land. After them will come seven years of famine; all the years of plenty in Egypt will
31 be forgotten, and the famine will ruin the country. The good years will not be remembered in the land because of the famine that follows; for it will be very severe.
32 The doubling of Pharaoh's dream means that God is already resolved to do this, and
33 he will very soon put it into effect. Pharaoh should now look for a shrewd and intel-
34 ligent man, and put him in charge of the country. This is what Pharaoh should do:
appoint controllers over the land, and take one fifth of the produce of Egypt during
35 the seven years of plenty. They should collect all this food produced in the good
years that are coming and put the corn under Pharaoh's control in store in the cities,
36 and keep it under guard. This food will be a reserve for the country against the seven
years of famine which will come upon Egypt. Thus the country will not be devastated by the famine.'

37, 38 The plan pleased Pharaoh and all his courtiers, and he said to them, 'Can we
39 find a man like this man, one who has the spirit of a god in him?' He said to Joseph,
'Since a god has made all this known to you, there is no one so shrewd and intelligent
40 as you. You shall be in charge of my household, and all my people will depend on
41 your every word. Only my royal throne shall make me greater than you.' Pharaoh
42 said to Joseph, 'I hereby give you authority over the whole land of Egypt.' He took off
his signet-ring[48] and put it on Joseph's finger, he had him dressed in fine linen, and
43 hung a gold chain round his neck. He mounted him in his viceroy's chariot and men
44 cried 'Make way!' before him. Thus Pharaoh made him ruler over all Egypt and said
to him, 'I am the Pharaoh. Without your consent no man shall lift hand or foot
45 throughout Egypt.' Pharaoh named him Zaphenath-paneah, and he gave him as wife

[48] **signet-ring:** The ring would give Pharaoh's authority to Joseph, since it could be used to stamp Pharaoh's "signature."

Asenath the daughter of Potiphera priest of On. And Joseph's authority extended
over the whole of Egypt.
46 Joseph was thirty years old when he entered the service of Pharaoh king of
Egypt. When he took his leave of the king, he made a tour of inspection through the
47, 48 country. During the seven years of plenty there were abundant harvests, and Joseph
gathered all the food produced in Egypt during those years and stored it in the cities,
49 putting in each the food from the surrounding country. He stored the grain in huge
quantities; it was like the sand of the sea, so much that he stopped measuring: it was
beyond all measure.
50 Before the years of famine came, two sons were born to Joseph by Asenath the
51 daughter of Potiphera priest of On. He named the elder Manasseh,[49] 'for,' he said,
52 'God has caused me to forget all my troubles and my father's family.' He named the
second Ephraim,[50] 'for,' he said, 'God has made me fruitful in the land of my hard-
53, 54 ships.' When the seven years of plenty in Egypt came to an end, seven years of famine
began, as Joseph had foretold. There was famine in every country, but throughout
55 Egypt there was bread. So when the famine spread through all Egypt, the people
appealed to Pharaoh for bread, and he ordered them to go to Joseph and do as he
56 told them. In every region there was famine, and Joseph opened all the granaries and
57 sold corn to the Egyptians, for the famine was severe. The whole world came to
Egypt to buy corn from Joseph, so severe was the famine everywhere.

42

1 When Jacob saw that there was corn in Egypt, he said to his sons, 'Why do you
2 stand staring at each other? I have heard that there is corn in Egypt. Go down and
3 buy some so that we may keep ourselves alive and not starve.' So Joseph's brothers,
4 ten of them, went down to buy grain from Egypt, but Jacob did not let Joseph's
brother Benjamin go with them, for fear that he might come to harm.
5 So the sons of Israel came down with everyone else to buy corn, because of the
6 famine in Canaan. Now Joseph was governor of all Egypt, and it was he who sold the
corn to all the people of the land. Joseph's brothers came and bowed to the ground
7 before him, and when he saw his brothers, he recognized them but pretended not to
know them and spoke harshly to them. 'Where do you come from?' he asked. 'From
8 Canaan,' they answered, 'to buy food.' Although Joseph had recognized his brothers,
9 they did not recognize him. He remembered also the dreams he had had about
them; so he said to them, 'You are spies; you have come to spy out the weak points in
10, 11 our defences.' They answered, 'No, sir: your servants have come to buy food. We are
12 all sons of one man. Your humble servants are honest men, we are not spies.' 'No,' he
13 insisted, 'it is to spy out our weaknesses that you have come.' They answered him,
'Sir, there are twelve of us, all brothers, sons of one man in Canaan. The youngest is
14 still with our father, and one has disappeared.' But Joseph said again to them, 'No, as
15 I said before, you are spies. This is how you shall be put to the proof: unless your

[49] **Manasseh:** Causing to forget.

[50] **Ephrain:** Fruit.

youngest brother[51] comes here, by the life of Pharaoh, you shall not leave this place.
16 Send one of your number to bring your brother; the rest will be kept in prison. Thus
your story will be tested, and we shall see whether you are telling the truth. If not,
17 then, by the life of Pharaoh, you must be spies.' So he kept them in prison for three
days.

18 On the third day Joseph said to the brothers, 'Do what I say and your lives will be
19 spared; for I am a God-fearing man: If you are honest men, your brother there shall
20 be kept in prison, and the rest of you shall take corn for your hungry households and
bring your youngest brother to me; thus your words will be proved true, and you will
not die.'

21 They said to one another, 'No doubt we deserve to be punished because of our
brother, whose suffering we saw; for when he pleaded with us we refused to listen.
22 That is why these sufferings have come upon us.' But Reuben said, 'Did I not tell you
not to do the boy a wrong? But you would not listen, and his blood is on our heads,
23 and we must pay. They did not know that Joseph understood, because he had used
24 an interpreter. Joseph turned away from them and wept. Then, turning back, he
25 played a trick on them. First he took Simeon and bound him before their eyes; then
he gave orders to fill their bags with grain, to return each man's silver, putting it in
26 his sack, and to give them supplies for the journey. All this was done; and they loaded
27 the corn on to their asses and went away. When they stopped for the night, one of
them opened his sack to give fodder to his ass, and there he saw his silver at the top of
28 the pack. He said to his brothers, 'My silver has been returned to me, and here it is in
my pack.' Bewildered and trembling, they said to each other, 'What is this that God
has done to us?'

29 When they came to their father Jacob in Canaan, they told him all that had hap-
30 pened to them. They said, 'The man who is lord of the country spoke harshly to us
31 and made out that we were spies. We said to him, "We are honest men, we are not
32 spies. There are twelve of us, all brothers, sons of one father. One has disappeared,
33 and the youngest is with our father in Canaan." This man, the lord of the country,
said to us, "This is how I shall find out if you are honest men. Leave one of your
34 brothers with me, take food for your hungry households and go. Bring your
youngest brother to me, and I shall know that you are not spies, but honest men.
Then I will restore your brother to you, and you can move about the country freely." '
35 But on emptying their sacks, each of them found his silver inside, and when they and
36 their father saw the bundles of silver, they were afraid. Their father Jacob said to
them, 'You have robbed me of my children. Joseph has disappeared; Simeon has dis-
37 appeared; and now you are taking Benjamin. Everything is against me.' Reuben said
to his father, 'You may kill both my sons if I do not bring him back to you. Put him in
38 my charge, and I shall bring him back.' But Jacob said, 'My son shall not go with you,
for his brother is dead and he alone is left. If he comes to any harm on the journey,
you will bring down my grey hairs in sorrow to the grave.'

---

[51] **brother:** Joseph makes his half-brothers uneasy by demanding to see Benjamin, his only full brother.

43

1, 2 The famine was still severe in the country. When they had used up the corn they
had brought from Egypt, their father said to them, 'Go back and buy a little more
3 corn for us to eat.' But Judah replied, 'The man plainly warned us that we must not
4 go into his presence unless our brother was with us. If you let our brother go with us,
5 we will go down and buy food for you. But if you will not let him, we will not go; for
the man said to us, "You shall not come into my presence, unless your brother is with
6 you."' Israel said, 'Why have you treated me so badly? Why did you tell the man that
7 you had yet another brother?' They answered, 'He questioned us closely about ourselves and our family: "Is your father still alive?" he asked, "Have you a brother?", and
we answered his questions. How could we possibly know that he would tell us to
8 bring our brother to Egypt?' Judah said to his father Israel, 'Send the boy with me;
then we can start at once. By doing this we shall save our lives, ours, yours, and our
9 dependants', and none of us will starve. I will go surety for him and you may hold me
responsible. If I do not bring him back and restore him to you, you shall hold me
10 guilty all my life. If we had not wasted all this time, by now we could have gone back
twice over.'

11 Their father Israel said to them, 'If it must be so, then do this: take in your baggage, as a gift for the man, some of the produce for which our country is famous: a
little balsam, a little honey, gum tragacanth, myrrh, pistachio nuts, and almonds.
12 Take double the amount of silver and restore what was returned to you in your
13 packs; perhaps it was a mistake. Take your brother with you and go straight back to
14 the man. May God Almighty make him kindly disposed to you, and may he send
back the one whom you left behind, and Benjamin too. As for me, if I am bereaved,
15 then I am bereaved.' So they took the gift and double the amount of silver, and with
Benjamin they started at once for Egypt, where they presented themselves to Joseph.
16 When Joseph saw Benjamin with them, he said to his steward, 'Bring these men
17 indoors, kill a beast and make dinner ready, for they will eat with me at noon.' He did
18 as Joseph told him and brought the men into the house. When they came in they
were afraid, for they thought, 'We have been brought in here because of that affair of
the silver which was replaced in our packs the first time. He means to trump up
19 some charge against us and victimize us, seize our asses and make us his slaves.' So
20 they approached Joseph's steward and spoke to him at the door of the house. They
21 said, 'Please listen, my lord. After our first visit to buy food, when we reached the
place where we were to spend the night, we opened our packs and each of us found
22 his silver in full weight at the top of his pack. We have brought it back with us, and
have added other silver to buy food. We do not know who put the silver in our packs.'
23 He answered, 'Set your minds at rest; do not be afraid. It was your God, the God of
your father, who hid treasure for you in your packs. I did receive the silver.' Then he
brought Simeon out to them.

24 The steward brought them into Joseph's house and gave them water to wash
25 their feet, and provided fodder for their asses. They had their gifts ready when
26 Joseph arrived at noon, for they had heard that they were to eat there. When Joseph
came into the house, they presented him with the gifts which they had brought,
27 bowing to the ground before him. He asked them how they were and said, 'Is your

28 father well, the old man of whom you spoke? Is he still alive?' They answered, 'Yes,
my lord, our father is still alive and well.' And they bowed low and prostrated them-
29 selves. Joseph looked and saw his own mother's son, his brother Benjamin, and
asked, 'Is this your youngest brother, of whom you told me?', and to Benjamin he
said, 'May God be gracious to you, my son!' Joseph was overcome; his feelings for his
30 brother mastered him, and he was near to tears. So he went into the inner room and
31 wept. Then he washed his face and came out; and, holding back his feelings, he
32 ordered the meal to be served. They served him by himself, and the brothers by
themselves, and the Egyptians who were at dinner were also served separately; for
33 Egyptians hold it an abomination to eat with Hebrews. The brothers were seated in
his presence, the eldest first according to his age and so on down to the youngest:
34 they looked at one another in astonishment. Joseph sent them each a portion from
what was before him, but Benjamin's was five times larger than any of the other portions. Thus they drank with him and all grew merry.

44

1 Joseph gave his steward this order: 'Fill the men's packs with as much food as
2 they can carry and put each man's silver at the top of his pack. And put my goblet,
my silver goblet, at the top of the youngest brother's pack with the silver for the
3 corn.' He did as Joseph said. At daybreak the brothers were allowed to take their asses
4 and go on their journey; but before they had gone very far from the city, Joseph said
to his steward, 'Go after those men at once, and when you catch up with them, say,
5 "Why have you repaid good with evil? Why have you stolen the silver goblet? It is the
one from which my lord drinks, and which he uses for divination. You have done a
6, 7 wicked thing."' When he caught up with them, he repeated all this to them, but they
replied, 'My lord, how can you say such things? No, sir, God forbid that we should do
8 any such thing! You remember the silver we found at the top of our packs? We
brought it back to you from Canaan. Why should we steal silver or gold from your
9 master's house? If any one of us is found with the goblet, he shall die; and, what is
10 more, my lord, we will all become your slaves.' He said, 'Very well, then; I accept what
you say. The man in whose possession it is found shall be my slave, but the rest of
11 you shall go free.' Each man quickly lowered his pack to the ground and opened it.
12 The steward searched them, beginning with the eldest and finishing with the
youngest, and the goblet was found in Benjamin's pack.
13 At this they rent their clothes; then each man loaded his ass and they returned to
14 the city. Joseph was still in the house when Judah and his brothers came in. They
15 threw themselves on the ground before him, and Joseph said, 'What have you done?
16 You might have known that a man like myself would practise divination.' Judah said,
'What shall we say, my lord? What can we say to prove our innocence? God has
found out our sin. Here we are, my lord, ready to be made your slaves, we ourselves
17 as well as the one who was found with the goblet.' Joseph answered, 'God forbid that
I should do such a thing! The one who was found with the goblet shall become my
slave, but the rest of you can go home to your father in peace.'
18 Then Judah went up to him and said, 'Please listen, my lord. Let me say a word

to your lordship, I beg. Do not be angry with me, for you are as great as Pharaoh.
19, 20 You, my lord, asked us whether we had a father or a brother. We answered, "We have
an aged father, and he has a young son born in his old age; this boy's full brother is
dead and he alone is left of his mother's children, he alone, and his father loves him."
21, 22 Your lordship answered, "Bring him down to me so that I may set eyes on him." We
told you, my lord, that the boy could not leave his father, and that his father would
23 die if he left him. But you answered, "Unless your youngest brother comes here with
24 you, you shall not enter my presence again." We went back to your servant our father,
25 and told him what your lordship had said. When our father told us to go and buy
26 food, we answered, "We cannot go down; for without our youngest brother we can-
27 not enter the man's presence; but if our brother is with us, we will go." Our father, my
28 lord, then said to us, "You know that my wife bore me two sons. One left me, and I
29 said, 'He must have been torn to pieces.' I have not seen him to this day. If you take
this one from me as well, and he comes to any harm, then you will bring down my
30 grey hairs in trouble to the grave." Now, my lord, when I return to my father without
31 the boy—and remember, his life is bound up with the boy's—what will happen is
this: he will see that the boy is not with us and will die, and your servants will have
32 brought down our father's grey hairs in sorrow to the grave. Indeed, my lord, it was I
who went surety for the boy to my father. I said, "If I do not bring him back to you,
33 then you shall hold me guilty all my life." Now, my lord, let me remain in place of the
34 boy as your lordship's slave, and let him go with his brothers. How can I return to my
father without the boy? I could not bear to see the misery which my father would
suffer.'

45

1 Joseph could no longer control his feelings in front of his attendants, and he
called out, 'Let everyone leave my presence.' So there was nobody present when
2 Joseph made himself known to his brothers, but so loudly did he weep that the
3 Egyptians and Pharaoh's household heard him. Joseph said to his brothers, 'I am
Joseph; can my father be still alive?' His brothers were so dumbfounded at finding
4 themselves face to face with Joseph that they could not answer. Then Joseph said to
his brothers, 'Come closer', and so they came close. He said, 'I am your brother
5 Joseph whom you sold into Egypt. Now do not be distressed or take it amiss that you
sold me into slavery here; it was God who sent me ahead of you to save men's lives.
6 For there have now been two years of famine in the country, and there will be
7 another five years with neither ploughing nor harvest. God sent me ahead of you to
ensure that you will have descendants on earth, and to preserve you all, a great band
8 of survivors. So it was not you who sent me here, but God, and he has made me a
9 father to Pharaoh, and lord over all his household and ruler of all Egypt. Make haste
and go back to my father and give him this message from his son Joseph: "God has
10 made me lord of all Egypt. Come down to me; do not delay. You shall live in the land
of Goshen and be near me, you, your sons and your grandsons, your flocks and
11 herds and all that you have. I will take care of you there, you and your household and
all that you have, and see that you are not reduced to poverty; there are still five years

12 of famine to come." You can see for yourselves, and so can my brother Benjamin, that
13 it is Joseph himself who is speaking to you. Tell my father of all the honour which I
enjoy in Egypt, tell him all you have seen, and make haste to bring him down here.'
14 Then he threw his arms round his brother Benjamin and wept, and Benjamin too
15 embraced him weeping. He kissed all his brothers and wept over them, and afterwards his brothers talked with him.
16 When the report that Joseph's brothers had come reached Pharaoh's house, he
17 and all his courtiers were pleased. Pharaoh said to Joseph, 'Say to your brothers:
18 "This is what you are to do. Load your beasts and go to Canaan. Fetch your father
and your households and bring them to me. I will give you the best that there is in
19 Egypt, and you shall enjoy the fat of the land."[52] You shall also tell them: "Take wagons from Egypt for your dependants and your wives and fetch your father and come.
20 Have no regrets at leaving your possessions, for all the best that there is in Egypt is
21 yours."' The sons of Israel did as they were told, and Joseph gave them wagons,
22 according to Pharaoh's orders, and food for the journey. He provided each of them
with a change of clothing, but to Benjamin he gave three hundred pieces of silver
23 and five changes of clothing. Moreover he sent his father ten asses carrying the best
that there was in Egypt, and ten she-asses loaded with grain, bread, and provisions
24 for his journey. So he dismissed his brothers, telling them not to quarrel among
25 themselves on the road, and they set out. Thus they went up from Egypt and came to
26 their father Jacob in Canaan. There they gave him the news that Joseph was still alive
27 and that he was ruler of all Egypt. He was stunned and could not believe it, but they
told him all that Joseph had said; and when he saw the wagons which Joseph had
28 sent to take him away, his spirit revived. Israel said, 'It is enough. Joseph my son is
still alive; I will go and see him before I die.'

46

1 So Israel set out with all that he had and came to Beersheba where he offered
2 sacrifices to the God of his father Isaac. God said to Israel in a vision by night, 'Jacob,
3 Jacob', and he answered, 'I am here.' God said, 'I am God, the God of your father. Do
4 not be afraid to go down to Egypt, for there I will make you a great nation. I will go
down with you to Egypt, and I myself will bring you back again without fail; and
5 Joseph shall close your eyes.' So Jacob set out from Beersheba. Israel's sons conveyed
their father Jacob, their dependants, and their wives in the wagons which Pharaoh
6 had sent to carry them. They took the herds and the stock which they had acquired
7 in Canaan and came to Egypt, Jacob and all his descendants with him, his sons and
their sons, his daughters and his sons' daughters: he brought all his descendants to
Egypt. [. . .]

[52] **land:** Ancient Egyptian sources relate the arrival of Asiatic nomads by such means.

Exodus

Moses and the Exodus[1]

11

1 Then the Lord said to Moses, 'One last plague I will bring upon Pharaoh and
Egypt. After that he will let you go; he will send you packing, as a man dismisses
2 a rejected bride. Let the people be told that men and women alike should ask their
3 neighbours for jewellery of silver and gold.' The Lord made the Egyptians well-
disposed towards them, and, moreover, Moses was a very great man in Egypt in the
eyes of Pharaoh's courtiers and of the people.
4 Moses then said, 'These are the words of the Lord: "At midnight I will go out
5 among the Egyptians. Every first-born creature in the land of Egypt shall die: the
first-born of Pharaoh who sits on his throne, the first-born of the slave-girl at the
6 hand-mill, and all the first-born of the cattle. All Egypt will send up a great cry of
anguish, a cry the like of which has never been heard before, nor ever will be again.
7 But among all Israel not a dog's tongue shall be so much as scratched, no man or
beast be hurt." Thus you shall know that the Lord does make a distinction between
8 Egypt and Israel. Then all these courtiers of yours will come down to me, prostrate
themselves and cry, "Go away, you and all the people who follow at your heels." After
that I will go away.' Then Moses left Pharaoh's presence hot with anger.
9 The Lord said to Moses, 'Pharaoh will not listen to you; I will therefore show
10 still more portents in the land of Egypt.' All these portents had Moses and Aaron
shown in the presence of Pharaoh, and yet the Lord made him obstinate, and he did
not let the Israelites leave the country.

The Book of Exodus. The composition of this book, like the Book of Genesis, is dated between 900 and 500 B.C.E.; the date of the exodus of a band or tribe of Hebrews from Egypt is sometime in the thirteenth century B.C.E. The events described in Exodus, which means "going out," establish an "exodus paradigm," a model for peoples yearning to escape bondage and reach a "promised land." Egypt represents the place of persecution or bondage; the Red Sea symbolizes the process of cleansing and rebirth. The wilderness, with its tests and trials, and the Ten Commandments provide reconditioning and direction. Palestine or Canaan symbolizes the goal, the Promised Land. Peoples who have experienced oppression and sought liberation and who knew the Bible have modeled themselves on the Israelites, says Thomas D'Evelyn. "Puritans in seventeenth-century England, black Baptists in the United States in the 1960s, Roman Catholic revolutionaries in Latin America, have all used—and are using—the Exodus story to gain and keep political power." The Mormons, who were persecuted in the East and the Midwest, also made an exodus, to Utah.

---

[1] **Exodus:** The first chapters of the Book of Exodus describe the hardships suffered by the Hebrew slaves and the birth of Moses. As a young man, Moses flees into the Midian desert after killing an Egyptian guard. God appears to Moses in a burning bush, identifies himself, and tells Moses to return to Egypt and lead the Hebrews out of slavery. When Pharaoh refuses to comply with Moses' request, ten plagues are sent against Egypt to force compliance: water turned into blood, frogs, gnats, flies, cattle-sickness, boils, hail, locusts, and darkness. Chapter 11 describes the tenth and last plague.

PASSOVER

12

1, 2 The LORD said to Moses and Aaron in Egypt: This month is for you the first of
3 months; you shall make it the first month of the year.[2] Speak to the whole community of Israel and say to them: On the tenth day of this month let each man take a
4 lamb or a kid[3] for his family, one for each household, but if a household is too small
for one lamb or one kid, then the man and his nearest neighbour may take one
between them. They shall share the cost, taking into account both the number of
5 persons and the amount each of them eats. Your lamb or kid must be without blem-
6 ish, a yearling male. You may take equally a sheep or a goat. You must have it in safe
keeping until the fourteenth day of this month, and then all the assembled commu-
7 nity of Israel shall slaughter the victim between dusk and dark. They must take some
of the blood and smear it on the two doorposts and on the lintel of every house in
8 which they eat the lamb. On that night they shall eat the flesh roast on the fire; they
9 shall eat it with unleavened cakes[4] and bitter herbs. You are not to eat any of it raw or
10 even boiled in water, but roasted, head, shins, and entrails. You shall not leave any of
it till morning; if anything is left over until morning, it must be destroyed by fire.

11 This is the way in which you must eat it: you shall have your belt fastened, your
sandals on your feet and your staff in your hand, and you must eat in urgent haste. It
12 is the LORD's Passover.[5] On that night I shall pass through the land of Egypt and kill
every first-born of man and beast. Thus will I execute judgement, I the LORD, against
13 all the gods of Egypt. And as for you, the blood will be a sign on the houses in which
you are: when I see the blood I will pass over you; the mortal blow shall not touch
you, when I strike the land of Egypt.

14 You shall keep this day as a day of remembrance, and make it a pilgrim-feast, a
festival of the LORD; you shall keep it generation after generation as a rule for all
15 time. For seven days you shall eat unleavened cakes. On the very first day you shall
rid your houses of leaven; from the first day to the seventh anyone who eats leavened
16 bread shall be outlawed from Israel. On the first day there shall be a sacred assembly
and on the seventh day there shall be a sacred assembly: on these days no work shall
be done, except what must be done to provide food for everyone; and that will be
17 allowed. You shall observe these commandments because this was the very day on
which I brought you out of Egypt in your tribal hosts. You shall observe this day
from generation to generation as a rule for all time.

---

[2] **year:** The first month of the year is reckoned as at Passover time, the month of Nisan (March–April), in keeping with the late, postexilic calendar.

[3] **a lamb or a kid:** The annual sacrifice of a lamb or goat at the coming of spring may have had its origins in a pre-Mosaic shepherds' festival, meant both to insure fertility and to preserve the newborn lambs during the nomadic pasturing.

[4] **unleavened cakes:** The festival of unleavened cakes, probably an ancient Canaanite agricultural rite to celebrate the barley harvest, is here joined to the pastoral Passover festival.

[5] **Passover:** The name *Passover,* whose original meaning is uncertain, is now connected with the impending deliverance from Egypt.

18 You shall eat unleavened cakes in the first month from the evening which be-
19 gins the fourteenth day until the evening which begins the twenty-first day. For
seven days no leaven may be found in your houses, for anyone who eats anything
fermented shall be outlawed from the community of Israel, be he foreigner or
20 native. You must eat nothing fermented. Wherever you live you must eat your cakes
unleavened.

21 Moses summoned all the elders of Israel and said to them, 'Go at once and get
22 sheep for your families and slaughter the Passover. Then take a bunch of marjoram,
dip it in the blood in the basin and smear some blood from the basin on the lintel
and the two door-posts. Nobody may go out through the door of his house till
23 morning. The LORD will go through Egypt and strike it, but when he sees the blood
on the lintel and the two door-posts, he will pass over that door and will not let the
24 destroyer enter your houses to strike you. You shall keep this as a rule for you and
25 your children for all time. When you enter the land which the LORD will give you as
26 he promised, you shall observe this rite. Then, when your children ask you, "What is
27 the meaning of this rite?" you shall say, "It is the LORD's Passover, for he passed over
the houses of the Israelites in Egypt when he struck the Egyptians but spared our
houses."' The people bowed down and prostrated themselves.

28 The Israelites went and did all that the LORD had commanded Moses and Aaron;
29 and by midnight the LORD had struck down every first-born in Egypt, from the first-
born of Pharaoh on his throne to the first-born of the captive in the dungeon, and
30 the first-born of cattle. Before night was over Pharaoh rose, he and all his courtiers
and all the Egyptians, and a great cry of anguish went up, because not a house in
31 Egypt was without its dead. Pharaoh summoned Moses and Aaron while it was still
night and said, 'Up with you! Be off, and leave my people, you and your Israelites. Go
32 and worship the LORD, as you ask; take your sheep and cattle, and go; and ask God's
33 blessing on me also.' The Egyptians urged on the people and hurried them out of the
34 country, 'or else', they said, 'we shall all be dead.' The people picked up their dough
before it was leavened, wrapped their kneading-troughs in their cloaks, and slung
35 them on their shoulders. Meanwhile the Israelites had done as Moses had told them,
36 asking the Egyptians for jewellery of silver and gold and for clothing. As the LORD
had made the Egyptians well-disposed towards them, they let them have what they
asked; in this way they plundered the Egyptians.

THE EXODUS FROM EGYPT

37 The Israelites set out from Rameses[6] on the way to Succoth, about six hundred
38 thousand men on foot,[7] not counting dependents. And with them too went a large
39 company of every kind, and cattle in great numbers, both flocks and herds. The
dough they had brought from Egypt they baked into unleavened cakes, because

---

[6] **Rameses:** One of the storage cities which the Hebrews had built.

[7] **foot:** Scholars state that this number is an exaggeration: 600,000 men suggests a total of some 2,500,000 people. The number might be based on a census list in the Book of Numbers, chapter 1.

there was no leaven; for they had been driven out of Egypt and allowed no time even to get food ready for themselves.

40, 41 The Israelites had been settled in Egypt for four hundred and thirty years. At the
end of four hundred and thirty years, on this very day, all the tribes of the LORD
42 came out of Egypt. This was a night of vigil as the LORD waited to bring them out of
Egypt. It is the LORD's night; all Israelites keep their vigil generation after generation.
[. . .]

13

17 Now when Pharaoh let the people go, God did not guide them by the road
towards the Philistines,[8] although that was the shortest; for he said, 'The people may
18 change their minds when they see war before them, and turn back to Egypt.' So God
made them go round by way of the wilderness towards the Red Sea;[9] and the fifth
generation of Israelites departed from Egypt.

19 Moses took the bones of Joseph with him, because Joseph had exacted an oath
from the Israelites: 'Some day', he said, 'God will show his care for you, and then, as
you go, you must take my bones with you.'

20 They set out from Succoth and encamped at Etham on the edge of the wilder-
21 ness. And all the time the LORD went before them, by day a pillar of cloud to guide
them on their journey, by night a pillar of fire to give them light, so that they could
22 travel night and day. The pillar of cloud never left its place in front of the people by
day, nor the pillar of fire by night.[10]

14

1, 2 The LORD spoke to Moses and said, 'Speak to the Israelites: They are to turn back
and encamp before Pi-hahiroth, between Migdol and the sea to the east of Baal-
3 zephon; your camp shall be opposite, by the sea. Pharaoh will then think that the
Israelites are finding themselves in difficult country, and are hemmed in by the
4 wilderness. I will make Pharaoh obstinate, and he will pursue them, so that I may
win glory for myself at the expense of Pharaoh and all his army; and the Egyptians
shall know that I am the LORD.' The Israelites did as they were bidden.

5 When the king of Egypt was told that the Israelites had slipped away, he and his
courtiers changed their minds completely, and said, 'What have we done? We have
6 let our Israelite slaves go free!' So Pharaoh put horses to his chariot, and took his
7 troops with him. He took six hundred picked chariots and all the other chariots of

[8] **Philistines:** The main route to the Philistines on the coast of Canaan was avoided, since it would have been guarded by garrisons of Egyptian troops.

[9] **Red Sea:** Literally, "Sea of Reeds," and hence a shallow papyrus marsh on the border of Egypt. The Red Sea is the name of the Gulf of Elath, much farther east.

[10] **by night:** It is uncertain whether the cloud and fire derive from ordinary practices in travel (such as the ancient custom of carrying a burning brazier at the head of a caravan) or are, instead, symbols of divine presence. [Other scholars suggest that Mt. Sinai or Mt. Horeb was volcanic or that Yahweh was an ancient storm god represented by lightning. Editors' note.]

8 Egypt, with a commander in each. Then Pharaoh king of Egypt, made obstinate by
9 the LORD, pursued the Israelites as they marched defiantly away. The Egyptians, all
Pharaoh's chariots and horses, cavalry and infantry, pursued them and overtook
10 them encamped beside the sea by Pi-hahiroth to the east of Baal-zephon. Pharaoh
was almost upon them when the Israelites looked up and saw the Egyptians close
11 behind. In their terror they clamoured to the LORD for help and said to Moses, 'Were
there no graves in Egypt, that you should have brought us here to die in the wilder-
12 ness? See what you have done to us by bringing us out of Egypt! Is not this just what
we meant when we said in Egypt, "Leave us alone; let us be slaves to the Egyptians"?
13 We would rather be slaves to the Egyptians than die here in the wilderness.' 'Have no
fear,' Moses answered; 'stand firm and see the deliverance that the LORD will bring
you this day; for as sure as you see the Egyptians now, you will never see them again.
14 The LORD will fight for you; so hold your peace.'

15 The LORD said to Moses, 'What is the meaning of this clamour? Tell the Israelites
16 to strike camp. And you shall raise high your staff, stretch out your hand over the sea
17 and cleave it in two, so that the Israelites can pass through the sea on dry ground. For
my part I will make the Egyptians obstinate and they will come after you; thus will I
win glory for myself at the expense of Pharaoh and his army, chariots and cavalry all
18 together. The Egyptians will know that I am the LORD when I win glory for myself at
the expense of their Pharaoh, his chariots and cavalry.'

19 The angel of God, who had kept in front of the Israelites, moved away to the
20 rear. The pillar of cloud moved from the front and took its place behind them and so
came between the Egyptians and the Israelites. And the cloud brought on darkness
and early nightfall, so that contact was lost throughout the night.

21 Then Moses stretched out his hand over the sea, and the LORD drove the sea
away all night with a strong east wind and turned the sea-bed into dry land.[11] The
22 waters were torn apart, and the Israelites went through the sea on the dry ground,
23 while the waters made a wall for them to right and to left. The Egyptians went in
24 pursuit of them far into the sea, all Pharaoh's horse, his chariots, and his cavalry. In
the morning watch the LORD looked down on the Egyptian army through the pillar
25 of fire and cloud, and he threw them into a panic. He clogged their chariot wheels
and made them lumber along heavily, so that the Egyptians said, 'It is the LORD
26 fighting for Israel against Egypt; let us flee.' Then the LORD said to Moses, 'Stretch
out your hand over the sea, and let the water flow back over the Egyptians, their
27 chariots and their cavalry.' So Moses stretched out his hand over the sea, and at daybreak the water returned to its accustomed place; but the Egyptians were in flight as
28 it advanced, and the LORD swept them out into the sea. The water flowed back and
covered all Pharaoh's army, the chariots and the cavalry, which had pressed the pur-
29 suit into the sea. Not one man was left alive. Meanwhile the Israelites had passed
along the dry ground through the sea, with the water making a wall for them to right
30 and to left. That day the LORD saved Israel from the power of Egypt, and the
31 Israelites saw the Egyptians lying dead on the sea-shore. When Israel saw the great

[11] **land:** The story may be based upon natural phenomena whereby the east wind drives back the waters of the shallow marsh.

power which the LORD had put forth against Egypt, all the people feared the LORD, and they put their faith in him and in Moses his servant.

THE TEN COMMANDMENTS

19

1 In the third month after Israel had left Egypt, they came to the wilderness of
2 Sinai. They set out from Rephidim and entered the wilderness of Sinai, where they
3 encamped, pitching their tents opposite the mountain. Moses went up the mountain
of God,[12] and the LORD called to him from the mountain and said, 'Speak thus to the
4 house of Jacob, and tell this to the sons of Israel: You have seen with your own eyes
what I did to Egypt, and how I have carried you on eagles' wings and brought you
5 here to me. If only you will now listen to me and keep my covenant, then out of all
6 peoples you shall become my special possession; for the whole earth is mine. You
shall be my kingdom of priests, my holy nation. These are the words you shall speak
to the Israelites.'
7 Moses came and summoned the elders of the people and set before them all
8 these commands which the LORD had laid upon him. The people all answered
together, 'Whatever the LORD has said we will do.' Moses brought this answer back to
9 the LORD. The LORD said to Moses, 'I am now coming to you in a thick cloud, so that
I may speak to you in the hearing of the people, and their faith in you may never fail.'
10 Moses told the LORD what the people had said, and the LORD said to him, 'Go to the
people and hallow them today and tomorrow and make them wash their clothes.
11 They must be ready by the third day, because on the third day the LORD will descend
12 upon Mount Sinai in the sight of all the people. You must put barriers round the
mountain and say, "Take care not to go up the mountain or even to touch the edge of
13 it." Any man who touches the mountain must be put to death.[13] No hand shall touch
him; he shall be stoned or shot dead: neither man nor beast may live. But when the
14 ram's horn sounds, they may go up the mountain.' Moses came down from the
15 mountain to the people. He hallowed them and they washed their clothes. He said to
16 the people, 'Be ready by the third day; do not go near a woman.' On the third day,
when morning came, there were peals of thunder and flashes of lightning, dense
cloud on the mountain and a loud trumpet blast; the people in the camp were all
terrified.
17 Moses brought the people out from the camp to meet God, and they took their
18 stand at the foot of the mountain. Mount Sinai was all smoking because the LORD
had come down upon it in fire; the smoke went up like the smoke of a kiln; all the
19 people were terrified, and the sound of the trumpet grew ever louder. Whenever
20 Moses spoke, God answered him in a peal of thunder. The LORD came down upon

[12] **mountain of God:** The idea that the gods dwell upon or reveal themselves upon high mountains is attested throughout the ancient world. Yahweh was believed to dwell in heaven and to come down to the mountaintop to meet with Moses.

[13] **death:** The place at which the deity reveals himself is holy, and holiness was regarded as a mysterious energy transmittable by a touch sometimes fatal to humans.

the top of Mount Sinai and summoned Moses to the mountain-top, and Moses went
21 up. The LORD said to Moses, 'Go down; warn the people solemnly that they must not
22 force their way through to the LORD to see him, or many of them will perish. Even
the priests, who have access to the LORD, must hallow themselves, for fear that the
23 LORD may break out against them.' Moses answered the LORD, 'The people cannot
come up Mount Sinai, because thou thyself didst solemnly warn us to set a barrier to
24 the mountain and so to keep it holy.' The LORD therefore said to him, 'Go down; then
come up and bring Aaron with you, but let neither priests nor people force their way
25 up to the LORD, for fear that he may break out against them.' So Moses went down to
the people and spoke to them.

20

1, 2 God spoke, and these were his words: I am the LORD your God who brought you
out of Egypt, out of the land of slavery.
3 You shall have no other god to set against me.
4 You shall not make a carved image for yourself nor the likeness of anything in
the heavens above, or on the earth below, or in the waters under the earth.
5 You shall not bow down to them or worship them; for I, the LORD your God, am
a jealous god. I punish the children for the sins of the fathers to the third and fourth
6 generations of those who hate me. But I keep faith with thousands, with those who
love me and keep my commandments.
7 You shall not make wrong use of the name of the LORD your God: the LORD will
not leave unpunished the man who misuses his name.
8, 9 Remember to keep the sabbath day holy. You have six days to labour and do all
10 your work. But the seventh day is a sabbath of the LORD your God; that day you shall
not do any work, you, your son or your daughter, your slave or your slave-girl, your
11 cattle or the alien within your gates; for in six days the LORD made heaven and earth,
the sea, and all that is in them, and on the seventh day he rested. Therefore the LORD
blessed the sabbath day and declared it holy.
12 Honour your father and your mother, that you may live long in the land which
the LORD your GOD is giving you.
13 You shall not commit murder.
14 You shall not commit adultery.
15 You shall not steal.
16 You shall not give false evidence against your neighbour.
17 You shall not covet your neighbour's house; you shall not covet your neighbour's wife, his slave, his slave-girl, his ox, his ass, or anything that belongs to him.
18 When all the people saw how it thundered and the lightning flashed, when they
heard the trumpet sound and saw the mountain smoking, they trembled and stood
19 at a distance. 'Speak to us yourself,' they said to Moses, 'and we will listen; but if
20 God speaks to us we shall die.' Moses answered, 'Do not be afraid. God has come
21 only to test you, so that the fear of him may remain with you and keep you from sin.'
So the people stood at a distance, while Moses approached the dark cloud where
God was. . . .

Job

Prologue[1]

1

1 There lived in the land of Uz[2] a man of blameless[3] and upright life named Job,[4] who
2 feared God and set his face against wrongdoing. He had seven sons and three daugh-
3 ters; and he owned seven thousand sheep and three thousand camels, five hundred
yoke of oxen and five hundred asses, with a large number of slaves. Thus Job was the
greatest man in all the East.[5]
4 Now his sons used to foregather and give, each in turn, a feast in his own house;
5 and they used to send and invite their three sisters to eat and drink with them. Then,
when a round of feasts was finished, Job sent for his children and sanctified them,
rising early in the morning and sacrificing a whole-offering for each of them; for he
thought that they might somehow have sinned against God and committed blasphemy in their hearts. This he always did.
6 The day came when the members of the court of heaven took their places in the
7 presence of the LORD, and Satan[6] was there among them. The LORD asked him where
8 he had been. 'Ranging over the earth', he said, 'from end to end.' Then the LORD asked
Satan, 'Have you considered my servant Job? You will find no one like him on earth,
a man of blameless and upright life, who fears God and sets his face against wrong-
9, 10 doing.' Satan answered the LORD, 'Has not Job good reason to be God-fearing? Have
you not hedged him round on every side with your protection, him and his family
and all his possessions? Whatever he does you have blessed, and his herds have

---

The Book of Job. The dates for the composition of Job are uncertain, but the sixth century B.C.E. seems to fit the language and culture of the tale; additions were interpolated sometime in the fifth century B.C.E. It is thought that the author of Job took an old folktale, possibly an Ugaritic story from Syria, and used parts of it for his introduction and conclusion, filling in the philosophical material in the middle. The Book of Job is divided into the Prologue (chapters 1–2), which sets up a situation between Satan and God; the Dialogues (chapters 3–31), speeches by friends and Job; the Hymn on Wisdom (chapter 28), which explores the sources of wisdom; Elihu's speeches (chapters 32–37), on the power and righteousness of God; the Theophany (chapters 38–42:6), God's answers to Job and Job's response; and the Epilogue (chapter 42:7–17), the resolution of Job's suffering.

---

[1] **Prologue:** Job, a devout and prosperous man, is tested for his integrity by calamity and disaster.

[2] **Uz:** Probably Edom, a region south of the Dead Sea.

[3] **blameless:** The import is not sinless perfection, but a whole person.

[4] **Job:** The etymology suggests either "inveterate foe" or the "penitent one."

[5] **East:** The wealth described is that of a seminomadic sheikh; seven sons and three daughters was considered ideal.

[6] **Satan:** For the ancients, human events were decided in divine councils. The literal meaning of *satan* is "adversary" or "accuser," and is apparently a legal term, not yet the proper name for an evil being it later became.

11 increased beyond measure. But stretch out your hand and touch all that he has, and
12 then he will curse you to your face.' Then the LORD said to Satan, 'So be it. All that he
has is in your hands; only Job himself you must not touch.' And Satan left the LORD's
presence.

13 When the day came that Job's sons and daughters were eating and drinking in
14 the eldest brother's house, a messenger came running to Job and said, 'The oxen
15 were ploughing and the asses were grazing near them, when the Sabaeans[7] swooped
down and carried them off, after putting the herdsmen to the sword; and I am the
16 only one to escape and tell the tale.' While he was still speaking, another messenger
arrived and said, 'God's fire flashed from heaven. It struck the sheep and the shep-
17 herds and burnt them up; and I am the only one to escape and tell the tale.' While he
was still speaking, another arrived and said, 'The Chaldaeans,[8] three bands of them,
have made a raid on the camels and carried them off, after putting the drivers to the
18 sword; and I am the only one to escape and tell the tale.' While this man was speaking, yet another arrived and said, 'Your sons and daughters were eating and drinking
19 in the eldest brother's house, when suddenly a whirlwind swept across from the
desert and struck the four corners of the house, and it fell on the young people and
20 killed them; and I am the only one to escape and tell the tale.' At this Job stood up
21 and rent his cloak; then he shaved his head and fell prostrate on the ground, saying:

Naked I came from the womb,
naked I shall return whence I came.
The LORD gives and the LORD takes away;
blessed be the name of the LORD.

22 Throughout all this Job did not sin; he did not charge God with unreason.

2

1 Once again the day came when the members of the court of heaven took their
2 places in the presence of the LORD, and Satan was there among them. The LORD
asked him where he had been. 'Ranging over the earth', he said, 'from end to end.'
3 Then the LORD asked Satan, 'Have you considered my servant Job? You will find no
one like him on earth, a man of blameless and upright life, who fears God and sets
his face against wrongdoing. You incited me to ruin him without a cause, but his
4 integrity is still unshaken.' Satan answered the LORD, 'Skin for skin![9] There is nothing
5 the man will grudge to save himself. But stretch out your hand and touch his bone
and his flesh, and see if he will not curse you to your face.'

6 Then the LORD said to Satan, 'So be it. He is in your hands; but spare his life.'
7 And Satan left the LORD's presence, and he smote Job with running sores from head
8 to foot, so that he took a piece of a broken pot to scratch himself as he sat among the
9 ashes. Then his wife said to him, 'Are you still unshaken in your integrity? Curse God

---

[7] **Sabaeans:** Nomads from Arabia.

[8] **Chaldaeans:** The biblical name for Babylonians.

[9] **Skin for skin!:** Value for value.

10 and die!' But he answered, 'You talk as any wicked fool of a woman might talk. If we
accept good from God, shall we not accept evil?' Throughout all this, Job did not
utter one sinful word.
11 When Job's three friends, Eliphaz of Teman, Bildad of Shuah, and Zophar of
Naamah,[10] heard of all these calamities which had overtaken him, they left their
12 homes and arranged to come and condole with him and comfort him. But when
they first saw him from a distance, they did not recognize him; and they wept aloud,
13 rent their cloaks and tossed dust into the air over their heads. For seven days and
seven nights they sat beside him on the ground, and none of them said a word to
him; for they saw that his suffering was very great.

Job's Complaint to God

3

1, 2 After this Job broke silence and cursed the day of his birth:

3 Perish the day when I was born
and the night which said, 'A man is conceived'!
4 May that day turn to darkness; may God above not look for it,
nor light of dawn shine on it.
5 May blackness sully it, and murk and gloom,
cloud smother that day, swift darkness eclipse its sun.
6 Blind darkness swallow up that night;
count it not among the days of the year,
reckon it not in the cycle of the months.
7 That night, may it be barren for ever,
no cry of joy be heard in it.
8 Cursed be it by those whose magic binds even the monster of the deep,
who are ready to tame Leviathan himself with spells.[11]
9 May no star shine out in its twilight;
may it wait for a dawn that never comes,
nor ever see the eyelids of the morning,
10 because it did not shut the doors of the womb that bore me
and keep trouble away from my sight.
11 Why was I not still-born,
why did I not die when I came out of the womb?
12 Why was I ever laid on my mother's knees
or put to suck at her breasts?

---

[10] **friends . . . Naamah:** Job's friends probably come from northwest Arabia.

[11] **spells:** Astrologers and magicians were reputed to have dominance, by means of incantations, over the dragon of chaos, Leviathan; the mythological monster, mentioned frequently in Canaanite literature, plays a prominent role in Israelite poetry as the embodiment of disorder. In the Babylonian creation story, the god Marduk slays the monster Tiamat.

16[12] Why was I not hidden like an untimely birth,
like an infant that has not lived to see the light?
13 For then I should be lying in the quiet grave,
asleep in death, at rest,
14 with kings and their ministers
who built themselves palaces,
15 with princes rich in gold
who filled their houses with silver.
17 There the wicked man chafes no more,
there the tired labourer rests;
18 the captive too finds peace there
and hears no taskmaster's voice;
19 high and low are there,
even the slave, free from his master.

20 Why should the sufferer be born to see the light?
Why is life given to men who find it so bitter?
21 They wait for death but it does not come,
they seek it more eagerly than hidden treasure.
22 They are glad when they reach the tomb,
and when they come to the grave they exult.
23 Why should a man be born to wander blindly,
hedged in by God on every side?
24 My sighing is all my food,
and groans pour from me in a torrent.
25 Every terror that haunted me has caught up with me,
and all that I feared has come upon me.
26 There is no peace of mind nor quiet for me;
I chafe in torment and have no rest.

First Cycle of Speeches[13]

4

1 Then Eliphaz the Temanite began:

2 If one ventures to speak with you, will you lose patience?
For who could hold his tongue any longer?
3 Think how once you encouraged those who faltered,
how you braced feeble arms,

---

[12] Verse 16 transposed to follow verse 12.

[13] **First cycle of speeches:** Gently Eliphaz broaches the central ideas that will recur throughout the friends' speeches: Man cannot be more righteous than God, and even celestial beings have no claim to purity in God's sight.

4 how a word from you upheld the stumblers
and put strength into weak knees.
5 But now that adversity comes upon you, you lose patience;
it touches you, and you are unmanned.
6 Is your religion no comfort to you?
Does your blameless life give you no hope?
7 For consider, what innocent man has ever perished?
Where have you seen the upright destroyed?
8 This I know, that those who plough mischief and sow trouble
reap as they have sown;
9 they perish at the blast of God
and are shrivelled by the breath of his nostrils.

10 The roar of the lion, the whimpering of his cubs, fall silent;
the teeth of the young lions are broken;
11 the lion perishes for lack of prey
and the whelps of the lioness are abandoned.

12 A word stole into my ears,
and they caught the whisper of it;
13 in the anxious visions of the night,
when a man sinks into deepest sleep,
14 terror seized me and shuddering;
the trembling of my body frightened me.
15 A wind brushed my face
and made the hairs bristle on my flesh;
16 and a figure stood there whose shape I could not discern,
an apparition loomed before me,
and I heard the sound of a low voice:
17 'Can mortal man be more righteous than God,
or the creature purer than his Maker?
18 If God mistrusts his own servants
and finds his messengers[14] at fault,
19 how much more those that dwell in houses[15] whose walls are clay,
whose foundations are dust,
which can be crushed like a bird's nest
20 or torn down between dawn and dark,
how much more shall such men perish outright and unheeded,
21 die, without ever finding wisdom?'

[14] **messengers:** Angels.

[15] **houses:** The human body.

5

1 Call if you will; is there any to answer you?
To which of the holy ones[16] will you turn?
2 The fool is destroyed by his own angry passions,
and the end of childish resentment is death.
3 I have seen it for myself: a fool uprooted,
his home in sudden ruin about him,
4 his children past help,
browbeaten in court with none to save them.
5 Their rich possessions are snatched from them;
what they have harvested others hungrily devour;
the stronger man seizes it from the panniers,
panting, thirsting for their wealth.
6 Mischief does not grow out of the soil
nor trouble spring from the earth;
7 man is born to trouble,
as surely as birds fly upwards.

8 For my part, I would make my petition to God
and lay my cause before him,
9 who does great and unsearchable things,
marvels without number.
10 He gives rain to the earth
and sends water on the fields;
11 he raises the lowly to the heights,
the mourners are uplifted by victory;
12 he frustrates the plots of the crafty,
and they win no success,
13 he traps the cunning in their craftiness,
and the schemers' plans are thrown into confusion.
14 In the daylight they run into darkness,
and grope at midday as though it were night.
15 He saves the destitute from their greed,
and the needy from the grip of the strong;
16 so the poor hope again,
and the unjust are sickened.

17 Happy the man whom God rebukes!
therefore do not reject the discipline of the Almighty.
18 For, though he wounds, he will bind up;
the hands that smite will heal.
19 You may meet disaster six times, and he will save you;

---

[16] **holy ones:** Members of the heavenly court.

seven times,[17] and no harm shall touch you.
20 In time of famine he will save you from death,
in battle from the sword.
21 You will be shielded from the lash of slander,
and when violence comes you need not fear.
22 You will laugh at violence and starvation
and have no need to fear wild beasts;
23 for you have a covenant with the stones to spare your fields,
and the weeds have been constrained to leave you at peace.
24 You will know that all is well with your household,
you will look round your home and find nothing amiss;
25 you will know, too, that your descendants will be many
and your offspring like grass, thick upon the earth.
26 You will come in sturdy old age to the grave
as sheaves come in due season to the threshing-floor.

27 We have inquired into all this, and so it is;
this we have heard, and you may know it for the truth.

6

1 Then Job answered:[18]

2 O that the grounds for my resentment might be weighed,
and my misfortunes set with them on the scales!
3 For they would outweigh the sands of the sea:
what wonder if my words are wild?
4 The arrows of the Almighty find their mark in me,
and their poison[19] soaks into my spirit;
God's onslaughts wear me away.
5 Does the wild ass bray when he has grass
or the ox low when he has fodder?
6 Can a man eat tasteless food unseasoned with salt,
or find any flavour in the juice of mallows?
7 Food that should nourish me sticks in my throat,
and my bowels rumble with an echoing sound.

8 O that I might have my request,
that God would grant what I hope for:
9 that he would be pleased to crush me,

[17] **seven times:** A frequent numerical device meaning "totality."

[18] **Job answered:** His distress has come from God, unjustly. He will not abstain from expressing his bitterness.

[19] **poison:** While fire arrows were used in the ancient Near East, there is no evidence of them in the Hebrew Scriptures outside this verse.

to snatch me away with his hand and cut me off!
10 For that would bring me relief,
and in the face of unsparing anguish I would leap for joy.
11 Have I the strength to wait?
What end have I to expect, that I should be patient?
12 Is my strength the strength of stone,
or is my flesh bronze?
13 Oh how shall I find help within myself?
The power to aid myself is put out of my reach.

14 Devotion is due from his friends
to one who despairs and loses faith in the Almighty;
15 but my brothers have been treacherous as a mountain stream,
like the channels of streams that run dry,
16 which turn dark with ice
or are hidden with piled-up snow;
17 or they vanish the moment they are in spate,
dwindle in the heat and are gone.
18 Then the caravans, winding hither and thither,
go up into the wilderness and perish;
19 the caravans of Tema look for their waters,
travelling merchants of Sheba hope for them;
20 but they are disappointed, for all their confidence,
they reach them only to be balked.
21 So treacherous have you now been to me:
you felt dismay and were afraid.
22 Did I ever say, 'Give me this or that;
open your purses to save my life;
23 rescue me from my enemy;
ransom me out of the hands of ruthless men'?

24 Tell me plainly, and I will listen in silence;
show me where I have erred.
25 How harsh are the words of the upright man!
What do the arguments of wise men prove?
26 Do you mean to argue about words
or to sift the utterance of a man past hope?
27 Would you assail an orphan?
Would you hurl yourselves on a friend?
28 So now, I beg you, turn and look at me:
am I likely to lie to your faces?
29 Think again, let me have no more injustice;
think again, for my integrity is in question.
30 Do I ever give voice to injustice?
Does my sense not warn me when my words are wild?

7

1 Has not man hard service on earth,
and are not his days like those of a hired labourer,
2 like those of a slave longing for the shade
or a servant kept waiting for his wages?
3 So months of futility are my portion,
troubled nights are my lot.
4 When I lie down, I think,
'When will it be day that I may rise?'
When the evening grows long and I lie down,
I do nothing but toss till morning twilight.
5 My body is infested with worms,
and scabs cover my skin.
6 My days are swifter than a shuttle
and come to an end as the thread runs out.

7 Remember, my life is but a breath of wind;
I shall never again see good days.
8 Thou wilt behold me no more with a seeing eye;
under thy very eyes I shall disappear.
9 As clouds break up and disperse,
so he that goes down to Sheol never comes back;
10 he never returns home again,
and his place will know him no more.

11 But I will not hold my peace;
I will speak out in the distress of my mind
and complain in the bitterness of my soul.
12 Am I the monster of the deep, am I the sea-serpent,
that thou settest a watch over me?
13 When I think that my bed will comfort me,
that sleep will relieve my complaining,
14 thou dost terrify me with dreams
and affright me with visions.
15 I would rather be choked outright;
I would prefer death to all my sufferings.
16 I am in despair, I would not go on living;
leave me alone, for my life is but a vapour.
17 What is man that thou makest much of him
and turnest thy thoughts towards him,
18 only to punish him morning by morning
or to test him every hour of the day?
19 Wilt thou not look away from me for an instant?
Wilt thou not let me be while I swallow my spittle?

20 If I have sinned, how do I injure thee,
thou watcher of the hearts of men?
Why hast thou made me thy butt,
and why have I become thy target?
21 Why dost thou not pardon my offence
and take away my guilt?
But now I shall lie down in the grave;
seek me, and I shall not be.

8

1 Then Bildad the Shuhite began:[20]

2 How long will you say such things,
the long-winded ramblings of an old man?
3 Does God pervert judgement?
Does the Almighty pervert justice?
4 Your sons sinned against him,
so he left them to be victims of their own iniquity.
5 If only you will seek God betimes
and plead for the favour of the Almighty,
6 if you are innocent and upright,
then indeed will he watch over you
and see your just intent fulfilled.
7 Then, though your beginnings were humble,
your end will be great.

8 Inquire now of older generations
and consider the experience of their fathers;
9 for we ourselves are of yesterday and are transient;
our days on earth are a shadow.
10 Will not they speak to you and teach you
and pour out the wisdom of their hearts?
11 Can rushes grow where there is no marsh?
Can reeds flourish without water?
12 While they are still in flower and not ready to cut,
they wither earlier than any green plant.
13 Such is the fate of all who forget God;
the godless man's life-thread breaks off;
14 his confidence is gossamer,
and the ground of his trust a spider's web.
15 He leans against his house but it does not stand;
he clutches at it but it does not hold firm.

[20] **Bildad the Shuhite began:** Bildad appeals not to his own experience, but to that of the human race.

16 His is the lush growth of a plant in the sun,
pushing out shoots over the garden;
17 but its roots become entangled in a stony patch
and run against a bed of rock.
18 Then someone uproots it from its place,
which disowns it and says, 'I have never known you.'
19 That is how its life withers away,
and other plants spring up from the earth.

20 Be sure, God will not spurn the blameless man,
nor will he grasp the hand of the wrongdoer.
21 He will yet fill your mouth with laughter,
and shouts of joy will be on your lips;
22 your enemies shall be wrapped in confusion,
and the tents of the wicked shall vanish away.

9

1 Then Job answered:

2 Indeed this I know for the truth,
that no man can win his case against God.
3 If a man chooses to argue with him,
God will not answer one question in a thousand.
4 He is wise, he is powerful;
what man has stubbornly resisted him and survived?
5 It is God who moves mountains, giving them no rest,
turning them over in his wrath;
6 who makes the earth start from its place
so that its pillars[21] are convulsed;
7 who commands the sun's orb not to rise
and shuts up the stars under his seal;
8 who by himself spread out the heavens
and trod on the sea-monster's back;
9 who made Aldebaran[22] and Orion,
the Pleiades and the circle of the southern stars;
10 who does great and unsearchable things,
marvels without number.

11 He passes by me, and I do not see him;
he moves on his way undiscerned by me;
12 if he hurries on, who can bring him back?

---

[21] **pillars:** The seven columns supporting the cosmic house.

[22] **Aldebaran:** A red star, the brightest in Taurus.

Who will ask him what he does?
13 God does not turn back his wrath;
the partisans of Rahab[23] lie prostrate at his feet.
14 How much less can I answer him
or find words to dispute with him?
15 Though I am right,[24] I get no answer,
though I plead with my accuser for mercy.
16 If I summoned him to court and he responded,
I do not believe that he would listen to my plea—
17 for he bears hard upon me for a trifle
and rains blows on me without cause;
18 he leaves me no respite to recover my breath
but fills me with bitter thoughts.
19 If the appeal is to force, see how strong he is;
if to justice, who can compel him to give me a hearing?
20 Though I am right, he condemns me out of my own mouth;
though I am blameless, he twists my words.
21 Blameless, I say; of myself
I reck nothing, I hold my life cheap.
22 But it is all one; therefore I say,
'He destroys blameless and wicked alike.'
23 When a sudden flood brings death,
he mocks the plight of the innocent.
24 The land is given over to the power of the wicked,
and the eyes of its judges are blindfold.

25 My days have been swifter than a runner,
they have slipped away and seen no prosperity;
26 they have raced by like reed-built skiffs,
swift as vultures swooping on carrion.
27 If I think, 'I will forget my griefs,
I will show a cheerful face and smile,'
28 I tremble in every nerve;
I know that thou wilt not hold me innocent.
29 If I am to be accounted guilty,
why do I labour in vain?
30 Though I wash myself with soap
or cleanse my hands with lye,
31 thou wilt thrust me into the mud
and my clothes will make me loathsome.

32 He is not a man as I am, that I can answer him
or that we can confront one another in court.

---

[23] **Rahab:** In mythology the ocean-chaos monster, elsewhere called Leviathan or Tannin, slain by the deity.

[24] **right:** Innocent.

33 If only there were one to arbitrate between us
and impose his authority on us both,
34 so that God might take his rod from my back,
and terror of him might not come on me suddenly.
35 I would then speak without fear of him;
for I know I am not what I am thought to be.

10

1 I am sickened of life;
I will give free rein to my griefs,
I will speak out in bitterness of soul.
2 I will say to God, 'Do not condemn me,
but tell me the ground of thy complaint[25] against me.
3 Dost thou find any advantage in oppression,
in spurning the fruit of all thy labour
and smiling on the policy of wicked men?
4 Hast thou eyes of flesh
or dost thou see as mortal man sees?
5 Are thy days as those of a mortal
or thy years as the life of a man,
6 that thou lookest for guilt in me
and dost seek in me for sin,
7 though thou knowest that I am guiltless
and have none to save me from thee?

8 'Thy hands gave me shape and made me;
and dost thou at once turn and destroy me?
9 Remember that thou didst knead me like clay;
and wouldst thou turn me back into dust?
10 Didst thou not pour me out like milk
and curdle me like cheese,
11 clothe me with skin and flesh
and knit me together with bones and sinews?
12 Thou hast given me life and continuing favour,
and thy providence has watched over my spirit.
13 Yet this was the secret purpose of thy heart,
and I know that this was thy intent:
14 that, if I sinned, thou wouldst be watching me
and wouldst not acquit me of my guilt.
15 If I indeed am wicked, the worse for me!
If I am righteous, even so I may lift up my head;
16 if I am proud as a lion, thou dost hunt me down
and dost confront me again with marvellous power;

---

[25] **complaint:** A lawsuit.

17 thou dost renew thy onslaught upon me,
and with mounting anger against me
bringest fresh forces to the attack.
18 Why didst thou bring me out of the womb?
O that I had ended there and no eye had seen me,
19 that I had been carried from the womb to the grave
and were as though I had not been born.
20 Is not my life short and fleeting?
Let me be, that I may be happy for a moment,
21 before I depart to a land of gloom,
a land of deep darkness, never to return,
22 a land of gathering shadows, of deepening darkness,
lit by no ray of light, dark upon dark.'

11

1 Then Zophar the Naamathite began:[26]

2 Should this spate of words not be answered?
Must a man of ready tongue be always right?
3 Is your endless talk to reduce men to silence?
Are you to talk nonsense and no one rebuke you?
4 You claim that your opinions are sound;
you say to God, 'I am spotless in thy sight.'
5 But if only he would speak
and open his lips to talk with you,
6 and expound to you the secrets of wisdom,
for wonderful are its effects!
[Know then that God exacts from you less than your sin deserves.]
7 Can you fathom the mystery of God,
can you fathom the perfection of the Almighty?
8 It is higher than heaven; you can do nothing.
It is deeper than Sheol; you can know nothing.
9 Its measure is longer than the earth
and broader than the sea.
10 If he passes by, he may keep secret his passing;
if he proclaims it, who can turn him back?
11 He surely knows which men are false,
and when he sees iniquity, does he not take note of it?
12 Can a fool grow wise?
can a wild ass's foal be born a man?
13 If only you had directed your heart rightly

[26] **Zophar the Naamathite began:** He rebukes Job for presuming to understand God's unfathomable character, and tries to persuade Job to repent.

and spread out your hands to pray to him!
14 If you have wrongdoing in hand, thrust it away;
let no iniquity make its home with you.
15 Then you could hold up your head without fault,
a man of iron, knowing no fear.
16 Then you will forget your trouble;
you will remember it only as flood-waters that have passed;
17 life will be lasting, bright as noonday,
and darkness will be turned to morning.
18 You will be confident, because there is hope;
sure of protection, you will lie down in confidence;
19 great men will seek your favour.
20 Blindness will fall on the wicked;
the ways of escape are closed to them,
and their hope is despair.

12

1 Then Job answered:[27]

2 No doubt you are perfect men
and absolute wisdom is yours!
3 But I have sense as well as you;
in nothing do I fall short of you;
what gifts indeed have you that others have not?
4 Yet I am a laughing-stock to my friend—
a laughing-stock, though I am innocent and blameless,
one that called upon God, and he answered.
5 Prosperity and ease look down on misfortune,
on the blow that fells the man who is already reeling,
6 while the marauders' tents are left undisturbed
and those who provoke God live safe and sound.

7 Go and ask the cattle,
ask the birds of the air to inform you,
8 or tell the creatures that crawl to teach you,
and the fishes of the sea to give you instruction.
9 Who cannot learn from all these
that the LORD's[28] own hand has done this?

---

[27] **Job answered:** Job replies that he is no less wise than his friends, for even dumb animals understand shallow matters. To lie on behalf of God is wrong, and will be punished no less. Let God directly confront Job and let Job speak.

[28] **LORD's:** Nowhere else in Job (except 28.28) does the poetry use the divine name Yahweh, whereas the prose prologue and epilogue employ it regularly.

11 (Does not the ear test what is spoken
as the palate savours food?
12 There is wisdom, remember, in age,
and long life brings understanding.)

10[29] In God's hand are the souls of all that live,
the spirits of all human kind.
13 Wisdom and might are his,
with him are firmness and understanding.
14 If he pulls down, there is no rebuilding;
if he imprisons, there is no release.
15 If he holds up the waters, there is drought;
if he lets them go, they turn the land upside down.
16 Strength and success belong to him,
deceived and deceiver are his to use.
17 He makes counsellors behave like idiots
and drives judges mad;
18 he looses the bonds imposed by kings
and removes the girdle of office from their waists;
19 he makes priests behave like idiots
and overthrows men long in office;
20 those who are trusted he strikes dumb,
he takes away the judgement of old men;
21 he heaps scorn on princes
and abates the arrogance of nobles.
22 He leads peoples astray and destroys them,
he lays them low, and there they lie.
23 He takes away their wisdom from the rulers of the nations
and leaves them wandering in a pathless wilderness;
24 they grope in the darkness without light
and are left to wander like a drunkard.
25 He uncovers mysteries deep in obscurity
and into thick darkness he brings light.

13

1 All this I have seen with my own eyes,
with my own ears I have heard it, and understood it.
2 What you know, I also know;
in nothing do I fall short of you.
3 But for my part I would speak with the Almighty
and am ready to argue with God,
4 while you like fools are smearing truth with your falsehoods,

[29] Verse 10 transposed to follow verse 12.

stitching a patchwork of lies, one and all.
5 Ah, if you would only be silent
and let silence be your wisdom!
6 Now listen to my arguments
and attend while I put my case.
7 Is it on God's behalf that you speak so wickedly,
or in his defence that you allege what is false?
8 Must you take God's part,
or put his case for him?
9 Will all be well when he examines you?
Will you quibble with him as you quibble with a man?
10 He will most surely expose you
if you take his part by falsely accusing me.
11 Will not God's majesty strike you with dread,
and terror of him overwhelm you?
12 Your pompous talk is dust and ashes,
your defences will crumble like clay.
13 Be silent, leave me to speak my mind,
and let what may come upon me!
14 I will put my neck in the noose
and take my life in my hands.
15 If he would slay me, I should not hesitate;
I should still argue my cause to his face.
16 This at least assures my success,
that no godless man may appear before him.
17 Listen then, listen to my words,
and give a hearing to my exposition.
18 Be sure of this: once I have stated my case
I know that I shall be acquitted.
19 Who is there that can argue so forcibly with me
that he could reduce me straightway to silence and death?

20 Grant me these two conditions only,
and then I will not hide myself out of thy sight:
21 take thy heavy hand clean away from me
and let not the fear of thee strike me with dread.
22 Then summon me, and I will answer;
or I will speak first, and do thou answer me.
23 How many iniquities and sins are laid to my charge?
let me know my offences and my sin.
24 Why dost thou hide thy face
and treat me as thy enemy?
25 Wilt thou chase a driven leaf,
wilt thou pursue dry chaff,
26 prescribing punishment for me

and making me heir to the iniquities of my youth,
27 putting my feet in the stocks
and setting a slave-mark on the arches of my feet?

14

1 Man born of woman is short-lived and full of disquiet.
2 He blossoms like a flower and then he withers;
he slips away like a shadow and does not stay;
he is like a wine-skin that perishes
or a garment that moths have eaten.
3 Dost thou fix thine eyes on such a creature,
and wilt thou bring him into court to confront thee?[30]
5 The days of his life are determined,
and the number of his months is known to thee;
thou hast laid down a limit, which he cannot pass.
6 Look away from him therefore and leave him alone
counting the hours day by day like a hired labourer.

7 If a tree is cut down,
there is hope that it will sprout again
and fresh shoots will not fail.
8 Though its roots grow old in the earth,
and its stump is dying in the ground,
9 if it scents water it may break into bud
and make new growth like a young plant.
10 But a man dies, and he disappears;
man comes to his end, and where is he?
11 As the waters of a lake dwindle,
or as a river shrinks and runs dry,
12 so mortal man lies down, never to rise
until the very sky splits open.
If a man dies, can he live again?
He shall never be roused from his sleep.
13 If only thou wouldst hide me in Sheol
and conceal me till thy anger turns aside,
if thou wouldst fix a limit for my time there, and then remember me!
14 Then I would not lose hope, however long my service,
waiting for my relief to come.
15 Thou wouldst summon me, and I would answer thee;
thou wouldst long to see the creature thou hast made.
16 But now thou dost count every step I take,
watching all my course.
17 Every offence of mine is stored in thy bag;

[30] Verse 4 deliberately excluded.

thou dost keep my iniquity under seal.
18 Yet as a falling mountain-side is swept away,
and a rock is dislodged from its place,
19 as water wears away stones,
and a rain-storm scours the soil from the land,
so thou hast wiped out the hope of frail man;
20 thou dost overpower him finally, and he is gone;
his face is changed, and he is banished from thy sight.
21 His flesh upon him becomes black,
and his life-blood dries up within him.
22 His sons rise to honour, and he sees nothing of it;
they sink into obscurity, and he knows it not.

Second Cycle of Speeches

15

Then Eliphaz the Temanite answered:

2 Would a man of sense give vent to such foolish notions
and answer with a bellyful of wind?
3 Would he bandy useless words
and arguments so unprofitable?
4 Why! you even banish the fear of God from your mind,
usurping the sole right to speak in his presence;
5 your iniquity dictates what you say,
and deceit is the language of your choice.
6 You are condemned out of your own mouth, not by me;
your own lips give evidence against you.

7 Were you born first of mankind?
were you brought forth before the hills?
8 Do you listen in God's secret council
or usurp all wisdom for yourself alone?
9 What do you know that we do not know?
What insight have you that we do not share?
10 We have age and white hairs in our company,[31]
men older than your father.
11 Does not the consolation of God suffice you,
a word whispered quietly in your ear?
12 What makes you so bold at heart,
and why do your eyes flash,
13 that you vent your anger on God
and pour out such a torrent of words?

[31] **company:** Job is apparently younger than his visitors; he has not reached the age of a grandfather.

14 What is frail man that he should be innocent,
or any child of woman that he should be justified?
15 If God puts no trust in his holy ones,
and the heavens are not innocent in his sight,
16 how much less so is man, who is loathsome and rotten
and laps up evil like water!

17 I will tell you, if only you will listen,
and I will describe what I have seen
18 [what has been handed down by wise men
and was not concealed from them by their fathers;
19 to them alone the land was given,
and no foreigner settled among them]:
20 the wicked are racked with anxiety all their days,
the ruthless man for all the years in store for him.
21 The noise of the hunter's scare rings in his ears,
and in time of peace the raider falls on him;
22 he cannot hope to escape from dark death;
he is marked down for the sword;
23 he is flung out as food for vultures;
such a man knows that his destruction is certain.
24 Suddenly a black day comes upon him,
distress and anxiety overwhelm him
[like a king ready for battle];
25 for he has lifted his hand against God
and is pitting himself against the Almighty,
26 charging him head down,
with the full weight of his bossed shield.

27 Heavy though his jowl is and gross,
and though his sides bulge with fat,
28 the city where he lives will lie in ruins,
his house will be deserted;
it will soon become a heap of rubble.
29 He will no longer be rich, his wealth will not last,
and he will strike no root in the earth;
30 scorching heat will shrivel his shoots,
and his blossom will be shaken off by the wind.[32]
31 He deceives himself, trusting in his high rank,
for all his dealings will come to nothing.
32 His palm-trees will wither unseasonably,
and his branches will not spread;

[32] **wind:** The traditional teaching held that the wicked who seem to prosper would be barren ("strike no root in the earth") or lose their children ("like blossoms shaken off by the wind").

33 he will be like a vine that sheds its unripe grapes,
like an olive-tree that drops its blossom.
34 For the godless, one and all, are barren,
and their homes, enriched by bribery, are destroyed by fire;
35 they conceive mischief and give birth to trouble,
and the child of their womb is deceit.

16

1 Then Job answered:

2 I have heard such things often before,
you who make trouble, all of you, with every breath,
3 saying, 'Will this windbag never have done?
What makes him so stubborn in argument?'
4 If you and I were to change places,
I could talk like you;
how I could harangue you
and wag my head[33] at you!
5 But no, I would speak words of encouragement,
and then my condolences would flow in streams.
6 If I speak, my pain is not eased;
if I am silent, it does not leave me.
7 Meanwhile, my friend wearies me with false sympathy;
8 they tear me to pieces, he and his fellows.
He has come forward to give evidence against me;
the liar testifies against me to my face,
9 in his wrath he wears me down, his hatred is plain to see;
he grinds his teeth[34] at me.

My enemies look daggers at me,
10 they bare their teeth to rend me,
they slash my cheeks with knives;
they are all in league against me.
11 God has left me at the mercy of malefactors
and cast me into the clutches of wicked men.
12 I was at ease, but he set upon me and mauled me,
seized me by the neck and worried me.
He set me up as his target;
13 his arrows rained upon me from every side;
pitiless, he cut deep into my vitals,

---

[33] **wag my head:** A sign of gloating over the misfortune of another.
[34] **grinds his teeth:** A sign of scornful hatred and hostility.

he spilt my gall on the ground.
14 He made breach after breach in my defences;
he fell upon me like a fighting man.

15 I stitched sackcloth together to cover my body
and I buried my forelock in the dust;[35]
16 my cheeks were flushed with weeping
and dark shadows were round my eyes,
17 yet my hands were free from violence
and my prayer was sincere.

18 O earth, cover not my blood
and let my cry for justice find no rest!
19 For look! my witness is in heaven;
there is one on high ready to answer for me.
20 My appeal will come before God,
while my eyes turn again and again to him.
21 If only there were one to arbitrate between man and God,
as between a man and his neighbour!
22 For there are but few years to come
before I take the road from which I shall not return.

17

1 My mind is distraught, my days are numbered,
and the grave is waiting for me.
2 Wherever I turn, men taunt me,
and my day is darkened by their sneers.
3 Be thou my surety with thyself,[36]
for who else can pledge himself for me?
4 Thou wilt not let those men triumph,
whose minds thou hast sunk in ignorance;
5 if such a man denounces his friends to their ruin,
his sons' eyes shall grow dim.

6 I am held up as a byword in every land,
a portent for all to see;
7 my eyes are dim with grief,
my limbs wasted to a shadow.
8 Honest men are bewildered at this,
and the innocent are indignant at my plight.

[35] **sackcloth . . . in the dust:** Sackcloth and dust or ashes are signs of grief and mourning.

[36] **Be thou . . . with thyself:** This is a key sentence in which Job shows his faith by asking God to be Job's pledge with the deity.

9 In spite of all, the righteous man maintains his course,
and he whose hands are clean grows strong again.

10 But come on, one and all, try again!
I shall not find a wise man among you.

11 My days die away like an echo;
my heart-strings are snapped.
12 Day is turned into night,
and morning light is darkened before me.
13 If I measure Sheol for my house,
if I spread my couch in the darkness,
14 if I call the grave my father
and the worm my mother or my sister,
15 Where, then, will my hope be,
and who will take account of my piety?
16 I cannot take them down to Sheol with me,
nor can they descend with me into the earth. [. . .]

Job's Final Survey of His Case[37]

29

1 Then Job resumed his discourse:

2 If I could only go back to the old days,
to the time when God was watching over me,
3 when his lamp shone above my head,
and by its light I walked through the darkness!
4 If I could be as in the days of my prime,
when God protected my home,
5 while the Almighty was still there at my side,
and my servants stood round me,
6 while my path flowed with milk,
and the rocks streamed oil!
7 If I went through the gate out of the town
to take my seat in the public square,
8 young men saw me and kept out of sight;
old men rose to their feet,
9 men in authority broke off their talk
and put their hands to their lips;
10 the voices of the nobles died away,

[37] **Job's . . . Case:** The round of speeches by Job's friends and his responses in chapters 20–28 generally repeats earlier arguments. With chapter 29 Job wishes to return to his past happiness, wealth, and prestige.

and every man held his tongue.
21[38] They listened to me expectantly
and waited in silence for my opinion.
22 When I had spoken, no one spoke again;
my words fell gently on them;
23 they waited for them as for rain
and drank them in like showers in spring.
24 When I smiled on them, they took heart;
when my face lit up, they lost their gloomy looks.
25 I presided over them, planning their course,
like a king encamped with his troops.

11 Whoever heard of me spoke in my favour,
and those who saw me bore witness to my merit,
12 how I saved the poor man when he called for help
and the orphan who had no protector.
13 The man threatened with ruin blessed me,
and I made the widow's heart sing for joy.
14 I put on righteousness as a garment and it clothed me;
justice, like a cloak or a turban, wrapped me round.
15 I was eyes to the blind
and feet to the lame;
16 I was a father to the needy,
and I took up the stranger's cause.
17 I broke the fangs of the miscreant
and rescued the prey from his teeth.
18 I thought, 'I shall die with my powers unimpaired
and my days uncounted as the grains of sand,[39]
19 with my roots spreading out to the water
and the dew lying on my branches,
20 with the bow always new in my grasp
and the arrow ever ready to my hand.'

30

1 But now I am laughed to scorn
by men of a younger generation,
men whose fathers I would have disdained
to put with the dogs who kept my flock.
2 What use were their strong arms to me,
since their sturdy vigour had wasted away?
3 They gnawed roots in the desert,

[38] Verses 21–25 transposed to follow verse 11.

[39] **grains of sand:** A variant reading of this phrase is "as those of the phoenix," which was the fabled bird that arose to new life from the ashes of its funeral pyre.

gaunt with want and hunger,
4 they plucked saltwort and wormwood
and root of broom[40] for their food.
5 Driven out from the society of men,
pursued like thieves with hue and cry,
6 they lived in gullies and ravines,
holes in the earth and rocky clefts;
7 they howled like beasts among the bushes,
huddled together beneath the scrub,
8 vile base-born wretches,
hounded from the haunts of men.
9 Now I have become the target of their taunts,
my name is a byword among them.
10 They loathe me, they shrink from me,
they dare to spit in my face.
11 They run wild and savage me;
at sight of me they throw off all restraint.
12 On my right flank they attack in a mob;
they raise their siege-ramps against me,
13 they tear down my crumbling defences to my undoing,
and scramble up against me unhindered;
14 they burst in through the gaping breach;
at the moment of the crash they come rolling in.
15 Terror upon terror overwhelms me,
it sweeps away my resolution like the wind,
and my hope of victory vanishes like a cloud.
16 So now my soul is in turmoil within me,
and misery has me daily in its grip.
17 By night pain pierces my very bones,
and there is ceaseless throbbing in my veins;
18 my garments are all bespattered with my phlegm,
which chokes me like the collar of a shirt.
19 God himself has flung me down in the mud,
no better than dust or ashes.

20 I call for thy help, but thou dost not answer;
I stand up to plead, but thou sittest aloof;
21 thou hast turned cruelly against me
and with thy strong hand pursuest me in hatred;
22 thou dost snatch me up and set me astride the wind,
and the tempest tosses me up and down.

[40] **saltwort . . . broom:** Saltwort is a plant in the goosefoot family that grows on the saline soils of seashores; wormwood is a bitter-tasting plant with yellow or white flowers; broom is probably the fungus on broom, a flowering shrub.

23 I know that thou wilt hand me over to death,
to the place appointed for all mortal men.

24 Yet no beggar held out his hand
but was relieved by me in his distress.
25 Did I not weep for the man whose life was hard?
Did not my heart grieve for the poor?
26 Evil has come though I expected good;
I looked for light but there came darkness.
27 My bowels are in ferment and know no peace;
days of misery stretch out before me.
28 I go about dejected and friendless;
I rise in the assembly, only to appeal for help.
29 The wolf is now my brother,
the owls of the desert have become my companions.
30 My blackened skin peels off,
and my body is scorched by the heat.
31 My harp has been tuned for a dirge,
my flute to the voice of those who weep.

31

2[41] What is the lot prescribed by God above,
the reward from the Almighty on high?
3 Is not ruin prescribed for the miscreant
and calamity for the wrongdoer?
4 Yet does not God himself see my ways
and count my every step?

5 I swear I have had no dealings with falsehood
and have not embarked on a course of deceit.
1 I have come to terms with my eyes,
never to take notice of a girl.
6 Let God weigh me in the scales of justice,
and he will know that I am innocent!
7 If my steps have wandered from the way,
if my heart has followed my eyes,
or any dirt stuck to my hands,
8 may another eat what I sow,
and may my crops be pulled up by the roots!
9 If my heart has been enticed by a woman
or I have lain in wait at my neighbour's door,

[41] Verse 1 transposed to follow verse 5.

10 may my wife be another man's slave,
and may other men enjoy her.
11 [But that is a wicked act, an offence before the law;
12 it would be a consuming and destructive fire,
raging among my crops.]
13 If I have ever rejected the plea of my slave
or of my slave-girl, when they brought their complaint to me,
14 what shall I do if God appears?
What shall I answer if he intervenes?
15 Did not he who made me in the womb make them?
Did not the same God create us in the belly?
16 If I have withheld their needs from the poor
or let the widow's eye grow dim with tears,
17 if I have eaten my crust alone,
and the orphan has not shared it with me—
18 the orphan who from boyhood honoured me like a father,
whom I guided from the day of his birth—
19 if I have seen anyone perish for lack of clothing,
or a poor man with nothing to cover him,
20 if his body had no cause to bless me,
because he was not kept warm with a fleece from my flock,
21 if I have raised my hand against the innocent,
knowing that men would side with me in court,
22 then may my shoulder-blade be torn from my shoulder,
my arm be wrenched out of its socket!
23 But the terror of God was heavy upon me,
and for fear of his majesty I could do none of these things.
24 If I have put my faith in gold
and my trust in the gold of Nubia,[42]
25 if I have rejoiced in my great wealth
and in the increase of riches;
26 if I ever looked on the sun in splendour
or the moon moving in her glory,
27 and was led astray in my secret heart
and raised my hand in homage;
28 this would have been an offence before the law,
for I should have been unfaithful to God on high.
38[43] If my land has cried out in reproach at me,
and its furrows have joined in weeping,
39 if I have eaten its produce without payment

[42] **Nubia:** Ethiopia.

[43] Verses 38–40 are transposed here to follow verse 28, except for the last line of verse 40 which concludes the section after verse 37 below.

and have disappointed my creditors,
40 may thistles spring up instead of wheat,
and weeds instead of barley!

29 Have I rejoiced at the ruin of the man that hated me
or been filled with malice when trouble overtook him,
30 even though I did not allow my tongue to sin
by demanding his life with a curse?
31 Have the men of my household never said,
'Let none of us speak ill of him!
32 No stranger has spent the night in the street'?
For I have kept open house for the traveller.
33 Have I ever concealed my misdeeds as men do,
keeping my guilt to myself,
34 because I feared the gossip of the town
or dreaded the scorn of my fellow-citizens?
35 Let me but call a witness in my defence!
Let the Almighty state his case against me!
If my accuser had written out his indictment,
I would not keep silence and remain indoors.
36 No! I would flaunt it on my shoulder
and wear it like a crown on my head;
37 I would plead the whole record of my life
and present that in court as my defence.

Job's speeches are finished.

God's Answer and Job's Submission[44]

38

1 Then the Lord answered Job out of the tempest:

2 Who is this whose ignorant words
cloud my design in darkness?
3 Brace[45] yourself and stand up like a man;
I will ask questions, and you shall answer.
4 Where were you when I laid the earth's foundations?
Tell me, if you know and understand.
5 Who settled its dimensions? Surely you should know.
Who stretched his measuring-line over it?
6 On what do its supporting pillars rest?

[44] **God's . . . Submission:** Chapters 32–37 are a series of speeches by Elihu, a new character; they seem to interrupt the text and repeat the arguments made by Job's friends. Beginning with chapter 38, Job finally has a hearing before God.

[45] **Brace:** Prepare for warfare.

Who set its corner-stone in place,
7 when the morning stars sang together
and all the sons of God shouted aloud?
8 Who watched over the birth of the sea,
when it burst in flood from the womb?—
9 when I wrapped it in a blanket of cloud
and cradled it in fog,
10 when I established its bounds,
fixing its doors and bars in place,
11 and said, 'Thus far shall you come and no farther,
and here your surging waves shall halt.'
12 In all your life have you ever called up the dawn
or shown the morning its place?
13 Have you taught it to grasp the fringes of the earth
and shake the Dog-star from its place;
14 to bring up the horizon in relief as clay under a seal,
until all things stand out like the folds of a cloak,
15 when the light of the Dog-star is dimmed
and the stars of the Navigator's Line[46] go out one by one?
16 Have you descended to the springs of the sea
or walked in the unfathomable deep?
17 Have the gates of death been revealed to you?
Have you ever seen the door-keepers of the place of darkness?
18 Have you comprehended the vast expanses of the world?
Come, tell me all this, if you know.
19 Which is the way to the home of light
and where does darkness dwell?
20 And can you then take each to its appointed bound
and escort it on its homeward path?
21 Doubtless you know all this; for you were born already,
so long is the span of your life!

22 Have you visited the storehouse of the snow
or seen the arsenal where hail is stored,
23 which I have kept ready for the day of calamity,
for war and for the hour of battle?
24 By what paths is the heat spread abroad
or the east wind carried far and wide over the earth?
25 Who has cut channels for the downpour
and cleared a passage for the thunderstorm,
26 for rain to fall on land where no man lives
and on the deserted wilderness,
27 clothing lands waste and derelict with green
and making grass grow on thirsty ground?

[46] **Navigator's Line:** One of the constellations, probably Ursa Major.

28 Has the rain a father?
Who sired the drops of dew?
29 Whose womb gave birth to the ice,
and who was the mother of the frost from heaven,
30 which lays a stony cover over the waters
and freezes the expanse of ocean?
31 Can you bind the cluster of the Pleiades
or loose Orion's belt?
32 Can you bring out the signs of the zodiac in their season
or guide Aldebaran and its train?
33 Did you proclaim the rules that govern the heavens,
or determine the laws of nature on earth?
34 Can you command the dense clouds
to cover you with their weight of waters?
35 If you bid lightning speed on its way,
will it say to you, 'I am ready'?
36 Who put wisdom in depths of darkness
and veiled understanding in secrecy?
37 Who is wise enough to marshal the rain-clouds
and empty the cisterns of heaven,
38 when the dusty soil sets hard as iron,
and the clods of earth cling together?
39 Do you hunt her prey for the lioness
and satisfy the hunger of young lions,
40 as they crouch in the lair
or lie in wait in the covert?
41 Who provides the raven with its quarry
when its fledglings croak for lack of food?

39

1 Do you know when the mountain-goats are born
or attend the wild doe when she is in labour?
2 Do you count the months that they carry their young
or know the time of their delivery,
3 when they crouch down to open their wombs
and bring their offspring to the birth,
4 when the fawns grow and thrive in the open forest,
and go forth and do not return?
5 Who has let the wild ass of Syria range at will
and given the wild ass of Arabia its freedom?—
6 whose home I have made in the wilderness
and its lair in the saltings;
7 it disdains the noise of the city
and is deaf to the driver's shouting;

8 it roams the hills as its pasture
and searches for anything green.
9 Does the wild ox consent to serve you,
does it spend the night in your stall?
10 Can you harness its strength with ropes,
or will it harrow the furrows after you?
11 Can you depend on it, strong as it is,
or leave your labour to it?
12 Do you trust it to come back
and bring home your grain to the threshing-floor?

13 The wings of the ostrich are stunted;
her pinions and plumage are so scanty
14 that she abandons her eggs to the ground,
letting them be kept warm by the sand.
15 She forgets that a foot may crush them,
or a wild beast trample on them;
16 she treats her chicks heartlessly as if they were not hers,
not caring if her labour is wasted
17 (for God has denied her wisdom
and left her without sense),
18 while like a cock she struts over the uplands,
scorning both horse and rider.
19 Did you give the horse his strength?
Did you clothe his neck with a mane?
20 Do you make him quiver like a locust's wings,
when his shrill neighing strikes terror?
21 He shows his mettle as he paws and prances;
he charges the armoured line with all his might.
22 He scorns alarms and knows no dismay;
he does not flinch before the sword.
23 The quiver rattles at his side,
the spear and sabre flash.
24 Trembling with eagerness, he devours the ground
and cannot be held in when he hears the horn;
25 at the blast of the horn he cries 'Aha!'
and from afar he scents the battle.
26 Does your skill teach the hawk to use its pinions
and spread its wings towards the south?
27 Do you instruct the vulture to fly high
and build its nest aloft?
28 It dwells among the rocks and there it lodges;
its station is a crevice in the rock;
29 from there it searches for food,
keenly scanning the distance,

30 that its brood may be gorged with blood;
and where the slain are, there the vulture is.

41[47]

1 Can you pull out the whale with a gaff
or can you slip a noose round its tongue?
2 Can you pass a cord through its nose
or put a hook through its jaw?
3 Will it plead with you for mercy
or beg its life with soft words?
4 Will it enter into an agreement with you
to become your slave for life?
5 Will you toy with it as with a bird
or keep it on a string like a songbird for your maidens?
6 Do trading-partners haggle over it
or merchants share it out?

40

1 Then the Lord said to Job:

2 Is it for a man who disputes with the Almighty to be stubborn?
Should he that argues with God answer back?

3 And Job answered the Lord:

4 What reply can I give thee, I who carry no weight?
I put my finger to my lips.
5 I have spoken once and now will not answer again:
twice have I spoken, and I will do so no more.

6 The the Lord answered Job out of the tempest:

7 Brace yourself and stand up like a man;
I will ask questions, and you shall answer.
8 Dare you deny that I am just
or put me in the wrong that you may be right?
9 Have you an arm like God's arm,
can you thunder with a voice like his?
10 Deck yourself out, if you can, in pride and dignity,
array yourself in pomp and splendour;
11 unleash the fury of your wrath,
look upon the proud man and humble him;

---

[47] Chapters 41:1–6 are transposed to this point.

12 look upon every proud man and bring him low,
throw down the wicked where they stand;
13 hide them in the dust together,
and shroud them in an unknown grave.
14 Then I in my turn will acknowledge
that your own right hand can save you.

15 Consider the chief of the beasts, the crocodile,[48]
who devours cattle as if they were grass:
16 what strength is in his loins!
what power in the muscles of his belly!
17 His tail is rigid as a cedar,
the sinews of his flanks are closely knit,
18 his bones are tubes of bronze,
and his limbs like bars of iron.
19 He is the chief of God's works,
made to be a tyrant over his peers;
20 for he takes the cattle of the hills for his prey
and in his jaws he crunches all wild beasts.
21 There under the thorny lotus he lies,
hidden in the reeds and the marsh;
22 the lotus conceals him in its shadow,
the poplars of the stream surround him.
23 If the river is in spate,[49] he is not scared,
he sprawls at his ease though the stream is in flood.
24 Can a man blind his eyes and take him
or pierce his nose with the teeth of a trap?

41.7

7 Can you fill his skin with harpoons
or his head with fish-hooks?
8 If ever you lift your hand against him,
think of the struggle that awaits you, and let be.

9 No, such a man is in desperate case,
hurled headlong at the very sight of him.
10 How fierce he is when he is roused!
Who is there to stand up to him?
11 Who has ever attacked him unscathed?
Not a man under the wide heaven.
12 I will not pass over in silence his limbs,

[48] **crocodile:** Other translations use "hippopotamus" or "Behemoth" here; the latter suggests a primeval monster of chaos—see note 22. [Editors' note.]

[49] **spate:** Flood.

his prowess and the grace of his proportions.
13 Who has ever undone his outer garment
or penetrated his doublet of hide?
14 Who has ever opened the portals of his face?
for there is terror in his arching teeth.
15 His back is row upon row of shields,
enclosed in a wall of flints;
16 one presses so close on the other
that air cannot pass between them,
17 each so firmly clamped to its neighbour
that they hold and cannot spring apart.
18 His sneezing sends out sprays of light,
and his eyes gleam like the shimmer of dawn.
19 Firebrands shoot from his mouth,
and sparks come streaming out;
20 his nostrils pour forth smoke
like a cauldron on a fire blown to full heat.
21 His breath sets burning coals ablaze,
and flames flash from his mouth.
22 Strength is lodged in his neck,
and untiring energy dances ahead of him.
23 Close knit is his underbelly,
no pressure will make it yield.
24 His heart is firm as a rock,
firm as the nether millstone.
25 When he raises himself, strong men take fright,
bewildered at the lashings of his tail.
26 Sword or spear, dagger or javelin,
if they touch him, they have no effect.
27 Iron he counts as straw,
and bronze as rotting wood.
28 No arrow can pierce him,
and for him sling-stones are turned into chaff;
29 to him a club is a mere reed,
and he laughs at the swish of the sabre.
30 Armoured beneath with jagged sherds,
he sprawls on the mud like a threshing-sledge.
31 He makes the deep water boil like a cauldron,
he whips up the lake like ointment in a mixing-bowl.
32 He leaves a shining trail behind him,
and the great river is like white hair in his wake.
33 He has no equal on earth;
for he is made quite without fear.
34 He looks down on all creatures, even the highest;
he is king over all proud beasts.

42

1 Then Job answered the LORD:

2 I know that thou canst do all things
and that no purpose is beyond thee.
3 But I have spoken of great things which I have not understood,
things too wonderful for me to know.
5 I knew of thee then only by report
but now I see thee with my own eyes.
6 Therefore I melt away;[50]
I repent in dust and ashes.

EPILOGUE[51]

7 When the LORD had finished speaking to Job, he said to Eliphaz the Temanite, 'I am
angry with you and your two friends, because you have not spoken as you ought
8 about me, as my servant Job has done. So now take seven bulls and seven rams, go to
my servant Job and offer a whole-offering for yourselves, and he will intercede for
you; I will surely show him favour by not being harsh with you because you have not
9 spoken as you ought about me, as he has done.' Then Eliphaz the Temanite and Bildad the Shuhite and Zophar the Naamathite went and carried out the LORD's com-
10 mand, and the LORD showed favour to Job when he had interceded for his friends. So
the LORD restored Job's fortunes and doubled all his possessions.
11 Then all Job's brothers and sisters and his former acquaintance came and
feasted with him in his home, and they consoled and comforted him for all the misfortunes which the LORD had brought on him; and each of them gave him a sheep
12 and a gold ring.[52] Furthermore, the LORD blessed the end of Job's life more than the
beginning; and he had fourteen thousand head of small cattle and six thousand
13 camels, a thousand yoke of oxen and as many she-asses. He had seven sons and three
14 daughters; and he named his eldest daughter Jemimah, the second Keziah and the
15 third Keren-happuch.[53] There were no women in all the world so beautiful as Job's
daughters; and their father gave them an inheritance with their brothers.
16 Thereafter Job lived another hundred and forty years, he saw his sons and his
17 grandsons to four generations, and died at a very great age.[54]

---

[50] **melt away:** Or "despise myself."

[51] **Epilogue:** The prose Epilogue, like the Prologue, probably represents an earlier story. [Editors' note.]

[52] **gold ring:** For the ear or nose.

[53] **Jemimah . . . Keren-happuch:** Jemimah means "dove"; Keziah means "cinnamon"; Keren-happuch means "horn of eye-shadow." The specific mention of daughters receiving an inheritance is unique in Hebrew Scriptures.

[54] **great age:** Job's lifespan becomes double the usual expectation. The language here is reminiscent of descriptions of the patriarchs in the Book of Genesis.

Psalm 23

1 The LORD is my shepherd; I shall want nothing.
2 He makes me lie down in green pastures,
and leads me beside the waters of peace;
3 he renews life within me,
and for his name's sake guides me in the right path.
4 Even though I walk through a valley dark as death
I fear no evil, for thou art with me,
thy staff and thy crook[1] are with my comfort.

5 Thou spreadest a table for me in the sight of my enemies;
thou hast richly bathed my head with oil,[2]
and my cup runs over.
6 Goodness and love unfailing, these will follow me
all the days of my life,
and I shall dwell in the house of the LORD
my whole life long.

Psalms. The Jewish law against idolatry forbade the creation of visual art, but there was no injunction against the ancient Hebrews being magnificent poets; one of the most treasured collections of lyrics or songs is Psalms. King David, who has the reputation of being a musician and a poet, is credited with composing seventy-three Psalms. Numerous other poets made contributions as well. Because of the references within the work, it is possible to date Psalm 137 between 586 and 538 B.C.E., as an exile lament, but most of the Psalms do not reference specific historical events or time periods.

The most common feature of Hebrew poetry is parallelism, and the two most common types of parallelism are when two lines are complementary (different words expressing similar ideas) or two lines are antithetical (lines in which two ideas oppose each other). An example of the first type is found in Psalm 104:

> The trees of the Lord are green and leafy,
> the cedars of Lebanon which he planted. . . .

Psalm 23 contains an example of antithetical parallelism:

> Even though I walk through a valley dark as death
> I fear no evil, for thou art with me. . . .

Psalm 121 illustrates two other poetic techniques common to Hebrew poetry: one is a version of parallelism in which a question is followed by an answer: ". . . where shall I find help? / Help comes only from the Lord. . . ." Hebrew verse also uses simple repetition in the form of a word or phrase repeated and woven into several lines, such as the repeated use of the words *guard* and *guardian* in the second half of Psalm 121.

---

[1] **staff . . . crook:** A staff was used to ward off wild animals and a crook was used for guiding sheep.

[2] **oil:** It was a Near Eastern tradition to anoint the head of an honored guest with oil.

Psalm 104[3]

1 Bless the LORD, my soul:
O LORD my God, thou art great indeed,
clothed in majesty and splendour,
2 and wrapped in a robe of light.
Thou hast spread out the heavens like a tent
3 and on their waters laid the beams of thy pavilion;
who takest the clouds for thy chariot,
riding on the wings of the wind;
4 who makest the winds thy messengers
and flames of fire thy servants;
5 thou didst fix the earth on its foundation
so that it never can be shaken;
6 the deep overspread it like a cloak,
and the waters lay above the mountains.
7 At thy rebuke they ran,
at the sound of thy thunder they rushed away,
8 flowing over the hills,
pouring down into the valleys
to the place appointed for them.
9 Thou didst fix a boundary which they might not pass;
they shall not return to cover the earth.

10 Thou dost make springs break out in the gullies,
so that their water runs between the hills.
11 The wild beasts all drink from them,
the wild asses quench their thirst;
12 the birds of the air nest on their banks
and sing among the leaves.

13 From thy high pavilion thou dost water the hills;
the earth is enriched by thy provision.
14 Thou makest grass grow for the cattle
and green things for those who toil for man,
bringing bread out of the earth
15 and wine to gladden men's hearts,
oil to make their faces shine
and bread to sustain their strength.
16 The trees of the LORD are green and leafy,
the cedars of Lebanon which he planted;

[3] **Psalm 104:** A creation hymn often compared to the Egyptian "Hymn to Aten" and to the Mesopotamian *Epic of Creation* (*Enuma Elish*) since it uses similar mythological language.

17 the birds build their nests in them,
the stork makes her home in their tops.
18 High hills are the haunt of the mountain-goat,
and boulders a refuge for the rock-badger.

19 Thou hast made the moon to measure the year
and taught the sun where to set.
20 When thou makest darkness and it is night,
all the beasts of the forest come forth;
21 the young lions roar for prey,
seeking their food from God.
22 When thou makest the sun rise, they slink away
and go to rest in their lairs;
23 but man comes out to his work
and to his labours until evening.
24 Countless are the things thou hast made, O LORD.
Thou hast made all by thy wisdom;
and the earth is full of thy creatures,
25 beasts great and small.

Here is the great immeasurable sea,
in which move creatures beyond number.
26 Here ships sail to and fro,
here is Leviathan[4] whom thou hast made thy plaything.

27 All of them look expectantly to thee
to give them their food at the proper time;
28 what thou givest them they gather up;
when thou opened thy hand, they eat their fill.
29 Then thou hidest thy face, and they are restless and troubled;
when thou takest away their breath, they fail
[and they return to the dust from which they came];
30 but when thou breathest into them, they recover;
thou givest new life to the earth.

31 May the glory of the LORD stand for ever
and may he rejoice in his works!
32 When he looks at the earth, it quakes;
when he touches the hills, they pour forth smoke.

33 I will sing to the LORD as long as I live,
all my life I will sing psalms to my God.

[4] **Leviathan:** A sea monster symbolizing primeval chaos. [Editors' note]

34 May my meditation please the LORD,
as I show my joy in him!
35 Away with all sinners from the earth
and may the wicked be no more!

Bless the LORD, my soul.

O praise the LORD.

Psalm 137[5]

1 By the rivers of Babylon[6] we set down and wept
when we remembered Zion.[7]
2 There on the willow-trees
we hung up our harps,
3 for there those who carried us off
demanded music and singing,
and our captors called on us to be merry:
'Sing us one of the songs of Zion.'
4 How could we sing the LORD's song
in a foreign land?

5 If I forget you, O Jerusalem,
let my right hand wither away;
6 let my tongue cling to the roof of my mouth
if I do not remember you,
if I do not set Jerusalem
above my highest joy.
7 Remember, O LORD, against the people of Edom[8]
the day of Jerusalem's fall,
when they said, 'Down with it, down with it,
down to its very foundations!'
8 O Babylon, Babylon the destroyer,
happy the man who repays you
for all that you did to us!
9 Happy is he who shall seize your children
and dash them against the rock.

[5] **Psalm 137:** A lament sung in the Exile, after the destruction of Jerusalem by the Babylonians in 587 B.C.E.
[6] **rivers of Babylon:** The Tigris and Euphrates Rivers.
[7] **Zion:** The hill in Jerusalem on which the Temple was built, considered the center of Jewish life.
[8] **Edom:** Southwest of Judah, and allied with the Babylonian defeat of Jerusalem in 587 B.C.E.

The Song of Songs

1

BRIDE:

1 I will sing the song of all songs[1] to Solomon
2 that he may smother me with kisses.

Your love is more fragrant than wine,
3 fragrant is the scent of your perfume,
and your name like perfume poured out;
for this the maidens love you.
4 Take me with you, and we will run together;
bring me into your chamber, O king.[2]

COMPANIONS:

Let us rejoice and be glad for you;
Let us praise your love more than wine,
    and your caresses more than any song.

BRIDE:

5 I am dark but lovely, daughters of Jerusalem,
    like the tents of Kedar
    or the tent-curtains of Shalmah.[3]
6 Do not look down on me; a little dark I may be
    because I am scorched by the sun.
My mother's sons were displeased with me,
they sent me to watch over the vineyards;
so I did not watch over my own vineyard.

The Song of Songs. In some translations this work is called the Song of Solomon since its first line ascribes authorship to King Solomon (r. 960–922 B.C.E.), who was considered a great poet like his father, King David. Solomon's name would lend prestige to the work, but in fact modern scholars believe that it was written down after he lived, between 350 and 250 B.C.E., although it might have existed orally for several centuries prior to that. This book is also called Canticles, or Canticle of Canticles; a canticle is a hymn that uses words from the Bible.

Not knowing exactly how to classify this piece of writing, some commentators have called it a wedding idyll. An idyl, or idyll, is a lyric poem that features picturesque, pastoral images that stress romantic rather than heroic elements. The images of doves, flowers, pomegranates, gardens, gazelles, goats, fawns, honey, raisins, apricots, and wheat not only create a natural setting for the songs but also have a long history of association with sexuality, the human body, and bliss.

---

[1] **song of all songs:** The best of songs. [2] **king:** Bridegroom. [3] **Shalmah:** Possibly it was near Kedar in northern Arabia.

7 Tell me, my true love,
where you mind your flocks,
where you rest them at midday,
that I may not be left picking lice
as I sit among your companions' herds.

BRIDEGROOM:

8 If you yourself do not know,
O fairest of women,
go, follow the tracks of the sheep
and mind your kids by the shepherds' huts.

9 I would compare you, my dearest,
to Pharaoh's chariot-horses.
10 Your cheeks are lovely between plaited tresses,
your neck with its jewelled chains.

COMPANIONS:

11 We will make you braided plaits of gold
set with beads of silver.

BRIDE:

12 While the king reclines on his couch,
my spikenard[4] gives forth its scent.
13 My beloved is for me a bunch of myrrh[5]
as he lies on my breast,
14 my beloved is for me a cluster of henna-blossom[6]
from the vineyards of En-gedi.[7]

BRIDEGROOM:

15 How beautiful you are, my dearest,
O how beautiful,
your eyes are like doves!

BRIDE:

16 How beautiful you are, O my love,
and how pleasant!

BRIDEGROOM:

Our couch is shaded with branches;
17 the beams of our house are of cedar,
our ceilings are all of fir.

[4] **spikenard:** A fragrant ointment popular in the ancient world. [Editors' note.]
[5] **myrrh:** A gum resin made from several plants in Arabia and used for incense and perfume. [Editors' note.]
[6] **henna-blossom:** Plant used for dyeing hair auburn or reddish-brown. [Editors' note.]
[7] **En-gedi:** On the western edge of the Dead Sea.

2

BRIDE:

1 I am an asphodel in Sharon,[8]
a lily growing in the valley.

BRIDEGROOM:

2 No, a lily among thorns
is my dearest among girls.

BRIDE:

3 Like an apricot-tree among the trees of the wood,
so is my beloved among boys.
To sit in its shadow was my delight,
and its fruit was sweet to my taste.
4 He took me into the wine-garden
and gave me loving glances.
5 He refreshed me with raisins, he revived me with apricots;
for I was faint with love.
6 His left arm was under my head, his right arm was round me.

BRIDEGROOM:

7 I charge you, daughters of Jerusalem,
by the spirits and the goddesses of the field:
Do not rouse her, do not disturb my love
until she is ready.

BRIDE:

8 Hark! My beloved! Here he comes,
bounding over the mountains, leaping over the hills.
9 My beloved is like a gazelle
or a young wild goat:
there he stands outside our wall,
peeping in at the windows, glancing through the lattice.

10 My beloved answered, he said to me:
Rise up, my darling;
my fairest, come away.
11 For now the winter is past,
the rains are over and gone;
12 the flowers appear in the countryside;
the time is coming when the birds will sing,
and the turtle-dove's cooing will be heard in our land;
13 when the green figs will ripen on the fig-trees
and the vines give forth their fragrance.

[8] **Sharon:** The coastal plain in north central Israel.

Rise up, my darling;
my fairest, come away.

BRIDEGROOM:

14 My dove, that hides in holes in the cliffs
or in crannies on the high ledges,
let me see your face, let me hear your voice;
for your voice is pleasant, your face is lovely.

COMPANIONS:

15 Catch for us the jackals, the little jackals,[9]
that spoil our vineyards, when the vines are in flower.

BRIDE:

16 My beloved is mine and I am his;
he delights in the lilies.
17 While the day is cool and the shadows are dispersing,
turn, my beloved, and show yourself
a gazelle or a young wild goat
on the hills where cinnamon grows.

3

1 Night after night on my bed
I have sought my true love;
I have sought him but not found him,
I have called him but he has not answered.
2 I said, 'I will rise and go the rounds of the city,
through the streets and the squares,
seeking my true love.'
I sought him but I did not find him,
I called him but he did not answer.
3 The watchmen, going the rounds of the city, met me,
and I asked, 'Have you seen my true love?'
4 Scarcely had I left them behind me
when I met my true love.
I seized him and would not let him go
until I had brought him to my mother's house,
to the room of her who conceived me.

BRIDEGROOM:

5 I charge you, daughters of Jerusalem,
by the spirits and the goddesses of the field:

[9] **jackals:** The import of the verse is unclear; it is directed against someone or something interfering with the lovers.

Do not rouse her, do not disturb my love
until she is ready.

COMPANIONS:

6 What is this coming up from the wilderness
like a column of smoke
from burning myrrh or frankincense,
from all the powdered spices that merchants bring?
7 Look; it is Solomon[10] carried in his litter;
sixty of Israel's chosen warriors
are his escort,
8 all of them skilled swordsmen,
all trained to handle arms,
each with his sword ready at his side
to ward off the demon of the night.

9 The Palanquin which King Solomon had made for himself
was of wood from Lebanon.
10 Its poles he had made of silver,
its head-rest of gold;
its seat was of purple stuff,
and its lining was of leather.

11 Come out, daughters of Jerusalem;
you daughters of Zion, come out and welcome King Solomon,
wearing the crown with which his mother has crowned him,
on his wedding day, on his day of joy.

4

BRIDEGROOM:

1 How beautiful you are, my dearest, how beautiful!
Your eyes behind your veil are like doves,
your hair like a flock of goats streaming down Mount Gilead.[11]
2 Your teeth are like a flock of ewes just shorn
which have come up fresh from the dipping;
each ewe has twins and none has cast a lamb.
3 Your lips are like a scarlet thread,
and your words are delightful;
your parted lips behind your veil
are like a pomegranate cut open.
4 Your neck is like David's tower,

[10] **Solomon:** The legendary style of Solomon was perhaps the model for every groom to aspire to.

[11] **Mount Gilead:** A mountain east of the Jordan.

which is built with winding courses;
a thousand bucklers hang upon it,
and all are warriors' shields.
5 Your two breasts are like two fawns,
twin fawns of a gazelle.
6 While the day is cool and the shadows are dispersing,
I will go to the mountains of myrrh
and to the hills of frankincense.[12]
7 You are beautiful, my dearest,
beautiful without a flaw.

8 Come from Lebanon, my bride;
come with me from Lebanon.
Hurry down from the top of Amana,
from Senir's top and Hermon's,[13]
from the lions' lairs, and the hills the leopards haunt.

9 You have stolen my heart, my sister,[14]
you have stolen it, my bride,
with one of your eyes, with one jewel of your necklace.
10 How beautiful are your breasts, my sister, my bride!
Your love is more fragrant than wine,
and your perfumes sweeter than any spices.
11 Your lips drop sweetness like the honeycomb, my bride,
syrup and milk are under your tongue,
and your dress has the scent of Lebanon.
13[15] Your two cheeks are an orchard of pomegranates,
an orchard full of rare fruits:
14 spikenard and saffron, sweet-cane and cinnamon
with every incense-bearing tree,
myrr and aloes
with all the choicest spices.
12 My sister, my bride, is a garden close-locked,[16]
a garden close-locked, a fountain sealed.

BRIDE:

15 The fountain in my garden is a spring of running water
pouring down from Lebanon.

---

[12] **frankincense:** A gum resin from Arabian and north African trees used for incense. [Editors' note.]

[13] **Hermon's:** Many commentators hold that this is an old poem from Lebanon, and hence the mention of Lebanese mountaintops.

[14] **sister:** A term of endearment as in ancient Egypt.

[15] Verse 12 transposed to follow verse 14.

[16] **close-locked:** Her charms are closed to all but her beloved.

16 Awake, north wind, and come, south wind;
blow upon my garden that its perfumes may pour forth,
that my beloved may come to his garden
and enjoy its rare fruits.

5

BRIDEGROOM:

1 I have come to my garden, my sister and bride,
and have plucked my myrrh with my spices;
I have eaten my honey and my syrup,
I have drunk my wine and my milk.
Eat, friends, and drink,
until you are drunk with love.

BRIDE:

2 I sleep but my heart is awake.
Listen! My beloved is knocking:

'Open to me, my sister, my dearest, my dove, my perfect one;
for my head is drenched with dew,
my locks with the moisture of the night.'

3 'I have stripped off my dress; must I put it on again?
I have washed my feet; must I soil them again?'

4 When my beloved slipped his hand through the latch-hole,[17]
my bowels stirred within me.
5 When I arose to open for my beloved,
my hands dripped with myrrh;
the liquid myrrh from my fingers
ran over the knobs of the bolt.
6 With my own hands I opened to my love,
but my love had turned away and gone by;
my heart sank when he turned his back.
I sought him but I did not find him,
I called him but he did not answer.
7 The watchmen, going the rounds of the city, met me;
they struck me and wounded me;
the watchman on the walls took away my cloak.
8 I charge you, daughters of Jerusalem,
if you find my beloved, will you not tell him
that I am faint with love?

[17] **latch-hole:** In the door.

COMPANIONS:

9 What is your beloved more than any other,
O fairest of women?
What is your beloved more than any other,
that you give us this charge?

BRIDE:

10 My beloved is fair and ruddy,
a paragon among ten thousand.
11 His head is gold, finest gold;
his locks are like palm-fronds.
12 His eyes are like doves beside brooks of water,
splashed by the milky water
as they sit where it is drawn.
13 His cheeks are like beds of spices or chests full of perfumes;
his lips are lilies, and drop liquid myrrh;
14 his hands are golden rods set in topaz;
his belly a plaque of ivory overlaid with lapis lazuli.
15 His legs are pillars of marble in sockets of finest gold;
his aspect is like Lebanon, noble as cedars.
16 His whispers are sweetness itself, wholly desirable.
Such is my beloved, such is my darling,
daughters of Jerusalem.

6

COMPANIONS:

1 Where has your beloved gone,
O fairest of women?
Which way did your beloved go,
that we may help you to seek him?

BRIDE:

2 My beloved has gone down to his garden,
to the beds where balsam grows,
to delight in the garden and to pick the lilies.
3 I am my beloved's, and my beloved is mine,
he who delights in the lilies.

BRIDEGROOM:

4 You are beautiful, my dearest, as Tirzah,[18]
lovely as Jerusalem.
5 Turn your eyes away from me;
they dazzle me.
Your hair is like a flock of goats streaming down Mount Gilead;

[18] **Tirzah:** The early residence of the northern kings of Israel.

6 your teeth are like a flock of ewes come up fresh from the dipping,
each ewe has twins and none has cast a lamb.
7 Your parted lips behind your veil
are like a pomegranate[19] cut open.
8 There may be sixty princesses,
eighty concubines, and young women past counting,
9 but there is one alone, my dove, my perfect one,
her mother's only child,
devoted to the mother who bore her;
young girls see her and call her happy,
princesses and concubines praise her.
10 Who is this that looks out like the dawn,
beautiful as the moon, bright as the sun,
majestic as the starry heavens?

11 I went down to a garden of nut-trees
to look at the rushes by the stream,
to see if the vine had budded
or the pomegranates were in flower.
12 I did not know myself;
she made me feel more than a prince
reigning over the myriads of his people.

COMPANIONS:

13 Come back, come back, Shulammite[20] maiden,
come back, that we may gaze upon you.

BRIDEGROOM:

How you love to gaze on the Shulammite maiden,
as she moves between the lines of dancers!

7

1 How beautiful are your sandalled feet, O prince's daughter!
The curves of your thighs are like jewels,
the work of a skilled craftsman.
2 Your navel is a rounded goblet
that never shall want for spiced wine.
Your belly is a heap of wheat
fenced in by lilies.
3 Your two breasts are like two fawns,
twin fawns of a gazelle.
4 Your neck is like a tower of ivory.

---

[19] **pomegranate:** Generally known in the ancient Mediterranean world as a symbol of the womb.

[20] **Shulammite:** The name occurs only here in the book. It seems related to the Hebrew for Solomon.

Your eyes are the pools in Heshbon,[21]
beside the gate of the crowded city.
Your nose is like towering Lebanon
that looks towards Damascus.
5 You carry your head like Carmel;[22]
the flowing hair on your head is lustrous black,
your tresses are braided with ribbons.
6 How beautiful, how entrancing you are,
my loved one, daughter of delights!
7 You are stately as a palm-tree,
and your breasts are the clusters of dates.
8 I said, 'I will climb up into the palm
to grasp its fronds.'
May I find your breasts like clusters of grape on the vine,
the scent of your breath like apricots,
9 and your whispers like spiced wine
flowing smoothly to welcome my caresses,
gliding down through lips and teeth.

BRIDE:

10 I am my beloved's, his longing is all for me.
11 Come, my beloved, let us go out into the fields
to lie among the henna-bushes;
12 let us go early to the vineyards
and see if the vine has budded or its blossom opened,
if the pomegranates are in flower.'
There will I give you my love,
13 when the mandrakes[23] give their perfume,
and all rare fruits are ready at our door,
fruits new and old
which I have in store for you, my love.

8

1 If only you were my own true brother
that sucked my mother's breasts!
Then, if I found you outside, I would kiss you,
and no man would despise me.
2 I would lead you to the room of the mother who bore me,
bring you to her house for you to embrace me;

[21] **Heshbon:** A city in Moab east of the Jordan.

[22] **Carmel:** A famous mountain on the coast, in the north.

[23] **mandrakes:** A plant of the nightshade family; because of its human shape, the root was thought to be an aphrodisiac. [Editors' note.]

I would give you mulled wine to drink
and the fresh juice of pomegranates,
3 your left arm under my head and your right arm round me.

BRIDEGROOM:

4 I charge you, daughters of Jerusalem:
Do not rouse her, do not disturb my love
until she is ready.

COMPANIONS:

5 Who is this coming up from the wilderness
leaning on her beloved?

BRIDEGROOM:

Under the apricot-trees I roused you,
there where your mother was in labour with you,
there where she who bore you was in labour.
6 Wear me as a seal upon your heart,
as a seal upon your arm;
for love is strong as death,
passion cruel as the grave;
it blazes up like blazing fire,
fiercer than any flame.
7 Many waters cannot quench love,
no flood can sweep it away;
if a man were to offer for love
the whole wealth of his house,
it would be utterly scorned.

COMPANIONS:

8 We have a little sister[24]
who has no breasts;
what shall we do for our sister
when she is asked in marriage?
9 If she is a wall,
we will build on it a silver parapet,
but if she is a door,
we will close it up with planks of cedar.

BRIDE:

10 I am a wall and my breasts are like towers;
so in his eyes I am as one who brings contentment.
11 Solomon has a vineyard at Baal-hamon;[25]
he has let out his vineyard to guardians,

[24] **little sister:** To her brothers who seek to protect her, the maiden responds with a statement of her chastity in verses 10–12.

[25] **Baal-hamon:** An unknown place.

and each is to bring for its fruit
a thousand pieces of silver.
12 But my vineyard is mine to give;
the thousand pieces are yours, O Solomon,
and the guardians of the fruit shall have two hundred.[26]

BRIDEGROOM:

13 My bride, you who sit in my garden,
what is it that my friends are listening to?
Let me also hear your voice.

BRIDE:

14 Come into the open, my beloved,
and show yourself like a gazelle or a young wild goat
on the spice-bearing mountains.

[26] **two hundred:** Possibly the dowry.

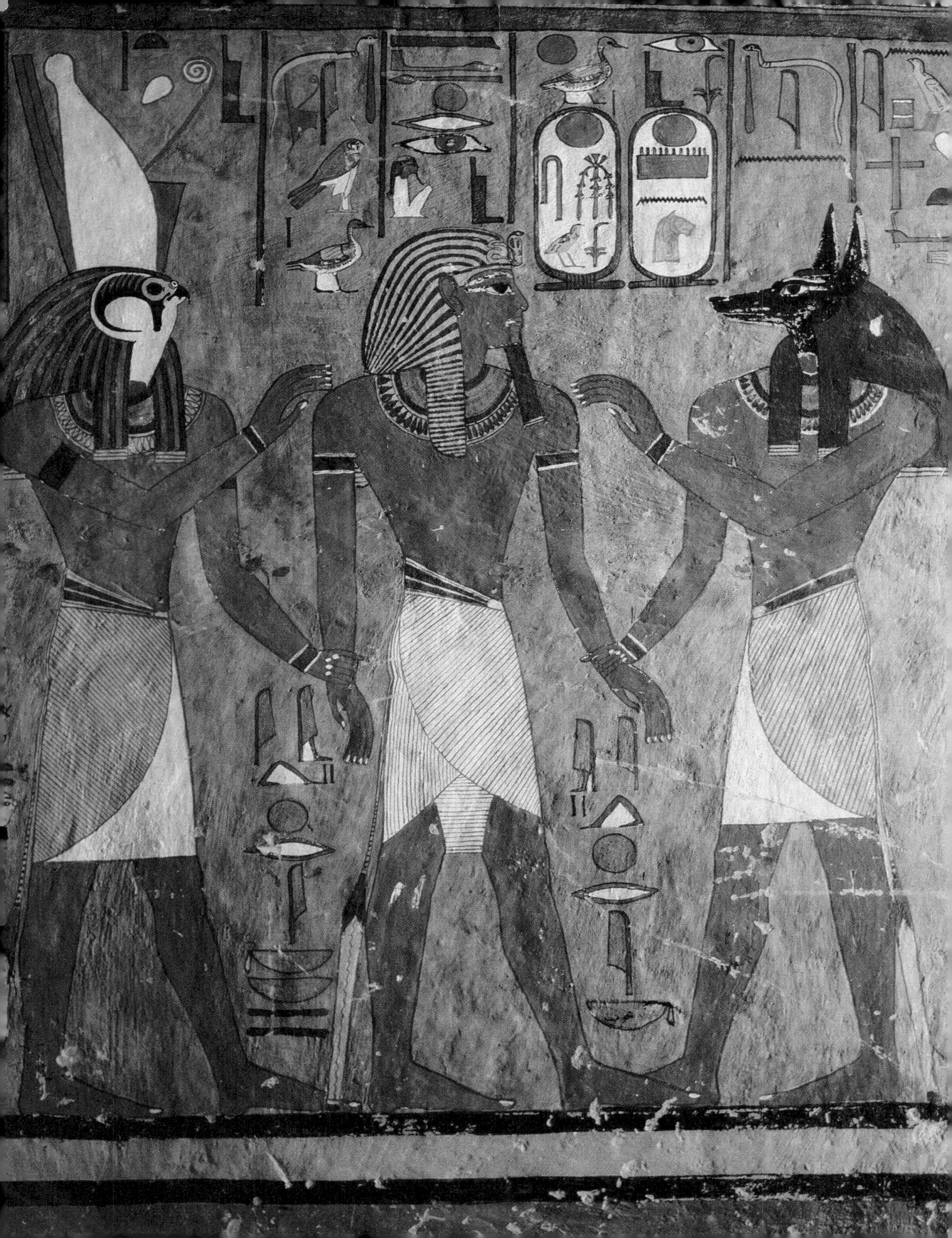

Creating Cosmogony

A remarkable revolution of culture and consciousness took place in Mesopotamia in the fourth millennium B.C.E. The early city-states along the Tigris and Euphrates Rivers tied their vision and understanding of the cosmos to a system or pattern of rulership on earth; in other words, the kingdom was synchronized with the cosmos. The core idea that the microcosm of the palace and temple should reflect or mirror the macrocosm of the celestial realm became the fundamental philosophy of urban civilizations throughout the world. The ancient Egyptians developed the concept of *MAAT,* meaning "right order" or "justice," which they saw as the ruling dynamic of the heavens and made it the social responsibility of both king and commoner, framing a moral society through laws, rules, and customs. The ancient Hebrews, using the idea of a contract or a covenant with their deity, Yahweh, formulated an elaborate regimen of rules for themselves to fulfill their obligation and imagined a bountiful future as their reward for righteousness and for having been especially chosen by God.

The first key ingredients to this relationship between cosmos and kingdom were the development of astronomy and the belief, based on astronomers' observations, that the heavens were orderly. From a careful and systematic study of the heavens, the Sumerians

Having remarked a mathematically calculable regularity in the passages of the planets through the constellations of the fixed stars, these first systematic observers [Mesopotamians] of the heavens conceived — in that specific period, in that specific place, for the first time in human history — the grandiose idea of a mathematically determined cosmic order of greater and lesser, ever-revolving cycles of celestial manifestation, disappearance and renewal, with which it would be prudent for man to put himself in accord.

—JOSEPH CAMPBELL, mythologist, 1974

◀ **Ramses I Flanked by Gods, fourteenth century B.C.E.**
Ancient Egyptian kings and pharaohs were worshiped as gods and received legitimacy for their rule from their association with powerful deities. This fresco from the tomb of Ramses I shows Ramses flanked by Horus, god of the sky, and Anubis, god of embalming. (The Art Archive/Dagli Orti)

Babylonian Tablet Calculating Jupiter's Movements, 500 B.C.E.

A revolution in human consciousness occurred when ancient cultures began studying the heavens and creating a systematic cosmogony. (British Museum, London, UK / The Bridgeman Art Library)

Somehow, [the Sumerian] study of the heavens and their search for a meaningful ordering of human affairs in the new city-states interpenetrated each other, and from this union came a fundamental conviction that we shall call the *cosmological conviction.*

– CORNELIUS LOEW, historian, 1967

had ascertained that the five visible planets followed regular patterns among the fixed stars. The next ingredient was the idea that the sociopolitical realm should somehow imitate the cosmic paradigm. So, like the sun at the center of the heavens, the king and later the pharaoh was the centerpiece of the realm, usually depicted as the representative of the gods, the founder of cities, and the symbol of the city's health. In ancient Egypt and later in Rome, the king or pharaoh actually became a god.

The palace temple, or ZIGGURAT, was at the ceremonial center of the walled city and was itself a symbol of the cosmos. The first architects were a combination of priest, astronomer, and astrologer, men who designed official buildings to reflect the religious dimensions of the universe. A religious calendar marking appropriate and regular ceremonies coordinated the life of the city with the seasons of the agricultural year, themselves related to the movement of the sun and moon among the heavenly constellations. The great family of deities and their roles were the model for the ritual dramas performed at the temple and court and the source of legal prescriptions for the commoners.

Full-time, professional temple priests oversaw this elaborate bilevel world. The priest might appoint or anoint the king; or he may have simply been his instrument in religious matters. The art of writing, developed at this time (c. 3200 B.C.E.), was usually under the control of the priesthood. Writing was necessary for documenting religious rituals and keeping records of taxes and the movement of food and goods from the royal depositories to outlying areas of the realm. Indeed, in addition to the technology necessary for construction and food production, the linchpin of social order in the earliest cities was writing.

For the ancient Egyptians, the concept of *maat* was personified in the sun-god Re, the "lord of *maat*"; each sunrise was an assertion of *maat,* of order over chaos and the serpent **Apophis** or Apep. The earthly but no less divine representative of this daily victory was the king or pharaoh. In the selection from the **Pyramid Texts** anthologized here, a deceased King Unas is resurrected from the dead and joins the company of gods in the sky.

uh-POH-fis

p. 226

As yet no ancient Egyptian laws have been found. There are, however, records of the development of a body of customary laws for urban centers in the Fertile Crescent during the third millennium B.C.E. This tradition later influenced the legal infrastructure of the Babylonian empire and the collections of laws in the Hebrew Scriptures in Israel. Although judges and the military enforced the law, rulers tended to attribute the origin of legal codes to their titular deities and to the idea of cosmic order. God-given law also involved the additional authorities of the temple and priests.

About 2000 B.C.E. the Sumerians of Mesopotamia were invaded by a succession of conquerors from the northern banks of the Euphrates River. Of these, the Babylonians gained control of the whole river valley, laying the foundation for their rule in a mythology dominated by patriarchal sky-deities who were represented on earth by monarchs and warriors. At the conclusion of the Babylonian *Epic of Creation,* or *Enuma Elish* (c. 1800 B.C.E.), the supreme cosmic deity, Marduk, who has conquered the forces of chaos in the form of the serpentine water-goddess Tiamat, assigns lesser deities to the care of the heavenly bodies. For the Babylonians as well, the heavenly hierarchy involving the sun, the moon, and various constellations was the primary model for the organization of political power, from

By what inner change did immemorial custom become written law, did the old village rituals become drama, and magical practices turn into an organized and unified religious cult, built upon cosmic myths that open up vast perspectives of time, space, power?

– LEWIS MUMFORD, critic and historian, 1956

the king down to the peasants as well as of the social classes themselves. An elaborate system of divinely inspired laws bridged the orderly cosmos and the harmonious, smoothly functioning populace. The code of laws associated with the Babylonians is attributed to King **Hammurabi** (p. 229) (r. c. 1792–1750 B.C.E.), who transformed a small city-state into an empire, constructing religious buildings and irrigation systems, and establishing law and order.

hah-moo-RAH-bee

p. 234

The selections from the **Upanishads** presented in this section state in a direct, condensed fashion that human beings live in an orderly and just universe that is sustained by what Hindus call ***DHARMA***. As the basis of human morality—as regulated by the caste system—and cosmic lawfulness, *dharma* is the foundation for the law of karma, which attests that good acts—either mental or physical—bear good fruit and evil actions produce evil. Unlike Hammurabi's Code, justice administrated by a legal system according to written laws, the universal law of karma plays itself out irrespective of human laws. Moreover, karmic cause and effect can carry over from previous lifetimes and have consequences in one's reincarnations.

The first five books of the Hebrew Scriptures—also called the Torah—portray Yahweh, the god of Israel, as the supreme lawgiver. Law is the core of Judaism and radiates into all aspects of Jewish life. In contrast to the Code of Hammurabi, which was administered by the king and his court, the legal imperatives in **Deuteronomy** were a covenant made by Yahweh with seminomadic Hebrew tribes. This covenant stated that the Hebrew people would prosper if they kept the laws. Deuteronomy also prescribes the appropriate treatment for the enemies of Israel.

p. 235

The Greek philosopher Plato (p. 238) (c. 427–347 B.C.E.) took the idea of divine or cosmic order one step further by saying it was a part of the essential nature of the human being. In his writings, he shifts attention away from legal codes to the soul or the psyche. According to Plato, by understanding and perfecting the inner self, the individual inevitably lives according to the universal plan for an ideal universe. In Chinese thought, the DAO, or the invisible order of the universe, is similar to *dharma:* Everything has its dao—its Way or path. Confucius (sixth century B.C.E.) tended to use related terms, *Heaven* or *the Will of Heaven,* to indicate the cosmic moral order. **Mencius** (p. 239) further developed this same idea—that nature and society were an extension of the heavenly order, the Will of Heaven—by linking the Will of Heaven and the inner person, much

MEN-shee-us

as Plato had; in effect, Mencius replaced the idea of dao with individual conscience, compassion, and sensitivity to right and wrong. This concept of human benevolence, known as *JEN* in Chinese, is translated as *Humanity* in the Mencius excerpts included here. Although humans are born with Humanity or *jen*, it still must be cultivated and can approach human perfection in the adult.

Finally, the excerpt from the **Dead Sea Scrolls** is a radical departure from and disillusionment with the belief in the symbiotic relationship between cosmos and kingdom, a loss of hope in the ability of governments to administer justice and alleviate oppression. The Dead Sea Scrolls were written during the Roman rule in Palestine by a Jewish monastic sect that despaired and withdrew into the desert on the northwest edge of the Dead Sea in the second century B.C.E. The selection "War of Sons of Light and Sons of Darkness" shows the apocalyptic nature of its teachings: The moral order has degenerated to such a point that only divine intervention by a messiah figure can restore righteousness. The approaching end of history, the sect writes, will culminate in a final messianic battle in which Yahweh and the forces of good will crush darkness and evil, laying the foundation for a New Jerusalem.

p. 243

■ CONNECTIONS

***Epic of Creation,* p. 44; "Creating the World and Defeating Apophis," p. 109; Bhagavad Gita, p. 1488; Confucius, *Analects,* p. 1594.** Early civilizations established a fixed principle in the universe to which humans could relate and around which patterns of change might cycle. These fixed principles were—and are—called "god" in some cultures. The following are core, cosmic principles: in Mesopotamian, *me;* in Egypt, *maat;* in India, *dharma;* and in China, *dao.* How are these principles similar? What roles do these core principles play in the literary works listed in this Connection?

Book of Job, p. 169; The Code of Hammurabi, p. 230; *Oedipus Rex,* p. 899. A society's codes of law reflect not only the prescribed rules for human behavior but a sense of whether the cosmos is fundamentally just or capricious. While Hammurabi's laws attempt to bring justice to the society of Babylon, the Book of Job and the play *Oedipus Rex* question whether justice pervades all levels of existence, from human to divine. Why does Hammurabi consider laws the inspiration of a deity? Why do Job and Oedipus question the legal frameworks of their worlds?

Primitive man was sustained by a sense of union with his world: stones, trees, animals, spirits, people, all spoke to him and responded to him; and he was in them and of them. Civilized man throve on struggle and opposition; he must master or be mastered, and the more formidable the struggle the greater his own sense of life.

– Lewis Mumford, critic and historian, 1956

■ PRONUNCIATION

Akhenaten: ah-kuh-NAH-tun
Amenhotep: ah-men-HOH-tep
Apophis: uh-POH-fis
Hammurabi: hah-moo-RAH-bee
Mencius: MEN-shee-us
Tutankhamen: too-tahn-KAH-mun

Pyramid Texts

c. 2350–2150 B.C.E.

Pyramid Texts represent the earliest body of recorded religious writings in the world. (Texts from Sumer in Mesopotamia are thought to come from an equally early period of history, since the existing texts are first-millennium-B.C.E. copies of earlier works.) Pyramid Texts is the name that has been given to the hieroglyphic inscriptions found in the corridors and burial chambers of the Pyramids of Saqqara (Sakkara). The following selection from the Pyramid of Unas is dated c. 2350 B.C.E. Pyramid Texts can be hymns, incantations, or prayers that promote the resurrection of the deceased king, a process that traditionally follows three stages: The king awakens from sleep in his tomb, ascends to the sky, and is admitted into a union with the gods somewhere in the heavens. The death ritual of the king was modeled after the myth of the god Osiris, who was killed by his brother, Seth. After Isis revives Osiris, she becomes pregnant with Horus; Osiris chooses to become ruler of the underworld. Each Egyptian king was a god, an incarnation of Horus. When a king died he became an "Osiris"; the new king became Horus. The texts inscribed in the Pyramids, recited by priests during the stages of the king's transformation, dealt with rites of purification, the offering of food and drink, and the worthiness of a specific king. The poems themselves are written in the "orational or incantational style," meaning that they make use of strong, regular rhythms and declarative syntax. The footnotes are the editors'.

Unas Pyramid Text 217

Translated by Miriam Lichtheim

King Unas Joins the Sun-god

Re-Atum,[1] this Unas comes to you,
A spirit[2] indestructible
Who lays claim to the place of the four pillars![3]
Your son comes to you, this Unas comes to you,
May you cross the sky united in the dark,
May you rise in lightland, the place in which you shine!

---

[1] **Re-Atum:** The sun-god.

[2] **spirit:** The word for the imperishable spirit is *akh* or *ankh,* which in Egyptian hieroglyphics is a "T" with a circle on top; this symbol represents the union of male and female and the sacred marriage of Osiris and Isis. When Egyptian gods carry it in their right hands, it stands for the gift of eternal life.

[3] **the four pillars:** The four pillars represent the four basic directions of the universe: north, south, east, and west.

King Unas,
c. 2494–2345 B.C.E.
Stele with hieroglyphics from the tomb of King Unas. (The Art Archive/ Dagli Orti)

Seth, Nephthys,[4] go proclaim to Upper Egypt's gods
And their spirits:
"This Unas comes, a spirit indestructible,
If he wishes you to die, you will die,
If he wishes you to live, you will live!"
Re-Atum, this Unas comes to you,
A spirit indestructible
Who lays claim to the place of the four pillars!
Your son comes to you, this Unas comes to you,
May you cross the sky united in the dark,
May you rise in lightland, the place in which you shine!
Osiris, Isis,[5] go proclaim to Lower Egypt's gods
And their spirits:
"This Unas comes, a spirit indestructible,

[4] **Seth, Nephthys:** Seth is the god of desert wastes and the murderer of his brother Osiris. Nephthys, the sister of Osiris, Isis, and Seth, is a goddess of the household.

[5] **Osiris, Isis:** Osiris is ruler of the underworld and the model for resurrection and immortality. Isis, the great mother goddess, is the sister and wife of Osiris and the mother of Horus.

Like the morning star above Hapy,[6]
Whom the water-spirits worship;
Whom he wishes to live will live,
Whom he wishes to die will die!"

Re-Atum, this Unas comes to you,
A spirit indestructible
Who lays claim to the place of the four pillars!
Your son comes to you, this Unas comes to you,
May you cross the sky united in the dark,
May you rise in lightland, the place in which you shine!
Thoth,[7] go proclaim to the gods of the west
And their spirits:
"This Unas comes, a spirit indestructible,
Decked above the neck as Anubis,[8]
Lord of the western height,
He will count hearts, he will claim hearts,
Whom he wishes to live will live,
Whom he wishes to die will die!"

Re-Atum, this Unas comes to you,
A spirit indestructible
Who lays claim to the place of the four pillars!
Your son comes to you, this Unas comes to you,
May you cross the sky united in the dark,
May you rise in lightland, the place in which you shine!
Horus,[9] go proclaim to the powers of the east
And their spirits:
"This Unas comes, a spirit indestructible,
Whom he wishes to live will live,
Whom he wishes to die will die!"
Re-Atum, your son comes to you,
Unas comes to you,
Raise him to you, hold him in your arms,
He is your son, of your body, forever!

[6] **Hapy:** God of the Nile.

[7] **Thoth:** God of scribes, literacy, and knowledge; a moon-god often portrayed as a baboon or an ibis.

[8] **Anubis:** God of embalming; often portrayed as a jackal.

[9] **Horus:** The falcon-god, ruler of the sky, protector of the king, and son of Osiris and Isis.

Hammurabi

r. 1792–1750 B.C.E.

Hammurabi, the sixth king of the first Babylonian dynasty, created an empire over a period of thirty years that extended from the Persian Gulf to the Mediterranean Sea and lasted some two hundred years. He was an unusual ruler; in addition to being a great builder of canals and temples, he promoted the collection and translation of scientific, religious, and literary texts. In order to unify and pacify his empire, he authored an extensive legal code. This code of laws, which cover public and political conduct as well as family life and work, is engraved in Akkadian, a Semitic language, on a black diorite stele, or pillar, that was discovered in Elam in 1902 and is now housed in the Louvre Museum in Paris. At the top of the stele, copies of which were distributed to Hammurabi's administrators throughout the empire, is an engraving showing the sun-god Shamash conferring on Hammurabi the power and knowledge to rule.

The Code of Hammurabi, r. 1792–1750 B.C.E. *The top of the stele on which is inscribed the Code of Hammurabi, one of the earliest extant examples of written laws, pictures Hammurabi receiving the blessing of the god Shamash for his rule. (Erich Lessing/Art Resource, NY)*

The stele was erected in a public place as a reminder of the laws themselves and of the divine sanction of Hammurabi's rule.

The very important Prologue to the Code of Hammurabi is a statement of the king's divine lineage extending back to Marduk, the local god of Babylon, who was elevated to national status with his earthly representative, Hammurabi, and the establishment of the empire. The laws are written in terms of particular situations: If such and such were to occur, the consequence would be as stated. *Lex talionis* or the law of retaliation—"an eye for an eye, a tooth for a tooth"—is quite evident in the Code and later shows up in Mosaic law in Israel. Particular notice should be taken of women's rights, laws regarding marriage, and the care of adoptive sons in the following small sample of Hammurabi's laws. The Epilogue to the Code is a tribute to the king himself, especially his protection of the weak and the poor and his concern for justice.

FROM

The Code of Hammurabi

Translated by Robert Francis Harper

Prologue

When the lofty Anu, king of the Anunnaki,[1] and Bel, lord of heaven and earth, he who determines the destiny of the land, committed the rule of all mankind to Marduk,[2] the chief son of Ea[3]; when they made him great among the Igigi[4]; when they pronounced the lofty name of Babylon; when they made it famous among the quarters of the world and in its midst established an everlasting kingdom whose foundations were firm as heaven and earth—at that time, Anu and Bel called me, Hammurabi, the exalted prince, the worshiper of the gods, to cause justice to prevail in the land, to destroy the wicked and the evil, to prevent the strong from oppressing the weak, to go forth like the Sun over the Black Head Race,[5] to enlighten the land and to further the welfare of the people. . . .

On Theft

6.

If a man steal the property of a god (temple) or palace, that man shall be put to death; and he who receives from his hand the stolen (property) shall also be put to death.

[1] **Anu . . . Anunnaki:** Anu is god of the sky or firmament; the Anunnaki are the deities of the underworld who judge the dead. [2] **Marduk:** A patron god of Babylon. [3] **Ea:** God of fresh water. [4] **Igigi:** The younger generation of sky gods. [5] **the Black Head Race:** The human race.

8.

If a man steal ox or sheep, ass or pig, or boat—if it be from a god (temple) or a palace, he shall restore thirtyfold; if it be from a freeman, he shall render tenfold. If the thief have nothing wherewith to pay he shall be put to death.

14.

If a man steal a man's son, who is a minor, he shall be put to death.

15.

If a man aid a male or female slave of the palace, or a male or female slave of a freeman to escape from the city gate, he shall be put to death.

16.

If a man harbor in his house a male or female slave who has fled from the palace or from a freeman, and do not bring him (the slave) forth at the call of the commandant, the owner of that house shall be put to death.

On Marriage

127.

If a man point the finger at a priestess or the wife of another and cannot justify it, they shall drag that man before the judges and they shall brand his forehead.

128.

If a man take a wife and do not arrange with her the (proper) contracts, that woman is not a (legal) wife.

129.

If the wife of a man be taken in lying with another man, they shall bind them and throw them into the water. If the husband of the woman would save his wife, or if the king would save his male servant (he may).

130.

If a man force the (betrothed) wife of another who has not known a male and is living in her father's house, and he lie in her bosom and they take him, that man shall be put to death and that woman shall go free.

131.

If a man accuse his wife and she has not been taken in lying with another man, she shall take an oath in the name of god and she shall return to her house.

On Assault

195.

If a son strike his father, they shall cut off his fingers.

196.

If a man destroy the eye of another man, they shall destroy his eye.

197.

If one break a man's bone, they shall break his bone.

199.

If one destroy the eye of a man's slave or break a bone of a man's slave he shall pay one-half his price.

200.

If a man knock out a tooth of a man of his own rank, they shall knock out his tooth.

Epilogue

The righteous laws, which Hammurabi, the wise king, established and (by which) he gave the land stable support and pure government. Hammurabi, the perfect king, am I. I was not careless, nor was I neglectful of the Black-Head people, whose rule Bel presented and Marduk delivered to me. [. . .]

The great gods proclaimed me and I am the guardian governor, whose scepter is righteous and whose beneficent protection is spread over my city. In my bosom I carried the people of the land of Sumer and Akkad; under my protection I brought their brethren into security; in my wisdom I restrained (hid) them; that the strong might not oppose the weak, and that they should give justice to the orphan and the widow, in Babylon, the city whose turrets Anu and Bel raised; in Esagila, the temple whose foundations are firm as heaven and earth, for the pronouncing of judgments in the land, for the rendering of decisions for the land, and for the righting of wrong, my weighty words I have written upon my monument, and in the presence of my image as king of righteousness have I established. . . .

THE UPANISHADS

NINTH CENTURY B.C.E.

The excerpts from the Brihad-Aranyaka and Chandogya Upanishads describe the cause-and-effect dynamic of a just universe: In both Buddhism and Hinduism, karma means that good thoughts or acts are rewarded with good consequences; bad results in bad. The word *karma* is used both for an individual's actions and the consequences of those actions as well as for the principle of cause and effect in the universe, a pattern which confirms *dharma,* the abiding order of the cosmos. The coupling of reincarnation with karma means that the consequences of actions in a previous life can be experienced in the present. For example, a murderer in one life can be punished in the next. Likewise, a doer of good deeds in one life can be rewarded in the next. Karma, like the Christian teachings about heaven and hell, transcends the legal system of any particular political or social entity and reaffirms larger principles that are integral to the workings of the universe. You might not be caught by the local police, but you will suffer the fruits of your acts, either in this lifetime or in the next. Another way to state this is: What goes around, comes around.

According as one acts, according as one conducts himself, so does he become. The doer of good becomes good. The doer of evil becomes evil.

– BRIHAD-ARANYAKA UPANISHAD

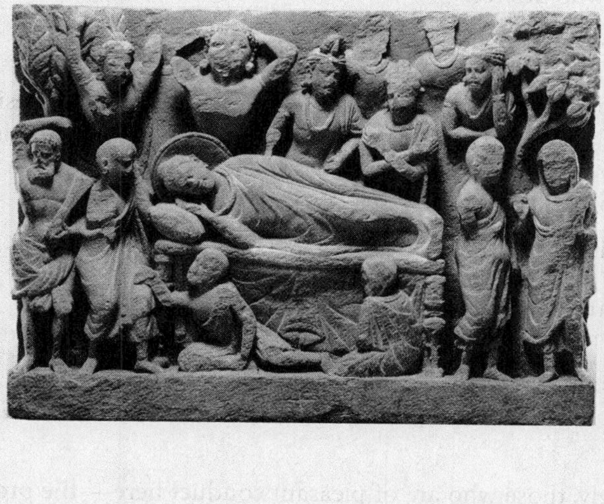

The Maha-pari-nirvana, second to third centuries B.C.E. Maha-pari-nirvana *is Buddha's physical passing from this world into a state beyond nirvana, that is, separating from the cycle of rebirths and merging with the absolute. Buddhist belief revolves around the concept of karma: Whatever one is now is a direct result of one's previous actions and determines what one will be. (Courtesy of the British Museum)*

FROM

Brihad-Aranyaka Upanishad and Chandogya Upanishad

Translated by Robert Ernest Hume

[Karma and Reincarnation]

According as one acts, according as one conducts himself, so does he become. The doer of good becomes good. The doer of evil becomes evil. One becomes virtuous by virtuous action, bad by bad action.

But people say: "A person is made [not of acts, but] of desires only." [In reply to this I say:] As is his desire, such is his resolve; as is his resolve, such the action he performs; what action *(karma)* he performs, that he procures for himself.

On this point there is this verse:—

Where one's mind is attached—the inner self
Goes thereto with action, being attached to it alone.

Obtaining the end of his action,
Whatever he does in this world,
He comes again from that world
To this world of action.

—So the man who desires.

The Soul of the Released

Now the man who does not desire.—He who is without desire, who is freed from desire, whose desire is satisfied, whose desire is the Soul—his breaths do not depart. Being very Brahma, he goes to Brahman.[1]

On this point there is this verse:—

When are liberated all
The desires that lodge in one's heart,
Then a mortal becomes immortal!
Therein he reaches Brahman!

As the slough of a snake lies on an ant-hill, dead, cast off, even so lies this body. But this incorporeal, immortal Life *(prāṇa)* is Brahman indeed, is light indeed. [. . .]

Accordingly, those who are of pleasant conduct here—the prospect is, indeed, that they will enter a pleasant womb, either the womb of a Brahman, or the womb of a Kshatriya,[2] or the womb of a Vaiśya.[3] But those who are of stinking conduct here—the prospect is, indeed, that they will enter a stinking womb, either the womb of a dog, or the womb of a swine, or the womb of an outcast *(caṇḍāla)*.

---

[1] **Brahman:** The eternal, unnamable Absolute. [2] **Kshatriya:** The warrior or administrator caste. [3] **Vaiśya:** The merchant or farmer caste.

HEBREW SCRIPTURES
EIGHTH–SEVENTH CENTURY B.C.E.

The name of the fifth book of the Hebrew Scriptures means "second law," which is a reference to how it repeats material found in the books of Exodus, Leviticus, and Numbers. In much of Deuteronomy, Moses, the leader of the Israelites, speaks in the first person in three farewell addresses given on the plains of Moab. The author of the book, called the "Deuteronomist" by scholars, is believed to have been a priest or prophet of the kingdom of Judah who was writing either in the late eighth century B.C.E. or during the reign of Manasseh (c. 687–642 B.C.E.). According to scriptures, Manasseh was a wicked king who turned away from the worship of Yahweh and led the people into idolatry. In 621 B.C.E., during the reign of Josiah in Judah, a book of law was discovered in the Jerusalem Temple now believed to be the essential chapters of Deuteronomy; the discovery led to a religious revival.

The author of Deuteronomy wanted to restore monotheistic worship in Judah by reiterating the legal tradition handed down by Moses. However, Deuteronomy does more than simply restate Mosaic law; it clearly ties together the God who actively led His people out of bondage in Egypt with the God who gave to them a land "flowing with milk and honey." Obedience to the law is spoken of as the people's obligation in the covenant that has provided them with the Promised Land. In the chapter that precedes the following selection, Moses recites the Ten Commandments.

You must not follow other gods, gods of the nations that are around you; if you do, the Lord your God who is in your midst will be angry with you, and he will sweep you away off the face of the earth, for the Lord your God is a jealous god.

– DEUTERONOMY 6:14–15

Deuteronomy

[GOD OF LAW AND VENGEANCE]

6

1 These are the commandments, statutes, and laws which the LORD[1] your God
commanded me to teach you to observe in the land into which you are passing to
2 occupy it, a land flowing with milk and honey, so that you may fear the LORD your
God and keep all his statutes and commandments which I am giving you, both you,
3 your sons, and your descendants all your lives, and so that you may live long. If you
listen, O Israel, and are careful to observe them, you will prosper and increase greatly
as the LORD the God of your fathers promised you.
4, 5 Hear, O Israel, the LORD is our God, one LORD, and you must love the LORD your

[1] **the LORD:** This translation uses *Lord* instead of the name of Israel's God, *Yahweh;* the first line of chapter six of Deuteronomy in the Jerusalem Bible reads: "These then are the commandments and the customs which Yahweh your God has instructed me to teach you. . . ."

6 God with all your heart and soul and strength.[2] These commandments which I give
7 you this day are to be kept in your heart; you shall repeat them to your sons, and
8 speak of them indoors and out of doors, when you lie down and when you rise. Bind
9 them as a sign on the hand and wear them as a phylactery[3] on the forehead; write
them up on the door-posts of your houses and on your gates.

10 The LORD your God will bring you into the land which he swore to your forefathers Abraham, Isaac, and Jacob that he would give you, a land of great and fine
11 cities which you did not build, houses full of good things which you did not provide,
rock-hewn cisterns which you did not hew, and vineyards and olive-groves which
12 you did not plant. When you eat your fill there, be careful not to forget the LORD
13 who brought you out of Egypt, out of the land of slavery. You shall fear the LORD
14 your God, serve him alone and take your oaths in his name. You must not follow
15 other gods, gods of the nations that are around you; if you do, the LORD your God
who is in your midst will be angry with you, and he will sweep you away off the face
of the earth, for the LORD your God is a jealous god.

16 You must not challenge the LORD your God as you challenged him at Massah.[4]
17 You must diligently keep the commandments of the LORD your God as well as the
18 precepts and statutes which he gave you. You must do what is right and good in the
LORD's eyes so that all may go well with you, and you may enter and occupy the rich
19 land which the LORD promised by oath to your forefathers; then you shall drive out
all your enemies before you, as the LORD promised.

20 When your son asks you in time to come, 'What is the meaning of the precepts,
21 statutes, and laws which the LORD our God gave you?,' you shall say to him, 'We were
Pharaoh's slaves in Egypt, and the LORD brought us out of Egypt with his strong
22 hand, sending great disasters, signs, and portents against the Egyptians and against
23 Pharaoh and all his family, as we saw for ourselves. But he led us out from there to
24 bring us into the land and give it to us as he had promised to our forefathers. The
LORD commanded us to observe all these statutes and to fear the LORD our God; it
25 will be for our own good at all times, and he will continue to preserve our lives. It
will be counted to our credit if we keep all these commandments in the sight of the
LORD our God, as he has bidden us.'

7

1 WHEN THE LORD YOUR GOD BRINGS YOU into the land which you are entering to
occupy and drives out many nations before you—Hittites, Girgashites, Amorites,
Canaanites, Perizzites, Hivites, and Jebusites, seven nations more numerous and
2 powerful than you—when the LORD your God delivers them into your power and
you defeat them, you must put them to death. You must not make a treaty with them

---

[2] **Hear . . . strength:** The verse beginning "Hear, O Israel" is called the Shama and is the common preface to private and public prayer among Jews.

[3] **phylactery:** A small leather box containing a slip of Hebrew Scripture worn by Orthodox and Conservative Jews during prayer.

[4] **Massah:** After the Exodus from Egypt, the Israelites doubted whether Yahweh would provide for them; at Massah Moses answered their doubt by striking a rock with his rod and producing water.

3 or spare them. You must not intermarry with them, neither giving your daughters to
4 their sons nor taking their daughters for your sons; if you do, they will draw your
sons away from the LORD and make them worship other gods. Then the LORD will be
5 angry with you and will quickly destroy you. But this is what you must do to them:
Pull down their altars, break their sacred pillars, hack down their sacred poles and
6 destroy their idols by fire, for you are a people holy to the LORD your God; the LORD
your God chose you out of all nations on earth to be his special possession.

7 It was not because you were more numerous than any other nation that the
8 LORD cared for you and chose you, for you were the smallest of all nations; it was
because the LORD loved you and stood by his oath to your forefathers, that he
brought you out with his strong hand and redeemed you from the land of slavery,
9 from the power of Pharaoh king of Egypt. Know then that the LORD your God is
God, the faithful God; with those who love him and keep his commandments he
10 keeps covenant and faith for a thousand generations, but those who defy him and
show their hatred for him he repays with destruction: He will not be slow to requite
any who so hate him.

11 You are to observe these commandments, statutes, and laws which I give you
this day, and keep them.

12 If you listen to these laws and are careful to observe them, then the LORD your
God will observe the sworn covenant[5] he made with your forefathers and will keep
13 faith with you. He will love you, bless you and cause you to increase. He will bless the
fruit of your body and the fruit of your land, your corn and new wine and oil, the
offspring of your herds, and of your lambing flocks, in the land which he swore to
14 your forefathers to give you. You shall be blessed above every other nation; neither
among your people nor among your cattle shall there be impotent male or barren
15 female. The LORD will take away all sickness from you; he will not bring upon you
any of the foul diseases of Egypt which you know so well, but will bring them upon
16 all your enemies. You shall devour all the nations which the LORD your God is giving
over to you. Spare none of them, and do not worship their gods; that is the snare
which awaits you.

17 You may say to yourselves, 'These nations outnumber us, how can we drive them
18 out?' But you need have no fear of them; only remember what the LORD your God did
19 to Pharaoh and to the whole of Egypt, the great challenge which you yourselves witnessed, the signs and portents, the strong hand and the outstretched arm by which the
LORD your God brought you out. He will deal thus with all the nations of whom you
20 are afraid. He will also spread panic among them until all who are left or have gone
21 into hiding perish before you. Be in no dread of them, for the LORD your God is in
22 your midst, a great and terrible god. He will drive out these nations before you little by
little. You will not be able to exterminate them quickly, for fear the wild beasts become
23 too numerous for you. The LORD your God will deliver these nations over to you and
24 will throw them into great panic in the hour of their destruction. He will put their
kings into your hands, and you shall wipe out their name from under heaven. When

[5] **the sworn covenant:** Yahweh's promise to Abraham to make his descendants "a great nation" was the beginning of the covenant between Yahweh and the Hebrews.

you destroy them, no man will be able to withstand you. Their idols you shall destroy by fire; you must not covet the silver and gold on them and take it for yourselves, or you will be ensnared by it; for these things are abominable to the LORD your God.

PLATO

C. 427–347 B.C.E.

> **There is of course only one way to look after anything and that is to give it its proper food and motions. And the motions in us that are akin to the divine are the thoughts and revolutions of the universe.**
>
> **– PLATO, *Timaeus***

The purpose of Plato's *Timaeus,* named after a Pythagorean philosopher, was to provide a religious and philosophical account of the origin of the cosmos and the laws that govern nature. There is a vast hierarchy of divine beings in Plato's COSMOGONY, beginning with the creator-god—the unnamed Zeus of Greek tradition—who acts like an architect or craftsman imposing order or form on a material world already in existence. This results in a world composed of four materials—earth, air, fire, and water—and an animating world-soul. As Frank Tilly describes it, the world-soul "is an intermediary between the world of ideas and the world of phenomena; it is the cause of all law, mathematical relations, harmony, order, uniformity, life, mind, and knowledge. It moves according to fixed laws and is the cause of the motion and distribution of matter in the heavenly spheres." Besides creating souls or gods for the planets, the creator-god or Demiurge created rational human souls. It is through the idea of soul, in fact, that the world-soul that animates the cosmos is identified with the human soul that animates the body. This correspondence between macrocosm and microcosm is the central theme of the following selection from *Timaeus.*

FROM

Timaeus

Translated by H. D. P. Lee

[THE DIVINE UNIVERSE WITHIN]

As we have said more than once, there are housed in us three distinct forms of soul,[1] each having its own motions. Accordingly we may now say, very briefly, that any of these forms that lives in idleness and fails to exercise its own proper motions is bound to become very feeble, while any that exercises them will become very

[1] **three . . . soul:** Plato divides the soul into a rational part, which resides in the head, and an irrational part, which is further subdivided into emotions, like anger and ambition, and desires, like food and wealth. Emotions and desires reside in the heart and the lower extremities, respectively.

strong; hence we must take care that these motions are properly proportioned to each other. We should think of the most authoritative part of our soul as a guardian spirit given by god, living in the summit of the body, which can properly be said to lift us from the earth towards our home in heaven; for we are creatures not of earth but of heaven, where the soul was first born, and our divine part attaches us by the head to heaven, like a plant by its roots, and keeps our body upright. If therefore a man's attention and effort is centred on appetite and ambition, all his thoughts are bound to be mortal, and he can hardly fail, in so far as it is possible, to become entirely mortal, as it is his mortal part that he has increased. But a man who has given his heart to learning and true wisdom and exercised that part of himself is surely bound if he attains to truth, to have immortal and divine thoughts, and cannot fail to achieve immortality as fully as is permitted to human nature; and because he has always looked after the divine element in himself and kept his guardian spirit in good order he must be happy above all men.[2] There is of course only one way to look after anything and that is to give it its proper food and motions. And the motions in us that are akin to the divine are the thoughts and revolutions of the universe. We should each therefore attend to these motions and by learning about the harmonious circuits of the universe repair the damage done at birth to the circuits in our head,[3] and so restore understanding and what is understood to their original likeness to each other. When that is done we shall have achieved the goal set us by the gods, the life that is best for this present time and for all time to come.

---

[2] **guardian . . . men:** There is a play on words at the end of the sentence: The word for guardian spirit is *daemon* and the Greek word for happy is *eudaemon.* (Translator's note.)

[3] **repair . . . head:** Since the rational soul preexists before birth and has complete knowledge of the world of ideas, birth in a mortal body interferes with what this soul knows. Education, then, becomes a process of reminiscence, recalling what the soul already knows.

MENCIUS (MENGZI)
c. 371–c. 288 B.C.E.

Very few details are known about Mencius' life, although it is said that his father died when he was young and that he was raised by his mother—identical circumstances to those of his philosophical mentor, Confucius. Mencius lived during the "Warring States Period" (c. 403–221 B.C.E.) in China, a time of great turbulence and uncertainty. Lacking a unified, central authority, China consisted of numerous internal factions battling for survival. Moreover, China was defending its borders against nomadic warriors of the Asian steppe, whose skills with the bow and arrow on horseback made the Chinese chariot warfare obsolete. The primary focus of Chinese philosophers of the Confucian era was the creation of an

***Mencius*, eighteenth century**
This portrait of the inward-looking Chinese philosopher Mencius was painted more than two thousand years after his death. (© Archivio Iconographico, S.A. / CORBIS)

orderly society, one in which everyone, from rulers to peasants, understood his or her essential role as mandated by Heaven. Confucius emphasized external behavior, decorum, and the proper ritual or gesture. Mencius looked inward.

The following selections from Mencius connect Heaven with the inner person and state that good conduct results from self-examination. The key terms in these selections, *T'ien, jen,* and *yi,* are the basic principles of Mencius's philosophy. *T'ien* means Heaven and refers to the impartial, divine intelligence that underlies the workings of the cosmos. *Jen,* translated as Humanity, is natural or instinctive feeling of kindness or love for another human being. Humans are born with *jen,* but one must also cultivate it in order to become a "True Gentleman," someone of wisdom and honor. The translation of *yi* is justice: doing what is right for oneself and for others. *Yi* then is the proper or expected expression of a person's *jen.* In the last saying, *jen* and *yi* shape the primary Confucian relationships: love and duty toward parents, respect for elder brothers.

[Heaven and Human Nature]

Translated by W. A. C. H. Dobson

Mencius said, "It is the man who has stretched his mind to the full who fully understands man's true nature. And understanding his true nature, he understands Heaven. To guard one's mind and to nourish one's true nature is to serve Heaven. Do not be in two minds about premature death or a ripe old age. Cultivate yourself and await the outcome. In this way you will attain to your allotted span."

Mencius said, "Nothing, but is preordained.[1] We should accept obediently our rightful lot. Therefore he who understands Heaven's ordinances does not walk below high walls, but when he dies in the full discharge of his principles he has fulfilled the lot that heaven has ordained for him. He who dies, however, in a felon's chains cannot be said to have fulfilled the lot that Heaven ordained for him."

Mencius said, "The functions of the body are the endowment of Heaven. But it is only a Sage who can properly manipulate them."

Mencius said, "All things are complete within ourselves. There is no joy that exceeds that of the discovery, upon self-examination, that we have acted with integrity. And we are never closer to achieving Humanity than when we seek to act, constrained by the principle of reciprocity."[2]

Mencius said, "Humanity is the mind of man. Justice, the path he follows. If by closing the way he fails to follow it, then he loses his mind and has no way of retrieving it. How sad this is! If a fowl or a dog stray we know how to find them again, but if the mind strays we have no such recourse. The whole purport of learning is nothing more than this: to regain the mind that has strayed."

Mencius said, "The True Gentleman pursues knowledge profoundly according to the Way,[3] wishing to appropriate it for himself. Having appropriated it, he abides with it in perfect assurance. Abiding with it in assurance, he stores it deeply, and storing it deeply he draws from it whichever way he moves, as though he were encountering a spring.

Mencius said, "The abilities men have which are not acquired by study are part of their endowment of good. The knowledge men have which is not acquired by deep thought is part of their endowment of good. Every baby in his mother's arms knows about love for his parents. When they grow up, they know about the respect they must pay to their elder brothers. The love for parents is Humanity. The respect for elders is Justice. It is nothing more than this, and it is so all over the world."

---

[1] **"Nothing . . . preordained":** Mencius does not resolve the conflict between preordination and free will here; on one hand, there are Heaven's ordinances, and on the other, it is possible to go against the prescribed order and become a felon.

[2] **principle of reciprocity:** This might be rephrased as, Do unto others what you would have them do to you. The original phrase could also be translated as the "principle of altruism," unselfish concern or selflessness.

[3] **the Way:** For Confucians, dao, or the Way, involves proper conduct according to universal ordinances.

Dead Sea Scrolls

SECOND CENTURY B.C.E. — FIRST CENTURY C.E.

In 1947, two young shepherds accidentally discovered a cave in the Qumran hills near the Dead Sea in present-day Palestine, and in the cave they found ancient scrolls in clay jars. When the archeological and biblical value of the scrolls was recognized, extensive exploration of other caves in the region turned up additional material. Then the task of editing and translating began. Ten complete scrolls were found along with thousands of fragments from some six hundred manuscripts. The documents contain biblical texts from the entire Hebrew Bible (except for the Book of Esther), many of which are the oldest biblical manuscripts extant. The complete scroll of the Book of Isaiah is 900 years older than the previous manuscript found for Isaiah. Most of the documents, however, are the nonbiblical writings of an ascetic Jewish sect, the Essenes, that flourished from c. 200 B.C.E. to 68 C.E. and left the writings behind when they were defeated by the Romans. Also called the Khirbet Qumran community after the location on the Dead Sea where they built their settlement, the Essenes withdrew from what they considered to be a sinful society into monastic piety sometime in the second half of the second century B.C.E. but were forced to abandon the site just before the destruction of the Temple and the fall of Jerusalem in 70 C.E. Both the Jewish historian Josephus and Pliny the Elder, a Roman, had made note of the existence of the Essenes, but until the discovery of the scrolls, information about their beliefs was incomplete.

Following the apocalyptic tradition of Daniel in the Hebrew Bible, the Qumran community interpreted the political unrest in Palestine in

The Dead Sea Scrolls, third century B.C.E. *The Dead Sea Scrolls, discovered in caves in the hills above the Dead Sea in present-day Palestine, include some of the earliest biblical fragments extant. They are also a treasure trove of information about the religious beliefs of the Essenes, an early Jewish ascetic sect. (© The Dead Sea Scrolls Foundation, Inc. / CORBIS)*

the first century B.C.E. as preparation for the final battle between the forces of good and evil, between the Sons of Light and the Sons of Darkness. This casting of the struggle between good and evil as the battle between light and dark originated with the Persian prophet Zoroaster in the twelfth century B.C.E., who predicted that a messiah named Saoshyant would lead the forces of light in a final cosmic battle against darkness and install the Kingdom of God for all time.

The following excerpt is taken from what is called the War Rule or the War Scroll. It describes military preparations for fighting the Kittim, the occupying Romans; the Romans here are also a symbol of the ultimate foe, the armies of Satan.

It has been surmised that John the Baptist, the precursor to Jesus of Nazareth in Christian Scriptures, was a member of the Qumran community. The Teacher of Righteousness whom the Essenes write of may be Jesus of Nazareth, who must have known about the community and might have visited it. Their apocalyptic view of history was reinforced by the Book of Revelation, the last book of the Christian Bible; its dualistic view of reality as a struggle between the forces of light and dark has been revived throughout time whenever Christians have felt that the end of the world was near and that Jesus was about to return in order to defeat the powers of Satan and establish a new heaven and a new earth. A number of contemporary Christian leaders maintain that the period around the year 2000 is the time of the Second Coming and that, therefore, the end of history is near.

The translator uses the following punctuation: "Lacunae impossible to complete with any measure of confidence are indicated by dots. Hypothetical but likely reconstructions are placed between [ ] and glosses necessary for fluency between ( ). Biblical quotations appearing in the text are printed in italics, as well as the titles and headings which figure in the manuscripts."

. . . [the trumpets of Summons shall sound for disposal in] . . . battle formations and to summon the foot-soldiers to advance when the gates of war shall open; and the trumpets of Alarm shall sound for massacre, and for ambush, and for pursuit when the enemy shall be smitten, and for withdrawal from battle.

– Dead Sea Scrolls

FROM

Dead Sea Scrolls

Translated by G. Vermes

[War of Sons of Light and Sons of Darkness]

1

For the M[aster. The Rule of] War on the unleashing of the attack of the sons of light against the company of the sons of darkness, the army of Satan: against the band of Edom, Moab, and the sons of Ammon,[1] *and [against the army of the sons of the East*

[1] ***Edom . . . Ammon:*** Lands south and east of the Dead Sea inhabited by traditional enemies of the Israelites.

and] the Philistines, and against the bands of the Kittim[2] *of Assyria and their allies the ungodly of the Covenant*

The sons of Levi, Judah, and Benjamin,[3] the exiles in the desert, shall battle against them in . . . all their bands when the exiled sons of light return from the Desert of the Peoples to camp in the Desert of Jerusalem; and after the battle they shall go up from there (to Jerusalem?).

[The king] of the Kittim [shall enter] into Egypt, and in his time he shall set out in great wrath to wage war against the kings of the north, that his fury may destroy and cut off the horn of [the nations].

This shall be a time of salvation for the people of God, an age of dominion for all the members of His company, and of everlasting destruction for all the company of Satan. The confusion of the sons of Japheth shall be [great] and Assyria[4] shall fall unsuccoured. The dominion of the Kittim shall come to an end and iniquity shall be vanquished, leaving no remnant; [for the sons] of darkness there shall be no escape. [The seasons of righteous]ness shall shine over all the ends of the earth; they shall go on shining until all the seasons of darkness are consumed and, at the season appointed by God, His exalted greatness shall shine eternally to the peace, blessing, glory, joy, and long life of all the sons of light.

On the day when the Kittim fall, there shall be battle and terrible carnage before the God of Israel, for that shall be the day appointed from ancient times for the battle of destruction of the sons of darkness. At that time, the assembly of gods and the hosts of men shall battle, causing great carnage; on the day of calamity, the sons of light shall battle with the company of darkness amid the shouts of a mighty multitude and the clamour of gods and men to [make manifest] the might of God. And it shall be a time of [great] tribulation for the people which God shall redeem; of all its afflications none shall be as this, from its sudden beginning until its end in eternal redemption.

On the day of their battle against the Kittim [they shall set out for] carnage. In three lots shall the sons of light brace themselves in battle to strike down iniquity, and in three lots shall Satan's host gird itself to thrust back the company [of God. And when the hearts of the detach]ments of foot-soldiers faint, then shall the might of God fortify [the heart of the sons of light]. And with the seventh lot, the mighty hand of God shall bring down [the army of Satan, and all] the angels of his kingdom, and all the members [of his company in everlasting destruction]. . . .

2

. . . the fifty-two heads of family in the congregation.

They shall rank the chief Priests below the High Priest and his vicar. And the twelve chief Priests shall minister at the daily sacrifice before God, whereas the twenty-six leaders of the priestly divisions shall minister in their divisions.

---

[2] ***Philistines . . . Kittim:*** The non-Semitic Philistines lived in southwest Palestine and warred repeatedly against Israel. The Kittim were either the Romans or the Seleucids.

[3] **Levi . . . Benjamin:** Tribes of Israel; the tribe of Levi was considered the priestly tribe.

[4] **Japheth . . . Assyria:** Japheth possibly refers to a non-Semitic tribe near the Black Sea. Assyria refers to the Mesopotamian conquerors on the Tigris River.

Below them, in perpetual ministry, shall be the chiefs of the Levites to the number of twelve, one for each tribe. The leaders of their divisions shall minister each in his place.

Below them shall be the chiefs of the tribes together with the heads of family of the congregation. They shall attend daily at the gates of the Sanctuary, whereas the leaders of their divisions, with their numbered men, shall attend at their appointed times, on new moons and on Sabbaths and on all the days of the year, their age being fifty years and over.

These are the men who shall attend at holocausts and sacrifices to prepare sweet-smelling incense for the good pleasure of God, to atone for all His congregation, and to satisfy themselves perpetually before Him at the table of glory. They shall arrange all these things during the season of the year of Release.[5]

During the remaining thirty-three years of the war, the men of renown, those summoned to the Assembly, together with all the heads of family of the congregation, shall choose for themselves fighting-men for all the lands of the nations. They shall arm for themselves warriors from all the tribes of Israel to enter the army year by year when they are summoned to war. But they shall arm no man for entry into the army during the years of Release, for they are Sabbaths of rest for Israel. In the thirty-five years of service, the war shall be fought during six; the whole congregation shall fight it together.

And during the remaining twenty-nine years the war shall be divided. During the first year they shall fight against Aram-Naharaim; during the second, against the sons of Lud; during the third, against the remnant of the sons of Aram, against Uz and Hul and Togar and Mesha[6] beyond the Euphrates; during the fourth and fifth, they shall fight against the sons of Arphakshad; during the sixth and seventh, against all the sons of Assyria and Persia and the East as far as the Great Desert; during the eighth year they shall fight against the sons of Elam; during the ninth, against the sons of Ishmael and Keturah.[7] In the ten years which follow, the war shall be divided against all the sons of Ham[8] according to [their clans and in their ha]bitations; and during the ten years which remain, the war shall be divided against all [the sons of Japhethin] their habitations.

[5] **the year of Release:** The seventh or sabbatical year, a sacred period like the Sabbath set aside from ordinary activities.

[6] **Aram-Naharaim . . . Mesha:** Names associated with peoples in Asia Minor and Africa.

[7] **Elam . . . Keturah:** Elam was east of Mesopotamia; the son of Abraham and Hagar, Ishmael is the traditional ancestor of Arabian tribes; Keturah was a wife of Abraham connected to Arabian tribes.

[8] **Ham:** One of the three sons of Noah; Ham has been linked to the Canaanites, certain Arabian tribes, and the Egyptians.

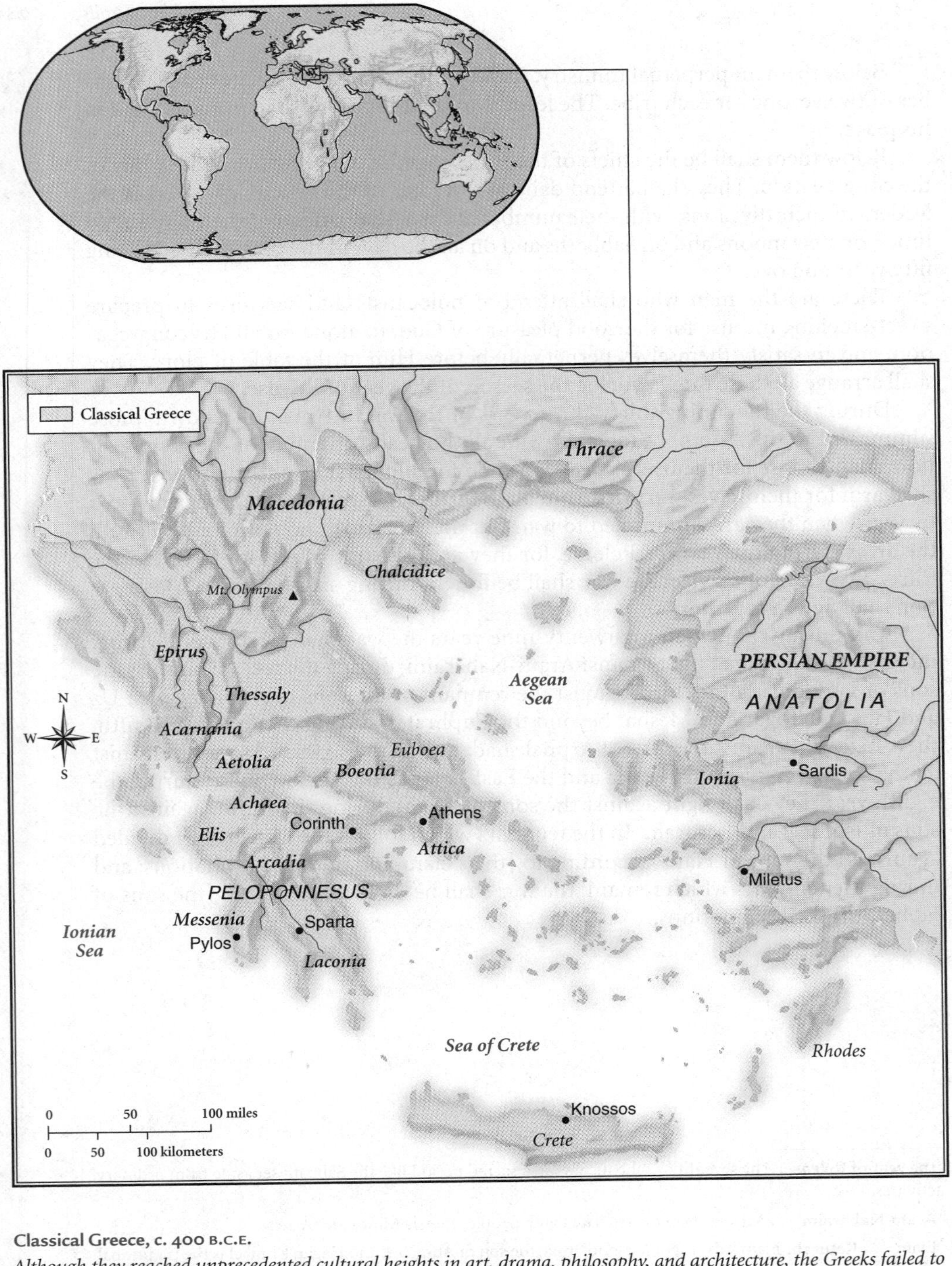

Classical Greece, c. 400 B.C.E.

Although they reached unprecedented cultural heights in art, drama, philosophy, and architecture, the Greeks failed to achieve political unity and harmony. Athens and Sparta, along with their respective allies, fought the bloody and costly Peloponnesian War (431–404 B.C.E.). Defeating the Athenians, the Spartans then tried to become an international power by sending campaigns east into Anatolia (present-day Turkey), threatening the Persians who then ruled most of Anatolia and resulting in ongoing turmoil in the Mediterranean.

GREECE

The Golden Age of Literature and Philosophy

While there are older civilizations than those of Greece and Israel—Mesopotamia and Egypt, for example—Greece and Israel are still thought of as the "cradle of Western civilization." It is possible to trace a line of development from their ancient cultures on the Mediterranean Sea to Europe and present-day America. In the hands of the Greek poets, Greece's early gods and goddesses became not so much objects of worship as idealized models of human behavior, extending the boundaries of human possibilities; their epic heroes exemplified the strength, courage, and honor of the warrior. The Greeks invented philosophy and drama, and they were among the first peoples to write history. While other ancient cultures were deeply involved in organizing and controlling the general populace through military might and religious doctrine, Greek art celebrated the intelligence and beauty of the individual. As the Hebrews debated what it meant to be the "chosen people of God," the Greeks conceived of their cities as places where individuals might grow into their full potential as human beings. The Greek counterpart to Moses receiving God's laws on Mt. Sinai is Socrates in the marketplace discussing self-knowledge with his students.

THE EARLY GREEKS

The Greeks, like other heroic societies, displayed an ongoing disposition for war; warfare was a continuous theme in their society, dating back to the invasion of the Greek peninsula in the second millennium B.C.E. when nomadic warriors called Achaeans brought with them male gods of war and a culture of domination. A different kind of influence on Greek culture came from the island of Crete, where, protected by the sea from the early invasions of the Indo-Europeans (or **ARYANS**), a prosperous goddess culture with labyrinthine palaces, bull rituals, and powerful priestesses developed from c. 3000–1500 B.C.E. The demise of that society, which has been called the Minoan civilization, around 1400 B.C.E. was probably caused by a combination of natural disasters—volcanic eruptions, earthquakes, and floods—and invasions from the mainland by a feudal, warrior people called the Myceneans. They took their name from the citadel at Mycenae, which was ruled by the legendary King Agamemnon sometime during the Mycenean Age (c. 1500–1100 B.C.E.).

These warriors were a blend of non-Hellenic, black-haired Cretans and Hellenic peoples from the north, Homer's "brown-haired Achaeans (Akhaians)." Their written language, labeled by scholars as Linear B, was an early form of Greek, and their religion integrated deities from Crete and northern Indo-European figures, resulting in a fusion of myths. The Myceneans lived in a series of fortress-cities, largely in the Peloponnesus, the southern portion of Greece. The Mycenean Age, also called the Heroic Age in Greek history, produced several warrior heroes of legendary stature. One of their most famous expeditions resulted in the destruction of Troy in northwestern Asia Minor about 1200 B.C.E.—the narrative material of Homer's great epics.

Shortly after the destruction of Troy, another group of Indo-Europeans, the Dorians, apparently conquered the Mycenean fortresses with their iron implements c. 1100 B.C.E., ending the Mycenean Age. A number of uprooted Greeks settled on the coast of Asia Minor, into regions that came to be known as Ionia and Aeolia, where the foundations were laid for one of Greece's most influential creations, the Greek city-state, or ***POLIS.***

THE ATHENIAN POLIS

Just as major rivers determined the location of the earliest civilizations, geography played an important role in the culture of the Greek city-state. Greece comprises a mountainous peninsula and 1,600 islands, 169 of which are inhabited. The relative independence of the Greek city-states, isolated by mountains or water, fostered the growth of individualism, self-sufficiency, and freedom, ideals consistent with the heroic outlook. The ancient Greeks used water routes for trade as well as adventure. During the eighth and seventh centuries B.C.E., Greeks colonized numerous parts of the Mediterranean. When the production of wine and olive oil stimulated the growth of shipping and trade among the colonies, a merchant class came into being. To allay the threat of strife between nobles and peasants over the ownership of land, the institution of the "tyrant" arose in city-states like Athens and Corinth. Originally *tyrant* simply meant an individual who seized and held power without constitutional authority. Some tyrants, however, like Peisistratus in Athens, were good rulers who resolved civil conflict and economic problems; others were tyrants in the modern sense, seizing power and brutally maintaining it.

Athens was fortunate with its rulers. Towards the end of the seventh century B.C.E., Draco reformed the criminal justice system by replacing blood feuds or extended vendettas between families or clans with public trials. In 594 B.C.E., threatened by a worsening economy and a possible rebellion, Athens elected an extraordinary leader, or **ARCHON**, the philosopher-poet Solon. With the goals of allowing all citizens to participate in government and legally protecting the weak majority from the wealthy and stronger minority, Solon moved Athens in the direction of a community of free men. He promoted the growth of olives by banning the export of all other agricultural produce and by making the cutting down an olive tree punishable by death. He then withdrew to Cyprus and Egypt to test whether his reforms would better Athenian life in his absence. When order broke down, Peisistratus, who traced his ancestry to Nestor—the Homeric king of Pylos—seized power and used force to protect Solon's reforms. He built temples and founded the great **DIONYSIAC FESTIVALS**, which probably led to the invention of drama. After a popular uprising brought Cleisthenes to power in 510 B.C.E., the Athenian city-state became a democracy. It was every citizen's duty to participate in the *polis;* citizenship, however, was limited to men and those born from citizen stock. Every citizen by definition was thought to be qualified for public office, and the use of slaves allowed wealthy citizens the time for public service. Under this model of democracy, which promoted a balance between communal commitment and personal freedom for male citizens, Athens prospered materially and artistically like no other Greek state.

THE GOLDEN AGE

After repulsing invasions by the Persians (490–479 B.C.E.), the Athenians grew confident in their military might and, dreaming of an empire, organized the Delian League, a naval confederacy. Supported by imperialism and tribute money from allies, the Golden Age of Athens dawned, an age characterized by an ingenious flowering of thought and culture. This Classical Age, with its sense of excellence and form, set standards in art and literature for generations to come. Pericles, who came to power in 461 B.C.E., began a building program to make Athens worthy of its international renown. A new Parthenon—or temple—with a towering statue of the goddess Athena crowned the Acropolis, the central citadel. Other buildings and works of art enhanced the beauty of schools and marketplaces. In his funeral oration (431 B.C.E.), Pericles described the qualities of judgment, harmony, and industry that characterized the Athenian ideal.

The rivalry between Athens and the city-state of Sparta in the southern Peloponnesus, stemming from a desire for economic and political control over the region, finally led to war. In the sixth century B.C.E., under the direction of its

A View of the Parthenon, 447–438 B.C.E.
Situated above Athens on the Acropolis, or "Sacred Rock," the Parthenon is an international symbol of the Golden Age of Greece and a reflection of its classical ideals. Dedicated to the goddess Athena, the Parthenon was built under the urging of Pericles and played important religious and civic roles in Greek society. (© Wolfgang Kaehler / CORBIS)

legendary lawgiver Lycurgus, Sparta had developed into a military state with a highly disciplined mercenary army supported by a serf class and became increasingly isolated from other city-states. By 500 B.C.E. Sparta dominated the Peloponnesus through a confederacy of allies called the Peloponnesian League. Although Sparta supported Athens in the wars against Persia, the competition with Athens heated up after the Persian navy was defeated at Plataea in 479 B.C.E. and Athens grew more powerful, finally resulting in the Peloponnesian War that lasted for some twenty-seven years, from 431–404 B.C.E. For the Athenians, Pericles' death, bad judgments, a disastrous invasion of Sicily, internal rebellions, and the desertion of allies all led to defeat in 404 B.C.E. Continuous warfare waged by thousands of Greek mercenaries led to the decline of the ideals of the *polis.* Despite its victory, Sparta eventually faded, defeated by Thebes in 371 B.C.E.

In 359 B.C.E. Philip II seized the royal reins of Macedonia, a region in the northern part of Greece. After defeating Athens at the battle of Chaeronea in 338 B.C.E.,

Philip controlled Greece through the Hellenic League until he was murdered in 336 B.C.E. Philip's plans were adopted by his twenty-year-old son Alexander, who led an army of four thousand men eastward, liberating the Greek cities of Asia Minor. He defeated the Persian army at the eastern Anatolian city of Issus in 333 B.C.E. and sent the King of Persia, Darius III, into a hasty retreat eastward across Persia. His brilliant military skills and heroic ambition led to the conquest of both Persia and Egypt. Although Alexander, whose favorite literary work was Homer's *Iliad,* died of a fever at the early age of thirty-two in Babylon, he did far more than simply reincarnate the mythical Achilles (Akhilleus) through his military triumphs in the ancient Near East. He opened wealthy Persia to Western trade and spread the Greek language and the ideals of Greek education and culture to the eastern Mediterranean world. He also founded the city of Alexandria in Egypt, whose libraries became extraordinarily important to philosophical and scientific learning.

LITERACY AND LITERATURE

The Greeks borrowed from the Western Semitic-Phoenician alphabet in the ninth century B.C.E. to create their own system of writing; their addition of vowels to these consonants became the basis of all Western alphabets; *alphabet* itself is a word combining the Greek terms *alpha* and *beta,* the first two letters of the Greek alphabet. An earlier script, termed "Linear A," has been found on clay tablets on the island of Crete; it is thought to be of Semitic origin but has not yet been deciphered. Its replacement, "Linear B," was used on the mainland c. 1450 B.C.E. and was deciphered by Michael Ventris, a British architect, in 1952. It turned out to be an earlier form of Greek, making modern-day Greek the second-longest written language in use after Chinese. The Greek alphabet, which was relatively easy to learn, was an economical, flexible form of expression used for recording patterns of speech and various kinds of literature on inexpensive papyrus sheets imported from Egypt.

In Greece as in most civilizations, literature arose from mythology and folklore, a repository of oral stories that became the cultural heritage of the culture's poets and artists. Even though the Greek historian Herodotus (fifth century B.C.E.) called Homer and Hesiod the fathers of Greek mythology, these poets in fact inherited the tradition of heroic **LAYS** or short narrative poems that they developed into **EPICS**. Typically, epics are long narrative poems that present the history of a people or nation as a series of grand episodes involving the extraordinary actions of gods and heroes. Epics that appear to be the culmination of an extended oral or folk tradition are called "**FOLK EPICS**" and include, besides the Greek *Iliad* and *Odyssey,* the Mesopotamian *Epic of Gilgamesh,* the Indian *Ramayana* and *Mahabharata,* the

Old English *Beowulf,* and the West African *Sunjata.* The "art" or **"LITERARY" EPIC**, by contrast, is born of a written literary tradition and has as much concern for artistry as for history. Examples of the literary epic are Virgil's *Aeneid,* Dante's *Divine Comedy* and John Milton's *Paradise Lost.* Some storytellers retold myth and folklore in short prose anecdotes or fables that taught moral lessons; the legendary founder of this genre is Aesop.

An early form of philosophical writing is found in the works of Hesiod, who combined folklore and philosophy in order to systematize the earliest stories of the deities. His *Theogony,* which describes how creation emerged from chaos and the earth, or **GAIA**, reflects shadowy issues within the Greek family structure in its portrayal of the generational conflicts between the gods. Hesiod's stories about the goddesses Styx and Hecate illustrate how a number of Greek deities had their roots in a much earlier age. Zeus himself evolved through several stages before he assumed his rather stable throne on Mt. Olympus. If Hesiod is primarily concerned with the generations of gods and goddesses in *Theogony,* Homer's attention is focused on the glories of a heroic society, creating warriors from one of the most important cycles of stories to be passed down from the oral tradition, the stories of the Trojan War.

The heroes of the Trojan War and all that they symbolized provided important themes for the whole of the classical age in Greece and Rome—be it for military, intellectual, or artistic endeavors. Homer's *Iliad* (eighth century B.C.E.), the most well-known account of the war and the literary standard for epics ever since, focuses on the exploits of Achilles. With some nostalgia Homer depicts a heroic age four to five hundred years in the past and celebrates the patriarchal, feudal lifestyles of the Achaean warlords. Although savage at times, Achilles is nevertheless the epitome of the Greek hero and the heroic view of life: someone with superior mental and physical abilities who uses conquest and adventure to achieve honor and glory—the ultimate goals of his life. Throughout *The Iliad* the reader is made aware that while groups of men or whole armies are fighting over Helen and Troy, the real measure of heroism rests with individual warriors and their achievements.

In *The Odyssey,* Homer expands the heroic model to include Odysseus's wily intelligence and imagination. Homer weaves Odysseus's return to Ithaca into a series of adventures and near-fatal encounters that test him both physically and mentally. Odysseus's affairs with Circe (Kirké) and Calypso (Kalypso) reveal both his strengths and frailties, a man whose desires sometimes conflict with his ideals. Odysseus never falters, however, when it comes to survival. Homer's Ionian audience from the west coast of Asia Minor was a **FEUDAL ARISTOCRACY** who are likely to have identified with Odysseus, Achilles, and the warrior culture of the Myceneans.

The subjects of fertility, sexuality, agriculture, and life after death, traditionally associated with goddesses and **CHTHONIC**, or underworld, rituals, were largely neglected by Homer; absent in his work also are most of the goddesses who had been prominent on Crete.

Centuries after Homer's heroic models first appeared they continued to inspire Greeks who strove for excellence and fame in the *polis* as well as on the battlefield. Initially linked to war, the heroic code of honor came to stand for seeing life as a series of challenges that one must courageously face and overcome, for meeting each day forthrightly, whether one's challenges were intellectual, material, or political. Such an approach is reflected in this statement from Pericles' funeral oration: "[. . . we] place the real disgrace of poverty not in owning to the fact but in declining the struggle against it."

In addition to the epic, Greek poets also achieved excellence in the **LYRIC**, poems that were accompanied by a lyre, employed a variety of meters, and expressed personal feelings about topics like love and death. The lyric, sung by a single performer, was distinguished from choral poetry, which was sung by a chorus and danced. The earliest Greek lyric poets, Sappho, Terpander, and Alcaeus, lived on the island of Lesbos in the seventh century B.C.E. Sappho's genius was recognized by her contemporaries and those who followed, who regarded her as the "Tenth Muse," after the nine muses of Greek mythology; unfortunately, like the work of other lyric poets, most of her poems have been lost. By the time Roman poets inherited the genre of the lyric, the lyre was no longer used for accompaniment; there is a large sampling of extant lyrics by Roman poets like Catullus, Horace, and Propertius.

AN AGE OF UNUSUAL CREATIVITY

The world's first generally literate society developed in the city-states of Greece and Ionia during the sixth and fifth centuries B.C.E. As a result, citizens involved in public life were increasingly expected to be able to read and write. Artists, thinkers, and writers were drawn in particular to the intellectual and creative ferment of Athens. Although the ancient Greeks undoubtedly borrowed habits of mind and systems of knowledge from earlier civilizations, such as the priestly wisdom of Egypt, theirs was a unique passion for thinking and philosophy, matched only perhaps by the "hundred philosophers" in China, c. fourth century B.C.E. Departing somewhat from the popular Greek stories of gods and goddesses and the folk festivals of the time, intellectuals began to examine the social and physical world, speculate about its composition, and arrive at theories independent of religious tradition or institutions. Greek writers largely invented new literary forms and executed them brilliantly. Herodotus and Thucydides, for example, invented the writing of history. Herodotus is considered the "Father of History" in the Western tradition, and Thucydides one of its earliest practitioners. Plato and Aristotle in the fourth century B.C.E. broadened the Greek tradition of philosophical and scientific writing begun by earlier thinkers of the sixth and fifth centuries like Heraclitus, Empedocles, and Pythagorus—the first man to call himself a *philosopher,* meaning a "lover of wisdom."

Two Views of the Theater at Epidaurus, fourth century B.C.E. *Spectacularly built into a hillside, the theater at Epidaurus offers fantastic views and excellent acoustics. With a seating capacity of approximately fourteen thousand, this was one of the larger theaters in antiquity and is still in use today. (Above: © Yann Arthus-Bertrand/CORBIS; below: © Bettman/CORBIS)*

In the fifth century B.C.E., Attic tragedy, with its roots in religious ritual, became central to the festival life of the city. Although the exact origins of Greek drama are still debated, Aristotle maintained it began with the **DITHYRAMB**, or choral ode, used in religious ceremonies focusing on the figure of Dionysus. Greek comedy (from *komos,* "revel") probably originated in phallic ceremonies and fertility rites, while tragedy (from *tragoidia,* meaning "goat-song") first had to do with the Dionysian themes of death and resurrection enacted by a chorus dressed as goats or satyrs—figures sacred to Dionysus. Drama evolved from a dialogue between a leader and a chorus that gradually introduced additional speakers and eliminated the chorus. Tradition holds that the Greek playwright Aeschylus (525–456 B.C.E.) added a second actor for genuine dialogue; he also brought in costumes, masks, and thick-soled boots to "elevate" the action.

On the stages of Athens, the heroic legacy of Homer was questioned, revised, and adjusted to fit urban responsibilities. The great themes of the Trojan War were the subjects of Greek plays that were performed at the two major Athenian festivals in honor of Dionysus: the Lenaea in January and February, and the Great Dionysia in March and April, at which dramatists were awarded prizes by a jury. Most Greek cities, even some small ones, had outdoor theaters and valued the psychological and social roles that drama could play in civic life.

Aeschylus, the first great tragedian, explored human suffering and the complexities of human relationships through the legends of the House of Atreus and its curse—the underlying family saga for the Trojan War. In *The Oresteia,* Aeschylus prepares his audience for civic duty by submitting Orestes' murder of his mother to a newly created court system, thus interrupting the cyclical pattern of blood revenge. The *Oresteia* ends with a hymn to the newly constituted political and judicial system, a patriarchal system that muffles the powerful feminine Furies by transforming them into the Eumenides—the "gracious ones." Sophocles (496–406 B.C.E.) uses a different cycle of stories to create a tragic hero in *Oedipus Rex* and a new kind of strong, proud heroine in *Antigone,* a play that explores the conflicting demands of loyalty to family and civic obedience. Ever since Homer, who depicted the glory as well as the suffering of combat, there had been an ambivalence about the personal and social consequences of war among Greece's artists and thinkers. With the character of Antigone, Sophocles showed how militarism could lead to personal tragedy.

Two playwrights in particular attacked the political weaknesses that had allowed the Athenians to drift into the disastrous war with Sparta. Disillusioned by the wars of his own time and the heroic posturing of its leaders, Euripides (c. 480–406 B.C.E.) exposed the dark and painful side of the Trojan story in *Trojan Women* (415 B.C.E.), showing the pettiness and cruelty of the Greek warriors

TIME AND PLACE

Ancient Greece: The Trojan War

Many stories from Greek mythology have become part of the West's cultural consciousness; heroes such as Odysseus and Achilles are still referred to in literature today, 2,500 to 3,000 years after their stories were first told. One of the most compelling and enduring stories is that of the Trojan War. The mythic origins of the war are traced to Eris, the goddess of discord, who, at the wedding of the nymph Thetis to the mortal Peleus, rolled a golden apple across the floor inscribed with the words "For the Fairest." Shrewdly, Zeus chose Paris, a prince of Troy, to judge the beauty contest of Hera, who offered him power; Athena, who offered him wisdom; and Aphrodite, who promised Paris the most beautiful woman in the world. Paris chose Aphrodite, and the two losers became hostile towards Troy. While visiting King Menelaus of Sparta, Paris abducted Menelaus's beautiful wife, Helen, the daughter of Zeus and Leda and sister to Clytemnestra, and a portion of the Spartan treasury, then fled to Troy.

Angered by the betrayal, Menelaus called on his brother, King Agamemnon of Mycenae, to put together an army to take revenge on Troy. The brothers were joined by the armies of nearby city-states, Helen's former suitors, and heroes like Achilles, Odysseus, and Ajax. The Greek ships congregated at Aulis on the east coast of Greece but were stalled there because of inadequate winds. Following an oracle, Agamemnon sacrificed his youngest daughter, Iphigenia, who had been lured to Aulis with the promise of marriage to Achilles. The winds were restored and the boats sailed for Troy, a fortress city in the northwest corner of Asia Minor.

***Scene from the Trojan War, seventh century* B.C.E.**
One of the most famous mythological stories of all time, the climactic moment in the story of the Trojan War occurs when the Greeks, hidden inside a huge gift horse and wheeled into the besieged city of Troy, emerge at nightfall and destroy the city. (Erich Lessing / Art Resource, NY)

For nine years this army attacked the outskirts of Troy—the final year of which is documented in Homer's *Iliad*—failing to reach the

alongside the extreme suffering and courage of the Trojan women. The heroine of *Medea* (431 B.C.E.) expresses outrage at being betrayed by her man. She challenges the patriarchal pattern of family relationships and commits outrageous acts toward her children as a way of asserting her power as a woman and punishing Jason, who tarnishes the heroic tradition with his vacillation and cowardice. In the same period, comedic dramatist Aristophanes (c. 450–386 B.C.E.), although a devoted

TIME AND PLACE

Ancient Greece: The Trojan War continued

city itself, which was protected by a wall. Achilles killed Hector, the most famous Trojan warrior, but Troy persisted. Odysseus and Diomedes sneaked into the city of Troy by night and stole the sacred statue of Athena, the Palladium, believed to be the source of Trojan strength. But even with its heroes dead and the Palladium stolen, Troy did not fall. Finally, guided by Odysseus, the Greeks resorted to deception. Epeius built a large wooden horse and the strongest warriors hid in its belly. When the rest of the Greeks sailed away leaving the horse behind them, the curious Trojans came out of the city and found Sinon, a lone Greek soldier, on the beach. Lying to the Trojans, he said he had been abandoned and that the horse was an atonement for the theft of the Palladium; however, it had been built too large to be pulled through the gates into Troy. Falling for the trick, the Trojans dragged the horse inside the walls. In the middle of the night, the Greek soldiers emerged from the horse, called their compatriots back from a nearby island, and then they sacked and burned Troy.

A number of Greek warriors reached their homes quickly and safely. Agamemnon arrived home with Cassandra only to be assassinated by his wife, Clytemnestra. Others took many years to return. Menelaus and Helen were detoured to Egypt, where they spent seven years before returning to Sparta. Most famous of the Greek wanderers, Odysseus of Homer's *The Odyssey* spent ten years filled with love and adventure making his way back to his wife, Penelope, and son, Telemachus, on the island of Ithaca. The most famous Trojan survivor was Aeneas, son of Aphrodite and Anchises, who set out from the ruins of Troy with his wife, Creusa, son, Iulus (also Ascanius), and his father, to fulfill his destiny by founding a new Troy in a distant land. After losing his wife and wandering the seas—much like Odysseus—he gained the Italian coast and founded a colony that later became Rome.

Although this story belongs to the realm of mythology and legend, it was probably influenced by a real war between the Greeks and the people of Troas around 1200 B.C.E. Histories of city-states and peoples and stories of conquest were crucial narratives in the ancient world, replete with mythological heroes and gods who intervened in the history of human beings. Greek myths provided the ancestry for Greek city-states, the stories for religious life, and the subjects of art and plays. In essence, mythology provided a cosmic context within which the drama of everyday life might be carried out.

citizen of Athens, castigated certain politicians and criticized the ethos of war that he saw as undermining the very fabric of civic life. It is a remarkable measure of the freedom in Athenian society that Aristophanes' plays were performed during wartime. *Lysistrata* exposes the folly of men at war by depicting a conspiracy by a council of women to deny men sexual favors until they make peace with Sparta. The women of Sparta carry out the same plan, and peace is finally achieved.

Although Sophocles' Antigone rivals any man with her courage and heroism in the face of death and the women in Aristophanes' *Lysistrata* use their powers to affect policy, generally speaking, the men and women in Greek art and literature live in separate worlds, with Athenian women mostly living secluded lives as housewives. The acceptance of homosexuality among Greek men further indicates the low status of women. The labor of women and slaves made it possible for Greek citizens—all male—to spend their time debating the great issues of the day and to develop the deep and lasting friendships praised in Hellenic poems and essays.

The Peloponnesian War brought about important changes in Athenian society. Disillusionment with the social upheaval resulting from the war upset the balance between the individual and the state by questioning whether democracy and the ideal city-state were indeed workable. Methods of argumentation taught by professional teachers, known as **Sophists**, were seen as undermining traditional, civic values and promoting individual cleverness and skepticism. The most renowned teacher of the time, Socrates (c. 470–399 B.C.E.), was seen as further weakening the appeal of civic responsibility through his teachings on personal knowledge and the inner voice, even though he himself had served in the army as a **hoplite** and had been elected to the Council, a body that prepared the political agenda for the general Assembly to which all citizens were welcome. In the unstable atmosphere of the war's aftermath and the decline of Athens, charges were brought against Socrates, who in *The Apology* questions whether personal honesty is compatible with public service. He was convicted and sentenced to death in 399 B.C.E. Socrates's most famous pupil, Plato (c. 427–347 B.C.E.), founded a school, Academy, in 387 B.C.E. His own star pupil was Aristotle (384–322 B.C.E.), the philosopher who conceived of logic and then used it to codify human knowledge.

www For more information about the culture and context of Greece in the ancient world, see *World Literature Online* at bedfordstmartins.com/worldlit.

HESIOD
EIGHTH CENTURY B.C.E.

Western culture owes a great debt to Hesiod, a Greek poet who lived in roughly the same era as Homer but who was interested in different kinds of myths and stories. Homer focused primarily on deities that became part of the Olympic PANTHEON,[1] a divine community gathered around Zeus and often resembling the heroic warrior culture of a past age with its patriarchal, feudal trappings; he avoided the types of stories Hesiod collected and preserved—stories about old, powerful goddesses like **Styx** and **Hecate**;[2] rebellions against Zeus and the creation of woman; about the chthonic, nocturnal worlds of sacrifice and spells; and sex, fertility, and death.

STIKS; HEH-kuh-tee

In the first of his two major works, *Theogony,* Hesiod created a rather unusual mythic world—what has been called a philosophical myth of creation—through an extensive genealogy of abstract qualities and deities. His second work, *Works and Days,* is a picture of peasant life in the eighth century B.C.E. that dispenses advice about the appropriate attitudes and rituals needed to appease the gods. In addition to being a kind of ancient farmer's almanac, *Works and Days* is the oldest source of myths about Prometheus, the first woman, Pandora, and the Golden Age. M. L. West assesses Hesiod's niche in literary history: "Hesiod is a less familiar name to the general reader than Homer, **Aeschylus**, or Plato,[3] and no one would claim that he is as great a writer as they. He was nevertheless one of the most famous poets of antiquity, often mentioned in the same breath as Homer as the other main representative of the early worldview."

ES-kuh-lus

A Farmer Becomes a Poet. Hesiod, who unlike Homer provided some information about himself and his family, is thought to have lived in the last third of the eighth century B.C.E. His father was a merchant seaman who moved to Ascra, northwest of Athens, in the province of Boeotia, to farm. Thebes, the home of Oedipus Rex, the character made famous in the Sophocles play of the same name, is Boeotia's central city; the port of Aulis, from which the Greeks sailed for Troy and the Trojan War, is also in the province. Hesiod and his brother Perses were born in Ascra, a favorite haunt of the Muses on the eastern side of Mt. Helicon. In *Theogony,*

WWW For links to information about Hesiod and a quiz on *Theogony* and *Works and Days,* see *World Literature Online* at bedfordstmartins.com/worldlit.

[1] **Olympic pantheon:** From Mt. Olympus, the highest mountain in Greece; home of the gods and goddesses.

[2] **Styx and Hecate:** Styx is an ancient goddess of oaths after whom the river in Hades is named. Hecate is an ancient moon-goddess and the oldest member of the female trinity, or the triple goddess: Persephone (maid), Demeter (mother), and Hecate (crone).

[3] **Aeschylus . . . Plato:** Aeschylus (525–456 B.C.E.), Greek tragedian known for *Oresteia.* The philosopher Plato (c. 427–347 B.C.E.) founded the Academy, where one of his pupils was the philosopher and naturalist Aristotle (384–322 B.C.E.).

Hesiod's vision of the realities of the Iron Age instructed and inspired some of the greatest social thinkers of Greece, such as Solon and Aeschylus. We today are still living in the Iron Age. From Hesiod we can gain insight not only into his life, but also into our own.

– Norman O. Brown, critic, 1953

Hesiod describes how the **Muses**[4] visited him while he was tending sheep on Mt. Helicon and ordered him "To sing the race of blessed ones who live / Forever. . . ." Other famous natives of this region are the poet Pindar (522–443 B.C.E.), the greatest lyric poet of his age and a major source of Greek myth, and Plutarch (46?–120? C.E.), the historian and biographer who is a prime source of the Egyptian myth of Osiris and Isis.[5] It is believed that Hesiod was murdered and buried at Oenoe, a fortress on Mt. Cithaeron.

Theogony. In *Theogony,* which means "the generations of the gods," Hesiod attempted to give coherence to a number of different creation stories and short sketches of deities. Although there were several creation myths holding sway in ancient Greece at the time, Hesiod's version served as the perfect complement to Homer's writings, since it traced the history of divine patriarchal rule from Earth, Gaia, to Sky, Ouranos (Uranus), to Ouranos's son Kronos (Cronus), the head of the Titans,[6] to the reign of Zeus, son of Kronos and undisputed ruler of the Olympian deities. Like Indra, the creator-god of the Rig-Veda, Zeus was originally a storm-god, whose major weapon was the lightning bolt.

Reflecting most ancient mythology, Hesiod believed that creation occurred within an existent material world that was in a state of disorder or chaos. **Gaia**, or Earth, as the physical world, gave birth to the first sky-god, **Ouranos**. Ouranos and Gaia mated and produced the Titans and many other deities. Hesiod further believed, based on the family dynamics of the first generations of the gods, that life is difficult and that women are dangerous to men; these views have their roots in Ouranos's hate for his children, which leads him to hide them in Gaia's body. Groaning in pain, Gaia devises revenge: Kronos, one of her sons, will castrate his father with a flint knife. A pattern of father-son conflict is repeated in succeeding generations, becoming a divine model for the patriarchal family and later a theme in Greek drama.

GIGH-yuh

YOO-ruh-nus

Becoming the next ruler of the universe, Kronos marries his sister Rhea and they create the first generation of Olympian deities. Because of the cycle of violence that he has initiated, Kronos fears the birth of a son and so swallows each of his children at birth. Rhea rebels and, assisted by Gaia and Ouranos, substitutes a stone for the baby Zeus, which Kronos swallows. The grown Zeus then overthrows his father and the Titans, and releases his siblings. Fearing a rebellious son of his own, Zeus swallows Metis, who is pregnant with the potential next ruler. Athena is born out of Zeus's head and joins forces with him. The important story of Prometheus's struggle with Zeus over the ritual of sacrifice and the possession of fire extends this story of rebellion and conflict into the human sphere.

---

[4] **the Muses:** The nine—or sometimes only three—daughters of Zeus and Mnemosyne who are the source of inspiration for poets and artists.

[5] **Osiris and Isis:** Important Egyptian deities (see pages 98–99).

[6] **Titans:** An early race of giants who represent the primitive forces of nature.

Hesiod added to the Greek cosmogony a myriad of children who were said to occupy every possible tree, river, spring, and mountain in Greece.[7] Hesiod's world is a reminder that Greek religion was not housed exclusively in temples, the residences of the deities, but was a part of the physical environment and marked by altars in specific locations scattered throughout the natural world. Hesiod's system is an **ANTHROPOCENTRIC** collection of deities ruled by King Zeus who intermingle with human society. While Homer fashioned godlike heroes, Hesiod, retooling theology, created deities that shared the faculties and frailties of humankind; as if to punctuate their commonality, Hesiod concludes *Theogony* with episodes of matings between gods and humans. In both Hesiod and Homer, the gods and the humans possess a willfulness and freedom totally absent from the mythic worlds of ancient Mesopotamia, Egypt, and India, in which humans were pawns, servants, or subjects of a priesthood.

Homer and Hesiod attributed to the gods all sorts of actions which when done by men are disreputable and deserving of blame—such lawless deeds as theft, adultery, and mutual deception.

–XENOPHANES OF COLOPHON, C. 570–478 B.C.E.

Works and Days. In *Works and Days,* a series of pastoral poems, Hesiod gives his brother Perses advice about living an upright life and records maxims about farming. Hesiod is the first poet in Greece to recognize the persuasive power of speaking directly to his audience, namely, the men of his time. He begins *Works and Days* with a continuation of the Prometheus myth from *Theogony* and the creation of Pandora, the first woman and the source of men's trouble. Then he names the five ages of humankind in terms of a succession of metals—from the golden age, which resembles paradise, through the silver, bronze, heroic, and iron ages—and describes a gradual devolution of behavior and living conditions. For his era, Hesiod sees little that is precious: "This is the race of iron. Now, by day / Men work and grieve unceasingly; by night, / They waste away and die." Often compared to the prophets of Israel, Hesiod warned his contemporaries of the consequences of conflict and injustice.

Hesiod's five ages are roughly the equivalent of the Hebrew story of the Fall of mankind in Eden, which resulted in expulsion from the garden. Traditionally, the Greek Golden Age and Eden were phenomena of the distant past, lost or abandoned. Writers referred to them as an irreplaceable, paradisal condition in man's past. But the Golden Age also came to represent a future place or condition toward which mankind might be striving. The Romans, for example, believed that they were entering the Golden Age with Caesar Augustus. Within the long cycles of creation and destruction in the Hindu tradition, the Golden Age is recoverable, even though it might take thousands of years to find again. The paradigm of the Golden Age, transmitted by Ovid,[8] a poet who later recreated Greek myths in Latin, had a tremendous influence on the Middle Period (first through the fourteenth centuries). The myth of a Golden Age spread throughout the Mediterranean region and served as an incentive for explorers who would one day search for Paradise in the West.

. . . it was Hesiod, in his . . . *Theogony* or *Descent of the Gods,* who first ventured to arrange all mythology into a comprehensive philosophical system.

–WERNER JAEGER, historian, 1939

[7] **every . . . Greece:** With its innumerable divinities and semidivinities, ancient Greece had an abundance of sacred sites.

[8] **Ovid** (43 B.C.E.–17 C.E.): Roman poet who reinterpreted Greek myth in *Metamorphoses.*

■ CONNECTIONS

***Epic of Creation*, p. 44; Hebrew Scriptures, p. 134.** From the Babylonian *Epic of Creation* to the Hebrew Scriptures, the transition from chaotic wilderness to first nomadic tribes to settled, organized cities is commonly portrayed as a conflict between gods and giants, fathers and sons, and brothers. In what ways are the Greek myths as presented by Hesiod similar to those of Mesopotamia and Israel? What type of society do Hesiod's myths describe?

India, p. 1323. Early deities often were associated with nature or weather. One of the most powerful deities in ancient India was Indra; how are Indra's qualities as a storm-god similar to those of the Greek Zeus, who carries a lightning bolt?

***Book of Songs*, p. 1573; Egyptian Hymns, p. 104; Hebrew Scriptures, p. 134.** In ancient literature, advances in civilization are often portrayed as gifts from the gods or miraculous creations of legendary heroes. China, for example, attributed the invention of agriculture to a legendary emperor, Shen Nung; the Greeks credited Prometheus with the gift of fire and medicinal plants; the ancient Hebrews attributed the invention of blacksmithing to the legendary Tubal-cain, and the Egyptians associated the first writing with Thoth. Why are inventions such as irrigation, writing, fire, and metallurgy so significant that they are attributed to legendary heroes or deities?

■ FURTHER RESEARCH

Translations and Editions

Hesiod. *The Works and Days, Theogony, and the Shield of Herakles.* Richard Lattimore, trans. 1991.

———. *Theogony.* Norman O. Brown, trans. 1953. An excellent introduction.

———. *Theogony.* M. L. West, ed. 1966. Lengthy introduction.

———. *Works and Days.* M. L. West, ed. 1978. Lengthy introduction.

Wender, Dorothea, trans. *Hesiod and Theognis.* 1973.

Background and Commentary

Burn, A. R. *The World of Hesiod.* 1936.

Frankel, H. *Early Greek Poetry and Philosophy.* 1975.

Jaeger, Werner. *Paideia: The Ideals of Greek Culture: Volume 1: Archaic Greece, The Mind of Athens.* 1965.

Lesky, A. *History of Greek Literature.* 1966.

Nelson, Stephanie. *God and the Land: The Metaphysics of Farming in Hesiod and Vergil.* 1998.

Penglase, Charles. *Greek Myths and Mesopotamia: Parallels and Influence in the Homeric Hymns and Hesiod.* 1994.

Solmsen, Friedrich. *Hesiod and Aeschylus.* 1949.

Walcott, P. *Hesiod and the Near East.* 1966.

■ PRONUNCIATION

Aeschylus: ES-kuh-lus
Chaeronea: kee-roh-NEE-uh
Chthonic: THAH-nik
Cithaeron: sih-THEE-run, kih-THIGH-rohn
Dithyramb: DITH-ih-ram
Gaia: GIGH-yuh
Hecate: HEK-uh-tee
Hecuba: HEH-kuh-bee
Neoptolemus: nee-up-TAH-luh-mus
Oresteia: oh-res-TIGH-uh
Ouranos: YOO-ruh-nus, yoo-RAY-nus
Peisistratus: pih-SIS-truh-tus
Philoctetes: fih-lahk-TEE-teez
Styx: STIKS

FROM

Theogony

Translated by Dorothea Wender

[The Castration of Uranus]

Chaos was first of all, but next appeared
Broad-bosomed Earth,[1] sure standing-place for all
The gods who live on snowy Olympus' peak,
And misty Tartarus,[2] in a recess
Of broad-pathed earth, and Love,[3] most beautiful
Of all the deathless gods. He makes men weak,
He overpowers the clever mind, and tames
The spirit in the breasts of men and gods.
From Chaos came black Night and Erebos.[4]
And Night in turn gave birth to Day and Space[5]
Whom she conceived in love to Erebos.
And Earth bore starry Heaven,[6] first, to be
An equal to herself, to cover her
All over, and to be a resting-place,
Always secure, for all the blessed gods.
Then she brought forth long hills, the lovely homes
Of goddesses, the Nymphs who live among
The mountain clefts. Then, without pleasant love,
She bore the barren sea with its swollen waves,
Pontus. And then she lay with Heaven, and bore
Deep-whirling Oceanus and Koios; then

Theogony. Probably composed in the latter half of the eighth century B.C.E. and written down shortly after that, Hesiod's creation myth describes the transition from female to male dominance in the cosmos in four major episodes: the emergence of Earth from Chaos and the first generation of gods; the castration of Sky (Ouranos); Kronos swallowing his children and Zeus escaping; and the victorious battle of Zeus and the Olympian gods against the Titans.

In *Theogony,* the rebellion of the younger gods against the fathers in each generation is reminiscent of the scenes in the Babylonian *Epic of Creation* in which the younger generation of gods plot against Tiamat, the female dragon, and her husband, Apsu. Family conflict also plays a central role in the stories of patriarchs and their families in the Bible's Book of Genesis.

---

[1] **Earth:** Called Gaea or Gaia (*Ge* in Greek); the Earth as a goddess.

[2] **Tartarus:** The lowest region of Hades where the most wicked were punished and the Titans confined.

[3] **Love:** The god Eros (Desire).

[4] **Erebos:** The mysterious darkness under the earth through which the dead pass en route to Hades.

[5] **Space:** Ether, the upper atmosphere.

[6] **Heaven:** Uranus (*Ouranos* in Greek); the Heaven or Sky as a god.

Kreius, Iapetos, Hyperion,
Theia, Rhea, Themis, Mnemosyne,
Lovely Tethys, and Phoebe, golden-crowned.
Last, after these, most terrible of sons,
The crooked-scheming Kronos[7] came to birth
Who was his vigorous father's enemy.
Again, she bore the Cyclopes, whose hearts
Were insolent, Brontes and Steropes
And proud-souled Arges,[8] those who found and gave
The thunder and the lightning-bolt to Zeus.
They were like other gods in all respects,
But that a single eye lay in the brow
Of each, and from this, they received the name,
Cyclopes, from the one round eye which lay
Set in the middle of each forehead.[9] Strength
And energy and craft were in their works.
Then Ouranos and Gaia bore three sons
Mighty and violent, unspeakable
Kottos and Gyes and Briareus,
Insolent children, each with a hundred arms
On his shoulders, darting about, untouchable,
And each had fifty heads, standing upon
His shoulders, over the crowded mass of arms,
And terrible strength was in their mighty forms.

And these most awful sons of Earth and Heaven
Were hated by their father from the first.
As soon as each was born, Ouranos hid
The child in a secret hiding-place in Earth
And would not let it come to see the light,
And he enjoyed this wickedness. But she,
Vast Earth, being strained and stretched inside her, groaned.
And then she thought of a clever, evil plan.
Quickly she made grey adamant,[10] and formed
A mighty sickle, and addressed her sons,
Urging them on, with sorrow in her heart,
'My sons, whose father is a reckless fool,
If you will do as I ask, we shall repay

[7] **Kronos:** The offspring of Earth and Heaven are the original Titans, twelve in number, Oceanus through Phoebe; in general, they are deifications of various aspects of nature; a few gain individual importance later.

[8] **Cyclopes . . . Arges:** Here, the one-eyed giants are sons of Heaven and Earth. In *The Odyssey,* the Cyclops Polyphemus is the son of Poseidon.

[9] **one . . . forehead:** *Cyclopes* means "round-eyed."

[10] **grey adamant:** A mythical metal, like flint.

Your father's wicked crime. For it was he
Who first began devising shameful acts.'

She spoke, but fear seized all of them, and none
Replied. Then crooked Kronos, growing bold,
Answered his well-loved mother with these words:
'Mother, I undertake to do the deed;
I do not care for my unspeakable
Father, for he first thought of shameful acts.'
He spoke, and giant Earth was glad at heart.
She set him in a hiding-place, and put
Into his hands the saw-toothed scimitar,
And told him all the plot she had devised.

Great Heaven came, and with him brought the night.
Longing for love, he lay around the Earth,
Spreading out fully. But the hidden boy
Stretched forth his left hand; in his right he took
The great long jagged sickle; eagerly
He harvested his father's genitals
And threw them off behind. They did not fall
From his hands in vain, for all the bloody drops
That leaped out were received by Earth; and when
The year's time was accomplished, she gave birth
To the Furies, and the Giants, strong and huge,
Who fought in shining armour, with long spears,
And the nymphs called Meliae[11] on the broad earth.

The genitals, cut off with adamant
And thrown from land into the stormy sea,
Were carried for a long time on the waves.
White foam surrounded the immortal flesh,
And in it grew a girl. At first it touched
On holy Cythera, from there it came
To Cyprus, circled by the waves. And there
The goddess came forth, lovely, much revered,
And grass grew up beneath her delicate feet.
Her name is Aphrodite among men
And gods, because she grew up in the foam,[12]
And Cytherea, for she reached that land,
And Cyprogenes from the stormy place

[11] **Meliae:** Ash-tree nymphs.

[12] **foam:** The root of Aphrodite's name is linked to *aphros,* meaning "foam." Aphrodite is the goddess of love.

Where she was born, and Philommedes[13] from
The genitals, by which she was conceived.
Eros is her companion; fair Desire[14]
Followed her from the first, both at her birth
And when she joined the company of the gods.
From the beginning, both among gods and men,
She had this honour and received this power:
Fond murmuring of girls, and smiles, and tricks,
And sweet delight, and friendliness, and charm.

But the great father Ouranos reproached
His sons, and called them Titans,[15] for, he said
They strained in insolence, and did a deed
For which they would be punished afterwards.

And Night bore frightful Doom and the black Ker,[16]
And Death, and Sleep, and the whole tribe of Dreams.

Again, although she slept with none of the gods,
Dark Night gave birth to Blame and sad Distress,
And the Hesperides, who, out beyond
The famous stream of Oceanus, tend
The lovely golden apples, and their trees.
She bore the Destinies and ruthless Fates,[17]
Goddesses who track down the sins of men
And gods, and never cease from awful rage
Until they give the sinner punishment.
Then deadly Night gave birth to Nemesis,
That pain to gods and men, and then she bore
Deceit and Love, sad Age, and strong-willed Strife.
And hateful Strife gave birth to wretched Work,
Forgetfulness, and Famine, tearful Pains,
Battles and Fights, Murders, Killings of men,
Quarrels and Lies and Stories and Disputes,
And Lawlessness and Ruin, both allied,
And Oath, who brings most grief to men on earth
When anyone swears falsely, knowing it. [. . .]

---

[13] **Philommedes:** Greek for "Genital loving."

[14] **fair Desire:** An abstraction elevated by Hesiod to a deity, similar to the other abstractions that follow.

[15] **Titans:** From *teino,* meaning "I strain"; probably a false etymology.

[16] **Ker:** A spirit of death.

[17] **Fates:** Called *Moerae* in Greek, the Fates were usually old women—three in number—who were present at every birth and determined one's fate. Lacheisis determines the length of life's thread, Clotho spins the thread, and Atropos uses shears to cut it off.

[Kronos Swallows His Children and the Birth of Zeus]

And Rhea, being forced by Kronos, bore
Most brilliant offspring to him: Hestia,
Demeter, golden-slippered Hera, strong
Hades,[18] who has his home beneath the earth,
The god whose heart is pitiless, and him
Who crashes loudly and who shakes the earth,[19]
And thoughtful Zeus, father of gods and men,
Whose thunder makes the wide earth tremble. Then,
As each child issued from the holy womb
And lay upon its mother's knees, each one
Was seized by mighty Kronos, and gulped down.
He had in mind that no proud son of Heaven
Should hold the royal rank among the gods
Except himself. For he had learned from Earth
And starry Heaven, that his destiny
Was to be overcome, great though he was,
By one of his own sons, and through the plans
Of mighty Zeus. Therefore he never dropped
His guard, but lay in wait, and swallowed down
His children. Rhea suffered endless grief;
But when she was about to bring forth Zeus,
Father of gods and men, she begged the Earth
And starry Heaven, her parents, to devise
A plan to hide the birth of her dear son
And bring the Fury down on Kronos, for
His treatment of his father and his sons
Whom mighty, crooked Kronos swallowed down.
They heard their daughter and agreed, and told
Her all that fate would bring upon the king
Kronos, and to his mighty-hearted son.
They sent her to the fertile land of Crete,
To Lyctus,[20] when she was about to bear
Her youngest child, great Zeus. And in broad Crete
Vast Earth received the child from her, to raise
And cherish. And she carried him, with speed,
Through the black night, and came to Lyctus first.
She took him in her arms and hid him, deep
Under the holy earth, in a vast cave,

---

[18] **Hestia . . . Hades:** The first four Olympian deities, usually twelve or thirteen in total.

[19] **him Who crashes . . . earth:** Poseidon, god of the sea and earthquakes.

[20] **Lyctus:** A site near the modern village of Xidas in central Crete.

On thickly-wooded Mount Aegeum.[21] Then,
To the great lord, the son of Heaven, the past
King of the gods, she handed, solemnly,
All wrapped in swaddling-clothes, a giant stone.
He seized it in his hands and thrust it down
Into his belly, fool! He did not know
His son, no stone, was left behind, unhurt
And undefeated, who would conquer him
With violence and force, and drive him out
From all his honours, and would rule the gods.

The strength and glorious limbs of the young lord
Grew quickly and the years went by, and Earth
Entrapped great clever Kronos with shrewd words
Advising him to bring his offspring back.
(His son, by craft and power, conquered him.)
And first he vomited the stone, which he
Had swallowed last. At holy Pytho,[22] Zeus
Set firm the stone in broad-pathed earth, beneath
Parnassus, in a cleft, to be a sign
In future days, for men to marvel at.

He freed his uncles from their dreadful bonds,
The sons of Heaven; his father, foolishly,
Had bound them. They remembered gratitude
And gave him thunder and the blazing bolt
And lightning, which, before, vast Earth had hid.
Trusting in them, he rules both men and gods.
And Klymene, the lovely-ankled nymph,
Daughter of Ocean, married Iapetos,
And went to bed with him, and bore a son,
Strong-hearted Atlas, then, notorious
Menoitios, and then, Prometheus[23]
Brilliant and shifty, Epimetheus
The foolish one, who first brought harm to men
Who live on bread, for he took Woman in,
The manufactured maiden, gift of Zeus.
Far-seeing Zeus cast proud Menoitios

[21] **Mount Aegeum:** "Goat's Mountain"; probably Mt. Dikte, in which there is a large cave.

[22] **the stone . . . Pytho:** The stone, called the omphalos, or navel stone, was located at Apollo's temple at Pytho, the ancient name of Delphi, on the slope of Mt. Parnassus.

[23] **Prometheus:** Meaning "forethought"; Prometheus is known as the champion of humanity for rebelling against Zeus.

Down into Erebos; he struck him with
The smoking thunderbolt, because he was
Insanely bold and reckless in his pride.
And Atlas, forced by hard necessity,
Holds the broad heaven up, propped on his head
And tireless hands, at the last ends of Earth,
In front of the clear-voiced Hesperides;
For Zeus the Counsellor gave him this fate.
Clever Prometheus was bound by Zeus
In cruel chains, unbreakable, chained round
A pillar, and Zeus roused and set on him
An eagle with long wings, which came and ate
His deathless liver. But the liver grew
Each night, until it made up the amount
The long-winged bird had eaten in the day.
Lovely Alcmene's son, strong Heracles,
Killing the eagle, freed Prometheus
From his affliction and his misery,
And Zeus, Olympian, who rules on high,
Approved, so that the fame of Heracles
The Theban might be greater than before
Upon the fruitful earth; he showed respect,
And gave the honour to his famous son.
And angry though he was, he checked the rage
He felt against Prometheus, who dared
To match his wits against almighty Zeus.

[Prometheus Steals Fire]

For at Mekone, once, there was a test
When gods and mortal men divided up
An ox; Prometheus audaciously
Set out the portions, trying to deceive
The mind of Zeus. Before the rest, he put
Pieces of meat and marbled inner parts
And fat upon the hide, and hid them in
The stomach of the ox; but before Zeus
The white bones of the ox, arranged with skill,
Hidden in shining fat. And then he spoke,
The father of gods and men, and said to him,
'Milord, most famous son of Iapetos,
The shares you've made, my friend, are most unfair!'
Thus Zeus, whose plans are everlasting, spoke
And criticized. But sly Prometheus
Did not forget his trick, and softly smiled

And said, 'Most glorious Zeus, greatest of all
The gods who live forever, choose your share,
Whichever one your heart leads you to pick.'
He spoke deceitfully, but Zeus who knows
Undying plans, was not deceived, but saw
The trick, and in his heart made plans
To punish mortal men in future days.
He took the fatted portion in his hands
And raged within, and anger seized his heart
To see the trick, the white bones of the ox.
(And from this time the tribes of men on earth
Burn, on the smoking altars, white ox-bones.)

But Zeus, the gatherer of clouds, enraged,
Said, 'Son of Iapetos, cleverest god
Of all: so, friend, you do not yet forget
Your crafty tricks!' So spoke the angry Zeus
Whose craft is everlasting. From that time
He bore the trick in mind, and would not give,
To wretched men who live on earth, the power
Of fire, which never wearies. The brave son
Of Iapetos deceived him, and he stole
The ray, far-seeing, of unwearied fire,
Hid in the hollow fennel stalk, and Zeus
Who thunders in the heavens ate his heart,
And raged within to see the ray of fire
Far-seeing, among men. Immediately
He found a price for men to pay for fire,
An evil: for the famous Limping God[24]
Moulded, from earth, the image of a girl
A modest virgin, through the plans of Zeus.
Grey-eyed Athene[25] made her belt and dressed
The girl in robes of silver; over her face
She pulled a veil, embroidered cleverly,
Marvellous to behold, and on her head
Pallas Athene set a lovely wreath
Of blossoms from spring grasses, and a crown
Of gold, made by the famous Limping God,
Worked with his hands, to please his father Zeus.
Upon it many clever things were worked,
Marvellous to behold: monsters which earth

[24] **the . . . Limping God:** Hephaistos, the divine craftsman.

[25] **Grey-eyed Athene:** Goddess of wisdom and patroness of Athens.

And sea have nourished, made to seem as real
As living, roaring creatures, miracles,
And beauty in abundance shone from it.

When he had made the lovely curse, the price
For the blessing of fire, he brought her to a place
Where gods and men were gathered, and the girl
Was thrilled by all her pretty trappings, given
By mighty Zeus's daughter with grey eyes.
Amazement seized the mortal men and gods,
To see the hopeless trap, deadly to men.

From her comes all the race of womankind,
The deadly female race and tribe of wives
Who live with mortal men and bring them harm,
No help to them in dreadful poverty
But ready enough to share with them in wealth.
As in the covered hive the honey-bees
Keep feeding drones, conspirators in wrong,
And daily, all day long, until the sun
Goes down, the workers hurry about their work
And build white honeycombs, while those inside
In the sheltered storeroom, fill their bellies up
With products of the toil of others, thus,
Women are bad for men, and they conspire
In wrong, and Zeus the Thunderer made it so.
He made a second evil as a price
Of fire, man's blessing: if a man avoids
Marriage and all the troubles women bring
And never takes a wife, at last he comes
To miserable old age, and does not have
Anyone who will care for the old man.
He has enough to live on, while he lives,
But when he dies, his distant relatives
Divide his property. The married man
Who gets a good wife, suited to his taste,
Gets good and evil mixed, but he who gets
One of the deadly sort, lives all his life
With never-ending pain inside his heart
And on his mind; the wound cannot be healed.
It is impossible to hoodwink Zeus
Or to surpass him, for Prometheus,
The son of Iapetos, kind though he was
And wise, could not escape his heavy rage
But he was bound by force, with heavy chains.

FROM

Works and Days

Translated by Dorothea Wender

[Prometheus and Pandora]

The gods desire to keep the stuff of life
Hidden from us. If they did not, you could
Work for a day and earn a year's supplies;
You'd pack away your rudder, and retire
The oxen and the labouring mules. But Zeus
Concealed the secret, angry in his heart
At being hoodwinked by Prometheus,
And so he thought of painful cares for men.
First he hid fire. But the son of Iapetos° Prometheus
Stole it from Zeus the Wise, concealed the flame
In a fennel stalk, and fooled the Thunderer.

Then, raging, spoke the Gatherer of Clouds:
'Prometheus, most crafty god of all,
You stole the fire and tricked me, happily,
You, plague on all mankind and on yourself.
They'll pay for fire: I'll give another gift
To men, an evil thing for their delight,
And all will love this ruin in their hearts.'
So spoke the father of men and gods, and laughed.

He told Hephaistos quickly to mix earth
And water, and to put in it a voice

Works and Days. A continuous theme in *Works and Days* is that life is a struggle; virtue results from meeting the challenge of adversity. Greece is mostly hills, mountains, and narrow valleys with rocky soil. There are very few large, easily cultivatable plains like those of northern Europe or the western United States. Greek civilization was built in large part through hard work. Unlike Homer, who writes about the world of aristocrats whose ideal is the warrior and whose activities include warring and playing games, Hesiod is concerned more with man's labor and is suspicious of any distraction from diligence. The Puritans in seventeenth-century New England would be similarly convinced of work's virtue.

The first excerpt from *Works and Days* expands on the story of Prometheus's rebellion against Zeus and the creation of the first woman, Pandora, as a punishment for Prometheus's transgression. Next, Hesiod describes the five ages of humanity, from the Golden to the Iron Age. This is the Greek story of the loss of Paradise and the accumulation of the ills associated with the present age: death, war, generational conflict, and deceit.

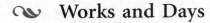

And human power to move, to make a face
Like an immortal goddess, and to shape
The lovely figure of a virgin girl.
Athene was to teach the girl to weave,
And golden Aphrodite to pour charm
Upon her head, and painful, strong desire,
And body-shattering cares. Zeus ordered, then,
The killer of Argos, Hermes, to put in
Sly manners, and the morals of a bitch.
The son of Kronos spoke, and was obeyed.
The Lame God moulded earth as Zeus decreed
Into the image of a modest girl,
Grey-eyed Athene made her robes and belt,
Divine Seduction and the Graces gave
Her golden necklaces, and for her head
The Seasons wove spring flowers into a crown.
Hermes the Messenger put in her breast
Lies and persuasive words and cunning ways;
The herald of the gods then named the girl
Pandora,[1] for the gifts which all the gods
Had given her, this ruin of mankind.

The deep and total trap was now complete;
The Father sent the gods' fast messenger
To bring the gift to Epimetheus.° hindsight
And Epimetheus forgot the words
His brother said, to take no gift from Zeus,
But send it back, lest it should injure men.
He took the gift, and understood, too late.

Before this time men lived upon the earth
Apart from sorrow and from painful work,
Free from disease, which brings the Death-gods in.
But now the woman opened up the cask,
And scattered pains and evils among men.
Inside the cask's hard walls remained one thing,
Hope, only, which did not fly through the door.
The lid stopped her, but all the others flew,
Thousands of troubles, wandering the earth.
The earth is full of evils, and the sea.
Diseases come to visit men by day

[1] **Pandora:** All the gifts.

And, uninvited, come again at night
Bringing their pains in silence, for they were
Deprived of speech by Zeus the Wise. And so
There is no way to flee the mind of Zeus.

[The Ages of Man]

And now with art and skill I'll summarize
Another tale, which you should take to heart,
Of how both gods and men began the same.
The gods, who live on Mount Olympus, first
Fashioned a golden race of mortal men;
These lived in the reign of Kronos, king of heaven,
And like the gods they lived with happy hearts
Untouched by work or sorrow. Vile old age
Never appeared, but always lively-limbed,
Far from all ills, they feasted happily.
Death came to them as sleep, and all good things
Were theirs; ungrudgingly, the fertile land
Gave up her fruits unasked. Happy to be
At peace, they lived with every want supplied,
[Rich in their flocks, dear to the blessed gods.]

And then this race was hidden in the ground.
But still they live as spirits of the earth,
Holy and good, guardians who keep off harm,
Givers of wealth: this kingly right is theirs.
The gods, who live on Mount Olympus, next
Fashioned a lesser, silver race of men:
Unlike the gold in stature or in mind.
A child was raised at home a hundred years
And played, huge baby, by his mother's side.
When they were grown and reached their prime, they lived
Brief, anguished lives, from foolishness, for they
Could not control themselves, but recklessly
Injured each other and forsook the gods;
They did not sacrifice, as all tribes must, but left
The holy altars bare. And, angry, Zeus
The son of Kronos, hid this race away,
For they dishonoured the Olympian gods.

The earth then hid this second race, and they
Are called the spirits of the underworld,
Inferior to the gold, but honoured, too.
And Zeus the father made a race of bronze,

Sprung from the ash tree,[2] worse than the silver race,
But strange and full of power. And they loved
The groans and violence of war; they ate
No bread; their hearts were flinty-hard; they were
Terrible men; their strength was great, their arms
And shoulders and their limbs invincible.
Their weapons were of bronze, their houses bronze;
Their tools were bronze; black iron was not known.
They died by their own hands, and nameless, went
To Hades' chilly house. Although they were
Great soldiers, they were captured by black Death,
And left the shining brightness of the sun.

But when this race was covered by the earth,
The son of Kronos made another, fourth,
Upon the fruitful land, more just and good,
A godlike race of heroes, who are called
The demi-gods — the race before our own.
Foul wars and dreadful battles ruined some;
Some sought the flocks of Oedipus,[3] and died
In Cadmus' land, at seven-gated Thebes;
And some, who crossed the open sea in ships,
For fair-haired Helen's sake,[4] were killed at Troy.
These men were covered up in death, but Zeus
The son of Kronos gave the others life
And homes apart from mortals, at Earth's edge.
And there they live a carefree life, beside
The whirling Ocean, on the Blessed Isles.
Three times a year the blooming, fertile earth
Bears honeyed fruits for them, the happy ones.
[And Kronos is their king, far from the gods,
For Zeus released him from his bonds and these,
The race of heroes, well deserve their fame.

Far-seeing Zeus then made another race,
The fifth, who live now on the fertile earth.]
I wish I were not of this race, that I
Had died before, or had not yet been born.
This is the race of iron. Now, by day,

[2] **Sprung . . . ash tree:** An ambiguous phrase that might mean "spears made of ash."

[3] **Oedipus:** King of Thebes; see the play *Oedipus Rex* by Sophocles on page 899.

[4] **For . . . Helen's sake:** The mythic cause of the Trojan War is said to be the abduction of Helen, Menelaus's wife, by Paris, who takes her to Troy. The Greeks then mount an expedition to retrieve her.

Men work and grieve unceasingly; by night,
They waste away and die. The gods will give
Harsh burdens, but will mingle in some good;
Zeus will destroy this race of mortal men,
When babies shall be born with greying hair.
Father will have no common bond with son,
Neither will guest with host, nor friend with friend;
The brother-love of past days will be gone.
Men will dishonour parents, who grow old
Too quickly, and will blame and criticize
With cruel words. Wretched and godless, they
Refusing to repay their bringing up,
Will cheat their aged parents of their due.
Men will destroy the towns of other men.
The just, the good, the man who keeps his word
Will be despised, but men will praise the bad
And insolent. Might will be Right, and shame
Will cease to be. Men will do injury
To better men by speaking crooked words
And adding lying oaths; and everywhere
Harsh-voiced and sullen-faced and loving harm,
Envy will walk along with wretched men.
Last, to Olympus from the broad-pathed Earth,
Hiding their loveliness in robes of white,
To join the gods, abandoning mankind,
Will go the spirits Righteousness and Shame.[5]
And only grievous troubles will be left
For men, and no defence against our wrongs.

And now, for lords who understand, I'll tell
A fable: once a hawk, high in the clouds,
Clutched in his claws a speckled nightingale.
She, pierced by those hooked claws, cried, 'Pity me!'
But he made scornful answer: 'Silly thing.
Why do you cry? Your master holds you fast,
You'll go where I decide, although you have
A minstrel's lovely voice, and if I choose,
I'll have you for a meal, or let you go.
Only a fool will match himself against
A stronger party, for he'll only lose,

[5] **Shame:** Considered a positive quality, since the fear of what people think was thought to promote honorable qualities.

And be disgraced as well as beaten.' Thus
Spoke the swift-flying hawk, the long-winged bird.

O Perses, follow right; control your pride.
For pride is evil in a common man.
Even a noble finds it hard to bear;
It weighs him down and leads him to disgrace.
The road to justice is the better way,
For Justice in the end will win the race
And Pride will lose: the simpleton must learn
This fact through suffering.

HOMER

EIGHTH CENTURY B.C.E.

The two outstanding heroic epics of ancient Greece, *The Iliad* and *The Odyssey,* are attributed to Homer. These two great works, which set the standard for all subsequent epic poetry in the West, tell different parts of a single story about a Greek military expedition to the distant city of Troy,[1] the war with the Trojans, and the return of the heroes to their cities and kingdoms. The legend of the Trojan War is not a fixed history with an unchanging set of facts; stories about the engagement between the Trojans and the Greeks, which were passed down in oral form from the time of the war until the eighth century B.C.E., when Homer created his own versions of the events, vary according to the storyteller and his time and place. The heroic ideals universally associated with the battlefield at Troy constitute one of the most important legacies of the Greek Heroic Age (c. 1500–1100 B.C.E.), which was known for its sea voyages and military adventures. Later Greeks believed that the Trojan stories were a blend of history and legend, and that Homer was writing about a period some four to five hundred years older than himself. While very few heroes from either ancient Mesopotamia or Egypt are known, Homer, at the end of a long oral tradition, created a grand catalog of Greek heroes that bridged history and mythology and served as a source of traditional knowledge and morality for several hundred years.

WWW For links to more information about Homer, quizzes on *The Iliad* and *The Odyssey,* and information about the twenty-first-century relevance of Homer, see *World Literature Online* at bedfordstmartins.com/worldlit.

Though a poet—not a priest or a prophet—Homer profoundly affected Greek religion, as Greek historian Herodotus (484–c. 424 B.C.E.) once commented: ". . . it was only—if I may so put it—the day before

[1] **Troy:** In ancient times Troy, or Ilium (Ilion), was a city on a hill in Asia Minor. The city, located today in the northwest corner of Turkey overlooking the Dardanelles (Hellespont), is now called Hissarlik.

Achilles Killing the Amazon Queen, 540–530 B.C.E.
A Greek amphora, or wine jar, detailing a scene from the Trojan War. (Courtesy of the British Museum)

yesterday that the Greeks came to know the origin and form of the various gods, and whether or not all of them had always existed; for Homer and Hesiod are the poets who composed our theogonies[2] and described the gods for us, giving them all their appropriate titles, offices, and powers, and they lived, as I believe, not more than four hundred years ago." Hesiod's *Theogony* and Homer's *Iliad* and *Odyssey* collectively have been called the Bible of the ancient Greeks: the basis for religious ceremony as well as public education.

As the oldest surviving European poems, *The Iliad* and *The Odyssey* were the models for later epic works by such poets as the Roman Virgil (70–19 B.C.E.), the Italian Dante (1265–1321), the English Milton (1608–1674), and, in modern times, the West Indian poet Derek Walcott, winner of the Nobel Prize in literature in 1992. Both *The Iliad* and *The Odyssey* are so filled with brilliant imagery that whole scenes come to life for the reader. This visualization of Greek deities made them accessible models for human behavior, unlike the mysterious and inscrutable Hebrew God, Yahweh,[3] a deity who was heard but not seen. Homer's

[2] **theogonies:** A theogony is an orderly description of the genealogies of the gods. Herodotus's dating puts both Hesiod and Homer in the eighth century B.C.E., roughly the same time period that modern scholars place them in. For an excerpt from Hesiod's *Theogony,* see page 263.

[3] **Yahweh:** The most common name given for God in the Hebrew Scriptures (Old Testament).

images were later translated into the glories of Greek drama, sculpture, and vase paintings; scenes from and allusions to classical art and literature have been depicted again and again, from the European Renaissance up to the present day.

The Iliad **and *The Odyssey* have been called the Bible of the Greeks. For centuries these two poems were the basis of Greek education, both of formal school education and of the cultural life of the ordinary citizen.**

– H. D. F. Kitto, classicist, 1951

The Homeric Mystery. Scholars have debated the Homeric question—who Homer was, where he came from in Greece, and exactly when he wrote—for some two hundred years. And not all scholars are convinced, to further complicate matters, that the same poet wrote both *The Iliad* and *The Odyssey.* As many as seven cities in Ionia, the region of Asia Minor on the east coast of the Aegean, have claimed to be Homer's birthplace.

Because there are elements of the Ionian dialect in the poems thought to be his, it is probable that Homer, whom the Greeks called *theios Homeros,* meaning "divine Homer," was a descendant of the early Greeks who migrated to Ionia after invaders from the north conquered the major city-states on mainland Greece, around 1100 B.C.E. Before the rise of Athens in the Classical Period, Ionia was the intellectual and cultural center of the Greek world. Ionian writer Hellanicus placed Homer in the twelfth century B.C.E., believing that Homer had to have been an eyewitness to the Trojan War to write such vivid descriptions of it. However, tradition suggests that Homer himself was blind. A blind bard, **Demodocus**, appears in *The Odyssey* (Book 8), and at the conclusion of the *Homeric Hymn to Delian Apollo,* a poem probably not written by Homer but dated in the seventh century B.C.E., the poet says to the maidens of Delos that a blind man from Chios[4] is the sweetest singer:

duh-MAH-duh-kus

> "O maidens, what man to you is the sweetest of singers
> Who frequent this place, and whose songs give you greatest delight?"
> Then all of you answer in unison, choosing felicitous words:
> "A blind man who lives on the rugged island of Chios,
> All of whose songs in aftertime will be known as the best."

Even before epic stories were written down and widely circulated, oral versions were considered property. Fraternities of poets, or bards, held their epic materials in common for use at royal feasts or weddings.

In the sixth century, a professional group of poets on Chios who called themselves *Homeridai* (Sons of Homer) recited Homeric poetry. Homer might have been a single poet who composed the epics, or the name "Homer" might have been associated with a series of poets who recited and modified oral epics for several hundred years until *The Iliad* and *The Odyssey* reached their final form sometime in the sixth century. A combination of these two possibilities probably approaches the truth.

It was once believed that epic poems such as Homer's were too long to be memorized and must therefore have originated in written form, meaning that *The Iliad* and *The Odyssey* would have been composed and written down between 750 and 650 B.C.E., about the time when writing was revived in Greece with the adoption of the Phoenician alphabet. But

[4] **Chios:** A small island just off the coast of Asia Minor (now Turkey).

[The Homeric age] did not erect any religious system but it remodelled its inheritance in accordance with two predominating lines of thought, anthropomorphism and rationalism. The latter played into the hands of the former by removing all the elements of the supernatural and the wonderful, and by refashioning the inherited myths in accordance with human standards.
– MARTIN P. NILSSON, *A History of Greek Religion*, classicist, 1949

studies in the 1930s by Milman Parry and his student Albert Lord in Yugoslavia, where an oral epic tradition still existed, substantiated that poems the length of *The Iliad,* about fifteen thousand verses, could indeed be memorized and recited. A number of factors made memorization possible. The verse was metered, and poets used a stringed instrument like a lyre to establish a rhythm. Most important, this kind of oral poetry featured poetic formulas, stock situations, and stock phrases used to set patterns. There is a set way, for example, of describing a feast or arrival at a palace. Stock epithets are used for describing nightfall, the sea, the sun, and major characters. Dawn comes with "her fingers of pink light," the sea is "winedark." Athena is the "grey-eyed goddess" or the "grey-eyed daughter of Zeus" and Poseidon is the "Earthshaker." Zeus, the "lord of storm and lightning" uses Hermes, the "Wayfinder" with a "golden wand," as his messenger. Odysseus is the "canniest of men" and the "raider of cities."

It is possible that for several hundred years Homer's epics were recited orally and a written text also existed, and that by the fifth century, the commercial reproductions of the texts finally canonized them and prevented further interpolation.

The Iliad. The most famous account of the Trojan War is found in Homer's *Iliad,* which means the "Tale of Ilios," or "Tale of Troy." In its present version, it is a work divided into twenty-four books, one for each letter of the Greek alphabet. *The Iliad* is based on a body of mythic stories known collectively as The Judgment of Paris, which themselves begin with the story of the wedding between Pêleus and Thetis. At this wedding, Eris, goddess of discord, rolls a golden apple inscribed with the words "For the Fairest" across the floor. The goddesses Hera, Athena, and Aphrodite[5] all claim the apple. Zeus chooses Paris, the handsome prince of Troy, to decide which of the three goddesses deserves the title. After the goddesses bribe him, Paris picks Aphrodite, who has promised him the most beautiful woman in the world in return: Helen, wife of **Menelaus** (Meneláos). While on a mission to Sparta, Paris falls in love with Helen and takes her and other Spartan treasures back to Troy. Seeking revenge, Greek kings under the leadership of **Agamemnon** (Agamémnon), Menelaus' brother, band together in ships at Aulis, but an absence of wind prevents them from sailing to Troy. Agamemnon is persuaded by a seer to sacrifice his youngest daughter, Iphigenia, as a means of restoring the winds. (This becomes an important event in Aeschylus's dramatic trilogy, *The Oresteia* (458 B.C.E.).) When at Troy a Greek embassy fails to secure the return of Helen and the stolen treasures, and the war settles into a ten-year siege. Then in the tenth year, the point at which *The Iliad* begins, the action comes to a climax with a quarrel between Agamemnon and Achilles, the death of **Achilles**' close friend **Patroclus** (Patróklus) and the death of Hector (Hektor), the Trojans' greatest warrior. Achilles himself is

meh-nuh-LAY-us

ag-uh-MEM-nahn

uh-KIL-eez

puh-TROH-klus

[5] **Hera . . . Aphrodite:** The goddesses of marriage, wisdom, and love, respectively.

then killed by Paris. The end of the war comes about when the Trojans are tricked into hauling a large wooden horse filled with **Achaeans**, or Greeks, into the city, precipitating Troy's destruction.

uh-KEE-uns

The Iliad, choosing amongst these tales, focuses on the exploits of Achilles during a brief period toward the end of the war. For Homer, the fortunes of this war are measured by individual encounters rather than group victories. In the intensity of war, individual decisions can mean life or death, and a single encounter can bring fame or infamy. Warriors such as Hector, Achilles, and Aias live in an elevated sphere where the demands of sacrifice and bravery seem to dwarf humdrum, ordinary peacetime.

At the heart of *The Iliad* is a celebration of heroes, men who rely on their own abilities to win battles and strive for the honor that comes with victory. Although savage at times, Achilles is the great hero of the Achaeans,[6] a man of formidable virtues as well as faults. The beginning of the epic announces the role that his passion will play in the poem:

Anger be now your song, immortal one,
Akhilleus' anger, doomed and ruinous,
that caused the Akhaians loss on bitter loss
and crowded brave souls into the undergloom.

It is possible to sympathize with Achilles' anger at Agamemnon for taking away the woman that Achilles had won and to appreciate his reasons for withdrawing from the battle. But Achilles' stubbornness about not returning to fight is excessive and causes his close friend Patroclus to risk his life. Patroclus's ensuing death forces Achilles to acknowledge the consequences of his choices. In the background is his mother's warning that he was fated for either a quiet, long life at home in Phthia[7] or a short, glorious life in the Trojan War. When Achilles decides to fight again, his head is crowned with a golden cloud of fire, and when he announces his return with three tremendous cries, panic runs through the Trojan warriors, causing twelve fighters to be trampled by their own chariots. Achilles is larger than life.

The ideal Trojan warrior is Hector, son of Priam. His role seems to be balanced by a sensitivity toward his wife, **Andromache**, and his son **Astyanax** (Astýnax) By modern standards, Hector represents the whole man. In one of the most poignant scenes in the epic, Andromache explains her fears about how his family will be abused should Hector be killed in battle. In response, Hector explains his duty as a warrior, then turns to his son:

an-DRAH-muh-kee
uh-STIGH-uh-naks

As he said this, Hektor held out his arms
to take his baby. But the child squirmed round
on the nurse's bosom and began to wail,
terrified by his father's great war helm—

[6] **Achaeans:** The principal peoples of ancient Greece were the Achaeans (Akhaians), the Dorians, the Aeolians, and the Ionians; Homer frequently called all the Greeks Akhaians.

[7] **Phthia:** A town in Thessaly, a region in the midsection of Greece.

Homer's anthropomorphism gave rise to the first criticism of religion. . . .
– MARTIN P. NILSSON, classicist, 1949

the flashing bronze, the crest with horsehair plume
tossed like a living thing at every nod.

In this brief scene, Homer deftly portrays the two sides of warfare: Hector's sentiments about defending his city are admirable, but the ugly consequences of the defeated, the surviving women and children, are terrifying. All of this is captured in Astyanax's fear of his father's military outfit. The settings of the two sides further the contrast: The stark masculine world of the Achaean warriors on the plains in front of Troy is contrasted with the beautiful, cultured city, which shelters men, women, and children. It is a tribute to Homer's breadth as an artist that he sympathizes with both worlds and both sides of the conflict, just as he apparently admires both Achilles and Hector.

After Hector is killed and Achilles desecrates his body, Hector's father risks his life by personally asking Achilles for his son's body. A more sympathetic side of Achilles is revealed during their meeting, when the two reminisce and weep over past sorrows. Hector's burial at the end of *The Iliad* provides a mixed message about the nature of war and the price men and women pay for heroism.

The Odyssey. The Greek title for Homer's *Odyssey* is *Odysseia,* which means "poetry about Odysseus." Though somewhat shorter than *The Iliad* at twelve thousand verses, *The Odyssey* is also divided into twenty-four books, again corresponding to the twenty-four letters of the Greek alphabet. It begins ***IN MEDIAS RES,*** or *in the middle of,* Odysseus's return to his home island of Ithaca at the close of the Trojan War. A number of important events have taken place, however, between the end of *The Iliad,* which concludes with the burning and burial of Hector, and Odysseus's heading home.

Achilles is killed by a poisoned arrow. When the seer Helenus, son of Priam, is captured by the Greeks, he tells them that Troy will fall only when Philoctetes reenters the war with Achilles' son, Neoptolemus. Using trickery, Odysseus and Neoptolemus lure the bowman Philoctetes from Lemnon to Troy, where he kills Paris with Herakles' bow. When the war still does not end, Odysseus and **Diomedes** sneak into the city of Troy by night and steal the sacred statue of Athena, the Palladium, believed to be the source of Trojan strength. But even with its heroes dead and the Palladium stolen, Troy does not fall. Finally, guided by Odysseus, the Greeks resort to deception. Epeios (Epeius) builds a large, hollow wooden horse and the Greeks' strongest warriors hide in its belly. When the rest of the Greeks sail away, leaving the horse behind, the curious Trojans come out of the city and find Sinon, a lone Greek soldier, on the beach. Sinon tells the Trojans he has been abandoned and that the horse is an atonement for the theft of the Palladium. Falling for the trick, the Trojans drag the horse inside the city walls, and in the middle of the night, the Greek soldiers emerge from the horse and call their compatriots back from a nearby island. The Greeks then sack and burn Troy.

digh-uh-MEE-deez

The victors divide the spoils. Menelaus retrieves Helen; Agamemnon claims Priam's daughter Cassandra; and Odysseus receives **Hecuba**. Hec-

HEH-kuh-bee

The Return of Odysseus, 460–450 B.C.E.
A Greek terracotta plaque depicting a scene from The Odyssey. *After many years away from home, Odysseus returns to Ithaka disguised as a beggar and confronts his faithful wife Penelope while his father, Laertes, his son Telemachus, and the swineherd Eumaios look on. (The Metropolitan Museum of Art, Fletcher Fund, 1930 (30.11.9). All rights reserved.)*

tor's wife, Andromache, is the prize of Neoptolemus. The Greeks then set sail for home. Some, like Nestor, Diomedes, Idomeneus, Philoctetes, and Neoptolemus, reach their homes quickly and safely. Agamemnon arrives home with Cassandra only to be assassinated by his wife, Clytemnestra (Klytaimnéstra) and her lover, Aegisthus. Others take many years to reach their destinations. Menelaus and Helen are detoured to Egypt, where they spend seven years before returning to Sparta. Odysseus, the best known of the Greek wanderers, leaves Troy with twelve ships and about six hundred men and, because of the anger of three deities, spends ten years making his way back to his wife, Penelope (Penélopê), and his son **Telemachus** (Telémakhos).

tuh-LEH-muh-kus

During that decade about one hundred suitors gather at Odysseus's palace in Ithaca and press Penelope to choose a husband from among them, a new king. Penelope delays in making a choice by telling the suitors that she must first weave a funeral shroud for her father-in-law, Laertes; she then unravels the day's weaving each night. The suitors, meanwhile, live off the food and drink of the palace and make fun of the youthful, inexperienced Telemachus, who lacks the stature to replace his father on the throne.

The Odyssey begins during the tenth year of Odysseus's journey, meaning about twenty years after he originally left Ithaca for the Trojan War. Unlike *The Iliad, The Odyssey* is not held together by a unifying plot. It is a series of episodes of Odysseus's protracted homeward voyage, which divide rather neatly into three parts, or songs. The first introduces Telemachus, who is now old enough to become king but who must undergo rites of passage before assuming that role. The second comprises Odysseus's adventures on his return journey. And in the third, Odysseus and Penelope reunite and Odysseus disposes of the suitors. It was Homer who brought these three stories together and made them into a single epic.

. . . it was only — if I may so put it — the day before yesterday that the Greeks came to know the origin and form of the various gods, and whether or not all of them had always existed; for Homer and Hesiod are the poets who composed our theogonies and described the gods for us, giving them all their appropriate titles, offices, and powers, and they lived, as I believe, not more than four hundred years ago.

– Herodotus, historian, fifth century B.C.E.

One way to read Odysseus's journey and his adventures is that Odysseus himself is gaining the necessary experience and self-knowledge to confront and finally defeat the hundred or so suitors who threaten his household and kingdom. The stories about the return of other chieftains to their kingdoms, especially Agamemnon's reception by his wife and her lover, serve as object lessons for Odysseus's own return. Quite another perspective on Odysseus is that he is the quintessential world traveler and that his adventures in various locales enable Homer to paint exotic pictures of the distant frontiers of the world while borrowing from the folklore of his day, including stories about lotus eating, the Cyclops (Kyklopês), island temptresses, rock-throwing giants, and water monsters. Seen in this light, Troy then symbolizes that exotic, seductive place on the threshold of consciousness that compels the wanderer in each of us to give up the security of the known and set out for uncharted territory. Although haunted by the *idea* of home, this Odysseus would have mixed feelings about actually returning home and having to admit to himself that the grand adventure of his life is over, that he now should be sensible and retire, leaving challenge and risk to the next generation, his son Telemachus.

The Odyssey is unique for its fascinating, strong women. Penelope keeps her hand on Ithaca's throne while holding off a hoard of suitors for years. A brief glimpse of Helen confirms her reputation for beauty and power; she still exercises her charms over the opposite sex. Both Calypso and Circe are beautiful. Although some of Homer's best writing celebrates the attributes of warriors, his portrayal of the lovely princess Nausicaa, Odysseus's final temptation before home, is tender and sympathetic, as are his treatments of the soldier **Elpénor**, the nurse Eurycleia, and the loyal swineherd.

el-PEE-nore

In *The Odyssey,* Homer's two epic heroes meet. When Odysseus visits Hades and meets the shade of Achilles, Odysseus speaks about the deified honor and fame associated with Achilles' deeds and his rank in the underworld; Achilles responds:

Let me hear no smooth talk
of death from you Odysseus, light of councils.
Better, I say, to break sod as a farm hand
for some poor country man, on iron rations,
than lord it over all the exhausted dead.

This speech somewhat undercuts the earlier image of a youthful Achilles who chooses glory regardless of the fatal consequences. Odysseus represents a more complicated, thoughtful warrior who will be honored by cultures that value mental as well as physical prowess. Although *The Iliad* was at one time considered by some scholars to be the superior poem, the complex character of Odysseus, his series of marvelous adventures, and the epic's strong, interesting women are likely to make *The Odyssey* the favorite with many modern readers.

■ CONNECTIONS

Hebrew Scriptures, p. 134. In some ancient religions, humans conversed readily with the gods. The God of the Hebrew Scriptures is most characteristically a voice: He is heard but not easily seen. How is an aural deity distinctively different from Homer's gods, who are identified visually as well as with a voice?

Virgil, *The Aeneid,* p. 1181. Historians distinguish between "folk epics," which have roots in the oral tradition of an indigenous culture, and "literary epics," which use the basic characteristics of the earlier epics but are also the product of a writer's imagination. Why is Virgil's *Aeneid* considered a "literary epic," and how is it different from Homer's epics, which were apparently derived from an oral tradition that had been passed down for generations?

***Ramayana* and *Mahabarata,* pp. 1351 and 1434; and *Beowulf* (Book 2).** Long epic poems typically arise from a period characterized as a Heroic Age, an age of warfare and conflict in which tribal loyalties are sorted out and legendary warriors become models for succeeding kings and rulers. What about the historical age in which India's epics, the *Ramayana* and *Mahabarata,* emerged might account for the fact that they are much longer than Homer's epics? What period in northern European history produced *Beowulf*? What aspects of the Trojan War influenced later generations of Greeks?

■ FURTHER RESEARCH

History and Background

Barr, Stringfellow. *The Will of Zeus: A History of Greece.* 1961.

Bowra, C. M. *Homer.* 1972.

Bury, J. B., and Russell Meiggs. *A History of Greece to the Death of Alexander the Great.* 1975.

Forsdyke, John. *Greece Before Homer: Ancient Chronology and Mythology.* 1964.

Nagy, Gregory. *The Best of the Achaeans: Concepts of the Hero in Archaic Greek Poetry.* 1999.

Nilsson, Martin P. *A History of Greek Religion.* 1964.

Rose, H. J. *A Handbook of Greek Literature: From Homer to the Age of Lucian.* 1996.

Homer and His Epics

Benardete, Seth. *The Bow and the Lyre: A Platonic Reading of the Odyssey.* 1997.

Clarke, Michael J. *Flesh and Spirit in the Songs of Homer: A Study of Words and Myths.* 1999.

Cohen, Beth. *The Distaff Side: Representing the Female in Homer's* Odyssey. 1995.

Griffin, Jasper. *The Odyssey.* 1987.

Hansen, William F. "The Homeric Epics and Oral Poetry," in Felix J. Oinas, ed., *Heroic Epic and Saga: An Introduction to the World's Great Folk Epics.* 1978.

Karydas, Helen Pournara. *Eurykleia and Her Successors: Female Figures of Authority in Greek Poetics.* 1998.
Kirk, G. S. *Homer and the Oral Tradition.* 1976.
Latacz, Joachim. *Homer, His Art and His World.* James P. Holoka. trans. 1996.
Mueller, Martin. *The Iliad.* 1984.
Steiner, George, and Robert Fagles, eds. *Homer: A Collection of Critical Essays.* 1962.

■ PRONUNCIATION

Achaeans (Akhaians): uh-KEE-unz
Achilles (Akhilleus): uh-KIL-eez
Aeneas (Aineías): uh-NEE-us
Aeolus (Aiolos): ee-YOH-lus
Agamemnon (Agamémnon): ag-uh-MEM-nahn
Aias (Aîas): IGH-yus
Alcinus (Alkínoos): al-KIN-oh-us
Alcmene (Alkmênê): alk-MEE-nee
Alcyone (Alkýonê): al-SIGH-uh-nee
Andromache: an-DRAH-muh-kee
Arete (Arêtê): AH-ri-tay
Astýanax: uh-STIGH-uh-naks
Calydon (Kálydôn): KAL-i-dahn
Calypso (Kalypso): kuh-LIP-soh
Charybdis (Kharybdis): kuh-RIB-dis
Circe (Kirkê): SUR-see
Clytemnestra (Klytaimnéstra): kligh-tum-NES-truh
Couretes (Kourêtês): koo-REE-teez
Cyclops (Kyklopês): sigh-KLOH-peez
Demóducus (Demódokos): duh-MAH-duh-kus
Diomêdês: digh-uh-MEE-deez
Elpénor (Elpênor): el-PEE-nore
Eumaios: yoo-MAY-us, yoo-MIGH-yus
Eunus (Euênos): yoo-EE-nus
Euryclea (Eurýkleia): yoo-rih-KLIGH-uh
Hecabe (Hékabê): HEH-kuh-bee
Laertes (Laërtês): luh-UR-teez, lay-UR-teez
Laistrygonians: leh-strih-GOH-nee-unz
Marpessê: mar-PESS-uh
Meneláos: meh-nuh-LAY-us
Mycenae (Mykênai): migh-SEE-nee
Myrmidons: MUR-muh-donz
Nausikaa: naw-SIK-ay-uh
Patróklus (Patróklos): puh-TROH-klus
Phaiakians: fee-EE-shunz
Phémios: FEE-mee-us
Polyphemos (Polyphêmos): pah-luh-FEE-mus
Scylla (Skylla): SIL-ah
Sirens (Seirênês): sigh-REE-neez
Sisyphus (Sísyphos): SIZ-uh-fus
Tatar: TAH-tar
Teiresias (Teirêsias): tigh-REE-seeus
Telemachus (Telémakhos): tuh-LEH-muh-kus

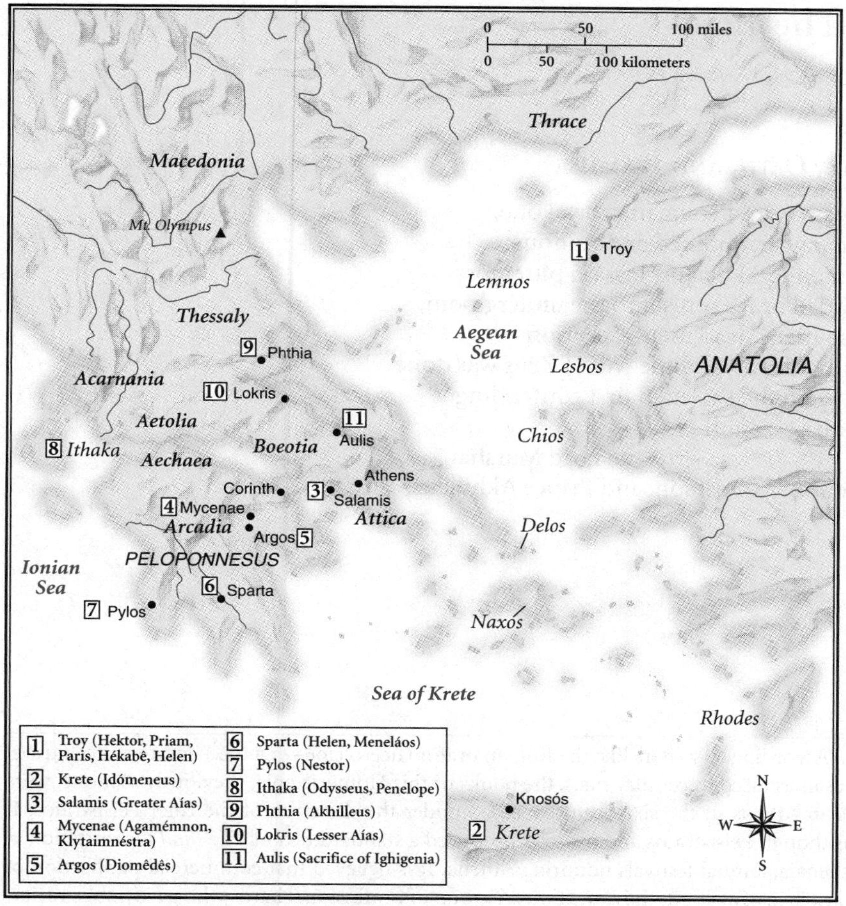

Major Sites and Characters in *The Iliad*

As with The Odyssey, *exact locations mentioned in* The Iliad *are difficult to pinpoint precisely. However, based on modern archaeological excavations, the information presented here and in the key should be useful in locating the major places discussed in* The Iliad *along with their associated heroes and heroines.*

The Iliad

Translated by Robert Fitzgerald[1]

Book 1
Quarrel, Oath, and Promise

Anger be now your song, immortal one,[2]
Akhilleus' anger, doomed and ruinous,
that caused the Akhaians[3] loss on bitter loss
and crowded brave souls into the undergloom,
leaving so many dead men—carrion
for dogs and birds; and the will of Zeus was done.
Begin it when the two men first contending
broke with one another—
the Lord Marshal
Agamémnon, Atreus' son, and Prince Akhilleus.

The Iliad. According to writers like the Roman orator Cicero (106–43 B.C.E.) and the Greek travel writer Pausanias (second century C.E.), the books of this Homeric epic, previously separate, were assembled in Athens in the sixth century B.C.E. under the direction of the ruler Peisistratos. It appears as though Peisistratos and his sons produced a standard text of *The Iliad* for recitation at the Panathenaia, annual festivals honoring Athena. It is believed that commercial publication of *The Iliad* also began at about the same time. A group of professional bards who gave public recitations of Homeric poetry, such as the Sons of Homer on Chios, may have been responsible for preserving the text from Homer's time until the sixth century.

The modern study of Homer's epics was transformed by the German archeologist Heinrich Schliemann, who in the twenty-year period between the 1870s and the 1890s uncovered the remains of the legendary city of Troy—actually, he unearthed several "Troys," one on top of the other—on the northwest coast of Turkey. Then, on the Greek mainland, he discovered Mycenae, the palace of the legendary King Agamemnon. In so doing, Schliemann had provided a historical

[1] **Robert Fitzgerald:** This translator does not use the more common Latinized spelling of names, such as Achilles and Achaeans, but versions closer to Greek spelling and pronunciation.

[2] **immortal one:** The Muse, spirit of inspiration.

[3] **Akhaians:** The Greek forces; also called Danaans and Argives.

Among the gods, who brought this quarrel on?
The son of Zeus by Lêto.° Agamémnon
angered him, so he made a burning wind
of plague rise in the army: rank and file
sickened and died for the ill their chief had done
in despising a man of prayer.
This priest, Khrysês,[4] had come down to the ships
with gifts, no end of ransom for his daughter;
on a golden staff he carried the god's white bands
and sued for grace from the men of all Akhaia,
the two Atreidai[5] most of all:
"O captains
Meneláos and Agamémnon, and you other
Akhaians under arms!
The gods who hold Olympos, may they grant you
plunder of Priam's town and a fair wind home,

° Apollo

world to which one could attach Homer's works. Modern readers can now better appreciate how the defeat of Troy provided Greece a legacy for hundreds of years. Important Greek families traced their descent from Achaean warriors, and Greek cities claimed they had been founded by warriors returning from Troy. Other peoples traced their lineage to the Trojans. In the great Roman epic, *The Aeneid,* Virgil makes use of the tradition of the Trojan warrior Aeneas, who survives the defeat of Troy and eventually guides a small band to the shores of Italy, where he establishes an ancestral line that leads to no less than Julius Caesar and the Roman Empire.

In *History of the Kings of Britain,* Geoffrey of Monmouth (twelfth century C.E.) links the Britons to the Trojan search for a homeland and to Brutus, the great-grandson of Aeneas, the mythical founder of Britain. The great Icelandic scholar Snorri Sturluson (thirteenth century C.E.) in *Prose Edda* traces some of the Norse gods back to one of Priam's daughters. According to Sturluson, sometime in the distant past, gods left Troy—located at the center of the world—and traveled to northern Europe. All warriors in later literature, all extended journeys to the edge of the world, are measured against Homer's epic portraits of divinity and humanity.

[4] **Khrysês:** His daughter is Khrysêis and his town is Khrysê.

[5] **the two Atreidai:** That is, sons of Atreus: Agamémnon and Meneláos.

but let me have my daughter back for ransom
as you revere Apollo, son of Zeus!"

Then all the soldiers murmured their assent:
"Behave well to the priest. And take the ransom!"

But Agamémnon would not. It went against his desire,
and brutally he ordered the man away:
"Let me not find you here by the long ships
loitering this time or returning later,
old man; if I do,
the staff and ribbons of the god will fail you.
Give up the girl? I swear she will grow old
at home in Argos,[6] far from her own country,
working my loom and visiting my bed.
Leave me in peace and go, while you can, in safety."

So harsh he was, the old man feared and obeyed him,
in silence trailing away
by the shore of the tumbling clamorous whispering sea,
and he prayed and prayed again, as he withdrew,
to the god whom silken-braided Lêto bore:
"O hear me, master of the silver bow,
protector of Ténedos[7] and the holy towns,
Apollo, Sminthian,[8] if to your liking
ever in any grove I roofed a shrine
or burnt thighbones in fat upon your altar—
bullock or goat flesh—let my wish come true:
your arrows on the Danáäns for my tears!"

Now when he heard this prayer, Phoibos Apollo
walked with storm in his heart from Olympos' crest,
quiver and bow at his back, and the bundled arrows
clanged on the sky behind as he rocked in his anger,
descending like night itself. Apart from the ships
he halted and let fly, and the bowstring slammed
as the silver bow sprang, rolling in thunder away.
Pack animals were his target first, and dogs,
but soldiers, too, soon felt transfixing pain
from his hard shots, and pyres burned night and day.
Nine days the arrows of the god came down
broadside upon the army. On the tenth,

---

[6] **Argos:** A region of southern Greece. [7] **Ténedos:** An island off the coast. [8] **Sminthian:** A name for Apollo meaning "mouse god."

Akhilleus called all ranks to assembly. Hêra,[9]
whose arms are white as ivory, moved him to it,
as she took pity on Danááns dying.
All being mustered, all in place and quiet,
Akhilleus, fast in battle as a lion,
rose and said:
"Agamémnon, now, I take it,
the siege is broken, we are going to sail,
and even so may not leave death behind:
if war spares anyone, disease will take him . . .
We might, though, ask some priest or some diviner,
even some fellow good at dreams — for dreams
come down from Zeus as well —
why all this anger of the god Apollo?

Has he some quarrel with us for a failure
in vows or hekatombs?[10] Would mutton burned
or smoking goat flesh make him lift the plague?"

Putting the question, down he sat. And Kalkhas,
Kalkhas Thestórides, came forward, wisest
by far of all who scanned the flight of birds.[11]
He knew what was, what had been, what would be,
Kalkhas, who brought Akhaia's ships to Ilion° Troy
by the diviner's gift Apollo gave him.
Now for their benefit he said:
"Akhilleus,
dear to Zeus, it is on me you call
to tell you why the Archer God is angry.
Well, I can tell you. Are you listening? Swear
by heaven that you will back me and defend me,
because I fear my answer will enrage
a man with power in Argos, one whose word
Akhaian troops obey.
A great man in his rage is formidable
for underlings: though he may keep it down,
he cherishes the burning in his belly
until a reckoning day. Think well
if you will save me."

Said Akhilleus:
"Courage.

[9] **Hêra:** Wife of Zeus; she supports the Greeks. [10] **hekatombs:** Sacrifices to the gods. [11] **all who . . . birds:** Seers used the flights of birds as oracles.

Tell what you know, what you have light to know.
I swear by Apollo, the lord god to whom
you pray when you uncover truth,
never while I draw breath, while I have eyes to see,
shall any man upon this beachhead dare
lay hands on you — not one of all the army,
not Agamémnon, if it is he you mean,
though he is first in rank of all Akhaians."

The diviner then took heart and said:
"No failure
in hekatombs or vows is held against us.
It is the man of prayer whom Agamémnon
treated with contempt: he kept his daughter,
spurned his gifts: for that man's sake the Archer
visited grief upon us and will again.
Relieve the Danáäns of this plague he will not
until the girl who turns the eyes of men
shall be restored to her own father — freely,
with no demand for ransom — and until
we offer up a hekatomb at Khrysê.
Then only can we calm him and persuade him."

He finished and sat down. The son of Atreus,
ruler of the great plain, Agamémnon,
rose, furious. Round his heart resentment
welled, and his eyes shone out like licking fire.
Then, with a long and boding look at Kalkhas,
he growled at him:
"You visionary of hell,
never have I had fair play in your forecasts.
Calamity is all you care about, or see,
no happy portents; and you bring to pass
nothing agreeable. Here you stand again
before the army, giving it out as oracle
the Archer made them suffer because of me,
because I would not take the gifts
and let the girl Khrysêis go; I'd have her
mine, at home. Yes, if you like, I rate her
higher than Klytaimnestra, my own wife!
She loses nothing by comparison
in beauty or womanhood, in mind or skill.

For all of that, I am willing now to yield her
if it is best; I want the army saved
and not destroyed. You must prepare, however,

a prize of honor for me, and at once,
that I may not be left without my portion—
I, of all Argives. It is not fitting so.
While every man of you looks on, my girl
goes elsewhere."

Prince Akhilleus answered him:
"Lord Marshal, most insatiate of men,
how can the army make you a new gift?
Where is our store of booty? Can you see it?
Everything plundered from the towns has been
distributed; should troops turn all that in?
Just let the girl go, in the god's name, now;
we'll make it up to you, twice over, three
times over, on that day Zeus gives us leave
to plunder Troy behind her rings of stone."

Agamémnon answered:
"Not that way
will I be gulled, brave as you are, Akhilleus.
Take me in, would you? Try to get around me?
What do you really ask? That you may keep
your own winnings, I am to give up mine
and sit here wanting her? Oh, no:
the army will award a prize to me
and make sure that it measures up, or if
they do not, I will take a girl myself,
your own, or Aías', or Odysseus'[12] prize!
Take her, yes, to keep. The man I visit
may choke with rage; well, let him.
But this, I say, we can decide on later.

Look to it now, we launch on the great sea
a well-found ship, and get her manned with oarsmen,
load her with sacrificial beasts and put aboard
Khrysêis in her loveliness. My deputy,
Aías, Idómeneus,[13] or Prince Odysseus,
or you, Akhilleus, fearsome as you are,
will make the hekatomb and quiet the Archer."

Akhilleus frowned and looked at him, then said:
"You thick-skinned, shameless, greedy fool!

[12] **Aías . . . Odysseus:** Two famous Greek warriors: Aías is known for bravery; Odysseus, hero of *The Odyssey*, is exceedingly clever. [13] **Idómeneus:** Ruler of Krete.

Can any Akhaian care for you, or obey you,
after this on marches or in battle?
As for myself, when I came here to fight,
I had no quarrel with Troy or Trojan spearmen:
they never stole my cattle or my horses,
never in the black farmland of Phthía[14]
ravaged my crops. How many miles there are
of shadowy mountains, foaming seas, between!
No, no, we joined for you, you insolent boor,
to please you, fighting for your brother's sake
and yours, to get revenge upon the Trojans.
You overlook this, dogface, or don't care,
and now in the end you threaten to take my girl,
a prize I sweated for, and soldiers gave me!

Agamemnon Says that he is going to take Achiles

Never have I had plunder like your own
from any Trojan stronghold battered down
by the Akhaians. I have seen more action
hand to hand in those assaults than you have,
but when the time for sharing comes, the greater
share is always yours. Worn out with battle
I carry off some trifle to my ships.
Well, this time I make sail for home.
Better to take now to my ships. Why linger,
cheated of winnings, to make wealth for you?"

To this the high commander made reply:
"Desért, if that's the way the wind blows. Will I
beg you to stay on my account? I will not.
Others will honor me, and Zeus who views
the wide world most of all.
No officer
is hateful to my sight as you are, none
given like you to faction, as to battle—
rugged you are, I grant, by some god's favor.
Sail, then, in your ships, and lord it over
your own battalion of Myrmidons.[15] I do not
give a curse for you, or for your anger.
But here is warning for you:
Khrysêis
being required of me by Phoibos Apollo,
she will be sent back in a ship of mine,

[14] **Phthía:** Akhilleus's home in northern Greece. [15] **Myrmidons:** Akhilleus's followers.

manned by my people. That done, I myself
will call for Brisêis at your hut, and take her,
flower of young girls that she is, your prize,
to show you here and now who is stronger
and make the next man sick at heart — if any
think of claiming equal place with me."

A pain like grief weighed on the son of Pêleus,[16]
and in his shaggy chest this way and that
the passion of his heart ran: should he draw
longsword from hip, stand off the rest, and kill
in single combat the great son of Atreus,
or hold his rage in check and give it time?
And as this tumult swayed him, as he slid
the big blade slowly from the sheath, Athêna[17]
came to him from the sky. The white-armed goddess,
Hêra, sent her, being fond of both,
concerned for both men. And Athêna, stepping
up behind him, visible to no one
except Akhilleus, gripped his red-gold hair.

Startled, he made a half turn, and he knew her
upon the instant for Athêna: terribly
her grey eyes blazed at him. And speaking softly
but rapidly aside to her he said:

"What now, O daughter of the god of heaven
who bears the stormcloud, why are you here? To see
the wolfishness of Agamémnon?
Well, I give you my word: this time, and soon,
he pays for his behavior with his blood."

The grey-eyed goddess Athêna said to him:
"It was to check this killing rage I came
from heaven, if you will listen. Hêra sent me,
being fond of both of you, concerned for both.
Enough: break off this combat, stay your hand
upon the sword hilt. Let him have a lashing
with words, instead: tell him how things will be.
Here is my promise, and it will be kept:
winnings three times as rich, in due season,

[16] **Pêleus:** Akhilleus's father. [17] **Athêna:** Virgin goddess, daughter of Zeus, patron of Athens, associated with crafts and wisdom; she strongly favors the Greeks.

you shall have in requital for his arrogance.
But hold your hand. Obey."

The great runner,
Akhilleus, answered:
"Nothing for it, goddess,
but when you two immortals speak, a man
complies, though his heart burst. Just as well.
Honor the gods' will, they may honor ours."

On this he stayed his massive hand
upon the silver pommel, and the blade
of his great weapon slid back in the scabbard.
The man had done her bidding. Off to Olympos,
gaining the air, she went to join the rest,
the powers of heaven in the home of Zeus.

But now the son of Pêleus turned on Agamémnon
and lashed out at him, letting his anger ride
in execration:
"Sack of wine,
you with your cur's eyes and your antelope heart!
You've never had the kidney to buckle on
armor among the troops, or make a sortie
with picked men—oh, no; that way death might lie.
Safer, by god, in the middle of the army—
is it not?—to commandeer the prize
of any man who stands up to you! Leech!
Commander of trash! If not, I swear,
you never could abuse one soldier more!

But here is what I say: my oath upon it
by this great staff: look: leaf or shoot
it cannot sprout again, once lopped away
from the log it left behind in the timbered hills;
it cannot flower, peeled of bark and leaves;
instead, Akhaian officers in council
take it in hand by turns, when they observe
by the will of Zeus due order in debate:
let this be what I swear by then: I swear
a day will come when every Akhaian soldier
will groan to have Akhilleus back. That day
you shall no more prevail on me than this
dry wood shall flourish—driven though you are,
and though a thousand men perish before

the killer, Hektor.[18] You will eat your heart out,
raging with remorse for this dishonor
done by you to the bravest of Akhaians."

He hurled the staff, studded with golden nails,
before him on the ground. Then down he sat,
and fury filled Agamémnon, looking across at him.
But for the sake of both men Nestor arose,
the Pylians' orator, eloquent and clear;
argument sweeter than honey rolled from his tongue.
By now he had outlived two generations
of mortal men, his own and the one after,
in Pylos[19] land, and still ruled in the third.
In kind reproof he said:
"A black day, this.
Bitter distress comes this way to Akhaia.
How happy Priam and Priam's sons would be,
and all the Trojans — wild with joy — if they
got wind of all these fighting words between you,
foremost in council as you are, foremost
in battle. Give me your attention. Both
are younger men than I, and in my time
men who were even greater have I known
and none of them disdained me. Men like those
I have not seen again, nor shall: Peiríthoös,
the Lord Marshal Dryas, Kaineus, Exádios,
Polyphêmos, Theseus — Aigeus' son,
a man like the immortal gods. I speak
of champions among men of earth, who fought
with champions, with wild things of the mountains,
great centaurs whom they broke and overpowered.
Among these men I say I had my place
when I sailed out of Pylos, my far country,
because they called for me. I fought
for my own hand among them. Not one man
alive now upon earth could stand against them.
And I repeat: they listened to my reasoning,
took my advice. Well, then, you take it too.
It is far better so.
Lord Agamémnon,
do not deprive him of the girl, renounce her.
The army had allotted her to him.

[18] **Hektor:** Son of Priam, the best of Trojan warriors. [19] **Pylos:** On the western edge of the Peloponnese.

Akhilleus, for your part, do not defy
your King and Captain. No one vies in honor
with him who holds authority from Zeus.
You have more prowess, for a goddess bore you;[20]
his power over men surpasses yours.

But, Agamémnon, let your anger cool.
I beg you to relent, knowing Akhilleus
a sea wall for Akhaians in the black waves of war."

Lord Agamémnon answered:
"All you say
is fairly said, sir, but this man's ambition,
remember, is to lead, to lord it over
everyone, hold power over everyone,
give orders to the rest of us! Well, one
will never take his orders! If the gods
who live forever made a spearman of him,
have they put insults on his lips as well?"

Akhilleus interrupted:
"What a poltroon,° coward
how lily-livered I should be called, if I
knuckled under to all you do or say!
Give your commands to someone else, not me!
And one more thing I have to tell you: think it
over: this time, for the girl, I will not
wrangle in arms with you or anyone,
though I am robbed of what was given me;
but as for any other thing I have
alongside my black ship, you shall not take it
against my will. Try it. Hear this, everyone:
that instant your hot blood blackens my spear!"

They quarreled in this way, face to face, and then
broke off the assembly by the ships. Akhilleus
made his way to his squadron and his quarters,
Patróklos[21] by his side, with his companions.

Agamémnon proceeded to launch a ship,
assigned her twenty oarsmen, loaded beasts
for sacrifice to the god, then set aboard

[20] **you:** Thetis, a nymph, was for a time a companion of Pêleus. [21] **Patróklos:** Akhilleus's closest friend.

Khrysêis in her loveliness. The versatile
Odysseus took the deck, and, all oars manned,
they pulled out on the drenching ways of sea.
The troops meanwhile were ordered to police camp
and did so, throwing refuse in the water;
then to Apollo by the barren surf
they carried out full-tally hekatombs,
and the savor curled in crooked smoke toward heaven.

That was the day's work in the army.
Agamémnon
had kept his threat in mind, and now he acted,
calling Eurýbatês and Talthýbios,
his aides and criers:
"Go along," he said
"both of you, to the quarters of Akhilleus
and take his charming Brisêis by the hand
to bring to me. And if he balks at giving her
I shall be there myself with men-at-arms
in force to take her—all the more gall for him."
So, ominously, he sent them on their way,
and they who had no stomach for it went
along the waste sea shingle toward the ships
and shelters of the Myrmidons. Not far
from his black ship and hut they found the prince
in the open, seated. And seeing these two come
was cheerless to Akhilleus. Shamefast, pale
with fear of him, they stood without a word;
but he knew what they felt and called out:
"Peace to you,
criers and couriers of Zeus and men!
Come forward. Not one thing have I against you:
Agamémnon is the man who sent you
for Brisêis. Here then, my lord Patróklos,
bring out the girl and give her to these men.
And let them both bear witness before the gods
who live in bliss, as before men who die,
including this harsh king, if ever hereafter
a need for me arises to keep the rest
from black defeat and ruin.
Lost in folly,
the man cannot think back or think ahead
how to come through a battle by the ships."
Patróklos did the bidding of his friend,
led from the hut Brisêis in her beauty

and gave her to them. Back along the ships
they took their way, and the girl went, loath to go.

Leaving his friends in haste, Akhilleus wept,
and sat apart by the grey wave, scanning the endless sea.
Often he spread his hands in prayer to his mother:
"As my life came from you, though it is brief,
honor at least from Zeus who storms in heaven
I call my due. He gives me precious little.
See how the lord of the great plains, Agamémnon,
humiliated me! He has my prize,
by his own whim, for himself."

Eyes wet with tears,
he spoke, and her ladyship his mother heard him
in green deeps where she lolled near her old father.[22]
Gliding she rose and broke like mist from the inshore
grey sea face, to sit down softly before him,
her son in tears; and fondling him she said:
"Child, why do you weep? What grief is this?
Out with it, tell me, both of us should know."
Akhilleus, fast in battle as a lion,
groaned and said:

"Why tell you what you know?
We sailed out raiding, and we took by storm
that ancient town of Eëtíôn called Thêbê,
plundered the place, brought slaves and spoils away.
At the division, later,
they chose a young girl, Khrysêis, for the king.
Then Khrysês, priest of the Archer God, Apollo,
came to the beachhead we Akhaians hold,
bringing no end of ransom for his daughter;
he had the god's white bands on a golden staff
and sued for grace from the army of Akhaia,
mostly the two Atreidai, corps commanders.
All of our soldiers murmured in assent:
'Behave well to the priest. And take the ransom!'
But Agamémnon would not. It went against his desire,
and brutally he ordered the man away.
So the old man withdrew in grief and anger.

[22] **her old father:** Nereus, father of the sea-nymphs.

Apollo cared for him: he heard his prayer
and let black bolts of plague fly on the Argives.

One by one our men came down with it
and died hard as the god's shots raked the army
broadside. But our priest divined the cause
and told us what the god meant by plague.

I said, 'Appease the god!' but Agamémnon
could not contain his rage; he threatened me,
and what he threatened is now done—
one girl the Akhaians are embarking now
for Khrysê beach with gifts for Lord Apollo;
the other, just now, from my hut—the criers
came and took her, Briseus' girl, my prize,
given by the army.
If you can, stand by me:
go to Olympos, pray to Zeus, if ever
by word or deed you served him—
and so you did, I often heard you tell it
in Father's house: that time when you alone
of all the gods shielded the son of Krónos[23]
from peril and disgrace—when other gods,
Pallas Athêna, Hêra, and Poseidon,[24]
wished him in irons, wished to keep him bound,
you had the will to free him of that bondage,
and called up to Olympos in all haste
Aigaion, whom the gods call Briareus,[25]
the giant with a hundred arms, more powerful
than the sea-god, his father. Down he sat
by the son of Krónos, glorying in that place.
For fear of him the blissful gods forbore
to manacle Zeus.
Remind him of these things,
cling to his knees and tell him your good pleasure
if he will take the Trojan side
and roll the Akhaians back to the water's edge,
back on the ships with slaughter! All the troops
may savor what their king has won for them,

---

[23] **Krónos:** Father of Zeus and previous ruler of the universe. [24] **Poseidon:** God of the ocean, Zeus's brother.
[25] **Briareus:** A giant, son of Poseidon.

and he may know his madness, what he lost
when he dishonored me, peerless among Akhaians."

Her eyes filled, and a tear fell as she answered:
"Alas, my child, why did I rear you, doomed
the day I bore you?[26] Ah, could you only be
serene upon this beachhead through the siege,
your life runs out so soon.
Oh early death! Oh broken heart! No destiny
so cruel! And I bore you to this evil!

But what you wish I will propose
To Zeus, lord of the lightning, going up
myself into the snow-glare of Olympos
with hope for his consent.
Be quiet now
beside the long ships, keep your anger bright
against the army, quit the war.
Last night
Zeus made a journey to the shore of Ocean
to feast among the Sunburned,[27] and the gods
accompanied him. In twelve days he will come
back to Olympos. Then I shall be there
to cross his bronze doorsill and take his knees.
I trust I'll move him."

Thetis left her son
still burning for the softly belted girl
whom they had wrested from him.
Meanwhile Odysseus
with his shipload of offerings came to Khrysê.
Entering the deep harbor there
they furled the sails and stowed them, and unbent
forestays to ease the mast down quickly aft
into its rest; then rowed her to a mooring.
Bow-stones were dropped, and they tied up astern,
and all stepped out into the wash and ebb,
then disembarked their cattle for the Archer,
and Khrysêis, from the deepsea ship. Odysseus,

[26] **doomed . . . bore you:** Akhilleus is fated to die at an early age. [27] **the Sunburned:** The Ethiopians, who lived at the edge of the world, which was surrounded by Ocean.

the great tactician, led her to the altar,
putting her in her father's hands, and said:
"Khrysês, as Agamémnon's emissary
I bring your child to you, and for Apollo
a hekatomb in the Danáäns' name.
We trust in this way to appease your lord,
who sent down pain and sorrow on the Argives."

So he delivered her, and the priest received her,
the child so dear to him, in joy. Then hastening
to give the god his hekatomb, they led
bullocks to crowd around the compact altar,
rinsed their hands and delved in barley baskets,
as open-armed to heaven Khrysês prayed:
"Oh hear me, master of the silver bow,
protector of Ténedos and the holy towns,
if while I prayed you listened once before
and honored me, and punished the Akhaians,
now let my wish come true again. But turn
your plague away this time from the Danáäns."

And this petition, too, Apollo heard.
When prayers were said and grains of barley strewn,
they held the bullocks for the knife, and flayed them,
cutting out joints and wrapping these in fat,
two layers, folded, with raw strips of flesh,
for the old man to burn on cloven faggots,
wetting it all with wine.
Around him stood
young men with five-tined forks in hand, and when
the vitals had been tasted, joints consumed,
they sliced the chines and quarters for the spits,
roasted them evenly and drew them off.
Their meal being now prepared and all work done,
they feasted to their hearts' content and made
desire for meat and drink recede again,
then young men filled their winebowls to the brim,
ladling drops for the god in every cup.
Propitiatory songs rose clear and strong
until day's end, to praise the god, Apollo,
as One Who Keeps the Plague Afar; and listening
the god took joy.
After the sun went down

and darkness came, at last Odysseus' men
lay down to rest under the stern hawsers.

When Dawn spread out her finger tips of rose
they put to sea for the main camp of Akhaians,
and the Archer God sent them a following wind.
Stepping the mast they shook their canvas out,
and wind caught, bellying the sail. A foaming
dark blue wave sang backward from the bow
as the running ship made way against the sea,
until they came offshore of the encampment.
Here they put in and hauled the black ship high,
far up the sand, braced her with shoring timbers,
and then disbanded, each to his own hut.

Meanwhile unstirring and with smoldering heart,
the godlike athlete, son of Pêleus, Prince
Akhilleus waited by his racing ships.
He would not enter the assembly
of emulous men, nor ever go to war,
but felt his valor staling in his breast
with idleness, and missed the cries of battle.

Now when in fact twelve days had passed, the gods
who live forever turned back to Olympos,
with Zeus in power supreme among them.
Thetis
had kept in mind her mission for her son,
and rising like a dawn mist from the sea
into a cloud she soared aloft in heaven
to high Olympos. Zeus with massive brows
she found apart, on the chief crest enthroned,
and slipping down before him, her left hand
placed on his knees and her right hand held up
to cup his chin, she made her plea to him:[28]
"O Father Zeus, if ever amid immortals
by word or deed I served you, grant my wish
and see to my son's honor! Doom for him
of all men came on quickest.
Now Lord Marshal
Agamémnon has been highhanded with him,
has commandeered and holds his prize of war.

[28] **her left hand . . . plea to him:** The posture of a supplicant.

But you can make him pay for this, profound
mind of Olympos!
Lend the Trojans power,
until the Akhaians recompense my son
and heap new honor upon him!"

When she finished,
the gatherer of cloud said never a word
but sat unmoving for a long time, silent.
Thetis clung to his knees, then spoke again:
"Give your infallible word, and bow your head,
or else reject me. Can you be afraid
to let me see how low in your esteem
I am of all the gods?"

Greatly perturbed,
Lord Zeus who masses cloud said:
"Here is trouble.
You drive me into open war with Hêra
sooner or later:
she will be at me, scolding all day long.
Even as matters stand she never rests
from badgering me before the gods: I take
the Trojan side in battle, so she says.

Go home before you are seen. But you can trust me
to put my mind on this; I shall arrange it.
Here let me bow my head, then be content
to see me bound by that most solemn act
before the gods. My word is not revocable
nor ineffectual, once I nod upon it."

He bent his ponderous black brows down, and locks
ambrosial of his immortal head
swung over them, as all Olympos trembled.
After this pact they parted: misty Thetis
from glittering Olympos leapt away
into the deep sea; Zeus to his hall retired.
There all the gods rose from their seats in deference
before their father; not one dared
face him unmoved, but all stood up before him,
and thus he took his throne.
But Hêra knew
he had new interests; she had seen
the goddess Thetis, silvery-footed daughter

of the Old One of the Sea, conferring with him,
and, nagging, she inquired of Zeus Kroníon:

"Who is it this time, schemer? Who has your ear?
How fond you are of secret plans, of taking
decisions privately! You could not bring yourself,
could you, to favor me with any word
of your new plot?"

The father of gods and men
said in reply:
"Hêra, all my provisions
you must not itch to know.
You'll find them rigorous, consort though you are.
In all appropriate matters no one else,
no god or man, shall be advised before you.
But when I choose to think alone,
don't harry me about it with your questions."
The Lady Hêra answered, with wide eyes:
"Majesty, what a thing to say. I have not
'harried' you before with questions, surely;
you are quite free to tell what you will tell.
This time I dreadfully fear—I have a feeling—
Thetis, the silvery-footed daughter
of the Old One of the Sea, led you astray.
Just now at daybreak, anyway, she came
to sit with you and take your knees; my guess is
you bowed your head for her in solemn pact
that you will see to the honor of Akhilleus—
that is, to Akhaian carnage near the ships."

Now Zeus the gatherer of cloud said:
"Marvelous,
you and your guesses; you are near it, too.
But there is not one thing that you can do about it,
only estrange yourself still more from me—
all the more gall for you. If what you say
is true, you may be sure it pleases me.
And now you just sit down, be still, obey me,
or else not all the gods upon Olympos
can help in the least when I approach your chair
to lay my inexorable hands upon you."
At this the wide-eyed Lady Hêra feared him,
and sat quite still, and bent her will to his.
Up through the hall of Zeus now all the lords

of heaven were sullen and looked askance. Hêphaistos,[29]
master artificer, broke the silence,
doing a kindness to the snowy-armed
lady, his mother Hêra.

He began:
"Ah, what a miserable day, if you two
raise your voices over mortal creatures!
More than enough already! Must you bring
your noisy bickering among the gods?
What pleasure can we take in a fine dinner
when baser matters gain the upper hand?
To Mother my advice is—what she knows—
better make up to Father, or he'll start
his thundering and shake our feast to bits.
You know how he can shock us if he cares to—
out of our seats with lightning bolts!
Supreme power is his. Oh, soothe him, please,
take a soft tone, get back in his good graces.
Then he'll be benign to us again."
He lurched up as he spoke, and held a winecup
out to her, a double-handed one,
and said:
"Dear Mother, patience, hold your tongue,
no matter how upset you are. I would not
see you battered, dearest.
It would hurt me,
and yet I could not help you, not a bit.
The Olympian is difficult to oppose.
One other time I took your part he caught me
around one foot and flung me
into the sky from our tremendous terrace.
I soared all day! Just as the sun dropped down
I dropped down, too, on Lemnos—nearly dead.
The island people nursed a fallen god."

He made her smile—and the goddess, white-armed Hêra,
smiling took the winecup from his hand.
Then, dipping from the winebowl, round he went
from left to right, serving the other gods
nectar of sweet delight.
And quenchless laughter

[29] **Hêphaistos:** God of fire and metallurgy.

broke out among the blissful gods
to see Hêphaistos wheezing down the hall.
So all day long until the sun went down
they spent in feasting, and the measured feast
matched well their hearts' desire.
So did the flawless harp held by Apollo
and heavenly songs in choiring antiphon
that all the Muses sang.
And when the shining
sun of day sank in the west, they turned
homeward each one to rest, each to that home
the bandy-legged wondrous artisan
Hêphaistos fashioned for them with his craft.
The lord of storm and lightning, Zeus, retired
and shut his eyes where sweet sleep ever came to him,
and at his side lay Hêra, Goddess of the Golden Chair.

From Book 6
Interludes in Field and City

[In Book 2, a council of Greek leaders decides to test the troops. Agamémnon suggests that they all go home and the men begin to leave. Inspired by Athêna, Odysseus convinces everyone to stay by reminding them of Kalkhas's prophecy of victory in the tenth year. In Book 3, both sides agree to a single combat between Meneláos and Paris to settle the war. Meneláos wins the duel, but Paris is saved from certain death by the goddess Aphrodite. In Book 4, Hêra wants to see Troy destroyed and Zeus agrees to let the war continue. In Book 5, Diomêdês performs heroic feats by slaying many Trojans and wounding others. Aeneas is wounded, but then rescued by Apollo and Aphrodite. Diomêdês finally wounds Arês, the god of war, who has been assisting the Trojans, and is now forced to withdraw, along with Hêra and Athêna. At the beginning of Book 6, the Trojans begin to retreat and Hektor is summoned back to Troy to tell the women to provide offerings to Athêna so that they might restrain Diomêdês, who is about to fight Glaukos. The two of them make an interesting discovery.]

[. . .] Meanwhile, driving into an open space
between the armies, Hippólokhos' son, Glaukos,
and Diomêdês advanced upon each other,
hot for combat. When the range was short,
Diomêdês, face to face with him, spoke up:
"Young gallant stranger, who are you?
I have not noticed you before in battle—
never before, in the test that brings men honor—
but here you come now, far in front of everyone,
with heart enough to risk my beam of spear.
A sorrowing old age they have whose children
face me in war! If you are a god from heaven,
I would not fight with any out of heaven.

No long life remained — far from it — for
Lykourgos,[30] Dryas' rugged son,
when he in his day strove with gods — that time
he chased the maenads on the sacred ridge
of manic Dionysos, on Mount Nysa.
Belabored by the ox-goad of Lykourgos,
killer that he was, they all flung down
their ivy-staves, while terrified Dionysos
plunged under a sea-surge. In her arms
Thetis received him, shaking from head to foot,
after that yelling man's pursuit.
And now the gods whose life is ease
turned on Lykourgos; Zeus put out his eyes;
his days were numbered, hated by them all.
I would not fight, not I, with gods in bliss,
but you, if you are man and mortal, one
who feeds on harvest of the grainland, take
one step nearer! and before you know it
you will come up against the edge of death."

Hippólokhos' distinguished son replied:
"Why ask my birth, Diomêdês? Very like leaves
upon this earth are the generations of men —
old leaves, cast on the ground by wind, young leaves
the greening forest bears when spring comes in.
So mortals pass; one generation flowers
even as another dies away.
My lineage?
If you are really bent on knowing all —
and many others know my story — listen.
Ephýra is a city on the gulf
of Argos: in Ephýra Sísyphos
Aiólidês, the craftiest of men,
lived once upon a time and fathered Glaukos,
father in turn of Prince Bellérophontês,
one to whom the gods had given beauty
with charm and bravery. But there came a day
when Proitos wished him ill — and Zeus had put him
under the power of Proitos. That strong king
now drove Bellérophontês out of Argos:
this because Ánteia, the queen,
lusted to couple with him secretly,

---

[30] **Lykourgos:** Lykourgos, king of the Edonians, used an ox-goad to drive away the wine-god Dionysos and his followers. Descriptions of Lykourgos's punishments vary.

but he was honorable, she could not lure him,
and in the king's ear hissed a lie:
                                        'Oh, Proitos,
I wish that you may die unless you kill
Bellérophontês: he desired to take me
in lust against my will.'
                                        Rage filled the king
over her slander, but being scrupulous
he shrank from killing him. So into Lykia
he sent him, charged to bear a deadly cipher,
magical marks Proitos engraved and hid
in folded tablets. He commanded him
to show these to his father-in-law,
thinking in this way he should meet his end.
Guided by gods he sailed, and came to Lykia,
high country, crossed by Xánthos' running stream;
and Lykia's lord received him well.
Nine days he honored him, nine revels led
with consecrated beasts. When Dawn with rosy
fingers eastward made the tenth day bright,
he questioned him, and asked at length to see
what sign he brought him from his son-in-law.
When he had read the deadly cipher, changing,
he gave his first command: his guest should fight
and quell a foaming monster, the Khimaira,
of ghastly and inhuman origin,
her forepart lionish, her tail a snake's,
a she-goat in between. This thing exhaled
in jets a rolling fire.
                                        Well, he killed her,
by taking heed of omens from the gods.
His second test was battle with Solýmoi,
formidable aborigines. He thought
this fight the worst he ever had with men.
A third mission was to slaughter Amazons,
women virile in war. On his return,
the king devised yet one more trap for him,
laying an ambush, with picked men of Lykia.
But not a single one went home again:
Bellérophontês killed them all.
                                        His eyes
opened at last to the young man's power, godly
from godly lineage, the king detained him,
offered him his daughter, gave him, too,
a moiety of royal privileges,

and Lykians for their part set aside
their finest land for him, vineyard and plowland,
fertile for wheatfields. The king's daughter bore
three children to Bellérophontês: Ísandros,
Hippólokhos, and Laodámeia.
Zeus the Profound lay with Laodámeia,
who bore Sarpêdôn, one of our great soldiers.
By now one day Bellérophontês too
incurred the gods' wrath—and alone he moped
on Alêïon plain, eating his heart out,
shunning the beaten track of men. His son
Ísandros in a skirmish with Solýmoi
met his death at insatiable Arês'[31] hands,
and angry Artemis[32] killed Laodámeia.
Hippólokhos it was who fathered me,
I am proud to say. He sent me here to Troy
commanding me to act always with valor,
always to be most noble, never to shame
the line of my progenitors, great men
first in Ephýra, then in Lykia.
That is the blood and birth I claim."

At this,
joy came to Diomêdês, loud in battle.
With one thrust in the field where herds had cropped
he fixed his long spear like a pole, and smiled
at the young captain, saying gently:
"Why,
you are my friend! My grandfather, Oineus,
made friends of us long years ago. He welcomed
Prince Bellérophontês in his hall,
his guest for twenty days. They gave each other
beautiful tokens of amity: Grandfather's
offering was a lion-guard sewn in purple,
Bellérophontês gave a cup of gold
two-handled; it is in my house; I left it there,
coming away to Troy. I cannot remember
Tydeus, my father—I was still too young
when he departed, when the Akhaian army
came to grief at Thebes.
I am your friend,
sworn friend, in central Argos. You are mine

[31] **Arês:** God of war. [32] **Artemis:** Goddess of the hunt.

in Lykia, whenever I may come.
So let us keep away from one another's
weapons in the spear-fights of this war.
Trojans a-plenty will be left for me,
and allies, as god puts them in my path;
many Akhaians will be left for you
to bring down if you can.
Each take the other's
battle-gear; let those around us know
we have this bond of friendship from our fathers."

Both men jumped down then to confirm the pact,
taking each other's hands. But Zeus
had stolen Glaukos' wits away—
the young man gave up golden gear for bronze,
took nine bulls' worth for armor worth a hundred!

Now, when Hektor reached the Skaian Gates[33]
daughters and wives of Trojans rushed to greet him
with questions about friends, sons, husbands, brothers.
"Pray to the gods!" he said to each in turn,
as grief awaited many. He walked on
and into Priam's palace, fair and still,
made all of ashlar,[34] with bright colonnades.
Inside were fifty rooms of polished stone
one by another, where the sons of Priam
slept beside their wives; apart from these
across an inner court were twelve rooms more
all in one line, of polished stone, where slept
the sons-in-law of Priam and their wives.
Approaching these, he met his gentle mother° Hékabê
going in with Laódikê, most beautiful
of all her daughters. Both hands clasping his,
she looked at him and said:
"Why have you come
from battle, child? Those fiends, the Akhaians, fighting
around the town, have worn you out; you come
to climb our Rock[35] and lift your palms to Zeus!
Wait, and I'll serve you honeyed wine.
First you may offer up a drop to Zeus,
to the immortal gods, then slake your thirst.

---

[33] **Skaian Gates:** The main entrance to Troy. [34] **ashlar:** Square stones used in building. [35] **our Rock:** The hill on which the city rests.

Wine will restore a man when he is weary
as you are, fighting to defend your own."

Hektor answered her, his helmet flashing:
"No, my dear mother, ladle me no wine;
You'd make my nerve go slack: I'd lose my edge.
May I tip wine to Zeus with hands unwashed?
I fear to—a bespattered man, and bloody,
may not address the lord of gloomy cloud.
No, it is you I wish would bring together
our older women, with offerings, and go visit
the temple of Athêna, Hope of Soldiers.
Pick out a robe, most lovely and luxurious,
most to your liking in the women's hall;
place it upon Athêna's knees; assure her
a sacrifice of heifers, twelve young ones
ungoaded ever in their lives, if in her mercy
relenting toward our town, our wives and children,
she keeps Diomêdês out of holy Troy.
He is a wild beast now in combat and pursuit.
Make your way to her shrine, visit Athêna,
Hope of Soldiers.
As for me, I go
for Paris, to arouse him, if he listens.
If only earth would swallow him here and now!
What an affliction the Olympian
brought up for us in him—a curse for Priam
and Priam's children! Could I see that man
dwindle into Death's night, I'd feel my soul
relieved of its distress!"

So Hektor spoke, and she walked slowly on
into the mégaron.[36] She called her maids,
who then assembled women from the city.
But Hékabê went down to the low chamber
fragrant with cedar, where the robes were kept,
embroidered work by women of Sidonia
Aléxandros° had brought, that time he sailed Paris
and ravished Helen, princess, pearl of kings.
Hékabê lifted out her loveliest robe,
most ample, most luxurious in brocade,
and glittering like starlight under all.

[36] **the mégaron:** The great hall.

This offering she carried to Athêna
with a long line of women in her train.
On the Akrópolis, Athêna's shrine
was opened for them by Theanô, stately
daughter of Kisseus, wife to Antênor,[37]
and chosen priestess of Athêna. Now
all crying loud stretched out their arms in prayer,
while Theanô with grace took up the robe
to place it on fair-haired Athêna's knees.
She made petition then to Zeus's daughter:
"Lady,
excellent goddess, towering friend of Troy,
smash Diomêdês' lance-haft! Throw him hard
below the Skaian Gates, before our eyes!
Upon this altar we'll make offering
of twelve young heifers never scarred!
Only show mercy to our town,
mercy to Trojan men, their wives and children."

These were Theanô's prayers, her vain prayers.
Pallas Athêna turned away her head.

During the supplication at the shrine,
Hektor approached the beautiful house Aléxandros
himself had made, with men who in that time
were master-builders in the land of Troy.
Bedchamber, hall, and court, in the upper town,
they built for him near Priam's hall and Hektor's.
Now Hektor dear to Zeus went in, his hand
gripping a spear eleven forearms long,
whose bronze head shone before him in the air
as shone, around the neck, a golden ring.
He found his brother in the bedchamber
handling a magnificent cuirass[38] and shield
and pulling at his bent-horn bow, while Helen
among her household women sat nearby,
directing needlecraft and splendid weaving.
At sight of him, to shame him, Hektor said:
"Unquiet soul, why be aggrieved in private?
Our troops are dying out there where they fight
around our city, under our high walls.
The hue and cry of war, because of you,
comes in like surf upon this town.

---

[37] **Antênor:** Trojan lord. [38] **cuirass:** Armor for breast and back.

You'd be at odds with any other man
you might see quitting your accursèd war.
Up; into action, before torches thrown
make the town flare!"

And shining like a god
Aléxandros replied:
"Ah, Hektor,
this call to order is no more than just.
So let me tell you something: hear me out.
No pettishness, resentment toward the Trojans,
kept me in this bedchamber so long,
but rather my desire, on being routed,
to taste grief to the full.
In her sweet way
my lady rouses me to fight again—
and I myself consider it better so.
Victory falls to one man, then another.
Wait, while I put on the wargod's gear,
or else go back; I'll follow, sure to find you."

For answer, Hektor in his shining helm
said not a word, but in low tones
enticing Helen murmured:
"Brother dear—
dear to a whore, a nightmare of a woman!
That day my mother gave me to the world
I wish a hurricane blast had torn me away
to wild mountains, or into tumbling sea
to be washed under by a breaking wave,
before these evil days could come!—or, granted
terrible years were in the gods' design,
I wish I had had a good man for a lover
who knew the sharp tongues and just rage of men.
This one—his heart's unsound, and always will be,
and he will win what he deserves. Come here
and rest upon this couch with me, dear brother.
You are the one afflicted most
by harlotry in me and by his madness,
our portion, all of misery, given by Zeus
that we may live in song for men to come."

Great Hektor shook his head, his helmet flashing,
and said:
"No, Helen, offer me no rest;
I know you are fond of me. I cannot rest.

Time presses, and I grow impatient now
to lend a hand to Trojans in the field
who feel a gap when I am gone. Your part
can be to urge him—let him feel the urgency
to join me in the city. He has time:
I must go home to visit my own people,
my own dear wife and my small son. Who knows
if I shall be reprieved again to see them,
or beaten down under Akhaian blows
as the immortals will."

He turned away
and quickly entered his own hall, but found
Princess Andrómakhê was not at home.
With one nursemaid and her small child, she stood
upon the tower of Ilion, in tears,
bemoaning what she saw.

Now Hektor halted
upon his threshold, calling to the maids:
"Tell me at once, and clearly, please,
my lady Andrómakhê, where has she gone?
To see my sisters, or my brothers' wives?
Or to Athêna's temple? Ladies of Troy
are there to make petition to the goddess."

The busy mistress of the larder answered:
"Hektor, to put it clearly as you ask,
she did not go to see your sisters, nor
your brothers' wives, nor to Athêna's shrine
where others are petitioning the goddess.
Up to the great square tower of Ilion
she took her way, because she heard our men
were spent in battle by Akhaian power.
In haste, like a madwoman, to the wall
she went, and Nurse went too, carrying the child."

At this word Hektor whirled and left his hall,
taking the same path he had come by,
along byways, walled lanes, all through the town
until he reached the Skaian Gates, whereby
before long he would issue on the field.
There his warmhearted lady
came to meet him, running: Andrómakhê,
whose father, Eëtiôn, once had ruled
the land under Mount Plakos, dark with forest,

at Thêbê under Plakos—lord and king
of the Kilikians. Hektor was her lord now,
head to foot in bronze; and now she joined him.
Behind her came her maid, who held the child
against her breast, a rosy baby still,
Hektoridês,[39] the world's delight, as fresh
as a pure shining star. Skamándrios
his father named him; other men would say
Astýanax, "Lord of the Lower Town,"
as Hektor singlehanded guarded Troy.
How brilliantly the warrior smiled, in silence,
his eyes upon the child! Andrómakhê
rested against him, shook away a tear,
and pressed his hand in both her own, to say:
"Oh, my wild one, your bravery will be
your own undoing! No pity for our child,
poor little one, or me in my sad lot—
soon to be deprived of you! soon, soon
Akhaians as one man will set upon you
and cut you down! Better for me, without you,
to take cold earth for mantle. No more comfort,
no other warmth, after you meet your doom,
but heartbreak only. Father is dead, and Mother.
My father great Akhilleus killed when he
besieged and plundered Thêbê, our high town,
citadel of Kilikians. He killed him,
but, reverent at last in this, did not
despoil him. Body, gear, and weapons forged
so handsomely, he burned, and heaped a barrow
over the ashes. Elms were planted round
by mountain-nymphs of him who bears the stormcloud.° Zeus
Then seven brothers that I had at home
in one day entered Death's dark place. Akhilleus,
prince and powerful runner, killed all seven
amid their shambling cattle and silvery sheep.
Mother, who had been queen of wooded Plakos,
he brought with other winnings home, and freed her,
taking no end of ransom. Artemis
the Huntress shot her in her father's house.
Father and mother—I have none but you,
nor brother, Hektor; lover none but you!
Be merciful! Stay here upon the tower!

[39] **Hektoridês:** The suffix *-ides* means "son of."

Do not bereave your child and widow me!
Draw up your troops by the wild figtree; that way
the city lies most open, men most easily
could swarm the wall where it is low:
three times, at least, their best men tried it there
in company of the two called Aías, with
Idómeneus, the Atreidai, Diomêdês—
whether someone who had it from the oracles
had told them, or their own hearts urged them on."

Great Hektor in his shimmering helmet answered:
"Lady, these many things beset my mind
no less than yours. But I should die of shame
before our Trojan men and noblewomen
if like a coward I avoided battle,
nor am I moved to. Long ago I learned
how to be brave, how to go forward always
and to contend for honor, Father's and mine.
Honor—for in my heart and soul I know
a day will come when ancient Ilion falls,
when Priam and the folk of Priam perish.
Not by the Trojans' anguish on that day
am I so overborne in mind—the pain
of Hékabê herself, or Priam king,
or of my brothers, many and valorous,
who will have fallen in dust before our enemies—
as by your own grief, when some armed Akhaian
takes you in tears, your free life stripped away.
Before another woman's loom in Argos
it may be you will pass, or at Messêis
or Hypereiê fountain, carrying water,
against your will—iron constraint upon you.
And seeing you in tears, a man may say:
'There is the wife of Hektor, who fought best
of Trojan horsemen when they fought at Troy.'
So he may say—and you will ache again
for one man who could keep you out of bondage.
Let me be hidden dark down in my grave
before I hear your cry or know you captive!"

As he said this, Hektor held out his arms
to take his baby. But the child squirmed round
on the nurse's bosom and began to wail,

terrified by his father's great war helm—
the flashing bronze, the crest with horsehair plume
tossed like a living thing at every nod.
His father began laughing, and his mother
laughed as well. Then from his handsome head
Hektor lifted off his helm and bent
to place it, bright with sunlight, on the ground.
When he had kissed his child and swung him high
to dandle him, he said this prayer:
"O Zeus
and all immortals, may this child, my son,
become like me a prince among the Trojans.
Let him be strong and brave and rule in power
at Ilion; then someday men will say
'This fellow is far better than his father!'
seeing him home from war, and in his arms
the bloodstained gear of some tall warrior slain—
making his mother proud."

After this prayer,
into his dear wife's arms he gave his baby,
whom on her fragrant breast
she held and cherished, laughing through her tears.
Hektor pitied her now. Caressing her,
he said:
"Unquiet soul, do not be too distressed
by thoughts of me. You know no man dispatches me
into the undergloom against my fate;
no mortal, either, can escape his fate,
coward or brave man, once he comes to be.
Go home, attend to your own handiwork
at loom and spindle, and command the maids
to busy themselves, too. As for the war,
that is for men, all who were born at Ilion,
to put their minds on—most of all for me."

He stooped now to recover his plumed helm
as she, his dear wife, drew away, her head
turned and her eyes upon him, brimming tears.
She made her way in haste then to the ordered
house of Hektor and rejoined her maids,
moving them all to weep at sight of her.
In Hektor's home they mourned him, living still

but not, they feared, again to leave the war
or be delivered from Akhaian fury.

Paris in the meantime had not lingered:
after he buckled his bright war-gear on
he ran through Troy, sure-footed with long strides.
Think how a stallion fed on clover and barley,
mettlesome, thundering in a stall, may snap
his picket rope and canter down a field
to bathe as he would daily in the river—
glorying in freedom! Head held high
with mane over his shoulders flying,
his dazzling work of finely jointed knees
takes him around the pasture haunts of horses.
That was the way the son of Priam, Paris,
ran from the height of Pergamos;[40] his gear
ablaze like the great sun,
and laughed aloud. He sprinted on, and quickly
met his brother, who was slow to leave
the place where he had discoursed with his lady.
Aléxandros was first to speak:
"Dear fellow,"
he said, "have I delayed you, kept you waiting?
Have I not come at the right time, as you asked?"

And Hektor in his shimmering helm replied:
"My strange brother! No man with justice in him
would underrate your handiwork in battle;
you have a powerful arm. But you give way
too easily, and lose interest, lose your will.
My heart aches in me when I hear our men,
who have such toil of battle on your account,
talk of you with contempt. Well, come along.
Someday we'll make amends for that, if ever
we drive the Akhaians from the land of Troy—
if ever Zeus permit us, in our hall,
to set before the gods of heaven, undying
and ever young, our winebowl of deliverance."

[40] **the height of Pergamos:** The citadel of Troy.

From Book 8
The Battle Swayed by Zeus

[In Book 7, Hektor and Aías battle to a standstill. The Trojans offer to return Helen's wealth to Meneláos, but the offer is rejected. The dead are buried during a truce. In Book 8, the battle resumes and by the end of the day the Trojans have driven the Akhaians back to their fortifications around their boats.]

[. . .] Now in the western Ocean
the shining sun dipped, drawing dark night on
over the kind grainbearing earth — a sundown
far from desired by Trojans; but the night
came thrice besought and blest by the Akhaians.
Hektor at once called Trojans to assembly,
leading the way by night back from the ships
to an empty field beside the eddying river —
a space that seemed free of the dead. The living
halted and dismounted there to listen
to a speech by Hektor, dear to Zeus. He held
his lance erect — eleven forearms long
with bronze point shining in the air before him
as shone, around the shank, a golden ring.
Leaning on this, he spoke amid the Trojans:
"Hear me, Trojans, Dardans, and allies!
By this time I had thought we might retire
to windy Ilion, after we had destroyed
Akhaians and their ships; but the night's gloom
came before we finished. That has saved them,
Argives and ships, at the sea's edge near the surf.
All right, then, let us bow to the black night,
and make an evening feast! From the chariot poles
unyoke the teams, toss fodder out before them;
bring down beeves and fat sheep from the city,
and lose no time about it — amber wine
and wheaten bread, too, from our halls. Go, gather
piles of firewood, so that all night long,
until the first-born dawn, our many fires
shall burn and send to heaven their leaping light,
that not by night shall the unshorn Akhaians
get away on the broad back of the sea.
Not by night — and not without combat, either,
taking ship easily, but let there be
those who take homeward missiles to digest,
hit hard by arrows or by spears as they
shove off and leap aboard. And let the next man
hate the thought of waging painful war

on Trojan master-horsemen.
Honored criers
throughout our town shall publish this command:
old men with hoary brows, and striplings, all
camp out tonight upon the ancient towers;
women in every mégaron kindle fires,
and every sentry keep a steady watch
against a night raid on the city, while
my troops are in the field. These dispositions,
Trojans, are to be taken as I command. And may
what I have said tonight be salutary;
likewise what I shall say at Dawn. I hope
with prayer to Zeus and other immortal gods
we shall repulse the dogs of war and death
brought on us in the black ships. Aye, this night
we'll guard ourselves, toward morning arm again
and whet against the ships the edge of war!
I'll see if Diomêdês has the power
to force me from the ships, back on the rampart,
or if I kill him and take home his gear,
wet with his blood. He will show bravery
tomorrow if he face my spear advancing!
In the first rank, I think, wounded he'll lie
with plenty of his friends lying around him
at sunup in the morning.
Would I were sure
of being immortal, ageless all my days,
and reverenced like Athêna and Apollo,
as it is sure this day will bring defeat
on those of Argos!"

This was the speech of Hektor,
and cheers rang out from the Trojans after it.
They led from under the yokes their sweating teams,
tethering each beside his chariot,
then brought down from the city beeves and sheep
in all haste—brought down wine and bread as well
out of their halls. They piled up firewood
and carried out full-tally hekatombs
to the immortals. Off the plain, the wind
bore smoke and savor of roasts into the sky.
Then on the perilous open ground of war,
in brave expectancy, they lay all night
while many campfires burned. As when in heaven
principal stars shine out around the moon

when the night sky is limpid, with no wind,
and all the lookout points, headlands, and mountain
clearings are distinctly seen, as though
pure space had broken through, downward from heaven,
and all the stars are out, and in his heart
the shepherd sings: just so from ships to river
shone before Ilion the Trojan fires.
There were a thousand burning in the plain,
and round each one lay fifty men in firelight.
Horses champed white barley, near the chariots,
waiting for Dawn to mount her lovely chair.

Book 9
A Visit of Emissaries

So Trojans kept their watch that night.
To seaward
Panic that attends blood-chilling Rout
now ruled the Akhaians. All their finest men
were shaken by this fear, in bitter throes,
as when a shifting gale
blows up over the cold fish-breeding sea,
north wind and west wind wailing out of Thrace
in squall on squall, and dark waves crest, and shoreward
masses of weed are cast up by the surf:
so were Akhaian hearts torn in their breasts.

By that great gloom hard hit, the son of Atreus
made his way amid his criers and told them
to bid each man in person to assembly
but not to raise a general cry. He led them,
making the rounds himself, and soon the soldiers
grimly took their places. Then he rose,
with slow tears trickling, as from a hidden spring
dark water runs down, staining a rock wall;
and groaning heavily he addressed the Argives:
"Friends, leaders of Argives, all my captains,
Zeus Kronidês entangled me in folly
to my undoing. Wayward god, he promised
solemnly that I should not sail away
before I stormed the inner town of Troy.
Crookedness and duplicity, I see now!
He calls me to return to Argos beaten
after these many losses. That must be
his will and his good pleasure, who knows why?

Many a great town's height has he destroyed
and will destroy, being supreme in power.
Enough. Now let us act on what I say:
Board ship for our own fatherland! Retreat!
We cannot hope any longer to take Troy!"

At this a stillness overcame them all,
the Akhaian soldiers. Long they sat in silence,
hearing their own hearts beat. Then Diomêdês
rose at last to speak. He said:
"My lord,
I must contend with you for letting go,
for losing balance. I may do so here
in assembly lawfully. Spare me your anger.
Before this you have held me up to scorn
for lack of fighting spirit; old and young,
everyone knows the truth of that. In your case,
the son of crooked-minded Krónos gave you
one gift and not both: a staff of kingship
honored by all men, but no staying power—
the greatest gift of all.
What has come over you, to make you think
the Akhaians weak and craven as you say?
If you are in a passion to sail home,
sail on: the way is clear, the many ships
that made the voyage from Mykênê[41] with you
stand near the sea's edge. Others here will stay
until we plunder Troy! Or if they, too,
would like to, let them sail for their own country!
Sthénelos[42] and I will fight alone
until we see the destined end of Ilion.
We came here under god."

When Diomêdês
finished, a cry went up from all the Akhaians
in wonder at his words. Then Nestor stood
and spoke among them:
"Son of Tydeus, formidable
above the rest in war, in council, too,
you have more weight than others of your age.
No one will cry down what you say, no true

[41] **Mykênê:** Mycenae, Agamémnon's fortress city. [42] **Sthénelos:** Diomêdês' charioteer.

Akhaian will, or contradict you. Still,
you did not push on to the end.
I know you are young; in years you might well be
my last-born son, and yet for all of that
you kept your head and said what needed saying
before the Argive captains. My own part,
as I am older, is to drive it home.
No one will show contempt for what I say,
surely not Agamémnon, our commander.
Alien to clan and custom and hearth fire
is he who longs for war—heartbreaking war—
with his own people.
Let us yield to darkness
and make our evening meal. But let the sentries
take their rest on watch outside the rampart
near the moat; those are my orders for them.
Afterward, you direct us, Agamémnon,
by right of royal power. Provide a feast
for older men, your counselors. That is duty
and no difficulty: your huts are full of wine
brought over daily in our ships from Thrace
across the wide sea, and all provender
for guests is yours, as you are high commander.
Your counselors being met, pay heed to him
who counsels best. The army of Akhaia
bitterly needs a well-found plan of action.
The enemy is upon us, near the ships,
burning his thousand fires. What Akhaian
could be highhearted in that glare? This night
will see the army saved or brought to ruin."

They heeded him and did his will. Well-armed,
the sentries left to take their posts, one company
formed around Thrasymêdês, Nestor's son,
another mustered by Askálaphos
and Iálmenos, others commanded by
Meríonês, Aphareus, Dêípyros,
and Kreion's son, the princely Lykomêdês.
Seven lieutenants, each with a hundred men,
carrying long spears, issued from the camp
for outposts chosen between ditch and rampart.
Campfires were kindled, and they took their meal.

The son of Atreus led the elder men
together to his hut, where he served dinner,

and each man's hand went out upon the meal.
When they had driven hunger and thirst away,
Old Nestor opened their deliberations—
Nestor, whose counsel had seemed best before,
point by point weaving his argument:
"Lord Marshal of the army, Agamémnon,
as I shall end with you, so I begin,
since you hold power over a great army
and are responsible for it: the Lord Zeus
put in your keeping staff and precedent
that you might gather counsel for your men.
You should be first in discourse, but attentive
to what another may propose, to act on it
if he speak out for the good of all. Whatever
he may initiate, action is yours.
On this rule, let me speak as I think best.
A better view than mine no man can have,
the same view that I've held these many days
since that occasion when, my lord, for all
Akhilleus' rage, you took the girl Brisêis
out of his lodge—but not with our consent.
Far from it; I for one had begged you not to.
Just the same, you gave way to your pride,
and you dishonored a great prince,
a hero to whom the gods themselves do honor.
Taking his prize, you kept her and still do.
But even so, and even now, we may
contrive some way of making peace with him
by friendly gifts, and by affectionate words."

Then Agamémnon, the Lord Marshal, answered:
"Sir, there is nothing false in your account
of my blind errors. I committed them;
I will not now deny it. Troops of soldiers
are worth no more than one man cherished by Zeus
as he has cherished this man and avenged him,
overpowering the army of Akhaians.
I lost my head, I yielded to black anger,
but now I would retract it and appease him
with all munificence. Here before everyone
I may enumerate the gifts I'll give.
Seven new tripods and ten bars of gold,
then twenty shining caldrons, and twelve horses,
thoroughbreds, who by their wind and legs

have won me prizes: any man who owned
what these have brought me could not lack resources,
could not be pinched for precious gold—so many
prizes have these horses carried home.
Then I shall give him seven women, deft
in household handicraft—women of Lesbos
I chose when he himself took Lesbos town,
as they outshone all womankind in beauty.
These I shall give him, and one more, whom I
took away from him then: Briseus' daughter.
Concerning her, I add my solemn oath
I never went to bed or coupled with her,
as custom is with men and women.
These will be his at once. If the immortals
grant us the plundering of Priam's town,
let him come forward when the spoils are shared
and load his ship with bars of gold and bronze.
Then he may choose among the Trojan women
twenty that are most lovely, after Helen.
If we return to Argos of Akhaia,
flowing with good things of the earth, he'll be
my own adopted son, dear as Orestês,
born long ago and reared in bounteous peace.
I have three daughters now at home, Khrysóthemis,
Laódikê, and Iphiánassa.
He may take whom he will to be his bride
and pay no bridal gift, leading her home
to Pêleus' hall. But I shall add a dowry
such as no man has given to his daughter.
Seven flourishing strongholds I'll give him:
Kardamylê and Enopê and Hirê
in the wild grassland; holy Phêrai too,
and the deep meadowland of Ántheia,
Aipeia and the vineyard slope of Pêdasos,
all lying near the sea in the far west
of sandy Pylos. In these lands are men
who own great flocks and herds; now as his liegemen,
they will pay tithes and sumptuous honor to him,
prospering as they carry out his plans.
These are the gifts I shall arrange if he
desists from anger. Let him be subdued!
Lord Death indeed is deaf to appeal, implacable;
of all gods therefore he is most abhorrent
to mortal men. So let Akhilleus bow to me,

considering that I hold higher rank
and claim the precedence of age."

To this

Lord Nestor of Gerênia replied:
"Lord Marshal of the army, Agamémnon,
this time the gifts you offer Lord Akhilleus
are not to be despised. Come, we'll dispatch
our chosen emissaries to his quarters
as quickly as possible. Those men whom I
may designate, let them perform the mission.
Phoinix,[43] dear to Zeus, may lead the way.
Let Aías follow him, and Prince Odysseus.
The criers, Hódios and Eurýbatês,
may go as escorts. Bowls for their hands here!
Tell them to keep silence, while we pray
that Zeus the son of Krónos will be merciful."

Nestor's proposal fell on willing ears,
and criers came at once to tip out water
over their hands, while young men filled the winebowls
and dipped a measure into every cup.
They spilt their offerings and drank their fill,
then briskly left the hut of Agamémnon.
Nestor accompanied them with final words
and sage looks, especially for Odysseus,
as to the effort they should make to bring
the son of Pêleus round.

Following Phoinix,

Aías and Odysseus walked together
beside the tumbling clamorous whispering sea,
praying hard to the girdler of the islands° Poseidon
that they might easily sway their great friend's heart.
Amid the ships and huts of the Myrmidons
they found him, taking joy in a sweet harp
of rich and delicate make—the crossbar set
to hold the strings being silver. He had won it
when he destroyed the city of Eëtíôn,
and plucking it he took his joy: he sang
old tales of heroes, while across the room
alone and silent sat Patróklos, waiting
until Akhilleus should be done with song.

[43] **Phoinix:** Akhilleus's tutor.

Phoinix had come in unremarked, but when
the two new visitors, Odysseus leading,
entered and stood before him, then Akhilleus
rose in wonderment, and left his chair,
his harp still in his hand. So did Patróklos
rise at sight of the two men. Akhilleus
made both welcome with a gesture, saying:

"Peace! My two great friends, I greet your coming.
How I have needed it! Even in my anger,
of all Akhaians, you are closest to me."
And Prince Akhilleus led them in. He seated them
on easy chairs with purple coverlets,
and to Patróklos who stood near he said:
"Put out an ampler winebowl, use more wine
for stronger drink,[44] and place a cup for each.
Here are my dearest friends beneath my roof."

Patróklos did as his companion bade him.
Meanwhile the host set down a carving block
within the fire's rays; a chine of mutton
and a fat chine of goat he placed upon it,
as well as savory pork chine. Automédôn
steadied the meat for him, Akhilleus carved,
then sliced it well and forked it on the spits.
Meanwhile Patróklos, like a god in firelight,
made the hearth blaze up. When the leaping flame
had ebbed and died away, he raked the coals
and in the glow extended spits of meat,
lifting these at times from the firestones
to season with pure salt. When all was done
and the roast meat apportioned into platters,
loaves of bread were passed round by Patróklos
in fine baskets. Akhilleus served the meat.
He took his place then opposite Odysseus,
back to the other wall, and told
Patróklos to make offering to the gods.
This he did with meat tossed in the fire,
then each man's hand went out upon the meal.
When they had put their hunger and thirst away,
Aías nodded silently to Phoinix,
but Prince Odysseus caught the nod. He filled

[44] **use more . . . drink:** Wine was usually mixed with water.

a cup of wine and lifted it to Akhilleus,
saying:
"Health, Akhilleus. We've no lack
of generous feasts this evening—in the lodge
of Agamémnon first, and now with you,
good fare and plentiful each time.
It is not feasting that concerns us now,
however, but a ruinous defeat.
Before our very eyes we see it coming
and are afraid. By a blade's turn, our good ships
are saved or lost, unless you arm your valor.
Trojans and allies are encamped tonight
in pride before our ramparts, at our sterns,
and through their army burn a thousand fires.
These men are sure they cannot now be stopped
but will get through to our good ships. Lord Zeus
flashes and thunders for them on the right,[45]
and Hektor in his ecstasy of power
is mad for battle, confident in Zeus,
deferring to neither men nor gods. Pure frenzy
fills him, and he prays for the bright dawn
when he will shear our stern-post beaks away
and fire all our ships, while in the shipways
amid that holocaust he carries death
among our men, driven out by smoke. All this
I gravely fear; I fear the gods will make
good his threatenings, and our fate will be
to die here, far from the pastureland of Argos.
Rouse yourself, if even at this hour
you'll pitch in for the Akhaians and deliver them
from Trojan havoc. In the years to come
this day will be remembered pain for you
if you do not. No remedy, no remedy
will come to hand, once the great ill is done.
While there is time, think how to keep this evil
day from the Danáäns!
My dear lad,
how rightly in your case your father, Pêleus,
put it in his farewell, sending you out
from Phthía to take ship with Agamémnon!
'Now as to fighting power, child,' he said,
'if Hêra and Athêna wish, they'll give it.

[45] **flashes . . . on the right:** A favorable omen.

Control your passion, though, and your proud heart,
for gentle courtesy is a better thing.
Break off insidious quarrels, and young and old,
the Argives will respect you for it more.'
That was your old father's admonition:
you have forgotten. Still, even now, abandon
heart-wounding anger. If you will relent,
Agamémnon will match this change of heart
with gifts. Now listen and let me list for you
what just now in his quarters he proposed:
seven new tripods, and ten bars of gold,
then twenty shining caldrons, and twelve horses,
thoroughbreds, that by their wind and legs
have won him prizes: any man who owned
what these have brought him would not lack resources,
could not be pinched for precious gold—so many
prizes have these horses carried home.
Then he will give you seven women, deft
in household handicraft: women of Lesbos
chosen when you yourself took Lesbos town,
as they outshone all womankind in beauty.
These he will give you, and one more, whom he
took away from you then: Briseus' daughter,
concerning whom he adds a solemn oath
never to have gone to bed or coupled with her,
as custom is, my lord, with men and women.
These are all yours at once. If the immortals
grant us the pillaging of Priam's town,
you may come forward when the spoils are shared
and load your ship with bars of gold and bronze.
Then you may choose among the Trojan women
twenty that are most lovely, after Helen.
And then, if we reach Argos of Akhaia,
flowing with good things of the earth, you'll be
his own adopted son, dear as Orestês,
born long ago and reared in bounteous peace.
He has three daughters now at home, Khrysóthemis,
Laódikê, and Iphiánassa.
You may take whom you will to be your bride
and pay no gift when you conduct her home
to your ancestral hall. He'll add a dowry
such as no man has given to his daughter.
Seven flourishing strongholds he'll give to you:
Kardamylê and Enopê and Hirê
in the wild grassland; holy Phêrai too,

and the deep meadowland of Ántheia,
Aipeia and the vineyard slope of Pêdasos,
all lying near the sea in the far west
of sandy Pylos. In these lands are men
who own great flocks and herds; now as your liegemen,
they will pay tithes and sumptuous honor to you,
prospering as they carry out your plans.
These are the gifts he will arrange if you
desist from anger.
Even if you abhor
the son of Atreus all the more bitterly,
with all his gifts, take pity on the rest,
all the old army, worn to rags in battle.
These will honor you as gods are honored!
And ah, for these, what glory you may win!
Think: Hektor is your man this time: being crazed
with ruinous pride, believing there's no fighter
equal to him among those that our ships
brought here by sea, he'll put himself in range!"

Akhilleus the great runner answered him:
"Son of Laërtês and the gods of old,
Odysseus, master soldier and mariner,
I owe you a straight answer, as to how
I see this thing, and how it is to end.
No need to sit with me like mourning doves
making your gentle noise by turns. I hate
as I hate Hell's own gate that man who hides
one thought within him while he speaks another.
What I shall say is what I see and think.
Give in to Agamémnon? I think not,
neither to him nor to the rest. I had
small thanks for fighting, fighting without truce
against hard enemies here. The portion's equal
whether a man hangs back or fights his best;
the same respect, or lack of it, is given
brave man and coward. One who's active dies
like the do-nothing. What least thing have I
to show for it, for harsh days undergone
and my life gambled, all these years of war?
A bird will give her fledglings every scrap
she comes by, and go hungry, foraging.
That is the case with me.

Many a sleepless night I've spent afield
and many a day in bloodshed, hand to hand
in battle for the wives of other men.
In sea raids I plundered a dozen towns,
eleven in expeditions overland
through Trojan country, and the treasure taken
out of them all, great heaps of handsome things,
I carried back each time to Agamémnon.
He sat tight on the beachhead, and shared out
a little treasure; most of it he kept.
He gave prizes of war to his officers;
the rest have theirs, not I; from me alone
of all Akhaians, he pre-empted her.
He holds my bride, dear to my heart. Aye, let him
sleep with her and enjoy her!
Why must Argives
fight the Trojans? Why did he raise an army
and lead it here? For Helen, was it not?
Are the Atreidai of all mortal men
the only ones who love their wives? I think not.
Every sane decent fellow loves his own
and cares for her, as in my heart I loved
Brisêis, though I won her by the spear.
Now, as he took my prize out of my hands,
tricked and defrauded me, he need not tempt me;
I know him, and he cannot change my mind.
Let him take thought, Odysseus, with you
and others how the ships may be defended
against incendiary attack. By god,
he has achieved imposing work without me,
a rampart piled up overnight, a ditch
running beyond it, broad and deep,
with stakes implanted in it! All no use!
He cannot hold against the killer's charge.
As long as I was in the battle, Hektor
never cared for a fight far from the walls;
his limit was the oak tree by the gate.
When I was alone one day he waited there,
but barely got away when I went after him.
Now it is I who do not care to fight.
Tomorrow at dawn when I have made offering
to Zeus and all the gods, and hauled my ships
for loading in the shallows, if you like

and if it interests you, look out and see
my ships on Hellê's waters in the offing,[46]
oarsmen in line making the sea-foam scud!
And if the great Earthshaker° gives a breeze, Poseidon
the third day out I'll make it home to Phthía.
Rich possessions are there I left behind
when I was mad enough to come here; now
I take home gold and ruddy bronze, and women
belted luxuriously, and hoary iron,
all that came to me here. As for my prize,
he who gave her took her outrageously back.
Well, you can tell him all this to his face,
and let the other Akhaians burn
if he in his thick hide of shamelessness
picks out another man to cheat. He would not
look me in the eye, dog that he is!
I will not share one word of counsel with him,
nor will I act with him; he robbed me blind,
broke faith with me: he gets no second chance
to play me for a fool. Once is enough.
To hell with him, Zeus took his brains away!
His gifts I abominate, and I would give
not one dry shuck for him. I would not change,
not if he multiplied his gifts by ten,
by twenty times what he has now, and more,
no matter where they came from: if he gave
what enters through Orkhómenos'[47] town gate
or Thebes of Egypt, where the treasures lie—
that city where through each of a hundred gates
two hundred men drive out in chariots.
Not if his gifts outnumbered the sea sands
or all the dust grains in the world could Agamémnon
ever appease me—not till he pays me back
full measure, pain for pain, dishonor for dishonor.
The daughter of Agamémnon, son of Atreus,
I will not take in marriage. Let her be
as beautiful as pale-gold Aphrodítê,
skilled as Athêna of the sea-grey eyes,
I will not have her, at any price. No, let him
find someone else, an eligible Akhaian,
kinglier than I.

[46] **Hellê's . . . offing:** Hellespont (or Dardanelles). [47] **Orkhómenos:** City north of Athens.

Now if the gods
preserve me and I make it home, my father
Pêleus will select a bride for me.
In Hellas[48] and in Phthía there are many
daughters of strong men who defend the towns.
I'll take the one I wish to be my wife.
There in my manhood I have longed, indeed,
to marry someone of congenial mind
and take my ease, enjoying the great estate
my father had acquired.
Now I think
no riches can compare with being alive,
not even those they say this well-built Ilion
stored up in peace before the Akhaians came.
Neither could all the Archer's shrine contains
at rocky Pytho,[49] in the crypt of stone.
A man may come by cattle and sheep in raids;
tripods he buys, and tawny-headed horses;
but his life's breath cannot be hunted back
or be recaptured once it pass his lips.
My mother, Thetis of the silvery feet,
tells me of two possible destinies
carrying me toward death: two ways:
if on the one hand I remain to fight
around Troy town, I lose all hope of home
but gain unfading glory; on the other,
if I sail back to my own land my glory
fails—but a long life lies ahead for me.
To all the rest of you I say: 'Sail home:
you will not now see Ilion's last hour,'
for Zeus who views the wide world held his sheltering
hand over that city, and her troops
have taken heart.
Return, then, emissaries,
deliver my answer to the Akhaian peers—
it is the senior officer's privilege—
and let them plan some other way, and better,
to save their ships and save the Akhaian army.
This one cannot be put into effect—
their scheme this evening—while my anger holds.
Phoinix may stay and lodge the night with us,

[48] **Hellas:** A region in northern Greece; later it means Greece itself. [49] **Pytho:** Apollo's sanctuary at Delphi.

then take ship and sail homeward at my side
tomorrow, if he wills. I'll not constrain him."

After Akhilleus finished, all were silent,
awed, for he spoke with power.
Then the old master-charioteer, Lord Phoinix,
answered at last, and let his tears come shining,
fearing for the Akhaian ships:
"Akhilleus,
if it is true you set your heart on home
and will not stir a finger to save the ships
from being engulfed by fire—all for this rage
that has swept over you—how, child, could I
be sundered from you, left behind alone?
For your sake the old master-charioteer,
Pêleus, made provision that I should come,
that day he gave you godspeed out of Phthía
to go with Agamémnon. Still a boy,
you knew nothing of war that levels men
to the same testing, nothing of assembly
where men become illustrious. That is why
he sent me, to instruct you in these matters,
to be a man of eloquence and action.
After all that, dear child, I should not wish
to be left here apart from you—not even
if god himself should undertake to smooth
my wrinkled age and make me fresh and young,
as when for the first time I left the land
of lovely women, Hellas. I went north
to avoid a feud with Father, Amyntor
Orménidês. His anger against me rose
over a fair-haired slave girl whom he fancied,
without respect for his own wife, my mother.
Mother embraced my knees and begged that I
make love to this girl, so that afterward
she might be cold to the aging man. I did it.
My father guessed the truth at once, and cursed me,
praying the ghostly Furies[50] that no son
of mine should ever rest upon his knees:
a curse fulfilled by the immortals—Lord
Zeus of undergloom and cold Perséphonê.[51]

[50] **Furies:** Feminine spirits of revenge, especially for blood crimes. [51] **Perséphonê:** Queen of the underworld, wife of Hades.

I planned to put a sword in him, and would have,
had not some god unstrung my rage, reminding me
of country gossip and the frowns of men;
I shrank from being called a parricide
among the Akhaians. But from that time on
I felt no tie with home, no love for lingering
under the rooftree of a raging father.
Our household and our neighbors, it is true,
urged me to stay. They made a handsome feast
of shambling cattle butchered, and fat sheep;
young porkers by the litter, crisp with fat,
were singed and spitted in Hêphaistos' fire,
rivers of wine drunk from the old man's store.
Nine times they spent the night and slept beside me,
taking the watch by turns, leaving a fire
to flicker under the entrance colonnade,
and one more in the court outside my room.
But when the tenth night came, starless and black,
I cracked the tight bolt on my chamber door,
pushed out, and scaled the courtyard wall, unseen
by household men on watch or women slaves.
Then I escaped from that place, made my way
through Hellas where the dancing floors are wide,
until I came to Phthía's fertile plain,
mother of flocks, and Pêleus the king.
He gave me welcome, treated me with love,
as a father would an only son, his heir
to rich possessions. And he made me rich,
appointing me great numbers of retainers
on the frontier of Phthía, where I lived
as lord of Dolopês. Now, it was I
who formed your manhood, handsome as a god's,
Akhilleus: I who loved you from the heart;
for never in another's company
would you attend a feast or dine in hall—
never, unless I took you on my knees
and cut your meat, and held your cup of wine.
Many a time you wet my shirt, hiccuping
wine-bubbles in distress, when you were small.
Patient and laborious as a nurse
I had to be for you, bearing in mind
that never would the gods bring into being
any son of mine. Godlike Akhilleus,
you were the manchild that I made my own

to save me someday, so I thought, from misery.
Quell your anger, Akhilleus! You must not
be pitiless! The gods themselves relent,
and are they not still greater in bravery,
in honor and in strength? Burnt offerings,
courteous prayer, libation, smoke of sacrifice,
with all of these, men can placate the gods
when someone oversteps and errs. The truth is,
prayers are daughters of almighty Zeus—
one may imagine them lame, wrinkled things
with eyes cast down, that toil to follow after
passionate Folly. Folly is strong and swift,
outrunning all the prayers, and everywhere
arriving first to injure mortal men;
still they come healing after. If a man
reveres the daughters of Zeus when they come near,
he is rewarded, and his prayers are heard;
but if he spurns them and dismisses them,
they make their way to Zeus again and ask
that Folly dog that man till suffering
has taken arrogance out of him.
Relent,
be courteous to the daughters of Zeus, you too,
as courtesy sways others, and the best.
If Agamémnon had no gifts for you,
named none to follow, but inveighed against you
still in fury, then I could never say,
'Discard your anger and defend the Argives—'
never, no matter how they craved your help.
But this is not so: he will give many things
at once; he promised others; he has sent
his noblest men to intercede with you,
the flower of the army, and your friends,
dearest among the Argives. Will you turn
their words, their coming, into humiliation?
Until this moment, no one took it ill
that you should suffer anger; we learned this
from the old stories of how towering wrath
could overcome great men; but they were still
amenable to gifts and to persuasion.
Here is an instance I myself remember
not from our own time but in ancient days:
I'll tell it to you all, for all are friends.

The Kourêtês were fighting a warlike race,[52]
Aitolians, around the walls of Kálydôn,
with slaughter on both sides: Aitolians
defending their beloved Kálydôn
while the Kourêtês longed to sack the town.
The truth is, Artemis of the Golden Chair
had brought the scourge of war on the Aitolians;
she had been angered because Oineus[53] made
no harvest offering from his vineyard slope.
While other gods enjoyed his hekatombs
he made her none, either forgetful of it
or careless—a great error, either way.
In her anger, the Mistress of Long Arrows
roused against him a boar with gleaming tusks
out of his wild grass bed, a monstrous thing
that ravaged the man's vineyard many times
and felled entire orchards, roots,
blooms, apples and all. Now this great boar
Meléagros, the son of Oineus, killed
by gathering men and hounds from far and near.
So huge the boar was, no small band could master him,
and he brought many to the dolorous pyre.
Around the dead beast Artemis set on
a clash with battlecries between Kourêtês
and proud Aitolians over the boar's head
and shaggy hide. As long, then, as Meléagros,
backed by the wargod, fought, the Kourêtês
had the worst of it for all their numbers
and could not hold a line outside the walls.
But then a day came when Meléagros
was stung by venomous anger that infects
the coolest thinker's heart: swollen with rage
at his own mother, Althaiê, he languished
in idleness at home beside his lady,
Kleopátrê.
This lovely girl was born
to Marpessê of ravishing pale ankles,[54]

---

[52] **Kourêtês . . . race:** The Kourêtês and the Aitolians were once friends, but now are enemies. [53] **Oineus:** King of Kálydôn. [54] **Marpessê . . . ankles:** A daughter of Euênos, Marpessê was wooed by Apollo, but a mortal, Idês, carried her off; when Apollo caught them, Idês and Apollo were about to fight, when Marpessê was allowed to choose between them and she chose Idês. They gave their daughter Kleopátrê a second name, Alkýonê, meaning a seabird that mourns for its mate.

Euênos' child, and Idês, who had been
most powerful of men on earth. He drew
the bow against the Lord Phoibos Apollo
over his love, Marpessê, whom her father
and gentle mother called Alkýonê,
since for her sake her mother gave that seabird's
forlorn cry when Apollo ravished her.
With Kleopátrê lay Meléagros,
nursing the bitterness his mother stirred,
when in her anguish over a brother slain[55]
she cursed her son. She called upon the gods,
beating the grassy earth with both her hands
as she pitched forward on her knees, with cries
to the Lord of Undergloom and cold Perséphonê,
while tears wetted her veils—in her entreaty
that death come to her son. Inexorable
in Érebos[56] a vampire Fury listened.
Soon, then, about the gates of the Aitolians
tumult and din of war grew loud; their towers
rang with blows. And now the elder men
implored Meléagros to leave his room,
and sent the high priests of the gods, imploring him
to help defend the town. They promised him
a large reward: in the green countryside
of Kálydôn, wherever it was richest,
there he might choose a beautiful garden plot
of fifty acres, half in vineyard, half
in virgin prairie for the plow to cut.
Oineus, master of horsemen, came with prayers
upon the doorsill of the chamber, often
rattling the locked doors, pleading with his son.
His sisters, too, and then his gentle mother
pleaded with him. Only the more fiercely
he turned away. His oldest friends, his dearest,
not even they could move him—not until
his room was shaken by a hail of stones
as Kourêtês began to scale the walls
and fire the city.
Then at last his lady
in her soft-belted gown besought him weeping,
speaking of all the ills that come to men

[55] **a brother slain:** Meléagros had killed one of his mother's brothers. [56] **Érebos:** A region in the underworld.

whose town is taken: soldiers put to the sword;
the city razed by fire; alien hands
carrying off the children and the women.
Hearing these fearful things, his heart was stirred
to action: he put on his shining gear
and fought off ruin from the Aitolians.
Mercy prevailed in him. His folk no longer
cared to award him gifts and luxuries,
yet even so he saved that terrible day.
Oh, do not let your mind go so astray!
Let no malignant spirit
turn you that way, dear son! It will be worse
to fight for ships already set afire!
Value the gifts; rejoin the war; Akhaians
afterward will give you a god's honor.
If you reject the gifts and then, later,
enter the deadly fight, you will not be
accorded the same honor, even though
you turn the tide of war!"

But the great runner
Akhilleus answered:
"Old uncle Phoinix, bless you,
that is an honor I can live without.
Honored I think I am by Zeus's justice,
justice that will sustain me by the ships
as long as breath is in me and I can stand.
Here is another point: ponder it well:
best not confuse my heart with lamentation
for Agamémnon, whom you must not honor;
you would be hateful to me, dear as you are.
Loyalty should array you at my side
in giving pain to him who gives me pain.
Rule with me equally, share half my honor,
but do not ask my help for Agamémnon.
My answer will be reported by these two.
Lodge here in a soft bed, and at first light
we can decide whether to sail or stay."

He knit his brows and nodded to Patróklos
to pile up rugs for Phoinix' bed — a sign
for the others to be quick about departing.
Aías, however, noble son of Télamôn
made the last appeal. He said:
"Odysseus,

master soldier and mariner, let us go.
I do not see the end of this affair
achieved by this night's visit. Nothing for it
but to report our talk for what it's worth
to the Danáäns, who sit waiting there.
Akhilleus hardened his great heart against us,
wayward and savage as he is, unmoved
by the affections of his friends who made him
honored above all others on the beachhead.
There is no pity in him. A normal man
will take the penalty for a brother slain
or a dead son. By paying much, the one
who did the deed may stay unharmed at home.
Fury and pride in the bereaved are curbed
when he accepts the penalty. Not you.
Cruel and unappeasable rage the gods
put in you for one girl alone. We offer
seven beauties, and much more besides!
Be gentler, and respect your own rooftree
whereunder we are guests who speak for all
Danáäns as a body. Our desire
is to be closest to you of them all."

Akhilleus the great runner answered him:
"Scion° of Télamôn and gods of old, Offspring
Aías, lord of fighting men, you seemed
to echo my own mind in what you said!
And yet my heart grows large and hot with fury
remembering that affair: as though I were
some riffraff or camp follower, he taunted me
before them all!
Go back, report the news:
I will not think of carnage or of war
until Prince Hektor, son of Priam, reaches
Myrmidon huts and ships in his attack,
slashing through Argives, burning down their ships.
Around my hut, my black ship, I foresee
for all his fury, Hektor will break off combat."
That was his answer. Each of the emissaries
took up a double-handed cup and poured
libation by the shipways. Then Odysseus
led the way on their return. Patróklos
commanded his retainers and the maids
to make at once a deep-piled bed for Phoinix.

Obediently they did so, spreading out
fleeces and coverlet and a linen sheet,
and down the old man lay, awaiting Dawn.
Akhilleus slept in the well-built hut's recess,
and with him lay a woman he had brought
from Lesbos, Phorbas' daughter, Diomêdê.
Patróklos went to bed at the other end,
and with him, too, a woman lay—soft-belted
Iphis, who had been given to him by Akhilleus
when he took Skyros, ringed by cliff, the mountain
fastness of Enyéus.
Now the emissaries
arrived at Agamémnon's lodge. With cups
of gold held up, and rising to their feet
on every side, the Akhaians greeted them,
curious for the news. Lord Agamémnon
put the question first:
"Come, tell me, sir,
Odysseus, glory of Akhaia—will Akhilleus
fight off ravenous fire from the ships
or does he still refuse, does anger still
hold sway in his great heart?"

That patient man,
the Prince Odysseus, made reply:
"Excellency,
Lord Marshal of the army, son of Atreus,
the man has no desire to quench his rage.
On the contrary, he is more than ever
full of anger, spurns you and your gifts,
calls on you to work out your own defense
to save the ships and the Akhaian army.
As for himself, he threatens at daybreak
to drag his well-found ships into the surf,
and says he would advise the rest as well
to sail for home. 'You shall not see,' he says,
'the last hour that awaits tall Ilion,
for Zeus who views the wide world held his sheltering
hand over the city, and her troops
have taken heart.' That was Akhilleus' answer.
Those who were with me can confirm all this,
Aías can, and the two clearheaded criers.
As to old Phoinix, he is sleeping there
by invitation, so that he may sail

to his own country, homeward with Akhilleus,
tomorrow, if he wills, without constraint."

When he had finished everyone was still,
sitting in silence and in perturbation
for a long time. At last brave Diomêdês,
lord of the warcry, said:
"Excellency,
Lord Marshal of the army, Agamémnon,
you never should have pled with him, or given
so many gifts to him. At the best of times
he is a proud man; now you have pushed him far
deeper into his vanity and pride.
By god, let us have done with him—
whether he goes or stays! He'll fight again
when the time comes, whenever his blood is up
or the god rouses him. As for ourselves,
let everyone now do as I advise
and go to rest. Your hearts have been refreshed
with bread and wine, the pith and nerve of men.
When the fair Dawn with finger tips of rose
makes heaven bright, deploy your men and horses
before the ships at once, and cheer them on,
and take your place, yourself, in the front line
to join the battle."

All gave their assent
in admiration of Diomêdês,
breaker of horses. When they had spilt their wine
they all dispersed, each man to his own hut,
and lying down they took the gift of sleep.

FROM BOOK 16
A SHIP FIRED, A TIDE TURNED

[In Book 10, Diomêdês and Odysseus volunteer to spy behind enemy lines, where they kill Rhesos, the Thracian king, and steal his horses. In Book 11, the Akhaians prevail the next day and drive the Trojans back to Troy's walls, then again lose ground. Nestor urges Patróklos to disguise himself in Akhilleus' armor and lead the Myrmidons into battle. In Book 12, Hektor breaks through the wall defending the Akhaian ships and the Trojans charge through the breach. In Book 13, Idomeneus and Aías heroically hold off the Trojans. In Book 14, Agamémnon recommends abandoning the war, but then the Akhaians force the Trojans to retreat. In Book 15, the Trojans regain their lost ground and are on the verge of burning the Akhaian ships and ending the war. Book 16 begins with a request from Patróklos to enter the war and fight in Akhilleus's armor. In order to defend the fifty ships that he brought to Troy, Akhilleus reluctantly gives his permission, and his troops, the Myrmidons, brace for battle.]

. . . Before them all
two captains stood in gear of war: Patróklos
and Automédôn, of one mind, resolved
to open combat in the lead.
Akhilleus
went to his hut. He lifted up the lid
of a seachest, all intricately wrought,
that Thetis of the silver feet had stowed
aboard his ship for him to take to Ilion,
filled to the brim with shirts, wind-breaking cloaks,
and fleecy rugs. His hammered cup was there,
from which no other man drank the bright wine,
and he made offering to no god but Zeus.
Lifting it from the chest, he purified it
first with brimstone, washed it with clear water,
and washed his hands, then dipped it full of wine.
Now standing in the forecourt, looking up
toward heaven, he prayed and poured his offering out,
and Zeus who plays in thunder heard his prayer:
"Zeus of Dôdôna,[57] god of Pelasgians,
O god whose home lies far! Ruler of wintry
harsh Dôdôna! Your interpreters,
the Selloi, live with feet like roots, unwashed,
and sleep on the hard ground. My lord, you heard me
praying before this, and honored me
by punishing the Akhaian army. Now,
again, accomplish what I most desire.
I shall stay on the beach, behind the ships,
but send my dear friend with a mass of soldiers,
Myrmidons, into combat. Let your glory,
Zeus who view the wide world, go beside him.
Sir, exalt his heart,
so Hektor too may see whether my friend
can only fight when I am in the field,
or whether singlehanded he can scatter them
before his fury! When he has thrown back
their shouting onslaught from the ships, then let him
return unhurt to the shipways and to me,
his gear intact, with all his fighting men."

That was his prayer, and Zeus who views the wide world
heard him. Part he granted, part denied:
he let Patróklos push the heavy fighting

[57] **Dôdôna:** Zeus's principal shrine is at Dôdôna.

back from the ships, but would not let him come
unscathed from battle.
Now, after Akhilleus
had made his prayer and offering to Zeus,
he entered his hut again, restored the cup
to his seachest, and took his place outside—
desiring still to watch the savage combat
of Trojans and Akhaians. Brave Patróklos'
men moved forward with high hearts until
they charged the Trojans—Myrmidons in waves,
like hornets that small boys, as boys will do,
the idiots, poke up with constant teasing
in their daub chambers on the road,
to give everyone trouble. If some traveler
who passes unaware should then excite them,
all the swarm comes raging out
to defend their young. So hot, so angrily
the Myrmidons came pouring from the ships
in a quenchless din of shouting. And Patróklos
cried above them all:
"O Myrmidons,
brothers-in-arms of Pêleus' son, Akhilleus,
fight like men, dear friends, remember courage,
let us win honor for the son of Pêleus!
He is the greatest captain on the beach,
his officers and soldiers are the bravest!
Let King Agamémnon learn his folly
in holding cheap the best of the Akhaians!"

Shouting so, he stirred their hearts. They fell
as one man on the Trojans, and the ships
around them echoed the onrush and the cries.
On seeing Menoitios' powerful son, and with him
Automédôn, aflash with brazen gear,
the Trojan ranks broke, and they caught their breath,
imagining that Akhilleus the swift fighter
had put aside his wrath for friendship's sake.
Now each man kept an eye out for retreat
from sudden death. Patróklos drove ahead
against their center with his shining spear,
into the huddling mass, around the stern
of Prôtesílaos' burning ship. He hit
Pyraikhmês, who had led the Paiônês
from Amydôn, from Áxios' wide river—
hit him in the right shoulder. Backward in dust

he tumbled groaning, and his men-at-arms,
the Paiônês, fell back around him. Dealing
death to a chief and champion, Patróklos
drove them in confusion from the ship,
and doused the tigerish fire. The hull half-burnt
lay smoking on the shipway. Now the Trojans
with a great outcry streamed away; Danáäns
poured along the curved ships, and the din
of war kept on. As when the lightning master,
Zeus, removes a dense cloud from the peak
of some great mountain, and the lookout points
and spurs and clearings are distinctly seen
as though pure space had broken through from heaven:
so when the dangerous fire had been repelled
Danáäns took breath for a space. The battle
had not ended, though; not yet were Trojans
put to rout by the Akhaian charge
or out of range of the black ships. They withdrew
but by regrouping tried to make a stand.
In broken
ranks the captains sought and killed each other,
Menoitios' son making the first kill.
As Arêilykos wheeled around to fight,
he caught him with his spearhead in the hip,
and drove the bronze through, shattering the bone.
He sprawled face downward on the ground.
Now veteran
Meneláos thrusting past the shield
of Thoas to the bare chest brought him down.
Rushed by Ámphiklos, the alert Mégês
got his thrust in first, hitting his thigh
where a man's muscles bunch. Around the spearhead
tendons were split, and darkness veiled his eyes.
Nestor's sons were in action: Antílokhos
with his good spear brought down Atýmnios,
laying open his flank; he fell headfirst.
Now Maris moved in, raging for his brother,
lunging over the dead man with his spear,
but Thrasymêdês had already lunged
and did not miss, but smashed his shoulder squarely,
tearing his upper arm out of the socket,
severing muscles, breaking through the bone.
He thudded down and darkness veiled his eyes.
So these two, overcome by the two brothers,
dropped to the underworld of Érebos.

They were Sarpêdôn's true brothers-in-arms
and sons of Amisôdaros, who reared
the fierce Khimaira,[58] nightmare to many men.
Aías,[59] Oileus' son, drove at Kleóboulos
and took him alive, encumbered in the press,
but killed him on the spot with a sword stroke
across his nape—the whole blade running hot
with blood, as welling death and his harsh destiny
possessed him. Now Pênéleos
and Lykón clashed; as both had cast and missed
and lunged and missed with spears,
they fought again with swords. The stroke of Lykôn
came down on the other's helmet ridge
but his blade broke at the hilt. Pênéleos
thrust at his neck below the ear and drove
the blade clear in and through; his head toppled,
held only by skin, and his knees gave way.
Meríonês on the run overtook Akámas
mounting behind his horses and hit his shoulder,
knocking him from the car. Mist swathed his eyes.
Idómeneus thrust hard at Erýmas' mouth
with his hard bronze. The spearhead passed on through
beneath his brain and split the white brain-pan.
His teeth were dashed out, blood filled both his eyes,
and from his mouth and nostrils as he gaped
he spurted blood. Death's cloud enveloped him.
There each Danáän captain killed his man.
As ravenous wolves come down on lambs and kids
astray from some flock that in hilly country
splits in two by a shepherd's negligence,
and quickly wolves bear off the defenseless things,
so when Danááns fell on Trojans, shrieking
flight was all they thought of, not of combat.
Aías the Tall[60] kept after bronze-helmed Hektor,
casting his lance, but Hektor, skilled in war,
would fit his shoulders under the bull's-hide shield,
and watch for whizzing arrows, thudding spears.
Aye, though he knew the tide of battle turned,
he kept his discipline and saved his friends.
As when Lord Zeus would hang the sky with storm,
a cloud may enter heaven from Olympos

[58] **Khimaira:** Also Chimera: a being with a lion's head, a goat's body, and a serpent's tail. [59] **Aías:** A different Aías from the earlier warrior. [60] **Aías the Tall:** The famous warrior from the earlier books.

out of crystalline space, so terror and cries
increased about the shipways. In disorder
men withdrew. Then Hektor's chariot team
cantering bore him off with all his gear,
leaving the Trojans whom the moat confined;
and many chariot horses in that ditch,
breaking their poles off at the tip, abandoned
war-cars and masters. Hard on their heels
Patróklos kept on calling all Danáäns
onward with slaughter in his heart. The Trojans,
yelling and clattering, filled all the ways,
their companies cut in pieces. High in air
a blast of wind swept on, under the clouds,
as chariot horses raced back toward the town
away from the encampment. And Patróklos
rode shouting where he saw the enemy mass
in uproar: men fell from their chariots
under the wheels and cars jounced over them,
and running horses leapt over the ditch—
immortal horses, whom the gods gave Pêleus,
galloping as their mettle called them onward
after Hektor, target of Patróklos.
But Hektor's battle-team bore him away.

As under a great storm black earth is drenched
on an autumn day, when Zeus pours down the rain
in scudding gusts to punish men, annoyed
because they will enforce their crooked judgments
and banish justice from the market place,
thoughtless of the gods' vengeance; all their streams
run high and full, and torrents cut their way
down dry declivities into the swollen sea
with a hoarse clamor, headlong out of hills,
while cultivated fields erode away—
such was the gasping flight of the Trojan horses.

When he had cut their first wave off, Patróklos
forced it back again upon the ships
as the men fought toward the city. In between
the ships and river and the parapet
he swept among them killing, taking toll
for many dead Akhaians. First,
thrusting past Prónoös' shield, he hit him
on the bare chest, and made him crumple: down
he tumbled with a crash. Then he rushed Thestôr,

Enop's son, who sat all doubled up
in a polished war-car, shocked out of his wits,
the reins flown from his hands—and the Akhaian
got home his thrust on the right jawbone, driving
through his teeth. He hooked him by the spearhead
over the chariot rail, as a fisherman
on a point of rock will hook a splendid fish
with line and dazzling bronze out of the ocean:
so from his chariot on the shining spear
he hooked him gaping and face downward threw him,
life going out of him as he fell.

Patróklos
now met Erýlaos' rush and hit him square
mid-skull with a big stone. Within his helm
the skull was cleft asunder, and down he went
headfirst to earth; heartbreaking death engulfed him.
Next Erýmas, Amphóteros, Epaltês,
Tlêpolemos Damastoridês, Ekhíos,
Pyris, Ipheus, Euíppos, Polymêlos,
all in quick succession he brought down
to the once peaceful pastureland.

Sarpêdôn,
seeing his brothers-in-arms in their unbelted
battle jackets downed at Patróklos' hands,
called in bitterness to the Lykians:
"Shame, O Lykians, where are you running?
Now you show your speed!

I'll take on this one,
and learn what man he is that has the power
to do such havoc as he has done among us,
cutting down so many, and such good men."

He vaulted from his car with all his gear,
and on his side Patróklos, when he saw him,
leapt from his car. Like two great birds of prey
with hooked talons and angled beaks, who screech
and clash on a high ridge of rock, these two
rushed one another with hoarse cries. But Zeus,
the son of crooked-minded Krónos, watched,
and pitied them. He said to Hêra:

"Ai!
Sorrow for me, that in the scheme of things
the dearest of men to me must lie in dust
before the son of Menoitios, Patróklos.

My heart goes two ways as I ponder this:
shall I catch up Sarpêdôn
out of the mortal fight with all its woe
and put him down alive in Lykia,[61]
in that rich land? Or shall I make him fall
beneath Patróklos' hard-thrown spear?"

Then Hêra
of the wide eyes answered him:
"O fearsome power,
my Lord Zeus, what a curious thing to say.
A man who is born to die, long destined for it,
would you set free from that unspeakable end?
Do so; but not all of us will praise you.
And this, too, I may tell you: ponder this:
should you dispatch Sarpêdôn home alive,
anticipate some other god's desire
to pluck a man he loves out of the battle.
Many who fight around the town of Priam
sprang from immortals; you'll infuriate these.
No, dear to you though he is, and though you mourn him,
let him fall, even so, in the rough battle,
killed by the son of Menoitios, Patróklos.
Afterward, when his soul is gone, his lifetime
ended, Death and sweetest Sleep can bear him
homeward to the broad domain of Lykia.
There friends and kin may give him funeral
with tomb and stone, the trophies of the dead."

To this the father of gods and men agreed,
but showered bloody drops upon the earth
for the dear son Patróklos would destroy
in fertile Ilion, far from his home.
When the two men had come in range, Patróklos
turned like lightning against Thrasydêmos,
a tough man ever at Sarpêdôn's side,
and gave him a death-wound in the underbelly.
Sarpêdôn's counterthrust went wide, but hit
the trace horse, Pêdasos, in the right shoulder.
Screaming harshly, panting his life away,
he crashed and whinnied in the dust; the spirit
left him with a wingbeat. The team shied

[61] **Lykia:** Lykia, south of Troy, ruled by Sarpêdôn.

and strained apart with a great creak of the yoke
as reins were tangled over the dead weight
of their outrider fallen. Automédôn,
the good soldier, found a way to end it:
pulling his long blade from his hip
he jumped in fast and cut the trace horse free.
The team then ranged themselves beside the pole,
drawing the reins taut, and once more,
devoured by fighting madness, the two men clashed.
Sarpêdôn missed again. He drove his spearhead
over the left shoulder of Patróklos,
not even grazing him. Patróklos then
made his last throw, and the weapon left his hand
with flawless aim. He hit his enemy
just where the muscles of the diaphragm
encased his throbbing heart. Sarpêdôn fell
the way an oak or poplar or tall pine
goes down, when shipwrights in the wooded hills
with whetted axes chop it down for timber.
So, full length, before his war-car lay
Sarpêdôn raging, clutching the bloody dust.
Imagine a greathearted sultry bull
a lion kills amid a shambling herd:
with choking groans he dies under the claws.
So, mortally wounded by Patróklos
the chief of Lykian shieldsmen lay in agony
and called his friend by name:
"Glaukos, old man,
old war-dog, now's the time to be a spearman!
Put your heart in combat! Let grim war
be all your longing! Quickly, if you can,
arouse the Lykian captains, round them up
to fight over Sarpêdôn. You, too, fight
to keep my body, else in later days
this day will be your shame. You'll hang your head
all your life long, if these Akhaians take
my armor here, where I have gone down fighting
before the ships. Hold hard; cheer on the troops!"

The end of life came on him as he spoke,
closing his eyes and nostrils. And Patróklos
with one foot on his chest drew from his belly
spearhead and spear; the diaphragm came out,
so he extracted life and blade together.

Myrmidons clung to the panting Lykian horses,
rearing to turn the car left by their lords.

But bitter anguish at Sarpêdôn's voice
had come to Glaukos, and his heart despaired
because he had not helped his friend. He gripped
his own right arm and squeezed it, being numb
where Teukros with a bowshot from the rampart
had hit him while he fought for his own men,[62]
and he spoke out in prayer to Lord Apollo:
"Hear me, O lord, somewhere in Lykian farmland
or else in Troy: for you have power to listen
the whole world round to a man hard pressed as I!
I have my sore wound, all my length of arm
a-throb with lancing pain; the flow of blood
cannot be stanched; my shoulder's heavy with it.
I cannot hold my spear right or do battle,
cannot attack them. Here's a great man destroyed,
Sarpêdôn, son of Zeus. Zeus let his own son
die undefended. O my lord, heal this wound,
lull me my pains, put vigor in me! Let me
shout to my Lykians, move them into combat!
Let me give battle for the dead man here!"

This way he prayed, and Phoibos Apollo heard him,
cutting his pain and making the dark blood dry
on his deep wound, then filled his heart with valor.
Glaukos felt the change, and knew with joy
how swiftly the great god had heard his prayer.
First he appealed to the Lykian captains, going
right and left, to defend Sarpêdôn's body,
then on the run he followed other Trojans,
Poulýdamas, Pánthoös' son, Agênor,
and caught up with Aineías and with Hektor,
shoulder to shoulder, urgently appealing:
"Hektor, you've put your allies out of mind,
those men who give their lives here for your sake
so distant from their friends and lands: you will not
come to their aid! Sarpêdôn lies there dead,
commander of the Lykians, who kept
his country safe by his firm hand, in justice!

[62] **Teukros . . . own men:** A reference to events in Book 12.

Arês in bronze has brought him down: the spear
belonged to Patróklos. Come, stand with me, friends,
and count it shame if they strip off his gear
or bring dishonor on his body—these
fresh Myrmidons enraged for the Danááns
cut down at the shipways by our spears!"

At this, grief and remorse possessed the Trojans,
grief not to be borne, because Sarpêdôn
had been a bastion of the town of Troy,
foreigner though he was. A host came with him,
but he had fought most gallantly of all.
They made straight for the Danááns, and Hektor
led them, hot with anger for Sarpêdôn.
Patróklos in his savagery cheered on
the Akhaians, first the two named Aías, both
already aflame for war:
"Aías and Aías,
let it be sweet to you to stand and fight!
You always do; be lionhearted, now.
The man who crossed the rampart of Akhaians
first of all lies dead: Sarpêdôn.[63] May we
take him, dishonor him, and strip his arms,
and hurl any friend who would defend him
into the dust with our hard bronze!"

At this they burned to throw the Trojans back.
And both sides reinforced their battle lines,
Trojans and Lykians, Myrmidons and Akhaians,
moving up to fight around the dead
with fierce cries and clanging of men's armor.
Zeus unfurled a deathly gloom of night
over the combat, making battle toil
about his dear son's body a fearsome thing.
At first, the Trojans drove back the Akhaians,
fiery-eyed as they were; one Myrmidon,
and not the least, was killed: noble Epeigeus,
a son of Agaklês. In Boudeion,
a flourishing town, he ruled before the war,
but slew a kinsman. So he came as suppliant
to Pêleus and to Thetis, who enlisted him
along with Lord Akhilleus, breaker of men,

[63] **Sarpêdôn:** In Book 12, it says that Hektor broke through the rampart first.

to make war in the wild-horse country of Ilion
against the Trojans. Even as he touched the dead man,
Hektor hit him square upon the crest
with a great stone: his skull split in the helmet,
and he fell prone upon the corpse. Death's cloud
poured round him, heart-corroding. Grief and pain
for this friend dying came to Lord Patróklos,
who pounced through spear-play like a diving hawk
that puts jackdaws and starlings wildly to flight:
straight through Lykians, through Trojans, too,
you drove, Patróklos, master of horse,
in fury for your friend. Sthenélaos
the son of Ithaiménês was the victim:
Patróklos with a great stone broke his nape-cord.

Backward the line bent, Hektor too gave way,
as far as a hunting spear may hurtle, thrown
by a man in practice or in competition
or matched with deadly foes in war. So far
the Trojans ebbed, as the Akhaians drove them.
Glaukos, commander of Lykians, turned first,
to bring down valorous Báthyklês, the son
of Khalkôn, one who had his home in Hellas,
fortunate and rich among the Myrmidons.
Whirling as this man caught him, Glaukos hit him
full in the breastbone with his spear, and down
he thudded on his face. The Akhaians grieved
to see their champion fallen, but great joy
came to the Trojans, and they thronged about him.
Not that Akhaians now forgot their courage,
no, for their momentum carried them on.
Meríonês brought down a Trojan soldier,
Laógonos, Onêtor's rugged son,
a priest of Zeus on Ida, honored there
as gods are. Gashed now under jaw and ear
his life ran out, and hateful darkness took him.
Then at Meríonês Aineías cast
his bronze-shod spear, thinking to reach his body
under the shield as he came on. But he
looked out for it and swerved, slipping the spear-throw,
bowing forward, so the long shaft stuck
in earth behind him and the butt quivered;
the god Arês deprived it of its power.
Aineías raged and sneered:
"Meríonês,

fast dodger that you are, if I had hit you
my spearhead would have stopped your dance for good!"
Meríonês, good spearman, answered him:
"For all your power, Aineías, you could hardly
quench the fighting spirit of every man
defending himself against you. You are made
of mortal stuff like me. I, too, can say,
if I could hit you square, then tough and sure
as you may be, you would concede the game
and give your soul to the lord of nightmare, Death."

Patróklos said to him sharply:
"Meríonês,
you have your skill, why make a speech about it?
No, old friend, rough words will make no Trojans
back away from the body. Many a one
will be embraced by earth before they do.
War is the use of arms, words are for council.
More talk's pointless now; we need more fighting!"

He pushed on, and godlike Meríonês
fought at his side. Think of the sound of strokes
woodcutters make in mountain glens, the echoes
ringing for listeners far away: just so
the battering din of these in combat rose
from earth where the living go their ways—the clang
of bronze, hard blows on leather, on bull's hide,
as longsword blades and spearheads met their marks.
And an observer could not by now have seen
the Prince Sarpêdôn, since from head to foot
he lay enwrapped in weapons, dust, and blood.
Men kept crowding around the corpse. Like flies
that swarm and drone in farmyards round the milkpails
on spring days, when the pails are splashed with milk:
just so they thronged around the corpse. And Zeus
would never turn his shining eyes away
from this mêlée, but watched them all and pondered
long over the slaughter of Patróklos—
whether in that place, on Sarpêdôn's body,
Hektor should kill the man and take his gear,
or whether he, Zeus, should augment the moil° turmoil
of battle for still other men. He weighed it
and thought this best: that for a while Akhilleus'
shining brother-in-arms should drive his foes
and Hektor in the bronze helm toward the city,

taking the lives of many. First of all
he weakened Hektor, made him mount his car
and turn away, retreating, crying out
to others to retreat: for he perceived
the dipping scales of Zeus.[64] At this the Lykians
themselves could not stand fast, but all turned back,
once they had seen their king struck to the heart,
lying amid swales of dead—for many
fell to earth beside him when Lord Zeus
had drawn the savage battle line. So now
Akhaians lifted from Sarpêdôn's shoulders
gleaming arms of bronze, and these Patróklos
gave to his soldiers to be carried back
to the decked ships. At this point, to Apollo
Zeus who gathers cloud said:
"Wipe away the blood mantling Sarpêdôn;
take him up, out of the play of spears,
a long way off, and wash him in the river,
anoint him with ambrosia, put ambrosial
clothing on him. Then have him conveyed
by those escorting spirits quick as wind,
sweet Sleep and Death, who are twin brothers. These
will set him down in the rich broad land of Lykia,
and there his kin and friends may bury him
with tomb and stone, the trophies of the dead."

Attentive to his father, Lord Apollo
went down the foothills of Ida[65] to the field
and lifted Prince Sarpêdôn clear of it.
He bore him far and bathed him in the river,
scented him with ambrosia, put ambrosial
clothing on him, then had him conveyed
by those escorting spirits quick as wind,
sweet Sleep and Death, who are twin brothers. These
returned him to the rich broad land of Lykia.

Patróklos, calling to his team, commanding
Automédôn, rode on after the Trojans
and Lykians—all this to his undoing,
the blunderer. By keeping Akhilleus' mandate,
he might have fled black fate and cruel death.
But overpowering is the mind of Zeus

[64] **dipping . . . Zeus:** Zeus's scales for measuring the progress of the war. [65] **Ida:** Mountain near Troy.

forever, matched with man's. He turns in fright
the powerful man and robs him of his victory
easily, though he drove him on himself.
So now he stirred Patróklos' heart to fury.

Whom first, whom later did you kill in battle,
Patróklos, when the gods were calling deathward?
First it was Adrêstos, Autônoös,
and Ekheklos; then Périmos Megadês,
Eristôr, Melánippos; afterward,
Elasos, Moulios, Pylartês. These
he cut down, while the rest looked to their flight.
Troy of the towering gates was on the verge
of being taken by the Akhaians, under
Patróklos' drive: he raced with blooded spear
ahead and around it. On the massive tower
Phoibos Apollo stood as Troy's defender,
deadly toward him. Now three times Patróklos
assaulted the high wall at the tower joint,
and three times Lord Apollo threw him back
with counterblows of his immortal hands
against the resplendent shield. The Akhaian then
a fourth time flung himself against the wall,
more than human in fury. But Apollo
thundered:
"Back, Patróklos, lordly man!
Destiny will not let this fortress town
of Trojans fall to you! Not to Akhilleus,
either, greater far though he is in war!"

Patróklos now retired, a long way off
and out of range of Lord Apollo's anger.
Hektor had held his team at the Skaian Gates,
being of two minds: should he re-engage,
or call his troops to shelter behind the wall?
While he debated this, Phoibos Apollo
stood at his shoulder in a strong man's guise:
Ásïos, his maternal uncle, brother
of Hékabê and son of Dymas, dweller
in Phrygia on Sangaríos river.
Taking his semblance now, Apollo said:
"Why break off battle, Hektor? You need not.
Were I superior to you in the measure
that I am now inferior, you'd suffer

from turning back so wretchedly from battle.
Action! Lash your team against Patróklos,
and see if you can take him. May Apollo
grant you the glory!"

And at this, once more
he joined the mêlée, entering it as a god.
Hektor in splendor called Kebríonês
to whip the horses toward the fight. Apollo,
disappearing into the ranks, aroused
confusion in the Argives, but on Hektor
and on the Trojans he conferred his glory.
Letting the rest go, Hektor drove his team
straight at Patróklos; and Patróklos faced him
vaulting from his war-car, with his spear
gripped in his left hand; in his right
he held enfolded a sparkling jagged stone.
Not for long in awe of the other man,
he aimed and braced himself and threw the stone
and scored a direct hit on Hektor's driver,
Kebríonês, a bastard son of Priam,
smashing his forehead with the jagged stone.
Both brows were hit at once, the frontal bone
gave way, and both his eyes burst from their sockets
dropping into the dust before his feet,
as like a diver from the handsome car
he plummeted, and life ebbed from his bones.
You jeered at him then, master of horse, Patróklos:
"God, what a nimble fellow, somersaulting!
If he were out at sea in the fishing grounds
this man could feed a crew, diving for oysters,
going overboard even in rough water,
the way he took that earth-dive from his car.
The Trojans have their acrobats, I see."

With this, he went for the dead man with a spring
like a lion, one that has taken a chest wound
while ravaging a cattle pen—his valor
his undoing. So you sprang, Patróklos,
on Kebríonês. Then Hektor, too, leapt down
out of his chariot, and the two men fought
over the body like two mountain lions
over the carcass of a buck, both famished,
both in pride of combat. So these two

fought now for Kebríonês, two champions,
Patróklos, son of Menoitios, and Hektor,
hurling their bronze to tear each other's flesh.
Hektor caught hold of the dead man's head and held,
while his antagonist clung to a single foot,
as Trojans and Danááns pressed the fight.
As south wind and the southeast wind, contending
in mountain groves, make all the forest thrash,
beech trees and ash trees and the slender cornel
swaying their pointed boughs toward one another
in roaring wind, and snapping branches crack:
so Trojans and Akhaians made a din
as lunging they destroyed each other. Neither
considered ruinous flight. Many sharp spears
and arrows trued by feathers from the strings
were fixed in flesh around Kebríonês,
and boulders crashed on shields, as they fought on
around him. And a dustcloud wrought
by a whirlwind hid the greatness of him slain,
minding no more the mastery of horses.
Until the sun stood at high noon in heaven,
spears bit on both sides, and the soldiers fell;
but when the sun passed toward unyoking time,
the Akhaians outfought destiny to prevail.
Now they dragged off gallant Kebríonês
out of range, away from the shouting Trojans,
to strip his shoulders of his gear. And fierce
Patróklos hurled himself upon the Trojans,
in onslaughts fast as Arês, three times, wild
yells in his throat. Each time he killed nine men.
But on the fourth demonic foray, then
the end of life loomed up for you, Patróklos.
Into the combat dangerous Phoibos came
against him, but Patróklos could not see
the god, enwrapped in cloud as he came near.
He stood behind and struck with open hand
the man's back and broad shoulders, and the eyes
of the fighting man were dizzied by the blow.
Then Phoibos sent the captain's helmet rolling
under the horses' hooves, making the ridge
ring out, and dirtying all the horsehair plume
with blood and dust. Never in time before
had this plumed helmet been befouled with dust,
the helmet that had kept a hero's brow

unmarred, shielding Akhilleus' head. Now Zeus
bestowed it upon Hektor, let him wear it,
though his destruction waited. For Patróklos
felt his great spearshaft shattered in his hands,
long, tough, well-shod, and seasoned though it was;
his shield and strap fell to the ground; the Lord
Apollo, son of Zeus, broke off his cuirass.
Shock ran through him, and his good legs failed,
so that he stood agape. Then from behind
at close quarters, between the shoulder blades,
a Dardan fighter speared him: Pánthoös' son,
Euphórbos, the best Trojan of his age
at handling spears, in horsemanship and running:
he had brought twenty chariot fighters down
since entering combat in his chariot,
already skilled in the craft of war. This man
was first to wound you with a spear, Patróklos,
but did not bring you down. Instead, he ran back
into the mêlée, pulling from the flesh
his ashen spear, and would not face his enemy,
even disarmed, in battle. Then Patróklos,
disabled by the god's blow and the spear wound,
moved back to save himself amid his men.
But Hektor, seeing that his brave adversary
tried to retire, hurt by the spear wound, charged
straight at him through the ranks and lunged for him
low in the flank, driving the spearhead through.
He crashed, and all Akhaian troops turned pale.
Think how a lion in his pride brings down
a tireless boar; magnificently they fight
on a mountain crest for a small gushing spring—
both in desire to drink—and by sheer power
the lion conquers the great panting boar:
that was the way the son of Priam, Hektor,
closed with Patróklos, son of Menoitios,
killer of many, and took his life away.
Then glorying above him he addressed him:
"Easy to guess, Patróklos, how you swore
to ravage Troy, to take the sweet daylight
of liberty from our women, and to drag them
off in ships to your own land—you fool!
Between you and those women there is Hektor's
war-team, thundering out to fight! My spear
has pride of place among the Trojan warriors,

keeping their evil hour at bay.
The kites[66] will feed on you, here on this field.
Poor devil, what has that great prince, Akhilleus,
done for you? He must have told you often
as you were leaving and he stayed behind,
'Never come back to me, to the deepsea ships,
Patróklos, till you cut to rags
the bloody tunic on the chest of Hektor!'
That must have been the way he talked, and won
your mind to mindlessness."

In a low faint voice,
Patróklos, master of horse, you answered him:
"This is your hour to glory over me,
Hektor. The Lord Zeus and Apollo gave you
the upper hand and put me down with ease.
They stripped me of my arms. No one else did.
Say twenty men like you had come against me,
all would have died before my spear.
No, Lêto's son and fatal destiny
have killed me; if we speak of men, Euphórbos.
You were in third place, only in at the death.
I'll tell you one thing more; take it to heart.
No long life is ahead for you. This day
your death stands near, and your immutable end,
at Prince Akhilleus' hands."

His own death
came on him as he spoke, and soul from body,
bemoaning severance from youth and manhood,
slipped to be wafted to the underworld.
Even in death Prince Hektor still addressed him:
"Why prophesy my sudden death, Patróklos?
Who knows, Akhilleus, son of bright-haired Thetis,
might be hit first; he might be killed by me."

At this he pulled his spearhead from the wound,
setting his heel upon him; then he pushed him
over on his back clear of the spear,
and lifting it at once sought Automédôn,
companion of the great runner, Akhilleus,
longing to strike him. But the immortal horses,
gift of the gods to Pêleus, bore him away.

[66] **kites:** Birds of the hawk family.

Book 18
The Immortal Shield

[In Book 17, Hektor claims Patróklos' armor, but the Akhaians succeed in bringing his body to their camp.–ED.]

While they were still in combat, fighting seaward
raggedly as fire, Antílokhos[67]
ran far ahead with tidings for Akhilleus.
In shelter of the curled, high prows he found him
envisioning what had come to pass,
in gloom and anger saying to himself:
"Ai! why are they turning tail once more,
unmanned, outfought, and driven from the field
back on the beach and ships? I pray the gods
this may not be the last twist of the knife!
My mother warned me once that, while I lived,
the most admirable of Myrmidons
would quit the sunlight under Trojan blows.
It could indeed be so. He has gone down,
my dear and wayward friend!
Push their deadly fire away, I told him,
then return! You must not fight with Hektor!"

And while he called it all to mind,
the son of gallant Nestor came up weeping
to give his cruel news:
"Here's desolation,
son of Pêleus, the worst for you—
would god it had not happened!—Lord Patróklos
fell, and they are fighting over his body,
stripped of armor. Hektor has your gear."

A black stormcloud of pain shrouded Akhilleus.
On his bowed head he scattered dust and ash
in handfuls and befouled his beautiful face,
letting black ash sift on his fragrant khiton.[68]
Then in the dust he stretched his giant length
and tore his hair with both hands.
From the hut
the women who had been spoils of war to him
and to Patróklos flocked in haste around him,
crying loud in grief. All beat their breasts,

[67] **Antílokhos:** Nestor's son. [68] **khiton:** A loose garment, like a tunic.

and trembling came upon their knees.
                                        Antílokhos
wept where he stood, bending to hold the hero's
hands when groaning shook his heart: he feared
the man might use sharp iron to slash his throat.
And now Akhilleus gave a dreadful cry.
                                        Her ladyship
his mother heard him, in the depths offshore
lolling near her ancient father. Nymphs
were gathered round her: all Nêrêïdês
who haunted the green chambers of the sea.
Glaukê, Thaleia, and Kymodokê,
Nesaiê, Speiô, Thoê, Haliê
with her wide eyes; Kymothoê, Aktaiê,
Limnôreia, Melitê, and Iaira,
Amphitoê, Agauê, Dôtô, Prôtô,
Pherousa, Dynaménê, Dexaménê,
Amphinomê, Kallianeira, Dôris,
Panopê, and storied Galateia,
Nêmertês and Apseudês, Kallianassa,
Klyméne, Ianeira, Ianassa,
Maira, Oreithyia, Amathyia,
and other Nêrêïdês of the deep sea,
filling her glimmering silvery cave. All these
now beat their breasts as Thetis cried in sorrow:
"Sisters, daughters of Nêreus, hear and know
how sore my heart is! Now my life is pain
for my great son's dark destiny! I bore
a child flawless and strong beyond all men.
He flourished like a green shoot, and I brought him
to manhood like a blossoming orchard tree,
only to send him in the ships to Ilion
to war with the Trojans. Now I shall never see him
entering Pêleus' hall, his home, again.
But even while he lives, beholding sunlight,
suffering is his lot. I have no power
to help him, though I go to him. Even so,
I'll visit my dear child and learn what sorrow
came to him while he held aloof from war."

On this she left the cave, and all in tears
her company swam aloft with her. Around them
a billow broke and foamed on the open sea.
As they made land at the fertile plain of Troy,
they went up one by one in line to where,

in close order, Myrmidon ships were beached
to right and left of Akhilleus. Bending near
her groaning son, the gentle goddess wailed
and took his head between her hands in pity,
saying softly:
"Child, why are you weeping?
What great sorrow came to you? Speak out,
do not conceal it. Zeus
did all you asked: Akhaian troops,
for want of you, were all forced back again
upon the ship sterns, taking heavy losses
none of them could wish."

The great runner
groaned and answered:
"Mother, yes, the master
of high Olympos brought it all about,
but how have I benefited? My greatest friend
is gone: Patróklos, comrade in arms, whom I
held dear above all others—dear as myself—
now gone, lost; Hektor cut him down, despoiled him
of my own arms, massive and fine, a wonder
in all men's eyes. The gods gave them to Pêleus
that day they put you in a mortal's bed—
how I wish the immortals of the sea
had been your only consorts! How I wish
Pêleus had taken a mortal queen! Sorrow
immeasurable is in store for you as well,
when your own child is lost: never again
on his homecoming day will you embrace him!
I must reject this life, my heart tells me,
reject the world of men,
if Hektor does not feel my battering spear
tear the life out of him, making him pay
in his own blood for the slaughter of Patróklos!"

Letting a tear fall, Thetis said:
"You'll be
swift to meet your end, child, as you say:
your doom comes close on the heels of Hektor's own."

Akhilleus the great runner ground his teeth
and said:
"May it come quickly. As things were,
I could not help my friend in his extremity.

Far from his home he died; he needed me
to shield him or to parry the death stroke.
For me there's no return to my own country.
Not the slightest gleam of hope did I
afford Patróklos or the other men
whom Hektor overpowered. Here I sat,
my weight a useless burden to the earth,
and I am one who has no peer in war
among Akhaian captains—
though in council
there are wiser. Ai! let strife and rancor
perish from the lives of gods and men,
with anger that envenoms even the wise
and is sweeter than slow-dripping honey,
clouding the hearts of men like smoke: just so
the marshal of the army, Agamémnon,
moved me to anger. But we'll let that go,
though I'm still sore at heart; it is all past,
and I have quelled my passion as I must.

Now I must go to look for the destroyer
of my great friend. I shall confront the dark
drear spirit of death at any hour Zeus
and the other gods may wish to make an end.
Not even Hêraklês escaped that terror
though cherished by the Lord Zeus. Destiny
and Hêra's bitter anger mastered him.
Likewise with me, if destiny like his
awaits me, I shall rest when I have fallen!
Now, though, may I win my perfect glory
and make some wife of Troy break down,
or some deep-breasted Dardan[69] woman sob
and wipe tears from her soft cheeks. They'll know then
how long they had been spared the deaths of men,
while I abstained from war!
Do not attempt to keep me from the fight,
though you love me; you cannot make me listen."

Thetis, goddess of the silvery feet,
answered:
"Yes, of course, child: very true.
You do no wrong to fight for tired soldiers

[69] **Dardan:** Allied with Troy.

and keep them from defeat. But still, your gear,
all shining bronze, remains in Trojan hands.
Hektor himself is armed with it in pride!—
Not that he'll glory in it long, I know,
for violent death is near him.
Patience, then.
Better not plunge into the moil of Arês
until you see me here once more. At dawn,
at sunrise, I shall come
with splendid arms for you from Lord Hêphaistos."

She rose at this and, turning from her son,
told her sister Nêrêïdês:
"Go down
into the cool broad body of the sea
to the sea's Ancient; visit Father's hall,
and make all known to him. Meanwhile, I'll visit
Olympos' great height and the lord of crafts,
Hêphaistos, hoping he will give me
new and shining armor for my son."

At this they vanished in the offshore swell,
and to Olympos Thetis the silvery-footed
went once more, to fetch for her dear son
new-forged and finer arms.
Meanwhile, Akhaians,
wildly crying, pressed by deadly Hektor,
reached the ships, beached above Hellê's water.
None had been able to pull Patróklos clear
of spear- and swordplay: troops and chariots
and Hektor, son of Priam, strong as fire,
once more gained upon the body. Hektor
three times had the feet within his grasp
and strove to wrest Patróklos backward, shouting
to all the Trojans—but three times the pair
named Aías in their valor shook him off.
Still he pushed on, sure of his own power,
sometimes lunging through the battle-din,
or holding fast with a great shout: not one step
would he give way. As from a fresh carcass
herdsmen in the wilds cannot dislodge
a tawny lion, famished: so those two
with fearsome crests could not affright the son
of Priam or repel him from the body.
He might have won it, might have won unending

glory, but Iris[70] running on the wind
came from Olympos to the son of Pêleus,
bidding him gird for battle. All unknown
to Zeus and the other gods she came, for Hêra
sent her down. And at his side she said:
"Up with you, Pêleidês, who strike cold fear
into men's blood! Protect your friend Patróklos,
for whom, beyond the ships, desperate combat
rages now. They are killing one another
on both sides: the Akhaians to defend him,
Trojans fighting for that prize
to drag to windy Ilion. And Hektor
burns to take it more than anyone—
to sever and impale Patróklos' head
on Trojan battlements. Lie here no longer.
It would be shameful if wild dogs of Troy
made him their plaything! If that body suffers
mutilation, you will be infamous!"

Prince Akhilleus answered:
"Iris of heaven,
what immortal sent you to tell me this?"
And she who runs upon the wind replied:
"Hêra, illustrious wife of Zeus,
but he on his high throne knows nothing of it.
Neither does any one of the gods undying
who haunt Olympos of eternal snows."

Akhilleus asked:
"And now how shall I go
into the fighting? Those men have my gear.
My dear mother allows me no rearming
until I see her again here.
She promises fine arms from Lord Hêphaistos.
I don't know whose armor I can wear,
unless I take Aías' big shield.
But I feel sure he's in the thick of it,
contending with his spear over Patróklos."

Then she who runs upon the wind replied:
"We know they have your arms, and know it well.
Just as you are, then, stand at the moat; let Trojans

[70] **Iris:** Messenger of the gods.

take that in; they will be so dismayed
they may break off the battle, and Akhaians
in their fatigue may win a breathing spell,
however brief, a respite from the war."

At this,
Iris left him, running downwind. Akhilleus,
whom Zeus loved, now rose. Around his shoulders
Athêna hung her shield[71] like a thunderhead
with trailing fringe. Goddess of goddesses,
she bound his head with golden cloud, and made
his very body blaze with fiery light.
Imagine how the pyre of a burning town
will tower to heaven and be seen for miles
from the island under attack, while all day long
outside their town, in brutal combat, pikemen
suffer the wargod's winnowing; at sundown
flare on flare is lit, the signal fires
shoot up for other islanders to see,
that some relieving force in ships may come:
just so the baleful radiance from Akhilleus
lit the sky. Moving from parapet
to moat, without a nod for the Akhaians,
keeping clear, in deference to his mother,
he halted and gave tongue. Not far from him
Athêna shrieked. The great sound shocked the Trojans
into tumult, as a trumpet blown
by a savage foe shocks an encircled town,
so harsh and clarion was Akhilleus' cry.
The hearts of men quailed, hearing that brazen voice.
Teams, foreknowing danger, turned their cars
and charioteers blanched, seeing unearthly fire,
kindled by the grey-eyed goddess Athêna,
brilliant over Akhilleus. Three great cries
he gave above the moat. Three times they shuddered,
whirling backward, Trojans and allies,
and twelve good men took mortal hurt
from cars and weapons in the rank behind.
Now the Akhaians leapt at the chance
to bear Patróklos' body out of range.
They placed it on his bed,
and old companions there with brimming eyes

[71] **her shield:** The famous aegis with the image of Medusa on it.

surrounded him. Into their midst Akhilleus
came then, and he wept hot tears to see
his faithful friend, torn by the sharp spearhead,
lying cold upon his cot. Alas,
the man he sent to war with team and chariot
he could not welcome back alive.
Her majesty,
wide-eyed Hêra, made the reluctant sun,
unwearied still, sink in the streams of Ocean.
Down he dropped, and the Akhaian soldiers
broke off combat, resting from the war.
The Trojans, too, retired. Unharnessing
teams from war-cars, before making supper,
they came together on the assembly ground,
every man on his feet; not one could sit,
each being still in a tremor — for Akhilleus,
absent so long, had once again appeared.
Clearheaded Poulýdamas, son of Pánthoös,
spoke up first, as he alone could see
what lay ahead and all that lay behind.
He and Hektor were companions-in-arms,
born, as it happened, on the same night; but one
excelled in handling weapons, one with words.
Now for the good of all he spoke among them:
"Think well of our alternatives, my friends.
What I say is, retire upon the town,
instead of camping on the field till dawn
here by ships. We are a long way
from our stone wall. As long as that man raged
at royal Agamémnon, we could fight
the Akhaians with advantage. I was happy
to spend last night so near the beach and think
of capturing ships today. Now, though, I fear
the son of Pêleus to my very marrow!
There are no bounds to the passion of that man.
He will not be contained by the flat ground
where Trojans and Akhaians share between them
raging war: he will strive on to fight
to win our town, our women. Back to Troy!
Believe me, this is what we face!
Now, starry night has made Akhilleus pause,
but when day comes, when he sorties in arms
to find us lingering here, there will be men
who learn too well what he is made of. Aye,
I daresay those who get away will reach

walled Ilion thankfully, but dogs and kites
of Troy will feed on many. May that story
never reach my ears! If we can follow
my battle plan, though galled by it, tonight
we'll husband strength, at rest in the market place.
Towers, high gates, great doors of fitted planking,
bolted tight, will keep the town secure.
Early tomorrow we shall arm ourselves
and man the walls. Worse luck then for Akhilleus,
if he comes looking for a head-on fight
on the field around the wall! He can do nothing
but trot back, after all, to the encampment,
his proud team in a lather from their run,
from scouring every quarter below the town.
Rage as he will, he cannot force an entrance,
cannot take all Troy by storm. Wild dogs
will eat him first!"

Under his shimmering helmet
Hektor glared at the speaker. Then he said:
"Poulýdamas, what you propose no longer
serves my turn. To go on the defensive
inside the town again? Is anyone
not sick of being huddled in those towers?
In past days men told tales of Priam's city,
rich in gold and rich in bronze, but now
those beautiful treasures of our home are lost.
Many have gone for sale to Phrygia
and fair Mêïonié, since Lord Zeus
grew hostile toward us.

Now when the son of Krónos
Crooked Wit has given me a chance
of winning glory, pinning the Akhaians
back on the sea—now is no time to publish
notions like these to troops, you fool! No Trojan
goes along with you, I will not have it!
Come, let each man act as I propose.
Take your evening meal by companies;
remember sentries; keep good watch; and any
Trojan tired of his wealth, who wants
to lose everything, let him turn it over
to the army stores to be consumed in common!
Better our men enjoy it than Akhaians.
At first light we shall buckle armor on

and bring the ships under attack. Suppose
the man who stood astern there was indeed
Akhilleus, then worse luck for him,
if he will have it so. Shall I retreat
from him, from clash of combat? No, I will not.
Here I'll stand, though he should win; I might
just win, myself: the battle-god's impartial,
dealing death to the death-dealing man."

This was Hektor's speech. The Trojans roared
approval of it — fools, for Pallas Athêna
took away their wits. They all applauded
Hektor's poor tactics, but Poulýdamas
with his good judgment got not one assent.
They took their evening meal now, through the army,
while all night long Akhaians mourned Patróklos.

Akhilleus led them in their lamentation,
laying those hands deadly to enemies
upon the breast of his old friend, with groans
at every breath, bereft as a lioness
whose whelps a hunter seized out of a thicket;
late in returning, she will grieve, and roam
through many meandering valleys on his track
in hope of finding him; heart-stinging anger
carries her away. Now with a groan
he cried out to the Myrmidons:
"Ah, god,
what empty prophecy I made that day
to cheer Menoitios in his mégaron!
I promised him his honored son, brought back
to Opoeis,[72] as pillager of Ilion
bearing his share of spoils.
But Zeus will not fulfill what men design,
not all of it. Both he and I were destined
to stain the same earth dark red here at Troy.
No going home for me; no welcome there
from Pêleus, master of horse, or from my mother,
Thetis. Here the earth will hold me under.
Therefore, as I must follow you into the grave,
I will not give you burial, Patróklos,

[72] **Opoeis:** A city in Greece, home of Menoitios, father of Patróklos.

until I carry back the gear and head
of him who killed you, noble friend.
Before your funeral pyre I'll cut the throats
of twelve resplendent children of the Trojans—
that is my murdering fury at your death.
But while you lie here by the swanlike ships,
night and day, close by, deep-breasted women
of Troy, and Dardan women, must lament
and weep hot tears, all those whom we acquired
by labor in assault, by the long spear,
pillaging the fat market towns of men."

With this Akhilleus called the company
to place over the campfire a big tripod
and bathe Patróklos of his clotted blood.
Setting tripod and caldron on the blaze
they poured it full, and fed the fire beneath,
and flames licked round the belly of the vessel
until the water warmed and bubbled up
in the bright bronze. They bathed him then, and took
sweet oil for his anointing, laying nard[73]
in the open wounds; and on his bed they placed him,
covering him with fine linen, head to foot,
and a white shroud over it.
So all that night
beside Akhilleus the great runner,
the Myrmidons held mourning for Patróklos.
Now Zeus observed to Hêra, wife and sister:
"You had your way, my lady, after all,
my wide-eyed one! You brought him to his feet,
the great runner! One would say the Akhaian
gentlemen were progeny of yours."

And Hêra with wide eyes replied:
"Dread majesty,
Lord Zeus, why do you take this tone? May not
an ordinary mortal have his way,
though death awaits him, and his mind is dim?
Would anyone suppose that I, who rank
in two respects highest of goddesses—
by birth and by my station, queen to thee,

[73] **nard:** Spikenard, from which ointment was made.

lord of all gods — that I should not devise
ill fortune for the Trojans whom I loathe?"

So ran their brief exchange. Meanwhile
the silvery-footed Thetis reached Hêphaistos'
lodging, indestructible and starry,
framed in bronze by the bandy-legged god.
She found him sweating, as from side to side
he plied his bellows; on his forge were twenty
tripods to be finished, then to stand
around his mégaron. And he wrought wheels
of gold for the base of each, that each might roll
as of itself into the gods' assembly,
then roll home, a marvel to the eyes.
The caldrons were all shaped but had no handles.
These he applied now, hammering rivets in;
and as he toiled surehandedly at this,
Thetis arrived.
Grace in her shining veil
just going out encountered her — that Grace
the bowlegged god had taken to wife.[74] She greeted
Thetis with a warm handclasp and said:
"My lady Thetis, gracious goddess, what
has brought you here? You almost never honor us!
Please come in, and let me give you welcome."

Loveliest of goddesses, she led the way,
to seat her guest on a silver-studded chair,
elaborately fashioned, with a footrest.
Then she called to Hêphaistos:
"Come and see!
Thetis is here, in need of something from you!"

To this the Great Gamelegs replied:
"Ah, then we have a visitor I honor.
She was my savior, after the long fall
and fractures that I had to bear, when Mother,° Hêra
bitch that she is, wanted to hide her cripple.
That would have been a dangerous time, had not
Thetis and Eurýnomê[75] taken me in —
Eurýnomê, daughter of the tidal Ocean.
Nine years I stayed, and fashioned works of art,

[74] **that Grace . . . to wife:** Hêphaistos was lame; usually his wife is Aphrodítê. [75] **Eurýnomê:** Thetis's aunt.

brooches and spiral bracelets, necklaces,
in their smooth cave, round which the stream of Ocean
flows with a foaming roar: and no one else
knew of it, gods or mortals. Only Thetis
knew, and Eurýnomê, the two who saved me.
Now she has come to us. Well, what I owe
for life to her ladyship in her soft braids
I must repay. Serve her our choicest fare
while I put up my bellows and my tools."

At this he left the anvil block, and hobbled
with monstrous bulk on skinny legs to take
his bellows from the fire. Then all the tools
he had been toiling with he stowed
in a silver chest.
That done, he sponged himself,
his face, both arms, bull-neck and hairy chest,
put on a tunic, took a weighty staff,
and limped out of his workshop. Round their lord
came fluttering maids of gold, like living girls:
intelligences, voices, power of motion
these maids have, and skills learnt from immortals.
Now they came rustling to support their lord,
and he moved on toward Thetis, where she sat
upon the silvery chair. He took her hand
and warmly said:
"My Lady Thetis, gracious
goddess, why have you come? You almost never honor us.
Tell me the favor that you have in mind,
for I desire to do it if I can,
and if it is a thing that one may do."

Thetis answered, tear on cheek:
"Hêphaistos,
who among all Olympian goddesses
endured anxiety and pain like mine?
Zeus chose me, from all of them, for this!
Of sea-nymphs I alone was given in thrall
to a mortal warrior, Pêleus Aiákidês,
and I endured a mortal warrior's bed
many a time, without desire. Now Pêleus
lies far gone in age in his great hall,
and I have other pain. Our son, bestowed
on me and nursed by me, became a hero
unsurpassed. He grew like a green shoot;

I cherished him like a flowering orchard tree,
only to send him in the ships to Ilion
to war with Trojans. Now I shall never see him
entering Pêleus' hall, his home, again.
But even while he lives, beholding sunlight,
suffering is his lot. I have no power
to help him, though I go to him. A girl,
his prize from the Akhaians, Agamémnon
took out of his hands to make his own,
and ah, he pined with burning heart! The Trojans
rolled the Akhaians back on the ship sterns,
and left them no escape. Then Argive officers
begged my son's help, offering every gift,
but he would not defend them from disaster.
Arming Patróklos in his own war-gear,
he sent him with his people into battle.
All day long, around the Skaian Gates,
they fought, and would have won the city, too,
had not Apollo, seeing the brave son
of Menoitios wreaking havoc on the Trojans,
killed him in action, and then given Hektor
the honor of that deed.
On this account
I am here to beg you: if you will, provide
for my doomed son a shield and crested helm,
good legging-greaves, fitted with ankle clasps,
a cuirass, too. His own armor was lost
when his great friend went down before the Trojans.
Now my son lies prone on the hard ground in grief."

The illustrious lame god replied:
"Take heart.
No trouble about the arms. I only wish
that I could hide him from the power of death
in his black hour—wish I were sure of that
as of the splendid gear he'll get, a wonder
to any one of the many men there are!"

He left her there, returning to his bellows,
training them on the fire, crying, "To work!"
In crucibles the twenty bellows breathed
every degree of fiery air: to serve him
a great blast when he labored might and main,
or a faint puff, according to his wish

and what the work demanded.
Durable
fine bronze and tin he threw into the blaze
with silver and with honorable gold,
then mounted a big anvil in his block
and in his right hand took a powerful hammer,
managing with his tongs in his left hand.

His first job was a shield, a broad one, thick,
well-fashioned everywhere. A shining rim
he gave it, triple-ply, and hung from this
a silver shoulder strap. Five welded layers
composed the body of the shield. The maker
used all his art adorning this expanse.
He pictured on it earth, heaven, and sea,
unwearied sun, moon waxing, all the stars
that heaven bears for garland: Plêïadês,
Hyadês, Oríôn in his might,
the Great Bear, too, that some have called the Wain,
pivoting there, attentive to Oríôn,
and unbathed ever in the Ocean stream.[76]

He pictured, then, two cities, noble scenes:
weddings in one, and wedding feasts, and brides
led out through town by torchlight from their chambers
amid chorales, amid the young men turning
round and round in dances: flutes and harps
among them, keeping up a tune, and women
coming outdoors to stare as they went by.
A crowd, then, in a market place, and there
two men at odds over satisfaction owed
for a murder done: one claimed that all was paid,
and publicly declared it; his opponent
turned the reparation down, and both
demanded a verdict from an arbiter,
as people clamored in support of each,
and criers restrained the crowd. The town elders
sat in a ring, on chairs of polished stone,
the staves of clarion criers in their hands,
with which they sprang up, each to speak in turn,

[76] **Great Bear . . . stream:** The Great Bear (Ursa Major) is the Big Dipper, which never descends below the horizon.

and in the middle were two golden measures
to be awarded him whose argument
would be the most straightforward.
                                        Wartime then;
around the other city were emplaced
two columns of besiegers, bright in arms,
as yet divided on which plan they liked:
whether to sack the town, or treat for half
of all the treasure stored in the citadel.
The townsmen would not bow either: secretly
they armed to break the siege-line. Women and children
stationed on the walls kept watch, with men
whom age disabled. All the rest filed out,
as Arês led the way, and Pallas Athêna,
figured in gold, with golden trappings, both
magnificent in arms, as the gods are,
in high relief, while men were small beside them.
When these had come to a likely place for ambush,
a river with a watering place for flocks,
they there disposed themselves, compact in bronze.
Two lookouts at a distance from the troops
took their posts, awaiting sight of sheep
and shambling cattle. Both now came in view,
trailed by two herdsmen playing pipes, no hidden
danger in their minds. The ambush party
took them by surprise in a sudden rush;
swiftly they cut off herds and beautiful flocks
of silvery grey sheep, then killed the herdsmen.
When the besiegers from their parleying ground
heard sounds of cattle in stampede, they mounted
behind mettlesome teams, following the sound,
and came up quickly. Battle lines were drawn,
and on the riverbanks the fight began
as each side rifled javelins at the other.
Here then Strife and Uproar joined the fray,
and ghastly Fate, that kept a man with wounds
alive, and one unwounded, and another
dragged by the heels through battle-din in death.
This figure wore a mantle dyed with blood,
and all the figures clashed and fought
like living men, and pulled their dead away.

Upon the shield, soft terrain, freshly plowed,
he pictured: a broad field, and many plowmen
here and there upon it. Some were turning

ox teams at the plowland's edge, and there
as one arrived and turned, a man came forward
putting a cup of sweet wine in his hands.
They made their turns-around, then up the furrows
drove again, eager to reach the deep field's
limit; and the earth looked black behind them,
as though turned up by plows. But it was gold,
all gold—a wonder of the artist's craft.

He put there, too, a king's field. Harvest hands
were swinging whetted scythes to mow the grain,
and stalks were falling along the swath
while binders girded others up in sheaves
with bands of straw—three binders, and behind them
children came as gleaners, proffering
their eager armfuls. And amid them all
the king stood quietly with staff in hand,
happy at heart, upon a new-mown swath.
To one side, under an oak tree his attendants
worked at a harvest banquet. They had killed
a great ox, and were dressing it; their wives
made supper for the hands, with barley strewn.

A vineyard then he pictured, weighted down
with grapes: this all in gold; and yet the clusters
hung dark purple, while the spreading vines
were propped on silver vine-poles. Blue enamel
he made the enclosing ditch, and tin the fence,
and one path only led into the vineyard
on which the loaded vintagers took their way
at vintage time. Lighthearted boys and girls
were harvesting the grapes in woven baskets,
while on a resonant harp a boy among them
played a tune of longing, singing low
with delicate voice a summer dirge. The others,
breaking out in song for the joy of it,
kept time together as they skipped along.

The artisan made next a herd of longhorns,
fashioned in gold and tin: away they shambled,
lowing, from byre to pasture by a stream
that sang in ripples, and by reeds a-sway.
Four cowherds all of gold were plodding after
with nine lithe dogs beside them.
On the assault,

in two tremendous bounds, a pair of lions
caught in the van a bellowing bull, and off
they dragged him, followed by the dogs and men.
Rending the belly of the bull, the two
gulped down his blood and guts, even as the herdsmen
tried to set on their hunting dogs, but failed:
no trading bites with lions for those dogs,
who halted close up, barking, then ran back.

And on the shield the great bowlegged god
designed a pasture in a lovely valley,
wide, with silvery sheep, and huts and sheds
and sheepfolds there.

A dancing floor as well
he fashioned, like that one in royal Knossos
Daidalos made for the Princess Ariadnê.[77]
Here young men and the most desired young girls
were dancing, linked, touching each other's wrists,
the girls in linen, in soft gowns, the men
in well-knit khitons given a gloss with oil;
the girls wore garlands, and the men had daggers
golden-hilted, hung on silver lanyards.
Trained and adept, they circled there with ease
the way a potter sitting at his wheel
will give it a practice twirl between his palms
to see it run; or else, again, in lines
as though in ranks, they moved on one another:
magical dancing! All around, a crowd
stood spellbound as two tumblers led the beat
with spins and handsprings through the company.

Then, running round the shield-rim, triple-ply,
he pictured all the might of the Ocean stream.

Besides the densely plated shield, he made
a cuirass, brighter far than fire light,
a massive helmet, measured for his temples,

[77] **Ariadnê:** The daughter of King Minos, who hired Daidalos to construct his great palace and a labyrinth at Knossos on Krete.

handsomely figured, with a crest of gold;
then greaves[78] of pliant tin.

Now when the crippled god
had done his work, he picked up all the arms
and laid them down before Akhilleus' mother,
and swift as a hawk from snowy Olympos' height
she bore the brilliant gear made by Hêphaistos.

Book 22
Desolation before Troy

[In Book 19, Akhilleus and Agamémnon are reconciled; turning his anger to the Trojans who caused Patróklos's death, Akhilleus asks his horses not to leave him dead on the battlefield, as they left Patróklos. Xánthos, one of the horses, prophesies that Akhilleus will not die in this battle, but soon. In Book 20, the gods actively take sides. Poseidon rescues Aineías from Akhilleus because Aineías is fated to survive the war. Akhilleus, however, kills many Trojans. In Book 21, the god of the River Xánthos is angered by the numerous corpses Akhilleus dumped in the river, and turns on Akhilleus. Akhilleus is saved by gods and goddesses, who then in the excitement of warfare begin to fight each other. The remaining Trojans retreat to the city.]

Once in the town, those who had fled like deer
wiped off their sweat and drank their thirst away,
leaning against the cool stone of the ramparts.
Meanwhile Akhaians with bright shields aslant
came up the plain and nearer. As for Hektor,
fatal destiny pinned him where he stood
before the Skaian Gates, outside the city.

Now Akhilleus heard Apollo calling
back to him:
"Why run so hard, Akhilleus,
mortal as you are, after a god?
Can you not comprehend it? I am immortal.
You are so hot to catch me, you no longer
think of finishing off the men you routed.
They are all in the town by now, packed in
while you were being diverted here. And yet
you cannot kill me; I am no man's quarry."
Akhilleus bit his lip and said:
"Archer of heaven, deadliest
of immortal gods, you put me off the track,

[78] **greaves:** Armor for legs.

turning me from the wall this way. A hundred
might have sunk their teeth into the dust
before one man took cover in Ilion!
You saved my enemies with ease and stole
my glory, having no punishment to fear.
I'd take it out of you, if I had the power."

Then toward the town with might and main he ran,
magnificent, like a racing chariot horse
that holds its form at full stretch on the plain.
So light-footed Akhilleus held the pace.
And aging Priam was the first to see him
sparkling on the plain, bright as that star
in autumn rising, whose unclouded rays
shine out amid a throng of stars at dusk—
the one they call Oríôn's dog,[79] most brilliant,
yes, but baleful as a sign: it brings
great fever to frail men. So pure and bright
the bronze gear blazed upon him as he ran.
The old man gave a cry. With both his hands
thrown up on high he struck his head, then shouted,
groaning, appealing to his dear son. Unmoved,
Lord Hektor stood in the gateway, resolute
to fight Akhilleus.
Stretching out his hands,
old Priam said, imploring him:
"No, Hektor!
Cut off as you are, alone, dear son,
don't try to hold your ground against this man,
or soon you'll meet the shock of doom, borne down
by the son of Pêleus. He is more powerful
by far than you, and pitiless. Ah, were he
but dear to the gods as he is dear to me!
Wild dogs and kites would eat him where he lay
so within the hour, and ease me of my torment.
Many tall sons he killed, bereaving me,
or sold them to far islands. Even now
I cannot see two sons of mine, Lykáôn
and Polydôros, among the Trojans massed
inside the town. A queen, Laóthoê,[80]
conceived and bore them. If they are alive
amid the Akhaian host, I'll ransom them

[79] **Oríôn's dog:** Sirius, the "dog star." [80] **Laóthoê:** One of Priam's concubines.

with bronze and gold: both I have, piled at home,
rich treasures that old Altês, the renowned,
gave for his daughter's dowry. If they died,
if they went under to the homes of Death,
sorrow has come to me and to their mother.
But to our townsmen all this pain is brief,
unless you too go down before Akhilleus.
Come inside the wall, child; here you may
fight on to save our Trojan men and women.
Do not resign the glory to Akhilleus,
losing your own dear life! Take pity, too,
on me and my hard fate, while I live still.
Upon the threshold of my age, in misery,
the son of Krónos will destroy my life
after the evil days I shall have seen—
my sons brought down, my daughters dragged away,
bedchambers ravaged, and small children hurled
to earth in the atrocity of war,
as my sons' wives are taken by Akhaians'
ruinous hands. And at the end, I too—
when someone with a sword-cut or a spear
has had my life—I shall be torn apart
on my own doorstep by the hounds
I trained as watchdogs, fed from my own table.
These will lap my blood with ravenous hearts
and lie in the entranceway.
Everything done
to a young man killed in war becomes his glory,
once he is riven by the whetted bronze:
dead though he be, it is all fair, whatever
happens then. But when an old man falls,
and dogs disfigure his grey head and cheek
and genitals, that is most harrowing
of all that men in their hard lives endure."

The old man wrenched at his grey hair and pulled out
hanks of it in both his hands, but moved
Lord Hektor not at all. The young man's mother
wailed from the tower across, above the portal,
streaming tears, and loosening her robe
with one hand, held her breast out in the other,
saying:
"Hektor, my child, be moved by this,
and pity me, if ever I unbound
a quieting breast for you. Think of these things,

dear child; defend yourself against the killer
this side of the wall, not hand to hand.
He has no pity. If he brings you down,
I shall no longer be allowed to mourn you
laid out on your bed, dear branch in flower,
born of me! And neither will your lady,
so endowed with gifts. Far from us both,
dogs will devour you by the Argive ships."

With tears and cries the two implored their son,
and made their prayers again, but could not shake him.
Hektor stood firm, as huge Akhilleus neared.
The way a serpent, fed on poisonous herbs,
coiled at his lair upon a mountainside,
with all his length of hate awaits a man
and eyes him evilly: so Hektor, grim
and narrow-eyed, refused to yield. He leaned
his brilliant shield against a spur of wall
and in his brave heart bitterly reflected:
"Here I am badly caught. If I take cover,
slipping inside the gate and wall, the first
to accuse me for it will be Poulýdamas,
he who told me I should lead the Trojans
back to the city on that cursed night
Akhilleus joined the battle. No, I would not,
would not, wiser though it would have been.
Now troops have perished for my foolish pride,
I am ashamed to face townsmen and women.
Someone inferior to me may say:
'He kept his pride and lost his men, this Hektor!'
So it will go. Better, when that time comes,
that I appear as he who killed Akhilleus
man to man, or else that I went down
before him honorably for the city's sake.
Suppose, though, that I lay my shield and helm
aside, and prop my spear against the wall,
and go to meet the noble Prince Akhilleus,
promising Helen, promising with her
all treasures that Aléxandros brought home
by ship to Troy—the first cause of our quarrel—
that he may give these things to the Atreidai?
Then I might add, apart from these, a portion
of all the secret wealth the city owns.
Yes, later I might take our counselors' oath
to hide no stores, but share and share alike
to halve all wealth our lovely city holds,

all that is here within the walls. Ah, no,
why even put the question to myself?
I must not go before him and receive
no quarter, no respect! Aye, then and there
he'll kill me, unprotected as I am,
my gear laid by, defenseless as a woman.
No chance, now, for charms from oak or stone
in parley with him — charms a girl and boy
might use when they enchant each other talking!
Better we duel, now at once, and see
to whom the Olympian awards the glory."

These were his shifts of mood. Now close at hand
Akhilleus like the implacable god of war
came on with blowing crest, hefting the dreaded
beam of Pêlian ash on his right shoulder.
Bronze light played around him, like the glare
of a great fire or the great sun rising,
and Hektor, as he watched, began to tremble.
Then he could hold his ground no more. He ran,
leaving the gate behind him, with Akhilleus
hard on his heels, sure of his own speed.
When that most lightning-like of birds, a hawk
bred on a mountain, swoops upon a dove,
the quarry dips in terror, but the hunter,
screaming, dips behind and gains upon it,
passionate for prey. Just so, Akhilleus
murderously cleft the air, as Hektor
ran with flashing knees along the wall.
They passed the lookout point, the wild figtree
with wind in all its leaves, then veered away
along the curving wagon road, and came
to where the double fountains well, the source
of eddying Skamánder. One hot spring
flows out, and from the water fumes arise
as though from fire burning; but the other
even in summer gushes chill as hail
or snow or crystal ice frozen on water.
Near these fountains are wide washing pools
of smooth-laid stone, where Trojan wives and daughters
laundered their smooth linen in the days
of peace before the Akhaians came. Past these
the two men ran, pursuer and pursued,
and he who fled was noble, he behind
a greater man by far. They ran full speed,
and not for bull's hide or a ritual beast

or any prize that men compete for: no,
but for the life of Hektor, tamer of horses.
Just as when chariot-teams around a course
go wheeling swiftly, for the prize is great,
a tripod or a woman, in the games
held for a dead man, so three times these two
at full speed made their course round Priam's town,
as all the gods looked on. And now the father
of gods and men turned to the rest and said:
"How sad that this beloved man is hunted
around the wall before my eyes! My heart
is touched for Hektor; he has burned thigh flesh
of oxen for me often, high on Ida,
at other times on the high point of Troy.
Now Prince Akhilleus with devouring stride
is pressing him around the town of Priam.
Come, gods, put your minds on it, consider
whether we may deliver him from death
or see him, noble as he is, brought down
by Pêleus' son, Akhilleus."

Grey-eyed Athêna
said to him:
"Father of the blinding bolt,
the dark stormcloud, what words are these? The man
is mortal, and his doom fixed, long ago.
Would you release him from his painful death?
Then do so, but not all of us will praise you."

Zeus who gathers cloud replied:
"Take heart,
my dear and honored child. I am not bent
on my suggestion, and I would indulge you.
Act as your thought inclines, refrain no longer."

So he encouraged her in her desire,
and down she swept from ridges of Olympos.
Great Akhilleus, hard on Hektor's heels,
kept after him, the way a hound will harry
a deer's fawn he has startled from its bed
to chase through gorge and open glade, and when
the quarry goes to earth under a bush
he holds the scent and quarters till he finds it;
so with Hektor: he could not shake off
the great runner, Akhilleus. Every time

he tried to sprint hard for the Dardan gates
under the towers, hoping men would help him,
sending missiles down, Akhilleus loomed
to cut him off and turn him toward the plain,
as he himself ran always near the city.
As in a dream a man chasing another
cannot catch him, nor can he in flight
escape from his pursuer, so Akhilleus
could not by swiftness overtake him,
nor could Hektor pull away. How could he
run so long from death, had not Apollo
for the last time, the very last, come near
to give him stamina and speed?
Akhilleus
shook his head at the rest of the Akhaians,
allowing none to shoot or cast at Hektor—
none to forestall him, and to win the honor.
But when, for the fourth time, they reached the springs,
the Father poised his golden scales.
He placed
two shapes of death, death prone and cold, upon them,
one of Akhilleus, one of the horseman, Hektor,
and held the midpoint, pulling upward. Down
sank Hektor's fatal day, the pan went down
toward undergloom, and Phoibos Apollo left him.
Then came Athêna, grey-eyed, to the son
of Pêleus, falling in with him, and near him,
saying swiftly:
"Now at last I think
the two of us, Akhilleus loved by Zeus,
shall bring Akhaians triumph at the ships
by killing Hektor—unappeased
though he was ever in his thirst for war.
There is no way he may escape us now,
not though Apollo, lord of distances,
should suffer all indignity for him
before his father Zeus who bears the stormcloud,
rolling back and forth and begging for him.
Now you can halt and take your breath, while I
persuade him into combat face to face."

These were Athêna's orders. He complied,
relieved, and leaning hard upon the spearshaft
armed with its head of bronze. She left him there
and overtook Lord Hektor—but she seemed

Dêíphobos in form and resonant voice,
appearing at his shoulder, saying swiftly:
"Ai! Dear brother, how he runs, Akhilleus,
harrying you around the town of Priam!
Come, we'll stand and take him on."

To this,
great Hektor in his shimmering helm replied:
"Dêíphobos, you were the closest to me
in the old days, of all my brothers, sons
of Hékabê and Priam. Now I can say
I honor you still more
because you dared this foray for my sake,
seeing me run. The rest stay under cover."

Again the grey-eyed goddess Athêna spoke:
"Dear brother, how your father and gentle mother
begged and begged me to remain! So did
the soldiers round me, all undone by fear.
But in my heart I ached for you.
Now let us fight him, and fight hard.
No holding back. We'll see if this Akhilleus
conquers both, to take our armor seaward,
or if he can be brought down by your spear."

This way, by guile, Athêna led him on.
And when at last the two men faced each other,
Hektor was the first to speak. He said:
"I will no longer fear you as before,
son of Pêleus, though I ran from you
round Priam's town three times and could not face you.
Now my soul would have me stand and fight,
whether I kill you or am killed. So come,
we'll summon gods here as our witnesses,
none higher, arbiters of a pact: I swear
that, terrible as you are,
I'll not insult your corpse should Zeus allow me
victory in the end, your life as prize.
Once I have your gear, I'll give your body
back to Akhaians. Grant me, too, this grace."

But swift Akhilleus frowned at him and said:
"Hektor, I'll have no talk of pacts with you,
forever unforgiven as you are.
As between men and lions there are none,

no concord between wolves and sheep, but all
hold one another hateful through and through,
so there can be no courtesy between us,
no sworn truce, till one of us is down
and glutting with his blood the wargod Arês.
Summon up what skills you have. By god,
you'd better be a spearman and a fighter!
Now there is no way out. Pallas Athêna
will have the upper hand of you. The weapon
belongs to me. You'll pay the reckoning
in full for all the pain my men have borne,
who met death by your spear."

He twirled and cast
his shaft with its long shadow. Splendid Hektor,
keeping his eye upon the point, eluded it
by ducking at the instant of the cast,
so shaft and bronze shank passed him overhead
and punched into the earth. But unperceived
by Hektor, Pallas Athêna plucked it out
and gave it back to Akhilleus. Hektor said:
"A clean miss. Godlike as you are,
you have not yet known doom for me from Zeus.
You thought you had, by heaven. Then you turned
into a word-thrower, hoping to make me lose
my fighting heart and head in fear of you.
You cannot plant your spear between my shoulders
while I am running. If you have the gift,
just put it through my chest as I come forward.
Now it's for you to dodge my own. Would god
you'd give the whole shaft lodging in your body!
War for the Trojans would be eased
if you were blotted out, bane that you are."

With this he twirled his long spearshaft and cast it,
hitting his enemy mid-shield, but off
and away the spear rebounded. Furious
that he had lost it, made his throw for nothing,
Hektor stood bemused. He had no other.
Then he gave a great shout to Dêiphobos
to ask for a long spear. But there was no one
near him, not a soul. Now in his heart
the Trojan realized the truth and said:
"This is the end. The gods are calling deathward.
I had thought

a good soldier, Dêíphobos, was with me.
He is inside the walls. Athêna tricked me.
Death is near, and black, not at a distance,
not to be evaded. Long ago
this hour must have been to Zeus's liking
and to the liking of his archer son.
They have been well disposed before, but now
the appointed time's upon me. Still, I would not
die without delivering a stroke,
or die ingloriously, but in some action
memorable to men in days to come."

With this he drew the whetted blade that hung
upon his left flank, ponderous and long,
collecting all his might the way an eagle
narrows himself to dive through shady cloud
and strike a lamb or cowering hare: so Hektor
lanced ahead and swung his whetted blade.
Akhilleus with wild fury in his heart
pulled in upon his chest his beautiful shield—
his helmet with four burnished metal ridges
nodding above it, and the golden crest
Hêphaistos locked there tossing in the wind.
Conspicuous as the evening star that comes,
amid the first in heaven, at fall of night,
and stands most lovely in the west, so shone
in sunlight the fine-pointed spear
Akhilleus poised in his right hand, with deadly
aim at Hektor, at the skin where most
it lay exposed. But nearly all was covered
by the bronze gear he took from slain Patróklos,
showing only, where his collarbones
divided neck and shoulders, the bare throat
where the destruction of a life is quickest.
Here, then, as the Trojan charged, Akhilleus
drove his point straight through the tender neck,
but did not cut the windpipe, leaving Hektor
able to speak and to respond. He fell
aside into the dust. And Prince Akhilleus
now exulted:

"Hektor, had you thought
that you could kill Patróklos and be safe?
Nothing to dread from me; I was not there.
All childishness. Though distant then, Patróklos'

comrade in arms was greater far than he—
and it is I who had been left behind
that day beside the deepsea ships who now
have made your knees give way. The dogs and kites
will rip your body. His will lie in honor
when the Akhaians give him funeral."

Hektor, barely whispering, replied:
"I beg you by your soul and by your parents,
do not let the dogs feed on me
in your encampment by the ships. Accept
the bronze and gold my father will provide
as gifts, my father and her ladyship
my mother. Let them have my body back,
so that our men and women may accord me
decency of fire when I am dead."

Akhilleus the great runner scowled and said:
"Beg me no beggary by soul or parents,
whining dog! Would god my passion drove me
to slaughter you and eat you raw, you've caused
such agony to me! No man exists
who could defend you from the carrion pack—
not if they spread for me ten times your ransom,
twenty times, and promise more as well;
aye, not if Priam, son of Dárdanos,
tells them to buy you for your weight in gold!
You'll have no bed of death, nor will you be
laid out and mourned by her who gave you birth.
Dogs and birds will have you, every scrap."

Then at the point of death Lord Hektor said:
"I see you now for what you are. No chance
to win you over. Iron in your breast
your heart is. Think a bit, though: this may be
a thing the gods in anger hold against you
on that day when Paris and Apollo
destroy you at the Gates, great as you are."

Even as he spoke, the end came, and death hid him;
spirit from body fluttered to undergloom,
bewailing fate that made him leave his youth
and manhood in the world. And as he died
Akhilleus spoke again. He said:

"Die, make an end. I shall accept my own
whenever Zeus and the other gods desire."

At this he pulled his spearhead from the body,
laying it aside, and stripped
the bloodstained shield and cuirass from his shoulders.
Other Akhaians hastened round to see
Hektor's fine body and his comely face,
and no one came who did not stab the body.
Glancing at one another they would say:
"Now Hektor has turned vulnerable, softer
than when he put the torches to the ships!"

And he who said this would inflict a wound.
When the great master of pursuit, Akhilleus,
had the body stripped, he stood among them,
saying swiftly:
"Friends, my lords and captains
of Argives, now that the gods at last have let me
bring to earth this man who wrought
havoc among us — more than all the rest —
come, we'll offer battle around the city,
to learn the intentions of the Trojans now.
Will they give up their strongpoint at this loss?
Can they fight on, though Hektor's dead?
But wait:
why do I ponder, why take up these questions?
Down by the ships Patróklos' body lies
unwept, unburied. I shall not forget him
while I can keep my feet among the living.
If in the dead world they forget the dead,
I say there, too, I shall remember him,
my friend. Men of Akhaia, lift a song!
Down to the ships we go, and take this body,
our glory. We have beaten Hektor down,
to whom as to a god the Trojans prayed."

Indeed, he had in mind for Hektor's body
outrage and shame. Behind both feet he pierced
the tendons, heel to ankle. Rawhide cords
he drew through both and lashed them to his chariot,
letting the man's head trail. Stepping aboard,
bearing the great trophy of the arms,
he shook the reins, and whipped the team ahead
into a willing run. A dustcloud rose

above the furrowing body; the dark tresses
flowed behind, and the head so princely once
lay back in dust. Zeus gave him to his enemies
to be defiled in his own fatherland.
So his whole head was blackened. Looking down,
his mother tore her braids, threw off her veil,
and wailed, heartbroken to behold her son.
Piteously his father groaned, and round him
lamentation spread throughout the town,
most like the clamor to be heard if Ilion's
towers, top to bottom, seethed in flames.
They barely stayed the old man, mad with grief,
from passing through the gates. Then in the mire
he rolled, and begged them all, each man by name:
"Relent, friends. It is hard; but let me go
out of the city to the Akhaian ships.
I'll make my plea to that demonic heart.
He may feel shame before his peers, or pity
my old age. His father, too, is old,
Pêleus, who brought him up to be a scourge
to Trojans, cruel to all, but most to me,
so many of my sons in flower of youth
he cut away. And, though I grieve, I cannot
mourn them all as much as I do one,
for whom my grief will take me to the grave—
and that is Hektor. Why could he not have died
where I might hold him? In our weeping, then,
his mother, now so destitute, and I
might have had surfeit and relief of tears."

These were the words of Priam as he wept,
and all his people groaned. Then in her turn
Hékabê led the women in lamentation:
"Child, I am lost now. Can I bear my life
after the death of suffering your death?
You were my pride in all my nights and days,
pride of the city, pillar of the Trojans
and Trojan women. Everyone looked to you
as though you were a god, and rightly so.
You were their greatest glory while you lived.
Now your doom and death have come upon you."

These were her mournful words. But Hektor's lady
still knew nothing; no one came to tell her
of Hektor's stand outside the gates. She wove

upon her loom, deep in the lofty house,
a double purple web with rose design.
Calling her maids in waiting,
she ordered a big caldron on a tripod
set on the hearthfire, to provide a bath
for Hektor when he came home from the fight.
Poor wife, how far removed from baths he was
she could not know, as at Akhilleus' hands
Athêna brought him down.
Then from the tower
she heard a wailing and a distant moan.
Her knees shook, and she let her shuttle fall,
and called out to her maids again:
"Come here.
Two must follow me, to see this action.
I heard my husband's queenly mother cry.
I feel my heart rise, throbbing in my throat.
My knees are like stone under me. Some blow
is coming home to Priam's sons and daughters.
Ah, could it never reach my ears! I die
of dread that Akhilleus may have cut off Hektor,
blocked my bold husband from the city wall,
to drive him down the plain alone! By now
he may have ended Hektor's deathly pride.
He never kept his place amid the chariots
but drove ahead. He would not be outdone
by anyone in courage."

Saying this, she ran
like a madwoman through the mégaron,
her heart convulsed. Her maids kept at her side.
On reaching the great tower and the soldiers,
Andrómakhê stood gazing from the wall
and saw him being dragged before the city.
Chariot horses at a brutal gallop
pulled the torn body toward the decked ships.
Blackness of night covered her eyes; she fell
backward swooning, sighing out her life,
and let her shining headdress fall, her hood
and diadem, her plaited band and veil
that Aphrodítê once had given her,
on that day when, from Eëtíôn's house,
for a thousand bridal gifts, Lord Hektor led her.
Now, at her side, kinswomen of her lord

supported her among them, dazed and faint
to the point of death. But when she breathed again
and her stunned heart recovered, in a burst
of sobbing she called out among the women:
"Hektor! Here is my desolation. Both
had this in store from birth—from yours in Troy
in Priam's palace, mine by wooded Plakos
at Thêbê in the home of Eëtíôn,
my father, who took care of me in childhood,
a man cursed by fate, a fated daughter.
How I could wish I never had been born!
Now under earth's roof to the house of Death
you go your way and leave me here, bereft,
lonely, in anguish without end. The child
we wretches had is still in infancy;
you cannot be a pillar to him, Hektor,
now you are dead, nor he to you. And should
this boy escape the misery of the war,
there will be toil and sorrow for him later,
as when strangers move his boundary stones.[81]
The day that orphans him will leave him lonely,
downcast in everything, cheeks wet with tears,
in hunger going to his father's friends
to tug at one man's cloak, another's khiton.
Some will be kindly: one may lift a cup
to wet his lips at least, though not his throat;
but from the board some child with living parents
gives him a push, a slap, with biting words:
'Outside, you there! Your father is not with us
here at our feast!' And the boy Astýanax
will run to his forlorn mother. Once he fed
on marrow only and the fat of lamb,
high on his father's knees. And when sleep came
to end his play, he slept in a nurse's arms,
brimful of happiness, in a soft bed.
But now he'll know sad days and many of them,
missing his father. 'Lord of the lower town'[82]
the Trojans call him. They know, you alone,
Lord Hektor, kept their gates and their long walls.
Beside the beaked ships now, far from your kin,
the blowflies' maggots in a swarm will eat you

[81] **move . . . stones:** Steal his land. [82] **'Lord . . . town':** The meaning of "Astýanax."

naked, after the dogs have had their fill.
Ah, there are folded garments in your chambers,
delicate and fine, of women's weaving.
These, by heaven, I'll burn to the last thread
in blazing fire! They are no good to you,
they cannot cover you in death. So let them
go, let them be burnt as an offering
from Trojans and their women in your honor."

Thus she mourned, and the women wailed in answer.

Book 24
A Grace Given in Sorrow

[In Book 23, Akhilleus and his followers participate in elaborate ceremonies for Patróklos, including a large funeral pyre, which is lit the next day. Funeral games are then held in his honor. The body of Hektor lies untended, but protected by Apollo and Aphrodítê.]

The funeral games were over. Men dispersed
and turned their thoughts to supper in their quarters,
then to the boon of slumber. But Akhilleus
thought of his friend, and sleep that quiets all things
would not take hold of him. He tossed and turned
remembering with pain Patróklos' courage,
his buoyant heart; how in his company
he fought out many a rough day full of danger,
cutting through ranks in war and the bitter sea.
With memory his eyes grew wet. He lay
on his right side, then on his back, and then
face downward—but at last he rose, to wander
distractedly along the line of surf.
This for eleven nights. The first dawn, brightening
sea and shore, became familiar to him,
as at that hour he yoked his team, with Hektor
tied behind, to drag him out, three times
around Patróklos' tomb. By day he rested
in his own hut, abandoning Hektor's body
to lie full-length in dust—though Lord Apollo,
pitying the man, even in death,
kept his flesh free of disfigurement.
He wrapped him in his great shield's flap of gold
to save him from laceration. But Akhilleus
in rage visited indignity on Hektor
day after day, and, looking on,
the blessed gods were moved. Day after day

they urged the Wayfinder[83] to steal the body—
a thought agreeable to all but Hêra,
Poseidon, and the grey-eyed one, Athêna.
These opposed it, and held out, since Ilion
and Priam and his people had incurred
their hatred first, the day Aléxandros
made his mad choice and piqued two goddesses,
visitors in his sheepfold: he praised
a third, who offered ruinous lust.[84]
Now when Dawn grew bright for the twelfth day,
Phoibos Apollo spoke among the gods:
"How heartless and how malevolent you are!
Did Hektor never make burnt offering
of bulls' thighbones to you, and unflawed goats?
Even in death you would not stir to save him
for his dear wife to see, and for his mother,
his child, his father, Priam, and his men:
they'd burn the corpse at once and give him burial.
Murderous Akhilleus has your willing help—
a man who shows no decency, implacable,
barbarous in his ways as a wild lion
whose power and intrepid heart
sway him to raid the flocks of men for meat.
The man has lost all mercy;
he has no shame—that gift that hinders mortals
but helps them, too. A sane one may endure
an even dearer loss: a blood brother,
a son; and yet, by heaven, having grieved
and passed through mourning, he will let it go.
The fates have given patient hearts to men.
Not this one: first he took Prince Hektor's life
and now he drags the body, lashed to his car,
around the barrow[85] of his friend, performing
something neither nobler in report
nor better in itself. Let him take care,
or, brave as he is, we gods will turn against him,
seeing him outrage the insensate earth!"

Hêra whose arms are white as ivory
grew angry at Apollo. She retorted:

---

[83] **the Wayfinder:** Hermês, messenger god and trickster. [84] **he praised . . . lust:** Zeus chose Aléxandros (Paris) to be the judge in a beauty contest; Paris chose the goddess Aphrodítê, who promised Paris the most beautiful woman in the world, over the goddesses Hêra and Athêna. [85] **barrow:** A grave mound.

"Lord of the silver bow, your words would be
acceptable if one had a mind to honor
Hektor and Akhilleus equally.
But Hektor suckled at a woman's breast,
Akhilleus is the first-born of a goddess—
one I nursed myself. I reared her, gave her
to Pêleus, a strong man whom the gods loved.
All of you were present at their wedding—
you too—friend of the base, forever slippery!—
came with your harp and dined there!"

Zeus the stormking

answered her:

"Hêra, don't lose your temper
altogether. Clearly the same high honor
cannot be due both men. And yet Lord Hektor,
of all the mortal men in Ilion,
was dearest to the gods, or was to me.
He never failed in the right gift; my altar
never lacked a feast
of wine poured out and smoke of sacrifice—
the share assigned as ours. We shall renounce
the theft of Hektor's body; there is no way;
there would be no eluding Akhilleus' eye,
as night and day his mother comes to him.
Will one of you now call her to my presence?
I have a solemn message to impart:
Akhilleus is to take fine gifts from Priam,
and in return give back Prince Hektor's body."

At this, Iris who runs on the rainy wind
with word from Zeus departed. Midway between
Samos and rocky Imbros,[86] down she plunged
into the dark grey sea, and the brimming tide
roared over her as she sank into the depth—
as rapidly as a leaden sinker, fixed
on a lure of wild bull's horn, that glimmers down
with a fatal hook among the ravening fish.
Soon Iris came on Thetis in a cave,
surrounded by a company of Nereids
lolling there, while she bewailed the fate
of her magnificent son, now soon to perish

[86] **Samos . . . Imbros:** Islands in the north Aegean.

on Troy's rich earth, far from his fatherland.
Halting before her, Iris said:
"Come, Thetis,
Zeus of eternal forethought summons you."

Silvery-footed Thetis answered:
"Why?
Why does the great one call me to him now,
when I am shy of mingling with immortals,
being so heavyhearted? But I'll go.
Whatever he may say will have its weight."

That loveliest of goddesses now put on
a veil so black no garment could be blacker,
and swam where windswift Iris led. Before them
on either hand the ground swell fell away.
They rose to a beach, then soared into the sky
and found the viewer of the wide world, Zeus,
with all the blissful gods who live forever
around him seated. Athêna yielded place,
and Thetis sat down by her father, Zeus,
while Hêra handed her a cup of gold
and spoke a comforting word. When she had drunk,
Thetis held out the cup again to Hêra.
The father of gods and men began:
"You've come
to Olympos, Thetis, though your mind is troubled
and insatiable pain preys on your heart.
I know, I too. But let me, even so,
explain why I have called you here. Nine days
of quarreling we've had among the gods
concerning Hektor's body and Akhilleus.
They wish the Wayfinder to make off with it.
I, however, accord Akhilleus honor
as I now tell you — in respect for you
whose love I hope to keep hereafter. Go, now,
down to the army, tell this to your son:
the gods are sullen toward him, and I, too,
more than the rest, am angered at his madness,
holding the body by the beaked ships
and not releasing it. In fear of me
let him relent and give back Hektor's body!
At the same time I'll send Iris to Priam,
directing him to go down to the beachhead

and ransom his dear son. He must bring gifts
to melt Akhilleus' rage."

Thetis obeyed,
leaving Olympos' ridge and flashing down
to her son's hut. She found him groaning there,
inconsolable, while men-at-arms
went to and fro, making their breakfast ready—
having just put to the knife a fleecy sheep.
His gentle mother sat down at his side,
caressed him, and said tenderly:
"My child,
will you forever feed on your own heart
in grief and pain, and take no thought of sleep
or sustenance? It would be comforting
to make love with a woman. No long time
will you live on for me: Death even now
stands near you, appointed and all-powerful.
But be alert and listen: I am a messenger
from Zeus, who tells me the gods are sullen toward you
and he himself most angered at your madness,
holding the body by the beaked ships
and not releasing it. Give Hektor back.
Take ransom for the body."

Said Akhilleus:
"Let it be so. Let someone bring the ransom
and take the dead away, if the Olympian
commands this in his wisdom."

So, that morning,
in camp, amid the ships, mother and son
conversed together, and their talk was long.
Lord Zeus meanwhile sent Iris to Ilion.

"Off with you, lightfoot, leave Olympos, take
my message to the majesty of Priam
at Ilion. He is to journey down
and ransom his dear son upon the beachhead.
He shall take gifts to melt Akhilleus' rage,
and let him go alone, no soldier with him,
only some crier, some old man, to drive
his wagon team and guide the nimble wagon,
and afterward to carry home the body
of him that Prince Akhilleus overcame.

Let him not think of death, or suffer dread,
as I'll provide him with a wondrous guide,
the Wayfinder, to bring him across the lines
into the very presence of Akhilleus.
And he, when he sees Priam within his hut,
will neither take his life nor let another
enemy come near. He is no madman,
no blind brute, nor one to flout the gods,
but dutiful toward men who beg his mercy."

Then Iris at his bidding ran
on the rainy winds to bear the word of Zeus,
until she came to Priam's house and heard
voices in lamentation. In the court
she found the princes huddled around their father,
faces and clothing wet with tears. The old man,
fiercely wrapped and hooded in his mantle,
sat like a figure graven—caked in filth
his own hands had swept over head and neck
when he lay rolling on the ground. Indoors
his daughters and his sons' wives were weeping,
remembering how many and how brave
the young men were who had gone down to death
before the Argive spearmen.
Zeus's courier,
appearing now to Priam's eyes alone,
alighted whispering, so the old man trembled:
"Priam, heir of Dárdanos, take heart,
and have no fear of me; I bode no evil,
but bring you friendly word from Zeus,
who is distressed for you and pities you
though distant far upon Olympos. He
commands that you shall ransom the Prince Hektor,
taking fine gifts to melt Akhilleus' rage.
And go alone: no soldier may go with you,
only some crier, some old man, to drive
your wagon team and guide the nimble wagon,
and afterward to carry home the body
of him that Prince Akhilleus overcame.
Put away thoughts of death, shake off your dread,
for you shall have a wondrous guide,
the Wayfinder, to bring you across the lines
into the very presence of Akhilleus.
He, for his part, seeing you in his quarters,
will neither take your life nor let another

enemy come near. He is no madman,
no blind brute, nor one to flout the gods,
but dutiful toward men who beg his mercy."

Iris left him, swift as a veering wind.
Then Priam spoke, telling the men to rig
a four-wheeled wagon with a wicker box,
while he withdrew to his chamber roofed in cedar,
high and fragrant, rich in precious things.
He called to Hékabê, his lady:

"Princess,
word from Olympian Zeus has come to me
to go down to the ships of the Akhaians
and ransom our dead son. I am to take
gifts that will melt Akhilleus' anger. Tell me
how this appears to you, tell me your mind,
for I am torn with longing, now, to pass
inside the great encampment by the ships."

The woman's voice broke as she answered:

"Sorrow,
sorrow. Where is the wisdom now that made you
famous in the old days, near and far?
How can you ever face the Akhaian ships
or wish to go alone before those eyes,
the eyes of one who stripped your sons in battle,
how many, and how brave? Iron must be
the heart within you. If he sees you, takes you,
savage and wayward as the man is,
he'll have no mercy and no shame. Better
that we should mourn together in our hall.
Almighty fate spun this thing for our son
the day I bore him: destined him to feed
the wild dogs after death, being far from us
when he went down before the stronger man.
I could devour the vitals of that man,
leeching into his living flesh! He'd know
pain then—pain like mine for my dead son.
It was no coward the Akhaian killed;
he stood and fought for the sweet wives of Troy,
with no more thought of flight or taking cover."

In majesty old Priam said:

"My heart

is fixed on going. Do not hold me back,
and do not make yourself a raven crying
calamity at home. You will not move me.
If any man on earth had urged this on me—
reader of altar smoke, prophet or priest—
we'd say it was a lie, and hold aloof.
But no: with my own ears I heard the voice,
I saw the god before me. Go I shall,
and no more words. If I must die alongside
the ships of the Akhaians in their bronze,
I die gladly. May I but hold my son
and spend my grief; then let Akhilleus kill me."

Throwing open the lids of treasure boxes
he picked out twelve great robes of state, and twelve
light cloaks for men, and rugs, an equal number,
and just as many capes of snowy linen,
adding a dozen khitons to the lot;
then set in order ten pure bars of gold,
a pair of shining tripods, four great caldrons,
and finally one splendid cup, a gift
Thracians had made him on an embassy.
He would not keep this, either—as he cared
for nothing now but ransoming his son.

And now, from the colonnade,
he made his Trojan people keep their distance,
berating and abusing them:
"Away,
you craven fools and rubbish! In your own homes
have you no one to mourn, that you crowd here,
to make more trouble for me? Is this a show,
that Zeus has crushed me, that he took the life
of my most noble son? You'll soon know what it means,
as you become child's play for the Akhaians
to kill in battle, now that Hektor's gone.
As for myself, before I see my city
taken and ravaged, let me go down blind
to Death's cold kingdom!"

Staff in hand,
he herded them, until they turned away
and left the furious old man. He lashed out
now at his sons, at Hélenos and Paris,

Agathôn, Pammôn, Antíphonos,
Polítês, Dêíphobos, Hippóthoös,
and Dios — to these nine the old man cried:
"Bestir yourselves, you misbegotten whelps,
shame of my house! Would god you had been killed
instead of Hektor at the line of ships.
How curst I am in everything! I fathered
first-rate men, in our great Troy; but now
I swear not one is left: Mêstôr, Trôïlos,
laughing amid the war-cars; and then Hektor —
a god to soldiers, and a god among them,
seeming not a man's child, but a god's.
Arês killed them. These poltroons are left,
hollow men, dancers, heroes of the dance,
light-fingered pillagers of lambs and kids
from the town pens!
Now will you get a wagon
ready for me, and quickly? Load these gifts
aboard it, so that we can take the road."

Dreading the rough edge of their father's tongue,
they lifted out a cart, a cargo wagon,
neat and maneuverable, and newly made,
and fixed upon it a wicker box; then took
a mule yoke from a peg, a yoke of boxwood
knobbed in front, with rings to hold the reins.
They brought out, too, the band nine forearms long
called the yoke-fastener, and placed the yoke
forward at the shank of the polished pole,
shoving the yoke-pin firmly in. They looped
three turns of the yoke-fastener round the knob
and wound it over and over down the pole,
tucking the tab end under. Next, the ransom:
bearing the weight of gifts for Hektor's person
out of the inner room, they piled them up
on the polished wagon. It was time to yoke
the mule-team, strong in harness, with hard hooves,
a team the Mysians had given Priam.
Then for the king's own chariot they harnessed
a team of horses of the line of Trôs,[87]
reared by the old king in his royal stable.

[87] **Trôs:** Great-grandfather of Priam.

So the impatient king and his sage crier
had their animals yoked in the palace yard
when Hékabê in her agitation joined them,
carrying in her right hand a golden cup
of honeyed wine, with which, before they left,
they might make offering. At the horses' heads
she stood to tell them:
"Here, tip wine to Zeus,
the father of gods. Pray for a safe return
from the enemy army, seeing your heart is set
on venturing to the camp against my will.
Pray in the second place to Zeus the stormking,
gloomy over Ida, who looks down
on all Troy country. Beg for an omen-bird,
the courier dearest of all birds to Zeus
and sovereign in power of flight,° eagle
that he appear upon our right in heaven.
When you have seen him with your own eyes, then,
under that sign, you may approach the ships.
If Zeus who views the wide world will not give you
vision of his bird, then I at least
cannot bid godspeed to your journey,
bent on it though you are."

In majesty
Priam replied:
"My lady, in this matter
I am disposed to trust you and agree.
It is an excellent thing and salutary
to lift our hands to Zeus, invoking mercy."

The old king motioned to his housekeeper,
who stood nearby with a basin and a jug,
to pour clear water on his hands. He washed them,
took the cup his lady held, and prayed
while standing there, midway in the walled court.
Then he tipped out the wine, looking toward heaven,
saying:
"Zeus, our Father, reigning from Ida,
god of glory and power, grant I come
to Akhilleus' door as one to be received
with kindliness and mercy. And dispatch
your courier bird, the nearest to your heart
of all birds, and the first in power of flight.
Let him appear upon our right in heaven

that I may see him with my own eyes
and under that sign journey to the ships."

Zeus all-foreseeing listened to this prayer
and put an eagle, king
of winged creatures, instantly in flight:
a swamp eagle, a hunter, one they call
the duskwing. Wide as a doorway in a chamber
spacious and high, built for a man of wealth,
a door with long bars fitted well, so wide
spread out each pinion. The great bird appeared
winging through the town on their right hand,
and all their hearts lifted with joy to see him.
In haste the old king boarded his bright car
and clattered out of the echoing colonnade.
Ahead, the mule-team drew the four-wheeled wagon,
driven by Idaíos,[88] and behind
the chariot rolled, with horses that the old man
whipped into a fast trot through the town.
Family and friends all followed weeping
as though for Priam's last and deathward ride.
Into the lower town they passed, and reached
the plain of Troy. Here those who followed after
turned back, sons and sons-in-law. And Zeus
who views the wide world saw the car and wagon
brave the plain. He felt a pang for Priam
and quickly said to Hermês, his own son:
"Hermês, as you go most happily
of all the gods with mortals, and give heed
to whom you will, be on your way this time
as guide for Priam to the deepsea ships.
Guide him so that not one of the Danáäns
may know or see him till he reach Akhilleus."

Argeiphontês[89] the Wayfinder obeyed.
He bent to tie his beautiful sandals on,
ambrosial, golden, that carry him over water
and over endless land on a puff of wind,
and took the wand with which he charms asleep—
or, when he wills, awake—the eyes of men.
So, wand in hand, the strong god glittering
paced into the air. Quick as a thought
he came to Hellê's waters and to Troy,
appearing as a boy whose lip was downy

[88] **Idaíos:** Priam's herald. [89] **Argeiphontês:** One of Hermês's names.

in the first bloom of manhood, a young prince,
all graciousness.
After the travelers
drove past the mound of Ilos,[90] at the ford
they let the mules and horses pause to drink
the running stream. Now darkness had come on
when, looking round, the crier
saw Hermês near at hand. He said to Priam:
"You must think hard and fast, your grace;
there is new danger; we need care and prudence.
I see a man-at-arms there—ready, I think,
to prey on us. Come, shall we whip the team
and make a run for it? Or take his knees
and beg for mercy?"

Now the old man's mind
gave way to confusion and to terror.
On his gnarled arms and legs the hair stood up,
and he stared, breathless. But the affable god
came over and took his hand and asked:
"Old father,
where do you journey, with your cart and car,
while others rest, below the evening star?
Do you not fear the Akhaians where they lie
encamped, hard, hostile outlanders, nearby?
Should someone see you, bearing stores like these
by night, how would you deal with enemies?
You are not young, your escort's ancient, too.
Could you beat off an attacker, either of you?
I'll do no hurt to you but defend you here.
You remind me of my father, whom I hold dear."

Old Priam answered him:
"Indeed, dear boy,
the case is as you say. And yet some god
stretched out his hand above me, he who sent
before me here—and just at the right time—
a traveler like yourself, well-made, well-spoken,
clearheaded, too. You come of some good family."

The Wayfinder rejoined:
"You speak with courtesy,
dear sir. But on this point enlighten me:
are you removing treasure here amassed

---

[90] **Ilos:** Founder of Iliom, or Ilium (Troy), grandfather of Priam.

for safety abroad, until the war is past?
Or can you be abandoning Ilion
in fear, after he perished, that great one
who never shirked a battle, your own princely son?"

Old Priam replied:
"My brave young friend, who are you?
Born of whom? How nobly you acknowledge
the dreadful end of my unfortunate son."

To this the Wayfinder replied:
"Dear sir,
you question me about him? Never surmise
I have not seen him with my very eyes,
and often, on the field. I saw him chase
Argives with carnage to their own shipways,
while we stood wondering, forbidden war
by the great anger that Akhilleus bore
Lord Agamémnon. I am of that company
Akhilleus led. His own ship carried me
as one of the Myrmidons. My father is old,
as you are, and his name's Polyktôr; gold
and other wealth he owns;
and I am seventh and last of all his sons.
When I cast lots among them, my lot fell
to join the siege against Troy citadel.
Tonight I've left the camp to scout this way
where, circling Troy, we'll fight at break of day;
our men are tired of waiting and will not stand
for any postponement by the high command."

Responded royal Priam:
"If you belong
to the company of Akhilleus, son of Pêleus,
tell me this, and tell me the whole truth:
is my son even now beside the ships?
Or has Akhilleus by this time dismembered him
and thrown him to the wild dogs?"

The Wayfinder
made reply again:
"Dear sir,
no dogs or birds have yet devoured your son.
Beside Akhilleus' ship, out of the sun,
he lies in a place of shelter. Now twelve days
the man has lain there, yet no part decays,

nor have the blowfly's maggots, that devour
dead men in war, fed on him to this hour.
True that around his dear friend's barrow tomb
Akhilleus drags him when dawn-shadows come,
driving pitilessly; but he mars him not.
You might yourself be witness, on the spot,
how fresh with dew he lies, washed of his gore,
unstained, for the deep gashes that he bore
have all closed up — and many thrust their bronze
into his body. The blest immortal ones
favor your prince, and care for every limb
even in death, as they so cherished him."

The old king's heart exulted, and he said:
"Child, it was well to honor the immortals.
He never forgot, at home in Ilion —
ah, did my son exist? was he a dream? —
the gods who own Olympos. They in turn
were mindful of him when he met his end.
Here is a goblet as a gift from me.
Protect me, give me escort, if the gods
attend us, till I reach Akhilleus' hut."

And in response Hermês the Wayfinder
said:
"You are putting a young man to test,
dear sir, but I may not, as you request,
accept a gift behind Akhilleus' back.
Fearing, honoring him, I could not lack
discretion to that point. The consequence, too,
could be unwelcome. As for escorting you,
even to Argos' famous land I'd ride
a deck with you, or journey at your side.
No cutthroat ever will disdain your guide."

With this, Hermês who lights the way for mortals
leapt into the driver's place. He caught up
reins and whip, and breathed a second wind
into the mule-team and the team of horses.
Onward they ran toward parapet and ships,
and pulled up to the moat.
Now night had fallen,
bringing the sentries to their supper fire,
but the glimmering god Hermês, the Wayfinder,
showered a mist of slumber on them all.
As quick as thought, he had the gates unbarred

and open to let the wagon enter, bearing
the old king and the ransom.
Going seaward
they came to the lofty quarters of Akhilleus,
a lodge the Myrmidons built for their lord
of pine trees cut and trimmed, and shaggy thatch
from mowings in deep meadows. Posts were driven
round the wide courtyard in a palisade,
whose gate one crossbar held, one beam of pine.
It took three men to slam this home, and three
to draw the bolt again—but great Akhilleus
worked his entryway alone with ease.
And now Hermês, who lights the way for mortals,
opened for Priam, took him safely in
with all his rich gifts for the son of Pêleus.
Then the god dropped the reins, and stepping down
he said:
"I am no mortal wagoner,
but Hermês, sir. My father sent me here
to be your guide amid the Akhaian men.
Now that is done, I'm off to heaven again
and will not visit Akhilleus. That would be
to compromise an immortal's dignity—
to be received with guests of mortal station.
Go take his knees, and make your supplication:
invoke his father, his mother, and his child;
pray that his heart be touched, that he be reconciled."

Now Hermês turned, departing for Olympos,
and Priam vaulted down. He left Idaíos
to hold the teams in check, while he went forward
into the lodge. He found Akhilleus, dear
to Zeus, there in his chair, with officers
at ease across the room. Only Automédôn
and Álkimos were busy near Akhilleus,
for he had just now made an end of dinner,
eating and drinking, and the laden boards
lay near him still upon the trestles.
Priam,
the great king of Troy, passed by the others,
knelt down, took in his arms Akhilleus' knees,
and kissed the hands of wrath that killed his sons.

When, taken with mad Folly in his own land,
a man does murder and in exile finds
refuge in some rich house, then all who see him

stand in awe.
So these men stood.
Akhilleus
gazed in wonder at the splendid king,
and his companions marveled too, all silent,
with glances to and fro. Now Priam prayed
to the man before him:
"Remember your own father,
Akhilleus, in your godlike youth: his years
like mine are many, and he stands upon
the fearful doorstep of old age. He, too,
is hard pressed, it may be, by those around him,
there being no one able to defend him
from bane of war and ruin. Ah, but he
may nonetheless hear news of you alive,
and so with glad heart hope through all his days
for sight of his dear son, come back from Troy,
while I have deathly fortune.
Noble sons
I fathered here, but scarce one man is left me.
Fifty I had when the Akhaians came,
nineteen out of a single belly, others
born of attendant women. Most are gone.
Raging Arês cut their knees from under them.
And he who stood alone among them all,
their champion, and Troy's, ten days ago
you killed him, fighting for his land, my prince,
Hektor.
It is for him that I have come
among these ships, to beg him back from you,
and I bring ransom without stint.
Akhilleus,
be reverent toward the great gods! And take
pity on me, remember your own father.
Think me more pitiful by far, since I
have brought myself to do what no man else
has done before—to lift to my lips the hand
of one who killed my son."

Now in Akhilleus
the evocation of his father stirred
new longing, and an ache of grief. He lifted
the old man's hand and gently put him by.
Then both were overborne as they remembered:
the old king huddled at Akhilleus' feet
wept, and wept for Hektor, killer of men,

while great Akhilleus wept for his own father
as for Patróklos once again; and sobbing
filled the room.
But when Akhilleus' heart
had known the luxury of tears, and pain
within his breast and bones had passed away,
he stood then, raised the old king up, in pity
for his grey head and greybeard cheek, and spoke
in a warm rush of words:
"Ah, sad and old!
Trouble and pain you've borne, and bear, aplenty.
Only a great will could have brought you here
among the Akhaian ships, and here alone
before the eyes of one who stripped your sons,
your many sons, in battle. Iron must be
the heart within you. Come, then, and sit down.
We'll probe our wounds no more but let them rest,
though grief lies heavy on us. Tears heal nothing,
drying so stiff and cold. This is the way
the gods ordained the destiny of men,
to bear such burdens in our lives, while they
feel no affliction. At the door of Zeus
are those two urns of good and evil gifts
that he may choose for us; and one for whom
the lightning's joyous king dips in both urns
will have by turns bad luck and good. But one
to whom he sends all evil—that man goes
contemptible by the will of Zeus; ravenous
hunger drives him over the wondrous earth,
unresting, without honor from gods or men.
Mixed fortune came to Pêleus. Shining gifts
at the gods' hands he had from birth: felicity,
wealth overflowing, rule of the Myrmidons,
a bride immortal at his mortal side.
But then Zeus gave afflictions too—no family
of powerful sons grew up for him at home,
but one child, of all seasons and of none.
Can I stand by him in his age? Far from my country
I sit at Troy to grieve you and your children.
You, too, sir, in time past were fortunate,
we hear men say. From Makar's isle of Lesbos
northward, and south of Phrygia and the Straits,
no one had wealth like yours, or sons like yours.
Then gods out of the sky sent you this bitterness:
the years of siege, the battles and the losses.
Endure it, then. And do not mourn forever

for your dead son. There is no remedy.
You will not make him stand again. Rather
await some new misfortune to be suffered."

The old king in his majesty replied:
"Never give me a chair, my lord, while Hektor
lies in your camp uncared for. Yield him to me
now. Allow me sight of him. Accept
the many gifts I bring. May they reward you,
and may you see your home again.
You spared my life at once and let me live."

Akhilleus, the great runner, frowned and eyed him
under his brows:
"Do not vex me, sir," he said.
"I have intended, in my own good time,
to yield up Hektor to you. She who bore me,
the daughter of the Ancient of the sea
has come with word to me from Zeus. I know
in your case, too — though you say nothing, Priam —
that some god guided you to the shipways here.
No strong man in his best days could make entry
into this camp. How could he pass the guard,
or force our gateway?
Therefore, *let me be.*
Sting my sore heart again, and even here,
under my own roof, suppliant though you are,
I may not spare you, sir, but trample on
the express command of Zeus!"

When he heard this,
the old man feared him and obeyed with silence.
Now like a lion at one bound Akhilleus
left the room. Close at his back the officers
Automédôn and Álkimos went out —
comrades in arms whom he esteemed the most
after the dead Patróklos. They unharnessed
mules and horses, led the old king's crier
to a low bench and sat him down.
Then from the polished wagon
they took the piled-up price of Hektor's body.
One khiton and two capes they left aside
as dress and shrouding for the homeward journey.
Then, calling to the women slaves, Akhilleus
ordered the body bathed and rubbed with oil —
but lifted, too, and placed apart, where Priam
could not see his son — for seeing Hektor

he might in his great pain give way to rage,
and fury then might rise up in Akhilleus
to slay the old king, flouting Zeus's word.
So after bathing and anointing Hektor
they drew the shirt and beautiful shrouding over him.
Then with his own hands lifting him, Akhilleus
laid him upon a couch, and with his two
companions aiding, placed him in the wagon.
Now a bitter groan burst from Akhilleus,
who stood and prayed to his own dead friend:
"Patróklos,
do not be angry with me, if somehow
even in the world of Death you learn of this—
that I released Prince Hektor to his father.
The gifts he gave were not unworthy. Aye,
and you shall have your share, this time as well."

The Prince Akhilleus turned back to his quarters.
He took again the splendid chair that stood
against the farther wall, then looked at Priam
and made his declaration:
"As you wished, sir,
the body of your son is now set free.
He lies in state. At the first sight of Dawn
you shall take charge of him yourself and see him.
Now let us think of supper. We are told
that even Niobê in her extremity
took thought for bread—though all her brood had perished,
her six young girls and six tall sons. Apollo,
making his silver longbow whip and sing,
shot the lads down, and Artemis with raining
arrows killed the daughters—all this after
Niobê had compared herself with Lêto,[91]
the smooth-cheeked goddess.
She has borne two children,
Niobê said, How many have I borne!
But soon those two destroyed the twelve.
Besides,
nine days the dead lay stark, no one could bury them,
for Zeus had turned all folk of theirs to stone.
The gods made graves for them on the tenth day,
and then at last, being weak and spent with weeping,
Niobê thought of food. Among the rocks
of Sipylos'[92] lonely mountainside, where nymphs

[91] **Lêto:** Mother of Apollo and Artemis. [92] **Sipylos:** Mountain with a legendary woman's weeping face.

who race Akhelôïos river go to rest,
she, too, long turned to stone, somewhere broods on
the gall immortal gods gave her to drink.

Like her we'll think of supper, noble sir.
Weep for your son again when you have borne him
back to Troy; there he'll be mourned indeed."

In one swift movement now Akhilleus caught
and slaughtered a white lamb. His officers
flayed it, skillful in their butchering
to dress the flesh, they cut bits for the skewers,
roasted, and drew them off, done to a turn.
Automédôn dealt loaves into the baskets
on the great board; Akhilleus served the meat.
Then all their hands went out upon the supper.
When thirst and appetite were turned away,
Priam, the heir of Dárdanos, gazed long
in wonder at Akhilleus' form and scale—
so like the gods in aspect. And Akhilleus
in his turn gazed in wonder upon Priam,
royal in visage as in speech. Both men
in contemplation found rest for their eyes,
till the old hero, Priam, broke the silence:
"Make a bed ready for me, son of Thetis,
and let us know the luxury of sleep.
From that hour when my son died at your hands
till now, my eyelids have not closed in slumber
over my eyes, but groaning where I sat
I tasted pain and grief a thousandfold,
or lay down rolling in my courtyard mire.
Here for the first time I have swallowed bread
and made myself drink wine.
Before, I could not."

Akhilleus ordered men and servingwomen
to make a bed outside, in the covered forecourt,
with purple rugs piled up and sheets outspread
and coverings of fleeces laid on top.
The girls went out with torches in their hands
and soon deftly made up a double bed.
Then Akhilleus, defiant of Agamémnon,
told his guest:
"Dear venerable sir,
you'll sleep outside tonight, in case an Akhaian
officer turns up, one of those men
who are forever taking counsel with me—

as well they may. If one should see you here
as the dark night runs on, he would report it
to the Lord Marshal Agamémnon. Then
return of the body would only be delayed.
Now tell me this, and give me a straight answer:
How many days do you require
for the funeral of Prince Hektor?—I should know
how long to wait, and hold the Akhaian army."

Old Priam in his majesty replied:
"If you would have me carry out the burial,
Akhilleus, here is the way to do me grace.
As we are penned in the town, but must bring wood
from the distant hills, the Trojans are afraid.
We should have mourning for nine days in hall,
then on the tenth conduct his funeral
and feast the troops and commons;
on the eleventh we should make his tomb,
and on the twelfth give battle, if we must."

Akhilleus said:
"As you command, old Priam,
the thing is done. I shall suspend the war
for those eleven days that you require."

He took the old man's right hand by the wrist
and held it, to allay his fear.

Now crier
and king with hearts brimful retired to rest
in the sheltered forecourt, while Akhilleus slept
deep in his palisaded lodge. Beside him,
lovely in her youth, Brisêis lay.
And other gods and soldiers all night long,
by slumber quieted, slept on. But slumber
would not come to Hermês the Good Companion,
as he considered how to ease the way
for Priam from the camp, to send him through
unseen by the formidable gatekeepers.
Then Hermês came to Priam's pillow, saying:
"Sir, no thought of danger shakes your rest,
as you sleep on, being great Akhilleus' guest,
amid men fierce as hunters in a ring.
You triumphed in a costly ransoming,
but three times costlier your own would be
to your surviving sons—a monarch's fee—
if this should come to Agamémnon's ear
and all the Akhaian host should learn that you are here."

The old king started up in fright, and woke
his herald. Hermês yoked the mules and horses,
took the reins, then inland like the wind
he drove through all the encampment, seen by no one.
When they reached Xánthos, eddying and running
god-begotten river, at the ford,
Hermês departed for Olympos. Dawn
spread out her yellow robe on all the earth,
as they drove on toward Troy, with groans and sighs,
and the mule-team pulled the wagon and the body.
And no one saw them, not a man or woman,
before Kassandra.[93] Tall as the pale-gold
goddess Aphrodítê, she had climbed
the citadel of Pergamos at dawn.
Now looking down she saw her father come
in his war-car, and saw the crier there,
and saw Lord Hektor on his bed of death
upon the mulecart. The girl wailed and cried
to all the city:
"Oh, look down, look down,
go to your windows, men of Troy, and women,
see Lord Hektor now! Remember joy
at seeing him return alive from battle,
exalting all our city and our land!"

Now, at the sight of Hektor, all gave way
to loss and longing, and all crowded down
to meet the escort and body near the gates,
till no one in the town was left at home.
There Hektor's lady and his gentle mother
tore their hair for him, flinging themselves
upon the wagon to embrace his person
while the crowd groaned. All that long day
until the sun went down they might have mourned
in tears before the gateway. But old Priam
spoke to them from his chariot:
"Make way,
let the mules pass. You'll have your fill of weeping
later, when I've brought the body home."

They parted then, and made way for the wagon,
allowing Priam to reach the famous hall.
They laid the body of Hektor in his bed,
and brought in minstrels, men to lead the dirge.
While these wailed out, the women answered, moaning.

[93] **Kassandra (Cassandra):** A seer who is not believed; the daughter of Priam and Hékabê.

Andrómakhê of the ivory-white arms
held in her lap between her hands
the head of Hektor who had killed so many.
Now she lamented:
"You've been torn from life,
my husband, in young manhood, and you leave me
empty in our hall. The boy's a child
whom you and I, poor souls, conceived; I doubt
he'll come to manhood. Long before, great Troy
will go down plundered, citadel and all,
now that you are lost, who guarded it
and kept it, and preserved its wives and children.
They will be shipped off in the murmuring hulls
one day, and I along with all the rest.

You, my little one, either you come with me
to do some grinding labor, some base toil
for a harsh master, or an Akhaian soldier
will grip you by the arm and hurl you down
from a tower here to a miserable death—
out of his anger for a brother, a father,
or even a son that Hektor killed. Akhaians
in hundreds mouthed black dust under his blows.
He was no moderate man in war, your father,
and that is why they mourn him through the city.
Hektor, you gave your parents grief and pain
but left me loneliest, and heartbroken.
You could not open your strong arms to me
from your deathbed, or say a thoughtful word,
for me to cherish all my life long
as I weep for you night and day."

Her voice broke,
and a wail came from the women. Hékabê
lifted her lamenting voice among them:

"Hektor, dearest of sons to me, in life
you had the favor of the immortal gods,
and they have cared for you in death as well.
Akhilleus captured other sons of mine
in other years, and sold them overseas
to Samos, Imbros, and the smoky island,
Lemnos. That was not his way with you.
After he took your life, cutting you down
with his sharp-bladed spear, he trussed and dragged you
many times round the barrow of his friend,
Patróklos, whom you killed—though not by this

could that friend live again. But now I find you
fresh as pale dew, seeming newly dead,
like one to whom Apollo of the silver bow
had given easy death with his mild arrows."

Hékabê sobbed again, and the wails redoubled.
Then it was Helen's turn to make lament:

"Dear Hektor, dearest brother to me by far!
My husband is Aléxandros,
who brought me here to Troy—God, that I might
have died sooner! This is the twentieth year
since I left home, and left my fatherland.
But never did I have an evil word
or gesture from you. No—and when some other
brother-in-law or sister would revile me,
or if my mother-in-law spoke to me bitterly—
but Priam never did, being as mild
as my own father—you would bring her round
with your kind heart and gentle speech. Therefore
I weep for you and for myself as well,
given this fate, this grief. In all wide Troy
no one is left who will befriend me, none;
they all shudder at me."

Helen wept,
and a moan came from the people, hearing her.
Then Priam, the old king, commanded them:
"Trojans, bring firewood to the edge of town.
No need to fear an ambush of the Argives.
When he dismissed me from the camp, Akhilleus
told me clearly they will not harass us,
not until dawn comes for the twelfth day."

Then yoking mules and oxen to their wagons
the people thronged before the city gates.
Nine days they labored, bringing countless loads
of firewood to the town. When Dawn that lights
the world of mortals came for the tenth day,
they carried greathearted Hektor out at last,
and all in tears placed his dead body high
upon its pyre, then cast a torch below.
When the young Dawn with finger tips of rose
made heaven bright, the Trojan people massed
about Prince Hektor's ritual fire.
All being gathered and assembled, first
they quenched the smoking pyre with tawny wine
wherever flames had licked their way, then friends

and brothers picked his white bones from the char
in sorrow, while the tears rolled down their cheeks.

In a golden urn they put the bones,
shrouding the urn with veiling of soft purple.
Then in a grave dug deep they placed it
and heaped it with great stones. The men were quick
to raise the death-mound, while in every quarter
lookouts were posted to ensure against
an Akhaian surprise attack. When they had finished
raising the barrow, they returned to Ilion,
where all sat down to banquet in his honor
in the hall of Priam king. So they performed
the funeral rites of Hektor, tamer of horses.

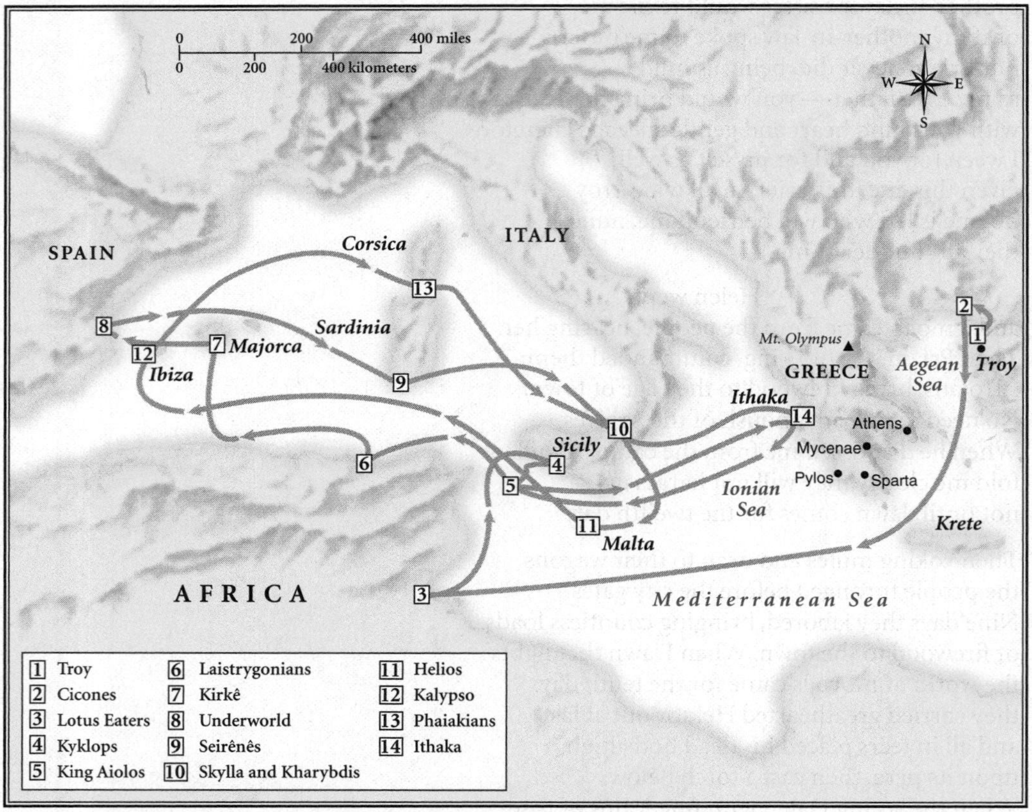

The Journeys of Odysseus

The Odyssey, *together with* The Iliad, *provides accounts of the Trojan War, the idea of the hero, and ancient Greek social and political customs. The journey of Odysseus is based on myth and legend; exact locations in* The Odyssey *presented here are based on the best but by no means definitive attempts to reconstruct his travels.*

The Odyssey

Translated by Robert Fitzgerald

Book 1
A Goddess Intervenes

Sing in me, Muse, and through me tell the story
of that man skilled in all ways of contending,
the wanderer, harried for years on end,
after he plundered the stronghold
on the proud height of Troy.
He saw the townlands
and learned the minds of many distant men,
and weathered many bitter nights and days
in his deep heart at sea, while he fought only
to save his life, to bring his shipmates home.
But not by will nor valor could he save them,
for their own recklessness destroyed them all—
children and fools, they killed and feasted on

The Odyssey. As described by the Greek philosopher Aristotle (384–322 B.C.E.) in his *Poetics,* the essential plot of *The Odyssey,* except for the mention of Poseidon, sounds very much like that of a modern novel:

> A certain man is absent from home for many years; he is jealously watched by Poseidon, and left desolate. Meanwhile his home is in a wretched plight—suitors are wasting his substance and plotting against his son. At length, tempest-tost, he himself arrives . . . he attacks the suitors with his own hand and is himself preserved while he destroys them.

A comparison with the Mesopotamian *Epic of Gilgamesh* (c. 1800 B.C.E.) suggests that either the author of *The Odyssey* knew of the epic or the Gilgamesh poet and Homer both drew from a common source. The intimate friendship between Gilgamesh and Enkidu seems to be a model for the bond between Achilles and Patroclus. The death of Enkidu sends Gilgamesh on an extended journey that ends in a visit to the nether world; Patroclus's death and the death of numerous Greek heroes precipitate Odysseus's travels and a visit to Hades. Both heroes are assisted by prescient women—Siduri and Circe—on journeys that prepare the men to be rulers.

It is unclear how *The Odyssey* originally ended. Two Alexandrian critics, Aristophanes (c. 257–180 B.C.E.) and Aristarchus (c. 217–c. 145 B.C.E.), responsible for the excellent editions of Homer in current use, maintained that the poem ended with Book 23, with the conjugal reunion of Odysseus and Penelope. Book 24, lacking in artistic merit, seems to have been added at a later date by someone other than the work's original author. Whether it was part of the original text or not, Book 24, which contains scenes in Hades, Odysseus's reunion with his father, and a debate about revenging the deaths of the suitors, nevertheless contributes to the whole of the epic by resolving issues about the reprisals.

A note on the translation: This translator does not use the more common Latinized spelling of names, such as Achilles and Achaeans, but versions closer to Greek spelling and pronunciation.

the cattle of Lord Hêlios,[1] the Sun,
and he who moves all day through heaven
took from their eyes the dawn of their return.

Of these adventures, Muse, daughter of Zeus,
tell us in our time, lift the great song again.
Begin when all the rest who left behind them
headlong death in battle or at sea
had long ago returned,[2] while he alone still hungered
for home and wife. Her ladyship Kalypso[3]
clung to him in her sea-hollowed caves—
a nymph, immortal and most beautiful,
who craved him for her own.
And when long years and seasons
wheeling brought around that point of time
ordained for him to make his passage homeward,
trials and dangers, even so, attended him
even in Ithaka,[4] near those he loved.
Yet all the gods had pitied Lord Odysseus,
all but Poseidon,[5] raging cold and rough
against the brave king till he came ashore
at last on his own land.
But now that god
had gone far off among the sunburnt races,
most remote of men, at earth's two verges,
in sunset lands and lands of the rising sun,
to be regaled by smoke of thighbones burning,
haunches of rams and bulls, a hundred fold.
He lingered delighted at the banquet side.

In the bright hall of Zeus upon Olympos
the other gods were all at home, and Zeus,
the father of gods and men, made conversation.
For he had meditated on Aigísthos, dead
by the hand of Agamémnon's son, Orestês[6]
and spoke his thought aloud before them all:
"My word, how mortals take the gods to task!
All their afflictions come from us, we hear.
And what of their own failings? Greed and folly

[1] **they killed . . . Hêlios:** This incident is found in Book 12. [2] **when all . . . returned:** From Troy. [3] **Kalypso:** Daughter of Atlas; a nymph is a lesser divinity, usually associated with nature, such as streams and springs. [4] **Ithaka:** Odysseus' island home off the western coast of Greece. [5] **Poseidon:** God of the ocean; lines 86–89 provide the reason for his rage. [6] **Orestês:** Aigísthos conspired with Klytaimnestra to kill Agamémnon when he returned from Troy; Orestês killed Aigísthos. See Book 11 of *The Odyssey.*

double the suffering in the lot of man.
See how Aigísthos, for his double portion,
stole Agamémnon's wife and killed the soldier
on his homecoming day. And yet Aigísthos
knew that his own doom lay in this. We gods
had warned him, sent down Hermês Argeiphontês,[7]
our most observant courier, to say:
'Don't kill the man, don't touch his wife,
or face a reckoning with Orestês
the day he comes of age and wants his patrimony.'
Friendly advice—but would Aigísthos take it?
Now he has paid the reckoning in full."

The grey-eyed goddess Athena replied to Zeus:
"O Majesty, O Father of us all,
that man is in the dust indeed, and justly.
So perish all who do what he had done.
But my own heart is broken for Odysseus,
the master mind of war, so long a castaway
upon an island in the running sea;
a wooded island, in the sea's middle,
and there's a goddess in the place, the daughter
of one whose baleful mind knows all the deeps
of the blue sea—Atlas,[8] who holds the columns
that bear from land the great thrust of the sky.
His daughter will not let Odysseus go,
poor mournful man; she keeps on coaxing him
with her beguiling talk, to turn his mind
from Ithaka. But such desire is in him
merely to see the hearthsmoke leaping upward
from his own island, that he longs to die.
Are you not moved by this, Lord of Olympos?
Had you no pleasure from Odysseus' offerings
beside the Argive[9] ships, on Troy's wide seaboard?
O Zeus, what do you hold against him now?"

To this the summoner of cloud replied:
"My child, what strange remarks you let escape you.
Could I forget that kingly man, Odysseus?
There is no mortal half so wise; no mortal
gave so much to the lords of open sky.

---

[7] **Hermês Argeiphontês:** Hermês is a messenger god; the meaning of *Argeiphontês* is uncertain, but it could signify "brightness." [8] **Atlas:** A Titan who supports the world on his shoulders; father of Kalypso. [9] **Argive:** A collective name for the Greeks fighting at Troy.

Only the god who laps the land in water,
Poseidon, bears the fighter an old grudge
since he poked out the eye of Polyphêmos,
brawniest of the Kyklopês.[10] Who bore
that giant lout? Thoösa, daughter of Phorkys,
an offshore sea lord: for this nymph had lain
with Lord Poseidon in her hollow caves.
Naturally, the god, after the blinding—
mind you, he does not kill the man;
he only buffets him away from home.
But come now, we are all at leisure here,
let us take up this matter of his return,
that he may sail. Poseidon must relent
for being quarrelsome will get him nowhere,
one god, flouting the will of all the gods."

The grey-eyed goddess Athena answered him:
"O Majesty, O Father of us all,
if it now please the blissful gods
that wise Odysseus reach his home again,
let the Wayfinder, Hermês, cross the sea
to the island of Ogýgia; let him tell
our fixed intent to the nymph with pretty braids,
and let the steadfast man depart for home.
For my part, I shall visit Ithaka
to put more courage in the son, and rouse him
to call an assembly of the islanders,
Akhaian[11] gentlemen with flowing hair.
He must warn off that wolf pack of the suitors
who prey upon his flocks and dusky cattle.
I'll send him to the mainland then, to Sparta
by the sand beach of Pylos;[12] let him find
news of his dear father where he may
and win his own renown about the world."

She bent to tie her beautiful sandals on,
ambrosial, golden, that carry her over water
or over endless land on the wings of the wind,
and took the great haft of her spear in hand—

[10] **Kyklopês (Cyclops):** The encounter with Polyphêmos, a Kyklopês, is told in Book 9. [11] **Akhaian:** Another name for the Greeks at Troy. [12] **Pylos:** A city in southern Greece ruled by Nestor.

that bronzeshod spear this child of Power can use
to break in wrath long battle lines of fighters.

Flashing down from Olympos' height she went
to stand in Ithaka, before the Manor,
just at the doorsill of the court. She seemed
a family friend, the Taphian[13] captain, Mentês,
waiting, with a light hand on her spear.
Before her eyes she found the lusty suitors
casting dice inside the gate, at ease
on hides of oxen — oxen they had killed.
Their own retainers made a busy sight
with houseboys mixing bowls of water and wine,
or sopping water up in sponges, wiping
tables to be placed about in hall,
or butchering whole carcasses for roasting.

Long before anyone else, the prince Telémakhos
now caught sight of Athena — for he, too,
was sitting there unhappy among the suitors,
a boy, daydreaming. What if his great father
came from the unknown world and drove these men
like dead leaves through the place, recovering
honor and lordship in his own domains?
Then he who dreamed in the crowd gazed out at Athena.

Straight to the door he came, irked with himself
to think a visitor had been kept there waiting,
and took her right hand, grasping with his left
her tall bronze-bladed spear. Then he said warmly:
"Greetings, stranger! Welcome to our feast.
There will be time to tell your errand later."

He led the way, and Pallas Athena followed
into the lofty hall. The boy reached up
and thrust her spear high in a polished rack
against a pillar where tough spear on spear
of the old soldier, his father, stood in order.
Then, shaking out a splendid coverlet,
he seated her on a throne with footrest — all
finely carved — and drew his painted armchair

[13] **Taphian:** A neighboring, seafaring people.

near her, at a distance from the rest.
To be amid the din, the suitors' riot,
would ruin his guest's appetite, he thought,
and he wished privacy to ask for news
about his father, gone for years.
A maid
brought them a silver finger bowl and filled it
out of a beautiful spouting golden jug,
then drew a polished table to their side.
The larder mistress with her tray came by
and served them generously. A carver lifted
cuts of each roast meat to put on trenchers
before the two. He gave them cups of gold,
and these the steward as he went his rounds
filled and filled again.
Now came the suitors,
young bloods trooping in to their own seats
on thrones or easy chairs. Attendants poured
water over their fingers, while the maids
piled baskets full of brown loaves near at hand,
and houseboys brimmed the bowls with wine.
Now they laid hands upon the ready feast
and thought of nothing more. Not till desire
for food and drink had left them were they mindful
of dance and song, that are the grace of feasting.
A herald gave a shapely cithern harp
to Phêmios,[14] whom they compelled to sing—
and what a storm he plucked upon the strings
for prelude! High and clear the song arose.

Telémakhos now spoke to grey-eyed Athena,
his head bent close, so no one else might hear:
"Dear guest, will this offend you, if I speak?
It is easy for these men to like these things,
harping and song; they have an easy life,
scot free, eating the livestock of another—
a man whose bones are rotting somewhere now,
white in the rain on dark earth where they lie,
or tumbling in the groundswell of the sea.
If he returned, if these men ever saw him,
faster legs they'd pray for, to a man,
and not more wealth in handsome robes or gold.

[14] **Phêmios:** The household bard.

But he is lost; he came to grief and perished,
and there's no help for us in someone's hoping
he still may come; that sun has long gone down.
But tell me now, and put it for me clearly—
who are you? Where do you come from? Where's your home
and family? What kind of ship is yours,
and what course brought you here? Who are your sailors?
I don't suppose you walked here on the sea.
Another thing—this too I ought to know—
is Ithaka new to you, or were you ever
a guest here in the old days? Far and near
friends knew this house; for he whose home it was
had much acquaintance in the world."

To this
the grey-eyed goddess answered:
"As you ask,
I can account most clearly for myself.
Mentês I'm called, son of the veteran
Ankhíalos; I rule seafaring Taphos.
I came by ship, with a ship's company,
sailing the winedark sea for ports of call
on alien shores—to Témesê, for copper,
bringing bright bars of iron in exchange.
My ship is moored on a wild strip of coast
in Reithron Bight, under the wooded mountain.
Years back, my family and yours were friends,
as Lord Laërtês[15] knows; ask when you see him.
I hear the old man comes to town no longer,
stays up country, ailing, with only one
old woman to prepare his meat and drink
when pain and stiffness take him in the legs
from working on his terraced plot, his vineyard.
As for my sailing here—
the tale was that your father had come home,
therefore I came. I see the gods delay him.
But never in this world is Odysseus dead—
only detained somewhere on the wide sea,
upon some island, with wild islanders;
savages, they must be, to hold him captive.
Well, I will forecast for you, as the gods
put the strong feeling in me—I see it all,

[15] **Laërtês:** Father of Odysseus.

and I'm no prophet, no adept in bird-signs.
He will not, now, be long away from Ithaka,
his father's dear land; though he be in chains
he'll scheme a way to come; he can do anything.

But tell me this now, make it clear to me:
You must be, by your looks, Odysseus' boy?
The way your head is shaped, the fine eyes—yes,
how like him! We took meals like this together
many a time, before he sailed for Troy
with all the lords of Argos in the ships.
I have not seen him since, nor has he seen me."

And thoughtfully Telémakhos replied:
"Friend, let me put it in the plainest way.
My mother says I am his son; I know not
surely. Who has known his own engendering?
I wish at least I had some happy man
as father, growing old in his own house—
but unknown death and silence are the fate
of him that, since you ask, they call my father."

Then grey-eyed Athena said:
"The gods decreed
no lack of honor in this generation:
such is the son Penélopê bore in you.
But tell me now, and make this clear to me:
what gathering, what feast is this? Why here?
A wedding? Revel? At the expense of all?
Not that, I think. How arrogant they seem,
these gluttons, making free here in your house!
A sensible man would blush to be among them."

To this Telémakhos answered:
"Friend, now that you ask about these matters,
our house was always princely, a great house,
as long as he of whom we speak remained here.
But evil days the gods have brought upon it,
making him vanish, as they have, so strangely.
Were his death known, I could not feel such pain—
if he had died of wounds in Trojan country
or in the arms of friends, after the war.
They would have made a tomb for him, the Akhaians,
and I should have all honor as his son.

Instead, the whirlwinds got him, and no glory.
He's gone, no sign, no word of him; and I inherit
trouble and tears—and not for him alone,
the gods have laid such other burdens on me.
For now the lords of the islands,
Doulíkhion and Samê, wooded Zakýnthos,
and rocky Ithaka's young lords as well,
are here courting my mother; and they use
our house as if it were a house to plunder.
Spurn them she dare not, though she hates that marriage,
nor can she bring herself to choose among them.
Meanwhile they eat their way through all we have,
and when they will, they can demolish me."

Pallas Athena was disturbed, and said:
"Ah, bitterly you need Odysseus, then!
High time he came back to engage these upstarts.
I wish we saw him standing helmeted
there in the doorway, holding shield and spear,
looking the way he did when I first knew him.
That was at our house, where he drank and feasted
after he left Ephyra, homeward bound
from a visit to the son of Mérmeris, Ilos.
He took his fast ship down the gulf that time
for a fatal drug to dip his arrows in
and poison the bronze points; but young Ilos
turned him away, fearing the gods' wrath.
My father gave it, for he loved him well.
I wish these men could meet the man of those days!
They'd know their fortune quickly: a cold bed.
Aye! but it lies upon the gods' great knees
whether he can return and force a reckoning
in his own house, or not.
If I were you,
I should take steps to make these men disperse.
Listen, now, and attend to what I say:
at daybreak call the islanders to assembly,
and speak your will, and call the gods to witness:
the suitors must go scattering to their homes.
Then here's a course for you, if you agree:
get a sound craft afloat with twenty oars
and go abroad for news of your lost father—
perhaps a traveller's tale, or rumored fame
issued from Zeus abroad in the world of men.

Talk to that noble sage at Pylos, Nestor,
then go to Meneláos,[16] the red-haired king
at Sparta, last man home of all the Akhaians.
If you should learn your father is alive
and coming home, you could hold out a year.
Or if you learn that he is dead and gone,
then you can come back to your own dear country
and raise a mound for him, and burn his gear,
with all the funeral honors due the man,
and give your mother to another husband.

When you have done all this, or seen it done,
it will be time to ponder
concerning these contenders in your house—
how you should kill them, outright or by guile.
You need not bear this insolence of theirs,
you are a child no longer. Have you heard
what glory young Orestês won
when he cut down that two-faced man, Aigísthos,
for killing his illustrious father?
Dear friend, you are tall and well set-up, I see;
be brave—you, too—and men in times to come
will speak of you respectfully.
Now I must join my ship;
my crew will grumble if I keep them waiting.
Look to yourself; remember what I told you."
Telémakhos replied:
"Friend, you have done me
kindness, like a father to his son,
and I shall not forget your counsel ever.
You must get back to sea, I know, but come
take a hot bath, and rest; accept a gift
to make your heart lift up when you embark—
some precious thing, and beautiful, from me,
a keepsake, such as dear friends give their friends."

But the grey-eyed goddess Athena answered him:
"Do not delay me, for I love the sea ways.
As for the gift your heart is set on giving,

[16] **Meneláos (Menelaus):** Brother of Agamémnon, husband of Helen of Troy.

let me accept it on my passage home,
and you shall have a choice gift in exchange."

With this Athena left him
as a bird rustles upward, off and gone.
But as she went she put new spirit in him,
a new dream of his father, clearer now,
so that he marvelled to himself
divining that a god had been his guest.
Then godlike in his turn he joined the suitors.

The famous minstrel still sang on before them,
and they sat still and listened, while he sang
that bitter song, the Homecoming of Akhaians—
how by Athena's will they fared from Troy;
and in her high room careful Penélopê,
Ikários' daughter, heeded the holy song.
She came, then, down the long stairs of her house,
this beautiful lady, with two maids in train
attending her as she approached the suitors;
and near a pillar of the roof she paused,
her shining veil drawn over across her cheeks,
the two girls close to her and still,
and through her tears spoke to the noble minstrel:
"Phêmios, other spells you know, high deeds
of gods and heroes, as the poets tell them;
let these men hear some other; let them sit
silent and drink their wine. But sing no more
this bitter tale that wears my heart away.
It opens in me again the wound of longing
for one incomparable, ever in my mind—
his fame all Hellas° knows, and midland Argos." Greece

But Telémakhos intervened and said to her:
"Mother, why do you grudge our own dear minstrel
joy of song, wherever his thought may lead?
Poets are not to blame, but Zeus who gives
what fate he pleases to adventurous men.
Here is no reason for reproof: to sing
the news of the Danaans![17] Men like best

[17] **Danaans:** Another name for the Greeks at Troy.

a song that rings like morning on the ear.
But you must nerve yourself and try to listen.
Odysseus was not the only one at Troy
never to know the day of his homecoming.
Others, how many others, lost their lives!"

The lady gazed in wonder and withdrew,
her son's clear wisdom echoing in her mind.
But when she had mounted to her rooms again
with her two handmaids, then she fell to weeping
for Odysseus, her husband. Grey-eyed Athena
presently cast a sweet sleep on her eyes.

Meanwhile the din grew loud in the shadowy hall
as every suitor swore to lie beside her,
but Telémakhos turned now and spoke to them:
"You suitors of my mother! Insolent men,
now we have dined, let us have entertainment
and no more shouting. There can be no pleasure
so fair as giving heed to a great minstrel
like ours, whose voice itself is pure delight.
At daybreak we shall sit down in assembly
and I shall tell you—take it as you will—
you are to leave this hall. Go feasting elsewhere,
consume your own stores. Turn and turn about,
use one another's houses. If you choose
to slaughter one man's livestock and pay nothing,
this is rapine; and by the eternal gods
I beg Zeus you shall get what you deserve:
a slaughter here, and nothing paid for it!"

By now their teeth seemed fixed in their under-lips,
Telémakhos' bold speaking stunned them so.
Antínoös, Eupeithês' son, made answer:
"Telémakhos, no doubt the gods themselves
are teaching you this high and mighty manner.
Zeus forbid you should be king in Ithaka,
though you are eligible as your father's son."

Telémakhos kept his head and answered him:
"Antínoös, you may not like my answer,
but I would happily be king, if Zeus
conferred the prize. Or do you think it wretched?
I shouldn't call it bad at all. A king
will be respected, and his house will flourish.

But there are eligible men enough,
heaven knows, on the island, young and old,
and one of them perhaps may come to power
after the death of King Odysseus.
All I insist on is that I rule our house
and rule the slaves my father won for me."

Eurýmakhos, Pólybos' son, replied:
"Telémakhos, it is on the gods' great knees
who will be king in sea-girt Ithaka.
But keep your property, and rule your house,
and let no man, against your will, make havoc
of your possessions, while there's life on Ithaka.
But no, my brave young friend,
a question or two about the stranger.
Where did your guest come from? Of what country?
Where does he say his home is, and his family?
Has he some message of your father's coming,
or business of his own, asking a favor?
He left so quickly that one hadn't time
to meet him, but he seemed a gentleman."

Telémakhos made answer, cool enough:
"Eurýmakhos, there's no hope for my father.
I would not trust a message, if one came,
nor any forecaster my mother invites
to tell by divination of time to come.
My guest, however, was a family friend,
Mentês, son of Ankhíalos.
He rules the Taphian people of the sea."

So said Telémakhos, though in his heart
he knew his visitor had been immortal.
But now the suitors turned to play again
with dance and haunting song. They stayed till nightfall,
indeed black night came on them at their pleasure,
and half asleep they left, each for his home.

Telémakhos' bedroom was above the court,
a kind of tower, with a view all round;
here he retired to ponder in the silence,
while carrying brands of pine alight beside him
Eurýkleia went padding, sage and old.
Her father had been Ops, Peisênor's son,
and she had been a purchase of Laërtês

when she was still a blossoming girl. He gave
the price of twenty oxen for her, kept her
as kindly in his house as his own wife,
though, for the sake of peace, he never touched her.
No servant loved Telémakhos as she did,
she who had nursed him in his infancy.
So now she held the light, as he swung open
the door of his neat freshly painted chamber.
There he sat down, pulling his tunic off,
and tossed it into the wise old woman's hands.
She folded it and smoothed it, and then hung it
beside the inlaid bed upon a bar;
then, drawing the door shut by its silver handle
she slid the catch in place and went away.
And all night long, wrapped in the finest fleece,
he took in thought the course Athena gave him.

Book 2
A Hero's Son Awakens

When primal Dawn spread on the eastern sky
her fingers of pink light, Odysseus' true son
stood up, drew on his tunic and his mantle,
slung on a sword-belt and a new-edged sword,
tied his smooth feet into good rawhide sandals,
and left his room, a god's brilliance upon him.
He found the criers with clarion voices and told them
to muster the unshorn Akhaians in full assembly.
The call sang out, and the men came streaming in;
and when they filled the assembly ground, he entered,
spear in hand, with two quick hounds at heel;
Athena lavished on him a sunlit grace
that held the eye of the multitude. Old men
made way for him as he took his father's chair.

Now Lord Aigýptios, bent down and sage with years,
opened the assembly. This man's son
had served under the great Odysseus, gone
in the decked ships with him to the wild horse country
of Troy—a spearman, Ántiphos by name.
The ravenous Kyklops in the cave destroyed him
last in his feast of men. Three other sons
the old man had, and one, Eurýnomos,
went with the suitors; two farmed for their father;

but even so the old man pined, remembering
the absent one, and a tear welled up as he spoke:
"Hear me, Ithakans! Hear what I have to say.
No meeting has been held here since our king,
Odysseus, left port in the decked ships.
Who finds occasion for assembly, now?
one of the young men? one of the older lot?
Has he had word our fighters are returning—
news to report if he got wind of it—
or is it something else, touching the realm?
The man has vigor, I should say; more power to him.
Whatever he desires, may Zeus fulfill it."

The old man's words delighted the son of Odysseus,
who kept his chair no longer but stood up,
eager to speak, in the midst of all the men.
The crier, Peisênor, master of debate,
brought him the staff and placed it in his hand;[18]
then the boy touched the old man's shoulder, and said:
"No need to wonder any more, Sir,
who called this session. The distress is mine.
As to our troops returning, I have no news—
news to report if I got wind of it—
nor have I public business to propose;
only my need, and the trouble of my house—
the troubles.

My distinguished father is lost,
who ruled among you once, mild as a father,
and there is now this greater evil still:
my home and all I have are being ruined.
Mother wanted no suitors, but like a pack
they came—sons of the best men here among them—
lads with no stomach for an introduction
to Ikários, her father across the sea;
he would require a wedding gift, and give her
to someone who found favor in her eyes.
No; these men spend their days around our house
killing our beeves and sheep and fatted goats,
carousing, soaking up our good dark wine,
not caring what they do. They squander everything.
We have no strong Odysseus to defend us,

[18] **placed it . . . hand:** The person holding the staff has permission to speak.

and as to putting up a fight ourselves—
we'd only show our incompetence in arms.
Expel them, yes, if I only had the power;
the whole thing's out of hand, insufferable.
My house is being plundered: is this courtesy?
Where is your indignation? Where is your shame?
Think of the talk in the islands all around us,
and fear the wrath of the gods,
or they may turn, and send you some devilry.
Friends, by Olympian Zeus and holy Justice
that holds men in assembly and sets them free,
make an end of this! Let me lament in peace
my private loss. Or did my father, Odysseus,
ever do injury to the armed Akhaians?
Is this your way of taking it out on me,
giving free rein to these young men?
I might as well—might better—see my treasure
and livestock taken over by you all;
then, if you fed on them, I'd have some remedy,
and when we met, in public, in the town,
I'd press my claim; you might make restitution.
This way you hurt me when my hands are tied."

And in hot anger now he threw the staff to the ground,
his eyes grown bright with tears. A wave of sympathy
ran through the crowd, all hushed; and no one there
had the audacity to answer harshly
except Antínoös, who said:
"What high and mighty
talk, Telémakhos! No holding you!
You want to shame us, and humiliate us,
but you should know the suitors are not to blame—
it is your own dear, incomparably cunning mother.
For three years now—and it will soon be four—
she has been breaking the hearts of the Akhaians,
holding out hope to all, and sending promises
to each man privately—but thinking otherwise.

Here is an instance of her trickery:
she had her great loom standing in the hall
and the fine warp of some vast fabric on it;
we were attending her, and she said to us:
'Young men, my suitors, now my lord is dead,
let me finish my weaving before I marry,
or else my thread will have been spun in vain.

It is a shroud I weave for Lord Laërtês,
when cold death comes to lay him on his bier.
The country wives would hold me in dishonor
if he, with all his fortune, lay unshrouded.'
We have men's hearts; she touched them; we agreed.
So every day she wove on the great loom—
but every night by torchlight she unwove it;
and so for three years she deceived the Akhaians.
But when the seasons brought the fourth around,
one of her maids, who knew the secret, told us;
we found her unraveling the splendid shroud.
She had to finish then, although she hated it.

Now here is the suitors' answer—
you and all the Akhaians, mark it well:
dismiss your mother from the house, or make her marry
the man her father names and she prefers.
Does she intend to keep us dangling forever?
She may rely too long on Athena's gifts—
talent in handicraft and a clever mind;
so cunning—history cannot show the like
among the ringleted ladies of Akhaia,
Mykênê with her coronet, Alkmênê, Tyro.[19]
Wits like Penélopê's never were before,
but this time—well, she made poor use of them.
For here are suitors eating up your property
as long as she holds out—a plan some god
put in her mind. She makes a name for herself,
but you can feel the loss it means for you.
Our own affairs can wait; we'll never go anywhere else,
until she takes an Akhaian to her liking."

But clear-headed Telémakhos replied:
"Antínoös, can I banish against her will
the mother who bore me and took care of me?
My father is either dead or far away,
but dearly I should pay for this
at Ikários' hands, if ever I sent her back.
The powers of darkness would requite it, too,
my mother's parting curse would call hell's furies[20]
to punish me, along with the scorn of men.

---

[19] **Mykênê . . . Tyro:** Mykênê, Alkmênê, and Tyro were famous women; Alkmênê was the mother of Heraklês and Tyro was the grandmother of Jason. [20] **furies:** Spirits who avenge crimes against women, especially mothers; their Greek name is Erinyes.

No: I can never give the word for this.
But if your hearts are capable of shame,
leave my great hall, and take your dinner elsewhere,
consume your own stores. Turn and turn about,
use one another's houses. If you choose
to slaughter one man's livestock and pay nothing,
this is rapine; and by the eternal gods
I beg Zeus you shall get what you deserve:
a slaughter here, and nothing paid for it!"

Now Zeus who views the wide world sent a sign to him,
launching a pair of eagles from a mountain crest
in gliding flight down the soft blowing wind,
wing-tip to wing-tip quivering taut, companions,
till high above the assembly of many voices
they wheeled, their dense wings beating, and in havoc
dropped on the heads of the crowd—a deathly omen—
wielding their talons, tearing cheeks and throats;
then veered away on the right hand through the city.
Astonished, gaping after the birds, the men
felt their hearts flood, foreboding things to come.
And now they heard the old lord Halithersês,
son of Mastor, keenest among the old
at reading birdflight into accurate speech;
in his anxiety for them, he rose and said:
"Hear me, Ithakans! Hear what I have to say,
and may I hope to open the suitors' eyes
to the black wave towering over them. Odysseus
will not be absent from his family long:
he is already near, carrying in him
a bloody doom for all these men, and sorrow
for many more on our high seamark, Ithaka.
Let us think how to stop it; let the suitors
drop their suit; they had better, without delay.
I am old enough to know a sign when I see one,
and I say all has come to pass for Odysseus
as I foretold when the Argives massed on Troy,
and he, the great tactician, joined the rest.
My forecast was that after nineteen years,
many blows weathered, all his shipmates lost,
himself unrecognized by anyone,
he would come home. I see this all fulfilled."

But Pólybos' son, Eurýmakhos, retorted:
"Old man, go tell the omens for your children

at home, and try to keep them out of trouble.
I am more fit to interpret this than you are.
Bird life aplenty is found in the sunny air,
not all of it significant. As for Odysseus,
he perished far from home. You should have perished with him—
then we'd be spared this nonsense in assembly,
as good as telling Telémakhos to rage on;
do you think you can gamble on a gift from him?
Here is what I foretell, and it's quite certain:
if you, with what you know of ancient lore,
encourage bitterness in this young man,
it means, for him, only the more frustration—
he can do nothing whatever with two eagles—
and as for you, old man, we'll fix a penalty
that you will groan to pay.
Before the whole assembly I advise Telémakhos
to send his mother to her father's house;
let them arrange her wedding there, and fix
a portion° suitable for a valued daughter. a dowry
Until he does this, courtship is our business,
vexing though it may be; we fear no one,
certainly not Telémakhos, with his talk;
and we care nothing for your divining, uncle,
useless talk; you win more hatred by it.
We'll share his meat, no thanks or fee to him,
as long as she delays and maddens us.
It is a long, long time we have been waiting
in rivalry for this beauty. We could have gone
elsewhere and found ourselves very decent wives."

Clear-headed Telémakhos replied to this:
"Eurýmakhos, and noble suitors all,
I am finished with appeals and argument.
The gods know, and the Akhaians know, these things.
But give me a fast ship and a crew of twenty
who will see me through a voyage, out and back.
I'll go to sandy Pylos, then to Sparta,
for news of Father since he sailed from Troy—
some traveller's tale, perhaps, or rumored fame
issued from Zeus himself into the world.
If he's alive, and beating his way home,
I might hold out for another weary year;
but if they tell me that he's dead and gone,
then I can come back to my own dear country
and raise a mound for him, and burn his gear,

with all the funeral honors that befit him,
and give my mother to another husband."

The boy sat down in silence. Next to stand
was Mentor, comrade in arms of the prince Odysseus,
an old man now. Odysseus left him authority
over his house and slaves, to guard them well.
In his concern, he spoke to the assembly:
"Hear me, Ithakans! Hear what I have to say.
Let no man holding scepter as a king
be thoughtful, mild, kindly, or virtuous;
let him be cruel, and practice evil ways;
it is so clear that no one here remembers
how like a gentle father Odysseus ruled you.
I find it less revolting that the suitors
carry their malice into violent acts;
at least they stake their lives
when they go pillaging the house of Odysseus—
their lives upon it, he will not come again.
What sickens me is to see the whole community
sitting still, and never a voice or a hand raised
against them—a mere handful compared with you."

Leókritos, Euênor's son, replied to him:
"Mentor, what mischief are you raking up?
Will this crowd risk the sword's edge over a dinner?
Suppose Odysseus himself indeed
came in and found the suitors at his table:
he might be hot to drive them out. What then?
Never would he enjoy his wife again—
the wife who loves him well; he'd only bring down
abject death on himself against those odds.
Madness, to talk of fighting in either case.
Now let all present go about their business!
Halithersês and Mentor will speed the traveller;
they can help him: they were his father's friends.
I rather think he will be sitting here
a long time yet, waiting for news on Ithaka;
that seafaring he spoke of is beyond him."

On this note they were quick to end their parley.
The assembly broke up; everyone went home—
the suitors home to Odysseus' house again.
But Telémakhos walked down along the shore
and washed his hands in the foam of the grey sea,

then said this prayer:
"O god of yesterday,
guest in our house, who told me to take ship
on the hazy sea for news of my lost father,
listen to me, be near me:
the Akhaians only wait, or hope to hinder me,
the damned insolent suitors most of all."

Athena was nearby and came to him,
putting on Mentor's figure and his tone,
the warm voice in a lucid flight of words:
"You'll never be fainthearted or a fool,
Telémakhos, if you have your father's spirit;
he finished what he cared to say,
and what he took in hand he brought to pass.
The sea routes will yield their distances
to his true son, Penélopê's true son,—
I doubt another's luck would hold so far.
The son is rare who measures with his father,
and one in a thousand is a better man,
but you will have the sap and wit
and prudence—for you get that from Odysseus—
to give you a fair chance of winning through.
So never mind the suitors and their ways,
there is no judgment in them, neither do they
know anything of death and the black terror
close upon them—doom's day on them all.
You need not linger over going to sea.
I sailed beside your father in the old days,
I'll find a ship for you, and help you sail her.
So go on home, as if to join the suitors,
but get provisions ready in containers—
wine in two-handled jugs and barley meal,
the staying power of oarsmen,
in skin bags, watertight. I'll go the rounds
and call a crew of volunteers together.
Hundreds of ships are beached on sea-girt Ithaka;
let me but choose the soundest, old or new,
we'll rig her and take her out on the broad sea."

This was the divine speech Telémakhos heard
from Athena, Zeus's daughter. He stayed no longer,
but took his heartache home,
and found the robust suitors there at work,
skinning goats and roasting pigs in the courtyard.

Antínoös came straight over, laughing at him,
and took him by the hand with a bold greeting:
"High-handed Telémakhos, control your temper!
Come on, get over it, no more grim thoughts,
but feast and drink with me, the way you used to.
The Akhaians will attend to all you ask for—
ship, crew, and crossing to the holy land
of Pylos, for the news about your father."

Telémakhos replied with no confusion:
"Antínoös, I cannot see myself again
taking a quiet dinner in this company.
Isn't it enough that you could strip my house
under my very nose when I was young?
Now that I know, being grown, what others say,
I understand it all, and my heart is full.
I'll bring black doom upon you if I can—
either in Pylos, if I go, or in this country.
And I will go, go all the way, if only
as someone's passenger. I have no ship,
no oarsmen: and it suits you that I have none."

Calmly he drew his hand from Antínoös' hand.
At this the suitors, while they dressed their meat,
began to exchange loud mocking talk about him.
One young toplofty gallant set the tone:
"Well, think of that!

Telémakhos has a mind to murder us.
He's going to lead avengers out of Pylos,
or Sparta, maybe; oh, he's wild to do it.
Or else he'll try the fat land of Ephyra—
he can get poison there, and bring it home,
doctor the wine jar and dispatch us all."

Another took the cue:
"Well now, who knows?
He might be lost at sea, just like Odysseus,
knocking around in a ship, far from his friends.
And what a lot of trouble that would give us,
making the right division of his things!
We'd keep his house as dowry for his mother—
his mother and the man who marries her."

That was the drift of it. Telémakhos
went on through to the storeroom of his father,
a great vault where gold and bronze lay piled

along with chests of clothes, and fragrant oil.
And there were jars of earthenware in rows
holding an old wine,
mellow, unmixed, and rare; cool stood the jars
against the wall, kept for whatever day
Odysseus, worn by hardships, might come home.
The double folding doors were tightly locked
and guarded, night and day, by the serving woman,
Eurýkleia, grand-daughter of Peisênor,
in all her duty vigilant and shrewd.
Telémakhos called her to the storeroom, saying:
"Nurse, get a few two-handled travelling jugs
filled up with wine—the second best, not that
you keep for your unlucky lord and king,
hoping he may have slipped away from death
and may yet come again—royal Odysseus.
Twelve amphorai will do; seal them up tight.
And pour out barley into leather bags—
twenty bushels of barley meal ground fine.
Now keep this to yourself! Collect these things,
and after dark, when mother has retired
and gone upstairs to bed, I'll come for them.
I sail to sandy Pylos, then to Sparta,
to see what news there is of Father's voyage."

His loving nurse Eurýkleia gave a cry,
and tears sprang to her eyes as she wailed softly:
"Dear child, whatever put this in your head?
Why do you want to go so far in the world—
and you our only darling? Lord Odysseus
died in some strange place, far from his homeland.
Think how, when you have turned your back, these men
will plot to kill you and share all your things!
Stay with your own, dear, do. Why should you suffer
hardship and homelessness on the wild sea?"

But seeing all clear, Telémakhos replied:
"Take heart, Nurse, there's a god behind this plan.
And you must swear to keep it from my mother,
until the eleventh day, or twelfth, or till
she misses me, or hears that I am gone.
She must not tear her lovely skin lamenting."

So the old woman vowed by all the gods,
and vowed again, to carry out his wishes;
then she filled up the amphorai with wine

and sifted barley meal into leather bags.
Telémakhos rejoined the suitors.
Meanwhile
the goddess with grey eyes had other business:
disguised as Telémakhos, she roamed the town
taking each likely man aside and telling him:
"Meet us at nightfall at the ship!" Indeed,
she asked Noêmon, Phronios' wealthy son,
to lend her a fast ship, and he complied.
Now when at sundown shadows crossed the lanes
she dragged the cutter to the sea and launched it,
fitted out with tough seagoing gear,
and tied it up, away at the harbor's edge.
The crewmen gathered, sent there by the goddess.
Then it occurred to the grey-eyed goddess Athena
to pass inside the house of the hero Odysseus,
showering a sweet drowsiness on the suitors,
whom she had presently wandering in their wine;
and soon, as they could hold their cups no longer,
they straggled off to find their beds in town,
eyes heavy-lidded, laden down with sleep.
Then to Telémakhos the grey-eyed goddess
appeared again with Mentor's form and voice,
calling him out of the lofty emptied hall:
"Telémakhos, your crew of fighting men
is ready at the oars, and waiting for you;
come on, no point in holding up the sailing."

And Pallas Athena turned like the wind, running
ahead of him. He followed in her footsteps
down to the seaside, where they found the ship,
and oarsmen with flowing hair at the water's edge.
Telémakhos, now strong in the magic, cried:
"Come with me, friends, and get our rations down!
They are all packed at home, and my own mother
knows nothing! — only one maid was told."

He turned and led the way, and they came after,
carried and stowed all in the well-trimmed ship
as the dear son of Odysseus commanded.
Telémakhos then stepped aboard; Athena
took her position aft, and he sat by her.
The two stroke oars cast off the stern hawsers
and vaulted over the gunnels to their benches.
Grey-eyed Athena stirred them a following wind,

soughing from the north-west on the winedark sea,
and as he felt the wind, Telémakhos
called to all hands to break out mast and sail.
They pushed the fir mast high and stepped it firm
amidships in the box, made fast the forestays,
then hoisted up the white sail on its halyards
until the wind caught, booming in the sail;
and a flushing wave sang backward from the bow
on either side, as the ship got way upon her,
holding her steady course.
Now they made all secure in the fast black ship,
and, setting out the winebowls all a-brim,
they made libation to the gods,
the undying, the ever-new,
most of all to the grey-eyed daughter of Zeus.
And the prow sheared through the night into the dawn.

Book 3
The Lord of the Western Approaches

The sun rose on the flawless brimming sea
into a sky all brazen—all one brightening
for gods immortal and for mortal men
on plowlands kind with grain.
And facing sunrise
the voyagers now lay off Pylos town,
compact stronghold of Neleus.[21] On the shore
black bulls were being offered by the people
to the blue-maned god° who makes the islands tremble: Poseidon
nine congregations, each five hundred strong,
led out nine bulls apiece to sacrifice,
taking the tripes to eat, while on their altars
thighbones in fat lay burning for the god.
Here they put in, furled sail, and beached the ship;
but Telémakhos hung back in disembarking,
so that Athena turned and said:
"Not the least shyness, now, Telémakhos.
You came across the open sea for this—
to find out where the great earth hides your father
and what the doom was that he came upon.

[21] **Neleus:** Son of Poseidon and father of Nestor.

Go to old Nestor, master charioteer,
so we may broach the storehouse of his mind.
Ask him with courtesy, and in his wisdom
he will tell you history and no lies."

But clear-headed Telémakhos replied:
"Mentor, how can I do it, how approach him?
I have no practice in elaborate speeches, and
for a young man to interrogate an old man
seems disrespectful—"

But the grey-eyed goddess said:
"Reason and heart will give you words, Telémakhos;
and a spirit will counsel others. I should say
the gods were never indifferent to your life."

She went on quickly, and he followed her
to where the men of Pylos had their altars.
Nestor appeared enthroned among his sons,
while friends around them skewered the red beef
or held it scorching. When they saw the strangers
a hail went up, and all that crowd came forward
calling out invitations to the feast.
Peisístratos in the lead, the young prince,
caught up their hands in his and gave them places
on curly lambskins flat on the sea sand
near Thrasymêdês, his brother, and his father;
he passed them bits of the food of sacrifice,
and, pouring wine in a golden cup,
he said to Pallas Athena, daughter of Zeus:
"Friend, I must ask you to invoke Poseidon:
you find us at this feast, kept in his honor.
Make the appointed offering then, and pray,
and give the honeyed winecup to your friend
so he may do the same. He, too,
must pray to the gods on whom all men depend,
but he is just my age, you are the senior,
so here, I give the goblet first to you."

And he put the cup of sweet wine in her hand.
Athena liked his manners, and the equity
that gave her precedence with the cup of gold,
so she besought Poseidon at some length:
"Earthshaker, listen and be well disposed.
Grant your petitioners everything they ask:

above all, honor to Nestor and his sons;
second, to every man of Pylos town
a fair gift in exchange for this hekatomb;[22]
third, may Telémakhos and I perform
the errand on which last night we put to sea."

This was the prayer of Athena—
granted in every particular by herself.
She passed the beautiful wine cup to Telémakhos,
who tipped the wine and prayed as she had done.
Meanwhile the spits were taken off the fire,
portions of crisp meat for all. They feasted,
and when they had eaten and drunk their fill, at last
they heard from Nestor, prince of charioteers:
"Now is the time," he said, "for a few questions,
now that our young guests have enjoyed their dinner.
Who are you, strangers? Where are you sailing from,
and where to, down the highways of sea water?
Have you some business here? or are you, now,
reckless wanderers of the sea, like those corsairs
who risk their lives to prey on other men?"

Clear-headed Telémakhos responded cheerfully,
for Athena gave him heart. By her design
his quest for news about his father's wandering
would bring him fame in the world's eyes. So he said:
"Nestor, pride of Akhaians, Neleus' son,
you ask where we are from, and I can tell you:
our home port is under Mount Neion, Ithaka.
We are not here on Ithakan business, though,
but on my own. I want news of my father,
Odysseus, known for his great heart, and I
will comb the wide world for it. People say
he fought along with you when Troy was taken.
As to the other men who fought that war,
we know where each one died, and how he died;
but Zeus allotted my father death and mystery.
No one can say for sure where he was killed,
whether some hostile landsmen or the sea,
the stormwaves on the deep sea, got the best of him.
And this is why I come to you for help.

[22] **hekatomb:** Literally, *hekatomb* means a sacrifice to the gods of one hundred animals, but it may also indicate any large, public sacrifice.

Tell me of his death, sir, if perhaps
you witnessed it, or have heard some wanderer
tell the tale. The man was born for trouble.
Spare me no part of it for kindness' sake,
but put the scene before me as you saw it.
If ever Odysseus my noble father
served you by promise kept or work accomplished
in the land of Troy, where you Akhaians suffered,
recall those things for me the way they were."

Then Nestor, prince of charioteers, made answer:
"Dear friend, you take me back to all the trouble
we went through in that country, we Akhaians:
rough days aboard ship on the cloudy sea
cruising away for pillage after Akhilleus;
rough days of battle around Priam's town.
Our losses, then—so many good men gone:
Arês' great Aias lies there, Akhilleus lies there,
Patróklos, too, the wondrous counselor,
and my own strong and princely son, Antílokhos[23]—
fastest man of them all, and a born fighter.
Other miseries, and many, we endured there.
Could any mortal man tell the whole story?
Not if you stayed five years or six to hear
how hard it was for the flower of the Akhaians;
you'd go home weary, and the tale untold.
Think: we were there nine years, and we tried everything,
all stratagems against them,
up to the bitter end that Zeus begrudged us.
And as to stratagems, no man would claim
Odysseus' gift for those. He had no rivals,
your father, at the tricks of war.
Your father?
Well, I must say I marvel at the sight of you:
your manner of speech couldn't be more like his;
one would say No; no boy could speak so well.
And all that time at Ilion,° he and I Troy
were never at odds in council or assembly—
saw things the same way, had one mind between us
in all the good advice we gave the Argives.

[23] **Antílokhos:** Great heroes of the Trojan War at Priam's city of Troy are listed here: Aías (or Ajax); Akhilleus, the central hero of *The Iliad,* who withdrew from battle, then returned to avenge the death of his friend Patróklos; and the clever Odysseus.

But when we plundered Priam's town and tower
and took to the ships, God scattered the Akhaians.
He had a mind to make homecoming hard for them,
seeing they would not think straight nor behave,
or some would not. So evil days came on them,
and she who had been angered,[24]
Zeus's dangerous grey-eyed daughter, did it,
starting a fight between the sons of Atreus.[25]
First they were fools enough to call assembly
at sundown, unheard of hour;
the Akhaian soldiers turned out, soaked with wine,
to hear talk, talk about it from their commanders:
Meneláos harangued them to get organized—
time to ride home on the sea's broad back, he said;
but Agamémnon wouldn't hear of it. He wanted
to hold the troops, make sacrifice, a hekatomb,
something to pacify Athena's rage.
Folly again, to think that he could move her.
Will you change the will of the everlasting gods
in a night or a day's time?
The two men stood there hammering at each other
until the army got to its feet with a roar,
and no decision, wanting it both ways.
That night no one slept well, everyone cursing
someone else. Here was the bane from Zeus.
At dawn we dragged our ships to the lordly water,
stowed aboard all our plunder
and the slave women in their low hip girdles.
But half the army elected to stay behind
with Agamémnon as their corps commander;
the other half embarked and pulled away.
We made good time, the huge sea smoothed before us,
and held our rites when we reached Ténedos,[26]
being wild for home. But Zeus, not willing yet,
now cruelly set us at odds a second time,
and one lot turned, put back in the rolling ships,
under command of the subtle captain, Odysseus;
their notion was to please Lord Agamémnon.

---

[24] **she . . . angered:** Athena was angry with the Greeks because her shrine had been violated when Kassandra tried to take refuge in it but was raped. [25] **sons of Atreus:** Agamémnon and Meneláos. [26] **But half the army . . . Ténedos:** Ténedos was an island off the Trojan coast. The question that troubled the various leaders was whether to hug the shoreline on the way home or take the more direct but dangerous route across the open water.

Not I. I fled, with every ship I had;
I knew fate had some devilment brewing there.
Diomêdês[27] roused his company and fled, too,
and later Meneláos, the red-haired captain,
caught up with us at Lesbos,
while we mulled over the long sea route, unsure
whether to lay our course northward of Khios,
keeping the Isle of Psyria off to port,
or inside Khios, coasting by windy Mimas.
We asked for a sign from heaven, and the sign came
to cut across the open sea to Euboia,
and lose no time putting our ills behind us.
The wind freshened astern, and the ships ran
before the wind on paths of the deep sea fish,
making Geraistos before dawn. We thanked Poseidon
with many a charred thighbone for that crossing.
On the fourth day, Diomêdês' company
under full sail put in at Argos port,
and I held on for Pylos. The fair wind,
once heaven set it blowing, never failed.

So this, dear child, was how I came from Troy,
and saw no more of the others, lost or saved.
But you are welcome to all I've heard since then
at home; I have no reason to keep it from you.
The Myrmidon[28] spearfighters returned, they say,
under the son of lionhearted Akhilleus;
and so did Poias' great son, Philoktêtês.[29]
Idómeneus brought his company back to Krete;
the sea took not a man from him, of all
who lived through the long war.
And even as far away as Ithaka
you've heard of Agamémnon—how he came
home, how Aigísthos waited to destroy him
but paid a bitter price for it in the end.
That is a good thing, now, for a man to leave
a son behind him, like the son who punished
Aigísthos for the murder of his great father.

[27] **Diomêdês:** One of the bravest chieftains in the Trojan War; his home was Argos. [28] **Myrmidon:** The Myrmidons were Akhilleus's warriors; his son, Neoptólemus, went to Troy to avenge his father's death. [29] **Philoktêtês:** Philoktêtês, who had been left behind on an island because of sickness, arrived at Troy for the conclusion of the war; Idómeneus was king of Krete.

You, too, are tall and well set-up, I see;
be brave, you too, so men in times to come
will speak well of you."

Then Telémakhos said:
"Nestor, pride of Akhaians, Neleus' son,
that was revenge, and far and wide the Akhaians
will tell the tale in song for generations.
I wish the gods would buckle his arms on me!
I'd be revenged for outrage
on my insidious and brazen enemies.
But no such happy lot was given to me
or to my father. Still, I must hold fast."

To this Lord Nestor of Gerênia said:
"My dear young friend, now that you speak of it,
I hear a crowd of suitors for your mother
lives with you, uninvited, making trouble.
Now tell me how you take this. Do the people
side against you, hearkening to some oracle?
Who knows, your father might come home someday
alone or backed by troops, and have it out with them.
If grey-eyed Athena loved you
the way she did Odysseus in the old days,
in Troy country, where we all went through so much—
never have I seen the gods help any man
as openly as Athena did your father—
well, as I say, if she cared for you that way,
there would be those to quit this marriage game."

But prudently Telémakhos replied:
"I can't think what you say will ever happen, sir.
It is a dazzling hope. But not for me.
It could not be—even if the gods willed it."

At this grey-eyed Athena broke in, saying:
"What strange talk you permit yourself, Telémakhos.
A god could save the man by simply wishing it—
from the farthest shore in the world.
If I were he, I should prefer to suffer
years at sea, and then be safe at home;
better that than a knife at my hearthside
where Agamémnon found it—killed by adulterers.
Though as for death, of course all men must suffer it:

the gods may love a man, but they can't help him
when cold death comes to lay him on his bier."

Telémakhos replied:
"Mentor, grievously though we miss my father, why
go on as if that homecoming could happen?
You know the gods had settled it already,
years ago, when dark death came for him.
But there is something else I imagine Nestor
can tell us, knowing as he does the ways of men.
They say his rule goes back over three generations,
so long, so old, it seems death cannot touch him.
Nestor, Neleus' son, true sage, say how
did the Lord of the Great Plains, Agamémnon, die?
What was the trick Aigísthos used
to kill the better man? And Meneláos,
where was he? Not at Argos[30] in Akhaia,
but blown off course, held up in some far country,
is that what gave the killer nerve to strike?"

Lord Nestor of Gerênia made answer:
"Well, now, my son, I'll tell you the whole story.
You know, yourself, what would have come to pass
if red-haired Meneláos, back from Troy,
had caught Aigísthos in that house alive.
There would have been no burial mound for him,
but dogs and carrion birds to huddle on him
in the fields beyond the wall, and not a soul
bewailing him, for the great wrong he committed.
While we were hard-pressed in the war at Troy
he stayed safe inland in the grazing country,
making light talk to win Agamémnon's queen.
But the Lady Klytaimnéstra, in the first days,
rebuffed him, being faithful still;
then, too, she had at hand as her companion
a minstrel Agamémnon left attending her,
charged with her care, when he took ship for Troy.
Then came the fated hour when she gave in.
Her lover tricked the poet and marooned him
on a bare island for the seabirds' picking,
and took her home, as he and she desired.

---

[30] **Argos:** A region in the Peloponnese ruled by Agamémnon.

Many thighbones he burned on the gods' altars
and many a woven and golden ornament
hung to bedeck them, in his satisfaction;
he had not thought life held such glory for him.

Now Meneláos and I sailed home together
on friendly terms, from Troy,
but when we came off Sunion Point[31] in Attika,
the ships still running free, Onêtor's son
Phrontis, the steersman of Meneláos' ship,
fell over with a death grip on the tiller:
some unseen arrow from Apollo hit him.
No man handled a ship better than he did
in a high wind and sea, so Meneláos
put down his longing to get on, and landed
to give this man full honor in funeral.
His own luck turned then. Out on the winedark sea
in the murmuring hulls again, he made Cape Malea,[32]
but Zeus who views the wide world sent a gloom
over the ocean, and a howling gale
came on with seas increasing, mountainous,
parting the ships and driving half toward Krete
where the Kydonians live by Iardanos river.
Off Gortyn's coastline in the misty sea there
a reef, a razorback, cuts through the water,
and every westerly piles up a pounding
surf along the left side, going toward Phaistos—
big seas buffeted back by the narrow stone.
They were blown here, and fought in vain for sea room;
the ships kept going in to their destruction,
slammed on the reef. The crews were saved. But now
those five that weathered it got off to southward,
taken by wind and current on to Egypt;
and there Meneláos stayed. He made a fortune
in sea traffic among those distant races,
but while he did so, the foul crime was planned
and carried out in Argos by Aigísthos,
who ruled over golden Mykênai[33] seven years.
Seven long years, with Agamémnon dead,

[31] **Sunion Point:** The southern tip of Attica, near Athens; their route lies westward around this point toward the Peloponnese. [32] **Cape Malea:** The southern cape of the Greek mainland; farther south is the island of Krete.
[33] **Mykênai:** Agamémnon's capital city, often used interchangeably by Homer with Argos.

he held the people down, before the vengeance.
But in the eighth year, back from exile in Attika,
Orestês killed the snake who killed his father.
He gave his hateful mother and her soft man
a tomb together, and proclaimed the funeral day
a festal day for all the Argive people.
That day Lord Meneláos of the great war cry
made port with all the gold his ships could carry.
And this should give you pause, my son:
don't stay too long away from home, leaving
your treasure there, and brazen suitors near;
they'll squander all you have or take it from you,
and then how will your journey serve?
I urge you, though, to call on Meneláos,
he being but lately home from distant parts
in the wide world. A man could well despair
of getting home at all, if the winds blew him
over the Great South Sea—that weary waste,
even the wintering birds delay
one winter more before the northward crossing.
Well, take your ship and crew and go by water,
or if you'd rather go by land, here are
horses, a car,° and my own sons for company chariot
as far as the ancient land of Lakedaimon° Sparta
and Meneláos, the red-haired captain there.
Ask him with courtesy, and in his wisdom
he will tell you history and no lies."

While Nestor talked, the sun went down the sky
and gloom came on the land,
and now the grey-eyed goddess Athena said:
"Sir, this is all most welcome and to the point,
but why not slice the bulls' tongues now, and mix
libations for Poseidon and the gods?
Then we can all retire; high time we did;
the light is going under the dark world's rim,
better not linger at the sacred feast."

When Zeus's daughter spoke, they turned to listen,
and soon the squires brought water for their hands,
while stewards filled the winebowls and poured out
a fresh cup full for every man. The company
stood up to fling the tongues and a shower of wine
over the flames, then drank their thirst away.
Now finally Telémakhos and Athena

bestirred themselves, turning away to the ship,
but Nestor put a hand on each, and said:
"Now Zeus forbid, and the other gods as well,
that you should spend the night on board, and leave me
as though I were some pauper without a stitch,
no blankets in his house, no piles of rugs,
no sleeping soft for host or guest! Far from it!
I have all these, blankets and deep-piled rugs,
and while I live the only son of Odysseus
will never make his bed on a ship's deck—
no, not while sons of mine are left at home
to welcome any guest who comes to us."

The grey-eyed goddess Athena answered him:
"You are very kind, sir, and Telémakhos
should do as you ask. That is the best thing.
He will go with you, and will spend the night
under your roof. But I must join our ship
and talk to the crew, to keep their spirits up,
since I'm the only senior in the company.
The rest are boys who shipped for friendship's sake,
no older than Telémakhos, any of them.
Let me sleep out, then, by the black hull's side,
this night at least. At daybreak I'll be off
to see the Kaukonians[34] about a debt they owe me,
an old one and no trifle. As for your guest,
send him off in a car, with one of your sons,
and give him thoroughbreds, a racing team."

Even as she spoke, Athena left them—seeming
a seahawk, in a clap of wings,—and all
the Akhaians of Pylos town looked up astounded.
Awed then by what his eyes had seen, the old man
took Telémakhos' hand and said warmly:
"My dear child, I can have no fears for you,
no doubt about your conduct or your heart,
if, at your age, the gods are your companions.
Here we had someone from Olympos—clearly
the glorious daughter of Zeus, his third child,
who held your father dear among the Argives.
O, Lady, hear me! Grant an illustrious name

[34] **the Kaukonians:** A tribe southwest of Pylos.

to me and to my children and my dear wife!
A noble heifer shall be yours in sacrifice,
one that no man has ever yoked or driven;
my gift to you — her horns all sheathed in gold."

So he ended, praying; and Athena heard him.
Then Nestor of Gerênia led them all,
his sons and sons-in-law, to his great house;
and in they went to the famous hall of Nestor,
taking their seats on thrones and easy chairs,
while the old man mixed water in a wine bowl
with sweet red wine, mellowed eleven years
before his housekeeper uncapped the jar.
He mixed and poured his offering, repeating
prayers to Athena, daughter of royal Zeus.
The others made libation, and drank deep,
then all the company went to their quarters,
and Nestor of Gerênia showed Telémakhos
under the echoing eastern entrance hall
to a fine bed near the bed of Peisístratos,
captain of spearmen, his unmarried son.
Then he lay down in his own inner chamber
where his dear faithful wife had smoothed his bed.

When Dawn spread out her finger tips of rose,
Lord Nestor of Gerênia, charioteer,
left his room for a throne of polished stone,
white and gleaming as though with oil, that stood
before the main gate of the palace; Neleus here
had sat before him — masterful in kingship,
Neleus, long ago a prey to death, gone down
to the night of the underworld.
So Nestor held his throne and scepter now,
lord of the western approaches to Akhaia.
And presently his sons came out to join him,
leaving the palace: Ekhéphron and Stratíos,
Perseus and Arêtós and Thrasymêdês,
and after them the prince Peisístratos,
bringing Telémakhos along with him.
Seeing all present, the old lord Nestor said:
"Dear sons, here is my wish, and do it briskly
to please the gods, Athena first of all,
my guest in daylight at our holy feast.
One of you must go for a young heifer

and have the cowherd lead her from the pasture.
Another call on Lord Telémakhos' ship
to invite his crewmen, leaving two behind;
and someone else again send for the goldsmith,
Laerkês, to gild the horns.
The rest stay here together. Tell the servants
a ritual feast will be prepared in hall.
Tell them to bring seats, firewood and fresh water."

Before he finished, they were about these errands.
The heifer came from pasture,
the crewmen of Telémakhos from the ship,
the smith arrived, bearing the tools of his trade—
hammer and anvil, and the precision tongs
he handled fiery gold with,—and Athena
came as a god comes, numinous, to the rites.

The smith now gloved each horn in a pure foil
beaten out of the gold that Nestor gave him—
a glory and delight for the goddess' eyes—
while Ekhéphron and Stratíos held the horns.
Arêtós brought clear lustral water
in a bowl quivering with fresh-cut flowers,
a basket of barley in his other hand.
Thrasymêdês who could stand his ground in war,
stood ready, with a sharp two-bladed axe,
for the stroke of sacrifice, and Perseus
held a bowl for the blood. And now Nestor,
strewing the barley grains, and water drops,
pronounced his invocation to Athena
and burned a pinch of bristles from the victim.
When prayers were said and all the grain was scattered
great-hearted Thrasymêdês in a flash
swung the axe, at one blow cutting through
the neck tendons. The heifer's spirit failed.
Then all the women gave a wail of joy—
daughters, daughters-in-law, and the Lady Eurydíkê,
Klyménos' eldest daughter. But the men
still held the heifer, shored her up
from the wide earth where the living go their ways,
until Peisístratos cut her throat across,
the black blood ran, and life ebbed from her marrow.
The carcass now sank down, and they disjointed
shoulder and thigh bone, wrapping them in fat,

two layers, folded, with raw strips of flesh.
These offerings Nestor burned on the split-wood fire
and moistened with red wine. His sons took up
five-tined forks in their hands, while the altar flame
ate through the bones, and bits of tripe went round.
Then came the carving of the quarters, and they spitted
morsels of lean meat on the long sharp tines
and broiled them at arm's length upon the fire.

Polykástê, a fair girl, Nestor's youngest,
had meanwhile given a bath to Telémakhos—
bathing him first, then rubbing him with oil.
She held fine clothes and a cloak to put around him
when he came godlike from the bathing place;
then out he went to take his place with Nestor.
When the best cuts were broiled and off the spits,
they all sat down to banquet. Gentle squires
kept every golden wine cup brimming full.
And so they feasted to their heart's content,
until the prince of charioteers commanded:
"Sons, harness the blood mares for Telémakhos;
hitch up the car, and let him take the road."

They swung out smartly to do the work, and hooked
the handsome horses to a chariot shaft.
The mistress of the stores brought up provisions
of bread and wine, with victuals fit for kings,
and Telémakhos stepped up on the painted car.
Just at his elbow stood Peisístratos,
captain of spearmen, reins in hand. He gave
a flick to the horses, and with streaming manes
they ran for the open country. The tall town
of Pylos sank behind them in the distance,
as all day long they kept the harness shaking.

The sun was low and shadows crossed the lanes
when they arrived at Phêrai.[35] There Dióklês,
son of Ortílokhos whom Alpheios fathered,
welcomed the young men, and they slept the night.
But up when the young Dawn's finger tips of rose

[35] **Phêrai:** Uncertain location; perhaps the modern Calamata.

opened in the east, they hitched the team
once more to the painted car,
and steered out eastward through the echoing gate,
whipping their fresh horses into a run.
That day they made the grainlands of Lakedaimon,
where, as the horses held to a fast clip,
they kept on to their journey's end. Behind them
the sun went down and all the roads grew dark.

Book 4
The Red-Haired King and His Lady

By vales and sharp ravines in Lakedaimon
the travellers drove to Meneláos' mansion,
and found him at a double wedding feast
for son and daughter.
Long ago at Troy
he pledged her to the heir[36] of great Akhilleus,
breaker of men—a match the gods had ripened;
so he must send her with a chariot train
to the town and glory of the Myrmidons.
And that day, too, he brought Alektor's daughter
to marry his tall scion, Megapénthês,
born of a slave girl during the long war—
for the gods had never after granted Helen
a child to bring into the sunlit world
after the first, rose-lipped Hermionê,
a girl like the pale-gold goddess Aphroditê.

Down the great hall in happiness they feasted,
neighbors of Meneláos, and his kin,
for whom a holy minstrel harped and sang;
and two lithe tumblers moved out on the song
with spins and handsprings through the company.
Now when Telémakhos and Nestor's son
pulled up their horses at the main gate,
one of the king's companions in arms, Eteóneus,
going outside, caught sight of them. He turned
and passed through court and hall to tell the master,

[36] **the heir:** Neoptólemos, son of Akhilleus.

stepping up close to get his ear. Said he:
"Two men are here—two strangers, Meneláos,
but nobly born Akhaians, they appear.
What do you say, shall we unhitch their team,
or send them on to someone free to receive them?"

The red-haired captain answered him in anger:
"You were no idiot before, Eteóneus,
but here you are talking like a child of ten.
Could we have made it home again—and Zeus
give us no more hard roving!—if other men
had never fed us, given us lodging?
Bring
these men to be our guests: unhitch their team!"

Eteóneus left the long room like an arrow,
calling equerries after him, on the run.
Outside, they freed the sweating team from harness,
stabled the horses, tied them up, and showered
bushels of wheat and barley in the feed box;
then leaned the chariot pole
against the gleaming entry wall of stone
and took the guests in. What a brilliant place
that mansion of the great prince seemed to them!
A-glitter everywhere, as though with fiery
points of sunlight, lusters of the moon.
The young men gazed in joy before they entered
into a room of polished tubs to bathe.
Maidservants gave them baths, anointed them,
held out fresh tunics, cloaked them warm; and soon
they took tall thrones beside the son of Atreus.
Here a maid tipped out water for their hands
from a golden pitcher into a silver bowl,
and set a polished table near at hand;
the larder mistress with her tray of loaves
and savories came, dispensing all her best,
and then a carver heaped their platters high
with various meats, and put down cups of gold.
Now said the red-haired captain, Meneláos,
gesturing:
"Welcome; and fall to; in time,
when you have supped, we hope to hear your names,
forbears and families—in your case, it seems,

no anonymities, but lordly men.
Lads like yourselves are not base born."

At this,
he lifted in his own hands the king's portion,
a chine of beef, and set it down before them.
Seeing all ready then, they took their dinner;
but when they had feasted well,
Telémakhos could not keep still, but whispered,
his head bent close, so the others might not hear:
"My dear friend, can you believe your eyes?—
the murmuring hall, how luminous it is
with bronze, gold, amber, silver, and ivory!
This is the way the court of Zeus must be,
inside, upon Olympos. What a wonder!"

But splendid Meneláos had overheard him
and spoke out on the instant to them both:
"Young friends, no mortal man can vie with Zeus.
His home and all his treasures are for ever.
But as for men, it may well be that few
have more than I. How painfully I wandered
before I brought it home! Seven years at sea,
Kypros, Phoinikia, Egypt, and still farther
among the sun-burnt races.
I saw the men of Sidon and Arabia
and Libya, too, where lambs are horned at birth.
In every year they have three lambing seasons,
so no man, chief or shepherd, ever goes
hungry for want of mutton, cheese, or milk—
all year at milking time there are fresh ewes.
But while I made my fortune on those travels
a stranger killed my brother, in cold blood,—
tricked blind, caught in the web of his deadly queen.
What pleasure can I take, then, being lord
over these costly things?
You must have heard your fathers tell my story,
whoever your fathers are; you must know of my life,
the anguish I once had, and the great house
full of my treasure, left in desolation.
How gladly I should live one third as rich
to have my friends back safe at home!—my friends
who died on Troy's wide seaboard, far

from the grazing lands of Argos.
But as things are, nothing but grief is left me
for those companions. While I sit at home
sometimes hot tears come, and I revel in them,
or stop before the surfeit makes me shiver.
And there is one I miss more than the other
dead I mourn for; sleep and food alike
grow hateful when I think of him. No soldier
took on so much, went through so much, as Odysseus.
That seems to have been his destiny, and this mine—
to feel each day the emptiness of his absence,
ignorant, even, whether he lived or died.
How his old father and his quiet wife,
Penélopê, must miss him still!
And Telémakhos, whom he left as a new-born child."

Now hearing these things said, the boy's heart rose
in a long pang for his father, and he wept,
holding his purple mantle with both hands
before his eyes. Meneláos knew him now,
and so fell silent with uncertainty
whether to let him speak and name his father
in his own time, or to inquire, and prompt him.
And while he pondered, Helen came
out of her scented chamber, a moving grace
like Artemis,[37] straight as a shaft of gold.
Beside her came Adrastê, to place her armchair,
Alkippê, with a rug of downy wool,
and Phylo, bringing a silver basket, once
given by Alkandrê, the wife of Pólybos,
in the treasure city, Thebes of distant Egypt.
He gave two silver bathtubs to Meneláos
and a pair of tripods, with ten pure gold bars,
and she, then, made these beautiful gifts to Helen:
a golden distaff, and the silver basket
rimmed in hammered gold, with wheels to run on.
So Phylo rolled it in to stand beside her,
heaped with fine spun stuff, and cradled on it
the distaff swathed in dusky violet wool.
Reclining in her light chair with its footrest,
Helen gazed at her husband and demanded:
"Meneláos, my lord, have we yet heard

[37] **Artemis:** Virgin goddess of the hunt and childbirth.

our new guests introduce themselves? Shall I
dissemble what I feel? No, I must say it.
Never, anywhere, have I seen so great a likeness
in man or woman—but it is truly strange!
This boy must be the son of Odysseus,
Telémakhos, the child he left at home
that year the Akhaian host made war on Troy—
daring all for the wanton that I was."

And the red-haired captain, Meneláos, answered:
"My dear, I see the likeness as well as you do.
Odysseus' hands and feet were like this boy's;
his head, and hair, and the glinting of his eyes.
Not only that, but when I spoke, just now,
of Odysseus' years of toil on my behalf
and all he had to endure—the boy broke down
and wept into his cloak."

Now Nestor's son,
Peisístratos, spoke up in answer to him:
"My lord marshal, Meneláos, son of Atreus,
this is that hero's son as you surmise,
but he is gentle, and would be ashamed
to clamor for attention before your grace
whose words have been so moving to us both.
Nestor, Lord of Gerênia, sent me with him
as guide and escort; he had wished to see you,
to be advised by you or assisted somehow.
A father far from home means difficulty
for an only son, with no one else to help him;
so with Telémakhos:
his father left the house without defenders."

The king with flaming hair now spoke again:
"His son, in my house! How I loved the man,
And how he fought through hardship for my sake!
I swore I'd cherish him above all others
if Zeus, who views the wide world, gave us passage
homeward across the sea in the fast ships.
I would have settled him in Argos, brought him
over with herds and household out of Ithaka,
his child and all his people. I could have cleaned out
one of my towns to be his new domain.
And so we might have been together often
in feasts and entertainments, never parted

till the dark mist of death lapped over one of us.
But God himself must have been envious,
to batter the bruised man so that he alone
should fail in his return."

A twinging ache of grief rose up in everyone,
and Helen of Argos wept, the daughter of Zeus,[38]
Telémakhos and Meneláos wept,
and tears came to the eyes of Nestor's son—
remembering, for his part, Antílokhos,
whom the son of shining Dawn had killed in battle.
But thinking of that brother, he broke out:
"O son of Atreus, when we spoke of you
at home, and asked about you, my old father
would say you have the clearest mind of all.
If it is not too much to ask, then, let us not
weep away these hours after supper;
I feel we should not: Dawn will soon be here!
You understand, I would not grudge a man
right mourning when he comes to death and doom:
what else can one bestow on the poor dead?—
a lock of hair sheared, and a tear let fall.
For that matter, I, too,
lost someone in the war at Troy—my brother,
and no mean soldier, whom you must have known,
although I never did,—Antílokhos.
He ranked high as a runner and fighting man."

The red-haired captain Meneláos answered:
"My lad, what you have said is only sensible,
and you did well to speak. Yes, that was worthy
a wise man and an older man than you are:
you speak for all the world like Nestor's son.
How easily one can tell the man whose father
had true felicity, marrying and begetting!
And that was true of Nestor, all his days,
down to his sleek old age in peace at home,
with clever sons, good spearmen into the bargain.
Come, we'll shake off this mourning mood of ours
and think of supper. Let the men at arms

[38] **Helen . . . daughter of Zeus:** Helen's mother was a mortal, Lêda, who was seduced by Zeus in the form of a swan.

rinse our hands again! There will be time
for a long talk with Telémakhos in the morning."

The hero Meneláos' companion in arms,
Asphalion, poured water for their hands,
and once again they touched the food before them.
But now it entered Helen's mind
to drop into the wine that they were drinking
an anodyne, mild magic of forgetfulness.
Whoever drank this mixture in the wine bowl
would be incapable of tears that day—
though he should lose mother and father both,
or see, with his own eyes, a son or brother
mauled by weapons of bronze at his own gate.
The opiate of Zeus's daughter bore
this canny power. It had been supplied her
by Polydamna, mistress of Lord Thôn,
in Egypt, where the rich plantations grow
herbs of all kinds, maleficent and healthful;
and no one else knows medicine as they do,
Egyptian heirs of Paian,[39] the healing god.
She drugged the wine, then, had it served, and said—
taking again her part in the conversation—
"O Meneláos, Atreus' royal son,
and you that are great heroes' sons, you know
how Zeus gives all of us in turn
good luck and bad luck, being all powerful.
So take refreshment, take your ease in hall,
and cheer the time with stories. I'll begin.
Not that I think of naming, far less telling,
every feat of that rugged man, Odysseus,
but here is something that he dared to do
at Troy, where you Akhaians endured the war.
He had, first, given himself an outrageous beating
and thrown some rags on—like a household slave—
then slipped into that city of wide lanes
among his enemies. So changed, he looked
as never before upon the Akhaian beachhead,
but like a beggar, merged in the townspeople;

[39] **Egyptian heirs of Paian:** *Paian* means "healer" and is another name for Apollo and Apollo's son Asclepius, god of healing. Egyptians were famous for their knowledge of herbs and drugs.

and no one there remarked him. But I knew him—
even as he was, I knew him,
and questioned him. How shrewdly he put me off!
But in the end I bathed him and anointed him,
put a fresh cloak around him, and swore an oath
not to give him away as Odysseus to the Trojans,
till he got back to camp where the long ships lay.
He spoke up then, and told me
all about the Akhaians, and their plans—
then sworded many Trojans through the body
on his way out with what he learned of theirs.
The Trojan women raised a cry—but my heart
sang—for I had come round, long before,
to dreams of sailing home, and I repented
the mad day Aphrodítê
drew me away from my dear fatherland,
forsaking all—child, bridal bed, and husband—
a man without defect in form or mind."

Replied the red-haired captain, Meneláos:
"An excellent tale, my dear, and most becoming.
In my life I have met, in many countries,
foresight and wit in many first rate men,
but never have I seen one like Odysseus
for steadiness and a stout heart. Here, for instance,
is what he did—had the cold nerve to do—
inside the hollow horse,[40] where we were waiting,
picked men all of us, for the Trojan slaughter,
when all of a sudden, you came by—I dare say
drawn by some superhuman
power that planned an exploit for the Trojans;
and Deïphobos,[41] that handsome man, came with you.
Three times you walked around it, patting it everywhere,
and called by name the flower of our fighters,
making your voice sound like their wives, calling.
Diomêdês and I crouched in the center
along with Odysseus; we could hear you plainly;
and listening, we two were swept
by waves of longing—to reply, or go.
Odysseus fought us down, despite our craving,

[40] **inside the hollow horse:** Appearing to have abandoned the fight against Troy, a group of warriors hid inside a wooden horse that the Trojans dragged inside the walls of their city, precipitating its downfall. [41] **Deïphobos:** A Trojan prince married to Helen after Paris's death.

and all the Akhaians kept their lips shut tight,
all but Antiklos. Desire moved his throat
to hail you, but Odysseus' great hands clamped
over his jaws, and held. So he saved us all,
till Pallas Athena led you away at last."

Then clear-headed Telémakhos addressed him:
"My lord marshal, Meneláos, son of Atreus,
all the more pity, since these valors
could not defend him from annihilation—
not if his heart were iron in his breast.
But will you not dismiss us for the night now?
Sweet sleep will be a pleasure, drifting over us."

He said no more, but Helen called the maids
and sent them to make beds, with purple rugs
piled up, and sheets outspread, and fleecy
coverlets, in the porch inside the gate.
The girls went out with torches in their hands,
and presently a squire led the guests—
Telémakhos and Nestor's radiant son—
under the entrance colonnade, to bed.
Then deep in the great mansion, in his chamber,
Meneláos went to rest, and Helen,
queenly in her long gown, lay beside him.

When the young Dawn with finger tips of rose
made heaven bright, the deep-lunged man of battle
stood up, pulled on his tunic and his mantle,
slung on a swordbelt and a new edged sword,
tied his smooth feet into fine rawhide sandals
and left his room, a god's brilliance upon him.
He sat down by Telémakhos, asking gently:
"Telémakhos, why did you come, sir, riding
the sea's broad back to reach old Lakedaimon?
A public errand or private? Why, precisely?"

Telémakhos replied:
"My lord marshal Meneláos, son of Atreus,
I came to hear what news you had of Father.
My house, my good estates are being ruined.
Each day my mother's bullying suitors come
to slaughter flocks of mine and my black cattle;
enemies crowd our home. And this is why
I come to you for news of him who owned it.

Tell me of his death, sir, if perhaps
you witnessed it, or have heard some wanderer
tell the tale. The man was born for trouble.
Spare me no part for kindness' sake; be harsh;
but put the scene before me as you saw it.
If ever Odysseus my noble father
served you by promise kept or work accomplished
in the land of Troy, where you Akhaians suffered,
recall those things for me the way they were."

Stirred now to anger, Meneláos said:
"Intolerable—that soft men, as those are,
should think to lie in that great captain's bed.
Fawns in a lion's lair! As if a doe
put down her litter of sucklings there, while she
quested a glen or cropped some grassy hollow.
Ha! Then the lord returns to his own bed
and deals out wretched doom on both alike.
So will Odysseus deal out doom on these.
O Father Zeus, Athena, and Apollo!
I pray he comes as once he was, in Lesbos,
when he stood up to wrestle Philomeleidês—
champion and Island King—
and smashed him down. How the Akhaians cheered!
If only that Odysseus met the suitors,
they'd have their consummation, a cold bed!
Now for your questions, let me come to the point.
I would not misreport it for you; let me
tell you what the Ancient of the Sea,
who is infallible, said to me—every word.

During my first try at a passage homeward
the gods detained me, tied me down to Egypt—
for I had been too scant in hekatombs,
and gods will have the rules each time remembered.
There is an island washed by the open sea
lying off Nile mouth—seamen call it Pharos—
distant a day's sail in a clean hull
with a brisk land breeze behind. It has a harbor,
a sheltered bay, where shipmasters
take on dark water for the outward voyage.
Here the gods held me twenty days becalmed.
No winds came up, seaward escorting winds
for ships that ride the sea's broad back, and so
my stores and men were used up; we were failing

had not one goddess intervened in pity—
Eidothea, daughter of Proteus,
the Ancient of the Sea. How I distressed her!
I had been walking out alone that day—
my sailors, thin-bellied from the long fast,
were off with fish hooks, angling on the shore—
then she appeared to me, and her voice sang:
'What fool is here, what drooping dunce of dreams?
Or can it be, friend, that you love to suffer?
How can you linger on this island, aimless
and shiftless, while your people waste away?'

To this I quickly answered:
'Let me tell you,
goddess, whatever goddess you may be,
these doldrums are no will of mine. I take it
the gods who own broad heaven are offended.
Why don't you tell me—since the gods know everything—
who has me pinned down here?
How am I going to make my voyage home?'

Now she replied in her immortal beauty:
'I'll put it for you clearly as may be, friend.
The Ancient of the Salt Sea haunts this place,
immortal Proteus of Egypt; all the deeps
are known to him; he serves under Poseidon,
and is, they say, my father.
If you could take him by surprise and hold him,
he'd give you course and distance for your sailing
homeward across the cold fish-breeding sea.
And should you wish it, noble friend, he'd tell you
all that occurred at home, both good and evil,
while you were gone so long and hard a journey.'

To this I said:
'But you, now—you must tell me
how I can trap this venerable sea-god.
He will elude me if he takes alarm;
no man—god knows—can quell a god with ease.'

That fairest of unearthly nymphs replied:
'I'll tell you this, too, clearly as may be.
When the sun hangs at high noon in heaven,
the Ancient glides ashore under the Westwind,
hidden by shivering glooms on the clear water,

and rests in caverns hollowed by the sea.
There flippered seals, brine children, shining come
from silvery foam in crowds to lie around him,
exhaling rankness from the deep sea floor.
Tomorrow dawn I'll take you to those caves
and bed you down there. Choose three officers
for company—brave men they had better be—
the old one has strange powers, I must tell you.
He goes amid the seals to check their number,
and when he sees them all, and counts them all,
he lies down like a shepherd with his flock.
Here is your opportunity: at this point
gather yourselves, with all your heart and strength,
and tackle him before he bursts away.
He'll make you fight—for he can take the forms
of all the beasts, and water, and blinding fire;
but you must hold on, even so, and crush him
until he breaks the silence. When he does,
he will be in that shape you saw asleep.
Relax your grip, then, set the Ancient free,
and put your questions, hero:
Who is the god so hostile to you,
and how will you go home on the fish-cold sea.'

At this she dove under a swell and left me.
Back to the ships in the sandy cove I went,
my heart within me like a high surf running;
but there I joined my men once more
at supper, as the sacred Night came on,
and slept at last beside the lapping water.
When Dawn spread out her finger tips of rose
I started, by the sea's wide level ways,
praying the gods for help, and took along
three lads I counted on in any fight.
Meanwhile the nereid° swam from the lap of Ocean sea nymph
laden with four sealskins, new flayed
for the hoax she thought of playing on her father.
In the sand she scooped out hollows for our bodies
and sat down, waiting. We came close to touch her,
and, bedding us, she threw the sealskins over us—
a strong disguise; oh, yes, terribly strong
as I recall the stench of those damned seals.
Would any man lie snug with a sea monster?
But here the nymph, again, came to our rescue,
dabbing ambrosia under each man's nose—

a perfume drowning out the bestial odor.
So there we lay with beating hearts all morning
while seals came shoreward out of ripples, jostling
to take their places, flopping on the sand.
At noon the Ancient issued from the sea
and held inspection, counting off the sea-beasts.
We were the first he numbered; he went by,
detecting nothing. When at last he slept
we gave a battlecry and plunged for him,
locking our hands behind him. But the old one's
tricks were not knocked out of him; far from it.
First he took on a whiskered lion's shape,
a serpent then; a leopard; a great boar;
then sousing water; then a tall green tree.
Still we hung on, by hook or crook, through everything,
until the Ancient saw defeat, and grimly
opened his lips to ask me:
'Son of Atreus,
who counselled you to this? A god: what god?
Set a trap for me, overpower me—why?'

He bit it off, then, and I answered:
'Old one,
you know the reason—why feign not to know?
High and dry so long upon this island
I'm at my wits' end, and my heart is sore.
You gods know everything; now you can tell me:
which of the immortals chained me here?
And how will I get home on the fish-cold sea?'

He made reply at once:
'You should have paid
honor to Zeus and the other gods, performing
a proper sacrifice before embarking:
that was your short way home on the winedark sea.
You may not see your friends, your own fine house,
or enter your own land again,
unless you first remount the Nile in flood
and pay your hekatomb to the gods of heaven.
Then, and then only,
the gods will grant the passage you desire.'

Ah, how my heart sank, hearing this—
hearing him send me back on the cloudy sea
in my own track, the long hard way of Egypt.

Nevertheless, I answered him and said:
'Ancient, I shall do all as you command.
But tell me, now, the others—
had they a safe return, all those Akhaians
who stayed behind when Nestor and I left Troy?
Or were there any lost at sea—what bitterness!—
any who died in camp, after the war?'

To this he said:
'For you to know these things
goes beyond all necessity, Meneláos.
Why must you ask?—you should not know my mind,
and you will grieve to learn it, I can tell you.
Many there were who died, many remain,
but two high officers alone were lost—
on the passage home, I mean; you saw the war.
One is alive, a castaway at sea;
the other, Aias,[42] perished with all hands—
though first Poseidon landed him on Gyrai
promontory, and saved him from the ocean.
Despite Athena's hate, he had lived on,
but the great sinner in his insolence
yelled that the gods' will and the sea were beaten,
and this loud brag came to Poseidon's ears.
He swung the trident in his massive hands
and in one shock from top to bottom split
that promontory, toppling into the sea
the fragment where the great fool sat.
So the vast ocean had its will with Aias,
drunk in the end on salt spume as he drowned.
Meanwhile your brother° left that doom astern — Agamémnon
in his decked ships—the Lady Hera[43] saved him;
but as he came round Malea
a fresh squall caught him, bearing him away
over the cold sea, groaning in disgust,
to the Land's End of Argos, where Thyestês
lived in the days of old, and then his son,
Aigísthos. Now, again, return seemed easy:
the high gods wound the wind into the east,
and back he sailed, this time to his own coast.

---

[42] **Aias:** The Lesser Aias who raped Kassandra in Athena's temple. [43] **Lady Hêra:** Wife and sister of Zeus.

He went ashore and kissed the earth in joy,
hot tears blinding his eyes at sight of home.
But there were eyes that watched him from a height—
a lookout, paid two bars of gold to keep
vigil the year round for Aigísthos' sake,
that he should be forewarned, and Agamémnon's
furious valor sleep unroused.
Now this man with his news ran to the tyrant,
who made his crooked arrangements in a flash,
stationed picked men at arms, a score of men
in hiding; set a feast in the next room;
then he went out with chariots and horses
to hail the king and welcome him to evil.
He led him in to banquet, all serene,
and killed him, like an ox felled at the trough;
and not a man of either company
survived that ambush in Aigísthos' house.'

Before the end my heart was broken down.
I slumped on the trampled sand and cried aloud,
caring no more for life or the light of day,
and rolled there weeping, till my tears were spent.
Then the unerring Ancient said at last:
'No more, no more; how long must you persist?
Nothing is gained by grieving so. How soon
can you return to Argos? You may take him
alive there still—or else meanwhile Orestês
will have despatched him. You'll attend the feast.'

At this my heart revived, and I recovered
the self command to question him once more:
'Of two companions now I know. The third?
Tell me his name, the one marooned at sea;
living, you say, or dead? Even in pain
I wish to hear.'

And this is all he answered:
'Laërtês' son, whose home is Ithaka.
I saw him weeping, weeping on an island.
The nymph Kalypso has him, in her hall.
No means of faring home are left him now;
no ship with oars, and no ship's company
to pull him on the broad back of the sea.
As to your own destiny, prince Meneláos,

you shall not die in the bluegrass land of Argos;
rather the gods intend you for Elysion[44]
with golden Rhadamanthos at the world's end,
where all existence is a dream of ease.
Snowfall is never known there, neither long
frost of winter, nor torrential rain,
but only mild and lulling airs from Ocean
bearing refreshment for the souls of men—
the West Wind always blowing.
For the gods
hold you, as Helen's lord, a son of Zeus.'

At this he dove under a swell and left me,
and I went back to the ship with my companions,
feeling my heart's blood in me running high;
but in the long hull's shadow, near the sea,
we supped again as sacred Night came on
and slept at last beside the lapping water.

When Dawn spread out her finger tips of rose,
in first light we launched on the courtly breakers,
setting up masts and yards in the well-found ships;
went all on board, and braced on planks athwart
oarsmen in line dipped oars in the grey sea.
Soon I drew in to the great stream[45] fed by heaven
and, laying by, slew bulls in the proper number,
until the immortal gods were thus appeased;
then heaped a death mound on that shore against
all-quenching time for Agamémnon's honor,
and put to sea once more. The gods sent down
a sternwind for a racing passage homeward.

So ends the story. Now you must stay with me
and be my guest eleven or twelve days more.
I'll send you on your way with gifts, and fine ones:
three chariot horses, and a polished car;
a hammered cup, too, so that all your days,

[44] **Elysion:** A portion of the afterworld located on the western edge of the world and reserved for heroes; ruled by Rhadamanthos, a son of Zeus. [45] **the great stream:** The river Nile was believed to have its source in the heavens; it was therefore sacred and related to Zeus.

tipping the red wine for the deathless gods,
you will remember me."

Telémakhos answered:
"Lord, son of Atreus, no, you must not keep me.
Not that a year with you would be too long:
I never could be homesick here—I find
your tales and all you say so marvellous.
But time hangs heavy on my shipmates' hands
at holy Pylos, if you make me stay.
As for your gift, now, let it be some keepsake.
Horses I cannot take to Ithaka;
let me bestow them back on you, to serve
your glory here. My lord, you rule wide country,
rolling and rich with clover, galingale
and all the grains: red wheat and hoary barley.
At home we have no level runs or meadows,
but highland, goat land—prettier than plains, though.
Grasses, and pasture land, are hard to come by
upon the islands tilted in the sea,
and Ithaka is the island of them all."

At this the deep-lunged man of battle smiled.
Then he said kindly, patting the boy's hand:
"You come of good stock, lad. That was well spoken.
I'll change the gift, then—as indeed I can.
Let me see what is costliest and most beautiful
of all the precious things my house contains:
a wine bowl, mixing bowl, all wrought of silver,
but rimmed with hammered gold. Let this be yours.
It is Hephaistos'[46] work, given me by Phaidimos,
captain and king of Sidon. He received me
during my travels. Let it be yours, I say."

This was their discourse on that morning. Meanwhile
guests were arriving at the great lord's house,
bringing their sheep, and wine, the ease of men,
with loaves their comely kerchiefed women sent,
to make a feast in hall.

At that same hour,

[46] **Hephaistos:** The god of fire and metallurgy.

before the distant manor of Odysseus,
the suitors were competing at the discus throw
and javelin, on a measured field they used,
arrogant lords at play. The two best men,
Antínoös and Eurýmakhos, presided.
Now Phronios' son, Noêmon, came to see them
with a question for Antínoös. He said:
"Do any of us know, or not, Antínoös,
what day Telémakhos will be home from Pylos?
He took my ship, but now I need it back
to make a cruise to Elis, where the plains are.
I have a dozen mares at pasture there
with mule colts yet unweaned. My notion is
to bring one home and break him in for labor."

His first words made them stare—for they knew well
Telémakhos could not have gone to Pylos,
but inland with his flocks, or to the swineherd.
Eupeithês' son, Antínoös, quickly answered:
"Tell the story straight. He sailed? Who joined him—
a crew he picked up here in Ithaka,
or his own slaves? He might have done it that way.
And will you make it clear
whether he took the ship against your will?
Did he ask for it, did you lend it to him?"

Now said the son of Phronios in reply:
"Lent it to him, and freely. Who would not,
when a prince of that house asked for it, in trouble?
Hard to refuse the favor, it seems to me.
As for his crew, the best men on the island,
after ourselves, went with him. Mentor I noted
going aboard—or a god who looked like Mentor.
The strange thing is, I saw Lord Mentor here
in the first light yesterday—although he sailed
five days ago for Pylos."

Turning away,
Noêmon took the path to his father's house,
leaving the two men there, baffled and hostile.
They called the rest in from the playing field
and made them all sit down, so that Antínoös
could speak out from the stormcloud of his heart,
swollen with anger; and his eyes blazed:

"A bad business. Telémakhos had the gall
to make that crossing, though we said he could not.
So the young cub rounds up a first rate crew
in spite of all our crowd, and puts to sea.
What devilment will he be up to next time?—
Zeus blast the life out of him before he's grown!
Just give me a fast ship and twenty men;
I'll intercept him, board him in the strait
between the crags of Samê and this island.
He'll find his sea adventure after his father
swamping work in the end!"

They all cried "Aye!"
and "After him!" and trailed back to the manor.

Now not much time went by before Penélopê
learned what was afoot among the suitors.
Medôn the crier told her. He had been
outside the wall, and heard them in the court
conspiring. Into the house and up the stairs
he ran to her with his news upon his tongue—
but at the door Penélopê met him, crying:
"Why have they sent you up here now? To tell
the maids of King Odysseus—'Leave your spinning:
Time to go down and slave to feed those men'?
I wish this were the last time they came feasting,
courting me or consorting here! The last!
Each day you crowd this house like wolves
to eat away my brave son's patrimony.
When you were boys, did your own fathers tell you
nothing of what Odysseus was for them?
In word and act impeccable, disinterested
toward all the realm—though it is king's justice
to hold one man abhorred and love another;
no man alive could say Odysseus wronged him.
But your own hearts—how different!—and your deeds!
How soon are benefactions all forgotten!"

Now Medôn, the alert and cool man, answered:
"I wish that were the worst of it, my Lady,
but they intend something more terrible—
may Zeus forfend and spare us!
They plan to drive the keen bronze through Telémakhos
when he comes home. He sailed away, you know,

to hallowed Pylos and old Lakedaimon
for news about his father."

Her knees failed,
and her heart failed as she listened to the words,
and all her power of speech went out of her.
Tears came; but the rich voice could not come.
Only after a long while she made answer:
"Why has my child left me? He had no need
of those long ships on which men shake out sail
to tug like horses, breasting miles of sea.
Why did he go? Must he, too, be forgotten?"

Then Medôn, the perceptive man, replied:
"A god moved him — who knows? — or his own heart
sent him to learn, at Pylos, if his father
roams the wide world still, or what befell him."

He left her then, and went down through the house.
And now the pain around her heart benumbed her;
chairs were a step away, but far beyond her;
she sank down on the door sill of the chamber,
wailing, and all her women young and old
made a low murmur of lament around her,
until at last she broke out through her tears:
"Dearest companions, what has Zeus given me?
Pain — more pain than any living woman.
My lord, my lion heart, gone, long ago —
the bravest man, and best, of the Danaans,
famous through Hellas and the Argive midlands —
and now the squalls have blown my son, my dear one,
an unknown boy, southward. No one told me.
O brute creatures, not one soul would dare
to wake me from my sleep; you knew
the hour he took the black ship out to sea!
If I had seen that sailing in his eyes
he should have stayed with me, for all his longing,
stayed — or left me dead in the great hall.
Go, someone, now, and call old Dólios,
the slave my father gave me before I came,
my orchard keeper — tell him to make haste
and put these things before Laërtês; he
may plan some kind of action; let him come

to cry shame on these ruffians who would murder
Odysseus' son and heir, and end his line!"

The dear old nurse, Eurýkleia, answered her:
"Sweet mistress, have my throat cut without mercy
or what you will; it's true, I won't conceal it,
I knew the whole thing; gave him his provisions;
grain and sweet wine I gave, and a great oath
to tell you nothing till twelve days went by,
or till you heard of it yourself, or missed him;
he hoped you would not tear your skin lamenting.
Come, bathe and dress your loveliness afresh,
and go to the upper rooms with all your maids
to ask help from Athena, Zeus's daughter.
She it will be who saves this boy from death.
Spare the old man this further suffering;
the blissful gods cannot so hate his line,
heirs of Arkêsios;[47] one will yet again
be lord of the tall house and the far fields."

She hushed her weeping in this way, and soothed her.
The Lady Penélopê arose and bathed,
dressing her body in her freshest linen,
filled a basket with barley, and led her maids
to the upper rooms, where she besought Athena:
"Tireless child of Zeus, graciously hear me!
If ever Odysseus burned at our altar fire
thighbones of beef or mutton in sacrifice,
remember it for my sake! Save my son!
Shield him, and make the killers go astray!"

She ended with a cry, and the goddess heard her.
Now voices rose from the shadowy hall below
where the suitors were assuring one another:
"Our so-long-courted Queen is even now
of a mind to marry one of us, and knows
nothing of what is destined for her son."

Of what was destined they in fact knew nothing,
but Antínoös addressed them in a whisper:

---

[47] **Arkêsios:** Father of Laërtês, grandfather of Odysseus.

"No boasting—are you mad?—and no loud talk:
someone might hear it and alarm the house.
Come along now, be quiet, this way; come,
we'll carry out the plan our hearts are set on."

Picking out twenty of the strongest seamen,
he led them to a ship at the sea's edge,
and down they dragged her into deeper water,
stepping a mast in her, with furled sails,
and oars a-trail from thongs looped over thole pins,
ready all; then tried the white sail, hoisting,
while men at arms carried their gear aboard.
They moored the ship some way off shore, and left her
to take their evening meal there, waiting for night to come.

Penélopê at that hour in her high chamber
lay silent, tasting neither food nor drink,
and thought of nothing but her princely son—
could he escape, or would they find and kill him?—
her mind turning at bay, like a cornered lion
in whom fear comes as hunters close the ring.
But in her sick thought sweet sleep overtook her,
and she dozed off, her body slack and still.

Now it occurred to the grey-eyed goddess Athena
to make a figure of dream in a woman's form—
Iphthimê, great Ikários' other daughter,
whom Eumêlos of Phêrai took as bride.
The goddess sent this dream to Odysseus' house
to quiet Penélopê and end her grieving.
So, passing by the strap-slit[48] through the door,
the image came a-gliding down the room
to stand at her bedside and murmur to her:
"Sleepest thou, sorrowing Penélopê?
The gods whose life is ease no longer suffer thee
to pine and weep, then; he returns unharmed,
thy little one; no way hath he offended."

Then pensive Penélopê made this reply,
slumbering sweetly in the gates of dream:

[48] **strap-slit:** By using a strap that passed through a slit in a door, a person on the outside could unbolt a door on the inside.

"Sister, hast thou come hither? Why? Aforetime
never wouldst come, so far away thy dwelling.
And am I bid be done with all my grieving?
But see what anguish hath my heart and soul!
My lord, my lion heart, gone, long ago—
the bravest man, and best, of the Danaans,
famous through Hellas and the Argive midlands—
and now my son, my dear one, gone seafaring,
a child, untrained in hardship or in council.
Aye, 'tis for him I weep, more than his father!
Aye, how I tremble for him, lest some blow
befall him at men's hands or on the sea!
Cruel are they and many who plot against him,
to take his life before he can return."

Now the dim phantom spoke to her once more:
"Lift up thy heart, and fear not overmuch.
For by his side one goes whom all men else
invoke as their defender, one so powerful—
Pallas Athena; in thy tears she pitied thee
and now hath sent me that I so assure thee."

Then said Penélopê the wise:
"If thou art
numinous and hast ears for divine speech,
O tell me, what of Odysseus, man of woe?
Is he alive still somewhere, seeth he day light still?
Or gone in death to the sunless underworld?"

The dim phantom said only this in answer:
"Of him I may not tell thee in this discourse,
alive or dead. And empty words are evil."

The wavering form withdrew along the doorbolt
into a draft of wind, and out of sleep
Penélopê awoke, in better heart
for that clear dream in the twilight of the night.

Meanwhile the suitors had got under way,
planning the death plunge for Telémakhos.
Between the Isles of Ithaka and Samê
the sea is broken by an islet, Asteris,
with access to both channels from a cove.
In ambush here that night the Akhaians lay.

Book 5
Sweet Nymph and Open Sea

Dawn came up from the couch of her reclining,
leaving her lord Tithonos'[49] brilliant side
with fresh light in her arms for gods and men.
And the master of heaven and high thunder, Zeus,
went to his place among the gods assembled
hearing Athena tell Odysseus' woe.
For she, being vexed that he was still sojourning
in the sea chambers of Kalypso, said:
"O Father Zeus and gods in bliss forever,
let no man holding scepter as a king
think to be mild, or kind, or virtuous;
let him be cruel, and practice evil ways,
for those Odysseus ruled cannot remember
the fatherhood and mercy of his reign.
Meanwhile he lives and grieves upon that island
in thralldom to the nymph; he cannot stir,
cannot fare homeward, for no ship is left him,
fitted with oars—no crewmen or companions
to pull him on the broad back of the sea.
And now murder is hatched on the high sea
against his son, who sought news of his father
in the holy lands of Pylos and Lakedaimon."

To this the summoner of cloud replied:
"My child, what odd complaints you let escape you.
Have you not, you yourself, arranged this matter—
as we all know—so that Odysseus
will bring these men to book, on his return?
And are you not the one to give Telémakhos
a safe route for sailing? Let his enemies
encounter no one and row home again."

He turned then to his favorite son and said:
"Hermês, you have much practice on our missions,
go make it known to the softly-braided nymph
that we, whose will is not subject to error,
order Odysseus home; let him depart.
But let him have no company, gods or men,
only a raft that he must lash together,

[49] **Tithonos:** The lover of Eos, the dawn goddess.

and after twenty days, worn out at sea,
he shall make land upon the garden isle,
Skhería,[50] of our kinsmen, the Phaiákians.
Let these men take him to their hearts in honor
and berth him in a ship, and send him home,
with gifts of garments, gold, and bronze—
so much he had not counted on from Troy
could he have carried home his share of plunder.
His destiny is to see his friends again
under his own roof, in his father's country."

No words were lost on Hermês the Wayfinder,
who bent to tie his beautiful sandals on,
ambrosial, golden, that carry him over water
or over endless land in a swish of the wind,
and took the wand with which he charms asleep—
or when he wills, awake—the eyes of men.
So wand in hand he paced into the air,
shot from Pieria[51] down, down to sea level,
and veered to skim the swell. A gull patrolling
between the wave crests of the desolate sea
will dip to catch a fish, and douse his wings;
no higher above the whitecaps Hermês flew
until the distant island lay ahead,
then rising shoreward from the violet ocean
he stepped up to the cave. Divine Kalypso,
the mistress of the isle, was now at home.
Upon her hearthstone a great fire blazing
scented the farthest shores with cedar smoke
and smoke of thyme, and singing high and low
in her sweet voice, before her loom a-weaving,
she passed her golden shuttle to and fro.
A deep wood grew outside, with summer leaves
of alder and black poplar, pungent cypress.
Ornate birds here rested their stretched wings—
horned owls, falcons, cormorants—long-tongued
beachcombing birds, and followers of the sea.
Around the smoothwalled cave a crooking vine
held purple clusters under ply of green;
and four springs, bubbling up near one another
shallow and clear, took channels here and there

[50] **Skhería:** Probably the island of Corcyra (Corfu), off the west coast of Greece. [51] **Pieria:** Near Mt. Olympos (Olympus).

through beds of violets and tender parsley.
Even a god who found this place
would gaze, and feel his heart beat with delight:
so Hermês did; but when he had gazed his fill
he entered the wide cave. Now face to face
the magical Kalypso recognized him,
as all immortal gods know one another
on sight—though seeming strangers, far from home.
But he saw nothing of the great Odysseus,
who sat apart, as a thousand times before,
and racked his own heart groaning, with eyes wet
scanning the bare horizon of the sea.
Kalypso, lovely nymph, seated her guest
in a bright chair all shimmering, and asked:
"O Hermês, ever with your golden wand,
what brings you to my island?
Your awesome visits in the past were few.
Now tell me what request you have in mind;
for I desire to do it, if I can,
and if it is a proper thing to do.
But wait a while, and let me serve my friend."

She drew a table of ambrosia near him
and stirred a cup of ruby-colored nectar—
food and drink for the luminous Wayfinder,
who took both at his leisure, and replied:
"Goddess to god, you greet me, questioning me?
Well, here is truth for you in courtesy.
Zeus made me come, and not my inclination;
who cares to cross that tract of desolation,
the bitter sea, all mortal towns behind
where gods have beef and honors from mankind?
But it is not to be thought of—and no use—
for any god to elude the will of Zeus.

He notes your friend, most ill-starred by renown
of all the peers who fought for Priam's town—
nine years of war they had, before great Troy was down.
Homing, they wronged the goddess with grey eyes,
who made a black wind blow and the seas rise,
in which his troops were lost, and all his gear,
while easterlies and current washed him here.
Now the command is: send him back in haste.
His life may not in exile go to waste.

His destiny, his homecoming, is at hand,
when he shall see his dearest, and walk on his own land."

That goddess most divinely made
shuddered before him, and her warm voice rose:
"Oh you vile gods, in jealousy supernal!
You hate it when we choose to lie with men—
immortal flesh by some dear mortal side.
So radiant Dawn once took to bed Orion
until you easeful gods grew peevish at it,
and holy Artemis, Artemis throned in gold,
hunted him down in Delos with her arrows.
Then Dêmêtêr of the tasseled tresses yielded
to Iasion, mingling and making love
in a furrow three times plowed;[52] but Zeus found out
and killed him with a white-hot thunderbolt.
So now you grudge me, too, my mortal friend.
But it was I who saved him—saw him straddle
his own keel board, the one man left afloat
when Zeus rent wide his ship with chain lightning
and overturned him in the winedark sea.
Then all his troops were lost, his good companions,
but wind and current washed him here to me.
I fed him, loved him, sang that he should not die
nor grow old, ever, in all the days to come.
But now there's no eluding Zeus's will.
If this thing be ordained by him, I say
so be it, let the man strike out alone
on the vast water. Surely I cannot 'send' him.
I have no long-oared ships, no company
to pull him on the broad back of the sea.
My counsel he shall have, and nothing hidden,
to help him homeward without harm."

To this the Wayfinder made answer briefly:
"Thus you shall send him, then. And show more grace
in your obedience, or be chastised by Zeus."

The strong god glittering left her as he spoke,
and now her ladyship, having given heed
to Zeus's mandate, went to find Odysseus

[52] **Then Dêmêter . . . three times plowed:** Perhaps symbolic of an agricultural ritual; Dêmêter is goddess of cereals.

in his stone seat to seaward—tear on tear
brimming his eyes. The sweet days of his life time
were running out in anguish over his exile,
for long ago the nymph had ceased to please.
Though he fought shy of her and her desire,
he lay with her each night, for she compelled him.
But when day came he sat on the rocky shore
and broke his own heart groaning, with eyes wet
scanning the bare horizon of the sea.
Now she stood near him in her beauty, saying:
"O forlorn man, be still.
Here you need grieve no more; you need not feel
your life consumed here; I have pondered it,
and I shall help you go.
Come and cut down high timber for a raft
or flatboat; make her broad-beamed, and decked over,
so you can ride her on the misty sea.
Stores I shall put aboard for you—bread, water,
and ruby-colored wine, to stay your hunger—
give you a seacloak and a following wind
to help you homeward without harm—provided
the gods who rule wide heaven wish it so.
Stronger than I they are, in mind and power."

For all he had endured, Odysseus shuddered.
But when he spoke, his words went to the mark:
"After these years, a helping hand? O goddess,
what guile is hidden here?
A raft, you say, to cross the Western Ocean,
rough water, and unknown? Seaworthy ships
that glory in god's wind will never cross it.
I take no raft you grudge me out to sea.
Or yield me first a great oath, if I do,
to work no more enchantment to my harm."

At this the beautiful nymph Kalypso smiled
and answered sweetly, laying her hand upon him:
"What a dog you are! And not for nothing learned,
having the wit to ask this thing of me!
My witness then be earth and sky
and dripping Styx[53] that I swear by—
the gay gods cannot swear more seriously—

[53] **Styx:** A river in Hades as well as the name of an underworld goddess by whom oaths were sworn.

I have no further spells to work against you.
But what I shall devise, and what I tell you,
will be the same as if your need were mine.
Fairness is all I think of. There are hearts
made of cold iron — but my heart is kind."

Swiftly she turned and led him to her cave,
and they went in, the mortal and immortal.
He took the chair left empty now by Hermês,
where the divine Kalypso placed before him
victuals and drink of men; then she sat down
facing Odysseus, while her serving maids
brought nectar and ambrosia to her side.
Then each one's hands went out on each one's feast
until they had had their pleasure; and she said:
"Son of Laërtês, versatile Odysseus,
after these years with me, you still desire
your old home? Even so, I wish you well.
If you could see it all, before you go —
all the adversity you face at sea —
you would stay here, and guard this house, and be
immortal — though you wanted her forever,
that bride for whom you pine each day.
Can I be less desirable than she is?
Less interesting? Less beautiful? Can mortals
compare with goddesses in grace and form?"

To this the strategist Odysseus answered:
"My lady goddess, here is no cause for anger.
My quiet Penélopê — how well I know —
would seem a shade before your majesty,
death and old age being unknown to you,
while she must die. Yet, it is true, each day
I long for home, long for the sight of home.
If any god has marked me out again
for shipwreck, my tough heart can undergo it.
What hardship have I not long since endured
at sea, in battle! Let the trial come."

Now as he spoke the sun set, dusk drew on,
and they retired, this pair, to the inner cave
to revel and rest softly, side by side.

When Dawn spread out her finger tips of rose
Odysseus pulled his tunic and his cloak on,

while the sea nymph dressed in a silvery gown
of subtle tissue, drew about her waist
a golden belt, and veiled her head, and then
took thought for the great-hearted hero's voyage.
A brazen axehead first she had to give him,
two-bladed, and agreeable to the palm
with a smooth-fitting haft of olive wood;
next a well-polished adze; and then she led him
to the island's tip where bigger timber grew—
besides the alder and poplar, tall pine trees,
long dead and seasoned, that would float him high.
Showing him in that place her stand of timber
the loveliest of nymphs took her way home.
Now the man fell to chopping; when he paused
twenty tall trees were down. He lopped the branches,
split the trunks, and trimmed his puncheons true.
Meanwhile Kalypso brought him an auger tool
with which he drilled through all his planks, then drove
stout pins to bolt them, fitted side by side.
A master shipwright, building a cargo vessel,
lays down a broad and shallow hull; just so
Odysseus shaped the bottom of his craft.
He made his decking fast to close-set ribs
before he closed the side with longer planking,
then cut a mast pole, and a proper yard,
and shaped a steering oar to hold her steady.
He drove long strands of willow in all the seams
to keep out waves, and ballasted with logs.
As for a sail, the lovely nymph Kalypso
brought him a cloth so he could make that, too.
Then he ran up his rigging—halyards, braces—
and hauled the boat on rollers to the water.

This was the fourth day, when he had all ready;
on the fifth day, she sent him out to sea.
But first she bathed him, gave him a scented cloak,
and put on board a skin of dusky wine
with water in a bigger skin, and stores—
boiled meats and other victuals—in a bag.
Then she conjured a warm landbreeze to blowing—
joy for Odysseus when he shook out sail!
Now the great seaman, leaning on his oar,
steered all the night unsleeping, and his eyes

picked out the Pleiadês, the laggard Ploughman,[54]
and the Great Bear, that some have called the Wain,
pivoting in the sky before Orion;[55]
of all the night's pure figures, she alone
would never bathe or dip in the Ocean stream.
These stars the beautiful Kalypso bade him
hold on his left hand as he crossed the main.
Seventeen nights and days in the open water
he sailed, before a dark shoreline appeared;
Skhería then came slowly into view
like a rough shield of bull's hide on the sea.

But now the god of earthquake,° storming home — Poseidon
over the mountains of Asia from the Sunburned land,
sighted him far away. The god grew sullen
and tossed his great head, muttering to himself:
"Here is a pretty cruise! While I was gone
the gods have changed their minds about Odysseus.
Look at him now, just offshore of that island
that frees him from the bondage of his exile!
Still I can give him a rough ride in, and will."

Brewing high thunderheads, he churned the deep
with both hands on his trident—called up wind
from every quarter, and sent a wall of rain
to blot out land and sea in torrential night.
Hurricane winds now struck from the South and East
shifting North West in a great spume of seas,
on which Odysseus' knees grew slack, his heart
sickened, and he said within himself:
"Rag of man that I am, is this the end of me?
I fear the goddess told it all too well—
predicting great adversity at sea
and far from home. Now all things bear her out:
the whole rondure of heaven hooded so
by Zeus in woeful cloud, and the sea raging
under such winds. I am going down, that's sure.
How lucky those Danaans were who perished

[54] **Ploughman:** The name of the constellation Boötes means "ploughman." [55] **the Wain . . . Orion:** The Great Bear, or Wain, refers to the Big Dipper, which in northern latitudes never sets. Orion, the Hunter, is another constellation.

on Troy's wide seaboard, serving the Atreidai!
Would God I, too, had died there—met my end
that time the Trojans made so many casts at me
when I stood by Akhilleus after death.
I should have had a soldier's burial
and praise from the Akhaians—not this choking
waiting for me at sea, unmarked and lonely."

A great wave drove at him with toppling crest
spinning him round, in one tremendous blow,
and he went plunging overboard, the oar-haft
wrenched from his grip. A gust that came on howling
at the same instant broke his mast in two,
hurling his yard and sail far out to leeward.
Now the big wave a long time kept him under,
helpless to surface, held by tons of water,
tangled, too, by the seacloak of Kalypso.
Long, long, until he came up spouting brine,
with streamlets gushing from his head and beard;
but still bethought him, half-drowned as he was,
to flounder for the boat and get a handhold
into the bilge—to crouch there, foiling death.
Across the foaming water, to and fro,
the boat careered like a ball of tumbleweed
blown on the autumn plains, but intact still.
So the winds drove this wreck over the deep,
East Wind and North Wind, then South Wind and West,
coursing each in turn to the brutal harry.

But Ino saw him—Ino, Kadmos' daughter,
slim-legged, lovely, once an earthling girl,
now in the seas a nereid, Leukothea.
Touched by Odysseus' painful buffeting
she broke the surface, like a diving bird,
to rest upon the tossing raft and say:
"O forlorn man, I wonder
why the Earthshaker, Lord Poseidon, holds
this fearful grudge—father of all your woes.
He will not drown you, though, despite his rage.
You seem clear-headed still; do what I tell you.
Shed that cloak, let the gale take your craft,
and swim for it—swim hard to get ashore
upon Skhería, yonder,
where it is fated that you find a shelter.
Here: make my veil your sash; it is not mortal;

you cannot, now, be drowned or suffer harm.
Only, the instant you lay hold of earth,
discard it, cast it far, far out from shore
in the winedark sea again, and turn away."

After she had bestowed her veil, the nereid
dove like a gull to windward
where a dark waveside closed over her whiteness.
But in perplexity Odysseus
said to himself, his great heart laboring:
"O damned confusion! Can this be a ruse
to trick me from the boat for some god's pleasure?
No I'll not swim; with my own eyes I saw
how far the land lies that she called my shelter.
Better to do the wise thing, as I see it.
While this poor planking holds, I stay aboard;
I may ride out the pounding of the storm,
or if she cracks up, take to the water then;
I cannot think it through a better way."

But even while he pondered and decided,
the god of earthquake heaved a wave against him
high as a rooftree and of awful gloom.
A gust of wind, hitting a pile of chaff,
will scatter all the parched stuff far and wide;
just so, when this gigantic billow struck
the boat's big timbers flew apart. Odysseus
clung to a single beam, like a jockey riding,
meanwhile stripping Kalypso's cloak away;
then he slung round his chest the veil of Ino
and plunged headfirst into the sea. His hands
went out to stroke, and he gave a swimmer's kick.
But the strong Earthshaker had him under his eye,
and nodded as he said:
"Go on, go on;
wander the high seas this way, take your blows,
before you join that race[56] the gods have nurtured.
Nor will you grumble, even then, I think,
for want of trouble."

Whipping his glossy team
he rode off to his glorious home at Aigai.[57]

---

[56] **that race:** The Phaiákians, who befriend Odysseus. [57] **Aigai:** An island off the east coast of Greece.

But Zeus's daughter Athena countered him:
she checked the course of all the winds but one,
commanding them, "Be quiet and go to sleep."
Then sent a long swell running under a norther
to bear the prince Odysseus, back from danger,
to join the Phaiákians, people of the sea.

Two nights, two days, in the solid deep-sea swell
he drifted, many times awaiting death,
until with shining ringlets in the East
the dawn confirmed a third day, breaking clear
over a high and windless sea; and mounting
a rolling wave he caught a glimpse of land.
What a dear welcome thing life seems to children
whose father, in the extremity, recovers
after some weakening and malignant illness:
his pangs are gone, the gods have delivered him.
So dear and welcome to Odysseus
the sight of land, of woodland, on that morning.
It made him swim again, to get a foothold
on solid ground. But when he came in earshot
he heard the trampling roar of sea on rock,
where combers, rising shoreward, thudded down
on the sucking ebb—all sheeted with salt foam.
Here were no coves or harborage or shelter,
only steep headlands, rockfallen reefs and crags.
Odysseus' knees grew slack, his heart faint,
a heaviness came over him, and he said:
"A cruel turn, this. Never had I thought
to see this land, but Zeus has let me see it—
and let me, too, traverse the Western Ocean—
only to find no exit from these breakers.
Here are sharp rocks off shore, and the sea a smother
rushing around them; rock face rising sheer
from deep water; nowhere could I stand up
on my two feet and fight free of the welter.
No matter how I try it, the surf may throw me
against the cliffside; no good fighting there.
If I swim down the coast, outside the breakers,
I may find shelving shore and quiet water—
but what if another gale comes on to blow?
Then I go cursing out to sea once more.
Or then again, some shark of Amphitritê's° sea nymph

may hunt me, sent by the genius of the deep.
I know how he who makes earth tremble hates me."

During this meditation a heavy surge
was taking him, in fact, straight on the rocks.
He had been flayed there, and his bones broken,
had not grey-eyed Athena instructed him:
he gripped a rock-ledge with both hands in passing
and held on, groaning, as the surge went by,
to keep clear of its breaking. Then the backwash
hit him, ripping him under and far out.
An octopus, when you drag one from his chamber,
comes up with suckers full of tiny stones:
Odysseus left the skin of his great hands
torn on that rock-ledge as the wave submerged him.
And now at last Odysseus would have perished,
battered inhumanly, but he had the gift
of self-possession from grey-eyed Athena.
So, when the backwash spewed him up again,
he swam out and along, and scanned the coast
for some landspit that made a breakwater.
Lo and behold, the mouth of a calm river
at length came into view, with level shores
unbroken, free from rock, shielded from wind—
by far the best place he had found.
But as he felt the current flowing seaward
he prayed in his heart:
"O hear me, lord of the stream:
how sorely I depend upon your mercy!
derelict as I am by the sea's anger.
Is he not sacred, even to the gods,
the wandering man who comes, as I have come,
in weariness before your knees, your waters?
Here is your servant; lord, have mercy on me."

Now even as he prayed the tide at ebb
had turned, and the river god made quiet water,
drawing him in to safety in the shallows.
His knees buckled, his arms gave way beneath him,
all vital force now conquered by the sea.
Swollen from head to foot he was, and seawater
gushed from his mouth and nostrils. There he lay,
scarce drawing breath, unstirring, deathly spent.

In time, as air came back into his lungs
and warmth around his heart, he loosed the veil,
letting it drift away on the estuary
downstream to where a white wave took it under
and Ino's hands received it. Then the man
crawled to the river bank among the reeds
where, face down, he could kiss the soil of earth,
in his exhaustion murmuring to himself:
"What more can this hulk suffer? What comes now?
In vigil through the night here by the river
how can I not succumb, being weak and sick,
to the night's damp and hoarfrost of the morning?
The air comes cold from rivers before dawn.
But if I climb the slope and fall asleep
in the dark forest's undergrowth—supposing
cold and fatigue will go, and sweet sleep come—
I fear I make the wild beasts easy prey."

But this seemed best to him, as he thought it over.
He made his way to a grove above the water
on open ground, and crept under twin bushes
grown from the same spot—olive and wild olive—
a thicket proof against the stinging wind
or Sun's blaze, fine soever the needling sunlight;
nor could a downpour wet it through, so dense
those plants were interwoven. Here Odysseus
tunnelled, and raked together with his hands
a wide bed—for a fall of leaves was there,
enough to save two men or maybe three
on a winter night, a night of bitter cold.
Odysseus' heart laughed when he saw his leaf-bed,
and down he lay, heaping more leaves above him.

A man in a distant field, no hearthfires near,
will hide a fresh brand in his bed of embers
to keep a spark alive for the next day;
so in the leaves Odysseus hid himself,
while over him Athena showered sleep
that his distress should end, and soon, soon.
In quiet sleep she sealed his cherished eyes.

Book 6
The Princess at the River

Far gone in weariness, in oblivion,
the noble and enduring man slept on;
but Athena in the night went down the land
of the Phaiákians, entering their city.
In days gone by, these men held Hypereia,[58]
a country of wide dancing grounds, but near them
were overbearing Kyklopês, whose power
could not be turned from pillage. So the Phaiákians
migrated thence under Nausíthoös
to settle a New World across the sea,
Skhería Island. That first captain walled
their promontory, built their homes and shrines,
and parcelled out the black land for the plow.
But he had gone down long ago to Death.
Alkínoös ruled, and Heaven gave him wisdom,
so on this night the goddess, grey-eyed Athena,
entered the palace of Alkínoös
to make sure of Odysseus' voyage home.
She took her way to a painted bedchamber
where a young girl lay fast asleep—so fine
in mould and feature that she seemed a goddess—
the daughter of Alkínoös, Nausikaa.
On either side, as Graces[59] might have slept,
her maids were sleeping. The bright doors were shut,
but like a sudden stir of wind, Athena
moved to the bedside of the girl, and grew
visible as the shipman Dymas' daughter,
a girl the princess' age, and her dear friend.
In this form grey-eyed Athena said to her:
"How so remiss, and yet thy mother's daughter?
leaving thy clothes uncared for, Nausikaa,
when soon thou must have store of marriage linen,
and put thy minstrelsy in wedding dress!
Beauty, in these, will make the folk admire,
and bring thy father and gentle mother joy.

[58] **Hypereia:** An unknown location. [59] **Graces:** Attendants of Aphroditê, the Graces personify beauty, youth, and modesty.

Let us go washing in the shine of morning!
Beside thee will I drub, so wedding chests
will brim by evening. Maidenhood must end!
Have not the noblest born Phaiákians
paid court to thee, whose birth none can excel?
Go beg thy sovereign father, even at dawn,
to have the mule cart and the mules brought round
to take thy body-linen, gowns and mantles.
Thou shouldst ride, for it becomes thee more,
the washing pools are found so far from home."

On this word she departed, grey-eyed Athena,
to where the gods have their eternal dwelling—
as men say—in the fastness of Olympos.
Never a tremor of wind, or a splash of rain,
no errant snowflake comes to stain that heaven,
so calm, so vaporless, the world of light.
Here, where the gay gods live their days of pleasure,
the grey-eyed one withdrew, leaving the princess.

And now Dawn took her own fair throne, awaking
the girl in the sweet gown, still charmed by dream.
Down through the rooms she went to tell her parents,
whom she found still at home: her mother seated
near the great hearth among her maids—and twirling
out of her distaff yarn dyed like the sea—;
her father at the door, bound for a council
of princes on petition of the gentry.
She went up close to him and softly said:
"My dear Papà, could you not send the mule cart
around for me—the gig with pretty wheels?
I must take all our things and get them washed
at the river pools; our linen is all soiled.
And you should wear fresh clothing, going to council
with counselors and first men of the realm.
Remember your five sons at home: though two
are married, we have still three bachelor sprigs;
they will have none but laundered clothes each time
they go to the dancing. See what I must think of!"

She had no word to say of her own wedding,
though her keen father saw her blush. Said he:
"No mules would I deny you, child, nor anything.

Go along, now; the grooms will bring your gig
with pretty wheels and the cargo box upon it."

He spoke to the stableman, who soon brought round
the cart, low-wheeled and nimble;
harnessed the mules, and backed them in the traces.
Meanwhile the girl fetched all her soiled apparel
to bundle in the polished wagon box.
Her mother, for their luncheon, packed a hamper
with picnic fare, and filled a skin of wine,
and, when the princess had been handed up,
gave her a golden bottle of olive oil
for softening girls' bodies, after bathing.
Nausikaa took the reins and raised her whip,
lashing the mules. What jingling! What a clatter!
But off they went in a ground-covering trot,
with princess, maids, and laundry drawn behind.
By the lower river where the wagon came
were washing pools, with water all year flowing
in limpid spillways that no grime withstood.
The girls unhitched the mules, and sent them down
along the eddying stream to crop sweet grass.
Then sliding out the cart's tail board, they took
armloads of clothing to the dusky water,
and trod them in the pits, making a race of it.
All being drubbed, all blemish rinsed away,
they spread them, piece by piece, along the beach
whose pebbles had been laundered by the sea;
then took a dip themselves, and, all anointed
with golden oil, ate lunch beside the river
while the bright burning sun dried out their linen.
Princess and maids delighted in that feast;
then, putting off their veils,
they ran and passed a ball to a rhythmic beat,
Nausikaa flashing first with her white arms.

So Artemis goes flying after her arrows flown
down some tremendous valley-side—
Taÿgetos, Erymanthos[60]—

[60] **Taÿgetos, Erymanthos:** Erymanthos is a mountain in Arcadia sacred to Artemis; Taÿgetos is a mountain range in southern Greece.

chasing the mountain goats or ghosting deer,
with nymphs of the wild places flanking her;
and Lêto's[61] heart delights to see them running,
for, taller by a head than nymphs can be,
the goddess shows more stately, all being beautiful.
So one could tell the princess from the maids.

Soon it was time, she knew, for riding homeward—
mules to be harnessed, linen folded smooth—
but the grey-eyed goddess Athena made her tarry,
so that Odysseus might behold her beauty
and win her guidance to the town.
It happened
when the king's daughter threw her ball off line
and missed, and put it in the whirling stream,—
at which they all gave such a shout, Odysseus
awoke and sat up, saying to himself:
"Now, by my life, mankind again! But who?
Savages, are they, strangers to courtesy?
Or gentle folk, who know and fear the gods?
That was a lusty cry of tall young girls—
most like the cry of nymphs, who haunt the peaks,
and springs of brooks, and inland grassy places.
Or am I amid people of human speech?
Up again, man; and let me see for myself."

He pushed aside the bushes, breaking off
with his great hand a single branch of olive,
whose leaves might shield him in his nakedness;
so came out rustling, like a mountain lion,
rain-drenched, wind-buffeted, but in his might at ease,
with burning eyes—who prowls among the herds
or flocks, or after game, his hungry belly
taking him near stout homesteads for his prey.
Odysseus had this look, in his rough skin
advancing on the girls with pretty braids;
and he was driven on by hunger, too.
Streaked with brine, and swollen, he terrified them,
so that they fled, this way and that. Only

[61] **Lêto:** Mother of Apollo and Artemis.

Alkínoös' daughter stood her ground, being given
a bold heart by Athena, and steady knees.

She faced him, waiting. And Odysseus came,
debating inwardly what he should do:
embrace this beauty's knees in supplication?
or stand apart, and, using honeyed speech,
inquire the way to town, and beg some clothing?
In his swift reckoning, he thought it best
to trust in words to please her—and keep away;
he might anger the girl, touching her knees.
So he began, and let the soft words fall:
"Mistress: please: are you divine, or mortal?
If one of those who dwell in the wide heaven,
you are most near to Artemis, I should say—
great Zeus's daughter—in your grace and presence.
If you are one of earth's inhabitants,
how blest your father, and your gentle mother,
blest all your kin. I know what happiness
must send the warm tears to their eyes, each time
they see their wondrous child go to the dancing!
But one man's destiny is more than blest—
he who prevails, and takes you as his bride.
Never have I laid eyes on equal beauty
in man or woman. I am hushed indeed.
So fair, one time, I thought a young palm tree
at Delos[62] near the altar of Apollo—
I had troops under me when I was there
on the sea route that later brought me grief—
but that slim palm tree filled my heart with wonder:
never came shoot from earth so beautiful.
So now, my lady, I stand in awe so great
I cannot take your knees. And yet my case is desperate:
twenty days, yesterday, in the winedark sea,
on the ever-lunging swell, under gale winds,
getting away from the Island of Ogýgia.
And now the terror of Storm has left me stranded
upon this shore—with more blows yet to suffer,
I must believe, before the gods relent.

[62] **Delos:** A small island in the Aegean Sea, south of the Greek mainland, and the birthplace of Apollo.

Mistress, do me a kindness!
After much weary toil, I come to you,
and you are the first soul I have seen — I know
no others here. Direct me to the town,
give me a rag that I can throw around me,
some cloth or wrapping that you brought along.
And may the gods accomplish your desire:
a home, a husband, and harmonious
converse with him — the best thing in the world
being a strong house held in serenity
where man and wife agree. Woe to their enemies,
joy to their friends! But all this they know best."

Then she of the white arms, Nausikaa, replied:
"Stranger, there is no quirk or evil in you
that I can see. You know Zeus metes out fortune
to good and bad men as it pleases him.
Hardship he sent to you, and you must bear it.
But now that you have taken refuge here
you shall not lack for clothing, or any other
comfort due to a poor man in distress.
The town lies this way, and the men are called
Phaiákians, who own the land and city.
I am daughter to the Prince Alkínoös,
by whom the power of our people stands."

Turning, she called out to her maids-in-waiting:
"Stay with me! Does the sight of a man scare you?
Or do you take this one for an enemy?
Why, there's no fool so brash, and never will be,
as to bring war or pillage to this coast,
for we are dear to the immortal gods,
living here, in the sea that rolls forever,
distant from other lands and other men.
No: this man is a castaway, poor fellow;
we must take care of him. Strangers and beggars
come from Zeus: a small gift, then, is friendly.
Give our new guest some food and drink, and take him
into the river, out of the wind, to bathe."

They stood up now, and called to one another
to go on back. Quite soon they led Odysseus
under the river bank, as they were bidden;
and there laid out a tunic, and a cloak,
and gave him olive oil in the golden flask.

"Here," they said, "go bathe in the flowing water."
But heard now from that kingly man, Odysseus:
"Maids," he said, "keep away a little; let me
wash the brine from my own back, and rub on
plenty of oil. It is long since my anointing.
I take no bath, however, where you can see me—
naked before young girls with pretty braids."

They left him, then, and went to tell the princess.
And now Odysseus, dousing in the river,
scrubbed the coat of brine from back and shoulders
and rinsed the clot of sea-spume from his hair;
got himself all rubbed down, from head to foot,
then he put on the clothes the princess gave him.
Athena lent a hand, making him seem
taller, and massive too, with crisping hair
in curls like petals of wild hyacinth,
but all red-golden. Think of gold infused
on silver by a craftsman, whose fine art
Hephaistos taught him, or Athena: one
whose work moves to delight: just so she lavished
beauty over Odysseus' head and shoulders.
Then he went down to sit on the sea beach
in his new splendor. There the girl regarded him,
and after a time she said to the maids beside her:
"My gentlewomen, I have a thing to tell you.
The Olympian gods cannot be all averse
to this man's coming here among our islanders.
Uncouth he seemed, I thought so, too, before;
but now he looks like one of heaven's people.
I wish my husband could be fine as he
and glad to stay forever on Skhería!

But have you given refreshment to our guest?"

At this the maids, all gravely listening, hastened
to set out bread and wine before Odysseus,
and ah! how ravenously that patient man
took food and drink, his long fast at an end.

The princess Nausikaa now turned aside
to fold her linens; in the pretty cart
she stowed them, put the mule team under harness,
mounted the driver's seat, and then looked down
to say with cheerful prompting to Odysseus:

"Up with you now, friend; back to town we go;
and I shall send you in before my father
who is wondrous wise; there in our house with him
you'll meet the noblest of the Phaiákians.
You have good sense, I think; here's how to do it:
while we go through the countryside and farmland
stay with my maids, behind the wagon, walking
briskly enough to follow where I lead.
But near the town—well, there's a wall with towers
around the Isle, and beautiful ship basins
right and left of the causeway of approach;
seagoing craft are beached beside the road
each on its launching ways. The agora,[63]
with fieldstone benches bedded in the earth,
lies either side Poseidon's shrine—for there
men are at work on pitch-black hulls and rigging,
cables and sails, and tapering of oars.
The archer's craft is not for the Phaiákians,
but ship designing, modes of oaring cutters
in which they love to cross the foaming sea.
From these fellows I will have no salty talk,
no gossip later. Plenty are insolent.
And some seadog might say, after we passed:
'Who is this handsome stranger trailing Nausikaa?
Where did she find him? Will he be her husband?
Or is she being hospitable to some rover
come off his ship from lands across the sea—
there being no lands nearer. A god, maybe?
a god from heaven, the answer to her prayer,
descending now—to make her his forever?
Better, if she's roamed and found a husband
somewhere else: none of our own will suit her,
though many come to court her, and those the best.'
This is the way they might make light of me.
And I myself should hold it shame
for any girl to flout her own dear parents,
taking up with a man, before her marriage.

Note well, now, what I say, friend, and your chances
are excellent for safe conduct from my father.
You'll find black poplars in a roadside park
around a meadow and fountain—all Athena's—

[63] **agora:** Greek for a place of assembly, especially a marketplace.

but Father has a garden in the place—
this within earshot of the city wall.
Go in there and sit down, giving us time
to pass through town and reach my father's house.
And when you can imagine we're at home,
then take the road into the city, asking
directions to the palace of Alkínoös.
You'll find it easily: any small boy
can take you there; no family has a mansion
half so grand as he does, being king.
As soon as you are safe inside, cross over
and go straight through into the mégaron[64]
to find my mother. She'll be there in firelight
before a column, with her maids in shadow,
spinning a wool dyed richly as the sea.
My father's great chair faces the fire, too;
there like a god he sits and takes his wine.
Go past him, cast yourself before my mother,
embrace her knees—and you may wake up soon
at home rejoicing, though your home be far.
On Mother's feeling much depends; if she
looks on you kindly, you shall see your friends
under your own roof in your father's country."

At this she raised her glistening whip, lashing
the team into a run; they left the river
cantering beautifully, then trotted smartly.
But then she reined them in, and spared the whip,
so that her maids could follow with Odysseus.
The sun was going down when they went by
Athena's grove. Here, then, Odysseus rested,
and lifted up his prayer to Zeus's daughter:
"Hear me, unwearied child of royal Zeus!
O listen to me now—thou so aloof
while the Earthshaker wrecked and battered me.
May I find love and mercy among these people."

He prayed for that, and Pallas Athena heard him—
although in deference to her father's brother
she would not show her true form to Odysseus,
at whom Poseidon smoldered on
until the kingly man came home to his own shore.

[64] **the mégaron:** The great hall.

Book 7
Gardens and Firelight

As Lord Odysseus prayed there in the grove
the girl rode on, behind her strapping team,
and came late to the mansion of her father,
where she reined in at the courtyard gate. Her brothers
awaited her like tall gods in the court,
circling to lead the mules away and carry
the laundered things inside. But she withdrew
to her own bedroom, where a fire soon shone,
kindled by her old nurse, Eurymedousa.
Years ago, from a raid on the continent,
the rolling ships had brought this woman over
to be Alkínoös' share—fit spoil for him
whose realm hung on his word as on a god's.
And she had schooled the princess, Nausikaa,
whose fire she tended now, making her supper.

Odysseus, when the time had passed, arose
and turned into the city. But Athena
poured a sea fog around him as he went—
her love's expedient, that no jeering sailor
should halt the man or challenge him for luck.
Instead, as he set foot in the pleasant city,
the grey-eyed goddess came to him, in figure
a small girl child, hugging a water jug.

Confronted by her, Lord Odysseus asked:
"Little one, could you take me to the house
of that Alkínoös, king among these people?
You see, I am a poor old stranger here;
my home is far away; here there is no one
known to me, in countryside or city."

The grey-eyed goddess Athena replied to him:
"Oh yes, good grandfer, sir, I know, I'll show you
the house you mean; it is quite near my father's.
But come now, hush, like this, and follow me.
You must not stare at people, or be inquisitive.
They do not care for strangers in this neighborhood;
a foreign man will get no welcome here.
The only things they trust are the racing ships

Poseidon gave, to sail the deep blue sea
like white wings in the sky, or a flashing thought."

Pallas Athena turned like the wind, running
ahead of him, and he followed in her footsteps.
And no seafaring men of Phaiákia
perceived Odysseus passing through their town:
the awesome one in pigtails barred their sight
with folds of sacred mist. And yet Odysseus
gazed out marvelling at the ships and harbors,
public squares, and ramparts towering up
with pointed palisades along the top.
When they were near the mansion of the king,
grey-eyed Athena in the child cried out:
"Here it is, grandfer, sir—that mansion house
you asked to see. You'll find our king and queen
at supper, but you must not be dismayed;
go in to them. A cheerful man does best
in every enterprise—even a stranger.
You'll see our lady just inside the hall—
her name is Arêtê; her grandfather
was our good king Alkínoös's father—
Nausíthoös by name, son of Poseidon
and Periboia. That was a great beauty,
the daughter of Eurymedon, commander
of the Gigantês[65] in the olden days,
who led those wild things to their doom and his.
Poseidon then made love to Periboia,
and she bore Nausíthoös, Phaiákia's lord,
whose sons in turn were Rhêxênor and Alkínoös.
Rhêxênor had no sons; even as a bridegroom
he fell before the silver bow of Apollo,
his only child a daughter, Arêtê.
When she grew up, Alkínoös married her
and holds her dear. No lady in the world,
no other mistress of a man's household,
is honored as our mistress is, and loved,
by her own children, by Alkínoös,
and by the people. When she walks the town

[65] **Gigantês:** Giants; as sons of Uranus and Gaia, they are similar if not identical to the Titans in Hesiod's *Theogony,* who battled unsuccessfully against the Olympians.

they murmur and gaze, as though she were a goddess.
No grace or wisdom fails in her; indeed
just men in quarrels come to her for equity.
Supposing, then, she looks upon you kindly,
the chances are that you shall see your friends
under your own roof, in your father's country."

At this the grey-eyed goddess Athena left him
and left that comely land, going over sea
to Marathon, to the wide roadways of Athens
and her retreat in the stronghold of Erekhtheus.[66]
Odysseus, now alone before the palace,
meditated a long time before crossing
the brazen threshold of the great courtyard.
High rooms he saw ahead, airy and luminous
as though with lusters of the sun and moon,
bronze-paneled walls, at several distances,
making a vista, with an azure molding
of lapis lazuli. The doors were golden
guardians of the great room. Shining bronze
plated the wide door sill; the posts and lintel
were silver upon silver; golden handles
curved on the doors, and golden, too, and silver
were sculptured hounds, flanking the entrance way,
cast by the skill and ardor of Hephaistos
to guard the prince Alkínoös's house—
undying dogs that never could grow old.
Through all the rooms, as far as he could see,
tall chairs were placed around the walls, and strewn
with fine embroidered stuff made by the women.
Here were enthroned the leaders of Phaiákia
drinking and dining, with abundant fare.
Here, too, were boys of gold on pedestals
holding aloft bright torches of pitch pine
to light the great rooms, and the night-time feasting.
And fifty maids-in-waiting of the household
sat by the round mill, grinding yellow corn,
or wove upon their looms, or twirled their distaffs,
flickering like the leaves of a poplar tree;
while drops of oil glistened on linen weft.

[66] **Marathon . . . Erekhtheus:** The tomb of Erekhtheus, the sixth king of Athens, was located in the Erekhtheum (or Erechtheum), a white marble temple sacred to Athena on the Acropolis. Marathon was the site of a famous battle at which the Athenians defeated the Persians in 490 B.C.E.

Skillful as were the men of Phaiákia
in ship handling at sea, so were these women
skilled at the loom, having this lovely craft
and artistry as talents from Athena.

To left and right, outside, he saw an orchard
closed by a pale—four spacious acres planted
with trees in bloom or weighted down for picking:
pear trees, pomegranates, brilliant apples,
luscious figs, and olives ripe and dark.
Fruit never failed upon these trees: winter
and summer time they bore, for through the year
the breathing Westwind ripened all in turn—
so one pear came to prime, and then another,
and so with apples, figs, and the vine's fruit
empurpled in the royal vineyard there.
Currants were dried at one end, on a platform
bare to the sun, beyond the vintage arbors
and vats the vintners trod; while near at hand
were new grapes barely formed as the green bloom fell,
or half-ripe clusters, faintly coloring.
After the vines came rows of vegetables
of all the kinds that flourish in every season,
and through the garden plots and orchard ran
channels from one clear fountain, while another
gushed through a pipe under the courtyard entrance
to serve the house and all who came for water.
These were the gifts of heaven to Alkínoös.

Odysseus, who had borne the barren sea,
stood in the gateway and surveyed this bounty.
He gazed his fill, then swiftly he went in.
The lords and nobles of Phaiákia
were tipping wine to the wakeful god, to Hermês—
a last libation before going to bed—
but down the hall Odysseus went unseen,
still in the cloud Athena cloaked him in,
until he reached Arêtê, and the king.
He threw his great hands round Arêtês knees,
whereon the sacred mist curled back;
they saw him; and the diners hushed amazed
to see an unknown man inside the palace.
Under their eyes Odysseus made his plea:
"Arêtê, admirable Rhêxênor's daughter,
here is a man bruised by adversity, thrown

upon your mercy and the king your husband's,
begging indulgence of this company—
may the gods' blessing rest on them! May life
be kind to all! Let each one leave his children
every good thing this realm confers upon him!
But grant me passage to my father land.
My home and friends lie far. My life is pain."

He moved, then, toward the fire, and sat him down
amid the ashes.[67] No one stirred or spoke
until Ekhenêos broke the spell—an old man,
eldest of the Phaiákians, an oracle,
versed in the laws and manners of old time.
He rose among them now and spoke out kindly:
"Alkínoös, this will not pass for courtesy:
a guest abased in ashes at our hearth?
Everyone here awaits your word; so come, then,
lift the man up; give him a seat of honor,
a silver-studded chair. Then tell the stewards
we'll have another wine bowl for libation
to Zeus, lord of the lightning—advocate
of honorable petitioners. And supper
may be supplied our friend by the larder mistress."

Alkínoös, calm in power, heard him out,
then took the great adventurer by the hand
and led him from the fire. Nearest his throne
the son whom he loved best, Laódamas,
had long held place; now the king bade him rise
and gave his shining chair to Lord Odysseus.
A serving maid poured water for his hands
from a gold pitcher into a silver bowl,
and spread a polished table at his side;
the mistress of provisions came with bread
and other victuals, generous with her store.
So Lord Odysseus drank, and tasted supper.
Seeing this done, the king in majesty
said to his squire:
"A fresh bowl, Pontónoös;

[67] **sat him down . . . ashes:** Since the hearth was the sacred center of the home, a guest who sits there has a safe refuge or sanctuary.

we make libation to the lord of lightning,
who seconds honorable petitioners."

Mixing the honey-hearted wine, Pontónoös
went on his rounds and poured fresh cups for all,
whereof when all had spilt they drank their fill.
Alkínoös then spoke to the company:
"My lords and leaders of Phaiákia:
hear now, all that my heart would have me say.
Our banquet's ended, so you may retire;
but let our seniors gather in the morning
to give this guest a festal day, and make
fair offerings to the gods. In due course we
shall put our minds upon the means at hand
to take him safely, comfortably, well
and happily, with speed, to his own country,
distant though it may lie. And may no trouble
come to him here or on the way; his fate
he shall pay out at home, even as the Spinners
spun for him on the day his mother bore him.
If, as may be, he is some god, come down
from heaven's height, the gods are working strangely:
until now, they have shown themselves in glory
only after great hekatombs—those figures
banqueting at our side, throned like ourselves.
Or if some traveller met them when alone
they bore no least disguise; we are their kin; Gigantês,
Kyklopês, rank no nearer gods than we."

Odysseus' wits were ready, and he replied:
"Alkínoös, you may set your mind at rest.
Body and birth, a most unlikely god
am I, being all of earth and mortal nature.
I should say, rather, I am like those men
who suffer the worst trials that you know,
and miseries greater yet, as I might tell you—
hundreds; indeed the gods could send no more.
You will indulge me if I finish dinner—?
grieved though I am to say it. There's no part
of man more like a dog than brazen Belly,
crying to be remembered—and it must be—
when we are mortal weary and sick at heart;
and that is my condition. Yet my hunger
drives me to take this food, and think no more

of my afflictions. Belly must be filled.
Be equally impelled, my lords, tomorrow
to berth me in a ship and send me home!
Rough years I've had; now may I see once more
my hall, my lands, my people before I die!"

Now all who heard cried out assent to this:
the guest had spoken well; he must have passage.
Then tipping wine they drank their thirst away,
and one by one went homeward for the night.
So Lord Odysseus kept his place alone
with Arêtê and the king Alkínoös
beside him, while the maids went to and fro
clearing away the wine cups and the tables.
Presently the ivory-skinned lady
turned to him—for she knew his cloak and tunic
to be her own fine work, done with her maids—
and arrowy came her words upon the air:
"Friend, I, for one, have certain questions for you.
Who are you, and who has given you this clothing?
Did you not say you wandered here by sea?"

The great tactician carefully replied:
"Ah, majesty, what labor it would be
to go through the whole story! All my years
of misadventures, given by those on high!
But this you ask about is quickly told:
in mid-ocean lies Ogýgia, the island
haunt of Kalypso, Atlas' guileful daughter,
a lovely goddess and a dangerous one.
No one, no god or man, consorts with her;
but supernatural power brought me there
to be her solitary guest: for Zeus
let fly with his bright bolt and split my ship,
rolling me over in the winedark sea.
There all my shipmates, friends were drowned, while I
hung on the keelboard of the wreck and drifted
nine full days. Then in the dead of night
the gods brought me ashore upon Ogýgia
into her hands. The enchantress in her beauty
fed and caressed me, promised me I should be
immortal, youthful, all the days to come;
but in my heart I never gave consent
though seven years detained. Immortal clothing

I had from her, and kept it wet with tears.
Then came the eighth year on the wheel of heaven
and word to her from Zeus, or a change of heart,
so that she now commanded me to sail,
sending me out to sea on a craft I made
with timber and tools of hers. She gave me stores,
victuals and wine, a cloak divinely woven,
and made a warm land breeze come up astern.
Seventeen days I sailed in the open water
before I saw your country's shore, a shadow
upon the sea rim. Then my heart rejoiced—
pitiable as I am! For blows aplenty
awaited me from the god who shakes the earth.
Cross gales he blew, making me lose my bearings,
and heaved up seas beyond imagination—
huge and foundering seas. All I could do
was hold hard, groaning under every shock,
until my craft broke up in the hurricane.
I kept afloat and swam your sea, or drifted,
taken by wind and current to this coast
where I went in on big swells running landward.
But cliffs and rock shoals made that place forbidding,
so I turned back, swimming off shore, and came
in the end to a river, to auspicious water,
with smooth beach and a rise that broke the wind.
I lay there where I fell till strength returned.
Then sacred night came on, and I went inland
to high ground and a leaf bed in a thicket.
Heaven sent slumber in an endless tide
submerging my sad heart among the leaves.
That night and next day's dawn and noon I slept;
the sun went west; and then sweet sleep unbound me,
when I became aware of maids—your daughter's—
playing along the beach; the princess, too,
most beautiful. I prayed her to assist me,
and her good sense was perfect; one could hope
for no behavior like it from the young,
thoughtless as they most often are. But she
gave me good provender and good red wine,
a river bath, and finally this clothing.
There is the bitter tale. These are the facts."

But in reply Alkínoös observed:
"Friend, my child's good judgment failed in this—

not to have brought you in her company home.
Once you approached her, you became her charge."

To this Odysseus tactfully replied:
"Sir, as to that, you should not blame the princess.
She did tell me to follow with her maids,
but I would not. I felt abashed, and feared
the sight would somehow ruffle or offend you.
All of us on this earth are plagued by jealousy."

Alkínoös' answer was a declaration:
"Friend, I am not a man for trivial anger:
better a sense of measure in everything.
No anger here. I say that if it should please
our father Zeus, Athena, and Apollo—
seeing the man you are, seeing your thoughts
are my own thoughts—my daughter should be yours
and you my son-in-law, if you remained.
A home, lands, riches you should have from me
if you could be contented here. If not,
by Father Zeus, let none of our men hold you!
On the contrary, I can assure you now
of passage late tomorrow: while you sleep
my men will row you through the tranquil night
to your own land and home or where you please.
It may be, even, far beyond Euboia—
called most remote by seamen of our isle
who landed there, conveying Rhadamanthos
when he sought Tītyos,[68] the son of Gaia.
They put about, with neither pause nor rest,
and entered their home port the selfsame day.
But this you, too, will see: what ships I have,
how my young oarsmen send the foam a-scudding!"

Now joy welled up in the patient Lord Odysseus
who said devoutly in the warmest tones:
"O Father Zeus, let all this be fulfilled
as spoken by Alkínoös! Earth of harvests
remember him! Return me to my homeland!"

In this manner they conversed with one another;
but the great lady called her maids, and sent them

[68] **Títyos:** A giant who tried to rape Lêto and who was killed by Apollo and Artemis and placed in Tartarus, the lowest region of Hades.

to make a kingly bed, with purple rugs
piled up, and sheets outspread, and fleecy
coverlets in an eastern colonnade.
The girls went out with torches in their hands,
swift at their work of bedmaking; returning
they whispered at the lord Odysseus' shoulder:
"Sir, you may come; your bed has been prepared."

How welcome the word "bed" came to his ears!
Now, then, Odysseus laid him down and slept
in luxury under the Porch of Morning,
while in his inner chamber Alkínoös
retired to rest where his dear consort lay.

Book 8
The Songs of the Harper

Under the opening fingers of the dawn
Alkínoös, the sacred prince, arose,
and then arose Odysseus, raider of cities.
As the king willed, they went down by the shipways
to the assembly ground of the Phaiákians.
Side by side the two men took their ease there
on smooth stone benches. Meanwhile Pallas Athena
roamed through the byways of the town, contriving
Odysseus' voyage home—in voice and feature
the crier of the king Alkínoös
who stopped and passed the word to every man:
"Phaiákian lords and counselors, this way!
Come to assembly: learn about the stranger,
the new guest at the palace of Alkínoös—
a man the sea drove, but a comely man;
the gods' own light is on him."

She aroused them,
and soon the assembly ground and seats were filled
with curious men, a throng who peered and saw
the master mind of war, Laërtês' son.
Athena now poured out her grace upon him,
head and shoulders, height and mass—a splendor
awesome to the eyes of the Phaiákians;
she put him in a fettle to win the day,
mastering every trial they set to test him.
When all the crowd sat marshalled, quieted,

Alkínoös addressed the full assembly:
"Hear me, lords and captains of the Phaiákians!
Hear what my heart would have me say!
Our guest and new friend—nameless to me still—
comes to my house after long wandering
in Dawn lands, or among the Sunset races.
Now he appeals to me for conveyance home.
As in the past, therefore, let us provide
passage, and quickly, for no guest of mine
languishes here for lack of it. Look to it:
get a black ship afloat on the noble sea,
and pick our fastest sailer; draft a crew
of two and fifty from our younger townsmen—
men who have made their names at sea. Loop oars
well to your tholepins, lads, then leave the ship,
come to our house, fall to, and take your supper:
we'll furnish out a feast for every crewman.
These are your orders. As for my older peers
and princes of the realm, let them foregather
in festival for our friend in my great hall;
and let no man refuse. Call in our minstrel,
Demódokos, whom God made lord of song,
heart-easing, sing upon what theme he will."

He turned, led the procession, and those princes
followed, while his herald sought the minstrel.
Young oarsmen from the assembly chose a crew
of two and fifty, as the king commanded,
and these filed off along the waterside
to where the ship lay, poised above open water.
They hauled the black hull down to ride the sea,
rigging a mast and spar in the black ship,
with oars at trail from corded rawhide, all
seamanly; then tried the white sail, hoisting,
and moored her off the beach. Then going ashore
the crew went up to the great house of Alkínoös.
Here the enclosures, entrance ways, and rooms
were filled with men, young men and old, for whom
Alkínoös had put twelve sheep to sacrifice,
eight tuskers and a pair of shambling oxen.
These, now, they flayed and dressed to make their banquet.
The crier soon came, leading that man of song
whom the Muse cherished; by her gift he knew

the good of life, and evil—
for she who lent him sweetness made him blind.
Pontónoös fixed a studded chair for him
hard by a pillar amid the banqueters,
hanging the taut harp from a peg above him,
and guided up his hands upon the strings;
placed a bread basket at his side, and poured
wine in a cup, that he might drink his fill.
Now each man's hand went out upon the banquet.

In time, when hunger and thirst were turned away,
the Muse brought to the minstrel's mind a song
of heroes whose great fame rang under heaven:
the clash between Odysseus and Akhilleus,
how one time they contended at the godfeast
raging, and the marshal, Agamémnon,
felt inward joy over his captains' quarrel;
for such had been foretold him by Apollo
at Pytho[69]—hallowed height—when the Akhaian
crossed that portal of rock to ask a sign—
in the old days when grim war lay ahead
for Trojans and Danaans, by God's will.
So ran the tale the minstrel sang. Odysseus
with massive hand drew his rich mantle down
over his brow, cloaking his face with it,
to make the Phaiákians miss the secret tears
that started to his eyes. How skillfully
he dried them when the song came to a pause!
threw back his mantle, spilt his gout of wine!
But soon the minstrel plucked his note once more
to please the Phaiákian lords, who loved the song;
then in his cloak Odysseus wept again.
His tears flowed in the mantle unperceived;
only Alkínoös, at his elbow, saw them,
and caught the low groan in the man's breathing.
At once he spoke to all the seafolk round him:
"Hear me, lords and captains of the Phaiákians.
Our meat is shared, our hearts are full of pleasure
from the clear harp tone that accords with feasting;

[69] **at Pytho:** Apollo's shrine at Delphi, on the slopes of Mt. Parnassos.

now for the field and track; we shall have trials
in the pentathlon. Let our guest go home
and tell his friends what champions we are
at boxing, wrestling, broadjump and foot racing."

On this he led the way and all went after.
The crier unslung and pegged the shining harp
and, taking Demódokos's hand,
led him along with all the rest — Phaiákian
peers, gay amateurs of the great games.
They gained the common where a crowd was forming,
and many a young athlete now came forward
with seaside names like Tipmast, Tiderace, Sparwood,
Hullman, Sternman, Beacher and Pullerman,
Bluewater, Shearwater, Runningwake, Boardalee,
Seabelt, son of Grandfleet Shipwrightson;
Seareach stepped up, son of the Launching Master,
rugged as Arês,° bane of men: his build god of war
excelled all but the Prince Laódamas;
and Laódamas made entry with his brothers,
Halios and Klytóneus, sons of the king.
The runners, first, must have their quarter mile.
All lined up tense; then Go! and down the track
they raised the dust in a flying bunch, strung out
longer and longer behind Prince Klytóneus.
By just so far as a mule team, breaking ground,
will distance oxen, he left all behind
and came up to the crowd, an easy winner.
Then they made room for wrestling — grinding bouts
that Seareach won, pinning the strongest men;
then the broadjump; first place went to Seabelt;
Sparwood gave the discus the mightiest fling,
and Prince Laódamas outboxed them all.
Now it was he, the son of Alkínoös,
who said when they had run through these diversions:
"Look here, friends, we ought to ask the stranger
if he competes in something. He's no cripple;
look at his leg muscles and his forearms.
Neck like a bollard;[70] strong as a bull, he seems;
and not old, though he may have gone stale under

[70] **bollard:** The posts on a dock used for mooring boats.

the rough times he had. Nothing like the sea
for wearing out the toughest man alive."

Then Seareach took him up at once, and said:
"Laódamas, you're right, by all the powers.
Go up to him, yourself, and put the question."

At this, Alkínoös' tall son advanced
to the center ground, and there addressed Odysseus:
"Friend, Excellency, come join our competition,
if you are practiced, as you seem to be.
While a man lives he wins no greater honor
than footwork and the skill of hands can bring him.
Enter our games, then; ease your heart of trouble.
Your journey home is not far off, remember;
the ship is launched, the crew all primed for sea."

Odysseus, canniest of men, replied:
"Laódamas, why do you young chaps challenge me?
I have more on my mind than track and field—
hard days, and many, have I seen, and suffered.
I sit here at your field meet, yes; but only
as one who begs your king to send him home."

Now Seareach put his word in, and contentiously:
"The reason being, as I see it, friend,
you never learned a sport, and have no skill
in any of the contests of fighting men.
You must have been the skipper of some tramp
that crawled from one port to the next, jam full
of chaffering hands: a tallier of cargoes,
itching for gold—not, by your looks, an athlete."

Odysseus frowned, and eyed him coldly, saying:
"That was uncalled for, friend, you talk like a fool.
The gods deal out no gift, this one or any—
birth, brains, or speech—to every man alike.
In looks a man may be a shade, a specter,
and yet be master of speech so crowned with beauty
that people gaze at him with pleasure. Courteous,
sure of himself, he can command assemblies,
and when he comes to town, the crowds gather.
A handsome man, contrariwise, may lack
grace and good sense in everything he says.

You now, for instance, with your fine physique—
a god's, indeed—you have an empty noddle.
I find my heart inside my ribs aroused
by your impertinence. I am no stranger
to contests, as you fancy. I rated well
when I could count on youth and my two hands.
Now pain has cramped me, and my years of combat
hacking through ranks in war, and the bitter sea.
Aye. Even so I'll give your games a trial.
You spoke heart-wounding words. You shall be answered."

He leapt out, cloaked as he was, and picked a discus,
a rounded stone, more ponderous than those
already used by the Phaiákian throwers,
and, whirling, let it fly from his great hand
with a low hum. The crowd went flat on the ground—
all those oar-pulling, seafaring Phaiákians—
under the rushing noise. The spinning disk
soared out, light as a bird, beyond all others.
Disguised now as a Phaiákian, Athena
staked it and called out:
"Even a blind man,
friend, could judge this, finding with his fingers
one discus, quite alone, beyond the cluster.
Congratulations; this event is yours;
not a man here can beat you or come near you."

That was a cheering hail, Odysseus thought,
seeing one friend there on the emulous field,
so, in relief, he turned among the Phaiákians
and said:
"Now come alongside that one, lads.
The next I'll send as far, I think, or farther.
Anyone else on edge for competition
try me now. By heaven, you angered me.
Racing, wrestling, boxing—I bar nothing
with any man except Laódamas,
for he's my host. Who quarrels with his host?
Only a madman—or no man at all—
would challenge his protector among strangers,
cutting the ground away under his feet.
Here are no others I will not engage,
none but I hope to know what he is made of.
Inept at combat, am I? Not entirely.
Give me a smooth bow; I can handle it,

and I might well be first to hit my man
amid a swarm of enemies, though archers
in company around me drew together.
Philoktêtês[71] alone, at Troy, when we
Akhaians took the bow, used to outshoot me.
Of men who now eat bread upon the earth
I hold myself the best hand with a bow—
conceding mastery to the men of old,
Heraklês, or Eurýtos[72] of Oikhalía,
heroes who vied with gods in bowmanship.
Eurýtos came to grief, it's true; old age
never crept over him in his long hall;
Apollo took his challenge ill, and killed him.
What then, the spear? I'll plant it like an arrow.
Only in sprinting, I'm afraid, I may
be passed by someone. Roll of the sea waves
wearied me, and the victuals in my ship
ran low; my legs are flabby."

When he finished,
the rest were silent, but Alkínoös answered:
"Friend, we take your challenge in good part,
for this man angered and affronted you
here at our peaceful games. You'd have us note
the prowess that is in you, and so clearly,
no man of sense would ever cry it down!
Come, turn your mind, now, on a thing to tell
among your peers when you are home again,
dining in hall, beside your wife and children:
I mean our prowess, as you may remember it,
for we, too, have our skills, given by Zeus,
and practiced from our father's time to this—
not in the boxing ring nor the palestra[73]
conspicuous, but in racing, land or sea;
and all our days we set great store by feasting,
harpers, and the grace of dancing choirs,
changes of dress, warm baths, and downy beds.
O master dancers of the Phaiákians!
Perform now: let our guest on his return
tell his companions we excel the world

[71] **Philoktêtês:** Inherited Heraklês' bow. [72] **Eurýtos:** Eurýtos challenged Apollo to an archery contest and lost; his bow was given to Odysseus, who uses it at the end of the epic. [73] **the palestra:** A public place for wrestling and other athletics.

in dance and song, as in our ships and running.
Someone go find the gittern[74] harp in hall
and bring it quickly to Demódokos!"

At the serene king's word, a squire ran
to bring the polished harp out of the palace,
and place was given to nine referees—
peers of the realm, masters of ceremony—
who cleared a space and smoothed a dancing floor.
The squire brought down, and gave Demódokos,
the clear-toned harp; and centering on the minstrel
magical young dancers formed a circle
with a light beat, and stamp of feet. Beholding,
Odysseus marvelled at the flashing ring.

Now to his harp the blinded minstrel sang
of Arês' dalliance with Aphroditê:
how hidden in Hephaistos' house they played
at love together, and the gifts of Arês,
dishonoring Hephaistos' bed—and how
the word that wounds the heart came to the master
from Hélios,° who had seen the two embrace; the sun
and when he learned it, Lord Hephaistos went
with baleful calculation to his forge.
There mightily he armed his anvil block
and hammered out a chain whose tempered links
could not be sprung or bent; he meant that they should hold.
Those shackles fashioned hot in wrath Hephaistos
climbed to the bower and the bed of love,
pooled all his net of chain around the bed posts
and swung it from the rafters overhead—
light as a cobweb even gods in bliss
could not perceive, so wonderful his cunning.
Seeing his bed now made a snare, he feigned
a journey to the trim stronghold of Lemnos,
the dearest of earth's towns to him.[75] And Arês?
Ah, golden Arês' watch had its reward
when he beheld the great smith leaving home.
How promptly to the famous door he came,
intent on pleasure with sweet Kythereia![76]

---

[74] **the gittern:** An early ancestor of the guitar. [75] **Lemnos . . . to him:** Hephaistos landed on the island of Lemnos when Zeus threw him off Olympos. [76] **Kythereia:** A name for Aphroditê taken from the island Kythera (Cythera), to which Aphroditê floated after her birth from sea foam.

She, who had left her father's side but now,
sat in her chamber when her lover entered;
and tenderly he pressed her hand and said:
"Come and lie down, my darling, and be happy!
Hephaistos is no longer here, but gone
to see his grunting[77] Sintian friends on Lemnos."

As she, too, thought repose would be most welcome,
the pair went in to bed—into a shower
of clever chains, the netting of Hephaistos.
So trussed they could not move apart, nor rise,
at last they knew there could be no escape,
they were to see the glorious cripple now—
for Hêlios had spied for him, and told him;
so he turned back this side of Lemnos Isle
sick at heart, making his way homeward.
Now in the doorway of the room he stood
while deadly rage took hold of him; his voice,
hoarse and terrible, reached all the gods:
"O Father Zeus, O gods in bliss forever,
here is indecorous entertainment for you,
Aphroditê, Zeus's daughter,
caught in the act, cheating me, her cripple,
with Arês—devastating Arês.
Cleanlimbed beauty is her joy, not these
bandylegs I came into the world with:
no one to blame but the two gods[78] who bred me!
Come see this pair entwining here
in my own bed! How hot it makes me burn!
I think they may not care to lie much longer,
pressing on one another, passionate lovers;
they'll have enough of bed together soon.
And yet the chain that bagged them holds them down
till Father sends me back my wedding gifts—
all that I poured out for his damned pigeon,
so lovely, and so wanton."

All the others
were crowding in, now, to the brazen house—
Poseidon who embraces earth, and Hermês
the runner, and Apollo, lord of Distance.

[77] **grunting:** Non-Greek speaking. [78] **the two gods:** Zeus and Hêra.

The goddesses stayed home for shame; but these
munificences ranged there in the doorway,
and irrepressible among them all
arose the laughter of the happy gods.
Gazing hard at Hephaistos' handiwork
the gods in turn remarked among themselves:
"No dash in adultery now."

"The tortoise tags the hare—
Hephaistos catches Arês—and Arês outran the wind."

"The lame god's craft has pinned him. Now shall he
pay what is due from gods taken in cuckoldry."

They made these improving remarks to one another,
but Apollo leaned aside to say to Hermês:
"Son of Zeus, beneficent Wayfinder,
would you accept a coverlet of chain, if only
you lay by Aphroditê's golden side?"

To this the Wayfinder replied, shining:
"Would I not, though, Apollo of distances!
Wrap me in chains three times the weight of these,
come goddesses and gods to see the fun;
only let me lie beside the pale-golden one!"

The gods gave way again to peals of laughter,
all but Poseidon, and he never smiled,
but urged Hephaistos to unpinion Arês,
saying emphatically, in a loud voice:
"Free him;
you will be paid, I swear; ask what you will;
he pays up every jot the gods decree."

To this the Great Gamelegs replied:
"Poseidon,
lord of the earth-surrounding sea, I should not
swear to a scoundrel's honor. What have I
as surety from you, if Arês leaves me
empty-handed, with my empty chain?"

The Earthshaker for answer urged again:
"Hephaistos, let us grant he goes, and leaves
the fine unpaid; I swear, then, I shall pay it."

Then said the Great Gamelegs at last:
                              "No more;
you offer terms I cannot well refuse."

And down the strong god bent to set them free,
till disencumbered of their bond, the chain,
the lovers leapt away—he into Thrace,[79]
while Aphroditê, laughter's darling, fled
to Kypros[80] Isle and Paphos, to her meadow
and altar dim with incense. There the Graces
390 bathed and anointed her with golden oil—
a bloom that clings upon immortal flesh alone—
and let her folds of mantle fall in glory.

So ran the song the minstrel sang.

                              Odysseus,
listening, found sweet pleasure in the tale,
among the Phaiákian mariners and oarsmen.
And next Alkínoös called upon his sons,
Halios and Laódamas, to show
the dance no one could do as well as they—
400 handling a purple ball carven by Pólybos.
One made it shoot up under the shadowing clouds
as he leaned backward; bounding high in air
the other cut its flight far off the ground—
and neither missed a step as the ball soared.
The next turn was to keep it low, and shuttling
hard between them, while the ring of boys
gave them a steady stamping beat.
Odysseus now addressed Alkínoös:
"O majesty, model of all your folk,
410 your promise was to show me peerless dancers;
here is the promise kept. I am all wonder."

At this Alkínoös in his might rejoicing
said to the seafarers of Phaiákia:
"Attend me now, Phaiákian lords and captains:
our guest appears a clear-eyed man and wise.
Come, let him feel our bounty as he should.
Here are twelve princes of the kingdom—lords

[handwritten margin note:] Tales of Trojan war made Odysseus wep.

---

[79] **Thrace:** A country north and east of Greece; Thrace was the home of Arês and a warlike people.   [80] **Kypros:** Aphroditê's shrine on Kypros (Cyprus) was at Paphos.

paramount, and I who make thirteen;
let each one bring a laundered cloak and tunic,
and add one bar of honorable gold.
Heap all our gifts together; load his arms;
let him go joyous to our evening feast!
As for Seareach — why, man to man
he'll make amends, and handsomely; he blundered."

Now all as one acclaimed the king's good pleasure,
and each one sent a squire to bring his gifts.
Meanwhile Seareach found speech again, saying:
"My lord and model of us all, Alkínoös,
as you require of me, in satisfaction,
this broadsword of clear bronze goes to our guest.
Its hilt is silver, and the ringed sheath
of new-sawn ivory — a costly weapon."

He turned to give the broadsword to Odysseus,
facing him, saying blithely:
"Sir, my best
wishes, my respects; if I offended,
I hope the seawinds blow it out of mind.
God send you see your lady and your homeland
soon again, after the pain of exile."

Odysseus, the great tactician, answered:
"My hand, friend; may the gods award you fortune.
I hope no pressing need comes on you ever
for this fine blade you give me in amends."

He slung it, glinting silver, from his shoulder,
as the light shone from sundown. Messengers
were bearing gifts and treasure to the palace,
where the king's sons received them all, and made
a glittering pile at their grave mother's side;
then, as Alkínoös took his throne of power,
each went to his own high-backed chair in turn,
and said Alkínoös to Arêtê:
"Lady, bring here a chest, the finest one;
a clean cloak and tunic; stow these things;
and warm a cauldron for him. Let him bathe,
when he has seen the gifts of the Phaiákians,
and so dine happily to a running song.
My own wine-cup of gold intaglio
I'll give him, too; through all the days to come,

tipping his wine to Zeus or other gods
in his great hall, he shall remember me."

Then said Arêtê to her maids:
"The tripod:
stand the great tripod legs about the fire."

They swung the cauldron on the fire's heart,
poured water in, and fed the blaze beneath
until the basin simmered, cupped in flame.
The queen set out a rich chest from her chamber
and folded in the gifts—clothing and gold
given Odysseus by the Phaiákians;
then she put in the royal cloak and tunic,
briskly saying to her guest:
"Now here, sir,
look to the lid yourself, and tie it down
against light fingers, if there be any,
on the black ship tonight while you are sleeping."

Noble Odysseus, expert in adversity,
battened the lid down with a lightning knot
learned, once, long ago, from the Lady Kirkê.[81]
And soon a call came from the Bathing Mistress
who led him to a hip-bath, warm and clear—
a happy sight, and rare in his immersions
after he left Kalypso's home—where, surely,
the luxuries of a god were ever his.
When the bath maids had washed him, rubbed him down,
put a fresh tunic and a cloak around him,
he left the bathing place to join the men
at wine in hall.

The princess Nausikaa,
exquisite figure, as of heaven's shaping,
waited beside a pillar as he passed
and said swiftly, with wonder in her look:
"Fare well, stranger; in your land remember me
who met and saved you. It is worth your thought."

The man of all occasions now met this:
"Daughter of great Alkínoös, Nausikaa,

[81] **Lady Kirkê (Circe):** A sorceress; Odysseus encounters Kirkê on her island in Book 12.

may Zeus the lord of thunder, Hêra's consort,
grant me daybreak again in my own country!
But there and all my days until I die
may I invoke you as I would a goddess,
princess, to whom I owe my life."

He left her
and went to take his place beside the king.

Now when the roasts were cut, the winebowls full,
a herald led the minstrel down the room
amid the deference of the crowd, and paused
to seat him near a pillar in the center—
whereupon that resourceful man, Odysseus,
carved out a quarter from his chine of pork,
crisp with fat, and called the blind man's guide:
"Herald! here, take this to Demódokos:
let him feast and be merry, with my compliments.
All men owe honor to the poets—honor
and awe, for they are dearest to the Muse
who puts upon their lips the ways of life."

Gentle Demódokos took the proffered gift
and inwardly rejoiced. When all were served,
every man's hand went out upon the banquet,
repelling hunger and thirst, until at length
Odysseus spoke again to the blind minstrel:
"Demódokos, accept my utmost praise.
The Muse, daughter of Zeus in radiance,
or else Apollo gave you skill to shape
with such great style your songs of the Akhaians—
their hard lot, how they fought and suffered war.
You shared it, one would say, or heard it all.
Now shift your theme, and sing that wooden horse
Epeios built, inspired by Athena—
the ambuscade Odysseus filled with fighters
and sent to take the inner town of Troy.
Sing only this for me, sing me this well,
and I shall say at once before the world
the grace of heaven has given us a song."

The minstrel stirred, murmuring to the god, and soon
clear words and notes came one by one, a vision
of the Akhaians in their graceful ships
drawing away from shore: the torches flung

and shelters flaring: Argive soldiers crouched
in the close dark around Odysseus: and
the horse, tall on the assembly ground of Troy.
For when the Trojans pulled it in, themselves,
up to the citadel, they sat nearby
with long-drawn-out and hapless argument—
favoring, in the end, one course of three:
either to stave the vault with brazen axes,
or haul it to a cliff and pitch it down,
or else to save it for the gods, a votive glory—
the plan that could not but prevail.
For Troy must perish, as ordained, that day
she harbored the great horse of timber; hidden
the flower of Akhaia lay, and bore
slaughter and death upon the men of Troy.
He sang, then, of the town sacked by Akhaians
pouring down from the horse's hollow cave,
this way and that way raping the steep city,
and how Odysseus came like Arês to
the door of Deïphobos, with Meneláos,
and braved the desperate fight there—
conquering once more by Athena's power.

The splendid minstrel sang it.

And Odysseus
let the bright molten tears run down his cheeks,
weeping the way a wife mourns for her lord
on the lost field where he has gone down fighting
the day of wrath that came upon his children.
At sight of the man panting and dying there,
she slips down to enfold him, crying out;
then feels the spears, prodding her back and shoulders,
and goes bound into slavery and grief.
Piteous weeping wears away her cheeks:
but no more piteous than Odysseus' tears,
cloaked as they were, now, from the company.
Only Alkínoös, at his elbow, knew—
hearing the low sob in the man's breathing—
and when he knew, he spoke:
"Hear me, lords and captains of Phaiákia!
And let Demódokos touch his harp no more.
His theme has not been pleasing to all here.
During the feast, since our fine poet sang,
our guest has never left off weeping. Grief

seems fixed upon his heart. Break off the song!
Let everyone be easy, host and guest;
there's more decorum in a smiling banquet!
We had prepared here, on our friend's behalf,
safe conduct in a ship, and gifts to cheer him,
holding that any man with a grain of wit
will treat a decent suppliant like a brother.
Now by the same rule, friend, you must not be
secretive any longer! Come, in fairness,
tell me the name you bore in that far country;
how were you known to family, and neighbors?
No man is nameless—no man, good or bad,
but gets a name in his first infancy,
none being born, unless a mother bears him!
Tell me your native land, your coast and city—
sailing directions for the ships, you know—
for those Phaiákian ships of ours
that have no steersman, and no steering oar,
divining the crew's wishes, as they do,
and knowing, as they do, the ports of call
about the world. Hidden in mist or cloud
they scud the open sea, with never a thought
of being in distress or going down.
There is, however, something I once heard
Nausíthoös, my father, say: Poseidon
holds it against us that our deep sea ships
are sure conveyance for all passengers.
My father said, some day one of our cutters
homeward bound over the cloudy sea
would be wrecked by the god, and a range of hills
thrown round our city. So, in his age, he said,
and let it be, or not, as the god please.
But come, now, put it for me clearly, tell me
the sea ways that you wandered, and the shores
you touched; the cities, and the men therein,
uncivilized, if such there were, and hostile,
and those godfearing who had kindly manners.
Tell me why you should grieve so terribly
over the Argives and the fall of Troy.
That was all gods' work, weaving ruin there
so it should make a song for men to come!
Some kin of yours, then, died at Ilion,
some first rate man, by marriage near to you,
next your own blood most dear?
Or some companion of congenial mind

and valor? True it is, a wise friend
can take a brother's place in our affection."

Book 9
New Coasts and Poseidon's Son

Now this was the reply Odysseus made:
"Alkínoös, king and admiration of men,
how beautiful this is, to hear a minstrel
gifted as yours: a god he might be, singing!
There is no boon in life more sweet, I say,
than when a summer joy holds all the realm,
and banqueters sit listening to a harper
in a great hall, by rows of tables heaped
with bread and roast meat, while a steward goes
to dip up wine and brim your cups again.
Here is the flower of life, it seems to me!
But now you wish to know my cause for sorrow—
and thereby give me cause for more.
What shall I
say first? What shall I keep until the end?
The gods have tried me in a thousand ways.
But first my name: let that be known to you,
and if I pull away from pitiless death,
friendship will bind us, though my land lies far.

I am Laërtês' son, Odysseus.
Men hold me
formidable for guile in peace and war:
this fame has gone abroad to the sky's rim.
My home is on the peaked sea-mark of Ithaka
under Mount Neion's wind-blown robe of leaves,
in sight of other islands—Doulíkhion,
Samê, wooded Zakynthos—Ithaka
being most lofty in that coastal sea,
and northwest, while the rest lie east and south.
A rocky isle, but good for a boy's training;
I shall not see on earth a place more dear,
though I have been detained long by Kalypso,
loveliest among goddesses, who held me
in her smooth caves, to be her heart's delight,
as Kirkê of Aiaia, the enchantress,
desired me, and detained me in her hall.
But in my heart I never gave consent.

Where shall a man find sweetness to surpass
his own home and his parents? In far lands
he shall not, though he find a house of gold.

What of my sailing, then, from Troy?
What of those years
of rough adventure, weathered under Zeus?
The wind that carried west from Ilion
brought me to Ísmaros, on the far shore,
a strongpoint on the coast of the Kikonês.[82]
I stormed that place and killed the men who fought.
Plunder we took, and we enslaved the women,
to make division, equal shares to all—
but on the spot I told them: 'Back, and quickly!
Out to sea again!' My men were mutinous,
fools, on stores of wine. Sheep after sheep
they butchered by the surf, and shambling cattle,
feasting—while fugitives went inland, running
to call to arms the main force of Kikonês.
This was an army, trained to fight on horseback
or, where the ground required, on foot. They came
with dawn over that terrain like the leaves
and blades of spring. So doom appeared to us,
dark word of Zeus for us, our evil days.
My men stood up and made a fight of it—
backed on the ships, with lances kept in play,
from bright morning through the blaze of noon
holding our beach, although so far outnumbered;
but when the sun passed toward unyoking time,
then the Akhaians, one by one, gave way.
Six benches were left empty in every ship
that evening when we pulled away from death.
And this new grief we bore with us to sea:
our precious lives we had, but not our friends.
No ship made sail next day until some shipmate
had raised a cry, three times, for each poor ghost
unfleshed by the Kikonês on that field.

Tells story about how odysseus and his men were attacked

Now Zeus the lord of cloud roused in the north
a storm against the ships, and driving veils
of squall moved down like night on land and sea.
The bows went plunging at the gust; sails

[82] **Kikonês:** Allies of Troy, the Kikonês lived on the northern coast of the Aegean Sea.

cracked and lashed out strips in the big wind.
We saw death in that fury, dropped the yards,
unshipped the oars, and pulled for the nearest lee:
then two long days and nights we lay offshore
worn out and sick at heart, tasting our grief,
until a third Dawn came with ringlets shining.
Then we put up our masts, hauled sail, and rested,
letting the steersmen and the breeze take over.

I might have made it safely home, that time,
but as I came round Malea the current
took me out to sea, and from the north
a fresh gale drove me on, past Kythera.[83]
Nine days I drifted on the teeming sea
before dangerous high winds. Upon the tenth
we came to the coastline of the Lotos Eaters,[84]
who live upon that flower. We landed there
to take on water. All ships' companies
mustered alongside for the mid-day meal.
Then I sent out two picked men and a runner
to learn what race of men that land sustained.
They fell in, soon enough, with Lotos Eaters,
who showed no will to do us harm, only
offering the sweet Lotos to our friends—
but those who ate this honeyed plant, the Lotos,
never cared to report, nor to return:
they longed to stay forever, browsing on
that native bloom, forgetful of their homeland.
I drove them, all three wailing, to the ships,
tied them down under their rowing benches,
and called the rest: 'All hands aboard;
come, clear the beach and no one taste
the Lotos, or you lose your hope of home.'
Filing in to their places by the rowlocks
my oarsmen dipped their long oars in the surf,
and we moved out again on our sea faring.

In the next land we found were Kyklopês,[85]
giants, louts, without a law to bless them.

[83] **Malea . . . Kythera:** Malea is at the southernmost tip of Greece; Kythera is an island farther south.
[84] **Lotos Eaters:** Usually identified with North Africans, perhaps near modern Libya; a wide range of interpretations exist for the lotus—from a mild narcotic or hallucinogen to an aphrodisiac.
[85] **Kyklopês:** According to ancient tradition, the Kyklopês (Cyclops) lived in Sicily.

In ignorance leaving the fruitage of the earth in mystery
to the immortal gods, they neither plow
nor sow by hand, nor till the ground, though grain—
wild wheat and barley—grows untended, and
wine-grapes, in clusters, ripen in heaven's rain.
Kyklopês have no muster and no meeting,
no consultation or old tribal ways,
but each one dwells in his own mountain cave
dealing out rough justice to wife and child,
indifferent to what the others do.
Well, then:
across the wide bay from the mainland
there lies a desert island, not far out,
but still not close inshore. Wild goats in hundreds
breed there; and no human being comes
upon the isle to startle them—no hunter
of all who ever tracked with hounds through forests
or had rough going over mountain trails.
The isle, unplanted and untilled, a wilderness,
pastures goats alone. And this is why:
good ships like ours with cheekpaint at the bows
are far beyond the Kyklopês. No shipwright
toils among them, shaping and building up
symmetrical trim hulls to cross the sea
and visit all the seaboard towns, as men do
who go and come in commerce over water.
This isle—seagoing folk would have annexed it
and built their homesteads on it: all good land,
fertile for every crop in season: lush
well-watered meads along the shore, vines in profusion,
prairie, clear for the plow, where grain would grow
chin high by harvest time, and rich sub-soil.
The island cove is landlocked, so you need
no hawsers out astern, bow-stones[86] or mooring:
run in and ride there till the day your crews
chafe to be under sail, and a fair wind blows.
You'll find good water flowing from a cavern
through dusky poplars into the upper bay.
Here we made harbor. Some god guided us
that night, for we could barely see our bows
in the dense fog around us, and no moonlight

[86] **bow-stones:** An anchor made out of stones knotted in rope and hung over the bow of a boat.

filtered through the overcast. No look-out,
nobody saw the island dead ahead,
nor even the great landward rolling billow
that took us in: we found ourselves in shallows,
keels grazing shore: so furled our sails
and disembarked where the low ripples broke.
There on the beach we lay, and slept till morning.

When Dawn spread out her finger tips of rose
we turned out marvelling, to tour the isle,
while Zeus's shy nymph daughters flushed wild goats
down from the heights—a breakfast for my men.
We ran to fetch our hunting bows and long-shanked
lances from the ships, and in three companies
we took our shots. Heaven gave us game a-plenty:
for every one of twelve ships in my squadron
nine goats fell to be shared; my lot was ten.
So there all day, until the sun went down,
we made our feast on meat galore, and wine—
wine from the ship, for our supply held out,
so many jars were filled at Ísmaros
from stores of the Kikonês that we plundered.
We gazed, too, at Kyklopês Land, so near,
we saw their smoke, heard bleating from their flocks.
But after sundown, in the gathering dusk,
we slept again above the wash of ripples.

When the young Dawn with finger tips of rose
came in the east, I called my men together
and made a speech to them:
'Old shipmates, friends,
the rest of you stand by; I'll make the crossing
in my own ship, with my own company,
and find out what the mainland natives are—
for they may be wild savages, and lawless,
or hospitable and god fearing men.'

At this I went aboard, and gave the word
to cast off by the stern. My oarsmen followed,
filing in to their benches by the rowlocks,
and all in line dipped oars in the grey sea.

As we rowed on, and nearer to the mainland,
at one end of the bay, we saw a cavern

yawning above the water, screened with laurel,
and many rams and goats about the place
inside a sheepfold — made from slabs of stone
earthfast between tall trunks of pine and rugged
towering oak trees.
A prodigious man
slept in this cave alone, and took his flocks
to graze afield — remote from all companions,
knowing none but savage ways, a brute
so huge, he seemed no man at all of those
who eat good wheaten bread; but he seemed rather
a shaggy mountain reared in solitude.
We beached there, and I told the crew
to stand by and keep watch over the ship;
as for myself I took my twelve best fighters
and went ahead. I had a goatskin full
of that sweet liquor that Euanthês' son,
Maron, had given me. He kept Apollo's
holy grove at Ísmaros; for kindness
we showed him there, and showed his wife and child,
he gave me seven shining golden talents[87]
perfectly formed, a solid silver winebowl,
and then this liquor — twelve two-handled jars
of brandy, pure and fiery. Not a slave
in Maron's household knew this drink; only
he, his wife and the storeroom mistress knew;
and they would put one cupful — ruby-colored,
honey-smooth — in twenty more of water,
but still the sweet scent hovered like a fume
over the winebowl. No man turned away
when cups of this came round.
A wineskin full
I brought along, and victuals in a bag,
for in my bones I knew some towering brute
would be upon us soon — all outward power,
a wild man, ignorant of civility.

We climbed, then, briskly to the cave. But Kyklops
had gone afield, to pasture his fat sheep,
so we looked round at everything inside:

[87] **talents:** Units of gold.

a drying rack that sagged with cheeses, pens
crowded with lambs and kids, each in its class:
firstlings apart from middlings, and the 'dewdrops,'
or newborn lambkins, penned apart from both.
And vessels full of whey were brimming there—
bowls of earthenware and pails for milking.
My men came pressing round me, pleading:
'Why not
take these cheeses, get them stowed, come back,
throw open all the pens, and make a run for it?
We'll drive the kids and lambs aboard. We say
put out again on good salt water!'

Ah,
how sound that was! Yet I refused. I wished
to see the caveman, what he had to offer—
no pretty sight, it turned out, for my friends.
We lit a fire, burnt an offering,
and took some cheese to eat; then sat in silence
around the embers, waiting. When he came
he had a load of dry boughs on his shoulder
to stoke his fire at suppertime. He dumped it
with a great crash into that hollow cave,
and we all scattered fast to the far wall.
Then over the broad cavern floor he ushered
the ewes he meant to milk. He left his rams
and he-goats in the yard outside, and swung
high overhead a slab of solid rock
to close the cave. Two dozen four-wheeled wagons,
with heaving wagon teams, could not have stirred
the tonnage of that rock from where he wedged it
over the doorsill. Next he took his seat
and milked his bleating ewes. A practiced job
he made of it, giving each ewe her suckling;
thickened his milk, then, into curds and whey,
sieved out the curds to drip in withy baskets,
and poured the whey to stand in bowls
cooling until he drank it for his supper.
When all these chores were done, he poked the fire,
heaping on brushwood. In the glare he saw us.

'Strangers,' he said, 'who are you? And where from?
What brings you here by sea ways—a fair traffic?

Or are you wandering rogues, who cast your lives
like dice, and ravage other folk by sea?'

We felt a pressure on our hearts, in dread
of that deep rumble and that mighty man.
But all the same I spoke up in reply:
'We are from Troy, Akhaians, blown off course
by shifting gales on the Great South Sea;
homeward bound, but taking routes and ways
uncommon; so the will of Zeus would have it.
We served under Agamémnon, son of Atreus—
the whole world knows what city
he laid waste, what armies he destroyed.
It was our luck to come here; here we stand,
beholden for your help, or any gifts
you give—as custom is to honor strangers.[88]
We would entreat you, great Sir, have a care
for the gods' courtesy; Zeus will avenge
the unoffending guest.'

He answered this
from his brute chest, unmoved:
'You are a ninny
or else you come from the other end of nowhere,
telling me, mind the gods! We Kyklopês
care not a whistle for your thundering Zeus
or all the gods in bliss, we have more force by far.
I would not let you go for fear of Zeus—
you or your friends—unless I had a whim to.
Tell me, where was it, now, you left your ship—
around the point, or down the shore, I wonder?'

He thought he'd find out, but I saw through this,
and answered with a ready lie:
'My ship?
Poseidon Lord, who sets the earth a-tremble,
broke it up on the rocks at your land's end.
A wind from seaward served him, drove us there.
We are survivors, these good men and I.'

[88] **as custom . . . strangers:** The laws of hospitality, protected by Zeus, included the giving of gifts.

Neither reply nor pity came from him,
but in one stride he clutched at my companions
and caught two in his hands like squirming puppies
to beat their brains out, spattering the floor.
Then he dismembered them and made his meal,
gaping and crunching like a mountain lion—
everything: innards, flesh, and marrow bones.
We cried aloud, lifting our hands to Zeus,
powerless, looking on at this, appalled;
but Kyklops went on filling up his belly
with manflesh and great gulps of whey,
then lay down like a mast among his sheep.
My heart beat high now at the chance of action,
and drawing the sharp sword from my hip I went
along his flank to stab him where the midriff
holds the liver. I had touched the spot
when sudden fear stayed me: if I killed him
we perished there as well, for we could never
move his ponderous doorway slab aside.
So we were left to groan and wait for morning.

When the young Dawn with finger tips of rose
lit up the world, the Kyklops built a fire
and milked his handsome ewes, all in due order,
putting the sucklings to the mothers. Then,
his chores being all dispatched, he caught
another brace of men to make his breakfast,
and whisked away his great door slab
to let his sheep go through—but he, behind,
reset the stone as one would cap a quiver.
There was a din of whistling as the Kyklops
rounded his flock to higher ground, then stillness.
And now I pondered how to hurt him worst,
if but Athena granted what I prayed for.
Here are the means I thought would serve my turn:

a club, or staff, lay there along the fold—
an olive tree, felled green and left to season
for Kyklops' hand. And it was like a mast
a lugger of twenty oars, broad in the beam—
a deep-sea-going craft—might carry:
so long, so big around, it seemed. Now I
chopped out a six foot section of this pole
and set it down before my men, who scraped it;
and when they had it smooth, I hewed again

to make a stake with pointed end. I held this
in the fire's heart and turned it, toughening it,
then hid it, well back in the cavern, under
one of the dung piles in profusion there.
Now came the time to toss for it: who ventured
along with me? whose hand could bear to thrust
and grind that spike in Kyklops' eye, when mild
sleep had mastered him? As luck would have it,
the men I would have chosen won the toss—
four strong men, and I made five as captain.

At evening came the shepherd with his flock,
his woolly flock. The rams as well, this time,
entered the cave: by some sheep-herding whim—
or a god's bidding—none were left outside.
He hefted his great boulder into place
and sat him down to milk the bleating ewes
in proper order, put the lambs to suck,
and swiftly ran through all his evening chores.
Then he caught two more men and feasted on them.
My moment was at hand, and I went forward
holding an ivy bowl of my dark drink,
looking up, saying:

'Kyklops, try some wine.
Here's liquor to wash down your scraps of men.
Taste it, and see the kind of drink we carried
under our planks. I meant it for an offering
if you would help us home. But you are mad,
unbearable, a bloody monster! After this
will any other traveller come to see you?'

He seized and drained the bowl, and it went down
so fiery and smooth he called for more:
'Give me another, thank you kindly. Tell me,
how are you called? I'll make a gift will please you.
Even Kyklopês know the wine-grapes grow
out of grassland and loam in heaven's rain,
but here's a bit of nectar and ambrosia!'

Three bowls I brought him, and he poured them down.
I saw the fuddle and flush come over him,
then I sang out in cordial tones:

'Kyklops,
you ask my honorable name? Remember
the gift you promised me, and I shall tell you.

My name is Nohbdy: mother, father, and friends,
everyone calls me Nohbdy.'

And he said:
'Nohbdy's my meat, then, after I eat his friends.
Others come first. There's a noble gift, now.'

Even as he spoke, he reeled and tumbled backward,
his great head lolling to one side: and sleep
took him like any creature. Drunk, hiccuping,
he dribbled streams of liquor and bits of men.

Now, by the gods, I drove my big hand spike
deep in the embers, charring it again,
and cheered my men along with battle talk
to keep their courage up: no quitting now.
The pike of olive, green though it had been,
reddened and glowed as if about to catch.
I drew it from the coals and my four fellows
gave me a hand, lugging it near the Kyklops
as more than natural force nerved them; straight
forward they sprinted, lifted it, and rammed it
deep in his crater eye, and I leaned on it
turning it as a shipwright turns a drill
in planking, having men below to swing
the two-handled strap that spins it in the groove.
So with our brand we bored that great eye socket
while blood ran out around the red hot bar.
Eyelid and lash were seared; the pierced ball
hissed broiling, and the roots popped.

In a smithy
one sees a white-hot axehead or an adze
plunged and wrung in a cold tub, screeching steam—
the way they make soft iron hale and hard—:
just so that eyeball hissed around the spike.
The Kyklops bellowed and the rock roared round him,
and we fell back in fear. Clawing his face
he tugged the bloody spike out of his eye,
threw it away, and his wild hands went groping;
then he set up a howl for Kyklopês
who lived in caves on windy peaks nearby.
Some heard him; and they came by divers ways
to clump around outside and call:

'What ails you,

Polyphêmos? Why do you cry so sore
in the starry night? You will not let us sleep.
Sure no man's driving off your flock? No man
has tricked you, ruined you?'

Out of the cave
the mammoth Polyphêmos roared in answer:
'Nohbdy, Nohbdy's tricked me, Nohbdy's ruined me!'

To this rough shout they made a sage reply:
'Ah well, if nobody has played you foul
there in your lonely bed, we are no use in pain
given by great Zeus. Let it be your father,
Poseidon Lord, to whom you pray.'

So saying
they trailed away. And I was filled with laughter
to see how like a charm the name deceived them.
Now Kyklops, wheezing as the pain came on him,
fumbled to wrench away the great doorstone
and squatted in the breach with arms thrown wide
for any silly beast or man who bolted—
hoping somehow I might be such a fool.
But I kept thinking how to win the game:
death sat there huge; how could we slip away?
I drew on all my wits, and ran through tactics,
reasoning as a man will for dear life,
until a trick came—and it pleased me well.
The Kyklops' rams were handsome, fat, with heavy
fleeces, a dark violet.

Three abreast
I tied them silently together, twining
cords of willow from the ogre's bed;
then slung a man under each middle one
to ride there safely, shielded left and right.
So three sheep could convey each man. I took
the woolliest ram, the choicest of the flock,
and hung myself under his kinky belly,
pulled up tight, with fingers twisted deep
in sheepskin ringlets for an iron grip.
So, breathing hard, we waited until morning.

When Dawn spread out her finger tips of rose
the rams began to stir, moving for pasture,

and peals of bleating echoed round the pens
where dams with udders full called for a milking.
Blinded, and sick with pain from his head wound,
the master stroked each ram, then let it pass,
but my men riding on the pectoral fleece
the giant's blind hands blundering never found.
Last of them all my ram, the leader, came,
weighted by wool and me with my meditations.
The Kyklops patted him, and then he said:
'Sweet cousin ram, why lag behind the rest
in the night cave? You never linger so,
but graze before them all, and go afar
to crop sweet grass, and take your stately way
leading along the streams, until at evening
you run to be the first one in the fold.
Why, now, so far behind? Can you be grieving
over your Master's eye? That carrion rogue
and his accurst companions burnt it out
when he had conquered all my wits with wine.
Nohbdy will not get out alive, I swear.
Oh, had you brain and voice to tell
where he may be now, dodging all my fury!
Bashed by this hand and bashed on this rock wall
his brains would strew the floor, and I should have
rest from the outrage Nohbdy worked upon me.'

He sent us into the open, then. Close by,
I dropped and rolled clear of the ram's belly,
going this way and that to untie the men.
With many glances back, we rounded up
his fat, stiff-legged sheep to take aboard,
and drove them down to where the good ship lay.
We saw, as we came near, our fellows' faces
shining; then we saw them turn to grief
tallying those who had not fled from death.
I hushed them, jerking head and eyebrows up,
and in a low voice told them: 'Load this herd;
move fast, and put the ship's head toward the breakers.'
They all pitched in at loading, then embarked
and struck their oars into the sea. Far out,
as far off shore as shouted words would carry,
I sent a few back to the adversary:
'O Kyklops! Would you feast on my companions?
Puny, am I, in a Caveman's hands?

How do you like the beating that we gave you,
you damned cannibal? Eater of guests
under your roof! Zeus and the gods have paid you!'

The blind thing in his doubled fury broke
a hilltop in his hands and heaved it after us.
Ahead of our black prow it struck and sank
whelmed in a spuming geyser, a giant wave
that washed the ship stern foremost back to shore.
I got the longest boathook out and stood
fending us off, with furious nods to all
to put their backs into a racing stroke—
row, row, or perish. So the long oars bent
kicking the foam sternward, making head
until we drew away, and twice as far.
Now when I cupped my hands I heard the crew
in low voices protesting:
'Godsake, Captain!
Why bait the beast again? Let him alone!'
'That tidal wave he made on the first throw
all but beached us.'

'All but stove us in!'

'Give him our bearing with your trumpeting,
he'll get the range and lob a boulder.'

'Aye

He'll smash our timbers and our heads together!'

I would not heed them in my glorying spirit,
but let my anger flare and yelled:
'Kyklops,
if ever mortal man inquire
how you were put to shame and blinded, tell him
Odysseus, raider of cities, took your eye:
Laërtês' son, whose home's on Ithaka!'

At this he gave a mighty sob and rumbled:
'Now comes the weird° upon me, spoken of old. destiny
A wizard, grand and wondrous, lived here—Télemos,
a son of Eurymos; great length of days
he had in wizardry among the Kyklopês,
and these things he foretold for time to come:

my great eye lost, and at Odysseus' hands.
Always I had in mind some giant, armed
in giant force, would come against me here.
But this, but you—small, pitiful and twiggy—
you put me down with wine, you blinded me.
Come back, Odysseus, and I'll treat you well,
praying the god of earthquake to befriend you—
his son I am, for he by his avowal
fathered me, and, if he will, he may
heal me of this black wound—he and no other
of all the happy gods or mortal men.'

Few words I shouted in reply to him:
'If I could take your life I would and take
your time away, and hurl you down to hell!
The god of earthquake could not heal you there!'

At this he stretched his hands out in his darkness
toward the sky of stars, and prayed Poseidon:
'O hear me, lord, blue girdler of the islands,
if I am thine indeed, and thou art father:
grant that Odysseus, raider of cities, never
see his home: Laërtês' son, I mean,
who kept his hall on Ithaka. Should destiny
intend that he shall see his roof again
among his family in his father land,
far be that day, and dark the years between.
Let him lose all companions, and return
under strange sail to bitter days at home.'

In these words he prayed, and the god heard him.
Now he laid hands upon a bigger stone
and wheeled around, titanic for the cast,
to let it fly in the black-prowed vessel's track.
But it fell short, just aft the steering oar,
and whelming seas rose giant above the stone
to bear us onward toward the island.
There
as we ran in we saw the squadron waiting,
the trim ships drawn up side by side, and all
our troubled friends who waited, looking seaward.
We beached her, grinding keel in the soft sand,
and waded in, ourselves, on the sandy beach.
Then we unloaded all the Kyklops' flock
to make division, share and share alike,

only my fighters voted that my ram,
the prize of all, should go to me. I slew him
by the sea side and burnt his long thighbones
to Zeus beyond the stormcloud, Kronos' son,
who rules the world. But Zeus disdained my offering;
destruction for my ships he had in store
and death for those who sailed them, my companions.
Now all day long until the sun went down
we made our feast on mutton and sweet wine,
till after sunset in the gathering dark
we went to sleep above the wash of ripples.

When the young Dawn with finger tips of rose
touched the world, I roused the men, gave orders
to man the ships, cast off the mooring lines;
and filing in to sit beside the rowlocks
oarsmen in line dipped oars in the grey sea.
So we moved out, sad in the vast offing,
having our precious lives, but not our friends.

Book 10
The Grace of the Witch

We made our landfall on Aiolia Island,
domain of Aiolos Hippotadês,[89]
the wind king dear to the gods who never die—
an isle adrift upon the sea, ringed round
with brazen ramparts on a sheer cliffside.
Twelve children had old Aiolos at home—
six daughters and six lusty sons—and he
gave girls to boys to be their gentle brides;
now those lords, in their parents' company,
sup every day in hall—a royal feast
with fumes of sacrifice and winds that pipe
'round hollow courts; and all the night they sleep
on beds of filigree beside their ladies.
Here we put in, lodged in the town and palace,
while Aiolos played host to me. He kept me
one full month to hear the tale of Troy,
the ships and the return of the Akhaians,

[89] **Aiolos Hippotadês (Aeolus)**: God of the winds; he inhabited a floating island off Sicily.

all which I told him point by point in order.
When in return I asked his leave to sail
and asked provisioning, he stinted nothing,
adding a bull's hide sewn from neck to tail
into a mighty bag, bottling storm winds;
for Zeus had long ago made Aiolos
warden of winds, to rouse or calm at will.
He wedged this bag under my afterdeck,
lashing the neck with shining silver wire
so not a breath got through; only the west wind
he lofted for me in a quartering breeze
to take my squadron spanking home.
No luck:
the fair wind failed us when our prudence failed.

Nine days and nights we sailed without event,
till on the tenth we raised our land. We neared it,
and saw men building fires along the shore;
but now, being weary to the bone, I fell
into deep slumber; I had worked the sheet
nine days alone, and given it to no one,
wishing to spill no wind on the homeward run.
But while I slept, the crew began to parley:
silver and gold, they guessed, were in that bag
bestowed on me by Aiolos' great heart;
and one would glance at his benchmate and say:
'It never fails. He's welcome everywhere:
hail to the captain when he goes ashore!
He brought along so many presents, plunder
out of Troy, that's it. How about ourselves—
his shipmates all the way? Nigh home we are
with empty hands. And who has gifts from Aiolos?
He has. I say we ought to crack that bag,
there's gold and silver, plenty, in that bag!'

Temptation had its way with my companions,
and they untied the bag.
Then every wind
roared into hurricane; the ships went pitching
west with many cries; our land was lost.
Roused up, despairing in that gloom, I thought:
'Should I go overside for a quick finish
or clench my teeth and stay among the living?'
Down in the bilge I lay, pulling my sea cloak

over my head, while the rough gale blew the ships
and rueful crews clear back to Aiolia.

We put ashore for water; then all hands
gathered alongside for a mid-day meal.
When we had taken bread and drink, I picked
one soldier, and one herald, to go with me
and called again on Aiolos. I found him
at meat with his young princes and his lady,
but there beside the pillars, in his portico,
we sat down silent at the open door.
The sight amazed them, and they all exclaimed:
'Why back again, Odysseus?'
'What sea fiend
rose in your path?'
'Did we not launch you well
for home, or for whatever land you chose?'

Out of my melancholy I replied:
'Mischief aboard and nodding at the tiller—
a damned drowse—did for me. Make good my loss,
dear friends! You have the power!'

Gently I pleaded,
but they turned cold and still. Said Father Aiolos:
'Take yourself out of this island, creeping thing—
no law, no wisdom, lays it on me now
to help a man the blessed gods detest—
out! Your voyage here was cursed by heaven!'

He drove me from the place, groan as I would,
and comfortless we went again to sea,
days of it, till the men flagged at the oars—
no breeze, no help in sight, by our own folly—
six indistinguishable nights and days
before we raised the Laistrygonian height
and far stronghold of Lamos.[90] In that land
the daybreak follows dusk, and so the shepherd
homing calls to the cowherd setting out;
and he who never slept could earn two wages,
tending oxen, pasturing silvery flocks,

[90] **Lamos:** King of the Laistrygonians, whose location is uncertain. The next lines seem to refer to the long summer days of northern latitudes.

where the low night path of the sun is near
the sun's path by day. Here, then, we found
a curious bay with mountain walls of stone
to left and right, and reaching far inland,—
a narrow entrance opening from the sea
where cliffs converged as though to touch and close.
All of my squadron sheltered here, inside
the cavern of this bay.
Black prow by prow
those hulls were made fast in a limpid calm
without a ripple, stillness all around them.
My own black ship I chose to moor alone
on the sea side, using a rock for bollard;
and climbed a rocky point to get my bearings.
No farms, no cultivated land appeared,
but puffs of smoke rose in the wilderness;
so I sent out two picked men and a herald
to learn what race of men this land sustained.

My party found a track—a wagon road
for bringing wood down from the heights to town;
and near the settlement they met a daughter
of Antiphatês the Laistrygon—a stalwart
young girl taking her pail to Artakía,
the fountain where these people go for water.
My fellows hailed her, put their questions to her:
who might the king be? ruling over whom?
She waved her hand, showing her father's lodge,
so they approached it. In its gloom they saw
a woman like a mountain crag, the queen—
and loathed the sight of her. But she, for greeting,
called from the meeting ground her lord and master,
Antiphatês, who came to drink their blood.
He seized one man and tore him on the spot,
making a meal of him; the other two
leaped out of doors and ran to join the ships.
Behind, he raised the whole tribe howling, countless
Laistrygonês—and more than men they seemed,
gigantic when they gathered on the sky line
to shoot great boulders down from slings; and hell's own
crashing rose, and crying from the ships,
as planks and men were smashed to bits—poor gobbets
the wildmen speared like fish and bore away.
But long before it ended in the anchorage—
havoc and slaughter—I had drawn my sword

and cut my own ship's cable. 'Men,' I shouted,
'man the oars and pull till your hearts break
if you would put this butchery behind!'
The oarsmen rent the sea in mortal fear
and my ship spurted out of range, far out
from that deep canyon where the rest were lost.
So we fared onward and death fell behind,
and we took breath to grieve for our companions.

Our next landfall was on Aiaia, island
of Kirkê,[91] dire beauty and divine,
sister of baleful Aiêtês, like him
fathered by Hêlios the light of mortals
on Persê, child of the Ocean stream.
We came
washed in our silent ship upon her shore,
and found a cove, a haven for the ship—
some god, invisible, conned us in. We landed,
to lie down in that place two days and nights,
worn out and sick at heart, tasting our grief.
But when Dawn set another day a-shining
I took my spear and broadsword and I climbed
a rocky point above the ship, for sight
or sound of human labor. Gazing out
from that high place over a land of thicket,
oaks and wide watercourses, I could see
a smoke wisp from the woodland hall of Kirkê.
So I took counsel with myself: should I
go inland scouting out that reddish smoke?
No: better not, I thought, but first return
to waterside and ship, and give the men
breakfast before I sent them to explore.
Now as I went down quite alone, and came
a bowshot from the ship, some god's compassion
set a big buck in motion to cross my path—
a stag with noble antlers, pacing down
from pasture in the woods to the riverside,
as long thirst and the power of sun constrained him.
He started from the bush and wheeled: I hit him
square in the spine midway along his back
and the bronze point broke through it. In the dust

[91] **Kirkê:** An enchantress who uses drugs and herbs to manipulate men.

he fell and whinnied as life bled away.
I set one foot against him, pulling hard
to wrench my weapon from the wound, then left it,
butt-end on the ground. I plucked some withies
and twined a double strand into a rope—
enough to tie the hocks of my huge trophy;
then pickaback I lugged him to the ship,
leaning on my long spearshaft; I could not
haul that mighty carcass on one shoulder.
Beside the ship I let him drop, and spoke
gently and low to each man standing near:
'Come, friends, though hard beset, we'll not go down
into the House of Death before our time.
As long as food and drink remain aboard
let us rely on it, not die of hunger.'

At this those faces, cloaked in desolation
upon the waste sea beach, were bared;
their eyes turned toward me and the mighty trophy,
lighting, foreseeing pleasure, one by one.
So hands were washed to take what heaven sent us.
And all that day until the sun went down
we had our fill of venison and wine,
till after sunset in the gathering dusk
we slept at last above the line of breakers.
When the young Dawn with finger tips of rose
made heaven bright, I called them round and said:
'Shipmates, companions in disastrous time,
O my dear friends, where Dawn lies, and the West,
and where the great Sun, light of men, may go
under the earth by night, and where he rises—
of these things we know nothing. Do we know
any least thing to serve us now? I wonder.
All that I saw, when I went up the rock
was one more island in the boundless main,
a low landscape, covered with woods and scrub,
and puffs of smoke ascending in mid-forest.'

They were all silent, but their hearts contracted,
remembering Antiphatês the Laistrygon
and that prodigious cannibal, the Kyklops.
They cried out, and the salt tears wet their eyes.
But seeing our time for action lost in weeping,
I mustered those Akhaians under arms,
counting them off in two platoons, myself

and my godlike Eurýlokhos commanding.
We shook lots in a soldier's dogskin cap
and his came bounding out — valiant Eurýlokhos! —
So off he went, with twenty-two companions
weeping, as mine wept, too, who stayed behind.

In the wild wood they found an open glade,
around a smooth stone house — the hall of Kirkê —
and wolves and mountain lions lay there, mild
in her soft spell, fed on her drug of evil.
None would attack — oh, it was strange, I tell you —
but switching their long tails they faced our men
like hounds, who look up when their master comes
with tidbits for them — as he will — from table.
Humbly those wolves and lions with mighty paws
fawned on our men — who met their yellow eyes
and feared them.
In the entrance way they stayed
to listen there: inside her quiet house
they heard the goddess Kirkê.
Low she sang
in her beguiling voice, while on her loom
she wove ambrosial fabric sheer and bright,
by that craft known to the goddesses of heaven.
No one would speak, until Politês — most
faithful and likable of my officers, said:
'Dear friends, no need for stealth: here's a young weaver
singing a pretty song to set the air
a-tingle on these lawns and paven courts.
Goddess she is, or lady. Shall we greet her?'

So reassured, they all cried out together,
and she came swiftly to the shining doors
to call them in. All but Eurýlokhos —
who feared a snare — the innocents went after her.
On thrones she seated them, and lounging chairs,
while she prepared a meal of cheese and barley
and amber honey mixed with Pramnian wine,
adding her own vile pinch, to make them lose
desire or thought of our dear father land.
Scarce had they drunk when she flew after them
with her long stick and shut them in a pigsty —
bodies, voices, heads, and bristles, all
swinish now, though minds were still unchanged.

So, squealing, in they went. And Kirkê tossed them
acorns, mast, and cornel berries—fodder
for hogs who rut and slumber on the earth.

Down to the ship Eurýlokhos came running
to cry alarm, foul magic doomed his men!
But working with dry lips to speak a word
he could not, being so shaken; blinding tears
welled in his eyes; foreboding filled his heart.
When we were frantic questioning him, at last
we heard the tale: our friends were gone. Said he:
'We went up through the oak scrub where you sent us,
Odysseus, glory of commanders,
until we found a palace in a glade,
a marble house on open ground, and someone
singing before her loom a chill, sweet song—
goddess or girl, we could not tell. They hailed her,
and then she stepped through shining doors and said,
"Come, come in!" Like sheep they followed her,
but I saw cruel deceit, and stayed behind.
Then all our fellows vanished. Not a sound,
and nothing stirred, although I watched for hours.'

When I heard this I slung my silver-hilted
broadsword on, and shouldered my long bow,
and said, 'Come, take me back the way you came.'
But he put both his hands around my knees
in desperate woe, and said in supplication:
'Not back there, O my lord! Oh, leave me here!
You, even you, cannot return, I know it,
I know you cannot bring away our shipmates;
better make sail with these men, quickly too,
and save ourselves from horror while we may.'

But I replied:
'By heaven, Eurýlokhos,
rest here then; take food and wine;
stay in the black hull's shelter. Let me go,
as I see nothing for it but to go.'

I turned and left him, left the shore and ship,
and went up through the woodland hushed and shady
to find the subtle witch in her long hall.
But Hermês met me, with his golden wand,

barring the way—a boy whose lip was downy
in the first bloom of manhood, so he seemed.
He took my hand and spoke as though he knew me:

'Why take the inland path alone,
poor seafarer, by hill and dale
upon this island all unknown?
Your friends are locked in Kirkê's pale;
all are become like swine to see;
and if you go to set them free
you go to stay, and never more make sail
for your old home upon Thaki.° Ithaka

But I can tell you what to do
to come unchanged from Kirkê's power
and disenthrall your fighting crew:
take with you to her bower
as amulet, this plant I know—
it will defeat her horrid show,
so pure and potent is the flower;
no mortal herb was ever so.

Your cup with numbing drops of night
and evil, stilled of all remorse,
she will infuse to charm your sight;
but this great herb with holy force
will keep your mind and senses clear:
when she turns cruel, coming near
with her long stick to whip you out of doors,
then let your cutting blade appear,

Let instant death upon it shine,
and she will cower and yield her bed—
a pleasure you must not decline,
so may her lust and fear bestead
you and your friends, and break her spell;
but make her swear by heaven and hell
no witches' tricks, or else, your harness shed,
you'll be unmanned by her as well.'

He bent down glittering for the magic plant
and pulled it up, black root and milky flower—
a *molü*[92] in the language of the gods—

[92] ***molü:*** The exact nature of the magical *molü,* or moly, is unknown.

fatigue and pain for mortals to uproot;
but gods do this, and everything, with ease.

Then toward Olympos through the island trees
Hermês departed, and I sought out Kirkê,
my heart high with excitement, beating hard.
Before her mansion in the porch I stood
to call her, all being still. Quick as a cat
she opened her bright doors and sighed a welcome;
then I strode after her with heavy heart
down the long hall, and took the chair she gave me,
silver-studded, intricately carved,
made with a low footrest. The lady Kirkê
mixed me a golden cup of honeyed wine,
adding in mischief her unholy drug.
I drank, and the drink failed. But she came forward
aiming a stroke with her long stick, and whispered:
'Down in the sty and snore among the rest!'

Without a word, I drew my sharpened sword
and in one bound held it against her throat.
She cried out, then slid under to take my knees,
catching her breath to say, in her distress:
'What champion, of what country, can you be?
Where are your kinsmen and your city?
Are you not sluggish with my wine? Ah, wonder!
Never a mortal man that drank this cup
but when it passed his lips he had succumbed.
Hale must your heart be and your tempered will.
Odysseus then you are, O great contender,
of whom the glittering god with golden wand° Hermês
spoke to me ever, and foretold
the black swift ship would carry you from Troy.
Put up your weapon in the sheath. We two
shall mingle and make love upon our bed.
So mutual trust may come of play and love.'

To this I said:
'Kirkê, am I a boy,
that you should make me soft and doting now?
Here in this house you turned my men to swine;
now it is I myself you hold, enticing
into your chamber, to your dangerous bed,

to take my manhood when you have me stripped.
I mount no bed of love with you upon it.
Or swear me first a great oath, if I do,
you'll work no more enchantment to my harm.'

She swore at once, outright, as I demanded,
and after she had sworn, and bound herself,
I entered Kirkê's flawless bed of love.

Presently in the hall her maids were busy,
the nymphs who waited upon Kirkê: four,
whose cradles were in fountains, under boughs,
or in the glassy seaward-gliding streams.
One came with richly colored rugs to throw
on seat and chairback, over linen covers;
a second pulled the tables out, all silver,
and loaded them with baskets all of gold;
a third mixed wine as tawny-mild as honey
in a bright bowl, and set out golden cups.
The fourth came bearing water, and lit a blaze
under a cauldron. By and by it bubbled,
and when the dazzling brazen vessel seethed
she filled a bathtub to my waist, and bathed me,
pouring a soothing blend on head and shoulders,
warming the soreness of my joints away.
When she had done, and smoothed me with sweet oil,
she put a tunic and a cloak around me
and took me to a silver-studded chair
with footrest, all elaborately carven.
Now came a maid to tip a golden jug
of water into a silver finger bowl,
and draw a polished table to my side.
The larder mistress brought her tray of loaves
with many savory slices, and she gave
the best, to tempt me. But no pleasure came;
I huddled with my mind elsewhere, oppressed.

Kirkê regarded me, as there I sat
disconsolate, and never touched a crust.
Then she stood over me and chided me:
'Why sit at table mute, Odysseus?
Are you mistrustful of my bread and drink?

Can it be treachery that you fear again,
after the gods' great oath I swore for you?'

I turned to her at once, and said:
'Kirkê,
where is the captain who could bear to touch
this banquet, in my place? A decent man
would see his company before him first.
Put heart in me to eat and drink—you may,
by freeing my companions. I must see them.'

But Kirkê had already turned away.
Her long staff in her hand, she left the hall
and opened up the sty. I saw her enter,
driving those men turned swine to stand before me.
She stroked them, each in turn, with some new chrism;
and then, behold! their bristles fell away,
the coarse pelt grown upon them by her drug
melted away, and they were men again,
younger, more handsome, taller than before.
Their eyes upon me, each one took my hands,
and wild regret and longing pierced them through,
so the room rang with sobs, and even Kirkê
pitied that transformation. Exquisite
the goddess looked as she stood near me, saying:
'Son of Laërtês and the gods of old,
Odysseus, master mariner and soldier,
go to the sea beach and sea-breasting ship;
drag it ashore, full length upon the land;
stow gear and stores in rock-holes under cover;
return; be quick; bring all your dear companions.'

Now, being a man, I could not help consenting.
So I went down to the sea beach and the ship,
where I found all my other men on board,
weeping, in despair along the benches.
Sometimes in farmyards when the cows return
well fed from pasture to the barn, one sees
the pens give way before the calves in tumult,
breaking through to cluster about their mothers,
bumping together, bawling. Just that way
my crew poured round me when they saw me come—

their faces wet with tears as if they saw
their homeland, and the crags of Ithaka,
even the very town where they were born.
And weeping still they all cried out in greeting:
'Prince, what joy this is, your safe return!
Now Ithaka seems here, and we in Ithaka!
But tell us now, what death befell our friends?'

And, speaking gently, I replied:
'First we must get the ship high on the shingle,
and stow our gear and stores in clefts of rock
for cover. Then come follow me, to see
your shipmates in the magic house of Kirkê
eating and drinking, endlessly regaled.'

They turned back, as commanded, to this work;
only one lagged, and tried to hold the others:
Eurýlokhos it was, who blurted out:
'Where now, poor remnants? is it devil's work
you long for? Will you go to Kirkê's hall?
Swine, wolves, and lions she will make us all,
beasts of her courtyard, bound by her enchantment.
Remember those the Kyklops held, remember
shipmates who made that visit with Odysseus!
The daring man! They died for his foolishness!'

When I heard this I had a mind to draw
the blade that swung against my side and chop him,
bowling his head upon the ground—kinsman[93]
or no kinsman, close to me though he was.
But others came between, saying, to stop me,
'Prince, we can leave him, if you say the word;
let him stay here on guard. As for ourselves,
show us the way to Kirkê's magic hall.'

So all turned inland, leaving shore and ship,
and Eurýlokhos—he, too, came on behind,
fearing the rough edge of my tongue. Meanwhile
at Kirkê's hands the rest were gently bathed,
anointed with sweet oil, and dressed afresh
in tunics and new cloaks with fleecy linings.
We found them all at supper when we came.

[93] **kinsman:** Related to Odysseus by marriage.

But greeting their old friends once more, the crew
could not hold back their tears, and now again
the rooms rang with sobs. Then Kirkê, loveliest
of all immortals, came to counsel me:
'Son of Laërtês and the gods of old,
Odysseus, master mariner and soldier,
enough of weeping fits. I know—I, too—
what you endured upon the inhuman sea,
what odds you met on land from hostile men.
Remain with me, and share my meat and wine;
restore behind your ribs those gallant hearts
that served you in the old days, when you sailed
from stony Ithaka. Now parched and spent,
your cruel wandering is all you think of,
never of joy, after so many blows.'

As we were men we could not help consenting.
So day by day we lingered, feasting long
on roasts and wine, until a year grew fat.
But when the passing months and wheeling seasons
brought the long summery days, the pause of summer,
my shipmates one day summoned me and said:
'Captain, shake off this trance, and think of home—
if home indeed awaits us,
if we shall ever see
your own well-timbered hall on Ithaka.'

They made me feel a pang, and I agreed.
That day, and all day long, from dawn to sundown,
we feasted on roast meat and ruddy wine,
and after sunset when the dusk came on
my men slept in the shadowy hall, but I
went through the dark to Kirkê's flawless bed
and took the goddess' knees in supplication,
urging, as she bent to hear:
'O Kirkê,
now you must keep your promise; it is time.
Help me make sail for home. Day after day
my longing quickens, and my company
give me no peace, but wear my heart away
pleading when you are not at hand to hear.'

The loveliest of goddesses replied:
'Son of Laërtês and the gods of old,
Odysseus, master mariner and soldier,

you shall not stay here longer against your will;
but home you may not go
unless you take a strange way round and come
to the cold homes of Death and pale Perséphonê.[94]
You shall hear prophecy from the rapt shade
of blind Teirêsias of Thebes,[95] forever
charged with reason even among the dead;
to him alone, of all the flitting ghosts,
Perséphonê has given a mind undarkened.'

At this I felt a weight like stone within me,
and, moaning, pressed my length against the bed,
with no desire to see the daylight more.
But when I had wept and tossed and had my fill
of this despair, at last I answered her:
'Kirkê, who pilots me upon this journey?
No man has ever sailed to the land of Death.'

That loveliest of goddesses replied:
'Son of Laërtês and the gods of old,
Odysseus, master of land ways and sea ways,
feel no dismay because you lack a pilot;
only set up your mast and haul your canvas
to the fresh blowing North; sit down and steer,
and hold that wind, even to the bourne of Ocean,
Perséphonê's deserted strand and grove,
dusky with poplars and the drooping willow.
Run through the tide-rip, bring your ship to shore,
land there, and find the crumbling homes of Death.[96]
Here, toward the Sorrowing Water, run the streams
of Wailing, out of Styx, and quenchless Burning[97]—
torrents that join in thunder at the Rock.
Here then, great soldier, setting foot obey me:
dig a well shaft a forearm square; pour out
libations round it to the unnumbered dead:
sweet milk and honey, then sweet wine, and last
clear water, scattering handfulls of white barley.
Pray now, with all your heart, to the faint dead;
swear you will sacrifice your finest heifer,

---

[94] **Perséphonê:** Queen of the Underworld. [95] **Teirêsias of Thebes:** A famous blind soothsayer in the legends of Thebes who plays important roles in Sophocles' Oedipus plays. [96] **homes of Death:** Homer locates Hades on the western and northern frontier of the Greek world; after Homer, Hades was ordinarily located beneath the earth, similar to the Christian Hell. [97] **Sorrowing Water . . . Burning:** The rivers of Hades are Sorrowing Water (Acheron), Wailing (Cocytus), and Burning (Phlegethon).

at home in Ithaka, and burn for them
her tenderest parts in sacrifice; and vow
to the lord Teirêsias, apart from all,
a black lamb, handsomest of all your flock—
thus to appease the nations of the dead.
Then slash a black ewe's throat, and a black ram,
facing the gloom of Erebos;[98] but turn
your head away toward Ocean. You shall see, now
souls of the buried dead in shadowy hosts,
and now you must call out to your companions
to flay those sheep the bronze knife has cut down,
for offerings, burnt flesh to those below,
to sovereign Death and pale Perséphonê.
Meanwhile draw sword from hip, crouch down, ward off
the surging phantoms from the bloody pit
until you know the presence of Teirêsias.
He will come soon, great captain; be it he
who gives you course and distance for your sailing
homeward across the cold fish-breeding sea.'

As the goddess ended, Dawn came stitched in gold.
Now Kirkê dressed me in my shirt and cloak,
put on a gown of subtle tissue, silvery,
then wound a golden belt about her waist
and veiled her head in linen,
while I went through the hall to rouse my crew.

I bent above each one, and gently said:
'Wake from your sleep: no more sweet slumber. Come,
we sail: the Lady Kirkê so ordains it.'

They were soon up, and ready at that word;
but I was not to take my men unharmed
from this place, even from this. Among them all
the youngest was Elpênor—
no mainstay in a fight nor very clever—
and this one, having climbed on Kirkê's roof
to taste the cool night, fell asleep with wine.
Waked by our morning voices, and the tramp
of men below, he started up, but missed
his footing on the long steep backward ladder
and fell that height headlong. The blow smashed

[98] **Erebos:** The darkest region of Hades.

the nape cord, and his ghost fled to the dark.
But I was outside, walking with the rest,
saying:
'Homeward you think we must be sailing
to our own land; no, elsewhere is the voyage
Kirkê has laid upon me. We must go
to the cold homes of Death and pale Perséphonê
to hear Teirêsias tell of time to come.'

They felt so stricken, upon hearing this,
they sat down wailing loud, and tore their hair.
But nothing came of giving way to grief.
Down to the shore and ship at last we went,
bowed with anguish, cheeks all wet with tears,
to find that Kirkê had been there before us
and tied nearby a black ewe and a ram:
she had gone by like air.
For who could see the passage of a goddess
unless she wished his mortal eyes aware?

Book 11
A Gathering of Shades

We bore down on the ship at the sea's edge
and launched her on the salt immortal sea,
stepping our mast and spar in the black ship;
embarked the ram and ewe and went aboard
in tears, with bitter and sore dread upon us.
But now a breeze came up for us astern—
a canvas-bellying landbreeze, hale shipmate
sent by the singing nymph with sun-bright hair;
so we made fast the braces, took our thwarts,
and let the wind and steersman work the ship
with full sail spread all day above our coursing,
till the sun dipped, and all the ways grew dark
upon the fathomless unresting sea.
By night
our ship ran onward toward the Ocean's bourne,
the realm and region of the Men of Winter,[99]
hidden in mist and cloud. Never the flaming

[99] **Men of Winter:** The fabled Cimmerians who live in perpetual darkness.

eye of Hêlios lights on those men
at morning, when he climbs the sky of stars,
nor in descending earthward out of heaven;
ruinous night being rove° over those wretches. stretched
We made the land, put ram and ewe ashore,
and took our way along the Ocean stream
to find the place foretold for us by Kirkê.
There Perimêdês and Eurýlokhos
pinioned the sacred beasts. With my drawn blade
I spaded up the votive pit, and poured
libations round it to the unnumbered dead:
sweet milk and honey, then sweet wine, and last
clear water; and I scattered barley down.
Then I addressed the blurred and breathless dead,
vowing to slaughter my best heifer for them
before she calved, at home in Ithaka,
and burn the choice bits on the altar fire;
as for Teirêsias, I swore to sacrifice
a black lamb, handsomest of all our flock.
Thus to assuage the nations of the dead
I pledged these rites, then slashed the lamb and ewe,
letting their black blood stream into the wellpit.
Now the souls gathered, stirring out of Erebos,
brides and young men, and men grown old in pain,
and tender girls whose hearts were new to grief;
many were there, too, torn by brazen lanceheads,
battle-slain, bearing still their bloody gear.
From every side they came and sought the pit
with rustling cries; and I grew sick with fear.
But presently I gave command to my officers
to flay those sheep the bronze cut down, and make
burnt offerings of flesh to the gods below—
to sovereign Death, to pale Perséphonê.
Meanwhile I crouched with my drawn sword to keep
the surging phantoms from the bloody pit
till I should know the presence of Teirêsias.

One shade came first—Elpênor, of our company,
who lay unburied still on the wide earth
as we had left him—dead in Kirkê's hall,
untouched, unmourned, when other cares compelled us.
Now when I saw him there I wept for pity
and called out to him:
'How is this, Elpênor,

how could you journey to the western gloom
swifter afoot than I in the black lugger?'

He sighed, and answered:
'Son of great Laërtês,
Odysseus, master mariner and soldier,
bad luck shadowed me, and no kindly power;
ignoble death I drank with so much wine.
I slept on Kirkê's roof, then could not see
the long steep backward ladder, coming down,
and fell that height. My neck bone, buckled under,
snapped, and my spirit found this well of dark.
Now hear the grace I pray for, in the name
of those back in the world, not here—your wife
and father, he who gave you bread in childhood,
and your own child, your only son, Telémakhos,
long ago left at home.
When you make sail
and put these lodgings of dim Death behind,
you will moor ship, I know, upon Aiaia Island;
there, O my lord, remember me, I pray,
do not abandon me unwept, unburied,
to tempt the gods' wrath, while you sail for home;
but fire my corpse, and all the gear I had,
and build a cairn for me above the breakers—
an unknown sailor's mark for men to come.
Heap up the mound there, and implant upon it
the oar I pulled in life with my companions.'

He ceased, and I replied:
'Unhappy spirit,
I promise you the barrow and the burial.'

So we conversed, and grimly, at a distance,
with my long sword between, guarding the blood,
while the faint image of the lad spoke on.
Now came the soul of Antikleía, dead,
my mother, daughter of Autólykos,
dead now, though living still when I took ship
for holy Troy. Seeing this ghost I grieved,
but held her off, through pang on pang of tears,
till I should know the presence of Teirêsias.
Soon from the dark that prince of Thebes came forward
bearing a golden staff; and he addressed me:
'Son of Laërtês and the gods of old,

Odysseus, master of land ways and sea ways,
why leave the blazing sun, O man of woe,
to see the cold dead and the joyless region?
Stand clear, put up your sword;
let me but taste of blood, I shall speak true.'

At this I stepped aside, and in the scabbard
let my long sword ring home to the pommel silver,
as he bent down to the sombre blood. Then spoke
the prince of those with gift of speech:
'Great captain,
a fair wind and the honey lights of home
are all you seek. But anguish lies ahead;
the god who thunders on the land prepares it,
not to be shaken from your track, implacable,
in rancor for the son whose eye you blinded.
One narrow strait may take you through his blows:
denial of yourself, restraint of shipmates.
When you make landfall on Thrinakia first
and quit the violet sea, dark on the land
you'll find the grazing herds of Hêlios
by whom all things are seen, all speech is known.
Avoid those kine, hold fast to your intent,
and hard seafaring brings you all to Ithaka.
But if you raid the beeves, I see destruction
for ship and crew. Though you survive alone,
bereft of all companions, lost for years,
under strange sail shall you come home, to find
your own house filled with trouble: insolent men
eating your livestock as they court your lady.
Aye, you shall make those men atone in blood!
But after you have dealt out death—in open
combat or by stealth—to all the suitors,
go overland on foot, and take an oar,
until one day you come where men have lived
with meat unsalted, never known the sea,
nor seen seagoing ships, with crimson bows
and oars that fledge light hulls for dipping flight.
The spot will soon be plain to you, and I
can tell you how: some passerby will say,
"What winnowing fan is that upon your shoulder?"
Halt, and implant your smooth oar in the turf
and make fair sacrifice to Lord Poseidon:
a ram, a bull, a great buck boar; turn back,
and carry out pure hekatombs at home

to all wide heaven's lords, the undying gods,
to each in order. Then a seaborne death
soft as this hand of mist will come upon you
when you are wearied out with rich old age,
your country folk in blessed peace around you.
And all this shall be just as I foretell.'

When he had done, I said at once,
'Teirêsias,
my life runs on then as the gods have spun it:
But come, now, tell me this; make this thing clear:
I see my mother's ghost among the dead
sitting in silence near the blood. Not once
has she glanced this way toward her son, nor spoken.
Tell me, my lord,
may she in some way come to know my presence?'

To this he answered:
'I shall make it clear
in a few words and simply. Any dead man
whom you allow to enter where the blood is
will speak to you, and speak the truth; but those
deprived will grow remote again and fade.'

When he had prophesied, Teirêsias' shade
retired lordly to the halls of Death;
but I stood fast until my mother stirred,
moving to sip the black blood; then she knew me
and called out sorrowfully to me:
'Child,
how could you cross alive into this gloom
at the world's end?—No sight for living eyes;
great currents run between, desolate waters,
the Ocean first, where no man goes a journey
without ship's timber under him.
Say, now,
is it from Troy, still wandering, after years,
that you come here with ship and company?
Have you not gone at all to Ithaka?
Have you not seen your lady in your hall?'

She put these questions, and I answered her:
'Mother, I came here, driven to the land of death
in want of prophecy from Teirêsias' shade;
nor have I yet coasted Akhaia's hills

nor touched my own land, but have had hard roving
since first I joined Lord Agamémnon's host
by sea for Ilion, the wild horse country,
to fight the men of Troy.
But come now, tell me this, and tell me clearly,
what was the bane that pinned you down in Death?
Some ravaging long illness, or mild arrows
a-flying down one day from Artemis?
Tell me of Father, tell me of the son
I left behind me; have they still my place,
my honors, or have other men assumed them?
Do they not say that I shall come no more?
And tell me of my wife: how runs her thought,
still with her child, still keeping our domains,
or bride again to the best of the Akhaians?'

To this my noble mother quickly answered:
'Still with her child indeed she is, poor heart,
still in your palace hall. Forlorn her nights
and days go by, her life used up in weeping.
But no man takes your honored place. Telémakhos
has care of all your garden plots and fields,
and holds the public honor of a magistrate,
feasting and being feasted. But your father
is country bound and comes to town no more.
He owns no bedding, rugs, or fleecy mantles,
but lies down, winter nights, among the slaves,
rolled in old cloaks for cover, near the embers.
Or when the heat comes at the end of summer,
the fallen leaves, all round his vineyard plot,
heaped into windrows, make his lowly bed.
He lies now even so, with aching heart,
and longs for your return, while age comes on him.
So I, too, pined away, so doom befell me,
not that the keen-eyed huntress° with her shafts Artemis
had marked me down and shot to kill me, not
that illness overtook me — no true illness
wasting the body to undo the spirit;
only my loneliness for you, Odysseus,
for your kind heart and counsel, gentle Odysseus,
took my own life away.'

I bit my lip,
rising perplexed, with longing to embrace her,
and tried three times, putting my arms around her,

but she went sifting through my hands, impalpable
as shadows are, and wavering like a dream.
Now this embittered all the pain I bore,
and I cried in the darkness:
'O my mother,
will you not stay, be still, here in my arms,
may we not, in this place of Death, as well,
hold one another, touch with love, and taste
salt tears' relief, the twinge of welling tears?
Or is this all hallucination, sent
against me by the iron queen, Perséphonê,
to make me groan again?'

My noble mother
answered quickly:
'O my child—alas,
most sorely tried of men—great Zeus's daughter,
Perséphonê, knits no illusion for you.
All mortals meet this judgment when they die.
No flesh and bone are here, none bound by sinew,
since the bright-hearted pyre consumed them down—
the white bones long exanimate—to ash;
dreamlike the soul flies, insubstantial.

You must crave sunlight soon.
Note all things strange
seen here, to tell your lady in after days.'

So went our talk; then other shadows came,
ladies in company, sent by Perséphonê—
consorts or daughters of illustrious men—
crowding about the black blood.
I took thought
how best to separate and question them,
and saw no help for it, but drew once more
the long bright edge of broadsword from my hip,
that none should sip the blood in company
but one by one, in order; so it fell
that each declared her lineage and name.

Here was great loveliness of ghosts! I saw
before them all, that princess of great ladies,

Tyro,[100] Salmoneus' daughter, as she told me,
and queen to Krêtheus, a son of Aiolos.
She had gone daft for the river Enipeus,
most graceful of all running streams, and ranged
all day by Enipeus' limpid side,
whose form the foaming girdler of the islands,
the god who makes earth tremble, took and so
lay down with her where he went flooding seaward,
their bower a purple billow, arching round
to hide them in a sea-vale, god and lady.
Now when his pleasure was complete, the god
spoke to her softly, holding fast her hand:
'Dear mortal, go in joy! At the turn of seasons,
winter to summer, you shall bear me sons;
no lovemaking of gods can be in vain.
Nurse our sweet children tenderly, and rear them.
Home with you now, and hold your tongue, and tell
no one your lover's name—though I am yours,
Poseidon, lord of surf that makes earth tremble.'

He plunged away into the deep sea swell,
and she grew big with Pelias and Neleus,
powerful vassals, in their time, of Zeus.
Pelias lived on broad Iolkos seaboard
rich in flocks, and Neleus at Pylos.
As for the sons borne by that queen of women
to Krêtheus, their names were Aison, Pherês,
and Amytháon, expert charioteer.

Next after her I saw Antiopê,
daughter of Ásopos. She too could boast
a god for lover, having lain with Zeus
and borne two sons to him: Amphion and
Zêthos, who founded Thebes, the upper city,
and built the ancient citadel. They sheltered
no life upon that plain, for all their power,
without a fortress wall.

And next I saw
Amphitrion's true wife, Alkmênê, mother,

[100] **Tyro:** A queen of Thessaly who fell in love with a river god—Poseidon in disguise; she bore him two sons, Pelias and Neleus, the father of Nestor.

as all men know, of lionish Heraklês,
conceived when she lay close in Zeus's arms;
and Megarê, high-hearted Kreon's daughter,
wife of Amphitrion's unwearying son.

I saw the mother of Oidipous, Epikastê,[101]
whose great unwitting deed it was
to marry her own son. He took that prize
from a slain father; presently the gods
brought all to light that made the famous story.
But by their fearsome wills he kept his throne
in dearest Thebes, all through his evil days,
while she descended to the place of Death,
god of the locked and iron door. Steep down
from a high rafter, throttled in her noose,
she swung, carried away by pain, and left him
endless agony from a mother's Furies.

And I saw Khloris, that most lovely lady,
whom for her beauty in the olden time
Neleus wooed with countless gifts, and married.
She was the youngest daughter of Amphion,
son of Iasos. In those days he held
power at Orkhómenos, over the Minyai.
At Pylos then as queen she bore her children—
Nestor, Khromios, Periklýmenos,
and Pêro, too, who turned the heads of men
with her magnificence. A host of princes
from nearby lands came courting her; but Neleus
would hear of no one, not unless the suitor
could drive the steers of giant Íphiklos
from Phylakê—longhorns, broad in the brow,
so fierce that one man only, a diviner,
offered to round them up. But bitter fate
saw him bound hand and foot by savage herdsmen.
Then days and months grew full and waned, the year
went wheeling round, the seasons came again,
before at last the power of Íphiklos,
relenting, freed the prisoner, who foretold
all things to him. So Zeus's will was done.

And I saw Lêda, wife of Tyndareus,
upon whom Tyndareus had sired twins

[101] **Epikastê:** Jocasta, mother and wife of Oidipous (Oedipus).

indomitable: Kastor, tamer of horses,
and Polydeukês, best in the boxing ring.[102]
Those two live still, though life-creating earth
embraces them: even in the underworld
honored as gods by Zeus, each day in turn[103]
one comes alive, the other dies again.
Then after Lêda to my vision came
the wife of Aloeus, Iphimedeia,
proud that she once had held the flowing sea
and borne him sons, thunderers for a day,
the world-renowned Otos and Ephialtês.
Never were men on such a scale
bred on the plowlands and the grainlands, never
so magnificent any, after Orion.
At nine years old they towered nine fathoms tall,
nine cubits in the shoulders, and they promised
furor upon Olympos, heaven broken by battle cries,
the day they met the gods in arms.
With Ossa's
mountain peak they meant to crown Olympos
and over Ossa Pelion's[104] forest pile
for footholds up the sky. As giants grown
they might have done it, but the bright son of Zeus° Apollo
by Lêto of the smooth braid shot them down
while they were boys unbearded; no dark curls
clustered yet from temples to the chin.

Then I saw Phaidra, Prokris; and Ariadnê,
daughter of Minos,[105] the grim king. Theseus took her
aboard with him from Krete for the terraced land
of ancient Athens; but he had no joy of her.
Artemis killed her on the Isle of Dia
at a word from Dionysos.
Maira, then,
and Klymênê, and that detested queen,
Eríphylê,[106] who betrayed her lord for gold . . .

---

[102] **Lêda . . . boxing ring:** By Zeus, Lêda was the mother of Helen and Polydeukês (Pollux); by Tyndareus, Lêda was the mother of Kastor and Klytaimnéstra (Clytemnestra), Agamémnon's wife. [103] **each day in turn:** Kastor and Polydeukês share one immortality between them. [104] **Ossa Pelion:** Ossa and Pelion are mountains near Olympos. [105] **Minos:** Minos, king of Krete, was the father of Phaidra (Phaedra) and Ariadnê. After Theseus, king of Athens, killed the Minotaur he took Ariadnê with him to Dia (Naxos). It is not clear why Dionysos wanted her killed. [106] **Eríphylê:** Polynices, Oidipous's son, bribed Eríphylê with a golden necklace; she persuaded her husband, Amphiaraus, to join the attack on Thebes, where he was killed.

but how name all the women I beheld there,
daughters and wives of kings? The starry night
wanes long before I close.
                                        Here, or aboard ship,
amid the crew, the hour for sleep has come.
Our sailing is the gods' affair and yours."

Then he fell silent. Down the shadowy hall
the enchanted banqueters were still. Only
the queen with ivory pale arms, Arêtê, spoke,
saying to all the silent men:
                                        "Phaiákians,
how does he stand, now, in your eyes, this captain,
the look and bulk of him, the inward poise?
He is my guest, but each one shares that honor.
Be in no haste to send him on his way
or scant your bounty in his need. Remember
how rich, by heaven's will, your possessions are."

Then Ekheneôs, the old soldier, eldest
of all Phaiákians, added his word:
"Friends, here was nothing but our own thought spoken,
the mark hit square. Our duties to her majesty.
For what is to be said and done,
we wait upon Alkínoös' command."

At this the king's voice rang:
                                        "I so command—
as sure as it is I who, while I live,
rule the sea rovers of Phaiákia. Our friend
longs to put out for home, but let him be
content to rest here one more day, until
I see all gifts bestowed. And every man
will take thought for his launching and his voyage,
I most of all, for I am master here."

Odysseus, the great tactician, answered:
"Alkínoös, king and admiration of men,
even a year's delay, if you should urge it,
in loading gifts and furnishing for sea—
I too could wish it; better far that I
return with some largesse of wealth about me—

I shall be thought more worthy of love and courtesy
by every man who greets me home in Ithaka."

The king said:
"As to that, one word, Odysseus:
from all we see, we take you for no swindler—
though the dark earth be patient of so many,
scattered everywhere, baiting their traps with lies
of old times and of places no one knows.
You speak with art, but your intent is honest.
The Argive troubles, and your own troubles,
you told as a poet would, a man who knows the world.
But now come tell me this: among the dead
did you meet any of your peers, companions
who sailed with you and met their doom at Troy?
Here's a long night—an endless night—before us,
and no time yet for sleep, not in this hall.
Recall the past deeds and the strange adventures.
I could stay up until the sacred Dawn
as long as you might wish to tell your story."

Odysseus the great tactician answered:
"Alkínoös, king and admiration of men,
there is a time for story telling; there is
also a time for sleep. But even so,
if, indeed, listening be still your pleasure,
I must not grudge my part. Other and sadder
tales there are to tell; of my companions,
of some who came through all the Trojan spears,
clangor and groan of war,
only to find a brutal death at home—
and a bad wife behind it.
After Perséphonê,
icy and pale, dispersed the shades of women,
the soul of Agamémnon, son of Atreus,
came before me, sombre in the gloom,
and others gathered round, all who were with him
when death and doom struck in Aegísthos' hall.
Sipping the black blood, the tall shade perceived me,
and cried out sharply, breaking into tears;
then tried to stretch his hands toward me, but could not,
being bereft of all the reach and power

he once felt in the great torque of his arms.
Gazing at him, and stirred, I wept for pity,
and spoke across to him:
'O son of Atreus,
illustrious Lord Marshal, Agamémnon,
what was the doom that brought you low in death?
Were you at sea, aboard ship, and Poseidon
blew up a wicked squall to send you under,
or were you cattle-raiding on the mainland
or in a fight for some strongpoint, or women,
when the foe hit you to your mortal hurt?'

But he replied at once:
'Son of Laërtês,
Odysseus, master of land ways and sea ways,
neither did I go down with some good ship
in any gale Poseidon blew, nor die
upon the mainland, hurt by foes in battle.
It was Aegísthos who designed my death,
he and my heartless wife, and killed me, after
feeding me, like an ox felled at the trough.
That was my miserable end—and with me
my fellows butchered, like so many swine
killed for some troop, or feast, or wedding banquet
in a great landholder's household. In your day
you have seen men, and hundreds, die in war,
in the bloody press, or downed in single combat,
but these were murders you would catch your breath at:
think of us fallen, all our throats cut, winebowl
brimming, tables laden on every side,
while blood ran smoking over the whole floor.
In my extremity I heard Kassandra,[107]
Priam's daughter, piteously crying
as the traitress Klytaimnéstra made to kill her
along with me. I heaved up from the ground
and got my hands around the blade, but she
eluded me, that whore. Nor would she close
my two eyes[108] as my soul swam to the underworld
or shut my lips. There is no being more fell,
more bestial than a wife in such an action,

[107] **Kassandra:** She was brought back from Troy by Agamémnon as a part of his booty. [108] **close my two eyes:** That is, perform the proper burial rites.

and what an action that one planned!
The murder of her husband and her lord.
Great god, I thought my children and my slaves
at least would give me welcome. But that woman,
plotting a thing so low, defiled herself
and all her sex, all women yet to come,
even those few who may be virtuous.'

He paused then, and I answered:
'Foul and dreadful.
That was the way that Zeus who views the wide world
vented his hatred on the sons of Atreus—
intrigues of women, even from the start.
Myriads
died by Helen's fault, and Klytaimnéstra
plotted against you half the world away.'

And he at once said:
'Let it be a warning
even to you. Indulge a woman never,
and never tell her all you know. Some things
a man may tell, some he should cover up.
Not that I see a risk for you, Odysseus,
of death at your wife's hands. She is too wise,
too clear-eyed, sees alternatives too well,
Penélopê, Ikários' daughter—
that young bride whom we left behind—think of it!—
when we sailed off to war. The baby boy
still cradled at her breast—now he must be
a grown man, and a lucky one. By heaven,
you'll see him yet, and he'll embrace his father
with old fashioned respect, and rightly.
My own
lady never let me glut my eyes
on my own son, but bled me to death first.
One thing I will advise, on second thought;
stow it away and ponder it.
Land your ship
in secret on your island; give no warning.
The day of faithful wives is gone forever.

But tell me, have you any word at all
about my son's life? Gone to Orkhómenos
or sandy Pylos, can he be? Or waiting

with Meneláos in the plain of Sparta?
Death on earth has not yet taken Orestês.'

But I could only answer:
'Son of Atreus,
why do you ask these questions of me? Neither
news of home have I, nor news of him,
alive or dead. And empty words are evil.'

So we exchanged our speech, in bitterness,
weighed down by grief, and tears welled in our eyes,
when there appeared the spirit of Akhilleus,
son of Peleus; then Patróklos' shade,
and then Antílokhos, and then Aias,
first among all the Danaans in strength
and bodily beauty, next to prince Akhilleus.
Now that great runner, grandson of Aíakhos,° Akhilleus
recognized me and called across to me:
'Son of Laërtês and the gods of old,
Odysseus, master mariner and soldier,
old knife, what next? What greater feat remains
for you to put your mind on, after this?
How did you find your way down to the dark
where these dimwitted dead are camped forever,
the after images of used-up men?'

I answered:
'Akhilleus, Peleus' son, strongest of all
among the Akhaians, I had need of foresight
such as Teirêsias alone could give
to help me, homeward bound for the crags of Ithaka.
I have not yet coasted Akhaia, not yet
touched my land; my life is all adversity.
But was there ever a man more blest by fortune
than you, Akhilleus? Can there ever be?
We ranked you with immortals in your lifetime,
we Argives did, and here your power is royal
among the dead men's shades. Think, then, Akhilleus:
you need not be so pained by death.'

To this
he answered swiftly:
'Let me hear no smooth talk
of death from you, Odysseus, light of councils.

Better, I say, to break sod as a farm hand
for some poor country man, on iron rations,
than lord it over all the exhausted dead.
Tell me, what news of the prince my son:° did he
come after me to make a name in battle
or could it be he did not? Do you know
if rank and honor still belong to Peleus
in the towns of the Myrmidons? Or now, may be,
Hellas and Phthia[109] spurn him, seeing old age
fetters him, hand and foot. I cannot help him
under the sun's rays, cannot be that man
I was on Troy's wide seaboard, in those days
when I made bastion for the Argives
and put an army's best men in the dust.
Were I but whole again, could I go now
to my father's house, one hour would do to make
my passion and my hands no man could hold
hateful to any who shoulder him aside.'

° Neoptólemos

Now when he paused I answered:
'Of all that—
of Peleus' life, that is—I know nothing;
but happily I can tell you the whole story
of Neoptólemos, as you require.
In my own ship I brought him out from Skyros
to join the Akhaians under arms.
And I can tell you,
in every council before Troy thereafter
your son spoke first and always to the point;
no one but Nestor and I could out-debate him.
And when we formed against the Trojan line
he never hung back in the mass, but ranged
far forward of his troops—no man could touch him
for gallantry. Aye, scores went down before him
in hard fights man to man. I shall not tell
all about each, or name them all—the long
roster of enemies he put out of action,
taking the shock of charges on the Argives.
But what a champion his lance ran through
in Eurýpulos[110] the son of Télephos! Keteians

[109] **Phthia:** Peleus's kingdom. [110] **Eurýpulos:** Leader of the Keteians, a group of warriors who fought on the side of the Trojans.

in throngs around that captain also died—
all because Priam's gifts had won his mother
to send the lad to battle; and I thought
Memnon[111] alone in splendor ever outshone him.

But one fact more: while our picked Argive crew
still rode that hollow horse Epeios built,
and when the whole thing lay with me, to open
the trapdoor of the ambuscade or not,
at that point our Danaan lords and soldiers
wiped their eyes, and their knees began to quake,
all but Neoptólemos. I never saw
his tanned cheek change color or his hand
brush one tear away. Rather he prayed me,
hand on hilt, to sortie, and he gripped
his tough spear, bent on havoc for the Trojans.
And when we had pierced and sacked Priam's tall city
he loaded his choice plunder and embarked
with no scar on him; not a spear had grazed him
nor the sword's edge in close work—common wounds
one gets in war. Arês in his mad fits
knows no favorites.'

But I said no more,
for he had gone off striding the field of asphodel,
the ghost of our great runner, Akhilleus Aiákidês,
glorying in what I told him of his son.

Now other souls of mournful dead stood by,
each with his troubled questioning, but one
remained alone, apart: the son of Télamon,
Aîas, it was—the great shade burning still
because I had won favor on the beachhead
in rivalry over Akhilleus' arms.[112]
The Lady Thetis, mother of Akhilleus,
laid out for us the dead man's battle gear,
and Trojan children, with Athena,

[111] **Memnon:** King of the Ethiopians; he took ten thousand men to Troy to assist the Trojans. [112] **in rivalry . . . arms:** After Akhilleus was killed, his armor was offered as a prize to Odysseus rather than to Aias, who then committed suicide.

named the Danaan fittest to own them. Would
god I had not borne the palm that day!
For earth took Aîas then to hold forever,
the handsomest and, in all feats of war,
noblest of the Danaans after Akhilleus.
Gently therefore I called across to him:
'Aîas, dear son of royal Télamon,
you would not then forget, even in death,
your fury with me over those accurst
calamitous arms?—and so they were, a bane
sent by the gods upon the Argive host.
For when you died by your own hand we lost
a tower, formidable in war. All we Akhaians
mourn you forever, as we do Akhilleus;
and no one bears the blame but Zeus.
He fixed that doom for you because he frowned
on the whole expedition of our spearmen.
My lord, come nearer, listen to our story!
Conquer your indignation and your pride.'

But he gave no reply, and turned away,
following other ghosts toward Erebos.
Who knows if in that darkness he might still
have spoken, and I answered?
But my heart
longed, after this, to see the dead elsewhere.
And now there came before my eyes Minos,
the son of Zeus, enthroned, holding a golden staff,
dealing out justice among ghostly pleaders
arrayed about the broad doorways of Death.

And then I glimpsed Orion, the huge hunter,
gripping his club, studded with bronze, unbreakable,
with wild beasts he had overpowered in life
on lonely mountainsides, now brought to bay
on fields of asphodel.
And I saw Títyos,
the son of Gaia, lying
abandoned over nine square rods of plain.
Vultures, hunched above him, left and right,
rifling his belly, stabbed into the liver,
and he could never push them off.
This hulk
had once committed rape of Zeus's mistress,

Lêto, in her glory, when she crossed
the open grass of Panopeus toward Pytho.

Then I saw Tántalos[113] put to the torture:
in a cool pond he stood, lapped round by water
clear to the chin, and being athirst he burned
to slake his dry weasand with drink, though drink
he would not ever again. For when the old man
put his lips down to the sheet of water
it vanished round his feet, gulped underground,
and black mud baked there in a wind from hell.
Boughs, too, drooped low above him, big with fruit,
pear trees, pomegranates, brilliant apples,
luscious figs, and olives ripe and dark;
but if he stretched his hand for one, the wind
under the dark sky tossed the bough beyond him.

Then Sísyphos[114] in torment I beheld
being roustabout to a tremendous boulder.
Leaning with both arms braced and legs driving,
he heaved it toward a height, and almost over,
but then a Power spun him round and sent
the cruel boulder bounding again to the plain.
Whereon the man bent down again to toil,
dripping sweat, and the dust rose overhead.
Next I saw manifest the power of Heraklês—
a phantom, this, for he himself has gone
feasting amid the gods, reclining soft
with Hêbê of the ravishing pale ankles,
daughter of Zeus and Hêra, shod in gold.
But, in my vision, all the dead around him
cried like affrighted birds; like Night itself
he loomed with naked bow and nocked arrow
and glances terrible as continual archery.
My hackles rose at the gold swordbelt he wore
sweeping across him: gorgeous intaglio
of savage bears, boars, lions with wildfire eyes,
swordfights, battle, slaughter, and sudden death—
the smith who had that belt in him, I hope
he never made, and never will make, another.

[113] **Tántalos:** The nature of Tántalos's crime is uncertain. He might have revealed secrets of the gods, or he might have served his son's flesh to the gods. [114] **Sísyphos:** A king of Corinth known for his teachery; it is not known what misdeed he is being punished for in this passage.

The eyes of the vast figure rested on me,
and of a sudden he said in kindly tones:
'Son of Laërtês and the gods of old,
Odysseus, master mariner and soldier,
under a cloud, you too? Destined to grinding
labors like my own in the sunny world?[115]
Son of Kroníon Zeus or not, how many
days I sweated out, being bound in servitude
to a man far worse than I, a rough master!
He made me hunt this place one time
to get the watchdog of the dead: no more
perilous task, he thought, could be; but I
brought back that beast, up from the underworld;
Hermês and grey-eyed Athena showed the way.'

And Heraklês, down the vistas of the dead,
faded from sight; but I stood fast, awaiting
other great souls who perished in times past.
I should have met, then, god-begotten Theseus
and Peirithoös,[116] whom both I longed to see,
but first came shades in thousands, rustling
in a pandemonium of whispers, blown together,
and the horror took me that Perséphonê
had brought from darker hell some saurian death's head.
I whirled then, made for the ship, shouted to crewmen
to get aboard and cast off the stern hawsers,
an order soon obeyed. They took their thwarts,
and the ship went leaping toward the stream of Ocean
first under oars, then with a following wind.

Book 12
Sea Perils and Defeat

The ship sailed on, out of the Ocean Stream,
riding a long swell on the open sea
for the Island of Aiaia.
                                        Summering Dawn
has dancing grounds there, and the Sun his rising;
but still by night we beached on a sand shelf

[115] **grinding labors . . . world:** Under the "rough master" Eurýstheus, Heraklês was made to perform his famous twelve labors, one of which was to fetch the dog Cerberus from Hades. [116] **Peirithoös:** A friend of Theseus; together they attempted to kidnap Perséphonê.

and waded in beyond the line of breakers
to fall asleep, awaiting the Day Star.

When the young Dawn with finger tips of rose
made heaven bright, I sent shipmates to bring
Elpênor's body from the house of Kirkê.
We others cut down timber on the foreland,
on a high point, and built his pyre of logs,
then stood by weeping while the flame burnt through
corse and equipment.
Then we heaped his barrow,
lifting a gravestone on the mound, and fixed
his light but unwarped oar against the sky.
These were our rites in memory of him. Soon, then,
knowing us back from the Dark Land, Kirkê came
freshly adorned for us, with handmaids bearing
loaves, roast meats, and ruby-colored wine.
She stood among us in immortal beauty
jesting:
'Hearts of oak, did you go down
alive into the homes of Death? One visit
finishes all men but yourselves, twice mortal!
Come, here is meat and wine, enjoy your feasting
for one whole day; and in the dawn tomorrow
you shall put out to sea. Sailing directions,
landmarks, perils, I shall sketch for you, to keep you
from being caught by land or water
in some black sack of trouble.'

In high humor
and ready for carousal, we agreed;
so all that day until the sun went down
we feasted on roast meat and good red wine,
till after sunset, at the fall of night,
the men dropped off to sleep by the stern hawsers.
She took my hand then, silent in that hush,
drew me apart, made me sit down, and lay
beside me, softly questioning, as I told
all I had seen, from first to last.
Then said the Lady Kirkê:
'So: all those trials are over.
Listen with care
to this, now, and a god will arm your mind.
Square in your ship's path are Seirênês,° crying Sirens
beauty to bewitch men coasting by;

woe to the innocent who hears that sound!
He will not see his lady nor his children
in joy, crowding about him, home from sea;
the Seirênês will sing his mind away
on their sweet meadow lolling. There are bones
of dead men rotting in a pile beside them
and flayed skins shrivel around the spot.
Steer wide;
keep well to seaward; plug your oarsmen's ears
with beeswax kneaded soft; none of the rest
should hear that song.
But if you wish to listen,
let the men tie you in the lugger, hand
and foot, back to the mast, lashed to the mast,
so you may hear those harpies' thrilling voices;
shout as you will, begging to be untied,
your crew must only twist more line around you
and keep their stroke up, till the singers fade.
What then? One of two courses you may take,
and you yourself must weigh them. I shall not
plan the whole action for you now, but only
tell you of both.
Ahead are beetling rocks
and dark blue glancing Amphitritê,[117] surging,
roars around them. Prowling Rocks,[118] or Drifters,
the gods in bliss have named them—named them well.
Not even birds can pass them by, not even
the timorous doves that bear ambrosia
to Father Zeus; caught by downdrafts, they die
on rockwall smooth as ice.
Each time, the Father
wafts a new courier to make up his crew.

Still less can ships get searoom of these Drifters,
whose boiling surf, under high fiery winds,
carries tossing wreckage of ships and men.
Only one ocean-going craft, the far-famed
Argo, made it, sailing from Aiêta;
but she, too, would have crashed on the big rocks
if Hêra had not pulled her through, for love
of Iêson, her captain.

[117] **Amphitritê:** A sea nymph; wife of Poseidon. [118] **Prowling Rocks:** Possibly the straits between Sicily and Italy.

A second course
lies between headlands. One is a sharp mountain
piercing the sky, with stormcloud round the peak
dissolving never, not in the brightest summer,
to show heaven's azure there, nor in the fall.
No mortal man could scale it, nor so much
as land there, not with twenty hands and feet,
so sheer the cliffs are—as of polished stone.
Midway that height, a cavern full of mist
opens toward Erebos and evening. Skirting
this in the lugger, great Odysseus,
your master bowman, shooting from the deck,
would come short of the cavemouth with his shaft;
but that is the den of Skylla, where she yaps
abominably, a newborn whelp's cry,
though she is huge and monstrous. God or man,
no one could look on her in joy. Her legs—
and there are twelve—are like great tentacles,
unjointed, and upon her serpent necks
are borne six heads like nightmares of ferocity,
with triple serried rows of fangs and deep
gullets of black death. Half her length, she sways
her heads in air, outside her horrid cleft,
hunting the sea around that promontory
for dolphins, dogfish, or what bigger game
thundering Amphitritê feeds in thousands.
And no ship's company can claim
to have passed her without loss and grief; she takes,
from every ship, one man for every gullet.

The opposite point seems more a tongue of land
you'd touch with a good bowshot, at the narrows.
A great wild fig, a shaggy mass of leaves,
grows on it, and Kharybdis lurks below
to swallow down the dark sea tide. Three times
from dawn to dusk she spews it up
and sucks it down again three times, a whirling
maelstrom; if you come upon her then
the god who makes earth tremble could not save you.
No, hug the cliff of Skylla, take your ship
through on a racing stroke. Better to mourn
six men than lose them all, and the ship, too.'

So her advice ran; but I faced her, saying:
'Only instruct me, goddess, if you will,

how, if possible, can I pass Kharybdis,
or fight off Skylla when she raids my crew?'

Swiftly that loveliest goddess answered me:
'Must you have battle in your heart forever?
The bloody toil of combat? Old contender,
will you not yield to the immortal gods?
That nightmare cannot die, being eternal
evil itself—horror, and pain, and chaos;
there is no fighting her, no power can fight her,
all that avails is flight.
Lose headway there
along that rockface while you break out arms,
and she'll swoop over you, I fear, once more,
taking one man again for every gullet.
No, no, put all your backs into it, row on;
invoke Blind Force, that bore this scourge of men,
to keep her from a second strike against you.

Then you will coast Thrinákia,° the island Sicily
where Hêlios' cattle graze, fine herds, and flocks
of goodly sheep. The herds and flocks are seven,
with fifty beasts in each.
No lambs are dropped,
or calves, and these fat cattle never die.
Immortal, too, their cowherds are—their shepherds—
Phaëthousa and Lampetía, sweetly braided
nymphs that divine Neaira bore
to the overlord of high noon, Hêlios.
These nymphs their gentle mother bred and placed
upon Thrinákia, the distant land,
in care of flocks and cattle for their father.

Now give those kine a wide berth, keep your thoughts
intent upon your course for home,
and hard seafaring brings you all to Ithaka.
But if you raid the beeves, I see destruction
for ship and crew.
Rough years then lie between
you and your homecoming, alone and old,
the one survivor, all companions lost.'

As Kirkê spoke, Dawn mounted her golden throne,
and on the first rays Kirkê left me, taking
her way like a great goddess up the island.

I made straight for the ship, roused up the men
to get aboard and cast off at the stern.
They scrambled to their places by the rowlocks
and all in line dipped oars in the grey sea.
But soon an off-shore breeze blew to our liking—
a canvas-bellying breeze, a lusty shipmate
sent by the singing nymph with sunbright hair.
So we made fast the braces, and we rested,
letting the wind and steersman work the ship.
The crew being now silent before me, I
addressed them, sore at heart:
'Dear friends,
more than one man, or two, should know those things
Kirkê foresaw for us and shared with me,
so let me tell her forecast: then we die
with our eyes open, if we are going to die,
or know what death we baffle if we can. Seirênês
weaving a haunting song over the sea
we are to shun, she said, and their green shore
all sweet with clover; yet she urged that I
alone should listen to their song. Therefore
you are to tie me up, tight as a splint,
erect along the mast, lashed to the mast,
and if I shout and beg to be untied,
take more turns of the rope to muffle me.'

I rather dwelt on this part of the forecast,
while our good ship made time, bound outward down
the wind for the strange island of Seirênês.
Then all at once the wind fell, and a calm
came over all the sea, as though some power
lulled the swell.
The crew were on their feet
briskly, to furl the sail, and stow it; then,
each in place, they poised the smooth oar blades
and sent the white foam scudding by. I carved
a massive cake of beeswax into bits
and rolled them in my hands until they softened—
no long task, for a burning heat came down
from Hêlios, lord of high noon. Going forward
I carried wax along the line, and laid it
thick on their ears. They tied me up, then, plumb
amidships, back to the mast, lashed to the mast,
and took themselves again to rowing. Soon,
as we came smartly within hailing distance,

the two Seirênês, noting our fast ship
off their point, made ready, and they sang:

This way, oh turn your bows,
Akhaia's glory,
As all the world allows—
Moor and be merry.

Sweet coupled airs we sing.
No lonely seafarer
Holds clear of entering
Our green mirror.

Pleased by each purling note
Like honey twining
From her throat and my throat,
Who lies a-pining?

Sea rovers here take joy
Voyaging onward,
As from our song of Troy
Greybeard and rower-boy
Goeth more learnèd.

All feats on that great field
In the long warfare,
Dark days the bright gods willed,
Wounds you bore there,

Argos' old soldiery
On Troy beach teeming,
Charmed out of time we see.
No life on earth can be
Hid from our dreaming.

The lovely voices in ardor appealing over the water
made me crave to listen, and I tried to say
'Untie me!' to the crew, jerking my brows;
but they bent steady to the oars. Then Perimêdês
got to his feet, he and Eurýlokhos,
and passed more line about, to hold me still.
So all rowed on, until the Seirênês
dropped under the sea rim, and their singing
dwindled away.
My faithful company
rested on their oars now, peeling off
the wax that I had laid thick on their ears;
then set me free.
But scarcely had that island

faded in blue air than I saw smoke
and white water, with sound of waves in tumult—
a sound the men heard, and it terrified them.
Oars flew from their hands; the blades went knocking
wild alongside till the ship lost way,
with no oarblades to drive her through the water.

Well, I walked up and down from bow to stern,
trying to put heart into them, standing over
every oarsman, saying gently,
'Friends,
have we never been in danger before this?
More fearsome, is it now, than when the Kyklops
penned us in his cave? What power he had!
Did I not keep my nerve, and use my wits
to find a way out for us?
Now I say
by hook or crook this peril too shall be
something that we remember.
Heads up, lads!
We must obey the orders as I give them.
Get the oarshafts in your hands, and lay back
hard on your benches; hit these breaking seas.
Zeus help us pull away before we founder.
You at the tiller, listen, and take in
all that I say—the rudders are your duty;
keep her out of the combers and the smoke;
steer for that headland; watch the drift, or we
fetch up in the smother, and you drown us.'

That was all, and it brought them round to action.
But as I sent them on toward Skylla, I
told them nothing, as they could do nothing.
They would have dropped their oars again, in panic,
to roll for cover under the decking. Kirkê's
bidding against arms had slipped my mind,
so I tied on my cuirass and took up
two heavy spears, then made my way along
to the foredeck—thinking to see her first from there,
the monster of the grey rock, harboring
torment for my friends. I strained my eyes
upon that cliffside veiled in cloud, but nowhere
could I catch sight of her.

And all this time,
in travail, sobbing, gaining on the current,
we rowed into the strait—Skylla to port
and on our starboard beam Kharybdis, dire
gorge of the salt sea tide. By heaven! when she
vomited, all the sea was like a cauldron
seething over intense fire, when the mixture
suddenly heaves and rises.
The shot spume
soared to the landside heights, and fell like rain.

But when she swallowed the sea water down
we saw the funnel of the maelstrom, heard
the rock bellowing all around, and dark
sand raged on the bottom far below.
My men all blanched against the gloom, our eyes
were fixed upon that yawning mouth in fear
of being devoured.
Then Skylla made her strike,
whisking six of my best men from the ship.
I happened to glance aft at ship and oarsmen
and caught sight of their arms and legs, dangling
high overhead. Voices came down to me
in anguish, calling my name for the last time.

A man surfcasting on a point of rock
for bass or mackerel, whipping his long rod
to drop the sinker and the bait far out,
will hook a fish and rip it from the surface
to dangle wriggling through the air:
so these
were borne aloft in spasms toward the cliff.

She ate them as they shrieked there, in her den,
in the dire grapple, reaching still for me—
and deathly pity ran me through
at that sight—far the worst I ever suffered,
questing the passes of the strange sea.
We rowed on.
The Rocks were now behind; Kharybdis, too,
and Skylla dropped astern.
Then we were coasting
the noble island of the god, where grazed

those cattle with wide brows, and bounteous flocks
of Hêlios, lord of noon, who rides high heaven.

From the black ship, far still at sea, I heard
the lowing of the cattle winding home
and sheep bleating; and heard, too, in my heart
the words of blind Teirêsias of Thebes
and Kirkê of Aiaia: both forbade me
the island of the world's delight, the Sun.
So I spoke out in gloom to my companions:
'Shipmates, grieving and weary though you are,
listen: I had forewarning from Teirêsias
and Kirkê, too; both told me I must shun
this island of the Sun, the world's delight.
Nothing but fatal trouble shall we find here.
Pull away, then, and put the land astern.'

That strained them to the breaking point, and, cursing,
Eurýlokhos cried out in bitterness:
'Are you flesh and blood, Odysseus, to endure
more than a man can? Do you never tire?
God, look at you, iron is what you're made of.
Here we all are, half dead with weariness,
falling asleep over the oars, and you
say "No landing"—no firm island earth
where we could make a quiet supper. No:
pull out to sea, you say, with night upon us—
just as before, but wandering now, and lost.
Sudden storms can rise at night and swamp
ships without a trace.
Where is your shelter
if some stiff gale blows up from south or west—
the winds that break up shipping every time
when seamen flout the lord gods' will? I say
do as the hour demands and go ashore
before black night comes down.
We'll make our supper
alongside, and at dawn put out to sea.'

Now when the rest said 'Aye' to this, I saw
the power of destiny devising ill.
Sharply I answered, without hesitation:
'Eurýlokhos, they are with you to a man.
I am alone, outmatched.

Let this whole company
swear me a great oath: Any herd of cattle
or flock of sheep here found shall go unharmed;
no one shall slaughter out of wantonness
ram or heifer; all shall be content
with what the goddess Kirkê put aboard.'

They fell at once to swearing as I ordered,
and when the round of oaths had ceased, we found
a halfmoon bay to beach and moor the ship in,
with a fresh spring nearby. All hands ashore
went about skillfully getting up a meal.
Then, after thirst and hunger, those besiegers,
were turned away, they mourned for their companions
plucked from the ship by Skylla and devoured,
and sleep came soft upon them as they mourned.

In the small hours of the third watch, when stars
that shone out in the first dusk of evening
had gone down to their setting, a giant wind
blew from heaven, and clouds driven by Zeus
shrouded land and sea in a night of storm;
so, just as Dawn with finger tips of rose
touched the windy world, we dragged our ship
to cover in a grotto, a sea cave
where nymphs had chairs of rock and sanded floors.
I mustered all the crew and said:
'Old shipmates,
our stores are in the ship's hold, food and drink;
the cattle here are not for our provision,
or we pay dearly for it.
Fierce the god is
who cherishes these heifers and these sheep:
Hêlios; and no man avoids his eye.'

To this my fighters nodded. Yes. But now
we had a month of onshore gales, blowing
day in, day out—south winds, or south by east.
As long as bread and good red wine remained
to keep the men up, and appease their craving,
they would not touch the cattle. But in the end,
when all the barley in the ship was gone,
hunger drove them to scour the wild shore
with angling hooks, for fishes and sea fowl,

whatever fell into their hands; and lean days
wore their bellies thin.

The storms continued.
So one day I withdrew to the interior
to pray the gods in solitude, for hope
that one might show me some way of salvation.
Slipping away, I struck across the island
to a sheltered spot, out of the driving gale.
I washed my hands there, and made supplication
to the gods who own Olympos, all the gods—
but they, for answer, only closed my eyes
under slow drops of sleep.
Now on the shore Eurýlokhos
made his insidious plea:
'Comrades,' he said,
'You've gone through everything; listen to what I say.
All deaths are hateful to us, mortal wretches,
but famine is the most pitiful, the worst
end that a man can come to.
Will you fight it?
Come, we'll cut out the noblest of these cattle
for sacrifice to the gods who own the sky;
and once at home, in the old country of Ithaka,
if ever that day comes—
we'll build a costly temple and adorn it
with every beauty for the Lord of Noon.
But if he flares up over his heifers lost,
wishing our ship destroyed, and if the gods
make cause with him, why, then I say: Better
open your lungs to a big sea once for all
than waste to skin and bones on a lonely island!'

Thus Eurýlokhos; and they murmured 'Aye!'
trooping away at once to round up heifers.
Now, that day tranquil cattle with broad brows
were grazing near, and soon the men drew up
around their chosen beasts in ceremony.
They plucked the leaves that shone on a tall oak—
having no barley meal—to strew the victims,
performed the prayers and ritual, knifed the kine
and flayed each carcass, cutting thighbones free
to wrap in double folds of fat. These offerings,

with strips of meat, were laid upon the fire.
Then, as they had no wine, they made libation
with clear spring water, broiling the entrails first;
and when the bones were burnt and tripes shared,
they spitted the carved meat.
Just then my slumber
left me in a rush, my eyes opened,
and I went down the seaward path. No sooner
had I caught sight of our black hull, than savory
odors of burnt fat eddied around me;
grief took hold of me, and I cried aloud:
'O Father Zeus and gods in bliss forever,
you made me sleep away this day of mischief!
O cruel drowsing, in the evil hour!
Here they sat, and a great work they contrived.'

Lampetía in her long gown meanwhile
had borne swift word to the Overlord of Noon:
'They have killed your kine.'

And the Lord Hêlios
burst into angry speech amid the immortals:
'O Father Zeus and gods in bliss forever,
punish Odysseus' men! So overweening,
now they have killed my peaceful kine, my joy
at morning when I climbed the sky of stars,
and evening, when I bore westward from heaven.
Restitution or penalty they shall pay—
and pay in full—or I go down forever
to light the dead men in the underworld.'

Then Zeus who drives the stormcloud made reply:
'Peace, Hêlios: shine on among the gods,
shine over mortals in the fields of grain.
Let me throw down one white-hot bolt, and make
splinters of their ship in the winedark sea.'

—Kalypso later told me of this exchange,
as she declared that Hermês had told her.
Well, when I reached the sea cave and the ship,
I faced each man, and had it out; but where
could any remedy be found? There was none.
The silken beeves of Hêlios were dead.

The gods, moreover, made queer signs appear:
cowhides began to crawl, and beef, both raw
and roasted, lowed like kine upon the spits.

Now six full days my gallant crew could feast
upon the prime beef they had marked for slaughter
from Hêlios' herd; and Zeus, the son of Kronos,
added one fine morning.
All the gales
had ceased, blown out, and with an offshore breeze
we launched again, stepping the mast and sail,
to make for the open sea. Astern of us
the island coastline faded, and no land
showed anywhere, but only sea and heaven,
when Zeus Kroníon piled a thunderhead
above the ship, while gloom spread on the ocean.
We held our course, but briefly. Then the squall
struck whining from the west, with gale force, breaking
both forestays, and the mast came toppling aft
along the ship's length, so the running rigging
showered into the bilge.
On the after deck
the mast had hit the steersman a slant blow
bashing the skull in, knocking him overside,
as the brave soul fled the body, like a diver.
With crack on crack of thunder, Zeus let fly
a bolt against the ship, a direct hit,
so that she bucked, in reeking fumes of sulphur,
and all the men were flung into the sea.
They came up 'round the wreck, bobbing a while
like petrels on the waves.
No more seafaring
homeward for these, no sweet day of return;
the god had turned his face from them.
I clambered
fore and aft my hulk until a comber
split her, keel from ribs, and the big timber
floated free; the mast, too, broke away.
A backstay floated dangling from it, stout
rawhide rope, and I used this for lashing
mast and keel together. These I straddled,
riding the frightful storm.
Nor had I yet
seen the worst of it: for now the west wind
dropped, and a southeast gale came on—one more

twist of the knife—taking me north again,
straight for Kharybdis. All that night I drifted,
and in the sunrise, sure enough, I lay
off Skylla mountain and Kharybdis deep.
There, as the whirlpool drank the tide, a billow
tossed me, and I sprang for the great fig tree,
catching on like a bat under a bough.
Nowhere had I to stand, no way of climbing,
the root and bole being far below, and far
above my head the branches and their leaves,
massed, overshadowing Kharybdis pool.
But I clung grimly, thinking my mast and keel
would come back to the surface when she spouted.
And ah! how long, with what desire, I waited!
till, at the twilight hour, when one who hears
and judges pleas in the marketplace all day
between contentious men, goes home to supper,
the long poles at last reared from the sea.

Now I let go with hands and feet, plunging
straight into the foam beside the timbers,
pulled astride, and rowed hard with my hands
to pass by Skylla. Never could I have passed her
had not the Father of gods and men, this time,
kept me from her eyes. Once through the straight,
nine days I drifted in the open sea
before I made shore, buoyed up by the gods,
upon Ogýgia Isle. The dangerous nymph
Kalypso lives and sings there, in her beauty,
and she received me, loved me.
But why tell
the same tale that I told last night in hall
to you and to your lady? Those adventures
made a long evening, and I do not hold
with tiresome repetition of a story."

Book 13
One More Strange Island

He ended it, and no one stirred or sighed
in the shadowy hall, spellbound as they all were,
until Alkínoös answered:
"When you came
here to my strong home, Odysseus, under

my tall roof, headwinds were left behind you.
Clear sailing shall you have now, homeward now,
however painful all the past.
                                        My lords,
ever my company, sharing the wine of Council,
the songs of the blind harper, hear me further:
garments are folded for our guest and friend
in the smooth chest, and gold
in various shaping of adornment lies
with other gifts, and many, brought by our peers;
let each man add his tripod and deep-bellied
cauldron: we'll make levy upon the realm
to pay us for the loss each bears in this."

Alkínoös had voiced their own hearts' wish.
All gave assent, then home they went to rest;
but young Dawn's finger tips of rose, touching
the world, roused them to make haste to the ship,
each with his gift of noble bronze. Alkínoös,
their ardent king, stepping aboard himself,
directed the stowing under the cross planks,
not to cramp the long pull of the oarsmen.
Going then to the great hall, lords and crew
prepared for feasting.
                                        As the gods' anointed,
Alkínoös made offering on their behalf—an ox
to Zeus beyond the stormcloud, Kronos' son,
who rules the world. They burnt the great thighbones
and feasted at their ease on fresh roast meat,
as in their midst the godlike harper sang—
Demódokos, honored by all that realm.
                                        Only Odysseus
time and again turned craning toward the sun,
impatient for day's end, for the open sea.
Just as a farmer's hunger grows, behind
the bolted plow and share, all day afield,
drawn by his team of winedark oxen: sundown
is benison° for him, sending him homeward   blessing
stiff in the knees from weariness, to dine;
just so, the light on the sea rim gladdened Odysseus,
and as it dipped he stood among the Phaiákians,
turned to Alkínoös, and said:
"O king and admiration of your people,
give me fare well, and stain the ground with wine;
my blessings on you all! This hour brings

fulfillment to the longing of my heart:
a ship for home, and gifts the gods of heaven
make so precious and so bountiful.
After this voyage
god grant I find my own wife in my hall
with everyone I love best, safe and sound!
And may you, settled in your land, give joy
to wives and children; may the gods reward you
every way, and your realm be free of woe."

Then all the voices rang out, "Be it so!"
and "Well spoken!" and "Let our friend make sail!"

Whereon Alkínoös gave command to his crier:
"Fill the winebowl, Pontónoös: mix and serve:
go the whole round, so may this company
invoke our Father Zeus, and bless our friend,
seaborne tonight and bound for his own country."

Pontónoös mixed the honey-hearted wine
and went from chair to chair, filling the cups;
then each man where he sat poured out his offering
to the gods in bliss who own the sweep of heaven.
With gentle bearing Odysseus rose, and placed
his double goblet in Arêtê's hands,
saying:
"Great Queen, farewell;
be blest through all your days till age comes on you,
and death, last end for mortals, after age.
Now I must go my way. Live in felicity,
and make this palace lovely for your children,
your countrymen, and your king, Alkínoös."

Royal Odysseus turned and crossed the door sill,
a herald at his right hand, sent by Alkínoös
to lead him to the sea beach and the ship.
Arêtê, too, sent maids in waiting after him,
one with a laundered great cloak and a tunic,
a second balancing the crammed sea chest,
a third one bearing loaves and good red wine.
As soon as they arrived alongside, crewmen
took these things for stowage under the planks,
their victualling and drink; then spread a rug
and linen cover on the after deck,
where Lord Odysseus might sleep in peace.

Now he himself embarked, lay down, lay still,
while oarsmen took their places at the rowlocks
all in order. They untied their hawser,
passing it through a drilled stone ring; then bent
forward at the oars and caught the sea
as one man, stroking.
Slumber, soft and deep
like the still sleep of death, weighed on his eyes
as the ship hove seaward.
How a four horse team
whipped into a run on a straightaway
consumes the road, surging and surging over it!
So ran that craft and showed her heels to the swell,
her bow wave riding after, and her wake
on the purple night-sea foaming.
Hour by hour
she held her pace; not even a falcon wheeling
downwind, swiftest bird, could stay abreast of her
in that most arrowy flight through open water,
with her great passenger—godlike in counsel,
he that in twenty years had borne such blows
in his deep heart, breaking through ranks in war
and waves on the bitter sea.
This night at last
he slept serene, his long-tried mind at rest.

When on the East the sheer bright star arose
that tells of coming Dawn, the ship made landfall
and came up islandward in the dim of night.
Phorkys, the old sea baron, has a cove
here in the realm of Ithaka; two points
of high rock, breaking sharply, hunch around it,
making a haven from the plunging surf
that gales at sea roll shoreward. Deep inside,
at mooring range, good ships can ride unmoored.
There, on the inmost shore, an olive tree
throws wide its boughs over the bay; nearby
a cave of dusky light is hidden
for those immortal girls, the Naiadês.[119]
Within are winebowls hollowed in the rock
and amphorai; bees bring their honey here;
and there are looms of stone, great looms, whereon

[119] **Naiadês:** Water nymphs who presided over rivers, lakes, springs, and fountains.

the weaving nymphs make tissues, richly dyed
as the deep sea is; and clear springs in the cavern
flow forever. Of two entrances,
one on the north allows descent of mortals,
but beings out of light alone, the undying,
can pass by the south slit; no men come there.

This cove the sailors knew. Here they drew in,
and the ship ran half her keel's length up the shore,
she had such way on her from those great oarsmen.
Then from their benches forward on dry ground
they disembarked. They hoisted up Odysseus
unruffled on his bed, under his cover,
handing him overside still fast asleep,
to lay him on the sand; and they unloaded
all those gifts the princes of Phaiákia
gave him, when by Athena's heart and will
he won his passage home. They bore this treasure
off the beach, and piled it close around
the roots of the olive tree, that no one passing
should steal Odysseus' gear before he woke.
That done, they pulled away on the homeward track.

But now the god that shakes the islands, brooding
over old threats of his against Odysseus,
approached Lord Zeus to learn his will. Said he:
"Father of gods, will the bright immortals ever
pay me respect again, if mortals do not?—
Phaiákians, too, my own blood kin?
I thought
Odysseus should in time regain his homeland;
I had no mind to rob him of that day—
no, no; you promised it, being so inclined;
only I thought he should be made to suffer
all the way.
But now these islanders
have shipped him homeward, sleeping soft, and put him
on Ithaka, with gifts untold
bronze and gold, and fine cloth to his shoulder.
Never from Troy had he borne off such booty
if he had got home safe with all his share."

Then Zeus who drives the stormcloud answered, sighing:
"God of horizons, making earth's underbeam
tremble, why do you grumble so?

The immortal gods show you no less esteem,
and the rough consequence would make them slow
to let barbs fly at their eldest and most noble.
But if some mortal captain, overcome
by his own pride of strength, cuts or defies you,
are you not always free to take reprisal?
Act as your wrath requires and as you will."

Now said Poseidon, god of earthquake:
"Aye,
god of the stormy sky, I should have taken
vengeance, as you say, and on my own;
but I respect, and would avoid, your anger.
The sleek Phaiákian cutter, even now,
has carried out her mission and glides home
over the misty sea. Let me impale her,
end her voyage, and end all ocean-crossing
with passengers, then heave a mass of mountain
in a ring around the city."

Now Zeus who drives the stormcloud said benignly:
"Here is how I should do it, little brother:
when all who watch upon the wall have caught
sight of the ship, let her be turned to stone—
an island like a ship, just off the bay.
Mortals may gape at that for generations!
But throw no mountain round the sea port city."

When he heard this, Poseidon, god of earthquake,
departed for Skhería, where the Phaiákians
are born and dwell. Their ocean-going ship
he saw already near, heading for harbor;
so up behind her swam the island-shaker
and struck her into stone, rooted in stone, at one
blow of his palm,
then took to the open sea.
Those famous ship handlers, the Phaiákians,
gazed at each other, murmuring in wonder;
you could have heard one say:
"Now who in thunder
has anchored, moored that ship in the seaway,
when everyone could see her making harbor?"

The god had wrought a charm beyond their thought.
But soon Alkínoös made them hush, and told them:
"This present doom upon the ship—on me—

my father prophesied in the olden time.
If we gave safe conveyance to all passengers
we should incur Poseidon's wrath, he said,
whereby one day a fair ship, manned by Phaiákians,
would come to grief at the god's hands; and great
mountains would hide our city from the sea.
So my old father forecast.
Use your eyes:
these things are even now being brought to pass.
Let all here abide by my decree:
We make
an end henceforth of taking, in our ships,
castaways who may land upon Skhería;
and twelve choice bulls we dedicate at once
to Lord Poseidon, praying him of his mercy
not to heave up a mountain round our city."

In fearful awe they led the bulls to sacrifice
and stood about the altar stone, those captains,
peers of Phaiákia, led by their king in prayer
to Lord Poseidon.

Meanwhile, on his island,
his father's shore, that kingly man, Odysseus,
awoke, but could not tell what land it was
after so many years away; moreover,
Pallas Athena, Zeus's daughter, poured
a grey mist all around him, hiding him
from common sight—for she had things to tell him
and wished no one to know him, wife or townsmen,
before the suitors paid up for their crimes.

The landscape then looked strange, unearthly strange
to the Lord Odysseus: paths by hill and shore,
glimpses of harbors, cliffs, and summer trees.
He stood up, rubbed his eyes, gazed at his homeland,
and swore, slapping his thighs with both his palms,
then cried aloud:
"What am I in for now?
Whose country have I come to this time? Rough
savages and outlaws, are they, or
godfearing people, friendly to castaways?
Where shall I take these things? Where take myself,
with no guide, no directions? These should be
still in Phaiákian hands, and I uncumbered,
free to find some other openhearted

prince who might be kind and give me passage.
I have no notion where to store this treasure;
first-comer's trove it is, if I leave it here.

My lords and captains of Phaiákia
were not those decent men they seemed, not honorable,
landing me in this unknown country—no,
by god, they swore to take me home to Ithaka
and did not! Zeus attend to their reward,
Zeus, patron of petitioners, who holds
all other mortals under his eye; he takes
payment from betrayers!
I'll be busy.
I can look through my gear. I shouldn't wonder
if they pulled out with part of it on board."

He made a tally of his shining pile—
tripods, cauldrons, cloaks, and gold—and found
he lacked nothing at all.
And then he wept,
despairing, for his own land, trudging down
beside the endless wash of the wide, wide sea,
weary and desolate as the sea. But soon
Athena came to him from the nearby air,
putting a young man's figure on—a shepherd,
like a king's son, all delicately made.
She wore a cloak, in two folds off her shoulders,
and sandals bound upon her shining feet.
A hunting lance lay in her hands.
At sight of her
Odysseus took heart, and he went forward
to greet the lad, speaking out fair and clear:
"Friend, you are the first man I've laid eyes on
here in this cove. Greetings. Do not feel
alarmed or hostile, coming across me; only
receive me into safety with my stores.
Touching your knees I ask it, as I might
ask grace of a god.
O sir, advise me,
what is this land and realm, who are the people?
Is it an island all distinct, or part
of the fertile mainland, sloping to the sea?"

To this grey-eyed Athena answered:
"Stranger,

you must come from the other end of nowhere,
else you are a great booby, having to ask
what place this is. It is no nameless country.
Why, everyone has heard of it, the nations
over on the dawn side, toward the sun,
and westerners in cloudy lands of evening.
No one would use this ground for training horses,
it is too broken, has no breadth of meadow;
but there is nothing meager about the soil,
the yield of grain is wondrous, and wine, too,
with drenching rains and dewfall.
There's good pasture
for oxen and for goats, all kinds of timber,
and water all year long in the cattle ponds.
For these blessings, friend, the name of Ithaka
has made its way even as far as Troy—
and they say Troy lies far beyond Akhaia."

Now Lord Odysseus, the long-enduring,
laughed in his heart, hearing his land described
by Pallas Athena, daughter of Zeus who rules
the veering stormwind; and he answered her
with ready speech—not that he told the truth,
but, just as she did, held back what he knew,
weighing within himself at every step
what he made up to serve his turn.

Said he:
"Far away in Krete I learned of Ithaka—
in that broad island over the great ocean.
And here I am now, come myself to Ithaka!
Here is my fortune with me. I left my sons
an equal part, when I shipped out. I killed
Orsílokhos, the courier, son of Idómeneus.
This man could beat the best cross country runners
in Krete, but he desired to take away
my Trojan plunder, all I had fought and bled for,
cutting through ranks in war and the cruel sea.
Confiscation is what he planned; he knew
I had not cared to win his father's favor
as a staff officer in the field at Troy,
but led my own command.
I acted: I
hit him with a spearcast from a roadside
as he came down from the open country. Murky

night shrouded all heaven and the stars.
I made that ambush with one man at arms.
We were unseen. I took his life in secret,
finished him off with my sharp sword. That night
I found asylum on a ship off shore
skippered by gentlemen of Phoinikia;° I gave Phoenicia
all they could wish, out of my store of plunder,
for passage, and for landing me at Pylos
or Elis Town,[120] where the Epeioi are in power.
Contrary winds carried them willy-nilly
past that coast; they had no wish to cheat me,
but we were blown off course.
Here, then, by night
we came, and made this haven by hard rowing.
All famished, but too tired to think of food,
each man dropped in his tracks after the landing,
and I slept hard, being wearied out. Before
I woke today, they put my things ashore
on the sand here beside me where I lay,
then reimbarked for Sidon, that great city.
Now they are far at sea, while I am left
forsaken here."

At this the grey-eyed goddess
Athena smiled, and gave him a caress,
her looks being changed now, so she seemed a woman,
tall and beautiful and no doubt skilled
at weaving splendid things. She answered briskly:
"Whoever gets around you must be sharp
and guileful as a snake; even a god
might bow to you in ways of dissimulation.
You! You chameleon!
Bottomless bag of tricks! Here in your own country
would you not give your stratagems a rest
or stop spellbinding for an instant?

You play a part as if it were your own tough skin.

No more of this, though. Two of a kind, we are,
contrivers, both. Of all men now alive
you are the best in plots and story telling.
My own fame is for wisdom among the gods—
deceptions, too.

[120] **Elis Town:** Elis was a famous city in the western Peloponnese.

Would even you have guessed
that I am Pallas Athena, daughter of Zeus,
I that am always with you in times of trial,
a shield to you in battle, I who made
the Phaiákians befriend you, to a man?
Now I am here again to counsel with you—
but first to put away those gifts the Phaiákians
gave you at departure—I planned it so.
Then I can tell you of the gall and wormwood
it is your lot to drink in your own hall.
Patience, iron patience, you must show;
so give it out to neither man nor woman
that you are back from wandering. Be silent
under all injuries, even blows from men."

His mind ranging far, Odysseus answered:
"Can mortal man be sure of you on sight,
even a sage, O mistress of disguises?
Once you were fond of me—I am sure of that—
years ago, when we Akhaians made
war, in our generation, upon Troy.
But after we had sacked the shrines of Priam
and put to sea, God scattered the Akhaians;
I never saw you after that, never
knew you aboard with me, to act as shield
in grievous times—not till you gave me comfort
in the rich hinterland of the Phaiákians
and were yourself my guide into that city.

Hear me now in your father's name, for I
cannot believe that I have come to Ithaka.
It is some other land. You made that speech
only to mock me, and to take me in.
Have I come back in truth to my home island?"

To this the grey-eyed goddess Athena answered:
"Always the same detachment! That is why
I cannot fail you, in your evil fortune,
coolheaded, quick, well-spoken as you are!
Would not another wandering man, in joy,
make haste home to his wife and children? Not
you, not yet. Before you hear their story
you will have proof about your wife.
I tell you,
she still sits where you left her, and her days

and nights go by forlorn, in lonely weeping.
For my part, never had I despaired; I felt
sure of your coming home, though all your men
should perish; but I never cared to fight
Poseidon, Father's brother, in his baleful
rage with you for taking his son's eye.

Now I shall make you see the shape of Ithaka.
Here is the cove the sea lord Phorkys owns,
there is the olive spreading out her leaves
over the inner bay, and there the cavern
dusky and lovely, hallowed by the feet
of those immortal girls, the Naiadês—
the same wide cave under whose vault you came
to honor them with hekatombs—and there
Mount Neion, with his forest on his back!"

She had dispelled the mist, so all the island
stood out clearly. Then indeed Odysseus'
heart stirred with joy. He kissed the earth,
and lifting up his hands prayed to the nymphs:
"O slim shy Naiadês, young maids of Zeus,
I had not thought to see you ever again!
O listen smiling
to my gentle prayers, and we'll make offering
plentiful as in the old time, granted I
live, granted my son grows tall, by favor
of great Athena, Zeus's daughter,
who gives the winning fighter his reward!"

The grey-eyed goddess said directly:
"Courage;
and let the future trouble you no more.
We go to make a cache now, in the cave,
to keep your treasure hid. Then we'll consider
how best the present action may unfold."

The goddess turned and entered the dim cave,
exploring it for crannies, while Odysseus
carried up all the gold, the fire-hard bronze,
and well-made clothing the Phaiákians gave him.
Pallas Athena, daughter of Zeus the storm king,
placed them, and shut the cave mouth with a stone,
and under the old grey olive tree those two
sat down to work the suitors death and woe.

Grey-eyed Athena was the first to speak, saying:
"Son of Laërtês and the gods of old,
Odysseus, master of land ways and sea ways,
put your mind on a way to reach and strike
a crowd of brazen upstarts.
Three long years
they have played master in your house: three years
trying to win your lovely lady, making
gifts as though betrothed. And she? Forever
grieving for you, missing your return,
she has allowed them all to hope, and sent
messengers with promises to each—
though her true thoughts are fixed elsewhere."

At this
the man of ranging mind, Odysseus, cried:
"So hard beset! An end like Agamémnon's
might very likely have been mine, a bad end,
bleeding to death in my own hall. You forestalled it,
goddess, by telling me how the land lies.
Weave me a way to pay them back! And you, too,
take your place with me, breathe valor in me
the way you did that night when we Akhaians
unbound the bright veil from the brow of Troy!
O grey-eyed one, fire my heart and brace me!
I'll take on fighting men three hundred strong
if you fight at my back, immortal lady!"

The grey-eyed goddess Athena answered him:
"No fear but I shall be there; you'll go forward
under my arm when the crux comes at last.
And I foresee your vast floor stained with blood,
spattered with brains of this or that tall suitor
who fed upon your cattle.
Now, for a while,
I shall transform you; not a soul will know you,
the clear skin of your arms and legs shriveled,
your chestnut hair all gone, your body dressed
in sacking that a man would gag to see,
and the two eyes, that were so brilliant, dirtied—
contemptible, you shall seem to your enemies,
as to the wife and son you left behind.

But join the swineherd first—the overseer
of all your swine, a good soul now as ever,

devoted to Penélopê and your son.
He will be found near Raven's Rock and the well
of Arethousa, where the swine are pastured,
rooting for acorns to their hearts' content,
drinking the dark still water. Boarflesh grows
pink and fat on that fresh diet. There
stay with him and question him, while I
am off to the great beauty's land of Sparta,
to call your son Telémakhos home again—
for you should know, he went to the wide land
of Lakedaimon, Meneláos' country,
to learn if there were news of you abroad."

Odysseus answered:
"Why not tell him, knowing
my whole history, as you do? Must he
traverse the barren sea, he too, and live
in pain, while others feed on what is his?"

At this the grey-eyed goddess Athena said:
"No need for anguish on that lad's account.
I sent him off myself, to make his name
in foreign parts—no hardship in the bargain,
taking his ease in Meneláos' mansion,
lapped in gold.
The young bucks here, I know,
lie in wait for him in a cutter, bent
on murdering him before he reaches home.
I rather doubt they will. Cold earth instead
will take in her embrace a man or two
of those who fed so long on what is his."

Speaking no more, she touched him with her wand,
shriveled the clear skin of his arms and legs,
made all his hair fall out, cast over him
the wrinkled hide of an old man, and bleared
both his eyes, that were so bright. Then she
clapped an old tunic, a foul cloak, upon him,
tattered, filthy, stained by greasy smoke,
and over that a mangy big buck skin.
A staff she gave him, and a leaky knapsack
with no strap but a loop of string.
Now then,

their colloquy at an end, they went their ways—
Athena toward illustrious Lakedaimon
far over sea, to join Odysseus' son.

Book 14
Hospitality in the Forest

He went up from the cove through wooded ground,
taking a stony trail into the high hills, where
the swineherd lived, according to Athena.
Of all Odysseus' field hands in the old days
this forester cared most for the estate;
and now Odysseus found him
in a remote clearing, sitting inside the gate
of a stockade he built to keep the swine
while his great lord was gone.
Working alone,
far from Penélopê and old Laërtês,
he had put up a fieldstone hut and timbered it
with wild pear wood. Dark hearts of oak he split
and trimmed for a high palisade around it,
and built twelve sties adjoining in this yard
to hold the livestock. Fifty sows with farrows
were penned in each, bedded upon the earth,
while the boars lay outside—fewer by far,
as those well-fatted were for the suitors' table,
fine pork, sent by the swineherd every day.
Three hundred sixty now lay there at night,
guarded by dogs—four dogs like wolves, one each
for the four lads the swineherd reared and kept
as under-herdsmen.
When Odysseus came,
the good servant sat shaping to his feet
oxhide for sandals, cutting the well-cured leather.
Three of his young men were afield, pasturing
herds in other woods; one he had sent
with a fat boar for tribute into town,
the boy to serve while the suitors got their fill.

The watch dogs, when they caught sight of Odysseus,
faced him, a snarling troop, and pelted out
viciously after him. Like a tricky beggar

he sat down plump, and dropped his stick. No use.
They would have rolled him in the dust and torn him
there by his own steading if the swineherd
had not sprung up and flung his leather down,
making a beeline for the open. Shouting,
throwing stone after stone,
he made them scatter; then turned to his lord
and said:
"You might have got a ripping, man!
Two shakes more and a pretty mess for me
you could have called it, if you had the breath.
As though I had not trouble enough already,
given me by the gods, my master gone,
true king hat he was. I hang on here,
still mourning for him, raising pigs of his
to feed foreigners, and who knows where the man is,
in some far country among strangers! Aye—
if he is living still, if he still sees the light of day.

Come to the cabin. You're a wanderer too.
You must eat something, drink some wine, and tell me
where you are from and the hard times you've seen."

The forester now led him to his hut
and made a couch for him, with tips of fir
piled for a mattress under a wild goat skin,
shaggy and thick, his own bed covering.
Odysseus,
in pleasure at this courtesy, gently said:
"May Zeus and all the gods give you your heart's desire
for taking me in so kindly, friend."

Eumaios—
O my swineherd![121] —answered him:
"Tush, friend,
rudeness to a stranger is not decency,
poor though he may be, poorer than you.
All wanderers
and beggars come from Zeus. What we can give
is slight but well-meant—all we dare. You know
that is the way of slaves, who live in dread

[121] **O my swineherd!:** The poet addresses Eumaios directly here, something he does only with Eumaios in *The Odyssey.* It may indicate a special feeling for the old swineherd.

of masters—new ones like our own.
I told you
the gods, long ago, hindered our lord's return.
He had a fondness for me, would have pensioned me
with acres of my own, a house, a wife
that other men admired and courted; all
gifts good-hearted kings bestow for service,
for a life work the bounty of god has prospered—
for it does prosper here, this work I do.
Had he grown old in his own house, my master
would have rewarded me. But the man's gone.
God curse the race of Helen and cut it down,
that wrung the strength out of the knees of many!
And he went, too—for the honor of Agamémnon
he took ship overseas for the wild horse country
of Troy, to fight the Trojans."

This being told,
he tucked his long shirt up inside his belt
and strode into the pens for two young porkers.
He slaughtered them and singed them at the fire,
flayed and quartered them, and skewered the meat
to broil it all; then gave it to Odysseus
hot on the spits. He shook out barley meal,
took a winebowl of ivy wood and filled it,
and sat down facing him, with a gesture, saying:
"There is your dinner, friend, the pork of slaves.
Our fat shoats[122] are all eaten by the suitors,
cold-hearted men, who never spare a thought
for how they stand in the sight of Zeus. The gods
living in bliss are fond of no wrongdoing,
but honor discipline and right behavior.
Even the outcasts of the earth, who bring
piracy from the sea, and bear off plunder
given by Zeus in shiploads—even those men
deep in their hearts tremble for heaven's eye.
But the suitors, now, have heard some word, some oracle
of my lord's death, being so unconcerned
to pay court properly or to go about their business.
All they want is to prey on his estate,
proud dogs: they stop at nothing. Not a day
goes by, and not a night comes under Zeus,

[122] **shoats:** Young, weaned pigs.

but they make butchery of our beeves and swine—
not one or two beasts at a time, either.
As for swilling down wine, they drink us dry.
Only a great domain like his could stand it—
greater than any on the dusky mainland
or here in Ithaka. Not twenty heroes
in the whole world were as rich as he. I know:
I could count it all up: twelve herds in Elis,
as many flocks, as many herds of swine,
and twelve wide ranging herds of goats, as well,
attended by his own men or by others—
out at the end of the island, eleven herds
are scattered now, with good men looking after them,
and every herdsman, every day, picks out
a prize ram to hand over to those fellows.
I too as overseer, keeper of swine,
must go through all my boars and send the best."

While he ran on, Odysseus with zeal
applied himself to the meat and wine, but inwardly
his thought shaped woe and ruin for the suitors.
When he had eaten all that he desired
and the cup he drank from had been filled again
with wine—a welcome sight—,
he spoke, and the words came light upon the air:
"Who is this lord who once acquired you,
so rich, so powerful, as you describe him?
You think he died for Agamémnon's honor.
Tell me his name: I may have met someone
of that description in my time. Who knows?
Perhaps only the immortal gods could say
if I should claim to have seen him: I have roamed
about the world so long."

The swineherd answered
as one who held a place of trust:

"Well, man,
his lady and his son will put no stock
in any news of him brought by a rover.
Wandering men tell lies for a night's lodging,
for fresh clothing; truth doesn't interest them.
Every time some traveller comes ashore
he has to tell my mistress his pretty tale,
and she receives him kindly, questions him,
remembering her prince, while the tears run

down her cheeks—and that is as it should be
when a woman's husband has been lost abroad.
I suppose you, too, can work your story up
at a moment's notice, given a shirt or cloak.
No: long ago wild dogs and carrion
birds, most like, laid bare his ribs on land
where life had left him. Or it may be, quick fishes
picked him clean in the deep sea, and his bones
lie mounded over in sand upon some shore.
One way or another, far from home he died,
a bitter loss, and pain, for everyone,
certainly for me. Never again shall I
have for my lot a master mild as he was
anywhere—not even with my parents
at home, where I was born and bred. I miss them
less than I do him—though a longing comes
to set my eyes on them in the old country.
No, it is the lost man I ache to think of—
Odysseus. And I speak the name respectfully,
even if he is not here. He loved me, cared for me.
I call him dear my lord, far though he be."

Now royal Odysseus, who had borne the long war,
spoke again:
"Friend, as you are so dead sure
he will not come—and so mistrustful, too—
let me not merely talk, as others talk,
but swear to it: your lord is now at hand.
And I expect a gift for this good news
when he enters his own hall. Till then I would not
take a rag, no matter what my need.
I hate as I hate Hell's own gate that weakness
that makes a poor man into a flatterer.
Zeus be my witness, and the table garnished
for true friends, and Odysseus' own hearth—
by heaven, all I say will come to pass!
He will return, and he will be avenged
on any who dishonor his wife and son."

Eumaios—O my swineherd!—answered him:
"I take you at your word, then: you shall have
no good news gift from me. Nor will Odysseus
enter his hall. But peace! drink up your wine.
Let us talk now of other things. No more
imaginings. It makes me heavy-hearted

when someone brings my master back to mind—
my own true master.
No, by heaven,
let us have no oaths! But if Odysseus
can come again god send he may! My wish
is that of Penélopê and old Laërtês
and Prince Telémakhos.
Ah, he's another
to be distressed about—Odysseus' child,
Telémakhos! By the gods' grace he grew
like a tough sapling, and I thought he'd be
no less a man than his great father—strong
and admirably made; but then someone,
god or man, upset him, made him rash,
so that he sailed away to sandy Pylos
to hear news of his father. Now the suitors
lie in ambush on his homeward track,
ready to cut away the last shoot of Arkêsios'
line, the royal stock of Ithaka.
No good
dwelling on it. Either he'll be caught
or else Kroníon's[123] hand will take him through.

Tell me, now, of your own trials and troubles.
And tell me truly first, for I should know,
who are you, where do you hail from, where's your home
and family? What kind of ship was yours,
and what course brought you here? Who are your sailors?
I don't suppose you walked here on the sea."

To this the master of improvisation answered:
"I'll tell you all that, clearly as I may.
If we could sit here long enough, with meat
and good sweet wine, warm here, in peace and quiet
within doors, while the work of the world goes on—
I might take all this year to tell my story
and never end the tale of misadventures
that wore my heart out, by the gods' will.

My native land is the wide seaboard of Krete
where I grew up. I had a wealthy father,
and many other sons were born to him

[123] **Kroníon:** Zeus, son of Kronos.

of his true lady. My mother was a slave,
his concubine; but Kastor Hylákidês,
my father, treated me as a true born son.
High honor came to him in that part of Krete
for wealth and ease, and sons born for renown,
before the death-bearing Kêrês drew him down
to the underworld. His avid sons thereafter
dividing up the property by lot
gave me a wretched portion, a poor house.
But my ability won me a wife
of rich family. Fool I was never called,
nor turn-tail in a fight.
My strength's all gone,
but from the husk you may divine the ear
that stood tall in the old days. Misery owns me
now, but then great Arês and Athena
gave me valor and man-breaking power,
whenever I made choice of men-at-arms
to set a trap with me for my enemies.
Never, as I am a man, did I fear Death
ahead, but went in foremost in the charge,
putting a spear through any man whose legs
were not as fast as mine. That was my element,
war and battle. Farming I never cared for,
nor life at home, nor fathering fair children.
I reveled in long ships with oars; I loved
polished lances, arrows in the skirmish,
the shapes of doom that others shake to see.
Carnage suited me; heaven put those things
in me somehow. Each to his own pleasure!
Before we young Akhaians shipped for Troy
I led men on nine cruises in corsairs
to raid strange coasts, and had great luck, taking
rich spoils on the spot, and even more
in the division. So my house grew prosperous,
my standing therefore high among the Kretans.
Then came the day when Zeus who views the wide world
drew men's eyes upon that way accurst
that wrung the manhood from the knees of many!
Everyone pressed me, pressed King Idómeneus
to take command of ships for Ilion.
No way out; the country rang with talk of it.
So we Akhaians had nine years of war.
In the tenth year we sacked the inner city,
Priam's town, and sailed for home; but heaven

dispersed the Akhaians. Evil days for me
were stored up in the hidden mind of Zeus.
One month, no more, I stayed at home in joy
with children, wife, and treasure. Lust for action
drove me to go to sea then, in command
of ships and gallant seamen bound for Egypt.
Nine ships I fitted out; my men signed on
and came to feast with me, as good shipmates,
for six full days. Many a beast I slaughtered
in the gods' honor, for my friends to eat.
Embarking on the seventh, we hauled sail
and filled away from Krete on a fresh north wind
effortlessly, as boats will glide down stream.
All rigging whole and all hands well, we rested,
letting the wind and steersmen work the ships,
for five days; on the fifth we made the delta.[124]
I brought my squadron in to the river bank
with one turn of the sweeps. There, heaven knows,
I told the men to wait and guard the ships
while I sent out patrols to rising ground.
But reckless greed carried them all away
to plunder the rich bottomlands; they bore off
wives and children, killed what men they found.

When this news reached the city, all who heard it
came at dawn. On foot they came, and horsemen,
filling the river plain with dazzle of bronze;
and Zeus lord of lightning
threw my men into blind panic: no one dared
stand against that host closing around us.
Their scything weapons left our dead in piles,
but some they took alive, into forced labor.
And I—ah, how I wish that I had died
in Egypt, on that field! So many blows
awaited me!—Well, Zeus himself inspired me;
I wrenched my dogskin helmet off my head,
dropped my spear, dodged out of my long shield,
ran for the king's chariot and swung on
to embrace and kiss his knees. He pulled me up,
took pity on me, placed me on the footboards,
and drove home with me crouching there in tears.

124 **the delta:** Of the Nile River.

Aye—for the troops, in battle fury still,
made one pass at me after another, pricking me
with spears, hoping to kill me. But he saved me,
for fear of the great wrath of Zeus that comes
when men who ask asylum are given death.

Seven years, then, my sojourn lasted there,
and I amassed a fortune, going about
among the openhanded Egyptians.
But when the eighth came round, a certain
Phoinikian adventurer came too,
a plausible rat, who had already done
plenty of devilry in the world.

This fellow
took me in completely with his schemes,
and led me with him to Phoinikia,
where he had land and houses. One full year
I stayed there with him, to the month and day,
and when fair weather came around again
he took me in a deepsea ship for Libya,
pretending I could help in the cargo trade;
he meant, in fact, to trade me off, and get
a high price for me. I could guess the game
but had to follow him aboard. One day
on course due west, off central Krete, the ship
caught a fresh norther, and we ran southward
before the wind while Zeus piled ruin ahead.
When Krete was out of sight astern, no land
anywhere to be seen, but sky and ocean,
Kroníon put a dark cloud in the zenith
over the ship, and gloom spread on the sea.
With crack on crack of thunder, he let fly
a bolt against the ship, a direct hit,
so that she bucked, in sacred fumes of sulphur,
and all the men were flung into the water.
They came up round the wreck, bobbing a while
like petrels on the waves. No homecoming
for these, from whom the god had turned his face!
Stunned in the smother as I was, yet Zeus
put into my hands the great mast of the ship—
a way to keep from drowning. So I twined
my arms and legs around it in the gale
and stayed afloat nine days. On the tenth night,

odysseus Tells another lie

a big surf cast me up in Thesprotia.[125]
Pheidon the king there gave me refuge, nobly,
with no talk of reward. His son discovered me
exhausted and half dead with cold, and gave me
a hand to bear me up till he reached home
where he could clothe me in a shirt and cloak.
In that king's house I heard news of Odysseus,
who lately was a guest there, passing by
on his way home, the king said; and he showed me
the treasure that Odysseus had brought:
bronze, gold, and iron wrought with heavy labor—
in that great room I saw enough to last
Odysseus' heirs for ten long generations.
The man himself had gone up to Dodona[126]
to ask the spelling leaves of the old oak
the will of God: how to return, that is,
to the rich realm of Ithaka, after so long
an absence—openly, or on the quiet.
And, tipping wine out, Pheidon swore to me
the ship was launched, the seamen standing by
to take Odysseus to his land at last.
But he had passage first for me: Thesprotians
were sailing, as luck had it, for Doulíkhion,[127]
the grain-growing island; there, he said,
they were to bring me to the king, Akastos.
Instead, that company saw fit to plot
foul play against me; in my wretched life
there was to be more suffering.
At sea, then,
when land lay far astern, they sprang their trap.
They'd make a slave of me that day, stripping
cloak and tunic off me, throwing around me
the dirty rags you see before you now.
At evening, off the fields of Ithaka,
they bound me, lashed me down under the decking
with stout ship's rope, while they all went ashore
in haste to make their supper on the beach.
The gods helped me to pry the lashing loose
until it fell away. I wound my rags
in a bundle round my head and eased myself

[125] **Thesprotia:** The west coast of the Greek mainland. [126] **Dodona:** Site of the most famous oracle of Zeus; the rustlings of oak leaves were interpreted as messages from the god. [127] **Doulíkhion:** An island off the west coast of Greece.

down the smooth lading plank into the water,
up to the chin, then swam an easy breast stroke
out and around, putting that crew behind,
and went ashore in underbrush, a thicket,
where I lay still, making myself small.
They raised a bitter yelling, and passed by
several times. When further groping seemed
useless to them, back to the ship they went
and out to sea again. The gods were with me,
keeping me hid; and with me when they brought me
here to the door of one who knows the world.
My destiny is yet to live awhile."

The swineherd bowed and said:
"Ah well, poor drifter,
you've made me sad for you, going back over it,
all your hard life and wandering. That tale
about Odysseus, though, you might have spared me;
you will not make me believe that.
Why must you lie, being the man you are,
and all for nothing?
I can see so well
what happened to my master, sailing home!
Surely the gods turned on him, to refuse him
death in the field, or in his friends' arms
after he wound up the great war at Troy.
They would have made a tomb for him, the Akhaians,
and paid all honor to his son thereafter. No,
stormwinds made off with him. No glory came to him.

I moved here to the mountain with my swine.
Never, now, do I go down to town
unless I am sent for by Penélopê
when news of some sort comes. But those who sit
around her go on asking the old questions—
a few who miss their master still,
and those who eat his house up, and go free.
For my part, I have had no heart for inquiry
since one year an Aitolian[128] made a fool of me.
Exiled from land to land after some killing,
he turned up at my door; I took him in.

[128] **Aitolian:** Aitolia is a section of central Greece.

My master he had seen in Krete, he said,
lodged with Idómeneus, while the long ships,
leaky from gales, were laid up for repairs.
But they were all to sail, he said, that summer,
or the first days of fall—hulls laden deep
with treasure, manned by crews of heroes.
This time
you are the derelict the Powers bring.
Well, give up trying to win me with false news
or flattery. If I receive and shelter you,
it is not for your tales but for your trouble,
and with an eye to Zeus, who guards a guest."

Then said that sly and guileful man, Odysseus:
"A black suspicious heart beats in you surely;
the man you are, not even an oath could change you.
Come then, we'll make a compact; let the gods
witness it from Olympos, where they dwell.
Upon your lord's homecoming, if he comes
here to this very hut, and soon—
then give me a new outfit, shirt and cloak,
and ship me to Doulíkhion—I thought it
a pleasant island. But if Odysseus
fails to appear as I predict, then Swish!
let the slaves pitch me down from some high rock,
so the next poor man who comes will watch his tongue."

The forester gave a snort and answered:
"Friend,
if I agreed to that, a great name
I should acquire in the world for goodness—
at one stroke and forever: your kind host
who gave you shelter and the hand of friendship,
only to take your life next day!
How confidently, after that, should I
address my prayers to Zeus, the son of Kronos!

It is time now for supper. My young herdsmen
should be arriving soon to set about it.
We'll make a quiet feast here at our hearth."

At this point in their talk the swine had come
up to the clearing, and the drovers followed
to pen them for the night—the porkers squealing

to high heaven, milling around the yard.
The swineherd then gave orders to his men:
"Bring in our best pig for a stranger's dinner.
A feast will do our hearts good, too; we know
grief and pain, hard scrabbling with our swine,
while the outsiders live on our labor."

Bronze
axe in hand, he turned to split up kindling,
while they drove in a tall boar, prime and fat,
planting him square before the fire. The gods,
as ever, had their due in the swineherd's thought,
for he it was who tossed the forehead bristles
as a first offering on the flames, calling
upon the immortal gods to let Odysseus
reach his home once more.
Then he stood up
and brained the boar with split oak from the woodpile.
Life ebbed from the beast; they slaughtered him,
singed the carcass, and cut out the joints.
Eumaios, taking flesh from every quarter,
put lean strips on the fat of sacrifice,
floured each one with barley meal, and cast it
into the blaze. The rest they sliced and skewered,
roasted with care, then took it off the fire
and heaped it up on platters. Now their chief,
who knew best the amenities, rose to serve,
dividing all that meat in seven portions—
one to be set aside, with proper prayers,
for the wood nymphs and Hermês, Maia's[129] son;
the others for the company. Odysseus
he honored with long slices from the chine—
warming the master's heart. Odysseus looked at him
and said:
"May you be dear to Zeus
as you are dear to me for this, Eumaios,
favoring with choice cuts a man like me."

And—O my swineherd!—you replied, Eumaios:
"Bless you, stranger, fall to and enjoy it
for what it is. Zeus grants us this or that,

[129] **Maia:** The goddess of spring is the oldest and loveliest of the Pleiades, the seven daughters of Atlas and Pleione.

or else refrains from granting, as he wills;
all things are in his power."

He cut and burnt
a morsel for the gods who are young forever,
tipped out some wine, then put it in the hands
of Odysseus, the old soldier, raider of cities,
who sat at ease now with his meat before him.
As for the loaves, Mesaúlios dealt them out,
a yard boy, bought by the swineherd on his own,
unaided by his mistress or Laërtês,
from Taphians, while Odysseus was away.
Now all hands reached for that array of supper,
until, when hunger and thirst were turned away
Mesaúlios removed the bread and, heavy
with food and drink, they settled back to rest.

Now night had come on, rough, with no moon,
but a nightlong downpour setting in, the rainwind
blowing hard from the west. Odysseus
began to talk, to test the swineherd, trying
to put it in his head to take his cloak off
and lend it, or else urge the others to.
He knew the man's compassion.

"Listen," he said,
"Eumaios, and you others, here's a wishful
tale that I shall tell. The wine's behind it,
vaporing wine, that makes a serious man
break down and sing, kick up his heels and clown,
or tell some story that were best untold.
But now I'm launched, I can't stop now.

Would god I felt
the hot blood in me that I had at Troy!
Laying an ambush near the walls one time,
Odysseus and Meneláos were commanders
and I ranked third. I went at their request.
We worked in toward the bluffs and battlements
and, circling the town, got into canebrakes,
thick and high, a marsh where we took cover,
hunched under arms.

The northwind dropped, and night
came black and wintry. A fine sleet descending
whitened the cane like hoarfrost, and clear ice
grew dense upon our shields. The other men,

all wrapt in blanket cloaks as well as tunics,
rested well, in shields up to their shoulders,
but I had left my cloak with friends in camp,
foolhardy as I was. No chance of freezing hard,
I thought, so I wore kilts and a shield only.
But in the small hours of the third watch, when stars
that rise at evening go down to their setting,
I nudged Odysseus, who lay close beside me;
he was alert then, listening, and I said:
'Son of Laërtês and the gods of old,
Odysseus, master mariner and soldier,
I cannot hold on long among the living.
The cold is making a corpse of me. Some god
inveigled me to come without a cloak.
No help for it now; too late.'

Next thing I knew
he had a scheme all ready in his mind—
and what a man he was for schemes and battles!
Speaking under his breath to me, he murmured:
'Quiet; none of the rest should hear you.'

Then,
propping his head on his forearm, he said:
'Listen, lads, I had an ominous dream,
the point being how far forward from our ships
and lines we've come. Someone should volunteer
to tell the corps commander, Agamémnon;
he may reinforce us from the base.'

At this,
Thoas jumped up, the young son of Andraimon,
put down his crimson cloak and headed off,
running shoreward.

Wrapped in that man's cloak
how gratefully I lay in the bitter dark
until the dawn came stitched in gold! I wish
I had that sap and fiber in me now!"

Then—O my swineherd!—you replied, Eumaios:
"That was a fine story, and well told,
not a word out of place, not a pointless word.
No, you'll not sleep cold for lack of cover,
or any other comfort one should give

to a needy guest. However, in the morning,
you must go flapping in the same old clothes.
Shirts and cloaks are few here; every man
has one change only. When our prince arrives,
the son of Odysseus, he will make you gifts—
cloak, tunic, everything—and grant you passage
wherever you care to go."

On this he rose
and placed the bed of balsam near the fire,
strewing sheepskins on top, and skins of goats.
Odysseus lay down. His host threw over him
a heavy blanket cloak, his own reserve
against the winter wind when it came wild.
So there Odysseus dropped off to sleep,
while herdsmen slept nearby. But not the swineherd:
not in the hut could he lie down in peace,
but now equipped himself for the night outside;
and this rejoiced Odysseus' heart, to see him
care for the herd so, while his lord was gone.
He hung a sharp sword from his shoulder, gathered
a great cloak round him, close, to break the wind,
and pulled a shaggy goatskin on his head.
Then, to keep at a distance dogs or men,
he took a sharpened lance, and went to rest
under a hollow rock where swine were sleeping
out of the wind and rain.

Book 15
How They Came to Ithaka

South into Lakedaimon
into the land where greens are wide for dancing
Athena went, to put in mind of home
her great-hearted hero's honored son,
rousing him to return.

And there she found him
with Nestor's lad in the late night at rest
under the portico of Meneláos,
the famous king. Stilled by the power of slumber
the son of Testor lay, but honeyed sleep
had not yet taken in her arms Telémakhos.
All through the starlit night, with open eyes,
he pondered what he had heard about his father,

until at his bedside grey-eyed Athena
towered and said:
"The brave thing now, Telémakhos,
would be to end this journey far from home.
All that you own you left behind
with men so lost to honor in your house
they may devour it all, shared out among them.
How will your journey save you then?
Go quickly
to the lord of the great war cry, Meneláos;
press him to send you back. You may yet find
the queen your mother in her rooms alone.
It seems her father and her kinsmen say
Eurýmakhos is the man for her to marry.
He has outdone the suitors, all the rest,
in gifts to her, and made his pledges double.
Check him, or he will have your lands and chattels
in spite of you.
You know a woman's pride
at bringing riches to the man she marries.
As to her girlhood husband, her first children,
he is forgotten, being dead—and they
no longer worry her.
So act alone.
Go back; entrust your riches to the servant
worthiest in your eyes, until the gods
make known what beauty you yourself shall marry.

This too I have to tell you: now take heed:
the suitors' ringleaders are hot for murder,
waiting in the channel between Ithaka
and Samê's rocky side; they mean to kill you
before you can set foot ashore. I doubt
they'll bring it off. Dark earth instead
may take to her cold bed a few brave suitors
who preyed upon your cattle.
Bear well out
in your good ship, to eastward of the islands,
and sail again by night. Someone immortal
who cares for you will make a fair wind blow.
Touch at the first beach, go ashore, and send
your ship and crew around to port by sea,
while you go inland to the forester,
your old friend, loyal keeper of the swine.
Remain that night with him; send him to town

to tell your watchful mother Penélopê
that you are back from Pylos safe and sound."

With this Athena left him for Olympos.
He swung his foot across and gave a kick
and said to the son of Nestor:
"Open your eyes,
Peisístratos. Get our team into harness.
We have a long day's journey."

Nestor's son
turned over and answered him:
"It is still night,
and no moon. Can we drive now? We can not,
itch as we may for the road home. Dawn is near.
Allow the captain of spearmen, Meneláos,
time to pack our car with gifts and time
to speak a gracious word, sending us off.
A guest remembers all his days
that host who makes provision for him kindly."

The Dawn soon took her throne of gold, and Lord
Meneláos, clarion in battle,
rose from where he lay beside the beauty
of Helen with her shining hair. He strode
into the hall nearby.
Hearing him come,
Odysseus' son pulled on his snowy tunic
over the skin, gathered his long cape
about his breadth of shoulder like a captain,
the heir of King Odysseus. At the door
he stood and said:
"Lord Marshal, Meneláos,
send me home now to my own dear country:
longing has come upon me to go home."

The lord of the great war cry said at once:
"If you are longing to go home, Telémakhos,
I would not keep you for the world, not I.
I'd think myself or any other host
as ill-mannered for over-friendliness
as for hostility.
Measure is best in everything.
To send a guest packing, or cling to him
when he's in haste—one sin equals the other.

'Good entertaining ends with no detaining.'
Only let me load your car with gifts
and fine ones, you shall see.
I'll bid the women
set out breakfast from the larder stores;
honor and appetite—we'll attend to both
before a long day's journey overland.
Or would you care to try the Argive midlands
and Hellas, in my company? I'll harness
my own team, and take you through the towns.
Guests like ourselves no lord will turn away;
each one will make one gift, at least,
to carry home with us: tripod or cauldron
wrought in bronze, mule team, or golden cup."

Clearheaded Telémakhos replied:
"Lord Marshal
Meneláos, royal son of Atreus,
I must return to my own hearth. I left
no one behind as guardian of my property.
This going abroad for news of a great father—
heaven forbid it be my own undoing,
or any precious thing be lost at home."

At this the tall king, clarion in battle,
called to his lady and her waiting women
to give them breakfast from the larder stores.
Eteóneus, the son of Boethoös, came
straight from bed, from where he lodged nearby,
and Meneláos ordered a fire lit
for broiling mutton. The king's man obeyed.
Then down to the cedar chamber Meneláos
walked with Helen and Prince Megapénthês.
Amid the gold he had in that place lying
the son of Atreus picked a wine cup, wrought
with handles left and right, and told his son
to take a silver winebowl.
Helen lingered
near the deep coffers filled with gowns, her own
handiwork.
Tall goddess among women,
she lifted out one robe of state so royal,
adorned and brilliant with embroidery,
deep in the chest it shimmered like a star.
Now all three turned back to the door to greet

Telémakhos. And red-haired Meneláos
cried out to him:
"O prince Telémakhos,
may Hêra's Lord of Thunder see you home
and bring you to the welcome you desire!
Here are your gifts—perfect and precious things
I wish to make your own, out of my treasure."

And gently the great captain, son of Atreus,
handed him the goblet. Megapénthês
carried the winebowl glinting silvery
to set before him, and the Lady Helen
drew near, so that he saw her cheek's pure line.
She held the gown and murmured:
"I, too,
bring you a gift, dear child, and here it is;
remember Helen's hands by this; keep it
for your own bride, your joyful wedding day;
let your dear mother guard it in her chamber.
My blessing: may you come soon to your island,
home to your timbered hall."

So she bestowed it,
and happily he took it. These fine things
Peisístratos packed well in the wicker carrier,
admiring every one. Then Meneláos
led the two guests in to take their seats
on thrones and easy chairs in the great hall.
Now came a maid to tip a golden jug
of water over a silver finger bowl,
and draw the polished tables up beside them;
the larder mistress brought her tray of loaves,
with many savories to lavish on them;
viands were served by Eteóneus, and wine
by Meneláos' son. Then every hand
reached out upon good meat and drink to take them,
driving away hunger and thirst. At last,
Telémakhos and Nestor's son led out
their team to harness, mounted their bright car,
and drove down under the echoing entrance way,
while red-haired Meneláos, Atreus' son,
walked alongside with a golden cup—
wine for the wayfarers to spill at parting.
Then by the tugging team he stood, and spoke

over the horses' heads:
"Farewell, my lads.
Homage to Nestor, the benevolent king;
in my time he was fatherly to me,
when the flower of Akhaia warred on Troy."

Telémakhos made this reply:
"No fear
but we shall bear at least as far as Nestor
your messages, great king. How I could wish
to bring them home to Ithaka! If only
Odysseus were there, if he could hear me tell
of all the courtesy I have had from you,
returning with your finery and your treasure."

Even as he spoke, a beat of wings went skyward
off to the right—a mountain eagle, grappling
a white goose in his talons, heavy prey
hooked from a farmyard. Women and men-at-arms
made hubbub, running up, as he flew over,
but then he wheeled hard right before the horses—
a sight that made the whole crowd cheer, with hearts
lifting in joy. Peisístratos called out:
"Read us the sign, O Meneláos, Lord
Marshal of armies! Was the god revealing
something thus to you, or to ourselves?"

At this the old friend of the god of battle
groped in his mind for the right thing to say,
but regal Helen put in quickly:
"Listen:
I can tell you—tell what the omen means,
as light is given me, and as I see it
point by point fulfilled. The beaked eagle
flew from the wild mountain of his fathers
to take for prey the tame house bird. Just so,
Odysseus, back from his hard trials and wandering,
will soon come down in fury on his house.
He may be there today, and a black hour
he brings upon the suitors."

Telémakhos
gazed and said:
"May Zeus, the lord of Hêra,

make it so! In far-off Ithaka, all my life,
I shall invoke you as a goddess, lady."

He let the whip fall, and the restive mares
broke forward at a canter through the town
into the open country.
All that day
they kept their harness shaking, side by side,
until at sundown when the roads grew dim
they made a halt at Pherai. There Dióklês
son of Ortílokhos whom Alpheios fathered,
welcomed the young men, and they slept the night.
Up when the young Dawn's finger tips of rose
opened in the east, they hitched the team
once more to the painted car
and steered out westward through the echoing gate,
whipping their fresh horses into a run.
Approaching Pylos Height at that day's end,
Telémakhos appealed to the son of Nestor:
"Could you, I wonder, do a thing I'll tell you,
supposing you agree?
We take ourselves to be true friends—in age
alike, and bound by ties between our fathers,
and now by partnership in this adventure.
Prince, do not take me roundabout,
but leave me at the ship, else the old king
your father will detain me overnight
for love of guests, when I should be at sea."

The son of Nestor nodded, thinking swiftly
how best he could oblige his friend.
Here was his choice: to pull the team hard over
along the beach till he could rein them in
beside the ship. Unloading Meneláos'
royal keepsakes into the stern sheets,
he sang out:
"Now for action! Get aboard,
and call your men, before I break the news
at home in hall to father. Who knows better
the old man's heart than I? If you delay,
he will not let you go, but he'll descend on you
in person and imperious; no turning

back with empty hands for him, believe me,
once his blood is up."

He shook the reins
to the lovely mares with long manes in the wind,
guiding them full tilt toward his father's hall.
Telémakhos called in the crew, and told them:
"Get everything shipshape aboard this craft;
we pull out now, and put sea miles behind us."

The listening men obeyed him, climbing in
to settle on their benches by the rowlocks,
while he stood watchful by the stern. He poured out
offerings there, and prayers to Athena.

Now a strange man came up to him, an easterner
fresh from spilling blood in distant Argos,
a hunted man. Gifted in prophecy,[130]
he had as forebear that Melampous, wizard
who lived of old in Pylos, mother city
of western flocks.

Melampous, a rich lord,
had owned a house unmatched among the Pylians,
until the day came when king Neleus, noblest
in that age, drove him from his native land.
And Neleus for a year's term sequestered
Melampous' fields and flocks, while he lay bound
hand and foot in the keep of Phylakos.
Beauty of Neleus' daughter put him there
and sombre folly the inbreaking Fury
thrust upon him. But he gave the slip
to death, and drove the bellowing herd of Iphiklos
from Phylakê to Pylos, there to claim
the bride that ordeal won him from the king.
He led her to his brother's house, and went on

[130] **a strange man . . . prophecy:** Melampous was a famous soothsayer; the purpose of the following complicated passage is to provide a genealogical connection between Melampous and Theoklýmenos, the young man who approaches Telémakhos. Melampous was imprisoned when he tried to steal Phylakos's cattle so that his brother could pay the bride-price for King Neleus's daughter. When Melampous prophesied the collapse of a roof, Phylakos released him and gave him the cattle. The bride-price was paid, the brother received the bride, and Melampous moved to Argos.

eastward into another land, the bluegrass
plain of Argos. Destiny held for him
rule over many Argives. Here he married,
built a great manor house, fathered Antíphatês
and Mantios, commanders both, of whom
Antíphatês begot Oikleiês
and Oikleiês the firebrand Amphiaraos.
This champion the lord of stormcloud, Zeus,
and strong Apollo loved; nor had he ever
to cross the doorsill into dim old age.
A woman, bought by trinkets, gave him over
to be cut down in the assault on Thebes.
His sons were Alkmáon and Amphílokhos.
In the meantime Lord Mantios begot
Polypheidês, the prophet, and
Kleitos—famous name! For Dawn in silks
of gold carried off Kleitos for his beauty
to live among the gods. But Polypheidês,
high-hearted and exalted by Apollo
above all men for prophecy, withdrew
to Hyperesia[131] when his father angered him.
He lived on there, foretelling to the world
the shape of things to come.
His son it was,
Theoklýmenos, who came upon Telémakhos
as he poured out the red wine in the sand
near his trim ship, with prayer to Athena:
and he called out, approaching:
"Friend, well met
here at libation before going to sea.
I pray you by the wine you spend, and by
your god, your own life, and your company;
enlighten me, and let the truth be known.
Who are you? Of what city and what parents?"

Telémakhos turned to him and replied:
"Stranger, as truly as may be, I'll tell you.
I am from Ithaka, where I was born;
my father is, or he once was, Odysseus.
But he's a long time gone, and dead, may be;

[131] **Hyperesia:** In the vicinity of Argos.

and that is what I took ship with my friends
to find out—for he left long years ago."

Said Theoklýmenos in reply:
"I too
have had to leave my home. I killed a cousin.
In the wide grazing lands of Argos live
many kinsmen of his and friends in power,
great among the Akhaians. These I fled.
Death and vengeance at my back, as Fate
has turned now, I came wandering overland.
Give me a plank aboard your ship, I beg,
or they will kill me. They are on my track."

Telémakhos made answer:
"No two ways
about it. Will I pry you from our gunnel
when you are desperate to get to sea?
Come aboard; share what we have, and welcome."

He took the bronze-shod lance from the man's hand
and laid it down full-length on deck; then swung
his own weight after it aboard the cutter,
taking position aft, making a place
for Theoklýmenos near him. The stern lines
were slacked off, and Telémakhos commanded:
"Rig the mast; make sail!" Nimbly they ran
to push the fir pole high and step it firm
amidships in the box, make fast the forestays,
and hoist aloft the white sail on its halyards.
A following wind came down from grey-eyed Athena,
blowing brisk through heaven, and so steady
the cutter lapped up miles of salt blue sea,
passing Krounoi abeam and Khalkis estuary
at sundown when the sea ways all grew dark.
Then, by Athena's wind borne on, the ship
rounded Pheai by night and coasted Elis,[132]
the green domain of the Epeioi; thence
he put her head north toward the running pack

[132] **passing Krounoi . . . Elis:** The exact location of Krounoi and Khalkis is not known; Elis is the site of the Olympics on the west coast of the Peloponnese.

of islets, wondering if by sailing wide
he sheered off Death, or would be caught.

That night
Odysseus and the swineherd supped again
with herdsmen in their mountain hut. At ease
when appetite and thirst were turned away,
Odysseus, while he talked, observed the swineherd
to see if he were hospitable still—
if yet again the man would make him stay
under his roof, or send him off to town.

"Listen," he said, "Eumaios; listen, lads.
At daybreak I must go and try my luck
around the port. I burden you too long.
Direct me, put me on the road with someone.
Nothing else for it but to play the beggar
in populous parts. I'll get a cup or loaf,
maybe from some householder. If I go
as far as the great hall of King Odysseus
I might tell Queen Penélopê my news.
Or I can drift inside among the suitors
to see what alms they give, rich as they are.
If they have whims, I'm deft in ways of service—
that I can say, and you may know for sure.
By grace of Hermês the Wayfinder, patron
of mortal tasks, the god who honors toil,
no man can do a chore better than I can.
Set me to build a fire, or chop wood,
cook or carve, mix wine and serve—or anything
inferior men attend to for the gentry."

Now you were furious at this, Eumaios,
and answered—O my swineherd!—
"Friend, friend,
how could this fantasy take hold of you?
You dally with your life, and nothing less,
if you feel drawn to mingle in that company—
reckless, violent, and famous for it
out to the rim of heaven. Slaves
they have, but not like you. No—theirs are boys
in fresh cloaks and tunics with pomade
ever on their sleek heads, and pretty faces.
These are their minions, while their tables gleam
and groan under big roasts, with loaves and wine.

Stay with us here. No one is burdened by you,
neither myself nor any of my hands.
Wait here until Odysseus' son returns.
You shall have clothing from him, cloak and tunic,
and passage where your heart desires to go."

The noble and enduring man replied:
"May you be dear to Zeus for this, Eumaios,
even as you are to me. Respite from pain
you give me—and from homelessness. In life
there's nothing worse than knocking about the world,
no bitterness we vagabonds are spared
when the curst belly rages! Well, you master it
and me, making me wait for the king's son.
But now, come, tell me:
what of Odysseus' mother, and his father
whom he took leave of on the sill of age?
Are they under the sun's rays, living still,
or gone down long ago to lodge with Death?"

To this the rugged herdsman answered:
"Aye,
that I can tell you; it is briefly told.
Laërtês lives, but daily in his hall
prays for the end of life and soul's delivery,
heartbroken as he is for a son long gone
and for his lady. Sorrow, when she died,
aged and enfeebled him like a green tree stricken;
but pining for her son, her brilliant son,
wore out her life.
Would god no death so sad
might come to benefactors dear as she!
I loved always to ask and hear about her
while she lived, although she lived in sorrow.
For she had brought me up with her own daughter,
Princess Ktimenê, her youngest child.
We were alike in age and nursed as equals
nearly, till in the flower of our years
they gave her, married her, to a Samian prince,
taking his many gifts. For my own portion
her mother gave new clothing, cloak and sandals,
and sent me to the woodland. Well she loved me.
Ah, how I miss that family! It is true
the blissful gods prosper my work; I have
meat and drink to spare for those I prize;

but so removed I am, I have no speech
with my sweet mistress, now that evil days
and overbearing men darken her house.
Tenants all hanker for good talk and gossip
around their lady, and a snack in hall,
a cup or two before they take the road
to their home acres, each one bearing home
some gift to cheer his heart."

The great tactician
answered:
"You were still a child, I see,
when exiled somehow from your parents' land.
Tell me, had it been sacked in war, the city
of spacious ways in which they made their home,
your father and your gentle mother? Or
were you kidnapped alone, brought here by sea
huddled with sheep in some foul pirate squadron,
to this landowner's hall? He paid your ransom?"

The master of the woodland answered:
"Friend,
now that you show an interest in that matter,
attend me quietly, be at your ease,
and drink your wine. These autumn nights are long,
ample for story-telling and for sleep.
You need not go to bed before the hour;
sleeping from dusk to dawn's a dull affair.
Let any other here who wishes, though,
retire to rest. At daybreak let him breakfast
and take the king's own swine into the wilderness.
Here's a tight roof; we'll drink on, you and I,
and ease our hearts of hardships we remember,
sharing old times. In later days a man
can find a charm in old adversity,
exile and pain. As to your question, now:

A certain island, Syriê by name—
you may have heard the name—lies off Ortýgia[133]
due west, and holds the sunsets of the year.
Not very populous, but good for grazing

[133] **Ortýgia:** The name of a small island on the east coast of Sicily, but Ortýgia might be the island of Delos.

sheep and kine; rich too in wine and grain.
No dearth is ever known there, no disease
wars on the folk, of ills that plague mankind;
but when the townsmen reach old age, Apollo
with his longbow of silver comes, and Artemis,
showering arrows of mild death.
Two towns
divide the farmlands of that whole domain,
and both were ruled by Ktêsios, my father,
Orménos' heir, and a great godlike man.

Now one day some of those renowned seafaring
men, sea-dogs, Phoinikians, came ashore
with bags of gauds for trading. Father had
in our household a woman of Phoinikia,
a handsome one, and highly skilled. Well, she
gave in to the seductions of those rovers.
One of them found her washing near the mooring
and lay with her, making such love to her
as women in their frailty are confused by,
even the best of them.
In due course, then,
he asked her who she was and where she hailed from:
and nodding toward my father's roof, she said:
'I am of Sidon town, smithy of bronze
for all the East. Arubas Pasha's daughter.
Taphian pirates caught me in a byway
and sold me into slavery overseas
in this man's home. He could afford my ransom.'

The sailor who had lain with her replied:
'Why not ship out with us on the run homeward,
and see your father's high-roofed hall again,
your father and your mother? Still in Sidon
and still rich, they are said to be.'

She answered:
'It could be done, that, if you sailors take
oath I'll be given passage home unharmed.'

Well, soon she had them swearing it all pat
as she desired, repeating every syllable,
whereupon she warned them:
'Not a word
about our meeting here! Never call out to me

when any of you see me in the lane
or at the well. Some visitor might bear
tales to the old man. If he guessed the truth,
I'd be chained up, your lives would be in peril.
No: keep it secret. Hurry with your peddling,
and when your hold is filled with livestock, send
a message to me at the manor hall.
Gold I'll bring, whatever comes to hand,
and something else, too, as my passage fee—
the master's child, my charge: a boy so high,
bright for his age; he runs with me on errands.
I'd take him with me happily; his price
would be I know not what in sale abroad.'

Her bargain made, she went back to the manor.
But they were on the island all that year,
getting by trade a cargo of our cattle;
until, the ship at length being laden full,
ready for sea, they sent a messenger
to the Phoinikian woman. Shrewd he was,
this fellow who came round my father's hall,
showing a golden chain all strung with amber,
a necklace. Maids in waiting and my mother
passed it from hand to hand, admiring it,
engaging they would buy it. But that dodger,
as soon as he had caught the woman's eye
and nodded, slipped away to join the ship.
She took my hand and led me through the court
into the portico. There by luck she found
winecups and tables still in place—for Father's
attendant counselors had dined just now
before they went to the assembly. Quickly
she hid three goblets in her bellying dress
to carry with her while I tagged along
in my bewilderment. The sun went down
and all the lanes grew dark as we descended,
skirting the harbor in our haste to where
those traders of Phoinikia held their ship.
All went aboard at once and put to sea,
taking the two of us. A favoring wind
blew from the power of heaven. We sailed on
six nights and days without event. Then Zeus
the son of Kronos added one more noon—and sudden
arrows from Artemis pierced the woman's heart.

Stone-dead she dropped
into the sloshing bilge the way a tern
plummets; and the sailors heaved her over
as tender pickings for the seals and fish.
Now I was left in dread, alone, while wind
and current bore them on to Ithaka.
Laërtês purchased me. That was the way
I first laid eyes upon this land."

Odysseus,
the kingly man, replied:
"You rouse my pity,
telling what you endured when you were young.
But surely Zeus put good alongside ill:
torn from your own far home, you had the luck
to come into a kind man's service, generous
with food and drink. And a good life you lead,
unlike my own, all spent in barren roaming
from one country to the next, till now."

So the two men talked on, into the night,
leaving few hours for sleep before the Dawn
stepped up to her bright chair.
The ship now drifting
under the island lee, Telémakhos'
companions took in sail and mast, unshipped
the oars and rowed ashore. They moored her stern
by the stout hawser lines, tossed out the bow stones,
and waded in beyond the wash of ripples
to mix their wine and cook their morning meal.
When they had turned back hunger and thirst, Telémakhos
arose to give the order of the day.

"Pull for the town," he said, "and berth our ship,
while I go inland across country. Later,
this evening, after looking at my farms,
I'll join you in the city. When day comes
I hope to celebrate our crossing, feasting
everyone on good red meat and wine."

His noble passenger, Theoklýmenos,
now asked:
"What as to me, my dear young fellow,
where shall I go? Will I find lodging here

with some one of the lords of stony Ithaka?
Or go straight to your mother's hall and yours?"

Telémakhos turned round to him and said:
"I should myself invite you to our hall
if things were otherwise; there'd be no lack
of entertainment for you. As it stands,
no place could be more wretched for a guest
while I'm away. Mother will never see you;
she almost never shows herself at home
to the suitors there, but stays in her high chamber
weaving upon her loom. No, let me name
another man for you to go to visit:
Eurýmakhos, the honored son of Pólybos.
In Ithaka they are dazzled by him now—
the strongest of their princes, bent on making
mother and all Odysseus' wealth his own.
Zeus on Olympos only knows
if some dark hour for them will intervene."

The words were barely spoken, when a hawk,
Apollo's courier, flew up on the right,
clutching a dove and plucking her—so feathers
floated down to the ground between Telémakhos
and the moored cutter. Theoklýmenos
called him apart and gripped his hand, whispering:
"A god spoke in this bird-sign on the right.
I knew it when I saw the hawk fly over us.
There is no kinglier house than yours, Telémakhos,
here in the realm of Ithaka. Your family
will be in power forever."

The young prince,
clear in spirit, answered:
"Be it so,
friend, as you say. And may you know as well
the friendship of my house, and many gifts
from me, so everyone may call you fortunate."

He called a trusted crewman named Peiraios,
and said to him:
"Peiraios, son of Klýtios,
can I rely on you again as ever, most
of all the friends who sailed with me to Pylos?

Take this man home with you, take care of him,
treat him with honor, till I come."

To this
Peiraios the good spearman answered:
"Aye,
stay in the wild country while you will,
I shall be looking after him, Telémakhos.
He will not lack good lodging."

Down to the ship
he turned, and boarded her, and called the others
to cast off the stern lines and come aboard.
So men climbed in to sit beside the rowlocks.
Telémakhos now tied his sandals on
and lifted his tough spear from the ship's deck;
hawsers were taken in, and they shoved off
to reach the town by way of the open sea
as he commanded them—royal Odysseus'
own dear son, Telémakhos.
On foot
and swiftly he went up toward the stockade
where swine were penned in hundreds, and at night
the guardian of the swine, the forester,
slept under arms on duty for his masters.

Book 16
Father and Son

But there were two men in the mountain hut—
Odysseus and the swineherd. At first light
blowing their fire up, they cooked their breakfast
and sent their lads out, driving herds to root
in the tall timber.
When Telémakhos came,
the wolvish troop of watchdogs only fawned on him
as he advanced. Odysseus heard them go
and heard the light crunch of a man's footfall—
at which he turned quickly to say:
"Eumaios,
here is one of your crew come back, or maybe
another friend: the dogs are out there snuffling

belly down; not one has even growled.
I can hear footsteps—"

But before he finished
his tall son stood at the door.
The swineherd
rose in surprise, letting a bowl and jug
tumble from his fingers. Going forward,
he kissed the young man's head, his shining eyes
and both hands, while his own tears brimmed and fell.
Think of a man whose dear and only son,
born to him in exile, reared with labor,
has lived ten years abroad and now returns:
how would that man embrace his son! Just so
the herdsman clapped his arms around Telémakhos
and covered him with kisses—for he knew
the lad had got away from death. He said:
"Light of my days, Telémakhos,
you made it back! When you took ship for Pylos
I never thought to see you here again.
Come in, dear child, and let me feast my eyes;
here you are, home from the distant places!
How rarely anyway, you visit us,
your own men, and your own woods and pastures!
Always in the town, a man would think
you loved the suitors' company, those dogs!"

Telémakhos with his clear candor said:
"I am with you, Uncle. See now, I have come
because I wanted to see you first, to hear from you
if Mother stayed at home—or is she married
off to someone and Odysseus' bed
left empty for some gloomy spider's weaving?"

Gently the forester replied to this:
"At home indeed your mother is, poor lady,
still in the women's hall. Her nights and days
are wearied out with grieving."

Stepping back
he took the bronze-shod lance, and the young prince
entered the cabin over the worn door stone.
Odysseus moved aside, yielding his couch,
but from across the room Telémakhos checked him:

"Friend, sit down; we'll find another chair
in our own hut. Here is the man to make one!"

The swineherd, when the quiet man sank down,
built a new pile of evergreens and fleeces—
a couch for the dear son of great Odysseus—
then gave them trenchers of good meat, left over
from the roast pork of yesterday, and heaped up
willow baskets full of bread, and mixed
an ivy bowl of honey-hearted wine.
Then he in turn sat down, facing Odysseus,
their hands went out upon the meat and drink
as they fell to, ridding themselves of hunger,
until Telémakhos paused and said:
"Oh, Uncle,
what's your friend's home port? How did he come?
Who ere the sailors brought him here to Ithaka?
I doubt if he came walking on the sea."

And you replied, Eumaios—O my swineherd—
"Son, the truth about him is soon told.
His home land, and a broad land, too, is Krete,
but he has knocked about the world, he says,
for years, as the Powers wove his life. Just now
he broke away from a shipload of Thesprotians
to reach my hut. I place him in your hands.
Act as you will. He wishes your protection."

The young man said:
"Eumaios, my protection!
The notion cuts me to the heart. How can I
receive your friend at home? I am not old enough
or trained in arms. Could I defend myself
if someone picked a fight with me?
Besides,
mother is in a quandary, whether to stay with me
as mistress of our household, honoring
her lord's bed, and opinion in the town,
or take the best Akhaian who comes her way—
the one who offers most.
I'll undertake,
at all events, to clothe your friend for winter,
now he is with you. Tunic and cloak of wool,
a good broadsword, and sandals—these are his.

I can arrange to send him where he likes
or you may keep him in your cabin here.
I shall have bread and wine sent up; you need not
feel any pinch on his behalf.
Impossible
to let him stay in hall, among the suitors.
They are drunk, drunk on impudence, they might
injure my guest—and how could I bear that?
How could a single man take on those odds?
Not even a hero could.
The suitors are too strong."

At this the noble and enduring man, Odysseus,
addressed his son:
"Kind prince, it may be fitting
for me to speak a word. All that you say
gives me an inward wound as I sit listening.
I mean this wanton game they play, these fellows,
riding roughshod over you in your own house,
admirable as you are. But tell me,
are you resigned to being bled? The townsmen,
stirred up against you, are they, by some oracle?
Your brothers—can you say your brothers fail you?
A man should feel his kin, at least, behind him
in any clash, when a real fight is coming.
If my heart were as young as yours, if I were
son to Odysseus, or the man himself,
I'd rather have my head cut from my shoulders
by some slashing adversary, if I
brought no hurt upon that crew! Suppose
I went down, being alone, before the lot,
better, I say, to die at home in battle
than see these insupportable things, day after
day the stranger cuffed, the women slaves
dragged here and there, shame in the lovely rooms,
the wine drunk up in rivers, sheer waste
of pointless feasting, never at an end!"

Telémakhos replied:
"Friend, I'll explain to you.
There is no rancor in the town against me,
no fault of brothers, whom a man should feel
behind him when a fight is in the making;

no, no — in our family the First Born
of Heaven, Zeus, made single sons the rule.
Arkeísios had but one, Laërtês; he
in his turn fathered only one, Odysseus,
who left me in his hall alone, too young
to be of any use to him.
And so you see why enemies fill our house
in these days: all the princes of the islands,
Doulíkhion, Samê, wooded Zakýnthos,
Ithaka too — lords of our island rock —
eating our house up as they court my mother.
She cannot put an end to it; she dare not
bar the marriage that she hates; and they
devour all my substance and my cattle,
and who knows when they'll slaughter me as well?
It rests upon the gods' great knees.
Uncle,
go down at once and tell the Lady Penélopê
that I am back from Pylos, safe and sound.
I stay here meanwhile. You will give your message
and then return. Let none of the Akhaians
hear it; they have a mind to do me harm."

To this, Eumaios, you replied:
"I know.
But make this clear, now — should I not likewise
call on Laërtês with your news? Hard hit
by sorrow though he was, mourning Odysseus,
he used to keep an eye upon his farm.
He had what meals he pleased, with his own folk.
But now no more, not since you sailed for Pylos;
he has not taken food or drink, I hear,
sitting all day, blind to the work of harvest,
groaning, while the skin shrinks on his bones."

Telémakhos answered:
"One more misery,
but we had better leave it so.
If men could choose, and have their choice, in everything,
we'd have my father home.
Turn back
when you have done your errand, as you must,
not to be caught alone in the countryside.

But wait—you may tell Mother
to send our old housekeeper on the quiet
and quickly; she can tell the news to Grandfather."

The swineherd, roused, reached out to get his sandals,
tied them on, and took the road.

Who else
beheld this but Athena? From the air
she walked, taking the form of a tall woman,
handsome and clever at her craft, and stood
beyond the gate in plain sight of Odysseus,
unseen, though, by Telémakhos, unguessed,
for not to everyone will gods appear.
Odysseus noticed her; so did the dogs,
who cowered whimpering away from her. She only
nodded, signing to him with her brows,
a sign he recognized. Crossing the yard,
he passed out through the gate in the stockade
to face the goddess. There she said to him:
"Son of Laërtês and the gods of old,
Odysseus, master of land ways and sea ways,
dissemble to your son no longer now.
The time has come: tell him how you together
will bring doom on the suitors in the town.
I shall not be far distant then, for I
myself desire battle."

Saying no more,
she tipped her golden wand upon the man,
making his cloak pure white and the knit tunic
fresh around him. Lithe and young she made him,
ruddy with sun, his jawline clean, the beard
no longer grew upon his chin. And she
withdrew when she had done.

Then Lord Odysseus
reappeared—and his son was thunderstruck.
Fear in his eyes, he looked down and away
as though it were a god, and whispered:

"Stranger,
you are no longer what you were just now!
Your cloak is new; even your skin! You are
one of the gods who rule the sweep of heaven!

Be kind to us, we'll make you fair oblation
and gifts of hammered gold. Have mercy on us!"

The noble and enduring man replied:
"No god. Why take me for a god? No, no.
I am that father whom your boyhood lacked
and suffered pain for lack of. I am he."

Held back too long, the tears ran down his cheeks
as he embraced his son.
Only Telémakhos,
uncomprehending, wild
with incredulity, cried out:
"You cannot
be my father Odysseus! Meddling spirits
conceived this trick to twist the knife in me!
No man of woman born could work these wonders
by his own craft, unless a god came into it
with ease to turn him young or old at will.
I swear you were in rags and old,
and here you stand like one of the immortals!"

Odysseus brought his ranging mind to bear
and said:
"This is not princely, to be swept
away by wonder at your father's presence.
No other Odysseus will ever come,
for he and I are one, the same; his bitter
fortune and his wanderings are mine.
Twenty years gone, and I am back again
on my own island.
As for my change of skin,
that is a charm Athena, Hope of Soldiers,
uses as she will; she has the knack
to make me seem a beggar man sometimes
and sometimes young, with finer clothes about me.
It is no hard thing for the gods of heaven
to glorify a man or bring him low."

When he had spoken, down he sat.
Then, throwing
his arms around this marvel of a father
Telémakhos began to weep. Salt tears

rose from the wells of longing in both men,
and cries burst from both as keen and fluttering
as those of the great taloned hawk,
whose nestlings farmers take before they fly.
So helplessly they cried, pouring out tears,
and might have gone on weeping so till sundown,
had not Telémakhos said:
"Dear father! Tell me
what kind of vessel put you here ashore
on Ithaka? Your sailors, who were they?
I doubt you made it, walking on the sea!"

Then said Odysseus, who had borne the barren sea:
"Only plain truth shall I tell you, child.
Great seafarers, the Phaiákians, gave me passage
as they give other wanderers. By night
over the open ocean, while I slept,
they brought me in their cutter, set me down
on Ithaka, with gifts of bronze and gold
and stores of woven things. By the gods' will
these lie all hidden in a cave. I came
to this wild place, directed by Athena,
so that we might lay plans to kill our enemies.
Count up the suitors for me, let me know
what men at arms are there, how many men.
I must put all my mind to it, to see
if we two by ourselves can take them on
or if we should look round for help."

Telémakhos
replied:
"O Father, all my life your fame
as a fighting man has echoed in my ears—
your skill with weapons and the tricks of war—
but what you speak of is a staggering thing,
beyond imagining, for me. How can two men
do battle with a houseful in their prime?
For I must tell you this is no affair
of ten or even twice ten men, but scores,
throngs of them. You shall see, here and now.
The number from Doulíkhion alone
is fifty-two picked men, with armorers,
a half dozen; twenty-four came from Samê,
twenty from Zakýnthos; our own island

accounts for twelve, high-ranked, and their retainers,
Medôn the crier, and the Master Harper,
besides a pair of handymen at feasts.
If we go in against all these
I fear we pay in salt blood for your vengeance.
You must think hard if you would conjure up
the fighting strength to take us through."

Odysseus
who had endured the long war and the sea
answered:
"I'll tell you now.
Suppose Athena's arm is over us, and Zeus
her father's, must I rack my brains for more?"

Clearheaded Telémakhos looked hard and said:
"Those two are great defenders, no one doubts it,
but throned in the serene clouds overhead;
other affairs of men and gods they have
to rule over."

And the hero answered:
"Before long they will stand to right and left of us
in combat, in the shouting, when the test comes—
our nerve against the suitors' in my hall.
Here is your part: at break of day tomorrow
home with you, go mingle with our princes.
The swineherd later on will take me down
the port-side trail—a beggar, by my looks,
hangdog and old. If they make fun of me
in my own courtyard, let your ribs cage up
your springing heart, no matter what I suffer,
no matter if they pull me by the heels
or practice shots at me, to drive me out.
Look on, hold down your anger. You may even
plead with them, by heaven! in gentle terms
to quit their horseplay—not that they will heed you,
rash as they are, facing their day of wrath.
Now fix the next step in your mind.

Attack the suitors with Athena's help

Athena,
counseling me, will give me word, and I
shall signal to you, nodding: at that point
round up all armor, lances, gear of war
left in our hall, and stow the lot away

back in the vaulted store room. When the suitors
miss those arms and question you, be soft
in what you say: answer:
'I thought I'd move them
out of the smoke. They seemed no longer those
bright arms Odysseus left us years ago
when he went off to Troy. Here where the fire's
hot breath came, they had grown black and drear.
One better reason, too, I had from Zeus:
suppose a brawl starts up when you are drunk,
you might be crazed and bloody one another,
and that would stain your feast, your courtship. Tempered
is iron can magnetize a man.'
Say that.
But put aside two broadswords and two spears
for our own use, two oxhide shields nearby
when we go into action. Pallas Athena
and Zeus All Provident will see you through,
bemusing our young friends.
Now one thing more.
If son of mine you are and blood of mine,
let no one hear Odysseus is about.
Neither Laërtês, nor the swineherd here,
nor any slave, nor even Penélopê.
But you and I alone must learn how far
the women are corrupted; we should know
how to locate good men among our hands,
the loyal and respectful, and the shirkers
who take you lightly, as alone and young."

His admirable son replied:
"Ah, Father,
even when danger comes I think you'll find
courage in me. I am not scatterbrained.
But as to checking on the field hands now,
I see no gain for us in that. Reflect,
you make a long toil, that way, if you care
to look men in the eye at every farm,
while these gay devils in our hall at ease
eat up our flocks and herds, leaving us nothing.

As for the maids I say, Yes: make distinction
between good girls and those who shame your house;

all that I shy away from is a scrutiny
of cottagers just now. The time for that
comes later — if in truth you have a sign
from Zeus the Stormking."

So their talk ran on,
while down the coast, and round toward Ithaka,
hove the good ship that had gone out to Pylos
bearing Telémakhos and his companions.
Into the wide bay waters, on to the dark land,
they drove her, hauled her up, took out the oars
and canvas for light-hearted squires to carry
homeward — as they carried, too, the gifts
of Meneláos round to Klýtios'[134] house.
But first they sped a runner to Penélopê.
They knew that quiet lady must be told
the prince her son had come ashore, and sent
his good ship round to port; not one soft tear
should their sweet queen let fall.
Both messengers,
crewman and swineherd — reached the outer gate
in the same instant, bearing the same news,
and went in side by side to the king's hall.
He of the ship burst out among the maids:
"Your son's ashore this morning, O my Queen!"

But the swineherd calmly stood near Penélopê
whispering what her son had bade him tell
and what he had enjoined on her. No more.
When he had done, he left the place and turned
back to his steading in the hills.

By now,
sullen confusion weighed upon the suitors.
Out of the house, out of the court they went,
beyond the wall and gate, to sit in council.
Eurýmakhos, the son of Pólybos,
opened discussion:
"Friends, face up to it;

[134] **Klýtios:** In Book 15 (l. 655), Telémakhos entrusts Theoklýmenos to Peiraios, son of Klýtios.

that young pup, Telémakhos, has done it;
he made the round trip, though we said he could not.
Well — now to get the best craft we can find
afloat, with oarsmen who can drench her bows,
and tell those on the island to come home."

He was yet speaking when Amphínomos,
craning seaward, spotted the picket ship
already in the roadstead under oars
with canvas brailed up; and this fresh arrival
made him chuckle. Then he told his friends:
"Too late for messages. Look, here they come
along the bay. Some god has brought them news,
or else they saw the cutter pass — and could not
overtake her."

On their feet at once,
the suitors took the road to the sea beach,
where, meeting the black ship, they hauled her in.
Oars and gear they left for their light-hearted
squires to carry, and all in company
made off for the assembly ground. All others,
young and old alike, they barred from sitting.
Eupeithês' son, Antínoös, made the speech:
"How the gods let our man escape a boarding,
that is the wonder.
We had lookouts posted
up on the heights all day in the sea wind,
and every hour a fresh pair of eyes;
at night we never slept ashore
but after sundown cruised the open water
to the southeast, patrolling until Dawn.
We were prepared to cut him off and catch him,
squelch him for good and all. The power of heaven
steered him the long way home.

Well, let this company plan his destruction,
and leave him no way out, this time. I see
our business here unfinished while he lives.
He knows, now, and he's no fool. Besides,
his people are all tired of playing up to us.
I say, act now, before he brings the whole
body of Akhaians to assembly —
and he would leave no word unsaid, in righteous

anger speaking out before them all
of how we plotted murder, and then missed him.
Will they commend us for that pretty work?
Take action now, or we are in for trouble;
we might be exiled, driven off our lands.
Let the first blow be ours.
If we move first, and get our hands on him
far from the city's eye, on path or field,
then stores and livestock will be ours to share;
the house we may confer upon his mother—
and on the man who marries her. Decide
otherwise you may—but if, my friends,
you want that boy to live and have his patrimony,
then we should eat no more of his good mutton,
come to this place no more.
Let each from his own hall
court her with dower gifts. And let her marry
the destined one, the one who offers most."

He ended, and no sound was heard among them,
sitting all hushed, until at last the son
of Nísos Aretíadês arose—
Amphínomos.
He led the group of suitors
who came from grainlands on Doulíkhion,
and he had lightness in his talk that pleased
Penélopê, for he meant no ill.
Now, in concern for them, he spoke:
"O Friends
I should not like to kill Telémakhos.
It is a shivery thing to kill a prince
of royal blood.
We should consult the gods.
If Zeus hands down a ruling for that act,
then I shall say, 'Come one, come all,' and go
cut him down with my own hand—
but I say Halt, if gods are contrary."

Now this proposal won them, and it carried.
Breaking their session up, away they went
to take their smooth chairs in Odysseus' house.
Meanwhile Penélopê the Wise,
decided, for her part, to make appearance
before the valiant young men.

She knew now
they plotted her child's death in her own hall,
for once more Medôn, who had heard them, told her.
Into the hall that lovely lady came,
with maids attending, and approached the suitors,
till near a pillar of the well-wrought roof
she paused, her shining veil across her cheeks,
and spoke directly to Antínoös:
"Infatuate,
steeped in evil! Yet in Ithaka they say
you were the best one of your generation
in mind and speech. Not so, you never were.
Madman, why do you keep forever knitting
death for Telémakhos? Have you no pity
toward men dependent on another's mercy?
Before Lord Zeus, no sanction can be found
for one such man to plot against another!
Or are you not aware that your own father
fled to us when the realm was up in arms
against him? He had joined the Taphian pirates
in ravaging Thesprotian folk, our friends.
Our people would have raided *him,* then—breached
his heart, butchered his herds to feast upon—
only Odysseus took him in, and held
the furious townsmen off. It is Odysseus'
house you now consume, his wife you court,
his son you kill, or try to kill. And me
you ravage now, and grieve. I call upon you
to make an end of it!—and your friends too!"

The son of Pólybos it was, Eurýmakhos,
who answered her with ready speech:
"My lady
Penélopê, wise daughter of Ikários,
you must shake off these ugly thoughts. I say
that man does not exist, nor will, who dares
lay hands upon your son Telémakhos,
while I live, walk the earth, and use my eyes.
The man's life blood, I swear,
will spurt and run out black around my lancehead!
For it is true of me, too, that Odysseus,
raider of cities, took me on his knees
and fed me often—tidbits and red wine.

Should not Telémakhos, therefore, be dear to me
above the rest of men? I tell the lad
he must not tremble for his life, at least
alone in the suitors' company. Heaven
deals death no man avoids."

Blasphemous lies
in earnest tones he told—the one who planned
the lad's destruction!
Silently the lady
made her way to her glowing upper chamber,
there to weep for her dear lord, Odysseus,
until grey-eyed Athena
cast sweet sleep upon her eyes.

At fall of dusk
Odysseus and his son heard the approach
of the good forester. They had been standing
over the fire with a spitted pig,
a yearling. And Athena coming near
with one rap of her wand made of Odysseus
an old old man again, with rags about him—
for if the swineherd knew his lord were there
he could not hold the news; Penélopê
would hear it from him.
Now Telémakhos
greeted him first:
"Eumaios, back again!
What was the talk in town? Are the tall suitors
home again, by this time, from their ambush,
or are they still on watch for my return?"

And you replied, Eumaios—O my swineherd:
"There was no time to ask or talk of that;
I hurried through the town. Even while I spoke
my message, I felt driven to return.
A runner from your friends turned up, a crier,
who gave the news first to your mother. Ah!
One thing I do know; with my own two eyes
I saw it. As I climbed above the town
to where the sky is cut by Hermês' ridge,
I saw a ship bound in for our own bay
with many oarsmen in it, laden down

with sea provisioning and two-edged spears,
and I surmised those were the men.
Who knows?"

Telémakhos, now strong with magic, smiled
across at his own father—but avoided
the swineherd's eye.
So when the pig was done,
the spit no longer to be turned, the table
garnished, everyone sat down to feast
on all the savory flesh he craved. And when
they had put off desire for meat and drink,
they turned to bed and took the gift of sleep.

Book 17
The Beggar at the Manor

When the young Dawn came bright into the East
spreading her finger tips of rose, Telémakhos,
the king's son, tied on his rawhide sandals
and took the lance that bore his handgrip. Burning
to be away, and on the path to town,
he told the swineherd:
"Uncle, the truth is
I must go down myself into the city.
Mother must see me there, with her own eyes,
or she will weep and feel forsaken still,
and will not set her mind at rest. Your job
will be to lead this poor man down to beg.
Some householder may want to dole him out
a loaf and pint. I have my own troubles.
Am I to care for every last man who comes?
And if he takes it badly—well, so much
the worse for him. Plain truth is what I favor."

At once Odysseus the great tactician
spoke up briskly:
"Neither would I myself
care to be kept here, lad. A beggar man
fares better in the town. Let it be said
I am not yet so old I must lay up
indoors and mumble, 'Aye, Aye' to a master.
Go on, then. As you say, my friend can lead me
as soon as I have had a bit of fire

and when the sun grows warmer. These old rags
could be my death, outside on a frosty morning,
and the town is distant, so they say."

Telémakhos
with no more words went out, and through the fence,
and down hill, going fast on the steep footing,
nursing woe for the suitors in his heart.

Before the manor hall, he leaned his lance
against a great porch pillar and stepped in
across the door stone.
Old Eurýkleia
saw him first, for that day she was covering
handsome chairs nearby with clean fleeces.
She ran to him at once, tears in her eyes;
and other maidservants of the old soldier
Odysseus gathered round to greet their prince,
kissing his head and shoulders.
Quickly, then,
Penélopê the Wise, tall in her beauty
as Artemis or pale-gold Aphroditê,
appeared from her high chamber and came down
to throw her arms around her son. In tears
she kissed his head, kissed both his shining eyes,
then cried out, and her words flew:
"Back with me!
Telémakhos, more sweet to me than sunlight!
I thought I should not see you again, ever,
after you took the ship that night to Pylos—
against my will, with not a word! you went
for news of your dear father. Tell me now
of everything you saw!"

But he made answer:
"Mother, not now. You make me weep. My heart
already aches—I came near death at sea.
You must bathe, first of all, and change your dress,
and take your maids to the highest room to pray.
Pray, and burn offerings to the gods of heaven,
that Zeus may put his hand to our revenge.

I am off now to bring home from the square
a guest, a passenger I had. I sent him
yesterday with all my crew to town.

Peiraios was to care for him, I said,
and keep him well, with honor, till I came."

She caught back the swift words upon her tongue.
Then softly she withdrew
to bathe and dress her body in fresh linen,
and make her offerings to the gods of heaven,
praying Almighty Zeus
to put his hand to their revenge.

Telémakhos
had left the hall, taken his lance, and gone
with two quick hounds at heel into the town,
Athena's grace in his long stride
making the people gaze as he came near.
And suitors gathered, primed with friendly words,
despite the deadly plotting in their hearts—
but these, and all their crowd, he kept away from.
Next he saw sitting some way off, apart,
Mentor, with Antiphos and Halithersês,
friends of his father's house in years gone by.
Near these men he sat down, and told his tale
under their questioning.
His crewman, young Peiraios,
guided through town, meanwhile, into the Square,
the Argive exile, Theoklýmenos.
Telémakhos lost no time in moving toward him;
but first Peiraios had his say:
"Telémakhos,
you must send maids to me, at once, and let me
turn over to you those gifts from Meneláos!"

The prince had pondered it, and said:
"Peiraios,
none of us knows how this affair will end.
Say one day our fine suitors, without warning,
draw upon me, kill me in our hall,
and parcel out my patrimony—I wish
you, and no one of them, to have those things.
But if my hour comes, if I can bring down
bloody death on all that crew,
you will rejoice to send my gifts to me—
and so will I rejoice!"

Then he departed,
leading his guest, the lonely stranger, home.

Over chair-backs in hall they dropped their mantles
and passed in to the polished tubs, where maids
poured out warm baths for them, anointed them,
and pulled fresh tunics, fleecy cloaks around them.
Soon they were seated at their ease in hall.
A maid came by to tip a golden jug
over their fingers into a silver bowl
and draw a gleaming table up beside them.
The larder mistress brought her tray of loaves
and savories, dispensing each.
In silence
across the hall, beside a pillar, propped
in a long chair, Telémakhos' mother
spun a fine wool yarn.
The young men's hands
went out upon the good things placed before them,
and only when their hunger and thirst were gone
did she look up and say:
"Telémakhos,
what am I to do now? Return alone
and lie again on my forsaken bed—
sodden how often with my weeping
since that day when Odysseus put to sea
to join the Atreidai[135] before Troy?
Could you not
tell me, before the suitors fill our house,
what news you have of his return?"

He answered:
"Now that you ask a second time, dear Mother,
here is the truth.
We went ashore at Pylos
to Nestor, lord and guardian of the West,
who gave me welcome in his towering hall.
So kind he was, he might have been my father
and I his long-lost son—so truly kind,

[135] **Atreidai:** As sons of Atreus, Agamémnon and Meneláos are known as Atreidai, or Atrides.

taking me in with his own honored sons.
But as to Odysseus' bitter fate,
living or dead, he had no news at all
from anyone on earth, he said. He sent me
overland in a strong chariot
to Atreus' son, the captain, Meneláos.
And I saw Helen there, for whom the Argives
fought, and the Trojans fought, as the gods willed.
Then Meneláos of the great war cry
asked me my errand in that ancient land
of Lakedaimon. So I told our story,
and in reply he burst out:
'Intolerable!
That feeble men, unfit as those men are,
should think to lie in that great captain's bed,
fawns in the lion's lair! As if a doe
put down her litter of sucklings there, while she
sniffed at the glen or grazed a grassy hollow.
Ha! Then the lord returns to his own bed
and deals out wretched doom on both alike.

So will Odysseus deal out doom on these.
O Father Zeus, Athena, and Apollo!
I pray he comes as once he was, in Lesbos,
when he stood up to wrestle Philomeleidês—
champion and Island King—
and smashed him down. How the Akhaians cheered!
If that Odysseus could meet the suitors,
they'd have a quick reply, a stunning dowry!
Now for your questions, let me come to the point.
I would not misreport it for you; let me
tell you what the Ancient of the Sea,
that infallible seer, told me.
On an island
your father lies and grieves. The Ancient saw him
held by a nymph, Kalypso, in her hall;
no means of sailing home remained to him,
no ship with oars, and no ship's company
to pull him on the broad back of the sea.'

I had this from the lord marshal, Meneláos,
and when my errand in that place was done
I left for home. A fair breeze from the gods
brought me swiftly back to our dear island."

The boy's tale made her heart stir in her breast,
but this was not all. Mother and son now heard
Theoklýmenos, the diviner, say:
"He does not see it clear—
O gentle lady,
wife of Odysseus Laërtiadês,
listen to me, I can reveal this thing.
Zeus be my witness, and the table set
for strangers and the hearth to which I've come—
the lord Odysseus, I tell you,
is present now, already, on this island!
Quartered somewhere, or going about, he knows
what evil is afoot. He has it in him
to bring a black hour on the suitors. Yesterday,
still at the ship, I saw this in a portent.
I read the sign aloud, I told Telémakhos!"

The prudent queen, for her part, said:
"Stranger,
if only this came true—
our love would go to you, with many gifts;
aye, every man who passed would call you happy!"

So ran the talk between these three.
Meanwhile,
swaggering before Odysseus' hall,
the suitors were competing at the discus throw
and javelin, on the level measured field.
But when the dinner hour drew on, and beasts
were being driven from the fields to slaughter—
as beasts were, every day—Medôn spoke out:
Medôn, the crier, whom the suitors liked;
he took his meat beside them.

"Men," he said,
"each one has had his work-out and his pleasure,
come in to Hall now; time to make our feast.
Are discus throws more admirable than a roast
when the proper hour comes?"

At this reminder
they all broke up their games, and trailed away
into the gracious, timbered hall. There, first,
they dropped their cloaks on chairs; then came their ritual:

putting great rams and fat goats to the knife—
pigs and a cow, too.
So they made their feast.

During these hours, Odysseus and the swineherd
were on their way out of the hills to town.
The forester had got them started, saying:
"Friend, you have hopes, I know, of your adventure
into the heart of town today. My lord
wishes it so, not I. No, I should rather
you stood by here as guardian of our steading.
But I owe reverence to my prince, and fear
he'll make my ears burn later if I fail.
A master's tongue has a rough edge. Off we go.
Part of the day is past; nightfall will be
early, and colder, too."

Odysseus,
who had it all timed in his head, replied:
"I know, as well as you do. Let's move on.
You lead the way—the whole way. Have you got
a staff, a lopped stick, you could let me use
to put my weight on when I slip? This path
is hard going, they said."

Over his shoulders
he slung his patched-up knapsack, an old bundle
tied with twine. Eumaios found a stick for him,
the kind he wanted, and the two set out,
leaving the boys and dogs to guard the place.
In this way good Eumaios led his lord
down to the city.
And it seemed to him
he led an old outcast, a beggar man,
leaning most painfully upon a stick,
his poor cloak, all in tatters, looped about him.

Down by the stony trail they made their way
as far as Clearwater, not far from town—
a spring house where the people filled their jars.
Ithakos, Nêritos, and Polýktor[136] built it,

[136] **Ithakos . . . Polýktor:** Early rulers of Ithaka.

and round it on the humid ground a grove,
a circular wood of poplars grew. Ice cold
in runnels from a high rock ran the spring,
and over it there stood an altar stone
to the cool nymphs, where all men going by
laid offerings.
Well, here the son of Dólios
crossed their path—Melánthios.
He was driving
a string of choice goats for the evening meal,
with two goatherds beside him; and no sooner
had he laid eyes upon the wayfarers
than he began to growl and taunt them both
so grossly that Odysseus' heart grew hot:
"Here comes one scurvy type leading another!
God pairs them off together, every time.
Swineherd, where are you taking your new pig,
that stinking beggar there, licker of pots?
How many doorposts has he rubbed his back on
whining for garbage, where a noble guest
would rate a cauldron or a sword?

Odysseus comes to his own house and catches Melanthios

Hand him
over to me, I'll make a farmhand of him,
a stall scraper, a fodder carrier! Whey
for drink will put good muscle on his shank!
No chance: he learned his dodges long ago—
no honest sweat. He'd rather tramp the country
begging, to keep his hoggish belly full.
Well, I can tell you this for sure:
in King Odysseus' hall, if he goes there,
footstools will fly around his head—good shots
from strong hands. Back and side, his ribs will catch it
on the way out!"

Enemy of Odysseus

And like a drunken fool
he kicked at Odysseus' hip as he passed by.
Not even jogged off stride, or off the trail,
the Lord Odysseus walked along, debating
inwardly whether to whirl and beat
the life out of this fellow with his stick,
or toss him, brain him on the stony ground.
Then he controlled himself, and bore it quietly.
Not so the swineherd.
Seeing the man before him,

he raised his arms and cried:
"Nymphs of the spring,
daughters of Zeus, if ever Odysseus
burnt you a thighbone in rich fat—a ram's
or kid's thighbone, hear me, grant my prayer:
let our true lord come back, let heaven bring him
to rid the earth of these fine courtly ways
Melánthios picks up around the town—
all wine and wind! Bad shepherds ruin flocks!"

Melánthios the goatherd answered:
"Bless me!
The dog can snap: how he goes on! Some day
I'll take him in a slave ship overseas
and trade him for a herd!
Old Silverbow
Apollo, if he shot clean through Telémakhos
in hall today, what luck! Or let the suitors
cut him down!
Odysseus died at sea;
no coming home for him."

He flung this out
and left the two behind to come on slowly,
while he went hurrying to the king's hall.
There he slipped in, and sat among the suitors,
beside the one he doted on—Eurýmakhos.
Then working servants helped him to his meat
and the mistress of the larder gave him bread.

Reaching the gate, Odysseus and the forester
halted and stood outside, for harp notes came
around them rippling on the air
as Phêmios picked out a song. Odysseus
caught his companion's arm and said:
"My friend,
here is the beautiful place—who could mistake it?
Here is Odysseus' hall: no hall like this!
See how one chamber grows out of another;
see how the court is tight with wall and coping;
no man at arms could break this gateway down!
Your banqueting young lords are here in force,
I gather, from the fumes of mutton roasting

and strum of harping—harping, which the gods
appoint sweet friend of feasts!"

And—O my swineherd!
you replied:
"That was quick recognition;
but you are no numbskull—in this or anything.
Now we must plan this action. Will you take
leave of me here, and go ahead alone
to make your entrance now among the suitors?
Or do you choose to wait?—Let me go forward
and go in first.
Do not delay too long;
someone might find you skulking here outside
and take a club to you, or heave a lance.
Bear this in mind, I say."

The patient hero
Odysseus answered:
"Just what I was thinking.
You go in first, and leave me here a little.
But as for blows and missiles,
I am no tyro at these things. I learned
to keep my head in hardship—years of war
and years at sea. Let this new trial come.
The cruel belly, can you hide its ache?
How many bitter days it brings! Long ships
with good stout planks athwart—would fighters rig them
to ride the barren sea, except for hunger?
Seawolves—woe to their enemies!"

While he spoke
an old hound, lying near, pricked up his ears
and lifted up his muzzle. This was Argos,
trained as a puppy by Odysseus,
but never taken on a hunt before
his master sailed for Troy. The young men, afterward,
hunted wild goats with him, and hare, and deer,
but he had grown old in his master's absence.
Treated as rubbish now, he lay at last
upon a mass of dung before the gates—
manure of mules and cows, piled there until
fieldhands could spread it on the king's estate.

Abandoned there, and half destroyed with flies,
old Argos lay.
But when he knew he heard
Odysseus' voice nearby, he did his best
to wag his tail, nose down, with flattened ears,
having no strength to move nearer his master.
And the man looked away,
wiping a salt tear from his cheek; but he
hid this from Eumaios. Then he said:
"I marvel that they leave this hound to lie
here on the dung pile;
he would have been a fine dog, from the look of him,
though I can't say as to his power and speed
when he was young. You find the same good build
in house dogs, table dogs landowners keep
all for style."

And you replied, Eumaios:
"A hunter owned him — but the man is dead
in some far place. If this old hound could show
the form he had when Lord Odysseus left him,
going to Troy, you'd see him swift and strong.
He never shrank from any savage thing
he'd brought to bay in the deep woods; on the scent
no other dog kept up with him. Now misery
has him in leash. His owner died abroad,
and here the women slaves will take no care of him.
You know how servants are: without a master
they have no will to labor, or excel.
For Zeus who views the wide world takes away
half the manhood of a man, that day
he goes into captivity and slavery."

Eumaios crossed the court and went straight forward
into the mégaron among the suitors;
but death and darkness in that instant closed
the eyes of Argos, who had seen his master,
Odysseus, after twenty years.

Long before anyone else
Telémakhos caught sight of the grey woodsman
coming from the door, and called him over
with a quick jerk of his head. Eumaios'

narrowed eyes made out an empty bench
beside the one the carver used—that servant
who had no respite, carving for the suitors.
This bench he took possession of, and placed it
across the table from Telémakhos
for his own use. Then the two men were served
cuts from a roast and bread from a bread basket.

At no long interval, Odysseus came
through his own doorway as a mendicant,
humped like a bundle of rags over his stick.
He settled on the inner ash wood sill,
leaning against the door jamb—cypress timber
the skilled carpenter planed years ago
and set up with a plumbline.

Now Telémakhos
took an entire loaf and a double handful
of roast meat; then he said to the forester:
"Give these to the stranger there. But tell him
to go among the suitors, on his own;
he may beg all he wants. This hanging back
is no asset to a hungry man."

The swineherd rose at once, crossed to the door,
and halted by Odysseus.

"Friend," he said,
"Telémakhos is pleased to give you these,
but he commands you to approach the suitors;
you may ask all you want from them. He adds,
your shyness is no asset to a beggar."

The great tactician, lifting up his eyes,
cried:
"Zeus aloft! A blessing on Telémakhos!
Let all things come to pass as he desires!"

Palms held out, in the beggar's gesture, he
received the bread and meat and put it down
before him on his knapsack—lowly table!—
then he fell to, devouring it. Meanwhile
the harper in the great room sang a song.

Not till the man was fed did the sweet harper
end his singing—whereupon the company
made the walls ring again with talk.

Unseen,
Athena took her place beside Odysseus
whispering in his ear:
"Yes, try the suitors.
You may collect a few more loaves, and learn
who are the decent lads, and who are vicious—
although not one can be excused from death!"

So he appealed to them, one after another,
going from left to right, with open palm,
as though his life time had been spent in beggary.
And they gave bread, for pity—wondering, though,
at the strange man. Who could this beggar be,
where did he come from? each would ask his neighbor;
till in their midst the goatherd, Melánthios,
raised his voice:
"Hear just a word from me,
my lords who court our illustrious queen!
This man,
this foreigner, I saw him on the road;
the swineherd here was leading him this way;
who, what, or whence he claims to be, I could not
say for sure."

At this, Antínoös
turned on the swineherd brutally, saying:
"You famous
breeder of pigs, why bring this fellow here?
Are we not plagued enough with beggars,
foragers and such rats?
You find the company
too slow at eating up your lord's estate—
is that it? So you call this scarecrow in?"

The forester replied:
"Antínoös,
well born you are, but that was not well said.
Who would call in a foreigner?—unless
an artisan with skill to serve the realm,
a healer, or a prophet, or a builder,
or one whose harp and song might give us joy.

All these are sought for on the endless earth,
but when have beggars come by invitation?
Who puts a field mouse in his granary? My lord,
you are a hard man, and you always were,
more so than others of this company—hard
on all Odysseus' people and on me.
But this I can forget
as long as Penélopê lives on, the wise and tender
mistress of this hall; as long
as Prince Telémakhos—"

But he broke off
at a look from Telémakhos, who said:
"Be still.
Spare me a long-drawn answer to this gentleman.
With his unpleasantness, he will forever make
strife where he can—and goad the others on."

He turned and spoke out clearly to Antínoös:
"What fatherly concern you show me! Frighten
this unknown fellow, would you, from my hall
with words that promise blows—may God forbid it!
Give him a loaf. Am I a niggard? No,
I call on you to give. And spare your qualms
as to my mother's loss, or anyone's—
not that in truth you have such care at heart:
your heart is all in feeding, not in giving."

Antínoös replied:
"What high and mighty
talk, Telémakhos! No holding you!
If every suitor gave what I may give him,
he could be kept for months—kept out of sight!"

He reached under the table for the footstool
his shining feet had rested on—and this
he held up so that all could see his gift.

But all the rest gave alms,
enough to fill the beggar's pack with bread
and roast meat.
So it looked as though Odysseus
had had his taste of what these men were like
and could return scot free to his own doorway—
but halting now before Antínoös

he made a little speech to him. Said he:
"Give a mite, friend. I would not say, myself,
you are the worst man of the young Akhaians.
The noblest, rather; kingly, by your look;
therefore you'll give more bread than others do.
Let me speak well of you as I pass on
over the boundless earth!
I, too, you know,
had fortune once, lived well, stood well with men,
and gave alms, often, to poor wanderers
like this one that you see — aye, to all sorts,
no matter in what dire want. I owned
servants — many, god knows — and all the rest
that goes with being prosperous, as they say.
But Zeus the son of Kronos brought me down.

No telling
why he would have it, but he made me go
to Egypt with a company of rovers —
a long sail to the south — for my undoing.
Up the broad Nile and in to the river bank
I brought my dipping squadron. There, indeed,
I told the men to stand guard at the ships;
I sent patrols out — out to rising ground;
but reckless greed carried my crews away
to plunder the Egyptian farms; they bore off
wives and children, killed what men they found.
The news ran on the wind to the city, a night cry,
and sunrise brought both infantry and horsemen,
filling the river plain with dazzle of bronze;
then Zeus lord of lightning
threw my men into a blind panic; no one dared
stand against that host closing around us.
Their scything weapons left our dead in piles,
but some they took alive, into forced labor,
myself among them. And they gave me, then,
to one Dmêtor, a traveller, son of Iasos,
who ruled at Kypros.° He conveyed me there. Cyprus
From that place, working northward, miserably —"

But here Antínoös broke in, shouting:
"God!
What evil wind blew in this pest?
Get over,
stand in the passage! Nudge my table, will you?

Egyptian whips are sweet
to what you'll come to here, you nosing rat,
making your pitch to everyone!
These men have bread to throw away on you
because it is not theirs. Who cares? Who spares
another's food, when he has more than plenty?"

With guile Odysseus drew away, then said:
"A pity that you have more looks than heart.
You'd grudge a pinch of salt from your own larder
to your own handy man. You sit here, fat
on others' meat, and cannot bring yourself
to rummage out a crust of bread for me!"

Then anger made Antínoös' heart beat hard,
and, glowering under his brows, he answered:
"Now!
You think you'll shuffle off and get away
after that impudence? Oh, no you don't!"

The stool he let fly hit the man's right shoulder
on the packed muscle under the shoulder blade—
like solid rock, for all the effect one saw.
Odysseus only shook his head, containing
thoughts of bloody work, as he walked on,
then sat, and dropped his loaded bag again
upon the door sill. Facing the whole crowd
he said, and eyed them all:
"One word only,
my lords, and suitors of the famous queen.
One thing I have to say.
There is no pain, no burden for the heart
when blows come to a man, and he defending
his own cattle—his own cows and lambs.
Here it was otherwise. Antínoös
hit me for being driven on by hunger—
how many bitter seas men cross for hunger!
If beggars interest the gods, if there are Furies
pent in the dark to avenge a poor man's wrong, then may
Antínoös meet his death before his wedding day!"

Then said Eupeithês' son, Antínoös:
"Enough.
Eat and be quiet where you are, or shamble elsewhere,
unless you want these lads to stop your mouth

pulling you by the heels, or hands and feet,
over the whole floor, till your back is peeled!"

But now the rest were mortified, and someone
spoke from the crowd of young bucks to rebuke him:
"A poor show, that—hitting this famished tramp—
bad business, if he happened to be a god.
You know they go in foreign guise, the gods do,
looking like strangers, turning up
in towns and settlements to keep an eye
on manners, good or bad."

But at this notion
Antínoös only shrugged.
Telémakhos,
after the blow his father bore, sat still
without a tear, though his heart felt the blow.
Slowly he shook his head from side to side,
containing murderous thoughts.
Penélopê
on the higher level of her room had heard
the blow, and knew who gave it. Now she murmured:
"Would god you could be hit yourself, Antínoös—
hit by Apollo's bowshot!"

And Eurýnomê
her housekeeper, put in:
"He and no other?
If all we pray for came to pass, not one
would live till dawn!"

Her gentle mistress said:
"Oh, Nan, they are a bad lot; they intend
ruin for all of us; but Antínoös
appears a blacker-hearted hound than any.
Here is a poor man come, a wanderer,
driven by want to beg his bread, and everyone
in hall gave bits, to cram his bag—only
Antínoös threw a stool, and banged his shoulder!"

So she described it, sitting in her chamber
among her maids—while her true lord was eating.
Then she called in the forester and said:
"Go to that man on my behalf, Eumaios,
and send him here, so I can greet and question him.

Abroad in the great world, he may have heard
rumors about Odysseus—may have known him!"

Then you replied—O swineherd!
"Ah, my queen,
if these Akhaian sprigs would hush their babble
the man could tell you tales to charm your heart.
Three days and nights I kept him in my hut;
he came straight off a ship, you know, to me.
There was no end to what he made me hear
of his hard roving and I listened, eyes
upon him as a man drinks in a tale
a minstrel sings—a minstrel taught by heaven
to touch the hearts of men. At such a song
the listener becomes rapt and still. Just so
I found myself enchanted by this man.
He claims an old tie with Odysseus, too—
in his home country the Minoan land
of Krete. From Krete he came, a rolling stone
washed by the gales of life this way and that
to our own beach.
If he can be believed
he has news of Odysseus near at hand
alive, in the rich country of Thesprotia,
bringing a mass of treasure home."

Then wise Penélopê said again:
"Go call him, let him come here, let him tell
that tale again for my own ears.
Our friends
can drink their cups outside or stay in hall,
being so carefree. And why not? Their stores
lie intact in their homes, both food and drink,
with only servants left to take a little.
But these men spend their days around our house
killing our beeves, our fat goats and our sheep,
carousing, drinking up our good dark wine;
sparing nothing, squandering everything.
No champion like Odysseus takes our part.
Ah, if he comes again, no falcon ever
struck more suddenly than he will, with his son,
to avenge this outrage!"

The great hall below
at this point rang with a tremendous sneeze—

"kchaou!" from Telémakhos — like an acclamation.
And laughter seized Penélopê.
Then quickly,
lucidly she went on:
"Go call the stranger
straight to me. Did you hear that, Eumaios?
My son's thundering sneeze at what I said!
May death come of a sudden so; may death
relieve us, clean as that, of all the suitors!
Let me add one thing — do not overlook it —
if I can see this man has told the truth,
I promise him a warm new cloak and tunic."

With all this in his head, the forester
went down the hall, and halted near the beggar,
saying aloud:
"Good father, you are called
by the wise mother of Telémakhos,
Penélopê. The queen, despite her troubles,
is moved by a desire to hear your tales
about her lord — and if she finds them true,
she'll see you clothed in what you need, a cloak
and a fresh tunic.
You may have your belly
full each day you go about this realm
begging. For all may give, and all they wish."

Now said Odysseus, the old soldier:
"Friend,
I wish this instant I could tell my facts
to the wise daughter of Ikários, Penélopê —
and I have much to tell about her husband;
we went through much together.
But just now
this hard crowd worries me. They are, you said
infamous to the very rim of heaven
for violent acts: and here, just now, this fellow
gave me a bruise. What had I done to him?
But who would lift a hand for me? Telémakhos?
Anyone else?
No; bid the queen be patient.
Let her remain till sundown in her room,
and then — if she will seat me near the fire —
inquire tonight about her lord's return.

My rags are sorry cover; you know that;
I showed my sad condition first to you."

The woodsman heard him out, and then returned;
but the queen met him on her threshold, crying:
"Have you not brought him? Why? What is he thinking?
Has he some fear of overstepping? Shy
about these inner rooms? A hangdog beggar?"

To this you answered, friend Eumaios:
"No:
he reasons as another might, and well,
not to tempt any swordplay from these drunkards.
Be patient, wait—he says—till darkness falls.
And, O my queen, for you too that is better:
better to be alone with him, and question him,
and hear him out."

Penélopê replied:
"He is no fool; he sees how it could be.
Never were mortal men like these
for bullying and brainless arrogance!"

Thus she accepted what had been proposed,
so he went back into the crowd. He joined
Telémakhos, and said at once in whispers—
his head bent, so that no one else might hear:
"Dear prince, I must go home to keep good watch
on hut and swine, and look to my own affairs.
Everything here is in your hands. Consider
your own safety before the rest; take care
not to get hurt. Many are dangerous here.
May Zeus destroy them first, before we suffer!"

Telémakhos said:
"Your wish is mine, Uncle.
Go when your meal is finished. Then come back
at dawn, and bring good victims for a slaughter.
Everything here is in my hands indeed—
and in the disposition of the gods."

Taking his seat on the smooth bench again,
Eumaios ate and drank his fill, then rose
to climb the mountain trail back to his swine,

leaving the mégaron and court behind him
crowded with banqueters.
These had their joy
of dance and song, as day waned into evening.

Book 18
Blows and a Queen's Beauty

Now a true scavenger came in—a public tramp
who begged around the town of Ithaka,
a by-word for his insatiable swag-belly,
feeding and drinking, dawn to dark. No pith
was in him, and no nerve, huge as he looked.
Arnaios, as his gentle mother called him,
he had been nicknamed "Iros" by the young
for being ready to take messages.[137]
This fellow
thought he would rout Odysseus from his doorway,
growling at him:
"Clear out, grandfather,
or else be hauled out by the ankle bone.
See them all giving me the wink? That means,
'Go on and drag him out!' I hate to do it.
Up with you! Or would you like a fist fight?"

Odysseus only frowned and looked him over,
taking account of everything, then said:
"Master, I am no trouble to you here.
I offer no remarks. I grudge you nothing.
Take all you get, and welcome. Here is room
for two on this doorslab—or do you own it?
You are a tramp, I think, like me. Patience:
a windfall from the gods will come. But drop
that talk of using fists; it could annoy me.
Old as I am, I might just crack a rib
or split a lip for you. My life would go

[137] **Arnaios . . . take messages:** Arnaios got his nickname "Iros" from Iris, goddess of the rainbow and a messenger for the goddess Hêra.

even more peacefully, after tomorrow,
looking for no more visits here from you."

Iros the tramp grew red and hooted:
"Ho,
listen to him! The swine can talk your arm off,
like an old oven woman! With two punches
I'd knock him snoring, if I had a mind to—
and not a tooth left in his head, the same
as an old sow caught in the corn! Belt up!
And let this company see the way I do it
when we square off. Can you fight a fresher man?"

Under the lofty doorway, on the door sill
of wide smooth ash, they held this rough exchange.
And the tall full-blooded suitor, Antínoös,
overhearing, broke into happy laughter.
Then he said to the others:
"Oh, my friends,
no luck like this ever turned up before!
What a farce heaven has brought this house!
The stranger
and Iros have had words, they brag of boxing!
Into the ring they go, and no more talk!"

All the young men got on their feet now, laughing,
to crowd around the ragged pair. Antínoös
called out:
"Gentlemen, quiet! One more thing:
here are goat stomachs ready on the fire
to stuff with blood and fat, good supper pudding.
The man who wins this gallant bout
may step up here and take the one he likes.
And let him feast with us from this day on:
no other beggar will be admitted here
when we are at our wine."

This pleased them all.
But now that wily man, Odysseus, muttered:
"An old man, an old hulk, has no business
fighting a young man, but my belly nags me;
nothing will do but I must take a beating.
Well, then, let every man here swear an oath

not to step in for Iros. No one throw
a punch for luck. I could be whipped that way."

So much the suitors were content to swear,
but after they reeled off their oaths, Telémakhos
put in a word to clinch it, saying:
"Friend,
if you will stand and fight, as pride requires,
don't worry about a foul blow from behind.
Whoever hits you will take on the crowd.
You have my word as host; you have the word
of these two kings, Antínoös and Eurýmakhos—
a pair of thinking men."

All shouted, "Aye!"
So now Odysseus made his shirt a belt
and roped his rags around his loins, baring
his hurdler's thighs and boxer's breadth of shoulder,
the dense rib-sheath and upper arms. Athena
stood nearby to give him bulk and power,
while the young suitors watched with narrowed eyes—
and comments went around:
"By god, old Iros now retires."

"Aye,
he asked for it, he'll get it—bloody, too."

"The build this fellow had, under his rags!"

Panic made Iros' heart jump, but the yard-boys
hustled and got him belted by main force,
though all his blubber quivered now with dread.
Antínoös' angry voice rang in his ears:
"You sack of guts, you might as well be dead,
might as well never have seen the light of day,
if this man makes you tremble! Chicken-heart,
afraid of an old wreck, far gone in misery!
Well, here is what I say—and what I'll do.
If this ragpicker can outfight you, whip you,
I'll ship you out to that king in Epeíros,[138]
Ékhetos—he skins everyone alive.

[138] **Epeíros:** North of Ithaka.

Let him just cut your nose off and your ears
and pull your privy parts out by the roots
to feed raw to his hunting dogs!"

Poor Iros
felt a new fit of shaking take his knees.
But the yard-boys pushed him out. Now both contenders
put their hands up. Royal Odysseus
pondered if he should hit him with all he had
and drop the man dead on the spot, or only
spar, with force enough to knock him down.
Better that way, he thought—gentle blow,
else he might give himself away.
The two
were at close quarters now, and Iros lunged
hitting the shoulder. Then Odysseus hooked him
under the ear and shattered his jaw bone,
so bright red blood came bubbling from his mouth,
as down he pitched into the dust, bleating,
kicking against the ground, his teeth stove in.
The suitors whooped and swung their arms, half dead
with pangs of laughter.
Then, by the ankle bone,
Odysseus hauled the fallen one outside,
crossing the courtyard to the gate, and piled him
against the wall. In his right hand he stuck
his begging staff, and said:
"Here, take your post
Sit here to keep the dogs and pigs away.
You can give up your habit of command
over poor waifs and beggarmen—you swab.
Another time you may not know what hit you."

When he had slung his rucksack by the string
over his shoulder, like a wad of rags,
he sat down on the broad door sill again,
as laughing suitors came to flock inside;
and each young buck in passing gave him greeting,
saying, maybe,
"Zeus fill your pouch for this!
May the gods grant your heart's desire!"

"Well done
to put that walking famine out of business."

"We'll ship him out to that king in Epéiros,
Ékhetos—he skins everyone alive."

Odysseus found grim cheer in their good wishes—
his work had started well.
Now from the fire
his fat blood pudding came, deposited
before him by Antínoös—then, to boot,
two brown loaves from the basket, and some wine
in a fine cup of gold. These gifts Amphínomos
gave him. Then he said:
"Here's luck, grandfather;
a new day; may the worst be over now."

Odysseus answered, and his mind ranged far:
"Amphínomos, your head is clear, I'd say;
so was your father's—or at least I've heard
good things of Nísos the Doulíkhion,
whose son you are, they tell me—an easy man.
And you seem gently bred.
In view of that,
I have a word to say to you, so listen.

Of mortal creatures, all that breathe and move,
earth bears none frailer than mankind. What man
believes in woe to come, so long as valor
and tough knees are supplied him by the gods?
But when the gods in bliss bring miseries on,
then willy-nilly, blindly, he endures.
Our minds are as the days are, dark or bright,
blown over by the father of gods and men.

So I, too, in my time thought to be happy;
but far and rash I ventured, counting on
my own right arm, my father, and my kin;
behold me now.
No man should flout the law,
but keep in peace what gifts the gods may give.

I see you young blades living dangerously,
a household eaten up, a wife dishonored—
and yet the master will return, I tell you,
to his own place, and soon; for he is near.

So may some power take you out of this,
homeward, and softly, not to face that man
the hour he sets foot on his native ground.
Between him and the suitors I foretell
no quittance, no way out, unless by blood,
once he shall stand beneath his own roof-beam."

Gravely, when he had done, he made libation
and took a sip of honey-hearted wine,
giving the cup, then, back into the hands
of the young nobleman. Amphínomos, for his part,
shaking his head, with chill and burdened breast,
turned in the great hall.
                    Now his heart foreknew
the wrath to come, but he could not take flight,
being by Athena bound there.
                    Death would have him
broken by a spear thrown by Telémakhos.
So he sat down where he had sat before.

And now heart-prompting from the grey-eyed goddess
came to the quiet queen, Penélopê:
a wish to show herself before the suitors;
for thus by fanning their desire again
Athena meant to set her beauty high
before her husband's eyes, before her son.
Knowing no reason, laughing confusedly,
she said:
          "Eurýnomê, I have a craving
I never had at all—I would be seen
among those ruffians, hateful as they are.
I might well say a word, then, to my son,
for his own good—tell him to shun that crowd;
for all their gay talk, they are bent on evil."

Mistress Eurýnomê replied:
                    "Well said, child,
now is the time. Go down, and make it clear,
hold nothing back from him.
                    But you must bathe
and put a shine upon your cheeks—not this way,
streaked under your eyes and stained with tears.
You make it worse, being forever sad,

and now your boy's a bearded man! Remember
you prayed the gods to let you see him so."

Penélopê replied:
"Eurýnomê,
it is a kind thought, but I will not hear it—
to bathe and sleek with perfumed oil. No, no,
the gods forever took my sheen away
when my lord sailed for Troy in the decked ships.
Only tell my Autonoë to come,
and Hippodameía; they should be attending me
in hall, if I appear there. I could not
enter alone into that crowd of men."

At this the good old woman left the chamber
to tell the maids her bidding. But now too
the grey-eyed goddess had her own designs.
Upon the quiet daughter of Ikários
she let clear drops of slumber fall, until
the queen lay back asleep, her limbs unstrung,
in her long chair. And while she slept the goddess
endowed her with immortal grace to hold
the eyes of the Akhaians. With ambrosia
she bathed her cheeks and throat and smoothed her brow—
ambrosia, used by flower-crowned Kythereia° Aphroditê
when she would join the rose-lipped Graces dancing.
Grandeur she gave her, too, in height and form,
and made her whiter than carved ivory.
Touching her so, the perfect one was gone.
Now came the maids, bare-armed and lovely, voices
breaking into the room. The queen awoke
and as she rubbed her cheek she sighed:
"Ah, soft
that drowse I lay embraced in, pain forgot!
If only Artemis the Pure would give me
death as mild, and soon! No heart-ache more,
no wearing out my lifetime with desire
and sorrow, mindful of my lord, good man
in all ways that he was, best of the Akhaians!"

She rose and left her glowing upper room,
and down the stairs, with her two maids in train,
this beautiful lady went before the suitors.
Then by a pillar of the solid roof
she paused, her shining veil across her cheek,

the two girls close to her and still;
and in that instant weakness took those men
in the knee joints, their hearts grew faint with lust;
not one but swore to god to lie beside her.
But speaking for her dear son's ears alone
she said:
"Telémakhos, what has come over you?
Lightminded you were not, in all your boyhood.
Now you are full grown, come of age; a man
from foreign parts might take you for the son
of royalty, to go by your good looks;
and have you no more thoughtfulness or manners?
How could it happen in our hall that you
permit the stranger to be so abused?
Here, in our house, a guest, can any man
suffer indignity, come by such injury?
What can this be for you but public shame?"

Telémakhos looked in her eyes and answered,
with his clear head and his discretion:
"Mother,
I cannot take it ill that you are angry.
I know the meaning of these actions now,
both good and bad. I had been young and blind.
How can I always keep to what is fair
while these sit here to put fear in me?—princes
from near and far whose interest is my ruin;
are any on my side?
But you should know
the suitors did not have their way, matching
the stranger here and Iros—for the stranger
beat him to the ground.
O Father Zeus!
Athena and Apollo! could I see
the suitors whipped like that! Courtyard and hall
strewn with our friends, too weak-kneed to get up,
chapfallen to their collarbones, the way
old Iros rolls his head there by the gate
as though he were pig-drunk! No energy
to stagger on his homeward path; no fight
left in his numb legs!"

Thus Penélopê
reproached her son, and he replied. Now, interrupting,
Eurýmakhos called out to her:

"Penélopê,
deep-minded queen, daughter of Ikários,
if all Akhaians in the land of Argos
only saw you now! What hundreds more
would join your suitors here to feast tomorrow!
Beauty like yours no woman had before,
or majesty, or mastery."

She answered:
"Eurýmakhos, my qualities — I know —
my face, my figure, all were lost or blighted
when the Akhaians crossed the sea to Troy,
Odysseus my lord among the rest.
If he returned, if he were here to care for me,
I might be happily renowned!
But grief instead heaven sent me — years of pain.
Can I forget? — the day he left this island,
enfolding my right hand and wrist in his,
he said:
'My lady, the Akhaian troops
will not easily make it home again
full strength, unhurt, from Troy. They say the Trojans
are fighters too; good lances and good bowmen,
horsemen, charioteers — and those can be
decisive when a battle hangs in doubt.
So whether God will send me back, or whether
I'll be a captive there, I cannot tell.
Here, then, you must attend to everything.
My parents in our house will be a care for you
as they are now, or more, while I am gone.
Wait for the beard to darken our boy's cheek;
then marry whom you will, and move away.'

The years he spoke of are now past; the night
comes when a bitter marriage overtakes me,
desolate as I am, deprived by Zeus
of all the sweets of life.
How galling, too,
to see newfangled manners in my suitors!
Others who go to court a gentlewoman,
daughter of a rich house, if they are rivals,
bring their own beeves and sheep along; her friends

ought to be feasted, gifts are due to her;
would any dare to live at her expense?"

Odysseus' heart laughed when he heard all this—
her sweet tones charming gifts out of the suitors
with talk of marriage, though she intended none.
Eupeithês' son, Antínoös, now addressed her:
"Ikários' daughter, O deep-minded queen!
If someone cares to make you gifts, accept them!
It is no courtesy to turn gifts away.
But we go neither to our homes nor elsewhere
until of all Akhaians here you take
the best man for your lord."

Pleased at this answer,
every man sent a squire to fetch a gift—
Antínoös, a wide resplendent robe,
embroidered fine, and fastened with twelve brooches,
pins pressed into sheathing tubes of gold;
Eurýmakhos, a necklace, wrought in gold,
with sunray pieces of clear glinting amber.
Eurýdamas' men came back with pendants,
ear-drops in triple clusters of warm lights;
and from the hoard of Lord Polýktor's son,
Peisándros, came a band for her white throat,
jewelled adornment. Other wondrous things
were brought as gifts from the Akhaian princes.
Penélopê then mounted the stair again,
her maids behind, with treasure in their arms.

And now the suitors gave themselves to dancing,
to harp and haunting song, as night drew on;
black night indeed came on them at their pleasure.
But three torch fires were placed in the long hall
to give them light. On hand were stores of fuel,
dry seasoned chips of resinous wood, split up
by the bronze hatchet blade—these were mixed in
among the flames to keep them flaring bright;
each housemaid of Odysseus took her turn.

Now he himself, the shrewd and kingly man,
approached and told them:

"Housemaids of Odysseus,
your master so long absent in the world,
go to the women's chambers, to your queen.
Attend her, make the distaff whirl, divert her,
stay in her room, comb wool for her.
I stand here
ready to tend these flares and offer light
to everyone. They cannot tire me out,
even if they wish to drink till Dawn.
I am a patient man."

But the women giggled,
glancing back and forth—laughed in his face;
and one smooth girl, Melántho, spoke to him
most impudently. She was Dólios' daughter,
taken as ward in childhood by Penélopê
who gave her playthings to her heart's content
and raised her as her own. Yet the girl felt
nothing for her mistress, no compunction,
but slept and made love with Eurýmakhos.
Her bold voice rang now in Odysseus' ears:
"You must be crazy, punch drunk, you old goat.
Instead of going out to find a smithy
to sleep warm in—or a tavern bench—you stay
putting your oar in, amid all our men.
Numbskull, not to be scared! The wine you drank
has clogged your brain, or are you always this way,
boasting like a fool? Or have you lost
your mind because you beat that tramp, that Iros?
Look out, or someone better may get up
and give you a good knocking about the ears
to send you out all bloody."

But Odysseus
glared at her under his brows and said:
"One minute:
let me tell Telémakhos how you talk
in hall, you slut; he'll cut your arms and legs off!"

This hard shot took the women's breath away
and drove them quaking to their rooms, as though
knives were behind: they felt he spoke the truth.
So there he stood and kept the firelight high

and looked the suitors over, while his mind
roamed far ahead to what must be accomplished.

They, for their part, could not now be still
or drop their mockery—for Athena wished
Odysseus mortified still more.
Eurýmakhos,
the son of Pólybos, took up the baiting,
angling for a laugh among his friends.

"Suitors of our distinguished queen," he said,
"hear what my heart would have me say.
This man
comes with a certain aura of divinity
into Odysseus' hall. He shines.
He shines
around the noggin, like a flashing light,
having no hair at all to dim his lustre."

Then turning to Odysseus, raider of cities,
he went on:
"Friend, you have a mind to work,
do you? Could I hire you to clear stones
from wasteland for me—you'll be paid enough—
collecting boundary walls and planting trees?
I'd give you a bread ration every day,
a cloak to wrap in, sandals for your feet.
Oh no: you learned your dodges long ago—
no honest sweat. You'd rather tramp the country
begging, to keep your hoggish belly full."

The master of many crafts replied:
"Eurýmakhos,
we two might try our hands against each other
in early summer when the days are long,
in meadow grass, with one good scythe for me
and one as good for you: we'd cut our way
down a deep hayfield, fasting to late evening.
Or we could try our hands behind a plow,
driving the best of oxen—fat, well-fed,
well-matched for age and pulling power, and say
four strips apiece of loam the share could break:
you'd see then if I cleft you a straight furrow.

Competition in arms? If Zeus Kroníon
rousèd up a scuffle now, give me a shield,
two spears, a dogskin cap with plates of bronze
to fit my temples, and you'd see me go
where the first rank of fighters lock in battle.
There would be no more jeers about my belly.
You thick-skinned menace to all courtesy!
You think you are a great man and a champion,
but up against few men, poor stuff, at that.
Just let Odysseus return, those doors
wide open as they are, you'd find too narrow
to suit you on your sudden journey out."

Now fury mounted in Eurýmakhos,
who scowled and shot back:
"Bundle of rags and lice!
By god, I'll make you suffer for your gall,
your insolent gabble before all our men."

He had his foot-stool out: but now Odysseus
took to his haunches by Amphínomos' knees,
fearing Eurýmakhos' missile, as it flew.
It clipped a wine steward on the serving hand,
so that his pitcher dropped with a loud clang
while he fell backward, cursing, in the dust.
In the shadowy hall a low sound rose—of suitors
murmuring to one another.

"Ai!" they said,
"This vagabond would have done well to perish
somewhere else, and make us no such rumpus.
Here we are, quarreling over tramps; good meat
and wine forgotten; good sense gone by the board."

Telémakhos, his young heart high, put in:
"Bright souls, alight with wine, you can no longer
hide the cups you've taken. Aye, some god
is goading you. Why not go home to bed?—
I mean when you are moved to. No one jumps
at my command."

Struck by his blithe manner,
the young men's teeth grew fixed in their under lips,
but now the son of Nísos, Lord Amphínomos
of Aretíadês, addressed them all:

"O friends, no ruffling replies are called for;
that was fair counsel.
Hands off the stranger, now,
and hands off any other servant here
in the great house of King Odysseus. Come,
let my own herald wet our cups once more,
we'll make an offering, and then to bed.
The stranger can be left behind in hall;
Telémakhos may care for him; he came
to Telémakhos' door, not ours."

This won them over.
The soldier Moulios, Doulíkhion herald,
comrade in arms of Lord Amphínomos,
mixed the wine and served them all. They tipped out
drops for the blissful gods, and drank the rest,
and when they had drunk their thirst away
they trailed off homeward drowsily to bed.

Book 19
Recognitions and a Dream

Now by Athena's side in the quiet hall
studying the ground for slaughter, Lord Odysseus
turned to Telémakhos.

"The arms," he said.
"Harness and weapons must be out of sight
in the inner room. And if the suitors miss them,
be mild; just say 'I had a mind to move them
out of the smoke. They seemed no longer
the bright arms that Odysseus left at home
when he went off to Troy. Here where the fire's
hot breath came, they had grown black and drear.
One better reason struck me, too:
suppose a brawl starts up when you've been drinking—
you might in madness let each other's blood,
and that would stain your feast, your courtship.
Iron
itself can draw men's hands.'"

Then he fell silent,
and Telémakhos obeyed his father's word.
He called Eurýkleia, the nurse, and told her:

"Nurse, go shut the women in their quarters
while I shift Father's armor back
to the inner rooms—these beautiful arms unburnished.
caked with black soot in his years abroad.
I was a child then. Well, I am not now.
I want them shielded from the draught and smoke."

And the old woman answered:
"It is time, child,
you took an interest in such things. I wish
you'd put your mind on all your house and chattels.
But who will go along to hold a light?
You said no maids, no torch-bearers."

Telémakhos
looked at her and replied:
"Our friend here.
A man who shares my meat can bear a hand,
no matter how far he is from home."

He spoke so soldierly
her own speech halted on her tongue. Straight back
she went to lock the doors of the women's hall.
And now the two men sprang to work—father
and princely son, loaded with round helms
and studded bucklers, lifting the long spears,
while in their path Pallas Athena
held up a golden lamp of purest light.
Telémakhos at last burst out:
"Oh, Father,
here is a marvel! All around I see
the walls and roof beams, pedestals and pillars,
lighted as though by white fire blazing near.
One of the gods of heaven is in this place!"

Then said Odysseus, the great tactician,
"Be still: keep still about it: just remember it.
The gods who rule Olympos make this light.
You may go off to bed now. Here I stay
to test your mother and her maids again.
Out of her long grief she will question me."

Telémakhos went across the hall and out
under the light of torches—crossed the court
to the tower chamber where he had always slept.

Here now again he lay, waiting for dawn,
while in the great hall by Athena's side
Odysseus waited with his mind on slaughter.

Presently Penélopê from her chamber
stepped in her thoughtful beauty.
So might Artemis
or golden Aphroditê have descended;
and maids drew to the hearth her own smooth chair
inlaid with silver whorls and ivory. The artisan
Ikmálios had made it, long before,
with a footrest in a single piece, and soft
upon the seat a heavy fleece was thrown.
Here by the fire the queen sat down. Her maids,
leaving their quarters, came with white arms bare
to clear the wine cups and the bread, and move
the trestle boards where men had lingered drinking.
Fiery ashes out of the pine-chip flares
they tossed, and piled on fuel for light and heat.
And now a second time Meléntho's voice
rang brazen in Odysseus' ears:
"Ah, stranger,
are you still here, so creepy, late at night
hanging about, looking the women over?
You old goat, go outside, cuddle your supper;
get out, or a torch may kindle you behind!"

At this Odysseus glared under his brows
and said:
"Little devil, why pitch into me again?
Because I go unwashed and wear these rags,
and make the rounds? But so I must, being needy;
that is the way a vagabond must live.
And do not overlook this: in my time
I too had luck, lived well, stood well with men,
and gave alms, often, to poor wanderers
like him you see before you—aye, to all sorts,
no matter in what dire want. I owned
servants—many, I say—and all the rest
that goes with what men call prosperity.
But Zeus the son of Kronos brought me down.
Mistress, mend your ways, or you may lose
all this vivacity of yours. What if her ladyship
were stirred to anger? What if Odysseus came?—
and I can tell you, there is hope of that—

or if the man is done for, still his son
lives to be reckoned with, by Apollo's will.
None of you can go wantoning on the sly
and fool him now. He is too old for that."

Penélopê, being near enough to hear him,
spoke out sharply to her maid:
"Oh, shameless,
through and through! And do you think me blind,
blind to your conquest? It will cost your life.[139]
You knew I waited — for you heard me say it —
waited to see this man in hall and question him
about my lord; I am so hard beset."

She turned away and said to the housekeeper:
"Eurýnomê, a bench, a spread of sheepskin,
to put my guest at ease. Now he shall talk
and listen, and be questioned."

Willing hands
brought a smooth bench, and dropped a fleece upon it.
Here the adventurer and king sat down;
then carefully Penélopê began:
"Friend, let me ask you first of all:
who are you, where do you come from, of what nation
and parents were you born?"

And he replied:
"My lady, never a man in the wide world
should have a fault to find with you. Your name
has gone out under heaven like the sweet
honor of some god-fearing king, who rules
in equity over the strong: his black lands bear
both wheat and barley, fruit trees laden bright,
new lambs at lambing time — and the deep sea
gives great hauls of fish by his good strategy,
so that his folk fare well.
O my dear lady,
this being so, let it suffice to ask me
of other matters — not my blood, my homeland.
Do not enforce me to recall my pain.
My heart is sore; but I must not be found

[139] **It will . . . life:** Melántho's affair with Eurýmakhos put her in league with the suitors.

sitting in tears here, in another's house:
it is not well forever to be grieving.
One of the maids might say—or you might think—
I had got maudlin over cups of wine."

And Penélopê replied:
"Stranger, my looks,
my face, my carriage, were soon lost or faded
when the Akhaians crossed the sea to Troy,
Odysseus my lord among the rest.
If he returned, if he were here to care for me,
I might be happily renowned!
But grief instead heaven sent me—years of pain.
Sons of the noblest families on the islands,
Doulíkhion, Samê, wooded Zakýnthos,
with native Ithakans, are here to court me,
against my wish; and they consume this house.
Can I give proper heed to guest or suppliant
or herald on the realm's affairs?
How could I?
wasted with longing for Odysseus, while here
they press for marriage.
Ruses served my turn
to draw the time out—first a close-grained web
I had the happy thought to set up weaving
on my big loom in hall. I said, that day:
'Young men—my suitors, now my lord is dead,
let me finish my weaving before I marry,
or else my thread will have been spun in vain.
It is a shroud I weave for Lord Laërtês
when cold Death comes to lay him on his bier.
The country wives would hold me in dishonor
if he, with all his fortune, lay unshrouded.'
I reached their hearts that way, and they agreed.
So every day I wove on the great loom,
but every night by torchlight I unwove it;
and so for three years I deceived the Akhaians.
But when the seasons brought a fourth year on,
as long months waned, and the long days were spent,
through impudent folly in the slinking maids
they caught me—clamored up to me at night;
I had no choice then but to finish it.
And now, as matters stand at last,
I have no strength left to evade a marriage,
cannot find any further way; my parents

Penelope telling odysseus everything

urge it upon me, and my son
will not stand by while they eat up his property.
He comprehends it, being a man full grown,
able to oversee the kind of house
Zeus would endow with honor.
But you too
confide in me, tell me your ancestry.
You were not born of mythic oak or stone."

And the great master of invention answered:
"O honorable wife of Lord Odysseus,
must you go on asking about my family?
Then I will tell you, though my pain
be doubled by it: and whose pain would not
if he had been away as long as I have
and had hard roving in the world of men?
But I will tell you even so, my lady.

One of the great islands of the world
in midsea, in the winedark sea, is Krete:
spacious and rich and populous, with ninety
cities and a mingling of tongues.
Akhaians there are found, along with Kretan
hillmen of the old stock, and Kydonians,
Dorians in three blood-lines, Pelasgians—[140]
and one among their ninety towns is Knossos.[141]
Here lived King Minos whom great Zeus received
every ninth year in private council—Minos,
the father of my father, Deukálion.
Two sons Deukálion had: Idómeneus,
who went to join the Atreidai before Troy
in the beaked ships of war; and then myself,
Aithôn by name—a stripling next my brother.
But I saw with my own eyes at Knossos once
Odysseus.
Gales had caught him off Cape Malea,
driven him southward on the coast of Krete
when he was bound for Troy. At Ámnisos,
hard by the holy cave of Eileithuía,[142]

[140] **Kydonians . . . Pelasgians:** Kydonians, Dorians, and Pelasgians represent the migrations of various peoples into the Greek peninsula. [141] **Knossos:** Knossos, the cultural center of the Minoan civilization on Krete (Crete), was also the name of the great palace of King Minos. [142] **Eileithuía:** The goddess of childbirth who had a shrine at Ámnisos, on the coast near Knossos.

he lay to, and dropped anchor, in that open
and rough roadstead riding out the blow.
Meanwhile he came ashore, came inland, asking
after Idómeneus: dear friends he said they were;
but now ten mornings had already passed,
ten or eleven, since my brother sailed.
So I played host and took Odysseus home,
saw him well lodged and fed, for we had plenty;
then I made requisitions—barley, wine,
and beeves for sacrifice—to give his company
abundant fare along with him.
Twelve days
they stayed with us, the Akhaians, while that wind
out of the north shut everyone inside—
even on land you could not keep your feet,
such fury was abroad. On the thirteenth,
when the gale dropped, they put to sea."

Now all these lies he made appear so truthful
she wept as she sat listening. The skin
of her pale face grew moist the way pure snow
softens and glistens on the mountains, thawed
by Southwind after powdering from the West,
and, as the snow melts, mountain streams run full:
so her white cheeks were wetted by these tears
shed for her lord—and he close by her side.
Imagine how his heart ached for his lady,
his wife in tears; and yet he never blinked;
his eyes might have been made of horn or iron
for all that she could see. He had this trick—
wept, if he willed to, inwardly.
Well, then,
as soon as her relieving tears were shed
she spoke once more:
"I think that I shall say, friend,
give me some proof, if it is really true
that you were host in that place to my husband
with his brave men, as you declare. Come, tell me
the quality of his clothing, how he looked,
and some particular of his company."

Odysseus answered, and his mind ranged far:
"Lady, so long a time now lies between,
it is hard to speak of it. Here is the twentieth year

since that man left the island of my father.
But I shall tell what memory calls to mind.
A purple cloak, and fleecy, he had on—
a double thick one. Then, he wore a brooch
made of pure gold with twin tubes for the prongs,
and on the face a work of art: a hunting dog
pinning a spotted fawn in agony
between his forepaws—wonderful to see
how being gold, and nothing more, he bit
the golden deer convulsed, with wild hooves flying.
Odysseus' shirt I noticed, too—a fine
closefitting tunic like dry onion skin,
so soft it was, and shiny.
Women there,
many of them, would cast their eyes on it.
But I might add, for your consideration,
whether he brought these things from home, or whether
a shipmate gave them to him, coming aboard,
I have no notion: some regardful host
in another port perhaps it was. Affection
followed him—there were few Akhaians like him.
And I too made him gifts: a good bronze blade,
a cloak with lining and a broidered shirt,
and sent him off in his trim ship with honor.
A herald, somewhat older than himself,
he kept beside him; I'll describe this man:
round-shouldered, dusky, woolly-headed;
Eurýbates, his name was—and Odysseus
gave him preferment over the officers.
He had a shrewd head, like the captain's own."

Now hearing these details—minutely true—
she felt more strangely moved, and tears flowed
until she had tasted her salt grief again.
Then she found words to answer:
"Before this
you won my sympathy, but now indeed
you shall be our respected guest and friend.
With my own hands I put that cloak and tunic
upon him—took them folded from their place—
and the bright brooch for ornament.
Gone now,
I will not meet the man again

returning to his own home fields. Unkind
the fate that sent him young in the long ship
to see that misery at Ilion, unspeakable!"

And the master improviser answered:
"Honorable
wife of Odysseus Laërtiadês,
you need not stain your beauty with these tears,
nor wear yourself out grieving for your husband.
Not that I can blame you. Any wife
grieves for the man she married in her girlhood,
lay with in love, bore children to—though he
may be no prince like this Odysseus,
whom they compare even to the gods. But listen:
weep no more, and listen:
I have a thing to tell you, something true.
I heard but lately of your lord's return,
heard that he is alive, not far away,
among Thesprótians in their green land
amassing fortune to bring home. His company
went down in shipwreck in the winedark sea
off the coast of Thrinákia. Zeus and Hêlios
held it against him that his men had killed
the kine of Hêlios. The crew drowned for this.
He rode the ship's keel. Big seas cast him up
on the island of Phaiákians, godlike men
who took him to their hearts. They honored him
with many gifts and a safe passage home,
or so they wished. Long since he should have been here,
but he thought better to restore his fortune
playing the vagabond about the world;
and no adventurer could beat Odysseus
at living by his wits—no man alive.
I had this from King Phaidôn of Thesprótia;
and, tipping wine out, Phaidôn swore to me
the ship was launched, the seamen standing by
to bring Odysseus to his land at last,
but I got out to sea ahead of him
by the king's order—as it chanced a freighter
left port for the grain bins of Doulíkhion.
Phaidôn, however, showed me Odysseus' treasure.
Ten generations of his heirs or more
could live on what lay piled in that great room.

The begger (odysseus) saying that Penelope will soon be reunited with her husband

The man himself had gone up to Dodona
to ask the spelling leaves of the old oak
what Zeus would have him do—how to return to Ithaka
after so many years—by stealth or openly.
You see, then, he is alive and well, and headed
homeward now, no more to be abroad
far from his island, his dear wife and son.
Here is my sworn word for it. Witness this,
god of the zenith, noblest of the gods,
and Lord Odysseus' hearthfire, now before me:
I swear these things shall turn out as I say.
Between this present dark and one day's ebb,
after the wane, before the crescent moon,
Odysseus will come."

Penélopê,
the attentive queen, replied to him:
"Ah, stranger,
if what you say could ever happen!
You would soon know our love! Our bounty, too:
men would turn after you to call you blessed.
But my heart tells me what must be.
Odysseus will not come to me; no ship
will be prepared for you. We have no master
quick to receive and furnish out a guest
as Lord Odysseus was.
Or did I dream him?

Maids, maids: come wash him, make a bed for him,
bedstead and colored rugs and coverlets
to let him lie warm into the gold of Dawn.
In morning light you'll bathe him and anoint him
so that he'll take his place beside Telémakhos
feasting in hall. If there be one man there
to bully or annoy him that man wins
no further triumph here, burn though he may.
How will you understand me, friend, how find in me,
more than in common women, any courage
or gentleness, if you are kept in rags
and filthy at our feast? Men's lives are short.
The hard man and his cruelties will be
cursed behind his back, and mocked in death.
But one whose heart and ways are kind—of him

strangers will bear report to the wide world,
and distant men will praise him."

Warily
Odysseus answered:
"Honorable lady,
wife of Odysseus Laërtiadês,
a weight of rugs and cover? Not for me.
I've had none since the day I saw the mountains
of Krete, white with snow, low on the sea line
fading behind me as the long oars drove me north.
Let me lie down tonight as I've lain often,
many a night unsleeping, many a time
afield on hard ground waiting for pure Dawn.
No: and I have no longing for a footbath
either: none of these maids will touch my feet,
unless there is an old one, old and wise,
one who has lived through suffering as I have:
I would not mind letting my feet be touched
by that old servant."

And Penélopê said:
"Dear guest, no foreign man so sympathetic
ever came to my house, no guest more likeable,
so wry and humble are the things you say.
I have an old maidservant ripe with years,
one who in her time nursed my lord. She took him
into her arms the hour his mother bore him.
Let her, then, wash your feet though she is frail.
Come here, stand by me, faithful Eurýkleia,
and bathe, bathe your master. I almost said,
for they are of an age, and now Odysseus'
feet and hands would be enseamed like his.
Men grow old soon in hardship."

Hearing this,
the old nurse hid her face between her hands
and wept hot tears, and murmured:
"Oh, my child!
I can do nothing for you! How Zeus hated you,
no other man so much! No use, great heart;
O faithful heart, the rich thighbones you burnt
to Zeus who plays in lightning—and no man

ever gave more to Zeus—with all your prayers
for a green age, a tall son reared to manhood.
There is no day of homecoming for you.
Stranger, some women in some far off place
perhaps have mocked my lord when he'd be home
as now these strumpets mock you here. No wonder
you would keep clear of all their whorishness
and have no bath. But here am I. The queen
Penélopê, Ikários' daughter, bids me;
so let me bathe your feet to serve my lady—
to serve you, too.
My heart within me stirs,
mindful of something. Listen to what I say:
strangers have come here, many through the years,
but no one ever came, I swear, who seemed
so like Odysseus—body, voice and limbs—
as you do."

Ready for this, Odysseus answered:
"Old woman, that is what they say. All who have seen
the two of us remark how like we are,
as you yourself have said, and rightly, too."

Then he kept still, while the old nurse filled up
her basin glittering in firelight; she poured
cold water in, then hot.
But Lord Odysseus
whirled suddenly from the fire to face the dark.
The scar: he had forgotten that. She must not
handle his scarred thigh, or the game was up.
But when she bared her lord's leg, bending near,
she knew the groove at once.
An old wound
a boar's white tusk inflicted, on Parnassos[143]
years ago. He had gone hunting there
in company with his uncles and Autólykos,
his mother's father—a great thief and swindler
by Hermês'[144] favor, for Autólykos pleased him
with burnt offerings of sheep and kids. The god
acted as his accomplice. Well, Autólykos
on a trip to Ithaka

[143] **Parnassos:** The mountains rising above Apollo's famous shrine at Delphi. [144] **Hermês:** In addition to his other tasks as messenger god, Hermês was patron of thieves and trickery.

arrived just after his daughter's boy was born.
In fact, he had no sooner finished supper
than Nurse Eurýkleia put the baby down
in his own lap and said:
"It is for you, now,
to choose a name for him, your child's dear baby;
the answer to her prayers."

Autólykos replied:
"My son-in-law, my daughter, call the boy
by the name I tell you. Well you know, my hand
has been against the world of men and women;
odium and distrust[145] I've won. Odysseus
should be his given name. When he grows up,
when he comes visiting his mother's home
under Parnassos, where my treasures are,
I'll make him gifts and send him back rejoicing."

Odysseus in due course went for the gifts,
and old Autólykos and his sons embraced him
with welcoming sweet words; and Amphithéa,
his mother's mother, held him tight and kissed him,
kissed his head and his fine eyes.
The father
called on his noble sons to make a feast,
and going about it briskly they led in
an ox of five years, whom they killed and flayed
and cut in bits for roasting on the skewers
with skilled hands, with care; then shared it out.
So all the day until the sun went down
they feasted to their hearts' content. At evening,
after the sun was down and dusk had come,
they turned to bed and took the gift of sleep.

When the young Dawn spread in the eastern sky
her finger tips of rose, the men and dogs
went hunting, taking Odysseus. They climbed
Parnassos' rugged flank mantled in forest,
entering amid high windy folds at noon
when Hêlios beat upon the valley floor
and on the winding Ocean whence he came.

[145] **odium and distrust:** By referring to himself as odious *(odyssamenos),* Autólykos is playing with the name Odysseus, meaning someone who is angry or wrathful.

with hounds questing ahead, in open order,
the sons of Autólykos went down a glen,
Odysseus in the lead, behind the dogs,
pointing his long-shadowing spear.
Before them
a great boar lay hid in undergrowth,
in a green thicket proof against the wind
or sun's blaze, fine soever the needling sunlight,
impervious too to any rain, so dense
that cover was, heaped up with fallen leaves.
Patter of hounds' feet, men's feet, woke the boar
as they came up — and from his woody ambush
with razor back bristling and raging eyes
he trotted and stood at bay. Odysseus,
being on top of him, had the first shot,
lunging to stick him; but the boar
had already charged under the long spear.
He hooked aslant with one white tusk and ripped out
flesh above the knee, but missed the bone.
Odysseus' second thrust went home by luck,
his bright spear passing through the shoulder joint;
and the beast fell, moaning as life pulsed away.
Autólykos' tall sons took up the wounded,
working skillfully over the Prince Odysseus
to bind his gash, and with a rune° they stanched — magic spell
the dark flow of blood. Then downhill swiftly
they all repaired to the father's house, and there
tended him well — so well they soon could send him,
with Grandfather Autólykos' magnificent gifts,
rejoicing, over sea to Ithaka.
His father and the Lady Antikleía
welcomed him, and wanted all the news
of how he got his wound; so he spun out
his tale, recalling how the boar's white tusk
caught him when he was hunting on Parnassos.

This was the scar the old nurse[146] recognized;
she traced it under her spread hands, then let go,
and into the basin fell the lower leg
making the bronze clang, sloshing the water out.
Then joy and anguish seized her heart; her eyes

[146] **the old nurse:** Nurse Eurýkleia, daughter of Ops, was bought by Laërtês to be Odysseus's nurse, and later became Telémakhos's nurse.

filled up with tears; her throat closed, and she whispered,
with hand held out to touch his chin:
"Oh yes!
You are Odysseus! Ah, dear child! I could not
see you until now—not till I knew
my master's very body with my hands!"

Her eyes turned to Penélopê with desire
to make her lord, her husband, known—in vain,
because Athena had bemused the queen,
so that she took no notice, paid no heed.
At the same time Odysseus' right hand
gripped the old throat; his left hand pulled her near,
and in her ear he said:
"Will you destroy me,
nurse, who gave me milk at your own breast?
Now with a hard lifetime behind I've come
in the twentieth year home to my father's island.
You found me out, as the chance was given you.
Be quiet; keep it from the others, else
I warn you, and I mean it, too,
if by my hand god brings the suitors down
I'll kill you, nurse or not, when the time comes—
when the time comes to kill the other women."

Eurýkleia kept her wits and answered him:
"Oh, what mad words are these you let escape you!
Child, you know my blood, my bones are yours;
no one could whip this out of me. I'll be
a woman turned to stone, iron I'll be.
And let me tell you too—mind now—if god
cuts down the arrogant suitors by your hand,
I can report to you on all the maids,
those who dishonor you, and the innocent."

But in response the great tactician said:
"Nurse, no need to tell me tales of these.
I will have seen them, each one, for myself.
Trust in the gods, be quiet, hold your peace."

Silent, the old nurse went to fetch more water,
her basin being all spilt.
When she had washed
and rubbed his feet with golden oil, he turned,
dragging his bench again to the fire side

for warmth, and hid the scar under his rags.
Penélopê broke the silence, saying:
"Friend,
allow me one brief question more. You know,
the time for bed, sweet rest, is coming soon,
if only that warm luxury of slumber
would come to enfold us, in our trouble. But for me
my fate at night is anguish and no rest.
By day being busy, seeing to my work,
I find relief sometimes from loss and sorrow;
but when night comes and all the world's abed
I lie in mine alone, my heart thudding,
while bitter thoughts and fears crowd on my grief.
Think how Pandáreos' daughter, pale forever,
sings as the nightingale[147] in the new leaves
through those long quiet hours of night,
on some thick-flowering orchard bough in spring;
how she rills out and tilts her note, high now, now low,
mourning for Itylos whom she killed in madness—
her child, and her lord Zêthos' only child.
My forlorn thought flows variable as her song,
wondering: shall I stay beside my son
and guard my own things here, my maids, my hall,
to honor my lord's bed and the common talk?
Or had I best join fortunes with a suitor,
the noblest one, most lavish in his gifts?
Is it now time for that?
My son being still a callow boy forbade
marriage, or absence from my lord's domain;
but now the child is grown, grown up, a man,
he, too, begins to pray for my departure,
aghast at all the suitors gorge on.

Listen:
interpret me this dream: From a water's edge
twenty fat geese have come to feed on grain
beside my house. And I delight to see them.
But now a mountain eagle with great wings
and crooked beak storms in to break their necks

[147] **sings as the nightingale:** Aedon, the daughter of Pandáreos, was married to Zethos. Jealous of her sister-in-law Niobe's several sons, Aedon intended to kill Niobe's eldest son but by mistake killed her own son, Itylos. Turned into a nightingale by Zeus, Aedon mourns her terrible deed through the nightingale's song.

and strew their bodies here. Away he soars
into the bright sky; and I cry aloud—
all this in dream—I wail and round me gather
softly braided Akhaian women mourning
because the eagle killed my geese.
Then down
out of the sky he drops to a cornice beam
with mortal voice telling me not to weep.
'Be glad,' says he, 'renowned Ikários' daughter:
here is no dream but something real as day,
something about to happen. All those geese
were suitors, and the bird was I. See now,
I am no eagle but your lord come back
to bring inglorious death upon them all!'
As he said this, my honeyed slumber left me.
Peering through half-shut eyes, I saw the geese
in hall, still feeding at the self-same trough."

The master of subtle ways and straight replied:
"My dear, how can you choose to read the dream
differently? Has not Odysseus himself
shown you what is to come? Death to the suitors,
sure death, too. Not one escapes his doom."

Penélopê shook her head and answered:
"Friend,
many and many a dream is mere confusion,
a cobweb of no consequence at all.
Two gates for ghostly dreams there are: one gateway
of honest horn, and one of ivory.
Issuing by the ivory gate are dreams
of glimmering illusion, fantasies,
but those that come through solid polished horn
may be borne out, if mortals only know them.
I doubt it came by horn, my fearful dream—
too good to be true, that, for my son and me.
But one thing more I wish to tell you: listen
carefully. It is a black day, this that comes.
Odysseus' house and I are to be parted.
I shall decree a contest for the day.
We have twelve axe heads. In his time, my lord
could line them up, all twelve, at intervals
like a ship's ribbing; then he'd back away

a long way off and whip an arrow through.[148]
Now I'll impose this trial on the suitors.
The one who easily handles and strings the bow
and shoots through all twelve axes I shall marry,
whoever he may be—then look my last
on this my first love's beautiful brimming house.
But I'll remember, though I dream it only."

Odysseus said:
"Dear honorable lady,
wife of Odysseus Laërtiadês,
let there be no postponement of the trial.
Odysseus, who knows the shifts of combat,
will be here: aye, he'll be here long before
one of these lads can stretch or string that bow
or shoot to thread the iron!"

Grave and wise,
Penélopê replied:
"If you were willing
to sit with me and comfort me, my friend,
no tide of sleep would ever close my eyes.
But mortals cannot go forever sleepless.
This the undying gods decree for all
who live and die on earth, kind furrowed earth.
Upstairs I go, then, to my single bed,
my sighing bed, wet with so many tears
after my Lord Odysseus took ship
to see that misery at Ilion, unspeakable.
Let me rest there, you here. You can stretch out
on the bare floor, or else command a bed."

So she went up to her chamber softly lit,
accompanied by her maids. Once there, she wept
for Odysseus, her husband, till Athena
cast sweet sleep upon her eyes.

[148] **whip an arrow through:** A number of theories have arisen to explain how this archery contest was performed. This translation suggests that the wooden handles are missing and that it is the empty sockets of ax heads that are lined up.

Book 20
Signs and a Vision

Outside in the entry way he made his bed—
raw oxhide spread on level ground, and heaped up
fleeces, left from sheep the Akhaians killed.
And when he had lain down, Eurýnomê
flung out a robe to cover him. Unsleeping
the Lord Odysseus lay, and roved in thought
to the undoing of his enemies.
Now came a covey of women
laughing as they slipped out, arm in arm,
as many a night before, to the suitors' beds;
and anger took him like a wave to leap
into their midst and kill them, every one—
or should he let them all go hot to bed
one final night? His heart cried out within him
the way a brach[149] with whelps between her legs
would howl and bristle at a stranger—so
the hackles of his heart rose at that laughter.
Knocking his breast he muttered to himself:
"Down; be steady. You've seen worse, that time
the Kyklops like a rockslide ate your men
while you looked on. Nobody, only guile,
got you out of that cave alive."

His rage
held hard in leash, submitted to his mind,
while he himself rocked, rolling from side to side,
as a cook turns a sausage, big with blood
and fat, at a scorching blaze, without a pause,
to broil it quick: so he rolled left and right,
casting about to see how he, alone,
against the false outrageous crowd of suitors
could press the fight.
And out of the night sky
Athena came to him; out of the nearby dark
in body like a woman; came and stood
over his head to chide him:

---

[149] **brach:** Female dog; bitch.

"Why so wakeful,
most forlorn of men? Here is your home,
there lies your lady; and your son is here,
as fine as one could wish a son to be."

Odysseus looked up and answered:
"Aye,
goddess, that much is true; but still
I have some cause to fret in this affair.
I am one man; how can I whip those dogs?
They are always here in force. Neither
is that the end of it, there's more to come.
If by the will of Zeus and by your will
I killed them all, where could I go for safety?
Tell me that!"

And the grey-eyed goddess said:
"Your touching faith! Another man would trust
some villainous mortal, with no brains—and what
am I? Your goddess-guardian to the end
in all your trials. Let it be plain as day:
if fifty bands of men surrounded us
and every sword sang for your blood,
you could make off still with their cows and sheep.
Now you, too, go to sleep. This all night vigil
wearies the flesh. You'll come out soon enough
on the other side of trouble."

Raining soft
sleep on his eyes, the beautiful one as gone
back to Olympos. Now at peace, the man
slumbered and lay still, but not his lady:
Wakeful again with all her cares, reclining
in the soft bed, she wept and cried aloud
until she had had her fill of tears, then spoke
in prayer first to Artemis:
"O gracious
divine lady Artemis, daughter of Zeus,
if you could only make an end now quickly,
let the arrow fly, stop my heart,
or if some wind could take me by the hair
up into running cloud, to plunge in tides of Ocean,

as hurricane winds took Pandareos' daughters[150]
when they were left at home alone. The gods
had sapped their parents' lives. But Aphroditê
fed those children honey, cheese, and wine,
and Hêra gave them looks and wit, and Artemis,
pure Artemis, gave lovely height, and wise
Athena made them practised in her arts—
till Aphroditê in glory walked on Olympos,
begging for each a happy wedding day
from Zeus, the lightning's joyous king, who knows
all fate of mortals, fair and foul—
but even at that hour the cyclone winds
had ravished them away
to serve the loathsome Furies.
Let me be
blown out by the Olympians! Shot by Artemis,
I still might go and see amid the shades
Odysseus in the rot of underworld.
No coward's eye should light by my consenting!
Evil may be endured when our days pass
in mourning, heavy-hearted, hard beset,
if only sleep reign over nighttime, blanketing
the world's good and evil from our eyes.
But not for me: dreams too my demon sends me.
Tonight the image of my lord came by
as I remember him with troops. O strange
exultation! I thought him real, and not a dream."

Now as the Dawn appeared all stitched in gold,
the queen's cry reached Odysseus at his waking,
so that he wondered, half asleep: it seemed
she knew him, and stood near him! Then he woke
and picked his bedding up to stow away
on a chair in the mégaron. The oxhide pad
he took outdoors. There, spreading wide his arms,

[150] **Pandareos' daughters:** Pandareos stole a golden dog made by Hephaistos from a shrine of Zeus. After Pandareos and his wife were killed by the gods, Aphroditê, Hêra, and Artemis brought up their three daughters, until they were killed for their father's offense by winds directed by the Furies. This story represents a different tradition from the one in Book 19, in which Pandareos's daughter was changed into a nightingale.

He prayed:
"O Father Zeus, if over land and water,
after adversity, you willed to bring me home,
let someone in the waking house give me good augury,
and a sign be shown, too, in the outer world."

He prayed thus, and the mind of Zeus in heaven
heard him. He thundered out of bright Olympos
down from above the cloudlands in reply—
a rousing peal for Odysseus. Then a token
came to him from a woman grinding flour
in the court nearby. His own handmills were there,
and twelve maids had the job of grinding out
whole grain and barley meal, the pith of men.
Now all the rest, their bushels ground, were sleeping;
one only, frail and slow, kept at it still.
She stopped, stayed her hand, and her lord heard
the omen from her lips:
"Ah, Father Zeus
almighty over gods and men!
A great bang of thunder that was, surely,
out of the starry sky, and not a cloud in sight.
It is your nod to someone. Hear me, then,
make what I say come true:
let this day be the last the suitors feed
so dainty in Odysseus' hall!
They've made me work my heart out till I drop,
grinding barley. May they feast no more!"

The servant's prayer, after the cloudless thunder
of Zeus, Odysseus heard with lifting heart,
sure in his bones that vengeance was at hand.
Then other servants, wakening, came down
to build and light a fresh fire at the hearth.
Telémakhos, clear-eyed as a god, awoke,
put on his shirt and belted on his sword,
bound rawhide sandals under his smooth feet,
and took his bronze-shod lance. He came and stood
on the broad sill of the doorway, calling Eurýkleia:
"Nurse, dear Nurse, how did you treat our guest?
Had he a supper and a good bed? Has he lain
uncared for still? My mother is like that,

perverse for all her cleverness:
she'd entertain some riff-raff, and turn out
a solid man."

The old nurse answered him:
"I would not be so quick to accuse her, child.
He sat and drank here while he had a mind to;
food he no longer hungered for, he said—
for she did ask him. When he thought of sleeping,
she ordered them to make a bed. Poor soul!
Poor gentleman! So humble and so miserable,
he would accept no bed with rugs to lie on,
but slept on sheepskins and a raw oxhide
in the entry way. We covered him ourselves."

Telémakhos left the hall, hefting his lance,
with two swift flickering hounds for company,
to face the island Akhaians in the square;
and gently born Eurýkleia the daughter
of Ops Peisenórides, called to the maids:
"Bestir yourselves! you have your brooms, go sprinkle
the rooms and sweep them, robe the chairs in red,
sponge off the tables till they shine.
Wash out the winebowls and two-handled cups.
You others go fetch water from the spring;
no loitering; come straight back. Our company
will be here soon, morning is sure to bring them;
everyone has a holiday today."

The women ran to obey her—twenty girls
off to the spring with jars for dusky water,
the rest at work inside. Then tall woodcutters
entered to split up logs for the hearth fire,
the water carriers returned; and on their heels
arrived the swineherd, driving three fat pigs,
chosen among his pens. In the wide court
he let them feed, and said to Odysseus kindly:
"Friend, are they more respectful of you now,
or still insulting you?"

Replied Odysseus:
"The young men, yes. And may the gods requite

those insolent puppies for the game they play
in a home not their own. They have no decency."

During this talk, Melánthios the goatherd
came in, driving goats for the suitors' feast,
with his two herdsmen. Under the portico
they tied the animals, and Melánthios
looked at Odysseus with a sneer. Said he:
"Stranger,
I see you mean to stay and turn our stomachs
begging in this hall. Clear out, why don't you?
Or will you have to taste a bloody beating
before you see the point? Your begging ways
nauseate everyone. There are feasts elsewhere."

Odysseus answered not a word, but grimly
shook his head over his murderous heart.
A third man came up now: Philoítios
the cattle foreman, with an ox behind him
and fat goats for the suitors. Ferrymen
had brought these from the mainland, as they bring
travellers, too—whoever comes along.
Philoítios tied the beasts under the portico
and joined the swineherd.

"Who is this," he said,
"Who is the new arrival at the manor?
Akhaian? or what else does he claim to be?
Where are his family and fields of home?
Down on his luck, all right: carries himself like a captain.
How the immortal gods can change and drag us down
once they begin to spin dark days for us!—
Kings and commanders, too."

Then he stepped over
and took Odysseus by the right hand, saying:
"Welcome, Sir. May good luck lie ahead
at the next turn. Hard times you're having, surely.
O Zeus! no god is more berserk in heaven
if gentle folk, whom you yourself begot,[151]
you plunge in grief and hardship without mercy!
Sir, I began to sweat when I first saw you,

[151] **you yourself begot:** Attributing fatherhood to Zeus was a way of paying a compliment.

and tears came to my eyes, remembering
Odysseus: rags like these he may be wearing
somewhere on his wanderings now—
I mean, if he's alive still under the sun.
But if he's dead and in the house of Death,
I mourn Odysseus. He entrusted cows to me
in Kephallênia,[152] when I was knee high,
and now his herds are numberless, no man else
ever had cattle multiply like grain.
But new men tell me I must bring my beeves
to feed them, who care nothing for our prince,
fear nothing from the watchful gods. They crave
partition of our lost king's land and wealth.
My own feelings keep going round and round
upon this tether: can I desert the boy
by moving, herds and all, to another country,
a new life among strangers? Yet it's worse
to stay here, in my old post, herding cattle
for upstarts.
I'd have gone long since,
gone, taken service with another king; this shame
is no more to be borne; but I keep thinking
my own lord, poor devil, still might come
and make a rout of suitors in his hall."

Odysseus, with his mind on action, answered:
"Herdsman, I make you out to be no coward
and no fool: I can see that for myself.
So let me tell you this. I swear by Zeus
all highest, by the table set for friends,
and by your king's hearthstone to which I've come,
Odysseus will return. You'll be on hand
to see, if you care to see it,
how those who lord it here will be cut down."

The cowman said:
"Would god it all came true!
You'd see the fight that's in me!"

Then Eumaios
echoed him, and invoked the gods, and prayed

[152] **Kephallênia:** An island near Ithaka, the modern Cephalonia.

that his great-minded master should return.
While these three talked, the suitors in the field
had come together plotting—what but death
for Telémakhos?—when from the left an eagle
crossed high with a rockdove in his claws.[153]

Amphínomos got up. Said he, cutting them short:
"Friends, no luck lies in that plan for us,
no luck, knifing the lad. Let's think of feasting."

A grateful thought, they felt, and walking on
entered the great hall of the hero Odysseus,
where they all dropped their cloaks on chairs or couches
and made a ritual slaughter, knifing sheep,
fat goats and pigs, knifing the grass-fed steer.
Then tripes were broiled and eaten. Mixing bowls
were filled with wine. The swineherd passed out cups,
Philoítios, chief cowherd, dealt the loaves
into the panniers, Melánthios poured wine,
and all their hands went out upon the feast.

Telémakhos placed his father to advantage
just at the door sill of the pillared hall,
setting a stool there and a sawed-off table,
gave him a share of tripes, poured out his wine
in a golden cup, and said:
"Stay here, sit down
to drink with our young friends. I stand between you
and any cutting word or cuffing hand
from any suitor. Here is no public house
but the old home of Odysseus, my inheritance.
Hold your tongues then, gentlemen, and your blows,
and let no wrangling start, no scuffle either."

The others, disconcerted, bit their lips
at the ring in the young man's voice. Antínoös,
Eupeithês' son, turned round to them and said:
"It goes against the grain, my lords, but still
I say we take this hectoring by Telémakhos.
You know Zeus balked at it, or else

[153] **an eagle crossed high . . . claws:** An ill omen.

we might have shut his mouth a long time past,
the silvery speaker."

But Telémakhos
paid no heed to what Antínoös said.

Now public heralds wound through Ithaka
leading a file of beasts for sacrifice, and islanders
gathered under the shade trees of Apollo,
in the precinct of the Archer° — while in hall Apollo
the suitors roasted mutton and fat beef
on skewers, pulling off the fragrant cuts;
and those who did the roasting served Odysseus
a portion equal to their own, for so
Telémakhos commanded.

But Athena
had no desire now to let the suitors
restrain themselves from wounding words and acts.
Laërtês' son again must be offended.
There was a scapegrace[154] fellow in the crowd
named Ktésippos, a Samian, rich beyond
all measure, arrogant with riches, early
and late a bidder for Odysseus' queen.
Now this one called attention to himself:
"Hear me, my lords, I have a thing to say.
Our friend has had his fair share from the start
and that's polite; it would be most improper
if we were cold to guests of Telémakhos —
no matter what tramp turns up. Well then, look here,
let me throw in my own small contribution.
He must have prizes to confer, himself,
on some brave bathman or another slave
here in Odysseus' house."

His hand went backward
and, fishing out a cow's foot from the basket,
he let it fly.

Odysseus rolled his head
to one side softly, ducking the blow, and smiled
a crooked smile with teeth clenched. On the wall

[154] **scapegrace:** Graceless; unprincipled.

the cow's foot struck and fell. Telémakhos
blazed up:
"Ktésippos, lucky for you, by heaven,
not to have hit him! He took care of himself,
else you'd have had my lance-head in your belly;
no marriage, but a grave instead on Ithaka
for your father's pains.
You others, let me see
no more contemptible conduct in my house!
I've been awake to it for a long time—by now
I know what is honorable and what is not.
Before, I was a child. I can endure it
while sheep are slaughtered, wine drunk up, and bread—
can one man check the greed of a hundred men?—
but I will suffer no more viciousness.
Granted you mean at last to cut me down:
I welcome that—better to die than have
humiliation always before my eyes,
the stranger buffeted, and the serving women
dragged about, abused in a noble house."

They quieted, grew still, under his lashing,
and after a long silence, Ageláos,
Damástor's son, spoke to them all:
"Friends, friends,
I hope no one will answer like a fishwife.
What has been said is true. Hands off this stranger,
he is no target, neither is any servant
here in the hall of King Odysseus.
Let me say a word, though, to Telémakhos
and to his mother, if it please them both:
as long as hope remained in you to see
Odysseus, that great gifted man, again,
you could not be reproached for obstinacy,
tying the suitors down here; better so,
if still your father fared the great sea homeward.
How plain it is, though, now, he'll come no more!
Go sit then by your mother, reason with her,
tell her to take the best man, highest bidder,
and you can have and hold your patrimony,
feed on it, drink it all, while she
adorns another's house."

Keeping his head,
Telémakhos replied:

"By Zeus Almighty,
Ageláos, and by my father's sufferings,
far from Ithaka, whether he's dead or lost,
I make no impediment to Mother's marriage.
'Take whom you wish,' I say, 'I'll add my dowry.'
But can I pack her off against her will
from her own home? Heaven forbid!"

At this,
Pallas Athena touched off in the suitors
a fit of laughter, uncontrollable.
She drove them into nightmare, till they wheezed
and neighed as though with jaws no longer theirs,
while blood defiled their meat, and blurring tears
flooded their eyes, heart-sore with woe to come.
Then said the visionary, Theoklýmenos:
"O lost sad men, what terror is this you suffer?
Night shrouds you to the knees, your heads, your faces;
dry retch of death runs round like fire in sticks;
your cheeks are streaming; these fair walls and pedestals
are dripping crimson blood. And thick with shades
is the entry way, the courtyard thick with shades
passing athirst toward Érebos, into the dark,
the sun is quenched in heaven, foul mist hems us in . . ."

The young men greeted this with shouts of laughter,
and Eurýmakhos, the son of Pólybos, crowed:
"The mind of our new guest has gone astray.
Hustle him out of doors, lads, into the sunlight;
he finds it dark as night inside!"

The man of vision looked at him and said:
"When I need help, I'll ask for it, Eurýmakhos.
I have my eyes and ears, a pair of legs,
and a straight mind, still with me. These will do
to take me out. Damnation and black night
I see arriving for yourselves: no shelter,
no defence for any in this crowd—
fools and vipers in the king's own hall."

With this he left that handsome room and went
home to Peiraios, who received him kindly.
The suitors made wide eyes at one another
and set to work provoking Telémakhos
with jokes about his friends. One said, for instance:

"Telémakhos, no man is a luckier host
when it comes to what the cat dragged in. What burning
eyes your beggar had for bread and wine!
But not for labor, not for a single heave—
he'd be a deadweight on a field. Then comes
this other, with his mumbo-jumbo. Boy,
for your own good, I tell you, toss them both
into a slave ship for the Sikels.° That would pay you." Sicilians

Telémakhos ignored the suitors' talk.
He kept his eyes in silence on his father,
awaiting the first blow. Meanwhile
the daughter of Ikários, Penélopê,
had placed her chair to look across and down
on father and son at bay; she heard the crowd,
and how they laughed as they resumed their dinner,
a fragrant feast, for many beasts were slain—
but as for supper, men supped never colder
than these, on what the goddess and the warrior
were even then preparing for the suitors,
whose treachery had filled that house with pain.

Book 21
The Test of the Bow

Upon Penélopê, most worn in love and thought,
Athena cast a glance like a grey sea
lifting her. Now to bring the tough bow out and bring
the iron blades. Now try those dogs at archery
to usher bloody slaughter in.
So moving stairward
the queen took up a fine doorhook of bronze,
ivory-hafted, smooth in her clenched hand,
and led her maids down to a distant room,
a storeroom where the master's treasure lay:
bronze, bar gold, black iron forged and wrought.
In this place hung the double-torsion bow
and arrows in a quiver, a great sheaf—
quills of groaning.
In the old time in Lakedaimon[155]

[155] **Lakedaimon:** The region of Sparta.

her lord had got these arms from Íphitos,
Eurýtos'[156] son. The two met in Messenia[157]
at Ortílokhos' table, on the day
Odysseus claimed a debt owed by that realm—
sheep stolen by Messenians out of Ithaka
in their long ships, three hundred head, and herdsmen.
Seniors of Ithaka and his father sent him
on that far embassy when he was young.
But Íphitos had come there tracking strays,
twelve shy mares, with mule colts yet unweaned.
And a fatal chase they led him over prairies
into the hands of Heraklês. That massive
son of toil and mortal son of Zeus
murdered his guest[158] at wine in his own house—
inhuman, shameless in the sight of heaven—
to keep the mares and colts in his own grange.
Now Íphitos, when he knew Odysseus, gave him
the master bowman's arm; for old Eurýtos
had left it on his deathbed to his son.
In fellowship Odysseus gave a lance
and a sharp sword. But Heraklês killed Íphitos
before one friend could play host to the other.
And Lord Odysseus would not take the bow
in the black ships to the great war at Troy.
As a keepsake he put it by:
it served him well at home in Ithaka.

Now the queen reached the storeroom door and halted.
Here was an oaken sill, cut long ago
and sanded clean and bedded true. Foursquare
the doorjambs and the shining doors were set
by the careful builder. Penélopê untied the strap
around the curving handle, pushed her hook
into the slit, aimed at the bolts inside
and shot them back. Then came a rasping sound
as those bright doors the key had sprung gave way—
a bellow like a bull's vaunt in a meadow—
followed by her light footfall entering
over the plank floor. Herb-scented robes

[156] **Eurýtos:** A famous archer; Íphitos provides the bow that Odysseus uses to slaughter the suitors. [157] **Messenia:** A coastal region in southwestern Greece. [158] **murdered his guest:** In a fit of madness and revenge Heraklês murdered Íphitos, angered because Eurýtos had refused to give him the prize, his daughter Iole, for an archery contest he had won.

lay there in chests, but the lady's milkwhite arms
went up to lift the bow down from a peg
in its own polished bowcase.
Now Penélopê
sank down, holding the weapon on her knees,
and drew her husband's great bow out, and sobbed
and bit her lip and let the salt tears flow.
Then back she went to face the crowded hall,
tremendous bow in hand, and on her shoulder hung
the quiver spiked with coughing death. Behind her
maids bore a basket full of axeheads, bronze
and iron implements for the master's game.
Thus in her beauty she approached the suitors,
and near a pillar of the solid roof
she paused, her shining veil across her cheeks,
her maids on either hand and still,
then spoke to the banqueters:
"My lords, hear me:
suitors indeed, you commandeered this house
to feast and drink in, day and night, my husband
being long gone, long out of mind. You found
no justification for yourselves — none
except your lust to marry me. Stand up, then:
we now declare a contest for that prize.
Here is my lord Odysseus' hunting bow.
Bend and string it if you can. Who sends an arrow
through iron axe-helve sockets, twelve in line?
I join my life with his, and leave this place, my home,
my rich and beautiful bridal house, forever
to be remembered, though I dream it only."

Then to Eumaios:
"Carry the bow forward.

Carry the blades."

Tears came to the swineherd's eyes
as he reached out for the big bow. He laid it
down at the suitors' feet. Across the room
the cowherd sobbed, knowing the master's weapon.
Antínoös growled, with a glance at both:
"Clods.
They go to pieces over nothing.
You two, there,
why are you sniveling? To upset the woman

even more? Has she not pain enough
over her lost husband? *Sit down.*
Get on with dinner quietly, or cry about it
outside, if you must. Leave us the bow.
A clean-cut game, it looks to me.
Nobody bends that bowstave easily
in this company. Is there a man here
made like Odysseus? I remember him
from childhood: I can see him even now."

That was the way he played it, hoping inwardly
to span the great horn bow with corded gut
and drill the iron with his shot—he, Antínoös,
destined to be the first of all to savor
blood from a biting arrow at his throat,
a shaft drawn by the fingers of Odysseus
whom he had mocked and plundered, leading on
the rest, his boon companions. Now they heard
a gay snort of laughter from Telémakhos,
who said then brilliantly:
"A queer thing, that!
Has Zeus almighty made me a half-wit?
For all her spirit, Mother has given in,
promised to go off with someone—and
is that amusing? What am I cackling for?
Step up, my lords, contend now for your prize.
There is no woman like her in Akhaia,
not in old Argos, Pylos, or Mykênê,
neither in Ithaka nor on the mainland,
and you all know it without praise of mine.
Come on, no hanging back, no more delay
in getting the bow bent. Who's the winner?
I myself should like to try that bow.
Suppose I bend it and bring off the shot,
my heart will be less heavy, seeing the queen my mother
go for the last time from this house and hall,
if I who stay can do my father's feat."

He moved out quickly, dropping his crimson cloak,
and lifted sword and sword belt from his shoulders.
His preparation was to dig a trench,
heaping the earth in a long ridge beside it
to hold the blades half-bedded. A taut cord
aligned the socket rings. And no one there
but looked on wondering at his workmanship,

for the boy had never seen it done.
He took his stand then
on the broad door sill to attempt the bow.
Three times he put his back into it and sprang it,
three times he had to slack off. Still he meant
to string that bow and pull for the needle shot.
A fourth try and he had it all but strung—
when a stiffening in Odysseus made him check.
Abruptly then he stopped and turned and said:
"Blast and damn it, must I be a milksop
all my life? Half-grown, all thumbs,
no strength or knack at arms, to defend myself
if someone picks a fight with me.
Take over,
O my elders and betters, try the bow,
run off the contest."

And he stood the weapon
upright against the massy-timbered door
with one arrow across the horn aslant,
then went back to his chair. Antínoös
gave the word:
"Now one man at a time
rise and go forward. Round the room in order;
left to right from where they dip the wine."

As this seemed fair enough, up stood Leódês
the son of Oinops. This man used to find
visions for them in the smoke of sacrifice.
He kept his chair well back, retired by the winebowl,
for he alone could not abide their manners
but sat in shame for all the rest. Now it was he
who had first to confront the bow,
standing up on the broad door sill. He failed.
The bow unbending made his thin hands yield,
no muscle in them. He gave up and said:
"Friends, I cannot. Let the next man handle it.
Here is a bow to break the heart and spirit
of many strong men. Aye. And death is less
bitter than to live on and never have
the beauty that we came here laying siege to
so many days. Resolute, are you still,
to win Odysseus' lady Penélopê?
Pit yourselves against the bow, and look

among Akhaians for another's daughter.
Gifts will be enough to court and take her.
Let the best offer win."

With this Leódês
thrust the bow away from him, and left it
upright against the massy-timbered door,
with one arrow aslant across the horn.
As he went down to his chair he heard Antínoös'
voice rising:

"What is that you say?
It makes me burn. You cannot string the weapon,
so 'Here is a bow to break the heart and spirit
of many strong men.' Crushing thought!
You were not born—you never had it in you—
to pull that bow or let an arrow fly.
But here are men who can and will."

He called out to the goatherd, Melánthios:
"Kindle a fire there, be quick about it,
draw up a big bench with a sheepskin on it,
and bring a cake of lard out of the stores.
Contenders from now on will heat and grease the bow.
We'll try it limber, and bring off the shot."

Melánthios darted out to light a blaze,
drew up a bench, threw a big sheepskin over it,
and brought a cake of lard. So one by one
the young men warmed and greased the bow for bending,
but not a man could string it. They were whipped.
Antínoös held off; so did Eurýmakhos,
suitors in chief, by far the ablest there.

Two men had meanwhile left the hall:
swineherd and cowherd, in companionship,
one downcast as the other. But Odysseus
followed them outdoors, outside the court,
and coming up said gently:

"You, herdsman,
and you, too, swineherd, I could say a thing to you,
or should I keep it dark?

No, no; speak,
my heart tells me. Would you be men enough
to stand by Odysseus if he came back?

Suppose he dropped out of a clear sky, as I did?
Suppose some god should bring him?
Would you bear arms for him, or for the suitors?"

The cowherd said:
"Ah, let the master come!
Father Zeus, grant our old wish! Some courier
guide him back! Then judge what stuff is in me
and how I manage arms!"

Likewise Eumaios
fell to praying all heaven for his return,
so that Odysseus, sure at least of these,
told them:
"I am at home, for I am he.
I bore adversities, but in the twentieth year
I am ashore in my own land. I find
the two of you, alone among my people,
longed for my coming. Prayers I never heard
except your own that I might come again.
So now what is in store for you I'll tell you:
If Zeus brings down the suitors by my hand
I promise marriages to both, and cattle,
and houses built near mine. And you shall be
brothers-in-arms of my Telémakhos.
Here, let me show you something else, a sign
that I am he, that you can trust me, look:
this old scar from the tusk wound that I got
boar hunting on Parnassos—
Autólykos' sons and I."

Shifting his rags
he bared the long gash. Both men looked, and knew,
and threw their arms around the old soldier, weeping,
kissing his head and shoulders. He as well
took each man's head and hands to kiss, then said—
to cut it short, else they might weep till dark—
"Break off, no more of this.
Anyone at the door could see and tell them.
Drift back in, but separately at intervals
after me.
Now listen to your orders:
when the time comes, those gentlemen, to a man,
will be dead against giving me bow or quiver.

Defy them. Eumaios, bring the bow
and put it in my hands there at the door.
Tell the women to lock their own door tight.
Tell them if someone hears the shock of arms
or groans of men, in hall or court, not one
must show her face, but keep still at her weaving.
Philoítios, run to the outer gate and lock it.
Throw the cross bar and lash it."

He turned back
into the courtyard and the beautiful house
and took the stool he had before. They followed
one by one, the two hands loyal to him.

Eurýmakhos had now picked up the bow.
He turned it round, and turned it round
before the licking flame to warm it up,
but could not, even so, put stress upon it
to jam the loop over the tip
though his heart groaned to bursting.
Then he said grimly:
"Curse this day.
What gloom I feel, not for myself alone,
and not only because we lose that bride.
Women are not lacking in Akhaia,
in other towns, or on Ithaka. No, the worst
is humiliation—to be shown up for children
measured against Odysseus—we who cannot
even hitch the string over his bow.
What shame to be repeated of us, after us!"

Antínoös said:
"Come to yourself. You know
that is not the way this business ends.
Today the islanders held holiday, a holy day,
no day to sweat over a bowstring.
Keep your head.
Postpone the bow. I say we leave the axes
planted where they are. No one will take them.
No one comes to Odysseus' hall tonight.
Break out good wine and brim our cups again,
we'll keep the crooked bow safe overnight,
order the fattest goats Melánthios has
brought down tomorrow noon, and offer thighbones burning

to Apollo, god of archers,
while we try out the bow and make the shot."

As this appealed to everyone, heralds came
pouring fresh water for their hands, and boys
filled up the winebowls. Joints of meat went round,
fresh cuts for all, while each man made his offering,
tilting the red wine to the gods, and drank his fill.
Then spoke Odysseus, all craft and gall:
"My lords, contenders for the queen, permit me:
a passion in me moves me to speak out.
I put it to Eurýmakhos above all
and to that brilliant prince, Antínoös. Just now
how wise his counsel was, to leave the trial
and turn your thoughts to the immortal gods! Apollo
will give power tomorrow to whom he wills.
But let me try my hand at the smooth bow!
Let me test my fingers and my pull
to see if any of the oldtime kick is there,
or if thin fare and roving took it out of me."

Now irritation beyond reason swept them all,
since they were nagged by fear that he could string it.
Antínoös answered, coldly and at length:
"You bleary vagabond, no rag of sense is left you.
Are you not coddled here enough, at table
taking meat with gentlemen, your betters,
denied nothing, and listening to our talk?
When have we let a tramp hear all our talk?
The sweet goad of wine has made you rave!
Here is the evil wine can do
to those who swig it down. Even the centaur[159]
Eurýtion, in Peiríthoös' hall
among the Lapíthai, came to a bloody end
because of wine; wine ruined him: it crazed him,
drove him wild for rape in that great house.
The princes cornered him in fury, leaping on him
to drag him out and crop his ears and nose.
Drink had destroyed his mind, and so he ended

[159] **centaur:** Half horse, half man, centaurs represent the uncivilized people of Thessaly. In this famous incident, centaurs were invited to the wedding of Peiríthoös; they got drunk and tried to rape the women. In this version of the story, a single centaur, Eurýtion, attempts to carry off the bride.

in that mutilation—fool that he was.
Centaurs and men made war for this,
but the drunkard first brought hurt upon himself.

The tale applies to you: I promise you
great trouble if you touch that bow. You'll come by
no indulgence in our house; kicked down
into a ship's bilge, out to sea you go,
and nothing saves you. Drink, but hold your tongue.
Make no contention here with younger men."

At this the watchful queen Penélopê
interposed:
"Antínoös, discourtesy
to a guest of Telémakhos—whatever guest—
that is not handsome. What are you afraid of?
Suppose this exile put his back into it
and drew the great bow of Odysseus—
could he then take me home to be his bride?
You know he does not imagine that! No one
need let that prospect weigh upon his dinner!
How very, very improbable it seems."

It was Eurýmakhos who answered her:
"Penélopê, O daughter of Ikários,
most subtle queen, we are not given to fantasy.
No, but our ears burn at what men might say
and women, too. We hear some jackal whispering:
'How far inferior to the great husband
her suitors are! Can't even budge his bow!
Think of it; and a beggar, out of nowhere,
strung it quick and made the needle shot!'
That kind of disrepute we would not care for."

Penélopê replied, steadfast and wary:
"Eurýmakhos, you have no good repute
in this realm, nor the faintest hope of it—
men who abused a prince's house for years,
consumed his wine and cattle. Shame enough.
Why hang your heads over a trifle now?
The stranger is a big man, well-compacted,
and claims to be of noble blood.
Ai!
Give him the bow, and let us have it out!

What I can promise him I will:
if by the kindness of Apollo he prevails
he shall be clothed well and equipped.
A fine shirt and a cloak I promise him;
a lance for keeping dogs at bay, or men;
a broadsword; sandals to protect his feet;
escort, and freedom to go where he will."

Telémakhos now faced her and said sharply:
"Mother, as to the bow and who may handle it
or not handle it, no man here
has more authority than I do—not one lord
of our own stony Ithaka nor the islands lying
east toward Elis: no one stops me if I choose
to give these weapons outright to my guest.
Return to your own hall. Tend your spindle.
Tend your loom. Direct your maids at work.
This question of the bow will be for men to settle,
most of all for me. I am master here."

She gazed in wonder, turned, and so withdrew,
her son's clearheaded bravery in her heart.
But when she had mounted to her rooms again
with all her women, then she fell to weeping
for Odysseus, her husband. Grey-eyed Athena
presently cast a sweet sleep on her eyes.

The swineherd had the horned bow in his hands
moving toward Odysseus, when the crowd
in the banquet hall broke into an ugly din,
shouts rising from the flushed young men:
"Ho! Where
do you think you are taking that, you smutty slave?"

"What is this dithering?"

"We'll toss you back alone
among the pigs, for your own dogs to eat,
if bright Apollo nods and the gods are kind!"

He faltered, all at once put down the bow, and stood
in panic, buffeted by waves of cries,
hearing Telémakhos from another quarter
shout:
"Go on, take him the bow!

Do you obey this pack?
You will be stoned back to your hills! Young as I am
my power is over you! I wish to God
I had as much the upper hand of these!
There would be suitors pitched like dead rats
through our gate, for the evil plotted here!"

Telémakhos' frenzy struck someone as funny,
and soon the whole room roared with laughter at him,
so that all tension passed. Eumaios picked up
bow and quiver, making for the door,
and there he placed them in Odysseus' hands.
Calling Eurýkleia to his side he said:
"Telémakhos
trusts you to take care of the women's doorway.
Lock it tight. If anyone inside
should hear the shock of arms or groans of men
in hall or court, not one must show her face,
but go on with her weaving."

The old woman
nodded and kept still. She disappeared
into the women's hall, bolting the door behind her.
Philoítios left the house now at one bound,
catlike, running to bolt the courtyard gate.
A coil of deck-rope of papyrus fiber
lay in the gateway; this he used for lashing,
and ran back to the same stool as before,
fastening his eyes upon Odysseus.
And Odysseus took his time,
turning the bow, tapping it, every inch,
for borings that termites might have made
while the master of the weapon was abroad.
The suitors were now watching him, and some
jested among themselves:

"A bow lover!"

"Dealer in old bows!"

"Maybe he has one like it
at home!"

"Or has an itch to make one for himself."

"See how he handles it, the sly old buzzard!"

And one disdainful suitor added this:
"May his fortune grow an inch for every inch he bends it!"

But the man skilled in all ways of contending,
satisfied by the great bow's look and heft,
like a musician, like a harper, when
with quiet hand upon his instrument
he draws between his thumb and forefinger
a sweet new string upon a peg: so effortlessly
Odysseus in one motion strung the bow.
Then slid his right hand down the cord and plucked it,
so the taut gut vibrating hummed and sang
a swallow's note.
In the hushed hall it smote the suitors
and all their faces changed. Then Zeus thundered
overhead, one loud crack for a sign.
And Odysseus laughed within him that the son
of crooked-minded Kronos had flung that omen down.
He picked one ready arrow from his table
where it lay bare: the rest were waiting still
in the quiver for the young men's turn to come.
He nocked it, let it rest across the handgrip,
and drew the string and grooved butt of the arrow,
aiming from where he sat upon the stool.
Now flashed
arrow from twanging bow clean as a whistle
through every socket ring, and grazed not one,
to thud with heavy brazen head beyond.
Then quietly
Odysseus said:
"Telémakhos, the stranger
you welcomed in your hall has not disgraced you.
I did not miss, neither did I take all day
stringing the bow. My hand and eye are sound,
not so contemptible as the young men say.
The hour has come to cook their lordships' mutton—
supper by daylight. Other amusements later,
with song and harping that adorn a feast."

He dropped his eyes and nodded, and the prince
Telémakhos, true son of King Odysseus,
belted his sword on, clapped hand to his spear,

and with a clink and glitter of keen bronze
stood by his chair, in the forefront near his father.

Book 22
Death in the Great Hall

Now shrugging off his rags the wiliest fighter of the islands
leapt and stood on the broad door sill, his own bow in his hand.
He poured out at his feet a rain of arrows from the quiver
and spoke to the crowd:
"So much for that. Your clean-cut game is over.
Now watch me hit a target that no man has hit before,
if I can make this shot. Help me, Apollo."

He drew to his fist the cruel head of an arrow for Antínoös
just as the young man leaned to lift his beautiful drinking cup,
embossed, two-handled, golden: the cup was in his fingers:
the wine was even at his lips: and did he dream of death?
How could he? In that revelry amid his throng of friends
who would imagine a single foe—though a strong foe indeed—
could dare to bring death's pain on him and darkness on his eyes?
Odysseus' arrow hit him under the chin
and punched up to the feathers through his throat.

Backward and down he went, letting the winecup fall
from his shocked hand. Like pipes his nostrils jetted
crimson runnels, a river of mortal red,
and one last kick upset his table
knocking the bread and meat to soak in dusty blood.
Now as they craned to see their champion where he lay
the suitors jostled in uproar down the hall,
everyone on his feet. Wildly they turned and scanned
the walls in the long room for arms; but not a shield,
not a good ashen spear was there for a man to take and throw.
All they could do was yell in outrage at Odysseus:
"Foul! to shoot at a man! That was your last shot!"

"Your own throat will be slit for this!"

"Our finest lad is down!

You killed the best on Ithaka."

"Buzzards will tear your eyes out!"

For they imagined as they wished that it was a wild shot,
an unintended killing—fools, not to comprehend
they were already in the grip of death.
But glaring under his brows Odysseus answered:
"You yellow dogs, you thought I'd never make it
home from the land of Troy. You took my house to plunder,
twisted my maids to serve your beds. You dared
bid for my wife while I was still alive.
Contempt was all you had for the gods who rule wide heaven,
contempt for what men say of you hereafter.
Your last hour has come. You die in blood."

As they all took this in, sickly green fear
pulled at their entrails, and their eyes flickered
looking for some hatch or hideaway from death.
Eurýmakhos alone could speak. He said:
"If you are Odysseus of Ithaka come back,
all that you say these men have done is true.
Rash actions, many here, more in the countryside.
But here he lies, the man who caused them all.
Antínoös was the ringleader; he whipped us on
to do these things. He cared less for a marriage
than for the power Kronion has denied him
as king of Ithaka. For that
he tried to trap your son and would have killed him.
He is dead now and has his portion. Spare
your own people. As for ourselves, we'll make
restitution of wine and meat consumed,
and add, each one, a tithe of twenty oxen
with gifts of bronze and gold to warm your heart.
Meanwhile we cannot blame you for your anger."

Odysseus glowered under his black brows
and said:
"Not for the whole treasure of your fathers,
all you enjoy, lands, flocks, or any gold
put up by others, would I hold my hand.
There will be killing till the score is paid.
You forced yourselves upon this house. Fight your way out,

or run for it, if you think you'll escape death.
I doubt one man of you skins by."

They felt their knees fail, and their hearts—but heard
Eurýmakhos for the last time rallying them.

"Friends," he said, "the man is implacable.
Now that he's got his hands on bow and quiver
he'll shoot from the big door stone there
until he kills us to the last man.
Fight, I say,
let's remember the joy of it. Swords out!
Hold up your tables to deflect his arrows.
After me, everyone: rush him where he stands.
If we can budge him from the door, if we can pass
into the town, we'll call out men to chase him.
This fellow with his bow will shoot no more."

He drew his own sword as he spoke, a broadsword of fine bronze,
honed like a razor on either edge. Then crying hoarse and loud
he hurled himself at Odysseus. But the kingly man let fly
an arrow at that instant, and the quivering feathered butt
sprang to the nipple of his breast as the barb stuck in his liver.
The bright broadsword clanged down. He lurched and fell aside,
pitching across his table. His cup, his bread and meat,
were spilt and scattered far and wide, and his head slammed on the ground.
Revulsion, anguish in his heart, with both feet kicking out,
he downed his chair, while the shrouding wave of mist closed on his eyes.

Amphínomos now came running at Odysseus,
broadsword naked in his hand. He thought to make
the great soldier give way at the door.
But with a spear throw from behind Telémakhos hit him
between the shoulders, and the lancehead drove
clear through his chest. He left his feet and fell
forward, thudding, forehead against the ground.
Telémakhos swerved around him, leaving the long dark spear
planted in Amphínomos. If he paused to yank it out
someone might jump him from behind or cut him down with a sword
at the moment he bent over. So he ran—ran from the tables
to his father's side and halted, panting, saying:

"Father let me bring you a shield and spear,
a pair of spears, a helmet.
I can arm on the run myself; I'll give
outfits to Eumaios and this cowherd.
Better to have equipment."

Said Odysseus:
"Run then, while I hold them off with arrows
as long as the arrows last. When all are gone
if I'm alone they can dislodge me."

Quick
upon his father's word Telémakhos
ran to the room where spears and armor lay.
He caught up four light shields, four pairs of spears,
four helms of war high-plumed with flowing manes,
and ran back, loaded down, to his father's side.
He was the first to pull a helmet on
and slide his bare arm in a buckler strap.
The servants armed themselves, and all three took their stand
beside the master of battle.
While he had arrows
he aimed and shot, and every shot brought down
one of his huddling enemies.
But when all barbs had flown from the bowman's fist,
he leaned his bow in the bright entry way
beside the door, and armed: a four-ply shield
hard on his shoulder, and a crested helm,
horsetailed, nodding stormy upon his head,
then took his tough and bronze-shod spears.
The suitors
who held their feet, no longer under bowshot,
could see a window high in a recess of the wall,
a vent, lighting the passage to the storeroom.
This passage had one entry, with a door,
at the edge of the great hall's threshold, just outside.

Odysseus told the swineherd to stand over
and guard this door and passage. As he did so,
a suitor named Ageláos asked the others:
"Who will get a leg up on that window
and run to alarm the town? One sharp attack
and this fellow will never shoot again."

His answer
came from the goatherd, Melánthios:
"No chance, my lord.
The exit into the courtyard is too near them,
too narrow. One good man could hold that portal
against a crowd. No: let me scale the wall
and bring your arms out of the storage chamber.
Odysseus and his son put them indoors,
I'm sure of it; not outside."

The goatish goatherd
clambered up the wall, toes in the chinks,
and slipped through to the storeroom. Twelve light shields,
twelve spears he took, and twelve thick-crested helms,
and handed all down quickly to the suitors.
Odysseus, when he saw his adversaries
girded and capped and long spears in their hands
shaken at him, felt his knees go slack,
his heart sink, for the fight was turning grim.
He spoke rapidly to his son:
"Telémakhos, one of the serving women
is tipping the scales against us in this fight,
or maybe Melánthios."

But sharp and clear
Telémakhos said:
"It is my own fault, Father,
mine alone. The storeroom door—I left it
wide open. They were more alert than I.
Eumaios, go and lock that door,
and bring back word if a woman is doing this
or Mélanthios, Dólios' son. More likely he."

Even as they conferred, Melánthios
entered the storeroom for a second load,
and the swineherd at the passage entry saw him.
He cried out to his lord:
"Son of Laërtês,
Odysseus, master mariner and soldier,
there he goes, the monkey, as we thought,
there he goes into the storeroom.
Let me hear your will:
put a spear through him—I hope I am the stronger—

or drag him here to pay for his foul tricks
against your house?"

Odysseus said:
"Telémakhos and I
will keep these gentlemen in hall, for all their urge to leave.
You two go throw him into the storeroom, wrench his arms
and legs behind him, lash his hands and feet
to a plank, and hoist him up to the roof beams.
Let him live on there suffering at his leisure."

The two men heard him with appreciation
and ducked into the passage. Melánthios,
rummaging in the chamber, could not hear them
as they came up; nor could he see them freeze
like posts on either side the door.
He turned back with a handsome crested helmet
in one hand, in the other an old shield
coated with dust—a shield Laërtês bore
soldiering in his youth. It had lain there for years,
and the seams on strap and grip had rotted away.
As Melánthios came out the two men sprang,
jerked him backward by the hair, and threw him.
Hands and feet they tied with a cutting cord
behind him, so his bones ground in their sockets,
just as Laërtês' royal son commanded.
Then with a whip of rope they hoisted him
in agony up a pillar to the beams,
and—O my swineherd—you were the one to say:
"Watch through the night up there, Melánthios.
An airy bed is what you need.
You'll be awake to see the primrose Dawn
when she goes glowing from the streams of Ocean
to mount her golden throne.
No oversleeping
the hour for driving goats to feed the suitors."

They stooped for helm and shield and left him there
contorted, in his brutal sling,
and shut the doors, and went to join Odysseus
whose mind moved through the combat now to come.
Breathing deep, and snorting hard, they stood
four at the entry, facing two score men.
But now into the gracious doorway stepped
Zeus's daughter Athena. She wore the guise of Mentor,

and Odysseus appealed to her in joy:
"O Mentor, join me in this fight! Remember
how all my life I've been devoted to you,
friend of my youth!"

For he guessed it was Athena,
Hope of Soldiers. Cries came from the suitors,
and Ageláos, Damástor's son, called out:
"Mentor, don't let Odysseus lead you astray
to fight against us on his side.
Think twice: we are resolved—and we will do it—
after we kill them, father and son,
you too will have your throat slit for your pains
if you make trouble for us here. It means your life.
Your life—and cutting throats will not be all.
Whatever wealth you have, at home, or elsewhere,
we'll mingle with Odysseus' wealth. Your sons
will be turned out, your wife and daughters
banished from the town of Ithaka."

Athena's anger grew like a storm wind as he spoke
until she flashed out at Odysseus:
"Ah, what a falling off!
Where is your valor, where is the iron hand
that fought at Troy for Helen, pearl of kings,
no respite and nine years of war? How many foes
your hand brought down in bloody play of spears?
What stratagem but yours took Priam's town?
How is it now that on your own door sill,
before the harriers of your wife, you curse your luck
not to be stronger?
Come here, cousin, stand by me,
and you'll see action! In the enemies' teeth
learn how Mentor, son of Álkimos,
repays fair dealing!"

For all her fighting words
she gave no overpowering aid—not yet;
father and son must prove their mettle still.
Into the smoky air under the roof
the goddess merely darted to perch on a blackened beam—
no figure to be seen now but a swallow.

Command of the suitors had fallen to Ageláos.
With him were Eurýnomos, Amphímedon,

Demoptólemos, Peisándros, Pólybos,
the best of the lot who stood to fight for their lives
after the streaking arrows downed the rest.
Ageláos rallied them with his plan of battle:
"Friends, our killer has come to the end of his rope,
and much good Mentor did him, that blowhard, dropping in.
Look, only four are left to fight, in the light there at the door.
No scattering of shots, men, no throwing away good spears;
we six will aim a volley at Odysseus alone,
and may Zeus grant us the glory of a hit.
If he goes down, the others are no problem."

At his command, then, "Ho!" they all let fly
as one man. But Athena spoiled their shots.
One hit the doorpost of the hall, another
stuck in the door's thick timbering, still others
rang on the stone wall, shivering hafts of ash.
Seeing his men unscathed, royal Odysseus
gave the word for action.

"Now I say, friends,
the time is overdue to let them have it.
Battlespoil they want from our dead bodies
to add to all they plundered here before."

Taking aim over the steadied lanceheads
they all let fly together. Odysseus killed
Demoptólemos; Telémakhos
killed Eurýadês; the swineherd, Élatos;
and Peisándros went down before the cowherd.
As these lay dying, biting the central floor,
their friends gave way and broke for the inner wall.
The four attackers followed up with a rush
to take spears from the fallen men.

Re-forming,
the suitors threw again with all their strength,
but Athena turned their shots, or all but two.
One hit a doorpost in the hall, another
stuck in the door's thick timbering, still others
rang on the stone wall, shivering hafts of ash.
Amphímedon's point bloodied Telémakhos'
wrist, a superficial wound, and Ktésippos'
long spear passing over Eumaios' shield
grazed his shoulder, hurtled on and fell.

No matter: with Odysseus the great soldier
the wounded threw again. And Odysseus raider of cities
struck Eurýdamas down. Telémakhos
hit Amphímedon, and the swineherd's shot
killed Pólybos. But Ktésippos, who had last evening thrown
a cow's hoof at Odysseus, got the cowherd's heavy cast
full in the chest — and dying heard him say:
"You arrogant joking bastard!
Clown, will you, like a fool, and parade your wit?
Leave jesting to the gods who do it better.
This will repay your cow's-foot courtesy
to a great wanderer come home."

The master
of the black herds had answered Ktésippos.
Odysseus, lunging at close quarters, put a spear
through Ageláos, Damastor's son. Telémakhos
hit Leókritos from behind and pierced him,
kidney to diaphragm. Speared off his feet,
he fell face downward on the ground.

At this moment that unmanning thunder cloud,
the aegis,[160] Athena's shield,
took form aloft in the great hall.

And the suitors mad with fear
at her great sign stampeded like stung cattle by a river
when the dread shimmering gadfly strikes in summer,
in the flowering season, in the long-drawn days.
After them the attackers wheeled, as terrible as falcons
from eyries in the mountains veering over and diving down
with talons wide unsheathed on flights of birds,
who cower down the sky in chutes and bursts along the valley —
but the pouncing falcons grip their prey, no frantic wing avails,
and farmers love to watch those beaked hunters.
So these now fell upon the suitors in that hall,
turning, turning to strike and strike again,
while torn men moaned at death, and blood ran smoking
over the whole floor.

Now there was one
who turned and threw himself at Odysseus' knees —
Leódês, begging for his life:

[160] **aegis:** The breastplate or shield with Medusa's head on it, used by Athena and Zeus; it caused panic among their enemies.

"Mercy,
mercy on a suppliant, Odysseus!
Never by word or act of mine, I swear,
was any woman troubled here. I told the rest
to put an end to it. They would not listen,
would not keep their hands from brutishness,
and now they are all dying like dogs for it.
I had no part in what they did: my part
was visionary—reading the smoke of sacrifice.
Scruples go unrewarded if I die."

The shrewd fighter frowned over him and said:
"You were diviner to this crowd? How often
you must have prayed my sweet day of return
would never come, or not for years!—and prayed
to have my dear wife, and beget children on her.
No plea like yours could save you
from this hard bed of death. Death it shall be!"

He picked up Ageláos' broadsword
from where it lay, flung by the slain man,
and gave Leódês' neck a lopping blow
so that his head went down to mouth in dust.

One more who had avoided furious death
was the son of Terpis, Phêmios, the minstrel,
singer by compulsion to the suitors.
He stood now with his harp, holy and clear,
in the wall's recess, under the window, wondering
if he should flee that way to the courtyard altar,
sanctuary of Zeus, the Enclosure God.
Thighbones in hundreds had been offered there
by Laërtês and Odysseus. No, he thought;
the more direct way would be best—to go
humbly to his lord. But first to save
his murmuring instrument he laid it down
carefully between the winebowl and a chair,
then he betook himself to Lord Odysseus,
clung hard to his knees, and said:
"Mercy,
mercy on a suppliant, Odysseus!
My gift is song for men and for the gods undying.
My death will be remorse for you hereafter.
No one taught me: deep in my mind a god

shaped all the various ways of life in song.
And I am fit to make verse in your company
as in the god's. Put aside lust for blood.
Your own dear son Telémakhos can tell you,
never by my own will or for love
did I feast here or sing amid the suitors.
They were too strong, too many; they compelled me."

Telémakhos in the elation of battle
heard him. He at once called to his father:
"Wait: that one is innocent: don't hurt him.
And we should let our herald live—Medôn;
he cared for me from boyhood. Where is *he?*
Has he been killed already by Philoítios
or by the swineherd? Else he got an arrow
in that first gale of bowshots down the room."

Now this came to the ears of prudent Medôn
under the chair where he had gone to earth,
pulling a new-flayed bull's hide over him.
Quiet he lay while blinding death passed by.
Now heaving out from under
he scrambled for Telémakhos' knees and said:
"Here I am, dear prince; but rest your spear!
Tell your great father not to see in me
a suitor for the sword's edge—one of those
who laughed at you and ruined his property!"

The lord of all the tricks of war surveyed
this fugitive and smiled. He said:
"Courage: my son has dug you out and saved you.
Take it to heart, and pass the word along:
fair dealing brings more profit in the end.
Now leave this room. Go and sit down outdoors
where there's no carnage, in the court,
you and the poet with his many voices,
while I attend to certain chores inside."

At this the two men stirred and picked their way
to the door and out, and sat down at the altar,
looking around with wincing eyes
as though the sword's edge hovered still.
And Odysseus looked around him, narrow-eyed,
for any others who had lain hidden

while death's black fury passed.
In blood and dust
he saw that crowd all fallen, many and many slain.

Think of a catch that fishermen haul in to a halfmoon bay
in a fine-meshed net from the white-caps of the sea:
how all are poured out on the sand, in throes for the salt sea,
twitching their cold lives away in Hêlios' fiery air:
so lay the suitors heaped on one another.

Odysseus at length said to his son:
"Go tell old Nurse I'll have a word with her.
What's to be done now weighs on my mind."

Telémakhos knocked at the women's door and called:
"Eurýkleia, come out here! Move, old woman.
You kept your eye on all our servant girls.
Jump, my father is here and wants to see you."

His call brought no reply, only the doors
were opened, and she came. Telémakhos
led her forward. In the shadowy hall
full of dead men she found his father
spattered and caked with blood like a mountain lion
when he has gorged upon an ox, his kill—
with hot blood glistening over his whole chest,
smeared on his jaws, baleful and terrifying—
even so encrimsoned was Odysseus
up to his thighs and armpits. As she gazed
from all the corpses to the bloody man
she raised her head to cry over his triumph,
but felt his grip upon her, checking her.
Said the great soldier then:
"Rejoice
inwardly. No crowing aloud, old woman.
To glory over slain men is no piety.
Destiny and the gods' will vanquished these,
and their own hardness. They respected no one,
good or bad, who came their way.
For this, and folly, a bad end befell them.
Your part is now to tell me of the women,
those who dishonored me, and the innocent."

His own old nurse Eurýkleia said:
"I will, then.

Child, you know you'll have the truth from me.
Fifty all told they are, your female slaves,
trained by your lady and myself in service,
wool carding and the rest of it, and taught
to be submissive. Twelve went bad,
flouting me, flouting Penélopê, too.
Telémakhos being barely grown, his mother
would never let him rule the serving women—
but you must let me go to her lighted rooms
and tell her. Some god sent her a drift of sleep."

But in reply the great tactician said:
"Not yet. Do not awake her. Tell those women
who were the suitors' harlots to come here."

She went back on this mission through his hall.
Then he called Telémakhos to his side
and the two herdsmen. Sharply Odysseus said:
"These dead must be disposed of first of all.
Direct the women. Tables and chairs will be
scrubbed with sponges, rinsed and rinsed again.
When our great room is fresh and put in order,
take them outside, these women,
between the roundhouse and the palisade,
and hack them with your swordblades till you cut
the life out of them, and every thought of sweet
Aphroditê under the rutting suitors,
when they lay down in secret."

As he spoke
here came the women in a bunch, all wailing,
soft tears on their cheeks. They fell to work
to lug the corpses out into the courtyard
under the gateway, propping one
against another as Odysseus ordered,
for he himself stood over them. In fear
these women bore the cold weight of the dead.
The next thing was to scrub off chairs and tables
and rinse them down. Telémakhos and the herdsman
scraped the packed earth floor with hoes, but made
the women carry out all blood and mire.
When the great room was cleaned up once again,
at swordpoint they forced them out, between
the roundhouse and the palisade, pell-mell
to huddle in that dead end without exit.

Telémakhos, who knew his mind, said curtly:
"I would not give the clean death of a beast
to trulls[161] who made a mockery of my mother
and of me too—you sluts, who lay with suitors."

He tied one end of a hawser to a pillar
and passed the other about the roundhouse top,
taking the slack up, so that no one's toes
could touch the ground. They would be hung like doves
or larks in springès triggered in a thicket,
where the birds think to rest—a cruel nesting.
So now in turn each woman thrust her head
into a noose and swung, yanked high in air,
to perish there most piteously.
Their feet danced for a little, but not long.

From storeroom to the court they brought Melánthios,
chopped with swords to cut his nose and ears off,
pulled off his genitals to feed the dogs
and raging hacked his hands and feet away.

As their own hands and feet called for a washing,
they went indoors to Odysseus again.
Their work was done. He told Eurýkleia:
"Bring me
brimstone and a brazier—medicinal
fumes to purify my hall. Then tell
Penélopê to come, and bring her maids.
All servants round the house must be called in."

His own old nurse Eurýkleia replied:
"Aye, surely that is well said, child. But let me
find you a good clean shirt and cloak and dress you.
You must not wrap your shoulders' breadth again
in rags in your own hall. That would be shameful."

Odysseus answered:
"Let me have the fire.
The first thing is to purify this place."

With no more chat Eurýkleia obeyed
and fetched out fire and brimstone. Cleansing fumes

[161] **trulls:** Calling the trulls harlots, Telémakhos refuses to use a sword to kill them, choosing instead the dishonorable method of hanging.

he sent through court and hall and storage chamber.
Then the old woman hurried off again
to the women's quarters to announce her news,
and all the servants came now, bearing torches
in twilight, crowding to embrace Odysseus,
taking his hands to kiss, his head and shoulders,
while he stood there, nodding to every one,
and overcome by longing and by tears.

Book 23
The Trunk of the Olive Tree

The old nurse went upstairs exulting,
with knees toiling, and patter of slapping feet,
to tell the mistress of her lord's return,
and cried out by the lady's pillow:
"Wake,
wake up, dear child! Penélopê, come down,
see with your own eyes what all these years you longed for!
Odysseus is here! Oh, in the end, he came!
And he has killed your suitors, killed them all
who made his house a bordel[162] and ate his cattle
and raised their hands against his son!"

Penélopê said:
"Dear nurse . . . the gods have touched you.
They can put chaos into the clearest head
or bring a lunatic down to earth. Good sense
you always had. They've touched you. What is this
mockery you wake me up to tell me,
breaking in on my sweet spell of sleep?
I had not dozed away so tranquilly
since my lord went to war, on that ill wind
to Ilion.
Oh, leave me! Back down stairs!
If any other of my women came in babbling
things like these to startle me, I'd see her
flogged out of the house! Your old age spares you that."

Eurýkleia said:
"Would I play such a trick on you, dear child?

[162] **bordel:** Bordello, or brothel.

It is true, true, as I tell you, he has come!
That stranger they were baiting was Odysseus.
Telémakhos knew it days ago—
cool head, never to give his father away,
till he paid off those swollen dogs!"

The lady in her heart's joy now sprang up
with sudden dazzling tears, and hugged the old one,
crying out:
"But try to make it clear!
If he came home in secret, as you say,
could he engage them singlehanded? How?
They were all down there, still in the same crowd."

To this Eurýkleia said:
"I did not see it,
I knew nothing; only I heard the groans
of men dying. We sat still in the inner rooms
holding our breath, and marvelling, shut in,
until Telémakhos came to the door and called me—
your own dear son, sent this time by his father!
So I went out, and found Odysseus
erect, with dead men littering the floor
this way and that. If you had only seen him!
It would have made your heart glow hot!—a lion
splashed with mire and blood.
But now the cold
corpses are all gathered at the gate,
and he has cleansed his hall with fire and brimstone,
a great blaze. Then he sent me here to you.
Come with me: you may both embark this time
for happiness together, after pain,
after long years. Here is your prayer, your passion,
granted: your own lord lives, he is at home,
he found you safe, he found his son. The suitors
abused his house, but he has brought them down."

The attentive lady said:
"Do not lose yourself
in this rejoicing: wait: you know
how splendid that return would be for us,
how dear to me, dear to his son and mine;
but no, it is not possible, your notion
must be wrong.

Some god has killed the suitors,
a god, sick of their arrogance and brutal
malice—for they honored no one living,
good or bad, who ever came their way.
Blind young fools, they've tasted death for it.
But the true person of Odysseus?
He lost his home, he died far from Akhaia."

The old nurse sighed:
"How queer, the way you talk!
Here he is, large as life, by his own fire,
and you deny he ever will get home!
Child, you always were mistrustful!
But there is one sure mark that I can tell you:
that scar left by the boar's tusk long ago.
I recognized it when I bathed his feet
and would have told you, but he stopped my mouth,
forbade me, in his craftiness.
Come down,
I stake my life on it, he's here!
Let me die in agony if I lie!"

Penélopê said:
"Nurse dear, though you have your wits about you,
still it is hard not to be taken in
by the immortals. Let us join my son, though,
and see the dead and that strange one who killed them."

She turned then to descend the stair, her heart
in tumult. Had she better keep her distance
and question him, her husband? Should she run
up to him, take his hands, kiss him now?
Crossing the door sill she sat down at once
in firelight, against the nearest wall,
across the room from the lord Odysseus.
There
leaning against a pillar, sat the man
and never lifted up his eyes, but only waited
for what his wife would say when she had seen him.
And she, for a long time, sat deathly still
in wonderment—for sometimes as she gazed
she found him—yes, clearly—like her husband,
but sometimes blood and rags were all she saw.
Telémakhos' voice came to her ears:

"Mother,
cruel mother, do you feel nothing,
drawing yourself apart this way from Father?
Will you not sit with him and talk and question him?
What other woman could remain so cold?
Who shuns her lord, and he come back to her
from wars and wandering, after twenty years?
Your heart is hard as flint and never changes!"

Penélopê answered:
"I am stunned, child.
I cannot speak to him. I cannot question him.
I cannot keep my eyes upon his face.
If really he is Odysseus, truly home,
beyond all doubt we two shall know each other
better than you or anyone. There are
secret signs we know, we two."

A smile
came now to the lips of the patient hero, Odysseus,
who turned to Telémakhos and said:
"Peace: let your mother test me at her leisure.
Before long she will see and know me best.
These tatters, dirt—all that I'm caked with now—
make her look hard at me and doubt me still.
As to this massacre, we must see the end.
Whoever kills one citizen, you know,
and has no force of armed men at his back,
had better take himself abroad by night
and leave his kin. Well, we cut down the flower of Ithaka,
the mainstay of the town. Consider that."

Telémakhos replied respectfully:
"Dear Father,
enough that you yourself study the danger,
foresighted in combat as you are,
they say you have no rival.
We three stand
ready to follow you and fight. I say
for what our strength avails, we have the courage."

And the great tactician, Odysseus, answered:
"Good.

Here is our best maneuver, as I see it:
bathe, you three, and put fresh clothing on,
order the women to adorn themselves,
and let our admirable harper choose a tune
for dancing, some lighthearted air, and strum it.
Anyone going by, or any neighbor,
will think it is a wedding feast he hears.
These deaths must not be cried about the town
till we can slip away to our own woods. We'll see
what weapon, then, Zeus puts into our hands."

They listened attentively, and did his bidding,
bathed and dressed afresh; and all the maids
adorned themselves. Then Phêmios the harper
took his polished shell and plucked the strings,
moving the company to desire
for singing, for the sway and beat of dancing,
until they made the manor hall resound
with gaiety of men and grace of women.
Anyone passing on the road would say:
"Married at last, I see—the queen so many courted.
Sly, cattish wife! She would not keep—not she!—
the lord's estate until he came."

So travellers'
thoughts might run—but no one guessed the truth.
Greathearted Odysseus, home at last,
was being bathed now by Eurýnomê
and rubbed with golden oil, and clothed again
in a fresh tunic and a cloak. Athena
lent him beauty, head to foot. She made him
taller, and massive, too, with crisping hair
in curls like petals of wild hyacinth
but all red-golden. Think of gold infused
on silver by a craftsman, whose fine art
Hephaistos taught him, or Athena: one
whose work moves to delight: just so she lavished
beauty over Odysseus' head and shoulders.
He sat then in the same chair by the pillar,
facing his silent wife, and said:
"Strange woman,
the immortals of Olympos made you hard,
harder than any. Who else in the world

would keep aloof as you do from her husband
if he returned to her from years of trouble,
cast on his own land in the twentieth year?

Nurse, make up a bed for me to sleep on.
Her heart is iron in her breast."

Penélopê
spoke to Odysseus now. She said:
"Strange man,
if man you are . . . This is no pride on my part
nor scorn for you—not even wonder, merely.
I know so well how you—how he—appeared
boarding the ship for Troy. But all the same . . .

Make up his bed for him, Eurýkleia.
Place it outside the bedchamber my lord
built with his own hands. Pile the big bed
with fleeces, rugs, and sheets of purest linen."

With this she tried him to the breaking point,
and he turned on her in a flash raging:
"Woman, by heaven you've stung me now!
Who dared to move my bed?
No builder had the skill for that—unless
a god came down to turn the trick. No mortal
in his best days could budge it with a crowbar.
There is our pact and pledge, our secret sign,
built into that bed—my handiwork
and no one else's!

An old trunk of olive
grew like a pillar on the building plot,
and I laid out our bedroom round that tree,
lined up the stone walls, built the walls and roof,
gave it a doorway and smooth-fitting doors.
Then I lopped off the silvery leaves and branches,
hewed and shaped that stump from the roots up
into a bedpost, drilled it, let it serve
as model for the rest. I planed them all,
inlaid them all with silver, gold and ivory,
and stretched a bed between—a pliant web
of oxhide thongs dyed crimson.

There's our sign!
I know no more. Could someone else's hand
have sawn that trunk and dragged the frame away?"

Their secret! as she heard it told, her knees
grew tremulous and weak, her heart failed her.
With eyes brimming tears she ran to him,
throwing her arms around his neck, and kissed him,
murmuring:
"Do not rage at me, Odysseus!
No one ever matched your caution! Think
what difficulty the gods gave: they denied us
life together in our prime and flowering years,
kept us from crossing into age together.
Forgive me, don't be angry. I could not
welcome you with love on sight! I armed myself
long ago against the frauds of men,
impostors who might come—and all those many
whose underhanded ways bring evil on!
Helen of Argos, daughter of Zeus and Leda,
would she have joined the stranger,[163] lain with him,
if she had known her destiny? known the Akhaians
in arms would bring her back to her own country?
Surely a goddess moved her to adultery,
her blood unchilled by war and evil coming,
the years, the desolation; ours, too.
But here and now, what sign could be so clear
as this of our own bed?
No other man has ever laid eyes on it—
only my own slave, Aktoris, that my father
sent with me as a gift—she kept our door.
You make my stiff heart know that I am yours."

Now from his breast into his eyes the ache
of longing mounted, and he wept at last,
his dear wife, clear and faithful, in his arms,
longed for
as the sunwarmed earth is longed for by a swimmer
spent in rough water where his ship went down
under Poseidon's blows, gale winds and tons of sea.

[163] **the stranger:** Paris was the guest of Helen and Meneláos.

Few men can keep alive through a big surf
to crawl, clotted with brine, on kindly beaches
in joy, in joy, knowing the abyss behind:
and so she too rejoiced, her gaze upon her husband,
her white arms round him pressed as though forever.
The rose Dawn might have found them weeping still
had not grey-eyed Athena slowed the night
when night was most profound, and held the Dawn
under the Ocean of the East. That glossy team,
Firebright and Daybright, the Dawn's horses
that draw her heavenward for men—Athena
stayed their harnessing.

Then said Odysseus:
"My dear, we have not won through to the end.
One trial—I do not know how long—is left for me
to see fulfilled. Teirêsias' ghost forewarned me
the night I stood upon the shore of Death, asking
about my friends' homecoming and my own.

But now the hour grows late, it is bed time,
rest will be sweet for us; let us lie down."

To this Penélopê replied:
"That bed,
that rest is yours whenever desire moves you,
now the kind powers have brought you home at last.
But as your thought has dwelt upon it, tell me:
what is the trial you face? I must know soon;
what does it matter if I learn tonight?"

The teller of many stories said:
"My strange one,
must you again, and even now,
urge me to talk? Here is a plodding tale;
no charm in it, no relish in the telling.
Teirêsias told me I must take an oar
and trudge the mainland, going from town to town,
until I discover men who have never known
the salt blue sea, nor flavor of salt meat—
strangers to painted prows, to watercraft
and oars like wings, dipping across the water.
The moment of revelation he foretold
was this, for you may share the prophecy:

some traveller falling in with me will say:
'A winnowing fan, that on your shoulder, sir?'
There I must plant my oar, on the very spot,
with burnt offerings to Poseidon of the Waters:
a ram, a bull, a great buck boar. Thereafter
when I come home again, I am to slay
full hekatombs to the gods who own broad heaven,
one by one.
Then death will drift upon me
from seaward, mild as air, mild as your hand,
in my well-tended weariness of age,
contented folk around me on our island.
He said all this must come."

Penélopê said:
"If by the gods' grace age at least is kind,
we have that promise—trials will end in peace."

So he confided in her, and she answered.
Meanwhile Eurýnomê and the nurse together
laid soft coverlets on the master's bed,
working in haste by torchlight. Eurýkleia
retired to her quarters for the night,
and then Eurýnomê, as maid-in-waiting,
lighted her lord and lady to their chamber
with bright brands.

She vanished.
So they came
into that bed so steadfast, loved of old,
opening glad arms to one another.
Telémakhos by now had hushed the dancing,
hushed the women. In the darkened hall
he and the cowherd and the swineherd slept.

The royal pair mingled in love again
and afterward lay revelling in stories:
hers of the siege her beauty stood at home
from arrogant suitors, crowding on her sight,
and how they fed their courtship on his cattle,
oxen and fat sheep, and drank up rivers
of wine out of the vats.
Odysseus told
of what hard blows he had dealt out to others

and of what blows he had taken — all that story.
She could not close her eyes till all was told.

His raid on the Kikonês, first of all,
then how he visited the Lotos Eaters,
and what the Kyklops did, and how those shipmates,
pitilessly devoured, were avenged.
Then of his touching Aiolos's isle
and how that king refitted him for sailing
to Ithaka; all vain: gales blew him back
groaning over the fishcold sea. Then how
he reached the Laistrygonians' distant bay
and how they smashed his ships and his companions.
Kirkê, then: of her deceits and magic,
then of his voyage to the wide underworld
of dark, the house of Death, and questioning
Teirêsias, Theban spirit.
Dead companions,
many, he saw there, and his mother, too.
Of this he told his wife, and told how later
he heard the choir of maddening Seirênês,
coasted the Wandering Rocks, Kharybdis' pool
and the fiend Skylla who takes toll of men.
Then how his shipmates killed Lord Hêlios' cattle
and how Zeus thundering in towering heaven
split their fast ship with his fuming bolt,
so all hands perished.
He alone survived,
cast away on Kalypso's isle, Ogýgia.
He told, then, how that nymph detained him there
in her smooth caves, craving him for her husband,
and how in her devoted lust she swore
he should not die nor grow old, all his days,
but he held out against her.
Last of all
what sea-toil brought him to the Phaiákians;
their welcome; how they took him to their hearts
and gave him passage to his own dear island
with gifts of garments, gold and bronze . . .
Remembering,
he drowsed over the story's end. Sweet sleep
relaxed his limbs and his care-burdened breast.

Other affairs were in Athena's keeping.
Waiting until Odysseus had his pleasure

of love and sleep, the grey-eyed one bestirred
the fresh Dawn from her bed of paling Ocean
to bring up daylight to her golden chair,
and from his fleecy bed Odysseus
arose. He said to Penélopê:
"My lady,
what ordeals have we not endured! Here, waiting
you had your grief, while my return dragged out—
my hard adventures, pitting myself against
the gods' will, and Zeus, who pinned me down
far from home. But now our life resumes:
we've come together to our longed-for bed.
Take care of what is left me in our house;
as to the flocks that pack of wolves laid waste
they'll be replenished: scores I'll get on raids
and other scores our island friends will give me
till all the folds are full again.
This day
I'm off up country to the orchards. I must see
my noble father, for he missed me sorely.
And here is my command for you—a strict one,
though you may need none, clever as you are.
Word will get about as the sun goes higher
of how I killed those lads. Go to your rooms
on the upper floor, and take your women. Stay there
with never a glance outside or a word to anyone."
Fitting cuirass and swordbelt to his shoulders,
he woke his herdsmen, woke Telémakhos,
ordering all in arms. They dressed quickly,
and all in war gear sallied from the gate,
led by Odysseus.
Now it was broad day
but these three men Athena hid in darkness,
going before them swiftly from the town.

Book 24
Warriors, Farewell

Meanwhile the suitors' ghosts were called away
by Hermês of Kyllênê,[164] bearing the golden wand
with which he charms the eyes of men or wakens
whom he wills.

[164] **Kyllênê:** The mountain birthplace of Hermês in Arcadia.

He waved them on, all squeaking
as bats will in a cavern's underworld,
all flitting, flitting criss-cross in the dark
if one falls and the rock-hung chain is broken.
So with faint cries the shades trailed after Hermês,
pure Deliverer.
He led them down dank ways,
over grey Ocean tides, the Snowy Rock,
past shores of Dream and narrows of the sunset,
in swift flight to where the Dead inhabit
wastes of asphodel at the world's end.

Crossing the plain they met Akhilleus' ghost,
Patróklos and Antílokhos, then Aias,
noblest of Danaans after Akhilleus
in strength and beauty. Here the newly dead
drifted together, whispering. Then came
the soul of Agamémnon, son of Atreus,
in black pain forever, surrounded by men-at-arms
who perished with him in Aigísthos' hall.

Akhilleus greeted him:
"My lord Atreidês,
we held that Zeus who loves the play of lightning
would give you length of glory, you were king
over so great a host of soldiery
before Troy, where we suffered, we Akhaians.
But in the morning of your life
you met that doom that no man born avoids.
It should have found you in your day of victory,
marshal of the army, in Troy country;
then all Akhaia would have heaped your tomb
and saved your honor for your son. Instead
piteous death awaited you at home."

And Atreus' son replied:
"Fortunate hero,
son of Pêleus, godlike and glorious,
at Troy you died, across the sea from Argos,
and round you Trojan and Akhaian peers
fought for your corpse and died. A dustcloud wrought
by a whirlwind hid the greatness of you slain,
minding no more the mastery of horses.
All that day we might have toiled in battle
had not a storm from Zeus broken it off.

We carried you out of the field of war
down to the ships and bathed your comely body
with warm water and scented oil. We laid you
upon your long bed, and our officers
wept hot tears like rain and cropped their hair.
Then hearing of it in the sea, your mother, Thetis,
came with nereids of the grey wave crying
unearthly lamentation over the water,
and trembling gripped the Akhaians to the bone.
They would have boarded ship that night and fled
except for one man's wisdom—venerable
Nestor, proven counselor in the past.
He stood and spoke to allay their fear: 'Hold fast,
sons of the Akhaians, lads of Argos.
His mother it must be, with nymphs her sisters,
come from the sea to mourn her son in death.'

Veteran hearts at this contained their dread
while at your side the daughters of the ancient
seagod wailed and wrapped ambrosial shrouding
around you.
Then we heard the Muses sing
a threnody[165] in nine immortal voices.
No Argive there but wept, such keening[166] rose
from that one Muse who led the song.
Now seven
days and ten, seven nights and ten, we mourned you,
we mortal men, with nymphs who know no death,
before we gave you to the flame, slaughtering
longhorned steers and fat sheep on your pyre.

Dressed by the nereids and embalmed with honey,
honey and unguent in the seething blaze,
you turned to ash. And past the pyre Akhaia's
captains paraded in review, in arms,
clattering chariot teams and infantry.
Like a forest fire the flame roared on, and burned
your flesh away. Next day at dawn, Akhilleus,
we picked your pale bones from the char to keep
in wine and oil. A golden amphora
your mother gave for this—Hephaistos' work,
a gift from Dionysos.[167] In that vase,

[165] **a threnody:** A dirge or lamentation. [166] **keening:** A wailing for the dead. [167] **Dionysos:** God of wine and ecstasy.

Akhilleus, hero, lie your pale bones mixed
with mild Patróklos' bones, who died before you,
and nearby lie the bones of Antílokhos,
the one you cared for most of all companions
after Patróklos.
We of the Old Army,
we who were spearmen, heaped a tomb for these
upon a foreland over Hellê's waters,[168]
to be a mark against the sky for voyagers
in this generation and those to come.
Your mother sought from the gods magnificent trophies
and set them down midfield for our champions. Often
at funeral games after the death of kings
when you yourself contended, you've seen athletes
cinch their belts when trophies went on view.
But these things would have made you stare—the treasures
Thetis on her silver-slippered feet
brought to your games—for the gods held you dear.
You perished, but your name will never die.
It lives to keep all men in mind of honor
forever, Akhilleus.
As for myself, what joy
is this, to have brought off the war? Foul death
Zeus held in store for me at my coming home;
Aigísthos and my vixen cut me down."

While they conversed, the Wayfinder° came near, Hermês
leading the shades of suitors overthrown
by Lord Odysseus. The two souls of heroes
advanced together, scrutinizing these.
Then Agamémnon recognized Amphímedon,
son of Meláneus—friends of his on Ithaka—
and called out to him:
"Amphimedon
what ruin brought you into this undergloom?
All in a body, picked men, and so young?
One could not better choose the kingdom's pride.
Were you at sea, aboard ship, and Poseidon
blew up a dire wind and foundering waves,
or cattle-raiding, were you, on the mainland,
or in a fight for some stronghold, or women,

[168] **Hellê's waters:** The Hellespont, which is the strait separating Asia Minor from Europe, just north of Troy; the modern Dardanelles.

when the foe hit you to your mortal hurt?
Tell me, answer my question. Guest and friend
I say I am of yours — or do you not remember
I visited your family there? I came
with Prince Meneláos, urging Odysseus
to join us in the great sea raid on Troy.
One solid month we beat our way, breasting
south sea and west, resolved to bring him round,
the wily raider of cities."

The new shade said:
"O glory of commanders, Agamémnon,
all that you bring to mind I remember well.
As for the sudden manner of our death
I'll tell you of it clearly, first to last.
After Odysseus had been gone for years
we were all suitors of his queen. She never
quite refused, nor went through with a marriage,
hating it, ever bent on our defeat.
Here is one of her tricks: she placed her loom,
her big loom, out for weaving in her hall,
and the fine warp of some vast fabric on it.
We were attending her, and she said to us:
'Young men, my suitors, now my lord is dead,
let me finish my weaving before I marry,
or else my thread will have been spun in vain.
This is a shroud I weave for Lord Laërtês
when cold Death comes to lay him on his bier.
The country wives would hold me in dishonor
if he, with all his fortune, lay unshrouded.'
We had men's hearts; she touched them; we agreed.
So every day she wove on the great loom —
but every night by torchlight she unwove it,
and so for three years she deceived the Akhaians.
But when the seasons brought the fourth around,
as long months waned, and the slow days were spent,
one of her maids, who knew the secret, told us.
We found her unraveling the splendid shroud,
and then she had to finish, willy nilly —
finish, and show the big loom woven tight
from beam to beam with cloth. She washed the shrouding
clean as sun or moonlight.

Then, heaven knows
from what quarter of the world, fatality
brought in Odysseus to the swineherd's wood

far up the island. There his son went too
when the black ship put him ashore from Pylos.
The two together planned our death-trap. Down
they came to the famous town — Telémakhos
long in advance: we had to wait for Odysseus.
The swineherd led him to the manor later
in rags like a foul beggar, old and broken,
propped on a stick. These tatters that he wore
hid him so well that none of us could know him
when he turned up, not even the older men.
We jeered at him, took potshots at him, cursed him.
Daylight and evening in his own great hall
he bore it, patient as a stone. That night
the mind of Zeus beyond the stormcloud stirred him
with Telémakhos at hand to shift his arms
from mégaron to storage room and lock it.
Then he assigned his wife her part: next day
she brought his bow and iron axeheads out
to make a contest. Contest there was none;
that move doomed us to slaughter. Not a man
could bend the stiff bow to his will or string it,
until it reached Odysseus. We shouted,
'Keep the royal bow from the beggar's hands
no matter how he begs!' Only Telémakhos
would not be denied.
So the great soldier
took his bow and bent it for the bowstring
effortlessly. He drilled the axeheads clean,
sprang, and decanted arrows on the door sill,
glared, and drew again. This time he killed
Antínoös.
There facing us he crouched
and shot his bolts of groaning at us, brought us
down like sheep. Then some god, his familiar,[169]
went into action with him round the hall,
after us in a massacre. Men lay groaning,
mortally wounded, and the floor smoked with blood.

That was the way our death came, Agamémnon.
Now in Odysseus' hall untended still
our bodies lie, unknown to friends or kinsmen

---

[169] **his familiar:** An attendant spirit.

who should have laid us out and washed our wounds
free of the clotted blood, and mourned our passing.
So much is due the dead."

But Agamémnon's
tall shade when he heard this cried aloud:
"O fortunate Odysseus, master mariner
and soldier, blessed son of old Laërtês!
The girl you brought home made a valiant wife!
True to her husband's honor and her own,
Penélopê, Ikários' faithful daughter!
The very gods themselves will sing her story
for men on earth — mistress of her own heart,
Penélopê!
Tyndáreus' daughter waited, too — how differently!
Klytaimnéstra, the adulteress,
waited to stab her lord and king. That song
will be forever hateful. A bad name
she gave to womankind, even the best."

These were the things they said to one another
under the rim of earth where Death is lord.

Leaving the town, Odysseus and his men
that morning reached Laërtês' garden lands,
long since won by his toil from wilderness —
his homestead, and the row of huts around it
where fieldhands rested, ate and slept. Indoors
he had an old slave woman, a Sikel, keeping
house for him in his secluded age.

Odysseus here took leave of his companions.
"Go make yourselves at home inside," he said.
"Roast the best porker and prepare a meal.
I'll go to try my father. Will he know me?
Can he imagine it, after twenty years?"

He handed spear and shield to the two herdsmen,
and in they went, Telémakhos too. Alone
Odysseus walked the orchard rows and vines.
He found no trace of Dólios and his sons
nor the other slaves — all being gone that day
to clear a distant field, and drag the stones
for a boundary wall.

But on a well-banked plot

Odysseus found his father in solitude
spading the earth around a young fruit tree.

He wore a tunic, patched and soiled, and leggings—
oxhide patches, bound below his knees
against the brambles; gauntlets on his hands
and on his head a goatskin cowl of sorrow.
This was the figure Prince Odysseus found—
wasted by years, racked, bowed under grief.
The son paused by a tall pear tree and wept,
then inwardly debated: should he run
forward and kiss his father, and pour out
his tale of war, adventure, and return,
or should he first interrogate him, test him?
Better that way, he thought—
first draw him out with sharp words, trouble him.
His mind made up, he walked ahead. Laërtês
went on digging, head down, by the sapling,
stamping the spade in. At his elbow then
his son spoke out:
"Old man, the orchard keeper
you work for is no townsman. A good eye
for growing things he has; there's not a nurseling,
fig tree, vine stock, olive tree or pear tree
or garden bed uncared for on this farm.
But I might add—don't take offense—your own
appearance could be tidier. Old age
yes—but why the squalor, and rags to boot?
It would not be for sloth, now, that your master
leaves you in this condition; neither at all
because there's any baseness in your self.
No, by your features, by the frame you have,
a man might call you kingly,
one who should bathe warm, sup well, and rest easy
in age's privilege. But tell me:
who are your masters? whose fruit trees are these
you tend here? Tell me if it's true this island
is Ithaka, as that fellow I fell in with
told me on the road just now? He had
a peg loose, that one: couldn't say a word
or listen when I asked about my friend,
my Ithakan friend. I asked if he were alive
or gone long since into the underworld.
I can describe him if you care to hear it:
I entertained the man in my own land

when he turned up there on a journey; never
had I a guest more welcome in my house.
He claimed his stock was Ithakan: Laërtês
Arkeísiadês, he said his father was.
I took him home, treated him well, grew fond of him—
though we had many guests—and gave him
gifts in keeping with his quality: seven
bars of measured gold, a silver winebowl
filigreed with flowers, twelve light cloaks,
twelve rugs, robes and tunics—not to mention
his own choice of women trained in service,
the four well-favored ones he wished to take."

His father's eyes had filled with tears. He said:
"You've come to that man's island, right enough,
but dangerous men and fools hold power now.
You gave your gifts in vain. If you could find him
here in Ithaka alive, he'd make
return of gifts and hospitality,
as custom is, when someone has been generous.
But tell me accurately—how many years
have now gone by since that man was your guest?
your guest, my son—if he indeed existed—
born to ill fortune as he was. Ah, far
from those who loved him, far from his native land,
in some sea-dingle° fish have picked his bones, valley
or else he made the vultures and wild beasts
a trove ashore! His mother at his bier
never bewailed him, nor did I, his father,
nor did his admirable wife, Penélopê,
who should have closed her husband's eyes in death
and cried aloud upon him as he lay.
So much is due the dead.
But speak out, tell me further:
who are you, of what city and family?
where have you moored the ship that brought you here,
where is your admirable crew? Are you a peddler
put ashore by the foreign ship you came on?"

Again Odysseus had a fable ready.
"Yes," he said, "I can tell you all those things.
I come from Rover's Passage where my home is,
and I'm King Allwoes' only son. My name
is Quarrelman.
Heaven's power in the westwind

drove me this way from Sikania,° Sicily
off my course. My ship lies in a barren
cove beyond the town there. As for Odysseus,
now is the fifth year since he put to sea
and left my homeland—bound for death, you say.
Yet landbirds flying from starboard crossed his bow—
a lucky augury. So we parted joyously,
in hope of friendly days and gifts to come."

A cloud of pain had fallen on Laërtês.
Scooping up handfuls of the sunburnt dust
he sifted it over his grey head, and groaned,
and the groan went to the son's heart. A twinge
prickling up through his nostrils warned Odysseus
he could not watch this any longer.
He leaped and threw his arms around his father,
kissed him, and said:
"Oh, Father, I am he!
Twenty years gone, and here I've come again
to my own land!
Hold back your tears! No grieving!
I bring good news—though still we cannot rest.
I killed the suitors to the last man!
Outrage and injury have been avenged!"

Laërtês turned and found his voice to murmur:
"If you are Odysseus, my son, come back,
give me some proof, a sign to make me sure."

His son replied:
"The scar then, first of all.
Look, here the wild boar's flashing tusk
wounded me on Parnassos; do you see it?
You and my mother made me go, that time,
to visit Lord Autólykos, her father,
for gifts he promised years before on Ithaka.
Again—more proof—let's say the trees you gave me
on this revetted[170] plot of orchard once.
I was a small boy at your heels, wheedling
amid the young trees, while you named each one.
You gave me thirteen pear, ten apple trees,

[170] **revetted:** Protected by a wall or embankment.

and forty fig trees. Fifty rows of vines
were promised too, each one to bear in turn.
Bunches of every hue would hang there ripening,
weighed down by the god of summer days."

The old man's knees failed him, his heart grew faint,
recalling all that Odysseus calmly told.
He clutched his son. Odysseus held him swooning
until he got his breath back and his spirit
and spoke again:
"Zeus, Father! Gods above!—
you still hold pure Olympos, if the suitors
paid for their crimes indeed, and paid in blood!
But now the fear is in me that all Ithaka
will be upon us. They'll send messengers
to stir up every city of the islands."

Odysseus the great tactician answered:
"Courage, and leave the worrying to me.
We'll turn back to your homestead by the orchard.
I sent the cowherd, swineherd, and Telémakhos
ahead to make our noonday meal."

Conversing
in this vein they went home, the two together,
into the stone farmhouse. There Telémakhos
and the two herdsmen were already carving
roast young pork, and mixing amber wine.
During these preparations the Sikel woman
bathed Laërtês and anointed him,
and dressed him in a new cloak. Then Athena,
standing by, filled out his limbs again,
gave girth and stature to the old field captain
fresh from the bathing place. His son looked on
in wonder at the godlike bloom upon him,
and called out happily:
"Oh, Father,
surely one of the gods who are young forever
has made you magnificent before my eyes!"

Clearheaded Laërtês faced him, saying:
"By Father Zeus, Athena and Apollo,
I wish I could be now as once I was,
commander of Kephallenians, when I took

the walled town, Nérikos,[171] on the promontory!
Would god I had been young again last night
with armor on me, standing in our hall
to fight the suitors at your side! How many
knees I could have crumpled, to your joy!"

While son and father spoke, cowherd and swineherd
attended, waiting, for the meal was ready.
Soon they were all seated, and their hands
picked up the meat and bread.

But now old Dólios
appeared in the bright doorway with his sons,
work-stained from the field. Laërtês' housekeeper,
who reared the boys and tended Dólios
in his bent age, had gone to fetch them in.
When it came over them who the stranger was
they halted in astonishment. Odysseus
hit an easy tone with them. Said he:
"Sit down and help yourselves. Shake off your wonder.
Here we've been waiting for you all this time,
and our mouths watering for good roast pig!"

But Dólios came forward, arms outstretched,
and kissed Odysseus' hand at the wrist bone,
crying out:
"Dear master, you returned!
You came to us again! How we had missed you!
We thought you lost. The gods themselves have brought you!
Welcome, welcome; health and blessings on you!
And tell me, now, just one thing more: Penélopê,
does she know yet that you are on the island?
or should we send a messenger?"

Odysseus gruffly said,
"Old man, she knows.
Is it for you to think of her?"

So Dólios
quietly took a smooth bench at the table
and in their turn his sons welcomed Odysseus,
kissing his hands; then each went to his chair

[171] **Kephallenians . . . Nérikos:** A town on the west coast of Greece whose exact location is unknown; the Kephallenians are Odysseus's subjects on the mainland.

beside his father. Thus our friends
were occupied in Laërtês' house at noon.

Meanwhile to the four quarters of the town
the news ran: bloody death had caught the suitors;
and men and women in a murmuring crowd
gathered before Odysseus' hall. They gave
burial to the piteous dead, or bore
the bodies of young men from other islands
down to the port, thence to be ferried home.
Then all the men went grieving to assembly
and being seated, rank by rank, grew still,
as old Eupeithês rose to address them. Pain
lay in him like a brand for Antínoös,
the first man that Odysseus brought down,
and tears flowed for his son as he began:
"Heroic feats that fellow did for us
Akhaians, friends! Good spearmen by the shipload
he led to war and lost—lost ships and men,
and once ashore again killed these, who were
the islands' pride.
Up with you! After him!—
before he can take flight to Pylos town
or hide at Elis, under Epeian law!
We'd be disgraced forever! Mocked for generations
if we cannot avenge our sons' blood, and our brothers'!
Life would turn to ashes—at least for me;
rather be dead and join the dead!
I say
we ought to follow now, or they'll gain time
and make the crossing."

His appeal, his tears,
moved all the gentry listening there;
but now they saw the crier and the minstrel
come from Odysseus' hall, where they had slept.
The two men stood before the curious crowd,
and Medôn[172] said:
"Now hear me, men of Ithaka.
When these hard deeds were done by Lord Odysseus
the immortal gods were not far off. I saw
with my own eyes someone divine who fought
beside him, in the shape and dress of Mentor;

[172] **Medôn:** A herald forced to serve the suitors but faithful to Odysseus.

it was a god who shone before Odysseus,
a god who swept the suitors down the hall
dying in droves."

At this pale fear assailed them,
and next they heard again the old forecaster,
Halithérsês Mastóridês. Alone
he saw the field of time, past and to come.
In his anxiety for them he said:
"Ithakans, now listen to what I say.
Friends, by your own fault these deaths came to pass.
You would not heed me nor the captain, Mentor;
would not put down the riot of your sons.
Heroic feats they did!—all wantonly
raiding a great man's flocks, dishonoring
his queen, because they thought he'd come no more.
Let matters rest; do as I urge; no chase,
or he who wants a bloody end will find it."

The greater number stood up shouting "Aye!"
But many held fast, sitting all together
in no mind to agree with him. Eupeithês
had won them to his side. They ran for arms,
clapped on their bronze, and mustered
under Eupeithês at the town gate
for his mad foray.

Vengeance would be his,
he thought, for his son's murder; but that day
held bloody death for him and no return.

At this point, querying Zeus, Athena said:
"O Father of us all and king of kings,
enlighten me. What is your secret will?
War and battle, worse and more of it,
or can you not impose a pact on both?"

The summoner of cloud replied:

"My child,
why this formality of inquiry?
Did you not plan that action by yourself—
see to it that Odysseus, on his homecoming,
should have their blood?

Conclude it as you will.
There is one proper way, if I may say so:
Odysseus' honor being satisfied,
let him be king by a sworn pact forever,

and we, for our part, will blot out the memory
of sons and brothers slain. As in the old time
let men of Ithaka henceforth be friends;
prosperity enough, and peace attend them."

Athena needed no command, but down
in one spring she descended from Olympos
just as the company of Odysseus finished
wheat crust and honeyed wine, and heard him say:
"Go out, someone, and see if they are coming."

One of the boys went to the door as ordered
and saw the townsmen in the lane. He turned
swiftly to Odysseus.
"Here they come,"
he said, "best arm ourselves, and quickly."

All up at once, the men took helm and shield—
four fighting men, counting Odysseus,
with Dólios' half dozen sons. Laërtês
armed as well, and so did Dólios—
greybeards, they could be fighters in a pinch.
Fitting their plated helmets on their heads
they sallied out, Odysseus in the lead.

Now from the air Athena, Zeus's daughter,
appeared in Mentor's guise, with Mentor's voice,
making Odysseus' heart grow light. He said
to put cheer in his son:
"Telémakhos,
you are going into battle against pikemen
where hearts of men are tried. I count on you
to bring no shame upon your forefathers.
In fighting power we have excelled this lot
in every generation."

Said his son:
"If you are curious, Father, watch and see
the stuff that's in me. No more talk of shame."

And old Laërtês cried aloud:
"Ah, what a day for me, dear gods!
to see my son and grandson vie in courage!"

Athena halted near him, and her eyes
shone like the sea. She said:

"Arkeísiadês,
dearest of all my old brothers-in-arms,
invoke the grey-eyed one and Zeus her father,
heft your spear and make your throw."

Power flowed into him from Pallas Athena,
whom he invoked as Zeus's virgin child,
and he let fly his heavy spear.
It struck
Eupeithês on the cheek plate of his helmet,
and undeflected the bronze head punched through.
He toppled, and his armor clanged upon him.
Odysseus and his son now furiously
closed, laying on with broadswords, hand to hand,
and pikes: they would have cut the enemy down
to the last man, leaving not one survivor,
had not Athena raised a shout
that stopped all fighters in their tracks.

"Now hold!"
she cried, "Break off this bitter skirmish;
end your bloodshed, Ithakans, and make peace."

Their faces paled with dread before Athena,
and swords dropped from their hands unnerved, to lie
strewing the ground, at the great voice of the goddess.
Those from the town turned fleeing for their lives.
But with a cry to freeze their hearts
and ruffling like an eagle on the pounce,
the lord Odysseus reared himself to follow—
at which the son of Kronos dropped a thunderbolt
smoking at his daughter's feet.

Athena
cast a grey glance at her friend and said:
"Son of Laërtês and the gods of old,
Odysseus, master of land ways and sea ways,
command yourself. Call off this battle now,
or Zeus who views the wide world may be angry."

He yielded to her, and his heart was glad.
Both parties later swore to terms of peace
set by their arbiter, Athena, daughter
of Zeus who bears the stormcloud as a shield—
though still she kept the form and voice of Mentor.

Changing Gods: From Religion to Philosophy

Historians have observed that a profound change of consciousness took place in Europe, the Middle East, and Asia around the sixth century B.C.E.: a shift of focus from myth to philosophy, from a concern with transcendent realities and explanations of the cosmos to the historical-political world of the senses. Although *myth* is today sometimes used to mean unscientific, fictitious, or false, in the context of ancient cultures the term is used to mean stories about gods, and how the cosmos was created and how it works, and about the relations between gods and humans. Most, if not all, ancient religions expressed their version of the sacred and found a narrative context for their rituals and beliefs in myths. *Philosophy,* by contrast, means a logical or rational analysis of the basic principles that underlie the nature of reality and human behavior. Although philosophy did emerge during this time, it is not true that most people abandoned religious stories altogether and became rationalists; myths constitute the core of world religions even today. Nevertheless, over this period of two to three hundred years there was a gradual growth in philosophical analysis during which influential thinkers and writers questioned the myths of their particular cultures and began to replace them with rational explanations, a process that has continued into the modern day with the development of science and technology.

This was the era that started with Zoroaster and the Magians of Persia, a relatively short era during which the most momentous events that started history proper on its course were concentrated — the age of Confucius, Lao-tzu, and the great Chinese schools of philosophy; the age of the Upanishads and the Buddha in India; of Socrates, Plato, and Periclean Athens; of the great Hebrew prophets in Palestine, Elijah, Isaiah, and Jeremiah — all between 800 and 200 B.C., the most deep-cut dividing line in history.

– Amaury de Riencourt, historian, 1974

Ancient India had a unique way of dealing with the two traditions of myth and philosophy: It treated them as parallel developments. The Vedas, the oldest collection of sacred writings in India, contain myths about gods, goddesses, and creation stories. The Upanishads (ninth to fifth centuries B.C.E.) are essentially books of

philosophy that reflect on the nature of reality, on what humans need to know and understand. A creation hymn from the Rig Veda (c. 1000 B.C.E.), "**In the Beginning, before the Gods**," seems to reflect the change from the Vedic Age (1500–500 B.C.E.) to the more philosophical world of the **UPANISHADS**. This creation hymn, called Nasadiya in Sanskrit, a title derived from the opening words, "Then neither Being nor Not-being was," searches for a primordial impulse, an intelligent abstraction, like desire or life force, that might account for creation and then comes face to face with the complexity of pondering creation in the questions, "Who knows truly? Who can here declare it? Who then knows whence it has arisen?" p. 776

The Upanishads developed the concept of **BRAHMAN** to explain ultimate reality, but the Brihadaranyaka Upanishad, a text from the eighth or seventh century B.C.E., states explicitly of the difficulty of answering questions about origins and the relationship of language to transcendent reality, and the consequent need to rely on metaphor. In this passage, translated by Wendy Doniger O'Flaherty, *he* is substituted for *Brahman,* as in the original Indian text: "At that time, all of this (world) was undifferentiated. By means of name and form it became differentiated—'This has this name; this has this form,' distinguishing by means of name and form. He entered in here, right up to the tips of his fingernails, as a razor is hidden in a razor sheath, or as fire is inside firewood. People do not see him, for (whatever they see) is incomplete. Whenever one breathes, he becomes breath; whenever one speaks, he is speech; seeing, he is the eye; hearing, the ear; thinking, the mind. These are just the names for his acts. Whoever worships one (aspect) or another does not understand, for he is incomplete in any one or another."

According to the **Buddhist Texts**, in the sixth century B.C.E. the Buddha further changed India's wisdom tradition by simply refusing to speculate about the nature of the universe—"Whether the world is eternal or not eternal, whether the world is finite or not, whether the soul is the same as the body or whether the soul is one thing and the body another. . . ." In Majjhima Nikaya, the Buddha patiently p. 778

◀ **Gandhara Buddha, third century**
Rather than spending time speculating on the nature of the universe, Buddhist teachings advocate concerning oneself with the here and now. (Eliot Elisofon / TimePix)

The terms axial period and axial religions have been used by the philosopher, Karl Jaspers, to describe a fact that various observers had intermittently noted during the last century: namely, . . . in Europe and Asia a profound change of a religious and moral nature took place more or less within the span of the sixth century B.C. at widely separated points. At that time, the earliest universal religions, Buddhism and Zoroastrianism, came forth, while those that appeared later, Christianity, Mithraism, Manichaeism, and Islam, continued the transformations begun then. With this a new kind of person and a new kind of community took form.

– Lewis Mumford, social historian, 1956

explains to the disciple who asks him about such matters that his attention is focused solely on the problem of suffering and how to deal with it. He tells a story about someone who has been wounded by a poisoned arrow and says that the person who is dying does not concern himself with speculation about the ways and means of the wound but rather is pragmatically concerned with healing.

As the Buddha's answer demonstrates, India's religious and philosophical traditions are rooted in language—and the inability to use words to describe some concepts such as reality and suffering. In China as well as in India, sophisticated poets and philosophers recognized at least two characteristics of language: Language is limited to and is inevitably a product of a particular culture; there is no universal language. The reality of any deity therefore transcends any particular combination of letters or symbols used to denote him or her. Moreover, different names in two languages and cultures might refer to the same deity, and that deity transcends both languages. The Chinese sage Laozi (Lao Tzu) (sixth to third century B.C.E.) makes the limitations of language the foundation for discussing the dao (Tao) in the Dao De Jing (Tao Te Ching):

> The Tao that can be told is not the eternal Tao.
> The name that can be named is not the eternal name.
> The nameless is the beginning of heaven and earth.
> The named is the mother of ten thousand things.

Like the Buddha's, Laozi's advice was to attend to this world and not get distracted by religious customs; one follows the Way, the **DAO**, by aligning oneself with the forces of nature.

The most influential social and political philosopher of China in the sixth century B.C.E. was Confucius, whose philosophy can be seen in this dialogue quoted in Book Eleven of *The Analects*: "Tzu-lu asked how one should serve ghosts and spirits. The Master said, 'Till you have learnt to serve men, how can you serve ghosts?' Tzu-lu then ventured upon a question about the dead. The Master said, 'Till you know about the living, how are you to know about the dead?'" Although Confucius promoted a fellowship between families and their ancestors, he played a significant role in shifting attention away from the worship of a deity or deities and toward a code of ethics for this world.

A number of Greek philosophers and scientists of the sixth and fifth centuries B.C.E. actively critiqued their traditional religion and

Confucius, nineteenth century
A modern Chinese engraving showing the Chinese philosopher on his travels. (The Art Archive/Bibliothèque Nationale, Paris/Dagli Orti)

wondered whether there might be more rational ways of conceiving of the cosmos. **Heraclitus** (c. 535–475 B.C.E.) observed that the various myths shared an abstract concept that could account for the basic condition of the cosmos—change or conflict; behind the figure of Zeus was war. The Greek philosopher Xenophanes of Colophon's (fl. c. 536 B.C.E.) definition of deity is similar to the Indian concept of Brahman. "There is one God," he wrote, "greatest among gods and men, neither in shape nor in thought like unto mortals . . . He is all sight, all mind, all ear . . . He abides ever in the same place motionless, and it befits him not to wander hither and thither. . . ." Xenophanes noted that deities of a particular religion mirror their peoples' culture and language: "Yet men imagine gods to be born, and to have raiment, voice, and body, like themselves . . .

heh-ruh-KLIGH-tus

The School of Philosophy, first century
Roman mosaic showing a group of philosophy students at Plato's Academy. (The Art Archive / Archaeological Museum Naples / Dagli Orti)

Even so the gods of the Ethiopians are swarthy and flat-nosed, the gods of the Thracians, fair-haired and blue-eyed . . . Even so Homer and Hesiod attributed to the gods all that is a shame and a reproach among men—theft, adultery, deceit, and other lawless acts. . . . Even so oxen, lions, and horses, if they had hands wherewith to carve images, would fashion gods after their own shapes and make them bodies like to their own."

Aristotle (384–322 B.C.E.), who believed that the world was intelligible and subject to rational inquiry, in *Against the Logicians* (***Adversus Dogmaticos***) applies logical analysis to the origins of religion. **Euhemerus** (fl. c. 300 B.C.E.) in *Sacred History* carries the critique of mythology and religion even further with his view that while some gods are eternal beings, others are actually humans who have been elevated to godhood. Myth then, according to Euhemerus, is history distorted or amplified by fanciful storytellers.

p. 782

yoo-HEE-muh-rus

The evolution of Greek religion from the Olympian deities like Zeus, Apollo, and Athena to philosophical principles and concepts had a profound effect on Roman writers of the first century B.C.E. like Horace and Ovid. The Roman poet and philosopher Lucretius (c. 99–c. 55 B.C.E.), in his didactic poem in six books, ***On the Nature***

p. 786

of Things (*De rerum natura*), draws on earlier Greek scientific theories to argue that the universe came into being through natural laws and to question the existence of mythic deities. As Lucretius explains away the deities, one wonders about the possible effects of secularization on those who formerly depended on religion for meaning. Lucretius himself does not seem to realize that demythologizing could be causing the depression and fear that he observes in his contemporaries.

In the fourth century B.C.E. Alexander the Great spread the gospel of **Hellenism**, with its emphasis on literacy, education, libraries, art, and tolerance, as far east as India and south to Egypt, where he founded Alexandria. The philosopher Philo Judaeus (c. 20 B.C.E.–c. 50 C.E.) was a member of the large Jewish population in Alexandria that had migrated to Egypt after the Babylonian captivity, as part of the **Diaspora**, the dispersion of Jews outside of Jerusalem. Philo was the foremost intellectual of the reconciliation of Greek thought with Judaism, or Hellenistic Judaism. The core of his synthesis, related in *On the Creation of the World,* was the association of God with *Logos,* or Rational Word; Logos is the creative agent that gives form and structure to the world. This **Platonic** idea was later picked up by the Christian author of the Gospel of John, who wrote, "In the beginning was the Word, and the Word was with God. . . ." Philo Judaeus and the Gospel of John represented a new direction for religious thought, which had evolved over several centuries from anthropomorphic deities associated with nature to highly abstract philosophical concepts. This evolution would later give a boost to the Western development of science and technology in the sixteenth century when the philosophical concepts associated with the cosmos were linked to physical principles.

Set loose from the mythical age with its calm and gentle stagnation, he [humans] set out on an anxiety-filled journey of exploration armed with the essential tools of masculinity: philosophic thought in Greece, cosmological thought in Iran, driving willpower among the Hebrews. Even in India and China, philosophers were basically unmythical in their creative intellectual power, although tolerant of surviving mythologies. . . .

– Amaury de Riencourt, historian, 1974

■ CONNECTIONS

***In the World:* The Spirit of Inquiry (Book 4).** The gradual transformation of deities from anthropomorphic figures with personalities to cosmic, abstract principles like Justice or Reason eventually led to the substitution of philosophical explanations about the workings of the cosmos for religious theories. How did this process in the ancient world set the stage for the later development of science and technology?

Greece, p. 247; Ancient Hebrews, p. 127; China, p. 1563. In several ancient civilizations, the authority of transcendent deities was at some time undercut by a concern with ethics and the transformation of society. How is this shift evident in the works of the Greek philosophers Socrates and Aristotle, the story of Job in Hebrew Scriptures, the laws of Hammurabi, and the concerns of Confucius?

■ **PRONUNCIATION**

Ephesus: EF-uh-sus
Euhemerus: yoo-HEE-muh-rus
Heraclitus: heh-ruh-KLIGH-tus
Malunkyaputta: muh-LOONG-kyuh-POO-tuh
Tathagata: tuh-TAH-guh-tuh
Tityos: TIT-ee-us

Rig Veda

c. 1000 B.C.E.

The sacred texts of the Hindus in India are collectively called the Veda or Vedas, which generally speaking refers to a large body of written literature dating from c. 1000 B.C.E. to c. 1500 C.E. Hindus refer to the Veda as *shruti,* meaning "that which is heard," suggesting that the sages who recorded the texts first *heard* them from the gods; it is thought that the materials were passed down orally for centuries, if not millennia, before being set down as text.

Composed around 1000 B.C.E., the Rig Veda, the earliest and probably the most important Vedic text, is made up of 1,028 hymns, prayers used for sacrificial rituals, and rules for daily living. A number of the hymns explore the origins and the sequence of creation. The following creation hymn is called a "metaphysical" text because it uses abstract or philosophical language to contemplate the nature of creation. In the sixth stanza, the writer dispenses with the notion that the gods are responsible for the birth of the world, since they "Only later [came to be]." The probing assertions of this hymn, whose primary purpose may be to challenge the reader to go beyond simple ideas about the nature of life and humankind's origins, have stimulated complex commentaries by both Indian and Western scholars.

The Rig Veda

Translated by Dominic Goodall

In the Beginning, before the Gods

1. Then neither Being nor Not-being was,
Nor atmosphere, nor firmament, nor what is beyond.
What did it encompass? Where? In whose protection?
What was the water, the deep, unfathomable?

2. Neither death nor immortality was there then,
No sign of night or day.
That One breathed, windless, by its own energy (*svadhā*):
Nought else existed then.

3. In the beginning was darkness swathed in darkness;
All this was but unmanifested water.
Whatever was, that One, coming into being,
Hidden by the Void,
Was generated by the power of heat (*tapas*).

4. In the beginning this [One] evolved,
Became desire, first seed of mind.
Wise seers, searching within their hearts,
Found the bond of Being in Not-being.

5. Their cord[1] was extended athwart:
Was there a below? Was there an above?
Casters of seed there were, and powers;[2]
Beneath was energy, above was impulse.

6. Who knows truly? Who can here declare it?
Whence it was born, whence is this emanation.
By the emanation of this the gods
Only later [came to be].[3]
Who then knows whence it has arisen?

7. Whence this emanation hath arisen,
Whether [God] disposed[4] it, or whether he did not,—
Only he who is its overseer in highest heaven knows.
[He only knows,] or perhaps he does not know!

[1] **cord:** A reference to either the "bond" spoken of in the previous stanza or a measuring cord for separating the elements.

[2] **Casters . . . powers:** This line and the next seem to suggest that there are male powers above—"casters of seed"—and female powers below.

[3] **Only . . . be:** Since the gods came afterwards, they cannot be the source of creation.

[4] **disposed:** Or "created." (Translator's note.)

Buddhist Texts

FIFTH–FIRST CENTURY, B.C.E.

The Majjhima Nikaya is a collection of Buddhist texts belonging to the second of three groups of canonized texts, or Pitaka. In the Pali version, texts written in a dialect of Sanscrit, this second group contains 152 sutras. In Sutra 63, excerpted here, the monk Malunkyaputta asks the Buddha for an explanation of eternity and life after death. The Buddha patiently explains that he is not concerned with metaphysical questions, that there is a pressing need to deal with the immediate condition of suffering in the world, as the parable of the poisoned arrow illustrates. The Buddha focuses on the practical concerns of being mortal. Although Buddhism takes various forms in different countries, it consistently requires great personal effort to diligently follow a path, devoid of the supernatural, that will get rid of suffering and lead ultimately to identification with the Universal Spirit.

FROM

Majjhima Nikaya

Translated by H. C. Warren

[On Metaphysical Questions]

Then the venerable Malunkyaputta arose at eventide from his seclusion, and drew near to where the Blessed One was; and having drawn near and greeted the Blessed One, he sat down respectfully at one side. And seated respectfully at one side, the venerable Malunkyaputta spoke to the Blessed One as follows:

"Reverend Sir, it happened to me, as I was just now in seclusion and plunged in meditation, that a consideration presented itself to my mind, as follows: 'These theories which the Blessed One has left unexplained, has set aside and rejected—that the world is eternal, that the world is not eternal . . . that the saint neither exists nor does not exist after death—these the Blessed One does not explain to me. And the fact that the Blessed One does not explain them to me does not please me nor suit me. I will draw near to the Blessed One and inquire of him concerning this matter. If the Blessed One will explain to me, either that the world is eternal, or that the world is not eternal . . . or that the saint neither exists nor does not exist after death, in that case will I lead the religious life under the Blessed One. If the Blessed One will not explain to me, either that the world is eternal, or that the world is not eternal . . . or that the saint neither exists nor does not exist after death, in that case will I abandon religious training and return to the lower life of a layman.' . . .

"Pray, Malunkyaputta, did I ever say to you, 'Come, Malunkyaputta, lead the religious life under me, and I will explain to you either that the world is eternal, or that the world is not eternal . . . or that the saint neither exists nor does not exist after death'?"

"Nay, verily, Reverend Sir."

"Or did you ever say to me, 'Reverend Sir, I will lead the religious life under the Blessed One, on condition that the Blessed One explain to me either that the world is eternal, or that the world is not eternal . . . or that the saint neither exists nor does not exist after death'?"

"Nay, verily, Reverend Sir." . . .

"Malunkyaputta, any one who should say, 'I will not lead the religious life under the Blessed One until the Blessed One shall explain to me either that the world is eternal, or that the world is not eternal . . . or that the saint neither exists nor does not exist after death';—that person would die, Malunkyaputta, before the Tathagata[1] had ever explained this to him.

"It is as if, Malunkyaputta, a man had been wounded by an arrow thickly smeared with poison, and his friends and companions, his relatives and kinsfolk, were to procure for him a physician or surgeon; and the sick man were to say, 'I will not have this arrow taken out until I have learnt whether the man who wounded me belonged to the warrior caste, or to the Brahmin caste, or to the agricultural caste, or to the menial caste.'

"Or again he were to say, 'I will not have this arrow taken out until I have learnt the name of the man who wounded me, and to what clan he belongs.'

"Or again he were to say, 'I will not have this arrow taken out until I have learnt whether the man who wounded me was tall, or short, or of the middle height.'

"Or again he were to say, 'I will not have this arrow taken out until I have learnt whether the man who wounded me was black, or dusky, or of a yellow skin.'

"Or again he were to say, 'I will not have this arrow taken out until I have learnt whether the man who wounded me was from this or that village, or town, or city.' . . .

[Many other possibilities are mentioned.]

"That man would die, Malunkyaputta, without ever having learnt this.

"In exactly the same way, Malunkyaputta, any one who should say, 'I will not lead the religious life under the Blessed One until the Blessed One shall explain to me either that the world is eternal, or that the world is not eternal . . . or that the saint neither exists nor does not exist after death';—that person would die, Malunkyaputta, before the Tathagata had ever explained this to him.

"The religious life, Malunkyaputta, does not depend on the dogma that the world is eternal; nor does the religious life, Malunkyaputta, depend on the dogma that the world is not eternal. Whether the dogma obtain, Malunkyaputta, that the world is eternal, or that the world is not eternal, there still remain birth, old age, death, sorrow, lamentation, misery, grief, and despair. . . .

"Accordingly, Malunkyaputta, bear always in mind what it is that I have not explained, and what it is that I have explained. And what, Malunkyaputta, have I not

[1] **Tathagata:** One of the ten titles for the Buddha, meaning "one who on his way to truth has achieved enlightenment."

explained? I have not explained, Malunkyaputta, that the world is eternal; I have not explained that the world is not eternal; I have not explained that the world is finite; I have not explained that the world is infinite; I have not explained that the soul and the body are identical; I have not explained that the soul is one thing and the body another; I have not explained that the saint exists after death; I have not explained that the saint does not exist after death; I have not explained that the saint both exists and does not exist after death; I have not explained that the saint neither exists nor does not exist after death. And why, Malunkyaputta, have I not explained this? Because, Malunkyaputta, this profits not, nor has to do with the fundamentals of religion, nor tends to aversion, absence of passion, cessation, quiescence, the supernatural faculties, supreme wisdom, and Nirvana;[2] therefore have I not explained it?

"And what, Malunkyaputta, have I explained? Misery,[3] Malunkyaputta, have I explained; the origin of misery have I explained; the cessation of misery have I explained; and the path leading to the cessation of misery have I explained. And why, Malunkyaputta, have I explained this? Because, Malunkyaputta, this does profit, has to do with the fundamentals of religion, and tends to aversion, absence of passion, cessation, quiescence, knowledge, supreme wisdom, and Nirvana; therefore have I explained it. Accordingly, Malunkyaputta, bear always in mind what it is that I have not explained, and what it is that I have explained." . . .

---

[2] **Nirvana:** A state of bliss beyond individual existence when one unites with the Universal Spirit.

[3] **Misery:** A more common translation is "suffering."

Heraclitus

fl. c. 535–475 B.C.E.

EF-uh-sus

heh-ruh-KLIGH-tus

Associated with the city of **Ephesus** on the western coast of what is now Turkey, **Heraclitus** was born to a noble family. Rejecting a hereditary role in politics, he chose instead the life of a philosopher. He wrote one book containing his views about life, politics, religion, and science of which only fragments survive. He died at the age of sixty. Along with other thinkers of his time, he searched for the ultimate nature of reality, for what made the world tick. Unwilling to ascribe cosmic control to a deity or group of deities, Heraclitus pointed at *change* as a prime principle of life and fire as the essential substance of the universe, though it is unclear exactly what he meant by fire. Because he was wrestling with somewhat mysterious issues that often confound reason and logic, his prose is filled with abbreviated assertions and paradoxes. He was part of a movement that in the Western world at the time was unique to Greece: the use of human reason in examining how to live and what to believe without recourse to a particular religious code or body of beliefs. Today these thinkers are known as philosophers, individuals who explored a path that gradually diverged from the authority of religious tradition, the priesthood, and political rule.

Two quotes from Greek philosophers follow the Heraclitus Fragments: one is from Theophrastus (c. 372–c. 287 B.C.E.), who succeeded Aristotle as the head of the Lyceum in Athens; the other is from Chrysippus (c. 280–c. 207 B.C.E.), a Greek stoic philosopher who succeeded Cleanthes as the head of Plato's Academy in Athens.

FROM

Fragments

Translated by Philip Wheelwright

[Change Runs the Universe]

20. Everything flows and nothing abides; everything gives way and nothing stays fixed.

21. You cannot step twice into the same river, for other waters and yet others go ever flowing on. (91, 12)

26. It should be understood that war is the common condition, that strife is justice, and that all things come to pass through the compulsion of strife. (80)

27. Homer was wrong in saying, "Would that strife might perish from amongst gods and men." For if that were to occur, then all things would cease to exist.

66. Immortals become mortals, mortals become immortals; they live in each other's death and die in each other's life. (62)

118. Listening not to me but to the Logos,[1] it is wise to acknowledge that all things are one. (50)

119. Wisdom is one and unique; it is unwilling and yet willing to be called by the name of Zeus. (32)

120. Wisdom is one—to know the intelligence by which all things are steered through all things. (41)

Hippasus of Metapontum and Heraclitus of Ephesus declare that reality is one and in motion and limited. Taking fire as the first-principle they explain all things as derived from fire and resolved again into fire through the complementary processes of condensation and rarefaction; for fire, they assert, is the one essential nature that underlies appearances. Whatever occurs, Heraclitus declares, is a transformation of fire; and in what occurs he finds a certain order and definite time, determined by fated necessity. –Theophrastus, *Physical Opinions*

Heraclitus says that war and Zeus are the same thing. (Chrysippus)

[1] **Logos:** Here, *Logos* means the transcendent Word as a principle of the universe.

Aristotle
384–322 B.C.E.

Two names are prominently associated with ancient Greek philosophy: Plato and Aristotle, two men whose use of reason to investigate the basic principles of knowledge, nature, ethics, and literature has influenced thought in the West up to the present day. Aristotle began his studies at Plato's Academy in Athens at seventeen and remained there for twenty years, until Plato's death in 347 B.C.E. For the next several years he traveled about and was the tutor of young Alexander of Macedonia, who became Alexander the Great and eventually spread the Greek culture and language throughout his empire. Aristotle returned to Athens in 335 B.C.E. to found a school called the Lyceum, the first research institution in Greece devoted to science, literature, and philosophy. Aristotle, whose sheer force of intellect and breadth of inquiry made him a genius, was devoted to the fundamental idea that the world is essentially rational and therefore subject to human reason and understanding. It was not necessary to resort to revelation from a god or gods. Through the rigors of rational inquiry, he set about to analyze and categorize human beings, nature, and the cosmos. In *Against the Logicians (Adversus Dogmaticos)*, an excerpt of which follows, Sextus Empiricus explains Aristotle's views on the origin of religion.

Sextus Empiricus, from *Adversus Dogmaticos*

Translated by Frederick C. Grant

The Origin of Religion

And Aristotle said that the conception of the gods arose among mankind from two sources, namely, from events which affect the soul and from the phenomena of the heavens. (1) It arose from events which affect the soul because of the things that occur in sleep, viz., its inspirations and its prophecies. For when, he says, the soul is alone in sleep, then it takes its real nature, and prophesies and predicts things to come. It is also in this same state when it is being separated from bodies [i.e., the body] at death. He certainly agrees with the observation of the poet Homer, for Homer told how the dying Patroclus predicted the slaying of Hector and how Hector foretold the end of Achilles [*Iliad* 16; 22]. For these reasons, then, he says, men came to suspect the existence of something divine, in itself like the soul and of all things the most intelligent. (2) But they also derived this conception from the phenomena of the heavens, or when they saw the sun circling about [the celestial poles] in the daytime and at night observed the orderly motion of the other stars, they assumed that some god was the cause of such motion and order.

Philosophic Conversation, fifth century B.C.E.
A red-figure vase showing two Greeks discussing philosophy. "Red-figure" refers to an ancient glazing technique that allowed the decorative motif to remain the color of the clay while the background turned black. (The Art Archive / Musée du Louvre, Paris / Dagli Orti)

EUHEMERUS

FL. C. 300 B.C.E.

The influential Euhemerus of Messene looked for the "truth" of myth in the "facts" of history. Euhemerus's *Sacred History* (c. 300 B.C.E.), which reportedly describes a political utopia and explains the origin of the gods, is no longer extant, but references to it appear in other texts, notably in *Library of History* by Diodorus (first century B.C.E.), a Sicilian historian. **Euhemerus** claimed that the Greek Olympian deities were originally royal families honored by their followers and called *theos* (god) while alive, a deification that was perpetuated in the increasingly embellished stories told of them after their deaths. Zeus, for example, was born and died on Crete, where he had been king. He married Hera, Demeter, and Themis and sired Curetes, Persephone, and Athena by each, respectively.

yoo-HEE-muh-rus

Euhemerism, used by the early Christian church fathers to discredit pagan religions, has been loosely defined as any attempt to rationalize myth as distorted history: that is, to explain how the stories of gods and goddesses might have resulted from a misreading of history. Euhemerism could also be seen as part of the process by which people or cultures reflect on past events and individuals and interpret their significance in the present. It is only in retrospect that legends are created, why not deities as well?

In the following excerpt, Euhemerus is quoted by various authors—Eusebius, John Malalas, Eustathius, Tertullian, and others. Modern editors have put these fragments together to form a cohesive text.

FROM

Sacred History

Translated by Frederick C. Grant

[On the Origin of the Gods]

Regarding the gods, the ancients have handed down to later generations two different ideas. They say that some of them are eternal and incorruptible, such as the sun and moon and other stars in the heavens, and also the winds and other things of similar nature, for each of these has an eternal generation and duration; but others, they say, are earthly beings who became gods, having received honor and glory because of their benefactions to mankind, and such are Heracles, Dionysus, Aristaeus, and the others who are like them. Concerning these terrestrial gods, many and various are the accounts (*logoi*) handed down by historians and mythographers. Among the historians Euhemerus, the author of *The Sacred History,* has devoted special attention to them; among the mythologists Homer and Hesiod and Orpheus and others of their ilk have fabricated the most marvel-laden myths about the gods. [. . .]

Euhemerus, who was a friend of King Cassander [of Macedonia, ca. 301–297 B.C.], and was required by him to perform certain matters of state and to make distant journeys, is said to have traveled southward as far as the ocean. For he set sail from Arabia Felix and voyaged many days across the ocean, and came upon islands in the open sea, one of which was called Panchaea. Here he saw how their inhabitants, the Panchaeans, excel in piety, and honor the gods with most magnificent sacrifices and praiseworthy votive offerings of silver and gold. The island is sacred to the gods. Besides this are many other marvelous things, remarkable for their antiquity and for the technical skill required in their construction; about these we have already said something in the preceding books. There is also a majestic sanctuary of Zeus Triphylius [i.e., of the three tribes], located upon a great hill; it was established by him while he was king of the whole inhabited earth and was still a man among men. In this temple there is a gold stele, on which is inscribed, in Panchaean characters, a summary of the deeds of Uranus, Kronos, and Zeus.

After this [Euhemerus] says that Uranus was the first king, a gentle and benevolent man, familiar with the movements of the stars; he was the first to honor the heavenly gods with sacrifices, and that is why he is called Uranus, or Heaven. By his wife Hestia he had two sons, Titan and Kronos, and two daughters, Rhea and Demeter. Kronos succeeded Uranus as king and, marrying Rhea, became the father of

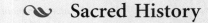

Zeus, Hera, and Poseidon. When Zeus succeeded to the kingship, he married Hera, Demeter, and Themis; his children by the first were the Curetes, by the second Persephone, by the third Athena. Journeying to Babylon, he was the guest of Belus and afterward visited the island of Panchaea, lying in the ocean, where he erected an altar to his own ancestor, Uranus. [. . .]

Ninus' brother Picus,[1] who was also called Zeus, ruled over Italy, being sovereign of the West for a hundred and twenty years. He had many sons and daughters by the most beautiful women, for he produced [in them] various mystical fantasies and then took advantage of them. These very women took him for a god, though they were corrupted by him. This same Picus, who is also Zeus, had a son named Faunus; he also called him Hermes after the wandering star [i.e., the planet Mercury]. And when Zeus was about to die, he ordered that his remains should be buried on the island of Crete; there his sons built a temple and buried him. The tomb still exists and bears this inscription: "Here lies Picus, who is also called Zeus." [. . .]

[1] **Picus:** Picus is an example from Roman mythology of Euhemerus's theory: Some Roman mythographers say that Picus was once a man, the son of Saturn and Venilia, the daughter of Janus.

Lucretius
c. 99–c. 55 B.C.E.

Born in Rome about 99 B.C.E., the poet Lucretius was an aristocrat who is known today by his only extant work, a long unfinished didactic poem titled *On the Nature of Things (De rerum natura).* This philosophical work in six books discusses the formation of the universe, the nature of matter and space, the movements of atoms, and the characteristics of mind, spirit, sense perceptions, thought, and emotions. The first excerpt is the opening prose paragraph of Book I: Matter and Space, which pays tribute to the Greek philosopher Epicurus (341–270 B.C.E.), whose ideas are the foundation for Lucretius's own beliefs. Epicurus was essentially a philosophical materialist: That is, he believed that there is no transcendent spiritual reality, that the material world of the senses is all there is. Humans have one life to live and that's it, so they should make the best of it while they can. For both Epicurus and Lucretius, philosophy replaced religion. In the second selection from Book III: Life and Mind, Lucretius makes the brilliant observation that the gods who were once said to populate the external, natural world have become fixtures in the internal landscape of the psyche, a connection that psychologists Sigmund Freud and Carl Jung would reiterate in the twentieth century.

FROM

On the Nature of Things

Translated by Ronald Latham

BOOK I

[The Greek Consciousness]

When human life lay grovelling in all men's sight, crushed to the earth under the dead weight of superstition whose grim features loured menacingly upon mortals from the four quarters of the sky, a man of Greece[1] was first to raise mortal eyes in defiance, first to stand erect and brave the challenge. Fables of the gods did not crush him, nor the lightning flash and the growling menace of the sky. Rather, they quickened his manhood, so that he, first of all men, longed to smash the constraining locks of nature's doors. The vital vigour of his mind prevailed. He ventured far out beyond the flaming ramparts of the world and voyaged in mind throughout infinity. Returning victorious, he proclaimed to us what can be and what cannot: how a limit is fixed to the power of everything and an immovable frontier post. Therefore superstition in its turn lies crushed beneath his feet, and we by his triumph are lifted level with the skies. [. . .]

BOOK III

[The Psychological Origin of the Underworld]

There is no wretched Tantalus,[2] as the myth relates, transfixed with groundless terror at the huge boulder poised above him in the air. But in this life there really are mortals oppressed by unfounded fear of the gods and trembling at the impending doom that may fall upon any of them at the whim of chance.

There is no Tityos[3] lying in Hell for ever probed by birds of prey. Assuredly they cannot find food by groping under those giant ribs to glut them throughout eternity. No matter to what length that titanic frame may lie outstretched, so that he covers not a paltry nine acres with his spread-eagled limbs but the whole extent of earth, he will not be able to suffer an eternity of pain nor furnish food from his body for evermore. But Tityos is here in our midst—that poor devil prostrated by love, torn indeed by birds of prey, devoured by gnawing jealousy or rent by the fangs of some other passion.

---

[1] **a man of Greece:** Epicurus.

[2] **Tantalus:** In Greek mythology, a man whose punishment in Hades consisted of having a great stone suspended over his head, threatening to overwhelm him, so that he was prevented from enjoying the banquet set before him. (Translator's note.)

[3] **Tityos:** In Greek mythology, a giant punished in Hades by having to lie bound while two vultures tore at his liver. (Translator's note.)

Sisyphus[4] too is alive for all to see, bent on winning the insignia of office, its rods and ruthless axes,[5] by the people's vote and embittered by perpetual defeat. To strive for this profitless and never-granted prize, and in striving toil and moil incessantly, this truly is to push a boulder laboriously up a steep hill, only to see it, once the top is reached, rolling and bounding down again to the flat levels of the plain.

By the same token, to be for ever feeding a malcontent mind, filling it with good things but never satisfying it—the fate we suffer when the circling seasons enrich us with their products and their ever-changing charms but we are never filled with the fruits of life—this surely exemplifies the story of those maidens in the flower of life for ever pouring water into a leaking vessel which can never by any sleight be filled.

As for Cerberus and the Furies[6] and the pitchy darkness and the jaws of Hell belching abominable fumes, these are not and cannot be anywhere at all. But life is darkened by the fear of retribution for our misdeeds, a fear enormous in proportion to their enormity, and by the penalties imposed for crime—imprisonment and ghastly precipitation from Tarpeia's Crag,[7] the lash, the block, the rack, the boiling pitch, the firebrand and the branding iron. Even though these horrors are not physically present, yet the conscience-ridden mind in terrified anticipation torments itself with its own goads and whips. It does not see what term there can be to its suffering nor where its punishment can have an end. It is afraid that death may serve merely to intensify pain. So at length the life of misguided mortals becomes a Hell on earth. [. . .]

Add the attendants of the Muses, among them Homer who in solitary glory bore the sceptre but has sunk into the same slumber as the rest. Democritus,[8] when ripe age warned him that the mindful motions of his intellect were running down, made his unbowed head a willing sacrifice to death. And the Master himself, when his daylit race was run, Epicurus himself died, whose genius outshone the race of men and dimmed them all, as the stars are dimmed by the rising of the fiery sun. And will *you* kick and protest against your sentence? You, whose life is next-door to death while you are still alive and looking on the light. You, who waste the major part of your time in sleep and, when you are awake, are snoring still and dreaming. You, who bear a mind hag-ridden by baseless fear and cannot find the commonest cause of your distress, hounded as you are, poor creature, by a pack of troubles and drifting in a drunken stupor upon a wavering tide of fantasy.

Men feel plainly enough within their minds, a heavy burden, whose weight depresses them. If only they perceived with equal clearness the causes of this depression, the origin of this lump of evil within their breasts, they would not lead such a

---

[4] **Sisyphus:** In Greek mythology, a man punished in Hades by being condemned eternally to roll a large stone to the top of a hill, from which it immediately rolled down and had to be rolled up again. (Translator's note.)

[5] **rods . . . axes:** In Rome the symbol of royal, and then of consular authority were the fasces, a bundle of rods fastened together with a red strap and enclosing an axe. (Translator's note.)

[6] **Cerberus . . . Furies:** In Greek mythology, the three-headed dog Cerberus watches over Hades. The Furies are ancient spirits who avenge violations of the natural order, like patricide or matricide.

[7] **Tarpeia's Crag:** Roman criminals were thrown to their death from a cliff called Tarpeia's Crag.

[8] **Democritus:** Fifth century B.C.E. Greek philosopher who believed that the universe was made up of atoms.

life as we now see all too commonly—no one knowing what he really wants and everyone for ever trying to get away from where he is, as though mere locomotion could throw off the load. Often the owner of some stately mansion, bored stiff by staying at home, takes his departure, only to return as speedily when he feels himself no better off out of doors. Off he goes to his country seat, driving his carriage and pair hot-foot, as though in haste to save a house on fire. No sooner has he crossed its doorstep than he starts yawning or retires moodily to sleep and courts oblivion, or else rushes back to revisit the city. In so doing the individual is really running away from himself. Since he remains reluctantly wedded to the self whom he cannot of course escape, he grows to hate him, because he is a sick man ignorant of the cause of his malady. If he did but see this, he would cast other thoughts aside and devote himself first to studying the nature of the universe. It is not the fortune of an hour that is in question, but of all time—the lot in store for mortals throughout the eternity that awaits them after death.

Philo Judaeus

c. 20 B.C.E.–c. 50 C.E.

The name *Philo Judaeus* is made up of the Greek word for "loving" and the Latin word for "Jew," uncannily reflecting the mindset of its bearer. Philo Judaeus was a prominent spokesman for the fusion of Jewish and Greek thought in Alexandria, Egypt, an intellectual and artistic center in the Near East, and his writings influenced both Jews and Christians. Few details are known about his life except that in 40 C.E. he traveled to Rome to represent the Jewish community penalized for not worshiping Caligula.

In his writings, only fragments of which remain, Philo consistently employs allegory to discover within Hebrew Scriptures the neo-Platonic substructure of the cosmos. The Greek word *logos* had traditionally meant both "word" and "the creative faculty in human beings"—or, reason—which expresses itself in language and speech. In *On the Creation of the World,* Philo connects this human faculty to the Mind of God that pervades the visible universe. According to Philo, the essential, intelligible infrastructure of the world was created by the divine *Logos,* the supreme Idea—a teaching common to Plato and the Greek Stoics. An analogy of the creator of the universe as an architectural planner of a city is used by Philo in the following excerpt.

On the Creation of the World

Translated by Nahum N. Glatzer

When any city is founded through the exceeding ambition of some king or leader who lays claim to absolute authority, and is at the same time a man of brilliant imagination, eager to display his good fortune, then it happens at times that some man coming up who, from his education, is skilful in architecture, and he, seeing the advantageous character and beauty of the situation, first of all sketches out in his own mind nearly all the parts of the city which is about to be completed—the temples, the gymnasia, the prytanea, the markets, the harbour, the docks, the streets, the arrangement of the walls, the situations of the dwelling houses, and of the public and other buildings. Then, having received in his own mind, as on a waxen tablet, the form of each building, he carries in his heart the image of a city, perceptible as yet only by the intellect, the images of which he stirs up in memory which is innate in him, and, still further, engraving them in his mind like a good workman, keeping his eyes fixed on his model, he begins to raise the city of stones and wood, making the corporeal substances to resemble each of the incorporeal ideas. Now we must form a somewhat similar opinion of God, who, having determined to found a mighty state, first of all conceived its form in his mind, according to which form he made a world perceptible only by the intellect, and then completed one visible to the external senses, using the first one as a model.

V. As therefore the city, when previously shadowed out in the mind of the man of architectural skill had no external place, but was stamped solely in the mind of the workman, so in the same manner neither can the world which existed in ideas have had any other local position except the divine reason which made them; for what other place could there be for his powers which should be able to receive and contain, I do not say all, but even any single one of them whatever, in its simple form? [. . .]

And if any one were to desire to use more undisguised terms, he would not call the world, which is perceptible only to the intellect, any thing else but the reason of God,[1] already occupied in the creation of the world; for neither is a city, while only perceptible to the intellect, anything else but the reason of the architect, who is already designing to build one perceptible to the external senses, on the model of that which is so only to the intellect—this is the doctrine of Moses, not mine. Accordingly he, when recording the creation of man, in words which follow, asserts expressly, that he was made in the image of God—and if the image be a part of the image, then manifestly so is the entire form, namely, the whole of this world perceptible by the external senses, which is a greater imitation of the divine image than the human form is. It is manifest also, that the archetypal seal, which we call that world

[1] **the reason of God:** Another translator uses "Word of God" here, referring to *Logos*.

which is perceptible only to the intellect, must itself be the archetypal model, the idea of ideas, the Reason of God. [. . .]

XXIII. So then after all the other things, as has been said before, Moses says that man was made in the image and likeness of God. And he says well; for nothing that is born on the earth is more resembling God than man. And let no one think that he is able to judge of this likeness from the characters of the body: for neither is God a being with the form of a man, nor is the human body like the form of God; but the resemblance is spoken of with reference to the most important part of the soul, namely, the mind: for the mind which exists in each individual has been created after the likeness of that one mind which is in the universe as its primitive model,[2] being in some sort the God of that body which carries it about and bears its image within it. In the same rank that the great Governor occupies in the universal world, that same as it seems does the mind of man occupy in man; for it is invisible, though it sees everything itself; and it has an essence which is indiscernible, though it can discern the essences of all other things, and making for itself by art and science all sorts of roads leading in divers directions, and all plain; it traverses land and sea, investigating everything which is contained in either element. And again, being raised up on wings, and so surveying and contemplating the air, and all the commotions to which it is subject, it is borne upwards to the higher firmament, and to the revolutions of the heavenly bodies. And also being itself involved in the revolutions of the planets and fixed stars according to the perfect laws of music, and being led on by love, which is the guide of wisdom, it proceeds onwards till, having surmounted all essence intelligible by the external senses, it comes to aspire to such as is perceptible only by the intellect: and perceiving in that, the original models and ideas of those things intelligible by the external senses which it saw here full of surpassing beauty, it becomes seized with a sort of sober intoxication like the zealots engaged in the Corybantian festivals,[3] and yields to enthusiasm, becoming filled with another desire, and a more excellent longing, by which it is conducted onwards to the very summit of such things as are perceptible only to the intellect, till it appears to be reaching the great King himself. And while it is eagerly longing to behold him pure and unmingled, rays of divine light are poured forth upon it like a torrent, so as to bewilder the eyes of its intelligence by their splendour. [. . .]

---

[2] **primitive model:** An original pattern or archetype.

[3] **zealots . . . festivals:** In ancient Asia Minor, the worshipers of the goddess Cybele were known for their irrational frenzies.

SAPPHO
C. 600 B.C.E.

Sappho, the female poet of sixth-century B.C.E. Greece whom Plato called "the tenth Muse" and upon whose work many poets of both sexes in ancient Greece and Rome modeled their own, was honored in ancient times as the foremost writer of the Greek lyric. Even though very little of her work remains, that reputation holds. Lyric poetry like Sappho's offers an invaluable glimpse into private emotions and everyday experience seldom seen in Greek epic and drama. Whereas epic writers and tragedians kept a certain distance from their subjects, the personal voice is central to the Greek LYRIC. Like Sei Shonagan, one of the earliest Japanese writers, who wrote in intimate detail of everyday life in the Japanese court, Sappho recorded life in ancient Greece from a woman's point of view. She too wrote in the first person about romantic love and lust, about celebrations and partings, about jealousy, betrayal, friendship, loss, death, and survival.

WWW For links to more information about Sappho and a quiz on her poetry, see *World Literature Online* at bedfordstmartins .com/worldlit.

An Obscure Life. Although a great body of legend and conjecture surrounds Sappho, little is known for certain about her. She was born to a well-to-do family sometime in the late seventh century B.C.E. on the Aegean island of Lesbos, off the coast of present-day Turkey, probably at Mytelene. Her mother was named **Cleis**; Sappho probably had two or three brothers. She is said to have been a small and dark-complected woman. Socrates called her beautiful, but others said he must have been thinking about her poetry, not her person. An anonymous commentator wrote that she was "like a nightingale with ill-shapen wings enfolding a tiny body." By a merchant husband or consort named Cercolis, Sappho apparently gave birth to a fair-haired daughter whom she named Cleis, after her mother; she addresses her child tenderly in a number of poems.

KLEE-is

The popular image of Sappho as a woman born before her time, a lonely poet dwelling with a few sympathetic female companions on a remote island outpost of Greek civilization is not corroborated by historical data. During Sappho's lifetime the Greek settlements on the Dodecanese Islands were lively trading centers, ports where people from Asia Minor, the eastern Mediterranean, and the Middle East freely met with Westerners from Greece, Italy, and the western Mediterranean. On these cosmopolitan islands there were enclaves of art and learning that valued women highly. Sixth-century Lesbos was probably a far better place for independent and creative women to live than "Golden Age" fifth-century Athens. By all evidence, Sappho for most of her life lived and wrote within an emotionally close community of women friends and companions. The exact nature of that community is uncertain; the *moisopolon domos,* or "house of the muses," Sappho refers to may have been anything ranging from an informal association of women friends to a quite formal religious and educational order devoted to **Aphrodite**, the Greek goddess of love, with Sappho as head priestess in charge of both religious rites and

AF-roh-digh-tee, AF-ruh-digh-tee

Female Author, 75 C.E.
A late Roman portrait of a female author previously thought to be Sappho, with stylus and tablet. (Erich Lessing/Art Resource, NY)

the training of young novices. There is a tradition that Sappho died a suicide, throwing herself off a cliff into the sea when her love for a ferryman named Phaon was not returned, but this sounds a lot like folklore. In one fragment of her work, possibly a poem written on her deathbed, Sappho reminds her daughter that grief is not becoming to a poet's household.

Censorship. Sappho is counted among a number of great writers whose works have been deliberately and successfully banned. Except for one complete poem and four stanzas of another, all that has been recovered of Sappho's writings are scattered lines and partial stanzas. Sappho's work disappeared not only because of the general neglect of ancient manuscripts during the Middle Ages but also because of specific acts of censorship. Owing to the lesbian themes of some of her poetry (the word *lesbian* derives from Sappho's Lesbos) and perhaps because she was an honored female writer who depicted women as lively, intelligent, and goddess-worshiping, Sappho incurred the all-out animosity of the Christian Church patriarchy during the Middle Ages, more so than any Greek or Roman male writer did. Her poems were twice singled out for destruction by church authorities: In the fourth century the Bishop of Constantinople decreed that her work should be destroyed, and in the eleventh century Pope Gregory VII ordered manuscripts of her poems to be thrown into public bonfires in Rome and Constantinople. Fragments of her work survive only because lines of her poetry were quoted by other poets, by praiseful critics such as Longinus,[1] and by Greek grammarians who wished to cite examples of the Aeolic dialect in which she wrote. In addition, bits and pieces of Sappho's work were found by nineteenth-century Egyptologists who discovered that strips of papyrus torn from manuscripts of her poems had been used to stuff the mouths of mummified crocodiles. It is a measure of the astonishing personal intensity and music of her voice that even fragments of her verse have had the power to move readers deeply, century after century, leaving them longing to possess more of the nine books of odes, elegies, wedding songs, and hymns Sappho is said to have written.

Celebrant of the Ordinary. Sappho was able to express in few words what passion and jealousy and lust and tenderness feel like, both physically and spiritually. In some instances these emotions so transcend the poet's gender, time, and circumstances that certain of Sappho's love poems have been translated or adapted again and again, assigned to male and female speakers alike, as in the poem beginning, "He is more than a hero," in which Sappho evokes the physiological sensations of lovesickness. She is also the first Western woman writer of lyrical and intimate accounts of experience that is particularly female—a woman's loss of virginity; a young woman's fear and anticipation of marriage when it is the only way open to her; the way women talk among themselves when

[1] **Longinus** (first century C.E.): Obscure author of one of the most influential works of classical literary criticism, the treatise *On the Sublime,* which discusses style in literature.

they are at ease; the volatile friendships and rivalries among women poets; the choice of an especially finely made pair of sandals; the young girl in love putting her weaving aside impatiently, unable to concentrate on the household task her mother has set her. Sappho's poetry celebrates not only the formal rites of Aphrodite but also the day-to-day rituals that mark continuities between generations of women, as when the poet dresses her daughter's fair hair and remembers what her own mother used to tell her about fashions in headbands.

Sappho is probably best known for lines such as those in "He is more than a hero" that relate intense, aching passion, but the West's earliest lyric poet was also a celebrant of the ordinary, of the way golden broom (a delicate flowering shrub) blossoms on the Greek coastline, of the pleasure of setting out fresh pillows for a welcome guest, of the shrilling of crickets, and of the smell of crushed grass.

The tenth Muse.

– Plato, describing Sappho

■ CONNECTIONS

Catullus, poems, p. 1168. The Roman poet Catullus, who admired and imitated Sappho's work, wrote on many of the same themes as his mentor. What qualities do the two poets' work have in common? Could the differences in their poetry be attributed to those between a man's and a woman's point of view?

Egyptian Love Poems, p. 121; Hebrew Scriptures, Song of Songs, p. 208; China, *Book of Songs*, p. 1573. Love is the perennial subject of poetry, and poets have found seemingly endless ways to describe it. Characterize the love poems from the ancient Egyptian, Hebrew, and Chinese cultures. In any given work, is the poet's voice male or female? Is the love more physical or more intellectual? What sort of imagery do the poets from each culture use?

The Kokinshu (Book 2). Japanese poetry is noted especially for its brevity and its ability to capture the transitory, fleeting nature of life in images. Sappho's poems, particularly in Mary Barnard's translations, share these qualities. How do Sappho's verses compare with the poems in *The Kokinshu,* one of the earliest collections of Japanese verse? Would it be appropriate to say that Sappho's poetry has a Japanese feel to it?

■ FURTHER RESEARCH

Barnstone, Willis. *Sappho: Lyrics in the Original Greek with Translations.* 1965.
Bowra, C. M. *Greek Lyric Poetry.* 1961.
DuBois, Page. *Sappho Is Burning.* 1995.
Foley, Helene P. *Reflections on Women in Antiquity.* 1981.
Greene, Ellen. *Reading Sappho: Contemporary Approaches.* 1996.
Raynor, Diane. *Sappho's Lyre; Archaic Lyric and Women Poets of Ancient Greece.* 1991.
Snyder, Jane M. *Lesbian Desire in the Lyrics of Sappho.* 1997.

■ PRONUNCIATION

Aphrodite: AF-roh-digh-tee, AF-ruh-digh-tee
Cleis: KLEE-is
Croesus: KREE-sus

It's no use

Translated by Mary Barnard

It's no use

Mother dear, I
can't finish my
weaving
          You may
blame Aphrodite

soft as she is

she has almost
killed me with
love for that boy

Sleep, darling

Translated by Mary Barnard

Sleep, darling

I have a small
daughter called
Cleis, who is
like a golden
flower
          I wouldn't

Selected Poems. Except for a very few poems, like "He is more than a hero," which were quoted in full by ancient commentators, only fragments of Sappho's lyrics remain. Of these, some were recorded by classical writers; many were discovered in the nineteenth century on pieces of papyrus used to stuff mummified Egyptian crocodiles. They often consist of single images or momentary perceptions that were originally part of longer works. Translator Mary Barnard does not try to re-create the original Greek verse structure or guess at the missing portions of the poems; she aims to represent Sappho's "fresh colloquial directness of speech" and seeks "to avoid . . . spinning the fragment out 'to make a poem.'"

take all Croesus'[1]
kingdom with love
thrown in, for her

[1] **Croesus:** Lydian king (r. 560–546 B.C.E.) proverbial for his wealth.

Don't ask me what to wear

Translated by Mary Barnard

Don't ask me what to wear

I have no embroidered
headband from Sardis to
give you, Cleis, such as
I wore
        and my mother
always said that in her
day a purple ribbon
looped in the hair was thought
to be high style indeed

but we were dark:
                    a girl
whose hair is yellower than
torchlight should wear no
headdress but fresh flowers

Lament for a Maidenhead

Translated by Mary Barnard

FIRST VOICE:
Like a quince-apple
ripening on a top
branch in a tree top

not once noticed by
harvesters or if
not unnoticed, not reached

SECOND VOICE:
Like a hyacinth in
the mountains, trampled
by shepherds until
only a purple stain
remains on the ground

He is more than a hero

Translated by Mary Barnard

He is more than a hero

He is a god in my eyes—
the man who is allowed
to sit beside you—he

who listens intimately
to the sweet murmur of
your voice, the enticing

laughter that makes my own
heart beat fast. If I meet
you suddenly, I can't

speak—my tongue is broken;
a thin flame runs under
my skin; seeing nothing,

hearing only my own ears
drumming, I drip with sweat;
trembling shakes my body

and I turn paler than
dry grass. At such times
death isn't far from me

You know the place: then

Translated by Mary Barnard

You know the place: then

Leave Crete and come to us
waiting where the grove is
pleasantest, by precincts

sacred to you; incense
smokes on the altar, cold
streams murmur through the

apple branches, a young
rose thicket shades the ground
and quivering leaves pour

down deep sleep; in meadows
where horses have grown sleek
among spring flowers, dill

scents the air. Queen! Cyprian![1]
Fill our gold cups with love
stirred into clear nectar

[1] **Queen! Cyprian!:** This poem is addressed to Aphrodite, who was conceived from the sea-foam of Uranus' severed genitals off the coast of Cyprus.

I have had not one word from her

Translated by Mary Barnard

I have had not one word from her

Frankly I wish I were dead.
When she left, she wept
a great deal; she said to

me, "This parting must be
endured, Sappho. I go unwillingly."

I said, "Go, and be happy
but remember (you know
well) whom you leave shackled by love

"If you forget me, think
of our gifts to Aphrodite
and all the loveliness that we shared

"all the violet tiaras,
braided rosebuds, dill and
crocus twined around your young neck

"myrrh poured on your head
and on soft mats girls with
all that they most wished for beside them

"while no voices chanted
choruses without ours,
no woodlot bloomed in spring without song . . ."

Aeschylus

c. 525–456 B.C.E.

ES-kuh-lus

Aeschylus is the earliest and, in company with his younger contemporaries Sophocles and Euripides,[1] one of the greatest tragedians of fifth-century Athens. Of the more than seventy plays Aeschylus is known to have written, only seven have survived. Nonetheless, these plays were influential in establishing the principles of Greek drama. By introducing a second actor to the Greek stage, Aeschylus moved dialogue to the forefront of drama, giving it a dynamic form approaching that found in modern theater. Above all, like Sophocles, Aeschylus placed before his audiences the life of Athens at a time of that city's transition, exploiting the elements of conflict and crisis that characterize drama to explore the competing and often contradictory social, political, and religious forces

[1] **Sophocles and Euripides:** Sophocles (496–406 B.C.E.) and Euripides (c. 480–406 B.C.E.), Greek playwrights noted for their tragedies. See pages 891 and 999.

at play in his fifth-century city. Aeschylus, whose high acclaim has never waned, used tragedies to probe the dynamic relationship among the gods, elemental forces of the earth, and human beings—the divine, the natural, and the human.

Soldier and Playwright. The son of a wealthy aristocrat who lived at Eleusis, a town near Athens, Aeschylus was born around 525 B.C.E. From his epitaph it is known that he fought in the celebrated battle at Marathon (490 B.C.E.), where Athenian forces roundly defeated the Persians, and it is likely that he also fought in the battles against the Persians at Salamis and Plataea (480–479 B.C.E.). In the annual drama competitions held during the Festivals of Dionysus,[2] Aeschylus won his first prize in 484, with his plays taking first place thirteen times after that. In 472, his play *The Persians,* financed by the then twenty-year-old Pericles[3] (c. 495–429 B.C.E.) serving as the production's *choregus,* or sponsor, won first prize and fixed Aeschylus's reputation as far as Sicily, where Hieron, the ruler of Syracuse, invited him to produce his play. After spending some time in Sicily, Aeschylus returned to Athens, where he continued to enter his dramas in competitions, losing to Sophocles in 468, winning first prize in 467 with a series of plays, including *Seven Against Thebes,* and again in 458 with the trilogy ***The Oresteia.*** Two years later in Gela, Sicily, Aeschylus died; his four-line epitaph, possibly composed by Aeschylus himself, subordinates his powerful role as one of the chief dramatists of his age to his participation in the battle of Marathon:

> Beneath this monument lies the son of Euphorion, Aeschylus
> The Athenian, who died among the rich wheatfields of Gela;
> Of his valor in battle the sacred plains of Marathon may tell
> And too the long-haired Persian who well remembers his worth.

Athens: A City in Flux. Aeschylus came of age during the twilight of the ancient tribal ways that had guided social and political affairs in Greece when it was primarily organized around decentralized rural clans, whose character and experiences were reflected in the myths they had handed down from before the eighth century. The *polis,* or city-state, that had been developing since the seventh century demanded a new system of law, however, a new code that would accommodate the concentration of individuals in a city, the exchange of goods and ideas, and a class system distinct from that of the old aristocracy; the ***POLIS*** also demanded a reworking of the older myths and legends that no longer mirrored but still influenced daily life.

WWW For links to more information about Aeschylus and a quiz on *The Oresteia,* see *World Literature Online* at bedfordstmartins .com/worldlit.

aw-ruh-STIGH-uh

[2] **Festivals of Dionysus:** Starting at about 530 B.C.E., Athenians held annual spring festivals in honor of Dionysus, the god of wine. During these festivals, among other activities, playwrights competed for prizes for the best tragedy and the best comedy. Tragedians presented three related dramas followed by a satyr, often a bawdy play serving to lighten the mood.

[3] **Pericles** (c. 495–429 B.C.E.): Athenian nobleman and statesman who became one of Athens' greatest leaders in 461 B.C.E. Under Pericles, whose rule lasted until 429 B.C.E., Athens broadened its democratic policies at home and expanded its empire abroad. The arts, including philosophy and drama, flourished in the Age of Pericles.

Mask of Agamemnon, sixteenth century B.C.E.
This golden mask of Agamemnon is thought to be a portrait of the legendary (and possibly historic) king of Mycenae. Agamemnon is the central character of the first play in Aeschylus's Oresteia *trilogy. (Bettman/CORBIS)*

After years of civil strife under leaders who unsuccessfully tried to serve the different classes of citizens in Athens, the constitutional reformer Cleisthenes (fl. 510 B.C.E.) gained power and restructured Athens' political system. Taking hold when Aeschylus was a young man, these reforms marked a major step toward democracy, enabling more citizens to participate in the political process. Most significant perhaps for *The Oresteia*, Cleisthenes had created ten artificial tribes drawn from geographically separate districts known as demes; each tribe contained members from the upper, middle, and lower classes. The effect was to extend citizenship to a great number of men; women were not citizens and did not participate in the political process, even under the democratic policies in the Age of Pericles. The creation of these artificial tribes accentuated the distinction between kinship ties and civic allegiances dramatized in the plays of Aeschylus and Sophocles.

Under Cleisthenes, all free men had full rights and could participate in political decision making by casting votes in the general Assembly. The

Council of 500, the main legislative body of Athens, ruled over the Assembly; above the Council were the ARCHONS, men drawn from among the wealthiest citizens, and a body of former archons known as the **Areopagus**. Dating back to the seventh century when it emerged as an advisory council to the top leadership of Athens, the Areopagus initially functioned as a court for high crimes like homicide and exercised broad authority over government policy. By Aeschylus's time, the powers of the Areopagus had been partially reduced, though it still regulated the appointment of officials and heard cases on homicide and some religious offenses. In 462 and 461, about four years before the first production of *The Oresteia,* controversy over the power of the Areopagus flared up when a group of reformers, including Pericles and the unlucky Ephialtes, assassinated for his role in the affair, severely limited the authority of the Areopagus by extending the powers of the Council of 500 and broadening its membership, effectively solidifying the democratic system in Athens. In *The* ***Eumenides,*** the final play of *The Oresteia* trilogy, Aeschylus takes up the issue of these reforms and provides a founding myth for the Areopagus as the guardian of justice perpetually seated "on Ares' Hill." Rather than the aristocratic council attacked by Pericles and Ephialtes, Aeschylus's Areopagus appears to be a court of citizens, suggesting that Aeschylus supported the reforms.

eh-ree-AH-puh-gus

yoo-MEN-ih-deez

Whatever his political position, Aeschylus's treatment of the Areopagus points to the larger philosophical, mythic, and religious ramifications of justice in fifth-century Athens. Despite its emphasis on the contrast between vengeance and justice, *The Oresteia* actually transcends its ostensible theme and may be seen as a work heralding the birth of enlightened civilization out of chaos and darkness. The lawgiving Areopagus becomes a symbol of civil society—the *polis* and its institutions—triumphing over and transforming the tribal institutions of the archaic past. This triumph was also one of patriarchy over the mythic and religious forces associated with the feminine.

The Plays. In addition to the three plays of *The Oresteia—Agamemnon, The Libation Bearers (The Choephori),* and *The Eumenides*—four other plays by Aeschylus have survived: *The Persians, Seven Against Thebes, The Suppliants,* and *Prometheus Bound. The Persians,* first produced in 472 B.C.E., is a topical historical play—the only one from this period in Greece—that celebrates the Athenian victory over the Persians at Salamis six years earlier. *Seven Against Thebes* and *The Suppliants,* both produced in the 460s, and *Prometheus Bound,* whose date is uncertain, draw from traditional myths and legends and from the works of Hesiod and Homer. Like Sophocles after him, Aeschylus refashioned the familiar stories of gods and heroes to dramatize both the disjunction and the union of the values and institutions of the older religious system and those of the new *polis* as well as to probe the age-old question of human suffering in a universe presided over by divine forces. *Prometheus Bound,* for example, takes up the myth of its title character, the Titan who stole "fire"—the source of all arts and sciences—from the gods and gave it to man; *The Suppliants* takes up the story of the Danaids, the descendants of

The uniqueness of Aeschylean drama seems to reside in this: it is expressed almost entirely in the immemorially old mythic-poetic idiom in which Aeschylus . . . had been raised; and yet it is heavily . . . engaged with the Athenian transition to a new world, a world that in many senses is still ours.
—John Herington, critic, 1986

Io, an Argive princess transformed into a cow and driven on extensive wanderings by a jealous Hera because Zeus had fallen in love with her. *Seven Against Thebes,* like Sophocles's *Oedipus Rex* and *Antigone,* draws on the story of the curse on the house of Laius that was visited upon Laius's son Oedipus and his family. Performed in 467, the play focuses on the conflict between Oedipus's two sons, Eteocles and Polyneices, in their rival claims to rule Thebes after their father's death. Like *The Oresteia,* the play questions the ancient prohibition against shedding the blood of one's kin as the chorus tries to persuade Eteocles to avoid face-to-face combat with his brother, thereby fulfilling the curse on the house of Oedipus. In all his plays Aeschylus reexamines the philosophical and moral core of myths and legends and asks how much of a voice citizens should have in the *polis,* to what degree individuals are responsible for their actions, and under what conditions, if any, they may challenge divine, legal, and political authority.

The Oresteia. *The Oresteia* is composed of three plays: *Agamemnon,* the story of Clytemnestra's murder of her husband, King Agamemnon, upon his return home from the Trojan War; *The Libation Bearers,* the story of Orestes' murder of his mother, Clytemnestra, to avenge his father's death; and *The Eumenides,* the story of Orestes' trial for matricide, held in the court of the Areopagus at Athens, to which he has fled. This trilogy dramatizes a society's transition from a tribal form of justice that enforced an ironclad prohibition of blood crimes against immediate kin to a civic system of justice that recognized mitigating factors in homicide cases—even those involving immediate family. In the course of the three plays, the Furies (the Erinyes), serpent-haired female monsters charged with avenging blood crimes against kin, serve as the ministers of the archaic law, while the gods Apollo and Athene represent the new law—one based on trial and persuasion.

Agamemnon. The trilogy opens with *Agamemnon,* a powerful, ritualistic drama that recounts the murder of King Agamemnon of Argos when he returns home triumphant from the Trojan War. Agamemnon returns with Cassandra, the daughter of the Trojan King Priam and Queen Hecuba, and a seer cursed with never being understood. Before Agamemnon's arrival, the monologue of the watchman and the exchange between **Clytemnestra** (kligh-tum-NES-truh) and the chorus establish a mood of foreboding, intimating the impending murder of the returning king at the hands of his wife and her accomplice and consort, Aegisthus, the king's nephew. The chorus also reminds the audience, as Cassandra's frantic prophecies also do later in the play, of horrors past afflicted on the descendants of Tantalus and Atreus.

Indeed, the murder of Agamemnon is linked to a bloody cycle of revenge unleashed on the descendants of the House of Atreus in the city of Argos going back several generations, to Tantalus, the great-grandfather of Agamemnon. To test the perceptiveness of the gods who had invited him to a banquet, Tantalus murdered his son Pelops and fed his body to them in a stew; the gods, discovering the trick at once, restored Pelops to life and condemned Tantalus to Hades, where he was eternally tempted to slake his thirst and satisfy his hunger from a pool and a bough of fruit that receded whenever he tried to reach them. Sent back to earth, Pelops eventually betrayed Myrtilus, his conspirator, in a scheme to win Hippodameia as his bride; before dying, Myrtilus cursed Pelops and his descendants, including both of his sons—Thyestes, the father of Aegisthus, and Atreus, the father of Menelaus and Agamemnon. Thyestes and Atreus became bitter enemies, and Atreus eventually repeated Tantalus's horrible crime, secretly murdering his brother's sons and serving them to Thyestes in a stew. Thyestes then cursed Atreus. **Aegisthus**, a later son of Thyestes, by the time of Agamemnon's return to Argos has joined as a consort and conspirator with Clytemnestra, who wants to murder her husband to avenge the death of her daughter, **Iphigenia**. (Advised by the seer Calchas, Agamemnon sacrificed his daughter to the goddess Artemis in order to raise the winds to launch the Greek fleet against Troy.)

ee-JIS-thus

ih-fuh-juh-NIGH-uh, ih-fuh-juh-NEE-uh

Having brooded for seven years on the murder of her daughter and enlisted an equally bitter Aegisthus into her service, Clytemnestra has prepared a cold homecoming for her husband. In a spectacular scene, Clytemnestra, with jealousy over Cassandra adding to her rage, lays out a lavish welcome fit only for the gods. As she goads and taunts the reluctant Agamemnon to step down on the blood-red ceremonial carpet, her words of welcome reek with irony and cloak threats of imminent violence. Despite her own cries about the atrocities visited upon the house of Atreus, Cassandra too goes into the palace where, along with Agamemnon, she falls victim to Clytemnestra and Aegisthus.

By the end of the play, Aegisthus and Clytemnestra appear before the horrified chorus, the citizens of the city, and celebrate what they call the justice of their actions. They also make clear that they will rule over Argos with a heavy hand, threatening to subject its citizens to arbitrary discipline. Under the tribal code of retributive justice, Clytemnestra's murder of her husband is justified because he is guilty of a blood-crime against their daughter. Moreover, Tantalus's original offense against the gods had set in motion a cycle of vengeance that had accumulated the force of fate itself. As the repeated pattern of crimes and curses makes clear, however, there can be no end to vengeance, and the chorus remains unconvinced of the righteousness of Clytemnestra and Aegisthus's deed and fears for its own civil liberties. Aeschylus scrutinizes the idea of justice in the trilogy's second and third plays.

The Libation Bearers. Although included only in part in this anthology (see p. 1134) this play is an important part of *The Oresteia.* In *The Libation Bearers,* Agamemnon's son **Orestes** returns to Argos to avenge his father's murder, but to do so not only must he kill his cousin Aegisthus, but he must also commit the worst crime of all—matricide. By acting out the tribal code of retribution, he becomes part of an endless cycle of revenge. Orestes, who was abetted in his plot by his surviving sister, Electra, is now

oh-RES-teez

How many of us . . . were taught that *The Oresteia* is about the establishment of justice for Western civilization, rather than that it is a great act of mythopoeia [mythmaking] in which politics are sexualized and where the idea of justice becomes defined as "masculine."

– Adrienne Munich, critic, 1985

plagued by the Furies. Following the advice of Apollo, who urged him to kill his mother, he flees from Argos to the Temple of Apollo at Delphi.

The Eumenides. The Temple of Apollo at Delphi is where the beleaguered Orestes is found at the beginning of the trilogy's final play, *The Eumenides.* The Furies, who visit their tortures with special intensity upon those who commit matricide, surround Orestes, who is polluted by his crime. Apollo, who has guided Orestes all along, sends him to Athens where he will be judged in a court of law presided over by none other than the guardian of the city herself, the goddess Athene. Meanwhile the Furies have already begun to make their case against Orestes, justifying their role as agents of a divine justice that takes precedence over that of the younger gods like Apollo who in the Furies' view "ride roughshod / Over elder Powers" and undermine the strict code of *lex talionis,* or retributive justice.

Further compounding this struggle among the gods, Aeschylus's plays align Clytemnestra and the Furies, and hence archaic law itself, with the feminine. Throughout *Agamemnon,* Clytemnestra is described as a woman who acts like a man, and the chorus warns that her dangerous behavior threatens to destabilize the city she governs. Furthermore she is associated with Helen, whose beauty led to the Trojan War and who is here described as a beast and a fiend bent on destruction. Linking the crossing of gender boundaries to a world order turned upside down, Cassandra envisions Clytemnestra's murder of her husband as an act defying nature itself: "Will cow gore bull?" she cries. Inventing a genealogy suited to his purposes, Aeschylus links the Furies to "brooding Night," or Nyx, the mother of doom, the Fates, and Nemesis. As it weighs the merits of two systems of justice, *The Oresteia* on the whole also reflects on the cosmic model of social order, which is based in part on the willingness of men and women, citizens and noncitizens to observe the societal roles they've been assigned. Whether the trilogy really challenges that order can be debated, but recent criticism suggests that the powerful voice of Clytemnestra in *Agamemnon* and even the argumentative skills of the Furies in *The Eumenides* are forerunners to such strong female characters as Euripides' Medea and Chaucer's Wife of Bath.

As *The Eumenides* proceeds, Athene, a female deity not of woman born, must shift the balance in favor of Orestes before a divided jury of Athenian citizens. As a result of Athene's intervention and vote, Clytemnestra's murder of Agamemnon, justified under the old law, is now condemned; Orestes' murder of his mother, on the other hand, is justified, in part because it is determined that the father's seed alone forms the blood of the offspring. Athene persuades the fearsome Furies to give up their role as avengers of blood crimes and assume the new title and role of Eumenides, or givers of blessings. The new civic order rests on a strict patriarchy whose values are supported by Athene's domestication of the Furies. The play concludes with a final procession of the chorus and the players singing a tribute to Athens and to "all-seeing Zeus," who in *Agamemnon* was described as a just god who ordered the world according to one principle: "Man must suffer to be wise."

■ CONNECTIONS

The Hebrew Scriptures, p. 134; The New Testament (Book 2). *The Oresteia* ponders the relationship between human beings and the gods, fate and free will, and justice and human suffering. So too do the Hebrew Bible and the New Testament. Agamemnon's sacrifice of his daughter, Iphigenia, precipitates Clytemnestra's revenge and renews a long chain of retribution that is resolved only in the establishment of the Areopagus and the acquittal of Orestes. Compare the code of justice in *Agamemnon* with that of the Hebrew Scriptures. Does the New Testament offer a resolution similar to that in *The Eumenides*?

Euripides, *Medea*, p. 1004; Chaucer, *The Wife of Bath* (Book 3). The struggle between the older and the younger gods in *The Oresteia* dramatizes the conflict between the female powers associated with earth and night and the male gods affiliated with the sky and the sun (light). The murder of the powerful queen Clytemnestra, who is said to have crossed or blurred gender boundaries, and the domestication of the female Furies associate the foundation of just order in fifth-century Athens with the subordination of women. How do Euripides' *Medea* and Chaucer's *The Wife of Bath* treat patriarchy and the subordination of women? How do Medea and Alisoun compare with Clytemnestra?

Bhagavad Gita, p. 1488. Like *The Oresteia*, the great Indian epic Mahabharata dramatizes a conflict between two systems of thought and action. In the Mahabharata, the conflict is between the code of the warrior and the principles of the Brahmin priests. Yudhishthira, the eldest of the Pandava brothers, seems to prefer peace and nonviolent resolution, whereas his brothers live by the principles of the warrior, or *kshatriya*. This clash climaxes in the Bhagavad Gita when the Pandava prince Arjuna pauses on the eve of battle and considers whether it is just to go to war against his kin. Compare the way *The Oresteia* and the Bhagavad Gita treat the issue of kinship ties and service or loyalty to a higher calling of justice than blood.

■ FURTHER RESEARCH

Goldhill, Simon. *Aeschylus: The Oresteia.* 1992.
Herington, John. *Aeschylus.* 1986.
Hogan, James. *A Commentary on the Complete Greek Tragedies: Aeschylus.* 1987.
McCall, Marsh H., ed. *Aeschylus: A Collection of Critical Essays.* 1972.
Munich, Adrienne. "Notorious Signs, Feminist Criticism, and Literary Tradition." In Gayle Green and Coppelia Kahn, eds., *Making a Difference: Feminist Literary Criticism.* 1985.
Podlecki, Anthony J. *The Political Background of Aeschylean Tragedy.* 1966.
Rocco, Christopher. "Democracy and Discipline in Aeschylus's *Oresteia.*" In *Tragedy and Enlightenment: Athenian Political Thought and the Dilemmas of Modernity.* 1997.
Zeitlin, Froma. "The Dynamics of Misogyny." In *Playing the Other: Gender and Society in Classical Greek Literature.* 1996.

■ PRONUNCIATION

Aegisthus: ee-JIS-thus
Aeschylus: ES-kuh-lus
Areopagus: eh-ree-AH-puh-gus
Clytemnestra: kligh-tum-NES-truh
Eumenides: yoo-MEN-ih-deez
Iphigenia: ih-fuh-juh-NIGH-uh, ih-fuh-juh-NEE-uh
Oresteia: aw-ruh-STIGH-uh, oh-ruh-STIGH-uh
Orestes: oh-RES-teez, uh-RES-teez

Agamemnon

Translated by Philip Vellacott

CHARACTERS:

A WATCHMAN
CHORUS *of twelve Elders of Argos*
CLYTEMNESTRA, *wife of Agamemnon*
A HERALD
AGAMEMNON, *King of Argos*
CASSANDRA, *a princess of Troy*
AEGISTHUS, *Clytemnestra's paramour, cousin to Agamemnon*
Soldiers attending Agamemnon; guards attending Aegisthus

It is night, a little before sunrise. On the roof of Atreus' palace a WATCHMAN *stands, or rises from a small mattress placed on the hewn stone. In front of the palace are statues of Zeus, Apollo, and Hermes; each with an altar before it.*

WATCHMAN:

O gods! grant me release from this long weary watch.
Release, O gods! Twelve full months now, night after night
Dog-like I lie here, keeping guard from this high roof
On Atreus' palace.[1] The nightly conference of stars,
Resplendent rulers, bringing heat and cold in turn,
Studding the sky with beauty—I know them all, and watch them
Setting and rising; but the one light I long to see
Is a new star, the promised sign, the beacon-flare
To speak from Troy and utter one word, 'Victory!'—

Agamemnon. Aeschylus's *Oresteia* was first performed at the Festival of Dionysus in 458 B.C.E., about five years after Pericles, Ephialtes, and other reformers reduced the power of the Areopagus, and after the Athenian alliance with Argos, to which the plays in the trilogy allude. The three plays of *The Oresteia* are *Agamemnon, The Libation Bearers,* and *The Eumenides,* the first and third of which are presented here.

In the foreground of *Agamemnon* is King Agamemnon, hero of the Trojan War. He has joined his brother, King Menelaus of Sparta, in raising an army of Greeks after Menelaus's wife, Helen, was stolen by Paris, son of King Priam of Troy. When his departure from Argos is frustrated by a becalmed sea, Agamemnon seeks a prophecy and discovers that the gods demand the sacrifice of his daughter, Iphigenia, in order for his ships to sail. He sacrifices his daughter and sets sail for Troy, leaving behind his wife, Clytemnestra, to mourn her daughter's death and plot her revenge.

As the play begins, Agamemnon returns to Argos and is greeted by Clytemnestra with more ceremony than he believes necessary. They argue, and then withdraw together. The Chorus, which

[1] **Atreus' palace:** In Homer, Atreus, the father of Agamemnon and Menelaus, was the king of Mycenae. Aeschylus shifts the location from Mycenae to Argos, in part to reflect recent historical events: In 463 B.C.E. Argos had overtaken Mycenae, after which, in 461, Argos joined Athens in an alliance against Sparta. Orestes' oath in *The Eumenides* vowing that no Argive king will ever rise up against Athens celebrates the alliance of these two cities. [Ed.]

Great news for Clytemnestra, in whose woman's heart
A man's will nurses hope.
Now once more, drenched with dew,
I walk about; lie down, but no dreams visit me.
Sleep's enemy, fear, stands guard beside me, to forbid
My eyes one instant's closing. If I sing some tune—
Since music's the one cure prescribed for heartsickness—
Why, then I weep, to think how changed this house is now
From splendour of old days, ruled by its rightful lord.
So may the gods be kind and grant release from trouble,
And send the fire to cheer this dark night with good news.

[*The beacon shines out.*]

O welcome beacon, kindling night to glorious day,
Welcome! You'll set them dancing in every street in Argos
When they hear your message. Ho there! Hullo! Call Clytemnestra!
The Queen must rise at once like Dawn from her bed, and welcome
The fire with pious words and a shout of victory,
For the town of Ilion's° ours—that beacon's clear enough! Troy
I'll be the first myself to start the triumphal dance.
Now I can say the gods have blessed my master's hand;
And for me too that beacon-light's a lucky throw.
Now Heaven bring Agamemnon safe to his home! May I
Hold his dear hand in mine! For the rest, I say no more;
My tongue's nailed down. This house itself, if walls had words,
Would tell its story plainly. Well, I speak to those
Who understand me; to the rest—my door is shut.

[*He descends. Lights begin to appear in the palace. A cry of triumph is heard from* CLYTEMNESTRA *within, and is echoed by other women. Then from the palace a messenger hurries out towards the city; attendants follow, going in various directions, and carrying jars and bowls with oil and incense for sacrifice. Then* CLYTEMNESTRA *enters from the palace, with two attendants; she casts incense on the altars, and prays before the statue of Zeus. Day begins to break. From the city enter the* ELDERS OF ARGOS. *They do not yet see* CLYTEMNESTRA.]

---

is constantly remembering and forgetting the crimes that lie heavy on the land, hears Agamemnon's prisoner and concubine, the Trojan prophetess Cassandra, predict what is about to happen but misinterprets her remarks. There is a scream from inside the door and Agamemnon's corpse is revealed. Clytemnestra and Aegisthus address the Chorus, giving their reasons for the murder. The play ends with members of the Chorus calling for the return of Orestes, the son of Agamemnon, to avenge his father's death and the usurpation of the state by Aegisthus.

A note on the translation: We are using the Philip Vellacott translation of *The Oresteia*, commissioned for a BBC production of the trilogy produced in 1956. The notes are a combination of the translator's notes, sometimes slightly modified for length, and notes from the editors, indicated as such in brackets.

CHORUS:

Ten years have passed since the strong sons of Atreus,
Menelaus and Agamemnon,[2] both alike
Honoured by Zeus with throned and sceptred power,
Gathered and manned a thousand Argive ships,
And with the youth of Hellas under arms
Sailed from these ports to settle scores with Priam.

Then loud their warlike anger cried,
As eagles cry, that wild with grief,
On some steep, lonely mountain-side
Above their robbed nest wheel and sail,
Oaring the airy waves, and wail
Their wasted toil, their watchful pride;
Till some celestial deity,
Zeus, Pan, Apollo,[3] hears on high
Their scream of wordless misery;
And pitying their forlorn estate
(Since air is Heaven's protectorate)
Sends a swift Fury[4] to pursue
Marauding guilt with vengeance due.

So against Paris's guilty boast
Zeus, witness between guest and host,[5]
Sends Atreus' sons for stern redress
Of his and Helen's wantonness.
Now Greece and Troy both pay their equal debt
Of aching limbs and wounds and sweat,
While knees sink low in gory dust,
And spears are shivered at first thrust.

Things are—as they are now; their end
Shall follow Fate's decree, which none can bend.

---

[2] **Menelaus and Agamemnon:** In the following lines, the Chorus alludes to the events of the Trojan War. The Trojan prince, Paris, abducted Menelaus's wife, Helen, precipitating a retaliative war led by the Greek (Argive) commanders, Menelaus and his brother, Agamemnon, against Troy, which was ruled by King Priam. Helen was Clytemnestra's half sister. [Ed.]

[3] **Zeus . . . Apollo:** The gods care for the helpless young of animals. Cf. Calchas's address to Artemis, below. The parallel between these two passages suggests that the rape of Helen and the sacrifice of Iphigenia were both abhorrent to the gods.

[4] **Fury:** The Furies are serpent-headed female creatures who avenge blood crimes against kin; their role becomes increasingly important throughout the trilogy. [Ed.]

[5] **Zeus . . . host:** Zeus, the chief of the Olympian gods, was said to uphold the code of hospitality, which Paris violated by running off with Helen, the wife of his host, King Menelaus of Sparta. [Ed.]

In vain shall Priam's altars burn,
His rich libations vainly flow
To gods above and powers below:
No gift, no sacrificial flame
Can soothe or turn
The wrath of Heaven from its relentless aim.

We were too old to take our share
With those who joined the army then.
We lean on sticks—in strength not men
But children; so they left us here.
In weakness youth and age are one:
The sap sleeps in the unripe bone
As in the withered. The green stalk
Grows without thorns: so, in the grey
And brittle years, old men must walk
Three-footed, weak as babes, and stray
Like dreams lost in the light of day.

[*Here the* CHORUS-LEADER *sees* CLYTEMNESTRA.]

Daughter of Tyndareos,[6] Queen Clytemnestra,
What have you heard? What has happened? Why have you ordered
Sacrifice through the city? Is there news?
Altars of all the gods who guard our State,
Gods of the sky, powers of the lower earth,
Altars of town and country, blaze with offerings;
On every hand heaven-leaping flames implore
Anger to melt in gentleness—a glare
Enriched with holy ointment, balm so rare
As issues only from a royal store!
Why are these things? Be gracious, Queen:
Tell what you can, or what you may;
Be healer of this haunting fear
Which now like an enemy creeps near,
And now again, when hope has seen
These altars bright with promise, slinks away—
Tell us, that hope may lift the load
Which galls our souls by night and day,
Sick with the evil which has been,
The evil which our hearts forebode.[7]

---

[6] **Tyndareos:** A former king of Sparta, Tyndareos was married to Leda, the mother of Clytemnestra and Helen, the latter of whom was fathered by Zeus. [Ed.]

[7] **The evil . . . forebode:** Past evil (the killing of Iphigenia) makes them apprehensive of the future. They now proceed to tell the story of the setting-out of the expedition.

[CLYTEMNESTRA *remains silent, her back turned to the* CHORUS.]
[*They continue, addressing the audience.*]

I am the man to speak, if you would hear
The whole tale from its hopeful starting-place—
That portent, which amazed our marching youth.
It was ten years ago—but I was there.[8]
The poet's grace, the singer's fire,
Grow with his years; and I can still speak truth
With the clear ring the gods inspire;—
How those twin monarchs of our warlike race,
Two leaders one in purpose, were sped forth—
Their vengeful spears in thousands pointing North
To Troy—by four wings' furious beat:
Two kings of birds, that seemed to bode
Great fortune to the kings of that great fleet.
Close to the palace, on spear-side of the road,
One tawny-feathered, one white in the tail,
Perched in full view, they ravenously tear
The body of a pregnant hare
Big with her burden, now a living prey
In the last darkness of their unborn day.[9]
Cry Sorrow, sorrow—yet let good prevail!
The army's learned Seer[10] saw this, and knew
The devourers of the hare
For that relentless pair—
Different in nature, as the birds in hue—
The sons of Atreus; and in council of war
Thus prophesied: 'Your army, it is true,
In time shall make King Priam's town their prey;
Those flocks and herds Troy's priests shall slay
With prayers for safety of her wall
Perish in vain—Troy's violent doom shall swallow all.
Only, see to it, you who go
To bridle Trojan pride, that no

---

[8] **It was . . . there:** This line is inserted by the translator to make the situation clearer. The Elders, too old to join the army, saw the soldiers off from Argos; some elders may even have accompanied them as far as Aulis.

[9] **Perched . . . unborn day:** The portent's primary meaning is the destruction of Troy, with its teeming population, by Agamemnon and Menelaus. This destruction, when accomplished, will be as abhorrent to the gods as the killing of the young in the womb; therefore it behooves the Greek army to be careful to avoid all further offence, such as desecration of temples in the captured city. There is also plainly a secondary allusion to the sacrifice of Iphigenia; as the hare dies before the fulfillment of birth, so Iphigenia dies before the fulfillment of marriage. She was offered to Artemis, but "Artemis abominates the eagles' feast."

[10] **Seer:** Calchas, who was with the army throughout the ten years. He prescribed human sacrifice again when Troy was captured.

Anger of gods benight your day
And strike before your hulls are under way.
For virgin Artemis, whom all revere,
Hates with a deadly hate
The swift-winged hounds of Zeus who swooped to assail
Their helpless victim wild with fear
Before her ripe hour came;
Who dared to violate
(So warning spoke the priest)
The awe that parenthood must claim,
As for some rite performed in Heaven's name;
Yes, Artemis abominates the eagles' feast!'
Cry Sorrow, sorrow—yet let good prevail!

Still spoke on the prophet's tongue:
'Lovely child of Zeus,[11] I pray,
You who love the tender whelp
Of the ravening lion, and care
For the fresh-wild sucking young
Of fox and rat and hind and hare;
If ever by your heavenly help
Hope of good was brought to flower,
Bless the sign we saw to-day!
Cancel all its presaged ill,
All its promised good fulfil!
Next my anxious prayers entreat
Lord Apollo's healing power,
That his Sister may not plan
Winds to chain the Hellene fleet;
That her grievance may not crave
Blood to drench another grave
From a different sacrifice
Hallowed by no festal joy—
Blood that builds a tower of hate,
Mad blood raging to destroy
Its self-source, a ruthless Fate
Warring with the flesh of man;
Bloodshed bringing in its train
Kindred blood that flows again,
Anger still unreconciled

[11] **Lovely child of Zeus:** Artemis. She and Apollo were the twin children of Leto by Zeus. As the virgin goddess of the hunt and guardian of childbirth and of wildlife, Artemis has been angered by the slaughter of the pregnant animals by the eagles, who represent the two kings who will similarly destroy the Trojans. Although Artemis is offended here, ironically Agamemnon's sacrifice of Iphigenia will be made in Artemis's name. [Ed.]

Poisoning a house's life
With darkness, treachery and strife,
Wreaking vengeance for a murdered child.'

So Calchas, from that parting prodigy
Auguring the royal house's destiny,
Pronounced his warning of a fatal curse,
With hope of better mingling fear of worse.
Let us too, echoing his uncertain tale,
Cry *Sorrow, sorrow—yet let good prevail!*

Let good prevail!
So be it! Yet, what is good? And who
Is God? How name him, and speak true?[12]
If he accept the name that men
Give him, Zeus I name him then.
I, still perplexed in mind,
For long have searched and weighed
Every hope of comfort or of aid:
Still I can find
No creed to lift this heaviness,
This fear that haunts without excuse—
No name inviting faith, no wistful guess,
Save only—Zeus.

The first of gods is gone,
Old Ouranos, once blown
With violence and pride;
His name shall not be known,
Nor that his dynasty once lived, and died.
His strong successor, Cronos, had his hour,
Then went his way, thrice thrown
By a yet stronger power.
Now Zeus is lord;[13] and he

[12] **How . . . true?:** This question is inserted to make clear the sequence of thought, which is that "Let good prevail" assumes an understanding of what "good" is, and leads back to the more fundamental problem of God and so to the theme of the stanza.

[13] **Now Zeus is lord:** These lines describe a succession of rebellions of younger gods against their fathers: The youngest of the gods, the Olympian Zeus, overthrew his father, Cronos, just as Cronos had overthrown Ouranos, the first and oldest of the gods. For Aeschylus, this sequence demonstrates a gradual move from violent and arbitrary justice to rule by law and order—a development among the gods correlating to the major theme of the trilogy. [Ed.]

Who loyally acclaims his victory
Shall by heart's instinct find the universal key:

Zeus, whose will has marked for man
The sole way where wisdom lies;
Ordered one eternal plan:
Man must suffer to be wise.
Head-winds heavy with past ill
Stray his course and cloud his heart:
Sorrow takes the blind soul's part—
Man grows wise against his will.
For powers who rule from thrones above
By ruthlessness commend their love.

So was it then. Agamemnon, mortified,
Dared not, would not, admit to error; thought
Of his great Hellene fleet, and in his pride
Spread sail to the ill wind he should have fought.
Meanwhile his armed men moped along the shores,
And cursed the wind, and ate his dwindling stores;
Stared at white Chalkis'[14] roofs day after day
Across the swell that churned in Aulis Bay.
And still from Strymon came that Northern blast,
While hulks and ropes grew rotten, mooring parted,
Deserters slunk away,
All ground their teeth, bored, helpless, hungry, thwarted.
The days of waiting doubled. More days passed.
The flower of warlike Hellas withered fast.

Then Calchas spoke again. The wind, he said,
Was sent by Artemis; and he revealed
Her remedy—a thought to crush like lead
The hearts of Atreus' sons, who wept, as weep they must,
And speechless ground their sceptres in the dust.

The elder king then spoke: 'What can I say?
Disaster follows if I disobey;
Surely yet worse disaster if I yield
And slaughter my own child, my home's delight,
In her young innocence, and stain my hand
With blasphemous unnatural cruelty,

[14] **Chalkis:** The city of Chalkis on the island of Euboea lies across the straits of Euripos from the port city of Aulis, where the Greeks have been stalled by unfavorable winds. [Ed.]

Bathed in the blood I fathered! Either way,
Ruin! Disband the fleet, sail home, and earn
The deserter's badge—abandon my command,
Betray the alliance—now! The wind must turn,
There must be sacrifice, a maid must bleed—
Their chafing rage demands it—they are right!
May good prevail, and justify my deed!'

Then he put on
The harness of Necessity.[15]
The doubtful tempest of his soul
Veered, and his prayer was turned to blasphemy,
His offering to impiety.
Hence that repentance late and long
Which, since his madness passed, pays toll
For that one reckless wrong.
Shameless self-willed infatuation
Emboldens men to dare damnation,
And starts the wheels of doom which roll
Relentless to their piteous goal.
So Agamemnon, rather than retreat,
Endured to offer up his daughter's life
To help a war fought for a faithless wife
And pay the ransom for a storm-bound fleet.

Heedless of her tears,
Her cries of 'Father!' and her maiden years,
Her judges valued more
Their glory and their war.
A prayer was said. Her father gave the word
Limp in her flowing dress
The priest's attendants held her high
Above the altar, as men hold a kid.
Her father spoke again, to bid
One bring a gag, and press
Her sweet mouth tightly with a cord,
Lest Atreus' house be cursed by some ill-omened cry.

Rough hands tear at her girdle, cast
Her saffron silks to earth. Her eyes

[15] **The harness of Necessity:** This is the central paradox of Fate and free will. In *The Oresteia* and in other plays, Aeschylus insists that although an inherited curse may make a person's choice desperately hard, choice is still possible.

Search for her slaughterers; and each,
Seeing her beauty, that surpassed
A painter's vision, yet denies
The pity her dumb looks beseech,
Struggling for voice; for often in old days,
When brave men feasted in her father's hall,
With simple skill and pious praise
Linked to the flute's pure tone
Her virgin voice would melt the hearts of all,
Honouring the third libation near her father's throne.

The rest I did not see,
Nor do I speak of it . . .
But this I know:
What Calchas prophesies will be fulfilled.
The scale of Justice falls in equity:
The killer will be killed.

But now, farewell foreboding! Time may show,
But cannot alter, what shall be.
What help, then, to bewail
Troubles before they fall?
Events will take their way
Even as the prophet's words foreshadowed all.
For what is next at hand,
Let good prevail!
That is the prayer we pray—
We, who alone now stand
In Agamemnon's place, to guard this Argive land.

[*The day has broken.* THE QUEEN *now turns and stands facing the* ELDERS.]

CHORUS:

We come obedient to your bidding, Clytemnestra.
Our king and leader absent, and his throne unfilled,
Our duty pays his due observance to his wife.
Have you received some message? Do these sacrifices
Rise for good news, give thanks for long hope re-assured?
I ask in love; and will as loyally receive
Answer or silence.

CLYTEMNESTRA:

Good news, if the proverb's true,
Should break with sunrise from the kindly womb of night.
But here's a richer joy than you dared ever hope:
Our Argive men have captured Priam's town.

CHORUS:

Have *what?*

I heard it wrong—I can't believe it!

CLYTEMNESTRA:

Troy is ours!

Is that clear speaking?

CHORUS:

Happiness fills my eyes with tears.

CLYTEMNESTRA:

They show your loyalty.

CHORUS:

Have you some sure proof of this?

CLYTEMNESTRA:

I have indeed; unless a god has played me false.

CHORUS:

A god! Was it some dream you had, persuaded you?

CLYTEMNESTRA:

Dream! Am I one to air drowsy imaginings?

CHORUS:

Surely you feed yourself on unconfirmed report?

CLYTEMNESTRA:

You choose to criticize me as an ignorant girl!

CHORUS:

Well, then, when was Troy captured?

CLYTEMNESTRA:

In this very night

That brought to birth this glorious sun.

CHORUS:

What messenger

Could fly so fast from Troy to here?

CLYTEMNESTRA:

The god of fire!

Ida first launched his blazing beam; thence to this palace
Beacon lit beacon in relays of flame. From Ida[16]
To Hermes' crag on Lemnos; from that island, third
To receive the towering torch was Athos, rock of Zeus;
There, as the blaze leapt the dark leagues, the watch in welcome

---

[16] **From Ida:** The passage that begins here describes a chain of beacon fires reaching from Ida, the mountains near Troy, across the Aegean island of Lemnos to Mt. Athos in northern Greece and southward to Mt. Makistos, Mt. Messapion, Mt. Kithairon, Mt. Aegiplanctus, and Mt. Arachneus, to, finally, the watch at Argos. The geography throughout this passage is associated with violence and danger, heightening the foreboding at the beginning of the play: Euripus's channel, for example, which divides the Greek mainland from Euboea, suggests Aulis, where Agamemnon sacrificed Iphigenia; Arachneus, which means "Spider Mountain," foreshadows the web Clytemnestra is spinning for Agamemnon. [Ed.]

Leapt too, and a twin tower of brightness speared the sky,
Pointing athwart the former course; and in a stride
Crossing the Aegean, like the whip-lash of lightning, flew
The resinous dazzle, molten-gold, till the fish danced,
As at sunrise, enraptured with the beacon's glow,
Which woke reflected sunrise on Makistos' heights.
The watchman there, proof against sleep, surprise or sloth,
Rose faithful to the message; and his faggots' flame
Swept the wide distance to Euripus' channel, where
Its burning word was blazoned to the Messapian guards.
They blazed in turn, kindling their pile of withered heath,
And passed the signal on. The strong beam, still undimmed,
Crossed at one bound Asopus' plain, and like the moon
In brilliance, lighted on Cithaeron's crags, and woke
Another watch, to speed the flying token on.
On still the hot gleam hurtled, past Gorgopis' lake;
Made Aegiplanctus, stirred those watching mountaineers
Not to stint boughs and brushwood; generously they fed
Their beacon, and up burst a monstrous beard of fire,
Leapt the proud headland fronting the Saronic Gulf,
To lofty Arachnaeus, neighbour to our streets;
Thence on this Atreid palace the triumphant fire
Flashed, lineal descendant of the flame of Ida.

Such, Elders, was the ritual race my torchbearers,
Each at his faithful post succeeding each, fulfilled;
And first and last to run share equal victory.
Such, Elders, is my proof and token offered you,
A message sent to me from Troy by Agamemnon.

CHORUS:

Madam, we will in due course offer thanks to Heaven;
But now we want to savour wonder to the full,
And hear you speak at length: tell us your news again!

CLYTEMNESTRA:

Today the Greeks hold Troy! Her walls echo with cries
That will not blend. Pour oil and vinegar in one vessel,
You'll see them part and swirl, and never mix: so, there,
I think, down narrow streets a discord grates the ear—
Screams of the captured, shouts of those who've captured them,
The unhappy and the happy. Women of Troy prostrate
Over dead husbands, brothers; aged grandfathers
Mourning dead sons and grandsons, and remembering
Their very cries are slaves' cries now. . . . And then the victors:
After a night of fighting, roaming, plundering,
Hungry to breakfast, while their hosts lie quiet in dust;

No rules to keep, no order of place; each with the luck
That fell to him, quartered in captured homes of Troy,
Tonight, at last, rolled in dry blankets, safe from frost—
No going on guard—blissfully they'll sleep from dusk to dawn.

If in that captured town they are reverencing the gods
Whose home it was, and not profaning holy places,
The victors will avoid being vanquished in their turn.
Only, let no lust of unlawful plunder tempt
Our soldiers' hearts with wealth, to their own harm—there still
Remains the journey home: God grant we see them safe!
If the fleet sails free from the taint of sin, the gods
May grant them safely to retrace their outward course—
Those whom no wakeful anger of the forgotten dead[17]
Waits to surprise with vengeance. . . .
These are a woman's words.
May good prevail beyond dispute, in sight of all!
My life holds many blessings; I would enjoy them now.

CHORUS:
Madam, your words are like a man's, both wise and kind.
Now we have heard trustworthy proof from your own lips,
We will prepare ourselves again to praise the gods,
Whose gracious acts call for our most devout response.

[CLYTEMNESTRA *goes into the palace.*]

CHORUS:
Zeus, supreme of heavenly powers!
Friendly night, whose fateful hours
Built for Argos' warlike name
Bright imperishable fame!
Night in which a net was laid
Fast about the Trojan towers
Such that none of mortal flesh,
Great or little, could evade
Grim annihilation's deadly mesh!
This is the hand of Zeus! Zeus we revere,
Whose lasting law both host and guest must fear;
Who long since against Paris[18] bent

---

[17] **the forgotten dead:** As soon as he reaches home, a returning warrior must undergo ritual purification to guard himself against the vengeance of the spirits of those he has killed. The "forgotten dead" Clytemnestra is thinking of is Iphigenia, whom Agamemnon on his return will seem to have forgotten.

[18] **against Paris:** While the chorus speaks explicitly of Paris here, most of what is said may also apply to Agamemnon and those in the House of Atreus whose crimes are visited upon their children. [Ed.]

His bow with careful aim, and sent
His vengeance flying not too near
Nor past the stars, but timed to pay
The debt of Justice on the appointed day.

'The hand of Zeus has cast
The proud from their high place!'
This we may say, and trace
That hand from first to last.
As Zeus foreknowing willed,
So was their end fulfilled.

One said, 'The gods disdain
To mark man's wanton way
Who tramples in the dust
Beauty of holy things.'
Impious! The truth shows plain:
Pride now has paid its debt, and they
Who laughed at Right and put their boastful trust
In arms and swollen wealth of kings,
Have gone their destined way.
A middle course is best,
Not poor nor proud; but this,
By no clear rule defined,
Eludes the unstable, undiscerning mind,
Whose aim will surely miss.
Thenceforth there is no way to turn aside;
When man has once transgressed,
And in his wealth and pride
Spurned the high shrine of Justice, nevermore
May his sin hope to hide
In that safe dimness he enjoyed before.[19]

Retreat cut off, the fiend Temptation[20]
Forces him onward, the unseen
Effectual agent of Damnation;
When his fair freshness once has been
Blotched and defiled with grime, and he,
Like worthless bronze, which testing blows
Have blackened, lies despoiled, and shows

[19] **May his sin . . . before:** The sinner is thought of as shunning the light, lest God should find him out.

[20] **Temptation:** The word is really *persuasion,* used here in the sense more often expressed by the English word *temptation.* But the same power that is here an agent of evil reappears in *The Eumenides* as an agent of good.

His baseness plain for all to see,
Then every cure renews despair;
A boy chasing a bird on wing,
He on his race and soil must bring
A deeper doom than flesh can bear;
The gods are deaf to every prayer;
If pity lights a human eye,
Pity by Justice's law must share
The sinner's guilt, and with the sinner die.
So, doomed, deluded, Paris came
To sit at his host's table, and seduce
Helen his wife, and shame
The house of Atreus and the law of Zeus.

Bequeathing us in Argos
Muster of shields and spears,
The din of forge and dockyard,
Lightly she crossed the threshold
And left her palace, fearless
Of what should wake her fears;
And took to Troy as dowry
Destruction, blood, and tears.
Here, in her home deserted,
The voice of guard and groom
With love and grief lamented:
'O house! O king! O pity!
O pillow softly printed
Where her loved head had rested!'
There lies her husband° fasting, Menelaus
Dumb in his stricken room.
His thought across sea reaches
With longings, not reproaches;
A ghost will rule the palace,
A home become a tomb!
Her statue's sweet perfection
Torments his desolation;
Still his eyes' hunger searches—
That living grace is hardened
And lost that beauty's bloom.

Visions of her beset him
With false and fleeting pleasure
When dreams and dark are deep.
He sees her, runs to hold her;
And, through his fingers slipping,

Lightly departs his treasure,
The dream he cannot keep,
Wafted on wings that follow
The shadowy paths of sleep.

Such are the searching sorrows
This royal palace knows,
While through the streets of Argos
Grief yet more grievous grows,
With all our manhood gathered
So far from earth of Hellas;
As in each home unfathered,
Each widowed bed, the whetted
Sword of despair assails
Hearts where all hope has withered
And angry hate prevails.
They sent forth men to battle,
But no such men return;
And home, to claim their welcome,
Come ashes in an urn.

For War's a banker, flesh his gold.
There by the furnace of Troy's field,
Where thrust meets thrust, he sits to hold
His scale, and watch the spear-point sway;
And back to waiting homes he sends
Slag from the ore, a little dust
To drain hot tears from hearts of friends;
Good measure, safely stored and sealed
In a convenient jar—the just
Price for the man they sent away.
They praise him through their tears, and say,
'He was a soldier!' or, 'He died
Nobly, with death on every side!'
And fierce resentment mutters low,
'Yes—for another's wife!' And so
From grief springs gall, which fear must hide—
Let kings and their revenges go!
But under Ilion's wall the dead,
Heirs of her earth, lie chambered deep;
While she, whose living blood they shed,
Covers her conquerors in sleep.

A nation's voice, enforced with anger,
Strikes deadly as a public curse.

I wait for word of hidden danger,
And fear lest bad give place to worse.
God marks that man with watchful eyes
Who counts his killed by companies;
And when his luck, his proud success,
Forgets the law of righteousness,
Then the dark Furies launch at length
A counter-blow to crush his strength
And cloud his brightness, till the dim
Pit of oblivion swallows him.
In fame unmeasured, praise too high,
Lies danger: God's sharp lightnings fly
To stagger mountains. Then, I choose
Wealth that invites no rankling hate;
Neither to lay towns desolate,
Nor wear the chains of those who lose
Freedom and life to war and Fate.

[*The sound of women's voices excitedly shouting and cheering is heard. One or two* ELDERS *go out, and return immediately to report. The following remarks are made severally by various members of the* CHORUS.]

Since the beacon's news was heard
Rumour flies through every street.
Ought we to believe a word?
Is it some inspired deceit?
Childish, crack-brained fantasy!
Wing your hopes with such a tale,
Soon you'll find that fire can lie,
Facts can change, and trust can fail.
Women all are hasty-headed:
Beacons blaze—belief rejoices;
All too easily persuaded.
Rumour fired by women's voices,
As we know, is quickly spread;
—As we know, is quickly dead!

[*The* CHORUS *depart; and an interval representing the lapse of several days now takes place. After the interval the* CHORUS *re-appear in great excitement.*]

CHORUS:

We shall soon know whether this relay-race of flame,
This midnight torch-parade, this beacon-telegraph,
Told us the truth, or if the fire made fools of us—
All a delightful dream! Look! There's a herald coming
Up from the shore, wearing a crown of olive-leaves!
And, further off, a marching column of armed men,

Sheathed in hot dust, tells me this herald won't stand dumb
Or light a pinewood fire to announce the smoke of Troy!
Either his news doubles our happiness, or else—
The gods forbid all else! Good shows at first appearance,
Now may the proof be good! He who prays otherwise
For Argos—let him reap the folly of his soul!

[*Enter a* HERALD.]

HERALD:

Argos! Dear earth my fathers trod! After ten years
Today I have come home! All other hopes were false,
But this proves true! I dared not think my own land would
In death receive me to my due and dearest rest.
Now blest be Argos, and the sun's sweet light, and Zeus,
God of this realm, and Pythian Apollo, who no more
Aims against us the shafts of his immortal bow.
You fought us, Phoebus,[21] by Scamander long enough:
Be Saviour now, be Healer; once, not twice, our death!
Gods of the city's gathering, hear my prayer; and thou,
Hermes, dear Guardian, Herald, every herald's god;
And you, heroes of old, whose blessing sent us forth,
Bless the returning remnant that the sword has spared!
O house of kings! Beloved walls! O august thrones!
You deities who watch the rising sun, watch now![22]
Welcome with shining eyes the royal architect
Of towering glories to adorn his ancient throne.
To you, and every Argive citizen, Agamemnon
Brings light in darkness; come, then, greet him royally,
As fits one in whose hands Zeus the Avenger's plough
Passed over Troy, to split her towers, scar and subdue
Her fields, and from her fair soil extirpate her seed.
So harsh a halter Atreus' elder son has thrown
Around Troy's neck, and now comes home victorious
To claim supremest honours among mortal men.
For neither Paris now, nor his accomplice town,
Can boast their deed was greater than their punishment.
Found guilty of theft and robbery, he has forfeited
His treasured spoil, destroyed his father's house and throne,
And made his people pay twice over for his sin.

[21] **Phoebus:** Apollo, the Bright One. Apollo had showered the Greeks with "arrows" of plague at the beginning of the Trojan War. [Ed.]

[22] **You deities . . . now!:** The statues of Zeus, Apollo, and Hermes stand on the eastern or southeastern facade of the palace, facing the direction from which Agamemnon arrives.

CHORUS:
Herald of the Greek army, greeting! Welcome home!
HERALD:
Thanks. For ten years I've prayed for life; now I can die.
CHORUS:
Longing for Argos, for your home, tormented you?
HERALD:
Cruelly; and now my cloak is wet with tears of joy.
CHORUS:
Your suffering had its happy side.
HERALD:
What do you mean?
CHORUS:
Your love and longing were returned. Is that not happy?
HERALD:
You mean that Argos longed for us, as we for her?
CHORUS:
Our hearts were dark with trouble. We missed and needed you.
HERALD:
What caused your trouble? An enemy?
CHORUS:
I learnt long ago,
Least said is soonest mended.
HERALD:
But was Argos threatened
In the king's absence?
CHORUS:
Friend, you said just now that death
Was dearly welcome. Our hearts echo what you felt.
HERALD:
Yes, I could die, now the war's over, and all well.
Time blurs the memory; some things one recalls as good,
Others as hateful. We're not gods; then why expect
To enjoy a lifetime of unbroken happiness?
To think what we went through! If I described it all,
The holes we camped in, dirt and weariness and sweat;
Or out at sea, with storms all night, trying to sleep
On a narrow board, with half a blanket; and all day,
Miserable and sick, we suffered and put up with it.
Then, when we landed, things were worse. We had to camp
Close by the enemy's wall, in the wet river-meadows,
Soaked with the dew and mist, ill from damp clothes, our hair
Matted like savages'. If I described the winter, when

In cruel snow-winds from Ida birds froze on the trees;
Or if I told of the fierce heat, when Ocean dropped
Waveless and windless to his noon-day bed, and slept . . .

Well, it's no time for moaning; all that's over now.
And those who died out there—it's over for them too;
No need to jump to orders; they can take their rest.
Why call the roll of those who were expendable,
And make the living wince from old wounds probed again?
Nor much hurrahing either, if we're sensible.
For us who've come safe home the good weighs heaviest,
And what we've suffered counts for less. The praise that's due,
Proudly inscribed, will show these words to the bright sun:
The Argive army conquered Troy,
And brought home over land and sea
These hard-won spoils, the pride and joy
Of ancient palaces, to be
Trophies of victory, and grace
The temples of the Hellene race.
Let Argos hear this, and receive her general home
With thanks and praise. Let Zeus, who gave us victory,
Be blest for his great mercy. I have no more to say.

CHORUS:
Well, I was wrong, I own it. Old and ready to learn
Is always young. But this great news is for the palace,
And chiefly Clytemnestra, whose wealth of joy we share.

[CLYTEMNESTRA *has appeared at the palace door.*]

CLYTEMNESTRA:
I sang for joy to hail this victory long ago,
When the first fiery midnight message told that Troy
Was sacked and shattered. Someone then took me to task:
'Beacons! So you believe them? Troy, you think, is taken?
Typical female hopefulness!' Remarks like these
Exposed my folly. Yet I made thankful sacrifice,
And throughout Argos women gathered to celebrate
Victory with songs of praise in temples of all the gods,
And feed their scented fires with rich flesh-offerings.
I have no need now to hear your detailed narrative;
I'll hear all from the king's own lips. But first, to greet,
Fitly and soon my honoured husband's home-coming—
For to a wife what day is sweeter than when she,
Receiving by God's mercy her lord safe home from war,

Flings wide the gates in welcome?—take to him this message:
Let him come quickly; Argos longs for him; and he
Will find at home a wife as faithful as he left,[23]
A watch-dog at his door; knowing one loyalty;
To enemies implacable; in all ways unchanged.
No seal of his have I unsealed in these ten years.
Of pleasure found with other men, or any breath
Of scandal, I know no more than how to dip hot steel.

[*Exit* CLYTEMNESTRA *to the palace.*]

HERALD:
That's a strange boast—and more strange, as more full of truth.
Is it not scandal that a queen should speak such words?

CHORUS:
Strange? No! Her style eludes you. We interpret her.
A very proper statement—unimpeachable!
Now, Herald, tell us of our loved King Menelaus:
Has he come? Did he sail with you? Is he safely home?

HERALD:
That false good news you ask for—I can't give it you,
My friends; delusion would not comfort you for long.

CHORUS:
Telling a fair tale falsely cannot hide the truth;
When truth and good news part, the rift shows plain enough.

HERALD:
Then here it is: Menelaus has vanished, ship and all!

CHORUS:
You mean, he sailed with you from Troy, and then a storm
Fell on the fleet, and parted his ship from the rest?

HERALD:
Good marksman! An age of agony pointed in three words.

CHORUS:
But Menelaus—what was it thought had happened to him?
Is he given up for lost? Or may he yet survive?

HERALD:
No one can tell, for no one knows; except, perhaps,
The Sun, who fosters every earthly creature's life.

CHORUS:
You mean, I think, that when this storm had scourged our fleet
Some anger of the heavenly powers was satisfied?

HERALD:
Can it be right to foul this fair and holy day,

---

[23] **Will find . . . left:** In this and the following lines, Clytemnestra uses her characteristic mixture of irony and extravagant lies, designed to baffle and disturb with innuendo.

Blurting bad news? After our thanksgiving to the gods,
Such speech is out of place. When a man stands recounting
With bloodshot stare catastrophe and horror, an army dead,
The body of State staggered and gored, homes emptied, men
Blasted, lashed out of life by fire and sword, War's whips—
If such tales were my wares, this triumph-song of disaster
I bring, would suit well. But my news is victory,
Brought to a jubilant city—how can I countervail
Such good with sorrow, tell of the murderous armed alliance
Fate forged with angry gods to pursue and harass us?
For fire and water, age-old enemies, made league,
And pledged good faith in combined slaughter of Greek men.
One night a vicious swell rose with a gale from Thrace;
The sky was a mad shepherd tearing his own flock;
Ship against ship butted like rutting rams; mountains
Of wind and water leapt, surge swallowed and rain threshed.
At dawn, where were the ships? The bright sun beamed—we saw
The Aegean flowering thick with faces of dead Greeks
And scraps of wrecks . . .

Our hull had held, and we came through.
It was no mortal hand that gripped our helm that night:
Some god, by guile or intercession, saved our lives.
Fortune sat smiling on our prow; we sprang no leak,
Nor ran aground on rocks. In the next morning's light,
Stunned, sickened, still incredulous of our own luck,
We brooded, thinking of our maimed and battered fleet.
And they, if any still draw breath, now speak of us
As caught in the same fate we picture theirs. . . . But yet,
May best prove truest! For Menelaus, more than all else
Expect him home. If any searching shaft of sun
Sees him alive and well, by the providence of Zeus
Not yet resolved to exterminate this house—there's hope
That Menelaus will yet come safe to his own home.
And every word you have heard me speak is the plain truth.

[*The* MESSENGER *goes, in the direction from which he came.*]

CHORUS:

Who was the unknown seer whose voice—
Uttered at venture, but instinct
With prescience of what Fate decreed—
Guessing infallibly, made choice
Of a child's name, and deftly linked
Symbol with truth, and name with deed,
Naming, inspired, the glittering bride
Of spears, for whom men killed and died,

Helen, the Spoiler?[24] On whose lips
Was born that fit and fatal name,
To glut the sea with spoil of ships,
Spoil souls with swords, a town with flame?
The curtained softness of her bed
She left, to hear the Zephyr breathe
Gigantic in tall sails; and soon
Comes hue and cry—armed thousands fly
Tracing her trackless oar, and sheathe
Their keels in Simois'[25] shingly bank,
Near fields where grass today grows rank
In soil by war's rich rain made red.

And anger—roused, relentless, sure—
Taught Troy that words have double edge,
That men and gods use *bond* and *pledge*
For love past limit, doom past cure:
Love seals the hearts of bride and groom;
And seal of love is seal of doom.
Loud rings the holy marriage-song
As kinsmen honour prince and bride;
The hour is theirs—but not for long.
Wrath, borne on Time's unhurrying tide,
Claims payment due for double wrong—
The outraged hearth, the god defied.[26]
And songs are drowned in tears, and soon
Must Troy the old learn a new tune;
On Paris, once her praise and pride,
She calls reproach, that his proud wooing
Has won his own and her undoing:
Her sons beset on every side,
Her life-blood mercilessly spilt—
Hers is the loss, and his the guilt.

There was a shepherd once who reared at home
A lion's cub.[27] It shared with sucking lambs
Their milk—gentle, while bone and blood were young.
The children loved it; the old watched and smiled.

---

[24] **Helen, the Spoiler:** The root *hele* means "destroying." This does not mean that the name *Helen* originally meant "a destroyer"; but fancied derivations were a Greek pastime and were felt to have dramatic significance.

[25] **Simois:** A river in Troy. [Ed.]

[26] **the god defied:** Zeus, guardian of the laws of hospitality, which Paris broke.

[27] **lion's cub:** The gentle young creature is a symbol of Helen, as Paris and the Trojans first saw her.

Often the shepherd held it like a child
High in his arms; and often it would seek
His hand with soft eyes and caressing tongue,
Tense with the force of hunger. But in time
It showed the nature of its kind. Repaying
Its debt for food and shelter, it prepared
A feast unbidden. Soon the nauseous reek
Of torn flesh filled the house; a bloody slime
Drenched all the ground from that unholy slaying,
While helpless weeping servants stood and stared.
The whelp once reared with lambs, now grown a beast,
Fulfils his nature as Destruction's priest!

And so to Troy there came
One in whose presence shone
Beauty no thought can name:
A still enchantment of sweet summer calm;
A rarity for wealth to dote upon;
Glances whose gentle fire
Bestowed both wound and balm;
A flower to melt man's heart with wonder and desire.
But time grew ripe, and love's fulfilment ran
Aside from that sweet course where it began.
She, once their summer joy,
Transmuted, now like a swift curse descended
On every home, on every life
Whose welcome once befriended
The outlaw wife;
A fiend sent by the god of host and guest,
Whose law her lover had transgressed,
To break his heart, and break the pride of Troy.

When Earth and Time were young,[28]
A simple ancient saw
Phrased on the common tongue
Declared that man's good fortune, once mature,
Does not die childless, but begets its heir;
That from life's goodness grows, by Nature's law,
Calamity past cure
And ultimate despair.
I think alone; my mind

[28] **When Earth . . . young:** In the following lines the Chorus, with some equivocation, questions the prevailing view of the time that excessive prosperity inevitably leads to calamity. Evil action and vice, they suggest, not good fortune, lead to grief, and justice and honesty reward even those who are poor. [Ed.]

Rejects this general belief.
Sin, not prosperity, engenders grief;
For impious acts breed their own kind,
And evil's nature is to multiply.
The house whose ways are just in word and deed
Still as the years go by
Sees lasting wealth and noble sons succeed.

So, by law of consequence,
Pride or Sin the Elder will,
In the man who chooses ill,
Breed a Younger Insolence.
Sin the Younger breeds again
Yet another unseen Power
Like the Powers that gave it birth:
Recklessness, whose force defies
War and violence, heaven and earth;
Whose menace like a black cloud lies
On the doomed house hour by hour,
Fatal with fear, remorse, and pain.

But Justice with her shining eyes
Lights the smoke-begrimed and mean
Dwelling; honours those who prize
Honour; searches far to find
All whose hearts and hands are clean;
Passes with averted gaze
Golden palaces which hide
Evil armed in insolence;
Power and riches close combined,
Falsely stamped with all men's praise,
Win from her no reverence.
Good and evil she will guide
To their sure end by their appointed ways.

[*Enter* AGAMEMNON *in his chariot, followed by another chariot bearing spoils of war and* CASSANDRA.]

CHORUS:

King! Heir of Atreus! Conqueror of Troy!
What greeting shall we bring? What shall we say
    To voice our hearts' devotion,
    Observe both truth and measure,
Be neither scant nor fulsome in our love?
Many, whose conscience is not innocent,
Attach high value to a show of praise.

As ill-luck finds on all sides
Eyes brimming with condolence
Where no true sting of sorrow pricks the heart,
So now some harsh embittered faces, forced
Into a seemly smile, will welcome you,
And hide the hearts of traitors
Beneath their feigned rejoicing.
Well, a wise shepherd knows his flock by face;
And a wise king can tell the flatterer's eye—
Moist, unctuous, adoring—
The expressive sign of loyalty not felt.
Now this I will not hide: ten years ago
When you led Greece to war for Helen's sake
You were set down as sailing
Far off the course of wisdom.
We thought you wrong, misguided, when you tried
To keep morale from sagging
In superstitious soldiers
By offering sacrifice to stop the storm.
Those times are past; you have come victorious home;
Now from our open hearts we wish you well.
Time and your own enquiries
Will show, among your people,
Who has been loyal, who has played you false.

AGAMEMNON:

First, Argos, and her native gods, receive from me
The conqueror's greeting on my safe return; for which,
As for the just revenge I wrought on Priam's Troy,
Heaven shares my glory. Supplications without end
Won Heaven's ear; Troy stood her trial; unfaltering
The immortals cast their votes into the urn of death,
Dooming Troy's walls to dust, her men to the sword's edge.
The acquitting urn saw hope alone come near, and pass,
Vanishing in each empty hand.[29] Smoke, rising still,
Marks great Troy's fall; flames of destruction's sacrifice
Live yet; and, as they die, stirs from the settled ash
The wind-borne incense of dead wealth and luxury.

Now for this victory let our pious thanksgiving
Tell and re-tell Heaven's favour. We have made Troy pay

[29] **The acquitting . . . hand:** In the Athenian courts, citizen jurors cast their votes into one of two urns—one for acquittal, one for conviction. See the judgment scene in *The Eumenides,* when the jurors cast their votes in the trial of Orestes. [Ed.]

For her proud rape a woman's price. The Argive beast,
The lion rampant on all our shields, at dead of night
Sprang from the womb of the horse[30] to grind that city's bones,
A ranked and ravening litter, that over wall and tower
Leaping, licked royal blood till lust was surfeited.

Thus to the gods I pay first my full salutation.
For your advice, I note it; I am of your mind,
And uphold your judgement. There are few whose inborn love
Warms without envy to a friend's prosperity.
Poison of jealousy laps the disappointed heart,
Doubling its grievance: pangs for its own losses match
With pangs for neighbours' wealth. Life and long observation
Taught me the look of men whose loving show, examined,
Proves but a shadow's shadow: I speak of what I know.
One man, Odysseus, who set sail unwillingly—
At this hour dead or living?—he alone, once yoked,
With good will shared my burden.

For affairs of State,
And this feared disaffection, we will set a day
For assembly and debate among our citizens,
And take wise counsel; where disease wants remedy,
Fire or the knife shall purge this body for its good.

Now to my home, to stand at my own altar-hearth
And give Heaven my first greeting, whose protecting power
Sent forth, and brought me home again. May Victory,
My guardian hitherto, walk constant at my side!

[*Enter* CLYTEMNESTRA *attended by maids holding a long drape of crimson silk.*]

CLYTEMNESTRA:

Elders and citizens of Argos! In your presence now
I will speak, unashamed, a wife's love for her husband.
With time dies diffidence. What I shall tell I learnt
Untaught, from my own long endurance, these ten years
My husband spent under the walls of Ilion.
First, that a woman should sit forlorn at home, unmanned,
Is a crying grief. Then, travellers, one on other's heels,
Dismay the palace, each with worse news than the last.
Why, if my lord received as many wounds as Rumour,

[30] **the horse:** Agamemnon refers here to the so-called Trojan horse, a hollow wooden horse by means of which the Greeks secretly entered Troy. [Ed.]

Plying from Troy to Argos, gave him, he is a net,
All holes! Or had he died each time report repeated
News of his death — see him, a second Geryon,[31]
Boasting his monstrous right, his thrice-spread quilt of earth —
A grave for each death, each body! Many times despair
At a cruel message noosed my throat in a hung cord,
Which force against my will untied.

These fears explain
Why our child is not here to give you fitting welcome,
Our true love's pledge, Orestes. Have no uneasiness.
He is Phocis, a guest of Strophius[32] your well-tried friend,
Who warned me of peril from two sources: first, the risk
Threatening your life at Troy; then, if conspiracy
Matured to popular revolt in Argos, fear
Of man's instinct to trample on his fallen lord.
Such was his reasoning — surely free from all suspicion.

For me — the springing torrents of my tears are all
Drawn dry, no drop left; and my sleepless eyes are sore
With weeping by the lamp long lit for you in vain.
In dreams, the tenuous tremors of the droning gnat
Roused me from dreadful visions of more deaths for you
Than could be compassed in the hour that slept with me.

There is no dearer sight than shelter after storm;
No escape sweeter than from siege of circumstance.
Now, after siege and storm endured, my happy heart
Welcomes my husband, faithful watch-dog of his home,
Our ship's firm anchor, towering pillar that upholds
This royal roof; as dear, as to a father's hope
His longed-for son, a spring to thirsty travellers,
Or sight of land unlooked-for to men long at sea.

Such praise I hold his due; and may Heaven's jealousy
Acquit us;[33] our past suffering has been enough.

---

[31] **Geryon:** Descended from the terrifying Gorgon Medusa, Geryon was a man with three heads (or three bodies) who was king of Erytheia in what is now Cadiz; he was slain by Hercules. [Ed.]

[32] **He is . . . Strophius:** The king of Phocis and ally of Agamemnon, Strophius is the father of Pylades, who helps Orestes when he returns to Argos to slay his father's killers. Orestes has been sent to Phocis, a region near Delphi, to keep him out of the way. [Ed.]

[33] **Acquit us:** She means, for the ears of the Chorus, "acquit Agamemnon and me for our abundant happiness in being reunited"; for the ears of the audience, "acquit Aegisthus and me for the success we hope to achieve by the removal of Agamemnon."

Now, dearest husband, come, step from your chariot.
But do not set to earth, my lord, the conquering foot
That trod down Troy. Servants, do as you have been bidden;
Make haste, carpet his way with crimson tapestries,
Spread silk before your master's feet; Justice herself
Shall lead him to a home he never hoped to see.
All other matters forethought, never lulled by sleep,
Shall order justly as the will of Heaven decrees.

[CLYTEMNESTRA*'s maids spread a path of crimson cloth from the chariot to the palace door.*]

AGAMEMNON:

Daughter of Leda, guardian of my house, your speech
Matches its theme, my absence; for both were prolonged.[34]
Praise fitly spoken should be heard on other lips.
And do not with these soft attentions woman me,
Nor prostrate like a fawning Persian mouth at me
Your loud addresses; not with your spread cloths invite
Envy of gods, for honours due to gods alone.[35]
I count it dangerous, being mortal, to set foot
On rich embroidered silks. I would be reverenced
As man, not god. The praise of fame rings clear without
These frills and fancy foot-rugs; and the god's best gift
Is a mind free from folly. Call him fortunate
Whom the end of life finds harboured in tranquility.

CLYTEMNESTRA:

There is the sea—who shall exhaust the sea?—which teems
With purple dye[36] costly as silver, a dark stream
For staining of fine stuffs, unceasingly renewed.
This house has store of crimson, by Heaven's grace, enough
For one outpouring; you are no king of beggary!
Had oracles prescribed it, I would have dedicated
Twenty such cloths to trampling, if by care and cost
I might ensure safe journey's end for this one life.
Now you are come to your dear home, your altar-hearth,
The tree, its root refreshed, spreads leaf to the high beams
To veil us from the dog-star's heat. Your loved return
Shines now like Spring warmth after winter; but when Zeus
From the unripe grape presses his wine, then through the house

[34] **your speech . . . prolonged:** The dramatic value of this vicious snub is not merely that it further whets Clytemnestra's appetite for revenge but that it establishes Agamemnon as a formidable person, a worthy antagonist even for Clytemnestra.

[35] **honours due to gods alone:** Agamemnon fears that stepping down onto these rich tapestries dyed blood-red would be an act of excessive insolence, overreaching the bounds of propriety. [Ed.]

[36] **purple dye:** The dye was from shellfish, hence the connection to the sea. [Ed.]

Heat dies, and coolness comes, as through this royal door
Enters its lord, perfected to receive his own.

AGAMEMNON:
I have said how I would enter with an easy mind.

CLYTEMNESTRA:
Tell me—not contrary to your resolve—one thing.

AGAMEMNON:
Be sure I shall do nothing against my resolve.

CLYTEMNESTRA:
Might you have vowed to the gods, in danger, such an act?

AGAMEMNON:
Yes, if someone with knowledge had prescribed it me.

CLYTEMNESTRA:
Imagine Priam conqueror: what would he have done?

AGAMEMNON:
Walked on embroidered satin, I have little doubt.

CLYTEMNESTRA:
Then why humble your heart to men's censorious tongue?

AGAMEMNON:
Why indeed? Yet the people's voice speaks with great power.

CLYTEMNESTRA:
Greatness wins hate. Unenvied is unenviable.

AGAMEMNON:
It does not suit a woman to be combative.

CLYTEMNESTRA:
Yet it suits greatness also to accept defeat.

AGAMEMNON:
Why, here's a battle! What would you not give to win?

CLYTEMNESTRA:
Yield! You are victor: give me too my victory.

AGAMEMNON:
Since you're resolved—[*to an attendant*] Come kneel; untie my shoes; dismiss
These leathern slaves that smooth my path. And as I tread
This deep-sea treasure, may no watchful envious god
Glance from afar. It offends modesty, that I
Should dare with unwashed feet to soil these costly rugs,
Worth weight for weight of silver, spoiling my own house!
But let that pass.

Take in this girl[37] and treat her well.
God will reward from heaven a gentle conqueror.

[37] **this girl:** Cassandra, the captive prophetess and daughter of King Priam of Troy; as seen in the Chorus's response to her (next page) though Cassandra was granted the gift of prophecy from Apollo, when she spurned his amorous advances he vowed that her prophecies would never be understood or believed. [Ed.]

Slavery is a yoke no one bears willingly; and she
Came to me by the army's gift, of all Troy's wealth
The chosen jewel.
Now, since I have been subdued to obedience in this matter,
Treading on purple I will go into my house.

CLYTEMNESTRA:
Elelelelеu!

[*a prolonged triumphant cry; which the* CHORUS *accept as a formal celebration of the victor's return, while only* CASSANDRA *understands its true meaning.* AGAMEMNON *walks alone along the purple path and enters the palace.*]

CLYTEMNESTRA:
Zeus, Zeus, Fulfiller! Now fulfil these prayers of mine;
And let thy will accomplish all that is thy will!

[CLYTEMNESTRA *enters the palace.* AGAMEMNON*'s chariot is taken away by attendants.* CASSANDRA *remains seated in the second chariot.*]

CHORUS:
What is this persistent dread
Haunting, hovering to show
Signs to my foreboding soul,
While unbidden and unpaid
Throbs the prophet in my veins,
While persuasive confidence
That should rule the heart, and scorn
Fantasies of cloudy dreams,
Trembles, and resigns her throne?
Once before, though far away,
My heart knew the pregnant hour,
When at Troy our sailors' shouts,
As they coiled their sheets astern,
Chimed with my triumphal song;
And the fleet set sail for home.

Then was guessing; now I see
With these eyes the fleet returned.
Yet my spirit knows again
The foreboding hour; again
Sings, by untaught instinct, that
Sad, familiar, fatal dirge;
Yields her kingdom in the flesh,
Daunted with surmise, and feels
Pang and pulse of groin and gut,
Blood in riot, brain awhirl,
Nerve and tissue taut, and knows
Truth must prick, where flesh is sore.

Yet I pray, may time and truth
Shame my fears; may prophecy
Vanish, and fulfilment fail!

When fortune flowers too lushly,
Decay, her envious neighbour,
Stands eager to invade;
Glory's brief hours are numbered,
And what has flowered must fade.
Bold in success, ambition
Sails on, where rocks lie hidden,
Strikes, and her debt is paid.
Yet, debts may be compounded:
When Thracian storm-winds threaten,
The merchant, for his silver,
With pious prayers devotes
A tithe in ample measure;
Into the sea he slings it,
And safe his vessel floats.
The house that offers to the envious Powers
Its wealthy surplus will not fail and die;
Zeus to their prayers will bounteously reply,
Bless each year's furrowed fields with sun and showers,
Bid harvests teem, and fear of famine fly.

But when, from flesh born mortal,
Man's blood on earth lies fallen,
A dark, unfading stain,
Who then by incantations
Can bid blood live again?
Zeus in pure wisdom ended
That sage's skill[38] who summoned
Dead flesh to rise from darkness
And live a second time;
Lest murder cheaply mended
Invite men's hands to crime.
Were I not sure that always
Events and causes hold
Sequence divinely ordered,
And next by last controlled,
Speech would forestall reluctance,

[38] **That sage's skill:** Asclepius, the legendary physician who was struck down by Zeus when he resurrected a dead man. [Ed.]

Voice thoughts I dare not fathom,
And leave no fear untold.
But now my tongue mutters in darkness, sharing
The heart's distress, tormented with desire
To achieve some timely word, and still despairing;
While my dumb spirit smoulders with deep fire.

[CLYTEMNESTRA *comes to the palace door.*]

CLYTEMNESTRA:

You too, Cassandra there, do you hear me? Get indoors.
You may thank Zeus, this palace bears you no ill-will;
You shall stand near our sovereign altar, and partake,
With many other slaves, the cleansing ritual.
Then leave that chariot; do not be proud. They say
Heracles[39] once was sold, and learnt to eat slaves' bread.
If such misfortune falls, and there's no help for it—
A house of long-established wealth is generous;
Where meagre hopes reap opulence, it goes hard with slaves.
Here you shall have your due—what's customary, and more.

CHORUS:

It was to you she spoke. She waits. Was it not clear?
Since you're a captive in the toils of destiny
Obey, if you understand. Or do you choose defiance?

CLYTEMNESTRA:

If she's not crazed, she will obey; unless she speaks
Some weird unheard-of tongue, like swallows twittering.

CHORUS:

Come, now; her bidding is the best that's possible.
Leave sitting in that chariot; obey, go in.

CLYTEMNESTRA:

I have no time to spend standing out here. Already
Victims for sacrifice wait at the central hearth.
If you understand what I have said, come in at once;
If not, [*to an attendant*] since she's a foreigner, explain by signs.

[*An attendant makes signs to* CASSANDRA *to enter the palace.*]

CHORUS:

It's clear enough the girl needs an interpreter.
She has the look of some wild creature newly trapped.

CLYTEMNESTRA:

Why, she is mad, hears only her own frenzied thoughts.
Has she not left her city levelled with the ground?—
Yet has not sense enough to accept her owner's bit

[39] **Heracles:** Hercules, the great hero who once had to serve as a slave to Queen Omphale of Lydia. [Ed.]

Till she has frothed her rage out from a bloody mouth.
I will spend words no longer, to be thus ignored.

[CLYTEMNESTRA *goes into the palace.*]

CHORUS:

I feel pity, not anger. Come, poor girl, step down;
Yield to this hard necessity; wear your new yoke.

[CASSANDRA *steps down. She sees the statue of Apollo.*]

CASSANDRA:

O Apollo! Oh, oh! No, no, no, no! O Earth! O Apollo!

CHORUS:

Why name Apollo with this wail of agony?
He is no god of mourning, to be so invoked.

CASSANDRA:

Oh, oh! O horror! O Earth! O Apollo, Apollo!

CHORUS:

Again she utters blasphemy, to call Apollo,
Whose godhead may not stand in the same house with grief.

CASSANDRA:

Apollo, Apollo! Leader of journeys, my destroyer!
All this way you have led me, to destroy me again!

CHORUS:

She is inspired to speak of her own sufferings.
The prophetic power stays with her even in slavery.

CASSANDRA:

Apollo, Apollo! Leader of journeys, my destroyer!
Where have you led me? Oh! what fearful house is this?

CHORUS:

Does not prophecy tell you this is Atreus' palace?
I tell you, then; so call it, and you will speak the truth.

CASSANDRA:

No! but a house that hates
The gods; whose very stones
Bear guilty witness to a bloody act;
That hides within these gates
Remnants of bodies hacked,
And murdered children's bones![40]

CHORUS:

This prophetess goes to it like a keen-scented hound;
We know the trail she follows, and it leads to blood.

[40] **murdered children's bones:** Cassandra here alludes to Atreus's murder of Thyestes' sons, from whose corpses he prepared a stew for their father to eat. She may also be alluding to the murder of Pelops, who was served up in a stew to the gods by his father Tantalus (see pages 802–803). Aegisthus tells the story of Thyestes in lines 1666–87. [Ed.]

CASSANDRA:

To blood—I know. See there,
The witness that they bear—
Those children weeping for their own blood shed,
For their own tender flesh,
That cruel, nameless dish
From which their father fed!

CHORUS:

We had all heard of your prophetic power; but this
Requires no prophecy to tell us of—

CASSANDRA:

Ah, ah!
Oh, shame! Conspiracy!
A heart obsessed with hate
And lurking to betray
Pollutes this house anew
With deadly injury
Where deepest love was due!
Surprised, unarmed, how can he fight with Fate?
And help is far away.

CHORUS:

The first we understand—all Argos speaks of it;
But to this second prophecy I have no key.

CASSANDRA:

Shame on her! She will stand—
Would there were room for doubt!—
To cleanse her lawful lord
From guilt of war—and then—
How can I speak the word?
This cleansing ritual
Shall serve his burial!
Despairing hands reach out,
Snared by a stronger hand!

CHORUS:

Still I am baffled by her riddling utterance;
What can one make of prophecy so recondite?

CASSANDRA:

There, there! O terror! What is this new sight?
A hunting-net, Death's weapon of attack!
And she who hunts is she who shared his bed.
Howl, Furies, howl, you bloody ravening pack,
Gorged with this house's blood, yet thirsting still;
The victim bleeds: come, Fiends, and drink your fill!

CHORUS:

What fiends are these you call to bay at Death?

Your ghastly hymn has paled your cheek; and pale
The blood shrinks to your heart, as when men die
Sword-struck in battle, pulse and vision fail,
And life's warm colours fly;
See, how her utterance chokes her laboured breath!

CASSANDRA:

Help! Look, a nightmare! What? will cow gore bull,
The black-horned monarch? Save him, drag him away!
The treacherous water's poured, the lustral bath is full;
She holds him in a trap made like a gown,—
She strikes! He crashes down!
Listen! It is treachery, treachery, I say!

CHORUS:

Although I claim no special skill in oracles,
Her words, I feel, augur no good. Yet, after all,
What good news ever comes to men through oracles?
Prophets find bad news useful. Why, the primary aim
Of all their wordy wisdom is to make men gape.

CASSANDRA:

O fear, and fear again!
O pity! Not alone
He suffers; with his pain
Mingled I mourn my own!
Cruel Apollo! Why,
Why have you led me here?
Only that I may share
The death that he must die!

CHORUS:

She is insane, poor girl, or god-possessed,
And for herself alone she makes this wail,
Unwearied in her tuneless song;
As the shrill nightingale
Unburdens her distracted breast,
Sobbing *Itun, Itun,*[41] remembering all her wrong.

CASSANDRA:

Bitter was her ordeal;
Yet by the kind gods' wish
The lovely robe she wears
Is feathered wings; and even
The plaint she pours to heaven,
Note answering note with tears,

---

[41] ***Itun:*** The accusative case of *itus,* usually spelled *Itys* in English. He was the son of Tereus and Procne, whom Procne herself killed to punish her husband for the rape of her sister Philomela. Philomela was afterwards turned into a nightingale, and "*Itun, Itun*" is supposed to represent her song.

Rings sweet. But I must feel
The parting of the flesh
Before the whetted steel.

CHORUS:
Whence come these violent miseries, god-inspired
Yet void of meaning? Why with voice like doom
Intone these horrors in heart-searing words?
Who marked the oracular road
Whose evil terms you trace?

CASSANDRA [*changing from the shrill declamation of prophecy to the quiet sadness of mourning*]:
O Paris and his passion!
O marriage-bed that slew
His family and city!
O sweet Scamander[42] river
Our thirsting fathers knew,
By whose loved banks I grew!
But soon the dark Cocytus
And Acheron[43] shall echo
My prophecies, and witness
Whether my words are true.

CHORUS:
Paris's marriage! This is at last clear
To any child. Yet in her muttered fear
Lies more than meets the sight:
With stunning pain, like a brute serpent's bite,
Her whispered cry crashes upon my ear.

CASSANDRA:
O Ilion and her passion!
O city burnt and rased!
O fires my father kindled
To keep his towers defiant!
O blood of beasts he offered
From every herd that grazed!
Yet no propitiation
Could save her sons from dying
As I foretold they would;
And I will join my brothers,
And soon the ground will welcome
My warm and flowing blood.

---

[42] **Scamander:** A river at Troy. [Ed.]

[43] **Cocytus . . . Acheron:** Two rivers of the lower world. The names mean respectively "river of wailing" and "river of grief."

CHORUS:

Once more her utterance adds like to like.
Tell us, what god is he, so merciless,
Whose grievous hand can strike
Such deathly music from your mournful soul,
Arrows of prophecy whose course and goal
I seek, but cannot guess?

CASSANDRA:

Then listen. Now my prophecy shall no more peep
From under shy veils like a new-made bride, but blow
A bounding gale towards the sunrise, on whose surge
A crime more fearful than my murder shall at once
Sweep into blazing light. Without more mystery
I will instruct you; but first testify how close
I scent the trail of bloody guilt incurred long since.
Under this roof live day and night a ghastly choir[44]
Venting their evil chant in hideous harmony;
Drunk with men's blood, boldly established here, they hold
Unbroken revel, Fiends of the blood royal, whom none
Can exorcize. Drinking they sit, and with their songs
Drive folly first to crime; the crime performed, in turn
They spew out the defiler of his brother's bed!
Do I miss? Or has my arrow found a mark you know?
Or am I 'lying prophet', 'gypsy', 'tale-spinner'?
Come, on your oath, bear witness: the foul history
Of Atreus' palace, sin for sin, is known to me!

CHORUS:

The holiest oath could help but little. Yet I marvel
That you, bred overseas in a foreign tongue, unfold
Our city's past as truly as if you had been here.

CASSANDRA:

Apollo, god of prophecy, gave me this office.

CHORUS:

Did *he* lust for your mortal body, though a god?

CASSANDRA:

Yes. Until now I was ashamed to speak of it.

CHORUS:

We all are more reserved when we are prosperous.

CASSANDRA:

He urged me hard, made warmest protest of his love.

CHORUS:

And did you lie together? Had you child by him?

[44] **a ghastly choir:** Cassandra means the Furies, who would naturally haunt a house so steeped in crime.

CASSANDRA:
I gave my word, and broke it—to the God of Words.[45]
CHORUS:
Already god-possessed with the prophetic art?
CASSANDRA:
I had foretold already the whole doom of Troy.
CHORUS:
Surely the god was angry? Did he punish you?
CASSANDRA:
After my sin, no one believed one word I spoke.
CHORUS:
To us your prophecies seem all too credible.
CASSANDRA:
Oh! Oh!
Horror and sin! Again the anguish of true vision—
Yes, sin and horror!—racks and ravages my brain.
Look! See them sit, there on the wall, like forms in dreams,
Children butchered like lambs by their own kindred. See,
What do they carry in their hands? O piteous sight!
It is their own flesh—limb and rib and heart they hold,
Distinct and horrible, the food their father ate!
I tell you, for this crime revenge grows hot: there lurks
In the home lair—as regent, say—a cowardly lion
Who plots against his master absent at the war;
While the Commander Lion[46] who uprooted Troy,
Met by the fawning tongue, the bright obsequious ear,
Of the vile plotting she-hound, does not know what wounds
Venomed with hidden vengeance she prepares for him.
Female shall murder male: what kind of brazenness
Is that? What loathsome beast lends apt comparison?
A basilisk? Or Scylla's[47] breed, living in rocks
To drown men in their ships—a raging shark of hell,
Dreaming of steel thrust at her husband's unarmed flesh?
You heard her superb bluff, that cry of triumph, raised
As if for a hard battle won, disguised as joy
At his safe home-coming? You are incredulous—
No matter—I say, no matter; what will come will come.
Soon you will see with your own eyes, and pity me,
And wish my prophecy had not been half so true.

[45] **God of Words:** A very common name for Apollo was Loxias, which has this meaning, being connected with the Greek *logos,* word, or *loxos,* ambiguous.

[46] **Commander Lion:** Agamemnon; the "cowardly lion" of line 1292 is Aegisthus. [Ed.]

[47] **Scylla:** Female sea monster with six heads who, along with her companion Charybdis, attacked sailors as they passed through the strait of Messina. (See Homer's *Odyssey,* Book 12.) [Ed.]

CHORUS:
Thyestes' feast of children's flesh we understand;
Horror gives place to wonder at your true account;
The rest outstrips our comprehension; we give up.

CASSANDRA:
I say Agamemnon shall lie dead before your eyes.

CHORUS:
Silence, you wretched outcast—or speak wholesome words!

CASSANDRA:
No wholesome word can purge the poison of that truth.

CHORUS:
None, if it is to be; but may the gods forbid!

CASSANDRA:
You turn to prayer; others meanwhile prepare to kill.

CHORUS:
What man can be the source of such polluting sin?

CASSANDRA:
What man? You miss the main point of my prophecies.

CHORUS:
How could such murder be contrived? This baffles me.

CASSANDRA:
Yet I speak good Greek—all too good.

CHORUS:
The oracles
Of Delphi are good Greek, but hard to understand.

CASSANDRA:
Oh, oh! For pity, Apollo! Where can I escape?
This death you send me is impatient, merciless!
She, this lioness in human form, who when her lord
Was absent paired with a wolf, will take my wretched life.
Like one who mixes medicine for her enemies,
Now, while she whets the dagger for her husband's heart,
She vows to drug his dram with a memory of me,
And make him pledge my safe arrival—in my blood.[48]

This robe—why should I wear what mocks me? Why still keep
This sceptre, these oracular garlands round my neck?
Before I die I'll make an end of you . . . and you . . .
Go, with my curse, go! Thus I pay my debt to you!

[*trampling them on the ground*]

Go, make some other woman rich in misery!

---

[48] **She vows . . . blood:** A safe arrival would be celebrated both by drinking and by libation to the gods. The cup Clytemnestra is preparing for Agamemnon is his death, mingled with Cassandra's.

And let Apollo see, and witness what I do—
He who once saw me in these same insignia
Scorned, jeered at like some gypsy quack, by enemies
And friends alike, called starveling, beggar, conjuror,
Pitiable wretch—all this I bore; and now Apollo,
Who gave a portion of his own prescience to me,
Brings me from Ilion here to this death-reeking porch,
Where I shall never court crass unbelief again,
Where not my father's hearthstone but the slaughterer's block
Waits for me, warm already with a victim's blood.

Yet we shall not die unregarded by the gods.
A third shall come to raise our cause, a son[49] resolved
To kill his mother, honouring his father's blood.
He, now a wandering exile, shall return to set
The apex on this tower of crime his race has built.
A great oath, sealed in sight of gods, binds him to exact
Full penance for his father's corpse stretched dead in dust.

Why then should I lament? Am I so pitiable?
I have watched Fate unfold her pattern: Troy endured
What she endured; her captor now, by Heaven's decree,
Ends thus. I have done with tears. I will endure my death.
O gates of the dark world, I greet you as I come!
Let me receive, I pray, a single mortal stroke,
Sink without spasm, feel the warm blood's gentle ebb,
Embrace death for my comfort, and so close my eyes.

CHORUS:
O woman deep in wisdom as in suffering,
You have told us much. Yet, if you have true foreknowledge
Of your own death, why, like an ox for sacrifice,
Move thus towards the altar with intrepid step?

CASSANDRA:
Friends, there is no escape, none—once the hour has come.

CHORUS:
Yet last to go gains longest time.

CASSANDRA:
This is the day.
Retreat wins little.

CHORUS:
Courage and destiny in you
Are proudly matched.

---

[49] **A third . . . son:** Orestes, the son of Agamemnon and Clytemnestra, who has been sent away to Phocis under the care of King Strophius. [Ed.]

CASSANDRA:

The happy never hear such praise.

CHORUS:

Yet a brave death lends brightness to mortality.

CASSANDRA:

O father! O my brothers! All your brightness dead! . . .
I go. Now in the land of the defeated I
Will mourn my end and Agamemnon's. I have lived.

[*She goes towards the door; then with a cry turns back.*]

CHORUS:

What is it? What do you see? What terror turns you back?

[CASSANDRA *gasps, with a sound of choking.*]

CHORUS:

You gasp, as if some nausea choked your very soul.

CASSANDRA:

There is a smell of murder. The walls drip with blood.

CHORUS:

The altar's ready. This is the smell of sacrifice.

CASSANDRA:

It is most like the air that rises from a grave.

CHORUS:

You mean the Syrian perfume sprinkled for the feast?

CASSANDRA:

I am not like a bird scared at an empty bush,
Trembling for nothing. Wait: when you shall see my death
Atoned with death, woman for woman; when in place
Of him whom marriage cursed another man shall fall:
Then witness for me—these and all my prophecies
Were utter truth. This I request before I die.

CHORUS:

To die is sad; sadder, to know death fore-ordained.

CASSANDRA:

Yet one word more, a prophecy—or, if a dirge,
At least not mine alone. In this sun's light—my last—
I pray: when the sword's edge requites my captor's blood,
Then may his murderers, dying, with that debt pay too
For her they killed in chains, their unresisting prey!

Alas for human destiny! Man's happiest hours
Are pictures drawn in shadow. Then ill fortune comes,
And with two strokes the wet sponge wipes the drawing out.
And grief itself is hardly more pitiable than joy.

[*She goes into the palace.*]

CHORUS:

Of fortune no man tastes his fill.
While pointing envy notes his store,
And tongues extol his happiness,
Man surfeited will hunger still.
For who grows weary of success,
Or turns good fortune from his door
Bidding her trouble him no more?

Our king, whom Fortune loves to bless,
By the gods' will has taken Troy,
And honour crowns his safe return.
If now, for blood shed long ago,
In penance due his blood must flow,
And if his murderers must earn
Death upon death, and Fate stands so,
I ask, what mortal man can claim
That he alone was born to enjoy
A quiet life, and an untarnished name?

[AGAMEMNON*'s voice is heard from inside the palace.*]

AGAMEMNON:

Help, help! I am wounded, murdered, here in the inner room!

CHORUS:

Hush, listen! Who cried 'Murder'? Do you know that voice?

AGAMEMNON:

Help, help again! Murder—a second, mortal blow!

CHORUS:

1. That groan tells me the deed is done. It was the king.
Come, let's decide together on the safest plan.
2. This is what I advise—to send a herald round
Bidding the citizens assemble here in arms.
3. Too slow. I say we should burst in at once, and catch
Murder in the act, before the blood dries on the sword.
4. I share your feeling—that is what we ought to do,
Or something of that kind. Now is the time to act.
5. It's plain what this beginning points to: the assassins
Mean to establish a tyrannical regime.
6. Yes—while we talk and talk; but action, spurning sleep,
Tramples the gentle face of caution in the dust.
7. I can suggest no plan that might prove practical.
I say, let those who took this step propose the next.
8. I'm of the same opinion. If the king is dead,
I know no way to make him live by argument.
9. Then shall we patiently drag out our servile years

Governed by these disgraces of our royal house?
10. No, no! Intolerable! Who would not rather die?—
A milder fate than living under tyranny!
11. Wait; not too fast. What is our evidence? Those groans?
Are we to prophesy from them that the king's dead?
12. We must be certain; this excitement's premature.
Guessing and certain knowledge are two different things.

CHORUS:
I find this view supported on all sides: that we
Make full enquiry what has happened to the king.

[*The palace doors open, revealing* CLYTEMNESTRA. *At her feet* AGAMEMNON *lies dead, in a silver bath, and wrapped in a voluminous purple robe. On his body lies* CASSANDRA, *also dead.*]

CLYTEMNESTRA:
I said, not long since, many things to match the time;
All which, that time past, without shame I here unsay.
How else, when one prepares death for an enemy
Who seems a friend—how else net round the deadly trap
High enough to forestall the victim's highest leap?
A great while I have pondered on this trial of strength.
At long last the pitched battle came, and victory:
Here where I struck I stand and see my task achieved.
Yes, this is my work, and I claim it. To prevent
Flight or resistance foiling death, I cast on him,
As one who catches fish, a vast voluminous net,
That walled him round with endless wealth of woven folds;
And then I struck him, twice. Twice he cried out and groaned;
And then fell limp. And as he lay I gave a third
And final blow, my thanks for prayers fulfilled, to Zeus,
Lord of the lower region, Saviour—of dead men!
So falling he belched forth his life; with cough and retch
There spurted from him bloody foam in a fierce jet,
And spreading, spattered me with drops of crimson rain;
While I exulted as the sown cornfield exults
Drenched with the dew of heaven when buds burst forth in Spring.

So stands the case, Elders of Argos. You may be
As you choose, glad or sorry; I am jubilant.
And, were it seemly over a *dead* man to pour
Thankoffering for safe journey, surely Justice here
Allows it, here demands it; so enriched a wine
Of wickedness this man stored in his house, and now
Returned, drains his own cursed cup to the last dregs.

CHORUS:
The brute effrontery of your speech amazes us.

To boast so shamelessly over your husband's corpse!

CLYTEMNESTRA:

You speak as to some thoughtless woman: you are wrong.
My pulse beats firm. I tell what you already know:
Approve or censure, as you will; all's one to me.
This is my husband, Agamemnon, now stone dead;
His death the work of my right hand, whose craftsmanship
Justice acknowledges. There lies the simple truth.

CHORUS:

Vile woman! What unnatural food or drink,
Malignant root, brine from the restless sea,
Transformed you, that your nature did not shrink
From foulest guilt? Argos will execrate
Your nameless murder with one voice of hate,
Revoke your portion with the just and free,
And drive you outlawed from our Argive gate.

CLYTEMNESTRA:

Yes! Now you righteously mulct *me* with banishment,
Award me public curses, roars of civic hate.
Why, once before, did you not dare oppose this man?
Who with as slight compunction as men butcher sheep,
When his own fields were white with flocks, must sacrifice
His child, and my own darling, whom my pain brought forth—
He killed her for a charm to stop the Thracian wind!
He was the one you should have driven from Argos; he,
Marked with his daughter's blood, was ripe for punishment.
But *my* act shocks your ears, whets your judicial wrath!
Your threats doubtless rely on force—you have your men
And weapons: try your strength in fair fight against mine.
Win, and you may command me. If—please Heaven—you lose,
Old as you are, you shall be taught some wisdom yet.

CHORUS:

Such boasts show folly in a crafty mind.
So surely as your robe blazons your crime
In those red drops, shall your own head bow low
Under a bloody stroke. Wait but the time:
Friendless, dishonoured, outcast, you shall find
Your debt fall due, and suffer blow for blow.

CLYTEMNESTRA:

Is it so? Then you shall hear the righteous oath I swear.
By Justice, guardian of my child, now perfected;
By her avenging Fury, at whose feet I poured
His blood: I have no fear that *his* avenger's tread
Shall shake this house, while my staunch ally now as then,
Aegisthus, kindles on my hearth the ancestral fire.

With such a shield, strength marches boldly on. Meanwhile,
He who was sweet to every Trojan Chryseis,[50]
And soured my life, lies here; with him his prisoner,
His faithful soothsayer, who shared his berth, and knew
Sailors' lasciviousness; their ends both richly earned.
He—as you see him; she first, like the dying swan,
Sang her death-song, and now lies in her lover's clasp.
Brought as a variant to the pleasures of my bed,
She lends an added relish now to victory.

CHORUS:

Come, look on him, and weep.
O that some merciful swift fate,
Not wasting-sick nor wry with pain,
Would bid me share his ever-endless sleep!
Low lies the kindly guardian of our State,
Who fought ten years to win
Redress for woman's sin;
Now by a woman slain.

Helen! Infatuate Helen! You who spilt
Beneath Troy's wall lives without number! You
Now on your house have fixed a lasting guilt
Which every age will tell anew.
Surely, that day you fled beyond recall,
A curse of grief already grew
Deep-rooted in this royal hall.

CLYTEMNESTRA:

Is fact so gross a burden?
Put up no prayers for death;
Nor turn your spleen on Helen,
As if her act had ordered
The fate of fighting thousands
And robbed their souls of breath;
Or from her fault alone
Such cureless grief had grown.

CHORUS:

Spirit of hate, whose strong curse weighs
Hard on the house and heirs of Tantalus,
Your power it is engenders thus
In woman's brain such evil art,
And darkens all my bitter days.

---

[50] **Chryseis:** The daughter of Khryse (Chryse), a priest of Apollo; Agamemnon refused to return this girl, taken as a war captive, to her father and claimed that he would rank her higher than Clytemnestra. See *The Odyssey*, Book 1. [Ed.]

It is your hateful form I see rejoice,
Standing like crow on carrion; your voice
Whose execrable song affronts both ear and heart.

CLYTEMNESTRA:

You now speak more in wisdom,
Naming the thrice-gorged Fury
That hates and haunts our race.
Hers is the thirst of slaughter,
Still slaked with feud and vengeance,
Till, with each wrong requited
A new thirst takes its place.

CHORUS:

This grievous power whose wrath you celebrate
With cursed truth, no royal house's fall,
No mad catastrophe, can ever sate.
O piteous mystery! Is Zeus not lord?
Zeus, Zeus, alas! doer and source of all?
Could even this horror be, without his sovereign word?

Sad, silent king! How shall I mourn your death?
How find the heart's true word, to prove me friend?
Here where you spent your dying breath,
Caught by the ruthless falsehood of a wife,
In the foul spider's web fast bound you lie.
Unholy rest, and most ignoble end—
That man like beast should die
Pierced with a two-edged knife!

CLYTEMNESTRA:

This murder's mine, you clamour.
I was his wife, but henceforth
My name from his be freed!
Dressed in my form, a phantom[51]
Of vengeance, old and bitter,
On that obscene host, Atreus,
For his abhorrent deed,
Has poured this blood in payment,
That here on Justice's altar
A man for babes should bleed.

CHORUS:

And are you guiltless? Some revengeful Power
Stood, maybe, at your side; but of this blood
Who will, who could absolve you? Hour by hour

[51] **Dressed . . . phantom:** That is, I am but an instrument of the living curse that haunts our house.

On his unyielding course the black-robed King,
Pressing to slaughter, swells the endless flood
Of crimson life by pride and hate released
From brothers' veins—till the due reckoning,
When the dried gore shall melt, and Ares° bring — the god of war
Justice at last for that unnatural feast.

Sad, silent king! How shall I mourn your death?
How find the heart's true word, to prove me friend?
Here where you spent your dying breath,
Caught by the ruthless falsehood of a wife,
In the foul spider's web fast bound you lie.
Unholy rest, and most ignoble end—
That man like beast should die
Pierced with a two-edged knife!

CLYTEMNESTRA:

The guile I used to kill him
He used himself the first,
When he by guile uprooted
The tender plant he gave me,
And made this house accurst.
When on my virgin daughter
His savage sword descended,
My tears in rivers ran;
If now by savage sword-thrust
His ageing days are ended,
Let shame and conscience ban
His boasts, where he pays forfeit
For wrong his guile began.

CHORUS:

Where, where lies Right? Reason despairs her powers,
Mind numbly gropes, her quick resources spent.
Our throne endangered, and disaster near,
Where can I turn? I fear
Thunder that cracks foundations, blood-red showers;
The light rain slacks—the deluge is in store.
Justice, in harmony with Fate's intent,
Hardens her hold to shake the earth once more.

O earth, O earth! Would that some timely chance
Had laid me in your lap, before my eyes
Had seen him laid so low,
Lord of this silver-walled inheritance!
Who will inter him? Who lament the dead?
Will *you* wear mourning for disguise?

Bewail the husband whom your own hand killed?
For his high glories offer gifts of lies?
Since Justice answers, No!
By whom shall tears of honest love be shed,
His graveside ritual of praise fulfilled?

CLYTEMNESTRA:

That question's not your business.
I felled him; I despatched him;
And I will earth his bones.
No troops from house or city
Shall beat their breasts and lay him
In vaults of bronze and marble
With seemly civic groans.
But, as is fit, his daughter
Shall meet him near the porchway
Of those who perished young;
His loved Iphigenia
With loving arms shall greet him,
And gagged and silent tongue.

CHORUS:

Reproach answers reproach; truth darkens still.
She strikes the striker; he who dared to kill
Pays the full forfeit. While Zeus holds his throne,
This maxim holds on earth: *the sinner dies.*
That is God's law. Oh, who can exorcize
This breeding curse, this canker that has grown
Into these walls, to plague them at its will?

CLYTEMNESTRA:

The sinner dies: you have reached the truth at last.
Now to the Powers that persecute
Our race I offer a sworn pact:
With this harsh deed and bitter fact
I am content; let *them* forget the past,
Leave us for ever, and oppress
Some other house with murderous wickedness.
I ask no weight of wealth;
For me it will suffice
To purchase, at this price,
For our long sickness, health.

[*Enter* AEGISTHUS.]

AEGISTHUS:

O happy day, when Justice comes into her own!
Now I believe that gods, who dwell above the earth,
See what men suffer, and award a recompense:

Here, tangled in a net the avenging Furies wove,
He lies, a sight to warm my heart; and pays his blood
In full atonement for his father's treacherous crime.

Here is the story plain. There was dispute between
Atreus, Agamemnon's father, who ruled Argos then,
And my father Thyestes, his own brother; whom
Atreus drove out from home and city. He came back;
Sat as a piteous suppliant at Atreus' hearth;
Gained his request—in part: his own blood did not stain
His childhood's home. But Atreus, this man's father, gave
His guest, my father, a host's gift; a gift more full
Of eagerness than love. He feigned a feasting-day,
And amidst lavish meats served him his own sons' flesh.
The feet and the splayed fingers he concealed, putting
The other parts, unrecognizably chopped small,
Above them. Each guest had his table; and this dish
Was set before my father. He, in ignorance,
At once took that which prompted no close scrutiny,
And tasted food from which, as you now see, our house
Has not recovered. Then he recognized, in all
Its loathsomeness, what had been done. With one deep groan,
Back from his chair, vomiting murdered flesh, he fell;
Cursed Pelops' race with an inexorable curse;
With his foot sent the table crashing wide, and screamed,
'So crash to ruin the whole house of Tantalus!'

That deed gave birth to what you now see here, this death.
I planned his killing, as was just: I was the third
Child of Thyestes, then a brat in baby-clothes;
Spared, and sent off with my distracted father, till,
Full-grown, Justice restored me to my native land.
I, from a distance, plotted this whole evil snare,
And caught my man. Thus satisfied, I could die now,
Seeing Agamemnon in the trap of Justice, dead.

CHORUS:

Aegisthus, we acquit you of insults to the dead.
But since you claim that you alone laid the whole plot,
And thus, though absent, took his blood upon your hands,
I tell you plainly, your own life is forfeited;
Justice will curse you, Argive hands will stone you dead.

AEGISTHUS:

So, this is how you lecture, from the lower deck,
The master on the bridge? Then you shall learn, though old,
How harsh a thing is discipline, when reverend years

Lack wisdom. Chains and the distress of hunger are
A magic medicine, of great power to school the mind.
Does not this sight bid you reflect? Then do not kick
Against the goad, lest you should stumble, and be hurt.

CHORUS:
You woman! While he went to fight, you stayed at home;
Seduced his wife meanwhile; and then, against a man
Who led an army, *you* could scheme this murder! Pah!

AEGISTHUS:
You still use words that have in them the seed of tears.
Your voice is most unlike the voice of Orpheus:[52] he
Bound all who heard him with delight; your childish yelps
Annoy us, and will fasten bonds on you yourselves.
With hard control you will prove more amenable.

CHORUS:
Control! Are we to see *you* king of Argos—you,
Who, after plotting the king's murder, did not dare
To lift the sword yourself?

AEGISTHUS:
To lure him to the trap
Was plainly woman's work; I, an old enemy,
Was suspect. Now, helped by his wealth, I will attempt
To rule in Argos. The refractory shall not
Be fed fat like show-horses, but shall feel the yoke—
A heavy one. Hunger and darkness joined will soon
Soften resistance.

CHORUS:
Then, if you're so bold, why not
Yourself with your own hands plunder your enemy?
Instead, a woman, whose life makes this earth unclean
And flouts the gods of Argos, helped you murder him!
Oh, does Orestes live? Kind Fortune, bring him home,
To set against these two his sword invincible!

AEGISTHUS:
Then, since your treason's militant, you shall soon learn
That it is foolish to insult authority.
Ready, there! Forward, guards! [*armed soldiers rush in*]
Here's work for you. Each man
Handle his sword.

CHORUS:
Our swords are ready. We can die.

---

[52] **Orpheus:** Legendary musician and poet from Thrace whose songs charmed all who heard them, including nature and the gods. [Ed.]

AEGISTHUS:
'Die'! We accept the omen. Fortune hold the stakes!

CLYTEMNESTRA:
Stop, stop, Aegisthus, dearest! No more violence!
When this first harvest ripens we'll reap grief enough.
Crime and despair are fed to bursting; let us not
Plunge deeper still in blood. Elders, I beg of you,
Yield in good time to Destiny; go home, before
You come to harm; what we have done was fore-ordained.
If our long agony finds here fulfilment, we,
Twice gored by Fate's long talons, welcome it. I speak
With woman's wisdom, if you choose to understand.

AEGISTHUS:
Then are these gross-tongued men to aim their pointed gibes
At random, and bluff out the fate they've richly earned?

CHORUS:
You'll find no Argive grovel at a blackguard's feet.

AEGISTHUS:
Enough! Some later day I'll settle scores with you.

CHORUS:
Not if Fate sets Orestes on the Argos road.

AEGISTHUS:
For men in exile hopes are meat and drink—I know.

CHORUS:
Rule on, grow fat defiling Justice—while you can.

AEGISTHUS:
You are a fool; in time you'll pay me for those words.

CHORUS:
Brag blindly on—a cock that struts before his hen!

[*During these last lines the* CHORUS *have gone out two by two, the last man vanishing with the last insult, leaving* CLYTEMNESTRA *and* AEGISTHUS *alone.*]

CLYTEMNESTRA:
Pay no heed to this currish howling. You and I,
Joint rulers, will enforce due reverence for our throne.

The Eumenides

Translated by Philip Vellacott

CHARACTERS:

THE PYTHIAN PRIESTESS
APOLLO
HERMES
ORESTES
THE GHOST OF CLYTEMNESTRA
CHORUS *of the Furies, or Eumenides*
ATHENE
Twelve Athenian Citizens
A number of Athenian women and girls

SCENE: *First at Delphi, at the Pythian*[1] *Oracle, or Temple of Apollo; then at Athens, in the Temple of Athene on the Acropolis.*

SCENE I: *Before the Pythian Oracle. The scene is curtained.* THE PYTHIAN PRIESTESS *enters below at one side, mounts by steps to the stage, and stands at the centre before the curtain.*

PRIESTESS:[2]

First in my prayer of all the gods I reverence
Earth, first author of prophecy; Earth's daughter then,
Themis; who, legend tells, next ruled this oracle;
The third enthroned, succeeding by good-will, not force,
Phoebe—herself another Titan child of Earth—
In turn gave her prerogative, a birthday gift,

The Eumenides. In *The Libation Bearers,* the play that precedes *The Eumenides,* Orestes returns to Argos. Spurred on by Apollo, he kills both his mother and Aegisthus. But a sense of guilt invades him: To avenge regicide, the murder of his father the king, he has committed matricide, the murder of his mother the queen. Furthermore, he has acted against the claims of both Aegisthus and Clytemnestra that *they* were in the right in murdering Agamemnon: Aegisthus in revenge against the House of Atreus for the murder of his brothers and pollution of his father, and Clytemnestra in revenge for the murder of her daughter, Iphigenia. Orestes, in killing the pair, is both an avenging hero and the perpetrator of fresh crimes.

The Eumenides, the final play of *The Oresteia* trilogy, opens at the temple of Apollo, where Orestes, his hands still dripping blood from the double killing, has gone seeking refuge from the

---

[1] **Pythian:** The word is applied to Apollo, to his oracle, and to his priestess. It is derived from the Greek word meaning "to find out by inquiry," and refers to Apollo's oracular function.

[2] **Priestess:** The Pythian priestess here provides a genealogy of the powers that presided over this site of prophecy. Like the succession of gods described in *Agamemnon,* lines 193 to 203, this history traces a line of progress from the female powers of Earth, the mother goddess; to her daughter Themis, the goddess of order and the mother of Dike (Justice); to Phoebe, another daughter of Earth and grandmother of Apollo; and finally to the male power of Phoebus Apollo, the god of prophecy, music, and healing. Unlike the succession from Ouranos to Zeus described in *Agamemnon,* this handing off of prophetic power takes place in a peaceful and orderly manner. Aeschylus deliberately suppresses an alternative myth that shows Apollo taking power over the oracle by killing the giant serpent Pytho, from which the Pythian Oracle derives its name. [Ed.]

To her young namesake, Phoebus. From the Delian lake[3]
Ringed with high rocks he came to the craft-crowded shores
Of Pallas; thence to Parnassus[4] and this holy seat.
And in his progress bands of Attic worshippers,
Hephaestus' sons,[5] builders of roads, escorted him,
Taming for pilgrims' passage ground untamed before.
So Phoebus came to Delphi; people and king alike
Paid him high honour; Zeus endowed his prescient mind
With heavenly wisdom, and established him as fourth
Successor to this throne, whence he, as Loxias,[6]
Interprets to mankind his father's word and will.

These first my piety invokes. And I salute
With holy words Pallas Pronaia,[7] and the nymphs

Furies, female monsters who are tormenting him for his crime. The Furies, the ancient upholders of vengeance and the externalization of Orestes' guilt, claim special jurisdiction in cases of blood crimes committed within a family. Apollo, whose powers are limited here, sends Orestes to the temple of Athene, the goddess of wisdom and the guardian of Athens. The Furies follow him and confront Athene with their case against him. They invite Athene to judge the case herself, but she decides instead to try the case in a court of the citizens of Athens at whose head she will preside. First performed only a few years after the original aristocratic Council of Areopagus had seen its powers curtailed under the reforms of Ephialtes, this play uses the new court, housed on the Areopagus, the "crag of Ares," as its political centerpiece. The trial itself weighs not only Orestes' crimes but also the relative merits of the old and new systems of justice, the old chthonic gods and the newer Olympian gods, whose values in the play are aligned with those of the *polis*.

Orestes confesses to the killing of Clytemnestra but pleads that he committed the act at the behest of Apollo. The rest of the case turns on the technical point of whether or not Orestes carries the blood of his mother, Clytemnestra, since the seed from which he was formed comes from the body of his father, Agamemnon. When the citizen jury divides evenly on the verdict, Athene casts the tiebreaking vote, in favor of Orestes. At the end of the play Athene makes peace with the Furies. Their traditional role is reconciled with the new system of law in Athens, and to placate them Athene renames them the Eumenides, meaning the "kindly ones." From that moment on they assume a new role as the guardians of marriage, while the courts are entrusted with matters of law. The conclusion of the trilogy celebrates the founding of a new system of justice and civic order at the cost of domesticating the powers of women, who are associated throughout the play with the chthonic powers of Earth, personified by Clytemnestra and the Furies.

---

[3] **the Delian lake:** Apollo's birthplace was thought to be the island of Delos in the Cyclades. [Ed.]

[4] **Parnassus:** The mountain that rises close to Delphi.

[5] **Hephaestus' sons:** Erichthonius, mythical founder of Athens, was a son of Hephaestus.

[6] **Loxias:** Apollo, in his role as Interpreter; from *loxos,* which means "ambiguous." [Ed.]

[7] **Pallas Pronaia:** Pallas before the temple, or of the precincts.

Of the Corycian cave,[8] where, in enchanted shelter,
Birds love to nest; where Bromius[9] too makes his home,
Since, once, he led his frenzied Bacchic army forth
To tear King Pentheus as a hare is torn by hounds.
Fountains of Pleistos, Delphi's river, next I name;
Poseidon;[10] and, last, the supreme Fulfiller, Zeus.

Now on the seat of prophecy I take my place;
Heaven grant that this day's service far surpass in blessing
All former days! Let any Greek enquirer here,
As custom is, cast lots for precedence, and come.
As Phoebus guides my lips, so I pronounce his truth.

[*The* PRIESTESS *goes in between the curtains. After a short pause, her voice is heard in a cry of terror, and she reappears.*]

A fearful sight, a thing appalling to describe,
Drives me staggering and helpless out of Apollo's house.
My legs give way and tremble; hands must hold me up.
How useless fear makes an old woman—like a child!
As I went towards the inner shrine, all hung with wreaths,
There on the navel-stone[11] a suppliant was sitting,
A man polluted—blood still wet on hands that grasp
A reeking sword; yet on his head fresh olive-leaves,
Twined thickly with white wool, show heedful reverence.[12]
So far I can speak plainly. But beside this man,
Stretched upon benches, sleeping, a strange company
Of women—no, not women; Gorgons—yet, again,
They are not like Gorgons. Harpies I saw painted once,
Monsters robbing King Phineus[13] of his feast; but these
Are wingless, black, utterly loathsome; their vile breath
Vents in repulsive snoring; from their eyes distils
A filthy rheum; their garb is wickedness to wear

[8] **Corycian cave:** A cave located above Delphi on Mt. Parnassus that was sacred to Pan, the god of shepherds, and the nymphs. [Ed.]

[9] **Bromius:** Dionysus, who presided over Delphi in the winter when Apollo was absent. Aeschylus alludes to the story of King Pentheus of Thebes who was ripped to pieces by his mother and other Bacchantes as punishment for suppressing the worship of Dionysus and for spying on the revel in which his mother was participating. [Ed.]

[10] **Poseidon:** The god of the sea, who once was associated with Delphi. [Ed.]

[11] **navel-stone:** The *Omphalos,* a stone in the forecourt of the Temple at Delphi that was said to be the center of the earth. [Ed.]

[12] **olive-leaves . . . reverence:** The proper equipment for a suppliant at an altar.

[13] **King Phineus:** The Priestess, who does not recognize the Furies, believes them to be either Gorgons, female creatures whose horrid features would turn those who looked upon them to stone, or Harpies, bird-like female creatures who tormented the Thracian King Phineus by stealing and fouling his food. [Ed.]

In sight of the gods' statues or in human homes.
They are creatures of no race I ever saw; no land
Could breed them and not bear the curse of God and man.
I will go. Loxias is powerful, and this temple's his.
Men's tainted walls wait for his purifying power:
Let him—Priest, Prophet, Healer—now protect his own.

[*The* PRIESTESS *returns by the way that she came. The curtains open, revealing the Temple of Apollo. In the centre* ORESTES *sits by a rough stone altar—the 'Navel-Stone'. Beside him stand* APOLLO *and* HERMES. *Around them, asleep on benches or on the floor, lie the twelve* FURIES.]

APOLLO:

I will not fail you. Near at hand or far away,
I am your constant guardian and your enemies' dread.
Now for this one brief hour you see these ragers quiet,
These hunters caught in sleep; these ancient, ageless hags,
Whose presence neither god nor man nor beast can bear.
For sake of evil they were born; and evil is
The dark they dwell in, subterranean Tartarus;[14]
Beings abhorred by men and by Olympian gods.
Then fly, and do not weaken. They will hound you yet
Through seas and island cities, over the vast continent,
Wherever the earth's face is hard with wanderers' feet.
Keep courage firm; nurse your appointed pain; and go
To Athens, city of Pallas.° There with suppliant hands Athene
Embrace her ancient image, and implore her help.
There I will set you judges; and with soothing pleas
I, who first bade you take your mother's life, will bring
From all your painful days final deliverance.

ORESTES:

Apollo, Lord! Knowledge of justice and of right
Is yours: let will prompt knowledge, and let care fulfil.
Your strength shall be my surety for your promised help.

APOLLO:

Remember, let no fear conquer your steadfast heart.
Go, Hermes,[15] brother, as his guardian, and fulfil
Your titular office. His protection is my care:
Shepherd him well. The outlaw has his sanctity,
Which Zeus regards, giving him Fortune for his guide.

[HERMES *leads* ORESTES *away;* APOLLO *retires into the temple. The* GHOST OF CLYTEMNESTRA *appears.*]

---

[14] **Tartarus:** The deepest region of Hades, or hell, where the Titans were imprisoned and punished. [Ed.]

[15] **Hermes:** The messenger god, here associated with his role as the god who guides spirits of the dead to Hades. [Ed.]

CLYTEMNESTRA:

Will you still sleep? Oh, wake! What use are you, asleep?
Since you so slight me, I am abused unceasingly
Among the other dead, for him I killed, and wander
Despised and shamed. I tell you truly, by them all
I am held guilty and condemned; while, for the blow
My own son struck, no angry voice protests. See here,
This wound under my heart, and say whose was the sword!
Look! For though daylight cannot see beyond the flesh,
The mind in sleep has eyes. Often for you my hand
Has poured wineless libations, sober soothing draughts;
Upon my hearth in midnight ritual—an hour
Given to no other god—banquets have burned for you.
Now all my gifts I see spurned underfoot; while he,
Like a fawn lightly leaping out of the sprung snare,
Has escaped away and gone, and mocks you to your shame.
Listen, you Powers of the deep earth, and understand!
Listen, I entreat you, for my plea is life and death!
Listen! In your dream I, Clytemnestra, call to you!

[*The* CHORUS *mutter restlessly, as dogs growl in sleep.*]

CLYTEMNESTRA:

You murmur; but your prey has vanished out of sight.
His friends are not like mine: they save him, while you sleep.

[*Again the* CHORUS *mutter.*]

CLYTEMNESTRA:

Will you not wake? Does grief not touch you? He has gone!
Orestes, who killed me, his mother, has escaped!

[*More excited cries come from the* CHORUS.]

CLYTEMNESTRA:

Still crying, still asleep? Quick now, wake and stand up!
To work! Evil's your province—evil waits for you!

[*The cries continue.*]

CLYTEMNESTRA:

Sleep and fatigue, two apt accomplices, have drained
All force from the she-dragons' rage.

CHORUS [*with still louder cries*]:

After him! Catch him, catch him, catch him, catch him, catch him! Take care, take care!

CLYTEMNESTRA:

In dreams you hunt your prey, baying like hounds whose thought
Will never rest; but what of deeds? Has weariness
Conquered and softened you with sleep, till you forget
My pain? Rise up, torment his heart with just reproach;

For whetted words goad the quick conscience. Storm at him
With hot blood-reeking blasts blown from your vaporous womb,
Wither his hope of respite, hunt him to the death!

[*As the* CHORUS *awake, the* GHOST OF CLYTEMNESTRA *vanishes.*]

CHORUS:

Come, wake; wake you too; wake each other; come, wake all!
Shake off your sleep, stand up. What could that warning mean?

[*They see that* ORESTES *has gone.*]

What has happened? Furies, we are foiled!
Who were ever mocked as we?
Who would bear such mockery?
Sleepless labour spent in vain!
Duty flouted, privilege despoiled!
See the empty snare—our prey
Vanished, fled, and free again!
While we slept our right was stolen away.

Phoebus, son of Zeus, are you a god?
You set honesty aside;
You, the younger, ride roughshod
Over elder Powers; you have defied
Justice for your altar's sake,
Saved a godless matricide
From appointed pain, to make
Mockery of motherhood:
Who can call such crooked dealing good?

Out of my dreams I heard
A sharp accusing word
That struck me to the deep heart's core,
As on an uphill road
The driver's firm-gripped goad
Strikes till the flesh is sore.
I feel the common scourge, Remorse,
Wielded in Fate's strong hand,
Whose cold and crushing force
None can withstand.

The fault's not ours. It lies
With younger gods who rise
In place of those that ruled before;
From stool to crown their throne
Is stained with gore.
See, how Earth's central sacred stone

Has taken for its own
A grim pollution Justice must abhor!

Phoebus, for all your prophet's skill,
Your holy wisdom, by this deed
You of your own unprompted will
Have sullied your own altar's flames,
Infringing laws by gods decreed
And Destiny's primeval claims,[16]
To grant some mortal's passing need.

Fate's enemy, my enemy too,
Shall not give sanctuary to sin.
Orestes is accurst, and he,
Though he seek refuge with the dead,
Shall find no place where guilt is free;
Soon there shall come, of his own kin,
A like Avenger, to renew
Fate's curse upon his branded head.

[*Enter* APOLLO *from within the temple, carrying his bow and quiver.*]

APOLLO:

Out of this temple! I command you, go at once!
Quit my prophetic sanctuary, lest you feel
The gleaming snake that darts winged from my golden bow,
And painfully spew forth the black foam that you suck
From the sour flesh of murderers. What place have you
Within these walls? Some pit of punishments, where heads
Are severed, eyes torn out, throats cut, manhood unmanned,
Some hell of maimings, mutilations, stonings, where
Bodies impaled on stakes melt the mute air with groans—
Your place is there! Such are the feasts you love, for which
Heaven loathes you. Is not this the truth, proclaimed in you
By every feature? Find some blood-gorged lion's den,
There make your seemly dwelling, and no more rub off
Your foulness in this house of prayer and prophecy.
Away! Graze other fields, you flock unshepherded!
No god loves such as you![17]

[16] Literally, the three Fates, or Morae; the three sisters—Clotho, Lachesis, and Atropos—who spin, measure, and snip off the thread of life. [Ed.]

[17] Apollo abuses the Furies as barbarous, and the barbarisms he mentions are horrors that Greeks usually associated with "foreign" despotism. He means simply that the function of the Furies is "un-Hellenic," in contrast to the Hellenic use of courts and juries.

CHORUS:

Now is my turn to speak.
You, Lord Apollo, you alone are answerable
To your own charge; what's done's your doing, first to last.

APOLLO:

How's this? So far inform me.

CHORUS:

It was your oracle
That bade him take his mother's life.

APOLLO:

My oracle
Bade him avenge his father.

CHORUS:

With his hand still red
He found you his protector.

APOLLO:

I commanded him
To fly for refuge to this temple.

CHORUS:

We are here
As his appointed escort. Why revile us then?

APOLLO:

Your presence here is outrage.

CHORUS:

But it is no less
Our duty and our office.

APOLLO:

A high office, this.
Come, with due pride proclaim it.

CHORUS:

We hound matricides
To exile.

APOLLO:

And when wife kills husband, what of her?

CHORUS:

They are not kin; therefore such blood is not self-spilt.

APOLLO:

Then you dishonour and annul the marriage-bond
Of Zeus and Hera, that confirms all marriage-bonds;
And by your argument the sweetest source of joy
To mortals, Aphrodite,[18] falls into contempt.

---

[18] **Aphrodite:** The goddess of love; Hera, above, was the wife of Zeus and the goddess of marriage and childbirth. [Ed.]

Marriage, that joins two persons in Fate's ordinance,
Guarded by justice, stands more sacred than an oath.
If, then, to one that kills the other you show grace,
All penalty remitted, and all wrath renounced,
You are unjust to persecute Orestes' life.
His crime, I know, you take most grievously to heart;
While for his mother's you show open leniency.
Pallas herself shall hear this case, and judge our pleas.

CHORUS:
I tell you, I will never let Orestes go.

APOLLO:
Pursue him, then; take all the pains you wish.

CHORUS:
Phoebus,
You shall not, even in word, curtail my privilege.

APOLLO:
Not as a gift would I accept your privilege.

CHORUS:
You are called great beside the throne of Zeus.
But I
Will trace him by his mother's blood, hound him to earth,
And sue for justice on him.

APOLLO:
He is my suppliant;
And I will stand by him and save him if I can.
Fierce anger stirs to action both in heaven and earth
If I forsake the guilty man who turned to me.

[*While* APOLLO *speaks the* CHORUS *have begun to leave the stage;* APOLLO *withdraws into the temple.*]

SCENE II: *The Temple of Athene in Athens, with a statue of the goddess before it.* ORESTES *enters and kneels before the statue.*

ORESTES:
Divine Athene! At Apollo's word I come.
Receive me graciously; though still a fugitive,
Not unclean now.[19] Long wandering through tribes and towns
Has cleansed my bloodstained hand, blunted the edge of guilt;
Welcoming homes have rubbed the foulness from my soul.
Now, my long journey over land and sea fulfilled,
Faithful to Loxias' bidding and his oracle,
Goddess, I approach your house, your holy effigy.
Here I will stay, to know the issue of my trial.

[19] **Not unclean now:** In the first scene, Orestes's hands and sword were still wet with blood. By now, Apollo has guided Orestes through a purification ritual. [Ed.]

[*The* CHORUS *enter, following the track of* ORESTES.]

CHORUS:

This is his trail, I have it clear. Come, follow, where
The silent finger of pollution points the way.
Still by the scent we track him, as hounds track a deer
Wounded and bleeding. As a shepherd step by step
Searches a mountain, so have we searched every land,
Flown wingless over sea, swifter than sailing ships,
Always pursuing, till we gasp with weariness.
Now he is here, I know, crouched in some hiding-place.
The scent of mortal murder laughs in my nostrils—

Look there! See him! See him at last!
Watch every doorway, lest the murderer
Steal away and escape unpunished!
Once again he has found protection;
Closely clinging to the immortal
Goddess's image, thus he offers
His life for trial, for the deed of his hand.

No hope can rescue him.
A mother's blood once spilt
None can restore again;
In dust the fresh stream lies,
A parched, accusing stain.
You shall, for your soul's guilt,
Give us your blood to drink
Red from the living limb,
Our dear and deadly food,
Our labour's lawful prize.
Yes, while you still draw breath,
Your withered flesh shall sink,
In payment for her blood,
In penance for her pain,
Down to the world of death.

Mark this: not only you,
But every mortal soul
Whose pride has once transgressed
The law of reverence due
To parent, god, or guest,
Shall pay sin's just, inexorable toll.

Deep in the nether sky
Death rules the ways of man
With stern and strong control;

And there is none who can,
By any force or art,
Elude Death's watchful eye
Or his recording heart.

ORESTES:

Long taught by pain, learned in cleansing ritual,
I know when speech is lawful, when to hold my tongue;
And in this case a wise instructor bade me speak.
The blood upon my hand is drowsed and quenched; the stain
Of matricide washed clean, exorcized while yet fresh
At Phoebus' hearth with purgative blood-offerings.
It would take long to tell of all the friends whose homes
And hands have given me welcome without harm or taint.
And now from holy lips, with pure words, I invoke
Athene, ruler of this country, to my aid.
Thus she shall gain, without one blow, by just compact,
Myself, my country, and my Argive citizens
In loyal, lasting, unreserved confederacy.[20]
Whether by the Tritonian lake, her Libyan home,
She stands—at rest, at war, a bulwark to her friends;[21]
Or with a warrior's eye in bold command surveys
The Phlegraean plain[22]—a god can hear me—let her now
Come in divine authority and save my soul!

CHORUS:

Neither Apollo nor Athene can have power
To save you. Lost, cast off, the very taste of joy
Forgotten, you will live the prey of vampire Powers,
A pale ghost. Do you spurn my words in silence—you,
To me assigned and dedicated? There's no need
To await knife and altar, for your living flesh
Shall feast us. Hear this song that binds you to our will.

Come, Furies, our resolve is set;
Let mime and measure tread their course,
That none who feels the maddening force
Of our dread music may forget
How all the varying fates that bind
Men's lives are by our will assigned.

[20] **Thus she . . . confederacy:** Through Orestes' speech here, Aeschylus refers to the recent alliance between Athens and Argos. [Ed.]

[21] **She stands . . . friends:** The Greek says "whether standing or sitting," and refers to statues of Athene, which were made sometimes in the one posture, sometimes in the other.

[22] **The Phlegraean plain:** The scene of the battle between gods and giants, in which Athene acted as a general and from which the Olympian gods, led by Zeus, emerged victorious. [Ed.]

We hold our judgement just and true:
The man whose open hands are pure
Anger of ours shall not pursue;
He lives untroubled and secure.
But when a sinner, such as he,
Burdened with blood so foully shed,
Covers his guilty hands for shame,
Then, bearing witness for the dead,
We at his judgement stand to claim
The price of blood unyieldingly.

Hear me, O brooding Night,[23]
My mother, from whose womb
I came for punishment
Of all who live in light
Or grope beyond the tomb.
Phoebus would steal away
My office and my right,
My trapped and cowering prey
Whose anguish must atone
For sin so violent,
For blood that bore his own.

Now, by the altar,
Over the victim
Ripe for our ritual,
Sing this enchantment:
A song without music,
A sword in the senses,
A storm in the heart
And a fire in the brain;
A clamour of Furies
To paralyse reason,
A tune full of terror,
A drought in the soul!

Fate, whose all-powerful sway
Weaves out the world's design,
Decreed for evermore
This portion to be mine:

---

[23] **Night:** Nyx, a chthonic goddess born out of Chaos, along with Ouranos and Ge (Earth). Here Aeschylus deepens the affiliation of the Furies, who were generally said to be born from Ge, with the older gods and with shadowy, underworld figures such as the Fates, Doom, Thanatos (Death), and Nemesis, who were also born from Mother Night. [Ed.]

When for some murderous blow
The pangs of guilt surprise
Man's folly, from that day
Close at his side we go
Until the day he dies;
And Hope, that says, 'Below
The earth is respite', lies.

Now, by the altar,
Over the victim
Ripe for our ritual,
Sing this enchantment:
A song without music,
A sword in the senses,
A storm in the heart
And a fire in the brain:
A clamour of Furies
To paralyse reason,
A tune full of terror,
A drought in the soul!

The day we were begotten
These rights to us were sealed,
That against sin of mortals
Our hand should be revealed.
Immortals need not fear us;
Our feasts no god can share;
When white robes throng the temples
The darkness that we wear
Forbids our presence there.
Our chosen part is torment,
And great ones' overthrow;
When War turns home, and kinsman
Makes kinsman's life-blood flow,
Then in his strength we hunt him
And lay his glory low.

Our zeal assumes this office,
Our care and pains pursue it,
That gods may be exempt;
Zeus, free from taint or question,
Repels our gory presence
With loathing and contempt.
For him our dreaded footfall,

Launched from the height, leaps downward
With keen and crushing force,
Till helpless guilt, despairing,
Falls in his headlong course.

And so men's glories, towering to the sky,
Soon at our black-robed onset, the advance
Of vengeance beating in our fateful dance,
Fade under earth, and in dishonour die.

And in man's downfall his own hand's pollution,
Hovering round him like a misty gloom,
Pours deeper darkness on his mind's confusion,
While groaning ghosts intone his house's doom.

For Law lives on; and we, Law's holy few,
Law's living record of all evil done,
Resourceful and accomplishing, pursue
Our hateful task unhonoured; and no prayer
Makes us relent. All other gods must shun
The sunless glimmer of those paths we strew
With rocks, that quick and dead may stumble there.

So, Heaven's firm ordinance has now been told,
The task which Fate immutably assigned
To our devotion. Who will then withhold
Due fear and reverence? Though our dwelling lie
In subterranean caverns of the blind,
Our ancient privilege none dares deny.

[*Enter* ATHENE *from her temple.*]

ATHENE:

From far away I heard my name loudly invoked,
Beside Scamander,[24] where I went in haste to claim
Land that the Achaean chieftains had allotted me,
An ample gift chosen from plunder won in war
And given entire to Theseus'[25] sons to hold for ever.
And quickly, without toil of foot or wing, I came

[24] **Scamander:** The major river on the plains of Troy. What follows is an allusion to a dispute between Athens and Mytilene concerning the possession of some territory near Troy, which took place about the time this play was produced. [Ed.]

[25] **Theseus:** Legendary king and hero of Athens. [Ed.]

Borne on my strident aegis,[26] with the galloping winds
Harnessed before me.

This strange company I see
Here in my precincts moves me—not indeed to fear,
But to amazement. Who are you? I speak to all—
This man who clasps my statue as a suppliant,
And you—beings like none I know that earth brings forth,
Either of those seen among gods and goddesses—
Nor yet are you like mortals.—But I am unjust;
Reason forbids to slander others unprovoked.

CHORUS:
Daughter of Zeus, you shall hear all, and briefly told.
We are the children of primeval Night; we bear
The name of Curses in our home deep under earth.

ATHENE:
Your race I know, also your names in common speech.

CHORUS:
Maybe. Next you shall hear our office.

ATHENE:
Willingly—
If you would speak plain words.

CHORUS:
We drive out murderers.

ATHENE:
And where can such a fugitive find rest and peace?

CHORUS:
Only where joy and comfort are not current coin.

ATHENE:
And to such end your hue and cry pursues this man?

CHORUS:
Yes. He chose to become his mother's murderer.

ATHENE:
Was there not some compulsive power whose wrath he feared?

CHORUS:
And who has power to goad a man to matricide?

ATHENE:
One plea is now presented; two are to be heard.

CHORUS:
But he would ask no oath from us, nor swear himself.[27]

[26] **aegis:** Athene's cape, worn in her role as warrior, on which appears the face of the Gorgon Medusa. [Ed.]

[27] **But he . . . swear himself:** In the preliminary inquiry, which an Athenian magistrate would conduct before referring the case to the appropriate court of law, the plaintiff would state on oath that he had suffered injury, and the defendant that he was innocent.

ATHENE:
You seek the form of justice, more than to be just.
CHORUS:
How so? Instruct me; you do not lack subtlety.
ATHENE:
Injustice must not win the verdict by mere oaths.
CHORUS:
Then try him fairly, and give judgement on the facts.
ATHENE:
You grant to me final decision in this case?
CHORUS:
We do; we trust your wisdom, and your father's name.
ATHENE:
It is your turn to speak, my friend. What will you say?
Your faith in justice sent you to my statue here,
A holy suppliant, like Ixion,[28] at my hearth;
Therefore tell first your country, birth, and history;
Then answer to this charge; and let your speech be plain.
ORESTES:
Divine Athene, first from your last words I will
Set one great doubt at rest. My hand is not unclean;
I do not sit polluted at your statue's foot.
And I will tell you weighty evidence of this.
To a blood-guilty man the law forbids all speech,
Till blood-drops from some suckling beast are cast on him
By one whose office is to purge from homicide.
Long since, these rituals were all performed for me
In other temples; beasts were slain, pure water poured.
That question, then, I thus dispose of. For my birth,
I am of Argos, and you know my father well,
For you and he joined league to make the city of Troy
No city—Agamemnon, leader of that warlike fleet.
When he came home, he met a shameful death, murdered
By my black-hearted mother, with a cunning snare
Which first hid, then proclaimed the bloody act that felled
My father as he washed away the stains of war.

When, later, after years of exile I came home,
I killed my mother—I will not deny it—in
Just retribution for my father, whom I loved.
For this Apollo equally is answerable;

[28] **Ixion:** The first Greek to murder his own kin, his father-in-law; although Zeus purified him and brought him to Olympus, Ixion then tried to seduce Hera and so was sentenced to eternal punishment enchained to a wheel of fire in Hades. [Ed.]

He told me of the tortures that would sear my soul
If I neglected vengeance on the murderers.
Whether or no I acted rightly, is for you
To judge; I will accept your word, for life or death.

ATHENE:

This is too grave a cause for any man to judge;
Nor, in a case of murder, is it right that I
Should by my judgement let the wrath of Justice loose;
The less so, since you came after full cleansing rites
As a pure suppliant to my temple, and since I
And Athens grant you sanctuary and welcome you.
But your accusers' claims are not to be dismissed;
And, should they fail to win their case, their anger falls
Like death and terror, blight and poison, on my land.
Hence my dilemma—to accept, or banish them;
And either course is peril and perplexity.
Then, since decision falls to me, I will choose out
Jurors of homicide, for a perpetual court,[29]
In whom I vest my judgement. Bring your evidence,
Call witnesses, whose oaths shall strengthen Justice's hand.
I'll pick my wisest citizens, and bring them here
Sworn to give sentence with integrity and truth.

[*Exit* ATHENE, *to the city;* ORESTES *retires into the temple.*]

CHORUS:

Now true and false must change their names,
Old law and justice be reversed,
If new authority put first
The wrongful right this murderer claims.
His act shall now to every man
Commend the easy path of crime;
And parents' blood in after time
Shall gleam on children's hands accurst,
To pay the debt this day began.

The Furies' watchful rage shall sleep,
No anger hunt the guilty soul;
Murder shall flout my lost control;
And neighbours talk of wrongs, and weep,
And ask how flesh can more endure,
Or stem the swelling flood of ill,

[29] **Jurors . . . perpetual court:** The Areopagus, the court that decided homicide cases in Aeschylus's time and which had been a bastion of aristocratic rule up to the time of the reforms of Ephialtes, enacted shortly before the first performance of the play. [Ed.]

Or hope for better times—while still
Each wretch commends some useless cure.

When stunned by hard misfortune,
On us let no man call,
Chanting the old entreaties,
'Come, swift, avenging Furies!
O sword of Justice, fall!'
Some parent, struck or slighted,
In loud and vain distress
Often will cry, a stranger
To the new wickedness,
Which soon shall reach and ruin
The house of Righteousness.

For fear, enforcing goodness,
Must somewhere reign enthroned,
And watch men's ways, and teach them,
Through self-inflicted sorrow,
That sin is not condoned.
What man, no longer nursing
Fear at his heart—what city,
Once fear is cast away,
Will bow the knee to Justice
As in an earlier day?

Seek neither licence, where no laws compel,
Nor slavery beneath a tyrant's rod;
Where liberty and rule are balanced well
Success will follow as the gift of God,
Though how He will direct it none can tell.
This truth is apt: the heart's impiety
Begets after its kind the hand's misdeed;
But when the heart is sound, from it proceed
Blessings long prayed for, and prosperity.

This above all I bid you: reverence
Justice's high altar; let no sight of gain
Tempt you to spurn with godless insolence
This sanctity. Cause and effect remain;
From sin flows sorrow. Then let man hold dear
His parents' life and honour, and revere
Each passing guest with welcome and defence.

Wealth and honour will attend
Love of goodness gladly held;

Virtue free and uncompelled
Fears no harsh untimely end.
But the man whose stubborn soul
Steers a rash defiant course
Flouting every law's control—
He in time will furl perforce,
Late repenting, when the blast
Shreds his sail and snaps his mast.

Helpless in the swirling sea,
Struggling hands and anguished cries
Plead with the unheeding skies;
And God smiles to note that he,
Changing folly for despair,
Boasts for fear, will not escape
Shipwreck on the stormy cape;
But, his former blessings thrown
On the reef of justice, there
Perishes unwept, unknown.

[ATHENE *returns, bringing with her twelve Athenian citizens.* APOLLO *comes from the temple, leading* ORESTES.]

ATHENE:
Summon the city, herald, and proclaim the cause;
Let the Tyrrhenian trumpet, filled with mortal breath,
Crack the broad heaven, and shake Athens with its voice.
And while the council-chamber fills, let citizens
And jurors all in silence recognize this court
Which I ordain today in perpetuity,
That now and always justice may be well discerned.

CHORUS:
Divine Apollo, handle what belongs to you.
Tell us, what right have you to meddle in this case?

APOLLO:
I came to answer that in evidence. This man
Has my protection by the law of suppliants.
I cleansed him from this murder; I am here to be
His advocate, since I am answerable for
The stroke that killed his mother. Pallas, introduce
This case, and so conduct it as your wisdom prompts.

ATHENE:
The case is open.
[*To the* LEADER OF THE CHORUS.] Since you are the accuser, speak.
The court must first hear a full statement of the charge.

CHORUS:
Though we are many, few words will suffice. [*To* ORESTES.] And you
Answer our questions, point for point. First, did you kill
Your mother?

ORESTES:
I cannot deny it. Yes, I did.

CHORUS:
Good; the first round is ours.

ORESTES:
It is too soon to boast:
I am not beaten.

CHORUS:
You must tell us, none the less,
How you dispatched her.

ORESTES:
With a sword I pierced her heart.

CHORUS:
On whose persuasion, whose advice?

ORESTES:
Apollo's. He
Is witness that his oracle commanded me.

CHORUS:
The god of prophecy commanded matricide?

ORESTES:
Yes; and he has not failed me from that day to this.

CHORUS:
If to-day's vote condemns you, you will change your words.

ORESTES:
I trust him. My dead father too will send me help.

CHORUS:
Yes, trust the dead now: your hand struck your mother dead.

ORESTES:
She was twice guilty, twice condemned.

CHORUS:
How so? Instruct
The court.

ORESTES:
She killed her husband, and my father too.

CHORUS:
Her death absolved her; you still live.

ORESTES:
But why was she
Not punished by you while she lived?

CHORUS:
The man she killed

Was not of her own blood.

ORESTES:

But I am of my mother's?

CHORUS:

Vile wretch! Did she not nourish you in her own womb?
Do you disown your mother's blood, which is your own?

ORESTES:

Apollo, now give evidence. Make plain to me
If I was right to kill her. That I struck the blow
Is true, I own it. But was murder justified?
Expound this point, and show me how to plead my cause.

APOLLO:

To you, august court of Athene, I will speak
Justly and truly, as befits a prophet-god.
I never yet, from my oracular seat, pronounced
For man, woman, or city any word which Zeus,
The Olympian Father, had not formally prescribed.
I bid you, then, mark first the force of justice here;
But next, even more, regard my father's will. No oath
Can have more force than Zeus, whose name has sanctioned it.[30]

CHORUS:

Then Zeus, you say, was author of this oracle
You gave Orestes—that his mother's claims should count
For nothing, till he had avenged his father's death?

APOLLO:

Zeus so ordained, and Zeus was right. For their two deaths
Are in no way to be compared. He was a king
Wielding an honoured sceptre by divine command.
A woman killed him: such death might be honourable—
In battle, dealt by an arrow from an Amazon's bow.
But you shall hear, Pallas and you who judge this case,
How Clytemnestra killed her husband. When he came
Home from the war, for the most part successful, and
Performed his ritual cleansing, she stood by his side;
The ritual ended, as he left the silver bath,
She threw on him a robe's interminable folds,
Wrapped, fettered him in an embroidered gown, and struck.

Such, jurors, was the grim end of this king, whose look
Was majesty, whose word commanded men and fleets.
Such was his wife who killed him—such that none of you,
Who sit to try Orestes, hears her crime unmoved.

[30] **No oath . . . it:** Zeus was the guardian of oaths.

CHORUS:
Zeus rates a father's death the higher, by your account.
Yet Zeus, when his own father Cronos became old,
Bound him with chains. Is there not contradiction here?
Observe this, jurors, on your oath.

APOLLO:
Execrable hags,
Outcasts of heaven! Chains may be loosed, with little harm,
And many ways to mend it. But when blood of man
Sinks in the thirsty dust, the life once lost can live
No more. For death alone my father has ordained
No healing spell; all other things his effortless
And sovereign power casts down or raises up at will.

CHORUS:
You plead for his acquittal: have you asked yourself
How one who poured out on the ground his mother's blood
Will live henceforth in Argos, in his father's house?
Shall he at public altars share in sacrifice?
Shall holy water lave his hands at tribal feasts?

APOLLO:
This too I answer; mark the truth of what I say.
The mother is not the true parent of the child
Which is called hers. She is a nurse who tends the growth
Of young seed planted by its true parent, the male.
So, if Fate spares the child, she keeps it, as one might
Keep for some friend a growing plant. And of this truth,
That father without mother may beget, we have
Present, as proof, the daughter of Olympian Zeus:
One never nursed in the dark cradle of the womb;
Yet such a being no god will beget again.

Pallas, I sent this man to supplicate your hearth;
He is but one of many gifts my providence
Will send, to make your city and your people great.
He and his city, Pallas, shall for ever be
Your faithful allies; their posterity shall hold
This pledge their dear possession for all future years.

ATHENE:
Shall I now bid the jurors cast each man his vote
According to his conscience? Are both pleas complete?

APOLLO:
I have shot every shaft I had; and wait to hear
The jurors' verdict.

ATHENE [*to the* CHORUS]:
Will this course content you too?

CHORUS [*to the jurors*]:
You have heard them and us. Now, jurors, as you cast
Your votes, let reverence for your oath guide every heart.

ATHENE:
Citizens of Athens! As you now try this first case
Of bloodshed, hear the constitution of your court.
From this day forward this judicial council shall
For Aegeus'[31] race hear every trial of homicide.
Here shall be their perpetual seat, on Ares' Hill.[32]
Here, when the Amazon army came to take revenge
On Theseus, they set up their camp, and fortified
This place with walls and towers as a new fortress-town
To attack the old, and sacrificed to Ares; whence
This rock is named Areopagus. Here, day and night,
Shall Awe, and Fear, Awe's brother, check my citizens
From all misdoing, while they keep my laws unchanged.
If you befoul a shining spring with an impure
And muddy dribble, you will come in vain to drink.
So, do not taint pure laws with new expediency.
Guard well and reverence that form of government
Which will eschew alike licence and slavery;
And from your polity do not wholly banish fear.
For what man living, freed from fear, will still be just?
Hold fast such upright fear of the law's sanctity,
And you will have a bulwark of your city's strength,
A rampart round your soil, such as no other race
Possesses between Scythia and the Peloponnese.
I here establish you a court inviolable,
Holy, and quick to anger, keeping faithful watch
That men may sleep in peace.

I have thus far extended
My exhortation, that Athens may remember it.
Now give your votes in uprightness, and judge this cause
With reverence for your oath. I have no more to say.

[*During the following dialogue the jurors rise in turn to vote. There are two urns, one of which is 'operative', the other 'inoperative'. Each juror has two pebbles, a black and a white. Into the 'operative' urn each drops a white pebble for acquittal or a black one for condemnation; then disposes of the other pebble in the other urn, and returns to his seat.*]

---

[31] **Aegeus:** An early king of Athens and the father of Theseus. [Ed.]

[32] **Ares' Hill:** That is, the Areopagus, which translates as the Crag or Hill of Ares, who according to legend had once been tried there for murder. It was also the site of Theseus's defeat of the Amazons, a tribe of women warriors. [Ed.]

CHORUS:
I too advise you: do not act in scorn of us,
Your country's visitants, or you will find us harsh.

APOLLO:
I bid you fear my oracle and the word of Zeus,
And not make both unfruitful.

CHORUS [*to* APOLLO]:
Deeds of blood are not
For your protection. Henceforth you will prophesy
From a polluted shrine.

APOLLO:
Then what of Zeus? Did he
Suffer pollution, when he willed to purify
His suppliant Ixion, the first murderer?

CHORUS:
You argue; but if we should fail to win this case
We will infest the land with plagues unspeakable.

APOLLO:
You have as little honour amongst elder gods
As amongst us, the younger. I shall win this case.

CHORUS:
This recalls your behaviour in Admetus' house:[33]
You bribed the Fates to let a mortal live again.

APOLLO:
Was it not right to help a man who worshipped me?
Undoubtedly; besides, Admetus' need was great.

CHORUS:
You mocked primeval goddesses with wine, to break
The ancient dispensation.

APOLLO:
Disappointment soon
Will make you vomit all your poison—harmlessly.

CHORUS:
You think your youth may tread my age into the dust.
When we have heard the verdict will be soon enough
To launch my anger against Athens. I will wait.

ATHENE:
My duty is to give the final vote. When yours
Are counted, mine goes to uphold Orestes' plea.
No mother gave me birth. Therefore the father's claim

[33] **your behaviour in Admetus' house:** The chorus of Furies recalls that Apollo tricked the three Fates, by making them drunk, into agreeing to postpone the death of Admetus on condition that he found a willing substitute—Admetus's wife, Alcestis. [Ed.]

And male supremacy in all things, save to give
Myself in marriage, wins my whole heart's loyalty.
Therefore a woman's death, who killed her husband, is,
I judge, outweighed in grievousness by his. And so
Orestes, if the votes are equal, wins the case.
Let those appointed bring the urns and count the votes.

[*Two of the jurors obey her.*]

ORESTES:

O bright Apollo, what verdict will be revealed?

CHORUS:

O Mother Night, O Darkness, look on us!

ORESTES:

To me
This moment brings despair and death, or life and hope.

CHORUS:

To us increase of honour, or disgrace and loss.

APOLLO:

The votes are out. Count scrupulously, citizens;
Justice is holy; in your division worship her.
Loss of a single vote is loss of happiness;
And one vote gained will raise to life a fallen house.

[*The votes are brought to* ATHENE. *The black and the white pebbles are even in number.* ATHENE *adds hers to the white.*]

ATHENE:

Orestes is acquitted of blood-guiltiness.
The votes are even.

ORESTES:

Pallas, Saviour of my house!
I was an exile; you have brought me home again.
Hellas° can say of me, 'He is an Argive, as — Greece
He used to be, and holds his father's house and wealth
By grace of Pallas and Apollo, and of Zeus
The Saviour, the Fulfiller.' Zeus has shown respect
For my dead father, seeing my mother's advocates,
And has delivered me.

So now, before I turn
My steps to Argos, hear the oath I make to you,
Your country, and your people, for all future time:
No Argive king shall ever against Attica
Lead his embattled spears. If any man transgress
This oath of mine, I will myself rise from the grave
In vengeance, to perplex him with disastrous loss,
Clogging his marches with ill omens and despair,

Till all his soldiers curse the day they left their homes.
But if my oath is kept, and my posterity
Prove staunch and faithful allies to the Athenian State,
They shall enjoy my blessing. So, Pallas, farewell;
Farewell, citizens of Athens! May each struggle bring
Death to your foes, to you success and victory!

[*Exeunt* APOLLO *and* ORESTES.]

CHORUS:

The old is trampled by the new!
Curse on you younger gods who override
The ancient laws and rob me of my due!
Now to appease the honour you reviled
Vengeance shall fester till my full heart pours
Over this land on every side
Anger for insult, poison for my pain—
Yes, poison from whose killing rain
A sterile blight shall creep on plant and child
And pock the earth's face with infectious sores.
Why should I weep? Hear, Justice, what I do!
Soon Athens in despair shall rue
Her rashness and her mockery.
Daughters of Night and Sorrow, come with me,
Feed on dishonour, on revenge to be!

ATHENE:

Let me entreat you soften your indignant grief.
Fair trial, fair judgement, ended in an even vote,
Which brings to you neither dishonour nor defeat.
Evidence which issued clear as day from Zeus himself,
Brought by the god who bade Orestes strike the blow,
Could not but save him from all harmful consequence.
Then quench your anger; let not indignation rain
Pestilence on our soil, corroding every seed
Till the whole land is sterile desert. In return
I promise you, here in this upright land, a home,
And bright thrones in a holy cavern, where you shall
Receive for ever homage from our citizens.

CHORUS:

The old is trampled by the new!
Curse on you younger gods who override
The ancient laws and rob me of my due!
Now to appease the honour you reviled
Vengeance shall fester till my full heart pours
Over this land on every side
Anger for insult, poison for my pain—
Yes, poison from whose killing rain

A sterile blight shall creep on plant and child
And pock the earth's face with infectious sores.
Why should I weep? Hear, Justice, what I do!
Soon Athens in despair shall rue
Her rashness and her mockery.
Daughters of Night and Sorrow, come with me,
Feed on dishonour, on revenge to be!

ATHENE:

None has dishonoured you. Why should immortal rage
Infect the fields of mortal men with pestilence?
You call on Justice: I rely on Zeus. What need
To reason further? I alone among the gods
Know the sealed chamber's keys where Zeus's thunderbolt
Is stored. But force is needless; let persuasion check
The fruit of foolish threats before it falls to spread
Plague and disaster. Calm this black and swelling wrath;
Honour and dignity await you: share with me
A home in Athens. You will yet applaud my words,
When Attica's wide fields bring you their firstfruit gifts,
When sacrifice for childbirth and for marriage-vows
Is made upon your altars in perpetual right.

CHORUS:

O shame and grief, that such a fate
Should fall to me, whose wisdom grew
Within me when the world was new!
Must I accept, beneath the ground,
A nameless and abhorred estate?
O ancient Earth, see my disgrace!
While anguish runs through flesh and bone
My breathless rage breaks every bound.
O Night, my mother, hear me groan,
Outwitted, scorned and overthrown
By new gods from my ancient place!

ATHENE:

Your greater age claims my forbearance, as it gives
Wisdom far greater than my own; though to me too
Zeus gave discernment. And I tell you this: if you
Now make some other land your home, your thoughts will turn
With deep desire to Athens. For the coming age
Shall see her glory growing yet more glorious.
You, here possessing an exalted sanctuary
Beside Erechtheus'[34] temple, shall receive from all,

[34] **Erechtheus:** The first king of Athens.

Both men and women, honours which no other land
Could equal. Therefore do not cast upon my fields
Whetstones of murder, to corrupt our young men's hearts
And make them mad with passions not infused by wine;
Nor plant in them the temper of the mutinous cock,
To set within my city's walls man against man
With self-destructive boldness, kin defying kin.
Let war be with the stranger, at the stranger's gate;
There let men fall in love with glory; but at home
Let no cocks fight.[35]

Then, goddesses, I offer you
A home in Athens, where the gods most love to live,
Where gifts and honours shall deserve your kind good-will.

CHORUS:

O shame and grief, that such a fate
Should fall to me, whose wisdom grew
Within me when the world was new!
Must I accept, beneath the ground,
A nameless and abhorred estate?
O ancient Earth, see my disgrace!
While anguish runs through flesh and bone
My breathless rage breaks every bound.
O Night, my mother, hear me groan,
Outwitted, scorned and overthrown
By new gods from my ancient place!

ATHENE:

I will not weary in offering you friendly words.
You shall not say that you, an elder deity,
Were by a younger Power and by these citizens
Driven dishonoured, homeless, from this land. But if
Holy Persuasion bids your heart respect my words
And welcome soothing eloquence, then stay with us!
If you refuse, be sure you will have no just cause
To turn with spleen and malice on our peopled streets.
A great and lasting heritage awaits you here;
Thus honour is assured and justice satisfied.

CHORUS:

What place, divine Athene, do you offer me?

ATHENE:

One free from all regret. Acceptance lies with you.

---

[35] **Therefore do not . . . fight:** The whole of this passage is plainly a stern warning against political disunity within Athens.

CHORUS:
Say I accept it: what prerogatives are mine?
ATHENE:
Such that no house can thrive without your favour sought.
CHORUS:
You promise to secure for me this place and power?
ATHENE:
I will protect and prosper all who reverence you.
CHORUS:
Your word is pledged for ever?
ATHENE:
Do I need to promise
What I will not perform?
CHORUS:
My anger melts. Your words
Move me.
ATHENE:
In Athens you are in the midst of friends.
CHORUS:
What blessings would you have me call upon this land?
ATHENE:
Such as bring victory untroubled with regret;
Blessing from earth and sea and sky; blessing that breathes
In wind and sunlight through the land; that beast and field
Enrich my people with unwearied fruitfulness,
And armies of brave sons be born to guard their peace.
Sternly weed out the impious, lest their rankness choke
The flower of goodness. I would not have just men's lives
Troubled with villainy. These blessings *you* must bring;
I will conduct their valiant arms to victory,
And make the name of Athens honoured through the world.
CHORUS:
I will consent to share Athene's home,
To bless this fortress of the immortal Powers
Which mighty Zeus and Ares
Chose for their habitation,
The pride and glory of the gods of Greece,
And guardian of their altars.
This prayer I pray for Athens,
Pronounce this prophecy with kind intent:
Fortune shall load her land with healthful gifts
From her rich earth engendered
By the sun's burning brightness.

ATHENE:

I will do my part, and win
Blessing for my city's life,
Welcoming within our walls
These implacable and great
Goddesses. Their task it is
To dispose all mortal ways.
He who wins their enmity
Lives accurst, not knowing whence
Falls the wounding lash of life.
Secret guilt his father knew
Hails him to their judgement-seat,
Where, for all his loud exclaims,
Death, his angry enemy,
Silent grinds him into dust.

CHORUS:

I have yet more to promise. No ill wind
Shall carry blight to make your fruit-trees fade;
No bud-destroying canker
Shall creep across your frontiers,
Nor sterile sickness threaten your supply.
May Pan give twin lambs to your thriving ewes
In their expected season;
And may the earth's rich produce
Honour the generous Powers with grateful gifts.

ATHENE:

Guardians of our city's wall,
Hear the blessings they will bring!
Fate's Avengers wield a power
Great alike in heaven and hell;
And their purposes on earth
They fulfil for all to see,
Giving, after their deserts,
Songs to some, to others pain
In a prospect blind with tears.

CHORUS:

I pray that no untimely chance destroy
Your young men in their pride;
And let each lovely virgin, as a bride,
Fulfil her life with joy.
For all these gifts, you sovereign gods, we pray,
And you, our sisters three,
Dread Fates, whose just decree

Chooses for every man his changeless way,
You who in every household have your place,
    Whose visitations fall
    With just rebuke on all—
Hear us, most honoured of the immortal race!

ATHENE:

Now, for the love that you perform
To this dear land, my heart is warm.
Holy Persuasion too I bless,
Who softly strove with harsh denial,
Till Zeus the Pleader came to trial
And crowned Persuasion with success.
Now good shall strive with good; and we
And they shall share the victory.

CHORUS:

Let civil war, insatiate of ill,
    Never in Athens rage;
Let burning wrath, that murder must assuage,
    Never take arms to spill,
    In this my heritage,
The blood of man till dust has drunk its fill.
    Let all together find
        Joy in each other;
And each both love and hate with the same mind
        As his blood-brother;
For this heals many hurts of humankind.

ATHENE:

These gracious words and promised deeds
Adorn the path where wisdom leads.
Great gain for Athens shall arise
From these grim forms and threatening eyes.
Then worship them with friendly heart,
For theirs is friendly. Let your State
Hold justice as her chiefest prize;
And land and city shall be great
And glorious in every part.

CHORUS:

City, rejoice and sing,
Who, blest and flourishing
With wealth of field and street,
Wise in your hour, and dear
To the goddess you revere,
Sit by the judgement-seat
Of heaven's all-judging king,

Who guards and governs well
Those favoured ones who dwell
Under her virgin wing.

ATHENE:

We wish you joy in turn. Now I must go
And guide you to your chambers in the rock,
Lit by the holy torches
Of these who shall escort you.
With eager haste and solemn sacrifice,
Come, enter this dear earth, there to repel
Harm from our homes and borders,
And bring us wealth and glory.
Sons of the Rock of Athens, lead their way,
Welcome these Residents within your walls;
They come to bless our city:
Let our good-will reward them.

CHORUS:

My blessings I repeat
On all whose homes are here,
To whom this rock is dear;
On temple and on street
Where gods and mortals meet.
And as with awe and fear
And humble hearts you greet
My presence as your guest,
So year succeeding year
Shall be more richly blest.

ATHENE:

I thank you for your prayers. Now by these torches' gleam
I and my maidens who attend my statue here
Come to escort you to your home beneath the ground.
Young women, children, a resplendent company,[36]
Flower of the land of Theseus, with a reverend troop
Of elder women, dressed in robes of purple dye,
Shall go with you. Honour the Friendly Goddesses;
And let the flaring lights move on, that our new guests
In coming years may grace our land with wealth and peace.

---

[36]**Young women . . . company:** This suggests the great Panathenaic procession, the culminating event of a quarterly Athenian festival that in part honored "resident aliens" such as the Eumenides. Athenians prided themselves on the liberal welcome they extended to immigrants from other cities. [The "robes of purple dye," the official dress of the resident aliens or "metics" during the Panathenean Festival, underscore the enlightened policy Athens had toward immigrants in Aeschylus's time. (Ed.)]

[*During the last three speeches a procession has been gathering, with music and lighted torches, to escort the* CHORUS *from the stage; as they go, all sing together:*]

Pass onward to your home,
Great ones, lovers of honour,
Daughters of ancient Night,
Led by the friends your peace has won;
(And let every tongue be holy!)

On to the deep of earth,
To the immemorial cavern,
Honoured with sacrifice,
Worshipped in fear and breathless awe;
(And let every tongue be holy!)

Come, dread and friendly Powers
Who love and guard our land;
And while devouring flame
Fills all your path with light,
Gather with gladness to your rest.
And let every voice
Crown our song with a shout of joy!

Again let the wine be poured
By the glare of the crackling pine;
Now great, all-seeing Zeus
Guards the city of Pallas;
Thus God and Fate are reconciled.
Then let every voice
Crown our song with a shout of joy!

Sophocles
496–406 B.C.E.

Sophocles is considered one of the three great Greek tragedians, along with Aeschylus and Euripides. In plays such as *Oedipus Rex* and ***Antigone,*** the noblest of human beings are brought under intense strain as their personal convictions and values come up against the rules of public life and the force of fate. Sophocles' plays question the limits of individual freedom and authority in the face of religious and civic laws, ethical and moral imperatives, and private obligations—the very stuff out of which later playwrights, such as William Shakespeare (1564–1616) in England and Chikamatsu Monzaemon[1] (1653–1724) in Japan, would shape their own great tragedies. Moreover, Sophocles' depiction of what the English poet Matthew Arnold (1822–1888) called the "ebb and flow / Of human misery" evokes sympathy and admiration even in modern audiences moved by the spectacle of dignified suffering conveyed by his plays.

an-TIG-uh-nee

Playwright/Citizen. Sophocles' life spanned the years of most of the Persian Wars (500–479 B.C.E.) to just beyond the Peloponnesian War (431–404 B.C.E.).[2] Between the two wars Athens rose to the height of its political and cultural power during the Age of Pericles (461–429 B.C.E.) and declined after the great plague of 429 B.C.E. that killed a third of its population. Sophocles was born at Colonus, a suburb of Athens, in 496. A general, a priest of Asclepius (god of medicine), and a model citizen, Sophocles served in various civic and administrative posts, participating fully in the rise and decline of his city. The first notice we have of his public life is his membership in the chorus celebrating the Athenian naval victory over the Persians at Salamis in 480. In 468, Sophocles won his first prize as a playwright, when his *Triptolemus* took first place over a play by Aeschylus at the Festival of Dionysus.[3] Sophocles was to enjoy twenty-four more such victories in the course of his career, during which he produced more than 120 plays—only seven of which have survived.

WWW For links to more information about Sophocles, quizzes on *Antigone* and *Oedipus Rex,* and information about Sophocles' twenty-first-century relevance, see *World Literature Online* at bedfordstmartins.com/worldlit.

Sophocles enjoyed the respect and admiration of his fellow Athenians, not only for his plays but also for his public service and reputation

[1] **Chikamatsu Monzaemon:** (1653–1724) Japan's greatest playwright, who wrote about history, domestic life, and *shinju,* or suicide, in such dramas as *The Battles of Coxinga, The Uprooted Pine,* and *The Love Suicides at Amijima.* (See Chikamatsu, Book 4.)

[2] **Persian Wars . . . Peloponnesian War:** The Persian Wars, between a coalition of Greek city-states and the Persian empire, were fought from 500 to 479 B.C.E.; the Greek victory set the stage for the flourishing of Greek culture. The Peloponnesian War between Athens and Sparta was fought from 431 to 404 B.C.E.; Athens surrendered to Sparta shortly after Lysander defeated the Athenian navy at the Battle of the Aegospotami in 405 and then attacked Athens.

[3] **Festival of Dionysus:** From about 530 B.C.E., Athenians held annual spring festivals in honor of Dionysus, the god of wine. Among other activities during these festivals, playwrights competed for prizes for the best tragedy and the best comedy. Tragedians put on three related plays followed by a satyr, often a bawdy play serving to lighten the mood.

for fairness and affability. His even temper won him the friendship of Herodotus and Aristophanes,[4] among others. Sophocles took charge of the imperial treasury in 443, was elected to be one of the ten *strategoi,* or generals, one of the highest positions of Athenian society, in 440, and served with Pericles in the Samian War.[5] During this time he was involved in forming a "company of the Educated" to promote the discussion and criticism of literature. In later life Sophocles served his state as a diplomat and an ambassador, and was a priest of Halon, a minor god associated with Asclepius whose cult increased following the plague of 429. Sophocles died in 406, less than two years before a starving Athens surrendered to Sparta when the Athenian fleet, once the pride of the Aegean, was defeated at the Battle of the Aegospotami.[6]

The Plays. In addition to the two plays included here, the surviving plays of Sophocles are *Ajax, The Women of Trachis, Electra, Philoctetes,* and *Oedipus at Colonus.* Drawing on the story of the Trojan War and its aftermath as well as on Greek myth and legend, the plays of Sophocles present archetypal men and women forced to measure their inner strength and principles against the formidable forces of society, history, and fate. Steering a course between the high religious themes of Aeschylus and the topical social criticism of Euripides, Sophocles' dramas focus on human beings caught between irreconcilable sets of values and confronted with the difficulty of acting consistently according to their principles. Noble in character and bold in action, characters such as Oedipus and Antigone are nonetheless human in their capacity for error and the psychological unawareness that leads them to intense suffering. In *Oedipus Rex,* for example, King Oedipus of Thebes, a model of piety and virtue, pursues an investigation that ultimately reveals he has unwittingly committed unspeakable crimes—he has killed his father, King Laius, and taken his mother, Jocasta, as his wife. In *Antigone,* the formidable Antigone, princess of Thebes, and Creon, the new king, adamantly refuse to compromise their equally legitimate but opposing positions regarding the burial of Polynices, leading to the downfall of both. Though Sophocles' characters are strongly affected by fate and the will of the gods, the plays invite one to question to what extent individuals are ultimately responsible for their actions, thus giving voice to the

[4] **Herodotus and Aristophanes:** Herodotus (c. 484–425 B.C.E.) was a Greek historian and the author of *The Persian Wars,* considered the first major narrative history in the Western world. Aristophanes (c. 450–c. 386 B.C.E.) was an Athenian dramatist known for satires and comedies; his plays include *The Clouds, Lysistrata,* and *The Frogs.*

[5] **Pericles . . . Samian War:** Pericles (c. 495–429 B.C.E.) was one of the great leaders of Athens under whose reign (461–429 B.C.E.) Athenian society and culture flourished until Athens suffered humiliating defeats in the Peloponnesian War. The Samian War (441–439 B.C.E.) between Athens and Samos was fought to bring the island of Samos, which had broken off from the league of Greek states led by Athens, back into the alliance and back into compliance with Athenian hegemony.

[6] **the Battle of the Aegospotami:** The battle that took place at the mouth of the Aegospotamos, a river flowing into the Hellespont, where Sparta defeated the Athenian fleet in 405 B.C.E., effectively decimating Athenian military power and leading to the defeat of Athens the following year.

enduring question of how much human beings are free to determine their life in the face of forces apparently beyond their control.

> [Oedipus's] destiny moves us only because it might have been ours — because the oracle laid the same curse upon us before our birth as upon him. It is the fate of all of us, perhaps, to direct our first sexual impulse towards our mother and our first hatred and our first murderous wish against our father. Our dreams convince us that is so. King Oedipus, who slew his father Laius and married his mother Jocasta, merely shows us the fulfillment of our own childhood wishes.
>
> – SIGMUND FREUD, founder of psychoanalysis, 1900

The Model Tragedy. As a playwright, Sophocles was a consummate craftsman and technical innovator. Aeschylus had already introduced a second actor into drama; Sophocles increased the number of players to three, thereby increasing the complexity of the interchanges. Moreover, Sophocles reduced the number of people in the chorus from fifty to twelve and introduced painted backdrops to the set. Such changes allowed for a more subtle and complex development of both plot and character, perhaps leading in part to Aristotle's tribute to Sophocles' craftsmanship in *Poetics,*[7] in which *Oedipus Rex,* Sophocles' greatest play, serves as the model tragedy. According to Aristotle, a great tragedy concentrates on a single dramatic conflict, a noble action that unfolds in the course of a single day. The purpose of the tragedy is to arouse both pity and terror in the audience in order to effect what he calls *katharsis,* a purgation of the emotions and a clarification of the mind that leads to a degree of equanimity, a lightening of the soul. To arouse pity and fear in the onlooker, a tragedy should depict the fall of a person of noble character and good fortune who unwittingly commits a grave error (*hamartia*) resulting from a tragic character flaw to which he or she is blind. As in the case of *Oedipus Rex,* it is important that the audience understand this reversal of fortune to be undeserved, resulting not from vice or depravity on the part of the hero but rather from some unintentional miscalculation. Thus, King Oedipus, who suffers along with his people and serves them well by seeking in good faith to root out the cause of the plague that besets their and his city, eventually learns that he has unwittingly committed the crimes for which they are being punished. In this moment of ***ANAGNORISIS***—self-awareness or recognition—Oedipus undergoes a tragic reversal of fortune, or ***PERIPETEIA.*** Though he has committed them unintentionally, he takes responsibility for his crimes; blinds himself; and goes into exile. For Aristotle, *Oedipus Rex* invokes fear because we identify with Oedipus's lack of self-knowledge and recognize our inability to fully determine the consequences of our actions; it also invokes pity, as the audience sympathizes with someone who undeservedly suffers misfortune. Although Oedipus is not without faults—the tragic hero must have some faults, according to Aristotle, in order for the audience to identify with and pity him or her—there are also cosmic and divine forces at work in his life that complicate the matter of his personal responsibility. In order to appreciate those forces, one must first know and understand the curse on the House of Thebes.

The House of Thebes. Both *Oedipus Rex* and *Antigone* invoke the story of the curse on the House of Thebes to dramatize the sweeping changes taking place in the fifth century B.C.E. in the political and cultural life of

[7] ***Poetics:*** One of the earliest works of literary criticism in the West, *Poetics* was compiled from the notes of students who had attended the lectures of the Greek philosopher Aristotle (384–322 B.C.E.).

Athens, especially the move toward democracy, the decline in the role of religion, and the changing relations between men and women. The story begins when Laius, the grandson of Cadmus, founder of Thebes, abducts Chrysippus, the beautiful though illegitimate son of Pelops, the king of Pisa, in the Peloponnese. Laius, who had been given refuge at the court of Pelops at the time, thus violates one of the most sacred of relationships—that between a guest and his host. After he is restored to the throne at Thebes, Laius marries Jocasta and eventually learns from the Delphic Oracle that his punishment for having abducted Chrysippus will be to die at the hand of his own son. To prevent the prophecy from being fulfilled, when Jocasta gives birth to a son, Laius hands over the infant, spiked through the ankles to lash its legs together, to shepherds. These men are supposed to leave the baby to die on Mt. Cithaeron. The good-hearted shepherds, however, deliver the boy to the king and queen of Corinth, Polybus and Merope, instead, who give him the name Oedipus, which means "swollen foot," and raise him as their own. What happens next is told in *Oedipus Rex.* Having discovered that he has indeed unwittingly killed his true father and married his mother, Jocasta, who gave him two sons, Eteocles and Polynices, and two daughters, Antigone and Ismene, Oedipus blinds himself and is banished. Jocasta kills herself in despair, and the throne of Thebes descends on Creon, who assumes the role of regent until **Eteocles** and **Polynices** are old enough to take power.

uh-TEE-uh-kleez; pah-lih-NIGH-seez

The story of Oedipus's banishment is told in *Oedipus at Colonus,* probably Sophocles' last play, written shortly before his death and performed posthumously. *Antigone* begins in the aftermath of the disagreement between Polynices and Eteocles over sharing power at Thebes, though the Chorus from time to time alludes to incidents from the larger legend of the House of Thebes. When Eteocles backs out of an agreement to rule in alternate years, Polynices returns with seven Argive leaders to kill his brother, a story told in Aeschylus's *Seven Against Thebes.* When *Antigone* opens, the two brothers are dead, and their uncle, Creon, has taken over now as king of Thebes. Because he perceives Polynices as a traitor to the *polis,* he refuses him a proper burial. Antigone, while recognizing that Polynices has violated the legal code, insists that a higher and more ancient code—one that honors blood ties over civic duties—demands that he be buried.

Oedipus Rex. This play, also known as *Oedipus the King,* has been perhaps the most influential of Sophocles' dramas, serving not only as the model for Aristotle's ideal tragedy but also as the basis for one of the key concepts of Freudian psychoanalysis, the Oedipus complex.[8] This story that was familiar to Sophocles' audience is, remarkably, imbedded in contemporary thought as well. Fated to kill his father, Laius, and marry his

[8] **Oedipus complex:** One of the most important theories advanced by the Viennese psychiatrist and theorist Sigmund Freud (1856–1939); it holds that children are sexually attracted to their parent of the opposite sex and harbor hostile feelings toward their parent of the same sex, whom they see as a rival in what has become known as the "family romance."

Louis-Edouard-Paul Fournier, *Mounet as Oedipus Rex*, 1890s
Sophocles' Oedipus Rex *has been staged for more than two millennia. In this painting, the late-nineteenth-century French actor Jean Sully Mounet is seen in his dressing room as the title character, Oedipus Rex, Mounet's most distinguished role. (The Art Archive / Musée Carnavalet, Paris / Dagli Orti)*

mother, **Jocasta**, the virtuous and resourceful Oedipus seeks to prevent the prophecy from being fulfilled only to have his determination lead him to the very circumstances he fears. In the play, Sophocles is less interested in retelling a familiar story than he is in presenting noble Oedipus, unaware of his crimes and still taking measures to avoid them, as he gradually comes under the strain of recognizing that his efforts have been in vain—that indeed his measures to avoid the crimes as well as his somewhat volatile character have in fact precipitated them. As is also true of the characters in *Antigone,* several interpretations of Oedipus's virtues and faults are possible. Indeed, Sophocles is one of the first of the Greek tragedians to show a keen interest in the development of complex characters.

joh-KAS-tuh, ee-oh-KAS-tee, yoh-KAS-tee

Oedipus Rex opens ***IN MEDIAS RES,*** long after Oedipus has killed his father and taken his mother as his wife, events foretold by the Oracle. The Oracle also reveals that only when the murderer of King Laius is banished from the city will the plague that has fallen on Thebes be lifted. As the play moves forward, Oedipus gradually uncovers more and more about his past, and his determined pursuit of the truth, conducted in part to relieve his city of its blight, leads him to discover that he is the guilty party. Although familiar with the story of Oedipus, Sophocles' audiences didn't know the steps Oedipus would take to solve the most important riddle of all—that of self-knowledge—nor did they have a complete sense of Oedipus's character. The action of the play consists primarily of the process by which Oedipus discovers his true identity, in time also revealing his inherent flaws and strengths. While Oedipus demonstrates great concern for his people, his penchant for anger and impetuosity complicates his actions and humanizes his character. In his public condemnation of the murderer of Laius, for example, he sets up the violence

tigh-REE-see-us

of his own fall. His unwarranted rage against **Tiresias** and hasty accusation of Creon lead the Chorus to worry that Oedipus's lack of prudence may do the city more harm than good and to caution him that "judgments too quickly formed are dangerous."

Yet Oedipus's compassion for his people softens his faults. In the hands of another playwright, Oedipus might be condemned for his crimes. Sophocles, however, gives a much more complex rendering of Oedipus and his situation. Even as evidence mounts against him, Oedipus follows the threads of self-incriminating evidence, committed to bringing the truth to light no matter the consequences. Moreover, the depth of Oedipus's response—his suffering and self-punishment—at the moment of full self-recognition makes him sympathetic. A critical moment in the play comes in the encounter between Oedipus and Tiresias, the blind seer who openly and rightly accuses Oedipus of being the murderer he seeks and, perhaps more important, of being totally ignorant of his crimes: "I say you live in hideous shame with those / Most dear to you. You can not see the evil." This scene evokes the issue of self-knowledge, and the rest of the play gradually shows that gaining a true understanding of the self comes only at the cost of great personal suffering. Once Oedipus recognizes that he has indeed murdered his father and committed incest with his mother, he blinds himself and goes into exile. Whatever one's judgment of Oedipus's crimes, the circumstances and facts of which are acknowledged but not dramatized in the play, *Oedipus Rex* speaks to the limits, perhaps even the folly, of human agency and knowledge, and suggests that human beings have no choice but to act, even in blindness, and to continue the quest for self-awareness no matter the outcome.

Antigone. This drama has often been read as a struggle between two antagonistic but clear-cut opposites, usually the individual and the state. Tied to her brother by the sacred bonds of kinship, Antigone in this reading subverts the decree of Creon, who in the interest of civic order must deny her demand that her offending brother Polynices receive a proper burial. Without a proper burial, however, a soul cannot cross over the river Styx into the underworld, so Antigone's concern for Polynices goes beyond a matter of mere formality or ritual. Her religious responsibility for the destiny of her brother's soul stands in opposition to the civic law that must punish enemies of the state.

By making [Oedipus] criminal in a small degree, and miserable in a very great one, by investing him with some excellent qualities, and some imperfections, he at once inclines us to pity and to condemn.
– Samuel Johnson, writer and critic, 1779

Antigone represents more than just the individual. She is also a symbol of a complex set of affiliations to the gods of the underworld and the household, to the ancient blood code of the family, and to women, who in fifth-century-B.C.E. Athens did not enjoy the rights of citizenship granted to men. Creon has his own set of affiliations to the sky gods, to the new legal code ushered in under the auspices of Athena in Aeschylus's *Eumenides,* and to the patriarchy. *Antigone* thus further dramatizes the transformations taking place in the democratization of Athens, which under Cleisthenes transferred power to districts established by law, not kinship ties.

The tragedy does not rest easily even on these more complex oppositions but rather encourages further scrutiny of Antigone's and Creon's positions. Both Creon and Antigone are right, and both are wrong—Creon, in light of the archaic laws honoring kinship relations; Antigone, in view of the new ***POLIS***, which honors civic allegiances. The spectator is left to question seriously the values that each represents. Although Antigone swears to be bound by the blood code associated with the family and with faint traces of a matriarchal lineage, she nonetheless cruelly dismisses **Ismene**, who is both her sister and a woman. Moreover, although Creon declares that he has the interests of the state at heart, he ignores the advice and warnings of his people (embodied by the Chorus), his son Haemon, and the prophet Tiresias. Creon's refusal to bend mirrors Antigone's; her unwillingness to compromise, though supported by the play, thus becomes suspect. Creon's unwillingness to listen to the voice of the people suggests that he is a tyrant, an outmoded political type who contradicts the democratic impetus of the new Athenian state. Yet despite his ultimate fall, his statements about the necessity of relinquishing the ties of blood in the interests of the *polis* were important to the very process of democratization that most Athenians supported. Thus, *Antigone* invited its spectators to place their cherished interests into the crucible of high tragic art. The questions of the play mirror before Athenian audiences their own uncertainty about the costs of patriarchy and the demise of more ancient aristocratic systems of justice and codes of honor subverted by the process of democratic reform.

is-MEE-nee

Further complicating the play is the issue of destiny. As the curse on the House of Thebes unfolds, both Antigone and Creon—and one might add Ismene, Haemon, and even Eurydice—seem to be endowed with freedom of choice and are therefore in some measure the shapers of their own lives. Antigone rejects Ismene's argument, for example, that women should not contend with men, that by nature they must obey the "stronger" sex. Similarly, Tiresias reminds Creon that all human beings will err, but that once they recognize their error they can make amends. It is not certain whether Creon rejects Tiresias's advice, though in the final scene of the play the Chorus seems to suggest that he does. Thus, Sophocles again poses two alternatives: Human destiny is not sealed—human actions and decisions may indeed alter the course of events—or, fate determines the course of human life. Either way may lead to tragic consequences.

■ CONNECTIONS

***The Epic of Gilgamesh*, p. 62; Hebrew Scriptures, Genesis, p. 140.** Many works of the ancient world describe what might be called the birth of a tragic understanding of the human predicament—a self-conscious awareness of suffering and death. Seeking to root out the cause of his city's troubles, for example, Oedipus learns that he himself is the culprit, and with this knowledge comes a blinding sense of guilt. Similarly, Gilgamesh, seeking the secret of immortality from Utnapishtim, learns that he, like all human beings, must die; and when Adam and Eve eat the forbidden fruit from the Tree of Knowledge, they experience guilt and sorrow. How do each of these texts define what it means to be human? What are the culturally specific aspects of those definitions?

Aeschylus, *The Oresteia*, pp. 806, 858, 1134; Bhagavad Gita, p. 1488. Like many fifth-century-B.C.E. Greek dramas, *Antigone* presents a clash between the values of kinship and those of the *polis,* in this case in the standoff between Antigone and Creon. *The Oresteia* similarly dramatizes such conflicts as a contest between the Furies and Apollo, between the old and the new gods. The Bhagavad Gita also weighs the values of kinship against a higher duty when it dramatizes Arjuna's doubts about entering into combat against his cousins. How might these texts be a reflection of the historical and cultural changes taking place in ancient Greece and India?

Kalidasa, *Shakuntala* (Book 2); Chikamatsu Monzaemon, *The Love Suicides at Amijima* (Book 4). In *Poetics,* Aristotle describes *Oedipus Rex* as the paradigmatic tragedy, culling from it a set of rules that other tragedies should follow. Compare the structure, form, and emplotment of Sophocles' play with these others. In what way might some of the differences you find result from culturally and/or historically distinct ideas about art and ritual, time and place, and action and character?

■ FURTHER RESEARCH

General Criticism

Knox, Bernard M. W. *The Heroic Temper. Studies in Sophoclean Tragedy.* 1964.
Ringer, Mark. *Electra and the Empty Urn: Metatheater and Role Playing in Sophocles.* 1998.
Scodel, Ruth. *Sophocles.* 1984.
Seale, David. *Vision and Stagecraft in Sophocles.* 1982.
Segal, Charles. *Tragedy and Civilization.* 1981.
Walton, J. Michael. *The Greek Sense of Theatre.* 1985.
Winnington-Ingram, R. P. *Sophocles: An Interpretation.* 1980.
Woodard, Thomas Marion, ed. *Sophocles: A Collection of Critical Essays.* 1966.

Oedipus

Ahl, Fredrick. *Sophocles' Oedipus.* 1992.
Berkowitz, Luci, and Theodore F. Brunner, eds. *Sophocles: Oedipus Tyrannus.* 1970.
Knox, Bernard M. W. *Oedipus at Thebes.* 1957.
Segal, Charles. *Oedipus Tyrannus: Tragic Heroism and the Limits of Knowledge.* 1993.

Antigone

Goheen, R. F. *The Imagery of Sophocles'* Antigone. 1951.
Griffith, Mark. *Antigone/Sophocles.* 1999.

■ PRONUNCIATION

Antigone: an-TIG-uh-nee
Cadmus (Kadmos): KAD-muhs
Eteocles: uh-TEE-uh-kleez
Eurydice: yoo-RIH-dih-see
Ismene: is-MEE-nee
Jocasta (Iocastê): joh-KAS-tuh, ee-oh-KAS-tee, yoh-KAS-tee
Laius (Laïos): LAY-uhs
Oedipus: ED-uh-pus
Polynices (Polyneices): pah-lih-NIGH-seez
Tiresias (Teiresias): tigh-REE-see-us

Oedipus Rex

Translated by Dudley Fitts and Robert Fitzgerald

PERSONS REPRESENTED:

OEDIPUS
A PRIEST
CREON
TEIRESIAS
IOCASTE
MESSENGER
SHEPHERD OF LAÏOS
SECOND MESSENGER
CHORUS OF THEBAN ELDERS

THE SCENE. *Before the palace of Oedipus, King of Thebes. A central door and two lateral doors open onto a platform which runs the length of the façade. On the platform, right and left, are altars; and three steps lead down into the "orchestra," or chorus-ground. At the beginning of the action these steps are crowded by suppliants who have brought branches and chaplets of olive leaves and who lie in various attitudes of despair.* OEDIPUS *enters.*

Prologue

OEDIPUS:

My children, generations of the living
In the line of Kadmos,[1] nursed at his ancient hearth:
Why have you strewn yourselves before these altars

Oedipus Rex. The dating of Sophocles' plays is an imprecise art. Scholars believe that *Oedipus Rex* was most likely first performed in the 430s B.C.E., sometime after *Antigone,* which dates from the late 440s, before 441, when Sophocles served as a general in the fighting against Samos. But because the events occurring in *Oedipus Rex* take place before those in *Antigone, Oedipus Rex* precedes *Antigone* in this anthology.

As the action begins, a plague has stirred up questions about the death of Laius (Laïos). Good king that he is, Oedipus sets out to unlock the secret of the former king's death. The action of the play essentially involves the sequential revelation of Oedipus's guilt, the disclosure of his true identity, and his banishment. Although Oedipus's curse on the killer of Laius and his misplaced anger against Tiresias (Teiresias) and Creon display his weaknesses, his shortcomings are outdone by his love for the people and his tireless efforts to lift the curse on Thebes. Ironically, the lack of self-knowledge Oedipus demonstrates in the beginning of the action returns as physical blindness at the end of the play. His moment of self-recognition quickly leads to a total reversal of his life, and his self-inflicted punishment and banishment reflect the unbearable pain of his situation. Yet for all that, one identifies and sympathizes with Oedipus, recognizing his blindness as a universal condition; though human beings cannot always know the consequences of their actions, they must, like Oedipus, strive to know and fulfill their destiny regardless of any suffering it might entail.

A note on the translation: This is the Dudley Fitts and Robert Fitzgerald translation of *Oedipus Rex,* which attempts to preserve the original Greek pronunciation of the characters' names and the poetic quality of the play. The notes are the editors'.

[1] **Kadmos:** Legendary founder of Thebes, originally called Kadmeia; he was the son of Agenor, king of Tyre (Sidon).

In supplication, with your boughs and garlands?
The breath of incense rises from the city
With a sound of prayer and lamentation.
Children,
I would not have you speak through messengers,
And therefore I have come myself to hear you—
I, Oedipus, who bear the famous name.

[*To a* PRIEST:]
You, there, since you are eldest in the company,
Speak for them all, tell me what preys upon you,
Whether you come in dread, or crave some blessing:
Tell me, and never doubt that I will help you
In every way I can; I should be heartless
Were I not moved to find you suppliant here.

PRIEST:
Great Oedipus, O powerful King of Thebes!
You see how all the ages of our people
Cling to your altar steps: here are boys
Who can barely stand alone, and here are priests
By weight of age, as I am a priest of God,[2]
And young men chosen from those yet unmarried;
As for the others, all that multitude,
They wait with olive chaplets in the squares,
At the two shrines of Pallas,[3] and where Apollo[4]
Speaks in the glowing embers.
Your own eyes
Must tell you: Thebes is tossed on a murdering sea
And can not lift her head from the death surge.
A rust consumes the buds and fruits of the earth;
The herds are sick; children die unborn,
And labor is vain. The god of plague and pyre
Raids like detestable lightning through the city,
And all the house of Kadmos is laid waste,
All emptied, and all darkened: Death alone
Battens upon the misery of Thebes.
You are not one of the immortal gods, we know;
Yet we have come to you to make our prayer
As to the man surest in mortal ways
And wisest in the ways of God. You saved us

[2] **God:** Zeus, the chief ruler of the Olympian gods; the son of the Titans Cronus and Rhea.

[3] **Pallas:** Pallas Athene, goddess of wisdom and knowledge.

[4] **Apollo:** The god of prophecy, music, and healing; the son of Zeus and Leto.

From the Sphinx,[5] that flinty singer, and the tribute
We paid to her so long; yet you were never
Better informed than we, nor could we teach you:
It was some god breathed in you to set us free.

Therefore, O mighty King, we turn to you:
Find us our safety, find us a remedy,
Whether by counsel of the gods or men.
A king of wisdom tested in the past
Can act in a time of troubles, and act well.
Noblest of men, restore
Life to your city! Think how all men call you
Liberator for your triumph long ago;
Ah, when your years of kingship are remembered,
Let them not say *We rose, but later fell*—
Keep the State from going down in the storm!
Once, years ago, with happy augury,
You brought us fortune; be the same again!
No man questions your power to rule the land:
But rule over men, not over a dead city!
Ships are only hulls, citadels are nothing,
When no life moves in the empty passageways.

OEDIPUS:

Poor children! You may be sure I know
All that you longed for in your coming here.
I know that you are deathly sick; and yet,
Sick as you are, not one is as sick as I.
Each of you suffers in himself alone
His anguish, not another's; but my spirit
Groans for the city, for myself, for you.
I was not sleeping, you are not waking me.
No, I have been in tears for a long while
And in my restless thought walked many ways.
In all my search, I found one helpful course,
And that I have taken: I have sent Creon,
Son of Menoikeus, brother of the Queen,
To Delphi,[6] Apollo's place of revelation,

[5] **Sphinx:** A female monster who feeds on young men who cannot answer her riddles; when Oedipus solved her riddle, the Sphinx killed herself. Her riddle for Oedipus was: What creature moves first on four legs, then on two, and then on three, and is weakest when it walks on all four? Oedipus's correct answer was "man," the creature who crawls as a baby, then walks, and finally walks with a cane in old age.

[6] **Delphi:** Creon has been sent to the Temple of Apollo at Delphi, presided over by a prophetess known as the Pythia (so named after the python, the snake slain by Apollo at the site of the shrine).

To learn there, if he can,
What act or pledge of mine may save the city.
I have counted the days, and now, this very day,
I am troubled, for he has overstayed his time.
What is he doing? He has been gone too long.
Yet whenever he comes back, I should do ill
To scant whatever duty God reveals.

PRIEST:
It is a timely promise. At this instant
They tell me Creon is here.

OEDIPUS:
O Lord Apollo!
May his news be fair as his face is radiant!

PRIEST:
It could not be otherwise: he is crowned with bay,
The chaplet is thick with berries.

OEDIPUS:
We shall soon know;
He is near enough to hear us now.

[*Enter* CREON]

O Prince:
Brother: son of Menoikeus:
What answer do you bring us from the god?

CREON:
A strong one. I can tell you, great afflictions
Will turn out well, if they are taken well.

OEDIPUS:
What was the oracle? These vague words
Leave me still hanging between hope and fear.

CREON:
Is it your pleasure to hear me with all these
Gathered around us? I am prepared to speak,
But should we not go in?

OEDIPUS:
Let them all hear it.
It is for them I suffer, more than for myself.

CREON:
Then I will tell you what I heard at Delphi.

In plain words
The god commands us to expel from the land of Thebes
An old defilement we are sheltering.
It is a deathly thing, beyond cure;

We must not let it feed upon us longer.

OEDIPUS:
What defilement? How shall we rid ourselves of it?

CREON:
By exile or death, blood for blood. It was
Murder that brought the plague-wind on the city.

OEDIPUS:
Murder of whom? Surely the god has named him?

CREON:
My lord: long ago Laïos was our king,
Before you came to govern us.

OEDIPUS:
I know;
I learned of him from others; I never saw him.

CREON:
He was murdered; and Apollo commands us now
To take revenge upon whoever killed him.

OEDIPUS:
Upon whom? Where are they? Where shall we find a clue
To solve that crime, after so many years?

CREON:
Here in this land, he said.
If we make enquiry,
We may touch things that otherwise escape us.

OEDIPUS:
Tell me: Was Laïos murdered in his house,
Or in the fields, or in some foreign country?

CREON:
He said he planned to make a pilgrimage.
He did not come home again.

OEDIPUS:
And was there no one,
No witness, no companion, to tell what happened?

CREON:
They were all killed but one, and he got away
So frightened that he could remember one thing only.

OEDIPUS:
What was that one thing? One may be the key
To everything, if we resolve to use it.

CREON:
He said that a band of highwaymen attacked them,
Outnumbered them, and overwhelmed the King.

OEDIPUS:
Strange, that a highwayman should be so daring—
Unless some faction here bribed him to do it.

CREON:
We thought of that. But after Laïos' death
New troubles arose and we had no avenger.

OEDIPUS:
What troubles could prevent your hunting down the killers?

CREON:
The riddling Sphinx's song
Made us deaf to all mysteries but her own.

OEDIPUS:
Then once more I must bring what is dark to light.
It is most fitting that Apollo shows,
As you do, this compunction for the dead.
You shall see how I stand by you, as I should,
To avenge the city and the city's god,
And not as though it were for some distant friend,
But for my own sake, to be rid of evil.
Whoever killed King Laïos might—who knows?—
Decide at any moment to kill me as well.
By avenging the murdered king I protect myself.

Come, then, my children: leave the altar steps,
Lift up your olive boughs!
One of you go
And summon the people of Kadmos to gather here.
I will do all that I can; you may tell them that.

[*Exit a* PAGE]

So, with the help of God,
We shall be saved—or else indeed we are lost.

PRIEST:
Let us rise, children. It was for this we came,
And now the King has promised it himself.
Phoibos[7] has sent us an oracle; may he descend
Himself to save us and drive out the plague.

[*Exeunt* OEDIPUS *and* CREON *into the palace by the central door. The* PRIEST *and the* SUPPLIANTS *disperse R and L. After a short pause the* CHORUS *enters the orchestra.*

PÁRADOS

[*Strophe 1*]

CHORUS:
What is God singing in his profound
Delphi of gold and shadow?
What oracle for Thebes, the sunwhipped city?

[7] **Phoibos:** Apollo the Bright One; this epithet associates Apollo with the sun.

Fear unjoints me, the roots of my heart tremble.

Now I remember, O Healer,[8] your power, and wonder:
Will you send doom like a sudden cloud, or weave it
Like nightfall of the past?

Speak, speak to us, issue of holy sound:
Dearest to our expectancy: be tender!

[*Antistrophe 1*]

Let me pray to Athenê,[9] the immortal daughter of Zeus,
And to Artemis[10] her sister
Who keeps her famous throne in the market ring,
And to Apollo, bowman at the far butts of heaven—

O gods, descend! Like three streams leap against
The fires of our grief, the fires of darkness;
Be swift to bring us rest!

As in the old time from the brilliant house
Of air you stepped to save us, come again!

[*Strophe 2*]

Now our afflictions have no end,
Now all our stricken host lies down
And no man fights off death with his mind;

The noble plowland bears no grain,
And groaning mothers can not bear—

See, how our lives like birds take wing,
Like sparks that fly when a fire soars,
To the shore of the god of evening.[11]

[*Antistrophe 2*]

The plague burns on, it is pitiless,
Though pallid children laden with death
Lie unwept in the stony ways,

[8] **Healer:** That is, Apollo, as the god of healing.

[9] **Athenê:** Goddess of wisdom, arts, and war; she is Apollo's half sister, having been born from Zeus's head.

[10] **Artemis:** Goddess of hunting and childbirth; she was Apollo's twin sister, the daughter of Zeus and Leto.

[11] **the god of evening:** Hades, the god of the underworld, who presides over the dead.

And old gray women by every path
Flock to the strand about the altars

There to strike their breasts and cry
Worship of Phoibos in wailing prayers:
Be kind, God's golden child!

[*Strophe 3*]

There are no swords in this attack by fire,
No shields, but we are ringed with cries.

Send the besieger plunging from our homes
Into the vast sea-room of the Atlantic
Or into the waves that foam eastward of Thrace—

For the day ravages what the night spares—

Destroy our enemy, lord of the thunder!
Let him be riven by lightning from heaven!

[*Antistrophe 3*]

Phoibos Apollo, stretch the sun's bowstring,
That golden cord, until it sing for us,
Flashing arrows in heaven!
Artemis, Huntress,
Race with flaring lights upon our mountains!

O scarlet god, O golden-banded brow,
O Theban Bacchos[12] in a storm of Maenads,[13]

[*Enter* OEDIPUS, *C.*]

Whirl upon Death, that all the Undying hate!
Come with blinding torches, come in joy!

Scene I

OEDIPUS:

Is this your prayer? It may be answered. Come,
Listen to me, act as the crisis demands,
And you shall have relief from all these evils.

---

[12] **Bacchos:** Or Dionysus, the god of wine and nature; he is associated with the woods and wild places.

[13] **Maenads:** The Bacchanals, female worshippers of Dionysus (Bacchos).

Until now I was a stranger to this tale,
As I had been a stranger to the crime.
Could I track down the murderer without a clue?
But now, friends,
As one who became a citizen after the murder,
I make this proclamation to all Thebans:
If any man knows by whose hand Laïos, son of Labdakos,[14]
Met his death, I direct that man to tell me everything,
No matter what he fears for having so long withheld it.
Let it stand as promised that no further trouble
Will come to him, but he may leave the land in safety.

Moreover: If anyone knows the murderer to be foreign,
Let him not keep silent: he shall have his reward from me.
However, if he does conceal it; if any man
Fearing for his friend or for himself disobeys this edict,
Hear what I propose to do:

I solemnly forbid the people of this country,
Where power and throne are mine, ever to receive that man
Or speak to him, no matter who he is, or let him
Join in sacrifice, lustration, or in prayer.
I decree that he be driven from every house,
Being, as he is, corruption itself to us: the Delphic
Voice of Zeus has pronounced this revelation.
Thus I associate myself with the oracle
And take the side of the murdered king.

As for the criminal, I pray to God—
Whether it be a lurking thief, or one of a number—
I pray that that man's life be consumed in evil and wretchedness.
And as for me, this curse applies no less
If it should turn out that the culprit is my guest here,
Sharing my hearth.
You have heard the penalty.
I lay it on you now to attend to this
For my sake, for Apollo's, for the sick
Sterile city that heaven has abandoned.
Suppose the oracle had given you no command:
Should this defilement go uncleansed for ever?
You should have found the murderer: your king,
A noble king, had been destroyed!

[14] **Labdakos:** Former king of Thebes and the father of Laïos, Oedipus's father.

Now I,
Having the power that he held before me,
Having his bed, begetting children there
Upon his wife, as he would have, had he lived—
Their son would have been my children's brother,
If Laïos had had luck in fatherhood!
(But surely ill luck rushed upon his reign)—
I say I take the son's part, just as though
I were his son, to press the fight for him
And see it won! I'll find the hand that brought
Death to Labdakos' and Polydoros' child,
Heir of Kadmos' and Agenor's line.[15]
And as for those who fail me,
May the gods deny them the fruit of the earth,
Fruit of the womb, and may they rot utterly!
Let them be wretched as we are wretched, and worse!

For you, for loyal Thebans, and for all
Who find my actions right, I pray the favor
Of justice, and of all the immortal gods.

CHORAGOS:
Since I am under oath, my lord, I swear
I did not do the murder, I can not name
The murderer. Might not the oracle
That has ordained the search tell where to find him?

OEDIPUS:
An honest question. But no man in the world
Can make the gods do more than the gods will.

CHORAGOS:
There is one last expedient—

OEDIPUS:
Tell me what it is.
Though it seem slight, you must not hold it back.

CHORAGOS:
A lord clairvoyant to the lord Apollo,
As we all know, is the skilled Teiresias.
One might learn much about this from him, Oedipus.

OEDIPUS:
I am not wasting time:
Creon spoke of this, and I have sent for him—

[15] **Labdakos' . . . line:** Oedipus gives a genealogy of the kings of Thebes, unwittingly tracing his own ancestry: Agenor, a king of Tyre in Phoenicia, was the father of Kadmos, the founder of Thebes. Kadmos, in turn, was the father of Polydorus, who fathered Labdakos. (See note 14.)

Twice, in fact; it is strange that he is not here.

CHORAGOS:

The other matter—that old report—seems useless.

OEDIPUS:

Tell me. I am interested in all reports.

CHORAGOS:

The King was said to have been killed by highwaymen.

OEDIPUS:

I know. But we have no witnesses to that.

CHORAGOS:

If the killer can feel a particle of dread,
Your curse will bring him out of hiding!

OEDIPUS:

No.
The man who dared that act will fear no curse.

[*Enter the blind seer* TEIRESIAS, *led by a* PAGE]

CHORAGOS:

But there is one man who may detect the criminal.
This is Teiresias, this is the holy prophet
In whom, alone of all men, truth was born.

OEDIPUS:

Teiresias: seer: student of mysteries,
Of all that's taught and all that no man tells,
Secrets of Heaven and secrets of the earth:
Blind though you are, you know the city lies
Sick with plague; and from this plague, my lord,
We find that you alone can guard or save us.
Possibly you did not hear the messengers?
Apollo, when we sent to him,
Sent us back word that this great pestilence
Would lift, but only if we established clearly
The identity of those who murdered Laïos.
They must be killed or exiled.
Can you use
Birdflight or any art of divination
To purify yourself, and Thebes, and me
From this contagion? We are in your hands.
There is no fairer duty
Than that of helping others in distress.

TEIRESIAS:

How dreadful knowledge of the truth can be
When there's no help in truth! I knew this well,
But made myself forget. I should not have come.

OEDIPUS:

What is troubling you? Why are your eyes so cold?

TEIRESIAS:
Let me go home. Bear your own fate, and I'll
Bear mine. It is better so: trust what I say.

OEDIPUS:
What you say is ungracious and unhelpful
To your native country. Do not refuse to speak.

TEIRESIAS:
When it comes to speech, your own is neither temperate
Nor opportune. I wish to be more prudent.

OEDIPUS:
In God's name, we all beg you—

TEIRESIAS:
You are all ignorant.
No; I will never tell you what I know.
Now it is my misery; then, it would be yours.

OEDIPUS:
What! You do know something, and will not tell us?
You would betray us all and wreck the State?

TEIRESIAS:
I do not intend to torture myself, or you.
Why persist in asking? You will not persuade me.

OEDIPUS:
What a wicked old man you are! You'd try a stone's
Patience! Out with it! Have you no feeling at all?

TEIRESIAS:
You call me unfeeling. If you could only see
The nature of your own feelings . . .

OEDIPUS:
Why,
Who would not feel as I do? Who could endure
Your arrogance toward the city?

TEIRESIAS:
What does it matter!
Whether I speak or not, it is bound to come.

OEDIPUS:
Then, if "it" is bound to come, you are bound to tell me.

TEIRESIAS:
No, I will not go on. Rage as you please.

OEDIPUS:
Rage? Why not!
And I'll tell you what I think:
You planned it, you had it done, you all but
Killed him with your own hands: if you had eyes,
I'd say the crime was yours, and yours alone.

TEIRESIAS:
So? I charge you, then,

Abide by the proclamation you have made:
From this day forth
Never speak again to these men or to me;
You yourself are the pollution of this country.

OEDIPUS:

You dare say that! Can you possibly think you have
Some way of going free, after such insolence?

TEIRESIAS:

I have gone free. It is the truth sustains me.

OEDIPUS:

Who taught you shamelessness? It was not your craft.

TEIRESIAS:

You did. You made me speak. I did not want to.

OEDIPUS:

Speak what? Let me hear it again more clearly.

TEIRESIAS:

Was it not clear before? Are you tempting me?

OEDIPUS:

I did not understand it. Say it again.

TEIRESIAS:

I say that you are the murderer whom you seek.

OEDIPUS:

Now twice you have spat out infamy. You'll pay for it!

TEIRESIAS:

Would you care for more? Do you wish to be really angry?

OEDIPUS:

Say what you will. Whatever you say is worthless.

TEIRESIAS:

I say you live in hideous shame with those
Most dear to you. You can not see the evil.

OEDIPUS:

It seems you can go on mouthing like this for ever.

TEIRESIAS:

I can, if there is power in truth.

OEDIPUS:

There is:
But not for you, not for you,
You sightless, witless, senseless, mad old man!

TEIRESIAS:

You are the madman. There is no one here
Who will not curse you soon, as you curse me.

OEDIPUS:

You child of endless night! You can not hurt me
Or any other man who sees the sun.

TEIRESIAS:

True: it is not from me your fate will come.

That lies within Apollo's competence,
As it is his concern.

OEDIPUS:

Tell me:
Are you speaking for Creon, or for yourself?

TEIRESIAS:

Creon is no threat. You weave your own doom.

OEDIPUS:

Wealth, power, craft of statesmanship!
Kingly position, everywhere admired!
What savage envy is stored up against these,
If Creon, whom I trusted, Creon my friend,
For this great office which the city once
Put in my hands unsought—if for this power
Creon desires in secret to destroy me!

He has bought this decrepit fortune-teller, this
Collector of dirty pennies, this prophet fraud—
Why, he is no more clairvoyant than I am!
Tell us:
Has your mystic mummery ever approached the truth?
When that hellcat the Sphinx was performing here,
What help were you to these people?
Her magic was not for the first man who came along:
It demanded a real exorcist. Your birds—
What good were they? or the gods, for the matter of that?
But I came by,
Oedipus, the simple man, who knows nothing—
I thought it out for myself, no birds helped me!
And this is the man you think you can destroy,
That you may be close to Creon when he's king!
Well, you and your friend Creon, it seems to me,
Will suffer most. If you were not an old man,
You would have paid already for your plot.

CHORAGOS:

We can not see that his words or yours
Have been spoken except in anger, Oedipus,
And of anger we have no need. How can God's will
Be accomplished best? That is what most concerns us.

TEIRESIAS:

You are a king. But where argument's concerned
I am your man, as much a king as you.
I am not your servant, but Apollo's.
I have no need of Creon to speak for me.

Listen to me. You mock my blindness, do you?
But I say that you, with both your eyes, are blind:
You can not see the wretchedness of your life,
Nor in whose house you live, no, nor with whom.
Who are your father and mother? Can you tell me?
You do not even know the blind wrongs
That you have done them, on earth and in the world below.
But the double lash of your parents' curse will whip you
Out of this land some day, with only night
Upon your precious eyes.
Your cries then—where will they not be heard?
What fastness of Kithairon[16] will not echo them?
And that bridal-descant of yours—you'll know it then,
The song they sang when you came here to Thebes
And found your misguided berthing.
All this, and more, that you can not guess at now,
Will bring you to yourself among your children.

Be angry, then. Curse Creon. Curse my words.
I tell you, no man that walks upon the earth
Shall be rooted out more horribly than you.

OEDIPUS:
Am I to bear this from him?—Damnation
Take you! Out of this place! Out of my sight!

TEIRESIAS:
I would not have come at all if you had not asked me.

OEDIPUS:
Could I have told that you'd talk nonsense, that
You'd come here to make a fool of yourself, and of me?

TEIRESIAS:
A fool? Your parents thought me sane enough.

OEDIPUS:
My parents again!—Wait: who were my parents?

TEIRESIAS:
This day will give you a father, and break your heart.

OEDIPUS:
Your infantile riddles! Your damned abracadabra!

TEIRESIAS:
You were a great man once at solving riddles.

OEDIPUS:
Mock me with that if you like; you will find it true.

---

[16] **Kithairon:** A mountain range near Thebes where Oedipus was abandoned in infancy and to which he returns when he is banished from Thebes.

TEIRESIAS:
It was true enough. It brought about your ruin.
OEDIPUS:
But if it saved this town?
TEIRESIAS:
[*To the* PAGE:]
Boy, give me your hand.
OEDIPUS:
Yes, boy; lead him away.
—While you are here
We can do nothing. Go; leave us in peace.
TEIRESIAS:
I will go when I have said what I have to say.
How can you hurt me? And I tell you again:
The man you have been looking for all this time,
The damned man, the murderer of Laïos,
That man is in Thebes. To your mind he is foreign-born,
But it will soon be shown that he is a Theban,
A revelation that will fail to please.
A blind man,
Who has his eyes now; a penniless man, who is rich now;
And he will go tapping the strange earth with his staff
To the children with whom he lives now he will be
Brother and father—the very same; to her
Who bore him, son and husband—the very same
Who came to his father's bed, wet with his father's blood.

Enough. Go think that over.
If later you find error in what I have said,
You may say that I have no skill in prophecy.
[*Exit* TEIRESIAS, *led by his* PAGE. OEDIPUS *goes into the palace.*]

ODE I

[*Strophe 1*]

CHORUS:
The Delphic stone of prophecies
Remembers ancient regicide
And a still bloody hand.
That killer's hour of flight has come.
He must be stronger than riderless
Coursers of untiring wind,
For the son of Zeus° armed with his father's thunder Apollo

Leaps in lightning after him;
And the Furies follow him, the sad Furies.[17]

[*Antistrophe 1*]

Holy Parnassos'[18] peak of snow
Flashes and blinds that secret man,
That all shall hunt him down:
Though he may roam the forest shade
Like a bull gone wild from pasture
To rage through glooms of stone.
Doom comes down on him; flight will not avail him;
For the world's heart calls him desolate,
And the immortal Furies follow, for ever follow.

[*Strophe 2*]

But now a wilder thing is heard
From the old man skilled at hearing Fate in the wingbeat of a bird.
Bewildered as a blown bird, my soul hovers and can not find
Foothold in this debate, or any reason or rest of mind.
But no man ever brought—none can bring
Proof of strife between Thebes' royal house,
Labdakos' line, and the son of Polybos;[19]
And never until now has any man brought word
Of Laïos' dark death staining Oedipus the King.

[*Antistrophe 2*]

Divine Zeus and Apollo hold
Perfect intelligence alone of all tales ever told;
And well though this diviner works, he works in his own night;
No man can judge that rough unknown or trust in second sight,
For wisdom changes hands among the wise.
Shall I believe my great lord criminal
At a raging word that a blind old man let fall?
I saw him, when the carrion woman faced him of old,
Prove his heroic mind! These evil words are lies.

---

[17] **Furies:** Serpent-haired female monsters who torment those who are guilty of blood crimes against their kin.

[18] **Holy Parnassos:** A mountain in Phocis and site of the Oracle at Delphi.

[19] **Labdakos' . . . Polybos:** That is, the people of Thebes and Oedipus; Polybos, the king of Corinth, was supposedly the father of Oedipus.

SCENE II

CREON:

Men of Thebes:
I am told that heavy accusations
Have been brought against me by King Oedipus.

I am not the kind of man to bear this tamely.

If in these present difficulties
He holds me accountable for any harm to him
Through anything I have said or done—why then,
I do not value life in this dishonor.
It is not as though this rumor touched upon
Some private indiscretion. The matter is grave.
The fact is that I am being called disloyal
To the State, to my fellow citizens, to my friends.

CHORAGOS:

He may have spoken in anger, not from his mind.

CREON:

But did you not hear him say I was the one
Who seduced the old prophet into lying?

CHORAGOS:

The thing was said; I do not know how seriously.

CREON:

But you were watching him! Were his eyes steady?
Did he look like a man in his right mind?

CHORAGOS:

I do not know.
I can not judge the behavior of great men.
But here is the King himself.

[*Enter* OEDIPUS]

OEDIPUS:

So you dared come back.
Why? How brazen of you to come to my house,
You murderer!
Do you think I do not know
That you plotted to kill me, plotted to steal my throne?
Tell me, in God's name: am I coward, a fool,
That you should dream you could accomplish this?
A fool who could not see your slippery game?
A coward, not to fight back when I saw it?
You are the fool, Creon, are you not? hoping
Without support or friends to get a throne?

Thrones may be won or bought: you could do neither.

CREON:

Now listen to me. You have talked; let me talk, too.
You can not judge unless you know the facts.

OEDIPUS:

You speak well: there is one fact; but I find it hard
To learn from the deadliest enemy I have.

CREON:

That above all I must dispute with you.

OEDIPUS:

That above all I will not hear you deny.

CREON:

If you think there is anything good in being stubborn
Against all reason, then I say you are wrong.

OEDIPUS:

If you think a man can sin against his own kind
And not be punished for it, I say you are mad.

CREON:

I agree. But tell me: what have I done to you?

OEDIPUS:

You advised me to send for that wizard, did you not?

CREON:

I did. I should do it again.

OEDIPUS:

Very well. Now tell me:
How long has it been since Laïos—

CREON:

What of Laïos?

OEDIPUS:

Since he vanished in that onset by the road?

CREON:

It was long ago, a long time.

OEDIPUS:

And this prophet,
Was he practicing here then?

CREON:

He was; and with honor, as now.

OEDIPUS:

Did he speak of me at that time?

CREON:

He never did;
At least, not when I was present.

OEDIPUS:

But . . . the enquiry?
I suppose you held one?

CREON:

We did, but we learned nothing.

OEDIPUS:

Why did the prophet not speak against me then?

CREON:

I do not know; and I am the kind of man
Who holds his tongue when he has no facts to go on.

OEDIPUS:

There's one fact that you know, and you could tell it.

CREON:

What fact is that? If I know it, you shall have it.

OEDIPUS:

If he were not involved with you, he could not say
That it was I who murdered Laïos.

CREON:

If he says that, you are the one that knows it!—
But now it is my turn to question you.

OEDIPUS:

Put your questions. I am no murderer.

CREON:

First, then: You married my sister?

OEDIPUS:

I married your sister.

CREON:

And you rule the kingdom equally with her?

OEDIPUS:

Everything that she wants she has from me.

CREON:

And I am the third, equal to both of you?

OEDIPUS:

That is why I call you a bad friend.

CREON:

No. Reason it out, as I have done.
Think of this first: Would any sane man prefer
Power, with all a king's anxieties,
To that same power and the grace of sleep?
Certainly not I.
I have never longed for the king's power—only his rights.
Would any wise man differ from me in this?
As matters stand, I have my way in everything
With your consent, and no responsibilities.
If I were king, I should be a slave to policy.

How could I desire a scepter more
Than what is now mine—untroubled influence?

No, I have not gone mad; I need no honors,
Except those with the perquisites I have now.
I am welcome everywhere; every man salutes me,
And those who want your favor seek my ear,
Since I know how to manage what they ask.
Should I exchange this ease for that anxiety?
Besides, no sober mind is treasonable.
I hate anarchy
And never would deal with any man who likes it.
Test what I have said. Go to the priestess
At Delphi, ask if I quoted her correctly.
And as for this other thing: if I am found
Guilty of treason with Teiresias,
Then sentence me to death! You have my word
It is a sentence I should cast my vote for—
But not without evidence!
You do wrong
When you take good men for bad, bad men for good.
A true friend thrown aside—why, life itself
Is not more precious!
In time you will know this well:
For time, and time alone, will show the just man,
Though scoundrels are discovered in a day.

CHORAGOS:
This is well said, and a prudent man would ponder it.
Judgments too quickly formed are dangerous.

OEDIPUS:
But is he not quick in his duplicity?
And shall I not be quick to parry him?
Would you have me stand still, hold my peace, and let
This man win everything, through my inaction?

CREON:
And you want—what is it, then? To banish me?

OEDIPUS:
No, not exile. It is your death I want,
So that all the world may see what treason means.

CREON:
You will persist, then? You will not believe me?

OEDIPUS:
How can I believe you?

CREON:
Then you are a fool.

OEDIPUS:
To save myself?

CREON:
In justice, think of me.

OEDIPUS:
You are evil incarnate.

CREON:
But suppose that you are wrong?

OEDIPUS:
Still I must rule.

CREON:
But not if you rule badly.

OEDIPUS:
O city, city!

CREON:
It is my city, too!

CHORAGOS:
Now, my lords, be still. I see the Queen,
Iocastê, coming from her palace chambers;
And it is time she came, for the sake of you both.
This dreadful quarrel can be resolved through her.

[*Enter* IOCASTE]

IOCASTE:
Poor foolish men, what wicked din is this?
With Thebes sick to death, is it not shameful
That you should rake some private quarrel up?

[*To* OEDIPUS:]
Come into the house.
—And you, Creon, go now:
Let us have no more of this tumult over nothing.

CREON:
Nothing? No, sister: what your husband plans for me
Is one of two great evils: exile or death.

OEDIPUS:
He is right.
Why, woman I have caught him squarely
Plotting against my life.

CREON:
No! Let me die
Accurst if ever I have wished you harm!

IOCASTE:
Ah, believe it, Oedipus!
In the name of the gods, respect this oath of his
For my sake, for the sake of these people here!

[*Strophe 1*]

CHORAGOS:
Open your mind to her, my lord. Be ruled by her, I beg you!

OEDIPUS:
What would you have me do?

CHORAGOS:
Respect Creon's word. He has never spoken like a fool,
And now he has sworn an oath.

OEDIPUS:
You know what you ask?

CHORAGOS:
I do.

OEDIPUS:
Speak on, then.

CHORAGOS:
A friend so sworn should not be baited so,
In blind malice, and without final proof.

OEDIPUS:
You are aware, I hope, that what you say
Means death for me, or exile at the least.

[*Strophe 2*]

CHORAGOS:
No, I swear by Helios,[20] first in Heaven!
May I die friendless and accurst,
The worst of deaths, if ever I meant that!
It is the withering fields
That hurt my sick heart:
Must we bear all these ills,
And now your bad blood as well?

OEDIPUS:
Then let him go. And let me die, if I must,
Or be driven by him in shame from the land of Thebes.
It is your unhappiness, and not his talk,
That touches me.
As for him—
Wherever he goes, hatred will follow him.

CREON:
Ugly in yielding, as you were ugly in rage!

[20] **Helios:** The god of the sun, often invoked in the swearing of oaths because in his daily journey across the heavens he can see all things.

Natures like yours chiefly torment themselves.

OEDIPUS:
Can you not go? Can you not leave me?

CREON:
I can.
You do not know me; but the city knows me,
And in its eyes I am just, if not in yours.

[*Exit* CREON]

[*Antistrophe 1*]

CHORAGOS:
Lady Iocastê, did you not ask the King to go to his chambers?

IOCASTE:
First tell me what has happened.

CHORAGOS:
There was suspicion without evidence; yet it rankled
As even false charges will.

IOCASTE:
On both sides?

CHORAGOS:
On both.

IOCASTE:
But what was said?

CHORAGOS:
Oh let it rest, let it be done with!
Have we not suffered enough?

OEDIPUS:
You see to what your decency has brought you:
You have made difficulties where my heart saw none.

[*Antistrophe 2*]

CHORAGOS:
Oedipus, it is not once only I have told you—
You must know I should count myself unwise
To the point of madness, should I now forsake you—
You, under whose hand,
In the storm of another time,
Our dear land sailed out free.
But now stand fast at the helm!

IOCASTE:
In God's name, Oedipus, inform your wife as well:
Why are you so set in this hard anger?

OEDIPUS:

I will tell you, for none of these men deserves
My confidence as you do. It is Creon's work,
His treachery, his plotting against me.

IOCASTE:

Go on, if you can make this clear to me.

OEDIPUS:

He charges me with the murder of Laïos.

IOCASTE:

Has he some knowledge? Or does he speak from hearsay?

OEDIPUS:

He would not commit himself to such a charge,
But he has brought in that damnable soothsayer
To tell his story.

IOCASTE:

Set your mind at rest.
If it is a question of soothsayers, I tell you
That you will find no man whose craft gives knowledge
Of the unknowable.

Here is my proof:

An oracle was reported to Laïos once
(I will not say from Phoibos himself, but from
His appointed ministers, at any rate)
That his doom would be death at the hands of his own son—
His son, born of his flesh and of mine!

Now, you remember the story: Laïos was killed
By marauding strangers where three highways meet;
But his child had not been three days in this world
Before the King had pierced the baby's ankles
And left him to die on a lonely mountainside.

Thus, Apollo never caused that child
To kill his father, and it was not Laïos' fate
To die at the hands of his son, as he had feared.
This is what prophets and prophecies are worth!
Have no dread of them.

It is God himself
Who can show us what he wills, in his own way.

OEDIPUS:

How strange a shadowy memory crossed my mind,
Just now while you were speaking; it chilled my heart.

IOCASTE:
What do you mean? What memory do you speak of?

OEDIPUS:
If I understand you, Laïos was killed
At a place where three roads meet.

IOCASTE:
So it was said;
We have no later story.

OEDIPUS:
Where did it happen?

IOCASTE:
Phokis, it is called: at a place where the Theban Way
Divides into the roads toward Delphi and Daulia.

OEDIPUS:
When?

IOCASTE:
We had the news not long before you came
And proved the right to your succession here.

OEDIPUS:
Ah, what net has God been weaving for me?

IOCASTE:
Oedipus! Why does this trouble you?

OEDIPUS:
Do not ask me yet.
First, tell me how Laïos looked, and tell me
How old he was.

IOCASTE:
He was tall, his hair just touched
With white; his form was not unlike your own.

OEDIPUS:
I think that I myself may be accurst
By my own ignorant edict.

IOCASTE:
You speak strangely.
It makes me tremble to look at you, my King.

OEDIPUS:
I am not sure that the blind man can not see.
But I should know better if you were to tell me—

IOCASTE:
Anything—though I dread to hear you ask it.

OEDIPUS:
Was the King lightly escorted, or did he ride
With a large company, as a ruler should?

IOCASTE:

There were five men with him in all: one was a herald,
And a single chariot, which he was driving.

OEDIPUS:

Alas, that makes it plain enough!
But who—
Who told you how it happened?

IOCASTE:

A household servant,
The only one to escape.

OEDIPUS:

And is he still
A servant of ours?

IOCASTE:

No; for when he came back at last
And found you enthroned in the place of the dead king,
He came to me, touched my hand with his, and begged
That I would send him away to the frontier district
Where only the shepherds go—
As far away from the city as I could send him.
I granted his prayer; for although the man was a slave,
He had earned more than this favor at my hands.

OEDIPUS:

Can he be called back quickly?

IOCASTE:

Easily.
But why?

OEDIPUS:

I have taken too much upon myself
Without enquiry; therefore I wish to consult him.

IOCASTE:

Then he shall come.
But am I not one also
To whom you might confide these fears of yours?

OEDIPUS:

That is your right; it will not be denied you,
Now least of all; for I have reached a pitch
Of wild foreboding. Is there anyone
To whom I should sooner speak?

Polybos of Corinth is my father.
My mother is a Dorian: Meropê.
I grew up chief among the men of Corinth

Until a strange thing happened—
Not worth my passion, it may be, but strange.

At a feast, a drunken man maundering in his cups
Cries out that I am not my father's son!

I contained myself that night, though I felt anger
And a sinking heart. The next day I visited
My father and mother, and questioned them. They stormed,
Calling it all the slanderous rant of a fool;
And this relieved me. Yet the suspicion
Remained always aching in my mind;
I knew there was talk; I could not rest;
And finally, saying nothing to my parents,
I went to the shrine at Delphi.
The god dismissed my question without reply;
He spoke of other things.
                                        Some were clear,
Full of wretchedness, dreadful, unbearable:
As, that I should lie with my own mother, breed
Children from whom all men would turn their eyes;
And that I should be my father's murderer.

I heard all this, and fled. And from that day
Corinth to me was only in the stars
Descending in that quarter of the sky,
As I wandered farther and farther on my way
To a land where I should never see the evil
Sung by the oracle. And I came to this country
Where, so you say, King Laïos was killed.

I will tell you all that happened there, my lady.

There were three highways
Coming together at a place I passed;
And there a herald came towards me, and a chariot
Drawn by horses, with a man such as you describe
Seated in it. The groom leading the horses
Forced me off the road at his lord's command;
But as this charioteer lurched over towards me
I struck him in my rage. The old man saw me
And brought his double goad down upon my head
As I came abreast.
                                        He was paid back, and more!
Swinging my club in this right hand I knocked him

Out of his car, and he rolled on the ground.
I killed him.

I killed them all.
Now if that stranger and Laïos were—kin,
Where is a man more miserable than I?
More hated by the gods? Citizen and alien alike
Must never shelter me or speak to me—
I must be shunned by all.
And I myself
Pronounced this malediction upon myself!

Think of it: I have touched you with these hands,
These hands that killed your husband. What defilement!

Am I all evil, then? It must be so,
Since I must flee from Thebes, yet never again
See my own countrymen, my own country,
For fear of joining my mother in marriage
And killing Polybos, my father.
Ah,
If I was created so, born to this fate,
Who could deny the savagery of God?

O holy majesty of heavenly powers!
May I never see that day! Never!
Rather let me vanish from the race of men
Than know the abomination destined me!

CHORAGOS:
We too, my lord, have felt dismay at this.
But there is hope: you have yet to hear the shepherd.

OEDIPUS:
Indeed, I fear no other hope is left me.

IOCASTE:
What do you hope from him when he comes?

OEDIPUS:
This much:
If his account of the murder tallies with yours,
Then I am cleared.

IOCASTE:
What was it that I said
Of such importance?

OEDIPUS:
Why, "marauders," you said,
Killed the King, according to this man's story.

If he maintains that still, if there were several,
Clearly the guilt is not mine: I was alone.
But if he says one man, singlehanded, did it,
Then the evidence all points to me.

IOCASTE:

You may be sure that he said there were several;
And can he call back that story now? He can not.
The whole city heard it as plainly as I.
But suppose he alters some detail of it:
He can not ever show that Laïos' death
Fulfilled the oracle: for Apollo said
My child was doomed to kill him; and my child—
Poor baby!—it was my child that died first.

No. From now on, where oracles are concerned,
I would not waste a second thought on any.

OEDIPUS:

You may be right.
But come: let someone go
For the shepherd at once. This matter must be settled.

IOCASTE:

I will send for him.
I would not wish to cross you in anything,
And surely not in this.—Let us go in.

[*Exeunt into the palace*]

ODE II

[*Strophe 1*]

CHORUS:

Let me be reverent in the ways of right,
Lowly the paths I journey on;
Let all my words and actions keep
The laws of the pure universe
From highest Heaven handed down.
For Heaven is their bright nurse,
Those generations of the realms of light;
Ah, never of mortal kind were they begot,
Nor are they slaves of memory, lost in sleep:
Their Father is greater than Time, and ages not.

[*Antistrophe 1*]

The tyrant is a child of Pride
Who drinks from his great sickening cup

Recklessness and vanity,
Until from his high crest headlong
He plummets to the dust of hope.
That strong man is not strong.
But let no fair ambition be denied;
May God protect the wrestler for the State
In government, in comely policy,
Who will fear God, and on His ordinance wait.

[*Strophe 2*]

Haughtiness and the high hand of disdain
Tempt and outrage God's holy law;
And any mortal who dares hold
No immortal Power in awe
Will be caught up in a net of pain:
The price for which his levity is sold.
Let each man take due earnings, then,
And keep his hands from holy things,
And from blasphemy stand apart—
Else the crackling blast of heaven
Blows on his head, and on his desperate heart;
Though fools will honor impious men,
In their cities no tragic poet sings.

[*Antistrophe 2*]

Shall we lose faith in Delphi's obscurities,
We who have heard the world's core
Discredited, and the sacred wood
Of Zeus at Elis[21] praised no more?
The deeds and the strange prophecies
Must make a pattern yet to be understood.
Zeus, if indeed you are lord of all,
Throned in light over night and day,
Mirror this in your endless mind:
Our masters call the oracle
Words on the wind, and the Delphic vision blind!
Their hearts no longer know Apollo,
And reverence for the gods has died away.

[21] **Elis:** An area in the northwestern part of the Peloponnese.

Scene III

[*Enter* IOCASTE]

IOCASTE:

Princes of Thebes, it has occurred to me
To visit the altars of the gods, bearing
These branches as a suppliant, and this incense.
Our King is not himself: his noble soul
Is overwrought with fantasies of dread,
Else he would consider
The new prophecies in the light of the old.
He will listen to any voice that speaks disaster,
And my advice goes for nothing.

[*She approaches the altar, R.*]

To you, then, Apollo,
Lycean lord, since you are nearest, I turn in prayer.
Receive these offerings, and grant us deliverance
From defilement. Our hearts are heavy with fear
When we see our leader distracted, as helpless sailors
Are terrified by the confusion of their helmsman.

[*Enter* MESSENGER]

MESSENGER:

Friends, no doubt you can direct me:
Where shall I find the house of Oedipus,
Or, better still, where is the King himself?

CHORAGOS:

It is this very place, stranger; he is inside.
This is his wife and mother of his children.

MESSENGER:

I wish her happiness in a happy house,
Blest in all the fulfillment of her marriage.

IOCASTE:

I wish as much for you: your courtesy
Deserves a like good fortune. But now, tell me:
Why have you come? What have you to say to us?

MESSENGER:

Good news, my lady, for your house and your husband.

IOCASTE:

What news? Who sent you here?

MESSENGER:

I am from Corinth.
The news I bring ought to mean joy for you,
Though it may be you will find some grief in it.

IOCASTE:

What is it? How can it touch us in both ways?

MESSENGER:

The word is that the people of the Isthmus
Intend to call Oedipus to be their king.

IOCASTE:

But old King Polybos—is he not reigning still?

MESSENGER:

No. Death holds him in his sepulchre.

IOCASTE:

What are you saying? Polybos is dead?

MESSENGER:

If I am not telling the truth, may I die myself.

IOCASTE:

[*To a* MAIDSERVANT:]

Go in, go quickly; tell this to your master.

O riddlers of God's will, where are you now!
This was the man whom Oedipus, long ago,
Feared so, fled so, in dread of destroying him—
But it was another fate by which he died.

[*Enter* OEDIPUS, *C.*]

OEDIPUS:

Dearest Iocastê, why have you sent for me?

IOCASTE:

Listen to what this man says, and then tell me
What has become of the solemn prophecies.

OEDIPUS:

Who is this man? What is his news for me?

IOCASTE:

He has come from Corinth to announce your father's death!

OEDIPUS:

Is it true, stranger? Tell me in your own words.

MESSENGER:

I can not say it more clearly: the King is dead.

OEDIPUS:

Was it by treason? Or by an attack of illness?

MESSENGER:

A little thing brings old men to their rest.

OEDIPUS:

It was sickness, then?

MESSENGER:

Yes, and his many years.

OEDIPUS:

Ah!
Why should a man respect the Pythian hearth, or
Give heed to the birds that jangle above his head?
They prophesied that I should kill Polybos,
Kill my own father; but he is dead and buried,
And I am here — I never touched him, never,
Unless he died of grief for my departure,
And thus, in a sense, through me. No. Polybos
Has packed the oracles off with him underground.
They are empty words.

IOCASTE:

Had I not told you so?

OEDIPUS:

You had; it was my faint heart that betrayed me.

IOCASTE:

From now on never think of those things again.

OEDIPUS:

And yet — must I not fear my mother's bed?

IOCASTE:

Why should anyone in this world be afraid,
Since Fate rules us and nothing can be foreseen?
A man should live only for the present day.

Have no more fear of sleeping with your mother:
How many men, in dreams, have lain with their mothers!
No reasonable man is troubled by such things.

OEDIPUS:

That is true; only —
If only my mother were not still alive!
But she is alive. I can not help my dread.

IOCASTE:

Yet this news of your father's death is wonderful.

OEDIPUS:

Wonderful. But I fear the living woman.

MESSENGER:

Tell me, who is this woman that you fear?

OEDIPUS:

It is Meropê, man; the wife of King Polybos.

MESSENGER:

Meropê? Why should you be afraid of her?

OEDIPUS:

An oracle of the gods, a dreadful saying.

MESSENGER:

Can you tell me about it or are you sworn to silence?

OEDIPUS:

I can tell you, and I will.
Apollo said through his prophet that I was the man
Who should marry his own mother, shed his father's blood
With his own hands. And so, for all these years
I have kept clear of Corinth, and no harm has come—
Though it would have been sweet to see my parents again.

MESSENGER:

And is this the fear that drove you out of Corinth?

OEDIPUS:

Would you have me kill my father?

MESSENGER:

As for that
You must be reassured by the news I gave you.

OEDIPUS:

If you could reassure me, I would reward you.

MESSENGER:

I had that in mind, I will confess: I thought
I could count on you when you returned to Corinth.

OEDIPUS:

No: I will never go near my parents again.

MESSENGER:

Ah, son, you still do not know what you are doing—

OEDIPUS:

What do you mean? In the name of God tell me!

MESSENGER:

—If these are your reasons for not going home.

OEDIPUS:

I tell you, I fear the oracle may come true.

MESSENGER:

And guilt may come upon you through your parents?

OEDIPUS:

That is the dread that is always in my heart.

MESSENGER:

Can you not see that all your fears are groundless?

OEDIPUS:

How can you say that? They are my parents, surely?

MESSENGER:

Polybos was not your father.

OEDIPUS:

Not my father?

MESSENGER:

No more your father than the man speaking to you.

OEDIPUS:

But you are nothing to me!

MESSENGER:
Neither was he.

OEDIPUS:
Then why did he call me son?

MESSENGER:
I will tell you:
Long ago he had you from my hands, as a gift.

OEDIPUS:
Then how could he love me so, if I was not his?

MESSENGER:
He had no children, and his heart turned to you.

OEDIPUS:
What of you? Did you buy me? Did you find me by chance?

MESSENGER:
I came upon you in the crooked pass of Kithairon.

OEDIPUS:
And what were you doing there?

MESSENGER:
Tending my flocks.

OEDIPUS:
A wandering shepherd?

MESSENGER:
But your savior, son, that day.

OEDIPUS:
From what did you save me?

MESSENGER:
Your ankles should tell you that.

OEDIPUS:
Ah, stranger, why do you speak of that childhood pain?

MESSENGER:
I cut the bonds that tied your ankles together.

OEDIPUS:
I have had the mark as long as I can remember.

MESSENGER:
That was why you were given the name you bear.

OEDIPUS:
God! Was it my father or my mother who did it?
Tell me!

MESSENGER:
I do not know. The man who gave you to me
Can tell you better than I.

OEDIPUS:
It was not you that found me, but another?

MESSENGER:
It was another shepherd gave you to me.

OEDIPUS:
Who was he? Can you tell me who he was?
MESSENGER:
I think he was said to be one of Laïos' people.
OEDIPUS:
You mean the Laïos who was king here years ago?
MESSENGER:
Yes; King Laïos; and the man was one of his herdsmen.
OEDIPUS:
Is he still alive? Can I see him?
MESSENGER:
These men here
Know best about such things.
OEDIPUS:
Does anyone here
Know this shepherd that he is talking about?
Have you seen him in the fields, or in the town?
If you have, tell me. It is time things were made plain.
CHORAGOS:
I think the man he means is that same shepherd
You have already asked to see. Iocastê perhaps
Could tell you something.
OEDIPUS:
Do you know anything
About him, Lady? Is he the man we have summoned?
Is that the man this shepherd means?
IOCASTE:
Why think of him?
Forget this herdsman. Forget it all.
This talk is a waste of time.
OEDIPUS:
How can you say that,
When the clues to my true birth are in my hands?
IOCASTE:
For God's love, let us have no more questioning!
Is your life nothing to you?
My own is pain enough for me to bear.
OEDIPUS:
You need not worry. Suppose my mother a slave,
And born of slaves: no baseness can touch you.
IOCASTE:
Listen to me, I beg you: do not do this thing!
OEDIPUS:
I will not listen; the truth must be made known.

IOCASTE:
Everything that I say is for your own good!
OEDIPUS:
My own good
Snaps my patience, then; I want none of it.
IOCASTE:
You are fatally wrong! May you never learn who you are!
OEDIPUS:
Go, one of you, and bring the shepherd here.
Let us leave this woman to brag of her royal name.
IOCASTE:
Ah, miserable!
That is the only word I have for you now.
That is the only word I can ever have.
[*Exit into the palace*]
CHORAGOS:
Why has she left us, Oedipus? Why has she gone
In such a passion of sorrow? I fear this silence:
Something dreadful may come of it.
OEDIPUS:
Let it come!
However base my birth, I must know about it.
The Queen, like a woman, is perhaps ashamed
To think of my low origin. But I
Am a child of Luck; I can not be dishonored.
Luck is my mother; the passing months, my brothers,
Have seen me rich and poor.
If this is so,
How could I wish that I were someone else?
How could I not be glad to know my birth?

Ode III

[*Strophe*]

CHORUS:
If ever the coming time were known
To my heart's pondering,
Kithairon, now by Heaven I see the torches
At the festival of the next full moon,
And see the dance, and hear the choir sing
A grace to your gentle shade:
Mountain where Oedipus was found,
O mountain guard of a noble race!
May the god who heals us lend his aid,

And let that glory come to pass
For our king's cradling-ground.

[*Antistrophe*]

Of the nymphs that flower beyond the years,
Who bore you, royal child,
To Pan[22] of the hills or the timberline Apollo,
Cold in delight where the upland clears,
Or Hermês[23] for whom Kyllenê's heights are piled?
Or flushed as evening cloud,
Great Dionysus,[24] roamer of mountains,
He—was it he who found you there,
And caught you up in his own proud
Arms from the sweet god-ravisher
Who laughed by the Muses' fountains?

Scene IV

OEDIPUS:
Sirs: though I do not know the man,
I think I see him coming, this shepherd we want:
He is old, like our friend here, and the men
Bringing him seem to be servants of my house.
But you can tell, if you have ever seen him.

[*Enter* SHEPHERD *escorted by servants*]

CHORAGOS:
I know him, he was Laïos' man. You can trust him.

OEDIPUS:
Tell me first, you from Corinth: is this the shepherd
We were discussing?

MESSENGER:
This is the very man.

OEDIPUS:

[*To* SHEPHERD:]

Come here. No, look at me. You must answer
Everything I ask.—You belonged to Laïos?

SHEPHERD:
Yes: born his slave, brought up in his house.

OEDIPUS:
Tell me: what kind of work did you do for him?

---

[22] **Pan:** God of the woods, mountains, and wild nature in general. [23] **Hermês:** The messenger of the gods, and the son of Zeus and Maia, a nymph who lived on Mt. Kyllenê in Arcadia. [24] **Dionysus:** Also known as Bacchos, the god of wine and of vegetation in general.

SHEPHERD:
I was a shepherd of his, most of my life.

OEDIPUS:
Where mainly did you go for pasturage?

SHEPHERD:
Sometimes Kithairon, sometimes the hills near-by.

OEDIPUS:
Do you remember ever seeing this man out there?

SHEPHERD:
What would he be doing there? This man?

OEDIPUS:
This man standing here. Have you ever seen him before?

SHEPHERD:
No. At least, not to my recollection.

MESSENGER:
And that is not strange, my lord. But I'll refresh
His memory: he must remember when we two
Spent three whole seasons together, March to September,
On Kithairon or thereabouts. He had two flocks;
I had one. Each autumn I'd drive mine home
And he would go back with his to Laïos' sheepfold.—
Is this not true, just as I have described it?

SHEPHERD:
True, yes; but it was all so long ago.

MESSENGER:
Well, then: do you remember, back in those days,
That you gave me a baby boy to bring up as my own?

SHEPHERD:
What if I did? What are you trying to say?

MESSENGER:
King Oedipus was once that little child.

SHEPHERD:
Damn you, hold your tongue!

OEDIPUS:
No more of that!
It is your tongue needs watching, not this man's.

SHEPHERD:
My King, my Master, what is it I have done wrong?

OEDIPUS:
You have not answered his question about the boy.

SHEPHERD:
He does not know . . . He is only making trouble . . .

OEDIPUS:
Come, speak plainly, or it will go hard with you.

SHEPHERD:
In God's name, do not torture an old man!

OEDIPUS:
Come here, one of you; bind his arms behind him.
SHEPHERD:
Unhappy king! What more do you wish to learn?
OEDIPUS:
Did you give this man the child he speaks of?
SHEPHERD:
I did.
And I would to God I had died that very day.
OEDIPUS:
You will die now unless you speak the truth.
SHEPHERD:
Yet if I speak the truth, I am worse than dead.
OEDIPUS:
Very well; since you insist upon delaying—
SHEPHERD:
No! I have told you already that I gave him the boy.
OEDIPUS:
Where did you get him? From your house? From somewhere else?
SHEPHERD:
Not from mine, no. A man gave him to me.
OEDIPUS:
Is that man here? Do you know whose slave he was?
SHEPHERD:
For God's love, my King, do not ask me any more!
OEDIPUS:
You are a dead man if I have to ask you again.
SHEPHERD:
Then . . . Then the child was from the palace of Laïos.
OEDIPUS:
A slave child? or a child of his own line?
SHEPHERD:
Ah, I am on the brink of dreadful speech!
OEDIPUS:
And I of dreadful hearing. Yet I must hear.
SHEPHERD:
If you must be told, then . . .
They said it was Laïos' child;
But it is your wife who can tell you about that.
OEDIPUS:
My wife!—Did she give it to you?
SHEPHERD:
My lord, she did.
OEDIPUS:
Do you know why?

SHEPHERD:
I was told to get rid of it.

OEDIPUS:
An unspeakable mother!

SHEPHERD:
There had been prophecies . . .

OEDIPUS:
Tell me.

SHEPHERD:
It was said that the boy would kill his own father.

OEDIPUS:
Then why did you give him over to this old man?

SHEPHERD:
I pitied the baby, my King,
And I thought that this man would take him far away
To his own country.
He saved him—but for what a fate!
For if you are what this man says you are,
No man living is more wretched than Oedipus.

OEDIPUS:
Ah God!
It was true!
All the prophecies!
—Now,
O Light, may I look on you for the last time!
I, Oedipus,
Oedipus, damned in his birth, in his marriage damned,
Damned in the blood he shed with his own hand!

[*He rushes into the palace*]

Ode IV

[*Strophe 1*]

CHORUS:
Alas for the seed of men.

What measure shall I give these generations
That breathe on the void and are void
And exist and do not exist?

Who bears more weight of joy
Than mass of sunlight shifting in images,
Or who shall make his thought stay on
That down time drifts away?

Your splendor is all fallen.

O naked brow of wrath and tears,
O change of Oedipus!
I who saw your days call no man blest—
Your great days like ghósts góne.

[*Antistrophe 1*]

That mind was a strong bow.

Deep, how deep you drew it then, hard archer,
At a dim fearful range,
And brought dear glory down!

You overcame the stranger—
The virgin with her hooking lion claws—[25]
And though death sang, stood like a tower
To make pale Thebes take heart.

Fortress against our sorrow!

True king, giver of laws,
Majestic Oedipus!
No prince in Thebes had ever such renown,
No prince won such grace of power.

[*Strophe 2*]

And now of all men ever known
Most pitiful is this man's story:
His fortunes are most changed, his state
Fallen to a low slave's
Ground under bitter fate.

O Oedipus, most royal one!
The great door that expelled you to the light
Gave at night—ah, gave night to your glory:
As to the father, to the fathering son.

All understood too late.

[25] **The virgin . . . claws:** The Sphinx. (See note 5.)

How could that queen whom Laïos won,
The garden that he harrowed at his height,
Be silent when that act was done?

[*Antistrophe 2*]

But all eyes fail before time's eye,
All actions come to justice there.
Though never willed, though far down the deep past,
Your bed, your dread sirings,
Are brought to book at last.

Child by Laïos doomed to die,
Then doomed to lose that fortunate little death,
Would God you never took breath in this air
That with my wailing lips I take to cry:

For I weep the world's outcast.

I was blind, and now I can tell why:
Asleep, for you had given ease of breath
To Thebes, while the false years went by.

Éxodos

[*Enter, from the palace,* SECOND MESSENGER]

SECOND MESSENGER:

Elders of Thebes, most honored in this land,
What horrors are yours to see and hear, what weight
Of sorrow to be endured, if, true to your birth,
You venerate the line of Labdakos!
I think neither Istros nor Phasis, those great rivers,[26]
Could purify this place of the corruption
It shelters now, or soon must bring to light—
Evil not done unconsciously, but willed.

The greatest griefs are those we cause ourselves.

CHORAGOS:

Surely, friend, we have grief enough already;
What new sorrow do you mean?

SECOND MESSENGER:

The Queen is dead.

---

[26] **Istros . . . rivers:** Istros was the name for the Danube River. Phasis is a river in Asia Minor that flows into the Black Sea.

CHORAGOS:
Iocastê? Dead? But at whose hand?
SECOND MESSENGER:
Her own.
The full horror of what happened you can not know,
For you did not see it; but I, who did, will tell you
As clearly as I can how she met her death.

When she had left us,
In passionate silence, passing through the court,
She ran to her apartment in the house,
Her hair clutched by the fingers of both hands.
She closed the doors behind her; then, by that bed
Where long ago the fatal son was conceived—
That son who should bring about his father's death—
We heard her call upon Laïos, dead so many years,
And heard her wail for the double fruit of her marriage,
A husband by her husband, children by her child.

Exactly how she died I do not know:
For Oedipus burst in moaning and would not let us
Keep vigil to the end: it was by him
As he stormed about the room that our eyes were caught.
From one to another of us he went, begging a sword,
Cursing the wife who was not his wife, the mother
Whose womb had carried his own children and himself.
I do not know: it was none of us aided him,
But surely one of the gods was in control!
For with a dreadful cry
He hurled his weight, as though wrenched out of himself,
At the twin doors: the bolts gave, and he rushed in.
And there we saw her hanging, her body swaying
From the cruel cord she had noosed about her neck.
A great sob broke from him, heartbreaking to hear,
As he loosed the rope and lowered her to the ground.

I would blot out from my mind what happened next!
For the King ripped from her gown the golden brooches
That were her ornament, and raised them, and plunged them down
Straight into his own eyeballs, crying, "No more,
No more shall you look on the misery about me,
The horrors of my own doing! Too long you have known
The faces of those whom I should never have seen,
Too long been blind to those for whom I was searching!
From this hour, go in darkness!" And as he spoke,

He struck at his eyes—not once, but many times;
And the blood spattered his beard,
Bursting from his ruined sockets like red hail.

So from the unhappiness of two this evil has sprung.
A curse on the man and woman alike. The old
Happiness of the house of Labdakos
Was happiness enough: where is it today?
It is all wailing and ruin, disgrace, death—all
The misery of mankind that has a name—
And it is wholly and for ever theirs.

CHORAGOS:
Is he in agony still? Is there no rest for him?

SECOND MESSENGER:
He is calling for someone to lead him to the gates
So that all the children of Kadmos may look upon
His father's murderer, his mother's—no,
I can not say it!
And then he will leave Thebes,
Self-exiled, in order that the curse
Which he himself pronounced may depart from the house.
He is weak, and there is none to lead him,
So terrible is his suffering.
But you will see:
Look, the doors are opening; in a moment
You will see a thing that would crush a heart of stone.

[*The central door is opened;* OEDIPUS, *blinded, is led in*]

CHORAGOS:
Dreadful indeed for men to see.
Never have my own eyes
Looked on a sight so full of fear.

Oedipus!
What madness came upon you, what daemon
Leaped on your life with heavier
Punishment than a mortal man can bear?
No: I can not even
Look at you, poor ruined one.
And I would speak, question, ponder,
If I were able. No.
You make me shudder.

OEDIPUS:
God. God.
Is there a sorrow greater?

Where shall I find harbor in this world?
My voice is hurled far on a dark wind.
What has God done to me?

CHORAGOS:

Too terrible to think of, or to see.

[*Strophe 1*]

OEDIPUS:

O cloud of night,
Never to be turned away: night coming on,
I can not tell how: night like a shroud!

My fair winds brought me here.
O God. Again
The pain of the spikes where I had sight,
The flooding pain
Of memory, never to be gouged out.

CHORAGOS:

This is not strange.
You suffer it all twice over, remorse in pain,
Pain in remorse.

[*Antistrophe 1*]

OEDIPUS:

Ah dear friend
Are you faithful even yet, you alone?
Are you still standing near me, will you stay here,
Patient, to care for the blind?
The blind man!
Yet even blind I know who it is attends me,
By the voice's tone—
Though my new darkness hide the comforter.

CHORAGOS:

Oh fearful act!
What god was it drove you to rake black
Night across your eyes?

[*Strophe 2*]

OEDIPUS:

Apollo. Apollo. Dear
Children, the god was Apollo.
He brought my sick, sick fate upon me.
But the blinding hand was my own!

How could I bear to see
When all my sight was horror everywhere?

CHORAGOS:

Everywhere; that is true.

OEDIPUS:

And now what is left?
Images? Love? A greeting even,
Sweet to the senses? Is there anything?
Ah, no, friends: lead me away.
Lead me away from Thebes.
Lead the great wreck
And hell of Oedipus, whom the gods hate.

CHORAGOS:

Your fate is clear, you are not blind to that.
Would God you had never found it out!

[*Antistrophe 2*]

OEDIPUS:

Death take the man who unbound
My feet on that hillside
And delivered me from death to life! What life?
If only I had died,
This weight of monstrous doom
Could not have dragged me and my darlings down.

CHORAGOS:

I would have wished the same.

OEDIPUS:

Oh never to have come here
With my father's blood upon me! Never
To have been the man they call his mother's husband!
Oh accurst! Oh child of evil,
To have entered that wretched bed—
the selfsame one!
More primal than sin itself, this fell to me.

CHORAGOS:

I do not know how I can answer you.
You were better dead than alive and blind.

OEDIPUS:

Do not counsel me any more. This punishment
That I have laid upon myself is just.
If I had eyes,
I do not know how I could bear the sight
Of my father, when I came to the house of Death,
Or my mother: for I have sinned against them both

So vilely that I could not make my peace
By strangling my own life.
                                        Or do you think my children,
Born as they were born, would be sweet to my eyes?
Ah never, never! Nor this town with its high walls,
Nor the holy images of the gods.
                                                For I,
Thrice miserable!—Oedipus, noblest of all the line
Of Kadmos, have condemned myself to enjoy
These things no more, by my own malediction
Expelling that man whom the gods declared
To be a defilement in the house of Laïos.
After exposing the rankness of my own guilt,
How could I look men frankly in the eyes?
No, I swear it,
If I could have stifled my hearing at its source,
I would have done it and made all this body
A tight cell of misery, blank to light and sound:
So I should have been safe in a dark agony
Beyond all recollection.
                                    Ah Kithairon!
Why did you shelter me? When I was cast upon you,
Why did I not die? Then I should never
Have shown the world my execrable birth.

Ah Polybos! Corinth, city that I believed
The ancient seat of my ancestors: how fair
I seemed, your child! And all the while this evil
Was cancerous within me!
                                        For I am sick
In my daily life, sick in my origin.

O three roads, dark ravine, woodland and way
Where three roads met: you, drinking my father's blood,
My own blood, spilled by my own hand: can you remember
The unspeakable things I did there, and the things
I went on from there to do?
                                          O marriage, marriage!
The act that engendered me, and again the act
Performed by the son in the same bed—
                                                        Ah, the net
Of incest, mingling fathers, brothers, sons,
With brides, wives, mothers: the last evil
That can be known by men: no tongue can say
How evil!

No. For the love of God, conceal me
Somewhere far from Thebes; or kill me; or hurl me
Into the sea, away from men's eyes for ever.

Come, lead me. You need not fear to touch me.
Of all men, I alone can bear this guilt.

[*Enter* CREON]

CHORAGOS:
We are not the ones to decide; but Creon here
May fitly judge of what you ask. He only
Is left to protect the city in your place.

OEDIPUS:
Alas, how can I speak to him? What right have I
To beg his courtesy whom I have deeply wronged?

CREON:
I have not come to mock you, Oedipus,
Or to reproach you, either.

[*To* ATTENDANTS:]

—You, standing there:
If you have lost all respect for man's dignity,
At least respect the flame of Lord Helios:
Do not allow this pollution to show itself
Openly here, an affront to the earth
And Heaven's rain and the light of day. No, take him
Into the house as quickly as you can.
For it is proper
That only the close kindred see his grief.

OEDIPUS:
I pray you in God's name, since your courtesy
Ignores my dark expectation, visiting
With mercy this man of all men most execrable:
Give me what I ask—for your good, not for mine.

CREON:
And what is it that you would have me do?

OEDIPUS:
Drive me out of this country as quickly as may be
To a place where no human voice can ever greet me.

CREON:
I should have done that before now—only,
God's will had not been wholly revealed to me.

OEDIPUS:
But his command is plain: the parricide
Must be destroyed. I am that evil man.

CREON:
That is the sense of it, yes; but as things are,

We had best discover clearly what is to be done.

OEDIPUS:

You would learn more about a man like me?

CREON:

You are ready now to listen to the god.

OEDIPUS:

I will listen. But it is to you
That I must turn for help. I beg you, hear me.

The woman in there—
Give her whatever funeral you think proper:
She is your sister.
—But let me go, Creon!
Let me purge my father's Thebes of the pollution
Of my living here, and go out to the wild hills,
To Kithairon, that has won such fame with me,
The tomb my mother and father appointed for me,
And let me die there, as they willed I should.
And yet I know
Death will not ever come to me through sickness
Or in any natural way: I have been preserved
For some unthinkable fate. But let that be.

As for my sons,[27] you need not care for them.
They are men, they will find some way to live.
But my poor daughters, who have shared my table,
Who never before have been parted from their father—
Take care of them, Creon; do this for me.
And will you let me touch them with my hands
A last time, and let us weep together?
Be kind, my lord,
Great prince, be kind!
Could I but touch them,
They would be mine again, as when I had my eyes.

[*Enter* ANTIGONE *and* ISMENE, *attended*]

Ah, God!
Is it my dearest children I hear weeping?
Has Creon pitied me and sent my daughters?

CREON:

Yes, Oedipus: I knew that they were dear to you
In the old days, and know you must love them still.

---

[27] **my sons:** Eteocles and Polynices, who will challenge each other over the rule of Thebes; Oedipus also leaves behind two daughters, Antigone and Ismene.

OEDIPUS:
May God bless you for this—and be a friendlier
Guardian to you than he has been to me!

Children, where are you?
Come quickly to my hands: they are your brother's—
Hands that have brought your father's once clear eyes
To this way of seeing—
Ah dearest ones
I had neither sight nor knowledge then, your father
By the woman who was the source of his own life!
And I weep for you—having no strength to see you—,
I weep for you when I think of the bitterness
That men will visit upon you all your lives.
What homes, what festivals can you attend
Without being forced to depart again in tears?
And when you come to marriageable age,
Where is the man, my daughters, who would dare
Risk the bane that lies on all my children?
Is there any evil wanting? Your father killed
His father; sowed the womb of her who bore him;
Engendered you at the fount of his own existence!
That is what they will say of you.

Then, whom
Can you ever marry? There are no bridegrooms for you,
And your lives must wither away in sterile dreaming.

O Creon, son of Menoikeus!
You are the only father my daughters have,
Since we, their parents, are both of us gone for ever.
They are your own blood: you will not let them
Fall into beggary and loneliness;
You will keep them from the miseries that are mine!
Take pity on them; see, they are only children,
Friendless except for you. Promise me this,
Great Prince, and give me your hand in token of it.

[CREON *clasps his right hand*]
Children:
I could say much, if you could understand me,
But as it is, I have only this prayer for you:
Live where you can, be as happy as you can—
Happier, please God, than God has made your father!

CREON:
Enough. You have wept enough. Now go within.

OEDIPUS:
I must; but it is hard.

CREON:
Time eases all things.

OEDIPUS:
But you must promise—

CREON:
Say what you desire.

OEDIPUS:
Send me from Thebes!

CREON:
God grant that I may!

OEDIPUS:
But since God hates me . . .

CREON:
No, he will grant your wish.

OEDIPUS:
You promise?

CREON:
I can not speak beyond my knowledge.

OEDIPUS:
Then lead me in.

CREON:
Come now, and leave your children.

OEDIPUS:
No! Do not take them from me!

CREON:
Think no longer
That you are in command here, but rather think
How, when you were, you served your own destruction.

[*Exeunt into the house all but the* CHORUS; *the* CHORAGOS *chants directly to the audience:*]

CHORAGOS:
Men of Thebes: look upon Oedipus.

This is the king who solved the famous riddle
And towered up, most powerful of men.
No mortal eyes but looked on him with envy,
Yet in the end ruin swept over him.

Let every man in mankind's frailty
Consider his last day; and let none
Presume on his good fortune until he find
Life, at his death, a memory without pain.

Antigone

Translated by Robert Fagles

CHARACTERS

ANTIGONE, *daughter of Oedipus and Jocasta*
ISMENE, *sister of Antigone*
A CHORUS *of old Theban citizens and their* LEADER
CREON, *king of Thebes, uncle of Antigone and Ismene*
A SENTRY
HAEMON, *son of Creon and Eurydice*
TIRESIAS, *a blind prophet*
A MESSENGER
EURYDICE, *wife of Creon*
Guards, attendants, and a boy

TIME AND SCENE: *The royal house of Thebes. It is still night, and the invading armies of Argos have just been driven from the city. Fighting on opposite sides, the sons of Oedipus, Eteocles and Polynices, have killed each other in combat. Their uncle,* CREON, *is now king of Thebes.*

[*Enter* ANTIGONE, *slipping through the central doors of the palace. She motions to her sister,* ISMENE, *who follows her cautiously toward an altar at the center of the stage.*]

ANTIGONE:

My own flesh and blood—dear sister, dear Ismene,
how many griefs our father Oedipus[1] handed down!
Do you know one, I ask you, one grief
that Zeus will not perfect for the two of us
while we still live and breathe? There's nothing,
no pain—our lives are pain—no private shame,

Antigone. The dating of Sophocles' plays, as noted in the headnote to *Oedipus Rex*, is an imprecise art. Scholars believe that *Antigone* dates from the late 440s B.C.E., some years before the production of *Oedipus Rex* in the 430s. However, because the events in *Antigone* follow after those in *Oedipus Rex, Antigone* follows *Oedipus Rex* in these pages, an exception to the usual chronological order of selections in this anthology.

On close examination, *Antigone* is more than a dramatization of the individual fighting the state. As in Aeschylus's *Oresteia,* two value systems clash in *Antigone:* one, a blood code that places preeminent value on honoring the family; the other, a legal code of the newly formed *polis,* or city-state, that gives the interests of the city preference over those of the family or individual. Tragedy comes about, however, not solely from these apparently irreconcilable oppositions but also from the unwillingness of either side to negotiate a compromise, if in fact such a compromise is possible.

Antigone, whose name means "born to oppose," remains fixed in her position throughout the play and experiences none of the dramatic crises visited on Creon. Yet Creon's inflexibility leads to

---

[1] **Oedipus:** Son of Laïos, king of Thebes, and Jocasta; through a series of events foretold in an oracle, Oedipus unknowingly kills his father, Laius, marries his mother, Jocasta, and replaces his father as king. Learning the truth, as Ismene explains, he blinds himself and goes into exile at Colonus. Jocasta's brother is Creon (Kreon). Notice that while the names and spellings of many of the names in this translation differ from those in the Fitts and Fitzgerald translation of *Oedipus Rex,* the characters are the same. (See pronunciation guide, on page 898.)

no public disgrace, nothing I haven't seen
in your griefs and mine. And now this:
emergency decree, they say, the Commander
has just declared for all of Thebes.
What, haven't you heard? Don't you see?
The doom reserved for enemies
marches on the ones we love the most.

ISMENE:

Not I, I haven't heard a word, Antigone.
Nothing of loved ones,
no joy or pain has come my way, not since
the two of us were robbed of our two brothers,
both gone in a day, a double blow—
not since the armies of Argos vanished,
just this very night. I know nothing more,
whether our luck's improved or ruin's still to come.

ANTIGONE:

I thought so. That's why I brought you out here,
past the gates, so you could hear in private.

ISMENE:

What's the matter? Trouble, clearly . . .
you sound so dark, so grim.

ANTIGONE:

Why not? Our own brothers' burial!
Hasn't Creon graced one with all the rites,
disgraced the other? Eteocles, they say,
has been given full military honors,
rightly so—Creon's laid him in the earth
and he goes with glory down among the dead.

---

the fall of his entire household. A dynamic character, Creon finally realizes that he has been too rigid; at this moment of recognition, or *anagnorisis,* Creon relents, but his reversal of fortune has already gone too far in its course for him to save those who are dear to him. Because Creon, more than Antigone, goes through the classic phases of the tragic plot—pride, reversal, and recognition—it is worth considering whether he, rather than Antigone, is the tragic hero of the play. Knowing that they could have prevented the deaths that befall their loved ones, both Antigone and Creon attain a considerable dignity that they would have lacked if they had been presented as mere playthings of the gods. In both characters Sophocles may be subtly questioning the consequences of secularization and the falling away from the gods that was taking place in his society. The greatest *hubris,* or tragic pride, may be to think that human beings can somehow sway the moral order of things.

A note on the translation: This is the fine translation of *Antigone* by Robert Fagles. The notes are the editors'.

But the body of Polynices, who died miserably—
why, a city-wide proclamation, rumor has it,
forbids anyone to bury him, even mourn him.
He's to be left unwept, unburied, a lovely treasure
for birds that scan the field and feast to their heart's content.

Such, I hear, is the martial law our good Creon
lays down for you and me—yes, me, I tell you—
and he's coming here to alert the uninformed
in no uncertain terms,
and he won't treat the matter lightly. Whoever
disobeys in the least will die, his doom is sealed:
stoning to death inside the city walls!

There you have it. You'll soon show what you are,
worth your breeding, Ismene, or a coward—
for all your royal blood.

ISMENE:

My poor sister, if things have come to this,
who am I to make or mend them, tell me,
what good am I to you?

ANTIGONE:

Decide.
Will you share the labor, share the work?

ISMENE:

What work, what's the risk? What do you mean?

ANTIGONE:

Raising her hands.

Will you lift up his body with these bare hands
and lower it with me?

ISMENE:

What? You'd bury him—
when a law forbids the city?

ANTIGONE:

Yes!
He is my brother and—deny it as you will—
your brother too.
No one will ever convict me for a traitor.

ISMENE:

So desperate, and Creon has expressly—

ANTIGONE:

No,
he has no right to keep me from my own.

ISMENE:

Oh my sister, think—

think how our own father died, hated,[2]
his reputation in ruins, driven on
by the crimes he brought to light himself
to gouge out his eyes with his own hands—
then mother . . . his mother and wife, both in one,
mutilating her life in the twisted noose—
and last, our two brothers dead in a single day,[3]
both shedding their own blood, poor suffering boys,
battling out their common destiny hand-to-hand.

Now look at the two of us, left so alone . . .
think what a death we'll die, the worst of all
if we violate the laws and override
the fixed decree of the throne, its power—
we must be sensible. Remember we are women,
we're not born to contend with men. Then too,
we're underlings, ruled by much stronger hands,
so we must submit in this, and things still worse.

I, for one, I'll beg the dead to forgive me—
I'm forced, I have no choice—I must obey
the ones who stand in power. Why rush to extremes?
It's madness, madness.

ANTIGONE:

I won't insist,
no, even if you should have a change of heart,
I'd never welcome you in the labor, not with me.
So, do as you like, whatever suits you best—
I will bury him myself.
And even if I die in the act, that death will be a glory.
I will lie with the one I love and loved by him—
an outrage sacred to the gods! I have longer
to please the dead than please the living here:
in the kingdom down below I'll lie forever.
Do as you like, dishonor the laws
the gods hold in honor.

ISMENE:

I'd do them no dishonor . . .

---

[2] **our own father . . . hated:** In *Oedipus at Colonus,* which Sophocles wrote after *Antigone,* Oedipus dies a mysterious but honorable death, unlike the one described here. The sisters are with Oedipus, their father, during his banishment from Thebes and witness his suffering and sorrow.

[3] **two brothers . . . day:** As the Chorus alludes to in succeeding lines, Polynices and Eteocles, the sons of Oedipus, fought over rightful rule of Thebes. Exiled by his brother, Polynices assembled an army under the leadership of seven commanders and attacked the city; in the ensuing battle, the brothers ended up killing each other.

but defy the city? I have no strength for that.

ANTIGONE:

You have your excuses. I am on my way,
I'll raise a mound for him, for my dear brother.

ISMENE:

Oh Antigone, you're so rash—I'm so afraid for you!

ANTIGONE:

Don't fear for me. Set your own life in order.

ISMENE:

Then don't, at least, blurt this out to anyone.
Keep it a secret. I'll join you in that, I promise.

ANTIGONE:

Dear god, shout it from the rooftops. I'll hate you
all the more for silence—tell the world!

ISMENE:

So fiery—and it ought to chill your heart.

ANTIGONE:

I know I please where I must please the most.

ISMENE:

Yes, if you can, but you're in love with impossibility.

ANTIGONE:

Very well then, once my strength gives out
I will be done at last.

ISMENE:

You're wrong from the start,
you're off on a hopeless quest.

ANTIGONE:

If you say so, you will make me hate you,
and the hatred of the dead, by all rights,
will haunt you night and day.
But leave me to my own absurdity, leave me
to suffer this—dreadful thing. I will suffer
nothing as great as death without glory.

[*Exit to the side.*]

ISMENE:

Then go if you must, but rest assured,
wild, irrational as you are, my sister,
you are truly dear to the ones who love you.

[*Withdrawing to the palace.*
Enter a CHORUS, *the old citizens of Thebes, chanting as the sun begins to rise.*]

CHORUS:

Glory!—great beam of the sun, brightest of all
that ever rose on the seven gates of Thebes,
you burn through night at last!
Great eye of the golden day,

mounting the Dirce's banks[4] you throw him back—
the enemy out of Argos, the white shield, the man of bronze—
he's flying headlong now
the bridle of fate stampeding him with pain!

And he had driven against our borders,
launched by the warring claims of Polynices—
like an eagle screaming, winging havoc
over the land, wings of armor
shielded white as snow,
a huge army massing,
crested helmets bristling for assault.

He hovered above our roofs, his vast maw gaping
closing down around our seven gates,
his spears thirsting for the kill
but now he's gone, look,
before he could glut his jaws with Theban blood
or the god of fire put our crown of towers to the torch.
He grappled the Dragon[5] none can master—Thebes—
the clang of our arms like thunder at his back!

Zeus hates with a vengeance all bravado,
the mighty boasts of men. He watched them
coming on in a rising flood, the pride
of their golden armor ringing shrill—
and brandishing his lightning
blasted the fighter[6] just at the goal,
rushing to shout his triumph from our walls.

Down from the heights he crashed, pounding down on the earth!
And a moment ago, blazing torch in hand—
mad for attack, ecstatic
he breathed his rage, the storm
of his fury hurling at our heads!
But now his high hopes have laid him low
and down the enemy ranks the iron god of war

[4] **Dirce's banks:** Dirce is a river to the west of Thebes.

[5] **the Dragon:** The people of Thebes were said to have descended from the teeth of a dragon slain by Cadmus, the city's legendary founder.

[6] **the fighter:** Capaneus, the fiercest commander of "the Seven" fighting against Thebes, who boasted that even Zeus could not stop him from toppling the city; as punishment for his vain outburst, Zeus struck him dead with a lightning bolt as he scaled the wall of the fortified city.

deals his rewards, his stunning blows—Ares[7]
rapture of battle, our right arm in the crisis.

Seven captains marshaled at seven gates
seven against their equals, gave
their brazen trophies up to Zeus,
god of the breaking rout of battle,
all but two: those blood brothers,
one father, one mother—matched in rage,
spears matched for the twin conquest—
clashed and won the common prize of death.

But now for Victory! Glorious in the morning,
joy in her eyes to meet our joy
she is winging down to Thebes,
our fleets of chariots wheeling in her wake—
Now let us win oblivion from the wars,
thronging the temples of the gods
in singing, dancing choirs through the night!
Lord Dionysus,[8] god of the dance
that shakes the land of Thebes, now lead the way!

[*Enter* CREON *from the palace, attended by his guard.*]
But look, the king of the realm is coming,
Creon, the new man for the new day,
whatever the gods are sending now . . .
what new plan will he launch?
Why this, this special session?
Why this sudden call to the old men
summoned at one command?

CREON:
My countrymen,
the ship of state is safe. The gods who rocked her,
after a long, merciless pounding in the storm,
have righted her once more.
Out of the whole city
I have called you here alone. Well I know,
first, your undeviating respect
for the throne and royal power of King Laius.
Next, while Oedipus steered the land of Thebes,
and even after he died, your loyalty was unshakable,
you still stood by their children. Now then,

[7] **Ares:** The god of war and a protector of Thebes.

[8] **Dionysus:** The god of wine and revels; his mother, Semele, hailed from Thebes.

since the two sons are dead—two blows of fate
in the same day, cut down by each other's hands,
both killers, both brothers stained with blood—
as I am next in kin[9] to the dead,
I now possess the throne and all its powers.

Of course you cannot know a man completely,
his character, his principles, sense of judgment,
not till he's shown his colors, ruling the people,
making laws. Experience, there's the test.
As I see it, whoever assumes the task,
the awesome task of setting the city's course,
and refuses to adopt the soundest policies
but fearing someone, keeps his lips locked tight,
he's utterly worthless. So I rate him now,
I always have. And whoever places a friend
above the good of his own country, he is nothing:
I have no use for him. Zeus my witness,
Zeus who sees all things, always—
I could never stand by silent, watching destruction
march against our city, putting safety to rout,
nor could I ever make that man a friend of mine
who menaces our country. Remember this:
our country *is* our safety.
Only while she voyages true on course
can we establish friendships, truer than blood itself.
Such are my standards. They make our city great.

Closely akin to them I have proclaimed,
just now, the following decree to our people
concerning the two sons of Oedipus.
Eteocles, who died fighting for Thebes,
excelling all in arms: he shall be buried,
crowned with a hero's honors, the cups we pour[10]
to soak the earth and reach the famous dead.

But as for his blood brother, Polynices,
who returned from exile, home to his father-city
and the gods of his race, consumed with one desire—
to burn them roof to roots—who thirsted to drink

[9] **I am . . . kin:** Creon was a first cousin of Laius, the king of Thebes whom Oedipus murdered, and he is the brother of Jocasta, the mother of Eteocles and Polynices.

[10] **the cups we pour:** Libations, the ritual offering of liquids to the dead. (See also line 479.)

his kinsmen's blood and sell the rest to slavery:
that man—a proclamation has forbidden the city
to dignify him with burial, mourn him at all.
No, he must be left unburied, his corpse
carrion for the birds and dogs to tear,
an obscenity for the citizens to behold!

These are my principles. Never at my hands
will the traitor be honored above the patriot.
But whoever proves his loyalty to the state—
I'll prize that man in death as well as life.

LEADER:
If this is your pleasure, Creon, treating
our city's enemy and our friend this way . . .
The power is yours, I suppose, to enforce it
with the laws, both for the dead and all of us,
the living.

CREON:
Follow my orders closely then,
be on your guard.

LEADER:
We're too old.
Lay that burden on younger shoulders.

CREON:
No, no,
I don't mean the body—I've posted guards already.

LEADER:
What commands for us then? What other service?

CREON:
See that you never side with those who break my orders.

LEADER:
Never. Only a fool could be in love with death.

CREON:
Death is the price—you're right. But all too often
the mere hope of money has ruined many men.

[*A* SENTRY *enters from the side.*]

SENTRY:
My lord,
I can't say I'm winded from running, or set out
with any spring in my legs either—no sir,
I was lost in thought, and it made me stop, often,
dead in my tracks, wheeling, turning back,
and all the time a voice inside me muttering,
"Idiot, why? You're going straight to your death."

Then muttering, "Stopped again, poor fool?
If somebody gets the news to Creon first,
what's to save your neck?"
And so,
mulling it over, on I trudged, dragging my feet,
you can make a short road take forever . . .
but at last, look, common sense won out,
I'm here, and I'm all yours,
and even though I come empty-handed
I'll tell my story just the same, because
I've come with a good grip on one hope,
what will come will come, whatever fate—

CREON:
Come to the point!
What's wrong—why so afraid?

SENTRY:
First, myself, I've got to tell you,
I didn't do it, didn't see who did—
Be fair, don't take it out on me.

CREON:
You're playing it safe, soldier,
barricading yourself from any trouble.
It's obvious, you've something strange to tell.

SENTRY:
Dangerous too, and danger makes you delay
for all you're worth.

CREON:
Out with it—then dismiss!

SENTRY:
All right, here it comes. The body—
someone's just buried it, then run off . . .
sprinkled some dry dust on the flesh,
given it proper rites.

CREON:
What?
What man alive would dare—

SENTRY:
I've no idea, I swear it.
There was no mark of a spade, no pickaxe there,
no earth turned up, the ground packed hard and dry,
unbroken, no tracks, no wheelruts, nothing,
the workman left no trace. Just at sunup
the first watch of the day points it out—
it was a wonder! We were stunned . . .
a terrific burden too, for all of us, listen:

you can't see the corpse, not that it's buried,
really, just a light cover of road-dust on it,
as if someone meant to lay the dead to rest
and keep from getting cursed.
Not a sign in sight that dogs or wild beasts
had worried the body, even torn the skin.

But what came next! Rough talk flew thick and fast,
guard grilling guard — we'd have come to blows
at last, nothing to stop it; each man for himself
and each the culprit, no one caught red-handed,
all of us pleading ignorance, dodging the charges,
ready to take up red-hot iron in our fists,
go through fire, swear oaths to the gods —
"I didn't do it, I had no hand in it either,
not in the plotting, not the work itself!"

Finally, after all this wrangling came to nothing,
one man spoke out and made us stare at the ground,
hanging our heads in fear. No way to counter him,
no way to take his advice and come through
safe and sound. Here's what he said:
"Look, we've got to report the facts to Creon,
we can't keep this hidden." Well, that won out,
and the lot fell to me, condemned me,
unlucky as ever, I got the prize. So here I am,
against my will and yours too, well I know —
no one wants the man who brings bad news.

LEADER:

My king,
ever since he began I've been debating in my mind,
could this possibly be the work of the gods?

CREON:

Stop —
before you make me choke with anger — the gods!
You, you're senile, must you be insane?
You say — why it's intolerable — say the gods
could have the slightest concern for that corpse?
Tell me, was it for meritorious service
they proceeded to bury him, prized him so? The hero
who came to burn their temples ringed with pillars,
their golden treasures — scorch their hallowed earth
and fling their laws to the winds.
Exactly when did you last see the gods
celebrating traitors? Inconceivable!

No, from the first there were certain citizens
who could hardly stand the spirit of my regime,
grumbling against me in the dark, heads together,
tossing wildly, never keeping their necks beneath
the yoke, loyally submitting to their king.
These are the instigators, I'm convinced—
they've perverted my own guard, bribed them
to do their work.
Money! Nothing worse
in our lives, so current, rampant, so corrupting.
Money—you demolish cities, root men from their homes,
you train and twist good minds and set them on
to the most atrocious schemes. No limit,
you make them adept at every kind of outrage,
every godless crime—money!
Everyone—
the whole crew bribed to commit this crime,
they've made one thing sure at least:
sooner or later they will pay the price.

[*Wheeling on the* SENTRY.]

You—
I swear to Zeus as I still believe in Zeus,
if you don't find the man who buried that corpse,
the very man, and produce him before my eyes,
simple death won't be enough for you,
not till we string you up alive
and wring the immorality out of you.
Then you can steal the rest of your days,
better informed about where to make a killing.
You'll have learned, at last, it doesn't pay
to itch for rewards from every hand that beckons.
Filthy profits wreck most men, you'll see—
they'll never save your life.

SENTRY:
Please,
may I say a word or two, or just turn and go?

CREON:
Can't you tell? Everything you say offends me.

SENTRY:
Where does it hurt you, in the ears or in the heart?

CREON:
And who are you to pinpoint my displeasure?

SENTRY:
The culprit grates on your feelings,

I just annoy your ears.

CREON:

Still talking?
You talk too much! A born nuisance—

SENTRY:

Maybe so,
but I never did this thing, so help me!

CREON:

Yes you did—
what's more, you squandered your life for silver!

SENTRY:

Oh it's terrible when the one who does the judging
judges things all wrong.

CREON:

Well now,
you just be clever about your judgments—
if you fail to produce the criminals for me,
you'll swear your dirty money brought you pain.

[*Turning sharply, reentering the palace.*]

SENTRY:

I hope he's found. Best thing by far.
But caught or not, that's in the lap of fortune:
I'll never come back, you've seen the last of me.
I'm saved, even now, and I never thought,
I never hoped—
dear gods, I owe you all my thanks!

[*Rushing out.*]

CHORUS:

Numberless wonders
terrible wonders walk the world but none the match for man—
that great wonder crossing the heaving gray sea,
driven on by the blasts of winter
on through breakers crashing left and right,
holds his steady course
and the oldest of the gods he wears away—
the Earth, the immortal, the inexhaustible—
as his plows go back and forth, year in, year out
with the breed of stallions turning up the furrows.

And the blithe, lightheaded race of birds he snares,
the tribes of savage beasts, the life that swarms the depths—
with one fling of his nets
woven and coiled tight, he takes them all,
man the skilled, the brilliant!

He conquers all, taming with his techniques
the prey that roams the cliffs and wild lairs,
training the stallion, clamping the yoke across
    his shaggy neck, and the tireless mountain bull.
And speech and thought, quick as the wind
and the mood and mind for law that rules the city—
    all these he has taught himself
and shelter from the arrows of the frost
when there's rough lodging under the cold clear sky
and the shafts of lashing rain—
        ready, resourceful man!
            Never without resources
never an impasse as he marches on the future—
only Death, from Death alone he will find no rescue
but from desperate plagues he has plotted his escapes.

Man the master, ingenious past all measure
past all dreams, the skills within his grasp—
    he forges on, now to destruction
now again to greatness. When he weaves in
the laws of the land, and the justice of the gods
that binds his oaths together
        he and his city rise high—
            but the city casts out
that man who weds himself to inhumanity
thanks to reckless daring. Never share my hearth
never think my thoughts, whoever does such things.

[*Enter* ANTIGONE *from the side, accompanied by the* SENTRY.]

Here is a dark sign from the gods—
what to make of this? I know her,
how can I deny it? That young girl's Antigone!
Wretched, child of a wretched father,
Oedipus. Look, is it possible?
They bring you in like a prisoner—
why? did you break the king's laws?
Did they take you in some act of mad defiance?

SENTRY:

She's the one, she did it single-handed—
we caught her burying the body. Where's Creon?

[*Enter* CREON *from the palace.*]

LEADER:

Back again, just in time when you need him.

CREON:

In time for what? What is it?

SENTRY:

My king,
there's nothing you can swear you'll never do—
second thoughts make liars of us all.
I could have sworn I wouldn't hurry back
(what with your threats, the buffeting I just took),
but a stroke of luck beyond our wildest hopes,
what a joy, there's nothing like it. So,
back I've come, breaking my oath, who cares?
I'm bringing in our prisoner—this young girl—
we took her giving the dead the last rites.
But no casting lots this time; this is *my* luck,
my prize, no one else's.

Now, my lord,
here she is. Take her, question her,
cross-examine her to your heart's content.
But set me free, it's only right—
I'm rid of this dreadful business once for all.

CREON:

Prisoner! Her? You took her—where, doing what?

SENTRY:

Burying the man. That's the whole story.

CREON:

What?
You mean what you say, you're telling me the truth?

SENTRY:

She's the one. With my own eyes I saw her
bury the body, just what you've forbidden.
There. Is that plain and clear?

CREON:

What did you see? Did you catch her in the act?

SENTRY:

Here's what happened. We went back to our post,
those threats of yours breathing down our necks—
we brushed the corpse clean of the dust that covered it,
stripped it bare . . . it was slimy, going soft,
and we took to high ground, backs to the wind
so the stink of him couldn't hit us;
jostling, baiting each other to keep awake,
shouting back and forth—no napping on the job,
not this time. And so the hours dragged by
until the sun stood dead above our heads,
a huge white ball in the noon sky, beating,
blazing down, and then it happened—
suddenly, a whirlwind!
Twisting a great dust-storm up from the earth,

a black plague of the heavens, filling the plain,
ripping the leaves off every tree in sight,
choking the air and sky. We squinted hard
and took our whipping from the gods.

And after the storm passed — it seemed endless —
there, we saw the girl!
And she cried out a sharp, piercing cry,
like a bird come back to an empty nest,
peering into its bed, and all the babies gone . . .
Just so, when she sees the corpse bare
she bursts into a long, shattering wail
and calls down withering curses on the heads
of all who did the work. And she scoops up dry dust,
handfuls, quickly, and lifting a fine bronze urn,
lifting it high and pouring, she crowns the dead
with three full libations.
Soon as we saw
we rushed her, closed on the kill like hunters,
and she, she didn't flinch. We interrogated her,
charging her with offenses past and present —
she stood up to it all, denied nothing. I tell you,
it made me ache and laugh in the same breath.
It's pure joy to escape the worst yourself,
it hurts a man to bring down his friends.
But all that, I'm afraid, means less to me
than my own skin. That's the way I'm made.

CREON:

[*Wheeling on* ANTIGONE.]

You,
with your eyes fixed on the ground — speak up.
Do you deny you did this, yes or no?

ANTIGONE:

I did it. I don't deny a thing.

CREON:

[*To the* SENTRY.]

You, get out, wherever you please —
you're clear of a very heavy charge.

[*He leaves;* CREON *turns back to* ANTIGONE.]

You, tell me briefly, no long speeches —
were you aware a decree had forbidden this?

ANTIGONE:

Well aware. How could I avoid it? It was public.

CREON:

And still you had the gall to break this law?

ANTIGONE:

Of course I did. It wasn't Zeus, not in the least,
who made this proclamation — not to me.
Nor did that Justice, dwelling with the gods
beneath the earth, ordain such laws for men.
Nor did I think your edict had such force
that you, a mere mortal, could override the gods,
the great unwritten, unshakable traditions.
They are alive, not just today or yesterday:
they live forever, from the first of time,
and no one knows when they first saw the light.

These laws — I was not about to break them,
not out of fear of some man's wounded pride,
and face the retribution of the gods.
Die I must, I've known it all my life —
how could I keep from knowing? — even without
your death-sentence ringing in my ears.
And if I am to die before my time
I consider that a gain. Who on earth,
alive in the midst of so much grief as I,
could fail to find his death a rich reward?
So for me, at least, to meet this doom of yours
is precious little pain. But if I had allowed
my own mother's son to rot, an unburied corpse —
that would have been an agony! This is nothing.
And if my present actions strike you as foolish,
let's just say I've been accused of folly
by a fool.

LEADER:

Like father like daughter,
passionate, wild . . .
she hasn't learned to bend before adversity.

CREON:

No? Believe me, the stiffest stubborn wills
fall the hardest; the toughest iron,
tempered strong in the white-hot fire,
you'll see it crack and shatter first of all.
And I've known spirited horses you can break
with a light bit — proud, rebellious horses.
There's no room for pride, not in a slave,
not with the lord and master standing by.

This girl was an old hand at insolence
when she overrode the edicts we made public.

But once she'd done it—the insolence,
twice over—to glory in it, laughing,
mocking us to our face with what she'd done.
I am not the man, not now: she is the man
if this victory goes to her and she goes free.

Never! Sister's child or closer in blood
than all my family clustered at my altar
worshiping Guardian Zeus—she'll never escape,
she and her blood sister, the most barbaric death.
Yes, I accuse her sister of an equal part
in scheming this, this burial.

[*To his attendants.*]

Bring her here!
I just saw her inside, hysterical, gone to pieces.
It never fails: the mind convicts itself
in advance, when scoundrels are up to no good,
plotting in the dark. Oh but I hate it more
when a traitor, caught red-handed,
tries to glorify his crimes.

ANTIGONE:

Creon, what more do you want
than my arrest and execution?

CREON:

Nothing. Then I have it all.

ANTIGONE:

Then why delay? Your moralizing repels me,
every word you say—pray god it always will.
So naturally all I say repels you too.

Enough.
Give me glory! What greater glory could I win
than to give my own brother decent burial?
These citizens here would all agree,

[*To the* CHORUS.]

they'd praise me too
if their lips weren't locked in fear.

[*Pointing to* CREON.]

Lucky tyrants—the perquisites of power!
Ruthless power to do and say whatever pleases *them.*

CREON:

You alone, of all the people in Thebes,
see things that way.

ANTIGONE:

They see it just that way

but defer to you and keep their tongues in leash.

CREON:
And you, aren't you ashamed to differ so from them?
So disloyal!

ANTIGONE:
Not ashamed for a moment,
not to honor my brother, my own flesh and blood.

CREON:
Wasn't Eteocles a brother too—cut down, facing him?

ANTIGONE:
Brother, yes, by the same mother, the same father.

CREON:
Then how can you render his enemy such honors,
such impieties in his eyes?

ANTIGONE:
He'll never testify to that,
Eteocles dead and buried.

CREON:
He will—
if you honor the traitor just as much as him.

ANTIGONE:
But it was his brother, not some slave that died—

CREON:
Ravaging our country!—
but Eteocles died fighting in our behalf.

ANTIGONE:
No matter—Death longs for the same rites for all.

CREON:
Never the same for the patriot and the traitor.

ANTIGONE:
Who, Creon, who on earth can say the ones below
don't find this pure and uncorrupt?

CREON:
Never. Once an enemy, never a friend,
not even after death.

ANTIGONE:
I was born to join in love, not hate—
that is my nature.

CREON:
Go down below and love,
if love you must—love the dead! While I'm alive,
no woman is going to lord it over me.

[*Enter* ISMENE *from the palace, under guard.*]

CHORUS:
Look,

Ismene's coming, weeping a sister's tears,
loving sister, under a cloud . . .
her face is flushed, her cheeks streaming.
Sorrow puts her lovely radiance in the dark.

CREON:

You—
in my own house, you viper, slinking undetected,
sucking my life-blood! I never knew
I was breeding twin disasters, the two of you
rising up against my throne. Come, tell me,
will you confess your part in the crime or not?
Answer me. Swear to me.

ISMENE:

I did it, yes—
if only she consents—I share the guilt,
the consequences too.

ANTIGONE:

No,
Justice will never suffer that—not you,
you were unwilling. I never brought you in.

ISMENE:

But now you face such dangers . . . I'm not ashamed
to sail through trouble with you,
make your troubles mine.

ANTIGONE:

Who did the work?
Let the dead and the god of death bear witness!
I have no love for a friend who loves in words alone.

ISMENE:

Oh no, my sister, don't reject me, please,
let me die beside you, consecrating
the dead together.

ANTIGONE:

Never share my dying,
don't lay claim to what you never touched.
My death will be enough.

ISMENE:

What do I care for life, cut off from you?

ANTIGONE:

Ask Creon. Your concern is all for him.

ISMENE:

Why abuse me so? It doesn't help you now.

ANTIGONE:

You're right—
if I mock you, I get no pleasure from it,
only pain.

ISMENE:

Tell me, dear one,
what can I do to help you, even now?

ANTIGONE:

Save yourself. I don't grudge you your survival.

ISMENE:

Oh no, no, denied my portion in your death?

ANTIGONE:

You chose to live, I chose to die.

ISMENE:

Not, at least,
without every kind of caution I could voice.

ANTIGONE:

Your wisdom appealed to one world—mine, another.

ISMENE:

But look, we're both guilty, both condemned to death.

ANTIGONE:

Courage! Live your life. I gave myself to death,
long ago, so I might serve the dead.

CREON:

They're both mad, I tell you, the two of them.
One's just shown it, the other's been that way
since she was born.

ISMENE:

True, my king,
the sense we were born with cannot last forever . . .
commit cruelty on a person long enough
and the mind begins to go.

CREON:

Yours did,
when you chose to commit your crimes with her.

ISMENE:

How can I live alone, without her?

CREON:

Her?
Don't even mention her—she no longer exists.

ISMENE:

What? You'd kill your own son's bride?

CREON:

Absolutely:
there are other fields for him to plow.

ISMENE:

Perhaps,
but never as true, as close a bond as theirs.

CREON:

A worthless woman for my son? It repels me.

ISMENE:

Dearest Haemon, your father wrongs you so!

CREON:

Enough, enough—you and your talk of marriage!

ISMENE:

Creon—you're really going to rob your son of Antigone?

CREON:

Death will do it for me—break their marriage off.

LEADER:

So, it's settled then? Antigone must die?

CREON:

Settled, yes—we both know that.

[*To the guards.*]

Stop wasting time. Take them in.
From now on they'll act like women.
Tie them up, no more running loose;
even the bravest will cut and run,
once they see Death coming for their lives.

[*The guards escort* ANTIGONE *and* ISMENE *into the palace.* CREON *remains while the old citizens form their* CHORUS.]

CHORUS:

Blest, they are the truly blest who all their lives
have never tasted devastation. For others, once
the gods have rocked a house to its foundations
the ruin will never cease, cresting on and on
from one generation on throughout the race—
like a great mounting tide
driven on by savage northern gales,
surging over the dead black depths
roiling up from the bottom dark heaves of sand
and the headlands, taking the storm's onslaught full-force,
roar, and the low moaning
echoes on and on
and now
as in ancient times I see the sorrows of the house,
the living heirs of the old ancestral kings,
piling on the sorrows of the dead
and one generation cannot free the next—
some god will bring them crashing down,
the race finds no release.
And now the light, the hope
springing up from the late last root
in the house of Oedipus, that hope's cut down in turn
by the long, bloody knife swung by the gods of death
by a senseless word

by fury at the heart.
Zeus,
yours is the power, Zeus, what man on earth
can override it, who can hold it back?
Power that neither Sleep, the all-ensnaring
no, nor the tireless months of heaven
can ever overmaster—young through all time,
mighty lord of power, you hold fast
the dazzling crystal mansions of Olympus.
And throughout the future, late and soon
as through the past, your law prevails:
no towering form of greatness
enters into the lives of mortals
free and clear of ruin.
True,
our dreams, our high hopes voyaging far and wide
bring sheer delight to many, to many others
delusion, blithe, mindless lusts
and the fraud steals on one slowly . . . unaware
till he trips and puts his foot into the fire.
He was a wise old man who coined
the famous saying: "Sooner or later
foul is fair, fair is foul
to the man the gods will ruin"—
He goes his way for a moment only
free of blinding ruin.

[*Enter* HAEMON *from the palace.*]
Here's Haemon now, the last of all your sons.[11]
Does he come in tears for his bride,
his doomed bride, Antigone—
bitter at being cheated of their marriage?

CREON:
We'll soon know, better than seers could tell us.

[*Turning to* HAEMON.]
Son, you've heard the final verdict on your bride?
Are you coming now, raving against your father?
Or do you love me, no matter what I do?

HAEMON:
Father, I'm your *son* . . . you in your wisdom
set my bearings for me—I obey you.

[11] **Haemon . . . sons:** Haemon was the youngest son of Creon and Eurydice; their first son was Megareus. (See note 34.)

No marriage could ever mean more to me than you,
whatever good direction you may offer.

CREON:

Fine, Haemon.
That's how you ought to feel within your heart,
subordinate to your father's will in every way.
That's what a man prays for: to produce good sons—
households full of them, dutiful and attentive,
so they can pay his enemy back with interest
and match the respect their father shows his friend.
But the man who rears a brood of useless children,
what has he brought into the world, I ask you?
Nothing but trouble for himself, and mockery
from his enemies laughing in his face.
Oh Haemon,
never lose your sense of judgment over a woman.
The warmth, the rush of pleasure, it all goes cold
in your arms, I warn you . . . a worthless woman
in your house, a misery in your bed.
What wound cuts deeper than a loved one
turned against you? Spit her out,
like a mortal enemy—let the girl go.
Let her find a husband down among the dead.
Imagine it: I caught her in naked rebellion,
the traitor, the only one in the whole city.
I'm not about to prove myself a liar,
not to my people, no, I'm going to kill her!
That's right—so let her cry for mercy, sing her hymns
to Zeus who defends all bonds of kindred blood.
Why, if I bring up my own kin to be rebels,
think what I'd suffer from the world at large.
Show me the man who rules his household well:
I'll show you someone fit to rule the state.
That good man, my son,
I have every confidence he and he alone
can give commands and take them too. Staunch
in the storm of spears he'll stand his ground,
a loyal, unflinching comrade at your side.

But whoever steps out of line, violates the laws
or presumes to hand out orders to his superiors,
he'll win no praise from me. But that man
the city places in authority, his orders
must be obeyed, large and small,
right and wrong.
Anarchy—

show me a greater crime in all the earth!
She, she destroys cities, rips up houses,
breaks the ranks of spearmen into headlong rout.
But the ones who last it out, the great mass of them
owe their lives to discipline. Therefore
we must defend the men who live by law,
never let some woman triumph over us.
Better to fall from power, if fall we must,
at the hands of a man — never be rated
inferior to a woman, never.

LEADER:

To us,
unless old age has robbed us of our wits,
you seem to say what you have to say with sense.

HAEMON:

Father, only the gods endow a man with reason,
the finest of all their gifts, a treasure.
Far be it from me — I haven't the skill,
and certainly no desire, to tell you when,
if ever, you make a slip in speech . . . though
someone else might have a good suggestion.

Of course it's not for you,
in the normal run of things, to watch
whatever men say or do, or find to criticize.
The man in the street, you know, dreads your glance,
he'd never say anything displeasing to your face.
But it's for me to catch the murmurs in the dark,
the way the city mourns for this young girl.
"No woman," they say, "ever deserved death less,
and such a brutal death for such a glorious action.
She, with her own dear brother lying in his blood —
she couldn't bear to leave him dead, unburied,
food for the wild dogs or wheeling vultures.
Death? She deserves a glowing crown of gold!"
So they say, and the rumor spreads in secret,
darkly . . .

I rejoice in your success, father —
nothing more precious to me in the world.
What medal of honor brighter to his children
than a father's growing glory? Or a child's
to his proud father? Now don't, please,
be quite so single-minded, self-involved,
or assume the world is wrong and you are right.
Whoever thinks that he alone possesses intelligence,

the gift of eloquence, he and no one else,
and character too . . . such men, I tell you,
spread them open—you will find them empty.
No,
it's no disgrace for a man, even a wise man,
to learn many things and not to be too rigid.
You've seen trees by a raging winter torrent,
how many sway with the flood and salvage every twig,
but not the stubborn—they're ripped out, roots and all
Bend or break. The same when a man is sailing:
haul your sheets too taut, never give an inch,
you'll capsize, and go the rest of the voyage
keel up and the rowing-benches under.

Oh give way. Relax your anger—change!
I'm young, I know, but let me offer this:
it would be best by far, I admit,
if a man were born infallible, right by nature.
If not—and things don't often go that way,
it's best to learn from those with good advice.

LEADER:
You'd do well, my lord, if he's speaking to the point,
to learn from him,

[*Turning to* HAEMON.]

and you, my boy, from him.
You both are talking sense.

CREON:
So,
men our age, we're to be lectured, are we?—
schooled by a boy his age?

HAEMON:
Only in what is right. But if I seem young,
look less to my years and more to what I do.

CREON:
Do? Is admiring rebels an achievement?

HAEMON:
I'd never suggest that you admire treason.

CREON:
Oh?—
isn't that just the sickness that's attacked her?

HAEMON:
The whole city of Thebes denies it, to a man.

CREON:
And is Thebes about to tell me how to rule?

HAEMON:
Now, you see? Who's talking like a child?
CREON:
Am I to rule this land for others — or myself?
HAEMON:
It's no city at all, owned by one man alone.
CREON:
What? The city *is* the king — that's the law!
HAEMON:
What a splendid king you'd make of a desert island —
you and you alone.
CREON:

[*To the* CHORUS.]
This boy, I do believe,
is fighting on her side, the woman's side.
HAEMON:
If you are a woman, yes —
my concern is all for you.
CREON:
Why, you degenerate — bandying accusations,
threatening me with justice, your own father!
HAEMON:
I see my father offending justice — wrong.
CREON:
Wrong?
To protect my royal rights?
HAEMON:
Protect your rights?
When you trample down the honors of the gods?
CREON:
You, you soul of corruption, rotten through —
woman's accomplice!
HAEMON:
That may be,
but you'll never find me accomplice to a criminal.
CREON:
That's what *she* is,
and every word you say is a blatant appeal for her —
HAEMON:
And you, and me, and the gods beneath the earth.
CREON:
You will never marry her, not while she's alive.
HAEMON:
Then she'll die . . . but her death will kill another.

CREON:

What, brazen threats? You go too far!

HAEMON:

What threat?
Combating your empty, mindless judgments with a word?

CREON:

You'll suffer for your sermons, you and your empty wisdom!

HAEMON:

If you weren't my father, I'd say you were insane.

CREON:

Don't flatter me with Father—you woman's slave!

HAEMON:

You really expect to fling abuse at me
and not receive the same?

CREON:

Is that so!
Now, by heaven, I promise you, you'll pay—
taunting, insulting me! Bring her out,
that hateful—she'll die now, here,
in front of his eyes, beside her groom!

HAEMON:

No, no, she will never die beside me—
don't delude yourself. And you will never
see me, never set eyes on my face again.
Rage your heart out, rage with friends
who can stand the sight of you.

[*Rushing out.*]

LEADER:

Gone, my king, in a burst of anger.
A temper young as his . . . hurt him once,
he may do something violent.

CREON:

Let him do—
dream up something desperate, past all human limit!
Good riddance. Rest assured,
he'll never save those two young girls from death.

LEADER:

Both of them, you really intend to kill them both?

CREON:

No, not her, the one whose hands are clean—
you're quite right.

LEADER:

But Antigone—
what sort of death do you have in mind for her?

CREON:
I'll take her down some wild, desolate path
never trod by men, and wall her up alive
in a rocky vault, and set out short rations,
just a gesture of piety
to keep the entire city free of defilement.[12]
There let her pray to the one god she worships:
Death[13]—who knows?—may just reprieve her from death.
Or she may learn at last, better late than never,
what a waste of breath it is to worship Death.

[*Exit to the palace.*]

CHORUS:
Love, never conquered in battle
Love the plunderer laying waste the rich!
Love standing the night-watch
guarding a girl's soft cheek,
you range the seas, the shepherds' steadings off in the wilds—
not even the deathless gods can flee your onset,
nothing human born for a day—
whoever feels your grip is driven mad.
Love!—
you wrench the minds of the righteous into outrage,
swerve them to their ruin—you have ignited this,
this kindred strife, father and son at war
and Love alone the victor—
warm glance of the bride triumphant, burning with desire!
Throned in power, side-by-side with the mighty laws!
Irresistible Aphrodite,[14] never conquered—
Love, you mock us for your sport.

[ANTIGONE *is brought from the palace under guard.*]
But now, even I'd rebel against the king,
I'd break all bounds when I see this—
I fill with tears, can't hold them back,
not any more . . . I see Antigone make her way
to the bridal vault where all are laid to rest.

ANTIGONE:
Look at me, men of my fatherland,
setting out on the last road

---

[12] **defilement:** In line 43, Antigone noted that the punishment for disobedience was death by stoning. Creon may hope here not only to save the citizens from participating in Antigone's death but to free his own hands from shedding the blood of kin as well.

[13] **god . . . Death:** The god Hades, king of the underworld.

[14] **Aphrodite:** The goddess of love.

looking into the last light of day
the last I'll ever see . . .
the god of death who puts us all to bed
takes me down to the banks of Acheron[15] alive—
denied my part in the wedding-songs,
no wedding-song in the dusk has crowned my marriage—
I go to wed the lord of the dark waters.

CHORUS:

Not crowned with glory, crowned with a dirge,
you leave for the deep pit of the dead.
No withering illness laid you low,
no strokes of the sword—a law to yourself,
alone, no mortal like you, ever, you go down
to the halls of Death alive and breathing.

ANTIGONE:

But think of Niobe[16]—well I know her story—
think what a living death she died,
Tantalus' daughter, stranger queen from the east:
there on the mountain heights, growing stone
binding as ivy, slowly walled her round
and the rains will never cease, the legends say
the snows will never leave her . . .
wasting away, under her brows the tears
showering down her breasting ridge and slopes—
a rocky death like hers puts me to sleep.

CHORUS:

But she was a god, born of gods,
and we are only mortals born to die.
And yet, of course, it's a great thing
for a dying girl to hear, just hear
she shares a destiny equal to the gods,
during life and later, once she's dead.

ANTIGONE:

O you mock me!
Why, in the name of all my fathers' gods
why can't you wait till I am gone—
must you abuse me to my face?
O my city, all your fine rich sons!

---

[15] **Acheron:** A river of sorrow in the underworld.

[16] **Niobe:** The daughter of the Titan Tantalus, Niobe was a Phrygian princess who married Amphion, an early king of Thebes. Niobe earned the wrath of the goddess Leto by boasting that Leto's two children—Apollo and Artemis—did not compare with Niobe's own fourteen children. To avenge the insult, Leto had Apollo and Artemis murder all of Niobe's children, and Niobe was turned into a weeping rock, shedding perpetual tears.

And you, you springs of the Dirce,
holy grove of Thebes where the chariots gather,
you at least, you'll bear me witness, look,
unmourned by friends and forced by such crude laws
I go to my rockbound prison, strange new tomb—
always a stranger, O dear god,
I have no home on earth and none below,
not with the living, not with the breathless dead.

CHORUS:

You went too far, the last limits of daring—
smashing against the high throne of Justice!
Your life's in ruins, child—I wonder . . .
do you pay for your father's terrible ordeal?

ANTIGONE:

There—at last you've touched it, the worst pain
the worst anguish! Raking up the grief for father
three times over, for all the doom
that's struck us down, the brilliant house of Laius.
O mother, your marriage-bed
the coiling horrors, the coupling there—
you with your own son, my father—doomstruck mother!
Such, such were my parents, and I their wretched child.
I go to them now, cursed, unwed, to share their home—
I am a stranger! O dear brother, doomed
in your marriage[17]—your marriage murders mine,
your dying drags me down to death alive!

[*Enter* CREON.]

CHORUS:

Reverence asks some reverence in return—
but attacks on power never go unchecked,
not by the man who holds the reins of power.
Your own blind will, your passion has destroyed you.

ANTIGONE:

No one to weep for me, my friends,
no wedding-song—they take me away
in all my pain . . . the road lies open, waiting.
Never again, the law forbids me to see
the sacred eye of day. I am agony!
No tears for the destiny that's mine,
no loved one mourns my death.

[17] **your marriage:** Polynices married the daughter of Adrastus, the king of Argos, in order to ensure Argive military support in the war against Thebes.

CREON:

Can't you see?
If a man could wail his own dirge *before* he dies,
he'd never finish.

[*To the guards.*]

Take her away, quickly!
Wall her up in the tomb, you have your orders.
Abandon her there, alone, and let her choose—
death or a buried life with a good roof for shelter.
As for myself, my hands are clean. This young girl—
dead or alive, she will be stripped of her rights,
her stranger's rights, here in the world above.

ANTIGONE:

O tomb, my bridal-bed—my house, my prison
cut in the hollow rock, my everlasting watch!
I'll soon be there, soon embrace my own,
the great growing family of our dead
Persephone[18] has received among her ghosts.

I,

the last of them all, the most reviled by far,
go down before my destined time's run out.
But still I go, cherishing one good hope:
my arrival may be dear to father,
dear to you, my mother,
dear to you, my loving brother, Eteocles—
When you died I washed you with my hands,
I dressed you all, I poured the cups
across your tombs. But now, Polynices,
because I laid your body out as well,
this, this is my reward. Nevertheless
I honored you—the decent will admit it—
well and wisely too.

Never, I tell you.
if I had been the mother of children
or if my husband died, exposed and rotting—
I'd never have taken this ordeal upon myself,
never defied our people's will. What law,
you ask, do I satisfy with what I say?
A husband dead, there might have been another.
A child by another too, if I had lost the first.
But mother and father both lost in the halls of Death,

[18] **Persephone:** Queen of the underworld.

no brother could ever spring to light again.
For this law alone I held you first in honor.
For this, Creon, the king, judges me a criminal
guilty of dreadful outrage, my dear brother!
And now he leads me off, a captive in his hands,
with no part in the bridal-song, the bridal-bed,
denied all joy of marriage, raising children—
deserted so by loved ones, struck by fate,
I descend alive to the caverns of the dead.

What law of the mighty gods have I transgressed?
Why look to the heavens any more, tormented as I am?
Whom to call, what comrades now? Just think,
my reverence only brands me for irreverence!
Very well: if this is the pleasure of the gods,
once I suffer I will know that I was wrong.
But if these men are wrong, let them suffer
nothing worse than they mete out to me—
these masters of injustice!

LEADER:
Still the same rough winds, the wild passion
raging through the girl.

CREON:
[*To the guards.*]
Take her away.
You're wasting time—you'll pay for it too.

ANTIGONE:
Oh god, the voice of death. It's come, it's here.

CREON:
True. Not a word of hope—your doom is sealed.

ANTIGONE:
Land of Thebes, city of all my fathers—
O you gods, the first gods of the race![19]
They drag me away, now, no more delay.
Look on me, you noble sons of Thebes—
the last of a great line of kings,
I alone, see what I suffer now
at the hands of what breed of men—
all for reverence, my reverence for the gods!

[*She leaves under guard: the* CHORUS *gathers.*]

---

[19] **Land . . . race:** The house of Thebes charted its lineage to the gods Aphrodite and Ares, whose daughter Harmonia married Cadmus, the legendary founder of Thebes.

CHORUS:

Danaë,[20] Danaë—
even she endured a fate like yours,
in all her lovely strength she traded
the light of day for the bolted brazen vault—
buried within her tomb, her bridal-chamber,
wed to the yoke and broken.
But she was of glorious birth
my child, my child
and treasured the seed of Zeus within her womb,
the cloudburst streaming gold!
The power of fate is a wonder,
dark, terrible wonder—
neither wealth nor armies
towered walls nor ships
black hulls lashed by the salt
can save us from that force.

The yoke tamed him too
young Lycurgus[21] flaming in anger
king of Edonia, all for his mad taunts
Dionysus clamped him down, encased
in the chain-mail of rock
and there his rage
his terrible flowering rage burst—
sobbing, dying away . . . at last that madman
came to know his god—
the power he mocked, the power
he hunted in all his frenzy
trying to stamp out
the women strong with the god—
the torch, the raving sacred cries—
enraging the Muses who adore the flute.

And far north where the Black Rocks
cut the sea in half
and murderous straits
split the coast of Thrace
a forbidding city stands

[20] **Danaë:** The daughter of Acrisius, an Argive king; because it was foretold that he would die at the hand of Danaë's son, Acrisius ordered Danaë to be shut up in a tower. Here Zeus comes to her in the form of a shower of golden rain, after which she gives birth to Perseus, who eventually kills Acrisius.

[21] **Lycurgus:** King of Thrace (or Edonia), who was imprisoned by the god Dionysus for trying to thwart the spread of the Dionysian sect.

where once, hard by the walls
the savage Ares thrilled to watch
a king's new queen, a Fury rearing in rage
against his two royal sons—
her bloody hands, her dagger-shuttle
stabbing out their eyes—cursed, blinding wounds—
their eyes blind sockets screaming for revenge![22]

They wailed in agony, cries echoing cries
the princes doomed at birth . . .
and their mother doomed to chains,
walled off in a tomb of stone—
but she traced her own birth back
to a proud Athenian line and the high gods
and off in caverns half the world away,
born of the wild North Wind
she sprang on her father's gales,
racing stallions up the leaping cliffs—
child of the heavens. But even on her the Fates
the gray everlasting Fates rode hard
my child, my child.

[*Enter* TIRESIAS, *the blind prophet, led by a boy.*]

TIRESIAS:
Lords of Thebes,
I and the boy have come together,
hand in hand. Two see with the eyes of one . . .
so the blind must go, with a guide to lead the way.

CREON:
What is it, old Tiresias? What news now?

TIRESIAS:
I will teach you. And you obey the seer.

CREON:
I will,
I've never wavered from your advice before.

TIRESIAS:
And so you kept the city straight on course.

CREON:
I owe you a great deal, I swear to that.

TIRESIAS:
Then reflect, my son: you are poised,
once more, on the razor-edge of fate.

[22] **And far north . . . revenge:** Lines 1066 to 1077 refer to the story of Phineas, a king of Thrace who supposedly divorced and imprisoned Cleopatra, daughter of Boreas (the north wind) and Athenian princess Orithyea. Phineas's new wife, Eidothea, blinded Cleopatra's two sons as Ares, the god of war, looked on.

CREON:
What is it? I shudder to hear you.
TIRESIAS:
You will learn
when you listen to the warnings of my craft.
As I sat on the ancient seat of augury,
in the sanctuary where every bird I know
will hover at my hands—suddenly I heard it,
a strange voice in the wingbeats, unintelligible,
barbaric, a mad scream! Talons flashing, ripping,
they were killing each other—that much I knew—
the murderous fury whirring in those wings
made that much clear!
I was afraid,
I turned quickly, tested the burnt-sacrifice,
ignited the altar at all points—but no fire,
the god in the fire never blazed.
Not from those offerings . . . over the embers
slid a heavy ooze from the long thighbones,
smoking, sputtering out, and the bladder
puffed and burst—spraying gall into the air—
and the fat wrapping the bones slithered off
and left them glistening white. No fire!
The rites failed that might have blazed the future
with a sign. So I learned from the boy here:
he is my guide, as I am guide to others.
And it's you—
your high resolve that sets this plague on Thebes.
The public altars and sacred hearths are fouled,
one and all, by the birds and dogs with carrion
torn from the corpse, the doomstruck son of Oedipus!
And so the gods are deaf to our prayers, they spurn
the offerings in our hands, the flame of holy flesh.
No birds cry out an omen clear and true—
they're gorged with the murdered victim's blood and fat.
Take these things to heart, my son, I warn you.
All men make mistakes, it is only human.
But once the wrong is done, a man
can turn his back on folly, misfortune too,
if he tries to make amends, however low he's fallen,
and stops his bullnecked ways. Stubbornness
brands you for stupidity—pride is a crime.
No, yield to the dead!
Never stab the fighter when he's down.
Where's the glory, killing the dead twice over?

I mean you well. I give you sound advice.
It's best to learn from a good adviser
when he speaks for your own good:
it's pure gain.

CREON:

Old man — all of you! So,
you shoot your arrows at my head like archers at the target —
I even have *him* loosed on me, this fortune-teller.
Oh his ilk has tried to sell me short
and ship me off for years. Well,
drive your bargains, traffic — much as you like —
in the gold of India, silver-gold of Sardis.[23]
You'll never bury that body in the grave,
not even if Zeus's eagles rip the corpse
and wing their rotten pickings off to the throne of god!
Never, not even in fear of such defilement
will I tolerate his burial, that traitor.
Well I know, we can't defile the gods —
no mortal has the power.
No,
reverend old Tiresias, all men fall,
it's only human, but the wisest fall obscenely
when they glorify obscene advice with rhetoric —
all for their own gain.

TIRESIAS:

Oh god, is there a man alive
who knows, who actually believes . . .

CREON:

What now?
What earth-shattering truth are you about to utter?

TIRESIAS:

. . . just how much a sense of judgment, wisdom
is the greatest gift we have?

CREON:

Just as much, I'd say,
as a twisted mind is the worst affliction going.

TIRESIAS:

You are the one who's sick, Creon, sick to death.

CREON:

I am in no mood to trade insults with a seer.

TIRESIAS:

You have already, calling my prophecies a lie.

---

[23] **Sardis:** A place in Asia Minor near the site where electrum, a mixture of silver and gold, was found.

CREON:

Why not?
You and the whole breed of seers are mad for money!

TIRESIAS:

And the whole race of tyrants lusts to rake it in.

CREON:

This slander of yours—
are you aware you're speaking to the king?

TIRESIAS:

Well aware. Who helped you save the city?

CREON:

You—
you have your skills, old seer, but you lust for injustice!

TIRESIAS:

You will drive me to utter the dreadful secret in my heart.

CREON:

Spit it out! Just don't speak it out for profit.

TIRESIAS:

Profit? No, not a bit of profit, not for you.

CREON:

Know full well, you'll never buy off my resolve.

TIRESIAS:

Then know this too, learn this by heart!
The chariot of the sun will not race through
so many circuits more, before you have surrendered
one born of your own loins, your own flesh and blood,
a corpse for corpses given in return, since you have thrust
to the world below a child sprung for the world above,
ruthlessly lodged a living soul within the grave—
then you've robbed the gods below the earth,
keeping a dead body here in the bright air,
unburied, unsung, unhallowed by the rites.

You, you have no business with the dead,
nor do the gods above—this is violence
you have forced upon the heavens.
And so the avengers, the dark destroyers late
but true to the mark, now lie in wait for you,
the Furies[24] sent by the gods and the god of death
to strike you down with the pains that you perfected!

[24] **Furies:** Female spirits who avenge crimes against blood kin, such as patricide or matricide.

There. Reflect on that, tell me I've been bribed.
The day comes soon, no long test of time, not now,
that wakes the wails for men and women in your halls.
Great hatred rises against you—
cities in tumult, all whose mutilated sons
the dogs have graced with burial, or the wild beasts
or a wheeling crow that wings the ungodly stench of carrion
back to each city, each warrior's hearth and home.

These arrows for your heart! Since you've raked me
I loose them like an archer in my anger,
arrows deadly true. You'll never escape
their burning, searing force.

[*Motioning to his escort.*]
Come, boy, take me home.
So he can vent his rage on younger men,
and learn to keep a gentler tongue in his head
and better sense than what he carries now.

[*Exit to the side.*]

LEADER:
The old man's gone, my king—
terrible prophecies. Well I know,
since the hair on this old head went gray,
he's never lied to Thebes.

CREON:
I know it myself—I'm shaken, torn.
It's a dreadful thing to yield . . . but resist now?
Lay my pride bare to the blows of ruin?
That's dreadful too.

LEADER:
But good advice,
Creon, take it now, you must.

CREON:
What should I do? Tell me . . . I'll obey.

LEADER:
Go! Free the girl from the rocky vault
and raise a mound for the body you exposed.

CREON:
That's your advice? You think I should give in?

LEADER:
Yes, my king, quickly. Disasters sent by the gods
cut short our follies in a flash.

CREON:
Oh it's hard,

giving up the heart's desire . . . but I will do it—
no more fighting a losing battle with necessity.

LEADER:

Do it now, go, don't leave it to others.

CREON:

Now—I'm on my way! Come, each of you,
take up axes, make for the high ground,
over there, quickly! I and my better judgment
have come round to this—I shackled her,
I'll set her free myself. I am afraid . . .
it's best to keep the established laws
to the very day we die.

[*Rushing out, followed by his entourage. The* CHORUS *clusters around the altar.*]

CHORUS:

God of a hundred names!
Great Dionysus—
Son and glory of Semele![25] Pride of Thebes—
Child of Zeus whose thunder rocks the clouds—
Lord of the famous lands of evening—
King of the Mysteries!
King of Eleusis,[26] Demeter's plain
her breasting hills that welcome in the world—
Great Dionysus!
Bacchus, living in Thebes
the mother-city of all your frenzied women[27]—
Bacchus
living along the Ismenus'[28] rippling waters
standing over the field sown with the Dragon's teeth!

You—we have seen you through the flaring smoky fires,
your torches blazing over the twin peaks
where nymphs of the hallowed cave climb onward
fired with you, your sacred rage—
we have seen you at Castalia's running spring[29]

---

[25] **Semele:** The mother of Bacchus (Dionysus) who died when Zeus visited her in the form of a thunderbolt; her as-yet-unborn child lived.

[26] **Eleusis:** On the coast of Attica, Eleusis was the site of mystery rites for Persephone, goddess of the underworld, and her mother, Demeter, goddess of grain and harvest.

[27] **frenzied women:** The Bacchae, or female worshippers of Bacchus (Dionysus).

[28] **Ismenus:** A river at Thebes.

[29] **Castalia's running spring:** A spring and pool on Mt. Parnassus, the waters of which were said to bring poetic inspiration.

and down from the heights of Nysa[30] crowned with ivy
the greening shore rioting vines and grapes
down you come in your storm of wild women
ecstatic, mystic cries—
Dionysus—
down to watch and ward the roads of Thebes!
First of all cities, Thebes you honor first
you and your mother, bride of the lightning—
come, Dionysus! now your people lie
in the iron grip of plague,
come in your racing, healing stride
down Parnassus'[31] slopes
or across the moaning straits.
Lord of the dancing—
dance, dance the constellations breathing fire!
Great master of the voices of the night!
Child of Zeus, God's offspring, come, come forth!
Lord, king, dance with your nymphs, swirling, raving
arm-in-arm in frenzy through the night
they dance you, Iacchus°— Dionysus
Dance, Dionysus
giver of all good things!

[*Enter a* MESSENGER *from the side.*]

MESSENGER:

Neighbors,
friends of the house of Cadmus and the kings,
there's not a thing in this mortal life of ours
I'd praise or blame as settled once for all.
Fortune lifts and Fortune fells the lucky
and unlucky every day. No prophet on earth
can tell a man his fate. Take Creon:
there was a man to rouse your envy once,
as I see it. He saved the realm from enemies,
taking power, he alone, the lord of the fatherland,
he set us true on course—he flourished like a tree
with the noble line of sons he bred and reared . . .
and now it's lost, all gone.
Believe me,
when a man has squandered his true joys,
he's good as dead, I tell you, a living corpse.

[30] **Nysa:** A mountain sacred to Dionysus.

[31] **Parnassus:** A mountain near Delphi whose two peaks were sacred to Apollo and Dionysus; the Corcyian Cave, located on the mountain, was sacred to Pan and the woodland nymphs.

Pile up riches in your house, as much as you like—
live like a king with a huge show of pomp,
but if real delight is missing from the lot,
I wouldn't give you a wisp of smoke for it,
not compared with joy.

LEADER:

What now?
What new grief do you bring the house of kings?

MESSENGER:

Dead, dead—and the living are guilty of their death!

LEADER:

Who's the murderer? Who is dead? Tell us.

MESSENGER:

Haemon's gone, his blood spilled by the very hand—

LEADER:

His father's or his own?

MESSENGER:

His own . . .
raging mad with his father for the death—

LEADER:

Oh great seer,
you saw it all, you brought your word to birth!

MESSENGER:

Those are the facts. Deal with them as you will.

[*As he turns to go,* EURYDICE *enters from the palace.*]

LEADER:

Look, Eurydice. Poor woman, Creon's wife,
so close at hand. By chance perhaps,
unless she's heard the news about her son.

EURYDICE:

My countrymen,
all of you—I caught the sound of your words
as I was leaving to do my part,
to appeal to queen Athena[32] with my prayers.
I was just loosing the bolts, opening the doors,
when a voice filled with sorrow, family sorrow,
struck my ears, and I fell back, terrified,
into the women's arms—everything went black.
Tell me the news, again, whatever it is . . .
sorrow and I are hardly strangers.
I can bear the worst.

[32] **Athena (Athene):** Goddess of war, wisdom, and arts and crafts.

MESSENGER:

I—dear lady,
I'll speak as an eye-witness. I was there.
And I won't pass over one word of the truth.
Why should I try to soothe you with a story,
only to prove a liar in a moment?
Truth is always best.
So,
I escorted your lord, I guided him
to the edge of the plain where the body lay,
Polynices, torn by the dogs and still unmourned.
And saying a prayer to Hecate of the Crossroads,
Pluto[33] too, to hold their anger and be kind,
we washed the dead in a bath of holy water
and plucking some fresh branches, gathering . . .
what was left of him, we burned them all together
and raised a high mound of native earth, and then
we turned and made for that rocky vault of hers,
the hollow, empty bed of the bride of Death.

And far off, one of us heard a voice,
a long wail rising, echoing
out of that unhallowed wedding-chamber,
he ran to alert the master and Creon pressed on,
closer—the strange, inscrutable cry came sharper,
throbbing around him now, and he let loose
a cry of his own, enough to wrench the heart,
"Oh god, am I the prophet now? going down
the darkest road I've ever gone? My son—
it's *his* dear voice, he greets me! Go, men,
closer, quickly! Go through the gap,
the rocks are dragged back—
right to the tomb's very mouth—and look,
see if it's Haemon's voice I think I hear,
or the gods have robbed me of my senses."

The king was shattered. We took his orders,
went and searched, and there in the deepest,
dark recesses of the tomb we found her . . .
hanged by the neck in a fine linen noose,
strangled in her veils—and the boy,

[33] **Hecate . . . Pluto:** Hecate, the queen of the underworld, is associated with night and burial; in her guise as Trivia, she is associated with crossroads. Pluto is another name for Hades, god of the underworld.

his arms flung around her waist,
clinging to her, wailing for his bride,
dead and down below, for his father's crimes
and the bed of his marriage blighted by misfortune.
When Creon saw him, he gave a deep sob,
he ran in, shouting, crying out to him,
"Oh my child—what have you done? what seized you,
what insanity? what disaster drove you mad?
Come out, my son! I beg you on my knees!"
But the boy gave him a wild burning glance,
spat in his face, not a word in reply,
he drew his sword—his father rushed out,
running as Haemon lunged and missed!—
and then, doomed, desperate with himself,
suddenly leaning his full weight on the blade,
he buried it in his body, halfway to the hilt.
And still in his senses, pouring his arms around her,
he embraced the girl and breathing hard,
released a quick rush of blood,
bright red on her cheek glistening white.
And there he lies, body enfolding body . . .
he has won his bride at last, poor boy,
not here but in the houses of the dead.

Creon shows the world that of all the ills
afflicting men the worst is lack of judgment.

[EURYDICE *turns and reenters the palace.*]

LEADER:

What do you make of that? The lady's gone,
without a word, good or bad.

MESSENGER:

I'm alarmed too
but here's my hope—faced with her son's death
she finds it unbecoming to mourn in public.
Inside, under her roof, she'll set her women
to the task and wail the sorrow of the house.
She's too discreet. She won't do something rash.

LEADER:

I'm not so sure. To me, at least,
a long heavy silence promises danger,
just as much as a lot of empty outcries.

MESSENGER:

We'll see if she's holding something back,
hiding some passion in her heart.

I'm going in. You may be right—who knows?
Even too much silence has its dangers.

[*Exit to the palace. Enter* CREON *from the side, escorted by attendants carrying* HAEMON*'s body on a bier.*]

LEADER:

The king himself! Coming toward us,
look, holding the boy's head in his hands.
Clear, damning proof, if it's right to say so—
proof of his own madness, no one else's,
no, his own blind wrongs.

CREON:

Ohhh,
so senseless, so insane . . . my crimes,
my stubborn, deadly—
Look at us, the killer, the killed,
father and son, the same blood—the misery!
My plans, my mad fanatic heart,
my son, cut off so young!
Ai, dead, lost to the world,
not through your stupidity, no, my own.

LEADER:

Too late,
too late, you see what justice means.

CREON:

Oh I've learned
through blood and tears! Then, it was then,
when the god came down and struck me—a great weight
shattering, driving me down that wild savage path,
ruining, trampling down my joy. Oh the agony,
the heartbreaking agonies of our lives.

[*Enter the* MESSENGER *from the palace.*]

MESSENGER:

Master,
what a hoard of grief you have, and you'll have more.
The grief that lies to hand you've brought yourself—

[*Pointing to* HAEMON*'s body.*]

the rest, in the house, you'll see it all too soon.

CREON:

What now? What's worse than this?

MESSENGER:

The queen is dead.
The mother of this dead boy . . . mother to the end—
poor thing, her wounds are fresh.

CREON:

No, no,
harbor of Death, so choked, so hard to cleanse!—
why me? why are you killing me?
Herald of pain, more words, more grief?
I died once, you kill me again and again!
What's the report, boy . . . some news for me?
My wife dead? O dear god!
Slaughter heaped on slaughter?

[*The doors open; the body of* EURYDICE *is brought out on her bier.*]

MESSENGER:

See for yourself:
now they bring her body from the palace.

CREON:

Oh, no,
another, a second loss to break the heart.
What next, what fate still waits for me?
I just held my son in my arms and now,
look, a new corpse rising before my eyes—
wretched, helpless mother—O my son!

MESSENGER:

She stabbed herself at the altar,
then her eyes went dark, after she'd raised
a cry for the noble fate of Megareus,[34] the hero
killed in the first assault, then for Haemon,
then with her dying breath she called down
torments on your head—you killed her sons.

CREON:

Oh the dread,
I shudder with dread! Why not kill me too?—
run me through with a good sharp sword?
Oh god, the misery, anguish—
I, I'm churning with it, going under.

MESSENGER:

Yes, and the dead, the woman lying there,
piles the guilt of all their deaths on you.

CREON:

How did she end her life, what bloody stroke?

MESSENGER:

She drove home to the heart with her own hand,
once she learned her son was dead . . . that agony.

[34] **Megareus:** Haemon's brother; Megareus committed suicide in order to fulfill a prophecy and save Thebes from destruction.

CREON:

And the guilt is all mine—
can never be fixed on another man,
no escape for me. I killed you,
I, god help me, I admit it all!

[*To his attendants.*]

Take me away, quickly, out of sight.
I don't even exist—I'm no one. Nothing.

LEADER:

Good advice, if there's any good in suffering.
Quickest is best when troubles block the way.

CREON:

[*Kneeling in prayer.*]

Come, let it come!—that best of fates for me
that brings the final day, best fate of all.
Oh quickly, now—
so I never have to see another sunrise.

LEADER:

That will come when it comes;
we must deal with all that lies before us.
The future rests with the ones who tend the future.

CREON:

That prayer—I poured my heart into that prayer!

LEADER:

No more prayers now. For mortal men
there is no escape from the doom we must endure.

CREON:

Take me away, I beg you, out of sight.
A rash, indiscriminate fool!
I murdered you, my son, against my will—
you too, my wife . . .
Wailing wreck of a man,
whom to look to? where to lean for support?

[*Desperately turning from* HAEMON *to* EURYDICE *on their biers.*]

Whatever I touch goes wrong—once more
a crushing fate's come down upon my head!

[*The* MESSENGER *and attendants lead* CREON *into the palace.*]

CHORUS:

Wisdom is by far the greatest part of joy,
and reverence toward the gods must be safeguarded.
The mighty words of the proud are paid in full
with mighty blows of fate, and at long last
those blows will teach us wisdom.

[*The old citizens exit to the side.*]

EURIPIDES
C. 480–406 B.C.E.

Euripides, Aeschylus, and Sophocles make up the triumvirate of the great Greek tragedians of the sixth and fifth centuries B.C.E. Of the three, Euripides was the most unconventional and consequently the least esteemed and most satirized in his own lifetime. But Greek playgoers venerated him after his death, and twenty-first-century audiences find his work eerily modern. His plays often shake themselves free of the formal conventions observed by Aeschylus and Sophocles; they are sometimes violent and shocking in the actions they depict; and they frequently concern themselves with human and divine aberration and irrationality. They feature fiery dramatic exchanges between opposing characters; they sharply question received ideas concerning war and justice, gods, and temporal rulers. Their endings are often tantalizingly ambiguous. More than any male Greek writer in any genre, Euripides gave great prominence to women. Whether courageous and nurturing like Hecuba in *The Trojan Women* (415 B.C.E.), witty and charming like the main character of *Helen* (412 B.C.E.), or terrifying like the title character of *Medea* (431 B.C.E.), Euripides' women are fully realized and powerful figures.

WWW For links to more information about Euripides and a quiz on *Medea,* see *World Literature Online* at bedfordstmartins .com/worldlit.

An Obscure Life. We know far fewer facts about Euripides than we do about Aeschylus and Sophocles, perhaps because he participated less in public life than they did. Aristotle does say that a Euripides was sent to negotiate a peace with Syracuse, and it may be the playwright he refers to, although Euripides by most accounts was a somber man who preferred to closet himself with his notable collection of books. Tradition has it that he was born on the day of the battle of Salamis in 480 B.C.E., but this date may represent the wishful thinking of a later biographer who wanted to render Euripides thoroughly Greek. If the plays are any indication, nationalism was scarcely Euripides' credo, and the dramatist seems to have understood well what it meant to be the underdog, the gadfly, the outsider.

A Prolific Playwright. Euripides' career was long and productive. His first play, *The Daughters of Pelias,* was produced in 455 B.C.E., and his last, *Bacchae,* in 405. Of the eighty or ninety plays he wrote, only five of his works won prizes for "best tragedy" at the Greater Dionysia[1]; in comparison, Sophocles won eighteen prizes in his lifetime. In 408 Euripides voluntarily left Athens and journeyed northeast to the court of Archelaus of Macedonia, where he was accorded great honor. Tradition has it that he died there, torn to pieces accidentally by his host's pack of hunting dogs

[1] **the Greater Dionysia:** Festivals in honor of the god Dionysus—the Lenaea in January and February and the Greater Dionysia in March and April—included dramatic performances. The best tragedy and comedy were awarded prizes by an Athenian jury.

999+1=1000

or else deliberately by a group of angry and vindictive women; a Macedonian admirer named Adaeus, however, tells a less dramatic story in the epitaph he composed for the playwright:

> Neither dogs slew thee, Euripides, nor the rage of women, . . . but death and old age, and under Macedonian Arethusa thou liest, honored by the friendship of Archelaus. Yet it is not this that I account thy tomb, but the altar of Dionysus, and the buskin-trodden stage.

Although Euripides' plays feature flying chariots drawn by dragons, as in *Medea,* strange prisoners transforming themselves into bulls, as in *Bacchae,* and gods descending from heaven to solve impasses, as in *Ion* (410), they are often described as more realistic than those of Aeschylus and Sophocles because their characters exhibit a wider and subtler range of human emotions. Among his contemporaries Euripides had the reputation of being able to make his kings, queens, gods, and warriors speak the language of everyday life, and he had a knack for making small homely details suggest a whole character. Among all the bedraggled, grieving, and thirsty prisoners of war in *The Trojan Women,* only Helen, a queen, contrives to get washwater so she can freshen up before she pleads for her life before Menelaus; at the beginning of ***Medea,*** a tutor describes how old men sit gossiping and playing at dice beside the fountain in the marketplace; in *Bacchae,* the elderly would-be orgiasts Tiresias and Cadmus wonder if it would be appropriate for them to ride up the steep mountain path to the wild Dionysian rites in their comfortable chariot. At such moments, one knows he or she is in a Euripidean universe.

muh-DEE-uh

Jason and the Argonauts. Nineteen of Euripides' plays survived. *Medea,* chosen to represent his work here, was produced in 431 B.C.E. Euripides could expect his audience to know by heart the earlier parts of the story of Medea and Jason, events he alludes to briefly throughout this play, which focuses on the violent end of Jason and Medea's mutual passion and adventures. In their earlier story, Jason's father, **Aeson**, is the rightful heir of the kingdom of Iolcus in Thessaly near the Black Sea. When Aeson's half-brother **Pelias** usurps the throne, Jason is sent away for safekeeping to be educated by the wise centaur Chiron. When he becomes a man, he journeys back to Iolcus to try to argue for his family's right to the kingdom. But Pelias has been forewarned that he will die at the hands of a young relative wearing only one shoe, and when Jason arrives, Pelias sees that he has lost a sandal in his travels. Pelias tries to strike a wily bargain by agreeing that he will certainly restore the throne to Jason's family if Jason will only prove his worthiness by performing an impossible task. He commands Jason to fetch the golden fleece of the sheep guarded by a ceaselessly vigilant dragon in Colchis, a land on the eastern coast of the Black Sea ruled by King **Aietes**. Jason sets about recruiting a company of sailor-heroes to accompany him on his quest. He gathers in his fifty-man crew heroes from other myth cycles, such as Heracles, Orpheus, the twins Castor and Polydeuces,[2] and assorted characters

EE-sun

PEE-lee-us

ee-EE-teez

[2] **Heracles . . . Polydeuces:** Heracles, a hero of ancient Greek myth who proved his strength and courage by performing the twelve labors of Heracles. Orpheus, a poet and musician of Thrace in Greek legend who can

from *The Odyssey.* Together they will come to be called the Argonauts after the *Argo,* the trim oared ship especially built for their long voyage.

> **Sophocles . . . drew men as they ought to be, and Euripides men as they are.**
> – Aristotle, philosopher, critic

When the Argonauts anchor at Colchis after many harrowing adventures, Medea, Aietes' daughter, falls instantly in love with Jason. Aietes says he will give Jason the fleece he's after if he can yoke two brazen-hoofed and fire-breathing bullocks, plow a field with them, and then sow the soil with the teeth of a dragon. From this strange seed will spring up a mighty army of men, whom the Argonauts will then have to defeat. Jason and his men are given a magical ointment by Medea that makes them invulnerable for a day and are able to accomplish Aietes' tasks. Aietes, growing alarmed at the prospect that he may actually have to give up the golden fleece, plots to ambush Jason and his men in the night, but Medea overhears the plan and quietly leads Jason to the dragon's lair and enchants the creature into sleep so Jason can easily kill it. Then the lovers gather up the golden fleece and flee Colchis with the Argonauts. Aietes soon sails after them in pursuit; to distract her father, Medea kills and dismembers her younger brother and tosses his body into the sea, piece by piece, in front of Aietes' ship.

Back in **Iolcus**, when Jason learns that his father Aeson has been killed by Pelias and that his mother has killed herself in her grief, he turns to Medea for revenge. She shows the daughters of Pelias an old ram, butchers it, and boils the meat with herbs in a cauldron. Soon a frisky lamb springs from the brew. She offers to rejuvenate Pelias in the same way, and his daughters eagerly cut him up and bring Medea his corpse; this time, however, when Medea prepares her brew, she leaves out the magical herbs and omits certain incantations, and Pelias remains quite dead. Pelias's son then drives Jason and Medea from Iolcus, and they make their way to Corinth, where Medea bears two sons. *Medea* begins just after Jason has announced his plans to put Medea aside and make a profitable marriage to Glauce, the daughter of Creon, king of Corinth.

ee-AWL-kus

Medea. Medea's story has figured into many misogynist writings over the centuries, as it would seem to confirm the belief that if a man gives woman power, especially magical powers, she will be a monster. Indeed, defenses of Medea as a hapless woman who has been seduced, torn from her homeland, and then abandoned by a condescending, heartless ingrate all seem somewhat weak, given her unconscionable acts of child-murder in Euripides' drama. It may be worthwhile to know that her character is derived from an even stronger figure, the mother-goddess of the Medes, an ancient Middle Eastern people who named themselves after her. As such a goddess, she presided over life as well as death; in her different aspects, she was the passionate lover, the tender, life-giving mother, and the death crone who leads human beings to the underworld. Perhaps some of her ancient significance is embodied in Euripides' Medea, who makes love, gives birth, and kills with equal energy.

---

charm with his music. He rescues his wife, Eurydice, from the underworld by so charming Pluto but loses her when she turns and looks back as they escape. Castor and Polydeuces, the twin brothers of Clytemnestra and Helen, are the offspring of Zeus and Leda.

Medea Kills Her Son, 340–320 B.C.E.
A detail from a Greek vase showing the shocking climactic scene of Euripides' Medea. *(Erich Lessing / Art Resource, NY)*

Similar stories of a wronged woman who kills her own children appear in many cultures, from ancient Mexico to Dravidian India to China; perhaps those stories are not so much about women's innate evil as they are reflections of the male fear of dependency on women as child-bearers and nurturers; what if Mother, that radiant source of life and warmth, were to turn bad? In these stories, the women are often depicted as outsiders to the culture, and the stories are often in part expressions of xenophobia. One insistent feature of the Medea story is its repeated contrast of West and East: Jason is a Westerner, a rational Greek, from a land where men rule; Medea is Eastern, exotic, from a magic-infused land noted for its strong women. "In all Hellas there is not one woman / Who could have done it," rages Jason in lines 1214–15, referring to Medea's string of murders, and it was probably very comforting for Greeks to think that that was so.

The play also calls attention to women's lack of rights and power under Greek marriage laws; as an alien and as a woman, Medea is especially without legal recourse, while Jason has the power to decide to dissolve their marriage and to do with their sons as he sees fit. Nevertheless, Athenian citizens probably were not leaving the theater engaged in heated discussions of women's rights. The delight and horror of the play really lie in the machinations of a powerful woman who gradually evolves a plan, executes it, and gets away with it, escaping in her sun-god grandfather's chariot while Jason is left with the bitter losses she has inflicted on him. In Greek myth Medea is not even punished in the afterlife but goes to Elysium, where she marries Achilles. Achilles, whose sense of personal honor also looms large, might be a quite fitting mate for Medea. For the Greeks, a hero was not necessarily a good, kind person, but rather a strong, larger-than-life figure whose deeds were somehow performed on a grand scale.

■ CONNECTIONS

Aeschylus, *The Oresteia*, pp. 806, 858, 1134. *The Oresteia* is usually seen as a series of plays about blood vengeance being replaced by a system of justice that utilizes courts and juries. In Aeschylus's plays, blood vengeance is insisted on by the feminine Furies and carried out by Clytemnestra — a woman — to avenge Agamemnon's sacrifice of Iphegenia, whereas the courts and juries that condone Orestes' murder of his mother are agencies of the male citizens of Athens. The contest, therefore, can be seen as one between a matriarchal system and an emerging patriarchy even though Athene administers the final decision, because Athene is a goddess not born of woman. Like Clytemnestra, Medea responds to her mistreatment by exacting blood revenge. Who represents the patriarchy in *Medea*? Is the patriarchal point of view represented as civilized? Does Euripides condemn or condone Medea's crimes?

Virgil, *The Aeneid*, p. 1811; Kalidasa, *Shakuntala* (Book 2); Alexander Pope, *The Rape of the Lock* (Book 4). *Medea* can be considered a treatment of the theme of "a woman scorned." Consider the different responses to rejection on the part of Dido in *The Aeneid*, Shakuntala in *Shakuntala*, and Belinda in *The Rape of the Lock*. How do their reactions reflect the different literary genres in which they appear and the varied cultures from which the works come?

Aristophanes, *Lysistrata*, p. 1049; Emilia Pardo Bazán, "The Revolver" (Book 5); Charlotte Perkins Gilman, "The Yellow Wallpaper" (Book 5). *Medea* and *Lysistrata* have both been called "feminist" literary works. In what ways might that term apply to the two plays? Do Euripides and Aristophanes seem to hold the same attitude toward the situation of women? Look at some later feminist works by nineteenth-century women writers, such as "The Revolver" and "The Yellow Wallpaper." Does the fact that they were written by women make their "feminism" different from that of these male authors?

■ FURTHER RESEARCH

McDermott, Emily A. *Euripides' Medea: The Incarnation of Disorder.* 1989.
Murray, Gilbert. *Euripides and His Age.* 1947.
Segal, Eric, ed. *Euripides: A Collection of Critical Essays.* 1968.
Webster, T. B. L. *The Tragedies of Euripides.* 1967.

■ **PRONUNCIATION**

Aegeus: ih-JEE-us
Aeson: EE-sun
Aietes: ee-EE-teez
Aphrodite: AF-roh-digh-tee, AF-ruh-digh-tee
Erechtheus: ih-REK-thee-us
Hecate: HEK-uh-tee
Iolcus: ee-AWL-kus, ee-OLE-kus
Medea: muh-DEE-uh, mee-DEE-uh
Pelias: PEE-lee-us
Symplegades: sim-PLEG-uh-deez

Medea

Translated by Philip Vellacott

CHARACTERS:

NURSE
TUTOR *to Medea's sons*
MEDEA
CHORUS *of Corinthian women*
CREON, *king of Corinth*
JASON
AEGEUS, *king of Athens*
MESSENGER
MEDEA'S TWO CHILDREN

SCENE: *Before Jason's house in Corinth*

NURSE:

If only they had never gone! If the Argo's hull
Never had winged out through the grey-blue jaws of rock
And on towards Colchis! If that pine on Pelion's slopes
Had never felt the axe, and fallen, to put oars

Medea. First produced in 431 B.C.E., this is one of Euripides' early heroic plays, but it is a heroic play with a difference. Instead of the usual male hero, the protagonist of *Medea* is a woman, and a woman's lack of station and her peripheral role in Greek society is magnified in Medea's case because she is also a foreigner. When she loses her one defining source of identity, her marriage to Jason, she strikes out in passionate rage and vengeance. Although the Chorus initially shows sympathy for her and her mistreatment, her revenge is so excessive that by the end she is as much abhorred as she was pitied.

In the figure of Medea Euripides exposes the wrongs against women; both Medea and the Chorus understand that her situation, though extreme, is consistent with the devaluation of women in Greek society. The destruction wrought by Medea, however, is out of proportion with her mistreatment. Euripides makes no attempt to restore balance to the situation; in the end Medea is "rescued" and taken away by the sun-god in a chariot, leaving the subject of ultimate justice in the universe open for discussion.

A note on the translation: Although less poetic than some other modern translations of *Medea,* Vellacott's version of the play is marked by a clarity and accuracy that has made it one of the most readable translations.

Into those heroes' hands, who went at Pelias' bidding
To fetch the golden fleece! Then neither would Medea,
My mistress, ever have set sail for the walled town
Of Iolcus, mad with love for Jason; nor would she,
When Pelias' daughters, at her instance, killed their father,
Have come with Jason and her children to live here
In Corinth; where, coming as an exile, she has earned
The citizens' welcome; while to Jason she is all
Obedience—and in marriage that's the saving thing,
When a wife obediently accepts her husband's will.[1]

But now her world has turned to enmity, and wounds her
Where her affection's deepest. Jason has betrayed
His own sons, and my mistress, for a royal bed,
For alliance with the king of Corinth. He has married
Glauce, Creon's daughter. Poor Medea! Scorned and shamed,
She raves, invoking every vow and solemn pledge
That Jason made her, and calls the gods as witnesses
What thanks she has received for her fidelity.
She will not eat; she lies collapsed in agony,
Dissolving the long hours in tears. Since first she heard
Of Jason's wickedness, she has not raised her eyes,
Or moved her cheek from the hard ground; and when her friends
Reason with her, she might be a rock or wave of the sea,
For all she hears—unless, maybe, she turns away
Her lovely head, speaks to herself alone, and wails
Aloud for her dear father, her own land and home,
Which she betrayed and left, to come here with this man
Who now spurns and insults her. Poor Medea! Now
She learns through pain what blessings they enjoy who are not
Uprooted from their native land. She hates her sons:
To see them is no pleasure to her. I am afraid
Some dreadful purpose is forming in her mind. She is
A frightening woman; no one who makes an enemy
Of her will carry off an easy victory.

Here come the boys, back from their running. They've no thought
Of this cruel blow that's fallen on their mother. Well,
They're young; young heads and painful thoughts don't go together.

[*Enter the* TUTOR *with* MEDEA'S TWO SONS.]

[1] **If only . . . husband's will:** The nurse alludes to the circumstances of Jason's voyage to capture the golden fleece and his early relationship with Medea.

TUTOR:
Old nurse and servant of my mistress's house, tell me,
What are you doing, standing out here by the door,
All alone, talking to yourself, harping on trouble?
Eh? What does Medea say to being left alone?

NURSE:
Old friend, tutor of Jason's sons, an honest slave
Suffers in her own heart the blow that strikes her mistress.
It was too much, I couldn't bear it; I had to come
Out here and tell my mistress's wrongs to earth and heaven.

TUTOR:
Poor woman! Has she not stopped crying yet?

NURSE:
Stopped crying?
I envy you. Her grief's just born—not yet half-grown.

TUTOR:
Poor fool—though she's my mistress and I shouldn't say it—
She had better save her tears. She has not heard the worst.

NURSE:
The worst? What now? Don't keep it from me. What has happened?

TUTOR:
Why, nothing's happened. I'm sorry I said anything.

NURSE:
Look—we're both slaves together: don't keep me in the dark.
Is it so great a secret? I can hold my tongue.

TUTOR:
I'd gone along to the benches where the old men play
At dice, next to the holy fountain of Peirene;
They thought I was not listening; and I heard one say
That Creon king of Corinth means to send these boys
Away from here—to banish them, and their mother too.
Whether the story's true I don't know. I hope not.

NURSE:
But surely Jason won't stand by and see his sons
Banished, even if he has a quarrel with their mother?

TUTOR:
Old love is ousted by new love. Jason's no friend
To this house.

NURSE:
Then we're lost, if we must add new trouble
To old, before we're rid of what we had already.

TUTOR:
But listen: it's no time to tell Medea this.
Keep quiet, say nothing about it.

NURSE:
Children, do you hear

What sort of father Jason is to you? My curse
On—No! No curse; he is my master. All the same,
He is guilty: he has betrayed those near and dear to him.

TUTOR:

What man's not guilty? It's taken you a long time to learn
That everybody loves himself more than his neighbour.
These boys are nothing to their father: he's in love.

NURSE:

Run into the house, boys. Everything will be all right.

[*The* CHILDREN *move away a little.*]

You do your best to keep them by themselves, as long
As she's in this dark mood; don't let them go to her.
I've watched her watching them, her eye like a wild bull's.
There's something that she means to do; and I know this:
She'll not relax her rage till it has found its victim.
God grant she strike her enemies and not her friends!

[MEDEA*'s voice is heard from inside the house.*]

MEDEA:

Oh, oh! What misery, what wretchedness!
What shall I do? If only I were dead!

NURSE:

There! You can hear; it is your mother
Racking her heart, racking her anger.
Quick, now, children, hurry indoors;
And don't go within sight of her,
Or anywhere near her; keep a safe distance.
Her mood is cruel, her nature dangerous,
Her will fierce and intractable.
Come on, now, in with you both at once.

[*The* CHILDREN *go in, and the* TUTOR *follows.*]

The dark cloud of her lamentations
Is just beginning. Soon, I know,
It will burst aflame as her anger rises.
Deep in passion and unrelenting,
What will she do now, stung with insult?

MEDEA [*indoors*]:

Do I not suffer? Am I not wronged? Should I not weep?
Children, your mother is hated, and you are cursed:
Death take you, with your father, and perish his whole house!

NURSE:

Oh, the pity of it! Poor Medea!
Your children—why, what have *they* to do
With their father's wickedness? Why hate *them*?
I am sick with fear for you, children, terror

Of what may happen. The mind of a queen
Is a thing to fear. A queen is used
To giving commands, not obeying them;
And her rage once roused is hard to appease.

To have learnt to live on the common level
Is better. No grand life for me,
Just peace and quiet as I grow old.
The middle way, neither great nor mean,
Is best by far, in name and practice.
To be rich and powerful brings no blessing;
Only more utterly
Is the prosperous house destroyed, when the gods are angry.

[*Enter the* CHORUS *of Corinthian women.*]

CHORUS:

I heard her voice, I heard
That unhappy woman from Colchis
Still crying, not calm yet.
Old Nurse, tell us about her.
As I stood by the door I heard her
Crying inside the palace.
And my own heart suffers too
When Jason's house is suffering;
For that is where my loyalty lies.

NURSE:

Jason's house? It no longer exists; all that is finished.
Jason is a prisoner in a princess's bed;
And Medea is in her room
Melting her life away in tears;
No word from any friend can give her comfort.

MEDEA [*still from indoors*]:

Come, flame of the sky,
Pierce through my head!
What do I gain from living any longer?
Oh, how I hate living! I want
To end my life, leave it behind, and die.

CHORUS:

O Zeus, and Earth, and Light,
Do you hear the chanted prayer
Of a wife in her anguish?

[*turning to the door and addressing* MEDEA]

What madness is this? The bed you long for —
Is it what others shrink from?
Is it death you demand?

Do not pray that prayer, Medea!
If your husband is won to a new love—
The thing is common; why let it anger you?
Zeus will plead your cause.
Check this passionate grief over your husband
Which wastes you away.

MEDEA:

Mighty Themis! Dread Artemis![2]
Do you see how I am used—
In spite of those great oaths I bound him with—
By my accursed husband?
Oh, may I see Jason and his bride
Ground to pieces in their shattered palace
For the wrong they have dared to do to me, unprovoked!
O my father, my city, you I deserted;
My brother I shamefully murdered!

NURSE:

Do you hear what my mistress is saying,
Clamouring to Themis, hearer of prayer,
And to Zeus, who is named guardian of men's oaths?
It is no trifling matter
That can end a rage like hers.

CHORUS:

I wish she would come out here and let us see her
And talk to her; if she would listen
Perhaps she would drop this fierce resentful spirit,
This passionate indignation.
As a friend I am anxious to do whatever I can.
Go, nurse, persuade her to come out to us.
Tell her we are all on her side.
Hurry, before she does harm—to those in there;
This passion of hers is an irresistible flood.

NURSE:

I will. I fear I shall not persuade her;
Still, I am glad to do my best.
Yet as soon as any of us servants
Goes near to her, or tries to speak,
She glares at us like a mad bull
Or a lioness guarding her cubs.

[*The* NURSE *goes to the door, where she turns.*]

The men of old times had little sense;

---

[2] **Themis . . . Artemis:** Themis is a goddess of justice. Artemis is the goddess of wild animals, hunting, and childbirth.

If you called them fools you wouldn't be far wrong.
They invented songs, and all the sweetness of music,
To perform at feasts, banquets, and celebrations;
But no one thought of using
Songs and stringed instruments
To banish the bitterness and pain of life.
Sorrow is the real cause
Of deaths and disasters and families destroyed.
If music could cure sorrow it would be precious;
But after a good dinner why sing songs?
When people have fed full they're happy already.

[*The* NURSE *goes in.*]

CHORUS:

I heard her sobbing and wailing,
Shouting shrill, pitiful accusations
Against her husband who has betrayed her.
She invokes Themis, daughter of Zeus,
Who witnessed those promises which drew her
Across from Asia to Hellas, setting sail at night,
Threading the salt strait,
Key and barrier to the Pontic Sea.

[MEDEA *comes out. She is not shaken with weeping, but cool and self-possessed.*]

MEDEA:

Women of Corinth, I would not have you censure me,
So I have come. Many, I know, are proud at heart,
Indoors or out; but others are ill spoken of
As supercilious, just because their ways are quiet.
There is no justice in the world's censorious eyes.
They will not wait to learn a man's true character;
Though no wrong has been done them, one look—and they hate.
Of course a stranger must conform; even a Greek
Should not annoy his fellows by crass stubbornness.
I accept my place; but this blow that has fallen on me
Was not to be expected. It has crushed my heart.
Life has no pleasure left, dear friends. I want to die.
Jason was my whole life; he knows that well. Now he
Has proved himself the most contemptible of men.

Surely, of all creatures that have life and will, we women
Are the most wretched. When, for an extravagant sum,
We have bought a husband, we must then accept him as
Possessor of our body. This is to aggravate
Wrong with worse wrong. Then the great question: will the man

We get be bad or good? For women, divorce is not
Respectable; to repel the man, not possible.

Still more, a foreign woman, coming among new laws,
New customs, needs the skill of magic, to find out
What her home could not teach her, how to treat the man
Whose bed she shares. And if in this exacting toil
We are successful, and our husband does not struggle
Under the marriage yoke, our life is enviable.
Otherwise, death is better. If a man grows tired
Of the company at home, he can go out, and find
A cure for tediousness. We wives are forced to look
To one man only. And, they tell us, we at home
Live free from danger, they go out to battle: fools!
I'd rather stand three times in the front line than bear
One child.
But the same arguments do not apply
To you and me. You have this city, your father's home,
The enjoyment of your life, and your friends' company.
I am alone; I have no city; now my husband
Insults me. I was taken as plunder from a land
At the earth's edge. I have no mother, brother, nor any
Of my own blood to turn to in this extremity.

So, I make one request. If I can find a way
To work revenge on Jason for his wrongs to me,
Say nothing. A woman's weak and timid in most matters;
The noise of war, the look of steel, makes her a coward.
But touch her right in marriage, and there's no bloodier spirit.

CHORUS:
I'll do as you ask. To punish Jason will be just.
I do not wonder that you take such wrongs to heart.

[CREON *approaches.*]
But look, Medea; I see Creon, King of Corinth;
He must have come to tell you of some new decision.

CREON:
You there, Medea, scowling rage against your husband!
I order you out of Corinth; take your sons and go
Into exile. Waste no time; I'm here to see this order
Enforced. And I'm not going back into my palace
Until I've put you safe outside my boundaries.

MEDEA:
Oh! this is the cruel end of my accursed life!

My enemies have spread full sail; no welcoming shore
Waits to receive and save me. Ill-treated as I am,
Creon, I ask: for what offence do you banish me?

CREON:
I fear you. Why wrap up the truth? I fear that you
May do my daughter some irreparable harm.
A number of things contribute to my anxiety.
You're a clever woman, skilled in many evil arts;
You're barred from Jason's bed, and that enrages you.
I learn too from reports, that you have uttered threats
Of revenge on Jason and his bride and his bride's father.
I'll act first, then, in self-defence. I'd rather make you
My enemy now, than weaken, and later pay with tears.

MEDEA:
My reputation, yet again! Many times, Creon,
It has been my curse and ruin. A man of any shrewdness
Should never have his children taught to use their brains
More than their fellows. What do you gain by being clever?
You neglect your own affairs; and all your fellow citizens
Hate you. Those who are fools will call you ignorant
And useless, when you offer them unfamiliar knowledge.
As for those thought intelligent, if people rank
You above *them*, that is a thing they will not stand.
I know this from experience: because I am clever,
They are jealous; while the rest dislike me. After all,
I am not so clever as all that.
So you, Creon,
Are afraid—of what? Some harm that I might do to you?
Don't let *me* alarm you, Creon. I'm in no position—
A woman—to wrong a king. You have done me no wrong.
You've given your daughter to the man you chose. I hate
My husband—true; but you had every right to do
As you have done. So now I bear no grudge against
Your happiness: marry your daughter to him, and good luck
To you both. But let me live in Corinth. I will bear
My wrongs in silence, yielding to superior strength.

CREON:
Your words are gentle; but my blood runs cold to think
What plots you may be nursing deep within your heart.
In fact, I trust you so much less now than before.
A woman of hot temper—and a man the same—
Is a less dangerous enemy than one quiet and clever.
So out you go, and quickly; no more arguing.
I've made my mind up; you're my enemy. No craft

Of yours will find a way of staying in my city.

MEDEA:

I kneel to you, I beseech you by the young bride, your child.

CREON:

You're wasting words; you'll never make me change my mind.

MEDEA:

I beg you! Will you cast off pity, and banish me?

CREON:

I will: I have more love for my family than for you.

MEDEA:

My home, my country! How my thoughts turn to you now!

CREON:

I love my country too—next only to my daughter.

MEDEA:

Oh, what an evil power love has in people's lives!

CREON:

That would depend on circumstances, I imagine.

MEDEA:

Great Zeus, remember who caused all this suffering!

CREON:

Go, you poor wretch, take all my troubles with you! Go!

MEDEA:

I know what trouble is; I have no need of more.

CREON:

In a moment you'll be thrown out neck and crop. Here, men!

MEDEA:

No, no, not that! But, Creon, I have one thing to ask.

CREON:

You seem inclined, Medea, to give me trouble still.

MEDEA:

I'll go. [*She still clings to him.*] It was not *that* I begged.

CREON:

Then why resist?

Why will you not get out?

MEDEA:

This one day let me stay,

To settle some plan for my exile, make provision
For my two sons, since their own father is not concerned
To help them. Show some pity: you are a father too,
You should feel kindly towards them. For myself, exile
Is nothing. I weep for them; their fate is very hard.

CREON:

I'm no tyrant by nature. My soft heart has often
Betrayed me; and I know it's foolish of me now;

Yet none the less, Medea, you shall have what you ask.
But take this warning: if tomorrow's holy sun
Finds you or them inside my boundaries, you die.
That is my solemn word. Now stay here, if you must,
This one day. You can hardly in one day accomplish
What I am afraid of.

[*Exit* CREON.]

CHORUS:

Medea, poor Medea!
Your grief touches our hearts.
A wanderer, where can you turn?
To what welcoming house?
To what protecting land?
How wild with dread and danger
Is the sea where the gods have set your course!

MEDEA:

A bad predicament all round — yes, true enough;
But don't imagine things will end as they are now.
Trials are yet to come for this new-wedded pair;
Nor shall those nearest to them get off easily.

Do you think I would ever have fawned so on this man,
Except to gain my purpose, carry out my schemes?
Not one touch, not one word: yet he — oh, what a fool!
By banishing me at once he could have thwarted me
Utterly; instead, he allows me to remain one day.
Today three of my enemies I shall strike dead:
Father and daughter, and *my* husband.
I have in mind so many paths of death for them,
I don't know which to choose. Should I set fire to the house,
And burn the bridal chamber? Or creep up to their bed
And drive a sharp knife through their guts? There is one fear:
If I am caught entering the house, or in the act,
I die, and the last laugh goes to my enemies.
The best is the direct way, which most suits my bent:
To kill by poison.

So — say they are dead: what city will receive me then?
What friend will guarantee my safety, offer land
And home as sanctuary? None. I'll wait a little.
If some strong tower of help appears, I'll carry out
This murder cunningly and quietly. But if Fate

Banishes me without resource, I will myself
Take sword in hand, harden my heart to the uttermost,
And kill them both, even if I am to die for it.

For, by Queen Hecate,[3] whom above all divinities
I venerate, my chosen accomplice, to whose presence
My central hearth is dedicated, no one of them
Shall hurt me and not suffer for it! Let me work:
In bitterness and pain they shall repent this marriage,
Repent their houses joined, repent my banishment.

Come! Lay your plan, Medea; scheme with all your skill.
On to the deadly moment that shall test your nerve!
You see now where you stand. Your father was a king,
His father was the Sun-god: you must not invite
Laughter from Jason and his new allies, the tribe
Of Sisyphus.[4] You know what you must do. Besides—

[*She turns to the* CHORUS.]

We were born women—useless for honest purposes,
But in all kinds of evil skilled practitioners.

CHORUS:

Streams of the sacred rivers flow uphill;
Tradition, order, all things are reversed:
    Deceit is *men's* device now,
    Men's oaths are gods' dishonour.
Legend will now reverse our reputation;
A time comes when the female sex is honoured;
    That old discordant slander
    Shall no more hold us subject.
Male poets of past ages, with their ballads
Of faithless women, shall go out of fashion;
    For Phoebus, Prince of Music,
Never bestowed the lyric inspiration
    Through female understanding—
    Or we'd find themes for poems,
We'd counter with our epics against man.
Oh, Time is old; and in his store of tales

[3] **Hecate:** A powerful moon goddess associated with the female trinity of maiden, mother, and crone.

[4] **Sisyphus:** An earlier king of Corinth and an ancestor of Creon.

Men figure no less famous
Or infamous than women.

So you, Medea, wild with love,
Set sail from your father's house,
Threading the Rocky Jaws of the eastern sea;
And here, living in a strange country,
Your marriage lost, your bed solitary,
You are driven beyond the borders,
An exile with no redress.
The grace of sworn oaths is gone;
Honour remains no more
In the wide Greek world, but is flown to the sky.
Where can you turn for shelter?
Your father's door is closed against you;
Another is now mistress of your husband's bed;
A new queen rules in your house.

[*Enter* JASON.]

JASON:

I have often noticed — this is not the first occasion —
What fatal results follow from ungoverned rage.
You could have stayed in Corinth, still lived in this house,
If you had quietly accepted the decisions
Of those in power. Instead, you talked like a fool; and now
You are banished. Well, your angry words don't upset *me;*
Go on as long as you like reciting Jason's crimes.
But after your abuse of the King and the princess
Think yourself lucky to be let off with banishment.
I have tried all the time to calm them down; but you
Would not give up your ridiculous tirades against
The royal family. So, you're banished. However, I
Will not desert a friend. I have carefully considered
Your problem, and come now, in spite of everything,
To see that you and the children are not sent away
With an empty purse, or unprovided. Exile brings
With it a train of difficulties. You no doubt
Hate me: but I could never bear ill-will to you.

MEDEA:

You filthy coward! — if I knew any worse name
For such unmanliness I'd use it — so, you've come!
You, my worst enemy, come to me! Oh, it's not courage,
This looking friends in the face after betraying them.

It is not even audacity; it's a disease,
The worst a man can have, pure shamelessness. However,
It is as well you came; to say what I have to say
Will ease my heart; to hear it said will make you wince.

I will begin at the beginning. When you were sent
To master the fire-breathing bulls, yoke them, and sow
The deadly furrow, then I saved your life; and that
Every Greek who sailed with you in the Argo knows.
The serpent that kept watch over the Golden Fleece,
Coiled round it fold on fold, unsleeping—it was I
Who killed it, and so lit the torch of your success.[5]
I willingly deceived my father; left my home;
With you I came to Iolcus by Mount Pelion,
Showing much love and little wisdom. There I put
King Pelias to the most horrible of deaths
By his own daughters' hands, and ruined his whole house.
And in return for this you have the wickedness
To turn me out, to get yourself another wife,
Even after I had borne you sons! If you had still
Been childless I could have pardoned you for hankering
After this new marriage. But respect for oaths has gone
To the wind. Do you, I wonder, think that the old gods
No longer rule? Or that new laws are now in force?
You must know you are guilty of perjury to me.

My poor right hand, which you so often clasped! My knees
Which you then clung to! How we are besmirched and mocked
By this man's broken vows, and all our hopes deceived!

Come, I'll ask your advice as if you were a friend.
Not that I hope for any help from you; but still,
I'll ask you, and expose your infamy. Where now
Can I turn? Back to my country and my father's house,
Which I betrayed to come with you? Or to Iolcus,
To Pelias' wretched daughters? What a welcome they
Would offer me, who killed their father! Thus it stands:
My friends at home now hate me; and in helping you
I have earned the enmity of those I had no right
To hurt. For my reward, you have made me the envy
Of Hellene women everywhere! A marvellous

[5] **I will begin . . . success:** Medea used her magic to assist Jason in his quest for the golden fleece.

Husband I have, and faithful too, in the name of pity;
When I'm banished, thrown out of the country without a friend,
Alone with my forlorn waifs. Yes, a shining shame
It will be to you, the new-made bridegroom, that your own sons,
And I who saved your life, are begging beside the road!

O Zeus! Why have you given us clear signs to tell
True gold from counterfeit; but when we need to know
Bad *men* from good, the flesh bears no revealing mark?

CHORUS:

The fiercest anger of all, the most incurable,
Is that which rages in the place of dearest love.

JASON:

I have to show myself a clever speaker, it seems.
This hurricane of recrimination and abuse
Calls for good seamanship: I'll furl all but an inch
Of sail, and ride it out. To begin with, since you build
To such a height your services to me, I hold
That credit for my successful voyage was solely due
To Aphrodite, no one else divine or human.
I admit, you have intelligence; but, to recount
How helpless passion drove you then to save my life
Would be invidious; and I will not stress the point.
Your services, so far as they went, were well enough;
But in return for saving me you got far more
Than you gave. Allow me, in the first place, to point out
That you left a barbarous land to become a resident
Of Hellas; here you have known justice; you have lived
In a society where force yields place to law.
Moreover, here your gifts are widely recognized,
You are famous; if you still lived at the ends of the earth
Your name would never be spoken. Personally, unless
Life brings me fame, I long neither for hoards of gold,
Nor for a voice sweeter than Orpheus![6] Well, *you* began
The argument about my voyage; and that's my answer.

As for your scurrilous taunts against my marriage with
The royal family, I shall show you that my action
Was wise, not swayed by passion, and directed towards
Your interests and my children's.—No, keep quiet! When I
Came here from Iolcus as a stateless exile, dogged

[6] **Orpheus:** A legendary musician; his playing gained him entrance into the underworld. See Ovid's *Metamorphoses,* Book 10.

And thwarted by misfortunes—why, what luckier chance
Could I have met, than marriage with the King's daughter?
It was not, as you resentfully assume, that I
Found your attractions wearisome, and was smitten with
Desire for a new wife; nor did I specially want
To raise a numerous family—the sons we have
Are enough, I'm satisfied; but I wanted to ensure
First—and the most important—that we should live well
And not be poor; I know how a poor man is shunned
By all his friends. Next, that I could bring up my sons
In a manner worthy of my descent; have other sons,
Perhaps, as brothers to your children; give them all
An equal place, and so build up a closely-knit
And prosperous family. *You* need no more children, do you?
While *I* thought it worth while to ensure advantages
For those I have, by means of those I hope to have.

Was such a plan, then, wicked? Even you would approve
If you could govern your sex-jealousy. But you women
Have reached a state where, if all's well with your sex-life,
You've everything you wish for; but when *that* goes wrong,
At once all that is best and noblest turns to gall.
If only children could be got some other way,
Without the female sex! If women didn't exist,
Human life would be rid of all its miseries.

CHORUS:

Jason, you have set your case forth very plausibly.
But to my mind—though you may be surprised at this—
You are acting wrongly in thus abandoning your wife.

MEDEA:

No doubt I differ from many people in many ways.
To me, a wicked man who is also eloquent
Seems the most guilty of them all. He'll cut your throat
As bold as brass, because he knows he can dress up murder
In handsome words. He's not so clever after all.
You dare outface me now with glib high-mindedness!
One word will throw you: if you were honest, you ought first
To have won me over, not got married behind my back.

JASON:

No doubt, if I had mentioned it, you would have proved
Most helpful. Why, even now you will not bring yourself
To calm this raging temper.

MEDEA:

That was not the point;
But you're an ageing man, and an Asiatic wife

Was no longer respectable.

JASON:

Understand this:
It's not for the sake of any woman that I have made
This royal marriage, but, as I've already said,
To ensure your future, and to give my children brothers
Of royal blood, and build security for us all.

MEDEA:

I loathe your prosperous future; I'll have none of it,
Nor none of your security—it galls my heart.

JASON:

You know—you'll change your mind and be more sensible.
You'll soon stop thinking good is bad, and striking these
Pathetic poses when in fact you're fortunate.

MEDEA:

Go on, insult me: you have a roof over your head.
I am alone, an exile.

JASON:

It was your own choice.
Blame no one but yourself.

MEDEA:

My choice? What did I do?
Did I make you my wife and then abandon you?

JASON:

You called down wicked curses on the King and his house.

MEDEA:

I did. On your house too Fate sends me as a curse.

JASON:

I'll not pursue this further. If there's anything else
I can provide to meet the children's needs or yours,
Tell me; I'll gladly give whatever you want, or send
Letters of introduction, if you like, to friends
Who will help you.—Listen: to refuse such help is mad.
You've everything to gain if you give up this rage.

MEDEA:

Nothing would induce me to have dealings with your friends,
Nor to take any gift of yours; so offer none.
A lying traitor's gifts carry no luck.

JASON:

Very well.
I call the gods to witness that I have done my best
To help you and the children. You make no response
To kindness; friendly overtures you obstinately
Reject. So much the worse for you.

MEDEA:

Go! You have spent
Too long out here. You are consumed with craving for
Your newly-won bride. Go, enjoy her!

[*Exit* JASON.]

It may be—
And God uphold my words—that this your marriage-day
Will end with marriage lost, loathing and horror left.

CHORUS:

Visitations of love that come
Raging and violent on a man
Bring him neither good repute nor goodness.
But if Aphrodite descends in gentleness
No other goddess brings such delight.
Never, Queen Aphrodite,
Loose against me from your golden bow,
Dipped in sweetness of desire,
Your inescapable arrow!

Let Innocence, the gods' loveliest gift,
Choose me for her own;
Never may the dread Cyprian[7]
Craze my heart to leave old love for new,
Sending to assault me
Angry disputes and feuds unending;
But let her judge shrewdly the loves of women
And respect the bed where no war rages.

O my country, my home!
May the gods save me from becoming
A stateless refugee
Dragging out an intolerable life
In desperate helplessness!
That is the most pitiful of all griefs;
Death is better. Should such a day come to me
I pray for death first.
Of all pains and hardships none is worse
Than to be deprived of your native land.

This is no mere reflection derived from hearsay;
It is something we have seen.

[7] **Cyprian:** One of Aphrodite's titles was "Cyprian" because Cyprus was a major center for her worship.

You, Medea, have suffered the most shattering of blows;
Yet neither the city of Corinth
Nor any friend has taken pity on you.
May dishonour and ruin fall on the man
Who, having unlocked the secrets
Of a friend's frank heart, can then disown him!
He shall be no friend of mine.

[*Enter* AEGEUS.]

AEGEUS:
All happiness to you, Medea! Between old friends
There is no better greeting.

MEDEA:
All happiness to you,
Aegeus, son of Pandion the wise! Where have you come from?

AEGEUS:
From Delphi, from the ancient oracle of Apollo.

MEDEA:
The centre of the earth, the home of prophecy:
Why did you go?

AEGEUS:
To ask for children; that my seed
May become fertile.

MEDEA:
Why, have you lived so many years
Childless?

AEGEUS:
Childless I am; so some fate has ordained.

MEDEA:
You have a wife, or not?

AEGEUS:
I am married.

MEDEA:
And what answer
Did Phoebus give you about children?

AEGEUS:
His answer was
Too subtle for me or any human interpreter.

MEDEA:
Is it lawful for me to hear it?

AEGEUS:
Certainly; a brain
Like yours is what is needed.

MEDEA:

Tell me, since you may.

AEGEUS:

He commanded me 'not to unstop the wineskin's neck'—

MEDEA:

Yes—until when?

AEGEUS:

Until I came safe home again.

MEDEA:

I see. And for what purpose have you sailed to Corinth?

AEGEUS:

You know the King of Troezen, Pittheus, son of Pelops?

MEDEA:

Yes, a most pious man.

AEGEUS:

I want to ask his advice
About this oracle.

MEDEA:

He is an expert in such matters.

AEGEUS:

Yes, and my closest friend. We went to the wars together.

MEDEA:

I hope you will get all you long for, and be happy.

AEGEUS:

But you are looking pale and wasted: what is the matter?

MEDEA:

Aegeus, my husband's the most evil man alive.

AEGEUS:

Why, what's this? Tell me all about your unhappiness.

MEDEA:

Jason has betrayed me, though I never did him wrong.

AEGEUS:

What has he done? Explain exactly.

MEDEA:

He has taken
Another wife, and made her mistress of *my* house.

AEGEUS:

But such a thing is shameful! He has never dared—

MEDEA:

It is so. Once he loved me; now I am disowned.

AEGEUS:

Was he tired of you? Or did he fall in love elsewhere?

MEDEA:

Oh, passionately. He's not a man his friends can trust.

AEGEUS:
Well; if—as you say—he's a bad lot, let him go.
MEDEA:
It's royalty and power he's fallen in love with.
AEGEUS:
What?
Go on. Who's the girl's father?
MEDEA:
Creon, King of Corinth.
AEGEUS:
I see. Then you have every reason to be upset.
MEDEA:
It is the end of everything! What's more, I'm banished.
AEGEUS:
Worse still—extraordinary! Why, who has banished you?
MEDEA:
Creon has banished me from Corinth.
AEGEUS:
And does Jason
Accept this? How disgraceful!
MEDEA:
Oh, no! He protests.
But he's resolved to bear it bravely.—Aegeus, see,
I touch your beard as a suppliant, embrace your knees,
Imploring you to have pity on my wretchedness.
Have pity! I am an exile; let me not be friendless.
Receive me in Athens; give me a welcome in your house.
So may the gods grant you fertility, and bring
Your life to a happy close. You have not realized
What good luck chance has brought you. I know certain drugs
Whose power will put an end to your sterility.
I promise you shall beget children.
AEGEUS:
I am anxious,
For many reasons, to help you in this way, Medea;
First, for the gods' sake, then this hope you've given me
Of children—for I've quite despaired of my own powers.
This then is what I'll do: once you can get to Athens
I'll keep my promise and protect you all I can.
But I must make this clear first: I do not intend
To take you with me away from Corinth. If you come
Yourself to Athens, you shall have sanctuary there;
I will not give you up to anyone. But first
Get clear of Corinth without help; the Corinthians too
Are friends of mine, and I don't wish to give offence.

MEDEA:

So be it. Now confirm your promise with an oath,
And all is well between us.

AEGEUS:

Why? Do you not trust me?
What troubles you?

MEDEA:

I trust you; but I have enemies—
Not only Creon, but the house of Pelias.
Once you are bound by oaths you will not give me up
If they should try to take me out of your territory.
But if your promise is verbal, and not sworn to the gods,
Perhaps you will make friends with them, and agree to do
What they demand. I've no power on my side, while they
Have wealth and all the resources of a royal house.

AEGEUS:

Your forethought is remarkable; but since you wish it
I've no objection. In fact, the taking of an oath
Safeguards me; since I can confront your enemies
With a clear excuse; while *you* have full security.
So name your gods.

MEDEA:

Swear by the Earth under your feet,
By the Sun, my father's father, and the whole race of gods.

AEGEUS:

Tell me what I shall swear to do or not to do.

MEDEA:

Never yourself to expel me from your territory;
And, if my enemies want to take me away, never
Willingly, while you live, to give me up to them.

AEGEUS:

I swear by Earth, and by the burning light of the Sun,
And all the gods, to keep the words you have just spoken.

MEDEA:

I am satisfied. And if you break your oath, what then?

AEGEUS:

Then may the gods do to me as to all guilty men.

MEDEA:

Go now, and joy be with you. Everything is well.
I'll reach your city as quickly as I can, when I
Have carried out my purpose and achieved my wish.

[AEGEUS *clasps her hand and hurries off.*]

CHORUS:

May Hermes, protector of travellers, bring you

Safe to your home, Aegeus; may you accomplish
All that you so earnestly desire;
For your noble heart wins our goodwill.

MEDEA:

O Zeus! O Justice, daughter of Zeus! O glorious Sun!
Now I am on the road to victory; now there's hope!
I shall see my enemies punished as they deserve.
Just where my plot was weakest, at that very point
Help has appeared in this man Aegeus; he is a haven
Where I shall find safe mooring, once I reach the walls
Of the city of Athens. Now I'll tell you all my plans:
They'll not make pleasant hearing.

[MEDEA'S NURSE *has entered; she listens in silence.*]

First I'll send a slave
To Jason, asking him to come to me; and then
I'll give him soft talk; tell him he has acted well,
Tell him I think this royal marriage which he has bought
With my betrayal is for the best and wisely planned.
But I shall beg that my children be allowed to stay.
Not that I would think of leaving sons of mine behind
On enemy soil for those who hate me to insult;
But in my plot to kill the princess they must help.
I'll send them to the palace bearing gifts, a dress
Of soft weave and a coronet of beaten gold.
If she takes and puts on this finery, both she
And all who touch her will expire in agony;
With such a deadly poison I'll anoint my gifts.

However, enough of that. What makes me cry with pain
Is the next thing I have to do. I will kill my sons.
No one shall take my children from me. When I have made
Jason's whole house a shambles,[8] I will leave Corinth
A murderess, flying from my darling children's blood.
Yes, I can endure guilt, however horrible;
The laughter of my enemies I will not endure.

Now let things take their course. What use is life to me?
I have no land, no home, no refuge from despair.
My folly was committed long ago, when I
Was ready to desert my father's house, won over
By eloquence from a Greek, whom with God's help I now

[8] **shambles:** A slaughterhouse.

Will punish. He shall never see alive again
The sons he had from me. From his new bride he never
Shall breed a son; she by my poison, wretched girl,
Must die a hideous death. Let no one think of me
As humble or weak or passive; let them understand
I am of a different kind: dangerous to my enemies,
Loyal to my friends. To such a life glory belongs.

CHORUS:
Since you have told us everything, and since I want
To be your friend, and also to uphold the laws
Of human life—I tell you, you must not do this!

MEDEA:
No other thing is possible. You have excuse
For speaking so: you have not been treated as I have.

CHORUS:
But—to kill your own children! Can you steel your heart?

MEDEA:
This is the way to deal Jason the deepest wound.

CHORUS:
This way will bring you too the deepest misery.

MEDEA:
Let be. Until it is done words are unnecessary.
Nurse! You are the one I use for messages of trust.
Go and bring Jason here. As you're a loyal servant,
And a woman, breathe no word about my purposes.

[*Exit* NURSE.]

CHORUS:
The people of Athens, sons of Erechtheus, have enjoyed their prosperity
Since ancient times. Children of blessed gods,
They grew from holy soil unscorched by invasion.
Among the glories of knowledge their souls are pastured;
They walk always with grace under the sparkling sky.
There long ago, they say, was born golden-haired Harmony,
Created by the nine virgin Muses[9] of Pieria.

They say that Aphrodite dips her cup
In the clear stream of the lovely Cephisus;[10]
It is she who breathes over the land the breath
Of gentle honey-laden winds; her flowing locks
She crowns with a diadem of sweet-scented roses,

[9] **Muses:** The nine divine muses were associated with the various arts; Pieria is a region of Mt. Olympus.

[10] **Cephisus:** A river that flows into the Saronic Gulf near Athens.

And sends the Loves to be enthroned beside Knowledge,
And with her to create excellence in every art.

Then how will such a city,
Watered by sacred rivers,
A country giving protection to its friends—
How will Athens welcome
You, the child-killer
Whose presence is pollution?
Contemplate the blow struck at a child,
Weigh the blood you take upon you.
Medea, by your knees,
By every pledge or appeal we beseech you,
Do not slaughter your children!

Where will you find hardness of purpose?
How will you build resolution in hand or heart
To face horror without flinching?
When the moment comes, and you look at them—
The moment for you to assume the role of murderess—
How will you do it?
When your sons kneel to you for pity,
Will you stain your fingers with their blood?
Your heart will melt; you will know you cannot.

[*Enter* JASON *from the palace. Two maids come from the house to attend* MEDEA.]

JASON:

You sent for me: I have come. Although you hate me, I
Am ready to listen. You have some new request; what is it?

MEDEA:

Jason, I ask you to forgive the things I said.
You must bear with my violent temper; you and I
Share many memories of love. I have been taking
Myself to task. 'You are a fool,' I've told myself,
'You're mad, when people try to plan things for the best,
To be resentful, and pick quarrels with the King
And with your husband; what he's doing will help us all.
His wife is royal; her sons will be my sons' brothers.
Why not throw off your anger? What is the matter, since
The gods are making kind provision? After all
I have two children still to care for; and I know
We came as exiles, and our friends are few enough.'
When I considered this, I saw my foolishness;
I saw how useless anger was. So now I welcome
What you have done; I think you are wise to gain for us

This new alliance, and the folly was all mine.
I should have helped you in your plans, made it my pleasure
To get ready your marriage-bed, attend your bride.
But we women—I won't say we are bad by nature,
But we are what we are. You, Jason, should not copy
Our bad example, or match yourself with us, showing
Folly for folly. I give in; I was wrong just now,
I admit. But I have thought more wisely of it since.
Children, children! Are you indoors? Come out here.

[*The* CHILDREN *come out. Their* TUTOR *follows.*]

Children,
Greet your father, as I do, and put your arms round him.
Forget our quarrel, and love him as your mother does.
We have made friends; we are not angry any more.
There, children; take his hand.

[*She turns away in a sudden flood of weeping.*]

Forgive me; I recalled
What pain the future hides from us.

[*After embracing* JASON *the* CHILDREN *go back to* MEDEA.]

Oh children! Will you
All your lives long, stretch out your hands to me like this?
Oh, my tormented heart is full of tears and terrors.
After so long, I have ended my quarrel with your father;
And now, see! I have drenched this young face with my tears.

CHORUS:
I too feel fresh tears fill my eyes. May the course of evil
Be checked now, go no further!

JASON:
I am pleased, Medea,
That you have changed your mind; though indeed I do not blame
Your first resentment. Only naturally a woman
Is angry when her husband marries a second wife.
You have had wiser thoughts; and though it has taken time,
You have recognized the right decision. This is the act
Of a sensible woman. As for you, my boys, your father
Has taken careful thought, and, with the help of the gods,
Ensured a good life for you. Why, in time, I'm sure,
You with your brothers will be leading men in Corinth.
Only grow big and strong. Your father, and those gods
Who are his friends, have all the rest under control.
I want to see you, when you're strong, full-grown young men,
Tread down my enemies.

[*Again* MEDEA *breaks down and weeps.*]

What's this? Why these floods of tears?
Why are you pale? Did you not like what I was saying?
Why do you turn away?

MEDEA:

It is nothing. I was thinking
About these children.

JASON:

I'll provide for them. Cheer up.

MEDEA:

I will. It is not that I mean to doubt your word.
But women—are women; tears come naturally to us.

JASON:

Why do you grieve so over the children?

MEDEA:

I'm their mother.
When you just now prayed for them to live long, I wondered
Whether it would be so; and grief came over me.
But I've said only part of what I had to say;
Here is the other thing. Since Creon has resolved
To send me out of Corinth, I fully recognize
That for me too this course is best. If I lived here
I should become a trouble both to you and him.
People believe I bear a grudge against you all.
So I must go. But the boys—I would like *them* to be
Brought up in your care. Beg Creon to let them stay.

JASON:

I don't know if I can persuade him; but I'll try.

MEDEA:

Then—get your wife to ask her father to let them stay.

JASON:

Why, certainly; I'm pretty sure she'll win him over.

MEDEA:

She will, if she's like other women. But I too
Can help in this. I'll send a present to your wife—
The loveliest things to be found anywhere on earth.
The boys shall take them.—One of you maids, go quickly, bring
The dress and golden coronet.—They will multiply
Her happiness many times, when she can call her own
A royal, noble husband, and these treasures, which
My father's father the Sun bequeathed to his descendants.

[*A slave has brought a casket, which* MEDEA *now hands to her sons.*]

Boys, hold these gifts. Now carry them to the happy bride,

The princess royal; give them into her own hands.
Go! She will find them all that such a gift should be.

JASON:

But why deprive yourself of such things, foolish woman?
Do you think a royal palace is in want of dresses?
Or gold, do you suppose? Keep them, don't give them away.
If my wife values me at all she will yield to *me*
More than to costly presents, I am sure of that.

MEDEA:

Don't stop me. Gifts, they say, persuade even the gods;
With mortals, gold outweighs a thousand arguments.
The day is hers; from now on *her* prosperity
Will rise to new heights. She is royal and young. To buy
My sons from exile I would give life, not just gold.
Come, children, go both of you into this rich palace;
Kneel down and beg your father's new wife, and my mistress,
That you may not be banished. And above all, see
That she receives my present into her own hands.
Go quickly; be successful, and bring good news back,
That what your mother longs for has been granted you.

[*Exit* JASON *followed by the* CHILDREN *and the* TUTOR.]

CHORUS:

Now I have no more hope,
No more hope that the children can live;
They are walking to murder at this moment.
The bride will receive the golden coronet,
Receive her merciless destroyer;
With her own hands she will carefully fit
The adornment of death round her golden hair.

She cannot resist such loveliness, such heavenly gleaming;
She will enfold herself
In the dress and the wreath of wrought gold,
Preparing her bridal beauty
To enter a new home—among the dead.
So fatal is the snare she will fall into,
So inevitable the death that awaits her;
From its cruelty there is no escape.

And you, unhappy Jason, ill-starred in marriage,
You, son-in-law of kings:
Little you know that the favour you ask
Will seal your sons' destruction
And fasten on your wife a hideous fate.

O wretched Jason!
So sure of destiny, and so ignorant!

Your sorrow next I weep for, pitiable mother;
You, for jealousy of your marriage-bed,
Will slaughter your children;
Since, disregarding right and loyalty,
Your husband has abandoned you
And lives with another wife.

[*The* TUTOR *returns from the palace with the two* CHILDREN.]

TUTOR:
Mistress! These two boys are reprieved from banishment.
The princess took your gifts from them with her own hand,
And was delighted. They have no enemies in the palace.

[MEDEA *is silent.*]

Well, bless my soul!
Isn't that good news? Why do you stand there thunderstruck?

MEDEA [*to herself*]:
How cruel, how cruel!

TUTOR:
That's out of tune with the news I brought.

MEDEA:
How cruel life is!

TUTOR:
Have I, without knowing it,
Told something dreadful, then? I thought my news was good.

MEDEA:
Your news is what it is. I am not blaming you.

TUTOR:
Then why stand staring at the ground, with streaming eyes?

MEDEA:
Strong reason forces me to weep, old friend. The gods,
And my own evil-hearted plots, have led to this.

TUTOR:
Take heart, mistress; in time your sons will bring you home.

MEDEA:
Before then, I have others to send home.—Oh, gods!

[*She weeps.*]

TUTOR:
You're not the only mother parted from her sons.
We are all mortal; you must not bear grief so hard.

MEDEA:
Yes, friend. I'll follow your advice. Now go indoors

And get things ready for them, as on other days.

[*Exit* TUTOR. *The* CHILDREN *come to* MEDEA.]

O children, children! You have a city, and a home;
And when we have parted, there you both will stay for ever,
You motherless, I miserable. And I must go
To exile in another land, before I have had
My joy of you, before I have seen you growing up,
Becoming prosperous. I shall never see your brides,
Adorn your bridal beds, and hold the torches high.
My misery is my own heart, which will not relent.
All was for nothing, then—these years of rearing you,
My care, my aching weariness, and the wild pains
When you were born. Oh, yes, I once built many hopes
On you; imagined, pitifully, that you would care
For my old age, and would yourselves wrap my dead body
For burial. How people would envy me my sons!
That sweet, sad thought has faded now. Parted from you,
My life will be all pain and anguish. You will not
Look at your mother any more with these dear eyes.
You will have moved into a different sphere of life.

Dear sons, why are you staring at me so? You smile
At me—your last smile: why?

[*She weeps. The* CHILDREN *go from her a little, and she turns to the* CHORUS.]

Oh, what am I to do?
Women, my courage is all gone. Their young, bright faces—
I can't do it. I'll think no more of it. I'll take them
Away from Corinth. Why should I hurt *them,* to make
Their father suffer, when I shall suffer twice as much
Myself? I won't do it. I won't think of it again.
What is the matter with me? Are my enemies
To laugh at me? Am I to let them off scot free?
I must steel myself to it. What a coward I am,
Even tempting my own resolution with soft talk.
Boys, go indoors.

[*The* CHILDREN *go to the door, but stay there watching her.*]

If there is any here who finds it
Not lawful to be present at my sacrifice,
Let him see to it. My hand shall not weaken.

Oh, my heart, don't, don't do it! Oh, miserable heart,
Let them be! Spare your children! We'll all live together
Safely in Athens; and they will make you happy. . . . No!
No! No! By all the fiends of hate in hell's depths, no!

I'll not leave sons of mine to be the victims of
My enemies' rage. In any case there is no escape,
The thing's done now. Yes, now—the golden coronet
Is on her head, the royal bride is in her dress,
Dying, I know it. So, since I have a sad road
To travel, and send these boys on a still sadder road,
I'll speak to them. Come, children; give me your hand, dear son;
Yours too. Now we must say goodbye. Oh, darling hand,
And darling mouth; your noble, childlike face and body!
Dear sons, my blessing on you both—but there, not here!
All blessing here your father has destroyed. How sweet
To hold you! And children's skin is soft, and their breath pure.
Go! Go away! I can't look at you any longer;
My pain is more than I can bear.

[*The* CHILDREN *go indoors.*]

I understand
The horror of what I am going to do; but anger,
The spring of all life's horror, masters my resolve.

[MEDEA *goes to stand looking towards the palace.*]

CHORUS:

I have often engaged in arguments,
And become more subtle, and perhaps more heated,
Than is suitable for women;
Though in fact women too have intelligence,
Which forms part of our nature and instructs us—
Not all of us, I admit, but a certain few
You might perhaps find, in a large number of women—
A few not incapable of reflection;

And this is my opinion: those men or women
Who never had children of their own at all
Enjoy the advantage in good fortune
Over those who are parents. Childless people
Have no means of knowing whether children are
A blessing or a burden; but being without them
They live exempt from many troubles.

While those who have growing up in their homes
The sweet gift of children I see always
Burdened and worn with incessant worry,
First, how to rear them in health and safety,
And bequeath them, in time, enough to live on;
And then this further anxiety:

They can never know whether all their toil
Is spent for worthy or worthless children.

And beyond the common ills that attend
All human life there is one still worse:
Suppose at last they are pretty well off,
Their children have grown up, and, what's more,
Are kind and honest: then what happens?
A throw of chance—and there goes Death
Bearing off your child into the unknown.

Then why should mortals thank the gods,
Who add to their load, already grievous,
This one more grief, for their children's sake,
Most grievous of all?

MEDEA:

Friends, I have long been waiting for a message from the palace.
What is to happen next? I see a slave of Jason's
Coming, gasping for breath. He must bring fearful news.

[*Enter a* MESSENGER.]

MESSENGER:

Medea! Get away, escape! Oh, what a thing to do!
What an unholy, horrible thing! Take ship, or chariot,
Any means you can, but escape!

MEDEA:

Why should I escape?

MESSENGER:

She's dead—the princess, and her father Creon too,
They're both dead, by your poisons.

MEDEA:

Your news is excellent.
I count you from today my friend and benefactor.

MESSENGER:

What? Are you sane, or raving mad? When you've committed
This hideous crime against the royal house, you're glad
At hearing of it? Do you not tremble at such things?

MEDEA:

I could make suitable reply to that, my friend.
But take your time now; tell me, how did they die? You'll give
Me double pleasure if their death was horrible.

MESSENGER:

When your two little boys came hand in hand, and entered
The palace with their father, where the wedding was,

We servants were delighted. We had all felt sorry
To hear how you'd been treated; and now the word went round
From one to another, that you and Jason had made it up.
So we were glad to see the boys; one kissed their hand,
Another their fair hair. Myself, I was so pleased,
I followed with them to the princess's room. Our mistress—
The one we now call mistress in your place—before
She saw your pair of boys coming, had eyes only
For Jason; but seeing them she dropped her eyes, and turned
Her lovely cheek away, upset that they should come
Into her room. Your husband then began to soothe
Her sulkiness, her girlish temper. 'You must not,'
He said, 'be unfriendly to our friends. Turn your head round,
And give up feeling angry. Those your husband loves
You must love too. Now take these gifts,' he said, 'and ask
Your father to revoke their exile for my sake.'
So, when she saw those lovely things, she was won over,
And agreed to all that Jason asked. At once, before
He and your sons were well out of the house, she took
The embroidered gown and put it round her. Then she placed
Over her curls the golden coronet, and began
To arrange her hair in a bright mirror, smiling at
Her lifeless form reflected there. Then she stood up,
And to and fro stepped daintily about the room
On white bare feet, and many times she would twist back
To see how the dress fell in clear folds to the heel.

Then suddenly we saw a frightening thing. She changed
Colour; she staggered sideways, shook in every limb.
She was just able to collapse on to a chair,
Or she would have fallen flat. Then one of her attendants,
An old woman, thinking that perhaps the anger of Pan[11]
Or some other god had struck her, chanted the cry of worship.
But then she saw, oozing from the girl's lips, white froth;
The pupils of her eyes were twisted out of sight;
The blood was drained from all her skin. The old woman knew
Her mistake, and changed her chant to a despairing howl.
One maid ran off quickly to fetch the King, another
To look for Jason and tell him what was happening
To his young bride; the whole palace was filled with a clatter
Of people running here and there.
All this took place

[11] **the anger of Pan:** It was thought that the old nature-god Pan frightened some people, causing "panic."

In a few moments, perhaps while a fast runner might run
A hundred yards; and she lay speechless, with eyes closed.
Then she came to, poor girl, and gave a frightful scream,
As two torments made war on her together: first
The golden coronet round her head discharged a stream
Of unnatural devouring fire: while the fine dress
Your children gave her—poor miserable girl!—the stuff
Was eating her clear flesh. She leapt up from her chair,
On fire, and ran, shaking her head and her long hair
This way and that, trying to shake off the coronet.
The ring of gold was fitted close and would not move;
The more she shook her head the fiercer the flame burned.
At last, exhausted by agony, she fell to the ground;
Save to her father, she was unrecognizable.
Her eyes, her face, were one grotesque disfigurement;
Down from her head dripped blood mingled with flame; her flesh,
Attacked by the invisible fangs of poison, melted
From the bare bone, like gum-drops from a pine-tree's bark—
A ghastly sight. Not one among us dared to touch
Her body. What we'd seen was lesson enough for us.

But suddenly her father came into the room.
He did not understand, poor man, what kind of death
Had struck his child. He threw himself down at her side,
And sobbed aloud, and kissed her, and took her in his arms,
And cried, 'Poor darling child, what god destroyed your life
So cruelly? Who robs me of my only child,
Old as I am, and near my grave? Oh, let me die
With you, my daughter!' Soon he ceased his tears and cries,
And tried to lift his aged body upright; and then,
As ivy sticks to laurel-branches, so he stuck
Fast to the dress. A ghastly wrestling then began;
He struggled to raise up his knee, she tugged him down.
If he used force, he tore the old flesh off his bones.
At length the King gave up his pitiful attempts;
Weakened with pain, he yielded, and gasped out his life.
Now, joined in death, daughter and father—such a sight
As tears were made for—they lie there.
                                        To you, Medea,
I have no more to say. You will yourself know best
How to evade reprisal. As for human life,
It is a shadow, as I have long believed. And this
I say without hesitation: those whom most would call
Intelligent, the propounders of wise theories—
Their folly is of all men's the most culpable.

Happiness is a thing no man possesses. Fortune
May come now to one man, now to another, as
Prosperity increases; happiness never.

[*Exit* MESSENGER.]

CHORUS:

Today we see the will of Heaven, blow after blow,
Bring down on Jason justice and calamity.

MEDEA:

Friends, now my course is clear: as quickly as possible
To kill the children and then fly from Corinth; not
Delay and so consign them to another hand
To murder with a better will. For they must die,
In any case; and since they must, then I who gave
Them birth will kill them. Arm yourself, my heart: the thing
That you must do is fearful, yet inevitable.
Why wait, then? My accursed hand, come, take the sword;
Take it, and forward to your frontier of despair.
No cowardice, no tender memories; forget
That you once loved them, that of your body they were born.
For one short day forget your children; afterwards
Weep: though you kill them, they were your beloved sons.
Life has been cruel to me.

[MEDEA *goes into the house.*]

CHORUS:

Earth, awake! Bright arrows of the Sun,
Look! Look down on the accursed woman
Before she lifts up a murderous hand
To pollute it with her children's blood!
For they are of your own golden race;
And for mortals to spill blood that grew
In the veins of gods is a fearful thing.
Heaven-born brightness, hold her, stop her,
Purge the palace of her, this pitiable
Bloody-handed fiend of vengeance!

All your care for them lost! Your love
For the babes you bore, all wasted, wasted!
Why did you come from the blue Symplegades[12]
That hold the gate of the barbarous sea?
Why must this rage devour your heart
To spend itself in slaughter of children?

---

[12] **the blue Symplegades:** Two rocks that form a gateway to the Black Sea. They were thought to open and shut to allow ships to pass through.

Where kindred blood pollutes the ground
A curse hangs over human lives;
And murder measures the doom that falls
By Heaven's law on the guilty house.

[*A child's scream is heard from inside the house.*]

CHORUS:

Do you hear? The children are calling for help.
O cursed, miserable woman!

CHILDREN'S VOICES:

Help, help! Mother, let me go!
Mother, don't kill us!

CHORUS:

Shall we go in?
I am sure we ought to save the children's lives.

CHILDREN'S VOICES:

Help, help, for the gods' sake! She is killing us!
We can't escape from her sword!

CHORUS:

O miserable mother, to destroy your own increase,
Murder the babes of your body!
Stone and iron you are, as you resolved to be.

There was but one in time past,
One woman that I have heard of,
Raised hand against her own children.
It was Ino,[13] sent out of her mind by a god,
When Hera, the wife of Zeus,
Drove her from her home to wander over the world.
In her misery she plunged into the sea
Being defiled by the murder of her children;
From the steep cliff's edge she stretched out her foot,
And so ended,
Joined in death with her two sons.

What can be strange or terrible after this?
O bed of women, full of passion and pain,
What wickedness, what sorrow you have caused on the earth!

[*Enter* JASON, *running and breathless.*]

JASON:

You women standing round the door there! Is Medea
Still in the house?—vile murderess!—or has she gone

[13] **Ino:** Because Ino helped to raise Dionysus, son of Zeus and Semele, Zeus's wife Hera drove Ino mad.

And escaped? I swear she must either hide in the deep earth
Or soar on wings into the sky's abyss, to escape
My vengeance for the royal house.—She has killed the King
And the princess! Does she expect to go unpunished?

Well, I am less concerned with her than with the children.
Those who have suffered at her hands will make her suffer;
I've come to save my sons, before Creon's family
Murder them in revenge for this unspeakable
Crime of their mother's.

CHORUS:
Jason, you have yet to learn
How great your trouble is; or you would not have spoken so.

JASON:
What trouble? Is Medea trying to kill me too?

CHORUS:
Your sons are dead. Their mother has killed both your sons.

JASON:
What? Killed my sons? That word kills me.

CHORUS:
They are both dead.

JASON:
Where are they? Did she kill them out here, or indoors?

CHORUS:
Open that door, and see them lying in their blood.

JASON:
Slaves, there! Unbar the doors! Open, and let me see
Two horrors: my dead sons, and the woman I will kill.

[JASON *batters at the doors.* MEDEA *appears above the roof, sitting in a chariot drawn by dragons, with the bodies of the two children beside her.*]

MEDEA:
Jason! Why are you battering at these doors, seeking
The dead children and me who killed them? Stop! Be quiet.
If you have any business with me, say what you wish.
Touch us you cannot, in this chariot which the Sun
Has sent to save us from the hands of enemies.

JASON:
You abomination! Of all women most detested
By every god, by me, by the whole human race!
You could endure—a mother!—to lift sword against
Your own little ones, to leave me childless, my life wrecked.
After such murder do you outface both Sun and Earth—
Guilty of gross pollution? May the gods blast your life!

I am sane now; but I was mad before, when I
Brought you from your palace in a land of savages
Into a Greek home—you, a living curse, already
A traitor both to your father and your native land.
The vengeance due for your sins the gods have cast on me.
You had already murdered your brother at his own hearth
When first you stepped on board my lovely Argo's hull.
That was your beginning. Then you became my wife, and bore
My children, now, out of mere sexual jealousy,
You murder them! In all Hellas there is not one woman
Who could have done it; yet in preference to them
I married you, chose hatred and murder for my wife—
No woman, but a tiger; a Tuscan Scylla[14]—but more savage.
Ah, what's the use? If I cursed you all day, no remorse
Would touch you, for your heart's proof against feeling. Go!
Out of my sight, polluted fiend, child-murderer!
Leave me to mourn over my destiny: I have lost
My young bride; I have lost the two sons I begot
And brought up; I shall never see them alive again.

MEDEA:

I would if necessary have answered at full length
Everything you have said; but Zeus the father of all
Knows well what service I once rendered you, and how
You have repaid me. You were mistaken if you thought
You could dishonour my bed and live a pleasant life
And laugh at me. The princess was wrong too, and so
Was Creon, when he took you for his son-in-law
And thought he could exile me with impunity.
So now, am I a tiger, Scylla?—Hurl at me
What names you please! I've reached your heart; and that is right.

JASON:

You suffer too; my loss is yours no less.

MEDEA:

It is true;
But my pain's a fair price, to take away your smile.

JASON:

O children, what a wicked mother Fate gave you!

MEDEA:

O sons, your father's treachery cost you your lives.

JASON:

It was not my hand that killed my sons.

---

[14] **Scylla:** A sea monster who attacked ships in the strait between Italy's mainland and Sicily.

MEDEA:
No, not your hand;
But your insult to me, and your new-wedded wife.

JASON:
You thought *that* reason enough to murder them, that I
No longer slept with you?

MEDEA:
And is that injury
A slight one, do you imagine, to a woman?

JASON:
Yes,
To a modest woman; but to you—the whole world lost.

MEDEA:
I can stab too: your sons are dead!

JASON:
Dead? No! They live—
To haunt your life with vengeance.

MEDEA:
Who began this feud?
The gods know.

JASON:
Yes—they know the vileness of your heart.

MEDEA:
Loathe on! Your bitter voice—how I abhor the sound!

JASON:
As I loathe yours. Let us make terms and part at once.

MEDEA:
Most willingly. What terms? What do you bid me do?

JASON:
Give me my sons for burial and mourning rites.

MEDEA:
Oh, no! I will myself convey them to the temple
Of Hera Acraea; there in the holy precinct I
Will bury them with my own hand, to ensure that none
Of my enemies shall violate or insult their graves.
And I will ordain an annual feast and sacrifice
To be solemnized for ever by the people of Corinth,
To expiate this impious murder. I myself
Will go to Athens, city of Erechtheus, to make my home
With Aegeus son of Pandion. You, as you deserve,
Shall die an unheroic death, your head shattered
By a timber from the Argo's hull. Thus wretchedly
Your fate shall end the story of your love for me.

JASON:
The curse of children's blood be on you!
Avenging Justice blast your being!

MEDEA:
What god will hear your imprecation,
Oath-breaker, guest-deceiver, liar?

JASON:
Unclean, abhorrent child-destroyer!

MEDEA:
Go home: your wife waits to be buried.

JASON:
I go—a father once; now childless.

MEDEA:
You grieve too soon. Old age is coming.

JASON:
Children, how dear you were!

MEDEA:
To their mother; not to you.

JASON:
Dear—and you murdered them?

MEDEA:
Yes, Jason, to break your heart.

JASON:
I long to fold them in my arms;
To kiss their lips would comfort me.

MEDEA:
Now you have loving words, now kisses for them:
Then you disowned them, sent them into exile.

JASON:
For God's sake, let me touch their gentle flesh.

MEDEA:
You shall not. It is waste of breath to ask.

JASON:
Zeus, do you hear how I am mocked,
Rejected, by this savage beast
Polluted with her children's blood?

But now, as time and strength permit,
I will lament this grievous day,
And call the gods to witness, how
You killed my sons, and now refuse
To let me touch or bury them.
Would God I had not bred them,

Or ever lived to see
Them dead, you their destroyer!

[*During this speech the chariot has moved out of sight.*]

CHORUS:
Many are the Fates which Zeus in Olympus dispenses;
Many matters the gods bring to surprising ends.
The things we thought would happen do not happen;
The unexpected God makes possible;
And such is the conclusion of this story.

ARISTOPHANES
c. 450–c. 386 B.C.E.

WWW For links to more information about Aristophanes and a quiz on *Lysistrata,* see *World Literature Online* at bedfordstmartins.com/worldlit.

Imagine an entrepreneur who convinces a colony of birds to establish a kingdom between earth and sky where they can intercept the smoke from ritual sacrifices and thus "starve" the gods into submission. Or a school run by an ivory-tower Socrates who spends his days suspended in a basket from the ceiling because he needs that rarefied atmosphere to enable him to think. Or a dramatic contest in which the tragic playwrights Aeschylus and Euripides weigh their best lines on a scale to determine which is the better dramatist. These are among the fantastic inventions of Aristophanes, the great comic dramatist of fifth-century-B.C.E. Athens whose works are the only surviving examples of what is known as Greek Old Comedy. Although Aristophanes used his comic inventiveness to satirize the politicians and cultural leaders of his day to comment on topical issues, and, especially, to attack the Peloponnesian War between Athens and Sparta, his plays transcend their topicality and still provide trenchant and extravagant commentary on human foibles.

An Antiwar Playwright. Aristophanes lived from about 450 to 386 B.C.E. and seems to have come from a well-to-do Athenian family, for his plays often take a traditional, aristocratic point of view as they criticize the democracy of his day. Most of Aristophanes' plays were written during the Peloponnesian War (431–404 B.C.E.), a war between Athens and Sparta that Aristophanes opposed, blaming the leaders of democratic Athens for causing and prolonging it. Several of his extant eleven plays directly take up the issue of the war. The earliest, *The Archarnians* (425 B.C.E.), attacks Athenian hawks as warmongers who persecute a farmer for making a private peace with the Spartans. *Peace* (421 B.C.E.) shows another countryman, disgusted and ruined by the war, who goes up to heaven on the back of a gigantic dung beetle and discovers that the gods are gone and that

War has imprisoned Peace in a cave and is about to grind up the Greek city-states in a mortar. The hero rescues Peace from the cave and takes back the Athenian council from the warmongers. ***Lysistrata*** (411 B.C.E.), the most famous of Aristophanes' antiwar plays, describes the first women's strike for peace, as the women of the Greek city-states band together to end the war by withholding sex from their warrior husbands. In several other plays, Aristophanes attacks Athenian politicians responsible for the war policy, especially Cleon, the ruling demagogue in Athens from 429 to 422. The attacks in *The Babylonians* (426 B.C.E.) and *The Archarnians* led to the writer being prosecuted by the government, perhaps for treason, but the punishment must have been light, for Aristophanes continued to write plays and again attacked Cleon in *The Knights* in 423.

lih-SIS-truh-tuh

Old Comedy. Aristophanes' best-known plays in modern times have been those on social and cultural themes, many of which are as current today as they were in Aristophanes' time. *The Clouds* (423 B.C.E.) ridicules the **Sophists**[1] for training their students in rhetorical cleverness and encouraging them to use their knowledge for selfish and dishonest ends. *The Wasps* (422 B.C.E.) satirizes Athenian litigiousness. In *The Frogs* (405 B.C.E.), Aristophanes makes literary controversy absurd. In the play, although Aeschylus finally wins the contest with Euripides over who is the greater tragedian, both playwrights are well criticized in the course of their debate. While the scheme of establishing a kingdom to challenge the gods in *The Birds* (414 B.C.E.) was based on the disastrous Athenian invasion of Sicily, it satirizes all grandiose imperialistic schemes and the jingoism, or extreme nationalism, that promotes them.

Aristophanes' best-known plays are examples of Old Comedy, a form that flourished in the fifth-century-B.C.E. Greek theater. Because Aristophanes' plays are the only examples of the form that have survived, they have come to define Old Comedy. These plays grew out of seasonal fertility rituals honoring Dionysus, the god of wine and vegetation, similar to those described by Euripides in *Bacchae.* The animal choruses in these plays (the wasps, frogs, and birds, for example) played an important role. Each of the three main actors in the drama, masked and dressed in grotesquely padded costumes, displayed a conspicuous leather phallus. Similarly, coarse sexual humor, fantastic plots, explicit political satire, songs, and musical comedy, sometimes compared to songs of Gilbert and Sullivan,[2] are all characteristic of Old Comedy.

The Graces were looking for an everlasting home; They found it in the soul of Aristophanes.
– attributed to Plato, philosopher

Old Comedy plays typically have six parts: the Prologue, in which the main character develops a "happy idea," such as Lysistrata's scheme to

[1] **Sophists:** Teachers who gave instruction for a fee; they gained a reputation for seeking victory rather than the truth in debates.

[2] **songs of Gilbert and Sullivan:** English playwright William Schwenck Gilbert (1836–1911) collaborated with composer Arthur Sullivan (1842–1900) on a series of popular satiric and comic operas, including *H. M. S. Pinafore* (1878) and *The Mikado* (1885).

organize the women against the war; the Parados, or entrance-song of the Chorus; the Agon, a debate between those for and against the protagonist's happy idea, ending with the defeat of the opposition; the Parabasis, a second choral song in which the playwright addresses the audience directly on the issues of the play or on other topics; Episodes, which explore and apply the happy idea; and the Exode, a formal song that often leads to a feast, dance, or scene of revelry to close the play.

Middle Comedy. Aristophanes' later plays, less successful than those written during the Peloponnesian War, are examples of Middle Com edy, more realistic plays in which the Chorus is less significant, or altogether absent, and the coarse humor and political satire are muted. One of these later plays, however, *Ecclesiazusae,* or *Women in Parliament* (392 B.C.E.), is similar to *Lysistrata,* for it describes the women of Athens disguising themselves as men and voting themselves into power in the Assembly. There they establish a new regime where equality of the sexes and the communal ownership of property are the guiding principles. Through this feminist fantasy, Aristophanes turns the world upside down and makes visible the shortcomings of the established order. *Lysistrata* uses a similar tack to attack the Athenian involvement in the Peloponnesian War.

The Peloponnesian War. By the time *Lysistrata* was written, the war had gone on for twenty years and neither Athenian naval power nor the Spartan land armies could gain the upper hand. The Athenians were tired of the fighting and the political turmoil brought on by the war. Athens was split into bitterly contending factions of "hawks" and "doves," and the democracy that Pericles, the Athenian statesman and political leader, so eloquently celebrated after the first year of the war had been undermined and replaced in 411 B.C.E by an oligarchy, or rule by the few. The war had also led to atrocities on both sides, to genocidal massacres and the enslavement of captured populations. In 413 B.C.E., the Athenian expedition to conquer Sicily and cut off Sparta from its allies to the west ended in failure. Two hundred Athenian ships were lost, virtually the whole navy, along with their crews of about thirty-five thousand men and a land army including four thousand Athenian soldiers. For Aristophanes, one of the moderate faction in Athens, the defeat in Sicily was a sure sign of the need to challenge the extremism of the war party.

Lysistrata. In characteristic fashion, Aristophanes begins with fantasy, imagining a new Athens ruled by women. Led by Lysistrata, the women take over the Acropolis, the "Capitol Hill" of Athens, and promote similar rebellions in other city-states. By doing so, they challenge the values of the male warrior culture and its sterile obsession with the war as "a serious business." The women propose an alternative set of values, expressed through the metaphor of weaving: They will wind the country and its citizens together into "a great ball, and then weave a stout cloak for the

***Lysistrata,* 2002**
Aristophanes' classic antiwar play Lysistrata *has resonated with theatergoers for more than two thousand years. Here, in a modern production, Cherry Jones (center) stars in the title role. (Richard Feldman)*

democracy." The women may scandalize the men by reducing state questions to matters of weaving, but they do alter the course of the war.

Once they gain control of the Acropolis, the women seek to end the war by refusing to have sex with their men until a peace is signed. In the episodes that follow the Parabasis, Aristophanes plays out the effects of this scheme on both the women and the men in a series of sexual confrontations not far removed from the phallic comedy of the Dionysian rites. The resolution, engineered by Lysistrata, takes place before the statue of the naked sex goddess Reconciliation, and the play ends with dancing and revelry in the Exode.

■ CONNECTIONS

Sophocles, *Antigone,* p. 952. In both *Antigone* and Aristophanes' *Lysistrata,* women try to influence the war policies of men. Aristophanes uses this situation to produce satiric comedy; Sophocles turns the conflict between Antigone and Creon into tragedy. Using these two plays, identify the differences between comedy and tragedy. How are the plays' heroines characterized? How does the emotional impact of the two plays differ?

Chaucer, *The Canterbury Tales* (Book 2); Rokeya Hossain, "Sultana's Dream" (Book 6). Aristophanes reverses conventional ideas about gender roles to expose the misguided war policies of Athens and Sparta. Chaucer's Wife of Bath, describing herself as the more aggressive partner in her several marriages, also challenges conventional gender expectations. Hossain, imagining a feminine utopia in twentieth-century India, places men in purdah, or seclusion, and gives women control of public life. To what extent is each of these works a critique of patriarchal hegemony? What feminine alternatives do the women in these works offer to the male point of view?

Molière, *Tartuffe* (Book 4); Tawfiq al-Hakim, *The Fate of a Cockroach* (Book 6). *Lysistrata, Tartuffe,* and *The Fate of a Cockroach* are satiric plays that come from very different places and times. What is satirized in each play, and who represents the reasonable alternative? Based on these three plays how would you define satire? Also, what do these plays tell you about the differences and similarities between classical Greece, seventeenth-century France, and twentieth-century Egypt?

■ FURTHER RESEARCH

Dover, K. J. *Aristophanic Comedy.* 1972.
MacDowell, Douglas M. *Aristophanes and Athens: An Introduction to the Plays.* 1995.
McLeish, Kenneth. *The Theatre of Aristophanes.* 1980.
Spatz, Lois. *Aristophanes.* 1978.
Taaffee, Lauren K. *Aristophanes and Women.* 1993.
Whitman, C. H. *Aristophanes and the Comic Hero.* 1964.

■ PRONUNCIATION

Acharnae: uh-KAR-nee
Aristogeiton: uh-ris-toh-GAY-tahn, uh-ris-toh-JIGH-tun
Aristophanes: eh-ris-TAH-fuh-neez
Calonice: kal-uh-NIGH-see
Cinesias: sih-NEE-see-us, -zee-us
Cleisthenes: KLIGH-sthuh-neez
Lacedaemon: las-ih-DEE-mun
Leipsydrion: layp-SID-ree-un
Lysistrata: lih-SIS-truh-tuh, ligh-sis-STRAH-tuh
Myrrhine: MIH-rih-nee (if noun)
Pherecrates: fih-REK-ruh-teez

Lysistrata[1]

Translated by Charles T. Murphy

CHARACTERS IN THE PLAY

LYSISTRATA, CALONICE, MYRRHINE — *Athenian women*
LAMPITO, *a Spartan woman*
LEADER OF THE CHORUS OF OLD MEN
CHORUS OF OLD MEN
LEADER OF THE CHORUS OF OLD WOMEN
CHORUS OF OLD WOMEN
ATHENIAN MAGISTRATE
THREE ATHENIAN WOMEN
CINESIAS, *an Athenian, husband of* MYRRHINE
SPARTAN HERALD
SPARTAN AMBASSADORS
ATHENIAN AMBASSADORS
TWO ATHENIAN CITIZENS
CHORUS OF ATHENIANS
CHORUS OF SPARTANS

SCENE: *in Athens, beneath the Acropolis. In the center of the stage is the Propylaea, or gate-way to the Acropolis; to one side is a small grotto, sacred to Pan. The Orchestra represents a slope leading up to the gate-way.*

It is early in the morning. LYSISTRATA *is pacing impatiently up and down.*

Lysistrata. First presented at the Lenaea, the winter drama festival, of 411 B.C.E., this work was written in the shadow of the disastrous Athenian defeat in Sicily in 413. Although Athenian leaders were still promulgating the war, the ultimate defeat of Athens was foreseen. Rather than attacking the poor policies that had produced the defeat, Aristophanes mocks militarism itself in *Lysistrata.* The fantastic invention he uses to do so, a political coup by the women of the Greek city-states, turns Athenian politics and society on its head. By putting women, who had virtually no influence in the public life of Athens, into positions of power, Aristophanes satirizes the masculine assumptions that produced the military policy in the first place, and by turning the war into a battle of the sexes, he dramatizes a peace process that arises from even stronger impulses than the impulse to kill.

The orgiastic Dionysian roots of Greek comedy are obvious in *Lysistrata.* The women's attempt at stopping the war by denying sexual favors has the comedic effect of turning every political discussion into a sexual one. Double entendre and sexual innuendo are pervasive as the young women fend off their more and more frustrated husbands and the two choruses of older men and older women enact a comic battle in which the men's attempt to penetrate the gates of the Acropolis is frustrated by the women's throwing cold water on them. As an alternative to war the women propose a policy of cooperation and reconciliation couched in the imagery of their domestic pursuits, particularly weaving.

The longer the war goes on, the greater the urgency on both sides. Lysistrata must keep her "troops" from surrendering to the enemy, while the men, greatly needing to relieve their sexual frustration, finally agree to their wives' terms and celebrate the naked goddess Reconciliation.

---

[1] ***Lysistrata***: As is usual in ancient comedy, the leading characters have significant names. Lysistrata is "She who disbands the armies"; Myrrhine's name is chosen to suggest *myrton,* a Greek word meaning *pudenda muliebria;* female sex organ; Lampito is a celebrated Spartan name; Cinesias, although a real name in Athens, is chosen to suggest a Greek verb *kinein, to move,* then *to make love, to have intercourse,* and the name of his deme, Paionidai, suggests the verb *paiein,* which has about the same significance. (Translator's note.)

LYSISTRATA: If they'd been summoned to worship the God of Wine, or Pan, or to visit the Queen of Love, why, you couldn't have pushed your way through the streets for all the timbrels. But now there's not a single woman here—except my neighbour; here she comes. [*Enter* CALONICE] Good day to you, Calonice.

CALONICE: And to you, Lysistrata. [*noticing* LYSISTRATA*'s impatient air*] But what ails you? Don't scowl, my dear; it's not becoming to you to knit your brows like that.

LYSISTRATA [*sadly*]: Ah, Calonice, my heart aches; I'm so annoyed at us women. For among men we have a reputation for sly trickery—

CALONICE: And rightly too, on my word!

LYSISTRATA: —but when they were told to meet here to consider a matter of no small importance, they lie abed and don't come.

CALONICE: Oh, they'll come all right, my dear. It's not easy for a woman to get out, you know. One is working on her husband, another is getting up the maid, another has to put the baby to bed, or wash and feed it.

LYSISTRATA: But after all, there are other matters more important than all that.

CALONICE: My dear Lysistrata, just what is this matter you've summoned us women to consider? What's up? Something big?

LYSISTRATA: Very big.

CALONICE [*interested*]: Is it stout, too?

LYSISTRATA [*smiling*]: Yes indeed—both big and stout.

CALONICE: What? And the women still haven't come?

LYSISTRATA: It's not what you suppose; they'd have come soon enough for *that.* But I've worked up something, and for many a sleepless night I've turned it this way and that.

CALONICE [*in mock disappointment*]: Oh, I guess it's pretty fine and slender, if you've turned it this way and that.

LYSISTRATA: So fine that the safety of the whole of Greece lies in us women.

CALONICE: In us women? It depends on a very slender reed then.

LYSISTRATA: Our country's fortunes are in our hands; and whether the Spartans shall perish—

CALONICE: Good! Let them perish, by all means.

LYSISTRATA: —and the Boeotians shall be completely annihilated.

CALONICE: Not completely! Please spare the eels.[2]

LYSISTRATA: As for Athens, I won't use any such unpleasant words. But you understand what I mean. But if the women will meet here—the Spartans, the Boeotians, and we Athenians—then all together we will save Greece.

CALONICE: But what could women do that's clever or distinguished? We just sit around all dolled up in silk robes, looking pretty in our sheer gowns and evening slippers.

LYSISTRATA: These are just the things I hope will save us: these silk robes, perfumes, evening slippers, rouge, and our chiffon blouses.

CALONICE: How so?

---

[2] **eels:** A delicacy from the Boeotian lakes.

LYSISTRATA: So never a man alive will lift a spear against the foe—
CALONICE: I'll get a silk gown at once.
LYSISTRATA: —or take up his shield—
CALONICE: I'll put on my sheerest gown!
LYSISTRATA: —or sword.
CALONICE: I'll buy a pair of evening slippers.
LYSISTRATA: Well then, shouldn't the women have come?
CALONICE: Come? Why, they should have *flown* here.
LYSISTRATA: Well, my dear, just watch: they'll act in true Athenian fashion—everything too late! And now there's not a woman here from the shore or from Salamis.[3]
CALONICE: They're coming, I'm sure; at daybreak they were laying—to their oars to cross the straits.
LYSISTRATA: And those I expected would be the first to come—the women of Acharnae[4]—they haven't arrived.
CALONICE: Yet the wife of Theagenes[5] means to come: she consulted Hecate about it. [*seeing a group of women approaching*] But look! Here come a few. And there are some more over here. Hurrah! Where do they come from?
LYSISTRATA: From Anagyra.[6]
CALONICE: Yes indeed! We've raised up quite a stink from Anagyra anyway.

[*Enter* MYRRHINE *in haste, followed by several other women.*]
MYRRHINE [*breathlessly*]: Have we come in time, Lysistrata? What do you say? Why so quiet?
LYSISTRATA: I can't say much for you, Myrrhine, coming at this hour on such important business.
MYRRHINE: Why, I had trouble finding my girdle in the dark. But if it's so important, we're here now; tell us.
LYSISTRATA: No. Let's wait a little for the women from Boeotia and the Peloponnesus.
MYRRHINE: That's a much better suggestion. Look! Here comes Lampito now.

[*Enter* LAMPITO *with two other women.*]
LYSISTRATA: Greetings, my dear Spartan friend. How pretty you look, my dear. What a smooth complexion and well-developed figure! You could throttle an ox.
LAMPITO: Faith, yes, I think I could. I take exercises and kick my heels against my bum. [*She demonstrates with a few steps of the Spartan "bottom-kicking" dance.*]
LYSISTRATA: And what splendid breasts you have.
LAMPITO: La! You handle me like a prize steer.
LYSISTRATA: And who is this young lady with you?
LAMPITO: Faith, she's an Ambassadress from Boeotia.
LYSISTRATA: Oh yes, a Boeotian, and blooming like a garden too.

---

[3] **Salamis:** An island off the coast of Piraeus, the port of Athens. [4] **Acharnae:** A town outside of Athens. [5] **Theagenes:** A notoriously superstitious man. [6] **Anagyra:** A foul-smelling marshy area south of Athens.

CALONICE [*lifting up her skirt*]: My word! How neatly her garden's weeded!

LYSISTRATA: And who is the other girl?

LAMPITO: Oh, she's a Corinthian swell.

MYRRHINE [*after a rapid examination*]: Yes indeed. She swells very nicely [*pointing*] here and here.

LAMPITO: Who has gathered together this company of women?

LYSISTRATA: I have.

LAMPITO: Speak up, then. What do you want?

MYRRHINE: Yes, my dear, do tell us what this important matter is.

LYSISTRATA: Very well, I'll tell you. But before I speak, let me ask you a little question.

MYRRHINE: Anything you like.

LYSISTRATA [*earnestly*]: Tell me: don't you yearn for the fathers of your children, who are away at the wars? I know you all have husbands abroad.

CALONICE: Why, yes; mercy me! my husband's been away for five months in Thrace keeping guard on — Eucrates.[7]

MYRRHINE: And mine for seven whole months in Pylus.

LAMPITO: And mine, as soon as ever he returns from the fray, readjusts his shield and flies out of the house again.

LYSISTRATA: And as for lovers, there's not even a ghost of one left. Since the Milesians revolted from us, I've not even seen an eight-inch dingus to be a leather consolation for us widows.[8] Are you willing, if I can find a way, to help me end the war?

MYRRHINE: Goodness, yes! I'd do it, even if I had to pawn my dress and — get drunk on the spot!

CALONICE: And I, even if I had to let myself be split in two like a flounder.

LAMPITO: I'd climb up Mt. Taygetus[9] if I could catch a glimpse of peace.

LYSISTRATA: I'll tell you, then, in plain and simple words. My friends, if we are going to force our men to make peace, we must do without —

MYRRHINE: Without what? Tell us.

LYSISTRATA: Will you do it?

MYRRHINE: We'll do it, if it kills us.

LYSISTRATA: Well then, we must do without sex altogether. [*general consternation*] Why do you turn away? Where go you? Why turn so pale? Why those tears? Will you do it or not? What means this hesitation?

MYRRHINE: I won't do it! Let the war go on.

CALONICE: Nor I! Let the war go on.

LYSISTRATA: So, my little flounder? Didn't you say just now you'd split yourself in half?

CALONICE: Anything else you like. I'm willing, even if I have to walk through fire. Anything rather than sex. There's nothing like it, my dear.

LYSISTRATA [*to* MYRRHINE]: What about you?

MYRRHINE [*sullenly*]: I'm willing to walk through fire, too.

---

[7] **Eucrates:** An Athenian general of questionable loyalty. [8] **leather . . . widows:** The Milesians, former allies of Athens, manufactured a leather dildo. [9] **Mt. Taygetus:** A mountain near Sparta.

LYSISTRATA: Oh vile and cursed breed! No wonder they make tragedies about us: we're naught but "love-affairs and bassinets." But you, my dear Spartan friend, if you alone are with me, our enterprise might yet succeed. Will you vote with me?

LAMPITO: 'Tis cruel hard, by my faith, for a woman to sleep alone without her nooky; but for all that, we certainly do need peace.

LYSISTRATA: O my dearest friend! You're the only real woman here.

CALONICE [*wavering*]: Well, if we do refrain from— [*shuddering*] what you say (God forbid!), would that bring peace?

LYSISTRATA: My goodness, yes! If we sit at home all rouged and powdered, dressed in our sheerest gowns, and neatly depilated, our men will get excited and want to take us; but if you don't come to them and keep away, they'll soon make a truce.

LAMPITO: Aye; Menelaus caught sight of Helen's naked breast and dropped his sword, they say.

CALONICE: What if the men give us up?

LYSISTRATA: "Flay a skinned dog," as Pherecrates says.

CALONICE: Rubbish! These make-shifts are no good. But suppose they grab us and drag us into the bedroom?

LYSISTRATA: Hold on to the door.

CALONICE: And if they beat us?

LYSISTRATA: Give in with a bad grace. There's no pleasure in it for them when they have to use violence. And you must torment them in every possible way. They'll give up soon enough; a man gets no joy if he doesn't get along with his wife.

MYRRHINE: If this is your opinion, we agree.

LAMPITO: As for our own men, we can persuade them to make a just and fair peace; but what about the Athenian rabble? Who will persuade them not to start any more monkey-shines?

LYSISTRATA: Don't worry. We guarantee to convince them.

LAMPITO: Not while their ships are rigged so well and they have that mighty treasure in the temple of Athene.

LYSISTRATA: We've taken good care for that too: we shall seize the Acropolis today. The older women have orders to do this, and while we are making our arrangements, they are to pretend to make a sacrifice and occupy the Acropolis.

LAMPITO: All will be well then. That's a very fine idea.

LYSISTRATA: Let's ratify this, Lampito, with the most solemn oath.

LAMPITO: Tell us what oath we shall swear.

LYSISTRATA: Well said. Where's our Policewoman? [*to a Scythian slave*] What are you gaping at? Set a shield upside-down here in front of me, and give me the sacred meats.

CALONICE: Lysistrata, what sort of an oath are we to take?

LYSISTRATA: What oath? I'm going to slaughter a sheep over the shield, as they do in Aeschylus.[10]

---

[10] **in Aeschylus:** In *Seven Against Thebes*, the warriors swear loyalty to each other and slaughter a bull so that the blood flows into the hollow of a shield.

CALONICE: Don't, Lysistrata! No oaths about peace over a shield.

LYSISTRATA: What shall the oath be, then?

CALONICE: How about getting a white horse somewhere and cutting out its entrails for the sacrifice?

LYSISTRATA: White horse indeed!

CALONICE: Well then, how shall we swear?

MYRRHINE: I'll tell you: let's place a large black bowl upside-down and then slaughter—a flask of Thasian wine.[11] And then let's swear—not to pour in a single drop of water.

LAMPITO: Lord! How I like that oath!

LYSISTRATA: Someone bring out a bowl and a flask.

[*A slave brings the utensils for the sacrifice.*]

CALONICE: Look, my friends! What a big jar! Here's a cup that 'twould give me joy to handle. [*She picks up the bowl.*]

LYSISTRATA: Set it down and put your hands on our victim. [*as* CALONICE *places her hands on the flask*] O Lady of Persuasion and dear Loving Cup, graciously vouchsafe to receive this sacrifice from us women. [*She pours the wine into the bowl.*]

CALONICE: The blood has a good colour and spurts out nicely.

LAMPITO: Faith, it has a pleasant smell, too.

MYRRHINE: Oh, let me be the first to swear, ladies!

CALONICE: No, by our Lady! Not unless you're allotted the first turn.

LYSISTRATA: Place all your hands on the cup, and one of you repeat on behalf of all what I say. Then all will swear and ratify the oath. *I will suffer no man, be he husband or lover,*

CALONICE: *I will suffer no man, be he husband or lover,*

LYSISTRATA: *To approach me all hot and horny.* [*as* CALONICE *hesitates*] Say it!

CALONICE [*slowly and painfully*]: *To approach me all hot and horny.* O Lysistrata, I feel so weak in the knees!

LYSISTRATA: *I will remain at home unmated,*

CALONICE: *I will remain at home unmated,*

LYSISTRATA: *Wearing my sheerest gown and carefully adorned,*

CALONICE: *Wearing my sheerest gown and carefully adorned,*

LYSISTRATA: *That my husband may burn with desire for me.*

CALONICE: *That my husband may burn with desire for me.*

LYSISTRATA: *And if he takes me by force against my will,*

CALONICE: *And if he takes me by force against my will,*

LYSISTRATA: *I shall do it badly and keep from moving.*

CALONICE: *I shall do it badly and keep from moving.*

LYSISTRATA: *I will not stretch my slippers toward the ceiling,*

CALONICE: *I will not stretch my slippers toward the ceiling,*

LYSISTRATA: *Nor will I take the posture of the lioness on the knife-handle.*

---

[11] **Thasian wine:** A strong wine from the island of Thasos.

CALONICE: *Nor will I take the posture of the lioness on the knife-handle.*

LYSISTRATA: *If I keep this oath, may I be permitted to drink from this cup,*

CALONICE: *If I keep this oath, may I be permitted to drink from this cup,*

LYSISTRATA: *But f I break it, may the cup be filled with water.*

CALONICE: *But if I break it, may the cup be filled with water.*

LYSISTRATA: Do you all swear to this?

ALL: I do, so help me!

LYSISTRATA: Come then, I'll just consummate this offering. [*She takes a long drink from the cup.*]

CALONICE [*snatching the cup away*]: Shares, my dear! Let's drink to our continued friendship.

[*A shout is heard from off-stage.*]

LAMPITO: What's that shouting?

LYSISTRATA: That's what I was telling you: the women have just seized the Acropolis. Now, Lampito, go home and arrange matters in Sparta; and leave these two ladies here as hostages. We'll enter the Acropolis to join our friends and help them lock the gates.

CALONICE: Don't you suppose the men will come to attack us?

LYSISTRATA: Don't worry about them. Neither threats nor fire will suffice to open the gates, except on the terms we've stated.

CALONICE: I should say not! Else we'd belie our reputation as unmanageable pests.

[LAMPITO *leaves the stage. The other women retire and enter the Acropolis through the Propylaea.*]
[*Enter the* CHORUS OF OLD MEN, *carrying fire-pots and a load of heavy sticks.*]

LEADER OF MEN:

Onward, Draces, step by step, though your shoulder's aching.
Cursèd logs of olive-wood, what a load you're making!

FIRST SEMI-CHORUS OF OLD MEN [*singing*]:

Aye, many surprises await a man who lives to a ripe old age;
For who could suppose, Strymodorus my lad, that the women we've
nourished (alas!),
Who sat at home to vex our days,
Would seize the holy image here,
And occupy this sacred shrine,
With bolts and bars, with fell design,
To lock the Propylaea?

LEADER:

Come with speed, Philourgus, come! to the temple hast'ning.
There we'll heap these logs about in a circle round them,
And whoever has conspired, raising this rebellion,
Shall be roasted, scorched, and burnt, all without exception,
Doomed by one unanimous vote—but first the wife of Lycon.[12]

---

[12] **the wife of Lycon:** A woman of dubious reputation.

SECOND SEMI-CHORUS [*singing*]:
No, no! by Demeter, while I'm alive, no woman shall mock at me.
Not even the Spartan Cleomenes,[13] our citadel first to seize,
Got off unscathed; for all his pride
And haughty Spartan arrogance,
He left his arms and sneaked away,
Stripped to his shirt, unkempt, unshav'd,
With six years' filth still on him.

LEADER:
I besieged that hero bold, sleeping at my station,
Marshalled at these holy gates sixteen deep against him.
Shall I not these cursèd pests punish for their daring,
Burning these Euripides-and-God-detested women?[14]
Aye! or else may Marathon overturn my trophy.[15]

FIRST SEMI-CHORUS [*singing*]:
There remains of my road
Just this brow of the hill;
There I speed on my way.
Drag the logs up the hill, though we've got no ass to help.
(God! my shoulder's bruised and sore!)
Onward still must we go.
Blow the fire! Don't let it go out
Now we're near the end of our road.

ALL [*blowing on the fire-pots*]: Whew! Whew! Drat the smoke!

SECOND SEMI-CHORUS [*singing*]:
Lord, what smoke rushing forth
From the pot, like a dog
Running mad, bites my eyes!
This must be Lemnos-fire.[16] What a sharp and stinging smoke!
Rushing onward to the shrine
Aid the gods. Once for all
Show your mettle, Laches my boy!
To the rescue hastening all!

ALL [*blowing on the fire-pots*]: Whew! Whew! Drat the smoke!

[*The chorus has now reached the edge of the orchestra nearest the stage, in front of the Propylaea. They begin laying their logs and fire-pots on the ground.*]

LEADER: Thank heaven, this fire is still alive. Now let's first put down these logs here and place our torches in the pots to catch; then let's make a rush for the gates

---

[13] **Cleomenes:** A Spartan king who interfered in an Athenian civil dispute in 508 B.C.E. and briefly occupied the Acropolis. [14] **Euripides . . . detested women:** Aristophanes frequently represents Euripides as a misogynist. [15] **I beseiged . . . trophy:** The old men are unbelievably boastful. If they were really alive at the time of Cleomenes' occupation in 508 B.C.E. and the Battle of Marathon in 490, they are very old men indeed. [16] **Lemnos-fire:** Lemnos is a volcanic island in the Aegean.

with a battering-ram. If the women don't unbar the gate at our summons, we'll have to smoke them out.

Let me put down my load. Ouch! That hurts! [*to the audience*] Would any of the generals in Samos[17] like to lend a hand with this log? [*throwing down a log*] Well, *that* won't break my back any more, at any rate. [*turning to his fire-pot*] Your job, my little pot, is to keep those coals alive and furnish me shortly with a red-hot torch.

O mistress Victory, be my ally and grant me to rout these audacious women in the Acropolis.

[*While the men are busy with their logs and fires, the* CHORUS OF OLD WOMEN *enters, carrying pitchers of water.*]

LEADER OF WOMEN:

What's this I see? Smoke and flames? Is that a fire ablazing?
Let's rush upon them. Hurry up! They'll find us women ready.

FIRST SEMI-CHORUS OF OLD WOMEN [*singing*]:

With wingèd foot onward I fly,
Ere the flames consume Neodice;
Lest Critylla be overwhelmed
By a lawless, accurst herd of old men.
I shudder with fear. Am I too late to aid them?
At break of the day filled we our jars with water
Fresh from the spring, pushing our way straight through the crowds. Oh, what a din!
Mid crockery crashing, jostled by slave-girls,
Sped we to save them, aiding our neighbours,
Bearing this water to put out the flames.

SECOND SEMI-CHORUS OF OLD WOMEN [*singing*]:

Such news I've heard: doddering fools
Come with logs, like furnace-attendants,
Loaded down with three hundred pounds,
Breathing many a vain, blustering threat,
That all these abhorred sluts will be burnt to charcoal.
O goddess, I pray never may they be kindled;
Grant them to save Greece and our men; madness and war help them to end.
With this as our purpose, golden-plumed Maiden,
Guardian of Athens, seized we thy precinct.
Be my ally, Warrior-maiden,
'Gainst these old men, bearing water with me.

[*The women have now reached their position in the orchestra, and their* LEADER *advances toward the* LEADER OF THE MEN.]

[17] **Samos:** An island off the coast of Asia Minor, headquarters for the Athenian fleet.

LEADER OF THE CHORUS OF OLD WOMEN: Hold on there! What's this, you utter scoundrels? No decent, God-fearing citizens would act like this.

LEADER OF THE CHORUS OF OLD MEN: Oho! Here's something unexpected: a swarm of women have come out to attack us.

LEADER OF THE CHORUS OF OLD WOMEN: What, do we frighten you? Surely you don't think we're too many for you. And yet there are ten thousand times more of us whom you haven't even seen.

LEADER OF THE CHORUS OF OLD MEN: What say, Phaedria? Shall we let these women wag their tongues? Shan't we take our sticks and break them over their backs?

LEADER OF THE CHORUS OF OLD WOMEN: Let's set our pitchers on the ground; then if anyone lays a hand on us, they won't get in our way.

LEADER OF THE CHORUS OF OLD MEN: By God! If someone gave them two or three smacks on the jaw, like Bupalus,[18] they wouldn't talk so much!

LEADER OF THE CHORUS OF OLD WOMEN: Go on, hit me, somebody! Here's my jaw! But no other bitch will bite a piece out of you before me.

LEADER OF THE CHORUS OF OLD MEN: Silence! or I'll knock out your—senility!

LEADER OF THE CHORUS OF OLD WOMEN: Just lay one finger on Stratyllis, I dare you!

LEADER OF THE CHORUS OF OLD MEN: Suppose I dust you off with this fist? What will you do?

LEADER OF THE CHORUS OF OLD WOMEN: I'll tear the living guts out of you with my teeth.

LEADER OF THE CHORUS OF OLD MEN: No poet is more clever than Euripides: "There is no beast so shameless as a woman."

LEADER OF THE CHORUS OF OLD WOMEN: Let's pick up our jars of water, Rhodippe.

LEADER OF THE CHORUS OF OLD MEN: Why have you come here with water, you detestable slut?

LEADER OF THE CHORUS OF OLD WOMEN: And why have you come with fire, you funeral vault? To cremate yourself?

LEADER OF THE CHORUS OF OLD MEN: To light a fire and singe your friends.

LEADER OF THE CHORUS OF OLD WOMEN: And I've brought water to put out your fire.

LEADER OF THE CHORUS OF OLD MEN: What? You'll put out my fire?

LEADER OF THE CHORUS OF OLD WOMEN: Just try and see!

LEADER OF THE CHORUS OF OLD MEN: I wonder: shall I scorch you with this torch of mine?

LEADER OF THE CHORUS OF OLD WOMEN: If you've got any soap, I'll give you a bath.

LEADER OF THE CHORUS OF OLD MEN: Give *me* a bath, you stinking hag?

LEADER OF THE CHORUS OF OLD WOMEN: Yes—a bridal bath!

LEADER OF THE CHORUS OF OLD MEN: Just listen to her! What crust!

LEADER OF THE CHORUS OF OLD WOMEN: Well, I'm a free citizen.

LEADER OF THE CHORUS OF OLD MEN: I'll put an end to your bawling. [*The men pick up their torches.*]

---

[18] **Bupalus:** A sixth-century-B.C.E. sculptor.

LEADER OF THE CHORUS OF OLD WOMEN: You'll never do jury-duty again. [*The women pick up their pitchers.*]

LEADER OF THE CHORUS OF OLD MEN: Singe her hair for her!

LEADER OF THE CHORUS OF OLD WOMEN: Do your duty, water! [*The women empty their pitchers on the men.*]

LEADER OF THE CHORUS OF OLD MEN: Ow! Ow! For heaven's sake!

LEADER OF THE CHORUS OF OLD WOMEN: Is it too hot?

LEADER OF THE CHORUS OF OLD MEN: What do you mean "hot"? Stop! What are you doing?

LEADER OF THE CHORUS OF OLD WOMEN: I'm watering you, so you'll be fresh and green.

LEADER OF THE CHORUS OF OLD MEN: But I'm all withered up with shaking.

LEADER OF THE CHORUS OF OLD WOMEN: Well, you've got a fire; why don't you dry yourself?

[*Enter an Athenian* MAGISTRATE, *accompanied by four Scythian policemen.*]

ATHENIAN MAGISTRATE: Have these wanton women flared up again with their timbrels and their continual worship of Sabazius?[19] Is this another Adonis-dirge upon the roof-tops—which we heard not long ago in the Assembly? That confounded Demostratus[20] was urging us to sail to Sicily, and the whirling women shouted, "Woe for Adonis!" And then Demostratus said we'd best enroll the infantry from Zacynthus, and a tipsy woman on the roof shrieked, "Beat your breasts for Adonis!" And that vile and filthy lunatic forced his measure through. Such license do our women take.

LEADER OF THE CHORUS OF OLD MEN: What if you heard of the insolence of these women here? Besides their other violent acts, they threw water all over us, and we have to shake out our clothes just as if we'd leaked in them.

ATHENIAN MAGISTRATE: And rightly, too, by God! For we ourselves lead the women astray and teach them to play the wanton; from these roots such notions blossom forth. A man goes into the jeweler's shop and says, "About that necklace you made for my wife, goldsmith: last night, while she was dancing, the fastening-bolt slipped out of the hole. I have to sail over to Salamis today; if you're free, do come around tonight and fit in a new bolt for her." Another goes to the shoemaker, a strapping young fellow with manly parts, and says, "See here, cobbler, the sandal-strap chafes my wife's little—toe; it's so tender. Come around during the siesta and stretch it a little, so she'll be more comfortable." Now we see the results of such treatment: here I'm a special Councillor and need money to procure oars for the galleys; and I'm locked out of the Treasury by these women.

---

[19] **worship of Sabazius:** A religious cult worshiping the Eastern deity Sabazius, similar to the Adonis cult. Both cults were suspect in the eyes of religious conservatives.

[20] **Demostratus:** One of the prominent supporters of the disastrous Athenian campaign in Sicily. He urged the Assembly to draft the inhabitants of the island of Zacynthus, allies of the Athenians, to the Athenian cause.

But this is no time to stand around. Bring up crow-bars there! I'll put an end to their insolence. [*to one of the policemen*] What are you gaping at, you wretch? What are you staring at? Got an eye out for a tavern, eh? Set your crow-bars here to the gates and force them open. [*retiring to a safe distance*] I'll help from over here.

[*The gates are thrown open and* LYSISTRATA *comes out followed by several other women.*]

LYSISTRATA: Don't force the gates; I'm coming out of my own accord. We don't need crow-bars here; what we need is good sound common-sense.

ATHENIAN MAGISTRATE: Is that so, you strumpet? Where's my policeman? Officer, arrest her and tie her arms behind her back.

LYSISTRATA: By Artemis, if he lays a finger on me, he'll pay for it, even if he is a public servant.

[*The policeman retires in terror.*]

ATHENIAN MAGISTRATE: You there, are you afraid? Seize her round the waist—and you, too. Tie her up, both of you!

FIRST WOMAN [*as the second policeman approaches* LYSISTRATA]: By Pandrosus,[21] if you but touch her with your hand, I'll kick the stuffings out of you.

[*The second policeman retires in terror.*]

ATHENIAN MAGISTRATE: Just listen to that: "kick the stuffings out." Where's another policeman? Tie *her* up first, for her chatter.

SECOND WOMAN: By the Goddess of the Light, if you lay the tip of your finger on her, you'll soon need a doctor.

[*The third policeman retires in terror.*]

ATHENIAN MAGISTRATE: What's this? Where's my policeman? Seize *her* too. I'll soon stop your sallies.

THIRD WOMAN: By the Goddess of Tauros,[22] if you go near her, I'll tear out your hair until it shrieks with pain.

[*The fourth policeman retires in terror.*]

ATHENIAN MAGISTRATE: Oh, damn it all! I've run out of policemen. But women must never defeat us. Others, let's charge them all together. Close up your ranks!

[*The policemen rally for a mass attack.*]

LYSISTRATA: By heaven, you'll soon find out that we have four companies of warrior-women, all fully equipped within!

ATHENIAN MAGISTRATE [*advancing*]: Twist their arms off, men!

LYSISTRATA [*shouting*]:

> To the rescue, my valiant women!
> O sellers-of-barley-green-stuffs-and-eggs,
> O sellers-of-garlic, ye keepers-of-taverns, and vendors-of-bread,

[21] **Pandrosus:** A mythical Athenian goddess. [22] **Goddess of Tauros:** Artemis.

Grapple! Smite! Smash!
Won't you heap filth on them? Give them a tongue-lashing!

[*The women beat off the policemen.*]

Halt! Withdraw! No looting on the field.

ATHENIAN MAGISTRATE: Damn it! My police-force has put up a very poor show.

LYSISTRATA: What did you expect? Did you think you were attacking slaves? Didn't you know that women are filled with passion?

ATHENIAN MAGISTRATE: Aye, passion enough—for a good strong drink!

LEADER OF THE CHORUS OF OLD MEN:

O chief and leader of this land, why spend your words in vain?
Don't argue with these shameless beasts. You know not how we've fared:
A soapless bath they've given us; our clothes are soundly soaked.

LEADER OF THE CHORUS OF OLD WOMEN:

Poor fool! You never should attack or strike a peaceful girl.
But if you do, your eyes must swell. For I am quite content
To sit unmoved, like modest maids, in peace and cause no pain;
But let a man stir up my hive, he'll find me like a wasp.

CHORUS OF MEN [*singing*]:

O God, whatever shall we do with creatures like Womankind?
This can't be endured by any man alive. Question them!
Let us try to find out what this means.
To what end have they seized on this shrine,
This steep and rugged, high and holy,
Undefiled Acropolis?

LEADER OF THE CHORUS OF OLD MEN:

Come, put your questions; don't give in, and probe her every statement.
For base and shameful it would be to leave this plot untested.

ATHENIAN MAGISTRATE: Well then, first of all I wish to ask her this: for what purpose have you barred us from the Acropolis?

LYSISTRATA: To keep the treasure safe, so you won't make war on account of it.

ATHENIAN MAGISTRATE: What? Do we make war on account of the treasure?

LYSISTRATA: Yes, and you cause all our other troubles for it too. Peisander[23] and those greedy office-seekers keep things stirred up so they can find occasions to steal. Now let them do what they like: they'll never again make off with any of this money.

ATHENIAN MAGISTRATE: What will you do?

LYSISTRATA: What a question! We'll administer it ourselves.

ATHENIAN MAGISTRATE: *You* will administer the treasure?

LYSISTRATA: What's so strange in that? Don't we administer the household money for you?

[23] **Peisander:** A corrupt politician and one of the leaders of the Athenian war party.

…THENIAN MAGISTRATE: That's different.

…YSISTRATA: How is it different?

…THENIAN MAGISTRATE: We've got to make war with this money.

LYSISTRATA: But that's the very first thing: you mustn't make war.

ATHENIAN MAGISTRATE: How else can we be saved?

LYSISTRATA: We'll save you.

ATHENIAN MAGISTRATE: *You?*

LYSISTRATA: Yes, we!

ATHENIAN MAGISTRATE: God forbid!

LYSISTRATA: We'll save you, whether you want it or not.

ATHENIAN MAGISTRATE: Oh! This is terrible!

LYSISTRATA: You don't like it, but we're going to do it none the less.

ATHENIAN MAGISTRATE: Good God! it's illegal!

LYSISTRATA: We *will* save you, my little man!

ATHENIAN MAGISTRATE: Suppose I don't want you to?

LYSISTRATA: That's all the more reason.

ATHENIAN MAGISTRATE: What business have you with war and peace?

LYSISTRATA: I'll explain.

ATHENIAN MAGISTRATE [*shaking his fist*]: Speak up, or you'll smart for it.

LYSISTRATA: Just listen, and try to keep your hands still.

ATHENIAN MAGISTRATE: I can't. I'm so mad I can't stop them.

FIRST WOMAN: Then you'll be the one to smart for it.

ATHENIAN MAGISTRATE: Croak to yourself, old hag! [*to* LYSISTRATA] Now then, speak up.

LYSISTRATA: Very well. Formerly we endured the war for a good long time with our usual restraint, no matter what you men did. You wouldn't let us say "boo," although nothing you did suited us. But we watched you well, and though we stayed at home we'd often hear of some terribly stupid measure you'd proposed. Then, though grieving at heart, we'd smile sweetly and say, "What was passed in the Assembly today about writing on the treaty-stone?"[24] "What's that to you?" my husband would say. "Hold your tongue!" And I held my tongue.

FIRST WOMAN: But I wouldn't have—not I!

ATHENIAN MAGISTRATE: You'd have been soundly smacked, if you hadn't kept still.

LYSISTRATA: So I kept still at home. Then we'd hear of some plan still worse than the first; we'd say, "Husband, how could you pass such a stupid proposal?" He'd scowl at me and say, "If you don't mind your spinning, your head will be sore for weeks. *War shall be the concern of Men.*"[25]

ATHENIAN MAGISTRATE: And he was right, upon my word!

LYSISTRATA: Why right, you confounded fool, when your proposals were so stupid and we weren't allowed to make suggestions?

"There's not a *man* left in the country," says one. "No, not one," says another.

[24] **treaty-stone:** Treaties were inscribed on a stone and displayed in a public place. [25] ***War . . . Men:*** The final sentence repeats Hector's words to Andromache in *The Iliad*, Book 6.

Therefore all we women have decided in council to make a common effort to save Greece. How long should we have waited? Now, if you're willing to listen to our excellent proposals and keep silence for us in your turn, we still may save you.

ATHENIAN MAGISTRATE: We men keep silence for you? That's terrible; I won't endure it!

LYSISTRATA: Silence!

ATHENIAN MAGISTRATE: Silence for *you,* you wench, when you're wearing a snood? I'd rather die!

LYSISTRATA: Well, if that's all that bothers you—here! take my snood and tie it round your head. [*During the following words the women dress up the* MAGISTRATE *in women's garments.*] And *now* keep quiet! Here, take this spinning-basket, too, and card your wool with robes tucked up, munching on beans. *War shall be the concern of Women!*

LEADER OF THE CHORUS OF OLD WOMEN:

Arise and leave your pitchers, girls; no time is this to falter.
We too must aid our loyal friends; our turn has come for action.

CHORUS OF WOMEN [*singing*]:

I'll never tire of aiding them with song and dance; never may
Faintness keep my legs from moving to and fro endlessly.
For I yearn to do all for my friends;
They have charm, they have wit, they have grace,
With courage, brains, and best of virtues—
Patriotic sapience.

LEADER OF THE CHORUS OF OLD WOMEN:

Come, child of manliest ancient dames, offspring of stinging nettles,
Advance with rage unsoftened; for fair breezes speed you onward.

LYSISTRATA: If only sweet Eros and the Cyprian Queen of Love shed charm over our breasts and limbs and inspire our men with amorous longing and priapic spasms, I think we may soon be called Peacemakers among the Greeks.

ATHENIAN MAGISTRATE: What will you do?

LYSISTRATA: First of all, we'll stop those fellows who run madly about the Marketplace in arms.

FIRST WOMAN: Indeed we shall, by the Queen of Paphos.[26]

LYSISTRATA: For now they roam about the market, amid the pots and greenstuffs, armed to the teeth like Corybantes.[27]

ATHENIAN MAGISTRATE: That's what manly fellows ought to do!

LYSISTRATA: But it's so silly: a chap with a Gorgon-emblazoned shield buying pickled herring.

FIRST WOMAN: Why, just the other day I saw one of those long-haired dandies who command our cavalry ride up on horseback and pour into his bronze helmet

[26] **Queen of Paphos:** Aphrodite. [27] **Corybantes:** Armed priests of the goddess Cybele.

the egg-broth he'd bought from an old dame. And there was a Thracian slinger too, shaking his lance like Tereus;[28] he'd scared the life out of the poor fig-peddler and was gulping down all her ripest fruit.

ATHENIAN MAGISTRATE: How can you stop all the confusion in the various states and bring them together?

LYSISTRATA: Very easily.

ATHENIAN MAGISTRATE: Tell me how.

LYSISTRATA: Just like a ball of wool, when it's confused and snarled: we take it thus, and draw out a thread here and a thread there with our spindles; thus we'll unsnarl this war, if no one prevents us, and draw together the various states with embassies here and embassies there.

ATHENIAN MAGISTRATE: Do you suppose you can stop this dreadful business with balls of wool and spindles, you nit-wits?

LYSISTRATA: Why, if *you* had any wits, you'd manage all affairs of state like our wool-working.

ATHENIAN MAGISTRATE: How so?

LYSISTRATA: First you ought to treat the city as we do when we wash the dirt out of a fleece: stretch it out and pluck and thrash out of the city all those prickly scoundrels; aye, and card out those who conspire and stick together to gain office, pulling off their heads. Then card the wool, all of it, into one fair basket of goodwill, mingling in the aliens residing here, any loyal foreigners, and anyone who's in debt to the Treasury; and consider that all our colonies lie scattered round about like remnants; from all of these collect the wool and gather it together here, wind up a great ball, and then weave a good stout cloak for the democracy.

ATHENIAN MAGISTRATE: Dreadful! Talking about thrashing and winding balls of wool, when you haven't the slightest share in the war!

LYSISTRATA: Why, you dirty scoundrel, we bear more than twice as much as you. First, we bear children and send off our sons as soldiers.

ATHENIAN MAGISTRATE: Hush! Let bygones be bygones!

LYSISTRATA: Then, when we ought to be happy and enjoy our youth, we sleep alone because of your expeditions abroad. But never mind us married women: I grieve most for the maids who grow old at home unwed.

ATHENIAN MAGISTRATE: Don't men grow old, too?

LYSISTRATA: For heaven's sake! That's not the same thing. When a man comes home, no matter how grey he is, he soon finds a girl to marry. But woman's bloom is short and fleeting; if she doesn't grasp her chance, no man is willing to marry her and she sits at home a prey to every fortune-teller.

ATHENIAN MAGISTRATE [*coarsely*]: But if a man can still get it up—

LYSISTRATA: See here, you: what's the matter? Aren't you dead yet? There's plenty of room for you. Buy yourself a shroud and I'll make you a honey-cake.[29] [*handing*

---

[28] **Tereus:** A mythical king of Thrace. [29] **honey-cake:** The dead were provided with a honey-cake to throw to Cerberus, the guardian of the entrance to the underworld.

him a copper coin for his passage across the Styx] Here's your fare! Now get yourself a wreath.

[*During the following dialogue the women dress up the* MAGISTRATE *as a corpse.*]

FIRST WOMAN: Here, take these fillets.

SECOND WOMAN: Here, take this wreath.

LYSISTRATA: What do you want? What's lacking? Get moving; off to the ferry! Charon is calling you; don't keep him from sailing.

ATHENIAN MAGISTRATE: Am I to endure these insults? By God! I'm going straight to the magistrates to show them how I've been treated.

LYSISTRATA: Are you grumbling that you haven't been properly laid out? Well, the day after tomorrow we'll send around all the usual offerings early in the morning.

[*The* MAGISTRATE *goes out still wearing his funeral decorations.* LYSISTRATA *and the women retire into the Acropolis.*]

LEADER OF THE CHORUS OF OLD MEN: Wake, ye sons of freedom, wake! 'Tis no time for sleeping. Up and at them, like a man! Let us strip for action.

[*The* CHORUS OF MEN *remove their outer cloaks.*]

CHORUS OF MEN [*singing*]:

Surely there is something here greater than meets the eye;
For without a doubt I smell Hippias'[30] tyranny.
Dreadful fear assails me lest certain bands of Spartan men,
Meeting here with Cleisthenes,[31] have inspired through treachery
All these god-detested women secretly to seize
Athens' treasure in the temple, and to stop that pay
Whence I live at my ease.

LEADER OF THE CHORUS OF OLD MEN: Now isn't it terrible for them to advise the state and chatter about shields, being mere women?

And they think to reconcile us with the Spartans—men who hold nothing sacred any more than hungry wolves. Surely this is a web of deceit, my friends, to conceal an attempt at tyranny. But they'll never lord it over me; I'll be on my guard and from now on, "The blade I bear / A myrtle spray shall wear." I'll occupy the market under arms and stand next to Aristogeiton.[32]

Thus I'll stand beside him. [*He strikes the pose of the famous statue of the tyrannicides, with one arm raised.*] And here's my chance to take this accurst old hag and— [*striking the* LEADER OF WOMEN] smack her on the jaw!

LEADER OF THE CHORUS OF OLD WOMEN: You'll go home in such a state your Ma won't recognize you!

Ladies all, upon the ground let us place these garments.

---

[30] **Hippias:** The last tyrant in Athens, who was overthrown in 510 B.C.E. [31] **Cleisthenes:** An effeminate Athenian, suspected of collaboration with the women. [32] **Aristogeiton:** One of the heroes of Athenian democracy; he had assassinated Hipparchus, brother of the tyrant Hippias.

[*The* CHORUS OF WOMEN *remove their outer garments.*]

CHORUS OF WOMEN [*singing*]:

Citizens of Athens, hear useful words for the state.
Rightly; for it nurtured me in my youth royally.
As a child of seven years carried I the sacred box;[33]
Then I was a Miller-maid, grinding at Athene's shrine;
Next I wore the saffron robe and played Brauronia's Bear;
And I walked as Basket-bearer, wearing chains of figs,
As a sweet maiden fair.

LEADER OF THE CHORUS OF OLD WOMEN: Therefore, am I not bound to give good advice to the city? Don't take it ill that I was born a woman, if I contribute something better than our present troubles. I pay my share; for I contribute MEN. But you miserable old fools contribute nothing, and after squandering our ancestral treasure, the fruit of the Persian Wars, you make no contribution in return. And now, all on account of you, we're facing ruin.

What, muttering, are you? If you annoy me, I'll take this hard, rough slipper and — [*striking the* LEADER OF MEN] smack you on the jaw!

CHORUS OF MEN [*singing*]:

This is outright insolence! Things go from bad to worse.
If you're men with any guts, prepare to meet the foe.
Let us strip our tunics off! We need the smell of male
Vigour. And we cannot fight all swaddled up in clothes!

[*They strip off their tunics.*]

Come then, my comrades, on to the battle, ye who once to Leipsydrion[34] came;
Then ye were MEN. Now call back your youthful vigour.
With light, wingèd footstep advance,
Shaking old age from your frame.

LEADER OF THE CHORUS OF OLD MEN: If any of us give these wenches the slightest hold, they'll stop at nothing: such is their cunning.

They will even build ships and sail against us, like Artemisia.[35] Or if they turn to mounting, I count our Knights as done for: a woman's such a tricky jockey when she gets astraddle, with a good firm seat for trotting. Just look at those Amazons that Micon painted, fighting on horseback against men!

But we must throw them all in the pillory — [*seizing and choking the* LEADER OF WOMEN] grabbing hold of yonder neck!

---

[33] **carried . . . box:** The religious duties of an Athenian girl included carrying a sacred box containing relics connected with the worship of Athena, grinding flour for religious wafers, and wearing a saffron robe and participating in the rites of Artemis.

[34] **Leipsydrion:** The site where the heroes of Athenian democracy gathered to challenge Hippias.

[35] **Artemisia:** Queen of Halicarnassus in Asia Minor, whose ships participated in Xerxes' invasion of Greece.

CHORUS OF WOMEN [*singing*]:

'Ware my anger! Like a boar 'twill rush upon you men.
Soon you'll bawl aloud for help, you'll be so soundly trimmed!
Come, my friends, let's strip with speed, and lay aside these robes;
Catch the scent of women's rage. Attack with tooth and nail!

[*They strip off their tunics.*]

Now then, come near me, you miserable man! you'll never eat garlic or black beans again.
And if you utter a single hard word, in rage I will "nurse" you as once
The beetle requited her foe.[36]

LEADER OF THE CHORUS OF OLD WOMEN: For you don't worry me; no, not so long as my Lampito lives and our Theban friend, the noble Ismenia.

You can't do anything, not even if you pass a dozen—decrees! You miserable fool, all our neighbours hate you. Why, just the other day when I was holding a festival for Hecate, I invited as playmate from our neighbours the Boeotians a charming, well-bred Copaic—eel. But they refused to send me one on account of your decrees.

And you'll never stop passing decrees until I grab your foot and—[*tripping up the* LEADER OF MEN] toss you down and break your neck!

[*Here an interval of five days is supposed to elapse.* LYSISTRATA *comes out from the Acropolis.*]

LEADER OF THE CHORUS OF OLD WOMEN [*dramatically*]: Empress of this great emprise and undertaking,

Why come you forth, I pray, with frowning brow?

LYSISTRATA: Ah, these cursèd women! Their deeds and female notions make me pace up and down in utter despair.

LEADER OF THE CHORUS OF OLD WOMEN: Ah, what sayest thou?

LYSISTRATA: The truth, alas! the truth.

LEADER OF THE CHORUS OF OLD WOMEN: What dreadful tale hast thou to tell thy friends?

LYSISTRATA: 'Tis shame to speak, and not to speak is hard.

LEADER OF THE CHORUS OF OLD WOMEN: Hide not from me whatever woes we suffer.

LYSISTRATA: Well then, to put it briefly, we want—laying!

LEADER OF THE CHORUS OF OLD WOMEN: O Zeus, Zeus!

LYSISTRATA: Why call on Zeus? That's the way things are. I can no longer keep them away from the men, and they're all deserting. I caught one wriggling through a hole near the grotto of Pan, and another sliding down a rope, another deserting her post; and yesterday I found one getting on a sparrow's back to fly off to Orsilochus,[37] and had to pull her back by the hair. They're digging up all sorts of excuses to get home. Look, here comes one of them now. [*A woman comes hastily out of the Acropolis.*] Here you! Where are you off to in such a hurry?

---

[36] **The beetle . . . foe:** In Aesop's fable, the beetle gets back at the eagle by breaking its eggs. [37] **Orsilochus:** Proprietor of a brothel.

FIRST WOMAN: I want to go home. My very best wool is being devoured by moths.

LYSISTRATA: Moths? Nonsense! Go back inside.

FIRST WOMAN: I'll come right back; I swear it. I just want to lay it out on the bed.

LYSISTRATA: Well, you won't lay it out, and you won't go home, either.

FIRST WOMAN: Shall I let my wool be ruined?

LYSISTRATA: If necessary, yes. [*Another woman comes out.*]

SECOND WOMAN: Oh dear! Oh dear! My precious flax! I left it at home all unpeeled.

LYSISTRATA: Here's another one, going home for her "flax." Come back here!

SECOND WOMAN: But I just want to work it up a little and then I'll be right back.

LYSISTRATA: No indeed! If you start this, all the other women will want to do the same. [*A third woman comes out.*]

THIRD WOMAN: O Eilithyia, goddess of travail, stop my labour till I come to a lawful spot![38]

LYSISTRATA: What's this nonsense?

THIRD WOMAN: I'm going to have a baby — right now!

LYSISTRATA: But you weren't even pregnant yesterday.

THIRD WOMAN: Well, I am today. O Lysistrata, do send me home to see a midwife, right away.

LYSISTRATA: What are you talking about? [*putting her hand on her stomach*] What's this hard lump here?

THIRD WOMAN: A little boy.

LYSISTRATA: My goodness, what have you got there? It seems hollow; I'll just find out. [*pulling aside her robe*] Why, you silly goose, you've got Athene's sacred helmet there. And you said you were having a baby!

THIRD WOMAN: Well, I *am* having one, I swear!

LYSISTRATA: Then what's this helmet for?

THIRD WOMAN: If the baby starts coming while I'm still in the Acropolis, I'll creep into this like a pigeon and give birth to it there.

LYSISTRATA: Stuff and nonsense! It's plain enough what you're up to. You just wait here for the christening of this — helmet.

THIRD WOMAN: But I can't sleep in the Acropolis since I saw the sacred snake.

FIRST WOMAN: And I'm dying for lack of sleep: the hooting of the owls[39] keeps me awake.

LYSISTRATA: Enough of these shams, you wretched creatures. You want your husbands, I suppose. Well, don't you think they want us? I'm sure they're spending miserable nights. Hold out, my friends, and endure for just a little while. There's an oracle that we shall conquer, if we don't split up. [*producing a roll of paper*] Here it is.

FIRST WOMAN: Tell us what it says.

LYSISTRATA: Listen.

---

[38] **lawful spot:** The Acropolis was sacred ground; to give birth there was considered sacrilegious.

[39] **owls:** The sacred birds of Athena.

"When in the length of time the Swallows shall gather together,
Fleeing the Hoopoe's amorous flight and the Cockatoo shunning,
Then shall your woes be ended and Zeus who thunders in heaven
Set what's below on top—"

FIRST WOMAN: What? Are we going to be on top?

LYSISTRATA: "But if the Swallows rebel and flutter away from the temple,
Never a bird in the world shall seem more wanton and worthless."

FIRST WOMAN: That's clear enough, upon my word!

LYSISTRATA: By all that's holy, let's not give up the struggle now. Let's go back inside. It would be a shame, my dear friends, to disobey the oracle.

[*The women all retire to the Acropolis again.*]

CHORUS OF MEN [*singing*]:

I have a tale to tell,
Which I know full well.
It was told me
In the nursery.

Once there was a likely lad,
Melanion they name him;
The thought of marriage made him mad,
For which I cannot blame him.

So off he went to mountains fair;
(No women to upbraid him!)
A mighty hunter of the hare,
He had a dog to aid him.

He never came back home to see
Detested women's faces.
He showed a shrewd mentality.
With him I'd fain change places!

ONE OF THE MEN [*to one of the women*]: Come here, old dame; give me a kiss.

WOMAN: You'll ne'er eat garlic, if you dare!

MAN: I want to kick you—just like this!

WOMAN: Oh, there's a leg with bushy hair!

MAN: Myronides and Phormio[40]
Were hairy—and they thrashed the foe.

CHORUS OF WOMEN [*singing*]

I have another tale,

[40] **Myronides . . . Phormio:** Athenian generals.

With which to assail
    Your contention
    'Bout Melanion.

Once upon a time a man
    Named Timon left our city.
To live in some deserted land.
    (We thought him rather witty.)

He dwelt alone amidst the thorn;
    In solitude he brooded.
From some grim Fury he was born:
    Such hatred he exuded.

He cursed you men, as scoundrels through
    And through, till life he ended.
He couldn't stand the sight of YOU!
    But women he befriended.

WOMAN [*to one of the men*]: I'll smash your face in, if you like.
MAN: Oh no, please don't! You frighten me.
WOMAN: I'll lift my foot—and thus I'll strike.
MAN: Aha! Look there! What's that I see?
WOMAN: Whate'er you see, you cannot say
  That I'm not neatly trimmed today.

[LYSISTRATA *appears on the wall of the Acropolis.*]

LYSISTRATA: Hello! Hello! Girls, come here quick!

[*Several women appear beside her.*]

WOMAN: What is it? Why are you calling?

LYSISTRATA: I see a man coming: he's in a dreadful state. He's mad with passion. O Queen of Cyprus, Cythera, and Paphos, just keep on this way!

WOMAN: Where is the fellow?

LYSISTRATA: There, beside the shrine of Demeter.

WOMAN: Oh yes, so he is. Who is he?

LYSISTRATA: Let's see. Do any of you know him?

MYRRHINE: Yes indeed. That's my husband, Cinesias.

LYSISTRATA: It's up to you, now: roast him, rack him, fool him, love him—and leave him! Do everything, except what our oath forbids.

MYRRHINE: Don't worry; I'll do it.

LYSISTRATA: I'll stay here to tease him and warm him up a bit. Off with you.

[*The other women retire from the wall. Enter* CINESIAS *followed by a slave carrying a baby.* CINESIAS *is obviously in great pain and distress.*]

CINESIAS [*groaning*]: Oh-h! Oh-h-h! This is killing me! O God, what tortures I'm suffering!

LYSISTRATA [*from the wall*]: Who's that within our lines?

CINESIAS: Me.

LYSISTRATA: A *man*?

CINESIAS [*pointing*]: A *man*, indeed!

LYSISTRATA: Well, go away!

CINESIAS: Who are you to send me away?

LYSISTRATA: The captain of the guard.

CINESIAS: Oh, for heaven's sake, call out Myrrhine for me.

LYSISTRATA: Call Myrrhine? Nonsense! Who are you?

CINESIAS: Her husband, Cinesias of Paionidai.

LYSISTRATA [*appearing much impressed*]: Oh, greetings, friend. Your name is not without honour here among us. Your wife is always talking about you, and whenever she takes an egg or an apple, she says, "Here's to my dear Cinesias!"

CINESIAS [*quivering with excitement*]: Oh, ye gods in heaven!

LYSISTRATA: Indeed she does! And whenever our conversations turn to men, your wife immediately says, "All others are mere rubbish compared with Cinesias."

CINESIAS [*groaning*]: Oh! Do call her for me.

LYSISTRATA: Why should I? What will you give me?

CINESIAS: Whatever you want. All I have is yours—and you see what I've got!

LYSISTRATA: Well then, I'll go down and call her. [*She descends.*]

CINESIAS: And hurry up! I've had no joy of life ever since she left home. When I go in the house, I feel awful: everything seems so empty and I can't enjoy my dinner. I'm in such a state all the time!

MYRRHINE [*from behind the wall*]: I *do* love him so. But he won't let me love him. No, no! Don't ask me to see him!

CINESIAS: O my darling, O Myrrhine honey, why do you do this to me? [MYRRHINE *appears on the wall.*] Come down here!

MYRRHINE: No, I won't come down.

CINESIAS: Won't you come, Myrrhine, when *I* call you?

MYRRHINE: No; you don't want me.

CINESIAS: *Don't want you?* I'm in agony!

MYRRHINE: I'm going now.

CINESIAS: Please don't! At least, listen to your baby. [*to the baby*] Here you, call your mamma! [*pinching the baby*]

BABY: Ma-ma! Ma-ma! Ma-ma!

CINESIAS [*to* MYRRHINE]: What's the matter with you? Have you no pity for your child, who hasn't been washed or fed for five whole days?

MYRRHINE: Oh, poor child; your father pays no attention to you.

CINESIAS: Come down then, you heartless wretch, for the baby's sake.

MYRRHINE: Oh, what it is to be a mother! I've got to come down, I suppose. [*She leaves the wall and shortly reappears at the gate.*]

CINESIAS [*to himself*]: She seems much younger, and she has such a sweet look about her. Oh, the way she teases me! And her pretty, provoking ways make me burn with longing.

MYRRHINE [*coming out of the gate and taking the baby*]: O my sweet little angel. Naughty papa! Here, let Mummy kiss you, Mamma's little sweetheart! [*She fondles the baby lovingly.*]

CINESIAS [*in despair*]: You heartless creature, why do you do this? Why follow these other women and make both of us suffer so? [*He tries to embrace her.*]

MYRRHINE: Don't touch me!

CINESIAS: You're letting all our things at home go to wrack and ruin.

MYRRHINE: I don't care.

CINESIAS: You don't care that your wool is being plucked to pieces by the chickens?

MYRRHINE: Not in the least.

CINESIAS: And you haven't celebrated the rites of Aphrodite for ever so long. Won't you come home?

MYRRHINE: Not on your life, unless you men make a truce and stop the war.

CINESIAS: Well then, if that pleases you, we'll do it.

MYRRHINE: Well then, if that pleases *you,* I'll come home—afterwards! Right now I'm on oath not to.

CINESIAS: Then just lie down here with me for a moment.

MYRRHINE: No—[*in a teasing voice*] and yet, I won't say I don't love you.

CINESIAS: You love me? Oh, do lie down here, Myrrhine dear!

MYRRHINE: What, you silly fool! in front of the baby?

CINESIAS [*hastily thrusting the baby at the slave*]: Of course not. Here—home! Take him, Manes! [*The slave goes off with the baby.*] See, the baby's out of the way. Now won't you lie down?

MYRRHINE: But where, my dear?

CINESIAS: Where? The grotto of Pan's a lovely spot.

MYRRHINE: How could I purify myself before returning to the shrine?

CINESIAS: Easily: just wash here in the Clepsydra.[41]

MYRRHINE: And then, shall I go back on my oath?

CINESIAS: On my head be it! Don't worry about the oath.

MYRRHINE: All right, then. Just let me bring out a bed.

CINESIAS: No, don't. The ground's all right.

MYRRHINE: Heavens, no! Bad as you are, I won't let you lie on the bare ground. [*She goes into the Acropolis.*]

CINESIAS: Why, she really loves me; it's plain to see.

MYRRHINE [*returning with a bed*]: There! Now hurry up and lie down. I'll just slip off this dress. But—let's see: oh yes, I must fetch a mattress.

CINESIAS: Nonsense! No mattress for me.

MYRRHINE: Yes indeed! It's not nice on the bare springs.

CINESIAS: Give me a kiss.

MYRRHINE [*giving him a hasty kiss*]: There! [*She goes.*]

---

[41] **Clepsydra:** A spring on the Acropolis.

CINESIAS [*in mingled distress and delight*]: Oh-h! Hurry back!

MYRRHINE [*returning with a mattress*]: Here's the mattress; lie down on it. I'm taking my things off now — but — let's see: you have no pillow.

CINESIAS: I don't *want* a pillow!

MYRRHINE: But I do. [*She goes.*]

CINESIAS: Cheated again, just like Heracles and his dinner!

MYRRHINE [*returning with a pillow*]: Here, lift your head. [*to herself, wondering how else to tease him*] Is that all?

CINESIAS: Surely that's all! Do come here, precious!

MYRRHINE: I'm taking off my girdle. But remember: don't go back on your promise about the truce.

CINESIAS: Hope to die, if I do.

MYRRHINE: You don't have a blanket.

CINESIAS [*shouting in exasperation*]: *I don't want one!* I WANT TO —

MYRRHINE: Sh-h! There, there, I'll be back in a minute. [*She goes.*]

CINESIAS: She'll be the death of me with these bed-clothes.

MYRRHINE [*returning with a blanket*]: Here, get up.

CINESIAS: I've got *this* up!

MYRRHINE: Would you like some perfume?

CINESIAS: Good heavens, no! I won't have it!

MYRRHINE: Yes, you shall, whether you want it or not. [*She goes.*]

CINESIAS: O lord! Confound all perfumes anyway!

MYRRHINE [*returning with a flask*]: Stretch out your hand and put some on.

CINESIAS [*suspiciously*]: By God, I don't much like this perfume. It smacks of shilly-shallying, and has no scent of the marriage-bed.

MYRRHINE: Oh dear! This is Rhodian perfume I've brought.

CINESIAS: It's quite all right, dear. Never mind.

MYRRHINE: Don't be silly! [*She goes out with the flask.*]

CINESIAS: Damn the man who first concocted perfumes!

MYRRHINE [*returning with another flask*]: Here, try this flask.

CINESIAS: I've got another one all ready for you. Come, you wretch, lie down and stop bringing me things.

MYRRHINE: All right; I'm taking off my shoes. But, my dear, see that you vote for peace.

CINESIAS [*absently*]: I'll consider it. [MYRRHINE *runs away to the Acropolis.*] I'm ruined! The wench has skinned me and run away! [*chanting, in tragic style*] Alas! Alas! Deceived, deserted by this fairest of women, whom shall I — lay? Ah, my poor little child, how shall I nurture thee? Where's Cynalopex?[42] I needs must hire a nurse!

LEADER OF THE CHORUS OF OLD MEN [*chanting*]: Ah, wretched man, in dreadful wise beguiled, betrayed, thy soul is sore distressed. I pity thee, alas! alas! What soul, what loins, what liver could stand this strain? How firm and unyielding he stands, with naught to aid him of a morning.

[42] **Cynalopex:** A brothel-keeper.

CINESIAS: O lord! O Zeus! What tortures I endure!

LEADER OF THE CHORUS OF OLD MEN: This is the way she's treated you, that vile and cursèd wanton.

LEADER OF THE CHORUS OF OLD WOMEN: Nay, not vile and cursèd, but sweet and dear.

LEADER OF THE CHORUS OF OLD MEN: Sweet, you say? Nay, hateful, hateful!

CINESIAS:

Hateful indeed! O Zeus, Zeus!
Seize her and snatch her away,
Like a handful of dust, in a mighty,
Fiery tempest! Whirl her aloft, then let her drop
Down to the earth, with a crash, as she falls—
On the point of this waiting
Thingummybob! [*He goes out.*]

[*Enter a Spartan* HERALD, *in an obvious state of excitement, which he is doing his best to conceal.*]

HERALD: Where can I find the Senate or the Prytanes?[43] I've got an important message.

[*The Athenian* MAGISTRATE *enters.*]

ATHENIAN MAGISTRATE: Say there, are you a man or Priapus?[44]

HERALD [*in annoyance*]: I'm a herald, you lout! I've come from Sparta about the truce.

ATHENIAN MAGISTRATE: Is that a spear you've got under your cloak?

HERALD: No, of course not!

ATHENIAN MAGISTRATE: Why do you twist and turn so? Why hold your cloak in front of you? Did you rupture yourself on the trip?

HERALD: By gum, the fellow's an old fool.

ATHENIAN MAGISTRATE [*pointing*]: Why, you dirty rascal, you're all excited.

HERALD: Not at all. Stop this tom-foolery.

ATHENIAN MAGISTRATE: Well, what's that I see?

HERALD: A Spartan message-staff.

ATHENIAN MAGISTRATE: Oh, certainly! That's just the kind of message-staff I've got. But tell me the honest truth: how are things going in Sparta?

HERALD: All the land of Sparta is up in arms—and our allies are up, too. We need Pellene.[45]

ATHENIAN MAGISTRATE: What brought this trouble on you? A sudden Panic?

HERALD: No, Lampito started it and then all the other women in Sparta with one accord chased their husbands out of their beds.

---

[43] **Prytanes:** The executive committee of the Athenian Assembly. [44] **Priapus:** A fertility god whose phallic statue guarded gardens and orchards. [45] **Pellene:** A city held by Athens and claimed by Sparta; also a famous Athenian prostitute.

ATHENIAN MAGISTRATE: How do you feel?

HERALD: Terrible. We walk around the city bent over like men lighting matches in a wind. For our women won't let us touch them until we all agree and make peace throughout Greece.

ATHENIAN MAGISTRATE: This is a general conspiracy of the women; I see it now. Well, hurry back and tell the Spartans to send ambassadors here with full powers to arrange a truce. And I'll go tell the Council to choose ambassadors from here; I've got a little something here that will soon persuade them!

HERALD: I'll fly there; for you've made an excellent suggestion.

[*The* HERALD *and the* MAGISTRATE *depart on opposite sides of the stage.*]

LEADER OF THE CHORUS OF OLD MEN:

No beast or fire is harder than womankind to tame,
Nor is the spotted leopard so devoid of shame.

LEADER OF THE CHORUS OF OLD WOMEN:

Knowing this, you dare provoke us to attack?
I'd be your steady friend, if you'd but take us back.

LEADER OF THE CHORUS OF OLD MEN:

I'll never cease my hatred keen of womankind.

LEADER OF THE CHORUS OF OLD WOMEN:

Just as you will. But now just let me help you find
That cloak you threw aside. You look so silly there
Without your clothes. Here, put it on and don't go bare.

LEADER OF THE CHORUS OF OLD MEN:

That's very kind, and shows you're not entirely bad.
But I threw off my things when I was good and mad.

LEADER OF THE CHORUS OF OLD WOMEN:

At last you seem a man, and won't be mocked, my lad.
If you'd been nice to me, I'd take this little gnat
That's in your eye and pluck it out for you, like that.

LEADER OF THE CHORUS OF OLD MEN:

So that's what's bothered me and bit my eye so long!
Please dig it out for me. I own that I've been wrong.

LEADER OF THE CHORUS OF OLD WOMEN:

I'll do so, though you've been a most ill-natured brat.
Ye gods! See here! A huge and monstrous little gnat!

LEADER OF THE CHORUS OF OLD MEN:

Oh, how that helps! For it was digging wells in me.
And now it's out, my tears can roll down hard and free.

LEADER OF THE CHORUS OF OLD WOMEN:

Here, let me wipe them off, although you're such a knave,
And kiss me.

LEADER OF THE CHORUS OF OLD MEN:

No!

LEADER OF THE CHORUS OF OLD WOMEN:

Whate'er you say, a kiss I'll have. [*She kisses him.*]

LEADER OF THE CHORUS OF OLD MEN:
Oh, confound these women! They've a coaxing way about them.
He was wise and never spoke a truer word, who said,
"We can't live with women, but we cannot live without them."
Now I'll make a truce with you. We'll fight no more; instead,
I will not injure you if you do me no wrong.
And now let's join our ranks and then begin a song.

COMBINED CHORUS [*singing*]:
Athenians, we're not prepared,
To say a single ugly word
About our fellow-citizens.
Quite the contrary: we desire but to say and to do
Naught but good. Quite enough are the ills now on hand.

Men and women, be advised:
If anyone requires
Money—minae two or three—,
We've got what he desires.

My purse is yours, on easy terms:
When Peace shall reappear,
Whate'er you've borrowed will be due.
So speak up without fear.

You needn't pay me back, you see,
If you can get a cent from me!

We're about to entertain
Some foreign gentlemen;
We've soup and tender, fresh-killed pork.
Come round to dine at ten.

Come early; wash and dress with care,
And bring the children, too.
Then step right in, no "by your leave."
We'll be expecting you.

Walk in as if you owned the place.
You'll find the door—shut in your face!

[*Enter a group of Spartan Ambassadors; they are in the same desperate condition as the Herald in the previous scene.*]

LEADER OF CHORUS: Here come the envoys from Sparta, sprouting long beards and looking for all the world as if they were carrying pig-pens in front of them.
Greetings, gentlemen of Sparta. Tell me, in what state have you come?

SPARTAN: Why waste words? You can plainly see what state we've come in!

LEADER OF CHORUS: Wow! You're in a pretty high-strung condition, and it seems to be getting worse.

SPARTAN: It's indescribable. Won't someone please arrange a peace for us—in any way you like.

LEADER OF CHORUS: Here come our own, native ambassadors, crouching like wrestlers and holding their clothes in front of them; this seems an athletic kind of malady.

[*Enter several Athenian Ambassadors.*]

ATHENIAN: Can anyone tell us where Lysistrata is? You see our condition.

LEADER OF CHORUS: Here's another case of the same complaint. Tell me, are the attacks worse in the morning?

ATHENIAN: No, we're always afflicted this way. If someone doesn't soon arrange this truce, you'd better not let me get my hands on—Cleisthenes!

LEADER OF CHORUS: If you're smart, you'll arrange your cloaks so none of the fellows who smashed the Hermae[46] can see you.

ATHENIAN: Right you are; a very good suggestion.

SPARTAN: Aye, by all means. Here, let's hitch up our clothes.

ATHENIAN: Greetings, Spartan. We've suffered dreadful things.

SPARTAN: My dear fellow, we'd have suffered still worse if one of those fellows had seen us in this condition.

ATHENIAN: Well, gentlemen, we must get down to business. What's your errand here?

SPARTAN: We're ambassadors about peace.

ATHENIAN: Excellent; so are we. Only Lysistrata can arrange things for us; shall we summon her?

SPARTAN: Aye, and Lysistratus too, if you like.

LEADER OF CHORUS: No need to summon her, it seems. She's coming out of her own accord.

[*Enter* LYSISTRATA *accompanied by a statue of a nude female figure, which represents Reconciliation.*]

Hail, noblest of women; now must thou be
A judge shrewd and subtle, mild and severe,
Be sweet yet majestic: all manners employ.
The leaders of Hellas, caught by thy love-charms,
Have come to thy judgment, their charges submitting.

LYSISTRATA: This is no difficult task, if one catch them still in amorous passion, before they've resorted to each other. But I'll soon find out. Where's Reconciliation? Go, first bring the Spartans here, and don't seize them rudely and violently, as our tactless husbands used to do, but as befits a woman, like an old, familiar

[46] **Hermae:** Small phallic statues of the god Hermes. Before the expedition to Sicily, rioters in Athens smashed many of these statues.

friend; if they won't give you their hands, take them however you can. Then go fetch these Athenians here, taking hold of whatever they offer you. Now then, men of Sparta, stand here beside me, and you Athenians on the other side, and listen to my words.

I am a woman, it is true, but I have a mind; I'm not badly off in native wit, and by listening to my father and my elders, I've had a decent schooling.

Now I intend to give you a scolding which you both deserve. With one common font you worship at the same altars, just like brothers, at Olympia, at Thermopylae, at Delphi—how many more might I name, if time permitted;—and the Barbarians stand by waiting with their armies; yet you are destroying the men and towns of Greece.

ATHENIAN: Oh, this tension is killing me!

LYSISTRATA: And now, men of Sparta,—to turn to you—don't you remember how the Spartan Pericleidas came here once as a suppliant, and sitting at our altar, all pale with fear in his crimson cloak, begged us for an army?[47] For all Messene had attacked you and the god sent an earthquake too? Then Cimon went forth with four thousand hoplites and saved all Lacedaemon. Such was the aid you received from Athens, and now you lay waste the country which once treated you so well.

ATHENIAN [*hotly*]: They're in the wrong, Lysistrata, upon my word, they are!

SPARTAN [*absently, looking at the statue of Reconciliation*]: We're in the wrong. What hips! How lovely they are!

LYSISTRATA: Don't think I'm going to let you Athenians off. Don't you remember how the Spartans came in arms when you were wearing the rough, sheepskin cloak of slaves and slew the host of Thessalians, the comrades and allies of Hippias?[48] Fighting with you on that day, alone of all the Greeks, they set you free and instead of a sheepskin gave your folk a handsome robe to wear.

SPARTAN [*looking at* LYSISTRATA]: I've never seen a more distinguished woman.

ATHENIAN [*looking at Reconciliation*]: I've never seen a more voluptuous body!

LYSISTRATA: Why then, with these many noble deeds to think of, do you fight each other? Why don't you stop this villainy? Why not make peace? Tell me, what prevents it?

SPARTAN [*waving vaguely at Reconciliation*]: We're willing, if you're willing to give up your position on yonder flank.

LYSISTRATA: What position, my good man?

SPARTAN: Pylus; we've been panting for it for ever so long.

ATHENIAN: No, by God! You shan't have it!

LYSISTRATA: Let them have it, my friend.

ATHENIAN: Then what shall we have to rouse things up?

LYSISTRATA: Ask for another place in exchange.

---

[47] **how the Spartan . . . army:** In 464 B.C.E. the Spartans secured Athenian aid to put down a rebellion following an earthquake in Sparta.

[48] **how the Spartans . . . Hippias:** The Spartans had aided Athenian exiles in overthrowing the tyrant Hippias, thus establishing Athenian democracy. Hippias had required the exiles to wear sheepskins.

ATHENIAN: Well, let's see: first of all [*pointing to various parts of Reconciliation's anatomy*] give us Echinus here, this Maliac Inlet in back there, and these two Megarian legs.

SPARTAN: No, by heavens! You can't have *everything*, you crazy fool!

LYSISTRATA: Let it go. Don't fight over a pair of legs.

ATHENIAN [*taking off his cloak*]: I think I'll strip and do a little planting now.

SPARTAN [*following suit*]: And I'll just do a little fertilizing, by gosh!

LYSISTRATA: Wait until the truce is concluded. Now if you've decided on this course, hold a conference and discuss the matter with your allies.

ATHENIAN: Allies? Don't be ridiculous! They're in the same state we are. Won't all our allies want the same thing we do—to jump in bed with their women?

SPARTAN: Ours will, I know.

ATHENIAN: Especially the Carystians,[49] by God!

LYSISTRATA: Very well. Now purify yourselves, that your wives may feast and entertain you in the Acropolis; we've provisions by the basketfull. Exchange your oaths and pledges there, and then each of you may take his wife and go home.

ATHENIAN: Let's go at once.

SPARTAN: Come on, where you will.

ATHENIAN: For God's sake, let's hurry!

[*They all go into the Acropolis.*]

CHORUS [*singing*]:

> Whate'er I have of coverlets
> And robes of varied hue
> And golden trinkets,—without stint
> I offer them to you.
>
> Take what you will and bear it home,
> Your children to delight,
> Or if your girl's a Basket-maid;
> Just choose whate'er's in sight.
>
> There's naught within so well secured
> You cannot break the seal
> And bear it off; just help yourselves;
> No hesitation feel.
>
> But you'll see nothing, though you try,
> Unless you've sharper eyes than I!
>
> If anyone needs bread to feed
> A growing family,

[49] **Carystians:** Allies of the Athenians who were thought to be primitive and uninhibited.

I've lots of wheat and full-grown loaves;
So just apply to me.

Let every poor man who desires
Come round and bring a sack
To fetch the grain; my slave is there
To load it on his back.

But don't come near my door, I say:
Beware the dog, and stay away!

[*An* ATHENIAN *enters carrying a torch; he knocks at the gate.*]

ATHENIAN: Open the door! [*to the* CHORUS, *which is clustered around the gate*] Make way, won't you! What are you hanging around for? Want me to singe you with this torch? [*to himself*] No; it's a stale trick, I won't do it! [*to the audience*] Still, if I've got to do it to please you, I suppose I'll have to take the trouble.

[*A* SECOND ATHENIAN *comes out of the gate.*]

SECOND ATHENIAN: And I'll help you.

FIRST ATHENIAN [*waving his torch at the* CHORUS]: Get out! Go bawl your heads off! Move on there, so the Spartans can leave in peace when the banquet's over.

[*They brandish their torches until the* CHORUS *leaves the Orchestra.*]

SECOND ATHENIAN: I've never seen such a pleasant banquet: the Spartans are charming fellows, indeed they are! And we Athenians are very witty in our cups.

FIRST ATHENIAN: Naturally: for when we're sober we're never at our best. If the Athenians would listen to me, we'd always get a little tipsy on our embassies. As things are now, we go to Sparta when we're sober and look around to stir up trouble. And then we don't hear what they say—and as for what they *don't* say, we have all sorts of suspicions. And then we bring back varying reports about the mission. But this time everything is pleasant; even if a man should sing the Telamon-song when he ought to sing "Cleitagoras," we'd praise him and swear it was excellent.

[*The two* CHORUSES *return, as a* CHORUS OF ATHENIANS *and a* CHORUS OF SPARTANS.]

Here they come back again. Go to the devil, you scoundrels!

SECOND ATHENIAN: Get out, I say! They're coming out from the feast.

[*Enter the Spartan and Athenian envoys, followed by* LYSISTRATA *and all the women.*]

SPARTAN [*to one of his fellow-envoys*]: My good fellow, take up your pipes; I want to do a fancy two-step and sing a jolly song for the Athenians.

ATHENIAN: Yes, do take your pipes, by all means. I'd love to see you dance.

SPARTAN [*singing and dancing with the* CHORUS OF SPARTANS]:

These youths inspire
To song and dance, O Memory;
Stir up my Muse, to tell how we

And Athens' men, in our galleys clashing
At Artemisium,[50] 'gainst foemen dashing
In godlike ire,
Conquered the Persian and set Greece free.

Leonidas
Led on his valiant warriors
Whetting their teeth like angry boars.
Abundant foam on their lips was flow'ring,
A stream of sweat from their limbs was show'ring.
The Persian was
Numberless as the sand on the shores.

O Huntress° who slayest the beasts in the glade, Artemis
O Virgin divine, hither come to our truce,
Unite us in bonds which all time will not loose.
Grant us to find in this treaty, we pray,
An unfailing source of true friendship today,
And all of our days, helping us to refrain
From weaseling tricks which bring war in their train.
Then hither, come hither! O huntress maid.

LYSISTRATA: Come then, since all is fairly done, men of Sparta, lead away your wives, and you, Athenians, take yours. Let every man stand beside his wife, and every wife beside her man, and then, to celebrate our fortune, let's dance. And in the future, let's take care to avoid these misunderstandings.

CHORUS OF ATHENIANS [*singing and dancing*]:
Lead on the dances, your graces revealing.
Call Artemis hither, call Artemis' twin,
Leader of dances, Apollo the Healing,
Kindly God—hither! let's summon him in!
Nysian Bacchus call,
Who with his Maenads, his eyes flashing fire,
Dances, and last of all
Zeus of the thunderbolt flaming, the Sire,
And Hera in majesty,
Queen of prosperity.

Come, ye Powers who dwell above
Unforgetting, our witnesses be

[50] **Artemisium:** Site of a naval battle where the Athenian fleet fought the Persians while the Spartans, led by Leonidas, fought the Persians on land at Thermopylae.

Of Peace with bonds of harmonious love—
The Peace which Cypris has wrought for me.
Alleluia! Io Paean!
Leap in joy—hurrah! hurrah!
'Tis victory—hurrah! hurrah!
Euoi! Euoi! Euai! Euai!

LYSISTRATA [*to the Spartans*]: Come now, sing a new song to cap ours.

CHORUS OF SPARTANS [*singing and dancing*]:
Leaving Taygetus fair and renown'd,
Muse of Laconia,[51] hither come:
Amyclae's[52] god in hymns resound,
Athene of the Brazen Home,[53]
And Castor and Pollux, Tyndareus' sons,
Who sport where Eurotas[54] murmuring runs.

On with the dance! Heia! Ho!
All leaping along,
Mantles a-swinging as we go!
Of Sparta our song.
There the holy chorus ever gladdens,
There the beat of stamping feet,
As our winsome fillies, lovely maidens,
Dance, beside Eurotas' banks a-skipping,—
Nimbly go to and fro
Hast'ning, leaping feet in measures tripping,
Like the Bacchae's revels, hair a-streaming.
Leda's child, divine and mild,
Leads the holy dance, her fair face beaming.
On with the dance! as your hand
Presses the hair
Streaming away unconfined.
Leap in the air
Light as the deer; footsteps resound
Aiding our dance, beating the ground.
Praise Athene, Maid divine, unrivalled in her might,
Dweller in the Brazen Home, unconquered in the fight.

[*All go out singing and dancing.*]

[51] **Laconia:** The region of Sparta. [52] **Amyclae:** Part of Sparta. [53] **Brazen Home:** The Temple of Athena in Sparta was bronze-plated. [54] **Eurotas:** The river in Sparta.

PLATO
C. 427–347 B.C.E.

Of the three great philosophers of classical Greece — Socrates, Plato, and Aristotle — only Plato's and Aristotle's teachings and theories and thoughts were written down. Socrates, a great teacher, didn't publish, so all that is known of his philosophy comes from others, especially from the writings of Plato, one of his students. For Plato, Socrates was a philosopher-hero who pursued truth through questioning, saw self-understanding as the beginning of knowledge, and had the integrity to live his philosophic principles. Following the maxim, "the unexamined life is not worth living," Socrates made his life his most important work. By living and dying for his beliefs, Socrates epitomized some of the most deeply held ideals of his culture, ideals that remain central to the Western tradition. Plato's *Dialogues,* most of which feature Socrates as the central figure, are an extended tribute to Plato's mentor and hero.

WWW For links to more information about Plato and a quiz on his *Apology,* see *World Literature Online* at bedfordstmartins.com/worldlit.

The Historical Socrates. Born about 470 B.C.E., Socrates' seventy years spanned a period of profound transformation in Athens. His early life was spent in the Golden Age of classical Athenian culture, the Age of Pericles.[1] Although not much is known about this period in Socrates' life, he seems to have come from a prosperous family, one that was able at least to indulge his interest in learning and philosophical speculation. During these years, he also may have studied the origin and nature of the universe, the traditional subject of philosophical speculation in ancient Greece. But by the beginning of the Peloponnesian War in 431, he began to focus on the study of conduct.

A "street teacher" known for his grotesque appearance — short and stout, with prominent eyes and a snub nose — and for such eccentricities as going barefoot year round, Socrates was sometimes linked with the **SOPHISTS**, freelance teachers who taught expedient and fashionable ideas to their pupils for a fee. In *Apology,* in which Plato writes in the first person as Socrates, Socrates is anxious to distinguish himself from these popular teachers. He has no art to teach, he claims, nor any rhetorical cleverness to model for his followers. He is just a gadfly asking plain questions and seeking plain answers. If he is the wisest man in Athens, as the Delphic Oracle stated, it is only because he knows that he does not know anything. His approach, perceived as naive arrogance, often annoys those he questions, especially when their conventional beliefs are challenged or held up to mockery. When Socrates questioned what justice or piety or wisdom was, he often arrived at answers different from those that had been previously generally accepted.

[1] **Age of Pericles:** The Golden Age of Athens in the fifth century B.C.E. when Pericles (c. 495–429 B.C.E.) was the city's leader. During this period, Athenian democracy reached its height, the Parthenon was constructed, and drama and music flourished.

Socrates Philosophizing, 150 B.C.E.
Detail from the Roman Sarcophagus (limestone burial structure) of the Muses. (The Art Archive / Musée du Louvre, Paris / Dagli Orti)

I . . . am a sort of gadfly, given to the state by God; and the state is a great and noble steed who is tardy in his motions owing to his very size, and requires to be stirred into life.

– SOCRATES, in *Apology*

Socrates' middle years coincided with the Peloponnesian War (431–404 B.C.E.), the struggle, led by Athens on one side and Sparta on the other, among the city-states of the Greek peninsula. Although Athens had some important victories along the way, Sparta was the eventual winner. The resultant political turmoil in Athens led to the fall of Athenian democracy and the emergence of oligarchic rule. In this tense political atmosphere, Socrates' inquiries into justice, loyalty, and piety were often viewed as unpatriotic or sacrilegious, even though he professed a belief in the gods and had served in the Athenian army and fought heroically in battle. Although Socrates tried to avoid political involvement, the years just before his death in 399 were especially troubled and he was unable to protect himself completely from the controversies of the times. Politics probably played a part in his final condemnation.

Socrates has often been compared to Jesus. Both were charismatic teachers who attracted followers. Both challenged the political and social institutions of their time and place, and were models of the moral and committed life. Both became martyrs for their ideals, choosing to die rather than compromise the principles by which they lived. They differed most significantly, perhaps, in those ideals: Jesus taught love, compassion, and salvation; Socrates taught self-knowledge, critical thinking, and good citizenship. Their teachings form two of the central threads in the tapestry of Western civilization.

The unexamined life is not worth living.
– Socrates, in *Apology*

Plato's Socrates. Just as Jesus is largely known through the biographies written of him in the four gospels of the New Testament, Socrates is known through Plato's *Dialogues.* Plato, one of Socrates' students, considered his teacher "of all the men of his time whom I have known . . . the wisest and justest, and best," and made him the hero of nearly all of his philosophic works. From a well-to-do and aristocratic family, Plato knew Socrates only at the end of the elder teacher's life. In *Apology* and ***Phaedo***, Plato presents Socrates' trial and execution, events that he witnessed himself as a young man. Disillusioned by Socrates' death, Plato left Athens and traveled abroad for several years. When he returned about fourteen years later, he took up Socrates' mantle as a teacher and founded the Academy, a school that flourished in Athens until 529 C.E., when it was closed by the Byzantine emperor Justinian. Plato taught "in the groves of Academe," the gardens at the school where he met with his students, for the remainder of his long life, writing down the dialogues for which he is known and revered. When he was eighty, after attending the wedding of one of his students, Plato retired to a corner to rest and died peacefully in his sleep.

FEE-doh

Plato's philosophic works are literary in character, "dialogues" in which the participants articulate different perspectives on the issues under discussion. The hero of nearly all of Plato's philosophic discussions is Socrates, who is seen employing a question-and-answer technique now known as "the Socratic method." He tests big ideas by analyzing assumptions and seeking clear definitions. When he asks in the *Euthyphro,* for example, "What is piety?", Euthyphro answers that piety "is that which is dear to the gods, and impiety is that which is not dear to them." Socrates then continues his questioning, getting Euthyphro to admit that because the gods disagree among themselves, there are contradictions in his definition. Moreover, he asserts, to define piety as "what is dear to the gods" does not identify what it is that makes something dear. By the end of their conversation Socrates has poked holes in Euthyphro's reasoning and challenged any conventional, untested belief in the gods. Although Socrates purges the definition of *piety* of its indefensible claims, he does not come up with a workable alternative. His approach to knowledge, his questioning, made room for not knowing, for acknowledging ignorance.

Apology. *Apology,* perhaps the most famous of Plato's writings, depicts mostly in summary Socrates' defense against charges of corrupting the youth of Athens and introducing new divinities. Socrates' three accusers,

MEL-ih-tus; AN-uh-tus

Meletus, **Anytus**, and Lycon, have made their case against him, and as *Apology* begins, Socrates is stating his response. He must convince a jury of 501 citizens to vote for his acquittal. After acknowledging the eloquence of his accusers and stating that his presentation will be informal since this is his first appearance in court and he is unaccustomed to orating, Socrates addresses some old charges against him, namely that he is a Sophist who is teaching for money and that he teaches COSMOLOGY.

Socrates responds directly to the current charges by recounting his quest to understand the meaning of the Delphic Oracle's[2] assertion that he, a man who only knows that he knows nothing, is the wisest man in Athens. He describes how those he has questioned—politicians, poets, and artisans—proved to have no greater knowledge than he did, even though they had professed to be able to answer questions that Socrates could not. Finally, he realized that his wisdom was that he *knew* he did not know, and he set out to show others that they were not as wise as they thought they were. His accusers were angry with him, he suggests, because they did not like having their ignorance revealed.

Defiant and uncompromising, Socrates refuses to give the court an excuse for dismissing or reducing the charges against him. He reaffirms his commitment to questioning and to teaching his fundamental truths that "virtue is knowledge" and that "the unexamined life is not worth living." He will not abandon his god-given role as a gadfly sent to sting the citizens of Athens to virtuous living, and he will make no deals in exchange for his life. If he is allowed to live, he will continue to urge his fellow citizens to "know themselves."

Some argue that Socrates takes an elitist stance, unwilling to make compromises that are necessary in a democratic society, thus bringing on himself a just punishment. The democrats in power in Athens in 399 B.C.E. considered Socrates dangerous. Some of the most prominent of Socrates' disciples—Alcibiades, Critias, Plato, and Xenophon,[3] for example—were members of the antidemocratic faction. Socrates' belief that government should be led by trained experts, his questioning, and his refusal to negotiate with the court threatened the party in power. Although at the time the government considered his execution justified, history has adopted Plato's view that Socrates' death was unjust, the martyrdom of a principled and courageous man. In *Phaedo,* Plato reflects on Socrates' execution, praising his hero's courageous integrity in facing death and his piety for dying for his convictions.

KRIGH-toh

The Allegory of the Cave. The critical side to the Socratic method is most apparent in Plato's early dialogues, works like *Euthyphro* and ***Crito,***

[2] **Delphic Oracle:** A shrine to the god Apollo at Delphi, near the foot of Mt. Parnassus. The priestess at the site delivered oracular messages, like the one through which Socrates learned that he was the wisest of men.

[3] **Alcibiades . . . Xenophon:** Alcibiades (c. 450–404 B.C.E.), an Athenian general and political leader; Critias (c. 460–403 B.C.E.), an aristocratic relative of Plato who was one of the thirty tyrants imposed on Athens by the Spartans; Xenophon (c. 430–c. 355 B.C.E.), an Athenian historian banished to Sparta who wrote about Socrates in several of his works.

in which Socrates the gadfly challenges the views of those he questions. In the great dialogues of Plato's middle period, such as *Symposium* or *The Republic,* a different Socrates seems to appear. He continues questioning, but he also has an agenda. It is impossible to know whether the historical Socrates held the views on politics, law, aesthetics, theology, psychology, education, and other topics that Plato discusses in later works or if using Socrates' voice had become more of a literary device for the philosophy. Classicist Edith Hamilton asserts that Plato "cannot be separated from Socrates. Almost all that Plato wrote professes to be a report of what Socrates said . . . and it is impossible to decide just what part belongs to each." In any case, the historical Socrates becomes less important in Plato's later works, disappearing altogether in some.

All European philosophy is but a footnote to Plato.

– Alfred North Whitehead, philosopher

The parable "Allegory of the Cave," from *The Republic,* gives mythological expression to one of Plato's central concepts, the doctrine of Ideas or Forms. In it, Socrates distinguishes four kinds of knowledge, two that are possible within the underground den, or cave, and two that are possible only outside it. In the cave, chained men can see only shadows of objects cast on the wall before them, for the objects casting the shadows are behind them. Were they unchained, they could also see the particular objects themselves that made the shadows, but, still inside the cave, they would not be aware of the larger world outside. They might know the shadows of a chair or a dog and, if unchained, might know the particular chair or dog casting the shadows, but they would not understand the general *idea* of a chair or a dog, which can only be comprehended in the daylight outside of the cave. An IDEALIST, Plato believed that these general Ideas or Forms existed independently of any particular embodiment of them. The highest ideas, symbolized in the parable by the sun, the concepts of the Good, the True, and the Beautiful informed all lesser realities. Thus the parable presents a hierarchical scheme of reality with four distinct levels. Only someone who grasped all four levels could fully comprehend the truth. Such men Plato called "philosopher-kings." Everyone else was caught to some extent in illusion.

■ CONNECTIONS

Homer, *The Iliad* and *The Odyssey,* pp. 288 and 421; *In the World:* Heroes and Citizens, p. 1117. In classical Greece, the idea of the hero changes from the military figures seen in Homer's epics to the civil and philosophical standouts of the Athenian Golden Age. Compare Socrates as a hero with Achilles in *The Iliad* and Odysseus in *The Odyssey.* Are there qualities in the epic heroes that Socrates would not admire? Does Socrates fulfill the notions of heroism developed by the writers presented in *In the World:* Heroes and Citizens? Is Diogenes Laertius's view of Socrates the same as Plato's?

The New Testament (Book 2). The story of Socrates' trial and martyrdom has often been compared to that of Jesus in the New Testament. Identify the principles for which each man died. Could Jesus or Socrates have saved himself from death? How? Is either of them in any way responsible for his fate? What do you consider the main differences between the two men and their teachings?

***The Descent of Inanna,* p. 28; Dante, *The Inferno* (Book 2); Joseph Conrad, *Heart of Darkness* (Book 6).** One of the archetypes of epic literature is a journey to the underworld, a journey beyond the usual boundaries of human experience to gain supernatural understanding of the human condition. Inanna, for example, dies and is reborn in the underworld; Dante is guided by Virgil through Hell, Purgatory, and Paradise; and Marlow, in *Heart of Darkness,* confronts evil in what is to him alien Africa. All three journeys are described as experiences of darkness. Plato's "Allegory of the Cave," by contrast, shows man gaining knowledge by emerging from the darkness of the cave and entering the light. In what ways does Plato's idea of reality or truth differ from that in the other works? Are different kinds of truth involved? How are the metaphors of descent and ascent and light and darkness used today in discussions of truth, learning, and understanding?

Voltaire, *Candide* (Book 4); Jean-Paul Sartre, *The Flies* (Book 6). Many writers have expressed philosophical ideas through literary works. Compare Plato's use of the dialogue form with Voltaire's use of the novella and Sartre's use of drama as vehicles for philosophy. Which genre is most successful? Why?

■ FURTHER RESEARCH

Brickhouse, Thomas C. *Socrates on Trial.* 1989.
Gooch, Paul W. *Reflections on Jesus and Socrates: Word and Silence.* 1996.
Gutherie, W. K. C. *The Greek Philosophers: From Thales to Aristotle.* 1950, 1975.
Levin, Richard L., and John Bremer. *The Question of Socrates.* 1961.
Phillopson, Coleman. *The Trial of Socrates.* 1928.
Reeve, C. D. C. *Socrates in the Apology: An Essay on Plato's Apology of Socrates.* 1989.
Richmond, William K. *Socrates and the Western World.* 1954.
Stone, I. F. *The Trial of Socrates.* 1988.
Versényi, Laszlo. *Socratic Humanism.* 1963, 1979.

■ PRONUNCIATION

Adeimantus: ad-ee-MAN-tus
Aeacus: EE-uh-kus
Aeantodorus: ee-an-tuh-DOH-rus
Amphipolis: am-FIP-uh-lis
Anytus: AN-uh-tus
Arginusae: ar-jih-NOO-see
Asclepius: us-KLEE-pee-us
Cebes: SEE-beez
Ceos: SEE-ahs
Cephisus: see-FIGH-sus
Chaerephon: KLEH-ruh-fahn
Clazomenian: kluh-ZAH-muh-NEE-un
Crito: KRIGH-toh
Critobulus: krigh-toh-BYOO-lus
Demodocus: duh-MAH-duh-kus
Echecrates: ih-KEK-ruh-teez
Epigenes: eh-PIJ-ih-neez
Evenus: ih-VEE-nus
Gorgias: GORE-jus, GORE-jee-us
Leontium: lee-AHN-shum, lee-AHN-tee-um
Meletus: MEL-ih-tus
Musaeus: myoo-ZEE-us, myoo-ZAY-us
Nicostratus: nigh-KAH-struh-tus
Palamedes: pal-uh-MEE-deez
Phaedo: FEE-doh, FAY-doh

Potidaea: pah-tih-DEE-uh
Prytanes: PRIT-uh-neez
Rhadamanthus: rad-uh-MAN-thus
Simmias: SIM-ee-us
Theages: THEE-uh-jeez
Theozdotides: thee-uz-DOH-tih-deez
Triptolemus: trip-TAH-lih-mus

Apology

Translated by Benjamin Jowett

How you, O Athenians, have been affected by my accusers, I cannot tell; but I know that they almost made me forget who I was—so persuasively did they speak; and yet they have hardly uttered a word of truth. But of the many falsehoods told by them, there was one which quite amazed me;—I mean when they said that you should be upon your guard and not allow yourselves to be deceived by the force of my eloquence. To say this, when they were certain to be detected as soon as I opened my lips and proved myself to be anything but a great speaker, did indeed appear to me most shameless—unless by the force of eloquence they mean the force of truth; for if such is their meaning, I admit that I am eloquent. But in how different a way from theirs! Well, as I was saying, they have scarcely spoken the truth at all; but from me you shall hear the whole truth: not, however, delivered after their manner in a set oration duly ornamented with words and phrases. No, by heaven! but I shall use the words and arguments which occur to me at the moment; for I am confident in the justice of my cause: at my time of life I ought not to be appearing before you, O men of Athens, in the character of a juvenile orator—let no one expect it of me. And I must beg of you to grant me a favour:—If I defend myself in my accustomed manner, and you hear me using the words which I have been in the habit of using in the agora[1] at the tables of the money-changers, or anywhere else, I would ask you not to be surprised, and not to interrupt me on this account. For I am more than seventy

---

***Apology* and *Phaedo*.** In these two works, Plato writes about Socrates' trial and execution. In *Apology,* Plato, writing in the first person as Sophocles, transcribes Socrates' own defense, which is what *apology* refers to in the title. Instead of appealing to the mercy of the court or the emotional sympathy of the jurors, Socrates makes a bold case for his actions. In doing so he defends not only himself but also the necessity for skeptical questioning and free inquiry in a self-governing society. Even after he fails to convince a majority of the 501 jurors of his innocence and is condemned to death, Socrates refuses to compromise and gain a lighter sentence. Instead he explains why such pleading would be dishonest and hence worse than the sentence he faces. In *Phaedo,* with his friends gathered round him at the time of his execution, Socrates reaffirms his belief in an afterlife and accepts his fate courageously.

[1] **agora:** The marketplace.

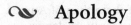

years of age, and appearing now for the first time in a court of law, I am quite a stranger to the language of the place; and therefore I would have you regard me as if I were really a stranger, whom you would excuse if he spoke in his native tongue, and after the fashion of his country:—Am I making an unfair request of you? Never mind the manner, which may or may not be good; but think only of the truth of my words, and give heed to that: let the speaker speak truly and the judge decide justly.

And first, I have to reply to the older charges and to my first accusers, and then I will go on to the later ones. For of old I have had many accusers, who have accused me falsely to you during many years; and I am more afraid of them than of Anytus and his associates, who are dangerous, too, in their own way. But far more dangerous are the others, who began when you were children, and took possession of your minds with their falsehoods, telling of one Socrates, a wise man, who speculated about the heaven above and searched into the earth beneath, and made the worse appear the better cause.[2] The disseminators of this tale are the accusers whom I dread; for their hearers are apt to fancy that such enquirers do not believe in the existence of the gods. And they are many, and their charges against me are of ancient date, and they were made by them in the days when you were more impressible than you are now—in childhood, or it may have been in youth—and the cause when heard went by default, for there was none to answer. And hardest of all, I do not know and cannot tell the names of my accusers; unless in the chance case of a Comic poet.[3] All who from envy and malice have persuaded you—some of them having first convinced themselves—all this class of men are most difficult to deal with; for I cannot have them up here, and cross-examine them, and therefore I must simply fight with shadows in my own defence, and argue when there is no one who answers. I will ask you then to assume with me, as I was saying, that my opponents are of two kinds; one recent, the other ancient: and I hope that you will see the propriety of my answering the latter first, for these accusations you heard long before the others, and much oftener.

Well, then, I must make my defence, and endeavor to clear away in a short time, a slander which has lasted a long time. May I succeed, if to succeed be for my good and yours, or likely to avail me in my cause! The task is not an easy one; I quite understand the nature of it. And so leaving the event with God, in obedience to the law I will now make my defence.

I will begin at the beginning, and ask what is the accusation which has given rise to the slander of me, and in fact has encouraged Meletus to prefer this charge against me. Well, what do the slanderers say? They shall be my prosecutors, and I will sum up their words in an affidavit: 'Socrates is an evil-doer, and a curious person, who searches into things under the earth and in heaven, and he makes the worse appear

---

[2] **speculated . . . cause:** Socrates is here answering older charges brought against him, specifically that he was a materialist who speculated about the physical world and that he was one of the Sophists who taught expeditious modes of argument rather than truth.

[3] **Comic poet:** Aristophanes, in *The Clouds,* satirized Socrates as a charlatan who promulgated extravagant theories about the physical world.

the better cause; and he teaches the aforesaid doctrines to others.' Such is the nature of the accusation: it is just what you have yourselves seen in the comedy of Aristophanes, who has introduced a man whom he calls Socrates, going about and saying that he walks in air, and talking a deal of nonsense concerning matters of which I do not pretend to know either much or little—not that I mean to speak disparagingly of any one who is a student of natural philosophy. I should be very sorry if Meletus could bring so grave a charge against me. But the simple truth is, O Athenians, that I have nothing to do with physical speculations. Very many of those here present are witnesses to the truth of this, and to them I appeal. Speak then, you who have heard me, and tell your neighbours whether any of you have ever known me hold forth in few words or in many upon such matters. . . . You hear their answer. And from what they say of this part of the charge you will be able to judge of the truth of the rest.

As little foundation is there for the report that I am a teacher, and take money; this accusation has no more truth in it than the other. Although, if a man were really able to instruct mankind, to receive money for giving instruction would, in my opinion, be an honour to him. There is Gorgias of Leontium, and Prodicus of Ceos, and Hippias of Elis,[4] who go the round of the cities, and are able to persuade the young men to leave their own citizens by whom they might be taught for nothing, and come to them whom they not only pay, but are thankful if they may be allowed to pay them. There is at this time a Parian[5] philosopher residing in Athens, of whom I have heard; and I came to hear of him in this way:—I came across a man who has spent a world of money on the Sophists, Callias, the son of Hipponicus, and knowing that he had sons, I asked him: 'Callias,' I said, 'if your two sons were foals or calves, there would be no difficulty in finding some one to put over them; we should hire a trainer of horses, or a farmer probably, who would improve and perfect them in their own proper virtue and excellence; but as they are human beings, whom are you thinking of placing over them? Is there any one who understands human and political virtue? You must have thought about the matter, for you have sons; is there any one?' 'There is,' he said. 'Who is he?' said I; 'and of what country? and what does he charge?' 'Evenus the Parian,' he replied; 'he is the man, and his charge is five minae.' Happy is Evenus, I said to myself; if he really has this wisdom, and teaches at such a moderate charge. Had I the same, I should have been very proud and conceited; but the truth is that I have no knowledge of the kind.

I dare say, Athenians, that some one among you will reply, 'Yes, Socrates, but what is the origin of these accusations which are brought against you; there must have been something strange which you have been doing? All these rumours and this talk about you would never have arisen if you had been like other men: tell us, then, what is the cause of them, for we should be sorry to judge hastily of you.' Now I regard this as a fair challenge, and I will endeavour to explain to you the reason why I am called wise and have such an evil fame. Please to attend then. And although some of you may think that I am joking, I declare that I will tell you the entire truth.

[4] **Gorgias . . . of Elis:** Famous Sophists who taught rhetoric and logic. [5] **Parian:** From Paros, an island in the Aegean.

Men of Athens, this reputation of mine has come of a certain sort of wisdom which I possess. If you ask me what kind of wisdom, I reply, wisdom such as may perhaps be attained by man, for to that extent I am inclined to believe that I am wise; whereas the persons of whom I was speaking have a superhuman wisdom, which I may fail to describe, because I have it not myself; and he who says that I have, speaks falsely, and is taking away my character. And here, O men of Athens, I must beg you not to interrupt me, even if I seem to say something extravagant. For the word which I will speak is not mine. I will refer you to a witness who is worthy of credit; that witness shall be the God of Delphi[6]—he will tell you about my wisdom, if I have any, and of what sort it is. You must have known Chaerephon; he was early a friend of mine, and also a friend of yours, for he shared in the recent exile of the people,[7] and returned with you. Well, Chaerephon, as you know, was very impetuous in all his doings, and he went to Delphi and boldly asked the oracle to tell him whether—as I was saying, I must beg you not to interrupt—he asked the oracle to tell him whether any one was wiser than I was, and the Pythian prophetess answered, that there was no man wiser. Chaerephon is dead himself; but his brother, who is in court, will confirm the truth of what I am saying.

Why do I mention this? Because I am going to explain to you why I have such an evil name. When I heard the answer, I said to myself, What can the god mean? and what is the interpretation of his riddle? for I know that I have no wisdom, small or great. What then can he mean when he says that I am the wisest of men? And yet he is a god, and cannot lie; that would be against his nature. After long consideration, I thought of a method of trying the question. I reflected that if I could only find a man wiser than myself, then I might go to the god with a refutation in my hand. I should say to him, 'Here is a man who is wiser than I am; but you said that I was the wisest.' Accordingly I went to one who had the reputation of wisdom, and observed him—his name I need not mention; he was a politician whom I selected for examination—and the result was as follows: When I began to talk with him, I could not help thinking that he was not really wise, although he was thought wise by many, and still wiser by himself; and thereupon I tried to explain to him that he thought himself wise, but was not really wise; and the consequence was that he hated me, and his enmity was shared by several who were present and heard me. So I left him, saying to myself, as I went away: Well, although I do not suppose that either of us knows anything really beautiful and good, I am better off than he is,—for he knows nothing, and thinks that he knows; I neither know nor think that I know. In this latter particular, then, I seem to have slightly the advantage of him. Then I went to another who had still higher pretensions to wisdom, and my conclusion was exactly the same. Whereupon I made another enemy of him, and of many others besides him.

Then I went to one man after another, being not unconscious of the enmity which I provoked, and I lamented and feared this: But necessity was laid upon

---

[6] **God of Delphi:** The Oracle of Apollo at Delphi.

[7] **exile of the people:** After the defeat of Athens by Sparta in 404 B.C.E., the democratic leaders of Athens had gone into exile, driven out of the city by the Thirty Tyrants who ruled briefly until democracy was reestablished in 403 B.C.E.

me,—the word of God, I thought, ought to be considered first. And I said to myself, Go I must to all who appear to know, and find out the meaning of the oracle. And I swear to you, Athenians, by the dog I swear!—for I must tell you the truth—the result of my mission was just this: I found that the men most in repute were all but the most foolish; and that others less esteemed were really wiser and better. I will tell you the tale of my wanderings and of the 'Herculean' labours, as I may call them, which I endured only to find at last the oracle irrefutable. After the politicians, I went to the poets; tragic, dithyrambic, and all sorts. And there, I said to myself, you will be instantly detected; now you will find out that you are more ignorant than they are. Accordingly, I took them some of the most elaborate passages in their own writings, and asked what was the meaning of them—thinking that they would teach me something. Will you believe me? I am almost ashamed to confess the truth, but I must say that there is hardly a person present who would not have talked better about their poetry than they did themselves. Then I knew that not by wisdom do poets write poetry, but by a sort of genius and inspiration; they are like diviners or soothsayers who also say many fine things, but do not understand the meaning of them. The poets appeared to me to be much in the same case; and I further observed that upon the strength of their poetry they believed themselves to be the wisest of men in other things in which they were not wise. So I departed, conceiving myself to be superior to them for the same reason that I was superior to the politicians.

At last I went to the artisans, for I was conscious that I knew nothing at all, as I may say, and I was sure that they knew many fine things; and here I was not mistaken, for they did know many things of which I was ignorant, and in this they certainly were wiser than I was. But I observed that even the good artisans fell into the same error as the poets;—because they were good workmen they thought that they also knew all sorts of high matters, and this defect in them overshadowed their wisdom; and therefore I asked myself on behalf of the oracle, whether I would like to be as I was, neither having their knowledge nor their ignorance, or like them in both; and I made answer to myself and to the oracle that I was better off as I was.

This inquisition has led to my having many enemies of the worst and most dangerous kind, and has given occasion also to many calumnies. And I am called wise, for my hearers always imagine that I myself possess the wisdom which I find wanting in others: but the truth is, O men of Athens, that God only is wise; and by his answer he intends to show that the wisdom of men is worth little or nothing; he is not speaking of Socrates, he is only using my name by way of illustration, as if he said, He, O men, is the wisest, who, like Socrates, knows that his wisdom is in truth worth nothing. And so I go about the world, obedient to the god, and search and make enquiry into the wisdom of any one, whether citizen or stranger, who appears to be wise; and if he is not wise, then in vindication of the oracle I show him that he is not wise; and my occupation quite absorbs me, and I have no time to give either to any public matter of interest or to any concern of my own, but I am in utter poverty by reason of my devotion to the god.

There is another thing:—young men of the richer classes, who have not much to do, come about me of their own accord; they like to hear the pretenders examined, and they often imitate me, and proceed to examine others; there are plenty of persons, as they quickly discover, who think that they know something, but really know little or nothing; and then those who are examined by them instead of being angry with themselves are angry with me: This confounded Socrates, they say; this villainous misleader of youth!—and then if somebody asks them, Why, what evil does he practice or teach? they do not know, and cannot tell; but in order that they may not appear to be at a loss, they repeat the ready-made charges which are used against all philosophers about teaching things up in the clouds and under the earth, and having no gods, and making the worse appear the better cause; for they do not like to confess that their pretence of knowledge has been detected—which is the truth; and as they are numerous and ambitious and energetic, and are drawn up in battle array and have persuasive tongues, they have filled your ears with their loud and inveterate calumnies. And this is the reason why my three accusers, Meletus and Anytus and Lycon, have set upon me; Meletus, who has a quarrel with me on behalf of the poets; Anytus, on behalf of the craftsmen and politicians; Lycon, on behalf of the rhetoricians: and as I said at the beginning, I cannot expect to get rid of such a mass of calumny all in a moment. And this, O men of Athens, is the truth and the whole truth; I have concealed nothing, I have dissembled nothing. And yet, I know that my plainness of speech makes them hate me, and what is their hatred but a proof that I am speaking the truth?—Hence has arisen the prejudice against me; and this is the reason of it, as you will find out either in this or in any future enquiry.

I have said enough in my defence against the first class of my accusers; I turn to the second class. They are headed by Meletus, that good man and true lover of his country, as he calls himself. Against these, too, I must try to make a defence:—Let their affidavit be read: it contains something of this kind: It says that Socrates is a doer of evil, who corrupts the youth; and who does not believe in the gods of the state, but has other new divinities of his own. Such is the charge; and now let us examine the particular counts. He says that I am a doer of evil, and corrupt the youth; but I say, O men of Athens, that Meletus is a doer of evil, in that he pretends to be in earnest when he is only in jest, and is so eager to bring men to trial from a pretended zeal and interest about matters in which he really never had the smallest interest. And the truth of this I will endeavour to prove to you.

Come hither, Meletus, and let me ask a question of you. You think a great deal about the improvement of youth?

Yes, I do.

Tell the judges, then, who is their improver; for you must know, as you have taken the pains to discover their corrupter, and are citing and accusing me before them. Speak, then, and tell the judges who their improver is.—Observe, Meletus, that you are silent, and have nothing to say. But is not this rather disgraceful, and a very considerable proof of what I was saying, that you have no interest in the matter? Speak up, friend, and tell us who their improver is.

The laws.

But that, my good sir, is not my meaning. I want to know who the person is, who, in the first place, knows the laws.

The judges, Socrates, who are present in court.

What, do you mean to say, Meletus, that they are able to instruct and improve youth?

Certainly they are.

What, all of them, or some only and not others?

All of them.

By the goddess Here,[8] that is good news! There are plenty of improvers, then. And what do you say of the audience,—do they improve them?

Yes, they do.

And the senators?

Yes, the senators improve them.

But perhaps the members of the assembly corrupt them?—or do they too improve them?

They improve them.

Then every Athenian improves and elevates them; all with the exception of myself; and I alone am their corrupter? Is that what you affirm?

That is what I stoutly affirm.

I am very unfortunate if you are right. But suppose I ask you a question: How about horses? Does one man do them harm and all the world good? Is not the exact opposite the truth? One man is able to do them good, or at least not many;—the trainer of horses, that is to say, does them good, and others who have to do with them rather injure them? Is not that true, Meletus, of horses, or any other animals? Most assuredly it is; whether you and Anytus say yes or no. Happy indeed would be the condition of youth if they had one corrupter only, and all the rest of the world were their improvers. But you, Meletus, have sufficiently shown that you never had a thought about the young: your carelessness is seen in your not caring about the very things which you bring against me.

And now, Meletus, I will ask you another question—by Zeus I will: Which is better, to live among bad citizens, or among good ones? Answer, friend, I say; the question is one which may be easily answered. Do not the good do their neighbours good, and the bad do them evil?

Certainly.

And is there any one who would rather be injured than benefited by those who live with him? Answer, my good friend, the law requires you to answer—does any one like to be injured?

Certainly not.

And when you accuse me of corrupting and deteriorating the youth, do you allege that I corrupt them intentionally or unintentionally?

Intentionally, I say.

But you have just admitted that the good do their neighbours good, and evil do them evil. Now, is that a truth which your superior wisdom has recognized thus early in life, and am I, at my age, in such darkness and ignorance as not to know that

---

[8] **Here:** Hera, the queen of the gods.

if a man with whom I have to live is corrupted by me, I am very likely to be harmed by him; and yet I corrupt him, and intentionally, too—so you say, although neither I nor any other human being is ever likely to be convinced by you. But either I do not corrupt them, or I corrupt them unintentionally; and on either view of the case you lie. If my offence is unintentional, the law has no cognizance of unintentional offences: you ought to have taken me privately, and warned and admonished me; for if I had been better advised, I should have left off doing what I only did unintentionally—no doubt I should; but you would have nothing to say to me and refused to teach me. And now you bring me up in this court, which is not a place of instruction, but of punishment.

It will be very clear to you, Athenians, as I was saying, that Meletus has no care at all, great or small, about the matter. But still I should like to know, Meletus, in what I am affirmed to corrupt the young. I suppose you mean, as I infer from your indictment, that I teach them not to acknowledge the gods which the state acknowledges, but some other new divinities or spiritual agencies in their stead. These are the lessons by which I corrupt the youth, as you say.

Yes, that I say emphatically.

Then, by the gods, Meletus, of whom we are speaking, tell me and the court, in somewhat plainer terms, what you mean! for I do not as yet understand whether you affirm that I teach other men to acknowledge some gods, and therefore that I do believe in gods, and am not an entire atheist—this you do not lay to my charge,—but only you say that they are not the same gods which the city recognizes—the charge is that they are different gods. Or, do you mean that I am an atheist simply, and a teacher of atheism?

I mean the latter—that you are a complete atheist.

What an extraordinary statement! Why do you think so, Meletus? Do you mean that I do not believe in the godhead of the sun or moon, like other men?

I assure you, judges, that he does not: for he says that the sun is stone, and the moon earth.[9]

Friend Meletus, you think that you are accusing Anaxagoras:[10] and you have but a bad opinion of the judges, if you fancy them illiterate to such a degree as not to know that these doctrines are found in the books of Anaxagoras the Clazomenian, which are full of them. And so, forsooth, the youth are said to be taught them by Socrates, when there are not unfrequently exhibitions of them at the theatre (price of admission one drachma at the most); and they might pay their money, and laugh at Socrates if he pretends to father these extraordinary views. And so, Meletus, you really think that I do not believe in any god?

I swear by Zeus that you believe absolutely in none at all.

Nobody will believe you, Meletus, and I am pretty sure that you do not believe yourself. I cannot help thinking, men of Athens, that Meletus is reckless and impudent, and that he has written this indictment in a spirit of mere wantonness and

---

[9] **sun . . . earth:** These are the older charges, that Socrates taught atheistic doctrines that challenged the worship of Apollo, god of the sun, and Artemis, goddess of the moon.

[10] **Anaxagoras:** A fifth-century-B.C.E. materialist philosopher from Clazomenae.

youthful bravado. Has he not compounded a riddle, thinking to try me? He said to himself:—I shall see whether the wise Socrates will discover my facetious contradiction, or whether I shall be able to deceive him and the rest of them. For he certainly does appear to me to contradict himself in the indictment as much as if he said that Socrates is guilty of not believing in the gods, and yet of believing in them—but this is not like a person who is in earnest.

I should like you, O men of Athens, to join me in examining what I conceive to be his inconsistency; and do you, Meletus, answer. And I must remind the audience of my request that they would not make a disturbance if I speak in my accustomed manner:

Did ever man, Meletus, believe in the existence of human things, and not of human beings? . . . I wish, men of Athens, that he would answer, and not be always trying to get up an interruption. Did ever any man believe in horsemanship, and not in horses? or in flute-playing, and not in flute-players? No, my friend; I will answer to you and to the court, as you refuse to answer for yourself. There is no man who ever did. But now please to answer the next question: Can a man believe in spiritual and divine agencies, and not in spirits or demigods?

He cannot.

How lucky I am to have extracted that answer, by the assistance of the court! But then you swear in the indictment that I teach and believe in divine or spiritual agencies (new or old, no matter for that); at any rate, I believe in spiritual agencies,—so you say and swear in the affidavit; and yet if I believe in divine beings, how can I help believing in spirits or demigods;—must I not? To be sure I must; and therefore I may assume that your silence gives consent. Now what are spirits or demigods? Are they not either gods or the sons of gods?

Certainly they are.

But this is what I call the facetious riddle invented by you: the demigods or spirits are gods, and you say first that I do not believe in gods, and then again that I do believe in gods; that is, if I believe in demigods. For if the demigods are the illegitimate sons of gods, whether by the nymphs or by any other mothers, of whom they are said to be the sons—what human being will ever believe that there are no gods if they are the sons of gods? You might as well affirm the existence of mules and deny that of horses and asses. Such nonsense, Meletus, could only have been intended by you to make trial of me. You have put this into the indictment because you had nothing real of which to accuse me. But no one who has a particle of understanding will ever be convinced by you that the same men can believe in divine and superhuman things, and yet not believe that there are gods and demigods and heroes.

I have said enough in answer to the charge of Meletus: any elaborate defence is unnecessary; but I know only too well how many are the enmities which I have incurred, and this is what will be my destruction if I am destroyed;—not Meletus, nor yet Anytus, but the envy and detraction of the world, which has been the death of many good men, and will probably be the death of many more; there is no danger of my being the last of them.

Some one will say: And are you not ashamed, Socrates, of a course of life which is likely to bring you to an untimely end? To him I may fairly answer: There you are mistaken: a man who is good for anything ought not to calculate the chance of living or dying; he ought only to consider whether in doing anything he is doing right or wrong—acting the part of a good man or of a bad. Whereas, upon your view, the heroes who fell at Troy were not good for much, and the son of Thetis[11] above all, who altogether despised danger in comparison with disgrace; and when he was so eager to slay Hector, his goddess mother said to him, that if he avenged his companion Patroclus, and slew Hector, he would die himself—'Fate,' she said, in these or the like words, 'waits for you next after Hector;' he, receiving this warning, utterly despised danger and death, and instead of fearing them, feared rather to live in dishonour, and not to avenge his friend. 'Let me die forthwith,' he replies, 'and be avenged of my enemy, rather than abide here by the beaked ships, a laughing-stock and a burden of the earth.' Had Achilles any thought of death and danger? For wherever a man's place is, whether the place which he has chosen or that in which he has been placed by a commander, there he ought to remain in hour of danger; he should not think of death or of anything but of disgrace. And this, O men of Athens, is a true saying.

Strange, indeed, would be my conduct, O men of Athens, if I who, when I was ordered by the generals whom you chose to command me at Potidaea and Amphipolis and Delium,[12] remained where they placed me, like any other man, facing death—if now, when, as I conceive and imagine, God orders me to fulfil the philosopher's mission of searching into myself and other men, I were to desert my post through fear of death, or any other fear; that would indeed be strange, and I might justly be arraigned in court for denying the existence of the gods, if I disobeyed the oracle because I was afraid of death, fancying that I was wise when I was not wise. For the fear of death is indeed the pretence of wisdom, and not real wisdom, being a pretence of knowing the unknown; and no one knows whether death, which men in their fear apprehend to be the greatest evil, may not be the greatest good. Is not this ignorance of a disgraceful sort, the ignorance which is the conceit that man knows what he does not know? And in this respect only I believe myself to differ from men in general, and may perhaps claim to be wiser than they are:—that whereas I know but little of the world below, I do not suppose that I know: but I do know that injustice and disobedience to a better, whether God or man, is evil and dishonourable, and I will never fear or avoid a possible good rather than a certain evil. And therefore if you let me go now, and are not convinced by Anytus, who said that since I had been prosecuted I must be put to death (or if not that I ought never to have been prosecuted at all); and that if I escape now, your sons will all be utterly ruined by listening to my words—if you say to me, Socrates, this time we will not mind Anytus, and you shall be let off, but upon one condition, that you are not to enquire and speculate in this way any more, and that if you are caught doing so again you shall die:—if this was the condition on which you let me go, I should reply: Men of Athens, I honour and love you; but I shall obey God rather than you, and while I

---

[11] **son of Thetis:** Achilles; the scene described here is in Book 28 of *The Iliad.*

[12] **Potidaea . . . Delium:** The sites of three battles in which Socrates fought as a soldier.

have life and strength I shall never cease from the practice and teaching of philosophy, exhorting any one whom I meet and saying to him after my manner: You, my friend,—a citizen of the great and mighty and wise city of Athens,—are you not ashamed of heaping up the greatest amount of money and honour and reputation, and caring so little about wisdom and truth and the greatest improvement of the soul, which you never regard or heed at all? And if the person with whom I am arguing, says: Yes, but I do care; then I do not leave him or let him go at once; but I proceed to interrogate and examine and cross-examine him, and if I think that he has no virtue in him, but only says that he has, I reproach him with undervaluing the greater, and overvaluing the less. And I shall repeat the same words to every one whom I meet, young and old, citizen and alien, but especially to the citizens, inasmuch as they are my brethren. For know that this is the command of God; and I believe that no greater good has ever happened in the state than my service to the God. For I do nothing but go around persuading you all, old and young alike, not to take thought for your persons or your properties, but first and chiefly to care about the greatest improvement of the soul. I tell you that virtue is not given by money, but that from virtue comes money and every other good of man, public as well as private. This is my teaching, and if this is the doctrine which corrupts the youth, I am a mischievous person. But if any one says that this is not my teaching, he is speaking an untruth. Wherefore, O men of Athens, I say to you, do as Anytus bids or not as Anytus bids, and either acquit me or not; but whichever you do, understand that I shall never alter my ways, not even if I have to die many times.

Men of Athens, do not interrupt, but hear me; there was an understanding between us that you should hear me to the end: I have something more to say, at which you may be inclined to cry out; but I believe that to hear me will be good for you, and therefore I beg that you will not cry out. I would have you know, that if you kill such an one as I am, you will injure yourselves more than you will injure me. Nothing will injure me, not Meletus nor yet Anytus—they cannot, for a bad man is not permitted to injure a better than himself. I do not deny that Anytus may, perhaps, kill him, or drive him into exile, or deprive him of civil rights; and he may imagine, and others may imagine, that he is inflicting a great injury upon him: but there I do not agree. For the evil of doing as he is doing—the evil of unjustly taking away the life of another—is greater far.

And now, Athenians, I am not going to argue for my own sake, as you may think, but for yours, that you may not sin against the God by condemning me, who am his gift to you. For if you kill me you will not easily find a successor to me, who, if I may use such a ludicrous figure of speech, am a sort of gadfly, given to the state by God; and the state is a great and noble steed who is tardy in his motions owing to his very size, and requires to be stirred into life. I am that gadfly which God has attached to the state, and all day long and in all places am always fastening upon you, arousing and persuading and reproaching you. You will not easily find another like me, and therefore I would advise you to spare me. I dare say that you may feel out of temper (like a person who is suddenly awakened from sleep), and you think that you might easily strike me dead as Anytus advises, and then you would sleep on for the remainder of your lives, unless God in his care of you sent you another gadfly. When I say that I am given to you by God, the proof of my mission is this:—if I had been like other men, I should not have neglected all my own concerns or patiently seen the neglect of them during all these years, and have been doing yours, coming to you individually like a father or elder brother, exhorting you to regard virtue; such conduct, I say, would be unlike human nature. If I had gained anything, or if my exhortations had been paid, there would have been some sense in my doing so; but now, as you will perceive, not even the impudence of my accusers dares to say that I have ever exacted or sought pay of any one; of that they have no witness. And I have a sufficient witness to the truth of what I say—my poverty.

Some one may wonder why I go about in private giving advice and busying myself with the concerns of others, but do not venture to come forward in public and advise the state. I will tell you why. You have heard me speak at sundry times and in divers places of an oracle or sign which comes to me, and is the divinity which Meletus ridicules in the indictment. This sign, which is a kind of voice, first began to come to me when I was a child; it always forbids but never commands me to do anything which I am going to do. This is what deters me from being a politician. And rightly, as I think. For I am certain, O men of Athens, that if I had engaged in politics, I should have perished long ago, and done no good either to you or to myself. And do not be offended at my telling you the truth: for the truth is, that no man who goes to war with you or any other multitude, honestly striving against the many lawless and unrighteous deeds which are done in a state, will save his life; he who will fight for the right, if he would live even for a brief space, must have a private station and not a public one.

I can give you convincing evidence of what I say, not words only, but what you value far more—actions. Let me relate to you a passage of my own life which will prove to you that I should never have yielded to injustice from any fear of death, and that 'as I should have refused to yield' I must have died at once. I will tell you a tale of the courts, not very interesting perhaps, but nevertheless true. The only office of state which I ever held, O men of Athens, was that of senator:[13] the tribe Antiochis, which is my tribe, had the presidency at the trial of the generals who had not taken up the bodies of the slain after the battle of Arginusae; and you proposed to try them in a body, contrary to law, as you all thought afterwards; but at the time I was the only one of the Prytanes who was opposed to the illegality, and I gave my vote against you; and when the orators threatened to impeach and arrest me, and you called and shouted, I made up my mind that I would run the risk, having law and justice with me, rather than take part in your injustice because I feared imprisonment and death. This happened in the days of the democracy.[14] But when the

[13] **office . . . senator:** The Athenian Assembly was composed of 500 members, 50 from each of ten tribes. Each tribe led the Assembly for one-tenth of the year, during which time of leadership its members were known as Prytanes. Socrates, from the tribe of Antiochis, was serving as Prytane following the naval battle of Arginusae in 406 B.C.E., when several Athenian naval commanders were accused of neglecting the dead. Socrates refused to participate in the trial, held in the Assembly, which he deemed to be unjust.

[14] **the trial . . . democracy:** Socrates is giving two examples of his opposition to the government, one democratic and one the oligarchy of the Thirty Tyrants who ruled after Athens fell to Sparta.

oligarchy of the Thirty was in power, they sent for me and four others into the rotunda,[15] and bade us bring Leon the Salaminian from Salamis,[16] as they wanted to put him to death. This was a specimen of the sort of commands which they were always giving with the view of implicating as many as possible in their crimes; and then I showed, not in word only but in deed, that, if I may be allowed to use such an expression, I cared not a straw for death, and that my great and only care was lest I should do an unrighteous or unholy thing. For the strong arm of that oppressive power did not frighten me into doing wrong; and when we came out of the rotunda the other four went to Salamis and fetched Leon, but I went quietly home. For which I might have lost my life, had not the power of the Thirty shortly afterwards come to an end. And many will witness to my words.

Now do you really imagine that I could have survived all these years, if I had led a public life, supposing that like a good man I had always maintained the right and had made justice, as I ought, the first thing? No indeed, men of Athens, neither I nor any other man. But I have been always the same in all my actions, public as well as private, and never have I yielded any base compliance to those who are slanderously termed my disciples, or to any other. Not that I have any regular disciples. But if any one likes to come and hear me while I am pursuing my mission, whether he be young or old, he is not excluded. Nor do I converse only with those who pay; but any one, whether he be rich or poor, may ask and answer me and listen to my words; and whether he turns out to be a bad man or a good one, neither result can be justly imputed to me; for I never taught or professed to teach him anything. And if any one says that he has ever learned or heard anything from me in private which all the world has not heard, let me tell you that he is lying.

But I shall be asked, Why do people delight in continually conversing with you? I have told you already, Athenians, the whole truth about this matter: they like to hear the cross-examination of the pretenders to wisdom; there is amusement in it. Now this duty of cross-examining other men has been imposed upon me by God; and has been signified to me by oracles, visions, and in every way in which the will of divine power has ever intimated to any one. This is true, O Athenians; or, if not true, would be soon refuted. If I am or have been corrupting the youth, those of them who are now grown up and become sensible that I gave them bad advice in the days of their youth should come forward as accusers, and take their revenge; or if they do not like to come themselves, some of their relatives, fathers, brothers, or other kinsmen, should say what evil their families have suffered at my hands. Now is their time. Many of them I see in the court. There is Crito, who is of the same age and of the same deme[17] with myself, and there is Critobulus his son, whom I also see. Then again there is Lysanias of Sphettus, who is the father of Aeschines—he is present; and also there is Antiphon of Cephisus, who is the father of Epigenes; and there are the brothers of several who have associated with me. There is Nicostratus the son of Theosdotides, and the brother of Theodotus (now Theodotus himself is dead, and

[15] **rotunda:** The circular building where the Prytanes met. [16] **Salamis:** An island off the coast near Athens, where Leon fled to escape prosecution. [17] **deme:** Precinct.

therefore he, at any rate, will not seek to stop him); and there is Paralus the son of Demodocus, who had a brother Theages; and Adeimantus the son of Ariston, whose brother Plato[18] is present; and Aeantodorus, who is the brother of Apollodorus, whom I also see. I might mention a great many others, some of whom Meletus should have produced as witnesses in the course of his speech; and let him still produce them, if he has forgotten—I will make way for him. And let him say, if he has any testimony of the sort which he can produce. Nay, Athenians, the very opposite is the truth. For all these are ready to witness on behalf of the corrupter, of the injurer of their kindred, as Meletus and Anytus call me; not the corrupted youth only—there might have been a motive for that—but their uncorrupted elder relatives. Why should they too support me with their testimony? Why, indeed, except for the sake of truth and justice, and because they know that I am speaking the truth, and that Meletus is a liar.

Well, Athenians, this and the like of this is all the defence which I have to offer. Yet a word more. Perhaps there may be some one who is offended at me, when he calls to mind how he himself on a similar, or even a less serious occasion, prayed and entreated the judges with many tears, and how he produced his children in court, which was a moving spectacle, together with a host of relations and friends; whereas I, who am probably in danger of my life, will do none of these things. The contrast may occur to his mind, and he may be set against me, and vote in anger because he is displeased at me on this account. Now if there be such a person among you,—mind, I do not say that there is,—to him I may fairly reply: My friend, I am a man, and like other men, a creature of flesh and blood, and not 'of wood or stone,' as Homer says,[19] and I have a family, yes, and sons, O Athenians, three in number, one almost a man, and two others who are still young; and yet I will not bring any of them hither in order to petition you for an acquittal. And why not? Not from any self-assertion or want of respect for you. Whether I am or am not afraid of death is another question, of which I will not now speak. But, having regard to public opinion, I feel that such conduct would be discreditable to myself, and to you, and to the whole state. One who has reached my years, and who has a name for wisdom, ought not to demean himself. Whether this opinion of me be deserved or not, at any rate the world has decided that Socrates is in some way superior to other men. And if those among you who are said to be superior in wisdom and courage, and any other virtue, demean themselves in this way, how shameful is their conduct! I have seen men of reputation, when they have been condemned, behaving in the strangest manner: they seemed to fancy that they were going to suffer something dreadful if they died, and that they could be immortal if you only allowed them to live; and I think that such are a dishonour to the state, and that any stranger coming in would have said of them that the most eminent men of Athens, to whom the Athenians themselves give honour and command, are no better than women. And I say that these things ought

[18] **Plato:** The author of *Apology.*

[19] **'of wood . . .' as Homer says:** In Book 19 of *The Odyssey,* Penélopê addresses these words to her husband, Odysseus, who is disguised as a beggar.

not to be done by those of us who have a reputation; and if they are done, you ought not to permit them; you ought rather to show that you are far more disposed to condemn the man who gets up a doleful scene and makes the city ridiculous, than him who holds his peace.

But, setting aside the question of public opinion, there seems to be something wrong in asking a favour of a judge, and thus procuring an acquittal, instead of informing him and convincing him. For his duty is, not to make a present of justice, but to give judgment; and he has sworn that he will judge according to the laws, and not according to his own good pleasure; and we ought not to encourage you, nor should you allow yourself to be encouraged, in this habit of perjury—there can be no piety in that. Do not then require me to do what I consider dishonourable and impious and wrong, especially now, when I am being tried for impiety on the indictment of Meletus. For if, O men of Athens, by force of persuasion and entreaty I could overpower your oaths, then I should be teaching you to believe that there are no gods, and in defending should simply convict myself of the charge of not believing in them. But that is not so—far otherwise. For I do believe that there are gods, and in a sense higher than that which any of my accusers believe in them. And to you and to God I commit my cause, to be determined by you as is best for you and me.[20]

There are many reasons why I am not grieved, O men of Athens, at the vote of condemnation. I expected it, and am only surprised that the votes are so nearly equal; for I had thought that the majority against me would have been far larger; but now, had thirty votes gone over to the other side, I should have been acquitted. And I may say, I think, that I have escaped Meletus. I may say more; for without the assistance of Anytus and Lycon, any one may see that he would not have had a fifth part of the votes,[21] as the law requires, in which case he would have incurred a fine of a thousand drachmae.

And so he proposes death as the penalty. And what shall I propose on my part, O men of Athens? Clearly that which is my due. And what is my due? What return shall be made to the man who has never had the wit to be idle during his whole life; but has been careless of what the many care for—wealth, and family interests, and military offices, and speaking in the assembly, and magistracies, and plots, and parties. Reflecting that I was really too honest a man to be a politician and live, I did not go where I could do no good to you or to myself; but where I could do the greatest good privately to every one of you, thither I went, and sought to persuade every man among you that he must look to himself, and seek virtue and wisdom before he looks to his private interests, and look to the state before he looks to the interests of the state; and that this should be the order which he observes in all his actions. What

[20] The jurors cast their votes, 280 for conviction and 220 against. Next the jury must determine the sentence. Meletus demands death. Socrates is given an opportunity to propose a lighter sentence.

[21] **fifth part of the votes:** A minimum vote of one-fifth of the Assembly, or 100 votes, was required to justify conducting a trial. By dividing the 280 votes among his three accusers, Socrates arrives at a figure that suggests his accusers have not met the minimum required.

shall be done to such an one? Doubtless some good thing, O men of Athens, if he has his reward; and the good should be of a kind suitable to him. What would be a reward suitable to a poor man who is your benefactor, and who desires leisure that he may instruct you? There can be no reward so fitting as maintenance in the Prytaneum,[22] O men of Athens, a reward which he deserves far more than the citizen who has won the prize at Olympia in the horse or chariot race, whether the chariots were drawn by two horses or by many. For I am in want, and he has enough; and he only gives you the appearance of happiness, and I give you the reality. And if I am to estimate the penalty fairly, I should say that maintenance in the Prytaneum is the just return.

Perhaps you think that I am braving you in what I am saying now, as in what I said before about the tears and prayers. But this is not so. I speak rather because I am convinced that I never intentionally wronged any one, although I cannot convince you—the time has been too short; if there were a law at Athens, as there is in other cities, that a capital cause should not be decided in one day, then I believe that I should have convinced you. But I cannot in a moment refute great slander; and, as I am convinced that I never wronged another, I will assuredly not wrong myself. I will not say of myself that I deserve any evil, or propose any penalty. Why should I? Because I am afraid of the penalty of death which Meletus proposes? When I do not know whether death is a good or an evil, why should I propose a penalty which would certainly be an evil? Shall I say imprisonment? And why should I live in prison, and be the slave of the magistrates of the year—of the Eleven?[23] Or shall the penalty be a fine, and imprisonment until the fine is paid? There is the same objection. I should have to lie in prison, for money I have none, and cannot pay. And if I say exile (and this may possibly be the penalty which you will affix), I must indeed be blinded by the love of life, if I am so irrational as to expect that when you, who are my own citizens, cannot endure my discourses and words, and have found them so grievous and odious that you will have no more of them, others are likely to endure me. No indeed, men of Athens, that is not very likely. And what a life should I lead, at my age, wandering from city to city, ever changing my place of exile, and always being driven out! For I am quite sure that wherever I go, there, as here, the young men will flock to me; and if I drive them away, their elders will drive me out at their request; and if I let them come, their fathers and friends will drive me out for their sakes.

Some one will say: Yes, Socrates, but cannot you hold your tongue, and then you may go into a foreign city, and no one will interfere with you? Now I have great difficulty in making you understand my answer to this. For if I tell you that to do as you say would be a disobedience to the God, and therefore that I cannot hold my tongue, you will not believe that I am serious; and if I say again that daily to discourse about virtue, and of those other things about which you hear me examining myself and others, is the greatest good of man, and that the unexamined life is not worth living,

[22] **Prytaneum:** The place where the Prytanes honored the benefactors of Athens. [23] **the Eleven:** The committee in charge of prisons and public executions.

you are still less likely to believe me. Yet I say what is true, although a thing of which it is hard for me to persuade you. Also, I have never been accustomed to think that I deserve to suffer any harm. Had I money I might have estimated the offence at what I was able to pay, and not have been much the worse. But I have none, and therefore I must ask you to proportion the fine to my means. Well, perhaps I could afford a mina, and therefore I propose that penalty: Plato, Crito, Critobulus, and Apollodorus, my friends here, bid me say thirty minae, and they will be the sureties. Let thirty minae be the penalty; for which sum they will be ample security to you.[24]

Not much time will be gained, O Athenians, in return for the evil name which you will get from the detractors of the city, who will say that you killed Socrates, a wise man; for they will call me wise, even although I am not wise, when they want to reproach you. If you had waited a little while, your desire would have been fulfilled in the course of nature. For I am far advanced in years, as you may perceive, and not far from death. I am speaking now not to all of you, but only to those who have condemned me to death. And I have another thing to say to them: You think that I was convicted because I had no words of the sort which would have procured my acquittal—I mean, if I had thought fit to leave nothing undone or unsaid. Not so; the deficiency which led to my conviction was not of words—certainly not. But I had not the boldness or impudence or inclination to address you as you would have liked me to do, weeping and wailing and lamenting, and saying and doing many things which you have been accustomed to hear from others, and which, as I maintain, are unworthy of me. I thought at the time that I ought not to do anything common or mean when in danger: nor do I now repent of the style of my defence; I would rather die having spoken after my manner, than speak in your manner and live. For neither in war nor yet at law ought I or any man to use every way of escaping death. Often in battle there can be no doubt that if a man will throw away his arms, and fall on his knees before his pursuers, he may escape death; and in other dangers there are other ways of escaping death, if a man is willing to say and do anything. The difficulty, my friends, is not to avoid death, but to avoid unrighteousness; for that runs faster than death. I am old and move slowly, and the slower runner has overtaken me, and my accusers are keen and quick, and the faster runner, who is unrighteousness, has overtaken them. And now I depart hence condemned by you to suffer the penalty of death,—they too go their ways condemned by the truth to suffer the penalty of villainy and wrong; and I must abide by my award—let them abide by theirs. I suppose that these things may be regarded as fated,—and I think that they are well.

And now, O men who have condemned me, I would fain prophesy to you; for I am about to die, and in the hour of death men are gifted with prophetic power. And I prophesy to you who are my murderers, that immediately after my departure punishment far heavier than you have inflicted on me will surely await you. Me you have killed because you wanted to escape the accuser, and not to give an account of your lives. But that will not be as you suppose: far otherwise. For I say that there will be more accusers of you than there are now; accusers whom hitherto I have

[24] The jury now casts another split vote on the sentence, ruling for the death penalty.

restrained: and as they are younger they will be more inconsiderate with you, and you will be more offended at them. If you think that by killing men you can prevent some one from censuring your evil lives, you are mistaken; that is not a way of escape which is either possible or honourable; the easiest and the noblest way is not to be disabling others, but to be improving yourselves. This is the prophecy which I utter before my departure to the judges who have condemned me.

Friends, who would have acquitted me, I would like also to talk with you about the thing which has come to pass, while the magistrates are busy, and before I go to the place at which I must die. Stay then a little, for we may as well talk with one another while there is time. You are my friends, and I should like to show you the meaning of this event which has happened to me. O my judges—for you I may truly call judges—I should like to tell you of a wonderful circumstance. Hitherto the divine faculty of which the internal oracle is the source has constantly been in the habit of opposing me even about trifles, if I was going to make a slip or error in any matter; and now as you see there has come upon me that which may be thought, and is generally believed to be, the last and worst evil. But the oracle made no sign of opposition, either when I was leaving my house in the morning, or when I was on my way to the court, or while I was speaking, at anything which I was going to say; and yet I have often been stopped in the middle of a speech, but now in nothing I either said or did touching the matter in hand has the oracle opposed me. What do I take to be the explanation of this silence? I will tell you. It is an intimation that what has happened to me is a good, and that those of us who think that death is an evil are in error. For the customary sign would surely have opposed me had I been going to evil and not to good.

Let us reflect in another way, and we shall see that there is great reason to hope that death is a good; for one of two things—either death is a state of nothingness and utter unconsciousness, or, as men say, there is a change and migration of the soul from this world to another. Now if you suppose that there is no consciousness, but a sleep like the sleep of him who is undisturbed even by dreams, death will be an unspeakable gain. For if a person were to select the night in which his sleep was undisturbed even by dreams, and were to compare with this the other days and nights of his life, and then were to tell us how many days and nights he had passed in the course of his life better and more pleasantly than this one, I think that any man, I will not say a private man, but even the great king will not find many such days or nights, when compared with the others. Now if death be of such a nature, I say that to die is gain; for eternity is then only a single night. But if death is the journey to another place, and there, as men say, all the dead abide, what good, O my friends and judges, can be greater than this? If indeed when the pilgrim arrives in the world below, he is delivered from the professors of justice in this world, and finds the true judges who are said to give judgment there, Minos and Rhadamanthus and Aeacus and Triptolemus,[25] and other sons of God who were righteous in their own life, that

[25] **Minos . . . Triptolemus:** The four judges of the dead.

pilgrimage will be worth making. What would not a man give if he might converse with Orpheus and Musaeus and Hesiod[26] and Homer? Nay, if this be true, let me die again and again. I myself, too, shall have a wonderful interest in there meeting and conversing with Palamedes, and Ajax the son of Telamon, and any other ancient hero who has suffered death through an unjust judgment; and there will be no small pleasure, as I think, in comparing my own sufferings with theirs. Above all, I shall then be able to continue my search into true and false knowledge; as in this world, so also in the next and I shall find out who is wise, and who pretends to be wise, and is not. What would not a man give, O judges, to be able to examine the leader of the great Trojan expedition; or Odysseus or Sisyphus,[27] or numberless others, men and women too! What infinite delight would there be in conversing with them and asking them questions! In another world they do not put a man to death for asking questions: assuredly not. For besides being happier than we are, they will be immortal, if what is said is true.

Wherefore, O judges, be of good cheer about death, and know of a certainty, that no evil can happen to a good man, either in life or after death. He and his are not neglected by the gods; nor has my own approaching end happened by mere chance. But I see clearly that the time had arrived when it was better for me to die and be released from trouble; wherefore the oracle gave no sign. For which reason, also, I am not angry with my condemners, or with my accusers; they have done me no harm, although they did not mean to do me any good; and for this I may gently blame them.

Still I have a favour to ask of them. When my sons are grown up, I would ask you, O my friends, to punish them; and I would have you trouble them, as I have troubled you, if they seem to care about riches, or anything more than about virtue; or if they pretend to be something when they are really nothing,—then reprove them, as I have reproved you, for not caring about that for which they ought to care, and thinking that they are something when they are really nothing. And if you do this, both I and my sons will have received justice at your hands.

The hour of departure has arrived, and we go our ways—I to die, and you to live. Which is better God only knows.

---

[26] **Orpheus . . . Hesiod:** Orpheus and Musaeus were legendary poets; Hesiod was a Greek poet of the eighth century B.C.E.

[27] **Odysseus or Sisyphus:** Both Odysseus and Sisyphus were noted for their cunning.

FROM

Phaedo

Translated by Benjamin Jowett

PERSONS OF THE DIALOGUE:

PHAEDO, *who is the narrator of the Dialogue to Echecrates of Phlius*
SOCRATES
APOLLODORUS
SIMMIAS
CEBES
CRITO
ATTENDANT OF THE PRISON

SCENE: *The Prison of Socrates; Place of the Narration: Phlius*

[In this excerpt from the final pages of the *Phaedo,* Plato describes the execution of Socrates. The narrator, Phaedo, and several other friends of Socrates listen to the philosopher prove the immortality of the soul. The excerpt begins as Socrates concludes by describing the virtuous person's hopes for an afterlife.–ED.]

. . . A man of sense ought not to say, nor will I be very confident, that the description which I have given of the soul and her mansions is exactly true. But I do say that, inasmuch as the soul is shown to be immortal, he may venture to think, not improperly or unworthily, that something of the kind is true. The venture is a glorious one, and he ought to comfort himself with words like these, which is the reason why I lengthen out the tale. Wherefore, I say, let a man be of good cheer about his soul, who having cast away the pleasures and ornaments of the body as alien to him and working harm rather than good, has sought after the pleasures of knowledge; and has arrayed the soul, not in some foreign attire, but in her own proper jewels, temperance, and justice, and courage, and nobility, and truth—in these adorned she is ready to go on her journey to the world below, when her hour comes. You, Simmias and Cebes, and all other men, will depart at some time or other. Me already, as a tragic poet would say, the voice of fate calls. Soon I must drink the poison; and I think that I had better repair to the bath first, in order that the women may not have the trouble of washing my body after I am dead.

When he had done speaking, Crito said: And have you any commands for us, Socrates—anything to say about your children, or any other matter in which we can serve you?

Nothing particular, Crito, he replied: only, as I have always told you, take care of yourselves; that is a service which you may be ever rendering to me and mine and to all of us, whether you promise to do so or not. But if you have no thought for yourselves, and care not to walk according to the rule which I have prescribed for you, not now for the first time, however much you may profess or promise at the moment, it will be of no avail.

We will do our best, said Crito: And in what way shall we bury you?

In any way that you like; but you must get hold of me, and take care that I do not run away from you. Then he turned to us, and added with a smile:—I cannot make Crito believe that I am the same Socrates who has been talking and conducting the argument; he fancies that I am the other Socrates whom he will soon see, a dead body—and he asks, How shall he bury me? And though I have spoken many words in the endeavour to show that when I have drunk the poison I shall leave you and go to the joys of the blessed,—these words of mine, with which I was comforting you and myself, have had, as I perceive, no effect upon Crito. And therefore I want you to be surety for me to him now, as at the trial he was surety to the judges for me: but let the promise be of another sort; for he was surety for me to the judges that I would remain, and you must be my surety to him that I shall not remain, but go away and depart; and then he will suffer less at my death, and not be grieved when he sees my body being burned or buried. I would not have him sorrow at my hard lot, or say at the burial, Thus we lay out Socrates, or, Thus we follow him to the grave or bury him; for false words are not only evil in themselves, but they infect the soul with evil. Be of good cheer then, my dear Crito, and say that you are burying my body only, and do with that whatever is usual, and what you think best.

When he had spoken these words, he arose and went into a chamber to bathe; Crito followed him and told us to wait. So we remained behind, talking and thinking of the subject of discourse, and also of the greatness of our sorrow; he was like a father of whom we were being bereaved, and we were about to pass the rest of our lives as orphans. When he had taken the bath his children were brought to him—(he had two young sons and an elder one); and the women of his family also came, and he talked to them and gave them a few directions in the presence of Crito; then he dismissed them and returned to us.

Now the hour of sunset was near, for a good deal of time had passed while he was within. When he came out, he sat down with us again after his bath, but not much was said. Soon the jailer, who was the servant of the Eleven, entered and stood by him, saying:—To you, Socrates, whom I know to be the noblest and gentlest and best of all who ever came to this place, I will not impute the angry feelings of other men, who rage and swear at me, when, in obedience to the authorities, I bid them drink the poison—indeed, I am sure that you will not be angry with me; for others, as you are aware, and not I, are to blame. And so fare you well, and try to bear lightly what must needs be—you know my errand. Then bursting into tears he turned away and went out.

Socrates looked at him and said: I return your good wishes, and will do as you bid. Then turning to us, he said, How charming the man is: since I have been in prison he has always been coming to see me, and at times he would talk to me, and was as good to me as could be, and now see how generously he sorrows on my account. We must do as he says, Crito; and therefore let the cup be brought, if the poison is prepared: if not, let the attendant prepare some.

Yet, said Crito, the sun is still upon the hilltops, and I know that many a one has taken the draught late, and after the announcement has been made to him, he has eaten and drunk, and enjoyed the society of his beloved; do not hurry—there is time enough.

Socrates said: Yes, Crito, and they of whom you speak are right in so acting, for they think that they will be gainers by the delay; but I am right in not following their example, for I do not think that I should gain anything by drinking the poison a little later; I should only be ridiculous in my own eyes for sparing and saving a life which is already forfeit. Please then to do as I say, and not to refuse me.

Crito made a sign to the servant, who was standing by; and he went out, and having been absent for some time, returned with the jailer carrying the cup of poison. Socrates said: You, my good friend, who are experienced in these matters, shall give me directions how I am to proceed. The man answered: You have only to walk about until your legs are heavy, and then to lie down, and the poison will act. At the same time he handed the cup to Socrates, who in the easiest and gentlest manner, without the least fear or change of colour or feature, looking at the man with all his eyes, Echecrates, as his manner was, took the cup and said: What do you say about making a libation out of this cup to any god? May I, or not? The man answered: We only prepare, Socrates, just so much as we deem enough. I understand, he said: but I may and I must ask the gods to prosper my journey from this to the other world—even so—and so be it according to my prayer. Then raising the cup to his lips, quite readily and cheerfully he drank off the poison. And hitherto most of us had been able to control our sorrow; but now when we saw him drinking, and saw too that he had finished the draught, we could no longer forbear, and in spite of myself my own tears were flowing fast; so that I covered my face and wept, not for him, but at the thought of my own calamity in having to part from such a friend. Nor was I the first; for Crito, when he found himself unable to restrain his tears, had got up, and I followed; and at that moment, Apollodorus, who had been weeping all the time, broke out in a loud and passionate cry which made cowards of us all. Socrates alone retained his calmness: What is this strange outcry? he said. I sent away the women mainly in order that they might not misbehave in this way, for I have been told that a man should die in peace. Be quiet then, and have patience. When we heard his words we were ashamed, and refrained our tears; and he walked about until, as he said, his legs began to fail, and then he lay on his back, according to the directions, and the man who gave him the poison now and then looked at his feet and legs; and after a while he pressed his foot hard, and asked him if he could feel; and he said, No; and then his leg, and so upwards and upwards, and showed us that he was cold and stiff. And he felt them himself, and said: When the poison reaches the heart, that will be the end. He was beginning to grow cold about the groin, when he uncovered his face, for he had covered himself up, and said—they were his last words—he said: Crito, I owe a cock to Asclepius; will you remember to pay the debt? The debt shall be paid, said Crito; is there anything else? There was no answer to this question; but in a minute or two a movement was heard, and the attendants uncovered him; his eyes were set, and Crito closed his eyes and mouth.

Such was the end, Echecrates, of our friend; concerning whom I may truly say, that of all the men of his time whom I have known, he was the wisest and justest and best.

FROM

The Republic

Translated by Benjamin Jowett

[The Allegory of the Cave]

SPEAKERS IN THE DIALOGUE:
SOCRATES GLAUCON

And now, I said, let me show in a figure how far our nature is enlightened or unenlightened: — Behold! human beings living in an underground den, which has a mouth open towards the light and reaching all along the den; here they have been from their childhood, and have their legs and necks chained so that they cannot move, and can only see before them, being prevented by the chains from turning round their heads. Above and behind them a fire is blazing at a distance, and between the fire and the prisoners there is a raised way; and you will see, if you look, a low wall built along the way, like the screen which marionette players have in front of them, over which they show the puppets.

I see.

And do you see, I said, men passing along the wall carrying all sorts of vessels, and statues and figures of animals made of wood and stone and various materials, which appear over the wall? Some of them are talking, others silent.

You have shown me a strange image, and they are strange prisoners.

Like ourselves, I replied; and they see only their own shadows, or the shadows of one another, which the fire throws on the opposite wall of the cave?

True, he said; how could they see anything but the shadows if they were never allowed to move their heads?

And of the objects which are being carried in like manner they would only see the shadows?

Yes, he said.

And if they were able to converse with one another, would they not suppose that they were naming what was actually before them?

"Allegory of the Cave." In this allegory from Book 7 of *The Republic,* Plato uses the metaphors of a cave and the world outside of a cave to illustrate the relation of appearances to reality. The shadows cast on the wall of the underground den, or cave, are insubstantial and distorted versions of their originals. Outside of the cave is a higher realm, where the light of the sun replaces the feeble firelight in the cave and enables a clearer perception of reality. Those capable of leaving the cave will be few in number; fewer still will be able to look at the sun itself, symbolic of the highest truths, the Ideas of Goodness, Truth, and Beauty. This small group of "philosopher-kings," Plato suggests, have a duty to guide and govern those who remain in the dark.

Very true.

And suppose further that the prison had an echo which came from the other side, would they not be sure to fancy when one of the passers-by spoke that the voice which they heard came from the passing shadow?

No question, he replied.

To them, I said, the truth would be literally nothing but the shadows of the images.

That is certain.

And now look again, and see what will naturally follow if the prisoners are released and disabused of their error. At first, when any of them is liberated and compelled suddenly to stand up and turn his neck round and walk and look towards the light, he will suffer sharp pains; the glare will distress him, and he will be unable to see the realities of which in his former state he had seen the shadows; and then conceive some one saying to him, that what he saw before was an illusion, but that now, when he is approaching nearer to being and his eye is turned towards more real existence, he has a clearer vision—what will be his reply? And you may further imagine that his instructor is pointing to the objects as they pass and requiring him to name them—will he not be perplexed? Will he not fancy that the shadows which he formerly saw are truer than the objects which are now shown to him?

Far truer.

And if he is compelled to look straight at the light, will he not have a pain in his eyes which will make him turn away to take refuge in the objects of vision which he can see, and which he will conceive to be in reality clearer than the things which are now being shown to him?

True, he said.

And suppose once more, that he is reluctantly dragged up a steep and rugged ascent, and held fast until he is forced into the presence of the sun himself, is he not likely to be pained and irritated? When he approaches the light his eyes will be dazzled, and he will not be able to see anything at all of what are now called realities.

Not all in a moment, he said.

He will require to grow accustomed to the sight of the upper world. And first he will see the shadows best, next the reflections of men and other objects in the water, and then the objects themselves; then he will gaze upon the light of the moon and the stars and the spangled heaven; and he will see the sky and the stars by night better than the sun or the light of the sun by day?

Certainly.

Last of all he will be able to see the sun, and not mere reflections of him in the water, but he will see him in his own proper place, and not in another; and he will contemplate him as he is.

Certainly.

He will then proceed to argue that this is he who gives the season and the years, and is the guardian of all that is in the visible world, and in a certain way the cause of all things which he and his fellows have been accustomed to behold?

Clearly, he said, he would first see the sun and then reason about him.

And when he remembered his old habitation, and the wisdom of the den and his fellow-prisoners, do you not suppose that he would felicitate himself on the change, and pity them?

Certainly, he would.

And if they were in the habit of conferring honours among themselves on those who were quickest to observe the passing shadows and to remark which of them went before, and which followed after, and which were together; and who were therefore best able to draw conclusions as to the future, do you think that he would care for such honours and glories, or envy the possessors of them? Would he not say with Homer,

> Better to be the poor servant of a poor master,

and to endure anything, rather than think as they do and live after their manner?

Yes, he said, I think that he would rather suffer anything than entertain these false notions and live in this miserable manner.

Imagine once more, I said, such an one coming suddenly out of the sun to be replaced in his old situation; would he not be certain to have his eyes full of darkness?

To be sure, he said.

And if there were a contest, and he had to compete in measuring the shadows with the prisoners who had never moved out of the den, while his sight was still weak, and before his eyes had become steady (and the time which would be needed to acquire this new habit of sight might be very considerable), would he not be ridiculous? Men would say of him that up he went and down he came without his eyes; and that it was better not even to think of ascending; and if any one tried to loose another and lead him up to the light, let them only catch the offender, and they would put him to death.

No question, he said.

This entire allegory, I said, you may now append, dear Glaucon, to the previous argument; the prison-house is the world of sight, the light of the fire is the sun, and you will not misapprehend me if you interpret the journey upwards to be the ascent of the soul into the intellectual world according to my poor belief, which, at your desire, I have expressed—whether rightly or wrongly God knows. But, whether true or false, my opinion is that in the world of knowledge the idea of good appears last of all, and is seen only with an effort; and, when seen, is also inferred to be the universal author of all things beautiful and right, parent of light and of the lord of light in this visible world, and the immediate source of reason and truth in the intellectual; and that this is the power upon which he who would act rationally either in public or private life must have his eye fixed.

I agree, he said, as far as I am able to understand you.

Moreover, I said, you must not wonder that those who attain to this beatific vision are unwilling to descend to human affairs; for their souls are ever hastening into the upper world where they desire to dwell; which desire of theirs is very natural, if our allegory may be trusted.

Yes, very natural.

And is there anything surprising in one who passes from divine contemplations to the evil state of man, misbehaving himself in a ridiculous manner; if, while his eyes are blinking and before he has become accustomed to the surrounding darkness, he is compelled to fight in courts of law, or in other places, about the images or the shadows of images of justice, and is endeavouring to meet the conceptions of those who have never yet seen absolute justice?

Anything but surprising, he replied.

Any one who has common sense will remember that the bewilderments of the eyes are of two kinds, and arise from two causes, either from coming out of the light or from going into the light, which is true of the mind's eye, quite as much as of the bodily eye; and he who remembers this when he sees any one whose vision is perplexed and weak, will not be too ready to laugh; he will first ask whether that soul of man has come out of the brighter life, and is unable to see because unaccustomed to the dark, or having turned from darkness to the day is dazzled by excess of light. And he will count the one happy in his condition and state of being, and he will pity the other; or, if he have a mind to laugh at the soul which comes from below into the light, there will be more reason in this than in the laugh which greets him who returns from above out of the light into the den.

That, he said, is a very just distinction.

But then, if I am right, certain professors of education must be wrong when they say that they can put a knowledge into the soul which was not there before, like sight into blind eyes.

They undoubtedly say this, he replied.

Whereas, our argument shows that the power and capacity of learning exists in the soul already; and that just as the eye was unable to turn from darkness to light without the whole body, so too the instrument of knowledge can only by the movement of the whole soul be turned from the world of becoming into that of being, and learn by degrees to endure the sight of being, and of the brightest and best of being, or in other words, of the good.

Very true.

And must there not be some art which will effect conversion in the easiest and quickest manner; not implanting the faculty of sight, for that exists already, but has been turned in the wrong direction, and is looking away from the truth?

Yes, he said, such an art may be presumed.

And whereas the other so-called virtues of the soul seem to be akin to bodily qualities, for even when they are not originally innate they can be implanted later by habit and exercise, the virtue of wisdom more than anything else contains a divine element which always remains, and by this conversion is rendered useful and profitable; or, on the other hand, hurtful and useless. Did you never observe the narrow intelligence flashing from the keen eye of a clever rogue—how eager he is, how clearly his paltry soul sees the way to his end; he is the reverse of blind, but his keen eye-sight is forced into the service of evil, and he is mischievous in proportion to his cleverness?

Very true, he said.

But what if there had been a circumcision of such natures in the days of their youth; and they had been severed from those sensual pleasures, such as eating and drinking, which, like leaden weights, were attached to them at their birth, and which drag them down and turn the vision of their souls upon the things that are below—if, I say, they had been released from these impediments and turned in the opposite direction, the very same faculty in them would have seen the truth as keenly as they see what their eyes are turned to now.

Very likely.

Yes, I said; and there is another thing which is likely, or rather a necessary inference from what has preceded, that neither the uneducated and uninformed of the truth, nor yet those who never make an end of their education, will be able ministers of State; not the former, because they have no single aim of duty which is the rule of all their actions, private as well as public; nor the latter, because they will not act at all except upon compulsion, fancying that they are already dwelling apart in the islands of the blest.

Very true, he replied.

Then, I said, the business of us who are the founders of the State will be to compel the best minds to attain that knowledge which we have already shown to be the greatest of all—they must continue to ascend until they arrive at the good; but when they have ascended and seen enough we must not allow them to do as they do now.

What do you mean?

I mean that they remain in the upper world: but this must not be allowed; they must be made to descend again among the prisoners in the den, and partake of their labours and honours, whether they are worth having or not.

But is not this unjust? he said; ought we to give them a worse life, when they might have a better?

You have again forgotten, my friend, I said, the intention of the legislator, who did not aim at making any one class in the State happy above the rest; the happiness was to be in the whole State, and he held the citizens together by persuasion and necessity, making them benefactors of the State, and therefore benefactors of one another; to this end he created them, not to please themselves, but to be his instruments in binding up the State.

True, he said, I had forgotten.

Observe, Glaucon, that there will be no injustice in compelling our philosophers to have a care and providence of others; we shall explain to them that in other States, men of their class are not obliged to share in the toils of politics: and this is reasonable, for they grow up at their own sweet will, and the government would rather not have them. Being self-taught, they cannot be expected to show any gratitude for a culture which they have never received. But we have brought you into the world to be rulers of the hive, kings of yourselves and of the other citizens, and have educated you far better and more perfectly than they have been educated, and you are better able to share in the double duty. Wherefore each of you, when his turn comes, must go down to the general underground abode, and get the habit of seeing in the dark. When you have acquired the habit, you will see ten thousand times better than the inhabitants of the den, and you will know what the several images are, and what they represent, because you have seen the beautiful and just and good in their truth. And thus our State which is also yours will be a reality, and not a dream only, and will be administered in a spirit unlike that of other States, in which men fight with one another about shadows only and are distracted in the struggle for power, which in their eyes is a great good. Whereas the truth is that the State in which the rulers are most reluctant to govern is always the best and most quietly governed, and the State in which they are most eager, the worst.

Quite true, he replied.

And will our pupils, when they hear this, refuse to take their turn at the toils of State, when they are allowed to spend the greater part of their time with one another in the heavenly light?

Impossible, he answered; for they are just men, and the commands which we impose upon them are just; there can be no doubt that every one of them will take office as a stern necessity, and not after the fashion of our present rulers of State.

Yes, my friend, I said; and there lies the point. You must contrive for your future rulers another and a better life than that of a ruler, and then you may have a well-ordered State; for only in the State which offers this, will they rule who are truly rich, not in silver and gold, but in virtue and wisdom, which are the true blessings of life. Whereas if they go to the administration of public affairs, poor and hungering after their own private advantage, thinking that hence they are to snatch the chief good, order there can never be; for they will be fighting about office, and the civil and domestic broils which thus arise will be the ruin of the rulers themselves and of the whole State.

Most true, he replied.

And the only life which looks down upon the life of political ambition is that of true philosophy. Do you know of any other?

Indeed, I do not, he said. . . .

Heroes and Citizens

People in the West often trace the idea of the hero back to the portraits of noblemen and warriors in Homer's epics (eighth century B.C.E.) in ***The Iliad*** and ***The Odyssey***, models based on an even earlier age of chivalry. In *The Iliad*, Achilles is portrayed as the ultimate superhuman figure known for his superior physical prowess, courage, and fighting skills. The driving purpose of his life is to achieve glory, fame, and honor. Symbolizing excellence in the Trojan War, Achilles was honored with marble memorials and celebrated in song and drama. Military prowess, however, while providing the cornerstone of city-states or empires, does not of itself lead to the sustained development of a civil society, which ultimately is dependent on responsible citizenship, not the energies and ideals of the warrior. Literature, on the other hand, does provide portraits of heroes and kings who contribute to the betterment of society through what might be called public works: slaying the dragons of chaos, harnessing wild rivers, eliminating floods, capturing outlaws, and building temples and palaces. Such achievements are often attributed to godlike monarchs who combine the roles of hero and king.

pp. 288, 421

The Zhou dynasty in China (c. 1027–221 B.C.E.) referred to the heroism of the third millennium B.C.E. in its history, a golden age during which legendary rulers became models of Confucian virtue, as a blueprint for later dynasties. Though the divine Yao was perhaps the most celebrated of the Zhou monarchs, it was the accomplishments of Shun, Yao's successor, that established a pattern for later rulers. Shun represented a true success story, since he had risen from the poor classes and was chosen to succeed Yao on the basis of merit,

Standing Warrior, 221–210 B.C.E.
This warrior in breastplate with a chariot horse is one of the Terracotta Warriors, a group of lifesize statues that guarded the tomb of the first emperor of China, the visionary yet brutal ruler Qin Shi Huangdi (Ch'in Shih Huang Ti). (The Art Archive / Dagli Orti)

not right of birth—establishing a Confucian ideal for later successions. Shun gained control of the region, regulated ritual and ceremony, established order through a system of rewards and punishments, and laid the foundation of filial piety in all relationships, from family to that of ruler and subject. **The Shu Jing (*Book of History*)** documents the life of Shun.

p. 1122

The most popular human hero in Greece to have earned immortality with his exploits and to have become a god was Heracles, clearly the working-class hero of his time. It was probably in retrospect that special heroes in the ancient world were said to have come from mixed parentage—one human parent and the other a deity. It was a practice the Greeks might have inherited from Mesopotamia, whose great hero Gilgamesh was born of a goddess mother. Apollodorus describes a few of Heracles' labors that earned him fame and deification in his ***Bibliotheca.*** The legends of Heracles' adventures in the netherworld especially enhanced his reputation. p. 1128

One tradition of the hero in ancient Greece probably predates Homer's warrior-heroes and is reflected in the root of the Greek word *heros,* which means "to watch over, protect." The oldest word for a hero in Greece was *daimon*[1]—or, in Latin, *daemon*—believed to mean a guardian spirit that existed halfway between the gods and humans, not unlike the Christian guardian angel. Like the ancient Egyptians and Chinese, the early Greeks associated heroes with a cult of the dead in which dead heroes were thought to reside in their tombs and watch over the living, bestowing blessings from the grave. In one form or another, cults of the dead, along with ancestor worship, are thought to be the oldest religions in the world—if not the origin of religion itself. A prayer in Aeschylus's play ***The Libation Bearers*** shows the tomb or grave as the threshold between two worlds, the place where contact can be made with the spirits of the dead. p. 1134

The challenge for all ancient civilizations during peacetime was to transform the concept of the hero from one of a warrior to one of a responsible citizen, a transition that was only partially successful during the Golden Age of Athens under Pericles. By the fifth century B.C.E. in Athens, the city-state (or *polis*) became an arena for a secular or civil religion in which the responsibilities of citizenship had a "sacred" importance superior to the priesthood. As **Pericles' Funeral Oration**, as recorded by Thucydides, indicates, the real heroes were now the citizens who sacrificed their lives for Athens,[2] the "school of Hellas." But when Athens fell to Sparta at the end of the Peloponnesian War, in 404 B.C.E., the citizen-hero went with it, p. 1136

[1] ***daimon:*** Though this Greek word originally meant "hero," in the Middle Ages in Europe, a fear of the connection between spirit and psyche led to the more frightening concept of *demon* as we know it today.

[2] **Athens:** The United States celebrates its "civil religion" through major holidays, or "holy days": the birthdays of Washington, Lincoln, and Martin Luther King Jr., as well as Memorial Day, Independence Day, Labor Day, and Thanksgiving.

Greek Warrior, fifth century B.C.E.
Vase detail of an armed warrior in a classic hero pose. (Erich Lessing/ Art Resource, NY)

replaced by a figure whose heroism was marked by the inner, spiritual qualities of self-discipline and a simple lifestyle rather than overt or public action. Out of this major cultural transformation came the famous schools of Greek philosophy: the Platonists, Cynics, and Stoics.

The ultimate citizen of Athens, ironically, was itinerant philosopher Socrates, the supreme example of the philosopher-hero who was sentenced to death for his honesty and outspokenness; his trial and death further tarnished Athens's already declining reputation for democracy and tolerance. In ***Apology***, the most well-known account of the seventy-year-old Socrates' defiant defense against charges of impiety and corruption of Athens' youth, Plato depicts Socrates as a man with exceptional mental and spiritual qualities, like leadership and extreme goodness. Diogenes Laertius, a third-century-C.E. Greek biographer who specialized in the lives of his country's philosophers, reflects in his writings about **Socrates** the idea of the ideal Greek philosopher as it must have been understood at the time.

p. 1089
p. 1142

Diogenes' details about Socrates' physique and home life tend to humanize the great teacher.

While the Greek thinkers focused on citizenship and morality, the founder of the Maurya dynasty that unified all of India, Chandragupta Maurya (r. 322–297 B.C.E.), a contemporary of Alexander the Great, was obsessed with maintaining control over his empire through an elaborate hierarchy of ministers, spies, and informers. Out of this period came an elaborate manual called ***The Treatise on Material Gain (Arthashastra),*** attributed to Kautilya (Kautalya), a minister of Chandragupta Maurya, which spells out in great detail the machinery of absolute control. Like the sixteenth-century Machiavelli in Italy who explained the manipulation of power to Florentine princes, Kautilya deals with the means and ends of government administration and indicates that the end of survival justifies most any means. The brief excerpts presented here instruct on how to test the loyalty of ministers and how to employ spies.

p. 1145

Today the word *hero* is applied to someone who models extraordinary valor or courage, often during war or other national crisis. Physical courage characterizes the heroes of the world wars in the twentieth century. The twentieth century, however, was also notable for its spiritual heroes, people like Mother Teresa of Calcutta, Nelson Mandela of South Africa, Mahatma Gandhi of India, and Martin Luther King Jr. of the United States. The great heroes in the aftermath of the attack on the World Trade Center in New York City on September 11, 2001, were the firefighters and policemen who gave their lives to save others, and Mayor Giuliani, who was an inspirational leader during the crisis.

■ CONNECTIONS

Homer and Kautilya, pp. 277 and 1145. The ongoing survival of a society is dependent on the participation of its citizens in its collective welfare. Often societies will glorify past legendary citizens, making them models of positive participation. Some societies enforce model behavior, using laws, punishments, and policing. A few take a laissez-faire approach, believing that educated individuals would *choose* to contribute to a society's well-being. Compare the approaches reflected by Homer and Kautilya in this *In the World* section. Which is closest to the model we know today?

Hebrew Scriptures, p. 134, 235; The Code of Hammurabi, p. 230. In the ancient Near East, the rule of law in controlling behavior was enforced through the gods and punishments for wrongdoing. Greek and Chinese philosophers such as Plato and Confucius stressed the role of education for changing behavior: They believed that once people understood the truths of morality their behavior would change. How is the Greek and Chinese use of inspirational models for shaping behavior different from the focus on law in Hebrew and Babylonian societies?

Shu Jing (Book of History)
c. 800 B.C.E.

Written down c. 800 B.C.E., the *Shu Jing* (*The Book of History*) became one of the five Confucian classics, works identified with the history, literature, religion, and worldview of ancient China. Although traditionally the authorship of the *Shu Jing* was attributed to Confucius, perhaps as a way of establishing a canon of Confucian works for posterity, the actual author is unknown. The period of time covered in the following selection is from about 2285 B.C.E. to the death of Shun, in about 2205 B.C.E. Shun not only regulated the physical boundaries of China, referred to as the Four Mountains, but also established the parameters of human behavior through enforcing the five punishments and modeling the five cardinal duties. The five punishments were branding, cutting off the feet, cutting off the nose, castration, and death. The five duties of filial piety involved appropriate attitudes and behavior between husband and wife, father and son, sovereign and subject, older and younger brothers, and friends.

The selection begins with the sovereign Yao beginning the process of choosing a successor; his successor ultimately is Shun.

A note on the translation: We use the standard translation by James Legge, modernized by Clae Waltham. The footnotes are the editors', except where translator's notes by Clae Waltham are indicated.

FROM

The Shu Jing

Translated by James Legge, modernized by Clae Waltham

[The Reign of Shun]

The sovereign said, "Who will search out for me a man according to the times, whom I can raise and employ?"

Fang Ch'i[1] said, "Your heir-son Chu is highly intelligent."

The sovereign said, "Alas! he is insincere and quarrelsome. Could he do?"

The sovereign said, "Who will search out for me a man equal to the exigency of my affairs?"

Huan Tou said, "Oh! the merits of the minister of Works have just been displayed on a wide scale."

The sovereign said, "Alas! when all is quiet, he talks; but when employed, his actions turn out differently. He is respectful only in appearance. See! the floods assail the heavens!"

[1] **Fang Ch'i:** Fang Ch'i, and later Huan Tou, are advisors.

Portrait of Confucius, nineteenth century
A French aquatint of the Chinese philosopher, teacher, and political theorist. (The Art Archive)

The sovereign said, "Oh! Chief of the Four Mountains,[2] the waters of the inundation are destructive in their overflow. In their vastness they embrace the hills and overtop great heights, threatening the heavens with their floods. The lower people groan and murmur! Is there a capable man to whom I can assign the correction of this calamity?"

All in the court said, "Ah! is there not Kun?"

The sovereign said, "Alas! how perverse is he! He is disobedient to orders and tries to injure his peers."

The Chief of the Four Mountains said, "Well, but try him—to see if he can accomplish the work."

Accordingly, Kun was employed.

The sovereign said to him, "Go; be reverent!"

For nine years Kun labored. But the work was not accomplished.

[2] **Chief of the Four Mountains:** The chief is an administrative officer. "The four mountains are Tai in the east, in present-day Shantung; Hua in the west, in present-day Shansi; Mt. Heng in the south, in present-day Hunan; and the northern Mt. Heng, in present-day Hopeh." (Translator's note.)

The sovereign said, "Oh! Chief of the Four Mountains, I have been on the throne for seventy years. You can carry out my commands. I will resign my throne to you."

The Chief said, "I have not the virtue; I should disgrace the imperial seat."

The sovereign said, "Show me someone among the illustrious, or set forth one from among the poor and mean."

All then said to the sovereign, "There is an unmarried man among the lower people called Shun of Yü."[3]

The sovereign said, "Yes, I have heard of him. What have you to say about him?"

The Chief said, "He is the son of a blind man. His father was obstinately unprincipled; his stepmother was insincere; his half brother Hsiang was arrogant. Shun has been able, however, by his filial piety to live in harmony with them and to lead them gradually to self-government, so that they no longer proceed to great wickedness."

The sovereign said, "I will try him; I will wive him and thereby see his behavior with my two daughters."

Accordingly he prepared and sent down his two daughters to the north of the Kuei, to be wives in the family of Shun in Yü. The sovereign said to his daughters, "Be reverent!"

[. . .]

Examining into antiquity, we find the sovereign Shun was styled Ch'ung Hua.[4] His character was entirely conformed to that of the former sovereign: he was profound, wise, accomplished, and intelligent. He was mild and courteous and truly sincere. The report of his mysterious virtue was heard on high and he was appointed to occupy the imperial seat.

Shun carefully set forth the beauty of the five cardinal duties and they came to be universally observed. Being appointed General Regulator, the affairs of every department were arranged in their proper seasons. Being charged to receive the princes from the four quarters of the land, they were all docilely submissive. Being sent to the great plains at the foot of the mountains amid violent wind, thunder, and rain, he did not go astray.

The sovereign said, "Come, you Shun. For three years I have consulted you on all affairs, examined your words, and found that they can be carried into practice. Now you ascend the seat of the sovereign."

Shun wished to decline in favor of someone more virtuous, and not to be Yao's successor. On the first day of the first month, however, he received Yao's retirement from the imperial duties in the temple of the Accomplished Ancestor.

Shun examined the pearl-adorned turning sphere with its transverse tube of jade and reduced to a harmonious system the movements of the Seven Directors.[5]

Thereafter, Shun sacrificed especially, but with the ordinary forms, to God;

---

[3] **Yü:** A principality.

[4] **Ch'ung Hua:** Unknown designation.

[5] **sphere . . . Seven Directors:** The examining instrument was probably a kind of armillary sphere representing the revolution of the heavens, with the transverse athwart the sphere for the purpose of celestial observation. Legge thought the Seven Directors designated the seven stars of the Big Dipper. (Translator's note.)

sacrificed with reverent purity to the Six Honored Ones;[6] offered appropriate sacrifices to the hills and rivers; and extended his worship to the host of spirits.

He called in all the five jade symbols of rank. And when the month was over, he gave daily audience to the Chief of the Four Mountains and all the Pastors, finally returning their symbols to the various princes.[7]

In the second month of the year he made a tour of inspection eastward as far as lofty Mount Tai, where he presented a burnt offering to Heaven and sacrificed to the hills and rivers in order. Thereafter he gave audience to the princes of the east. He set in accord their seasons and months and regulated the days. He made uniform the standard tubes, the measures of length and of capacity, and the steelyards.[8] He regulated the five classes of ceremonies. As to the several articles of introduction: the five symbols of jade, the three kinds of silk, the two living animals and the one dead one: when all was over he returned the five symbols of jade.

In the fifth month he made a similar tour southward as far as the mountain of the south, where he observed the same ceremonies as at Mount Tai.

In the eighth month he made a tour westward as far as the mountain of the west, where he did as before.

In the eleventh month he made a tour northward as far as the mountain of the north, where he observed the same ceremonies as in the west. He then returned to the capital, went to the temple of the Accomplished Ancestor, and sacrificed a single bull.

In five years there was one tour of inspection, and there were four appearances of the princes at court. They gave a report of their government in words. This was clearly tested by their works. They received chariots and robes according to their merits.

Shun divided the land into twelve provinces, raising altars upon twelve hills in them. He also deepened the rivers.

He exhibited to the people the statutory punishments, enacting banishment as a mitigation of the five great inflictions; with the whip to be employed in the magistrates' courts, the stick to be employed in the schools for officers, and fines to be paid for redeemable offenses. Inadvertent offenses and those which might be ascribed to misfortune were to be pardoned. Those who transgressed presumptuously and repeatedly were to be punished with death. "Let me be reverent! Let me be reverent!" he said to himself. "Let compassion rule in punishment!"

---

[6] **Six Honored Ones:** Unknown identity.

[7] **various princes:** When appointed the princes received tokens that fit a form in the imperial treasury. An impostor might thus be detected. Shun, in returning the five jade symbols of rank, was confirming the appointments of the princes. They were called pastors because, under the direction of the Chief of the Mountains, they were shepherds of men. (Translator's note.)

[8] **tubes . . . steelyards:** Standard tubes, made of bamboo, were twelve in number and approximated the chromatic scale. They were used not only in music but also to regulate measures of length. *Steelyard* refers to a weighing device of that generic name and does not imply that such a device was made of steel as we know that metal. (Translator's note.)

Shun banished the minister of Works to Yu island; confined Huan Tou on Mount Ch'ung; drove the chief of San Miao and his people into San-wei and kept them there; and held Kun a prisoner until death on Mount Yü. These four criminals being thus dealt with, all under heaven acknowledged the justice of his administration.

After twenty-eight years the sovereign Yao deceased. The people mourned for him as for a parent for three years. Within the four seas all the eight kinds of instruments of music were stopped and hushed.

On the first day of the first month of the next year, Shun went to the temple of the Accomplished Ancestor.

He deliberated with the Chief of the Four Mountains how to throw open the doors of communication between himself and the four quarters of the land, and how he could see with the eyes and hear with the ears of all.

He consulted with the twelve Pastors and said to them, "The food: it depends on observing the seasons. Be kind to the distant and cultivate the ability of the near. Give honor to the virtuous and your confidence to the good, while you discountenance the artful. So shall the barbarous tribes lead on one another to make their submission."

Shun said, "Oh! Chief of the Four Mountains, is there any one who can with vigorous service attend to all the affairs of the sovereign? Whom I may appoint General Regulator to assist me in all affairs and manage each department according to its nature?"

All in the court replied, "There is Yü, the minister of Works."

The sovereign said, "Yes. Oh! Yü, you have regulated the water and the land. In this new office exert yourself."

Yü did obeisance with his head to the ground, and wished to decline in favor of Ch'i, minister of Agriculture, or Hsieh, or Kao Yao.

The sovereign said, "Yes, but let you go and undertake the duties."

The sovereign said, "Ch'i, the black-haired people are still suffering from famine. Let you, O prince, as minister of Agriculture, continue to sow for them the various kinds of grain."

The sovereign said, "Hsieh, the people are still wanting in affection for one another and do not docilely observe the five orders of relationship. It is yours, as minister of Instruction, reverently to set forth the lessons of duty belonging to those five orders. Do so with gentleness."

The sovereign said, "Kao Yao, the barbarous tribes trouble our great land. There are also robbers, murderers, insurgents, and traitors. It is yours, as minister of Crime, to use the five punishments to deal with their offenses. For the infliction of these there are the three appointed places. There are the five cases in which banishment in the appropriate places is to be resorted to, to which three localities are assigned. Perform your duties with intelligence and you will secure a sincere submission."

The sovereign said, "Who can superintend my works as they require?"

All in the court replied, "Is there not Ch'uei?"

The sovereign said, "Yes. Oh! Ch'uei, you must be minister of Works."

Ch'uei did obeisance with his head to the ground, and wished to decline in favor of Shu, Ch'iang, or Po Yü. The sovereign said, "Yes, but let you go and undertake the duties. Effect a harmony in all the departments."

The sovereign said, "Who is equal to the duty of superintending the grass and the trees, with the birds and beasts, on my mountains and in my marshes?"

All in the court replied, "Is there not Yi?"

The sovereign said, "Yes. Oh! Yi, let you be my Forester."

Yi did obeisance with his head to the ground and wished to decline in favor of Chu, Hu, Hsiung, or P'i.

The sovereign said, "Yes, but let you go and undertake the duties. You must manage them harmoniously."

The sovereign said, "Oh! Chief of the Four Mountains, is there any one able to direct my three religious ceremonies?"[9]

All in the court answered, "Is there not Po-i?"

The sovereign said, "Yes. Oh! Po, you must be the Arranger in the Ancestral Temple. Morning and night be reverent. Be upright, be pure."

Po did obeisance with his head to the ground, and wished to decline in favor of K'uei or Lung. The sovereign said, "Yes, but let you go and undertake the duties. Be reverent!"

The sovereign said, "K'uei, I appoint you to be Director of Music and to teach our sons, so that the straightforward shall yet be mild; the gentle, dignified; the strong, not tyrannical; and the impetuous, not arrogant. Poetry is the expression of earnest thought; singing is the prolonged utterance of that expression; the notes accompany that utterance and are harmonized by the standard tubes. In this way the eight different kinds of musical instruments can be adjusted so that one shall not take from or interfere with another, and spirits and men are brought into harmony."

K'uei said, "I smite the musical stone, I gently strike it, and the various animals lead on one another to dance."[10]

The sovereign said, "Lung, I abominate slanderous speakers and destroyers of the right ways who agitate and alarm my people. I appoint you minister of Communication. Early and late give forth my orders and report to me, seeing that everything is true."

The sovereign said, "Oh! you twenty and two men, be reverent; so shall you be helpful to the business entrusted to me by Heaven."

Every three years there was an examination of merits, and after three examinations the undeserving were degraded and the deserving advanced. By this arrangement the duties of all the departments were fully discharged. The people of San Miao were discriminated and separated.

In the thirtieth year of his age, Shun was called to employment. Thirty years he was on the throne with Yao. Fifty years afterwards he went on high and died.

---

[9] **three religious ceremonies:** Rites for the spirits of heaven, earth, and humans.

[10] **"I smite . . . dance":** Musical stones were made of jade cut in an L shape and suspended from a hole at the apex of the right angle. When struck, they gave off a pleasing tone. (Translator's note.)

~ APOLLODORUS

FL. SECOND CENTURY B.C.E.

Very little is known about Apollodorus's life, which is usually dated the second century B.C.E., sometimes later. By reputation Apollodorus was an Athenian grammarian; he is known to have written a prose treatise on Greek deities called *On the Gods. Bibliotheca (The Library),* which is attributed to Apollodorus and which contains the story of Heracles' twelve labors, is a compendium of Greek mythology and history; in the words of translator Sir James G. Frazer, it is a "history of the world as it was conceived by the Greeks."

Heracles, whose name means the "glory of Hera," began his life under the shadow of the goddess Hera's wrath, since her husband, Zeus, had fathered Heracles with a mortal, Alcmene. Wearing a lion skin and swinging a club, Heracles was a hero of the people who battled with humans and monsters. Though with so much brute strength he did make mistakes and accidentally kill people, he was nevertheless the first mortal who achieved

Heracles and Greek Heroes, 475–450 B.C.E. *Detail from a red-figure vase showing clothed and semiclothed Greek heroes striking various heroic poses. (Heracles is in the middle of the top row.) (Musée du Louvre, Paris/Peter Willi, Bridgeman Art Library)*

divinity through suffering and hard work. He represented hope for the ordinary man, who placed the following charm over his threshold:

> The son of Zeus, the Conqueror dwells here,
> Heracles. Let no evil thing come near.

The following *Bibliotheca* excerpts detail four of the twelve (or ten) labors assigned to Heracles by the Delphic Oracle after Heracles, in a fit of madness, kills his own children. In the first, he is to conquer the Nemean lion with brute strength. In the second, he will need cleverness for besting the Lernaean hydra. In another of Heracles' labors he is to travel to the edge of the world and steal golden apples from the Hesperides, an ultimate prize akin to acquiring the knowledge held by immortals. The fourth labor described here, actually Heracles' last, involves fetching the hound Cerberus from the underworld; this story belongs to a general type known as the "harrowing of hell," in which a hero descends into the underworld in order to steal, plunder, learn something, or rescue someone, feats carried out by such ancient heroes as Theseus, Orpheus, and Aeneas. It is said that Jesus, too, harrowed hell when, according to the Gospel of Nicodemus, he rescues the souls of the righteous from the underworld. After Heracles returns Cerberus to Hades, he has completed his labors and earns immortality, as predicted by the Delphic Oracle. The translation is by Sir James G. Frazer; all of the footnotes are the editors'.

The Pythian priestess then first called him Heracles, for hitherto he was called Alcides. And she told him to dwell in Tiryns, serving Eurystheus for twelve years and to perform the ten labours imposed on him, and so, she said, when the tasks were accomplished, he would be immortal.

– Apollodorus, historian

FROM

Bibliotheca

Translated by Sir James G. Frazer

Now it came to pass that after the battle with the Minyans Heracles was driven mad through the jealousy of Hera and flung his own children, whom he had by Megara, and two children of Iphicles into the fire; wherefore he condemed himself to exile, and was purified by Thespius, and repairing to Delphi he inquired of the god where he should dwell. The Pythian priestess then first called him Heracles, for hitherto he was called Alcides.[1] And she told him to dwell in Tiryns, serving Eurystheus for twelve years and to perform the ten labours[2] imposed on him, and so, she said, when the tasks were accomplished, he would be immortal.

When Heracles heard that, he went to Tiryns and did as he was bid by Eurystheus. First, Eurystheus ordered him to bring the skin of the Nemean lion; now that was an invulnerable beast begotten by Typhon.[3] On his way to attack the lion he

[1] **he was called Alcides:** Heracles had been called Alcides, after his grandfather, Alcaeus. Delphi's former name was Pytho, probably named after the monster Python, which was killed by Apollo. Apollo's priestess at Delphi was called the Pythia.

[2] **the ten labours:** There is disagreement about whether there were ten or twelve labors assigned to Heracles, although in this version there are actually twelve.

[3] **Typhon:** An ancient monster with one hundred burning heads.

came to Cleonae and lodged at the house of a day-labourer, Molorchus; and when his host would have offered a victim in sacrifice, Heracles told him to wait for thirty days, and then, if he had returned safe from the hunt, to sacrifice to Saviour Zeus, but if he were dead, to sacrifice to him as to a hero. And having come to Nemea and tracked the lion, he first shot an arrow at him, but when he perceived that the beast was invulnerable, he heaved up his club and made after him. And when the lion took refuge in a cave with two mouths, Heracles built up the one entrance and came in upon the beast through the other, and putting his arm round its neck held it tight till he had choked it; so laying it on his shoulders he carried it to Cleonae. And finding Molorchus on the last of the thirty days about to sacrifice the victim to him as to a dead man, he sacrificed to Saviour Zeus and brought the lion to Mycenae. Amazed at his manhood, Eurystheus forbade him thenceforth to enter the city, but ordered him to exhibit the fruits of his labours before the gates. They say, too, that in his fear he had a bronze jar made for himself to hide in under the earth, and that he sent his commands for the labours through a herald, Copreus, son of Pelops the Elean. This Copreus had killed Iphitus and fled to Mycenae, where he was purified by Eurystheus and took up his abode.

As a second labour he ordered him to kill the Lernaean hydra. That creature, bred in the swamp of Lerna, used to go forth into the plain and ravage both the cattle and the country. Now the hydra had a huge body, with nine heads, eight mortal, but the middle one immortal. So mounting a chariot driven by Iolaus, he came to Lerna, and having halted his horses, he discovered the hydra on a hill beside the springs of the Amymone, where was its den. By pelting it with fiery shafts he forced it to come out, and in the act of doing so he seized and held it fast. But the hydra wound itself about one of his feet and clung to him. Nor could he effect anything by smashing its heads with his club, for as fast as one head was smashed there grew up two. A huge crab also came to the help of the hydra by biting his foot. So he killed it, and in his turn called for help on Iolaus who, by setting fire to a piece of the neighbouring wood and burning the roots of the heads with the brands, prevented them from sprouting. Having thus got the better of the sprouting heads, he chopped off the immortal head, and buried it, and put a heavy rock on it, beside the road that leads through Lerna to Elaeus. But the body of the hydra he slit up and dipped his arrows in the gall. However, Eurystheus said that this labour should not be reckoned among the ten because he had not got the better of the hydra by himself, but with the help of Iolaus. [. . .]

When the labours had been performed in eight years and a month, Eurystheus ordered Heracles, as an eleventh labour, to fetch golden apples from the Hesperides, for he did not acknowledge the labour of the cattle of Augeas[4] nor that of the hydra. These apples were not, as some have said, in Libya, but on Atlas among the Hyperboreans.[5] They were presented by Earth to Zeus after his marriage with Hera, and

[4] **the labour . . . Augeas:** Heracles cleaned Augeas's stables, which had never been cleaned, by diverting two rivers through them, thus washing out the manure.

[5] **Hyperboreans:** Here Apollodorus departs from the usual version, which placed the gardens of the Hesperides in the far west, not the far north. (Translator's note.) The Hesperides, the garden of the gods situated beside Mt. Atlas, was guarded by a huge serpent.

guarded by an immortal dragon with a hundred heads, offspring of Typhon and Echidna, which spoke with many and divers sorts of voices. . . .

. . . And going on foot through Illyria and hastening to the river Eridanus he came to the nymphs, the daughters of Zeus and Themis. They revealed Nereus to him, and Heracles seized him while he slept, and though the god turned himself into all kinds of shapes, the hero bound him and did not release him till he had learned from him where were the apples and the Hesperides. Being informed, he traversed Libya. That country was then ruled by Antaeus, son of Poseidon, who used to kill strangers by forcing them to wrestle. Being forced to wrestle with him, Heracles hugged him, lifted him aloft, broke and killed him; for when he touched earth so it was that he waxed stronger, wherefore some said that he was a son of Earth. . . .

And passing by Arabia he slew Emathion, son of Tithonus, and journeying through Libya to the outer sea he received the goblet from the Sun. And having crossed to the opposite mainland he shot on the Caucasus the eagle, offspring of Echidna and Typhon, that was devouring the liver of Prometheus, and he released Prometheus,[6] after choosing for himself the bond of olive,[7] and to Zeus he presented Chiron,[8] who, though immortal, consented to die in his stead.

Now Prometheus had told Heracles not to go himself after the apples but to send Atlas, first relieving him of the burden of the sphere; so when he was come to Atlas in the land of the Hyperboreans, he took the advice and relieved Atlas. But when Atlas had received three apples from the Hesperides, he came to Heracles, and not wishing to support the sphere <he said that he would himself carry the apples to Eurystheus, and bade Heracles hold up the sky in his stead. Heracles promised to do so, but succeeded by craft in putting it on Atlas instead. For at the advice of Prometheus he begged Atlas to hold up the sky till he should>[9] put a pad on his head. When Atlas heard that, he laid the apples down on the ground and took the sphere from Heracles. And so Heracles picked up the apples and departed. But some say that he did not get them from Atlas, but that he plucked the apples himself after killing the guardian snake. And having brought the apples he gave them to Eurystheus. But he, on receiving them, bestowed them on Heracles, from whom Athena got them and conveyed them back again; for it was not lawful that they should be laid down anywhere.

A twelfth labour imposed on Heracles was to bring Cerberus from Hades. Now this Cerberus had three heads of dogs, the tail of a dragon, and on his back the heads

[6] **Prometheus:** Imprisoned by Zeus for stealing the gift of fire and giving it to humanity.

[7] **bond of olive:** The ancients had a curious notion that the custom of wearing crowns or garlands on the head and rings on the fingers was a memorial of the shackles once worn for their sake by their great benefactor Prometheus among the rocks and snows of the Caucasus. (Translator's note.)

[8] **Chiron:** Or Cheiron, an extremely wise and learned man; unfortunately, he was accidentally wounded by one of Heracles's poisoned arrows. The pain was so great he wished to die, even though he was an immortal. Prometheus agreed to take on Chiron's immortality so that Chiron could happily die.

[9] **<he . . . should>:** The passage in angular brackets is missing from Apollodorus's manuscript but is reconstructed from an earlier version of the story in Apollonius Rhodius's *Argonautica* (third century B.C.E.) that quotes as its authority Pherecydes, the writer here seemingly followed by Apollodorus. (Translator's note.)

of all sorts of snakes. When Heracles was about to depart to fetch him, he went to Eumolpus at Eleusis,[10] wishing to be initiated. However it was not then lawful for foreigners to be initiated: since he proposed to be initiated as the adoptive son of Pylius. But not being able to see the mysteries because he had not been cleansed of the slaughter of the centaurs, he was cleansed by Eumolpus and then initiated. And having come to Taenarum in Laconia, where is the mouth of the descent to Hades, he descended through it. But when the souls saw him, they fled, save Meleager and the Gorgon Medusa.[11] And Heracles drew his sword against the Gorgon, as if she were alive, but he learned from Hermes that she was an empty phantom. And being come near to the gates of Hades he found Theseus and Pirithous,[12] him who wooed Persephone in wedlock and was therefore bound fast. And when they beheld Heracles, they stretched out their hands as if they should be raised from the dead by his might. And Theseus, indeed, he took by the hand and raised up, but when he would have brought up Pirithous, the earth quaked and he let go. And he rolled away also the stone of Ascalaphus.[13] And wishing to provide the souls with blood, he slaughtered one of the kine of Hades. But Menoetes, son of Ceuthonymus, who tended the kine, challenged Heracles to wrestle, and, being seized round the middle, had his ribs broken; howbeit, he was let off at the request of Persephone. When Heracles asked Hades for Cerberus, Hades ordered him to take the animal provided he mastered him without the use of the weapons which he carried. Heracles found him at the gates of Acheron,[14] and, cased in his cuirass and covered by the lion's skin, he flung his arms round the head of the brute, and though the dragon in its tail bit him, he never relaxed his grip and pressure till it yielded. So he carried it off and ascended through Troezen.[15] But Demeter turned Ascalaphus into a short-eared owl, and Heracles, after showing Cerberus to Eurystheus, carried him back to Hades.

[10] **Eleusis:** For some 2,000 years Eleusis was the site of a mystery religion centering on the worship of Demeter and Persephone. Eumolpus was one of the founders of the Eleusinian Mysteries and possibly a priest.

[11] **the Gorgon Medusa:** The Gorgons were three frightful sisters with snakes for hair; their glance turned men to stone.

[12] **Theseus and Pirithous:** The two friends Theseus and Pirithous journeyed to the underworld so that Pirithous could ask Persephone, queen of Hades, to be his bride. Hades, Persephone's husband, then seated Theseus and Pirithous on stone chairs, to which they were stuck.

[13] **the stone of Ascalaphus:** Ascalaphus, a resident of the underworld, told Hades when Persephone ate pomegranate seeds, which symbolized the consummation of the marriage, Hades could then claim Persephone's presence part of the year in the underworld. Demeter, Persephone's mother, punished Ascalaphus by placing a heavy stone on him. When Heracles frees Ascalaphus, Demeter changes him into an owl.

[14] **Acheron:** One of the five rivers of the underworld.

[15] **Troezen:** An ancient city in the Peloponnesus where Theseus had been born.

Aeschylus
c. 525–456 B.C.E.

The second play in Aeschylus's classic trilogy, *The Oresteia,* explores the role of the spirit world in human affairs. After a long absence fighting in the Trojan War, Agamemnon, the king, returns to Argos and is killed by his wife, Clytemnestra, in collusion with her lover, Aegisthus. According to popular tradition, the dead Agamemnon then resided in his tomb. In the prayer excerpted here, Electra, Agamemnon's daughter, invokes the power of Agamemnon to curse her mother and Aegisthus and to bring blessings on her and her brother, Orestes. Electra believes that her mother has gotten away with murder and is clinging to a throne that is rightfully hers or her brother's. This passage is a fine illustration of the Greek belief that heroes could influence affairs from the other side of mortality. For more on Aeschylus, please see page 798.

I myself pour these lustral waters to the dead, / and speak, and call upon my father.

– Electra, in *The Libation Bearers*

Electra and Orestes, 133–131 B.C.E.
Electra drapes herself over her brother, Orestes, in a Roman statue copied from the Greek original. (The Art Archive / Archaeological Museum, Naples / Dagli Orti)

FROM

The Libation Bearers

Translated by Richmond Lattimore

[Prayer to the Dead]

ELECTRA:

Almighty herald of the world above, the world
below: Hermes, lord of the dead, help me; announce
my prayers to the charmed spirits underground, who watch
over my father's house, that they may hear. Tell Earth
herself, who brings all things to birth, who gives them strength,
then gathers their big yield into herself at last.
I myself pour these lustral waters to the dead,
and speak, and call upon my father: Pity me;
pity your own Orestes. How shall we be lords
in our house? We have been sold, and go as wanderers
because our mother bought herself, for us, a man,
Aegisthus, he who helped her hand to cut you down.
Now I am what a slave is, and Orestes lives
outcast from his great properties, while they go proud
in the high style and luxury of what you worked
to win. By some good fortune let Orestes come
back home. Such is my prayer, my father. Hear me; hear.
And for myself, grant that I be more temperate
of heart than my mother; that I act with purer hand.

Such are my prayers for us; but for our enemies,
father, I pray that your avenger come, and they
who killed you shall be killed in turn, as they deserve.
Between my prayer for good and prayer for good I set
this prayer for evil; and I speak it against Them.
For us, bring blessings up into the world. Let Earth
and conquering Justice,[1] and all gods beside, give aid.

Such are my prayers; and over them I pour these drink
offerings. Yours the strain now, yours to make them flower
with mourning song, and incantation for the dead.

---

[1] **Justice:** Dice or Dike, goddess of justice.

THUCYDIDES

c. 460–c. 399 B.C.E.

Along with Herodotus (c. 480–c. 424 B.C.E.), Thucydides is the great historian of classical Greece, one of the two "Fathers of History." His *History of the Peloponnesian War* describes Athens at the high point of its democratic golden age and traces its decline as the sustained conflict with Sparta and its allies weakened Athenian alliances and undermined its democratic ideals.

Herodotus had written in *Histories* a sweeping account of the emergence of Greece as a nation and of its struggle to separate itself from Asia, from the time of the Trojan War (c. 1200 B.C.E.) to the Persian Wars in the fifth century. Thucydides took a different approach. Rather than creating a panorama of the past, he wrote a detailed record of his own time. His *History of the Peloponnesian War* is a strictly chronological account of the wars between the Athenian empire and Sparta and its allies between 431 and 404 B.C.E. Thucydides did not finish his history, however, for it breaks off abruptly in 411, more than six years before the end of the war.

Legend has it that this sudden conclusion resulted from Thucydides' death by assassination, but in truth little is known of Thucydides' life beyond what he alludes to in his history. He did command the Athenian naval forces at the Battle of Amphipolis in 424, and as a result of

Bust of Pericles, 495–429 B.C.E.
The citizen-hero of Athenian democracy. (The Art Archive, JFB)

the defeat he suffered there was banished from Athens for twenty years. During this period in exile, presumably, he had time to write his history of the war.

Thucydides was a more documentary historian than Herodotus. Writing about the events of his own time, he seems to have kept careful notes of things as they happened, and, even though he lacked the news accounts and tape recorders of the contemporary historian, he re-created speeches and debates from memory and from oral sources, which he included verbatim in his record. As an exile, he was also in the unusual position of having access to sources from both sides of the conflict, so he was able to achieve an extraordinary degree of objectivity. Because he was writing before the end of the war, without the prejudice of hindsight, Thucydides produced a dramatic and objective narrative of the events and controversies of the period, with insightful portraits of the statesmen and generals as well as analyses of the psychological, economic, and moral forces at work.

The passage that follows, Pericles's famous Funeral Oration commemorating the Athenian dead after the first year of the war (430 B.C.E.), illustrates Thucydides's dramatic method. Even though he had to reconstruct it, he presents the speech in Pericles's own words. The speech itself is much more than a funeral oration. Pericles uses the occasion to celebrate Athens and its democratic ideals, for which he is remembered as the great champion during the Age of Pericles (461–429 B.C.E.). His defense of majority rule, political equality, the recognition of merit, tolerance, and individualism have made this speech a classic statement of democratic values.

FROM

The Peloponnesian War

Translated by Benjamin Jowett

[Pericles' Funeral Oration]

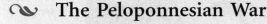

In the same winter the Athenians gave a funeral at the public cost to those who had first fallen in this war. It was a custom of their ancestors, and the manner of it is as follows. Three days before the ceremony, the bones of the dead are laid out in a tent which has been erected; and their friends bring to their relatives such offerings as they please. In the funeral procession cypress coffins are borne on wagons, one for each tribe, the bones of the deceased being placed in the coffin of their tribe. Among these is carried one empty bier decked for the missing, that is, for those whose bodies could not be recovered. Any citizen or stranger who pleases joins in the procession: and the female relatives are there to wail at the burial. The dead are laid in the public sepulchre in the most beautiful suburb of the city, in which those who fall in war are always buried—with the exception of those slain at Marathon, who for their singular and extraordinary valour were interred on the spot where they fell. After the bodies have been laid in the earth, a man chosen by the state, of approved wisdom and eminent reputation, pronounces over them an appropriate panegyric, after which all retire. Such is the manner of the burying; and throughout the whole of the war, whenever the occasion arose, the established custom was observed. Meanwhile these were the first that had fallen, and Pericles, son of Xanthippus, was chosen to pronounce their eulogium. When the proper time arrived, he advanced from the sepulchre to an elevated platform in order to be heard by as many of the crowd as possible, and spoke as follows:

"Most of my predecessors in this place have commended him who made this speech part of the law, telling us that it is well that it should be delivered at the burial of those who fall in battle. For myself, I should have thought that the worth which had displayed itself in deeds would be sufficiently rewarded by honours also shown by deeds, such as you now see in this funeral prepared at the people's cost. And I could have wished that the reputations of many brave men were not to be imperilled in the mouth of a single individual, to stand or fall according as he spoke well or ill. For it is hard to speak properly upon a subject where it is even difficult to convince your hearers that you are speaking the truth. On the one hand, the friend who is familiar with every fact of the story may think that some point has not been set forth with that fullness which he wishes and knows it to deserve; on the other, he who is a stranger to the matter may be led by envy to suspect exaggeration if he hears anything above his own nature. For men can endure to hear others praised only so long as they can severally persuade themselves of their own ability to equal the actions recounted: when this point is passed, envy comes in and with it incredulity. However, since our ancestors have stamped this custom with their approval, it becomes my duty to obey the law and to try to satisfy your several wishes and opinions as best I may.

"I shall begin with our ancestors: it is both just and proper that they should have the honour of the first mention on an occasion like the present. They dwelt in the country without break in the succession from generation to generation, and handed it down free to the present time by their valour. And if our more remote ancestors deserve praise, much more do our own fathers, who added to their inheritance the empire which we now possess, and spared no pains to be able to leave their acquisitions to us of the present generation. Lastly, there are few parts of our dominions that have not been augmented by those of us here, who are still more or less in the vigour of life; and the mother country has been furnished by us with everything that can enable her to depend on her own resources whether for war or for peace. That part of our history which tells of the military achievements which gave us our several possessions, or of the ready valour with which either we or our fathers stemmed the tide of Hellenic or foreign aggression, is a theme too familiar to my hearers for me to dilate on, and I shall therefore pass it by. But by what road we reached our position, under what form of government our greatness grew, out of what national habits it sprang—these are subjects which I may pursue before I proceed to my panegyric upon these men; for I think them to be themes upon which on the present occasion a speaker may properly dwell, and to which the whole assemblage, whether citizens or foreigners, may listen with advantage.

"Our constitution does not copy the laws of neighbouring states; we are rather a pattern to others than imitators ourselves. Its administration favours the many instead of the few; this is why it is called a democracy. If we look to the laws, they afford equal justice to all in their private differences; if to social standing, advancement in public life falls to reputation for capacity, class considerations not being allowed to interfere with merit; nor again does poverty bar the way: if a man is able to serve the state, he is not hindered by the obscurity of his condition. The freedom which we enjoy in our government extends also to our ordinary life. There, far from exercising a jealous surveillance over each other, we do not feel called upon to be angry with our neighbour for doing what he likes, or even to indulge in those injurious looks which cannot fail to be offensive, although they inflict no positive penalty. But all this ease in our private relations does not make us lawless as citizens. Against this fear is our chief safeguard, teaching us to obey the magistrates and the laws, particularly such as regard the protection of the injured, whether they are actually on the statute book, or belong to that code which, although unwritten, yet cannot be broken without acknowledged disgrace.

"Further, we provide plenty of means for the mind to refresh itself from business. We celebrate games and sacrifices all the year round, and the elegance of our private establishments forms a daily source of pleasure and helps to banish our cares; and the magnitude of our city draws the produce of the world into our harbour, so that to the Athenian the fruits of other countries are as familiar a luxury as those of his own.

"If we turn to our military policy, there also we differ from our antagonists. We throw open our city to the world, and never by alien acts exclude foreigners from any opportunity of learning or observing, although the eyes of an enemy may occasionally profit by our liberality; we trust less in system and policy than in the native spirit of our citizens; and in education, where our rivals from their very cradles by a painful discipline seek after manliness, at Athens we live exactly as we please, and yet are just as ready to encounter every legitimate danger. In proof of this it may be noticed that the Lacedæmonians[1] do not invade our country alone, but bring with them all their confederates, while we Athenians advance unsupported into the territory of a neighbour, and fighting upon a foreign soil usually vanquish with ease men who are defending their homes. Our united force was never yet encountered by any enemy, because we have at once to attend to our marine and to despatch our citizens by land upon a hundred different services; thus wherever they engage with some such fraction of our strength, a success against a detachment is magnified into a victory over the nation, and a defeat into a reverse suffered at the hands of our entire people. And yet if with habits not of labour but of ease, and courage not of art but of nature, we are still willing to encounter danger, we have the double advantage of escaping the experience of hardships in anticipation and of facing them in the hour of need as fearlessly as those who are never free from them.

---

[1] **Lacedæmonians:** The Spartans.

"Nor are these the only points in which our city is worthy of admiration. We cultivate refinement without extravagance and knowledge without effeminacy; wealth we employ more for use than for show, and place the real disgrace of poverty not in owning to the fact but in declining the struggle against it. Our public men have, besides politics, their private affairs to attend to, and our ordinary citizens, though occupied with the pursuits of industry, are still fair judges of public matters; for, unlike any other nation, regarding him who takes no part in these duties not as unambitious but as useless, we Athenians are able to judge at all events if we cannot originate, and instead of looking on discussion as a stumbling-block in the way of action, we think it an indispensable preliminary to any wise action at all. Again, in our enterprises we present the singular spectacle of daring and deliberation, each carried to its highest point, and both united in the same persons, although usually decision is the fruit of ignorance, hesitation of reflection. But the palm of courage will surely be adjudged most justly to those who best know the difference between hardship and pleasure and yet are never tempted to shrink from danger. In generosity we are equally singular, acquiring our friends by conferring, not by receiving, favours. Yet, of course, the doer of the favour is the firmer friend of the two, in order by continued kindness to keep the recipient in his debt, while the debtor feels less keenly from the very consciousness that the return he makes will be a payment, not a free gift. And it is only the Athenians who, fearless of consequences, confer their benefits not from calculations of expediency, but in the confidence of liberality.

"In short, I say that as a city we are the school of Hellas;[2] and I doubt if the world can produce a man, who where he has only himself to depend upon, is equal to so many emergencies, and graced by so happy a versatility as the Athenian. And that this is no mere boast thrown out for the occasion, but plain matter of fact, the power of the state acquired by these habits proves. For Athens alone of her contemporaries is found when tested to be greater than her reputation, and alone gives no occasion to her assailants to blush at the antagonist by whom they have been worsted, or to her subjects to question her title by merit to rule. Rather, the admiration of the present and succeeding ages will be ours, since we have not left our power without witness, but have shown it by mighty proofs; and far from needing a Homer for our panegyrist, or other of his craft whose verses might charm for the moment only for the impression which they gave to melt at the touch of fact, we have forced every sea and land to be the highway of our daring, and everywhere, whether for evil or for good, have left imperishable monuments behind us. Such is the Athens for which these men, in the assertion of their resolve not to lose her, nobly fought and died; and well may every one of their survivors be ready to suffer in her cause.

"Indeed if I have dwelt at some length upon the character of our country, it has been to show that our stake in the struggle is not the same as theirs who have no such blessings to lose, and also that the panegyric of the men over whom I am now

---

[2] **as a city . . . school of Hellas:** A much-quoted phrase indicating that Athens is the model for the rest of Greece and the world.

speaking might be by definite proofs established. That panegyric is now in a great measure complete; for the Athens that I have celebrated is only what the heroism of these and their like have made her, men whose fame, unlike that of most Hellenes, will be found to be only commensurate with their deserts. And if a test of worth be wanted, it is to be found in their closing scene, and this not only in the cases in which it set the final seal upon their merit, but also in those in which it gave the first intimation of their having any. For there is justice in the claim that steadfastness in his country's battles should be as a cloak to cover a man's other imperfections; for the good action has blotted out the bad, and his merit as a citizen more than outweighed his demerits as an individual. But none of these allowed either wealth with its prospect of future enjoyment to unnerve his spirit, or poverty with its hope of a day of freedom and riches to tempt him to shrink from danger. No, holding that vengeance upon their enemies was more to be desired than any personal blessings, and reckoning this to be the most glorious of hazards, they joyfully determined to accept the risk, to make sure of their vengeance and to let their wishes wait; and while committing to hope the uncertainty of final success, in the business before them they thought fit to act boldly and trust in themselves. Thus choosing to die resisting, rather than to live submitting, they fled only from dishonour, but met danger face to face, and after one brief moment, while at the summit of their fortune, escaped, not from their fear, but from their glory.

"So died these men as became Athenians. You, their survivors, must determine to have as unaltering a resolution in the field, though you may pray that it may have a happier issue. And not contented with ideas derived only from words of the advantages which are bound up with the defence of your country, though these would furnish a valuable text to a speaker even before an audience so alive to them as the present, you must yourselves realize the power of Athens, and feed your eyes upon her from day to day, till love of her fills your hearts; and then when all her greatness shall break upon you, you must reflect that it was by courage, sense of duty, and a keen feeling of honour in action that men were enabled to win all this, and that no personal failure in an enterprise could make them consent to deprive their country of their valour, but they laid it at her feet as the most glorious contribution that they could offer. For this offering of their lives made in common by them all they each of them individually received that renown which never grows old, and for a sepulchre, not so much that in which their bones have been deposited, but that noblest of shrines wherein their glory is laid up to be eternally remembered upon every occasion on which deed or story shall call for its commemoration. For heroes have the whole earth for their tomb; and in lands far from their own, where the column with its epitaph declares it, there is enshrined in every breast a record unwritten with no tablet to preserve it, except that of the heart. These take as your model, and judging happiness to be the fruit of freedom and freedom of valour, never decline the dangers of war. For it is not the miserable that would most justly be unsparing of their lives; these have nothing to hope for: it is rather they to whom continued life may bring reverses as yet unknown, and to whom a fall, if it came, would be most tremendous in its consequences. And surely, to a man of spirit, the degradation of cowardice must be immeasurably more grievous than the unfelt death which strikes him in the midst of his strength and patriotism!

"Comfort, therefore, not condolence, is what I have to offer to the parents of the dead who may be here. Numberless are the chances to which, as they know, the life of man is subject; but fortunate indeed are they who draw for their lot a death so glorious as that which has caused your mourning, and to whom life has been so exactly measured as to terminate in the happiness in which it has been passed. Still I know that this is a hard saying, especially when those are in question of whom you will constantly be reminded by seeing in the homes of others blessings of which once you also boasted: for grief is felt not so much for the want of what we have never known, as for the loss of that to which we have been long accustomed. Yet you who are still of an age to beget children must bear up in the hope of having others in their stead; not only will they help you to forget those whom you have lost, but will be to the state at once a reinforcement and a security; for never can a fair or just policy be expected of the citizen who does not, like his fellows, bring to the decision the interests and apprehensions of a father. And those of you who have passed your prime must congratulate yourselves with the thought that the best part of your life was fortunate, and that the brief span that remains will be cheered by the fame of the departed. For it is only the love of honour that never grows old; and honour it is, not gain, as some would have it, that rejoices the heart of age and helplessness.

"Turning to the sons or brothers of the dead, I see an arduous struggle before you. When a man is gone, all are wont to praise him, and should your merit be ever so transcendent, you will still find it difficult not merely to overtake, but even to approach their renown. The living have envy to contend with, while those who are no longer in our path are honoured with a goodwill into which rivalry does not enter. On the other hand, if I must say anything on the subject of female excellence to those of you who will now be in widowhood, it will be all comprised in this brief exhortation. Great will be your glory in not falling short of your natural character; and greatest will be hers who is least talked of among the men whether for good or for bad.

"My task is now finished. I have performed it to the best of my ability, and in words, at least, the requirements of the law are now satisfied. If deeds be in question, those who are here interred have received part of their honours already, and for the rest, their children will be brought up till manhood at the public expense: the state thus offers a valuable prize as the garland of victory in this race of valour, for the reward both of those who have fallen and their survivors. And where the rewards for merit are greatest, there are found the best citizens.

"And now that you have brought to a close your lamentations for your relatives, you may depart."

DIOGENES LAERTIUS

FL. EARLY THIRD CENTURY C.E.

Diogenes Laertius was a Greek biographer and historian whose *Lives of Eminent Philosophers* is a work in ten volumes that discusses the lives and teachings of Greek philosophers, from Thales in the seventh century B.C.E. to Epicurus in the third century B.C.E. In the case of Socrates, Diogenes Laertius, in a series of anecdotes, bits of narrative, and random teachings, provides the kind of information that later generations would find relevant and interesting about the great philosopher. Plato and Xenophon (c. 431–c. 354 B.C.E.), both disciples of Socrates, also wrote about Socrates, but as a philosopher, describing and defending his ideas about morality and politics (see pages 1083–1116). Diogenes Laertius captures Socrates in informal moments of ordinary conversation, and supplies homey details about Socrates' regard for his body and his need for exercise. He also includes Socrates' dealings with his first wife, Xanthippe, which are especially interesting.

FROM

Lives of Eminent Philosophers

Translated by R. D. Hicks

[SOCRATES]

Demetrius of Byzantium relates that Crito removed [Socrates] from his workshop and educated him, being struck by his beauty of soul; that he discussed moral questions in the workshops and the market-place, being convinced that the study of nature is no concern of ours; and that he claimed that his inquiries embraced

Whatso'er is good or evil in an house[1];

that frequently, owing to his vehemence in argument, men set upon him with their fists or tore his hair out; and that for the most part he was despised and laughed at, yet bore all his ill-usage patiently. [. . .] when [. . .] some one expressed surprise at his taking it so quietly, Socrates rejoined, "Should I have taken the law of a donkey, supposing that he had kicked me?" Thus far Demetrius.

Unlike most philosophers, he had no need to travel, except when required to go on an expedition. The rest of his life he stayed at home and engaged all the more keenly in argument with anyone who would converse with him, his aim being not to alter his opinion but to get at the truth. They relate that Euripides gave him the treatise of Heraclitus and asked his opinion upon it, and that his reply was, "The part I

[1] **Whatso'er is . . . house:** See *The Odyssey*, Book 4.

understand is excellent, and so too is, I dare say, the part I do not understand; but it needs a Delian[2] diver to get to the bottom of it."

He took care to exercise his body and kept in good condition. At all events he served on the expedition to Amphipolis; and when in the battle of Delium Xenophon had fallen from his horse, he stepped in and saved his life. For in the general flight of the Athenians he personally retired at his ease, quietly turning round from time to time and ready to defend himself in case he were attacked. Again, he served at Potidaea, whither he had gone by sea, as land communications were interrupted by the war; and while there he is said to have remained a whole night without changing his position, and to have won the prize of valour. [. . .]

His strength of will and attachment to the democracy are evident from his refusal to yield to Critias and his colleagues when they ordered him to bring the wealthy Leon of Salamis[3] before them for execution, and further from the fact that he alone voted for the acquittal of the ten generals;[4] and again from the facts that when he had the opportunity to escape from the prison he declined to do so, and that he rebuked his friends for weeping over his fate, and addressed to them his most memorable discourses in the prison.

He was a man of great independence and dignity of character. Pamphila in the seventh book of her *Commentaries* tells how Alcibiades once offered him a large site on which to build a house; but he replied, "Suppose, then, I wanted shoes and you offered me a whole hide to make a pair with, would it not be ridiculous in me to take it?" Often when he looked at the multitude of wares exposed for sale, he would say to himself, "How many things I can do without!" And he would continually recite the lines:

> The purple robe and silver's shine
> More fits an actor's need than mine.[5]

. . .

Aristotle says that he married two wives: his first wife was Xanthippe, by whom he had a son, Lamprocles; his second wife was Myrto, the daughter of Aristides the Just, whom he took without a dowry. By her he had Sophroniscus and Menexenus. [. . .]

He could afford to despise those who scoffed at him. He prided himself on his plain living, and never asked a fee from anyone. He used to say that he most enjoyed the food which was least in need of condiment, and the drink which made him feel the least hankering for some other drink; and that he was nearest to the gods in that he had the fewest wants. [. . .]

---

[2] **Delian:** From the island of Delos.

[3] **Leon of Salamis:** In 404 B.C.E., Athens was led by a group called the Thirty, led by Critias and Charmides, who began to terrorize citizens. Socrates was one of five citizens ordered to produce Leon of Salamis, a resident alien who was executed.

[4] **the acquittal . . . generals:** In a battle against the Peloponnesians in 406 B.C.E., a number of generals were accused of criminal negligence. Socrates voted against their conviction.

[5] **The purple . . . mine:** Probably these lines are falsely quoted, since they appear to be by the dramatist Philemon, who wrote them after Socrates' death.

Moreover, in his old age he learnt to play the lyre, declaring that he saw no absurdity in learning a new accomplishment. As Xenophon relates in the *Symposium,* it was his regular habit to dance, thinking that such exercise helped to keep the body in good condition. He used to say that his supernatural sign warned him beforehand of the future; that to make a good start was no trifling advantage, but a trifle turned the scale; and that he knew nothing except just the fact of his ignorance. He said that, when people paid a high price for fruit which had ripened early, they must despair of seeing the fruit ripen at the proper season. And, being once asked in what consisted the virtue of a young man, he said, "In doing nothing to excess." He held that geometry should be studied to the point at which a man is able to measure the land which he acquires or parts with. [. . .]

He had invited some rich men and, when Xanthippe said she felt ashamed of the dinner, "Never mind," said he, "for if they are reasonable they will put up with it, and if they are good for nothing, we shall not trouble ourselves about them." He would say that the rest of the world lived to eat, while he himself ate to live. [. . .]

When Xanthippe first scolded him and then drenched him with water, his rejoinder was, "Did I not say that Xanthippe's thunder would end in rain?" When Alcibiades declared that the scolding of Xanthippe was intolerable, "Nay, I have got used to it," said he, "as to the continued rattle of a windlass. And you do not mind the cackle of geese." "No," replied Alcibiades, "but they furnish me with eggs and goslings." "And Xanthippe," said Socrates, "is the mother of my children." When she tore his coat off his back in the market-place and his acquaintances advised him to hit back, "Yes, by Zeus," said he, "in order that while we are sparring each of you may join in with 'Go it, Socrates!' 'Well done, Xanthippe!' " He said he lived with a shrew, as horsemen are fond of spirited horses, "but just as, when they have mastered these, they can easily cope with the rest, so I in the society of Xanthippe shall learn to adapt myself to the rest of the world."

These and the like were his words and deeds, to which the Pythian priestess bore testimony when she gave Chaerephon the famous response:

> Of all men living Socrates most wise.

. . .

The affidavit in the case,[6] which is still preserved, says Favorinus, in the *Metroön,* ran as follows: "This indictment and affidavit is sworn by Meletus, the son of Meletus of Pitthos, against Socrates, the son of Sophroniscus of Alopece: Socrates is guilty of refusing to recognize the gods recognized by the state, and of introducing other new divinities. He is also guilty of corrupting the youth. The penalty demanded is death." The philosopher then, after Lysias had written a defence for him, read it through and said: "A fine speech, Lysias; it is not, however, suitable to me." For it was plainly more forensic than philosophical. Lysias said, "If it is a fine speech, how can it fail to suit you?" "Well," he replied, "would not fine raiment and fine shoes be just as unsuitable to me?"

Justus of Tiberias in his book entitled *The Wreath* says that in the course of the trial Plato mounted the platform and began: "Though I am the youngest, men of

---

[6] **the case:** The trial of Socrates.

Athens, of all who ever rose to address you"—whereupon the judges shouted out, "Get down! Get down!" When therefore he was condemned by 281 votes more than those given for acquittal, and when the judges were assessing what he should suffer or what fine he should pay, he proposed to pay 25 drachmae. Eubulides indeed says he offered 100. When this caused an uproar among the judges, he said, "Considering my services, I assess the penalty at maintenance in the Prytaneum at the public expense."

Sentence of death was passed, with an accession of eighty fresh votes. He was put in prison, and a few days afterwards drank the hemlock, after much noble discourse which Plato records in the *Phaedo.* [. . .]

So he was taken from among men; and not long afterwards the Athenians felt such remorse that they shut up the training grounds and gymnasia. They banished the other accusers but put Meletus to death; they honoured Socrates with a bronze statue, the work of Lysippus, which they placed in the hall of processions. [. . .]

Kautilya

fl. third century b.c.e.

Because Kautilya's name is used in the text *The Treatise on Material Gain,* scholars assume that he was associated with its authorship and assign c. 300 B.C.E. to an early version of the work. It is possible that it then was revised over a period of several hundred years. As a manual on how to control people, it presents the ultimate picture of a police state or dictatorship and as such bears directly on authoritarian measures used from Kautilya's day to the present time.

The present edition is divided into fifteen books; the following excerpts are taken from Book 1, chapters 10 and 12. The translator encloses words or phrases in brackets that provide better understanding of the translation. The footnotes are the editors'.

from

The Treatise on Material Gain (Arthashastra)

Translated by R. P. Kangle

[Loyalty Tests]

1 After appointing ministers to ordinary offices in consultation with the councillors and the chaplain, he should test their integrity by means of secret tests.

2 The king should (seemingly) discard the chaplain on the ground that he showed resentment when appointed to officiate at the sacrifice of a person not entitled to the privilege of a sacrifice or to teach (such a person). 3 He should (then)

get each minister individually instigated, through secret agents, under oath, (in this manner): 'This king is impious; well, let us set up another pious (king), either a claimant from his own family or a prince in disfavour or a member of the (royal) family or a person who is the one support of the kingdom or a neighbouring prince or a forest chieftain or a person suddenly risen to power; this is approved by all; what about you?' 4 If he repulses (the suggestion), he is loyal.

This is the test of piety.

5 The commander of the army, (seemingly) dismissed by reason of support given to evil men, should get each minister individually instigated, through secret agents, to (bring about) the king's destruction, with (the offer of) a tempting material gain, (saying): 'This is approved by all; what about you?' 6 If he repulses (the suggestion), he is upright.

This is the test of material gain.

7 A wandering nun, who has won the confidence (of the different ministers) and is treated with honour in the palace, should secretly suggest to each minister individually: 'The chief queen is in love with you and has made arrangements for a meeting (with you); besides, you will obtain much wealth.' 8 If he repulses (the proposal), he is pure.

This is the test of lust.

9 On the occasion of a festive party, one minister should invite all the (other) ministers. 10 Through (seeming) fright at this (conspiracy), the king should put them in prison. 11 A sharp pupil, imprisoned there earlier, should secretly suggest to each of those ministers individually, when they are deprived of property and honour, (in this manner): 'This king is behaving wickedly; well, let us kill him and install another; this is approved by all; what about you?' 12 If he repulses (the suggestion), he is loyal.

This is the test of fear.

13 From among them, he should appoint those proved loyal by the test of piety to posts in the judiciary and for suppression of criminals, those proved upright by the test of material gain to offices of the Administrator and in the stores of the Director of Stores, those proved pure by the test of lust to guardianship of (places of) recreation inside (the palace) as well as outside, those proved loyal by the test of fear to duties near the (person of the) king. 14 Those proved honest by all tests, he should make (his) councillors. 15 Those (found) dishonest by every test, he should employ in mines, in forests for material produce, in elephant-forests and in factories.

16 'He should appoint ministers, who have been cleared by the (tests of the) group of three (goals of life)[1] and fear, to duties appropriate to them in accordance with their integrity;' thus have the (ancient) teachers laid down.

17 'However, under no circumstances must the king make himself or the queen the target for the sake of ascertaining the probity of ministers;' this is the opinion of Kautilya.

---

[1] **three (goals of life):** The three goals are usually defined as *dharma* (lawful order or moral virtue), *artha* (power and success), and *kama* (love and pleasure). A fourth, *moksha,* is sometimes mentioned as an ultimate release from the previous three.

18 He should not effect the corruption of the uncorrupted as of water by poison; for, it may well happen that a cure may not be found for one corrupted.

19 And the mind, perverted by the fourfold secret tests, may not turn back without going to the end, remaining fixed in the will of spirited persons.

[Informers]

1 And those who are without relations and have to be necessarily maintained, when they study the (science of the interpretation of) marks, the science of (the touch of) the body, the science of magic, that pertaining to (the creation of) illusions, the duties of the *āśramas,* (the science of) omens, the 'wheel with the spaces' and so on, are the secret agents; or, (when they study) the art of association (with men).

2 Those in the land who are brave, have given up all (thought of) personal safety (and) would fight, for the sake of money, an elephant or a wild animal, are the bravoes.

3 Those who are without affection for their kinsmen and are cruel and indolent are the poison-givers.

4 A wandering nun, seeking a (secure) livelihood, poor, widowed, bold, Brahmin (by caste) and treated with honour in the palace, should (frequently) go to the houses of high officers. 5 By her (office) are explained (similar offices for) the shaven nuns of heretical sects.

These are the roving spies.

6 The king should employ these with a credible disguise as regards country, dress, profession, language and birth, to spy, in conformity with their loyalty and capability, on the councillor, the chaplain, the commander-in-chief, the crown-prince, the chief palace usher, the chief of the palace guards, the director, the administrator, the director of stores, the magistrate, the commandant, the city-judge, the director of factories, the council of ministers, the superintendents, the chief of the army staff, the commandant of the fort, the commandant of the frontier-fort and the forest chieftain, in his own territory.

7 Bravoes,[2] (serving as) bearers of umbrella, water-vessel, fan, shoes, seat, carriage and riding animal, should (spy on and) ascertain the out-of-door activity of those (officers). 8 Secret agents should communicate that (information) to the (spy-) establishments.

9 Poison-givers, serving as cooks, waiters, bath-attendants, shampooers, bed-preparers, barbers, valets and water-servers, those appearing as hump-backs, dwarfs, Kirātas,[3] dumb, deaf, idiotic or blind persons, (and) actors, dancers, singers, musicians, professional story-tellers and minstrels as well as women should (spy on and) ascertain the indoor activity (of those officers). 10 Nuns should communicate that (information) to the (spy-) establishments.

11 Assistants of the establishments should carry out the transmission of spied out news by means of sign-alphabets. 12 And neither the establishments nor these (assistants) should know one another.

13 In case of prohibition (of entry into the house) for nuns, (secret agents)

---

[2] **Bravoes:** Hired killers. [3] **Kirātas:** Hunters.

appearing at the door one after another (or) appearing as the mother or father (of servants in the house), or posing as female artists, singers or female slaves, should get the secret information that is spied out conveyed outside by means of songs, recitations, writings concealed in musical instruments or signs. 14 Or, a secret get-away (from the house should be made by the spies) by (taking advantage of a pretended) long illness or madness or by setting (something) on fire or administering poison (to someone).

15 When there is agreement in the reports of three (spies), credence (should be given). 16 In case of continuous mistakes on their part, 'silent' punishment is (the means of) their removal.

17 And spies mentioned in 'The Suppression of Criminals' should live with enemies receiving wages from them, in order to find out secret information, without associating with one another. 18 They are 'persons in the pay of both.'

19 And he should appoint 'persons in the pay of both,' after taking charge of their sons and wives. And he should know such agents when they are employed by the enemies. And (he should ascertain) their loyalty through (spies of) their type.

20 Thus he should sow spies among the enemy, the ally, the middle king, the neutral king, as well as among the eighteen high officers of (each of) those (kings).

ARISTOTLE
384–322 B.C.E.

Plato and Aristotle built on a tradition of rational inquiry that began in the sixth century B.C.E. in Greece when individuals attempted to *understand* the world and not merely to *explain* it through myth or religion. The key assumption for this intellectual pursuit was that the world was essentially rational and knowable, that human reason could grasp its workings. Aristotle's genius consisted of his developing the tools of analysis—in particular, logic and taxonomy[1]—which made the inquiry into the nature of social and material reality both possible and rewarding. Aristotle's works, about four hundred in number, covered nearly all the known fields of knowledge of his time: from astronomy and mathematics to physics, biology, ethics, politics, and literature. There is no doubt that Aristotle laid the foundation for the development of modern science and is therefore a recognizable influence on the modern world.

Bust of Aristotle
Though considered one of the founders of modern science, Aristotle's contributions were not limited to the realm of science but extended to the fields of literature, philosophy, and art as well. (Erich Lessing/ Art Resource, NY)

A Life of Study and Teaching. Aristotle was born the son of a physician in the north of Greece, in the town of Stagira in Macedonia. When he was seventeen, Aristotle studied at Plato's Academy in Athens, remaining there twenty years until Plato's death in 347 B.C.E. For the next several years Aristotle traveled about and in 342 B.C.E. became the tutor of young Alexander of Macedon,[2] returning to Athens to found the Lyceum, a school of philosophy, in 335. Known also as the Peripatetic School because the students walked about on the grounds while Aristotle taught, this school was the first research institution in Greece devoted to science, literature, and philosophy. After Alexander's death in 323, anti-Macedonian feelings in Athens led Aristotle to retire on Macedonia's Chalcidian peninsula, where he died a year later, in 322 B.C.E.

It was typical of Aristotle's gentle, generous thoughtfulness that in his will he provided for all his relatives and dependents—including his slaves. He thanked his wife, Herpyllis, for her goodness and provided a dowry for her. He asked, however, that his bones be placed in the grave of his first wife, Pythias, the adoptive daughter or niece of his close friend Hermias; Aristotle had rescued Pythias from robbers.

WWW For links to more information about Aristotle and quizzes on *Metaphysics* and *Poetics,* see *World Literature Online* at bedfordstmartins .com/worldlit.

A Sampling of Writings. In the excerpt from *Metaphysics* that follows, Aristotle discusses the importance of reasoning. A selection from *Poetics,* the first extended piece of literary criticism written in the West, also

[1] **logic and taxonomy:** Logic is a system of reasoning in which statements lead to sound conclusions. Taxonomy is the science of classification and labeling. Aristotle believed in a grand hierarchy of being in which every thing and every idea had its place.

[2] **Alexander of Macedon:** Alexander the Great (356–323 B.C.E.) became king of Macedon after the death of his father. Considered the most brilliant general of the ancient, Western world, Alexander extended his empire while spreading the culture of ancient Greece through Egypt, Palestine, Persia, and northern India before he tragically died in Babylon in 323 B.C.E.

Although his debt to Plato is visible throughout his work, Aristotle rejected his master's Forms for a thoroughgoing empiricism: the world of experience is what one needs to understand, and therefore that is what one starts with — all experience, for he had an intellectual energy and curiosity that have never been surpassed and rarely been approached.

– M. I. Finley, historian, 1964

follows. In *Poetics,* Aristotle sets out to describe the general nature of Greek literature. As with other fields of knowledge, Aristotle systematizes, distinguishing among various kinds of literature and describing their basic principles and aims. In contrast to Plato, who questioned the moral impact of art, Aristotle discussed the positive influence of literature on human beings, especially the healthy effect of ***CATHARSIS,*** the purgation of the emotions.

Aristotle's influence on Western culture has been immense, although at first it took a rather circuitous route. Of the few philosophical works by Aristotle published in his lifetime, only brief fragments remain. Aristotle's lectures on scientific matters, however, recorded by his students and lost from the time of his death until the first century B.C.E., were published in Rome and preserved by Byzantine scholars for several hundred years until they were passed on to great Islamic scholars like Avicenna (980–1037) in Persia and Averroës (1126–1198) in Spain and Morocco, renowned for their studies in medicine and philosophy. Aristotle's treatises were then passed back to Europe where they influenced that continent's revival of learning in the twelfth and thirteenth centuries.

Thomas Aquinas (c. 1225–1274) used Aristotelian philosophy to construct the theoretical basis of Medieval Christianity by reconciling the Greek texts of Aristotle with the doctrines of Christianity. Dante, the fourteenth-century Italian poet and creator of *The Divine Comedy,* borrowed from Aristotle's hierarchical thinking and called him "the Master of those who know." After the rise of modern science, Aristotle's importance declined, but the example of his intellect and the compelling nature of his methodology have continued to inspire thinkers to the present day. We might not all be Platonists or Aristotelians,[3] as British Romantic Samuel Taylor Coleridge maintained in the early nineteenth century, but it is still common for modern intellectuals to seek refuge in the basic tenets of the humanism fostered by these men.

■ CONNECTIONS

Plato, *Apology, Phaedo, The Republic,* pp. 1089, 1108, and 1111. Plato and Aristotle represent two different approaches to the acquisition of knowledge: Plato assumed that meaning lay beyond external sensual phenomena; physical matter was an imperfect reflection of a perfect spiritual Idea. Aristotle, on the contrary, turned to the physical world itself. How might Plato have influenced the evolution of religion and Aristotle the development of the sciences?

Upanishads and Bhagavad Gita, pp. 233, 1346; 1488. Ancient religions and philosophies tended to view the physical world either as an arena of engagement in which individual choices could effect change or as a place of suffering and illusion from which one would do best to escape or withdraw. Indian philosophical inquiry in the Upanishads and the Bhagavad Gita directs its attention on either the inner world of the soul or the transcendent world of avatars, always within a framework of universal, invisible principles like *karma* and *maya.* How does Aristotle's thought differ from Indian philosophy?

[3] **Platonists or Aristotelians:** Coleridge (1772–1834) was referring to two of the major directions of modern Western thought, which seem to originate with Plato and Aristotle: a concern with the spiritual world, the inner world of feelings and beliefs, and a desire to describe and understand the external phenomenal world.

Confucius, *Analects*, p. 1594; Laozi (Lao Tzu), Dao De Jing (Tao Te Ching) pp. 1525, 1605. Like Plato's belief in the perfection of Ideas, the Daoists of China acknowledged a hidden reality, the dao, that shaped experience. Confucius, however, refused to become involved with metaphysical speculation about the origins of the cosmos; he concerned himself instead with behavior and how it could contribute to a harmonious society. Toward which school of philosophy, the Daoists or the Confucians, would Aristotle, with his focus on reason and an intelligible universe, have been most sympathetic?

■ FURTHER RESEARCH

Background and Criticism

Hardison Jr., O. B. *Aristotle's Poetics.* 1968.

Irwin, Terence. *Aristotle's First Principles.* 1989.

Jaeger, Werner. *Paideia: The Ideals of Greek Culture.* 1939–44.

Olson, Elder, ed. *Aristotle's Poetics and English Literature: A Collection of Critical Essays.* 1965.

Zeller, Eduard. *Outlines of the History of Greek Philosophy.* 1955.

FROM

Metaphysics

Translated by Philip Wheelwright

[On Philosophical Wisdom]

All men by nature desire to know. An indication of this is the joy we take in our perceptions; which we cherish for their own sakes, quite apart from any benefits they may yield to us. It is especially true of sight, which we tend to prefer to all the other senses even when it points to no action, and even indeed when no action is in prospect; a preference explained by the greater degree to which sight promotes knowledge by revealing so many differences among things.

The Evolution of Reason

But while the other animals live by means of impressions and memories, with only a small amount of general experience, the human race lives also by art and reasoning. Memory is what gives rise to experience in men, for it is by having repeated memories of the same thing that our ability to have a single whole experience arises. At first sight experience seems much like knowledge and art, but it is truer to say that

Metaphysics. Sulla, a Roman leader, collected Aristotle's extant treatises in Athens in 78 B.C.E. and presided over the current editions of his writings. The title *Metaphysics* was given to the treatises that dealt with what Aristotle called "First Philosophy," those problems "after the *Physics,*" that go beyond the scientific knowledge of the natural world. In the excerpts reprinted here, Aristotle discusses the origins of reason in the human capacity to wonder and how wisdom results from speculation about ultimate principles.

experience is the means through which science and art can be acquired; thus Polus rightly declares that "experience has produced art, inexperience chance."

No doubt the first discoverer of any art that went beyond man's ordinary sense-perceptions was admired by his fellows, not merely for whatever utility his discoveries may have had, but because his wisdom seemed to set him above others. And as further arts were discovered, some supplying the necessities of life, others its leisure moments, the discoverers of the latter were always considered wiser than the discoverers of the former, because theirs was a sort of knowledge that did not aim at utility. The next step, when all such discoveries had been made, was the discovery of the sciences that do not aim either at pleasure or at the necessities of life; and this first occurred in those places where men enjoyed leisure: which explains why the mathematical disciplines first arose in Egypt, because in that country the priestly caste was permitted to live in leisure.

The Nature of Wisdom

The aim of our present discussion is to inquire about wisdom, which is generally understood to deal with the basic determining factors and initiating principles. For the man of experience is agreed to be wiser than one who is limited to mere sense-awareness, the artist than the man of experience, the master-craftsman than the manual worker, and the contemplative sciences to partake of more wisdom than the productive sciences. From this progressive relation it becomes clear that wisdom is that kind of knowledge which concerns ultimate principles and reasons-why.[1]

The Motive of Philosophy

It is through wonder that men begin to philosophize, whether in olden times or today. First their wonder is stirred by difficulties of an obvious sort, and then gradually they proceed to inquire about weightier matters, like the changes of the moon, sun and stars, and the origin of the universe. Now the result of wonderment and perplexity is to feel oneself ignorant. If, then, it was to escape ignorance that men began to philosophize, it is evident that they were pursuing this sort of study in order to know and not from any motive of utility. An incidental confirmation of this view is that thinking began to be undertaken as a pastime and recreation at a period when all the main necessities of life had been supplied. Clearly, then, knowledge of the kind that is under discussion is not sought for the sake of any external advantage; but rather, as we call that man free who exists in and for himself and not for another, so we pursue this as the one free and independent study, because it is the only one that exists for the sake of itself.

The Paradox of Philosophy

Let it be noted, however, that the acquisition of such knowledge leads to a point of view which is in a way the reverse of that from which we began. Everyone begins, as we remarked earlier, by wondering that things should be as they are—whether

[1] **reasons-why:** Usually translated as "cause."

the movements of marionettes, or the solstices, or the incommensurability of the diameter of a square with its side; because it seems remarkable to those who have not yet fathomed the reason-why, that there should exist no smallest common unit by which any two lengths could be measured. But in the end we come to the opposite point of view—which moreover is the better one, for surely the adage that "second thoughts are better thoughts" is most applicable in these cases where learning takes place. From the new standpoint there is nothing a geometer would so greatly wonder at as if the diameter *were* to be found commensurable.

The study of philosophic truth is difficult in one respect, easy in another. This is shown by the double fact that while no individual can grasp truth adequately, yet collectively we do not entirely fail. Each individual makes some report on the nature of things, and while this by itself contributes very little to the inquiry a combination of all such reports amounts to a good deal. In so far as truth can be likened to the proverbial big door which even the poorest marksman cannot miss, it is easy; but the fact that we can know a large general truth and still not grasp some particular part of it shows how difficult truth-seeking really is. However, there are roughly two ways of accounting for a difficulty, and it may be that in the present case the reason for it lies not in the subject-matter but in ourselves, and that as bats' eyes are dimmed by daylight so the power of reason in our souls is dimmed by what is intrinsically most self-evident.

FROM

Poetics

Translated by Samuel Henry Butcher

[On Tragedy]

Tragedy, then, is an imitation of an action that is serious, complete, and of a certain magnitude; in language embellished with every kind of artistic ornament, the several kinds being found in separate parts of the play; in the form of dramatic action, not of narrative; through pity and fear effecting the proper purification of these emotions.[1] By "language embellished," I mean language into which rhythm,

Poetics. Aristotle's classic work of literary criticism, written in the form of rather condensed lecture notes, is probably his most popular work among students of literature today. Aristotle was fortunate enough to have a substantial body of classical literature on which to base his analysis, resulting in principles that became for many Western writers and critics the measure of a well-made piece of literature. The essential mechanism of the Aristotelian analysis of literature—like his previous analyses of wisdom and ethics—is the separation of a whole subject into its constituent parts and the formation of suitable definitions. *Poetics* begins with a general discussion of poetry and then moves on to epics and tragedies. These excerpts are taken from the sections that deal with tragedy, which according to Aristotle is made up of six parts: plot, character, diction, thought, spectacle, and melody. The soul of tragedy, he says, is plot, or action.

[1] **Tragedy . . . emotions:** The Greeks did not require an unhappy or "tragic" ending for their tragedies.

harmony, and song enter. By "the several kinds of separate parts," I mean that some parts are rendered through the medium of verse alone, others again with the aid of song.

Now as tragic imitation implies persons acting, it necessarily follows, in the first place, that spectacular equipment will be a part of tragedy. Next, song and diction, for these are the medium of imitation. By diction, I mean the metrical arrangement of the words: as for song, it is a term whose sense everyone understands.

Again, tragedy is the imitation of an action, and an action implies personal actors, who necessarily possess certain distinctive qualities of character and thought; for it is by these that we form our estimate of their actions and these two—thought and character—are the natural causes from which their actions spring, and on their actions all success or failure depends. Now, the imitation of the action is the plot; by plot I here mean the arrangement of the incidents. By character I mean that because of which we ascribe certain qualities to the actors. Thought is needed whenever they speak to prove a statement or declare a general truth. Every tragedy, therefore, must have six parts, which parts determine its quality—namely, plot, character, diction, thought, spectacle, song. . . .

But most important of all is the structure of the incidents. For tragedy is an imitation, not of men, but of action and life, of happiness and misery. And life consists of action, and its end is a mode of activity, not a quality. Now character determines men's qualities, but it is their actions that make them happy or wretched. The purpose of action in the tragedy, therefore, is not the representation of character: character comes in as contributing to the action. Hence the incidents and the plot are the end of the tragedy; and the end is the chief thing of all. So without action there cannot be a tragedy; there may be one without character. . . .

Again, you may string together a set of speeches expressive of character, and well finished in point of diction and thought, and not produce the essential tragic effect nearly so well as with a play which, however deficient in these respects, yet has a plot and artistically constructed incidents. Besides which, the most powerful elements of emotional interest in tragedy—reversal of the situation and recognition scenes—are parts of the plot. A further proof is that novices in the art attain to finish of diction and precision of portraiture before they can construct the plot. It is the same with almost all the early poets.

The plot, then, is the first principle, and, as it were, the soul of a tragedy: character holds the second place. A similar statement is true of painting. The most beautiful colors, laid on confusedly, will not give as much pleasure as a simple chalk outline of a portrait. Thus tragedy is the imitation of an action, and of actors mainly with a view to the action. . . .

The spectacle is, indeed, an attraction in itself, but of all the parts it is the least artistic, and connected least with the art of poetry. For the power of tragedy is felt even apart from representation and actors. Besides, the production of scenic effects is more a matter for the property man than for the poet.

These principles being established, let us now discuss the proper structure of the plot, since this is the first and most important thing in tragedy.

Now, according to our definition, tragedy is an imitation of an action that is complete and whole and of a certain magnitude; for there may be a whole that is wanting in magnitude. A whole is that which has a beginning, a middle, and an end. A beginning is that which does not have to follow anything else, but after which something else naturally takes place. An end, on the contrary, is that which itself naturally follows something else, either by necessity or as a general rule, but has nothing coming after it. A middle is that which follows something else as some other thing follows it. A well-constructed plot must neither begin nor end at haphazard, but conform to these principles.

Again, a beautiful object, whether it be a living organism or any whole composed of parts, must not only have an orderly arrangement of parts, but must also be of a certain magnitude; for beauty depends on magnitude and order. Hence a very tiny creature cannot be beautiful; for the view of it is confused, the object being seen in an almost imperceptible moment of time. Nor, again, can one of vast size be beautiful; for as the eye cannot take it all in at once, the unity and sense of the whole is lost for the spectator; as it would be if there were a creature a thousand miles long. As, therefore, in the case of living bodies and organisms, a certain magnitude is necessary, and a magnitude which may be easily embraced in one view; so in the plot, a certain length is necessary, and length which can be easily embraced by the memory. . . . And to state the matter roughly, we may say that the proper length is such as to allow for a sequence of necessary or probable events that will bring about a change from calamity to good fortune, or from good fortune to calamity.

Unity of plot does not, as some persons think, consist of having a single man as the hero. For infinitely various are the incidents in one man's life which cannot be reduced to unity; and so, too, there are many actions of one man out of which we cannot make one action. Hence the error, as it appears, of all poets who have composed a Heracleid, a Theseid,[2] or other poems of the kind. They imagine that as Heracles was one man, the story of Heracles must also be a unity. But Homer, as in all else he is of surpassing merit, here too—whether from art or natural genius—seems to have happily discerned the truth. In composing the *Odyssey* he did not include all the adventures of Odysseus—such as his wound on Parnassus, or his feigned madness at the mustering of the host[3]—incidents between which there was no necessary or probable connection: but he made the *Odyssey* and likewise the *Iliad* center around an action that in our sense of the word is one. As therefore, in the other imitative arts, the imitation is one when the object imitated is one, so the plot, being an imitation of an action, must imitate one action and that a whole, the structural union of the parts being such that, if any one of them is displaced or removed, the whole will be disjointed and disturbed. For a thing whose presence or absence makes no visible difference is not an organic part of the whole.

[2] **Heracleid . . . Theseid:** Long narrative poems about the adventures of a figure such as Heracles or Theseus.

[3] **such as . . . host:** Incidents that occurred before the opening of *The Iliad.*

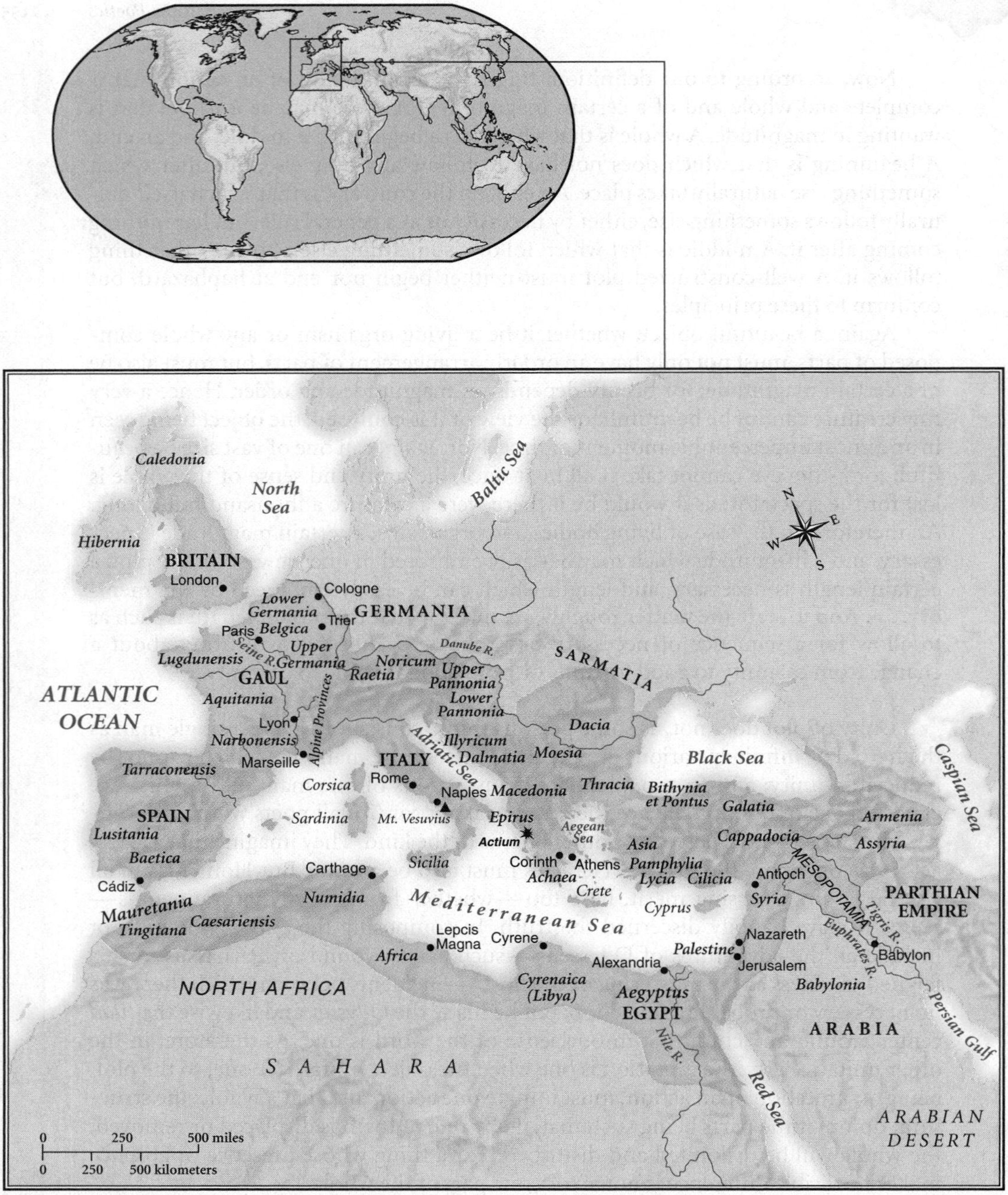

The Roman Empire, 117 C.E.

For close to one hundred fifty years, Rome steadily expanded its borders. In 30 B.C.E. Octavian (the future emperor Augustus) captured Egypt following the suicides of Mark Antony and Cleopatra. Imperial conquest reached its height in 114–117 C.E., when Emperor Trajan seized southern Mesopotamia, the farthest east Rome had yet extended.

ROME
Creating the Myth of Empire in the Land of the Caesars

According to legend, Romulus, the mythic son of Mars and Rhea Silvia, founded Rome in 753 B.C.E., but the Romans ultimately traced their ancestry to a survivor of the Trojan War, Aeneas, who wandered the Mediterranean Sea and eventually arrived on Italy's shores, a journey recounted in Virgil's classic epic, *The Aeneid.* From the eighth to the third centuries B.C.E., Rome's history was characterized by rivalries among various factions and the conquest of neighboring armies. By using alliances and military might, Rome gained control of the entire Italian peninsula by 270 B.C.E. Beyond its borders, Rome became involved in a protracted hundred-year war (264–146 B.C.E.) with the nearby North African city of Carthage, known as the **Punic Wars**. The term *punic* comes from the Greek for Phoenicians, who were the original settlers at Carthage under the leadership of Hamilcar Barca and his two sons, Hannibal and Hasdrubal.

Victory over Carthage, which had dominated the central Mediterranean since the seventh century B.C.E., made Rome the undisputed ruler of the western Mediterranean. Rome then began to look further beyond its shores and became an empire by conquering Sicily, Sardinia, Corsica, Spain, and North Africa as well as a section of Macedonia. Unlike Athens, Rome had a rather enlightened foreign policy; it encouraged the residents of conquered tribes and cities to become Roman citizens with all the privileges and protections that that entailed.

THE REPUBLIC

According to legend, Rome was ruled by a succession of seven kings from 753 to 509 B.C.E. Although details of this period are lacking, it is known that the kings created an advisory body, the Senate, which survived for two thousand years—through monarchy, a republic, and imperial rule. A legend of rape and revolt is told in connection with the creation of a Roman republic in 509 B.C.E.: the son of King

Tarquin is said to have raped a socialite named Lucretia, who then committed suicide. Led by Lucius Junius Brutus, the Liberator, Lucretia's family and friends drove out King Tarquin and established a republic to prevent further abuse of power. Rome was then a republic ruled by twin consuls, a Senate and a popular Assembly. The two consuls served for one year and took turns ruling, alternating monthly. A fasces, a bundle of rods enclosing an ax, was used in consul processions, symbolizing the consuls' power to scourge and execute. (Fasces later became the symbol of the twentieth-century Italian Fascists.) Ancient Roman society was divided into two classes. The elite **PATRICIANS** (from *patres,* meaning "fathers") were the heads of the oldest families who occupied the Senate. The **PLEBEIANS**, the general populace and lower class, made up the Assembly. The next two hundred years saw a power struggle between these two classes. With the patricians numbering only about one hundred thirty families in the early republic, the plebeians sometimes exploited their majority status to gain power by refusing services, such as serving their time in the army. It wasn't until 287 B.C.E. that the Assembly gained the power to make laws. The uneven distribution of wealth and power led to civil wars and slave revolts that threatened the growing empire from within.

Finally, in the first century B.C.E., a civil war resulted in a division of power between Pompey, whose power lay in the east, and Julius Caesar, who had spread Roman rule to the west with his Gallic wars. These two leaders were temporarily joined by Crassus to make up the First Triumvirate in 60 B.C.E. A war between Pompey, favored by the senatorial party, and Caesar, leader of the popular party, ended with Caesar's victory at Pharsala in 48 B.C.E. The Roman historian Suetonius (75–160 C.E.) credited Julius Caesar with correcting the calendar—the Julian calendar—and with numerous public projects, but praised him above all for his brilliance as a military commander: "He was perfect in the use of arms, an accomplished rider, and able to endure fatigue beyond all belief."

Shortsighted conspirators, upset by Caesar's aggregation of power and dreaming of the return of the old republic, arranged for Caesar's assassination in 44 B.C.E., plunging Rome into another thirteen years of civil war. Caesar's nephew and adopted son, Gaius Julius Caesar Octavianus, joined forces with Mark Antony and Lepidus to form the Second Triumvirate in 43 B.C.E. Together they ventured into Greece to defeat Caesar's murderers, Brutus and Cassius, at Philippi in 42 B.C.E., resulting in a division of the Roman world between the east and the west. Mixing love and politics, Antony joined forces with Cleopatra, queen of Egypt, while Octavian eliminated his rivals and consolidated his forces in the west. The seemingly inevitable battle between Antony and Cleopatra and Octavian occurred at Actium in 31 B.C.E.; defeated, Antony and Cleopatra fled to Egypt, where they committed suicide. Uniting an empire that stretched from the Straits of Gibraltar to

Pont du Gard, 19 B.C.E.
A happy result of the Roman love of water and building, the Pont du Gard straddles the river Gard, and is an outstanding example of Roman engineering. Water was brought into Nimes (a Roman city in what is now southern France) via an aquaduct, of which the Pont du Gard is only a small part, through a series of aboveground and underground channels. (© Adam Woolfitt/CORBIS)

Palestine, Octavian took the name Augustus, established a constitutional monarchy, and inaugurated the Augustan Age, a golden age of art and literature.

PAX ROMANA AND ROMAN SOCIETY

The term ***Pax Romana*** refers to the unprecedented two hundred years of relative peace that began with Augustus and ended with the emperor Marcus Aurelius (161–180 C.E.), a time when resources could be devoted to peaceful projects rather than to armaments and war. Throughout their vast empire, the Romans built roads, bridges, aqueducts, baths, sewers, and public buildings. Undergirding their bureaucratic system was a concept of universal law rooted in Nature, which declared the equality of all men and protected the individual against the state. This ideal of law lifted justice from the prerogative of local or tribal powers to an impersonal, universal legal structure that included all inhabitants of an expanding

Model of Ancient Rome

In its ancient heyday, Rome was a remarkably modern city with restaurants, cafés, public baths, theaters, and apartments and houses with indoor plumbing, heat, and running water. (The Art Archive/Museo della Civiltà Romana, Rome/Dagli Orti)

empire. This law, which embraced the ideal of a free society, was Rome's greatest contribution to Western civilization. The Romans systematized education, inculcating the Latin virtues of ***PIETAS*** (duty), ***GRAVITAS*** (seriousness), and ***AMOR IMPERII*** (love of empire). Symbolizing this state religion was the emperor Augustus, who was given the title *pater patriae,* Father of the Country, in 2 B.C.E. This Roman religion of patriotism produced the man of letters, the man of politics, the man of the world embodied in such figures as the great statesman and philosopher Cicero (106–43 B.C.E.), the poet Horace (65–8 B.C.E.), and the writer and statesman Pliny the Younger (c. 62–c. 113 C.E.).

Romans appeared to be as organized in the home as they were in the public arena. They valued family life highly and made the eldest male in every household—the *pater familias*—the authority over all important matters, including marriage, religion, fidelity, dowries—even life and death. As in Greece, it was a civic duty in the empire to have children. Although upper-class women played subordinate roles to men, they were not sequestered in their homes as Athenian women seem to have been. Through birth control and abortion, they freed themselves from bearing children continuously and developed lives outside the home. They shopped in markets and attended festivals and dinner parties with their husbands. Women were allowed to attend elementary school; some were educated by

Female Artist, 50–79 B.C.E.
Women had many freedoms in Roman society. Here, a female artist paints a portrait under the watchful gaze of two friends. (The Art Archive / Archaeological Museum Naples / Dagli Orti)

private tutors to become musicians, poets, and artists. Although they were given no true political positions and only honorary titles, they were sometimes highly influential behind the scenes. By the second century C.E., women were involved in business, sports, and the arts; they also chose their own marriage partners.

Under Rome's later rulers, Tiberius, Caligula, and Claudius I (first century C.E.), the empire stretched from Britain to Mesopotamia, the largest empire in the history of the West up to that time. Nevertheless, the period between 14 C.E. and 96 C.E. was filled with the insanity of Emperors Nero and Caligula, the burning of Rome, the defeat of a Jewish uprising, the destruction of Jerusalem, and the ongoing persecution of a new religious sect calling themselves Christians. The period from 96 to 180 C.E.—under the reigns of Nerva, Trajan, Hadrian, Antoninus Pius, and Marcus Aurelius—was a peaceful period. Something, however, seems to have been missing in the personal lives of the people, many of whom increasingly turned to imported mystery religions for spiritual purpose and direction. These religions promised communion with a messiah and a future paradise as compensation for suffering and despair.

In the third century, the empire was weakened by an internal east-west division. Constantine, who granted official tolerance to the new Christian sect in 313 and later converted to Christianity himself, moved his capital to Constantinople in the east. Invaders from the north increasingly penetrated the frontiers of the empire, until finally Rome was sacked by Alaric and his Visigoths in 410. The Roman Empire in the west formally came to an end when the barbarian Odoacer replaced the last emperor, Romulus Augustulus, in 476 C.E.

LITERATURE

The Latin alphabet, which was to become the script for English and other Western European languages, was developed from the Greek language by way of the Etruscans around the sixth century B.C.E. The Etruscans adjusted a number of Greek vowels and consonants in order to spell the many names and words borrowed from the Greek during the imperial Roman period. Latin became the dominant language in Europe for some two millennia. As the official liturgical language of Christianity until the Reformation in the sixteenth century and the language of scholars, Latin was spread throughout medieval Europe through the agency of the Roman Catholic Church.

In literature as well as in their **PANTHEON** of deities, Rome was indebted to ancient Greece and to the many cultures it encountered throughout its empire. Lucretius (c. 99–c. 55 B.C.E.), for example, wrote his lengthy poem, *On the Nature of Things,* using the theories of the Greek philosopher Epicurus (c. 341–270 B.C.E.). From the time of his *Eclogues* (37 B.C.E.), Virgil, the most famous poet of the Roman Empire, was well known at Augustus's court and was probably beginning to plan the epic poem that would do for Rome what Homer's epics had done for Greece—namely, the creation of mythic-historic roots. In *The Aeneid,* Virgil seeks to create a founding myth of Rome's origins that will celebrate Augustus's accomplishments and support a vision of Rome's world mission. Though modeled after Homer's *Odyssey,* the travails of Aeneas's own journey through the Mediterranean reflect in miniature the labors undertaken by Roman Senators, legions, and slaves to create the empire. Understanding the anxiety that Roman intellectuals felt about the impending end of an age, Virgil attempts to allay the fears of his Roman audience through Jupiter, who says: "I set no limits to their fortunes and / no time; I give them empire without end." Later, in Book 4, Virgil creates a new hero by

www For more information about the culture of Rome in the ancient world, see *World Literature Online* at bedfordstmartins.com/worldlit.

TIME AND PLACE

Augustus Caesar and the Golden Age

From the first century B.C.E. onward, intellectuals throughout the Greco-Roman world commonly believed that the cosmos operated in long cycles of time, that an era or age inevitably came to an end so that a new period of history might begin. The Greek writer Hesiod (c. 800 B.C.E.) wrote about the degeneration of time from a golden age to a silver, bronze, and, finally, an iron age. In *Politicus* (fourth century B.C.E.), Plato explains how the earth will change directions at the end of a final age and turn in the opposite direction, causing cataclysms at first and then a regeneration of all life and the advent of a new ruler.

Romans viewed Romulus's founding of Rome (c. 753 B.C.E.) and his sighting of twelve birds as omens indicating that Rome would endure twelve centuries. Seven centuries later with the reign of Augustus, they dared to hope that they could pass from one age to another, from the Iron Age to a new Golden Age, without a cosmic catastrophe, or *ekpyrosis,* "destruction by fire."

On the tenth anniversary of Augustus's regime, he inaugurated the Secular Games, a three-day festival meant to purify Rome from past pollution and represent a transition to a world renewed, a messianic Golden Age. With the death of Lepidus in 12 B.C.E., Augustus became Rome's Chief Priest *(pontifex maximus).* Officially, he could not become a god until he died, but in 2 B.C.E. he became "Father of the Fatherland" *(pater patriae),* a title that supported his claim that he was the son of the deified Julius Caesar, the *divi filius.*

In *The Aeneid,* Virgil, the poet laureate of Rome, unveils Rome's destiny and predicts that Rome will regenerate itself indefinitely through Julius's line and under the glorious reign of Augustus. Ruler worship spread throughout the empire, with temples dedicated to Rome and tributes to Augustus as Savior, Benefactor, and the God Epiphanes (Manifest). Especially in the eastern provinces, Augustus's gradual deification became a binding political force.

Augustus, r. 27 B.C.E.–14 C.E. *The Roman Empire enjoyed a period of relative peace and stability under the long reign of Augustus (a religious title meaning "revered") Caesar (63 B.C.E.–14 C.E.). (The Art Archive / Musée du Louvre, Paris / Dagli Orti)*

After Augustus's death in 14 C.E., a special priesthood was established to care for his cult.

portraying Aeneas with psychological depth and complexity in his relationship with Dido, the queen of Carthage. After the publication of *The Aeneid,* Augustus was designated the second founder of Rome, a realm that for a time was called the *urbs aeterna* (the eternal city). The Greek ***POLIS*** had been expanded by Rome into a grand **COSMOPOLIS.**

Both Catullus (c. 84–c. 54 B.C.E.) and Ovid (43 B.C.E.–17 C.E.) wrote personal poems as well as poems on mythical subjects. Catullus, in particular, is remembered for his love poems, with their expression of sensitive feeling and their portrayal of the pangs of rejection and despair. Ovid, the first century poet laureate of love under Augustus, is best known for his *Metamorphoses,* a compendium of Greek and Roman myths. The ancient stories of gods and goddesses that had once been used to illustrate the spiritual mysteries of life became, in Ovid's skillful hands, the marvelously entertaining materials of literature. He concluded the *Metamorphoses* with the prediction, "My fame shall live to all eternity"; and so far he has not been proven wrong, influencing a long line of poets, including Dante, Petrarch, Chaucer, Shakespeare, Alexander Pope, and T. S. Eliot.

CATULLUS
C. 84–C. 54 B.C.E.

www For links to more information about Catullus and a quiz on his poetry, see *World Literature Online* at bedfordstmartins.com/worldlit.

The voice of the Roman lyric poet Catullus speaks directly across some two thousand years in startlingly colloquial language, his tone ranging from leering to loving, from scornful sarcasm to warm affection to bitter grief. From the first century B.C.E. he reports on daily life among his friends, the rich and fast-living younger set in Rome. While he gossips wickedly about bathhouse scandals, back-alley doings, and bisexual politics in the capital, telling who is incestuous or adulterous, there are private and tender moments, too, as when he thanks friends who have stood by him; chronicles his aching love affair with Lesbia, the older woman whose flamboyance both enchants him and breaks his heart; and stands over the lonely grave of his beloved elder brother, who has died in the remote province of Bithynia. Like Sappho,[1] the predecessor he revered and imitated, Catullus is a poet whose love poetry has inspired almost every succeeding generation of poets in the west to translate him anew.

[1] **Sappho** (early sixth century B.C.E.): Greek lyric poet from the island of Lesbos; her love lyrics, some of which Catullus translated into Latin, have been widely influential (see p. 791).

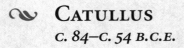

Lovers, first century
In this erotic scene from a fresco in the ancient city of Pompeii, Italy, two lovers coyly approach each other. (Erich Lessing/Art Resource, NY)

From Verona to Rome. Like Sappho, Catullus grew up far from the intellectual center of the culture he lived in. He was born about 84 B.C.E. in Verona, a city in the northern Italian province of Cisalpine Gaul. The second son of a prosperous contractor for the Roman legions, Gaius Valerius, Catullus was taken in by the circle gathered around the brilliant teacher, poet, and Hellenist Valerius Cato, one of the leaders of the *Neoteri,* or New Poets, who emphasized the craft of poetry. In one of his own poems Catullus claims that he began to write when he was about sixteen. Brilliant, handsome, witty, and with a keen appetite for experience, at some point Catullus made his way to Rome and from that time on regarded it as his home. There he found companions among both the intellectuals and the most avid pleasure-seekers; if the great statesman and orator Marcus Tullius Cicero (106–43 B.C.E.) was his friend, so were the full array of Gelliuses, Quintiuses, and Balbuses who lust, drink, and carouse in his poems. One person whom he and his friends seem to have regarded with mild dislike was Julius Caesar (102–44 B.C.E.) himself, seemingly on the grounds of personality rather than politics: "Caesar? What Caesar?" Catullus jokes in one fragment.

Formally innovative, intellectually and emotionally sophisticated, Catullus and his colleagues created a poetics of the subjective, the ironic, the erotic. To their contemporaries, who referred to them in Latin as "the new poets" *(Poetae novi)* and in Greek as "the modernists" *(hoi neoteroi)*, it must have seemed as though these writers, known today as the neoterics, had come out of nowhere, for they were almost without precedent in Roman literature.

– CHARLES MARTIN, critic, 1992

Lesbia. Clodia Metelli, whom Catullus addresses in his poems as Lesbia in tribute to Sappho, was the wife of Metellus Celer, the governor of Cisalpine Gaul. It is very likely that she came into Catullus's life while he was still living in Verona. She was more than five years older than Catullus, and already notorious for her commanding air, her charm, her caprices, and her sexual appetites; when her husband died in 59 B.C.E., rumors circulated that she had poisoned him to clear the way for an incestuous affair with her brother. Cicero wrote a polemic against her when one of his favorite pupils was accused of trying to poison her. Cicero, who believed Roman women should be quiet, stately matrons, must have been galled to no end by the outspoken Metelli, who lived only a few houses away from him and enjoyed staging riotous salons for politicians opposed to him. The very qualities in Metelli that so irked Cicero made Catullus fall helplessly in love with her. Their affair is chronicled in about forty poems that trace their relationship from its playful, ecstatic beginning through betrayal, jealousy, recriminations, reconciliations, and, finally, contempt. Yet with all the heartbreak, it seems that Catullus does not wish to have forgone meeting and loving Clodia/Lesbia; she is the great experience of his life.

Bithynia and Mortality. In the year 57, very likely at about the time that Catullus's love affair was ending, he received word that his much-loved elder brother had died while on a diplomatic mission in Bithynia, in what is now Turkey. Catullus arranged for a political appointment and traveled to Bithynia in the entourage of the magistrate Caius Memmius Gemellus. At some time during his tour of duty, Catullus visited his brother's grave, an occasion commemorated movingly in one of his finest poems, 101, famous for its salutation to the dead, *Ave atque vale* ("Hail and farewell," here translated as "Goodbye, goodbye"). This death, perhaps linked in his mind with the death of his relationship with Lesbia, affected Catullus deeply. He had always lived at a riotous pace, as though he sensed death were close and he needed to cram in quickly all the experience he could. His brother's death seems to have confirmed what he had guessed about mortality. He writes in another poem addressed to his brother, "You have darkened my mind."

Catullus remained in Bithynia for about a year, and then, homesick, he returned to his family villa on the shores of Lake Garda. He visited Rome one last time, where he may have resumed his affair with Lesbia. Soon after, though exactly when or how is not known, Catullus died. He was about thirty years old.

The Poetry. As a young poet Catullus belonged to the bright group of Roman writers known as the Neoterics. While a few of their names are known, Catullus's is the only body of work that has survived. The Neoterics were impatient with the ponderous high-mindedness and patriotic and mythological themes that characterized a good deal of Roman literature. They were far more taken by the racy, breezy Roman comedy that mocked pretentiousness and celebrated in colloquial language the everyday life of gossipy servants, lovesick young folk, feasting, and drinking. Such a shift from the high seriousness of earlier Roman poetry effected a revolution in poetics and in sensibility. Contemporary critic Charles Martin characterizes this new poetry as groundbreaking: "Formally innovative, intellectually and emotionally sophisticated, Catullus and his colleagues created a poetics of the subjective, the ironic, the erotic. To their contemporaries, who referred to them in Latin as 'the new poets' *(Poetae novi)* and in Greek as 'the modernists' *(hoi neoteroi)*, it must have seemed as though these writers, known today as the neoterics, had come out of nowhere, for they were almost without precedent in Roman literature."

Catullus turned his poems away from epic themes and looked to the sophisticated urban life that teemed before his eyes for his subject. Candor, wit, intimacy, and an astonishing range characterize Catullus's work. That range is discernible even in the brief selection presented here. Lightly, lovingly, in poem 2 Catullus describes his beloved sensuously playing with her tame sparrow—teasing it, cuddling it, feeding it; he says he wishes he might be her, able for a while to forget the pains of love, but it is clear that it is the petted sparrow he envies as well. And in poem 3, when the sparrow dies, his elegy for it begins in the mock-heroic tone of one making a great fuss over a trivial thing, but the poem deepens within a few lines into a genuine rage against the mortality that in the end will devour all lovely things, whether they are trivial or of great importance. Lesbia and her sparrow alike will one day be "lost in darkness / . . . a sad place / from which no one returns." Extravagantly, in poem 5, in the exuberance of first love, he and his sweetheart defy death with their wealth of infinitely multiplied embraces. Finally, in poem 101 the poet stands stricken beside a lonely grave in a far country, death offerings in his hands, surrounded by a vast silence. It may in fact have been Catullus's keen intuition of death's constant presence that enabled him to write poems that spill over with all the beauty and decadence of Roman life.

■ CONNECTIONS

Sappho, poems, p. 791; *In the Tradition:* Courtly Love Lyrics (Book 2). Romantic love is one of the enduring themes of world literature, and Catullus's poetry embodies its full experience—from tender affection to bitter disappointment, from deference to a lover to snarling defiance. As such, Catullus's poetry can be compared to that of Sappho, a writer he revered and imitated, as well as to the love lyrics of later generations of European poets whose work Catullus influenced. How does the poetry of Arabic writers Ibn Zaydun and Wallada (*In the Tradition:* Courtly Love Lyrics), which expresses the love-hate motif also found in Catullus, compare? What are the cultural and historical characteristics of these writings?

Francesco Petrarch, *Canzoniere* (Book 3). Catullus treats love from a variety of perspectives and is capable of expressing deep affection. The secular nature of that love, however, contrasts strikingly with that in the Italian poet Petrarch's lyrics, which draw on the language and motifs of Christian devotion. How are Catullus's and Petrarch's love lyrics a measure of the cultural distance between Catullus's Rome and Renaissance Italy?

Basavanna (Book 3); *The Kokinshu* (Book 2). While love is often thought to be a universal phenomenon, the "language of love," as expressed in literature, is guided by culturally specific norms and conventions. Consider Catullus's love lyrics in the context of the devotional lyrics of the Indian and Kannada poets and the poems in the Japanese collection *The Kokinshu.* What in all these love poems might be said to be universal? What is culturally specific?

■ **FURTHER RESEARCH**

Havelock, E. A. *The Lyric Genius of Catullus.* 1964.
Martin, Charles. *Catullus.* 1992.
Quinn, Kenneth. *Catullus: An Interpretation.* 1973.
Wiseman, T. P. *Catullus and His World: A Reappraisal.* 1985.

2: Sparrow, O, sweet sparrow

Translated by Horace Gregory

Sparrow, O, sweet sparrow,
love of my lady love,
she who's always nursing
you between her breasts and
feeding you her finger-tips;

Selected Poems. In his day, Catullus sang and read aloud his poetry before privileged audiences eager to hear him scandalize their friends and acquaintances. Some of his poems may have been collected into a book, but the poems that have survived were found in a copyist's manuscript. Around 1300 C.E. a rolled-up manuscript of Catullus's poems was found in a jar; the manuscript, containing 115 poems ranging from two hundred to nearly four hundred lines of verse, was copied by hand at least three times and then disappeared. One of Catullus's poems, number 62, exists from an earlier manuscript dated in the ninth century. Several of the poems presented here deal with the poet's at-times-turbulent love affair with Clodia Metelli, addressed as "Lesbia." As noted in the headnote to Catullus, Metelli, a married woman, was known for her intelligence, beauty, and sexual intrigues. While many editors rearrange the poems to reflect what is supposed to be the rise and fall of Catullus's relationship with Metelli, Catullus's poems are printed here in the order in which they appear in the manuscripts; it is quite possible that their relationship did not follow an even path from passionate intensity to bitter disillusionment. Poems 2, 3, 5, 8, 11, 51, 76, and 85 all concern the love affair; poem 101 is a tribute to Catullus's brother, written after visiting his grave in the Troad, near the site of the ancient city of Troy in what is now Turkey.

A note on the translation: We are using the lively translations of Catullus's poems by the classicist Horace Gregory; notes are the editors'.

she, that radiant lady,
delicious in her play with you,
for a while forgetting
all the deeper wounds of love . . .
I envy her. This pastime
would raise my heart from darkness.

3: Dress now in sorrow, O all

Translated by Horace Gregory

Dress now in sorrow, O all
your shades of Venus,[1]
and your little cupids weep.

My girl has lost her darling sparrow;
he is dead, her precious toy
that she loved more than her two eyes,
O, honeyed sparrow following her
as a girl follows her mother,
never to leave her breast, but tripping
now here, now there, and always singing
his sweet falsetto
song to her alone.

Now he is gone; poor creature,
lost in darkness,
to a sad place
from which no one returns.

O ravenous hell!
My evil hatred rises against your power,
you that devour
all things beautiful;
and now this pitiful, broken sparrow,
who is the cause of my girl's grief,
making her eyes weary and red with sorrow.

[1] **Venus:** Roman goddess of love (Aphrodite in Greek mythology).

5: Come, Lesbia, let us live and love

Translated by Horace Gregory

Come, Lesbia, let us live and love,
nor give a damn what sour old men say.
The sun that sets may rise again
but when our light has sunk into the earth,
it is gone forever.
Give me a thousand kisses,
then a hundred, another thousand,
another hundred
and in one breath
still kiss another thousand,
another hundred.
O then with lips and bodies joined
many deep thousands;
confuse
their number,
so that poor fools and cuckolds (envious
even now) shall never
learn our wealth and curse us
with their
evil eyes.

8: Poor damned Catullus, here's no time for nonsense

Translated by Horace Gregory

Poor damned Catullus, here's no time for nonsense,
open your eyes, O idiot, innocent boy, look at what has happened:
once there were sunlit days when you followed after
where ever a girl would go, she loved with greater
love than any woman knew.
Then you took your pleasure
and the girl was not unwilling. Those were the bright days, gone;
now she's no longer yielding; you must be, poor idiot,
more like a man! not running after
her your mind all tears; stand firm, insensitive.
say with a smile, voice steady, "Good-bye, my girl," Catullus
strong and manly no longer follows you, nor comes when you are calling

him at night and you shall need him.
You whore! Where's your man to cling to, who will praise your beauty,
where's the man that you love and who will call you his,
and when you fall to kissing, whose lips will you devour?
But always, your Catullus will be as firm as rock is.

11: Furius, Aurelius, bound to Catullus

Translated by Horace Gregory

Furius, Aurelius, bound to Catullus
though he marches piercing farthest India
where echoing waves of the Eastern Oceans
    break upon the shores:

Under Caspian seas, to mild Arabia,
east of Parthia,[1] dark with savage bowmen,
or where the Nile, sevenfold and uprising,
    stains its leveled sands,—

Even though he marches over Alps to gaze on
great Caesar's monuments: the Gallic Rhine and
Britons who live beyond torn seas, remotest
    men of distant lands—

Friends who defy with me all things, whatever
gods may send us, go now, friends, deliver
these words to my lady, nor sweet—flattering,
    nor kind nor gentle:

Live well and sleep with adulterous lovers,
three hundred men between your thighs, embracing

Poem 11. In this poem as in Poem 51, which introduces his love for "Lesbia," Catullus uses a Sapphic meter. Latin poetry, like Greek, was based on precise metrical forms and thus demanded rigorous attention to the number and patterns of accented and unaccented, long and short, syllables. The Sapphic meter calls for three lines of eleven syllables each, followed by a fourth line of five syllables. To produce lines of uneven numbers of syllables, the meter calls for a spondee, or one short and two long syllables, in each line, a combination not easily arrived at in English. The poem signals Catullus's infelicitous break with his lover.

[1] **east of Parthia:** A country in what is now northeastern Iran; Catullus's point here is that his wandering has taken him to the remote periphery of the Roman Empire.

all love turned false, again, again, and breaking
their strength, now sterile.

She will not find my love (once hers) returning;
she it was who caused love, this lonely flower,
tossed aside, to fall by the plough dividing
blossoming meadows.

51: He is changed to a god he who looks on her

Translated by Horace Gregory

He is changed to a god he who looks on her,
godlike he shines when he's seated beside her,
immortal joy to gaze and hear the fall of
her sweet laughter.

All of my senses are lost and confounded;
Lesbia rises before me and trembling
I sink into earth and swift dissolution
seizes my body.

Limbs are pierced with fire and the heavy tongue fails,
ears resound with noise of distant storms shaking
this earth, eyes gaze on stars that fall forever
into deep midnight.

This languid madness destroys you Catullus,
long day and night shall be desolate, broken,
as long ago ancient kings and rich cities
fell into ruin.

Poem 51. Like Poem 11, the original Latin verse of this poem is also written in Sapphic meter (see note to Poem 11) and is in part a translation of one of Sappho's lyrics. Here, the use of Sapphic meter underscores the powerful love Catullus feels for "Lesbia."

76: If man can find rich consolation . . .

Translated by Horace Gregory

If man can find rich consolation, remembering his good deeds and all he has done,
if he remembers his loyalty to others, nor abuses his religion by heartless betrayal
of friends to the anger of powerful gods,
then, my Catullus, the long years before you shall not sink in darkness with all hope gone,
wandering, dismayed, through the ruins of love.
All the devotion that man gives to man, you have given, Catullus,
your heart and your brain flowed into a love that was desolate, wasted, nor can it return.
But why, why do you crucify love and yourself through the years?
Take what the gods have to offer and standing serene, rise forth as a rock against darkening skies;
and yet you do nothing but grieve, sunken deep in your sorrow, Catullus,
for it is hard, hard to throw aside years lived in poisonous love that has tainted your brain
and must end.
If this seems impossible now, you must rise
to salvation. O gods of pity and mercy, descend and witness my sorrow, if ever
you have looked upon man in his hour of death, see me now in despair.
Tear this loathsome disease from my brain. Look, a subtle corruption has entered my bones,
no longer shall happiness flow through my veins like a river. No longer I pray
that she love me again, that her body be chaste, mine forever.
Cleanse my soul of this sickness of love, give me power to rise, resurrected, to thrust love aside,
I have given my heart to the gods, O hear me, omnipotent heaven,
and ease me of love and its pain.

85: I hate and love

Translated by Horace Gregory

I hate and love.
    And if you ask me why,
I have no answer, but I discern,
can feel, my senses rooted in eternal torture.

101: Dear brother, I have come these many miles

Translated by Horace Gregory

Dear brother, I have come these many miles, through strange lands to this
 Eastern Continent
to see your grave, a poor sad monument of what you were, O brother.
And I have come too late; you cannot hear me; alone now I must speak
to these few ashes that were once your body and expect no answer.
I shall perform an ancient ritual over your remains, weeping,
(this plate of lentils for dead men to feast upon, wet with my tears)
O brother, here's my greeting: here's my hand forever welcoming you
and I forever saying: good-bye, good-bye.

Virgil

70–19 B.C.E.

Virgil achieved fame in his lifetime as the poet of *The Eclogues,* ten pastoral poems about the lives of shepherds, and *The Georgics,* a patriotic poem about methods of farming and the dignity of country life. His works, including his greatest work, *The Aeneid,* a twelve-book epic left unfinished at his death, exerted a profound influence on later European literature and culture. Like Homer's ***Iliad*** and ***Odyssey*** and the great Sanskrit epic ***Mahabharata,*** *The Aeneid* has inspired generations of subsequent writers and artists, providing them with a rich mine of heroic themes and tragic scenes—**Aeneas** leaving Troy, carrying his father on his shoulders and holding his son by the hand; **Dido** sacrificing herself on a blazing pyre as Aeneas sails away from Carthage; the death of Turnus. Virgil's *Eclogues* and *Georgics* elevated and invigorated the genres of pastoral and didactic poetry, leading to countless imitations produced from his time to the present day. Most significant, his *Aeneid* was a powerful reassessment of the cost of singleminded heroic enterprise. While this story of the founding of Rome by descendants of the conquered city of Troy recalls the Greek epics of Homer, it goes beyond them to stress the theme of *pietas,* public virtue or duty, which Virgil thought lay at the core of Roman civilization and which he saw as attainable only through great suffering and loss.

pp. 288, 421
p. 1434

uh-NEE-us
DIGH-doh

The Poet from Mantua. Publius Vergilius Maro was born in 70 B.C.E. in or near Mantua, a city in Cisalpine Gaul, a northern province of Italy, where his family owned land in the country. Virgil was educated at nearby Cremona and Milan before moving to Rome for a short time; there is some (disputed) evidence that he may also have studied at Naples. A shy and retiring figure, Virgil was never actively engaged in politics, though he circulated among some of the most important and influential people of his time, eventually winning the notice of Octavian[1] himself. However, as we see clearly in *The Aeneid,* Virgil, who had grown up during a time of civil strife, celebrated in his poetry the consolidation of Roman rule. Virgil witnessed the bloody rivalry between Pompey (106–48 B.C.E.) and Julius Caesar (102–44 B.C.E.), the rioting of mobs in Rome, the assassination of Caesar, and the divisive war between Octavian (63 B.C.E.–14 C.E.) and his rival for control over the Roman Empire, Marc Antony (83 B.C.E.–30 C.E.).[2] When Octavian's forces defeated those of Antony and Cleopatra in the battle of Actium (31 B.C.E.), which led to the suicides of the famous couple, Virgil, like most Romans, welcomed the new possibilities for peace under the capable rule of Octavian, soon to be named Augustus Caesar. During the period of civil war, Virgil had already begun to devote himself to the main business of his life: writing poetry of a national character. Having spent most of his life writing poetry while living on his family's property near Mantua, Virgil died at the coastal town of Brundisium on 21 September 19 B.C.E. Although he had asked his friends to destroy the unfinished *Aeneid,* Octavian himself ordered that the manuscript be saved and entrusted it to Varius Rufus, a poet and playwright who saw it through to publication.

WWW For links to more information about Virgil, a quiz on the Aeneid, and information about the twenty-first century relevance of Virgil, see *World Literature Online* at bedfordstmartins.com/worldlit.

***The Eclogues* and *The Georgics*.** Between 42 and 37 B.C.E., Virgil wrote *The Eclogues,* also known as *The Bucolics.* Modeled on the pastoral poetry of Theocritus, a Greek Alexandrian poet from the third century B.C.E., *The Eclogues* depicts the idyllic lives of shepherds against an ominous backdrop of rural dispossession and loss. Taking the form of dialogues, poetic contests, and elegiac complaints, these poems celebrate the virtues

[1] **Octavian:** Caius Octavius (63 B.C.E.–14 C.E.), who became Augustus Caesar. After the death of Julius Caesar, Augustus's great uncle, Octavian formed the Second Triumvirate with Marc Antony and Lepidus. Octavian's defeat of his rivals, including Antony and Cleopatra, helped to stabilize Rome and led to the Senate's appointing him emperor and giving him the honorific title "Augustus." During his era, Roman art, culture, and society flourished.

[2] **Pompey . . . Julius Caesar . . . Marc Antony:** Three Roman generals and statesmen who became rivals for power. In 60 B.C.E., Pompey, Cneius Pompeius Magnus (106–48 B.C.E.), and Julius Caesar (102–44 B.C.E.) joined Marcus Licinius Crassus to form the First Triumvirate. After the death of Crassus, Marc Antony (c. 83–30 B.C.E.), a tribune with ties to Caesar, joined with Caesar in a campaign against Pompey, who now opposed his former ally. Pompey was defeated in 48 B.C.E. and later killed in Egypt, where he had taken refuge. Caesar became dictator and consul in 46 B.C.E. but was assassinated by jealous lieutenants just two years later, on 15 March 44 B.C.E. After the assassination, Antony joined Caesar's great-nephew Octavian (later Augustus Caesar) and Lepidus to form the Second Triumvirate, before making his way in 37 B.C.E. to Alexandria, Egypt, where he carried on a celebrated love affair with Queen Cleopatra. A breach between Antony and Octavian led to another civil war, culminating in the naval battle at Actium in 31 B.C.E., in which Octavian's fleet roundly defeated the combined forces of Antony and Cleopatra. A year later, with Octavian's troops entering Alexandria, Antony committed suicide, followed soon after by Cleopatra, who refused to be taken captive.

of an idealized rustic life filled with love, music, and poetry, while at the same time alluding to real events and people in Virgil's time when lands in his own region of Italy were being confiscated from their original owners and handed over as rewards to the military heroes from the wars against Julius Caesar. Virgil's own lands were expropriated and eventually returned to him, presumably due to the influence of several important people he names in the poems. The idealized rural scenes of *The Eclogues,* then, offer a stark contrast to the contested lands of his own Cisalpine Gaul; sometimes invoking the mythical Greek land of Arcadia, a rural paradise, the countryside in the poems is also a contrast to Rome, the seat of strife. After Virgil, the dichotomy between the country and the city would become an important motif in poetry and art throughout Europe, especially in the revival of pastoral and **GEORGIC POETRY** during and after the Renaissance, when people began to crowd into urban areas, creating a nostalgia for the supposedly quiet and peaceful life of the country. The celebrated *Fourth Eclogue,* which predicts the coming of a new age of peace and justice signaled by the birth of a divinely gifted child, was thought by later Christian interpreters to have heralded the coming of Christ.

As someone who had grown up in the country, Virgil was well aware of the importance of the rural countryside, not only as a scene for poetic idylls but also as a place of labor and production. From about 36 to 29 B.C.E., he worked on *The Georgics,* a didactic poem in four books that has often been described as a handbook for farmers. Modeled in part on ***Works and Days*** by the eighth-century Greek poet Hesiod, *Georgics* offers a vision of the importance of agriculture and the quiet nobility of country life. While its poems focus minutely on horticulture, animal husbandry, and beekeeping, they also celebrate, without sentimentality, human labor in general, including the arts of war, statesmanship, and poetry; more problematically today than in Virgil's time, they also praise human dominion over nature. *The Georgics,* which celebrates the civilizing potential of human labor, anticipates the great theme of *The Aeneid:* the founding of cities and the birth of the Roman Empire.

p. 272

***The Aeneid* — Style.** Just as *The Eclogues* and *The Georgics* revitalized and innovated the genres of pastoral and georgic poetry, *The Aeneid* announced a new advance in the long tradition of epic poetry. Virgil looked to Homer's *Iliad* and *Odyssey* for his epic poem that commemorates even as it invents and embellishes the mythic and historical origins of Rome. Written in dactylic hexameters like his previous two works, Virgil's twelve-book *Aeneid* consists of nearly ten thousand lines in the original Latin. This verse form, consisting of six-foot lines of mixed dactyls (a long followed by two short syllables: – ⏑ ⏑) and spondees (two long syllables: – –), the traditional metrical form for Greek and Latin epic poetry, can be seen in the first two lines of Virgil's poem:

Arma virumque cano, Troiae qui primus ab oris
Italiam, fato profugus, Laviniaque venit
(My song is of arms and a man, the first of Troy
to come to Italy and Lavinian shores.)

As many scholars have pointed out, Virgil masterfully exploits the hexameter line, making it supple and varied, playing the rhythms of spoken Latin against the formal demands of the meter. Moreover, in contrast to previous Latin epics, the most notable of which is the *Annales* by Ennius (239–169 B.C.E.), *The Aeneid* uses colloquial, even playful, diction, and combinations of words that would have sounded novel to Virgil's contemporaries. Virgil made innovations in the epic devices of oral poetry found in Homer's works—the epithets, epic similes, repetitions, and catalogs—and exploited the possibilities of written language to produce what some call a "literary epic"—a work of great subtlety and a high degree of self-conscious artistry. Some critics think of Homer as the poet of nature, unselfconsciously holding a mirror up to life, and Virgil as the poet of civilization, reflecting upon his world with a critical eye.

But the word *pietas* with Virgil has much wider associations of meaning: it implies an attitude towards the individual, towards the family, towards the region, and towards the imperial destiny of Rome. And finally Aeneas is "pious" also in his respect towards the gods, and in his punctilious observance of rites and offerings. It is an attitude towards all these things, and therefore implies a unity and an order among them: it is in fact an attitude towards life.

– T. S. ELIOT, poet, 1943

***The Aeneid* — Structure and Content.** *The Aeneid* divides rather neatly into two halves of six books each: The first half, self-consciously rooted in *The Odyssey,* tells the story of the legendary flight of Aeneas, son of Anchises, from the doomed city of Troy and his eventual arrival on the shores of Latium, in what would become Italy; the second half, self-consciously rooted in *The Iliad,* tells of the war between the Trojan exiles led by Aeneas and the people of Latium led by the formidable Turnus. While *The Iliad* and *The Odyssey* describe the fall of Troy and the return home of an Achaean war hero, Odysseus, *The Aeneid* describes the journey of Aeneas away from the fallen city of Troy and the founding of new cities—Alba Longa, the first capital of the Latins, and Rome, founded many generations later by Romulus, a descendant of Aeneas. In linking the founding of Rome to the fall of Troy, Virgil was working a prevailing myth that the Romans were descended from the Trojans into his national epic. Furthermore, he links Aeneas to Octavian, who was named Augustus Caesar in 27 B.C.E., about two years after Virgil began writing *The Aeneid.* Virgil had already lavished praise on Octavian in *The Georgics,* which in several digressions tracks Octavian's rise to power and praises him as the champion of Roman unity and peace. Combining the martial prowess of Achilles with the keen intelligence and foresight of Odysseus, Virgil's Aeneas exhibits the strengths of a warrior-statesman like Octavian, a powerful general and an astute politician. Yet Aeneas is not Octavian, and *The Aeneid* is not merely a historical epic; in its broad scope, its depth of feeling, and its recognition of and emphasis on the heavy costs of selfless devotion to a cause, however noble, *The Aeneid* is one of the world's great tragedies—a tragicomedy, really, depicting the great suffering and sacrifice that accompany a great accomplishment.

***The Aeneid* — The Story of Aeneas.** Books 1 through 4 and Book 6 were chosen to represent Virgil's epic poem in this anthology. The poet's invocation in Book 1 finds him singing of "arms and a man," acts of war and the career of Aeneas, whose destiny brings him to the shores of Italy to found Lavinium. The poet puts the question immediately: Why must this prince, famed for his goodness, have to suffer so much to accomplish his goal? The opening lines thus brilliantly set the stage for the great themes

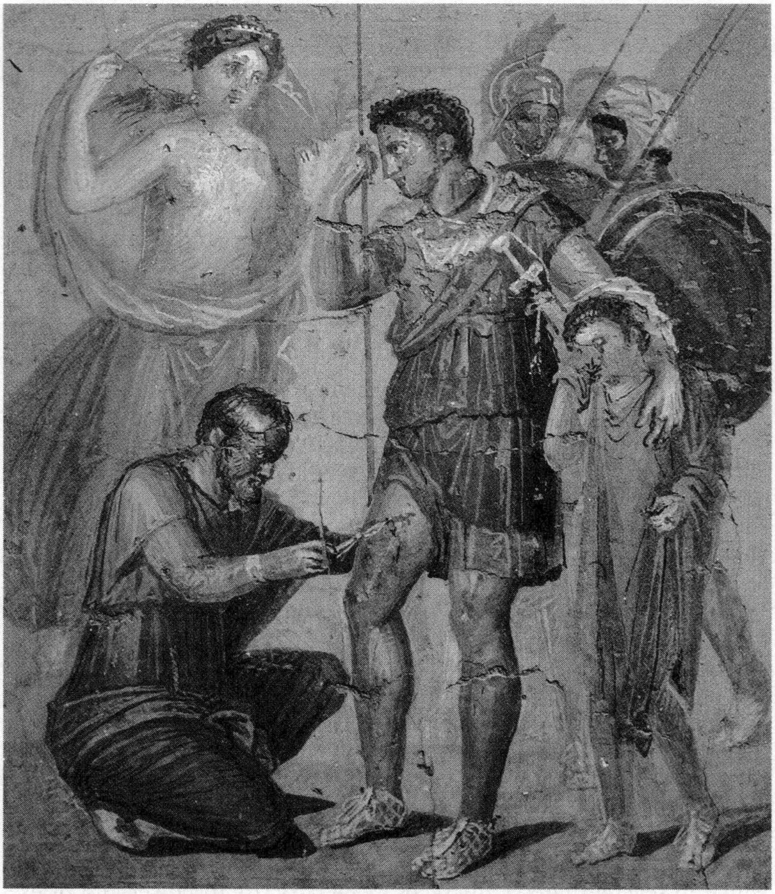

Aeneas Wounded, first century
A fresco from Pompeii illustrates a scene from Virgil's Aeneid. (The Art Archive / Archaeological Museum, Naples / Dagli Orti)

of the work: Aeneas's destiny, his moral virtue, and the suffering he must endure.

That suffering comes about in part because Aeneas is destined to subordinate even his most profound and passionate desires to the higher goods of family, state, and religion. Through the character of Aeneas, Virgil explores one of the principal Roman virtues, *pietas,* which comprises the concepts of piety, public virtue, and duty. Aeneas must set aside all that is dear to him in the world—including the great passion of his life, his love for Dido, queen of Carthage—in order to follow the single purpose of the founding of Lavinium, the ancient site and first city of Roman civilization. The modernist poet and critic T. S. Eliot (1888–1965) sums up the range of associations of *pietas* in *The Aeneid:* "[*Pietas*] implies an attitude towards the individual, towards the family, towards the region, and towards the imperial destiny of Rome [and towards the gods]. . . . It is an attitude towards all these things, and therefore implies a unity and an order among them: it is in fact an attitude towards life." The expression of sorrow and loss for which Virgil's epic has been celebrated, manifest from the very beginning of the poem, when the sacking of Troy is told from the perspective of the defeated, results in part from the stern dictates of *pietas,* which move the sometimes reluctant Aeneas toward his goal. The hero's only comfort is the confident vision he receives from his father, **Anchises**, who in Book 6 shows Aeneas the future glory of Rome. ang-KIGH-zeez

The story begins when the Trojans, under Aeneas, sail from Sicily to Italy on what appears to be the last leg of their fateful journey. Because of the goddess Juno's wrath, however, they encounter a storm at sea and are forced to land on the northern tip of Africa. Aeneas, battered by the storm, meets Queen Dido, who has recently led her people out of tribulation to this same shore to found the city of Carthage. Through a trick of the gods, Dido is made to fall in love with Aeneas. In Books 2 and 3, Aeneas tells Dido and her companions of his adventures, some of which follow those of Odysseus, from the fall of Troy to his landing at Carthage. Hearing of his exploits while under the magical spell, Dido loves him all the more.

Dido is at the center of the action in Book 4. After she and Aeneas fall in love, both slacken in their duties. Dido, herself the builder of a great city and a powerful, even visionary, leader, roams Carthage like a stricken deer, wounded by love and careless of her commitment to her subjects. Aeneas too deviates from his responsibilities, forcing Jove to send his messenger Mercury to remind him of his great charge. When Aeneas regains his determination to continue his voyage and sails away, Dido commits suicide. The poet reminds all that ever since then there has been enmity between Rome and Carthage.

In Book 6 Aeneas lands at Cumae, the home of the prophetic Sibyl, from whom he learns how to enter Hades, the land of the dead. In Hades he meets those who have helped him along the way, including Dido and his father, from whom he receives the vision of Rome's future. In the moving scene when Aeneas meets Dido, he attempts to console her by assuring her that his love was genuine; she turns from him, her eyes to the ground, and vanishes into the darkness where she joins the shade of her first husband, **Sychaeus**. In this heartrending moment, Virgil dramatizes the dual desires of personal fulfillment and public duty, the relationship between private suffering and—as seen in his father's vision—public joy. When Aeneas meets Anchises, the ghost of his father shows him a long line of Roman heroes as yet unborn, from Sylvius, founder of Alba Longa, and Romulus, founder of Rome, to Augustus Caesar. Moreover, Anchises tells him that the principal art of the Romans is the rule of nations and the business of peace. With this vision firmly planted in his mind and his ambition and commitment to his destiny restored, Aeneas returns to his ships to renew his fateful voyage. Thus, Book 6 does not simply conclude the story of Aeneas and Dido by showing Aeneas's intense suffering over the loss of his love, but begins a new story of the hero's reward for his suffering: the magnificence of Rome under the rule of Augustus Caesar. *Pietas* has won the day, but the price of great achievement, Virgil suggests, may well be the subordination of personal desires

sih-KEE-us

and immediate attachments to friends and family in pursuit of larger, more public goals.

■ CONNECTIONS

The Book of Exodus, p. 162. Virgil's *Aeneid* is an epic about the founding of a nation. Aeneas must undertake a journey from the ruins of Troy to strange lands where he faces numerous trials and doubts before he finally sets foot on the land that has been shown to him in a vision. Similarly, in Exodus, Moses leads his people from captivity in Egypt through the arid wilderness, where they meet with trials and doubt, and finally to the Promised Land. Compare Moses and Aeneas as heroes whose destiny involves the founding or affirmation of nations and national identities.

Homer, *The Odyssey,* p. 421; Euripides, *Medea,* p. 1004; Kalidasa, *Shakuntala* (Book 2). One of the most celebrated tragic love stories in Western literature is that of Dido and Aeneas. Depicted as a woman who threatens Aeneas's heroic duty, Dido takes her place among other female figures such as Nausicaa or Circe in *The Odyssey* and Medea in Euripides' play of the same name. Similarly, Kalidasa's *Shakuntala* tells the story of a king who marries a forest girl then leaves her behind, subordinating his love for her to his sovereign duties. How do these stories depict the relationship between duty—especially the duty of males—and private life or love? How are they different?

***The Descent of Inanna,* p. 28; Homer, *The Odyssey,* p. 421; Dante, *The Inferno* (Book 2).** Among the heroic feats undertaken by epic heroes such as Inanna, Odysseus, and Aeneas, none is perhaps more important than the dangerous but self-affirming journey to the underworld. In creating the elaborate structure of the underworld in *The Divine Comedy,* Dante drew on Virgil's *Aeneid.* Compare the underworlds of these various texts. What do they say about the cultural backgrounds of their writers?

■ FURTHER RESEARCH

Anderson, W. S. *The Art of the* Aeneid. 1969.
Bloom, Harold, ed. *Modern Critical Interpretations of the Aeneid.* 1987.
Camps, W. A. *An Introduction to Virgil's* Aeneid. 1969.
Grandsen, K. W. *Virgil, the Aeneid.* 1990.
Griffin, Jasper. *Virgil.* 1986.
Horsfall, Nicholas, ed. *A Companion to the Study of Virgil.* 2000.
Johnson, W. R. *Darkness Visible: A Study of Virgil's* Aeneid. 1976.
Lyne, R. O. A. M. *Further Voices in Virgil's* Aeneid. 1987.
Otis, Brooks. *Virgil: A Study in Civilized Poetry.* 1963, 1985.

■ PRONUNCIATION

Aeneas: uh-NEE-us
Anchises: ang-KIGH-zeez, -seez
Andromache: an-DRAH-muh-kee
Danaans: duh-NAY-unz
Deiphobus: dee-IF-oh-bus, -uh-bus
Dido: DIGH-doh
Dionysus: digh-uh-NIGH-sus
Hecate: HEK-uh-tee
Peneleus: pih-NEE-lee-us
Pirithous: pih-RITH-oos
Sychaeus: sih-KEE-us

FROM

The Aeneid

Translated by Frank O. Copley

Book 1
[Arriving in Carthage]

My song is arms and a man,[1] the first of Troy
to come to Italy and Lavinian shores,[2]
a fated fugitive, harried on land and sea
by heaven's huge might and Juno's endless hate,[3]
pommeled by wars, till he could found the City

The Aeneid. Virgil began writing this epic in about 29 B.C.E., shortly after completing work on *The Georgics.* The poem remained unfinished at his death ten years later, and in his last days he had requested that the poem be destroyed. At the intervention of Augustus Caesar himself, the poem was saved. The poet and playwright Varius Rufus saw the work through to publication. The Romans immediately praised *The Aeneid* as one of the greatest works of all Latin literature, and its reputation only grew in time. Its influence on Western literature and art has been immense.

As mentioned in the headnote to Virgil, *The Aeneid* divides thematically into two parts: Books 1 through 6 describe the wanderings of Aeneas; Books 7 through 12 tell of the battles between Aeneas and Turnus over Latium, or Italy. Here, parts of Books 1 through 4 and Book 6 are presented; Book 5, which primarily describes the athletic contests held on the island of Sicily in honor of Anchises, Aeneas's father, who had died there before Aeneas reached Carthage, has been left out. Book 1 describes the wrath of Juno, who took sides with the Achaeans during the war against Troy. In her anger Juno sends a storm to batter Aeneas's ships, and the hero finds refuge on the shores of Carthage, Dido's home. In Books 2 and 3, Aeneas, now a guest of the widow Dido, tells of the fall of Troy, his flight from the city, and his hazardous journey across the seas. In these books Aeneas also describes how he has learned of his destiny to play a role in the founding of a new city. Book 4 focuses on the love between Dido and Aeneas and its tragic consequences; this book also addresses the struggle between duty and desire that both Dido and Aeneas experience. Finally, Book 6 recounts Aeneas's descent into the underworld, where he, like Odysseus, meets people from his past, including Dido and Anchises. Intensifying the conflict between duty and desire, these two meetings in particular heighten Aeneas's intense personal suffering as well as his awareness of great public good.

---

[1] **a man:** Aeneas, the son of Anchises, king of Dardania, and Venus, the goddess of love; Aeneas was a member of the royal house of Troy. Anchises' uncle was Laomedon, a king of Troy, and the Dardanians were allies of the Trojans in the war against the Greeks.

[2] **Lavinian shores:** Refers to Lavinium, a city just south of Rome named after the daughter of King Latinus, Lavinia, who marries Aeneas after he arrives in Latium, the southwestern coastal plain of Italy settled by the exiled Trojans.

[3] **Juno's . . . hate:** Known as Hera in Greek mythology, Juno is the queen of the gods and the wife of Jove. Because the Trojan prince Paris praised Venus's (Aphrodite's) beauty above hers, Juno bitterly resented the Trojans and aided their enemies.

and bring his gods to Latium, whence the race
of Latins, our Alban[4] sires, and towering Rome.

Muse, tell me the causes: how was godhead wronged,
how injured the queen of heaven that she must force
through many a fall of fate and many a toil
that great, good man: can heaven hold such ill will?

A city once stood, a colony of Tyre,
Carthage,[5] across from Italy and far
from Tiber's mouth,[6] rich and agog for war,
a spot that Juno loved more than all worlds,
more even than Samos:[7] here stood her arms and here
her chariot; throne of mankind it was to be
if Fate allowed; this was her cherished aim.
But men would spring of Trojan blood, she'd heard,
and some day lay her Carthage in the dust—
a race of world-wide kings, whose pride was war
and death for Libya: so ran the thread of Fate.

This she feared, remembering, too, that war
when first she fought for her dear Greece at Troy.
Still she recalled the anger and the pain
that sent her there: deep in her heart lay stored
the judgment of Paris,[8] the insult to her beauty,
a hated people, a Ganymede[9] raped to heaven.
Her anger flared; she drove all over the deep
the Trojan few that Achilles and Greece had spared,
and kept them far from Latium; year on year

[4] **Alban:** Refers to Alba Longa, the city founded by Aeneas's son Ascanius and the home of Romulus, the legendary founder of Rome.

[5] **Tyre, Carthage:** Tyre, a city on the coast of Syria (Lebanon), was home to the Phoenicians; Carthage, settled by Phoenician colonists, is a city on the northern coast of Africa near today's Tunis. Carthage was a traditional enemy of Rome against whom Rome fought a succession of three wars known as the Punic Wars (264–241, 218–201, and 149–146 B.C.E.). Carthage is associated in Virgil's epic with Libya and the Libyan people, natives of the land in which Dido and her Phoenicians have settled.

[6] **Tiber's mouth:** The Tiber, or Tiberus, is a river that flows through Rome; it was at the mouth of the Tiber that the Trojan exiles landed when they arrived in Latium.

[7] **Samos:** An Aegean island known for its worship of Juno (Hera).

[8] **judgment of Paris:** Paris was the son of King Priam of Troy; when Paris judged Juno's beauty to be inferior to that of Aphrodite (Venus), the insulted Juno turned her wrath against the Trojans. Paris's judgment had been influenced by Aphrodite's promise that she would grant him the love of the beautiful Helen, the wife of King Menelaus of Sparta. Paris's abduction of Helen precipitated the Trojan War.

[9] **Ganymede:** A Trojan youth whose beauty won the favor of Jupiter (Zeus), who appointed him to be the cupbearer to the gods, a position held by Juno's daughter Hebe.

they wandered, dogged by Fate, across the seas.
Such matter it was to found our Roman race. [. . .]

[In the section omitted here from the text, the goddess Juno, who is hostile to Aeneas and the Trojans, persuades Aeolus, the god of the winds, to visit a storm upon Aeneas's fleet. Seeing the devastation that ensues, Neptune, the god of the sea, calms the waters, but not before many ships have been wrecked. With seven surviving ships, Aeneas puts in at a harbor on the coast of Libya, the land of the great city of Carthage, ruled by Dido. As Aeneas and his crew rest and ponder their fate, his mother, the goddess Venus, appeals on his behalf to Jove, who assures Venus that her son will prevail in his quest to sail to Italy and found a great city and nation. As the text picks up the story again, Jove has just sent the messenger Mercury to ensure that the people of Carthage, the Tyrians, will give Aeneas a friendly welcome and Aeneas ventures forth.]

Faithful Aeneas lay thinking all night long,
determined, soon as daylight came, to search
this unfamiliar land: Where had the wind
brought him? Who lived here? man? (he saw no homes)
or beast? He must find out and tell his men!
In a wooded cave beneath an overhang
he hid his ships where they were screened by trees
above and behind. Then with one friend, Achates,[10]
he went forth, clasping in each hand a spear.
Out in the woods his mother came to meet him.
She seemed a girl; her face and garb were those
of a Spartan maid or Thracian Harpalyce[11]
whipping her horses to outrun Hebrus' current.
Over her shoulder a bow hung ready to hand;
her hair lay loose and scattered by the wind,
her flowing gown belted to bare her knee.
She hailed the men: "Tell me, sirs, have you seen
one of my sisters wandering down this way?
She'd have a quiver and spotted lynx-hide cape;
perhaps she was hot on the trail of a foam-flecked boar."

So Venus; and Venus' son replied to her:
"None of your sisters have I seen or heard,
O—what shall I call you? That's no mortal face,
that voice no girl's. You are a goddess, sure!
Sister of Phoebus?[12] One of the Nymphs' descent?

[10] **Achates:** Achates, as will become evident, is Aeneas's most "faithful friend."

[11] **Thracian Harpalyce:** Harpalyce was a legendary huntress and warrior princess from Thrace, a region in the northwest of Greece. What is crucial here is that Venus appears to her son in disguise, one of the many sources of sadness for the hero. Hebrus, in the next line, is one of the chief rivers of Thrace.

[12] **Sister of Phoebus:** Phoebus Apollo, the brother of Venus (Aphrodite); the epithet means "bright" or "shining."

Blessed be your name, whatever it is! But help us!
What land is this? On what coasts of the world
have we been tossed? Tell us, for we are lost.
Vast waves and winds have sent us hapless here.
We'll offer prayer and rich blood-sacrifice!"

Then Venus: "I am not worthy of such honor.
We girls of Tyre by custom bear the bow
and lace the scarlet boot high on the leg.
This land is Punic; of Tyre, our city and name;
around us are Libyans, people untamed by war.
Our queen is Dido; she left the city of Tyre
to escape her brother — a long and tortured tale
of cruel deception. Hear while I tell it briefly.
Her husband, Sychaeus, held the richest lands
in all Phoenicia; he was the man she loved,
her first, to whom her father gave her, a bride,
a virgin. But her brother, the king of Tyre,
Pygmalion,[13] had no peer in monstrous crime.
The two men quarreled; blind for love of wealth
Pygmalion murdered Sychaeus at the altar,
catching him off his guard; his sister's love
left him unmoved. He kept the deed long hidden
and cheated the heartsick girl with empty hopes.
But as she slept, her husband's unlaid ghost
came to her, showing a face all strange and pale.
He told of the murder, bared his wounded breast,
and brought the whole foul story to the light.
'Hurry! Run! Leave your fatherland!' he urged,
'and for your help, look, here a treasure buried —
silver and gold, more than you ever knew!'
His words led Dido to prepare for flight.
She brought together those who loathed the tyrant
or feared him. Ships, it happened, stood complete;
they seized them, put the treasure aboard. To sea
went greedy Pygmalion's gold. A woman led them!
They came to the place where you shall see the walls
huge rising and the towers of Carthage-town.
Here they bought land — 'as much as one bull's hide
enclosed' — for this is the place called 'The Purse.'
But who are you? From what coasts have you come?

[13] **Pygmalion:** Pygmalion, Dido's brother, was a king of Tyre. (He is not the Pygmalion, king of Cyprus, who fashions his ideal image of a woman into a statue that is given life by Venus, as told in Ovid's *Metamorphoses.*)

Where are you going?" Aeneas at these words
heaved a deep sigh and drew speech from his heart:
"My lady, if I began with first-beginnings,
and you were free to hear our tale of toil,
day would lie locked in heaven before the end!
We are from ancient Troy—if to your ears has come
the name of Troy?—We'd traveled many a sea
when storms by sheer chance drove us to Libyan shores.
I am Aeneas the good; the gods I saved
ride in my ships. My name is known in heaven.
My goal is Italy, land of my fathers' line.
With twice ten ships I put to sea from Troy
to follow the path my goddess-mother showed me;
just seven, battered by wind and wave, remain.
I walk these Libyan wastes a helpless stranger
exiled by East and West." Venus could bear
no more, but spoke to end his sad account:

"Whoever you are, the love of heaven saved you
and brought you living to this Tyrian land.
Go now, and make your way to Dido's court.
Your men are safe, and changing winds have blown
your ships to safety. This I can tell you now,
unless I was taught to read the birds all wrong.
See there: twelve swans flying in joyful ranks;
Jove's eagle, swooping down from open sky
frightened and scattered them; now with lines new-formed
they've settled to earth or hover over the land.
As they in safety flapped their whistling wings
or soared in a flock to wreathe the sky with song,
just so your ships and men have come to port
or under full sail have reached the harbor's mouth.
Go now, and let this pathway guide your steps."

She turned to leave; a glow of light shone out
behind her head; her hair sent forth perfume
ambrosial; she let her train fall full-length down,
and walked in majesty divine! He knew
his mother, and as she hastened off he cried,
"What? Your son? Again so heartless to mock him—
you, too—with empty shows? Why was your hand
not laid in mine? Why could we not speak true?"
With this reproach he turned toward Dido's town.
But Venus walled the two in lightless air
and clothed them all about in heavy mist

so none could see them and no man had power
to hold them back or question why they came.
Then she flew off to Paphos, and with smiles
came home again, where incense wreathes her shrine
and hundred altars sweet with fresh-plucked blooms.

The two men meanwhile hurried down the path
and soon were climbing the highest hill that hangs
over the town and looks down on its walls.
Aeneas was awed: so vast, where once was camp-ground!
The wonder of gates, and avenues paved, and crowds!
Working like mad, those Tyrians; some at walls,
some toiled at forts, surveying, or hauling stone;
some marked out homesites and drew boundary lines.
They had their laws, their courts, their councilmen.
Here they were dredging a harbor; there they laid
a theater's undercroft, and cut tall columns
out of a quarry cliff to adorn the stage.
Like bees in June out in the blooming fields
busy beneath the sun, some teasing out
the new young workers, others pressing down
clear honey or making nectar burst the cells,
still others taking the loads brought in, while others
police the hive and drive off lazy drones:
the work hums on; the combs are sweet with thyme.
"O blessed by Fate! Your walls are building now!"
Aeneas said, as he watched the ramparts rise.
Walled in the cloud (a miracle!), he walked
among the workmen, and no one saw him come.

In mid-town was a pleasant, shady park,
marking the spot where Tyrians, tempest-tossed,
had dug to find, as Juno had foretold,
a horse's head—a sign that they should be
great soldiers and good farmers down the years.
Here Dido of Sidon built a temple to Juno
a huge vault filled with wealth and holiness.
Above its steps the doorway was of bronze,
the beams bronze-nailed, the doors and hinges brazen.
Here in the park Aeneas saw a sight
that eased his fears and made him first dare hope
for safety, and take heart for all his troubles.
As he searched over the temple, stone by stone,
awaiting the queen, and wondering how this town
had come to be, amazed at the workmen's zeal

and skill, he saw, scene after scene, the war
at Troy, battles now famed through all the world:
the Atrides, Priam, and, savage to both, Achilles.[14]
His tears welled up. "What place, Achates, now,"
he said, "what land does not know all we suffered?
See: Priam! Here too the brave have their reward!
The world has tears; man's lot does touch the heart.
Put off your fears: our story will save us yet!"
Aeneas spoke, and let this empty show
nourish his grief and flood his face with tears.
He saw how men had fought the fight for Troy:
here Greeks retreating, here Trojans pressing hard,
here their allies, here plumed Achilles' car.
Nearby were Rhesus'[15] snowy-canvassed tents—
(he knew them and wept!) his men, just fallen to sleep,
betrayed and butchered by bloody Diomede;
gone, too, his fiery team before they knew
the taste of Trojan feed or Xanthus' waters.
And here was Troilus,[16] running, his weapons lost
(poor boy! he was no man to meet Achilles!),
his horses pulled him clinging to his car,
still gripping the reins; his head and shoulders dragged
over the ground; his spear wrote in the dust.
And here the women of Troy in sad parade
were bringing the robe to cruel Athena's temple
with humble prayer, beating their breasts in grief:
with stony eyes the goddess stared them down.
And there Achilles peddled the lifeless corpse
of Hector, dragged three times around Troy-walls.
Aeneas could not hold back a cry of pain
to see the car, the ransom, his dead friend,
and Priam stretching out defenseless hands.
He saw himself, surrounded by great Greeks,
and Memnon the Moor,[17] with his Arabian troops.
And leading her crescent-shielded Amazons
Penthesilea[18] fought madly amid the host.

The Trojans would save the Aeneas

[14] **Atrides . . . Achilles:** The Atrides (Atreides) are the brothers Menelaus and Agamemnon who joined forces against the Trojans after the Trojan prince Paris abducted Menelaus's wife, Helen. Achilles, the principal hero of the Achaeans, is "savage to both [sides]" because he holds a grudge against Agamemnon, leader of the Achaean forces. [15] **Rhesus:** A Thracian king allied with the Trojans; it was said that if Rhesus's horses would taste "Trojan feed" or drink from the waters of the river Xanthus, Troy would not fall. As described here, Diomede and Odysseus drag the horses away before they can do so. [16] **Troilus:** One of King Priam's sons who was killed by Achilles. [17] **Memnon the Moor:** An Ethiopian king allied with the Trojans. [18] **Penthesilea:** The queen of the Amazons who supported the Trojans in the war; she was killed by Achilles.

One breast lay bare above the sword-belt clasp—
a warrior-maiden who dared to fight with men.

As Aeneas of Troy stood marveling at these sights,
unable to speak or turn his eyes away,
into the temple came Dido the beautiful,
the queen, with all her bodyguard around her.
As by Eurotas or on the height of Cynthus[19]
Diana leads her dancing mountain-maids,
a thousand ringed about her; there she goes
quiver on back, head-high above them all
(no word betrays her mother's heartfelt joy)—
just so was Dido, and just so her joy
to see her people working, building, planning.
She entered the temple; under its central dome
she took her place enthroned, walled by armed men.
There she sat judging, framing laws, assigning
work to her men by fair shares or by lot,
when all at once a crowd came rushing in.
Aeneas saw they had Sergestus, Antheus,
Cloanthus, and others whom the storm at sea
had scattered and carried away to distant shores.
Aeneas was speechless; Achates was struck hard
by joy and fear at once: they were afire
to greet their friends—but still, what did this mean?
Pretending calm, clothed in their cloud, they watched.
What had these men endured? Where were their ships?
Why were they here? Each ship had sent her man
to beg for mercy. Pleading, the group moved on.

Once they had entered and gained the right to speak,
Ilioneus, the oldest, pled in peace:
"My lady, Jove has let you found your city
and bring both right and rule to savage tribes.
We're Trojans, helpless, blasted by wind and wave.
We beg you: do us no wrong, nor burn our ships.
Spare a good people! Be merciful! Hear our plea!
We have not come in arms to scorch the earth
of Libya, to plunder your homes and load our ships.
The vanquished have no heart for such presumption.

[19] **Eurotas . . . Cynthus:** Eurotas is a river running near Sparta where Diana (Artemis in Greek mythology), the goddess of the hunt and guardian of animals and birth, was worshiped. Cynthus is a mountain in Delos, where Diana was born.

There is a place called 'Westland'[20] by the Greeks,
an ancient country, powerful, warlike, rich;
the Oenotri[21] settled it; now, we hear, their sons
are calling it 'Italy' for their founder's name.[22]
This was our goal.
But all of a sudden waves and rain and wind
drove us on unseen banks; squalls from the south
scattered our ships. Some sank; some hung on reefs
uncharted. We few swam here to your shores.
What kind of people are you? Civilized?
What laws are these? We have been kept from shore,
forbidden to land, and met with shows of force.
If men and mortal arms arouse your scorn,
be sure the gods take note of right and wrong.
Aeneas was our chief; he had no peer
in justice, goodness, and the arts of war.
If fate has saved him, if he lives and breathes,
and has not fallen to rest in heartless dark,
we have no fears. However great your kindness,
you'll not regret it. In Sicily, we have towns
and arms, for Acestes[23] boasts his Trojan blood.
We're badly damaged: let us beach our craft,
shape timbers in your woods, and strip out oars;
then if we find our friends and chief, we'll sail
for Italy, Latium—Italy with a will!
But if it's finished, if our well-loved lord
is lost at sea, and hope of Iulus[24] gone,
then let us cross to Sicily, whence we came.
Acestes will take us; he shall be our king."
Thus spoke Ilioneus; with one great shout
the sons of Troy assented.

Then with a gracious nod, Queen Dido answered:
"Put fear from your hearts, Trojans; dismiss your cares.
Our lot is hard, our kingdom new; for this
our laws are stern, our whole land under guard.
Who knows not Troy, knows not Aeneas' people,

[20] **'Westland':** Hesperia, the land of Evening or the West Land, was what the Greeks called Italy, which lay to their west. [21] **the Oenotri:** The original inhabitants of southern Italy. [22] **their founder's name:** Italus, the legendary father of Italy. [23] **Acestes:** A king of Sicily whose mother was from Troy; he offered the Trojans refuge in his lands on their journey. [24] **Iulus:** Also called Ascanius, Iulus is the son of Aeneas and Creusa. He represents the hope of the future in that he succeeds his father as the ruler of Lavinium, the first city established by the Trojans in Latium, and also founds Alba Longa. In Iulus, Virgil establishes the origin of the Julian emperors of Rome, including Julius Caesar and Augustus.

those brave fighters, and that great holocaust?
We Punic folk are not so dull of heart;
the sun starts not his course so far from Tyre.
You're bound for the Westland, Saturn's wide domain?
or Sicily, and Acestes for your king?
I'll help you, keep you safe, and send you on.
Or will you settle here and share my realm?
The city I build is yours: pull up your ships.
Trojan, Tyrian, all shall be one to me.
If only that same storm had forced your chief,
Aeneas, here too! I'll send out men to search
the shores and all the ends of Libyan land:
he may be safe, but in some backwood lost."

Her words set hearts a-beating in Achates
the brave and Lord Aeneas; they longed to burst
their cloud. Achates first was moved to speak:
"My lord, what thought arises in your heart?
Here we are safe; our ships and men are found.
One only is missing, but far at sea we saw
him drowned. The rest is as your mother told us."
Scarce had he spoken when their veiling cloud
burst all at once and turned to clearest air.
There stood Aeneas, splendid in bright light,
grand as a god, for Venus breathed on him
to give him strength and vigor, the glow of youth,
and made his eyes shine out with power and joy—
like ivory carved to beauty, like some work
of silver or Parian marble[25] chased with gold.
His presence and his words burst on the queen
and all her men: "You want me? Here I am,
Aeneas the Trojan, saved from Libyan seas.
You pitied, you only, the terrible toil of Troy.
We few that Greece had left on land and sea
have suffered every blow, lost everything,
yet you would share your city, your home, with us!
My lady, how can we thank you, we and all
the sons of Troy, now scattered across the earth?
Oh, if the gods note goodness, if there are
such things as justice and hearts that know the right,
you shall be richly blessed. What happy year
bore you? What noble parents got you so?

[25] **Parian marble:** A kind of marble noted for its particular beauty and found on the island of Paros.

While rivers run to sea, while shadows cross
the curving hills and fires feed the stars,
your name will live in honor and in praise
wherever the world may call me." With these words
he turned to greet Ilioneus, Serestus,
and the others, Gyas the brave, and brave Cloanthus.

Dido of Tyre, struck speechless at the sight
and at the man's misfortune, spoke at last:
"What happened, my lord? What ill luck dogged you here?
What dangers forced you onto rock and reef?
Are you Aeneas of Troy, Anchises' son?
Whom Venus in Phrygia bore by Simois' wave?
Yes! I remember! Teucer[26] came to Tyre
driven from Salamis, searching for new realms:
'Would Belus help?' (Belus—my father—was then
reducing fertile Cyprus to his power.)
And since that time I've known the tale of Troy,
the city, your name, and all the Argive kings.
Teucer, who fought the Teucri, praised them high,
and loved to claim descent from Teucrian stock.[27]
Enter my home! My welcome to you all!
My fate, like yours, has harried me through great toil
and trouble, at last to place me in this land.
By evil schooled, I know what mercy means."

With that she led Aeneas to her palace
and called for prayers of thanks to all the gods.
Nor did she forget his men: down to the beach
she sent off twenty steers, a hundred hogs
(fat tuskers all), a hundred lambs and ewes,
and wine, god's gift of joy.
In the great hall splendor to ease a king
was set out, and a banquet was prepared;
the cloths were royal red, embroidered fine;
on tables massive plate, and golden cups

[26] **Teucer:** The half brother of Telamon Ajax, Teucer was a Greek warrior who was banished from his home because he did not bring Ajax back with him from the Trojan War; in his exile he founded Salamis on the island of Cyprus. He was the first to bring Dido news of the Trojan War. (Not to be confused with Teucer, the founder of Troy; see note 27.)

[27] **Teucrian stock:** Dido is here playing on names, for the legendary founder of Troy was also named Teucer, whose descendants, the Trojans, were sometimes called "Teucri." Dido is speaking directly of Teucer, the Greek warrior. (See note 26.)

chased with historic scenes, the long, long line
of deeds heroic since the race began.

Aeneas, whose father-heart could not rest easy,
dispatched Achates to the ships, to tell
Ascanius[28] the news and bring him back;
his every thought was for the son he loved.
"We need gifts, too," he said. "Bring what we saved
when Ilium[29] fell—that coat all worked in gold,
the scarf bordered with yellow acanthus leaves
that Argive Helen[30] wore, brought from Mycenae
when she set sail for Troy and wedded bliss
unlawful—they were her mother Leda's[31] gifts;
yes, and the staff Ilione used to bear—
oldest of Priam's daughters—and her chain
of beads, her golden coronet, thick with gems."
Achates ran to the ships to speed compliance.

But Venus had new schemes at heart, new plans
devised: Cupid should change his face and form
and take Ascanius' place, to set the queen
afire with love and wrap her heart in flames.
(Who could have faith in Tyre, the double-tongued?
Who could sleep sound with Juno on the rage?)
And so to winged Love she turned and spoke:
"Son, my strength, my power and might, dear son,
who only scorn our father's giant bolt,
help me, I beg you; grant me your godly aid.
Your brother, Aeneas—how on every sea
and strand he has been harried by Juno's hate,
you know, and you have often shared my grief.
Now Punic Dido holds him by her charms
entranced. I fear where Juno's gentleness
may end. Fate hinges here: she'll not be idle.
I shall prevent her schemes and ring the queen
with flames of passion, past all power to change;
love for Aeneas shall bind her to my side.

[28] **Ascanius:** Also called Iulus; Aeneas's son by Creusa. (See note 24.) [29] **Ilium:** Another name for Troy. [30] **Argive Helen:** Helen, the wife of the Argive leader King Menelaus of Sparta. In return for Paris's favorable judgment in a beauty contest between herself, Juno (Hera), and Athena, Venus (Aphrodite) offers Helen as a bribe to the Trojan prince Paris. Paris soon after wins Helen's love and takes her from Sparta to Troy, setting off the Trojan War. [31] **Leda:** The wife of the exiled king of Sparta, Tyndareüs, who lived in Aetolia. From a sexual union with Jove (Zeus), who transformed her into a swan for the purpose, Leda bore Helen, who was hatched from an egg.

How may you help? Hear now what I have planned.
The little prince, my darling, soon will go
to Tyrian town at his dear father's call,
with gifts saved from the sea and flaming Troy.
He'll sleep; I'll hide him sleeping in my shrine
on Mount Cythera or holy Idalium:[32]
he must not know our plan, nor intervene.
You change yourself—for just one night, no more—
to look like him, take his young face for yours:
when Dido smiles and holds you in her arms
(while princes feast and drink their royal wines)
and clasps you close to give a perfumed kiss,
breathe soft on her the poisoned flame of love."
Cupid obeyed his mother's word, stripped off
his wings, and gayly mocked Iulus' stride.
But Venus on Ascanius poured the peace
of sleep and took him cradled in her arms
to Mount Idalium, where soft marjoram
with blossoms breathing nectar wrapped him round.

Obeying his mother, Cupid carried gifts
to the Tyrians, happy to walk with good Achates.
When he arrived, Dido had found her place,
her golden couch, all hung with royal red;
then Lord Aeneas, and then the men of Troy
came in and took their seats on purpled thrones.
Slaves brought water for washing, put out bread
in baskets, and offered soft and fleecy napkins.
In kitchen fifty maids prepared the food,
each dish in order, and kept the hearth-fires bright;
a hundred others, paired with men to match,
waited on table and set the wine cups out.
The Tyrians came, too, crowding through the doors
to take their places and make holiday.
They admired Aeneas' gifts, admired Iulus
(his glow was a god's, his charming speech a show)
and the coat and scarf with yellow acanthus leaves.
Above all, the Punic queen, already doomed
to suffer much, looked and could not be filled;
both gifts and lad alike stirred up the flames.
The boy, his arms around Aeneas' neck,

[32] **Mount Cythera . . . Idalium:** Venus was said to have been born from the sea foam on the island of Cythera, thus associating Mount Cythera with her birth; Idalium was the name of a mountain on Cyprus associated with the worship of Venus.

kissed him and filled him with false-fathered love,
then ran to the queen; she looked and loved, and loved
again, and held him to her, unaware
what power to hurt lay there. He, with a mind
to Venus' orders, gently began to drive
Sychaeus out, and fill with a living love
a heart long unaroused and half forgetful.

As soon as the feasting lulled, they cleared the board,
set out the mixing bowls, and crowned the wine.
The noise of voices rose and filled the hall
to the gilded ceiling where the lamps hung down
alight, and flaming wicks drove out the dark.
Then Dido took her golden jeweled cup
and filled it full — the one that Belus[33] used
and all his children. Silence fell. She prayed:
"Jove, whom we name the god of guest and host,
hallow this day for Tyre and Troy alike,
and bid our children keep its memory fresh!
Bless us, good Juno! Bacchus,[34] give us joy!
Come, Tyrians, join us in our holiday!"
She spoke and poured libation on the table,
then — only then — just wet her lip with wine,
and passed to Bitias: "Drink!" He drained the cup,
wine, froth, and all, down to its golden base,
and handed it on. Iopas struck his lyre
a golden note, as Atlas[35] the great had taught.
He sang the wandering moon, the toiling sun;
whence came mankind and beast, whence rain and fire,
Arcturus, the rain-stars, and the twin Triones,
why the sun hurries to dip below the seas
in winter, and why the nights must limp and lag.
The Tyrians cheered aloud; the Trojans joined them.
And Dido, too, prolonged the night with talk
and to her sorrow drank long draughts of love:
"Tell me of Priam,[36] tell me! And Hector, too!
The son of Dawn — how blazoned was his shield?
Diomede's team — what breed? How tall Achilles? —
No, no, my lord! From the beginning tell

[33] **Belus:** Dido's father and once king of Tyre. [34] **Bacchus:** The god of wine; Dionysus in Greek mythology. [35] **Atlas:** Iopas, the bard, is singing a song about the cosmos. Atlas, the sky-bearing Titan, was the father of the Pleiades and was associated with astronomy. [36] **Priam:** The king of Troy. The next few lines name heroes from the Trojan War, including the great Trojan warrior Hector, the son of Priam and Hecuba, who was killed by Achilles. The "son of Dawn" is Memnon, son of Aurora and Tithonus; he was a Trojan ally also slain by Achilles.

how the Greeks tricked you, how your city fell,
and how you lost your way—full seven years
have seen you wandering over land and sea."

Book 2
[The Fall of Troy]

All talking stopped; all faces turned to watch.
Aeneas looked out on the hall and then began:
"What? Know that sorrow again, my lady? What words
can tell how royal Troy, the throne of tears,
fell to the Greeks? I saw that tragedy
and in it played great part. Who'd tell that tale—
Myrmidon, Thracian, or cruel Ulysses'[37] man—
and keep from tears? Now dewy night is fading
from heaven; the setting stars warn men to sleep.
But if you want so much to learn our fate,
to hear in a word how Troy travailed and died,
though memory makes me shrink and shudder with grief,
I'll try.
    "Broken by war, forced back by fate,
the Argive kings watched year on year slip by,
then built with help of Pallas'[38] holy hand
a horse tall as a mountain, ribbed with pine—
'For a safe trip home,' they said. (The lie spread fast.)
They threw dice for a crew and slipped them in,
locking them deep inside that lightless cave
to fill the monster's womb with men-at-arms.

"Offshore lies Tenedos,[39] famed and storied island,
rich and a power while Priam's throne held firm,
now only a bay where keels ride rough to anchor;
thus far they sailed, to hide by moldering piers.
We thought them gone with the wind and homeward bound.
All Troy shook off her shackled years of pain,
threw open the gates, ran out in joy to see

---

[37] **Myrmidon . . . Ulysses:** Ulysses is the Roman name for Odysseus, the son of Laertes, king of Ithaca; one of the greatest of the Greek heroes, known for his cunning and quick-wittedness, Odysseus is the hero of Homer's *Odyssey.* The Myrmidons were the warriors led by Achilles. [38] **Pallas:** Pallas Athena, the goddess of wisdom; known as Minerva in Roman mythology. [39] **Tenedos:** An island in the Aegean, near the coast of the Troad, the region around Troy, where the Greeks sailed to deceive the Trojans into thinking they had given up the battle. They returned, as described here, to wreak havoc on the city of Troy, which had been penetrated by the so-called Trojan Horse, in which an advance team of Greek warriors hid and slipped into the city unbeknownst to the Trojans.

the empty Dorian[40] camp, the vacant shore:
here tented the Thracians, here the cruel Achilles;
here lay the fleet, here ranged the ranks of war.
Some stopped to stare at Pallas' deadly gift,
amazed at a horse so huge. Up spoke Thymoetes:
'Inside the walls with it! Station it in our fort!'
(Treason? Or just the turn of fate for Troy?)
But Capys and all our wiser heads bade throw
this Grecian trick and generosity suspect
into the sea, or bring up fire and burn it,
or pierce it and see what hollow wombs might hide.
Divided, bewildered, the people turned here, turned there.

"Laocoon[41] strode to the front. (With a crowd of priests
he'd run in fury and haste from Castle Hill.)
He shouted, 'You fools! You wretched, raving fools!
You think the enemy gone? Who left this 'gift'?
Greeks? And you trust it? This is our 'friend,' Ulysses?
That wooden thing holds Argives locked inside,
or else it's an engine built to attack our walls,
to spy on our homes and fall from above on us all.
There's treachery here. A horse? Don't trust it, Trojans!
Whatever it is, I fear Greeks even with gifts.'

"So speaking he heaved and hurled his heavy spear
against the creature's flank and vaulted paunch;
the shaft stood trembling; from that wounded womb
came a sound of moaning cavernous and hollow.
And had Fate and our hearts not been perverse,
we would have bloodied that Argive hiding-hole,
and Troy and Priam's towers would still be standing.

"Up came a man, hands bound behind his back,
dragged on by shepherds shouting, 'Where's the king?
We're Trojan; this stranger met us and surrendered!'
(He'd plotted and planned it so, to open Troy
to the Greeks—sure of himself—prepared both ways:
to turn his trick, or keep his day with death.)

---

[40] **Dorian:** Greek; the Dorians were a major branch of the early Greek people who moved into northern Greece from Thessaly, eventually moving south to occupy the Peloponnese. [41] **Laocoon:** A Trojan priest and follower of Neptune. When Laocoon warned the Trojans not to accept the wooden horse offered by the Greeks at Troy, he and his two sons were killed by giant sea-snakes. Thinking Laocoon had insulted the gods by refusing the gift, the Trojans brought the horse inside the city walls, enabling the Greek warriors hidden inside the horse to penetrate their defenses.

From all sides, eager to see, our Trojan men
came rushing to ring the captive round with taunts.
Now hear how Greeks can lie; from this one crime
learn of them all!
We watched him. There he stood, unarmed and frightened,
looking from face to hostile Phrygian face:
'O gods!' he cried, 'what land will take me in?
What sea? What's left for one like me? What's left?
I have no place among the Greeks, and now
the Trojans call for my blood to slake their hate.'
His pitiful cry softened our hearts and dulled
our every impulse. What was his name? we asked.
What did he want? How dared he trust to capture?
At last he laid his fear aside and spoke:

"'I'll tell it all, my lord, yes, all, and tell
it true,' he said. 'I'm Greek. Be that confessed
first off. If Fortune molded Sinon luckless,
she shall not mold him foul and a liar, too.[42]
Has anyone told you—has word reached your ears
of Belus' son, Palamedes?[43] Fame has called him
"the great." He hated war; for this, the Greeks
slandered, harried, and hounded the saintly man
down to his death. Now that he's gone, they mourn him.
I was his cousin. My father, a humble man,
sent me, no more than a boy, to be his aide.
While he stood king among the kings, full-fledged,
full-powered, I held my small lieutenancy
with honor; but Ulysses' craft and hate
(you know them!) sent him from this world of men.
That crushed me. I lived in darkness and in sorrow,
privately cursing my cousin's unjust fate.
Then like a fool I talked and swore revenge
if ever my luck should bring me home to Argos.
My silly boasting won me harsh ill will.
That was my downfall; from that hour Ulysses
brought charge after frightening charge, and spread dark hints
among the people, determined to see me dead.
He knew no rest until with Calchas'[44] help—

[42] **Sinon . . . liar, too:** A Greek master of deceit whose supposed kinship with Palamedes, the warrior who advised Agamemnon to abandon the war against Troy and was executed after Ulysses (Odysseus) brought false charges against him, is strategically designed to win over the Trojans, as is his bluff soldier's speech. [43] **Belus' son, Palamedes:** Palamedes' father, Belus, as a Greek, is not King Belus of Tyre who is Dido's father. (See note 33.) [44] **Calchas:** A Greek seer and priest serving with the Greek forces during the Trojan War.

but this is waste! Why tell unwelcome tales?
Why wait? If "Greek" means but one thing to you,
and the name is enough, exact the penalty now!
Ulysses would cheer, Agamemnon pay you well!'

"Then how we burned to question and inquire,
unschooled in crime so vile and Argive craft.
He trembled but talked on, with feigned concern:

"'Many times the Greeks had longed to abandon Troy
and run away home from the weary years of war;
and oh, that they had! Many times a blustery sea
blocked them, and storm winds frighted their departure.
And worst: when the wooden fabric stood complete—
that horse—all heaven flashed and roared and rained.
Worried, we sent Eurypylus off to seek
Apollo's will; and the word he brought was grim:
"With blood of a virgin slain[45] you won the winds
when you set sail, you Greeks, for Trojan shores;
with blood you'll buy return: an Argive soul's
the price to pay." When this word reached the ranks
men's hearts went numb; an icy tremor ran
down through their bones: whom had Apollo claimed?
Riot was near when the Ithacan° drew Calchas Ulysses
into our midst. "Speak, priest," he said, "and tell
God's will." (Men prophesied that murder plot
was aimed at me. They watched but said no word.)
Ten days he held his tongue, guarding against
one word that might send some man to his death.
At last Ulysses' bluster brought him round
to speak, as planned, and mark me for the altar.
No one protested; indignation died,
now that one wretch was scape for all their fears.

The dreadful day drew near; the rites were readied—
salt meal and sacred ribbons for my head.
I ran from death—yes, ran. I broke my bonds
by dark of night; in muddy marsh and reeds
I lay and waited, praying that they would sail.
Now I've no hope to see the hills of home,
my little sons, the father that I love—
the Greeks may well assess on them the price

[45] **Eurypylus . . . virgin slain:** Iphigenia, the daughter of Agamemnon and Clytemnestra, was sacrificed in order to win favorable winds from the gods and launch the Greek fleet against Troy. Eurypylus was a Greek commander.

of my escape—their deaths acquit my sin.
And so, sir, by God's name and power and truth,
by all the honor that still lives unstained
in mortal man, have mercy on my pain;
have mercy on a heart unjustly used!"

"His tears won him a pardon and our pity.
Priam at once commanded him relieved
of shackle and chain, then spoke as to a friend:
'Whoever you are, you've lost your Greeks: forget them!
Be one of us! Now speak out, tell the truth:
Why the huge horse? Who moved to place it here?
What is it? An act of worship? A siege machine?'
Sinon had learned his lines; with Argive art
he sloughed his irons and raised his hands to heaven:
'O fires eternal, O power beyond blaspheme,
be witness,' he cried; 'O altar and unblessed blade
that I escaped, O ribbons I wore to die:
I solemnly renounce my Argive oaths
and curse the Greeks. No law, no loyalty
bids me beware of telling all I know.
And if I keep Troy free, then keep your word
and promise—if I speak truth and give full measure.
The Greeks went off to war with hope and trust
based full and forever on Pallas' help; then crime
and crime's inventor—Diomede and Ulysses—
sinfully wrested from her hallowed shrine
Pallas the Less.[46] They killed the temple guards,
pulled down her idol, and with hands all blood
dared touch the virgin goddess' holy bands.
Thereafter nothing was certain. Argive hopes
faltered, their strength was gone, their goddess angry.
No room for doubt! Tritonia[47] gave clear sign:
scarce was her image based in camp, when fire
flashed from her staring eyes and salty sweat
ran over her limbs, and thrice (wonder to tell!)
she leaped up, shield in hand, and shook her spear.
"Run!" Calchas warned them. "Take to the seas at once!"—
Never could Argive power cut Troy down
till they went home to learn God's will, and brought

[46] **Pallas the Less:** The Palladium, a small statue of Minerva (Pallas Athena) that was said to guarantee the safety of Troy so long as it remained in place at Minerva's shrine. Ulysses and Diomede stole the Palladium and desecrated the goddess's shrine, so angering her that she wreaked revenge on the Greek forces she had thitherto supported. [47] **Tritonia:** An epithet for Minerva (Athena) associating her with Lake Tritonis in Libya, her birthplace.

his blessing anew in curved keels over the sea.
And home they've gone, riding the wind to Greece.
They'll win God's favor again, recross the water,
and land here unforeseen — so spoke the prophet.
This horse is payment for their heinous crime:
for godhead wronged, for Pallas the Less defiled.
And Calchas bid them build it massive, tall,
beam upon beam, to tower toward the sky —
too wide for the gates, too huge to pass the walls
and by some ancient covenant save your people.
For if your hand should harm Minerva's gift
then death (on Calchas' head may that doom fall!)
would come to Priam's Trojans and his power.
But if by your hand it climbed within your city
then Asia would some day march on Grecian walls,
and in that war our grandsons groan and die.'

"Strategy, perjury vile! Sinon by craft
won our belief; tricks and counterfeit tears
took captive men whom Diomede, Achilles,
ten years, and a thousand ships had never tamed!

"Here something worse and far more frightful rose
to meet us and trouble our unsuspecting hearts.
Laocoon, chosen by lot as Neptune's priest,
was killing a great bull at his sacred shrine,
when out from Tenedos, over the quiet floods
(I shudder to tell it) two snakes, coil on huge coil
breasting the sea, came slithering toward the shore.
Their necks rose high in the troughs, their blood-red manes
crested the waves; their other parts behind
slid through the water, twin bodies winding vast.
The salt sea gurgled and foamed. Now they reached land.
Hot were their eyes, bloodshot and flecked with flame;
through hissing lips their tongues flicked in, flicked out.
Bloodless we fled the sight; they never wavered
but went for Laocoon; first his two young sons —
poor little boys! — they hugged in their twin coils
wrapping them round and tearing at leg and arm.
Laocoon leaped to the rescue, sword in hand;
the great snakes seized him, wrapped him round and round,
two scaly coils at his waist, two at his throat.
Above his head, their heads and necks rose high.
With his hands he tried to pry the loops apart,
while blood and venom soaked his sacred bands.

He screamed to make high heaven shudder—screamed
like a bloodied bull run roaring from the altar
to shake free of his neck an ill-aimed ax.
But those twin snakes slipped off toward Castle Hill
and escaped. They made for cruel Tritonia's shrine
and hid at her feet behind her circled shield.

"We stood and shook while into every heart
fresh terror crept. 'He sinned and paid fair price,'
we said. 'Laocoon stabbed a sacred thing;
sin rode the spear he hurled against that flank.
Bring the horse home,' we cried, 'and let us pray,
pray to our lady of might.'
We cut through walls and flung our ramparts down.
All stripped for the work; under the horse's feet
we slipped rollers, and from its neck we rove
hempen halyards. Up rode the death machine,
big with armed men, while boys and virgin girls
sang hymns and joyed to lay hand to the lines.
Into mid-city the menacing mass rolled on.
O homeland, god-land, Troy! O Dardan walls
famed for your soldier sons! Four times it balked
at the sill, four times its belly rang with arms,
but we pushed on, forgetful, blind, and mad,
to set the luckless monster in our fort.
Even then Cassandra[48] cried, 'Death! Men will die!'
but Apollo had bid the Trojans never heed her.
In festive mood (poor souls! this day would be
our last!), we banked our hallowed shrines with flowers.

"The vault of heaven turned; night rushed from Ocean
enfolding in vast darkness earth and sky
and Myrmidon guile; on the walls our sentries lay
scattered, wordless, weary, sound asleep.
Now came the Argive ships in battle line
from Tenedos under a silent, friendly moon,
heading for well-known shores. A torch flamed out
from the royal ship. Sinon, by unkind fates
preserved, slipped softly back the bolts of pine
and freed the Greeks from the womb. The opened horse
released them; glad from that wooden cave they poured.
Thessander, Sthenelus—lords—and dire Ulysses

[48] **Cassandra:** A prophetess and daughter of King Priam and Queen Hecuba of Troy; because she offended Apollo by spurning his advances, he put a curse on her that her prophecies would never be believed.

let down a rope and slid, then Acamas, Thoas,
Machaon, next Neoptolemus, son of Achilles,
Menelaus, and he who laid the plot, Epeus.
They fell on a city buried in sleep and wine,
murdered the watch, threw open the gate, let in
their friends—a column of schemers, hand in hand.

"It was the hour when gentle sleep first comes,
welcome, by God's grace, welcome to weary men.
I dreamed, and there before my eyes stood Hector,
sorrowed and sad, his face a flood of tears.
He seemed as when the chariot dragged him: bruised,
bloody, dusty, thongs through his swollen feet.
O God! How he looked! How changed from that great man,
the Hector who wore Achilles' armor home,
who hurled into Argive ships our Trojan fire.
His beard all dirt, his hair was stiff with blood;
he wore each wound he'd earned before our walls—
our fathers' walls. I dreamed that I wept, too,
and hailed the man and let my grief pour out:
'O light of Troy! Dardania's[49] hope unfailing!
What held you, Hector? Where have you been? How long
we waited! Your people—so many of them are dead;
our men, our city have borne so many trials!
We are weary! We see you—but what is wrong? Your face
is clouded dark: Why? Why do I see these wounds?'
He said no word, nor heeded my vain questions,
but with a groan drawn deep from a burdened heart,
'Run, goddess-born,' he cried; 'run from these flames!
Greece owns our walls; the towers of Troy are tumbling!
To country and king all debts are paid; my hand
had saved them, if any hand had power to save.
Her holy things, her gods, Troy trusts to you.
Take them to share your fate; find walls for them:
wander the wide sea over, then build them great.'
He spoke, and in my hands laid mighty Vesta,
her ribbons, and—from her inmost shrine—her fire.[50]

"And now from the walls came screams and cries and groans.
Louder and louder, although my father's house

[49] **Dardania:** Another name for Troy, so called after King Dardanus, the legendary founder of the city.
[50] **Vesta . . . fire:** The ghost of Hector appears before Aeneas and bids him to take the household gods, the Penates, and flee the city. Vesta is the goddess of the hearth and fire who holds an eternal flame.

was set far off, apart, well screened by trees,
came the noise of battle, the terrible clash of arms.
I shook off sleep, and to the highest peak
of the roof I climbed, and stopped and strained to hear:
as when a flame by wild winds driven falls
on a grain field, or a mountain stream in flood
sweeps farms, sweeps crops away and plowman's toil,
and topples trees; high on his cliff the shepherd,
hearing the thunderous noise, sits blank with fear.
Then all — the word of honor, the Argive lie —
came clear. Deiphobus'[51] palace crashed and fell
in a holocaust roof-high; Ucalegon's next
caught fire; the straits reflected back the flames.
I heard men shouting, heard the trumpet-call.
Like a fool I seized my sword — what sense had swords?
But I was ablaze to round up men for war
and with them rush to the fort; a senseless wrath
propelled me: 'Glory!' I thought. 'To die in battle!'

"But here came Panthus escaping from Greek spears —
Panthus, priest of Apollo on Castle Hill —
arms full of holy things and beaten gods,
trailed by his grandson, panicking toward the gates.
'Panthus, how do we stand? What have we gained?'
He cut me off and answered with a groan:
'Dardania's end, her scapeless hour has come.
Trojan and Troy, we've had our day, our power,
our glory. A heartless Jove has handed all
to the Greeks. Our city is ashes! Greece is lord!
Tall stands the horse inside our fort, and births
her soldiers. Sinon, prancing his glory-dance,
sets fire on fire. Through gates flung wide, they come,
those myriads — all who marched from great Mycenae.[52]
Posts have been set, spear locked with spear, to block
our streets; they stand, a line of shining steel,
blades ready for blood. Our first-line watch can scarce
form battle rank; they fight without command.'

"The words of Panthus and God's holy will
sent me toward flames and fighting, where Mars[53] roared
his challenge, and battle cries rose up to heaven.

[51] **Deiphobus:** One of the sons of King Priam of Troy. Ucalegon in the next line is also a Trojan. [52] **Mycenae:** Agamemnon's home city in Greece. [53] **Mars:** The Roman god of war and agriculture; Ares in Greek mythology.

Friends joined me: Rhipeus and that champion,
Epytus, guided by moonlight; Hypanis, Dymas
fell in at my side, and young Coroebus, too,
the son of Mygdon, just now come to Troy,
fired with foolish passion for Cassandra
(accepted, he fought for Priam and his people—
unlucky youth, who would not heed the word
of his prophetic princess!).
I watched them boldly form a battle group,
then spoke to them: 'Good men, brave hearts—but brave
for nothing! If you feel you must fight on
and dare to the end, you see how fortune stands.
They've gone from every temple, every shrine,
the gods who blessed our power. You seek to save
a city in flames. But on to war! We'll die!
Sole hope of the vanquished is their hopelessness!'
This fired their mad young hearts afresh. Like wolves
hot for a kill at murky midnight, blind,
driven by horrid belly-lust—their cubs
are waiting with blood-parched throats—through hostile arms
we rushed to death undoubted, held our way
through mid-town; night swung sable wings around us.
That night of ruin, night of death—who'd tell
its story or match our sorrows with his tears?
An ancient city, queen of the ages, fell;
the dead men lay by thousands in her streets,
in home and palace, at the hallowed gates
of gods. Nor only Trojans paid their lives;
sometimes courage returned to beaten hearts,
and Danaan victors died. Here grief heartrending,
terror, and death over all in countless forms.

"Androgeos first approached us, at the head
of a crowd of Greeks; mistakenly he thought
us comrades in arms and spoke to us as friends:
'Hurry, men! You are late! What held you back
so long? The rest have ripped and stripped and fired
Troy. Have you just now left the tall-sparred ships?'
He broke off then (our answers seemed not made
for trust) and sensed he'd fallen amid his foes.
He stopped, clapped hand to mouth, and stumbled back.
As one who, feeling his way through brambles, steps
on a sudden snake, jumps and shudders and runs
from head held high to strike, and hood spread wide—
just so Androgeos saw and jumped and fled.

Shield lapped to shield, we charged and hemmed them in.
On unknown ground, they panicked; one by one
we killed them. Fortune blessed our first assault.
Our luck now made Coroebus' heart beat high;
'Look! Fortune,' he said, 'has shown us how to win!
Success lies where she points the way: let's follow!
Let's take their shields and wear the Greek device
ourselves. Deceit or daring, who'd ask a foe?
Arms are here for the taking.' He spoke, and seized
Androgeos' plumed helmet and his shield
with its proud device, and buckled on his sword.
Rhipeus, Dymas and all their company
laughed as they took the spoil to arm themselves.
Under false signs we mingled with the Greeks
and many a battle joined while night was blind,
and sent to Orcus[54] many a man of Greece.
Still others scattered and ran for trusted ship
and shore, while others in shame and terror climbed
the horse again, to cower in its vast belly.

"'Man, trust not the gods except with their consent!'
Here, dragged by her long, long hair, came Priam's daughter,[55]
holy and virgin, torn from Minerva's[56] shrine;
in vain toward heaven she turned her burning eyes—
eyes, for her soft, young hands were bound with chains.
This sight Coroebus could not bear; his heart
went wild; he rushed against their ranks to die.
Behind him we charged in a body, sword by sword.
And now—disaster! Down from the temple's top
came Trojan spears to spill our wretched blood:
our arms and plumes had wrongly marked us Greeks.
Then—for we'd seized the girl—the Argives roared
with fury, formed ranks and charged: Ajax the chief,[57]
the twin Atridae, the whole Thessalian host;
as when sometimes the winds whirl till they burst
then crash head-on: Westerly, South, and East
rich with his Orient steeds; the woodlands wail
and Nereus[58] stirs his deeps to foam and fury.

---

[54] **Orcus:** The Roman underworld, or land of the dead. [55] **Priam's daughter:** Cassandra, the prophetess. [56] **Minerva:** The Roman name for Pallas Athena, goddess of wisdom. (See notes 38 and 46.) [57] **Ajax the chief:** Ajax the lesser, son of Oileus, who was punished by the gods for desecrating Minerva's shrine and kidnapping and raping Cassandra; the Atridae of the next line are Agamemnon and Menelaus. [58] **Nereus:** A sea-god whose fifty daughters with the sea-goddess Doris were known as the Nereids.

And those whom darkness and our stratagem
had put to flight pell-mell down every street
now showed themselves; they first detected shields
and swords not ours, and caught our foreign speech.
Sheer numbers crushed us; first Coroebus fell
by hand of Peneleus at Minerva's altar;
and Rhipeus died, the justest man that lived
in Troy, unwavering servant of the right
(yet heaven forsook him); Hypanis died, and Dymas
transfixed by friends; not all your piety,
Panthus, could save you, nor Apollo's bands.
Ashes of Troy! Last flame of all I loved!
Bear witness that at your death I never shrank
from sword or sorrow, and had Fate so decreed
I had earned a death at Grecian hands! We ran,
Iphitus, Pelias, and I—one old and tired,
the other limping from Ulysses' wound—
straight toward the sound of war by Priam's palace.

"Here was huge battle to make all other strife
and death through all the city seem like nothing.
Here Mars ran wild, and Argives rushed the walls;
we saw them march the 'tortoise' toward the gates.[59]
Up went the ladders next to the very doors;
men climbed the rungs; their left hands held their shields,
bulwark to blows; their right hands seized the roof.
Our Trojans on their side ripped loose and flung
whole towers and rooftrees; seeing the end had come,
as death approached they made these weapons serve.
Gilt beams, the glory that roofed their sires of old,
they tumbled down, while others bared their blades
and stood to the doors, a barricade of men.
Our strength came back; we ran toward Priam's walls
to help our friends and give the vanquished valor.

"There was a secret hall and door, a passage
between the royal mansions—a gate that none
would notice; often, while our throne held firm,
Andromache[60]—poor thing!—had walked this way
taking her son to grandsire or to uncle.
Here I slipped in and climbed to the roof; there stood
our Trojans, hurling spear on useless spear.

[59] **march the 'tortoise' . . . gates:** Refers to the Romans' practice of holding shields over their heads when attacking fortified walls. [60] **Andromache:** Hector's wife and the mother of his son, Astyanax.

On a steep gable stood a tower, the peak
of the palace, where we were wont to keep the watch
over Troy and Grecian fleet and Argive camp.
We hacked at this where tower and rooftop joined—
the fabric's weakest spot—and tore it loose
from its base and pushed it over; down it went
to crack and shatter and scatter its fragments far
over Argive troops. But more marched up, though stones
and weapons of every kind rained down.

"At the very door of the palace Pyrrhus[61] pranced
with a flourish and brazen flash of spear and blade—
like a snake on foul herbs fed, come from his hole
all puffed from a long, cold winter under the soil.
Stripping his skin he turns out sleek and young
and ripples his liquid coils; he lofts his head
up toward the sun and flicks his three-forked tongue.
Periphas and Achilles' charioteer,
the squire Automedon, all the Scyrians,[62] too,
charged the palace and tossed fire toward the roof.
Pyrrhus was leader; he seized a double ax,
chopped through the threshold and ripped out post and hinge,
fittings and all, then hacked at oaken beam
and panel to make a huge hole gaping wide.
There stood the house revealed, there stood its halls,
the home of Priam, of a long line of kings;
there at his doorway stood his bodyguard.
Inside the house rose cries and screams of terror
commingled, while the caverned inmost vaults
shrieked with the women; the outcry struck the stars.
Mothers in fright ran madly round the halls,
threw arms about the columns and kissed them close.
On pressed Pyrrhus, strong as his father; nor bolts
nor guards could hold him back. Crash! came the ram;
down fell the door; down tumbled post and hinge.
Force paved a way; in burst the Greeks to slaughter
the guard and fill the palace, wall to wall.
Not so from a broken dam a stream bursts forth
that foams and swirls and sweeps the dikes away;
its crest runs raging over field and plain
to bear off beast and barn. I saw blood drive
men mad: Achilles' son, the twin Atridae;

[61] **Pyrrhus:** Also known as Neoptolomus, the son of Achilles. [62] **Scyrians:** Fighters from the island of Scyros, where Pyrrhus was born.

I saw Hecuba[63] her hundred daughters: Priam
fouling with blood the altar flame he'd blessed.
His fifty rooms, rich hope of a line of sons—
pillars of Orient gold, girt proud with spoils—
all fell. Where fire failed, the Argive ruled.

"Perhaps you wish to know how Priam died.
There lay his city—lost, there lay the ruin
that was his palace, there at his hearth, a foe.
The old king threw his armor, long unused,
on his shaking shoulders—useless gesture!—bound
his sword at his waist, and rushed to fight and die.
Within the close, beneath heaven's naked pole,
stood a high altar; nearby an old bay tree
leaned toward it and wrapped the household gods in shade.
Here Hecuba and her daughters vainly fled
headlong (like doves before the black rain cloud)
and tight in a ring sat suppliant round the gods.
Then she saw Priam dressed in his young man's arms
and said, 'What dreadful madness, my poor lord,
led you to wear those weapons? Where will you charge?
This is no hour for help like yours, no time
for such defense—no, even were Hector here.
Come, stand by me; this altar shall shield us all,
or you will die with us.' So saying, she placed
the old man at her side on holy ground.

"Here now, escaped from Pyrrhus' blade, Polites,
a son of Priam, dashed through enemy lines,
ran down the cloisters and round the empty halls,
wounded. Enraged at having missed his aim,
Pyrrhus pursued him, caught him, and stabbed him down.
He crawled on, till before his parents' eyes
he fell, and with his blood coughed out his life.
Then Priam, though death already gripped him round,
could not hold back or check his angry words:
'You murderer!' he cried. 'You foul blasphemer!
If heaven has righteous gods to mark such acts,
oh, may they thank you well and pay the price
you've earned, who made me watch my own son die,
and with his death befouled a father's eyes.
Achilles—you lie, to say you are his son!—

[63] **Hecuba:** The queen of Troy, wife of Priam, and mother of Hector.

never treated me so! I came a suppliant,
an enemy, yet he honored me and gave me
Hector's corpse to bury and sent me home.'
With that, the old king hurled his harmless spear
to touch and clang against the shield; it stopped
and dangled useless from the brazen boss.
Then Pyrrhus: 'Be my enemy! Tell your tale
to my father! Remember: call me barbarous
and name me "Neoptolemus, son unworthy"!
Now die!' He dragged him to the altar, faint
and slipping in the blood his son had shed.
His left hand gripped the old man's hair; his right
drew out a sword and sank it in his side.
So Priam died. His final, fated glance
fell on a Troy in ashes, on the ruins
of Pergama° — sometime proud imperial power, Troy
'of Asia, king.' On the strand his vast frame lies,
head torn from shoulders, a corpse without a name.

"For the first time then, a savage fear closed round me.
I froze. My own dear father's form rose up
as I watched the old king through that horrid wound
gasp out his life. Creusa — alone! — rose up:
my house — in ruins! My son, Iulus — where?
I turned about: What forces still remained?
Not a man! Heartsick and beaten, they had leaped
to the street or thrown themselves into the flames.

"I alone survived — but no! By Vesta's[64] shrine,
lurking wordless, in a dark corner hiding —
Helen! I saw her lighted by the flames
as I searched the ruins, looking everywhere.
She feared the fury of a vanquished Troy,
Greek vengeance, a deserted husband's wrath.
A fiendish curse alike to friend and foe,
hated, she'd sought asylum at the altar.
Flame burst in my heart as anger cried, 'Revenge,
for a country lost! Penalty, for her crimes!
Shall she, unscathed, see Sparta? Shall she march
in royal triumph through Mycenae's streets?
She, see her husband, her father's house, her children,
trailed by the women of Troy, her Orient slaves?

[64] **Vesta:** Roman goddess of the hearth and guardian of the family and community (Hestia in Greek mythology).

Yet death by the sword for Priam? Troy in flames?
A shore so often drenched in Trojan blood?
Never! Although men win no fame or glory
for woman punished (such victory earns no praise),
still to have stamped out sin, and made it pay
due price, is good; good, too, to fill the heart
with vengeful flame and vindicate the dead.'
Such the wild thoughts that swept my heart along
when — never before so clear for eye to see —
a vision shone through darkness, pure and bright:
my loving mother, goddess confessed, her form
and stature as in heaven. She seized my hand
and held me hard; her sweet lips spoke to me:
'My son, what pain has roused such unchecked wrath?
Are you mad, or have you lost all thought of me?
What? Not look first where your old father waits,
Anchises? See if yet Creusa lives,
your wife? Your son, Ascanius? All around them
Greeks walk their lines at will; but for my care,
flames or an enemy blade had borne them off.
No blame to Helen of Sparta's hated face;
no, nor to Paris: gods, the pitiless gods,
threw down the might and golden towers of Troy.
Look, for I'll rip it all away — the cloud
that blocks and blunts your mortal sight, hung dank
and dark around you; you must never fear
a mother's precept or disobey her word.
Here where you see the masonry all tumbled,
stone upon stone, where dust and smoke boil up,
Neptune is rocking our walls, and with his trident
knocking their base-blocks loose; our homes and halls
he'll pull to the ground. There, at the Scaean gates,[65]
Juno in blood-lust waves her columns on
from the ships with her drawn sword.
Look back! On Castle Hill Tritonia sits
in a cloud of flame, flashing her Gorgon head.[66]
Our father himself gives comfort, power, and strength
to the Greeks — yes, hurls the gods against our arms.
Hurry, my son! Take flight! Call this work done!
I am always with you, to guide you safely home!'

[65] **Scaean gates:** One of the main gates at Troy, outside of which in *The Iliad* the battle between Achilles and Hector took place. [66] **Gorgon head:** The head of Medusa, a hideous monster with snakes for hair whose visage would turn people to stone; after the hero Perseus decapitated Medusa, he gave the head to Minerva who attached it to her shield.

She spoke, and hid herself in night's black shades.
There rose up faces full of death and hate
for Troy—a ghastly glory of gods.

"Then came collapse, I saw all Ilium fall
in flames—saw Neptune's Troy come crashing down.
As when on mountain top an ancient ash
is hacked by the steel; blow after blow falls
as farmers vie at the felling. The old tree leans,
her foliage shakes, she bows her stricken crown,
till bit by bit her wounds win out. She groans
her last and falls and strews the ridge with wreckage.

"Divine grace led me down through flame and foe
with ease; swords made away and flames fell back.

"Soon as I stepped inside my father's house
and ancient home, I sought him out and begged
he'd let me carry him off to the high hills.
He answered, No: his Troy was lost, and life
in exile not for him. 'You young in years
and blood,' said he, 'who yet own strength and sinew,
do you take thought for flight.
If heaven had wished me further years of life
they'd saved my home for me. Enough that once
I lived to see my city fall and die.
Just let me lie here; say farewell and leave me.
I'll find death by myself. The foe will say
"Too bad!" and strip my corpse. A grave's well lost.
I've lived unloved of heaven,[67] useless, old,
for years, since Jove, the father of gods and men,
touched and scorched me with lightning's fiery breath.'

"He spoke and stood his ground, unmoved, unmoving.
But we burst out in tears—my wife Creusa,
Ascanius, our whole house—'He must not ruin
us all, or hasten the death that threatens us.'
He would not change, or leave his chosen spot.
I turned to my arms with bitter prayer to die.
What plans could be; what fortune granted now?
'You think, sir, I could take one step and leave
you here? Monstrous! This, from a father's lips?

[67] **unloved of heaven:** Jove (Zeus) crippled Anchises with a lightning bolt because Anchises broke his promise to keep secret that his son, Aeneas, was Venus's child.

If by God's law our city must be destroyed,
and you are resolved to cap the death of Troy
with death of you and yours, that door stands wide:
Pyrrhus is coming bathed in Priam's blood—
son before father, father by altar slain.
For this you haled me, mother, through steel and flame,
that I might see the enemy in my house,
and you, Ascanius, and Creusa too,
heaped in one bloody sacrificial pile?
Arms, men! To arms! We're lost! Our last day calls us!
Back to the Greeks! I'll see the fight renewed
once more. We shall not all die unavenged!'

"I buckled my sword again and strapped my shield
to my left arm with care, then moved outside.
But there at the door my wife fell at my feet
and kissed them, and held Iulus out to me:
'You go to die? Take us, too—anywhere!
But if experience gives you faith in arms,
guard first your home. Abandon us? Your son,
your father, me—once called your wife? To whom?'

"While thus she pled and filled the house with sobs—
wonder to tell!—a miracle occurred.
There in our arms, before his parents' eyes,
Iulus' little cap, right at its peak,
seemed to shed light. A harmless flame licked down
to touch his hair and play about his brow.
In panic terror we slapped at his burning hair
and tried to quench the holy flame with water.
But Father Anchises smiled, and raising eyes
toward heaven, spread out his hands, and spoke in prayer:
'Almighty Jove, if any prayer can bend you,
look down and for our merit grant just this:
a sign, father! Confirm this omen for us!'

"Scarce had he spoken when with sudden crash
came thunder on the left; down the dark sky
a meteor fell in a burst of sparks and flame.
We watched it glide high over roof and hall
—so bright!—then bury itself in Ida's woods,[68]
its path marked clear. Behind it, furrow and line

[68] **Ida's woods:** Ida was a mountain in Phrygia, in the vicinity of Troy.

shed light and left a smoking reek of sulphur.
My father now was certain; he turned toward heaven,
hailed godhead, and adored the holy star:
'No hesitation now! Lead on! I'll follow,
gods of my fathers! Oh, save my house and line!
Yours was that sign; your will embraces Troy.
I yield, my son; I'll gladly share your way.'

"Just then through our walls we heard a louder noise
of fire and closer rolled the holocaust.
'Come then, dear father, and climb upon my back.
Ride on my shoulders; the load will not be heavy.
Whatever may happen, we'll share a single risk,
a single rescue. Iulus, little son,
walk by me! Wife, stay back, but trace my steps!
And all you others, listen to my words!
Outside the city is a hill and shrine
of Ceres,[69] long unused; nearby, a cypress,
gnarled, and for years held sacred by our fathers.
Each go your way; we'll meet at that one spot.
You, father, carry our holies and household gods.
Fresh come from all the fighting, blood, and death,
I dare not touch them till in running stream
I wash myself.'
With that I spread across my neck and shoulders
a cloak, and over that a lion's skin,
and lifted my burden; little Iulus seized
my right hand, following two steps to my one;
behind us, my wife. We moved through pitch-black plazas,
and I was afraid, though minutes before no spear
nor prowling Greek patrol had worried me.
I started at every breeze; at every sound
I stiffened, fearful alike for father and son.
And now I was near the gate, and clear, I thought,
of the streets, when all at once I caught the sound
of many marching feet. My father peered
through the night, and cried out, 'Hurry, son; they're coming.
I see their shields alight and the flash of blades.'
I panicked then, as some strange, unkind power
left me confused and mindless. Hurrying down
byways, I'd left familiar streets behind,

[69] **Ceres:** Roman goddess of grain and the harvest; Demeter in Greek mythology. She appears here in her capacity as Ceres the Bereft, who mourns the loss of her daughter Proserpina (Persephone).

when Creusa—she was gone! Did cruel death take her?
Or had she lost her way? Or stopped to rest?
We've never known, nor ever seen her since.
I had not turned around nor marked her lost
until we reached the hill and ancient shrine
of Ceres. Here as we called the roll we found
her missing. Son nor husband—none had seen her.
Half mad, I railed at everyone, god and man:
What had I seen in captured town more cruel?
My son, my father, the household gods of Troy,
I left to my men, deep hidden in the hills.
I turned back to the city, armed again,
determined to take my chances, to go back
through all of Troy, and risk my life once more.
First to the walls and that half-hidden gate
where I'd gone out, I turned, and traced my steps
back through the night, my eyes' own light my guide;
no sound relieved the prickling sense of fear.
Then on to my house: Had she—had she perhaps
gone there? All doors were down, Greeks everywhere.
My house was wrapped in flames; wind-whipped they licked
at the roof, then raced in triumph toward the sky.
I ran to Priam's palace and the fort:
there on the empty porch of Juno's temple
a squad of sentries with Phoenix and Ulysses
were guarding the spoils. Here all the wealth of Troy,
ripped from her burning temples—holy tables,
wine bowls of solid gold, and captured vestments—
were heaped. Mothers and children, a long, long line,
terrified, stood nearby.
I even dared to shout. I filled the night
and dark streets with my sobbing cries: 'Creusa!'
No answer! 'Creusa!' I called, again, again.
I was pressing my search from house to endless house
when a luckless ghost, Creusa's very shade,
rose to my sight—her likeness, taller than life.
My hair stood up in terror; my voice stuck fast.
But then she spoke and banished all my fears:
'Why such indulgence of a pointless pain,
dear husband? Nothing but by the will of God
has happened. You were not meant to take Creusa
with you; so rules the lord of tall Olympus.
Go into exile; furrow the empty sea
to a western land of men and fertile fields

where Tiber pours his gentle Tuscan stream.[70]
There is your birthright: wealth, a throne, a queen.
You loved Creusa; but brush away your tears.
I'll catch no sight of Thessaly's haughty halls—
not I!—nor humbly serve the dames of Greece,
I, child of Dardanus, wife of Venus' son.
No; the mother of gods detains me here.
Farewell, and always love the son we share.'
With that, for all my tears, for all I hoped
to say, she turned to emptiness and air.
Three times I tried to fold her in my arms,
three times for nothing! The ghost-thing fled my grasp,
light as a breeze, most like the wings of sleep.
The night was gone when I rejoined my friends.

"And here I stood in wonder at the crowd
of people newly come—mothers and men,
children, huddled for exile—poor, lost souls.
They'd brought what they could save; they'd brought their courage;
they'd follow the course I set, no matter where.
And now the dawn star rose from Ida's heights
to bring the day. Greek guards were everywhere,
at every gate. We knew no help could come.
Bearing my father, I started toward the hills."

Book 3
[Helenus's Prophecy and Andromache's Sorrow]

"With Asian power and Priam's tribe uprooted,
though blameless, by heaven's decree; with Ilium's pride
fallen, and Neptune's Troy all smoke and ash,
God's oracles drove us on to exile, on
to distant, lonely lands. We built a fleet
down by Antander and Ida's Phrygian peaks,
uncertain which way Fate led or where to stop.
We marshaled our men. When summer first came on
Anchises bade us trust our sails to fate.
With tears I left the shores and ports of home,
the land that once was Troy, and sailed away
with friends and son, with gods both small and great. [. . .]

[70] **Tuscan stream:** The Tiber is a river in Italy that runs through Rome and was the site of Etruscan settlements, hence the "Tuscan stream."

[In the omitted lines, Aeneas continues his story of his hazardous journey from Troy to Carthage, describing how he and his men overcame countless obstacles, including some of the same ones Odysseus met with on his journey home from the war to Ithaca, as told in Homer's *Odyssey.* As the story picks up here, Aeneas has landed at Chaonia, near Buthrotum, a city founded by Priam's son Helenus, a prophet, and Hector's widow, Andromache. Helenus here foretells the founding of Rome, and the still-grieving Andromache sees in the face of Ascanius a reminder of her lost son, Astyanax, killed at Troy.]

Soon, too, Leucata's clouded mountain peaks
and Apollo,[71] terror of sailors, came to view.
Here we sought rest, close by a little town.
The anchors went out; the fleet lay stern to shore.

"Thus, unexpectedly, we came to land;
we purged our stain and payed our vows to Jove,
then, there at Actium,[72] staged the Trojan games.
Stripped and anointed, my men took part in sports
ancestral. (Joy! We'd slipped past all those towns
of Greeks! We'd escaped, though enemies hemmed us in!)
Meanwhile the sun rolled his great circle round,
and a wintry North Wind roughened and froze the waves.
On an entryway I nailed the curved bronze shield
huge Abas[73] carried, and marked it with a verse:
This shield Aeneas, from the conquering Greeks,
then ordered, 'Man the thwarts and put to sea!'
My men vied at the stroke and swept the waters.
Phaeacia's airy towers soon dropped behind;
we skirted Epirus' shores and made the port
of Chaonia, near Buthrotum in the hills.

"Here came report, incredible to our ears,
that Helenus, Priam's son, was king in Greece,
possessing the throne of Pyrrhus and his wife—
Andromache gone to a man of Troy once more![74]

---

[71] **Leucata's clouded . . . Apollo:** Leucata was a high promontory on the island of Leucas in the Ionian Sea near the northwestern coast of Greece. A temple of Apollo, god of music, poetry, and prophecy, was located there. [72] **Actium:** A promontory on the northwestern coast of Greece where Octavian defeated the forces of Marc Antony and Cleopatra in 31 B.C.E. [73] **Abas:** A Greek warrior killed in the Trojan War. The places named in the following lines show that Aeneas is tracking a course from the Ionian islands to reach Chaonia, a region near what today would be the border of Albania and Greece. Phaeacia, which Ulysses visited in *The Odyssey,* may be the island of Corfu. [74] **Andromache . . . once more:** Pyrrhus, son of Achilles, killed King Priam of Troy and took Priam's son, Helenus the prophet, and Andromache, wife of the fallen Trojan warrior Hector, as captives in the sack of Troy. Virgil has it that when Pyrrhus married Hermione, the daughter of Menelaus and Helen, he gave Andromache to Helenus. Not long after, Orestes, to whom Menelaus had first promised Hermione, killed Pyrrhus. After Pyrrhus's death, Helenus received some of his lands and eventually founded the port town of Buthrotum.

Speechless, my heart afire with passion strange
to address the king and hear so great a tale,
I walked from the harbor, leaving ship and shore.
At the city gates I chanced on funeral foods
and gifts in a grove by a counterfeit Simois;
Andromache there made offering to the dead
and called the ghosts to Hector's grass-grown mound—
empty, with twin altars—cause of her tears.
She saw me coming, saw my Trojan arms,
and thought me a phantom of madness and of fear.
She looked and stiffened; the warmth fled from her limbs,
she tottered, but at long last she came to speech:
'Is this your face? Is this your voice I hear,
Aeneas? Are you alive? Or if you've lost
the light of life, where is Hector?' She burst out
in a flood of tears and frenzied sobs; I scarce
could put in a stumbling word, now here, now there:
'Living, yes—and a life of endless peril.
Never doubt: you see reality.
What fate caught you and cast you from estate
so regal? What fitting fortune came to you,
Hector's Andromache? Still the wife of Pyrrhus?'
She bowed her head and spoke as if in shame:
'Of Priam's daughters, call her only blessed
who died beneath the lofty walls of Troy
on hostile tomb. No lots were cast for her;
she was no war prize for some victor's bed.[75]
From a home in flames I sailed through many a sea
and bore, the merest slave, the proud contempt
of Achilles' half-grown son. Then he pursued
Hermione, Spartan princess, child of Leda,
and passed me on to Helenus—slave to slave.
Orestes, for his stolen bride enflamed
with love, and fury-driven for his crimes,
caught Pyrrhus and killed him at his father's shrine.
At Pyrrhus' death, a share in power passed
to Helenus; he has called this land "Chaonia"
for Chaon of Troy, these plains "Chaonian,"
and built in the hills a fort called "Ilium."
But say what winds, what fates have stayed your course?
You could not know the way: what guided you?

[75] **call her only . . . bed:** Andromache refers to her daughter, Polyxena, whom the Greeks (in some versions of the story, Pyrrhus) sacrificed at the tomb of Achilles.

Your son — does he still draw the breath of life?
In Troy you kept him by you.
And does the boy still miss his poor lost mother?
Does he feel drawn toward ancient strength and courage
by Aeneas, his father, and by his uncle, Hector?'
She spoke in a flood of tears, and as she sobbed
long and in vain, down from the wall he came —
King Helenus, Priam's son, with all his guard.
He knew his kin and joyed to lead them home
with a word — then tears — then a word — then floods of tears.
As I walked, I saw it: a little Troy, a fort
just like the great one, and a dried-up stream
called 'Xanthus,' a Scaean Gate[76] — I kissed that gate!
My people, too, all shared the city's welcome.
The king received them in his ample halls,
then in mid-court they drank a toast of wine,
and ate from golden plates, and raised their cups.

"One day and then a second passed; then breezes
called to our canvas; a Southerly swelled our sails.
I went to our prophet and prince and thus inquired:
'Scion of Troy, God's prophet, who sense the will
of Phoebus in tripod and laurel, who know the stars
and the speech of birds, and the word of winged flight,
tell me (for all sound prophecy foretells
travel, and heaven's universal will
bids me seek Italy and her far-off lands;
only the Harpy sang of sacrilege
and strange forebodings, telling a carrion tale
of wrath and hunger), where lie my greatest dangers?
What course will carry me past all obstacles?'
Then Helenus, killing first the ritual calves,
prayed for God's peace, and from his hallowed head
untied the ribbons. He took me by the hand
and led me, filled with awe, to Phoebus' temple,
then spoke — a priest and voice of God — these words:

" 'Aeneas, we dare not doubt some greater power
sends you across the sea: so Jove allots
men's fate and turns the wheel of history.
I'll tell you a little, to help you cross strange waters
more safely to Ausonia, and come there

[76] **'Xanthus' . . . Gate:** The river Xanthus, also called Scamander, that flowed through Troy; the Scaean Gate was one of the gates of Troy. (See note 65.)

to harbor; all the rest the Fates forbid
me to know, or Juno says I may not tell.
To begin: This Italy, which you think so close,
whose nearby ports you may invade at will,
lies land past distant land, down trackless ways.
First you must bend oar in Sicilian wave
and sail the circuit of Ausonian seas,
the pools of hell, and Circe's Aeaean isle,[77]
before you'll see your city safely founded.
I'll tell you the signs; you lay them to your heart:
In an hour of trouble, beside a far-off stream
where oaks grow on the shore, you'll find a sow,
huge lying, having borne her thirty young—
white she will be, white babies at her teats.
Here build your city, find peace and labor's end.[78]
For fated "gnawing of tables," have no fears:
Apollo will hearken, and fate will find a way.
But all these lands, these coasts of Italy
nearby, washed by this ocean and this tide:
Shun them! Vile Greeks infest their every town.
Here Locrians[79] of Naryx laid their walls,
and here Idomeneus sat his army down
on plains Salentine; here on ramparts rises
Petelia, Philoctetes' modest home.
No—cross the water, and when you come to land,
build altars on the shore and pay your vows;
but with a purple shawl veil head and hair,
that while the fires of holy office burn
no view of hostile face confuse the signs.
(Preserve this way of prayer, you and your people;
so may your sons in purity keep the rite.)
Then sail away; the wind will bring you close
to Sicily. Where Pelorus[80] opens out,
bear off to port and follow coast and sea
the long way round. Shun starboard waves and shore.
These lands were once by earthquake ripped and riven
(long, long ago; such change time has wrought!).

[77] **Circe's . . . isle:** Circe was a sorceress who lived on the island of Aeaea off the western coast of Italy and who transformed Odysseus's men into swine (*Odyssey*, Book 10). [78] **In an hour . . . labor's end:** A prophecy that comes to pass in Book 8. [79] **Locrians:** Originally from the northern part of Greece, the Locrian people founded Naryx on the eastern tip of Italy. Helenus goes on to warn Aeneas to avoid other Greek settlements in Italy, including that of Philoctetes, a Greek commander who founded Petelia. [80] **Pelorus:** A headland in the northeast of Sicily marking the straits of Messina, a dangerous sea passage that gave rise to the myth of Scylla and Charybdis.

They leaped apart, men say, though they had been
one mass before; in rushed a roaring sea
to cut Hesperian from Sicilian shores.
Now narrow waters ebb and flow between them.
The right shore Scylla guards; the left, Charybdis
insatiate. Thrice, in her maelstrom pit, she gulps
the floods deep down, then belches them again
up to the air, to splash the very stars.
But Scylla hides in lightless, caverned lair;
her lips reach out to suck ships to the reefs.
Human her face, her lovely breast a girl's—
so to her waist. Below, a shapeless fish,
a womb of wolves, tapered to dolphin's tail.
Better to pass the pillars of Pachynus,[81]
taking the time to make the long course round,
than catch one glimpse of that vast-vaulted monster,
Scylla, and of the reefs where blue dogs bark.
Further, if Helenus has prophetic powers
worthy of trust, if God's truth fills his heart,
one thing, Aeneas, one thing before all else
I'll tell and advise you, again and again the same:
To Juno the queen make your first adorations;
to Juno, lady of power, chant willing prayers
and win her with humble gifts. So shall you gain
passage to Italy from Sicilian shores.
Once set down there, move on to Cumae's[82] town,
her hallowed pools, Avernus'[83] rustling groves.
There you'll find a prophetess: under a cliff
she sings of fate and writes her runes on leaves.
The leaves, with their recorded songs, she lays
in order and stores them deep within her cave;
they stay in place and never change their sequence.
But when some door is opened and a breeze,
the merest whisper, stirs the fragile leaves,
they flutter all over the cave. She never tries
to catch them, sort them out, or match the lines.
Men leave no wiser, and curse the Sibyl's see.
Count not too high the cost of tarrying here.
Though men complain, though breezes call you brisk
to sea and you could fill your canvas full,

[81] **Pachynus:** A headland on the southeastern point of Sicily. [82] **Cumae:** In Book 6 Aeneas will meet the Sibyl, who directs him to the entrance of the underworld at Cumae, a city on the west coast of Italy near what today is Naples. [83] **Avernus:** A wood near Cumae, near the entrance to the underworld.

still go to the lady, humbly beg her speak
and sing her runes, and let her words flow free.
The peoples of Italy, wars that are to be,
how best to shun each trial, or to bear,
she'll tell, and map your course to victory.
Thus far my voice may guide you. Go your way
and by your works exalt great Troy to heaven.'

"Thus spoke the prophet with the voice of love,
then ordered gifts heavy with ivory carved
and gold, sent to the ships, and crammed the holds
with silver ingots, cauldrons from Dodona,[84]
a suit of mail, hook-linked and twilled with gold,
a shining helmet, peaked with horsehair plumes—
Neoptolemus'[85] arms. Gifts for my father, too,
and horses he gave, and guides;
new oars for the ships, new armor for my men.

"Meanwhile Anchises bade the fleet make sail
to catch each minute of a favoring breeze.
With deep respect, Apollo's priest addressed him:
'Anchises, whom proud Venus deigned to wed,
heaven-blessed, twice rescued from a ruined Troy,
there lies your land, Ausonia! Sail there now!
But slip on down that coastline, as you must:
the shores Apollo names lie far beyond.
Blessed in the goodness of your son, sail on!
I'll say no more, nor block the rising winds.'
Andromache, too, sad at this last farewell,
brought garments pictured with a weft of gold;
for Ascanius, Trojan coats (he too was honored)
and piles of gifts of her weaving. Thus she spoke:
'These are for you, to call my hand to mind,
dear child, and witness to the lasting love
of Hector's wife. Take, them, our parting gifts,
O image of Astyanax,[86] all that's left me:
the eyes, the hands, the face—he bore them so,
and he'd be your age now, a boy like you.'
I turned to go, and tears flowed as I spoke:

[84] **Dodona:** A town in northwestern Greece and a center for the worship of Jove (Zeus); prophecies were told from the rustling of Dodonan oak trees. [85] **Neoptolemus:** Another name for Pyrrhus, the son of Achilles and murderer of King Priam. [86] **Astyanax:** The Greeks had murdered Astyanax, the son of Andromache and Hector, by throwing him from the walls of Troy; some say it was Pyrrhus who killed Astyanax.

'Be happy! Your trials are over, and you know
your fortune. We're hurried on from fate to fate.
You have found peace; you need not plow the sea
nor seek Ausonia, land that ever drops
below the horizon. You see Troy and Xanthus—
their likeness—built by your hands, and blessed, I pray,
more richly, and less in the path of Greeks.
If ever I enter Tiber and the lands
by Tiber, and see my people's promised walls,
that day shall see our towns, our nations, kin:
Hesperia to Epirus[87]—one in blood
and one in fate; our hearts will build them both
one Troy. Be that our mandate to our sons!' [. . .]

Book 4
[Aeneas and Dido]

Now Dido had felt the heavy slash of care,
the wound that grows in the vein, the lightless flame.
Aeneas' great courage, the glory of his people,
coursed through her mind; fast in her heart lay fixed
his face, his words. She knew no rest or peace.
The next day's lamp of sun was lighting earth,
and Dawn had cleared the sky of dew and dark,
when she, sick soul, spoke to her loving sister:
"Anna! My dreams! They leave me tense with fear!
What strange outsider has come here to our home?
How proud his bearing! How brave his heart and hand!
I believe—not lightly—he is a child of gods.
Fear proves the soul debased; but he, though battered
by Fate, tells how he fought war after war.
Had I not fixed it firm within my heart
never to yield myself to marriage bond
since that first love left me cheated by death,
did I not sicken at thought of bed and torch,[88]
to this one sin, this once, I might succumb.
No, Anna, I'll speak: Since poor Sychaeus died,
since brother[89] drenched my house with husband's blood,

[87] **Hesperia to Epirus:** That is, from Italy (the Westland, or Hesperia) to the region that is now western Greece and parts of Albania along the Adriatic Sea; during Virgil's time, Epirus was part of the Roman Empire.
[88] **bed and torch:** Used in wedding rituals, the torch was a symbol of marriage. Dido is associated with fire and flames throughout Book 4, from her first marriage with Sychaeus to her false marriage with Aeneas, her rage against Aeneas, and finally her suicide on a burning pyre. [89] **brother:** Pygmalion of Tyre, who killed Dido's husband Sychaeus in order to have his riches; Book 1, lines 69–97 tell the story of Dido's escape from Tyre.

Aeneas alone has moved my heart and shaken
resolve. I mark the trace of long-dead flame.
But, oh, may the earth gape wide and deep for me,
or the father almighty blast me down to death,
to the paling ghosts of hell and the pit of night,
before I play honor false or break her laws.
The man who first knew union with me stole
my heart; let him keep and guard it in the tomb."
She spoke; the well of her tears filled and ran over.

Then Anna: "Your sister loves you more than life:
why squander youth on endless, lonely grief
with no sweet sons, without the gifts of love?
You think mere ashes, ghosts in the grave, will care?
So be it! You've mourned; you've turned all suitors down
in Libya, and Tyre before. You've scorned Iarbas
and all the chiefs that Africa, proud and rich,
parades: why battle a love that you've found good?
Have you forgotten whose lands you've settled here?
This side, Gaetulians (race untamed by war),
savage Numidians, and a barrier sea;
that side, the desert, thirst, the wild nomads
of Barca.[90] Why tell of wars that rise in Tyre
or how your brother threatens?
I'm sure the gods have blessed the Trojans' course,
and Juno favored the wind that blew their ships.
Oh, what a city you'll see, what kingdoms rise,
with such a man! Allied with Trojan arms
Carthage will raise her glory to the sky.
Pray for the gods' forgiveness; give them gifts.
Be kind to our guest; weave tissues of delay:
'Winter—the sea is wild—the rains have come—
your ships are damaged—you cannot read the skies.'"

Such talk inflamed her heart with uncurbed love,
gave hope to doubt, and let restraint go free.
First they went to altar and shrine to beg
God's peace; they made due rite of sacrifice:
sheep to Ceres, to Phoebus, to Father Bacchus,
and most to Juno, lady of marriage bonds.
Dido the beautiful lifted a cup of wine

[90] **wild nomads of Barca:** The Gaetulians, Numidians, and Barcaeans were the peoples of North Africa near Carthage.

and poured it between the horns of a pure white cow,
or danced where the gods watch over blood-rich altars.
Each day began with victims; she slit their throats,
and hung over living vitals to read the signs.
But priests are fools! What help from shrine and prayer
for her madness? Flames devoured her soft heart's-flesh;
the wound in her breast was wordless, but alive.
Fevered and ill-starred, Dido wandered wild
through all the town, like a doe trailing an arrow
that she, heedless in Cretan forest, caught
from a shepherd who shot but never knew his bolt
had flown to the mark; she ranges field and grove
of Dicte;[91] the shaft of death clings to her flank.
Now Dido escorted Aeneas from wall to wall,
showed him her Tyrian wealth, her city all built—
she'd start to speak, but in mid-word fall mute.
Again, at wane of day, she'd fill her hall
and ask to hear once more of Troy's travail,
and hang once more, madly, upon each word.
Then when they'd parted and the shadowed moon
had paled, and fading stars warned men to sleep,
in the empty hall she'd lie where he had lain,
hearing him, seeing him—gone, and she alone;
or hold Ascanius close, caught by his father's
likeness, in hope of eluding a sinful love.
Her towers grew no taller; her army ceased
maneuvers and worked no more to strengthen port
and bastion for war: work hung half-done, walls stood
huge but unsteady; bare scaffolds met the sky.

As soon as Jove's dear wife knew Dido gripped
by the plague and grown too mad to heed report,
she, daughter of Saturn,[92] spoke harsh words to Venus:
"What glorious praise, what rich return you've gained,
you and your son; such might, such fabled power,
now that by godhead twain one woman's conquered!
I'm not deceived: you feared my city, and me,
and hence held Carthage and her halls suspect.
Is there no limit? Why this vast rivalry?
Why not make peace for good, and carry through
the match you planned? You've gained your heart's desire:

[91] **Dicte:** A mountain in Crete. [92] **Saturn:** The father of the gods Jove, Juno, Pluto, and Neptune was said to have settled in Italy after Jove ousted him from power; Saturnia is another name used for Juno.

Dido has drawn love's flame deep as her bones.
Why not join hands, join peoples, share the rule
between us? Let Dido serve her Trojan prince
and lay her dower—her Tyrians—in your hand."

Venus knew Juno spoke with veiled intent
to turn Italian power aside to Carthage.
Thus she replied: "To that, who but the mad
could object? Who'd choose to go to war with you?
If only success may crown our stratagem!
But I'm not sure of fate: would Jove allow
a single city for people of Tyre and Troy?
Approve such mingled blood, such rule conjoint?
You are his wife: seek out his will. You may.
You lead, I'll follow." To her then Juno spoke:
"That shall be my concern. How best to meet
the need of the moment, hear, while I briefly tell.
A hunt is planned. Aeneas, and Dido with him,
are off to the woods soon as tomorrow's sun
rises and with his ray reveals the world.
They'll see the clouds turn black with hail and rain;
then as their beaters rush to encircle a dell,
I'll pour down floods and shake all heaven with thunder.
Their men will scatter in darkness and disappear.
Your prince of Troy and Dido both will come
to a cave. I'll be there, too. With your consent,
I'll join them in marriage and name her 'lawful wife.'
Their wedding this shall be." No adverse word
spoke Venus, but nodded. Such tactics made her smile.

Meanwhile the Dawn arose and left the sea.
Out from the gates at sunrise young men ran
with nets and snares and broad-tipped hunting spears;
out galloped Moors with packs of keen-nosed hounds.
The queen was late; beside her hall the lords
of Carthage waited; there stood her horse, in gold
and purple caparison, nervous, champing the bit.
At last she came, surrounded by her vast guard,
wrapped in a scarlet cloak broidered with lace.
Gold was her quiver; gold held her plaited hair;
a brooch of gold fastened her purple gown.
In marched a Trojan group, Iulus too,
smiling and eager. Then, towering over all,
Aeneas joined them and brought their ranks together.
Like Apollo, leaving Lycia and streams of Xanthus,

in winter, to visit Delos, his mother's home!
He starts the dancing; gathering round his shrine,
islanders, mountaineers, painted plainsmen sing,
while he climbs Cynthus.[93] He braids his flowing hair
and holds it in place with laurel and crown of gold;
his arrows clang at his back. So fresh, alive,
was Aeneas, so matchless the glory of his face.
They rode to the hills, to the wayless woods and marches.
Look! Down from a rocky ridge leaped mountain goats
to race downhill; on this side, where the plains
lay open, a line of antelopes flashed past
away from the hillsides, trailing a swirl of dust.
Ascanius—boy on a lively pony—loped
up hill, down dale, with a laugh past these, past those.
Such nerveless beasts! He wished a foam-flecked boar
might come his way, or a lion charge from the hills.

Now thunder roared and rumbled across the sky;
soon came black clouds, the hailstorm, and the rain.
The Tyrian people and men of Troy broke ranks,
and with them Venus' grandson° ran for shelter— Ascanius
anywhere! Rivers in spate rushed down the slopes.
The prince of Troy and Dido both had come
to a cave. The bride's attendants, Earth and Juno,
gave signal: lightning and empyrean flamed
in witness; high in the hills Nymphs made their moan.
That was the day, the first of death and first
of evil. Repute, appearance, nothing moved
the queen; she laid no plan to hide her love,
but called it marriage, with this word veiled her shame.

At once Rumor went out through Libya's towns—
Rumor, than whom no evil thing is faster:
speed is her life; each step augments her strength.
Small, a shiver, at first, she soon rears high.
She walks aground; her head hides in the clouds.
Men say that Earth, in fury at the gods,
bore this last child, a sister to the Giants.
She is swift of foot and nimble on the wing,
a horror, misshapen, huge. Beneath each feather
there lies a sleepless eye (wonder to tell!),
and a tongue, and speaking lips, and ears erect.

[93] **Cynthus:** A mountain in Delos, said to be the birthplace of Apollo and Diana.

By night she flies far over the shadowed world
gibbering; sleep never comes to rest her eyes.
By day she sits at watch high on a roof
or lofty tower, and terrifies great cities,
as much a vessel of slander as crier of truth.
This time she filled men's minds with varied gossip,
chuckling and chanting alike both false and true:
Aeneas had come, born of the blood of Troy;
Dido had deemed him worthy mate and man.
Now they were warming the winter with rich exchange,
forgetful of thrones, ensnared by shameful lust.
Such tales foul Rumor spread upon men's lips,
then turned her course straight off to King Iarbas,
heaped fire into his heart and raked his wrath.

Iarbas, son of a Nymph by Hammon[94] raped,
had raised in his broad realms a hundred shrines
to Jove, a hundred altars and vigil fires
with priests at endless prayer; the blood of beasts
fattened the soil, the doors were decked with flowers.
Maddened at heart, enflamed by bitter rumor
he stood at the altar amid the powers of heaven,
raised hands in suppliance, and prayed aloud:

"Almighty Jove, to whom the Moorish kind
on purple couches serve rich food and wine,
do you see this? Or are we fools to fear
your lightning bolt? Are cloud and fire blind,
that frighten our hearts, mere noise devoid of strength?
This woman, this immigrant in my bounds, who paid
to build her little town, to whom I granted
tidewater land on terms, rejects my hand
but takes my lord Aeneas to her throne.
And now that Paris and his half-male crew,
with perfumed hair and Persian caps chin-tied,
keeps what he stole, while I bring gifts to shrines—
your shrines—and worship empty shams of glory."

As with hand on altar he made this prayer
the almighty heard; his eye turned toward the palace,
toward two in love forgetting their better fame.

---

[94] **Hammon:** Jove; King Iarbas, Dido's chief Libyan suitor, claims to be descended from Hammon, or Ammon, a Libyan-Egyptian deity who came to be associated with Jove.

He spoke to Mercury then with this command:
"Go, son, summon the Zephyrs[95] and take flight.
Our prince of Troy dawdles in Carthage now
and takes no thought for cities assigned by fate.
Fly with the wind, bring him my word, and speak:
'Such not the man his lovely mother promised,
nor such twice saved by her from Argive arms,
but one to rule a country big with power—
Italy, land of the war cry—to pass on
the blood of Teucer, and bring worlds under law.'
If none of these great glories fires his heart
and for his own renown he'll spend no toil,
does he begrudge his son a fortress Rome?
What plans, what hopes hold him on foreign soil,
blind to Ausonia and Lavinia's land?[96]
'Sail on!' That is all. Bring him this word from me."

He ended. Mercury moved to carry out
the father's command. First he put on his sandals
golden, winged, that bear him swift as the wind
high over land and high above the sea,
then took his wand. With this he calls the ghosts
pale out of Orcus,[97] or sends them sorrowing down,
grants sleep, withdraws it, unseals the eyes of death.
With it he drives the winds and sails the clouds.
Now flying he saw the cap and rugged flanks
of Atlas, whose granite shoulders prop the sky—
Atlas: his pine-clad head, forever crowned
with clouds, is buffeted by wind and rain.
A glacier clothes his back, and cascades course
down over his face; his beard bristles with ice.
Here Mercury hovering on both wings alike
stopped, then plummeted headlong toward the sea
just like a gull that, round the beaches, round
fish-haunted reefs, skims low across the waves.
So between earth and sky he flew along
toward Libya's sandy shore, cleaving the wind
eastward from Atlas—Mercury, son of Maia.
Soon as his winged feet touched settlement ground,
he saw Aeneas footing down forts and raising

[95] **Zephyrs:** The winds; the Zephyr is the warm, west wind. [96] **Ausonia . . . Lavinia's land:** Italy; Lavinia, whom Aeneas will later marry, is the daughter of Latinus, king of Latium. Ausonia is another name for Italy.
[97] **Orcus:** The land of the dead, or the underworld.

new homes. The sword he wore was yellow-starred
with jasper, a cape of glowing Tyrian scarlet
hung from his shoulders—gifts the wealthy queen
had given, and broidered the cloth with thread of gold.
Up stepped the god: "Aeneas! In Carthage now
do you lay foundations and plan a handsome town
for a wife? *Your* throne, *your* state—are they forgotten?
From shining Olympus *he* has sent me down—
the king of gods, whose nod makes heaven roll.
He bade me fly with the wind to bring his word:
what plans, what hopes hold you at leisure here?
If nothing of promised glory moves your heart,
and for your own renown you'll spend no toil,
what of your son? He's growing! Your heir, Iulus:
what of his hopes? A kingdom—Italy—Rome:
these are his due!" With this, the Cyllenian god[98]
left mortal sight, nor waited for reply;
beyond the eye he vanished into air.

Aeneas was frightened out of speech and mind;
his hair stood up in terror, his voice stuck fast.
He burned to go, to flee this pleasant land;
God's word, God's great commands had struck him hard.
But what should he do? How dare he tell the queen?
She was mad for love: how could he start his plea?
His mind turned quickly here, turned quickly there,
darting in different ways all round about.
As he weighed the matter this seemed the better course:
he called Sergestus, Mnestheus, Serestus the brave:
"Not a word! Prepare to sail! Call out our people!
To battle stations, all: coin some excuse
for these new orders." Meanwhile, let gentle Dido
know nothing, suspect no rupture of their love:
he now would test approaches, seek the time
and kindest way to tell her. Quickly all
in joy at his command obeyed his orders.

But still the queen (who can deceive a lover?)
foretold the scheme, caught contemplated moves,
feared even where all was safe. Then Rumor came
to report the fleet outfitted and ready to sail.

---

[98] **the Cyllenian god:** Mercury (Hermes) is so called because Mt. Cyllene, in Arcadia, was home to his mother, the nymph Maia, as well as his own birthplace.

Her passion burst control; savage, aflame,
she raced through town, as, at an elevation,
the Thyiad who feels the spur of Bacchic hymns
and dances, and hears Cithaeron shout by night.[99]
At last she addressed Aeneas; her words burst forth:

"You lied! You thought you could conceal a wrong
so vast, and leave my land without one word?
Our love, your right hand given in pledge that day,
a Dido to suffer and die—are these no check?
What? Fit out your fleet beneath a winter sun,
and hurry across the sea while north winds howl,
hard-hearted man? Were it no foreign land,
no unknown home you sought, but Troy still stood,
would you send ships through storms like these to Troy?
You run from *me*? In tears, I seize your hand
(what other solace have I left myself?)
and beg you recall our marriage, our wedding day:
if I have served you well, if you have found
delight in me, have mercy! My house is crumbling!
If prayer can still be heard, change, change your heart!
You made the Libyan tribes, the Nomad kings,
yes, my own Tyrians, hate me; lost for you
were honor and good repute, my only path
to glory. Cast off, fit only to die, who'll have me,
you whom I entertained—no more say, 'married.'
What now? Wait till Pygmalion levels my walls,
or the Moor Iarbas drags me off in chains?
If only before your flight I had conceived
your child, if only a baby Aeneas played
here in my court, whose face might mirror yours,
I'd feel less like one taken and discarded."
She finished. Aeneas, strengthened by Jove's words,
gazed steadily at her and suppressed his pain.
At last he briefly replied, "Speak! List them all—
your favors and courtesies! There is not one
I won't confess. I'll think of you with joy
long as I think at all, and live, and breathe.
But now to the point. I did not mean (believe me!)
to slip away by stealth, nor ever feigned
the wedding torch, or made such league with you.

[99] **the Thyiad . . . night:** Virgil compares Dido here to a Bacchante (Thyiad), a female devotee of Bacchus driven into an ecstatic, uncontrollable passion.

If fate had let me govern my own life
and heal my troubles in the way I willed,
I would be living in Troy with what remained
of my people; Priam's halls would still be standing;
and we, though beaten, had built our walls anew.
But Apollo Grynean[100] sent me to Italy;
'Find Italy! Win her!' declared the oracles.
My love, my home, lie there. You are of Tyre,
yet Libyan Carthage holds you, hall and wall:
why take it ill that Trojans look for homes
in Italy? Strange lands we too may seek.
Whenever dewy night enshrouds the world
and fiery stars arise, Anchises' ghost,
murky and fearful, warns me in my dreams.
Ascanius, well-loved son: see how I wrong him,
cheating him of Hesperian land and throne!
Now comes a messenger from Jove himself
(I swear it!); he sped through air to bring command.
In the clear light of day I saw that god;
he entered these walls; my ears drank in his words.
Cease to enflame my heart and yours with plaints:
not by my choice I go to Italy."

Even as he spoke she turned her face away.
Glancing now here, now there, she viewed the man
from head to foot, wordless. Then speech flared out:
"No goddess your mother, no Dardanus sired your kind,
you liar! No! Caucasus[101] got you on those cliffs
of jagged granite, and tigers suckled you there!
Dissemble? Why? To await some greater wrong?
I wept; he made no sound, nor turned an eye.
I loved him; where were his tears, his sympathy?
What else shall I say? Juno, lady and queen,
Jove, son of Saturn, can be unmoved no longer.
Good faith is folly! I saved him, castaway
and helpless, I made him partner to my power.
He'd lost his ships, his men; I rescued them.
My madness flames like fire: 'Apollo' now,
'the oracles' now; now 'sent by Jove himself
a messenger comes through air with dread commands.'

[100] **Apollo Grynean:** So called after Gryneum, a city in Asia Minor with a major shrine to Apollo. [101] **Caucasus:** Dido here personifies the Caucasus Mountains, the site of the torture of Prometheus near the Caspian Sea, to characterize the origin of Aeneas's cruelty.

This is the gods' life work! Such cares disturb
their peace! You're free; I'll not refute your claims.
Go! Find your Italian throne by wind and wave!
Midway, I trust, if God has power, you'll drink
requital on a reef and scream for Dido!
There'll be no Dido, but a funeral flame
will follow, and when death sunders soul from flesh
my shade will haunt you till my price is paid.
I'll know! Report will reach my ghost in hell!"
She broke off in mid-speech and, sickened, fled
the light of day—ran from his sight, from him,
while he stood trembling, groping, conning a flood
of words. She fainted. Her people raised her up
and bore her to her room and to her bed.

Aeneas the good, though longing to ease her pain
with words of comfort and turn aside her care
(his groans came deep, for love had racked his heart),
obeyed God's orders and sought his fleet again.
Then truly his men fell to; the shore was filled
with hauling of ships. Out swam fresh-painted keels;
men loaded oars still green, and from the woods
brought spars half-hewn in haste.
"Move out!" they heard. "All hands!" "Look lively, now!"
(As when the ants, mindful of winter, attack
a heap of grain and carry it home across
the fields: black goes the column; they bear their prize
down narrow grassy lanes. Some push big kernels
with heave of shoulders; some close the line of march
and hurry stragglers. The path is a froth of toil.)
Dido! What did you feel to see all this?
What cries did you utter when from tower's top
you saw the shore all seething, saw the sea
churned up before your eyes, and heard the shouts!
Shameless love, where do you not drive men's hearts?
Again she went and wept and begged, for try
she must; her pride must bend the knee to love,
lest for failing to move she die in vain.

"Anna, you see them rushing round the shore:
the crews are mustered; the canvas calls the breeze;
the men have cheered as garlands dressed the spar.
Could I have known such sorrow was to come,
I could have borne it; but now in tears I beg
one favor, Anna, of you: that faithless man

was always with you, told you his secret thoughts;
you knew, as no one else, his gentler moods.
Go, bring to our heartless guest this humble plea:
I joined no Greeks; I took no oath at Aulis[102]
of death to Trojans, I sent no ships to Troy,
I never harried his father Anchises' ghost.
Why will he lock his ears against my words?
Why haste? Let a broken heart win one last grace:
Await a safer passage and favoring winds!
I'll not ask now for the wedlock he betrayed,
or that he resign his darling Latin throne;
I beg for time, an hour of rest from madness,
till fortune teach me how to lose and grieve.
This favor the last your sister asks: be kind!
I'll pay my debt with death to make full measure."[103]

Such was her plea; such sorrows her grieving sister
reported, reported again. But nothing moved him;
no tears nor words could teach his heart to hear.
(Fate blocked the way; God closed his ears to pity.)
Like an oak tree, ancient, toughened by the years,
blasted by Alpine winds this way and that
contesting to uproot it; the North Wind howls,
the trunk is shaken, foliage strews the ground.
The tree holds hard; its crown lifts up toward heaven
far as its root grows down toward Tartarus.[104]
Just so Aeneas, by pleas this side and that
assaulted, felt in his heart the thrust of care.
His mind stood firm; tears came, but came in vain.[105]

Then Dido, luckless, by fortune terrified,
invited death: to view heaven's vault was pain.
To strengthen her resolve to leave the light,
she saw, when she offered her gifts and censed the altars
(dreadful to tell!), the holy water turn black
and the wine pour down in horrid clots of gore.
She told none, not even Anna, what she'd seen.
Besides, in her house there stood a marble shrine

[102] **Aulis:** The port in Boeotia from which the Greeks set sail for Troy after having sacrificed Iphigenia, Agamemnon's daughter, to stir up favorable winds. [103] **I'll pay . . . full measure:** The last line here is deliberately ambiguous: It could anticipate Dido's suicide or revenge on Aeneas. [104] **Tartarus:** The lowest region of the underworld where punishments are meted out to sinners. [105] **tears . . . in vain:** An ambiguous line. Whose tears are these? Some readers, including St. Augustine, have seen them as the concealed tears of the stoic Aeneas.

to her former husband, which she kept sacrosanct,
festooned with white wool bands and feast-day flowers:
from it she thought she heard her husband's voice
calling her, calling, when darkness gripped the world.
And on her roof a lonesome owl sang songs
of death; its mournful cry trailed off in sobs.
Then warnings of seers long dead came crowding back
to fill her with fright. She dreamed herself gone mad,
with Aeneas in wild pursuit; then left alone
to travel, forever friendless, a long, long road,
seeking her Tyrians in an empty world,
like maddened Pentheus[106] seeing the rank of Furies,
seeing twin suns and a double Thebes displayed;
or like Orestes racing across the stage
to escape a mother armed with torch and serpent—
and at Agamemnon's door the Dirae[107] wait.

Filled with madness and prisoner of her pain,
she determined to die; and now, with how and when
planned in her mind, she addressed her tearful sister
(concealing intent behind a cloudless brow):
"Anna, I've found a way—applaud your sister!—
that will bring him back, or free me from my love.
Near to the ocean's edge and setting sun
lies African land's-end, where giant Atlas
bears on his back the spinning star-tricked wheel.
I've found a religious of that place—a Moor;
she served the Hesperides' temple, fed the snake,
and guarded the holy branches on the tree;
with honey and poppy she made the elixir of sleep.
She swears she can release what hearts she will
with spells, and freight still other hearts with care,
can stop the rivers and reverse the stars,
and raise the dead by night: you'll see the earth
groan at her feet and trees climb down the hills.
Sister, I tell you, by your life, by all
that's holy, I take to witchcraft against my will.
Slip into our inner courtyard and build there

[106] **maddened Pentheus:** A king of Thebes who aroused the wrath of Bacchus by opposing his rites; Bacchus took revenge by driving Pentheus mad and having him murdered by his own mother and other Bacchantes in an ecstatic frenzy. The Furies were not part of the earlier myth or of Euripides' play *The Bacchae,* which tells the story of Pentheus. [107] **Dirae:** After killing his mother, Clytemnestra, to avenge the death of his father, Agamemnon, Orestes was pursued by the Furies (the Dirae), female creatures who punish those who commit blood-crimes against their kin.

a pyre; pile on it the arms that perjured man
hung in my house—take all he left, the bed
of marriage that brought me sorrow. I must destroy
his every devilish trace: so says my Moor."
This much, then silence, and her face turned pale.
Yet Anna did not suspect that these strange rites
were cover for death; her mind conceived no thought
so mad. Than when Sychaeus died: she feared
no worse, and did as asked.

In the inner court beneath the open sky
the pyre stood huge with pitch pine and with oak.
The queen hung garlands and wreathed the place with boughs
of death; atop, she laid his sword, his garments—
yes, and his image: she knew what she would do.
Ringed by altars the Moor let down her hair,
intoned the gods three hundred, Chaos, and Hell,
the Hecates three, Diana the triform virgin.[108]
She sprinkled water labeled "from Avernus,"[109]
selected hairy leaves by moonlight reaped
with brazen sickle (their milky juice turns black),
pulled out the membrane torn from a newborn foal
and snatched from its mother's mouth.
Dido stepped to an altar, blessed her hands,
took meal, slipped off one shoe, unlatched her gown,
then, ready to die, begged gods and stars prophetic
to hear her prayer to any power just
and mindful, that cares for lovers wrongly matched.

It was night; all over the world the weary flesh
found peace in sleep; forests and savage seas
rested; in middle course the stars rolled on.
No sound from field, from herd, from painted birds
that swarm the liquid lakes or love the thorn
and thicket: they slept in silence of the night,
healing the heart of care, forgetting pain.
But never the broken-hearted, luckless queen
slipped off to sleep or took the night to eyes
and heart. Her torment doubled; desire rose

---

[108] **Chaos . . . virgin:** Dido calls up all those associated with the underworld: Chaos, Hell, the Hecates (here meaning the three Furies), and Diana, in her role as the goddess of sorcery and the moon. [109] **"from Avernus":** Avernus is the lake and wood near Cumae in southern Italy where the entrance to the underworld was said to be; it is from here that Aeneas, in Book 6, begins his descent into the land of the dead.

raging; she ebbed and flowed on waves of wrath.
At last she paused and pondered inner thoughts:
"What shall I do? I'm scorned! Shall I turn and try
my earlier suitors, and beg a Nomad's bed?
I have disdained their hand, how many times?
Well, then, to the Trojan fleet? Hurry to catch
their final word? Because they prized my help
and remember that musty favor with gratitude?
Granted the will, who'd let an unloved woman
tread his proud deck? You fool! You still don't know,
don't see, how the sons of Laomedon can lie?
Well—? Trail his jeering crews, a lovesick girl?
Or board ship with my Tyrians, rank on rank,
around me—men whom just now I saved from Sidon:
bid them make sail and put to sea once more?
No! Die as you've earned! Take steel and end your pains!
You, Anna, hurt by my tears, you topped my folly
with wrongful acts; you tossed me to our foe!
I had not the will to pass my life unwed,
unstained, like some wild creature, untouched by guilt.
I did not keep my oath to dead Sychaeus."
Such were the sorrows that broke forth from her breast.

Aeneas knew he would go; on his tall ship,
his preparations made, he took his rest.
In his dreams a godly form appeared again,
just as before, and seemed to warn once more
(in all like Mercury, in voice, complexion,
in the flaxen hair and graceful limbs of youth):
"Goddess-born, can you sleep at such an hour,
and fail to see the dangers that surround you—
madman!—nor hear the favoring West Wind blow?
Dido devises malice and foul crime
(she knows she'll die) and roils her anger's waves.
Run! Leave in haste, while haste's within your power.
Soon you will see the ocean churned by ships,
the shore ablaze with savage torch and flames,
if Dawn shall touch you tarrying in this land.
Hurry, now! Ever a various, changeful thing
is woman." He spoke and mingled with black night.

This apparition terrified Aeneas.
He tore himself from sleep and harried his men
to haste: "Look lively, there, and man the thwarts!
Off buntlines! Quick! A god from heaven's height

again has bid us speed away and cut
our anchor-lines. We come, O sacred presence,
whoever you are! Again we obey your word.
Be with us in peace! Bless us! Show helpful stars
in heaven!" He spoke, and ripped his flashing sword
from sheath, and with the bared blade slashed the lines.
Like ardor held them all. They seized, they ran,
they emptied the beach; their vessels hid the sea.
Men heaved, churned up the foam, and swept the blue.

And now Aurora brought the dawn's new light
to earth, and left Tithonus'[110] golden couch.
Dido was watching, and with the first pale gleam
she saw the fleet, yards squared and outward bound,
and marked the emptiness of shore and pier.
Three times and four she beat her lovely breast
and tore her golden hair: "What? Shall he go,"
she said, "and mock my power—that foreigner!
There'll be no general muster? No pursuit?
Will no one hurry to launch my ships? Quick, men,
bring torches, hand out arms, lean on your oars!
What's this? Where am I? What madness warps my mind?
Fool! Has your sacrilege just struck you now?
It should have, the day you offered a throne! Such honor!
And he, they say, brings with him his fathers' gods;
his shoulders carried Anchises, tired and old!
Why couldn't I hack his flesh, tear it, and strew
the sea with it? Slaughter his people and his son—
serve up Ascanius at his father's table?
But battle had been uncertain? Grant it so,
why fear, when I meant to die? I'd have thrown fire
and filled their camp with flame: father and son
and people had burned to death to make my pyre.
O Sun, who with your flame light all men's works;
you, Juno, who know my troubles and read them true;
Hecate, hailed at night by town and crossroad;
Dirae, gods of a Dido soon to die,
receive my prayer; turn sanction meet and right
upon these wrongs; hear me! If touch he must
on promised port and land—that man accursed!—

[110] **Tithonus:** The beloved companion of Aurora, goddess of the dawn; Aurora won eternal life for Tithonus but forgot to ask also for eternal youth, so Tithonus grew weak and feebleminded. In some versions of the story, he was shut away from his former lover. Virgil's imagery suggests a more positive outcome.

and so Jove's laws demand, this end is fixed.
But let brave people harass him with war.
Driven from home, torn from Iulus' arms,
let him beg for help, and see his people die
disgraced. Make him surrender under terms
unjust, and know no happy years of rule,
but die untimely, untombed, in miles of sand.
This is my final prayer, poured with my blood.
And you, my Tyrians, hate his race, his kind,
all and always. On my remains bestow
this office: no love, no peace between our peoples!
And from my grave let some avenger rise
to harry the Trojan settlers with fire and sword—
now, some day, whenever we have the power.
Shore against shore, I pray, wave against sea,
sword against sword, fight, father and son, forever!"[111]

So said she, and turned her thoughts this way and that,
seeking how soonest to end an unloved life.
To Barce then she spoke—Sychaeus' nurse
(her own lay buried in the fatherland):
"Dear nurse, bring Anna, my sister, here to me.
Tell her to hurry and wash in a running stream,
then bring the victims and holy things I showed her.
Come, both, with sacred ribbons in your hair
I wish to do my office to Stygian Jove[112]
(all duly prepared) to put an end to care
and lay that Trojan soul on funeral flames."

This much. In joy, the old nurse hobbled off.
Savage design drove Dido mad with fright.
Her eyes were wild and bloodshot; on her cheek
flush faded to pallor in terror of death so near.
She rushed to the inner court; madly she climbed
up the tall pyre and drew that Trojan sword,
gift that was never meant for such a use.

[111] **no love . . . forever:** Dido's curse anticipates the historical conflict between Carthage and Rome, most pointedly during the Punic Wars of 264–241, 218–201, and 149–146 B.C.E. The "avenger" may refer to the great general Hannibal (247–c. 182 B.C.E.) who invaded Italy by crossing over the Alps using elephants to carry equipment and supplies. After many successful victories against the Romans, Hannibal eventually was forced to withdraw his forces from Italy. [112] **Stygian Jove:** Pluto (Hades in Greek mythology), the ruler of the underworld, associated with the key river of hell, the Styx.

She saw his Trojan garment and their bed
well-known; then after a moment's tearful thought
lay down on the couch and spoke these final words:
"Here, trophies that I loved, while God allowed!
Oh, take my life and free me from my sorrow.
I've lived, and run the course that fate assigned;
in glory my shade now goes beneath the earth.
I built a splendid city and saw it walled,
avenged my husband, and made my brother pay—
blessed beyond measure, if only Dardan craft
had never touched upon these shores of mine."
She kissed the couch. "I'll die without revenge,
but die, and pass to darkness undismayed.
From shipboard let the heartless Trojan see
my flames! My death ride with him as he sails!"

While she yet spoke, her people saw her fall
crumpled upon the sword, the blade all frothed
with blood, her hands spattered. A scream rose high
in the hall; the city was stricken; Rumor ran wild.
Houses were filled with sobs and lamentations,
with keening of women: the din rose to the skies—
as if an enemy had burst in, and all
Carthage or ancient Tyre were falling, while flames
rolled to the roofs, through homes of gods and men.
Anna, half-dead with fear, came running fast:
her fingers tore her face; she beat her breast.
She pushed through the crowd, calling her sister's name:
"Dido, was this what it meant? You lied? to *me*?
Was this the purpose of pyre, altar, and flame?
You left me! What shall I say? You died, but scorned
to take me? You might have let me share your death:
one hour, one stroke of pain had served for two.
These hands helped build—this voice of mine helped call
our gods—oh, cruel!—that I must fail you now!
You've killed yourself and me, your people, the lords
of Sidon, and your own city! Oh, let me wash
your wounds, and if some faltering breath remains,
let my lips take it!" With that, she climbed the pyre
and cradled her dying sister in her arms,
cried as she used her dress to stop the blood.
Dido would open her heavy eyes again,
but failed. The gash hissed in her wounded breast.
Three times she raised herself up on one arm,

three times fell back, then with an errant eye
sought light in heaven, and moaned that she had found it.

Then Juno in pity for her lingering pain
and laggard death, sent Iris down from heaven
to free her struggling soul from limbs entwined.
(For not at her earned and fated hour she died,
but in a flash of fury, before her days:
Proserpina[113] had not yet cut the lock
from her head, nor sentenced her to life below.)
But Iris flew down, dewy and golden-winged,
trailing against the sun a thousand colors.
She stopped over Dido's head: "This sacred lock
I carry to Dis,[114] and from the flesh I free you."
With that she cut the wisp; at once all warmth
dispersed, and life retreated to the winds.

Book 6
[Aeneas Visits the Underworld]

[In Book 5, Aeneas, ignorant of Dido's death, sails to Sicily, where to commemorate his father's death he holds athletic games. In a succession of contests he demonstrates his fairness and concern for all his company, especially through the dispensing of gifts. Meanwhile, on the beaches, the Trojan women are beguiled by the goddess Iris into burning their men's ships so they may sail no more. Aeneas puts out the fires and decides to leave the dissenters behind in Sicily. Aeneas and his men finally sail for Italy, assured of safe passage by the gods, except for the helmsman Palinurus, who falls overboard and is lost at sea. Now, in Book 6, Aeneas prepares to descend to the Underworld.]

He spoke, and wept, and gave the ships free rein
until they raised Euboean Cumae's[115] coasts.
Seaward the bows were swung; the anchor's tooth
grounded the ships, their curving quarterdecks
curtained the strand. The young men dashed like flame
to Hesperian shores. Part sought the seeds of fire
hidden in veins of flint, part raided forests,
the wild beasts' homes, found brooks, and marked them out.
But Aeneas the good looked for Apollo's hill

[113] **Proserpina:** The queen of the underworld, wife of Dis, or Pluto, the god of the underworld, to whom Proserpina offers a lock of hair from persons about to die. Since Dido has unexpectedly committed suicide, Proserpina must send Iris, the goddess of the rainbow and a messenger of the gods, to obtain a lock of Dido's hair.
[114] **Dis:** Another name for the underworld; also a name for the god of the underworld. [115] **Euboean Cumae:** Cumae, the Italian town that was home to the Sibyl, priestess of Apollo, the "Delian seer" of line 12. Cumae is called Euboean here after the people from the city of Chalcis on the island of Euboea who colonized Cumae.

and castle, and near it the awesome cave where hid
the Sibyl, the terrifier, whose heart and mind
the Delian seer filled with prophetic speech.
They came to Trivia's[116] grove and golden halls.

Men say that Daedalus,[117] fleeing Minos' power,
dared put his trust in air and widespread wings.
He sailed unwonted ways toward Arctic cold,
and settled lightly, at last, on Cumae's heights.
Safe landed, he made thank-offering first to Phoebus—
the wings he'd used—and built an awesome shrine:
on one door, Androgeos'[118] death; the penalty, next,
paid by a sorrowing Athens every year:
seven of her sons; the urn and lots were shown.
On the other side, the isle of Crete rose high;
here a bull's cruel and furtive act of love
with Minos' daughter, their twoform hybrid child,
the Minotaur, monument to love profaned.
Next came that winding, wearying, hopeless house;
but Daedalus pitied a princess lost for love[119]
and solved the riddle and puzzle of those halls,
with thread to guide blind feet. You, Icarus, too,
had shared in the masterpiece, had grief allowed.
Twice Daedalus tried to carve your fate in gold,
twice fell a father's hands.
They had perused
each last detail, had not Achates joined them,
and with him the seer of Phoebus and Trivia,
Deiphobë,[120] Glaucus' daughter. She hailed Aeneas:
"The hour allows no time for seeing sights!
Far better from virgin herd to slaughter bullocks
seven, and seven sheep, and make due prayer."

---

[116] **Trivia:** An epithet of Hecate, the patroness of sorcery and a goddess of the underworld, so named for her association with crossroads. [117] **Daedalus:** The architect of the Labyrinth on Crete. Daedalus was exiled to Crete after murdering his nephew, whose skill rivaled his own. He built the labyrinth to harbor the Minotaur, a creature half human and half bull fathered on King Minos's wife, Pasiphae, by a bull. To end the annual sacrifice of his fellow Athenians to the Minotaur, the hero Theseus killed the monster with the help of Ariadne, Minos's daughter. Daedalus was then imprisoned in the labyrinth for helping Ariadne and Theseus but escaped with his son, Icarus, by fashioning wings for them and flying away. Icarus perished after approaching too close to the sun; Daedalus flew on to Cumae and constructed the temple with the carvings described here. [118] **Androgeos:** The son of King Minos of Crete, whose murder by the Athenians led to the sacrifice of seven young men and seven virgins each year to the Minotaur. (See note 117.) [119] **princess lost for love:** Ariadne. (See note 117.) [120] **Deiphobë:** The Cumaean Sibyl.

So speaking (the men at once performed the rites
as ordered), she called the Trojans to her shrine.

From Cumae's cliff was hewn a monstrous cave,
with hundred gaping mouths and hundred doors,
whence poured out hundred words, the Sibyl's answers.
As they entered, the priestess cried, "Now hear your dooms!
'Tis the hour! Behold my god!" And as she spoke
there at the door her face and color changed,
her hair fell in a tangle; she choked, she gasped,
her heart swelled wild and savage; she seemed to grow
and utter inhuman sounds, as on her breathed
the power of God. "Trojan," she cried, "you lag?
Aeneas, you lag at prayers? No other power
can blast agape these temple doors." She spoke
no further word. Through hardened Trojan hearts
ran shock and chill; Aeneas was roused to pray:
"Phoebus, help ever-present in Troy's dark days,
who guided the Dardan shaft and hand of Paris
against Achilles,[121] through countless seas that block
vast lands you led me, and to frontier tribes
Massylian—tracts that border on the Syrtes.[122]
At last we've reached elusive Italy's coasts:
so far, no farther, let Troy's fate pursue us.
You too may lawfully show us mercy now,
you heavenly powers who hated Troy and all
our Dardan glory. And you, most holy seer,
who know the future, grant (the power I ask
is not unsanctioned) that for Trojan gods,
errant and battered, I find a Latin home.
To Phoebus and Trivia then I'll build a shrine
of marble, and name a day 'The Feast of Phoebus.'
You too shall find a temple in my realm;
there I will place your lots and arcane dooms
proclaimed to my people, and men shall be ordained,
lady, to serve you.[123] Write no more on leaves,

---

[121] **who guided . . . Achilles:** As god of archery, Apollo guided Paris's spear toward Achilles' heel, the only vulnerable spot on his body. [122] **Massylian . . . Syrtes:** The Massylians were a North African tribe; the Syrtes were dangerous shoals off the northern coast of Africa, near Tripoli and Tunis. [123] **You too . . . serve you:** Aeneas's promise to build the Sibyl a holy shrine alludes to the collection of Sibylline books containing prophetic oracles that were housed in a succession of Roman temples built over time by several rulers.

lest wanton winds make nonsense of your songs:
let your lips speak!" He said no further word.

Not yet possessed by Phoebus, the weird fay danced
wild in the cave, if she might shake the god
free of her heart, he harassed all the more
her lips, her savage soul, suppressing, molding.
And now the temple's hundred mouths gaped wide
of themselves; the Sibyl's answer rode the air:
"My son, you have passed all perils of the sea,
but ashore still worse await. To Latium's land
the sons of Troy shall come (this care dismiss),
but coming shall find no joy. War, terror, war,
I see, and Tiber foaming red with blood.
You'll face a Simois, Xanthus, Greeks encamped;
in Latium now a new Achilles lives,
he, too, a goddess' son.[124] Troy's burden, Juno,
will never leave you; humble, in need, you'll plead
with every Italian tribe and town for help.
Cause of disaster again a foreign bride,
a match with a woman not of Troy.[125]
Still, never retreat! Gain boldness from disaster!
Where chance allows, march on! Salvation's path
(where least you'd think) a Greek town will reveal."[126]

In words like these the Sibyl from her shrine
sang riddles of terror and bellowed in her cave,
wrapping the truth in darkness; such the rein
and spur Apollo gave her maddened heart.
Soon as her lips, deranged and wild, found rest,
Aeneas began "Lady, no face of peril
will strike me strange or rise up unforetold;
I've seized and pondered all things in advance.
One favor! Men say the infernal king has here
his gate; here hell's dark, swampy rivers rise:

[124] **a goddess' son:** The prophecy compares the war to come in Latium, where the Trojan exiles will land at the mouth of the Tiber River, to the Trojan War; Simois and Xanthus are rivers at Troy. The new Achilles is Turnus, the Rutulian leader who will oppose Aeneas. [125] **a woman not of Troy:** In keeping with the comparison of the war in Latium to the Trojan War (see note 124), here Virgil compares Lavinia, Aeneas's future wife, to Helen of Troy. [126] **a Greek town will reveal:** The town is Pallanteum, a colony founded on the Tiber River, at the site of Rome, by the Arcadian Evander. Evander's son, Pallas, will fight with Aeneas against Turnus, who kills Pallas in Book 10.

allow me to see my well-loved father's face;
show me the way, spread wide the holy doors.
Through flames and thousand flying spears I saved him
on these shoulders, with enemies all around.
He shared the route through all those seas with me
and bore the threats of ocean and of sky,
more than the old and ill have strength to bear.
Still more: he used to plead that I seek out
your door in humble access. Lady, have mercy
on father and son! All power is yours; not idly
did Hecate[127] lay Avernus to your charge:
Orpheus could hale a wife's poor ghost from hell
by power of music and his Thracian lyre,
and Pollux, saving his twin by altern death,
could pass and repass that road. Why tell of Theseus
or Hercules?[128] I too am of Jove's line."

So he petitioned, with hand on altar laid.
The Sibyl replied: "O child of blood divine,
Anchises' son, descent to hell is easy:
all night, all day black Pluto's[129] door stands wide.
To recall the step, escape to air and sky—
this, this is task and toil! Some few—those loved
of Jove, those heavenward rapt by valor's flame,
the sons of God—have done it. Between, all's forest
wrapped round with black Cocytus'[130] coiling streams.
But if you have at heart such love and lust
twice to cross over Styx, hell's darkness twice
to behold, and this mad project gives you joy,
hear what is first to do. A dark tree hides
a bough whose pliant withes and leaves are gold,
to hell's queen sacred. Curtained by a grove
it lies locked in a shadowy, lightless vale.

[127] **Hecate:** The patroness of sorcery and a goddess of the underworld; Hecate governs over Avernus, the lake and wood near Cumae where the entrance to the underworld was said to be. [128] **Orpheus . . . Hercules:** Aeneas recites the names of heroes who have been allowed to enter the underworld and return. By means of his enchanting music, Orpheus entered Hades and persuaded Proserpina (Persephone) to allow him to bring his dead wife, Eurydice, back to the land of the living so long as he did not turn back to look at her on their ascent; he did, and she vanished from him. Pollux and his brother Castor, the Dioscuri, were allowed to alternate days between the underworld and the land of the living. The Athenian hero Theseus was trapped in Hades when he tried to help Pirithous abduct Proserpina, the queen of Hades. Theseus was rescued when Hercules, performing one of his labors, came to the underworld to steal the guardian of the gate, the three-headed dog Cerberus. [129] **Pluto:** The god of the underworld; known as Hades in Greek mythology. [130] **Cocytus:** The wailing river; one of the rivers of hell.

But none may pass beneath this covering earth
till he has plucked the tree's gold-sprouted branch.
This must be brought to Pluto's lovely queen[131]
as offering due. (Break one, a second grows
like it, with leaves and stems of purest gold.)
Search then the treetops; when you find it, pray
and pluck. The branch will come away with ease
if you are elect of Fate. If not, no force
of yours will break it, no cold steel hack it free.
Lastly: a friend lies now a lifeless corpse
(you did not know!); his death stains all your fleet
while you hang at my door to ask advice.
Now bring him home and lay him in the tomb.
Over black beasts; be this your first atonement.
Then shall you see the grove of Styx, those realms
where the living never tread." She spoke no more.

Aeneas, with saddened face and downcast eye,
stepped from the cave, revolving in his heart
events beyond men's sight. Beside him walked
Achates the loyal, step by troubled step.
They spoke of many things, conjecturing much
what friend had died, whose body they must bury.
But high on the beach as they came in they found
Misenus, untimely taken off by death—
Misenus, son of Aeolus, best of all
at sounding the reveille or call to arms.
He had been Hector's man; by Hector's side
he'd marched to glory with trumpet and with spear.
But once Achilles had stripped his chief of life,
he'd joined Aeneas' corps, for he was brave
and a fighter, and would obey no lesser man.
But now with a conch he'd blared across the waves—
the fool!—and dared the gods contest his tunes.
Triton accepted and, if the tale be true,
caught him on foaming reefs and drowned him there.[132]
Now, circling round, the company mourned his death,
Aeneas leading. Then, with tears, they turned
to the Sibyl's orders. Quickly they built a mound

[131] **Pluto's lovely queen:** Proserpina, the queen of Hell; also known as Persephone in Greek mythology.
[132] **Triton . . . drowned him there:** Misenus, the Trojan trumpeter and the son of Aeolus, god of the winds, challenged Triton, a sea-god famous for blowing the conch shell, to a trumpeting contest; for his arrogance Misenus was drowned in the sea. Triton was the son of Neptune (Poseidon), the chief sea-god of the Romans.

and altar, and piled on logs to reach the sky.
They went to a wood, the wild beasts' mountain lair:
down came the pine, the oak rang to the ax,
the beech and holm were hewn and split to rail
and billet; great elms came rolling from the hills.

In this work, too, Aeneas took the lead,
urged on his men, and shared their tools and toil.
And yet discouragement circled through his heart
as he viewed the wood — so vast! He fell to prayer:
"Now be the golden bough revealed to us,
here in this endless wood! For all was true
that the seer has prophesied of poor Misenus."
Scarce had he spoken when before his face
a pair of doves came flying down the sky
and settled on the turf. Aeneas knew
his mother's birds, and said a joyful prayer:
"If path there be, lead me! Direct your flight
into the woods, where on the rich soil falls
the shade of the tree of wealth. Resolve my fears,
mother in heaven!" With that, he checked his pace
to see what signs they'd give, which way they'd go.
They stopped to feed, then flew on just so far
as could be seen by those who followed them.
Then as they reached Avernus'[133] stinking throat,
they rose with a swoop and sailed through brighter air
to perch on the tree they loved, a pair at home;
but — strange! — through the branches came a flash of gold!
As in the winter's cold the mistletoe
grows leafy and green (no child of its parent tree)
and with its yellow fruit loops treetrunks round,
so in the darkness of the oak shone leaves
of gold, thin foil that tinkled in the breeze.
Aeneas seized the branch; it clung; he wrenched
it free and brought it to the Sibyl's home.

Meanwhile down on the shore the Trojans mourned
Misenus in thankless office for the dead.
They built his pyre with pitch pine and split oak,
like one great torch, and then with dull dark leaves

[133] **Avernus:** This lake, the entrance to the underworld, was given its name, which means "birdless," because the vapors rising from it would kill any bird that flew over it; hence Venus's birds swerve upon their approach to the lake.

they screened its sides. In front they set the cypress,
the death tree; shining armor graced the top.
Some set bronze pots of water over flame
to boil, then washed the body and embalmed it.
They wailed the dead, then laid him on the bier,
and covered him with the purple robe he'd known
and loved. They lifted high his heavy bed—
sad office—and in our fathers' way applied
the torch with face averted. Up went the pyre:
incense, food, and oil and wine commingled.
When cinders crumbled and the flames died down,
they quenched the dust and thirsty ash with wine.
Corynaeus gathered the bones in a brazen urn;
he bore pure water three times round his friends,
sprinkling them with hyssop of fertile olive,
to wash them clean, then said the last farewell.
Aeneas the good piled high a mounded tomb
(placing upon it the man's arms, oar, and trumpet)
beneath the crag that men now call, for him,
"Mount Misenus," to keep his name forever.

This done, they turned to do the Sibyl's bidding.
There was a cave, deep, huge, and gaping wide,
rocky, guarded by night-black pools and woods;
above it hardly a bird could wing its way
safely, such were the vapors that poured forth
from that black throat, and rose toward heaven's vault
(and hence the Greeks have named it "Birdless Cavern").[134]
Here the Sibyl began by bringing oxen
four, black-hided. She sluiced their heads with wine;
between their horns she snipped the tips of bristles
to lay as first fruits on her altar fires,
then called on Hecate, power of heaven and hell.
Acolytes plunged their knives and caught the blood
hot in their salvers. Aeneas killed a lamb,
black-fleeced, for the mother of Furies and her sister,
and for the queen of hell,[135] a barren cow.
He built night-altars to the Stygian king
and laid bull's vitals whole upon the flames,
drenching the sizzling meats with olive oil.

[134] **"Birdless Cavern":** Refers to Avernus, or Aornos in Greek mythology. (See note 133.) [135] **mother of Furies . . . hell:** The mother of the Furies was Nox, or Night (Nyx), and her sister was Earth (Ge or Gaea). The queen of Hell was Proserpina (Persephone).

Just before sunrise and the dawn's first light,
the earth beneath them bawled, the wooded hills
opened, and in the shadows she-wolves howled.
"Here comes our lady![136] Fall back, unhallowed souls!"
the seer cried. "Out of the grove! Out! Out with you!
Aeneas, start down the road! Unsheathe your sword!
Now you need courage and now a steadfast heart!"
With one mad shriek she entered the cavern's mouth;
she led, he followed, step for fearless step.

O gods who rule all souls! O silent shades!
Phlegethon,[137] Chaos, regions of voiceless night!
Grant me apocalypse! Grant me right and power
to show things buried deep in earth and darkness!

They walked obscure through night's dark loneliness
past Pluto's empty halls and vacant thrones:
as one might walk through wood beneath a moon
malign and blotched, when Jove has hidden heaven
in shadow, and black night robs the world of color.
Right at the entrance, where hell's throat begins,
Sorrow, Vengeance, and Care have pitched their tents;
there live Diseases pale, and grim Old Age,
Fear, evil-counseling Hunger, shameful Want—
shapes terrible to see—and Death and Toil,
and Death's blood brother, Sleep, and Pleasures vile
even in thought. War, dealer of death, stands watch,
and Furies chambered in steel, while mad Sedition
leers through her bedlam braids of snakes and blood.

Midst all, an elm spreads wide her ancient boughs,
opaque and huge; men say this is the home
of Foolish Dreams: they cling beneath each leaf.
And there are wild beasts, monsters of mixed breed;
Centaurs and two-formed Scyllas haunt the doors,
Briareus hundred-handed, savage Hydra
horribly hissing, Chimaera armed with flame,
Gorgons, Harpies, the ghost of bodies three.[138]

---

[136] **our lady:** Hecate, who often appears accompanied by hell-hounds, here described as she-wolves. (See note 127.) [137] **Phlegethon:** A river of fire in the underworld. [138] **Centaurs . . . three:** A catalog of mythical monsters who guard the entrance of hell: Centaurs are half man, half horse; Scyllas are creatures with six heads; Briareus is a giant with fifty heads and one hundred hands; Hydra is a gigantic nine-headed serpent; Chimaera is a dragonlike creature who is part lion, part goat, and part snake; Gorgons are snake-haired female monsters who turn men to stone with their gaze; Harpies are birdlike monsters who carry souls to Hell; and the three-bodied Geryon is the son of the Gorgon Medusa.

In sudden terror Aeneas drew his sword
and showed the charging creatures his bare blade;
and had his guide, who knew, not warned that these
were lives unsubstanced, flitting empty shapes,
he had attacked and wasted blows on shadows.

Here leads the road toward hell and Acheron,
that mud-dark stream, wide, swirling, sucking down,
sinking and rising to belch Cocytus'[139] sands.
A frightful ferryman keeps the river-watch,
Charon,[140] a ragged horror, whose thick white beard
lies matted upon his chin. His eyes are flames,
and knotted rags hang filthy from his frame.
He poles his craft himself, he tends its sail,
and in its rusty hull he freights the dead—
old, but a god's old age is raw and green.
Toward him the whole crowd rushed to the river bank—
mothers and husbands, those that had lived the lives
of bold, brave fighters, boys, unmarried girls,
young men cremated before a father's face—
as many as forest leaves that flutter down
at the first autumn frost, or as the birds
that flock to earth from sea when winter's cold
drives them across the deep to sunny lands.
They stood there begging to be first to cross,
their hands outstretched in love of the other shore.
The glowering boatman took now these, now those,
but drove back others and blocked them from the strand.
Aeneas, amazed and by the tumult moved,
said, "Tell me, why this gathering at the river?
What do the souls want? Why do some fall back
from shore, while others cross the lead-gray stream?"
Briefly the aged priestess spoke to him:
"Son of Anchises, prince of blood divine,
you see dark, deep Cocytus and swampy Styx,
names not even the gods dare take in vain.
The boatman: Charon; his passengers: the entombed.
Those others are all unburied, a hapless host;
they may not pass the shore, the hoarse, wild waters,
until their bones have found a home and rest.
A hundred years they flutter round this beach;
then finally they may approach the longed-for stream."
The son of Anchises checked his pace and stopped,

[139] **Cocytus:** Like the Acheron, a river of the underworld. [140] **Charon:** The ferryman in Hell.

puzzled and grieved at death's inequities.
He saw, embittered for lack of funeral rites,
Orontes, the Lycian admiral, and Leucaspis.
These two, sailing the wind-swept seas from Troy,
were lost when a Norther sank them, ship and crew.

Then toward them came the helmsman, Palinurus
(plotting his course from Libya by the stars
he'd slipped from his quarterdeck far out at sea);
Aeneas scarce recognized his face, so dark
and bitter. He spoke: "Palinurus, what god did this?
Who stole you from us and drowned you in mid-sea?
Tell me! I've never known Apollo lie
till this one message that betrayed my trust.
He said you'd be unharmed afloat, and come
to Italy. Is this then his word, his promise?"
Palinurus answered: "Apollo told no lie,
my lord Aeneas. I was not drowned at sea.
In a sudden lurch, the helm was cast adrift,
with me fast to it, for it was in my charge.
Overside I carried it. By all storms I swear
that for myself I feared not half so much
as that your ship, with helm and helmsman lost
overboard, might founder in the rising seas.
Three winter nights I drifted endless miles
of wind-torn water; when the fourth dawn came
from crest of a wave I raised the Italian coast.
I floated ashore by inches, made it safe,
and was clawing my way, slowed by dripping clothes,
uphill across sharp rocks, when tribesmen killed me.
(They did not know me, but thought I was fair game.)
And now I lie awash in wind and surf.
And so, by the sky, the light, the air we love,
by Anchises, by all you hope for young Iulus,
rescue me from this misery. Find the bay
of Velia[141] and—for you can!—toss earth upon me.
Or, if your goddess mother show some way
(for not without the nod of heaven, I'm sure,
you sail the boundless pools and streams of hell),
give me a hand to cross the waves with you,
that here at last I find my peace, and rest."

[141] **the bay of Velia:** A bay to the south of Naples, near what is called Point Palinuro, after Aeneas's drowned helmsman.

Such was his plea, and this the seer's reply:
"Palinurus, whence this blasphemous desire?
Shall you, unburied, look on Styx, the stream
of stern requital—you, pass this beach unbidden?
Think not to change the law of God by prayer.
But hear! Note well! Be solaced, injured soul!
A nearby people, frightened by signs from heaven
all up and down their land, will bury your bones,
raise you a mound, do office for the dead,
and name that spot 'Palinurus' for all time."
These words resolved his care; for a time he ceased
to grieve, in joy that earth should bear his name.

They resumed their journey then and neared the stream.
But when the boatman saw them from the Styx
moving through voiceless trees on toward the shore,
he started up and challenged them, and shouted:
"You with the sword, who trespass toward my river,
halt! What are you doing here? Stop where you are!
This is the vale of Shades, Dreams, Night, and Sleep.
By law, no flesh may ride the boat of hell.
Alcides? Theseus? Pirithous?[142] 'Twas no joy
to me to see them come and cross my swamp—
'Son of the gods'? 'Unconquered heroes'? Hah!
That first one snapped hell's watchdog to a leash
and dragged him whimpering from the royal door;
the others tried to kidnap Pluto's bride."
To him the Amphrysian seer[143] gave brief reply:
"Here are no schemes like those (cease your concern),
nor does that sword mean war. Your ghostly guard
may bark forever to frighten bloodless ghosts,
your queen keep undefiled her uncle's house.
Aeneas of Troy, the good, the great in arms,
has come to the shadowy pit to find his father.
If goodness and greatness leave you unconcerned,
this bough" (she showed it, hidden in her gown)
"you'll know." His hostile, puffed-up fury died,
and with it, debate. He stood amazed and humbled
to see the wand of fate so long unseen;

[142] **Alcides . . . Pirithous:** All mortals who passed through the gates of Hell while still alive; Alcides is another name for Hercules. (See note 128.) [143] **Amphrysian seer:** The Cumaean Sibyl, priestess of Apollo. Virgil here makes an obscure allusion to Apollo, who had once spent a year in the service of King Admetus in Thessaly, where the river Amphrysia was located.

he swung his dead-blue craft stern-on to shore.
The other souls who sat along the thwarts
he herded out and cleared the decks, then called
Aeneas aboard. With groans at his weight, the scow
took water at every ragged, gaping seam.
Slowly it ferried them, seer and man; still whole
it dropped them in foul muck and dry, grey reeds.

At once the world burst round them with wild barking,
for Cerberus[144] crouched there, huge beside his cave.
But when the seer observed his snake-ruff rise,
she tossed him sleeping drugs tucked in a ball
of crumbs and honey. He stretched three greedy throats
and wildly gulped; his weird dog's-body crumpled
and sprawled from wall to wall across his cave.
Quickly Aeneas passed the sleeping guard,
and hurried away from the waters of no return.

Now they heard voices, sobs, a strange vast noise
of ghostly babies crying: just at the door
of life they'd lost their share; pulled from the breast
they'd sunk in darkness down to bitter death.
Next, those whom perjured witness sent to die.
(Due process, here, and justice fix their homes:
Minos[145] is judge; he draws the lots and holds
assize of the dead, to hear defense and charge.)
Next came the gloom-filled strip of suicides.
Sinless, they'd tossed their own dear lives away
for loathing of the light. Now, just to see
the sky, they'd gladly work for beggar's bread.
The law says no; the grim and loveless stream
prisons them: Styx enfolds them nine times round.

Nearby, the plains ran wide in all directions;
these were the Fields of Mourning—such their name.
Here dwell Love's lepers: wasted, ulcered cruel,
they slink down private paths, and hide in thickets
of myrtle; even death brings them no cure.

[144] **Cerberus:** The three-headed dog who guards the gates of Hell. [145] **Minos:** Former king of Crete who became judge over the dead after he was killed.

Aeneas saw Phaedra, Procris, Eriphylë
(tearfully showing the gash her son had made),
Evadne, Pasiphaë, Laodamia too,
all in a group, and Caeneus[146] (once a boy,
but now by fate returned to woman's shape).
There too among tall trees walked Punic Dido,
faltering, for her wound still bled. Soon as
the lord of Troy came near and saw her darkly,
midst shadows—as one sees the young new moon
(or thinks he saw it) rising through the clouds—
he dropped a tear and spoke with gentle love:
"Poor Dido! Then the news I heard was true,
that with a sword you'd made an end of life?
Your death—was I its cause? By heaven and gods
I swear, by every oath that hell can muster,
unwillingly, Lady, I parted from your shore.
The law of God—the law that sends me now
through darkness, bramble, rot, and night profound—
imperious, drove me; nor could I have dreamed
that in my leaving I would hurt you so.
Wait! Let me see you! Do not shrink from me!
Why run? Fate will not let us speak again."
He talked; she watched him, but with eyes of hate
and scorn, for all his soothing words and tears,
then looked away, her gaze fixed on the ground.
He tried to plead; her face remained unchanged
as if she were carved of granite or of flint.
At last she drew erect and turned unsmiling
back to the shadowed grove where her first love,
Sychaeus, gave her comfort in his arms.
Aeneas, hard-struck by unkind fate, still watched her
and pitied and wept until she disappeared.

The Sibyl led him farther. Soon they reached
Plain's-End, preserve where meet the great in arms.

[146] **Phaedra . . . Caeneus:** Women who died from causes related to love and jealousy. Phaedra, wife of the Athenian king Theseus, committed suicide after falling in love with her stepson Hippolotus; Procris, wife of the Phocian Cephalus, was killed by her husband, who mistook her for prey as she spied on him while he was hunting; Eriphylë, wife of Amphiaraüs, was bribed to send her husband off to certain death and was then killed by her own son; Evadne, wife of Capaneus, gave her life on her husband's funeral pyre; Pasiphaë, wife of King Minos, gave birth to the Minotaur and suffered jealousy over her husband's amours, casting a spell on him so that he would infect his lovers with a fatal poison; Laodamia, wife of Protesilaüs, who died at Troy, voluntarily accompanied her husband to the underworld. Caeneus was Caenis, the daughter of King Elatus from Thessaly; when she was raped by Neptune, who afterwards granted her a wish, she asked to be turned into a man so that she would never suffer such a fate again.

Here Tydeus ran up, Parthenopaeus, too,
and Adrastus[147] (poor, pale ghost!)—famed soldiers, all;
here, much bewailed on earth, the sons of Troy
fallen in war. Aeneas wept to see
that long parade: Glaucus, Thersilochus, Medon
(Antenor's sons), Polyboetes, priest of Ceres,
Idaeus, armed and gripping his chariot pole.
The souls thronged round him, pressing left and right.
Nor was one look enough; they tried to stop him,
to walk with him and learn why he had come.
But the Argive chiefs, Agamemnon's fighting men,
soon as they saw Aeneas and caught the flash
of arms, panicked. Some turned their backs and ran,
as once they ran to the ships; some gibbered and squeaked:
a jaw slack-fallen was all their battle cry.

Here too he saw Deiphobus, Priam's son,
his body one bloody wound, his lips hacked off—
his lips and both his hands; his ears were torn
from his head, his nose was lopped—unkindest cut.
He hardly knew him, for he cowered and tried
to hide his gashes. Aeneas addressed him gently:
"Deiphobus! Captain! Prince of Teucer's line!
Who felt impelled to such bloodthirsty blows?
Who thought himself so free? On that last night,
I heard, you killed Greeks till you fell exhausted
to die on your dead all helter-skelter piled.
On Cape Rhoeteum I raised your cenotaph—
I took that time—and thrice invoked your ghost.
Your name and armor mark the spot; I found
no trace of you to bury before I sailed."
Deiphobus answered: "You left no work undone;
you paid me every due the dead may ask.
Fate and that murdering she-devil from Sparta[148]
gave me these wounds: these are her souvenirs.
That final night: you know how gay we were,
such fools! You must remember all too well.
Even as that deadly horse came bounding up

[147] **Tydeus . . . Adrastus:** Three of the famous Argive warriors known as the Seven against Thebes. They aided Polyneices in his attempt to wrest power from his brother, Eteocles, who had violated their pact, formed after their father the former king Oedipus was banished, to share the rule of Thebes. [148] **she-devil from Sparta:** Helen, the wife of Menelaus who was abducted by the Trojan prince Paris, leading to the Trojan War; after Paris's death, the Trojans gave Helen to Deiphobus, who was eventually killed by Menelaus.

Troy's hill, its belly big with men-at-arms,
she led our women in the fire dance round,
'to honor God.' She held the biggest torch
and from a high point signaled to the Greeks.
I'd come home tired, worried, dead for rest,
to my ill-starred bedroom; there I lay in sleep
so sweet, so deep—most like the peace of death.
My noble wife now stripped my house of weapons;
from under my pillow she even slipped my sword.
She called Menelaus in, threw wide my door—
thinking this lovely gift would please her darling
and make him forget old tales and ugly talk.
In short, the two burst in (he had a friend
to abet his crime, Ulysses): God give the Greeks
as much, if I may justly ask revenge!
But you're alive! Come, tell me now: What chance
has brought you? Did you lose your course at sea?
Did God command? Tell, by what blow of fate
you've come to this grim, sunless, fogbound place?"

As they talked, Aurora with her rosy team
had passed the mid-point of her course in heaven,
and the time allowed might all have been so spent,
had not the Sibyl uttered admonition:
"Night's coming, Aeneas; we're wasting time on tears.
The road splits here and leads in two directions.
The right fork stretches beneath the wall of Dis
to Elysium: this is our route. Left runs the road
to Tartarus,[149] where the vile atone their crimes."
Deiphobus then: "Don't chide me, reverend lady!
I'm going—back to my company, back to night.
Go, glory of Troy! Have better luck than I!"
With that last word he turned and walked away.

Aeneas looked quickly round. To the left, he saw
a cliff; at its base, broad battlements triple-walled.
A river of swirling flame flowed all around—
Phlegethon, rolling a rubble of grinding rocks.
A gate rose huge, by granite columns flanked;
no mortal power—not even gods at war—

---

[149] **Elysium . . . Tartarus:** Elysium is the region of the underworld where the righteous and virtuous lead a pleasant existence; Tartarus is the part of Hell in which the Titans are confined and where sinners are meted out harsh punishments.

had strength to force it. Its tower of steel stood tall,
and at its gate, Tisiphone,[150] bloody-garbed,
kept sleepless watch eternal, night and day.
From here came forth wild screams, the savage whistle
of whips, the hiss of irons, the rattle of chains.
Aeneas stopped short. He listened and turned pale:
"What shapes of sin are here? Speak, Sibyl! What pains
pursue them? The noise is deafening to my ears!"
Then spoke the holy seer: "Great prince of Troy,
no guiltless man may pass the door of sin.
When Hecate laid Avernus to my charge
she showed me the place, and how God punishes.
This kingdom of torment Rhadamanthus[151] rules;
he hears and chastens fraud; all must confess
their sins committed on earth and tucked away
for atonement (death seemed pleasantly remote).
At the word 'Guilty!' Tisiphone lifts her lash
and leaps to snap it; her left hand holds out snakes
poised to strike; she summons her savage sisters.[152]
Then only the hellish gates are opened wide
on shrieking hinges. You see what kind of guard
sits at the entry? What shape patrols the door?
Inside is the Hydra's post; her fifty mouths
gape still more black and monstrous. Then the pit
opens toward darkness downward twice as far
as eye looks up toward heaven and Olympus.
Down at the bottom the ancient sons of Earth,
the Titans, wallow where the lightning hurled them.
I saw the sons of Aloeus, giant twins,
who attacked high heaven and tried to tear it down
barehanded, and pull Jove from his royal throne—
saw Salmoneus in torment of the damned
for mocking the flame and thunderbolt of Jove.
Driving a four-horse team and shaking a torch
he'd marched in pride through Greece and down the streets
of Elis, demanding honors due a god,
the fool: he'd made a lightning bolt of brass
and fashioned his horses' hooves to drum like thunder.
But the father almighty massed his clouds and whirled
his bolt—no pitch pine and no smoky flame
of torch; a fireball rode the pretender down.

---

[150] **Tisiphone:** One of the Furies, female creatures who punish those who commit blood-crimes against their kin. [151] **Rhadamanthus:** The brother of King Minos of Crete and, like him, a judge in hell. [152] **savage sisters:** Alecto and Megaera, sister Furies who also inflict punishment on the sinners here. (See note 150.)

Tityus,[153] too, the child of Earth all-mother,
was there to see: his body filled a field
nine acres broad; with curving beak, a vulture
fed on his deathless liver (fertile food
for pain), probing his vitals, making his ribs
her home; his flesh, reborn, could never rest.
Why tell of the Lapiths, Pirithous, and Ixion,[154]

. . .

over whom a black flint, ever about to fall,
hangs menacing. Brightly shines the wedding couch,
deep-cushioned, gilded; royal is the feast
he sees laid out. But there she lies, the worst
of the Furies, and will not let him touch the food:
she jumps to her feet, lifts up her torch, and snarls.

"They too come here who, living, loathed a brother,
drove out a father, or tricked a poor man's trust;
who, finding wealth, sat lonely brooding on it
with never a share for a neighbor (legion, they!);
and those for adultery killed, and those who raised
rebellion, heedless of oath and service due;
here they are jailed and wait their dooms. Don't ask
what doom, what shape, what lot entraps them there.
Some roll great boulders; some, spread-eagled, hang
on whirling wheels. One sits, forever sits:
Theseus the luckless; one—poor, wretched Phlegyas[155]—
repeats in the gloom his warning to all men:
'Hear this: learn justice; never scorn the gods!'
Here is the man who for a tyrant's gold
enslaved his country; here, the peddler of laws;
here, one who raped his child and called it marriage:
all monsters of insolence, monsters in success.
Had I a hundred tongues, a hundred mouths,
and chords of steel, I could not tell the forms
of all their crimes, nor list the penalties."

When Phoebus' aged seer had thus concluded,
"Come now," she said. "Move on! Complete your task!

---

[153] **Tityus:** Virgil has been describing the key sinners of Tartarus: the Titans, the race of giants who fought against the Olympian Jove in his successful war against the god Saturn (Cronos, in Greek). They are the giants Otus and Ephialtes, the sons of Aloeus, who fought against the Olympian gods; Simoneus, who wrongly imitated Jove's power by creating false lightning; and Tityus, who attempted to rape the goddess Latona (Leto in Greek). [154] **Lapiths . . . Ixion:** Ixion, the king of the Lapiths, a notoriously violent people from Thessaly, was the father of Pirithous. Father and son were punished for similar crimes—the first for having attempted to rape Juno, the second for attempting to kidnap Proserpina. [155] **Theseus . . . Phlegyas:** With the help of Pirithous, Theseus tried unsuccessfully to kidnap Proserpina; Phlegyas set fire to the temple of Apollo at Delphi.

Let's hurry! I see the walls forged on the hearths
of the Cyclops. There's the arch and there the gate,
where we must place our gift, as we were ordered."
Then, walking together over a lightless road,
they covered the mid-space and approached the door.
Aeneas stood close and with fresh water sprinkled
his body, then set the bough against the door.

Thus with their liturgy to the goddess ended,
they came to the place of joy, the pleasant lawns,
the groves of the lucky, and the blessed homes.[156]
These lands are clothed in larger air and light
the color of life; they see their sun, their stars.
Here, figures were training on the grassy grounds,
some playing games, some wrestling in the ring,
and some were treading the dance and singing songs.
There stood, in his poet's gown, the priest of Thrace,
playing his instrument of seven strings
(he plucked with fingers now, and now with plectrum).
Here, Teucer's ancient line, his splendid sons,
greathearted heroes, born in happier days:
Ilus, Assaracus, Dardanus,[157] founder of Troy.
Aeneas was startled: there lay cars and arms
at rest, spears stacked, and horses running free
grazing the field. The joy the living knew
in arms and car, their love of grooming horses
to sleekness, followed them beyond the grave.
Aeneas saw others about him on the grass,
feasting and singing cheerful songs of praise.
Above them hung sweet bays, and from a hill
Eridanus[158] tumbled his waters through the grove.

Here were the band who for their country bled,
here priests who in the world led saintly lives,
prophets of truth, who spoke as God would speak,
those whose discoveries made a better world,
those who by doing good earned men's remembrance.
Each one wore snow-white bands about his head.
The Sibyl addressed them as they gathered round,

[156] **place of joy . . . homes:** Aeneas and the Sibyl reach Elysium, the place of eternal happiness and home to Anchises; the "priest of Thrace" in line 645 is Orpheus. [157] **Ilus . . . Dardanus:** Ilus, the father of Laomedon, and his brother Assaracus were early kings of Troy; Dardanus, son of Jove (Zeus) and Electra, was the legendary founder of Troy. [158] **Eridanus:** A river sometimes identified in legend as the source of the Italian river Po.

Musaeus[159] first (the crowd surrounded him
and watched him towering shoulder-high above them):
"Tell us, O blessed souls, tell, best of bards,
where we may find Anchises? To see him
we came and crossed the floods of Erebus."
Then from the great man came this brief reply:
"None has a place assigned. We live in groves;
our beds are the riverbanks and fields made fresh
by springs. But if you wish so much to find him,
climb up this hill; I'll set you on your way."
He walked ahead, and from the hilltop showed them
the garden land. They left the summit then.

Deep in a grassy valley stood the souls
mustered for life on earth. With eye alert
Anchises surveyed them, checking off the roll
of all his cherished line: his sons, their sons,
their luck, their destinies, their works and ways.
But when, across the fields, he saw Aeneas
coming, he stretched out both his hands for joy;
tears washed his cheeks; words tumbled from his lips:
"You've come at last! Your father waited long
for love to conquer hardship! Oh, my son!
Do I see your face? And may we talk once more?
I knew it would happen! In my heart I knew!
I reckoned the hours with care and told them right.
Over what lands, what endless seas you traveled,
harried by countless dangers, and now you've come!
In Libya, disaster was close: I feared for you."
Aeneas replied: "Father, your tear-stained face,
so often in my mind, compelled me here.
Our fleet is in Tuscan waters! Give me your hand,
let me embrace you, father: don't slip away!"
So speaking, he let the tears course down his face.
Three times he tried to fold him in his arms;
three times an empty shade escaped his grasp,
light as the air, most like the wings of sleep.

Just then, far down a slope, Aeneas saw
a grove apart, with foliage thick and rustling:
this was the haven of peace, where Lethe[160] flowed:

[159] **Musaeus:** Legendary poet of Thrace. [160] **Lethe:** The river of forgetfulness in the underworld, through which all reborn souls must pass on their way to the upper world.

about it flitted the nations of mankind
like bees in a meadow on a summer's day
(they stop at bright-hued blooms and cluster close
around white lilies; their humming fills the field).
At the sight Aeneas was puzzled and stopped short:
"What did this mean? What river," he asked, "was that?
Who were those people that swarmed about its banks?"
Then Lord Anchises: "Those are souls whose fate
binds them to flesh once more. At Lethe's wave
they drink and forget past years of care and fear.
I've longed to show them to you and tell their names—
the line of my children, the number of my heirs—
that you may rejoice with me for Italy found."
"What, father? Must I think men's souls rise up
from here to the air, and to the sluggish flesh
return? Poor fools! Whence this mad lust for life?"
"I'll, speak at once, dear son, and ease your mind,"
Anchises answered, and told the order of things.

"To begin: the heavens, the earth, the watery wastes,
the lucent globe of moon, the sun, the stars,
exist through inward spirit. Their total mass
by mind is permeated: hence their motion.
From mind and spirit comes life—of man, of beast,
of bird, of monsters under the foam-flecked seas.
Life is from heaven—a seed of fire that glows
bright, so far as flesh cannot repress it,
or earthly, death-bound bodies dull its glow.
From flesh come fear, desire, pain, and joy:
its pitch-dark prison blinds us to the light.
And even on that last day when life departs,
not all our evil, all the body's foul
corruption leaves us: deep ingrained, in ways
past comprehension, much has hardened fast.
Our souls, then, suffer pain, and pay the price
for wrongs done years before: some, like a cloak
laid off, hang to the winds; some lose their stains
by flood and swirl, or cautery of fire.
We suffer, each, our ghostly selves, then pass—
some few—to gain Elysium's fields of joy.
The years go by; Time makes his cycle just,
our hardened filth is sloughed; intelligence
pure, as of heaven, is left, and breath, and fire.
After a thousand circling years, God calls
these souls to Lethe in a long parade

to gain forgetfulness, then view the sky
once more, and wish to put on flesh again."

Anchises spoke no more, and led his son
and the Sibyl, too, deep into the rustling throng,
then up on a mound where they could see the files
approaching and watch the faces as they passed.

"Now you shall see the glory that awaits
the children of Troy and their Italian sons—
all souls of splendor, who shall bear our name.
Hear their story, and learn your destiny.
That young man—see him, leaning on his staff?—
by lot will be the first to rise to light
and air with blood of Italy in his veins.
His name is Alban, 'Silvius,'[161] your last child,
born in your old age to your wife, Lavinia,
bred in the forest, king and sire of kings;
through him our line shall rule in Alba Longa.
Next him is Procas, pride of the race of Troy,
and Capys and Numitor and—named after you—
Aeneas Silvius, famed alike for valor
and goodness—if ever he gain the Alban throne.
What fine young men! Look at the strength they show!
See how they wear the oak-leaf civil crown!
They'll found Fidenae, Gabii, Nomentum,
and build Collatia's castle on the hills,
Bola, Cora, Pometii, and Castrum.[162]
(Great names they'll be; now they are land unnamed.)

"There's Romulus, son of Mars; with Numitor[163]
he'll take his stand (through Ilia, his mother,
he's of our blood): see, on his head, twin plumes,

---

[161] **'Silvius':** In lines 756 through 776 Anchises gives Aeneas a vision of the genealogy linking Troy to Rome, from Silvius, the early ruler of Alba Longa and Aeneas's son by the Latium princess Lavinia, to the legendary founder of Rome, Romulus (see notes 21 and 22). Procas, Capys, Numitor, and Aeneas Silvius were all kings of Alba Longa. [162] **Fidenae . . . Castrum:** Towns near Rome. [163] **Romulus . . . Numitor:** Anchises here gives Aeneas a vision of the glory of Rome from the founding of Rome by Romulus to the age of Augustus Caesar. Romulus and Remus were the twin sons of the Roman god of war, Mars, and Ilia (in some versions, Rea Silvia), whose uncle, Amulius, hoping to secure his power over the throne at Alba Longa, had the boys exposed in the Tiber. Raised in the woods by a she-wolf and a woodpecker, animals sacred to Mars, the boys eventually joined forces with their exiled grandfather, Numitor, the deposed king of Alba Longa, and won back the city. Eventually, after the death of Remus resulting from a quarrel, Romulus went on to found Rome. Numitor had been restored to power by his legendary grandsons.

sign of a father's favor, mark divine.
With him Rome will begin her march to glory,
to world-wide rule, to spirit that rivals heaven.
She'll throw one wall around her seven hills;
she shall be rich in sons, like that great mother
who, mural-crowned, rides through the Eastern world,
god-bearer triumphant; a hundred sons of sons,
all gods, a heavenly host, are in her arms.
But look, now! Look! Here comes your family,
your Roman children: Caesar and all the sons
of Iulus who'll come beneath the vault of heaven.
Here is the man you've heard so often promised:
Augustus, son of godhead.[164] He'll rebuild
a golden age in Latium, land where once
Saturn was king. Past India, past the Moor
he'll spread his rule to zones beyond the stars,
beyond the ecliptic, where Adas carries heaven,
and bears on his back the spinning, star-tricked wheel.
Against Augustus' advent, even now
God's oracles have panicked Eastern steppes
and roiled the outlets of the seven-twinned Nile.
Not even Hercules crossed so much land
to shoot the bronze-hoofed hind, or bring back peace
to Erymanthan groves, or frighten Lerna;
nor Bacchus, when he drove his tiger team,
with vines for reins, in glory down from Nysa.[165]
(And still we hesitate to fight and win,
or fear to make our stand in Italy?)

"But who is that? He wears the olive crown
and carries hallows. White hair and beard — I know him:
that king whose code gave Rome a base of law.[166]
He'll come from little Cures, poor-man's land,
but rise to royal heights. Succeeding him,
Tullus will shatter our peace and lead to war
a people soft, unused to battle line
and glory. Ancus next — a boastful man,

[164] **son of godhead:** Augustus, the grand-nephew and later the adopted son and heir of Julius Caesar, who had been deified upon his death. [165] **Erymanthan groves . . . Nysa:** Hercules' labors took him to Cerynaia (where he killed the Cerynaian hind), Erymantha, and Lerna, all sites in Greece; Nysa, the birthplace of Bacchus, has been located, depending on the tradition, in Ethiopia, Libya, India, and Thrace. With these allusions Virgil elaborates on the extent of the Roman Empire. [166] **that king . . . law:** Numa Pompilias, from the Sabine city of Cures, was the second king of Rome; his reign was marked by law and peace. Tullus (Tullus Hostilius) and Ancus (Ancus Marcius), described in the following lines, were the second and third kings of Rome.

too much enamored of the people's whims.
And there the Tarquins—see?—and their avenger,
Brutus[167] the proud, who'll give us back our power.
He first will rule as consul, first will take
the axes; when his sons rise in revolt,
in liberty's name he'll see them put to death
(unhappy father, however the tale be told!)
bested by love of country and lust for praise.

"See—back there!—Decius, Drusus, and Torquatus
the savage headsman, Camillus[168] with his standards,
and, just this way, two souls in armor bright,[169]
full of good will while night entombs them here;
but oh, if they see the light, what wars, what strife
they'll set afoot, what battle lines and death:
from Gaul and the Alps the father-in-law will march
against the son with Eastern legions massed.
(Children, never grow hardened to wars like those;
against your homeland raise no hostile hand!
Oh, take the lead, show mercy, child of heaven,
throw down that sword, son of my blood!)

"That man[170] will slaughter Greeks and conquer Corinth,
then ride in triumph up high Capitol Hill;
this one[171] will pull Agamemnon's Argos down,
and a king who boasts the blood of brave Achilles—
vengeance for Troy and Pallas' fane defiled!
Who'd pass by Cato[172] or Cossus without a word?
Who the Gracchi, or those twin thunderbolts,

[167] **Brutus:** Brutus (not the betrayer of Julius Caesar) avenged the rape of Lucretia by Sextus, son of the Roman king Tarquinus Superbus (Tarquin the Proud), expelling the king and establishing the first Roman republic in 509 B.C.E. [168] **Decius . . . Camillus:** Roman heroes from the fourth and third centuries B.C.E.; Drusus was head of the family whose line led to Livia, the second wife of Augustus. [169] **two souls . . . bright:** Julius Caesar and his rival, General Pompey; they fought against each other during the civil war (49–45 B.C.E.). [170] **That man:** Mummius, a Roman general who conquered Corinth in 167 B.C.E. [171] **this one:** Aemilius Paulus, who defeated the Macedonian king Perseus, who claimed to have blood ties to Achilles, in 168 B.C.E. [172] **Cato:** Anchises names several figures from Rome's history: Cato, the great Roman orator from the second century B.C.E.; Cossus, a general who vanquished the Etruscan king Tolumnius in 437 B.C.E.; the Gracchi, two brothers who lost their lives while fighting for constitutional reform in the second century B.C.E.; the two Scipios, Publius Cornelius and Publius Scipio Aemilianus, who fought against Carthage in the second and third Punic Wars, respectively; Fabricius, a Roman general who fought against Macedonia in the third century B.C.E.; the Fabii, a powerful family whose numbers include Quintus Fabius Maximus, the "Delayer," whose strategic delaying tactics helped defeat Hannibal in the second Punic War; and finally Marcellus, a Roman general who defeated the Gauls in 222 B.C.E. and fought against Hannibal in the second Punic War. Anchises also alludes to the curse of Dido (end of Book 4), which calls for endless conflict between Carthage and Rome.

the Scipios, bane of Libya? Who Fabricius,
whose need spelled might, or Regulus, sower of seed?
The Fabii rush me, yet he'll be their greatest
'who lone by laggard tactics saves our state.'
Others will forge the bronze to softer breath,
no doubt, and bring the sculptured stone to life,
show greater eloquence, and with their rule
map out the skies and tell the rising stars:
you, Roman, remember: Govern! Rule the world!
These are your arts! Make peace man's way of life;
spare the humble but strike the braggart down."
So Lord Anchises; then to their wonder, added:
"See, there: Marcellus, splendid in the spoils
of war, in victory tall above his troops.
In the great conflict, he'll set Rome aright
once more, bring down rebellious Gaul and Carthage,
and a third time offer captured arms to Mars."

Beside him, Aeneas saw, there walked a man[173]
handsome and young, with armor shining bright,
but brow not joyful, face and eyes downcast.
"Who, father, walks there at Marcellus' side?
His son? Some other of his glorious line?
See how his friends press close! There's greatness there,
yet shadows black as night hang round his head."

Anchises answered as tears rose in his eyes:
"Seek not to know your people's vastest grief!
The world will see him—only that, for Fate
will grant no more. The gods had deemed
our power too great, if we had kept this gift.
Mars' people, in his field, beside his city—
how they will grieve! What mourners you will see,
Tiber, as you glide past that new-raised mound![174]
No child of Trojan blood will raise such hopes
among his Latin sires, nor rouse such pride
of offspring in the land of Romulus.
Ah, loyalty, ancient honor, hand unbeaten
in battle! If he'd gone out to fight, no man
had dared to face him, whether he went on foot

[173] **a man:** Marcellus the Younger, the nephew and son-in-law of Augustus Caesar. Destined to succeed Augustus, the young man died when he was only nineteen, hence Anchises' comment in line 869. [174] **that new-raised mound:** The Campus Martius, or Field of Mars, where Marcellus's tomb was located.

or spurred a foaming horse against the foe.
Poor boy! If you should break the bars of fate,
you'll be Marcellus. Bring lilies! Fill my hands!
I'll scatter scarlet blooms: so much, at least,
I'll give a grandson's ghost, and do my office,
though vain." Thus over all that place they walked,
through broad and airy fields, and saw the sights.
After Anchises had shown his son each thing
and fired his heart with love of fame to come,
then he recounted wars that must be waged,
told of the Rutuli, of Latium's city,
and how he'd bear, or how escape, each blow.

Twin are the gates of sleep; men say that one
is of horn, a ready exit for real shades;
the other is white, of flawless ivory:
this way the dead send false dreams to the world.
Anchises' tale was told. Taking his son
and the Sibyl, he sent them through the ivory gate.
Aeneas made for the ships and joined his friends.
Then straight upshore he sailed to Port Caieta.
Out went the anchors; the fleet lay stern to shore.

Ovid
43 B.C.E.–17 C.E.

Ovid was the last of a new wave of Roman poets who challenged the assumptions of previous writers whose works focused primarily on serious matters of the state and religion. Like Catullus, the greatest lyric poet of the earlier generation, Ovid turned to love and private feeling for his subject matter. Most important, however, Ovid was a great storyteller. When he decided to retell the major Greek and Roman myths about transformation and love, he produced one of the most influential and readable works of all Latin literature, *Metamorphoses.* This encyclopedic collection of tales, loosely organized around the motif of changing form, has served readers from his time to the present day as a sourcebook of stories about figures such as Apollo and Daphne, Echo and Narcissus, **Orpheus** and **Eurydice**, Midas, and even the heroes of the Trojan War. Despite his somewhat cavalier attitude toward the "serious" poets of the

ORE-fee-us; yoo-RID-uh-see

My intention is to tell of bodies changed / To different forms
– OVID, *Metamorphoses*

earlier age, Ovid brilliantly managed to satisfy what Horace[1] claimed was the highest purpose of poetry: to please and to instruct.

Born a Poet. Publius Ovidius Naso was born in Sulmo (now Sulmona), a town just east of Rome, on 20 March 43 B.C.E. into a family of distinction and nobility. Ovid was born just a year after Julius Caesar's assassination on the celebrated Ides of March in 44 B.C.E. Ovid's father, hoping that his son would pursue a career in public service, sent Ovid to the finest schools in Rome, where he studied grammar and rhetoric, the refined arts of public speaking highly valued in the political forums of Rome. After completing his education, Ovid made a brief tour of Greece, then returned to Rome where he held some minor government posts before turning to poetry at the age of twenty-four. As he writes in *Tristia*, the **MUSE** visited him voluntarily: "Whatever I tried to say came out in verse." Living on the small but respectable family fortune, Ovid went through two very brief and disastrous marriages. (At forty, Ovid found a compatible marriage partner.) In Rome, the young poet became part of a literary circle that included the elegiac love poets C. Cornelius Gallus (c. 69–26 B.C.E.), Albius Tibullus (c. 54–19 B.C.E.), and Sextus Propertius (c. 50 B.C.E.–c. 16 C.E.), whom he describes as his models and his sometime companions. Virgil and Horace, who were older than Ovid, were also in Rome at this time, but Ovid's relationship to them—other than that he respected their work even as he departed from their style—is unclear.

Love, Poetry, and Exile. Like Catullus's circle in Verona a generation earlier, Ovid and his Roman peers were seeking to redefine Roman poetry, turning to the technically refined and learned poetry of the Greek Alexandrian poets such as Callimachus (fl. third century B.C.E.) for instruction. Gallus, Tibullus, and Propertius, in particular, realized the potential of the erotic love elegy inherited from Catullus, but it was Ovid above all who caught the attention of his contemporaries by making the form a vehicle for ever more detached and playfully wanton expression. In *Amores (Loves)*, a collection of forty-nine poems written in **ELEGIAC COUPLETS**,[2] Ovid brings nuance to the genre of elegiac love poetry, celebrating not love for one woman but amorous adventures with many, and portraying himself as an armed participant in the game of love, a voyeur who muses on the trials of the spurned suitor rather than the hapless victim of unrequited love. Rejecting the high seriousness of Virgilian epic and Horatian satire, Ovid calls on Venus to be his Muse and takes love as

WWW For links to more information about Ovid and a quiz on *Metamorphoses*, see *World Literature Online* at bedfordstmartins.com/worldlit.

[1] **Horace:** Quintus Horatius Flaccus (65–8 B.C.E.), Roman poet of the Augustan Age who wrote highly polished lyrics and odes; his *The Art of Poetry (Ars Poetica)* is an important document of literary criticism in verse.

[2] **elegiac couplets:** The conventional strophic form of Latin elegiac love poetry, consisting of one dactylic hexameter line followed by one dactylic pentameter line. A dactylic hexameter line is composed of six feet, each foot comprising one long (accented) and two short (unaccented) syllables; the sixth foot may be shortened by one or two syllables. A dactylic pentameter line consists of five such feet. The elegiac couplet is also known as a "distich."

Europa and the Bull *Ovid's* Metamorphoses *retells the classic stories of Greek mythology. Here, a Roman glass vase depicts a scene from the tale of Europa and the Bull in which Zeus, the King of the Gods, takes on the shape of a bull to woo the mortal Europa. (Musée Guimet, Paris, France / Peter Willi / Bridgeman Art Library)*

his dominion. Ovid took this cavalier attitude further in the didactic *Art of Love (Ars Amatoria)* and its sequel, *The Cure for Love (Remedia Amores).* The first work, written sometime at the turn of the century, consists of two books that show men how to seduce and keep their lovers and a third that advises women on how to seduce men. *Remedia Amores,* written around the same time, again goes against elegiac convention by offering ways to *overcome* the melancholy of love rather than focusing on melancholy itself. Ovid produced several other works during this period, including *Heroides,* a collection of verse epistles to absent lovers written

I am on fire, and my heart owns the dominion of love, / So let my work arise in the manner called elegiac: Good riddance, iron wars; good riddance, hexameters!
– OVID, *Amores* I

in the voices of famous heroines from Greek myth, and the unfinished *Feast Days (Fasti),* a twelve-book elegiac meditation on Roman festivals. This last work was interrupted in 8 C.E., when Augustus, an ardent moral reformer who cast a cold eye on Ovid's light treatment of love, banished the poet from Rome.

Ovid spent the last ten years of his life in Tomi, a town on the Black Sea on the outer periphery of the Roman Empire in what is today Romania. While the reasons for Ovid's exile are still unclear, Augustus likely had more than Ovid's erotic verse in mind when he banished the poet; Ovid was involved directly or indirectly with a scandal involving Augustus's daughter Julia. At Tomi, Ovid wrote the four-book *Sorrows (Tristia); Ibis,* a long elegiac poem; and the *Letters from the Pontus (Epistulae ex Ponto).* The poems written at Tomi, which Ovid hoped would earn him a pardon, are a reflective, if sometimes bitter, account of his life and a defense of his reputation as a poet. Despite his efforts, Ovid remained in exile and died in Tomi in 17 C.E.

Metamorphoses. Ovid tends to be appreciated today for his masterpiece, *Metamorphoses,* written sometime between 1 C.E. and 8 C.E. Written in HEXAMETER COUPLETS,[3] this epic-length poem of fifteen books contains nearly two hundred fifty stories, loosely held together by the thematic thread of metamorphosis—the changing of form. Absent the central hero and unifying plot of epics such as ***The Odyssey*** and ***The Aeneid,*** Ovid's opus is a series of short tales drawn from mythology and history, beginning with the story of creation and ending with the apotheosis, or deification, of Caesar. Ovid's treatment of myth and history in this work is playful and novel; his interest in the gods and goddesses, nymphs, satyrs, and naiads who frolic in his stories is clearly literary. He takes great pleasure in embellishing a story when it suits his purpose, elaborating and fabricating when necessary to produce lively and entertaining tales out of the stock mythological material of the past.

p. 421
p. 1181

As a work focusing thematically on transformation, Ovid's *Metamorphoses* engages structurally and stylistically with change. Plays on words, surprising metaphors, shifts in narration, and interruptions and digressions abound throughout the text, presenting readers with a delightful array of points of view and challenging them to chart a course through a sea of stories. At the base of these playful stories, however—as in *The Thousand and One Nights*[4]—is an awareness of the violence of natural

[3] **hexameter couplets:** The conventional strophic form of Greek and Latin epic poetry consisting of two dactylic hexameter lines; a dactylic hexameter line is composed of six feet, each foot comprising one long (accented) and two short (unaccented) syllables; the final foot is known as a catalectic foot, for it is generally shortened by one or two syllables.

[4] ***The Thousand and One Nights:*** Also known as *Arabian Nights,* a collection of Indian, Arabic, and Persian tales dating from the ninth century C.E. or earlier to the fourteenth century C.E. The wide array of tales, fables, and anecdotes in *The Thousand and One Nights* are framed by the story of Scheherezade, the wife of jealous King Shahryar of Samarkand who tells her husband a story every night for 1,001 nights in order to prevent him from killing her as he has previous wives. Her stories include the tales of Sinbad the Sailor, Ali Baba and the Forty Thieves, and Aladdin and His Magic Lamp.

and historical processes of change and the fragility of life. Much of the violence in the work is sexual in nature, as in the stories of Daphne and Apollo and Venus and Adonis, with the latter's embedded tale of **Atalanta**. Relations of passionate desire and love, Ovid recognizes, are not isolated from those of power. Sexual relationships, as in the fiction of contemporary Czech writer Milan Kundera,[5] can involve issues of power and control, or even violence and death. Thus, the stories in Ovid's *Metamorphoses* still have acute meaning today, and the genius of Ovid's storytelling is measured in part by how his comic approach to his subject draws readers close to mutability in all its manifestations, be they dangerous or delightful.

at-uh-LAN-tuh

■ CONNECTIONS

***The Epic of Gilgamesh*, p. 62; The Book of Genesis, p. 140.** In *Metamorphoses,* Ovid tells a story of a great flood. Consider how Ovid's version of this story differs from that in the ancient Akkadian and Hebrew texts named above, focusing especially on the way each text represents the relationship between the gods and human beings in the story. Does Ovid's treatment of the flood story suggest a secularization, a distancing from myth? What do these stories suggest about the cultures in which they originated?

The Ancient Mexicans, *Myths of Creation* (Book 3); The Book of Genesis, p. 140. Creation myths are key stories in the foundation of a culture's identity, often presenting not only a story of the origin of the cosmos and human beings but a scheme of history. Ovid's stories about flux and change begin with an account of creation as well as an account of the "four ages"—a mytho-historical scheme of the decline of civilizations from a perfect "golden age." Genesis, with its story of creation and man and woman's expulsion from the Garden of Eden, also tells a story of decline, one that may be compared to the Aztec myths of creation and the Aztec calendar. What do these various creation stories reveal about the cultures they helped to define?

***The Descent of Inanna*, p. 28; Homer, *The Odyssey*, p. 421; Virgil, *The Aeneid*, p. 1181; The Ancient Mexicans, *Myths of Creation* (Book 3).** The hero's journey to the underworld, the land of the dead, is an important topos, or traditional theme, throughout the literatures of the ancient world. In each of the texts listed here, a hero—Inanna, Odysseus, Aeneas, and Quetzalcoatl—undertakes a journey to the underworld in order to renew his or her strength, attain special powers, and/or to receive a boon, a special insight or vision of the future. Compare Ovid's version of Orpheus's journey to the underworld with one or more of these other journeys to the underworld. How is it different?

■ FURTHER RESEARCH

Fraenkel, H. *Ovid: A Poet Between Two Worlds.* 1945.

Galinsky, G. K. *Ovid's* Metamorphoses: *An Introduction to the Basic Aspects.* 1974.

Mack, Sara. *Ovid.* 1988.

Solodow, Joseph B. *The World of Ovid's* Metamorphoses. 1988.

Tissol, Garth. *The Face of Nature: Wit, Narrative, and Cosmic Origins in Ovid's* Metamorphoses. 1997.

Wilkinson, L. P. *Ovid Surveyed.* 1962.

[5] **Milan Kundera** (b. 1929): Czech writer best known for such works as the three-volume collection of short stories *Laughable Loves* (1963, 1965, 1969) and novels such as *The Joke* (1967) and *The Unbearable Lightness of Being* (1984). Most of his stories explore the machinations of power in sex and love.

PRONUNCIATION

Adonis: uh-DAH-nis
Atalanta: at-uh-LAN-tuh
Cybele: sigh-BEE-lee
Eurydice: yoo-RID-uh-see
Hippomenes: hip-AH-muh-neez
Lycaon: ligh-KAY-ahn
Orpheus: ORE-fee-us
Persephone: pur-SEF-uh-nee
Pygmalion: pig-MAY-lee-un
Sisyphus: SIZ-uh-fus

Metamorphoses

Translated by Rolfe Humphries

FROM

Book 1

My intention is to tell of bodies changed
To different forms; the gods, who made the changes,
Will help me—or I hope so—with a poem
That runs from the world's beginning to our own days.[1]

The Creation

Before the ocean was, or earth, or heaven,
Nature was all alike, a shapelessness,
Chaos, so-called, all rude and lumpy matter,
Nothing but bulk, inert, in whose confusion
Discordant atoms warred: there was no sun
To light the universe; there was no moon
With slender silver crescents filling slowly;

Metamorphoses. Ovid began his greatest work around the year 1 C.E., and completed it around 8 C.E. While epic in length and in versification—Ovid uses the hexameter couplets of epic poetry for this work—*Metamorphoses* does not narrate the adventures of a single hero whose presence provides unity for the whole of the text. Rather, *Metamorphoses* is held together thematically: All its stories, however loosely linked in action, engage the theme of physical transformation. While this work is modeled in part on the mini-epics, or *epyllion,* of Alexandrian poetry, Ovid's intention seems truly epic in scope. Indeed, his poem sweeps from the very creation of the world to the apotheosis of Caesar—what for Ovid's contemporaries would have been the beginning of the world to the very present. While many critics have sought to identify structural unities within

[1] **to our own days:** In Book 15, Julius Caesar, assassinated in 44 B.C.E., is transformed into a star.

No earth hung balanced in surrounding air;
No sea reached far along the fringe of shore.
Land, to be sure, there was, and air, and ocean,
But land on which no man could stand, and water
No man could swim in, air no man could breathe,
Air without light, substance forever changing,
Forever at war: within a single body
Heat fought with cold, wet fought with dry, the hard
Fought with the soft, things having weight contended
With weightless things.
Till God, or kindlier Nature,
Settled all argument, and separated
Heaven from earth, water from land, our air
From the high stratosphere, a liberation
So things evolved, and out of blind confusion
Found each its place, bound in eternal order.
The force of fire, that weightless element,
Leaped up and claimed the highest place in heaven;
Below it, air; and under them the earth
Sank with its grosser portions; and the water,
Lowest of all, held up, held in, the land.

Whatever god it was, who out of chaos
Brought order to the universe, and gave it
Division, subdivision, he molded earth,
In the beginning, into a great globe,
Even on every side, and bade the waters
To spread and rise, under the rushing winds,
Surrounding earth; he added ponds and marshes,
He banked the river-channels, and the waters
Feed earth or run to sea, and that great flood
Washes on shores, not banks. He made the plains
Spread wide, the valleys settle, and the forest

Metamòrphoses, the connections between the stories for the most part are arbitrary; perhaps Ovid's self-conscious pointing to the artifice of the work.

The selections presented here attempt to give a sense of the range of the stories in *Metamorphoses,* beginning with the most fundamental transformation of all, the formation of the world out of the raw stuff of chaos; moving through the story of the transformation of civilizations from a golden to an iron age; the story of a flood; and then four stories drawn from mythological tales about the transformations effected by love: the stories of Apollo and Daphne, Orpheus and Eurydice, Pygmalion, and Venus and Adonis. The stories of Orpheus and Pygmalion also involve the transformation of art. Rolfe Humphries' translation conveys the vibrant, witty, and economical style of Ovid's original Latin verse, a work of powerful momentum.

Be dressed in leaves; he made the rocky mountains
Rise to full height, and as the vault of Heaven
Has two zones, left and right, and one between them
Hotter than these, the Lord of all Creation
Marked on the earth the same design and pattern.
The torrid zone too hot for men to live in,
The north and south too cold, but in the middle
Varying climate, temperature and season.
Above all things the air, lighter than earth,
Lighter than water, heavier than fire,
Towers and spreads; there mist and cloud assemble,
And fearful thunder and lightning and cold winds,
But these, by the Creator's order, held
No general dominion; even as it is,
These brothers brawl and quarrel; though each one
Has his own quarter, still, they come near tearing
The universe apart. Eurus is monarch
Of the lands of dawn, the realms of Araby,
The Persian ridges under the rays of morning.
Zephyrus holds the west that glows at sunset,
Boreas, who makes men shiver, holds the north,
Warm Auster governs in the misty southland,
And over them all presides the weightless ether,
Pure without taint of earth.
These boundaries given,
Behold, the stars, long hidden under darkness,
Broke through and shone, all over the spangled heaven,
Their home forever, and the gods lived there,
And shining fish were given the waves for dwelling
And beasts the earth, and birds the moving air.

But something else was needed, a finer being,
More capable of mind, a sage, a ruler,
So Man was born, it may be, in God's image,
Or Earth, perhaps, so newly separated
From the old fire of Heaven, still retained
Some seed of the celestial force which fashioned
Gods out of living clay and running water.
All other animals look downward; Man,
Alone, erect, can raise his face toward Heaven.

The Four Ages

The Golden Age was first, a time that cherished
Of its own will, justice and right; no law.
No punishment, was called for; fearfulness

Was quite unknown, and the bronze tablets held
No legal threatening; no suppliant throng
Studied a judge's face; there were no judges,
There did not need to be. Trees had not yet
Been cut and hollowed, to visit other shores.
Men were content at home, and had no towns
With moats and walls around them; and no trumpets
Blared out alarums; things like swords and helmets
Had not been heard of. No one needed soldiers.
People were unaggressive, and unanxious;
The years went by in peace. And Earth, untroubled,
Unharried by hoe or plowshare, brought forth all
That men had need for, and those men were happy,
Gathering berries from the mountain sides,
Cherries, or blackcaps, and the edible acorns.
Spring was forever, with a west wind blowing
Softly across the flowers no man had planted,
And Earth, unplowed, brought forth rich grain; the field,
Unfallowed, whitened with wheat, and there were rivers
Of milk, and rivers of honey, and golden nectar
Dripped from the dark-green oak-trees.
After Saturn[2]
Was driven to the shadowy land of death,
And the world was under Jove, the Age of Silver
Came in, lower than gold, better than bronze.
Jove made the springtime shorter, added winter,
Summer, and autumn, the seasons as we know them.
That was the first time when the burnt air glowed
White-hot, or icicles hung down in winter.
And men built houses for themselves; the caverns,
The woodland thickets, and the bark-bound shelters
No longer served; and the seeds of grain were planted
In the long furrows, and the oxen struggled
Groaning and laboring under the heavy yoke.

Then came the Age of Bronze, and dispositions
Took on aggressive instincts, quick to arm,
Yet not entirely evil. And last of all
The Iron Age succeeded, whose base vein
Let loose all evil: modesty and truth
And righteousness fled earth, and in their place
Came trickery and slyness, plotting, swindling,

[2] **Saturn:** An ancient Roman fertility god, ruler of the Golden Age and father of Jove, who overthrew him.

Violence and the damned desire of having.
Men spread their sails to winds unknown to sailors,
The pines came down their mountain-sides, to revel
And leap in the deep waters, and the ground,
Free, once, to everyone, like air and sunshine,
Was stepped off by surveyors. The rich earth,
Good giver of all the bounty of the harvest,
Was asked for more; they dug into her vitals,
Pried out the wealth a kinder lord had hidden
In Stygian[3] shadow, all that precious metal,
The root of evil. They found the guilt of iron,
And gold, more guilty still. And War came forth
That uses both to fight with; bloody hands
Brandished the clashing weapons. Men lived on plunder.
Guest was not safe from host, nor brother from brother,
A man would kill his wife, a wife her husband,
Stepmothers, dire and dreadful, stirred their brews
With poisonous aconite, and sons would hustle
Fathers to death, and Piety lay vanquished,
And the maiden Justice, last of all immortals,
Fled from the bloody earth.
Heaven was no safer.
Giants attacked the very throne of Heaven,
Piled Pelion on Ossa,[4] mountain on mountain
Up to the very stars. Jove struck them down
With thunderbolts, and the bulk of those huge bodies
Lay on the earth, and bled, and Mother Earth,
Made pregnant by that blood, brought forth new bodies,
And gave them, to recall her older offspring,
The forms of men. And this new stock was also
Contemptuous of gods, and murder-hungry
And violent. You would know they were sons of blood.

Jove's Intervention

And Jove was witness from his lofty throne
Of all this evil, and groaned as he remembered
The wicked revels of Lycaon's[5] table,
The latest guilt, a story still unknown
To the high gods. In awful indignation

[3] **Stygian:** In the underworld; associated with the Styx, the river that marks the threshold to Hades.

[4] **Pelion . . . Ossa:** Mountains in Thessaly, in central Greece.

[5] **Lycaon:** A king of Arcadia, the primitive and mountainous region of the Peloponnese.

He summoned them to council. No one dawdled.
Easily seen when the night skies are clear,
The Milky Way shines white. Along this road
The gods move toward the palace of the Thunderer,
His royal halls, and, right and left, the dwellings
Of other gods are open, and guests come thronging.
The lesser gods live in a meaner section,
An area not reserved, as this one is,
For the illustrious Great Wheels of Heaven.
(Their Palatine Hill,[6] if I might call it so.)

They took their places in the marble chamber
Where high above them all their king was seated,
Holding his ivory sceptre, shaking out
Thrice, and again, his awful locks, the sign
That made the earth and stars and ocean tremble,
And then he spoke, in outrage: "I was troubled
Less for the sovereignty of all the world
In that old time when the snake-footed giants
Laid each his hundred hands on captive Heaven.
Monstrous they were, and hostile, but their warfare
Sprung from one source, one body. Now, wherever
The sea-gods roar around the earth, a race
Must be destroyed, the race of men. I swear it!
I swear by all the Stygian rivers gliding
Under the world, I have tried all other measures.
The knife must cut the cancer out, infection
Averted while it can be, from our numbers.
Those demigods, those rustic presences,
Nymphs, fauns, and satyrs, wood and mountain dwellers,
We have not yet honored with a place in Heaven,
But they should have some decent place to dwell in,
In peace and safety. Safety? Do you reckon
They will be safe, when I, who wield the thunder,
Who rule you all as subjects, am subjected
To the plottings of the barbarous Lycaon?"
They burned, they trembled. Who was this Lycaon,
Guilty of such rank infamy? They shuddered
In horror, with a fear of sudden ruin,
As the whole world did later, when assassins
Struck Julius Caesar down, and Prince Augustus
Found satisfaction in the great devotion

[6] **Palatine Hill:** The hill in Rome where Caesar Augustus lived.

That cried for vengeance, even as Jove took pleasure,
Then, in the gods' response. By word and gesture
He calmed them down, awed them again to silence,
And spoke once more:

The Story of Lycaon

"He has indeed been punished.
On that score have no worry. But what he did,
And how he paid, are things that I must tell you.
I had heard the age was desperately wicked,
I had heard, or so I hoped, a lie, a falsehood,
So I came down, as man, from high Olympus,
Wandered about the world. It would take too long
To tell you how widespread was all that evil.
All I had heard was grievous understatement!
I had crossed Maenala, a country bristling
With dens of animals, and crossed Cyllene,
And cold Lycaeus'[7] pine woods. Then I came
At evening, with the shadows growing longer,
To an Arcadian palace, where the tyrant
Was anything but royal in his welcome.
I gave a sign that a god had come, and people
Began to worship, and Lycaon mocked them,
Laughed at their prayers, and said: 'Watch me find out
Whether this fellow is a god or mortal,
I can tell quickly, and no doubt about it.'
He planned, that night, to kill me while I slumbered;
That was his way to test the truth. Moreover,
And not content with that, he took a hostage,
One sent by the Molossians,[8] cut his throat,
Boiled pieces of his flesh, still warm with life,
Broiled others, and set them before me on the table.
That was enough. I struck, and the bolt of lightning
Blasted the household of that guilty monarch.
He fled in terror, reached the silent fields,
And howled, and tried to speak. No use at all!
Foam dripped from his mouth; bloodthirsty still, he turned
Against the sheep, delighting still in slaughter,
And his arms were legs, and his robes were shaggy hair,
Yet he is still Lycaon, the same grayness,

[7] **Maenala . . . Lycaeus:** Maenala, Cyllene, and Lycaeus are mountains in Arcadia.

[8] **Molossians:** A tribe from Epeirus, along the Adriatic coast of Greece, noted for its barbarism.

The same fierce face, the same red eyes, a picture
Of bestial savagery. One house has fallen,
But more than one deserves to. Fury reigns
Over all the fields of Earth. They are sworn to evil,
Believe it. Let them pay for it, and quickly!
So stands my purpose."
Part of them approved
With words and added fuel to his anger,
And part approved with silence, and yet all
Were grieving at the loss of humankind,
Were asking what the world would be, bereft
Of mortals: who would bring their altars incense?
Would earth be given the beasts, to spoil and ravage?
Jove told them not to worry; he would give them
Another race, unlike the first, created
Out of a miracle; he would see to it.

He was about to hurl his thunderbolts
At the whole world, but halted, fearing Heaven
Would burn from fire so vast, and pole to pole
Break out in flame and smoke, and he remembered
The fates had said that some day land and ocean,
The vault of Heaven, the whole world's mighty fortress,
Besieged by fire, would perish. He put aside
The bolts made in Cyclopean[9] workshops; better,
He thought, to drown the world by flooding water.

The Flood

So, in the cave of Aeolus,[10] he prisoned
The North-wind, and the West-wind, and such others
As ever banish cloud, and he turned loose
The South-wind, and the South-wind came out streaming
With dripping wings, and pitch-black darkness veiling
His terrible countenance. His beard is heavy
With rain-cloud, and his hoary locks a torrent,
Mists are his chaplet, and his wings and garments
Run with the rain. His broad hands squeeze together
Low-hanging clouds, and crash and rumble follow
Before the cloudburst, and the rainbow, Iris,

[9] **Cyclopean:** Refers to one-eyed giants who worked under Vulcan, the artisan god of fire, as metalworkers.

[10] **Aeolus:** King of Aeolia, an island northeast of Sicily, in charge of governing the winds; he eventually came to be identified as the god of the winds.

Draws water from the teeming earth, and feeds it
Into the clouds again. The crops are ruined,
The farmers' prayers all wasted, all the labor
Of a long year, comes to nothing.
And Jove's anger,
Unbounded by his own domain, was given
Help by his dark-blue brother. Neptune[11] called
His rivers all, and told them, very briefly,
To loose their violence, open their houses,
Pour over embankments, let the river horses
Run wild as ever they would. And they obeyed him.
His trident struck the shuddering earth; it opened
Way for the rush of waters. The leaping rivers
Flood over the great plains. Not only orchards
Are swept away, not only grain and cattle,
Not only men and houses, but altars, temples,
And shrines with holy fires. If any building
Stands firm, the waves keep rising over its roof-top,
Its towers are under water, and land and ocean
Are all alike, and everything is ocean,
An ocean with no shore-line.
Some poor fellow
Seizes a hill-top; another, in a dinghy,
Rows where he used to plough, and one goes sailing
Over his fields of grain or over the chimney
Of what was once his cottage. Someone catches
Fish in the top of an elm-tree, or an anchor
Drags in green meadow-land, or the curved keel brushes
Grape-arbors under water. Ugly sea-cows
Float where the slender she-goats used to nibble
The tender grass, and the Nereids° come swimming sea nymphs
With curious wonder, looking, under water,
At houses, cities, parks, and groves. The dolphins
Invade the woods and brush against the oak-trees;
The wolf swims with the lamb; lion and tiger
Are borne along together; the wild boar
Finds all his strength is useless, and the deer
Cannot outspeed that torrent; wandering birds
Look long, in vain, for landing-place, and tumble,
Exhausted, into the sea. The deep's great license
Has buried all the hills, and new waves thunder
Against the mountain-tops. The flood has taken

[11] **Neptune:** God of the sea, recognized typically by his trident, a three-pronged spear.

All things, or nearly all, and those whom water,
By chance, has spared, starvation slowly conquers. [. . .]

Apollo and Daphne

Now the first girl Apollo loved was Daphne,
Whose father was the river-god Peneus,
And this was no blind chance, but Cupid's malice.
Apollo, with pride and glory still upon him
Over the Python slain, saw Cupid bending
His tight-strung little bow. "O silly youngster,"
He said, "What are you doing with such weapons?
Those are for grown-ups! The bow is for my shoulders;
I never fail in wounding beast or mortal,
And not so long ago I slew the Python
With countless darts; his bloated body covered
Acre on endless acre, and I slew him!
The torch, my boy, is enough for you to play with,
To get the love-fires burning. Do not meddle
With honors that are mine!" And Cupid answered:
"Your bow shoots everything, Apollo—maybe—
But mine will fix you! You are far above
All creatures living, and by just that distance
Your glory less than mine." He shook his wings,
Soared high, came down to the shadows of Parnassus,
Drew from his quiver different kinds of arrows,
One causing love, golden and sharp and gleaming,
The other blunt, and tipped with lead, and serving
To drive all love away, and this blunt arrow
He used on Daphne, but he fired the other,
The sharp and golden shaft, piercing Apollo
Through bones, through marrow, and at once he loved
And she at once fled from the name of lover,
Rejoicing in the woodland hiding places
And spoils of beasts which she had taken captive,
A rival of Diana,[12] virgin goddess.
She had many suitors, but she scorned them all;
Wanting no part of any man, she travelled
The pathless groves, and had no care whatever
For husband, love, or marriage. Her father often
Said; "Daughter, give me a son-in-law!" and "Daughter,
Give me some grandsons!" But the marriage torches

[12] **Diana:** A goddess of wild animals eventually associated with the Greek Artemis, goddess of the hunt.

Were something hateful, criminal, to Daphne,
So she would blush, and put her arms around him,
And coax him: "Let me be a virgin always;
Diana's father said she might. Dear father!
Dear father—please!" He yielded, but her beauty
Kept arguing against her prayer. Apollo
Loves at first sight; he wants to marry Daphne,
He hopes for what he wants—all wishful thinking!—
Is fooled by his own oracles. As stubble
Burns when the grain is harvested, as hedges
Catch fire from torches that a passer-by
Has brought too near, or left behind in the morning,
So the god burned, with all his heart, and burning
Nourished that futile love of his by hoping.
He sees the long hair hanging down her neck
Uncared for, says, "But what if it were combed?"
He gazes at her eyes—they shine like stars!
He gazes at her lips, and knows that gazing
Is not enough. He marvels at her fingers,
Her hands, her wrists, her arms, bare to the shoulder,
And what he does not see he thinks is better.
But still she flees him, swifter than the wind,
And when he calls she does not even listen:
"Don't run away, dear nymph! Daughter of Peneus,
Don't run away! I am no enemy,
Only your follower: don't run away!
The lamb flees from the wolf, the deer the lion,
The dove, on trembling wing, flees from the eagle.
All creatures flee their foes. But I, who follow,
Am not a foe at all. Love makes me follow,
Unhappy fellow that I am, and fearful
You may fall down, perhaps, or have the briars
Make scratches on those lovely legs, unworthy
To be hurt so, and I would be the reason.
The ground is rough here. Run a little slower,
And I will run, I promise, a little slower.
Or wait a minute: be a little curious
Just who it is you charm. I am no shepherd,
No mountain-dweller, I am not a ploughboy,
Uncouth and stinking of cattle. You foolish girl,
You don't know who it is you run away from,
That must be why you run. I am lord of Delphi
And Tenedos and Claros and Patara.[13]

[13] **Delphi . . . Patara:** These are oracular shrines associated with Apollo.

Jove is my father. I am the revealer
Of present, past and future; through my power
The lyre and song make harmony; my arrow
Is sure in aim—there is only one arrow surer,
The one that wounds my heart. The power of healing
Is my discovery; I am called the Healer
Through all the world: all herbs are subject to me.
Alas for me, love is incurable
With any herb; the arts which cure the others
Do me, their lord, no good!"
He would have said
Much more than this, but Daphne, frightened, left him
With many words unsaid, and she was lovely
Even in flight, her limbs bare in the wind,
Her garments fluttering, and her soft hair streaming,
More beautiful than ever. But Apollo,
Too young a god to waste his time in coaxing,
Came following fast. When a hound starts a rabbit
In an open field, one runs for game, one safety,
He has her, or thinks he has, and she is doubtful
Whether she's caught or not, so close the margin,
So ran the god and girl, one swift in hope,
The other in terror, but he ran more swiftly,
Borne on the wings of love, gave her no rest,
Shadowed her shoulder, breathed on her streaming hair.
Her strength was gone, worn out by the long effort
Of the long flight; she was deathly pale, and seeing
The river of her father, cried "O help me,
If there is any power in the rivers,
Change and destroy the body which has given
Too much delight!" And hardly had she finished,
When her limbs grew numb and heavy, her soft breasts
Were closed with delicate bark, her hair was leaves,
Her arms were branches, and her speedy feet
Rooted and held, and her head became a tree top,
Everything gone except her grace, her shining.
Apollo loved her still. He placed his hand
Where he had hoped and felt the heart still beating
Under the bark; and he embraced the branches
As if they still were limbs, and kissed the wood,
And the wood shrank from his kisses, and the god
Exclaimed: "Since you can never be my bride,
My tree at least you shall be! Let the laurel
Adorn, henceforth, my hair, my lyre, my quiver:
Let Roman victors, in the long procession,
Wear laurel wreaths for triumph and ovation.

Beside Augustus' portals let the laurel
Guard and watch over the oak, and as my head
Is always youthful, let the laurel always
Be green and shining!" He said no more. The laurel,
Stirring, seemed to consent, to be saying *Yes.*

There is a grove in Thessaly, surrounded
By woodlands with steep slopes; men call it Tempe.
Through this the Peneus River's foamy waters
Rise below Pindus mountain. The cascades
Drive a fine smoky mist along the tree tops,
Frail clouds, or so it seems, and the roar of the water
Carries beyond the neighborhood. Here dwells
The mighty god himself,° his holy of holies — Peneus
Is under a hanging rock; it is here he gives
Laws to the nymphs, laws to the very water.
And here came first the streams of his own country
Not knowing what to offer, consolation
Or something like rejoicing: crowned with poplars
Sperchios came, and restless Enipeus,
Old Apidanus, Aeas, and Amphrysos[14]
The easy-going. And all the other rivers
That take their weary waters into oceans
All over the world, came there, and only one
Was absent, Inachus,[15] hiding in his cavern,
Salting his stream with tears, oh, most unhappy,
Mourning a daughter lost. Her name was Io,
Who might, for all he knew, be dead or living,
But since he can not find her anywhere
He thinks she must be nowhere, and his sorrow
Fears for the worst. [. . .]

FROM

Book 10

The Story of Orpheus and Eurydice

So Hymen left there, clad in saffron robe,
Through the great reach of air, and took his way
To the Ciconian country, where the voice
Of Orpheus called him, all in vain.[16] He came there,
True, but brought with him no auspicious words,

---

[14] **Sperchios . . . Amphrysos:** All rivers in Thessay. [15] **Inachus:** The main river of Argos. [16] **So Hymen . . . vain:** Hymen, god of marriage, has just left Greece and arrived in Ciconia, a territory in Thrace.

No joyful faces, lucky omens. The torch
Sputtered and filled the eyes with smoke; when swung,
It would not blaze: bad as the omens were,
The end was worse, for as the bride went walking
Across the lawn, attended by her naiads,
A serpent bit her ankle, and she was gone.
Orpheus mourned her to the upper world,
And then, lest he should leave the shades untried,
Dared to descend to Styx, passing the portal
Men call Taenarian.[17] Through the phantom dwellers,
The buried ghosts, he passed, came to the king
Of that sad realm, and to Persephone,
His consort, and he swept the strings, and chanted:
"Gods of the world below the world, to whom
All of us mortals come, if I may speak
Without deceit, the simple truth is this:
I came here, not to see dark Tartarus,[18]
Nor yet to bind the triple-throated monster[19]
Medusa's offspring, rough with snakes. I came
For my wife's sake, whose growing years were taken
By a snake's venom. I wanted to be able
To bear this; I have tried to. Love has conquered.
This god is famous in the world above,
But here, I do not know. I think he may be
Or is it all a lie, that ancient story
Of an old ravishment,[20] and how he brought
The two of you together? By these places
All full of fear, by this immense confusion,
By this vast kingdom's silences, I beg you,
Weave over Eurydice's life, run through too soon.
To you we all, people and things, belong,
Sooner or later, to this single dwelling
All of us come, to our last home; you hold
Longest dominion over humankind.
She will come back again, to be your subject,
After the ripeness of her years; I am asking
A loan and not a gift. If fate denies us
This privilege for my wife, one thing is certain:
I do not want to go back either; triumph

[17] **Taenarian:** Taenarum, a cape on the southern Peloponnesus, thought to be an entrance to Hades, the underworld. [18] **Tartarus:** The farthest region in Hades, where the rebellious Titans were imprisoned. [19] **triple-throated monster:** Cerberus, the three-headed dog that guarded the entrance to Hades. Hercules once bound Cerberus and carried him to the upper world. [20] **an old ravishment:** Ovid alludes to the story of Pluto's abduction of Proserpina told in Book 5.

In the death of two."
And with his words, the music
Made the pale phantoms weep: Ixion's wheel
Was still, Tityos' vultures left the liver,
Tantalus tried no more to reach for the water,
And Belus' daughters rested from their urns,
And Sisyphus[21] climbed on his rock to listen.
That was the first time ever in all the world
The Furies[22] wept. Neither the king nor consort
Had harshness to refuse him, and they called her,
Eurydice. She was there, limping a little
From her late wound, with the new shades of Hell.
And Orpheus received her, but one term
Was set: he must not, till he passed Avernus,[23]
Turn back his gaze, or the gift would be in vain.

They climbed the upward path, through absolute silence,
Up the steep murk, clouded in pitchy darkness,
They were near the margin, near the upper land,
When he, afraid that she might falter, eager to see her,
Looked back in love, and she was gone, in a moment.
Was it he, or she, reaching out arms and trying
To hold or to be held, and clasping nothing
But empty air? Dying the second time,
She had no reproach to bring against her husband,
What was there to complain of? One thing, only:
He loved her. He could hardly hear her calling
Farewell! when she was gone.
The double death
Stunned Orpheus, like the man who turned to stone
At sight of Cerberus, or the couple of rock,
Olenos and Lethaea,[24] hearts so joined
One shared the other's guilt, and Ida's mountain,
Where rivers run, still holds them, both together.

---

[21] **Ixion . . . Sisyphus:** These are all sinners facing eternal tortures. Ixion was chained to a fiery wheel that turned endlessly; Tityos suffered the pain of vultures constantly feeding on his liver; Tantalus stood chin deep in water that receded whenever he tried to drink it, while above him fruit dangled just out of reach; Belus's daughters had to carry water in pitchers punctured with holes; and Sisyphus continually pushed a huge boulder to the top of a hill only to see it roll back down.

[22] **Furies:** Female spirits who avenged crimes against blood kin, especially against fathers and mothers; sometimes thought to inflict the tortures in Hades.

[23] **Avernus:** A poisonous lake and a wood near the entrance to the underworld.

[24] **the couple . . . Lethaea:** When Olenos, Lethaea's husband, offered to take on her punishment for offending the gods by bragging of her beauty, both were turned to stone.

In vain the prayers of Orpheus and his longing
To cross the river once more; the boatman Charon
Drove him away. For seven days he sat there
Beside the bank, in filthy garments, and tasting
No food whatever. Trouble, grief, and tears
Were all his sustenance. At last, complaining
The gods of Hell were cruel, he wandered on
To Rhodope and Haemus,[25] swept by the north winds,
Where, for three years, he lived without a woman
Either because marriage had meant misfortune
Or he had made a promise. But many women
Wanted this poet for their own, and many
Grieved over their rejection. His love was given
To young boys only, and he told the Thracians
That was the better way: *enjoy that springtime,*
Take those first flowers!
There was a hill, and on it
A wide-extending plain, all green, but lacking
The darker green of shade, and when the singer
Came there and ran his fingers over the strings,
The shade came there to listen. The oak-tree came,
And many poplars, and the gentle lindens,
The beech, the virgin laurel, and the hazel
Easily broken, the ash men use for spears,
The shining silver-fir, the ilex bending
Under its acorns, the friendly sycamore,
The changing-colored maple, and the willows
That love the river-waters, and the lotus
Favoring pools, and the green boxwood came,
Slim tamarisks, and myrtle, and viburnum
With dark-blue berries, and the pliant ivy,
The tendrilled grape, the elms, all dressed with vines,
The rowan-trees, the pitch-pines, and the arbute
With the red fruit, the palm, the victor's triumph,
The bare-trunked pine with spreading leafy crest,
Dear to the mother of the gods since Attis[26]
Put off his human form, took on that likeness,
And the cone-shaped cypress joined them, now a tree,
But once a boy, loved by the god Apollo
Master of lyre and bow-string, both together. [. . .]

[25] **Rhodope and Haemus:** Mountains in Thrace.

[26] **Attis:** A youth associated with the Phrygian mother goddess Cybele; in a fit of madness inspired by the jealous goddess, he castrated himself and was transformed into a pine tree.

The Story of Pygmalion

One man, Pygmalion, who had seen these women
Leading their shameful lives, shocked at the vices
Nature has given the female disposition
Only too often, chose to live alone,
To have no woman in his bed. But meanwhile
He made, with marvelous art, an ivory statue,
As white as snow, and gave it greater beauty
Than any girl could have, and fell in love
With his own workmanship. The image seemed
That of a virgin, truly, almost living,
And willing, save that modesty prevented,
To take on movement. The best art, they say,
Is that which conceals art, and so Pygmalion
Marvels, and loves the body he has fashioned.
He would often move his hands to test and touch it,
Could this be flesh, or was it ivory only?
No, it could not be ivory. His kisses,
He fancies, she returns; he speaks to her,
Holds her, believes his fingers almost leave
An imprint on her limbs, and fears to bruise her.
He pays her compliments, and brings her presents
Such as girls love, smooth pebbles, winding shells,
Little pet birds, flowers with a thousand colors,
Lilies, and painted balls, and lumps of amber.
He decks her limbs with dresses, and her fingers
Wear rings which he puts on, and he brings a necklace,
And earrings, and a ribbon for her bosom,
And all of these become her, but she seems
Even more lovely naked, and he spreads
A crimson coverlet for her to lie on,
Takes her to bed, puts a soft pillow under
Her head, as if she felt it, calls her *Darling,*
My darling love!
"And Venus' holiday
Came round, and all the people of the island
Were holding festival, and snow-white heifers,
Their horns all tipped with gold, stood at the altars,
Where incense burned, and, timidly, Pygmalion
Made offering, and prayed: 'If you can give
All things, O gods, I pray my wife may be—
(He almost said, *My ivory girl,* but dared not)—
One like my ivory girl.' And golden Venus
Was there, and understood the prayer's intention,
And showed her presence, with the bright flame leaping

Thrice on the altar, and Pygmalion came
Back where the maiden lay, and lay beside her,
And kissed her, and she seemed to glow, and kissed her,
And stroked her breast, and felt the ivory soften
Under his fingers, as wax grows soft in sunshine,
Made pliable by handling. And Pygmalion
Wonders, and doubts, is dubious and happy,
Plays lover again, and over and over touches
The body with his hand. It is a body!
The veins throb under the thumb. And oh, Pygmalion
Is lavish in his prayer and praise to Venus,
No words are good enough. The lips he kisses
Are real indeed, the ivory girl can feel them,
And blushes and responds, and the eyes open
At once on lover and heaven, and Venus blesses
The marriage she has made. The crescent moon
Fills to full orb, nine times, and wanes again,
And then a daughter is born, a girl named Paphos,
From whom the island later takes its name. [. . .]

The Story of Adonis

Time, in its stealthy gliding, cheats us all
Without our notice; nothing goes more swiftly
Than do the years. That little boy, whose sister
Became his mother, his grandfather's son,
Is now a youth, and now a man, more handsome
Than he had ever been, exciting even
The goddess Venus, and thereby avenging
His mother's passion. Cupid, it seems, was playing,
Quiver on shoulder, when he kissed his mother,
And one barb grazed her breast; she pushed him away,
But the wound was deeper than she knew; deceived,
Charmed by Adonis' beauty, she cared no more
For Cythera's shores nor Paphos' sea-ringed island,
Nor Cnidos, where fish teem, nor high Amathus,[27]
Rich in its precious ores. She stays away
Even from Heaven, Adonis is better than Heaven.
She is beside him always; she has always,
Before this time, preferred the shadowy places,
Preferred her ease, preferred to improve her beauty
By careful tending, but now, across the ridges,

[27] **Cythera's shores . . . Amathus:** These places were the favorite earthly haunts of Venus.

Through woods, through rocky places thick with brambles,
She goes, more like Diana than like Venus,
Bare-kneed and robes tucked up. She cheers the hounds,
Hunts animals, at least such timid creatures
As deer and rabbits; no wild boars for her,
No wolves, no bears, no lions. And she warns him
To fear them too, as if there might be good
In giving him warnings. 'Be bold against the timid,
The running creatures, but against the bold ones
Boldness is dangerous. Do not be reckless.
I share whatever risk you take; be careful!
Do not attack those animals which Nature
Has given weapons, lest your thirst for glory
May cost me dear. Beauty and youth and love
Make no impression on bristling boars and lions,
On animal eyes and minds. The force of lightning
Is in the wild boar's tusks, and tawny lions
Are worse than thunderbolts. I hate and fear them.'
He asks her why. She answers, 'I will tell you,
And you will wonder at the way old crime
Leads to monstrosities. I will tell you sometime,
Not now, for I am weary, all this hunting
Is not what I am used to. Here's a couch
Of grassy turf, and a canopy of poplar,
I would like to lie there with you.' And she lay there,
Making a pillow for him of her breast,
And kisses for her story's punctuation.

Venus Tells Adonis the Story of Atalanta

You may have heard (she said) about a girl
Who could outrun the swiftest men. The story
Is very true: she really could outrun them.
It would be hard to say, though, whether her speed
Or beauty earned more praise. She was very lovely.
She asked the oracle, one day, to give her
Advice on marriage. "You don't need a husband,"
The god replied, "Avoid that habit! Still,
I know you will not: you will keep your life,
And lose yourself." So Atalanta, frightened,
Lived in the shadowy woods, a single woman,
Harshly rejecting urgent throngs of suitors.
"No one gets me who cannot beat me running,
Race me!" she told them, "Wife and marriage-chamber
Go to the winner, but the slow ones get

The booby-prize of death. Those are my terms."
The terms were harsh, but beauty has such power
That those harsh terms were met by many suitors,
Foolhardy fellows. Watching the cruel race,
Hippomenes had some remarks to make:
"Is any woman worth it? These young men
Strike me as very silly." But when he saw her,
Her face, her body naked, with such beauty
As mine is, or as yours would be, Adonis,
If you were woman, he was struck with wonder,
Threw up his hands and cried: "I beg your pardon,
Young men, I judged you wrongly; I did not know
The value of the prize!" And he caught fire
From his own praising, hoped that no young runner
Would beat her, feared they might, was worried, jealous.
"Why don't I try?" he thought, "God helps the bold."
And, swifter than his thought, the girl sped by
On winged feet, swifter than Scythian arrow,
Yet not too swift for a young man's admiration,
And running made her lovelier: the breeze
Bore back the streaming pinions of her sandals,
Her hair was tossed back over ivory shoulders,
The colored ribbons fluttered at her knees,
And a light flush came over her girlish body
The way a crimson awning, over marble,
Tints it in pastel color. As he watched her,
She crossed the finish line, received the crown
Of victory, and the beaten suitors, groaning,
Were led away to death.
'Hippomenes,
Undaunted, came from the crowd; he fixed his eyes
On Atalanta, and he made his challenge:
"This is too easy, beating all these turtles!
Race against me!" he said, "If you are beaten
It will be no disgrace. Megareus is my father,
Whose grandfather was Neptune, and that makes me
Great-grandson of the king of all the oceans.
Nor is my worth inferior to my race.
Beat me, and you will have something to boast of!"
Listening, looking almost tenderly
At that young man, she wondered, in confusion,
Which would be better, to win or lose. "What god"
She thought, "So hates the young and handsome
He wants to ruin this one, tempting him
To risk his precious life to marry me?

I do not think I am worth it. I am not moved
By his beauty (though I could be); I am moved
Because he seems so young: he does not move me,
Only his age. What of his manly courage,
His nerve, his claim to proud descent, his love
For me, so great a love that death, he claims,
Is an advantage if he cannot have me?
Go while you may, O stranger, flee this marriage,
There is too much blood upon it. Any girl
Would marry you, and wisely. Why do I care,
Why worry for him, when I have slain so many?
Let him look out for himself, or let him die
Since the death of all those others has not warned him,
Since life is such a bore! Is he to die
Because he wants to live with me? Is death
To be the price of love? I shall be hated
In victory. It is not my fault. Poor fellow,
I wish you would forget it but, since you are crazy,
I wish at least you could run a little faster!
He looks like a girl, almost. I wish he had never
Laid eyes on me. He should have lived. If I
Were luckier, if the fates allowed me marriage,
He was the only one I would have taken
To bed with any pleasure." Atalanta
Was green in love, untutored—she did not know
What she was doing, and loved, and did not know it.
Meanwhile the people and her father, restless,
Were clamoring for the race. Hippomenes
Called me in supplication: "O, may Venus
Be near, I pray, assist my daring, favor
The love she gave me!" And a gentle breeze
Bore this soft prayer my way; it moved my heart,
I own, and there was little time to aid him.
There is a field the natives call Tamasus,
The richest part of Cyprus, which the ancients
Hallowed for me, and built my temples there,
And in a field there stands a golden tree,
Shining with golden leaves and branches rustling
With the soft click of gold, and golden apples
Are the fruit of that golden tree. I came from there
With three such apples in my hand, and no one
Saw me except Hippomenes, and I
Told him how he should use them.
'The trumpets sounded
The start: the pair, each crouching low, shot forward,

Skimming the sand with flying feet, so lightly
They could run on waves and never wet their sandals,
They could run on fields of grain and never bend them.
He heard them cheering: "Go, Hippomenes,
Lean to the work, use all your strength: go, go,
You are sure to win!" I could not tell you whether
The cheering pleased him more, or Atalanta.
How many times, when she could have passed, she lingered,
Slowed down to see his face, and, most unwilling,
Sprinted ahead! And now his breathing labored,
Came in great sobbing gasps, and the finish line
Was a long way off, and he tossed one golden apple,
The first one, down. She looked at it with wonder,
Eager to have the shining fruit, she darted
Out of the course, and picked it up, still rolling,
The golden thing. He gained the lead again
As all the people roared applause. She passed him
Again, and once again lost ground to follow
The toss of the second apple, and once more
Caught up and sprinted past him. "O be near me,
Gift-bringing Goddess, help me now!" he cried,
And this time threw the last third apple farther,
Angling it off the course, way to one side.
She hesitated, only for a moment,
Whether to chase it, but I made her do it,
And made the fruit weigh more, so she was hindered
Both by the burden and her own delay.
To run my story quickly, as the race
Was run, the girl was beaten, and the winner
Led off his prize.
'Do you not think, Adonis,
He should have brought me incense, or at least
Given me thanks? He did not. I was angry:
Once slighted, I should not again be slighted.
I told myself I would make examples of them.
One day they were going by a temple, hidden
In the deep woods; in ancient times Echion
Had consecrated this to Cybele
In payment of a vow. Their trip was long,
And they were tired, or thought so, but I drove
Hippomenes half crazy with the passion
To take his wife. He saw, beside the temple,
A dimly-lighted cavern, roofed with rock,
A chapel it was, really, where the priesthood
Had placed for worship their old wooden idols.

He could not wait, here he took Atalanta,
And the gods turned their eyes away; Cybele,
The tower-crowned Mother, had at first the impulse
To drown them, for their guilt, in the Stygian waters,
But that seemed much too easy. So their necks
Grew rough with tawny manes, their fingers, hooked,
Were claws, their arms were legs, their chests grew heavy,
Their tails swept over the sandy ground, and anger
Blazed in their features, they conversed in growling,
Took to the woods to couple: they were lions,
Frightful to all but Cybele, whose bridle
And bit they champed in meekness. Do not hunt them,
Adonis: let all beasts alone, which offer
Breasts to the fight, not backs, or else your daring
Will be the ruin of us both.'

The Fate of Adonis

"Her warning
Was given, and the goddess took her way,
Drawn by her swans through air. But the young hunter
Scorned all such warnings, and one day, it happened,
His hounds, hard on the trail, roused a wild boar,
And as he rushed from the wood, Adonis struck him
A glancing blow, and the boar turned, and shaking
The spear from the side, came charging at the hunter,
Who feared, and ran, and fell, and the tusk entered
Deep in the groin, and the youth lay there dying
On the yellow sand, and Venus, borne through air
In her light swan-guided chariot, still was far
From Cyprus when she heard his groans, and, turning
The white swans from their course, came back to him,
Saw, from high air, the body lying lifeless
In its own blood, and tore her hair and garments,
Beat her fair breasts with cruel hands, came down
Reproaching Fate. 'They shall not have it always
Their way,' she mourned, 'Adonis, for my sorrow,
Shall have a lasting monument: each year
Your death will be my sorrow, but your blood
Shall be a flower. If Persephone
Could change to fragrant mint the girl called Mentha,
Cinyras' son, my hero, surely also
Can be my flower.' Over the blood she sprinkled
Sweet-smelling nectar, and as bubbles rise
In rainy weather, so it stirred, and blossomed,

Before an hour, as crimson in its color
As pomegranates are, as briefly clinging
To life as did Adonis, for the winds
Which gave a name to the flower, anemone,
The wind-flower, shake the petals off, too early,
Doomed all too swift and soon."

PETRONIUS
D. 66 C.E.

A clichéd view of classical art sees the Greeks as idealists who portray human beings as they ought to be and the Romans as realists who describe men as they are. Probably no work of Latin literature provides more support for the latter portion of this assessment than *The Satyricon* of **Petronius**, a work of fiction that is unusually realistic even in the canon of Latin literature. *The Satyricon* is not about great historical events or mythological subjects, as so many of the Latin classics are; it treats instead trivial and commonplace subjects, and it does so in a colloquial language found almost nowhere else in Latin literature. It is so unusual that it is often referred to as "the first novel," more often compared to the PICARESQUE novels[1] of seventeenth-century Europe than to other works of classical literature.

pih-TROH-nee-us

An Obscure Author. Although scholars are generally agreed that the Petronius who wrote *The Satyricon* was named either **Gaius** or Titus, they do not know when Petronius, who died in 66 C.E., was born or much about his life. Almost all the facts of his life are supplied by the Roman historian Tacitus (c. 55–c. 117 C.E.), who reports that Petronius served as governor and consul of Bithynia and identifies Petronius's most notable role as friend of the emperor Nero (37–68 C.E.), the emperor's unofficial advisor on the pursuit of pleasure, his "arbiter of elegance" *(arbiter-elegantiae)*. Hence, Petronius is often called "Petronius Arbiter." Of Petronius, Tacitus wrote: "His days he passed in sleep, his nights in the business and pleasures of life. Indolence had raised him to fame, as energy raises others, and he was reckoned not a debauchee and spendthrift, like most of those who squander their substance, but a man of refined luxury." Petronius's favor with Nero sparked the jealousy of Tigellinus, a rival for

GIGH-yus

WWW For links to more information about Petronius and a quiz on *The Satyricon*, see *World Literature Online* at bedfordstmartins.com/worldlit.

[1] **picaresque novels:** Realistic novels that tell of the escapades of a *picaro*, a rogue who lives by his wits, using stratagems and trickery to survive. In European literature these works first appear in sixteenth-century Spain, such as the anonymous *Lazarillo de Tormes* (c. 1554). The genre now encompasses any "road novel" with a rogue hero and an episodic structure.

Banquet Scene, first century C.E.
The ancient Romans loved a good dinner party. Much like the characters in The Satyricon, *the Romans depicted in this Pompeiian fresco share a bountiful dinner and (perhaps) interesting conversation. (Erich Lessing/Art Resource, NY)*

Nero's favor who justly accused Petronius of conspiring against the emperor. After writing a catalog of Nero's debaucheries that he sent to the emperor, Petronius committed suicide.

Menippian Satire. Though unique, *The Satyricon* (a book of **SATYR**-like adventures) is not unrelated to other works of classical literature. Ancient commentators traced its stories to Milesian tales, collections of anecdotes, jests, and racy stories from Miletus in Asia Minor (Turkey), and to the satires of the Greek writer and philosopher Menippus (early third century B.C.E.). Although none of these earlier works survive, reports about and fragments of them appear in the Menippian satires of Roman writer Marcus Terentius Varro (116 B.C.E.–27 B.C.E.). From those works it is known that the genre mixed prose and verse materials and made extensive use of imitation, parody, and farce. The tradition of **MENIPPIAN SATIRE**[2]

[2] **Menippian satire:** Named for its originator, the Greek Cynic philosopher Menippus (first half of the third century B.C.E.), Menippian satire uses a mixture of prose, dialogue, and verse to make ludicrous a whole social class or a broad spectrum of social types. The form is sometimes called "an anatomy" because it catalogs the many social and intellectual types who constitute the social group it ridicules.

that derives from these writers uses character "types" to moralize or give a corrective turn to stories and verses.

The Satyricon. With only about ten percent of the original text to go by, judgments about the whole of *The Satyricon* call for a fair degree of speculation. Enough of the original survives to know that the story is a journey narrative, a tale of three young men who take to the road. The narrator, **Encolpius**, a student of rhetoric whose name translates roughly as "the crotch," and his fellow student Ascyltus ("scot-free"), are accompanied by Giton ("neighbor"), a boy who is their servant and the object of their sexual attentions. Their journey begins in southern Italy, near Naples, and was apparently intended to end at Marseilles.

eng-KOLE-pee-us

Enough of the original remains also to indicate its mixture of genres and styles. It contains anecdotal stories, sustained adventures, character sketches, mock-heroic poems, and literary discussions. Several passages indicate that the work as a whole was intended as a parody of ***The Odyssey***. Just as Odysseus's journey home is prolonged by the wrath of the sea-god Poseidon, Encolpius is tormented by Priapus, the classical god of lust whom he has offended by spying on the god's secret rites. Throughout his adventures, Encolpius is humiliated and stricken with impotence by the angry god.

p. 421

"Dinner with Trimalchio." The longest and most intact section of what remains of *The Satyricon* is the account of Trimalchio's banquet. This account may have been meant to satirize earlier classical narratives in which banquets offer an occasion for philosophical discussion, such as Plato's "Symposium," in which Socrates and his friends discuss over dinner the nature of love. Petronius paints a realistic portrait of those who gather at the feast, particularly the host, **Trimalchio**. A former slave who is now a rich freedman, Trimalchio is a character type who has appeared over and over again in satiric writing, the *nouveau riche,* the *parvenu.* His boastfulness, self-absorption, vulgarity, and grandiosity are standard characteristics of the type. As he conceived of the dinner scene, Petronius may have had the character sketches of the Greek writer and philosopher Theophrastus (c. 371–c. 288 B.C.E.) in mind, whose *Characters* includes sketches of various moral types. However, if Petronius did begin with such a "type," he managed to eliminate the moralistic point of view and add a great deal of individualizing realistic detail. In doing so he transcended moralism and created satiric comedy.

trih-MAL-kee-oh

Encolpius's objective narration allows his observations to speak for themselves. The students may observe Trimalchio with a certain snobbish disdain, but they are nonetheless amused by his excesses. Encolpius gives detailed descriptions of the food served at the banquet and the people in attendance, and he reports their conversation in an extraordinarily colloquial language.

The dinner is a microcosm of the self-indulgent Roman society of the first century. As the guests talk about food and money, and tell of how they escaped slavery, made money, and evaded taxes, the materialism of the time comes to light. There are no discussions of philosophy or religion

***The Satyricon* is beyond compare, the most brilliant piece of prose fiction left by antiquity; there is nothing like its easy and masterly drawing of gross and common or preposterous human nature, and nothing like its caustic wit, before the finest of the modern picaresque novelists.**

– Ernest A. Baker, critic

taking place; these men are far more interested in gladitorial games and the spectacle of men fighting animals. As the banquet reaches its climax, Trimalchio, its lord of misrule, reads his last will to those assembled. The document, an absurd exaggeration of his materialistic worldview, is a reminder of the transience of worldly pleasures and the imminence of death.

■ CONNECTIONS

Virgil, *The Aeneid,* p. 1181. In classical literature a banquet is often an occasion for philosophical discussion or storytelling, whose ideas and stories are enhanced by the characterizations of the guests at the meal. In Virgil's *Aeneid,* Books 2 and 3, at Dido's banquet Aeneas tells the story of the fall of Troy and of his adventures, revealing his heroism and arousing Dido's admiration and love. Petronius's portrayal of Trimalchio's feast satirizes such occasions, concentrating on the weaknesses and foibles of Trimalchio's invitees. Which elements in Dido's feast elevate Aeneas's character and which in Trimalchio's reveal the host's foolishness?

Geoffrey Chaucer, *The Canterbury Tales* (Book 2). Literary characters often entertain and instruct the reader by revealing more about themselves than they intend or realize. Trimalchio inadvertently reveals his vulgarity and materialism, and his story may suggest to the reader that what is valuable is not the influence and wealth that Trimalchio treasures. Chaucer's Wife of Bath is also delightfully frank, disclosing much about her marital history and her expectations of her husbands. What do we learn from each of these characters, and how do they entertain us?

Farid ud-Din Attar, *The Conference of the Birds* (Book 2). In *The Conference of the Birds,* the Hoopoe challenges the ostentatious bird's materialism by reminding him of his mortality and by telling the stories "A King Who Built a Splendid Palace" and "A Merchant Gives a Party." What might these stories have to say to Trimalchio? Are there any reminders of human mortality in Petronius's account of Trimalchio's dinner?

Gustave Flaubert, "A Simple Heart" (Book 5). Realists use an objective point of view to make the people and places they describe real. Flaubert, in "A Simple Heart," uses detailed description to create a convincing portrait of a servant woman. Petronius allows Trimalchio to reveal himself as he talks about his life. How do these Realists influence their readers' perceptions of their characters? What does Petronius do, for example, to make Trimalchio a satiric figure?

■ FURTHER RESEARCH

Arrowsmith, William. Introduction to *The Satyricon of Petronius.* Translated by William Arrowsmith. 1977.

Auerbach, Erich. "Fortunata," in *Mimesis: The Representation of Reality in Western Literature.* 1946.

Courtney, Edward. *A Companion to Petronius.* 2002.

Sullivan, J. P. Introduction to *Petronius: The Satyricon.* Translated by J. P. Sullivan. 1977.

Sullivan, J. P. *The "Satyricon" of Petronius: A Literary Study.* 1969.

■ PRONUNCIATION

Encolpius: eng-KOLE-pee-us, eng-KAHL-pee-us
Gaius: GIGH-yus
Petronius: pih-TROH-nee-us
Scintilla: sin-TIL-uh
Trimalchio: trih-MAL-kee-oh

The Satyricon

Translated by William Arrowsmith

FROM
DINNER WITH TRIMALCHIO

At last the third day had come with its prospect of a free meal and perhaps our last meal on this earth. But by now our poor bodies were so bruised and battered that escape, even if it cost us a meal, seemed preferable to staying where we were. While we were gloomily wondering how we could avoid the orgy in store for us with Quartilla, one of Agamemnon's[1] slaves came up and dispelled our despair. "What's eating you?" he asked. "Have you forgotten where you're going tonight? Trimalchio's[2] giving the meal. He's real swank. Got a great big clock in his dining room and a uniformed bugler who blows a horn every hour so the old man won't forget how fast his time is slipping away." Needless to say, we forgot our troubles fast when we heard this. We slipped into our best clothes, and when Giton very sweetly offered to act as our servant, we told him to attend us to the baths.

There we wandered around at first without getting undressed. Or rather we went joking around, mixing with various groups of bathers at their games. Suddenly we caught sight of an old, bald man in a long red undershirt, playing ball with a bunch of curly-headed slave boys. It wasn't so much the boys who took our eyes—though they were worth looking at—as the old man himself. There he stood, rigged

---

The Satyricon. Of the small portion of this work that remains (about one-tenth of the original), "Dinner with Trimalchio" is the longest and most intact section. These chapters, part of a manuscript that was discovered in a monastery in the former Yugoslavia in the seventeenth century, provide a detailed account of a dinner given by a rich former slave for his friends and associates. Petronius may have begun with the idea of writing a character sketch of a stereotypical figure, the *parvenu,* but the wealth of detail in his account individualizes Trimalchio, his wife, Fortunata, and several of the guests at the feast.

The narrator, Encolpius, an adventurer who appears to come from a more elevated social station than his host, describes Trimalchio's vulgarity, ostentation, affectation, and lack of taste with detailed objectivity rather than moralistic commentary. Indeed, Encolpius and his comrades are more amused than scandalized by Trimalchio's excesses. Petronius's eye for detail and the objectivity of his point of view have prompted literary historians to describe him as "the first novelist." His work, particularly "Dinner with Trimalchio," bears comparison to the picaresque novels of seventeenth-century Spain and to the work of such nineteenth-century realists as Honoré de Balzac, Gustave Flaubert, and Charles Dickens.

William Arrowsmith's translation adapts the colloquial, conversational style of the original to a similar modern American idiom. The notes, unless otherwise indicated, are the translator's.

---

[1] **Agamemnon:** A tutor in rhetoric. Encolpius, the narrator, is one of his students. (Editors' note.)

[2] **Trimalchio:** The name seems to be of Semitic origin and to mean "great and rich" or "triply fortunate."

out in undershirt and sandals, nothing else, bouncing a big green ball the color of a leek. When he dropped one ball, moreover, he never bothered to stoop for it, but simply took another from a slave who stood beside him with a huge sack tossing out fresh balls to the players. This was striking enough, but the real refinement was two eunuchs standing on either side of the circle, one clutching a chamber pot of solid silver, the other ticking off the balls. He was not, however, scoring the players' points, but merely keeping count of any balls that happened to drop on the ground. While we were gawking at these elegant gymnastics, Menelaus[3] came rushing up. "That's *him!*" he whispered, "that's the fellow who's giving the meal. What you're seeing now is just the prelude to the show." These words were hardly out when Trimalchio gave a loud snap with his fingers. The eunuch came waddling up with the chamber pot, Trimalchio emptied his bladder and went merrily on with his game. When he was done, he shouted for water, daintily dipped the tips of his fingers and wiped his hands in the long hair of a slave.

But the details of his performance would take too long to tell. We quickly undressed, went into the hot baths, and after working up a sweat, passed on to the cold showers. There we found Trimalchio again, his skin glistening all over with perfumed oil. He was being rubbed down, not with ordinary linen, but with cloths of the purest and softest wool. During this rubdown, right before his eyes, the three masseurs were guzzling away at the finest of his rare Falernian wines.[4] In a minute, moreover, they were squabbling and in the next second the wine had spilled all over the floor. "Tut, a mere trifle," said Trimalchio, "they were merely pouring me a toast."[5] He was then bundled into a blazing scarlet wrapper, hoisted onto a litter and trundled off. Before him went four runners in spangled harness and a little wheelbarrow in which the old man's favorite rode, a little boy with a wrinkled face and bleary, crudded eyes, even uglier than his master. A musician with a miniature flute trotted along at Trimalchio's head and during the entire trip played into his master's ear as though whispering him little secrets.

Drunk with admiration, we brought up the rear and Agamemnon joined us when we reached Trimalchio's door. Beside the door we saw a sign:

ANY SLAVE LEAVING THE PREMISES
WITHOUT AUTHORIZATION FROM THE MASTER
WILL RECEIVE ONE HUNDRED LASHES!

At the entrance sat the porter, dressed in that same leek-green that seemed to be the livery of the house. A cherry-colored sash was bound around his waist and he was busily shelling peas into a pan of solid silver. In the doorway hung a cage, all gold, and in it a magpie was croaking out his welcome to the guests.

[3] **Menelaus:** Agamemnon's assistant, the junior rhetorician. [4] **Falernian wines:** One of the more esteemed Roman wines. [5] **they were . . . toast:** It was Roman custom, when drinking someone's health, to pour some of the wine under the table as an offering to the gods. In this way, one procured the good will of the gods for the proposed toast.

I was gaping at all this in open-mouthed wonder when I suddenly jumped with terror, stumbled, and nearly broke my leg. For there on the left as you entered, in fresco, stood a huge dog straining at his leash. In large letters under the painting was scrawled:

BEWARE OF THE DOG!

The others burst out laughing at my fright. But when I'd recovered from the shock, I found myself following the rest of the frescoes with fascination. They ran the whole length of the wall. First came a panel showing a slave market with everything clearly captioned. There stood Trimalchio as a young man, his hair long and curly in slave fashion; in his hand he held a staff[6] and he was entering Rome for the first time under the sponsorship of Minerva.[7] In the next panel he appeared as an apprentice accountant, then as a paymaster—each step in his career portrayed in great detail and everything scrupulously labeled. At the end of the portico you came to the climax of the series: a picture of Mercury grasping Trimalchio by the chin and hoisting him up to the lofty eminence of the official's tribunal.[8] Beside the dais stood the goddess Fortuna with a great cornucopia and the three Fates, busily spinning out Trimalchio's life in threads of gold, while in the background a group of runners were shown working out with their trainer. In the corner at the end of the portico was a huge wardrobe with a small built-in shrine. In the shrine were silver statuettes of the household gods, a Venus in marble, and a golden casket containing, I was told, the clippings from Trimalchio's first beard.[9] I began questioning the attendant about some other frescoes in the middle. "Scenes from the *Iliad* and the *Odyssey*," he explained, "and the gladiator games given by Laenas."[10] But there was far too little time to ask about everything that took my eye.

We approached the dining room next where we found the steward at the door making up his accounts. I was particularly struck by the doorposts. For fixed to the jamb were *fasces*,[11] bundles of sticks with axes protruding from them; but on the

[6]**a staff:** The *caduceus* of Mercury, the god of trade and Trimalchio's special patron. [7]**sponsorship of Minerva:** As goddess of crafts (and Wisdom?), Minerva conducts Trimalchio to Rome. [8]**the official's tribunal:** The seat to which Mercury hoists Trimalchio is the throne allotted to the Sevirs, i.e., the officials appointed in the municipalities to carry out the worship of the deified emperor. Election to this office was normally purchased, and Trimalchio was proud of having been appointed without payment. [9]**first beard:** The first trimming of the beard was regarded by Romans as symbolic of a boy's having attained to his manhood and was usually the preliminary to his donning the man's garb, the *toga virilis*. [10]**"Scenes from . . . Laenas":** Laenas's gladiator games are otherwise unknown. Their presence here, however, is deliberately incongruous, an exposure of the vulgarity of taste of a man who could juxtapose scenes from Homer with others from mere gladiatorial games. The modern analogy would be the case of that book-collecting millionaire who claimed to specialize in "twelfth-century *incunabula* and first editions of Zane Grey." [11]***fasces:*** In Republican times *fasces* were symbols of authority, borne by lictors (or bearers) in attendance upon a magistrate possessing the *imperium*. The rods signified the magistrate's power of administering a flogging; the ax, the power of life and death. Under the Empire, however, *fasces* were made available even to the Sevirs, each of whom was allowed two lictors.

lower side the bundles terminated in what looked like the brass ram of a ship,[12] and on the brass this inscription had been engraved:

TO GAIUS POMPEIUS TRIMALCHIO,
OFFICIAL OF THE IMPERIAL CULT,[13]
FROM HIS STEWARD
CINNAMUS.

[. . .]

At last we took our places. Immediately slaves from Alexandria came in and poured ice water[14] over our hands. These were followed by other slaves who knelt at our feet and with extraordinary skill pedicured our toenails. Not for an instant, moreover, during the whole of this odious job, did one of them stop singing. This made me wonder whether the whole menage was given to bursts of song, so I put it to the test by calling for a drink. It was served immediately by a boy who trilled away as shrilly as the rest of them. In fact, anything you asked for was invariably served with a snatch of song, so that you would have thought you were eating in a concert-hall rather than a private dining room.

Now that the guests were all in their places, the *hors d'oeuvres* were served, and very sumptuous they were. Trimalchio alone was still absent, and the place of honor—reserved for the host in the modern fashion—stood empty. But I was speaking of the *hors d'oeuvres.* On a large tray stood a donkey made of rare Corinthian bronze; on the donkey's back were two panniers, one holding green olives, the other, black. Flanking the donkey were two side dishes, both engraved with Trimalchio's name and the weight of the silver, while in dishes shaped to resemble little bridges there were dormice,[15] all dipped in honey and rolled in poppyseed. Nearby, on a silver grill, piping hot, lay small sausages, while beneath the grill black damsons and red pomegranates had been sliced up and arranged so as to give the effect of flames playing over charcoal.

We were nibbling at these splendid appetizers when suddenly the trumpets blared a fanfare and Trimalchio was carried in,[16] propped up on piles of miniature

[12] **brass . . . ship:** The meaning of these brass rams is uncertain. It may be merely that Trimalchio is again guilty of pretentious bad taste, or that he liked this imposing, semiofficial suggestion of naval triumph. As a man who had made enormous wealth from merchant-shipping, he could think of himself as having won some sort of naval triumph. And to get from that to the notion of himself as almost an admiral would not be beyond the limits of *his* ingenuity or pretensions. His only problem is to know how close he can sail to the letter of the law, without incurring its penalties. [13] **OFFICIAL . . . CULT:** That is, a *sevir.* Cf. notes 8 and 11 above. [14] **ice water:** Three seasons out of the year, especially in Roman times, ice water would be a great luxury. During the Italian winter, however, it is supplied in bitter abundance. [15] **dormice:** Small rodents intermediate between the mouse and the squirrel; they were regarded as a great delicacy in antiquity. [16] **Trimalchio was carried in:** Trimalchio's entrance deserves comment. It is primarily the elaborate incongruity of his dress that accounts for the amusement of the more sophisticated guests. Thus, while the close-cropped haircut is typical of the slave or the recently manumitted slave, the broad purple stripe was a privilege permitted only to the Senatorial class. The gold rings, on the other hand, are the prerogative of the equestrian order. Trimalchio, having the right to neither the broad purple stripe nor the equestrian ring, does the next best thing, wearing an imitation

pillows in such a comic way that some of us couldn't resist impolitely smiling. His head, cropped close in a recognizable slave cut, protruded from a cloak of blazing scarlet; his neck, heavily swathed already in bundles of clothing, was wrapped in a large napkin bounded by an incongruous senatorial purple stripe with little tassels dangling down here and there. On the little finger of his left hand he sported an immense gilt ring; the ring on the last joint of his fourth finger looked to be solid gold of the kind the lesser nobility wear, but was actually, I think, an imitation, pricked out with small steel stars. Nor does this exhaust the inventory of his trinkets. At least he rather ostentatiously bared his arm to show us a large gold bracelet and an ivory circlet with a shiny metal plate.

He was picking his teeth with a silver toothpick when he first addressed us. "My friends," he said, "I wasn't anxious to eat just yet, but I've ignored my own wishes so as not to keep you waiting. Still, perhaps you won't mind if I finish my game." At these words a slave jumped forward with a board of juniper wood and a pair of crystal dice. I noticed one other elegant novelty as well: in place of the usual black and white counters, Trimalchio had substituted gold and silver coins. His playing, I might add, was punctuated throughout with all sorts of vulgar exclamations.

We, meanwhile, were still occupied with the *hors d'oeuvres* when a tray was carried in and set down before us. On it lay a basket, and in it a hen, carved from wood, with wings outspread as though sitting on her eggs. Then two slaves came forward and, to a loud flourish from the orchestra, began rummaging in the straw and pulling out peahen's eggs[17] which they divided among the guests. Trimalchio gave the whole performance his closest attention. "Friends," he said, "I ordered peahen eggs to be set under that hen, but I'm half afraid they may have hatched already. Still, let's see if we can suck them." We were handed spoons—weighing at least half a pound apiece—and cracked open the eggs, which turned out to be baked from rich pastry. To tell the truth, I had almost tossed my share away, thinking the eggs were really addled. But I heard one of the guests, obviously a veteran of these dinners, say, "I wonder what little surprise we've got in here." So I cracked the shell with my hand and found inside a fine fat oriole,[18] nicely seasoned with pepper.

By this time Trimalchio had finished his game. He promptly sent for the same dishes we had had and with a great roaring voice offered a second cup of mead to anyone who wanted it. Then the orchestra suddenly blared and the trays were snatched away from the tables by a troupe of warbling waiters. But in the confusion a silver side dish fell to the floor and a slave quickly stooped to retrieve it. Trimalchio, however, had observed the accident and gave orders that the boy's ears should be boxed and the dish tossed back on the floor. Immediately the servant in charge of the

---

steel ring and transferring the purple stripe from the toga to the napkin. Presumably, those who adopted insignia to which they had no legal right could be punished. For this reason Trimalchio specifies that the statue of himself on his tomb is to be shown wearing "five gold rings": the fraud would be unpunishable after death. The tassels may be a sign of effeminacy. The silver toothpick, of course, is sheer extravagance. [17] **peahen's eggs:** A fabulous delicacy. [18] **oriole:** Actually, the Latin gives *ficedula,* the modern Italian *beccafico* or fig-eater, a brilliantly colored bird whose habit of stuffing itself on ripe figs endeared it to Roman epicures. Since the fig-eater is unknown in America, I have translated it as "oriole," to which family it belongs.

dishware came pattering up with a broom and swept the silver dish out the door with the rest of the rubbish. Two curly-haired Ethiopian slaves followed him as he swept, both carrying little skin bottles like the circus attendants who sprinkle the arena with perfume, and poured wine over our hands. No one was offered water.

We clapped enthusiastically for this fine display of extravagance. "The god of war," said Trimalchio, "is a real democrat.[19] That's why I gave orders that each of us should have a table to himself. Besides, these stinking slaves will bother us less than if we were all packed in together."

Glass jars carefully sealed and coated were now brought in. Each bore this label:

GENUINE FALERNIAN WINE
GUARANTEED ONE HUNDRED YEARS
OLD!
BOTTLED
IN THE CONSULSHIP
OF
OPIMIUS.[20]

While we were reading the labels, Trimalchio clapped his hands for attention. "Just think, friends, wine lasts longer than us poor suffering humans. So soak it up, it's the stuff of life. I give you, gentlemen, the genuine Opimian vintage. Yesterday I served much cheaper stuff and the guests were much more important." While we were commenting on it and savoring the luxury, a slave brought in a skeleton,[21] cast of solid silver, and fastened in such a way that the joints could be twisted and bent in any direction. The servants threw it down on the table in front of us and pushed it into several suggestive postures by twisting its joints, while Trimalchio recited this verse of his own making:

Nothing but bones, that's what we are.
Death hustles us humans away.
Today we're here and tomorrow we're not,
so live and drink while you may!

The course that followed our applause failed, however, to measure up to our expectations of our host, but it was so unusual that it took everybody's attention.

[19] **"The god . . . democrat":** The proverb means simply that in war (where all men face death alike), social distinctions vanish. Trimalchio, as usual, misapplies his proverbs. [20] **GENUINE . . . OPIMIUS:** Trimalchio's attempts to impress his guests commonly founder on ignorance. Here either his chronology or his knowledge of wines is at fault; probably both. Opimius was consul in 121 B.C.E., and assuming the date of the dinner is sometime during the reign of Nero, the wine—if Opimian—could not be much less than 170 years old. Opimian, in any case, was not a wine which kept well; like any other good Falernian, it began to deteriorate after twenty years. [21] **a skeleton:** The *memento mori* was a common part of Roman feasts or even of the decoration of the dining room. We still possess, for instance, a number of vivid mosaics portraying skeletons with eating-vessels or food and a moralizing inscription. The point of these mementos, of course, was: "Eat, drink and be merry, for tomorrow we die." Trimalchio's memento is, one suspects, rather more vivid than usual, and the silver joints of the skeleton show the master's touch.

Spaced around a circular tray were the twelve signs of the zodiac, and over each sign the chef had put the most appropriate food.[22] Thus, over the sign of Aries were chickpeas, over Taurus a slice of beef, a pair of testicles and kidneys over Gemini, a wreath of flowers over Cancer, over Leo an African fig, virgin sowbelly on Virgo, over Libra a pair of scales with a tartlet in one pan and a cheesecake in the other, over Scorpion a crawfish, a lobster on Capricorn, on Aquarius a goose, and two mullets over the sign of the Fishes. The centerpiece was a clod of turf with the grass still green on top and the whole thing surmounted by a fat honeycomb. Meanwhile, bread in a silver chafing dish was being handed around by a black slave with long hair who was shrilling in an atrocious voice some song from the pantomime called *Asafoetida*. With some reluctance we began to attack this wretched fare, but Trimalchio kept urging us, "Eat up, gentlemen, eat up!"

Suddenly the orchestra gave another flourish and four slaves came dancing in and whisked off the top of the tray. Underneath, in still another tray, lay fat capons and sowbellies and a hare tricked out with wings to look like a little Pegasus.[23] At the corners of the tray stood four little gravy boats, all shaped like the satyr Marsyas,[24] with phalluses for spouts and a spicy hot gravy dripping down over several large fish swimming about in the lagoon of the tray. The slaves burst out clapping, we clapped too and turned with gusto to these new delights. [. . .]

At this point Trimalchio heaved himself up from his couch and waddled off to the toilet. Once rid of our table tyrant, the talk began to flow more freely. Damas called for larger glasses and led off himself. "What's one day? Bah, nothing at all. You turn round and it's dark. Nothing for it, I say, but jump right from bed to table. Brrrr. Nasty spell of cold weather we've been having. A bath hardly warmed me up. But a hot drink's the best overcoat of all; that's what I always say. Whoosh, I must have guzzled gallons. I'm tight and no mistake. Wine's gone right to my head . . ."

"As for me," Seleucus broke in, "I don't take a bath every day. Your bath's a fuller; the water's got teeth like a comb. Saps your vital juices. But once I've had a slug of mead, then bugger the cold. Couldn't have had a bath today anyway. Had to go to poor old Chrysanthus' funeral. Yup, he's gone for good, folded his tent forever. And a grand little guy he was; they don't make 'em any better these days. I might almost be talking to him now. Just goes to show you. What are men anyway but balloons on legs, a lot of blown-up bladders? Flies, that's what we are. No, not even flies. Flies have something inside. But a man's a bubble, all air, nothing else. And, you know, Chrysanthus might still be with us if he hadn't tried that starvation diet. Five days and not a crumb of bread, not a drop of water, passed his lips. Tch, tch. And now he's gone, joined the great majority. Doctors killed him. Maybe not doctors, call it fate.

---

[22] **appropriate food:** In almost all cases, the link between the zodiacal sign and the food placed upon it is a pun or some farfetched resemblance. Thus beef is appropriate to Taurus (the Bull); thus over the Ram (*Aries*), one finds chickpeas *(cicer arietinus)*, etc. [23] **Pegasus:** The famous winged horse that Bellerophon rode when he killed the Chimera. [24] **Marsyas:** The satyr Marsyas took part in a musical contest against Apollo and lost; in punishment, Apollo tied him to a tree and flayed him alive. The erection, of course, comes naturally to the Satyr, for the Satyrs were spirits of fertility. Marsyas, however, seems to have been domesticated; at least his statue appears to have been a frequent gathering place for the whores of ancient Rome.

What good's a doctor but for peace of mind? But the funeral was fine, they did it up proper: nice bier, fancy drapes, and a good bunch of mourners turned out too. Mostly slaves he'd set free, of course.[25] But his old lady was sure stingy with the tears. Not that he didn't lead her a hard life, mind. But women, they're a race of kites. Don't deserve love. You might as well drop it down a well. And old love's a real cancer . . ."

He was beginning to be tiresome and Phileros shouted him down. "Whoa there," he cut in, "let's talk about the living. He got what was coming to him. He lived well, he died well. What the hell more did he want? And got rich from nothing too. And no wonder, I say. That boy would have grubbed in the gutter for a coin and picked it out with his teeth too. God knows what he had salted away. Just got fatter and fatter, bloated with the stuff. Why, that man oozed money the way a honeycomb oozes honey. But I'll give you the lowdown on him, and no frills either. He talked tough, sure, but he was a born gabber. And a real scrapper too, regular pair of fists on legs. But you take his brother: now that's a real man for you, friendly and generous as they come, and what's more, he knows how to put on a spread. Anyway, as I was saying, what does our boy do but flop on his first big deal and end up eating crow? But come the vintage and he got right back on his feet and sold his wine at his own figure. What really gave him a boost was some legacy he got. And I don't mind telling you, he milked that legacy for all it was worth and then some. So what does the sap do next but pick a fight with his own brother and leave everything to a total stranger? I mean, it just shows you. Run from your kin and you run a damn long ways, as the saying goes. Well, you know, he had some slaves and he listened to them as though they were a lot of oracles, so naturally they took him in the end. It's like I always say, a sucker gets screwed. And that goes double when a man's in business. But there's a saying, it isn't what you're given, but what you can get that counts. Well, he got the meat out of that one all his life. He was Lady Luck's fair-haired boy and no mistake. Lead turned to gold in his hand. Of course, it's easy when the stuff comes rolling in on its own. And you know how old he was when he died? Seventy and then some. But carried it beautifully, hard as nails and his hair as black as a crow. I knew him for ages, and he was horny, right to the end. By god, I'll bet he even pestered the dog. Boys were what he really liked, but he wasn't choosy: he'd jump anything with legs. I don't blame him a bit, you understand. He won't have any fun where he's gone now."

But Ganymedes struck in, "Stuff like that doesn't matter a bit to man or beast. But nobody mentions the real thing, the way the price of bread is pinching. God knows, I couldn't buy a mouthful of bread today. And this damn drought goes on and on. Nobody's had a bellyful for years now. It's those rotten officials, you take my word for it. They're in cahoots with the bakers: you scratch me and I'll scratch you. So the little people get it in the neck, but in the rich man's jaws it's jubilee all year. By god, if we only had the kind of men we used to have, the sort I found here when I arrived from Asia. Then life was something like living. Man, milk and honey day

[25] **Mostly slaves . . . of course:** As an act of kindness, slaves were commonly manumitted [freed] in a man's will.

in and day out, and the way they'd wallop those blood-sucking officials, you'd have thought old Jupiter was having himself a tantrum. I remember old Safinius now. He used to live down by the old arch when I was a boy. More peppercorn than man. Singed the ground wherever he went. But honest and square and a real friend! Why, you could have matched coins with him in the dark. And in the townhall he'd lay it right on the line, no frills at all, just square on the target. And when he made a speech in the main square, he'd let loose like a bugle blowing. But neat as a pin all the time, never ruffled, never spat: there was something Asiatic about him. And you know, he always spoke to you, even remembered your name, just as though he were one of us. And bread was dirt-cheap in his day. For a penny you got a loaf that two men couldn't finish. Nowadays bulls' eyes come bigger than bread. But that's what I mean, things are just getting worse and worse. Why, this place is running downhill like a heifer's ass. You tell me, by god, the good of this three-fig official of ours who thinks more of his graft than what's happening to us. Why, that boy's just living it up at home and making more in a day than most men ever inherit. If we had any balls, let me tell you, he'd be laughing out of the other side of his face. But not us. Oh no, we're big lions at home and scared foxes in public. Why, I've practically had to pawn my clothes and if bread prices don't drop soon, I'll have to put my houses on the market.[26] Mark my words, we're in for bad times if some man or god doesn't have a heart and take pity on this place. I'll stake my luck on it, the gods have got a finger in what's been happening here. And you know why? Because no one believes in the gods, that's why. Who observes the fast days any more, who cares a rap for Jupiter? One and all, bold as brass, they sit there pretending to pray, but cocking their eyes on the chances and counting up their cash. Once upon a time, let me tell you, things were different. The women would dress up in their best and climb barefoot up to the temple on the hill. Their hair was unbound and their hearts were pure and they went to beg Jupiter for rain. And you know what happened? Then or never, the rain would come sloshing down by the bucket, and they'd all stand there like a pack of drowned rats, just grinning away. Well, that's why the gods have stuffed their ears, because we've gotten unreligious. The fields are lying barren and . . ."

"For god's sake," the ragseller Echion broke in, "cut out the damned gloom, will you? 'Sometimes it's good, sometimes it's bad,' as the old peasant said when he sold the spotted pig. Luck changes. If things are lousy today, there's always tomorrow. That's life, man. Sure, the times are bad, but they're no better anywhere else. We're all in the same boat, so what's the fuss? If you lived anywhere else, you'd be swearing the pigs here went waddling around already roasted. And don't forget, there's a big gladiator show coming up the day after tomorrow. Not the same old fighters either; they've got a fresh shipment in and there's not a slave in the batch. You know how old Titus works. Nothing's too good for him when he lets himself go. Whatever it is, it'll be something special. I know the old boy well, and he'll go whole hog. Just wait. There'll be cold steel for the crowd, no quarter, and the amphitheater will end up looking like a slaughterhouse. He's got what it takes too. When the old man died—and a nasty

[26] **if bread . . . market:** Exaggeration intended to be ironic: he is eating, after all, at Trimalchio's.

way to die, I'm telling you—he left Titus a cool million. Even if he spent ten thousand, he'd never feel it, and people won't forget him in a hurry either. He's already raked together a troupe of whirling dervishes, and there's a girl who fights from a chariot. And don't forget that steward that Glyco caught in bed with his wife. You just wait, there'll be a regular free-for-all between the lovers and the jealous husbands. But that Glyco's a cheap bastard. Sent the steward down to be pulled to pieces by the wild beasts, you know. So that just gave his little secret away, of course. And what's the crime, I'd like to know, when the poor slave is told to do it? It's that piss-pot-bitch of his that ought to be thrown to the bulls, by god! Still, those who can't beat the horse must whop the saddle. But what stumps me is why Glyco ever thought old Hermogenes' brat would turn out well anyway. The old man would have pared a hawk's claws in mid-air, and like father, like daughter, as I always say. But Glyco's thrown away his own flesh and blood; he'll carry the marks of this mess as long as he lives and only hell will burn it away. Yes sir, that boy has dug his own grave and no mistake.

"Well, they say Mammaea's going to put on a spread. Mmmm, I can sniff it already. There'll be a nice little handout all around. And if he does, he'll knock old Norbanus out of the running for good. Beat him hands down. And what's Norbanus ever done anyway, I'd like to know. A lot of two-bit gladiators and half-dead at that: puff at them and they'd fall down dead. Why, I've seen better men tossed to the wild animals. A lot of little clay statues, barnyard strutters, that's what they were. One was an old jade, another was a clubfoot, and the replacement they sent in for him was half-dead and hamstrung to boot. There was one Thracian with some guts but he fought by the book. And after the fight they had to flog the whole lot of them the way the mob was screaming, 'Let 'em have it!' Just a pack of runaway slaves. Well, says Norbanus, at least I gave you a show. So you did, says I, and you got my cheers for it. But tot it up and you'll see you got as much as you gave. So there too, and tit for tat, says I.

"Well, Agamemnon, I can see you're thinking, 'What's that bore blabbing about now?' You're the professor here, but I don't catch you opening your mouth. No, you think you're a cut above us, don't you, so you just sit sit there and smirk at the way we poor men talk. Your learning's made you a snob. Still, let it go. I tell you what. Someday you come down to my villa and look it over. We'll find something to nibble on, a chicken, a few eggs maybe. This crazy weather's knocked everything topsy-turvy, but we'll come up with something you like. Don't worry your head about it, there'll be loads to eat.

"You remember that little shaver of mine? Well, he'll be your pupil one of these days. He's already doing division up to four, and if he comes through all right, he'll sit at your feet someday. Every spare minute he has, he buries himself in his books. He's smart all right, and there's good stuff in him. His real trouble is his passion for birds. I killed three of his pet goldfinches the other day and told him the cat had got them. He found some other hobby soon enough. And, you know, he's mad about painting. And he's already started wading into Greek and he's keen on his Latin. But the tutor's a little stuck on himself and won't keep him in line. The older boy now, he's a bit slow. But he's a hard worker and teaches the others more than he knows.

Every holiday he spends at home, and whatever you give him, he's content. So I bought him some of those big red lawbooks. A smattering of law, you know, is a useful thing around the house. There's money in it too. He's had enough literature, I think. But if he doesn't stick it out in school, I'm going to have him taught a trade. Barbering or auctioneering, or at least a little law. The only thing that can take a man's trade away is death. But everyday I keep pounding the same thing into his head: 'Son, get all the learning you can. Anything you learn is money in the bank. Look at Lawyer Phileros. If he hadn't learned his law, he'd be going hungry and chewing on air. Not so long ago he was peddling his wares on his back; now he's running neck and neck with old Norbanus. Take my word for it, son, there's a mint of money in books, and learning a trade never killed a man yet.' "

Conversation was running along these lines when Trimalchio returned, wiping the sweat from his brow. He splashed his hands in perfume and stood there for a minute in silence. "You'll excuse me, friends," he began, "but I've been constipated for days and the doctors are stumped. I got a little relief from a prescription of pomegranate rind and resin in a vinegar base. Still, I hope my tummy will get back its manners soon. Right now my bowels are bumbling around like a bull. But if any of you has any business that needs attending to, go right ahead; no reason to feel embarrassed. There's not a man been born yet with solid insides. And I don't know any anguish on earth like trying to hold it in. Jupiter himself couldn't stop it from coming.—What are you giggling about, Fortunata? You're the one who keeps me awake all night with your trips to the potty. Well, anyone at table who wants to go has my permission, and the doctors tell us not to hold it in. Everything's ready outside—water and pots and the rest of the stuff. Take my word for it, friends, the vapors go straight to your brain. Poison your whole system. I know of some who've died from being too polite and holding it in." We thanked him for his kindness and understanding, but we tried to hide our snickers in repeated swallows of wine.

As yet we were unaware that we had slogged only halfway through this "forest of refinements," as the poets put it. But when the tables had been wiped—to the inevitable music, of course—servants led in three hogs rigged out with muzzles and bells. According to the headwaiter, the first hog was two years old, the second three, but the third was all of six. I supposed that we would now get tumblers and rope dancers and that the pigs would be put through the kind of clever tricks they perform for the crowds in the street. But Trimalchio dispelled such ideas by asking, "Which one of these hogs would you like cooked for your dinner? Now your ordinary country cook can whip you up a chicken or make a Bacchante mincemeat[27] or easy dishes of that sort. But my cooks frequently broil calves whole." With this he had the cook called in at once, and without waiting for us to choose our pig, ordered the oldest slaughtered. Then he roared at the cook, "What's the number of your corps, fellow?"

"The fortieth, sir," the cook replied.

[27] **Bacchante mincemeat:** Pentheus, the king of Thebes, was torn to pieces by the Bacchantes (i.e., Maenads, the god-possessed female followers of Dionysus).

"Were you born on the estate or bought?"

"Neither, sir. Pansa left me to you in his will."

"Well," barked Trimalchio, "see that you do a good job or I'll have you demoted to the messenger corps."

The cook, freshly reminded of his master's power, meekly led the hog off toward the kitchen, while Trimalchio gave us all an indulgent smile. "If you don't like the wine," he said, "we'll have it changed for you. I'll know by the amount you drink what you think of it. Luckily too I don't have to pay a thing for it. It comes with a lot of other good things from a new estate of mine near town. I haven't seen it yet, but I'm told it adjoins my lands at Terracina and Tarentum.[28] Right now what I'd really like to do is buy up Sicily. Then I could go to Africa without ever stepping off my own property."

"But tell me," he said, turning to Agamemnon, "what was the subject of your debate today? Of course, I'm no orator myself, but I've learnt a thing or two about law for use around the place. And don't think I'm one of those people who look down on learning. No sir, I've got two libraries, one Greek and the other Latin. So tell us, if you will, what your debate was about."

"Well," said Agamemnon, "it seems that a rich man and a poor man had gone to court . . ."

"A *poor* man?" Trimalchio broke in, "what's that?"

"Very pretty, very pretty," chuckled Agamemnon and then launched out into an exposition of god knows which of his debating topics.

But Trimalchio immediately interrupted him: "If that's the case, there's no argument; if it isn't the case, then what does it matter?" Needless to say, we pointedly applauded all of Trimalchio's sallies.

"But tell me, my dear Agamemnon," continued our host, "do you remember the twelve labors of Hercules or the story about Ulysses and how the Cyclops broke his thumb trying to get the log out of his eye? When I was a kid, I used to read all those stories in Homer.[29] And, you know, I once saw the Sybil of Cumae[30] in person. She was hanging in a bottle, and when the boys asked her, 'Sybil, what do you want?' she said, 'I want to die.' "

He was still chattering away when the servants came in with an immense hog on a tray almost the size of the table. We were, of course, astounded at the chef's speed

---

[28] **Terracina and Tarentum:** The suspicion that Trimalchio's geography is weak should not be allowed to detract from the sublimity of the boast. Tarentum is in the extreme south of Italy; Terracina lies about midway between Naples and Rome. The distance between them would be more than two hundred miles. The hope of buying up Sicily clearly confirms that Trimalchio has been boasting.

[29] **stories in Homer:** Trimalchio's learning is somewhat lacking. For the standard version of the story of Ulysses and the Cyclops, see Homer, *Odyssey,* Book 9. The twelve labors of Hercules as such are not, of course, recounted by Homer, though several of them are sketched in or used allusively.

[30] **Sibyl of Cumae:** The famous Sibyl who prophesied to Aeneas. It was believed of Sibyls that they were immortal; they shared with men, however, the curse of growing old. Evidently, the Sibyl of Cumae had simply withered away of her own antiquity until she was so small that she spent her days in a jug. In the circumstances, no one will marvel at her wish to die. Cumae was situated on the extreme western edge of the Phlegraean Fields, a few miles to the north and west of Naples, along the sea. The town was very early colonized by Greeks, a fact that probably explains why the boys' question to the Sibyl and her answer are both in Greek [in the original].

and swore it would have taken longer to roast an ordinary chicken, all the more since the pig looked even bigger than the one served to us earlier. Meanwhile Trimalchio had been scrutinizing the pig very closely and suddenly roared, "What! What's this? By god, this hog hasn't even been gutted! Get that cook in here on the double!"

Looking very miserable, the poor cook came shuffling up to the table and admitted that he had forgotten to gut the pig.

"You *forgot?*" bellowed Trimalchio. "*You forgot to gut a pig?* And I suppose you think that's the same thing as merely forgetting to add salt and pepper. Strip that man!"

The cook was promptly stripped and stood there stark naked between two bodyguards, utterly forlorn. The guests to a man, however, interceded for the chef. "Accidents happen," they said, "please don't whip him. If he ever does it again, we promise we won't say a word for him." My own reaction was anger, savage and unrelenting. I could barely restrain myself and leaning over, I whispered to Agamemnon, "Did you ever hear of anything worse? Who could forget to gut a pig? By god, you wouldn't catch me letting him off, not if it was just a fish he'd forgotten to clean."

Not so Trimalchio, however. He sat there, a great grin widening across his face, and said: "Well, since your memory's so bad, you can gut the pig here in front of us all." The cook was handed back his clothes, drew out his knife with a shaking hand and then slashed at the pig's belly with crisscross cuts. The slits widened out under the pressure from inside, and suddenly out poured, not the pig's bowels and guts, but link upon link of tumbling sausages and blood puddings. [. . .]

Ascyltus, however, was no longer able to swallow his snickers [at the excesses of their host] and he finally tossed back his head and roared and guffawed until he was almost in tears. At this one of Trimalchio's freedmen friends, the man just above me at the table, took offense and flared out in wild rage. "You cheap muttonhead," he snarled, "what are you cackling about? Entertainment isn't good enough for the likes of you, I suppose? You're richer, huh? And eat better too? I'll bet! So help me, if you were down here by me, I'd stop your damn bleating!

"Some nerve he's got, laughing at us. Stinking runaway, that's what he is. A burglar. A bum. Bah, he's not worth a good boot in the ass. By god, if I tangle with him, he won't know where he's headed! So help me, I don't often fly off the handle like this. Still, if the flesh is soft, I say, the worms will breed.

"Still cackling, are you? Who the hell are you to snicker? Where'd your daddy buy you? Think you're made out of gold, eh? So that's it, you're a Roman knight?[31] That makes me a king's son. Then why was I a slave? Because I wanted to be. Because I'd rather be a Roman slave than a tax-paying savage.[32] And as I live and breathe, I hope no man thinks I'm funny. I walk like a free man. I don't owe any man a thing. I've never been hauled into court. That's right: no man ever had to tell me to pay up.

[31] **Roman knight:** Ascyltus is evidently wearing the gold ring that was the privilege of the equestrian class.

[32] **tax-paying savage:** A foreigner who became a slave could look forward to the prospect of someday being freed and achieving citizenship. After the fall of the Republic, Roman citizens were not taxed; hence, one of the major inducements to achieve citizenship was the prospect of relief from taxation.

I've bought a few little plots of land and a nice bit of silver plate. I feed twenty stomachs, not counting the dog. I bought my wife's freedom so no man could put his dirty paws on her. I paid a good two hundred for my own freedom. Right now, I'm on the board for the emperor's worship,[33] and I hope when I die, I won't have to blush for anything. But you're so damn busy sneering at us, you don't look at your own behind. You see the lice on us but not the ticks on yourself. Nobody but you thinks we're funny. Look at your old professor there: he appreciates us. Bah, you're still sucking tit; you're limp leather, limper, no damn better. Oh, you're rich, are you? Then cram down two lunches; bolt two suppers, sonny. As for me, I'd rather have my credit than all your cash. Who ever had to dun me twice? Forty years, boy and man, I spent as a slave, but no one could tell now whether I was slave or free. I was just a curly-headed kid when I came to this place. The town hall wasn't even built then. But I did everything I could to please my master. He was a good man, a real gentleman, whose fingernail was worth more than your whole carcass. And there were some in that house who would have liked to see me stumble. But thanks to my master I gave them the slip. Those are real trials, those are real triumphs. But when you're born free everything's as easy as saying, 'Hurry on down.' Well, what are you gaping at now, like a goat in vetch?"[34]

At these last words, Giton, who was sitting at our feet, went rudely off into a great gale of whooping laughter which he had been trying to stifle for some time. Ascyltus' tormentor promptly trained his fire on the boy. "So you're snorting too, are you, you frizzle-headed scallion? You think it's time for capers, do you, carnival days and cold December?[35] When did you pay your freedom tax,[36] eh? Well, what are you smirking at, you little gallowsbird? Look, birdbait, I'll give it to you proper and the same for that master who won't keep you in line. May I never eat bread again, if I let you off for anyone except our host here; if it weren't for him, I'd fix you right now. We were all feeling good, nice happy party, and then those half-baked masters of yours let you cut out of line. Like master, like slave, I always say.

"Damnation, I'm so hopping mad, I can't stop. I'm no sorehead either, but when I let go, I don't give a damn for my own mother. Just you wait, I'll catch you out in the street someday. You mouse, you little potato! And when I do, if I don't knock your master into the cabbage patch, my name's not Hermeros. You can holler for Jupiter on Olympus as loud as you like, and it won't help you one little bit. By god, I'll fix those frizzle-curls of yours, and I'll fix your two-bit master too! You'll

---

[33] **on the board . . . worship:** That is, like Trimalchio, he is a *sevir.*

[34] **goat in vetch:** For a goat, vetch is good grazing. Hermeros means that Ascyltus is so startled by his torrent of abuse that he looks like a goat who found himself in a field of vetch, i.e., overwhelmed by his *embarras de choix.* Readers may note that there is a real dignity in Hermeros's angry tirade, as well as real social resentment against Ascyltus and his friends.

[35] **time for . . . December:** During the winter Carnival, slaves were permitted the same licence allowed to the free.

[36] **freedom tax:** When a slave was freed, his owner was required to pay a 5 per cent freedom tax on his assessed value.

feel my teeth, sonny boy. And you won't snicker then, or I don't know who I am. No, not if your beard were made out of gold! By god, I'll give you Athena's own anger, and that goes for the blockhead who set you free! I never learned geometry or criticism or hogwash of that kind, but I know how to read words carved in stone and divide up to a hundred, money, measure, or weights. Come on, I'll lay you a little bet. I'll stake a piece of my silver set. You may have learned some rhetoric in school, but let me prove your daddy wasted his money educating you. Ready? Then answer me this: 'I come long and I come broad. What am I?' I'll give you a clue. One of us runs, the other stays put. One grows bigger; the other stays small.[37] Well, that's you, skittering around, bustling and gaping like a mouse in a jug. So either shut up or don't bother your elders and betters who don't know you exist. Or do you think I'm impressed by those phony gold rings of yours? Swipe them from your girl? Sweet Mercury, come down to the main square in town and try to take out a loan. Then you'll see this plain iron ring of mine makes plenty of credit. Hah, that finished you. You look like a fox in the rain. By god, if I don't pull up my toga and hound you all over town, may I fail in my business and die broke! So help me! And isn't he something, that professor who taught you your manners? Him a professor? A bum, that's what he is. In my time, a teacher was a teacher. Why, my old teacher used to say, 'Now, boys, is everything in order? Then go straight home. No dawdling, no gawking on the way. And don't be sassy to your elders.' But nowadays teachers are trash. Not worth a damn. As for me, I'm grateful to my old teacher for what he taught me . . ." [. . .]

Meanwhile someone was hammering at the door and before long a carouser dressed in a splendid white robe and accompanied by a throng of slaves made his entrance. His face was dignified and stern, so stern in fact that I took him for the praetor,[38] slammed my bare feet onto the cold floor and made ready to run for it. But Agamemnon laughed at my fright and said, "Relax, you idiot, it's only Habinnas. He's an official of the imperial cult and a mason by trade. They say he makes first-rate tombstones."

Somewhat reassured, I sat down again but continued to observe Habinnas' entrance with mounting amazement. He was already half-drunk and was propping himself up by holding on to his wife's shoulders with both hands. He was literally draped in garlands of flowers and a stream of perfumed oil was running down his forehead and into his eyes. When he reached the place reserved for the praetor, he sat down and called for wine and warm water. Trimalchio was delighted to see his friend in such spirits and called for bigger glasses before asking him how he had eaten.

"Only one thing was missing," Habinnas smiled, "and that was you. My heart was really here the whole time. But, by god, Scissa did it up brown. She put on one

[37] **One of us runs . . . small:** The answer to the riddle is unknown, despite some ingenious guesses. I have, I confess, slightly tampered with the riddle in order to give it some point in its context.

[38] **the praetor:** The praetor in a municipality combined roughly the functions of both police and judiciary. For obvious reasons, neither Encolpius nor Ascyltus is anxious for a collision with the praetor.

fine spread for that poor slave's funeral, I'll say that for her. What's more, she set him free after his death. And what with the 5 per cent tax,[39] I'll bet that gesture cost her a pretty penny. The slave himself was valued at about two thousand. Still, it was very nice, though it cut across my grain to have to pour out half my drinks as an offering to the poor boy's bones."

"But what did they give you to eat?" Trimalchio pressed him.

"If I can remember, I'll tell you," said Habinnas. "But my memory's so bad these days, I sometimes can't even remember my own name. Let's see, first off we had some roast pork garnished with loops of sausage and flanked with more sausages and some giblets done to a turn. And there were pickled beets and some wholewheat bread made without bleach. I prefer it to white, you know. It's better for you and less constipating too. Then came a course of cold tart with a mixture of some wonderful Spanish wine and hot honey. I took a fat helping of the tart and scooped up the honey generously. Then there were chickpeas and lupins, no end of filberts, and an apple apiece. I took two apples and I've got one wrapped up in my napkin here. If I forgot to bring a little present to my pet slave, I'd be in hot water. And oh yes, my wife reminds me: the main course was a roast of bear-meat. Scintilla was silly enough to try some and almost chucked up her supper. But it reminds me of roast boar, so I put down about a pound of it. Besides, I'd like to know, if bears eat men, why shouldn't men eat bears? To wind up, we had some soft cheese steeped in fresh wine, a snail apiece, some tripe hash, liver in pastry boats and eggs topped with more pastry and turnips and mustard and beans boiled in the pod and—but enough's enough. Oh yes, and they passed around a dish of olives pickled in caraway, and some of the guests had the nerve to walk off with three fistfuls. But we sent the ham back untasted. See here, Gaius, why isn't Fortunata eating?"

"You know how she is," said Trimalchio. "Until she's put the silver away and divided the leftovers among the servants, she won't touch even a drop of water."

"Well, if she doesn't come and eat right now," said Habinnas, "I'm leaving."

With that he started to rise and probably would have left if Trimalchio had not signaled and the whole corps of slaves shouted four or five times in chorus: "FORTUNATA!" She promptly appeared, her dress bound up so high by a pale green sash that beneath her cherry-colored tunic I could glimpse her massive ankle-rings of twisted gold and a pair of golden slippers. She wiped her fingers on the handkerchief she wore around her neck and sat down on the couch beside Habinnas' wife, Scintilla. Scintilla clapped her hands, Fortunata kissed her and burst out, "Why, darling, it's been just ages since I've seen you!"

In this way the two women chattered on for some time. The next thing I knew Fortunata was undoing the bracelets on her grotesquely fat arms and showing them off for Scintilla to admire. Then she undid her anklets and finally her hair net, which she kept insisting was woven of pure gold. Trimalchio, who was observing this byplay with interest, ordered all her jewelry brought to him. "Gentlemen," he said, "I want you to see the chains and fetters our women load themselves with; this is how

[39] **5 per cent tax:** That is, the manumission tax.

we poor bastards are bankrupted. By god, she must be wearing six and a half pounds of solid gold. Still, I must admit I've got a bracelet that weighs a good ten pounds on its own. That was the value of two or three thousandths of my profits for the year, the same amount I give to Mercury as the patron-god of business."[40] To prove his boast, he ordered a pair of scales brought in and the weights passed around for us to test. For her part, Scintilla was not to be outdone and took off the large locket which she wore around her neck and called her "lucky piece." Out of it she drew a pair of golden earrings and handed them over for Fortunata's inspection. "They're a present from my husband," she said. "Thanks to his generosity, no woman on earth has a finer pair."

"Generosity, my ass," snorted Habinnas. "You'd pester the life out of me to get a couple of glass beans. If I had a daughter, so help me, I'd have her ears chopped off. If it weren't for the women, things would be as cheap as dirt. But money—they waste it like water. Swallow it cold and good and piss it hot and useless."

By this time both the women were high and sat there giggling and exchanging little hugs and kisses, Fortunata boasting about her abilities as a housekeeper and Scintilla complaining of her husband's favorites and his indifference to her. At one point during this tender scene Habinnas rose stealthily to his feet, tiptoed over behind their couch and, grabbing Fortunata by the knees, toppled her over backwards onto the couch. As she fell her tunic slipped up above her knees. Fortunata gave a piercing shriek, threw herself into Scintilla's arms and tried to hide her blushes in her handkerchief.

Once the confusion had died down, Trimalchio ordered the dessert brought on. The servants immediately removed not merely the dirty dishes but the tables themselves and replaced them with fresh ones. The floor was sprinkled with saffron sawdust and powdered mica, something I had never seen used for this purpose before. "Behold your dessert, gentlemen, these fresh tables," said Trimalchio. "I've made a clean sweep of everything, and that's all you get. That's what you deserve; that's your dessert. Haw, haw. But if there's still anything in the kitchen worth eating, boys, bring it on." Meanwhile an Alexandrian slave was passing us hot water for our wine and at the same time doing an imitation of a nightingale, but Trimalchio kept muttering, "Change that stinking tune." Then the slave seated at Habinnas' feet and clearly acting on his master's orders started to chant a passage from Vergil, the one beginning:

> Meanwhile Aeneas' fleet still rode the heavy swell . . .[41]

Altogether it was the most atrocious sound that ever fell on my ears. Not only was his pronunciation barbarous, a kind of singsong rising and falling of the pitch, but he

---

[40] **the same amount . . . business:** It was customary for men of commerce or business to dedicate at stated intervals a tithe of several tenths of 1 per cent of their profits to Mercury, patron god of trade. Even if we assume that Trimalchio had paid all of 1 per cent for the period, it would have required a profit of at least 1,000 pounds of gold to produce a gold bracelet that weighed ten pounds.

[41] **Meanwhile Aeneas' . . . heavy swell:** *Aeneid,* Book 1.

also jumbled in verses from some obscene farce,[42] so that for the first time in my life Vergil actually jarred on me. At the end, however, Habinnas clapped enthusiastically and said: "You wouldn't believe it, but he's never had any formal training. I sent him off to learn from the hawkers at the fairs, and he can't be beat at imitating muledrivers and barkers. And he's real smart, does everything: makes shoes, cooks, bakes . . . In fact, he'd be perfect if he didn't have two bad points: he's been circumcised and he snores. He's cross-eyed too, but I don't mind that. Venus has a bit of a squint, they say. And I bought him for next to nothing . . ."

"You haven't mentioned all the little bugger's tricks," broke in Scintilla angrily. "He's a little pimp and a fairy, that's what he is, and someday I'll see he's branded for it."[43]

Trimalchio guffawed at this. "Come on, Scintilla, don't be jealous. We know what the score is with you too. And why not, I'd like to know. Cross my heart and hope to die, if I didn't have a few tussles in the sheets with my old master's wife too. In fact, the old man got suspicious, so much so that he shipped me off to a farm in the country. But stop wagging, tongue, and I'll give you some bread to munch."

At this point that damned slave of Habinnas, obviously under the impression that we had been praising him, pulled a clay lamp with a spout out of his tunic and for a full half hour sat there mimicking a bugler while Habinnas hummed and fiddled his lower lip up and down in a kind of jew's harp accompaniment. Then, to crown all this, the slave stepped out before us all and first parodied with two straws the flutists at the plays and next, waving a whip and twisting himself in his cloak, did an imitation of a muledriver. Habinnas called him over finally, gave him a kiss and a glass of wine and said, "Nice work, Massa. I'll see that you get a pair of shoes for this."

This deadly entertainment would never have ended if the servants had not brought on another course, consisting of pastry thrushes with raisin and nut stuffing, followed by quinces with thorns stuck in them to resemble sea urchins. We could have put up with these dishes, if the last and most sickening course of all had not killed our appetites completely. When it was first brought in, we took it for a fat goose surrounded by fish and little birds of all kinds. But Trimalchio declared, "My friends, everything you see on that platter has been made from one and the same substance." I, of course, not the man to be deceived by appearances, had to turn and whisper to Agamemnon, "I'd be very surprised if everything there hadn't been made out of plain mud or clay. At the Carnival in Rome, I've seen whole meals made from stuff like that."

I was still whispering when Trimalchio said, "As surely as I hope to get richer—but not fatter, please god—my cook baked all that junk out of roast pork. In fact, I doubt if there's a more valuable chef in the whole world. Just say the word, and he'll

[42] **some obscene farce:** An Atellan farce, a primitive, rather crude variety of early Italian comedy much in vogue with Roman audiences.

[43] **branded for it:** Slaves guilty of misconduct (but especially those guilty of running away) were punished by being branded with a hot iron on the forehead.

whip you up a fish out of sowbelly, pigeons out of bacon, doves from ham and chicken from pigs' knuckles. That's why I've named him Daedalus,[44] and it suits him to a *T.* And because he's an inventor and a genius, I've brought him back some fine cutlery from Rome." He then ordered the knives brought in and passed around for us to admire and inspect. He also gave us permission to test the blades on the stubble of our cheeks.

Suddenly two slaves came rushing in looking as though they'd had an argument while drawing water at the well; at least they were carrying large jars on their backs and were obviously furious with each other. Trimalchio offered to act as arbiter of their argument but they refused to abide by his decision and began to pummel each other with their sticks. We were appalled by this drunken insolence but nonetheless kept our eyes glued to the fight. Suddenly we noticed that oysters and mussels were sloshing over from the jugs and a slave caught them as they fell and handed them around in a dish. Unwilling to be outstripped in extravagance, the clever chef matched the oysters by bringing around hot buttered snails on a silver grill and singing all the time in a hideously dismal, quavering voice.

What happened next was an extravagance so fantastic that I am almost embarrassed to mention it. However, young slaves with long flowing curls came around to each of us in turn, wreathed our legs and ankles with garlands of flowers and anointed our feet with perfume from a silver bowl. Then a generous amount of this same perfume was poured into the oil lamps and even into the wine bowl.

By now Fortunata was almost desperate to dance and Scintilla was clapping her hands even more frequently than she opened her mouth. Suddenly Trimalchio had an idea. "You there, Philargyrus," he called out to a slave, "I know you're a fan of the Greens[45] in the races, but come and sit with us anyway. You too, Cario, and tell your wife to do the same." Well, you can imagine what happened. The dining room was by now so packed with slaves that in the rush for seats the guests were almost shoved bodily from the couches. For my part, I had to endure seeing the cook—the one who had made the goose out of pork and who reeked of pickles and hot sauce—installed just above me on the couch. Worst of all, not content with a place at the table, he had to do an imitation of the tragic actor Ephesus[46] and then had the brass to bet his master that the Greens would win the next race in the Circus.

But Trimalchio was charmed by the challenge. "My friends," he brayed, "slaves are human too. They drink the same mother's milk that we do, though an evil fate grinds them down. But I swear that it won't be long—if nothing happens to me—before they all taste the good water of freedom. For I plan to free them all in my will.

---

[44] **Daedalus:** The famous legendary craftsman who made the wooden cow for Pasiphae and the famous artificial wings on which he and his ill-fated son, Icarus, attempted to flee from Minos's anger. He was regarded as the inventor of carpentry and of most of its tools.

[45] **the Greens:** In the chariot races at the circus, horses and drivers were distinguished by their colors. At this time there were four colors: Red, White, Blue and Green. But partisanship ran high, and supporters passionately identified themselves with their favorite charioteer and his color. Trimalchio's color is, I would infer, Red.

[46] **Ephesus:** Otherwise unknown.

To Philargyrus here I leave a farm and his woman. Cario inherits a block of flats and the tax on his freedom and his bed and bedding. To my dear Fortunata I leave everything I have, and I commend her to the kindness of my friends. But I'm telling you the contents of my will so my whole household will love me as much when I'm still alive as after I'm dead."

Once the slaves heard this, of course, they burst out with cheers and effusive thanks. But Trimalchio suddenly began to take the whole farce quite seriously and ordered his will brought out and read aloud from beginning to end while the slaves sat there groaning and moaning. At the close of the reading, he turned to Habinnas. "Well, old friend, will you make me my tomb exactly as I order it? First, of course, I want a statue of myself. But carve my dog at my feet, and give me garlands of flowers, jars of perfume and every fight in Petraites' career. Then, thanks to your good offices, I'll live on long after I'm gone. In front, I want my tomb one hundred feet long, but two hundred feet deep. Around it I want an orchard with every known variety of fruit tree. You'd better throw in a vineyard too. For it's wrong, I think, that a man should concern himself with the house where he lives his life but give no thought to the home he'll have forever. But above all I want you to carve this notice:

THIS MONUMENT DOES NOT PASS INTO
THE POSSESSION OF MY HEIRS.[47]

In any case I'll see to it in my will that my grave is protected from damage after my death. I'll appoint one of my ex-slaves to act as custodian to chase off the people who might come and crap on my tomb. Also, I want you to carve me several ships with all sail crowded[48] and a picture of myself sitting on the judge's bench in official dress[49] with five gold rings[50] on my fingers and handing out a sack of coins to the people. For it's a fact, and you're my witness, that I gave a free meal to the whole town and a cash handout to everyone. Also make me a dining room, a frieze maybe, but however you like, and show the whole town celebrating at my expense. On my right I want a statue of Fortunata with a dove in her hand. And oh yes, be sure to have her pet dog tied to her girdle. And don't forget my pet slave. Also I'd like huge jars of wine, well

---

[47] THIS . . . HEIRS: Presumably as a precaution against their selling it. Trimalchio has no faith in the *pietas* of his heirs.

[48] **several ships . . . crowded:** In token of Trimalchio's merchantmen.

[49] **sitting . . . official dress:** Upon ceremonial occasions the priests of Augustus (i.e., the *sevirs*) possessed the right to sit on a throne (see note 8 for *tribunal*) or judicial tribunal. When seated on this throne, the *sevirs* wore the *toga praetexta*.

[50] **five gold rings:** So far as one can tell, Trimalchio had no right to the gold ring of the equestrian order. Indeed, his very insistence on "five gold rings" after death is fairly convincing evidence of his disability—not to speak of his desire. Posthumously, of course, he may wear the rings with impunity, and Trimalchio typically proposes to go whole hog.

stoppered so the wine won't slosh out. Then sculpt me a broken vase with a little boy sobbing out his heart over it.[51] And in the middle stick a sundial so that anyone who wants the time of day will have to read my name. And how will this do for the epitaph?

HERE LIES GAIUS POMPEIUS TRIMALCHIO
MAECENATIANUS,[52]
VOTED IN ABSENTIA AN OFFICIAL OF THE
IMPERIAL CULT.
HE COULD HAVE BEEN REGISTERED
IN ANY CATEGORY OF THE CIVIL SERVICE AT ROME[53]
BUT CHOSE OTHERWISE.
PIOUS AND COURAGEOUS,
A LOYAL FRIEND,
HE DIED A MILLIONAIRE,
THOUGH HE STARTED LIFE WITH NOTHING.
LET IT BE SAID TO HIS ETERNAL CREDIT
THAT HE NEVER LISTENED TO PHILOSOPHERS.
PEACE TO HIM.
FAREWELL.

At the end he burst into tears. Then Fortunata started wailing, Habinnas began to cry, and every slave in the room burst out sobbing as though Trimalchio were dying then and there. [. . .]

"My friends," said Trimalchio, apropos of nothing, "my pet slave is having his first shave today. He's a good boy and a model of thrift. So let's celebrate. We'll drink until dawn!"

Pat to these last words, a cock ominously crowed somewhere. Alarmed by the coincidence, Trimalchio superstitiously ordered the servants to pour some wine under the table and even to sprinkle the lamps with wine. Then he slipped his ring from his left hand to his right and said, "Buglers don't bugle for kicks, and that cockcrow

[51] **broken vase . . . over it:** It is sometimes suggested that this touching scene is to be referred to an incident during the dinner, when a slaveboy dropped a silver dish and was punished. Actually, I suspect it is nothing more than a piece of simple funerary symbolism, whose sentimentality would be quite in keeping with Trimalchio's tastes. The broken vase would be the "smashed vessel" of Trimalchio's life, while the boy who mourns him would be the world of the living or Life, etc.

[52] HERE LIES . . . MAECENATIANUS: Freedmen commonly formed their cognomens from the name of their patron. Thus Trimalchio Maecenatianus would mean that Trimalchio's patron had been Maecenas. From this we have no right to infer that the patron must have been the famous Maecenas, Augustus's friend and chief of state-patronage. The name "Pompeius" would indicate that Trimalchio had also been a slave in the family of the Pompeii.

[53] HE COULD . . . ROME: Trimalchio boasts, that is, that had he gone to Rome, he could have been enrolled in any of the guilds (or *decuriae*) from which the lower echelons of the civil service were normally staffed. Either from indifference or lack of ambition (!), however, he chose otherwise.

means there's a fire nearby or somebody's died. Don't let it be bad luck for us, please heaven. Whoever fetches me that calamity-crowing rooster first, gets a fat reward." In half a minute, somebody had brought in the rooster from somewhere, and Trimalchio promptly ordered it cooked. The chef, Daedalus, that culinary genius who had whisked up birds and fish from the leg of pork, beheaded the bird and tossed it into a pot. And while the cook drew off the boiling broth, Fortunata ground up the pepper in a little wooden mill.

We were sampling this unexpected snack, when Trimalchio suddenly remembered that the servants had not yet eaten. "What?" he roared, "you haven't eaten yet? Then off with you. Go eat and send in another shift to take your places." So a fresh shift of slaves soon appeared at the door, all shouting, "Greetings, Gaius!" while the first shift went out with a cry of "Goodbye, Gaius!"

At this moment an incident occurred on which our little party almost foundered. Among the incoming slaves there was a remarkably pretty boy. Trimalchio literally launched himself upon him and, to Fortunata's extreme annoyance, began to cover him with rather prolonged kisses. Finally, Fortunata asserted her rights and began to abuse him. "You turd!" she shrieked, "you hunk of filth." At last she used the supreme insult: "Dog!" At this Trimalchio exploded with rage, reached for a wine cup and slammed it into her face. Fortunata let out a piercing scream and covered her face with trembling hands as though she'd just lost an eye. Scintilla, stunned and shocked, tried to comfort her sobbing friend in her arms, while a slave solicitously applied a glass of cold water to her livid cheek. Fortunata herself hunched over the glass heaving and sobbing.

But Trimalchio was still shaking with fury. "Doesn't that slut remember what she used to be? By god, *I* took her off the sale platform and made her an honest woman. But she blows herself up like a bullfrog. She's forgotten how lucky she is. She won't remember the whore she used to be. People in shacks shouldn't dream of palaces, I say. By god, if I don't tame that strutting Cassandra,[54] my name isn't Trimalchio! And to think, sap that I was, that I could have married an heiress worth half a million. And that's no lie. Old Agatho, who sells perfume to the lady next door, slipped me the word: 'Don't let your line die out, old boy,' he said. But not me. Oh no, I was a good little boy, nothing fickle about me. And now I've gone and slammed the axe into my shins good and proper.—But someday, slut, you'll come scratching at my grave to get me back! And just so you understand what you've done, I'll remove your statue from my tomb. That's an order, Habinnas. No sir, I don't want any more domestic squabbles in my grave. And what's more, just to show her I can dish it out too, I won't have her kissing me on my deathbed."

After this last thunderbolt, Habinnas begged him to calm himself and forgive her. "None of us is perfect," he said, "we're men, not gods." Scintilla burst into tears, called him her dear dear Gaius and implored him by everything holy to forgive Fortunata. Finally, even Trimalchio began to blubber. "Habinnas," he whined, "as you

[54] **Cassandra:** Literally, *Cassandra caligaria.* Cassandra was the mad priestess of Troy; *caligaria* means "dressed in high army boots," i.e., "masculine, brutal, raving virago."

hope to make a fortune, tell me the truth; if I've done anything wrong, spit right in my face. So I admit I kissed the boy, not because of his looks, but because he's a good boy, a thrifty boy, a boy of real character. He can divide up to ten, he reads at sight, he's saved his freedom price from his daily allowance and bought himself an armchair and two ladles out of his own pocket. Now doesn't a boy like that deserve his master's affection? But Fortunata says no.—Is that your idea, you high-stepping bitch? Take my advice, vulture, and keep your own nose clean. Don't make me show my teeth, sweetheart, or you'll feel my anger. You know me. Once I make up my mind, I'm as stubborn as a spike in wood.

"But the hell with her. Friends, make yourselves comfortable. Once I used to be like you, but I rose to the top by my ability. Guts are what make the man; the rest is garbage. I buy well, I sell well. Others have different notions. But I'm like to bust with good luck.—You slut, are you still blubbering? By god, I'll give you something to blubber about.

"But like I was saying, friends, it's through my business sense that I shot up. Why, when I came here from Asia, I stood no taller than that candlestick there. In fact, I used to measure myself by it every day; what's more, I used to rub my mouth with lamp oil to make my beard sprout faster. Didn't do a bit of good, though. For fourteen years I was my master's pet. But what's the shame in doing what you're told to do? But all the same, if you know what I mean, I managed to do my mistress a favor or two. But mum's the word: I'm none of your ordinary blowhards.

"Well, then heaven gave me a push and I became master in the house. I was my master's brains. So he made me joint heir with the emperor[55] to everything he had, and I came out of it with a senator's fortune.[56] But we never have enough, and I wanted to try my hand at business. To cut it short, I had five ships built. Then I stocked them with wine—worth its weight in gold at the time—and shipped them off to Rome. I might as well have told them to go sink themselves since that's what they did. Yup, all five of them wrecked. No kidding. In one day old Neptune swallowed down a cool million. Was I licked? Hell, no. That loss just whetted my appetite as though nothing had happened at all. So I built some more ships, bigger and better and a damn sight luckier. No one could say I didn't have guts. But big ships make a man feel big himself. I shipped a cargo of wine, bacon, beans, perfume and slaves. And then Fortunata came through nicely in the nick of time: sold her gold and the clothes off her back and put a hundred gold coins in the palm of my hand. That was the yeast of my wealth. Besides, when the gods want something done, it gets done in a jiffy. On that one voyage alone, I cleared about five hundred thousand. Right away

[55] **joint heir . . . emperor:** It was not uncommon during the Empire for rich men to list the emperor as one of their heirs. The reason was fear as much as snobbery. Thus, although the snobbish might feel that inheritance established a personal relationship between themselves and the Emperor, the legacy was a wise precaution in an age when the provisions of a will could be set aside at the Emperor's pleasure. The legacy, that is, was little more than a bribe in return for which the other dispensations of the will would presumably be left unaltered.

[56] **a senator's fortune:** A senatorial income was classed by law as consisting of at least 400,000 sesterces. It is difficult, for obvious reasons, to translate this figure into dollars; suffice it to say that in Rome it represented an upper-class fortune.

I bought up all my old master's property. I built a house, I went into slave-trading and cattle-buying. Everything I touched just grew and grew like a honeycomb. Once I was worth more than all the people in my home town put together, I picked up my winnings and pulled out. I retired from trade and started lending money to ex-slaves. To tell the truth, I was tempted to quit for keeps, but on the advice of an astrologer who'd just come to town, I decided to keep my hand in. He was a Greek, fellow by the name of Serapa, and clever enough to set up as consultant to the gods. Well, he told me things I'd clean forgotten and laid it right on the line from A to Z. Why, that man could have peeked into my tummy and told me everything except what I'd eaten the day before. You'd have thought he'd lived with me all his life.

"Remember what he said, Habinnas? You were there, I think, when he told my fortune. 'You have bought yourself a mistress and a tyrant,' he said, 'out of your own profits. You are unlucky in your friends. No one is as grateful to you as he should be. You own vast estates. You nourish a viper in your bosom.' There's no reason why I shouldn't tell you, but according to him, I have thirty years, four months, and two days left to live. And soon, he said, I am going to receive an inheritance. Now if I could just add Apulia[57] to the lands I own, I could die content.

"Meanwhile, with Mercury's help, I built this house. As you know, it used to be a shack; now it's a shrine. It has four dining rooms, twenty bedrooms, two marble porticoes, an upstairs dining room, the master bedroom where I sleep, the nest of that viper there, a fine porter's lodge, and guestrooms enough for all my guests. In fact, when Scaurus[58] came down here from Rome, he wouldn't put up anywhere else, though his father has lots of friends down on the shore who would have been glad to have him. And there are lots of other things I'll show you in a bit. But take my word for it: money makes the man. No money and you're nobody. But big money, big man. That's how it was with yours truly: from mouse to millionaire.

"In the meantime, Stichus," he called to a slave, "go and fetch out the clothes I'm going to be buried in. And while you're at it, bring along some perfume and a sample of that wine I'm having poured on my bones."

Stichus hurried off and promptly returned with a white grave-garment and a very splendid robe with a broad purple stripe. Trimalchio told us to inspect them and see if we approved of the material. Then he added with a smile, "See to it, Stichus, that no mice or moths get into them, or I'll have you burned alive. Yes sir, I'm going to be buried in such splendor that everybody in town will go out and pray for me." He then unstoppered a jar of fabulously expensive spikenard and had us all anointed with it. "I hope," he chuckled, "I like this perfume as much after I'm dead as I do now." Finally he ordered the slaves to pour the wine into the bowl and said, "Imagine that you're all present at my funeral feast."

---

[57] **Apulia:** Apulia would be an understandably desirable acquisition for a man who claimed that he owned property "from Terracina to Tarentum." Apulia (modern Italian *Puglia*) occupied the heel of the Italian boot. Possession of it would give Trimalchio control of most of southern Italy.

[58] **Scaurus:** Trimalchio is name dropping in order to make an invidious comparison. The family of Scaurus was one of the greatest families of Rome.

The whole business had by now become absolutely revolting. Trimalchio was obviously completely drunk, but suddenly he had a hankering for funeral music too and ordered a brass band sent into the dining room. Then he propped himself on piles of cushions and stretched out full length along the couch. "Pretend I'm dead," he said, "say something nice about me." The band blared a dead march, but one of the slaves belonging to Habinnas—who was, incidentally, one of the most respectable people present—blew so loudly that he woke up the entire neighborhood. Immediately the firemen assigned to that quarter of town, thinking that Trimalchio's house was on fire, smashed down the door and rushed in with buckets and axes to do their job. Utter confusion followed, of course, and we took advantage of the heaven-sent opportunity, gave Agamemnon the slip, and rushed out of there as though the place were really in flames.

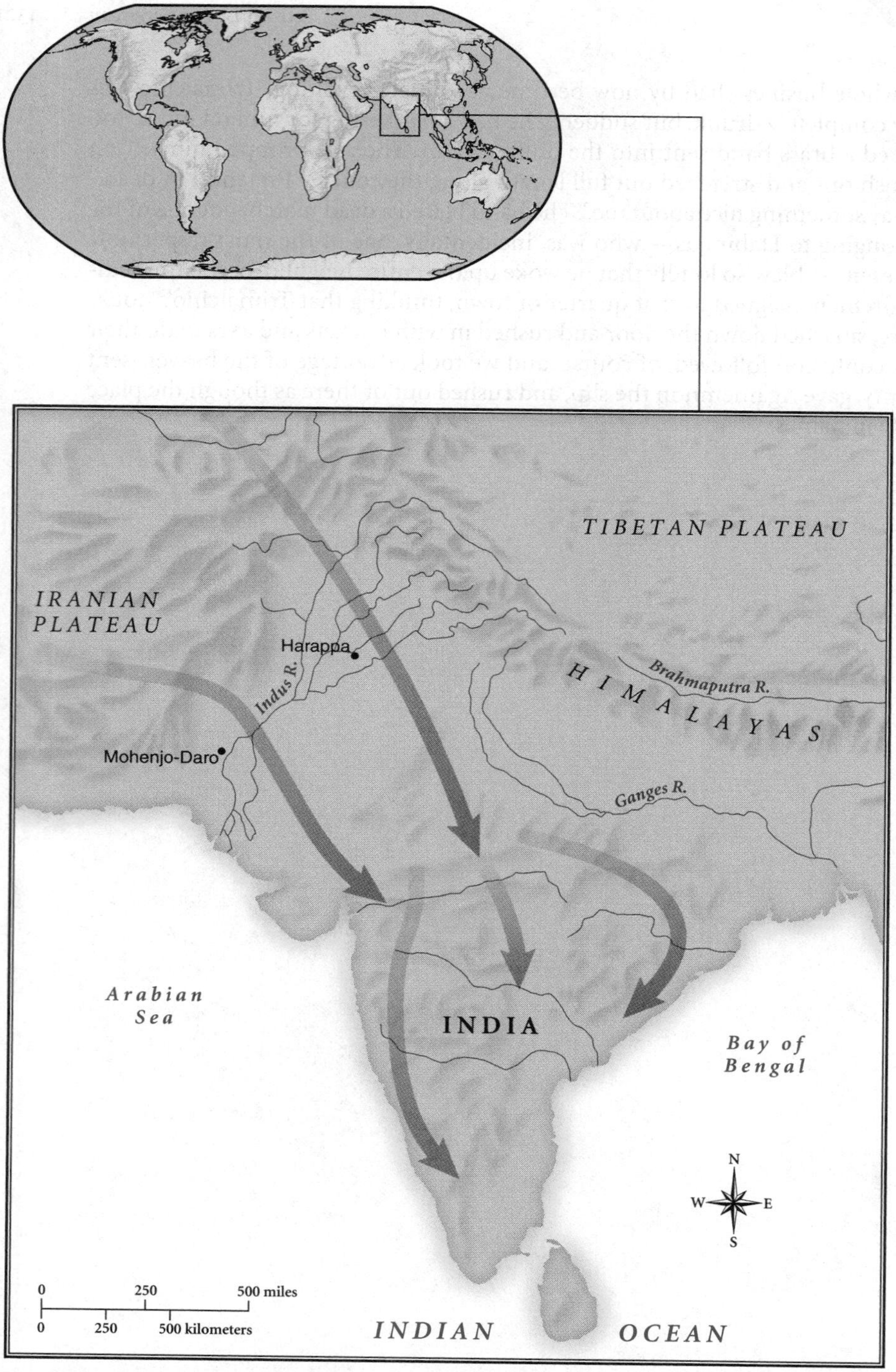

Aryan Migration into India, c. 1500–c. 700 B.C.E.

Two early Indian cities, Harappa and Mohenjo-Daro, located along the Indus River, underwent first a gradual decay and then sudden destruction around 1500 B.C.E. Although archaeologists still search for explanations for these civilizations' demise, they do know it was hastened by the arrival of the Aryans from Central Asia. After 1000 B.C.E., the Aryans continued to migrate into India, mixing with and replacing indigenous peoples.

INDIA

The Timeless Worlds of Priests, Warriors, and Caste

Developing in the Indus Valley around 2600 B.C.E., somewhat later than the birth of Mesopotamia and Egypt, Indian civilization became home to a complex and influential culture, including three major religions. India's largest body of artistic and literary material is associated with **HINDUISM**, both a religion and a total way of life with an extended history of some 3,000 years that is still part of a living culture today—probably the longest continuous religious tradition in the world. Hinduism, which originated with the Vedas—a sacred collection of hymns and rituals—is not a single religion, but a large, loose confederation of beliefs and practices ranging from simple fertility rites to a highly sophisticated philosophical **MONISM**, a belief that tries to explain things in terms of a single principle.

Great diversity in India resulted from an unusual mix of Aryan invaders and indigenous cultures in the second millennium B.C.E. A large **PANTHEON** of deities and an elaborate **COSMOLOGY** were coordinated with a unique, highly structured society that has largely remained the same throughout millennia. When doctrines and practices during the **BRAHMANIC PERIOD** (c. 1000–600 B.C.E.) became too rigid, two additional world religions were spawned, **BUDDHISM** and **JAINISM**, founded by Gautama Buddha (563–483 B.C.E.) and Mahavira (died c. 468 B.C.E.), respectively. A substantial body of religious literature has sustained the people of the Indian subcontinent; magnificent hymns and epics, which, like the Greek epics of Homer, have been continuing sources of plot and characters as retold and reinvented in plays, poems, film, fiction, and comic books even to the present day.

The influence of Indian thought spread beyond India in the nineteenth and twentieth centuries when Hindu scriptures were finally translated into European languages, including English. The great German writer Johann Wolfgang von Goethe (1749–1832) was a student of Indian literature. The American poets and

Recumbent Vishnu, 950–1050
The world's third largest religion, Hinduism is also one of the oldest, with adherents in India, Nepal, and Sri Lanka. Vishnu the Preserver is one of the three most important Hindu gods (along with Brahma the Creator and Shiva the Destroyer). Some consider Hinduism a monotheistic religion because this trinity is visualized as one within the universal principle of Brahman. (Borromeo / Art Resource, NY)

philosophers Ralph Waldo Emerson (1803–1882) and Henry David Thoreau (1817–1862) were devoted to the Bhagavad Gita. The modern Irish poet William Butler Yeats translated the **Upanishads** into English, and T. S. Eliot quotes from the Upanishads at the conclusion of his poem, *The Waste Land.*

THE INDUS VALLEY

The earliest civilization in India took hold along the Indus River in northwestern India in an area that today is mostly part of Pakistan. The Indus Valley civilization occupied a territory about the size of Texas, stretching almost a thousand miles from the Arabian Sea north to the Himalayan foothills and east to today's city of New Delhi. There are only archaeological remains left of this civilization's highly structured and deeply spiritual people, who developed a standardized system of weights and measures, brick architecture, elaborate granaries, drainage systems, a pictographic script, and a number of thriving villages. Its two most famous cities, some three hundred fifty miles apart, are Mohenjo-Daro in the south and Harappa in the north—a name borrowed from a modern town. Both of these cities are thought to have flourished about the same time, from 2600 to 1500 B.C.E., and had approximately thirty-five thousand inhabitants each, although some recent archaeology now dates the founding of Harappa around 3300 B.C.E.

Terracotta Vase with Goat, 2000 B.C.E.
Although not much is known about the Indus Valley civilization, this beautifully crafted and painted vase from the ancient city of Mohenjo-Daro suggests a highly advanced culture. (The Art Archive)

The people of ancient India supplemented their living from the land and an agricultural surplus with sea trade, especially with Mesopotamia. Like Mesopotamia a few centuries earlier, the Indus cities developed a writing system, of which thousands of samples have been unearthed but so far undeciphered—a fact that accounts for the scarcity of information about Harappan culture. The absence of great temples and tombs in the civilization's remains such as were found in Mesopotamia and Egypt suggest a corresponding absence of a powerful kingship. Moreover, few weapons and no representations of warfare have been found, indicating the sense of security felt by this civilization, which lasted more than a thousand years. Based on the similarity of its men's and women's graves, scholars have speculated that Harappa was an egalitarian, middle-class society made up of traders, merchants, craftsmen, and artists. As in other agricultural societies, Harappa's religion appears to have focused on fertility. Seals found at Harappa show a god wearing bull's horns seated in a yogic position with an erect phallus, a prototype for the later god Shiva, the lord of yoga in Hinduism. Images of fertility goddesses depict plants growing out of the wombs of the female deities.

THE ARYAN INVASION AND THE VEDIC AGE (c. 1500–c. 700 B.C.E.)

Early in the second millennium B.C.E. Aryans, nomadic tribes from the steppes of southern Russia and the grasslands of central Asia, swept in waves across ancient settlements. One group descended southeast into the Indus Valley. Historians originally called these tribes "Aryans" because the people who spoke Sanskrit were known as "Aryas"; Sanskrit was thought to be the parent language of all languages in the West. Later it was decided that there had to be an older language, called Indo-European or Indo-Germanic, from which Sanskrit had been derived. Other Indo-European groups, called Achaeans and Dorians, migrated northwest and invaded Greece in the second millennium B.C.E. They later moved into Italy and, finally, England.

The Aryans were light-skinned, hard-drinking warriors who used bows and arrows, bronze axes, and chariots drawn by pairs of horses to overrun the Harappan civilization and conquer a people who spoke a non–Indo-European language known as Dravidian, which includes the Tamil and Malayalam tongues. The Aryans called these indigenous people by the derogatory name *Dashyus,* which at first meant "enemies" but thereafter consistently meant "dark skinned." Aryans borrowed and assimilated parts of the Dravidian culture, which was superior to their own. Large numbers of the dark-skinned Dravidians were driven south into the Indian peninsula and Sri Lanka, where their descendants live today.

Ancient scriptures called the Vedas, which means "sacred knowledge," are the only known source of information about the next thousand years. Composed in Sanskrit, the Aryans' language, the Vedas describe a pantheon of warrior deities led by the god Indra, the wielder of the thunderbolt, whose roots were in nature but who were models for warrior chieftains. The Aryans had brought with them their language, a strongly patriarchal culture, and a sense of superiority; embodied in Vedic mythology is the imperative of racial separation and the "caste" system, which eventually became fixed in the social fabric of India. Initially, the Kshatriyas, or warriors, who occupied the top rung of the social ladder, were the governing caste. Next were the Brahmins, or the priestly caste; the Vaishya, the financial caste of merchants, farmers, and producers; and the Shudras, the laboring caste—the hands and feet for all those above them. Caste determined (and determines) not only one's occupation but one's dietary laws and one's circle of friends as well; it determines how and whom one may marry. Over centuries, the number of societal groups multiplied with the creation of several thousand subgroups.

THE BRAHMINS AND LITERACY

The warriors eventually relinquished control of the Vedas to the priestly class, the Brahmins, who took charge of religious ritual by singing the appropriate hymns contained in the Rig Veda—the oldest Veda dating from c. 1000 B.C.E.

The **Brahmanic Period** (c. 1000–600 b.c.e.) refers to the latter part of the Vedic Age when the Brahmins grew more powerful and gradually rose to the top of the caste system. Brahmins became the official guardians of the Vedas, and for a time they forbade the writing down of the texts. The hymns themselves were passed down orally from father to son for a thousand years. The Brahmins adapted the Aramaic alphabet, a branch of Phoenician, to Sanskrit, and produced what is called the Brahmi script. They then violently kept other castes from having contact with written texts. A Shudra convicted of reciting the Vedas would have his tongue split; if he possessed a written text, he was cut in two.

Shiva, 800–1000 c.e. *Shiva the Destroyer is here represented as Lord of the Dance. The ring of fire that surrounds him represents the cosmos, and the dwarf that he's stepping on represents ignorance. (The Art Archive / Musée Guimet, Paris / Dagli Orti)*

The Brahmins also became the official interpreters of the Vedas by writing the *Brahmanas,* or *Works of the Brahmins,* the earliest of which is dated about 800 B.C.E. In the *Brahmanas,* the Vedas are elevated to eternal truths that can be understood only by the Brahmins themselves. Earlier nature deities were redefined and arranged into a new hierarchy. At the same time there was a search for the supreme deity and a questioning of whether the new deity, Brahma, was one of the old gods or a truly new one. Eventually a trinity took over: Brahman, the universal spirit, comprises Brahma, the creator; Vishnu, the preserver; and Shiva, the destroyer.

During attempts to systematize the divine pantheon, the numbers of deities actually increased; it seems as if no deity was ever really discarded. The Brahmins became the medium through which the bounty of the gods flowed. The core of their religion, Hinduism, involved the recitation of the Vedas and the performance of fire-sacrifices involving the sacred drug soma. Later, milk and curds were added. During the Brahmanic Period sacrifices changed from acts of reverence to essential acts ensuring the continuance of the cosmos.

UPANISHADS

In addition to the four books of the Vedas, Indian spirituality rests on the foundation of the Upanishads (ninth to fifth centuries B.C.E.). From the time of the Rig Veda to the Upanishads, one can sense a transformation in Indian spiritual thought from a practical, this-worldly approach to a metaphysical and otherworldly orientation. The Rig Veda focuses on rituals, sacrifices, and prayers that seek to reconcile this life with deities who embody natural forces. Vedic hymns celebrate Indra, the ancient storm-god, and Agni, the god of fire. The Upanishads, in contrast, advocate a renunciation of the world and a focus on the inner life of the individual and the transcendental spirit. Poems in the Upanishads speculate about Brahman, the universal spirit, and Atman, the individual soul that participates in Brahman; about Vishnu, the preserver; and Shiva, the destroyer.

THE HEROIC AGE (c. 550 B.C.E.–100 C.E.)

The Heroic Age gave rise to two great literary epics that paint a vivid picture of Indian life from 1000 to 500 B.C.E., when the Aryans ceased to live as nomads and created villages. Written in Sanskrit, the *Ramayana* and the *Mahabharata* were edited and revised for a period of some nine hundred years, from c. 550 B.C.E. to 400 C.E. Called *itihasa* (historical narrative), these works deal with the period when settlements eastward, along the Ganges River, slowly expanded into numerous small kingdoms and the foundations of rule in Indian royal houses were laid. The *Ramayana* of Valmiki, an epic of twenty-four thousand verses, is the story of prince Rama of Kosala, his exile and adventures. The *Mahabharata (War of the*

Descendants of Bharata) by Vyasa, in about one hundred thousand verses (ten times longer than *The Iliad* and *The Odyssey* combined), tells the story of a civil war between clans while interweaving extensive legends, royal histories, and caste law. The *Mahabharata* includes the very popular Bhagavad Gita, or *Song of the Gods.* Like Homer's epics, the *Ramayana* and the *Mahabharata* have conveyed values as well as themes for art and literature—most recently, for television and film. Unlike the Homeric epics, however, the *Ramayana* and *Mahabharata* are considered sacred texts, providing religious and moral guidance for Hindus even today.

BUDDHISM AND JAINISM

At about the same time that the Brahmin class gained exclusive control of the social machinery of Hinduism in the sixth and fifth centuries B.C.E., a group of sages instigated a reform movement to challenge the dominance of Hinduism. Coming to the fore during a time of great ferment and change in the northeastern provinces of Bihar and Uttar Pradesh, these men criticized the Brahmin priests and their preoccupation with ceremony and sacrifice, teaching instead that knowledge and austerities could lead directly to identification with the universal spirit or world soul. Two great religions were born in India during this period, Buddhism and Jainism. Buddhism was founded by Siddhartha Gautama, or the Buddha (563–483 B.C.E.), and Jainism by Mahavira (c. 539–468 B.C.E.).

The goals of Hinduism and Buddhism are similar: deliverance from the cycle of death and rebirth and absorption into the universal or world soul. The major difference between the two systems lies in the means used for achieving those goals. In Hinduism, caste is the essential framework for educating the soul and moving it along the cycles of rebirth toward ***MOKSHA,*** or deliverance. The Buddha broke through the strictures of caste by focusing on a single lever for deliverance: detachment from this world. His fourfold truth and eightfold path are discussed in the introduction to Buddhist texts beginning on p. 1543. Jainism, founded by Mahavira, a contemporary of the Buddha, rejected the authority of the Vedas and promoted a path of austerity and ***AHIMSA,*** meaning "no harm to living things." Buddhism became the dominant religion among the ruling classes for the next thousand years. A popularized form of Buddhism that developed its own mythology, complete with a messianic promise and heavenly rewards, spread among the lower classes.

THE MAURYA EMPIRE (c. 322–c. 185 B.C.E.)

After his death, the Buddha's teachings spread throughout India. One of Buddhism's high points occurred during the reign of the emperor Ashoka (c. 273–232 B.C.E.). India was first unified by Chandragupta Maurya (r. 322–297 B.C.E.), whose movement originated in the state of Magadha, in the Ganges basin. Ashoka, the

Hindu Divinities Pay Homage to Buddha, second century B.C.E.
With the founding of Buddhism in the fifth century B.C.E., a new world religion was born. In this relief, Hindu gods venerate Buddha, represented as the enthroned wheel of law. (Victoria and Albert Museum, London / Art Resource, NY)

third ruler of the Maurya empire, converted to Buddhism, erected monasteries, and sent missionaries to Syria, Egypt, and Greece. With its abundant prosperity and a flourishing of art, Ashoka's reign was considered a golden age in ancient India. In 185 B.C.E. the Maurya empire fell and fragmented into small states; India would not be united again until the Gupta dynasty (320–c. 550 C.E.). The third Gupta king, Chandragupta II, brought about India's second golden age.

WWW For more information about the culture and context of India in the ancient world, see *World Literature Online* at bedfordstmartins.com/worldlit.

TIME AND PLACE

Ancient India: Cycles of Time

The concept of time in Indian literature is very different from time as it was depicted in ancient Mesopotamia, Egypt, and Israel. In those earlier cultures, a mythic or primordial time precedes history and is the occasion for the creation of a mythic cosmology. This is always followed by a transitional period when myth and legend merge with history—a linear or progressive concept of time—and are blended into the culture. Time in Indian myth is a larger beast; it consists of immense, nearly innumerable cycles of years and eons—probably the longest cycles of time ever conceived by any religion. In Indian thought, the world is presently in the last of four epochs, or *Yugas,* the Kali Yuga. According to some calculations, it began Friday, February 18, 3102 B.C.E. and will last 432,000 years. A different expert says that the Kali Yuga will last 10,800,000 years.

***Woman Making Offering to Brahma,* 1720.** *The Hindu creator god Brahma is shown in this Indian miniature with four faces, symbolizing the four* Yugas *(epochs), the four Vedas (sacred writings), and the four* varnas *(castes or social classes). (The Art Archive / Marco Polo Gallery Paris / Dagli Orti)*

The three previous Yugas—the *Krita,* the *Treta,* and the *Dvapara*—are spoken of in the present tense since they repeat endlessly. They represent a process of decline, ages during which life grows worse. In the Krita Yuga, the golden age associated with fullness, men and women are virtuous and all social classes act according to ideals. It lasts 1,728,000 years. In the Treta Yuga virtue diminishes slightly (by one quarter); the four castes begin to decay, and duties are not spontaneous but have to be learned. It lasts 1,296,000 years. In the Dvapara Yuga there is a dangerous balance between darkness and light, good and evil. People grow mean and greedy. It lasts 864,000 years. The Kali Yuga, the present age, is the dark age. Each age ends with darkness, but in the Kali Yuga, darkness deepens. A complete cycle of four Yugas is called *Maha Yuga,* or the Great Yuga, after which is *Pralaya,* meaning "dissolution." A single day of Brahma, the god of creation, or a single *kalpa,* equals 1,000 *Mahayugas* (4,320,000,000 human years); after one *kalpa,* everything is dissolved. After one hundred years of Brahma days and nights, which constitute the gods' existence, all spheres of being and existence sink into the primordial Substance, a condition that remains for a Brahma century, after which the creation-destruction cycle begins anew.

In the context of these great cycles, individual human existence is inconsequential; there is really no need to promote change or reform, to rid society of inequities or oppression; life's goal is contained in the idea of *dharma,* doing one's sacred duty.

■ **PRONUNCIATION**

Bhagavad Gita: bah-guh-vahd-GEE-tuh, buh-guh-vud-GEE-tuh
Brahmanas: BRAH-hmuh-nuhz
Dasyus: DUS-yooz
Itihasa: ih-tee-HAH-suh
Mahabharata: muh-huh-BAH-ruh-tuh, muh-hah-BAH-ruh-tuh
Mahavira: muh-hah-VEE-ruh
Malayalam: mal-uh-YAH-lum
Moksha: MOKE-shuh
Ramayana: ruh-MAH-yuh-nuh
Shiva: SHEE-vuh, SEE-vuh, SHIH-vuh
Upanishads: oo-PUN-ih-shudz, oo-PAHN-ih-shahdz
Vedas: VAY-duhz
Vishnu: VISH-noo
Vyasa: VYAH-suh, vee-YAH-suh

Vedic Literature

c. 1000–First Century B.C.E.

www For quizzes on the Rig Veda and the Upanishads, see *World Literature Online* at bedfordstmartins .com/worldlit.

Only Mesopotamian and Egyptian literatures are dated earlier than the works that make up the Vedas, which are the foundation of Hinduism. The word ***veda*** means "knowledge," knowledge about how the world works, about superhuman powers and how to influence them. In the Hindu tradition there are four Vedas—Rig Veda, Yayur Veda, Sama Veda, and Atharva Veda—that feature a wide variety of literatures. The Rig Veda contains creation stories, sacrificial rites, and formulas for priests. The Yayur Veda includes priest chants, litanies, and the ritual sacrifices necessary to maintain the favor of the gods, who were dependent on sacrifices for their well-being. The Sama Veda is known for its songs of praise, and the Atharva Veda focuses on spells and magic. The Vedas and some of the Upanishads, which are commentaries or philosophical reflections on the Vedas, are thought to be divinely revealed works. Such texts are known as ***shruti*** (***sruti***), revelation, in contrast to ***smirti*** (***smṛti***), secondary revelation or tradition. Although they are difficult to date, it is believed that the Vedas were revealed in a series of visions to ***rishi*** (***ṛṣi***) (poet-seers or sages), who began to recite them c. 1200 B.C.E., although they may have originated earlier. These revelations were passed down orally to succeeding generations by Brahmins, members of the priestly class, collected into a whole c. 1000 B.C.E., and written down c. 600 B.C.E.

Most of the deities in the Vedas, as with most deities in other ancient mythologies, were originally linked to natural forces. The hymns in the Vedas pay tribute to the beauty and power of the natural world—to fire and water, winds and storms, the rising and the setting sun. The Vedas, written in highly structured verse forms in Sanskrit, are memorized word for word by priests and storytellers. They are meant to be chanted and are

Vishnu Trivikrama, tenth century
The myth of Vishnu Trivikrama appears in the Rig Veda, one of the earliest Hindu texts. It tells the story of how Vishnu, in the guise of the dwarf Vamana, defeats the demon-king Bali by tricking Bali into granting him all he could encompass in three steps (trivikrama). *In this sculpted panel, Vishnu's foot is raised high, where it is worshiped by a small figure of Brahma. (Courtesy of The British Museum)*

The caste system held India together for more than two thousand years, through all the vicissitudes of foreign conquest, civil war, and political chaos. . . . In short, this institution represents the most astonishing attempt in history to maintain social stability and arrest change.

– HERBERT J. MULLER, historian, 1952

thought to have a powerful psychological effect. Similar to the Hebrew account of creation in the first chapter of Genesis, in which the breath of God passes over the waters and is instrumental in the subsequent creation, the breath of the Supreme Being of Hinduism is synonymous with the creation and sustenance of the world, the transmission of the Vedas, the recitation of the Vedas, and yogic breathing.[1]

The role of the Vedas in village life is shown in twenty-first-century Indian novelist and essayist R. K. Narayan's description of the typical storyteller in an Indian village. Known as a Pandit, the Indian storyteller has memorized the 24,000 stanzas of the *Ramayana,* the 100,000 stanzas of the *Mahabharata,*[2] and the 18,000 stanzas of the Bhagavad Gita. He obeys the ***SHASTRAS***—the ancient scriptures—in the details of his daily life: "He has unquestioned faith in the validity of the Vedas, which he commenced learning when he was seven years old. It took him twelve years to master the intonation of the Vedas. He had also to acquire precise knowledge of Sanskrit's grammar, syllabification, meaning of words . . . He has no doubt whatever that the Vedas were created out of the breath of God, and contain within them all that a man needs for his salvation at every level."

Indra Slays the Dragon. The Rig Veda, which means the "knowledge" *(veda)* laid down in "verses" *(rig),* is the earliest known Indo-European document and the oldest Veda. It contains more than a thousand hymns arranged in ten sections or "song cycles." With more than 250 hymns dedicated to him, Indra is the chief deity in the Rig Veda; one of the most popular creation myths in the Rig Veda is the story of Indra's defeat of the demon-dragon Vritra. Similar to the Greek god Zeus, whose Indo-European origin was a rain or weather god, Indra was originally a rain and fertility deity. Like Zeus, Indra carries a thunderbolt; he is also known as "he with a thousand testicles." His first and greatest deed is slaying the dragon Vritra, an act that symbolizes the freeing of the waters or rain that Vritra has swallowed. The earliest meaning of Vritra is the primeval water itself, which is pregnant with the sun. In the mythic drama of the Veda, Vritra becomes the demon of drought who in some fashion holds back all fertilizing waters. In one hymn, Vritra imprisons the rain cow in his cloud castle. Vritra belongs to a group of spirit beings called the *Danava,* meaning "restraint." Another similar name for this group is *rakshas,* or demons, who are imagined as serpents or dragons. The positive *Asuras,* or powers, are called ***Aditya,*** meaning "release."

AH-dit-yuh

The creation myth involving Indra begins with the *Adityas* at war with the *Danavas* over releasing the waters of creation. When the *Adityas* begin to lose the battle they call on Indra, whose epithet means "son of might." If Indra wins, he will be king of gods. With his weapon, the lightning bolt, Indra drinks three beakers of soma, fills the sky, and intervenes

[1] **the breath of . . . yogic breathing:** The English language makes these connections in the word *inspiration,* whose roots denote creativity, divinity, and breathing.

[2] ***Ramayana* . . . *Mahabharata*:** The great Indian epics from c. sixth century B.C.E. to the fifth century C.E. See pages 1351 and 1434.

in the battle, defeating the *Danavas* or *rakshas* led by Vritra, the arch-demon. There are striking similarities between this myth and the Mesopotamian story of Marduk's defeat of the dragon Tiamat. The Indian myth also shares characteristics with the ancient Egyptian story of the battle between the sun-god Re and the serpent Apophis.

> **In the songs of the *Vedas* we find the wonder of man before nature: fire and water, the winds and the storms, the sun and the rising of the sun are sung with adoration.**
>
> **–Juan Mascaró, translator and critic, 1965**

Hymn to the Sun. "Hymn to the Sun God," one of many such hymns, is an example of literature of the early Vedic period (c. 1500–1000 B.C.E.) when the sun-god Surya was an important member of the pantheon. The Sun in this hymn, included here for its lyric beauty, drives a chariot across the sky like the Greek god Helios. A prayer in the Vedas addressed to Savitri, another name for Surya, has been recited every morning for more than three millennia by millions of Indians:

TAT SAVITUR VARENIAM
BHARGO DEVASYA DHIMAHI
DHIYO YO NAH PRACODA YAT

"Let our meditation be on the glorious light of Savitri.
May this light illumine our minds."

The Dismemberment of Purusha. During the Brahmanic Age (c. 1000–600 B.C.E.), as the Indian culture became more settled and stable, the Brahmins, the priestly caste, began to assume the power of the superior caste once held by warriors. The Brahmins controlled the recitation of the Vedas and performed the sacrifices thought to sustain the life of the gods and the workings of the cosmos. The Indian archetypal model for the cosmic significance of sacrifice is the dismemberment of Purusha described in the hymn "Purusha-Sukta" ("The Song of Purusha"), another creation story. **Purusha** is the primordial being—translated as "Man" in the translation used here—whom the gods dismember in a Vedic sacrifice in order to create the world. Dismemberment is a common element of mythological stories around the world: Tiamat was dismembered to make the physical world in Mesopotamia; Ymir was dismembered in Nordic mythology; "Grandmother" was dismembered in the Okanagon creation story from western Canada. Typically in these stories, parts of the body become distinct features of the earth's landscape: flesh becomes soil, bone becomes rock, blood becomes rivers, breath becomes wind, and so on.

poo-ROO-shuh

There are at least two remarkable consequences of what might be called "dismemberment psychology." First, the sacrifice of a primordial being or a god or godlike being for the benefit of the world and human beings promotes reverence and subservience. Sacrifice becomes the threshold between the mortal and the divine. Second, such a creation by dismemberment means that the world is not only made by god, the world is god: It is alive, sacred stuff. Every tree and rock and breath of wind is dynamically alive. In the Indian myth, Purusha is the god to whom the sacrifice is dedicated as well as the victim that is sacrificed.

"The Song of Purusha" is the first and the only hymn to describe the caste system, the four social classes, or ***VARNAS,*** introduced by the Aryans

He [the village storyteller in India] has unquestioned faith in the validity of the *Vedas,* which he commenced learning when he was seven years old. It took him twelve years to master the intonation of the *Vedas.* He had also to acquire precise knowledge of Sanskrit's grammar, syllabification, meaning of words. . . . He has no doubt whatever that the *Vedas* were created out of the breath of God, and contain within them all that a man needs for his salvation at every level.

– R. K. Narayan, novelist, 1964

when they invaded India. The four *varnas* are the Brahmin (the priestly and learned); the *Kshatriya* (warriors and administrators); the *Vaishya* (merchants, farmers, and other producers); and the *Shudra* (laborers). In the caste system, a person must perform the duties appropriate to his or her social class, even if it goes against personal desires or needs; the caste system has held India together for more than two thousand years while also inhibiting social change. When the primordial Man, Purusha, is described in cosmic terms as "whatever has been and whatever is to be . . . the ruler of immortality," he sounds very much like Brahman, the Universal Spirit of the Upanishads. Later, in Hinduism, Purusha is replaced by the god Brahma in the creation story, and Brahma becomes the eternal validation for the caste system.

Hymn to the Horse. The horse sacrifice, which in various forms was practiced all over the ancient world, was the most elaborate ritual in Vedic times, created exclusively for kings. Like the elaborate calendric rituals involving the Jerusalem Temple found in Hebrew Scriptures, a detailed manual for sacrifices in the Vedas was provided. A major sacrifice required four different chief priests; a high priest was in charge of the whole ceremony. The *hotar,* or caller, at a sacrifice invoked the participation of the appropriate deities using hymns in the Rig Veda. The *udgatar,* or singer, accompanied the offering of the *soma* with songs from the Sama Veda. The *adhvaryu,* or general priest, performed the sacred ritual using texts from the Yayur Veda.

The detailed rites of the horse sacrifice took place over the period of one year and involved special prayers, the sacrifice of a dog, dances, recitations of epic poems, and sexual mimicry involving the consecrated horse, who represented the god Varuna, and the king's chief queen. The literature then describes how the horse is cooked on a spit over a fire and how the gods themselves partake in the sacrificial meal with special bowls and utensils. The horse's ribs are consecrated: one each to the sun and moon, five to the planets, and twenty-seven to the constellations. The ritual concludes with the prayer: "Let this racehorse bring us good cattle and good horses, male children, and all-nourishing wealth. Let **Aditi**[3] make us free from sin. Let the horse with our offerings achieve sovereign power for us."

AH-dit-tee

The Upanishads. The best known of the later metaphysical hymns of the Rig Veda, "In the Beginning, before the Gods" (p. 776), called the "Nasadiya," takes its title from the opening words of the poem that begins: "Then neither Being nor Not-being was." With its skeptical inquiry into beginnings, this hymn reflects the transition from the Vedic Age to the more philosophical world of the Upanishads. The Upanishads number about 112 hymns when published in Sanskrit. The oldest were composed from the ninth to the fifth centuries B.C.E., while some are dated as late as the fifteenth century C.E. Translator and scholar Juan Mascaró calls the Upanishads "spiritual treatises" since they do not present a unified philo-

[3] **Aditi:** Aditi, whose name means "boundless" or "infinite consciousness," is the mother of the group of early gods called *Adityas.*

sophical system but rather are viewed as interpreting and completing the Vedas. The oldest Upanishad, for example, the Brhadaranyaka Upanishad (c. 900–800 B.C.E.), contains an interpretation of the horse sacrifice that associates parts of the horse with relevant aspects of the cosmos.

The spiritual tradition represented by the Upanishads supplanted Brahmanic ritual with knowledge, with an understanding that the particular elements of the sacrifice are identical with the metaphysical reality of the universe. The Brhadaranyaka Upanishad teaches the most significant concept, one that runs throughout the other Upanishads as well: that *atman* equals *brahman*—that is, the immortal self of each individual partakes in the underlying, spiritual reality of the universe. The purpose of life is to realize this connection. The Upanishads, which represent a spiritual path that bypasses caste and is open to every individual, is more easily translatable to other cultures and other times than the Vedas.

A sampling of teachings from the various Upanishads follows. The first two selections, from the Maitri and Kena Upanishads, assert the omnipresence of *brahman,* that being that cannot be known by the human mind and that cannot be grasped by thought or speech. The third excerpt, from the Katha Upanishad, uses a horse-drawn chariot as a metaphor for the self. The last two selections, from the Chandogya Upanishad, highlight the role of the sacred syllable *Om* and tell of the nature of *atman* in a charming parable.

■ CONNECTIONS

Egypt, hymns, p. 104. The sun plays an important role in the mythologies of ancient Egypt and India and is celebrated in lovely hymns in both cultures. In Egypt under Akhenaten, the sun was the primary deity. Consider the sun's role in desert climates, where water is scarce to nonexistent. What does the Indian "Hymn to the Sun God" (p. 1340) reveal about the importance of the sun in India's climate?

Hebrew Scriptures, p. 134. All ancient religions sought to name the essential or key element that characterized the divine; was it power or kindness or justice? The breath that sweeps across the waters, the holy wind in the Book of Genesis is similar to the breath found in the Vedas. What are the characteristics of breath that link it to wind, and why is wind such a potent symbol of god?

Homer, *The Odyssey,* p. 421. In ancient times, sky-gods symbolized the essential fertilizing powers of the sun and rain; the power of these weather gods was represented in thunder, lightning, and earthquakes. Comparisons can be made among the Indo-European sky-god Dyaus, the Greek god Zeus, and the Indian god Indra. Why are the characteristics of a weather god suitable for a warrior culture, for conquering tribes or settlements?

■ FURTHER RESEARCH

Texts

de Bary, William Theodore, ed. *Sources of Indian Tradition.* 1958.
Goodall, Dominic. *Hindu Scriptures.* 1996.
Hume, R. E. *The Thirteen Principal Upanishads.* 1931.
Mascaró, Juan. *The Upanishads.* 1965.
O'Flaherty, Wendy Doniger. *Hindu Myths: A Sourcebook Translated from the Sanskrit.* 1975.
———. *The Rig Veda: An Anthology.* 1981.
———. *Textual Sources for the Study of Hinduism.* 1988.

Commentary
Campbell, Joseph. *The Masks of God: Oriental Mythology.* 1962.
Ions, Veronica. *Indian Mythology.* 1967.
Klostermaier, Klaus K. *A Concise Encyclopedia of Hinduism.* 1998.
Kramer, Samuel Noah, ed. *Mythologies of the Ancient World.* 1961.
Muller, Herbert J. *The Uses of the Past: Profiles of Former Societies.* 1954.
Schuhmacher, Stephen, and Gert Woerner, eds. *The Encyclopedia of Eastern Philosophy and Religion.* 1994. An indispensable guide to deities, documents, and concepts.
Sharma, Arvind. *Classical Hindu Thought: An Introduction.* 2000.
Shattuck, Cybelle. *Hinduism.* 1999.
Zimmer, Heinrich. *Myths and Symbols in Indian Art and Civilization.* 1946.

■ **PRONUNCIATION**
Purusha: poo-ROO-shuh
Agni: UG-nee, AHG-nee
Aditya: AH-dit-yuh

The Rig Veda [c. 1000 B.C.E.]

Translated by Wendy Doniger O'Flaherty

Indra Slays the Dragon Vritra

1 Let me now sing the heroic deeds of Indra, the first that the thunderbolt-wielder performed. He killed the dragon and pierced an opening for the waters; he split open the bellies of mountains.[1]

2 He killed the dragon who lay upon the mountain; Tvaṣṭṛ[2] fashioned the roaring thunderbolt for him. Like lowing cows, the flowing waters rushed straight down to the sea.

Indra Slays the Dragon Vritra. Since this text is not a narrative but a hymn, the story lies behind the text itself. The dense poetic lines of the hymn contain several layers of meaning. The name Vritra (Vṛtra) in Sanskrit means "storm cloud," in the sense of a cloud containing or holding back the rain, making Vritra the demon of drought. This cloud is also symbolically the cloud of ignorance, that which holds someone back from knowledge. Indra is the god of light, and of enlightenment—the knowledge that extinguishes the darkness of ignorance. In terms of spirituality, Vritra is a dry period, a time of confusion when someone loses his or her way; Indra represents the spirit of renewal, a new path opening up.

A note on the translation: All selections from the Rig Veda are taken from Wendy Doniger O'Flaherty's translation. Translators treat Sanskrit names in different ways, as you'll see in the selections included here; some anglicize them more than others. We reprint the texts as the translator intended, but our editorial notes use the more accessible, anglicized spellings.

---

[1] **He killed . . . mountains:** Indra's thunderbolt is a phallic club, symbolic of fertility.
[2] **Tvaṣṭṛ:** The artisan of the gods.

3 Wildly excited like a bull, he took the Soma for himself and drank the extract from the three bowls in the three-day Soma ceremony.[3] Indra the Generous seized his thunderbolt to hurl it as a weapon; he killed the first-born of dragons.

4 Indra, when you killed the first-born of dragons and overcame by your own magic the magic of the magicians, at that very moment you brought forth the sun, the sky, and dawn.[4] Since then you have found no enemy to conquer you.

5 With his great weapon, the thunderbolt, Indra killed the shoulderless Vṛtra,[5] his greatest enemy. Like the trunk of a tree whose branches have been lopped off by an axe, the dragon lies flat upon the ground.

6 For, muddled by drunkenness like one who is no soldier, Vṛtra challenged the great hero who had overcome the mighty and who drank Soma to the dregs. Unable to withstand the onslaught of his weapons, he found Indra an enemy to conquer him and was shattered, his nose crushed.

7 Without feet or hands he fought against Indra, who struck him on the nape of the neck with his thunderbolt. The steer who wished to become the equal of the bull bursting with seed, Vṛtra lay broken in many places.

8 Over him as he lay there like a broken reed the swelling waters flowed for man.[6] Those waters that Vṛtra had enclosed with his power—the dragon now lay at their feet.

9 The vital energy of Vṛtra's mother ebbed away, for Indra had hurled his deadly weapon at her. Above was the mother, below was the son; Dānu[7] lay down like a cow with her calf.

10 In the midst of the channels of the waters which never stood still or rested, the body was hidden. The waters flow over Vṛtra's secret place; he who found Indra an enemy to conquer him sank into long darkness.

11 The waters who had the Dāsa[8] for their husband, the dragon for their protector, were imprisoned like the cows imprisoned by the Paṇis.[9] When he killed Vṛtra he split open the outlet of the waters that had been closed.

---

[3] **the . . . Soma ceremony:** The juice from a psychotropic plant was used in Vedic ceremonies. The exact plant is unknown today; it has been suggested that it was the hallucinogenic mushroom *Amanita muscaria.*

[4] **brought forth . . . dawn:** The sun lay hidden in the primeval waters.

[5] **shoulderless Vṛtra:** Vritra, a serpent or dragon without shoulders.

[6] **flowed for man:** Flowed for the sake of mankind.

[7] **Dānu:** The archdemon mother of Vritra, who belongs to a group of demons called *Danavas.*

[8] **Dāsa:** Another name for Vritra.

[9] **the Paṇis:** A group of demonic enemies who stole the primordial cows and imprisoned them.

12 Indra, you became a hair of a horse's tail when Vṛtra struck you on the corner of the mouth.[10] You, the one god, the brave one, you won the cows; you won the Soma; you released the seven streams so that they could flow.

13 No use was the lightning and thunder, fog and hail that he[11] had scattered about, when the dragon and Indra fought. Indra the Generous remained victorious for all time to come.

14 What avenger of the dragon did you see, Indra, that fear entered your heart when you had killed him? Then you crossed the ninety-nine streams like the frightened eagle[12] crossing the realms of earth and air.

15 Indra, who wields the thunderbolt in his hand, is the king of that which moves and that which rests, of the tame and of the horned.[13] He rules the people as their king, encircling all this as a rim encircles spokes.

---

[10] **you became . . . mouth:** With magic, Indra made himself think as horse's hair would and thus became a hair of a horse's tail.

[11] **he:** Vritra.

[12] **the frightened eagle:** Possibly the eagle (Indra in disguise) that stole the Soma. [. . .] (Translator's note.)

[13] **the tame and of the horned:** According to Sayana [a fourteenth-century Vedic scholar], the "tame" are animals that do not attack, such as horses and donkeys, while the "horned" are fierce animals like buffaloes and bulls. (Translator's note.)

Hymn to the Sun God

1 His brilliant banners draw upwards the god who knows all creatures, so that everyone may see the sun.

2 The constellations, along with the nights, steal away like thieves, making way for the sun who gazes on everyone.

3 The rays that are his banners have become visible from the distance, shining over mankind like blazing fires.

Hymn to the Sun God. It is impossible to overemphasize the importance of sun symbolism in ancient mythologies. Some folklorists and philologists at the end of the nineteenth century believed that all mythology grew out of the day and night, that all heroes from Heracles to Beowulf to King Arthur embodied the same solar deity and were perpetually involved with one plot, the struggle of the sun against darkness. The prime support for this theory came from Vedic literature and Sanskrit, and the aboriginal god of the sky, Dyaus. Although the solar hypothesis seems to be an oversimplification today, the relationship of the sun to aspects of everyday life is manifold: from the centrality of the sun in the solar system and the analogies to kingship to the importance of fire and heat, and all the associations that exist between light and consciousness.

For all ancient peoples the phenomena in the heavens were a source of wonder: the heat from the sun, the changing nature of the moon, thunder and lightning, the unchanging patterns of the

4 Crossing space, you are the maker of light, seen by everyone, O sun. You illumine the whole, wide realm of space.

5 You rise up facing all the groups of gods, facing mankind, facing everyone, so that they can see the sunlight.

6 He is the eye with which, O Purifying Varuṇa, you look upon the busy one[1] among men.

7 You cross heaven and the vast realm of space, O sun, measuring days by nights, looking upon the generations.

8 Seven bay mares carry you in the chariot, O sun god with hair of flame, gazing from afar.

9 The sun has yoked the seven splendid daughters of the chariot; he goes with them, who yoke themselves.

10 We have come up out of darkness, seeing the higher light around us, going to the sun, the god among gods, the highest light.

11 As you rise today, O sun, you who are honoured as a friend, climbing to the highest sky, make me free of heartache and yellow pallor.[2]

12 Let us place my yellow pallor among parrots and thrushes, or let us place my yellow pallor among other yellow birds in yellow trees.

13 This Āditya[3] has risen with all his dominating force, hurling my hateful enemy down into my hands. Let me not fall into my enemy's hands!

---

constellations. Although it is doubtful these objects or powers were ever worshiped directly, gods of the sun and goddesses of the moon around the world have always been plentiful.

Although the sun is addressed here as if it were *the* god, the hymn is directed to Surya, the chief sun-god in the Vedas. Not surprisingly, he has golden hair and drives a gold chariot pulled by seven mares, or a single mare with seven heads. The sun is compared to a chariot drawn by horses for the simple reason that the chariot was the fastest mode of locomotion known to ancient peoples. The sun's rays, called banners, also refer to the seven mares pulling the chariot.

---

[1] **Varuṇa . . . the busy one:** The god Varuna is the universal monarch, the sustainer of creation and the guardian of cosmic law; here he uses the sun as his eye. The "busy one" is probably Agni, the god of sacrificial fires; he is at once the fire itself and the consumer of the sacrifice.

[2] **yellow pallor:** Yellow is a color associated with jaundice and sickness.

[3] **Āditya:** Adityas are solar deities, sons of the goddess Aditi.

The Song of Purusha

1 The Man has a thousand heads, a thousand eyes, a thousand feet. He pervaded the earth on all sides and extended beyond it as far as ten fingers.

2 It is the Man who is all this, whatever has been and whatever is to be. He is the ruler of immortality, when he grows beyond everything through food.[1]

3 Such is his greatness, and the Man is yet more than this. All creatures are a quarter of him; three quarters are what is immortal in heaven.

4 With three quarters the Man rose upwards, and one quarter of him still remains here.[2] From this he spread out in all directions, into that which eats and that which does not eat.

5 From him Virāj[3] was born, and from Virāj came the Man. When he was born, he ranged beyond the earth behind and before.

6 When the gods spread[4] the sacrifice with the Man as the offering, spring was the clarified butter, summer the fuel, autumn the oblation.

7 They anointed the Man, the sacrifice born at the beginning, upon the sacred grass.[5] With him the gods, Sādhyas,[6] and sages sacrificed.

8 From that sacrifice in which everything was offered, the melted fat[7] was collected, and he[8] made it into those beasts who live in the air, in the forest, and in villages.

The Song of Purusha. The Sanskrit title of this poem is "Purusha-Sukta," which literally means the "song of Purusha." In Wendy Doniger O'Flaherty's translation, "Purusha" is translated as "Man," meaning the first man. Others have suggested that the Universal Spirit took the form of a giant or Primal Person. "Man" needs to be understood in terms of a primordial setting, as Cosmic Man whose body becomes the parts of the world. Besides meaning "man" or "person," *Purusha* also means the Self or God-consciousness. In this context, the dismemberment of Purusha becomes an allegory of the soul's dispersion into the material world. The reference to the three Vedas in stanza nine and to the four social classes or *varnas* in stanza twelve indicate that this hymn comes rather late in the composition of the Rig Veda and is thought by some to form its conclusion.

[1] **He is the ruler . . . food:** An obscure statement possibly meaning that Purusha transcends the world of eating and being eaten.

[2] The first four stanzas emphasize the fact that the Man is the whole universe.

[3] **Virāj:** The female or material creative principle.

[4] **spread:** This is the word used to indicate the performance of a Vedic sacrifice, "spread" or "stretched out" (like the earth spread upon the cosmic waters). [. . .] (Translator's note.)

[5] **sacred grass:** Special grasses upon which the gods sit.

[6] **Sādhyas:** Meaning "those who are yet to be fulfilled": a class of demigods.

[7] **melted fat:** Literally a mixture of butter and sour milk used in the sacrifice; figuratively, the fat that drained from the sacrificial victim. (Translator's note.)

[8] **he:** Purusha or the creator-god; later in Hinduism, the creator Brahma replaces Purusha.

9 From that sacrifice in which everything was offered, the verses and chants were born, the metres were born from it, and from it the formulas were born.[9]

10 Horses were born from it, and those other animals that have two rows of teeth;[10] cows were born from it, and from it goats and sheep were born.

11 When they divided the Man, into how many parts did they apportion him? What do they call his mouth, his two arms and thighs and feet?

12 His mouth became the Brahmin; his arms were made into the Warrior, his thighs the People, and from his feet the Servants were born.[11]

13 The moon was born from his mind; from his eye the sun was born. Indra and Agni[12] came from his mouth, and from his vital breath the Wind was born.

14 From his navel the middle realm of space arose; from his head the sky evolved. From his two feet came the earth, and the quarters of the sky from his ear. Thus they[13] set the worlds in order.

15 There were seven enclosing-sticks[14] for him, and thrice seven fuel-sticks, when the gods, spreading the sacrifice, bound the Man as the sacrificial beast.

16 With the sacrifice the gods sacrificed to the sacrifice.[15] These were the first ritual laws.[16] These very powers reached the dome of the sky where dwell the Sādhyas, the ancient gods.

---

[9] **the verses . . . born:** Verses, chants, metres, and formulas are ways of referencing the Vedas.

[10] **two rows of teeth:** Incisors above and below, like cats and dogs.

[11] **His mouth . . . born:** The four social classes of Indian society: Brahmin (priests); *Kshatriya* (warriors and administrators); *Vaishya* (merchants, farmers, producers); and *Shudra* (laborers). The "Untouchables" are outside caste.

[12] **Indra and Agni:** The god of light and fertility and the god of fire.

[13] **they:** The gods.

[14] **seven enclosing-sticks:** The enclosing-sticks are green twigs that keep the fire from spreading; the fuel sticks are seasoned wood used for kindling. (Translator's note.)

[15] **With the . . . sacrifice:** Purusha was both the victim of the sacrifice and the divinity to whom the sacrifice was directed.

[16] **the first ritual laws:** Literally, the *dharmas,* a protean word that here designates the archetypal patterns of behavior established during this first sacrifice to serve as a model for all future sacrifices. (Translator's note.)

Hymn to the Horse

1 When you whinnied for the first time, as you were born coming forth from the ocean or from the celestial source,[1] with the wings of an eagle and the forelegs of an antelope—that, Swift Runner, was your great and awesome birth.

2 Yama gave him and Trita harnessed him; Indra was the first to mount him, and the Gandharva[2] grasped his reins. You gods fashioned the horse out of the sun.

3 Swift Runner, you are Yama; you are Āditya;[3] you are Trita, through the hidden design.[4] You are like and not like Soma. They say you have three bonds in the sky.[5]

4 They say you have three bonds in the sky, three in the waters, and three within the ocean.[6] And to me you appear, Swift Runner, like Varuṇa,[7] that is said to be your highest birth.

5 These are the places where they rubbed you down when you were victorious; here are the marks where you put down your hooves. Here I saw your lucky reins, which the Guardians of the Order keep safely.

6 From afar, in my heart I recognized your soul, the bird[8] flying below the sky. I saw your winged head snorting on the dustless paths easy to travel.

7 Here I saw your highest form eager for nourishment in the place of the cow.[9] As soon as a mortal gets the food that you enjoy, the great devourer of plants awakens him.[10]

Hymn to the Horse. Every aspect of the horse sacrifice has a cosmic referent. The symbolism of the horse alone is far-reaching and complex. First and foremost, the horse, which probably replaced the bull in rituals, symbolizes sexual energy; the power and might of a special stallion of a pure breed represents fertility, masculine virility, and in a larger context, the supreme power of the king over his kingdom. The horse and chariot played a central military role. Men also raced horses for recreation. The horse's name is analogous to the rays of the sun, to the ocean's waves. The speed of the horse associates it with fire and light. The winged horse can represent intellect and consciousness. Varuna, one of the oldest Vedic gods, rose out of the primordial waters as the cosmic horse.

[1] **the celestial source:** Probably a reference to the sun's birth from the primordial waters.

[2] **Yama . . . Gandharva:** Yama is god of the dead. Trita is one of the storm-gods associated with Indra, who is king of the gods but was originally a weather god. Gandharva is a solar deity in charge of dispensing soma.

[3] **Āditya:** A solar deity whose name means "release," as in releasing the sun from the primordial waters—Vritra.

[4] **the hidden design:** The magic, secret power of the sacrifice.

[5] **Soma . . . in the sky:** Soma was the ambrosial—probably psychotropic—offering to the gods that sustained their immortality. The "three bonds" are the three gods mentioned just previously: Yama, Aditya, and Trita.

[6] **in the sky . . . ocean:** The sky, rivers, and oceans are residences of various deities.

[7] **Varuṇa:** God of rivers, oceans, and cosmic order.

[8] **the bird:** The sun as a bird, but also the winged horse as the sun.

[9] **the cow:** The sacred cow symbolizes nourishment, the bounty of the earth.

[10] **the great . . . awakens him:** An ambiguous phrase; it might refer to the awakening effects of the sacrifice on a participant. The "great devourer" could be the horse but is most likely Agni, the god of the sacrificial fire.

8 The chariot follows you, Swift Runner; the young man follows, the cow follows, the love of young girls follows. The troops follow your friendship.[11] The gods entrusted virile power to you.

9 His mane is golden; his feet are bronze. He is swift as thought, faster than Indra. The gods have come to eat the oblation of the one who was the first to mount the swift runner.[12]

10 The celestial coursers, revelling in their strength, fly in a line like wild geese, the ends held back while the middle surges forward, when the horses reach the racecourse of the sky.

11 Your body flies, Swift Runner; your spirit rushes like wind. Your mane, spread in many directions, flickers and jumps about in the forests.

12 The racehorse has come to the slaughter, pondering with his heart turned to the gods. The goat, his kin,[13] is led in front; behind come the poets, the singers.

13 The swift runner has come to the highest dwelling-place, to his father and mother. May he go to the gods today and be most welcome, and then ask for the things that the worshipper wishes for.

---

[11] **The troops . . . friendship:** The sacrificial procession.

[12] **the one . . . swift runner:** The earthly king who mounted the sacrificial horse, even as Indra rides the solar horse.

[13] **The goat, his kin:** Either the scapegoat for the sacrificial horse or a sacrificial companion to the horse.

The Upanishads [ninth century–first century B.C.E.]

Translated by Juan Mascaró

FROM

Maitri Upanishad

[In the Beginning]

In the beginning all was Brahman, ONE and infinite. He is beyond north and south, and east and west, and beyond what is above or below. His infinity is everywhere. In him there is neither above, nor across, nor below; and in him there is neither east nor west.

The Spirit supreme is immeasurable, inapprehensible, beyond conception, never-born, beyond reasoning, beyond thought. His vastness is the vastness of space.

At the end of the worlds, all things sleep: he alone is awake in Eternity. Then from his infinite space new worlds arise and awake, a universe which is a vastness of thought. In the consciousness of Brahman the universe is, and into him it returns.

He is seen in the radiance of the sun in the sky, in the brightness of fire on earth, and in the fire of life that burns the food of life. Therefore it has been said:

He who is in the sun, and in the fire and in the heart of man is ONE. He who knows this is one with the ONE.

The Upanishads. The first two selections from Maitri and Kena Upanishads deal with the difficulties of speaking about Brahman or Absolute Being, since the idea of Brahman can be grasped neither by reason nor speech. The first piece, "In the beginning," asserts the absolute sovereignty of Brahman and the ultimate oneness of all creation. The second piece, "Brahman," attempts the impossible task of capturing the reality of Brahman in analogies: for example, Brahman cannot be seen or heard, but Brahman lies behind or beneath the capacity for sight or sound. Several stanzas conclude with the phrase, "and not what people here adore." This phrase indicates that whenever someone tries to think about Brahman it is necessary to give the concept form and a name, and this is Ishvara, a personal god equal to the personal deities of Christianity and Islam. The Katha Upanishad tells the story of a young boy, Nachiketas, who pesters his father with the question, "To whom will you give me in sacrifice?" Nachiketas's angry father offers him to Death. Nachiketas waits three days in the realm of Death for the arrival of Yama, the god of death, who grants him three boons. Nachiketas asks for the forgiveness of his father and instructions for the fire sacrifice that leads to heaven. These two boons are granted. Nachiketas then asks what happens to humans after they die. By way of testing the boy, Yama tells him that even the gods have trouble with this question and offers substitutes. Nachiketas persists, and finally Yama teaches him the secret of immortality. This results in the threefold boons or the threefold fire of Nachiketas.

The Chandogya Upanishad, dated c. 900–800 B.C.E., is the second oldest Upanishad. Its eight chapters contain ideas about the origin of the cosmos, the connection between the individual soul and the universal soul, and life in the afterworld. It is famous for locating God not as something

FROM

Kena Upanishad

[Brahman]

Who sends the mind to wander afar? Who first drives life to start on its journey? Who impels us to utter these words? Who is the Spirit behind the eye and the ear?

It is the ear of the ear, the eye of the eye, and the Word of words, the mind of mind, and the life of life. Those who follow wisdom pass beyond and, on leaving this world, become immortal.

There the eye goes not, nor words, nor mind. We know not, we cannot understand, how he can be explained: He is above the known and he is above the unknown. Thus have we heard from the ancient sages who explained this truth to us.

What cannot be spoken with words, but that whereby words are spoken: Know that alone to be Brahman, the Spirit; and not what people here adore.

What cannot be thought with the mind, but that whereby the mind can think: Know that alone to be Brahman, the Spirit; and not what people here adore.

What cannot be seen with the eye, but that whereby the eye can see: Know that alone to be Brahman, the Spirit; and not what people here adore.

What cannot be heard with the ear, but that whereby the ear can hear: Know that alone to be Brahman, the Spirit; and not what people here adore.

What cannot be indrawn with breath, but that whereby breath is indrawn: Know that alone to be Brahman, the Spirit; and not what people here adore.

FROM

Katha Upanishad

[Driving the Chariot]

In the secret high place of the heart there are two beings who drink the wine of life in the world of truth. Those who know Brahman, those who keep the five sacred fires[1] and those who light the three-fold fire of Nachiketas[2] call them 'light' and 'shade'.

May we light the sacred fire of Nachiketas, the bridge to cross to the other shore where there is no fear, the supreme everlasting Spirit!

"out there" and far away, but within. In a charming parable about banyan fruit and salt, the nature of God is expressed in a simple formula, *TAT TVAM ASI*, "Thou are That."

A note on the translation: Juan Mascaró's excellent translation captures the subtle meanings of the texts. All footnotes are the editors'.

---

[1] **the five sacred fires:** The five sacred fires refers to an arduous spiritual exercise called the penance of the "Five Fires." Four fires symbolizing the four points of the compass are placed close around the penitent; the intense heat of the Indian sun is the "fifth fire."

[2] **three-fold . . . Nachiketas:** See note on p. 1346.

Know the Atman as Lord of a chariot; and the body as the chariot itself. Know that reason is the charioteer; and the mind indeed is the reins.

The horses, they say, are the senses; and their paths are the objects of sense. When the soul becomes one with the mind and the senses he is called 'one who has joys and sorrows'.

He who has not right understanding and whose mind is never steady is not the ruler of his life, like a bad driver with wild horses.

But he who has right understanding and whose mind is ever steady is the ruler of his life, like a good driver with well-trained horses.

He who has not right understanding, is careless and never pure, reaches not the End of the journey; but wanders on from death to death.

But he who has understanding, is careful and ever pure, reaches the End of the journey, from which he never returns.

The man whose chariot is driven by reason, who watches and holds the reins of his mind, reaches the End of the journey, the supreme everlasting Spirit.

Beyond the senses are their objects, and beyond the objects is the mind. Beyond the mind is pure reason, and beyond reason is the Spirit in man.

Beyond the Spirit in man is the Spirit of the universe, and beyond is Purusha,[3] the Spirit Supreme. Nothing is beyond Purusha: He is the End of the path.

The light of the Atman, the Spirit, is invisible, concealed in all beings. It is seen by the seers of the subtle, when their vision is keen and is clear.

The wise should surrender speech in mind, mind in the knowing self, the knowing self in the Spirit of the universe, and the Spirit of the universe in the Spirit of peace.

Awake, arise! Strive for the Highest, and be in the Light! Sages say the path is narrow and difficult to tread, narrow as the edge of a razor.

The Atman is beyond sound and form, without touch and taste and perfume. It is eternal, unchangeable, and without beginning or end: indeed above reasoning. When consciousness of the Atman manifests itself, man becomes free from the jaws of death.

The wise who can learn and can teach this ancient story of Nachiketas, taught by Yama, the god of death, finds glory in the world of Brahman.

He who, filled with devotion, recites this supreme mystery at the gathering of Brahmins, or at the ceremony of the Sradha[4] for the departed, prepares for Eternity, he prepares in truth for Eternity.

---

[3] **Purusha:** The cosmic being out of which the cosmos was created; see note on page 1342.

[4] **the Sradha:** The faithful; those who believe and trust.

FROM

Chandogya Upanishad

[Banyan Fruit and Salt]

Prajapati,[5] the Creator of all, rested in life-giving meditation over the worlds of his creation; and from them came the three *Vedas.*[6] He rested in meditation and from those came the three sounds: BHUR, BHUVAS, SVAR,[7] earth, air, and sky. He rested in meditation and from the three sounds came the sound OM.[8] Even as all leaves come from a stem, all words come from the sound OM. OM is the whole universe. OM is in truth the whole universe.

OM. There lived once a boy, Svetaketu Aruneya by name. One day his father spoke to him in this way: 'Svetaketu, go and become a student of sacred wisdom. There is no one in our family who has not studied the holy *Vedas* and who might only be given the name of Brahman by courtesy.'

The boy left at the age of twelve and, having learnt the *Vedas*, he returned home at the age of twenty-four, very proud of his learning and having a great opinion of himself.

His father, observing this, said to him: 'Svetaketu, my boy, you seem to have a great opinion of yourself, you think you are learned, and you are proud. Have you asked for that knowledge whereby what is not heard is heard, what is not thought is thought, and what is not known is known?'

'What is that knowledge, father?' asked Svetaketu.

'Just as by knowing a lump of clay, my son, all that is clay can be known, since any differences are only words and the reality is clay;[9]

Just as by knowing a piece of gold all that is gold can be known, since any differences are only words and the reality is only gold;

And just as by knowing a piece of iron all that is iron is known, since any differences are only words and the reality is only iron.'

Svetaketu said: 'Certainly my honoured masters knew not this themselves. If they had known, why would they not have told me? Explain this to me, father.'

'So be it, my child.'

[5] **Prajapati:** A title used in the Vedas to mean Indra; later the title was used for Brahma in his role as creator. The two other gods in the Brahmanic trinity are Vishnu (preserver) and Shiva (destroyer).

[6] **the three *Vedas:*** The first three Vedas—Rig, Yayur, and Sama—were thought to have preceded creation at the time of the Upanishads.

[7] **BHUR, BHUVAS, SVAR:** Sanskrit for "earth, air, sky."

[8] **OM:** *OM*, or *AUM*, is not a word but a sound that represents the composite sound of all of reality; as such it is a sound that powerfully unifies the physical, mental, and spiritual realms. It is commonly used in mantras by both Hindus and Buddhists. The meanings and uses of *OM* are manifold.

[9] **the reality is clay:** Clay commonly symbolizes Brahman since it is made into many common objects; if a clay cup represents the individual, the clay itself is Universal Being.

'Bring me a fruit from this banyan tree.'

'Here it is, father.'

'Break it.'

'It is broken, Sir.'

'What do you see in it?'

'Very small seeds, Sir.'

'Break one of them, my son.'

'It is broken, Sir.'

'What do you see in it?'

'Nothing at all, Sir.'

Then his father spoke to him: 'My son, from the very essence in the seed which you cannot see comes in truth this vast banyan tree.

Believe me, my son, an invisible and subtle essence is the Spirit of the whole universe. That is Reality. That is Atman. THOU ART THAT.'[10]

'Explain more to me, father,' said Svetaketu.

'So be it, my son.

Place this salt in water and come to me tomorrow morning.'

Svetaketu did as he was commanded, and in the morning his father said to him: 'Bring me the salt you put into the water last night.'

Svetaketu looked into the water, but could not find it, for it had dissolved.

His father then said: 'Taste the water from this side. How is it?'

'It is salt.'

'Taste it from the middle. How is it?'

'It is salt.'

'Taste it from that side. How is it?'

'It is salt.'

'Look for the salt again and come again to me.'

The son did so, saying: 'I cannot see the salt. I only see water.'

His father then said: 'In the same way, O my son, you cannot see the Spirit. But in truth he is here.

An invisible and subtle essence is the Spirit of the whole universe. That is Reality. That is Truth. THOU ART THAT.'

'Explain more to me, father.'

'So be it, my son.

Even as a man, O my son, who had been led blindfolded from his land of the Gandharas[11] and then left in a desert place, might wander to the East and North and South, because he had been taken blindfolded and left in an unknown place, but if a good man took off his bandage and told him "In that direction is the land of the Gandharas, go in that direction," then, if he were a wise man, he would go asking

[10] THOU ART THAT: *Tat tvam asi.* The essential connection between the universe and the individual cannot be grasped by the understanding, but only realized in a moment of consciousness. The use of the repeated phrase "Thou art that" is an attempt to pierce understanding with an immediate intimation of this connection.

[11] **Gandharas:** Gandhara is a region in the northwest of India that today includes parts of Afghanistan and Pakistan. It is a center of Buddhist art.

from village to village until he would have reached his land of the Gandharas; so it happens in this world to a man who has a Master to direct him to the land of the Spirit. Such a man can say: "I shall wander in this world until I attain liberation; but then I shall go and reach my Home."

This invisible and subtle essence is the Spirit of the whole universe. That is Reality. That is Truth. THOU ART THAT.'

THE RAMAYANA

C. 550 B.C.E.–C. 400 C.E.

While the sacred texts known as the Vedas and the Upanishads appeared between about 1200 and 400 B.C.E., the advent of narrative literature in India dates from the time of its two great epics, the *Ramayana* and the *Mahabharata,* begun between the sixth and fifth centuries B.C.E. Like Homer's *Iliad* and *Odyssey,* both the ***Ramayana*** and the *Mahabharata* contain stories, myths, and legends taken from an oral tradition of philosophical poems and ballads, hymns and prayers, and fables and tales. These legends and tales concern an earlier era of history, dating back to the time between 1500 and 1000 B.C.E. when **ARYAN** invaders established centers of power in the Punjab region of India in their advance eastward. At that time, the conquerors were divided among themselves over the distribution of their newly acquired territories, and both the *Ramayana* and the ***Mahabharata*** center on the stories of heroic figures involved in attempts to regain patrimonial kingdoms unjustly denied them. The *Ramayana,* said to be the "first poem," concerns the adventures of the exiled prince Rama, from the kingdom of **Kosala**, and his beloved Sita. The *Mahabharata* tells the story of a great war between two rival sets of cousins descended from the legendary king Bharata over a disputed inheritance.

ruh-MAH-yuh-nuh

muh-huh-BAH-ruh-tuh

KOH-suh-luh

As is the case with Homer's epics, the *Ramayana* and the *Mahabharata* have served as rich lodes of lore. The Indian epics have been mined by Indian and Southeast Asian dramatists, poets, fiction writers, dancers and choreographers, and—most recently—television and film artists. Unlike the Homeric epics, however, in India the *Ramayana* and *Mahabharata,* especially the **Bhagavad Gita** in Book 6 of the *Mahabharata,* play a vital role in Hindu life, providing religious and moral guidance even today. Thus, in contrast to the Greco-Roman mythology found in the epics of Homer and Virgil, which largely belongs to the past, the myths and legends of the Indian epics constitute fundamental elements of a cultural and spiritual tradition that is very much alive today throughout India and Southeast Asia.

p. 1492

Dating the Epics. The dating of the *Ramayana* and the *Mahabharata* is uncertain, and scholars continue to disagree even over which epic

WWW For a quiz on the *Ramayana,* see *World Literature Online* at bedfordstmartins.com/worldlit.

appeared first. The story that forms the core of *Ramayana* appeared sometime in the sixth century B.C.E., while the core of the *Mahabharata* probably formed sometime in the fourth century B.C.E. By that time the Aryans who had invaded the northwestern region of India were beginning to form kingdoms, centers of rule that eventually led to the Maurya (c. 322–185 B.C.E.) and Gupta (c. 320–550 C.E.) empires. The Gupta era was a period of great cultural efflorescence in India, during which time the epics were completed; it was also the era of Kalidasa (fourth century), India's greatest classical playwright and author of *Shakuntala*. The historical geography alluded to in the epics indicates that the *Ramayana* in its final version may be later than its counterpart, because **Ayodhya**, Rama's capital city, is located much farther east than Hastinapura and Indraprastha, the chief cities of the Kauravas and the Pandavas in the *Mahabharata*, which were settled later. Whichever text came first, both epics were revised over time by several hands, though the *Ramayana* is attributed to a legendary author named **Valmiki** and the *Mahabharata* to a legendary author named Vyasa, which means the "compiler" or "arranger."

uh-YOH-dyah

VAHL-mih-kee

Ramayana as Sacred Text. The *Ramayana* is the most influential and popular work in India and Southeast Asia, and its legendary author, Valmiki, is known as India's "first poet" or *adivaki*. The tragic and romantic story of Prince **Rama** and his wife, **Sita**, has been retold in many versions and languages throughout the region. In addition to the fourth-century B.C.E. Sanskrit version of Valmiki, there is an eleventh-century C.E. Tamil version by Kamban; a fifteenth-century Bengali version by Krittivasa; and, perhaps the most well known, a sixteenth-century Hindi version, the *Ramcaritmanas*, by Tulsidas (c. 1543–1623). Most recently, Indian novelist R. K. Narayan, working from the Tamil text, has produced an abridged modern version of the *Ramayana* in English.

RAH-muh; SEE-tah

The *Ramayana* has come to play a significant role in the Hindu religion; its protagonist, Prince Rama, came to be worshiped as an incarnation of the god **Vishnu** (the Preserver). By the fifteenth century, the divinity of Rama was well established, and devotion to Rama remains an important aspect of Hindu culture today. The Diwali, festival of lights, celebrates the return of Rama to Ayodhya, and remains an important festival throughout India and parts of Southeast Asia.

VISH-noo

Rama the Virtuous Hero. Consisting of seven books, or *kandas*, totaling 24,000 verses, the *Ramayana* is about one fourth the length of the *Mahabharata*. As in the *Mahabharata*, the core story of the *Ramayana* revolves around a dispute over rightful succession to the throne. Like its cousin epic, the *Ramayana* contains elements of the fantastic and marvelous, and descriptive accounts of heroic feats and war; more so than the *Mahabharata*, it contains moving descriptions of longing, love, and tragic separation, specifically between the lovers Rama and Sita. Unlike the *Mahabharata*, with its vast compendium of lore and its hundreds of tales within tales, the *Ramayana* displays more self-conscious unity and literary craftsmanship. It focuses primarily on the adventures of Prince Rama, the son of King **Dasharatha** and his primary queen, Kausalya,

duh-shuh-RUH-tuh

who live in Ayodhya, the capital city of Kosala, a kingdom in the northeastern region of central India now known as Bihar. Like Virgil's *Aeneid,* the *Ramayana* may be described as a **LITERARY EPIC**,[1] and the self-conscious determination of Rama to act in accordance with ***DHARMA***, sacred duty or law, may be compared to the virtue of "pious Aeneas," the hero of Virgil's epic.

In striking contrast to the sometimes self-conflicted heroes of the *Mahabharata,* Rama never goes astray from his duty nor fails to do what is right according to the sacred law (dharma). Similarly, his wife, Sita, exemplifies right action for married women, so that she and Rama are the ideal couple representing the perfect marriage. Like Penelope in Homer's *Odyssey,* Sita shows that she is devoted to her husband, succeeding in preserving her chastity when she is captured by the demon-king Ravana. Moreover, both Rama and Sita endure great suffering as they give up their individual desires for the greater good of following their principles. With their moral integrity and heroic self-control, Rama and Sita represent the embodiment of right action and sacred duty on earth.

The perfect relationship of husband and wife is illustrated by the relationship of Rama and Sita in the *Ramayana*. The husband is all tenderness and kindly consideration, the wife all humble duty, submissiveness, and self-effacing, self-sacrificing love.

– R. C. ZAEHNER, critic, 1962

A Tale of Origins. The epic begins with a preamble of four chapters that describe the invention of poetry by the sage and poet Valmiki. The story of Rama, like that of the Pandavas and Kauravas in the *Mahabharata,* begins with a tale of origins. In Book 1, the Bala Kanda, King Dasharatha, who is without a son and heir, summons a Brahmin ascetic to help him. The king's three wives then bear him four sons: Rama, Bharata, and the twins, **Lakshmana** and **Shatrughna**. Each of these sons is invested with a portion of the god Vishnu, who has taken human form in order to defeat the ten-headed demon Ravana who has angered the gods.

LUKSH-muh-nuh; shuh-TROOG-nuh

Forest Exile. As the boys grow older, Rama and his loyal brother Lakshmana leave for the forest, where they have been summoned to protect the hermitage of the sage Vishvamitra from *rakshasas,* or demons. His errand completed, Rama moves on to Mithila, the capital city of King Janaka of Videha. Here, like Odysseus on his return home to Ithaca, Rama bends a mighty bow, proving his strength and virtue. In return, King Janaka gives Rama the hand of his daughter Sita; Lakshmana marries another of the king's daughters, Urmula, and all the newlyweds head back to Ayodhya where they hope to live in peace.

In Book 2, the Ayodhya Kanda, complications arise when Kaikeyi, King Dasharatha's second wife, blocks Rama's impending appointment to the throne. Although the retiring king wants Rama to take over as

[1] **literary epic:** An epic may be defined as a long narrative poem written in an elevated style, usually focusing on the adventures of a larger-than-life hero of great significance to a culture or nation. In contrast to folk epics, such as the *Mahabharata* and *The Iliad,* which may consist of somewhat loosely linked episodes that closely follow oral conventions, the "literary epic" is written with self-conscious artistry, possesses a more tightly knit organic unity, and reflects a style rooted in a literate culture. In actuality, the great epics often blur the distinctions between the oral or folk epic and the literary epic.

Sita's Marriage Procession, 1260
The adventures of the hero Rama as he tries to regain his beloved wife, Sita, from the demon Ravana are at the center of the Ramayana, *which is Sanskrit for* "Romance of Rama." *(Somnathpur, Karnataka, India / Dinodia Picture Agency, Bombay / Bridgeman Art Library)*

acting regent, **Kaikeyi** (kigh-KAY-yee) wants that honor to go to her son, Bharata. Having promised to honor his wife's wishes, King Dasharatha has to banish Rama from Ayodhya; Bharata, in protest to his mother's cruelty to Rama, sets up his regency in a nearby village, refusing to set foot in the capital city until his brother returns. Accompanied by Sita and Lakshmana, Rama dutifully exiles himself from Ayodhya, leaving behind his grief-stricken father.

Book 3, the Aranya Kanda, describes the events that take place during Rama's exile in the Dandaka Forest, where Rama and his companions battle several bands of demons, kill the giant demon Viradha, and encounter **Shurpanakha** (shoor-puh-NUH-kah), a demon woman who tries to seduce the men and kill Sita. After Lakshmana scars Shurpanakha, word of Rama and Lakshmana's successes against the *rakshasas* reaches the archdemon **Ravana** (RAH-vuh-nuh), who takes revenge by kidnapping Sita and taking her to his fortress at Lanka, an island kingdom that some scholars identify as Sri Lanka (Ceylon).

The War against Ravana. Following Sita's abduction, Rama meets the monkey-king Sugriva, the ruler of the *vanaras,* or ape-people, at **Kishkindha** (kish-KIN-duh). Here, as told in Book 4, the Kishkindha Kanda, Rama wins the alliance of Hanuman, the greatest of the ***vanara*** (VAH-nuh-ruh) warriors, by slaying the monkey-king Valin, Sugriva's rival. The next two books—the Sundara Kanda and the Yuddha Kanda—describe the great Hanuman's siege of archdemon Ravana's fortress at **Lanka** (LAHNG-kuh) and the war against Ravana. First Hanuman, the son of the wind-god Vayu, leaps across the waterway dividing the continent from Lanka, spies on Ravana's city, and finds Sita. Because she refuses to be touched by any man other than her husband,

Sita refuses to go back with **Hanuman**, who is captured by Ravana's forces but later escapes and sets fire to the city. The great war takes place when the *vanaras* build a giant causeway across the strait to Lanka and besiege the city. Rama eventually slays Ravana and rescues Sita, whose virtue is proved when the fire-god Agni refuses to consume her when she throws herself into a sacrificial fire.

HUH-noo-mahn

The Return of Rama. In Book 7, the Uttara Kanda, the triumphant heroes return to Ayodhya only to meet further disappointment and tragedy. After several years of peace during which Rama and Sita live in happiness, the people of the city begin to doubt that Sita remained chaste while she was in Ravana's clutches. Although Rama is certain of his wife's innocence, he must banish Sita, pregnant with his twin children, in order to honor his duties as king. Sita goes to live in the ashram of Valmiki, the purported author of the epic. Many years after the heartbreaking separation, two poets arrive in Ayodhya and tell the story of the *Ramayana.* Learning that the poets are his twin sons, **Kusha** and Lava, Rama sends for Sita, who refuses to return. Instead, she calls on her mother, Earth, to take her away from the world of suffering. The disappointed Rama lives out his life as king and eventually divides his kingdom between his sons before reentering heaven as Vishnu, whose earthly role as avatar has been completed.

KOO-shuh

Rama achieves his life's goal because he unflaggingly follows in the path of *dharma,* his sacred duty: When Rama willingly follows his father's orders and goes into exile, he acts according to filial piety; when he avenges the abduction of Sita, he fulfills his duties as a husband and warrior; and when he exiles Sita even though he is certain of her purity, he upholds his responsibilities as king. The Ayodhya Kanda says that Rama wins the respect of his people because he is the ideal ruler, "fit to rule the three worlds, not just this one." That is, Rama is fit to rule the lower, middle, and upper worlds—to lead politically, morally, and spiritually. As the embodiment of perfection, Rama is the *sat-purusha,* "the ideal man devoted to truth, the fountain of righteousness and welfare."

■ CONNECTIONS

Homer, *The Odyssey,* p. 421. *Ramayana,* like Homer's *Odyssey,* is an epic poem that recounts the adventures of a hero who goes into exile and eventually returns home to regain his rightful throne. While away from the place of the familiar, Rama and Odysseus meet strangers who help or threaten them, who endow them with powers or test their strength and virtue. Consider the many similarities between Rama and Odysseus. What makes them both epic heroes? How do their encounters with the unfamiliar or their wanderings test and help to form their character?

Virgil, *The Aeneid,* p. 1181. As a literary epic drawing on and alluding to earlier written texts, the elaborately polished *Aeneid* contrasts with the *Mahabharata* and the *Ramayana,* which, like Homer's epics, were born of an oral tradition. Yet, like *The Aeneid,* the *Ramayana* displays a unity of purpose and focuses on the moral integrity of its protagonist, Rama. How does the virtue of "pious Aeneas" compare with Rama's strict observance of his *dharma,* or sacred duty? How do both heroes enact the founding of a civilization or culture?

Shakespeare, *The Tempest* (Book 3). Shakespeare's *The Tempest* depicts a Renaissance prince betrayed by his brother and exiled to the island of Setebos. In exile, the prince, Prospero, cultivates his mastery over the elements and orchestrates a plan to recover his lost dominion. Unlike Rama, Prospero cannot claim any share of divine origin, yet he strives after godlike powers. What do the differences between Prospero and Rama suggest about the culture of the European Renaissance and that of ancient India, especially with regard to the sacred and the secular nature of those cultures?

■ FURTHER RESEARCH

Literary History/Background

Dimock, Edward C. Jr., et al. *The Literatures of India: An Introduction.* 1974.

Flood, Gavin. *An Introduction to Hinduism.* 1996.

Zaehner, R. C. *Hinduism.* 1962, 1966.

Criticism

Alles, Gregory D. *The* Iliad, *The* Ramayana, *and the Work of Religion: Failed Persuasion and Religious Mystification.* 1994.

Brockington, J. L. *Righteous Rama: The Evolution of an Epic.* 1984.

Richman, Paula, ed. *Many Ramayanas: The Diversity of a Narrative Tradition in South Asia.* 1991.

Translations / Abridgements

Buck, William. *Ramayana.* 1976.

Coomaraswamy, Ananda K., and Sister Nivedita. *Ramayana.* In *Myths of the Hindus and Buddhists.* 1967.

Goldman, Robert P., and Sally J. Sutherland, eds. *The Ramayana of Valmiki: An Epic of Ancient India.* 7 vols. 1984–present.

Narayan, R. K. *The Ramayana: A Shortened Modern Prose Version of the Indian Epic.* 1972.

Shastri, Hari Prasad. *The Ramayana of Valmiki.* 3 vols. 1957.

Venkatesananda, Swami. *The Concise Ramayana.* 1988.

■ PRONUNCIATION

Aditi: AH-dih-tee, UH-dih-tee
Agastya: uh-GUS-tyuh
Aksha: UK-shuh
Ayodhyā: uh-YOH-dyah
Brahmā: BRAH-hmuh
Dasharatha (Daśaratha): duh-shuh-RUH-tuh
Dushana (Dūṣaṇa): DOO-shuh-nuh
Hanumān: HUH-noo-mahn
Jaṭāyu: juh-TAH-yoo
Kaikeyī: kigh-KAY-yee
Kausalyā: KOW-sul-yah
Kishkindha: kish-KIN-duh
Kosala: KOH-suh-luh
Kusha (Kuśa): KOO-shuh
Lakshmana (Lakṣmaṇa): LUKSH-muh-nuh
Laṅkā: LAHNG-kuh
Mārīca: MAH-rih-chah
Pañcavaṭī: pun-chuh-VUH-tee
Rāma: RAH-muh

Rāmāyaṇa: ruh-MAH-yuh-nuh
Rāvaṇa: RAH-vuh-nuh
Rishiashringa (Ṛṣyaśṛṅga): rish-yuh-SHRING-guh, ur-shyuh-SHURNG-guh
Sarayū: suh-RAH-yoo, SUH-ruh-yoo
Shatrughna (Śatrughna): shuh-TROOG-nuh, SHUT-roog-nuh
Shurpanakha (Sūrpaṇakha): shoor-puh-NUH-kah
Sita (Sītā): SEE-tah
Sumitrā: soo-MIH-truh
Vālmīki: VAHL-mih-kee
vānara: VAH-nuh-ruh
Vasishtha (Vasiṣṭha): vuh-SISH-tuh
Vishvamitra: vish-VAH-mih-truh
Vishnu (Viṣṇu): VISH-noo

***FROM* BOOK 1**

Bala Kanda: Boyhood of Rama

Translated by Swami Venkatesananda

BALA 13–14

A year had gone by: as enjoined by the scriptures, the king was ready to commence the horse-rite. Humbly he approached his preceptor Vasiṣṭha[1] and said: "You are a dear friend to me, my supreme preceptor, too: you alone can bear the burden of the proper execution of this rite." The sage Vasiṣṭha immediately assumed charge.

At Vasiṣṭha's behest, a whole new township sprang up on the northern bank of the holy river Sarayū[2] with ritual pits, palaces for royal guests, mansions for the officiating priests, stables for horses, elephants and so on, wells and markets, all of them

Ramayana. Like the *Mahabharata,* this text exists in several versions, or rescensions, texts compiled and edited from earlier sources. Attributed to Valmiki, considered by some to be India's "first poet," the *Ramayana* was revised by many hands over a five-hundred-year period from the sixth century B.C.E. to the fourth century C.E. As in the case of the *Mahabharata,* later editors added layers of Brahminic doctrine to the text and may have added the first and last chapters concerning Rama's origins and his death. The epic as it has come down to us is divided into seven books, or *kandas,* each divided into several chapters, or *sargas.* The original Sanskrit is written in a verse form known as the *shloka* meter, which consists of two sixteen-syllable lines, each line separated into two eight-syllable parts. Considered to be the most poetic of all ancient verse forms, the *shloka* provides a supple and rich medium for heroic epithets and similes, such as those found in Homeric epic poetry.

The selections from the *Ramayana* presented here begin with a brief episode from Book 1, the Bala Kanda (Boyhood), which describes the miraculous circumstances of Rama's birth. In Book 2,

[1] **Vasiṣṭha (Vasishtha):** A Brahmin sage who serves as King Daśaratha's spiritual guide.

[2] **Sarayū:** A river near Ayodhyā.

properly equipped to supply the needs of the numerous guests expected to grace the occasion. Vasiṣṭha personally instructed: "Every house should be well provided with food and other necessities. Ensure that the people of all the communities are nicely fed and attended to, with respect—never without respect and reverence. No one shall show the least disrespect or displeasure, leave alone anger, towards the guests." All those in charge humbly accepted the charge. Vasiṣṭha asked Sumantra[3] to invite

---

the Ayodhya Kanda (Life in Ayodhya), Queen Kaikeyi forces her husband, King Dasharatha, to appoint her son, Bharata, as crown regent and to exile Rama, another of the king's sons and the epic's hero, to the forest. Book 3, the Aranya Kanda (The Forest Life), recounts Rama's adventures in the forest, which climax when the demon-woman Shurpanakha tries to seduce both Rama and his brother Lakshmana and kill Sita, Rama's wife. Toward that end, Shurpanakha seeks help from the ten-headed demon Ravana, who kidnaps Sita and takes her to his island fortress at Lanka. After many harrowing days of searching for Sita, Rama and Lakshmana meet with the *vanaras,* the monkeys who will help them defeat Ravana and rescue Sita. Rama's life among the *vanaras* in their kingdom of Kishkindha is described in Book 4, which is omitted here. In Book 5, the Sundara Kanda (Beautiful Exploits), the monkey-general Hanuman leaps across the waters dividing the mainland from Lanka, where he spies on the demons and attempts to bring Sita back alone. She, however, refuses to be touched by a man other than her husband, even if he's her rescuer, and so it remains in Book 6, the Yuddha Kanda (The Great War), for Rama to bring her home after he kills Ravana in combat. Rama then returns with his wife to his home city of Ayodhya, where he rules in peace and happiness for several years until he learns that his people have begun questioning his wife's virtue. Setting his duties as king above his responsibilities—and desires—as a husband in Book 7, the Uttara Kanda (The Period after Coronation), Rama banishes his wife, not to hear of her again until her two sons by Rama, Lava and Kusa, show up one day at Ayodhya and tell the story of Rama, the *Ramayana,* which they learned from the sage Valmiki. Shortly thereafter, Sita commits herself to the earth instead of returning home to Rama, who follows her in death after dividing his kingdom between his two sons.

A note on the translations: The abridged prose version of the *Ramayana* used here, translated by Swami Venkatesananda, is a highly readable English retelling of Prince Rama's exile, his war against Ravana, and his return to Ayodhya. In addition, *Sargas* 1 and 2 of the Ayodhya Kanda, from an unabridged translation by Sheldon I. Pollock, edited by Robert P. Goldman, are presented to give readers a sense of the poetic character of the Sanskrit *Ramayana* as well as an idea of what is lost in the abridged versions. Although also written in prose, Pollock's translation is a fine example of the poetic character of the original *Ramayana,* giving full voice to the amplitude of the text, with its extended similes, heroic epithets, and other poetic devices.

Other abridged versions in English include those of Ananda K. Coomaraswamy and Sister Nivedita (1967), William Buck (1976), and R. K. Narayan (1972). For the complete *Ramayana,* readers should consult the ongoing, multivolume translation and critical edition under the general editorship of Robert P. Goldman (1984–present), or the translations of Hari Prasad Shastri (1957) and N. Raghunathan (1981–82).

All notes are the editors'. The spellings of names in the translation have not been romanized. Refer to the pronunciation guide for romanized spellings.

---

[3] **Sumantra:** One of King Daśaratha's retainers and advisors. He is the one who remembers the prophecy that the sage Ṛṣyaśṛṅga would somehow be involved in helping King Daśaratha produce heirs.

the princely neighbours, the kings of neighbouring kingdoms as also those afar, to attend the sacred rite. Very soon they began to arrive with rich presents for king Daśaratha. Everyone concerned reported back to Vasiṣṭha that the duty allotted to them had been accomplished. Once again, Vasiṣṭha warned them: "Serve and give all that is necessary to our guests, but give with respect; do not serve with disrespect or playfully; disrespectful service destroys the giver."

At the conclusion of the year of consecration, the sacred horse had also returned. With Ṛṣyaśṛṅga[4] at their head the priests now commenced the horse-rite, which proceeded in strict accordance with scriptural injunctions. In fact, the priests in their eagerness not to let a flaw creep in, exceeded even the scriptural demands in the performance of the rite. There was no flaw in the rite, the mantras were correctly recited and the ordained procedure was strictly adhered to. Vasiṣṭha had said: "Give, give food and clothes to all," and those in charge literally fulfilled this command. All the guests were thoroughly satisfied and blessed the king. The various beasts through whom the different deities were to be worshipped had been brought to the hall. The horse itself was richly decked and worshipped by the queens. Delighted that the horse-rite had concluded without an obstacle, the king gave away the land to the priests who, however, returned it to the king and accepted more useful monetary gifts from the king. They were all highly pleased.

The king fell at the feet of Ṛṣyaśṛṅga and the sage reassured the king that his wish would be fulfilled.

Bala 15–16

The holy sage Ṛṣyaśṛṅga contemplated deeply for a few minutes and then said to king Daśaratha: "I shall perform a sacred rite prescribed in the Atharva Veda,[5] adopting the method of the perfected heavenly beings, for the sake of securing the boon of progeny for you." As the sage commenced this sacred rite, the gods and the siddhas (demi-gods) descended upon the hall of worship in their ethereal forms. They worshipfully addressed Brahmā[6] the creator as follows: "Lord, relying on a boon you had conferred upon him, the demon Rāvaṇa[7] is oppressing all of us. According to that boon he cannot be killed by gods, demi-gods and demons: and so we are powerless

[4] **Ṛṣyaśṛṅga (Rishiashringa):** The Brahmin sage who has been summoned to guide the king through the horse sacrifice so that it will bring him a male heir.

[5] **Atharva Veda:** One of four ancient sacred texts known as the Vedas, which provide ritual incantations, hymns, and instructions for performing ritual sacrifices, such as the horse sacrifice, which is being performed here to invoke fertility for the king.

[6] **Brahmā:** The four-headed creator of the universe; one of the gods of the Hindu trinity, which includes Brahmā, the creator; Viṣṇu, the preserver: and Śiva, the destroyer.

[7] **Rāvaṇa:** The ten-headed *rakṣasa* or demon-king and archenemy of Rāma; he resides in the island kingdom of Lanka in a magnificent, well-fortified palace. Rāvaṇa, who represents the forces of disorder, is invincible to all supernatural powers, including gods, but he can be killed by a human being. Viṣṇu, therefore, takes human form to put an end to Rāvaṇa's evil.

against him. Even the natural elements function in obedience to him. Pray, find some means of putting an end to our tormentor."

The creator was sorely distressed to hear this and replied: "Rāvaṇa, proud and haughty that he was, only prayed that the gods, demi-gods and demons should not kill him: he held man in such utter contempt that he did not include man in the list! Hence, he can only be killed by a human being." As Brahmā said this, the lord Viṣṇu descended upon the scene. The gods now turned to him in heartfelt prayer: "Lord, we lay the burden of our misery upon your shoulders. Pray, incarnate yourself as a human being and destroy this Rāvaṇa who is an enemy of the world; who is invincible by gods. All of us—gods, demi-gods, demons, sages and hermits seek your refuge for protection: you are indeed the supreme refuge for us all." The lord Viṣṇu assured them that he would do the needful.

Lord Viṣṇu quickly decided that he would become the son of Daśaratha, at the same time fulfilling the wish of the gods. The lord at once became invisible to them all.

At the same time, a divine being emerged from the sacred fire, holding in his hands a golden bowl containing pāyasaṁ (a preparation of milk and rice). He said to king Daśaratha: "I am a messenger of Viṣṇu. With this sacred rite you have propitiated the lord. This pāyasaṁ which has been prepared by the gods is capable of conferring the boon of progeny upon you; take it and give it to your wives." Saying thus, that messenger disappeared into the sacred fire. King Daśaratha at once gave the pāyasaṁ to his wives. Half of it he gave to Kausalyā, half of what remained he gave to Sumitrā, half of the rest to Kaikeyī,[8] and what remained he gave again to Sumitrā. Such indeed was the potency of this divine pāyasaṁ that all of them instantly shone with the radiance appropriate to the presence of a divine being in their wombs.

Bala 17–18

Brahmā, the creator, commanded the gods: "Project part of your energies into the mortal world so that mighty beings may be born of you, in order to aid the Lord."

Thus commanded by the creator, the gods begot through vānara-women offspring mighty, powerful and strong and with the form and the external appearance of their celestial parent. Hanumān, the offspring of the wind-god, was the cleverest and the ablest of them all.

A year had rolled by. At the end of the twelfth month after quaffing the celestial pāyasaṁ, on the ninth day of the lunar (bright) fortnight in the month of Caitra (April-May), Kausalyā gave birth to the resplendent Rāma, the Lord of the universe, adored by all, who was indeed the manifestation of one half of lord Viṣṇu. After this, Kaikeyī gave birth to Bharata who was a quarter-manifestation of lord Viṣṇu. Sumi-

[8] **Kausalyā . . . Kaikeyī:** The three wives of King Daśaratha who give birth to Rāma, Lakṣmaṇa and Śatrughna, and Bharata, respectively.

trā gave birth to twins Lakṣmaṇa and Śatrughna, who, together formed the other quarter of lord Viṣṇu.

This was an occasion for great rejoicing not only in Ayodhyā and in the kingdom of Kosala, but in the celestial realm, for the Lord incarnate as the son of man would put an end to the reign of terror of the demon Rāvaṇa. The citizens gave the fullest reins to their eagerness to celebrate the event.

The preceptor of the king, Vasiṣṭha, christened the four sons Rāma, Lakṣmaṇa, Bharata and Śatrughna, and also lavished gifts upon all, on behalf of the king. Lakṣmaṇa became an inseparable companion to Rāma; they were one life in two bodies, and without Lakṣmaṇa Rāma would not even go to sleep. Even so, Bharata and Śatrughna were dear to each other.

All of them grew up into intelligent and wise young men, learned in the scriptures, exemplary in their conduct and devoted to the welfare of all. The king was supremely happy to see them thus grow into young men. [. . .]

[In the chapters omitted here from the Bāla Kānda, Rāma and Lakṣmaṇa go to the forest hermitage of Viśvāmitra, where they protect their host from demons. After successfully defending the sage, they go to Mithilā, the capital city of the kingdom of Videha. Here, Rāma wins the hand of Sītā, the daughter of King Janaka, by performing the superhuman feat of bending and breaking a mighty celestial bow. Rāma, Sītā, Lakṣmaṇa, and Lakṣmaṇa's new bride, Urmila, return to Ayodhyā, which is the point at which the narrative picks up; see page 1362.]

***FROM* BOOK 2**

Ayodhya Kanda: Life in Ayodhya°

Translated by Swami Venkatesananda

Queen Kausalyā was filled with supreme delight to behold beloved Rāma of unexcelled excellence grow into a young prince, even as Aditi rejoiced to see Indra.[9] Rāma was a perfectly perfect young man. He had all the noble qualities. He was fully self-controlled. He was patient with others' wrongs, but would do no wrong himself. He sought the company of elders and wise men. He had a highly cultivated mind, and his behaviour was highly cultured, too. His actions were governed by the highest code of righteousness; and he was not interested in unworthy conduct. In the science of warfare he was a pastmaster. He knew when to use violence, and when to restrain himself. Even his body was perfect, healthy, strong and handsome. He was alert in mind and was able to read the mind and the intentions of everyone that came to him. He was highly learned in the scriptures, and was therefore well versed in the injunctions and prohibitions concerning the three pursuits of life[10] (dharma, material wealth, and also pursuit of pleasure). He did not display his pleasure or displeasure in relation to others, and hence he earned the friendship of all. He was indeed the repository of all the good qualities, and he was, as it were, the very life of the people, moving outside their bodies.

King Daśaratha was delighted with all this: he was quite proud and fond of Rāma. At this time he noticed omens portending terrible evil. And he was growing old, too: naturally, therefore, he thought his own end was near. He mused: "How can I ensure that Rāma ascends the throne even while I am alive? Truly, he is more than worthy of being king. I am very old and have lived long enough. It would be the greatest blessing to see Rāma, the beloved of all, rule the earth before I go to heaven."

He did not lose much time before telling his ministers, preceptors and others about his wish. Since Rāma was extremely popular with all his subjects as well as with the ministers and preceptors there was really no problem, nor any impediment in the way of his ascending the throne. The king then invited to his court, the leaders of the community from all the towns and cities of his kingdom, to ascertain their view. He also invited the kings and rulers of all the neighbouring kingdoms and states, to ensure their approval, too, so that Rāma would be assured not only of the loyalty of his subjects but of the friendliness of all his neighbours. By an oversight, however, king Daśaratha had omitted to invite his own father-in-law the king of Kekayas and his son's father-in-law, king Janaka. All the invitees arrived, and assembled in the court.

---

[9] **as Aditi . . . Indra:** The goddess Aditi, mother of the universe and the gods, including the warrior-god Indra.
[10] **the three pursuits of life:** Hinduism recognizes three pursuits or goals of life: *kama,* or pleasure; *artha,* or wealth; and *dharma,* or duty, righteous living.

°Note: For the purpose of comparison, we've included an alternate translation of the part of the story on this page on the two pages that follow. This translation, by Sheldon I. Pollock and edited by Robert P. Goldman (pp. 1363–64), gives a sense of the poetic character of the original Sanskrit. Swami Venkatesananda's translation resumes on p. 1364.

***FROM* BOOK 2**

Ayodhya Kanda: Ayodhya

Alternate translation by Sheldon I. Pollock

12 Following his father's orders, righteous Rāma did all that was required to please and benefit the people of the city.

13 He scrupulously did all that his mothers required of him and attended to his gurus' requirements with strict punctuality.

14 Thus Daśaratha was pleased with Rāma's conduct and character, as were the brahmans, the merchants, and all who lived in the realm.

15 Rāma was always even-tempered and kind-spoken. Even if he were to be harshly addressed, he would not answer back.

16 He would be satisfied with a single act of kindness, whatever its motive, and would ignore a hundred injuries, so great was his self-control.

17 With good men — men advanced in years, virtue, and wisdom — he would converse at every opportunity, even during breaks in his weapons practice.

18 He was of noble descent on both sides of his family, he was upright and cheerful, truthful, and honest. Aged brahmans had seen to his training, men who were wise in the ways of righteousness and statecraft.

19 And thus he understood the true nature of righteousness, statecraft, and personal pleasure. He was retentive and insightful, knowledgeable and adept in the social proprieties.

20 He was learned in the sciences and skilled in the practice of them as well. He was an excellent judge of men and could tell when it was appropriate to show his favor or withhold it.

21 He knew the right means for collecting revenue and the accepted way of regulating expenditure. He had achieved preeminence in the sum total of the sciences, even the most complex.

22 Only after satisfying the claims of righteousness and statecraft would he give himself up to pleasure, and then never immoderately. He was a connoisseur of the fine arts and understood all aspects of political life.

23 He was proficient in training and riding horses and elephants, eminently knowledgeable in the science of weapons, and esteemed throughout the world as a master chariot fighter.

24 He could head a charge and give battle and lead an army skillfully. He was invincible in combat, even if the gods and *asuras* themselves were to unite in anger against him.

25 He was never spiteful, haughty, or envious, and he had mastered his anger. He would never look down on any creature nor bow to the will of time.

26 By his eminent virtues the prince won the esteem of people throughout all the three worlds, for he was patient as the earth, wise as Bṛhaspati, and mighty as Indra, Śacī's lord.

27 Rāma's virtues were prized by all the people, a source of joy to his father, and lent the prince himself such splendor as the sun derives from its shining beams.

28 His conduct and invincible valor made him so like one of the gods who guard the world that Earth herself desired to have him as her master.

29 Now, as King Daśaratha, slayer of enemies, observed the many incomparable virtues of his son, he fell to thinking.

30 In his heart he cherished this single joyous thought: "When shall I see my dear son consecrated?

31 "His one desire is that the world should prosper, he shows compassion to all creatures and is loved in the world even more than I, like a cloud laden with rain.

32 "He is as mighty as Yama or Śakra, wise as Bṛhaspati, steady as a mountain, and far richer in virtues than I.

33 "O that at my age I might go to heaven seeing my son holding sway over this entire land."

34 Recognizing that his son was endowed with these consummate virtues, the great king consulted with his advisers and chose him to be prince regent.

35 The lord of earth then convened the chief men of the land from the various cities and provinces in which they lived.

36 The nobles arrived and in the different places he assigned to them they solemnly took their seats, facing the king.

37 The lord of men paid his respects to the nobles and the men of the city and provinces, and as they sat deferentially around him he resembled Indra, the thousand-eyed lord, surrounded by the deathless gods.

Ayodhya 2–3

King Daśaratha addressed the assembly in the following words: "I have lived long and shouldered the onerous duties of king for a very long time. This body is aged and fatigued. I wish to appoint my son to protect my people, and give this body its much-needed and well-earned rest in retirement. I am convinced that he will excel me and all my ancestors and that his rule will be a great good fortune to the earth. Is this acceptable to you all?" The assembly heartily applauded the king's proposal. Its spokesman said: "King, indeed you have ruled us well and for long. It is time that Rāma, the beloved of all of us, is enthroned."

The king addressed them, again: "I am pleased with your spontaneous response. But, tell me, pray, why is it that you wish to have Rāma enthroned even while I am alive?" The response was instantaneous and spontaneous again. The assembly assured the king that they were not displeased with him, but they adored Rāma. The spokesman spoke up again: "Rāma is a sat-puruṣa, the ideal man devoted to truth, the fountain of righteousness and welfare. He is richly endowed with knowledge, wisdom, valour, compassion, self-control, every good quality that the ideal man should possess, and he totally identifies himself with the joys and sorrows of the people and as such, is the ideal ruler. He is fit to rule the three worlds,[11] not just this one: and neither his anger nor his pleasure is purposeless. We feel that the kingdom is eager to have Rāma installed on the throne. We know that all the people, especially the womenfolk, daily pray that he should become their king." King Daśaratha was highly pleased and thanked them for their concurrence in his proposal.

After the assembly had dispersed, King Daśaratha humbly submitted to the sage Vasiṣṭha: "Holy sir, let everything needed be quickly done, to install Rāma on the throne." Vasiṣṭha in turn instructed the ministers. They reported back to the king that all had been arranged.

The king thereupon sent for Rāma who, on arrival, fell prostrate on the ground at the feet of his father. After embracing him, the king announced his intention: "You are my eldest and most beloved son; and you are the beloved of all our people. Hence ascend the throne as the yuvarājā (crown prince). You are excellent in every way: but on the eve of your enthronement I shall tender this friendly advice: 'Shun vices and adhere to righteousness. Do what is pleasing to your friends and the people, and they will be devoted to you.'" In the meantime, some of Rāma's friends went to his mother Kausalyā and conveyed the exceedingly glad tidings to her. She and all the citizens who heard it prayed to God for the success of the enthronement. [. . .]

Ayodhya 6–7

[. . .] Everywhere in the city, people were congregating and discussing the glorious event of the day. Troupes of artistes were performing, some of them enacting plays based on the lives of Rāma and his ancestors. Everywhere people had also erected 'dīpa-vṛkṣa' (trees with decorative lamps). Everybody was singing the glories of Rāma.

Somehow, Kaikeyī (the last wife of Daśaratha) had not been informed of all this. Her maid-servant Mantharā happened to see the festivities and the celebrations in the city, and also she noticed that Kausalyā's maid-servants were expensively dressed. On enquiry, she discovered the cause of all this. She rushed to Kaikeyī who had retired to bed and violently shook her saying in great agitation: "Get up! How can you rest? A great calamity awaits you. The person you love most, the person who pretends to love you dearly and whom you trust implicitly, is about to betray you and plunge you into misery." Calmly Kaikeyī asked her: "Are you sick? What are you saying?" Getting still more agitated Mantharā said: "Your ruin is at hand. King Daśaratha is going to crown Rāma tomorrow."

---

[11] **He . . . the three worlds:** The three worlds are the heavens, the earth, and the atmosphere (sometimes the underworld). In other words, Rāma is fit to rule the universe.

Mantharā went on: "You are the daughter of a king. You are the beloved consort of a great king. Yet, you do not realise the intricacies of palace intrigues. I am only your maid-servant who is devoted to your welfare. I can clearly see your downfall when Rāma and therefore his own mother Kausalyā, will become all-powerful, and your good fortune, and therefore mine, too, will come to an end. Oh, what a tragedy: you trusted and loved the king, not realising that you were holding a venomous reptile close to your bosom. You and your son Bharata have been deceived by the king. Awake, Kaikeyī, and act quickly to save yourself."

Pleased with the good news and not responding to Mantharā's panic, Kaikeyī gave rich and valuable presents to the maid-servant, saying "I do not see any difference between Rāma and Bharata; therefore, I am delighted to hear that the king is going to crown Rāma."

AYODHYA 8–9

Contemptuously throwing away the precious royal gifts, Mantharā continued: "How foolish of you to rejoice at the success of your enemy! Lucky Kausalyā! Very soon she will have you as her chief maid-servant. And, your beloved son Bharata who could be king, who has every right to be king, who is as much eligible to be king as Rāma is, might even be banished from the kingdom, if not from this earth!" Disgusted with the way Mantharā went on, Kaikeyī said firmly: "What has come over you, O Mantharā? Rāma is as dear to me as Bharata. Rāma, too, treats me with greater devotion and serves me more than he serves Kausalyā. If Rāma is crowned king, it is as good as if Bharata is crowned king, for Rāma treats Bharata as his own self." But Mantharā could not be silenced: she went on and on.

Mantharā's persistence paid off. Her evil counsel worked. Kaikeyī's anger was roused. She said: "Kindly devise a plan: what can I do?" Exulting over her victory, Mantharā quickly answered: "Of course, I have the plan ready. You yourself told me that during a war between Indra and the demons, king Daśaratha lay wounded and unconscious on the field, and you saved his life, and that he then offered you two boons which, however, you did not choose at that time. Probably you have forgotten: because I love you, I remember that story. First make the king promise that he will now honour his offer and give the two boons of your choice. And these should be: first, Bharata should be installed on the throne, and second, Rāma should be banished from the kingdom for fourteen years. If Rāma goes away for fourteen years, Bharata who has all the qualities of a monarch, can win the confidence of the people and consolidate his position. The king loves you dearly and will not refuse the boons. He might, however, offer gold and jewels instead: refuse to accept them. Let nothing deflect you from this twofold purpose. Do not be content with Bharata's coronation: insist on Rāma's banishment."

Mantharā's persuasiveness made evil appear to be good! Kaikeyī fell for it. She even glorified Mantharā: "They say that deformed people are sinful and wicked, but in your case, the hunchback is packed with wonderful tricks. I should worship the hump which enhances your most charming form." Mantharā returned to her theme: "No one builds a dam after the water has flowed away! Do it now." Entering 'the chamber of displeasure' Kaikeyī threw around herself the jewelry that had adorned her and flung herself on the floor, and said to Mantharā: "Rāma shall go to the forest; Bharata shall be king or you will inform the king that I am dead." Finally, once more, Mantharā reminded Kaikeyī of the danger ahead and counselled her to stand fast on her decision.

Ayodhya 10–11

When all the arrangements for the coronation had been made the king wanted to convey the happy news to his beloved wife Kaikeyī. He entered her palace which shone like a celestial mansion. He did not find her in the bed-chamber: overcome by an intense desire to be with her, he enquired about her whereabouts. Never before had she failed to lovingly greet him at that hour! A maid-servant informed the king: "In great anger, the queen is lying in the chamber of displeasure." Greatly distressed by this information, the king rushed to that chamber and saw his most beloved queen lying on the floor, with all her jewelry flung around her person. Sitting by her side, taking her hand into his, the king addressed her in the following consoling words: "My beloved, are you not well? Tell me: I shall have you served by the best and most able doctors. Has someone insulted you? Or, do you wish that someone should be killed who does not deserve to be killed, or do you wish a condemned person to be freed? Do you wish that I should enrich a pauper or deprive a wealthy man of his wealth? Myself and all that belongs to me are yours, and I cannot go against your wishes. Please get up and tell me what the matter is."

Thus comforted, Kaikeyī resolved to torment her husband still further. She said: "First, promise that you will do what I ask you to do; and then I shall let you know what I want." Delighted at the prospect of reconciliation, the king said: "In the name of Rāma whom I love most and without whom I cannot live even for a moment, I promise to do whatever you wish." And he thus promised thrice, and once again prayed to her to name her wish.

Taking the fullest and immediate advantage of this, Kaikeyī called the very gods to witness the proceedings, in the following words: "You are a righteous monarch: let the gods bear witness to your most solemn vow." Then, she proceeded: "Do you remember that on the battlefield when I saved your life, you offered me two boons? I said then that I would ask for them later. I want them now." The king patiently waited for her to name the boons. He was bound by his own vow. Kaikeyī continued: "You have made elaborate preparations to install Rāma on the throne. Using the same preparations, my son Bharata should be installed on the throne. This is my first boon. And the second boon is: let Rāma immediately proceed to Daṇḍaka forest and live there as a hermit for fourteen years. Wearing the bark of trees and deer skin, let Rāma become a hermit; and let Bharata enjoy the sovereignty of the kingdom. You are devoted to truth, and the wise say that truthfulness is the key to heaven. Therefore, adhere to your promise."

AYODHYA 12

Hit by the cruel shafts of Kaikeyī's words, the king was stupefied for a few moments. He wondered: "Am I fancying all this, or is my mind deranged, or is my mind re-enacting a past event or am I sick?" But a look at Kaikeyī convinced him that it was none of these. It was real. He promptly fainted. When he came to, he spoke to Kaikeyī in great anger and anguish: "Wicked woman, what has Rāma done to you that you are so cruel to him? He is more devoted to you, than to his mother: and you yourself used to praise him to me. The whole world sings his glory; for what fault shall I exile him? Oh, no: I shall abandon Kausalyā, Sumitrā, all my wealth, and even my life: but I shall not abandon my beloved Rāma. If you wish, I shall crown Bharata."

But Kaikeyī was unyielding. She said: "Ah, well, if you wish to go back on your word, if you wish to disgrace the fame of your dynasty, if you wish to be the laughing stock of wise and noble men, do so! Forsaking righteousness would you like to enjoy life with Kausalyā and Rāma? Shame on you. If my boons are not granted, I shall take poison and die!" Daśaratha began to wail and rave: but Kaikeyī did not even seem to listen. Seeing her determination and the terrible promise made by him, Daśaratha thought of Rāma and fell down like a felled tree.

Daśaratha pleaded again: "If I agree to your demands, people will say of me: 'For the sake of a woman, the king banished the noble and righteous Rāma; how could such a fool rule Ayodhyā for so long?' For your sake I ignored all the loving service that Kausalyā rendered to me, though to me she was a servant, a friend, a wife, a sister and a mother all in one, and she is the mother of my pet son. Ah, I did not realise that I was harbouring in you a venomous cobra in the shape of a wife! If I send Rāma away, Lakṣmaṇa also will go with him. Unable to bear his separation I shall die. You will rule as a widow: and how cruelly you will govern my beloved people! If I tell Rāma, 'Go to the forest', he will instantly obey me. He is incarnate dharma. How can you even conceive of this tender and glorious prince going to the forest, living on roots and fruits, wearing coarse apparel and roaming the forest on foot? If Bharata is pleased with this proposal to banish Rāma, he should not even perform my obsequies. Cruel woman, when you uttered those cruel words, your teeth should have broken into pieces and fallen from your mouth. I do not care if you faint, burn yourself, die, or enter the bowels of the earth: I will not do as you ask me to do. I bow down to you. I even touch your feet. Please bless me and save me." Daśaratha fell down, though his hands could not reach Kaikeyī's outstretched feet.

AYODHYA 13–14

But, Kaikeyī was unmoved, and repeated: "I am only claiming the boons which I had already earned and which are due to me. You promise, you break your promise, and you also boast that you are righteous!" Once again, Daśaratha lost his consciousness. On regaining consciousness, he once again pleaded: "Surely I shall die when Rāma leaves Ayodhyā. If the gods question me in the other world, if I reply: 'On account of my love for Kaikeyī, Rāma went to the forest' even that would be untruth. How can I ask my beloved Rāma to go to Daṇḍaka forest? If I die before inflicting this undeserved pain on Rāma, that will indeed be better for me." Kaikeyī was unmoved; but time moved on.

It was getting close to dawn. The palace musicians began to play the music with which they usually awoke the king; but the king stopped them that day. He was awake, distressed and restless. Seeing this, Kaikeyī declared: "You have promised the boons; why are you lying down like this? You should get busy fulfilling your promise. The knowers of righteous conduct declare that truth alone is the highest dharma; standing firmly on truth I prompt you to do what is right. The king Sibi attained to the supreme state by adhering to truth and sacrificing his very body. By parting with his very eyes and giving them to a brāhmaṇa, the king Alārka[12] attained fame. Adhering to truth and in fulfilment of its promise, the ocean does not transgress its bounds. Stick to truth. Send your son to the forest. If you do not, I shall die here in front of you."

Daśaratha clearly saw that he was bound by his own word. He cried: "I disown you and your son. When I die, let Rāma offer the libations. The libations should not be offered by you or your son. I have seen the joy on the faces of my people; how shall I see their grief-stricken faces on Rāma's departure to the forest?" But, Kaikeyī urged him: "Time is passing. Instead of wailing thus, call Rāma; when you send him away to the forest and install Bharata on the throne, you will have discharged your duty." Daśaratha agreed: "I am bound by the cords of dharma; I have lost my sense. I wish to see Rāma."

Eager to commence the auspicious ceremonies, Vasiṣṭha and his retinue arrived at the palace. He sent Sumantra to the king to announce his arrival and that everything was ready for the installation ceremony. Sumantra approached the room where the king was and in sublime words awakened him. They were hurtful to the agonised king who stopped him. The king could not speak: hence, Kaikeyī said on his behalf: "The king was awake the whole night and he is tired. He wishes to see Rāma." Puzzled, Sumantra looked at the king who confirmed: "Go and fetch Rāma." He left.

Ayodhya 15–16

The brāhmaṇas had got everything ready for the coronation ceremonies. Gold pots of holy water from all the sacred rivers, most of them gathered at their very source, were ready. All the paraphernalia like the umbrella, the chowries, an elephant and a white horse, were ready, too.

But, the king did not emerge, though the sun had risen and the auspicious hour was fast approaching. The priests and the people wondered: "Who can awaken the king, and inform him that he had better hurry up!" At that moment, Sumantra emerged from the palace. Seeing them, he told them: "Under the king's orders I am going to fetch Rāma." But, on second thought, knowing that the preceptors and the priests commanded even the king's respect, he returned to the king's presence to

[12] **king Alārka:** In *Mahabharata,* Alārka is said to be a just king and ruler of the Kasikaurusas.

announce that they were awaiting him. Standing near the king, Sumantra sang: "Arise, O king! Night has flown. Arise and do what should be done." The weary king asked: I ordered you to fetch Rāma, and I am not asleep. Why do you not do as you are told to do?" This time, Sumantra hurried out of the palace and sped to Rāma's palace.

Entering the palace and proceeding unobstructed through the gates and entrances of the palace, Sumantra beheld the divine Rāma, and said to him: "Rāma, the king who is in the company of queen Kaikeyī desires to see you at once." Immediately Rāma turned to Sītā and announced: "Surely, the king and mother Kaikeyī wish to discuss with me some important details in connection with the coronation ceremony. I shall go and return soon." Sītā, for her part, offered a heartfelt prayer to the gods: "May I have the blessing of humbly serving you during the auspicious coronation ceremony!"

As Rāma emerged from his palace there was great cheer among the people who hailed and applauded him. Ascending his swift chariot he proceeded to the king's palace, followed by the regalia. Women standing at the windows of their houses and richly adorned to express their joy, showered flowers on Rāma. They praised Kausalyā, the mother of Rāma; they praised Sītā, Rāma's consort: "Obviously she must have done great penance to get him as her husband." The people rejoiced as if they themselves were being installed on the throne. They said to one another: "Rāma's coronation is truly a blessing to all the people. While he rules, and he will rule for a long time, no one will even have an unpleasant experience, or ever suffer." Rāma too was happy to see the huge crowds of people, the elephants and the horses—indicating that people had come to Ayodhyā from afar to witness the coronation.

Ayodhya 17–18

As Rāma proceeded in his radiant chariot towards his father's palace, the people were saying to one another: "We shall be supremely happy hereafter, now that Rāma will be king. But, who cares for all this happiness? When we behold Rāma on the throne, we shall attain eternal beatitude!" Rāma heard all this praise and the people's worshipful homage to him, with utter indifference as he drove along the royal road. The chariot entered the first gate to the palace. From there on Rāma went on foot and respectfully entered the king's apartments. The people who had accompanied him eagerly waited outside.

Rushing eagerly and respectfully to his father's presence, Rāma bowed to the feet of his father and then devoutly touched the feet of his mother Kaikeyī, too. "O Rāma!" said the king: he could not say anything more, because he was choked with tears and grief. He could neither see nor speak to Rāma. Rāma sensed great danger: as if he had trodden on a most poisonous serpent. Turning to Kaikeyī, Rāma asked her: "How is it that today the king does not speak kindly to me? Have I offended him in any way? Is he not well? Have I offended prince Bharata or any of my mothers? Oh, it is agonising: and incurring his displeasure I cannot live even for an hour. Kindly reveal the truth to me."

In a calm, measured and harsh tone, Kaikeyī now said to Rāma: "The king is neither sick nor angry with you. What he must tell you he does not wish to, for fear of displeasing you. He granted me two boons. When I named them, he recoiled. How can a truthful man, a righteous king, go back on his own word? Yet that is his predicament at the moment. I shall reveal the truth to you if you assure me that you will honour your father's promise." For the first time Rāma was distressed: "Ah, shame! Please do not say such things to me! For the sake of my father I can jump into fire. And, I assure you, Rāma does not indulge in double talk. Hence, tell me what the king wants to be done."

Kaikeyī lost no time. She said: "Long ago I rendered him a great service, and he granted me two boons. I claimed them now: and he promised. I asked for these boons: that Bharata should be crowned, and that you should go away to Daṇḍaka forest now. If you wish to establish that both you and your father are devoted to truth, let Bharata be crowned with the same paraphernalia that have been got ready for you, and go away to the forest for fourteen years. Do this, O best of men, for that is the word of your father; and thus would you redeem the king."

Ayodhya 19–20

Promptly and without the least sign of the slightest displeasure, Rāma said: "So be it! I shall immediately proceed to the forest, to dwell there clad in bark and animal skin. But why does not the king speak to me, nor feel happy in my presence? Please do not misunderstand me; I shall go, and I myself will gladly give away to my brother Bharata the kingdom, wealth, Sītā and even my own life, and it is easier when all this is done in obedience to my father's command. Let Bharata be immediately requested to come. But it breaks my heart to see that father does not say a word to me directly."

Kaikeyī said sternly: "I shall attend to all that, and send for Bharata. I think, however, that you should not delay your departure from Ayodhyā even for a moment. Even the consideration that the father does not say so himself, should not stop you. Till you leave this city, he will neither bathe nor eat." Hearing this, the king groaned, and wailed aloud: "Alas, alas!" and became unconscious again. Rāma decided to leave at once and he said to Kaikeyī: "I am not fond of wealth and pleasure: but even as the sages are, I am devoted to truth. Even if father had not commanded me, and you had asked me to go to the forest I would have done so! I shall presently let my mother and also Sītā know of the position and immediately leave for the forest."

Rāma was not affected at all by this sudden turn of events. As he emerged from the palace, with Lakṣmaṇa, the people tried to hold the royal umbrella over him: but he brushed them aside. Still talking pleasantly and sweetly with the people, he entered his mother's apartment. Delighted to see him, Kausalyā began to glorify and bless him and asked him to sit on a royal seat. Rāma did not, but calmly said to her: "Mother, the king has decided to crown Bharata as the yuvarājā and I am to go to the forest and live there as a hermit for fourteen years." When she heard this, the queen fell down unconscious and grief-stricken. In a voice choked with grief, she said: "If I had been barren, I would have been unhappy; but I would not have had to endure this terrible agony. I have not known a happy day throughout my life. I have had to endure the taunts and the insults of the other wives of the king. Nay, even he did not treat me with kindness or consideration: I have always been treated with less affection and respect than Kaikeyī's servants were treated. I thought that after your birth, and after your coronation my luck would change. My hopes have been shattered. Even death seems to spurn me. Surely, my heart is hard as it does not break into pieces at this moment of the greatest misfortune and sorrow. Life is not worth living without you; so if you have to go to the forest, I shall follow you."

Ayodhya 21

Lakṣmaṇa said: "I think Rāma should not go to the forest. The king has lost his mind, overpowered as he is by senility and lust. Rāma is innocent. And, no righteous man in his senses would forsake his innocent son. A prince with the least knowledge of statesmanship should ignore the childish command of a king who has lost his senses." Turning to Rāma, he said: "Rāma, here I stand, devoted to you, dedicated to your cause. I am ready to kill anyone who would interfere with your coronation—even if it is the king! Let the coronation proceed without delay."

Kausalyā said: "You have heard Lakṣmaṇa's view. You cannot go to the forest because Kaikeyī wants you to. If, as you say, you are devoted to dharma, then it is your duty to stay here and serve me, your mother. I, as your mother am as much worthy of your devotion and service as your father is: and I do not give you permission to go to the forest. If you disobey me in this, terrible will be your suffering in hell. I cannot live here without you. If you leave, I shall fast unto death."

Rāma, devoted as he was to dharma, spoke: "Among our ancestors were renowned kings who earned fame and heaven by doing their father's bidding. Mother, I am but following their noble example." To Lakṣmaṇa he said: "Lakṣmaṇa, I know your devotion to me, love for me, your prowess and your strength. The universe rests on truth: and I am devoted to truth. Mother has not understood my view of truth, and hence suffers. But I am unable to give up my resolve. Abandon your resolve based on the principle of might; resort to dharma; let not your intellect become aggressive. Dharma, prosperity and pleasure are the pursuit of mankind here; and prosperity and pleasure surely follow dharma: even as pleasure and the birth of a son follow a dutiful wife's service of her husband. One should turn away from that action or mode of life which does not ensure the attainment of all the three goals of life, particularly of dharma; for hate springs from wealth and the pursuit of pleasure is not praiseworthy. The commands of the guru, the king, and one's aged father, whether uttered in anger, cheerfully, or out of lust, should be obeyed by one who is not of despicable behaviour, with a view to the promotion of dharma. Hence, I cannot swerve from the path of dharma which demands that I should implicitly obey our father. It is not right for you, mother, to abandon father and follow me to the forest, as if you are a widow. Therefore, bless me, mother, so that I may have a pleasant and successful term in the forest."

Ayodhya 22–23

Rāma addressed Lakṣmaṇa again: "Let there be no delay, Lakṣmaṇa. Get rid of these articles assembled for the coronation. And with equal expedition make preparations for my leaving the kingdom immediately. Only thus can we ensure that mother Kaikeyī attains peace of mind. Otherwise she might be worried that her wishes may not be fulfilled! Let father's promise be fulfilled. Yet, so long as the two objects of Kaikeyī's desire are not obtained, there is bound to be confusion in everyone's mind. I must immediately leave for the forest; then Kaikeyī will get Bharata here and have him installed on the throne. This is obviously the divine will and I must honour it without delay. My banishment from the kingdom as well as my return are all the fruits of my own doing (kṛtānta: end of action). Otherwise, how could such an unworthy thought enter the heart of noble Kaikeyī? I have never made any distinction between her and my mother; nor has she ever shown the least disaffection for me so far. The 'end' (reaction) of one's own action cannot be foreseen: and this which we call 'daiva' (providence or divine will) cannot be known and cannot be avoided by anyone. Pleasure, pain, fear, anger, gain, loss, life and death—all these are brought about by 'daiva'. Even sages and great ascetics are prompted by the divine will to give up their self-control and are subjected to lust and anger. It is unforeseen and inviolable. Hence, let there be no hostility towards Kaikeyī; she is not to blame. All this is not her doing, but the will of the divine."

Lakṣmaṇa listened to all this with mixed feelings: anger at the turn events had taken, and admiration for Rāma's attitude. Yet, he could not reconcile himself to the situation as Rāma had done. In great fury, he burst forth: "Your sense of duty is misdirected, O Rāma. Even so is your estimation of the divine will. How is it, Rāma, that being a shrewd statesman, you do not see that there are self-righteous people who merely pretend to be good for achieving their selfish and fraudulent ends? If all these boons and promises be true, they could have been asked for and given long ago! Why did they have to wait for the eve of coronation to enact this farce? You ignore this aspect and bring in your argument of the divine will! Only cowards and weak people believe in an unseen divine will: heroes and those who are endowed with a strong mind do not believe in the divine will. Ah, people will see today how my determination and strong action set aside any decrees of the divine will which may be involved in this unrighteous plot. Whoever planned your exile will go into exile! And you will be crowned today. These arms, Rāma, are not handsome limbs, nor are these weapons worn by me ornaments: they are for your service."

AYODHYA 24–25

Kausalyā said again: "How can Rāma born of me and the mighty emperor Daśaratha live on food obtained by picking up grains and vegetables and fruits that have been discarded? He whose servants eat dainties and delicacies—how will he subsist on roots and fruits? Without you, Rāma, the fire of separation from you will soon burn me to death. Nay, take me with you, too, if you must go."

Rāma replied: "Mother, that would be extreme cruelty towards father. So long as father lives, please serve him: this is the eternal religion. To a woman her husband is verily god himself. I have no doubt that the noble Bharata will be very kind to you and serve you as I serve you. I am anxious that when I am gone, you should console the king so that he does not feel my separation at all. Even a pious woman who is otherwise righteous, if she does not serve her husband, is deemed to be sinner. On the other hand, she who serves her husband attains blessedness even if she does not worship the gods, perform the rituals or honour the holy men."

Seeing that Rāma was inflexible in his resolve, Kausalyā regained her composure and blessed him. "I shall eagerly await your return to Ayodhyā, after your fourteen years in the forest," said Kausalyā.

Quickly gathering the articles necessary, she performed a sacred rite to propitiate the deities and thus to ensure the health, safety, happy sojourn and quick return of Rāma. "May dharma which you have protected so zealously protect you always," said Kausalyā to Rāma. "May those to whom you bow along the roads and the shrines protect you! Even so, let the missiles which the sage Viśvāmitra gave you ensure your safety. May all the birds and beasts of the forest, celestial beings and gods, the mountains and the oceans, and the deities presiding over the lunar mansions, natural phenomena and the seasons be propitious to you. May the same blessedness be with you that Indra enjoyed on the destruction of his enemy Vṛtra, that Vinata bestowed upon her son Garuḍa, that Aditi pronounced upon her son Indra when he was fighting the demons, and that Viṣṇu enjoyed while he measured the heaven and earth. May the sages, the oceans, the continents, the Vedas and the heavens be propitious to you."

As Rāma bent low to touch her feet, Kausalyā fondly embraced him and kissed his forehead, and then respectfully went round him before giving him leave to go.

Ayodhya 26–27

Taking leave of his mother, Rāma sought the presence of his beloved wife, Sītā. For her part, Sītā who had observed all the injunctions and prohibitions connected with the eve of the coronation and was getting ready to witness the auspicious event itself, perceived her divine spouse enter the palace and with a heart swelling with joy and pride, went forward to receive him. His demeanour, however, puzzled her: his countenance reflected sorrow and anxiety. Shrewd as she was she realised that something was amiss, and hence asked Rāma: "The auspicious hour is at hand; and yet what do I see! Lord, why are you not accompanied by the regalia, by men holding the ceremonial umbrella, by the royal elephant and the horses, by priests chanting the Vedas, by bards singing your glories? How is it that your countenance is shadowed by sorrow?"

Without losing time and without mincing words, Rāma announced: "Sītā, the king has decided to install Bharata on the throne and to send me to the forest for fourteen years. I am actually on my way to the forest and have come to say good-bye to you. Now that Bharata is the yuvarājā, nay king, please behave appropriately towards him. Remember: people who are in power do not put up with those who sing others' glories in their presence: hence do not glorify me in the presence of Bharata. It is better not to sing my praises even in the presence of your companions. Be devoted to your religious observances and serve my father, my three mothers and my brothers. Bharata and Śatrughna should be treated as your own brothers or sons. Take great care to see that you do not give the least offence to Bharata, the king. Kings reject even their own sons if they are hostile, and are favourable to even strangers who may be friendly. This is my counsel."

Sītā feigned anger, though in fact she was amused. She replied to Rāma: "Your advice that I should stay here in the palace while you go to live in the forest is unworthy of a heroic prince like you, Lord. Whereas one's father, mother, brother, son and daughter-in-law enjoy their own good or misfortune, the wife alone shares the life of her husband. To a woman, neither father nor son nor mother nor friends but the husband alone is her sole refuge here in this world and in the other world, too. Hence I shall accompany you to the forest. I shall go ahead of you, clearing a path for you in the forest. Life with the husband is incomparably superior to life in a palace, or an aerial mansion, or a trip to heaven! I have had detailed instructions from my parents on how to conduct myself in Ayodhyā! But I shall not stay here. I assure you, I shall not be a burden, an impediment, to you in the forest. Nor will I regard life in the forest as exile or as suffering. With you it will be more than heaven to me. It will not be the least hardship to me; without you, even heaven is hell."

Ayodhya 28–29

Thinking of the great hardships they would have to endure in the forest, however, Rāma tried to dissuade Sītā in the following words: "Sītā, you come of a very wealthy family dedicated to righteousness. It is therefore proper that you should stay behind and serve my people here. Thus, by avoiding the hardships of the forest and by lovingly serving my people here, would you gladden my heart. The forest is not a place for a princess like you. It is full of great dangers. Lions dwell in the caves; and it is frightening to hear their roar. These wild beasts are not used to seeing human beings; the way they attack human beings is horrifying even to think about. Even the paths are thorny and it is hard to walk on them. The food is a few fruits which might have fallen on their own accord from the trees: living on them, one has to be contented all day. Our garments will be bark and animal skins: and the hair will have to be matted and gathered on the top of the head. Anger and greed have to be given up, the mind must be directed towards austerity and one should overcome fear even where it is natural. Totally exposed to the inclemencies of nature, surrounded by wild animals, serpents and so on, the forest is full of untold hardships. It is not a place for you, my dear."

This reiteration on the part of Rāma moved Sītā to tears. "Your gracious solicitude for my happiness only makes my love for you more ardent, and my determination to follow you more firm. You mentioned animals: they will never come anywhere near me while you are there. You mentioned the righteousness of serving your people: but, your father's command that you should go to the forest demands I should go, too; I am your half: and because of this, again I cannot live without you. In fact you have often declared that a righteous wife will not be able to live separated from her husband. And listen! This is not new to me: for even when I was in my father's house, long before we were married, wise astrologers had rightly predicted that I would live in a forest for some time. If you remember, I have been longing to spend some time in the forest, for I have trained myself for that eventuality. Lord, I feel actually delighted at the very thought that I shall at last go to the forest, to serve you constantly. Serving you, I shall not incur the sin of leaving your parents: thus have I heard from those who are well-versed in the Vedas and other scriptures, that a devoted wife remains united with her husband even after they leave this earth-plane.

There is therefore no valid reason why you should wish to leave me here and go. If you still refuse to take me with you, I have no alternative but to lay down my life."

Ayodhya 30–31

To the further persuasive talk of Rāma, Sītā responded with a show of annoyance, courage and firmness. She even taunted Rāma in the following words: "While choosing you as his son-in-law, did my father Janaka realise that you were a woman at heart with a male body? Why, then are you, full of valour and courage, afraid even on my account? If you do not take me with you I shall surely die; but instead of waiting for such an event, I prefer to die in your presence. If you do not change your mind now, I shall take poison and die." In sheer anguish, the pitch of her voice rose higher and higher, and her eyes released a torrent of hot tears.

Rāma folded her in his arms and spoke to her lovingly, with great delight: "Sītā, I could not fathom your mind and therefore I tried to dissuade you from coming with me. Come, follow me. Of course I cannot drop the idea of going to the forest, even for your sake. I cannot live having disregarded the command of my parents. Indeed, I wonder how one could adore the unmanifest god, if one were unwilling to obey the commands of his parents and his guru whom he can see here. No religious activity nor even moral excellence can equal service of one's parents in bestowing supreme felicity on one. Whatever one desires, and whatever region one desires to ascend to after leaving this earth-plane, all this is secured by the service of parents. Hence I shall do as commanded by father; and this is the eternal dharma. And you have rightly resolved, to follow me to the forest. Come, and get ready soon. Give away generous gifts to the brāhmaṇas and distribute the rest of your possessions to the servants and others."

Lakṣmaṇa now spoke to Rāma: "If you are determined to go, then I shall go ahead of you." Rāma, however, tried to dissuade him: "Indeed, I know that you are my precious and best companion. Yet, I am anxious that you should stay behind and look after our mothers. Kaikeyī may not treat them well. By thus serving our mothers, you will prove your devotion to me." But Lakṣmaṇa replied quickly: "I am confident, Rāma, that Bharata will look after all the mothers, inspired by your spirit of renunciation and your adherence to dharma. If this does not prove to be the case, I can exterminate all of them in no time. Indeed, Kausalyā is great and powerful enough to look after herself: she gave birth to you! My place is near you; my duty to serve you."

Delighted to hear this, Rāma said: "Then let us all go. Before leaving I wish to give away in charity all that I possess to the holy brāhmaṇas. Please get them all together. Take leave of your friends and get our weapons ready, too." [. . .]

[Rāma, Sītā, Lakṣmaṇa, and Urmila have left Ayodhyā, its people stricken with grief upon the departure of the man (Rāma) they recognize as their "sole refuge and protector." Though Kaikeyī finally persuades Bharata to serve as crown regent, he, horrified by the injustice of his mother's actions, refuses to set foot in Ayodhyā and sets up rule from a nearby village. As the selection from Book 3 begins, the Āraṇya Kāṇḍa, Rāma, Sītā, and Lakṣmaṇa are on their way to Pañcavati, where they will build their ashram, or refuge, in the Daṇḍaka Forest.]

***FROM* BOOK 3**

Aranya Kanda: The Forest Life

Aranya 14–15

Rāma, Lakṣmaṇa and Sītā were proceeding towards Pañcavaṭī.[13] On the way they saw a huge vulture. Rāma's first thought was that it was a demon in disguise. The vulture[14] said: "I am your father's friend!" Trusting the vulture's words, Rāma asked for details of its birth and ancestry.

The vulture said: "You know that Dakṣa Prajāpati[15] had sixty daughters and the sage Kaśyapa married eight of them. One day Kaśyapa said to his wives: 'You will give birth to offspring who will be foremost in the three worlds.' Aditi, Diti, Danu and Kālaka listened attentively; the others were indifferent. As a result, the former four gave birth to powerful offspring who were superhuman. Aditi gave birth to thirty-three gods. Diti gave birth to demons. Danu gave birth to Aśvagrīva. And, Kālaka had Naraka and Kālikā. Of the others, men were born of Manu, and the sub-human species from the other wives of Kaśyapa. Tāmra's daughter was Sukī whose granddaughter was Vinatā who had two sons, Garuḍa and Aruṇa. My brother Sampāti and I are the sons of Aruṇa. I offer my services to you, O Rāma. If you will be pleased to accept them, I shall guard Sītā when you and Lakṣmaṇa may be away from your hermitage. As you have seen, this formidable forest is full of wild animals and demons, too."

Rāma accepted this new friendship. All of them now proceeded towards Pañcavaṭī in search of a suitable place for building a hermitage. Having arrived at Pañcavaṭī, identified by Rāma by the description which the sage Agastya had given, Rāma said to Lakṣmaṇa: "Pray, select a suitable place here for building the hermitage. It should have a charming forest, good water, firewood, flowers and holy grass." Lakṣmaṇa submitted: "Even if we live together for a hundred years, I shall continue to be your servant. Hence, Lord, you select the place and I shall do the needful." Rejoicing at Lakṣmaṇa's attitude, Rāma pointed to a suitable place, which satisfied all the requisites of a hermitage. Rāma said: "This is holy ground; this is charming; it is frequented by beasts and birds. We shall dwell here." Immediately Lakṣmaṇa set about building a hermitage for all of them to live in.

Rāma warmly embraced Lakṣmaṇa and said: "I am delighted by your good work and devoted service: and I embrace you in token of such admiration. Brother, you divine the wish of my heart, you are full of gratitude, you know dharma; with such a man as his son, father is not dead but is eternally alive."

---

[13] **Pañcavaṭī:** A banyan-tree grove where the sage Agastya has suggested Rāma establish his dwelling in the forest.

[14] **The vulture:** The vulture's name, as is revealed later, is Jaṭāyu; he comes to Sītā's aid when she is abducted by Rāvaṇa.

[15] **Dakṣa Prajāpati:** The "lord of creatures," a creator-god who, as told here, through his progeny is the grandfather of demigods, demons, and humans.

Entering that hermitage, Rāma, Lakṣmaṇa and Sītā dwelt in it with great joy and happiness.

Aranya 16

Time rolled on. One day Lakṣmaṇa sought the presence of Rāma early in the morning and described what he had seen outside the hermitage. He said: "Winter, the season which you love most, has arrived, O Rāma. There is dry cold everywhere; the earth is covered with foodgrains. Water is uninviting; and fire is pleasant. The first fruits of the harvest have been brought in; and the agriculturists have duly offered some of it to the gods and the manes, and thus reaffirmed their indebtedness to them. The farmer who thus offers the first fruits to gods and manes is freed from sin.

"The sun moves in the southern hemisphere; and the north looks lustreless. Himālaya, the abode of snow, looks even more so! It is pleasant to take a walk even at noon. The shade of a tree which we loved in summer is unpleasant now. Early in the morning the earth, with its rich wheat and barley fields, is enveloped by mist. Even so, the rice crop. The sun, even when it rises, looks soft and cool like the moon. Even the elephants which approach the water, touch it with their trunk but pull the trunk quickly away on account of the coldness of the water.

"Rāma, my mind naturally thinks of our beloved brother Bharata. Even in this cold winter, he who could command the luxury of a king, prefers to sleep on the floor and live an ascetic life. Surely, he, too, would have got up early in the morning and has perhaps had a cold bath in the river Sarayū. What a noble man! I can even now picture him in front of me: with eyes like the petals of a lotus, dark brown in colour, slim and without an abdomen, as it were. He knows what dharma is. He speaks the truth. He is modest and self-controlled, always speaks pleasantly, is sweet-natured, with long arms and with all his enemies fully subdued. That noble Bharata has given up all his pleasures and is devoted to you. He has already won his place in heaven, Rāma. Though he lives in the city; yet, he has adopted the ascetic mode of life and follows you in spirit.

"We have heard it said that a son takes after his mother in nature: but in the case of Bharata this has proved false. I wonder how Kaikeyī, in spite of having our father as her husband, and Bharata as her son, has turned out to be so cruel."

When Lakṣmaṇa said this, Rāma stopped him, saying: "Do not speak ill of our mother Kaikeyī, Lakṣmaṇa. Talk only of our beloved Bharata. Even though I try not to think of Ayodhyā and our people there, when I think of Bharata, I wish to see him."

Aranya 17–18

After their bath and morning prayers, Rāma, Lakṣmaṇa and Sītā returned to their hermitage. As they were seated in their hut, there arrived upon the scene a dreadful demoness. She looked at Rāma and immediately fell in love with him! He had a handsome face; she had an ugly face. He had a slender waist; she had a huge abdomen. He had lovely large eyes; she had hideous eyes. He had lovely soft hair; she had red hair. He had a lovable form; she had a terrible form. He had a sweet voice; hers resembled the barking of a dog. He was young; she was haughty. He was able; her speech was crooked. He was of noble conduct; she was of evil conduct. He was beloved; she had a forbidding appearance. Such a demoness spoke to Rāma: "Who are you, young men; and what are both of you doing in this forest, with this lady?"

Rāma told her the whole truth about himself, Lakṣmaṇa and Sītā, about his banishment from the kingdom, etc. Then Rāma asked her: "O charming lady, now tell me who you are." At once the demoness replied: "Ah, Rāma! I shall tell you all about myself immediately. I am Śūrpaṇakhā, the sister of Rāvaṇa. I am sure you have heard of him. He has two other brothers, Kumbhakarṇa and Vibhīsaṇa. Two other brothers Khara and Dūṣaṇa live in the neighbourhood here. The moment I saw you, I fell in love with you. What have you to do with this ugly, emaciated Sītā? Marry me. Both of us shall roam about this forest. Do not worry about Sītā or Lakṣmaṇa: I shall swallow them in a moment." But, Rāma smilingly said to her: "You see I have my wife with me here. Why do you not propose to my brother Lakṣmaṇa who has no wife here?" Śūrpaṇakhā did not mind that suggestion. She turned to Lakṣmaṇa and said: "It is all right. You please marry me and we shall roam about happily." She was tormented by passion.

Lakṣmaṇa said in a teasing mood: "O lady, you see that I am only the slave of Rāma and Sītā. Why do you choose to be the wife of a slave? You will only become a servant-maid. Persuade Rāma to send away that ugly wife of his and marry you." Śūrpaṇakhā turned to Rāma again. She said: "Unable to give up this wife of yours, Sītā, you turn down my offer. See, I shall at once swallow her. When she is gone you will marry me; and we shall roam about in this forest happily." So saying, she actually rushed towards Sītā. Rāma stopped her in time, and said to Lakṣmaṇa: "What are you doing, Lakṣmaṇa? It is not right to jest with cruel and unworthy people. Look at the plight of Sītā. She barely escaped with her life. Come, quickly deform this demoness and send her away.

Lakṣmaṇa drew his sword and quickly cut off the nose and the ears of Śūrpaṇakhā. Weeping and bleeding she ran away. She went to her brother Khara and fell down in front of him. [. . .]

[Khara and Dūṣaṇa, the brothers of Śūrpaṇakhā, lead a troop of demons from Janasthāna against Rāma and Lakṣmaṇa, who rout their attackers and kill both Khara and Dūṣaṇa. The story begins again as Śūrpaṇakhā goes to Laṅkā to ask Rāvaṇa, the king of demons, to avenge her injury and the deaths of her brothers.]

Aranya 32–33

Śūrpaṇakhā witnessed the wholesale destruction of the demons of Janasthāna,[16] including their supreme leader Khara. Stricken with terror, she ran to Laṅkā.[17] There

[16] **Janasthāna:** The region of the forest where the demons, including Khara and Dūṣaṇa, live.

[17] **Laṅkā:** The capital of the island kingdom where Rāvaṇa, the king of the *rakṣasas* (demons), has his magnificent, fortified palace.

she saw her brother Rāvaṇa, the ruler of Laṅkā, seated with his ministers in a palace whose roof scraped the sky. Rāvaṇa had twenty arms, ten heads, was broad chested and endowed with all the physical qualifications of a monarch. He had previously fought with the gods, even with their chief Indra. He was well versed in the science of warfare and knew the use of the celestial missiles in battle. He had been hit by the gods, even by the discus[18] of lord Viṣṇu, but he did not die. For, he had performed breath-taking austerities for a period of ten thousand years, and offered his own heads in worship to Brahmā the creator and earned from him the boon that he would not be killed by any superhuman or subhuman agency (except by man). Emboldened by this boon, the demon had tormented the gods and particularly the sages.

Śūrpaṇakhā entered Rāvaṇa's presence, clearly displaying the physical deformity which Lakṣmaṇa had caused to her. She shouted at Rāvaṇa in open assembly: "Brother, you have become so thoroughly infatuated and addicted to sense-pleasure that you are unfit to be a king any longer. The people lose all respect for the king who is only interested in his own pleasure and neglects his royal duties. People turn away from the king who has no spies, who has lost touch with the people and whom they cannot see, and who is unable to do what is good for them. It is the employment of spies that makes the king 'far-sighted' for through these spies he sees quite far. You have failed to appoint proper spies to collect intelligence for you. Therefore, you do not know that fourteen thousand of your people have been slaughtered by a human being. Even Khara and Dūṣaṇa have been killed by Rāma. And, Rāma has assured the ascetics of Janasthāna which is your territory, that the demons shall not do them any harm. They are now protected by him. Yet, here you are; revelling in little pleasures!

"O brother, even a piece of wood, a clod of earth or just dust, has some use; but when a king falls from his position he is utterly useless. But that monarch who is vigilant, who has knowledge of everything, through his spies, who is self-controlled, who is full of gratitude and whose conduct is righteous—he rules for a long time. Wake up and act before you lose your sovereignty."

This made Rāvaṇa reflect.

Aranya 34–35

And, Rāvaṇa's anger was roused. He asked Śūrpaṇakhā: "Tell me, who is it that disfigured you thus? What do you think of Rāma? Why has he come to Daṇḍaka forest?"

Śūrpaṇakhā gave an exact and colourful description of the physical appearance of Rāma. She said: "Rāma is equal in charm to Cupid himself. At the same time, he is a formidable warrior. When he was fighting the demons of Janasthāna, I could not see what he was doing; I only saw the demons falling dead on the field. You can easily

[18] **discus:** A celestial weapon; Rāvaṇa has received a boon that protects him from injury from gods and other demons; only humans, to whom he incorrectly believes he is superior, can harm him.

understand when I tell you that within an hour and a half he had killed fourteen thousand demons. He spared me, perhaps because he did not want to kill a woman. He has a brother called Lakṣmaṇa who is equally powerful. He is Rāma's right hand man and alter ego; Rāma's own life-force moving outside his body. Oh, you must see Sītā, Rāma's wife. I have not seen even a celestial nymph who could match her in beauty. He who has her for his wife, whom she fondly embraces, he shall indeed be the ruler of gods. She is a fit bride for you; and you are indeed the most suitable suitor for her. In fact, I wanted to bring that beautiful Sītā here so that you could marry her: but Lakṣmaṇa intervened and cruelly mutilated my body. If you could only look at her for a moment, you would immediately fall in love with her. If this proposal appeals to you, take some action quickly and get her here."

Rāvaṇa was instantly tempted. Immediately he ordered his amphibian vehicle to be got ready. This vehicle which was richly adorned with gold, could move freely wherever its owner willed. Its front part resembled mules with fiendish heads. Rāvaṇa took his seat in this vehicle and moved towards the seacoast. The coastline of Laṅkā was dotted with hermitages inhabited by sages and also celestial and semi-divine beings. It was also the pleasure resort of celestials and nymphs who went there to sport and to enjoy themselves. Driving at great speed through them, Rāvaṇa passed through caravan parks scattered with the space vehicles of the celestials. He also drove through dense forests of sandal trees, banana plantations and cocoanut palm groves. In those forests there were also spices and aromatic plants. Along the coast lay pearls and precious stones. He passed through cities which had an air of opulence.

Rāvaṇa crossed the ocean in his amphibian vehicle and reached the hermitage where Mārīca[19] was living in ascetic garb, subsisting on a disciplined diet. Mārīca welcomed Rāvaṇa and questioned him about the purpose of his visit.

Aranya 36–37

Rāvaṇa said to Mārīca: "Listen, Mārīca. You know that fourteen thousand demons, including my brother Khara and the great warrior Triśira have been mercilessly killed by Rāma and Lakṣmaṇa who have now promised their protection to the ascetics of Daṇḍaka forest, thus flouting our authority. Driven out of his country by his angry father, obviously for a disgraceful action, this unrighteous and hard-hearted prince Rāma has killed the demons without any justification. And, they have even dared to disfigure my beloved sister Śūrpaṇakhā. I must immediately take some action to avenge the death of my brother and to restore our prestige and our authority. I need your help; kindly do not refuse this time.

"Disguising yourself as a golden deer of great beauty, roam near the hermitage of Rāma. Sītā would surely be attracted, and she would ask Rāma and Lakṣmaṇa to capture you. When they go after you, leaving Sītā alone in the hermitage, I shall

---

[19] **Mārīca:** Rāvaṇa's uncle; he is also a *rakṣasa*.

easily abduct Sītā." Even as Rāvaṇa was unfolding this plot, Mārīca's mouth became dry and parched with fear. Trembling with fear, Mārīca said to Rāvaṇa:

"O king, one can easily get in this world a counsellor who tells you what is pleasing to you; but hard it is to find a wise counsellor who tells you the unpleasant truth which is good for you—and harder it is to find one who heeds such advice. Surely, your intelligence machine is faulty and therefore you have no idea of the prowess of Rāma. Else, you would not talk of abducting Sītā. I wonder: perhaps Sītā has come into this world to end your life, or perhaps there is to be great sorrow on account of Sītā, or perhaps maddened by lust, you are going to destroy yourself and the demons and Laṅkā itself. Oh, no, you were wrong in your estimation of Rāma. He is not wicked; he is righteousness incarnate. He is not cruel hearted; he is generous to a fault. He has not been disgraced and exiled from the kingdom. He is here to honour the promise his father had given his mother Kaikeyī, after joyously renouncing his kingdom.

"O king, when you entertain ideas of abducting Sītā you are surely playing with fire. Please remember: when you stand facing Rāma, you are standing face to face with your own death. Sītā is the beloved wife of Rāma, who is extremely powerful. Nay, give up this foolish idea. What will you gain by thus gambling with your sovereignty over the demons, and with your life itself? Please consult the noble Vibhīṣaṇa and your virtuous ministers before embarking upon such unwise projects. They will surely advise you against them." [. . .]

Aranya 42

Rāvaṇa was determined, and Mārīca knew that there was no use arguing with him. Hence, after the last-minute attempt to avert the catastrophe, Mārīca said to Rāvaṇa: "What can I do when you are so wicked? I am ready to go to Rāma's āśrama. God help you!" Not minding the taunt, Rāvaṇa expressed his unabashed delight at Mārīca's consent. He applauded Mārīca and said: "That is the spirit, my friend: you are now the same old Mārīca that I knew. I guess you had been possessed by some evil spirit a few minutes ago, on account of which you had begun to preach a different gospel. Let us swiftly get into this vehicle and proceed to our destination. As soon as you have accomplished the purpose, you are free to go and to do what you please!"

Both of them got into the amphibian vehicle which behaved like an aerial car (for it was in fact a hovercraft), and quickly left the hermitage of Mārīca. Once again they passed forests, hills, rivers and cities: and soon they reached the neighbourhood of the hermitage of Rāma. They got down from that hovercraft which had been embellished with gold. Holding Mārīca by the hand, Rāvaṇa said to him: "Over there is the hermitage of Rāma, surrounded by banana plantations. Well, now, get going with the work for which we have come here." Immediately Mārīca transformed himself into an attractive deer. It was extraordinary, totally unlike any deer that inhabited the forest. It was unique. It dazzled like a huge gem stone. Each part of its body had a different colour. The colours had an unearthly brilliance and charm. Thus embellished by the colours of all the precious stones, the deer which was the demon Mārīca in disguise, roamed about near the hermitage of Rāma, nibbling at the grass now and then. At one time it came close to Sītā; then it ran away and joined the other deer grazing at a distance. It was very playful, jumping about and chasing its tail and spinning around. Sītā went out to gather flowers. She cast a glance at that extraordinary and unusual deer. As she did so, the deer too, sensing the accomplishment of the mission, came closer to her. Then it ran away, pretending to be afraid. Sītā marvelled at the very appearance of this unusual deer the like of which she had not seen before and which had the hue of jewels.

Aranya 43

From where she was gathering flowers, Sītā, filled with wonder to see that unusual deer, called out to Rāma: "Come quick and see, O Lord; come with your brother. Look at this extraordinary creature. I have never seen such a beautiful deer before." Rāma and Lakṣmaṇa looked at the deer, and Lakṣmaṇa's suspicions were aroused: "I am suspicious; I think it is the same demon Mārīca in disguise. I have heard that Mārīca could assume any form at will, and through such tricks he had brought death and destruction to many ascetics in this forest. Surely, this deer is not real: no one has heard of a deer with rainbow colours, each one of its limbs shining resplendent with the colour of a different gem! That itself should enable us to understand that it is a demon, not an animal."

Sītā interrupted Lakṣmaṇa's talk, and said: "Never mind, one thing is certain; this deer has captivated my mind. It is such a dear. I have not seen such an animal near our hermitage! There are many types of deer which roam about near the hermitage; this is just an extraordinary and unusual deer. It is superlative in all respects: its colour is lovely, its texture is lovely, and even its voice sounds delightful. It would be a wonderful feat if it could be caught alive. We could use it as a pet, to divert our minds. Later we could take it to Ayodhyā: and I am sure all your brothers and mothers would just adore it. If it is not possible to capture it alive, O Lord, then it can be killed, and I would love to have its skin. I know I am not behaving myself towards both of you: but I am helpless; I have lost my heart to that deer. I am terribly curious."

In fact, Rāma was curious, too! And so, he took Sītā's side and said to Lakṣmaṇa: "It is beautiful, Lakṣmaṇa. It is unusual. I have never seen a creature like this. And, princes do hunt animals and cherish their skins. By sporting and hunting kings acquire great wealth! People say that that is real wealth which one pursues without premeditation. So, let us try to get the deer or its skin. If, as you say, it is a demon in disguise, then surely it ought to be killed by me, just as Vātāpi who was tormenting and destroying sages and ascetics was justly killed by the sage Agastya.[20] Vātāpi fooled the ascetics till he met the sage Agastya. This Mārīca, too, has fooled the ascetics so far: till coming to me today! The very beauty of his hide is his doom. And, you, Lakṣmaṇa, please guard Sītā with great vigilance, till I kill this deer with just one shot and bring the hide along with me."

---

[20] **Agastya:** The Brahmin sage Agastya tricked the *rakṣasa* Vātāpi, who killed guests by shrinking himself and hiding in their food. After they had consumed their meals, Vātāpi would rip open their stomachs. Agastya accelerated his digestion and so rid himself of the demon before he could be harmed.

Aranya 44–45

Rāma took his weapons and went after the strange deer. As soon as the deer saw him pursuing it, it started to run away. Now it disappeared, now it appeared to be very near, now it ran fast, now it seemed confused—thus it led Rāma far away from his hermitage. Rāma was fatigued, and needed to rest. As he was standing under a tree, intrigued by the actions of the mysterious deer, it came along with other deer and began to graze not far from him. When Rāma once again went for it, it ran away. Not wishing to go farther nor to waste more time, Rāma took his weapon and fitted the missile of Brahmā to it and fired. This missile pierced the illusory deer-mask and into the very heart of the demon. Mārīca uttered a loud cry, leapt high into the sky and then dropped dead onto the ground. As he fell, however, he remembered Rāvaṇa's instructions and, assuming the voice of Rāma cried aloud: "Hey Sītā; Hey Lakṣmaṇa."

Rāma saw the dreadful body of the demon. He knew now that Lakṣmaṇa was right. And, he was even more puzzled by the way in which the demon wailed aloud before dying. He was full of apprehension. He hastened towards the hermitage.

In the hermitage, both Sītā and Lakṣmaṇa heard the cry. Sītā believed it was Rāma's voice. She was panic-stricken. She said to Lakṣmaṇa: "Go, go quickly: your brother is in danger. And, I cannot live without him. My breath and my heart are both violently disturbed." Lakṣmaṇa remembered Rāma's admonition that he should stay with Sītā and not leave her alone. He said to her: "Pray, be not worried." Sītā grew suspicious and furious. She said to him: "Ah, I see the plot now! You have a wicked eye on me and so have been waiting for this to happen. What a terrible enemy of Rāma you are, pretending to be his brother!" Distressed to hear these words, Lakṣmaṇa replied: "No one in the three worlds can overpower Rāma, blessed lady! It was not his voice at all. These demons in the forest are capable of simulating the voice of anyone. Having killed that demon disguised as a deer, Rāma will soon be here. Fear not." His calmness even more annoyed Sītā, who literally flew into a rage. She said again: "Surely, you are the worst enemy that Rāma could have had. I know now that you have been following us, cleverly pretending to be Rāma's brother and friend. I know now that your real motive for doing so is either to get me or you are Bharata's accomplice. Ah, but you will not succeed. Presently, I shall give up my life. For I cannot live without Rāma." Cut to the quick by these terrible words, Lakṣmaṇa said: "You are worshipful to me: hence I cannot answer back. It is not surprising that women should behave in this manner: for they are easily led away from dharma; they are fickle and sharp-tongued. I cannot endure what you said just now. I shall go. The gods are witness to what took place here. May those gods protect you. But I doubt if when Rāma and I return, we shall find you." Bowing to her, Lakṣmaṇa left.

Aranya 46

Rāvaṇa was looking for this golden opportunity. He disguised himself as an ascetic, clad in ochre robes, carrying a shell water-pot, a staff and an umbrella, and approached Sītā who was still standing outside the cottage eagerly looking for Rāma's return. His very presence in that forest was inauspicious: and even the trees and the waters of the rivers were frightened of him, as it were. In a holy disguise, Rāvaṇa stood before Sītā: a deep well covered with grass; a death-trap.

Gazing at the noble Sītā, who had now withdrawn into the cottage and whose eyes were raining tears, Rāvaṇa came near her, and though his heart was filled with lust, he was chanting Vedic hymns. He said to Sītā in a soft, tender and affectionate tone: "O young lady! Pray, tell me, are you the goddess of fortune or the goddess of modesty, or the consort of Cupid[21] himself?" Then Rāvaṇa described her incomparable beauty in utterly immodest terms, unworthy of an anchorite whose form he had assumed. He continued: "O charming lady! You have robbed me of my heart. I have not seen such a beautiful lady, neither a divine or a semi-divine being. Your extraordinary form and your youthfulness, and your living in this forest, all these together agitate my mind. It is not right that you should live in this forest. You should stay in palaces. In the forest monkeys, lions, tigers and other wild animals live. The forest is the natural habitat of demons who roam freely. You are living alone in this dreadful forest: are you not afraid, O fair lady? Pray, tell me, why are you living in this forest?"

Rāvaṇa was in the disguise of a brāhmaṇa. Therefore, Sītā offered him the worship and the hospitality that it was her duty to offer a brāhmaṇa. She made him sit down; she gave him water to wash his feet and his hands. Then she placed food in front of him.

Whatever she did only aggravated his lust and his desire to abduct her and take her away to Laṅkā.

Aranya 47–48

Sītā, then, proceeded to answer his enquiry concerning herself. He appeared to be a brāhmaṇa; and if his enquiry was not answered, he might get angry and curse her. Sītā said: "I am a daughter of the noble king Janaka; Sītā is my name. I am the beloved consort of Rāma. After our marriage, Rāma and I lived in the palace of Ayodhyā for twelve years." She then truthfully narrated all that took place just prior to Rāma's exile to the forest. She continued: "And so, when Rāma was twenty-five and I was eighteen, we left the palace and sought the forest-life. And so the three of us dwell in this forest. My husband, Rāma, will soon return to the hermitage gathering various animals and also wild fruits. Pray, tell me who you are, O brāhmaṇa, and what you are doing in this forest roaming all alone."

Rāvaṇa lost no time in revealing his true identity. He said: "I am not a brāhmaṇa, O Sītā: I am the lord of demons, Rāvaṇa. My very name strikes terror in the hearts of gods and men. The moment I saw you, I lost my heart to you; and I derive no pleasure from the company of my wives. Come with me, and be my queen, O Sītā. You will love Laṅkā. Laṅkā is my capital, it is surrounded by the ocean and it is situated on the top of a hill. There we shall live together, and you will enjoy your life, and never even once think of this wretched forest-life."

---

[21] **Cupid:** Cupid, the boyish god of love in Roman mythology, is not a part of the Hindu pantheon.

Sītā was furious to hear this. She said: "O demon-king! I have firmly resolved to follow Rāma who is equal to the god of gods, who is mighty and charming, and who is devoted to righteousness. If you entertain a desire for me, his wife, it is like tying yourself with a big stone and trying to swim across the ocean: you are doomed. Where are you and where is he: there is no comparison. You are like a jackal; he the lion. You are like base metal; he gold."

But Rāvaṇa would not give up his desire. He repeated: "Even the gods dare not stand before me, O Sītā! For fear of me even Kubera the god of wealth abandoned his space vehicle and ran away to Kailāsa.[22] If the gods, headed by Indra, even sense I am angry, they flee. Even the forces of nature obey me. Laṅkā is enclosed by a strong wall; the houses are built of gold with gates of precious stones. Forget this Rāma, who lives like an ascetic, and come with me. He is not as strong as my little finger!" Sītā was terribly angered: "Surely you seek the destruction of all the demons, by behaving like this, O Rāvaṇa. It cannot be otherwise since they have such an unworthy king with no self-control. You may live after abducting Indra's wife, but not after abducting me, Rāma's wife."

Aranya 49–50

Rāvaṇa made his body enormously big and said to Sītā: "You do not realise what a mighty person I am. I can step out into space, and lift up the earth with my arms; I can drink up the waters of the oceans; and I can kill death itself. I can shoot a missile and bring the sun down. Look at the size of my body." As he expanded his form, Sītā turned her face away from him. He resumed his original form with ten heads and twenty arms. Again he spoke to Sītā: "Would you not like to be renowned in the three worlds? Then marry me. And, I promise I shall do nothing to displease you. Give up all thoughts of that mortal and unsuccessful Rāma."

Rāvaṇa did not wait for an answer. Seizing Sītā by her hair and lifting her up with his arm, he left the hermitage. Instantly the golden space vehicle appeared in front of him. He ascended it, along with Sītā. Sītā cried aloud: "O Rāma." As she was being carried away, she wailed aloud: "O Lakṣmaṇa, who is ever devoted to the elder brother, do you not know that I am being carried away by Rāvaṇa?" To Rāvaṇa, she said: "O vile demon, surely you will reap the fruits of your evil action: but they do not manifest immediately." She said as if to herself: "Surely, Kaikeyī would be happy today." She said to the trees, to the river Godāvarī, to the deities dwelling in the forest, to the animals and birds: "Pray, tell Rāma that I have been carried away by the wicked Rāvaṇa." She saw Jaṭāyu and cried aloud: "O Jaṭāyu! See, Rāvaṇa is carrying me away."

Hearing that cry, Jaṭāyu woke up. Jaṭāyu introduced himself to Rāvaṇa: "O Rāvaṇa, I am the king of vultures, Jaṭāyu. Pray, desist from this action unworthy of a

[22] **Kailāsa:** The dwelling place of Śiva, the destroyer.

king. Rāma, too, is a king; and his consort is worthy of our protection. A wise man should not indulge in such action as would disgrace him in the eyes of others. And, another's wife is as worthy of protection as one's own. The cultured and the common people often copy the behaviour of the king. If the king himself is guilty of unworthy behaviour what becomes of the people? If you persist in your wickedness, even the prosperity you enjoy will leave you soon.

"Therefore, let Sītā go. One should not get hold of a greater load than one can carry; one should not eat what he cannot digest. Who will indulge in an action which is painful and which does not promote righteousness, fame or permanent glory? I am sixty thousand years old and you are young. I warn you. If you do not give up Sītā, you will not be able to carry her away while I am alive and able to restrain you! I shall dash you down along with that space vehicle."

Aranya 51

Rāvaṇa could not brook this insult: he turned towards Jaṭāyu in great anger. Jaṭāyu hit the spacecraft and Rāvaṇa; Rāvaṇa hit Jaṭāyu back with terrible ferocity. This aerial combat between Rāvaṇa and Jaṭāyu looked like the collision of two mountains endowed with wings. Rāvaṇa used all the conventional missiles, the Nālikas, the Nārācas and the Vikarṇis. The powerful eagle shrugged them off. Jaṭāyu tore open the canopy of the spacecraft and inflicted wounds on Rāvaṇa himself.

In great anger, Jaṭāyu grabbed Rāvaṇa's weapon (a cannon) and broke it with his claws. Rāvaṇa took up a more formidable weapon which literally sent a shower of missiles. Against these Jaṭāyu used his own wings as an effective shield. Pouncing upon this weapon, too, Jaṭāyu destroyed it with his claws. Jaṭāyu also tore open Rāvaṇa's armour. Nay, Jaṭāyu even damaged the gold-plated propellers of Rāvaṇa's spacecraft, which had the appearance of demons, and thus crippled the craft which would take its occupant wherever he desired and which emitted fire. With his powerful beak, Jaṭāyu broke the neck of Rāvaṇa's pilot.

With the spacecraft thus rendered temporarily useless, Rāvaṇa jumped out of it, still holding Sītā with his powerful arm. While Rāvaṇa was still above the ground, Jaṭāyu again challenged him: "O wicked one, even now you are unwilling to turn away from evil. Surely, you have resolved to bring about the destruction of the entire race of demons. Unknowingly or wantonly, you are swallowing poison which would certainly kill you and your relations. Rāma and Lakṣmaṇa will not tolerate this sinful act of yours: and you cannot stand before them on the battlefield. The manner in which you are doing this unworthy act is despicable: you are behaving like a thief not like a hero." Jaṭāyu swooped on Rāvaṇa and violently tore at his body.

Then there ensued a hand-to-hand fight between the two. Rāvaṇa hit Jaṭāyu with his fist; but Jaṭāyu tore Rāvaṇa's arms away. However, new ones sprang up instantly. Rāvaṇa hit Jaṭāyu and kicked him. After some time, Rāvaṇa drew his sword and cut off the wings of Jaṭāyu. When the wings were thus cut, Jaṭāyu fell, dying. Looking at the fallen Jaṭāyu, Sītā ran towards him in great anguish, as she would to the side of a fallen relation. In inconsolable grief, Sītā began to wail aloud.

Aranya 52–53

As Sītā was thus wailing near the body of Jaṭāyu, Rāvaṇa came towards her. Looking at him with utter contempt, Sītā said: "I see dreadful omens, O Rāvaṇa. Dreams as also the sight and the cries of birds and beasts are clear indicators of the shape of things to come. But you do not notice them! Alas, here is Jaṭāyu, my father-in-law's friend who is dying on my account. O Rāma, O Lakṣmaṇa, save me, protect me!"

Once again Rāvaṇa grabbed her and got into the spacecraft which had been made airworthy again. The Creator, the gods and the celestials who witnessed this, exclaimed: "Bravo, our purpose is surely accomplished." Even the sages of the Daṇḍaka forest inwardly felt happy at the thought, "Now that Sītā has been touched by this wicked demon, the end of Rāvaṇa and all the demons is near." As she was carried away by Rāvaṇa, Sītā was wailing aloud: "O Rāma, O Lakṣmaṇa."

Placed on the lap of Rāvaṇa, Sītā was utterly miserable. Her countenance was full of sorrow and anguish. The petals of the flowers that dropped from her head fell and covered the body of Rāvaṇa for a while. She was of beautiful golden complexion; and he was of dark colour. Her being seated on his lap looked like an elephant wearing a golden sash, or the moon shining in the midst of a dark cloud, or a streak of lightning seen in a dense dark cloud.

The spacecraft streaked through the sky as fast as a meteor would. On the earth below, trees shook as if to reassure Sītā: "Do not be afraid," the waterfalls looked as if mountains were shedding tears, and people said to one another, "Surely, dharma has come to an end, as Rāvaṇa is carrying Sītā away."

Once again Sītā rebuked Rāvaṇa: "You ought to feel ashamed of yourself, O Rāvaṇa. You boast of your prowess; but you are stealing me away! You have not won me in a duel, which would be considered heroic. Alas, for a long, long time to come, people will recount your ignominy, and this unworthy and unrighteous act of yours will be remembered by the people. You are taking me and flying at such speed: hence no one can do anything to stop you. If only you had the courage to stop for a few moments, you would find yourself dead. My lord Rāma and his brother Lakṣmaṇa will not spare you. Leave me alone, O demon! But, you are in no mood to listen to what is good for your own welfare. Even as, one who has reached death's door loves only harmful objects. Rāma will soon find out where I am and ere long you will be transported to the world of the dead."

Rāvaṇa flew along, though now and then he trembled in fear.

Aranya 54–55

The spacecraft was flying over hills and forests and was approaching the ocean. At that time, Sītā beheld on the ground below, five strong vānaras[23] seated and watching the craft with curiosity. Quickly, Sītā took off the stole she had around her shoul-

[23] **vānaras:** Monkeys (or apes) ruled by the monkey-king Sugrīva in the forest kingdom of Kiṣkindhā; their military leader, Hanumān, will become one of Rāma's greatest allies.

ders and, removing all her jewels and putting them in that stole, bundled them all up and threw the bundle into the midst of the vānaras, in the hope that should Rāma chance to come there they would give him a clue to her whereabouts.

Rāvaṇa did not notice this but flew on. And now the craft, which shot through space at great speed, was over the ocean; a little while after that, Rāvaṇa entered Laṅkā along with his captive Sītā. Entering his own apartments, Rāvaṇa placed Sītā in them, entrusting her care to some of his chief female attendants. He said to them: "Take great care of Sītā. Let no male approach these apartments without my express permission. And, take great care to let Sītā have whatever she wants and asks for. Any neglect on your part means instant death."

Rāvaṇa was returning to his own apartments: on the way he was still considering what more could be done to ensure the fulfilment of his ambition. He sent for eight of the most ferocious demons and instructed them thus: "Proceed at once to Janasthāna. It was ruled by my brother Khara; but it has now been devastated by Rāma. I am filled with rage to think that a mere human being could thus kill Khara, Dūṣaṇa and all their forces. Never mind: I shall put an end to Rāma soon. Keep an eye on him and keep me informed of his movements. You are free to bring about the destruction of Rāma." And, the demons immediately left.

Rāvaṇa returned to where Sītā was and compelled her to inspect the apartments. The palace stood on pillars of ivory, gold, crystal and silver and was studded with diamonds. The floor, the walls, the stairways—everything was made of gold and diamonds. Then again he said to Sītā: "Here at this place there are over a thousand demons ever ready to do my bidding. Their services and the entire Laṅkā I place at your feet. My life I offer to you; you are to me more valuable than my life. You will have under your command even the many good women whom I have married. Be my wife. Laṅkā is surrounded by the ocean, eight hundred miles on all sides. It is unapproachable to anybody; least of all to Rāma. Forget the weakling Rāma. Do not worry about the scriptural definitions of righteousness: we shall also get married in accordance with demoniacal wedding procedure. Youth is fleeting. Let us get married soon and enjoy life."

Aranya 56

Placing a blade of grass[24] between Rāvaṇa and herself, Sītā said: "O demon! Rāma, the son of king Daśaratha, is my lord, the only one I adore. He and his brother Lakṣmaṇa will surely put an end to your life. If they had seen you lay your hands on me, they would have killed you on the spot, even as they laid Khara to eternal rest. It may be that you cannot be killed by demons and gods; but you cannot escape being killed at the hands of Rāma and Lakṣmaṇa. Rāvaṇa, you are doomed, beyond doubt. You have already lost your life, your good fortune, your very soul and your senses, and on account of your evil deeds Laṅkā has attained widowhood. Though you do not perceive this, death is knocking at your door, O Rāvaṇa. O sinner, you cannot

[24] **a blade of grass:** This fragile barrier symbolizes the power of Sītā's chastity.

under any circumstances lay your hands on me. You may bind this body, or you may destroy it: it is after all insentient matter, and I do not consider it worth preserving, nor even life worth living—not in order to live a life which will earn disrepute for me."

Rāvaṇa found himself helpless. Hence, he resorted to threat. He said: "I warn you, Sītā. I give you twelve months in which to make up your mind to accept me as your husband. If within that time you do not so decide, my cooks will cut you up easily for my breakfast." He had nothing more to say to her. He turned to the female attendants surrounding her and ordered them: "Take this Sītā away to the Aśoka grove. Keep her there. Use every method of persuasion that you know of to make her yield to my desire. Guard her vigilantly. Take her and break her will as you would tame a wild elephant."

The demonesses thereupon took Sītā away and confined her to the Aśoka grove, over which they themselves mounted guard day and night. Sītā did not find any peace of mind there, and stricken with fear and grief, she constantly thought of Rāma and Lakṣmaṇa.

It is said that at the same time, the creator Brahmā felt perturbed at the plight of Sītā. He spoke to Indra, the chief of gods: "Sītā is in the Aśoka grove. Pining for her husband, she may kill herself. Hence, go reassure her, and give her the celestial food to sustain herself till Rāma arrives in Laṅkā." Indra, thereupon, appeared before Sītā. In order to assure her of his identity he showed that his feet did not touch the ground and his eyes did not wink. He gave her the celestial food, saying: "Eat this, and you will never feel hunger or thirst, nor will fatigue overpower you." While Indra was thus talking to Sītā, the goddess of sleep (Nidrā) had overpowered the demonesses. [. . .]

[Book 4, the Kiṣkindhā Kāṇḍa, describes Rāma's search for Sītā and his meeting with the monkey-king Sugrīva who rules over the vānaras, the monkey- or ape-people. Rāma slays Sugrīva's rival, his brother Vāli, and wins the support of both Sugrīva and the greatest of the *vānara* warriors, Hanumān. The vānaras help in the search for Sītā, and learn from the vulture Sampatī, the brother of Jaṭāyu, that she is being held at Laṅkā by Rāvaṇa. When the story picks up again, Hanumān has agreed to cross over the waters dividing Laṅkā from the mainland to search for Sītā.]

***FROM* BOOK 5**

Sundara Kanda: Beautiful Exploits of Hanuman

Hanumān was preparing to jump into the ocean and to cross the ocean to go to Laṅkā. Before undertaking this momentous and vital adventure, he offered prayers to the sun-god, to Indra, to the wind-god, to the Creator and to the elements. He turned to the east and offered his salutations to the wind-god, his own divine parent. He turned his face now to the south, in order to proceed on his great mission.

As he stood there, with his whole being swelling with enthusiasm, fervour and determination, and as he pressed his foot on the mountain before taking off from there, the whole mountain shook. And the shock caused the trees to shed their flowers, birds and beasts to leave their sheltered abodes, subterranean water to gush forth, and even the pleasure-loving celestials and the peace-loving ascetics to leave the mountain resorts, to fly into the sky and watch Hanumān's adventure from there. Giving proof of their scientific skill and knowledge, these celestials and sages remained hovering over the hill, eager to witness Hanumān's departure to Laṅkā. They said to one another: "This mighty Hanumān who is the god-child of the wind-god himself, will swiftly cross this ocean; for he desires to cross the ocean in order to achieve the mission of Rāma and the mission of the vānaras."

Hanumān crouched on the mountain, ready to go. He tensed his body in an effort to muster all the energy that he had. He held his breath in his heart and thus charged himself with even more energy.

He said to the vānaras who surrounded him: "I shall proceed to Laṅkā with the speed of the missile discharged by Rāma. If I do not find Sītā there, I shall with the same speed go to the heaven to search for her. And, if I do not see her even there, I shall get hold of Rāvaṇa, bind him and bring him over to the presence of Rāma. I shall definitely return with success. If it is difficult to bind Rāvaṇa and bring him, I shall uproot Laṅkā itself and bring it to Rāma."

After thus reassuring the vānaras, Hanumān took to the sky. The big trees that stood on the mountain were violently drawn into the slip-stream. Some of these trees flew behind Hanumān; others fell into the ocean; and yet others shed their blossoms on the hill tops, where they lay as a colourful carpet, and on the surface of the ocean where they looked like stars in the blue sky.

Sundara 1

The mighty Hanumān was on his way to Laṅkā. He flew in the southerly direction, with his arms outstretched. One moment it looked as if he would soon drink the ocean; at another as if he desired to drink the blue sky itself. He followed the course of wind, his eyes blazing like fire, like lightning.

Hanumān flying in the air with his tail coiled up behind looked like a meteor with its tail flying from north to the south. His shadow was cast on the surface of the ocean: this made it appear as if there were a big ship on the ocean. As he flew over the surface of the ocean, the wind generated by his motion greatly agitated the ocean. He actually dashed the surface of the ocean with his powerful chest. Thus the sea was churned by him as he flew over it. Huge waves arose in his wake with water billowing high into fine spray which looked like clouds. Flying thus in the sky, without any visible support, Hanumān appeared to be a winged mountain.

Hanumān was engaged in the mission of Rāma: hence the sun did not scorch him. Rāma was a descendant of the solar dynasty. The sages who were present there in their ethereal forms showered their blessings upon him.

Sāgara, the deity presiding over the ocean, bethought to himself: "In days of yore, Rāma's ancestors, the sons of king Sāgara, rendered an invaluable service to me.[25] And it therefore behoves me to render some service to this messenger of Rāma who is engaged in the service of Rāma. I should see that Hanumān does not tire himself and thus fail in his mission. I should arrange for him to have some rest before he proceeds further."

Thus resolved, Sāgara summoned the deity presiding over the mountain named Maināka which had been submerged in the ocean, and said to Maināka: "O Maināka, Indra the chief of gods has established you here in order to prevent the denizens from the subterranean regions from coming up. You have the power to extend yourself on all sides. Pray, rise up and offer a seat to Hanumān who is engaged on an important mission on behalf of Rāma, so that he can refresh himself before proceeding further."

Readily agreeing to this request, the mountain Maināka rose from the bed of the ocean. As Hanumān flew towards Laṅkā he saw this mountain actually emerge from the ocean and come into his view. However, he considered that it was an obstacle to his progress towards Laṅkā, an obstruction on his path, to be quickly overcome. Hanumān actually flew almost touching the peak of the mountain and by the force of the motion, the peak was actually broken.

Assuming a human-form the deity presiding over the Maināka mountain addressed Hanumān who was still flying: "O Hanumān, pray accept my hospitality. Rest a while on my peak. Refresh yourself. The ocean was extended by the sons of king Sāgara, an ancestor of Rāma. Hence the deity presiding over the ocean wishes to return the service as a token of gratitude: thus to show one's gratitude is the eternal dharma. With this end in view, the ocean-god has commanded me to rise to the surface and offer you a resting place. It is our tradition to welcome and to honour guests, even if they are ordinary men; how much more important it is that we should thus honour men like you! There is yet another reason why I plead that you should accept my hospitality! In ancient times, all the mountains were endowed with wings. They used to fly around and land where they liked; thus, they terrorised sages and other beings. In answer to their prayer, Indra the chief of gods, wielded his thunderbolt and clipped off the wings of the mountains. As Indra was about to strike me, the wind-god bore me violently away and hid me in the ocean—so that I escaped Indra's wrath. I owe a debt of gratitude to the wind-god who is your god-father. Pray, allow me to discharge that debt by entertaining you."

Hanumān replied politely: "Indeed, I accept your hospitality, in spirit. Time is passing; and I am on an urgent mission. Moreover, I have promised not to rest till my task is accomplished. Hence, forgive my rudeness and discourtesy: I have to be on my way." As a token acceptance of Maināka's hospitality, Hanumān touched the mountain with his hand and was soon on his way. The gods and the sages who witnessed this scene were greatly impressed with Maināka's gesture of goodwill and

[25] **the sons . . . me:** When a sacrificial horse was stolen from King Sagara, former ruler of Ayodhyā, his 60,000 sons enlarged the ocean basin by digging out the earth in their search for the thief. The story is told in the Bāla Kāṇḍa, Sargas 37 and 38.

Hanumān's unflagging zeal and determination. Indra, highly pleased with the Maināka mountain, conferred upon it the boon of fearlessness.

The gods and the sages overseeing Hanumān's flight to Laṅkā had witnessed his first feat of strength when he took off from the Mahendra mountain, and his second feat of strength and enthusiasm when he declined even to rest and insisted on the accomplishment of the mission. They were eager to assure themselves still more conclusively of his ability to fulfil the task he had undertaken.

The gods and the sages now approached Surasā (mother of the Nāgas[26]) and said to her: "Here is Hanumān, the god-child of the wind-god, who is flying across the ocean. Pray, obstruct his path just a short while. Assume a terrible demoniacal form, with the body as big as a mountain, with terrible looking teeth and eyes, and mouth as wide as space. We wish to ascertain Hanumān's strength. And we therefore wish to see whether when he is confronted by you, he triumphs over you or becomes despondent."

In obedience to their command, Surasā assumed a terrible form and confronted Hanumān with her mouth wide open. She said to him, as he approached her mouth while flying in the air: "Ah, fate has decreed that you should serve as my food today! Enter my mouth and I shall eat you up."

Hanumān replied: "O lady, I am on an important mission. Rāma, the son of king Daśaratha, came to the forest to honour his father's promise. While he was in the forest with his wife, Sītā, and his brother, Sītā was abducted by Rāvaṇa, the ruler of Laṅkā. I am going to Laṅkā to find her whereabouts. Do not obstruct my path now. Let me go. If the gods have ordained that I should enter your mouth, I promise that as soon as I discover Sītā and inform Rāma of her whereabouts, I shall come back and enter your mouth."

But, Surasā could not be put off. She repeated: "No one can escape me; and it has been decreed that you shall enter my mouth." She opened her mouth wide. Hanumān, by his yogic power, made himself minute, quickly entered her mouth and as quickly got out! He then said to her: "O lady, let me now proceed. I have fulfilled your wish and honoured the gods' decree: I have entered your mouth! Salutations to you! I shall go to where Sītā is kept in captivity."

Surasā abandoned her demoniacal form and resumed her own form which was pleasant to look at. She blessed Hanumān: "Go! You will surely find Sītā and re-unite her with Rāma." The gods and the sages were thrilled to witness this third triumph of Hanumān.

Hanumān continued to fly towards Laṅkā, along the aerial route which contains rain-bearing clouds, along which birds course, where the masters of music[27] move about, and along which aerial cars which resemble lions, elephants, tigers, birds and

---

[26] **Nāgas:** Snake beings.

[27] **the masters of music:** *Gandharvas,* the heavenly musicians.

snakes, fly—the sky which is also the abode of holy men and women with an abundant store of meritorious deeds, which serves as a canopy created by the creator Brahmā to protect living beings on earth, and which is adorned with planets, the moon, the sun and the stars.

As he flew onwards, he left behind him a black trail which resembled black clouds, and also trails which were red, yellow and white. He often flew through cloud-formations.

A demoness called Simhikā saw Hanumān flying fearlessly in the sky and made up her mind to attack him. She said to herself: "I am hungry. Today I shall swallow this big creature and shall appease my hunger for some time." She caught hold of the shadow cast by Hanumān on the surface of the ocean. Immediately, Hanumān's progress was arrested and he was violently pulled down. He wondered: "How is it that suddenly I am dragged down helplessly?" He looked around and saw the ugly demoness Simhikā. He remembered the description which Sugrīva had given of her and knew it was Simhikā without doubt.

Hanumān stretched his body and the demoness opened her mouth wide. He saw her mouth and her inner vital organs through it. In the twinkling of an eye, he reduced himself to a minute size and dropped into her mouth. He disappeared into that wide mouth. The gods and the sages witnessing this were horrified. But with his adamantine nails he tore open the vital parts of the demoness and quickly emerged from her body. Thus, with the help of good luck, firmness and dexterity Hanumān triumphed over this demoness. The gods applauded this feat and said: "He in whom are found (as in you) these four virtues (firmness, vision, wisdom and dexterity) does not despair in any undertaking."

Hanumān had nearly covered the eight hundred miles, to his destination. At a short distance he saw the shore of Laṅkā. He saw thick forests. He saw the mountains known as Lamba. And he saw the capital city Laṅkā built on the mountains. Not wishing to arouse suspicion, he softly landed on the Lamba mountains which were rich in groves of Ketaka Uddalaka[28] and cocoanut trees.

Sundara 2

Though Hanumān had crossed the sea, covering a distance of eight hundred miles, he felt not the least fatigue nor exhaustion. Having landed on the mountain range close to the shore of the ocean, Hanumān roamed the forests for some time. In them he saw trees of various kinds, bearing flowers and fruits. He saw the city of Laṅkā situated on the top of a hill, surrounded by wide moats and guarded by security forces of demons. He approached the northern gate to the city and quietly surveyed it. That gate was guarded by the most ferocious looking demons armed to the teeth with the most powerful weapons. Standing there, he thought of Rāvaṇa, the abductor of Sītā.

[28] **Ketaka Uddalaka:** A green-leaved plant with yellowish-orange flowers *(pandanus odoratissimus)* that grows in the hottest regions of India.

Hanumān thought: "Even if the vānara forces do come here, of what use would that be? For Rāvaṇa's Laṅkā cannot be conquered even by the gods. Only four of us can cross the ocean and come here—Aṅgada, Nīla, Sugrīva and myself. And that is totally useless. One cannot negotiate with these demons and win them over by peaceful means. Anyhow, I shall first find out if Sīta is alive or not, and only then consider the next step."

In order to find out where Sītā was kept in captivity, he had to enter Laṅkā. The wise Hanumān considered that aspect of his mission. He thought: "Surely, I must be very careful, cautious and vigilant. If I am not, I might ruin the whole mission. An undertaking even after it has been carefully deliberated and decided upon will fail if it is mishandled by an ignorant or inefficient messenger. Therefore I should consider well what should be done and with due regard to all the pros and cons, I should vigilantly ensure that I do nothing which ought not to be done. I should enter the city in such a way that my presence and my movements are not detected; and I see that Rāvaṇa's security forces are so very efficient that it will not be easy to escape detection."

Thus resolved, Hanumān reduced himself to a small size, to the size of a cat as it were, and when darkness had fallen, proceeded towards the city. Even from a distance he could see the affluence that the city enjoyed. It had buildings of many storeys. It had archways made of gold. It was brilliantly lit and tastefully decorated. The city was of unimaginable beauty and glory. When Hanumān saw it, he was filled with a mixture of feelings, feelings of despondence, and joy—joy at the prospect of seeing Sītā, and despondency at the thought of the difficulty involved in it.

Unnoticed by the guards, Hanumān entered the gateway.

Sundara 3

Hanumān was still contemplating the difficulties of the imminent campaign for the recovery of Sītā. Conquering Laṅkā by force seemed to him to be out of the question. He thought: "Possibly only Kumuda, Aṅgada, Suṣena, Mainda, Dvivida, Sugrīva, Kuśaparva, Jāmbavān[29] and myself may be in a position to cross the ocean and come here. However, in spite of the heavy odds against such a campaign, there is the immeasurable prowess of Rāma and Lakṣmaṇa: surely they can destroy the demons without any difficulty whatsoever."

As he was entering the city, he was intercepted by Laṅkā, the guardian of the city. She questioned him: "Who are you, O vānara? This city of Laṅkā cannot be entered by you!" Hanumān was in no mood to reveal his identity: and he questioned her, in his turn: "Who are you, O lady? And why do you obstruct my path?" Laṅkā replied: "At the command of the mighty Rāvaṇa, I guard this city. No one can ignore me and enter this city: and you, O vānara, will soon enter into eternal sleep, slain at my hands!"

---

[29] **Kumuda . . . Jāmbavān:** Aṅgada is the son of Vāli, Sugrīva's evil brother, who has become an important ally of his uncle's forces; Jāmbavān, another ally of Rāma's, is the leader of a tribe of bears; the others are *vānaras.*

Hanumān said to her: "I have come as a visitor to this city, to see what is to be seen here. When I have seen what I wish to see, I shall duly return to where I have come from. Pray, let me proceed." But Laṅkā continued to say: "You cannot enter without overpowering me or winning my permission," and actually hit Hanumān on his chest with her hand.

Hanumān's anger was aroused. Yet, he controlled himself: for he did not consider it right to kill a woman! He clenched his fist and struck Laṅkā. She fell down, and then revealed: "Compose yourself, O vānara! Do not kill me. The truly strong ones do not violate the code of chivalry, and they do not kill a woman. I am Laṅkā, and he who has conquered me has conquered Laṅkā. That was what Brahmā the creator once said: 'When a vānara overpowers you, know that then the demons have cause for great fear.' I am sure that this prophecy refers to you, O vānara! I realise now that the inevitable destruction of the demons of Laṅkā has entered the territory in the form of Sītā who has been forcibly brought here by Rāvaṇa. Go, enter the city: and surely you will find Sītā and accomplish all that you desire to accomplish."

SUNDARA 4–5

Hanumān did not enter the city through the heavily guarded main gate, but climbed over the wall. Then he came to the main road and proceeded towards his destination—the abode of Rāvaṇa. On the way Hanumān saw the beautiful mansions from which issued the sound of music, and the sound of the citizens' rejoicing. He saw, too, prosperous looking mansions of different designs calculated to bring happiness and greater prosperity to the owners of the mansions. He heard the shouts of wrestling champions. Here and there he heard bards and others singing the glories of Rāvaṇa, and he noticed that these bards were surrounded by citizens in large numbers, blocking the road.

Right in the heart of the city, Hanumān saw in the main square numerous spies of Rāvaṇa: and these spies looked like holy men, with matted hair, or with shaven heads, clad in the hides of cows or in nothing at all. In their hands they carried all sorts of weapons, right from a few blades of grass to maces and sticks. They were of different shapes and sizes and of different appearance and complexions. Hanumān also saw the garrison with a hundred thousand soldiers right in front of the inner apartments of Rāvaṇa.

Hanumān approached the palace of Rāvaṇa himself. This was a truly heavenly abode. Within the compound of the palace and around the building there were numerous horses, chariots, and also aeroplanes. The palace was built of solid and pure gold and the inside was decorated with many precious stones, fragrant with incense and sandalwood which had been sprinkled everywhere: Hanumān entered the palace.

It was nearly midnight. The moon shone brilliantly overhead. From the palace wafted the strains of stringed musical instruments; good-natured women were asleep with their husbands; the violent night-stalkers also emerged from their dwellings to amuse themselves. In some quarters, Hanumān noticed wrestlers training themselves. In some others, women were applying various cosmetic articles to themselves. Some other women were sporting with their husbands. Others whose husbands were away looked unhappy and pale, though they were still beautiful. Hanumān saw all these: but he did not see Sītā anywhere.

Not seeing Sītā, the beloved wife of Rāma, Hanumān felt greatly distressed and unhappy and he became moody and dejected.

Sundara 6, 7, 8

Hanumān was greatly impressed by the beauty and the grandeur of Rāvaṇa's palace which he considered to be the crowning glory of Laṅkā itself. He did not all at once enter Rāvaṇa's inner apartments. First he surveyed the palaces of the other members of the royal family and the leaders of the demons, like Prahasta. He surveyed the palaces of Rāvaṇa's brothers Kumbhakarṇa and Vibhīṣaṇa, as also that of Rāvaṇa's son Indrajit. He was greatly impressed by the unmistakable signs of prosperity that greeted him everywhere. After thus looking at the palaces of all these heroes, Hanumān reached the abode of Rāvaṇa himself.

Rāvaṇa's own inner apartments were guarded by terrible looking demons, holding the most powerful weapons in their hands. Rāvaṇa's own private palace was surrounded by more armed forces; and even these garrisons were embellished by gold and diamonds. Hanumān entered the palace and saw within it palanquins, couches, gardens and art galleries, special chambers for enjoying sexual pleasures and others for indulging in other pastimes during the day. There were also special altars for the performance of sacred rituals. The whole palace was resplendent on account of the light emitted by precious stones which were found everywhere. Everywhere the couches, the seats and the dining vessels were of gold; and the floor of the whole palace was fragrant with the smell of wine and liquor. In fact Hanumān thought that the palace looked like heaven on earth, resplendent with the wealth of precious gems, and fragrant with the scent of a variety of flowers which covered its dome making it look like a flower-covered hill.

There were swimming pools with lotuses and lilies. In one of them there was the carved figure of a lordly elephant offering worship to Lakṣmī, the goddess of wealth.

Right in the centre of the palace stood the best of all aeroplanes, known as Puṣpaka. It had been painted with many colours and provided with numerous precious gems. It was decorated with lovely figures of snakes, birds, and horses fashioned of gems, silver and coral. Every part of that aeroplane had been carefully engineered, only the very best materials had been used, and it had special features which even the vehicles of the gods did not have—in fact, in it had been brought together only special features! Rāvaṇa had acquired it after great austerities and effort.

Hanumān saw all this. But, he did not see Sītā anywhere!

Sundara 9

Hanumān ascended the aeroplane Puṣpaka from which he could easily look into the inner apartments of Rāvaṇa! As he stood on the aeroplane, he smelt the extraordinary odour emanating from Rāvaṇa's dining room—the odour of wines and liquors, the smell of excellent food. The smell was appetising and Hanumān thought the food should be nourishing. And, he saw at the same time the beautiful hall of Rāvaṇa which had crystal floors, with inlaid figures made of ivory, pearls, diamonds, corals, silver and gold. The hall was resplendent with pillars of gems. There was on the floor, a carpet of extraordinary beauty and design. On the walls were murals of several countries' landscapes. This hall thus provided all the five senses with the objects for their utmost gratification! A soft light illumined this hall.

On the carpet beautiful women lay asleep. With their mouths and their eyes closed, they had fallen asleep, after drinking and dancing, and from their bodies issued the sweet fragrance of lotuses. Rāvaṇa, sleeping there surrounded by these beautiful women, looked like the moon surrounded by the stars in the night sky. They were all asleep in beautiful disorder. Some were using their own arms as the pillow, others used the different parts of yet others' bodies as their pillow. Their hair was in disarray. Their dress was in disarray, too. But none of these conditions diminished the beauty of their forms. From the breath of all the women there issued the smell of liquor.

These women had come from different grades of society. Some of them were the daughters of royal sages, others those of brāhmaṇas, yet others were the daughters of gandharvas (celestial artists), and, of course, some were the daughters of demons: and all of them had voluntarily sought Rāvaṇa, for they loved him. Some he had won by his valour; others had become infatuated with him. None of these women had been carried away by Rāvaṇa against their wish. None of them had been married before. None of them had desire for another man. Rāvaṇa had never before abducted any woman, except Sītā.

Hanumān thought for a moment: Rāvaṇa would indeed have been a good man if he had thus got Sītā too, to be his wife: that is, before she had married Rāma and if he had been able to win her by his valour or by his charm. But, Hanumān contemplated further: by abducting the wife of Rāma, Rāvaṇa had certainly committed a highly unworthy action.

Sundara 10–11

In the centre of that hall, Hanumān saw the most beautiful and the most luxurious bed: it was celestial in its appearance, built entirely of crystal and decked with gems. The lord of the demons, Rāvaṇa himself was asleep on it. The sight of this demon was at first revolting to Hanumān; so he turned his face away from Rāvaṇa. But then he turned his gaze again to Rāvaṇa. He saw that the two arms of Rāvaṇa were strong and powerful, and they were adorned with resplendent jewelry. His face, his chest, in fact his whole body was strong and radiant. His limbs shone like the lightning.

Around this bed were others on which the consorts of Rāvaṇa were asleep. Many of them had obviously been entertaining the demon with their music; and they had fallen asleep with the musical instruments in their arms. On yet another bed was asleep the most charming of all the women in that hall: she surpassed all the others in beauty, in youth and in adornment. For a moment Hanumān thought it was Sītā: and the very thought that he had seen Sītā delighted him.

But that thought did not last long. Hanumān realised: "It cannot be. For, separated from Rāma, Sītā will not sleep, nor will she enjoy herself, adorn herself or drink anything. Nor will Sītā ever dwell with another man, even if he be a celestial: for truly there is none equal to Rāma." He turned away from the hall, since he did not see Sītā there.

Next, Hanumān searched the dining hall and the kitchen: there he saw varieties of meats and other delicacies, condiments and a variety of drinks. The dining hall floor had been strewn with drinking vessels, fruits and even anklets and armlets which had obviously fallen from their wearers as they were drinking and getting intoxicated.

While he was thus inspecting the palace and searching for Sītā, a thought flashed in Hanumān's mind: was he guilty of transgressing the bounds of morality, in as much as he was gazing at the wives of others, while they were asleep with their ornaments and clothes in disarray? But, he consoled himself with the thought: "True, I have seen all these women in Rāvaṇa's apartment. But, no lustful thought has entered my mind! The mind alone is the cause of good and evil actions performed by the senses; but my mind is devoted to and established in righteousness. Where else can I look for Sītā, except among the womenfolk in Rāvaṇa's palace: shall I look for a lost woman among a herd of deer? I have looked for Sītā in this place with a pure mind; but she is not to be seen."

Sundara 12–13

Hanumān had searched the whole palace of Rāvaṇa. But he could not find Sītā. He reflected: "I shall not yield to despair. For, it has been well said that perseverance alone is the secret of prosperity and great happiness; perseverance alone keeps all things going, and crowns all activities with success. I shall search those places which I have not yet searched." He then began to search for Sītā in other parts of the palace. He saw many, many other women, but not Sītā.

Hanumān then searched for Sītā outside the palace. Yet, he could not find her. Once again dejection gripped him. He thought: "Sītā is to be found nowhere; yet Sampāti did say that he saw Rāvaṇa and he saw Sītā, too. Perhaps it was mistaken identity. It may be that slipping from the control of Rāvaṇa, Sītā dropped her body into the sea. Or, it may be she died of shock. Or, perhaps when she did not yield to him, Rāvaṇa killed her and ate her flesh. But it is impossible that she had consented to be Rāvaṇa's consort. Whether she is lost, or she has perished or has died, how can I inform Rāma about it? On the other hand, to inform Rāma and not to inform Rāma—both these appear to be objectionable. What shall I do now?" He also reflected on the consequence of his returning to Kiṣkindhā with no news of Sītā. He felt certain that: "When Rāma hears the bad news from me, he will give up his life. So will Lakṣmaṇa. And then their brothers and mothers in Ayodhyā. Nor could Sugrīva live after Rāma departs from this world. He will be followed to the other world by all the vānaras of Kiṣkindhā. What a terrible calamity will strike Ayodhyā and Kiṣkindhā if I return without news of Sītā's safety!" He resolved: "It is good that I should not return to Kiṣkindhā. Like an ascetic I shall live under a tree here. Or, I can commit suicide by jumping into the sea. However, the wise ones say that suicide is the root of many evils, and that if one lives one is sure to find what one seeks."

The consciousness of his extraordinary strength suddenly seized Hanumān! He sprang up and said to himself: "I shall at once kill this demon Rāvaṇa. Even if I cannot find Sītā, I shall have avenged her abduction by killing her abductor. Or, I shall kidnap him and take him to Rāma." Then he thought of a few places in Laṅkā he had not yet searched; one of them was Aśoka-grove. He resolved to go there. Before doing so, he offered a prayer: "Salutations to Rāma and Lakṣmaṇa; salutations to Sītā, the daughter of Janaka. Salutations to Rudra, Indra, Yama, the wind-god, to the moon, fire, and the Maruts." He turned round in all directions and invoked the blessings of all. He knew he needed them for he felt that demons of superhuman strength were guarding the Aśoka-grove.

Sundara 14–15

Hanumān then climbed the palace wall and jumped into the Aśoka-grove. It was most beautiful and enchanting, with trees and creepers of innumerable types.

In that grove, Hanumān also saw the bird sanctuary, the ponds and artificial swimming pools hemmed by flights of steps which had been paved with expensive precious and semi-precious stones. He also saw a hill with a waterfall flowing from its side. Not far from there, he saw a unique Aśoka or Simśapā tree which was golden in its appearance. The area around this tree was covered with trees which had golden leaves and blossoms, giving the appearance that they were ablaze.

Climbing up that unique Simśapā tree, Hanumān felt certain that he would soon see Sītā. He reasoned: "Sītā was fond of the forests and groves, according to Rāma. Hence, she will doubtless come to this yonder lotus-pond. Rāma did say that she was fond of roaming the forest: surely, then, she would wish to roam this grove, too. It is almost certain that the grief-stricken Sītā would come here to offer her evening prayers. If she is still alive, I shall surely see her today."

Seated on that Aśoka or Simśapā tree, Hanumān surveyed the whole of the grove. He was enthralled by the beauty of the grove, of the trees, and of the blossoms which were so colourful that it appeared as if the whole place were afire. There were numerous other trees, too, all of which were delightful to look at. While he was thus surveying the scene, he saw a magnificent temple, not far from him. This temple had a hall of a thousand pillars, and looked like the Kailāsa.[30] The temple had been painted white. It had steps carved out of coral. And its platforms were all made of pure gold.

And, then, Hanumān saw a radiant woman with an ascetic appearance. She

[30] **Kailāsa:** The Himalayan dwelling of Śiva.

was surrounded by demonesses who were apparently guarding her. She was radiant though her garments were soiled. She was beautiful in form, though emaciated through sorrow, hunger and austerity. Hanumān felt certain that it was Sītā, and that it was the same lady whom he had momentarily seen over the Ṛṣymūka hill. She was seated on the ground. And, she was frequently sighing, surely on account of her separation from Rāma. With great difficulty, Hanumān recognised her as Sītā: and in this he was helped only by the graphic and vivid description that Rāma had given him.

Looking at her, thus pining for Rāma, and recollecting Rāma's love for her, Hanumān marvelled at the patience of Rāma in that he could live without Sītā even for a short while.

Sundara 16–17

Hanumān contemplated the divine form of Sītā for a few minutes; and he once again gave way to dejection. He reflected: "If even Sītā who is highly esteemed by the noble and humble Lakṣmaṇa, and who is the beloved of Rāma himself, could be subjected to such sorrow, indeed one should conclude that Time is all-powerful. Surely, Sītā is utterly confident in the ability of Rāma and Lakṣmaṇa to rescue her; and hence she is tranquil even in this misfortune. Only Rāma deserves to be her husband, and she to be Rāma's consort." How great was Rāma's love for Sītā! And, what an extraordinary person Sītā was! Hanumān continued to 'weigh' her in his own mind's balance: "It was for the sake of Sītā that thousands of demons in the Daṇḍaka forest were killed by Rāma. It was for her sake alone that Rāma killed Vāli and Kabandha. Khara, Dūṣaṇa, Triśira—so many of these demons met their end because of her. And, why not: she is such a special person that if, for her sake, Rāma turned the whole world upside down it would be proper. For, she was of extraordinary birth, she is of extraordinary beauty and she is of extraordinary character. She is unexcelled in every way. And, what an extraordinary love she has for Rāma, in that she patiently endures all sorts of hardships living, as she does, as a captive in Laṅkā. Again, Rāma pines for her and is eagerly waiting to see her, to regain her. Here she is, constantly thinking of Rāma: she does not see either these demonesses guarding her, nor the trees, flowers or fruits, but with her heart centred in Rāma, she sees him alone constantly." He was now certain that that lady was in fact Sītā.

The moon had risen. The sky was clear and the moonlight enabled Hanumān to see Sītā clearly. He saw the demonesses guarding Sītā. They were hideous-looking and deformed in various parts of their bodies. Their lips, breasts and bellies were disproportionately large and hanging. Some were very tall; others were very short. They were mostly dark-complexioned. Some of them had ears, etc., that made them look like animals. They were querulous, noisy, and fond of flesh and liquor. They had smeared their bodies with meat and blood; and they ate meat and blood. Their very sight was revolting and frightening. There in their midst was Sītā.

Sītā's dress and her appearance reflected her grief. At the foot of the tree whose name, Aśoka, meant free of sorrow, was seated Sītā immersed in an ocean of sorrow, surrounded by these terrible demonesses! It was only her confidence in the prowess and the valour of her lord Rāma that sustained her life. Hanumān mentally prostrated to Rāma, to Lakṣmaṇa and to Sītā and hid himself among the branches of the tree.

Sundara 18, 19, 20

Night was drawing to a close. In his palace, Rāvaṇa was being awakened by the Vedic recitation of brāhmaṇa-demons who were well versed in the Vedas and other scriptural texts, and also by musicians and bards who sang his praises. Even before he had time to adorn himself properly, Rāvaṇa thought of Sītā and longed intensely to see her. Quickly adorning himself with the best of ornaments and clad in splendid garments, he entered the Aśoka-grove, accompanied by a hundred chosen women who carried golden torches, fans, cushions and other articles. They were still under the influence of alcohol: and Rāvaṇa, though mighty and powerful, was under the influence of passion for Sītā.

Hanumān recognised the person he had seen asleep in the palace the previous night.

Seeing him coming in her direction, the frightened Sītā shielded her torso with her legs and hands, and began to weep bitterly. Pining for Rāma, distressed on account of her separation from him and stricken with grief, the most beautiful and radiant Sītā resembled eclipsed fame, neglected faith, enfeebled understanding, forlorn hope, ruined prospect, disregarded command, and obstructed worship; eclipsed moon, decimated army, fuelless flame, river in drought. She was constantly engaged in the prayer that Rāma might soon triumph over Rāvaṇa and rescue her.

Rāvaṇa appeared to be chivalrous in his approach to Sītā, and his words were meaningful and sweet: he said to Sītā, "Pray, do not be afraid of me, O charming lady! It is natural for a demon to enjoy others' wives and abduct them forcibly; it is the demon's own dharma. But, I shall not violate you against your wishes. For, I want to win your love; I want to win your esteem. I have enough strength to restrain myself. Yet, it breaks my heart to see you suffer like this; to see you, a princess, dressed like this in tattered and dirty garments. You are born to apply the most delightful cosmetic articles, to wear royal attire, and to adorn yourself with the most expensive jewels. You are young, youthful: this is the time to enjoy yourself, for youth is passing. There is none in the three worlds who is as beautiful as you are, O princess: for, having fashioned you, the Creator has retired. You are so beautiful that no one in the three worlds — not even Brahmā the creator — could but be overcome by passion. When you accept me, all that I have will become yours. Even my chief wives will become your servants. Let me warn you: no one in the three worlds is my match in strength and valour. Rāma, even if he is alive, does not even know where you are: he has no hope of regaining you. Give up this foolish idea of yours. Let me behold you appropriately dressed and adorned. And, let us enjoy life to your heart's content."

Sundara 21–22

Rāvaṇa's words were extremely painful to the grief-stricken Sītā. She placed a blade of grass in front of her, unwilling even to speak to Rāvaṇa directly, and said: "You cannot aspire for me any more than a sinful man can aspire for perfection! I will not do what is unworthy in the eyes of a chaste wife. Surely, you do not know dharma, nor do you obviously listen to the advice of wise counsellors. Set an example to your subjects, O demon: and consort with your own wives; desire for others' wives will lead to infamy. The world rejoices at the death of a wicked man: even so it will, soon, on your death. But do not desire for me. You cannot win me by offering me power or wealth: for I am inseparable from Rāma even as light from the sun. He is the abode of righteousness, of dharma; take me back to him and beg his pardon. He loves those who seek his refuge. If you do not, you will surely come to grief: for no power on earth can save you from Rāma's weapon. His missiles will surely destroy the entire Laṅkā. In fact, if you had not stolen me in the absence of Rāma and Lakṣmaṇa, you would not be alive today: you could not face them, you coward!"

Rāvaṇa's anger was roused, and he replied: "Normally, women respond to a pleasant approach by a man. But you seem to be different, O Sītā. You rouse my anger; but my desire for you subdues that anger. My love for you prevents me from killing you straight away; though you deserve to be executed, for all the insulting and impudent words you utter. Well, I had fixed one year as the time-limit for you to make up your mind. Ten months have elapsed since then. You have two more months in which to decide to accede to my wish. If you fail to do so, my cooks will prepare a nice meal of your flesh for me to eat."

But, Sītā remained unmoved. She said to Rāvaṇa: "You are prattling, O wicked demon: I can by my own spiritual energy reduce you to ashes: but I do not do so on account of the fact that I have not been so ordered by Rāma and I do not want to waste my own spiritual powers."

The terrible demon was greatly enraged by these words of Sītā. He threatened her: "Wait, I shall destroy you just now." But he did not do so. However, he said to the demonesses guarding Sītā: "Use all your powers to persuade Sītā to consent to my proposal." Immediately, Rāvaṇa's consorts embraced him and pleaded: "Why don't you enjoy our company, giving up your desire for Sītā? For, a man who seeks the company of one who has no love for him comes to grief, and he who seeks the company of one who loves him enjoys life." Hearing this and laughing aloud, Rāvaṇa walked away.

Sundara 23–24

After Rāvaṇa had left the grove, the demonesses said: "How is it that you do not value Rāvaṇa's hand? Perhaps you do not know who he is. Of the six Prajāpatis who were the sons of the creator himself, Pulastya is the fourth; of Pulastya was the sage Viśrava born, and he was equal to Pulastya himself in glory. And this Rāvaṇa is the son of Viśrava. He is known as Rāvaṇa because he makes his enemies cry. It is a great honour to accept his proposal. Moreover, this Rāvaṇa worsted in battle the thirty-three deities presiding over the universe. Hence he is superior even to the gods. And, what is most important: he surely loves you so much that he is prepared to abandon his own favourite wives and give you all his love."

Sītā was deeply pained by these words uttered by the demonesses. She said: "Enough of this vulgar and sinful advice. A human being should not become the wife of a demon. But, even that is irrelevant. I shall not under any circumstance abandon my husband and seek another." The demonesses were enraged and began to threaten Sītā. And, Hanumān was witnessing all this.

The demonesses said again: "You have shown enough affection to the unworthy Rāma. Excess of anything is undesirable and leads to undesirable result. You have so far conformed to the human rules of conduct. It is high time that you abandoned that code, abandoned the human Rāma and consented to be Rāvaṇa's wife. We have so far put up with the rude and harsh words you have uttered; and we have so far offered you loving and wholesome advice, intent as we are on your welfare. But you seem to be too stupid to see the truth. You have been brought here by Rāvaṇa; you have crossed the ocean. Others cannot cross the ocean and come to your rescue. We tell you this, O Sītā: even Indra cannot rescue you from here. Therefore, please do as we tell you, in your interest. Enough of your weeping. Give up this sorrow which is destructive. Abandon this wretched life. Attain love and pleasure. Make haste, O Sītā: for youth, especially of women, is but momentary and passes quickly. Make up your mind to become Rāvaṇa's wife. If, however, you are obstinate, we shall ourselves tear your body and eat your heart."

Other demonesses took up the cue and began to threaten Sītā. They said: "When I first saw this lovely woman brought into Laṅkā by Rāvaṇa the desire arose in me that I should eat her liver and spleen, her breasts and her heart. I am waiting for that day. . . . What is the delay? Let us report to the king that she died and he will surely ask us to eat her flesh! . . . We should divide her flesh equally and eat it, there should be no quarrel amongst us. . . . After the meal, we shall dance in front of the goddess Bhadrakāli."[31]

Sundara 25–26

In utter despair, Sītā gave vent to her grief by thinking aloud: "The wise ones have rightly said that untimely death is not attained here either by man or a woman. Hence though I am suffering intolerable anguish on account of my separation from my beloved husband, I am unable to give up my life. This grief is slowly eating me. I can neither live nor can I die. Surely, this is the bitter fruit of some dreadful sin committed in a past birth. I am surrounded by these demonesses: and how can Rāma reach me here? Fie upon human birth, and fie upon the state of dependence upon others, as a result of which I cannot even give up my life.

[31] **Bhadrakāli:** The fearsome, eight-armed goddess of destruction, often depicted dancing.

"What a terrible misfortune it was that even though I was living under the protection of Rāma and Lakṣmaṇa, I was abducted by Rāvaṇa, in their absence. Even more terrible it is that having been separated from my beloved husband I am confined here surrounded by these terrible demonesses. And, the worst part of it is: in spite of all these misfortunes, my heart does not burst with anguish thus letting me die. Of course, I shall never allow Rāvaṇa to touch me, so long as I am alive.

"I wonder why Rāma has not taken steps to come to my aid. For my sake he killed thousands of demons while we were in the forest. True I am on an island; but Rāma's missiles have no difficulty crossing oceans and finding their target. Surely, he does not know where I am. Alas, even Jaṭāyu who could have informed Rāma of what had happened was killed by Rāvaṇa. If only he knew I was here, Rāma would have destroyed Laṅkā and dried up the ocean with his missiles. All the demonesses of Laṅkā would weep then, as I am weeping now; all the demons would be killed by Rāma. Laṅkā would be one huge crematorium.

"I see all sorts of evil portents. I shall be re-united with Rāma. He will come. He will destroy all these demons. If only Rāma comes to know where I am, Laṅkā will be turned desolate by him, burnt by his terrible missiles. On the other hand, the time is fast running out: the time limit that Rāvaṇa had fixed for me to decide. Two more months: and I shall be cut into pieces for Rāvaṇa's meal. May it be that Rāma himself is no more, having succumbed to grief on account of my separation? Or, may it be that he has turned an ascetic? Usually, people who love each other forget each other when they are separated; but not so Rāma whose love is eternal. Blessed indeed are the holy sages who have reached enlightenment and to whom the pleasant and the unpleasant are non-different. I salute the holy ones. And, fallen into this terrible misfortune, I shall presently give up my life."

Sundara 27

Hearing the words of Sītā, some of the demonesses grew terribly angry. They threatened: "We shall go and report all this to Rāvaṇa; and then we shall be able to eat you at once." Another demoness named Trijaṭā just then woke up from her slumber and announced: "Forget all this talk about eating Sītā, O foolish ones! I have just now dreamt a dream which forewarns that a terrible calamity awaits all of you." The demonesses asked: "Tell us what the dream was."

Trijaṭā narrated her dream in great detail: "I saw in my dream Rāma and Lakṣmaṇa, riding a white space vehicle. Sītā was sitting on a white mountain, clad in shining white robes. Rāma and Sītā were re-united. Rāma and Lakṣmaṇa then got on a huge elephant which Sītā, too, mounted. Sītā held out her arms and her hands touched the sun and the moon. Rāma, Lakṣmaṇa and Sītā later mounted the Puṣpaka space vehicle and flew away in a northerly direction. From all these I conclude that Rāma is divine and invincible.

"Listen to me further. In another dream I saw Rāvaṇa. His head had been shaven. He was covered with oil. He wore crimson clothes. He was drunk. He had fallen from the Puṣpaka space vehicle. Later, I saw him dressed in black but smeared in a red pigment and dragged by a woman riding a vehicle drawn by donkeys. He fell down from the donkey. He was prattling like a mad man. Then he entered a place which was terribly dark and foul-smelling. Later a dark woman with body covered in mud, bound Rāvaṇa's neck and dragged him away in a southerly direction. I saw Kumbhakarṇa as also the sons of Rāvaṇa in that dream; all of them undergoing the same or similar treatment. Only Vibhiṣaṇa's luck was different. He was clad in white garment, with white garlands, and had a royal white umbrella held over his head.

"I also saw in that dream that the whole of Laṅkā had been pushed into the sea, utterly destroyed and ruined. I also saw a rather strange dream. I saw Laṅkā burning furiously: though Laṅkā is protected by Rāvaṇa who is mighty and powerful, a vānara was able to set Laṅkā ablaze, because the vānara was a servant of Rāma.

"I see a clear warning in these dreams. O foolish women! Enough of your cruelty to Sītā; I think it is better to please her and win her favour. I am convinced that Sītā will surely achieve her purpose and her desire to be re-united with Rāma."

Hearing this, Sītā felt happy and said: "If this comes true, I shall certainly protect all of you."

Sundara 28, 29, 30

But, the demonesses did not pay heed to Trijaṭā. And, Sītā thought:

"Truly have the wise ones declared that death never comes to a person before the appointed time. My time has come. Rāvaṇa has said definitely that if I do not agree to him I will be put to death. Since I can never, never love him, it is certain that I shall be executed. Hence, I am condemned already. I shall, therefore, incur no blame if I voluntarily end my life today. O Rāma! O Lakṣmaṇa! O Sumitrā! O Kausalyā! O Mother! Caught helplessly and brought to this dreadful place, I am about to perish. Surely it was my own 'bad-time' that approached me in the form of that golden deer, and I, a foolish woman sent the two princes in search of it. Maybe, they were killed by some demon. Or, maybe they are alive and do not know where I am.

"Alas, whatever virtue I practised and the devotion with which I served my own lord and husband, all these have come to naught; I shall presently abandon this ill-fated life of mine. O Rāma, after you complete the fourteen-year term of exile, you will return to Ayodhyā and enjoy life with the queens you might marry. But, I who loved you and whose heart is forever fastened to you, shall soon be no more.

"How shall I end this life? I have no weapon; nor will anyone here give me a weapon or poison to end my life. Ah, I shall use this string with which my hair has been tied and hang myself from this tree."

Thinking aloud in this manner, Sītā contemplated the feet of Rāma and got ready to execute herself. At the same time, however, she noticed many auspicious omens which dissuaded her from her wish to end her life. Her left eye, left arm and left thigh throbbed. Her heart was gladdened, her sorrow left her for the moment, her despair abated, and she became calm and radiant once again.

Hanumān, sitting on the tree, watched all this. He thought: "If I meet Sītā in the midst of these demonesses, it would be disastrous. In fact, she might get frightened and cry and before I could make the announcement concerning Rāma, I might be caught. I can fight all the demons here; but then I might be too weak to fly back. I could speak to her in the dialect of the brāhmaṇa; but she might suspect a vānara speaking Sanskrit to be Rāvaṇa himself! To speak to Sītā now seems to be risky; yet, if I do not, she might commit suicide. If one does not act with due regard to place and time, the contrary results ensue. I shall sing the glories of Rāma softly and thus win Sītā's confidence. Then I shall deliver Rāma's message to her in a manner which will evoke her confidence."

Sundara 31, 32, 33

After deep deliberation, Hanumān decided upon the safest and the wisest course! Softly, sweetly, clearly and in cultured accents, he narrated the story of Rāma. He said: "A descendant of the noble Ikṣvāku was the emperor Daśaratha, who was a royal sage in as much as he was devoted to asceticism and righteousness, while yet ruling his kingdom. His eldest son Rāma was equally powerful, glorious and righteous. To honour his father's promise to his step-mother, Rāma went to the Daṇḍaka forest along with his brother Lakṣmaṇa, and his wife Sītā. There, Rāma killed thousands of demons. A demon disguised as a deer tricked Rāma and Lakṣmaṇa away, and at that time, the wicked Rāvaṇa abducted Sītā. Rāma went searching for her; and while so wandering the forest cultivated the friendship of the vānara Sugrīva. Sugrīva commissioned millions of vānaras to search for Sītā. Endowed with extraordinary energy, I crossed the ocean; and blessed I am that I am able to behold that Sītā."

Sītā was supremely delighted to hear that speech. She looked up and down, around and everywhere, and saw the vānara Hanumān. But, seeing the vānara seated on the tree, Sītā was frightened and suspicious. She cried aloud: "O Rāma, O Lakṣmaṇa." She was terror-stricken as the vānara approached her; but she was pleasantly surprised to see that he came humbly and worshipfully. She thought: "Am I dreaming? I hope not; it forebodes ill to dream of a vānara. Nay, I am not dreaming. Maybe, this is hallucination. I have constantly been thinking of Rāma. I have constantly uttered his name, and talked about him. Since my whole being is absorbed in him, I am imagining all this. But, I have reasoned out all this carefully within myself; yet, this being here is not only clearly seen by me, but it talks to me, too! I pray to the gods, may what I have just heard be true."

With his palms joined together in salutation over his head, Hanumān humbly approached Sītā and asked: "Who are you, O lady? Are you indeed the wife of that blessed Rāma?"

Highly pleased with this question, Sītā thereupon related her whole story: "I am the daughter-in-law of king Daśaratha, and the daughter of king Janaka. I am the wife of Rāma. We lived happily in Ayodhyā for twelve years. But when Rāma was about to be crowned, his step-mother Kaikeyī demanded the boon from her husband that Rāma should be banished to the forest. The king swooned on hearing this; but Rāma took it upon himself to fulfil that promise. I followed him; and Lakṣmaṇa, too, came with us. One day when they were away, Rāvaṇa forcibly carried me and brought me here. He has given me two more months to live; after which I shall meet my end."

SUNDARA 34–35

Once again bowing down to Sītā, Hanumān said to her: "O divine lady, I am a messenger sent by Rāma. He, as also his brother Lakṣmaṇa, send their greetings and hope that you are alive and well." Sītā rejoiced and thought to herself: "Surely, there is a lot of truth in the old adage: 'Happiness is bound to come to the man who lives, even though after a long time.'" But, as Hanumān came near her, she grew suspicious and would not even look at him: she thought, and said to him: "O Rāvaṇa! Previously you assumed the disguise of a mendicant and abducted me. Now, you have come to torment me in the guise of a vānara! Pray, leave me alone." But, on the other hand, she reasoned to herself: "No this cannot be; for on seeing this vānara, my heart rejoices."

Hanumān, however, reassured her: "O blessed Sītā, I am a messenger sent by Rāma who will very soon kill these demons and rescue you from their captivity. Rāma and Lakṣmaṇa constantly think of you. So does king Sugrīva whose minister Hanumān, I am. Endowed with extraordinary energy I crossed the sea. I am not what you suspect me to be!"

At her request, Hanumān recounted the glories of Rāma: "Rāma is equal to the gods in beauty, charm and wisdom. He is the protector of all living beings, of his own people, of his work and of his dharma; he is the protector of people of different occupations, of good conduct, and he himself adheres to good conduct and makes others do so, too. He is mighty, friendly, well-versed in scriptures and devoted to the holy ones. He is endowed with all the characteristics of the best among men, which are: broad shoulders, strong arms, powerful neck, lovely face, reddish eyes, deep voice, dark-brown coloured skin; he has firm chest, wrist and fist; he has long eyebrows, arms and scrotum; he has symmetrical locks, testicles and knees; he has strong bulging chest, abdomen and rim of the navel; reddish in the corner of his eyes, nails, palms and soles; he is soft in his glans, the lines of his feet and hair; he has deep voice, gait and navel; three folds adorn the skin of his neck and his abdomen; the arch of his feet, the lines on his soles, and the nipples are deep; he has short generative organ, neck, back and shanks; three spirals adorn the hair on his head; there are four lines at the root of his thumb; and four lines on his forehead; he is four cubits tall; the four pairs of his limbs (cheeks, arms, shanks and knees) are symmetrical; even so the other fourteen pairs of limbs; his limbs are long. He is excellent in every way. Lakṣmaṇa, Rāma's brother, is also full of charm and excellences."

SUNDARA 35–36

Hanumān then narrated in great detail all that had happened. He mentioned in particular how Rāma was moved to tears when Hanumān showed him the pieces of jewelry that Sītā had dropped on the hill. He concluded that narrative by affirming: "I shall certainly attain the glory of having seen you first; and Rāma too will soon come here to take you back." He also revealed to Sītā his own identity: "Kesari, my father, lived on the mountain known as Malayavān. Once he went to the Gokarṇa mountain at the command of the sages to fight and to kill a demon named Sāmbasadana who tormented the people. I was born of the wind-god and my mother Añjanā. I tell you again, O divine lady, that I am a vānara, and I am a messenger sent by Rāma; here, behold the ring which has been inscribed with the name of Rāma. Whatever might have been the cause of your suffering captivity, it has almost come to an end."

When she saw the signet ring, Sītā felt the presence of Rāma himself; she was filled with joy. Her attitude to Hanumān, too, immediately and dramatically changed. She exclaimed: "You are heroic, capable, and wise, too, O best among vānaras. What a remarkable feat you have accomplished by crossing this vast ocean, a distance of eight hundred miles. Surely, you are not an ordinary vānara in that you are not afraid of even Rāvaṇa. I am delighted to hear that Rāma and Lakṣmaṇa are well. But why has he not rescued me yet: he could dry up the ocean, in fact he could even destroy the whole earth with his missiles if he wanted to. Perhaps, they had to wait for the propitious moment, and that moment which would mean the end of my suffering has not yet arrived.

"O Hanumān, tell me more about Rāma. Does he continue to rely on both self-effort and divine agency in all that he undertakes? Tell me, O Hanumān, does he still love me as before? And, I also hope that, pining for me, he does not waste away. And also tell me: how will Rāma rescue me from here. Will Bharata send an army? When he renounced the throne and when he took me to the forest, he displayed extraordinary firmness: is he still as firm in his resolves? Oh, I know that he loves me more than anyone else in this world."

Hanumān replied: "You will soon behold Rāma, O Sītā! Stricken with grief on account of his separation from you, Rāma does not eat meat, nor drink wine; he does not even wish to ward off flies and mosquitoes that assail him. He thinks of you constantly. He hardly sleeps; and if he does, he wakes up calling out 'Ah Sītā'. When he sees a fruit or flower, he thinks of you." Hearing the glories of Rāma, Sītā was rid of sorrow; hearing of his grief, Sītā grew equally sorrowful.

SUNDARA 37

Sītā replied to Hanumān: "Your description of Rāma's love for me comes to me like nectar mixed with poison. In whatever condition one may be, whether one is enjoying unlimited power and prosperity or one is in dreadful misery, the end of one's action drags a man as if he were tied with a rope. Look at the way in which Rāma, Lakṣmaṇa and I have been subjected to sorrow: surely, no one can overcome destiny. I wonder when the time will come when I shall be united with Rāma once again. Rāvaṇa gave me one year, of which ten months have passed and only two are left. At the end of those two months, Rāvaṇa will surely kill me. There is no alternative. For, he does not fancy the thought of taking me back to Rāma. In fact, such a course was suggested by Rāvaṇa's own brother Vibhīṣaṇa: so his own daughter Kalā told me. But Rāvaṇa turns a deaf ear upon such wise counsel."

Hanumān said to Sītā: "I am sure that Rāma will soon arrive here, with an army of forest-dwellers and other tribes, as soon as I inform him of your whereabouts. But, O divine lady, I have another idea. You can rejoin your husband this very day. I can enable you to end this sorrow instantly. Pray, do not hesitate; get on my back, and seek union (yogam) with Rāma now. I have the power to carry you, or even Laṅkā, Rāvaṇa and everything in it! No one will be able to pursue me or to overcome me. What a great triumph it will be if I return to Kiṣkindhā with you on my back!"

For a moment Sītā was thrilled at this prospect. But she remarked almost in jest: "You are speaking truly like a vānara, an ignorant tribesman. You are so small: and you think you can carry me over the ocean!" Hanumān, thereupon, showed Sītā his real form. Seeing him stand like a mountain in front of her, Sītā felt sure that his confidence was justified, but said to him: "O mighty Hanumān, I am convinced that you can do as you say. But I do not think it is proper for me to go with you. You may proceed at great speed; but I may slip and fall into the ocean. If I go with you, the demons will suspect our relationship and give it an immoral twist. Moreover, many demons will pursue you: how will you, unarmed as you are, deal with them and at the same time protect me? I might once again fall into their hands. I agree you have the power to fight them: but if you kill them all, it will rob Rāma of the glory of killing them and rescuing me. Surely, when Rāma and Lakṣmaṇa come here with you, they will destroy the demons and liberate me. I am devoted to Rāma; and I will not of my own accord touch the body of another man. Therefore, O Hanumān, enable Rāma and Lakṣmaṇa to come here with greatest expedition."

Sundara 38

Hanumān, the wise vānara, was highly impressed and thoroughly convinced of the propriety of Sītā's arguments. He applauded them, and prayed: "If you feel you should not come, pray, give me a token which I might take back with me and which Rāma might recognise."

This suggestion revived old memories and moved Sītā to tears. She said to Hanumān: "I shall give you the best token. Please remind my glorious husband of a delightful episode in our forest-life which only he and I know. This happened when we were living near Citrakooṭa hill. We had finished our bath; and we had had a lot of fun playing in water, Rāma was sitting on my lap. A crow began to worry me. I kept it away threatening it with stones. It hid itself. When I was getting dressed and when my skirt slipped a little, the crow attacked me again: but I defended myself angrily. Looking at this Rāma laughed, while sweetly pacifying me.

"Both of us were tired. I slept on Rāma's lap for sometime. Later Rāma slept with his head resting on my lap. The crow (who was Indra's son in disguise) attacked me again and began to inflict wounds on my body. A few drops of blood trickled from my chest and fell on Rāma who awoke. Seeing the vicious crow perched on a nearby tree, Rāma picked up the missile named after the creator and hurled it at the crow. That crow flew round to the three worlds but found no asylum anywhere else.

"Eventually it sought refuge with Rāma himself. Rāma was instantly pacified. Yet, the missile could not be neutralised. The crow sacrificed its right eye and saved its life." As she was narrating the story, Sītā felt the presence of Rāma and addressed him: "O Rāma, you were ready to use the Brahmā-missile towards a mere crow for my sake; why do you suffer my abduction with patience? Though I have you as my lord and master, yet I live here like a destitute! Have you no compassion for me: it was from you I learnt that compassion is the greatest virtue!" She said to Hanumān again: "No power on earth can confront Rāma. It is only my ill-luck that prevents them from coming to my rescue."

Hanumān explained: "It was only ignorance of your whereabouts that has caused this delay, O divine lady. Now that we know where you are, the destruction of the demons is at hand." Sītā said: "The fulfilment of this mission depends upon you; with your aid, Rāma will surely succeed in his mission. But, please tell Rāma that I shall be alive only for a month more." Then as a further token, Sītā took off a precious jewel from her person and gave it to Hanumān. Receiving that jewel, and with Sītā's blessings Hanumān was ready to depart.

SUNDARA 39–40

Once again Sītā reminded Hanumān: "I had kept with me this jewel which was to me the very presence of Rāma. Whenever I looked at it, it was as if Rāma were with me. It will remind Rāma of me, of my mother and of king Daśaratha. Pray, tell Rāma all that you have seen here, how I live, how I pine for him and how I remain alive only in the hope of seeing him again. Say all this in such a way that Rāma will rescue me alive; and thus shall you have earned the merit of using the power of speech aright. What, when and how Rāma does now depends entirely upon what and how you say to him when you meet him." Hanumān reassured her.

But, fear and doubt haunted Sītā who said: "I am haunted by a doubt, O Hanumān. How will the hordes of the hill-tribes cross the ocean and come here? Of course it will be glorious if Rāma kills Rāvaṇa and his demon followers and returns with me to Ayodhyā. But, how do you think this can be achieved?"

To reassure her, Hanumān said: "It is easy for us vānaras, O divine lady. The vānaras are very powerful. They have often gone round the world along the aerial routes. Sugrīva's army consists of vānaras equal to me and far superior to me: in fact none in that army is inferior to me in power. Surely, it is obvious that no wise leader will send a superior hero as a messenger; only inferior ones are sent as messengers. Have no misgivings, O Sītā. I shall myself carry Rāma and Lakṣmaṇa on my back and bring them here. The rest of the work is easy."

Once again Sītā said to Hanumān as he was about to depart: "Pray, give that jewel to Rāma; it is something I have cherished and considered a most precious memento. Also remind him: once when the auspicious mark on my forehead had got wiped out, he himself applied it once again and laughed. Remind him of the story of the crow which I have already narrated to you. And, please do not forget to tell him that I can keep myself alive here—and that, too, only for his sake—only for a month more."

And, once again, Hanumān said to Sītā: "I swear that even as you are constantly thinking of him, Rāma, too is constantly thinking of you, O Sītā. And there will be no delay at all in his arrival here."

Sītā felt unhappy when Hanumān got ready to leave and put in the last word: "You have the best tokens of my love for Rāma. Pray, tell him everything in detail. Ensure that Rāma is able to end my agony in the shortest possible time." [. . .]

[After leaving Sītā, Hanumān does not leave Laṅkā; instead, he stays in Laṅkā, destroys Rāvaṇa's pleasure gardens, and begins ransacking one of Rāvaṇa's favorite monuments. After fierce fighting in which Hanumān kills several powerful demon commanders and Rāvaṇa's son Akṣa, Rāvaṇa's other son Indrajit captures Hanumān, who now faces Rāvaṇa.]

Sundara 49, 50, 51

Hanumān gazed at the resplendent Rāvaṇa who was excellent in every way. Rāvaṇa was seated on a crystal throne which was inlaid with jewels and had the most expensive covering. Hanumān looked at him and thought: "What charm, what heroism, what nobility of being, and what splendour; Rāvaṇa is wonderfully endowed with all the excellences. If only he were not devoted to unrighteousness, he could well be the ruler of heaven, nay even of its ruler."

Rāvaṇa was struck by the majesty of Hanumān's appearance and the strength which was evident. He commanded his ministers to ascertain the purpose of his visit to Laṅkā and why he had laid the Aśoka-grove to waste. The ministers addressed their questions to Hanumān and cautioned him: "Tell us the truth, and you will be released. If you utter falsehood you will not live!"

Hanumān replied: "I am not a messenger of the gods or demi-gods. But I am a messenger from Sugrīva. As I wished to meet Rāvaṇa in person, I pulled down the trees in his pet grove. And, when the demons attacked me, I killed them in self-defence."

Turning to Rāvaṇa himself, Hanumān said: "I have a message from Sugrīva. You know Sugrīva and he is like a brother to you." Hanumān then narrated the story of Rāma's birth and exile, the loss of Sītā in the forest, Rāma's friendship with Sugrīva, and the search for Sītā organised by Sugrīva.

"O King! I tell you what is good in the past, present and future. Accept my advice. Restore Sītā to Rāma. A glorious king like you should not stoop to such unrighteous conduct and abduct another's wife. No one in the three worlds can face the terrible power of Rāma and his brother Lakṣmaṇa: Rāma killed the mighty Vāli with just one shot. I have done a difficult task: I have discovered the whereabouts of Sītā. Soon, Rāma will complete this task.

"You cannot persuade Sītā to accept you, any more than a virulent poison can be digested. Listen to me, and do not forfeit the fruits of merits acquired by you in your previous birth. Sītā is surely the terrible Kālarātri[32] who has been brought here for your own destruction. Restore her to Rāma. Else, you will see Laṅkā burning and all the demons killed. No one, not even you, not even Indra the god of gods can escape Rāma's wrath. Rāma can destroy all the worlds and create them again! I am a humble servant of Rāma and his messenger: what I have said to you is the truth, listen to me."

[32] **Kālarātri:** The goddess Kālī, goddess of destruction, in her form as "black night."

SUNDARA 52–53

Rāvaṇa was furious with uncontrollable rage on hearing Hanumān's words. He ordered Hanumān's immediate execution. However, Rāvaṇa's brother Vibhīṣaṇa intervened and counselled Rāvaṇa as follows:

"O mighty King! If even you can be overpowered by anger, then surely knowledge of scriptures is a useless burden. Be composed; and let proper punishment be meted out to this vānara after due deliberation.

"The scriptures forbid the killing of a messenger or an ambassador. For, he is merely advocating his master's cause and he is entirely dependent upon his master. Yet, it is also true that this vānara has destroyed the grove and killed many of your soldiers.

"The proper punishment for such crimes is mutilation of the body, flogging, shaving the head and branding—disgrace which is worse than death. They who sent this messenger here, however, deserve the death penalty. And, if you kill this vānara then the episode might come to an end there, because no one else on the enemy's side will be able to cross the ocean and come here, and you will not be able to destroy your enemy."

The mighty Rāvaṇa appreciated the counsel and accepted it with his intelligence. He modified his order: "They say that the tail is the most important ornament of a vānara; set fire to it. Let this vānara return afterwards. With his tail ablaze take him round the city so that he and his comrades might know that such mischief as he has been guilty of will not go unpunished in Laṅkā."

The demons bound Hanumān, soaked his tail in oil and set it ablaze. Hanumān thought: "For the sake of Rāma's cause I shall endure even this. When they drag me around the city, I shall be able to take a better note of its military strength and gather more military information. It is good that I see Laṅkā in daylight, too." The demons dragged Hanumān around the city. They announced him as Rāma's spy. Some of the demonesses went to Sītā and informed her of Hanumān's predicament. Sītā prayed to the god of fire: "If I have been faithful to my husband and if I have served my husband; if I have performed any austerities at all, O God, be cool to Hanumān." An icy cold wind began to blow.

Hanumān, too, was intrigued to see that the fire did not burn him nor hurt him. He concluded: "Surely, Sītā's grace, Rāma's glory, and the friendship of wind and fire, have mitigated the heat; and fire does not affect me." Hanumān quickly freed himself from the bonds, picked up an iron mace and killed the demons guarding the city. And he began to inspect Laṅkā once more, with his tail ablaze.

SUNDARA 54–55

Hanumān reflected again: "I have destroyed the Aśoka-grove, killed the demons and met Rāvaṇa. I have done all that I wanted to do except the destruction of the fortress of Rāvaṇa. What more can I do here, before I return to Rāma?" He thought: "My tail is burning; with it I shall burn down the houses of the chiefs of Laṅkā."

Hanumān flew up and set ablaze, one after the other, all the houses of the foremost among the warriors of Laṅkā. Flying over Laṅkā, Hanumān thundered along like a cloud at the time of cosmic destruction. A fierce wind spread the fire. All the state houses were ablaze. Molten metals like gold etc., flowed from the houses carrying precious stones which had adorned the doors and the walls. The demons ran from the buildings thoroughly confused and frightened.

The entire city of Laṅkā was burnt down by Hanumān. The terrified demons and demonesses said to one another: "Surely he is the chief of the gods; or maybe he is Death itself. Or perhaps he is the embodiment of the power of lord Viṣṇu himself." Everywhere there was weeping and wailing. Tongues of fire reached the sky. The whole mountain on which the city stood was afire. As Hanumān stood on the shore of the ocean and quenched the fire on his own tail, the gods and the sages sang his glories and praised him for his exploits.

Hanumān's joy did not last long. A question arose in his heart: "What about Sītā? Was she also consumed by the fire?" Hanumān said to himself: "What a dreadful tragedy it is that blinded by anger I have unwittingly destroyed Sītā herself! What sin does man not commit while in the influence of anger; he might even kill his own guru and insult holy men! Surely, he who is able to subdue his anger by patience, he alone is Man. No doubt Sītā has been consumed by this fire. What shall I do now? Surely, it is wiser for me to jump into this ocean and perish, too. For, if Rāma hears of Sītā having been burnt in the fire, he will die; so will Lakṣmaṇa, Sugrīva and all the people in Ayodhyā. What a dreadful sequel to my anger!"

But, Hanumān experienced auspicious omens. And, he reflected: "But, surely, Sītā cannot be consumed by this fire. Fire does not burn fire! No doubt it was Rāma's grace and Sītā's power that ordained that the fire did not burn me! I am sure that on account of her austerities, truthfulness and chastity, Sītā is immune to the effects of fire. At the same time, the demi-gods and sages who were roaming the sky announced: "Hanumān has indeed burnt the whole of Laṅkā; but Sītā is safe." Delighted to hear this, Hanumān got ready to return to Rāma.

Sundara 56–57

Hanumān wished to make sure that Sītā was in fact safe and well. He went to the Aśoka-grove to see her: he said: "I am supremely blessed that you are safe, O divine lady!" Knowing that he was about to depart, Sītā felt unhappy: and in a manner characteristic of women, she repeated her own misgivings concerning the power of the vānaras to cross the ocean, and the likelihood of Rāvaṇa putting an end to her life before she could rejoin her lord. And, she reiterated that she should not escape along with Hanumān, but that Hanumān should do everything in such a way that Rāma destroyed the demons and attained glory and regained her.

Hanumān too once again reassured the noble Sītā that all would be well and that soon she would find Rāma in Laṅkā and that her sorrow would soon come to an end. After receiving Sītā's blessings, Hanumān went up the mountain named Ariṣṭa, ready to take off, for he was eager to behold Rāma and he was delighted that the mission had been accomplished. Hanumān, the god-son of the wind-god, flew northwards like a huge cloud floating in space. It looked as if as he took off the mountain sank into the bowels of the earth; trees shook and rocks flew from hill tops. A terrible roar was heard in his wake. [. . .]

[After Hanumān's return, Rāma decides to lead an attack on Laṅkā. As the story resumes, Rāma wonders how the monkey troops will be able to cross over the ocean dividing the mainland from Rāvaṇa's island kingdom.]

***FROM* BOOK 6**

Yuddha Kanda: The Great War

Yuddha 21–(22)

On a grass mat with his arm alone as his pillow, Rāma reclined, vowing to propitiate the god of the ocean and thus to secure his help to cross over to Laṅkā. The arm that had gifted thousands of cows, the arm that had been adorned by unguents and ornaments, the arm that Sītā had used as her pillow, the arm whose strength inspired fear in the enemy-hearts—that arm was the sole support for the head of Rāma, the ascetic, as he lay down on the sea-shore praying to the god of the ocean to show his grace. Rāma resolved: "I should now cross this ocean; or I shall dry up the ocean."

He lay there for three days and nights, without any sign of the ocean-god's pleasure. Rāma was seized with impatience and anger. He said to Lakṣmaṇa: "Here is an example, O Lakṣmaṇa, of how the wicked misinterpret the noble man's virtue: they think it is his weakness! The world respects only the man who is loud and noisy, vain and aggressive! Neither fame nor victory is won by a peaceful approach, O Lakṣmaṇa. See what I do now. Bring my weapon and bring the missiles. I shall dry up the ocean so that the vānaras may walk to Laṅkā."

Rāma got hold of his formidable weapon and took a few terrible missiles and discharged them at the ocean. These caused such a violent commotion that they whipped tidal waves of huge proportions. The creatures of the ocean, the huge snakes and other deep-sea creatures were disturbed and distressed. Mountainous waves rose in the sea. There was a terrifying roar from the ocean. Even Lakṣmaṇa was frightened.

Rāma looked at the ocean and said in great anger: "I shall dry up the entire ocean! Utterly deprived of your essence, O ocean, only a sand-bed will remain." He took the most powerful missile endowed with the powers of the Creator himself and hurled it at the ocean. The effect of this was unimaginable and beyond description. Mountains began to shake. There was an earthquake. There was dense darkness everywhere. The course of the sun, the moon and the planets was disturbed. The sky was illumined as if by the sudden appearance of thousands of meteors. Accompanied by deafening thunderclaps, the sky shone with lightning. Gale-force winds swept the surface of the earth and the ocean. Even the peaks of mountains were dislodged.

Living beings everywhere cried in agony. The waters of the ocean were stirred up so suddenly and with such force that it appeared as though the ocean would overstep its bounds and submerge the land.

YUDDHA 22–23

The deity presiding over the ocean then rose from the ocean and meekly approached Rāma. To Rāma who was standing burning with anger, his weapon ready to discharge the most deadly missile, the Ocean said:

"Rāma, everything in nature is governed by the immutable law which alone determines the inherent characteristic of every element in nature. In accordance with that law, it is natural for the ocean to be unfathomable and impassable. Yet, I shall suggest a way out, and I shall indicate the path by which the vānaras will be able to go over to Laṅkā."

Rāma asked the Ocean: "Against whom shall I direct this unfailing missile which has been readied for the purpose of drying the ocean?" And the Ocean pointed to the well-known Drumakulya inhabited by sinners: directed to this spot, Rāma's missile dried up the ocean there, and, in order to compensate for this action, Rāma blessed that piece of land: "You will be fertile and you will be full of fruit-bearing trees."

The Ocean said: "Rāma, here is Nala who is the son of the great Viśvakarma (the architect of all). Let him construct a bridge across these waters, for he is as good as his father. I shall gladly support that bridge."

Nala at once voluntarily offered: "What the Ocean has said is indeed true. I shall construct the bridge across these waters: and I am as proficient as my father. Actually, the Ocean owes a debt of gratitude to Rāma, for a great service was rendered by Rāma's ancestors to the Ocean. Yet, it was not gratitude that inspired the Ocean to give way; fear did it! The ungrateful man in this world recognises only punishment, not love or affection."

At Rāma's command, thousands of vānaras got ready for the mighty undertaking. They cut down logs of wood; they rolled away huge rocks and stones. They threw all these into the ocean which was greatly agitated by this. Some of the vānaras held a plumbline so that the rocks could be placed in a straight line. With the help of the vānaras of immeasurable strength and mighty deeds, Nala put up the bridge across the ocean, using logs of wood, rocks and stones. The eight hundred mile long bridge took five days to build. Celestial beings (devas or beings of light) and Gandharvas (celestial musicians) watched this marvellous feat.

As soon as the bridge was completed, Vibhīṣaṇa stood guard at the southern (Laṅkā) end, to prevent sabotage by the enemy. Sugrīva then said to Rāma: "Let Hanumān take you and let Aṅgada take Lakṣmaṇa, to Laṅkā." They were ready to depart. [. . .]

[After crossing over the causeway, the vānara and the rakṣasas engage in fierce fighting. They have been joined by Vibhīṣaṇa, Rāvaṇa's brother, who recognizes Rāma's virtue and who will become king of Laṅkā when Rāvaṇa is defeated. Now Rāma and Rāvaṇa face off against each other.]

YUDDHA 109, 110, 111

When Rāma and Rāvaṇa began to fight, their armies stood stupefied, watching them! Rāma was determined to win; Rāvaṇa was sure he would die: knowing this, they fought with all their might. Rāvaṇa attacked the standard on Rāma's car; and

Rāma similarly shot the standard on Rāvaṇa's car. While Rāvaṇa's standard fell; Rāma's did not. Rāvaṇa next aimed at the 'horses' (engines) of Rāma's car: even though he attacked them with all his might, they remained unaffected.

Both of them discharged thousands of missiles: these illumined the skies and created a new heaven, as it were! They were accurate in their aim and their missiles unfailingly hit the target. With unflagging zeal they fought each other, without the least trace of fatigue. What one did the other did in retaliation.

Rāvaṇa shot at Mātali[33] who remained unaffected by it. Then Rāvaṇa sent a shower of maces and mallets at Rāma. Their very sound agitated the oceans and tormented the aquatic creatures. The celestials and the holy brāhmaṇas witnessing the scene prayed: "May auspiciousness attend to all the living beings, and may the worlds endure forever. May Rāma conquer Rāvaṇa." Astounded at the way in which Rāma and Rāvaṇa fought with each other, the sages said to one another: "Sky is like sky, ocean is like ocean; the fight between Rāma and Rāvaṇa is like Rāma and Rāvaṇa—incomparable."

Taking up a powerful missile, Rāma correctly aimed at the head of Rāvaṇa; it fell. But another head appeared in its place. Every time Rāma cut off Rāvaṇa's head, another appeared! Rāma was puzzled. Mātali, Rāma's driver, said to Rāma: "Why do you fight like an ordinary warrior, O Rāma? Use the Brahmā-missile; the hour of the demon's death is at hand."

Rāma remembered the Brahmā-missile which the sage Agastya had given him. It had the power of the wind-god for its 'feathers'; the power of fire and sun at its head; the whole space was its body; and it had the weight of a mountain. It shone like the sun or the fire of nemesis. As Rāma took it in his hands, the earth shook and all living beings were terrified. Infallible in its destructive power, this ultimate weapon of destruction shattered the chest of Rāvaṇa, and entered deep into the earth.

Rāvaṇa fell dead. And the surviving demons fled, pursued by the vānaras. The vānaras shouted in great jubilation. The air resounded with the drums of the celestials. The gods praised Rāma. The earth became steady, the wind blew softly and the sun was resplendent as before. Rāma was surrounded by mighty heroes and gods who were all joyously felicitating him on the victory.

Yuddha 112, 113

Seeing Rāvaṇa lying dead on the battlefield, Vibhīṣaṇa[34] burst into tears. Overcome by brotherly affection, he lamented thus: "Alas, what I had predicted has come true: and my advice was not relished by you, overcome as you were by lust and delusion. Now that you have departed, the glory of Laṅkā has departed. You were like a tree firmly established in heroism with asceticism for its strength, spreading out firmness in all aspects of your life: yet you have been cut down. You were like an elephant with

[33] **Mātali:** The charioteer of Indra, king of the gods; Indra has sent Mātali to pilot Rāma's chariot.

[34] **Vibhīṣaṇa:** Rāvaṇa's brother, who has become an ally of Rāma's and has played a key role in defeating his wicked brother.

splendour, noble ancestry, indignation, and pleasant nature for parts: yet you have been killed. You, who were like blazing fire have been extinguished by Rāma."

Rāma approached the grief-stricken Vibhīṣaṇa and gently and lovingly said to him: "It is not right that you should thus grieve, O Vibhīṣaṇa, for a mighty warrior fallen on the battlefield. Victory is the monopoly of none: a hero is either slain in battle or he kills his opponent. Hence our ancients decreed that the warrior who is killed in combat should not be mourned. Get up and consider what should be done next."

Vibhīṣaṇa regained his composure and said to Rāma: "This Rāvaṇa used to give a lot in charity to ascetics; he enjoyed life; he maintained his servants well; he shared his wealth with his friends, and he destroyed his enemies. He was regular in his religious observances; learned he was in the scriptures. By your grace, O Rāma, I wish to perform his funeral in accordance with the scriptures, for his welfare in the other world." Rāma was delighted and said to Vibhīṣaṇa: "Hostility ends at death. Take steps for the due performance of the funeral rites. He is your brother as he is mine, too."

The womenfolk of Rāvaṇa's court, and his wives, hearing of his end, rushed out of the palace, and, arriving at the battlefield, rolled on the ground in sheer anguish. Overcome by grief they gave vent to their feelings in diverse heart-rending ways. They wailed: "Alas, he who could not be killed by the gods and demons, has been killed in battle by a man standing on earth. Our beloved lord! Surely when you abducted Sītā and brought her to Laṅkā, you invited your own death! Surely it was because death was close at hand that you did not listen to the wise counsel of your own brother Vibhīṣaṇa, and you ill-treated him and exiled him. Even later if you had restored Sītā to Rāma, this evil fate would not have overtaken you. However, it is surely not because you did what you liked, because you were driven by lust, that you lie dead now: God's will makes people do diverse deeds. He who is killed by the divine will dies. No one can flout the divine will, and no one can buy the divine will nor bribe it." [. . .]

Yuddha 115, 116

Rāma returned to the camp where the vānara troops had been stationed. He turned to Lakṣmaṇa and said: "O Lakṣmaṇa, install Vibhīṣaṇa on the throne of Laṅkā and consecrate him as the king of Laṅkā. He has rendered invaluable service to me and I wish to behold him on the throne of Laṅkā at once."

Without the least loss of time, Lakṣmaṇa made the necessary preparations and with the waters of the ocean consecrated Vibhīṣaṇa as king of Laṅkā, in strict accordance with scriptural ordinance. Rāma, Lakṣmaṇa and the others were delighted. The demon-leaders brought their tributes and offered them to Vibhīṣaṇa who in turn placed them all at Rāma's feet.

Rāma said to Hanumān: "Please go, with the permission of king Vibhīṣaṇa, to Sītā and inform her of the death of Rāvaṇa and the welfare of both myself and Lakṣmaṇa." Immediately Hanumān left for the Aśoka-grove. The grief-stricken Sītā was happy to behold him. With joined palms Hanumān submitted Rāma's message and added: "Rāma desires me to inform you that you can shed fear, for you are in your own home as it were, now that Vibhīṣaṇa is king of Laṅkā." Sītā was speechless for a moment and then said: "I am delighted by the message you have brought, O Hanumān: and I am rendered speechless by it. I only regret that I have nothing now with which to reward you; nor is any gift equal in value to the most joyous tidings you have brought me." Hanumān submitted: "O lady, the very words you have uttered are more precious than all the jewels of the world! I consider myself supremely blessed to have witnessed Rāma's victory and Rāvaṇa's destruction." Sītā was even more delighted: she said, "Only you can utter such sweet words, O Hanumān, endowed as you are with manifold excellences. Truly you are an abode of virtues."

Hanumān said: "Pray, give me leave to kill all these demonesses who have been tormenting you so long." Sītā replied: "Nay, Hanumān, they are not responsible for their actions, for they were but obeying their master's commands. And, surely, it was my own evil destiny that made me suffer at their hands. Hence, I forgive them. A noble man does not recognise the harm done to him by others: and he never retaliates, for he is the embodiment of goodness. One should be compassionate towards all, the good and the wicked, nay even towards those who are fit to be killed: who is free from sin?" Hanumān was thrilled to hear these words of Sītā, and said: "Indeed you are the noble consort of Rāma and his peer in virtue and nobility. Pray, give me a message to take back to Rāma." Sītā replied: "Please tell him that I am eager to behold his face." Assuring Sītā that she would see Rāma that very day, Hanumān returned to Rāma.

Yuddha 117, 118, 119

Hanumān conveyed Sītā's message to Rāma who turned to king Vibhīṣaṇa and said: "Please bring Sītā to me soon, after she has had a bath and has adorned herself." Immediately Vibhīṣaṇa went to Sītā and compelled her to proceed seated in a palanquin, to where Rāma was. Vānaras and demons had gathered around her, eager to look at Sītā. And Vibhīṣaṇa, in accordance with the tradition, wished to ensure that Sītā was not seen by these and rebuked them to go away. Restraining him, Rāma said: "Why do you rebuke them, O Vibhīṣaṇa? Neither houses nor clothes nor walls constitute a veil for a woman; her character alone is her veil. Let her descend from the palanquin and walk up to me." So she did.

Rāma said sternly: "My purpose has been accomplished, O Sītā. My prowess has been witnessed by all. I have fulfilled my pledge. Rāvaṇa's wickedness has been punished. The extraordinary feat performed by Hanumān in crossing the ocean and burning Laṅkā has borne fruit. Vibhīṣaṇa's devotion has been rewarded." Rāma's heart was in a state of conflict, afraid as he was of public ridicule. Hence, he continued: "I wish to let you know that all this was done not for your sake, but for the sake of preserving my honour. Your conduct is open to suspicion, hence even your sight is displeasing to me. Your body was touched by Rāvaṇa: how then can I, claiming to belong to a noble family, accept you? Hence I permit you to go where you like and live with whom you like—either Lakṣmaṇa, Bharata, Śatrughna, Sugrīva or even

Vibhīṣaṇa. It is difficult for me to believe that Rāvaṇa, who was so fond of you, would have been able to keep away from you for such a long time."

Sītā was shocked. Rāma's words wounded her heart. Tears streamed down her face. Wiping them, she replied: "O Rāma, you are speaking to me in the language of a common and vulgar man speaking to a common woman. That which was under my control, my heart, has always been yours; how could I prevent my body from being touched when I was helpless and under another person's control? Ah, if only you had conveyed your suspicion through Hanumān when he came to meet me, I would have killed myself then and saved you all this trouble and the risk involved in the war." Turning to Lakṣmaṇa, she said: "Kindle the fire, O Lakṣmaṇa: that is the only remedy. I shall not live to endure this false calumny." Lakṣmaṇa looked at Rāma and with his approval kindled the fire. Sītā prayed: "Even as my heart is ever devoted to Rāma, may the fire protect me. If I have been faithful to Rāma in thought, word or deed, may the fire protect me. The sun, the moon, the wind, earth and others are witness to my purity; may the fire protect me." Then she entered into the fire, even as an oblation poured into the fire would. Gods and sages witnessed this. The women who saw this screamed.

Yuddha 120, 121

Rāma was moved to tears by the heart-rending cries of all those women who witnessed the self-immolation of Sītā. At the same time, all the gods, including the trinity—the Creator, the Preserver, and the Redeemer[35]—arrived upon the scene in their personal forms. Saluting Rāma, they said: "You are the foremost among the gods, and yet you treat Sītā as if you were a common human being!"

Rāma replied to these divinities: "I consider myself a human being, Rāma the son of Daśaratha. Who I am, and whence I am, may you tell me!"

Brahmā the creator said: "You are verily lord Nārāyaṇa.[36] You are the imperishable cosmic being. You are the truth. You are eternal. You are the supreme dharma of the worlds. You are the father even of the chief of the gods, Indra. You are the sole refuge of perfected beings and holy men. You are the Om,[37] and you are the spirit of sacrifice. You are that cosmic being[38] with infinite heads, hands and eyes. You are the support of the whole universe. The whole universe is your body. Sītā is Lakṣmi[39] and you are lord Viṣṇu, who is of a dark hue, and who is the creator of all beings. For the sake of the destruction of Rāvaṇa you entered into a human body. This mission of

---

[35] **the Creator . . . Redeemer:** The gods of the Hindu trinity: Brahmā, Viṣṇu, and Śiva. (See note 6.)

[36] **Nārāyaṇa:** "The divine" or cosmic form of the god Viṣṇu.

[37] **Om:** The sacred sound or mantra associated in the Upaniṣads with Brahman, the universal spirit that permeates the cosmos.

[38] **that cosmic being:** Puruṣa, from a creation hymn in the Ṛg Veda; Puruṣa (Purusha) is the original cosmic "Man" offered up in the first sacrifice, which led to creation. From his mouth came the *Brahmins,* or priests; from his arms the *Kṣatriya,* the warriors; from his thighs the *Vaiṣya,* the merchants and farmers; and from his feet, the *Śūdra,* or servants.

[39] **Lakṣmi:** A goddess and the wife of Viṣṇu.

ours has been fully accomplished by you. Blessed it is to be in your presence; blessed it is to sing your glories; they are truly blessed who are devoted to you, for their life will be attended with success."

As soon as Brahmā finished saying this, the god of fire emerged from the fire in his personal form, holding up Sītā in his hands. Sītā shone in all her radiance. The god of fire who is the witness of everything that takes place in the world, said to Rāma: "Here is your Sītā, Rāma. I find no fault in her. She has not erred in thought, word or deed. Even during the long period of her detention in the abode of Rāvaṇa, she did not even think of him, as her heart was set on you. Accept her: and I command you not to treat her harshly."

Rāma was highly pleased at this turn of events. He said: "Indeed, I was fully aware of Sītā's purity. Even the mighty and wicked Rāvaṇa could not lay his hands upon her with evil intention. Yet, this baptism by fire was necessary, to avoid public calumny and ridicule, for though she was pure, she lived in Laṅkā for a long time. I knew, too, that Sītā would never be unfaithful to me: for we are non-different from each other even as the sun and its rays are. It is therefore impossible for me to renounce her."

After saying so, Rāma was joyously reunited with Sītā.

Yuddha 122, 123

Lord Śiva then said to Rāma: "You have fulfilled a most difficult task. Now behold your father, the illustrious king Daśaratha who appears in the firmament to bless you and to greet you."

Rāma along with Lakṣmaṇa saw that great monarch, their father, clad in a raiment of purity and shining by his own lustre. Still seated in his celestial vehicle, Daśaratha lifted up Rāma and placing him on his lap, warmly embraced him and said: "Neither heaven nor even the homage of the gods is as pleasing to me as to behold you, Rāma. I am delighted to see that you have successfully completed the period of your exile and that you have destroyed all your enemies. Even now the cruel words of Kaikeyī haunt my heart; but seeing you and embracing you, I am rid of that sorrow, O Rāma. You have redeemed my word and thus I have been saved by you. It is only now that I recognise you to be the supreme person incarnated as a human being in this world in order to kill Rāvaṇa."

Rāma said: "You remember that you said to Kaikeyī, 'I renounce you and your son'? Pray, take back that curse and may it not afflict Kaikeyī and Bharata." Daśaratha agreed to it and then said to Lakṣmaṇa: "I am pleased with you, my son, and you have earned great merit by the faithful service you have rendered to Rāma."

Lastly, king Daśaratha said to Sītā: "My dear daughter, do not take to heart the fire ordeal that Rāma forced you to undergo: it was necessary to reveal to the world your absolute purity. By your conduct you have exalted yourself above all women." Having thus spoken to them, Daśaratha ascended to heaven.

Before taking leave of Rāma, Indra prayed: "Our visit to you should not be fruitless, O Rāma. Command me, what may I do for you?" Rāma replied: "If you are really pleased with me, then I pray that all those vānaras who laid down their lives for my sake may come back to life. I wish to see them hale and hearty as before. I also wish to see the whole world fruitful and prosperous." Indra replied: "This indeed is an extremely difficult task. Yet, I do not go back on my word, hence I grant it. All the vānaras will come back to life and be restored to their original form, with all their wounds healed. Even as you had asked, the world will be fruitful and prosperous."

Instantly, all the vānaras arose from the dead and bowed to Rāma. The others who witnessed this marvelled and the gods beheld Rāma who had all his wishes fulfilled. The gods returned to their abodes. [. . .]

[After celebrating Vibhīṣaṇa's coronation, Rāma, Sītā, and Lakṣmaṇa, along with Vibhīṣaṇa, Sugrīva, Hanumān, and the vānaras, return to Ayodhyā, where Bharata has prepared a celebration.]

Yuddha 130

Bharata immediately made the reception arrangements. He instructed Śatrughna: "Let prayers be offered to the gods in all temples and houses of worship with fragrant flowers and musical instruments."

Śatrughna immediately gave orders that the roads along which the royal procession would wend its way to the palace should be levelled and sprinkled with water, and kept clear by hundreds of policemen cordoning them. Soon all the ministers, and thousands of elephants and men on horse-back and in cars went out to greet Rāma. The royal reception party, seated in palanquins, was led by the queen-mother Kausalyā herself; Kaikeyī and the other members of the royal household followed—and all of them reached Nandigrāma.[40]

From there Bharata headed the procession with the sandals of Rāma placed on his head,[41] with the white royal umbrella and the other regalia. Bharata was the very picture of an ascetic though he radiated the joy that filled his heart at the very thought of Rāma's return to the kingdom.

Bharata anxiously looked around but saw no signs of Rāma's return! But, Hanumān reassured him: "Listen, O Bharata, you can see the cloud of dust raised by the vānaras rushing towards Ayodhyā. You can now hear the roar of the Puṣpaka aircraft."

"Rāma has come!"—these words were uttered by thousands of people at the same time. Even before the Puṣpaka[42] landed, Bharata humbly saluted Rāma who was standing on the front side of the aircraft. The Puṣpaka landed. As Bharata approached it, Rāma lifted him up and placed him on his lap. Bharata bowed down to Rāma and also to Sītā and greeted Lakṣmaṇa. And he embraced Sugrīva, Jāmbavān,

[40] **Nandigrāma:** The village outside of Ayodhyā from where Bharata ruled. As a protest against his mother's palace intrigue, he refused to set foot in Ayodhyā until his brother Rāma returned to take over rightful power of the capital.

[41] **sandals . . . on his head:** A sign of deference to and respect for Rāma.

[42] **Puṣpaka:** The flying chariot, here translated as "aircraft," of Rāvaṇa, who took it from its original owner, Kubera, the god of wealth. Rāma flies home on this chariot.

Aṅgada, Vibhīṣaṇa and others. He said to Sugrīva: "We are four brothers, and with you we are five. Good deeds promote friendship, and evil is a sign of enmity."

Rāma bowed to his mother who had become emaciated through sorrow, and brought great joy to her heart. Then he also bowed to Sumitrā and Kaikeyī. All the people thereupon said to Rāma: "Welcome, welcome back, O Lord."

Bharata placed the sandals in front of Rāma, and said: "Rāma here is your kingdom which I held in trust for you during your absence. I consider myself supremely blessed in being able to behold your return to Ayodhyā. By your grace, the treasury has been enriched tenfold by me, as also the storehouses and the strength of the nation." Rāma felt delighted. When the entire party had disembarked, he instructed that the Puṣpaka aircraft be returned to its original owner, Kubera.[43]

Yuddha 131

The coronation proceedings were immediately initiated by Bharata. Skilled barbers removed the matted locks of Rāma. He had a ceremonial bath and he was dressed in magnificent robes and royal jewels. Kausalyā herself helped the vānara ladies to dress themselves in royal robes; all the queens dressed Sītā appropriately for the occasion. The royal chariot was brought; duly ascending it, Rāma, Lakṣmaṇa and Sītā, went in a procession to Ayodhyā, Bharata himself driving the chariot. When he had reached the court, Rāma gave his ministers and counsellors a brief account of the events during his exile, particularly the alliance with the vānara chief Sugrīva, and the exploits of Hanumān. He also informed them of his alliance with Vibhīṣaṇa.

At Bharata's request, Sugrīva despatched the best of the vānaras to fetch water from the four oceans, and all the sacred rivers of the world. The aged sage Vasiṣṭha thereupon commenced the ceremony in connection with the coronation of Rāma. Rāma and Sītā were seated on a seat made entirely of precious stones. The foremost among the sages thereupon consecrated Rāma with the appropriate Vedic chants. First the brāhmaṇas, then the virgins, then the ministers and warriors, and later the businessmen poured the holy waters on Rāma. After that the sage Vasiṣṭha placed Rāma on the throne made of gold and studded with precious stones, and placed on his head the dazzling crown which had been made by Brahmā the creator himself. The gods and others paid their homage to Rāma by bestowing gifts upon him. Rāma also gave away rich presents to the brāhmaṇas and others, including the vānara chiefs like Sugrīva. Rāma then gave to Sītā a necklace of pearls and said: "You may give it to whom you like, Sītā." And, immediately Sītā bestowed that gift upon Hanumān.

After witnessing the coronation of Rāma, the vānaras returned to Kiṣkindhā. So did Vibhīṣaṇa return to Laṅkā. Rāma looked fondly at Lakṣmaṇa and expressed the wish that he should reign as the prince regent. Lakṣmaṇa did not reply: he did not want it. Rāma appointed Bharata as prince regent. Rāma thereafter ruled the earth for a very long time.

---

[43] **Kubera:** The god of wealth; see note 42.

During the period of Rāma's reign, there was no poverty, no crime, no fear, and no unrighteousness in the kingdom. All the people constantly spoke of Rāma; the whole world had been transformed into Rāma. Everyone was devoted to dharma. And Rāma was highly devoted to dharma, too. He ruled for eleven thousand years.

Yuddha 131

Rāma's rule of the kingdom was characterised by the effortless and spontaneous prevalence of dharma. People were free from fear of any sort. There were no widows in the land: people were not molested by beasts and snakes, nor did they suffer from diseases. There was no theft, no robbery nor any violence. Young people did not die making older people perform funeral services for them. Everyone was happy and everyone was devoted to dharma; beholding Rāma alone, no one harmed another. People lived long and had many children. They were healthy and they were free from sorrow. Everywhere people were speaking all the time about Rāma; the entire world appeared to be the form of Rāma. The trees were endowed with undying roots, and they were in fruition all the time and they flowered throughout the year. Rain fell whenever it was needed. There was a pleasant breeze always. The brāhmaṇas (priests), the warriors, the farmers and businessmen, as also the members of the servant class, were entirely free from greed, and were joyously devoted to their own dharma and functions in society. There was no falsehood in the life of the people who were all righteous. People were endowed with all auspicious characteristics and all of them had dharma as their guiding light. Thus did Rāma rule the world for eleven thousand years, surrounded by his brothers.

This holy epic Rāmāyaṇa composed by the sage Vālmīki, promotes dharma, fame, long life and in the case of a king, victory. He who listens to it always is freed from all sins. He who desires sons gets them, and he who desires wealth becomes wealthy, by listening to the story of the coronation of Rāma. The king conquers the whole world, after overcoming his enemies. Women who listen to this story will be blessed with children like Rāma and his brothers. And they, too, will be blessed with long life, after listening to the Rāmāyaṇa. He who listens to or reads this Rāmāyaṇa propitiates Rāma by this; Rāma is pleased with him; and he indeed is the eternal lord Viṣṇu.

LAVA AND KUŚA[44] said: Such is the glorious epic, Rāmāyaṇa. May all recite it and thus augment the glory of dharma, of lord Viṣṇu. Righteous men should regularly listen to this story of Rāma, which increases health, long-life, love, wisdom and vitality.

---

[44] **LAVA AND KUŚA:** Lava and Kuśa are Rāma and Sītā's twin sons, born after Sītā was banished from Ayodhyā when its citizens began to doubt that she was chaste while in captivity at Laṅkā. Lava and Kuśa have been the tellers of this tale, which they learned from the sage Vālmīki, who sheltered Sītā in her exile. Most scholars believe the original epic ends here. The story of Sītā's banishment and of the deaths of Sītā, Lakṣmaṇa, and Rāma is told in Book 7, the Uttara Kāṇḍa.

***FROM* BOOK 7**

Uttara Kanda: The Period after Coronation

[Rāma and Sītā have enjoyed peace and happiness for some years in Ayodhyā. In this final selection from Book 7, the Uttara Kāṇḍa, Rāma is forced to send Sītā, who is pregnant with his twin sons, into exile at the hermitage of the sage Vālmīki, the author of the *Ramayana.* After several years, Rāma's sons, Lava and Kuśa, return to Ayodhyā and recite the epic, as seen at the end of Book 6, and Rāma sends for Sītā, who refuses to return.]

UTTARA 43–45

In Rāma's court, the clowns were entertaining Rāma and the other princes and dignitaries with humorous stories. Later, Rāma asked the spies and secret agents: "Tell me, what do people say about me, about Sītā, about my brothers? Tell me everything without any reservation."

After much hesitation Bhadra conveyed to the king what some citizens were saying: "Rāma has done what no one else has done: he built a bridge over the ocean, went over to Laṅkā with the vānara forces and others, killed Rāvaṇa and regained Sītā. I do not know how he still loves Sītā so much, after her abduction by Rāvaṇa who placed her on his lap and kept her in the Aśoka forest for such a long time. Well, well, I suppose that hereafter we cannot object to such conduct on the part of our wives, too."

Rāma's face showed deep concern and anxiety. He dismissed the court, and asked his messengers to request his brothers to come to his presence at once. Thus urgently summoned, the three brothers rushed to the court and were bewildered to see Rāma's anxious face. They bowed to him and stood respectfully at a distance.

Rāma gravely turned towards them and said as follows: "Pray, listen to what I have just heard. Public scandal is eating my heart. For I belong to the great Ikṣvāku dynasty. Sītā, too, belongs to a respectable family. You know how she was abducted by Rāvaṇa from the Daṇḍaka forest and how I eventually regained her. In order to convince me of her purity, Sītā even entered the fire; Lakṣmaṇa, you were witness to the declaration by the fire-god himself that Sītā is pure. In my own innermost being I know she is pure. Hence I brought her back to Ayodhyā with me.

"Yet, there is public scandal concerning her. He who is thus subjected to public scandal in this world goes down to the lower worlds so long as the scandal lasts. Infamy is ridiculed by the gods, and fame is adored in this world. Indeed it is for the sake of fame that people undertake various activities. For fear of scandal I can even give up my life and all of you, my dear brothers; what to speak of Sītā? Hence, do as I tell you and do not even counsel me against it. Take Sītā immediately and leave her in a far-off place: take her to the hermitage of the sage Vālmīki and leave her there. In fact, she herself wanted to go to visit those hermitages.

"I swear by my own feet, I will not change my mind, and please do not even try to make me change my mind."

Uttara 46–47

When that night was past and the next day dawned, Lakṣmaṇa asked Sumantra to get ready the royal chariot. When the chariot was ready, Lakṣmaṇa said to Sītā: "You had requested the king Rāma to let you visit the hermitages of the sages on the banks of the river Gaṅgā. The king has been graciously pleased to accede to that request and has commanded me to take you thither. Hence, O Sītā, ascend this chariot."

With a joyous heart, Sītā ran into her apartments, gathered clothes and jewels and other presents which she wished to give the sages and their consorts, and returned to where the chariot stood ready. The chariot sped forward.

However, Sītā noticed ill omens and was anxious on account of her husband and her mothers-in-law: she offered a prayer for their safety.

They spent the first night on the bank of the river Gautami in an Aśrama. The next morning they continued the journey. When they neared the river Gaṅgā, Lakṣmaṇa looking at the river wailed aloud, to the surprise of Sītā. She asked him: "Why do you cry thus, O Lakṣmaṇa? Surely, because you miss your brother Rāma so much. So do I. We shall visit the hermitages and spend tonight there and return to Ayodhyā as soon as possible."

Sītā and Lakṣmaṇa got into the ferry to cross the river Gaṅgā. Lakṣmaṇa began to weep and wail once again. He said to Sītā: "My heart is heavy, O Sītā. I know that the world will blame me for this. In fact, I would have preferred death at this very moment. Be gracious, for it is not my fault." Saying so, he fell at the feet of Sītā, weeping bitterly.

Sītā grew anxious and was greatly worried. She requested Lakṣmaṇa to tell her everything without reserve. Lakṣmaṇa got up and continued to address Sītā: "In the presence of the members of his assembly, Rāma heard a terrible public scandal. It is something which the citizens of Ayodhyā and the country are saying. Rāma was greatly upset and he told me something and retired to his apartment. I cannot repeat those words to you. It is on account of that scandal that the king has decided to abandon you. Pray, bear in mind that he does not accuse you, but he is afraid of public scandal. This is the command of the king: I should take you to the hermitage of the sage Vālmīki and leave you there. The sage is a great friend of our father and he will surely look after you very well."

Uttara 48–49

When Sītā heard Lakṣmaṇa's terrible words, she fainted, overwhelmed by grief. After a considerable time, she regained consciousness and in a sorrowful tone spoke to Lakṣmaṇa thus:

"My body has surely been created for suffering; and I am an embodiment of endless suffering. What great sin should I have committed in a previous birth, and whom did I deprive of his spouse, that I should be subjected to this fate though I am pure and innocent? Earlier in life I lived in the forest, but then I had my lord Rāma with me. Now deprived of him how shall I live in this forest?

"When I enter the hermitages of these sages, what shall I tell them; for what reason have I been banished by Rāma? It would have been better for me to drown myself in the Gaṅgā; but my lord would accuse me of having destroyed his dynasty, for I am with his child.

"O Lakṣmaṇa, do as you have been commanded by the Lord to do. When you return to Ayodhyā convey my prostrations to lord Rāma and also to my mothers-in-law, and assure him of my eternal devotion to him, of my purity. I am quite sure that I have been thus banished only on account of public scandal and not because my lord suspects my chastity. Indeed, the husband is the god, relative and guru for a chaste woman; he is dearer to her than even her life; hence his mission is all-important to her. It is in this spirit that I give you leave: you may now go." When he went out of sight, Sītā burst into tears, sitting on the bank of the Gaṅgā.

Vālmīki came to the bank of the Gaṅgā and greeted Sītā with due respect and honour. He said: "I know that you are Sītā, the daughter of king Janaka and the daughter-in-law of Daśaratha; you are the beloved queen of Rāma. I knew that you would be coming; and I also know the reason why you are here. By the eye of intuition gained by the practice of intense austerities I know that you are utterly chaste. I know all that happens in the three worlds. Come: at a little distance from here you will see a convent of female ascetics who will look after you from now on. Grieve not. Treat this as your own home."

Vālmīki led Sītā to the hermitage of the female ascetics and introduced her to them and entrusted her care to them. [. . .]

[Several years have passed since Sītā's banishment. Celebrations are under way for the great horse sacrifice that Rāma has ordered.]

UTTARA 92–93

When all the arrangements had been completed, Rāma let go a beautiful horse which was in the charge of Lakṣmaṇa. Then he entered the place in Naimiṣaṁ[45] where the sacred rite was to be held, along with his retinue.

The sacred rite commenced and lasted a whole year. Food, drinks, clothes, gold and ornaments flowed ceaselessly in that place. Bharata and Śatrughna were in charge of these and they ensured that no one who expressed the least inclination was denied anything. The vānaras spared themselves no pain in the service of all the guests. And, the noble Vibhīṣaṇa served the holy sages zealously.

No one was weak, dirty, or in want. No need remained unfulfilled. Before the need was expressed it was supplied. They who wanted gold, got gold; they who wanted clothes, got clothes. Sweets and other delicacies were always available to all.

All the guests said to one another: "We have not seen the like of this, neither Indra, nor Soma, nor Varuṇa,[46] no one else has performed a rite like this."

---

[45] **Naimiṣaṁ:** The forest where Rāma celebrates the Aṣvamedha sacrifice, the horse sacrifice.

[46] **Indra . . . Varuṇa:** Indra is the chief of gods; Soma is the god of the moon; Varuṇa is the god of the oceans.

Elsewhere, escorted by Lakṣmaṇa, the horse continued to roam the earth.

To this great sacred rite came the sage Viśvāmitra along with his disciples. Among the latter were the two boys Kuśa and Lava. The sage had told them: "Joyously sing the great epic poem Rāmāyaṇam which I have taught you. Sing it in the presence of sages or brāhmaṇas, in the palaces of princes and along the main roads. Sing it at the gates of Rāma's palace, and in front of the priests officiating at the sacred rite. Here, take these fruits: these will prevent fatigue and keep your voices from getting tired.

"Should Rāma call upon you to sing the poem, please do so without hesitation. Do not even expect a reward; for of what use is gold or wealth. Should Rāma ask you whose sons you are, merely reply: 'We are the disciples of Vālmīki.' Take this musical instrument and sing the poem to its accompaniment."

Thus instructed by the sage, the young sons of Sītā eagerly awaited the opportunity to sing the Rāmāyaṇam.

Uttara 94–95

The two boys got up early the next morning and offered their morning prayers. Just as the sage had instructed them, they began to sing; and Rāma made them sing the poem. The king assembled all the holy men, kings, heroes, pandits, storytellers, grammarians and all other brāhmaṇas who were interested in hearing the great poem, and requested the two boys to sing the poem in their presence. All the members of this august assembly drank the nectarine poem with their ears, and the beautiful personality of the two young boys with their eyes. They said to one another: "These two boys are very much like Rāma, like the very image of Rāma. Had they not been clad in ascetic garments, with matted locks and so on, we would have concluded that they were in fact Rāma's sons."

When they had completed the twenty chapters according to the instruction of sage Vālmīki, they paused; and the king asked his brother to give them a bag of gold—which they politely declined to accept, saying: "We are forest-dwellers, and gold is useless to us."

Rāma asked them who the author of the poem was and whether it was authentic; and they devoutly replied that it was the composition of sage Vālmīki and it was entirely truthful.

At the end of the day, Rāma gave them leave to return to the sage's camp. The next day again he had them recite the poem. Thus very many days passed. Rāma made them recite the poem in the presence of the sages and kings. And from the way in which it was recited, he concluded that they were the children of Sītā.

Rāma then sent messengers to the sage Vālmīki with the message: "If Sītā is free from unchaste conduct, then let her come here, escorted by the sage Vālmīki and prove her purity. Let her therefore present herself tomorrow morning here in this august assembly."

This message was duly conveyed to the sage Vālmīki who replied to the messengers: "Surely, Sītā would agree to do as instructed by Rāma; for she regards her husband as God himself."

When this was conveyed to Rāma, he addressed the sages and kings, and said: "You will witness tomorrow the purity of Sītā." And they, in their turn, applauded his decision: "This is entirely in accordance with your glorious and pure nature, O Rāma."

Uttara 96–97

When the night was past, and the day dawned, Rāma assembled all the sages and the holy men like Vasiṣṭha, Vāmadeva, Jābāli, Kaśyapa, Viśvāmitra, Dhīrghatamā and Durvāsa, and others. All of them were eagerly awaiting the developments, and looked forward to witness the noble Sītā prove her chastity.

Sage Vālmīki entered the assembly followed by Sītā. There was instant restlessness in the assembly, as everyone noticed the picture of sorrow and grief that Sītā was.

Vālmīki spoke: "Here, O Rāma, is Sītā who is devoted to her marital vows and whose conduct is perfectly righteous. Abandoned on account of public scandal she has been living near my hermitage. These two sons of Sītā are your sons, O Rāma: I speak the truth. I do not remember having uttered falsehood in my life. I have practised austerities for a very long time: I swear by them that Sītā is pure."

Rāma said: "I am also convinced of Sītā's purity, O sage. However, mighty is public scandal on account of which I had to abandon Sītā, even though I myself knew that she was pure. I know, too, that these two boys are my sons."

In the meantime, even the gods entered the assembly.

Sītā then said: "If I never even mentally thought of another, other than Rāma, then O Earth, receive me. If in thought, word and deed I have always worshipped Rāma, then O Earth, receive me."

When Sītā said these words, a celestial throne arose from the earth. In it was mother Earth; she received Sītā in her arms, and embracing her with great love, re-entered the earth.

All beings — the gods, the sages, the brāhmaṇas, the priests who had assembled to conduct the Aśvamedha rite, the birds, the beasts, and even the trees and insentient beings — all of them expressed their admiration, their devotion and their wonder in their own way. They were all wonderstruck, stunned, by the miraculous way in which Sītā disappeared into the earth.

Some praised and glorified Rāma; some praised and glorified Sītā. Everyone was filled with awe and wonder.

Uttara 98–99

When Rāma saw the descent of Sītā into the earth, he was completely overwhelmed with grief. He wept aloud. He cried: "Alas, even as I was looking, Sītā has been taken away. I rescued her from Laṅkā years ago; why should I not bring her back from the bowels of the earth? O Earth! Return Sītā to me immediately; or I will let you taste my anger. Wherever Sītā may be now, bring her back to me at once; if you do not, I shall destroy you along with the hills and forests, and the whole earth will be covered with water."

Seeing Rāma's anger, Brahmā the creator said: "O Rāma, do not lose your temper. The chaste and devoted Sītā has naturally gone ahead of you to the other world; and you will soon be reunited with her. Hear, again, O Rāma: your story till this period has been beautifully narrated in the great poem by the sage Vālmīki. There is some more left which concerns what is to come. Listen to that section, too." After saying so, Brahmā departed for his abode.

Rāma requested Vālmīki to recite the story of coming events. This was later recited by Kuśa and Lava.

Not seeing Sītā, Rāma regarded the world as empty, and overwhelmed by sorrow, he did not enjoy peace of mind. He did not consider looking upon another as wife, and for the performance of religious rites, he therefore used a golden image of Sītā.

Rāma ruled the earth for a very long time. During this entire period, all beings enjoyed health and long life. There was justice and righteousness everywhere. The earth was prosperous. There was adequate and timely rain. No one suffered any kind of misfortune.

After enjoying her life with Rāma, his children and his grandchildren, Rāma's mother Kausalyā ascended to heaven. After leading a righteous life, Sumitrā and Kaikeyī also went to heaven. All of them were reunited in heaven with the king Daśaratha. And, Rāma propitiated them all by the due and regular performance of the anniversary ceremonies performed for the welfare of the departed ancestors. [. . .]

Uttara 102–103

Then Rāma desired to establish the two sons of Lakṣmaṇa (Angada and Candraketu) as the rulers of two suitable principalities. Rāma said to Lakṣmaṇa: "These two sons of yours, O Lakṣmaṇa, are strong and valiant and are fit to be rulers of their own principalities. I shall anoint them kings; think of a suitable territory for each of them. It should be such that the rulers are free from trouble, and the hermitages are free from molestation."

As soon as such territories were found Rāma himself anointed the two boys kings: the territory ruled by Angada was known as Angada; and Candraketu was installed on the throne of Candrakānti. Lakṣmaṇa stayed for some time with them, and when the administration was functioning smoothly, he returned to Ayodhyā and to Rāma.

As Rāma was thus administering his empire, Time (or Death) appeared at the gate of Rāma's palace in the guise of an ascetic. The ascetic said to Lakṣmaṇa: "Pray, inform Rāma that a messenger from one who is supremely powerful has arrived and that I would like to speak to Rāma."

Lakṣmaṇa informed Rāma of the arrival of the ascetic. Upon Rāma's instructions Lakṣmaṇa led the ascetic to Rāma's presence. Rāma received the ascetic with great reverence and made him sit on a golden seat. Then, Rāma requested the ascetic to convey the message he had.

But the ascetic replied: "I can only reveal the message in private, O Rāma. And, whoever hears it or observes the two of us talking should be immediately put to death."

Rāma consented to this condition. He installed Lakṣmaṇa outside the chamber with the strict instruction: "Do not let anyone come in and interrupt this important conversation; anyone who enters the chamber will suffer death." He then turned to the ascetic: "Pray, convey the important message that you have for me."

UTTARA 104–105

When they were alone, the ascetic revealed his true identity as Time (or Death) and submitted to Rāma: "O Lord, the creator Brahmā sent me to you with this message: Once upon a time, you had withdrawn the universe into yourself and were resting on the great ocean. By your own Māyā you then created the two powerful beings, Madhu and Kaiṭabha.[47] Upon their destruction, this earth was fashioned from their own flesh. You yourself entrusted the work of protecting this world, to me who was born of the lotus that had sprung from your navel. And I have endeavoured to do my duty, placing the burden upon your shoulders. In course of time, for the destruction of the demons like Rāvaṇa, you incarnated on the earth, along with other divine beings. All that has been accomplished and the time for your return is at hand. If, however, you wish to continue to live on the earth, of course you can. If you wish to return to heaven so that heaven could have you as its sovereign, may it be so."

When Rāma heard this, he replied: "My manifestation is for the protection of the three worlds, not only of this earth; hence I shall soon depart from this earth. I shall do exactly as the creator, Brahmā, says."

As they were thus engaged in the conversation, there appeared at the entrance to the chamber Durvāsa, the great sage of terrible anger. He demanded of Lakṣmaṇa: "Take me to Rāma at once." When Lakṣmaṇa humbly questioned: "May I take a message to Rāma, for he is engaged in an important meeting? Or, would you care to wait for a few minutes?" the sage grew terribly angry and said: "Tell Rāma this moment that I am here. If you do not, I will curse him, you, your brothers and the whole royal family. I cannot contain my anger."

Hearing these terrible words, Lakṣmaṇa reflected for a moment: "It is better that I die rather than that this sage should curse the entire royal family." Having thus made up his mind, Lakṣmaṇa entered the chamber where Rāma and the ascetic were engaged in their conversation, and informed Rāma of Durvāsa's visit.

Rāma dismissed the ascetic and came out, bowed to the sage who said to him: "I have fasted for a thousand years; I wish to break the fast just now. Give me food." Rāma worshipfully served him with food. He ate and went away.

Thinking of his own terrible promise to the ascetic (that anyone interrupting the conversation would die), Rāma became moody.

---

[47] **Madhu and Kaiṭabha:** Two demons born from the ear of Viṣṇu; when they stole the Vedas from Brahmā, Viṣṇu took the form of the horse Hayagriva to destroy them. *Māyā* here means creative power; it is also the force that creates illusions.

Uttara 106–107

Lakṣmaṇa understood Rāma's predicament and approached him reverently and said: "Do not be worried on my account; all this is predestined to happen. Throw me out, O Rāma, and honour your promise; for when people dishonour their promise they go to hell."

Rāma summoned the ministers and the sages in council and informed them of all that had happened. The sage Vasiṣṭha then said: "O Rāma, I see that the end is coming: and now even Lakṣmaṇa has to be banished. It has to be done, for the sake of dharma. If dharma is abandoned, there will be universal destruction."

Rāma then said to Lakṣmaṇa: "Banishment is equal to execution, O Lakṣmaṇa. I banish you from the kingdom." Without even entering his house, Lakṣmaṇa went away. He reached the bank of the river Sarayū, ready to give up his life, sighing again and again. All the gods appeared in the heaven. Unseen by any human being, Indra took Lakṣmaṇa bodily to heaven. The gods were delighted that Lakṣmaṇa, who was inseparable from Rāma, had returned to heaven, thus indicating that Rāma would soon be with them.

Rāma was inconsolable with grief and he said: "I wish to abdicate the throne and retire to the forest; I wish to follow Lakṣmaṇa." He asked Bharata to ascend the throne.

But the noble Bharata replied: "Oh, no, Rāma, I have no desire for the kingdom without you. Install your sons Kuśa and Lava on the throne. Let Śatrughna also be informed of our decision."

Vasiṣṭha said to Rāma again: "Rāma, look at these citizens who are all grief-stricken." Rāma was overcome by sorrow and sighed: "Ah, what shall I do?" All of them with one voice said to Rāma: "With our wives and children, we shall all go where Rāma goes; we shall follow him."

Reflecting over the devotion of the citizens and also the imminent end of his career on earth, Rāma that very day installed Kuśa and Lava on the throne, apportioning to them suitable territory. He also sent fast messengers to inform Śatrughna of his decision.

Uttara 108–109

The messengers conveyed to Śatrughna all the news of the events in Ayodhyā: "Rāma has abdicated his throne, having installed Kuśa and Lava on the throne; Kuśa rules from his capital Kuśavati, and Lava from his capital Śṛavasti. All the citizens of Ayodhyā have decided to follow Rāma: the capital is therefore totally deserted. Rāma asked us to convey all this to you."

Hearing of the destruction of the family, Śatrughna instantly installed his sons on the throne and, alone on his vehicle, drove in great haste to meet Rāma. Upon reaching Rāma's presence, Śatrughna said: "I have enthroned my two sons on the throne, O Rāma, and I have decided to follow you." Rāma saw the firmness of his determination and acquiesced.

Coming to know of Rāma's abdication and of his imminent ascension to heaven, all the vānaras came, led by Sugrīva, and even so the gods and the sages rushed to where Rāma was. Sugrīva had installed Aṅgada on the throne and decided to follow Rāma.

When Vibhīṣaṇa arrived, Rāma quickly said to him: "O Vibhīṣaṇa, rule the kingdom of Laṅkā so long as the people wish you to do so, so long as the sun and the moon shine, and so long as my story is narrated in this world. Pray, do not argue." Vibhīṣaṇa consented.

Rāma blessed Hanumān: "Live and rejoice in this world as long as my story is narrated, and adhere to my instructions, O Hanumān." Hanumān bowed his acceptance.

All of them, thereupon, began to move out of Ayodhyā. All the weapons, the sages, the brāhmaṇas, the goddess of wealth, the holy scriptures, the holy mantras—all these followed Rāma. Bharata and Śatrughna went. All the ministers and the civil servants went. And all the citizens went, too. Not even the smallest creature stayed behind in Ayodhyā: all of them followed Rāma.

Uttara 110–111

Rāma approached the river Sarayū and touched its waters with his feet. To witness this most glorious and auspicious ascension of Rāma, all the gods had come in their space vehicles, and the creator Brahmā himself came in person in his own celestial vehicle.

Then, the Creator said to Rāma: "Come, O Viṣṇu, enter your own divine bodies along with your brothers. Whatever be the form which you wish to assume, that you may assume. Freed from the Māyā[48] with which you had covered yourself, you are once again beyond the reach of mind and speech. Pray, ascend to your own abode."

Rāma then entered into the spirit of lord Viṣṇu, along with his brothers. Hence, the gods and the sages worship Rāma as lord Viṣṇu himself.

Rāma said to Brahmā the creator: "Assign a celestial region for these, my devotees and followers, O Brahmā." Accordingly, Brahmā ordained a celestial region known as Śantanaka (or Śaantanaka), and decreed: "Even subhuman creatures that leave their physical body thinking of you, O Lord, will reach this celestial region."

Sugrīva entered the orb of the sun. And the other vānaras who were born of the various divinities re-entered their source. All the citizens and devotees of Rāma entered the river Sarayū and were instantly transported to heaven.

Brahmā the creator and all the gods in heaven were delighted at the return of Rāma and all the divine beings.

This is the Rāmāyana; the main parts of it were composed by the sage Vālmīki and approved by Brahmā the creator. It is extremely auspicious, and it destroys the sins of one who is able to read even a small part of it. In fact, this Rāmāyana is recited and listened to even in heaven. One who reads this daily obtains whatever he desires.

[48] **the Māyā:** The world of phenomena as illusion; the material world as a world of illusion from which Rāma has now been freed, released into the realm of spirit, which is the true reality.

THE MAHABHARATA
C. 400 B.C.E.–C. 400 C.E.

The longest epic in any language, the *Mahabharata,* the book of the "Great Bharata," consists of nearly one hundred thousand stanzas, almost eight times the length of *The Iliad* and *The Odyssey* combined. Unlike the Homeric epics or the *Ramayana,* which center on one main story line, the ***Mahabharata*** is an encyclopedic assemblage of many closely related stories, with interspersed mythic, genealogical, and philosophical tales about the descendants of King **Bharata**, a legendary ancestor of the Indo-Aryans.[1] As a compendium of stories fundamental to the later literatures of India and Southeast Asia, the *Mahabharata* has been called "the founding library of Brahmin-Indian civilization." Like Homer's *Iliad,* an eighth-century B.C.E. epic depicting the events of a war fought some four to five hundred years earlier, the *Mahabharata* tells of events that took place earlier in history—around 1000 B.C.E., during the period of the Aryan conquest. As described in the epic, a war takes place between two sets of cousins, the five sons of Pandu, known as the Pandavas, and the hundred sons of **Dhritarashtra**, known as the Kauravas. Less than half the text actually concerns this main story of patrimonial war; the rest consists of interwoven stories on myth, history, philosophy, and religion. Many of these tales, such as the stories of Savitri, of Shakuntala, and of King Nala and the princess Damayanti, are intricate and engaging tales in their own right. One of the most important of these, the Bhagavad Gita, added sometime between the first century B.C.E. and the first century C.E., often stands alone as one of India's most influential sacred texts.

muh-huh-BAH-ruh-tuh
BAH-ruh-tuh
drih-tuh-RAH-shtruh

The dating of the *Mahabharata* in relation to the *Ramayana* is uncertain. While the core story of the *Ramayana* appeared sometime in the sixth century B.C.E., the core of the *Mahabharata* most likely coalesced about two hundred years later. The historical geography alluded to in these epics suggests that in its final version the *Ramayana* was composed after its counterpart; Rama's capital city, Ayodhya, is located much farther east and so was settled earlier than either the chief city of the **Kauravas**, **Hastinapura** (near today's Delhi), or **Indraprastha**, the chief city of Pandavas. Both epics were revised over time by several hands, though like the ***Ramayana***, which is attributed to a single legendary author named Valmiki, the *Mahabharata* is attributed to a **Vyasa**, whose name means "compiler" or "arranger." It was not until the fourth century C.E. that the epics attained their final form, and even the later texts exist in several versions.

KOW-ruh-vuz
hus-tih-NAH-poo-ruh;
in-druh-PRAH-stuh
ruh-MAH-yuh-nuh
VYAH-suh

The Warrior Code and the Heroic Character. The core story of the war between the **Pandavas** and the Kauravas is reminiscent of Homer's *Iliad,* and like the heroes in that epic the heroes of the *Mahabharata* fol-

PAHN-duh-vuz

[1] **Aryans:** Tribal peoples from what is now the steppe region of Central Asia and Siberia who, moving south across the Hindu Kush, invaded India around 1500 B.C.E.

Sanskrit Text, nineteenth century
Sanskrit, the literary language of ancient India, was the written and spoken language of the Aryan peoples who invaded the Indian subcontinent around 1500 B.C.E. Classical Sanskrit has survived as a literary language into modern times. The Vedas—the Upanishads, the Sutras, and the Ramayana *and* Mahabharata*—were composed in Sanskrit. (The Art Archive / British Library)*

low a code of the warrior, the ***DHARMA*** of the ***KSHATRIYA*** (*KṢATRIA*), one of the original four classes[2] of ancient Indian society. Although the Brahmin or priestly class stood above the Kshatriya in the social hierarchy, the Kshatriya were not only warriors but the effective rulers of the worldly estate; their dharma, or sacred duty, was to master the use of weapons and to protect their people. Even though the Brahmins were the interpreters and guardians of the sacred texts of the Vedas, the Kshatriya were also trained in the sacred traditions and were expected to abide by their doctrines. In the *Mahabharata,* the values and duties of these two classes sometimes clash, and often the warriors must be reminded of their specific duties.

KSHUH-tree-yuh

[2] **four classes:** In Hindu tradition, humankind is created in four classes, or *varna:* in descending order they are the *Brahmins* (priests), the *Kshatriya* (warriors), the *Vaishya* (merchants and farmers), and the *Shudra* (laborers and servants).

The heroes and heroines of the *Mahabharata* are larger than life and have divine or miraculous origins. Nonetheless, as our translator, Chakravarthi V. Narasimhan, points out, each character is subject to human failings. Each of the Pandavas, in particular, has certain strengths that complement those of his brothers, while each also has certain weaknesses. The eldest brother, **Yudhishthira**, for example, who is the son of the god Dharma (Sacred Law), exhibits judicious conduct and acts according to high principles. His Brahminic ideals of peace and nonviolence sometimes conflict with the Kshatriya code that his brothers follow more strictly. At the same time he is a compulsive gambler who, as seen in the dice game with his foe Duryodhana, abandons all principles and even common sense in the heat of a game. Similarly, Bhima, the second born who excels in martial arts and physical strength, like Homer's Ajax or Achilles gives in to rash judgment and excessive violence, illustrated most poignantly when he drinks the blood of his enemy Duhsasana. Similarly, the third-born son, **Arjuna**, the main protagonist of the epic, demonstrates wisdom and virtue, but like Virgil's Aeneas sometimes wavers in his resolution, most famously on the night before the war begins. Indeed, Arjuna's internal struggle, the subject of the Bhagavad Gita, occasions one of the greatest scenes of instruction in all of world literature, when **Krishna**, the avatar of the god **Vishnu**, the Preserver, guides Arjuna toward accepting his duties as a warrior.

yoo-DISH-tih-ruh

AR-joo-nuh

KRISH-nuh; VISH-noo

On the Kaurava side, **Duryodhana**, though an effective leader, is undermined by jealousy and pride. Moreover, as in the Homeric epics, while women play a subordinate role overall, characters like Gandhari and particularly **Draupadi**, the wives of **Dhritarashtra** and the Pandava brothers, respectively, are not merely stock characters, allegories for female virtue or vice. Rather, they are strong willed and intelligent individuals guided in their judgment by a keen understanding of dharma. Like Queen Hecuba of Troy in *The Iliad,* **Gandhari** is a grieving mother and widow, and her evenhanded judgment contrasts sharply with the criminal manipulations of her husband. Yet, she is helpless to prevent the wrongdoing or to forestall the war that will lay waste to all of her sons and her husband. In contrast, Draupadi displays righteous indignation when she is humiliated in public by the Kauravas and principled judgment when she berates her husbands for their failure to defend her.

door-YOH-duh-nuh

DROW-puh-dee; drih-tuh-RAH-shtruh

gun-DAH-ree

The Pandavas and Kauravas struggle to exercise a just and righteous way of life—at least as they define it—in the face of delusion, vanity, and passion in the forms of envy, anger, greed, lust, and gluttony. Each follows what he thinks of as his sacred duty, but not without conflict. Yudhishthira cannot accept the bloody consequences of the Kshatriya code, which places high value on martial prowess, personal reputation, and decisive action. Arjuna, too, must be convinced that warfare can be a just means of bringing about peace. Thus, as in Homer's fifth-century B.C.E. treatment of heroes, in which the remnant values of a tribal system giving way to the city-state came under scrutiny, the *Mahabharata* weighs the relative merits of a culture founded on force versus a culture founded on rational discourse and diplomacy. Through its host of characters—warrior heroes, Brahmins, ascetics, sorcerers, demons, and more—the

Mahabharata presents a variety of perspectives on society, religion, and the cosmos, and suggests that in a world in which every strength is also a weakness and every virtue, especially if pressed too far, a potential vice, true salvation may be the ultimate release from the world, which is inherently flawed and fraught with illusion.

WWW For a quiz on the *Mahabharata,* see *World Literature Online* at bedfordstmartins .com/worldlit.

The Story of the Pandavas and Kauravas. The *Mahabharata* consists of eighteen books (Parvas), plus a final book of three parts called the *Harivamsa (Dynasty of Hari),* which was added late in the work's evolution. Book 1, Adi Parva (The Book of Origins), accounts for the miraculous and divine origins of the sons of Pandu, King of Hastinapura, and the Kauravas, the sons of Dhritarashtra, Pandu's brother. A curse on Pandu prevents him from having children with his wives, **Kunti** and **Madri**. To produce heirs for the king, Kunti summons the gods Dharma (sacred law), Vayu (wind), and Indra (the chief of gods), from whom she bears Yudhishthira, Bhima, and Arjuna, respectively. With Kunti's assistance, Madri similarly summons the Asvins, twin gods known as the "horsemen," with whom she bears the twins **Nakula** and **Sahadeva**. Though their true fathers are the gods, the five sons of Kunti and Madri are known as the Pandavas, the sons of **Pandu**. Around the same time, Dhritarashtra's wife Gandhari delivers a ball of flesh that miraculously produces one daughter and one hundred sons; these are the Kauravas, the eldest of whom is Duryodhana. The rivalry between the Pandavas and the Kauravas, who contest the rights to royal succession, leads to war.

KOON-tee

MAH-dree

NUH-koo-luh; suh-huh-DAY-vuh

PAHN-doo

Jealousy. After Pandu's death, Pandu's blind brother Dhritarashtra takes command of Hastinapura, which by rights should pass to Pandu's oldest son, Yudhishthira, once he comes of age. Meanwhile, under the leadership of their uncle Bhishma, the cousins undergo a rigorous program of education and training in martial arts. The godlike Pandavas, who have inherited certain gifts from their divine fathers, excel over the Kauravas. Hoping to outwit the Pandavas and to prevent Yudhishthira from inheriting the throne, Duryodhana and his brothers devise various schemes to keep power in the hands of their father, even plotting to murder the Pandavas.

To escape the plots of the Kauravas, the Pandavas go into exile in the forest for several years, where they study the Vedas and meet magical forest creatures. Eventually, they make their way to Pancala, where Arjuna, in a scene reminiscent of Odysseus's display of skill upon his return to Ithaca, wins Draupadi, the beautiful daughter of King Drupada, in an archery contest. By dint of their mother's injunction for the sons to share equally whatever prize Arjuna wins in the contest, Draupadi becomes the wife of all five brothers. Following the advice of Bhishma and Drona, King Dhritarashtra agrees to divide the kingdom in half to forestall hostilities between the two bands of cousins. Thus, the Pandavas settle at Indraprastha where Yudhishthira takes command of the new kingdom and rules from a magnificent palace built with the assistance of the architect and sorcerer Maya. From Indraprastha, the Pandavas expand their territory, subduing lesser kingdoms and exacting tribute from them.

. . . the composer of the *Mahabharata* has portrayed the actions of the warriors in both a heroic and a moral context, and it should be understood as a reenactment of a cosmic moral confrontation, not simply as an account of a battle. Unlike our Western historical philosophy, which looks for external causes — such as famine, population pressure, drought — to explain the phenomena of war and conquest, the epic bard views the events of war as prompted by observances and violations of the laws of morality.

– B. A. Van Nooten, critic, 1973

Arjuna meets and marries Subhadra, the sister of Krishna, who will become Arjuna's closest ally and spiritual counselor. These further successes of the Pandavas serve only to intensify the jealousy of Duryodhana, who is ever more determined to strip the Pandavas of their glory. His strategy is to challenge Yudhishthira, a compulsive but unskilled gambler, to a game of dice. Here the war between the cousins begins, and it is at this point that the selections from the *Mahabharata* found in the following pages begins.

The Dice Game and Exile of the Pandavas. Book 2, the Sabha Parva, relates the story of the dice game between Duryodhana and Yudhishthira. During the game, Duryodhana, aided by his uncle Sakuni Saubala, cheats Yudhishthira out of his entire fortune, including the freedom of his brothers and Draupadi. Moved by the righteous indignation of Draupadi, King Dhritarashtra returns to the Pandavas all they have lost, but the relentless Duryodhana gets his father to consent to holding yet another match, with the stakes that the Pandavas will go into exile if they lose. When the compulsive or reckless Yudhishthira loses the toss of the dice, the Pandavas go into a twelve-year exile, wandering through the forests and making a pilgrimage to the river Ganges. Their sojourn is related in Book 3, the Forest Book (Aranyaka Parva), in which Arjuna visits his true father, Indra, chief of the gods, from whom he receives celestial weapons. In the thirteenth year of exile, the subject of Book 4, the Book of Virata (Virata Parva), the Pandavas live in disguise in the court of King Virata and help to save the kingdom from an attack by the Kauravas.

When their period of exile is over, the Pandavas return to regain their lost kingdom, at first trying diplomacy, the subject of Book 5, Udyoga Parva. When all efforts at a peaceful resolution fail, the opposing cousins engage in a bloody and costly war. In a poignant moment, Kunti, the mother of the Pandavas, appeals to her firstborn son, Karna, now a powerful ally of the Kauravas, to make peace with his half brother Arjuna. Abandoned at birth by his mother, Karna came to despise the Pandavas, who once humiliated him. Thus, Karna, now a loyal friend to Duryodhana, refuses his mother's embassy for peace; his vow to fight to the death against his half-brother Arjuna anticipates and contrasts with Arjuna's crisis of faith in Book 6, when Arjuna pauses to question whether it is just to fight against his cousins.

koo-rook-SHAY-truh

BEESH-muh

The Great War. The story of the eighteen-day war on the fields of **Kurukshetra** occupies Books 6 through 10. The Book of Bhishma (Bhishma Parva), relates the story of the downfall of **Bhishma**, the Kauravas' first commander. Here, too, appears the text of the Bhagavad Gita, describing Arjuna's despondency and Krishna's council. After Bhishma's death, the command of the Kauravas goes successively to Drona, Karna, and Salya. By the end of the eighteenth day, all the Kauravas have been killed except Duryodhana, who is eventually caught and killed by Bhima. On the night of his death, as told in Book 10, the Sauptika Parva, some of Duryodhana's supporters slip into the Pandava camp and massacre almost the entire Pandava force while they sleep. The five Pandava brothers, Krishna, and Satyaki, a kinsman of Krishna and key ally of the Pandavas, manage to escape.

Peace and the Ascent to Heaven. After hunting down Asvatthama, the son of Drona and leader of the surprise assault on the sleeping Pandava forces, the war finally ends. The survivors observe a period of grieving, and the Pandavas finally regain their rightful rule over the kingdom. The final books of the *Mahabharata* recount the deaths of the old king Dhritarashtra, Krishna, and the Pandavas, who after ruling for twenty-one years go into the Himalayas to die. In Book 18, the Svarga-Arohanika Parva, Indra, the chief of the gods, persuades Yudhishthira to join his brothers in heaven. When his soul arrives there, to his dismay Yudhishthira finds his former enemy Duryodhana sitting on a lavish throne and his own brothers nowhere in sight. Guided by a celestial messenger, Yudhishthira enters the foul-smelling, corpse-ridden halls of Hell, where he finds his brothers. Indignant at the injustice of it all, Yudhishthira swears never to return to heaven, and just at that moment the gods appear to him and the illusion of Hell that he had been witnessing dissolves away. Like Odysseus or Aeneas, Yudhishthira has had to undertake a ritual descent into Hell; in the Indian hero's case, Hell is ***MAYA***, or illusion, and once the illusion departs, he attains his ultimate goal—***MOKSHA***, or release from the world of desire and suffering. Bathed in the heavenly Ganges, his purified soul is restored to the right way of seeing and he joins his brothers and cousins who, having been freed of earthly desire and deception, are finally reconciled in peace.

Thus, the Bharata war, which has cost many lives and caused great suffering, ends with a vision of spiritual peace and reconciliation. In depicting a war for paternal lands fought among cousins as well as the internal strife of characters like Yudhishthira and Arjuna, the *Mahabharata* tells the story both of the dharma of Kshatriya warriors who dominated the heroic culture of ancient India and of dharma as the universal force that orders the structure of society and the heavens. The epic is, therefore, more than a war story; it is the story of human conflict, both between social groups and within individuals. In later versions, the epic reads like a great comedy, the story of the successful victory of the human soul—personified by the five Pandava brothers with their complementary physical, intellectual, and spiritual attributes—over ***SAMSARA***, the cycle of death and rebirth. That triumph occurs only when an embodied spirit masters the dharma of his or her class, which is the message of the Bhagavad Gita.

> **The *Mahabharata* became the founding library of Brahmin-Indian civilization. It is necessary to understand the epic as an encyclopedia of that civilization.**
> **– EDWARD C. DIMOCK, critic, 1974**

■ CONNECTIONS

Homer, *The Iliad*, p. 288; *Beowulf* (Book 2). As epics based on an oral tradition, *The Iliad* and the *Mahabharata* both recount stories of a heroic age dominated by the code of the warrior. Moreover, both works retain stylistic remnants from the oral tradition: heroic similes, epithets, and formulaic expressions. As is true for the Pandava brothers, the heroic qualities of the Greek leaders Agamemnon, Menelaus, Achilles, Odysseus, and Nestor complement one another and together create a kind of composite ideal warrior. The epithets used to describe these heroes reveal their character. What picture of the warrior code emerges from these Greek and Indian epics, and how do the Greek heroes compare with their Indian counterparts? How does the warrior code of the Anglo-Saxons as depicted in *Beowulf* compare with the vestiges of that code in the *Mahabharata*?

Aeschylus, *The Oresteia*, pp. 806, 858, 1134. The works of fifth-century B.C.E. Athenian dramatists such as Aeschylus dramatize a society's transition from a tribal culture to city-states. So, too, the *Mahabharata* portrays a culture's changing from a tribal system to a number of kingdoms in northern India. Looking at the internal conflicts in the *Mahabharata*'s characters (such as Arjuna) and at the clash of values between the characters (between, say, Yudhishthira and Bhima), what do you see as the strategies by which the ancient Indian epic and the fifth-century B.C.E. Greek drama attempt to resolve the contradictions within their emergent social systems?

Sophocles, *Antigone*, p. 952; Chaucer, *The Wife of Bath* (Book 2). One of the issues raised by the *Mahabharata* (as well as the *Ramayana*), is the place of women in ancient Indian society. While the Penelope-like Sita of the *Ramayana* represents a woman who subordinates her will to the customs imposed on her by her culture, Draupadi of the *Mahabharata* challenges the actions of the men around her and, in the name of a higher justice, makes claims on them. How is Draupadi similar or dissimilar to other strong-willed women who defy the status quo in early literature, such as Antigone in Sophocles' play or the Wife of Bath in Chaucer's poem?

■ FURTHER RESEARCH

Literary History/Background
Dimock, Edward C. Jr., et al. *The Literatures of India: An Introduction.* 1974.
Flood, Gavin. *An Introduction to Hinduism.* 1996.
Zaehner, R. C. *Hinduism.* 1962, 1966.

Criticism
Sukthankar, V. S. *The Meaning of the Mahabharata.* 1957.
van Nooten, Barend A. *Mahabharata: Attributed to Krsna Dvaipayana Vyasa.* 1971.

Translations/Abridgements
Buck, William. *Mahabharata.* 1973.
Dutt, Manmatha Nath. *A Prose English Translation of the Mahabharata.* 6 vols. 1895–1905.
Narasimhan, Chakravarthi V. *The Mahabharata.* 1965; rev. 1998.
Narayan, R. K. *The Mahabharata: A Shortened Modern Prose Version of the Indian Epic.* 1978.

■ PRONUNCIATION

Abhimanyu: uh-bee-MUN-yoo
Arjuna: AR-joo-nuh
Ashvatthama (Aśvatthāmā): ush-vuh-TAH-muh
Bharata: BAH-ruh-tuh
Bishma (Bhīṣma): BEESH-muh
Brāhmaṇa: BRAH-hmuh-nuh
Dhirtarashtra (Dhṛtarāṣṭra): drih-tuh-RAH-shtruh
Draupadī: DROW-puh-dee
Duryodhana: door-YOH-duh-nuh
Gāndhārī: gun-DAH-ree, ghan-DAH-ree
Hāstinapura: hus-tih-NAH-poo-ruh
Indra: IN-druh

Indraprastha: in-druh-PRAH-stuh
Karṇa: KAR-nuh
Kauravas: KOW-ruh-vuz
Krishna (Kṛṣṇa): KRISH-nuh
Kshatriya (Kṣatriya): KSHUH-tree-yuh
Kuntī: KOON-tee
Kuru: KOO-roo
Kurukshetra (Kurukṣetra): koo-rook-SHAY-truh
Lakshmana (Lakṣmaṇa); LUKSH-muh-nuh
Madri (Mādrī): MAH-dree
Mahābhārata: muh-huh-BAH-ruh-tuh, muh-hah-BAH-ruh-tuh
Nakula: NUH-koo-luh, NAH-koo-luh
Pāñcāla: pun-CHAH-luh
Pāṇḍavas: PAHN-duh-vuz
Pāṇḍu: PAHN-doo
Rishi (Ṛṣi): RIH-shee, REE-shee
Sahadeva: suh-huh-DAY-vuh
Shiva (Śiva): SHEE-vuh, SEE-vuh, SHIH-vuh
Sūrya: SOOR-yuh
Vaishampayana (Vaiśampayana): vigh-shum-PAH-yuh-nuh
Vasishtha (Vasiṣṭha): vuh-SISH-tuh
Vāyu: VAH-yoo
Vidura: VIH-doo-ruh, VID-yoo-ruh
Vishnu (Viṣṇu): VISH-noo
Vyāsa: VYAH-suh, vee-YAH-suh
Yudhishthira (Yudhiṣṭhira): yoo-DISH-tih-ruh

***FROM* BOOK 2**

Sabha Parva [The Dice Game]

Translated by Chakravarthi V. Narasimhan

XX

When the Pāṇḍavas[1] decided to erect a splendid hall in Iṅdraprastha, Maya, the chief architect of the Dānavas,[2] volunteered his services. Lord Kṛṣṇa[3] said to Maya, "Build a hall which will be unique in the whole world, and will astound all men who see it." Maya happily accepted this command and designed for the Pāṇḍavas a hall in the form of an aerial car. He then marked out a site ten thousand cubits[4] square, well suited to all the seasons and very picturesque, on which he constructed the hall.

The assembly hall, which covered the entire area of the site, had golden pillars. It was very graceful, radiant as fire, so bright as to dim even the rays of the sun, and sparkled with a heavenly light, like the moon. In that hall Maya built a magnificent tank embellished with lotuses that had leaves made of vaiḍurya and stalks of bril-

---

Mahabharata. The *Mahabharata* exists in several versions, or rescensions, as they are called—texts compiled or produced from earlier sources. Though said to be written by one Vyasa, who appears as a Brahmin sage in the story, the *Mahabharata* was revised by many hands starting sometime in the fourth century B.C.E. and continuing through the fourth century C.E. The later editors or "arrangers," in particular, added layers of Brahminic doctrine to the text, including the Bhagavad Gita, which reflect transformations in religious and philosophical thinking over the period of the text's development. Like the *Ramayana,* the *Mahabharata* was written for the most part in the *shloka* verse form—a thirty-two syllable couplet, divided into four parts. Some parts of the *Mahabharata* use another Sanskrit verse form known as the *trishtubh* meter, consisting of four lines of eleven syllables each. Each quatrain of the trishtubh follows a strict, four-part pattern of short and long syllables. Like the *Ramayana,* the *Mahabharata* contains many epic similes, heroic epithets, and formulaic expressions—stylistic devices common to much epic poetry of the ancient world.

Book 1, the Adi Parva, summarized in the headnote, gives the genealogical background of the Pandavas and Kauravas and tells of the Kauravas' increasing jealousy of their godlike cousins, the

---

[1] **the Pāṇḍavas:** The five sons of Pāṇḍu, each of whom actually was fathered by one of the gods on Pāṇḍu's two wives, Kuṅtī and Mādrī. The sons of Kuṅtī are Yudhiṣṭhira, fathered by Dharma (god of law); Bhīma, by Vāyu (wind); and Arjuna, by Iṅdra (the chief of gods). The sons of Mādrī are the twins Nakula and Sahadeva, fathered by the Aśvins (physicians of heaven).

[2] **Maya . . . the Dānavas:** Those born of Dānu, an *asura,* or demon, are called the Dānavas; Maya is a legendary magician-builder who once constructed dwellings for demons.

[3] **Lord Kṛṣṇa:** The incarnation of the god Viṣṇu, the preserver god, who intermittently returns to earth in bodily form in order to restore order; he is a principal ally of the Pāṇḍavas and serves as the charioteer of and advisor to Arjuna. In the epic, he is the son of Vāsudeva (Kuṅtī's brother) and Devakī.

[4] **cubits:** Units of measure approximately eighteen to twenty-two inches long; originally, the length measured from the elbow to the end of the middle finger. Thus, the site measures more than 15,000 square feet.

liant gems. It was redolent with the fragrance of lotuses and was stocked with different birds, as well as with tortoises and fish. Having completed the construction of this unique assembly hall in fourteen months, Maya informed Yudhiṣṭhira that the work was done.

When the high-souled Pāṇḍavas were holding court in the assembly hall, the illustrious sage Nārada visited them, accompanied by other sages, in the course of his peregrinations all over the world. Nārada said: "O king! monarchs who perform the rājasūya sacrifice[5] rejoice with Iṅdra.[6] It is said that this sacrifice is full of hurdles. The Brahma-rākṣasas[7] like to hinder it. Any small incident may start a war that will destroy the whole world. O king of kings, ponder all this, and do what is beneficial. Be determined in protecting the four castes.[8] Be happy and please the Brāhmaṇas with gifts." After thus advising Yudhiṣṭhira, Nārada departed. Thereupon Yudhiṣṭhira began to consult with his brothers regarding the performance of that most illustrious and difficult of sacrifices, the rājasūya.

After much reflection, Yudhiṣṭhira decided to make preparations for the performance. Thinking that Kṛṣṇa would be the best person to decide the question, he mentally communed with him. Kṛṣṇa immediately came to Yudhiṣṭhira, who received him affectionately, like a brother. Kṛṣṇa was also happy to see his aunt Kuṅtī, as well as Bhīma.

Pandavas. Book 2, the Sabha Parva, begins just after the five Pandava brothers, all married to Draupadi, have settled in the city of Indraprastha, which they gained when King Dhritarashtra partitioned his kingdom in two. Following the story of the dice games, in which Yudhishthira's weakness and lack of skill in gambling lead the Pandavas into exile, the stories of their exile and disguise are omitted, and the story picks up again with the preparations for war, the Udyoga Parva, and continues through the war to its aftermath.

A note on the translation: The abridged prose version presented here, translated by Chakravarthi V. Narasimhan, offers a very readable, English retelling of the story about the war between the Pandavas and the Kauravas. The first section of the Bhisma Parva, chapter LXVIII, which contains the abridgment of what is the Bhagavad Gita, has been included; comparing this brief chapter with the Bhagavad Gita selections that follow the *Mahabharata* (see p. 1488) is a good way to see what is lost in the abridged versions of the epic and what the poetic character of the original Sanskrit text is like. Other abridgements and translations of the *Mahabharata* include those of William Buck (1973) and R. K. Narayan (2000). Those who wish to experience the *Mahabharata* in its full range of complexity, with its multiple narrators and dozens of subplots and digressions should consult the six-volume translation of the entire epic by Manmatha Nath Dutt (1895–1905) or the translation of the first five books by J. A. B. van Buitenen (1973). All notes are the editors'. As in the *Ramayana,* the spellings of names have not been romanized. See the pronunciation guide for a comparison of spellings.

---

[5] **rājasūya sacrifice:** The ritual sacrifice and celebration held for the king's coronation.

[6] **Iṅdra:** The king of the gods and a benefactor to men.

[7] **Brahma-rākṣasas:** The demon spirit of a wicked Brahmin (Brāhmaṇa), a member of the priestly class.

[8] **the four castes:** The four castes or classes *(varna),* in order of superiority, are the *Brahmins* (*Brāhmaṇa,* or priests), the *Kṣhatriya* (warriors), the *Vaiṣhya* (merchants and farmers), and the *Śhūdra* (laborers and servants).

"O Kṛṣṇa," said Yudhiṣṭhira, "I would like to perform the rājasūya sacrifice, but it cannot be accomplished by a mere wish. You know well how it can be done. My friends suggest that I should perform the rājasūya, but your advice on this matter will be final."

"O best of the Bharatas,"[9] Kṛṣṇa replied, "you are endowed with the attributes of an emperor. It is fitting that you should establish your dominion over all the Kṣatriyas.[10] At the same time, I do not believe that you will be able to perform the rājasūya sacrifice as long as the powerful Jarāsaṅdha[11] remains alive. He cannot be defeated in battle by all the asuras[12] and all the celestials. But I believe he can be overcome in single combat. If you have faith in me, give me Bhīma and Arjuna to help me overcome this obstacle."

Yudhiṣṭhira said, "For the fulfilment of our objective let Arjuna follow the best of the Yadus,[13] Kṛṣṇa, and let Bhīma follow Arjuna. Let us hope that tact coupled with prowess will bring about success." Thus blessed by Yudhiṣṭhira, Kṛṣṇa left for Magadha along with Arjuna and Bhīma. In time they entered the kingdom of the great King Jarāsaṅdha, like Himālayan lions entering a cattle pen. When the people of Magadha saw those heroes with broad chests, resembling elephants, they were greatly surprised.

Kṛṣṇa said to Jarāsaṅdha, "O king of Magadha, we challenge you to a duel. Either release all the kings whom you have unjustly imprisoned, or go to the abode of Yama.[14]" Jarāsaṅdha replied: "I have never imprisoned any king wrongfully. Who is kept prisoner whom I have not conquered? I am ready to fight on any terms, an army against an army, or alone against any one, any two, or all three of you."

Kṛṣṇa then said, "O king, name the one amongst us three whom you wish to fight. Who amongst us should be prepared to fight with you?" In reply to Kṛṣṇa, the king of Magadha, Jarāsaṅdha, chose to fight with Bhīma. The combat began on the first day of the month of Kārtika, and continued without any respite, day and night, for thirteen days. On the night of the fourteenth day the Magadha king stopped from exhaustion.

Taking advantage of Jarāsaṅdha's weariness, Bhīma caught hold of him, whirled him by his shoulders a hundred times, dashed him on the ground, and shattered his back. Then he roared in triumph. All the citizens, headed by the Brāhmaṇas, approached Bhīma respectfully and honoured him with every due rite. The liberated kings also offered their respects to Kṛṣṇa and spoke to him in peace. Kṛṣṇa consoled all those who were afraid and at once crowned the son of Jarāsaṅdha as his father's successor to the throne. The Pāṇḍavas and Kṛṣṇa then returned to Iṅdraprastha, and

---

[9] **the Bharatas:** King Bharata is the ancestor of both the Pāṇḍavas and the Kauravas, who are often referred to throughout the epic by this name.

[10] **Kṣatriyas:** See note 8.

[11] **Jarāsaṅdha:** The king of Magada, a kingdom to the east, and an enemy of the Pāṇḍavas.

[12] **asuras:** One of several types of demons.

[13] **the best of the Yadus:** An epithet for Kṛṣṇa, derived from one of the names of his clan, Yadu (also Yādava).

[14] **Yama:** The god of death.

Kṛṣṇa informed Yudhiṣṭhira, "O best among kings, providentially the powerful Jarāsaṅdha was defeated by Bhīma and the imprisoned kings have been released. You may therefore proceed with your plans for the great sacrifice."

Arjuna said to Yudhiṣṭhira: "O best among kings, I think that we should now add to our wealth and exact tribute from other kings." Yudhiṣṭhira approved of this, and Arjuna, accompanied by a large army, set forth on the divine and wonderful chariot given to him by Agni. Similarly the twins Nakula and Sahadeva, and Bhīma, after having been blessed by Yudhiṣṭhira, left with their respective armies. Arjuna reduced the north, Bhīma the east, Sahadeva the south, and Nakula the west. Meanwhile Yudhiṣṭhira stayed at Iṅdraprastha.

After praising his virtues, Kṛṣṇa said to Yudhiṣṭhira, "O emperor, you alone are worthy of performing the great sacrifice. If you complete it satisfactorily and obtain its benefit, then we shall all be happy." Thus advised by Kṛṣṇa, Yudhiṣṭhira, assisted by his brothers, completed the arrangements for the performance of the rājasūya. Vyāsa[15] himself officiated as its high priest, and Susāma, best among the Dhanañjayas, chanted the Sāma Veda.[16] Then Yudhiṣṭhira sent Nakula to Hāstinapura to invite Bhīṣma, Droṇa, Dhṛtarāṣṭra, Vidura, Kṛpa,[17] and all his brothers and relatives, to attend the great sacrifice.

Rivalling Varuṇa in splendour, Yudhiṣṭhira began the sacrifice marked by six sacrificial fires. He propitiated all the visitors with ceremonial offerings and many rich gifts. The mighty Kṛṣṇa, armed with the bow, the cakra, and the club, stood guard over the great sacrifice until its completion. Thereafter Kṛṣṇa and Yudhiṣṭhira took leave of each other and departed to their respective homes. After Kṛṣṇa had left for Dvārakā, only King Duryodhana[18] and his uncle Śakuni stayed on in that celestial hall.

XXI

Lingering in that hall, Duryodhana inspected it at leisure along with Śakuni. He saw many unique things such as he had never beheld in the city of Hāstinapura. Once he

---

[15] **Vyāsa:** The son of Satyavati and Parasara, a sage. Vyāsa, the father of Dhṛtarāṣṭra and Pāṇḍu, is the great-grandfather of the Pāṇḍavas and the Kauravas; he is a sage and the purported author of the epic.

[16] **Susāma . . . Sāma Veda:** Susāma is a priest of the Dhananjaya sect; the Sāma Veda is one of the four scriptures known as the Vedas. Written in verse and composed of strophes from the Rig Veda, the Sāma Veda is chanted by priests in conjunction with sacrifices.

[17] **Bhīṣma . . . Kṛpa:** Bhīṣma, the son of King Santanu and Gaṅgā, is the great-uncle of the Pāṇḍavas and Kauravas; the Brahmin Droṇa is the teacher who instructed the cousins in martial arts. Dhṛtarāṣṭra, the son of Vyāsa and Aṁbīka, is the father of the one hundred brothers known as the Kauravas, the eldest of whom is Duryodhana. Vidura is the son of Vyāsa and one of Aṁbīka's maids, and so the half brother of Pāṇḍu and Dhṛtarāṣṭra; he serves as a counselor to Dhṛtarāṣṭra. Kṛpa is Droṇa's brother-in-law. All of these men are associated with Hāstinapura, the original capital city of the Kurus, now governed nominally by Dhṛtarāṣṭra and effectively by his son Duryodhana.

[18] **King Duryodhana:** The eldest of the one hundred sons of Dhṛtarāṣṭra and Gāṅdhārī and the archrival of the Pāṇḍavas. His uncle Śakuni is Gāṅdhārī's brother.

reached a transparent surface and, mistaking it for water, drew up his clothes and went around the hall; when he discovered his error he felt ashamed and unhappy. Then he mistook a pond with crystal-clear water, adorned with lotuses, for land and fell into the water fully clothed. The servants laughed at this, but provided him with dry clothes at the royal command of Yudhiṣṭhira. The mighty Bhīma, Arjuna, the twins, and everybody else laughed at Duryodhana's discomfiture.

Duryodhana could not forgive their derision but, to save appearances, he ignored it. He then took leave of the Pāṇḍavas, but having witnessed the wonderful opulence displayed at the great rājasūya sacrifice, he returned to the city of Hāstinapura sad at heart. On his return, Śakuni said, "O Duryodhana, why are you going about sighing like this?" Duryodhana replied, "O uncle, I have observed the whole world brought under the sovereignty of Yudhiṣṭhira by the great Arjuna's skill in the use of arms. I have also seen the great sacrifice of Yudhiṣṭhira, which can be compared only to that performed by the glorious Iṅdra among the gods. Because of this, I am filled with envy which burns me day and night, and I feel dried up like a small pond in the summer."

"O Duryodhana," said Śakuni, "you should not envy Yudhiṣṭhira. After all, the Pāṇḍavas are enjoying their own good fortune." This was no consolation to Duryodhana, who replied: "If you will let me do so, I shall conquer them with your help and that of the great car-warriors who are our allies. Then the world will be mine, including that opulent assembly hall of great wealth, while all the kings will do me homage." Śakuni said, "The Pāṇḍavas cannot be defeated in battle even by the gods; they are great car-warriors, expert bowmen, learned in the science of arms, and eager for battle. But I know how Yudhiṣṭhira can be overcome."

Duryodhana's spirits picked up on hearing this. He said, "O uncle, tell me how they can be defeated without risk to our friends." Śakuni said, "Yudhiṣṭhira is fond of gambling, though he is no expert at throwing the dice. If he is invited to a game, he will not be able to resist the temptation. I am an expert gambler, without equal in the three worlds. Therefore ask Yudhiṣṭhira to play a game of dice. But, Duryodhana, you must inform the king, your father, about this. With his permission, I shall defeat Yudhiṣṭhira without a doubt."

Duryodhana readily agreed to this plan. Śakuni then went up to Dhṛtarāṣṭra and said, "O great king, you should know that Duryodhana has become pallid, wasted, weak, and absent-minded." Dhṛtarāṣṭra sent for his son and said to him, "O my son, why are you so sad? If you can confide in me, tell me why." "O king," replied Duryodhana, "I am unhappy on seeing the boundless wealth of the enemy. I am obsessed with this thought, so that I cannot obtain any peace of mind."

Śakuni then said, "O king, listen to the stratagem by which you can gain the matchless wealth of Yudhiṣṭhira which you have seen. I am adept in the art of throwing the dice. Yudhiṣṭhira likes to gamble, though he does not know how to throw the dice. If invited to play, he will surely respond. Therefore, ask him to a game." Dhṛtarāṣṭra said, "The wise Vidura is my adviser on whose counsel I act. I shall first consult him and I shall then know how to decide this issue." Duryodhana said, "If Vidura is consulted, this plan will not go through, and, O king of kings, if you stop this, I shall certainly commit suicide."

On hearing these sad words of his beloved son, Dhṛtarāṣṭra ordered his servants, "Let the masons quickly build a commodious and beautiful hall with a thousand pillars and a hundred doors. It must be well built and easily accessible, adorned with gems all over and provided with dice. Let me know when the hall is completed."

When the hall was ready, King Dhṛtarāṣṭra said to Vidura, his chief adviser, "Go to Prince Yudhiṣṭhira and request him on my behalf to come here quickly, along with his brothers, to see this wonderful assembly hall of mine, adorned with costly jewels and furnished with luxurious couches. We shall also have a friendly game of dice."

Vidura said, "O king, I do not like your message. Do not act thus. I apprehend the destruction of the family, for I fear there will soon be a quarrel amongst the brothers." Dhṛtarāṣṭra said, "O Vidura, if fate so ordains, such a quarrel will not trouble me. This world does not act on its own, but only at the will of the Creator and under the influence of fate. Therefore, go to the king as I have directed, and quickly fetch here the invincible Yudhiṣṭhira."

Thus Vidura was forced by Dhṛtarāṣṭra to go to fetch the wise Pāṇḍavas. When he reached Yudhiṣṭhira, the latter said, "I can see that you are unhappy. Vidura, is your mission one of peace? Are the sons of Dhṛtarāṣṭra behaving well? Are the subjects docile?" Vidura replied sorrowfully, "The king is well, as are his sons, but he is obstinate and selfish, and bent on self-aggrandisement. The king of the Kurus[19] asked me to tell you, having first made kind enquiries after your happiness and welfare, 'This hall matches yours in appearance, my son; so come and visit it along with your brothers. In it, O Yudhiṣṭhira, have an enjoyable game of dice with your brothers. We will be delighted if you can come, and so will all the Kurus assembled here.'"

After giving this message, Vidura continued, "You will see gamblers and cheats placed there by King Dhṛtarāṣṭra. I have come to give you this message. Do as you think fit." After considering the situation, Yudhiṣṭhira replied, "Terrible cheats and deceitful gamblers will be there. But we all have to submit to fate and the will of the Creator. I do not wish to play with cheats, and I am reluctant to gamble with Śakuni unless that insolent one challenges me in the hall. If challenged, however, I shall never disregard it. This is my firm vow."

Having said this to Vidura, Yudhiṣṭhira quickly ordered everybody to get ready to depart. The next day he started for Hāstinapura with his family and servants, and also the ladies, led by Draupadī. Having reached Hāstinapura, they spent the night happily. Then, early the next morning, they all completed their daily rites and entered the splendid hall full of gamblers.

XXII

Śakuni said, "O king, here are people gathered to capacity in this hall and ready to play. O Yudhiṣṭhira, now is the time to cast the dice and to agree on the rules of the game." "I have vowed that I shall not refuse to play if I am challenged," replied

[19] **The king of the Kurus:** Kuru, like Bharata, was a distant ancestor of the Pāṇḍavas and the Kauravas, and his name was given to the clan from which they come. Hence, his name, like "Bharata," is invoked in epithets, like "the king of the Kurus," referring to Dhṛtarāṣṭra, for any of the descendants of Kuru.

Yudhiṣṭhira. "O king, destiny is powerful and I am in its grip. Tell me, whom should I take on in this assembly? Who among these players can match my stakes? Answer me, and then let the game begin."

Duryodhana said, "O king, I shall furnish the gems and riches needed for stakes and my uncle Śakuni will play on my behalf." Yudhiṣṭhira replied, "It seems to me that it is wrong for one to play for another. I am sure even you will accept that. However, let it be as you wish." He continued, "O king, this expensive chain, rich with gems and adorned with the finest gold, and obtained from the ocean, this is my stake. What is the stake with which you will match it? I am going to win this stake." So saying, he cast the dice. Then Śakuni, who knew the secret of gambling, grabbed the dice. He cast them and then said to Yudhiṣṭhira, "I have won."

Yudhiṣṭhira said, "You won that stake by cheating. Fie on you, O Śakuni! Let us play staking thousands. I now stake these hundred jars, each filled with a thousand gold coins." They played, and again Śakuni claimed, "I have won." When the game had gone on for a while and Yudhiṣṭhira had lost again and again, Śakuni said, "O Yudhiṣṭhira, you have lost the greater part of the wealth of the Pāṇḍavas. Tell me if you have any assets left." Yudhiṣṭhira said, "O king, my city, my kingdom, my lands, the property that does not belong to the Brāhmaṇas, and the subjects who are not Brāhmaṇas[20]—these are my remaining assets. With this as my stake, O king, I shall now play against you." Once more Śakuni cheated when casting the dice and said to Yudhiṣṭhira, "I have won."

Having lost all his wealth, Yudhiṣṭhira said, "This dark young man with crimson eyes, who looks like a lion and is endowed with mighty shoulders, Nakula, is now my stake." Thereupon, Śakuni cast the dice again and claimed that he had won. Yudhiṣṭhira then said, "Sahadeva dispenses justice and has earned a reputation for wisdom throughout the world; though he does not deserve this and is dear to me, I shall stake him." Again Śakuni cheated when casting the dice, and told Yudhiṣṭhira, "I have won."

"O king," said Śakuni, "I have won both the sons of Mādrī, who are dear to you. Apparently Bhīma and Arjuna are even dearer to you, since you do not wish to stake them." Thus taunted, Yudhiṣṭhira said, "I shall now stake Arjuna who enables us to sail through a battle like a boat, who is the conqueror of enemies, who is a vigorous prince and the hero of the world." Having heard this, Śakuni again cheated when casting the dice, and told Yudhiṣṭhira, "I have won."

"O king," Yudhiṣṭhira said, "I shall now offer as my stake Bhīma, our leader, who leads us singlehanded in battle, who has straight eyes and close-set eyebrows, who has the shoulders of a lion and who never forgives an insult, whose strength is unmatched among humans, who is foremost among club-fighters, and who destroys his enemies." Śakuni, cheating while casting the dice, again said to Yudhiṣṭhira, "I have won."

Yudhiṣṭhira then said, "The only person left is myself, dear to my brothers. If I,

---

[20] **subjects . . . Brāhmaṇas:** Brahmins, members of the priest class, by their elevated status cannot be put up as stakes by Yudhiṣṭhira.

too, am won we shall accept our misfortune and the lot of the vanquished." Having heard this, Śakuni cheated again when casting the dice, and told Yudhiṣṭhira, "I have won."

Śakuni then said, "There is one stake left that has not been won as yet—your beloved queen. Stake Draupadī, the daughter of the Pāñcāla king,[21] and win back freedom along with her." "O wretch," replied Yudhiṣthira, "I shall now stake the slender-waisted and beautiful Draupadī, the princess of Pāñcāla, and play with you." When Yudhiṣthira said these words, the assembled elders voiced their disapproval. But, flushed with victory and mad with conceit, Śakuni cast the dice once more and said, "I have won."

Duryodhana said, "O Vidura, go and fetch Draupadī, the beloved spouse of the Pāṇḍavas. Let her clean this house and be one of our servant maids." Vidura said, "O fool, you cannot see that by these words you are binding yourself with cords. You do not realize that you are hanging on a precipice. You do not know that you are behaving like a child, like a deer rousing tigers."

Drunk with pride, Duryodhana ignored this warning, saying, "Fie on Vidura." He noticed Prātikāmī[22] in the hall and told him, in the midst of the venerable assembly, "Prātikāmī, fetch Draupadī here, since you are not afraid of the Pāṇḍavas. Vidura speaks in fear, and he never wished us well."

Accordingly, Prātikāmī went to the Pāṇḍavas' residence and told Draupadī of his errand. Draupadī then said, "O son of a charioteer, go and ascertain from the gambler in the hall whether he lost himself, or me, first. When you have this information, return to me and then lead me there." When Prātikāmī returned with this message from Draupadī, Duryodhana said, "O Duḥśāsana,[23] this son of my charioteer is weak-minded and afraid of Bhīma. Go yourself to Draupadī and seize and bring her here. What can these husbands of hers do, having lost their freedom?"

XXIII

His eyes red with anger, Prince Duḥśāsana rose at his brother's words, and entered the residence of those great car-warriors, the Pāṇḍavas. There he said to the Princess Draupadī, "Come, O Pāñcālī, you have been won. Discard your shyness and look at Duryodhana. O lady whose eyes are like lotus petals, respect the Kurus, who have won you fairly, and enter the hall." On hearing these words, the miserable Draupadī rose up in sorrow and, covering her pale face with her hands, she ran to the ladies' quarters in the palace of the old king. Thereupon Duḥśāsana ran after her in hot pursuit, roaring in anger, and caught hold of her by her long blue wavy tresses. He roughly dragged the defenceless Draupadī by her hair to the hall, while she quivered pitiably like a plantain tree in a storm.

---

[21] **Pāñcāla king:** King Drupada, Draupadī's father and the ruler of the kingdom of Pāñcāla.

[22] **Prātikāmī:** One of Duryodhana's servants.

[23] **Duḥśāsana:** A younger brother of Duryodhana; he is one of the hundred Kaurava brothers, sons of Dhṛtarāṣṭra and Gāndhārī.

With her hair dishevelled and her dress in disarray, the bashful Draupadī said deliberately, in anger, "O shame! The moral standards of the Bhāratas and of the Kṣatriya code have perished. In this hall everybody assembled looks on while the bounds of virtue are transgressed." So saying, she looked at her helpless husbands. While she was thus invoking virtue, Duḥśāsana shook her with even greater force, repeatedly calling her a slave and laughing aloud. Except for Duryodhana, Duḥśāsana, Śakuni, and Karṇa,[24] all those present felt very sad on seeing Draupadī thus dragged into the hall.

Bhīma then said to Yudhiṣṭhira, "All the tribute and other wealth you took from the king of Kāśī, all the gems the other kings presented to you, our chariots, our armour and weapons, our kingdom, and even our own selves, have all been lost in gambling. None of this provoked my anger, since you are our lord. But I think you went too far when you played with Draupadī as a stake."

Meanwhile, the evil Duḥśāsana began to pull at Draupadī's clothes, intending to disrobe her by force in the middle of the hall. But as her clothes were thus being pulled off, many similar clothes appeared in their place. There were loud acclamations from all the kings who saw that most miraculous spectacle.

Even as Duḥśāsana was engaged in his effort to remove Draupadī's clothing by force, she remembered that the great sage Vasiṣṭha had taught her a long time ago to meditate upon the Lord when she was in great peril. She began to recall again and again in her mind Lord Kṛṣṇa, in his various manifestations, as Goviṅda, as Nārāyaṇa, as the denizen of Dvāraka,[25] beloved of the cowherdesses. In her mind she appealed to him for succour even as she was being shamed by the Kauravas. Without revealing his presence, Kṛṣṇa saved Draupadī from humiliation. As one piece of cloth was stripped, another piece of cloth covered her, and hundreds of cloths of different colours littered the floor. The royal personages present in the hall were astonished by this miracle. They applauded Draupadī, and condemned the action of Duḥśāsana.

Then Bhīma swore in a loud voice in the presence of those kings, with his lower lip trembling in anger, and squeezing one hand in the other, "O kings, O men, listen to these my words which have never yet been uttered by any man and which will never be said by anyone else. If I do not drink the blood of this sinful, lowborn wretch Duḥśāsana in battle after rending apart his chest, let me forego the path of my ancestors!" Hearing his vow, which astonished everybody, many in the hall acclaimed Bhīma vigorously and condemned Duḥśāsana. When finally a mass of clothes was heaped in the midst of the assembly, Duḥśāsana, tired and abashed, gave up his evil design and sat down.

Draupadī then said, "I, who was seen only in the svayaṁvara arena by the assembled kings, and was never seen elsewhere in public, have been brought by force

---

[24] **Karṇa:** The firstborn son of Kuṅtī, fathered by the sun-god Sūrya before Kuṅtī married Pāṇḍu. Abandoned by his mother, Karṇa was raised by a charioteer; he has become a close friend and ally of Duryodhana and the other Kauravas. Despite his parentage, Karṇa is affiliated with the lower Vaiṣya class because he was raised by a charioteer.

[25] **Dvāraka:** A city in the kingdom of Anarta; Lord Kṛṣṇa's capital city.

to the assembly hall today. I think that these are evil times when the Kurus allow their daughter-in-law to be thus tormented. O Kauravas, say whether this wife of Yudhiṣṭhira, born like him of a royal family, is a slave or not. I shall accept your verdict."

Upon this, Duryodhana said to Yudhiṣṭhira, "Bhīma, Arjuna, and the twins are subject to your command. Reply to Draupadī's question, whether you deem her won or not." Having said this, and with the purpose of encouraging Karṇa and annoying Bhīma, before Draupadī's very eyes Duryodhana bared his left thigh. Bhīma then vowed, "Let me forego the regions of my ancestors if I do not break that thigh of yours in the great battle that is to come."

Meanwhile, thoroughly abashed by Draupadī's appeal, Dhṛtarāṣṭra said, "O Pāñcālī, ask any boon you wish of me. Virtuous and devoted to Dharma as you are, I regard you as the foremost of my daughters-in-law." Draupadī said, "O best of the Bhāratas, if you would give me a boon, I pray that the ever dutiful Yudhiṣṭhira may be set free." Dhṛtarāṣṭra granted her wish and said, "O blessed one, my heart goes out to you. You deserve more than one boon. I wish to give you a second boon; ask of me whatever you want." Draupadī then said, "Let Bhīma and Arjuna, Nakula and Sahadeva be given their chariots and bows: this is my second wish."

Dhṛtarāṣṭra then said, "Ask of me a third boon, for two boons are not enough for you. Truly you are the most virtuous and illustrious of my daughters-in-law." Draupadī said, "O best of kings, avarice kills virtue; I do not wish to be greedy and I do not deserve a third boon. These my husbands, having been rescued from the miserable state of slavery, will win prosperity by their good deeds."

"O king," said Yudhiṣṭhira, "command us and tell us what we should do, for you are our lord. We wish to obey your commands at all times." Dhṛtarāṣṭra said, "O Yudhiṣṭhira, I wish you everlasting prosperity! I give you leave to go in safety and rule your own kingdom with all your wealth intact." Then Yudhiṣṭhira saluted and took leave of everybody, and left with his brothers. Accompanied by Draupadī, they mounted their cars, and with happy minds they left for the most splendid of cities, Iṅdraprastha.

XXIV

After the departure of the Pāṇḍavas, Duḥśāsana said to Duryodhana, Karṇa, and Śakuni, "O great car-warriors, the old man has ruined what was achieved with so much effort and difficulty. The wealth has returned to the enemy." Then Duryodhana said to Dhṛtarāṣṭra, "O father, having got back their weapons and cars, the Pāṇḍavas will kill us like angry serpents. O best of the Bhāratas, there is only one solution: we should again gamble with the Pāṇḍavas, the penalty for the losers being exile to the forest, and we shall thus be able to control them. Either one of us, having lost at dice, shall enter the thick forest, dressed in skins, and live there for twelve years. In the thirteenth year the losers shall live in hiding amid the people. If recognized during this period, they shall return to the forest for another twelve years."

"One or the other of us shall live in this way," Duryodhana continued. "Therefore let the game commence once more. Let the dice be cast, and let the Pāṇḍavas be invited again to play. O king, this is our most important task. You know that Śakuni is skilled in the art of gambling. O king, if at the end of the thirteenth year the Pāṇḍavas return after having kept the vow, we can easily conquer them. By then we will be firmly established in our kingdom, and meanwhile we shall have gained allies and built up a strong, big, and invincible army. O destroyer of foes, consider this." Dhṛtarāṣṭra said, "Ask the Pāṇḍavas quickly to come back, even if they have gone some distance. Let them return and play again."

Prātikāmī was then dispatched to invite Yudhiṣṭhira to come and play again. Prātikāmī said, "O King Yudhiṣṭhira, the assembly is gathered and your father has asked me to invite you again to come and play at dice." "All creatures receive good or evil at the command of the Creator," said Yudhiṣṭhira. "If I have to play once more, it is inevitable. I know that this command of the king, this fresh invitation to a game of dice, will cause desolation all round. But even so, I am not able to disregard it." So saying, he returned to the gambling hall.

Śakuni then said, "The old king returned your wealth, and that is truly commendable. But listen to me carefully, for I am going to propose another very high stake. If you defeat us at dice we shall be exiled in the forest for twelve years, clad in deerskins, and shall live in hiding during the thirteenth year. If recognized during this period, we shall go into exile in the forest for another twelve years. On the other hand, if we defeat you, you shall likewise live in exile in the forest for twelve years, dressed in deerskins, and accompanied by Draupadī. At the end of the thirteenth year, one or the other shall regain his own kingdom. O Yudhiṣṭhira, with this compact between us, cast the dice for the game, and let us play."

"O Śakuni," said Yudhiṣṭhira, "how can a dutiful king like me refuse to accept such a challenge? I shall play with you." Thereupon Śakuni, casting the dice again, said to Yudhiṣṭhira, "I have won."

Then the defeated Pāṇḍavas prepared to go to the forest. They wore upper garments of deerskin, according to the compact. When the Pāṇḍavas were leaving the hall the foolish Duryodhana imitated the gait of Bhīma who walked like a lion. Bhīma said, "I shall kill Duryodhana, and Arjuna shall slay Karṇa, while Sahadeva will kill the deceitful Śakuni. I shall kill the evil Duryodhana in a club-fight. I shall stand with my foot on his head while he lies on the ground. Like a lion I shall drink the blood of the sinful Duḥśāsana, who is brave only in words."

When the Pāṇḍavas were getting ready to leave, Vidura said: "It is not right that the revered Princess Kuṅtī should go to the forest. She is delicate and aged, and should ever be comfortable. The blessed Kuṅtī will live in my house as an honoured and welcome guest. Know this, O Pāṇḍavas, and I bless you that you may always be safe!"

As she was about to depart, Draupadī was oppressed by sadness. She took leave of the illustrious Kuṅtī and the other ladies there. Kuṅtī, also greatly disturbed on seeing Draupadī ready to leave, spoke a few sad words with difficulty. "Good women are never worried about the future," she said. "Your great virtue will protect you and you will soon gain prosperity." Having consoled the weeping Kuṅtī and saluted her, the unhappy Pāṇḍavas left for the forest. When they had gone, King Dhṛtarāṣṭra's mind was overcome with worry. He asked Vidura to join him immediately.

[In Books 3 and 4, Āraṇyaka Parva and Virāta Parva, the Pāṇḍavas serve out their twelve years of exile in the forest and thirteenth year in disguise at the court of King Virāta. Arjuna marries princess Uttara, King Virāta's daughter, forming an alliance between the Matysas and the Bharatas and conceiving a son named Abhimanyu. The Pāṇḍavas then return to their homeland, hoping for a peaceful settlement and restoration of their kingdom. Despite the intervention of Kṛṣṇa as a mediator, the obstinate and still-jealous Duryodhana, preferring war, refuses to relinquish control over the Pāṇḍavas' share of the kingdom. Early in Book 5, the Udyoga Parva, Duryodhana and Arjuna meet with Kṛṣṇa who gives them a choice between enlisting his aid or the aid of the Narayanas, an army of ten million soldiers. Arjuna, making the first choice, asks Kṛṣṇa to join him, and Kṛṣṇa agrees so long as he plays a noncombatant role. Though both Bhīsma and Dhṛtarāṣṭra advise Duryodhana against war, he insists on fighting his cousins to the death.]

***FROM* BOOK 5**

Udyoga Parva [The Breakdown of a Peaceful Settlement]

XL

Meanwhile, at the Pāṇḍava camp, Yudhiṣṭhira said to Kṛṣṇa, "Relying on you, O Kṛṣṇa, we have without fear demanded our share of the kingdom from the son of Dhṛtarāṣṭra who is filled with vain pride, as are all his advisers. You have heard what Dhṛtarāṣṭra and his son intend to do. It is exactly as Sañjaya[26] told me. He wants to make peace with us without restoring our kingdom to us; the greedy man, moved by his sinful heart, shows bias towards his own son. We said to him, 'Give us, O sire, five villages or towns where we may live together; for we do not desire the destruction of the Bhāratas.' Even this the wicked-souled son of Dhṛtarāṣṭra does not permit, thinking that he is the sole lord. What is more deplorable than this?"

"Wealth is said to be the best virtue," Yudhiṣṭhira continued. "Everything is established on wealth; and rich men live in this world, while poor men are practically dead. Poverty is a greater danger to a man than death; for it destroys his prosperity, which is the source of his virtue as well as his pleasures. A man who is born poor does not suffer so much as one who, after having enjoyed great prosperity and a life of great happiness, is deprived of it. We have many cousins, and our elders are our allies on both sides. Their slaughter would be extremely sinful. One may well ask: what then is the good of engaging in battle? A Kṣatriya kills another Kṣatriya; a fish lives on another fish; a dog kills another dog. See how each follows his rule of life, O Kṛṣṇa. In all cases war is evil. Who that strikes is not struck in return? Victory and defeat, O Kṛṣṇa, are the same to one who is killed. Defeat is not very much better than death, I think; but he whose side gains victory also surely suffers some loss."

---

[26] **Sañjaya:** One of King Dhṛtarāṣṭra's advisors who had been sent as a messenger to the Pāṇḍava camp.

Yudhiṣṭhira asked him, "What then do you think, O Kṛṣṇa, to be appropriate to the occasion? How shall I find a way out without deviating from virtue as well as from worldly good? In such a predicament, whom else but yourself is it proper for us to consult, O best among men?" In reply, Kṛṣṇa said to Yudhiṣṭhira, "For the good of both of you I shall go to the Kuru camp. If I succeed in ensuring peace without sacrificing your interests, then I shall have performed a virtuous and fruitful act."

"As it pleases you, O Kṛṣṇa!" said Yudhiṣṭhira. "May good come out of it! May I see you return from the Kurus with your object gained, and in good health!" Kṛṣṇa said, "Going to the Kurus, I shall seek to make peace without any sacrifice of your interests; and I shall also observe their intentions. After noting the conduct of the sons of Kuru and ascertained their preparations for war, I shall return to make victory yours, O Bhārata."

Having come to know through his spies of the departure of Kṛṣṇa, Dhṛtarāṣṭra said to Bhīṣma,[27] after paying him due honour, "The powerful scion of the Dāśārha race is coming here for the sake of the Pāṇḍavas; he is at all times worthy of our respect and regard. Prepare for his worship and erect pavilions on the way, filled with all needed articles." Then at many places on the way, at spots of great beauty, pavilions were constructed and decked with all kinds of gems. The king sent there comfortable seats, girls, perfumes, ornaments, fine fabrics, excellent viands and drinks, and several kinds of fragrant garlands.

Vidura[28] addressed Dhṛtarāṣṭra, "O king, the five Pāṇḍavas desire only five villages. If you do not give them even those, who will conclude peace? You wish to win over Kṛṣṇa by wealth; and by this means you want to separate him from the Pāṇḍavas. Let me tell you this: he cannot be separated from Arjuna by wealth, or by efforts, or by accusations and complaints against the Pāṇḍavas."

Duryodhana said, "What Vidura has said just now regarding Kṛṣṇa has been truly spoken; for he is firmly attached to the Pāṇḍavas and inseparable from them. Listen to this great idea which I am determined to carry out. I shall imprison Kṛṣṇa, the refuge of the Pāṇḍavas. On his imprisonment, the Vṛṣṇis[29] and the Pāṇḍavas, in fact the whole world, will be at my disposal. Kṛṣṇa will be here tomorrow morning."

Hearing these words of terrible significance, the plan of making Kṛṣṇa a captive, Dhṛtarāṣṭra and his ministers were much pained. Dhṛtarāṣṭra then said to Duryodhana, "Do not say such foolish things, O my son. This is against eternal virtue. Kṛṣṇa is an ambassador, and he is also our kinsman. He has done no wrong to the Kurus. How then is it right that he should be made prisoner?"

Bhīṣma said, "This son of yours, Dhṛtarāṣṭra, has been seized by folly. He chooses evil rather than good, despite the entreaties of his well-wishers. I wish never to listen to the risk-laden words of this sinful and wicked wretch who has abandoned all virtue." Having said these words, the old chief of the Bhāratas, the truthful Bhīṣma, rose in a towering rage and left the court.

---

[27] **Bhīṣma:** See note 17.

[28] **Vidura:** See note 17.

[29] **Vṛṣṇis:** The members of Kṛṣṇa's clan.

XLI

In honour of Kṛṣṇa the city was well decorated and the streets were adorned with various gems. The people, with their heads bowed low to the ground, were in the streets when Kṛṣṇa entered the city. That lotus-eyed hero entered the ash-coloured palace of Dhṛtarāṣṭra, graced with many buildings. He was duly honoured by Dhṛtarāṣṭra and then came out with the permission of the king. Having exchanged greetings with the Kurus in the assembly, Kṛṣṇa went to the enchanting abode of Vidura. The virtuous Vidura completed the rites of hospitality for Kṛṣṇa, and then asked him about the welfare of the Pāṇḍavas.

After his visit to Vidura, Kṛṣṇa went in the afternoon to visit his aunt Kuṅtī.[30] Seeing Kṛṣṇa approach, shining like the radiant sun, Kuṅtī clasped his neck with her arms, and poured forth her lamentations, remembering her sons whom she had not seen for so long. Kṛṣṇa said to her, "Your sons, along with Draupadī,[31] salute you. They are well and have asked me to inquire about your welfare. You will soon see the Pāṇḍavas, in good health, with all their objects gained, their enemies killed and themselves surrounded by prosperity." Bidding her farewell, and respectfully circumambulating her, the mighty-armed Kṛṣṇa then left for Duryodhana's mansion.

During the night, after he had dined and refreshed himself, Vidura said to him, "O Kṛṣṇa, this mission of yours is not a well-considered act. The sons of Dhṛtarāṣṭra and Karṇa are convinced that the Pāṇḍavas are not capable even of gazing at an army under the leadership of Bhīṣma and Droṇa.[32] The idea of your going and speaking in the midst of all those misguided, impure, and evil-minded men does not please me. All the sons of Dhṛtarāṣṭra have come to the conclusion, O Kṛṣṇa, that they can give battle to Iṅdra himself along with the other gods. Your words, though wise in themselves, will be of no avail against those who are thus inclined, and who follow the dictates of desire and anger."

Kṛṣṇa said, "You have spoken wisely—you have spoken as a man of insight, and even as one friend to another. When there is a dispute between cousins, the wise men say that the friend who does not serve them as a mediator by all his efforts is not a true friend. If I can bring about peace with the Kurus without sacrificing the interests of the Pāṇḍavas, then my conduct will have been meritorious and very significant; and the Kurus will have been freed from the shackles of death."

In such talk the two wise men spent that starlit and beautiful night. At dawn many professional bards and singers endowed with good voices awakened Kṛṣṇa with the sound of conch and cymbal. Duryodhana and Śakuni[33] came to Kṛṣṇa while he was still performing his morning rites, and said to him, "King Dhṛtarāṣṭra has come to the assembly hall, and so have the other Kurus, headed by Bhīṣma and all

---

[30] **Kuṅtī:** The wife of Pāṇḍu, Kuṅtī is the mother of Karṇa (out of wedlock), and the mother of the first of the five Pāṇḍavas—Yudhiṣṭhira, Bhīma, and Arjuna.

[31] **Draupadī:** The daughter of King Drupada and the wife of the five Pāṇḍava brothers.

[32] **Droṇa:** See note 17.

[33] **Śakuni:** See note 18.

the rulers of the earth. They are waiting for you, O Kṛṣṇa, as the gods in heaven may await Iṅdra's arrival." Kṛṣṇa received them courteously, and in due course proceeded to the assembly hall.

When all the kings and courtiers had taken their seats and perfect stillness prevailed, Kṛṣṇa said in a voice like a drum, "I have come so that there may be peace between the Kurus and Pāṇḍavas, O Bhārata, without the slaughter of heroes on either side. However, your sons, headed by Duryodhana, are acting impiously, putting behind them all considerations of morality and earthly good. As boys the Pāṇḍavas lost their father and were brought up by you; protect them in accordance with justice, as you would your own sons, O king. The Pāṇḍavas salute you, and have sent you this message: 'At your command our followers and we ourselves have suffered untold misery. We have spent twelve years in banishment in the forest and the thirteenth year in disguise. We did not break our word, truly believing that our father would not break his pledge towards us. The Brāhmaṇas who accompanied us know this. Therefore abide by your pledge as we have done by ours, O best of the Bhārata race. We have suffered long, and now we desire to get our share of the kingdom.'"

Having given this message, Kṛṣṇa continued, "Restore to the Pāṇḍavas their due share of the ancestral kingdom, and enjoy the blessings of life, along with your sons. As for me, O Bhārata, I desire your welfare as much as that of the others. In the interests of virtue, profit, and happiness, O king, I adjure you not to allow the destruction of your subjects. Restrain your sons, who regard evil as good and good as evil, and who, moved by greed, have gone too far. The Pāṇḍavas are as ready to serve you dutifully as to fight. O king, adopt that course which seems wisest to you."

XLII

Dhṛtarāṣṭra said to Kṛṣṇa, "O Kṛṣṇa, I agree with what you have said to me. It will lead to the attainment of heaven, besides being beneficial to the world, as well as virtuous and just. But I am not my own master and I cannot do what I would like to do. O Kṛṣṇa, try and persuade my wicked son Duryodhana, who disregards the injunctions of the scriptures. Then you will have discharged a great duty as a friend."

So Kṛṣṇa addressed himself to the wrathful Duryodhana, in sweet words pregnant with virtue and worldly profit, "O Duryodhana, listen to these words of mine, which are meant for your benefit and that of your followers. Born as you are in a family of very wise men, and endowed as you are with learning and good conduct and with all good qualities, it is right and proper that you should behave honourably. In this case your obstinacy is perverse and unrighteous, and it will result in great and terrible loss of life. O tiger among men, be reconciled with the Pāṇḍavas, who are wise, heroic, energetic, self-restrained, and greatly learned. It is beneficial to you, and will be appreciated by the wise Dhṛtarāṣṭra, as well as by the grandfather Bhīṣma, Droṇa, and the intelligent Vidura. Let there be some survivors of the Kuru race and let not the whole race be destroyed, and do not let yourself, O king, become notorious as the exterminator of the race."

Duryodhana became enraged on hearing the words of Kṛṣṇa. Bhīṣma said to him, "Kṛṣṇa has spoken as a friend wishing peace; listen to his words, my dear son, and do not follow the lead of anger." But Duryodhana did not heed Bhīṣma's advice. He remained under the influence of wrath, breathing hard. Then Droṇa told him, "Kṛṣṇa said words to you which are filled with virtue and profit, my dear son; so did Bhīṣma, the son of Śantanu; heed them, O ruler of men." At the end of Droṇa's speech, Vidura spoke in similar terms to Duryodhana, the irate son of Dhṛtarāṣṭra. "Duryodhana," he said, "I do not grieve for you, but for these two old people, your father and Gāndhārī your mother." Dhṛtarāṣṭra then said to Duryodhana, who was seated along with his brothers and surrounded by other kings, "O Duryodhana, listen to this advice given by the great-souled Kṛṣṇa; accept his words which are beneficial, of eternal validity and conducive to our salvation."

So, among the assembled Kurus, Duryodhana had to listen to this counsel which he little liked. Finally he said in reply to Kṛṣṇa, "No doubt, as is proper, you have spoken to me after due consideration; but you find fault only with me. I have not committed the slightest fault, nor do I see even the smallest misconduct on my side after a searching examination. I may recall that the Pāṇḍavas were defeated at a game of dice in which they engaged of their own free will and in the course of which their kingdom was won by Śakuni; what misconduct was there on my part? Indeed, you will remember that I ordered at the time the return of the wealth which the Pāṇḍavas had lost. It is not our fault that the Pāṇḍavas were defeated at another game of dice and were then banished to the forest. The principal duty of a Kṣatriya is that he should lie down on a bed of arrows in the battlefield. I am ready to do so. I shall not, during my lifetime, allow the Pāṇḍavas to regain the share of the kingdom that was given them by our ancestors in early days."

After reflecting on Duryodhana's speech, Kṛṣṇa, his eyes red with anger, spoke these words to Duryodhana in that assembly of the Kurus: "It is your desire to get the bed of a hero, and it will be fulfilled; you and your advisers will not have to wait long. Soon there will be a great massacre. O fool, you think that there is nothing blameworthy in your conduct towards the Pāṇḍavas. All the kings here know the truth of what I am now going to say. Being jealous of the prosperity of the great Pāṇḍavas, you arranged for a game of dice in evil cabal with Śakuni. Who save yourself could have treated the wife of your brothers in the way you did? After dragging Draupadī to the council hall, who else could have spoken to her as you did? You went to great trouble to burn the Pāṇḍavas alive when they were mere boys, and were staying with their mother at Vāraṇāvata, but that attempt of yours did not succeed. By poison, by snake, and by rope, in fact by every means, you have attempted the destruction of the sons of Pāṇḍu, but you have not been successful. You have been urged again and again, by your mother and by your father and also by Bhīṣma, Droṇa, and Vidura, to make peace but you do not wish to do so."

When Kṣṛṇa had thus charged the wrathful Duryodhana, Duḥśāsana[34] said these words in the assembly of the Kurus, "If you do not make peace of your own free will with the Pāṇḍavas, it looks as if the Kauravas will make you over to Yudhiṣṭhira

[34] **Duḥśāsana:** One of the Kauravas, the hundred sons of King Dhṛtarāṣṭra and Gāndhārī.

bound hand and foot." Hearing these words of his brother, Duryodhana could no longer restrain himself. He got up from his seat hissing like a huge serpent. Disregarding all those present—Vidura, King Dhṛtarāṣṭra, Bāhlika,[35] Kṛpa, Somadatta, Bhīṣma, Droṇa, and Kṛṣṇa—that shameless and wicked prince walked out of the court.

XLIII

Dhṛtarāṣṭra then said to Vidura, "Go, my friend, to the wise Gāṅdhārī; get her here; along with her I shall try to persuade our son." In response to the request of Dhṛtarāṣṭra, Vidura brought the farsighted Gāṅdhārī. By command of Dhṛtarāṣṭra and also at the request of Gāṅdhārī, Vidura had the wrathful Duryodhana brought back. Seeing her son, who was following the wrong course, Gāṅdhārī spoke these significant words, "O Duryodhana, my dear son, listen to these words of mine which will be to your benefit and that of your followers, and which will bring you all happiness. It is my fond and earnest wish, as well as that of Bhīṣma, your father, and other well-wishers, the chief of whom is Droṇa, that you should make peace."

Disregarding those sensible words spoken by his mother, the obstinate Duryodhana again went to his own palace burning with rage. Then he consulted King Śakuni, the expert in the game of dice, as well as Karṇa and Duḥśāsana. The four, namely, Duryodhana, Karṇa, Śakuni, and Duḥśāsana, reached the following conclusion: "Kṛṣṇa means to waste no time, and wants to capture us first in concert with Dhṛtarāṣṭra and Bhīṣma. We shall, however, capture Kṛṣṇa by force, before he can carry out his plan."

Coming to know of this plan through Sātyaki,[36] Vidura said to Dhṛtarāṣṭra, "O king, your sons are approaching the hour of doom, because they are ready to perpetrate an infamous act, even though they are incapable of doing it." He then informed the king of Duryodhana's nefarious plot. On hearing this, Dhṛtarāṣṭra said to Vidura, "Bring here again the sinful Duryodhana, who covets the kingdom." Therefore Vidura made the reluctant Duryodhana return once more to the council chamber, along with his brothers.

King Dhṛtarāṣṭra addressed Duryodhana, Karṇa, Duḥśāsana, and the kings who surrounded them, "O you of inhuman conduct, of exceeding sinfulness, having for your supporters only petty men, I know of your secret desire to commit a wicked deed. Kṛṣṇa cannot be captured by force, even as air cannot be held by the hand, as the moon cannot be touched, and as the earth cannot be supported on the head." Vidura's warning was: "If you try to use force on the mighty Kṛṣṇa, you, along with your advisers, will perish like an insect falling into the flame."

When Vidura had finished speaking, Kṛṣṇa said to Duryodhana, "O Duryodhana! since, out of your folly, you suppose me to be alone, you think you can effect my capture by overpowering me." So saying, he laughed aloud. And at his laughter

---

[35] **Bāhlika:** Bāhlika and Somadatta are allies of the Kauravas.

[36] **Sātyaki:** A kinsman of Kṛṣṇa and a key ally of the Pāṇḍavas.

the body of the great-souled one became like lightning. From his body issued forth gods only as big as the thumb but bright as rays of fire. Brahmā was found to be on his brow and Rudra[37] on his breast. On his arms appeared the regents of the earth and from his mouth issued forth the god of fire. When Kṛṣṇa thus showed himself on the floor of the assembly hall, celestial drums were sounded and there was a shower of flowers. After a moment he discarded that celestial and wonderful form. Taking Sātyaki by the hand, Kṛṣṇa went out, with the permission of the sages present in the court.

As he was about to depart on the chariot which was ready for him, the great king Dhṛtarāṣṭra again said to Kṛṣṇa, "You have seen, O Kṛṣṇa, what little influence I wield over my sons; you have been a witness to that; nothing has happened behind your back." Then Kṛṣṇa said to Dhṛtarāṣṭra, and to Droṇa and the grandfather Bhīṣma, and to Vidura, and to Bāhlika and Kṛpa, "Your exalted selves are witnesses to what went on in the assembly of the Kurus; how today that fool, like an uneducated and unmannerly fellow, walked out. Now you have heard the ruler of the earth Dhṛtarāṣṭra say that he is powerless in the matter. With the permission of all of you I shall go to Yudhiṣṭhira."

Then in that large, white chariot, furnished with tinkling bells, Kṛṣṇa went first to see his aunt Kuṅtī. Entering her abode, he bowed at her feet, after which he briefly described to her what had happened in the assembly of the Kurus. Having completed his report he respectfully circumambulated her, and took leave of her.

When Kṛṣṇa had left, Bhīṣma and Droṇa said to Duryodhana, "The sons of Kuṅtī will do what Kṛṣṇa advises, and they will not be pacified without the restoration of the kingdom. The Pāṇḍavas and Draupadī too were persecuted by you in the assembly hall, but they were bound by the ties of virtue at that time. Now they have in Arjuna a master of all weapons and in Bhīma a giant of firm determination. They have the Gāṇḍīva bow and the two quivers and the chariot and the flag, and they have Kṛṣṇa as their ally. The Pāṇḍavas will not forgive the past."

XLIV

Before leaving Hāstinapura, Kṛṣṇa met Karṇa and said to him: "O Karṇa, you know the eternal instruction of the holy books and are fully conversant with all their subtleties. The two classes of sons called Kānīna and Sahoḍha who are borne by a girl before her marriage have for their father the man who marries their mother subsequently—so it is said by people conversant with the holy books. You were born in that way and you are therefore morally the son of Pāṇḍu; so come with me and be a king in your own right. Let us go together to the Pāṇḍava camp, and let the sons of Pāṇḍu know you to be the son of Kuṅtī born before Yudhiṣṭhira. The five Pāṇḍava brothers will clasp your feet, as will the five sons of Draupadī, and the invincible son

[37] **Brahmā . . . Rudra:** Brahmā is the god of creation; Rudra, another name for Śiva, is the god of destruction. The third god of the Hindu trinity is Viṣṇu, the preserver, of whom Kṛṣṇa is an incarnation. Thus, Kṛṣṇa here presents an awesome spectacle of divine powers.

of Subhadrā.[38] Enjoy the kingdom in company with your brothers, the sons of Pāṇḍu, who are ever engaged in prayer and sacrifice and other auspicious ceremonies. Let your friends rejoice and in the same way let your enemies suffer; be reconciled today with your brothers, the sons of Pāṇḍu."

Karṇa replied: "I have no doubt, O Kṛṣṇa, that you have spoken these words out of good will, love, and friendship, and also out of the desire to do me good. Before her wedding with Pāṇḍu, Kuṅtī conceived me by the Sun-god, and at his command she abandoned me as soon as I was born. I know I was born in this way and I am therefore morally the son of Pāṇḍu. I was however left destitute at birth by Kuṅtī, who had no thought of my welfare. On the other hand, I have been practically a member of the family of Dhṛtarāṣṭra and, under the protection of Duryodhana, I have enjoyed sovereignty for thirteen years without let or hindrance. Relying on me, Duryodhana has made preparations for war with the Pāṇḍavas. At this stage, I cannot behave treacherously towards Duryodhana out of fear of being slain or captured, or from covetousness."

Kṛṣṇa said, "I fear that this world will surely come to an end, O Karṇa, since my advice does not seem acceptable to you." "O Kṛṣṇa," replied Karṇa, "I shall see you again if I survive this great battle which has come upon us. Otherwise we shall surely meet in heaven. I now feel that I shall meet you only there, O sinless one."

Having learnt of the failure of Kṛṣṇa's mission, Kuṅtī decided to make a personal appeal to Karṇa. Thus resolved, she went towards the river Gaṅgā for the attainment of her object. On the banks of the river she heard the sound of the chanting of hymns by her son, the kind and truthful Karṇa. That austere lady waited behind Karṇa, whose arms were raised and whose face was turned to the east, till the end of his devotions, which continued till his back had been scorched by the rays of the sun. Karṇa then turned and, seeing Kuṅtī, did her honour by saluting her and folding his hands before her, according to proper form.

Karṇa first introduced himself, by saying, "I am Karṇa, the son of Rādhā and of Adhiratha,[39] and I salute you. Why are you come here? Tell me what I may do for you." Kuṅtī replied, "You are the son of Kuṅtī and not the son of Rādhā; nor is Adhiratha your father. O Karṇa, you are not born in the race of Sūta; know this word of mine to be true. I conceived you illegitimately when I was an unmarried girl and you were the first in my womb; you were born in the palace of Kuṅtibhoja, my dear son. The maker of brightness, the Sun-god, begot you on me, O Karṇa. O my son, you were born in my father's palace, wearing earrings, clad in a coat of mail, like a divine being. But, owing to ignorance of your true birth, you are now serving the sons of Dhṛtarāṣṭra, without recognizing your brothers. That is not proper, my son. Let the Kurus witness today the union between Karṇa and Arjuna; and seeing that true reconciliation among brothers let dishonest men bow down!"

---

[38] **son of Subhadrā:** Abhimanyu, the son of Arjuna and his wife, Subhadrā, who is Kṛṣṇa's sister.

[39] **Adhiratha:** The charioteer who, with his wife, Rādhā, found and raised Karṇa after Kuṅtī, in a fit of desperation, abandoned him in the river Ganges.

Then Karṇa heard an affectionate voice issue from the solar disc from afar. It was Sūrya himself, speaking with the affection of a father. The voice said, "O Karṇa, Kuṅtī has spoken the truth. Act according to the advice of your mother; by doing so, you will benefit greatly." But in spite of this entreaty both by his mother and by his father, Karṇa's attitude did not waver.

"O Kṣatriya lady," he said, "I cannot heed the words you have spoken and I do not feel that the way to virtue lies in my doing as you urge me to do. What you did to me was sinful, and I have thereby suffered what is tantamount to the destruction of my fame. Though I was born as a Kṣatriya I did not get the baptismal rites of a Kṣatriya; it was all your sinful doing; what enemy can possibly do me a greater injury? Without having shown me any mercy at that time, you come today to urge me, who was deprived of the rites of my order as a Kṣatriya at birth, to be reconciled to my brothers. You did not think as a mother of my good and you have now come to me purely out of desire for your own good. Unknown as a brother before, and recognized as such now, by whom shall I be called a Kṣatriya if I go over to the side of the Pāṇḍavas on the eve of battle?

"This is the time for those who have obtained their living from Duryodhana to show their fidelity," Karṇa continued, "and I shall do so even at the risk of my life. I shall stay on the side of the sons of Dhṛtarāṣṭra, and I shall fight your sons with all my might and prowess; I do not speak falsely to you. I promise you this: it is with Arjuna alone, among all the forces of Yudhiṣṭhira, that I shall fight. Killing Arjuna in battle, I shall obtain great merit. Slain by him, I shall obtain great glory. O illustrious lady, you will thus always be left with five sons; with Arjuna dead and me alive, or with me slain and Arjuna alive."

When she heard Karṇa's words, Kuṅtī trembled with grief. Embracing her son, who was unmoved in his fortitude, she said, "Indeed what you say is possible. As you say, fate is all-powerful." Before leaving him, Kuṅtī said to Karṇa, "May you be blessed and may all be well with you." Karṇa also saluted her, and the two went their own ways.

XLV

Kṛṣṇa returned to Yudhiṣṭhira and reported the failure of his mission. The virtuous and just Yudhiṣṭhira, after hearing Kṛṣṇa's account, said to his brothers, "You have heard what happened in that assemblage of the Kurus and you have no doubt understood what Kṛṣṇa has said. Therefore let us make a division of our army; here are the seven Akṣauhiṇis which are gathered for our victory. Listen to the names of those famous men who are to be their respective commanders. Drupada, Virāṭa, Dhṛṣṭadyumna and Śikhaṇḍī, Sātyaki, Cekitāna, and Bhīma endued with strength, these heroes, who are prepared to sacrifice their lives if necessary, will be the commanders of my army."

There was a speedy gathering of the soldiers and there was everywhere the trumpeting of elephants, the neighing of horses, and the clatter of chariot wheels, which mingled with the noise caused by the blare of the conch and the sound of the drum. The mobilization of that army caused a roar like that of the sea at high tide. Indeed, the tumult of those happy warriors seemed to reach the very heavens.

Forty thousand chariots, five times that number of horses, ten times that number of foot soldiers, and sixty thousand elephants were gathered there. Anādhṛṣṭi and Cekitāna, the king of Cedi, and Sātyaki surrounded Yudhiṣṭhira along with Kṛṣṇa and Arjuna. Finally, they reached Kurukshetra[40] with their army ready for action and they then blew their conches. All the soldiers of the army became cheerful on hearing the thunderous sound of Kṛṣṇa's conch, the Pāñcajanya.

The next morning, King Duryodhana surveyed his forces, which consisted of eleven Akṣauhiṇis. Dividing his men, elephants, chariots, and horses into superior, inferior, and indifferent, he distributed them among his forces. He selected men who were wise and also heroic to be the leaders of his army. They were Kṛpa, Droṇa, Śalya, Jayadratha the king of the Siṅdhus, Sudakṣiṇa the king of the Kāṁbojas, Kṛtavarmā, Aśvatthāmā the son of Droṇa, Karṇa, Bhūriśravas, Śakuni the son of Subala, and Bāhlika the great car-warrior.

Then, with clasped hands, Duryodhana went to Bhīṣma along with the other kings, and said to him, "Without a commander in chief even a large army is broken up like a swarm of ants when engaged in battle. You are like the sun among the luminous bodies, the moon among deciduous herbs,[41] Kubera among the Yakṣas,[42] Iṅdra among the gods. If you lead and protect us, we shall be like the gods protected by Iṅdra, and we shall surely be invincible even if faced by the denizens of heaven."

Bhīṣma replied, "I am at your disposal, O Duryodhana; but as you are dear to me, so are the Pāṇḍavas. It is my duty to look after their welfare too, but I shall fight on your side since I have promised to do so. In a moment I can make this world destitute of men, gods, asuras, and rākṣasas by the strength of my weapons. But I cannot kill these sons of Pāṇḍu. Instead, I shall slay ten thousand of the opposing warriors every day. In this way, I shall try to bring about their defeat, if indeed they do not kill me before I have time to carry out my plans in the battle."

"There is another condition," Bhīṣma continued, "on which I shall be commander in chief of your army; it is only fair that I should tell you about it now. Either let Karṇa fight first or I myself, but not both, since Karṇa always compares his prowess in battle with mine." Karṇa replied, "O king, I shall not fight as long as Bhīṣma the son of Gaṅgā lives. Should Bhīṣma be slain, I shall fight with Arjuna, the wielder of the Gāṇḍīva bow."

Meanwhile, in the Pāṇḍava camp, Yudhiṣṭhira summoned before him Drupada, Virāṭa, Sātyaki, Dhṛṣṭadyumna, Dhṛṣṭaketu, Śikhaṇḍī, and the king of Magadha, and made these heroes, who were eager for battle, the leaders of his army. Finally he installed Dhṛṣṭadyumna,[43] who had emerged from the sacrificial fire for causing the

---

[40] **Kurukshetra:** The field where the battle will be fought.

[41] **the moon . . . herbs:** The moon here is referred to in its capacity as lord of plants.

[42] **Yakṣas:** Kubera, the god of wealth, is the lord over the demigods known as Yakṣas.

[43] **Dhṛṣṭadyumna:** King Drupada's son, born like his sister Draupadī from a sacrificial fire, whom King Drupada summoned in order to have a son who could take revenge on his archenemy, Droṇa.

death of Droṇa, as commander in chief. The curly-haired Arjuna was made supreme commander over all those great men, while Kṛṣṇa was chosen as the guide of Arjuna and the driver of his horses.

Seeing that a very destructive battle was about to take place, Balarāma, elder brother of Kṛṣṇa, entered the encampment of the royal Pāṇḍavas. He said, "There will be a very fierce massacre; it is surely ordained by fate and cannot be averted. Both these heroes, Bhīma and Duryodhana, well skilled in fighting with the mace, are my pupils and I bear the same affection for both of them. I shall now go on a pilgrimage to the sacred waters of the Sarasvatī for ablutions, for I cannot stay and look on with indifference while this destruction of the Kurus takes place." [. . .]

[The first two chapters of Narasimhan's abridged translation of Book 6, the Bhīsma Parva, present the essential plot and dramatic conflict of what is known as the Bhagavad Gita. To get some idea of the magnitude of the *Mahabharata* and of the fullness of the poetic version, these chapters should be compared with the poetic translation of the Bhagavad Gita by Barbara Stoler Miller beginning on p. 1492.]

FROM BOOK 6

Bhisma Parva [The Defeat of Bhisma]

XLVIII

Before the fighting began, the Kurus, the Pāṇḍavas, and the Somakas entered into certain covenants regarding the different kinds of combat. Thus it was agreed that a car-warrior should fight only with a car-warrior. He who rode on an elephant could fight only with another such combatant. A horseman might fight with a horseman and a foot soldier with a foot soldier. It was also agreed that a combatant who was engaged in fighting with another, one seeking refuge, one retreating, one whose weapon was broken, and one who was not clad in armour should never be attacked. Likewise charioteers, animals, men engaged in carrying weapons, drummers, and conch-blowers should not be attacked.

When the two armies were ready for battle, the holy Vyāsa, foremost of all learned men, grandfather of the Pāṇḍavas and the Kurus, who was gifted with divine vision, spoke in private to Dhṛtarāṣṭra, who was distressed by the evil policy of his sons. "O king," said Vyāsa, "the last moments of your sons and of other kings have come. They have gathered to fight and they will kill one another. If you wish to witness the fighting, I shall bestow sight on you."

Dhṛtarāṣṭra replied, "O foremost of sages! I have no desire to see the slaughter of my kinsmen. Through your grace, however, I would like to hear a full account of this battle." Thereupon Vyāsa bestowed a boon on Sañjaya,[44] saying, "O king, Sañjaya will give you an account of this great battle. He will be able to see everything that takes place over the entire battlefield."

[44] **Sañjaya:** A bard, or poet, and one of Dhṛtarāṣṭra's advisors; he is the narrator of this portion of the epic.

Vyāsa then made a last appeal for peace. He said, "O king, Death himself has been born in the form of your son, Duryodhana. Slaughter is never praised in the Vedas. It can never produce any good. Save your good name and fame, and your virtue. Let the Pāṇḍavas have their kingdom and let the Kauravas have peace. You will thereby assure yourself of a place in heaven." Having made this final and fruitless appeal, Vyāsa went away, while Dhṛtarāṣṭra reflected in silence.

Meanwhile both sides prepared to give battle. When the troops were arrayed according to rule, Duryodhana said to Duḥśāsana, "O Duḥśāsana, let chariots be quickly directed so as to assure the protection of Bhīṣma. Make haste in urging all our troops to advance. What I have been wishing for a number of years has at last come to pass: the clash of the Pāṇḍavas and the Kurus at the head of their respective armies."

At sunrise the next day, the armies of the Kurus and the Pāṇḍavas completed all their arrangements. The eleventh division of the Kuru army stood in advance of all others; at the head of these troops stood Bhīṣma. On one side were the eleven splendid divisions of the Kaurava army. On the other side were the seven divisions of the Pāṇḍava army, protected by the foremost of men. The two armies facing each other looked like two mighty oceans agitated by fearful makaras.

Sañjaya reported to Dhṛtarāṣṭra: "When placed in battle array, the two armies, full of elephants, cars, and horses, looked like two woods in blossom. Both of them seemed as if they could conquer the very heavens. Both of them were commanded by excellent men. The Kaurava armies stood facing the west while the Pāṇḍavas stood facing the east—all ready for battle."

XLIX

Then Arjuna, whose flag bore the figure of an ape, looked at the Kauravas drawn up in battle array; as the fighting was about to begin, he took up his bow and said to Kṛṣṇa, "I wish to see my opponents who are eager for battle and whom I have to fight in the great struggle. Station my chariot, O Kṛṣṇa, between the two armies!" As requested by Arjuna, Kṛṣṇa drove the chariot to a position between the two armies.

Arjuna saw his closest kinsmen, related to him as father or grandfather, uncle or brother, son or grandson, preceptor as well as companion and friend, on both sides. Overcome by this sight, he said in sorrow and compassion, "O Kṛṣṇa, when I see my own people ready to fight and eager for battle, my limbs shudder, my mouth is dry, my body shivers, and my hair stands on end. Furthermore, I see evil portents, and I can see no good in killing my own kinsmen. It is not right and proper that we should kill our own kith and kin, the Kauravas. How can we be happy if we slay our own people?" Having said these words, Arjuna threw away his bow and arrows, and sat down sorrowfully on the seat of his car.

When he observed that Arjuna was overcome with compassion and that tears were welling up in his eyes, Kṛṣṇa said these words to him who was thus troubled and dejected: "O Arjuna, why have you become so depressed in this critical hour? Such dejection is unknown to noble men; it does not lead to the heavenly heights, and on earth it can only cause disgrace. Do not yield to cowardice, for it is not worthy of you. Cast away this faintness of heart and arise."

Arjuna said, "O Kṛṣṇa, how can I strike with my arrows people like the grandsire Bhīṣma and the preceptor Droṇa, who are worthy of my respect?" After such reflection, he finally told Kṛṣṇa, "I will not fight."

Kṛṣṇa smiled at Arjuna, so troubled in mind and dejected in spirit, and said, "You grieve for those for whom you should not grieve. The wise do not lament the dead or pine for the living. Anyone who believes that this kills, or thinks that this is killed, fails to understand that one neither kills nor is killed. The embodied soul merely casts off old bodies and enters new ones, just as a person discards used garments and puts on new clothes."

"The soul that lives in every human body is eternal and immortal," Kṛṣṇa went on to say. "Therefore do not grieve for any creature. As a Kṣatriya, your duty is to fight a righteous battle. This is the highest good for you, and you should not falter at this hour. Such a fight is an open door to heaven, and happy are they who engage in such a battle. Either you will win a victory and enjoy the earth, or be killed and go to heaven. Therefore arise, O Arjuna, and be determined to fight. Get ready for battle without thought of pleasure and pain, gain and loss, victory and defeat. In this way, you will not incur any sin. Remember that you have a right to action alone, but not to the fruits thereof. Be not motivated by the desire for the fruits of action. At the same time, do not pursue a policy of inaction."

"O Arjuna," he continued, "in this world I have taught a twofold way of life: the way of knowledge for men who engage in contemplation, and the way of works for men of action. One cannot maintain even one's physical life without action. Therefore, do your allotted work regardless of results, for men attain the highest good by doing work without attachment to its results. Resign yourself to me and fix your consciousness in the self, without desire or egoism, and then fight, freed from your fever."

Arjuna replied, "My confusion has been dispelled by this supreme discourse concerning the self, which you have given me out of your grace." Kṛṣṇa said, "I am Time itself, grown mature, capable of destroying the world, and now engaged in subduing it. Even without your effort, all the opposing warriors shall cease to exist. Therefore arise and win great glory, conquer your enemies, and enjoy a prosperous kingdom. They are already slain by me and you, O Arjuna, are merely the occasion. Kill Droṇa, Bhīṣma, Jayadratha, Karṇa, and all the other great warriors whom I have already doomed. Do not fear, but fight and conquer your enemies in battle."

"O Lord," said Arjuna, "I desire to know the true nature of 'renunciation' and of 'relinquishment.'" Kṛṣṇa replied, "The wise understand 'renunciation' to mean the giving up of those works which are prompted by desire. 'Relinquishment' means the abandonment of the fruits of all works. It is not right to renounce one's duty, but when one performs a prescribed duty, with detachment and without thought of the fruit thereof, that is 'relinquishment.' Courage, vigour, resourcefulness, steadfastness in battle, generosity, and leadership are the natural duties of a Kṣatriya.

"The Lord dwells in the hearts of all men and causes them to turn round by his power as if they were mounted on a machine," Kṛṣṇa concluded. "Seek shelter in him with your whole being, and you shall attain supreme peace and the eternal station by his grace." "My bewilderment is gone," said Arjuna. "By your grace, O Kṛṣṇa, I have been made to realize my true duties. My doubts have been dispelled and I stand ready to do your bidding."

L

When the two armies, which resembled two oceans, were ready for battle and surging continuously, the brave King Yudhiṣṭhira doffed his armour and cast aside his excellent weapon. Quickly alighting from his chariot, he proceeded on foot, with joined hands and with restrained speech, in the direction of the hostile host, towards his grandfather, Bhīṣma, whom he addressed thus: "O invincible one, I salute you. We shall fight with you. Give us your permission and your blessings." Bhīṣma replied, "O son, I am pleased with you. Fight and triumph. Whatever else you may have desired, may you obtain it in this battle! O king, man is the slave of wealth, though wealth is no one's slave. And I am bound to the Kurus by wealth." To this, Yudhiṣṭhira answered, "O wise one, I pray that, desiring my welfare from day to day, you may keep my interests in mind, while you fight for the Kurus."

Then, in the midst of the army, Yudhiṣṭhira loudly proclaimed, "Whoever will choose us, him I shall accept as our ally." Thereupon Yuyutsu[45] said with a cheerful heart to Yudhiṣṭhira, "I shall fight against the Kauravas in this battle, O king! I shall fight on your side, if you will accept me." So, abandoning the Kurus, Yuyutsu went over to the Pāṇḍava army to the accompaniment of kettledrums.

On the forenoon of that awful day the terrible battle began. The Kurus and the Sṛñjayas, both desirous of victory in battle, roared like lions and made both the sky and the earth resound with their war cries. In that general melee thousands of single combats took place between car-warriors, horsemen, and foot soldiers. Just for a short while that engagement was a beautiful sight. Soon, however, the fighting became confused and fierce in the extreme, with heroes rushing against each other in the melee.

In the afternoon Durmukha, Kṛtavarmā, Kṛpa, Śalya, and Viviṁśati surrounded Bhīṣma and began to protect him. Thus sheltered by those five mighty car-warriors, Bhīṣma penetrated the Pāṇḍava host. With his bow stretched to a circle, he shot therefrom blazing arrows that resembled virulent poison. Creating continuous lines of arrows in all directions, that hero slew many Pāṇḍava car-warriors, naming each victim beforehand. When the troops of the Pāṇḍavas were routed and crushed all over the field, the sun set and nothing could be seen. Then, while Bhīṣma proudly stood surveying the battlefield, the Pāṇḍavas withdrew their forces for the night.

LI

On the second day Yudhiṣṭhira said to the commander of his army, Drupada, "Form the array known by the name of Krauñcāruṇa. It is destructive of all foes and was suggested by Bṛhaspati to Indra in days of old when the gods and the asuras fought."

[45] **Yuyutsu:** A son of Dhṛtarāṣṭra by a Vaiṣya wife; a half brother of the Kauravas.

Then Bhīṣma and Droṇa formed a mighty array to resist that of the Pāṇḍavas. Surrounded by a large body of troops Bhīṣma advanced, like the chief of the celestials himself.

There was, however, no man in the Kaurava army who could advance against the heroic Arjuna in battle. Whoever tried to do so was pierced by Arjuna's sharp shafts and dispatched to the other world. Bhīṣma, seeing the Kaurava host thus routed, smilingly said to Droṇa, "This mighty and heroic Arjuna, accompanied by Kṛṣṇa, is dealing with our troops as he alone can deal with them. He is incapable of being vanquished in battle today by any means; he is like the Destroyer himself at the end of the Yuga!"[46] Bhīṣma then caused the Kaurava army to be withdrawn. About the same time the sun set, and the withdrawal of both armies took place in the twilight.

When the night had passed and the dawn brought the third day of fighting Bhīṣma gave the order for the Kaurava army to prepare for battle. Desirous of victory, he formed the mighty array known as Garuḍa.[47] The beak of that Garuḍa was Bhīṣma himself, and its two eyes were Droṇa and Kṛtavarmā. In opposition to the Garuḍa array Yudhiṣṭhira formed the fierce array in the shape of the half-moon.

In the afternoon, when the tide of battle was running in favour of the Pāṇḍavas, Bhīṣma rushed towards the Pāṇḍava host. Displaying his extreme lightness of touch, as if he were dancing along the track of his car, he seemed to be present everywhere like a circle of fire. In consequence of the speed of his movements, the embattled Pāṇḍavas saw that hero multiplied a thousandfold. Everyone regarded Bhīṣma as having made counterparts of himself by illusion because, having seen him now in the east, the next moment they saw him in the west; and having seen him in the north, the next moment they saw him in the south. There was no one amongst the Pāṇḍavas capable of even looking at Bhīṣma. What they saw were only the countless shafts shot from his bow. The vast host of the just King Yudhiṣṭhira, thus slaughtered by Bhīṣma, gave way in a thousand directions.

Beholding the Pāṇḍava army thus routed, Kṛṣṇa said unto Arjuna, "The hour is now come, O Pārtha, which you desired all along! Strike Bhīṣma, O tiger among men!" Kṛṣṇa urged those steeds of silvery hue towards the dazzling car of Bhīṣma. Taking up his celestial bow, whose twang resembled the roar of the clouds, Arjuna caused Bhīṣma's bow to drop, cutting it off with his keen shafts. In the twinkling of

---

[46] **Yuga:** According to Hindu doctrine, worldly time is marked by a great cycle of one thousand *manvantaras,* each lasting 4,320,000 years and each divided into a four-part succession of ages known as *yugas.* At the end of one thousand *manvantaras,* the universe is destroyed in a great cataclysm of fire or flood, and after a long age of night, the thousand manvantaras begin again. Each manvantara commences with an age of perfection (the *Kṛta Yuga*) ushered in by Kalki, an incarnation of Viṣṇu, followed by three progressively degenerate ages: the *Tretā Yuga,* the *Dvāpara Yuga,* and the *Kali Yuga.* The present day is considered part of the *Kali Yuga,* characterized by a breakdown of dharma, the binding or balancing force of the universe. This *Kali Yuga* is said to have begun with the era described in the *Mahabharata.*

[47] **Garuḍa:** Named after a mythic bird-god that figures into earlier stories in the *Mahabharata* and earlier legend; an eagle-like bird and carrier of Viṣṇu, the Garuḍa's golden feathers shine as bright as the sun and it can attack other creatures with beams of fire.

an eye, Bhīṣma took up another bow and struck both Kṛṣṇa and Arjuna with keen shafts all over their bodies.

Then the mighty Kṛṣṇa, beholding the prowess of Bhīṣma in battle, as well as the mildness with which Arjuna fought, abandoned the reins of the steeds. He jumped down from the car, whirling on his right arm his cakra which was sharp as a razor, bright as the sun, and powerful as a thousand heavenly bolts. And making the earth tremble under his tread, the high-souled Kṛṣṇa ran impetuously towards Bhīṣma, like a lion blinded with fury rushing upon an elephant.

Beholding that foremost of men, the divine Kṛṣṇa, advancing against him armed with the cakra, Bhīṣma fearlessly said, "Come, O Lord, the universe is your abode! I bow to you, who are armed with mace, sword, and bow! O Lord of the universe, who are the refuge of all creatures in this battle, throw me down from this car! Slain here by you, O Kṛṣṇa, great will be my good fortune both in this world and the next! Great is the honour you show me, O lord! My fame will be celebrated in the three worlds!"

Meanwhile, jumping down from his car, Arjuna quickly ran on foot after Kṛṣṇa and seized him by his two hands. And when Kṛṣṇa, decked as he was with a beautiful garland of gold, stopped, Arjuna bowed to him and said, "Control this wrath of yours, O lord! You are the refuge of the Pāṇḍavas. I swear to you, by my sons and brothers, that I will not withdraw from the action to which I have pledged myself! At your command I will certainly annihilate the Kurus!"

Hearing that promise, Kṛṣṇa was gratified. And ever bent as he was on doing what was agreeable to Arjuna, he once more mounted his car, cakra on arm. Arjuna drew his beautiful bow Gāṇḍīva, of immeasurable energy, with great force and invoked with proper mantras the wonderful and terrible Mahendra weapon, causing it to appear in the sky. That mighty weapon produced a great shower of arrows and Arjuna was thus able to check the entire Kaurava host. [. . .]

LV

On the ninth day Bhīṣma disposed his own troops in a mighty array called sarvatobhadra. Then King Yudhiṣṭhira, Bhīma, Nakula, and Sahadeva, clad in mail, took up their position in the van of the Pāṇḍava array, at the very head of all their troops.

At midday, a fierce battle raged between Bhīṣma and the Somakas, resulting in terrible carnage. That foremost of car-warriors, Bhīṣma, began to consume the ranks of the Pāṇḍavas by hundreds and thousands. Then Dhṛṣṭadyumna, Śikhaṇḍī,[48] Virāṭa, and Drupada fell upon Bhīṣma and discharged numberless arrows at him.

[48] **Dhṛṣṭadyumna, Śikhaṇḍī:** Dhṛṣṭadyumna, the son of the Pāñcāla king, Drupada, was born in a sacrificial fire summoned by the king in order to produce a son fit to kill his archenemy Droṇa in battle. Śikhaṇḍī is the male incarnation of Aṁbā, a daughter of the king of Kāśī and sister of Aṁbālikā and Aṁbikā, the grandmothers of the Pāṇḍavas and the Kauravas, respectively. Bearing enmity toward Bhīṣma, who had kidnapped her and her sisters, Aṁbā was reborn as a son of King Drupada in order to bring about Bhīṣma's downfall. Aware of Śikhaṇḍī's origins, Bhīṣma continues to think of him as a woman.

Even though Śikhaṇḍī pierced the grandsire with many shafts, Bhīṣma of unfading glory, regarding his foe as a female, did not strike back.

Surrounded on all sides, yet unvanquished by that large body of car-warriors, Bhīṣma blazed like a fire in the midst of a forest. His car was his hearth; his bow constituted the flames, his swords, darts, and his maces, the fuel; his shafts were the sparks of that fire. He took the lives of the opposing warriors like the sun sucking the energies of all things with his rays during summer. He broke the Pāṇḍava ranks, and the routed soldiers, helpless and fainthearted, unable even to look at him in battle, were slaughtered in their thousands by Bhīṣma.

While they were thus battling, the sun set, and there came the dreadful hour of twilight when the fighting could no longer be seen. Then King Yudhiṣṭhira, seeing how his own troops had been decimated by Bhīṣma, and how the mighty car-warriors of the Somakas had been vanquished, despaired and ordered the troops to be withdrawn for the day.

Late that night the Pāṇḍavas, the Vṛṣṇis, and the invincible Sṛñjayas[49] sat down for a consultation. Yudhiṣṭhira said, "Even before this conflict began, I made an agreement with Bhīṣma. He said, 'I will give you counsel, but I cannot fight for you, since I shall have to fight for Duryodhana.' Therefore, O Kṛṣṇa, all of us, together with you, will once more go to Bhīṣma, and ask him about the means of his own death."

Having thus deliberated, the heroic Pāṇḍavas and the valiant Kṛṣṇa proceeded together to Bhīṣma's quarters, casting aside their armour and weapons. Entering his tent, they all bowed low to him, and sought his protection. The mighty Bhīṣma, grandsire of the Kurus, greeted them and said, "Welcome, O Kṛṣṇa, welcome O Arjuna. Welcome to you, O King Yudhiṣṭhira the Just, and to you, O Bhīma. Welcome to you also, twins. What can I do now to make you happy? However difficult of achievement, I will yet do it with all my heart."

Unto Bhīṣma, who spoke to them with such affection, King Yudhiṣṭhira, with love in his heart, said these words, "You are conversant with everything. Tell us how we may obtain victory and acquire sovereignty. Tell us also how this destruction may be stopped. Tell us, O lord, the means of your own death. How can we cope with you in battle?"

Bhīṣma replied, "O son of Pāṇḍu, as you say, I am invincible. When I take my weapons and my large bow in hand, I am incapable of being defeated in battle by the very gods with Iṅdra at their head. If, however, I lay aside my weapons, almost any car-warrior can slay me. That mighty car-warrior, the son of Drupada, who fights on your side, and who is known by the name of Śikhaṇḍī, was once a woman but subsequently obtained manhood. You may know how all this took place. I therefore suggest this: let Arjuna, brave in battle and clad in mail, keep Śikhaṇḍī before him, and attack me from behind with his sharp shafts. When I see that inauspicious omen, in the form of one who was a woman before, I will never seek to strike back. Taking

[49] **Vṛṣṇis . . . Sṛñjayas:** Allies of the Pāṇḍavas; see also note 29.

advantage of that opportunity, let Arjuna quickly pierce me on all sides with his shafts. Except the blessed Kṛṣṇa and Arjuna, I do not see anyone in the three worlds who is capable of killing me in battle."

After Bhīṣma had blessed them again, the Pāṇḍavas saluted their high-souled grandsire and returned to their own tents.

LVI

The tenth day of the battle dawned. Soon afterwards the Pāṇḍavas, to the sound of drums and cymbals and the blare of conches, set forth to give battle, placing Śikhaṇḍī in front. But the Pāṇḍava army was torn into pieces by Bhīṣma who let loose his shafts by hundreds and thousands. The Pāṇḍavas seemed incapable of defeating in battle the great bowman Bhīṣma who resembled the Destroyer himself.

Beholding the prowess of Bhīṣma in battle, Arjuna said to Śikhaṇḍī, "Proceed towards the grandsire! Do not entertain the slightest fear of Bhīṣma today. I shall dislodge him from his excellent car by means of my sharp arrows." Thus urged by Pārtha, Śikhaṇḍī rushed at Bhīṣma.

Approaching Bhīṣma, Śikhaṇḍī struck him in the centre of the chest with ten broad-headed arrows. Bhīṣma did not retaliate but looked at Śikhaṇḍī with wrath, as if he would consume the Pāñcāla prince with that look.

Then all the Pāṇḍavas, placing themselves behind Śikhaṇḍī, attacked Bhīṣma in that battle repeatedly from all sides. Śikhaṇḍī himself, protected as he was by the diadem-decked Arjuna, pierced Bhīṣma with ten shafts. And he struck Bhīṣma's charioteer with other arrows and cut off his standard with one well-aimed shaft. Then Bhīṣma took up another bow that was tougher, which was cut off by Arjuna with three sharp shafts. Indeed, the ambidextrous Arjuna, excited with rage, cut off one by one all the bows that Bhīṣma took up.

When his bows were thus cut off, Bhīṣma, excited with rage, took up a dart that was capable of riving a hill, and hurled it at Arjuna's car. Seeing it coursing towards him like the blazing bolt of heaven Arjuna fixed five sharp broad-headed arrows on his bowstring. And with those five arrows he cut into five fragments that dart hurled by Bhīṣma, which fell down like a flash of lightning separated from a mass of clouds.

Beholding his dart cut off, Bhīṣma became filled with rage. Soon he calmed down a little, and began to reflect. And he said to himself, "With only a single bow I could slay all the Pāṇḍavas, if the mighty Viṣṇu himself were not their protector. Moreover, I will not fight with the Pāṇḍavas because of the femininity of Śikhaṇḍī. Formerly, when my father married Satyavatī, he gave me two boons, that I should be incapable of being slain in battle and that my death should depend on my own choice. I think this is the proper hour for me to wish my own death."

Ascertaining this to be the resolve of the great Bhīṣma, the Ṛṣis and the Vasus stationed in the firmament said, "O son, we approve of your resolve. Act accordingly and withdraw from battle!" When they had said these words, a fragrant and auspicious breeze began to blow. The celestial cymbals were sounded, and a shower of flowers fell upon Bhīṣma.

Then Arjuna, drawing his Gāṇḍīva bow, pierced the son of Gaṅgā with twenty-five arrows. Once more he drew closer to Bhīṣma and cut off his bow. Bhīṣma took up another bow that was stronger. However, within the twinkling of an eye, Arjuna cut that bow into three fragments with three broad-headed shafts.

After that, Bhīṣma, the son of Śaṅtanu, no longer desired to battle with Arjuna. Deeply pierced by Arjuna with keen shafts, Bhīṣma addressed Duḥśāsana with a smile, saying, "These arrows coursing towards me in one continuous line are surely not Śikhaṇḍī's. Except for Arjuna, all other kings united together cannot cause me pain!"

Bhīṣma had slain ten thousand warriors on that day, the tenth day of the battle, and now he stood on the field with his vitals pierced. There was not a space even two fingers wide in all his body that was free from arrow wounds. A little before sunset the heroic Bhīṣma fell down from his car on the field, with his head towards the east, in the very sight of the Kauravas. When he fell, loud lamentations of "Alas!" and "Oh!" were heard everywhere, among the kings and among the celestials in heaven. The heroic combatants of both armies laid down their weapons and withdrew from battle. Meanwhile Bhīṣma betook himself to yoga as taught in the great Upaniṣads and remained quiet, engaged in prayer.

LVII

When Bhīṣma was overthrown from his car and fell, he lay on a bed of arrows so that his body did not touch the earth. Informed by Duḥśāsana of the fall of Bhīṣma, Droṇa immediately fell down from his car in a faint. But he soon regained consciousness and ordered his own troops to stop fighting. Thereupon the Pāṇḍavas, sending out messengers riding fleet horses, ordered their own armies to stop fighting.

When the troops of both armies had ceased fighting everywhere, all the kings took off their armour and went to see Bhīṣma. The virtuous Bhīṣma spoke these words to the Pāṇḍavas and the Kauravas who, after saluting him, were standing at the head of the various kings. He said, "Hail, O great heroes, hail, O mighty car-warriors. I am indeed pleased to see you."

Having thus greeted them, he said, "My head needs support; give me a pillow." Thereupon the kings fetched many soft pillows made of delicate fabrics. But the grandsire did not like them. Smiling, he said to the kings, "These pillows do not suit a hero's bed." Then seeing Arjuna, Bhīṣma said to him, "O mighty Arjuna, my head needs support; give me a suitable pillow!" Arjuna said, "So be it." Determined to do Bhīṣma's bidding, he took up the Gāṇḍīva bow and some fine shafts, which he purified with maṅtras. He then discharged three sharp arrows with great velocity into the earth, so that they supported Bhīṣma's head.

Seeing that Arjuna had rightly divined his thoughts, Bhīṣma became greatly pleased. He praised Arjuna, foremost of warriors, for having given him a warrior's pillow, after which he spoke these words to all the kings and princes assembled there, along with the Pāṇḍavas, "I shall lie on this bed until the sun rolls back. When the maker of the day, the resplendent illuminator of the world, mounted on his brilliant chariot, proceeds towards the point of the compass occupied by Vaiśravaṇa,[50] then I shall yield up my vital breath, like one bidding adieu to his dear friends.

"My body is burning," Bhīṣma continued, "and I feel faint because of the wounds caused by the arrows. I need something to drink." Then the kings came with excellent viands and several pitchers of cold water. Seeing what they had brought, Bhīṣma said, "It is not possible for me to partake of any article of human enjoyment." In a weak voice, he addressed the mighty Arjuna, "My body is burning, and I am covered with arrows. I am in great pain all over and my mouth is dry. Give me water, O Arjuna, for the refreshment of my body. You alone are capable of providing me with water which is ritually clean."

Thereupon the heroic Arjuna mounted on his chariot. He first circumambulated that prostrate chief of the Bhāratas, Bhīṣma. Then he fixed on his bowstring an effulgent arrow inspired with mantras for the Parjanya weapon. Before the eyes of all the people present he penetrated the earth a little to the south of the spot where Bhīṣma lay. Thereupon there gushed out a pure jet of water, cool and nectar-like and filled with celestial fragrance and taste. Thus Arjuna quenched Bhīṣma's thirst. Seeing this feat of Arjuna's, which resembled that of Indra himself, all the kings were struck with wonder.

Bhīṣma then observed, "You have seen, even now, O Duryodhana, how the intelligent Arjuna created that jet of water, cool and fragrant as nectar. No one else in the universe could achieve such a feat. The weapons of which the presiding deities respectively are Agni, Varuṇa, Soma, Vāyu, Viṣṇu, Indra, Paśupati, Parameṣṭhi, Prajāpati, Dhātā, Tvaṣṭā, and Savitā, all these celestial weapons are known among all men only to Arjuna and to Kṛṣṇa, the son of Devakī, and to no one else. You can therefore never hope to win a victory against them in battle, my son. Renounce your anger. Make peace with the Pāṇḍavas. Let friendship be restored with the death of Bhīṣma. Give half of your kingdom to the Pāṇḍavas. Let Yudhiṣṭhira rule over Indraprastha. Do not create internal dissensions among the rulers of the earth." But Duryodhana was deaf even to this last appeal of Bhīṣma.

LVIII

Then Karṇa approached that hero lying with his eyes closed, and fell at his feet. His voice choked with weeping as he said, "I am Rādhā's son, O foremost of the Kurus. Whenever I became the object of your sight, you looked upon me with enmity." Bhīṣma replied, "You are the son of Kuntī, and not of Rādhā; there is no doubt about this; I have heard all this from Nārada, as well as from Vyāsa and Kṛṣṇa. I tell you in all truth that I bear you no malice, but used harsh words against you only to curb your impetuosity. I know your prowess in battle, your devotion to the Brāhmaṇas, your bravery, and your great capacity for charity. Among men there is none to rival you, and indeed you resemble an immortal. I spoke to you harshly only in the hope

[50] **Vaiśravaṇa:** Also known as Kubera, the god of wealth, whose domain is in the north.

of avoiding internal dissensions. You know the Pāṇḍavas are your brothers. If you desire to do what is agreeable to me, then be reconciled to them. O Karṇa, let hostilities end with my fall, and let all the kings of the earth be freed of danger."

Karṇa replied, "I know all this to be true, O hero! As you say, I am Kuṅtī's son, and not the son of a charioteer. I was, however, disowned by Kuṅtī, and brought up by a charioteer. Having enjoyed Duryodhana's bounty for so long, I cannot disappoint his hopes at this stage. O sire, with your full heart permit me to fight. I intend to fight only with your permission. I also pray you to forgive me for any unworthy expression I may have uttered against you at any time, and also for any act injurious to you that I may have done through malice or fickleness."

"If you cannot renounce the fierce hostility you have against the Pāṇḍavas," said Bhīṣma, "then, O Karṇa, I give you my permission. Be actuated by a desire to attain heaven. Free from wrath and malice, carry out the commissions of the king to the best of your ability and energy. Be observant of the conduct of the righteous. Engage in fighting without arrogance, depending on your prowess and strength. There is nothing more desirable to a Kṣatriya than a righteous battle."

Bhīṣma concluded, "Long and strenuously I strove to bring about peace, but I failed to accomplish the task. Where justice is, there victory shall be!" After Bhīṣma had spoken thus, Karṇa saluted him, mounted his chariot, and proceeded towards the camp of Duryodhana.

[In Book 7, the Droṇa Parva, or the Book of Droṇa, the war rages on, with Droṇa appointed as the commander of the Kaurava troops. In Book 8, the Kauravas manage to distract Arjuna from the battle, and in his father's absence Arjuna's son, Abhimanyu, is slain. In a series of events reminiscent of Achilles' revenge of the death of Patroclus, Arjuna returns to battle and repays the Kauravan forces for his son's murder. After five days King Drapuda's son Dhṛṣṭadyumna, born miraculously from a sacrificial fire, slays Droṇa, the purpose for which he was born.]

***FROM* BOOK 8**

Karna Parva [The Death of Karna]

LXVII

When the mighty bowman Droṇa was slain, the Kaurava host became pale-faced and gloomy. Seeing his own forces standing as if paralysed and lifeless, King Duryodhana said to them, "Relying on the strength of your arms, I have challenged the Pāṇḍavas to this battle. Victory or death is the lot of all warriors. Why wonder then at the fall of Droṇa? Let us resume the fighting in all directions, encouraged by the sight of the lofty-minded Karṇa, the son of Vikartana,[51] mighty bowman and wielder of celestial weapons, who is roving about in the field of battle. Permit me to remind you that it was he who slew Ghaṭotkaca,[52] that creator of illusions, with the

[51] **Vikartana:** Another name for Sūrya, the sun-god and Karṇa's father with Kuṅtī.

[52] **Ghaṭotkaca:** A rakṣasa, demon.

indomitable Śakti weapon." Then all those kings, headed by Duryodhana, quickly installed Karṇa as commander in chief, and bathed him according to rites with golden and earthen pitchers of holy water.

As the sixteenth day dawned, Karṇa summoned the Kaurava forces to battle with loud blasts on his conch. He arranged his army in the form of a makara,[53] and proceeded to attack the Pāṇḍavas, desirous of victory. On the Pāṇḍava side, Arjuna, whose car was drawn by white horses, formed a counter-array in the shape of a half-moon.

The day's fighting was marked by many duels, between Bhīma and Aśvatthāmā,[54] Sahadeva and Duḥśāsana, Nakula and Karṇa, Ulūka and Yuyutsu, Kṛpa and Dhṛṣṭadyumna, and Śikhaṇḍī and Kṛtavarmā. While they were thus engaged, the sun disappeared behind the western mountains. Then both sides retired from the field and proceeded to their own encampments.

Before the fighting began on the seventeenth day, Karṇa said to Duryodhana, "Today, O king, I will go forth and battle with the famous Pāṇḍava, Arjuna. Either I shall slay that hero, or he shall slay me. You are aware of his energy, weapons, and resources. My bow, known by the name of Vijaya, is the greatest of all weapons. It was made by Viśvakarmā[55] in accordance with Indra's wishes, and is a celestial and excellent weapon. On this count I believe I am superior to Arjuna."

"Now you must know," continued Karṇa, "in what respect Arjuna is superior to me. Kṛṣṇa, born of the Dāśārha race, who is revered by all people, is the holder of the reins of his horses. He who is verily the creator of the universe thus guards Arjuna's car. On our side Śalya,[56] who is the ornament of all assemblies, is of equal heroism. Should he take over the duties of my charioteer, then victory will surely be yours. Let the irresistible Śalya, therefore, act as my charioteer."

Duryodhana thereupon went to see Śalya. Humbly approaching the Madra prince, he affectionately spoke these words to him: "You have heard what Karṇa has said, namely that he chooses you, foremost of princes, as his charioteer. Therefore, for the destruction of the Pāṇḍavas, and for my own good, be pleased to become Karṇa's charioteer. As that foremost of charioteers, Kṛṣṇa, counsels and protects Arjuna, so should you support Karṇa at all times."

Śalya replied, "You are insulting me, O Duryodhana, or surely you must doubt my loyalty, since you so readily request me to do the work of a charioteer. You praise Karṇa and consider that he is superior to us. But I do not consider him to be my equal in the field of battle. Knowing that I can strike down the enemy, why do you wish to employ me in the office of charioteer to the lowborn Karṇa?"

Duryodhana replied to Śalya with great affection and high respect. Desirous of

---

[53] **makara:** That is, in the shape of a crocodile.

[54] **Aśvatthāmā:** Droṇa's son, who will figure prominently in Book 10, the Sauptika Parva, as the leader of a night assault on the sleeping Pāṇḍava forces.

[55] **Viśvakarmā:** Viśvakarmā, the god of fashioning things, somewhat like the metalworking god Hephaestus in the Greek panoply.

[56] **Śalya:** The king of Madra and a key ally of the Kauravas; after the death of Karṇa, Śalya will lead the Kurus on the very last day of battle, a scene described in Book 9, the Śalya Parva.

achieving his main objective, he addressed him in a friendly manner, saying sweetly, "O Śalya, what you say is doubtless true. However, in making this request I have a certain purpose. Even as Karṇa is reckoned to be superior to Arjuna in many ways so are you, in the opinion of the whole world, superior to Kṛṣṇa. As the high-souled Kṛṣṇa is expert in the handling of horses, even so, O Śalya, are you doubly skilled. There is no doubt about it."

Thus flattered, Śalya said, "O Duryodhana! As you tell me that amongst all these troops there is none but myself who is more accomplished than Kṛṣṇa, I am pleased with you. I therefore agree to act as the charioteer of the famous Karṇa while he is engaged in battle with Arjuna, foremost of the Pāṇḍavas. But there is one condition on which I accept your proposal: that I shall give vent in Karṇa's presence to such expressions as I may wish." Duryodhana, who was accompanied by Karṇa, readily accepted this condition, saying, "So be it."

LXVIII

After Śalya had taken over as his charioteer, Karṇa said to him, "Today I shall fearlessly fight Kṛṣṇa and Arjuna, foremost among all wielders of weapons. My mind is, however, troubled by the curse of Paraśurāma,[57] that best of Brāhmaṇas. In my early days, desirous of obtaining a celestial weapon, I lived with him in the disguise of a Brāhmaṇa. But, O Śalya, in order to benefit Arjuna, Indra, the king of the gods, took on the horrible form of an insect and stung my thigh. Even so, I remained motionless for fear of disturbing my preceptor. When he woke up, he saw what had happened. He subsequently learnt the deception I had practised on him, and cursed me, that the invocation for the weapon I had obtained by such trickery would not come to my memory at the time of dire need."

"Once while wandering in the forest," Karṇa continued, "I accidentally killed the sacrificial cow of a Brāhmaṇa. Although I offered him seven hundred elephants with large tusks, and many hundreds of male and female slaves, the best of Brāhmaṇas was still not pleased, and although I begged for forgiveness, he said: 'O sūta, what I have prophesied will happen. It cannot be otherwise.' He had said, 'Your wheel shall fall into a hole.' In this battle, while I am fighting, that will be my only fear."

During the fighting on that day there was a dreadful and thrilling battle between Karṇa and the Pāṇḍavas which increased the domain of the god of Death. After that terrible and gory combat only a few of the brave Samśaptakas survived. Then Dhṛṣṭadyumna and the rest of the Pāṇḍavas rushed towards Karṇa and attacked him. As a mountain receives heavy rainfall, so Karṇa received those warriors in battle. Elsewhere on the battlefield Duḥśāsana boldly went up to Bhīma and shot many arrows at him. Bhīma leapt like a lion attacking a deer, and hurried towards him. The struggle that took place between those two, incensed against each other and careless of life, was truly superhuman.

---

[57] **Paraśurāma:** An incarnation of Rāma in the form of a Brāhmaṇa empowered with magic weapons who makes war against the Kṣatriyas, or warrior classes, who have been harassing the Brahmins.

Fighting fiercely, Prince Duḥśāsana achieved many difficult feats in that duel. With a single shaft he cut off Bhīma's bow; with six shafts he pierced Bhīma's driver. Then, without losing a moment, he pierced Bhīma himself with many shafts discharged with great speed and power, while Bhīma hurled his mace at the prince. With that weapon, from a distance of ten bow-lengths, Bhīma forcibly dislodged Duḥśāsana from his car. Struck by the mace, and thrown to the ground, Duḥśāsana began to tremble. His charioteer and all his steeds were slain, and his car too was smashed to pieces by Bhīma's weapon.

Then Bhīma remembered all the hostile acts of Duḥśāsana towards the Pāṇḍavas. Jumping down from his car, he stood on the ground, looking steadily on his fallen foe. Drawing his keen-edged sword, and trembling with rage, he placed his foot upon the throat of Duḥśāsana and, ripping open the breast of his enemy, drank his warm lifeblood, little by little. Then, looking at him with wrathful eyes, he said, "I consider the taste of this blood superior to that of my mother's milk, or honey, or ghee, or wine, or excellent water, or milk, or curds, or buttermilk."

All those who stood around Bhīma and saw him drink the blood of Duḥśāsana fled in terror, saying to each other, "This one is no human being!" Bhīma then said, in the hearing of all those heroes, "O wretch among men, here I drink your lifeblood. Abuse us once more now, 'Beast, beast,' as you did before!"

Having spoken these words, the victorious Bhīma turned to Kṛṣṇa and Arjuna, and said, "O you heroes, I have accomplished today what I had vowed in respect of Duḥśāsana! I will soon fulfil my other vow by slaying that second sacrificial beast, Duryodhana! I shall kick the head of that evil one with my foot in the presence of the Kauravas, and I shall then obtain peace!" After this speech, Bhīma, drenched with blood, uttered loud shouts and roared with joy, even as the mighty Iṅdra of a thousand eyes after slaying Vṛtra.[58]

LXIX

Fleeing in the face of Arjuna's onslaught, the broken divisions of the Kauravas saw Arjuna's weapon swelling with energy and careering like lightning. But Karṇa destroyed that fiery weapon of Arjuna with his own weapon of great power which he had obtained from Paraśurāma. The encounter between Arjuna and Karṇa became very fierce. They attacked each other with arrows like two fierce elephants attacking each other with their tusks.

Karṇa then fixed on his bowstring the keen, blazing, and fierce shaft which he had long polished and preserved with the object of destroying Arjuna. Placing in position that shaft of fierce energy and blazing splendour, that venomous weapon which had its origin in the family of Airāvata[59] and which lay within a golden quiver covered by sandal dust, Karṇa aimed it at Arjuna's head. When he saw Karṇa aim

[58] **Vṛtra:** A demon slain by Iṅdra, the chief of the gods.

[59] **Airāvata:** In Hindu mythology, Airāvata is the king of all celestial elephants and the one upon whom Iṅdra rides. The name suggests "out of the water" and in this context may suggest a water serpent.

that arrow, Śalya said, "O Karṇa, this arrow will not succeed in hitting Arjuna's neck! Aim carefully, and discharge another arrow that may succeed in striking the head of your enemy!" His eyes burning in wrath, Karṇa replied, "O Śalya, Karṇa never aims an arrow twice!"

Thereupon Karṇa carefully let loose that mighty snake in the form of an arrow, which he had worshipped for many long years, saying, "You are slain, O Arjuna!" Seeing the snake aimed by Karṇa, Kṛṣṇa, strongest among the mighty, exerted his whole strength and pressed down Arjuna's chariot with his feet into the earth. When the car itself had sunk into the ground the steeds, too, bent their knees and laid themselves down upon the earth. The arrow then struck and dislodged Arjuna's diadem, that excellent ornament celebrated throughout the earth and the heavens.

The snake said, "O Kṛṣṇa! Know me as one who has been wronged by Arjuna. My enmity towards him stems from his having slain my mother!"

Then Kṛṣṇa said to Arjuna, "Slay that great snake which is your enemy." Thus urged by Kṛṣṇa, Arjuna asked, "Who is this snake that advances of his own accord against me, as if right against the mouth of Garuḍa?"[60] Kṛṣṇa replied, "While you were worshipping the fire-god at the Khāndava forest, this snake was ensconced within his mother's body, which was shattered by your arrows." As the snake took a slanting course across the sky, Arjuna cut it to pieces with six keen shafts, so that it fell down on the earth.

Then, because of the curse of the Brāhmaṇa, Karṇa's chariot wheel fell off, and his car began to reel. At the same time; he forgot the invocation for the weapon he had obtained from Paraśurāma. Unable to endure these calamities, Karṇa waved his arms and began to rail at righteousness, saying, "They that are conversant with virtue say that righteousness protects the righteous! But today righteousness does not save me."

Speaking thus, he shed tears of wrath, and said to Arjuna, "O Pāṇḍava! Spare me for a moment while I extricate my wheel from the earth! You are on your car while I am standing weak and languid on the ground. It is not fair that you should slay me now! You are born in the Kṣatriya order. You are the scion of a high race. Recollect the teachings of righteousness, and give me a moment's time!"

Then, from Arjuna's chariot, Kṛṣṇa said, "It is fortunate, O Karṇa, that you now remember virtue. It is generally true that those who are mean rail at Providence when they are afflicted by distress, but forget their own misdeeds. You and Duryodhana and Duḥśāsana and Śakuni caused Draupadī, clad in a single garment, to be brought into the midst of the assembly. On that occasion, O Karṇa, this virtue of yours was not in evidence! When Śakuni, skilled in dicing, vanquished Yudhiṣṭhira who was unacquainted with it, where was this virtue of yours? Out of covetousness, and relying on Śakuni, you again summoned the Pāṇḍavas to a game of dice. Whither then had this virtue of yours gone?"

When Kṛṣṇa thus taunted Karṇa, Arjuna became filled with rage. Remembering the incidents to which Kṛṣṇa alluded, he blazed with fury and, bent upon Karṇa's

---

[60] **"Who is . . . Garuḍa?":** See footnote 47; the eagle preys on snakes.

speedy destruction, took out of his quiver an excellent weapon. He then fixed on his bow that unrivalled arrow, and charged it with mantras. Drawing his bow Gāṇḍīva, he quickly said, "Let this shaft of mine be a mighty weapon capable of speedily destroying the body and heart of my enemy. If I have ever practised ascetic austerities, gratified my preceptors, and listened to the counsels of well-wishers, let this sharp shaft, so long worshipped by me, slay my enemy Karṇa by that Truth!"

Having uttered these words, Arjuna discharged for the destruction of Karṇa, that terrible shaft, that blazing arrow fierce and efficacious as a rite prescribed in the Atharva of Aṅgiras,[61] and invincible against the god of Death himself in battle. Thus sped by that mighty warrior, the shaft endowed with the energy of the Sun caused all the points of the compass to blaze with light. The head of the commander of the Kaurava army, splendid as the Sun, fell like the Sun disappearing in the blood-red sunset behind the western hills. Cut off by Arjuna's arrow and deprived of life, the tall trunk of Karṇa, with blood gushing from every wound, fell down like the thunder-riven summit of a mountain of red chalk with crimson streams running down its sides after a shower of rain.

Then from the body of the fallen Karṇa a light, passing through the atmosphere, illumined the sky. This wonderful sight was seen by all the warriors on the battlefield. After the heroic Karṇa was thus thrown down and stretched on the earth, pierced with arrows and bathed in blood, Śalya, the king of the Madras, withdrew with Karṇa's car. The Kauravas, afflicted with fear, fled from the field, frequently looking back on Arjuna's lofty standard which blazed in splendour.

[61] **Atharva of Aṅgiras:** The priest Aṅgiras is said to be the author of the Atharva Veda, which contains ritual incantations.

***FROM* BOOK 9**

Salya Parva [The End of the War and Death of Duryodhana]

LXX

After Karṇa's death the Kaurava forces were again without a leader. Then Aśvatthāmā said to Duryodhana, "Let Śalya become the commander of our army. In birth, in prowess, in energy, in fame, in beauty, and in every other accomplishment, he is qualified to lead us. He has joined us out of gratitude, having abandoned his own nephews. He has a large army of his own, and in personal valour he is without a rival. With Śalya as our commander, O king, we will be able to gain victory, as did the celestials after they made the invincible Skanda[62] their commander."

Duryodhana, alighting from his car, respectfully folded his hands and, approach-

[62] **Skanda:** The son of Śiva and Umā; he is a god of war.

ing Śalya, who was on his car, he said, "O brave hero! Become our commander in chief! When you go to battle, the Pāṇḍavas and their counsellors will lose heart, and the Pāñcālas will be depressed." Śalya answered, "O king of the Kurus, I will do as you desire. My life, my kingdom, my wealth, and everything else that belongs to me are at your disposal."

On the eighteenth day, the Kaurava soldiers led by Śalya once more rushed with great impetuosity into battle against the Pāṇḍavas. Śalya performed a wonderful feat in fighting the whole Pāṇḍava army singlehanded and slaying the opposing forces on all sides. When he saw his soldiers thus being killed by the king of the Madras, Yudhiṣṭhira was seized with rage. He swore: "Either Śalya shall kill me in battle today or I shall kill him."

Having made that vow, Yudhiṣṭhira proceeded against the king of the Madras. He took up a shining dart whose handle was made of gold and set with gems, and having inspired it with terrible mantras, and charged it with tremendous velocity by the exercise of great power and care, he hurled it along the best trajectory for the destruction of Śalya. The dart cut through his very vitals to penetrate his fair and broad chest, and then entered the earth as easily as if it were diving into water. Slain by Yudhiṣṭhira in fair fight, Śalya appeared like the dying embers of a sacrificial fire.

In the course of that day's battle Śakuni proceeded against Sahadeva. As Śakuni rushed quickly towards him, the valiant Sahadeva discharged at him veritable showers of quick-coursing arrows like a swarm of insects. Ulūka[63] struck Bhīma with ten arrows. Meanwhile Śakuni gave Sahadeva a mighty blow on the head with a lance. Stunned, Sahadeva sat down on the platform of his car.

Desirous of rescuing his father, Ulūka again attacked Bhīma with seven arrows and Sahadeva with seventy. Bhīma retaliated by hitting Ulūka with many keen arrows and Śakuni with sixty-four. At this stage the heroic and brave Sahadeva cut off Ulūka's head with a broad-headed arrow.

Seeing his son slain, Śakuni's voice was choked with tears. Sighing heavily, he recollected the words of Vidura. Filled with anger, he rushed, singlehanded, against Sahadeva and, eager to kill him, attacked him with a lance ornamented with gold. Sahadeva aimed at him a broad-headed arrow made of hard iron, adorned with wings of gold, capable of penetrating every armour. Shot with great force and care, the arrow cut off Śakuni's head from his trunk. Thereupon the Pāṇḍava forces were filled with joy. Rejoicing with Kṛṣṇa, they blew their conches. All of them praised Sahadeva and said, "By good luck, O hero, you have killed the wicked Śakuni of evil ways, along with his son."

LXXI

After the fall of Ulūka and Śakuni, their followers were enraged. Prepared to sacrifice their lives in that fierce encounter, they began to oppose the Pāṇḍavas. Duryodhana too was filled with rage. Collecting his remaining chariots, still many hundreds in number, as well as his elephants, horses, and foot soldiers, he said these words to

[63] **Ulūka:** The son of Śakuni, Gāndhārī's brother, and so a cousin of the Kauravas.

those warriors: "Kill the Pāṇḍavas with their friends and allies in this battle, and also the Pāñcāla prince with his own army. Then you may turn back from the field."

Respectfully obeying that mandate, the invincible warriors proceeded once more against the Pāṇḍavas. But because it had no leader, that army was destroyed in an instant by those great warriors the Pāṇḍavas. Thus all the eleven akṣauhiṇis of troops which had been collected by Duryodhana were killed by the Pāṇḍavas and the Sṛñjayas.

Looking on all sides, Duryodhana saw the field empty, and himself deprived of all his troops. Meanwhile the Pāṇḍavas, greatly pleased at having attained all their objects, were roaring aloud in joy. Overcome by despair, and bereft of troops and animals, Duryodhana decided to flee from the field. Taking up his mace, he fled on foot towards a lake.

In Duryodhana's army, which had consisted of many hundreds of thousands of warriors, not one single car-warrior was alive, save Aśvatthāmā the heroic son of Droṇa, Kṛtavarmā, Kṛpa, and Duryodhana himself. Duryodhana said to Sañjaya, "Tell the blind king that his son Duryodhana has entered into a lake." He then entered the waters of the lake, which he charmed by his power of wizardry.

Then the old men, who had been engaged to look after the ladies of the royal household, started for the city, followed by the princesses, who wept aloud when they heard of the destruction of the whole army. After the flight of the royal ladies the Kaurava camp was entirely empty, except for the three car-warriors. Filled with anxiety, and hoping to rescue Duryodhana, they too proceeded towards the lake.

Meanwhile Yudhiṣṭhira and his brothers felt happy, and ranged over the field with the desire to kill Duryodhana. Though they searched carefully for him everywhere, they could not discover the Kuru king who, mace in hand, had fled quickly from the field of battle, entered the lake, and solidified the water by his magic.

Not seeing Duryodhana who had thus concealed himself, and wishing to put an end to that sinful man's evil courses, the Pāṇḍavas sent spies in all directions on the field of battle. Some hunters brought news of Duryodhana's whereabouts to Bhīma. Rewarding them with immense wealth, Bhīma disclosed this news to the righteous King Yudhiṣṭhira, saying, "Duryodhana, O king, has been found by the hunters who supply me with meat. He for whom you feel sorry now lies within a lake whose waters have been turned solid by him."

Thereupon, with Kṛṣṇa in the lead, Yudhiṣṭhira proceeded toward that lake, accompanied by Arjuna, the twins, Dhṛṣṭadyumna, the invincible Śikhaṇḍī, Uttamaujas, Yudhāmanyu, the great car-warrior Sātyaki, the five sons of Draupadī, and those amongst the Pāñcālas who had survived, with all their elephants, and infantry by the hundreds.

LXXII

Having arrived at the banks of the Dvaipāyana lake, they saw the reservoir enchanted by Duryodhana. Then Yudhiṣṭhira said to Kṛṣṇa, "Behold, the son of Dhṛtarāṣṭra has charmed these waters by his power of wizardry, and lives within them, without fear of injury." Kṛṣṇa replied, "With your own power of wizardry, O Bhārata, destroy this illusion of Duryodhana."

Then Yudhiṣṭhira derisively said to Duryodhana, who was still within the waters of the lake, "Why, O Duryodhana, have you charmed these waters, after having caused the death of all the Kṣatriyas, as well as your own family? Why have you entered this lake today, in order to save your own life? Arise and fight us, O Suyodhana!"[64]

From the depths of the lake, Duryodhana replied, "It was not for the sake of saving my life, nor from fear, nor from grief, that I entered this lake. It was only out of fatigue that I did so. The Kurus for whose sake I desired sovereignty, those brothers of mine, all lie dead on the battlefield. This empty earth is now yours. Who could wish to rule a kingdom bereft of allies? As for myself, clad in deerskins I shall retire to the forest. Friendless as I am, I have no desire to live."

"You may now be willing, O Suyodhana," said Yudhiṣṭhira, "to make a gift of the earth to me. However, I do not wish to rule the earth as a gift from you. Before this, you would not agree to give me even so much of the earth as could be covered by the point of a needle. Either rule the earth after having defeated us, or go to the celestial regions after being slain by us."

Duryodhana said, "You Pāṇḍavas have friends, cars, and animals. I, however, am alone now, without a car or a mount. Alone as I am, and devoid of weapons, how can I venture to fight on foot against countless foes, all well armed and having cars? O Yudhiṣṭhira, fight one at a time with me. It is not fair that one should be called upon to fight with many, especially when that one is without armour, tired and wounded, and devoid of both animals and troops."

Thus challenged, Yudhiṣṭhira replied, "Fight any one of us, choosing whatever weapon you like. The rest of us will remain spectators. I grant you also this other wish of yours, that if you kill any one of us, you shall then become king. Otherwise, you shall be killed, and go to heaven."

"Brave as you are," answered Duryodhana, "if you allow me the option of fighting only one of you, I choose to fight with this mace that I have in my hand. Let any of you who thinks that he is a match for me come forward and fight me on foot, armed with mace." So saying, Duryodhana emerged from the water and stood there, mace in hand, his limbs covered with blood.

At the conclusion of this parley Kṛṣṇa, worked up with wrath, said to Yudhiṣṭhira, "Planning to kill Bhīma, O king, Duryodhana has practised with the mace upon a statue of iron for thirteen years. Except for Bhīma, I do not at this moment see any match for Duryodhana. However, Bhīma has not practised as hard as Duryodhana. I do not see any man in the world today, nor even a god, who can defeat the mace-armed Duryodhana in battle. In a fair fight between Duryodhana and Bhīma, our victory will be in doubt because Duryodhana is powerful, practised, and skilful."

Bhīma was, however, more confident. He said, "I shall surely kill Duryodhana in battle. I feel that the victory of the righteous Yudhiṣṭhira is certain. This mace of

[64] **Suyodhana:** Duryodhana.

mine is one and a half times as heavy as Duryodhana's. Do not give way to anxiety. I dare to fight him, selecting the mace as the weapon. All of you, O Kṛṣṇa, witness this encounter!"

After Bhīma had said these words, Kṛṣṇa joyfully applauded him and said, "Thanks to you, O mighty Bhīma, the righteous King Yudhiṣṭhira will regain prosperity after achieving the destruction of all his foes. You should, however, always fight with care against Duryodhana. He is endowed with skill and strength and loves to fight."

When the fierce duel was about to start, and when all the great Pāṇḍavas had taken their seats, Balarāma[65] came there, having heard that a battle between those two heroes, both of whom were his disciples, was about to start. Seeing him, the Pāṇḍavas and Kṛṣṇa were filled with joy. They greeted him and saluted him with due rites. They then said to him, "Witness, O Rāma, the skill in battle of your two disciples."

LXXIII

The duel then began. Duryodhana and Bhīma fought like two bulls attacking each other with their horns. The clash of their maces produced loud peals like those of thunderbolts. After the fierce and terrible battle had lasted for some time, both contenders were exhausted. They rested for some time and then, taking up their maces, they once again began to ward off each other's attacks.

While the fight was thus raging between those two heroes, Arjuna said to Kṛṣṇa, "Who, in your opinion, is the better of these two? What is their respective merit? Tell me this, O Kṛṣṇa!"

Kṛṣṇa replied, "They are equally well instructed. Bhīma is possessed of greater strength while Duryodhana has greater skill and has practised harder. If he fights fairly, Bhīma will never succeed in gaining victory. If, however, he fights unfairly, he will surely be able to kill Duryodhana. At the time of the gambling Bhīma promised to break the thighs of Duryodhana with his mace in battle. Let him now fulfil his vow. Let him, by deception, kill the Kuru king who is the master of deception! If Bhīma does not kill him by unfair means, the son of Dhṛtarāṣṭra will surely retain the kingdom!"

Thereupon Arjuna, before Bhīma's sight, struck his own left thigh. Understanding that sign, Bhīma began to move about with his mace raised, making many kinds of manoeuvres. Seeing the energetic and angry Bhīma rushing towards him and desiring to thwart his blow, Duryodhana thought of the manoeuvre called avasthāna, and prepared to jump upwards.

Bhīma fully understood the object of his opponent. Rushing at him, with a loud roar, he fiercely hurled his mace at Duryodhana's thighs, as the latter jumped into the air. The mace, hurled by Bhīma, broke the thighs of Duryodhana, and he fell down, so that the earth resounded.

---

[65] **Balarāma:** A brother of Kṛṣṇa.

Having struck Duryodhana down, Bhīma approached the Kuru chief and said, "O wretch, formerly you laughed at Draupadī who had only one bit of cloth in the midst of the assembly, and you called us cows. Bear now the consequences of that insult." Saying this, he kicked the head of his fallen foe with his left foot.

Balarāma became highly incensed when he saw Duryodhana thus brought down by a blow aimed at his thighs. Raising his arms, he sorrowfully said in the midst of those kings, "Oh, fie on Bhīma, that in such a fair fight a blow should have been inflicted below the navel! Never before has such a foul blow been seen in an encounter with the mace!

"Having unfairly killed the righteous King Duryodhana," Balarāma continued, "Bhīma shall be known in the world as an unfair fighter! The righteous Duryodhana, on the other hand, shall acquire eternal blessedness!"

Kṛṣṇa then said to Yudhiṣṭhira, "O king of virtue, why do you permit such a wrong act? Why do you suffer the head of the insensible and fallen Duryodhana to be thus kicked by Bhīma with his foot? Conversant as you are with the rules of morality, why do you look on this deed with indifference?"

Yudhiṣṭhira said, "O Kṛṣṇa, Bhīma's action in angrily touching the head of the fallen king with his foot does not please me, nor am I glad at this extermination of my race! But remember how we were cheated by the sons of Dhṛtarāṣṭra! Remember too the many harsh words they addressed to us, and how they sent us in exile into the forest. On account of all those things Bhīma has been nursing a great grief in his heart! Bearing all this in mind, O Kṛṣṇa, I looked on his actions with indifference!" [. . .]

[In Book 10, the Sauptika Parva, Aśvatthāmā, the son of Droṇa, leads an attack on the Pāṇḍava forces while they are sleeping in their encampment. All the warriors except for the five brothers are killed. Hunted down by the Pāṇḍavas, Aśvatthāmā eventually faces off against Arjuna, both of whom brandish celestial weapons. Kṛṣṇa intervenes to forestall further bloodshed, and Aśvatthāmā is forced into 3,000 years of companionless exile.]

***FROM* BOOK 11**

Stri Parva [The Grief of the Survivors]

LXXXI

Having lost all his sons, King Dhṛtarāṣṭra was grief-stricken. Looking like a tree shorn of its branches, he was overcome by depression and lost his power of speech. The wise Sañjaya approached the king and said to him, "Why do you grieve, O monarch? Forget your sorrow, and arrange for the due performance of the obsequial rites of your fathers, sons, grandsons, kinsmen, preceptors, and friends."

Dhṛtarāṣṭra lamented, "Deprived as I am of sons and counsellors and all my friends, I shall have to wander in sorrow over the earth. In the midst of the assembly, Kṛṣṇa told me what was for my good. He said, 'Let us end hostilities, O king! Let your son take the entire kingdom, except for five villages.' Foolishly I disregarded that advice, and I am now forced to repent. I must have committed great sins in my previous births, and hence the Creator has made me suffer such grief in this life. Ask the Pāṇḍavas to come and see me this very day, determined as I am upon following the long way that leads to the regions of Brahmā."

Though he too was grief-stricken because of the death of his own sons, Yudhiṣṭhira, accompanied by his brothers, set out to see Dhṛtarāṣṭra. He was followed by Kṛṣṇa and Sātyaki, and by Yuyutsu.[66] The grieving princess Draupadī too, accompanied by the Pāñcāla ladies, sorrowfully followed.

Having duly saluted their sire, the Pāṇḍavas announced themselves to him, each uttering his own name. Dhṛtarāṣṭra first greeted the eldest son of Pāṇḍu, Yudhiṣṭhira, who was the cause of the slaughter of all his sons. Having embraced Yudhiṣṭhira and spoken a few comforting words to him, the wicked Dhṛtarāṣṭra sought Bhīma, like a fire ready to burn everything that would approach it. Understanding his wicked intentions towards Bhīma, Kṛṣṇa dragged away the real Bhīma, and presented an iron statue of the second son of Pāṇḍu to the old king. Grasping with his two arms that iron statue, the powerful king broke it into pieces, taking it for the real Bhīma.

His passion gone, the king then cast off his anger and became normal. Overcome by grief, he began to weep aloud, "Alas, O Bhīma! Alas!" Knowing that he was no longer under the influence of anger, and that he was truly sorry for having, as he believed, slain Bhīma, Kṛṣṇa said, "Do not grieve, O Dhṛtarāṣṭra, for you have not killed Bhīma. What you broke was only an iron statue."

LXXXII

Then, at the request of Dhṛtarāṣṭra, the Pāṇḍava brothers, accompanied by Kṛṣṇa, went to see Gāndhārī. The innocent Gāndhārī was grief-stricken at the death of her hundred sons. Recalling that Yudhiṣṭhira had killed all his enemies, she wished to curse him. Knowing her evil intentions, Vyāsa prepared to keep them from being fulfilled.

He said to her, "Do not be angry with the Pāṇḍavas, O Gāndhārī! May you have peace! Control the words you are about to say! Listen to my counsel." Gāndhārī said, "Thanks to the folly of Duryodhana and Śakuni, of Karṇa and Duḥśāsana, this extinction of the Kurus has taken place. But in the very presence of Kṛṣṇa, Bhīma did something that excites my anger. Having challenged Duryodhana to a deadly duel with the mace, and knowing that my son was superior to him in skill, he struck him below the navel. It is this that provokes my wrath. Why should heroes forget their duties to save their lives?"

Hearing these words of Gāndhārī, Bhīma was afraid, and tried to soothe her. He said, "Whether the deed was fair or unfair, I did it through fear and to protect my own self! Please forgive me now! Your son was incapable of being killed by anybody in a fair fight. And therefore I did what was unfair."

---

[66] **Yuyutsu:** A younger son of Dhṛtarāṣṭra by a Vaiṣya woman; hence not one of the hundred Kaurava brothers, all of whom have been slain in the war.

Gāṅdhārī then said, "When Vṛṣasena had deprived Nakula of his horses, you drank Duḥśāsana's blood in battle. That was an act of cruelty which is censured by the good, becoming only to an unworthy person. It was an evil act, O Bhīma!"

"It is wrong to drink the blood of even a stranger," Bhīma replied. "One's brother is like one's own self, and there is no difference between them. The blood, however, did not pass my lips and teeth, as Karṇa knew well. Only my hands were covered with Duḥśāsana's blood. When Draupadī was seized by the hair after the gambling match, in my anger I gave vent to certain words which I still remember. For all the years to come I would have been deemed to have neglected the duties of a Kṣatriya if I had left that promise unfulfilled. It was for this reason, O queen, that I committed that act." Gāṅdhārī wailed, "You have killed a hundred sons of this old man [Dhṛtarāṣṭra]! Why did you not spare even one son of this old couple, deprived of their kingdom, who had committed only a minor offence?"

LXXXIII

Filled with anger at the slaughter of all her sons and grandsons, Gāṅdhārī then inquired after Yudhiṣṭhira, saying, "Where is the king?" After she had asked for him, Yudhiṣṭhira approached her, trembling and with joined hands, and said these soft words, "Here is Yudhiṣṭhira, O queen, that cruel destroyer of your sons! I deserve your curses, for I am the real cause of this universal destruction! Curse me! I do not care for life, for kingdom, or for wealth, having killed such friends."

Sighing heavily, Gāṅdhārī could say nothing to Yudhiṣṭhira as, overcome with fear, he stood in her presence. When Yudhiṣṭhira, with body bent, was about to prostrate himself at her feet, the far-sighted Kuru queen, conversant as she was with righteousness, directed her eyes from within the folds of the cloth that covered them to the tip of Yudhiṣṭhira's toe. Thereupon, the king whose nails had till then been perfect came to have a scorched nail on his toe.

Seeing this, Arjuna moved behind Kṛṣṇa, and the other Pāṇḍavas too became restless. Meanwhile Gāṅdhārī shook off her anger, and comforted the Pāṇḍavas as a mother should. With her permission those heroes then proceeded to see their mother.

Seeing her sons after a long time, Kuṅtī, who had been filled with anxiety for them, covered her face with a fold of her garment and shed copious tears. She then repeatedly embraced and patted each of her sons. Next she consoled Draupadī who had lost all her children and who was lying on the bare earth, wailing piteously. Raising the grief-stricken princess of Pāñcāla who was weeping thus, Kuṅtī began to comfort her.

Accompanied by Draupadī, and followed by her sons, Kuṅtī then proceeded towards the sorrowful Gāṅdhārī, though she herself was in greater sorrow. Seeing that illustrious lady with her daughter-in-law, Gāṅdhārī said, "Do not grieve thus, O daughter. I too am much afflicted with grief. I think this universal destruction has been caused by the irresistible course of Time. Since it was not brought about by human agency, this dreadful slaughter was inevitable. What the wise Vidura foretold, after Kṛṣṇa's supplication for peace had failed, has now come to pass!"

Gāṅdhārī then said to Kṛṣṇa, "The Pāṇḍavas and the sons of Dhṛtarāṣṭra have destroyed each other. Why did you look on while they were thus exterminating each other? Because you were deliberately indifferent to their destruction, you shall obtain the fruit of this act. O Kṛṣṇa, by constant service to my husband I have acquired a little merit. By that merit, which was so difficult to obtain, I now curse you. Since you remained indifferent while the Kauravas and Pāṇḍavas slew each other, O Kṛṣṇa, you shall be the slayer of your own kinsmen. Thirty-six years hence you shall, after causing the death of your kinsmen, friends, and son, perish by ignoble means in the wilderness."

BOOK 12

Santi Parva [The Pandavas Return]

LXXXIV

Along with Vidura, Dhṛtarāṣṭra, and all the Bhārata ladies, the Pāṇḍavas offered oblations of water to all their departed kinsmen and friends. The noble descendants of the Kurus then passed a month of purification outside the city. Many famous sages came there to see the virtuous King Yudhiṣṭhira. Among them were Vyāsa, Nārada, the great sage Devala, Devasthāna, and Kaṇva, and their worthy disciples.

Yudhiṣṭhira said, "I am haunted by grief because of the death in battle of young Abhimanyu, the sons of Draupadī, Dhṛṣṭadyumna, Virāṭa, King Drupada, Vasuṣeṇa, King Dhṛṣṭaketu, and other kings coming from various countries. I feel that, through my desire to recover my kingdom, I caused the destruction of my kinsmen and the extermination of my own race. I am an evil-doer and a sinner and the cause of the destruction of the earth. Seated as I am now, I shall starve myself to death."

Vyāsa consoled Yudhiṣṭhira, saying, "You should not, O king, grieve so. I shall repeat what I have once said. All this is Destiny. Do what you have been created to do by your Maker. That is your fulfilment. Remember, O king, you are not your own master.

"O king, do not indulge in grief!" Vyāsa continued. "Remember the duties of a Kṣatriya. All those fighters were killed while performing their legitimate duties. You too have performed the duties of a Kṣatriya and obtained the kingdom blamelessly. Do your duty now, O son of Kuṅtī, and you shall obtain happiness in the next world." Thus was Yudhiṣṭhira comforted, and persuaded to return to his kingdom.

When the Pāṇḍavas reentered the city, many thousands of citizens came out to greet them. Entering the interior of the palace, the illustrious Yudhiṣṭhira approached the deities and worshipped them with offerings of gems and incense and garlands of all kinds.

Freed of his grief and his sickness of heart, Yudhiṣṭhira cheerfully sat facing eastward on an excellent seat made of gold. Those two heroes, Sātyaki and Kṛṣṇa, sat facing him on a seat covered by a rich carpet. On either side of the king sat the great-minded Bhīma and Arjuna upon two soft seats set with gems. Upon a white ivory couch, decked with gold, sat Kuṅtī with Sahadeva and Nakula.

Then by Kṛṣṇa's leave the priest Dhaumya consecrated, according to rule, an altar facing the east and the north. He next seated the great Yudhiṣṭhira and Draupadī upon a soft seat covered with a tiger-skin, called Sarvatobhadra. Thereafter he began to pour libations of clarified butter upon the sacrificial fire while chanting the prescribed incantations. King Dhṛtarāṣṭra was first to anoint Yudhiṣṭhira and all the others followed him. Thus worshipped by those pious men, Yudhiṣṭhira the king of virtue, with his friends, was restored to his kingdom.

Accepting the greetings of his subjects, King Yudhiṣṭhira answered them, saying: "Blessed are the sons of Pāṇḍu, whose merits, deservedly or otherwise, are thus recited in this world by the foremost of Brāhmaṇas assembled together. King Dhṛtarāṣṭra, however, is our father and supreme deity. Those who wish to please me should obey his commands and respect his every wish. The whole world is his, as are the Pāṇḍavas, and everybody else. These words of mine should be borne in mind by all of you."

Having given the citizens and the villagers leave to depart, the Kuru king appointed his brother Bhīma as yuvarāja.[67] He gladly appointed the highly intelligent Vidura to help him with advice and to look after the sixfold requirements[68] of the state. The venerable Sañjaya, wise and thoughtful and endued with every accomplishment, was designated as the superintendent of finances.

Nakula was placed in charge of the forces, to give them food and pay and to look after the other affairs of the army. Yudhiṣṭhira made Arjuna responsible for resisting hostile forces and punishing the wicked. Dhaumya, the foremost of priests, was asked to attend to the Brāhmaṇas and to perform all Vedic rites and all other rites. Sahadeva was always to remain by Yudhiṣṭhira's side, as his protector.

[In the final books of the epic, not included here, Dhṛtrāṣṭra remains the nominal king while Yudhiṣṭhira wields effective power. After about fifteen years, the old king, his wife Gāṅdhārī, and Kuṅtī renounce the world and go into the forest where they meet the old sage Vyāsa. Vyāsa brings about a reconciliation between the Pāṇḍavas and the Kauravas by summoning the spirits of the dead warriors by the waters of the Gaṅgā. Soon after, the old king, his wife, and Kuṅtī die in a forest fire. About twenty-one years later, the Gāṅdhārī's curse on Krṣṇa comes to pass (see Stri Parva, Chapter 83), and he dies at the hands of a hunter who mistakes him for a deer. In the last two books of the epic, Yudhiṣṭhira and his brothers leave the world.]

---

[67] **yuvarāja:** The crown prince.

[68] **the sixfold requirements:** Peace, war, parade, cease-fire, inciting divisions among enemies, and defense.

Bhagavad Gita

C. First Century B.C.E.–First Century C.E.

WWW For a quiz on the Bhagavad Gita, see *World Literature Online* at bedfordstmartins .com/worldlit.

Tucked into the Bhishma Parva, Book 6 of the *Mahabharata,* appears one of India's most important and influential sacred texts, the Bhagavad Gita. Added to the *Mahabharata* sometime between the first century B.C.E. and the first century C.E., this seven-hundred-verse poem of eighteen chapters or "teachings" has been called "a compendium of the whole Vedic doctrine" of earlier sacred texts such as the Vedas and the Upanishads,[1] and it is often treated as an independent text. Indeed, the Gita, or Song of God as it is often called, is well known throughout the world as an important guide to moral and spiritual action. American writer and naturalist Henry David Thoreau (1817–1862) and Indian spiritual leader Mohandas (Mahatma) Gandhi (1869–1948) were among the work's admirers.

The Bhagavad Gita attempted to weave together the various philosophical strands of the Vedas and the Upanishads, which had been unraveling for centuries, as well as accommodate some of the ideas of the two relatively new religions of Buddhism and Jainism. Just as Greek thinkers and writers of the fifth century B.C.E. aimed to square the mythology and customs of a tribal society with the philosophical needs of a new social formation, the city-state, the Gita sought to synthesize the older teachings of the Vedic tradition with the new demands of the changing Indian society. One of the most influential aspects of the newer religions was the idea of ***ahimsa,*** or nonviolence, by means of which individuals from any class could achieve spiritual liberation. This concept was a problem for the warrior class, the ***Kshatriya*** (Kṣatria), of course, who according to the Vedas fulfilled the duties of their caste by engaging in war. This clash of values provides the basic conflict of the Bhagavad Gita, as the **Pandava** hero Arjuna weighs whether or not it is just to wage war against his kinsmen, the Kauravas.

PAHN-duh-vuh

The Bhagavad Gita takes the form of an extended dialogue between **Arjuna** and **Krishna**, the incarnation of **Vishnu**, just before the war between the cousins begins. Arjuna, who has lost his heart for battle, surveys the field of **Kuru** with his charioteer, Krishna. Looking out in "strange pity" at his cousins and uncles, his former mentors and friends, Arjuna anticipates imminent carnage and is filled with doubt about the wisdom of engaging in war. Krishna counsels him about his spiritual and moral obligation to engage in combat and prosecute the war according to the sacred duty of the warrior class into which he was born. At the same time Krishna teaches Arjuna that in order to free himself from worldly attachment, Arjuna must perform his duties without desire for reward and with the understanding that all action should be undertaken as a

AR-joo-nuh; KRISH-nuh; VISH-noo

KOO-roo

[1] **Vedas and Upanishads:** The Vedas, dating from c. 1000 B.C.E., are a group of the earliest sacred texts, written in Sanskrit, from India; they contain hymns and ritual lore considered to be revelation (*sruti*). The Upanishads, dating from the ninth century B.C.E., are sacred texts that are a mystical development of and commentary on the earlier Vedic texts.

Temple of Vishnu, 500
A principal Hindu deity, Vishnu (the four-armed figure at left), in the guise of Krishna, serves as Arjuna's charioteer and counselor in the Bhagavad Gita. (Borromeo/Art Resource, NY)

form of devotion to Vishnu, whose cosmic plan comprehends all that we do. Action taken out of duty, without desire for reward, with devotion to Krishna, and with consciousness of the divinity of all things leads to the ultimate goal of ***MOKSHA***, release from ***SAMSARA***, or the cycle of death and rebirth.

Arjuna's dilemma stems in part from a desire to renounce the world and a belief that violent action will keep his spirit tied to the material world. The solution to Arjuna's problem is given in stages throughout the dialogue, which in Book 11 culminates in a marvelous revelation of Krishna's divinity. The key teaching is that Arjuna must fulfill his duties as a warrior but with total disregard for the immediate or future consequences. First, he must recognize that the human spirit that acts is not separate from the universal and immortal spirit, Brahman. Once Arjuna

[The *Bhagavad-Gita*] is the focal point around which all later Hinduism was to revolve, and so all-embracing is its appeal that it has commanded not only the allegiance of the orthodox but also that of modern and modernist Hindus, and not least of [whom was] Mahatma Gandhi himself. It is the sacred fount from which the popular cults of rapt devotion to God (whether it be Vishnu or Siva) naturally flow.

– R. C. ZAEHNER, critic, 1962

realizes that the human soul is in fact a portion of the universal soul that is constantly interacting with the world, Krishna points out that renouncing worldly action goes against the divine scheme of things. To act according to the ***DHARMA*** of one's class, then, is to act in accordance with *Dharma* understood as divine law. In other words, in acting out their duties, human beings participate in the divine plan. Thus, Arjuna learns that action is necessary, but that action must be undertaken with discipline and understanding.

Given the immortality of the soul, actions have consequences in the spiritual realm, which is timeless, as well as in the world of historical time. The law of ***KARMA***, already articulated in the Upanishads, states that all individuals are locked into a chain of consequences that determines one's status in a future life and that may free one from *samsara*. According to the Gita, one way to liberate the soul from the cycle of death and rebirth is by means of ***KARMA-YOGA***, the path of disciplined action. In the Gita, the greatest happiness comes from action performed with detachment from gain and in strict accordance with one's station in life. Any longing for results, or confusion of roles, as Krishna advises Arjuna, subverts the moral and spiritual order. "Your own duty done imperfectly / is better than another man's done well," the teacher tells the warrior. Thus, from Krishna, Arjuna learns that when the warrior or any other class member gives himself up to *dharma* without desire, though his actions have consequences in historical time, they will in fact further the progress of his soul toward *moksha*, a release to a oneness with the supreme spirit, or Brahman, and an escape from the cycle of rebirth. Moreover, what makes possible such liberation, Arjuna learns, is not only the actions one performs but also one's moral and philosophical relation to and understanding of those actions. In other words, it is not just what one does—so long as individuals abide by their sacred duty—it is also how one thinks about what one does that matters.

■ CONNECTIONS

Hebrew Scriptures, p. 134. As a drama of spiritual and ethical crisis, the Bhagavad Gita takes its place among the great works of wisdom literature and sacred writings, including the Bible. In some ways, the Gita is a theodicy, a work that attempts to explain or justify the ways of God to man. Consider how the Book of Job in the Hebrew Scriptures raises ethical and spiritual issues similar to those in the Gita. What do Job and Arjuna suggest about their cultures' approach to suffering and/or to the relationship between God and man?

Homer, *The Iliad*, p. 288. The Bhagavad Gita forms a small part of the great epic poem *Mahabharata*, in which, as in Homer's *Iliad*, the gods oversee the warriors' actions and even intervene to shift the balance of the war. Though only a small part of the epic, the Gita is an extended reflection on the meaning and purpose of a warrior's actions and their consequences, on the battlefield as well as within the larger context of spiritual life. Compare Arjuna's thoughts about duty to the reasons Achilles gives for returning to the war. What does this comparison suggest about the Greek idea of the warrior-hero in Homer's time and the Indian concept of the warrior-hero in the first century?

Chikamatsu Monzaemon, *The Love Suicides at Amijima* (Book 4); Sophocles, *Antigone*, p. 952. As a work dramatizing self-doubt, the Bhagavad Gita portrays Arjuna's conflict between his allegiance to his kinsmen and his sacred duty to affirm and follow a higher purpose. Like many of the great dramas of world literature, Chikamatsu's *Love Suicides at Amijima* also portrays an individual whose pursuit of a higher set of values complicates allegiances to kin and obligations to the rule of law. In Chikamatsu's play, Kamiya Jihei and his lover, Koharu, sever their worldly ties to family and work in order to immortalize their love. Sophocles' *Antigone* pits Antigone's sacred duty to her kin against the rule of law, represented by Creon. Compare Arjuna's situation to Jihei's and Antigone's. What do the differences suggest about the cultures represented in the texts?

■ FURTHER RESEARCH

Literary History/Background

Dimock, Edward C. Jr., et al. *The Literatures of India: An Introduction.* 1974.
Flood, Gavin. *An Introduction to Hinduism.* 1996.
Zaehner, R. C. *Hinduism.* 1962, 1966.

Criticism

Minor, Robert. *Modern Interpreters of the Bhagavadgita.* 1986.
Sharpe, Eric. *The Universal Gita: Western Images of the Bhagavad Gita.* 1985.

Translations

Johnson, W. J. *The Bhagavad Gita.* 1994.
Mascaró, Juan. *The Bhagavad Gita.* 1962.
Prabhavananda, Swami, and Christopher Isherwood. *The Song of God: Bhagavad-Gita.* 1944.
Miller, Barbara Stoler. *The Bhagavad Gita: Krishna's Counsel in Time of War.* 1986.

■ PRONUNCIATION

Arjuna: AR-joo-nuh
Bhagavad Gita: bah-guh-vahd-GEE-tuh, buh-guh-vud-GEE-tuh
Bhima: BEE-muh
Bhishma: BEESH-muh
Brahma: BRAH-hmuh
Dhritarashtra: drih-tuh-RAH-shtruh
Drishtadyumna: drish-tuh-DYOOM-nuh
Drona: DROH-nuh
Drupada: DROO-puh-duh
Duryodhana: door-YOH-duh-nuh
Karna: KAR-nuh
Kauravas: KOW-ruh-vuhz
Krishna: KRISH-nuh
Kripa: KRIH-puh
Pandava: PAHN-duh-vuh
Pandu: PAHN-doo
Prajapati: pruh-JAH-puh-tee
Sanjaya: SUN-juh-yuh
Satyaki: SAH-tyuh-kee
Virata: vih-RAH-tuh
Vishnu: VISH-noo
Yudhishthira: yoo-DISH-tih-ruh

FROM

Bhagavad Gita

Translated by Barbara Stoler Miller

THE FIRST TEACHING: ARJUNA'S DEJECTION

DHRITARASHTRA:[1]

Sanjaya, tell me what my sons
and the sons of Pandu[2] did when they met,
wanting to battle on the field of Kuru,[3]
1 on the field of sacred duty?

SANJAYA:[4]

Your son Duryodhana,[5] the king,
seeing the Pandava forces arrayed,
approached his teacher Drona[6]
2 and spoke in command.

Bhagavad Gita. The Bhagavad Gita was added to Book 6, the Bhishma Parva, of the *Mahabharata* sometime between the first centuries B.C.E. and C.E. The Gita was first translated into a European language by Charles Wilkins in 1785. From that time on the work became well known in the West, undergoing translation into many languages. A poem in eighteen books, called "teachings," the Gita is a dramatic dialogue between the warrior hero Arjuna and his divine charioteer, Krishna. The dialogue takes place on the evening before Arjuna, the third-born of the five Pandava brothers, must make war against his cousins, the Kauravas, on the field of Kuru. While engaging the most subtle philosophical points about sacred duty *(dharma)*, right action *(yoga)*, the consequences of actions *(karma)*, and devotion *(bhakti)*, the dialogue itself never loses sight of the dramatic situation in which it occurs. Thus, the Gita embraces both the epic and heroic realm of action even as it demonstrates that action ultimately takes its meaning in the transcendental realm of Brahman, the one soul or spirit that permeates all things. As the conversation between Arjuna and Krishna unfolds, Arjuna learns the importance of dharma and its relationship to karma; he comes to see action as one of the ways human beings participate in Krishna's cosmic or divine

---

[1] **Dhritarashtra:** The son of Vyasa and Ambika (Kansalya), now the blind king at Hastinapurna and the father of the one hundred brothers known as the Kauravas.

[2] **Pandu:** The son of Vyasa and Ambalika and the father of the five brothers known as the Pandavas.

[3] **field of Kuru:** Kurukshetra, the field where the eighteen-day battle between the Pandavas and the Kauravas is fought.

[4] **Sanjaya:** Dhritarashtra's advisor and the narrator of the Bhagavad Gita.

[5] **Duryodhana:** The eldest of the Kaurava brothers; his jealousy of the great success of the Pandavas has led to the war.

[6] **Drona:** Mentor in the martial arts to the Kauravas and the Pandavas.

"My teacher, see
the great Pandava army arrayed
by Drupada's son,[7]
3 your pupil, intent on revenge.

Here are heroes, mighty archers
equal to Bhima and Arjuna[8] in warfare,
Yuyudhana, Virata, and Drupada,[9]
4 your sworn foe on his great chariot.

Here too are Dhrishtaketu, Cekitana,
and the brave king of Benares;
Purujit, Kuntibhoja,
5 and the manly king of the Shibis.

Yudhamanyu is bold,
and Uttamaujas is brave;
the sons of Subhadra and Draupadi
6 all command great chariots.

Now, honored priest, mark
the superb men on our side
as I tell you the names
7 of my army's leaders.

---

scheme. By the end of the Gita, Arjuna understands his duty as a warrior and decides to engage in combat against his kin.

The First Teaching sets the scene of Arjuna's state of mind, his dejection. The visionary poet Sanjaya is the narrator of the poem, describing what he sees to King Dhritarashtra (Dhṛtarāṣṭra), the father of the Kauravas. Excerpts from the Second, Third, and Sixth Teachings follow the exchange between Arjuna and Krishna. Responding to Arjuna's questions, Krishna, the incarnation of the preserver-god Vishnu, gradually imparts the meaning of sacred duty and right action while slowly revealing his own divinity. This revelation culminates in The Eleventh Teaching when, like the pilgrim Dante in the *Paradiso* of *The Divine Comedy,* Arjuna receives a spectacular vision—a theophany—in this case, of Krishna's boundless being in all its fullness and light.

A note on the translation: We are using for our selection the highly readable and lucid verse translation by the late Sanskrit scholar Barbara Stoler Miller. Notes are the editors'.

---

[7] **Drupada's son:** Dhrishtadyumna, the commander of the Pandavas and brother of Draupadi, the wife of the five Pandavas.

[8] **Bhima and Arjuna:** Nominally, the second and third sons of Pandu; they are actually the sons of Pandu's wife Kunti and the gods Vayu (the wind god) and Indra (the chief of the gods), respectively. Yudhishthira, the first-born son of Pandu, is actually the son of Kunti and Dharma (the god of sacred duty and law).

[9] **Yuyudhana . . . Drupada:** These names and those in verse five catalog the chief allies of the Pandavas.

They are you and Bhishma,[10]
Karna[11] and Kripa,[12] a victor in battles,
your own son Ashvatthama,
8 Vikarna, and the son of Somadatta.

Many other heroes also risk
their lives for my sake,
bearing varied weapons
9 and skilled in the ways of war.

Guarded by Bhishma, the strength
of our army is without limit;
but the strength of their army,
10 guarded by Bhima, is limited.

In all the movements of battle,
you and your men,
stationed according to plan,
11 must guard Bhishma well!"

Bhishma, fiery elder of the Kurus,
roared his lion's roar
and blew his conch horn,
12 exciting Duryodhana's delight.

Conches and kettledrums,
cymbals, tabors, and trumpets
were sounded at once
13 and the din of tumult arose.

Standing on their great chariot
yoked with white stallions,
Krishna and Arjuna, Pandu's son,
14 sounded their divine conches.

Krishna blew Pancajanya, won from a demon;
Arjuna blew Devadatta, a gift of the gods;

---

[10] **Bhishma:** The son of King Santanu and Ganga; as the great-uncle of both Duryodhana and Arjuna, he tried to avert war through negotiations but found on the side of the Kauravas.

[11] **Karna:** The first son of Kunti by the sun-god Surya; born before Kunti married Pandu, Karna was abandoned by his mother and raised by a charioteer. Though a half brother of the Pandavas, Karna fights for the Kauravas out of loyalty to his friend Duryodhana.

[12] **Kripa:** Drona's brother-in-law; the list that follows, similar to lists in the Homeric epics, catalogs the chief allies of the Kauravas.

fierce wolf-bellied Bhima blew Paundra,
15 his great conch of the east.

Yudhishthira,[13] Kunti's son, the king,
blew Anantavijaya, conch of boundless victory;
his twin brothers Nakula and Sahadeva[14]
16 blew conches resonant and jewel toned.

The king of Benares, a superb archer,
and Shikhandin on his great chariot,
Drishtadyumna, Virata, and indomitable Satyaki,[15]
17 all blew their conches.

Drupada, with his five grandsons,
and Subhadra's strong-armed son,[16]
each in his turn blew
18 their conches, O King.

The noise tore the hearts
of Dhritarashtra's sons,
and tumult echoed
19 through heaven and earth.

Arjuna, his war flag a rampant monkey,
saw Dhritarashtra's sons assembled
as weapons were ready to clash,
20 and he lifted his bow.

He told his charioteer:[17]
"Krishna,
halt my chariot
21 between the armies!

Far enough for me to see
these men who lust for war,

[13] **Yudhishthira:** See note 8.

[14] **Nakula and Sahadeva:** Nominally, the twin sons of Pandu by his wife, Madri; actually fathered by the Asvins (physicians of heaven), they are the fourth and fifth Pandava brothers. (See also note 8.)

[15] **Drishtadyumna . . . Satyaki:** Drishtadyumna is the son of King Drupada and the brother of Draupadi, the wife of the five Pandavas. Virata is the king of the Matsyas and Satyaki is a kinsman of Krishna. All are fighting for the Pandavas.

[16] **Subhadra's strong-armed son:** Abhimanyu, son of Arjuna and his wife, Subhadra, Krishna's sister.

[17] **his charioteer:** Krishna, the incarnation of the preserver-god Vishnu, is Arjuna's spiritual guide and charioteer.

ready to fight with me
22 in the strain of battle.

I see men gathered here,
eager to fight,
bent on serving the folly
23 of Dhritarashtra's son."

When Arjuna had spoken,
Krishna halted
their splendid chariot
24 between the armies.

Facing Bhishma and Drona
and all the great kings,
he said, "Arjuna, see
25 the Kuru men assembled here!"

Arjuna saw them standing there:
fathers, grandfathers, teachers,
uncles, brothers, sons,
26 grandsons, and friends.

He surveyed his elders
and companions in both armies,
all his kinsmen
27 assembled together.

Dejected, filled with strange pity,
he said this:
"Krishna, I see my kinsmen
28 gathered here, wanting war.

My limbs sink,
my mouth is parched,
my body trembles,
29 the hair bristles on my flesh.

The magic bow[18] slips
from my hand, my skin burns,

[18] **The magic bow:** Gandiva, a weapon Arjuna won from Agni, the god of fire.

I cannot stand still,
30 my mind reels.

I see omens of chaos,
Krishna; I see no good
in killing my kinsmen
31 in battle.

Krishna, I seek no victory,
or kingship or pleasures.
What use to us are kingship,
32 delights, or life itself?

We sought kingship, delights,
and pleasures for the sake of those
assembled to abandon their lives
33 and fortunes in battle.

They are teachers, fathers, sons,
and grandfathers, uncles, grandsons,
fathers and brothers of wives,
34 and other men of our family.

I do not want to kill them
even if I am killed, Krishna;
not for kingship of all three worlds,
35 much less for the earth!

What joy is there for us, Krishna,
in killing Dhritarashtra's sons?
Evil will haunt us if we kill them,
36 though their bows are drawn to kill.

Honor forbids us to kill
our cousins, Dhritarashtra's sons;
how can we know happiness
37 if we kill our own kinsmen?

The greed that distorts their reason
blinds them to the sin they commit
in ruining the family, blinds them
38 to the crime of betraying friends.

How can we ignore the wisdom
of turning from this evil

when we see the sin
39 of family destruction, Krishna?

When the family is ruined,
the timeless laws of family duty
perish; and when duty is lost,
40 chaos overwhelms the family.

In overwhelming chaos, Krishna,
women of the family are corrupted;
and when women are corrupted,
41 disorder is born in society.[19]

This discord drags the violators
and the family itself to hell;
for ancestors fall when rites
42 of offering rice and water lapse.

The sins of men who violate
the family create disorder in society
that undermines the constant laws
43 of caste and family duty.

Krishna, we have heard
that a place in hell
is reserved for men
44 who undermine family duties.

I lament the great sin
we commit when our greed
for kingship and pleasures
45 drives us to kill our kinsmen.

If Dhritarashtra's armed sons
kill me in battle when I am unarmed
and offer no resistance,
46 it will be my reward."

Saying this in the time of war,
Arjuna slumped into the chariot
and laid down his bow and arrows,
47 his mind tormented by grief.

---

[19] **disorder . . . society:** That is, the social order of the castes—Brahmin, *Kshatriya* (warrior), *Vaishya* (merchant and farmer), and *Shudra* (laborer and servant)—will be overthrown.

FROM

The Second Teaching: Philosophy and Spiritual Discipline

SANJAYA:
Arjuna sat dejected,
filled with pity,
his sad eyes blurred by tears.
1 Krishna gave him counsel. [. . .]

LORD KRISHNA:
You grieve for those beyond grief,
and you speak words of insight;
but learned men do not grieve
11 for the dead or the living.

Never have I not existed,
nor you, nor these kings;
and never in the future
12 shall we cease to exist.

Just as the embodied self
enters childhood, youth, and old age,
so does it enter another body;
13 this does not confound a steadfast man.

Contacts with matter make us feel
heat and cold, pleasure and pain.
Arjuna, you must learn to endure
14 fleeting things—they come and go!

When these cannot torment a man,
when suffering and joy are equal
for him and he has courage,
15 he is fit for immortality.

Nothing of nonbeing comes to be,
nor does being cease to exist;
the boundary between these two
16 is seen by men who see reality.

Indestructible is the presence[20]
that pervades all this;

[20] **the presence:** Krishna means Brahman, the universal spirit that permeates all creation. What Arjuna perceives as mutable and limited is in fact part of the unchanging and infinite soul.

no one can destroy
17 this unchanging reality.

Our bodies are known to end,
but the embodied self is enduring,
indestructible, and immeasurable;
18 therefore, Arjuna, fight the battle!

He who thinks this self a killer
and he who thinks it killed,
both fail to understand;
19 it does not kill, nor is it killed.

It is not born,
it does not die;
having been,
it will never not be;
unborn, enduring,
constant, and primordial,
it is not killed
20 when the body is killed.

Arjuna, when a man knows the self
to be indestructible, enduring, unborn,
unchanging, how does he kill
21 or cause anyone to kill?

As a man discards
worn-out clothes
to put on new
and different ones,
so the embodied self
discards
its worn-out bodies
22 to take on other new ones.

Weapons do not cut it,
fire does not burn it,
waters do not wet it,
23 wind does not wither it.

It cannot be cut or burned;
it cannot be wet or withered;
it is enduring, all-pervasive,
24 fixed, immovable, and timeless.

It is called unmanifest,
inconceivable, and immutable;
since you know that to be so,
25 you should not grieve!

If you think of its birth
and death as ever-recurring,
then too, Great Warrior,
26 you have no cause to grieve!

Death is certain for anyone born,
and birth is certain for the dead;
since the cycle is inevitable,
27 you have no cause to grieve!

Creatures are unmanifest in origin,
manifest in the midst of life,
and unmanifest again in the end.
28 Since this is so, why do you lament?

Rarely someone
sees it,
rarely another
speaks it,
rarely anyone
hears it—
even hearing it,
29 no one really knows it.

The self embodied in the body
of every being is indestructible;
you have no cause to grieve
30 for all these creatures, Arjuna!

Look to your own duty;
do not tremble before it;
nothing is better for a warrior
31 than a battle of sacred duty.[21]

The doors of heaven open
for warriors who rejoice

---

[21] **sacred duty:** That is, *dharma;* in Arjuna's case, the responsibilities of the *Kshatriya* class.

to have a battle like this
32 thrust on them by chance.

If you fail to wage this war
of sacred duty,
you will abandon your own duty
33 and fame only to gain evil.

People will tell
of your undying shame,
and for a man of honor
34 shame is worse than death.

The great chariot warriors will think
you deserted in fear of battle;
you will be despised
35 by those who held you in esteem.

Your enemies will slander you,
scorning your skill
in so many unspeakable ways—
36 could any suffering be worse?

If you are killed, you win heaven;
if you triumph, you enjoy the earth;
therefore, Arjuna, stand up
37 and resolve to fight the battle!

Impartial to joy and suffering,
gain and loss, victory and defeat,
arm yourself for the battle,
38 lest you fall into evil.

Understanding is defined in terms of philosophy;
now hear it in spiritual discipline.
Armed with this understanding, Arjuna,
39 you will escape the bondage of action.[22] [. . .]

Be intent on action,
not on the fruits of action;

[22] **the bondage of action:** That is, the cycle of death and rebirth in the world of embodied action; to escape the cycle of rebirth *(samsara)* is to attain *moksha,* spiritual liberation and oneness with Brahman.

avoid attraction to the fruits
47 and attachment to inaction!

Perform actions, firm in discipline,
relinquishing attachment;
be impartial to failure and success—
48 this equanimity is called discipline.

Arjuna, action is far inferior
to the discipline of understanding;[23]
so seek refuge in understanding—pitiful
49 are men drawn by fruits of action.

Disciplined by understanding,
one abandons both good and evil deeds;
so arm yourself for discipline—
50 discipline is skill in actions.

Wise men disciplined by understanding
relinquish the fruit born of action;
freed from these bonds of rebirth,
51 they reach a place beyond decay.

When your understanding passes beyond
the swamp of delusion,
you will be indifferent to all
52 that is heard in sacred lore.[24]

When your understanding turns
from sacred lore to stand fixed,
immovable in contemplation,
53 then you will reach discipline.

ARJUNA:

Krishna, what defines a man
deep in contemplation whose insight
and thought are sure? How would he speak?
54 How would he sit? How would he move?

[23] **discipline of understanding:** Disciplined understanding means something like pure consciousness or intuition as opposed to instrumental or practical reason, which acts on objects in the world.

[24] **sacred lore:** That is, the Vedas and Upanishads, according to which strict observance of ritual sacrifice alone leads to *moksha.* Krishna guides Arjuna to understand that the Brahminic recitation of scriptures does not stem from or lead to understanding and hence does not lead to liberation.

LORD KRISHNA:

When he gives up desires in his mind,
is content with the self within himself,[25]
then he is said to be a man
55 whose insight is sure, Arjuna.

When suffering does not disturb his mind,
when his craving for pleasures has vanished,
when attraction, fear, and anger are gone,
56 he is called a sage whose thought is sure.

When he shows no preference
in fortune or misfortune
and neither exults nor hates,
57 his insight is sure.

When, like a tortoise retracting
its limbs, he withdraws his senses
completely from sensuous objects,
58 his insight is sure.

Sensuous objects fade
when the embodied self abstains from food;
the taste lingers, but it too fades
59 in the vision of higher truth.

Even when a man of wisdom
tries to control them, Arjuna,
the bewildering senses
60 attack his mind with violence.

Controlling them all,
with discipline he should focus on me;
when his senses are under control,
61 his insight is sure.

Brooding about sensuous objects
makes attachment to them grow;
from attachment desire arises,
62 from desire anger is born.

[25] **the self within himself:** According to Samkhya theory, within each person lies the immortal, universal self *(purusha);* this pure self is distinct from the "I" or consciousness. When embodied in the realm of matter, the self loses sight of its immortal soul. Through disciplined understanding, the self can know its true nature.

From anger comes confusion;
from confusion memory lapses;
from broken memory understanding is lost;
63 from loss of understanding, he is ruined.

But a man of inner strength
whose senses experience objects
without attraction and hatred,
64 in self-control, finds serenity. [. . .]

FROM

The Third Teaching: Discipline of Action

ARJUNA:

If you think understanding
is more powerful than action,
why, Krishna, do you urge me
1 to this horrific act?

You confuse my understanding
with a maze of words;
speak one certain truth
2 so I may achieve what is good.

LORD KRISHNA:

Earlier I taught the twofold
basis of good in this world—
for philosophers, disciplined knowledge;
3 for men of discipline, action.

A man cannot escape the force
of action by abstaining from actions;
he does not attain success
4 just by renunciation.

No one exists for even an instant
without performing action;
however unwilling, every being is forced
5 to act by the qualities of nature.[26]

[26] **the qualities of nature:** The principles of nature *(praktri)* derive from the three *gunas* (qualities or strands); they are *sattva,* the quality of pure light; *rajas,* the quality of passion or energy; and *tamas,* the quality of inertia. The first quality frees the self from its bondage to matter; the second forces it to act in the world; the third binds it in ignorance.

When his senses are controlled
but he keeps recalling
sense objects with his mind,
6 he is a self-deluded hypocrite.

When he controls his senses
with his mind and engages in the discipline
of action with his faculties of action,
7 detachment sets him apart.

Perform necessary action;
it is more powerful than inaction;
without action you even fail
8 to sustain your own body.

Action imprisons the world
unless it is done as sacrifice;
freed from attachment, Arjuna,
9 perform action as sacrifice!

When creating living beings and sacrifice,
Prajapati,[27] the primordial creator, said:
"By sacrifice will you procreate!
10 Let it be your wish-granting cow!

Foster the gods with this,
and may they foster you;
by enriching one another,
11 you will achieve a higher good.

Enriched by sacrifice, the gods
will give you the delights you desire;
he is a thief who enjoys their gifts
12 without giving to them in return."

Good men eating the remnants
of sacrifice are free of any guilt,
but evil men who cook for themselves
13 eat the food of sin.

Creatures depend on food,
food comes from rain,

[27] **Prajapati:** As the "lord of creatures," Prajapati is the guardian of living beings.

rain depends on sacrifice,
14 and sacrifice comes from action.

Action comes from the spirit of prayer,
whose source is OM,[28] sound of the imperishable;
so the pervading infinite spirit
15 is ever present in rites of sacrifice.

He who fails to keep turning
the wheel here set in motion
wastes his life in sin,
16 addicted to the senses, Arjuna.

But when a man finds delight
within himself and feels inner joy
and pure contentment in himself,
17 there is nothing more to be done.

He has no stake here
in deeds done or undone,
nor does his purpose
18 depend on other creatures.

Always perform with detachment
any action you must do;
performing action with detachment,
19 one achieves supreme good. [. . .]

ARJUNA:

Krishna, what makes a person
commit evil
against his own will,
36 as if compelled by force?

LORD KRISHNA:

It is desire and anger, arising
from nature's quality of passion;
know it here as the enemy,
37 voracious and very evil!

As fire is obscured by smoke
and a mirror by dirt,

---

[28] **OM:** The sacred sound or mantra, associated in the *Upanishads* with *brahman,* the universal spirit that underlies the cosmos.

as an embryo is veiled by its caul,
38 so is knowledge obscured by this.

Knowledge is obscured
by the wise man's eternal enemy,
which takes form as desire,
39 an insatiable fire, Arjuna.

The senses, mind, and understanding
are said to harbor desire;
with these desire obscures knowledge
40 and confounds the embodied self.

Therefore, first restrain
your senses, Arjuna,
then kill this evil
41 that ruins knowledge and judgment.

Men say that the senses are superior
to their objects, the mind superior to the senses,
understanding superior to the mind;
42 higher than understanding is the self.

Knowing the self beyond understanding,
sustain the self with the self.
Great Warrior, kill the enemy
43 menacing you in the form of desire!

FROM

The Sixth Teaching: The Man of Discipline

[LORD KRISHNA]:
A man of discipline[29] should always
discipline himself, remain in seclusion,
isolated, his thought and self well controlled,
10 without possessions or hope.

He should fix for himself
a firm seat in a pure place,

[29] **man of discipline:** Discipline is *yoga,* from the Sanskrit for "yoking" or binding; the man of discipline is known as a *yogi.* Through certain disciplined action, knowledge, and devotion individuals may align themselves more perfectly to the divine purpose of Krishna.

neither too high nor too low,
11 covered in cloth, deerskin, or grass.

He should focus his mind and restrain
the activity of his thought and senses;
sitting on that seat, he should practice
12 discipline for the purification of the self.

He should keep his body, head,
and neck aligned, immobile, steady;
he should gaze at the tip of his nose
13 and not let his glance wander.

The self tranquil, his fear dispelled,
firm in his vow of celibacy, his mind restrained,
let him sit with discipline,
14 his thought fixed on me, intent on me.

Disciplining himself,
his mind controlled,
a man of discipline finds peace,
15 the pure calm that exists in me.

Gluttons have no discipline,
nor the man who starves himself,
nor he who sleeps excessively
16 or suffers wakefulness.

When a man disciplines his diet
and diversions, his physical actions,
his sleeping and waking,
17 discipline destroys his sorrow.

When his controlled thought
rests within the self alone,
without craving objects of desire,
18 he is said to be disciplined.

"He does not waver, like a lamp sheltered
from the wind" is the simile recalled
for a man of discipline, restrained in thought
19 and practicing self-discipline.

When his thought ceases,
checked by the exercise of discipline,

he is content within the self,
20 seeing the self through himself.

Absolute joy beyond the senses
can only be grasped by understanding;
when one knows it, he abides there
21 and never wanders from this reality.

Obtaining it, he thinks
there is no greater gain;
abiding there, he is unmoved,
22 even by deep suffering.

Since he knows that discipline
means unbinding the bonds of suffering,
he should practice discipline resolutely,
23 without despair dulling his reason.

He should entirely relinquish
desires aroused by willful intent;
he should entirely control
24 his senses with his mind.

He should gradually become tranquil,
firmly controlling his understanding;
focusing his mind on the self,
25 he should think nothing.

Wherever his faltering mind
unsteadily wanders,
he should restrain it
26 and bring it under self-control.

When his mind is tranquil, perfect joy
comes to the man of discipline;
his passion is calmed, he is without sin,
27 being one with the infinite spirit.

Constantly disciplining himself,
free from sin, the man of discipline
easily achieves perfect joy
28 in harmony with the infinite spirit.

Arming himself with discipline,
seeing everything with an equal eye,

he sees the self in all creatures
29 and all creatures in the self.

He who sees me everywhere
and sees everything in me
will not be lost to me,
30 and I will not be lost to him.

I exist in all creatures,
so the disciplined man devoted to me
grasps the oneness of life;
31 wherever he is, he is in me.

When he sees identity in everything,
whether joy or suffering,
through analogy with the self,
32 he is deemed a man of pure discipline. [. . .]

FROM

The Eleventh Teaching: The Vision of Krishna's Totality

ARJUNA:

To favor me you revealed
the deepest mystery of the self,
and by your words
1 my delusion is dispelled.

I heard from you in detail
how creatures come to be and die,
Krishna, and about the self
2 in its immutable greatness.

Just as you have described
yourself, I wish to see your form
in all its majesty,
3 Krishna, Supreme among Men.

If you think I can see it,
reveal to me
your immutable self,
4 Krishna, Lord of Discipline.

LORD KRISHNA:

Arjuna, see my forms

in hundreds and thousands;
diverse, divine,
5 of many colors and shapes.

See the sun gods, gods of light,
howling storm gods, twin gods of dawn,
and gods of wind, Arjuna,
6 wondrous forms not seen before.

Arjuna, see all the universe,
animate and inanimate,
and whatever else you wish to see;
7 all stands here as one in my body.

But you cannot see me
with your own eye;
I will give you a divine eye to see
8 the majesty of my discipline.

SANJAYA:
O King, saying this, Krishna,
the great lord of discipline,
revealed to Arjuna
9 the true majesty of his form.

It was a multiform, wondrous vision,
with countless mouths and eyes
and celestial ornaments,
10 brandishing many divine weapons.

Everywhere was boundless divinity
containing all astonishing things,
wearing divine garlands and garments,
11 anointed with divine perfume.

If the light of a thousand suns
were to rise in the sky at once,
it would be like the light
12 of that great spirit.

Arjuna saw all the universe
in its many ways and parts,
standing as one in the body
13 of the god of gods. [. . .]

[ARJUNA]:
I bow to you,

I prostrate my body,
I beg you to be gracious,
Worshipful Lord—
as a father to a son,
a friend to a friend,
a lover to a beloved,
44 O God, bear with me.

I am thrilled,
and yet my mind
trembles with fear
at seeing
what has not been seen before.
Show me, God, the form I know—
be gracious, Lord of Gods,
45 Shelter of the World.

I want to see you
as before,
with your crown and mace,
and the discus in your hand.
O Thousand-Armed God,
assume the four-armed form[30]
embodied
46 in your totality.

LORD KRISHNA:

To grace you, Arjuna,
I revealed
through self-discipline
my higher form,
which no one but you
has ever beheld—
brilliant, total,
47 boundless, primal.

Not through sacred lore
or sacrificial ritual
or study or charity,
not by rites
or by terrible penances
can I be seen in this form

[30] **the four-armed form:** Having seen a vision of divinity in its totality, Arjuna asks Krishna to return to his form as Vishnu, a four-armed god.

in the world of men
48 by anyone but you, Great Hero.

Do not tremble
or suffer confusion
from seeing
my horrific form;
your fear dispelled,
your mind full of love,
see my form again
49 as it was.

SANJAYA:

Saying this to Arjuna,
Krishna once more
revealed
his intimate form;
resuming his gentle body,
the great spirit
let the terrified hero
50 regain his breath.

ARJUNA:

Seeing your gentle human form,
Krishna, I recover
my own nature,
51 and my reason is restored.

LORD KRISHNA:

This form you have seen
is rarely revealed;
the gods are constantly craving
52 for a vision of this form.

Not through sacred lore,
penances, charity, or sacrificial rites
can I be seen in the form
53 that you saw me.

By devotion alone
can I, as I really am,
be known and seen
54 and entered into, Arjuna.

Acting only for me, intent on me,
free from attachment,
hostile to no creature, Arjuna,
55 a man of devotion comes to me.

War, Rulers, and Empire

War has been a key ingredient in the development of civilization, from the very first cities to the present day. Walls were erected around early cities to protect riches such as surplus food from wandering "barbarians." Armies were created to mind the walls and protect the granaries. Then armies discovered they could raid other cities. Confucius, the great philosopher from ancient China, dealt with issues of warfare by focusing on the morality of rulers; he proposed that with an upright ruler following the tenets of Confucianism, cruelty and slaughter would be done away with. The goal of several thinkers in ancient India and China was to eliminate war and create a state of perpetual peace and harmony. Since this condition was rarely achievable in ordinary political life, adherents to this ideal became marginal sects who lived somewhat outside of ordinary society, later developing into monasteries of one kind or another. The Greek philosopher Heraclitus (sixth century B.C.E.), far from seeking to eliminate warfare, believed that war was the essential condition of reality and the origin of all great things. War was normal; it created courageous heroes and it was the duty of kings and rulers.

War and peace were two of the most important themes of ancient literature. The dramatic conflict of opposing armies and ideals held a special interest for early poets and writers. The model for all Western epic poets is the Greek Homer, whose extended poems about the Trojan War and its aftermath exposed the ironies and tragedies of warfare; while war elevated certain heroes to greatness, it also involved pettiness and betrayal. In war there was no clear-cut right and wrong; even the gods in Homer's works were divided in their sympathies between the Greeks and the Trojans.

Warfare for the ancient Hebrews in the Middle East was associated with a particular god, Yahweh. The conquest of Canaan, the Promised Land, is portrayed in the Hebrew Scriptures as a sweeping devastation of the existing settlements and cities. In the books of Deuteronomy and Joshua, Yahweh is a single-minded, ruthless conqueror. Probably the longest war epic, however, depicting the struggles between two powerful families, comes from India. The ***Mahabharata***, "Book of the Great War of the Sons of Bharata," is a work of 106,000 verses in eighteen books. War in these early works was a dramatic setting in which the artist could study individual virtue and the relative loyalties and strengths of deities.

p. 1434

In the ancient world, the simplest solution for dealing with the defeated was eradication. According to the testimony of Greek writers, Troy was burnt to the ground, its men slain, and its women and children taken into captivity. The Semitic-Bedouin policy toward the Canaanites differed only slightly. In Deuteronomy 20:10–18, Yahweh instructs his Hebrew followers to slay the males but to take the women, children, cattle, and goods as booty. In Joshua 6:21, however, Jericho is totally annihilated: ". . . they destroyed everything in the city; they put everyone to the sword, men and women, young and old, and also cattle, sheep, and asses" (New English Bible). Captured enemies were commonly offered as a sacrifice to a deity. The debate about the morality of war would come much later.

War became increasingly complex when it became the instrument for extending the rule of early city-states into fledgling empires. Warfare, with its strategies and weapons technology, contributed to the arts of governance and raised questions about what was to be done with surviving enemies and conquered territories. In the Middle East, the Assyrians, with the first great war machine, created the first international empire, beginning c. 1300 B.C.E. and lasting for the next seven centuries. By the ninth century B.C.E., the empire extended from the eastern shore of the Mediterranean south to Egypt and east to the territory north of the Persian Gulf. The

◀ **King Ashurbanipal, 650 B.C.E.**
The Assyrians created the first international empire, chiefly through excellence in warfare. Here the powerful king Ashurbanipal is shown on a chariot with archers, a frightening sight for any army. (The Art Archive / British Museum / Dagli Orti (A))

Assyrians, however, though able soldiers, were ineffectual administrators. The governors appointed to oversee subjugated lands could not maintain control for long; the Assyrian military eventually was exhausted by having to reconquer and repacify the same regions time and again. Tiglath Pilesar III (r. 745–727 B.C.E.) invented a new policy for establishing order: instead of massacres there were to be massive exchanges of populations: The defeated exchanged locations with followers of the conqueror. In **The Fall of Samaria**, King Sargon II (r. 721–705 B.C.E.) describes the exchange that took place after the capture of Samaria, capital of the northern Hebrew kingdom. The Ten Hebrew Tribes, deported to Mesopotamia where most likely they were absorbed into the populace, became the "Lost Tribes"; certain religious groups speculate that they eventually settled in Africa, while others believe they became the early inhabitants of America. In the Middle East, this policy of deportation lasted into the sixth century B.C.E., when the Babylonian king Nebuchadnezzar conquered Jerusalem in 586 B.C.E. and deported most of the Jews to Babylon. The Assyrian model of military might for sustaining an empire came to an end with the Persian Cyrus the Great, who conquered the Babylonians in 539 B.C.E. and instituted yet another policy: instead of massacre or population exchanges, Cyrus governed the conquered peoples through the careful appointment of rulers chosen from the conquered population itself.

During this same era in China and India, discussions about the nature of rulership went far beyond the use of force and "might makes right." The history of China from the sixth century to the third century B.C.E. is filled with feuding kingdoms and the rise and fall of petty chieftains. But this was also the period of the Golden
p. 1525
Age of Philosophy. A very thin volume, the **Dao De Jing** (Tao Te Ching), attributed to Laozi (Lao Tzu), gave rise to Daoism (Taoism). Although Daoism is an optimistic philosophy suited to individual practice, a number of the writings in the Dao De Jing deal with the principles of rulership. Poem 30 expresses the Daoist precepts that war is futile and wasteful and that everyone, including the king, should adapt to the essential spiritual harmony of nature and follow the dao, an approach that usually leads to withdrawal from political life rather than political reformation. Confucianism, by contrast, provided a great deal of practical advice for rulers as well as for other members of the social hierarchy. **Mencius** (fourth century B.C.E.)

was a disciple of Confucius (Kongfuzi) who attempted to spread Confucianism by traveling through Chinese states advising rulers on proper conduct. Mencius tied the concept of rulership to what he perceived as the essential goodness of human nature. In the excerpt from his writings included here, Mencius instructs a ruler to use compassion as his directive for governance.

The Jain religion of India, which shares certain attitudes with Buddhism, was founded by Mahavira, a contemporary of the Buddha. Jainism developed the most radical doctrine of ***AHIMSA*** (literally, "nonharming"), extending it to every living being. Vegetarians, Jains must not kill or hurt any being. The Jain selection is a parable that compares the traditional roles of a warrior-king and the worldview of a monk. In the third century B.C.E. Ashoka Maurya became an influential king of the Maurya empire, which comprised all of India. While engaged in the ordinary bloodshed and devastation of a war on the eastern frontier, Ashoka experienced a radical

Head of a Jain Tirthankara, third to fourth century B.C.E. *Jains believe in the cyclical nature of the universe, which has no beginning, end, or creator. A* tirthankara *is a Jain saint. (Ashmolean Museum, Oxford, UK/Bridgeman Art Library)*

change of consciousness. He converted to Buddhism, gave up warring, and committed his reign to nonviolence and kindness to all humans and animals. An inscription by King Ashoka, the *Asokavadana,* found on a piece of rock, shows the ruler's remarkable tolerance for different belief systems and cultures.

The Greek philosophers Plato and Aristotle both upheld the importance of reason in politics—perhaps as optimistic and idealistic as Mencius's faith in human compassion. In the ***Republic,*** a lengthy treatise on the ideals of statehood, Plato describes the merging of philosopher and ruler into the ultimate monarch, the philosopher-king. Alexander the Great (Alexander III of Macedon, 356–323 B.C.E.) was actively aspiring to the role of the philosopher-ruler when he became ill and died prematurely. By the year 330 B.C.E., having gained control of the Persian empire by defeating Darius III, Alexander's kingdom stretched from the Mediterranean to the Indus River in south Asia. His liberal treatment of the Persians, including his acceptance of intermarriage, alienated his soldiers, who were unable to appreciate Alexander's ethic of tolerance and his vision of a unified humanity that transcended national differences. Plutarch, in ***Moralia,*** sings Alexander's exceptional qualities.

p. 1111

p. 1535

Like China before national unity and empire, Rome went through a long period of civil war, settling down under the expansion and consolidation of power under Augustus, a title that in 27 B.C.E. the Senate conferred on Octavian, whose rule as the first Roman emperor continued until 14 C.E. A period of relative peace and prosperity, which lasted until 235 C.E., has thus been called the ***Pax Romana,*** *Pax Augusta,* or Augustan Age (27 B.C.E.–235 C.E.). During the early Augustan Age, it was the task of writers—both literary and historical—to support and legitimize the empire. While the physical or material magnificence of Rome was evident in its armies, wealth, architecture, civic events, and engineering feats, there was, as with all world powers, a dark side to Roman rule having to do with the legitimacy and administering of vast frontiers, competition with Hellenism and the heritage of Greece, debauchery and immorality, free food and outrageous spectacles ("bread and circuses"), and Rome's potential fall amid prophecies of the end of an age. Virgil, the "poet laureate" of Rome, mimicking Homer's epics, established a mythic and legendary foundation for the founding of Rome in his epic ***The Aeneid,*** thus elevating the political and mate-

p. 1181

Warrior Fresco, fourth century B.C.E. *The Romans were great empire-builders, using their famous legionnaires to conquer much of the known world of the time. At its height the Roman Empire encompassed nearly all the lands bordering the Mediterranean, stretching into parts of England and central Europe to the north, and deep into southern Egypt to the south. (The Art Archive / Archaeological Museum, Naples / Dagli Orti (A))*

rial city to the level of destiny and the will of the gods. In these famous lines from *The Aeneid,* myth allows Virgil to invest Augustus with cosmic features:

> And here, here is the man, the promised one you know of—
> Caesar Augustus, son of a god, destined to rule
> Where Saturn ruled of old in Latium, and there
> Bring back the age of gold: his empire shall expand
> Past Garamants and Indians to a land beyond the zodiac.
>
> —TRANSLATED BY C. DAY-LEWIS

Virgil's renowned contemporary, Horace, used a formal, allegorical rhetoric to describe the new age of Augustus: "Now Faith and Peace and Honor and Antique Modesty and neglected Virtue dare return, and Plenty appears in view, rich with her overflowing horn."

It was the task of Roman historians like Polybius, Livy, and **Suetonius** not only to describe actual events associated with the building of the empire but also to articulate the intangibles of the

soo-ih-TOH-nee-us

formation and maintenance of an empire, that meeting ground of powerful individuals, governments, and destiny. These historical accounts promoted a vision of sociopolitical stability, the restoration of morality, and the celebration of service. Although Suetonius had a tendency to mix gossip with facts, his portrait of Julius Caesar as a divine being reveals some of the extraordinary qualities of this dictator, who ruled Rome from 49 to 44 B.C.E. As Suetonius makes clear, in **Lives of the Twelve Caesars**, Julius Caesar had a genius for leadership that far exceeded his military prowess.

p. 1540 The concluding excerpt from Flavius Josephus's ***The Jewish War*** depicts in painful eyewitness detail a pivotal event in the history of Judaism: the insurrection of Jews against Roman rule and the suppression of those Jews by Roman legions in 66–73 C.E., including the destruction of the Third Temple, the laying waste of Jerusalem, and the suffering of its inhabitants. This event led to the protracted exile of the Jews and their dispersal into the surrounding territories, a pattern begun with Babylonian exile (sixth century B.C.E.) and known as the ***DIASPORA***.

■ CONNECTIONS

***In the World:* East and West (Book 5).** The creation of empire in the ancient world required more complex military actions than simple physical might. In addition to larger armies and sophisticated military strategy, empire builders in the West had to develop ways of administering empire through force, persuasion, and rewards. How did the various philosophies and religions from Asia—such as Daoism, Confucianism, Jainism, and Buddhism—shift the emphasis from external might to the inner, spiritual development of the individual ruler?

Greece (p. 247); Rome (p. 1157); and India (p. 1323). Certain individuals in the ancient world achieved lasting fame through their unusual leadership qualities. Consider the portraits of Julius Caesar, Alexander, and Ashoka in the readings: What qualities led to their success as leaders and human beings?

■ PRONUNCIATION

Flavius Josephus: FLAY-vee-us joh-ZEE-fus, joh-SEE-fus
Suetonius: soo-ih-TOH-nee-us

Sargon II

r. 721–705 B.C.E.

The ancient history of Mesopotamia, the fertile lands around and between the Tigris and Euphrates Rivers, in what today is Iraq, involved a succession of city-states, kingdoms, and empires that went under the names of Sumer, Akkad, Assyria, and Babylonia. The last two in particular struggled for dominance of the region from c. 2000 B.C.E. to 539 B.C.E., when the last Babylonian empire fell to Cyrus the Great of Persia. Sargon II was one of several Assyrian kings who gradually expanded the Assyrian empire. Within the history of Judaism he is particularly known for capturing Samaria in 721 B.C.E., the capital of the northern Israelite kingdom, which was made up of ten tribes. After crushing the enemy, Sargon deported the remaining population, which came to be known as the Lost Tribes of Israel, to Assyria. The inscription titled "The Fall of Samaria" was found in 1843 by French scholar Paul Emile Botta,

Sargon II, eighth century B.C.E.
The Assyrians administered one of the first international empires. In this relief from the palace of Sargon II at Khorsabad (in present-day Iraq), the ruler conducts official business with a vizier, a high official. (Giraudon / Bridgeman Art Library)

who unearthed Sargon's palace at Khorsabad, Iraq, on the walls of which were inscribed invaluable historical texts.

Sargon's description of his conquests, taken from the first year's annals, supports the Assyrians' reputation for ruthlessness. The towns mentioned in the text, like Ashdod and Hamath, were in Palestine or Syria. Brackets are used around restorations to the text, here translated by A. Leo Oppenheim; parentheses enclose material added for understanding. Missing material is indicated by ellipses.

FROM

The Fall of Samaria

Translated by A. Leo Oppenheim

From Annalistic Reports

At the begi[nning of my royal rule, I . . . the town of the Sama]rians [I besieged, conquered] (2 lines destroyed) [for the god . . . who le]t me achieve (this) my triumph. . . . I led away as prisoners [27,290 inhabitants of it (and) [equipped] from among [them (soldiers to man)] 50 chariots for my royal corps. . . . [The town I] re[built] better than (it was) before and [settled] therein people from countries which [I] myself [had con]quered. I placed an officer of mine as governor over them and imposed upon them tribute as (is customary) for Assyrian citizens.

Iamani from Ashdod, afraid of my armed force (lit.: weapons), left his wife and children and fled to the frontier of M[usru] which belongs to Meluhha (i.e., Ethiopia) and hid (lit.: stayed) there like a thief. I installed an officer of mine as governor over his entire large country and its prosperous inhabitants, (thus) aggrandizing (again) the territory belonging to Ashur,[1] the king of the gods. The terror (-inspiring) glamor of Ashur, my lord, overpowered (however) the king of Meluhha and he threw him (i.e. Iamani) in fetters on hands and feet, and sent him to me, to Assyria. I conquered and sacked the towns Shinuhtu (and) Samaria, and all Israel (lit.: "Omri-Land" *Bît Ḫu-um-ri-ia*). I caught, like a fish, the Greek (Ionians) who live (on islands) amidst the Western Sea.

Ia'ubidi from Hamath, a commoner without claim to the throne, a cursed Hittite, schemed to become king of Hamath, induced the cities Arvad, Simirra, Damascus *(Di-maš-qa)* and Samaria to desert me, made them collaborate and fitted out an army. I called up the masses of the soldiers of Ashur and besieged him and his warriors in Qarqar, his favorite city. I conquered (it) and burnt (it). Himself I flayed; the rebels I killed in their cities and established (again) peace and harmony. A contingent of 200 chariots and 600 men on horseback I formed from among the inhabitants of Hamath and added them to my royal corps.

Upon a trust(-inspiring oracle given by) my lord Ashur, I crushed the tribes of

---

[1] **Ashur:** The national god of Assyria; he replaces Marduk in the Assyrian version of *The Epic of Creation.*

Tamud, Ibadidi, Marsimanu, and Haiapa, the Arabs who live, far away, in the desert (and) who know neither overseers nor official(s) and who had not (yet) brought their tribute to any king. I deported their survivors and settled (them) in Samaria.

From Pir'u, the king of Musru, Samsi, the queen of Arabia, It'amra, the Sabaean,—the(se) are the kings of the seashore and from the desert—I received as their presents, gold in the form of dust, precious stones, ivory, ebony-seeds, all kinds of aromatic substances, horses (and) camels.

LAOZI (LAO TZU)

C. SIXTH–THIRD CENTURY B.C.E.

As the traditional founder of the ancient spiritual path called Daoism, Laozi (Lao Tzu) proposed a radically different use of force and goals of governing than those that appear in Sargon II's inscriptions. Laozi is credited with the series of eighty-one poems known as the Dao De Jing (Tao Te Ching), which promote following the overall direction of life, or following the dao. Rather than seeking control over others through the use of force, Daoism pursues harmonies that might coalesce around a ruler and promote the good life for his or her subjects. Laozi understood that "the use of arms for conquest" inevitably led to a constant need to control one's subjects, since force tends to call forth force in return; subjugation creates rebellion. The last line of Poem 30 stresses the danger of going against the flow of life, the dao.

FROM

Dao De Jing (Tao Te Ching)

Translated by Witter Bynner

30: ONE WHO WOULD GUIDE A LEADER OF MEN

One who would guide a leader of men in the uses of life
Will warn him against the use of arms for conquest.
Weapons often turn upon the wielder,
An army's harvest is a waste of thorns,
Conscription of a multitude of men
Drains the next year dry.
A good general, daring to march, dares also to halt,
Will never press his triumph beyond need.

What he must do he does but not for glory,
What he must do he does but not for show,
What he must do he does but not for self;
He has done it because it had to be done,
Not from a hot head.
Let life ripen and then fall,
Force is not the way at all:
Deny the way° of life and you are dead. dao

Mencius (Mengzi)

c. 371–c. 288 B.C.E.

Very little is known about Mencius's life other than that he was a Chinese philosopher devoted to interpreting and teaching the wisdom tradition of Confucius (Kongfuzi). Mencius expanded on the philosophy of Confucius and contributed to its pervasive influence by adding to it a very optimistic view of human nature. At the center of Mencius's teachings was a belief that human beings were naturally good, known as *jên.* The cornerstone of goodness is compassion, a state in which a person cannot bear that another should suffer. According to Mencius, a person is responsible for showing benevolence toward others, a principle he extends to political policy and the idea of "compassionate government."

In this excerpt from his writings, Mencius says that motivation for ethical action comes from within; he argues that human sensitivity to the suffering of others should lead to a life of benevolence, duty, and wisdom. In contrast, other ethical systems locate the motivation for good behavior outside of the self, in the form of rewards and punishments.

FROM

Mencius

Translated by D. C. Lau

[Compassion]

6. Mencius said, "No man is devoid of a heart sensitive to the suffering of others. Such a sensitive heart was possessed by the Former Kings and this manifested itself in compassionate government. With such a sensitive heart behind compassionate government, it was as easy to rule the Empire as rolling it on your palm.

"My reason for saying that no man is devoid of a heart sensitive to the suffering

Tomb of Confucius, 551–479 B.C.E. *The Chinese philosopher Confucius had many followers, but perhaps the most well known was Mencius. With his emphasis on the natural goodness of human nature, or* jên, *Mencius helped extend and popularize traditional Confucianism. (Private Collection / Bridgeman Art Library)*

of others is this. Suppose a man were, all of a sudden, to see a young child on the verge of falling into a well. He would certainly be moved to compassion, not because he wanted to get in the good graces of the parents, nor because he wished to win the praise of his fellow villagers or friends, nor yet because he disliked the cry of the child. From this it can be seen that whoever is devoid of the heart of compassion is not human, whoever is devoid of the heart of shame is not human, whoever is devoid of the heart of courtesy and modesty is not human, and whoever is devoid of the heart of right and wrong is not human. The heart of compassion is the germ of benevolence; the heart of shame, of dutifulness; the heart of courtesy and modesty, of observance of the rites; the heart of right and wrong, of wisdom. Man has these four germs[1] just as he has four limbs. For a man possessing these four germs to deny his own potentialities is for him to cripple himself; for him to deny the potentialities of his prince is for him to cripple his prince. If a man is able to develop all these four germs that he possesses, it will be like a fire starting up or a spring coming through. When these are fully developed, he can take under this protection the whole realm within the Four Seas, but if he fails to develop them, he will not be able even to serve his parents."

[1] **four germs:** Natural capabilities.

7. Mencius said, "Is the maker of arrows really more unfeeling than the maker of armour? He is afraid lest he should fail to harm people, whereas the maker of armour is afraid lest he should fail to protect them. The case is similar with the sorcerer-doctor and the coffin-maker. For this reason one cannot be too careful in the choice of one's calling.

"Confucius said, "The best neighbourhood is where benevolence is to be found. Not to live in such a neighbourhood when one has the choice cannot by any means be considered wise." Benevolence is the high honour bestowed by Heaven and the peaceful abode of man. Not to be benevolent when nothing stands in the way is to show a lack of wisdom. A man neither benevolent nor wise, devoid of courtesy and dutifulness, is a slave. A slave ashamed of serving is like a maker of bows ashamed of making bows, or a maker of arrows ashamed of making arrows. If one is ashamed, there is no better remedy than to practice benevolence. Benevolence is like archery: an archer makes sure his stance is correct before letting fly the arrow, and if he fails to hit the mark, he does not hold it against his victor. He simply seeks the cause within himself."

Jainism

SIXTH CENTURY B.C.E.–FIRST CENTURY C.E.

The religion of Jainism was founded by Mahavira, a saint who established a religious community based on the extreme asceticism of Jain doctrines in the sixth century B.C.E. Although similar to Hinduism in many of its teachings, Jainism arose — like Buddhism — as a protest against the over-ritualized practices of Hinduism at the time. At present there are approximately two million Jains in the world.

The ultimate goal of Jainism is to escape the endless cycle of reincarnation imposed on every living thing, including humans. The core doctrine is *ahimsa,* Sanskrit for "nonharming" — practicing no harm in thought, word, or deed toward any living being. At one time extreme measures were taken, such as wearing cloth over the mouth so as not to kill any flying insects when inhaling. In one Jain legend, two merchants were fined their entire fortunes for killing fleas. Since it is impossible not to do some harm to living things during normal human activity, it was the practice of Jain saints to fast until they died in order to minimize their time of inflicting injury. This excerpt from the Jain text Uttaradhyayana Sutra is about the semilegendary king of Mithila, Nami, in northeastern India who severs his ties to the world to become a monk. Ordinarily, in the Jain and Buddhist traditions, such a choice brings relief to the participant; nevertheless the ascetic role of the monk is seen as a continuous struggle, equal in courage and commitment to the role of king.

Carving from the Vimala Sha Temple, 1032
The Jain temple at Vimala Sha is dedicated to Rishabhanatha, a Jain tirthankara, *or saint. (Mount Abu, Rajasthan, India / Dinodia Picture Agency, Bombay, India / Bridgeman Art Library)*

FROM

Uttaradhyayana Sutra

Translated by A. L. Basham

Two Ways of Life: King and Monk

With the fair ladies of his harem King Nami enjoyed pleasures like those of heaven,
And then he saw the light and gave up pleasure. . . .
In Mithilā, when the royal sage Nami left the world
And took to the life of a monk, there was a great uproar.
To the royal sage came the god Indra,[1] disguised as a brāhman,

[1] **Indra:** As king of the gods, the most important sky-deity in early Hinduism.

And spoke these words:
"There is fire and storm, your palace is burning!
Good sir, why don't you take care of your harem?"
Nami replied:
"Happy we dwell, happy we live, who call nothing whatever our own.
Though Mithilā burn, nothing of mine is burned!
When a monk has left his children and wives, and has given up worldly actions,
Nothing is pleasant to him, nothing unpleasant.
There is much that is good for the sage, the houseless monk
Set free from all ties, who knows himself to be alone."
Indra said:
"Build a wall, with gates and turrets,
And a moat and siege-engines;[2] then you will be a true warrior."
Nami replied:
"With faith as his city, hardship and self-control the bolt of the gate,
Patience its strong wall, impregnable in three ways.[3]
With effort as his bow, circumspection in walking its string,
And endurance as its tip, with truth he should bend his bow,
And pierce with the arrow of penance the mail of his enemy, karma.[4]
Thus the sage will conquer in battle, and be free [from samsāra]!"[5]
Indra said:
"By punishing thieves and burglars, pickpockets and robbers,
Keep the city in safety; then you will be a true warrior."
Nami replied:
"Often men punish unjustly,
And the guiltless are put in prison, the guilty set free."
Indra said:
"Bring under your yoke, O lord of men, those kings
Who do not bow before you; then you will be a true warrior."
Nami replied:
"Though a man conquer a thousand thousand brave foes in battle,
If he conquers only himself, this is his greatest conquest.

---

[2] **siege-engines:** Such as large catapults for storming fortress walls.

[3] **impregnable . . . three ways:** The three defenses are self-control in thought, word, and deed.

[4] **karma:** The moral cycle of cause and effect in one's life: All actions have consequences, if not in this life, then in the next.

[5] **samsāra:** The cycle of one life after another that results from an attachment to the world of one's senses.

Battle with yourself! Of what use is fighting others?
He who conquers himself by himself will win happiness." . . .

Throwing off his disguise, and taking his real shape,
Indra bowed before him and praised him with sweet words:
"Well done! You have conquered anger!
Well done! You have vanquished pride!
Well done! You have banished delusion!
Well done! You have put down craving!
Hurrah for your firmness!
Hurrah for your gentleness!
Hurrah for your perfect forbearance!
Hurrah for your perfect freedom! . . ."
Thus act the enlightened, the learned, the discerning.
They turn their backs on pleasure, like Nami the royal sage.

ASHOKA

C. 292–C. 232 B.C.E.

Early in the third century B.C.E., the Maurya empire was created through treaties and conquest, the first empire to include all of India. Upon the death of King Bindusara, a struggle for the throne ensued among his sons, and after four years of conflict, Ashoka emerged as the victor, around 269 B.C.E. Tradition has it that Ashoka succeeded because he was ruthless, having killed ninety-nine brothers. After several years of rule, King Ashoka went to war in the eastern province of India, in what became known as the Kalinga. The bloodshed and lives wasted in that war brought about a profound change in the sovereign: Ashoka converted to Buddhism and promoted a reign of peace and kindness, rejecting warfare for the rest of his rule.

The account in *Asokavadana,* which survived as an inscription carved into rock, was intended as a body of teachings for the populace. The inscription not only describes Ashoka's conversion in his own words but also displays the extraordinary tolerance that Ashoka showed to other religions. He believed that his subjects could learn from the essential doctrine common to all religions: *dharma* in Sanskrit, *dhamma* in Pali (human and cosmic lawfulness).

FROM

Asokavadana

Translated by John Strong

When he had been consecrated eight years the Beloved of the Gods, the king Piyadassi,[1] conquered Kaliṅga. A hundred and fifty thousand people were deported, a hundred thousand were killed and many times that number perished. Afterwards, now that Kaliṅga was annexed, the Beloved of the Gods[2] very earnestly practised *Dhamma,* desired *Dhamma,* and taught *Dhamma.*[3] On conquering Kaliṅga the Beloved of the Gods felt remorse, for, when an independent country is conquered the slaughter, death, and deportation of the people is extremely grievous to the Beloved of the Gods, and weighs heavily on his mind. What is even more deplorable to the Beloved of the Gods, is that those who dwell there, whether brahmans, *śramaṇas,*[4] or those of other sects, or householders who show obedience to their superiors, obedience to mother and father, obedience to their teachers and behave well and devotedly towards their friends, acquaintances, colleagues, relatives, slaves, and servants—all suffer violence, murder, and separation from their loved ones. Even those who are fortunate to have escaped, and whose love is undiminished [by the brutalizing effect of war], suffer from the misfortunes of their friends, acquaintances, colleagues, and relatives. This participation of all men in suffering, weighs heavily on the mind of the Beloved of the Gods. Except among the Greeks, there is no land where the religious orders of brahmans and *śramaṇas* are not to be found, and there is no land anywhere where men do not support one sect or another. Today if a hundredth or a thousandth part of those people who were killed or died or were deported when Kaliṅga was annexed were to suffer similarly, it would weigh heavily on the mind of the Beloved of the Gods.

The Beloved of the Gods believes that one who does wrong should be forgiven as far as it is possible to forgive him. And the Beloved of the Gods conciliates the forest tribes of his empire, but he warns them that he has power even in his remorse, and he asks them to repent, lest they be killed. For the Beloved of the Gods wishes that all beings should be unharmed, self-controlled, calm in mind, and gentle. . . .

The Beloved of the Gods, the king Piyadassi, honours all sects and both ascetics and laymen, with gifts and various forms of recognition. But the Beloved of the Gods does not consider gifts or honour to be as important as the advancement of the essential doctrine of all sects. This progress of the essential doctrine takes many

[1] **the king Piyadassi:** One of the royal names for Ashoka meaning "of gracious appearance."

[2] **Beloved of the Gods:** Ashoka.

[3] ***Dhamma:*** The norms of behavior consistent with the lawful order of the universe.

[4] ***śramaṇas:*** A category of Brahmin priests.

forms, but its basis is the control of one's speech, so as not to extoll one's own sect or disparage another's on unsuitable occasions, or at least to do so only mildly on certain occasions. On each occasion one should honour another man's sect, for by doing so one increases the influence of one's own sect and benefits that of the other man; while by doing otherwise one diminishes the influence of one's own sect and harms the other man's. Again, whosoever honours his own sect or disparages that of another man, wholly out of devotion to his own, with a view to showing it in a favourable light, harms his own sect even more seriously. Therefore, concord is to be commended, so that men may hear one another's principles and obey them. This is the desire of the Beloved of the Gods, that all sects should be well-informed, and should teach that which is good, and that everywhere their adherents should be told, 'The Beloved of the Gods does not consider gifts or honour to be as important as the progress of the essential doctrine of all sects.' Many are concerned with this matter—the officers of *Dhamma,* the women's officers, the managers of the state farms, and other classes of officers. The result of this is the increased influence of one's own sect and glory to *Dhamma*. . . .

The Beloved of the Gods, Piyadassi the king, has had this inscription on *Dhamma* engraved. Here, no living thing having been killed, is to be sacrificed; nor is the holding of a festival permitted. For the Beloved of the Gods, the king Piyadassi, sees much evil in festivals, though there are some of which the Beloved of the Gods, the king Piyadassi, approves.

Formerly in the kitchens of the Beloved of the Gods, the king Piyadassi, many hundreds of thousands of living animals were killed daily for meat. But now, at the time of writing this inscription on *Dhamma,* only three animals are killed, two peacocks and a deer, and the deer not invariably. Even these three animals will not be killed in future. . . .

Everywhere in the empire of the Beloved of the Gods, the king Piyadassi, and even in the lands on its frontiers . . . the two medical services of the Beloved of the Gods, the king Piyadassi, have been provided. These consist of the medical care of man and the care of animals. Medicinal herbs whether useful to man or to beast, have been brought and planted wherever they did not grow; similarly, roots and fruit have been brought and planted wherever they did not grow. Along the roads wells have been dug and trees planted for the use of men and beasts.

Thus speaks the Beloved of the Gods, Asoka: I have been a Buddhist layman for more than two and a half years, but for a year I did not make much progress. Now for more than a year I have drawn closer to the Order and have become more ardent. The gods, who in India up to this time did not associate with men, now mingle with them, and this is the result of my efforts. Moreover this is not something to be obtained only by the great, but it is also open to the humble, if they are earnest and they can even reach heaven easily. This is the reason for this announcement—that both humble and great should make progress and that the neighbouring peoples also should know that the progress is lasting. And this investment will increase and increase abundantly, and increase to half as much again. . . .

PLUTARCH
C. 46–C. 120 C.E.

Plutarch was a Greek biographer who taught moral lessons about leadership and character through his portraits of Greek and Roman political and military heroes in *Parallel Lives.* In *Moralia,* Plutarch writes on a wide variety of subjects, including marriage, children, and anger, as well as Alexander the Great, of whom he paints an extremely flattering portrait, thus contributing to what might be called the legend of Alexander. Plutarch attributes to Alexander, whom he says was both a brilliant military commander *and* a visionary, the belief that behind the differences of race and culture human beings are essentially the same and should be treated accordingly. The legend of Alexander in the West is an interesting complement to the legend of King Ashoka in the East.

Alexander the Great, second to first century B.C.E. *Alexander III of Macedon (356–323 B.C.E.) is considered one of the top military commanders of all time. Under his leadership the Greek empire extended from the Mediterranean to India. His life and legend captured the world's imagination, even that of the Romans, as is evident in this highly idealized mosaic portrait. (The Art Archive/ Archaeological Museum, Naples/ Dagli Orti (A))*

FROM

Moralia

Translated by Frank Cole Babbitt

[On the Fortune of Alexander]

If, then, philosophers take the greatest pride in civilizing and rendering adaptable the intractable and untutored elements in human character, and if Alexander has been shown to have changed the savage natures of countless tribes, it is with good reason that he should be regarded as a very great philosopher.

6. Moreover, the much-admired *Republic* of Zeno,[1] the founder of the Stoic sect, may be summed up in this one main principle: that all the inhabitants of this world of ours should not live differentiated by their respective rules of justice into separate cities and communities, but that we should consider all men to be of one community and one polity, and that we should have a common life and an order common to us all, even as a herd that feeds together and shares the pasturage of a common field. This Zeno wrote, giving shape to a dream or, as it were, shadowy picture of a well-ordered and philosophic commonwealth; but it was Alexander who gave effect to the idea. For Alexander did not follow Aristotle's advice to treat the Greeks as if he were their leader, and other peoples as if he were their master; to have regard for the Greeks as for friends and kindred, but to conduct himself toward other peoples as though they were plants or animals; for to do so would have been to cumber his leadership with numerous battles and banishments and festering seditions. But, as he believed that he came as a heaven-sent governor to all, and as a mediator for the whole world, those whom he could not persuade to unite with him, he conquered by force of arms, and he brought together into one body all men everywhere, uniting and mixing in one great loving-cup, as it were, men's lives, their characters, their marriages, their very habits of life. He bade them all consider as their fatherland the whole inhabited earth, as their stronghold and protection his camp, as akin to them all good men, and as foreigners only the wicked; they should not distinguish between Grecian and foreigner by Grecian cloak and targe, or scimitar and jacket; but the distinguishing mark of the Grecian should be seen in virtue, and that of the foreigner in iniquity; clothing and food, marriage and manner of life they should regard as common to all, being blended into one by ties of blood and children.

7. [. . .] But methinks I would gladly have been a witness of that fair and holy marriage-rite, when he brought together in one golden-canopied tent an hundred Persian brides and an hundred Macedonian and Greek bridegrooms, united at a common hearth and board. He himself, crowned with garlands, was the first to raise the marriage hymn as though he were singing a song of truest friendship over the union of the two greatest and most mighty peoples; for he, of one maid the bridegroom, and at the same time of all the brides the escort, as a father and sponsor

---

[1] **Zeno** (334?–261? B.C.E.): The Greek founder of Stoicism.

united them in the bonds of wedlock. Indeed at this sight I should have cried out for joy, "O dullard Xerxes,[2] stupid fool that spent so much fruitless toil to bridge the Hellespont! This is the way that wise kings join Asia with Europe; it is not by beams nor rafts, nor by lifeless and unfeeling bonds, but by the ties of lawful love and chaste nuptials and mutual joy in children that they join the nations together."

8. Considering carefully this order of affairs, Alexander did not favour the Median raiment, but preferred the Persian,[3] for it was much more simple than the Median. Since he deprecated the unusual and theatrical varieties of foreign adornment, such as the tiara and the full-sleeved jacket and trousers, he wore a composite dress adapted from both Persian and Macedonian fashion, as Eratosthenes[4] has recorded. As a philosopher what he wore was a matter of indifference, but as sovereign of both nations and benevolent king he strove to acquire the goodwill of the conquered by showing respect for their apparel, so that they might continue constant in loving the Macedonians as rulers, and might not feel hate toward them as enemies. [. . .] For he did not overrun Asia like a robber nor was he minded to tear and rend it, as if it were booty and plunder bestowed by unexpected good fortune, after the manner in which Hannibal later descended upon Italy, or as earlier the Treres descended upon Ionia and the Scythians upon Media. But Alexander desired to render all upon earth subject to one law of reason and one form of government and to reveal all men as one people, and to this purpose he made himself conform. But if the deity that sent down Alexander's soul into this world of ours had not recalled him quickly, one law would govern all mankind, and they all would look toward one rule of justice as though toward a common source of light. But as it is, that part of the world which has not looked upon Alexander has remained without sunlight.

[2] **Xerxes:** In the year 330 B.C.E., Alexander the Great defeated Darius, the Persian king, and extended the Greek empire into northern India. Xerxes was an earlier Persian king (r. 485–465 B.C.E.) who had burned down Athens but then was defeated by the Greeks at sea.

[3] **Median raiment . . . Persian:** Media was an ancient kingdom that became part of Iran; some of Alexander's soldiers resented his use of Persian dress.

[4] **Eratosthenes:** Lived sometime around 200 B.C.E.; the head of the library in Alexandria, Egypt, that had the largest collection of writings in the Western world, approximately 700,000 scrolls.

SUETONIUS

75–160 C.E.

Suetonius's *Lives of the Twelve Caesars* covers the Roman rulers from Julius Caesar to Domitian. As secretary to the emperor Hadrian, who ruled Rome from 117 to 138 C.E., Suetonius had access to official records and was privy to the conversations of important people. Although Suetonius seems to get personally involved with his material and therefore is not always objective, his collection of facts and anecdotes about the personal lives of the emperors is unique. Suetonius's treatment of Julius Caesar, who ruled Rome for only five years, 49–44 B.C.E., contributes to the conclusion that the emperor was a most unusual ruler whose talent for running an empire went far beyond military conquest and might. In addition to correcting the official calendar, Julius Caesar was committed to public projects that would enhance the beauty and power of Rome, as recounted in this excerpt.

Bust of Julius Caesar
One of the most interesting and prominent of the Roman emperors, Julius Caesar ruled Rome for only five years before he was assassinated by a group of nobles in the Senate. He was known not only as a great conqueror but as an able administrator as well. (Alinari / Art Resource, NY)

FROM

The Lives of the Twelve Caesars

Translated by Alexander Thomson

Julius Caesar

His thoughts were now fully employed from day to day on variety of great projects for the embellishment and improvement of the city, as well as for guarding and extending the bounds of the empire. In the first place, he meditated the construction of a temple to Mars, which should exceed in grandeur every thing of that kind in the world. For this purpose, he intended to fill up the lake on which he had entertained the people with the spectacle of a sea-fight. He also projected a most spacious theater adjacent to the Tarpeian mount; and also proposed to reduce the civil law to a reasonable compass, and out of that immense and undigested mass of statutes to extract the best and most necessary parts into a few books; to make as large a collection as possible of works in the Greek and Latin languages, for the public use; the province of providing and putting them in proper order being assigned to Marcus Varro. He intended likewise to drain the Pomptine marshes, to cut a channel for the discharge of the waters of the lake Fucinus, to form a road from the Adriatic through the ridge of the Apennine to the Tiber; to make a cut through the isthmus of Corinth, to reduce the Dacians, who had over-run Pontus and Thrace, within their proper limits, and then to make war upon the Parthians, through the Lesser Armenia, but not to risk a general engagement with them, until he had made some trial of their prowess in war. But in the midst of all his undertakings and projects, he was carried off by death; before I speak of which, it may not be improper to give an account of his person, dress, and manners, together with what relates to his pursuits, both civil and military.

It is said that he was tall, of a fair complexion, round limbed, rather full faced, with eyes black and piercing; and that he enjoyed excellent health, except toward the close of his life, when he was subject to sudden fainting-fits, and disturbance in his sleep. He was likewise twice seized with the falling sickness while engaged in active service. He was so nice in the care of his person, that he not only kept the hair of his head closely cut and had his face smoothly shaved, but even caused the hair on other parts of the body to be plucked out by the roots, a practice for which some persons rallied him. His baldness gave him much uneasiness, having often found himself upon that account exposed to the jibes of his enemies. He therefore used to bring forward the hair from the crown of his head; and of all the honors conferred upon him by the senate and people, there was none which he either accepted or used with greater pleasure, than the right of wearing constantly a laurel crown. It is said that he was particular in his dress. For he used the Latus Clavus[1] with fringes about the wrists, and always had it girded about him, but rather loosely. This circumstance gave origin to the expression of Sulla, who often advised the nobles to beware of "the ill-girt boy." [. . .]

He was perfect in the use of arms, an accomplished rider, and able to endure fatigue beyond all belief. On a march, he used to go at the head of his troops, sometimes on horseback, but oftener on foot, with his head bare in all kinds of weather. He would travel post in a light carriage without baggage, at the rate of a hundred miles a day; and if he was stopped by floods in the rivers, he swam across, or floated on skins inflated with wind, so that he often anticipated intelligence of his movements.

In his expeditions, it is difficult to say whether his caution or his daring was most conspicuous. He never marched his army by roads which were exposed to ambuscades, without having previously examined the nature of the ground by his scouts. Nor did he cross over to Britain, before he had carefully examined, in person,

[1] **Latus Clavus:** A broad stripe of purple worn on tunics by Senators.

the navigation, the harbors, and the most convenient point of landing in the island. When intelligence was brought to him of the siege of his camp in Germany, he made his way to his troops, through the enemy's stations, in a Gaulish dress. He crossed the sea from Brundisium to Dyrrachium, in the winter, through the midst of the enemy's fleets; and the troops, under orders to join him, being slow in their movements, notwithstanding repeated messages to hurry them, but to no purpose, he at last went privately, and alone, aboard a small vessel in the night time, with his head muffled up; nor did he make himself known, or suffer the master to put about, although the wind blew strong against them, until they were ready to sink.

Flavius Josephus

37–C. 100 C.E.

Flavius Josephus (Joseph ben Mattias), born into a Jewish priestly family in Judaea, was a well-educated man. As a Pharisee he preserved Jewish law while accommodating Rome politically, a strategy reinforced by a visit to Rome in 64 C.E. After witnessing firsthand Rome's military strengths, he devoted himself to preventing a Palestinian insurrection. When political revolt nonetheless occurred, led by Jewish extremists known as Zealots, Josephus was captured by the Romans under Vespasian and subsequently acted as a mediator between Romans and Jews.

When Vespasian was made emperor by the army in 69 C.E., Josephus retired to a secure living in Rome and wrote. His *Antiquities of the Jews* (c. 93–94 C.E.) covers the historical period between the creation of the world and the war with Rome. *The Jewish War* is an eyewitness, pro-Roman account of the defeat of Jewish rebels and the destruction of the Jerusalem Temple in 70 C.E. It took four years for the Romans to crush the Jewish revolt. The emperor Augustus (r. 27 B.C.E.–14 C.E.) hadn't forced matters with the Jews in Palestine, who refused to worship the emperor, but the Zealots fomented the rebellion that was finally subdued on September 7, 70, by the emperor Vespasian and his son, Titus. Titus ordered the complete destruction of the capital city, Jerusalem. Great numbers of people were killed and some one hundred thousand were taken as slaves to the mines of Egypt. Titus decided that the remaining Jews could not be allowed to administer their own internal affairs, as had been the policy for more than one hundred years. All marks of Judaism were erased from the city; the high priesthood was abolished. Similar to the Assyrian treatment of Samaria in the eighth century B.C.E., a colony of Roman citizens were imported to settle Jerusalem. Josephus's fine writing imparts the human dimension of this major event in Israel's history.

FROM

The Jewish War

Translated by G. A. Williamson

[The Destruction of Jerusalem]

As the legions charged in, neither persuasion nor threat could check their impetuosity: passion alone was in command. Crowded together round the entrances many were trampled by their friends, many fell among the still hot and smoking ruins of the colonnades and died as miserably as the defeated. As they neared the Sanctuary they pretended not even to hear Caesar's commands and urged the men in front to throw in more firebrands. The partisans were no longer in a position to help; everywhere was slaughter and flight. Most of the victims were peaceful citizens, weak and unarmed, butchered wherever they were caught. Round the Altar the heap of corpses grew higher and higher, while down the Sanctuary[1] steps poured a river of blood and the bodies of those killed at the top slithered to the bottom. The soldiers were like men possessed and there was no holding them, nor was there any arguing with the fire. Caesar therefore led his staff inside the building and viewed the Holy Place of the Sanctuary with its furnishings, which went far beyond the accounts circulating in foreign countries, and fully justified their splendid reputation in our own. The flames were not yet effecting an entry from any direction but were feeding on the chambers built round the Sanctuary; so realizing that there was still time to save the glorious edifice, Titus dashed out and by personal efforts strove to persuade his men to put out the fire, instructing Liberalius, a centurion of his bodyguard of spearmen, to lay his staff across the shoulders of any who disobeyed.[2] But their respect for Caesar and their fear of the centurion's staff were powerless against their fury, their detestation of the Jews, and an uncontrollable lust for battle. Most of them were also spurred on by the expectation of loot, being convinced that the interior was bursting with money and seeing that everything outside was of gold. But they were forestalled by one of those who had gone in. When Caesar dashed out to restrain the troops, that man pushed a firebrand into the hinges of the gate. Then from within a flame suddenly shot up, Caesar and his staff withdrew, and those outside were free to start what fires they liked. Thus the Sanctuary was set on fire in defiance of Caesar's wishes.

Grief might well be bitter for the destruction of the most wonderful edifice ever seen or heard of, both for its size and construction and for the lavish perfection of detail and the glory of its holy places; yet we find very real comfort in the thought that Fate is inexorable, not only towards living beings but also towards buildings and sites. We may wonder too at the exactness of the cycle of Fate: she kept, as I said, to

---

[1] **Sanctuary:** Possibly the Holy of Holies in the Temple.

[2] **Titus dashed . . . disobeyed:** Josephus attempts to absolve Titus of responsibility for the destruction of the Temple.

the very month and day which centuries before had seen the Sanctuary burnt by the Babylonians.[3] From its first foundation by King Solomon to its present destruction, which occurred in the second year of Vespasian's reign, was a period of 1,130 years, 7 months and 15 days; from its rebuilding in the second year of King Cyrus, for which Haggai was responsible, to its capture under Vespasian was 639 years and 45 days.[4]

While the Sanctuary was burning, looting went on right and left and all who were caught were put to the sword. There was no pity for age, no regard for rank; little children and old men, laymen and priests alike were butchered; every class was held in the iron embrace of war, whether they defended themselves or cried for mercy. Through the roar of the flames as they swept relentlessly on could be heard the groans of the falling: such were the height of the hill and the vastness of the blazing edifice that the entire city seemed to be on fire, while as for the noise, nothing could be imagined more shattering or more horrifying. There was the war-cry of the Roman legions as they converged; the yells of the partisans encircled with fire and sword; the panic flight of the people cut off above into the arms of the enemy, and their shrieks as the end approached. The cries from the hill were answered from the crowded streets; and now many who were wasted with hunger and beyond speech found strength to moan and wail when they saw the Sanctuary in flames. Back from Peraea and the mountains round about came the echo in a thunderous bass.

Yet more terrible than the din were the sights that met the eye. The Temple Hill, enveloped in flames from top to bottom, appeared to be boiling up from its very roots; yet the sea of flame was nothing to the ocean of blood, or the companies of killers to the armies of killed: nowhere could the ground be seen between the corpses, and the soldiers climbed over heaps of bodies as they chased the fugitives. The terrorist horde pushed the Romans back, and by a violent struggle burst through into the outer court of the Temple and from there into the City, the few surviving members of the public taking refuge on the outer colonnade. Some of the priests at first tore up from the Sanctuary the spikes with their lead sockets and threw them at the Romans. Then as they were no better off and the flames were leaping towards them, they retired to the wall, which was twelve feet wide, and stayed there. However, two men of note, in a position either to save their lives by going over to the Romans or to face with the others whatever came their way, threw themselves into the fire and were burnt to ashes with the Sanctuary—Meirus, son of Belgas, and Joseph, son of Dalaeus.

The Romans, judging it useless to spare the outbuildings now that the Sanctuary was in flames, set fire to them all—what remained of the colonnades and all the gates except two, one on the east end, the other on the south, both of which they later demolished. They also burnt the treasuries which housed huge sums of money, huge quantities of clothing, and other precious things; here, in fact, all the wealth of the Jews was piled up, for the rich had dismantled their houses and brought the contents here for safe keeping. Next they came to the last surviving colonnade of the outer

[3] **centuries before . . . Babylonians:** In 586 B.C.E.

[4] **1,130 years . . . 45 days:** Actually the first period was about 1,040 years and the second 589. (Editors' note.)

court. On this women and children and a mixed crowd of citizens had found a refuge—6,000 in all. Before Caesar could reach a decision about them or instruct his officers, the soldiers, carried away by their fury, fired the colonnade from below; as a result some flung themselves out of the flames to their death, others perished in the blaze: of that vast number there escaped not one. Their destruction was due to a false prophet who that very day had declared to the people in the City that God commanded them to go up into the Temple to receive the signs of their deliverance. A number of hireling prophets had been put up in recent days by the party chiefs to deceive the people by exhorting them to await help from God, and so to reduce the number of deserters and buoy up with hope those who were above fear and anxiety. Man is readily persuaded in adversity: when the deceiver actually promises deliverance from the miseries that envelop him, then the sufferer becomes the willing slave of hope. So it was that the unhappy people were beguiled at that stage by cheats and false messengers of God, while the unmistakable portents that foreshadowed the coming desolation they treated with indifference and incredulity, disregarding God's warnings as if they were moonstruck, blind and senseless. First a star stood over the city, very like a broadsword, and a comet that remained a whole year. Then before the revolt and the movement to war, while the people were assembling for the Feast of Unleavened Bread, on the 8th of Xanthicos at 3 a.m. so bright a light shone round the Altar and the Sanctuary that it might have been midday. This lasted half an hour. The inexperienced took it for a good omen, but the sacred scribes at once gave an interpretation which the event proved right. During the same feast a cow brought by someone to be sacrificed gave birth to a lamb in the middle of the Temple courts, while at midnight it was observed that the East Gate of the inner court had opened of its own accord—a gate made of bronze and so solid that every evening twenty strong men were required to shut it; it was fastened with iron-bound bars and secured by bolts which were lowered a long way into a threshold fashioned from a single slab of stone. The temple-guards ran with the news to the Captain,[5] who came up and by a great effort managed to shut it. This like the other seemed to the laity to be the best of omens: had not God opened to them the gate of happiness? But the learned perceived that the security of the Sanctuary was dissolving of its own accord, and that the opening of the gate was a gift to the enemy; and they admitted in their hearts that the sign was a portent of desolation.

A few days after the Feast, on the 21st of Artemisios,[6] a supernatural apparition was seen, too amazing to be believed. What I have to relate would, I suppose, have been dismissed as an invention, had it not been vouched for by eyewitnesses and followed by disasters that bore out the signs. Before sunset there were seen in the sky, over the whole country, chariots and regiments in arms speeding through the clouds and encircling the towns. [. . .]

[5] **the Captain:** Of the Temple.

[6] **the 21st of Artemisios:** Five or six weeks later, if the date is correct. (Editors' note.)

Buddhist Texts

FOURTH CENTURY B.C.E.–FIRST CENTURY C.E.

Two great religions were born in India in the sixth century B.C.E., Buddhism and Jainism. **Buddhism**, founded by Siddhartha Gautama, the Buddha (563–483 B.C.E.), and **Jainism**,[1] started by Mahavira (539–468 B.C.E.), arose during a time of great ferment and change in the northeastern provinces of Bihar and Uttar Pradesh. Rival princes and clans in northern India were warring at a time when old tribal structures were breaking down. Simultaneously, urban centers were developing along with a growing middle class. Conditions were ripe for a rebellion against **Hinduism**, the entrenched religious system of the priestly caste, the **Brahmins**,[2] which was becoming more and more rigid in terms of social caste, religious ritual, and the hierarchy of privilege. The gap between rich and poor, literate and illiterate, widened. A sense of hopelessness and dissatisfaction spread among ordinary people.

Both Jainism and Buddhism came into being as part of a heretic tradition of sages who challenged the **Vedic** tradition behind Hinduism, offering alternatives to urban merchants by shifting the dialogue from social class to personal conduct. Both Buddhism and Jainism promoted a new ethic of compassion—noninjury to all living things—and salvation from ***samsara***, the endless round of death and birth, through understanding the basic truths of the universe. In effect they taught that knowledge, the disciplined practice of meditation and learning, and the path of austerity could lead directly to ***moksha***, or identification with the universal spirit or world soul; this approach bypassed the role of the priests—an old story in world religion.

Buddhism has had an enormous influence on art, architecture, literature, and institutions for some two millennia. The image of the Buddha as a spiritual being, especially, continues to attract admirers, followers, and imitators. The texts that follow describe both the Buddha's life and his early teachings. A famous biography of the Buddha, written by Ashvaghosha, a Buddhist poet of the first century C.E., covers the major events of the holy man's life. The Buddha's "Sermon at Benares" contains the basic truths of his path to salvation. Another selection deals with the proper mental attitude required for following his recommendations. The Buddha's last instructions before he died reduced his teachings to very simple but extremely difficult to follow lessons. The Buddha was a

[Buddha] was undoubtedly one of the greatest rationalists of all time, resembling in this respect no one as much as Socrates. Every problem that came his way was automatically subjected to the cold, analytical glare of his intellect. . . . The remarkable fact, however, was the way this objective, critical component of his character was balanced by a Franciscan tenderness so strong as to have caused his message to be subtitled "a religion of infinite compassion."

– Huston Smith, philosopher, 1958

---

[1] **Buddhism . . . Jainism:** Buddhism spread throughout the world and has grown to about 400 million followers. Jainism, derived from the word *Jina,* meaning "conqueror," advocates overcoming all human passions and practicing *ahimsa,* or noninjury to all living creatures. There are between one and two million Jains in India.

[2] **Brahmins:** Members of the priestly class in the caste system of India; the other three original classes were *Kshatriya* (warriors and administrators), *Vaishya* (merchants, farmers, producers), and *Shudra* (laborers).

www For a quiz on Buddhist texts, see *World Literature Online* at bedfordstmartins .com/worldlit.

unique blend of head and heart, whose rational approach to problem-solving resembled that of the Greek philosopher Socrates.[3]

Beginning Life as a Prince. Typically the biographies of great religious prophets are written only after they die, when fame and spiritual fervor become intertwined with their historical legacy. As with nearly all founders of world religions in the ancient world—Moses, Zoroaster, Jesus, Laozi, and Mohammed—the Buddha's life story has become a confusing mix of myth, folklore, beliefs, and history. The earliest written accounts of Buddha's life are dated about 200 years after his death.

Siddhartha Gautama was born in 563 B.C.E. at Lumbini, near the town of Kapilavatthu in the Himalayan foothills of southern Nepal, about a hundred miles north of Benares. His father was King or Rajah **Shuddhodana** of the **Sakya** Clan, of the ***Kshatriya,*** or warrior, caste. Later in life Siddhartha would be called, among several other names, Sakyamuni, meaning "the sage of the Sakyas." Siddhartha's mother was Maya, described by Ashvaghosha in the excerpt presented here as pure and immaculate. According to legend, Siddhartha was born miraculously: He descended from the Tushita heaven,[4] entered the womb of his mother, Maya, as a wondrous white elephant, and was born painlessly from her side. He came forth "Like the sun bursting from a cloud in the morning . . . with his rays which dispelled the darkness."

shoo-DOH-duh-nuh; SAH-kyuh; KSHUH-tree-yuh

The Four Signs. A wise man told Siddhartha's father that his son would be either a king or a wandering holy man. His father wanted Siddhartha to be a king, so he raised his son in great physical comfort, shielding him from human suffering and any other unpleasant reality. Siddhartha eventually married Yashodhara, and together they had a son, Rahula. One day, however, at age twenty-nine, the prince desired to go outside the palace gates. There he met four men who changed his life: an old man, a sick man, a dead man, and an ascetic—a man who had renounced the world. This series of encounters, known as the "Four Signs," represented a time of awakening for Siddhartha, who had known only the sensuous pleasures provided by his father. He learned about the reality of suffering and death, and realized that he would not be young and beautiful forever. He left the luxurious life of the palace, and his wife and child, and ventured into the world to find answers to questions raised by his awareness of mortality.

The Path of Asceticism. Following the path taken by the ascetic, or holy man, Siddhartha tried sitting for long periods of time in yoga postures meditating. Dissatisfied, he turned to fasting and disciplining his body. After coming close to death, he took food and seated himself beneath a fig tree (a *ficus religiosa*) at Bodh Gaya, sixty miles south of

[3] **Socrates:** Socrates (469–399 B.C.E.), a philosopher of ancient Greece, examined common knowledge with a step-by-step questioning of accepted truths. See p. 1083.

[4] **Tushita heaven:** The heaven of all the buddhas who are awaiting rebirth on earth.

Siddhartha Goes to School, second–fourth century
The Buddha began life as a privileged member of the Indian aristocracy. Here he is shown in relief being escorted to school by various servants and retainers. Siddhartha's early years were extremely sheltered, as his father tried to protect him from the harsh realities of the world. (Victoria and Albert Museum, London / Art Resource, NY)

Patna and one of the four holy places of Buddhism. It was here that he made his famous pronouncement: "I will not rise from this position on the earth until I have obtained my utmost aim."

Enlightenment. He sat under the "Bodhi tree" (*bodhi* is Sanskrit for "enlightenment") for forty-nine days. (According to legend the original tree was destroyed by the Bengali king Shashanka in the seventh century. An offshoot of the tree still exists today beside the Mahabodhi Temple in Bodh Gaya.) After being attacked by Mara, the Buddhist demon, who tempted him with sexuality and threats of physical harm, Siddhartha learned about the condition of all beings, the causes of birth and rebirth. He recalled his own previous existences, patterns of cause and effect. He understood what caused human pain and how to alleviate it. When the next morning came, the ***BODHISATTVA***—someone en route to buddhahood who assists others—at age thirty-five was enlightened. He had attained perfect illumination. Just as Jesus of Nazareth became the Christ—meaning the "anointed one"—so Siddhartha Gautama became the Buddha—the "awakened one." There are ten titles that the Buddha used for himself and other buddhas, one of which is **TATHAGATA**, Sanskrit for "he who has arrived at the truth."

[Buddhism] has the honorable distinction of being the most tolerant, in theory and history, of the world-faiths.

– E. ROYSTON PIKE, theologian, 1958

Gautama the Buddha seems to have combined in high degree two qualities that are rarely found together and each of which is rarely exemplified in high degree. On the one hand he was a man of rich and responsive human sympathy, of unfailing patience, strength, gentleness, and good will . . . On the other hand, he was a thinker, of unexcelled philosophic power. . . . Buddhism is the only one of the great religions of the world that is consciously and frankly based on a systematic rational analysis of the problem of life, and of the way to its solution.

– E. A. Burtt, philosopher, 1955

The Wandering Teacher and Preacher. Instead of entering NIRVANA[5] immediately, Buddha decided to remain on earth to teach others his new understanding of human suffering and thus lead them to salvation.[6] He preached his first sermon on the fundamentals of what became Buddhism north of Benares at Sarnath, in a deer park at Isipatana, to five ascetics who became his first disciples. There he proclaimed the Middle Way, or Path, a road between the extremes of sensuous indulgence and senseless mortification. Although Buddhism takes various forms in various countries, all varieties preserve the same basic doctrines, which are psychological rather than theological. The Four Noble Truths are: Suffering and pain exist (old age, sickness, death, etc.); pain and suffering is caused by our attachments or desires; one can become freed from suffering; and freedom can be gained by following the Eightfold Path. The Eightfold Path is a practical, day-by-day plan for self-improvement: Right Belief,[7] Right Resolve, Right Speech, Right Behavior, Right Occupation, Right Effort, Right Mindfulness, and Right Concentration. The core teachings also include an injunction against killing, forgiveness of enemies, the importance of motive in ethics, and tolerance.

The Buddha then spent forty-five years wandering and teaching, spending time in monasteries donated by wealthy followers to his *SANGHA*, or communities of monks. He had indeed become the wandering holy man, not a king, the two possible destinies divined as possibilities for him in his childhood. After a last message to his followers to work out their salvation with diligence, Buddha died in the arms of his beloved disciple Ananda at the age of eighty. He was cremated, and his ashes were distributed amongst eight shrines, or *stupas*.

Buddhism Spreads throughout Asia. The Buddha's teachings spread throughout India, and for a millennium they were favored among the ruling classes. One of Buddhism's high points occurred during the reign of the emperor Ashoka (c. 273–c. 232 B.C.E.), the third ruler of the Maurya dynasty (c. 322–c. 185 B.C.E.), which had unified India for the first time. Ashoka converted to Buddhism, erected monasteries, and sent missionaries to Syria, Egypt, and Greece. With its prosperity and the flourishing of art, Ashoka's reign was considered a golden age in ancient India. After hundreds of years, Buddhism gradually died out in India, however, especially after the Muslim invasion in the twelfth century. In the meantime it had spread into Sri Lanka, Burma, and Indonesia in the form of Hinayana or Theravada[8] (School of the Elders) and into China, Japan,

[5] **Nirvana:** From *nirva,* meaning "to blow," thus an extinguishing of the individual flame of life. In both Hinduism and Buddhism, Nirvana represents a release from the endless transmigration of the soul. In Hinduism, Nirvana is a reunion with Brahma; Buddhism sees Nirvana as a state of blissful nonbeing.

[6] **salvation:** The *bodhisattva* remains on earth to lead others to salvation.

[7] **Right Belief:** The Sanskrit word for *right* is *samma,* which can mean both right as opposed to wrong and right as in completed or perfected.

[8] **Hinayana or Theravada:** Basic to this branch of Buddhism is a concern with becoming enlightened personally. The principal guide is one's mind or understanding, not ritual or prayer. Buddha is a saint and teacher.

Korea, Nepal, and Tibet in the form of Mahayana[9] (Great Career or Great Vehicle). Through time Buddhism has proved to be unimpeded by cultural lines, diverse environments, and changing world conditions.

The enduring influence of Buddhism has extended to some 400 million Buddhists worldwide. Some consider it to be a form of meditation or yoga, and Buddhist meditation centers have sprung up in all parts of the world. Some value Buddhism's ethical system and relate it to ecology. Still others view it as a cosmology, a way of viewing the world. Although originally it was antiauthoritarian, antiritualistic, and nontheistic, some followers nevertheless view Buddhist doctrine as a form of authority, practice Buddhist ritual, and believe the Buddha to be a savior.

Buddhist Texts. Ashvaghosha (c. 100 C.E.), one of the great Buddhist poets, wrote two long poems, three plays, and various hymns. Tradition suggests that he lived his life in the court of King Kanishka I (first century C.E.) in northern India. One of Ashvaghosha's long Sanskrit poems is *The Life of Buddha (Buddhacarita).* **Ashvaghosha** employs rich metaphors and imagery in this work to create a divine or supernatural context for Gautama's journey to enlightenment.

ush-vuh-GOH-shuh

The early Buddhists apparently distinguished themselves from the Brahmins and Brahmanic Sanskrit by speaking Pali, a colloquial Indian dialect derived from Sanskrit. Buddhist teachings and commentaries, passed down orally for several hundred years, were written down in Pali by Buddhists in south India and Ceylon in the first century B.C.E. and collected in the Pali Canon. The second division *(Pitaka)* of the Pali Canon, called *The Dhamma* ("Doctrine"), is a collection of sermons and discourses, including commentaries by the Buddha's disciples. "The Sermon at Benares: The Four Noble Truths" is part of the Pali Canon. "Right Mindfulness" tells of the seventh stage of the Noble Eightfold Path; though it comes seventh, it is the basis for all the previous stages since it involves the extension of awareness into every thought and deed. "The Last Instructions of the Buddha" is a thoughtful, personal description of the Buddha's last days, his last conversations with his disciples, and his death.

■ CONNECTIONS

Confucius (Kongfuzi), *The Analects,* pp. 1594 and 1631. During the period 700–400 B.C.E. several schools of thought were developed that had a lasting effect on particular cultures and on the world. The great philosopher from China, Confucius, directed his teachings to the reformation of society, providing guidelines for coordinating the various social classes. Buddhism is directed at the salvation of the individual. Why do you think the Buddha thought that that focus was quite enough for one lifetime?

[9] **Mahayana:** This branch of Buddhism is more social in nature, concerned not only with saving the self but also with reaching out to others. The principal guide is one's heart or compassion as strengthened by complex ritual and prayer. Buddha is the savior.

Laozi (Lao Tzu), Dao De Jing (Tao Te Ching), pp. 1525, 1605; Zhuangzi (Chuang Tzu) Basic Writings, p. 1613. Several philosophies from Asia appear to advocate a withdrawal from public life and a focus on personal salvation. Whether one is a ruler or a private citizen, Daoism advocates following the dao and using one's intuition. What is the attitude of Buddhism toward worldly roles such as king and warrior?

The New Testament (Book 2). Religious prophets and founders of new religions react to past doctrines while devising a new program for the future. The teachings of Jesus of Nazareth, the founder of Christianity, proposed changes to Judaism. In what way were the Buddha and his teachings a rebellion against the legalism of contemporary religious conditions in ancient India? Jesus and the Buddha share a reputation for personal goodness. How are their teachings similar?

■ FURTHER RESEARCH

The Buddha

Foucher, C. A. *The Life of the Buddha.* 1963.
Johnston, E. H., trans. *Aśvaghoṣa's Buddhacarita or Acts of the Buddha.* 1978.
Oldenberg, Hermann. *Buddha: His Life, His Doctrine, His Order.* 1971.
Thomas, Edward Joseph. *The Life of Buddha as Legend and History.* 1952.

Buddhism

Conze, Edward. *Buddhist Scriptures.* 1959.
De Bary, William Theodore, ed. *The Buddhist Tradition in India, China, and Japan.* 1969.
Gombrich, Richard. *Theravada Buddhism.* 1988.
Ishikawa, Jun. *The Bodhisattva.* 1990.
Kalupahana, David J. *Buddhist Thought and Ritual.* 1991.
Ray, Reginald A. *Buddhist Saints in India: A Study in Buddhist Values and Orientations.* 1994.
Sadakata, Akira. *Buddhist Cosmology: Philosophy and Origins.* 1997.
Tsomo, Karma Lekshe, ed. *Buddhist Women Across Cultures.* 1999.

■ PRONUNCIATION

Ashvaghosha (Asvagosha): ush-vuh-GOH-shuh
Dīgha Nikāya: DEE-guh nih-KAH-yuh
Kshatriya: KSHUH-tree-yuh
Mahāparinibbāna Sutta: muh-huh-pah-rih-nee-BAH-nuh SOO-tuh
Majjhima Nikāya: MUH-jih-muh nih-KAH-yuh
Sakya: SAH-kyuh, SHAH-kyuh
Samyutta Nikāya: sum-YOO-tuh nih-KAH-yuh
Shuddhodana (Suddhodana): shoo-DOH-duh-nuh

Ashvaghosha
c. 100 C.E.

FROM

The Life of Buddha

Translated by E. B. Cowell

[Birth and Childhood]

There was a city, the dwelling-place of the great saint Kapila, having its sides surrounded by the beauty of a lofty broad table-land as by a line of clouds, and itself, with its high-soaring palaces, immersed in the sky. [. . .]

A king, by name Suddhodana, of the kindred of the sun, anointed to stand at the head of earth's monarchs,—ruling over the city, adorned it, as a bee-inmate a full-blown lotus.

The very best of kings with his train ever near him,—intent on liberality yet devoid of pride; a sovereign, yet with an ever equal eye thrown on all,—of gentle nature and yet with wide-reaching majesty. [. . .]

He, the monarch of the Sâkyas,[1] of native pre-eminence, but whose actual pre-eminence was brought about by his numberless councillors of exalted wisdom, shone forth all the more gloriously, like the moon amidst the stars shining with a light like its own.

To him there was a queen, named Mâyâ, as if free from all deceit (mâyâ)—an effulgence proceeding from his effulgence, like the splendour of the sun when it is free from all the influence of darkness,—a chief queen in the united assembly of all queens.

Like a mother to her subjects, intent on their welfare,—devoted to all worthy of reverence like devotion itself,—shining on her lord's family like the goddess of prosperity,—she was the most eminent of goddesses to the whole world. [. . .]

Then falling from the host of beings in the Tushita heaven,[2] and illumining the three worlds, the most excellent of Bodhisattvas suddenly entered at a thought into her womb, like the Nâga-king[3] entering the cave of Nandâ.

The Life of Buddha. Seventeen cantos, or books, of the original *The Life of Buddha* by Ashvaghosha remain. Significant happenings in the Buddha's life—his miraculous birth, The Four Signs, his search for answers among the ascetics, sitting underneath the Bodhi tree, and the moment of enlightenment—are recounted in this prose translation of a poetic text that is dated around 100 C.E.

A note on the translation: The E. B. Cowell translation is very readable. All notes are the editors'. The excerpts are designated by ellipses.

---

[1] **Sâkyas:** The Sakya clan of the *Kshatriya,* or warrior, caste; later in his life the Buddha was referred to as Sakyamuni, meaning "the sage of the Sakyas."

[2] **Tushita heaven:** A special heavenly abode for buddhas awaiting incarnation.

[3] **Nâga-king:** King of the serpents or dragons.

Assuming the form of a huge elephant white like Himâlaya, armed with six tusks, with his face perfumed with flowing ichor, he entered the womb of the queen of king Suddhodana, to destroy the evils of the world. [. . .]

Then one day by the king's permission the queen, having a great longing in her mind, went with the inmates of the gynaeceum into the garden Lumbinî.

As the queen supported herself by a bough which hung laden with a weight of flowers, the Bodhisattva suddenly came forth, cleaving open her womb.

At that time the constellation Pushya was auspicious, and from the side of the queen, who was purified by her vow, her son was born for the welfare of the world, without pain and without illness.

Like the sun bursting from a cloud in the morning,—so he too, when he was born from his mother's womb, made the world bright like gold, bursting forth with his rays which dispelled the darkness. [. . .]

Having thus in due time issued from the womb, he shone as if he had come down from heaven, he who had not been born in the natural way,—he who was born full of wisdom, not foolish,—as if his mind had been purified by countless aeons of contemplation.

With glory, fortitude, and beauty he shone like the young sun descended upon the earth; when he was gazed at, though of such surpassing brightness, he attracted all eyes like the moon. [. . .]

[The Prophecy of a Wandering Sage]

Then having learned by signs and through the power of his penances this birth of him who was to destroy all birth, the great seer Asita[4] in his thirst for the excellent Law came to the palace of the Sâkya king.

Him shining with the glory of sacred knowledge and ascetic observances, the king's own priest,—himself a special student among the students of sacred knowledge,—introduced into the royal palace with all due reverence and respect.

He entered into the precincts of the king's gynaeceum, which was all astir with the joy arisen from the birth of the young prince,—grave from his consciousness of power, his pre-eminence in asceticism, and the weight of old age.

Then the king, having duly honoured the sage, who was seated in his seat, with water for the feet and an arghya offering,[5] invited him (to speak) with all ceremonies of respect [. . .]

The sage, being thus invited by the king, filled with intense feeling as was due, uttered his deep and solemn words, having his large eyes opened wide with wonder: [. . .]

'But hear now the motive for my coming and rejoice thereat; a heavenly voice

[4] **Asita:** Asita is a wandering sage who predicts that the son of Suddhodana "will shine forth as a sun of knowledge to destroy the darkness of illusion in the world." King Suddhodana, who is growing old, wants his son to succeed him.

[5] **arghya offering:** An offering to a divinity involving the use of flowers, sandalwood paste, grass, and rice.

has been heard by me in the heavenly path, that thy son has been born for the sake of supreme knowledge. [. . .]

'Having forsaken his kingdom, indifferent to all worldly objects, and having attained the highest truth by strenuous efforts, he will shine forth as a sun of knowledge to destroy the darkness of illusion in the world.

'He will deliver by the boat of knowledge the distressed world, borne helplessly along, from the ocean of misery which throws up sickness as its foam, tossing with the waves of old age, and rushing with the dreadful onflow of earth. [. . .]

Having heard these words, the king with his queen and his friends abandoned sorrow and rejoiced; thinking, 'such is this son of mine,' he considered that his excellence was his own.

But he let his heart be influenced by the thought, 'he will travel by the noble path,'—he was not in truth averse to religion, yet still he saw alarm at the prospect of losing his child. [. . .]

When he had passed the period of childhood and reached that of middle youth, the young prince learned in a few days the various sciences suitable to his race, which generally took many years to master.

But having heard before from the great seer Asita his destined future which was to embrace transcendental happiness, the anxious care of the king of the present Sâkya race turned the prince to sensual pleasures.

Then he sought for him from a family of unblemished moral excellence a bride possessed of beauty, modesty, and gentle bearing, of wide-spread glory, Yasodharâ by name, having a name well worthy of her, a very goddess of good fortune. [. . .]

In course of time to the fair-bosomed Yasodharâ,—who was truly glorious in accordance with her name,—there was born from the son of Suddhodana a son named Râhula, with a face like the enemy of Râhu.[6]

Then the king who from regard to the welfare of his race had longed for a son and been exceedingly delighted [at his coming],—as he had rejoiced at the birth of his son, so did he now rejoice at the birth of his grandson. [. . .]

[Awakening to Age, Disease, and Death]

On a certain day he heard of the forests carpeted with tender grass, with their trees resounding with the kokilas, adorned with lotus-ponds, and which had been all bound up in the cold season.

Having heard of the delightful appearance of the city groves beloved by the women, he resolved to go out of doors, like an elephant long shut up in a house.

The king, having learned the character of the wish thus expressed by his son, ordered a pleasure-party to be prepared, worthy of his own affection and his son's beauty and youth.

He prohibited the encounter of any afflicted common person in the highroad;

[6] **Râhu:** A demon who causes eclipses by seizing the sun and the moon.

'heaven forbid that the prince with his tender nature should even imagine himself to be distressed.'

Then having removed out of the way with the greatest gentleness all those who had mutilated limbs or maimed senses, the decrepit and the sick and all squalid beggars, they made the highway assume its perfect beauty. [. . .]

But then the gods, dwelling in pure abodes, having beheld that city thus rejoicing like heaven itself, created an old man to walk along on purpose to stir the heart of the king's son.

The prince having beheld him thus overcome with decrepitude and different in form from other men, with his gaze intently fixed on him, thus addressed his driver with simple confidence:

'Who is this man that has come here, O charioteer, with white hair and his hand resting on a staff, his eyes hidden beneath his brows, his limbs bent down and hanging loose,—is this a change produced in him or his natural state or an accident?'

Thus addressed, the charioteer revealed to the king's son the secret that should have been kept so carefully, thinking no harm in his simplicity, for those same gods had bewildered his mind:

'That is old age by which he is broken down,—the ravisher of beauty, the ruin of vigour, the cause of sorrow, the destruction of delights, the bane of memories, the enemy of the senses.

'He too once drank milk in his childhood, and in course of time he learned to grope on the ground; having step by step become a vigorous youth, he has step by step in the same way reached old age.'

Being thus addressed, the prince, starting a little, spoke these words to the charioteer, 'What! will this evil come to me also?' and to him again spoke the charioteer:

'It will come without doubt by the force of time through multitude of years even to my long-lived lord; all the world knows thus that old age will destroy their comeliness and they are content to have it so.' [. . .]

Drawing a long sigh and shaking his head, and fixing his eyes on that decrepit old man, and looking round on that exultant multitude he then uttered these distressed words:

'Old age thus strikes down all alike, our memory, comeliness, and valour; and yet the world is not disturbed, even when it sees such a fate visibly impending.

'Since such is our condition, O charioteer, turn back the horses,—go quickly home; how can I rejoice in the pleasure-garden, when the thoughts arising from old age overpower me?'

Then the charioteer at the command of the king's son turned the chariot back, and the prince lost in thought entered even that royal palace as if it were empty.

But when he found no happiness even there, as he continually kept reflecting, 'old age, old age,' then once more, with the permission of the king, he went out with the same arrangement as before.

Then the same deities created another man with his body all afflicted by disease; and on seeing him the son of Suddhodana addressed the charioteer, having his gaze fixed on the man:

'Yonder man with a swollen belly, his whole frame shaking as he pants, his arms and shoulders hanging loose, his body all pale and thin, uttering plaintively the word "mother," when he embraces a stranger,—who, pray, is this?'

Then his charioteer answered, 'Gentle Sir, it is a very great affliction called sickness, that has grown up, caused by the inflammation of the (three) humours, which has made even this strong man no longer master of himself.'

Then the prince again addressed him, looking upon the man compassionately, 'Is this evil peculiar to him or are all beings alike threatened by sickness?'

Then the charioteer answered, 'O prince, this evil is common to all; thus pressed round by diseases men run to pleasure, though racked with pain.'

Having heard this account, his mind deeply distressed, he trembled like the moon reflected in the waves of water; and full of sorrow he uttered these words in a low voice:

'Even while they see all this calamity of diseases mankind can yet feel tranquillity; alas for the scattered intelligence of men who can smile when still not free from the terrors of disease!

'Let the chariot, O charioteer, be turned back from going outside, let it return straight to the king's palace; having heard this alarm of disease, my mind shrinks into itself, repelled from pleasures.' [. . .]

Then the royal road being specially adorned and guarded, the king once more made the prince go out, having ordered the charioteer and chariot to proceed in a contrary direction (to the previous one).

But as the king's son was thus going on his way, the very same deities created a dead man, and only the charioteer and the prince, and none else, beheld him as he was carried dead along the road.

Then spoke the prince to the charioteer, 'Who is this borne by four men, followed by mournful companions, who is bewailed, adorned but no longer breathing?'

Then the driver,—having his mind overpowered by the gods who possess pure minds and pure dwellings,—himself knowing the truth, uttered to his lord this truth also which was not to be told:

'This is some poor man who, bereft of his intellect, senses, vital airs and qualities, lying asleep and unconscious, like mere wood or straw, is abandoned alike by friends and enemies after they have carefully swathed and guarded him.'

Having heard these words of the charioteer he was somewhat startled and said to him, 'Is this an accident peculiar to him alone, or is such the end of all living creatures?'

Then the charioteer replied to him, 'This is the final end of all living creatures; be it a mean man, a man of middle state, or a noble, destruction is fixed to all in this world.'

Then the king's son, sedate though he was, as soon as he heard of death, immediately sank down overwhelmed, and pressing the end of the chariot-pole with his shoulder spoke with a loud voice,

'Is this end appointed to all creatures, and yet the world throws off all fear and is infatuated! Hard indeed, I think, must the hearts of men be, who can be self-composed in such a road.

'Therefore, O charioteer, turn back our chariot, this is no time or place for a pleasure-excursion; how can a rational being, who knows what destruction is, stay heedless here, in the hour of calamity?' [. . .]

[The Path of Asceticism]

Then one day accompanied by some worthy sons of his father's ministers, friends full of varied converse,—with a desire to see the glades of the forest and longing for peace, he went out with the king's permission.

Having mounted his good horse Kamthaka, decked with bells and bridle-bit of new gold, with beautiful golden harness and the chowrie waving, he went forth like the moon mounted on a comet.

Lured by love of the wood and longing for the beauties of the ground, he went to a spot near at hand on the forest-outskirts; and there he saw a piece of land being ploughed, with the path of the plough broken like waves on the water. [. . .]

There he sat down on the ground covered with leaves, and with its young grass bright like lapis lazuli; and, meditating on the origin and destruction of the world, he laid hold of the path that leads to firmness of mind.

Having attained to firmness of mind, and being forthwith set free from all sorrows such as the desire of worldly objects and the rest, he attained the first stage of contemplation, unaffected by sin, calm, and 'argumentative.' [. . .]

Thus did this pure passionless meditation grow within the great-souled one; and unobserved by the other men, there crept up a man in a beggar's dress.

The king's son asked him a question,—he said to him, 'Tell me, who art thou?' and the other replied, 'Oh bull of men, I, being terrified at birth and death, have become an ascetic for the sake of liberation.

'Desiring liberation in a world subject to destruction, I seek that happy indestructible abode,—isolated from mankind, with my thoughts unlike those of others, and with my sinful passions turned away from all objects of sense.

'Dwelling anywhere, at the root of a tree, or in an uninhabited house, a mountain or a forest,—I wander without a family and without hope, a beggar ready for any fare, seeking only the highest good.'

When he had thus spoken, while the prince was looking on, he suddenly flew up to the sky; it was a heavenly inhabitant who, knowing that the prince's thoughts were other than what his outward form promised, had come to him for the sake of rousing his recollection.

When the other was gone like a bird to heaven, the foremost of men was rejoiced and astonished; and having comprehended the meaning of the term dharma,[7] he set his mind on the manner of the accomplishment of deliverance. [. . .]

Then the prince whose form was like the peak of a golden mountain,—whose eye, voice, and arm resembled a bull, a cloud, and an elephant,—whose countenance and prowess were like the moon and a lion,—having a longing aroused for something imperishable,—went into his palace.

Then stepping like a lion he went towards the king who was attended by his

[7] **dharma:** The ideal order; the way things should be.

numerous counsellors, like Sanatkumâra in heaven waiting on Indra resplendent in the assembly of the Maruts.

Prostrating himself, with folded hands, he addressed him, 'Grant me graciously thy permission, O lord of men,—I wish to become a wandering mendicant for the sake of liberation, since separation is appointed for me.'

Having heard his words, the king shook like a tree struck by an elephant, and having seized his folded hands which were like a lotus, he thus addressed him in a voice choked with tears:

'O my son, keep back this thought, it is not the time for thee to betake thyself to dharma; they say that the practice of religion is full of evils in the first period of life when the mind is still fickle. [. . .]

'As separation is inevitable to the world, but not for Dharma, this separation is preferable; will not death sever me helplessly, my objects unattained and myself unsatisfied?'

The monarch, having heard this resolve of his son longing for liberation, and having again exclaimed, 'He shall not go,' set guards round him and the highest pleasures.

Then having been duly instructed by the counsellors, with all respect and affection, according to the sâstras, and being thus forbidden with tears by his father, the prince, sorrowing, entered into his palace. [. . .]

[The Search for Answers]

Having awakened his horse's attendant, the swift Khamdaka, he thus addressed him: 'Bring me quickly my horse Kamthaka, I wish to-day to go hence to attain immortality.

'Since such is the firm content which to-day is produced in my heart, and since my determination is settled in calm resolve, and since even in loneliness I seem to possess a guide,—verily the end which I desire is now before me. [. . .]

The city-roads which were closed with heavy gates and bars, and which could be with difficulty opened even by elephants, flew open of their own accord without noise, as the prince went through.

Firm in his resolve and leaving behind without hesitation his father who turned ever towards him, and his young son, his affectionate people and his unparalleled magnificence, he then went forth out of his father's city.

Then he with his eyes long and like a full-blown lotus, looking back on the city, uttered a sound like a lion, 'Till I have seen the further shore of birth and death I will never again enter the city called after Kapila.' [. . .]

Then Yasodharâ fell upon the ground, like the ruddy goose parted from her mate, and in utter bewilderment she slowly lamented, with her voice repeatedly stopped by sobs:

'If he wishes to practise a religious life after abandoning me his lawful wife widowed,—where is his religion, who wishes to follow penance without his lawful wife to share it with him? [. . .]

'Even if I am unworthy to look on my husband's face with its long eyes and bright smile, still is this poor Râhula never to roll about in his father's lap?

'Alas! the mind of that wise hero is terribly stern,—gentle as his beauty seems, it is pitilessly cruel,—who can desert of his own accord such an infant son with his inarticulate talk, one who would charm even an enemy. [. . .]

For six years, vainly trying to attain merit, [Siddhartha] practised self-mortification, performing many rules of abstinence, hard for a man to carry out.

At the hours for eating, he, longing to cross the world whose farther shore is so difficult to reach, broke his vow with single jujube fruits, sesame seeds, and rice.

But the emaciation which was produced in his body by that asceticism, became positive fatness through the splendour which invested him. [. . .]

Then the seer, having his body evidently emaciated to no purpose in a cruel self-mortification,—dreading continued existence, thus reflected in his longing to become a Buddha:

'This is not the way to passionlessness, nor to perfect knowledge, nor to liberation; that was certainly the true way which I found at the root of the Gambu tree.[8]

'But that cannot be attained by one who has lost his strength,'—so resuming his care for his body, he next pondered thus, how best to increase his bodily vigour: [. . .]

'True meditation is produced in him whose mind is self-possessed and at rest,—to him whose thoughts are engaged in meditation the exercise of perfect contemplation begins at once.

'By contemplation are obtained those conditions through which is eventually gained that supreme calm, undecaying, immortal state, which is so hard to be reached.'

Having thus resolved, 'this means is based upon eating food,' the wise seer of unbounded wisdom, having made up his mind to accept the continuance of life, [. . .]

Now at that time Nandabalâ, the daughter of the leader of the herdsmen, impelled by the gods, with a sudden joy risen in her heart, had just come near,

Her arm gay with a white shell, and wearing a dark blue woollen cloth, like the river Yamunâ, with its dark blue water and its wreath of foam.

She, having her joy increased by her faith, with her lotus-like eyes opened wide, bowed down before him and persuaded him to take some milk.

By partaking that food having made her obtain the full reward of her birth, he himself became capable of gaining the highest knowledge, all his six senses being now satisfied, [. . .]

Accompanied only by his own resolve, having fixed his mind on the attainment of perfect knowledge, he went to the root of an Asvattha tree,[9] where the surface of the ground was covered with young grass.

Then Kâla,[10] the best of serpents, whose majesty was like the lord of elephants, having been awakened by the unparalleled sound of his feet, uttered this praise of the great sage, being sure that he was on the point of attaining perfect knowledge: [. . .]

'Inasmuch as lines of birds fluttering in the sky offer thee reverential salutation,

---

[8] **Gambu tree:** A rose apple tree *(Eugenia jambos)* belonging to the myrtle family; it is an ornamental tree.

[9] **Asvattha tree:** A fig tree, which has come to be known as the Bo tree (from *Bodhi,* enlightenment).

[10] **Kâla:** Naga king.

O lotus-eyed one, and inasmuch as gentle breezes blow in the sky, thou shalt certainly to-day become the Buddha.' [. . .]

Then he sat down on his hams in a posture, immovably firm and with his limbs gathered into a mass like a sleeping serpent's hood, exclaiming, 'I will not rise from this position on the earth until I have obtained my utmost aim.'

Then the dwellers in heaven burst into unequalled joy; the herds of beasts and the birds uttered no cry; the trees moved by the wind made no sound, when the holy one took his seat firm in his resolve.

[Enlightenment]

When the great sage, sprung from a line of royal sages, sat down there with his soul fully resolved to obtain the highest knowledge, the whole world rejoiced; but Mâra,[11] the enemy of the good law, was afraid. [. . .]

Then Mâra called to mind his own army, wishing to work the overthrow of the Sâkya saint; and his followers swarmed round, wearing different forms and carrying arrows, trees, darts, clubs, and swords in their hands;

Having the faces of boars, fishes, horses, asses, and camels, of tigers, bears, lions, and elephants,—one-eyed, many-faced, three-headed,—with protuberant bellies and speckled bellies;

Blended with goats, with knees swollen like pots, armed with tusks and with claws, carrying headless trunks in their hands, and assuming many forms, with half-mutilated faces, and with monstrous mouths;

Copper-red, covered with red spots, bearing clubs in their hands, with yellow or smoke-coloured hair, with wreaths dangling down, with long pendulous ears like elephants, clothed in leather or wearing no clothes at all; [. . .]

But the great sage having beheld that army of Mâra thus engaged in an attack on the knower of the Law, remained untroubled and suffered no perturbation, like a lion seated in the midst of oxen.

But a woman named Meghakâlî, bearing a skull in her hand, in order to infatuate the mind of the sage, flitted about unsettled and stayed not in one spot, like the mind of the fickle student over the sacred texts.

Another, fixing a kindling eye, wished to burn him with the fire of his glance like a poisonous serpent; but he saw the sage and lo! he was not there, like the votary of pleasure when true happiness is pointed out to him. [. . .]

[Acquiring Knowledge]

Then, having conquered the hosts of Mâra by his firmness and calmness, he the great master of meditation set himself to mediate, longing to know the supreme end.

And having attained the highest mastery in all kinds of meditation, he remembered in the first watch the continuous series of all his former births.

---

[11] **Mâra:** A Hindu demon who brings temptations and threats to the Buddha.

'In such a place I was so and so by name, and from thence I passed and came hither,' thus he remembered his thousands of births, experiencing each as it were over again.

And having remembered each birth and each death in all those various transmigrations, the compassionate one then felt compassion for all living beings. [. . .]

When the second watch came, he, possessed of unequalled energy, received a pre-eminent divine sight, he the highest of all sight-gifted beings.

Then by that divine perfectly pure sight he beheld the whole world as in a spotless mirror.

As he saw the various transmigrations and rebirths of the various beings with their several lower or higher merits from their actions, compassion grew up more within him. [. . .]

FROM

Samyutta Nikaya

Translated by A. L. Basham

The Sermon at Benares: The Four Noble Truths

Thus I have heard. Once the Lord was at Vārānasī,[1] at the deer park called Isipatana. There he addressed the five monks:

There are two ends not to be served by a wanderer. What are these two? The pursuit of desires and of the pleasure which springs from desire, which is base, common, leading to rebirth, ignoble, and unprofitable; and the pursuit of pain and hardship, which is grievous, ignoble, and unprofitable. The Middle Way of the Tathāgata avoids both these ends. It is enlightened, it brings clear vision, it makes for wisdom, and leads to peace, insight, enlightenment, and Nirvāna. What is the Middle Way? . . . It is the Noble Eightfold Path—Right Views, Right Resolve, Right Speech, Right Conduct, Right Livelihood, Right Effort, Right Mindfulness,[2] and Right Concentration. This is the Middle Way. . . .

And this is the Noble Truth of Sorrow. Birth is sorrow, age is sorrow, disease is sorrow, death is sorrow; contact with the unpleasant is sorrow, separation from the pleasant is sorrow, every wish unfulfilled is sorrow—in short all the five components of individuality[3] are sorrow.

The Sermon at Bernares. This address comes from a collection of shorter discourses in the Buddhist Canon (Pali Canon) called *Samyutta Nikaya,* or *Connected Group.* According to tradition the Buddha's first sermon was given to five ascetics who had earlier abandoned him when he gave up self-mortification and starvation. The Buddha redirects the attention of the five listeners from physical practices to questions of consciousness or understanding.

---

[1] **Vārānasī:** The ancient name of Benares, also spelled Banaras.

[2] **Right Mindfulness:** Becoming fully conscious of one's thoughts and deeds.

[3] **five components of individuality:** Forms, sensations, perceptions, psychic dispositions, and consciousness.

And this is the Noble Truth of the Arising of Sorrow. It arises from craving, which leads to rebirth, which brings delight and passion, and seeks pleasure now here, now there—the craving for sensual pleasure, the craving for continued life, the craving for power.

And this is the Noble Truth of the Stopping of Sorrow. It is the complete stopping of that craving, so that no passion remains, leaving it, being emancipated from it, being released from it, giving no place to it.

And this is the Noble Truth of the Way which Leads to the Stopping of Sorrow. It is the Noble Eightfold Path—Right Views, Right Resolve, Right Speech, Right Conduct, Right Livelihood, Right Effort, Right Mindfulness, and Right Concentration.

FROM

Majjhima Nikaya

Translated by A. L. Basham

Right Mindfulness

The Lord was staying at Sāvatthī at the monastery of Anāthapindaka in the Grove of Jeta. One morning he dressed, took his robe and bowl, and went into Sāvatthī for alms, with the Reverend Rāhula[1] following close behind him. As they walked the Lord, . . . without looking round, spoke to him thus:

"All material forms, past, present, or future, within or without, gross or subtle, base or fine, far or near, all should be viewed with full understanding—with the thought 'This is not mine, this is not I, this is not my soul.'"

"Only material forms, Lord?"

"No, not only material forms, Rāhula, but also sensation, perception, the psychic constructions, and consciousness."[2]

"Who would go to the village to collect alms today, when he has been exhorted by the Lord himself?" said Rāhula. And he turned back and sat cross-legged, with body erect, collected in thought.

Then the Venerable Sāriputta,[3] seeing him thus, said to him: "Develop concentration on inhalation and exhalation, for when this is developed and increased it is very productive and helpful."

Right Mindfulness. The instruction called "Right Mindfulness," from the *Majjhima Nikaya,* or *Medium Group,* shorter discourses in the Pali Canon, deals with the transience of all life. It's a good example of the Buddha's teaching techniques.

[1] **Rāhula:** The Buddha's son, who entered the *sangha,* or community of monks, at age seven. He is considered one of the ten great disciples of the Buddha.

[2] **not only . . . consciousness:** That is, the five components of individuality.

[3] **Sāriputta:** A chief disciple.

Towards evening Rāhula rose and went to the Lord, and asked him how he could develop concentration on inhalation and exhalation. And the Lord said:

"Rāhula, whatever is hard and solid in an individual, such as hair, nails, teeth, skin, flesh, and so on, is called the personal element of earth. The personal element of water is composed of bile, phlegm, pus, blood, sweat, and so on. The personal element of fire is that which warms and consumes or burns up, and produces metabolism of food and drink in digestion. The personal element of air is the wind in the body which moves upwards or downwards, the winds in the abdomen and stomach, winds which move from member to member, and the inhalation and exhalation of the breath. And finally the personal element of space comprises the orifices of ears and nose, the door of the mouth, and the channels whereby food and drink enter, remain in, and pass out of the body. These five personal elements, together with the five external elements, make up the total of the five universal elements. They should all be regarded objectively, with right understanding, thinking 'This is not mine, this is not me, this is not my soul.' With this understanding attitude a man turns from the five elements and his mind takes no delight in them.

"Develop a state of mind like the earth, Rāhula. For on the earth men throw clean and unclean things, dung and urine, spittle, pus and blood, and the earth is not troubled or repelled or disgusted. And as you grow like the earth no contacts with pleasant or unpleasant will lay hold of your mind or stick to it.

"Similarly you should develop a state of mind like water, for men throw all manner of clean and unclean things into water and it is not troubled or repelled or disgusted. And similarly with fire, which burns all things, clean and unclean, and with air, which blows upon them all, and with space, which is nowhere established.

"Develop the state of mind of friendliness, Rāhula, for, as you do so, ill-will will grow less; and of compassion, for thus vexation will grow less; and of joy, for thus aversion will grow less; and of equanimity,[4] for thus repugnance will grow less.

"Develop the state of mind of consciousness of the corruption of the body, for thus passion will grow less; and of the consciousness of the fleeting nature of all things, for thus the pride of selfhood will grow less.

"Develop the state of mind of ordering the breath, . . . in which the monk goes to the forest, or to the root of a tree or to an empty house, and sits cross-legged with body erect, collected in thought. Fully mindful he inhales and exhales. When he inhales or exhales a long breath he knows precisely that he is doing so, and similarly when inhaling or exhaling a short breath. While inhaling or exhaling he trains himself to be conscious of the whole of his body, . . . to be fully conscious of the components of his mind, . . . to realize the impermanence of all things, . . . or to dwell on passionlessness . . . or renunciation. Thus the state of ordered breathing, when developed and increased, is very productive and helpful. And when the mind is thus developed a man breathes his last breath in full consciousness, and not unconsciously."

[4] **friendliness . . . equanimity:** The four cardinal virtues of Buddhism are friendliness, compassion, joy, and equanimity.

FROM

Mahaparinibbana Sutta

Translated by A. L. Basham

The Last Instructions of the Buddha

Soon after this the Lord began to recover, and when he was quite free from sickness he came out of his lodging and sat in its shadow on a seat spread out for him. The Venerable Ānanda went up to him, paid his respects, sat down to one side, and spoke to the Lord thus:

"I have seen the Lord in health, and I have seen the Lord in sickness; and when I saw that the Lord was sick my body became as weak as a creeper, my sight dimmed, and all my faculties weakened. But yet I was a little comforted by the thought that the Lord would not pass away until he had left his instructions concerning the Order."

"What, Ānanda! Does the Order expect that of me? I have taught the truth without making any distinction between exoteric and esoteric doctrines; for . . . with the Tathāgata there is no such thing as the closed fist of the teacher who keeps some things back. If anyone thinks 'It is I who will lead the Order,' or 'The Order depends on me,' he is the one who should lay down instructions concerning the Order. But the Tathāgata has no such thought, so why should he leave instructions? I am old now, Ānanda, and full of years; my journey nears its end, and I have reached my sum of days, for I am nearly eighty years old. Just as a worn out cart can only be kept going if it is tied up with thongs, so the body of the Tathāgata can only be kept going by bandaging it. Only when the Tathāgata no longer attends to any outward object, when all separate sensation stops and he is deep in inner concentration, is his body at ease.

"So, Ānanda, you must be your own lamps, be your own refuges. Take refuge in nothing outside yourselves. Hold firm to the truth as a lamp and a refuge, and do not look for refuge to anything besides yourselves. A monk becomes his own lamp and refuge by continually looking on his body, feelings, perceptions, moods, and ideas in such a manner that he conquers the cravings and depressions of ordinary men and is always strenuous, self-possessed, and collected in mind. Whoever among my monks does this, either now or when I am dead, if he is anxious to learn, will reach the summit."

"All composite things must pass away. Strive onward vigilantly."[1]

The Last Instructions of the Buddha. The material devoted to the last days and the death of the Buddha comes from *Discourse of the Great Passing-away (Mahaparinibbana Sutta),* which is collected in the *Digha Nikaya,* or the *Long Group,* long discourses in the Pali Canon. This extended document describes the last years of the Buddha's life, his return to the hills where he was born, and his last meal in which poisonous mushrooms were accidentally included. After he died he was cremated and his relics were distributed to shrines. His final instructions came after he briefly recovered from illness. Ananda, which means "absolute joy," was one of the ten great disciples of the Buddha. Because of Ananda, the Buddha consented to founding an order of nuns.

---

[1] **"All composite . . . vigilantly":** The Buddha's last words are sometimes translated as, "Work out your salvation with diligence."

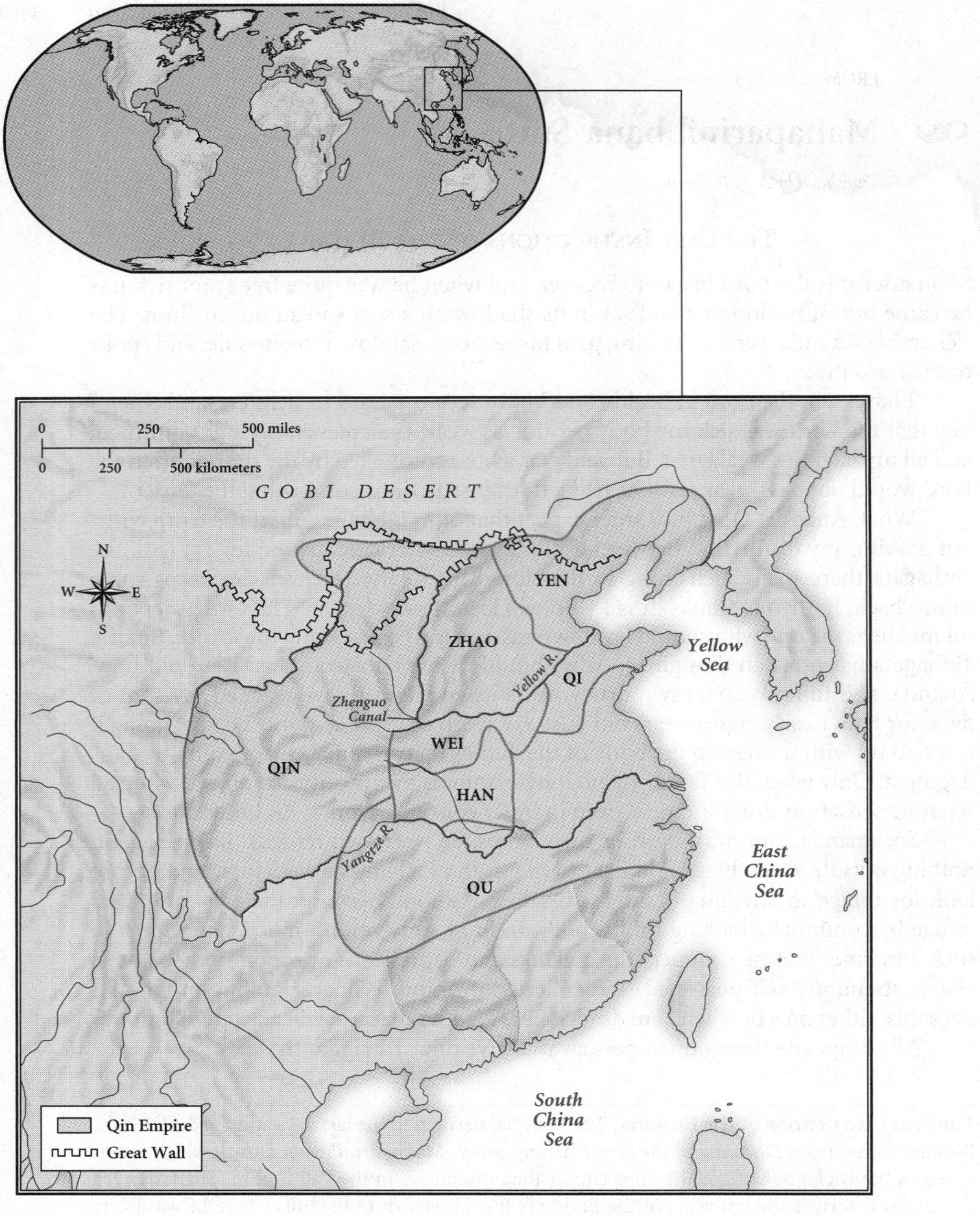

The Unification of China, 221 B.C.E.

About 250 B.C.E., political power in China was dispersed among the seven so-called warring states: Han, Wei, Zhao, Qin, Qu, Yen, and Qi. All maintained fortifications and engaged in intermittent conflict, but Qin emerged as the most technologically and militarily powerful state. In 221 B.C.E., after a decade of war, all seven states were united under the conquering Qin.

CHINA

The Ancient Way: Ancestors, Emperors, and Society

The richness of China's cultural heritage stems from the vast country's numerous past tribes, languages, and dialects. Nevertheless, early in its history China began to develop a national identity centered around the Chinese language, the world's oldest surviving tongue. Because written Chinese remained constant while the phonetic or spoken value of the Chinese characters varied, people from different regions of the country who might speak various dialects could nonetheless share a common written language and therefore a common body of literature. Sometime around the first millennium B.C.E. a Chinese identity first took shape through the continuous reworking of a literary tradition that through the centuries created and preserved cultural coherence. That revising of texts has presented a problem for historians: Although there are written historical records prior to Confucius in the sixth century B.C.E., there was such doctoring of texts that it has been difficult to reconstruct with accuracy ancient Chinese history.

Calling themselves the **Zhong Guo**, meaning "Central or Middle Kingdom," the Chinese perceived themselves as having a special destiny; outside the frontiers of the kingdom were barbarians. The Chinese speak of their history in terms of a series of dynasties, which can refer to the governments that ruled by the Mandate of Heaven or the years in which particular groups ruled; *Heaven,* or *t'ien,* appears to have signified a universal moral order that actively shaped history. Each dynasty began with a powerful family that established a strong government; when the dynasty lost favor because of its evil practices, it was overthrown. The Zhou rulers of the eleventh century B.C.E. explained the overthrow of the previous Shang dynasty, for example, by saying that when that dynasty ruled with an absence of virtue, it became the will of Heaven to change rulers. Dynastic stability was also at times undermined by peasant revolts and nomadic invasions from the Asian steppes.

The Chinese have some of the oldest literature in the world, with an oral folk

Mourners, ***twelfth century*** **B.C.E.**
Excavated from an ancient Chinese tomb, these beautifully abstract yet powerfully evocative figurines, all in various attitudes of mourning, were made shortly after the death of Confucius, the seminal Chinese philosopher and teacher. As a reformer and educator, Confucius disapproved of the use of figurines in burials, believing it too akin to the earlier Shang dynasty practice of sacrificing human slaves. (Laurie Platt Winfrey, Inc.)

tradition that reaches back to the second millennium B.C.E. Some of the earliest literature deals with dynastic histories, the myths and stories of early rulers. Stories about ghosts and the supernatural were popular from an early time. Other forms of ancient Chinese literature include folk ballads, diaries, shamanistic hymns, and letters. The large volume of philosophical literature is devoted to morality and the examination of government, and to how education might promote social and political harmony. Daoist and Buddhist priests used stories and parables in religious instruction. Chinese poetry, in particular, with its 3,000-year history, is exemplary for its variety and influence. The sheer volume of Chinese literature is overwhelming.

THE LEGENDARY PAST

Chinese civilization is thought to have developed in the Yellow River basin and along the river's tributaries, completely separate from other riverine civilizations on the Tigris and Euphrates, Nile, and Indus Rivers. Because of mountains, deserts, and seas, China was relatively isolated from the rest of Asia. Millet, a hardy grain, was the basis of an agricultural surplus that provided for the growth of cities and the rudiments of political organization. Unlike the civilizations of Mesopotamia, Egypt, Israel, Greece, and India, China set down no myths about the creation of the cosmos or stories about deities who informed the primordial origins of Chinese civilization. Instead, the cultural histories are accounts of a legendary or mythic past that tell of the earliest men, fabled emperors and cultural heroes from a golden age of China, figures who became the cultural models or paradigms for succeeding generations. One such figure, the sage Fu Xi (Fu Hsi), is believed to have invented fishing nets and the basic symbols of the *I Jing (I Ching),* the *Book of Changes,* the central collection of oracles, which connect the basic principles of the cosmos to individual decisions. Emperor Huangdi, the so-called Yellow Emperor (c. 2700 B.C.E.), drove an ivory chariot drawn by six dragons and represented the ideal ruler, a model similar to Rama in the great Indian epic the *Ramayana* (c. 400 B.C.E.). Huangdi is said to have driven out the wild beasts from China and to have invented cattle-breeding; his twenty-five sons provided the ancestry for at least twelve feudal families during the Zhou dynasty. The Great Yu, founder of the Xia (Hsia) dynasty (early second millennium B.C.E.), solved the problem of the flooding of the Yellow River by devising an elaborate irrigation system. The philosopher Mencius (Mengzi) fourth century B.C.E.) explains: "Yü dug the soil and led the water to the sea; drove out the snakes and dragons, relegating them to the marshes. The waters then had their courses through the middle of the land: the rivers Hsiang, Huai, Ho and Han." Jie (Chieh), the last ruler of the Xia dynasty, became the model of the bad ruler, and the reason for the ascendancy of the Shang dynasty, the first historical dynasty.

THE SHANG DYNASTY (c. 1600–c. 1028 B.C.E.)

The Shang people were a complex agricultural society that developed an aristocracy, a bureaucracy, a writing system, and the rudiments of ancestor worship—the core religion of the Chinese household. The basis of ancestor worship, which is common to other parts of the world, is the belief that individuals live on as spirits after they die and can influence for good or ill the affairs of the living. Attention to ancestral spirits usually involves prayers, ceremonies, gifts. Neglected ancestor souls become ghosts who make mischief. In ancient China, the names of the deceased, along with their birth and death dates, were inscribed on wooden tablets and kept

Votive Offering of Laozi and Two Attendants, 587
Ancestor worship is a core Chinese belief and is still practiced today. The Chinese philosopher Laozi (Lao Tzu) is pictured in this small carved limestone votive stele, used to hold candles at shrines. 24 × 15 × 11.5 cm. (Special Chinese and Japanese Fund. Courtesy of the Museum of Fine Arts, Boston. Reproduced with permission. © 2000 Museum of Fine Arts, Boston. All rights reserved.)

in a household shrine, or in an ancestral hall if the family could afford one. Like gravestones in a cemetery, these tablets became the residence of the spirits—at least during special periods of remembrance. The Chinese incorporated ancestral worship into the concept of filial piety—the reverence of children for their parents—by making the male head of the family or clan responsible for periodic ceremonies and offerings of food before the ancestral tablets, such as on the anniversaries of the passing of the deceased. Later, the philosopher Confucius

(Kongfuzi, 551–479 B.C.E.) defined filial piety as the worship of parents (alive or dead) and made it the foundation of both family and civic life. The aristocrats of the Shang dynasty built temples or ancestral halls to house ancestral tablets; ancestral spirits were invoked for good harvests, military victories, and healthy children. Apparently, the origin of writing in the Shang dynasty was connected to consultations with ancestral spirits for the purposes of prophecy or divination.

The earliest examples of PICTOGRAPHIC writing, from c. 1400 B.C.E., are inscriptions on ox bones and tortoise shells used for divination; inscriptions found on bronze vessels are dated c. 1200 B.C.E. Chinese writing evolved from pictograms into a logographic system in which characters could represent individual sounds, or phonemes, as well as ideas, objects, actions, etc. This made it very versatile but also extremely difficult to learn; scholars have identified about 3,000 characters from the Shang period, of which only 800 have been deciphered. Today the larger Chinese dictionaries contain approximately 14,000 signs, with some 4,000 individual characters in widespread use. Since meaning resides in the characters themselves, not in their pronunciation, the Chinese writing system could be exported to all parts of the realm as well as to Japan and Korea, where the pronunciation might be entirely different but the meaning would remain essentially the same.

ZHOU DYNASTY (c. 1027–221 B.C.E.)

The Zhou people came from western China and, guided by the founders of the Zhou dynasty—King Wu and King Cheng—took control of the Yellow River basin, consolidating the region into a central state. Duke Zhou, King Wu's younger brother and regent to King Cheng, instituted feudalism by appointing "lords" to rule over large plots of land in return for military service to the emperor. For the next few centuries a strong central government prevailed in the region. To avoid conflict, very strict rules about the succession of rulers were drawn up; only the first son of a legal wife could succeed his father. The emperor as the "father" of the Chinese people had a divine Mandate of Heaven to govern, as long as he was a virtuous leader; the Zhou leaders had been able to overthrow the previous Shang dynasty because of its corruption. Legends and laws that later inspired Confucian thinkers accumulated under the Zhou rulers.

In contrast to the Vedic culture in India, with its powerful priests and worship of gods associated with the natural world, Chinese feudalism centered on kings, the descendants of the very ancestors who provided blessings from the spirit world who were therefore worshiped by the family. The higher the official in the social and feudal hierarchy, the more ancestors he could legally worship and benefit from. Ancestor tablets were even carried into battle as an invocation for victory.

The central authority of the Zhou court enjoyed stability until about 722 B.C.E., when it was driven to the eastern city of Luoyang. For the next 500 years its kings reigned in name only, preserving the idea of a central state while in fact the country divided into several warring kingdoms. The feudal system became decentralized when local lords took control of the armies and became more powerful than the emperor. And two new "weapons" changed the nature of warfare. The nomads of the Asian steppe introduced the mounted archer, who with his speed and flexibility over rough terrain proved more effective than men in chariots. Meanwhile, the crossbow, with its deadly accuracy, changed the tactics of fighters on the ground.

Zhou Literature. The earliest great work of literature from this period is the *Book of Songs (Shi jing),* sometimes called the *Book of Odes.* Comparable to the Indian Vedas in importance, the *Book of Songs* is an anthology of 305 poems compiled during the period 1000–600 B.C.E. All but five pieces, attributed to the Shang dynasty, belong to Zhou. In addition to hymns to the Zhou ancestors, the collection pays tribute to the history of the Zhou people. Used by Confucius in his teachings, the *Book of Songs* became one of the canonical "Five Classics" of Chinese education. King Wen, the father of King Wu, the founder of the Zhou dynasty, organized the original symbols of the *Book of Changes* into the sixty-four hexagrams that became the basis of an elaborate machinery for divination used by rulers and commoners alike. Duke Zhou provided a basic commentary; later Confucius provided an additional commentary. The *Book of Changes* is widely used today in China and in the West.

Chinese historians refer to the years c. 403 to 221 B.C.E. as the Warring States Period; an extended period of political and social upheaval as well as philosophical controversy, it was also a time of great productivity. This was the time of the "hundred philosophers," an era of intellectual ferment. The same period in India saw innovative thinkers retreat from society into personal salvation; China's philosophical systems, however, were divided over the methods of effective government, whether political systems could be repaired or not. On one hand there was Confucius and Confucian teachers like Mencius (Mengzi, c. 371–c. 288 B.C.E.), thinkers who developed an ideal social theory consisting of a hierarchical structure held together by duty and authority. In Confucius's collected sayings, *The Analects (Lun Yu),* the philosopher explains the fundamental structure of harmonious, respectful family relationships, a model that can then be applied to the realm of rulers and subjects. Mencius further believed that the innate goodness of human beings could provide the basis for a caring society if governments established a moral context for that possibility.

Ritual Vessel, 500–450 B.C.E.
The ding, a three-legged vessel, held food offered to ancestral spirits. Symbols and written characters were usually cast onto its surface. This particular example from the early Warring States Period shows highly abstract and stylized animal-like and geometric elements. (Los Angeles County Museum of Art, Gift of Mr. and Mrs. Lidow. Photograph © 2003 Museum Associates / LACMA)

On the other hand, the philosopher Mozi (Mo Tzu), from the fifth century B.C.E., preached universal love, proposing that love for one's family could be the glue that held society together. But the real radical alternative philosophy to Confucian public service was Daoism. The basic texts of Daoism are the five-thousand-character Dao De Jing by Laozi (c. sixth to third century B.C.E.), called the Bible of Daoism, and the writings of Zhuangzi (fourth century B.C.E.). Often mystical and private, Daoism is committed to a spontaneous and individual adherence to nature's path, the dao or sacred Way. By the time of Zhuangzi, the Daoist disdain for political power and public office was overtly competitive with Confucianism. Daoist reaction to the endless wars and political intrigue of the time was to declare war futile and wasteful. The philosopher Hanfeizi (d. 233 B.C.E.) accused the Daoists of "quietism" and avoiding public responsibility: "They preach the doctrine of Quietism, but their exposition of it is couched in baffling and mysterious terms. . . . I submit that man's duty in life is to serve his prince and to nourish his parents, neither of which things can be done by quietness." Hanfeizi was associated with a school known as the Legalists, who believed in the strict enforcement of laws.

QIN (CH'IN) AND HAN DYNASTIES

The king who reunified China in 221 B.C.E., founded the Qin dynasty, and became the first emperor of China assumed the title Qin Shi Huangdi (Ch'in Shih Huang

TIME AND PLACE

Ancient China: The Five Confucian Classics

Ancient stories from all cultures aim to identify the powerful figures who provided the rudiments of civilization, like the use of fire, the creation of a ceremonial calendar, and the invention of agriculture and writing. These stories deal with the first humans, rituals, the existence of holy places, the reason for death, and the existence of evil. It is supposed that the stories first belonged to small groups, local tribes or communities, and that they were transmitted orally by designated bards or storytellers, by parents and grandparents. As the stories became associated with the history of large segments of a population—national groups—through the introduction of writing, there came a time when the literary materials were edited and organized into an acceptable or standard collection of stories, rituals, and laws. This collection is known as a canon. The works that define ancient Chinese myth, legend, and history, the Chinese canon, are the Five Classics or the Five Confucian Classics, the *Wu jing*. They are the *Yi jing* or *I Ching* (the *Book of Changes*); the *Shu jing* (the *Book of History* or *Book of Documents*); the *Shi jing* (the *Book of Songs* or *Book of Odes*); the *Li ji* (the *Book of Rites*); and the *Chun qiu* (the *Spring and Autumn Annals*). Although by tradition Confucius is credited with having written or at least edited these classics, only the last one, *Spring and Autumn Annals,* is from his period. Studied and memorized for more than two millennia, these texts were the primary works

Confucian Classics, 596–679 C.E. *The Five Confucian Classics have been an important part of Chinese culture for more than two millennia. Here is a seventh-century example, with calligraphy by the early Tang dynasty scholar and minister Chu Zui Liang. (Werner Forman / Art Resource, NY)*

TIME AND PLACE

Ancient China: The Five Confucian Classics continued

used to educate the upper or ruling classes in China.

The *Book of Changes,* attributed to the Shang dynasty (c. 1523–1027 B.C.E.), is a compilation of diagrams that represent the sixty-four basic patterns of existence, such as the relations between the characteristics of heaven and earth. These diagrams can be used either in divination or simply for inspiration. In addition to the diagrams the *Book of Changes* includes extensive commentaries, including a set by Confucius, that describe the basic functions of the universe and human nature. The *Book of History,* attributed primarily to the middle period (c. 800 B.C.E.) of the Zhou dynasty, is a collection of political and legal documents that delineate the proper ways to run a government. The *Book of Songs,* largely from the Zhou dynasty, is a collection of 305 poems divided into four sections about a broad range of subjects, from the early sage-kings Yao, Shun, and Yü to war and courtship. The *Book of Ritual,* edited during the Han dynasty (c. 202 B.C.E.–220 C.E.) is a collection of prayers and religious rites used by the ancient Chinese. The *Spring and Autumn Annals* is the history of a Chinese province, the old state of Lu, from the period 722 to 481 B.C.E. The annals describe natural disasters, provide a summary of events, and tell about Lu's relationships with other feudal states. Because Confucius lived in Lu, it is thought that he had a hand in editing the *Annals.*

Ti). The first half of that title, in the old spelling—Ch'in Shih—became the namesake for the region known today as China; the last half of the name, Huang Ti, invoked the legendary Yellow Emperor of the golden age—*di* or *ti,* which is often translated as "god." Almost immediately Huangdi began construction on the Great Wall, a fifteen- to thirty-foot-high and 1,500-mile-long structure, to keep out warring nomadic barbarians. Following the advice of the Legalists, the emperor created a strong, centralized bureaucracy fed by extensive roads and other means of communication. Despite the fact that the Chinese spoke about eight languages and numerous dialects in the third century B.C.E., their universal writing system brought a sense of national cohesion. Universal taxation, a unified currency, and a standardized written language became the model for the imperial system and is still in place today. In 213 B.C.E. Huangdi tightened the reins of government control by issuing an edict for the burning of books—books by philosophers like Confucius who might object to Huangdi's "politics of despotism." Scholars found to be

www For more information about the culture and context of China in the ancient world, see *World Literature Online* at bedfordstmartins.com/worldlit.

reading or discussing the Chinese classics thirty days after the announcement of the ban were condemned to work on the Great Wall, where they were often buried alive. Huangdi died in 210 B.C.E. and by 207 the Qin dynasty had collapsed.

The Han dynasty, which replaced the Qin, is a notable period in Chinese history known for *promoting* Confucianism and the arts and lasting from 206 B.C.E. to 220 C.E. A highly centralized bureaucratic state controlled by the emperor, the Han rule shifted power from the family to the state while upholding the Confucian ideal of filial piety. In the Han dynasty, respect for the elderly increased, as did ancestor worship. Emperor Wu (140–85 B.C.E.) confiscated lands from the aristocracy and distributed them to the poor. The state took over the production of salt, iron, and wine. The need for bureaucrats led to the creation of a competitive system for entrance into civil service. Men were selected from the lower classes of society, educated in universities, and trained for government entrance exams based on Confucian teachings. The Old Silk Road opened c. 100 B.C.E. and joined China to India, Persia, and Rome; along it ideas flowed from the East to the West and from the West to the East. It was probably in the first century C.E. that a major foreign influence arrived, Buddhism; Buddhism did not become powerful, however, until the period of chaos following the demise of the Han dynasty in 220 C.E.

It was also during the Han dynasty that a Chinese dictionary was compiled. And an advisor in Emperor Wu's court, Sima Qian (Ssu-ma Ch'ien, c. 145–85 B.C.E.) wrote the first extensive history of China, *Historical Records,* which begins with the sage-kings of the golden age, Yao, Shun, and Yu. In his history, Sima Qian includes legendary information about the life of Laozi, the founder of Daoism, and an amazing, almost certainly apocryphal encounter between Laozi (Lao Tzu) and Confucius. According to Sima Qian, Confucius visited Laozi to inquire about ritual and ancient heroes. After being scolded by Laozi about the uselessness of his concerns, Confucius reported to his students: "I know that birds can fly and fish can swim and beasts can run. Snares are set for things that run, nets for those that swim and arrows for whatever flies. But dragons! I shall never know how they ride wind and cloud up into the sky. Today I saw Lao Tzu. What a dragon!"

THE BOOK OF SONGS
c. 1000–600 B.C.E.

The collection of poems called the *Book of Songs (Shi jing)* is a classic work of literature on which all subsequent lyric poetry in China was modeled. The earliest name for the collection was simply *Shi,* meaning "song-words"; the later name, ***Shi jing,*** means "song-word scripture," suggesting a more revered work than a "book of songs." It has also been called the *Book of Odes* and *The Confucian Odes,* since at one time it was thought that Confucius had edited the whole collection, choosing the text's 305 poems from some 3,000 verses. The earliest literatures of most ancient cultures tend to be myths in prose or poetry about the origins of the world, epic poems that celebrate gods and heroes, and hymns to various deities. The equivalent in ancient China is the *Book of Songs,* but instead of focusing on the powerful influence of heavenly beings, this work speaks of earthly experiences in dynastic legends; ritual hymns; warrior ballads; songs for the gathering of clans, sacrifices, and feasting; and lyrics of courtship and grieving.

shur-JING

Although it is impossible to date precisely the individual poems, it is thought that five of them came from the Shang dynasty (c. 1600–c. 1028 B.C.E.) while the majority originated with the Zhou dynasty, the longest, and were collected between 1000 and 600 B.C.E. Certain names and events associated with the invasions of the Hsien-yün tribes help to date several poems at c. 800 B.C.E., but the themes of love and feasting in other verses are too general to associate with any particular period. The great variety of poems provided an ancestry and history for the Zhou dynasty, which itself became the cultural repository for succeeding generations of Chinese. In the fourth century B.C.E., the *Book of Songs* became one of the Five Confucian Classics.

Public Roles for the *Book of Songs.* Like Homer's epics in Greece, the Chinese songs were a major segment of the educational material the upper class was expected to know, especially with regard to the poems that described proper attitudes toward ancestors and the foundations of the Zhou people. The poems also could be cited by scholars in support of opinions and by diplomats to validate policy. The official histories of China provide examples of the use of particular poems. A nobleman in the sixth century B.C.E. attempts to persuade an estranged duke to return home by reciting lines from poem 122: "How few of us are left, how few! / Why do we not go back?" Elsewhere, someone at a banquet analyzes the emotional dispositions of the other guests by the songs that they recite. Poem 268, about the allegiance of brothers, was used by a diplomat who sought ties between his region and another. An envoy to Lu, not recognizing the poem, which was recited at his arrival, totally failed in his mission.

WWW For a quiz on the *Book of Songs,* see *World Literature Online* at bedfordstmartins.com/worldlit.

Confucius envisioned an educational role for the songs. In his teachings, the *Analects,* he explains how the songs provide insight into the

Bronze Bell, sixth–third century B.C.E. *Music played an important role in ancient Chinese culture. Confucius believed music to be one of the highest expressions of human virtue and thus fundamental to human society. (© The Seattle Art Museum, Eugene Fuller Memorial Collection)*

nature of feelings: how to regulate feelings and how to use them to influence other people. He also thought the songs would support dutiful behavior toward parents and the prince, and help people remember the names of birds, animals, plants, and trees. Confucius also believed that the songs had private value, for through them an individual could experience feelings unacceptable in any public setting: feelings of distrust and betrayal, illicit longing and estrangement, political unrest and social discord.

Besides being a repository of Confucian values, *The Songs* are "pure poetry" in that they present us an image, more rather than less full, of the people that wrote and sang them and of the period in which they were written and sung.
– William McNaughton, critic, 1971

Variety of Voices. The individual songs presented here represent a broad array of poetic voices exploring the many facets of human experience—that of soldiers, kings, noblemen, peasants, men, and women. Several love poems deal with courtship, secret meetings, betrayals, and heartache. The warrior songs either glorify war by pointing to specific battles and the value of comrades or lament warfare and being far from home. Many of the poems share a rural setting; some have to do specifically with the passing of seasons, the harvest, feasting, and the necessary sacrifices and ancestral ceremonies. The final poems have to do with dynastic legends and history.

Although these poems appear simple, their spare imagery and careful arrangement convey emotional depth and passion. The typical line in these songs is made up of four Chinese characters, each of which can be translated as a single word; often auxiliary words are needed in English for sense. The result is a compact line in which a simple image might comprise several meanings. As with other writings in China and Japan, both prose and poetry, a single word or a small gesture might represent an intricate complex of events such as adultery or divorce. It is common for a poem to begin with an image from nature that later has emotional resonance. Poem 75, which begins, "Tossed is that cypress boat, / Wave-tossed it floats," explores the many ways in which the speaker is affected by a "plight," one that is not named directly but is causing distress. The speaker imagines her emotions or her state of being in terms of a simple object, but not simply: "Sorrow clings to me / Like an unwashed dress." The consistent theme underlying the many different kinds of verses in the *Book of Songs* is the orderly and harmonious functioning of society as dictated by the Will or the Mandate of Heaven.

The great place of lyric poetry in Chinese literature was established by this anthology. Metaphors that connect problems of the human heart with the world of nature are not common in early Western poetry, and the broad range of topics in the *Book of Songs* is extraordinary.

– G. L. Anderson, critic, 1961

Grouping the Poems. Chinese editions of the *Shi jing (Book of Songs)* do not typically group the poems according to subject; translator Arthur Waley, however, concluded that there were distinct advantages to grouping the poems according to themes, and that grouping is used here. The first two groups of poems deal with courtship and romantic love; the first few poems generally show the sunny side of love affairs, while those that follow explore betrayal and loss. The third group is about the life of a soldier—the hardships of warfare, the bond between comrades, and the longing for home. The fourth group focuses on farm life: the work involved with planting and harvesting, the rituals and ceremonies for giving thanks and celebrating the end of a season. The last two poems, which probably should come first, provide an ancestral, cultural context for the entire group of poems by describing the legendary origins of the Zhou people.

■ CONNECTIONS

Egyptian Love Poems, p. 121. Love poems from various cultural traditions make use of images from nature to express feelings or to describe a loved one. Love poems from ancient Egypt use birds as metaphorical agencies for the expression of love. What roles does nature imagery play in the courtship poems of the Chinese *Book of Songs,* especially as associated with passion and urgency?

Hebrew Scriptures, p. 134. Patriarchs commonly provide models of wisdom and are credited for inventions like writing and agriculture in ancient cultures. The patriarchs in the Book of Genesis interpret dreams and establish a dialogue with the Hebrew God, Yahweh. How do the dynastic patriarchs in the *Book of Songs* differ in their cultural roles from the Hebrew patriarchs?

Rumi, poems (Book 2). When lyric poems use sensuous imagery it is not always clear whether those images carry a spiritual meaning or whether they are simply meant to evoke human courtship. Rumi is famous for discovering his Beloved deity in everyday experience. Even though the "Harvest Poems" in the Chinese *Book of Songs* are not about a direct experience of a deity or an ancestor, how do they point to ways of connecting with the spirit world?

■ **FURTHER RESEARCH**

Literary Texts

Karlgren, Bernhard. *The Book of Odes.* 1950.
Legge, James. *The Chinese Classics.* vol. 3. 1960.
McNaughton, William. *The Book of Songs.* 1971.
Waley, James. *The Book of Songs.* 1960.

Background and Commentary

Yu, Pauline. *The Reading of Imagery in the Chinese Tradition.* 1987.
Wang, Ching-hsien. *The Bell and the Drum: Shih Ching as Formulaic Poetry in an Oral Tradition.* 1974.
Watson, Burton. *Early Chinese Literature.* 1962.

The Book of Songs

Translated by Arthur Waley

17: Plop fall the plums

Plop fall the plums; but there are still seven.[1]
Let those gentlemen that would court me
Come while it is lucky!

Plop fall the plums; there are still three.
Let any gentleman that would court me
Come before it is too late!

Plop fall the plums; in shallow baskets we lay them.
Any gentleman who would court me
Had better speak while there is time.

Love Poems. According to translator Arthur Waley, "Plop fall the plums" is similar "to love-divinations of the type, 'Loves me, loves me not' and 'This year, next year, some time, never.'" Poem 24 draws on the tradition of secret nighttime visits between lovers, with the expectation that the visiting paramour will leave discreetly before daybreak, a common scene in ballads around the world. In the poem a women entreats her lover not to damage the garden, sneak into her home, and invite the disapproval of family and village, while at the same time expressing her love. Her unspoken message might even be an invitation to risk everything for their reunion. Poems 25 and 26, also written from a woman's point of view and having a similar theme and setting to Poem 24, speak of quite a different outcome. The second stanza of Poem 25 contains a pair of magical lines: after the woman tells her lover to bring home game to be dressed and eaten, she says, "And when I have dressed them we will drink wine / And I will be yours till we are old." The banquet becomes the setting for their union. In Poem 26, written as a dialogue, the poet captures the woman's

---

[1] **seven:** A lucky number for the Chinese.

24: I beg of you, Chung Tzu

I BEG of you, Chung Tzu,
Do not climb into our homestead,
Do not break the willows we have planted.
Not that I mind about the willows,
But I am afraid of my father and mother.
Chung Tzu I dearly love;
But of what my father and mother say
Indeed I am afraid.

I beg of you, Chung Tzu,
Do not climb over our wall,
Do not break the mulberry-trees we have planted.
Not that I mind about the mulberry-trees,
But I am afraid of my brothers.
Chung Tzu I dearly love;
But of what my brothers say
Indeed I am afraid.

I beg of you, Chung Tzu,
Do not climb into our garden,
Do not break the hard-wood we have planted.
Not that I mind about the hard-wood,
But I am afraid of what people will say.
Chung Tzu I dearly love;
But of all that people will say
Indeed I am afraid.

25: The lady says: "The cock has crowed"

THE lady says: "The cock has crowed";
The knight says: "Day has not dawned."
"Rise, then, and look at the night;
The morning star is shining.

---

anxiety about her lover's presence being discovered. Poem 30, which extols the qualities of a beloved, makes excellent use of contrasting lines as the narrator explains the effects of her lover's absence. Two poems explore unsuccessful affairs of the heart.

A note on the translation: Arthur Waley does a fine job of translating Chinese poetry into English. Unless otherwise indicated, all notes are the editors'.

You must be out and abroad,
Must shoot the wild-duck and wild-geese.

When you have shot them, you must bring them home
And I will dress them for you,
And when I have dressed them we will drink wine
And I will be yours till we are old.
I will set your zitherns before you;
All shall be peaceful and good.

Did I but know those who come to you,
I have girdle-stones of many sorts to give them;
Did I but know those that have followed you,
I have girdle-stones of many sorts as presents for them.
Did I know those that love you,
I have girdle-stones of many sorts to requite them."

26: The Lady: The cock has crowed

THE LADY: The cock has crowed;
    It is full daylight.
THE LOVER: It was not the cock that crowed,
    It was the buzzing of those green flies.
THE LADY: The eastern sky glows;
    It is broad daylight.
THE LOVER: That is not the glow of dawn,
    But the rising moon's light.
    The gnats fly drowsily;
    It would be sweet to share a dream with you.
THE LADY: Quick! Go home!
    Lest I have cause to hate you!

30: Shu is away in the hunting-fields

Shu is away in the hunting-fields,
There is no one living in our lane.
Of course there *are* people living in our lane;
But they are not like Shu,
So beautiful, so good.

Shu has gone after game.
No one drinks wine in our lane.
Of course people *do* drink wine in our lane

But they are not like Shu,
So beautiful, so loved.

Shu has gone to the wilds,
No one drives horses in our lane.
Of course people *do* drive horses in our lane.
But they are not like Shu,
So beautiful, so brave.

63: In the wilds there is a dead doe

In the wilds there is a dead doe;
With white rushes we cover her.
There was a lady longing for the spring;
A fair knight seduced her.

In the wood there is a clump of oaks,
And in the wilds a dead deer
With white rushes well bound;
There was a lady fair as jade.

"Heigh, not so hasty, not so rough;
Heigh, do not touch my handkerchief.[1]
Take care, or the dog will bark."

75: Tossed is that cypress boat

Tossed is that cypress boat,
Wave-tossed it floats.
My heart is in turmoil, I cannot sleep.
But secret is my grief.
Wine I have, all things needful
For play, for sport.

My heart is not a mirror,
To reflect what others will.

Love's Betrayal. These poems have to do with unsuccessful affairs of the heart. Poem 63 is about a seduction in which a woman is poignantly compared to a dead doe. The images of the boat and the sea in Poem 75 complement the turbulent feelings of the female speaker. As she compares her heart to several objects, she draws a picture of the criticism she has received for her romance.

---

[1] **handkerchief:** Worn on a sash around the waist; to touch the handkerchief is flirtatious.

Brothers too I have;
I cannot be snatched away.
But lo, when I told them of my plight
I found that they were angry with me.

My heart is not a stone;
It cannot be rolled.
My heart is not a mat;
It cannot be folded away.
I have borne myself correctly
In rites more than can be numbered.

My sad heart is consumed, I am harassed
By a host of small men.
I have borne vexations very many,
Received insults not few.
In the still of night I brood upon it;
In the waking hours I rend my breast.

O sun, ah, moon,
Why are you changed and dim?
Sorrow clings to me
Like an unwashed dress.
In the still of night I brood upon it,
Long to take wing and fly away.

131: We plucked the bracken

We plucked the bracken,[1] plucked the bracken
While the young shoots were springing up.
Oh, to go back, go back!
The year is ending.
We have no house, no home

Warrior Songs. These poems are about the invasion by the Hsien-yün, a fierce enemy from the northeastern region of China, c. 800 B.C.E. In Poem 131, a warrior feels caught between memories of home—images of peacetime—and loyalty to his lord and the fight. The campaign, which began in the spring, has lasted into the winter and worn down the soldiers. Poem 132 mentions Nan-chung, a general who is thought to have served King Hsüan (827–782 B.C.E.), one of a succession of Zhou kings. Poem 148 evokes a soldier's feelings for a comrade-in-arms through simple gestures.

[1] **bracken:** Coarse, weedy ferns.

Because of the Hsien-yün.[2]
We cannot rest or bide
Because of the Hsien-yün.

We plucked the bracken, plucked the bracken
While the shoots were soft.
Oh, to go back, go back!
Our hearts are sad,
Our sad hearts burn,
We are hungry and thirsty,
But our campaign is not over,
Nor is any of us sent home with news.

We plucked the bracken, plucked the bracken;
But the shoots were hard.
Oh, to go back, go back!
The year is running out.
But the king's business never ends;
We cannot rest or bide.
Our sad hearts are very bitter;
We went, but do not come.

What splendid thing is that?
It is the flower of the cherry-tree.
What great carriage is that?
It is our lord's chariot,
His war-chariot ready yoked,
With its four steeds so eager.
How should we dare stop or tarry?
In one month we have had three alarms.

We yoke the teams of four,
Those steeds so strong,
That our lord rides behind,
That lesser men protect.
The four steeds so grand,
The ivory bow-ends, the fish-skin quiver.
Yes, we must be always on our guard;
The Hsien-yün are very swift.

Long ago, when we started,
The willows spread their shade.

---

[2] **Hsien-yün:** A non-Chinese people who raided the Zhou lands.

Now that we turn back
The snowflakes fly.
The march before us is long,
We are thirsty and hungry,
Our hearts are stricken with sorrow,
But no one listens to our plaint.

132: We bring out our carts

We bring out our carts
On to those pasture-grounds.
From where the Son of Heaven[3] is
Orders have come that we are to be here.
The grooms are told
To get the carts loaded up.
The king's service brings many hardships;
It makes swift calls upon us.

We bring out our carts
On to those outskirts.
Here we set up the standards,
There we raise the ox-tail banners,
The falcon-banner and the standards
That flutter, flutter.
Our sad hearts are very anxious;
The grooms are worn out.

The king has ordered Nan-chung
To go and build a fort on the frontier.
To bring out the great concourse of chariots,
With dragon banners and standards so bright.
The Son of Heaven has ordered us
To build a fort on that frontier.
Terrible is Nan-chung;
The Hsien-yün are undone.

Long ago, when we started,
The wine-millet and cooking-millet were in flower.
Now that we are on the march again
Snow falls upon the mire.
The king's service brings many hardships.
We have no time to rest or bide.

---

[3] **the Son of Heaven:** King Hsüan.

We do indeed long to return;
But we fear the writing on the tablets.[4]

"Dolefully cry the cicadas,
Hop and skip go the grasshoppers.
Before I saw my lord
My heart was full of grief.
But now that I have seen my lord
My heart is still."[5]
Terrible is Nan-chun;
Lo, he has stricken the warriors of the West!

The spring days are drawn out;
All plants and trees are in leaf.
Tuneful is the oriole's song.
The women gather aster[6] in crowds.
We have bound the culprits; we have captured the chieftains,
And here we are home again!
Terrible is Nan-chung;
The Hsien-yün are levelled low.

148: How can you plead that you have no wraps?

How can you plead that you have no wraps?
I will share my rug with you.
The king is raising an army;
I have made ready both axe and spear;
You shall share them with me as my comrade.

How can you plead that you have no wraps?
I will share my under-robe with you.
The king is raising an army,
I have made ready both spear and halberd;[7]
You shall share them with me when we start.

How can you plead that you have no wraps?
I will share my skirt[8] with you.

---

[4] **the writing . . . tablets:** The king's command. (Translator's note.)

[5] **"Dolefully . . . still":** Bridal-hymn formula, spoken by the wives. (Translator's note.)

[6] **aster:** For use in the ancestral temple. (Translator's note.)

[7] **halberd:** Battle-ax.

[8] **I will . . . skirt:** As a rug at night. (Translator's note.)

The king is raising an army,
I have made ready both armour and arms;
You shall share them with me on the march.

157: THEY CLEAR AWAY THE GRASS, THE TREES

THEY clear away the grass, the trees;
Their ploughs open up the ground.
In a thousand pairs they tug at weeds and roots,
Along the low grounds, along the ridges.
There is the master and his eldest son,
There the headman and overseer.
They mark out, they plough.
Deep the food-baskets that are brought;
Dainty are the wives,
The men press close to them.
And now with shares so sharp
They set to work upon the southern acre.
They sow the many sorts of grain,
The seeds that hold moist life.
How the blade shoots up,
How sleek, the grown plant;
Very sleek, the young grain!
Band on band, the weeders ply their task.
Now they reap, all in due order;
Close-packed are their stooks[1]—
Myriads, many myriads and millions,
To make wine, make sweet liquor,
As offering to ancestor and ancestress,
For fulfilment of all the rites.
"When sweet the fragrance of offering,
Glory shall come to the fatherland.
When pungent the scent,
The blessed elders are at rest."
Not only here is it like this,
Not only now is it so.
From long ago it has been thus.

Harvest Poems. In beautifully concrete images, Poems 157 and 162 trace the process of agriculture, from the clearing of the fields to harvesting to the manufacture of offerings to the ancestors. Lines 25 to 28 of Poem 157 seem to be a ritual saying used during the actual offering ceremony; the poem's conclusion is an affirmation of tradition. Poem 195 is about the need for celebration.

[1] **stooks:** Shocks, or stacks of grain sheaves.

162: The big field brings a heavy crop

The big field brings a heavy crop.
We have chosen the seed, have seen to our tools;
We have got everything ready for you.[2]
With our sharp ploughs
Let us begin on the southern acre.
Now we sow our many crops;
They grow straight and tall;
The Descendant[3] is well pleased.

There are no bare patches, everywhere our crops sprout,
They are firm, they are good,
There is no foxtail, no weeds.
Avaunt, all earwigs and pests,
Do not harm our young crops.
The Field Grandad[4] has holy power,
He can take you and offer you to the flaming fire.

A damp air comes chill,
Brings clouds that gather,
Raining on our lord's fields
And then on our private plots.
There stand some backward blades that were not reaped,
Here some corn that was not garnered,
There an unremembered sheaf,
Here some littered grain—
Gleanings for the widowed wife.

Here is the Descendant
With his wife and children
Bringing dinner to the southern acres.
The labourers come to take good cheer.
Then he makes offering to the quarters,
Smoke-offering and sacrifice,
With his red bull and his black,
With his wine-millet and cooking-millet,
Makes offering and sacrifice,
That blessings may be ours for evermore.

---

[2] **you:** The overseer or lord.

[3] **The Descendant:** The sacrificer in the harvest ritual.

[4] **The Field Grandad:** A remnant from the previous harvest kept as a talisman for the new crop.

195: Ting, ting goes the woodman's axe

Ting, ting goes the woodman's axe;
Ying, ying cry the birds,
Leave the dark valley,
Mount to the high tree.
"Ying" they cry,
Each searching its mate's voice.

Seeing then that even a bird
Searches for its mate's voice,
How much the more must man
Needs search out friends and kin.
For the spirits are listening
Whether we are all friendly and at peace.

"Heave ho," cry the woodcutters.
I have strained my wine so clear,
I have got a fatted lamb
To which I invite all my fathers.[5]
Even if they choose not to come
They cannot say I have neglected them.

Spick and span I have sprinkled and swept,
I have set out the meats, the eight dishes of grain.
I have got a fatted ox,
To which I invite all my uncles,
And even if they choose not to come
They cannot hold me to blame.

They are cutting wood on the bank.
Of strained wine I have good store;
The dishes and trays are all in rows.
Elder brothers and younger brothers, do not stay afar!
If people lose the virtue that is in them,
It is a dry throat that has led them astray.

When we have got wine we strain it, we!
When we have none, we buy it, we!
Bang, bang we drum, do we!
Nimbly step the dance, do we!
And take this opportunity
Of drinking clear wine.

[5] **all . . . my fathers:** Paternal uncles.

238: She who in the beginning gave birth to the people

She who in the beginning gave birth to the people,
This was Chiang Yüan.[1]
How did she give birth to the people?
Well she sacrificed and prayed
That she might no longer be childless.
She trod on the big toe of God's footprint,
Was accepted and got what she desired.
Then in reverence, then in awe
She gave birth, she nurtured;
And this was Hou Chi.[2]

Indeed, she had fulfilled her months,
And her first-born came like a lamb
With no bursting or rending,
With no hurt or harm.
To make manifest His magic power
God[3] on high gave her ease.
So blessed were her sacrifice and prayer
That easily she bore her child.

Indeed, they put it in a narrow lane;
But oxen and sheep tenderly cherished it.

Dynastic Legends. Poem 238 describes the legendary origins of the Zhou people, created from a woman whose barrenness is healed miraculously. She gives birth to Hou Chi, the ancestor of the Zhou people who survives infancy despite being left alone in the wild. Stories of barren women becoming fertile is a common motif in the Book of Genesis (Hebrew Scriptures), and unusually strong and blessed infants are found in a number of ancient traditions, namely the Mesopotamian Gilgamesh and Sargon, the Hebrew Moses, the Greek Oedipus and Heracles, the Roman Romulus and Remus, the Christian Jesus, and the Teutonic Sigurd or Siegfried. Like other heroes, Hou Chi is assisted by the animal world and people close to nature, like woodcutters. Hou Chi is a culture-bringer: He becomes the father of agriculture—hence his name, Lord Millet—and the originator of sacrifices to ancestors.

Poem 241 is about King Wên, a founder of the Zhou (Chou) dynasty. It reiterates a theme repeated throughout Chinese literature: A dynasty exists only as long as it has the favor of Heaven; the Shang dynasty, which preceded the Zhou, lost Heaven's charge and was replaced. The last section of the poem is a warning about the temporary nature of rulership.

---

[1] **Chiang Yüan:** The mother who miraculously conceives and gives birth to the ancestor of the Zhou people.

[2] **Hou Chi:** Lord Millet.

[3] **God:** This translation uses "God" for the Chinese *ti*, which might also be translated as "the deified ancestor or spirit of a former king who resides on high"; *God* seems simpler.

Indeed, they[4] put it in a far-off wood;
But it chanced that woodcutters came to this wood.
Indeed, they put it on the cold ice;
But the birds covered it with their wings.
The birds at last went away,
And Hou Chi began to wail.

Truly far and wide
His voice was very loud.
Then sure enough he began to crawl;
Well he straddled, well he reared,
To reach food for his mouth.
He planted large beans;
His beans grew fat and tall.
His paddy-lines were close set,
His hemp and wheat grew thick,
His young gourds teemed.

Truly Hou Chi's husbandry
Followed the way that had been shown.[5]
He cleared away the thick grass,
He planted the yellow crop.
It failed nowhere, it grew thick,
It was heavy, it was tall,
It sprouted, it eared,
It was firm and good,
It nodded, it hung—
He made house and home in T'ai.

Indeed, the lucky grains were sent down to us,
The black millet, the double-kernelled,
Millet pink-sprouted and white.
Far and wide the black and the double-kernelled
He reaped and acred;[6]
Far and wide the millet pink and white
He carried in his arms, he bore on his back,
Brought them home, and created the sacrifice.

Indeed, what are they, our sacrifices?
We pound the grain, we bale it out,

[4] **they:** The ballad does not tell us who exposed the child. According to one version it was the mother herself; according to another, her husband. (Translator's note.)

[5] **had been shown:** By Heaven.

[6] **acred:** The yield was reckoned per acre (100 ft. square). (Translator's note.)

We sift, we tread,
We wash it—soak, soak;
We boil it all steamy.
Then with due care, due thought
We gather southernwood, make offering of fat,
Take lambs for the rite of expiation,
We roast, we broil,
To give a start to the coming year.

High we load the stands,
The stands of wood and of earthenware.
As soon as the smell rises
God on high is very pleased:
'What smell is this, so strong and good?'
Hou Chi founded the sacrifices,
And without blemish or flaw
They have gone on till now.

241: King Wên is on high

King Wên is on high;
Oh, he shines in Heaven!
Chou is an old people,
But its charge is new.
The land of Chou became illustrious,
Blessed by God's[7] charge.
King Wên ascends and descends
On God's left hand, on His right.

Very diligent was King Wên,
His high fame does not cease;
He spread his bounties in Chou,
And now in his grandsons and sons,
In his grandsons and sons
The stem has branched
Into manifold generations,
And all the knights of Chou
Are glorious in their generation.

Glorious in their generation,
And their counsels well pondered.
Mighty were the many knights
That brought this kingdom to its birth.

[7] **God's:** See note 3 for Poem 238.

This kingdom well they bore;
They were the prop of Chou.
Splendid were those many knights
Who gave comfort to Wên the king.

August is Wên the king;
Oh, to be reverenced in his glittering light!
Mighty the charge that Heaven gave him.
The grandsons and sons of the Shang,[8]
Shang's grandsons and sons,
Their hosts were innumerable.
But God on high gave His command,
And by Chou they were subdued.

By Chou they were subdued;
Heaven's charge is not for ever.
The knights of Yin,[9] big and little,
Made libations and offerings at the capital;
What they did was to make libations
Dressed in skirted robe and close cap.
O chosen servants of the king,
May you never thus shame your ancestors!

May you never shame your ancestors,
But rather tend their inward power,
That for ever you may be linked to Heaven's charge[10]
And bring to yourselves many blessings.
Before Yin lost its army
It was well linked to God above.
In Yin you should see as in a mirror
That Heaven's high charge is hard to keep.

The charge is not easy to keep.
Do not bring ruin on yourselves.
Send forth everywhere the light of your good fame;
Consider what Heaven did to the Yin.
High Heaven does its business
Without sound, without smell.
Make King Wên your example,
In whom all the peoples put their trust.

---

[8] **grandsons . . . Shang:** The dynasty overthrown by the Zhou.

[9] **Yin:** Another name for Shang.

[10] **Heaven's charge:** Kings rule in virtue of a charge *(ming)*, an appointment assigned to them by Heaven, just as barons hold their fiefs in virtue of a *ming* from their overlord. (Translator's note.)

Confucius (Kongfuzi)

551–479 B.C.E.

Like Socrates, Buddha, and Jesus, Confucius[1] left behind no writings of his own. What is known in English as *The Analects of Confucius,* as their first major translator into English, James Legge, called them, is a compendium of collected aphoristic tales and sayings handed down from Confucius's earliest followers and students; *Lun Yu,* as this same collection is known in Chinese, literally means "selected sayings." Confucius was the most profoundly influential thinker in Asia, for his teachings gave rise to a sociophilosophical system that has endured for more than 2,000 years. Confucius developed his system of morality during an era called the Period of the Hundred Philosophers, the classical age of Chinese philosophy that included such sages as Confucius; Laozi (Lao Tzu, sixth–third century B.C.E.); Mozi (Mo Tzu, c. 468–376 B.C.E.); Mengzi (Mencius, c. 371–c. 288 B.C.E.); Zhuangzi (Chuang Tzu, c. 369–286 B.C.E.); and Hui Shih (c. 370–310 B.C.E.). Daoism in particular offered an alternative to the social reform recommended by teachers like Confucius; Daoists favored a retreat from public duty and dedication to a life of meditation and spiritual growth.

By the second century B.C.E., Confucianism had become official doctrine in China, and it remains so today, having survived attempts to discredit it or to reduce it to rigid, unworkable dogma. Despite the inherent conservatism of Confucianism, which emphasizes filial piety (respect and loyalty on the part of children for their parents and ancestors), dutiful respect for authority, and deference to tradition, it has influenced various democratic movements in the East as well as the West. Sun Yat-sen,[2] for example, called Confucius and his best-known disciple, Mencius, fathers of the Chinese Revolution. Concerning Confucianism, modern historian Kevin Reilly asserts: "Whether practiced or honored in the breach, interpreted in various ways, enshrined as official orthodoxy, or sometimes vilified, probably no set of ideas has influenced so many people in the history of the world."

Portrait of Confucius
As the preeminent Chinese philosopher, teacher, and political theorist, Confucius has influenced Eastern and Western political and religious thought for more than two millennia. (Bettmann / CORBIS)

The Making of a Strong Mind. The life story of Confucius has been obscured by layers of legend that have accrued around his name. It is known that he was born in 551 B.C.E. in the feudal province of Lu, in eastern China north of the Yangtze River, probably to a family of the lower aristocracy, although legend has it that he sprung from more humble origins. Orphaned at an early age, Kongfuzi, or Master Kung (Latinized to "Confucius"), became a philosopher-teacher after intensive study of the

WWW For links to more information about Confucius and a quiz on the *Analects,* see *World Literature Online* at bedfordstmartins .com/worldlit.

[1] **Confucius:** The Chinese name for Confucius is Kongfuzi, but the Latinized version, Confucius, is so ingrained in the tradition of Chinese studies that it is the preferred name—at least for the time being.

[2] **Sun Yat-sen** (1866–1925): A Chinese revolutionary who in 1911 supported the overthrow of the Manchu dynasty and the establishment of a republic in China.

All Chinese philosophy is essentially the study of how men can best be helped to live together in harmony and good order.

– ARTHUR WALEY, historian and translator, 1949

traditional Five Classics,[3] a collection of poems, lore, and documents rooted in the ancient history of China. As *The Analects* report him to have said, "At fifteen I wanted to learn. At thirty I had a foundation. At forty, a certitude. At fifty, knew the orders of heaven. At sixty, was ready to listen to them. At seventy, could follow my own heart's desire without overstepping the law" (II.4). Apparently, Confucius began teaching before he knew certitude, for he began teaching just before his mother's death, when he was twenty-three. After a three-year period of grieving, he resumed his teaching and traveled from court to court as a wandering sage trying to teach the way of "Right Government" and "Right Living."

JOH

Political Instability. Confucius lived during the political decline of the **Zhou** dynasty (c. 770–256 B.C.E.), an age of great importance to Chinese culture. It was a time of unprecedented social and technological change during which the arts and letters flourished despite the lack of a strong central government. The power of feudal lords had come to overshadow that of the kings descended from the Zhou invaders, who had overthrown the ancient Shang dynasty.[4] Once the center of political power, these traditional leaders had been reduced to nominal roles as spiritual leaders. Most important for Confucianism, it was a time of instability when the feudal system that had held China intact began to break down; with a weakened central power, rivalries arose among the competing provincial lords. In the last years of his life, Confucius traveled to the courts of these once subordinate lords, unsuccessfully trying to convince them to accept his ways and to convert them into philosopher-kings, an ideal he held in common with Plato. Thus the practical piety, filial obligation, and respect for tradition that Confucius taught arose in part from his intention to preserve the failing integrity of Chinese society. Confucius returned home at the age of sixty-nine and devoted himself to writing. Books attributed to him include the *Book of Songs* (***Shi jing***) and the *Book of Writings (Shu jing)*. He died in 479 B.C.E. an apparent failure; he had not become the valued advisor to a great prince who might have restored the legendary Golden Age of **Yao** (third millennium B.C.E.).

shur-JING

YOW

The Analects. The selections from *The Analects* here give a fair sample of the basic tenets of Confucius's thought: its focus on the matters of this world; its celebration of the family as the central pillar of political and social life; and its emphasis on practicing a "middle way" that leads to moral propriety and social responsibility. Confucius did not consider himself the originator of his ideas, as he clearly states in Book VII: "I have transmitted what was taught to me without making up anything of my own. I have been faithful to and loved the Ancients." At the center of Con-

[3] **the Five Classics:** The Five Classics, memorized by educated Chinese for some two thousand years, include the *Book of Songs*, the *Book of Historical Documents*, the *Book of Changes* (the *I Ching*), the *Spring and Autumn Annals*, and the *Records of Ritual*.

[4] **Shang dynasty** (c. 1600–c. 1028 B.C.E.): An early feudal period in Chinese history.

fucianism, indeed of most Chinese thought, is the idea of the dao, or Way, which in *The Analects* means the virtuous life, the Way of Heaven. For Confucius, following the Way takes effort, a conscious striving for betterment and, above all, instruction. The dao in Daoism is the direct opposite, however; effort as well as ego must be laid aside in Daoism in order to move quietly and harmoniously in the eternal flow of life. Confucius's main teaching was that people should set aside self-interest for the good of others—their immediate family, their province, and their state.

The power that sustains relationships is benevolence, or *jen* (also spelled *ren*); the Chinese ideogram for *jen* is a combination of a sign meaning "human" and the sign for "two"—a respectful relationship based on human feeling, or benevolence. Right conduct at home, achieved through observing ritual and basing action in moral principle, leads ultimately to a balanced individual, family, and state.

According to Confucianism, the daily task of dealing with social affairs in human relations is not something alien to the sage. Carrying on this task is the very essence of the development of the perfection of his personality. He performs it not only as a citizen of society, but also as a "citizen of the universe," ***t'ien min,*** **as Mencius called it.**

–Yu-Lan Fung, philosopher, 1948

■ CONNECTIONS

Hebrew Scriptures, p. 134. The two most famous lawgivers in the East and in the West are Confucius and Moses. The writings associated with their pronouncements represent two totally different cultural traditions. Drawing on the tradition of law in the ancient Near East and on the Code of Hammurabi, Moses' teachings are exceedingly orderly and coherent. How would you characterize *The Analects*? What might account for the nature of their compilation?

Zhuangzi (Chuang Tzu), Chuang Tzu: Basic Writings, p. 1613; Laozi (Lao Tzu), Dao De Jing (Tao Te Ching), p. 1605. Confucius and the Daoists Laozi and Zhuangzi take two fundamentally different approaches to the ethical life. How is the use of poetry and anecdote in the writings of Laozi and Zhuangzi appropriate for a mystical approach to ethics and a concern for the transformation of consciousness? How is Confucius's legalistic approach to setting guidelines for proper conduct represented in his writings?

Bhagavad Gita, p. 1488. Behind the moral systems of the ancient world were concepts of cosmic order and justice that provided continuity. The Bhagavad Gita validates religion and assesses Indian heroes through *dharma* (duty). Why does Confucius need to invoke the dao as a cosmic law that reinforces a secular ethic of duty?

The Book of Job, p. 169. There is a vast difference between the idea of the personal deity of Western religions and the rather abstract, metaphysical principle of the dao in China. The Book of Job represents the wisdom tradition of the ancient Hebrews, with their personalized God who sits in judgment of humankind. How is the Hebrew god different from the principle of filial piety in Confucius?

I have read the books of Confucius with attention, I have made extracts from them; I found that they spoke only the purest morality. . . . He appeals only to virtue, he preaches no miracles, there is nothing in them of religious allegory.

–Voltaire

■ FURTHER RESEARCH

Background

Ames, R. T. *Thinking Through Confucius.* 1987.
Creel, H. G. *Confucius: The Man and the Myth.* 1951.
Fingarette, Herbert. *Confucius: The Sacred as Secular.* 1972.
Wu-chi, Liu. *An Introduction to Chinese Literature.* 1966.

Editions with Commentary

Dawson, Raymond, trans. *Confucius: The Analects.* 1993.
Lau, D. C., trans. *Confucius: The Analects.* 1979.
Waley, Arthur, trans. *The Analects of Confucius.* 1958.

■ **PRONUNCIATION**

Jan Ch'iu: jahn-CHYOO, jahn-CHOO
P'êng: BUNG
Shi jing: shur-JING
Tsêng: DZUNG
Tzu-kung: dzuh-GOHNG
Tzu-hsia: dzuh-SHAH
Tzu-yu: dzuh-YOO
Yao: YOW
Zhou: JOH

FROM

The Analects

Translated by Arthur Waley

[On Confucius the Man]

Book VII

4 In his leisure hours the Master's manner was very free-and-easy, and his expression alert and cheerful.

15 The 'Duke of Shê'[1] asked Tzu-lu about Master K'ung (Confucius). Tzu-lu did not reply. The Master said, Why did you not say 'This is the character of the man: so intent upon enlightening the eager that he forgets his hunger, and so happy in doing so, that he forgets the bitterness of his lot and does not realize that old age is at hand.[2] That is what he is.'

26 The Master fished with a line but not with a net; when fowling he did not aim at a roosting bird.

The Analects. This text is a compilation of the sayings or teachings of Confucius gathered by his students, which according to tradition numbered some three thousand. Although there is no certain date for their composition, it is thought that the teachings were written down several hundred years after Confucius's death. At some point the writings were organized into their present edition of twenty books. The sayings and anecdotes, which together do not possess the coherence of philosophical essays, seem to answer particular questions or situations. Their terse, truncated style is reminiscent of the verses in the Book of Proverbs in the Hebrew Scriptures.

Ordinarily, *The Analects* are published in their original sequence. The chapters of selected books have been rearranged here, however, according to the basic themes of Confucianism, to aid readers' understanding.

A note on the translation: Arthur Waley's original footnotes have been edited for length and style.

---

[1] **The 'Duke of Shê':** An adventurer, known originally as Shên Chu-liang; first mentioned in 523 B.C.E. and still alive in 475. The title 'Duke of Shê' was one which he had invented for himself.

[2] **old age . . . hand:** According to the traditional chronology Confucius was sixty-two at the time when this was said.

31 When in the Master's presence anyone sang a song that he liked, he did not join in at once, but asked for it to be repeated and then joined in.

37 The Master's manner was affable yet firm, commanding but not harsh, polite but easy.

Book X

7, 8 When preparing himself for sacrifice he must wear the Bright Robe,[3] and it must be of linen. He must change his food and also the place where he commonly sits. But there is no objection to his rice being of the finest quality, nor to his meat being finely minced. Rice affected by the weather or turned he must not eat, nor fish that is not sound, nor meat that is high. He must not eat anything discoloured or that smells bad. He must not eat what is overcooked nor what is undercooked, nor anything that is out of season. He must not eat what has been crookedly cut, nor any dish that lacks its proper seasoning. The meat that he eats must at the very most not be enough to make his breath smell of meat rather than of rice. As regards wine, no limit is laid down; but he must not be disorderly. He may not drink wine bought at a shop or eat dried meat from the market. He need not refrain from such articles of food as have ginger sprinkled over them; but he must not eat much of such dishes.[4]

After a sacrifice in the ducal palace, the flesh must not be kept overnight. No sacrificial flesh may be kept beyond the third day. If it is kept beyond the third day, it may no longer be eaten. While it is being eaten, there must be no conversation, nor any word spoken while lying down after the repast. Any article of food, whether coarse rice, vegetables, broth or melon, that has been used as an offering must be handled with due solemnity.

12 When the stables were burnt down, on returning from Court, he said, Was anyone hurt? He did not ask about the horses.

[On Education]

Book II

15 The Master said, 'He who learns but does not think, is lost.' He who thinks but does not learn is in great danger.[5]

17 The Master said, Yu,[6] shall I teach you what knowledge is? When you know a thing, to recognize that you know it, and when you do not know a thing, to recognize that you do not know it. That is knowledge.[7]

---

[3] **the Bright Robe:** *Ming I,* the 'spirit robe' used during the period of purification.

[4] **When preparing . . . dishes:** All the above refers to periods of preparation for sacrifice.

[5] **'He who . . . danger:** I imagine that the first clause is a proverbial saying, and that Confucius meets it with the second clause. The proverb says: 'To learn without thinking is fatal.' Confucius says: To think but not to learn (i.e., study the Way of the ancients) is equally dangerous.

[6] **Yu:** Familiar name of the disciple Tzu-lu.

[7] **That is knowledge:** That knowledge consists in knowing that one does not know is a frequent theme in early Chinese texts.

Book VII

1, 2 The Master said, I have 'transmitted what was taught to me without making up anything of my own.' I have been faithful to and loved the Ancients. In these respects, I make bold to think, not even our old P'êng[8] can have excelled me. The Master said, I have listened in silence and noted what was said, I have never grown tired of learning nor wearied of teaching others what I have learnt.

Book XIII

9 When the Master was going to Wei, Jan Ch'iu drove him. The Master said, What a dense population! Jan Ch'iu said, When the people have multiplied, what next should be done for them? The Master said, Enrich them. Jan Ch'iu said, When one has enriched them, what next should be done for them? The Master said, Instruct them.

Book XV

35 The Master said, When it comes to Goodness one need not avoid competing with one's teacher.

[On Goodness]

Book IV

15 The Master said, Shên! My Way has one (thread) that runs right through it. Master Tsêng said, Yes. When the Master had gone out, the disciples asked, saying What did he mean? Master Tsêng said, Our Master's Way is simply this: Loyalty, consideration.[9]

Book VI

28 Tzu-kung said, If a ruler not only conferred wide benefits upon the common people, but also compassed the salvation of the whole State, what would you say of him? Surely, you would call him Good? The Master said, it would no longer be a matter of 'Good.' He would without doubt be a Divine Sage. Even Yao and Shun could hardly criticize him. As for Goodness—you yourself desire rank and standing; then help others to get rank and standing. You want to turn your own merits to account; then help others to turn theirs to account—in fact, the ability to take one's own feelings as a guide—that is the sort of thing that lies in the direction of Goodness.

[8] **our old P'êng:** It is the special business of old men to transmit traditions.

[9] **Loyalty, consideration:** Loyalty to superiors; consideration for the feelings of others, 'not doing to them anything one would not like to have done to oneself.'

Book VII

15 The Master said, He who seeks only coarse food to eat, water to drink and bent arm for pillow, will without looking for it find happiness to boot. Any thought of accepting wealth and rank by means that I know to be wrong is as remote from me as the clouds that float above.

Book VIII

10 The Master said, One who is by nature daring and is suffering from poverty will not long be law-abiding. Indeed, any men, save those that are truly Good, if their sufferings are very great, will be likely to rebel.

Book XII

2 Jan Jung asked about Goodness.[10] The Master said, Behave when away from home[11] as though you were in the presence of an important guest. Deal with the common people as though you were officiating at an important sacrifice. Do not do to others what you would not like yourself. Then there will be no feelings of opposition to you, whether it is the affairs of a State that you are handling or the affairs of a Family.[12]

Jan Yung said, I know that I am not clever; but this is a saying that, with your permission, I shall try to put into practice.

Book XV

23 Tzu-kung asked saying, Is there any single saying that one can act upon all day and every day? The Master said, Perhaps the saying about consideration: 'Never do to others what you would not like them to do to you.'

28 The Master said, A man can enlarge his Way; but there is no Way that can enlarge a man.[13]

[On Filial Piety]

Book II

5 Mêng I Tzu asked about the treatment of parents. The Master said, Never disobey! When Fan Ch'ih[14] was driving his carriage for him, the Master said, Mêng asked me about the treatment of parents and I said, Never disobey! Fan Ch'ih said, In what sense did you mean it? The Master said, While they are alive, serve them

[10] **Goodness:** That is, ruling by Goodness, not by force.

[11] **when away from home:** That is, in handling public affairs.

[12] **a Family:** A ruling clan.

[13] **there is no Way . . . man:** Without effort on his part. Play on 'Way' and 'road.'

[14] **Fan Ch'ih:** A disciple.

according to ritual. When they die, bury them according to ritual and sacrifice to them according to ritual.[15]

7 Tzu-yu[16] asked about the treatment of parents. The Master said, 'Filial sons' nowadays are people who see to it that their parents get enough to eat. But even dogs and horses are cared for to that extent. If there is no feeling of respect, wherein lies the difference?

8 Tzu-hsia asked about the treatment of parents. The Master said, It is the demeanour that is difficult. Filial piety does not consist merely in young people undertaking the hard work, when anything has to be done, or serving their elders first with wine and food. It is something much more than that.

Book IV

18 The Master said, In serving his father and mother a man may gently remonstrate with them. But if he sees that he has failed to change their opinion, he should resume an attitude of deference and not thwart them; may feel discouraged, but not resentful.

Book XIII

18 The 'Duke' of Shê addressed Master K'ung saying, In my country there was a man called Upright Kung.[17] His father appropriated a sheep, and Kung bore witness against him. Master K'ung said, In my country the upright men are of quite another sort. A father will screen his son, and a son his father—which incidentally does involve a sort of uprightness.

Book XVII

21 Tsai Yü asked about the three years' mourning,[18] and said he thought a year would be quite long enough: 'If gentlemen suspend their practice of the rites[19] for three years, the rites will certainly decay; if for three years they make no music, music will certainly be destroyed.'[20] (In a year) the old crops have already vanished, the new crops have come up, the whirling drills have made new fire.[21] Surely a year would be enough?

---

[15] **Never . . . ritual:** Evidently by 'disobey' Confucius meant 'disobey the rituals.' The reply was intended to puzzle the enquirer and make him think. Here and elsewhere 'sacrifice' means offerings in general and not only animal sacrifice.

[16] **Tzu-yu:** A disciple.

[17] **Upright Kung:** A legendary paragon of honesty.

[18] **three years' mourning:** For parents. Three years is often interpreted as meaning 'into the third year,' i.e., twenty-five months.

[19] **practice . . . rites:** The mourning for parents entailed complete suspension of all ordinary activities.

[20] **'If gentlemen . . . destroyed':** A traditional saying.

[21] **new fire:** The ritualists describe four 'fire-changing' rites, one for each season, the new fire being in each case kindled on the wood of a tree appropriate to the season.

The Master said, Would you then (after a year) feel at ease in eating good rice and wearing silk brocades? Tsai Yü said, Quite at ease. (The Master said) If you would really feel at ease, then do so. But when a true gentleman is in mourning, if he eats dainties, he does not relish them, if he hears music, it does not please him, if he sits in his ordinary seat, he is not comfortable. That is why he abstains from these things. But if you would really feel at ease, there is no need for you to abstain.

When Tsai Yü had gone out, the Master said, How inhuman Yü is! Only when a child is three years old does it leave its parents' arms. The three years' mourning is the universal mourning everywhere under Heaven.[22] And Yü—was he not the darling of his father and mother for three years?

[On Ritual and Music]

Book III

3 The Master said, A man who is not Good, what can he have to do with ritual? A man who is not Good, what can he have to do with music?

4 Lin Fang asked for some main principles in connexion with ritual. The Master said, A very big question. In ritual at large it is a safe rule always to be too sparing rather than too lavish; and in the particular case of mourning-rites, they should be dictated by grief rather than by fear.

Book VIII

2 The Master said, Courtesy not bounded by the prescriptions of ritual becomes tiresome. Caution not bounded by the prescriptions of ritual becomes timidity, daring becomes turbulence, inflexibility becomes harshness.

8 The Master said, Let a man be first incited by the *Songs,* then given a firm footing by the study of ritual, and finally perfected by music.

[On Religion]

Book III

11 Someone asked for an explanation of the Ancestral Sacrifice. The Master said, I do not know. Anyone who knew the explanation could deal with all things under Heaven as easily as I lay this here; and he laid his finger upon the palm of his hand.

[22] **three years' . . . Heaven:** The whole object of this paragraph is to claim Confucius as a supporter of the three years' mourning. This custom was certainly far from being 'universal,' and was probably not ancient.

Book V

12 Tzu-kung said, Our Master's views concerning culture[23] and the outward insignia of goodness, we are permitted to hear; but about Man's nature[24] and the ways of Heaven[25] he will not tell us anything at all.

Book VII

20 The Master never talked of prodigies, feats of strength, disorders[26] or spirits.

34 When the Master was very ill, Tzu-lu asked leave to perform the Rite of Expiation. The Master said, Is there such a thing?[27] Tzu-lu answered saying, There is. In one of the Dirges it says, 'We performed rites of expiation for you, calling upon the sky-spirits above and the earth-spirits below.' The Master said, My expiation began long ago![28]

Book XI

11 Tzu-lu asked how one should serve ghosts and spirits. The Master said, Till you have learnt to serve men, how can you serve ghosts? Tzu-lu then ventured upon a question about the dead. The Master said, Till you know about the living, how are you to know about the dead?[29]

[On Morality in Government]

Book I

5 The Master said, A country of a thousand war-chariots cannot be administered unless the ruler attends strictly to business, punctually observes his promises, is economical in expenditure, shows affection towards his subjects in general, and uses the labour of the peasantry only at the proper times of year.[30]

Book II

3 The Master said, Govern the people by regulations, keep order among them by chastisements, and they will flee from you, and lose all self-respect. Govern them by

---

[23] **culture:** *Chang* ('insignia') means literally 'emblems' (usually representations of birds, beasts, or plants) figuring on banners or dresses to show the rank of the owner. Hence metaphorically, the outward manifestations of an inner virtue.

[24] **Man's nature:** As it is before it has been embellished with 'culture.'

[25] **the ways of Heaven:** T'ien Tao. The Tao taught by Confucius only concerned human behaviour ('the ways of man'); he did not expound a corresponding Heavenly Tao, governing the conduct of unseen powers and divinities.

[26] **disorders:** Disorders of nature; such as snow in summer, owls hooting by day, or the like.

[27] **Is there . . . thing?:** That is, is there any ancient authority for such a rite?

[28] **My expiation . . . ago!:** What justifies me in the eyes of Heaven is the life I have led. There is no need for any rite now.

[29] **to know . . . dead:** For example, whether they are conscious, which was a much debated problem.

[30] **uses the labour . . . year:** That is, not when they ought to be working in the fields.

moral force, keep order among them by ritual and they will keep their *self-respect* and come to you of their own accord.

Book XII

11 Duke Ching of Ch'i[31] asked Master K'ung about government. Master K'ung replied saying, ... prince be a prince, the minister a minister, the father a father and the son ... The Duke said, How true! For indeed when the prince is not a prince, the minister not a minister, the father not a father, the son not a son, one may have millet in front of one and yet not know if one will live to eat it.[32]

Book XIII

The Master said, If the ruler himself is upright, all will go well even though he does not give orders. But if he himself is not upright, even though he gives orders, they will not be obeyed.

[31] **Duke Ching of Ch'i:** Died 490 B.C.E. The last of a long line of powerful and successful dukes.

[32] **one may have . . . eat it:** Figure of speech denoting utter insecurity.

Laozi (Lao Tzu)

c. Sixth–Third Century B.C.E.

The collection of poems called the **Dao De Jing (Tao Te Ching)** is one of the most popular literary and religious classics in the world; in numbers of translations it is exceeded only by the Bible and the Bhagavad Gita. There are more than a hundred different translations of the Dao De Jing in English alone. It is almost impossible to date this text, just as it is difficult to pinpoint the origins of Daoism (Taoism), the influential religion associated with the Dao De Jing. Furthermore, **Laozi** (Lao Tzu), the legendary author of the Dao De Jing and founder of Daoism, remains a mystery. According to one legend, Laozi was an older contemporary of Confucius (551–479 B.C.E.). They each created very different schools of thought to address the social and political upheaval of the Warring States Period (c. 403–221 B.C.E.), a time when feudalism was decaying, the commoner was emerging, and divisive wars among individual states were prevalent throughout China.

dow-duh-JING; tow-tay-CHING

low-DZUH

WWW For links to more information about Laozi and a quiz on the Dao De Jing, see *World Literature Online* at bedfordstmartins.com/worldlit.

The ideas of Confucius and Laozi are almost totally opposite. Confucius's teachings are generally accessible; he emphasizes observing a hierarchy of loyalties, living deliberately according to prescribed ethical standards, and transforming society through political action. Laozi is more mysterious; he believes in individual, subjective truth, inaction, and

moral force, keep order among them by ritual and they will keep their self-respect and come to you of their own accord.

Book XII

11 Duke Ching of Ch'i[31] asked Master K'ung about government. Master K'ung replied saying, Let the prince be a prince, the minister a minister, the father a father and the son a son. The Duke said, How true! For indeed when the prince is not a prince, the minister not a minister, the father not a father, the son not a son, one may have a dish of millet in front of one and yet not know if one will live to eat it.[32]

Book XIII

6 The Master said, If the ruler himself is upright, all will go well even though he does not give orders. But if he himself is not upright, even though he gives orders, they will not be obeyed.

[31] **Duke Ching of Ch'i:** Died 490 B.C.E. The last of a long line of powerful and successful dukes.

[32] **one may have . . . eat it:** Figure of speech denoting utter insecurity.

LAOZI (LAO TZU)

C. SIXTH–THIRD CENTURY B.C.E.

The collection of poems called the **Dao De Jing** (**Tao Te Ching**) is one of the most popular literary and religious classics in the world; in numbers of translations it is exceeded only by the Bible and the Bhagavad Gita. There are more than a hundred different translations of the Dao De Jing in English alone. It is almost impossible to date this text, just as it is difficult to pinpoint the origins of Daoism (Taoism), the influential religion associated with the Dao De Jing. Furthermore, **Laozi** (Lao Tzu), the legendary author of the Dao De Jing and founder of Daoism, remains a mystery. According to one legend, Laozi was an older contemporary of Confucius (551–479 B.C.E.). They each created very different schools of thought to address the social and political upheaval of the Warring States Period (c. 403–221 B.C.E.), a time when feudalism was decaying, the commoner was emerging, and divisive wars among individual states were prevalent throughout China.

dow-duh-JING; tow-tay-CHING

low-DZUH

WWW For links to more information about Laozi and a quiz on the Dao De Jing, see *World Literature Online* at bedfordstmartins.com/worldlit.

The ideas of Confucius and Laozi are almost totally opposite. Confucius's teachings are generally accessible; he emphasizes observing a hierarchy of loyalties, living deliberately according to prescribed ethical standards, and transforming society through political action. Laozi is more mysterious; he believes in individual, subjective truth, inaction, and

Next to the Bible and the Bhagavad Gita, the Tao Te Ching is the most translated book in the world. Well over a hundred different renditions of the Taoist classic have been made into English alone, not to mention the dozens in German, French, Italian, Dutch, Latin, and other European languages. There are several reasons for the superabundance of translations. The first is that the Tao Te Ching is considered to be the fundamental text of both philosophical and religious Taoism. Indeed, the Tao or Way . . . is also the centerpiece of all Chinese religion and thought.

– Victor H. Mair, translator, 1990

a life lived in harmony with the DAO (the Way). Confucius was a pragmatist; he sought to impose order on the prevailing sociopolitical chaos through a system of guidelines and rules. Laozi, following in the tradition of **Quietism**,[1] was a mystic who thought that war was futile and that individuals should withdraw from conflict in order to develop inner resources.

Daoism. Some scholars believe that Daoism arose in the fifth century B.C.E. as a response to the dominance of Confucian philosophy and politics in China and out of a desire to return to an earlier period of Chinese history when life was simpler and people lived close to nature. The history of Daoism becomes further complicated in the second century C.E. when a split occurred between philosophical Daoism, which is personal, contemplative, and nonsectarian, and religious Daoism, which is cultic and which uses divination and alchemy in an attempt to achieve immortality. The sampling of writings from the Dao De Jing presented here belong to philosophical Daoism, which is brought into focus by Witter Bynner: "Laotzu's quietism is nothing but the fundamental sense commonly inherent in mankind, a common-sense so profound in its simplicity that it has come to be called mysticism. . . . While most of us, as we use life, try to open the universe to ourselves, Laotzu opens himself to the universe."

The Mysterious Old Master. No details are known with certainty about Laozi's life. Nothing is known about his parents, his childhood, or his education. There is no agreement about when he lived. One legend states that he was immaculately conceived and another that he was born already an old man with white hair and a beard. It was thought that for most of his existence he lived a secluded life as an ordinary bookkeeper of the imperial archives in the province of Honan. The most famous incident of his life occurs near the end of it. Sima Qian, in *Historical Records* (first century B.C.E.), summarizes his career:

> Lao Tzu practiced the Way and its Virtue. He learned to do his work in self-effacement and anonymity. For a long time he lived in Chou, and when he saw that it was breaking up, he left [riding a water buffalo]. At the frontier, the official Yin Hsi said: "Since, sir, you are retiring, I urge you to write me a book." So Lao Tzu wrote a book in two parts, explaining the Way and its Virtue in something over five thousand words. Then he went away. No one knows where he died.

The "book in two parts" is the Dao De Jing, which originally was called simply Laozi. Since the name Laozi means "the old philosopher" or "the old master," it is possible that Laozi was a generic name used for several poets who contributed to the Daoist collection for several hundred years until it was completed in the fourth century B.C.E. and written down in the third century B.C.E.

[1] **Quietism:** Scholars use this term to characterize thinkers in the fourth century B.C.E. who advocated withdrawal from the turbulence of society and concentration on inner peace and harmony.

Reading the Dao De Jing. One of the difficulties of the poems in the Dao De Jing is that they do not provide explanations or definitions. The Dao De Jing begins with what seems to be a series of conclusions about the dao, a word and a concept for which we have no English equivalent.

The Chinese written character for dao is a combination of two characters, one for "head" and the other for "going." Together they have been translated as the "conscious path," "the way," "the flow," and even "God." The second word in the collection's title, *de,* means "virtue" and the third, *Jing,* means "classic" or "text." Altogether the title is something like *The Classic of the Way and Its Virtue,* or simply *The Way of Life.* The first two lines of the first poem in the book have been translated here as "The Tao that can be told is not the eternal Tao." A literal translation would be, "Dao can dao not eternal Dao," or "Way can speak-about not eternal Way." Other translations include:

> The Way that can be described is not the eternal Way.
>
> The Flow that can be followed is not the real Flow.
>
> God (the great everlasting infinite First Cause from whom all things in heaven and earth proceed) can neither be defined nor named.
>
> There are ways but the Way is uncharted.

The complexity of Daoism's central tenet is not a deliberate attempt to mystify and confuse the reader, but a recognition of the nature of consciousness and the human tendency to reduce reality to words and definitions in order to conceptualize and categorize it. Language is a distinctly human construct that can only approximate or point to the ultimate, ineffable reality.

Laozi's first poem concludes with, "Darkness within darkness. / The gate to all mystery." This kind of writing is akin to proverbs and aphorisms, kernels of truth meant for meditation and contemplation. Pithy sayings were used in the wisdom tradition of the Middle East and are characteristic of the way that Jesus speaks in the New Testament. Although the truths of Daoism are stated simply, their meaning tends to be personal and subjective; the statements are not necessarily meant to be easily understood the first time one hears or reads them. Most of Laozi's poems demand repeated readings; furthermore, their meaning changes as one's circumstances change or as one grows older and gains more experience. Explaining Laozi's poems to others can be difficult.

The dao has often been compared to the flow of water. The ancient Chinese described the two poles of this natural rhythm, the ebb and flow, as *yin* and *yang: Yin* is associated with darkness and enclosure, withdrawal and winter; *yang* is associated with light and openness, expansiveness and summer. At times *yin* is linked to the feminine and *yang* to the masculine, but in fact neither is strictly tied to gender or sex. *Yin* and *yang* are simply metaphors for describing a changing, reciprocal flow from one side to another, just as day flows from light to dark and back again, and the seasons flow from life to death to life again. *Yin* and *yang* are not

If there is one book in the whole of Oriental literature which should be read above all others, it is, in my opinion, Laotzu's *Book of Tao* . . . It is one of the profoundest books in world philosophy . . . profound and clear, mystic and practical.

– Lin Yutang, philosopher, 1955

irreconcilable opposites in the Christian sense of *good* and *evil.* Daoism recognizes a necessity of embracing both poles of the rhythm, both the light and the dark, both the external and the internal. It is essentially a question of merging with this rhythm that is at the heart of the universe, as if life were a dance.

If the Way is simple, why then does there appear to be such disharmony and unhappiness in life? The early Daoist philosophers suggested that people get into trouble when they actively try to control their lives by making arbitrary choices and dominating their surroundings instead of going with the flow. Because human consciousness perceives only a small portion, a fragment of the whole, people do not see how everything is connected and meaningful. People attempt to make adjustments in the world system without understanding it. When one steps outside of the natural flow of nature and attempts to manipulate and construct a better system, one introduces conflicting systems of values and, ultimately, confusion and disorder. The ancient Daoists prized the state of *wu wei,* which literally means "inaction," a way of doing without egotistical effort or motives of gain.

Instead of modeling their lives after symbols of strength and hierarchy—the warrior, the mountain, the spear, the blacksmith, the king—the founders of Daoism valued supple images that illustrate participating or assimilating: water, infants, females, valleys, dancing, swimming. In Witter Bynner's translation,

> Man, born tender and yielding,
> Stiffens and hardens in death.
> All living growth is pliant,
> Until death transfixes it. (#76)

■ CONNECTIONS

Bhagavad Gita, p. 1488. Ethical systems developed in ancient times tended to emphasize high standards and strict discipline. The Gita speaks of *dharma* (duty) as well as deities, rituals, and proper attitudes. In contrast, Daoism advocates "letting go" or relaxation. In what way might "letting go" represent a significant or challenging lifestyle?

The Book of Job, p. 169. Wisdom literature often discusses the principles of "the good life" and its rewards. The Book of Job, which represents the wisdom tradition of the ancient Hebrews, is a debate about God's justice. How does the personal god of the Hebrews differ from the idea of following the dao?

St. Augustine, *Confessions* (Book 2). The concept of sin in Christianity adds to the difficulty of living a righteous life; in the New Testament St. Paul writes, "The good I would do, I do not; the evil that I do not want to do, this I do." In *Confessions,* St. Augustine is seen wrestling with his human nature. Do the poems of Laozi take into account the psychological complexities of being human?

■ FURTHER RESEARCH

Background

Gaer, Joseph. *What the Great Religions Believe.* 1963.
Smith, Huston. *The Religions of Man.* 1958.

Laozi
Chan, Wing-tsit, ed. *The Way of Lao Tzu.* 1963.
Chen, Ellen M. *The Tao Te Ching: A New Translation with Commentary.* 1989.
Henricks, Robert G. *Te-tao Ching: Translated from the Ma-wang-tui Texts.* 1993.
Mair, Victor H. *Tao Te Ching: An Entirely New Translation Based on the Recently Discovered Ma-Wang-Tui Manuscripts.* 1990.

PRONUNCIATION

Dao De Jing: dow-duh-JING
Laozi: low-DZUH
Tao Te Ching: tow-tay-CHING
Zhuangzi: jwahng-DZUH

Dao De Jing (Tao Te Ching)

Translated by Gia-Fu Feng and Jane English

ONE

The Tao that can be told is not the eternal Tao.
The name that can be named is not the eternal name.
The nameless is the beginning of heaven and earth.
The named is the mother of ten thousand things.
Ever desireless, one can see the mystery.
Ever desiring, one can see the manifestations.

Dao De Jing (Tao Te Ching). The exact dates for this text, like the dates for Laozi, are unknown. The text, which makes no reference to historical persons or events, was once thought to have originated as early as 500 B.C.E., but recently scholars have dated it in the fourth or third century B.C.E. The earliest known manuscript of the work comes from the Tang dynasty, about a thousand years later. It was probably in the fourth or third century B.C.E. that the text was edited to 5,000 characters divided into eighty-one verses.

One way to approach the idea of the dao is to imagine that life is an interrelated system, that all the parts fit together harmoniously, and that this whole system is moving through time, simply flowing along like a vast river, just about the way it should be, with overall purpose and meaning. This flow might be called "the natural way"; Laozi advises: "Tao in the world is like a river flowing home to the sea." The Daoists thought of water as a close analogy for the dao. Water has tremendous power to support objects and carry them along, and with a strong current one learns not to thrash about or to try to go upstream but to swim with the flow, adjusting one's movements to those of the current. The only thing a person must do to be happy is to go along with this grand movement or flow, to let the flow in and out. The Chinese character for a swimmer means "one who knows the nature of water."

A note on the translation: Translators Gia-Fu Feng and Jane English combine a spare poetic line with lively imagery. They use the older spelling of dao, *Tao.* The two spellings exemplify two different Western transcription systems for writing Chinese using the Roman alphabet; *dao* is closer to the actual Chinese pronunciation of the word.

These two spring from the same source but differ in name; this appears as darkness.
Darkness within darkness.
The gate to all mystery.

Fifteen

The ancient masters were subtle, mysterious, profound, responsive.
The depth of their knowledge is unfathomable.
Because it is unfathomable,
All we can do is describe their appearance.
Watchful, like men crossing a winter stream.
Alert, like men aware of danger.
Courteous, like visiting guests.
Yielding, like ice about to melt.
Simple, like uncarved blocks of wood.
Hollow, like caves.
Opaque, like muddy pools.

Who can wait quietly while the mud settles?
Who can remain still until the moment of action?
Observers of the Tao do not seek fulfillment.
Not seeking fulfillment, they are not swayed by desire for change.

Sixteen

Empty yourself of everything.
Let the mind rest at peace.
The ten thousand things rise and fall while the Self watches their return.
They grow and flourish and then return to the source.
Returning to the source is stillness, which is the way of nature.
The way of nature is unchanging.
Knowing constancy is insight.
Not knowing constancy leads to disaster.
Knowing constancy, the mind is open.
With an open mind, you will be openhearted.
Being openhearted, you will act royally.
Being royal, you will attain the divine.
Being divine, you will be at one with the Tao.
Being at one with the Tao is eternal.
And though the body dies, the Tao will never pass away.

Nineteen

Give up sainthood, renounce wisdom,
And it will be a hundred times better for everyone.

Give up kindness, renounce morality,
And men will rediscover filial piety and love.

Give up ingenuity, renounce profit,
And bandits and thieves will disappear.

These three are outward forms alone; they are not sufficient in themselves.
It is more important
To see the simplicity,
To realize one's true nature,
To cast off selfishness
And temper desire.

TWENTY

Give up learning, and put an end to your troubles.

Is there a difference between yes and no?
Is there a difference between good and evil?
Must I fear what others fear? What nonsense!
Other people are contented, enjoying the sacrificial feast of the ox.
In spring some go to the park, and climb the terrace,
But I alone am drifting, not knowing where I am.
Like a newborn babe before it learns to smile,
I am alone, without a place to go.

Others have more than they need, but I alone have nothing.
I am a fool. Oh, yes! I am confused.
Other men are clear and bright,
But I alone am dim and weak.
Other men are sharp and clever,
But I alone am dull and stupid.
Oh, I drift like the waves of the sea,
Without direction, like the restless wind.

Everyone else is busy,
But I alone am aimless and depressed.
I am different.
I am nourished by the great mother.

TWENTY-EIGHT

Know the strength of man,
But keep a woman's care!
Be the stream of the universe!

Being the stream of the universe,
Ever true and unswerving,
Become as a little child once more.

Know the white,
But keep the black!
Be an example to the world!
Being an example to the world,
Ever true and unwavering,
Return to the infinite.

Know honor,
Yet keep humility.
Be the valley of the universe!
Being the valley of the universe,
Ever true and resourceful,
Return to the state of the uncarved block.

When the block is carved, it becomes useful.
When the sage uses it, he becomes the ruler.
Thus, "A great tailor cuts little."

Twenty-nine

Do you think you can take over the universe and improve it?
I do not believe it can be done.

The universe is sacred.
You cannot improve it.
If you try to change it, you will ruin it.
If you try to hold it, you will lose it.

So sometimes things are ahead and sometimes they are behind;
Sometimes breathing is hard, sometimes it comes easily;
Sometimes there is strength and sometimes weakness;
Sometimes one is up and sometimes down.

Therefore the sage avoids extremes, excesses, and complacency.

Thirty-six

That which shrinks
Must first expand.

That which fails
Must first be strong.
That which is cast down
Must first be raised.
Before receiving
There must be giving.

This is called perception of the nature of things.
Soft and weak overcome hard and strong.

Fish cannot leave deep waters,
And a country's weapons should not be displayed.

FORTY-TWO

The Tao begot one.
One begot two.
Two begot three.
And three begot the ten thousand things.

The ten thousand things carry yin and embrace yang.
They achieve harmony by combining these forces.

Men hate to be "orphaned," "widowed," or "worthless,"
But this is how kings and lords describe themselves.

For one gains by losing
And loses by gaining.

What others teach, I also teach; that is:
"A violent man will die a violent death!"
This will be the essence of my teaching.

FORTY-THREE

The softest thing in the universe
Overcomes the hardest thing in the universe.
That without substance can enter where there is no room.
Hence I know the value of non-action.

Teaching without words and work without doing
Are understood by very few.

Forty-seven

Without going outside, you may know the whole world.
Without looking through the window, you may see the ways of heaven.
The farther you go, the less you know.

Thus the sage knows without traveling;
He sees without looking;
He works without doing.

Seventy-four

If men are not afraid to die,
It is of no avail to threaten them with death.

If men live in constant fear of dying,
And if breaking the law means that a man will be killed,
Who will dare to break the law?

There is always an official executioner.
If you try to take his place,
It is like trying to be a master carpenter and cutting wood.
If you try to cut wood like a master carpenter, you will only hurt your hand.

Eighty-one

Truthful words are not beautiful.
Beautiful words are not truthful.
Good men do not argue.
Those who argue are not good.
Those who know are not learned.
The learned do not know.

The sage never tries to store things up.
The more he does for others, the more he has.
The more he gives to others, the greater his abundance.
The Tao of heaven is pointed but does no harm.
The Tao of the sage is work without effort.

ZHUANGZI (CHUANG TZU)
C. 369–286 B.C.E.

Like Laozi (Lao Tzu), the legendary founder of Daoism and author of the Dao De Jing, in his writings **Zhuangzi** addressed the turbulent times in China, the Warring States Period (403–221 B.C.E.), characterized by social and political upheaval. There were at least two basic approaches to conflict during this era, political reform and withdrawal into personal development. Confucius (551–479 B.C.E.), Mo Tzu (470–391 B.C.E.), and the so-called Legalists were thinkers who sought concrete social and political reforms that would bring about stability and peace. As a major interpreter of Daoism, Zhuangzi's attention was not on society as a whole but on the reformation of the individual through conforming to the Dao—the invisible, unifying flow that is reality. In a word, Zhuangzi's answer, as Burton Watson explains, was freedom.

jwahng-DZUH

Little Is Known about Zhuangzi's Life. Sima Qian (c. 145–85 B.C.E.) writes in his *Historical Records* that Zhuangzi (Chuang Tzu) was a native of Meng, in what is now Honan province. He was married, served as an official in the lacquer garden, and was a contemporary of King Hui of Liang (370–319 B.C.E.). He was certainly acquainted with the Daoism of Laozi and was a constant critic of Confucianism. His attitude toward government officials and high-paying positions is illustrated in the piece called "The Job Offer," in which he tells representatives of the king who have offered him an important position in the realm that he would rather be a tortoise dragging his tail in the mud than be "wrapped and boxed" by the king. His writings constitute a rather small book, some 100,000 words, mostly in the forms of fables, anecdotes, parables, and aphorisms that editors divided into thirty-three sections.

Merging with the Dao. Zhuangzi's ideas about the dao are similar to Laozi's, but Zhuangzi's emphasis is more psychological in the sense that the goal of his writings seems to be to free his readers from all the mental baggage that keeps them from merging with the grand scheme of nature (or Nature). By changing individual consciousness, Zhuangzi expects to change individual lives. He tells the story of a man who visits Laozi seeking help in his life. When Laozi asks the man why he brought a crowd of people along with him, the man turns around and sees no one behind him. The implication was that people carry negative experiences with them: old ideas, childhood training, bad advice, stereotypes, prejudice, guilt, shame—almost as if they were literally accompanied by parents, teachers, priests, and rulers forming a long procession behind them. It is this psychological burden that must be left behind in order to be free.

The analogy most often used by Taoists to describe the "actionless activity" of *wu-wei* is water; as it follows the line of least resistance down a dry river bed, it pushes and recedes, it effortlessly penetrates every crack and crevice. When it meets resistance it merely rushes by, giving way and then filling up around hardness.

– RAYMOND VAN OVER, psychologist, 1973

Zhuangzi's Writings. In order to entice readers into a freer state, Zhuangzi uses humor, illogical perceptions, debates, and incisive metaphors. Zhuangzi's swimmer explains that he is able to stay afloat in rough

The central theme of the *Chuang Tzu* may be summed up in a single word: freedom. Essentially, all the philosophers of ancient China addressed themselves to the same problem: How is man to live in a world dominated by chaos, suffering, and absurdity? Nearly all of them answered with some concrete plan of action designed to reform the individual, to reform society, and eventually to free the world from its ills . . . Chuang Tzu's answer to the question: free yourself from the world.

– BURTON WATSON, historian and translator, 1964

waters because of his nature, not because of some special technique. An entirely different analogy is provided by the butcher who does not hack at the ox carcass but finds "the spaces between the joints" for cutting up the ox and preserving the edge on his knives. As in the story of the swimmer, the butcher's technique has a literal meaning, but it also symbolizes how one might live, with least effort and with self-care rather than by exerting a lot of energy fighting with tough, unyielding elements. In addition to the swimmer and the butcher, Zhuangzi's heroes are the woodcutter, the Yüan-ch'u bird, even the gamecock. In "The Wasted Gourd" and "The Ailanthus Tree," the focus is on imagination and intelligence, and the fact that, as the old saying goes, a person might not see the forest for the trees. Lacking imagination, individuals are involved in the incidentals and never envision the larger picture, the image of the One into which all particulars merge. Imagination is also the issue when Hui Tzu questions Zhuangzi about his intuition about the activities of fish in "What Fish Enjoy." In "Happiness," Zhuangzi stresses the importance of inaction; "I take inaction to be true happiness," he says. The Chinese word for inaction is *wu-wei,* which does not mean *no* action and withdrawal from life but rather refers to a lack of striving. As Burton Watson explains, inaction is ". . . a course of action that is not founded upon any purposeful motives of gain or striving. In such a state, all human actions become as spontaneous and mindless as those of the natural world." Daoist philosophy meets a critical test with the death of Zhuangzi's wife; when one might expect only grief and protestations about fate, Zhuangzi responds with both honesty and clarity. "The Death of Lao Tan" contains similar insights, as does "Transformations," in which men experience the physical changes brought on by growing old. Both aging and death are part of the grand scheme of Nature. An individual can choose to fight against the continuous transformation of all living things or can learn to adjust and, finally, to accept change. After Zhuangzi's wife died, the philosopher's attitude ultimately changed from grief to a celebration of his and his wife's participation in the larger pattern of the dao.

■ CONNECTIONS

Confucius, *The Analects*, p. 1594. Confucius and Zhuangzi represent two fundamentally different interpretations of ethical life. Confucius takes a legalistic approach, advising obedience to authority and offering rules for proper conduct. What is Zhuangzi's alternative to external guidelines for behavior?

The methods of Chuang Tzu are those of the poet, and in the case of poetry analysis is useless.

– ARTHUR WALEY, translator, 1939

The Book of Job, p. 169. Ethical codes tend to explain the consequences for "breaking the rules." The Book of Job represents the wisdom tradition of the ancient Hebrews, which assumes the reality of a personalized God who sits in judgment of humankind. According to Zhuangzi, what seem to be the consequences for not following the dao?

Machiavelli, *The Prince* (Book 2). There are different ways to teach about the good life. In *The Prince,* Machiavelli writes directly about the best ways for rulers to create policy, drawing on examples from history. Are Zhuangzi's parables and anecdotes an alternative to didactic instruction?

■ FURTHER RESEARCH

Background

Graham, A. C. *Disputers of the Tao: Philosophical Argument in Ancient China.* 1989.
Waley, Arthur. *Three Ways of Thought in Ancient China.* 1939.

Criticism

Giles, Herbert. *Chuang Tzu: Taoist Philosopher and Chinese Mystic.* 1961.
Wu, Kuang-ming. *The Butterfly as Companion: Meditations on the First Three Chapters of the Chuang Tzu.* 1990.

www For links to more information about Zhuangzi and a quiz on his writings, see *World Literature Online* at bedfordstmartins.com/worldlit.

Chuang Tzu: Basic Writings

Translated by Burton Watson

[The Wasted Gourd]

Hui Tzu[1] said to Chuang Tzu, "The king of Wei gave me some seeds of a huge gourd. I planted them, and when they grew up, the fruit was big enough to hold five piculs.[2] I tried using it for a water container, but it was so heavy I couldn't lift it. I split it in half to make dippers, but they were so large and unwieldy that I couldn't dip them into anything. It's not that the gourds weren't fantastically big—but I decided they were no use and so I smashed them to pieces."

Chuang Tzu said, "You certainly are dense when it comes to using big things! In Sung there was a man who was skilled at making a salve to prevent chapped hands, and generation after generation his family made a living by bleaching silk in water. A traveler heard about the salve and offered to buy the prescription for a hundred measures of gold. The man called everyone to a family council. 'For generations we've been bleaching silk and we've never made more than a few measures of gold,' he said. 'Now, if we sell our secret, we can make a hundred measures in one morning. Let's let him have it!' The traveler got the salve and introduced it to the king of Wu, who was having trouble with the state of Yüeh. The king put the man in charge of his troops, and that winter they fought a naval battle with the men of Yüeh and gave them a bad beating. A portion of the conquered territory was awarded to the man as a fief. The salve had the power to prevent chapped hands in either case;[3] but one man used it to get a fief, while the other one never got beyond silk bleaching—because they used it in different ways. Now you had a gourd big enough to hold five piculs. Why didn't you think of making it into a great tub so you could go floating around the rivers and lakes, instead of worrying because it was too big and unwieldy to dip into things! Obviously you still have a lot of underbrush in your head!"

---

[1] **Hui Tzu:** Stands for logical reasoning rather than imagination.

[2] **piculs:** A unit of weight used in Asia; one picul equals about 132 lbs.

[3] **case:** Preventing chapped hands allows for handling weapons.

[The Ailanthus Tree]

Hui Tzu said to Chuang Tzu, "I have a big tree named ailanthus. Its trunk is too gnarled and bumpy to apply a measuring line to, its branches too bent and twisty to match up to a compass or square. You could stand it by the road and no carpenter would look at it twice. Your words, too, are big and useless, and so everyone alike spurns them!"

Chuang Tzu said, "Maybe you've never seen a wildcat or a weasel. It crouches down and hides, watching for something to come along. It leaps and races east and west, not hesitating to go high or low—until it falls into the trap and dies in the net. Then again there's the yak, big as a cloud covering the sky. It certainly knows how to be big, though it doesn't know how to catch rats. Now you have this big tree and you're distressed because it's useless. Why don't you plant it in Not-Even-Anything Village, or the field of Broad-and-Boundless, relax and do nothing by its side, or lie down for a free and easy sleep under it? Axes will never shorten its life, nothing can ever harm it. If there's no use for it, how can it come to grief or pain?"

[Walking Two Roads]

What is acceptable we call acceptable; what is unacceptable we call unacceptable. A road is made by people walking on it; things are so because they are called so. What makes them so? Making them so makes them so. What makes them not so? Making them not so makes them not so. Things all must have that which is so; things all must have that which is acceptable. There is nothing that is not so, nothing that is not acceptable.

For this reason, whether you point to a little stalk or a great pillar, a leper or the beautiful Hsi-shih, things ribald and shady or things grotesque and strange, the Way makes them all into one. Their dividedness is their completeness; their completeness is their impairment. No thing is either complete or impaired, but all are made into one again. Only the man of far-reaching vision knows how to make them into one. So he has no use [for categories], but relegates all to the constant. The constant is the useful; the useful is the passable; the passable is the successful; and with success, all is accomplished. He relies upon this alone, relies upon it and does not know he is doing so. This is called the Way.

But to wear out your brain trying to make things into one without realizing that they are all the same—this is called "three in the morning." What do I mean by "three in the morning"? When the monkey trainer was handing out acorns, he said, "You get three in the morning and four at night." This made all the monkeys furious. "Well, then," he said, "you get four in the morning and three at night." The monkeys were all delighted. There was no change in the reality behind the words, and yet the monkeys responded with joy and anger. Let them, if they want to. So the sage harmonizes with both right and wrong and rests in Heaven the Equalizer. This is called walking two roads.

[Penumbra and Shadow]

Penumbra said to Shadow, "A little while ago you were walking and now you're standing still; a little while ago you were sitting and now you're standing up. Why this lack of independent action?"

Shadow said, "Do I have to wait for something before I can be like this? Does what I wait for also have to wait for something before it can be like this? Am I waiting for the scales of a snake or the wings of a cicada? How do I know why it is so? How do I know why it isn't so?"[4]

[The Dream and the Butterfly]

Once Chuang Chou[5] dreamt he was a butterfly, a butterfly flitting and fluttering around, happy with himself and doing as he pleased. He didn't know he was Chuang Chou. Suddenly he woke up and there he was, solid and unmistakable Chuang Chou. But he didn't know if he was Chuang Chou who had dreamt he was a butterfly, or a butterfly dreaming he was Chuang Chou. Between Chuang Chou and a butterfly there must be *some* distinction! This is called the Transformation of Things.

[Cutting Up the Ox]

Cook Ting was cutting up an ox for Lord Wen-hui. At every touch of his hand, every heave of his shoulder, every move of his feet, every thrust of his knee—zip! zoop! He slithered the knife along with a zing, and all was in perfect rhythm, as though he were performing the dance of the Mulberry Grove or keeping time to Ching-shou music.

"Ah, this is marvelous!" said Lord Wen-hui. "Imagine skill reaching such heights!"

Cook Ting laid down his knife and replied, "What I care about is the Way, which goes beyond skill. When I first began cutting up oxen, all I could see was the ox itself. After three years I no longer saw the whole ox. And now—now I go at it by spirit and don't look with my eyes. Perception and understanding have come to a stop and spirit moves where it wants. I go along with the natural makeup, strike in the big hollows, guide the knife through the big openings, and follow things as they are. So I never touch the smallest ligament or tendon, much less a main joint.

"A good cook changes his knife once a year—because he cuts. A mediocre cook changes his knife once a month—because he hacks. I've had this knife of mine for nineteen years and I've cut up thousands of oxen with it, and yet the blade is as good

---

[4] **so:** That is, to ordinary men the shadow appears to depend upon something else for its movement, just as the snake depends on its scales (according to Chinese belief) and the cicada on its wings. But do such causal views of action really have any meaning? (Translator's note.)

[5] **Chuang Chou:** Another name for Zhuangzi (Chuang Tzu).

as though it had just come from the grindstone. There are spaces between the joints, and the blade of the knife has really no thickness. If you insert what has no thickness into such spaces, then there's plenty of room—more than enough for the blade to play about in. That's why after nineteen years the blade of my knife is still as good as when it first came from the grindstone.

"However, whenever I come to a complicated place, I size up the difficulties, tell myself to watch out and be careful, keep my eyes on what I'm doing, work very slowly, and move the knife with the greatest subtlety, until—flop! the whole thing comes apart like a clod of earth crumbling to the ground. I stand there holding the knife and look all around me, completely satisfied and reluctant to move on, and then I wipe off the knife and put it away."

"Excellent!" said Lord Wen-hui. "I have heard the words of Cook Ting and learned how to care for life!"

[The Death of Lao Tan]

When Lao Tan[6] died, Ch'in Shih went to mourn for him; but after giving three cries, he left the room.

"Weren't you a friend of the Master?" asked Lao Tan's disciples.

"Yes."

"And you think it's all right to mourn him this way?"

"Yes," said Ch'in Shih. "At first I took him for a real man, but now I know he wasn't. A little while ago, when I went in to mourn, I found old men weeping for him as though they were weeping for a son, and young men weeping for him as though they were weeping for a mother. To have gathered a group like *that,* he must have done something to make them talk about him, though he didn't ask them to talk, or make them weep for him, though he didn't ask them to weep. This is to hide from Heaven, turn your back on the true state of affairs, and forget what you were born with. In the old days, this was called the crime of hiding from Heaven. Your master happened to come because it was his time, and he happened to leave because things follow along. If you are content with the time and willing to follow along, then grief and joy have no way to enter in. In the old days, this was called being freed from the bonds of God.

"Though the grease burns out of the torch, the fire passes on, and no one knows where it ends."[7]

[Transformations]

Master Ssu, Master Yü, Master Li, and Master Lai were all four talking together. "Who can look upon inaction as his head, on life as his back, and on death as his

[6] **Lao Tan:** Laozi (Lao Tzu, fourth to third century B.C.E.), reputed author of the Dao De Jing.

[7] **ends:** A possible interpretation: Though the fuel is consumed in this particular torch, the fire of knowledge is passed on.

rump?" they said. "Who knows that life and death, existence and annihilation, are all a single body? I will be his friend!"

The four men looked at each other and smiled. There was no disagreement in their hearts and so the four of them became friends.

All at once Master Yü fell ill. Master Ssu went to ask how he was. "Amazing!" said Master Yü. "The Creator is making me all crookedy like this! My back sticks up like a hunchback and my vital organs are on top of me. My chin is hidden in my navel, my shoulders are up above my head, and my pigtail points at the sky. It must be some dislocation of the yin and yang!"

Yet he seemed calm at heart and unconcerned. Dragging himself haltingly to the well, he looked at his reflection and said, "My, my! So the Creator is making me all crookedy like this!"

"Do you resent it?" asked Master Ssu.

"Why no, what would I resent? If the process continues, perhaps in time he'll transform my left arm into a rooster. In that case I'll keep watch on the night. Or perhaps in time he'll transform my right arm into a crossbow pellet and I'll shoot down an owl for roasting. Or perhaps in time he'll transform my buttocks into cartwheels. Then, with my spirit for a horse, I'll climb up and go for a ride. What need will I ever have for a carriage again?

"I received life because the time had come; I will lose it because the order of things passes on. Be content with this time and dwell in this order and then neither sorrow nor joy can touch you. In ancient times this was called the 'freeing of the bound.' There are those who cannot free themselves, because they are bound by things. But nothing can ever win against Heaven—that's the way it's always been. What would I have to resent?"

Suddenly Master Lai grew ill. Gasping and wheezing, he lay at the point of death. His wife and children gathered round in a circle and began to cry. Master Li, who had come to ask how he was, said, "Shoo! Get back! Don't disturb the process of change!"

Then he leaned against the doorway and talked to Master Lai. "How marvelous the Creator is! What is he going to make out of you next? Where is he going to send you? Will he make you into a rat's liver? Will he make you into a bug's arm?"

Master Lai said, "A child, obeying his father and mother, goes wherever he is told, east or west, south or north. And the yin and yang—how much more are they to a man than father or mother! Now that they have brought me to the verge of death, if I should refuse to obey them, how perverse I would be! What fault is it of theirs? The Great Clod burdens me with form, labors me with life, eases me in old age, and rests me in death. So if I think well of my life, for the same reason I must think well of my death. When a skilled smith is casting metal, if the metal should leap up and say, 'I insist upon being made into a Mo-yeh!'[8] he would surely regard it as very inauspicious metal indeed. Now, having had the audacity to take on human

[8] **Mo-yeh:** A famous sword of King Ho-lü of Wu (r. 514–496 B.C.E.).

form once, if I should say, 'I don't want to be anything but a man! Nothing but a man!', the Creator would surely regard me as a most inauspicious sort of person. So now I think of heaven and earth as a great furnace, and the Creator as a skilled smith. Where could he send me that would not be all right? I will go off to sleep peacefully, and then with a start I will wake up."

[The Job Offer]

Once, when Chuang Tzu was fishing in the P'u River, the king of Ch'u sent two officials to go and announce to him: "I would like to trouble you with the administration of my realm."

Chuang Tzu held on to the fishing pole and, without turning his head, said, "I have heard that there is a sacred tortoise in Ch'u that has been dead for three thousand years. The king keeps it wrapped in cloth and boxed, and stores it in the ancestral temple. Now would this tortoise rather be dead and have its bones left behind and honored? Or would it rather be alive and dragging its tail in the mud?"

"It would rather be alive and dragging its tail in the mud," said the two officials.

Chuang Tzu said, "Go away! I'll drag my tail in the mud!"

[Yuan-Chu Bird]

When Hui Tzu was prime minister of Liang, Chuang Tzu set off to visit him. Someone said to Hui Tzu, "Chuang Tzu is coming because he wants to replace you as prime minister!" With this Hui Tzu was filled with alarm and searched all over the state for three days and three nights trying to find Chuang Tzu. Chuang Tzu then came to see him and said, "In the south there is a bird called the Yüan-ch'u—I wonder if you've ever heard of it? The Yüan-ch'u rises up from the South Sea and flies to the North Sea, and it will rest on nothing but the Wu-t'ung tree, eat nothing but the fruit of the Lien, and drink only from springs of sweet water. Once there was an owl who had gotten hold of a half-rotten old rat, and as the Yüan-ch'u passed by, it raised its head, looked up at the Yüan-ch'u, and said, 'Shoo!' Now that you have this Liang state of yours, are you trying to shoo me?"

[What Fish Enjoy]

Chuang Tzu and Hui Tzu were strolling along the dam of the Hao River when Chuang Tzu said, "See how the minnows come out and dart around where they please! That's what fish really enjoy!"

Hui Tzu said, "You're not a fish—how do you know what fish enjoy?"

Chuang Tzu said, "You're not I, so how do you know I don't know what fish enjoy?"

Hui Tzu said, "I'm not you, so I certainly don't know what you know. On the other hand, you're certainly not a fish—so that still proves you don't know what fish enjoy!"

Chuang Tzu said, "Let's go back to your original question, please. You asked me *how* I know what fish enjoy—so you already knew I knew it when you asked the question. I know it by standing here beside the Hao."

[Happiness]

Is there such a thing as supreme happiness in the world or isn't there? Is there some way to keep yourself alive or isn't there? What to do, what to rely on, what to avoid, what to stick by, what to follow, what to leave alone, what to find happiness in, what to hate?

This is what the world honors: wealth, eminence, long life, a good name. This is what the world finds happiness in: a life of ease, rich food, fine clothes, beautiful sights, sweet sounds. This is what it looks down on: poverty, meanness, early death, a bad name. This is what it finds bitter: a life that knows no rest, a mouth that gets no rich food, no fine clothes for the body, no beautiful sights for the eye, no sweet sounds for the ear.

People who can't get these things fret a great deal and are afraid—this is a stupid way to treat the body. People who are rich wear themselves out rushing around on business, piling up more wealth than they could ever use—this is a superficial way to treat the body. People who are eminent spend night and day scheming and wondering if they are doing right—this is a shoddy way to treat the body. Man lives his life in company with worry, and if he lives a long while, till he's dull and doddering, then he has spent that much time worrying instead of dying, a bitter lot indeed! This is a callous way to treat the body.

Men of ardor[9] are regarded by the world as good, but their goodness doesn't succeed in keeping them alive. So I don't know whether their goodness is really good or not. Perhaps I think it's good—but not good enough to save their lives. Perhaps I think it's no good—but still good enough to save the lives of others. So I say, if your loyal advice isn't heeded, give way and do not wrangle. Tzu-hsü wrangled and lost his body. But if he hadn't wrangled, he wouldn't have made a name. Is there really such a thing as goodness or isn't there?

What ordinary people do and what they find happiness in—I don't know whether such happiness is in the end really happiness or not. I look at what ordinary people find happiness in, what they all make a mad dash for, racing around as though they couldn't stop—they all say they're happy with it. I'm not happy with it and I'm not unhappy with it. In the end is there really happiness or isn't there?

I take inaction to be true happiness, but ordinary people think it is a bitter thing. I say: the highest happiness has no happiness, the highest praise has no praise. The world can't decide what is right and what is wrong. And yet inaction can decide this. The highest happiness, keeping alive—only inaction gets you close to this!

[9] **Men of ardor:** Men who are willing to sacrifice their lives in order to preserve their honor or save the lives of others.

Let me try putting it this way. The inaction of Heaven is its purity, the inaction of earth is its peace. So the two inactions combine and all things are transformed and brought to birth. Wonderfully, mysteriously, there is no place they come out of. Mysteriously, wonderfully, they have no sign. Each thing minds its business and all grow up out of inaction. So I say, Heaven and earth do nothing and there is nothing that is not done. Among men, who can get hold of this inaction?

[Death of Chuang Tzu's Wife]

Chuang Tzu's wife died. When Hui Tzu went to convey his condolences, he found Chuang Tzu sitting with his legs sprawled out, pounding on a tub and singing. "You lived with her, she brought up your children and grew old," said Hui Tzu. "It should be enough simply not to weep at her death. But pounding on a tub and singing—this is going too far, isn't it?"

Chuang Tzu said, "You're wrong. When she first died, do you think I didn't grieve like anyone else? But I looked back to her beginning and the time before she was born. Not only the time before she was born, but the time before she had a body. Not only the time before she had a body, but the time before she had a spirit. In the midst of the jumble of wonder and mystery a change took place and she had a spirit. Another change and she had a body. Another change and she was born. Now there's been another change and she's dead. It's just like the progression of the four seasons, spring, summer, fall, winter.

"Now she's going to lie down peacefully in a vast room. If I were to follow after her bawling and sobbing, it would show that I don't understand anything about fate. So I stopped."

[Gamecocks]

Chi Hsing-tzu was training gamecocks for the king. After ten days the king asked if they were ready.

"Not yet. They're too haughty and rely on their nerve."

Another ten days and the king asked again.

"Not yet. They still respond to noises and movements."

Another ten days and the king asked again.

"Not yet. They still look around fiercely and are full of spirit."

Another ten days and the king asked again.

"They're close enough. Another cock can crow and they show no sign of change. Look at them from a distance and you'd think they were made of wood. Their virtue is complete. Other cocks won't dare face up to them, but will turn and run."

[The Swimmer]

Confucius was seeing the sights at Lü-liang, where the water falls from a height of thirty fathoms and races and boils along for forty li, so swift that no fish or other water creature can swim in it. He saw a man dive into the water and, supposing that the man was in some kind of trouble and intended to end his life, he ordered his disciples to line up on the bank and pull the man out. But after the man had gone a couple of hundred paces, he came out of the water and began strolling along the base of the embankment, his hair streaming down, singing a song. Confucius ran after him and said, "At first I thought you were a ghost, but now I see you're a man. May I ask if you have some special way of staying afloat in the water?"

"I have no way. I began with what I was used to, grew up with my nature, and let things come to completion with fate. I go under with the swirls and come out with the eddies, following along the way the water goes and never thinking about myself. That's how I can stay afloat."

Confucius said, "What do you mean by saying that you began with what you were used to, grew up with your nature, and let things come to completion with fate?"

"I was born on the dry land and felt safe on the dry land—that was what I was used to. I grew up with the water and felt safe in the water—that was my nature. I don't know why I do what I do—that's fate."

[Woodworker]

Woodworker Ch'ing carved a piece of wood and made a bell stand, and when it was finished, everyone who saw it marveled, for it seemed to be the work of gods or spirits. When the marquis of Lu saw it, he asked, "What art is it you have?"

Ch'ing replied, "I am only a craftsman—how would I have any art? There is one thing, however. When I am going to make a bell stand, I never let it wear out my energy. I always fast in order to still my mind. When I have fasted for three days, I no longer have any thought of congratulations or rewards, of titles or stipends. When I have fasted for five days, I no longer have any thought of praise or blame, of skill or clumsiness. And when I have fasted for seven days, I am so still that I forget I have four limbs and a form and body. By that time, the ruler and his court no longer exist for me. My skill is concentrated and all outside distractions fade away. After that, I go into the mountain forest and examine the Heavenly nature of the trees. If I find one of superlative form, and I can see a bell stand there, I put my hand to the job of carving; if not, I let it go. This way I am simply matching up 'Heaven' with 'Heaven.'[10] That's probably the reason that people wonder if the results were not made by spirits."

[10] **matching . . . 'Heaven' with 'Heaven':** Matching his innate nature with the nature of the tree.

The Good Life

In contemporary times, the good life has been associated with material things like money, houses, and cars; it also has been linked to success and power. When religions speak of the good life, however, they tend to stress spiritual attributes like peace of mind, hope, love, and compassion. All religions and ancient philosophies address what it means to live the good life and what one's chief aim in life should be. Some look to external, physical rewards, others to an inner state of being associated with the spirit or the soul. Some prophets spoke of eternal reward or punishment and how each was precipitated by one's beliefs and actions in this life. The traditional view of the good life in the wisdom tradition of the ancient Near East focused on the benefits of a life of hard work and good fortune, like riches, a long life, a faithful wife, and children who would care for their parents in old age. The root definition of *prosperity* includes both the notion of wealth and the idea of destiny or fate; this double meaning also applies to the word *fortune.* Ancient peoples clearly recognized that individuals were not entirely in control of their lives, that, in fact, there were larger forces at work influencing one's existence, no matter how clever or diligent the individual.

The tension between the determining factors of individual character and destiny is played out in the Book of Job in the Hebrew Scriptures, which asks, essentially, whether the "good life" is possible after someone is stripped of his health, family, and goods. How does one handle an enormous catastrophe like the death of one's child, for example, when one has made every effort to be a good parent and person? In **"The Persian Wars,"** the Greek historian Herodotus describes an incident involving a wise man named Solon, Athens's

p. 1626

Playing Cithara, first century
For some cultures and religions the good life meant material comforts but for others spiritual needs were more important. From this fresco, painted at the height of the Roman Empire, one might assume that the good life for these women consisted of a certain earthy pleasure in relaxing, and in listening to and playing music. (The Art Archive / Archaeological Museum, Naples / Dagli Orti (A))

ruler in the sixth century B.C.E. Solon adopted the traditional position on the good life by linking it with prosperity: "health, freedom from trouble, fine children, and good looks." But he acknowledged that destiny can reverse a person's good fortune at any time and concluded that life's happiness could be measured only in retrospect, at the time of death.

The selection from the **Svetasvatara Upanishad** represents the ancient wisdom tradition of India, which shifts the focus of what is important from the external measures of Solon and Job to the quality of an individual's inner life. In Western terminology, the underlying teaching of the Upanishads—a collection of spiritual essays—is that the good life is first and primarily a rapprochement with God, but not God in the sense of a father figure residing somewhere in the heavens. In the Upanishads, God is the underlying spiritual condition—the "god-ness"—of all creation; individuals connect with this God, Brahman, through the personal discovery of their own divine nature, deep within the self.

p. 1629

A third concept of the good life comes from ancient China and the teachings of Confucius in the sixth century B.C.E. Confucius developed an ethics of duty that wove together all classes and members of society. For Confucius the good life was synonymous with conforming to an ethical code, like being a good citizen, obeying laws, holding a job, and providing for one's family and the common good. The focus was not one's state of mind or the accumulation of wealth but rather how one performed one's role in the essential relationships of family, public life, and governance.

Various teachers and prophets — Eastern *and* Western — have shifted attention away from social values and material goods to individual spiritual consciousness and a simple, unadorned life — in Buddhist terms, an ethic of nonattachment to external realities. Greek philosophers in the fourth century B.C.E. attempted to separate "the good life" from politics, economics, and the wiles of fortune when the democratic ***POLIS*** in Athens collapsed after being defeated by Sparta in the Peloponnesian War in 404 B.C.E. Two very influential philosophies arose from that rather desperate social situation: **EPICUREANISM** and **STOICISM**. Epicurus concludes in **"Letter to a Friend"** p. 1634 that the measure of the good life is the experience of pleasure and the avoidance of pain. This principle has often been misinterpreted as the self-indulgent pursuit of pleasure at any cost, an attitude more properly labeled "hedonism." Such pleasure-seeking can result in extremely painful consequences. In contrast, Epicurus promoted a simple life, conquering one's desires through self-discipline and creating community through friendship; by avoiding pain and fear, a person would gain the lasting pleasures, what Epicurus called the "sweetness of life."

Zeno developed the philosophy of Stoicism toward the end of the fourth century B.C.E. It received its name from the *stoa,* or colonnade, in Athens under which Zeno taught. The foundation of Zeno's thought was the belief that there is an overall rational purpose to life that is revealed in nature, or Nature. A person's task, therefore, is to assess one's own life and then discover how to conform to Nature. **Cleanthes** (klee-AN-theez) was one of Zeno's students; in **"Invocation"** and **"Hymn to Zeus,"** p. 1667 the relationship between the individual and the larger forces of Destiny or Zeus is captured in lovely, vital metaphors, suggesting the nobility of the stoic life. With an emphasis on duty and the overall purpose of the cosmos, Stoicism was the most adaptable of Greek philosophies to the Roman world. Cicero, the eminent orator and statesman, was one of the Romans who espoused Stoicism; **Marcus Aurelius** (MAR-kus aw-REH-lee-us) — Roman emperor and Stoic philosopher — weighed the attractions of wealth and power against individual conscience. His ***Meditations*** p. 1640 is a kind of spiritual diary in which he explores the dimensions of the virtuous life and the purpose of reality.

■ CONNECTIONS

The Book of Job, p. 169; Confucius, *The Analects*, p. 1594; Plato, The Allegory of the Cave, p. 1111. One way to distinguish among the teachings of religions and philosophies regarding the "good life" is to differentiate between doing and being, between those teachings that suggest individuals act a particular way and those that focus on a state of consciousness or a condition of awareness. Consider the readings in this section. Do they favor being or doing as a means to the good life?

***In the World:* Heroes and Citizens, p. 1117; Bhagavad Gita, p. 1488.** How does one know when he or she has achieved the "good life"? Consider the readings in this section as well as those in *In the World:* Heroes and Citizens and the Bhagavad Gita. Which identify external validations for the good life, such as wealth or fame, and which internal validations, such as peace of mind?

■ PRONUNCIATION

Epicureanism: eh-pih-KYOO-ree-un-izm
Cleanthes: klee-AN-theez
Marcus Aurelius: MAR-kus aw-REH-lee-us, MAR-kus aw-RAY-lee-us
eudaemonia: yoo-digh-MOH-nee-uh, yoo-digh-muh-NEE-uh, yoo-day-muh-NEE-uh

HERODOTUS

C. 480–C. 425 B.C.E.

The Greek historian Herodotus is famous for including personal anecdotes in his writings. In this piece he describes the meeting in 594 B.C.E. between Solon, the father of Athenian democracy, and Croesus, the king of Lydia. After instituting democratic reforms in Athens, Solon traveled to various foreign countries while Athens attempted to conduct itself according to his new program. Since Solon was reputedly a wise man—indeed, one of the ancient sages—Croesus, after showing Solon his wealth, asked the sage to name the happiest man he had ever met. Solon's reply echoes the wisdom tradition of the ancient Near East, namely that the good life is measured by earthly abundance: a faithful wife, healthy and abundant children to care for you in old age, material wealth, and longevity. But, Solon cautions, these "blessings," finally, cannot be assessed until someone has actually died, since Destiny can intervene at any moment to destroy a person's reputation and belongings. Croesus, therefore, was not Solon's first choice since Croesus was still alive and subject to the unknowable designs of Fate.

He who unites the greatest number of advantages, and retaining them to the day of his death, then dies peaceably, that man alone, sire, is, in my judgment, entitled to bear the name of "happy."
– HERODOTUS

FROM

The Persian Wars

Translated by George Rawlinson

[Solon on Happiness]

When all these conquests had been added to the Lydian empire, and the prosperity of Sardis was now at its height, there came thither, one after another, all the sages of Greece living at the time, and among them Solon, the Athenian. He was on his travels, having left Athens to be absent ten years, under the pretense of wishing to see the world, but really to avoid being forced to repeal any of the laws which, at the request of the Athenians, he had made for them. Without his sanction the Athenians could not repeal them, as they had bound themselves under a heavy curse to be governed for ten years by the laws which should be imposed on them by Solon.

On this account, as well as to see the world, Solon set out upon his travels, in the course of which he went to Egypt to the court of Amasis, and also came on a visit to Croesus at Sardis. Croesus received him as his guest, and lodged him in the royal palace. On the third or fourth day after, he bade his servants conduct Solon over his treasuries, and show him all their greatness and magnificence. When he had seen them all, and, so far as time allowed, inspected them, Croesus addressed this question to him. "Stranger of Athens, we have heard much of thy wisdom and of thy travels through many lands, from love of knowledge and a wish to see the world. I am curious therefore to inquire of thee, whom, of all the men that thou hast seen, thou deemest the most happy?" This he asked because he thought himself the happiest of mortals: but Solon answered him without flattery, according to his true sentiments, "Tellus of Athens, sire." Full of astonishment at what he heard, Croesus demanded sharply, "And wherefore dost thou deem Tellus happiest?" To which the other replied, "First, because his country was flourishing in his days, and he himself had sons both beautiful and good, and he lived to see children born to each of them, and these children all grew up; and further because, after a life spent in what our people look upon as comfort, his end was surpassingly glorious. In a battle between the Athenians and their neighbors near Eleusis,[1] he came to the assistance of his countrymen, routed the foe, and died upon the field most gallantly. The Athenians gave him a public funeral on the spot where he fell, and paid him the highest honors."

Thus did Solon admonish Croesus by the example of Tellus, enumerating the manifold particulars of his happiness. When he had ended, Croesus inquired a second time, who after Tellus seemed to him the happiest, expecting that at any rate, he would be given the second place. "Cleobis and Bito," Solon answered; "they were of Argive race; their fortune was enough for their wants, and they were besides endowed with so much bodily strength that they had both gained prizes at the Games.

[1] **Eleusis:** A small town some fifteen miles northwest of Athens; home of the Eleusinian Mysteries, the most famous mysteries of the ancient Mediterranean world, which used the story of Demeter and Persephone as the pathway to happiness in the afterlife.

Also this tale is told of them:—There was a great festival in honor of the goddess Hera at Argos, to which their mother must needs be taken in a car.[2] Now the oxen did not come home from the field in time: so the youths, fearful of being too late, put the yoke on their own necks, and themselves drew the car in which their mother rode. Five and forty furlongs[3] did they draw her, and stopped before the temple. This deed of theirs was witnessed by the whole assembly of worshipers, and then their life closed in the best possible way. Herein, too, God showed forth most evidently, how much better a thing for man death is than life. For the Argive men, who stood around the car, extolled the vast strength of the youths; and the Argive women extolled the mother who was blessed with such a pair of sons; and the mother herself, overjoyed at the deed and at the praises it had won, standing straight before the image, besought the goddess to bestow on Cleobis and Bito, the sons who had so mightily honored her, the highest blessing to which mortals can attain. Her prayer ended, they offered sacrifice and partook of the holy banquet, after which the two youths fell asleep in the temple. They never woke more, but so passed from the earth. The Argives, looking on them as among the best of men, caused statues of them to be made, which they gave to the shrine at Delphi."

When Solon had thus assigned these youths the second place, Croesus broke in angrily, "What, stranger of Athens, is my happiness, then, so utterly set at nought by thee, that thou dost not even put me on a level with private men?"

"Oh! Croesus," replied the other, "thou askedst a question concerning the condition of man, of one who knows that the power above us is full of jealousy, and fond of troubling our lot. A long life gives one to witness much, and experience much oneself, that one would not choose. Seventy years I regard as the limit of the life of man. In these seventy years are contained, without reckoning intercalary[4] months, twenty-five thousand and two hundred days. Add an intercalary month to every other year, that the seasons may come round at the right time, and there will be, besides the seventy years, thirty-five such months, making an addition of one thousand and fifty days. The whole number of the days contained in the seventy years will thus be twenty-six thousand two hundred and fifty, whereof not one but will produce events unlike the rest. Hence man is wholly accident. For thyself, oh! Croesus, I see that thou art wonderfully rich, and art the lord of many nations; but with respect to that whereon thou questionest me, I have no answer to give, until I hear that thou hast closed thy life happily. For assuredly he who possesses great store of riches is no nearer happiness than he who has what suffices for his daily needs, unless it so hap that luck attend upon him, and so he continue in the enjoyment of all his good things to the end of life. For many of the wealthiest men have been unfavored of fortune, and many whose means were moderate have had excellent luck.

---

[2] **car:** Chariot.

[3] **furlongs:** A furlong is one-eighth of a mile, or 220 yards.

[4] **intercalary:** *Intercalary* refers to periods of time added to the regular calendar to equal one solar year. A solar year takes 365 days, five hours, forty-eight minutes, and forty-six seconds, or one revolution of the earth around the sun.

Men of the former class excel those of the latter but in two respects; these last excel the former in many. The wealthy man is better able to content his desires, and to bear up against a sudden buffet of calamity. The other has less ability to withstand these evils (from which, however, his good luck keeps him clear), but he enjoys all these following blessings: he is whole of limb, a stranger to disease, free from misfortune, happy in his children, and comely to look upon. If, in addition to all this, he end his life well, he is of a truth the man of whom thou art in search, the man who may rightly be termed happy. Call him, however, until he die, not happy but fortunate. Scarcely, indeed, can any man unite all these advantages: as there is no country which contains within it all that it needs, but each, while it possesses some things, lacks others, and the best country is that which contains the most; so no single human being is complete in every respect—something is always lacking. He who unites the greatest number of advantages, and retaining them to the day of his death, then dies peaceably, that man alone, sire, is, in my judgment, entitled to bear the name of 'happy.' But in every matter it behoves[5] us to mark well the end: for oftentimes God gives men a gleam of happiness, and then plunges them into ruin."

Such was the speech which Solon addressed to Croesus, a speech which brought him neither largess[6] nor honor. The king saw him depart with much indifference, since he thought that a man must be an arrant fool who made no account of present good, but bade men always wait and mark the end.

[5] **behoves:** To be necessary.
[6] **largess:** A generous gift.

Svetasvatara Upanishad

Ninth Century B.C.E.

The following excerpt from the Svetasvatara Upanishad deals with religious experience or religious practice, as opposed to religious belief or creed. In Part 2 of this ancient Vedic writing, the end of the yogic path is spelled out in the last few paragraphs: After one has discovered the Spirit within, then the soul is free to connect with the eternal Brahman, the Great Soul that sustains all of creation. In order to know this connection, the writer of the Upanishad recommends a spiritual practice or discipline that can control the "wild horses" of the mind and bring one's focus on the heart. In this practice, the universal sound "OM" is usually chanted; rhythmic chanting provides the occasion for shifting one's attention away from ordinary life to one of several spiritual practices—all of which can be grouped under the name "yoga." Yoga, which means simply "union" in Sanskrit, can be practiced through ordinary activities such as walking or praying or through prescribed yogic postures, like standing on

Ascetic Yogis, seventeenth century
Yoga has been practiced as a spiritual and physical discipline for more than two thousand years. Here yogis are pictured in various positions by a seventeenth-century Italian artist. (The Art Archive / Navy Historical Service, Vincennes, France / Dagli Orti)

one's head. After the body is under control, there is potential for health and spiritual growth. The purpose of this teaching is to reveal to the reader what is already the human condition but is hidden or confused—that the inner Spirit and Brahman are one.

Part 2: The Yogic Path

Translated by Juan Mascaró

Savitri,[1] the god of inspiration, sent the mind and its powers to find truth. He saw the light of the god of fire and spread it over the earth.

By the grace of god Savitri, our mind is one with him and we strive with all our power for light.

Savitri gives life to our souls and then they shine in great light. He makes our mind and its powers one and leads our thoughts to heaven.

The seers of the god who sees all keep their mind and their thoughts in oneness. They sing the glory of god Savitri who has given every man his work.

I sing the songs of olden times with adoration: may my own songs follow the path of the sun. Let all the children of immortality hear me, even those who are in the highest heaven.

Where the fire of the Spirit[2] burns, where the wind of the Spirit blows, where the Soma-wine of the Spirit[3] overflows, there a new soul is born.

Inspired then by Savitri let us find joy in the prayers of olden times: for if we make them our rock we shall be made pure of past sins.

---

[1] **Savitri:** A name for the sun god.

[2] **Spirit:** The Spirit of the universe, or Brahman.

[3] **Soma-wine of the Spirit:** Soma-wine is an intoxicating beverage thought to provide sacred powers or visions; it was offered to the gods and drunk by Brahmin priests.

With upright body, head, and neck lead the mind and its powers into thy heart; and the OM[4] of Brahman will then be thy boat with which to cross the rivers of fear.

And when the body is in silent steadiness, breathe rhythmically through the nostrils with a peaceful ebbing and flowing of breath. The chariot of the mind is drawn by wild horses, and those wild horses have to be tamed.

Find a quiet retreat for the practice of Yoga, sheltered from the wind, level and clean, free from rubbish, smouldering fires, and ugliness, and where the sound of waters and the beauty of the place help thought and contemplation.

These are the imaginary forms that appear before the final vision of Brahman: a mist, a smoke, and a sun; a wind, fire-flies, and a fire; lightnings, a clear crystal, and a moon.

When the Yogi has full power over his body composed of the elements of earth, water, fire, air, and ether, then he obtains a new body of spiritual fire which is beyond illness, old age, and death.

The first fruits of the practice of Yoga are: health, little waste matter, and a clear complexion; lightness of the body, a pleasant scent, and a sweet voice; and an absence of greedy desires.

Even as a mirror of gold, covered by dust, when cleaned well shines again in full splendour, when a man has seen the Truth of the Spirit he is one with him, the aim of his life is fulfilled and he is ever beyond sorrow.

Then the soul of man becomes a lamp by which he finds the Truth of Brahman. Then he sees God,[5] pure, never-born, everlasting; and when he sees God he is free from all bondage.

This is the God whose light illumines all creation, the Creator of all from the beginning. He was, he is and for ever he shall be. He is in all and he sees all.

Glory be to that God who is in the fire, who is in the waters, who is in plants and in trees, who is in all things in this vast creation. Unto that Spirit be glory and glory.

---

[4] **OM:** A sacred sound used as a mantra that represents the congruence of the inner world and the external spiritual and material worlds.

[5] **God:** Brahman.

Confucius
551–479 B.C.E.

Confucius's body of sayings, *The Analects,* so instrumental in shaping Chinese society for more than 2,000 years, are primarily concerned with morality: how to act in society. Like the Buddha in India, Confucius did not seem concerned with explaining the nature of god or the workings of the cosmos. In the following selection of sayings grouped under the subject of "Goodness," Confucius downplays the importance of characteristics like cleverness and pretension, traits that might distinguish an individual from a crowd, and recommends qualities that edify family life and, consequently, help one to fit into all groups beyond the family. The hierarchy of dutiful relationships within the family provides the model, according to Confucianism, on which society itself might be structured.

In this Arthur Waley translation, the Chinese word *xiao,* whose Chinese written character is made up of the symbol for "old" over the symbol for "the child," implying a younger person paying respect and honor to his or her elders, is rendered as *filial piety.* Similar to the connotation of *piety* in the West, where the word is linked to religious practices, *xiao* was originally associated with the prayers and offerings of ancestor worship. Only later was *xiao* connected with living parents; nevertheless, it would seem that some of the religious overtones of ancestor worship were transferred to attitudes toward parents.

The continuous focus in these Confucius sayings is on pleasing other people. The final imperative is a version of the "golden rule," which shows up some five centuries later in the teachings of Jesus of Nazareth (Matthew 7:12; Luke 6:31): Treat others as you would have them treat you.

FROM

The Analects

Translated by Arthur Waley

[On Goodness]

Book I

3 The Master said, 'Clever talk and a pretentious manner' are seldom found in the Good.

4 Master Tsêng[1] said, Every day I examine myself on these three points: in acting on behalf of others, have I always been loyal to their interests? In intercourse with my friends, have I always been true to my word? Have I failed to repeat the precepts that have been handed down to me?

[1] **Master Tsêng:** A disciple of Confucius who was important to the early development of Confucianism.

6 The Master said, A young man's duty is to behave well to his parents at home and to his elders abroad, to be cautious in giving promises and punctual in keeping them, to have kindly feelings towards everyone, but seek the intimacy of the Good. If, when all that is done, he has any energy to spare, then let him study the polite arts.[2]

Book IV

3, 4 Of the adage 'Only a Good Man knows how to like people, knows how to dislike them,' the Master said, He whose heart is in the smallest degree set upon Goodness will dislike no one.

6 The Master said, I for my part have never yet seen one who really cared for Goodness, nor one who really abhorred wickedness. One who really cared for Goodness would never let any other consideration come first. One who abhorred wickedness would be so constantly doing Good that wickedness would never have a chance to get at him. Has anyone ever managed to do Good with his whole might even as long as the space of a single day? I think not. Yet I for my part have never seen anyone give up such an attempt because he had not the *strength* to go on. It may well have happened, but I for my part have never seen it.[3]

Book XII

3 Ssu-ma Niu asked about Goodness. The Master said, The Good *(jên)* man is chary *(jên)* of speech. Ssu-ma Niu said, So that is what is meant by Goodness—to be chary of speech? The Master said, Seeing that the doing of it is so difficult, how can one be otherwise than chary of talking about it?[4]

---

[2] **the polite arts:** To recite texts, and to practice archery and manners.

[3] **because he had . . . seen it:** It is the will not the way that is wanting. (Translator's note.)

[4] **The Good . . . about it?:** He first puns on *jên*, "chary," and *jên*, "goodness"; and then in his second reply answers as though his first reply had meant "Goodness is a thing one ought to be chary of talking about." The implication is that the questioner had not yet reached a stage at which the mysteries of *jên* could be revealed to him. (Translator's note.)

EPICURUS

C. 341–270 B.C.E.

Epicurus was born on the island of Samos and taught in Asia Minor before going to Athens in 306 B.C.E., where his followers gave him the Garden—his home and his school, equivalent in some respects to Plato's Academy and Aristotle's Lyceum. Residing in the Garden, Epicurus taught his philosophy and created a religious community of **Epicureans**, which included slaves and women as well as philosophers. They lived a simple, healthy life, avoiding both meat and wine, with the goal of "securing the health of the body and tranquillity of the soul."

eh-pih-KYOO-ree-uns

Epicurus's mature teachings about enduring hardship and travail and his search for the possibilities of happiness in a troubled world apparently resulted from a childhood filled with poverty, suffering, and poor health. The key idea in Epicurus's teachings is that the basis of all knowledge is sensation; the mind is responsible for interpreting sensations and choosing actions that cause sensations of pleasure as opposed to those that cause pain to both the mind and the body. This means that an individual must learn to assess the consequences of actions, since a short-term pleasure might cause long-term pain. It is also necessary to differentiate between lasting and temporal pleasures, and between mental and bodily pleasures in order to make sensible choices. In his "Letter to a Friend," Epicurus does not advocate pursuing pleasures of the body that might be fleeting and that might result, finally, in pain. Rather he counsels one to seek the condition denoted by the Greek words *ataraxia*, meaning "serenity," and ***eudaemonia***, meaning "happiness" or "well-being." As opposed to the "pleasure of prodigals and sensualists," lasting pleasures are spiritual or psychological.

yoo-digh-MOH-nee-uh

Greek Bathing and Hunting Scene
Epicurean philosophy promoted not only the soundness of the mind but also the soundness and health of the physical body. (The Art Archive / Bibliothèque des Arts Decoratifs, Paris / Dagli Orti (A))

Letter to a Friend

Translated by Philip Wheelwright

We must consider that of desires some are natural, others empty; that of the natural some are necessary, others not; and that of the necessary some are necessary for happiness, others for bodily comfort, and others for life itself. A right understanding of these facts enables us to direct all choice and avoidance toward securing the health of the body and tranquillity of the soul; this being the final aim of a blessed life. For the aim of all actions is to avoid pain and fear; and when this is once secured for us the tempest of the soul is entirely quelled, since the living animal no longer needs to wander as though in search of something he lacks, hunting for that by which he can fulfill some need of soul or body. We feel a need of pleasure only when we grieve over its absence; when we stop grieving we are in need of pleasure no longer. Pleasure, then, is the beginning and end of the blessed life. For we recognize it as a good which is both primary and kindred to us. From pleasure we begin every act of choice and avoidance; and to pleasure we return again, using the feeling as the standard by which to judge every good.

Now since pleasure is the good that is primary and most natural to us, for that very reason we do not seize all pleasures indiscriminately; on the contrary we often pass over many pleasures, when greater discomfort accrues to us as a result of them. Similarly we not infrequently judge pains better than pleasures, when the long endurance of a pain yields us a greater pleasure in the end. Thus every pleasure because of its natural kinship to us is good, yet not every pleasure is to be chosen; just as every pain also is an evil, yet that does not mean that all pains are necessarily to be shunned. It is by a scale of comparison and by the consideration of advantages and disadvantages that we must form our judgment on these matters. On particular occasions we may have reason to treat the good as bad, and the bad as good.

Independence of circumstance we regard as a great good: not because we wish to dispense altogether with external advantages, but in order that, if our possessions are few, we may be content with what we have, sincerely believing that those enjoy luxury most who depend on it least, and that natural wants are easily satisfied if we are willing to forego superfluities. Plain fare yields as much pleasure as a luxurious table, provided the pain of real want is removed; bread and water can give exquisite delight to hungry and thirsty lips. To form the habit of a simple and modest diet, therefore, is the way to health: it enables us to perform the needful employments of life without shrinking, it puts us in better condition to enjoy luxuries when they are offered, and it renders us fearless of fortune.

Accordingly, when we argue that pleasure is the end and aim of life, we do not mean the pleasure of prodigals and sensualists, as some of our ignorant or prejudiced critics persist in mistaking us. We mean the pleasure of being free from pain of body and anxiety of mind. It is not a continual round of drunken debauches and lecherous delights, nor the enjoyment of fish and other delicacies of a wealthy table, which produce a pleasant life; but sober reasoning, searching out the motives of choice and avoidance, and escaping the bondage of opinion, to which the greatest disturbances of spirit are due.

The first step and the greatest good is prudence—a more precious thing than philosophy even, for all the other virtues are sprung from it. By prudence we learn that we can live pleasurably only if we live prudently, honorably, and justly, while contrariwise to live prudently, honorably, and justly guarantees a life that is pleasurable as well. The virtues are by nature bound up with a pleasant life, and a pleasant life is inseparable from them in turn.

Is there any better and wiser man than he who holds reverent beliefs about the gods, is altogether free from the fear of death, and has serenely contemplated the basic tendencies *(telê)* of natural law? Such a man understands that the limit of good things is easy to attain, and that evils are slight either in duration or in intensity. He laughs at Destiny, which so many accept as all-powerful. Some things, he observes, occur of necessity, others by chance, and still others through our own agency. Necessity is irresponsible, chance is inconstant, but our own actions are free, and it is to them that praise and blame are properly attached. It would be better even to believe the myths about the gods than to submit to the Destiny which the natural philosophers teach. For the old superstitions at least offer some faint hope of placating the gods by worship, but the Necessity of the scientific philosophers is absolutely unyielding. As to chance, the wise man does not deify it as most men do; for if it were divine it would not be without order. Nor will he accept the view that it is a universal cause even though of a wavering kind; for he believes that what chance bestows is not the good and evil that determine a man's blessedness in life, but the starting-points from which each person can arrive at great good or great evil. He esteems the misfortune of the wise above the prosperity of a fool; holding it better that well chosen courses of action should fail than that ill chosen ones should succeed by mere chance.

Meditate on these and like precepts day and night, both privately and with some companion who is of kindred disposition. Thereby shall you never suffer disturbance, waking or asleep, but shall live like a god among men. For a man who lives constantly among immortal blessings is surely more than mortal.

Cleanthes
331–233 B.C.E.

Cleanthes was a disciple of Zeno (c. 334–c. 261 B.C.E.), the founder of Stoicism. The basic teaching of Stoicism is that although people cannot control the external world—Fortune or Destiny—they can control their attitudes, the courage or cowardice with which they face life's challenges. Zeno did not sweeten his position by promising that virtue would be rewarded in the afterlife; the virtuous life was its own reward. Metaphors of the theater are commonly used in conjunction with Stoicism: Everyone is given a part to play in the great cosmic drama. Although the overall plot of the play is vaguely discernible, the particulars of everyday life and the time of the end are unknown. Each individual must act out his or her part in the best way possible, irrespective of life's hardships and ultimate outcome. Another metaphor sometimes used with stoicism is that of a card game: Everyone is dealt certain cards, which represent all those qualities of mind and body with which one is born—tall or short, bright or slow, beautiful or plain. What counts in life are not the cards one is dealt—these can't be changed—but how one plays out his or her individual hand.

Hera and Zeus, fifth century B.C.E. *In Greek and Roman mythology, Zeus (known as Jupiter to the Romans), the sky- and weather-god, was the chief deity. Hera (Juno to the Romans), his sister and wife, was queen of the Olympian gods. (Nimatallah / Art Resource, NY)*

Cleanthes succeeded Zeno as head of the Stoic school. In the following thoughtful "Invocation" Cleanthes attests to the power of Destiny. Although a few of the lines in Cleanthes's "Hymn to Zeus" might suggest an older, anthropomorphic Zeus who controls the cosmos, the Stoic Zeus is much closer to the laws of physics or the ultimate concept of Reason, which is accessible to human beings through understanding. In the hymn, the poet warns against pursuing fame, wealth, and pleasure rather than nobility of soul.

Invocation

Translated by Frederick C. Grant

Lead me, O Zeus, and thou, O Destiny, to the end that ye have ordained for me. I will follow without reluctance. Were I a fool, and refused, I should nevertheless have to follow!

Hymn to Zeus

Translated by Frederick C. Grant

Most glorious of immortals, Zeus
The many-named, almighty evermore,
Nature's great Sovereign, ruling all by law—
Hail to thee! On thee 'tis meet and right
That mortals everywhere should call.
From thee was our begetting; ours alone
Of all that live and move upon the earth
The lot to bear God's likeness.
Thee will I ever chant, thy power praise!

For thee this whole vast cosmos, wheeling round
The earth, obeys, and where thou leadest
It follows, ruled willingly by thee.
In thy unconquerable hands thou holdest fast,
Ready prepared, that two-tined flaming blast,
The ever-living thunderbolt:[1]
Nature's own stroke brings all things to their end.
By it thou guidest aright the sense instinct

[1] **The ever-living thunderbolt:** A reminder that Zeus was originally a weather-god.

Which spreads through all things, mingled even
With stars in heaven, the great and small—
Thou who art King supreme for evermore!

Naught upon earth is wrought in thy despite, O God,
Nor in the ethereal sphere aloft which ever winds
About its pole, nor in the sea—save only what
The wicked work, in their strange madness.
Yet even so thou knowest to make the crooked straight,
Prune all excess, give order to the orderless;
For unto thee the unloved still is lovely—
And thus in one all things are harmonized,
The evil with the good, that so one Word
Should be in all things everlastingly.

One Word—which evermore the wicked flee!
Ill-fated, hungering to possess the good
They have no vision of God's universal law,[2]
Nor will they hear; though if obedient in mind
They might obtain a noble life, true wealth.
Instead, they rush unthinking after ill:
Some with a shameless zeal for fame,
Others pursuing gain, disorderly;
Still others folly, or pleasures of the flesh.
[But evils are their lot,] and other times
Bring other harvests, all unsought—
For all their great desire, its opposite!

But, Zeus, thou giver of every gift,
Who dwellest within the dark clouds, wielding still
The flashing stroke of lightning, save, we pray,
Thy children from this boundless misery.
Scatter, O Father, the darkness from their souls,
Grant them to find true understanding—
On which relying thou justly rulest all—
While we, thus honored, in turn will honor thee,
Hymning thy works forever, as is meet
For mortals, while no greater right
Belongs even to the gods than evermore
Justly to praise the universal law!

[2] **God's universal law:** The unwritten law that everything in the cosmos belongs and fits together.

Marcus Aurelius

121–180 C.E.

The nobleman Marcus Aurelius was the emperor of Rome for the last two decades of his life, from 161 to 180 C.E. During that time he led his troops into battle against Germanic tribes in northern Europe. The twelve books of his *Meditations* are a kind of spiritual diary addressed to himself about his private, personal existence; they never mention his powerful role as emperor. Marcus Aurelius has been praised for saintliness, a devotion to conscience, and selflessness. In this excerpt from Book XII of *Meditations,* Marcus Aurelius explains a basic tenet of Stoicism: that Nature or the gods have designed a just universe and an appropriate role for each individual to play. The "good life" results from conforming to one's designated role; guidance is provided by one's *daemon*—one's inner voice or spirit.

Marcus Aurelius, 121–180
The Roman emperor Marcus Aurelius was a great general whose Meditations *reveal a philosophic and introspective nature unusual in such a powerful ruler. (The Art Archive / Museo Capitolino, Rome / Dagli Orti (A))*

FROM

Meditations

Translated by George Long

To Himself

1. All those things at which you wish to arrive by a circuitous road you can have now, if you do not refuse them to yourself. And this means, if you will take no notice of all the past, and trust the future to providence, and direct the present only conformably to piety and justice. Conformably to piety, that you may be content with the lot which is assigned to you, for nature designed it for you and you for it. Conformably to justice, that you may always speak the truth freely and without disguise, and do the things which are agreeable to law and according to the worth of each. And let neither another man's wickedness hinder you, nor opinion nor voice, nor yet the sensations of the poor flesh which has grown about you; for the passive part will look to this. If then, whatever the time may be when you shall be near to your departure, neglecting everything else you shall respect only your ruling faculty and the divinity within you, and if you shall be afraid not because you must some time cease to live, but if you shall fear never to have begun to live according to nature—then you will be a man worthy of the universe which has produced you, and you will cease to be a stranger in your native land, and to wonder at things which happen daily as if they were something unexpected, and to be dependent on this or that.

2. God sees the ruling principles of all men bared of the material vesture and rind and impurities. For with his intellectual part alone he touches the intelligence only which has flowed and been derived from himself into these bodies. And if you also use yourself to do this, you will rid yourself of much trouble. For he who regards not the poor flesh which envelops him, surely will not trouble himself by looking after raiment and dwelling and fame and such like externals and show.

3. The things are three of which you are composed—a little body, a little breath, intelligence. Of these the first two are yours, so far as it is your duty to take care of them; but the third alone is properly yours. Therefore if you shall separate from yourself, that is, from your understanding, whatever others do or say, and whatever you have done or said yourself, and whatever future things trouble you because they may happen, and whatever in the body which envelops you or in the breath which is by nature associated with the body and attached to you independent of your will, and whatever the external circumfluent vortex whirls round, so that the intellectual power exempt from the things of fate can live pure and free by itself, doing what is just and accepting what happens and saying the truth: if you will separate, I say, from this ruling faculty the things which are attached to it by the impressions of sense,

and the things of time to come and of time that is past, and will make yourself like Empedocles' sphere,[1]

> All round, and in its joyous rest reposing;

and if you shall strive to live only what is really your life, that is, the present—then you will be able to pass that portion of life which remains for you up to the time of your death, free from perturbations, nobly, and obedient to your own daemon.[2]

4. I have often wondered how it is that every man loves himself more than all the rest of men, but yet sets less value on his own opinion of himself than on the opinion of others. If then a god or a wise teacher should present himself to man and bid him to think of nothing and to design nothing which he would not express as soon as he conceived it, he could not endure it even for a single day. So much more respect have we to what our neighbors shall think of us than to what we shall think of ourselves.

5. How can it be that the gods after having arranged all things well and benevolently for mankind, have overlooked this alone, that some men and very good men, and men who, as we may say, have had most communion with the divinity, and through pious acts and religious observances have been most intimate with the divinity, when they have once died should never exist again, but should be completely extinguished?

But if this is so, be assured that if it ought to have been otherwise, the gods would have done it. For if it were just, it would also be possible; and if it were according to nature, nature would have had it so. But because it is not so, if in fact it is not so, be convinced that it ought not to have been so. You see even of yourself that in this inquiry you are disputing with the deity; and we should not thus dispute with the gods, unless they were most excellent and most just; but if this is so, they would not have allowed anything in the ordering of the universe to be neglected unjustly and irrationally. [. . .]

31. What do you wish? To continue to exist? Well, do you wish to have sensation? movement? growth? and then again to grow? to use your speech? to think? What is there of all these things which seems to you worth desiring? But if it is easy to set little value on all these things, turn to that which remains, which is to follow reason and God. But it is inconsistent with honoring reason and God to be troubled because by death a man will be deprived of the other things.

32. How small a part of boundless and unfathomable time is assigned to every man? for it is very soon swallowed up in the eternal. And how small a part of the

---

[1] **Empedocles' sphere:** Empedocles (fifth century B.C.E.) was a Greek philosopher and scientist who conceived of a spherical universe.

[2] **daemon:** The divine guardian spirit within that provides guidance.

whole substance? and how small a part of the universal soul? and on what a small clod of the whole earth you creep? Reflecting on all this consider nothing to be great, except to act as your nature leads you, and to endure that which the common nature brings.

33. How does the ruling faculty make use of itself? for all lies in this. But everything else, whether it is in the power of your will or not, is only lifeless ashes and smoke.

34. This reflection is most adapted to move us to contempt of death—that even those who think pleasure to be a good and pain an evil still have despised it.

35. The man to whom the only good is that which comes in due season, and to whom it is the same thing whether he has done more or fewer acts conformable to right reason, and to whom it makes no difference whether he contemplates the world for a longer or a shorter time—for this man neither is death a terrible thing.

36. Man, you have been a citizen in this great world state: what difference does it make to you whether for five years or three? for that which is conformable to the laws is just for all. Where is the hardship then, if no tyrant nor yet an unjust judge sends you away from the state, but nature who brought you into it? the same as if a praetor[3] who has employed an actor dismisses him from the stage. "But I have not finished the five acts, but only three of them." You say well, but in life the three acts are the whole drama; for what shall be a complete drama is determined by him who was once the cause of its composition, and now of its dissolution: but you are the cause of neither. Depart then satisfied, for he also who releases you is satisfied.

[3] **praetor:** A ranking magistrate in ancient Rome.

GLOSSARY OF LITERARY AND CRITICAL TERMS

Accent The emphasis given to a syllable or word, especially in poetry, that stresses a particular word in a line and may be used to define a poetic foot.

Acropolis The most fortified part of a Greek city, located on a hill; the most famous acropolis is in Athens, the site of the Parthenon.

Act A major division in the action of a play. In many full-length plays, acts are further divided into SCENES, which often mark a point in the action when the location changes or when a new character enters.

Adab An Islamic literary genre distinguished by its humanistic concerns on a variety of subjects that highlights the sensibilities and interests of authors and flourished throughout the tenth and eleventh centuries.

Aeneas The hero of Virgil's *Aeneid,* the Trojan Aeneas wanders for years after the Greek destruction of Troy before reaching the shores of Italy, where his descendants would later found the city of Rome.

The Aeneid The great epic poem of Virgil that tells of the adventures of its hero, Aeneas, after the Trojan War and provides illustrious historical background for the Roman Empire.

Age of Pericles The golden age of Athens in the fifth century B.C.E. when Pericles (c. 495–429 B.C.E.) was the head of the Athenian government. During this period, Athenian democracy was at its apex; the Parthenon was constructed and drama and music flourished.

Ahimsa The Buddhist belief that all life is one and sacred, resulting in the principle of nonviolence toward all living things.

Akam In Indian Tamil poetry, *akam* are "inner" poems, chiefly concerning passion and personal emotions.

Allegory A narrative in which the characters, settings, and episodes stand for something else. Traditionally, most allegories come in the form of stories that correlate to spiritual concepts; examples of these can be found in Dante's *Divine Comedy* (1321). Some later allegories allude to political, historical, and sociological ideas.

Alliteration The repetition of the same consonant sound or sounds in a sequence of words, usually at the beginning of a word or stressed syllable: "*d*escen*d*ing *d*ew *d*rops"; "*l*uscious *l*emons." Alliteration derives from the sounds, not the spelling of words; for example, "*k*een" and "*c*ar" alliterate, but "*c*ar" and "*c*ite" do not. Used sparingly, alliteration can intensify ideas by emphasizing key words.

Allusion A brief reference, sometimes direct, sometimes indirect, to a person, place, thing, event, or idea in history or literature. Such references could be to a scene in one of Shakespeare's plays, a historic figure, a war, a great love story, a biblical authority, or anything else that might enrich an author's work. Allusions, which function as a kind of shorthand, imply that the writer and the reader share similar knowledge.

Ambiguity Allows for two or more simultaneous interpretations of a word, phrase, action, or situation, all of whose meanings are supported by the work. Deliberate ambiguity can contribute to the effectiveness and richness of a piece of writing; unintentional ambiguity obscures meaning and may confuse readers.

Amor imperii Latin for love of power.

Anagnorisis The discovery or recognition that takes place in a tragedy, resulting in the protagonist's *PERIPETEIA*, or reversal of fortune.

Anagram A word or phrase made up of the same letters as another word or phrase; *heart* is an anagram of *earth*. Often considered merely an exercise of one's ingenuity, anagrams are sometimes used by writers to conceal proper names, veil messages, or suggest an important connection between words, such as that between *hated* and *death*.

Antagonist The character, force, or collection of forces in fiction or drama that opposes the PROTAGONIST and gives rise to the conflict in the story; an opponent of the protagonist, such as Caliban in Shakespeare's play *The Tempest*.

Anthropocentric Human-centered. A point of view that considers everything in the world or universe in terms of its relation to or value for human beings.

Apocalypse A prophetic revelation, particularly one that predicts the destruction of the world, as in the final battle between good and evil foreseen in Zoroastrianism and in the Revelation of St. John the Divine; the time when God conquers the powers of evil.

Apostrophe A statement or address made to an implied interlocutor, sometimes a nonhuman figure, or PERSONIFICATION. Apostrophes often provide a speaker with the opportunity to reveal his or her thoughts.

Archetype A universal symbol that evokes deep and sometimes unconscious responses in a reader. In literature, characters, images, and themes that symbolize universal meanings and basic human experiences are considered archetypes. Common literary archetypes include quests, initiations, scapegoats, descents to the underworld, and ascents to heaven.

Archon The chief ruler of Athens during the classical era.

Aryans A people who settled in Iran (Persia) and northern India in prehistoric times. Gradually, they spread through India in the first millennium B.C.E., extending their influence to southern India in the first three centuries C.E. Through their early writings in the Sanskrit language, the VEDAS, they established the basis of Hinduism and Indian culture.

Aside In drama, a speech directed to the audience that supposedly is not audible to the other characters onstage.

Assonance The repetition of vowel sounds in nearby words, as in "asl*ee*p under a tr*ee*" or "*ea*ch *e*vening." When words also share similar endings, as in "asl*eep* in the d*eep*," RHYME occurs. Assonance is an effective means of emphasizing important words.

Autobiography A narrative form of biography in which an author accounts for his or her own life and character to a public audience. As a literary genre, autobiography developed differently in several cultures: the *Confessions* of St. Augustine, written in Latin in the fifth century, served as a model in Europe; Ibn Ishaq's biography of Muhammad, written in Arabic in the eighth century, served as the model for both biographies and autobiographies by later Arabic writers.

Ballad A narrative verse form originally meant to be sung; it generally tells a dramatic tale or a simple story. Ballads are associated with the oral traditions or folklore of common people. The folk ballad stanza usually consists of four lines of alternating tetrameter (four accented syllables) and trimeter (three accented syllables) and follows a rhyme scheme of *abab* or *abcb*.

Ballad stanza A four-line stanza, known as a QUATRAIN, consisting of alternating eight- and six-syllable lines. Usually, only the second and fourth lines rhyme (an *abcb* pattern). Samuel Taylor Coleridge adapted the ballad stanza in *The Rime of the Ancient Mariner* (1798).

Baroque A style found in architecture, art, and literature from the late sixteenth century through the early eighteenth century, characterized by extravagance of theme, language, and form; striking and abrupt turns of line and logic; and ingenious and dynamic imagery. The English poet John Donne (1572–1631) and the Spanish-American poet Sor Juana Inés de la Cruz (c. 1648–1695) often employ what may be considered baroque styles.

Bhagavad Gita An ancient text of Hindu wisdom from the first century B.C.E. or first century C.E. inserted into the epic poem *Mahabharata.*

Bhakti From the Sanskrit for *devotion,* refers to the popular mystical movement stemming from Hinduism. In contrast to forms of Hinduism that stress knowledge, ritual, and good works, Bhakti cults emphasize that personal salvation may be achieved through the loving devotion and ecstatic surrender of an individual to a chosen deity, such as Shiva, Vishnu, and their consorts, often worshiped as a child, parent, beloved, or master.

Bible A collection of writings sacred to Christianity made up of the Hebrew Scriptures (also known as the Old Testament), containing the history, teachings, and literature of the ancient Hebrews and Jews, and the New Testament, the history, teachings, and literature associated with Jesus of Nazareth and his followers.

Biography A nonfiction literary genre that provides the history of an individual's life, detailing not only the facts of that life but also insights into the individual's personality and character. Biography is distinguished from autobiography in that it is written by someone other than the person who is the subject of the work. Biography became popular as a form beginning in the Renaissance.

Black Death The bubonic plague, a devastating disease that swept through Europe in the fourteenth century, leaving a trail of death in its wake.

Blank verse Unrhymed IAMBIC PENTAMETER. Blank verse is often considered the form closest to the natural rhythms of English speech and is therefore the most common pattern found in traditional English narrative and dramatic poetry, from Shakespeare to the writers of the early twentieth century.

Blazon A catalog of similes or metaphors drawn from nature wherein the fair parts of the lover's body are compared to what eventually came to be a stock set of images drawn from nature, seen in the Song of Songs, and earlier love poems. Shakespeare's "My mistress's eyes are nothing like the sun" parodies this convention.

Bodhisattva In Buddhism, a person who temporarily puts off nirvana in order to assist others on earth; one who has achieved great moral and spiritual enlightenment and is en route to becoming a Buddha.

Book of History An ancient collection of documents on Chinese history and politics written in prose dating back to the early years of the Zhou dynasty (c. 1027–221 B.C.E.), if not earlier. It is one of the oldest works of history and was a foundation for Confucian ideas; among other things it describes history as a process of change, and delineates the important "Mandate of Heaven," which said that emperors ruled by divine right, but if or when an emperor violated his office, the mandate would pass to another.

Book of Songs Also known as the *Poetry Classic, Book of Poems,* or *Book of Odes,* this is the oldest Chinese anthology of poems, dating from the ninth through the sixth centuries B.C.E. Written primarily in four-character verse, these poems treat a variety of subjects and form the foundation of later Chinese verse.

Brahman In the UPANISHADS—sacred Hindu texts—Brahman is the ultimate reality, the single unifying essence of the universe that transcends all names and descriptions. A Brahman, or Brahmin, is also a Hindu priest and thus of the highest caste in the traditional Hindu caste system.

Brahmanic period The period in ancient India (c. 1000–600 B.C.E.), in which VEDIC society was dominated by the Brahmins and every aspect of Aryan life was under the control of religious rituals. Both heroic epics of Indian culture, the *Mahabharata* and the *Ramayana*, were originally formulated and told in this period, though transcribed to written form much later, between 400 B.C.E. and 400 C.E.

Brahmin The priestly caste, the highest in the traditional Hindu caste system; a Hindu priest. Also spelled *BRAHMAN*.

Buddhism A religion founded in India in the sixth century B.C.E. by Siddhartha Gautama, the Buddha. While Buddhism has taken different forms in the many areas of the world to which it has spread, its central tenet is that life is suffering caused by desire. In order to obtain salvation, or nirvana, one must transcend desire through following an eightfold path that includes the practice of right action and right mindfulness.

Bunraku New name for *joruri*, traditional Japanese puppet theater.

Bushido The code of honor and conduct of the Japanese SAMURAI class. *Bushido* emphasizes self-discipline and bravery.

Cacophony In literature, language that is discordant and difficult to pronounce. Cacophony (from the Greek for "bad sound") may be unintentional, or it may be used for deliberate dramatic effect; also refers to the combination of loud, jarring sounds.

Caesura A pause within a line of poetry that contributes to the line's RHYTHM. A caesura can occur anywhere within a line and need not be indicated by punctuation. In scansion, caesuras are indicated by two vertical lines.

Caliph The chief civil and religious leader of a Muslim state, as a successor of Muhammad.

Caliphate Both the reign or term of a caliph as well as the area over which he rules.

Calvinists A Protestant denomination whose adherents follow the beliefs originally outlined by French Protestant reformer, John Calvin (1509-1564), especially predestination and salvation of the elect through God's grace alone.

Canon The works generally considered by scholars, critics, and teachers to be the most important to read and study and that collectively constitute the masterpieces of literature. Since the 1960s, the traditional English and American literary canons, consisting mostly of works by white male writers, have been expanding to include many female writers and writers of varying ethnic backgrounds. At the same time the world literature canon, as constructed in the West, has been broadened to include many works from non-Western literatures, especially those of Asia and Africa.

Canzoniere Medieval Italian lyric poetry. Masters of the form included Petrarch, Dante, Tasso, and Cavalcanti.

Carpe diem Latin phrase meaning "seize the day." This is a common literary theme, especially in lyric poetry, conveying that life is short, time is fleeting, and one should make the most of present pleasures. Andrew Marvell's poem "To His Coy Mistress" is a good example.

Caste The hereditary class to which a member of Hindu society belongs; stemming from the teachings of the VEDAS, Hindu society observes a strict hierarchy with the Brahmins, or priests, at the top; followed by the *KSHATRIYAS*, or warriors and rulers; and the Vaishyas, or farmers, merchants, and artisans; and a fourth class, added later than the others, the Shudras, servants. Only members of the first three "twice-born" castes could study the VEDAS and take part in religious rituals. Outside of this system were the outcastes, known as Untouchables.

Catechumen In the early Christian church, an individual officially recognized as a Christian and admitted to religious instruction required for full membership in the church.

Catharsis Meaning "purgation," or the release of the emotions of pity and fear by the audience at the end of a tragedy. In *Poetics*, Aristotle discusses the importance of catharsis.

The audience faces the misfortunes of the PROTAGONIST, which elicit pity and compassion. Simultaneously, the audience confronts the protagonist's failure, thus receiving a frightening reminder of human limitations and frailties.

Character, characterization A character is a person presented in a dramatic or narrative work; characterization is the process by which a writer presents a character to the reader.

Chin-Shi Examinations First begun in the Sui dynasty in China (581–618 C.E.) under Yang Jian and formalized during the Tang era, the system of chin-shi examinations brought bright and talented men from all over China into the government bureaucracy.

Chivalric romances Idealized stories from the medieval period that espoused the values of a sophisticated courtly society. These tales centered around the lives of knights who were faithful to God, king, and country and willing to sacrifice themselves for these causes and for the love and protection of women. Chivalric romances were highly moral and fanciful, often pitting knights against dark or supernatural forces.

Choka A Japanese form of an ode associated with Kakinomoto Hitomaro (late seventh century); a long poem often inspired by public occasions but also full of personal sentiment.

Chorus In Greek tragedies, a group of people who serve mainly as commentators on the play's characters and events, adding to the audience's understanding of a play by expressing traditional moral, religious, and social attitudes. Choruses are occasionally used by modern playwrights.

Christianity A world religion founded in Palestine in the first millennium C.E. upon the teachings of Jesus Christ, whose followers believe he is the Messiah prophesied in the Hebrew Scriptures (Old Testament). The central teachings of Christianity are that Jesus of Nazareth was the son of God, that his crucifixion and resurrection from the dead provide atonement for the sins of humanity, and that through faith in Jesus individuals might attain eternal life. Christianity has played a central role in the history of Europe and the Americas.

Chthonic From the Greek *chthonios,* meaning "in the earth," *chthonic* refers to the underworld spirits and deities in ancient religion and mythology.

Cliché An idea or expression that has become tired and trite from overuse.

Closet drama A play that is to be read rather than performed onstage. In closet dramas, literary art outweighs all other considerations.

Colloquial Informal diction that reflects casual, conversational language and often includes slang expressions.

Comedy A work intended to interest, involve, and amuse readers or an audience, in which no terrible disaster occurs and which ends happily for the main characters.

Comic relief A humorous scene or incident that alleviates tension in an otherwise serious work. Often these moments enhance the thematic significance of a story in addition to providing humor.

Comitatus Arrangement whereby young warriors attached themselves to the leader of a group and defended him in return for his economic and legal protection. Also, the bond among warriors attached to such a leader.

Conceit A figure of speech elaborating a surprising parallel between two dissimilar things. It was a favorite poetic device of the Petrarchan sonneteers and the English metaphysical poets of the seventeenth century.

Conflict In a literary work, the struggle between opposing forces. The PROTAGONIST is engaged in a conflict with the antagonist.

Confucianism A religious philosophy that has influenced Chinese and East Asian spirituality and culture for more than two thousand years. Based on the writings of Confucius (Kongfuzi; 551–479 B.C.E.), Confucianism asserts that humans can improve and even perfect themselves through education and moral reform. In its various manifestations, Confucianism has affected the social and political evolution of China and East Asia while providing a spiritual and moral template.

Connotation Implications going beyond the literal meaning of a word that derive from how the word has been commonly used and from ideas or things associated with it. For example, the word *eagle* in the United States connotes ideas of liberty and freedom that have little to do with the term's literal meaning.

Consonance A common type of near-rhyme or half rhyme created when identical consonant sounds are preceded by different vowel sounds: *home, same; worth, breath.*

Convention A characteristic of a literary genre that is understood and accepted by readers and audiences because it has become familiar. For example, the division of a play into acts and scenes is a dramatic convention, as are SOLILOQUIES and ASIDES.

Cosmogony An explanation for the origins of the universe and how the functioning of the heavens is related to the religious, political, and social organization of life on earth. The primary function of creation myths, such as the Hebrew Book of Genesis and the Mesopotamian *Epic of Creation,* is to depict a cosmogonic model of the universe.

Cosmology The metaphysical study of the origin and nature of the universe.

Cosmopolis A large city inhabited by people from many different countries.

Counter-Reformation The period of Catholic revival and reform from the beginning of the pontificate of Pope Pius IV in 1560 to the end of the Thirty Years' War in 1648 in response to the Protestant Reformation. Spearheaded in great part by members of the Society of Jesus (the Jesuits), it was a period in which the Roman Catholic church reaffirmed the veneration of saints and the authority of the pope and initiated many institutional reforms.

Couplet A two-line stanza.

Creation myth A symbolic narrative of the beginning of the world as configured by a particular society or culture. Examples of creation myths range from the Mesopotamian classic *Epic of Creation* to the Book of Genesis in Hebrew Scriptures to the creation myths of the Ancient Mexicans of the Americas.

Crisis The moment in a work of drama or fiction in which the elements of the conflict reach the point of maximum tension. The crisis is is not necessarily the emotional crescendo, or climax.

Cultural criticism An approach to literature that focuses on the historical, social, political, and economic contexts of a work. Cultural critics use widely eclectic strategies, such as anthropology, NEW HISTORICISM, psychology, gender studies, and DECONSTRUCTION, to analyze not only literary texts but everything from radio talk shows to comic strips, calendar art, advertising, travel guides, and baseball cards.

Cuneiform The wedge-shaped writing characters that stood for syllables or sounds and not letters in ancient Akkadian, Assyrian, Persian, and Babylonian inscriptions.

Daoism (Taoism) A religion/philosophy based on the Dao De Jing (Tao Te Ching) of Laozi (Lao Tzu) that emphasizes individual freedom, spontaneity, mystical experience, and self-transformation, and is the antithesis of CONFUCIANISM. In pursuit of the dao, or the Way—the eternal creative reality that is the essence of all things—practitioners embrace simplicity and reject learned wisdom. The Daoist tradition has flourished in China and East Asia for more than two thousand years.

Deconstructionism An approach to literature that suggests that literary works do not yield single, fixed meanings because language can never say exactly what one intends it to mean. Deconstructionism seeks to destabilize meaning by examining the gaps in and ambiguities of a text's language. Deconstructionists pay close attention to language in order to discover and describe how a variety of close readings of any given work can be generated.

Denouement French term meaning "unraveling" or "unknotting" used to describe the resolution of a PLOT following the action's climax.

Deus ex machina Latin for "god from the machine," a phrase originally applied to Greek plays, especially those by Euripides, in which resolution of the conflict was achieved by the intervention of a god who was lowered onto the stage mechanically. In its broader use, the phrase is applied to any plot that is resolved by an improbable or fortuitous device from outside the action.

Dharma Cosmic order or law in the Hindu tradition that includes the natural and moral laws that apply to all beings and things.

Dhimmi See THE PEOPLE OF THE BOOK.

Dialect A type of informal diction. Dialects are spoken by definable groups of people from a particular geographic region, economic group, or social class. Writers use dialect to express and contrast the education, class, and social and regional backgrounds of their characters.

Dialogue Verbal exchange between CHARACTERS. Dialogue reveals firsthand characters' thoughts, responses, and emotional states.

Diaspora From the Greek for "dispersion," this term was initially applied to the Jews exiled to Babylonia after the destruction of the Temple of Jerusalem in 586 B.C.E. and again forced into exile after the Romans defeated Jerusalem in 70 C.E. The term now refers to other peoples who have been forced from their homelands, such as the Africans uprooted by the slave trade.

Diction A writer's choice of words, phrases, sentence structure, and figurative language, which combine to help create meaning.

Didactic Literature intended to teach or convey instruction, especially of a moral, ethical, or religious nature, such as a didactic essay or poem.

Digressions In epics such as *Beowulf,* these are narratives imbedded in the story to illustrate a point or recall another situation. Digressions may consist of conventional wisdom; suggest how one is supposed to behave; or remind the audience of events occurring either before or after those treated in the story.

Dionysiac festival In Athens, plays were performed during two major festivals in honor of the god Dionysus: the Lenaea during January and February, and the Great Dionysia in March and April.

Dionysus The god of wine in Greek mythology whose cult originated in Thrace and Phrygia, north and east of the Greek peninsula. Dionysus was often blamed for people's irrational behavior and for chaotic situations. However, many Greeks also believed that Dionysus taught them good farming skills, especially those related to wine production. Greek tragedy evolved from a ceremony that honored Dionysus, and the theater in Athens was dedicated to him.

Dithyramb Originally a highly passionate, lyrical hymn sung during the rites of Dionysius in Greece, dithyramb now refers to any impassioned sequence of verse or prose, often characterized by irregular or unrestrained rhythms and extravagant imagery.

Divine Comedy Dante Alighieri's fourteenth-century narrative poem that deals with the poet's imaginary journey through hell, purgatory, and paradise.

Doggerel A derogatory term for poetry whose subject is trite and whose rhythm and sounds are monotonously heavy-handed.

Drama Derived from the Greek word *dram,* meaning "to do" or "to perform," *drama* may refer to a single play, a group of plays, or to plays in general. Drama is designed to be performed in a theater: Actors take on the roles of CHARACTERS, perform indicated actions, and deliver the script's DIALOGUE.

Dramatic monologue A type of lyric or narrative poem in which a speaker addresses an imagined and distinct audience in such a way as to reveal a dramatic situation and, often unintentionally, some aspect of his or her temperament or personality.

Dravidians A group of dark-skinned peoples of India who were either ancient occupants of the southern peninsula, refugees of earlier tribes pushed down from the north, or late arrivals to India from the Mediterranean seacoast.

Edo The ancient name for Tokyo. During the Tokugawa period (1600–1868), Edo became the imperial capital of Japan.

Elegiac couplets The conventional strophic form of Latin elegiac love poetry, consisting of one dactylic hexameter line followed by one dactylic pentameter line. A dactylic hexameter line is composed of six feet, each foot comprising one long, or accented, and two short, or unaccented, syllables; the sixth foot may be shortened by one or two syllables; a pentameter line consists of five such feet. The elegiac couplet is also known as a "distich."

Elegy A mournful, contemplative lyric poem often ending in consolation, written to commemorate someone who has died. *Elegy* may also refer to a serious, meditative poem that expresses a speaker's melancholy thoughts.

Elizabethan Of or characteristic of the time when Elizabeth I (1558–1603) was the queen of England. This era was perhaps the most splendid literary period in the history of English literature in that it encompassed the works of Sidney, Spenser, Marlowe, and Shakespeare, among many others, and saw the flourishing of such genres as poetry, especially the SONNET, and was a golden age of drama of all forms.

Elysian Fields In Greek mythology, some fortunate mortals spend their afterlife in the bliss of these Islands of the Blest, rather than in Hades, the underworld.

End-stopped line A line in a poem after which a pause occurs. End-stopped lines reflect normal speech patterns and are often marked by punctuation.

Enjambment In poetry, a line continuing without a pause into the next line for its meaning; also called a run-on line.

Ennead The group of nine primary deities in the religion of ancient Egypt.

Epic A long narrative poem told in a formal, elevated style that focuses on a serious subject and chronicles heroic deeds and events important to a culture or nation. It usually includes a supernatural dimension, like the gods in Homer. Most epics follow established conventions, such as beginning *in medias res* (in the middle of things); employing elaborate comparisons known as epic similes; and identifying characters with repeated epithets, such as "wily Odysseus." Oral or folk epics, recited tales told for many generations before being written down, such as *The Iliad* and *Sunjata,* are sometimes distinguished from literary epics like *The Aeneid* or *Paradise Lost,* whose original creation was the work of a single poet.

Epicureanism The doctrines of Epicurus (c. 341–270 B.C.E.), the Greek philosopher who espoused a life of pleasure and the avoidance of pain; commonly thought of as a license for indulgence, Epicureanism actually stipulates a life of simplicity and morality.

Essays A literary form that is an analytical, interpretive, or critical composition usually shorter and less formal than a dissertation or thesis and more personal in nature. The term was coined in the Renaissance by the master of the form, Montaigne (1533–1592), who chose it to underscore that his writings (from the French word *essai,* literally meaning "trial," or "test") were attempts toward understanding.

Euphony From the Greek for "good sound"; refers to language that is smooth and musically pleasant to the ear.

Exposition A narrative device often used at the beginning of a work to provide necessary background information about characters and their circumstances. Exposition explains such matters as what has gone on before; the relationships between characters; theme; and conflict.

Fabliau Although the *fabliau* originated in France as a comic or satiric tale in verse, by the time of Giovanni Boccaccio (1313–1375) and Geoffrey Chaucer (1340–1400) the term also stood for bawdy and ribald prose tales like "The Miller's Tale" in Chaucer's *Canterbury Tales* or Boccaccio's "Rustico and Alibech."

Farce A form of humor based on exaggerated, improbable incongruities. Farce involves rapid shifts in action and emotion as well as slapstick comedy and extravagant dialogue.

Feminist criticism An approach to literature that seeks to correct or supplement a predominantly male-dominated critical perspective with a feminist consciousness. Feminist criticism places literature in a social context and uses a broad range of disciplines, including history, sociology, psychology, and linguistics, to provide interpretations that are sensitive to feminist issues.

Feudal aristocracy, Feudalism A system of government that existed with some variations in Europe, China, and Japan in the Middle Period. The feudal system refers to a mode of agricultural production in which peasants worked for landowners, or lords, in return for debt forgiveness, food, and military protection.

Fiction Literature created from the imagination and not presented as fact, though it may be based on a true story or real-life situation. Genres of fiction include the short story, the novella, and the novel.

Figures of speech Ways of using language that deviate from the literal, denotative meanings of words, through comparison, exaggeration, or other verbal devices in order to suggest additional meanings or effects.

Fixed form A poem characterized by a fixed pattern of lines, syllables, or METER. A SONNET is a fixed form of poetry because it must have fourteen lines.

Flashback A literary or dramatic device that allows a past occurrence to be inserted into the chronological order of a narrative.

Flying Dutchman The legend of a ghostly ship doomed to sail for eternity. If a vision of it appears to sailors, it signals imminent disaster. Most versions of the story have the captain of the ill-fated ship playing dice or gambling with the devil.

Foil A character in a literary work or drama whose behavior or values contrast with those of another character, typically the PROTAGONIST.

Foot A poetic foot is a poem's unit of measurement, defined by an accented syllable and a varying number of unaccented syllables. In English, the iambic foot, an accented syllable followed by an unaccented syllable, is the most common.

Foreshadowing Providing hints of what is to happen in order to build suspense.

Formalism A type of criticism dominant in the early twentieth century that emphasizes the form of an artwork. Two of its prominent schools are Russian formalism, which favors the form of an artwork over its content and argues that it is necessary for literature to defamiliarize the ordinary objects of the world, and American NEW CRITICISM, which treats a work of art as an object and seeks to understand it through close, careful analysis.

Founding myth A story that explains how a particular nation or culture came to be, such as Virgil's *Aeneid*, which describes the founding of Rome. Many epic poems, sometimes called national epics, are founding myths.

Four classes In Hindu tradition, humans are created as one of four classes, or VARNA: in descending order, the BRAHMINS (priests), the *KSHATRIYA* (warriors), the *Vaishya* (merchants and farmers), and the *Shudra* (laborers and servants).

Framed narration Also called *framed tale.* A story within a story. In Chaucer's *Canterbury Tales*, each pilgrim's story is framed by the story of the pilgrimage itself. This device, used by writers from ancient times to the present, enjoyed particular popularity during the thirteenth, fourteenth, and fifteenth centuries and was most fully developed in *The Arabian Nights*, a work in which the framing is multilayered.

Free verse Highly irregular poetry, typically, free verse employs varying line patterns and rhythms and does not rhyme.

Freudian criticism A method of literary criticism associated with Freud's theories of psychoanalysis. Early Freudian critics sought to illustrate how literature is shaped by the unconscious desires of the author, but the term now more broadly encompasses many schools of thought that link psychoanalysis to the interpretation of literature.

Fu A mixed-genre Chinese literary form developed during the Han dynasty (206 B.C.E.–220 C.E.) that combines elements of prose and poetry; it begins with a prose introduction followed by lines of poetry of various metrical lengths.

Gaia From the Greek *Ge* meaning "earth," Gaia or Gaea was an earth goddess, mother of the Titans in Greek mythology.

Gay and lesbian criticism School of literary criticism that focuses on the representation of homosexuality in literature; also interested in how homosexuals read literature and to what extent sexuality and gender is culturally constructed.

Gender criticism Literary school that analyzes how an author's or a reader's sex affects the writing and reading experiences.

Genre A category of artistic works or literary compositions that have a distinctive style or content. Poetry, fiction, and drama are genres. Different genres have dominated at various times and places. Traditional genres include tragedy, comedy, romance, novel, epic, and lyric.

Georgic poetry Poetry dealing with the practical aspects of agriculture and rural affairs as first seen in the work of the Greek poet Nicander of Colophon (second century B.C.E.) and practiced by later poets such as Virgil (70–19 B.C.E.).

Ghazal A form of lyric poetry composed of three to seven couplets, called *sh'ir,* that follow the strict rhyme scheme of *aa ba ca da,* and so on, known as the *qafiyah.* Strict adherence to the form requires the use of the *radif,* a word that is repeated in a pattern dictated by the first couplet, throughout the poem. Literally meaning "dialogue with the beloved," the *ghazal,* as practiced in Arabia, Persia, Turkey, and India beginning around 1200, became the predominant form for love poetry.

Gnostics Members of an ancient sect in the Middle East who believed that hidden knowledge held the key to the universe. Throughout history there have been Gnostics who have formed secret societies with secret scriptures and who have believed they understood the workings of the cosmos.

Golden Age of Arabic science The period of the Abbassid caliphs, between 750 and 945 C.E., particularly the reigns of Harun al-Rashid (786–809) and al-Ma'mun (813–833). Al-Ma'mun founded a scientific academy in Baghdad, collected and had translated many ancient Greek and Indian manuscripts upon which Arab scholars built, and encouraged scholarship of all kinds, resulting in major advances in mathematics, astronomy, medicine, and geography.

Golden Age of Spain The "Siglo de Oro" period from the early sixteenth century to the end of the seventeenth century that is considered the high point of Spain's literary history. The age began with the political unification of Spain around 1500 and extended through 1681, the year in which Pedro Calderon (1600–1681) died. In addition to Calderon, this period saw the flourishing of such writers as Cervantes (1547–1616) and Lope de Vega (1562–1635).

Gothic A style of literature (especially novels) in the late eighteenth and early nineteenth centuries that reacted against the mannered decorum of earlier literature. Gothic novels explore the darker side of human experience; they are often set in the past and in foreign countries, and they employ elements of horror, mystery, and the supernatural.

Gravitas Formality in bearing and appearance; a reserved dignity of behavior and speech, especially in a leader or a ruler.

Great Chain of Being A conception of the universal order of things derived from Greek philosophy that exerted considerable influence on the European understanding of nature and the universe from the Renaissance through the eighteenth century. The Great Chain of Being posits that God ordered the universe so as to create the greatest possible diversity, continuity, and order, and envisions a hierarchical structure whereby every being, according to its nature, occupies a designated place on a ladder reaching from the basest matter to the highest spiritual entity, or God. This metaphor offered the assurance that degree, proportion, and place would be, or should be, observed in the social and natural order. Human beings occupy the middle position on this ladder or chain, sharing the spiritual potentials of "higher" beings as well as the material limits of the "lower" beings.

Greater Dionysia In ancient Greece, dramas were performed at festivals that honored the god Dionysus: the Lenaea during January and February and the Greater Dionysia in March and April. The best tragedies and comedies were awarded prizes by an Athenian jury.

Griot A storyteller in West Africa who perpetuates the oral traditions of a family or village.

Gupta dynasty The time of the reign of the Gupta emperors (320–c. 550), considered the golden age of classical Indian history. The dynasty, established by Chandragupta I (r. 320–35), disintegrated in the middle of the sixth century. It was during this period that the great poetry of Kalidasa was written.

Gushi In Chinese literature, a verse form that consists of even-numbered, alternately rhymed lines of five syllables each. Referred to as "old-style verse."

Hadith Islamic source of religious law and moral guidance. According to tradition, the Hadith were passed down orally to the prophet Muhammad, and today they are critical to the study of the early development of Islam.

Hajj The pilgrimage to Mecca, Saudi Arabia, one of the five pillars of Islam and the duty of every Muslim at least once in his or her lifetime.

Hamartia A tragic flaw or error that in ancient Greek tragedies leads to the hero's reversal of fortune, known as the *peripeteia.*

Hebrew Scriptures A collection of thirty-nine books sacred to Judaism sometimes called the Hebrew Bible, these writings contain the history, teachings, and literature of the ancient Hebrews and Jews; called the Old Testament by Christians.

Hellene The name for a Greek, dating from the inhabitants of ancient Greece, who took their name from Hellen, the son of the legendary Deucalion and Pyrrha.

Hellenism The language, thought, art, customs, and literature characteristic of classical Greece.

Heroic couplet A rhymed, iambic-pentameter stanza of two lines that completes its thought within the two-line form. Alexander Pope (1688–1744), the most accomplished practitioner of the form in English, included this couplet in his *Essay on Criticism:* "True wit is nature to advantage dressed, / What oft was thought, but ne'er so well expressed."

Heroic poetry Narrative verse that is elevated in mood and uses a dignified, dramatic, and formal style to describe the deeds of aristocratic warriors and rulers. Typically, it was transmitted orally over several generations and written down at a later date. Examples of the form include *The Iliad* and *The Odyssey.*

Hexameter couplets The conventional strophic form of Greek and Latin epic poetry consisting of two dactylic hexameter lines; each line is composed of six feet, and each foot comprises one long (accented) and two short (unaccented) syllables. The final foot is known as a catalectic foot, for it is generally shortened by one or two syllables.

Hieroglyphic writing A writing system using picture symbols to represent sounds, words, or images instead of alphabetical letters. It was used by the ancient Egyptians, Mexicans, and others.

Hieros gamos Literally, "sacred marriage"; a fertility ritual in which the god-king or priest-king is united with the goddess or priestess-queen in order to provide a model for the kingdom and establish the king's right to rule.

Hinduism The major religion of India based on the ancient doctrines found in the SANSKRIT texts known as the VEDAS and the UPANISHADS, dating from 1000 B.C.E.

Historical criticism An approach to literature that uses history as a means of understanding a literary work. Such criticism moves beyond both the facts of an author's life and the text itself to examine the social and intellectual contexts in which the author composed the work.

Homeric Hymns At one time attributed to Homer, the *Homeric Hymns* (seventh through sixth centuries B.C.E.) are now believed to have been created by poets from a Homeric school or simply in the style of Homer. Five of the longer hymns contain important stories about gods such as Demeter, DIONYSUS, Apollo, Aphrodite, and Hermes.

Homo viator Latin for "man the traveler," used by Augustine to signify man's pilgrimage through life toward God.

Hoplite The name used to designate the foot soldiers of ancient Greece.

Hubris Exaggerated pride or arrogance; in Greek tragedies, hubris causes fatal errors.

Huguenots French Protestant members of the Reformed Church established in France by John Calvin in about 1555. Due to religious persecution, many Huguenots fled to other countries in the sixteenth and seventeenth centuries.

Humanism The learning or cultural impulse that flourished during the European Renaissance characterized by a revival of classical letters, an individualistic and critical spirit, and a shift from religious to secular concerns.

Hundred Years' War A series of wars between the English and the French that lasted from 1337 to 1453 in which England lost all of its possessions in France except Calais, also eventually lost in 1565.

Hymn A form of lyric poetry, characterized by solemnity and high religious feeling, intended to be sung in praise of gods or heroic men and women.

Hyperbole A figure of speech; using overstatement or extravagant exaggeration.

Iambic pentameter A poetic line made up of five feet, or iambs, or a ten-syllable line.

Idealism Philosophical Idealism in its various forms holds that objects of perception are in reality mental constructs and not the material objects themselves.

Ideogram A pictorial symbol used in writing that stands for an idea or concept.

Image A verbal representation of a sensory phenomenon—visual, auditory, olfactory, etc. The two types of images are literal and figurative. Literal images are very detailed, almost photographic; figurative images are more abstract and often use symbols.

Imam The leader of prayer in a Muslim mosque; also a title indicating respect for a man of learning.

In medias res Literally, "in the midst of things"; a term used to characterize the beginning of epic poems, which typically start at a crucial point far along in the story. Earlier details are conveyed by means of flashbacks and digressions.

Inquisition A medieval institution established by the Fourth Lateran Council of the Roman Catholic Church, which met in 1215 and was presided over by Pope Innocent III. The Inquisition was formed largely to combat heresy in the aftermath of the Albigensian Crusade in Spain (1209–1229). Punishments included death by burning at the stake and long imprisonment as well as forfeiture of land and property. One of the late and most notorious results of the Inquisition was the trial and execution of Joan of Arc in France in 1456.

Irony A device used in writing and speech to deliberately express ideas so they can be understood in two ways. In drama, irony occurs when a character does not know something that the other characters or the audience knows.

Islam A world religion founded in the seventh century C.E. on the teachings of the prophet Muhammad, whose followers believe that the Qur'an (Koran), the holy book of Islam, contains the revelations of Allah. The Five Pillars of Islam are: to recite the creed, "There is no God but Allah, and Muhammad is his Prophet"; to acknowledge the oneness of Allah in prayer five times each day by reciting the opening verses of the Qur'an; to practice charity and help the needy; to fast in the month of Ramadan; and to make the *hajj,* or pilgrimage to Mecca, at least once in a lifetime if possible. Islam has played a major role in the history of the Middle East and Asia.

Jainism A religion founded in India by Mahavira (d. 468 B.C.E.), a contemporary of the Buddha. In reaction to the rigid and hierarchical structure of traditional Hinduism, Jainism teaches that divinity resides within each individual. Salvation is achieved through the ascetic renunciation of the world and through the practice of *AHIMSA*, nonviolence toward all living beings.

Jen (Ren) As a basic element of CONFUCIANISM, *jen* means "benevolence" or "love for fellow humans"; Mencius (fourth century B.C.E.) argued that all humans are endowed with *jen*; also spelled *ren*.

Jesuits A Roman Catholic religious order founded in 1540 by Ignatius Loyola (1491–1556) under the title the Society of Jesus as part of the wider Counter-Reformation.

Jewish mysticism Like all forms of mysticism, Jewish mysticism focuses on learning and practices that lead to unity with the creator; its teachings are contained in the Cabala (Kabala, Kabbalah).

Jihad From the Arabic *jahada*, meaning "striving," "struggle," or "exertion," this term came to mean a holy war conducted by Muslims against unbelievers or enemies of Islam carried out as a religious duty. After the death of Muhammad in 632, Muslim conquests extended beyond Arabia until early into the next century. *Jihad* also denotes a spiritual struggle for perfection and self-control by practicing Muslims, as well as a struggle for the faith conducted peacefully with unbelievers.

Judgment of Paris In Greek legend, Paris (Alexandros) was selected by the god Zeus to judge which of three goddesses was the most beautiful. He chose Aphrodite, who had bribed him by agreeing to help him seduce Helen, the most beautiful woman in the world. Paris' abduction of Helen and refusal to return her was the cause of the Trojan War.

Ka'ba (ka'bah) The sacred Muslim shrine at Mecca, toward which believers turn when praying.

Kana The portion of the Japanese writing system that represents syllables.

Karma In Hindu and Buddhist philosophy, the totality of a person's actions in any one of the successive states of that person's existence, thought to determine the fate of the next stage. More generally, fate or destiny.

Karma-yoga One of four types of yoga; the practitioner of karma-yoga strives to serve humanity selflessly and without ego, a practice that purifies the heart and prepares the heart and mind for the reception of divine light, or the attainment of knowledge of the self.

Kharja The short, two- or four-line tag ending of an Arabic *muwashshah*, a long, formal beginning to a poem consisting of five or six end-rhymed stanzas. The *Kharja* was often written in MOZARABIC, the spoken language of Andalusia (Spain) that included elements of Arabic, Spanish, and Hebrew. It was often conceived of as a direct, provocative remark made by a servant girl or other uneducated person.

Kshatriya The second highest of the four primary Hindu castes, the military or warrior caste just below the Brahmin class.

Lacunae Spaces where something has been left out; particularly, a gap or missing portion of a text.

Laisses In Medieval poetry, stanzas composed of a variable number of ten-syllable lines; the concluding line of the first stanza is repeated as a refrain at the end of subsequent stanzas.

Lay (Lai) A song or musical interlude; by extension, a poem accompanied by a musical instrument. Marie de France, a popular Anglo-Norman poet of the twelfth century, composed what she called "Breton Lais," short versions of courtly romances suitable for recitation.

Leitmotifs Themes, brief passages, or single words repeated within a work.

Line A sequence of words. In poetry, lines are typically measured by the number of feet they contain.

Lingam The phallic symbol through which Shiva is worshipped in his personification as the creative and reproductive power in the universe.

Literary epic A literary epic—as distinguished from folk epics such as the *Mahabharata* or *The Iliad,* which are made up of somewhat loosely linked episodes and closely follow oral conventions—is written with self-conscious artistry, has a tightly knit organic unity, and is stylistically rooted in a written, literate culture. In actuality, great epics often blur the distinction between the oral or folk epic and the literary epic.

Loa In Spanish and Spanish American drama, a prologue that sets the scene and adumbrates the themes of a play.

Logos In ancient Greece, philosophers such as Aristotle (384–322 B.C.E.) used *logos* to mean reason or thought as opposed to pathos or feeling and emotion. Logos was thought of as the controlling principle of the universe made manifest in speech or rhetoric.

Lushi A highly structured Chinese form of poetry consisting of eight lines of five or seven syllables each. Also referred to as "regulated verse."

Lyric Originally, poetry composed to the accompaniment of a lyre (a stringed musical instrument). By extension, lyric is any poetry that expresses intense personal emotion in a manner suggestive of a song, as opposed to narrative poetry that relates the events of a story. Short poems, often on the subject of love, exist in most of the world's cultures and can fall under the common designation of lyric.

Maat An ancient Egyptian word for the idea of "right order" or justice, the basis of both cosmic order and a civil society. *Maat* was associated with either the sun-god Re or the creator Ptah.

Maghazi Legendary accounts of "the raids of the Prophet" in Islamic literature, examples of which can be found in Ibn Ishaq's *The Biography of the Prophet,* which depicts events of Muhammad's embattled later life.

Mahabharata One of the two great epics of ancient India and the longest poem in world literature, consisting of nearly 100,000 stanzas—more than seven times longer than *The Iliad* and *The Odyssey* combined. Attributed to Vyasa, whose name means the "compiler" or "arranger," the *Mahabharata* was composed between the fifth century B.C.E. and the fourth century C.E.; written in Sanskrit, the epic appeared in its final written form sometime in the fourth century C.E.

Manicheanism A dualistic religion founded by Mani, a Persian philosopher, in the third century C.E. Combining Christian, Buddhist, and Zoroastrian elements, Mani taught that there were two gods, one good and one evil, a school of belief that affected such later church thinkers as Augustine of Hippo, as seen in his *Confessions.*

Manuscript illumination The elaborate illustration of manuscripts (handwritten and handmade books) in the Middle Ages with beautiful images, borders, and letters, embellished with luminous color, especially gold.

Marathi A Sanskritic language of western India spoken by the Marathas, known as the SAMURAI of western India for their defense of Hinduism against the onslaught of the Muslim invaders of India.

Marxist criticism Literary criticism that evolved from Karl Marx's political and economic theories. In the view of Marxist critics, texts must be understood in terms of the social class and the economic and political positions of their characters.

Masque Developed in the Renaissance, masques are highly stylized and structured performances with an often mythological or allegorical plot, combining drama, music, song, and dance in an elaborate display.

Materialism A worldview that explains the nature of reality in terms of physical matter and material conditions rather than by way of ideas, emotions, or the supernatural.

Mathnavi Persian poetic form used for romantic, epic, didactic, and other types of poems whose subjects demand a lengthy treatment;

its verse structure is similar to that of the Western heroic couplet, but with two rhyming halves in a single line.

Mauryan The Indian empire that existed between c. 322 and c. 185 B.C.E. Established by Chandragupta Maurya (r. 322–296 B.C.E.), the dynasty eventually united all of India except for the extreme south under one imperial power. During this period trade flourished, agriculture was regulated, weights and measures were standardized, and money first came into use.

Maya From the Sanskrit for "deception" or "illusion," *maya* is the veil drawn over the ultimate, eternal reality of BRAHMAN and therefore represents the phenomenal world of appearances that humans misinterpret as the only reality.

Me According to Sumerian philosophers, the *me* were the divine laws and rules that governed the universe as well as the cultural elements, like metalworking and the arts, that constituted urban life. In Sumerian mythology, the *me* are the gift of the goddess Inanna to humankind.

Medieval Romances See CHIVALRIC ROMANCES.

Menippian satire Named for its originator, the Greek Cynic philosopher Menippus (first half of the third century B.C.E.), Menippian satire uses a mixture of prose, dialogue, and verse to make ludicrous a whole social class or a broad spectrum of social types. The form is sometimes called an "anatomy" because it catalogs the many social and intellectual types who constitute the social group it satirizes.

Mestizos Peoples in the Americas of mixed ethnic or cultural heritage, usually a combination of Spanish and Native American.

Metaphor A comparison of two things that does not use the words *like* or *as.* For example, "love is a rose."

Metaphysical poetry Poetry written primarily in seventeenth-century England that has as its focus the analysis of feeling. Its chief characteristics are complexity and subtlety of thought, frequent use of paradox, often deliberate harshness or rigidity of expression, and the use of bold and ingenious conceits—sometimes forced comparisons of unlike ideas or things that startle the reader into a closer analysis of the argument of the poem. John Donne and Andrew Marvell are known as metaphysical poets; the term is sometimes also used with other poetry of this type.

Meter The RHYTHM of a poem based on the number of syllables in each line and which syllables are accented. See also FOOT.

Middle Ages A term applied specifically to Europe, dating from the decline of the Roman Empire in the fourth to sixth centuries to the revival of learning and the arts in the Early Modern or Renaissance period in the late fourteenth and fifteenth centuries.

Millenarianism A utopian belief that the end of time is imminent, after which there will be a thousand-year era of perfect peace on earth.

Ming dynasty (1368–1644) Founded by Zhu Yuan-zhang, who restored native Chinese rule from the Mongols who had ruled China during the previous Yuan dynasty (1271–1368) established by Kubla Khan. The Ming dynasty saw a flourishing of Chinese culture, the restoration of CONFUCIANISM, and the rise of the arts, including porcelain, architecture, drama, and the novel.

Miyabi A Japanese term denoting a delicate taste for the beautiful—a refined sensibility for subtle nuances of style and form in art, literature, and social conduct.

Moira In Greek mythology, the deity who assigns to every person his or her lot.

Moksha In the Hindu tradition, the *moksha* is the highest goal for all humans; it means the final liberation from all earthly, material existence and complete union with God or the ultimate reality.

Monism A unitary conception of the world in which everything that is—the whole of reality—constitutes an inseparable self-inclusive whole, as opposed to dualism, which sees reality as made up of opposing elements, such as mind and matter, and good and evil.

Monogatari Loosely translated from the Japanese as "tale" or the "telling of things," *monogatari* refers to the genre of fiction; as in the case of *NIKKI*, *monogatari* were written in KANA and often contained poetic passages in the form of *WAKA*. Lady Murasaki's *The Tale of Genji* is perhaps the greatest example of the *monogatari* in Japanese literature.

Monologue A speech of significant length delivered by one person; in drama, speech in which a CHARACTER talks to himself or herself or reveals personal secrets without addressing another character.

Monotheism The doctrine or belief that there is only one deity or God, such as Allah or Yaweh, as opposed to the polytheistic religions of ancient Greece and Rome that involved the worship of numerous gods.

Mozarabic Pertaining to Spanish Christians and Jews who were permitted to practice their religions during the period of Muslim rule in Andalusia. Also refers to the vernacular language spoken in Andalusia, a combination of Arabic, Christian, and Hebrew elements.

Mullah (Mulla) A Muslim teacher or interpreter of Muslim religious law; the more current usage is as a general title of respect for a learned person.

Muse In ancient Greek mythology, any of the nine daughters of Zeus who presided over the arts; current usage denotes a muse as the spirit that inspires a poet or artist to create.

Muwashshah A conventional Andalusian love poem, usually written in Arabic but occasionally in Hebrew, consisting of five or six end-rhymed stanzas followed by a brief "tag" ending called a *KHARJA*, usually written in MOZARABIC.

Mystery religions Mystery cults were very popular in ancient Greece and Rome for at least one thousand years, beginning around 1000 B.C.E. The details of each cult were kept a secret, but all cults shared a rigorous rite of initiation, a concern about death, and a hope for immortality centered on a deity who had personal knowledge of the afterlife. The most popular Greek versions were the Orphic and Eleusinian mysteries. The mysteries of Isis and Mithra were favored in the Roman world.

Mysticism The belief that communion with God can be achieved intuitively through contemplation and meditation on the divine spirit akin to an act of faith rather than through the intellect.

Mythological criticism A type of literary criticism that focuses on the archetypal stories common to all cultures. Initiated by Carl Jung in the early twentieth century, mythological criticism seeks to reveal how the psychological impulses and patterns lodged deep in human consciousness take the form of ARCHETYPAL stories and are the basis for literature.

Narrative poem A poem that tells a story. Ballads, epics, and romances are typically narrative poems.

Narrator The voice that in fiction describes the PLOT or action of a story. The narrator can speak in the first, second, or third person and, depending on the effect the author wishes to create, can be very visible or almost invisible (an explicit or an implicit narrator); he or she also can be involved in the action or be removed from it. See also POINT OF VIEW and SPEAKER.

Nasib The prelude or introductory stanzas of a *qasidah*, the Arabic lyric form comparable to the ode.

Nataka In Sanskrit drama, the heroic romance with an idealized warrior king as its central figure and a comic story concentrating on heroic and erotic themes.

Necropolis Literally meaning "city of the dead," *necropolis* was the name given to a cemetery in the ancient world.

Neo-Confucianism Refers generally to the philosophical tradition in China and Japan based on the thought of Confucius (Kongfuzi, 551–479 B.C.E.) and his commentators, particularly Mencius (Mengzi, c. 371–c. 280 B.C.E.) and Zhu Xi (Chu Hi, 1130–1200). Neo-Confucianism, which arose during the Sung dynasty (960–1279), asserts that an understanding of things must be based on their underlying principles; in moral and political philosophy, it emphasizes the study of history, loyalty to family and nation, and order.

Neoplatonism Considered the last great Greek philosophy, Neoplatonism was developed by Plotnus (204–270 C.E.), based on his reading of the works of Plato. This school of philosophy espouses a single source from which all forms of existence emanate and with which the soul seeks a mystical union.

New Criticism A type of formalist literary criticism that disregards historical and biographical information to focus on the text. The New Critics perform a close reading of a work and give special attention to technical devices such as irony and ambiguity.

New Historicism A school of literary criticism developed in the 1980s in part as a reaction to NEW CRITICISM and other formalist methods of literary analysis. In contrast to formalism, which focuses strictly on internal relations of form and structure in a text, New Historicism emphasizes the relation of the text to its historical and cultural contexts. New Historicists make a self-conscious attempt to place their own critical practice within the political and historical framework of their own time, and align the language, rhetorical strategies, and other features of the texts they study with those of works not usually considered literary.

New Testament The sacred writings of Christianity, which tell the life of Jesus in the Gospels, the history of the establishment of the early church in Paul's Epistles, and the prophesy of the ultimate fulfillment of Christian history in the Revelation of St. John the Divine. From the Christian perspective, the New Testament fulfills the prophesies of the Hebrew Scriptures, known to Christians as the Old Testament.

Nikki An important genre of Japanese literature, the prose diary, which flourished among women writers in the Heian period; these diaries were written primarily in KANA, the woman's form of writing, which formed the basis of the vernacular literary tradition in Japan, and, like *The Tale of Genji,* contained poetic passages in the form of *WAKA*.

Nirgun In Indian devotional tradition, or *glakti,* the idea that God is transcendent, having no physical or material attributes.

Nirvana In Buddhism, the state of perfect blessedness achieved by the extinction of individual existence and absorption of the soul into the supreme spirit, or by the extinction of all earthly passions and desires.

Nō The highly elaborate and ritualistic classical theater of Japan, known for its minimalist approach to plot, scenery, and stage effects and the stately performance and Zen-like mastery of its actors; *Nō* means "talent" or "accomplishment."

Novel An extended work of fictional prose narrative. The novel is a modern outgrowth of earlier genres such as the romance. There is considerable debate as to the origins of the novel; some critics trace it to Cervantes' *Don Quixote* (1605), others to Lady Murasaki's *The Tale of Genji* (c. 1022).

Octave A STANZA of eight lines in poetry.

Ode An elevated form of LYRIC generally written on a single theme, using varied metric and rhyme patterns. With the ode, poets working within classical schemes can introduce considerable innovation. There are three major types of odes in English: the Pindaric, or Regular; the Horatian; and the Irregular. The Pindaric ode is structured by three-strophe divisions, modulating between the strophe, antistrophe, and epode, which vary in tone. The Horatian ode uses only one STANZA type; variation is introduced within each stanza. The Irregular ode, sometimes called the English ode, allows wide variety among stanza forms, rhyme schemes, and metrical patterns. Related forms adopted by particular cultures include the Arabic *QASIDAH* as practiced by the pre-Muslim poet Imru al-Qays, and the ancient Japanese *CHOKA* as practiced by Kakinomoto Hitomaro.

Oedipus complex Sigmund Freud's conception of the unconscious male desire to kill one's own father and sleep with one's own mother. The term derives from the Greek myth of Oedipus, who unknowingly murdered his father and married his mother; his self-inflicted punishment was to blind himself. FREUDIAN CRITICS do not take the complex or the story literally, but frequently use the concept to examine in literature the guilt associated with sexual desire and with competition with or hostility toward one's father.

Onomatopoeia The quality of a word that sounds like the thing it refers to: for example, the *buzz* of bees.

Open form Also known as *free verse*. A type of poetry that does not follow established conventions of METER, RHYME, and STANZA.

Opera A musical drama in which the dialogue is sung to orchestral accompaniment. As a form, it has its origins in the liturgical drama of the Middle Ages. In sixteenth-century Italy, opera rose to grand musical productions marked by elaborate costuming, scenery, and choreography.

Organic form The concept that the structure of a literary work develops according to an internal logic. The literary work grows and becomes an organic whole that follows the principles of nature, not mechanics. The created work of art is akin to a growing plant that relies on all of its parts working together.

Ottava rima Italian stanza form composed of eleven-syllable lines, rhyming *ab ab ab cc* that originated in the late thirteenth and early fourteenth centuries in Italy. The early master of the form was Giovanni Boccaccio (1313–1375), who established it as the standard form for epic and narrative verse in his time, but later poets continued to make use of it.

Oxymoron A rhetorical figure of speech in which contradictory terms are combined, such as *jumbo shrimp* and *deafening silence.*

Panegyric An oration or eulogy in praise of some person or achievement. Primarily associated with classical antiquity, panegyrics continued to be written through the Middle Ages and Renaissance, especially in Elizabethan England, the Spanish Golden Age, and in France under Louis XIV.

Pantheism Literally, "God everywhere," the belief that God is immanent throughout the universe—that God is manifest in all things.

Pantheon Generally, all the deities of a particular religion considered collectively; also, a temple dedicated to all the gods; specifically, the temple built in Rome by Agrippa in 27 C.E. and rebuilt by Hadrian in the second century C.E.

Paraphrase To rewrite or say the same thing using different words.

Parataxis Literally, "placing one thing after another." The term refers to linear narrative, often employed in storytelling, consisting of a series of sentences or clauses joined by a coordinator (that happened…, then this happened…).

Parody A humorous imitation of another, usually serious, work. Parody can be a form of literary criticism that exposes defects in a work, or it can function as an acknowledgement of a work's cultural and literary importance.

Pastoral poetry A poem or a play dealing with the lives of shepherds or rural life in general and usually depicting shepherds as representative of a simple life of innocence and serenity as opposed to the misery and corruption of city or court life. An early example of the form is Virgil's *Eclogues,* which greatly influenced the Renaissance work of such writers as Dante, Petrarch, Boccaccio, and Shakespeare.

Patois A regional dialect of a language.

Patrician Originally, the hereditary aristocracy and nobility of ancient Rome. Later the term referred to any person who by birth or special compensation belonged to the nobility. More current usage denotes a person of high birth or a person of refined upbringing and manners.

Pax Romana Literally meaning "Roman peace," this is the long period of comparative peace enforced on states in the Roman Empire between the years 27 B.C.E. and 180 C.E.

People of the Book (Dhimmi) The Muslim name for Jews and Christians, followers of the teachings of the prophets of Hebrew Scriptures and the New Testament. Under normal conditions Islamic authorities granted Jews and Christians religious tolerance.

Peloponnesian War (431–404 B.C.E.) War between the Athenian and Spartan alliance systems that encompassed most of the Greek world. The war set new standards for warfare—Athens used its navy to support the land offensive, for instance—but the new tactics also prolonged the fighting; instead of there being one decisive battle, the war dragged on for three decades. Eventually, Athens was defeated, and Sparta took over the defeated power's overseas empire.

Peripeteia (Peripety) A character's reversal of fortune in the denouement of a plot. In tragedy, it means the hero's destruction, in comedy his or her happy resolution.

Persian Wars A series of wars between a coalition of Greek city-states and the Persian empire fought between 500 and 449 B.C.E.; the Greek victory set the stage for the flourishing of Greek culture.

Persona Literally, persona means "mask." In literature, a persona is a speaker created by a writer to tell a story or to speak in a poem. A persona is not a character in a story or narrative, nor does it necessarily directly reflect the author's personal voice.

Personification A figure of speech in which abstractions or inanimate objects are given human qualities or form.

Petrarchan conceit From *concept* or *conception,* this was an originally novel form of metaphor in which the speaker of a poem compared his or her beloved to something else, such as a doe, a rose, a summer's day, or even a newly discovered land. Originating with the Italian poet Petrarch, the freshness of this device soon wore off and the Petrarchan conceit became a stale convention, revitalized by only the most ingenious poets.

Petrarchan sonnet A fourteen-line lyric poem. The Petrarchan SONNET was the first basic sonnet form. It is divided into an eight-line octet and a six-line sestet, each with a specific but varied pattern of rhymes, for example *ab ba cd ec de.*

Philistines A powerful non-Semitic tribe that in biblical times inhabited the tract of land between Judea and Egypt; in almost perpetual war with the Israelites, they were ultimately conquered by the Romans.

Phonogram A letter, character, or mark used to represent a sound.

Picaresque A novel loosely structured around an episodic succession of adventures of a rogue hero—a *picaro*—who is on an aimless journey. The picaresque tale often provides a sweeping and satiric view of society and its customs. Examples include Petronius's *The Satyricon* and Voltaire's *Candide.*

Pictograh A picture used to represent an idea; hieroglyphics are pictographs.

Pieta A representation in painting or sculpture of the Virgin Mary mourning over the dead body of Jesus after the Crucifixion.

Pietas In ancient Roman Stoic philosophy, *pietas* is respect for authority.

Platonic Characteristic of the philosophy of Plato, essentially connoting idealistic or visionary outlooks.

Platonic love A pure, spiritual love between a man and a woman that is based on intellectual appreciation of the other person and is unmixed with sexual desire.

Platonist One who adheres to the philosophy of Plato, especially the doctrine that holds that things exist only as ideas in the mind rather than as material objects independent of the mind.

Plebeians Members of the ancient Roman lower class or common people, as opposed to PATRICIANS.

Plot The pattern of events told in a narrative or drama. Plot has a causal sequence and a unifying theme, in contrast to story, which is the simple narrative of the action.

Point of view The perspective from which the author, SPEAKER, or NARRATOR presents a story. A point of view might be localized within a CHARACTER, in which case the story is told from a first-person point of view. There is a range of possibilities between first-person point of view and omniscience, wherein a story is told from a perspective unlimited by time, place, or character.

Polis Greek term meaning "city"; designates the Greek city-states, such as Athens and Sparta, that arose in the sixth century B.C.E.

Polytheism The belief in or worship of many gods as opposed to monotheism, which is the doctrine or worship of a single god.

Pragmatism A philosophical approach that evaluates ideas and beliefs in terms of their usefulness and applicability to practical action.

Prologue Text that typically is placed prior to an introduction or that replaces a traditional introduction; often discusses events of importance for the general understanding of the work. See also LOA.

Protagonist A leading figure or the main character in a drama or other literary work.

Protestant Reformation See REFORMATION.

Psychological criticism An approach to literature that draws on psychoanalytic theories, especially those of Sigmund Freud (1856–1939) and Jacques Lacan (1901–1981), to understand more fully a text, its writer, and readers.

Pun A play on words that relies on a word's having more than one meaning or sounding like another word.

Punic Wars The series of wars between Rome and Carthage during the third and second centuries B.C.E.—the first taking place between 264 and 241 B.C.E., the second between 218 and 201, and the third between 149 and 146—which the Romans ultimately won.

Purdah Practice adopted by some Muslims and Hindus that obscures women from public sight by mandating that they wear concealing clothing, especially veils. The custom originated in the seventh century C.E. and is still common in Islamic countries, though it has largely disappeared in Hinduism.

Purim A Jewish holiday, also known as the Feast of Lots, celebrating the deliverance of the Jews by Esther from the planned massacre plotted by Haman.

Qasidah An Arabic form of lyric poetry, comparable to the ode, originally composed orally and consisting of several dozen to some sixty rhymed couplets, expressing reflection and sentiment while evoking scenes of desert life, romantic memories, and a tone of despair or self-glorification. Later literary versions of the *qasidah* often lost their desert setting but retained their reflective, romantic character.

Quatrain A stanza of four lines in a poem.

Quetzalcoatl The most important god of Mesoamerica, whose name means Plumed Serpent or Precious Twin. As a god, he was instrumental in creating the four previous worlds; as a hero-ruler of Tollan, he assumed the mantle of the priesthood of Quetzalcoatl, fell from grace, and delivered a messianic promise to return home.

Quietism Scholars use this term to characterize Chinese thinkers in the fourth century B.C.E. who advocated withdrawal from the turbulence of society and concentration on inner peace and harmony.

Quixotic Like Don Quixote, or having the characteristics of being romantic in the extreme, absurdly chivalrous, or foolishly idealistic.

Qur'an The sacred writings of Islam revealed by Allah to the prophet Muhammad.

Rahil That part of a QASIDAH's (or ode's) structure in Persian poetry — the "disengagement" — that tells of a solitary journey on horseback or camelback, or more metaphorically, of the separation of the poet from the source of his sorrowful memory.

Rasa Indian dramatic theory identifies eight *rasas* (aesthetic emotions) that can focus a drama: the erotic, the heroic, the disquieting, the furious, the comic, the marvelous, the horrible, and the pathetic. Only two are appropriate for the *NATAKA* form, the erotic and the heroic.

Reader-response criticism A critical approach to literature in which the primary focus falls on the reader or the process of reading, not on the author. Reader-response critics believe that a literary work does not possess a fixed idea or meaning; meaning is a function of the perspective of the reader.

Realism Most broadly defined, realism is the attempt to represent the world accurately in literature. As a literary movement, Realism flourished in Russia, France, England, and America in the latter half of the nineteenth century. It emphasized not only accurate representation but the "truth," usually expressed as the consequence of a moral choice. Realist writers deemphasized the shaping power of the imagination and concerned themselves with the experiences of ordinary, middle-class subjects and the dilemmas they faced.

Realpolitik Foreign policy based on practical political expediency rather than moral or ideological considerations.

Recognition Based on the Greek concept of tragedy, recognition, or ANAGNORISIS, is the point in a story when the PROTAGONIST discovers the truth about his or her situation. Usually this results in a drastic change in the course of the plot.

Reformation Also known as the Protestant Reformation, this sixteenth-century challenge to the authority of the Catholic Church caused a permanent rift in the Christian world, with those loyal to the pope remaining Catholic and those rejecting papal authority forming new Protestant faiths such as the Anglican, Lutheran, Calvinist, Anabaptist, and Presbyterian. The Reformation originated—and was most successful—in Northern Europe, especially Germany; its notable leaders include Martin Luther and John Calvin.

Renaissance The revival of art, literature, and learning in Europe in the fourteenth, fifteenth, and sixteenth centuries based on classical Greek and Roman sources. The movement began in Italy, spread throughout Europe, and marked the transition from the medieval to the modern Western world.

Renaissance man A term used to describe someone accomplished in many disciplines, especially in both science and the arts, like Leonardo da Vinci and other figures of the European Renaissance.

Resolution The point in the plot of a narrative work or drama that occurs after the climax and generally establishes a new understanding; also known as *falling action*.

Reversal The point in the plot of a story or drama when the fortunes of the PROTAGONIST change unexpectedly; also known as the *PERIPITEIA*.

Rhyme The repetition of identical or similar-sounding words or syllables, usually accented, in lines of poetry. Rhymes may occur within or at the end of lines.

Rhythm The pattern of stressed and unstressed syllables in prose and especially in poetry that can lend emphasis, reinforce a sound association, or suggest regularity or recurrence. The rhythm of a literary work can affect the emotional response of the reader or listener.

Rishi (Rṣi) Sanskrit for sage or holy man.

Romance A medieval tale based on heroic conduct, adventure, or chivalric love, sometimes in a supernatural setting. Medieval romances were composed in France in the twelfth century, spreading to Germany, Spain, England, and other countries in the next several centuries. Later, in the seventeenth century, the romance form was parodied in Miguel de Cervantes' literary masterpiece, *Don Quixote*.

Romantic hero The PROTAGONIST of a romance, novel, or poem who is shaped by experiences that frequently take the form of combat, love, or adventure. The Romantic hero is judged by his actions more than his thoughts, and he is often on a journey that will affect his moral development.

Ruba'i (plural, Ruba'iyat) Equivalent to the quatrain in Western poetry, a *ruba'i* is a very intricate Persian poetic line structure consisting of four lines of equal length, divided into half lines, with the first, second, and fourth lines rhyming.

St. Francis (c. 1181–1226) Founder of the Franciscan religious order, beloved for his gentleness and humility. An account of his life and teachings, *The Little Flowers of Saint Francis,* was published in the century after his death.

Samsara A Hindu term for the cycle of birth, life, death, and rebirth; many Hindu practices are aimed at obtaining release, or *moksha,* from the otherwise endless repetition of life and death.

Samurai Japanese feudal aristocrat and member of the hereditary warrior class. Denied recognition during the Meiji period (1867–1912).

Sangha The Sanskrit word for a fraternity or association often formed out of spiritual or learning communities.

Sanskrit The classical language of ancient India, in which many of the major Hindu religious and literary texts were written.

Satire A literary or dramatic genre whose works, such as Petronius's *Satyricon* and Jonathan Swift's (1667–1745) *Gulliver's Travels,* ridicule human behavior.

Satyr In classical mythology, a minor woodland deity represented as part man and part goat whose chief characteristics are riotous merriment and lasciviousness.

Scansion A system of poetic analysis that involves dividing lines into feet and examining patterns of stressed and unstressed syllables. Scansion is a mechanical way of breaking down verse in order to understand the regularities and irregularities of its METER.

Scene In drama, a subdivision of an ACT.

Scholasticism The dominant philosophical system of the twelfth to fourteenth centuries in Europe, based on the writings of Aristotle and his commentators, including Avicenna (Ibn Sina) and Averroes (Ibn Rushdi). The great Christian Scholastic philosopher, St. Thomas Aquinas, completed his *Summa Theologica* in 1273.

Script The written version or text of a play or movie that is used by the actors.

Sentimentality Extravagant emotion; T. S. Eliot defined this as "emotion in excess of the facts."

Septuagint A Greek version of the Hebrew Scriptures (Old Testament), so called because the ancient tradition was that it was completed in seventy or seventy-two days by seventy-two Palestinian Jews, for Ptolemy II of Egypt.

Sestet A STANZA of six lines; the last stanza of a Petrarchan SONNET is a sestet.

Setting The time, place, and social environment in a narrative or a drama.

Shastra A treatise for authoritative instruction among the Hindu, especially a treatise explaining the VEDAS.

Shi In China, the term used to designate poetry in general.

Shi'ite One of the two great branches of the Muslim faith. Shi'ites insisted on a strict line of family succession from Muhammad and rejected interpretations of Islam construed after the death of Muhammad. They soon were considered heretical by the majority branch, Sunnite (Sunna) Muslims. Present-day Shi'ites primarily occupy Iran and southern Iraq.

Shintoism The indigenous polytheistic religion of Japan, the beliefs of which stress the worship of nature, ancestors, and ancient heroes, and the divinity of the emperor.

Shite The PROTAGONIST or main character in a Japanese *Nō* play.

Shiva (Śiva) The Hindu god of destruction and creation and a member of the supreme Hindu trinity of Shiva, Brahma, and Vishnu.

Shogun A military ruler of feudal Japan between 1192 and 1867. The shogunate was an inherited position in the military that operated under the nominal control of the emperor.

Sikhism The beliefs of those who belong to the Hindu religious sect founded in northern India around 1500 C.E., based on a belief in one God and on a rejection of the caste system and idolatry.

Simile A figure of speech, introduced by *like* or *as,* in which two things are compared as equals.

Smirti (Smṛti) One of the two major classifications of Hindu sacred texts. *Smirti,* which means "memory," comprises Hindu texts other than the VEDAS, which are considered SRUTI, or revealed (heard) texts. *Smirti* may be thought of as a secondary category of sacred literature that includes the Sutras, the Puranas, and the Indian epics the *Ramayana* and the *Mahabharata.*

Sociological criticism School of literary criticism that seeks to place a work of art in its social context and define the relationship between the two. Like Marxist critics, sociological critics are oriented toward social class, political ideology, gender roles, and economic conditions in their analyses.

Soliloquy A dramatic speech in which a character speaks his or her inner thoughts aloud before the audience.

Sonnet A fourteen-line lyric poem. The first basic sonnet form is the Italian or Petrarchan sonnet, which is divided into an eight-line octet and a six-line SESTET (see PETRARCHAN SONNET). The English or Shakespearean sonnet is divided into three four-line QUATRAINS followed by a two-line couplet; the quatrains are rhymed *abab cdcd efef* and the couplet is also end-rhymed, *gg.*

Sophists Literally, "wise men." Greek teachers who provided instruction in logic and rhetoric to pupils who could afford their expensive fees. Rhetoric was a new discipline whose study was observed to provide an advantage in politics and in the courts. *Sophist* came to mean one who used argumentation to undermine traditional beliefs.

Speaker The person or PERSONA who speaks in a poem, often a created identity who cannot be equated with the poet.

Spiritual autobiography An autobiography that gives special importance to self-examination, interpretation of Scripture, and belief in predestination. St. Augustine's *Confessions* (c. 400), detailing a life of sin, conversion, and spiritual rebirth, is generally regarded as the archetypal spiritual autobiography.

Sprezzatura An Italian term that has no equivalent in English, *sprezzatura* suggests a quality of perfect composure and nonchalance, the ability to act with studied artifice while giving the appearance of effortless spontaneity.

Sruti One of the two major classifications of Hindu sacred texts. *Sruti,* which means "hearing," is reserved for the primary sacred texts of Hinduism, the VEDAS, including the Smahtas, the Brahmanas, and the Aranyakas, the most important of which is the UPANISHADS.

Stage directions Written directions explaining how actors are to move onstage. See also SCRIPT.

Stanza A poetic verse of two or more lines, sometimes characterized by a common pattern of RHYME and METER.

Stock responses Predictable responses to language and symbols. See also CLICHÉ.

Stoicism A school of thought founded by the Greek philosopher Zeno c. 308 B.C.E. Stoicism advocated the view that virtue is the ultimate goal of life and that the virtuous seek happiness within by overcoming their passions and emotions while remaining independent of the external natural world, which follows immutable laws.

Stress A syllable receiving emphasis in accordance with a metrical pattern.

Style The distinctive manner in which an author writes and thus makes his or her work unique. A style provides a kind of literary signature for the writer.

Subplot A PLOT subordinate to the main plot of a literary work or drama.

Sufism A devotional movement among certain Muslims emphasizing the union of the devotee with God through ritual and ascetic practices, who hold to a kind of PANTHEISM and practice extreme asceticism in their lives.

Suspense The anxious emotion of an audience or reader anticipating the outcome of a story or drama, typically having to do with the fate of the PROTAGONIST or another character with whom a sympathetic attachment has been formed.

Symbol A representative of something by association. Though a symbol is often confused with a metaphor, a metaphor compares two dissimilar things while a symbol associates two things. For example, the *word* "tree" is a symbol for an *actual* tree. Some symbols have values that are accepted by most people. A flag, for instance, is for many a symbol of national pride, just as a cross is widely seen as a symbol of Christianity. Knowledge of a symbol's cultural context is sometimes necessary to understand its meaning; an apple pie is an American symbol of innocence that a Japanese person, for example, would not necessarily recognize.

Syncretism Combining disparate philosophical or religious beliefs, such as the blending of Christianity or Islam with indigenous religions.

Synoptic Gospels The first three gospels of the New Testament, which give a similar account of the life, death, and Resurrection of Jesus.

Syntax The way parts of speech are arranged in a sentence.

TANAK An acronym used to describe three groupings in Hebrew Scriptures: the Torah (Pentateuch, or first five books), the Nebi'im, (the Prophets), and Ketubim (the Writings); also spelled TENACH.

Tanka A Japanese verse form of thirty-one syllables in five unrhymed lines, the first and third having five syllables each, the second, fourth, and fifth having seven. See also WAKA.

Tantrism A minor Hindu tradition written down in scriptures called Tantras. Tantrism holds the supreme deity to be feminine and teaches that spiritual liberation can be won through erotic practices.

Taoism See DAOISM.

Tathagata An epithet for the Buddha that means "thus gone," having attained enlightenment.

Tercets A unit or group of three lines of verse, usually rhymed.

Terza rima A verse form composed of iambic three-line stanzas, with lines of ten or eleven syllables. Terza rima employed most brilliantly in Dante's (1265–1321) *Divine Comedy.*

Tetragrammaton The four consonants of the Hebrew alphabet, YHWH, used to approximate God's secret name; this name and its utterances are believed to contain special powers.

Tezcatlipoca In Aztec mythology, he was the warrior god of the north and the god of sin and misery with an obsidian knife. In Toltec mythology, he was also the brother and/or antithesis of Quetzalcoatl.

Thanatos "Death" in Greek. According to Sigmund Freud, our two primary drives are Eros (love) and Thanatos (death).

Theme A topic of discussion or a point of view embodied in a work of art.

Theocracy Government of the state by God or a god as represented by a person or persons claiming to have divine authority.

Tolkappiyam The formal grammar developed in literary assemblies in and around the Indian city of Madurai between 100 and 250 C.E. created to classify aspects of Tamil poetry.

Tone A manner of expression in writing that indicates a certain attitude toward the subject or the implied audience.

Tour de force A masterly or brilliant creation, production, or performance; the phrase translates literally from the original French as "feat of strength."

Tragedy A dramatic or literary form originating in Greece that deals with serious human actions and issues. The actions are meant to create feelings of fear and compassion in the spectator that are later released (CATHARSIS). Typically, the main character is of a high stature or rank, so his or her fall is substantial. Even though tragedies are sad, they seem both just and believable. The tragedy raises serious moral and philosophical questions about the meaning of life and fate.

Tragicomedy A drama that combines tragedy and comedy and in which moral values are particularly questioned or ridiculed.

Travel narratives Also known as travel literature, a form of narrative that recounts the incidents that occur and the people and things that the narrator meets and sees while visiting a place with which she or he is typically unfamiliar. Prose and poetic accounts about exploration and adventure in unfamiliar lands and places as well as in more or less familiar locations are considered travel narratives. Examples of the genre include the travels of Marco Polo and the travels of Ibn Battuta.

Triplet In poetry, a group of three rhyming lines of verse.

Trobairitz Female troubadours, both members of the nobility and independent artists. See TROUBADOURS.

Troubadours Lyric poets and composers, sometimes of aristocratic rank but more often artists attached to regional courts, who flourished in the south of France in the twelfth and thirteenth centuries. Their compositions in the Provencal language centered on the subject of love. Their work derived in part from Arabic sources in Andalusia, and their influence spread throughout Europe in the thirteenth and fourteenth centuries.

Umrah Known as the "lesser pilgrimage"; in contrast to the *hajj,* which must be performed in the last month of the Islamic calendar year, *umrah* is a pilgrimage to Mecca that can be undertaken at any time.

Understatement A figure of speech that says less than what is intended. In Anglo-Saxon poetry, a special form of understatement known as the litote is an ironic form of address in which the full importance of something is concealed in order to force the listener to discover it by paying close attention.

Upanishads A body of sacred texts dating from the ninth century B.C.E. that provide a mystical development of and commentary on earlier VEDIC texts.

Urdu An Indo-European language closely related to Hindi. Urdu is the official language of Pakistan and is also spoken in India and Bangladesh.

Utopia In literature, a romance or other work describing an ideal place whose inhabitants live under seemingly perfect conditions. Though the term did not exist until coined by Sir Thomas More in 1516, earlier works such as Plato's *Republic* and Bacon's *New Atlantis* can be termed utopias due to the societies they depict.

Vandals Fierce warriors from near the Russian steppes who invaded Roman Gaul (France) in the fifth century C.E. and advanced through Spain to North Africa. They were notorious for their destruction of cities.

Varna Sanskrit word for "color" used in the sense of "class" to indicate the four classes or castes of Hinduism in India.

Vedas The earliest Indian sacred texts, written in Sanskrit, dating from sometime between 1000 and 500 B.C.E.; they contain hymns and ritual lore considered to be revelation, or SRUTI.

Vedic The Old Indic language of the VEDAS, it was an early form of Sanskrit.

Vernacular fiction Fiction that attempts to capture accurately the typical speech, mannerisms, or dialect of a region. The *Satyricon* of the Roman author Petronius is often considered the first work of vernacular fiction.

Waka Traditional Japanese poetry based on Chinese models that rose to prominence in the Heian Period (794–1195). The *waka* is a short five-line lyric consisting of thirty-one syllables with 5-7-5-7-7 syllables to a line. Writing *waka* was an important activity of the Heian aristocracy as well as their court followers. The poetry anthology *Kokinshu* (c. 905) is the most celebrated collection of *waka.* Now generally called *tanka,* these poems are still written today.

Waki Refers to the secondary PROTAGONIST or antagonist in Japanese *Nō* plays; the primary character is known as the shite.

Xiaopin A Chinese form of autobiographical essay that became an important medium in China in the late sixteenth century.

Yahweh A form of the Hebrew name for God in the Hebrew Scriptures.

Yin and yang A pair of opposites derived from a dualistic system of ancient Chinese philosophy; symbolically representing the sun and the moon, *yang* is positive, active, and strong, while *yin* is negative, passive, and weak. All things in the universe are formed from the dynamic interaction of these forces.

Yoni A representation of the vulva, a symbol used in the worship of the goddess Shakti in Hiduism.

Yuefu Chinese folk ballads that, during the Han dynasty, evolved into literary ballads written in quatrains of five-word lines. The ballad typically presented a monologue of dialogue presenting, in dramatic form, some misfortune.

Yugen From the Japanese meaning mystery or profound beauty, *yugen* refers to the aura of spiritual depth and beauty that is the aim of *Nō* drama.

Zajal One of two poetic forms that came to dominate the performance of the GHAZAL, or love poem, which consisted of elaborately rhymed strophes or stanzas in MOZARABIC, without the *KHARJA* ending.

Zen prominent school of Buddhism that seeks to reveal the essence of the enlightened mind. Zen teaches that everyone has the potential to attain enlightenment but that most are unaware of this potential because they are ignorant. The way to attain enlightenment is through transcending the boundaries of common thought, and the method of study is most frequently the intense, personal instruction of a student by a Zen master.

Zhong Guo The translation of the Chinese characters for "Middle Kingdom," which denotes what today is translated as China.

Ziggurat A temple tower of the ancient Akkadians and Babylonians in the form of a terraced pyramid with each story smaller than the one below it.

Zoroastrianism A dualistic religion founded in ancient Persia by Zoroaster (c. 12th century–7th century B.C.E.). It teaches that two powerful forces—light and darkness, good and evil—are engaged in a struggle that will eventually erupt into a cataclysmic war in which good will prevail, leading to the destruction of the earth.

Zuihitsu Japanese for "following the brush" and translated as "occasional writing" or "essays," *zuihitsu* denotes a genre of Japanese writing mixing poetry and prose that arose primarily among women writers during the Heian Period. Sei Shonagon's *Pillow Book* is an example of *zuihitsu.*

Acknowledgments (continued from p. iv)

Aeschylus, "Prayer to the Dead" from *The Libation Bearers,* translated by Richmond Lattimore, from *The Complete Greek Tragedies, Volume I.* Copyright © 1960 by the University of Chicago. Reprinted with the permission of The University of Chicago Press.

Aristophanes, "Lysistrata" from *Greek Literature in Translation,* by Whitney Jennings Oates and Charles T. Murphy. Copyright 1944 by Longman Publishing Group. Reprinted with the permission of Pearson Education.

Aristotle, "The Origin of Religion" from *Hellenistic Religions,* translated by Frederick C. Grant. Copyright 1953. Reprinted with the permission of Pearson Education, Inc., Upper Saddle River, NJ.

Aristotle, excerpts from "Metaphysics" from *The Way of Philosophy,* translated by Phillip Wheelwright. Copyright © 1960 by Macmillan Publishing Company. Reprinted with the permission of Pearson Education, Upper Saddle River, NJ.

Asoka Maurya, excerpt from "Asokavadana," translated by John Strong from Romila Thapar, *Asoka and the Decline of the Mauryas.* Copyright © 1961. Reprinted with the permission of Oxford University Press, New Delhi.

A. L. Basham (trans.), "The Ideal King" from "Nitivakyamrta," "The Four Noble Truths" from "Samyutta Nikaya," "Right Mindfulness" from "Majjhima Nikaya," "The Simile of the Chariot" from "Milindapañha," and "The Last Instructions of the Buddha" from "Mahaparinibbana Sutra" from *Sources of Indian Tradition,* compiled by William Theodore de Bary et al. Copyright © 1958 by Columbia University Press. Reprinted with the permission of the publisher.

Bible, excerpts from *The New English Bible.* Copyright © 1961, 1970 by Oxford University Press and Cambridge University Press. Reprinted by permission.

Catullus, poems from *The Poems of Catullus,* translated by Horace Gregory. Copyright © 1956 by Horace Gregory. Reprinted with the permission of Grove/Atlantic, Inc.

Chuang Tzu, excerpts from *Chuang Tzu: Basic Writings,* translated by Burton Watson. Copyright © 1963 by Columbia University Press. Reprinted with the permission of the publisher.

Cleanthes, "Invocation" and "Hymn to Zeus," translated by Frederick C. Grant from *Hellenistic Religions.* Copyright 1953. Reprinted with the permission of Pearson Education, Inc., Upper Saddle River, NJ.

Confucius, excerpts from *The Analects of Confucius,* translated by Arthur Waley. Copyright © 1938 by George Allen & Unwin, Ltd. Reprinted with the permission of Scribner, an imprint of Simon & Schuster Adult Publishing Group, and the Estate of Arthur Waley.

Stephanie Dalley (trans.), excerpts from "The Epic of Creation" and "The Descent of Ishtar" from *Myths from Mesopotamia.* Copyright © 1989 by Stephanie Dalley. Reprinted with the permission of Oxford University Press, Ltd.

Diogenes Laertius, "Socrates" from *Lives of Eminent Philosophers,* translated by R. D. Hicks. Reprinted with the permission of Harvard University Press and the Trustees of the Loeb Classical Library. The Loeb Classical Library™ is a registered trademark of the President and Fellows of Harvard College.

Epicurus, excerpt from "Letter to Menoeceus," translated by Philip Wheelwright, *The Way of Philosophy.* Copyright © 1960. Reprinted with the permission of Pearson Education, Inc., Upper Saddle River, NJ.

Euhemerus, excerpts from "On the Origin of the Gods" from *Hellenistic Religions,* translated by Frederick C. Grant. Copyright 1953. Reprinted with the permission of Pearson Education, Inc., Upper Saddle River, NJ.

Euripides, "Medea" from *Medea and Other Plays,* translated by Philip Vellacott. Copyright © 1963 by Philip Vellacott. Reprinted with the permission of Penguin Books, Ltd.

Flavius Josephus, "The Destruction of Jerusalem" from *The Jewish War,* translated by G. A. Williamson, revised by E. Mary Smallwood. Copyright © 1959, 1969 by G. A. Williamson. Reprinted with the permission of Penguin Books, Ltd.

Dominic Goodall (trans.), "In the Beginning" from "The Rig Veda" from *Hindu Scriptures,* edited and translated by Dominic Goodall. Copyright © 1996 by J. M. Dent. Reprinted with the permission of the University of California Press.

Heraclitus, "Change Runs the Universe" from *The Presocratics,* edited by Philip Wheelwright. Copyright © 1966. Reprinted with the permission of Pearson Education, Upper Saddle River, NJ.

Hesiod, "The Castration of Uranus," "Kronos Swallows His Children and the Birth of Zeus," "Prometheus Steals Fire," "Prometheus and Pandora," and "The Ages of Man" from *Theogony and Works and Days,* translated by Dorothea Wender. Copyright © 1973 by Dorothea Wender. Reprinted with the permission of Penguin Books, Ltd.

Homer, excerpts from *The Iliad,* translated by Robert Fitzgerald. Copyright © 1974 by Robert Fitzgerald. Reprinted with the permission of Doubleday, a division of Random House, Inc. Entire text (Books 1–24) from Homer: *The Odyssey* translated by Robert Fitzgerald. Copyright © 1961, 1963 by Robert Fitzgerald, renewed 1989 by Benedict R. C. Fitzgerald, on behalf of the Fitzgerald children. Reprinted with the permission of Farrar Straus & Giroux, LLC.

R. E. Hume (trans.), excerpt from "Brihad Aranyaka Upanishad" and excerpt from "Chandogya Upanishad" from *The Thirteen Principal Upanishads.* Reprinted with the permission of Oxford University Press India, New Delhi.

R. P. Kangle (trans.), Chapters 10 and 12 from *The Kautilíya Arthashastra.* Reprinted with the permission of Motilal Banarsidass, Publishers, India.

Lao Tzu, excerpts from *The Way of Life According to Lao Tzu,* translated by Witter Bynner. Copyright 1944 by Witter Bynner, renewed © 1972 by Dorothy Chauvenet and Paul Horgan. Reprinted with the permission of HarperCollins Publishers, Inc. Poems 1, 15, 16, 19, 20, 28, 29, 30, 36, 42, 43, 47, 74, 81 from *The Tao Te Ching,* translated by Gia-Fu Feng and Jane English. Copyright © 1972 by Gia-Fu Feng and Jane English. Reprinted with the permission of Alfred A. Knopf, a division of Random House, Inc.

Miriam Lichtheim (trans.), "King Unas Joins the Sun-God" (Utterance 217) from *Ancient Egyptian Literature: A Book of Readings.* Copyright © 1973–1980 by the Regents of the University of California. Reprinted with the permission of the University of California Press.

Lucretius, "The Psychological Origin of the Underworld" from *Lucretius: The Nature of the Universe, Book III,* translated by Ronald Latham, revised by John Goodwin. Copyright 1951 by R. E. Latham, revisions, introduction and notes © 1994 by John Goodwin. Reprinted with the permission of Penguin Books, Ltd.

Juan Mascaró (trans.), excerpts from *The Upanishads.* Copyright © 1965 by Juan Mascaró. Reprinted with the permission of Penguin Books, Ltd.

Mencius, "Compassion" from *Mencius,* translated by D. C. Lau. Copyright © 1970 by D. C. Lau. Reprinted with the permission of Penguin Books, Ltd. "Heaven and Human Nature" from *Mencius,* translated by W. A. C. H. Dobson. Reprinted with the permission of the University of Toronto Press.

Barbara Stoler Miller (trans.), excerpts from *The Bhagavad Gita: Krishna's Council in Time of War.* Copyright © 1986 by Barbara Stoler Miller. Reprinted with the permission of Columbia University Press.

Chakravarthi V. Narasimhan (trans.), excerpts from *The Mahabharata.* Copyright © 1965 by Columbia University Press. Reprinted with the permission of the publisher.

Wendy Doniger O'Flaherty (trans.), "Indra Slays the Dragon Vritra," "Hymn to the Sun," "The Song of Purusha," and "Hymn to the Horse" from *The Rig Veda: An Anthology.* Copyright © 1981 by Wendy Doniger O'Flaherty. Reprinted with the permission of Penguin Books, Ltd.

Ovid, excerpts from *Metamorphoses,* translated by Rolfe Humphries. Copyright © 1955 by Rolfe Humphries. Reprinted with the permission of Indiana University Press.

Petronius, "Dinner with Trimalchio" from *The Satyricon,* translated by William Arrowsmith. Copyright © 1959 by William Arrowsmith. Reprinted with the permission of The University of Michigan Press.

Philo Judeaus, "On the Creation of the World," translated by Nahum N. Glatzer, from *The Essential Philo,* edited by Nahum N. Glatzer. Copyright © 1971 by Schocken Books. Reprinted with the permission of Schocken Books, a division of Random House, Inc.

Plato, "The Divine Universe Within" from *Timaeus,* translated by H. D. P. Lee. Copyright © 1971 by H. D. P. Lee. Reprinted with the permission of Penguin Books, Ltd.

Plutarch, "On the Fortune of Alexander" from *Moralia,* translated by Frank Cole Babbitt. Reprinted with the permission of Harvard University Press and the Trustees of the Loeb Classical Library. The Loeb Classical Library™ is a registered trademark of the President and Fellows of Harvard College.

N. K. Sandars (trans.), "The Epic of Gilgamesh" from *The Epic of Gilgamesh, Second Revised Edition.* Copyright © 1960, 1964, 1972 by N. K. Sandars. Reprinted with the permission of Penguin Books, Ltd.

Sappho, selections from *Sappho: A New Translation,* by Mary Barnard. Copyright © 1958 by The Regents of the University of California, renewed 1986 by Mary Barnard. Reprinted with the permission of the University of California Press.

Sargon II, excerpt from "Annalistic Reports," translated by A. Leo Oppenheim from *The Ancient Near East,* edited by James B. Pritchard. Copyright © 1958 by Princeton University Press. Reprinted with the permission of the publisher.

William Kelly Simpson (trans.), "Hymn to Aten," "If I am [not] with you, where will you set your heart?," "My love for you is mixed throughout my body," "My heart is not yet happy with your love," "I sail downstream in the ferry by the pull of the current," "My god, my [lover . . .]," "I embrace her," "I wish I were her washerman," and "Seven days have passed, I've not seen my lady love," and "Please come quick to the lady love" from "Egyptian Love Poems" in *Literature of Ancient Egypt: An Anthology of Stories, Instructions, and Poetry,* edited by William Kelly Simpson. Copyright © 1972 by Yale University. Reprinted with the permission of Yale University Press.

Sophocles, "Antigone" from *Three Theban Plays: Antigone, Oedipus the King, Oedipus at Colonus,* translated by Theodore Howard Banks. Copyright © 1956 by Theodore Howard Banks, renewed 1984 by Marian C. Banks. Reprinted with the permission of Oxford University Press. *Oedipus Rex: An English Version,* translated by Dudley Fitts and Robert Fitzgerald. Copyright 1949 by Harcourt, Inc., renewed © 1977 by Cornelia Fitts and Robert Fitzgerald. Reprinted with the permission of Harcourt, Inc. All rights, including professional, amateur, motion picture, recitation, lecturing, public reading, radio broadcasting, and television, are strictly reserved. Inquiries on all rights should be addressed to Harcourt, Inc., Permissions Department, Orlando, FL 32887-6777.

Valmiki, excerpts from *The Concise Ramayana of Valmiki,* translated by Swami Venkatesanada. Copyright © 1988. Reprinted with the permission of SUNY Press.

Geza Vermes (trans.), "War of Sons of Light and Sons of Darkness" from *The Dead Sea Scrolls, Third Edition.* Copyright © 1962, 1965, 1968, 1975, 1987 by G. Vermes. Reprinted with the permission of Penguin Books, Ltd.

Virgil, excerpts from *The Aeneid,* translated by F. O. Copley and Brooks Otis. Copyright © 1965 by Macmillan Publishing Company. Reprinted with the permission of Macmillan Publishing Company.

INDEX